81st Association for Information Science and Technology Annual Meeting

Building and Sustaining and Ethical Future with Emerging Technology

Proceedings of the Association for Information Science and Technology Volume 55

Vancouver, Canada
10-14 November 2018

Editor:

Lydia S. Middleton

ISBN: 978-1-5108-8444-1

Printed from e-media with permission by:

Curran Associates, Inc.
57 Morehouse Lane
Red Hook, NY 12571

Printed by Curran Associates, Inc. (2019)

For permission requests, please contact Association for Information Science and Technology (ASIS&T) at the address below.

Association for Information Science and Technology (ASIS&T)
8555 16th Street, Suite 850
Silver Spring, Maryland 20910
USA

Phone: 301-495-0900
Fax: 301-495-0810

asist@asist.org

Additional copies of this publication are available from:

Curran Associates, Inc.
57 Morehouse Lane
Red Hook, NY 12571 USA
Phone: 845-758-0400
Fax: 845-758-2633
Email: curran@proceedings.com
Web: www.proceedings.com

PROCEEDINGS OF THE 81ST ANNUAL MEETING

BUILDING & SUSTAINING AN ETHICAL FUTURE WITH EMERGING TECHNOLOGY

10 - 14 NOVEMBER 2018
81st ANNUAL MEETING

WWW.ASIST.ORG/AM18

asis&t
81st ANNUAL MEETING
NOVEMBER 10-14, 2018
VANCOUVER, CANADA

Managing Editor
Lydia S. Middleton, MBA, CAE

Association for Information Science and Technology
8555 16th Street, Suite 850, Silver Spring, Maryland 20910

ASIS&T BOARD OF DIRECTORS

ABOUT THE MEETING

The Annual Meeting of the Association for Information Science and Technology is the premier international conference dedicated to the study of information, people, and technology in contemporary society. The meeting gathers leading professionals and faculty from around the globe to share innovations, ideas, research, and insights regarding how information and technology mediate the creation and use of knowledge within and across cultures.

The theme of the ASIS&T 2018 Annual Meeting is focused on the ethical implications of the rapid and dynamic transformation of technology and its use in the collection and dissemination of information.

The educational sessions push the boundaries of information studies, exploring core concepts and ideas, and creating new technological and conceptual configurations — all situated in interdisciplinary discourses.

THIS YEAR, WE EXPLORE:

- Alt-Metrics and Bibliometrics: Textual and Network Approaches
- Cross-Disciplinary Scholarly Impact
- Data Communities and Institutions
- Data Practices and Digital Curation
- Data Sharing
- Evaluating Systems
- Everyday Information Behavior
- Knowledge and Information Organization
- Language and Information Science
- Learning, Literacies, and Information Behavior
- Media and Communication
- Privacy and Policy Matters
- Scholarly Community Formation and Maintenance
- Scholarly Practices in Biomedical Research
- Searching Behaviors and Contexts (Info Behav)

VOLUME 55

PROCEEDINGS EDITOR
Luanne Freund, University of British Columbia, Canada

PUBLISHED FOR THE ASSOCIATION FOR INFORMATION SCIENCE & TECHNOLOGY
BY
JOHN WILEY & SONS, INC.
SOMERSET, NJ

2018 ANNUAL MEETING TECHNICAL PROGRAM COMMITTEE:

CONFERENCE CHAIR
Luanne Freund, University of British Columbia, Canada

PAPER CO-CHAIRS
Christopher Lueg, University of Tasmania, Australia
Kalpana Shankar, University College Dublin, Ireland

PANEL & WORKSHOP CO-CHAIRS
Rajesh Singh, St. John's University, USA
Catherine L. Smith, Kent State University, USA

VISUAL PRESENTATION CO-CHAIRS
Julia Hersberger, University of North Carolina Greensboro, USA
Maayan Zhitomirsky-Geffet, Bar Ilan University, Israel

DOCTORAL COLLOQUIUM CO-CHAIRS
Howard Rosenbuam, Indiana University, USA
Pnina Fichman, Indiana University, USA

STUDENT DESIGN COMPETITION CO-CHAIRS
Rachel Ivy Clarke, Syracuse University, USA
Rebekah Willson, University of Strathclyde Glasgow, Scotland

CHAIR'S MESSAGE

It is an honour to serve as General Chair of the 2018 Annual Meeting of the Association of Information Science & Technology (AM18), a gathering that has served as a pillar of the information science community for the past 81 years. We meet this year in Vancouver, which is situated in the traditional and unceded territory of the Coast Salish Peoples, the Squamish, Musqueam and Tsleil-Waututh First Nations, and I would like to acknowledge and thank them for their hospitality.

The theme of AM18 poses a challenge for the information science community: how can we build and sustain an ethical future with emerging technology? The annual meeting will provide an exceptional platform for the joint exploration of this question with a broad and inclusive program selected through a rigorous peer review process. We accepted 69 of 142 full papers (49%); 26 of 46 panels (57); and 100 of 203 visual presentations (49%). Many submissions connect to the conference theme and others reflect longtime areas of focus and emerging issues in our field, cutting across research and practice. Areas of particular emphasis in AM18 are: human information behaviour, social media, informetrics and altmetrics, data science and curation, knowledge organization, libraries and cultural institutions, and information ethics.

Framing the meeting are two outstanding keynote speakers, who will address the impacts of emerging technologies on society from critical and international perspectives. These talks by Dr. Ramesh Srinivasan, UCLA (opening plenary) and Dr. Zeynep Tufekci, University of North Carolina (closing plenary) are must-see events that will provide food for thought and debate throughout the meeting.

Many thanks go to the members of the AM18 Organizing Committee: Paper Co-Chairs – Kalpana Shankar, University College Dublin, Ireland and Christopher Lueg, University of Tasmania, Australia; Panel Co-Chairs - Catherine L. Smith, Kent State University, USA and Rajesh Singh, St. John's University, USA; Visual Presentation Co-Chairs - Maayan Zhitomirsky-Geffet, Bar Ilan University, Israel and Julia Hersberger, University of North

CHAIR'S MESSAGE

Carolina Greensboro, USA; and Doctoral Colloquium Chairs – Pnina Fichman and Howard Rosenbaum, both of Indiana University, USA. This international group coordinated the review of submissions and prepared the technical program for the AM, drawing upon the contributions and commitment of 255 reviewers who, collectively, completed almost 1000 reviews. We are grateful to all the reviewers who volunteered their time and expertise to this enormous task. In addition to the technical program, student attendees will have the opportunity to participate in the exciting Student Design Competition, thanks to event Co-Chairs: Rebekah Willson, University of Strathclyde, Scotland and Rachel Ivy Clarke, Syracuse University, USA.

I would also like to thank President Lisa M. Given and members of the ASIS&T Board, for trusting me with the opportunity to chair this event, and the capable ASIS&T staff who do so much of the work that makes the annual meeting possible, especially Lydia Middleton, ASIS&T Executive Director and DeVonne Parks, Director of Meetings and Events. This year, in consultation with the ASIS&T staff and board members, we made a number of changes to the traditional annual meeting structure, intended to streamline the event and open up time for informal networking and for new ideas and activities. Please connect to the conference app and the website for information, as AM18 has gone paperless, and join us for the many enticing social events and tours, and the rich program of meetings, panels, and presentations. Finally, a meeting of this scale cannot take place without support, and we are extremely grateful to all of the sponsors who have made AM18 possible.

Luanne Freund, PhD
Associate Professor & Director
University of British Columbia iSchool

TABLE OF CONTENTS

PAPERS

TABLE OF CONTENTS

TABLE OF CONTENTS

TABLE OF CONTENTS

TABLE OF CONTENTS ▶

PANELS

TABLE OF CONTENTS

TABLE OF CONTENTS

VISUAL PRESENTATIONS

TABLE OF CONTENTS

TABLE OF CONTENTS

TABLE OF CONTENTS

TABLE OF CONTENTS

TABLE OF CONTENTS

TABLE OF CONTENTS ▶

REVIEWERS

Our heartfelt thanks to all of the reviewers who gave their time and talents to ensuring the exceptional quality of this year's presentations. Those reviewers who were voted by the Planning Committee as **Top Reviewers** are indicated with an asterisk.

June Abbas, University of Oklahoma, USA
Muhammad Abdul-Mageed, University of British Columbia, Canada
Denice Adkins, University of Missouri, USA
Naresh Kumar Agarwal, Simmons College, USA
Noa Aharony, Bar-Ilan University, Israel
Robert Allen, Yonsei University, Republic of Korea
Kanwal Ameen, University of the Punjab, Pakistan
Jack Andersen, University of Copenhagen, Denmark
Tatjana Aparac, University of Zadar, Croatia
Richard Arias-Hernandez, University of British Columbia, Canada
Diana Ascher, University of California, Los Angeles, USA
Tariq Ashraf, University of Delhi South Campus, India
Shimelis Assefa, University of Denver, USA
Toluwase Victor Asubiaro, University of Western Ontario, Canada
Judit Bar-Ilan, Bar-Ilan University, Israel
Marguerite Barry, University College Dublin, Ireland
David Bawden, City University London, United Kingdom
Denise Bedford, Georgetown University, USA
Gerald Benoit, Simmons College, USA
Dania Bilal, U niversity of Tennessee, USA
Wade Bishop, University of Tennessee, USA
Jenny Bossaller, University of Missouri, USA
Matt Bouchard, University of Toronto, Canada
Leanne Bowler, Pratt Institute, USA
*Cecelia Brown, University of Oklahoma, USA
Yi Bu, Indiana University, USA
Sarah Buchanan, University of Missouri, USA
John Budd, University of Missouri, USA
Julia Bullard, University of British Columbia, Canada
Jacquelyn Burkell, University of Western Ontario, Canada
Gary Burnett, Florida State University, USA
Kathleen Burnett, Florida State University, USA
Sean Burns, University of Kentucky, USA
Joseph Busch, Taxonomy Strategies, USA
Brian Butler, University of Maryland, USA
Tiffany Chao, University of Illinois, USA
Hsin-liang Chen, University of Massachusetts Boston, USA
Sam Chu, University of Hong Kong, Hong Kong
Charles Cole, McGill University, Canada
Kevin Comerford, University of New Mexico, USA
Andrea Copeland, Indiana University at Indianapolis, USA
Edward Corrado, Naval Postgraduate School, USA
Andrew Cox, University of Sheffield, United Kingdom
Amber Cushing, University College Dublin, Ireland
Lyne Da Sylva, Université de Montréal, Canada
Mats Dahlstrom, University of Boras, Sweden
*Keren Dali, University of Alberta, Canada
Shengli Deng, Wuhan University, China
Nic DePaula, University at Albany, SUNY, USA
Ying Ding, Indiana University, USA
Brian Dobreski, Syracuse University, USA

REVIEWERS

Samuel Dodson, University of British Columbia, Canada

Isabelle Dorsch, Heinrich Heine University Düsseldorf, Germany

Philip Doty, University of Texas at Austin, USA

Jennifer Douglas, University of British Columbia, Canada

Virginia Dressler, Kent State University, USA

Tina Du, University of South Australia, Australia

Sanda Erdelez, University of Missouri, USA

Kristin Eschenfelder, University of Wisconsin-Madison, USA

Yuanyuan Feng, Drexel University, USA

Katrina Fenlon, University of Illinois, USA

Pnina Fichman, Indiana University, USA

Erin Fields, University of British Columbia, Canada

*Sean Fitzhugh, U.S. Army Research Laboratory, USA

Ken Fleischmann, University of Texas at Austin, USA

Schubert Foo Shou Boon, Nanyang Technological University, Singapore

Eric Forcier, Swinburne University of Technology, Australia

Melodie Fox, University of Wisconsin-Milwaukee, USA

Rob Fox, University of Notre Dame, USA

Norbert Fuhr, University of Duisburg-Essen, Germany

Henry Gabb, University of Illinois at Urbana-Champaign, USA

Rich Gazan, University of Hawaii, USA

Isha Ghosh, Rutgers University, USA

Twyla Gibson, University of Missouri, USA

Sarah Ann Gilbert, University of British Columbia, Canada

Anne Gilliland, University of California, USA

Dean Giustini, University of British Columbia, Canada

Tim Gorichanaz, Drexel University, USA

Juan Gorraiz, University of Vienna, Austria

Jane Greenberg, Drexel University, USA

Devon Greyson, University of Massachusettes at Amherst

Ekatarina Grguric, McGill University, Canada

Joachim Griesbaum, University of Hildesheim, Germany

Gussun Gunes, Marmara University, Turkey

Jacek Gwizdka, University of Texas at Austin, USA

Jim Hahn, University of Illinois at Urbana-Champaign, USA

Noriko Hara, Indiana University, USA

Jenna Hartel, University of Toronto, Canada

Stefanie Haustein, University of Ottawa, Canada

Blake Hawkins, University of British Columbia, Canada

Caroline Haythornthwaite, Syracuse University, USA

Tamara Heck, University of Southern Queensland, Australia

Donal Heidenblad, University Of Maryland, USA

Bradley Hemminger, University of North Carolina Chapel Hill, USA

Darra Hofman, University of British Columbia, Canada

Mary Horman, Renison University College, Canada

Eva Hourihan Jansen, University of Toronto, Canada

Lynne Howarth, University of Toronto, Canada

TsungMing Hsiao, National Taiwan University, Taiwan

Xiao Hu, University of Hong Kong, Hong Kong

Mu-hsuan Huang, National Taiwan University, Taiwan

REVIEWERS

Isto Huvila, Uppsala University, Sweden
*Aylin Ilhan, Heinrich Heine University, Germany
Md Anwarul Islam, University of Dhaka, Bangladesh
Jenna Jacobson, University of Toronto, Canada
Jim Jansen, Qatar Computing Research Institute, Quatar
Cary K. Jim, University of North Texas, USA
Kyle M. L. Jones, Indiana University-Indianapolis (IUPUI), USA
Boryung Ju, Louisiana State University, USA
Charles-Antoine Julien, McGill University, Canada
Amir Karami, University of South Carolina, USA
Diane Kelly, University of Tennessee, USA
Kyung-Sun Kim, University of Wisconsin-Madison, USA
Youngseek Kim, University of Kentucky, USA
Vanessa Lynn Kitzie, University of South Carolina, USA
Frauke Kling, Heinrich-Heine-University Düsseldorf, Germany
Emily Knox, University of Illinois at Urbana-Champaign, USA
Rick Kopak, University of British Columbia, Canada
Pei-Yi Kuo, University of Michigan, USA
Barbara Kwasnik, Syracuse University, USA
Kathryn La Barre, University of Illinois, USA
Vincent Lariviere, Université de Montréal, Canada
Jin Ha Lee, University of Washington, USA
Victoria Lemieux, University of British Columbia, Canada
Noah Lenstra, University of North Carolina at Greensboro, USA
Dirk Lewandowski, Hamburg University of Applied Sciences, Germany
Ping Li, Queens College, City University of New York, USA
Zack Lischer-Katz, University of Oklahoma, USA
Ying-Hsang Liu, Charles Sturt University, Australia
Irene Lopatovska, Pratt Institute, USA
Kun Lu, University of Oklahoma, USA
Pablo Lucas, University College Dublin, Ireland
Anna Lundh, Curtin University, Australia
Lai Ma, University College Dublin, Ireland
Millicent Mabi, University of British Columbia, Canada
Stephann Makri, City University London, United Kingdom
Thomas Mandl, University of Hildesheim, Germany
Zinaida Manžuch, Vilnius University, Lithuania
Laura Marcial, RTI International, USA
Betsy Martens, University of Oklahoma, USA
*Konstantina Martzoukou, Robert Gordon University, United Kingdom
*Matt Mayernik, National Center for Atmospheric Research (NCAR), USA
Philipp Mayr, GESIS - Leibniz Institute for the Social Sciences, Germany
Dana Mckay, University of Melbourne, Australia
Shane McLoughlin, Maynooth University, Ireland
David McMenemy, University of Strathclyde, United Kingdom
Bharat Mehra, University of Tennessee, USA
David Melero-Fuentes, Universidad Católica de Valencia San Vicente Mártir, Spain
Eric Meyer, University of Oxford, United Kingdom
*Eric Matthew Meyers, University of British Columbia, Canada
Lyndsey Middleton, Edinburgh Napier University, United Kingdom
Shawne Miksa, University of North Texas, USA
A.J. Million, University of Michigan, USA
Stasa Milojevic, Indiana University Bloomington, USA

REVIEWERS

Lorri Mon, Florida State University, USA
Philippe Mongeon, Leiden University, Netherlands
Javed Mostafa, University of North Carolina, USA
Heather Moulaison, University of Missouri, USA
Angela Murillo, Indiana University - Purdue University Indianapolis, USA
Jinfang Niu, University of South Florida, USA
Lorraine Normore, Normore Reseach Group, USA
Heather O'Brien, University of British Columbia, Canada
Melissa G. Ocepek, University of Illinois, USA
Fatih Oguz, University of North Carolina at Greensboro, USA
Tami Oliphant, University of Alberta, Canada
Shannon Oltmann, University of Kentucky, USA
Peter Organisciak, University of Illinois at Urbana-Champaign, USA
Tuulevi Ovaska, University of Eastern Finland, Finland
Anindita Paul, Indian Institute of Management Kozhikode, India
Isabella Peters, ZBW Leibniz Information Centre for Economics, Germany
Vivien Petras, Humboldt-Universität zu Berlin, Germany
Heather Pfeiffer, TRADOC Analysis Center, TRAC-WSMR, USA
Christina Pikas, Johns Hopkins University Applied Physics Laboratory, USA
Sarah Polkinghorne, University of Alberta, Canada
Angela Pollak, University of Alberta, Canada
Devendra Potnis, University of Tennessee at Knoxville, USA
Muhammad Qayyum, Charles Sturt University, Australia
Anabel Quan-Haase, Western University, Canada
Marie Radford, Rutgers University, USA
Muhammad Rafiq, University of the Punjab, Lahore, India
Diane Rasmussen Pennington, University of Strathclyde, United Kingdom
Edie Rasmussen, University of British Columbia, Canada
Soo Young Rieh, University of Michigan, USA
Marc Rittberger, DIPF - Deutsches Institut für Pädagogische Forschung, Germany
Michelle Rogers, Drexel, USA
Abebe Rorissa, University at Albany, State University of New York, USA
Howard Rosenbaum, Indiana University, USA
Ellen Rubenstein, University of Oklahoma, USA
Steve Sawyer, Syracuse University, USA
Christian Schloegl, University of Graz, Austria
Paul Scifleet, Swinburne University of Technology, Australia
Michael Seadle, Humboldt-Universität zu Berlin, Germany
Aravind Sesagiri Raamkumar, Nanyang Technological University, Singapore
Saguna Shankar, University of British Columbia, Canada
Ryan Shaw, University of North Carolina at Chapel Hill, USA
Patrick Shih, Indiana University Bloomington, USA
Ali Shiri, University of Alberta, Canada
Elisabeth Shook, Vanderbilt University, USA
Vivek Singh, Rutgers University, USA
Laura Skouvig, University of Copenhagen, Denmark
Richard Smiraglia, University of Wisconsin Milwaukee, USA
Dagobert Soergel, University at Buffalo, USA
Xiaoxuan Song, Peking University, China
Emma Spiro, University of Washington, USA

REVIEWERS

*Beth St. Jean, University of Maryland, USA
Suzanne Stauffer, Louisiana State University, USA
Marielle St-Germain, Université de Montréal, Canada
Wolfgang Stock, Heinrich Heine University Düsseldorf, Germany
Emma Stuart, University of Wolverhampton, United Kingdom
Besiki Stvilia, Florida State University, USA
Shigeo Sugimoto, University of Tsukuba, Japan
Honglei Sun, Nanjing University, China
Sue Yeon Syn, Catholic University of America, USA
Muh-Chyun Tang, National Taiwan University, Taiwan
Rong Tang, Simmons College, USA
Natalie Taylor, University of South Florida, USA
Joseph Tennis, University of Washington, USA
Andrea Karoline Thomer, University of Michigan, USA
Emma Tonkin, King's College, London, United Kingdom
Yasar Tonta, Hacettepe University, Turkey
Sandra Toze, Dalhousie University, Canada
Tien-I Tsai, National Taiwan University, Taiwan
Giannis Tsakonas, Library & Information Center, University of Patras, Greece
Kristine Unsworth, Stockton University, USA
Christine Urquhart, Aberystwyth University, United Kingdom
Olga Vechtomova, University of Waterloo, Canada
Diane Velasquez, University of South Australia, Australia
Andre Vellino, University of Ottawa, Canada
Sirje Virkus, Tallinn University, Estonia
Nina Wacholder, Rutgers University, USA
Peiling Wang, University of Tennessee, USA
Julian Warner, Queen's University Belfast, United Kingdom
Nicholas Weber, University of Washington, USA
Rosina Weber, Drexel University, USA
Rachel Williams, Simmons College, USA
Rebekah Willson, University of Strathclyde, United Kingdom
Christine T. Wolf, IBM Research, Almaden, USA
Christian Wolff, University of Regensburg, Germany
Dietmar Wolfram, University of Wisconsin Milwaukee, USA
Christa Womser-Hacker, University of Hildesheim, Germany
*Adam Worrall, University of Alberta, Canada
Shuheng Wu, Queens College, City University of New York, USA
Yejun Wu, Louisiana State University, USA
Judith Wusteman, University College Dublin, Ireland
Iris Xie, Univeristy of Wisconsin-Milwaukee, USA
Erjia Yan, Drexel University, USA
Kwan Yi, Eastern Kentucky University, USA
Ayoung Yoon, Indiana University Indianapolis (IUPUI), USA
Cindy Yu, University of Southern Mississippi, USA
Xiajun Yuan, University of Albany, SUNY, USA
Md Hassan Zamir, Dominican University, USA
Yi Zhang, University of Technology Sydney, Australia
Quan Zhou, Nanyang Technological University, Singapore
Xiaohua Zhu, University of Tennessee, USA
Maja Zumer, University of Ljubljana, Slovenia

Ascertaining the Place of Library & Information Science in Knowledge Management Research

Naresh Kumar Agarwal
Simmons School of Library & Information Science, USA.
agarwal@simmons.edu

Md. Anwarul Islam
University of Dhaka, Bangladesh
anwar@du.ac.bd

ABSTRACT

In the past few years, many researchers and practitioners have shown the value of applying knowledge management (KM) in libraries and other information settings – so as to serve the patron better and to innovate services. However, it is unclear to what extent has mainstream KM literature embraced LIS research as a domain within KM. In this research, we seek to ascertain the place of the LIS field in KM journals by analysing what the top KM journals – as identified by Google Scholar – have published on LIS in the last two decades since the year 2000. We analysed the publication trends, and the distribution of these articles by LIS-related terms used, region/country and information setting type. We also identified the top-cited LIS articles from within these and their coverage in different journals and in different years. 83 LIS-related articles were found within the 4601 research articles published in top KM journals. Only 1.8% of the KM articles were LIS-related. By showing the relatively low coverage of LIS within KM research, the study demonstrates that LIS researchers/practitioners need to do more to be recognized as an important area within KM. KM journals can also enable greater synergies with LIS for mutual benefit.

KEYWORDS

Knowledge management, LIS, KM in information settings, LIS in KM research, publishing trends in KM literature

INTRODUCTION

Over the last two decades, Knowledge Management (KM) has been widely accepted in many organizations. KM is a process adopted by organizations – both for-profit and non-profit – to address challenges, increase efficiency and effectiveness, and to achieve organizational goals, by applying various strategies, technologies, and tools in the business process (Abell & Oxbrow, 2001), and by harnessing the knowledge potential of its employees and other resources. Nonaka &Takeuchi (1995) define KM as the capability of "a company or any other organization…to create new knowledge, disseminate it throughout the organization, and embody it in products, services and systems" (p. 3). After examining over hundred definitions, Dalkir (2017) identified that KM is a multidisciplinary field – including organizational science, computer science, library and information science (LIS), education, business and many more. From the business perspective, KM is a business activity; from the cognitive science perspective, knowledge refers to insights and understanding; and from the process/technology perspective, information is turned into actionable knowledge (Dalkir, 2017). Wen (2005) identified KM's emergence first in the business sector, where it received most attention, then in higher education, and now in library management.

In the last few years, there has been an increasing call for the adoption of KM in libraries and other information settings which are primarily non-profit and service-oriented in nature, as opposed to business that are for-profit organizations. This is because the value proposition of KM in helping achieve the goals of the business, can also apply to information settings, where the goals is to provide better and innovative services to the patron, and to also increase the well-being and retention of its employees. Many researchers in the past two decades (e.g. Abell and Oxbrow, 2001; Southon and Todd, 2001; Sarrafzadeh, 2008; Agarwal and Islam, 2014; Islam, Agarwal and Ikeda, 2015) have argued for greater involvement of LIS practitioners in KM. Many scholars, through different scholarly activities, have argued for involving KM in libraries, in LIS education, and for improving services and operations. Some of these arguments are found in dissertations e.g. the implications of KM for LIS professions (Sarrafzadeh, 2008); when existing and emerging disciplines meet: LIS versus KM (Roknuzzaman, 2009); e-learning in academia from the viewpoint of KM: a case study of LIS schools (Islam, 2012); and Knowledge Management for Innovation in Academic Library Services (Islam, 2016). Most other arguments have been made in published journal articles, where researchers strongly advocated the adoption of KM in libraries. Examples of recent articles where the researchers gathered empirical data to support their arguments include: effect of KM and service innovation in academic libraries (Islam, Agarwal and Ikeda, 2017); are academic libraries ready for knowledge management? (Marouf, 2017); KM practices in some selected higher educational libraries in Europe (Balagué, Düren and Saarti, 2016) and a conceptual model of open access institutional repository in Indonesia academic libraries: viewed from the KM perspective (Farida, *et.al.*, 2015). In a panel discussion at the 2016 Annual Meeting of the Association for Information Science & Technology (ASIS&T), Dalkir, Bedord & Miller (2015) discussed the need for bridging research and practice on KM in LIS education.

As seen from the studies above, while many LIS researchers, academics and professionals are calling for KM in libraries and other information settings, and a substantial amount of KM-related work is published each year in LIS journals, there are no studies till date looking at the extent to which mainstream KM literature (which focuses on business and interdisciplinary areas) has embraced LIS and LIS-centered studies. In other words, while we find research in recent years in 'KM in LIS', we don't see any work on 'LIS in KM'. While most recent work has been about why libraries and LIS should adopt KM, we are looking at this differently. To what extent has KM accepted libraries and LIS? This study is first step in seeking answers to this.

Thus, in this study, we were interested in this overarching research question: *What is the place of LIS in KM research?* In order to answer this question, we looked a few specific research questions: RQ1) *How many LIS-related papers have been published in the top KM journals since the year 2000? What is the percentage of LIS articles among the overall KM articles from different disciplines published in this period?;* RQ2) *What are the publishing trends of these LIS-related articles a) by year; and b) by journal?;* RQ3) *Which areas of LIS research are gaining importance in these journals? In the LIS-related articles in top journals during this period, what are the a) LIS-related terms used; b) regions/countries investigated; c) information setting/library type investigated; and d) type of research methods used?;*RQ4) *Which are the top-cited articles within the identified LIS-related articles in top KM journals during this period? What is the coverage of these top-cited articles in a) different journals, and in b) different years? Which are the 5 top-ranked articles based on number of citations and average citations per year?*

The rest of the article is organized as follows: We provide a brief literature review. The other sections are on the methodology we followed, the data analysis and findings, discussion and implications, conclusions, limitations, and future work.

LITERATURE REVIEW

A number of prior researchers have reviewed the KM published literature for different purposes. These researchers have largely focused on bibliometric studies to trace the trends and themes of KM research. Yu (2009) examined the status of contemporary KM studies in the prior decade before 2009 with citation and co-citation analysis. The study identified the most important publications and the most influential scholars and journals in KM, and then mapped the major research paradigms in KM research. It aimed to profile the invisible network of knowledge production in KM. Serenko, *et.al.* (2010) conducted a scientometric analysis of KM and intellectual capital (IC) literature in 11 major KM and IC peer reviewed journals and identified KM/IC as a different scientific field. Using citation and co-citation analysis, Ma & Yu (2010) looked at the research trends of current KM studies and mapped the knowledge flows, relationships and evolution of KM research. Based on data from Web of Science, Sedighi & Jalalimanesh (2014) mapped the research trends of KM and found that KM has expanded dynamically during the 2004-2010 period. Serenko & Dumay (2015) carried out a KM research citation analysis to examine KM research trends as rising, steady or deteriorating. They found a bimodal citation distribution peak and an increase in the citations for all KM research. They also noted that more citations are affected by Google Scholar. Taking a sample of 500 articles, Akhavan *et.al.* (2016) carried out bibliometric and text mining analyses to study the major trends in KM literature from 1980 to 2014. They found that the most cited articles of KM are from the United States and the United Kingdom. The highest numbers of articles were published in 2009, and the highest number of citations was in 2012.

While all these studies described above analysed KM literature, they were all outside the LIS area. Lowry (2013) emphasized that analysis of research trends helps to identify gaps in the existing literature for selecting potential areas for future research. Examining the LIS-research trends in KM literature will help us ascertain where LIS-within-KM is now and get some insight into where it might be heading. Analysing these publishing trends will help us get some sense of the place LIS researchers are making in the KM field. This study will contribute to the KM and LIS fields from the bibliometric research perspective as well.

METHODOLOGY

Our primary aim in this research was to determine the number of LIS papers published in the 21st century in the top KM journals. To determine the top journals, we used the list of the top 20 publications matching knowledge management ranked by Google Scholar (2018). Of these, we excluded those that pertained to conference proceedings and were not journals. We excluded one journal (KMAE, ranked 6), as it was specific to a particular field and was not a general KM journal. We excluded one publication (ranked 20) as the articles were not in English. This left us with a list of top 10 journals among the 20 top publications identified by Google Scholar (see Table 1). The ten identified journals are all peer-reviewed publications dedicated to the exchange of the latest academic research and practical information on all aspects of managing knowledge in organizations. The Journal of Knowledge Management is the top-ranked in the KM field with a 2016 Impact Factor of 2.053 and a 5-year Impact Factor (2016) of 3.293 (JKM, 2018). Table 1 lists the ranking, as well as the h5-index and h5-median (productivity and citation metrics developed by Google Scholar) of these journals. H5-index is the h-index for articles published in the last 5 complete years. It is the largest number h such that h articles published in the last 5 years have at least h citations each (Journal-level impact, 2018). Thus, e.g., for JKM, the h5 index is 46. It is the largest number such that 46 articles published in the last 5 years have at least 46 citations each. H5-median is based on h5-index, but instead measures the median (or middle) value of citations for the h number of citations (Journal-level impact, 2018). For JKM, with an h5-index of 46 and h5-median of 59 means that, of 46 articles with 46 or more citations, the median of those citation values is 59.

Rank	Journal name	h5-index	h5-median	Remarks
1	Journal of Knowledge Management (JKM)	46	59	
2	ACM International Conference on Information and Knowledge Management	43	61	excluded
3	Knowledge Management Research & Practice (KMRP)	18	26	
4	Knowledge Engineering and Management by the Masses (EKAW)	17	33	excluded
5	VINE: The journal of information and knowledge management systems	16	25	
6	Knowledge and Management of Aquatic Ecosystems (KMAE)	16	20	excluded
7	Knowledge and Process Management (KPM)	15	25	
8	International Journal of Data Mining & Knowledge Management Process (IJDKP)	14	23	
9	Knowledge Management & E-Learning: An International Journal (KM&EL)	14	23	
10	International Conference on Information Processing and Management of Uncertainty in Knowledge-Based Systems	13	19	excluded
11	Electronic Journal of Knowledge Management (EJKM)	12	29	
12	Journal of Knowledge Management, Economics and Information Technology (JKMEIT)	10	13	
13	Journal of Information & Knowledge Management (JIKM)	9	14	
14	International Conference on Knowledge Management in Organizations (KMO)	8	10	excluded
15	International Conference on Knowledge Management and Information Sharing	8	9	excluded
16	Knowledge Science, Engineering and Management	7	10	excluded
17	Management Dynamics in the Knowledge Economy (MDKE)	7	10	
18	International Conference on Futuristic Trends on Computational Analysis and Knowledge Management	6	7	excluded
19	International Conference on Software, Knowledge, Information Management and Applications	6	6	excluded
20	Studies & Proceedings Polish Association for Knowledge Management	5	6	excluded

Table 1. Top ten Knowledge Management journals included in the study from the twenty ranked by Google Scholar

Table 2 provides more information on the top-10 KM journals. It lists the publisher, country, its frequency of publishing, and the reputed databases indexing the journal. EBSCO, SCOPUS, SSCI (Social Science Citation Index), ProQuest etc. are leading providers that index and abstract journals. DOAJ is the Directory of Open Access Journals.

Rank	Journal	Publisher (country)	Frequency	Indexed by
1	JKM	Emerald Insight (UK)	Quarterly	EBSCO, SCOPUS, SSCI (2016 impact factor 2.053)
3	KMRP	Palgrave Macmillan (UK)	Quarterly	SCOPUS, SSCI (2016 impact factor 1.013)
5	VINE	Emerald Insight (UK)	Quarterly	SCOPUS
7	KPM	Wiley Online Library (USA)	Quarterly	SCOPUS, ProQuest
8	IJDKP	AIRCC Publishing Corporation (India)	Bi-monthly	EBSCO, ProQuest
9	KM&EL	Academic Conferences & Publishing (UK)	Quarterly	SCOPUS, DOAJ
11	EJKM	The University of Hong Kong (Hong Kong)	Continuous	EBSCO, DOAJ
12	JKMEIT	Scientific Papers Publishing (Romania)	Quarterly	DOAJ
13	JIKM	World Scientific (Singapore)	Quarterly	Scopus, Google Scholar
17	MDKE	The National University of Political Studies and Public Administration (Romania)	Quarterly	EBSCO, DOAJ, ProQuest

Table 2. Rank, publisher, frequency and indexing database for top ten Knowledge Management journals

From the journals identified, we accessed the individual issues of each journal from the years 2000 – 2018. For each issue, we scanned the article title looking for any relationship with 'library and information science' (e.g. LIS, library, archives, LIS education, academic libraries, digital libraries, public libraries, information centers, reference service, information seeking behavior, etc.) or any relationship with LIS even if the term was not specifically mentioned. For further clarification to look for this relationship, we read the abstracts of specific articles. Also see Table 5.

From each LIS-related article identified, we entered its bibliographic information, number of times it was cited (as per Google Scholar), its objectives and research questions, findings, type of research method used, region, type of information setting for the study, and main keywords from the study. We compiled all this information in an Excel spreadsheet for all articles that we identified. We carried out the work of journal selection, combing of all articles, and analysis of identified LIS-related articles over a four-month period from December 2017 to March 2018.

DATA ANALYSIS AND FINDINGS

When analyzing the gathered data from the 83 LIS-related articles from top ten KM journals over an 18-year period, we found several interesting trends addressing the four research questions. We discuss the findings for each question below.

RQ1) How many LIS-related papers have been published in the top KM journals since the year 2000? What is the percentage of LIS articles among the overall KM articles from different disciplines published in this period?

Table 3 below shows the number of LIS-related articles published over the past 18 years in the top 10 KM journals. The years are arranged in the reverse chronological order (starting from most recent). Each row shows the total number of articles published by the KM journal per year, and the total number of LIS-related articles (within brackets) published by that journal that year. The shaded column (second from left) shows the total number of articles published by each journal from 2000-2018, and the LIS-related articles published by that journal during the same period. The shaded row at the bottom shows the total number of KM articles published each year across the top 10 journals, and the LIS-related articles published that year across all those journals. In total, we found that of the 4,601 articles published by the top 10 KM journals from 2000-2018, 83 were LIS-related.

Name of journal ↓ Year →	Tot. per jrnl	'18	'17	'16	'15	'14	'13	'12	'11	'10	'09	'08	'07	'06	'05	'04	'03	'02	'01	'00
JKM	1058 (3)	0	84	70	68 (2)	64	56	57	58	58	73	70	66	62	59 (1)	57	51	40	33	32
KMRP	571 (1)	0	49	52	40	41	39	37	37	35	41	44	39 (1)	40	33	28	16	0	0	0
VINE	585 (54)	8	29	28	27 (1)	28 (2)	23 (1)	23 (3)	25 (1)	24 (1)	22	41	42 (2)	42	38 (3)	28 (9)	26 (5)	29 (3)	57 (16)	45 (7)
KPM	430 (2)	6 (1)	23	24	27	27 (1)	25	20	21	18	16	25	27	26	24	23	23	23	23	29
IJDKP	173 (0)	1	8	23	22	24	50	29	16	0	0	0	0	0	0	0	0	0	0	0
KM&EL	321 (1)	0	32 (1)	39	44	32	34	42	45	32	21	0	0	0	0	0	0	0	0	0
EJKM	411 (2)	0	22	23 (1)	23	28	32	24	32	31 (1)	50	16	55	22	13	12	28	0	0	0
JKMEIT	381 (0)	0	0	26	37	54	71	83	110	0	0	0	0	0	0	0	0	0	0	0
JIKM	512 (20)	0	41 (2)	46 (2)	36 (2)	37 (4)	41 (5)	31	30	30 (1)	28	28 (1)	28	30	26 (1)	28	33 (2)	19	0	0
MDKE	159 (0)	0	33	32	36	29	29	0	0	0	0	0	0	0	0	0	0	0	0	0
Total per year	**4601 (83)**	15 (1)	321 (3)	363 (3)	360 (5)	364 (7)	400 (6)	346 (3)	374 (1)	228 (3)	251 (0)	224 (1)	257 (3)	222 (0)	193 (5)	176 (9)	177 (7)	111 (3)	113 (16)	106 (7)

Table 3. Total number of articles publisher per year per journal, and LIS-related articles within those (2000-2018)

Name of journal /Year	% per jrnl	'18	'17	'16	'15	'14	'13	'12	'11	'10	'09	'08	'07	'06	'05	'04	'03	'02	'01	'00
JKM	0.284				2.94										1.69					
KMRP	0.002												2.56							
VINE	9.231				3.70	7.14	4.35	13.04	4.00	4.17			4.76		7.89	32.14	19.23	10.34	28.07	15.56
KPM	0.465	16.67				3.70														
IJDKP	0.000																			
KM&EL	0.312		3.13																	
EJKM	0.487			4.35						3.23										
JKMEIT	0.000																			
JIKM	3.906		4.88	4.35	5.56	10.81	12.20			3.33		3.57			3.85		6.06			
MDKE	0.000																			
% per year	**1.804**	6.67	0.93	0.83	1.39	1.92	1.50	0.87	0.27	1.32	0	0.45	1.17	0	2.59	5.11	3.95	2.7	14.16	6.60

Table 4. Percentage of LIS-related articles among KM articles in top 10 KM journals (2000-2018)

Table 4 shows the percentage of LIS-related articles published among all KM articles in top KM journals since the year 2000. Each cell of the table represents a particular journal in a given year. Only those cells where LIS-related articles were published in a certain year for that journal are populated. The values in those cells represent the percentage of LIS-related articles published that year in that journal with respect to the total number of KM articles published that year by that journal. For example, in 2015, 2.94% of the articles published in the Journal of Knowledge Management (JKM) were LIS-related. In total, in the last 18 years, 1.8% of the KM articles were LIS-related.

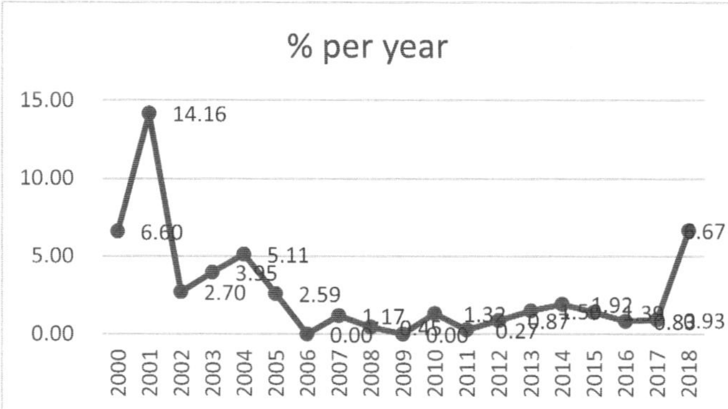

Figure 1. Percentage of LIS-related articles (among all KM articles) per year across the top-10 KM journals

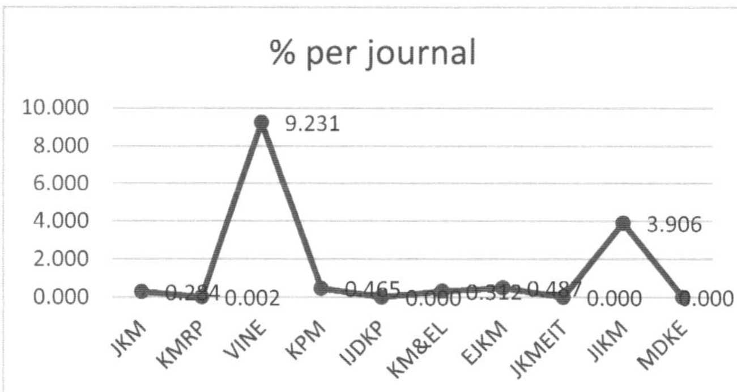

Figure 2. Percentage of LIS-related articles (among all KM articles) per journal for 2000-2018

RQ2) What are the publishing trends of these LIS-related articles a) by year; and b) by journal?

The last row in Table 4 shows the percentage of LIS-related articles published per year across the top-ten KM journals (see Figure 1). From the figure, we can see that the year 2001 was the most productive in terms of the place of LIS in KM research, with 14.16 percent of all KM articles published across journals being LIS-related. From Table 4, we can see that this contribution was by VINE, when it accepted 16 LIS-articles for publication that year out of its total of 57 KM articles that it published that year.

Figure 2 shows the publishing trends of LIS-related articles in KM journals per journal during the period from 2000-2018. The first shaded column in Table 4 shows the percentage of LIS-related articles published by each journal from 2000 – 2018. From Figure 2, we can see that VINE: The journal of information and knowledge management systems published the most number of articles in the LIS area (9.231%) during the eighteen-year period from 2000-2018, while in the top KM journal 'Journal of Knowledge Management', only 0.284% of the articles were LIS-related during the same period.

RQ3) Which areas of LIS research are gaining importance in these journals? In the LIS-related articles in top journals during this period, what are the a) LIS-related terms used; b) regions/countries investigated; c) information setting/library type investigated; and d) type of research methods used?

Table 5 shows the LIS-related terms found in the top 10 KM journal article titles and/or abstracts from 2000-2018. Where there were related terms of a particular category, the frequency of these is listed in brackets in the first column of the table. Of the 81 unique LIS-related articles identified, the total frequency of LIS-related terms was 165 (a particular article was found to touch-upon 1-3 terms listed in the table).

LIS terms appearing in KM journal articles	Frequency
library types – university / academic (28); special (5); national (4); public (1); hybrid (1)	39
setting – library (21); archives (3)	24
technology – library management system / information system (12); social media / Internet (3); new technology (3); content management (2); QR codes (1); taxonomy (1)	22
digital library / digital repository / online portal	20
library / information service	18
collections – e-book / e-journal (5); special collections (5); print and electronic resources (3)	13
employees – training and learning (5); systems librarian (3); library recruitment (2); information professionals (1)	11
LIS / LIS education	7
user –library user (5); use (2)	7
catalog / bibliographic records / OPAC	4
Total	165

Table 5. LIS-related terms identified in the KM journal articles (2000 – 2018)

Table 6 lists the distribution of LIS articles in KM journals by regions/countries, by information setting/library type and by the type of research method used. In the articles where regions/countries were identified, the most are from the UK, followed by the USA. Slightly more than half (42 of 83) articles pertained to academic libraries within a university. From the table, we can see that majority of LIS studies in KM journals were either reviews of the literature, opinion papers or theoretical papers. 18 of the 83 studies described surveys that were carried out.

Region/country	region/country not applicable (30); The UK (15); USA (8); Global (6); Bangladesh (3); Europe (2); Kuwait (2); Trinidad & Tobago, Croatia, RSA, Netherland, Scotland, Nordic, Oman, Western, Pakistan, North America, Iran, Nigeria, India, South Africa, Canada, Qatar and Singapore (1) for each.
Information setting type	academic library (42); special library (5); public library (3); national library (5); other information setting (28)
Research method type	literature review / opinion paper / theoretical paper (56); survey (18); interviews / case study (6); mixed methods (3)

Table 6. LIS articles in KM journals– distribution by a) region/country, b) information setting/library type and c) research method type (N = 83)

RQ4) Which are the top-cited articles within the identified LIS-related articles in top KM journals during this period? What is the coverage of these top-cited articles in a) different journals, and in b) different years? Which are the 5 top-ranked articles based on number of citations and average citations per year?

Table 7 below lists the top cited LIS-related articles published in KM journals since the year 2000. Only those articles with at least 10 citations each were included in the table, leading to a total of 22 articles (out of the overall total of 83 articles identified). The second column in the table shows the number of citations (as per Google Scholar) received till date for each of these articles. The third column shows the ranking of these articles (from 1 to 22) based on the total number of citations received (the top five ranks are shaded). However, some articles received citations in many years, while others were highly cited within a shorter period. To take this into consideration, the fourth column lists the year since publication (2018 – the year of publication). The fifth column shows the average citations received by each article per year (no. of citations / years since publication). The last column shows the rank received by the article (from 1 to 22) based on the average citations per year (the top five ranks are shaded). An overall ranking was then calculated based on the average of these two rankings (columns 3 and 6). This was used to arrive at the list of the most influential LIS articles in KM journals (from 2000-2018). The number at the start of the first column shows this ranking, and articles are arranged in order of influence, with the most influential articles listed on top. A few ranks (3, 6, 11, 14, 16, and 21) are repeated when they had the same overall ranking. The top five most influential articles are shaded.

Overall rank / Article	No. of citations	Rank based on no. of citations	Year since publication	Average citations per year	Rank based on average citations per year
1. Rah, Gul, & Ashraf Wani (2010)	27	**3**	8	3.38	**4**
2. Agarwal & Islam (2014)	20	7	4	5.00	**1**
3. Oltmans & Van Wijngaarden (2004)	33	**1**	14	2.36	9
3. Daneshgar & Bosanquet (2010)	25	**4**	8	3.13	6
5. Islam & Ikeda (2014)	17	11	4	4.25	**3**
6. Ebenezer (2002)	28	**2**	16	1.75	13
6. Daneshgar & Parirokh (2007)	23	**5**	11	2.09	10
8. De Sarkar (2012)	18	10	6	3.00	7
9. Agarwal & Islam (2015)	14	17	3	4.67	**2**
10. Forcier, Rathi, & Given (2013)	16	15	5	3.20	**5**
11. Cox (2003)	22	6	15	1.47	15
11. Roknuzzaman & Umemoto (2008)	19	9	10	1.90	12
13. In□s Cordeiro & de Carvalho (2002)	19	8	16	1.19	16
14. Doctor (2007)	17	12	11	1.55	14
14. Shiri & Rathi (2013)	14	18	5	2.80	8
16. Oliver (2003)	17	13	15	1.13	18
16. De Jager (2004)	16	14	14	1.14	17
18. Jain (2013)	10	22	5	2.00	11
19. Caplan (2004)	15	16	14	1.07	19
20. Malhan & Rao (2005)	13	19	13	1.00	20
21. Stubbings (2003)	11	20	15	0.73	22
21. Warren & Alsmeyer (2005)	10	21	13	0.77	21

Table 7. Top-ranked LIS articles – with 10 or more citations (from across top 10 KM journals, 2000-2018)

The 22 articles listed in Table 7 were analyzed for the journals in which they were published, and the years in which these articles were published (see Table 8). We found that VINE: The journal of information and knowledge management systems published most of these top-cited LIS-articles. Of these 22 top-cited articles, 3 were published in 2013, and 3 each in 2003-04.

	Name of journals (no. of top-cited articles)
Journals (no. of articles)	VINE (13); JIKM (6); KMRP(1); EJKM (1); JKM (1)
Years (no. of articles)	2013(3); 2004(3); 2003(3); 2014(2); 2010(2); 2007(2); 2005(2); 2002(2); 2015(1); 2012(1); 2008(1)

Table 8. Coverage of top-cited articles – in different journals and in different years (n = 22)

In Table 7, we identified the 5 top-ranked LIS articles in KM journals published between 2000 and 2018 based on the number of citations and average citations per year. In Table 9, further details on these top articles are listed – the region or country where the study population was drawn from, the information setting or library type for the particular research, primary stakeholder that the study focuses on, the methodology used in the study, and keywords describing the study.

Rank	Article	Region/ country	Information setting type	Primary stakeholder	Method	Keywords
1	Rah, Gul, & Ashraf Wani (2010)	not applicable	academic library	users	survey	WWW, university libraries, artificial intelligence, KM
2	Agarwal & Islam (2014)	not applicable	library in general	employees	theory	libraries, technology acceptance model, diffusion of innovation, KM cycle, KM tools, technologies
3	Oltmans & Van Wijngaarden (2004)	Netherlands	national library	employees	theory	digital storage, electronic media, libraries, archives, the Netherlands
3	Daneshar & Bosanquet (2010)	Australia	academic library	users	interview	knowledge taxonomy, customer KM, KM in library, evaluation of customer knowledge, innovative services, academic libraries
5	Islam & Ikeda (2014)	Developing countries	academic library	employees	interview	KM, library services, digital library, online services, WWW

Table 9. Five top-ranked LIS-related articles in KM journals (2000-2018)

DISCUSSION AND IMPLICATIONS

We set out to ascertain the place of LIS as a field in KM research. In terms of influence, we see that LIS still has a long way to go to make itself known in the KM field, as less than 2% of all research in KM is LIS-related. Of the more than 4,500 articles KM articles published in top journals in the past two decades, only 83 of these were LIS-related. While the percentage of LIS research in KM journals showed a spike in the year 2001 (more than 14%), and relatively high levels (above 5%) in 2000, 2005 and in 2018, it has remained quite low overall. A big reason for this might be that KM is still largely business-and-for profit focused, where a large majority of its audience resides, which might be affecting acceptance rates of LIS-related articles submitted to KM journals. Another reason could be that LIS researchers (even those who are doing KM-related research) are publishing more in LIS journals, and less in KM journals. This could be because LIS-researchers might be wanting to get to their primary LIS audience for more practical usage and citation impact, as opposed to publishing in multidisciplinary KM journals which their audience may not read as much. Of the ten top journals examined, 'VINE: The journal of information and knowledge management systems' and 'the Journal of Information & Knowledge Management (JIKM)' had a larger percentage of LIS-related articles compared to other top KM journals. 9% of the articles in VINE and almost 4% in JIKM were LIS-related. As compared to the other journals (which only had the word 'knowledge' in their names), these two journals had both 'information' and 'knowledge' in their titles. Thus, they might be more accepting of library and information science related research, as compared to the other top KM journals in the list.

An analysis of the LIS-terms identified in the KM journal articles shows that university libraries are the primary focus of KM studies. This might be because of the knowledge-creation culture and research culture in universities, which can be higher than that in other information settings. Getting students as research participants is also easier for researchers, as compared to working people. More articles focused on libraries than on archives, which might reflect their relative number in the real world, as there are more libraries than archives. The terms also reflect that KM is applied for either adopting/innovating new technologies, in providing improved services, and in helping employees in areas of training, learning, recruitment, etc. These provide an insight into the value propositions for KM in libraries and other information settings. While a number of studies applied to libraries in general, the UK and USA had more studies as compared to developing countries. This reflects the relative-level of adoption of KM in the information centers of these countries/regions. This aligns with the overall KM adoption trends (in areas outside of LIS), where the more developed countries have been at the forefront of adopting KM as compared to developing countries. This can be seen from the listing of 100 companies that matter in KM (Haimila, 2018), where most companies in the list are headquartered in developed countries such as the US and the UK. A huge majority of the LIS-related research articles were theoretical and position papers, as a lot of research is still devoted to advocating KM in library settings. Surveys are easier to administer to a large number of people, which could be the reason why more articles involving data gathering have adopted the survey method. This is also the common trend in most studies in LIS, where surveys are the most popular research method (Agarwal, 2018). In terms of citation impact, VINE and JIKM are good avenues for LIS-researchers in the KM area, as these two journals had most of the top-cited articles. Looking at the areas of focus in top 5 most-cited articles shows that adoption of technology tools and innovation in services is a major focus of interest to other researchers. This goes well with the general direction of innovation in library and other information settings as they adapt to changing patron preferences and changes in the external environment.

CONCLUSIONS, LIMITATIONS AND FUTURE WORK

What is the place of one research field within another? This research has determined that LIS accounts for about 2% within the KM field. By showing the relatively low coverage of LIS within KM research, the study demonstrates that LIS researchers and practitioners need to do more to be recognized as an important area within KM. KM journals can also enable ways for greater synergies with LIS, so that both the interdisciplinary fields can benefit mutually from each other. The study has a number of limitations. First, while the study investigated the place of LIS within KM, future research must dwell further into why LIS deserves to have a place within KM, and what are the synergies within the two fields. Second, only Google Scholar was used to determine top journal rankings. Future studies should also consider other databases such as SSCI, Scopus, and Web of Science. Third, within the Google Scholar ranking of KM publications, we excluded conference proceedings. Future research can include these to see if the overall percentage of LIS within KM changes when proceedings are included. Lastly, this research looked at LIS-within-KM. We should also study KM-within-LIS to get a greater sense of the relationship shared between LIS and KM. Future research must examine KM research in top LIS journals, so that we get an overall sense of the LIS-and-KM related research that has been published in the last two decades.

REFERENCES

Abell, A. & Oxbrow, N. (2001). Competing with Knowledge: The Information Professionals in the Knowledge Management Age, London: Library Association Publishing.

Agarwal, N. K., & Islam, M. A. (2015). Knowledge retention and transfer: how libraries manage employees leaving and joining, VINE: Journal of Information and Knowledge Management Systems, 45(2), 150-171.

Agarwal, N. K. (2018). Exploring Context in Information Behavior: Seeker, situation, surroundings, and shared identities. In G. Marchionini (Series Editor) Synthesis Lectures on Information Concepts, Retrieval, and Services. San Rafael, California: Morgan & Claypool Publishers.

Agarwal, N. K., & Islam, M. A (2014). Knowledge management implementation in a library: mapping tools and technologies to phases of the KM cycle, VINE: Journal of Information and Knowledge Management Systems, 44(3), 322-344.

Akhavan, P., Ebrahim, N. A., Fetrati, M. A., & Pezeshkan, A. (2016). Major trends in knowledge management research: a bibliometric study. Scientometrics, 107(3), 1249-1264.

Balagué, N., Düren, P., & Saarti, J. (2016). Comparing the knowledge management practices in selected European higher education libraries, Library Management, 37(4/5), 182-194.

Caplan, P. (2004). Building a digital preservation archive: Tales from the front, VINE: Journal of Information and Knowledge Management Systems, 34(1), 38-42.

Cox, A. (2003). Choosing a library portal system, VINE: Journal of Info. and Knowledge Management Systems, 33(1), 37-41.

Dalkir, K (2017). Knowledge management in theory and practice, MIT: Cambridge.

Dalkir, K. Bedord, D. A & Miller, K. (2015). Knowledge management in LIS education: Bridging research and practice. Proceedings of the Association for Information Science and Technology, 52(1), 1-4.

Daneshgar, F., & Bosanquet, L. (2010). Organizing Customer Knowledge in Academic Libraries. Electronic Journal of Knowledge Management, 8(1), 21-32.

Daneshgar, F., & Parirokh, M. (2007). A knowledge schema for organizational learning in academic libraries, Electronic Journal of Knowledge Management, 5(1), 22-33.

De Jager, K. (2004). Navigators and guides: the value of peer assistance in student use of electronic library facilities, VINE: Journal of Information and Knowledge Management Systems, 34(3), 99-106.

De Sarkar, T. (2012). Introducing podcast in library service: an analytical study, VINE: Journal of Information and Knowledge Management Systems, 42(2), 191-213.

Doctor, G. (2007). Knowledge sharing: developing the digital repository of SIPS, VINE: Journal of Information and Knowledge Management Systems, 37(1), 64-73.

Ebenezer, C. (2002). Trends in integrated library systems, VINE: Journal of Info. and Knowledge Mgmt. Sys., 32(4), 19-45.

Farida, I., Tjakraatmadja, J. H., Firman, A., & Basuki, S. (2015). A conceptual model of Open Access Institutional Repository in Indonesia academic libraries: Viewed from knowledge management perspective, Library Management, 36(1/2), 168-181.

Forcier, E., Rathi, D., & Given, L. M. (2013). Knowledge management and social media: A case study of two public libraries in Canada, Journal of Information and Knowledge Management, 12(04), 1350039.

Google Scholar (2018). Top 20 publications matching knowledge management. Retrieved March 22, 2018 from https://scholar.google.com/citations?hl=en&view_op=search_venues&vq=knowledge+management

Haimila, S. (2018). KMWorld 100 companies that matter in knowledge management 2018. KMWorld, 27(2), March 8, 2018. Retrieved March 22, 2018 from http://www.kmworld.com/Articles/Editorial/Features/KMWorld-100-Companies-That-Matter-in-Knowledge-Management-2017-116508.aspx

Inês Cordeiro, M., & de Carvalho, J. (2002). Web services: what they are and their importance for libraries, VINE: Journal of Information and Knowledge Management Systems, 32(4), 46-62.

Islam, M. A. (2016). Knowledge management for service innovation in academic libraries, Unpublished PhD Dissertation, School of Knowledge Science, Japan Advanced Institute of Science and Technology (JAIST), Japan.

Islam, M. A., Agarwal, N. K. & Ikeda, M. (2015). Knowledge management for service innovation in academic libraries: A qualitative study, Library Management, 36(1/2), 40-57.

Islam, M. A., & Ikeda, M. (2014). Convergence issues of knowledge management in digital libraries: steps towards state-of-the-art digital libraries, VINE: Journal of Information and Knowledge Management Systems, 44(1), 140-159.

Islam, M. A., Agarwal, N. K & Ikeda, M. (2017). Effect of knowledge management on service innovation in academic libraries, IFLA Journal, 43(3), 266-281

Islam, M. S. (2012). An analysis on e-learning in academia from the viewpoint of knowledge management: A case study of library and information science schools, Unpublished PhD Dissertation, School of Knowledge Science, Japan Advanced Institute of Science and Technology, Japan.

Jain, P. (2013). Knowledge management in academic libraries and information centres: A case of university libraries, Journal of Information and Knowledge Management, 12(04), 1350034.

JKM (2018). Journal of Knowledge Management. Emerald Publishing. Retrieved March 22, 2018 from http://www.emeraldgrouppublishing.com/products/journals/journals.htm?id=jkm

Journal-level impact (2018). Scholarly Research Impact Metrics. American University Library. Retrieved March 22, 2018 from https://subjectguides.library.american.edu/c.php?g=175335&p=1154177

Lowry, P. et al. (2013). Evaluating journal quality and the association for information systems senior scholars' journal basket via bibliometric measures: Do expert journal assessments add value?, MIS Quarterly, 37(4), 993-1012.

Ma, Z., & Yu, K. H. (2010). Research paradigms of contemporary knowledge management studies: 1998-2007, Journal of Knowledge Management, 14(2), 175-189.

Malhan, I. V., & Rao, S. (2005). From library management to knowledge management: a conceptual change, Journal of Information and Knowledge Management, 4(04), 269-277.

Marouf, L. (2017). Are academic libraries ready for knowledge management? The Electronic Library, 35(1), 137-151.

Nonaka, I. & Takeuchi, H. (1995), The Knowledge Creating Company: How Japanese Companies Create the Dynamics of Innovation, New York: Oxford University Press.

Oliver, G. (2003). Cultural dimensions of information management, Journal of Info. and Knowledge Mgmt., 2(01), 53-61.

Oltmans, E., & Van Wijngaarden, H. (2004). Digital preservation in practice: the e-Depot at the KoninklijkeBibliotheek. VINE, Journal of Information and Knowledge Management Systems 34(1), 21-26.

Rah, J. A., Gul, S., & Ashraf Wani, Z. (2010). University libraries: step towards a web based knowledge management system, VINE: Journal of Information and Knowledge Management Systems, 40(1), 24-38.

Roknuzzaman, M. (2009). When existing and emerging disciplines meet: Library and information science vs knowledge management. Unpublished PhD Dissertation, School of Knowledge Science, JAIST, Japan.

Roknuzzaman, M., & Umemoto, K. (2008). Knowledge management's relevance to library and information science: an interdisciplinary approach, Journal of Information and Knowledge Management, 7(04), 279-290.

Sarrafzadeh, M. (2008). The implications of knowledge management for the library and information professions, Unpublished PhD Dissertation, School of Business Information Technology, RMIT University, Australia.

Sedighi, M., & Jalalimanesh, A. (2017). Mapping research trends in the field of knowledge management, Malaysian Journal of Library & Information Science, 19(1), 71-85

Serenko, A., & Dumay, J. (2015). Citation classics published in Knowledge Management journals. Part II: studying research trends and discovering the Google Scholar Effect, Journal of Knowledge Management, 19(6), 1335-1355.

Serenko, A., Bontis, N., Booker, L., Sadeddin, K., & Hardie, T. (2010). A scientometric analysis of knowledge management and intellectual capital academic literature (1994-2008), Journal of knowledge management, 14(1), 3-23.

Shiri, A., & Rathi, D. (2013). Twitter content categorization: A public library perspective, Journal of Information and Knowledge Management, 12(04), 1350035.

Southon, G., & Todd, R. (2001). Library and information professionals and knowledge management: conceptions, challenges and conflicts, The Australian Library Journal, 50(3), 259-281.

Stubbings, R. (2003). MetaLib and SFX at Loughborough University library, VINE: Journal of Information and Knowledge Management Systems, 33(1), 25-32.

Warren, P., & Alsmeyer, D. (2005). The digital library: a case study in intelligent content management, Journal of Knowledge Management, 9(5), 28-39.

Wen, S. (2005). Implementing knowledge management in academic libraries: a pragmatic approach, Proceedings of the third China-US Library Conference, Shanghai, 22-25 March, Retrieved March 22, 2018 from http://www.white-clouds.com/iclc/cliej/cl19wen.htm

Yu, K. H. (2009). Current research paradigms in knowledge management studies: Themes, concepts and relationships, Journal of Far East University, 1(1), 1-1.

Distraction to Illumination: Mining Biomedical Publications for Serendipity in Research

Carla M. Allen
School of Information Sciences & Learning Technologies, University of Missouri-Columbia, USA.
AllenCar@health.missouri.edu

Sanda Erdelez
School of Library and Information Science, Simmons University, MA, USA.
Erdelez@simmons.edu

ABSTRACT

As our technological capabilities for filling information needs improve, developers seek to more effective ways to support different aspects of the users' experience. One aspect that is gaining attention as an emerging support area is serendipity. However, supporting serendipity within a recommender system is difficult because the experience is unexpected and, therefore unpredictable. While researchers agree that algorithms to support serendipity need to be able to provide a balance of surprise and value to the end user (Niu & Abbas, 2017), an understanding of how to provide that balance has not yet been realized. Information that could be puzzling or distracting to someone as they go about their research activities may provide the trigger someone else needs to make a serendipitous connection in their research. Reports of serendipitous occurrences in research settings have been identified in research commentaries (Campanario, 1996) and within full-text research articles (Allen, Erdelez, & Marinov, 2013). This paper investigates the feasibility of automating the identification of information encounters in full-text research articles. This study contributes to the development of algorithms for supporting serendipity in information systems. We identified four variables that are useful for predicting information encounters in 25-35% of the instances. While we should continue to search for additional predictive variables, these findings present a novel approach to undertaking the support of serendipity in information systems.

KEYWORDS

serendipity; information behavior; recommender systems; information encountering; human-centered information retrieval; research reporting.

INTRODUCTION

In the history of scientific research, 'serendipitous' events, or 'happy accidents', are known to have played significant roles in the advancement of innumerable fields. From the development of Post-it® notes (Schwager, 2000) and Super-glue® (Raja, 2016) to the discovery of x-rays (Shapiro, 1986) and the development of Viagra (Lesko, 2017), society has benefitted from these 'pleasant surprises'. The process of serendipity connects seemingly unrelated concepts in what can appear to be a highly subjective manner and relies on unique characteristics of the encountering individual to make these fortunate connections (Iaquinta et al., 2008; Maccatrozzo, van Everdingen, Aroyo, & Schreiber, 2017). When viewed from an information behavior perspective, however, it becomes evident that serendipity involves behaviors that are much more purposeful than mere accidents. Makri and Blandford (2012) note that realization of 'serendipity' requires insight and contemplation to make connections between disparate ideas. The unexpected circumstances must occur in the presence of someone who has the intellectual background and capacity to understand the significance of the event. That individual must possess an understanding of the context in which the unexpected event occurs and must also be able to apply that understanding to a different problem. In addition to being unexpected, the user must deem the information interesting (Ge, Delgado-Battenfeld, & Jannach, 2010). The individual must both perceive and attend to the unanticipated information for it to be useful in making connections between concepts. These characteristics are defining features of information encountering (Erdelez, 1997). Information encountering is the process of noticing and making note of unexpected information that, while not relevant to the most immediate information need, addresses a background need or an unrealized future information need. Information that is encountered rather than sought presents the user with features that are not only surprising but also are salient in a way that allows the user to make loose associations (Kefalidou & Sharples, 2016) between the presented information and distant concepts. The idea of 'loose associations' is particularly relevant to information encountering as additional, purposeful information search is required to build solid connections between the concepts. These associations are the starting point for making the concrete connections necessary for achieving 'serendipitous' outcomes. Serendipity forms the foundation for linking seemingly unrelated ideas and using that connection to improve either or both processes. At the heart of serendipity is a unique type of information behavior – information encountering. By understanding and identifying the ways in which information encountering is described in published research literature, we may be able to develop better methods of supporting serendipity within our information systems and catalyze the positive outcomes of serendipity.

Serendipity and Information Recommender systems

With the ubiquity of electronic resources, information systems have evolved from mere retrieval of information records to recommender systems which seek to supply end users with the most relevant and salient resources from the vast array of indexed information. Such recommender systems are powered by carefully developed algorithms (Kefalidou & Sharples, 2016; Wu, He, & Yang, 2012). While most algorithms focus on the accuracy of the retrieved results, there has been increased interest in the development of algorithms that will go beyond accuracy to support novelty, diversity and serendipity with the retrieved results. Development of recommender systems that focus on providing 'serendipitous' encounters have been the focus of several information behavior studies (Erdelez, 2004; Makri, Toms, McCay-Peet, & Blandford, 2011; McCay-Peet & Toms, 2011; Wopereis & Braam, 2018) and human computer interaction studies (Dahroug et al., 2017; Fazeli et al., 2017; Maccatrozzo et al., 2017; Niu & Abbas, 2017) in recent years. One challenge to the development of recommender systems that support serendipity is identifying the type of information that end users will find surprising but also useful. Iaquinta et al. (2008) found that the concept of serendipity in recommendations is highly subjective, and that serendipity as a quality of recommended information is difficult to assess. Many developers (Herlocker, Konstan, Terveen, & Riedl, 2004; Maccatrozzo et al., 2017; Niu & Abbas, 2017) have defined serendipity in returned results as those items which hold both surprise and value for the end user. Ge et al (2010) identified key features of serendipitous results as items which have not been previously discovered or expected by the user and are considered to be interesting, relevant and useful to the user. Other researchers have described serendipity in recommender systems as a user experience rather than a feature of the information presented (McNee, Riedl, & Konstan, 2006). While it has been widely accepted that recommender systems need to support serendipity, the development of a mechanism for identifying which items may be deemed both surprising and valuable remains elusive.

Identifying the Information Encounter

In a qualitative study of full-text research journal articles by Allen et al. (2013), it was found that serendipitous information encounters during the research process can be identified by examining the context of synonyms for surprising research findings. This study revealed that synonyms for serendipity were sometimes used to describe the final fortuitous outcome, i.e. the application of an information encounter to a new context in a beneficial way. Other times, synonyms for serendipity were used to describe an information encounter that had not yet been explored or applied to a different situation. These instances described the recognition of surprising or unexpected data during the research process and were termed 'mentioned findings'. As recommender systems for the support of serendipity requires identifying information that users will find surprising, these 'mentioned findings' articles that contain information that the author has already described as surprising may provide a mechanism for fulfilling that aspect of the serendipitous experience. This finding bears further investigation.

RATIONALE AND CONTRIBUTION

This paper investigates features of the ways researchers use terms related to serendipity in their research publications as a mechanism for identifying characteristics within indexed information resources that may be useful for supplying both surprising and valuable search results to recommender system end-users. By performing a quantitative analysis on the relationship between reports of actual information encounters and the synonyms for serendipity used by the author and the location of the report within the research article, we will look for predictive variables that may enable the creation of algorithms to automate the identification of these reports. Using logistic regression, this quantitative project addresses the research question:

What characteristics of author reporting are useful for predicting references to actual serendipitous events?

At this stage in the research, serendipity will generally be defined as a process or experience beginning with an information encounter which is followed up on by an individual with related knowledge, skills and understanding that allows them to realize a valuable outcome.

BACKGROUND

Serendipity in research and technological development has been analyzed in numerous and disparate fields, including chemistry (Giesy, Newsted, & Oris, 2013), environmental science (Wilkinson & Weitkamp, 2013), and psychiatry (Siris, 2011), and is a widespread topic of interest. Because it crosses disciplinary boundaries and approaches problems in novel ways, serendipity is a phenomenon that has the potential to connect disparate ideas and produce outcomes that improve our quality of life. McCay-Peet and Toms (2018) have advanced a model of serendipity that consists of 3 major stages (See Figure 1). This model was synthesized from five different conceptions (Corneli, Jordanous,

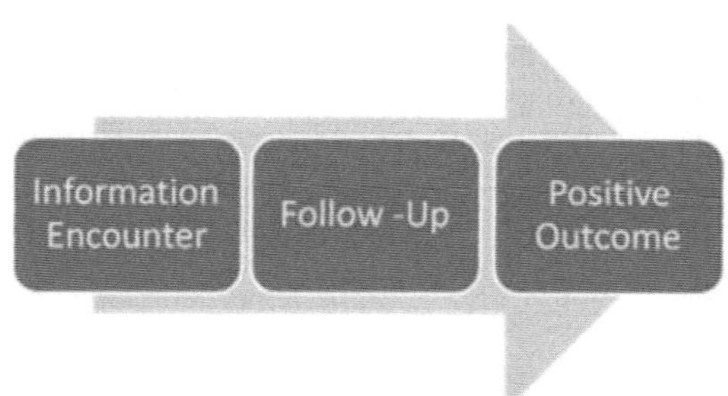

Figure 1:Basic Model of Serendipitous Experiences

Guckelsberger, Pease, & Colton, 2014; Makri & Blandford, 2012; McCay-Peet & Toms, 2015; Rubin, Burkell, & Quan-Haase, 2011; Sun, Sharples, & Makri, 2011) and provides a framework for understanding the experience of serendipity. In this model, a serendipitous experience begins with a triggering event that is unexpected and is coupled with insight by the subject that identifies the encounter as valuable. In order to capitalize on this value, the subject must follow up the finding until positive results are achieved. For this experience to reach the public as serendipitous, the the subject must also go through a period of reflection, where they acknowledge the unexpectedness of the trigger and view the process as fortuitous, describing it to others as such. It is known that disciplinary culture and the expectations of funding bodies may supress reports of serendipity, especially for early-career researchers and those whose observations may not fit with commonly accepted models of understanding. This model of serendipity holds true for those unexpected circumstances that are subsequently explored and their value brought to fruition.

Serendipity can be defined as a fortuitous experience that can occur in any realm of personal or professional occupation. Key aspects of a complete serendipitous experience include information that is acted upon, an element of unexpectedness, and a beneficial outcome. Serendipity is a process that starts with an observation which, when combined with an element of insight, brings about a beneficial outcome (McCay-Peet & Toms, 2015). The unexpectedness may arise at any point in the process. The initial observation may provide unexpected information. An unexpected information encounter may trigger a fortuitous insight. The process of observing and acting upon information may lead to an unexpected outcome. These unexpected aspects of information behavior that occur during the serendipitous experience are information encounters.

Information encountering was first described as a model of information behavior by Sanda Erdelez (1997) and has been analyzed in contexts ranging from news reading (Yadamsuren & Erdelez, 2016) to information literacy (Erdelez, Basic, & Levitov, 2011). Because serendipity is associated with positive outcomes, there is interest in supporting these types of information experiences in multimedia interfaces (McCay-Peet & Toms, 2018), with the expectation that increased information encounters will foster novel and creative leaps of understanding. Some work has been done fostering information encountering in music listening (Wopereis & Braam, 2018) and in multi-media recommender systems (Khalili, van Andel, van den Besselaar, & de Graaf, 2017; Kumpulainen & Kautonen, 2017; Rubin et al., 2011).

METHODOLOGY

As a starting point for investigating how biomedical researchers use terms related to serendipity in their research publications, we looked first to published research accounts as indexed in PubMed Central. To identify the representation of serendipity within the language of research articles, we began with a content analysis of full-text articles.

Unit of Analysis

The first step of a content analysis involves the identification of the sampling units, i.e., the synonyms related to the idea of serendipity. Search for these synonyms was undertaken through a process of chaining – identifying the synonyms of serendipity, and then identifying the synonyms of the synonyms until the possibilities were exhausted. Terms identified through this chaining process include: accidental, chance, fortuitous, happenstance, incidental, serendipitous, serendipity, surprising, unanticipated, unexpected, and unforeseen.

Study Population

The analysis sample was drawn from full text journal articles indexed in PubMed Central. PubMed Central was selected for its extensive collection of over two million full-text, primary research reports. Articles indexed in PubMed Central serve as the population for this study. PubMed Central acts as a free full-text archive of biomedical and life sciences journal literature at the U.S. National Institutes of Health's National Library of Medicine, currently archiving over 4.3 million articles. In addition to full text searching, PubMed Central offers users the ability to search by Medical Subject Headings, or MeSH terms. MeSH headings are frequently used to narrow literature searches to the user's key ideas. However, the MeSH category designation requires the documents to be classified with these terms by an expert examiner and assigned MeSH terms are limited to 10 to 12 terms per document, so minor ideas contained within the articles are not indexed by the MeSH terms. The current PubMed Central ontology includes the MeSH term "incidental findings," which includes the identified synonyms for serendipity: "incidental finding(s)", "finding(s), incidental", "incidental discovery(ies)", and "discovery(ies), incidental". A search of PubMed Central by usage of this MeSH heading returned only 303 articles. As you can see, while PubMed Central has a MeSH term that is mapped to serendipity, use of the MeSH heading failed to adequately return instances of serendipity, revealing the necessity of full text search for the related terms.

Population Strata

A full text search was performed for each of the identified terms with results filtered to include only research and review articles. The population for this study, consisting of all research or review articles containing a synonym for serendipity in the full-text article, includes 552,288 articles returned with frequencies as indicated in Table 1.

Instances of use of the terms serendipitous and serendipity, which were identified as synonyms in the chaining procedure, were combined into a single truncated search of serendipit*.

Random Stratified Sampling

In order to most accurately represent the population of articles, a proportional stratified random sampling method was employed. PASS 11 software was used to estimate the proportion of reported serendipity for the population of 552,288 (total over all strata) with 95% confidence, and a precision (half-width of the interval) of 0.1. A sample of 400 articles is necessary to estimate the true proportions within the population. SAS 9.2 Proc SurveySelect was used to proportionally allocate the sample among the strata for the total sample of 400 articles. Table 1, above, details the proportion of the sample drawn from each stratum.

Within each stratum, each article was assigned a number from 1 to the total number of articles. Article numbers were assigned based on the default order generated by PubMed Central. SAS was used to randomly identify the designated number of articles for review within each stratum according to the assigned article number.

Search Term	Incidence	Sample Size	Search Details
accidental	31669	23	accidental[Body - All Words] AND "research and review articles"[filter]
chance	144141	104	chance[Body - All Words] AND "research and review articles"[filter]
fortuitous	11572	8	fortuitous[Body - All Words] AND "research and review articles"[filter]
happenstance	314	1	happenstance[Body - All Words] AND "research and review articles"[filter]
incidental	20820	15	incidental[Body - All Words] AND "research and review articles"[filter]
serendipit*	3029	2	serendipit*[Body - All Words] AND "research and review articles"[filter]
surprising	205758	149	surprising[Body - All Words] AND "research and review articles"[filter]
unanticipated	8756	6	unanticipated[Body - All Words] AND "research and review articles"[filter]
unexpected	122334	89	unexpected[Body - All Words] AND "research and review articles"[filter]
unforeseen	3895	3	unforeseen[Body - All Words] AND "research and review articles"[filter]
Total	552288	400	

Table 1: Article frequency within full-text articles indexed by PubMed Central by serendipity term use, and associated sample size.

Categorization of Term Use

Term use was coded following the coding scheme described by Allen, et al. (2013), where four categories of term use were of particular interest to our investigation of serendipity. These categories include 'Inspiration' where unexpected information formed the basis for the research design, 'Research Focus' where the entire article is devoted to describing the unexpected information and its evaluation, 'Systematic Reviews' which provide overviews of serendipitous contributions in a field and 'Mentioned Findings' where unexpected or surprising information is presented briefly but is not the focus of the study. The articles coded into the 'Inspiration' and 'Research Focus' categories typically describe the ways in which the researcher followed up on the information encounter and applied information gleaned from the encounter to a new context or in a novel way. The 'Systematic Reviews' articles reflect on the impact that serendipitous outcomes have had on a discipline. It is the 'Mentioned Findings' category that is intriguing because it presents surprising information, but investigators have not yet identified salience of the information to a particular problem context. In achieving a serendipitous outcome, the surprising information needs to be connected to researchers with the sagacity necessary to apply that information in a novel way. For example, Roentgen's discovery of x-rays is a commonly noted serendipitous discovery. Most accounts, however, fail to mention that several other scientists experimenting with Crookes Tubes had noted the same glow from phosphoric plates, yet failed to connect the significance of that distant glow to the diagnostic tool that has revolutionized medical diagnostics (Harris, 1995, p. 1). When seeking to populate a recommender system with surprising information, it is the 'Mentioned Findings' category that we feel will prove most useful, as these orphaned findings need to have their salience and application revealed. Accuracy of the coding was evaluated on 10% of the sample, using independent coding by two researchers. Inter-coder reliability was calculated for a subset of 100 articles, returning a KALPHA = .9001, indicating a high level of agreement between the coders. All disagreements were resolved by independently recoding units in disagreement or, failing that, by consensus.

Coding Procedures

PubMed Central's search tool was used to identify all articles with instances serendipity-related term use. Full-text versions of each of those articles were uploaded into NVivo 11 for Windows. Each term was tagged within the articles, then individually analyzed to determine the meaning conveyed by the term. While the particular synonym for serendipity used to select the article for analysis was noted, all synonyms appearing within the text were coded.

From this examination, 10 categories of term use were identified and 3 of those categories were classified as indicating a serendipitous event, as described by Allen, et al. (2013). The reporting of serendipitous experiences as 'Inspiration' for a research study closely follows current models of the experience of serendipity. The research reported in these instances was inspired by an information encounter and the current study was subsequently undertaken (followed up) resulting in a positive outcome (research findings to report). The 'Research Focus' category reports a traditionally designed study (not arising as follow up to previous observations) where the positive result of the study presents in a way that is completely unexpected. This, likewise, is consistent with models of serendipitous experiences. The third way that terms can be used to indicate a serendipitous experience is as a 'Mentioned Findings'. In this category, the anomalous observations are reported, but they have not yet undergone the follow-up process. It is unknown why follow up is yet to occur. Perhaps the researcher does not have the time or funding to pursue this observation further. Perhaps they do not possess the sagacity to capitalize on the finding. Regardless, this type of reporting has yet to realize the possible positive outcomes. This category, in particular, may present opportunities for information systems to connect such findings with investigators with the education and experiences necessary to bring the process to fruition.

RESULTS

Descriptive statistics

The 400 sampled articles yielded 1,228 unique uses of a synonym for serendipity. Each of those instances was independently coded for term use regardless of the strata for which the article was selected. Following coding of the term use, it was found that 26% of the terms referred to some aspect of serendipity or information encountering and 74% had other semantic meanings (See Figure 2). Of the terms relating serendipitous experiences, 5% indicated using another researcher's unexpected finding as inspiration for their study. Twenty-three percent (23%) focused on describing or further applying serendipitously encountered information. Seventy-one percent (71%) of the terms that were relevant to serendipity fell into the 'Mentioned Findings' category. In these instances, authors reported unexpected or surprising observations made in the course of an investigation, but do not further explore the observation or attempt to apply the observation to another context. None of the articles sampled included terms that fell into the 'Systematic Reviews' category.

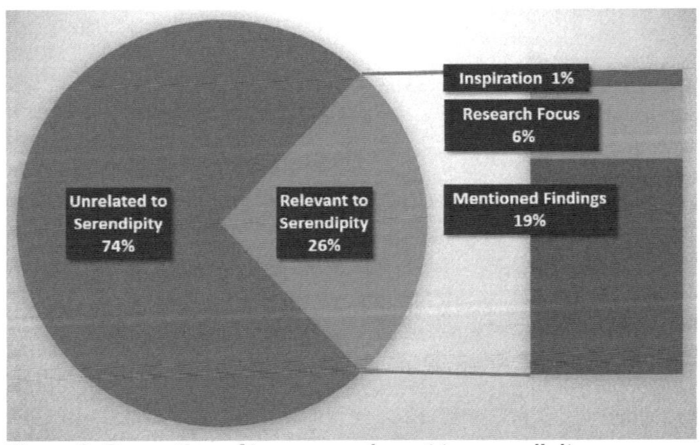

Figure 2: Proportion of term use relevant to serendipity or information encountering within the sample.

When extrapolated to the population of 552,288 articles within PubMed containing synonyms for serendipity, over 143,000 articles are estimated to contain mentions of actual serendipitous events, with nearly 102,000 of those indicating information encounters where the author noted the information as surprising and valuable but had not yet followed up on the application of that information.

Predictive statistics

Predictive statistics are key to identifying features that will be useful in creating algorithms for a recommender system. Because we have a dichotomous dependent variable (relevant to a serendipitous event or not) and categorical independent variables (serendipity synonym used and location within the article), a binary logistic regression is the preferred predictive analysis. In this analysis, both serendipity synonym used and location of the term within the article were also analyzed for their relationship to actual instances of serendipity. The first step in performing this predictive analysis is to conduct a chi-square analysis to determine if significant relationships exist to support performance of binary logistic regression. In this study the test for overall relationships between search term, location within the article and relationship to actual serendipitous events that was performed was a Fisher's Exact Test. A Fisher's Exact Test is a type of Chi-Square analysis that is performed when one or more cells have a count of 5 or less. The Fisher's Exact Test showed a significant interaction between location and relevance to serendipitous events, with a significance of .000 with a 95% confidence interval. The Fisher's Exact Test on the relationship between synonym used and relevance to serendipitous events also showed a significant interaction, with a significance of .000 with a 95% confidence interval. This test of bivariate relationships was necessary to verify that the data were suitable for performing the binary logistic regression. Because the chi-square test was significant, we know that both variables can be included in the binary logistic regression. Based on these results from the bivariate tests, we can then choose the variables to include in the final model.

When performing the binary logistic regression, we begin by performing a null analysis, or "null model," where the analysis is performed without including any predictors. The results, when the independent variables are included, are compared to the model when they are not included to see if including the variable significantly impacts the predictive value of the model. For the relationship between synonyms for serendipity and actual serendipitous events, this analysis returned a Wald chi-square statistic of 232.04, which is significant at $p < .05$. This indicates that the coefficients for the variables not in the model are significantly different from zero. This implies that the addition of one or more of these variables to the model will significantly affect its predictive power. The significant search terms in the single model were 'Accidental' and 'Incidental'. Likewise, a null analysis Wald chi-square statistic was performed for the relationship between location within the document and relationship to actual serendipitous events. The residual chi-square statistic for this analysis was 37.804, which is significant at $p < .05$ indicating that the coefficients for the variables not in the model are significantly different from zero. This implies that the addition of one or more of these variables to the model will significantly affect its predictive power. The significant locations in the single model were Abstract and Discussion.

Finally, an overall test of the predicting model was performed. The results of this analysis, which summarizes the relative importance of the explanatory variables individually, can be seen in Table 3. An Enter method was selected and the overall test of the model was statistically significant, indicating that the independent variables in our model are a significant improvement over those seen in the null model. The independent variables of serendipity synonym and location within the article can accurately predict the whether the author is describing an actual serendipitous event 25-35% of the time. Within that model, the only variables that contribute to this predictive value are the synonyms 'Accidental' and 'Serendipity' and the locations Abstract and Discussion. Location is directly related to the relationship to actual serendipitous events, with terms located in the abstract or discussion sections of the paper being 4 times more likely to refer to actual serendipitous events than terms located in other areas of the article. Interestingly, the relationship between serendipitous events and the synonym used to describe them was actually inverse. The term 'Accidental' was 8.85 times more likely to refer to something other than serendipity; and the term 'Serendipity' was 4.4 times more likely to refer to something else.

DISCUSSION AND CONCLUSIONS

The descriptive statistics show that there is a sizeable population of articles that contain references to serendipity. The majority of those references are in an early stage, where the researcher noticed unusual or unexpected information in the course of their research and valued that information enough to include it in their research publication. As an information behavior, this triggering episode is termed an information encounter. While information encountering is integral to serendipity, additional factors impact the realization of positive benefits from the information encounter. The large population of 'Mentioned Findings' – type reports of serendipity foreshadow the possibility of using this pool of surprising or unexpected information to support serendipity within information systems. In order to effectively incorporate these instances into an information system, the identification and cataloging of these reports must be automated.

The results of the binomial logistic regression allowed us to identify four variables that contribute to the effective identification of information encounters. The location of the report within the research article is very useful for predicting whether the author is relating an information encounter. As research articles tend to follow a similar format, automating the identification of these segments of the articles should be fairly straightforward. It was interesting that the terminology used to convey the information encounters was not an effective positive predictor of information encountering reports. Perhaps this is due to the varied scientific fields indexed by PubMed Central. Analysis of term use as it relates to serendipity and information encountering in a narrow disciplinary field is necessary to understanding the linguistic indicators of serendipity.

It was most interesting that 'serendipity' was negatively correlated with references to an active serendipitous experience. Perhaps this is due to the reflective nature of serendipity. It is possible that it is not until after the experience is seasoned and some perspective is gained that the experience is classified as serendipitous. In the midst of experiencing the unexpected, authors experience the confusion and distraction, but have not yet achieved illumination. Overall, this study contributes to the information sciences and human computer interaction literature by identifying a novel way for identifying items that users of information systems may find both surprising and valuable. Furthermore, analysis of ways in which authors represent these information encounters in their research journal articles provides predictive evidence for the development of recommender algorithms.

Challenges and Limitations

While the current study identified two significant variables to predicting reports of serendipity, these variables only account for 25-35% of the variability in the reports of serendipity. Further research is needed to identify additional characteristics that can facilitate the identification of these reports. Initial qualitative analysis hints at the possible existence of domain-specific terminology that could account for greater proportions of the variability in the reports of serendipity. Furthermore, as PubMed Central indexes multiple academic disciplines within the biomedical spectrum, it is possible that the variables identified in this study account for a much greater percentage of the variability in some fields but are not significant at all in others. In depth qualitative analysis of articles with identified reports of serendipity could prove fruitful.

While this quantitative model holds true for the articles indexed in PubMed Central, it may not be applicable to fields not indexed by PubMed Central. Furthermore, the cross-section of disciplines within PubMed Central may have masked predictive variables by combining competing disciplinary languages. For example, 'accidental' findings that indicate serendipity in a field like chemistry or genetics may be hidden by the use of 'accidental' to discuss traumatic injury in fields like orthopedics, pediatrics, or rehabilitation sciences.

Another challenge to populating information systems with information encounters reported in full-text journal articles is the limited accessibility to the published content. This study was performed using PubMed Central because it provides a large archive of freely accessible full text research articles. Accessing articles indexed through subscription services may prove cost prohibitive and inhibit access to information encounters in fields that are primarily indexed in subscription-based archives. Furthermore, PubMed Central already incorporates an option for full-text search within their user interface. Identifying the articles for initial screening is much more challenging without the option for full text search. Comparison of article identification through archives that are equipped for full-text search to the secondary article identification process that would be necessary to analyzing the contents of archives without a full-text search feature could be warranted.

Possibilities and Future Directions

In addition to connecting researchers to unexpected information, information systems that support serendipity may be helpful in identifying interdisciplinary collaborators. But research funding mechanisms, and thus the landscape of the research arena, are changing (Aagaard, 2017; Whitley, 2018; Kenney, 2017). Successful research programs are expected to bring in $5-8 for every dollar invested in their infrastructure. Such returns on investment are impossible to achieve by independent researchers bringing in single project grants. To maintain economic viability, research programs are increasingly moving away from the approach of research as a solitary, isolated pursuit, to an interdisciplinary, center-based model that is underpinned by computational informatics (Goecks, Nekrutenko, & Taylor, 2010; Myers et al., 2004) and leverages academic and industry resources to find solutions for complex, ill-defined problems (Bozeman, 2004; Whitley, 2018). They require a team of researchers pooling their efforts around a collective problem, sharing resources and building synergy, where they accomplish more together than any of them could individually. Building economically viable research teams requires the development of collaborations across disciplinary, organizational and institutional boundaries. Institutions currently approach the development of these teams rather haphazardly. Holding conferences can provide opportunities to develop these serendipitous connections, but success is far from guaranteed. In fact, many of the most successful research teams note that their partnerships seem to arise serendipitously. Information systems that mine and report information encounters would connect users not only to new, surprising and valuable information, but also to new researchers from diverse fields whose perspectives could enhance and amplify research productivity. By focusing on the information behaviors involved in serendipity, we can capitalize on the observations of others, connecting those observations and illuminating connections for the individuals who are best suited to bring about positive outcomes from them.

REFERENCES

Allen, C., Erdelez, S., & Marinov, M. (2013). Looking for Opportunistic Discovery of Information in Recent Biomedical Research – A Content Analysis. In Proceedings of the 76th ASIS&T Annual Meeting (Vol. 49). Montreal: Richard B. Hill.

Campanario, J. M. (1996). UsingCitation Classics to study the incidence of serendipity in scientific discovery. Scientometrics, 37(1), 3–24. https://doi.org/10.1007/BF02093482

Corneli, J., Jordanous, A., Guckelsberger, C., Pease, A., & Colton, S. (2014). Modelling serendipity in a computational context. ArXiv:1411.0440 [Cs]. Retrieved from http://arxiv.org/abs/1411.0440

Dahroug, A., López-Nores, M., Pazos-Arias, J. J., González-Soutelo, S., Reboreda-Morillo, S. M., & Antoniou, A. (2017). Exploiting relevant dates to promote serendipity and situational curiosity in cultural heritage experiences. In 2017 12th International Workshop on Semantic and Social Media Adaptation and Personalization (SMAP) (pp. 84–88). https://doi.org/10.1109/SMAP.2017.8022673

Erdelez, S. (1997). Information encountering: a conceptual framework for accidental information discovery (pp. 412–421). Presented at the ISIC '96: Proceedings of an international conference on Information seeking in context, Taylor Graham Publishing. Retrieved from http://portal.acm.org/citation.cfm?id=267217

Erdelez, S. (2004). Investigation of information encountering in the controlled research environment. Information Processing & Management, 40(6), 1013–1025. https://doi.org/10.1016/j.ipm.2004.02.002

Erdelez, S., Basic, J., & Levitov, D. D. (2011). Potential for inclusion of information encountering within information literacy models. Information Research, 16(3).

Fazeli, S., Drachsler, H., Bitter-Rijpkema, M., Brouns, F., Vegt, W. van der, & Sloep, P. B. (2017). User-centric Evaluation of Recommender Systems in Social Learning Platforms: Accuracy is Just the Tip of the Iceberg. IEEE Transactions on Learning Technologies, PP(99), 1–1. https://doi.org/10.1109/TLT.2017.2732349

Ge, M., Delgado-Battenfeld, C., & Jannach, D. (2010). Beyond accuracy: evaluating recommender systems by coverage and serendipity (p. 257). ACM Press. https://doi.org/10.1145/1864708.1864761

Giesy, J., Newsted, J., & Oris, J. (2013). Photo-enhanced toxicity: serendipity of a prepared mind and flexible program management. Environmental Toxicology and Chemistry, 32(5), 969–971. https://doi.org/10.1002/etc.2211

Goecks, J., Nekrutenko, A., & Taylor, J. (2010). Galaxy: a comprehensive approach for supporting accessible, reproducible, and transparent computational research in the life sciences. Genome Biology, 11, R86. https://doi.org/10.1186/gb-2010-11-8-r86

Harris, E. L. (1995). The shadowmakers: A history of radiologic technology (1st edition). Albuquerque, N.M: American Society of Radiologic Technologists.

Herlocker, J. L., Konstan, J. A., Terveen, L. G., & Riedl, J. T. (2004). Evaluating collaborative filtering recommender systems. ACM Transactions on Information Systems, 22(1), 5–53. https://doi.org/10.1145/963770.963772

Iaquinta, L., Gemmis, M. d, Lops, P., Semeraro, G., Filannino, M., & Molino, P. (2008). Introducing Serendipity in a Content-Based Recommender System. In 2008 Eighth International Conference on Hybrid Intelligent Systems (pp. 168–173). https://doi.org/10.1109/HIS.2008.25

Kefalidou, G., & Sharples, S. (2016). Encouraging serendipity in research: Designing technologies to support connection-making. International Journal of Human-Computer Studies, 89, 1–23. https://doi.org/10.1016/j.ijhcs.2016.01.003

Khalili, A., van Andel, P., van den Besselaar, P., & de Graaf, K. A. (2017). Fostering Serendipitous Knowledge Discovery Using an Adaptive Multigraph-based Faceted Browser. In Proceedings of the Knowledge Capture Conference (pp. 15:1–15:4). New York, NY, USA: ACM. https://doi.org/10.1145/3148011.3148037

Kumpulainen, S. W., & Kautonen, H. (2017). Accidentally Successful Searching: Users' Perceptions of a Digital Library (pp. 257–260). ACM Press. https://doi.org/10.1145/3020165.3022124

Lesko, L. (2017). Efficacy from Strange Sources. Clinical Pharmacology & Therapeutics, 103(2), 253–261. https://doi.org/10.1002/cpt.916

Maccatrozzo, V., van Everdingen, E., Aroyo, L., & Schreiber, G. (2017). Everybody, More or Less, likes Serendipity (pp. 29–34). ACM Press. https://doi.org/10.1145/3099023.3099064

Makri, S., & Blandford, A. (2012). Coming across information serendipitously – Part 1: A process model. Journal of Documentation, 68(5), 684–705. https://doi.org/10.1108/00220411211256030

Makri, S., Toms, E. G., McCay-Peet, L., & Blandford, A. (2011). Encouraging Serendipity in Interactive Systems. In Human-Computer Interaction – INTERACT 2011 (pp. 728–729). Springer, Berlin, Heidelberg. https://doi.org/10.1007/978-3-642-23768-3_136

McCay-Peet, L., & Toms, E. (2011). Measuring the dimensions of serendipity in digital environments. Usos y Gratificaciones: La Medición de Las Dimensiones de La Serendipia En Entornos Digitales., 16(3), 6–6.

McCay-Peet, L., & Toms, E. (2015). Investigating serendipity: How it unfolds and what may influence it. Journal of the Association for Information Science and Technology, 66(7), 1463–1476. https://doi.org/10.1002/asi.23273

McCay-Peet, L., & Toms, E. G. (2018). Researching serendipity in digital information environments. San Rafael, California: Morgan & Claypool Publishers.

McNee, S. M., Riedl, J., & Konstan, J. A. (2006). Being Accurate is Not Enough: How Accuracy Metrics Have Hurt Recommender Systems. In CHI '06 Extended Abstracts on Human Factors in Computing Systems (pp. 1097–1101). New York, NY, USA: ACM. https://doi.org/10.1145/1125451.1125659

Myers, J. D., Allison, T. C., Bittner, S., Didier, B., Frenklach, M., Green, W. H., … Yang, C. (2004). A collaborative informatics infrastructure for multi-scale science. In Proceedings of the Second International Workshop on Challenges of Large Applications in Distributed Environments, 2004. CLADE 2004. (pp. 24–33). https://doi.org/10.1109/CLADE.2004.1309089

Niu, X., & Abbas, F. (2017). A Framework for Computational Serendipity. In Adjunct Publication of the 25th Conference on User Modeling, Adaptation and Personalization (pp. 360–363). New York, NY, USA: ACM. https://doi.org/10.1145/3099023.3099097

Raja, P. R. (2016). Cyanoacrylate Adhesives: A Critical Review. Reviews of Adhesion and Adhesives, 4(4), 398–416. https://doi.org/10.7569/RAA.2016.097315

Rubin, V. L., Burkell, J., & Quan-Haase, A. (2011). Facets of serendipity in everyday chance encounters: a grounded theory approach to blog analysis. Information Research, 16(3), 27–27.

Schwager, E. (2000). Little-known facts about little-known people. Drug News and Perspectives, 13(2), 126–128.

Shapiro, G. (1986). A skeleton in the darkroom: stories of serendipity in science (1st ed). San Francisco: Harper & Row.

Siris, S. G. (2011). Searching for Serendipity. The Journal of Clinical Psychiatry, 72(8), 1156–1157. https://doi.org/10.4088/JCP.11lr07077

Sun, X., Sharples, S., & Makri, S. (2011). A user-centred mobile diary study approach to understanding serendipity in information research. Information Research-An International Electronic Journal, 16(3). Retrieved from http://informationr.net/ir/16-3/paper492.html

Wilkinson, C., & Weitkamp, E. (2013). A Case Study in Serendipity: Environmental Researchers Use of Traditional and Social Media for Dissemination. PLOS ONE, 8(12), e84339. https://doi.org/10.1371/journal.pone.0084339

Wopereis, I., & Braam, M. (2018). Seeking Serendipity: The Art of Finding the Unsought in Professional Music. In S. Kurbanoğlu, J. Boustany, S. Špiranec, E. Grassian, D. Mizrachi, & L. Roy (Eds.), Information Literacy in the Workplace (pp. 503–512). Springer International Publishing.

Wu, W., He, L., & Yang, J. (2012). Evaluating recommender systems. In Seventh International Conference on Digital Information Management (ICDIM 2012) (pp. 56–61). https://doi.org/10.1109/ICDIM.2012.6360092

Yadamsuren, B., & Erdelez, S. (2016). Incidental Exposure to Online News. Synthesis Lectures on Information Concepts, Retrieval, and Services, 8(5), i–73. https://doi.org/10.2200/S00744ED1V01Y201611ICR054

A Word-Level Language Identification Strategy for Resource-Scarce Languages

Toluwase Asubiaro
University of Western Ontario, Canada.
tasubiar@uwo.ca

Robert Mercer
University of Western Ontario, Canada.
rmercer@uwo.ca

Tunde Adegbola
African Languages Technology Initiative, Nigeria.
taintransit@hotmail.com

Isola Ajiferuke
University of Western Ontario, Canada.
iajiferu@uwo.ca

ABSTRACT

This study is based on the premise that it is possible to train computers to predict the language of a word (textual or audio) by learning from its character n-gram pattern, without recourse to the language's dictionary. With the growth of multilingual collections and a need for automatic means of cleaning textual datasets, this paper presents a strategy for language identification of individual words in a body of texts. This strategy is suitable for resource-scarce languages that do not have large electronic datasets that are required for machine learning and natural language processing studies and whose dictionaries may not be available. In this study, we focused on three African languages, namely Hausa, Igbo, and Yoruba. A training corpus in each of these languages was used to obtain the probabilities of character trigrams in the language. Given that English is a common language that is often mixed with these resource-scarce languages in texts, we also obtained the probabilities of trigrams in an English training corpus. These probabilities were then used in identifying the language of each word in test corpora containing bilingual texts. Our strategy achieved average precision, recall and F1 values of about 97%, 91% and 94% respectively.

KEYWORDS

Word-level language identification, resource-scarce languages, machine learning, character n-grams, textual pattern analysis

INTRODUCTION

The languages featured in the study are three West African languages- Hausa, Igbo, and Yoruba which are resource-scarce like most other African languages. Speakers of politically and economically relevant global and regional languages such as English can access information on the computer because of the availability of different computer software, hardware and resources in/for these languages. Conversely, resource-scarce languages such as the Hausa, Igbo and Yoruba belong to the *have-not* of the information divide because they lack computer software, hardware and information resources with which their speakers can access information on the computer. For instance, the *have* languages enjoy array of complex artificial intelligent (AI) and natural language processing (NLP) tools such as note-taking apps which can convert speech to text, digital personal assistants like Microsoft Cortana that can interpret speech and perform complex task digitally and article summarization apps in/for English through which English speakers can interact with the computer and access information online. The resource-scarce languages grapple with the problem of basic NLP tools such as language-dependent keyboards that cater to their orthographic needs.

Estimates based on the statistics from the Central Intelligence Agency (2017a) and the Ethnologue, (Simons, Gary F. and Charles D. Fennig (eds.), 2017), show that the native speakers of Hausa, Igbo and Yoruba languages in Nigeria alone constitute over 70%, that is 130 million, of the country's population of 186 million. Speakers of these three languages also live in other African countries such as Niger Republic, Benin Republic, Togo, Mali, Sierra Leone and Cote d'Ivoire (Central Intelligence Agency, 2017b), (News Agency of Nigeria, 2016). There are millions of undocumented speakers of these languages in other parts of the world. Yoruba, for instance is used for religious worship of Orischa or Sentaria in South American and the Caribbean countries like Cuba, Trinidad and Tobago, and Brazil (Falola & Childs, 2005), (Rauhut, 2014).

NLP based on data-driven approaches depend on large bodies of texts. Unfortunately, sufficiently large bodies of text are not readily available for the resource-scarce African languages. Experience in gathering corpora for Hausa, Igbo and Yoruba languages through text harvesting from the Internet has shown that such texts usually contain a significant number of foreign words which can be attributed to three main factors. These are colonization, religious proselytization and interaction with neighboring cultures. Consequently, a significant number of foreign words mostly from English and a few from other languages like French, Hebrew and Arabic may be found in the texts. In Yoruba, for instance, through the influence of English colonization in countries such as Nigeria and French colonization in Benin Republic where Yoruba is spoken, code mixing and code switching of Yoruba with the colonial languages is prevalent. Also, the dominance of English as the Internet language is another factor that has influenced its infiltration into the internet Yoruba texts. The presence of Arabic and Hebrew words in the Yoruba texts is attributable to the influences of Islam and Christianity respectively. Other languages that contribute words to Yoruba are the Hausa and Igbo languages, which are the languages that are spoken by Yoruba neighboring communities.

A major problem facing resource development for these languages is corpus gathering. Corpus gathering could be manually undertaken or gathered online. The Internet remains the most viable source of text harvesting for these languages but the online textual datasets for these languages are mostly infiltrated significantly with foreign words from the already mentioned sources and there is a need to automatically clean these texts. Manual typing of the texts of these languages into the computer is another method of corpus development. However, manual typing of the texts is a challenge because of the scarcity of keyboards that can cater to the orthography of the languages which involve heavy use of diacritics on some of the Latin alphabets. The Latin alphabets with diacritics such as ***ɓ, ụ, ẹ, ọ*** which are used in writing these languages are not represented on the conventional keyboards. Diacritics used in these languages are either used for tone marking, as sub-dots or hooks. The sub-dots, which are appended on some characters extend the functionality of the Latin alphabets because certain Hausa, Igbo or Yoruba speech sounds that cannot be properly represented by the Latin alphabets alone are instead expressed with the simple addition of sub-dots, as in ***ị, ẹ*** and ***ṣ***. Like the sub-dots, the hooks extend the functionality of the Latin alphabets by simple addition of hooks to the upper parts of certain alphabets, as in ***ɓ, ƙ, ƴ*** and ***ɗ***. Secondly, some forms of tonal information are provided by the tone marks, which are appended on some characters. In Yoruba for instance, they are appended on vowels or nasal consonants *n* and *m*. For example, vowel ***a*** can bear tone information in three modes; ***à***-LOW tone, ***a***-MID tone and ***á***-HIGH tone. The challenges of the scarcity of large bodies of text for NLP have been reported by many NLP studies of these languages (Adegbola & Odilinye, 2012; De Pauw, Wagacha, & De Schryver, 2007; Asahiah, Ajadi Odejobi, & Adagunodo, 2017; Scannell, 2011).

With the increasing development of multilingual information systems (MIS), identifying the language of each word in the MIS has become imperative. There are many well studied methods that have been developed for multi-lingual collections for English, global, regional and European languages. On the other hand, there are resource-scarce languages that require the application of word-level automatic language identification (LID) for basic natural language processing (NLP) processes, such as textual data collection, because of the presence of foreign words in their online textual data. Code mixing and code switching present a problem for online harvesting of large textual datasets for the resource-scarce languages because of the significantly large amount of foreign words in the available online corpora which may interfere with the true behavior of the main language when such datasets are used for language modelling and subsequently affect the veracity of statistical models. Human beings are usually employed to clean such texts by manual editing. This usually involves significant costs of time and monetary resources, and particularly for large corpora, it is known to be subject to human error. Hence, a need for automatic word-level language identification for the resource-scarce languages.

Word-level automatic LID are mostly done using the lexicon or dictionary-based methods and the n-grams modelling, and these methods are mostly used alone or in combination with each other, i.e., a hybrid of the dictionary-based method and the character n-grams modelling. These methods are language-dependent and require large annotated datasets or comprehensive dictionary of the target languages. For instance, some of the recent studies such as (Barman, Wagner, Vyas, Gella, Sharma, Bali, & Choudhury, 2014; Chrupala, & Foster, 2014; Dias Cardoso & Roy, 2016; Gella, Sharma, & Bali, 2013; Lavergne, Adda, Adda-Decker, & Lamel, 2014; Piergallini, Shirvani, Gautam, & Chouikha, 2016; Rijhwani, Sequiera, Choudhury, Bali, & Maddila, 2017; Barman, Das, Wagner, & Foster, 2014) used dictionary-based methods for LID at word level. While other studies such as (Banerjee et al., 2014, 2014; Chittaranjan, Vyas, Bali, & Choudhury, 2014; Dahiya, 2017; Das & Gambäck, 2014; Gella, Bali, & Choudhury, 2014; Jaech, Mulcaire, Hathi, Ostendorf, & Smith, 2016; Jhamtani, Bhogi, & Raychoudhury, 2014; King & Abney, 2013; Mandal, Banerjee, Naskar, Rosso, & Bandyopadhyay, 2015; Nguyen & Dogruoz, 2013; Řehůřek & Kolkus, 2009) used a combination of at least two of the following methods: dictionary-based methods, rule-based methods, character n-gram modelling and heuristics based on word level features modelling.

Dictionary-based LID and the earlier proposed methods of word-level LID have some limitations which make them unsuitable for resource-scarce languages. First, dictionary-based methods require large body of texts for generating the lexicon, which are most times not available for resource-scarce language (Selamat & Akosu, 2016). Second, the methods used in earlier studies are mostly language-dependent and therefore can only work for the targeted languages.

This study presents a language-independent strategy for word level LID through the textual character trigrams pattern analysis which can cater to the resource-scarce languages. The method proposed in this research has some advantages because it does not require the use of dictionary and large datasets for machine learning. Hence, this is potentially more suitable for the resource-scarce languages. This study could contribute towards other NLP research for resource-scarce LID, e.g., mapping the language in which a document is written (Goldszmidt, Najork, & Paparizos, 2013). LID is fundamental to many NLP applications like optical character recognition (Prasanthkumar & Dileesh, 2014), text mining (Lui, Lau, & Baldwin, 2014), information retrieval (Ali & Akosu, 2015), information extraction, document modelling and machine translation.

METHODOLOGY

Theoretical Approach

Human beings can identify words as valid in a language if such words are frequently encountered in the language or the validity of such words can be inferred by some morphological transformation. Humans can also guess the validity of words in a language with appreciable accuracy based on their conformity to observable patterns of sounds in the language. For example, patterns of sounds such as clicks in some Southern African languages, velar fricatives in Arabic, and nasal vowels in Mandarin are common observable patterns in languages. Differences in these observable patterns of sounds in various languages express the possibility of using statistical analysis of the occurrence of these patterns to identify foreign words in a document.

The Hausa, Igbo and Yoruba languages, like all languages, manifest certain articulatory peculiarities which result in specific phonological patterns. For example, Yoruba phonology abhors consonant clusters and vowel hiatus. Hence, words that contain consonant clusters or involve vowel hiatus are not likely to be Yoruba words. These articulatory and phonological sound patterns are reflected in written texts and this provides a theoretical basis for using pattern analysis of texts to reveal features by which words from foreign languages can be automatically identified.

The Datasets

Four clean, unilingual training datasets, one training dataset each for English, Hausa, Igbo and Yoruba languages, were used in this study. The datasets were saved in **utf-8** so that the digital encoding system of all the languages could be captured. This was particularly necessary for Igbo and Yoruba datasets as they contain diacritic marks. The datasets were cleaned manually of code-switched and code-mixed words and special characters that were potentially irrelevant to the study. Fully diacritically marked electronic Igbo and Yoruba texts for NLP studies are scarce, hence parts of the Igbo and Yoruba datasets for this study were obtained exclusively for the research and the copyright permission to make these texts available to the public has not been granted. However, the Hausa, Igbo and Yoruba texts which were mined from the internet are available on the GitHub repository (https://github.com/Toluwase/Word-Level-Language-Identification-for-Resource-Scarce-) as part of this research. The English training dataset was collected from American National Corpus on the internet through the web address: http://www.anc.org/data/masc/downloads/data-download/. The Hausa training corpus does not contain diacritics used in standard Hausa orthography; the diacritically marked characters were replaced with their ANSI equivalents in the texts. The Igbo training corpus contains Igbo published literature, which cannot be made public, and internet data from a Christian religious organization which is available through the GitHub repository. The Yoruba training corpus contains published literature, which cannot be made public, as well as students' research projects, which are available on the GitHub repository. The research projects did not conform to Yoruba orthographic rules originally because diacritically marked Yoruba characters were transliterated in the body of texts. Transliteration occurs when specific character(s) are used in place of others. To make the texts from the projects useful for this research work, the transliterated characters were replaced with the appropriate (diacritically marked) characters. The word frequency list along with other results of the analysis such as the trigrams and their probabilities and the python computer program code for this study are also available on the GitHub repository.

It was stated earlier that foreign words in Hausa, Igbo and Yoruba texts are mostly from English and neighboring languages. Hence, the three bilingual test datasets are as follows: Hausa (without diacritics) texts that contain English words; Yoruba diacritically marked texts that contain Igbo diacritically marked texts; and Yoruba diacritically marked texts that contain English words. In other words, the test data contain three bilingual or language encoding pairs: diacritically unmarked pair (Hausa-English); diacritically marked pair (Yoruba-Igbo); and diacritically marked and diacritically unmarked pair (Yoruba-English). The number of words and tokens contained in the training and test datasets are provided in Table 1.

	Training Corpus		
S/N	Language	No of Words	No of Tokens
1	English	308,746	23,455
2	Hausa	190,833	9,247
3	Igbo	125,690	6,737
4	Yoruba	282,146	14,290
	Test Corpus		
	Language Pair	No of Words	No of Tokens
1	Yoruba-English	11,918	2,003
2	Yoruba-Igbo	13,390	2,707
3	Hausa-English	7,368	1,771

Table 1. Number of words/tokens in the Training and Test Corpora

Trigrams and Weights

The first stage of this study involved generating the trigrams and the trigram weights from the unilingual training corpora (English, Hausa, Igbo and Yoruba). Character trigrams for every word in each of the training corpus whose length is equal to or greater than three were obtained. The character trigrams also used interchangeably as trigrams in this study were categorized based on their positions in a word. For words that are longer than four characters, the positions of the trigrams could either be the beginning, ending or middle of the words, while four-character words contain only start and end trigrams and three-character words has single trigrams; n-2 number of trigrams is obtainable from each word, where n is the number of characters a word has. The start trigrams are the first three characters of a word, the middle trigrams occur between the start and end trigrams, and the end trigrams are the last three characters of a word. Obtaining the start, middle and end trigrams of words is important because it has been observed that words of languages have unique start and end features which could be useful as a distinguishing factor. Similarly, certain character(s) or sounds that start or end words of some languages are not found in the middle and vice versa. For instance, a Yoruba word cannot end with a consonant or start with letter '*u*', whereas the letter '*u*' can occur in the middle or end of a Yoruba word. One-trigram words were categorized as single trigrams, because they cannot be categorized as beginning, ending or middle trigrams. Therefore, four categories of trigrams were obtained from every training corpus; single, start, middle and ending trigrams (see details in Table 2 below).

In this study, start, middle, end and single trigrams are regarded as the positional categories of trigrams. The probability of occurrence of every trigram was also obtained as the ratio of the number of times a trigram occurs to the total number of times for all the trigrams that occurred in the training corpus. The training corpora were paired for training the computer so that the paired corpora represent the two languages in a (bilingual) test corpus. In other words, there were Yoruba-English, Hausa-English and Yoruba-Igbo pairs. For each paired training corpora, a language was regarded as the main language while the other was regarded as the foreign language. For instance, the Yoruba language was regarded as the main language for the Yoruba-English training corpora pair while English was regarded as the foreign language, and the Yoruba-English pair was meant for training the computer for identifying words in the Yoruba-English bilingual corpus. The main or foreign language labelling is inconsequential as either language can be labelled as the main or foreign language. This convention was only adopted for the operation of the proposed method in this study. The trigrams that existed in each pair of unilingual training corpora were also obtained and regarded as the neutral trigrams. Hence, if '*fẹrin*' is a word from the Yoruba training corpus, it then contains the following start, middle and end trigrams- '*fẹr*', '*ẹri*', '*rin*' respectively. Since *'rin',* exist both in Yoruba and English trigrams, '*rin*', is a neutral end trigram.

The **trigram weights** (TW) of every trigram in a training corpus was obtained based on its probability and the function of the training corpus in the training corpora pair. TW was regarded as the ability of the trigram to contribute to the identification of the language of the word in which the trigram was obtained. The TW can be zero (neutral), positive or negative; this reflects the three functions of the trigrams. The TW for a (single, start, middle or end) trigram from the main language's training corpus was obtained by multiplying the probability of occurrence of the trigram by +1. Similarly, the TW for a (single, start, middle or end) trigram from the foreign language's training corpus was obtained by multiplying the probability of occurrence of the trigram by -1. On the other hand, the TW for a (single, start, *middle* and end) neutral or overlapping trigrams between the main and foreign languages from the training corpora pair was obtained by multiplying the probability of occurrence of the trigram by zero.

Twenty lists were generated from each of the unilingual training corpora pairs for the subsequent step of word-level language identification. Four lists from each of the two training corpora, that is, single, start, middle and end trigrams with four lists of their corresponding TWs were generated. For example, for the Yoruba-English pair of training corpora, single, start, middle and end trigrams as well as their corresponding TWs were generated from the Yoruba unilingual training corpus, and stored as lists. This step was repeated for the English unilingual corpus as well. In addition, four lists of the overlapping or neutral single, start, middle and end trigrams between the English and Yoruba unilingual corpora were also generated.

Hausa and English, and Yoruba and Igbo training corpora pairs were used for training the computer for the Hausa-English and Yoruba-Igbo bilingual test corpora where Hausa and Yoruba were the main languages and English and Igbo were the foreign languages respectively. The lexical similarity between two languages will determine the proportion of the neutral trigrams between them; the more similar the two languages, the larger the proportion of neutral trigrams. This is potentially one of the limitations of this study as the proportion of the shared trigrams is the discriminating factor between two languages. This nevertheless could be alleviated with the inclusion of some morphological rules and possibly semantic analytics in the adoption of this method. The phenomenon of neutral trigrams is not uncommon as two languages often share some words in their lexicons though the shared words may be semantically uncorrelated. For instance, words like '*Akin*', '*aye*', '*fun*', '*fare*' are both English and Yoruba words though they do not have the same meanings in the two languages. The trigrams of these words and others that are shared by these languages do not contribute to the ability of a computer to identify the language of a word.

Unique	All	Begin-ning	Middle	Ending	Single
English	5,640	2,383	4,654	2,086	857
Hausa	3,334	1,362	2,708	1,156	302
Igbo	3,987	1402	3198	1060	449
Yoruba	9,102	3,820	6,982	2,810	940
Overlapping					
Hausa-English	2,241	804	1,671	574	78
Igbo-Yoruba-	958	333	734	195	56
English-Yoruba	1,017	468	806	185	27

Table 2. Number of Unique and Overlapping Trigrams in the Training Corpora

Semantics or context may be required to distinguish the language of such words that occur in the two languages. The number of unique and overlapping trigrams found in different positions in words in the training corpora are displayed in Table 2.

Word-level Language Identification and Discrimination

This is the second stage of the study and it involved the use of lists of trigrams and trigram weights, which were generated in the first stage of the study. This stage involved matching the trigrams from the test corpus with the trigrams from the training corpus and obtaining the corresponding trigram weights from the training corpus. To identify the language of a word in the bilingual test corpus, the trigrams as well as their positional categories in the word were obtained. For each trigram, an appropriate list of the overlapping trigrams was first checked based on the position of the trigram, and if the trigram was found, its TW was recorded as zero. If the trigram was not found in the list of overlapping trigrams, then an appropriate list of the training corpora of the main language was checked based on its position, and if it was found, its corresponding TW was obtained. Otherwise, an appropriate list of the training corpora of the foreign language was checked based on its position, and if it was found, its corresponding TW was obtained. The language identification index (LID index) was then calculated for each word. The LID index is the addition of the TWs of all the trigrams in the word as obtained from the training corpora and normalized using the length of the word. In other words, for words that are more than four-character long, the TW of the beginning, middle and ending trigrams are added and divided by the length of the word. Words that are three-character long are single trigram words while words that are four-character long have only the beginning and ending trigrams. (See Appendix 1 for details of the steps used in calculating the LID index). For instance, if *'dàńsáakin'* is a word from the Yoruba-English bilingual test corpus, its trigrams and their TWs from the training corpora pair of Yoruba (main language) and English (foreign language) are displayed in Table 3.

Mathematically, $LID\ index\ of\ Word\ Z\ = \frac{(TW_1+TW_2+\cdots+TW_{L-2})}{L}$

Which equals to $\frac{1}{L} X \sum_{i=1}^{L-2}(TW_i)$

Where L= length of the word.

TW_1 and TW_{L-2} are the TW for the beginning and ending trigrams for word Z respectively.

Therefore, the LID index of *dàńsáakin*=$\frac{8.91E-06+7.12E-06+5.34E-06+7.12E-06+8.91E-06+0+0}{8}$

If the LID index of a word is greater than zero, then the word is predicted to belong to the main language. On the other hand, if the LID index of a word is less than zero, then the word is predicted to be a foreign word. Otherwise, if the LID index is zero, the word could exist in the two languages or the word cannot be predicted to belong to either languages. The words in this category are mostly words that exist in the two languages or words that contain character trigrams (neutral) from both languages that do not contribute to the discrimination or identification process.

Word	Tri-grams	TWs	Position of Trigram	Trigram Lang & Function
Dàńsáákì	dàń	8.91E-06	Beginning	Main, +
	àńs	7.12E-06	Middle	Main, +
	ńsá	5.34E-06	Middle	Main, +
	sáá	7.12E-06	Middle	Main, +
	áak	8.91E-06	Middle	Main, +
	aki	0	Middle	Neutral, 0
	kin	0	Ending	Neutral, 0

Table 3. Word-Level Discrimination Process for the word *'dàńsáakin'*

The choice of character n-grams where n=3 (that is, trigrams) and not n>3 is based on the consideration of the sparseness of data. For instance, at 4-grams, exponential amount of data will be required to obtain the same number of trigrams that were used in this study. Also, previous research has shown that performances of similar experiments using different values of n usually peak at 3, i.e. trigrams (Choong, Mikami, Marasinghe, & Nandasara, 2009; Suzuki, Mikami, Ohsato, & Chubachi, 2002; Jhamtani, Bhogi, & Raychoudhury, 2014; Chittaranjan, Vyas, Bali, & Choudhury, 2014).

Language Pair	Precision	Recall	Accuracy
Hausa- English	94.18%	83.45%	88.49%
Yoruba-English	99.40%	95.83%	97.79%
Yoruba-Igbo	98.23%	93.98%	96.10%
Average	97.27%	91.09%	94.13%

Table 4: Evaluation of the Strategy

RESULTS

The results are presented in three sub-sections. First, the analysis of the ranking of the words from one of the test corpora by the LID index; this is presented in the first subsection. The results of the evaluation of this strategy based on precision, recall and F1 score are then presented in sub-section 2 while the error analysis is presented in sub-section 3.

Word Ranking by LID Index

The three test corpora produced identical results, therefore one of the results was visualized in a graph. The words in the Yoruba-English corpus were arranged in ascending order by the LID index and presented in Figure 1. The graph is identical in shape to a tangential graph, with three noted regions (marked with letters A-D on the graph). The first region A-B is the sub-zero level, which contains the words from the foreign language. The second region B-C, which is the zero region, contains the unclassified words, that is, words that belong to the two languages. The third region C-D is the positive region, which contains the words that belong to the main language of the text.

Evaluation of the Strategy

The evaluation of this strategy, which is based on precision, recall and F1 score, is displayed in Table 4 below. The precision was calculated as the ratio of the number of correctly classified words to the number of classified words. The recall was calculated as the ratio of the classified words to the total number of words. The accuracy was obtained as the F1 score. The strategy worked best for the Yoruba-English bilingual texts, followed by the Yoruba-Igbo, and then Hausa-English texts. Maybe the difference in the character sets used in writing Yoruba and English contributed to the ability of the computer to distinguish between words of the two languages. However, Yoruba and Igbo languages were also written in their standard orthographies (with full diacritics) and the accuracy was above 95%. The Hausa language was not written in its full orthography, maybe this has a negative effect in identifying the words in the language. There is a need for further research to find out the effect of the encoding standard on the accuracy of this method.

Error Analysis

Based on the analysis of the errors made by the strategy adopted in this study, we will like to make a few observations. First, introducing rules will improve the method that this study proposed. For instance, specifying that a language does not contain certain characters will potentially help. For example, some Yoruba words were wrongly classified as English because they had strong English codons, however, specifying that Yoruba words do not contain ***c,z,x***, and ***q*** while English words do not contain ***ɓ, ụ, ẹ, ọ*** should improve word discrimination. Secondly, specifying that Yoruba words do not start with u can also help. For example, some of the words that were wrongly classified as Yoruba were found to contain some strong Yoruba words but with a few starting with a u. The unclassified words could also be identified through context analysis since most of them exist in the two languages or they could be left for humans to identify. Thirdly, there is not enough evidence to conclude that the size of the training corpus has an effect on the performance of the Hausa-English test corpus, rather the proportion of the overlaps between English and Hausa is high, possibly because of the wrong use of characters to represent the speech sounds in Hausa, where **ɓ, ƙ, ɗ, ƴ** were replaced with ***b, k, d*** and ***y*** respectively.

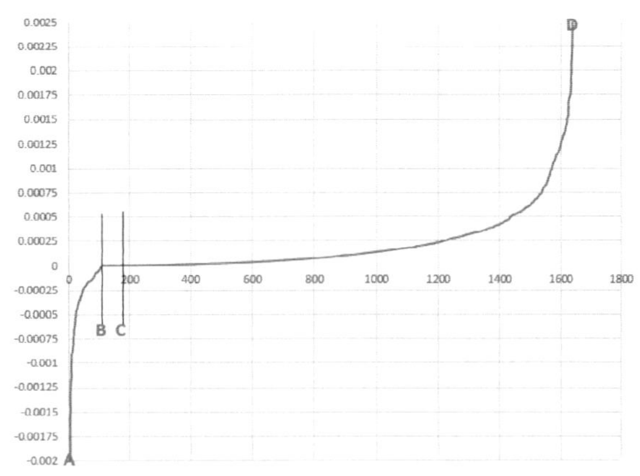

Figure 1: Graphical Presentation of the Yoruba-English Bilingual Text Result

CONCLUSION

This study developed a strategy for automatically identifying and discriminating the languages of words in a bilingual text. The results have shown that the proposed strategy is language-independent, and it requires a small corpus to achieve excellent precision and recall. Hence, the proposed strategy is suitable for resource-scarce languages, which are at a disadvantage in using dictionary-based methods for word-level identification. The essence of this study was to present an automatic means of identifying the language of individual words in a text, which potentially could be applied to corpora cleaning, language identification, multilingual information retrieval and machine translation

Scholarly and Practical Significance

This research work is a language-independent word-level language identification method with the potential of working for languages that use alphabet-based writing systems. Therefore, the application of this strategy could be extended to other languages of the world. The featured languages in this study (Hausa, Igbo and Yoruba) are geographically close; it will be interesting to see how accurate this strategy will be for lexically similar languages. The strategy could also be used for audio word-level language identification. In fact, the strategy has a greater prospect of working for word level language identification of spoken languages than written texts. This is because written texts often do not reflect the speech sounds that are made when words of language are spoken. For example, writing ought or owl in English does not reflect the sounds made when either word is pronounced.

One key practical application of the study is in corpora cleaning. In NLP studies that require the sentence structures in a language, the foreign words identified can be replaced with the main language's translated words. On the other hand, for NLP studies that require the lexicon alone, the foreign words may just be removed. Another practical application is the language identification of texts in multilingual collections to enhance language identification of under-represented languages in digital environment.

Limitations of the Study

Words with less than one trigram were not included in this strategy. It is therefore proposed that these words could be identified based on classical logic in systems where this strategy is implemented. The probability of occurrence for a one or two letter words could be set at either 0 or 1; therefore, if a one or two-character word is in the training corpus of a language, it belongs to the language.

REFERENCES

Adegbola, T., & Odilinye, L. U. (2012). Quantifying the effect of corpus size on the quality of automatic diacritization of Yorùbá texts. In Third Workshop on Spoken Language Technologies for Under-Resourced Languages (pp. 48-53). Cape Town, South Africa.

Ali, S., & Akosu, N. (2015). Word-length algorithm for language identification of under-resourced languages. Journal of King Saud University-Computer and Information Sciences, 28, 457–469.

Asahiah, F. O., Odejobi, A. O., & Adagunodo, R. E. (2017). Restoring Tone-marks in Standard Yoruba Electronic Text: Improved Model. Computer Science, 18(3), 305. https://doi.org/10.7494/csci.2017.18.3.2128

Banerjee, S., Kuila, A., Roy, A., Naskar, S. K., Rosso, P., & Bandyopadhyay, S. (2014). A hybrid approach for transliterated word-level language identification: Crf with post-processing heuristics. In Proceedings of the Forum for Information Retrieval Evaluation (pp. 54–59). ACM.

Barman, U., Das, A., Wagner, J., & Foster, J. (2014). Code mixing: A challenge for language identification in the language of social media. In Proceedings of The First Workshop on Computational Approaches to Code Switching (pp. 13–23). Retrieved from http://www.aclweb.org/website/old_anthology/W/W14/W14-39.pdf#page=21

Barman, U., Wagner, J., Chrupala, G., & Foster, J. (2014). Dcu-uvt: Word-level language classification with code-mixed data. In Proceedings of the First Workshop on Computational Approaches to Code Switching (pp. 127–132).

Central Intelligence Agency. (2017a). The World Factbook — Central Intelligence Agency: Benin. Retrieved April 28, 2017, from https://www.cia.gov/library/publications/the-world-factbook/geos/bn.html

Central Intelligence Agency. (2017b). The World Factbook — Central Intelligence Agency: Nigeria. Retrieved April 27, 2017, from https://www.cia.gov/library/publications/the-world-factbook/geos/ni.html

Chittaranjan, G., Vyas, Y., Bali, K., & Choudhury, M. (2014). Word-level language identification using CRF: Code-switching shared task report of MSR India system. In Proceedings of The First Workshop on Computational Approaches to Code Switching (pp. 73–79).

Choong, C. Y., Mikami, Y., Marasinghe, C., & Nandasara, S. (2009). Optimizing n-gram Order of an n-gram Based Language Identification Algorithm for 68 Written Languages. International Journal on Advances in ICT for Emerging Regions (ICTer), 2(2), 21. https://doi.org/10.4038/icter.v2i2.1385

Dahiya, M. (2017). Word-Level Language Identification in Bilingual Text and Back-Transliteration. International Journal of Advanced Research in Computer Engineering and Technology, 6(6), 887–889.

Das, A., & Gambäck, B. (2014). Identifying languages at the word level in code-mixed Indian social media text. In Proceedings of the 11th International Conference on Natural Language Processing, Goa, India (pp. 169–178). Citeseer. Retrieved from http://citeseerx.ist.psu.edu/viewdoc/download?doi=10.1.1.728.5180&rep=rep1&type=pdf

De Pauw, G., Wagacha, P. W., & De Schryver, G.-M. (2007). Automatic diacritic restoration for resource-scarce languages. In International Conference on Text, Speech and Dialogue (pp. 170–179). Springer. Retrieved from http://link.springer.com/chapter/10.1007/978-3-540-74628-7_24

Dias Cardoso, P. M., & Roy, A. (2016). Language Identification for Social Media: Short Messages and Transliteration (pp. 611–614). ACM Press. https://doi.org/10.1145/2872518.2890560

Falola, T., & Childs, M. D. (2005). The Yoruba Diaspora in the Atlantic World. Indiana University Press.

Gella, S., Bali, K., & Choudhury, M. (2014). "ye word kis lang ka hai bhai?" Testing the Limits of Word level Language Identification. In Proceedings of the 11th International Conference on Natural Language Processing (pp. 368–377).

Gella, S., Sharma, J., & Bali, K. (2013). Query word labeling and back transliteration for Indian languages: Shared task system description. FIRE Working Notes, 3.

Goldszmidt, M., Najork, M., & Paparizos, S. (2013). Boot-strapping language identifiers for short colloquial postings. In Joint European Conference on Machine Learning and Knowledge Discovery in Databases (pp. 95–111). Springer. Retrieved from http://link.springer.com/chapter/10.1007/978-3-642-40991-2_7

Jaech, A., Mulcaire, G., Hathi, S., Ostendorf, M., & Smith, N. A. (2016). Hierarchical character-word models for language identification. ArXiv Preprint ArXiv:1608.03030.

Jhamtani, H., Bhogi, S. K., & Raychoudhury, V. (2014). Word-level language identification in bi-lingual code-switched texts. In Proceedings of the 28th Pacific Asia Conference on Language, Information and Computing.

King, B., & Abney, S. (2013). Labeling the Languages of Words in Mixed-Language Documents using Weakly Supervised Methods. In Proceedings of NAACL-HLT 2013 (p. 1110=1119). Atlanta, Georgia: Association for Computational Linguistics.

Lavergne, T., Adda, G., Adda-Decker, M., & Lamel, L. (2014). Automatic language identity tagging on word and sentence-level in multilingual text sources: a case-study on Luxembourgish. In LREC (pp. 3300–3304).

Lui, M., Lau, J. H., & Baldwin, T. (2014). Automatic detection and language identification of multilingual documents. Transactions of the Association for Computational Linguistics, 2, 27–40.

Mandal, S., Banerjee, S., Naskar, S. K., Rosso, P., & Bandyopadhyay, S. (2015). Adaptive Voting in Multiple Classifier Systems for Word Level Language Identification. In FIRE Workshops (pp. 47–50).

Mathur, P., Misra, A., & Budur, E. (2015). Language Identification from Text Documents. Retrieved from http://cs229.stanford.edu/proj2015/324_report.pdf

News Agency of Nigeria. (2016, March 3). Yoruba Becomes Second Official Language In Benin Republic. Newsbreak.Ng. Retrieved from https://www.newsbreak.ng/2016/03/yoruba-becomes-second-official-language-in-benin-republic/

Nguyen, D.-P., & Dogruoz, A. S. (2013). Word level language identification in online multilingual communication. Association for Computational Linguistics. Retrieved from http://eprints.eemcs.utwente.nl/24092/

Piergallini, M., Shirvani, R., Gautam, G., & Chouikha, M. (2016). Word-Level Language Identification and Predicting Codeswitching Points in Swahili-English Language Data. In Proceedings of the Second Workshop on Computational Approaches to Code Switching, (pp. 21–29). Austin, Texas, USA: Association for Computational Linguistics.

Prasanthkumar, P. V., & Dileesh, E. D. (2014). Word level Script and Language identification for Unconstrained handwritten document images. In Eco-friendly Computing and Communication Systems (ICECCS), 2014 3rd International Conference on (pp. 14–18). IEEE. Retrieved from http://ieeexplore.ieee.org/abstract/document/7208958/

Rauhut, C. (2014). A Transatlantic Restoration of Religion: Of the Re-Construction of Yoruba and Lucumi in Cuban Santeria. In I. Kummels, C. Rauhut, S. Rinke, & B. Timm (Eds.), Transatlantic Caribbean: Dialogues of People, Practices, Ideas (pp. 181–200). Retrieved from www.lai.fu-berlin.de/homepages/.../Rauhut_A-Transatlantic-restauration-of-Religion....

Řehůřek, R., & Kolkus, M. (2009). Language identification on the web: Extending the dictionary method. In International Conference on Intelligent Text Processing and Computational Linguistics (pp. 357–368). Springer.

Rijhwani, S., Sequiera, R., Choudhury, M., Bali, K., & Maddila, C. S. (2017). Estimating code-switching on twitter with a novel generalized word-level language detection technique. In Proceedings of the 55th Annual Meeting of the Association for Computational Linguistics (Volume 1: Long Papers) (Vol. 1, pp. 1971–1982).

Scannell, K. P. (2011). Statistical unicodification of African languages. Language Resources and Evaluation, 45(3), 375.

Selamat, A., & Akosu, N. (2016). Word-length algorithm for language identification of under-resourced languages. Journal of King Saud University - Computer and Information Sciences, 28(4), 457–469. https://doi.org/10.1016/j.jksuci.2014.12.004

Simons, Gary F. and Charles D. Fennig (eds.). 2017. Ethnologue: Languages of the World, Twentieth edition. Dallas, Texas: SIL International. Online version: https://www.ethnologue.com/country/NG/languages

Suzuki, I., Mikami, Y., Ohsato, A., & Chubachi, Y. (2002). A language and character set determination method based on N-gram statistics. ACM Transactions on Asian Language Information Processing, 1(3), 269–278. https://doi.org/10.1145/772755.772759

Vyas, Y., Gella, S., Sharma, J., Bali, K., & Choudhury, M. (2014). POS Tagging of English-Hindi Code-Mixed Social Media Content. In EMNLP (Vol. 14, pp. 974–979).

APPENDIX 1: STEPS IN CALCULATING THE LID INDEX

	Training Corpus A from Language A=main language, Training Corpus B from language B=foreign language
Input 1	Unilingual training corpus A
Step 1	From unilingual training corpus A, generate single, start, middle and end trigrams and the probability of occurrence of the single, start, middle and end trigrams
Output 1	Lists of single, start, middle and end trigrams and the probability of occurrence of the single, start, middle and end trigrams for training corpus A
Input 2	Unilingual training corpus B
Step 2	Repeat step 1 for the training corpus B
Output 2	Lists of single, start, middle and end trigrams and the probability of occurrence of the single, start, middle and end trigrams for training corpus B
Input 3	the probability of occurrence of the single, start, middle and end trigrams for training corpus A
Step 3	From the probability of occurrence of the single, start, middle and end trigrams for training corpus A, calculate the trigram weights (TWs) by multiplying the probabilities with +1
Output 3	TWs for the single, start, middle and end trigrams for training corpus A
Input 4	The probability of occurrence of the single, start, middle and end trigrams for training corpus B
Step 4	From the probability of occurrence of the single, start, middle and end trigrams for training corpus B, calculate the TWs by multiplying the probabilities with -1
Output 4	TWs for the single, start, middle and end trigrams for training corpus B
Input 5	Single, start, middle and end trigrams from training corpus A and Single, start, middle and end trigrams from training corpus B
Step 5	generate the overlapping or neutral single, start, middle and end trigrams from the two training corpora
Output 5	neutral single, start, middle and end trigrams from the two training corpora
Input 6	Test corpus
Step 6a	From the bilingual test corpus, for each word generate the single, start, middle and end trigrams.
Step 6b	To calculate the LID index for each word, a. If word is three characters long (**single** trigram) i. Check if the **single** trigram is in the **single** neutral trigram list If yes, its LID index= 0 If no, go to ii ii. If, the **single** trigram is not in the **single** neutral list, check if it is in the **single** trigram list of training corpus A If yes, LID index =TW of the **single** trigram If no, go to iii iii. If the **single** trigram is not in the single neutral list, and **single** trigram list for corpus A, check is if it is the **single** trigram list of training Corpus B If yes, LID index=TW of the **single** trigram b. If word is more than three characters long (multiple trigrams with **start**, **middle** and **end** trigrams) i. Check if the **start** trigram is in the **start** neutral trigram list If yes, its LID index= 0 If no, go to ii ii. If, the **start** trigram is not in the **start** neutral list, check if it is in the **start** trigram list of training corpus A If yes, record the TW of the **start** trigram of the word If no, go to iii iii. If the **start** trigram is not in the **start** neutral list, and **start** trigram list for corpus A, check is if it is the **start** trigram list of training Corpus B If yes, record the TW of the **start** trigram of the word iv. Repeat the steps b.i, b.ii and b.iii for the **middle** (if they exist) and **end** trigrams to obtain their TWs Add all the TWs obtained for the word to generate the LID index for word.
Step 7	If the LID is greater than zero, the word is predicted to belong to language A Else if the LID is less than zero, the word is predicted to belong to language B Else if LID is zero, the word is predicted not be identifiable

Analyzing Scientific Collaboration with "Giants" based on the Milestones of Career

Yi Bu
Indiana University, USA. buyi@iu.edu

Dakota S. Murray
Indiana University, USA.dakmurra@iu.edu

Jian Xu *
Sun Yat-sen University, China. issxj@mail.sysu.edu.cn

Ying Ding
Indiana University, USA. dingying@indiana.edu

Peng Ai
University of Wisconsin-Madison, USA. pai6@wisc.edu

Jinhua Shen
Tongji University, China. shenjinhua111@126.com

Fan Yang
Peking University, China. jansky@pku.edu.cn

ABSTRACT

This paper explores how the patterns of collaboration change throughout a scientist's career, especially their collaboration with so-called "giants"—well-known elite scholars with very high scientific impact. We divide scientist's careers into five stages based on the number of years since obtaining their PhD, and for each stage, we calculate a number of indicators, such as publication count, normalized citation count, count of collaborations, count of collaborations with "giants," and percentage of uninterrupted and continuous presence. Our analysis shows that although collaborating with "giants" may benefit a young scholar, they are more likely to achieve greater scientific success if they first work independently and only collaborate with "giants" later in their career. Meanwhile, high-impact authors tend to work with "giants" early in their career, but not in the later stages, which forces us to reconsider the established notions of when is best to collaborate with elite scholars. Moreover, we find that high-impact authors tend to have fewer co-authors per article, regardless of the stage of their careers, indicating that collaboration is important, but the size of collaborations also matters.

KEYWORDS

Scientific collaboration, scientific career, authoritative author, pattern, scientometrics

INTRODUCTION

A professional career tends not to be uniform—different career stages may bring changes to a person's tasks, behavior, and work strategies. For example, at the beginning of the career, a promising junior entrepreneur might be eager to learn how to bring newly designed products to market or acquire venture funding, while senior businesspeople may be more likely to identify trading opportunities instead of indulging in specific product development or marketing tactics. To achieve success throughout each stage of a professional career, diverse strategies are *de facto* required. Similarly, in academia, successful scholars employ distinct strategies at each stage of their career, such as changing their collaboration patterns (Kumar & Ratnavelu, 2016).

Scientific collaboration has become increasingly prevalent in many fields of science (Zhang, Bu, Ding, & Xu, 2018). Collaborations may even lend to some scholar's success, having been shown to often result in more impactful products (Wuchty, Jones, & Uzzi, 2007), and also breed innovation (Camarinha-Matos & Afsarmanesh, 2005). Nevertheless, while successful scholars may be motivated to collaborate widely, the nature of their collaborations may change over the course of their scientific career. For example, young scholars might take the responsibility to write papers and do empirical studies (Baker & Pifer, 2011; Holgate, 2012), but will gradually start to lead research projects after several years, perhaps taking the role of a corresponding author in their collaborations (Du & Tang, 2013). Alternatively, at the beginning of their careers they may seek to collaborate with so-called "giants", who are well-known and elite authors in their field (Amjad *et al.*, 2017), but might later work more with students.

"Standing on the shoulders of giants" is a phrase repeated so often and nestled so deeply in the cultural lexicon of science that scholars have authored entire books tracing its attributions and uses (Merton, 1993). Often when scholars employ this adage it is in to reference the cumulative nature of science, with these "giants" taking the shape of famous yet long-gone scholars such as Isaac Newton and Albert Einstein; but others imply that modern scholars also stand on the shoulders of still-living "giants". Adegbola (2013) described a phenomenon wherein young scholars achieve career success by networking and benefiting from the expertise of their mentors and professional partners. Some scholars, by effort, luck, or both, gain access to the expertise and mentorship of so-called "giants" within their field of study (also referred to as authoritative authors, or AAs, in this paper). Working with AAs provides young scholars the unique opportunity to learn from elites, grow their professional networks, and help them achieve more (Amjad *et al.*, 2017), allowing them to better compete with others for resources, recognition, and employment (Kram & Isabella, 1985; Quatman & Chelladurai, 2008; Adegbola, 2010). Both metaphorically and practically, standing of the shoulders of individual "giants" is considered valuable which might motivate young scholars to seek out and collaborate with these giants.

While past research has examined the benefit of working with authoritative authors for a young scholar, little previous research has explored whether scholars should also collaborate with authoritative authors later in their career; answering this question could be crucial to help us identify successful collaboration patterns from a career-long perspective. This paper addresses this question by analyzing the entire career of researchers in the field of computer science who collaborate with authoritative authors (AAs), and examines the relationships between these collaborations and their scientific impact at each career stage.

RELATED STUDIES

Different Stages of Scientific Careers

Most researchers start their scientific careers by joining a mentor-mentee program such as doctoral training (Subramanyam, 1983; Hart, 2000), where they publish more papers than those who do not (Muschallik & Pull, 2016). Compared with other career stages, junior researchers are more likely to take the responsibility for writing manuscripts, conducting empirical studies, and implementing ideas (Pachalen & Bhattacharya, 2015) and are less likely to lead the entire research team (DeCastro, Sambuco, Ubel, Stewart, & Jaqsi, 2013). Meanwhile, young scholars during their doctoral studies tend to have more first-authored publications (Costas & Bordons, 2011). A number of researchers are interested in providing feedback to young scholars to help them achieve professional success and evaluate their career development; for example, Buddeberg-Fischer, Stamm, Buddeberg, and Klaghofer (2008) designed a one-dimensional career-success scale targeted to young researchers in the field of physics and proposed several approaches on guiding them towards high achievement. At this early stage of their career, scholars are meant to be gaining experience and preparing themselves for greater achievement later in their careers (Barbuto, Story, Fritz, & Schinstock, 2011; Schlosser & Gelso, 2001).

Having completed coursework, passed candidacy exams (e.g. qualifying exams) and defended their dissertation, junior researcher are ready to transit from doctoral students into independent scholars (Baker & Pifer, 2011). After they start their new careers, they might have research assistants or postdoctoral scholars working under them (Kumar & Ratnavelu, 2016). Nevertheless, their focus switches from purely publishing articles to writing research proposals, applying for funding, and supervising young scholars (Gulbradsen & Smeby, 2005; Price & Cotton, 2006). At this stage of career, scholars may also begin to experience stress related to productivity, promotion, and tenure—being pushed towards activities that more directly benefit their institutions (Raelin, 1985). When researchers advance to a senior or tenured position, they often serve as interpreters and interveners (Jaeger, Sandmann, & Kim, 2011) and may begin to lead research teams (Rowlands & Nicholas, 2006). Gingras, Larivière, Macaluso, and Robitaille (2008) found that senior researchers have a smaller ratio of first-authored articles, indicating that they might be managing research teams rather than executing the work. Meanwhile, senior researchers tend to spend less time on research (Kanda & Tomizawa, 2015), finding their research time limited by an increasing load of administrative duties (Barham, Foltz, & Prager, 2014; Kawaguchi, Kondo, & Saito, 2016) and teaching/service commitments (Taylor, Fender, & Burke, 2006). During this period, researchers tend not to seek mentors in an institutionalized or official way, as is usually the case while completing their education (Kram, 1985), but those wishing to cultivate mentor-mentee relationships for career progression purposes still may "seek mentors from within their organizations" (van Eck Peluchette & Jeanquart, 2000, p. 552), allowed for by the strong commitment they have given their institutional, and the shared organizational culture and values (Raelin, 1985). This later career and life stage was also found to have greater stability and less interest in relocation (van Eck Peluchette & Jeanquart, 2000). Each stage of a researcher's career brings with it distinct focuses, behaviors, and activities.

Scientific Collaboration and Career

Scientific collaboration is often considered as crucial to research in most disciplines and regardless of career stage (Wuchty *et al.*, 2007). However, the nature and frequency of collaborations varies between different career stages. For example, an international survey of 581 researchers in economics found that those who joined their current institution less than one year before have the highest proportion of multi-authored papers, which is untrue for researchers who have stayed with their current institution for ten years or more (Kumar and Ratnavelu, 2016). This study also found that researchers aged 56 or older have significantly fewer multi-authored publications than researchers do aged 45 or younger. Moreover, senior researchers show greater variation in the number of co-authors per publication than younger scholars who tend to have similar numbers of co-authors across articles (Hamermesh, 2015). Bu *et al.* (2018b) divided the high-impact researchers' careers into two parts: before and after Ph.D graduation, and found different collaboration patterns in each stage, corresponding to findings of previous research (Krapt, 2015). Moreover, in different stages of career, the division of tasks in a collaboration is also different; specifically, as pointed out by Kumar and Ratnavelu (2016), the load of tasks is "predominantly on the shoulders of the mentees" (p. 14) (or junior researchers) instead of mentors (or senior researchers) who instead provide guidance to their research assistants, postdoctoral scholars, and PhD students.

Scientific Collaboration with "Giants" (Authoritative Authors)

We often see that scholars try to meet and work with "giants" in a domain because they might provide knowledge, experience, and resources (Adegbola, 2013). Kumar and Ratnavelu (2016) found that for junior researchers, increasing their productivity is the most important reason to collaborate with "giants"; other reasons are those such as helping young scholars increase the article's likelihood of acceptance (Bhopal *et al.*, 1997; Bennett & Taylor, 2003). Some scholars have demonstrated the benefits of collaborating with "giants". For instance, Ebadi and Schiffauerova (2015) highlighted the significant role of social networking to collaboration, demonstrating that a scholar is more likely to secure more funding if they join a large research team and get connected to productive researchers who "have also a good control over the collaboration network and the flow of information" (p. 1). Packalen and Bhattacharya (2015) found that in biomedical sciences, young scholars are more likely to try out new ideas when encouraged and guided by the mentorship of more experienced researchers.

Newton claimed to have stood on the shoulders of giants; Adegbola (2013) used this as a starting point to argue that scholars in the field of healthcare could achieve success by working with "giants" in their domains. Amjad *et al.* (2017) expanded this concept and studied how working with giants influences the success of young scholars. They divided authors into two groups, those who have at any point collaborated with "giants" in their domain and those who had not. They further partitioned the first group into those who had worked with "giants" at the start of their career, and those who collaborated with "giants" later in their career. Their results showed that although collaboration with top researchers has significant positive impact on a future rising star, working alone or with "average" researchers first and then later collaborating with elite authors can also lead to success and high achievement. Based on Amjad *et al.* (2017)'s work, this paper aims to analyze the influence of scientific collaboration with "giants" in different careers using various bibliometric indicators.

METHODOLOGY

Data and Processing

The dataset is a part of ArnetMiner dataset (Tang *et al.*, 2008) including the Association for Computing Machinery (ACM) publications in the field of computer science. ArnetMiner has been widely used and considered as one of the best-curated databases for computer science articles (Dong, Johnson, & Chawla, 2016). We obtained 2,092,356 papers published between 1936 and 2014 that contain 1,207,061 unique authors and 8,024,869 citations. Author name disambiguation was performed according to the algorithms proposed by Tong, Fang, Wang, and Zhang (2012). Figure 1 outlines the procedures of data processing. Our analyses are conducted on scholars whose first publication was published between years 2000 and 2004. For each paper in this dataset, we count the number of citations each paper receives from other papers within ArnetMiner. An author's h-index (Hirsch, 2005), which has been widely used to evaluate a scholar's scientific achievements (Lacasse, Hodge, & Bean, 2011; Ciriminna & Pagliaro, 2013), is derived according to the number of his/her publications recorded in the dataset and the number of citations received.

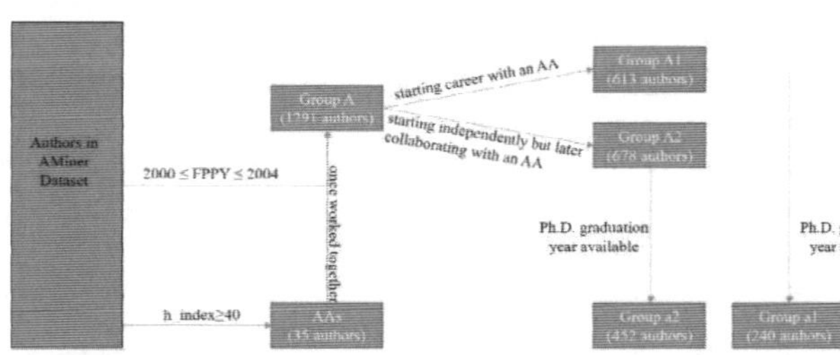

Figure 1. Procedures of data processing. (Note: FPPY = first paper published year).

Defining a "giant" is crucial in this research. As the h-index distribution for all authors is strongly skewed, we refer to Amjad *et al.* (2017) and define "giants" as those with an h-index of 40 or more and name them "authoritative authors" (AAs); there are 35 AAs in our dataset (0.002% out of all authors). In order to examine the difference of performance between scholars who have collaborated with AAs and those who have not, we partition the authors into two groups: group A contains those authors who collaborated with an AA at least once in their career (1,291 authors) and group B contains the remainder. To explore more granular patterns in their career paths, we further divide Group A authors into two sub-groups: Group A1, which includes 613 authors who published their first articles with an AA, and Group A2, which includes those who did not publish first with an AA, but later collaborated at least once with an AA. By identifying the exact year these authors obtained their doctoral degrees, we can approximate the time they start their scientific careers (Subramanyam, 1983; Hart, 2000). We manually obtain the PhD graduation year of all authors in Group A; we could only find such information for 240 and 452 authors in Groups A1 and A2; we name these two new groups with authors' PhD graduation years as Groups a1 and a2, which comprises our final population for analysis.

To indicate the research performance of authors and better analyze how their careers have been developed, we refer to Amjad *et al.* (2017) and divide all of the authors in Group a1 and a2 into three types: high-impact authors (h-index≥10), medium-impact authors (5≤h-index<10), and low-impact authors (h-index<5) based on their h-indices. Table 1 shows that the percentage of researchers with h-indices five or more in Group a2 is greater than that in Group a1, indicating that researchers who work alone at the beginning of their career and then collaborate with authoritative authors tend to have better research achievements, supporting the conclusions of Amjad *et al.* (2017).

author types		high-impact authors (h-index≥10)	medium-impact authors (10>h-index≥5)	low-impact authors (h-index<5)	total
Group a1	Number (%)	50 (20.8%)	76 (31.7%)	114 (47.5%)	240 (100%)
Group a2	Number (%)	158 (35.0%)	189 (41.8%)	105 (23.2%)	452 (100.0%)

Table 1. Impact categories of authors in Groups a1 and a2.

Methods

In the United States, many doctoral students majoring in computer science are expected to obtain their degrees in four to six years. Doctoral students tend to spend the first years of their study focused on coursework, leaving the last several years before graduation more devoted to research. After graduating with their PhD, researchers are likely to work as a postdoctoral scholar, assistant professor, or junior researchers. If they work in universities as faculty members, tenure promotion usually happens during the fourth to sixth year. If they work in industries or research institutions, they are likely to be promoted to senior researchers. Therefore, we define five stages (milestones) among the researchers' whole careers:

- Four years before PhD graduation to PhD graduation (annotated as Year -4-0): they are likely doctoral students;
- One to five years after PhD graduation (Year 1-5): they are likely to be postdocs, assistant professors, or junior researchers (Kawaguchi et al., 2016; University of California Berkley Career Center, 2017);
- Six to ten years after PhD graduation (Year 6-10): they might be assistant professors/researchers or tenured associate professors/researchers;
- 11 to 15 years after PhD graduation (Year 11-15): they might be associate professors/researchers, full professors, or senior researchers (The Princeton Overview, 2017); and
- 16 to 20 years after PhD graduation (Year 16-20): they tend to be more senior and experience, some of whom are likely to reach the end of their careers (Kawaguchi *et al.*, 2016).

For each of these periods, we calculate several bibliometric indicators. The number of publications and citations are traditional indicators to measure the scholars' research performance (de Solla Price, 1976), thus we incorporate them in this study. The number of publications is simply the number of citable items published by an author during each period. For each period, we then calculate the number of all citations made by other publications in the dataset to citable items published by the author during a given time period. For example, consider an author who publishes two journal articles, paper1 in years one-five, and paper2 during years six-ten; he/she does not publish in years 11-15. In years one-five, paper1 received ten citations. For years six-ten, paper1 received five additional citations, and paper2 received twenty citations. In years 11-15, both papers receive six citations. When calculating the author's citation count, they would have 21 (=10+5+6) citation in years one-five, 26 (=20+6) citations in years six-ten, and zero citations in years 11-15. After that, we normalize the citation count by using the product of the number of publications and the time difference between the published time and the year of 2014, i.e., the paper's age in 2014, in order to mitigate the potential biases caused by the productivity of the author's and the paper's age.

Another of our research goals is to explore scientific collaboration with authoritative authors and how it impacts a scholar's career; Hence, we will also explore relationships between career stage and the number of distinct collaborators (an indicator or collaboration), distinct AA collaborators (indicating authoritative collaborators), and average h-index of collaborators (indicating the performance of collaborators). Moreover, we are also interested in a scholar's total number of collaborators. We use these indicators to analyze the career trajectory of each author in Groups a1 and a2 along different career stages:

- the number of papers published;
- the number of citations received, normalized by each paper's age;
- the number of distinct collaborators;
- the number of distinct AA collaborators;
- the average h-index of the distinct collaborators; and
- the average number of collaborators per article published.

For each of these indicators, we perform median-based tests of statistical significance on using raw values because of the skewness distribution. We also use an indicator of uninterrupted and continuous presence (UCP) to measure the consistency of a researcher's achievements. Here, degree of UCP is defined as publishing at least one/three/five paper(s) in any consecutive five years. Ioannidis *et al.* (2014) argued that researchers maintaining UCP in publications could achieve higher citation impacts than those who cannot, and that UCP is a latent indicator for measuring scholars' research activity and professional sociability. Hence, the higher UCP a researcher has, the more achievements and stability they might achieve in their scientific career.

RESULTS

Figures 2-4 show the results of career analyses on different indicators of Group a1 and a2. Table 2 lists the statistical significance test results for all indicators. Some publications are excluded from these calculations because they are in some way an "extreme", such as having 15 or more co-authors or more than 10,000 citations. We also exclude certain extreme authors, such as those who have published more than 200 publications within any of the five-year time windows. For some groups there is no value for years 11-15 because no data is available for later period(s). For instance, authors who obtain their PhD after 2003 would enter into years 16-20 after 2014, which is not included in our analysis.

From the perspective of the number of papers one author had in different career stages (Figure 2 left and Table 2), we can see difference emerge between Groups a1 and a2 only after year 0, their PhD graduation. This indicates that although the similar-impact authors in Groups a1 and a2 publish similar number of papers before PhD graduation, a2 tends to be more productive after graduation, and thus more active in scientific activities (de Solla Price, 1976). Specifically, the gap in the number of publications between high-impact authors in these two groups increases as authors become older. Meanwhile, within 15 years of obtaining their doctoral degrees, authors with similar impact tend to publish fewer articles in Group a1 than in a2. However, compared with a1, authors in a2 seem more diligent when they become older. Therefore, although Group a1 was lucky enough to work with AAs at the beginning of their careers, they tended not to be as consistently productive as those in Group a2; on the contrary, a2 authors' hard work may have attracted the attentions of AAs who then began to collaborate with them.

It is also worth noting that high-impact authors in Group a2 publish more papers in years 16-20 than in years 11-15. During years 16-20, many researchers could have obtained their tenured position, some perhaps being promoted to full professors. Although previous studies have shown that a researcher's productivity tends to decrease in the later parts of their careers (Kanda & Tomizawa, 2015), our finding demonstrates that high-impact authors in Group a2, those who started their career independently and later have the chance to work with "giants", continuously publish and make consistent scientific contributions. Regardless of group, low impact authors have the fewest publications while the high-impact authors have the most, likely resulting from the fact that the h-index, our measure of impact, is dependent on the number of publications (Hirsch, 2005).

indicator	high	medium	low	indicator	high	medium	low
no. of publications	***	**	**	no. of distinct AA collaborators	**	*	***
normalized no. of citations	**	*	**	average no. of h-index of collaborators	*	**	***
no. of distinct collaborators	***	***	**	average no. of collaborators per article	***	***	*

Table 2. Statistical significance test for indicators in Groups a1 and a2 among high-, medium-, and low-impact groups (Note: *: <0.05; **: <0.01; ***: <0.001.).

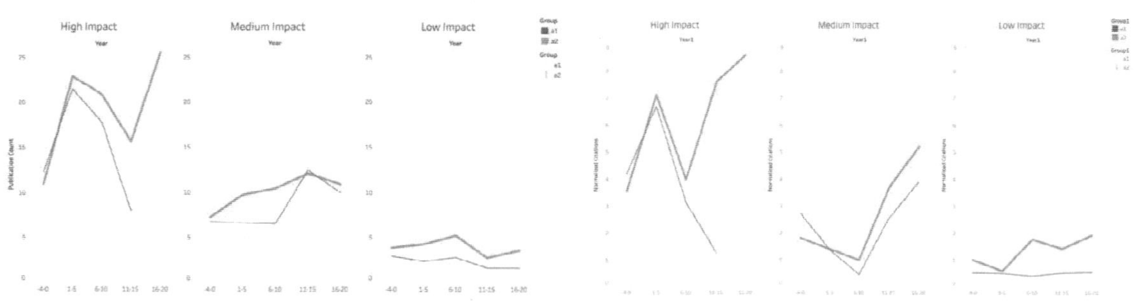

Figure 2. Average number of publications (left) and average normalized number of citations (right) for Groups a1 and a2.

As for the normalized number of citations (Figure 2 right and Table 2), the publications of Group a2 authors tend to receive more citations after we remove the biases of authors' productivity and papers' ages. After receiving their doctoral degrees, authors in Group a2 tend to receive slightly more citations than authors in Group a1, indicating greater scientific success during and immediately after their PhD, perhaps a precursor to a successful career. During later career stages, there is greater disparity between high-impact authors of both groups, with high-impact authors in Group a2 vastly outperforming authors in Group a1. These findings are consistent to the results of Amjad *et al.* (2017) who found that Group a2 authors have a tendency to receive more citations than Group a1 authors and such difference becomes larger as their careers progress. Meanwhile, we see a high number of citations in years 16-20 for high-impact authors in Group a2, consistent with the indicator of publication count shown in Figure 2 left. This not only demonstrates the career-long diligence of these authors but also suggests consistent quality of published papers throughout their scientific careers. We can also examine the number of collaborators of authors in each group, as in Figure 3 left (see significance test results in Table 2, the same below), and we see that the higher the impact of an author, the more collaborators they have, again demonstrating the importance of collaboration (Wuchty *et al.*, 2007). High-impact authors have twice the average number of collaborators than low-impact authors.

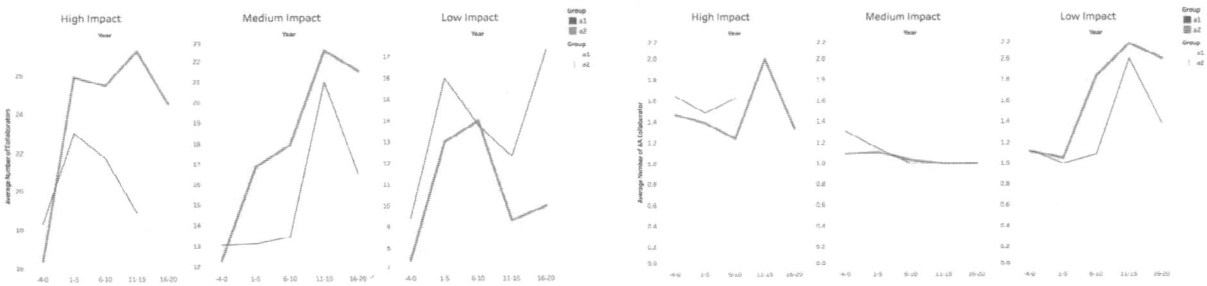

Figure 3. Average number of collaborators (left) and average number of AA collaborators (right) for Groups a1 and a2.

Figure 3 right shows that high-impact authors in these two groups have relatively more AA collaborators before their PhD graduations than after. Collaborating with AAs enables young scholars the chance to "stand on the shoulder" of the giants (Amjad *et al.*, 2017, p. 307), giants who might guide them on how to conduct research and prepare for future work. However, it does not seem that the more collaborations with AAs, the more successful the authors, especially five and ten years after their PhD graduation. One of the interpretations concerning this finding is that there is potential for the "halo effects" of AAs to "outshine" junior scholars and to some extent fetter their development (Bu *et al.*, 2018b). This finding warns us that collaborations with "giants" are not always as beneficial as we might think, especially at the beginning of our careers. Figure 4 left depicts the average h-index of collaborators for Groups a1 and a2 of authors in order to examine the impact of their collaborators. The result shows that the average h-index of collaborators declines as their careers progress, regardless of which group an author is in. This finding confirms our intuitive assumptions: At the beginning of their career, a scholar is likely to be a student, with their main collaborator being their advisor, supervisor, or mentor, who will tend to have a higher h-index than themselves; as time goes by, they may become an established researcher and their collaborators could include more students or junior researchers, decreasing the average h-index of their collaborators. The average number of collaborators per article, shown in Figure 4 right, ranges between two and five. Krapf (2015) points out that the skills and research capability of researchers can be exercised and enhanced by performing different types of tasks, such as designing research, conducting empirical studies, reviewing literature, writing manuscripts, and analyzing data. Exercise and experience with these distinct tasks could help them achieve their future success (Krapf, 2015). Nevertheless, low-impact authors, no matter which group they belong, are found to have more co-authors per article, suggesting a point where too many co-authors ceases to be beneficial.

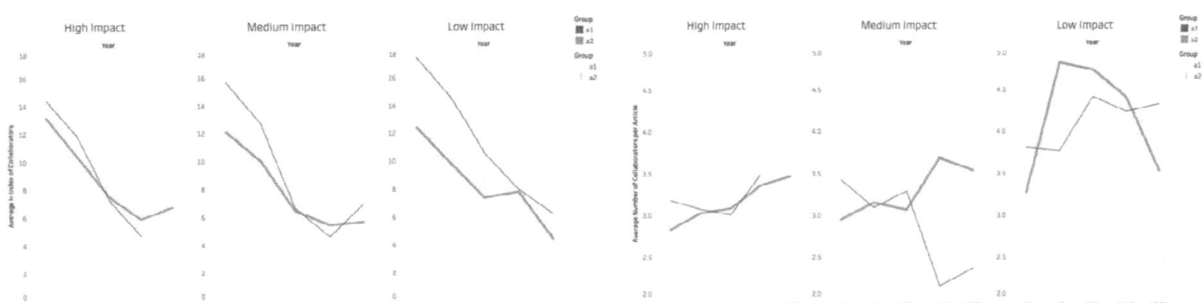

Figure 4. Average h-index of collaborators (left) and average number of collaborators per article (right) for Groups a1 and a2.

Figure 5 shows the UCP results based on different criteria (one, three, and five papers per year), in which we can see that the authors' UCP percentage in Group a2 is almost twice as many as that in Group a1. Specifically, about 70%, 28%, and 12% of the Group a2 authors can maintain a UCP publication flow for one, three, and five papers per year, while only 39%, 12%, and 5% of Group a1 authors can do so. This high value for UCP indicates that Group a2 has more consistent scholarly activities throughout their careers, corroborating the results of Amjad *et al.* (2017). For all of the authors satisfying UCP criteria in these two groups, we partition them into one of three categories based on whether they achieve their UCP status before, during, or after their PhD graduations. *Before PhD graduation* is defined as the periods before obtaining their PhD, including any publications made before they obtain their doctoral degree. *After PhD graduation* includes all papers published by an authors after their PhD graduation. The period of *during PhD graduation* overlaps with before/after PhD graduation; the starting time of during PhD graduation should be before the graduation year of doctoral degree and the ending time should be after the graduation year of doctoral degree. That is to say, the period of *during PhD graduation* should cover one author's PhD graduation year. For example, if an author begins his/her PhD in 2005 and completes it in 2010, then *before PhD graduation* would be defined as any time before 2010, *during PhD graduation* would be defined as the period that covers 2010, and *after PhD graduation* as any time after 2010. Figure 6 shows a low percentage of author UCP *before PhD graduation* in both groups. *During the PhD,* the percentage of author UCP in Group a2 is more than that in Group a1, and after graduating with their PhD, the gap doubles or even triples. This large discrepancy indicates dramatic variations of career trajectories between groups. Researchers without a UCP record are found more likely to leave academia and research (Ioannidis *et al.*, 2014); hence, Group a2 tends to be successful probably due to their "stable" scientific careers.

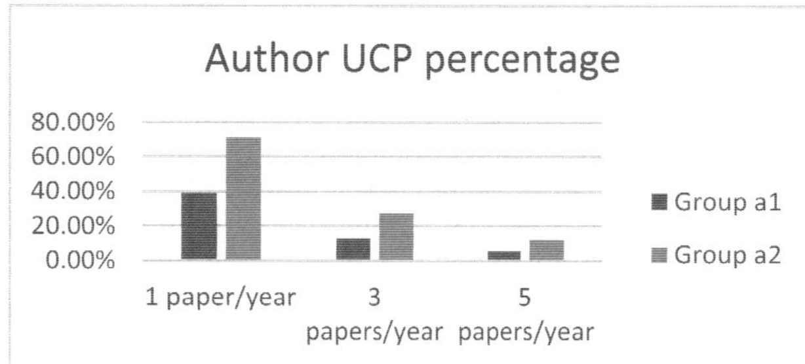

Figure 5. Authors' uninterrupted and continuous presence (UCP) percentage in Groups a1 and a2.

DISCUSSION AND CONCLUSIONS

Robert Merton detailed the "halo effect" (1968), which implies that the prestige and respect of successful scholars may "rub off" on their close counterparts, but our findings paint a more complicated image. This paper investigates the dimension of time in regard to collaborating with authoritative authors, or "giants", and explores how working with giants at different stages of a scientific career might lead to distinct outcomes. We divide the careers of researchers into different stages and calculate a number of indicators for each stage (e.g. number of publications, normalized number of citations, number of collaborations, and UCP percentage, etc.). Our results show that although working with "giants" may have benefits and appeal for ambit ious young scholars who prioritize career achievement and productivity; it is hardly a requirement for long-term success. Instead, working hard to become an established researcher, and only later attracting the attention of "giants" to work with and learn from tends to lead to greater professional achievement. The greater determinant of career success seems to be persistent hard work and continuous scientific contribution, evidenced by both our work and that of past researchers (Ioannidis *et al.*, 2014).

The Matthew effect in science (Merton, 1968) implies that if a young scholar dreams of success and prestige, then they would benefit from building cumulative advantage early in their career by finding and working with an elite and prestigious "giant" in their field. Our findings provide evidence that shows this may not be the case. While prestige has benefits, attentive mentorship may be more important for a young scholar just starting their research career. A "giant" may have little time for careful guidance of in dividuals, and is instead likely has many professional engagements, such as giving external lectures, serving on professional organization committees, mentoring doctoral students, and tending to heavy teaching and service loads (Barham *et al.*, 2014; Taylor, Fender, & Burke, 2006). In such circumstances, a young scholar may benefit from a more junior mentor who can devote more time to individual mentorship.

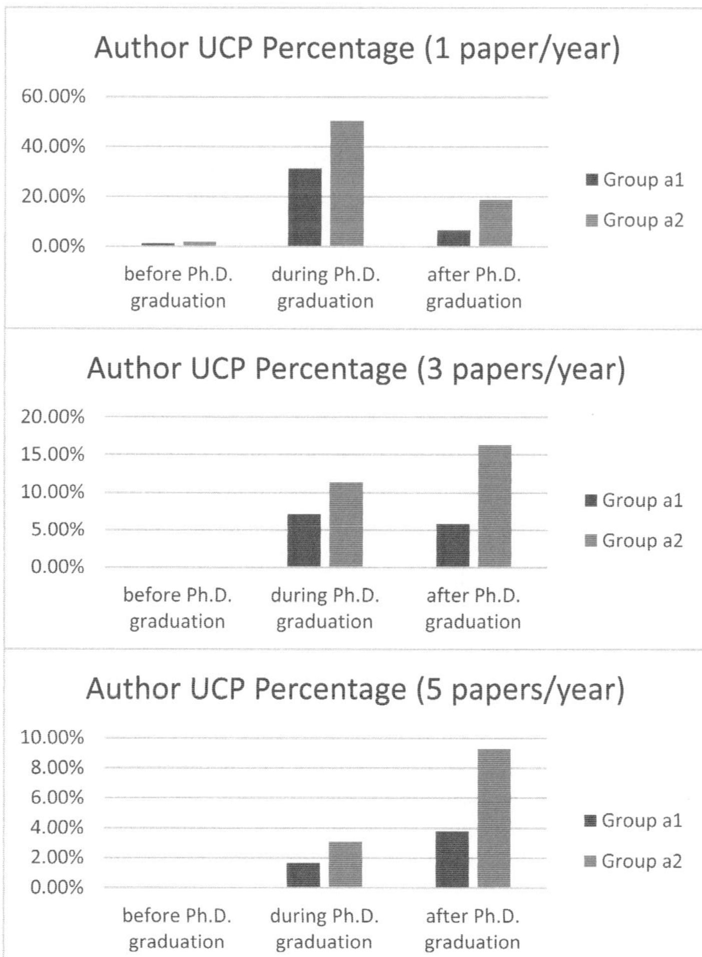

Figure 6. Author UCP percentage in different periods with different criteria: 1, 3, and 5 paper(s)/year

We need to reconsider the traditional wisdom of academia, and instead realize that there is a right time to prioritize prestige, and a right time to prioritize mentorship. Working with an authoritative author at the right time, when a scholar is still young but with an established career can position them to most benefit from the prestige and experience of such collaborations. Timing "forcefully moves them from inertia to dynamic and explosive scholarly heights" (Adegbola, 2013, p.17). Mentor-mentee program directors and conference organizers may be able to use these findings so that they can design conferences, workshops, and other opportunities that allow beginning, junior, and senior scholars to communicate and interact in a way that most benefits them. When it come s to mentorship and collaboration, there is no universal prescription; rather, policies and programs should reflect the fact that for best results, one must do the right thing at the right time.

This paper also explored the shifting styles of collaboration between levels of impact and throughout a career. We found that high-impact authors tend to have fewer coauthors per article than do medium- and low-impact authors, regardless of the stage of their career; while collaboration is important, this finding also indicates that the total number of collaborations also seems to have an effect. Too many collaborators in a research project may dilute the effectiveness of the team and result in a weaker publication. The increasing of the number of coauthors in one publication also hints at decreasing relative workloads for each author (Schneider & Doyen, 2005). As noted by Curral, Forrester, Dawson, and West (2011), too large of a team may limit performance, which then could limit the quality of the paper. Conducting research in large teams and on many projects may lead team-members to be less engaged with each individual project, and the loss efficiency by spending a disproportionate amount of time organizing the team, rather than improving the research (Vrabie, 2013). This finding adds to the literature of collaboration and offers the insight that more is not always better, a truism that seems to hold throughout a scholar's career.

This study is one of the first to explore the idea of "doing the right thing at the right time" in academia, and being an exploratory study, suffers from several limitations—most of which result from its scale. Identifying the collaborators of authoritative authors along with their career milestones, such as PhD graduation requires lengthy manual work, and limits the samples size of researchers to only a few hundred. With such a small sample, we cannot control for many of the confounding factors in our work. For example, researchers defined in Group a1, those who begin their career with giants, may be working on their PhD but after graduation may pursue a non-research-intensive career, publishing less or not at all, and thus lowering the average of the group's indicators. Conversely, researchers in Group a2, those who collaborate with giants later in their career are likely to be those who stay in academia and research enough to catch the attention of these giants and are therefore, almost by definition, likely to be stronger and more committed researchers. Differences in sub-discipline may also play a role; we were forced to define a cutoff with which to identify "giants", however different subfields vary greatly in the number of citations and publications they may receive (Qian, Rong, Jiang, Tang, & Xiong, 2017). A threshold at an h-index of 40 may restrict the number of "giants" in our sample; in the future, we plan to refer to Hohberger (2016) and define "giants" by using the top one and/or two percentile h-index authors. The h-index of 40 threshold might limit the sources of "giants" to a small number of highly productive or high-citation sub-fields which may have distinct patterns of collaboration, mentorship, and career trajectories after PhD graduation; these patterns are likely to diverge even more so between disciplines, such as in the life sciences or humanities. Moreover, because we simply aim to analyze collaboration with "giants" in various careers, this paper does not set as a baseline those authors who never have had any opportunities to work with "giants". Also, the citation count and h-index are both based on the records within the dataset, which might cause some biases. These limitations lead us to make our conclusions cautiously; while our findings offer evidence for distinct trends and nuances in collaboration over a career, more work is necessary to present a thorough understanding of the field.

Failing to take other co-authors into consideration is one of the limitations of the current paper. It is likely that the papers completed by a certain research and an AA are also co-authored with others. We will try to address this problem in the near future. On the other hand, ignoring the asymmetry between two co-authors is also imperfect. A potential approach to deal with it is to consider the preferred partners of a given author, such as employing Affinity Index and Probabilistic Affinity Index (Chinchilla-Rodríguez *et al.*, 2018). Meanwhile, we hope to work to increase and diversify our sample of researchers and control for these confounding factors. We also hope to expand the range of disciplines in order to understand whether the patterns of collaboration we find in the careers of computer scientists are similar in other fields. Moreover, we will expand our suite of indicators, which while presently useful for creating a rough understanding of a scholar's career achievement, do not capture the nuances of scientific impact. More indicators will also allow us to explore other aspects of collaboration and career stage, such as changes in impact diversity, research topic, collaborator diversity, and the degree of persistence (Bu *et al.*, 2018a) and stability (Bu *et al.*, 2018c) regarding scientific collaborations. This work lays the foundation for future exploration of how collaboration and other aspects of a researcher's career may affect future success, and to identity not only how to shape a successful career, but also when to prioritize different tasks and behaviors.

ACKNOWLEDGEMENT

The authors would like to thank three anonymous reviewers for their improving the quality of this paper.

REFERENCES

Adegbola, M. (2010). Nurses collaborating with cross disciplinary networks: starting to integrate genomics into practice. *Journal of National Black Nurses Association*, 21(1), 46-49.

Adegbola, M. (2013). Scholarly tailgating defined: A diverse, giant network. The ABNF Journal: *Official Journal of the Association of Black Nursing Faculty in Higher Education, Inc*, 24(1), 17-20.

Amjad, T., Ding, Y., Xu, J., Zhang, C., Daud, A., Tang, J., & Song, M. (2017). Standing on the shoulders of giants. *Journal of Informetrics*, 11(1), 307-323.

Baker, V.L., & Pifer, M.J. (2011). The role of relationships in the transition from doctoral student to independent scholar. Studies in Continuing Education, 33(1), 5–17.

Barbuto, J.E., Jr., Story, J.S., Fritz, S.M., & Schinstock, J.L. (2011). Full range advising: Transforming the advisor-advisee experience. *Journal of College Student Development*, 52(6), 656-670.

Barham, B.L., Foltz, J.D., & Prager, D.L. (2014). Making time for science. *Research Policy*, 43(1), 21-31.

Bennett, D.M., & Taylor, D.M. (2003). Unethical practices in authorship of scientific papers. *Emergency Medicine Australasia*, 15(3), 263-270.

Bhopal, R., Rankin, J., ..., & Rodgers, H. (1997). The vexed question of authorship: Views of researchers in a British medical faculty. *British Medical Journal*, 314(7086), 1009-1012.

Bu, Y., Ding, Y., Liang, X., & Murray, D.S. (2018a). Understanding persistent scientific collaboration. *Journal of the Association for Information Science and Technology*, 69(3), 438-448.

Bu, Y., Ding, Y., Xu, J., Liang, X., Gao, G., & Zhao, Y. (2018b). Understanding success through the diversity of collaborators and the milestone of career. *Journal of the Association for Information Science and Technology*, 69(1), 87-97.

Bu, Y., Murray, D.S., Ding, Y., Huang, Y., & Zhao, Y. (2018c). Measuring the stability of scientific collaboration. *Scientometrics*, 114(2), 463-479.

Camarinha-Matos, L.M., & Afsarmanesh, H. (2005). Collaborative networks: A new scientific discipline. Journal of Intelligent Manufacturing, 16(4-5), 439-452.

Chinchilla-Rodríguez, Z., Bu, Y., Robinson-García, N., Costas, R., & Sugimoto, C. R. (2018). Travel bans and scientific mobility: Utility of asymmetry and affinity indexes to inform science policy. Scientometrics.

Ciriminna, R., & Pagliaro, M. (2013). On the use of the h-index in evaluating chemical research. Chemistry Central Journal, 7(1), 132.

Costas, R., & Bordons, M. (2011). Do age and professional rank influence the order of authorship in scientific publications? Some evidence from a micro-level perspective. Scientometrics, 88(1), 145-161.

Curral, L.A., Forrester, R.H., Dawson, J.F., & West, M.A. (2001). It's what you do and the way that you do it: Team task, team size, and innovation-related group processes. European Journal of Work and Organizational Psychology, 10(2), 187-204.

DeCastro, R., Sambuco, D., Ubel, P.A., Stewart, A., & Jaqsi, R. (2013). Mentor networks in academic medicine: Moving beyond a dyadic conception of mentoring for junior faculty researchers. Journal of the Association of American Medical Colleges, 88(4), 488-496.

Dong, Y., Johnson, R.A., & Chawla, N.V. (2016). Can scientific impact be predicted? IEEE Transactions on Big Data, 2(1), 18–30.

Du, J., & Tang, X. (2013). Perceptions of author order versus contribution among researchers with different professional ranks and the potential of harmonic counts for encouraging ethical co-authorship practices. Scientometrics, 96(1), 277-295.

Ebadi, A., & Schiffauerova, A. (2015). How to receive more funding for your research? Get connected to the right people! PLoS One, 10(7), e0133061.

Gingras, Y., Larivière, V., Macaluso, B., & Robitaille, J.-P. (2008). The effects of aging on researchers' publication and citation patterns. PLoS One, 3(12), e0004048.

Gulbradsen, M., & Smeby, J.-C. (2005). Industry funding and university professors' research performance. Research Policy, 34(6), 932-950.

Hamermesh, D.S. (2015). Age, cohort and co-authorship. Cambridge, MA: National Bureau of Economic Research.

Hart, R.L. (2000). Co-authorship in the academic library literature: A survey of attitudes and behaviors. Journal of Academic Librarianship, 26(5), 339-345.

Hirsch, J.E. (2005). An index to quantify an individual's scientific research output. Proceedings of the National Academy of Sciences of the United States of America, 102(46), 16569-16572.

Hohberger, J. (2016). Does it pay to stand on the shoulders of giants? An analysis of the inventions of star inventors in the biotechnology sector. Research Policy, 45(3), 682-698.

Holgate, S.A. (2012) How to collaborate. Science (Careers), DOI: 10.1126/science.caredit.a1200082.

Ioannidis, J.P.A., Boyack, K.W., & Klavans, R. (2014). Estimates of the continuously publishing core in the scientific workforce. PLoS One, 9(7), e101698.

Jaeger, A.J., Sandmann, L.R., & Kim, J. (2011). Advising graduate students doing community-engaged dissertation research: The advisor-advisee relationship. Journal of Higher Education Outreach and Engagement, 15(4), 5-25.

Kanda, Y., & Tomizawa, H. (2015). Changes in the ratio of time spent on work activities by university and college faculty members: A comparison of results of the ''Survey of full-time equivalency data at universities and colleges'' of 2002, 2008 and 2013. NISTEP Research Material 236 (in Japanese). Retrieval from http://data.nistep.go.jp/dspace/handle/11035/3027.

Kawaguchi, D., Kondo, A., & Saito, K. (2016). Researchers' career transitions over the life cycle. Scientometrics, 109(3), 1435-1454.

Kram, K.E., & Isabella, L.A. (1985). Mentoring alternatives: The role of peer relationships in career development. Academy of Management Journal, 28(1), 110-132.

Koch, C.G. (2007). The science of success: How market-based management built the world's largest private company. Hoboken, NJ: Wiley.

Kumar S., & Ratnavelu, K. (2016). Perceptions of scholars in the field of Economics on co-authorship associations: Evidence from an international survey. PLoS One, 11(6), e0157633.

Lacasse, J.R., Hodge, D.R., & Bean, K.F. (2011). Evaluating the productivity of social work scholars using the h-index. Research on Social Work Practice, 21(5), 599-607.

Merton, R.K. (1968). The Matthew Effect in science. Science, 159(3810), 56-63.

Merton, R.K. (1993). On the Shoulders of Giants. Chicago: University of Chicago Press.

Muschallik, J., & Pull, K. (2016). Mentoring in higher education: Does it enhance mentees' research productivity? Education Economics, 24(2), 210-223.

Packalen, M., & Bhattacharya, J. (2015). Age and the trying out of new ideas. National Bureau of Economic Research. DOI: 10.3386/w20920.

Qian, Y., Rong, W., Jiang, N., Tang, J., & Xiong, Z. (2017). Citation regression analysis of computer science publications in different ranking categories and subfields. Scientometrics, 110(3), 1351-1374.

Quatman, C., & Chelladurai, P. (2008). Social network theory and analysis: A complementary lens for inquiry. Journal of Sport Management, 22(3), 338-360.

Raelin, J. (1985). The clash of cultures. Boston: Harvard Business School Press.

Rowlands, I., & Nicholas, D. (2006). The changing scholarly communication landscape: an international survey of senior researchers. Learned Publishing, 19(1), 31-55.

Schlosser, L.Z., & Gelso, C.J. (2001). Measuring the working alliance in advisor–advisee relationships in graduate school. Journal of Counseling Psychology, 48(2), 157-167.

Schneider, M.E., & Doyen, B. (2005). The everything guide to writing a book proposal: Insider advice on how to get your work published. San Diego, California: Adams Media Corporation.

de Solla Price, J. (1976). A general theory of bibliometric and other cumulative advantage processes. Journal of the American Society for Information Science, 27(5), 292-306.

de Solla Price, J., & Cotten, S.R. (2006). Teaching, research, and service: Expectations of assistant professors. The American Sociologist, 37(1), 5-21.

Subramanyam, K. (1983). Bibliometric studies of research collaboration: A review. Journal of Information Science, 6(1), 33-38.

Tang, J., Fong, A.C.M., Wang, B., & Zhang, J. (2012). A unified probabilistic framework for name disambiguation in digital library. IEEE Transaction on Knowledge and Data Engineering, 24(6), 975-987.

Tang, J., Zhang, J., Yao, L., Li, J., Zhang, L., & Su, Z. (2008). ArnetMiner: Extraction and mining of academic social networks. In Proceedings of the fourteenth ACM SIGKDD International Conference on Knowledge Discovery and Data Mining, pp.990-998, August 24-27, 2008, Las Vegas, NV., U.S.A.

Taylor, W., Fender, B., & Burke, K. (2006). Unraveling the academic productivity of economists: The opportunity costs of teaching and service. Southern Economic Journal, 72(4), 846-859.

The Princeton Overview. (2017). A day in the life of a professor. Retrieved from https://www.princetonreview.com/careers/127/professor.

University of California Berkley Career Center. (2017). The transition from graduate student to assistant professor. Retrieved from https://career.berkeley.edu/PhDs/PhDtransition.

van Eck Peluchette, J., & Jeanquart, S. (2000). Professionals' use of different mentor sources at various career stages: Implications for career success. The Journal of Social Psychology, 140(5), 549-564.

Vrabie, A. (2013). Productivity and team size: Less is more. Retrieved from http://blog.sandglaz.com/productivity-and-team-size-less-is-more/

Wuchty, S., Jones, B. F., & Uzzi, B. (2007). The increasing dominance of teams in production of knowledge. Science, 316(5827), 1036-1039.

Zhang, C., Bu, Y., Ding, Y., & Xu, J. (2018). Understanding scientific collaboration: Homophily, transitivity, and preferential attachment. *Journal of the Association for Information Science and Technology*, 69(1), 72-86.

Leader of the Pack: On Plagiarism Prevention Through Research Group Enculturation

George Buchanan
University of Melbourne, Australia. george.buchanan@unimelb.edu.au

Dana McKay
University of Melbourne, Australia. danamckay@gmail.com

ABSTRACT

Mispractice by researchers—plagiarism in particular—is, according to the research evidence enculturated within research groups. We interview a small sample of senior academics with a clean record regarding plagiarism, to investigate what has influenced their practice, and how they in turn influence the research groups and research students that they oversee. Our aim is to understand what strategies enculturate good practice. We point to surprisingly complex interactions between technology and culture.

KEYWORDS

Academic mispractice, plagiarism, cultural studies, open access, research ethics, information ethics

INTRODUCTION

There is a broad body of literature on plagiarism by university students, addressing causes, prevention, prevalence and management. Less common is literature on researcher plagiarism, though some studies have begun to examine prevalence and investigate PhD practice e.g. (Bretag & Mahmud, 2009; Gray & Jordan, 2012).

Research mispractice and plagiarism prevention are increasingly an area of interest both for research and practice. One factor in this interest is open access repositories, which make it easier for would-be plagiarists to access source material—which they demonstrably do (Buchanan & McKay, 2017)—but may also make plagiarism detection easier (Harnad, 1998). While uptake has been slow, some publication venues are now using TurnItIn-like plagiarism detection software (e.g. Elsevier and Springer are involved in the Similarity Check Initiative). Stacked against the increased opportunity for detection is an increasing mandate to 'publish or perish' that may promote plagiarism (Crace, 2003; Larivière & Gingras, 2010). Both the size of the academic literature and the number of papers read grew substantially in the 30 years to 2009 (Tenopir, et al., 2009); a trend that has likely continued. In this time plagiarism also appears to have increased, though the evidence for this is mixed (Larivière & Gingras, 2010; Miller et al., 2011).

The discovery of academic misconduct can be career-ending—as seen in a recent Australian case (Ketchell, 2012)—it is embarrassing for both the academic and the institution. Further self-archiving of infringing publications in institutional repositories could lead to copyright infringement claims against the institution (*University IT Systems: Managing Liability for Transmitting, Caching, Hosting and Linking to Copyright Material* 2007). Preventing plagiarism is in the best interest of everyone but plagiarists: plagiarism promotes bad science (Supak-Smolčić & Bilić-Zulle, 2013), stale conference material (Ison, 2012), and inappropriate allocation of academic credit (Bruton, 2014). How to promote *good* practice—what the influencers are and how to leverage them—is less clear.

One possible influence is enculturation; a study of PhD student attitudes to ethics and academic misconduct demonstrated high correlation with supervisor attitudes (Gray & Jordan, 2012). Further, supported we know that that personality traits affect tolerance for and propensity to plagiarism (Etter, Cramer, & Finn, 2006). A small-sample study of Australian academics' evaluation of varying levels of self-plagiarism revealed a near-dichotomy between those who do and those who don't (Bretag & Carapiet, 2007). Our own previous work on plagiarism provides further significant evidence for enculturation as a factor, demonstrating that plagiarism is clustered within research groups: those groups that have engaged in plagiarism are multiple offenders, whereas there is little evidence for isolated incidences within 'clean' research groups (Buchanan & McKay, 2017). Given that prevention is better than cure when it comes to plagiarism (Carroll, 2004; Gray & Jordan, 2012; Kara & MacAlister, 2010; Miller et al., 2011), understanding the drivers and influencers of this enculturation is important. As, such, we interviewed a sample of senior academics from research groups where there was no evidence of plagiarism. We asked about their experiences of plagiarism and how they manage the risk within their groups. From their responses, we identify several technological and social influences.

The paper is divided as follows: first we survey the literature on plagiarism, enculturation and academic misconduct. Then we describe our method and the results of our study, focusing on social and technical enculturation. Next, we discuss our results in the context of the current literature. Finally, we draw conclusions, and suggest future research.

BACKGROUND

In this section we first examine the concept of enculturation, drawing on the literature from cultural studies, then we make a case against plagiarism, addressing the complex issue of self-plagiarism. We then examine the prevalence of plagiarism; finally, we discuss plagiarism prevention, and the relationship between plagiarism and open access.

Cultural Theory and Enculturation

Recent years have seen a growth in interest in the theories of cultural studies (Bardzell, 2009; Harper & Mentis, 2013) by researchers in both human-computer interaction and information science. Previous research has concluded that senior personnel in a research group have influence their junior colleagues, and shape the ethos and practice of the group (Gray & Jordan, 2012), meaning cultural studies are a relevant lens for studies of research practice.

How ideas are created, spread and guarded within communities is a major strand of research on culture, flowing right from the beginning of the discipline. There are many theories of how cultures and values are diffuse through groups. One classic approach is to portray a single, culturally exclusive and dominant viewpoint as the norm. Commonly termed the 'high' view of culture, an elite group defines what is desirable behaviour, and other groups mimic this with varying degrees of authenticity and success. An example of this is Pierre Bourdieu's conception of taste and how it is used to define and defend a cultural elite (Bourdieu, 1984). Bourdieu himself, however, both criticised the social dynamic he examined and questioned the theoretical validity of relying on a single hierarchy. High culture theory, though, has numerous limitations: it presumes a single norm, and a single hierarchy of power and exclusivity, e.g. see (Dimaggio & Ostrower, 1990). It is poor at explaining how alternative groups generate their influence and power, and multiple competing social groups can co-exist with individuals having greater or lesser power within each group. For example, a person interested in music could be elite in their knowledge of jazz but be relatively ignorant of punk.

It is not clear whether research groups are best understood as diverse and heterogeneous, or as being aligned towards an elite on a single spectrum. This issue is particularly relevant to the question of the dissemination of norms: heterogeneous contexts lead to lower levels of conformity than elite contexts. Even within the heterogeneous model in a specific cultural field, some individuals will be seen as more authoritative. Where there is a hierarchical dynamic, they will have a strong local influence (Triandis, 1995). An individual's contextual cultural capital grows with accumulated knowledge, prestige and seniority within a group. Academic research is seen as a culturally significant product by those within it, thus we should expect to see a strong influence from the existing elite. This general theory would corroborate the speculation by previous researchers that behavioural norms are led by the senior members of research teams and suggests that senior people will refer to their own influencers and current status to validate their viewpoints.

Cultural studies researchers have also examined how culture influences how individuals conform or diverge from community norms. This is pointedly relevant in criminology, where breaking the law is known to often become a prevalent pattern in a person, and there are very strong correlations between different criminal behaviours, for example (Akers, 2011). In classrooms, students rapidly identify as high- or low-achieving against their peers, low achievers often engage in disruptive behaviour as a response to their status (Chemers, Hu &Garcia, 2001). Similar patterns of conformance & deviance from the norm can be found throughout human society. Within their own communities of choice, narratives emerge that reinforce and validate the responses, and the behaviours of contrasting approaches are reinterpreted within the individual's immediate group (Akers, 2011; Dimaggio & Ostrower, 1990).

In the context of plagiarism, this dynamic could be predicted to result in plagiarizers believing that their behaviours are normal and prevalent, even if not ideal. Conversely, 'honest' groups will believe that broaches of good practice are predominantly inadvertent errors. We certainly see both of these suggestions being made as causes of student plagiarism; the real factors are complex and include both inadvertent and deliberate plagiarism (Ashworth & Bannister, 1997). Deliberate plagiarism ranges from occurring out of desperation related to time, financial and knowledge pressure, to arrogance, with some students saying 'to do it the hard [honest] way is stupid' (Devlin & Gray, 2007). Just as there is evidence that mispractice is enculturated, there is clear evidence that good practice, e.g. citation is also enculturated (Cronin, 1998). There are also reported to be disciplinary microcultures around citation, with reasons for citation including demonstrating field knowledge and managing reviewer expectations, in addition to the more common and mechanical reasons of supporting an argument or arguing against one.

The Case Against (Self) Plagiarism

To discuss why plagiarism is problematic, we must first define it: not all text re-use is plagiarism. Legitimate forms of re-use include extending a conference publication into a journal article with appropriate citation, or quoting a section of text written by another academic in quotation marks and with citation (Samuelson, 1994). What is appropriate varies from field to field, but almost always includes the use of a citation to highlight previous publication (Bretag & Mahmud, 2009). By 'plagiarism', we do not mean these accepted forms of re-use. Rather, we mean re-using text written by another academic without citation or acknowledgement or (more contentiously) re-using one's own words without acknowledgement that they have been previously used, called self-plagiarism. How much text must be re-used for plagiarism to occur is open to question: some set the bar at six consecutive words (Masic, 2012), others at 20% of the total text (Walker, 2010). While it seems obvious that plagiarism is wrong, it is also surprisingly difficult to deal with it (Collberg & Kobourov, 2005; Kock, 1999). One author described academics discussing plagiarism 'like they discussed the weather' (Gotterbarn, 2006): something that affected them but about which they could do little.

While plagiarism of others is near universally condemned, attitudes to self-plagiarism are more heterogeneous (Collberg & Kobourov, 2005). This is perhaps understandable; Bruton points out that if plagiarism is conceived as theft, self-plagiarism is a victimless crime (Bruton, 2014). He offers an alternative framing—plagiarism is dishonesty, laying claim to a certain credit where none is due—that counters all forms of plagiarism. This credit, as noted in the introduction, can, in a climate that rewards increasing numbers of high quality publications (Bretag & Carapiet, 2007), see undeserving academics promoted faster than their more honest peers. Plagiarism of all forms is not just dishonest, it is unethical: it has been described as 'rip[ping] off readers' (Stokes, 2015), it results in presentation of stale content at conferences (Ison, 2012), it wastes reviewers' and editors' time (Bretag & Mahmud, 2009; Stokes, 2015), and it can be quite distressing and frustrating to victims (Collberg & Kobourov, 2005; Gotterbarn, 2006; Kock, 1999).

There are also legal and statutory arguments against plagiarism. Plagiarism is against the research codes of many countries and funding bodies. An examination of every research conduct code listed by the International Council for Science (http://www.icsu.org/freedom-responsibility/research-integrity/statements-codesreports) shows all (27) prohibit plagiarism of others; and 19 prohibit self-plagiarism as well. Not only does plagiarism contravene research codes, it often constitutes copyright infringement, resulting in potential claims against authors who do it (Samuelson, 1994).

Frequency of Plagiarism

The vast majority of plagiarism research focuses on student plagiarism. At the undergraduate level and below the proportion of students engaging in plagiarism ranged from 70% of high school students (Ercegovac, 2005) to 13% among second year university students (Walker, 2010). An early Australian study cited in (Carroll, 2004) measured undergraduate plagiarism found that 8.8% of the surveyed assignments contained plagiarism, however plagiarism has been steadily increasing since then, despite the normalisation of TurnItIn use (Walker, 2010). Reasons given for student plagiarism include time pressure, lack of understanding, linguistic problems and even disrespect for the rules of academic practice (Ashworth & Bannister, 1997; Devlin & Gray, 2007; Ercegovac, 2005).

Bordering on scholarly plagiarism is graduate student plagiarism: a study of online dissertations showed that 60% contained at least some plagiarism. This is much higher than the rate detected in studies of scholarly plagiarism (Larivière & Gingras, 2010; Sorokina, Gehrke, Warner, & Ginsparg, 2006), which show rates of between 3% (in arXiv.org) and 22.3% in surgical publications. It has been suggested that a third of researchers engage in plagiarism, but this statistic has not yet appeared in the scientific literature (Crace, 2003). Both plagiarism and self-plagiarism are increasing over time (Larivière & Gingras, 2010; Waldron, 1992), but outside of personality traits (Etter et al., 2006) the causes of plagiarism have not been addressed in the literature.

Plagiarism is less likely to be conducted by senior academics and less likely to be found in high impact publications (Buchanan & McKay, 2017; Larivière & Gingras, 2010; Sorokina et al., 2006), which is reassuring about the integrity of science. The high cultural capital of both the authors and the venues that are relatively free of plagiarism further suggests that there is some cultural effect on prevalence that has thus far remained unexamined.

Open Access and Plagiarism

The rise of open access has a fraught relationship with plagiarism. Many researchers have cited fear of plagiarism as a reason to avoid making their papers available via open access (Allen, 2005), and our earlier work shows this fear to be grounded (Buchanan & McKay, 2017). Open access is claimed to facilitate plagiarism detection (Harnad, 1998), however our work showed that publications containing illegitimately re-used text were less likely to be available via open access, mitigating against easy detection effect in favour of plagiarists. A further complication is the fact that open access repositories could put institutions in the legal position of publishers, making them liable for any infringing material contained within repositories (*University IT Systems: Managing Liability for Transmitting, Caching, Hosting and Linking to Copyright Material* 2007). The open access movement is now 15 years old, long enough to have has a significant impact on plagiarism, but that impact remains a mixed bag in terms of reduction

Plagiarism Prevention

Plagiarism prevention research has focused primarily on detection, most of which has resulted in algorithms work, e.g. (Brin et al., 1995; Meuschke & Gipp, 2013). These algorithms are not yet in common use, however, suggesting that plagiarism prevention is about more than technical difficulty. It is widely acknowledged that prevention is better than cure (Carroll, 2004; Miller et al., 2011; Walker, 2010), but how to prevent plagiarism remains an open question. One approach is education coupled with substantial monitoring to prevent recurrence (Carroll, 2004). Another approach is to use algorithms to formatively warn authors that their work contains plagiarism (Walker, 2010). A more 'cultural' suggestion is to use a restorative justice approach to eliminate recidivism (Kara & MacAlister, 2010). The discomfort of facing up to 'cheating' in a 'circle of one's peers' is likely to have a strong preventative effect, however, it may be impractical to implement this approach among scholars. It is clear that to prevent plagiarism it is necessary to change the attitudes of would-be plagiarists (Miller et al., 2011). PhD supervisors may influence their students (Gray & Jordan, 2012) but the mechanism and effect of that influence is unclear. Our work aims to address this gap.

METHOD

In (Buchanan & McKay, 2017), we investigated the publications of a random selection of ten major research groups in digital libraries. We used a conservative approach to automated detection of text re-use, considering only spans of twenty words that contained fewer than three changes. Using this metric, we processed the text of all publications of these research groups in the past 5 years. We checked for re-use of others' text, re-use of their own text, and re-use of their text by others on a random sampling. Self-plagiarism was only noted when the percentage of reused text exceeded the requirements of the host venue (venues require from 30% to 90% new material); this was checked manually.

We chose the digital library field as our knowledge of it allowed us to easily assess characteristics such as author seniority. The field's focus—the study of information & libraries—means researchers might be expected to have a better than average knowledge of plagiarism issues. The domain is relatively small allowing a better chance of arriving at a clear picture of cultural and behavioural norms. Other qualitative research on ethical issues in scholarship has typically taken a similarly focused approach for similar reasons (Ashworth & Bannister, 1997; Devlin & Gray, 2007).

We use the term 'group' to represent an ongoing research team at a given university that includes one or more senior academics. Groups are identified by co-authorship in papers published over at least five years. Groups may sporadically collaborate with other groups, but primarily maintain a separate identity: within the domain published collaborations between groups form less than 5% of publications. In our previous work (Buchanan & McKay, 2017) we used the broadly accepted figure of 10% (Bretag & Mahmud, 2009; Ison, 2012; Samuelson, 1994) as our bar for plagiarism. In the study presented here we did not offer participants a fixed percentage, instead choosing to let them define for themselves where the bar lay, and—as we will see in results—many of them considered as little as a sentence an issue.

Pre-Study Screening

There were two complementary ethical and practical issues in our choice of participants. First, we wished to ensure that our respondents were examples of good practice; thus, we needed to screen out groups that were identifiable as being prone to text re-use. Second, if a group had engaged in mispractice, there was a risk of self-implication that would lead to ethically compromised situations either for the participant or for our research. We screened several further groups beyond those examined in our earlier work. We drew our participants exclusively from groups that had been determined to have no scholarly mispractice, i.e. no detected reuse of other groups' text, bar quotations and standard definitions, and very limited reuse of their own–less than 3%. Even that reuse stems from recurring phrases or definitions that are likely either necessary for clarity, or unconscious.

Ethical approval was obtained for this research before we began screening research groups and covered both the screening and the interviews. We approached a single senior academic from each of the research groups we knew to be free of scholarly mispractice; this paper is based on eight interviews.

Interview Structure

Interviews followed four main themes: training, including their own experiences and their approach to training within their group; their assessment of the risk of the plagiarism of others by their group; the risk of self-plagiarism by the group; and any experiences of plagiarism by others, including that found during review, or due to their own work being infringed. The interviews were primarily conducted remotely due to geographical distance. Four interviews were conducted using Skype, two by phone and two in person. The interviews lasted 20-45 minutes, including briefing and debriefing of the participants to obtain their consent and discuss the future use of the data that they contributed. In our results, we refer to our participants by the form Pn (e.g. P3 being the third participant).

FINDINGS

Our participants had from seventeen to 'nearly forty' years of research. All had supervised over ten PhDs to completion, and each currently supervised two or more PhD students and one or more post-doctoral researchers. All were at associate- or full professor level. The pool was international, reflecting the the digital library domain. North America and Europe are the dominant research regions: three currently work in Europe, three in North-America, two elsewhere.

Ethical Training

Five researchers—none with less than 20 years' research experience—had experienced no formal ethics or academic practice training in their own time as a student, or subsequently. The other three, more recent graduates, had received some training in research ethics during their PhD. This training was always about 'research ethics as a whole' (P2), with only a limited amount on plagiarism 'maybe a lesson' (P2) and 'one brief paper' P3 (i.e. a single short assessment). P2 and P7 had received further training, but only in the context of a management role with responsibility for research oversight. That consisted of two one-day meetings on 'not just plagiarism but research practices in general'.

A lack of personal training was associated with neither a lack of awareness, nor a lack of action on the part of untrained academics. All participants bar one reported that their institutions now included ethical training, including plagiarism specifically. As we shall see, all in fact undertook some role in training or monitoring their students.

Plagiarism of Others

As noted in the introduction, the plagiarism of other groups' work is certainly seen as scholarly misconduct. We asked each participant to characterise their assessment of the risk that their group might use other researchers' words. There was a consistent theme that the general risk was small, but not negligible. P4 described the risks as 'generally, I think, low'. There were regular caveats to this point, however—as in P4's use of 'generally'. P2 mirrored P4's tone of caution with 'I hope it's slim', and P6 'Hmmm... small?', followed soon by 'you need to keep an eye on things.' While the perceived risk was small, there was also caution.

Participants varied far more in the factors they considered to contribute to plagiarism than in their assessment of the size of the risk. P2 pointed to students below PhD level, with 'problems with undergrads' and in masters' theses. They also identified an institutional issue that 'We get a lot of [PhD] students who didn't do their undergrad here, so we have to be careful', particularly when the students came 'from other countries'. This was specifically tied to experience of the onus being on them to show they had done 'everything you could' to train the student during taught programs. Students from elsewhere may not have been trained in the same way, so may have different levels of awareness. P6's concerns were similar, noting that 'we get quite a varied ... set of backgrounds now. More international [PhD] students...' and that this reflected a pattern in demographic changes in the discipline in general. While there were 'more incidents with international students' they were clear that 'you can't be sure, even with [PhD] students from your own school'—the issue was more about higher variation of practice, than ascribing particular blame to foreigners.

Length of time in study was also a factor. While P4 felt that there were two risk groups: visitors and new PhD students. P6 also said that 'early students' were a risk, and P5 had experienced a close call when a (new) PhD student extended a previous paper (that they, but not the group, had contributed to) and 'when I read the draft I thought "this looks very familiar"'. Fortunately, P5's recognition of the text avoided the use of another team's words. Here, there was both a move between universities and a move to a research degree. P1 referred to new students arriving with 'bad habits'.

A final influence on the perceived risk was disciplinary. P3's work is primarily qualitative and the 'smaller community' and the fact that the discipline 'seldom do[es] the same study twice' meant that it was easier to identify any replication. P3 also expressed a view that their peers would 'be harsh if they saw the same material again'. In contrast, P2 knew that students of another lab often started via 'cut-and-paste a previous paper', as this was seen as saving time.

All eight academics took steps to monitor these risks. A common strategy was to monitor new PhD students: 'by reading everything we send out' (P5) 'I'll read over a paper before we submit' (P2) and 'I ...check [the work of] each new student the first time they write' (P1). Other risks were managed at the same time, including novelty: e.g. P1 said that PhDs would often use 'their own words, but not their own ideas', while P3 sought to ensure a personal voice and avoid 'meaningless' repetition of existing ideas. P8 had a more structured strategy, explaining that 'I get uncomfortable when I don't see a paper early [in the writing process]'. They also tracked the writing process. The habit P2 noted above of starting with older text was one P8 avoided as 'I don't like cut-and-paste starts to papers'. A paper was expected to steadily improve as it developed. P8 said 'I can spot I think when something looks new and too perfect', and took this as a warning sign of material being misappropriated. Text was trusted when first seen in a draft form. P7 similarly explained that in general 'I would focus my attention on the issue of creativity rather than efficiency' in writing. However, they were wary of applying this universally as over-working some text 'is not a good expenditure of my time as a scientist', particularly where the text was 'not the point of the contribution.' Similarly, P1 started by ensuring that 'our researchers write each paper from the beginning' and reviewing repeatedly as the paper developed.

Formal training was also seen as taking a valuable role. P4 expressed the view that addressing plagiarism is 'an important part of training [PhD] students'...and that central university processes ensured that 'research students would undertake formal assessed research training'. P5 said their institutional training was now 'quite polished, though you can never be too sure that it's enough' and so locally: 'I keep telling the group to avoid doing it [plagiarising]. We don't want to be accused...'. Similarly, P2 explained that 'a lot is teaching and advice from the advisory panel'.

Self-Plagiarism

The issue of the reuse of one's own research text is a debated topic in computing science (Collberg & Kobourov, 2005). P5's near miss when a new PhD student transferring from another university reused text from a paper co-authored at a previous institution would represent a complex case that combined both self- and traditional plagiarism.

While plagiarism of others was seen as a rare, but high-impact, risk, self-plagiarism was perceived as a greater, though P3 thought it was 'In my own area [qualitative research] ...not so much' of a problem. P1 more typically reported that 'this happens often'. P4 explained that their group would reuse material because 'sometimes you need the same material to make clear what you're doing', but that this was undesirable unless absolutely necessary. P1 noted that 'sometimes it's just a phrase' that authors reuse often, but when reviewing 'one or twice' a year they'd encounter a paper with extensive reuse. Both P1 and P5 reported the importance of providing enough new material when extending a conference paper to journal format, but that this practice necessarily involved repetition of the earlier output's text. However, the greater risk of poor practice emerged from short-cuts being taken when writing new papers. P6 explained that this led to their group insisting that '[PhD] students start each paper from scratch' and then monitoring the early drafts for reuse, and P1 reported the same strategy as it would avoid the risk of 'a bad reputation' of recycling their own work. P1 indeed had encountered 'a [PhD] student try[ing] to add old words of mine' and they 'had to stop that'. This approach was supported by checks on early drafts, as with the management of the risk of plagiarism.

These strategies again had multiple purposes. P1 sought to ensure that each paper would appear as novel and fresh as possible, rather than another 'me too' paper in a chain. They also were concerned to ensure that new students really understood the literature they were reporting – a goal shared by P6, who worried 'did they understand it correctly?' when reusing the group's existing text, and P2 worried that in each paper 'you should be telling a different story.'

Reviewing

We asked the participants about their experiences of plagiarism as reviewers. All had encountered some issues, but the severity varied considerably. For example, P5 had encountered an article that 'looked *very* familiar' and that turned out to be two previous papers that had been combined; while P6 had once been given the same paper to review at the same time (by different authors). Not all was at large scale though: P2's experience was more of 'paragraphs and phrases' rather than entire papers, and this appeared to be more often the case, from the researchers' reporting.

The reaction of other reviewers and editors to these problems was mixed. P5's fused paper was contested, the editor trying to 'find a way around it' without rejecting the paper or contacting the authors. In the end, despite the 'reluctance to take it on', the paper was rejected. P6's duplicate paper led to one conference rejecting the paper immediately, while the other 'delayed – they questioned if anything could be done' before it was rejected. Neither paper was original.

P1's experience was that 'many people get embarrassed...they find it difficult'. They had recently detected a paper using text they frequently cited. While the first author was junior, a senior figure was involved. The editor of the journal was hesitant to take action due to the involvement of the senior academic. Eventually, the article was rejected. While formally it was taken no further, the editor asked P1 to suggest to the authors 'that they not submit anything for a year' and that future submissions would be closely scrutinised. Less prestigious venues, such as workshops, were perceived to receive a higher proportion of problematic material, but responses were more frequently decisive. P3 encountered a workshop submission that infringed their teams' work. When the organisers were contacted, they 'just rejected it' straightaway. This swift response was consistently reported as the norm in minor venues. In contrast P5 reported mispractice in a PhD thesis. There was again a reluctance to take action 'due to the severity of the consequences'. There were 'a lot of discussions' and 'it was a long fight to get it resolved'. Despite the student's insistence that their reuse was legitimate, P5 was obliged to make the ultimate decision as the chair; the examiners could not agree. The dispute took over a year, despite 'no one involved [being] satisfied with [the candidate's] explanation'.

Time

Time was commonly perceived as a risk factor in plagiarism and self-plagiarism. Both P5 and P6 used the accessibility of web material to speed up investigations when reviewing. However, time is not always on the reviewer's side. P2 believed that 'reviewers spend less time on reviews' due to the general increase in academic workload. To them, this limited the relative effectiveness of steps to counter plagiarism, in a context of increased ease of plagiarism.

P5's incident with the duplicate papers was a further example of time being a factor. The professor responsible for the plagiarism explained that they 'had to cut corners because there was so much pressure to publish a lot'. P2's observation about researchers starting a new paper with cut-and-paste was that 'a few people do that a lot, to save time'. P1 perceived that self-plagiarism was on the rise as 'so many groups hurry to submit'. They also believed it was possible that the time-cost of polishing text was a factor with 'new research countries' where 'they often copy older text because...they do not think they can write well...' especially combined with the urgency of publishing.

The Role of Technology

While we did not specifically ask participants about the role of technology in plagiarism, it came up a lot. One dominant theme was open access: it was seen to facilitate both plagiarism and detection. An extreme example of this came from P5's time in charge of their faculty's research. A professor was found to have 'submitted four papers that were identical except one paragraph in each paper'. This had emerged as the university was 'setting up open-access...we were testing, and the four papers matched the same search'. This was initially thought to be a mistake in the uploading of papers., 'but, no, it was just the same paper'. This led to considerable work addressing the situation.

The utility of technology to assist detection also arose: e.g. P2 would search the web for 'incongruous' phrases, and P4 and P7 would Google suspected cases of self-plagiarism, relying on open-access copies of the authors' work to match queries. P6 used P4's strategy for locating text that 'seems familiar or out of character', regularly uncovering plagiarism. P5 noted that 'being on the editorial board of [a journal] we can use TurnItIn now...that turns stuff up'. Another theme around technology was risk: while technology can aid detection, it can increase the risk of plagiarism. P6 worried how 'copy-and-paste is a real risk...when you can download in flash'. Six participants believed the risk of plagiarism was largely due to the ready availability of material, though P1 noted 'I hope we are more cautious than when I was younger'. P4 and P5 both noted that there was an increased risk to plagiarists that balanced the risk of plagiarism: 'easier to copy, easier to pick up', but P5 and P6 were doubted whether the rate of detection had kept up.

DISCUSSION

This section addresses our findings in comparison with other work on plagiarism and with respect to the role of culture in plagiarism prevention. We further speculate on how information science and technology may affect plagiarism.

On Plagiarism

One striking feature of our findings is how similar the reasons given for plagiarism are to those given for student work: time, language issues, different cultural practices and ignorance are all issues that appear regularly in the literature on student plagiarism (Ashworth & Bannister, 1997; Devlin & Gray, 2007; Ercegovac, 2005). Given this, perhaps some of the suggested responses to student plagiarism, such across-the-board electronic monitoring, longitudinal oversight of offenders, regular training, and restorative justice could reduce plagiarism prevalence among academics, too.

A second finding is the difficulties in dealing with plagiarism, which mirror Kock's own experience (Kock, 1999) and Gotterbarn's description of academics' feelings and approaches (Gotterbarn, 2006). The severity of the consequences serve as a deterrent to action (though likely not to plagiarism (Miller et al., 2011)); perhaps plagiarism, particularly by junior academics, needs to be treated more as an educational issue and less as an offence for which the appropriate response is 'a public flogging' (Collberg & Kobourov, 2005). Less severe punishment for first offences would be in line with suggestions for managing undergraduate plagiarism in an effective manner (Carroll, 2004; Walker, 2010).A finding that dovetails with the work on undergraduates is variation in the perception of venues. Less prestigious venues were seen as more likely to attract questionable submissions (again, this is borne out by (Buchanan & McKay, 2017)), but transgressions were more swiftly dealt with. This mirrors how students vary their attitudes to plagiarism in different assessment types, and in light of the assessment's perceived validity (Hayes & Introna, 2005).

Previous literature on plagiarism suggests, conservatively, that 10% of papers contain plagiarism, including self-plagiarism, that exceeds 70% of the paper, and 20% of papers have more than 50%. Our respondents review dozens of papers each year: a reviewer at a major conference will review about five. There are two prestigious conferences, half-a-dozen others, and several journals in the field. It is thus likely that each participant will have encountered several papers with extensive plagiarism, but often unwittingly. Topic clustering may be an effect: as P3 noted, they work in a clear sub-field, reviewing and being reviewed by a small network of peers. As mispractice is concentrated in a few groups, some will see almost no mispractice, while others are may encounter it regularly. As two researchers in the field, we recognize the likelihood that we will have missed plagiarism while we review. As P4 said, 'I wonder how much [plagiarism] I miss'. Without systematic plagiarism detection mechanisms this situation is likely to continue.

On Culture

By mentoring students, supervising junior researchers, and serving on steering committees and editorial boards the academics in our study act as arbiters of culture (Bourdieu, 1984). By far the best prevention strategy employed is enculturation of academic standards by mentorship. The literature shows that prevention of plagiarism is better than cure (Carroll, 2004; Miller et al., 2011). This process depends on relationships, so cannot be entirely replaced by (e.g.) online instruction. Insofar as relationships can be supported via online technology, technology could still play a role. Previous researchers argued that libraries have a role in enculturation at undergraduate and graduate levels (Buranen, 2009), but this likely is also a role to be filled at the doctoral level of study. The issue of enculturation becomes particularly clear when we note that our participants believed those at highest risk of engaging in plagiarism were PhD students and visitors—those new to the group and not yet au fait with group cultural norms.

One facet of this enculturation was an emphasis on novel content and originality of thought with those who our senior researchers oversee. This emphasis is backed up by monitoring publications within their team, which are then 'jumped on' if mispractice of either thought or ideas is detected. This chimes with earlier research, which shows that honest PhD supervisors tend to have honest students (Gray & Jordan, 2012), and further solidifies the suggestion that the relationship is causal. Not all PhD students come to these supervisors with perfect understanding of good academic practice, but these academics actively monitor for and correct any lapses. While didactic approaches to instruction on academic honesty are rare among our participants, this is likely down to the mentor-mentee relationship that usually accompanies supervision: didacticism is a poor approach for apprentice researchers moving toward independence.

The difficulties in monitoring for and dealing with lapses—especially persistent lapses, as seen in our earlier work (Buchanan & McKay, 2017)—are amply demonstrated by our participants: they are concerned that they don't catch every incidence of plagiarism, and there is not a systematic approach to dealing with it when it is found. This allows two cultures to exist within the field: one of academic integrity, and one that might be termed pragmatically risky at best. Determining the culture of an overall field is up to the people within it (Bourdieu, 1984), but support for managing behaviours that deviate from the cultural norm is needed. As (Williams & Williams, 2012) observed in student plagiarism, there is evidence that behaviours are repeated, and come from shared values towards transgressing norms. Rules against plagiarism are not on their own a sufficient deterrent: as so aptly put by a student participant in (Devlin & Gray, 2007) 'there are not enough obstructions to [plagiarism], it's too easy'. This reflects a value set that the rules are not important. Likewise, (Hayes & Introna, 2005) posits that alienation from the values that dominate the university system can also increase the acceptance of plagiarism. Thus, enculturation into the mainstream cannot be taken for granted, and may be supported by other actors, for example via clear guidelines from academic publishers and venues.

On Technology

The increasing use of technology in disseminating academic research appears to have had a number of effects on the process itself. The increased availability of digital text has increased the opportunity for both self- and simple plagiarism. (Wood, 2004) reported these issues in the context of undergraduate study. The increased availability of text is also described as a factor in scholarly plagiarism by both our own participants and one of the students in (Devlin & Gray, 2007). In contrast, search engines allow researchers to track suspicious text to its source with greater ease.

It is perhaps surprising that there is little routine use of plagiarism detection software in academic publishing. Its use could substantially reduce the risk of plagiarised text making it to publication. Technology could support the private-but-cross-field listing and monitoring of known offenders, enabling systematic, rather than piecemeal, handling and avoiding repeat behaviour. Given the similarities between student- and scholarly-plagiarism, these suggestions are grounded in (Carroll, 2004). In contrast, our participants used Google ad-hoc, relying on open-access text sources.

Technology is less likely to be useful in training novice academics: while universities offer online materials on plagiarism to undergraduates, these often go unused either due to accessibility problems or because they are simply not seen by students as useful (Ashworth & Bannister, 1997; Carroll, 2004; Devlin & Gray, 2007; Ercegovac, 2005). It seems likely that the cultural practices around plagiarism and mentorship used by every participant are effective, but this type of relationship is difficult to transfer online. Technology alone cannot solve academic plagiarism.

CONCLUSIONS

For everyone but plagiarists, plagiarism is the bane of academia. It results in inappropriate credit, poor science, and an atmosphere of distrust. Libraries—as supporters of open access—have a significant role to play in setting a no-tolerance culture. Similarly, as information scientists, it is our responsibility to not just enculturate our own research groups into good practice, but to understand how best to prevent plagiarism. This paper is a step in the direction of understanding how plagiarism prevention at the research level works in practice. It reports a preliminary study on how senior academics in the digital library field mentor PhD students, monitor for, and address issues of plagiarism. We have seen their perception of risk and identified how risk is mediated and moderated by technology.

The pivotal strategy employed in plagiarism-averse groups is mentorship. While technology can support those relationships, it is not a substitute. Academics use technology to detect plagiarism, but the approach is piecemeal. Consistent application of plagiarism detection software could reduce both the risk of undetected plagiarism and the time-cost of reviewer checks. Technology could support monitoring plagiarism across a domain, institution or community. With the rise of open-access, university repositories are a potential trip-wire to identify poor practice.

Our work generates many avenues for future work: while participants gave multiple reasons why plagiarism happens, this was not a focus of our research. Understanding the reasons for plagiarism could help address the dichotomous culture we saw in our earlier work: understanding an alternative perspective is, after all, the first step in addressing it. Similarly, trials of technology that supports plagiarism reduction in research writing would produce vital practical and theoretical knowledge. The problem of scholarly plagiarism is far from solved: it remains both an issue for future research and as an important consideration for scholarship as a whole.

REFERENCES

Akers, R. L. (2011). Social learning and social structure: A general theory of crime and deviance: Transaction Publishers.

Allen, J. (2005). Interdisciplinary Differences in Attitudes Towards Deposit in Institutional Repositories. (Masters Thesis), Manchester Metropolitan University, Manchester. Retrieved from http://eprints.rclis.org/6957/

Ashworth, P., & Bannister, P. (1997). Guilty in Whose Eyes? University Students' Perceptions of Cheating and Plagiarism in Academic Work and Assessment. Studies In Higher Education, 22(2), 187-204.

Bardzell, J. (2009). Interaction criticism and aesthetics. Paper presented SIGCHI 09, Boston, MA.

Bourdieu, P. (1984). Distinction: A social critique of the judgement of taste: Harvard University Press.

Bretag, T., & Carapiet, S. (2007). A Preliminary Study to Identify the Extent of Self-Plagiarism in Australian Academic Research. Plagiary: Cross-Disciplinary Studies in Plagiarism, Fabrication, and Falsification, 2(5), 1-15.

Bretag, T., & Mahmud, S. (2009). Self-Plagiarism or Appropriate Textual Re-use? Journal of Academic Ethics, 7(3), 193.

Brin, S., Davis, J., Garcia-Molina, H. (1995). Copy detection mechanisms for digital documents. Paper presented at SIGMOD 95, San Jose, CA.

Bruton, S. V. (2014). Self-Plagiarism and Textual Recycling: Legitimate Forms of Research Misconduct. Accountability in Research, 21(3), 176-197.

Buchanan, G., & McKay, D. (2017). The Lowest Form of Flattery: Characterising Text Re-use and Plagiarism Patterns in a Digital Library Corpus. Paper presented at JCDL '17, Toronto, Canada.

Buranen, L. (2009). A safe place: The role of librarians and writing centers in addressing citation practices and plagiarism. Knowledge Quest, 37(3), 24-34.

Carroll, J. (2004). Institutional Issues in Deterring, Detecting, and Dealing with Student Plagiarism. JISC Report.

Chemers M. M., Hu L., Garcia B. F. (2001). Academic self-efficacy and first-year college student performance and adjustment. Journal of Educational Psychology 93, 55–64.

Collberg, C., & Kobourov, S. (2005). Self-plagiarism in computer science. Commun. ACM, 48(4), 88-94. doi:10.1145/1053291.1053293

Crace, J. (2003). Peer Trouble. The Guardian. Retrieved from https://www.theguardian.com/education/2003/feb/11/highereducation.research

Cronin, B. (1998). Metatheorizing citation. Scientometrics, 43(1), 45-55.

Devlin, M., & Gray, K. (2007). In their own words: a qualitative study of the reasons Australian university students plagiarize. Higher Education Research & Development, 26(2), 181-198.

Dimaggio, P., & Ostrower, F. (1990). Participation in the Arts by Black and White Americans. Social Forces, 68(3), 753.

Ercegovac, Z. (2005). What Students Say They KNOW, FEEL and DO About Cyber-Plagiarism and Academic Dishonesty? A Case Study. Paper presented at the 68th ASIST Annual Meeting, Charlotte, NC.

Etter, S., Cramer, J. J., & Finn, S. (2006). Origins of Academic Dishonesty. Journal of Research on Technology in Education, 39(2), 133-155.

Gotterbarn, D. (2006). The shinning face of plagiarism: the graying of an issue. SIGCSE Bull., 38(2), 7-8.

Gray, P. W., & Jordan, S. R. (2012). Supervisors and Academic Integrity: Supervisors as Exemplars and Mentors. Journal of Academic Ethics, 10(4), 299-311.

Harnad, S. (1998). Learned inquiry and the Net: the role of peer review, peer commentary and copyright. Learned Publishing, 11(4), 283-292.

Harper, R., & Mentis, H. (2013). The mocking gaze: the social organization of kinect use. Paper presented at thCSCW 13, San Antonio, TX.

Hayes, N., & Introna, L. D. (2005). Cultural Values, Plagiarism, and Fairness: When Plagiarism Gets in the Way of Learning. Ethics & Behavior, 15(3), 213-231.

Ison, D. C. (2012). Plagiarism Among Dissertations: Prevalence at Online Institutions. Journal of Academic Ethics, 10(3), 227-236.

Kara, F., & MacAlister, D. (2010). Responding to academic dishonesty in universities: a restorative justice approach. Contemporary Justice Review, 13(4), 443-453.

Ketchell, M. (2012). Vice-chancellor resigns amid claims of plagiarism. Sydney Morning Herald. Retrieved from http://www.smh.com.au/articles/2002/07/11/1026185088581.html

Kock, N. (1999). A case of academic plagiarism. Communications of the ACM, 42(7), 96-104.

Larivière, V., & Gingras, Y. (2010). On the prevalence and scientific impact of duplicate publications in different scientific fields (1980-2007). Journal of Documentation, 66(2), 179-190.

Masic, I. (2012). Plagiarism in scientific publishing. Acta Informatica Medica, 20(4), 208-213.

Meuschke, N., & Gipp, B. (2013). State-of-the-art in detecting academic plagiarism. International Journal for Educational Integrity, 9(1).

Miller, A., Shoptaugh, C., & Wooldridge, J. (2011). Reasons Not to Cheat, Academic-Integrity Responsibility, and Frequency of Cheating. The Journal of Experimental Education, 79(2), 169-184.

Samuelson, P. (1994). Self-plagiarism or fair use. Communications of the ACM, 37(8), 21-25.

Sorokina, D., Gehrke, J., Warner, S., & Ginsparg, P. (2006). Plagiarism Detection in arXiv. Paper presented at ICDM'06, Hong Kong.

Stokes, P. (2015). Feeding the beast: why plagiarism rips off readers too. Retrieved from https://theconversation.com/feeding-the-beast-why-plagiarism-rips-off-readers-too-37702

Supak-Smolčić, V., & Bilić-Zulle, L. (2013). How do we handle self-plagiarism in submitted manuscripts? Biochemia Medica, 23(2), 150-153.

Tenopir, C., King, D. W., Edwards, S., & Wu, L. (2009). Electronic journals and changes in scholarly article seeking and reading patterns. Aslib Proceedings, 61(1), 5-32.

Triandis, H. C. (1995). Individualism & collectivism: Westview Press.

University IT Systems: Managing Liability for Transmitting, Caching, Hosting and Linking to Copyright Material (2007). Retrieved from https://www.universitiesaustralia.edu.au/ArticleDocuments/419/University%20IT%20Systems%20AVCC%202007.pdf.aspx

Waldron, T. (1992). Is duplicate publishing on the increase? BMJ : British Medical Journal, 304(6833), 1029-1029.

Walker, J. (2010). Measuring plagiarism: researching what students do, not what they say they do. Studies In Higher Education, 35(1), 41-59.

Williams, M. W. M., & Williams, M. N. (2012). Academic Dishonesty, Self-Control, and General Criminality: A Prospective and Retrospective Study of Academic Dishonesty in a New Zealand University. Ethics & Behavior, 22(2), 89-112.

Wood, G. (2004). Academic original sin: Plagiarism, the internet, and librarians. Journal of Academic Librarianship, 30(3), 237-242.

Funding for Retracted Research and Categorization of Retractions in the Biomedical Literature

John M. Budd
University of Missouri, USA. buddj@missoui.edu

ABSTRACT
The retraction of scientific publications (particularly in biomedical fields) is a continuing problem for the progress of science. The present study examines retractions that occurred in the calendar year 2016, with particular attention to whether the retracted papers indicate that the authors received external funding to complete their research. In addition to examination of funding support, the reasons for retraction are also determined. As is the case with previous studies, this work is situated within the context of scientific communication.

KEYWORDS
Scientific communication; misconduct; external sources of research funding; retraction of publication

INTRODUCTION
The problem related to the need for retraction of scientific articles is not new; the review of literature will detail some of the major studies (this will not be an exhaustive list but will point to the need to study the present phenomenon). The problematic nature of the need for retractions takes several forms. At times there are, and will continue to be, unavoidable errors that call for the retraction of some papers. For example, researchers may need to acquire tissue or other samples from a third party. Sometimes those samples, unbeknownst to the researchers, are tainted or contaminated in some way. The contamination may not be discovered until after the research is completed, requiring the authors to retract the article(s). No misconduct is evident, and none is suspected in these kinds of instances.

To reiterate what many have said about retractions in general, there are times when something occurs (such as the errors just described) that warrants the retraction of a published paper. Reasons other than error will be detailed in a moment. As Budd, Coble, and Abritis (2016) describe, when something has been determined to be seriously problematic with a published article, that article might be officially retracted. This action means that the article should no longer be considered as valid research. A paper may be retracted by one or more of the authors, by the journal's editor or publisher, or by a third party. When retraction occurs, the paper is marked as being retracted in databases such as MEDLINE. Any search—by subject, keyword, title word, or author—word usually yields the paper clearly marked as being retracted, usually along with the statement of retraction. The act of retraction signals to anyone retrieving the document that the research conducted should not be treated as valid.

Other reasons that can lead to a paper being retracted include overt misconduct, presumed misconduct, plagiarism, duplication of published articles and other things. The reasons are almost always fully evident in the retraction statement. Later in this paper there will be a classification of retractions for the set of papers under review here.

In brief, the present study examines retraction statements published in the year 2016. This is an exploratory study of the instances of funding, so only one year of retractions is analyzed. The first order of business is to determine whether the retracted work received funding from any external entities. The common expectation is that research that receives funding, particularly from governmental sources, would adhere to principles and practices of research integrity. This study also studies the stated reasons for retraction and categorizes them according to what is indicated in the retraction statements. This works builds upon previous investigations into retractions and adds the dimension of funding for the research undertaken.

RETRACTION AS A PHENOMENON
The examination of retracted publications extends back a few decades. One study of papers written by John Darsee, whose works were reviewed by his own institution and by the Office of Research Integrity, was reported by Kochan and Budd (1992). Darsee's case made news in the popular press as well as the professional literature and it turns out that his tainted work was cited long after the retractions were made public. More recently, there has been attention to misconduct in social science fields (see, for example, Budd, 2014), but the vast majority of examination has been devoted to the biomedical sciences.

There are guidelines that exist for retracting publications provided by the Committee on Publication Ethics (COPE). "COPE is a group of more than 10,000 members worldwide, including editors of academic journals and others interested and involved in publication ethics. They provide guidance on publication ethics with a particular focus on how to address cases of research and publication misconduct" (Riegelman and Bakker, 2018, p. 40). Journals and their editors are to follow the guidelines.

The number of retractions has increased in recent years, and it is something of an open question as to why. Oransky and Marcus (2016) write, it helps to know why retractions have been on the rise in recent years. The reasons are manifold, but they start with technology. Technology has provided ever-clever fraudsters new ways to pull the wool over the eyes of editors and reviewers. Some cheats use Photoshop to splice together parts of images to misrepresent the results of an experiment. Others take advantage of the fact that many journals ask authors to provide suggestions on who they would like to conduct peer review of their submissions (p. 41).

They make the point that, since retractions are relatively rare there is little impetus for researchers to admit to error or misconduct at this time. The presumption that guides this, and other, work is that the existence of the need for retraction necessitates attention through formal study.

Some writers have taken various serious approaches to the import of retractions, especially when misconduct is a factor. Menezes (2016), for example, says, "Imagine using the wrong treatment protocols, an unnecessary investigation modality or the wrong drug to treat patients based on unethical research. Therefore, it is imperative for us as a scientific body to realize the importance of not only being aware and reporting such articles but also ensuring that it never occurs in the first place" (p. 604).

Hesselmann and colleagues (2017) write, "Over the past decade, retraction of scientific articles have developed into the main format through which scientific misconduct is made visible" (p. 815). During that recent decade, there have been many studies of retractions. These have been undertaken even though, as Hesselmann, et al. (2017) further state, "Retractions are rare compared with other publication types, with a share among all articles in the biomedical database PubMed no higher than 0.02% (Amos, 2014; Wager and Williams, 2011) or considerably lower (Cokol et al., 2007, 2008; Redman et al., 2008)" (p. 817). In recent years a substantial amount of attention and analysis has been devoted to retractions, their categorization, and their subsequent citations. A major concern has been on the ethics of producing works requiring retraction. S. M. Yentis (2010), editor of the journal, *Anaesthesia*, says that this is something related to, but distinct from research ethics; it is a matter of publication ethics. The two forms of ethics are, however, ineluctably connected; in most instance the research lapses are related to the desire, or perceived need, to publish. Therefore, it is difficult to make a clear distinction between the two sub-branches of ethics. Budd, Coble, and Anderson (2011) cited Steen (2011) who concentrated on one particular retracted work, by Wakefield and colleagues, in which a connection between certain vaccines is related to instances of autism. Steen (2011) points out,

In the United Kingdom, there were no mumps cases in 2003 but widespread vaccine rejection led to 63,500 mumps cases in 2005. In the United States, the MMR [mumps-measles-rubella] vaccination rate decreased from 93% before the publicity to 79% in 2003. Subsequently, there was a mumps outbreak in the United States, and the number of cases in 2006 was 21-fold higher than in the prior year (p. 2).

SOME PREVIOUS WORK

There have been some rather extensive studies of the phenomenon of retraction and also the numbers and kinds of citations received by those retracted articles. Budd and colleagues (1999) examined retraction revealed by a search of the MEDLINE database (of papers published from 1966 through 1997). The 235 retracted articles were cited more than 2,000 times, and very few acknowledged that papers had been retracted. A substantial number were positive citations that treated the retracted papers as substantively valid. More recent work by Budd and colleagues (2011) extends the study, particularly of retraction statements, to the year 2009. Misconduct and presumed misconduct accounted for 58% of the retractions. Results regarding citations to retracted articles mirrored those of the earlier study; foe acknowledged the retraction, and many were substantively positive.

Wager and Williams (2011) have also analysed retractions to biomedical papers. Their study Reports an increase in the number of retractions (year-to-year) from 1988 to 2008). As is the case with the present study, the authors use the language of the retraction statements to arrive at the categorization of retractions (see below for a description of the method used in this study).

THE PRESENT STUDY

This study extends the previous studies, noted above, in some specific ways Retraction statement published in the year 2016 are examined. Again, this study is exploratory; one purpose is to determine if further examination is called for. The retracted articles are studied in order to determine if any of the authors obtained external funding to complete the research. As will be shown, some of the funding will be presented in detail. Further, the nations from which the authors hail will be noted. Lastly, the reasons for retraction will be indicated. The last of these aspects of the examination will be compared to some previous studies.

SOURCES OF FUNDING

All of the retracted papers in 2016 were analysed to determine whether authors received funding for the research that led to publication of the articles (from government or other sources). What follows is a list of the countries of the authors and the numbers of works that received funding and the numbers that did not receive funding.

Country	Funded	Not Funded
China	29	22
US	34	7
Japan	8	4
India	5	3
Italy	2	5
Singapore	4	0
Australia	2	1
Brazil	1	2
Canada	3	0
Germany	0	3
Iran	1	2
South Korea	3	0
Netherlands	0	2
Sweden	2	0
Turkey	0	2
Others	4	2

Table 1

It must be noted that twenty-five of the 183 retracted articles were not available for examination. Also, thirteen articles were removed from the publishers' Web sites, and could not be analysed. Of the 145 papers that could be examined, a total of 96 indicated that authors did receive funding, and 49 pointed to authors not receiving funding for the work. When the papers with authors from China are isolated, it can be determined that 63.4% of the articles had funding attached to them. When those from United States authors are studied, 82.9% received funding.

As it happens, there is some consistency regarding the sources of funding for work conducted by Chinese and US scientists. For example, seventeen of the retracted articles from China were funded by the National Natural Science Foundation of China. Other funding sources include regional science foundations and universities. When it comes to US scientists, eighteen received funding from the National Institutes of Health. Another three were funded by the National Institute of Mental Health and three from the National Science Foundation. One researcher gained funding from the Macarthur Foundation. The upshot is that much of the work published has been funded by prestigious outlets.

It is possible to determine the amounts of money funded through the National Institutes of Health (NIH). The NIH site has a tool called the Research Portfolio Online Reporting Tools (RePORTER, available at https:/ /projectreporter.nih.gov/reporter.cfm). The researcher's name, plus the NIH grant number, can be searched, and one element of the results is the amount of the grant, in US dollars. Some examples will be illustrated here to show the amounts of money received by authors of retracted papers. Pamela J. McLean received an NIH grant in 2011 in the amount of $383,317. This funding supporting the retracted work. Additionally, John W. Hollingsworth received two NIH grants, one in the amount of $419,332 and the other for $235,500 in 2010 and 2011. It should be noted that, in the aftermath of the retracted work, McLean and Hollingsworth continued to receive NIH funding. These examples

Grant No.	Amount
CA1555297 (2012)	$571,147 – 2011
MH087214 (2013)	$509,157 – 2011 $574,843 – 2012
NS063963 (2012)	$383,317 – 2010 $379,444 – 2011
ES016126 (2011)	$556,753 – 2009 $419,332 – 2010
ES016347 (2011)	$340,416 – 2009 $337,012 – 2010
HL081825 (2011)	$364,125 – 2009 $364,125 – 2010
MH41479 (2000)	$205,450 – 1998
CP010150 (2012)	$911,869 – 2011
CA124787 (2010)*	$206,792 – 2008 $325,799 – 2009
ES011961 (2009)	$113,509 – 2006 $194,699 – 2007
ES016347 (2009)	$340,416 – 2008
GM66778 (2007)	$231,345 – 2005 $225,908 – 2006
NS44232 (2007)	$1,422,730 – 2005 $1,565,283 – 2006
NS45713 (2007)	$715,166 – 2005 $751,765 – 2006
GM066777 (2007)	$293,355 – 2005 $286,461 – 2006
HL081205 (2008)	$399,144 – 2006 $388,754 – 2007
HL084945 (2008)	$362,597 – 2007
HL084948 (2008)	$490,173 – 2007
ES015903 (2009)	$410,000 – 2007
GM105386 (2015)	$756,600 – 2013 $780,000 – 2014
HD040404 (2014)	$319,661 – 2011
HD040444 (2014)	$597,508 – 2011
CE000906 (2014)	$294,000 – 2007 $294,137 – 2008
MH077026 (2014)	$219,767 – 2010 $211,767 – 2011
AG031259 (2014)	$304,866 – 2010 $684,454 – 2011
AG005842 (2014)	$118,438 – 2008
HD051152 (2014)	$530,909 – 2008

Table 2

are presented here as indicators of the level of support researchers included in the present study have received for their research. What follows is a table of specific grants (by number) and the amounts of the grants; the information has been located in the NIH RePORTER (These are not all of the NIH grants received but are the ones that could be located in the RePORTER.).

*One researcher, Bharat Aggarwal, was responsible for several works being retracted. His work was funded, in part, by NIH.

It must be noted that the above list is partial; not all NIH projects could be located using RePORTER. That said, the table represents a substantial amount (millions of dollars) of funded research.

REASONS FOR RETRACTION

Previous studies, some noted in the "Background" section, have delineated reasons why papers have been retracted. The following describes the reasons why articles have been retracted in 2016. It should be noted that the total adds up to 162, instead of 145. This is because for some items that were not available, or the articles had been removed, there were abstracts detailing the retraction reasons.

The list is arranged by presumed absence of misconduct (the first three reasons), which add up to 59 papers, or 36.4%. The remaining reasons indicate some form of misconduct related to the articles. These add up to 103, or 63.6%. By way of comparison, Budd et al. (1999) found that 37% of retracted works were due to misconduct. The category "Unintended Error" is self-explanatory. Something occurred in the research process, which can include tissue samples arriving with contamination, statistical mistakes being made, or other errors that were not the researchers' fault or responsibility. Absence of misconduct also includes failure to gain Institutional Review Board (or the national equivalent) permission. It is assumed that the failure to gain permission was not a deliberate act (with the lack of any evidence that this did constitute a deliberate act in the retraction statement). Further, lack of confidence in results is also presumed to be absence of intent to deceive (again, because of a lack of evidence of deliberate action in the statements).

Reason	Number
Unintended Error	46
No IRB Clearance	4
No Confidence in Results	9
Misconduct	14
Potential Misconduct	18
Plagiarism	19
Duplication of Publication	25
Faked Referee Reports	9
Duplication of Data	7
Manipulation of Images	4
Conflict of Authorship	3
Conflict of Interest	2
Copyright Issues	2

Table 3

The evidence of misconduct, as is the case for the rest of the papers, is garnered from the retraction statements. In the instances of overt misconduct, the reasons tended to be the fabrication of data or the falsification of data or results. The category "Potential Misconduct," as has been the case with the classification in previous studies, can be explained by the disappearance of data and data integrity questions. The latter reason applied to all articles by the researcher B. B. Aggarwal whose works were retracted. "Plagiarism" refers to instances where authors appropriated substantial segments of work done by other researchers and included it as their own. The category in which a plurality of items fall—"Duplication"—is applied when the retraction statement indicates that the researchers published the same paper prior to the retraction. Sometimes the original paper was published in the same journal as the retracted one and sometimes the original was published in a different journal. Regardless, the content of two or more papers was the same. In some cases, the categorization explains the problems; for example, data used in a previous study were duplicated in the retracted paper.

One category, faked or problematic referee reports, is a relatively new difficulty. The Web site Retraction Watch explains the phenomenon:

Elsevier has retracted 13 papers—and says it will retract 13 more—after discovering they were accepted because of fake reviews. A spokesperson for Elsevier told us that the journals are in the process of retracting all 26 papers affected by the "peer-review manipulation" and "unexplained authorship irregularities." Most share one corresponding author, a physical science researcher based in Iran.

Retraction Watch further reports, "We asked the publisher how the fake reviews were missed during peer review, as well as how (and when) the peer review manipulation was discovered. A spokesperson explained that the editors of two of the journals alerted Elsevier 'when they could not validate the email addresses of reviewers suggested by the authors upon submission:' Elsevier then conducted a thorough investigation of all historical submissions from this author group to all Elsevier journals. Based on the evidence provided, the various Editors decided that retraction was appropriate in 26 cases where the peer review process had been compromised. In addition, in several cases, the authorship lists had been changed without agreement with the Editor" (Elsevier retracting).

RETRACTIONS AND MISCONDUCT

As is stated above, some retracted are made because of unavoidable error that has taken place in the course of the research. This error is not the fault of the research team, but the ramifications are sufficiently serious to warrant retraction. The following is a statement that indicates this kind of retraction:

Consistent with the Committee on Publication Ethics guidelines, we the above authors are initiating the retraction of our paper: Young DA, Blake DF, Brown LH: Transcutaneous oximetry measurement: normal values for the upper limb. Diving Hyperb Med. 2012;42(4):208-213. We wish to make the following statement: "The authors voluntarily retract this article after discovering a critical error associated with the instrumentation used in the study, namely the fitting of incorrect sensor membranes on the electrodes of the transcutaneous oximetry device used in the study. This resulted in transcutaneous oxygen tension (PtcO2) measurements that were consistently lower than those that would have been recorded with the correct electrode membranes in place. We recently confirmed this by comparing the two membrane types once we discovered the error. We are in the process of replicating our work using the correct PtcO2 specific membranes.

The categorization of misconduct is derived directly from the statements that are published in the retracting journals. An example of a clear statement of retraction is:

The above article from European Journal of Neuroscience, published online on 5 March 2013 in Wiley Online Library (http://onlinelibrary.wiley.com.proxy.mul.missouri.edu/d...), has been retracted by agreement between the Editors-in-Chief, Paul Bolam and John Foxe, the authors and John Wiley & Sons Ltd. The retraction has been agreed as Dr Phillip Barber has informed the publisher that he had seen neither the original data nor any version of the manuscript and had not been involved in the work reported. A subsequent Institutional investigation found evidence of misconduct on the part of the submitting author. Reference Wang, L.-M., Wang, Y.-J., Cui, M., Luo, W.-J., Wang, X.-J., Barber, P.A. & Chen, Z.-Y. (2013) A dietary polyphenol resveratrol acts to provide neuroprotection in recurrent stroke models by regulating AMPK and SIRT1 signaling, thereby reducing energy requirements during ischemia.

At times the "presumed misconduct" category contains statements that indicate actual misconduct:

At the request of the authors, the Editors and Publisher retract the article "Nonsteroidal Anti-Inflammatory Drugs Cause Inhibition of the Growth Plate in Cultured Rat Metatarsal Bones" by Park et al, published ahead of print on July 2, 2015 in the Journal of Pediatric Orthopaedics. The corresponding author, Hyun Woo Kim, MD, has requested retraction of this report due to unresolvable issues regarding authorship.

At time there is clear evidence of plagiarism; here is an example:

The above article from European Journal of Neuroscience, published online on 4 February 2014 in Wiley Online Library (http://onlinelibrary.wiley.com.proxy.mul.missouri.edu/d...), has been retracted by agreement between the Editors-in-Chief, Paul Bolam and John Foxe, the authors and John Wiley & Sons Ltd. The retraction has been agreed as the above article has been found to overlap substantially with the article 'Chiou, L.-C., Hu, S. S.-J., and Ho, Y.-C. (2013), Targeting the cannabinoid system for pain relief? Acta Anaesthesiologica Taiwanica, Volume 51, Issue 4: 161 - 170. doi: 10.1016/j.aat.2013.10.004', which was submitted after the European Journal of Neuroscience article but was published first. Reference Hu, S.S.-J., Ho, Y.-C. & Chiou, L.-C. (2014) No more pain upon Gq-protein-coupled receptor activation: role of endocannabinoids.

In addition to plagiarism, there were numerous instances of duplication of entire documents. This statement indicates just such a case:

This manuscript has been retracted by the Editorial Board of Molecular Medicine Reports, following an investigation prompted by the authors of the article mentioned below and the Editor of the Journal, Inflammation. Fig. 1 in this manuscript was reproduced in its entirety from the following study: Gyurkovska V, Stefanova T, Dimitrova P, Danova S, Tropcheva R and Ivanovska N: Tyrosine kinase inhibitor tyrphostin AG490 retards chronic joint inflammation in mice. Inflammation 37: 995-1005, 2014. Every effort was made on the part of the publisher to contact the authors on the Molecular Medicine Reports paper but were unable to do so. As a result, this article has been retracted by the Editorial Board of Molecular Medicine Reports. [The original article was published in Molecular Medicine Reports 11: 2071-2075, 2015 DOI: 10.3893/mmr.2014.2983].

The cases where there were difficulties with peer review present specific challenges. It is apparent that something serious has occurred that renders some articles necessary of retraction. The following is a statement that details such a case:

The above article, published online on 28(th) November 2015 in Wiley Online Library (http://onlinelibrary.wiley.com.proxy.mul.missouri.edu/d...), and in volume 81, pp. 174-185, has been retracted by agreement between the authors, the journal Editor in Chief, Professor A Cohen, and John Wiley & Sons Limited. The retraction has been agreed owing to evidence indicating that the peer review of this paper was compromised. The authors were unaware of the actions of the third party responsible for compromising the peer review. Reference Lv M-Y, Deng S-L, Long X-F. rhBNP therapy can improve clinical outcomes and reduce in-hospital mortality compared with dobutamine in heart failure patients: a meta-analysis. Br J Clin Pharmacol 2016; 81: 174-85. doi:10.1111/bcp.12788.

One of the categories of retraction has to do with failing to obtain appropriate permissions and validations to conduct the research. A statement pertinent to this category reads as follows:

The above article from the Journal of Pharmacy and Pharmacology, published online on 14 February 2015 in Wiley Online Library (wileyonlinelibrary.com), and in Volume 67, pp. 972-979, has been retracted by agreement between the authors, the journal Editor-in-Chief, Professor David Jones, and John Wiley & Sons Ltd. The retraction has been agreed following an investigation by the Research Advisory Council at King Faisal Specialist Hospital and Research Centre, because the manuscript (including all of its content and authorship) was published without obtaining clearance from the Office of Research Affairs.

Budd, Coble, & Abritis (2016) write, "Every statement of retraction is carefully examined so that the classification of the retractions can be made with confidence. This is a time-consuming process, but there is no alternative to the close reading of the statements. In many ways, this mode of classification relies upon content analysis (p. 9).

SOME FUTURE WORK

Future work, particularly on retractions (and retractions), is still needed. For one thing, as is suggested above, more data should be analyzed to determine whether funding for research constitutes a problem (including continued funding awarded to authors of papers retracted because of misconduct). For another thing, there are individuals, such as Joachim Boldt, who have had nearly 100 of their articles retracted, mainly due to scientific misconduct. His works continue to be cited, even after reviews of his work have indicated the problems with his research. That kind of inquiry—examination of individuals' misconduct—needs to be conducted. It is hoped that researchers undertake this work.

John M. Budd is a Professor Emeritus with the University of Missouri. He has worked on retractions to scientific literature, as well as citations to the retracted items, for a number of years.

REFERENCES

Amos, K.A. (2014). The ethics of scholarly publishing: Exploring differences in plagiarism and duplicate publication across nations. *Journal of the Medical Library Association, 102*(2), 87-91.

Budd, J.M. (2014). The Stapel case: An object lesson in research integrity and its lapses. *Synthese, 4*, G47-G53.

Budd, J.M., Sievert, M.E., Schultz, T.R. & Scoville, C. (1999). Effects of article retraction on citation and practice in medicine. *Bulletin of the Medical Library Association*, *87*(4), 437-43.

Budd, J.M., Coble, Z. & Abritis, A. (2016). An investigation of retracted articles in the biomedical literature. *Proceedings of the 79th ASIS&T Annual Meeting,* asist.org/files/meetings/am16/proceedings/openpage16.html.

Budd, J.M., Coble, Z.C. & Anderson, K.M. (2011). Retracted publications in biomedicine: Cause for concern. Philadelphia, PA: Association of College & Research Libraries National Conference, http://www.ala.org/acrl/sites/ala.org.acrl/files/content/conferences/confsandpreconfs/national/2011/papers/retracted_publicatio.pdf.

Cokol, M., Iossifov, I., Rodriguez-Esteban, R. et al. (2007). How many scientific papers should be retracted? *EMBO Reports, 8*(5), 422-23.

Cokol, M., Ozbay, F. & Rodriguez-Esteban, R. (2008). Retraction rates are on the rise. *EMBO Reports, 9*(1), 2.

Corbyn, Z. (2009). Retraction up tenfold. *Times Higher Education*, https://www.timeshighereducation.com/news/retractions-up-tenfold/407838.article.

Elsevier retracting 26 papers accepted because of fake reviews. http://retractionwatch.com/2017/12/21/elsevier-retracting-26-papers-accepted-fake-reviews/.

Hesselmann, F., Graf, V., Schmidt, M. & Reinhart, M. (2017). The visibility of scientific misconduct: A review of the literature on retracted journal articles. *Current Sociology Review, 65*(6), 814-45.

Kochan, C. A. & Budd, J. M. (1992). The persistence of fraud in the literature: The Darsee case. *Journal of the American Society for Information Science, 43*, 488-93.

Menezes, R.G., Ram, P., Fatima. H. & Sathian, B. (2016). Honesty is the best policy: A brief overview of retraction notices. *Nepal Journal of epidemiology, 6*(4), 603-04.

Oransky, I. & Marcus, A. (2016). Two cheers for the retraction boom. *New Atlantis: A Journal of Technology and Society, 49*, 41-45.

Redman, B.K., Yarandi, H.N. &Merz, J.F. (2008). Empirical developments in retraction. *Journal of Medical Ethics, 34*(11), 807-09.

Riegelman, A. & Bakker, C. (2018). Understanding the complexities of retractions: Recommended resources. *College and Research Libraries News, 79*(1), 38-42.

Steen, R. G. (2011). Retractions in the medical literature: Who is responsible for scientific integrity? *AMWA Journal*, *26*(1), 2-7.

81st Annual Meeting of the Association for Information Science & Technology | Vancouver, Canada | 10 – 14 November 2018

Language Investigations of Children's Information Sources: A Research Agenda

Maria Cahill
University of Kentucky, USA. maria.cahill@uky.edu

Kathleen Campana
Kent State University, USA. kcampan2@kent.edu

Soohyung Joo
University of Kentucky, USA. soohyung.joo@uky.edu

ABSTRACT

When coupled with other qualitative approaches, textual analysis serves as a promising method for exploring the potential contributions of various children's information sources toward the language and vocabulary development of young children. We first identify theoretical frameworks relevant for guiding investigations that seek to understand the potential contributions of various information sources for young children. We next identify information sources that conceivably contribute to the language and vocabulary development of young children. We then explain through presentation of preliminary findings how textual analysis techniques might be applied to investigate these sources. Finally, we point to potential contextual factors worthy of consideration within these examinations. Findings from this line of research have the potential to contribute to both information practice with young children as well as information theory.

KEYWORDS

Textual analysis, children's information sources, library programs for children, language learning, vocabulary development

INTRODUCTION

For nearly three decades, school readiness has been on the radar of policy makers and politicians (Kagan & Rigby, 2003), yet in some states as many as two-thirds of all children continue to enter kindergarten lacking foundational skills linked to academic success (Mississippi Department of Education, 2014). Oral language skills, a primary indicator of school readiness, enable children to use spoken words to receive and express ideas, and they function as building blocks for both reading development (Metsala, 1999; Ricketts, Nation & Bishop, 2004) and broader cognitive processes such as reading comprehension (Beck, Perfetti, & McKeown, 1982).

Even before school entry, the language skills of children from families with fewer economic advantages lag behind those of peers in more highly resourced families (Farkas & Beron, 2004; Hart & Risley, 1995; Vasileyva, Waterfall, & Huttenlocher, 2008). Gaps in vocabulary size among children from different backgrounds are particularly concerning given that once established, differences tend to persist across the school years (Biemiller, 2001; Juel, 1988; National Early Literacy Panel, 2009) eventually bearing out in high school achievement (Cunningham & Stanovich, 1997) and even the likelihood of high school dropout or graduation (Alexander, Entwisle, & Horsey, 1997).

While much attention has been given to differences in the quantity of language exposure of children from various types of families (Hart & Risley, 1995), the quality of the language children hear is equally important (Dickinson & Porche, 2011; Hoff, 2003; Pan, Rowe, Singer & Snow, 2005) since children need knowledge of thousands of complex words to be successful academically (Biemiller 2006). Yet, everyday conversations in the home (Cunningham & Stanovich, 1998; Hayes & Ahrens, 1988) and preschool classrooms (Dickinson & Porsche, 2011) tend to be fairly modest in terms of language complexity and vary greatly in terms of interactional quality (Hirsh-Pasek et al., 2015a). This is especially troubling for children in the lowest socioeconomic conditions who suffer a "double dose of disadvantage" in both home and school environments (Neuman, Kaefer, & Pinkham, 2017).

Fortunately, a number of information sources beyond child-directed conversations are available to support the information needs of young children. Naturally, public and school libraries serve as both providers of multiple forms of information and promoters of knowledge building for children and youth (Mills, Romeijn-Stout, Campbell, & Koester, 2015; Ralli & Payne; Subramaniam, 2016), and library expenditures on materials and programming for children and youth relate favorably to circulation and program attendance rates (Joo & Cahill, 2017).

Yet for many years, researchers in the information sciences (Smardo, 1984; Stewart, 2016; Walter, 2003) have lamented the scarcity of empirical examinations, from an information perspective. Walter (2003) stated, "We have almost no good data about library services to very young children and their families and caregivers in spite of the fact that this is a growing element in public library services, with more and more public libraries entering the early childhood arena" (p. 581). The Board of Directors of the Association for Library Service to Children (2017), recognizing the existing gaps in research and theory, recently appointed a research agenda task force "To create a division-wide and subject-specific articulation of current research trends, areas of further exploration, and current needs in the field that might be addressed through research; and to recommend avenues for pursuing this research."

In addition to a paucity of empirical research, a dearth of theory related to children's information needs and behaviors has also hampered the discipline. Shenton and Dixon (2003) long ago argued for development of more nuanced theories focused on children's information seeking, in particular, development of theory that considered the role of other people in children's information seeking. The lack of information theory is even more pronounced when considering very young children whose literacy is still emerging (Teale & Sulzby, 1989), that is, children who "take in large quantities of information but much of it is still not from the abstract symbolism of textual sources because they are not yet facile with this means of communication" (Cooper, 2002, p. 904). For example, a recent publication concentrated on the information seeking behaviors of children is focused exclusively on children and youth already engaged in formal schooling (Chelton & Cool, 2007). On the other hand, as researchers have begun focusing more broadly on information behavior, theory building around young children's information behaviors has captured some attention (Agarwal, 2014; Byrnes & Bernacki, 2013; Spink & Heinstrom, 2011).

This paper proposes that, when coupled with other qualitative approaches, textual analysis serves as a promising method for exploring the potential contributions of various children's information sources toward the language and vocabulary development of young children. Within this agenda, we first identify theoretical frameworks from the fields of education, developmental psychology, and language and literacy that are relevant for guiding investigations that seek to understand the potential contributions of various information sources for young children. We next identify several information sources that conceivably contribute to the language and vocabulary development of young children. We then identify how textual analysis techniques might be applied to investigate these sources. Finally, we point to potential contextual factors worthy of consideration within these examinations. We believe findings from this line of research have the potential to contribute to both information practice with young children as well as information theory.

RELEVANT THEORETICAL FRAMEWORKS

This agenda draws on theoretical frameworks from the fields of education and language and literacy. When considering how information sources might support language learning and vocabulary growth, it is important to consider the innate systems and the agency of the individual as well as the contextual factors and learning situations that influence how the child learns and interacts.

Bioecological systems theory

Bioecological systems theory (Bronfenbrenner & Morris, 1998; 2006) proposes that child development is best conceptualized and understood through the lens of four nested and interacting contextual systems that affect progress and learning: microsystem, mesosystem, exosystem, and macrosystem. Within this contextual framework, the microsystem consists of those contexts in which the child is a member such as the child's family, school, and informal playgroup. The mesosystem encompasses the intersection of two or more microsystems, for example, the communication between the child's parent and teacher. The exosystem consists of those contexts in which the child is not a participating member but is indirectly affected such as parents' microsystems that impact the emotional state of the parent which in turn impacts the child. Finally, the macrosystem consists of social and cultural factors such as language, cultural norms, the economy, and policies. Within the microsystem the child's personal attributes and characteristics influence interactions that, in turn, impact development. Additionally, the child's attributes and interactions affect the contextual systems making the whole model reciprocal in nature. In short, the interactions, or proximal processes, in a microsystem are influenced by the child's own attributes, collective surrounding systems, and time, all of which impact development and affect both the microsystem itself and the other surrounding systems.

Emergenist coalition model

The emergentist coalition model (Hollich et al., 2000) of language acquisition and word learning bridges several seemingly oppositional theories of language development by acknowledging that certain aspects of language learning are biological in nature while also recognizing the social nature of language learning and the essential role of interaction with others. Further the model posits that a developing child's reliance on different inputs, for example, social vs. attentional cues, varies over time based on the existing knowledge brought to bear on the situation. Thus, the model identifies the importance of the biological systems, accounts for the importance of environmental components that facilitate learning and recognizes the importance of different strategies for children's subsequent language learning based on their existing language development and vocabulary knowledge.

INFORMATION SOURCES FOR YOUNG CHILDREN

We identify three potential information sources for young children that could be investigated using textual analysis methods alone or coupled with qualitative methods.

Children's books

Librarians, teachers, and parents use professional ratings (i.e. reviews) and awards to guide purchases and selection of books for children and young adults. Professional associations, such as the American Library Association (ALA) and the International Reading Association, and state-level affiliates have similarly created book awards to distinguish the best of the best. Members of book award committees serve with the intention of assisting children, teachers, and librarians with selection choices (Cohen & Andronik, 2012). Yet, award-winning books are not necessarily favored by children (Ujie & Krashen, 2006), and young children are particularly enamored with books portraying favorite television and media personalities (Anderson, 2016).

A number of studies in library and information science have examined qualities and characteristics of children's books. For example, protagonists in Newbery Award titles tend to display resiliency (Houdyshell & Martin, 2010; Lathey, 2005), while a study of Caldecott Award books identified a tendency for sex-role stereotyping (Weitzman, Eifler, Hokada, & Ross, 1972). More recently library scholars and practitioners have focused attention on diversity, or lack thereof, in children's literature (Hughes-Hassell, & Cox, 2010; Kurz, 2012; Mabbott, 2017). Yet, within the fields of library and information science, less attention has been devoted to language and vocabulary aspects of children's literature. Research proposed in this agenda would complement other studies conducted in education fields (e.g. Hayes, 1988; Massaro, 2015) to fill that gap. Investigations of the language of children's books might better support librarians', parents', and caregivers' selections for shared reading experiences.

Public library storytime programming

Public libraries are positioned to provide rich learning opportunities that support school readiness through programs for young children and their caregivers (IMLS, 2013). Prime among these programs is storytime. Libraries have been offering storytimes for young children since the 1940s with school readiness as one of several goals (Albright, Delecki, & Hinkle, 2009) and have since evolved to include a much greater focus on early literacy (Campana et al., 2016). Nearly all public libraries in the U.S. offer storytime programming for young children (Hughes-Hassell, Agosto, & Sun, 2007). Further, in the U.S., half of all children and youth who visit a public library do so to attend a program (Miller, Zickuhr, Raine, & Purcell, 2013).

Despite the popularity of public library storytimes, they have been largely understudied. Findings from the few studies that have examined public library storytimes, suggest they do contribute to young children's school readiness (Campana, 2018), and particularly in the domain of language and literacy (e.g. Campana et al., 2016; Mills et al., 2018; Neuman, Moland, & Celano, 2017). Storytimes have also been found to promote family engagement and interactions (Neuman, Moland, & Celano, 2017; McKenzie & Stooke, 2007). Investigations of the language that children hear and express in storytime might provide further direction for how these programs might be tweaked to better facilitate language learning and vocabulary growth.

Television programs designed for preschoolers

Despite cautions from the American Academy of Pediatrics (2016) to limit screen media for children under 18 months of age, approximately 40% of babies begin regular television viewing by 3 months of age, and 90% are regularly watching television by two years of age (Zimmerman, Christakis, & Meltzoff, 2007). On average, children between two- and four years of age watch more than two hours of television and video programming per day (Rideout, 2017). It is widely recognized that the content of the programs children watch is immensely important: children's consumption of programming produced for adults tends to be associated with adverse outcomes, while viewing educational programming produced for young children tends to have positive impacts on children's cognitive development (Anderson, Huston, Schmitt, Linebarger, & Wright, 2001).

Thus, television programming might be an ideal venue to enhance the language exposure and oral language development of a broad range of young children. Indeed, multimedia, such as television programming have been posited as one means for enriching the learning of young children at risk for poor academic outcomes (Neuman, 2008). While it is understood that television can influence language development (Moses, 2008), there have been only a limited number of investigations of the language landscape of television programs produced for children. Collectively, the results are promising with some findings suggesting that children make gains in their vocabulary knowledge of certain words (Rice & Woodsmall 1988). However, scholars have called for updated research on the language used in children's television (Gola, Mayeux, & Naigles, 2012) with a particular need for further research focused on entertainment content (beyond educational programming) produced for young children (Anderson & Subrahmanyam, 2017). Textual analysis is an ideal method for initial investigations of the language, and coupled with other qualitative methods, could contribute much to the understanding of how television programming, both educational and entertainment, supports or inhibits children's language development.

USE OF TEXTUAL ANALYSIS

To provide evidence for learning support provided by the information sources identified above, it is imperative to investigate the content of those sources. Textual analysis serves as a compelling method for exploring one important aspect of the content used in various information sources commonly accessed by children: the nature and sophistication of language. A variety of textual analysis methods are available for analyzing unstructured text data, particularly natural language processing and text mining. With the exponential increase of computational power, it has become possible for researchers to analyze larger sets of text data with more complex analytical methods in recent decades. Computational text analysis techniques have been employed to subdisciplines in information sciences to understand various contexts of text data, ranging from social media mining, news media analysis, bibliometrics, bioinformatics, and the like (e.g., Bae & Lee, 2012; Hung, 2012; Bleik et al., 2013; Wang et al., 2014). Yet, these methods have not been widely exercised in the context of children's information sources. Understanding the nature of language with which children interact is an essential step in explaining the environment provided by children's information sources.

In this paper, we present preliminary findings from the analysis of two information environments for young children to illustrate how textual analysis might serve as a beneficial method for investigations of children's information sources. We applied natural language analysis techniques to a partial data set from the IMLS funded Project VIEWS2 (http://views2.ischool.uw.edu/), a project aimed at investigating public library storytime programs in Washington state: the data set we used included video recordings of twenty-two storytime sessions intended for children ages 3-5. The second set of preliminary findings are based on transcripts of 140 episodes of television programs designed for young children.

In the first set of findings, we demonstrate how textual analysis might be used to understand the complexity of spoken language in natural contexts. In the second set of findings we focus exclusively on vocabulary complexity to demonstrate how textual analysis might be used to understand the sophistication of words used in information sources for children.

Several different indicators of vocabulary complexity are applicable to the context of children's information sources including Biemiller's (2010) *Words Worth Teaching,* the Corpus of Contemporary American English (COCA) (2015), and the Dale-Chall Word List (Chall & Dale, 1995). For the second pilot analysis, we adopted the Biemiller's word list to demonstrate the language sophistication of words spoken in public library storytimes and children's television programming. Biemiller's list prioritizes words for school education, and it categorizes words based on the importance of teaching within a formal learning context. Categories include as "E" as easy enough for children to learn without explicit teaching, "T2" denotes sophisticated high priority words to teach in the primary grades, "L2" signifies sophisticated low priority words for primary grade teaching, "T6" designates a word as useful to teach in upper elementary grades, and "D" means too difficult for most elementary children.

The presentation of these preliminary results is intended only to demonstrate how textual analysis could be used for investigations of various information sources intended for young children. Because the contextual factors surrounding each of these analyses are not comparable, it would be inappropriate to compare the results of the storytime programming analysis and the television programming analysis, and we are not suggesting that the results be used in that manner. Rather, we believe that textual analysis is an appropriate methodology for investigating a variety of information sources for young children when coupled with other qualitative methodologies that account for important contextual factors such as subject matter, child appeal, interactional quality, and more.

Public library storytime programming

From the video recordings of twenty-two preschool storytime sessions, we transcribed all language utterances spoken by children, storytime librarians, and other adult participants respectively. In this investigation, we employed term frequency analysis, part-of-speech tagging, and language complexity analysis. For data analysis, we constructed two sets of transcribed text corpus: one from the children's speech and the other from the librarians' speech. For term frequency analysis, we carried out tokenization and lemmatization. Each individual token observed was transformed to a lemma, which is an abstract form shared across word forms having the same stem (Jackson & Moulinier, 2007; Manning et al., 2008). Unlike conventional information retrieval research, stopwords were included in the analysis as we intended to analyze natural language use including all grammar components. Part-of-speech tagging analysis, which is the process of assigning a word class marker to each term in the sentence was then applied (Jackson & Moulinier, 2007).

Across the twenty-two sessions, we observed 67,285 tokens and 2,642 unique types from the librarian corpus and 13,308 tokens and 1,191 unique types from the children's corpus. Term frequency analysis revealed that during the storytime session, librarians spoke (3058.41 tokens per session) around five times more than children did (604.91 tokens per session). Most frequent terms from the two groups were mostly comprised of so-called stopwords, such as determiners (e.g., the, a), pronouns (e.g., I, you, it), and basic auxiliary verbs (e.g., go, do, have).

	Children	Librarians
Verb	18.24%	22.28%
Noun	18.68%	16.14%
Pronoun	13.89%	15.12%
Determiner	8.96%	8.85%
Adverb	5.92%	7.88%
Preposition	4.33%	6.05%
Adjective	4.04%	5.89%
Conjunction	2.95%	4.24%
Name	6.19%	3.46%
Interjection	8.69%	2.44%

Table 1. Grammar elements spoken by children and librarians respectively (most frequent ten elements

Part-of-speech tagging analysis explicitly revealed the different patterns of grammar element proportions between children and librarians (Table 1). Librarians were likely to use more verbs, adjectives, prepositions, adverbs, and conjunctions than children, suggesting their language tends to be comprised of more complete, complex sentences. On the contrary, children's language included more nouns, names, and interjections, implying that the storytime setting supports children's reception of complex sentences while interacting with librarians.

More importantly, we attempted to analyze the vocabulary sophistication of storytimes using Biemiller's word list. One limitation of the Biemiller taxonomy is that different definitions of the same words are categorized across different levels, and it is not easy to discern word meaning in the textual analysis. Despite this limitation, a higher-level category tends to involve more sophisticated words in general than the lower one does. Because the storytimes involved preschool children, we adopted the T2 level list, which consists of priority words for primary grades, as the reference vocabulary list as a measure for how storytimes support school readiness. As shown in Figure 1, we found that the tokens spoken by librarians contained significantly more T2 level words (29.95%) than those by children (20.91%), accounting for about 9% gap between them. When examining types in the T2 category, the gap becomes bigger. Only about 13.9% of the types generated by children were in the T2 list while 31.5% of the types by librarians were in the T2 list. This finding implies that the language environment is supportive of children's vocabulary learning, with an appropriate gap between children's and librarians' sophisticated vocabulary use, and suggests that for language purposes, storytimes may serve as a supportive information source for young children.

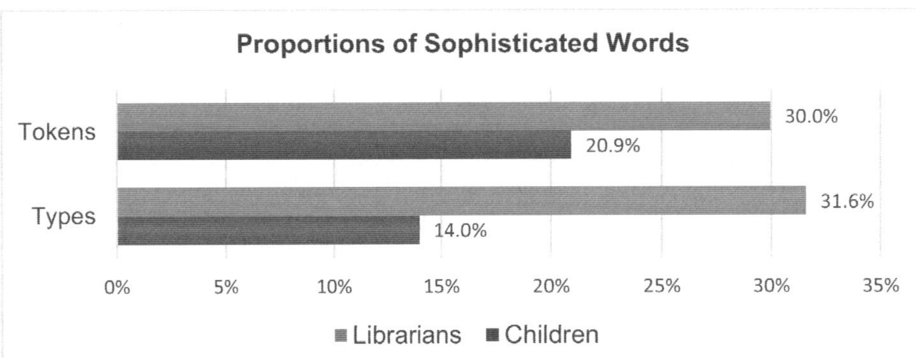

Figure 1. Proportions of sophisticated words spoken by children and librarians respectively

Television programs designed for children

For the pilot analysis involving television programs for young children, we analyzed the closed caption transcripts of a total of 140 episodes from 15 randomly selected programs aired on three popular channels for children, PBS Kids, Nick Jr., and Disney. The dataset consists of a total runtime of 104,255 seconds, or approximately 29 hours. We employed two different categories of Biemiller's taxonomy: T2 and T6 levels. In total, approximately 30.6% of the observed tokens were categorized as T2. As shown in Table 2, the amount of sophisticated words differed by program, with *Martha Speaks*, *Wild Kratts*, and *Sofia the First* exhibiting higher frequencies of T2 tokens per minute. These results point to the potential value of television programs for young children in terms of language development.

Channel	Program	T2 tokens per minute Mean (SD)	T6 tokens per minute Mean (SD)
PBS Kids	Arthur	35.86 (6.79)	23.31(5.31)
	Martha Speaks	38.67 (5.61)	28.23 (4.84)
	Nature Cat	29.31 (4.32)	20.15 (4.78)
	Thomas and friends	30.39 (4.17)	22.16 (3.71)
	Wild Kratts	35.62 (5.82)	25.57 (3.57)
Nick Jr.	Peppa Pig	25.57 (4.16)	15.61 (3.56)
	Team Umizoomi	28.79 (3.54)	21.82 (4.36)
	Tickety Toc	22.77 (3.31)	12.88 (2.78)
	Wonder Pets	27.71 (3.61)	16.77 (2.45)
	Zack and Quack	22.70 (2.28)	14.37 (1.58)
	Lion Guard	35.06 (2.43)	25.00 (2.33)
Disney	Little Einsteins	18.69 (3.36)	15.74 (6.00)
	Mickey Mouse Clubhouse	26.50 (5.55)	19.29 (3.96)
	Octonauts	31.27 (3.60)	21.05 (3.26)
	Sofia the First	39.45 (0.71)	24.55 (1.74)

Table 2. Language sophistication of television programing for children

FUTURE RESEARCH: INVESTIGATION OF CHILDREN'S INFORMATION ENVIRONMENTS

This paper proposes the application of textual analysis in the analysis of children's information sources. Specifically, we demonstrate through pilot analyses of language sophistication in two different children's information environments (Campana, 2018), public library storytimes and television programs produced for young children, the potential benefits as well as the methodological feasibility of using textual analysis for the investigation of children's information environments. Again, the presentation of results was not intended to be used for comparison purposes: we don't suggest that either information source is a better support for young children's language development. Rather, we purport that the method could be used more widely across children's information sources as a means for measuring the complexity of the language that children are exposed to when interacting with these sources.

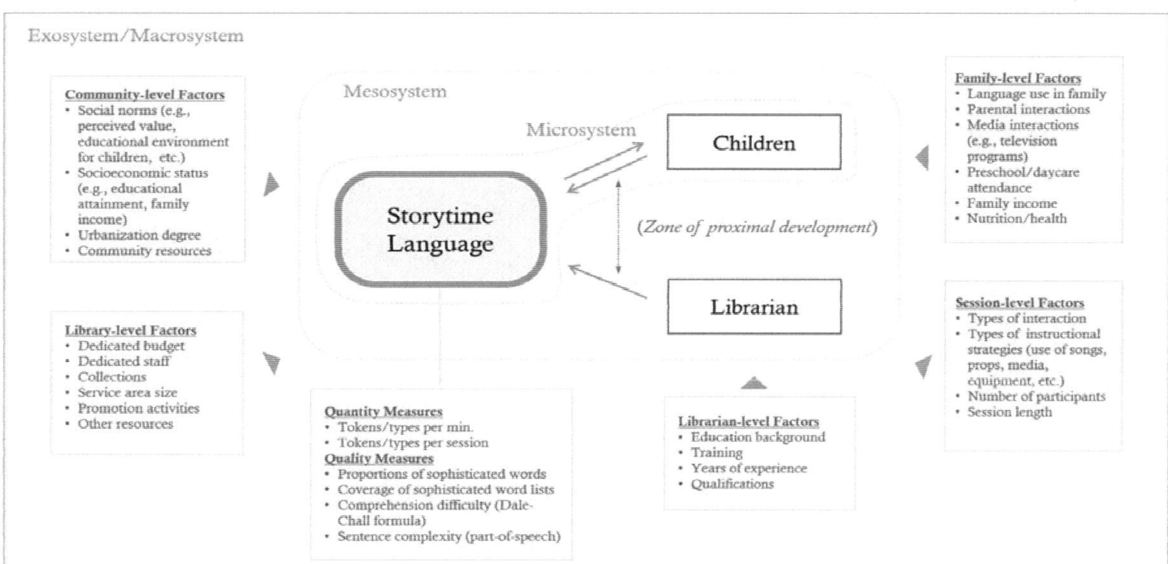

Figure 2. A Conceptual Model of the Storytime Information Environment

To build on the textual analysis work discussed here, we propose two conceptual-level research models as a comprehensive framework to investigate information environments for children, specifically storytimes and television programs, focusing on language development. We first identify various dimensions of factors associated with the information environments, and then, we propose a model to investigate the environment comprehensively.

First, we propose a conceptual research model for public library storytime analysis based on the bioecological systems theory (Bronfenbrenner & Morris, 1998; 2006). In the core of the model, our concern is the quantity and quality of the language and the interactions between children and the language at the microsystem level. Then, we plan to examine how, if at all, mesosystem and macrosystem factors influence the language use at the microsystem level via five hierarchical levels of potential contextual factors, including session-level, family-level, librarian-level, library-level, and community-level, to be considered in storytime settings.

Second, Figure 3 describes the conceptual research model suggested for investigating the television program environment as an information source for children. We recognize that the learning possibilities from television programs are dependant on a variety of other factors but for this model we position the direction of the research to serve as the basis for understanding the language context of television programs produced for young children and to offer insight into the potential of television programming as a basis for interventions to enhance the language development and school readiness of young children.

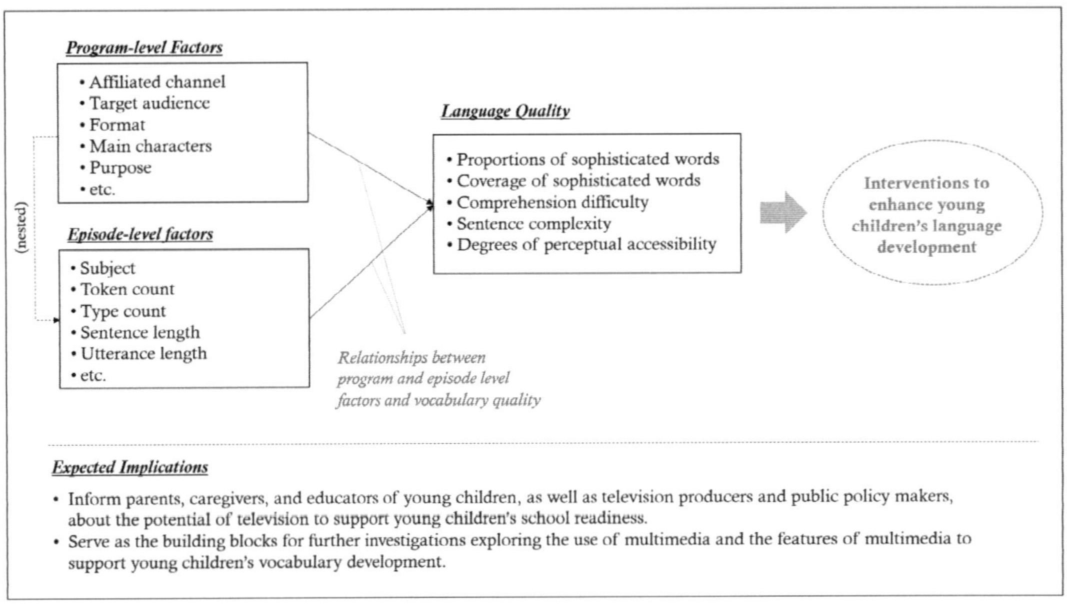

Figure 3. A Conceptual Model of the Television Program Information Environment

These conceptual research models can be used to guide further investigations into public library storytimes and television program information environments, as well as other information environments in which children exist. We plan to construct more specific, high-fidelity research designs, based on these models, by identifying measurable factors and variables. This line of research is important as it extends the foci of children's language learning research to diverse information environments. Future investigations into these models can and should include a variety of methodologies to explore the different factors, including textual analysis and complementary qualitative and quantitative methods. We plan both qualitative and quantitative analyses to probe the effectiveness of different information sources on children's development, but we posit that textual analysis should serve as a core method for understanding the nature of language use and complexity in different information sources used by young children.

REFERENCES

Agarwal, N. K. (2014). Use of touch devices by toddlers or preschoolers: Observations and findings from a single-case study. In D. Bilal & J. Beheshti (Eds.), *New directions in children's and adolescents' information behavior research* (pp. 3-37). Bingley, UK: Emerald Group Publishing Limited.

Albright, M., Delecki, K., & Hinkle, S. The evolution of early literacy: A history of best practices in storytime. *Children and Libraries, v(n)*, 13-18.

Alexander, K. L., Entwisle, D. R., & Horsey, C. (1997). From first grade forward: Early foundation of high school dropout. *Sociology of Education, 70*(2), 87-107.

American Association of Pediatrics Council on Communications and Media. (2016). *Media and young minds*. Pediatrics. 138(5), 1-6.

Anderson, D. R, Huston, A. C., Schmitt, K. L., Linebarger, D. L., & Wright, J. C. (2001). Early childhood television viewing and adolescent behavior: the recontact study. *Monographs of the Society for Research in Child Development, 66*(1), 1-147.

Anderson, D. R., & Subrahmanyam, K. (2017). Digital screen media and cognitive development. *Pediatrics, 140*(S2), S57-S61.

Anderson, P. (2016, November 1). Children's book summit: Nielsen on kids, their trends, and their parents. Retrieved from https://publishingperspectives.com/2016/11/nielsen-childrens-book-summit-2016/

Association for Library Service to Children. (2017). Research agenda task force. Retrieved from http://www.ala.org/alsc/research-agenda-task-force

Bae, Y., & Lee, H. (2012). Sentiment analysis of twitter audiences: Measuring the positive or negative influence of popular twitterers. Journal of the Association for Information Science and Technology, 63(12), 2521-2535.

Beck, I. L., Perfetti, C. A., McKeown, M. G. (1982). Effects of long-term vocabulary instruction on lexical access and reading comprehension. Journal of Educational Psychology, 74(4), 506-521.

Biemiller, A., & Slonim, N. (2001). Estimating root word vocabulary growth in normative and advantaged populations: Evidence for a common sequence of vocabulary acquisition. Journal of Educational Psychology, 93, 498–520.

Biemiller, A. (2006). Vocabulary development and instruction: A prerequisite for school learning. In D. Dickinson & S. B. Neuman (Eds.), Handbook of early literacy research (Vol. 2, pp. 41–51). New York: Guilford.

Biemiller, A. (2010). Words worth teaching: Closing the vocabulary gap. Columbus, OH: SRA/McGrawHill.

Bleik, S., Mishra, M., Huan, J., & Song, M. (2013). Text categorization of biomedical data sets using graph kernels and a controlled vocabulary. IEEE/ACM transactions on computational biology and bioinformatics, 10(5), 1211-1217.

Bronfenbrenner, U., & Morris, P.A. (1998). The bioecological model of human development. In W. Damon (Series Ed.) & R.M. Lerner (Vol. Ed.), Handbook of child psychology. Vol. 1 (pp. 993–1027). New York, NY: Wiley & Sons.

Bronfenbrenner, U., & Morris, P.A. (2006). The bioecological model of human development. In W. Damon (Series Ed.) & R.M. Lerner (Vol. Ed.), Handbook of child psychology. Vol. 1 (pp. 793–828). New York, NY: Wiley & Sons.

Byrnes, J. P., & Bernacki, M. L. (2013). Cognitive development and information behavior. In J. Beheshti & A. Large (Eds.), The information behavior of a new generation: Children and teens in the 21st century (pp. 23-43). Plymouth, UK: The Scarecrow Press.

Campana, K. (2018). The multimodal power of storytime: Exploring an information environment for young children (Doctoral dissertation). Retrieved from ProQuest Dissertations & Theses.

Campana, K., Mills, J. E., Capps, J. L., Dresang, E. T., Carlyle, A., et al. (2016). Early literacy in library storytimes: A study of measures of effectiveness. *Library Quarterly, 86*(4), 369-388.

Chall, J. S., & Dale, E. (1995). Readability revisited: The new Dale-Chall readability formula. Brookline Books.

Chelton, M. K., & Cool, C. (2007). Youth information-seeking behavior II: Context, theories, models, and issues. Lanham, MD: Scarecrow Press.

Cohen, J. W., & Andronik, C. (2012). Listening for the best: amazing audiobooks for teens. *Young adult library services, 10(3), 30-31.*

Cooper, L. Z. (2002). Methodology for a project examining cognitive categories for library information in young children. Journal of the American Society for Information Science and Technology, 53(14), 1223-1231.

Corpus of Contemporary American English (COCA). (1990-2015). Words added between 1990 and 2015. Retrieved October 20, 2016 http://corpus.byu.edu/coca/

Cunningham, A. E., & Stanovich, K., E. (1997). Early reading acquisition and its relation to reading experience and ability 10 years later. *Developmental Psychology, 33*, 934-945.

Dickinson, D. K., & Porche, M. V. (2011). Relation between language experiences in preschool classrooms and children's kindergarten and fourth-grade language and reading abilities. *Child Development, 82*(3), 870-886.

Farkas, G., & Beron, K. (2004). The detailed age trajectory of oral vocabulary knowledge: Differences by class and race. Social Science Research, 33, 464-497.

Gola, A. A. H., Mayeux, L., & Naigles, L. R. (2012). Electronic media as incidental language teachers. In D. G. Singer & J. L Singer (Eds.), *Handbook of Children and the Media (2nd ed)* (pp. 139-157). Thousand Oaks, CA: Sage.

Hart, B. & Risley, T. (1995). Meaningful differences in the everyday experience of young American children. Baltimore: Paul H. Brookes Publishing.

Hayes, D. P. (1988). Speaking and writing: Distinct patterns of word choice. *Journal of Memory and Language, 27*, 572-585.

Hayes, D. P., & Ahrens, M. (1988). Vocabulary simplification for children: A special case of "Motherese"? Journal of Child Language, 15, 395-410.

Hirsch-Pasek, K., Adamson, L. B., Bakeman, R., Owen, M. T., Golinkoff, R. M., et al. (2015). The contribution of early communication quality to low-income children's language success. Psychological Science, 26(7), 1071-1083.

Hoff, E. (2003). The specificity of environmental influence: Socieconomic status affects early vocabulary development via maternal speech. Child Development, 74, 1368–1378.

Hollich, G. J., Hirsh-Pasek, K., Golinkoff, R. M., Brand, R. J., Brown, E., Chung, H. L., & Bloom, L. (2000). Breaking the language barrier: An emergentist coalition model for the origins of word learning. *Monographs of the Society for Research in Child Development, 65*(3).

Houdyshell, M. L., & Martin, C.M. (2010). You go, girl! *Children & Libraries, 8*(1), 25-31.

Hughes-Hassell, S., & Cox, E. J. (2010). Inside board books: Representations of people of color. Library Quarterly 80(3), 211-230.

Hughes-Hassell, S., Agosto, D. E., & Sun, X. (2007). Making storytime available to children of working parents: Public libraries and the scheduling of children's literacy programs. *Children and Libraries, 5*(2), 43-48.

Hung, J. L. (2012). Trends of e-learning research from 2000 to 2008: Use of text mining and bibliometrics. British Journal of Educational Technology, 43(1), 5-16.

Institute of Museum and Library Services. (2013). *Growing young minds: How museums and libraries create lifelong learners*. Washington, DC: Author.

Jackson, P., & Moulinier, I. (2007). Natural language processing for online applications: Text retrieval, extraction and categorization (Vol. 5). John Benjamins Publishing.

Joo, S., & Cahill, M. (2017). The relationships between library resources and children's use of public libraries: An exploratory analysis of IMLS public library statistics data. Journal of Librarianship & Information Science. Retrieved from http://journals.sagepub.com/doi/full/10.1177/0961000617709057

Juel, C. (1988). Learning to read and write: A longitudinal study of 54 children from first through fourth grades. Journal of Educational Psychology, 80, 243-255.

Kagan, S. L., & Rigby, E. (2003). Policy matters: Setting and measuring benchmarks for state policies. Washington, DC: Center for the Study of Social Policy.

Kurz, R. F. (2012). Missing faces, beautiful places: The lack of diversity in South Carolina picture book award nominees. New Review of Children's Literature & Librarianship, 18(2), 128-145.

Lathey, J. (2005). Challenges then and now: A survey of protagonists in Newbery Award books, 1950s and 1990s. *Children & Libraries, 3*(3), 20-24.

Manning, C.D., Raghavan, P, & Schütze, H. (2008). Introduction to Information Retrieval. Cambridge, England: Cambridge University Press.

Mabbott, C. (2017). The We Need Diverse Books campaign and critical race theory: Charlemae Rollins and the call for diverse children's books. Library Trends, 65(4), 508-522.

McKenzie, P. J., & Stooke, R. K. (2007). Producing storytime: A collectivist analysis of work in a complex communicative space. *The Library Quarterly: Information, Communication, Policy, 77*, 3-20.

Metsala, J. L. (1999). Young children's phonological awareness and nonword repetition as a function of vocabulary development. Journal of Educational Psychology, 91(1), 3-19.

Mills, J. E., Campana, K., Carlyle, A., Kotrla, B., Dresang, E. T., Urban, I. B., Capps, J.L., Metoyer, C., Feldman, E., Brouwer, M., & Burnett, K. (2018). Early Literacy in Library Storytimes, Part 2: A Quasi-Experimental Study and Intervention with Children's Storytime Providers. Library Quarterly, 88(2), 160-176.

Mills, J. E., Romeijn-Stout, E., Campbell, C., & Koester, A. (2015). Results from the young children, new media, and libraries survey: What did we learn?. Children and Libraries, 13(2), 26-35.

Mississippi Department of Education. (2014). Kindergarten readiness assessment results October 2014. Retrieved from http://www.mde.k12.ms.us/docs/student-assessment/k-readiness-results-public_20141021113851_378676.pdf?sfvrsn=2

Moses, A. M. (2008). Impacts of television viewing on young children's literacy development in the USA: A review of the literature. Journal of Early Childhood Literacy, 8, 67-102.

National Early Literacy Panel. (2008). Developing early literacy: Report of the National Early Literacy Panel. Washington, DC: National Center for Family Literacy. Retrieved from http://lincs.ed.gov/publications/pdf/NELPReport09.pdf

Neuman, S. B. (Ed.). (2008). *Educating the other America: Top experts tackle poverty, literacy, and achievement in our schools*. Baltimore, MD: Paul H. Brooks.

Neuman, S. B., Kaefer, T., & Pinkham, A. M. (2018). A double dose of disadvantage: Language experiences for low-income children in home and school. Journal of Educational Psychology, 110(1), 102-118.

Neuman, S. B., Moland, N., Celano, D. (2017). Bringing literacy home: An evaluation of the Every Child Ready to Read program. Chicago: American Library Association.

Pan, B. A., Rowe, M. L., Singer, J. D., & Snow, C. E.(2005). Maternal correlates of growth in toddler vocabulary production in low-income families. Child Development, 76, 763–782.

Ralli J, & Payne RG (2016). Let's play at the library: Creating innovative play experiences for babies and toddlers. Library Trends 65(1): 41-64.

Rice, M. L., Woodsmall, L. (1988). Lessons for television: Children's word learning when viewing. *Child Development, 59*(2), 420-429.

Ricketts, J., Nation, K., & Bishop, D. V. M. (2007). Vocabulary is important for some, but not all reading skills. Scientific Studies of Reading, 11(3), 235-257.

Rideout, V. (2017). The Common Sense census: Media use by kids age zero to eight. San Francisco: Common Sense Media.

Shenton, A. K., & Dixon, P. (2003). Youngsters' use of other people as an information-seeking method. Journal of Librarianship and Information Science, 35(4), 219-233.

Smardo, F. A. (1983). A comparison of the impact of three methods of storyhour presentation upon children's listening skills. Public Library Quarterly, 4(1), 33–42.

Spink, A., & Heinstrom, J. (2011). Information behavior development in early childhood. In A. Spink & J. Heinstrom (Eds.), New directions in information behaviour (pp. 245-256). Bingley, UK: Emerald Group Publishing Limited.

Stewart, S. N. (2016). Understanding the information seeking of pre-kindergarten students: An ethnographic exploration of their seeking behaviors in a preschool setting (unpublished doctoral dissertation). University of North Texas, Denton, TX.

Subramaniam M (2016) Designing the library of the future for and with teens: librarians as the "connector" in connected learning. The Journal of Research on Libraries and Young Adults 7(2): 1-18.

Teale, W. H., & Sulzby, E. (1989). Emergent literacy: New perspectives. In D. S. Strickland & L. M. Morrow (Eds.), Emerging literacy: Young children learn to read and write. Newark, DE: International Reading Association.

Ujie, J. and Krashen, S. (January/February 2006). Are prize-winning books popular among children? An analysis of public library circulation. Knowledge Quest. 34(3), 33-35.

Vasilyeva, M., Waterfall, H., & Huttenlocher, J. (2008). Emergence of syntax: commonalities and differences across children. Developmental Science, 11(1), 84-97.

Walter, V. A. (2003). Public library service to children and teens: A research agenda. Library Trends, 51(4), 571-589.

Wang, Y., Joo, S., & Lu, K. (2014). Exploring topics in the field of data science by analyzing wikipedia documents: A preliminary result. Proceedings of the Association for Information Science and Technology, 51(1), 1-4.

Weitzman, L. J., Eifler, D., Hokada, E., & Ross, C. (1972). Sex role socialization in picture books for preschool children. American Journal of Sociology 77 (6), 1125-1150.

Zimmerman, F. J., Christakis, D. A., & Meltzoff, A. N. (2007). Television and DVD/video viewing in children younger than 2 years. *Archives of Pediatric and Adolescent Medicine, 161*, 473-479.

Re-examining Students' Reading Experience in a Gamified Context from a Self-determination Perspective: A Multiple-case Study

Xinyu Chen
The University of Hong Kong, Hong Kong. chen-xyxy@connect.hku.hk

Shum Yi Cameron Lee
The University of Hong Kong, Hong Kong
sycamlee@connect.hku.hk

Xiuhan Li
The University of Hong Kong, Hong Kong.
u3003557@hku.hk

Samuel K.W. Chu
The University of Hong Kong, Hong Kong.
samchu@hku.hk

ABSTRACT

The present study re-examines the reading experiences of eight primary school students in Hong Kong. Framed around theories of gamification and self-determination, the study looks at how these students developed as readers on an online gamified reader known as RB. An electronic extension to a reading database that contains more than 15,000 comprehension questions made from around 500 popular children's books, RB is found to enable the students feel competent, autonomous and connected with their family and friends during their game play. These feelings can be explained away by the three psychological needs of self -determination literature. For instance, after a period of time playing on RB, the students displayed competence in that they did well on their academics, increased their reading speed, expanded their vocabulary, and further developed their learning and problem-solving skills in school. They also showed autonomy in their learning, manifested in the expansion of the scope of their reading choices, a diversity of their reading methods, an increase in their reading frequency, and a boost to their drive in picking up a book for leisure read. Finally, they felt more connected now with their family and friends than before they used RB, for the bondage they formed over RB lasted well beyond their game play. Based on a re-evaluation of their success stories from gamification and self-determination perspectives, the study concludes that RB is an effective early English learners' tool in Hong Kong.

KEYWORDS

Educational technologies; Gamification; Learner's motivation; Self-determination theory

INTRODUCTION

Nowadays, the relations between technologies and learning are inseparable. With the development of educational technologies, our learning becomes expedited across wide-ranging contexts: business, charity, health and fitness, and education (Martens, 2014). Considering that a technologically literate population is a hallmark of any nation in pursuit of a sustainable and effective development, reading plays an essential role in that context because: (1) it is fundamental for anyone hoping to learn a skill; (2) it helps individuals to stay on top of current affairs; and (3) it steers life trajectories and empowers civic engagement in the broader community (Li & Wilhelm, 2008; Mullis, Martin, Foy & Drucker, 2011). In other words, living in the 21st century means that as much as digital connection afforded by technologies transforms our life, we all share a stake in shaping our milieu. It is thus paramount that a literate person should be able to identify, access, read, evaluate, synthesize, organize, use and communicate information effectively, as to make a contribution to their immediate locale (HKSAR, 2005; Mckee, 2012; Westby, 2004). Education researchers share that ideal. In their endeavor of expanding the field of their expertise, they never stop studying about and finding ways to improve one's reading abilities (Baker, 2004; Fajardo, 1996; Mckee, 2012; Mokhtari & Richard, 2002; Mullis, Martin, Foy & Drucker, 2011). To further their mantle, the present study hones in on literacy development in children, studying on the impact of gamification on school-aged children's English learning. Towards that end, a qualitative research method is designed to re-examine the accounts of how eight primary school students in Hong Kong developed as readers. Looking through the lenses of gamification and self-determination theories, the study is geared towards answering two questions: (1) In what ways has the online gamified reader 'RB' helped the eight students learn English? And (2) What have cognitively changed in the way those students learn English since they started using RB? But what is RB?

BACKGROUND

Encouraging children to read more is fundamental to improving the literacy rate of a population in the long run. Premising on this notion, the Education Bureau of Hong Kong spearheads various reading programmes in primary and secondary schools that are aimed at increasing youth literacy. One of their efforts in recent years is to integrate technologies into language learning.

This, in effect, mirrors a growing trend in education practices around the world where elements of gameplay are tactfully merged into curriculum design as to help children master a language in a fun and easy-going fashion (a process known as gamification) (Hanus & Fox, 2015). The ‘Chinese and English Extensive Reading Schemes’ in Hong Kong are examples of gamification. Both programmes require students to read a certain number of English books during and outside of class time as to promote active reading habits (The Government of the Hong Kong Special Administrative Region, 2016). Similarly, the “Chinese Octopus” (「中文百達通」) and “A Passage A Day” (「每日一篇網上閱讀計劃」) reading programmes also galvanize students to read Chinese books. To keep up with the pace of development in education technologies, a new online reader called ‘RB’ was recently developed in Hong Kong by a team of researchers at the University of Hong Kong, Faculty of Education (Chan, Chu, Mok & Tam, 2016; Fung, 2016; Wu, Chu, Chan & Mok, 2014). Designed to improve youth literacy, RB is an electronic extension to a reading database that contains more than 15,000 comprehension questions made from around 500 popular children’s books (Centre for Information Technology in Education, 2014). After reading a book suggested by RB, the student user would be prompted to take a corresponding comprehension quiz called ‘battle’ that tests their understanding of the book. At the end of each battle, instantaneous grading and system-generated lesson feedback would be provided for the student user to keep track of their progress and learning milestones. The reading record also enables the game system to rank its users, allowing those with a competitive mind to feel motivated about raising their ranks. Pitting one student against another through the number of books they read and the number of battles they “fought” and won, every year those who score in the top ten will be awarded a learning certificate and a print book that testify their achievement (“RB”, n.d.).

LITERATURE REVIEW

Reading literacy

In designing RB, a major pedagogical framework informing the game designers is the Progress in International Reading Literacy Study. Designed to test the reading competence of primary school children, this study sets a globally-accepted educational benchmark against which educators can review and revamp existing practices. According to the study, reading literacy is defined as “the ability to understand and use those written language forms required by society and/or valued by the individual. Readers can construct meaning from texts in a variety of forms. They read to learn, to participate in communities of readers in school and everyday life, and for enjoyment” (Mullis et al., 2016, p.12). This definition is further elaborated for a general audience by Leu and others (2004), Rosell and Pahl (2010), and Reuda (2013). Highlighting the importance of reading in schools, these authors call to attention the growing variety of lessons that merge texts with multimedia. Moreover, their studies drive home the point that reading is as much of a co-constructive experience by teachers and students as an interactive process where readers need to actively construct meanings in text with the tripartite inputs of their own linguistic skills, cognitive strategies, and background knowledge. Other researchers expand on this notion with psychological models. Guthrie and Wigfield (2000), in particular, find that cognitions, social environment, and intrinsic motivation are three areas that can further develop a person’s literacy skills if stimulated tactfully. In sum, if the right input is provided for a child at the right places, the research shows, the child can become an effective English learner.

Gamification in Learning

One increasingly popular site for English learning is an online gamified reader, an educational channel that makes use of game play mechanics for non-game applications as to help users reach designated learning goals. A main attraction of it is that it arouses players’ curiosity, stimulating them to learn as they play and compete against other players (Huotari & Hamari, 2012; Muntean, 2011; Nicholson, 2012). Characterized by a study as ‘fun’, ‘interactive’ and ‘challenging’, learning through games enables students to proactively solve problems they see (Deterding, Dixon, Khaled, & Nacke, 2011; Hanus & Fox, 2015). Specific gaming features that bring about that proactivity include learning targets or challenges, competitions, scoreboards, and badges and trophies. These elements align players’ desires to win with a set of age-appropriate learning goals embedded strategically throughout the game by designers (Chen, Teng, & Lee, 2011). When learning is planned in this way, learners are able to absorb the knowledge faster, understand easier, and improve their logical reasoning skills ((King, 1994; McDaniel & Donnelly, 1996). These desirable outcomes form the tenets of RB.

Self-determination theory in learner’s motivation: autonomy, competence, and relatedness

Although gamification can lead to desirable outcomes, getting there depends largely on players’ motivation and their in-game behaviors. The causal link between motivation and behavior can be best understood by self-determination theory (SDT). SDT is a psychological theory that studies human motivation, emotion and development. Unlike other psychological theories that are concerned with processes directing behaviours toward desired outcomes (e.g., Bandura, 1977; Dweck, 1986; Eccles 1983), SDT focuses on why only certain outcomes are desirable for and easily learnt by humans (Deci, Vallerand, Pelletier & Ryan, 1991). Three main intrinsic needs, positulated by Deci and Ryan (1991), provide an explanation of such a phenomenon: (1) a feeling of competence, which refers to the experience of behaviour as effectively enacted; (2) a feeling of autonomy, which refers to the experience of behaviour as volitional and reflectively self-endorsed; and (3) a feeling of relatedness, which refers to the urge to interact or to be connected with others. Scores of studies (e.g., Deci, 1971; Amabile, DeJong & Lepper, 1976, and Frodi, Bridges & Grolnick, 1985) confirm this. In the context of education, SDT provides a road map with which to guides teachers to come up with strategies for learning (Niemiec & Ryan, 2009). Studies by Grolnick and others (1991), Niemiec and others (2006), and Black and Deci (2000) find that desired academic outcomes can be explained by SDT and that successful learning depends on a satisfaction of those three needs. An analytical framework based on SDT in gamification was recently developed by Aparicio and others (2012), who outline the reasons behind the use of gamification by educators, what intrinsically motivating factors are present in their gamification design, what game mechanics are applied, and how SDT can be evaluated in the game system. This analytical framework, albeit timely, seems to lack rigor in its design and contain a major shortcoming that chimes with Katie and Deborah's research in 2015: a large majority (87%) of SDT-grounded gamification studies have loosely defined theoretical foundations. Hoping to eliminate major pitfalls in the present study, the theoretical scope and methodological approach of the study are discussed in detail next.

THEORETICAL FRAMEWORK

Since gamification is an underexplored research area in Hong Kong, to better understand the link between gamification and English learning, a theoretical framework as shown in Figure 1 is conceived. Although some studies (Chan, Chu, Mok & Tam, 2016; Fung, 2016; Wu, Chu, Chan & Mok, 2014) already confirmed the effectiveness of RB on literacy development (see Process 2 in Figure 1), there remains a lack of attention devoted to explaining what cognitively happened when a student reads under a gamified context. By looking at their learning experiences through the SDT model, the present study can scrutinize specific contextual conditions (see Process 1 in Figure 1) under which students are provided with scaffold in their learning. The results that emerge thereafter can become valuable insights for future research and reading programme designs in Hong Kong.

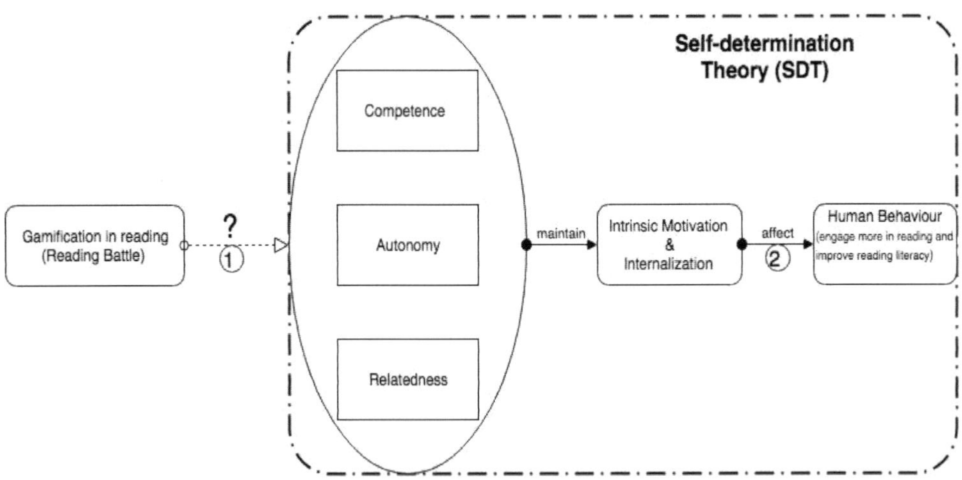

Figure 1. The theoretical framework of this study

METHODOLOGY

Before delving into the methodology of the present study, it is important to understand how the initial data were sourced. In the previous study in which the reading habits of high-performing RB students[1] were first examined, adult-oriented semi-structured interviews were arranged. The rationale was three-fold: 1. to explore different user experiences, the feedback from whom could further make RB more user-friendly; 2. to gain in-depth accounts of those who not only developed long-term reading habits but also made substantial improvements on their academics; and 3. to help establish the link between their top performance in the game and the reality of what they actually did to get there, their assumptions about the game, English learning and reading in general, and the discourses that informed their actions. Each interview took place in a room where an interviewer could speak privately with a student and his/her accompanying parent. The interview lasted around 15-20 minutes in an open, non-directive manner as to ensure the child was not guided to answer lead-in questions. Before the interview took

[1] Those invited for interviews were between the ages of 6 and 12, scored in the top ten on RB across all primary schools in Hong Kong, and showed substantial improvements on their school grades in the six months preceding the interviews.

place, the founder of RB headed down to the schools where the students were studying and discussed with the students, the parents, librarian teachers and school principals about RB, its research significance, and its impact on student learning.

In the present study, not all interview data were analysed from the previous study; only eight sets (from eight students) were scrutinized based on their relevance to self-determination theory. The select data were parsed with the qualitative data-analysis software NVivo 11.0 in a bid to answer two main questions: (1) In what ways has the online gamified reader 'RB' helped these students learn English? And (2) What have cognitively changed in the way those students learn English since they started using RB? The traditional self-determination model (Deci and Ryan, 1991) only identifies three needs of motivation: competence, autonomy, and relatedness. While the model is versatile, in this study to firmly establish the link between literacy development and gamification, a second-level categorization (shown Table 1) is conceived to further evaluate the data. As Table 1 further reveals, five second-level categories pertaining to competence, four categories pertaining to autonomy and three categories pertaining to relatedness are devised.

First Level Category	Definition	Second Level Category (Definition)	Sample Contents (Participant number)
Competence	the experience of behavior as effectively enacted	Vocabulary (experiences related to the change of their vocabulary)	...I have learnt more vocabularies since using RB. (Participant 8)
		Problem-solving skill (experiences when they meet challenge)	The book is challenging ... would never give up. (Participant 4)
		Academic performance (experiences related to the significant change of exam marks or another received award)	I have improved from around 70 marks to around 80 marks... (Participant 2)
		Reading speed (experiences related to the change in of their reading speed)	I can read faster now... (Participant 7)
		Learning ability (experiences related to the development of learning abilities and thinking)	...his advancement in logical thinking judging from the smooth and organized flow in his summaries ... (Participant 4)
Autonomy	the experience of behavior as volitional and reflectively self-endorsed	Reading material (experiences related to varied book choice)	...she has become an avid reader of a variety of genres, like history, science, detective novels etc. (Participant 3)
		Reading proactivity (experiences that show their reading initiative)	...he has borrowed many books about magic from the library. (Participant 4)
		Reading frequency (experiences related to how often they read)	Reading at least 2 books per week... (Participant 3)
		Reading method (experiences related to having more flexible reading methods)	He will skim through the beginning and the ending of the books to grasp the gist of the concept before diving into the details. (Participant 4)
Relatedness	The experience of interacting or being connected with others.	Connection with parents	...started to share more of this thoughts with his mother. (Participant 6)
		Connection with siblings	...my two brothers would read the books, and answer the RB questions together with me. (Participant 1)
		Connection with friends/classmates	...told his classmates: "Borrow it! It is fantastic, but I am not going to tell you the story... (Participant 4)

Table 1. Categories generated by the qualitative analysis based on self-determination theory

FINDINGS AND DISCUSSION

Overall result

A total of 57 textual references are identified and grouped according to the three needs of SDT. Among these references, 20 are associated with a need for competence, 22 with a need for autonomy, and 12 with a need for relatedness. The number of coded references and their corresponding percentage distributions relative to each other are summarized in Table 2. Results show that 40.36% of student feedback are tied in with the need for autonomy, followed closely by the need for competence (36.83%) and relatedness (22.81%). An interesting find is that every participant has made at least one reference to each need, as evidenced by the number of coded references for each individual participant in Table 3. This confirms that RB is an effective tool in learning English. The following discussion explores what cognitive changes have been observed in those primary students.

Basic needs	Experiences of behavior	Number of coded references (%)	Sub-Total
Competence	Vocabulary	3 (5.26%)	21 (36.83%)
	Problem-solving skill	3 (5.26%)	
	Academic performance	5 (8.77%)	
	Reading Speed	5 (8.77%)	
	Learning abilities	5 (8.77%)	
Autonomy	Reading material	7 (12.28%)	23 (40.36%)
	Reading frequency	4 (7.02%)	
	Reading method	7 (12.28%)	
	Reading proactivity	5(8.78%)	
Relatedness	Connection with parents	6 (10.53%)	13 (22.81%)
	Connection with siblings	2 (3.51%)	
	Connection with friends/classmates	5 (8.77%)	
Total		57(100%)	57 (100%)

Table 2. All categories of changed experiences found in the eight cases

	Partici-pant 1	Partici-pant 2	Partici-pant 3	Partici-pant 4	Partici-pant 5	Partici-pant 6	Partici-pant 7	Partici-pant 8	Sub-total
Competence	1	2	4	3	4	2	3	2	21
Autonomy	4	2	4	3	1	1	4	4	23
Relatedness	3	1	1	3	2	1	1	1	13
Sub-total	8	5	9	9	7	4	8	7	57

Table 3. The number of changed experienced related to three needs for all cases

Competence

RB motivates students to read by stimulating their need for competence. In gamified context, it is said that learners often have ample opportunities to acquire new knowledge, be optimally challenged, and receive positive feedback (Aparicio et al., 2012). This improves their perceived level of competition among other players. As the interviews reveal, the eight high-performing students on RB all share one thing: They all feel compelled to win. And the results are: Their academic performance improved, reading speed increased, vocabulary expanded, and learning abilities and problem-solving skills enhanced.

With the use of RB, the students first amp up their learning abilities. Participant 6, for instance, shares that he has acquired higher-order skills such as 'critique' and 'evaluation'. He said, "I have learnt that 'critique' is something like commenting on characters' personalities or the meaning behind the story." In a similar vein, Participant 4 notices that he is more logical in his organization and that he can summarize what he reads when he shares books with others. In his experience, RB helps fulfill his need for relatedness as he now connected more with his parents and friends when talking about books.

The students' improved reading skills also translate into their various forms of achievement. Grade-wise, Participant 2 states that "I have improved from around 70 marks to around 80 marks in [my] English [Language subject]", while Participant 4 also sees his grade for Chinese writing jumps from an average of less than 75 to now 88, a solid mark above the cut-off score for distinction (85% out of 100). Award-wise, Participant 3 serves a case in point. She can now write creatively, which is a skill that she picked up while playing RB, and has helped her win numerous writing contests, such as scoring in the top three of her school's writing competition 'New Fairy Tale' and receiving an award in a district-wide creative writing competition.

Along with an improved academic performance, another significant change is an increase in reading speed and an expansion of vocabulary, both of which are also connected to an increase in reading proactivity. For Participant 2, the well-chosen book list on RB and questions have turned the student into a keen reader by arousing her interest to read. Not only is she more willing now, but she reads at a blistering pace: "In the past, I used to read word by word [and I think that was done quite] slowly, [but] now I read faster." Like many other children who have a disinterest in reading, Participant 4 student only reads either at his mother's behest or passively in the form of his mother reading out stories to him. After using RB, he is now a fervent reader and is able to finish a dictionary-sized book on a 30-minute train commute. What motivates him to read is no longer a nudge by his parents or teachers, but his self-described "search for knowledge."

Lastly, the students acquire critical problem-solving skills. For example, in the summer of 2016, Participant 4 chanced upon a thick English book about magic. The book was a challenging read even to secondary school students, given the book's jargon. However, the student did not give up; he fully immersed himself in the book and occasionally asked for help from his mother. In this experience, he not only felt gratification from finishing the book. He also felt relatedness from working with his mother on overcoming a difficult book.

Autonomy

Other than competence, RB also satiates students' need for autonomy, as evidenced in the expansion of their book choices, the diversification of reading methods, an increase in their reading frequency, and a boost in their reading proactivity. According to Ryan, Rigby, and Przybylski (2006), when activities are performed out of personal interests, perceived autonomy is high. In a gamified environment, learners enjoy autonomy when they are given opportunities to choose and receive positive feedback. The more they are in control of their learning, the more intrinsically-motivated they are in overcoming adversity presented to them while learning. The eight students all share this aspect.

The most frequently mentioned item is the expansion of book choices. Participant 1, for example, never reads English books before RB. It is not because she hated reading or learning English, but because she has no idea how enjoyable an experience it can be to read books of a different language than the language she speaks at home. Her mother shares this sentiment as well, "In the past, when we went to the library, we used to borrow 8 books, and most of the time she chose to read Chinese books only. Now she is willing to try reading some English books too." Other students also broaden their reading choices. Participant 7 "now [reads] a greater variety of books." And because of the gaming environment where one student is pitted against another, he "literally [has] to read every kind of books in order to increase [his] ranking and marks on the Leaderboard." And that, as a result, extends his reading list from comics to the sciences and English novels. Applying the SDT model to this, as this student reads more books to realize his competence, he also internalizes his motivation to read out of intrinsic interest in other subjects. This pattern also finds its parallel in Participant 3 who dabbles in other book genres owing to the well-compiled list of books that RB provided. Thereafter, the battles she took on RB motivate her to explore further, pushing her to read titles that were once boring to her. And in that process, she becomes a voracious reader who tries to get her hands on a variety of subjects, such as history and science.

The other frequently mentioned item is the diversification of reading methods. For instance, to overcome a challenging book, Participant 4 develops his own reading method in that he would skim through the beginning and end of a book to get the gist of it, then he would delve into key parts in the book for textual details. In this case, devising reading strategies to overcome adversity proves a learner's need for competence, while the lesson (i.e. the reading method) the learner slowly makes out of becomes a transferable skill beyond the screen of RB (the learner's autonomy). In another case, autonomy and relatedness work hand in hand; Participant 8 recounts her experience, "I read page by page from the beginning to the end…And sometimes, I ask my mother [for the uncertain part] and she helps me understand it." His mother confirms, "He now goes over the details of stories. Perhaps it's because of RB, he pays more attention to the details of the content, rather than just finishing a book".

The third evidence for RB's fulfillment in students' need for autonomy is an increase in their reading frequency. Participant 1 explains that RB has affected her reading habits by providing her the joy and excitement to overcome her usual laziness in English reading. "In the past, I was lazy. I only read 1 book in a month. Now, in my own record, two books a month is the worst record and in my best month, I managed to read four to six books." In this case, the student has become motivated to read when the fun and entertaining aspects of RB prompt her to take up more book titles. Her motivation becomes the causal agent of her actions, an optimal development of the learner's autonomy.

Lastly, students have become proactive readers. Participant 8's mother praises her son in this regard: "Reading has become easier [for him]. He is more proactive about reading. He used to choose books with me but now he can pick suitable ones himself independently." Similarly, for Participant 4, he now enjoys magic books so much that he borrows many from the library himself. In both Participants 8 and 4, as the habit of reading gets easier, both feel a sense of competence, which transpires into proactivity.

Relatedness

Lastly, RB fulfills the need for relatedness. Most of the students feel that they are more connected to their family and friends.

Six students, in particular, have found that they have grown closer to their parents. Participant 6, who is not particularly talkative, has opened up himself more to his mother since he started playing RB. "I often talk about the game with my mother." His mother, too, notices a change in their bond. "The communication between us got better," the mother said, "my child was rather passive in the past, but after joining this reading scheme, he is more willing to open up and talk with me about the book contents. I feel that the way we interacted in the past was sort of plain and uninspiring but now there's something more...I will ask him a bit more about the books, like what in particular inside this book has fascinated him, and he'll answer back to me enthusiastically". Interestingly, although in most cases a child's bond with the mother has strengthened, nobody comments on their bond with the father.

Parents aside, sibling relations also improve by leaps and bounds. For instance, participant 1 student shares her stories with her two brothers: "Sometimes, my two brothers would read books with me, and after that, we'd all try to answer questions on RB". Furthermore, she now visits the local library with her two elder brothers, since she and her brothers enjoy reading even more than they have been. "Yes, [my brothers and I] become much closer now," she reflected happily during the interview. "[This is especially true] with her second eldest brother," the mother chimed in on this point, discussing how her daughter and sons now share a common ground. "Yes, she would discuss with her brothers. Sometimes, when she encountered a difficult English word or question on RB, she would consult her brothers. And if her brothers were busy, she would look it up online herself."

In addition, the students also see changes in their friendship with classmates. Participant 8, for example, the student, who was a quiet boy before playing RB, now talks more with his friends in class about RB. "I have more chances to talk with friends about books we like and we share our individual opinions towards them." His mother added that he now interacts more with his classmates, especially when he wants to borrow detective novels from his friends.

All cognitive changes observed in the students are visually presented in Figure 2.

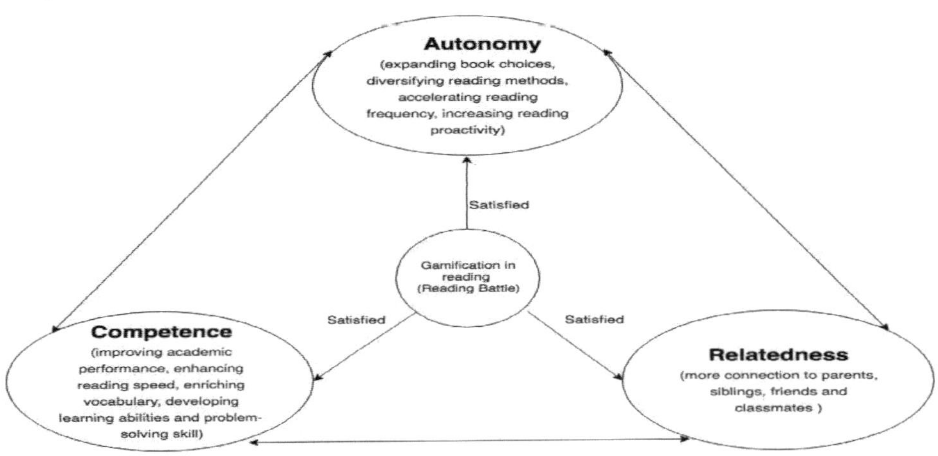

Figure 2. The cognitive changes that happened in the students since they used RB

CONCLUSION

In this study, the reading experiences of eight Hong Kong primary school students are examined through a self-determination framework. In re-examining their accounts of how RB changed their reading habits, these students find that they are motivated to read because RB has helped fulfill their needs for competence, autonomy and relatedness. In terms of competence, students are reported to have improved their academic performance, gained a faster reading speed, expanded their vocabulary, and developed their learning and problem-solving skills. Autonomy-wise, students expanded their book choices, diversified their reading methods, increased reading frequency and boosted their reading proactivity. Finally, students believed RB has helped them bond with their family and friends. As these stories pan out, it is evident that the needs for competence, autonomy and relatedness work to reinforce one another in a student's literacy development, and that no single aspect alone can bring about the results observed on the students. Considering the fact that reading literacy is a skill that takes a long to develop and mature, future studies need to have a longitudinal basis in its design. In the present study, two forms of limitation exist. The first is that the success stories of high-performing RB students were based on a publication in print, which precludes the researchers from accessing the original story scripts and organising necessary follow-up discussions with the students concerned. The second is that because interview participants tend to give desirable answers, data reliability may have been compromised.

REFERENCES

Alexander, P. & Jetton, T. (2000). Learning from text: A multidimensional and developmental perspective. In M. Kamil, P. Mosenthal, P. Pearson, & R. Barr (Eds.), *Handbook of reading research* (Vol. 3, pp. 285–310). Mahwah, NJ: Lawrence Erlbaum Associates.

Amabile, T. M., DeJong, W., & Lepper, M. R. (1976). Effects of externally imposed deadlines on subsequent intrinsic motivation. *Journal of personality and social psychology*, *34*(1), 92.

Aparicio, A.F., Vela, F.L.G., Sánchez, J.L.G., Montes, J.L.I., 2012. Analysis and application of gamification. In: Proceedings of the 13th International Conference on Interacción Persona-Ordenador. Presented at INTERACTION'12, ACM, Elche, Spain, p. 17.

Bandura, A. (1977). Self-efficacy: Toward a unifying theory of behavioral change. *Psychological Review, 84*, 191-21 5.

Black, A. E., & Deci, E. L. (2000). The effects of instructors' autonomy support and students' autonomous motivation on learning organic chemistry: A self-determination theory perspective. *Science education*, *84*(6), 740-756.

Chall, J. (1983). *Stages of reading development.* New York: McGraw-Hill.

Chan, M. Y .H., Chu, S. K. W., Mok, S. W. S. & Tam, F. (2016). Fostering Interest in Reading and Strengthening Reading Comprehension Ability of Primary School Students Using a Children's Literature E-quiz Bank on the Cloud. Paper presented at Social Media 2016, The 25th International Education and Technology Conference, Hong Kong.

Chen, N. S., Teng, D. C. E., & Lee, C. H. (2011). Augmenting paper-based reading activity with direct access to digital materials and scaffolded questioning. *Computers & Education*, 57(2), 1705-1715.

Chu, S. K. W., Chan, C. K. K., & Tiwari, A. F. Y. (2001). Using blogs to support learning during internship. *Computers & Education, 58*(3), 989-1000.

Chu, S. K. W., Chan. H. M. Y, Mok J. C. Y., Tse R. C. F, Leung, K. C. K. & Lee., C. W. Y. (2017). *Stories of Eight 300's*. Hong Kong: Academy 22.

Deci, E. L. (1971). Effects of externally mediated rewards on intrinsic motivation. *Journal of personality and Social Psychology*, *18*(1), 105.

Deci, E., & Ryan, R. (1991). A motivational approach to self: Integration in personality'. In R. Dienstbier (Ed.), *Nebraska symposium on motivation: Vol. 38. Perspectives on motivation*. Lincoln: University of Nebraska Press. p. 237–288.

Deci, E. L., & Ryan, R. M. (2000). The" what" and" why" of goal pursuits: Human needs and the self-determination of behavior. *Psychological inquiry, 11*(4), 227-268.

Deci, E. L., Vallerand, R. J., Pelletier, L. G., & Ryan, R. M. (1991). Motivation and education: The self-determination perspective. *Educational psychologist*, *26*(3-4), 325-346.

Deterding, S., Sicart, M., Nacke, L., O'Hara, K., and Dixon, D. (2011) Gamification. using game-design elements in non-gaming contexts. In Proceedings of CHI Extended Abstracts, 2425-2428

Dweck, C. S. (1986). Motivational processes affecting learning. *American Psychologist*, 41, 1040-1048.

Eccles, J. S. (1983). Expectancies, values, and academic behaviors. In J. T. Spence (Ed.), *Achievement and achievement motivation*. San Francisco: Freeman. 75-146.

Frodi, A., Bridges, L., & Grolnick, W. (1985). Correlates of mastery-related behavior: A short-term longitudinal study of infants in their second year. *Child development*, 1291-1298.

Fu, H., Chu, S.K.W. & Kang, W. (2013). Affordances and Constraints of Wiki for Primary-school Students' Group Projects. *Educational Technology & Society, 16*(4), 85–96

Fung, W. (2016). A study on intrinsic motivation, extrinsic motivation, reading efficacy, reading motivation in relation to the reading competency of top-performing and low- performing primary students in Hong Kong: a gamified reading perspective. (Thesis). University of Hong Kong, Pokfulam, Hong Kong SAR.

Ge, S., & Land, S. M. (2004). A conceptual framework for scaffolding ill-structured problem-solving processes using question prompts and peer interactions. *Educational Technology Research and Development, 52*(2), 5–22.

Grolnick, W. S., Ryan, R. M., & Deci, E. L. (1991). Inner resources for school achievement: Motivational mediators of children's perceptions of their parents. *Journal of educational psychology*, *83*(4), 508

Hanus, M. D., & Fox, J. (2015). Assessing the effects of gamification in the classroom: A longitudinal study on intrinsic motivation, social comparison, satisfaction, effort, and academic performance. *Computers & Education, 80*, 152-161.

Hong Kong Special Administrative Region of the People's Republic of China, Education and Manpower Bureau (2005). Information literacy framework for Hong Kong: Building the capacity of learning to learn in the information age.

Huotari, K., & Hamari, J. (2012). Defining gamification: a service marketing perspective. In Proceeding of the 16th International Academic MindTrek Conference (pp. 17-22). ACM.

Kapp, K. M. (2012). *The gamification of learning and instruction: Game-based methods and strategies for training and education.* San Francisco, CA: Pfeiffer.

Katie Seaborn & Deborah I. Fels. (2015). Gamification in theory and action: A survey. *International Journal of human-computer studies*, *74*, 14-31.

King, A. (1994). Guiding Knowledge Construction in the Classroom: Effects of Teaching Children How to Question and How to Explain. *American Educational Research Journal, 31*(2), 338-368.

Lee, E. Y. C., Chan, C. K. K., & van Aalst, J. (2006). Students assessing their own collaborative knowledge building. *International Journal of Computer-Supported Collaborative Learning, 1*(1), 57-87.

Lepper, M. K., Greene, D., & Nisbett, R. (1973). Undermining children's intrinsic interest with extrinsic reward: A test of the "overjustification" hypothesis. *Journal of Personality and Social Psychology*, *28*, 129–137.

Lepper, M. R., & Greene, D. (1975). Turning play into work: Effects of adult surveillance and extrinsic rewards on children's intrinsic motivation. *Journal of Personality and Social Psychology*, 3(1), 479-486.

Leu, D. J., Kinzer, C. K., Coiro, J. L., & Cammack, D. W. (2004). Toward a theory of new literacies emerging from the Internet and other information and communication technologies. *Theoretical models and processes of reading, 5*(1), 1570-1613.

Li, H., & Wilhelm, K. H. (2008). Exploring pedagogical reasoning: Reading strategy instruction from two teachers' perspectives. *The Reading Matrix, 8*(1), 96-110.

Martens, M. (2014). Reading and "Gamification". Children & Libraries: The Journal of the Association for Library Service to Children, 12(4), 19.

McDaniel, M. A., & Donnelly, C. M. (1996). Learning with analogy and elaborative interrogation. *Journal of Educational Psychology, 88*(3), 508-519.

Mckee, S. (2012). Reading Comprehension, What We Know: A Review of Research 1995 to 2011. *Language Testing in Asia*, 2(1), 1-14

Mullis, I. V. S., Martin, M. O., Kennedy, A. M., Trong, K. L. & Sainsbury, M. (2009). PIRLS 2011 assessment framework. Chestnut Hill, MA: TIMSS & PIRLS International Study Center, Lynch School of Education, Boston College. p.12

Muntean, C. I. (2011, October). Raising engagement in e-learning through gamification. In Proc. 6th International Conference on Virtual Learning ICVL (pp. 323-329).

Nicholson, S. (2012). A user-centered theoretical framework for meaningful gamification. Paper presented at Games+ Learning+ Society 8.0 conference, Madison, Wisconsin, June 2012

Niemiec, C. P., Lynch, M. F., Vansteenkiste, M., Bernstein, J., Deci, E. L., & Ryan, R. M. (2006). The antecedents and consequences of autonomous self-regulation for college: A self-determination theory perspective on socialization. *Journal of adolescence*, *29*(5), 761-775.

Niemiec, C. P., & Ryan, R. M. (2009). Autonomy, competence, and relatedness in the classroom: Applying self-determination theory to educational practice. *School Field*, *7*(2), 133-144.

Perfetti, C. (2007). Reading ability: Lexical quality to comprehension. *Scientific Studies of Reading, 11*(4), 357–383.

PIRLS 2011 Assessment framework. International Association for the Evaluation of Educational Achievement. Herengracht 487, Amsterdam, 1017 BT, The Netherlands.

RB. (n.d.) Library@RCHK. Retrieved from: http://lirc.rchk.edu.hk/reading-battle.html

Reuda, R. (2013). 21st-century skills: Cultural, linguistic, and motivational perspectives. In D. Alvermann, N. Unrau, & R. Ruddell (Eds.), *Theoretical models and processes of reading*, 6th edition Newark, DE: International Reading Association, pp. 1241–1268.

Rosell, J. & Pahl, K. (2010). The materials and the situated: What multimodality and new literacy studies do for literacy research. In D. Lapp & D. Fisher (Eds.), *Handbook of research on teaching the English language arts, third edition*, Newark, DE: International Reading Association, pp. 1462–1521.

Ryan, R. M., & Deci, E. L. (2000). Self-determination theory and the facilitation of intrinsic motivation, social development, and well-being. *American psychologist, 55*(1), 68.

Ryan, R. M., & Deci, E. L. (2000b). Intrinsic and extrinsic motivations: Classic definitions and new directions. *Contemporary educational psychology, 25*(1), 54-67.

Ryan, R. M., Rigby, C. S. & Przybylski, A. (2006) The Motivational Pull of Video Games: A Self-Determination Theory Approach. *Motivation and Emotion, 30*(4):344–360

Su, C., & Cheng, C. (2015). A mobile gamification learning system for improving the learning motivation and achievements. *Journal of Computer Assisted Learning*, 31(3), 268-286. doi:10.1111/jcal.12088

The Government of the Hong Kong Special Administrative Region. (2016, November 23). *Promoting Reading Culture* [Press Release]. Retrieved from: http://www.info.gov.hk/gia/general/201611/23/P2016112300401.htm

Walter, P. (1999). Defining literacy and its consequences in the developing world. *Journal of Lifelong Education, 18*(1), 31–48.

Westby, C. (2004). 21st Century literacy of a diverse world. *Folia Phoniatrica et Logopaedica, 56*(4), 254-271.

Wu, W. W. Y., Chu, S. K. W., Chan, H., Wong, J., Tse, S. K., Tavares, & Mok, S. W. S. (2014). Strengthening students' reading comprehension ability (both Chinese and English) through developing children's literature e-quiz bank on the cloud. Paper presented at 19th International Education & Technology Conference, Hong Kong.

"Being a Butt While on the Internet": Perceptions of What Is and Isn't Internet Trolling

Yimin Chen
University of Western Ontario, Canada.
ychen582@uwo.ca

ABSTRACT

The term "internet trolling" has come to encompass a wide range of behaviours, ranging from abusive speech and hacking to sarcastic humour and friendly teasing. While some of these behaviours are clearly antisocial and, in extreme cases, criminal, others are harmless and may even have potential prosocial functions. This study is an attempt to disambiguate some of the competing and contrary interpretations of internet trolling by examining the perspectives of avid internet users for whom trolling is a familiar part of their online lives. Through data collected from in-depth, semi-structured interviews, a multifaceted picture of trolling emerges that is at odds with previous media characterizations of internet trolls as merely hateful bullies. On the contrary, most participants in this study did not consider trolling to be a serious problem and many did not consider harmful interactions to be trolling at all. This paper describes some of the defining characteristics of internet trolling in order to differentiate the harmful behaviours from the harmless. This work aims to contribute to the growing body of literature on internet trolling in the hopes of informing regulatory policy and educational initiatives concerning internet use and safety.

KEYWORDS

Trolling, antisocial internet behaviour, internet communication, internet memes, internet culture, digital literacy.

INTRODUCTION

In conventional terms, a "troll" is a supernatural creature that has its origins in folklore. Some modern depictions of these creatures have characterized them as being cute and benign, such as in the case of the popular line of Troll dolls. These depictions, however, are the minority: from traditional folk tales like The Three Billy Goats Gruff to modern fantasy fiction like The Hobbit and Harry Potter, trolls have predominantly been cast in antagonistic roles as brutish, dim-witted monsters. Like the creatures of folklore, trolls on the internet are often characterized as hostile and belligerent. When it is reported at all, the news often latches onto the darkest stories about trolling: hate speech (Brady, 2018), death threats (McKnight & Bishop, 2018), and abuse (West, 2015). From this perspective, the troll is an internet bully – lashing out and harassing innocent victims for their own satisfaction. However, there is an alternative perspective that takes a less damning view of internet trolls and trolling.

Writing in the context of Usenet newsgroups, Judith Donath was among the first to describe trolling behaviour as "a game of identity deception, albeit one that is played without the consent of most of the players" (1999). She cites a newsgroup posting from 1995, which suggests this etymology of "trolling":

Are you familiar with fishing? Trolling is where you set your fishing lines in the water and then slowly go back and forth dragging the bait and hoping for a bite. Trolling on the Net is the same concept – someone baits a post and then waits for the bite on the line and then enjoys the ensuing fight. (Donath, 1999)

As opposed to the unthinking, reactionary nastiness described in media reports, Donath's view of trolling suggests that their intentions are more mischievous than abusive and more akin to pranking and mockery than to harassment.

How can these widely disparate concepts of trolling be reconciled? As more and more public attention is focused on the uses and abuses of online communications platforms, it is imperative both for governments and service providers to craft policies and standards to protect the safety of internet users, and for educational institutions to update information literacy programs to incorporate new best practices. But to do so effectively, we must better understand what constitutes "use" and "abuse". The aim of this research is to take a closer look at the types of negative online experiences reported by so many internet users. In doing so, the intent is to differentiate the harmful actions from the harmless and to help distinguish between the multitude of different meanings "trolling" has come to encompass.

Malicious online behaviour

In the years since Judith Donath's pioneering work, much of the academic discourse around trolling has been focused on its harmful aspects: as "questionable, dangerous and possibly deadly" (Harmon & Metaxas, 2010), "symbolic violence" (Lumsden

& Morgan, 2017), and "everyday sadism" (Buckels, Trapnell, & Paulhus, 2014). Several studies have examined the effect of trolling across a wide variety of communities, including feminist discussion forums (Herring, Job-Sluder, Scheckler, & Barab, 2002), magazine websites (Binns, 2012), and Wikipedia (Shachaf & Hara, 2010). In these cases, trolls were found to have a disruptive and destabilizing influence: trolls undermine trust, sabotage social interactions, and can even cause legal problems for the websites (Binns, 2012). Victims of trolling were reported to have withdrawn "not only from on-line engagement but from off-line public spheres as well" (Jane, 2012).

Beyond examples of "recreational nastiness" (Jane, 2012) on a personal scale, governments and corporations have also suffered at the hands of internet trolls, although in these cases, these malicious behaviours are usually labeled "hacktivism" (Sanfilippo, Yang, & Fichman, 2017). Arguably the most well-known instance of hacktivism, "the creative use of computer technology for the purposes of facilitating online protests, performing civil disobedience in cyberspace and disrupting the flow of information" (Gunkel, 2005), was the disclosure of thousands of confidential American diplomatic cables by Wikileaks in 2010, which the White House called a "reckless and dangerous action" with the potential to "deeply impact not only U.S. foreign policy interests, but those of our allies and friends around the world" (Kessler, 2010). While Wikileaks maintains an air of professionalism, other hacktivist groups, most famously Anonymous, embrace the sort of theatrics typical of trolling culture. Characterized by their "now-iconic Guy Fawkes masks ... anarchic wit and portentous (and, many would argue, pretentious) videos" (Mansfield-Devine, 2011),[1] Anonymous has most famously been involved in campaigns against the Church of Scientology and in support of Wikileaks and Occupy Wall Street. LulzSec and AntiSec, splinter groups of Anonymous, have been linked to attacks on Sony Corporation, stealing customer login credentials, and to the leak of emails from the U.S. Department of Homeland Security (Mansfield-Devine, 2011). More recently, spurred by allegations of Russian interference in the 2016 US presidential election, the concept of trolling has now expanded to include "influencing strategic and tactical outcomes via cyber-personas" (Hart & Klink, 2017) as a form of information warfare between nations (Hellman & Wagnsson, 2017).

Countercultural trolling

In contrast to prevailing notions of trolling as malicious abuse, trolling behaviour within some online communities has historically been seen as a means of gatekeeping. Early virtual communities, such as the WELL, were founded upon the visions of anti-establishmentarians and the Free Speech movement, as well as the techno-libertarian ethos of computer hackers (Levy, 1984). In these communities, as well as on Usenet newsgroups, trolling "serve[d] the dual purpose of enforcing community standards and of increasing community cohesion by providing a game that all those who know the rules can play against those who do not" (Tepper, 1997, p. 40). Operating within the grey area at "the boundaries between acceptable and unacceptable social behaviour" (Kirman, Lineham, & Lawson, 2012), tech-savvy internauts[2] created strong in-group/out-group distinctions through trolling. Memes and in-jokes marked their online territory as distinct from the mainstream and provided a means to quickly identify naïve trespassers. These internaut communities nurtured an "audacious politics of pranking, transgression, and mockery" (Coleman, 2012) where joking, irreverent styles of trolling flourished.

While the majority of current trolls likely have only weak, if any, ties to the internet's countercultural past, they have adopted many of its attitudes, rituals, and aesthetics. According to Coleman:

Trolls have transformed what were more occasional and sporadic acts, often focused on virtual arguments called flaming or flame wars, into a full-blown set of cultural norms and set of linguistic practices ... Trolls work to remind the 'masses' that have lapped onto the shores of the Internet that there is still a class of geeks who, as their name suggests, will cause Internet grief. (Coleman, 2012)

In this respect, trolling can be seen as a reaction to the "September that never ended,"[3] that is, the period of time since September 1993, when America Online first provided Usenet access to tens of thousands of their customers. Once the domain of scientists, researchers, and hackers (i.e., nerds and geeks), this opening up of the internet triggered what seemed like an endless wave of digital immigrants who proved impossible to acculturate into the prevailing netiquette. Instead, the mainstream masses took over.

From this perspective, trolling is more a form of protest than an act of random hostility; it is a show of resistance against the gentrification of online spaces that had once been safe haven to technologically-sophisticated subcultures who felt disenfranchised by the greater society. As described by Phillips and Milner (2017), subcultural trolling can minimize and marginalize

---

[1] For more on Anonymous, see: Coleman, G. (2015). Hacker, Hoaxer, Whistleblower, Spy. Brooklyn, NY: Verso

[2] A user of the Internet, especially a habitual or skilled one: https://en.oxforddictionaries.com/definition/internaut

[3] http://www.catb.org/jargon/html/S/September-that-never-ended.html

vulnerable perspectives, but it can also provide an outlet for those same groups to push back against oppressive norms. From this perspective, trolling represents the "tensions between dominant and subordinate groups" (Hebdige, 1979) played out all across cyberspace.

So, in the end, what are we to think of internet trolls? Unfortunately, the clash of definitions in the public and academic discourse has led to confusion and controversy over what "trolling" actually means. Is trolling just another name for online harassment or does it refer to a game of deception? What behaviours or actions constitute trolling and are the consequences harmful or harmless?

Purpose of this study

As computers and internet services become ever more ingrained in people's day to day lives, the idea of "disconnecting" and removing yourself from the online world and its associated technologies becomes steadily less appealing. In a study commemorating the 25th anniversary of the World Wide Web, the Pew Internet and American Life Project reported that 87% of American adults are online, of which 53% agree that the internet is an essential part of their life and 76% say that it has had a positive effect on society (Fox & Rainie, 2014). However, later surveys have tempered this positivity. A recent Pew report indicates that 41% of all American adults have personally experienced some sort of internet harassment and 62% consider online harassment to be a major problem (Duggan, 2017). At the same time, a majority of Americans also believe that offensive content online is taken too seriously – that it's "just trolls being trolls, nothing to worry about" (Duggan, 2017). How are we to reconcile these two seemingly contradictory viewpoints?

A review of the literature identifies two linked, but conflicting narratives conceptualizing online trolling. The first is a majority view that casts trolls as villainous, antagonistic users whose actions are harmful to online individuals and communities. Notably, this is the perspective that most frequently informs mainstream news reporting on trolling. The second is a minority view that casts trolls as edgy, but (mostly) harmless pranksters who push the boundaries of taste and sensibility – acting upon the ethos that online interactions should not be taken seriously. Representations of this perspective arise mostly from the accounts of self-described trolls and works on cyberculture. This study approaches the question of internet trolling from a third perspective: that of avid internet users who are familiar with internet trolling, but do not necessarily identify as trolls themselves.

This work follows in the footsteps of Dick Hebdige as an exploration of a subculture that is "alternately dismissed, denounced and canonized; treated at different times as threats to public order and as harmless buffoons" (1979). The intent is to understand and contextualize some of these subcultural practices at the boundary of what is acceptable and what is unacceptable. Social norms are not fixed and unchanging but may be challenged and eventually supplanted by new ideas and practices. This study is an examination of this negotiation centered on the phenomenon of online trolling and is guided by the following research questions:

How is trolling discussed and characterized by avid internet users in three areas:

a. Types of behaviours and actions?

b. Motivations behind those behaviours and actions?

c. Attitudes towards those behaviours and actions?

METHODOLOGY

Data for this study was collected in spring of 2016 through individual in-depth, semi-structured interviews lasting around one hour each. The study was advertised through posters on campus at a large public university in Ontario, Canada and twenty participants were recruited[4]. Inclusion criteria were that participants considered themselves to be avid internet users and were familiar with trolling. Participants in this study were mostly undergraduate students (n=16) from 18 to 23 years in age in fields of study ranging from business to computer science to sociology to anthropology. Two staff members (ages 43, 54) and two graduate students (ages 22, 27) were also interviewed. Fifteen participants identified as female and five as male. All participants reported that they had been internet users for at least 5 years and, while all reported regular internet use (ranging from 2-12 hours daily), over half (n=11) did not tend to engage publicly with online communities or conversations and limited their online interactions mostly to their personal social media accounts. Several of these participants described themselves as "lurkers," i.e. people who read or follow online conversations, but do not personally participate.

---

[4] A total of twenty-two participants were recruited, but two did not meet the inclusion criteria and were not included in this analysis

Interviews were structured around four main topics, based on the research questions:

1. Participant internet use history and habits.
2. Definitions and examples of internet trolling.
3. Attitudes toward internet trolling.
4. Motivations for trolling behaviour.

Interviews were audio recorded and transcribed, and then analyzed using qualitative analysis software.[5] Coding of the interview transcripts was conducted according to the Thematic Analysis approach (Braun & Clarke, 2006).[6] Although the limited sample size of this study denies generalizability of the results, these interviews nonetheless represent rich, diverse reflections on internet trolling from people for whom trolling is a familiar part of their online lives.

RESULTS AND DISCUSSION

Trolling Definitions

Based on participant responses, it is apparent that trolling is a complex and multifaceted phenomenon. When asked about what trolling means to them, participants described a variety of different behaviours and actions. Nonetheless, five major themes can be identified.

Provocation

The point on which every participant agreed was that trolling was a behaviour intended to elicit a reaction or response from others. All 20 participants touched upon this aspect of trolling in some way. Some participants described this provocation using aggressive terms: "trying to start sh*t" (P3), "people who are out to get you" (P6), and "someone who goes out of their way to leave comments and just leave hate" (P14). More frequently, participants offered some variant of "saying things that are intentionally meant to generate a reaction" (P16).

Both implicitly and explicitly, each participant indicated that they were confident that they could recognize trolling when it occurs, and so, would not be susceptible to the provocation. One participant even complained that she feels "a little bit of a frustration that people are falling for this stuff" (P3). None of the participants reported feeling seriously hurt by any trolling that they had personally encountered. P5 had this to say on the matter:

P5: "I know to some people, it's a big deal. Personally, it's not to me – I rather compare it to having little sisters, which I do, it's annoying, but you ignore it – don't feed the trolls and they go away."

Deception

Another defining feature that most of the participants (n=15) mentioned was that trolling involves some level of misdirection or deception. According to P14, "[trolls'] comments don't necessarily reflect how they feel, it's just that they know it's going to upset people". These participants gave examples of trolls disrupting online conversations by posting intentionally inflammatory or ridiculous messages:

P9: "On Facebook, I have a really strong vegan activist friend, and my other friend commented on one of her statuses saying, "I love bacon" or something. Or he'll post pictures just to get a reaction out of her"

Interviewer: "And does this typically get a reaction from your vegan friend?"

P9: "Yeah, like a 200 comments kind of thing."

While participants typically saw these sorts of disruptions as undesirable, some did speak about more positive examples of deception – especially in the context of playful trickery. P17 talked about trolling as "almost a bit of subversive behaviour … presenting false or misleading information with the intended effect of someone's amusement". In this vein, he described an instance where he and his classmates in an engineering program worked together on social media to play a prank on rival students:

---

[5] HyperRESEARCH: http://www.researchware.com

[6] Thematic Analysis involves six steps: (1) familiarizing yourself with your data, (2) generating initial codes, (3) searching for themes, (4) reviewing themes, (5) defining and naming themes, (6) producing the report.

P17: "We've posted in our main group and coordinated to make something that sounds legitimate from an engineering standpoint that is ridiculous, so we're leading along students from other engineering disciplines. It's a relatively harmless way of trolling, it's not like we're giving them wrong answers, it's more like trying to confuse them for fun."

Bullying

Every one of the participants described trolling behaviours as falling on a spectrum in terms of seriousness. On one end were the more benign, humorous forms of trolling; on the other, serious, harmful behaviours. Of these negative behaviours, bullying (or cyberbullying) was mentioned at some point by all of the interviewers. Sixteen of the participants saw trolling and bullying as related behaviours (2 of these 16 claimed that they were essentially synonymous). According to P11, trolling may have even worse connotations that bullying:

P11: "I think essentially, pretty much all the examples, trolling and bullying, they are the same thing, I almost wonder if the term bullying has just been so over used that you don't really think twice about it it's like oh well that happens to everyone, but trolling seems to have more serious consequences, like the intent is worse, almost."

Conversely, five participants saw trolling and bullying as clearly different. P22, for example, connects trolling with much more lighthearted behaviours:

P22: "To me trolling is, funny, there is a difference between trolling someone and bullying someone online, and I think trolling is more of a joke, kind of thing ... I think bullying is when you are deliberately attacking someone's opinion or choice, or calling them out on things they have no control over"

Joking

While all of the participants agreed that trolling could be funny at least some of the time, thirteen mentioned humour, specifically, as a defining feature. According to these participants, a comment or interaction only counts as trolling if it is motivated by a sense of fun. For P10, who self-identifies as a troll, "[trolls] are funny, or they don't make any lasting bad impressions on people". In the context of online gaming, he associates trolling with good-natured joking and playing around:

P10: "If we're playing League of Legends and we're playing a custom match, everyone knows each other, people are gonna troll, and there's gonna be a lot of good times. Especially with this group I mentioned earlier, we play Diablo III. There will be shenanigans, there always will be, but no one has ever come out of it feeling like the game was made worse, only that it was made better."

However, trolling jokes are not always good natured, and the humour may be one-sided. In these cases, trolling can be more like "a modern schadenfreude" (P1) where one party derives pleasure at the expense of another by "causing grief for fun" (P20).

Memes

The joking aspect of trolling is also strongly associated with internet memes, which can act as markers or signals that a particular joke or interaction is intended to be humorous. Thirteen of the participants brought up memes in relation to trolling, either using the term directly or by describing a specific meme. P9 gave the example of a meme based on American singer/actress Demi Lovato known as "Poot":[7]

P9: "It's just a picture and she doesn't look very flattering in it, and they said that this was her twin sister, from the basement, I don't know. It was kind of like trolling because they just wanted to be funny to see a reaction from her."

P9 described mixed feelings with respect to this example. While she was empathetic toward Lovato and felt that "it was kind of sad because [the meme] is targeting her," she also felt that the meme "made her more famous to people who don't really listen to music" (P9).

For some participants, the link between internet memes and trolling is quite a strong one. P22 cites a popular meme from late 2015 as a defining example of trolling:

P22: "Have you seen that thread between those two friends on Facebook? One is always making jokes about the other's status, because he'll usually be saying something... he'll usually be doing something contradictory, so then this person will always point out the contradictions and what not, so to me that's what trolling is, it's joking and there's no harm intended."

---

[7] For more on Poot, see: http://knowyourmeme.com/memes/poot-lovato

Interviewer: "Five out of seven perfect guy? Is that what you're talking about?"

In this (presumably staged) series of conversations between two Facebook friends, one friend consistently makes questionable, typo-ridden assertions, while the other friend replies with sarcastic, teasing remarks.[8] In this case, the spirit of trolling is found both in nature of the banter between these two friends and the later proliferation of the "5/7" as a meme referencing and celebrating the original Facebook conversation.

Attitudes towards trolling

Reflecting the variation in definitions, the attitudes toward trolling voiced by the interview participants were split. Nine of the participants expressed ambivalent feelings towards trolling, seeing both positive and negative sides. Six participants saw trolling as mostly positive and only five saw trolling as mostly negative (Figure 1). Furthermore, all twenty participants agreed that trolling could be funny, at least some the time. As mentioned above, humour was a defining characteristic of trolling for thirteen of the participants, but seven further stated that trolling must be funny for everyone involved. All but one of these seven participants had a positive interpretation of trolling. It seems clear that each participant's definition of trolling strongly shapes how they perceive it. All the participants drew a line between negative bullying and positive joking; the differences in opinion arise based on whether a participant sees one or the other or both types of behaviours as trolling.

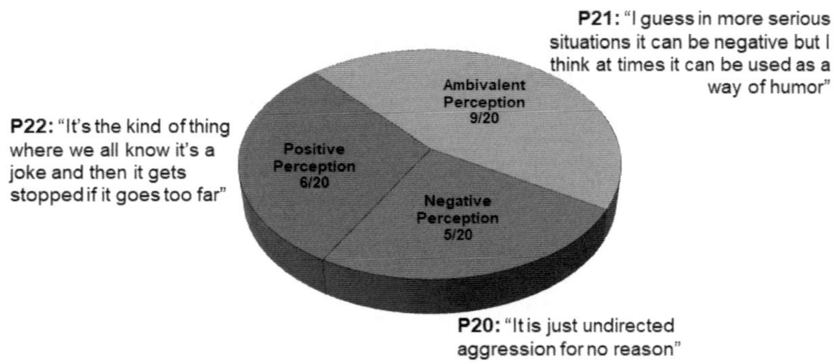

Figure 1. Participant attitudes toward trolling

Although trolling was not generally regarded as a very serious problem, in the grand scheme of things, all participants were keen on seeing the more obviously negative behaviours addressed in social media and gaming spaces. Many were not optimistic about the chances of stamping out trolling, though, as they considered the impetus to engage in mischievous behaviours as being an intrinsic part of human nature. The prevalence of trolling, for these participants, may be attributed to the disinhibition effect of the internet, which makes it easier for people to indulge their transgressive urges (Suler, 2004). Surprisingly, three participants also said that trolling is one of the features that they enjoy about the internet. According to P14: "I kind of appreciate it [trolling] because it makes the internet what it is; it is a very interesting place to be."

Motivations for trolling

Based on participants' stated attitudes toward trolling behaviours, we can similarly map trolling motivations onto broad categories: positive, neutral, and negative (Figure 2).

The neutral orientation of trolling can be read as a sort of computer-mediated solipsism: "the extreme preoccupation with and indulgence of one's own inclinations" (Foster, 1997). Early internet scholars worried that "the connectivity that CMC virtual communities confer upon us blinds the observer to the real character of the technology – all of its users exist as individuals extending their selves through the computer network" (Foster, 1997). Staring at pseudonyms and avatars on a screen, it can be all too easy to lose sight of the real people behind each profile. This process of online dehumanization makes it much easier for trolls to rationalize their virtual actions as disconnected from "real life," and therefore "not serious," all the while ignoring the fact that there may be real consequences (Dibbel, 1998).

---

[8] For details of this meme, see: http://knowyourmeme.com/memes/57

For the majority of the study participants, trolling occupies this ambiguous neutral space. Skilled absurdist performers like "Ken M"[9] might delight some onlookers with his trolling comments, but thoroughly confuse others. However, trolls can often be less funny than they imagine, and whereas the troll might not believe that they are causing any real harm, their antics can easily be interpreted as hateful rather than humorous.

The negative aspect of trolling most closely matches that of the trolls featured in news stories. These are, perhaps, the personalities most representative of the link between trolling and the dark tetrad (Buckels, et al. 2014).[10] In particular, some trolls seem to display everyday sadism, "an intrinsic appetitive motivation to inflict suffering on innocent others" (Buckels, et al. 2013). These are the bullies of the trolling world, bent on inflicting emotional and psychological harm on their victims, or worse. Labelled as haters, cyberbullies, and "misogynistic a**holes" (P12), these trolls are seen as "causing grief to people without reason" (P20). As described above, several of the study participants did not consider this category of people trolls at all, claiming that this behaviour clearly crosses all lines of acceptability. Unfortunately, precisely where that line actually is remains subjective, contextual, and contested.

Far on the opposite side of the spectrum, the positive troll is interested in contributing to the wellbeing of others. Perhaps the best example of this type of trolling is the "wholesome memes" phenomenon where, instead of the typical sarcastic or ironic captions, uplifting and supportive messages are placed over online images. Another example is the sharing of self-deprecating humour among friends: "it's positive when it's like joking … like you scrolling and you find funny pages and you're clicking through and you're like hahah that's me [and you share with] someone that you know is on that same level as you and would get the joke" (P19). Given the close association between trolling and internet memes, positive trolling may be seen as performing identity-signalling and community-building functions, as suggested by Bernstein, et al (2011).

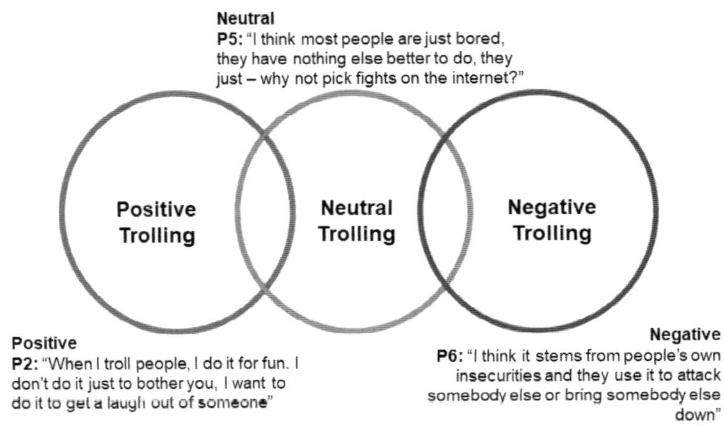

Figure 2. Positive, neutral, and negative trolling

Although trolling is discussed here as three distinct categories, the reality of the matter is rather more complicated. While the distinction between a positively intentioned act of trolling and a negative one is usually be fairly clear, intent and effect may not always align. Consider the example of a joke that misses its mark: while the intentions of the joker may have been friendly, a recipient could misinterpret the joke as hurtful or offensive. As illustrated in Figure 2, positivity can cross into neutrality into negativity. A joke may be funny if told once, but repeated a dozen times, it can quickly become annoying. Repeated a hundred times, the once-funny joke transforms into a means for harassment. Where an act of trolling falls on this spectrum is necessarily negotiated between the troll and the target and is highly contextual. However, we must consider that it is ultimately the perspective of the target that holds the most weight in this determination. After all, it is the target who experiences the direct consequences of an act of trolling.

Trolling targets

One recurring theme is that there is a difference between anonymous, impersonal trolling and targeted, personal trolling. The former is usually directed at no-one in particular and closely follows the bait and fishing metaphor of trolling (or, as P20 put

[9] For more on Ken M, see: http://knowyourmeme.com/memes/ken-m

[10] The dark tetrad of personality traits include: narcissism, Machiavellianism, psychopathy, and sadistic personality

it, "throwing sh*t at the wall and seeing what sticks"). This type of trolling is prevalent in more public spaces on the internet: on YouTube, Reddit threads, or newspaper comment sections. This type of trolling can be seen as performative – the troll is acting out in order to draw the attention of an audience. The target(s) are inconsequential to the troll and function mainly as an object to instigate and facilitate a sort of public spectacle. The latter type of trolling is usually focused on a specific target and shares much in common with traditional definitions of bullying in that it is aggressive, intentional, and repetitive (Görzig & Ólafsson, 2013).

Determining the consequences of trolling requires that we consider the intent of the troll, but must be largely dependent upon the impact on the target. Even the best-intentioned joke may go awry if misinterpreted by its recipient, just as the most pointed invective may be blunted if someone chooses not to acknowledge it. The vast majority of the study participants reported that their standard response to trolling was not to engage. Several recited the adage "don't feed the trolls" as the most practical course of action, in general. While such advice may be useful in dealing with cases of impersonal trolling, it may actually be harmful in cases of personal trolling. In situations where someone is the victim of a targeted cyberbullying campaign, non-engagement and avoidance may simply encourage the abusers further. Although there have been steps towards criminalization of extreme instances of negative trolling, study participants said they would like to see more initiative on the part of online platforms/service providers in addressing these behaviours.

CONCLUSION

More than simply the practice of "being a butt while on the internet" (P5), the accounts from these interviews suggest that trolling comes in many different varieties, echoing perspectives from a growing number of trolling scholars (Hardaker, 2010; Phillips, 2015; Sanfilippo, Fichman, & Yang, 2018). Unfortunately, this study was not able to arrive at a clear, single definition of internet trolling – in fact, rather the opposite: trolling seems to be highly subjective, contextual, and contested. While this study does provide further evidence that the prevailing media narrative of trolling as a *necessarily* harmful and antisocial phenomenon is oversimplified, it is nonetheless still true that trolling can *sometimes* be harmful or antisocial. Given the persistent definitional confusion over trolling, it may be wise for policymakers intending to crack down on problematic online behaviours to avoid framing guidelines around trolling and opt instead for more specific terms – like bullying and harassment.

As for solutions to those problematic online behaviours, there is a perception among the study participants that governments and social media platforms are both still woefully underequipped to deal with persistent and malicious online activity. For now, the most pragmatic solution may likely be a continued emphasis on educating internet users that online actions can have real consequences. On the part of trolls, it is imperative that they are able to read cues and respect boundaries: "trolling is one of those things where it's like most other social interactions, where it depends on the circumstances, the people, and the atmosphere" (P10). An ideal troll, perhaps, is one who recognises the norms of the spaces where they perform and understands the potential consequences of their actions. Trolling may indeed be "a art,"[11] as the saying goes, and the trolls who add value to a community may be those who are able to push boundaries enough to be provocative in a creative or thoughtful way, but not so much as to be distasteful.

The general internet-going public would benefit from trolling education as well. Advising people not to "feed the trolls" is all well and good, but people must first be able to recognize when they are being trolled. Just as there are guides and checklists detailing ways we can identify fake news,[12] libraries, schools, and other educational institutions are well-positioned to lead information literacy initiatives on how to spot trolls. The one consistent feature of trolling found in this study was its provocative nature. Identifying and documenting the ways in which trolls seek to provoke their targets may offer clues towards combatting their behaviour, but work in this area is presently sparse. This present study is one step towards that goal, but further research is required to ensure the efficacy of anti-trolling campaigns.

REFERENCES

Barak, A. (2007). Phantom emotions: Psychological determinants of emotional experiences on the internet. In A. Joinson, K.Y.A. McKenna, T. Postmes, U-D, Reips (Eds.), *The Oxford handbook of internet psychology* (pp. 303-329). New York, NY: Oxford

Bernstein, M., Monroy-Hernández, A., Harry, D., André, P., Panovich, K., & Vargas, G. (2011). 4chan and /b/: An analysis of anonymity and ephemerality in a large online community. *Proceedings of AAAI*, 50–57.

[11] For more information, see: https://www.urbandictionary.com/define.php?term=trolling%20is%20a%20art

[12] For example, the IFLA infographic on how to spot fake news: https://www.ifla.org/publications/node/11174

Binns, A. (2012). DON'T FEED THE TROLLS! Managing troublemakers in magazines' online communities. *Journalism Practice*, *6*(4), 547-562.

Brady, K. (2018, March 24). We need to get tough on sickening Twitter abuse. *The Sun*. Retrieved from https://www.thesun.co.uk/news/5892820/karren-brady-twitter-abuse-trolls

Braun, V., & Clarke, V. (2006). Using thematic analysis in psychology. *Qualitative research in psychology, 3*(2), 77-101.

Buckels, E. E., Jones, D. N., & Paulhus, D. L. (2013). Behavioral confirmation of everyday sadism. *Psychological science, 24*(11), 2201-2209.

Buckels, E. E., Trapnell, P. D., & Paulhus, D. L. (2014). Trolls just want to have fun. *Personality and Individual Differences*, *67*, 97-102.

Coleman, G. (2012). Phreaks, hackers, and trolls: The politics of transgression and spectacle. In Mandiberg, M. (Ed), *The social media reader* (pp. 99-119). New York, NY: New York University Press.

Dibbell, J. (1998). *A rape in cyberspace*. Retrieved from http://www.juliandibbell.com/articles/a-rape-in-cyberspace

Donath, J. (1999). Identity and deception in the virtual community. In Smith, M. & Kollock, P. (Eds.), *Communities in cyberspace* (pp. 29-59). London, UK: Routledge.

Duggan, M. (2017). *Online harassment 2017*. Pew Research Center. Retrieved from http://www.pewinternet.org/2017/07/11/online-harassment-2017

Foster, D (1997). Community and identity in the electronic village. In David Porter (Ed.), Internet culture (pp. 23-37). New York, NY: Routledge.

Fox, S., & Rainie, L. (2014). *The Web at 25 in the U.S.* Pew Research Center. Retrieved from http://www.pewinternet.org/files/2014/02/PIP_25th-anniversary-of-the-Web_0227141.pdf

Görzig, A., & Ólafsson, K. (2013). What makes a bully a cyberbully? Unravelling the characteristics of cyberbullies across twenty-five European countries. *Journal of Children and Media*, *7*(1), 9-27.

Gunkel, D. J. (2005). Introduction to hacking and hacktivism. *New Media & Society*, *7*(5), 595-597.

Hardaker, C. (2010). Trolling in asynchronous computer-mediated communication: From user discussions to academic definitions. *Journal of Politeness Research, 6*, 215–242.

Harmon, A.H. & Metaxas, P. (2010). How to create a Smart Mob: Understanding a social network capital. *e-Democracy Conference*, Germany. Retrieved from http://cs.wellesley.edu/~pmetaxas/How-to-create-Smart-Mobs%20eDem2010.pdf

Hart, S. W., & Klink, M. C. (2017, November). 1st Troll Battalion: Influencing military and strategic operations through cyber-personas. In *Cyber Conflict (CyCon US), 2017 International Conference on* (pp. 97-104). IEEE.

Hebdige, D. (1979). *Subculture: The meaning of style*. New York, NY: Methuen

Hellman, M., & Wagnsson, C. (2017). How can European states respond to Russian information warfare? An analytical framework. *European Security*, *26*(2), 153-170.

Herring, S. C., Job-Sluder, K., Scheckler, R., & Barab, S. (2002). Searching for safety: Managing "trolling" in a feminist discussion forum. *The Information Society*, *18* (5), pp. 371-383.

Jane, E. A. (2014). "Your a Ugly, Whorish, Slut" Understanding E-bile. *Feminist Media Studies*, *14*(4), 531-546.

Kessler, G. (2010, November 29). WikiLeaks's unveiling of secret State Department cables exposes U.S. diplomacy. *The Washintong Post*. Retrieved from http://www.washingtonpost.com/wp-dyn/content/article/2010/11/28/AR2010112802395.html

Kirman, B., Lineham, C., & Lawson, S. (2012, May). Exploring mischief and mayhem in social computing or: how we learned to stop worrying and love the trolls. In *CHI'12 Extended Abstracts on Human Factors in Computing Systems* (pp. 121-130). ACM.

Levy, S. (1984). *Hackers: Heroes of the computer revolution*. Garden City, NY: Anchor Press/Doubleday.

Lumsden, K., & Morgan, H. (2017). Media framing of trolling and online abuse: silencing strategies, symbolic violence, and victim blaming. *Feminist Media Studies*, *17*(6), 926-940.

Mansfield-Devine, S. (2011). Anonymous: serious threat or mere annoyance? *Network Security*, *2011*(1), 4-10.

McKnight, M. & Bishop, G. (2018, March 29). Inside the dark world of trolling. *Sports Illustrated*. Retrieved from https://www.si.com/more-sports/2018/03/29/twitter-internet-trolls-sports-athletes

Phillips, W. (2015). *This is why we can't have nice things: Mapping the relationship between online trolling and mainstream culture*. Cambridge, MA: MIT Press.

Phillips, W. & Milner, R. (2017). *The ambivalent internet*. Malden, MA: Polity.

Sanfilippo, M. R., Fichman, P., & Yang, S. (2018). Multidimensionality of online trolling behaviors. *The Information Society*, *34*(1), 27-39.

Sanfilippo, M. R., Yang, S., & Fichman, P. (2017). Managing online trolling: From deviant to social and political trolls. In *Proceedings of the 50th Hawaii International Conference on System Sciences*.

Shachaf, P. & Hara, N. (2010). Beyond vandalism: Wikipedia trolls. *Journal of Information Science, 36*(3), pp. 357-370.

Suler, J. (2004). The online disinhibition effect. *International Journal of Applied Psychoanalytic Studies, 2* (2), pp. 184-188.

Tepper, M. (1997). Usenet Communities and the Cultural Politics of Information. In David Porter (Ed.), *Internet culture* (pp. 39-54). New York, NY: Routledge.

West, L. (Writer). (2015, January 23). Ask not for whom the bell trolls; it trolls for thee. *This American Life*. Retrieved from https://www.thisamericanlife.org/545/if-you-dont-have-anything-nice-to-say-say-it-in-all-caps/act-one

Edge Perspectives in Online Scholarly Communities: A Network Analysis of #critlib

Philip Espinola Coombs
Simmons College, USA, coombsp@simmons.edu

Colin Rhinesmith
Simmons College, USA, crhinesmith@simmons.edu

ABSTRACT

The use of Twitter by scholars for public engagement is well-established in the literature. However, fewer studies have looked into the composition of users engaged in scholarly communication on Twitter. This paper considers the degree to which Twitter chats are dominated by established versus emerging or amateur scholars through an investigation of #critlib, a hashtag around which library and information scholars and practitioners have congregated. #critlib Tweets over a period of three months are examined using social network analysis to determine the users most central to the conversation. The findings show that #critlib serves as an important space for emerging and amateur scholars to participate in the co-creation of knowledge alongside experts in the field of LIS across a dispersed global network. The paper contributes to our knowledge of the #critlib community itself, suggests an impact of social media on the composition of scholarly communities, and deepens our understanding of networked participatory scholarship through the introduction of the idea of *edge perspectives*.

KEYWORDS

Critical librarianship, Twitter, networked participatory scholarship, scholarly communication, social justice.

INTRODUCTION

In the field of library and information science (LIS), critical librarianship is one area that has embraced Twitter as a platform for communication, engagement, and reflection. The critical librarianship community on Twitter, known as #critlib, is made up of LIS practitioners and scholars who seek to interrogate library practices through the lens of social justice (critlib.org, 2018). The critical librarianship approach not only considers the impacts of social inequalities on library practice, but also how the field of LIS itself may potentially contribute to further deepening such inequities in society. #critlib conversation topics have included: endangered data; academic libraries and the student loan crisis; and power, privilege, and oppression in library job search and hiring processes.

Often #critlib and the critical librarianship community are conflated, but they are distinct communities, albeit with many overlapping members (Almeida, 2018). In this paper, we focus on the #critlib community specifically. #critlib can be considered a community of practice (Hathcock, 2017), a community of activists (Almeida, 2018), and a community of scholars (Inefuku, H. & Roh, C., 2016). Here, we examined #critlib in its role as a community of scholars. While the significance of #critlib as an activist community (Almeida, 2018), as well as a space of intellectual ferment have been noted (Hathcock, 2017), the #critlib community's role within LIS scholarship is not yet fully understood. It is worthwhile to apprehend the role of #critlib within LIS scholarship because of its position outside of institutionally-sanctioned scholarly space and its deep engagement with the theory and practice of LIS.

LITERATURE REVIEW

Critical Librarianship on Twitter

The Twitter hashtag "#critlib" is short for critical librarianship. The critical librarianship community is an important segment of LIS scholarship. The critlib.org website defines critical librarianship as "a movement of library workers dedicated to bringing social justice principles into our work in libraries" (critlib.org). #critlib has become one of the most organized and vibrant LIS community on Twitter. The critlib hashtag first emerged on November 17, 2012 as a conference hashtag for the Critical Librarianship Symposium, held at Brandeis University and sponsored by the Boston Radical Reference Collective (Critical Librarianship Symposium, 2012). However, the hashtag really took off in 2014, when Nicole Pagowsky, Emily Drabinski, Annie Pho, Violet Fox, Jenna Freedman, and Kelly McElroy began organizing twice-monthly chats on critical librarianship topics (Pagowsky, 2015b). As of April 2, 2018, there have been 102 chats, all of which are available to view on the critlib.org website, where they were captured and organized into a coherent thread via the Storify tool (critlib, 2018b). #critlib is active outside of the organized chats as well.

While there has been reams of material produced within critical librarianship, few have examined the critical librarianship community itself—its members, practices, its role in the LIS intellectual landscape—and even fewer have examined the #critlib community specifically. When reviewing the extant literature, a few common threads emerge regarding the roles and nature of #critlib:

1. #critlib is described as a welcoming, accessible community (Fister, 2015; Inefuku, H. & Roh, C., 2016);
2. #critlib is described as an important space for members' professional and intellectual development (Fister, 2015; Randall, 2015; Pagowsky & McElroy, 2016);
3. #critlib is described as a space of significant intellectual ferment within LIS (Fister, 2015; Pagowsky, 2015a; Randall, 2015);
4. #critlib is described as exclusive; it does not live up to its goal of providing an inclusive space with diverse voices (Drabinski, 2016; Absher & Cardenas-Dow, 2016; Almeida, 2018).

In a blog post written for a #critlib chat, titled "#feelings: why we critlib," Sheldon-Hess (2015) spoke to thread #4 and recommended examining the demographics of #critlib participants. The existence of threads #1 and #4 suggest conflicting experiences with and understandings of #critlib. This disjuncture was deemed worthy of investigation. Examining the participants in the #critlib community through social network analysis and other methods might shed light and answer questions to help researchers better understand the role #critlib plays within LIS scholarship. Who are the most central figures within the #critlib network? Who is most active? Are these individuals established, emerging, or amateur scholars? The gaps in the #critlib literature dovetailed with those in the literature around scholarly communication on Twitter.

Social Media and Scholarly Communication

While there appears to be great variation among Twitter use by scholars depending on discipline (Sugimoto, et al., 2017), Twitter's importance within the modern scholarly communication landscape has been established (Fransman, 2013; Mahrt, et al., 2014; Veletsianos & Kimmons, 2016). Scholars use Twitter for a variety of reasons, including: to request and offer assistance to others; critique and comment upon published work; to curate a professional digital identity; and to stay abreast of developments in their fields (Veletsianos, 2012; Mahrt, et al., 2014).

Social media tools have been heralded for their ability to "disrupt knowledge hierarchies" (Battista, 2012, p. 4) and "change the way academics engage in scholarship" (Greenhow, Robelia, & Hughes, 2009, p. 252). These claims echo many earlier claims regarding the ability of technology to reshape scholarly knowledge-production. For example, Binkley (1935) saw the development of microphotography and near-print replication as steps towards the revitalization of the amatuer scholar, due to the potential of these technologies to lower access barriers to scholarship. Garnet and Ecclesfield (2011) suggested that changes to the landscape of scholarly communication and knowledge production have given birth to a new dimension of scholarly co-creation. Within this new landscape, scholars engage in collaborative knowledge building to a much greater degree than ever before. In this new landscape, knowledge is in "permanent beta," (a phrase which Garnet and Ecclesfield pulled from O'Reilly's description of the web 2.0), and knowledge production is a more fluid and dynamic process, rather than the more linear traditional view.

In this line of thought, tools like Twitter have the potential to reshape scholarly communication and knowledge production. Alternately, they may simply amplify the voices of the most active users (Mewburn & Thompson, 2013), or established scholars, at the expense of emerging or amateur scholars.

Scholarly communities on Twitter have received significant attention in the literature over the last few years. Specific fields have included science (Weller & Puschmann, 2011), education (Veletsianos, 2012; Veletsianos & Kimmons, 2016), and the digital humanities (Quan-Haase, et al., 2015; Grandjean, 2016). At the end of their study of Twitter use by education scholars, Veletsianos and Kimmons (2016) noted areas for future research, including "the comparison of traditional scholarly output measures to Twitter impact metrics [and] the analysis of role, gender, race, and age differences regarding hashtag use" (p. 9). While there have been many investigations published within the LIS field regarding scholarly communities on Twitter, markedly fewer have examined Twitter use in scholarly communities *within* the LIS field (e.g., see Sugimoto, et al., 2014.)

METHODOLOGY

Research Question

Considering the gaps in the literature regarding LIS scholarly communities on Twitter, we developed the following research question: *To what degree is the #critlib community dominated by established versus emerging or amateur scholars?* Drawing on digital scholarship research in the higher education literature, we used the framework of "networked participatory scholarship" (Veletsianos & Kimmons, 2012a) to examine whether #critlib can be understood as part of a complex "techno-cultural system" (p. 773) allowing diverse voices and perspectives to shape scholarly communication in LIS.

Theoretical Framework

Networked Participatory Scholarship

Our study's theoretical framework draws from and seeks to build upon the concepts of the "networked public" (boyd, 2010) and "networked participatory scholarship" (Veletsianos & Kimmons, 2012a). The networked public is best described as "the space constructed through networked technologies, and the imagined collective that emerges as a result of the intersection of people, technology, and practice" (boyd, 2010, p. 39). We agree with Veletsianos (2012), who argued that social media platforms are "emerging and evolving network[s] of scholar-learners where scholarly practices may be created, refined, performed, shared, discussed, and negotiated" (p. 2). Veletsianos and Kimmons worked off this idea of the networked public to come to the concept of networked participatory scholarship (NPS). "NPS refers to scholars' use of online social networks to share, reflect upon, critique, improve, validate, and otherwise develop their scholarship" (Veletsianos & Kimmons, 2012a, p. 2). These networked spaces lack formal membership and have the potential to draw participants from around the globe into conversation with one another. With this in mind, we used our study to examine the extent to which participants in #critlib might be considered members of a networked public participating in a process of networked participatory scholarship.

Social Network Analysis

In our study it was integral to identify the most prominent members of the #critlib community on Twitter. We chose to do this by way of social network analysis (SNA). SNA is not just a methodology, but a social science, with its own emblematic theoretical concepts (Borgatti, 2013). When we speak of "centrality," we are referring to the SNA concept of centrality. One could think about centrality "in terms of the contribution the node makes to the structure of the network" (Borgatti, 2013, p. 164). Centrality is not one thing, but a family of concepts (Borgatti, 2013). We specifically utilized degree centrality in determining the most prominent members of #critlib, following established conventions in similar studies (Grandjean, 2016; Riddell, et al., 2017; Tremayne, 2014). Degree centrality is the sum of a node's ties. In a weighted network such as ours, this represents the sum of all tie weights for a specific node.

Data Collection

The dataset is comprised of approximately three months of tweets, which included the hashtag #critlib. This amounted to 2,193 tweets, posted between July 23, 2017 9:11 AM Pacific Time to November 6, 2017 10:34 PM. Due to user error on our side, the dataset excludes tweets posted between August 18, 2017 8:41 PM and September 5, 2017 10:04 PM. The tweets were collected over a period of approximately three months using a Google Sheets add-on, Twitter Archiver. Twitter Archiver works through Twitter's API to collect tweets in real-time, situating the tweet, plus 15 fields of metadata, neatly into a Google Sheet.

Analysis

We processed the raw dataset using a homemade Python script, which counted the number of times each user communicated with another user by replying or retweeting. We treated replying and retweeting as communication forms on equal footing, with consideration towards the understanding of retweeting outlined in boyd, Golder, Lotan (2010): "a means of participating in a diffuse conversation" (p. 1) rather than solely a means of rebroadcasting. We conducted social network analyses, using the UCINET program, on the network of users which appeared in the dataset. The network was comprised of 972 nodes (users). The links represented the number of times a user communicated with another user.

Using UCINET, we calculated the degree centrality figures for each node in the network. We then zoomed in on the nodes which appeared in the top 5% (excluding isolates) of the degree centrality ranking. This subset included 40 users. We also zoomed in on the top 5% of those users with the most followers, as follower count has been a well-established measure of the influence of a user in the community (Dubois & Gaffney, 2014; Sugimoto, et al., 2017). These two subgroups—the most central users and the most followed users—were then compared. Using homemade Python scripts and the data analysis tools contained in Google Sheets, we created lists of the top 50 most retweeted tweets and the top 50 most favorited tweets, as well as calculated the number of tweets each user posted.

We compared our two subgroups on the frequency in which users appeared on the lists of most retweeted tweets and most favorited tweets, the volume of tweets produced, and the number of citations each user had in Google Scholar, as of December 1, 2017. It was possible to connect users to their full names thanks to the fact that the Twitter Archiver tool included a metadata field called "full name." This corresponded to the full name as listed on users' Twitter profiles. We used the tool Publish or Perish (PoP) to search Google Scholar for each of the users in each subgroup. Disambiguating among similarly named authors involved finding our author's CV or list of publications on personal websites and unchecking material by similarly-named individuals from the PoP search.

We also looked at the relationship between degree centrality and citation count in our degree centrality subgroup. We divided the subgroup into emerging scholars versus established scholars based on citation count. We considered "emerging" scholars to represent those individuals with fewer than 20 citations and "established" scholars to be those with 20 or more citations. We then analyzed the two subsets of our degree centrality subgroup: users which had 20 or more citations (established scholars) and users which had 0 citations (the least emergent of those emerging scholars). We compared these two subgroups, looking at the frequency users in our subgroups appeared on the lists of most retweeted tweets and most favorited tweets, to uncover their contributions to the #critlib conversation.

Limitations

We identified three significant limitations: (1) Google Scholar is not thorough in capturing citations from books and book chapters, or articles in languages other than English; (2) our study is limited to a small subset of a subfield of scholars; and (3) we had hoped to be able to examine a gap which was articulated both in the #critlib literature, as well as by Veletsianos and Kimmons (2016) in their study, which looked at the demographic landscape of a scholarly community, such as #critlib. While we had hoped to analyze information contained in Twitter users' profile "bio," (comprised of up to 160 characters of free text), we quickly found that the amount of wordplay and abbreviations contained in the bios severely constrained our ability to conduct analysis. Demographic information would likely have to be solicited directly from users in the form of an online survey. Such a survey, combined with a social network analysis, would be especially illuminating.

RESULTS

Through our analysis of the #critlib Twitter data we found that a small number of users dominated the conversation. However, these same users were generally not well-established scholarly figures in the LIS field (as we determined by high follower counts or high citations counts). In addition, those in the top followers' subgroup had higher citations counts than those in the degree centrality subgroup. Lastly, we found that those in the top followers' subgroup made a less significant contribution to the #critlib conversation than those with fewer followers overall on Twitter. Of the 972 nodes (users) in the #critlib network, 172 were isolates. These 172 users tweeted using #critlib, but they did not use the hashtag to communicate with another user by retweeting or replying. The average number of users communicated with by one user—as measured by degree—came out to 1.9. Only three users overlapped between our two subgroups: the top 5% of users ranked by degree centrality and the top 5% of users by follower count.

Degree Centrality Subgroup

The top 5% of users ranked by degree centrality produced significantly more tweets and significantly more of the tweets produced by the subgroup appeared in the Top 50 Retweeted Tweets and Top 50 Favorited Tweets lists.

The top 5% of users ranked by degree centrality produced:

- 32% of tweets within the dataset (701 out of 2193)
- 62% of the most favorited tweets (31 out of 50)
- 72% of the most retweeted tweets (36 out of 50)

We found that the degree centrality subgroup had the following characteristics: (1) a higher percentage of users with 0 citations to their name in Google Scholar; (2) a higher percentage of users with under 20 citations, and (3) a significantly lower median of citations, when compared to the top follower subgroup.

Citation Counts

When examining citation counts, we found that 4 out of 40 in the degree centrality subgroup were not people, so these users were given "NA." These were generally LIS organizations and were not included in the following calculations. 3 out of 40 were unidentifiable people, so they were given "Unknown." These were included in the following calculations.

We found that for the top 5% of users ranked by degree centrality:

- 27.8% (10 out of 36) had 0 citations
- 61.0% (22 out of 36) had at least 1 citation
- 27.8% (10 out of 36) had at least 20 citations
- 13.9% (5 out of 36) had at least 100 citations
- 3.8% (1 out 36) had at least 300 citations

72.2% had fewer than 20 citations, versus 28.8% with 20 or more citations. The median of the 33 identifiable human users: 5 citations. If unidentifiable users are included and considered to have 0 citations, the median is 3.5 citations.

When comparing the users with at least 20 citations to the users with 0 citations, we found that those with at least 20 citations appeared slightly more frequently in the lists of most retweeted tweets and most favorited tweets. 60% of users in the degree centrality subgroup with 20 citations or more appeared at least once in the lists of most retweeted tweets or most favorited tweets. The greatest number of appearances on the lists for a user with at least 20 citations was 8. 50% of users in the degree centrality subgroup with 0 citations appeared at least once in the lists. The greatest number of appearances for a user with 0 citations was 13.

Top Followers Subgroup

The top 5% of users ranked by follower count produced:

- 5.4% of tweets within the dataset (118 out of 2193)
- 18% of the most favorited tweets (9 out of 50)
- 18% of the most retweeted tweets (9 out of 50)

Citation Counts

When examining citation counts, we found 16 out of 40 in the top followers' subgroup were not people, so they were given "NA." These were a variety of things from LIS organizations (ALA LITA), to bots (EdTech), to institutions (Maryland Institute College of Art). These were not included in the following calculations. 2 out of 40 were unidentifiable people, so were given "Unknown." These were included in the following calculations.

We found that for the top 5% of users ranked by follower count:

- 16.7% (4 out of 24) had 0 citations
- 75% (18 out of 24) had at least 1 citation
- 58% (14 out of 24) had at least 20 citations
- 37.5% (9 out of 24) had at least 100 citations
- 20.8% (5 out of 24) had at least 300 citations

The median of the 24 users who were identifiable people: 43 citations. If the unidentifiable users are included and considered to have 0 citations, the median is 27.5 citations.

DISCUSSION

Veletsianos and Kimmons (2012b) argued that "networked participatory scholarship" provides a lens through which to understand how scholars use digital technologies to support their work (p. 768). The findings from our study contribute additional perspectives to this phenomenon by showing that the most important participants in the #critlib network on Twitter do not necessarily represent the most well-known or well-established members of the LIS scholarly community. The fact that there was very little overlap between our two subgroups (i.e., those with the highest degree centrality v. those with the most followers) is significant. It is not surprising then that the top 5% of users by degree centrality produced an outsized chunk of the #critlib corpus. However, the disparity between the degree centrality subgroup's high number of appearances on the lists of top retweeted and favorited tweets versus that of the top followers' subgroup is perhaps consequential. This is because it further shows that the most well-known users are not the most active participants in #critlib. While follower count has been established as a useful metric for measuring influence on Twitter, the findings from our study contribute additional evidence to suggest that follower count is not always the most accurate measure of influence in a particular Twitter community.

Edge Perspectives

In considering the impact of the degree centrality subgroup in #critlib during the period in which our study was conducted, one could assume that these users might simply be part of a less influential group of scholars, particularly with the low citation numbers. Yet, the importance of #critlib in the LIS landscape suggests that those users most central in the #critlib network are likely producing worthwhile commentary. With this in mind, we argue that these Twitter users are playing an important role in shaping networked participatory scholarship in LIS. More concretely, this group of users contribute what we are calling *edge perspectives*. Here, we mean perspectives from individuals who are either new to, less well-known within, or outside of academia altogether, yet remain core to shaping scholarship in networked participatory environments. We maintain that these edge perspectives offer the potential to significantly impact scholarly communication, particularly as established scholars use digital technologies "to circumvent established systems that are neither designed to value nor equipped to support such approaches to reflection and inquiry" (Veletsianos & Kimmons, 2012b, p. 771). In other words, as scholars use digital technologies to reflect and seek insights to further their ideas, edge perspectives can influence scholars open to seeking feedback and gaining insights to further their work through networked participatory platforms.

The influence of edge perspectives speaks back to other questions related to the demographic makeup of the #critlib community and more specifically to the perception that #critlib is dominated by an academic, theoretical voice. Given the relatively low citation levels for many of the most central members of the #critlib community, this suggests that this may be more of a perception than a reality. This disjuncture was itself noted in a 2015 #critlib chat entitled, "critiquing #critlib," by two participants, @elliehearts and @violetbfox. @elliehearts remarked in three successive tweets: "I'm noticing many that I consider most active in #critlib are saying they don't have theory backgrounds...Wondering how much is the more you know the more you realize you don't know…So are 'insiders' more steeped than they realize, or 'outsiders' getting false impression?" To which @violetbfox replied: "My impression is the latter and that the lack of an easy entry point...contributes to that," (Fox, 2015). Assuming that users are newly emerging into their scholarly identity certainly does not preclude them from speaking in an overly theoretical voice. However, the results from our study do give credence to the idea that it may be a misperception.

Our results also speak back to longstanding claims within the literature regarding the potential—or lack thereof—of social media technologies to reshape the spaces where scholarly communication and knowledge production occurs. When Veletsianos and Kimmons (2016) concluded that Twitter may not necessarily be the equalizing force it has been claimed to be, it was in response to their findings that "a scholar's power to disseminate meaningful work in a digitally connected culture is mediated (and therefore can be manipulated) by effective social media strategies" (p. 6). Our results do not dispute this aspect of Twitter. Rather, our results suggest that participating in a scholarly community like #critlib allows individuals to develop their scholarly identity in a space which might otherwise be unavailable or inaccessible. Different from a professional conference venue, #critlib offers a public space to which one does not need to travel or pay a registration fee to attend. It also provides a space for those who, as one #critlib participant has written, "feel alienated from more traditional...professional gatherings" (Fister, 2015, para. 8). In this way, Twitter offers a valuable space in which LIS practitioners and scholars across a diverse range of settings and backgrounds can develop their scholarly identities and/or contribute to scholarly conversations in the field.

CONCLUSION

In this paper, we sought to fill in gaps within the literature regarding the nature and role of the #critlib community within the greater LIS scholarly landscape by investigating the degree to which #critlib is dominated by established versus emerging or amateur scholars. We considered #critlib as an example of networked participatory scholarship. Through our study of #critlib Twitter chats within the three month period in which we analyzed, our findings showed the following: (1) the most central members of #critlib are not those with the top followers; (2) the most central members of #critlib have low citation numbers; and (3) the frequency by which the most central members of #critlib with 0 citations and those with more than 20 citation appeared in the lists of top retweets and favorited tweets was nearly the same: 50% versus 60%. In considering these findings, we introduced the concept of "edge perspectives" and suggested their role in shaping networked participatory scholarship in #critlib. We defined edge perspectives as perspectives from individuals who are either new to, less well-known within, or outside of academia altogether, yet remain core to shaping scholarship in online environments. This lens offers a way to view the role of #critlib within the LIS scholarly landscape, as a space for those who may be early in their careers or outside established scholarly circles to engage with and critique LIS theory and practice. This study is limited to a small group of scholars; we hope that future studies will further explore the relevance of edge perspectives. If our study of #critlib is taken as example of the relationship between online scholarly communities and their broader disciplines, edge perspectives may be playing a significant and unacknowledged role in the modern scholarly landscape.

REFERENCES

Absher, L. & Cardenas-Dow, M. (2016). Collaborative librarianship: A minority opinion. *Collaborative Librarianship*, *8*(4). Retrieved from http://digitalcommons.du.edu/collaborativelibrarianship/vol8/iss4/3

Almeida, N. (2018). Interrogating the Collective: #Critlib and the Problem of Community. In Karen P. Nicholson and Maura Seale (Eds), The Politics of Theory and the Practice of Critical Librarianship. Sacramento, CA: Library Juice Press.

Battista, A. (2012). From a "Crusade against Ignorance" to a "Crisis of Authenticity": Cultivating Information Literacy for a 21st Century Democracy. *LOEX Quarterly*, 38(4). Available at: http://commons.emich.edu/loexquarterly/vol38/iss4/3

Binkley, R. C. (1935). New tools for men of letters. *The Yale Review*, *24*, 519–537. Retrieved from https://www.wallandbinkley.com/rcb/works/new-tools-for-men-of-letters

Borgatti, S., Everett, M., Freeman, L.C. (2002). *Ucinet for Windows: Software for social network analysis*. Harvard, MA: Analytic Technologies.

Borgatti, S., Everett, M., & Johnson, J. (2013). *Analyzing Social Networks.* Thousand Oaks, CA: SAGE Publications.

Boyd, D. (2010). Social network sites as networked publics: Affordances, dynamics, and implications. In Z. Papacharissi (Ed.), *Networked self: Identity, community, and culture on social network sites*, pp. 39-58.

Boyd, D., Golder, S., Lotan, G. (2010). Tweet, tweet, retweet: Conversational aspects of retweeting on Twitter. *HICSS-43*. 1 - 10. 10.1109/HICSS.2010.412.

critlib.org. (2018a). *about / join the discussion*. Retrieved from http://critlib.org/about/

critilib.org (2018b). *Previous Twitter chats*. Retrieved from http://critlib.org/twitter-chats/previous-twitter-chats/

Critical Librarianship Symposium. (2012). Retrieved from http://radicalreference.info/PracticalChoices#About

Drabinski, E. (2016) What collaboration means to me: The infrastructure of welcome. *Collaborative Librarianship*, *8*(1). Retreived from http://digitalcommons.du.edu/collaborativelibrarianship/vol8/iss1/3

Dubois, E., & Gaffney, D. (2014). The multiple facets of influence: Identifying political influentials and opinion leaders on Twitter. *American Behavioral Scientist*, *58*(10), 1260 - 1277.

Fister, B. (2015). Some thoughts on #whyicritlib. Retrieved from https://www.insidehighered.com/blogs/library-babel-fish/some-thoughts-whyicritlib

Fox, V. [@violetbfox]. (2015). My impression is the latter and. [tweet]. Retrieved from https://twitter.com/violetbfox/status/616057285371039744

Fransman, J. (2013). Researching academic literacy practices around Twitter: performative methods and their onto-ethical implications. In R. Goodfellow & M. Lea (Eds.), *Literacy in the digital university: Critical perspectives on learning, scholarship, and technology*. London: Routledge, 27-41.

Garnet, F., & Ecclesfield, N. (2011). Towards a framework for co-creating open scholarship. *Research in Learning Technology*, *19*(1).

Grandjean, M. (2016). A social network analysis of Twitter: Mapping the digital humanities community. *Cogent Arts & Humanities*, *3*(1), 1171458.

Greenhow, C., Robelia, B., & Hughes, J. (2009). Learning, teaching, and scholarship in a digital age: Web 2.0 and classroom research: What path should we take now? *Educational Researcher*, *38*(4), 233–245.

Hathcock, A. (2017). Cultivating critical dialogue on Twitter. In S. Young & D. Rossmann (Eds), *Using social media to build library communities: A LITA guide,* pp. 137-150.

Harzing, A. (2007). *Publish or perish*. Retrieved from http://www.harzing.com/pop.htm

Holmberg, K., & Thelwall, M. (2014). Disciplinary differences in Twitter scholarly communication. *Scientometrics*, *101*, 1027–1042.

Inefuku, H. & Roh, C. (2016). Agents of Diversity and Social Justice: Librarians and Scholarly Communication. (2016). Digital Scholarship and Initiatives Publications. Retrieved from https://lib.dr.iastate.edu/digirep_pubs/5

Mahrt, M., Weller, K., & Peters, I. (2014). Twitter in scholarly communication. In K. Weller, A. Bruns, J. Burgess, M. Mahrt, & C. Puschmann (Eds.), *Twitter and society* (pp. 399–410). New York, NY: Peter Lang.

Mewburn, I., & P. Thompson. (2013). *Academic blogging is part of a complex online academic attention economy, Leading to unprecedented readership*. Retrieved from http://blogs.lse.ac.uk/impactofsocialsciences/2013/12/12/academic-attention-economy/

O'Reilly, T. (2005). *What is Web 2.0?* Retrieved from http://oreilly.com/web2/archive/what-is-web-20.html

Pagowsky, N. (2015a). Transforming our image through a compass of critical librarianship. Retrieved from http://nicolepagowsky.info/documents/PagowskyWAAL2015Transcript.pdf

Pagowsky, N. (2015b). *Why I #critlib*. Retrieved from http://pumpedlibrarian.blogspot.com/2015/12/why-i-critlib.html

Pagowsky, N. & McElroy, K. (2016). *Critical library pedagogy handbook*. Chicago, IL: Association of College and Research Libraries.

Quan-Haase, A., Martin, K., & McCay-Peet, L. (2015). Networks of digital humanities scholars: The informational and social uses and gratifications of Twitter. *Big Data & Society*, *2*(1), 1-12.

Randall, R. (2015). critlib #feelings. Retrieved from http://ryanpatrickrandall.com/2015/critlib-feelings/

Riddell, J., Brown, A., Kovic, I., & Jauregui, J. (2017). Who Are the Most Influential Emergency Physicians on Twitter?. Western Journal Of Emergency Medicine: Integrating Emergency Care With Population Health, 18(2), 281-287. doi:10.5811/westjem.2016.11.31299

Sheldon-Hess, C. (2015). #critlib #feelings (or #whyicritlib). Retrieved from http://www.sheldon-hess.org/coral/2015/12/critlib/

Sugimoto, C., Tsou, A., Naslund, S., Hauser, A., Brandon, M, Winter, D., Behles, C. & Finlay, S. (2014). Beyond gatekeepers of knowledge: Scholarly communication practices of academic librarians and archivists at ARL institutions. *College & Research Libraries*, 75(2), 145-161.

Sugimoto, C., Work, S., Larivière, V., & Haustein, S. (2017). Scholarly use of social media and altmetrics: A review of the literature. *Journal Of The Association For Information Science & Technology*, *68*(9), 2037-2062.

Tremayne, M. (2014). Anatomy of Protest in the Digital Era: A Network Analysis of Twitter and Occupy Wall Street. Social Movement Studies, 13(1), 110-126. doi:10.1080/14742837.2013.830969

Twitter Archiver. Retrieved from https://chrome.google.com/webstore/detail/twitter-archiver/pkanpfekacaojdncfgbjadedbggbbphi?hl=e

Veletsianos, G. (2012). Higher education scholars' participation and practices on Twitter. *Journal Of Computer Assisted Learning*, *28*(4), 336-349.

Veletsianos, G. & Kimmons, R. (2012a). Assumptions and challenges of open scholarship. *The International Review Of Research In Open And Distance Learning*, *13*(4), 166-189.

Veletsianos, G. & Kimmons, R. (2012b). Networked Participatory Scholarship: Emergent techno-cultural pressures toward open and digital scholarship in online networks. *Computers & Education*, *58*, 766-774.

Veletsianos, G., & Kimmons, R. (2016). Scholars in an increasingly open and digital world: How do education professors and students use Twitter? *The Internet and Higher Education*, 301-10. doi:10.1016/j.iheduc.2016.02.002

Weller, K., Puschmann, C. (2011). Twitter for scientific communication: How can citations/references be identified and measured? Retrieved from http://citeseerx.ist.psu.edu/viewdoc/download?doi=10.1.1.398.330&rep=rep1&type=pdf

Towards Linked Data: Some Consequences for Researchers in the Social Sciences and Humanities

Lyne Da Sylva
Université de Montréal, Canada. Lyne.Da.Sylva@UMontreal.CA

ABSTRACT

This paper addresses the introduction of Semantic Web and Linked Data technology in Social Science and Humanities research. On the basis of a sample of existing research projects, we examine the impact that the technology has on the research methodology. Three main points of impact were observed. The first is the epistemological foundations of the research, including a focus on individual entities in the research area (or "atomization"), the reification of research objects, and the favouring of analytical skills from researchers. Secondly, in the data analysis phase, research relies more heavily on technical skills during data discovery and processing, and the technology induces growing confusion between data and metadata. Thirdly, we show how the types of models that are built often imply a new encoding of already existing information.

KEYWORDS

Linked Data, Semantic Web, research methods, Social Science and Humanities

INTRODUCTION

Within the global movement of data-driven science (Borgman 2015; Kitchin 2014; Hey, Tansley, & Tolle 2009), there has been an increasing amount of research in the Social Sciences and Humanities (SSH) which makes use of Semantic Web technology – specifically, Linked Data (Berners-Lee, 2006). It has already been recognized that Big Data is causing an epistemological shift in the way research is carried out (Borgman, 2012; Boyd & Crawford, 2012). A similar case can be made about Linked Data. The goal of this paper is to discuss certain implications of the Semantic Web (specifically Linked Data) for researchers in the Social Sciences and Humanities (SSH), on the basis of selected case studies.

This paper proceeds as follows. We first give brief descriptions of Semantic Web and Linked Data (SW/LD) technology and a schematic representation of SSH methodology. We then report on related work. In the methodology section, we present our case study approach, in which we have selected a sample of research projects in the SSH which make use of SW/LD technology; against the backdrop of the methodology outlined for research in the SSH, we identify within the case studies steps or areas which are affected by the SW/LD methods and tools. The conclusion provides some additional thoughts on the study.

BASIC CONCEPTS – METHODOLOGICAL TOOLS

We first briefly define the Semantic Web and Linked Data and provide a description of SSH research methodology.

Semantic Web and Linked Open Data

The goal of the Semantic Web (Berners-Lee, Hendler, & Lassila 2001) is to make explicit the meaning of information on the Web, in order to allow complex automated processing of the data. The first such application would be semantic search: to perform information retrieval on the meaning of a word and not on a character string, e.g. "file" as in "computer file" and not "nail file"; or "Gandhi" as in "Mahatma Gandhi" and not "Indira Gandhi". This is possible only if the targeted documents have an explicit representation of the meaning of the "file" and "Gandhi" occurrences which they contain. Thus, the Semantic Web relies on the identification and naming of entities on the Web: unique entities such as people ("Gandhi"), places ("Paris") and dates, but also concepts such as "file" or "beauty". It also requires the explicit representation of relationships among entities, such as "is-used-for", "is-the-author-of" or "knows". Such explicit encoding allows computer agents (devoid of real understanding) to manipulate and process data appropriately, according to their algorithms. This is the meaning of "Semantic" in "Semantic Web".

Another example of complex automated processing of semantic data is the manipulation of different sets of data, to be combined in complex ways. For instance, one could create a personalized sightseeing tour for a city, using information from various sources: a list of tourist attractions; a database of museums with their opening hours and their intended audience; attendance statistics for each of these venues; a current weather forecast; routes and timetables for public transportation to these venues. Appropriate technology could combine this information (and perhaps more, notably user profiles) to produce daily suggestions for sightseeing. Note that this may only be possible if (i) the data sources are sufficiently explicit and disambiguated, (ii) the exchange of data between them is made easy by strict adherence to a shared standard, and (iii) appropriate rules are provided for reasoning on the data. This is the essence of the Semantic Web.

Transferring this example to a context of research in the SSH, one can envision a data-driven application which would provide background for an analysis of a historical event: given for example a list of locations, time periods, a database of people, their roles and the relationships among them, a number of time-situated events (natural phenomena such as earthquakes or human-created ones such as the 2018 Winter Olympics), one could imagine providing possible factors which may help contextualize a specific event or state of affairs. Alternatively, this data could be used to uncover heretofore undetected relationships among people, places or events. Some such research projects have been developed, as will be shown in the following sections. Again, to make this possible, the data must be explicit, easily accessible and uniformly represented. And so, an important part of the Semantic Web is the Linked Data, which we describe below.

Brief description of Linked Data

The basic notions of Linked Data (LD) (https://www.w3.org/wiki/LinkedData; http://linkeddata.org/) include: identifiers to represent distinct entities uniquely; relation names which will be used to make explicit links among these entities; RDF triples which encode the relations among pairs of entities; vocabularies and ontologies which encode regular, productive relationships among sets of data and can enforce constraints on their use; and triplestores, the databases used to store the sets of triples. Each is described below.

Identifiers are alphanumeric strings (such as numbers or « codes ») used to represent entities in a unique manner. For instance, ISBN (International Standard Book Numbers) are identifiers for books in the physical world; in the virtual world the work corresponding to a book can be unambiguously identified with an identifier that can be a URL which leads to a description of it. An example is found in the French national library catalogue (Catalogue de la Bibliothèque nationale de France), where the novel "War and Peace" has as its identifier "ark:/12148/cb31478402c", declared at the following URL: http://catalogue.bnf.fr/ark:/12148/cb31478402c.

Identifiers are also used for people, e.g. 0000-0001-2242-4494 for Leo Tolstoy and 0000-0001-2138-6043 for Mahatma Gandhi in the International Standard Name Identifier (ISNI) database; or https://orcid.org/0000-0003-2125-060X for Albert Einstein in the ORCID (Open Researcher and Contributor ID) registry. Identifiers may also designate places (e.g. http://id.dbpedia.org/page/Vancouver), and various other entities. They are a shorthand for any entity which can be described and mentioned on the Web. In the Semantic Web, identifier syntax is governed by the URI (Uniform Resource Identifier) standard (https://www.w3.org/wiki/URI). Very often, identifiers for LD are the by-now familiar URLs (Uniform Resource Locators). Identifiers are usually associated with names, labels that may vary across languages: Leo Tolstoy, Léon Tolstoï, Толстой, Лев Николаевич, etc.; or Mahatma Gandhi, Mohandas Karamchand Gandhi, મોહનદાસ કરમચંદ ગાંધી, etc.

To allow automatic processing, relevant **relations** among entities are encoded explicitly. For example: "is-the-father-of" or "has-written-to" may be relations between persons or corporate bodies; "is-situated-in" can relate two geographical entities such as a city and a country. Persons may also be linked to entities such as works or other concepts, with relations such as "is-the-author-of" (conversely, "has-author") or "is-the-president-of". Other types of relations are those which express properties of a given entity: "has-publication-date-of", or "is-the-family-name-of". Intuitive relations such as "is-the-author-of", "knows" or "is-the-family-name-of" are defined formally and publicly in so-called **vocabularies** or **ontologies**: "Vocabularies are the basic building blocks for inference techniques on the Semantic Web" (https://www.w3.org/standards/semanticweb/ontology). They allow uniform encoding of relations. Some examples are given in Table 1.

The sameAs relation plays a special role in LD. It is used to relate two identifiers, defined in different datasets, that actually denote the same entity.

As the vocabularies and ontologies are defined on the Web, the relations are assigned identifiers: URIs which uniquely define them. And so not only entities, but also relations, are encoded with identifiers in the Semantic Web: http://purl.org/dc/terms/creator for "creator" and http://xmlns.com/foaf/spec/knows for "knows".

All data in the Web of data are represented by binary relations between two entities. The two entities and their relation are referred to as a **triple**, consisting of a subject (the first entity), the predicate (i.e. the relation) and the object (the second entity). Thus "Leo Tolstoy is-the-author-of War and Peace", or "Leo Tolstoy has-written-to Mahatma Gandhi" are examples of triples, as well as: "War and Peace has-publication-date-of 1869". Librarians will recognize some of these as metadata, but relations are of a more general nature. In the Semantic Web, triples use a uniform encoding, provided by the **RDF** (Resource Description Framework -- https://www.w3.org/RDF/) standard: it expresses a binary relation between the subject and the object, where the subject and the relation are represented by URIs, and the object may be another URI or a literal (i.e. a string of characters); the latter option is the obvious one to represent titles or names. Thus, the triples above are represented as in Table 2, once with human-readable strings, and once using RDF-compliant URIs.

Vocabulary	Main use	Sample relations
Dublin Core	Documents	creator date rights
FOAF (Friend of a friend)	People and relationships	firstName familyName knows
SKOS (Simple Knowledge Organization System)	Thesauri	broader narrower prefLabel
OWL (Web Ontology Language)	Ontologies	sameAs

Table 1: Sample relations from vocabularies or ontologies used in RDF triples

Subject	Relation	Object
War and Peace http://catalogue.bnf.fr/ark:/12148/cb31478402c	has-author http://purl.org/dc/terms/creator	Leo Tolstoy urn:ISNI:0000-0001-2242-4494
Leo Tolstoy urn:ISNI:0000-0001-2242-4494	knows http://xmlns.com/foaf/spec/knows	Mahatma Gandhi urn:ISNI: 0000-0001-2138-6043

Table 2: Sample relations from vocabularies or ontologies used in RDF triples

Triplestores are databases used to store the triples (they are basically relational databases optimized to process triples). Ideally, these databases are "open", meaning that their data are freely accessible in reusable formats. In this case they hold not only Linked Data (LD), but Linked Open Data (LOD), which ensures accessibility and access.

Note that the Semantic Web involves more than simply Linked (Open) Data; but our focus on LD suffices for the purpose of our study. LD defines the Web of data, which is an extension of the Web of documents.

Web of data vs Web of documents

The Web of data and the Web of documents are complementary. Triplestores hold triples of data; this data may designate documents themselves and may also represent references to entities mentioned within documents. Some implicit relationships among documents may be made explicit given that they share occurrences of the same entities. Different technologies may be used to extract, analyze and abstract entities from documents (to add to the Web of data), or they may be used to help create new documents from the entities in the Web of data.

The Web itself is the product of contributions from all Internet users: corporate bodies, government, individuals, various organizations, etc. For the present discussion, however, it is important to note that some of the documents are authored by researchers, and some of the data constitute the output of research projects. This means that research contributes new information to the Web of documents and to the Web of data – and is doing increasingly so; it is this research output and this new research material which we consider in our study. In fact, a document-centric discipline such as History has seen several developments incorporating LD and ontologies to analyze, structure and display historical information.

State of the LOD cloud

As a final introduction to SW/LD technology, we note the impressive growth of the LOD datasets available. In 2017 the LOD cloud was described as containing about 1139 datasets (http://lod-cloud.net/), divided among different categories, the main ones being geography, government, life sciences, linguistics, media, publications, and social networking. Many of these are RDF versions of highly-valued, dependable databases produced by recognized authorities. For instance, there are RDF versions of thesauri, subject headings and classification schemes from various national libraries (the USA, France, Germany, the UK, Canada, Australia, etc.). There are lists of geographical names from the world over, registries of authors, works, and artists; vocabularies for describing time, genes, drugs, etc. The most important perhaps, in terms of links to other datasets, is DBpedia (which encodes, in RDF format, triples of information extracted from Wikipedia). Given the size and growth of Wikipedia and the fact that it gradually contains more and more verified information, one can only expect DBpedia to grow as well; eventually, DBpedia, and consequently the LOD cloud, will encode large amounts of data deemed relevant for scholarly research.

A schematic representation of research methodology

Many publications, aimed at budding researchers or seasoned researchers alike, detail the steps for conducting research in the SSH (e.g. Bryman 2015; van Peer, Hakemulder, & Zyngier 2012). Abstracting from the particulars of each, we present the following outline for stages of a research project:

1. Defining the research problem: formulating research questions and hypotheses; performing the conceptual analysis; assessing feasibility. This is where the epistemological stance of the research becomes apparent, assuming a conceptual framework such as described in Baronov (2004), including positivism (or a variation thereof), structuralism and hermeneutics.

2. Designing the methodology: choosing an inquiry method, whether direct (using an "informant") or indirect (using documents or data), and whether quantitative or qualitative; and then, choosing a specific technique among several options (in direct methods: in situ observation, interviews, think-aloud protocols, questionnaires/surveys, diaries, focus groups, experimentation, etc.; in indirect methods: content analysis, statistics analysis, analysis of output from previous experiments, etc.).

3. Collecting data: choosing a sample and applying the data collection tools.

4. Analyzing and interpreting data: this stage begins with various types of qualitative, statistical or other quantitative processing of the data. This leads to interpretations and, it is hoped, conclusions which support the initial research hypotheses and answer the research questions. Included in this stage should be the creation of some type of model emerging from the research. Arsham (2015) identifies four types of models: verbal, physical, analytical and simulation models. The first type is usually developed, as a resulting thesis or article is a verbal model of the problem investigated, the data analyzed, and the conclusions drawn. It may be the case that other models are created as well: an analytical model in form of a graph or LD, or a simulation model (especially in fields related to Computer Science).

Unsurprisingly, we will see that the data collection and analysis phases of research are strongly impacted by SW/LD methodology; we will also see how the very definition of the research problem (or rather, the epistemological stance of the research) is also affected.

RELATED WORK

The use of SW/LD technology in SSH research is fairly recent; for instance, as of July 2018, few of the datasets that can be accessed via the datahub platform (https://old.datahub.io/), which lists some 11,300 datasets, are relevant to SSH. However, close to 1,000 of its datasets are tagged with "publications" and represent corpora of documents (digital libraries, national bibliographies, etc.), many of which are relevant for SSH scholars. Some (11) are identified with cultural heritage: e.g. LD from museums, such as the Rijksmuseum (https://old.datahub.io/), the British Museum Collection (https://old.datahub.io/) and Europeana (https://old.datahub.io/dataset/europeana-lod-v1). Also, 37 datasets are retrieved by a search using "Digital Humanities". Only two bear the "arts and humanities" tag or the "social science" tag. There is a much greater number of datasets tagged for biomedicine (249), science (133), earth science (68), biology (33) or physical sciences (13).

Among important ontologies for SSH, one can cite CIDOC-CRM, the Conceptual Reference Model from CIDOC (ICOM International Committee on Documentation). It "provides definitions and a formal structure for describing the implicit and explicit concepts and relationships used in cultural heritage documentation" (http://www.cidoc-crm.org/). The latter has been widely used already: Eide et al. (2008) describe the production of CIDOC-CRM compliant datasets from diverse collections of source data. Also, noteworthy is the Records in Contexts-Conceptual Model (RiC-CM) (https://www.ica.org/en/egad-ric-conceptual-model), "the new standard for the description of records based on archival principles" and the soon-to-be-released related RiC-O, Records in Context Ontology.

Some other notable work includes the following: in Literary Studies, Brando, Frontini, & Ganascia (2016) use LD (from DBpedia and *Bibliothèque nationale de France* Linked Data) to help disambiguate authors' mentions in a corpus of French literary criticism; in Linguistics, Chiarcos, Nordhoff, & Hellmann (2012) explore LD for language data and metadata; Hyvönen (2012) gives an overview on the motivations and the methods for using SW/LD technology for publishing cultural heritage collections and other content on the Web. Unsworth (2016) recognizes the role which the SW will play in Digital Humanities (DH) and the need for researchers within humanities to participate in the definition of ontologies, given their expertise. Additionally, a careful study of papers presented at the Digital Humanities conference in 2017 (Lewis, Raynor, Forest, Sinatra, & Sinclair, 2017) reveals a number of projects which use LD in the humanities, as shown in Table 3.

Discipline	Authors	Data encoded as LD
Art History	Bégnis & Mendes da Silva	Images and descriptive metadata (place names, building names)
Cultural Studies	Kameda & Hara	Documents and "words"
Digital Libraries	Dussault et al. Hardy et al	Document metadata from catalogue entries
	Page et al.	Document metadata, genre attributes
History	Beals	"Historical evidences", document provenance, rhetorical relationships
	Goto & Shibutani	Resources (i.e. documents), spatial information
	Grossner et al.	"Data about the movement of people, ideas, cultural practices, and commodities between places" (e.g. routes, people, commodities, information, places, paths, time)
Literary Studies	Bauer et al.	"Readings" represented by annotations
	Laiacona	Places, events, artwork, people, texts
	Malta et al.	Units of analysis in poetry
Musicology	Craig-McFeely et al.	Digital imaging of musical scores, cataloguing metadata, semantic notation (e.g. time, proportion, duration, roles of people/organizations)
	Nurmikko-Fuller et al.	Musicians and their properties, details of solos within performances (including pitch, key and chord changes), recordings
	Page, Lewis & Weigl	Audio recordings, musicological relationships
Philology	Lorenzini & Sanna	Document contents (e.g. events, activities)
Sociology	Brown et al.	Socio-demographic data related to authors or themes in texts

Table 3. LD projects at DH2017.

At the same conference, Brown et al. held a panel called "Advancing Linked Open Data in the Humanities", where questions were raised regarding the impact of LD-based research on scholars, and which tools would be most needed. A study similar to our own has addressed epistemological considerations of research using Big Data (Boyd & Crawford, 2012); indeed, Big Data entail important changes to the manner in which science is conducted (Hey et al., 2009) and in the very definition of knowledge (Boyd & Crawford 2012, 665). The observations encoded in the data suggest an objective character and a precision that actually obscure the subjectivity and inaccuracy inherent in the selection and preparation of data (Boyd & Crawford, 2012, pp. 666–668). This may very well apply to Linked Data as well. Epistemological aspects of the Semantic Web and of its Linked Data have been addressed by d'Aquin & Motta (2016, p. 53), who highlight among other things the illusion of uniformity or homogeneity among data, as suggested by the very regular format of RDF:

> Somehow, there is one aspect of scalability which is much harder to address by means of purely technical means. In d'Aquin et al. [2014a] we called it *diversity*: the fact that data and knowledge not only come in different formats and subscribe to different modeling principles, but also that they originate from different sources, might be of different scope and quality, and might be distributed under different constraints, with different regulations applying to them...

Baronov (2004) addresses the conceptual foundations underlying research methods, especially in the social sciences. Four methodological orientations are defined and contrasted: positivism (in three phases, embryonic positivism, logical positivism and postpositivism); structuralism; hermeneutics; and antifoundationalism. This discussion has been useful for framing some of the epistemological consequences presented below.

DATA: SSH RESEARCH USING SEMANTIC WEB AND LINKED DATA TECHNOLOGY

We focus now on a sample of research projects in SSH using Linked Data in disciplines well represented in Table 3: Literary Studies, Music and History. They were retained here for their variety, for the way their data or the ontologies used were clearly presented, and, for case #3, because it was well-documented. We briefly present the LD used in the research or resulting from it, as was gathered from the publications. The main focus of the descriptions is the use made of SW/LD technology.

Case #1: Literary Studies

Curado Malta, González-Blanco, Martínez Cantón, & Del Rio (2017) use LD in a literary project which explores poetry: "...our work is interested in a structural and formal approach that looks at poetry into discrete units, categories, and their relationships. Thus, we are involved in analyzing how metrical repertoires in digital form model those structures" (p. 210). It aims to bridge the gap between alternative, linguistically diverse databases called "repertoires of poetry metrics", i.e. catalogues that "give an account of the metrical and rhythmical schemes of either a poetical tradition, a period or school, gathering a corpus of poems that are defined and classified by their main characteristics" (p. 210). Already existing repertoires (currently in various formats: MySQL or XML databases and files, Perl scripts and Worksheet files) will be published as LD, allowing heretofore closed silos to become interoperable. Thus, the linking of all this data should make it possible to compare poetic traditions and to create new repertoires, among other benefits.

Case #2: Music

The second case studied involves Music Informatics ("the study of information related to, or [which] is a result of, musical activity" (Humphrey, Bello, & LeCun, 2013, p. 461)), an interdisciplinary research area dealing with the production, distribution, consumption, and analysis of music through technology (especially in digital formats). Cannam et al. (2010) present the Sonic Visualiser, an application to visualize, annotate, and automate the analysis of audio recordings. It is a "highly customisable play-back and visualisation environment that includes such features as variable-speed playback, looping, and the ability to annotate the recording, for instance to identify specific points of reference"[1]. This research project makes use of a variety of existing ontologies, including the Music Ontology[2]; the Similarity Ontology which provides concepts and properties for describing similarities between things in the RDF/OWL framework; the Audio Features Ontology, "a descriptive framework for expressing different conceptual-isations of and designing linked data formats for content-based audio features" (Allik, Fazekas, & Sandler, 2016, p. 73). More ontologies have been created within the project: The Chord Ontology, "intended to provide a common, versatile vocabulary for describing chords and chord sequences in RDF"[3] and the Timeline Ontology which "used with the Event ontology, can be used to annotate sections of a signal, a video, or any temporal object"[4]. They encode, in this new format, information which previously existed in another form. The heavy use of ontologies by the project makes it of particular interest for our study. Great emphasis is put on individual, low-level structures which participate in music production, analysis and visualisation. The paper claims that with their tool, the interchange of data, the analysis of experimental results, and resulting outputs are rendered relatively easy. The underlying requirement is the use of standardized, uniform data. This is a case where vocabularies and ontologies provide readily available, standardized descriptions for the building blocks of the application.

This project creates and uses technology possibly applicable to the data alluded to in the Musicology examples in Table 3.

Case #3: History

The use of Linked Data in History research has been well documented in the work of Michon (2016); the author's rich descriptions of existing projects as well as the insightful analysis of their consequences provided valuable material for this case study. The specific case used here stems from the work of historian Tim Sherratt, who uses LD in various projects. One of them presents findings on a specific character, Inigo Jones, who was a meteorologist and farmer in Queensland, Australia. The research project resulted in not only a book (Sherratt 2007), but also an enriched document on the Web, which told the story of Inigo Jones while making use of various datasets from the LOD cloud to provide outgoing links to material related to the document: source documents, as well as links to people, places, events, etc. External datasets used included archives of newspaper articles from Trove, "Australia's national discovery service", which "provides access to more than 300 million resources managed by more than 1000 Australian and international organisations, and by members of the public" (Ayres, 2012). Data from Wikipedia and DBpedia were also used. Data encoding used Dublin Core and FOAF vocabularies. In the author's own words, he proceeded to "create narratives that embed Linked Open Data" (Sherratt, 2015). Thus, in his research methodology, data collection included LD sources as well as traditional print materials (the mainstay of History research). The research output combined not only the addition of LD to a document (a purely formal result), but also additional links made between existing data, based on the researcher's analysis of existing data and documents (novel associations which embody a new model of the phenomenon under study).

This is an illustration of how technology (LD) can modify the way research is conducted (data gathering, collection and analysis) as well as the product of the project.

Case #4: Classics

Classics studies are akin to History in relying heavily on documents (ancient ones in fact) and so might be deemed quite similar to our latest case. The SPQR ('Supporting Productive Queries") project (Blanke et al., 2012) was retained nonetheless as highly relevant to our study, as it presents itself as "Linked data for humanities research".

---

[1] http://www.charm.rhul.ac.uk/analysing/p9_0_1.html
[2] http://musicontology.com/
[3] http://motools.sourceforge.net/chord_draft_1/chord.html
[4] http://motools.sourceforge.net/timeline/timeline.html

The project investigated the potential of a SW/LD approach "for linking and integrating datasets related to classical antiquity, focusing on certain targeted datasets as test cases". In the field of Classics research, ancient texts are an important source of information. Even though a large amount of digital material has been created, it can be difficult to access due to its being distributed across locations, stored in diverse and incompatible formats, and either not available online or made available only in isolation (Blanke et al., 2012). The SPQR project uses LD principles and technology to link the existing datasets, "to deliver an integrated data landscape through which researchers can explore and so seek to understand this data" (Blanke et al., 2012, p. 1). Specifically, three datasets were transformed into RDF: the Heidelberger Gesamtverzeichnis der griechischen Papyrusurkunden Aegyptens (HGV), a collection of metadata records for 65,000 Greek papyri from Egypt (300 BC to 700 AD); the Inscriptions of Aphrodisias (InsAph), a corpus of 2,000 ancient Greek inscriptions from the Roman city of Aphrodisias in modern Turkey (200 BC to 700 AD); the Inscriptions of Tripolitania (IRT), a corpus of over 1,000 inscriptions from modern Libya (100 BC to 700 AD). Also, a SPQR-specific ontology was created: "The SPQR ontology consisted of URIs for a range of epigraphic concepts. The subject of a triple can be an epigraph, a date of origin, a person or a location." (Blanke et al., 2012, p. 3). Entities in their ontology were linked to other external sources, using the OWL 'sameAs' relationship described above. The result was deemed to offer "an intuitive and usable means of exploring and understanding the data, exceeding the capabilities offered by current online portals to classics data" (Blanke et al., 2012, p. 1). The goal of the project was thus the very creation of this LD resource.

The projects we have described claim that access to new datasets in a standardized form and in easily accessible places allow for new discoveries and new opportunities. Our goal here is not to question these efforts. It is simply to observe what implications this research agenda may have on research in the SSH.

DATA ANALYSIS: IMPLICATIONS OF SW/LD TECHNOLOGY FOR RESEARCH IN SSH

We have found that three aspects of the research methodology are especially impacted by the introduction of LD and SW technology: first, the epistemological stance of SW/LD-driven research; secondly, data collection and analysis; and thirdly, the nature of models created by this type of research.

Impact on epistemological stance

The adoption and use of LD and SW technology prove to have important consequences in the very outlook on research and on how they determine the orientation of a research project. We explain here: (i) how they change the focus of research (how they tend to "atomize" it), (ii) how they reify the research objects themselves, and (iii) how they may affect the terminology of all concerned disciplines.

Focus of research: "atomization" of research objects

Research based on LD favours the analysis of piecemeal information, as opposed to whole documents or overviews of a given situation. First and foremost are the individual entities which are assigned identifiers. Each and every entity participating in the research problem must be represented as a URI. In the case of the Inigo Jones project, this includes not only authors of documents and important historical figures, but also weather events, meteorology itself, different place names, etc. Note that there is no hierarchy *per se* in linked datasets (apart from the importance that can be attached to an entity which is linked to very many others); all are represented by identical-looking identifiers, which all become equally-small singular entities in the research space.

Another example of piecemeal information of major importance in the Semantic Web is the relations defined by individual triples. These are very specific, linking exactly two entities with a precise, named relation. Note that non-binary relations cannot be represented by triples. And yet most interesting phenomena are not binary. For example, an act of buying involves a seller, a buyer, some goods and some type of currency. This simple example requires many triples to represent it completely. One can only imagine what is required to describe the most basic historical event or musical form. In all cases, however, individual triples are the units that are stored in triplestores. Although triples related to the same entity can be grouped when displayed for a user, they are individually encoded, stored and processed.

LD-driven research favours a methodological orientation in line with a form of positivism – i.e. assuming that the entities defined in the Web of data represent objective, shared knowledge. A structuralist approach is not excluded: if one considers the totality of datasets and their links, together with the relations defined within ontologies, one may arrive at a description of the system as a whole and each piece's role within it. It is hoped that future work will allow a more holistic approach, but in these rather initial stages of the Semantic Web endeavour, the focus of research has been to define the URIs, to declare the ontologies and to create the datasets. And so, to focus on individual entities.

This is contrary to the usual synthetical approach of some disciplines. In disciplines such as History, Literature, Linguistics or Anthropology, the traditional approach is for the researcher to study the primary data, which include documents, phenomena (e.g. speech production) and observations (in field studies, for example). The researcher's important contribution is his or her analysis of this complex corpus of data; the relationships that are identified and the information that is abstracted allow a better understanding of the research question. The research results take the form of documents which provide a synthesis or a narrative of the data and phenomena under study. In a SW/LD approach, in addition to traditional sources, a researcher uses datasets that have been encoded by others. These datasets are typically isolated silos of (piecemeal) information. Then, the researcher's contribution must include the selection of relevant datasets (thus the evaluation of existing datasets), the encoding of any new data uncovered by his or her analysis of the entire corpus of documents, data and observations, and finally the process of adding any relevant new links in the final data. Among the research results, then, must figure the addition of more Linked Data. In a word: whereas the traditional approach requires more synthesis and abstraction from the researcher, a SW/LD-driven approach includes a strong analytical component, to decompose observations into individual data and triples – what we call here the "atomization" of research objects. "Big data is made up of many small acts of living" (Sherratt, 2016).

Reification of research objects

Interestingly, the creation of identifiers and triples entails the reification of research objects, i.e. raising to the status of some type of concrete object something that may in fact be abstract. All entities are represented by identifiers: weather events, musical chords, time, languages such as Greek, etc. It actually may not seem unnatural for researchers to reify their research objects (this may well be a natural process in a researcher's work); but it may be surprising to treat relations as reified entities. How does one interpret "is-the-author-of" as an entity? Or "has-date-of-birth"? And yet this is what is done in a sense when these relations are assigned identifiers. This may raise interesting new research questions.

One that has already received attention is the identity relation, through the definition of the "sameAs" relation in the OWL ontology. Different issues related to the (abusive) use of the sameAs relationship have been identified. Davis (2009) has noted the influence of time on the validity of the identity relationship (for example, three different datasets may give different populations for the same city, which may be due to the time when the population was counted). Halpin, Herman, & Hayes (2010) specifically looked at different notions of "is the same as," distinguishing four subtypes (valid but opaque references, context-variable similarity, representation, and quasi-identity).

Levelling of terminology

While terminology and concepts are more stable in the so-called Exact or Pure Sciences, they show less consensus in SSH (this has been widely documented in the construction of documentary thesauri). One can expect a greater number of competing terminological databases, in other words, of competing ontologies. This may have a number of possible consequences. One of them can be the proliferation of sameAs-based triples: a growing number of entities in different ontologies may be recognized as actually being the same entity – or at least similar enough to warrant a sameAs link. Eventually this can lead to more and more links between entities that are increasingly dissimilar. A different consequence of competing ontologies may actually be a tendency towards standardization: the fact that the data is linked allows interconnections (and a potential for standardization) that are not observed or required when competing research teams work independently. And in fact, work on ontologies may turn out to have a significant effect on the definition of the basic concepts of the disciplines and the attempts at bridging across disciplines. Work in terminology and thesaurus design could have a major impact in cross-disciplinary (as well as basic disciplinary) research.

Impact on data collection and analysis

In our study of SW/LD-based research, we have identified two main impacts on data collection and analysis. First, there are technical implications associated with the efforts required to gather data, and the skills necessary to process them. Secondly, a SW/LD-driven research method leads to a blurred distinction between data and metadata.

Technical implications

The efforts required to gather data in the SSH is much greater than it is the Pure Sciences. For SSH, where large amounts of data still lie in historical documents, in music partitions, in dictionaries, in field manuals, in legal documents (let alone the tacit, undocumented data in social practice), data must be gathered manually, by intellectual methods: reading, interpretation, observation. This is in sharp contrast to the Pure and Applied Sciences, where large amounts of data are being gathered today by automatic means: by probes or sensors, by extraction from databases, by computer generation. So the data-driven science craze has very different implications and may suffer more resistance in the SSH.

The technical computer skills needed to tackle a research project where LD plays an important role are not mastered by all researchers. It requires a formal and analytical approach which may be at odds with some research methods or indeed with some entire fields of study. Specific training must be provided regarding the basics of Semantic Web technologies. New skills will be needed – on "elements of mathematics, logic, engineering, and computer science" (Unsworth, 2016, p. 46). This may be disconcerting. For instance, the historian will need to concern himself with the structure of the data and no longer simply with their delivery (Michon, 2016, p. 17).

Blurred distinction between data and metadata

As suggested by the examples above, some triples are clearly metadata (e.g. Tolstoy is-the-author-of War and Peace). Others introduce true relationships between two entities with an equivalent status (e.g. Tolstoy has-written-to Ghandi). Yet they are treated in the same manner by the RDF triples. If triples are created by extracting data from primary documents, then in a sense all such encoding becomes metadata. But if all is metadata, what is the data? Do the data disappear? Or is it rather the concept of metadata which disappears?

Impact on resulting model

Our observations lead to what French researchers (Pédauque, 2007) have described as « Redocumenting » (« Redocumentarisation »). This refers to the process, in the late 20th and early 21st century, of large-scale digitization of existing print documents: "redocumenting" is performing anew the process of documenting human endeavours. A similar process took place with the invention of the printing press, when handwritten documents were gradually typeset and printed. And so the encoding of triples in RDF is, in fact, another process of taking existing information (contained in narrative or unstructured documents already on the Web) and transcoding it into a new form. The output of research then includes an analytical model consisting of Linked Data. This new form is deemed necessary to allow the sophisticated automated semantic processing by software agents. It is thus seen as somewhat unavoidable. And, given the simple binary nature of RDF triples, this redocumenting leads to the atomization of research described above.

CONCLUSION

We have examined some research projects which take advantage of possibilities afforded by SW/LD technology. Our goal was to pinpoint aspects of the research methodology which are impacted by the technology. Our examination of these cases has revealed three main points of impact. The first is the epistemological foundations of the research; the focus is on individual entities in the research area, leading to what we have called the "atomization" of research. This in turn favours analytical skills in the researcher rather than his or her ability to synthesize and abstract away from specific phenomena. In addition, all research phenomena are reified – raised to a concrete status in their representation by URIs, regardless of their original characteristics. Secondly, and unsurprisingly, it is the data analysis phase which is affected the most; it relies more heavily on technical skills during data discovery and processing. It obscures the distinction between data and metadata, thus requiring even more analytical skills from the researcher to diligently differentiate between the two as necessary. Thirdly, we have shown how the model-building aspect of research is affected by SW/LD-driven approaches, in the sense that existing models of knowledge (i.e. existing documents) require a transcoding into this new format in order to facilitate further research.

The scale of the efforts to produce LD datasets is such that it cannot be ignored, and research in SSH must take it into account, as so much useful data are now available. Transformations to the conduct of research is inevitable. But it is important to understand how this shift may affect research methodology. What is needed then is new solutions for new challenges.

Some additional thoughts: the implications vary for different disciplines. Data-oriented disciplines, such as Economics or Demography may see little change. For metadata-oriented disciplines (Library Science, Museum Studies, etc.), the shift entails fairly straightforward transformations (with the caveat that data and metadata may be difficult to distinguish). It is the document-oriented disciplines that should see the greatest change – History, Literature or Sociology, for instance. And yet it can be argued that the basis of data analysis is at the heart of such disciplines. In the words of (Sherratt 2015):

> *Let's think for a moment about the work of a historian — identifying actors, defining relationships, documenting the complex networks that bring together people, places and events over time. It's painstaking, exhilarating and potentially soul-destroying work. It's also an exercise in data modelling. Whether the results are preserved in a triplestore, a spreadsheet, or on a drawer full of index cards — it's nodes and edges, it's entities and relationships, it's data.*

REFERENCES

Allik, A., Fazekas, G., & Sandler, M. (2016). An Ontology for Audio Features. In *Proceedings of the 17th ISMIR Conference* (pp. 73–79). New York (NY).

Arsham, H. (2015). *Applied Management Science: Making Good Strategic Decisions*. Retrieved from http://home.ubalt.edu/ntsbarsh/opre640/opre640.htm

Ayres, M.-L. (2012). *Digging deep in Trove: Success, challenge and uncertainty*. National Library of Australia. Retrieved 29 March 2018, from https://www.nla.gov.au/our-publications/staff-papers/digging-deep-in-trove-success-challenge-and-uncertainty

Baronov, D. (2004). *Conceptual foundations of social research methods*. Boulder; London: Paradigm Publishers.

Berners-Lee, T. (2006, July 27). *Linked Data - Design Issues*. Retrieved 3 April 2018, from https://www.w3.org/DesignIssues/LinkedData.html

Berners-Lee, T., Hendler, J., & Lassila, O. (2001). The Semantic Web. *Scientific American*, 28–37.

Blanke, T., Bodard, G., Bryant, M., Dunn, S., Hedges, M., Jackson, M., & Scott, D. (2012). Linked data for humanities research: The SPQR experiment. In *6th IEEE International Conference on Digital Ecosystems and Technologies (DEST)* (pp. 1–6). https://doi.org/10.1109/DEST.2012.6227932

Borgman, C. L. (2012). The conundrum of sharing research data. *Journal of the American Society for Information Science and Technology*, 63(6), 1059–1078. https://doi.org/10.1002/asi.22634

Borgman, C. L. (2015). *Big Data, Little, Data, No Data. Scholarship in the Networked World*. Cambridge, MA: MIT Press.

Boyd, D., & Crawford, K. (2012). Critical Questions for Big Data. Information, *Communication & Society*, 15(5), 662–679. https://doi.org/10.1080/1369118X.2012.678878

Brando, C., Frontini, F., & Ganascia, J.-G. (2016). REDEN: Named Entity Linking in Digital Literary Editions Using Linked Data Sets. *Complex Systems Informatics and Modeling Quarterly*, 60–80. https://doi.org/10.7250/csimq.2016-7.04

Bryman, A. (2015). *Social Research Methods*. Oxford University Press.

Cannam, C., Sandler, M., Jewell, M. O., Rhodes, C., & d'Inverno, M. (2010). Linked Data and You: Bringing Music Research Software into the Semantic Web. *Journal of New Music Research*, 39(4), 313–325. https://doi.org/10.1080/09298215.2010.522715

Chiarcos, C., Nordhoff, S., & Hellmann, S. (Eds.). (2012). *Linked data in linguistics: representing and connecting language data and language metadata*. Berlin ; New York: Springer.

Curado Malta, M., González-Blanco, E., Martínez Cantón, C., & Del Rio, G. (2017). A Common Conceptual Model for the Study of Poetry in the Digital Humanities. In *Digital Humanities 2017 Conference Abstracts* (pp. 210–213). Montréal: ADHO.

d'Aquin, M., & Motta, E. (2016). *The epistemology of intelligent semantic web systems*. San Rafael, California: Morgan & Claypool. Retrieved from http://www.morganclaypool.com/doi/pdf/10.2200/S00708ED1V01Y201603WBE014

Davis, I. (2009). *Representing Time in RDF Part 1*. Retrieved 1 February 2017, from http://blog.iandavis.com/2009/08/representing-time-in-rdf-part-1/

Eide, O., Felicetti, A., Ore, C. E., D'Andrea, A., & Holmen, J. (2008). Encoding Cultural Heritage Information for the Semantic Web. Procedures for Data Integration through CIDOC-CRM Mapping. In D. Arnold, F. Niccolucci, D. Pletinckx, & L. Van Gool (Eds.), *Open Digital Cultural Heritage Systems Conference* (pp. 47–53). Budapest: Archeolingua. Retrieved from http://culturalinformatics.org.uk/sites/culturalinformatics.org.uk/files/Rome_Pro_20111012.pdf#page=47

Halpin, H., Herman, I., & Hayes, P. J. (2010). When owl:sameAs isn't the Same: An Analysis of Identity Links on the Semantic Web. In *RDF Next Steps Workshop*. Palo Alto, CA. Retrieved from https://www.w3.org/2009/12/rdf-ws/papers/ws21

Hey, T., Tansley, S., & Tolle, K. (2009). *The Fourth Paradigm: Data-Intensive Scientific Discovery*. Redmond, VA: Microsoft Research.

Humphrey, E. J., Bello, J. P., & LeCun, Y. (2013). Feature learning and deep architectures: New directions for music informatics. *Journal of Intelligent Information Systems*, 41(3), 461–481.

Hyvönen, E. (2012). Publishing and Using Cultural Heritage Linked Data on the Semantic Web. *Synthesis Lectures on the Semantic Web: Theory and Technology*, 2(1), 1–159. https://doi.org/10.2200/S00452ED1V01Y201210WBE003

Kitchin, R. (2014). *The Data Revolution: Big Data, Open Data, Data Infrastructures and Their Consequences*. SAGE Publications.

Lewis, R., Raynor, C., Forest, D., Sinatra, M., & Sinclair, S. (Eds.). (2017). *Digital Humanities 2017 Conference Abstracts*. McGill; University; Université de Montréal: ADHO. Retrieved from https://dh2017.adho.org/abstracts/DH2017-abstracts.pdf

Michon, P. (2016). *Vers une nouvelle architecture de l'information historique : L'impact du Web sémantique sur l'organisation du Répertoire du patrimoine culturel du Québec*. Master's thesis. Université de Sherbrooke, Sherbrooke. Retrieved from http://hdl.handle.net/11143/8776

Pédauque, R. T. (2007). *La Redocumentarisation du monde*. Paris: Éditions Cépadues.

Sherratt, T. (2007). *Inigo Jones : the weather prophet*. [Melbourne] : Bureau of Meteorology. Retrieved from https://trove.nla.gov.au/version/38963121

Sherratt, T. (2015, April 10). *Stories for Machines - Data for Humans*. Retrieved from http://discontents.com.au/stories-for-machines-data-for-humans/

Sherratt, T. (2016, August 25). *Telling stories with data – discontents*. Retrieved 29 March 2018, from http://discontents.com.au/telling-stories-with-data/

Unsworth, J. (2016). What is Humanities Computing and What is Not? In M. Terras, J. Nyhan, & E. Vanhoutte, *Defining Digital Humanities. A Reader* (pp. 35–47). London: Routledge.

van Peer, W., Hakemulder, F., & Zyngier, S. (2012). *Scientific methods for the humanities*. Amsterdam: John Benjamins Publishing Company.

Gender differences in Music Search Behaviour on Social Q&A Sites: A Case Study on Zhihu

Shengli Deng
Wuhan university, China. victorydc@sina.com

Ruhua Huang*
Wuhan university, China. rhhuang@whu.edu.cn

Anqi zhao
Wuhan university, China. zaq.12345@foxmail.com

ABSTRACT

In spite of ample studies on music information behaviour, little is known on how music search behaviour is performed on social question and answer (social Q&A) sites by considering gender differences. Based on a collection of 12,331 music questions collected from Zhihu, the study adopted a mixed research methodology and performed both quantitative analysis and qualitative content analysis to explore gender differences in music search behaviour on social Q&A sites. The results show that males are associated with more questions, answers and followers than females. Males asked question on social Q&A sites mainly for seeking ready reference, whereas females often asked question to promote a discussion. When formulating questions, females tend to use second pronouns and interrogative words like "what" more often than males. In contrast, questions from males tend to include more words and are thus longer than the questions from females. In addition, questions asked by males tend to attract more answers than those from females. Our results shed light to current music information behaviour studies and contribute new insights to the development of a better music service system.

KEYWORDS

Gender differences, music information behaviour, Social Q&A.

INTRODUCTION

Along with a rapid advance of network bandwidth and Internet services, listening to music online is becoming more and more popular in people's daily life. The number of online music users is reported to reach 524 million, or 69.8% of all Chinese Internet users, in June 2017 (Iresearch, 2017). About 80% of Chinese online music users listen to music every day, and 40.9% of them listen to music more than an hour per day (CNNIC, 2017).

Noticeably, music information demands are complex and diversified in nature. In this vein, social Q&A sites, such as Zhihu, Quora and Yahoo Answers, provide new instruments for users to obtain music information. Specifically, social Q&A sites allow users to ask questions using their own natural language and obtain answers from other users. Social Q&A has attracted many studies on the topics like what information users ask, how users describe their information requirements, and how to choose high-quality answers (e.g. Choi et al., 2016; Kim, 2010). In this light, music information behaviour in social Q&A has become an important research topic in the field (e.g. Hertzum et al., 2017).

Gender makes people's identity and differs their behaviours. Past studies discerned that gender differences affect user's friend-making motivations in social networking (Therwall, 2008), emotional perception (Pennebaker et al., 2011) and language performance (Large et al., 2002). Whereas ample studies have investigated gender differences in information behaviour (Lim et al., 2010; Rowley et al., 2015), little is known on whether and how gender difference manifested itself in the context of music information behaviour. Understanding the gender differences in music information behaviour can not only add new insights to gender-incurred information behaviour, but also offer reference for practitioners to manage music information system in a more effective manner.

In this study, we manually categorized 12,331music questions collected from Zhihu, a popular social Q&A site in China, and explore the gender differences embodied in the questions. Specifically, the study endeavours to address the following research question:

RQ: What are the differences in questioner's motivations, emotional expression and questioning style between males and females?

---

* Corresponding author: rhhuang@whu.edu.cn

The remainder of the paper is structured as follow: Section 2 provides a literature review on music information behaviour, information behaviour on social Q&A sites and gender differences in information behaviour. Section 3 discusses the methodology while Section 4 explains data analysis. Results are discussed in Section 5. Thereafter, we conclude the paper, highlight limitations and discuss directions for further research in Section 6.

LITERATURE REVIEW

Music information users, needs, and acquisition

Past studies have been mostly focused on two kinds of online music users: i) general online music information users (Lee et al., 2004; Laplante et al., 2006; Hu et al., 2014), and ii) music professionals who has a good knowledge of music, including music performers, music students, and musicians (Liew et al., 2006; Hunter et al., 2006; Korfiatis et al., 2015; Baharuddin, 2016). For example, the study of Kostagiolas (2017) explored the relationship between musicians' personality traits and their information seeking behaviour.

Individuals seeking for music information have reported a diversity of motivations. Most music information demands are relevant to music itself. For instance, a study shows that users who asked music-relevant questions on Google Answers were mainly for the purpose of identifying works, artists and recordings (e.g., album, LP, CD, audiotape) (Lee, 2010). Some studies alleged that seeking for identification, recommendation or evaluation on music is key motivations of music information behaviour (Downie et al., 2002; Lee et al., 2005). In addition, music information demands may be relevant to bibliographic information like music title and artists (Lee et al., 2016), or musical knowledge such as musical theories (Fu et al., 2016).

Recent studies started to explore natural language queries in attempt to understand the characteristics of queries across different music information retrieval systems. For instance, Bainbridge et al. (2003) explored how users express their music information demand by analysing 502 real-world music queries. They found that users often provided some form of bibliographic metadata when describing their information request, and the most common bibliographic metadata are relevant to the name of the performers and the title of a work. Laplante et al. (2011) reported that satisfaction with a music information retrieval system could depend on both hedonic (i.e., experiencing pleasure) and utilitarian outcomes in the context of everyday life.

Information behaviour on social Q&A sites

The popularity of social Q&A sites offers a new channel for people to acquire and share music information. Especially, Yahoo answers (Adamic et al., 2008; Bowler et al., 2012; Cunningham et al., 2014) and Google answers (Lee et al. 2007) are the popular social Q&A sites widely utilized to study information behaviour.

Recent studies on information behaviour on social Q&A sites are mainly focused on two streams of topics, including user behaviour and information content, respectively. Researches on user behaviour normally focused on user profiles, motivations and participations in information behaviour. Wang et al. (2016) identified four collaborative roles (starter, answerer, technical editor and follower) of users in Zhihu.com. Nam et al. (2009) analysed user behaviour on Naver Knowledge, the largest question-answering online community in South Korea. They found that altruism, learning, and competency motivated users to provide knowledge services for others. Choi et al. (2016) alleged that Wiki Answers users more often ask fact-related questions, whereas Yahoo Answers users tend to ask for opinion and advice.

In the studies on information content, scholars often investigated question types and answer features. In line with the study of Harper et al. (2010), Hertzum et al. (2017) categorized music-related questions on Yahoo answers into six types, including advice, identification, (dis)approval, quality, prescriptive, and factual. Bae et al. (2017) investigated the features of the answers that questioners want on social Q&A.

Gender influence on information behaviour

As a cultural and social dimension of personality, gender manifested itself in various behaviours of males and females. Many studies have related gender to information behaviour. For instance, Lim et al. (2010) found that male students used Wikipedia more frequently compared to their female counterparts. Males have more positive attitudes, emotions, and behaviours toward unconventional information source than females. Regarding the online health information-seeking behaviour, women were found to consult more sources than men did (Rowley et al., 2015).

Gender differs people's motivation of performing information behaviour alike. Based on a large-scale questionnaire survey, Steinerová et al. (2007) found that the main purpose of using online information resources for females was to learn, while males preferred to publish information. Lim et al. (2010) reported that male students used Wikipedia for entertainment or idle reading more than female counterparts.

Research reported gender differences in people's language expression behaviour. Males were found to formulate queries using fewer keywords than females when searching in web (Large et al., 2002). Otterbacher (2010) noted that female movie reviewers written in a more involved style and often in first person voice. In contrast, men often use a re-porting style, discussing "the movie" or "a film" and making use of the third person pronouns "his" and "it". It is noteworthy that, despite ample studies on gender differences in information behaviour, there is a paucity of studies on how gender affects music information behaviour on social Q&A platforms.

As the number of music information users are increasing rapidly and the demand of users become more diversified, social Q&A sites have been an important place for users to obtain information. In addition, given the evidence of gender differences in previous studies, male and female users may have different motivations, emotional expression and question style. Whereas that current researches have been performed on information behaviour of social Q&A sites, little studies have explored gender differences under the background of music information behaviour. This article addresses this research gap and contributes to understanding the gender influence on shaping music information search behaviour, which may aid in the development of music information system.

METHODOLOGY

Study Site: Zhihu

With 69 million users by 2017, Zhihu is one of the most popular social Q&A sites in China. It has accumulated 15 million questions, 55 million answers and 250 thousand topics by March 2017, drawing over 9 billion monthly visits (Wang et al., 2017). In Zhihu, users are able to ask questions, discuss and interact with others on the site. A question in Zhihu can be "fol-lowed" by users so that they would receive notifications about this question, e.g. when the question is answered. Concerning "music" topic, Zhihu currently hosts 174 thousand questions followed by 12 million users. Zhihu associates questions with one or several tags to indicate the domain of the question.

Data Collection

We performed a mixed-method design to explore gender differences in music search behaviour on Zhihu. Considering the types of analyses, we adopted qualitative content analysis to extract the characteristics of questioner's motivations, emotional ex-pression and question style. To compare the characteristics between males and females, it was indispensable to conduct a follow-up quantitative statistical analysis to calculate if the observation was statistically significant or just by accident.

Developed under OSI-approved open source license, Python is freely usable and hosts thousands of third-party modules. By using Python network crawler, we downloaded all the questions that are included in the "music" tag and published between May 2017 and November 2017. For each question, we collected the data of question text, question-posting date, answer count, and questioners' profile. For each profile, the data regarding questioner's gender and numbers of answers, questions and fol-lowers pertaining to the questioner are collected. In the data, 18,880 questions out of 39,228 total questions (48.13%) are from those who specified their gender in the profiles. After removing irrelevant and duplicate questions, the final data is comprised of 12,331questions, of which 5,170 are from males in comparison to 7,161 from females. Among the remaining 12331 ques-tions, we found 10814 unique users, and 4477(41.40%) of them were males whereas 6337(58.60%) were females.

Coding Scheme Development

Questioner's motivations

Classification	Definitions and examples
Description	Questions asking for a description of something (e.g., description of artist, album). ● What kind of person is Kim Hee Chul?
Recommendation	Questions asking for a list of music related information objects. ● Are there any particularly good Tibetan songs recommended?
Evaluation	Questions asking for opinions on songs, singers, musical activities, etc. ● How to evaluate the twelfth album of Wang Feng?
Ready Reference	Questions asking for simple, objective or factual information. ● What does the C tone mean?
Guidance	Questions asking for a solution, or a plan to complete a practice of music. ● How to join the Chinese rock association?
Discussion	Questions seeking to establish a communication or discussion with others on a given topic relevant to music. ● Is it really meaningful to be a starstruck?
Resources	Questions seeking for musical resources such as lyrics, photos etc. ● Who knows the download address of this song?

Table 1. Coding categories of questioner's motivation

Past studies discerned that the question-asking behaviours on social Q&A sites are driven by various motivations. Lee (2010) categorized the questions into nine types, including identification, location, verification, recommendation, evaluation, ready reference, reproduction, description, and research. Built upon the work of Lee (2010), we merged the "location" and "reproduction" categories into one category of "resources", because they both point to an effort to obtain musical resources. To simplify the classification, we incorporated the "identification" and "verification" categories into a "ready reference" category, because they both seek to ask for factual information describe factual questions. Considering the unique nature of Zhihu, we included two categories, "guidance" and "discussion", which is in line with the work of Harper et al. (2010) and Fu et al. (2016). As a result, the coding scheme consists of seven types of motivations, including description, recommendation, evaluation, ready reference, guidance, discussion and resources, as shown in Table 1.

Emotional expression

Music, as an art of emotion, can have a strong emotional impact on the audience, create imagination, and trigger the resonance of spirit. When listening to music, users may establish a subjective psychological feeling. In both eastern and western cultures, women have been considered to be more emotional (Belk et al.,1986). Robinson et al. (1998) reported that males were more willing to convey more socially desirable self-oriented emotions such as pride, whereas females tend to express the opposition such as guilty. Past studies indicated that emotion plays an essential role in affecting the users' information behaviour. Stieglitz et al. (2013) pointed out that the positive or negative sentiment in political Twitter messages are significantly related to retweet behaviour not only the quantity but also the speed. Hertzum et al. (2017) examined senso-emotional experience user experience conveyed in the questions on social Q&A sites. They found that 12% of the 3897 music questions on Yahoo Answers embodied the questioner's personal emotion, albeit unrelated to gender differences. Past studies have shown that the influence of emotion on music processing varied with gender (e.g. Gutiérrez et al., 2009).

We were interested in whether emotional expression differs by gender, so we identified the emotions expressed in individual questions. As a result, 1,755 (14.23%) questions are found to express personal emotions. Based on the existing and current framework (e.g. Pletea et al., 2014), the questions are further classified into 4 mutually exclusive categories of positive, negative, neutral and multiple emotion, as defined in Table 2.

Classification	Definitions and examples
Positive	Questions are associated with positive emotional expressions like happy, enthusiastic, excited, elated, peppy, euphoric, aspirated, persistent etc. ● Wang Lihong do have a lovely and magnetic voice. What do you think of his voice characteristics?
Neutral	Questions are associated with neither positive nor negative emotional expressions, such as curiosity. ● Compared to discuss the result of program named Hip-Hop in China, I am more curious about who can be competent for the producers in the second season.
Negative	Questions are associated with negative expressions like sadness, nervousness, jittery, anxiety, angry, hopelessness and disappointment, etc. ● What are the songs that people in a bad mood can listen to?
Multiple	Questions are associated with both positive and negative emotions, or emotions have changed over time, for example, from positive to negative. ● I can listen to a song for infinite times because I love it so much before. But I can't find the feeling now, sometimes even a little bitter. Have you ever felt that?

Table 2. Coding categories of emotional expression

Question style

The third classification concerns the style of questions, such as the use of personal pronouns, interrogative words, the words to show politeness, and the length of the question, as shown in Table 3.

Classification	Definitions and examples
Pronouns	Pronouns used in the questions, including: First person pronouns: I, me, we, us, etc. Second person pronouns: you, your, etc. Third person pronouns: he, him, she, her, etc.
Interrogative words	Whether interrogative words are used in the question text, such as "what", "where", "when", "who", "why", "how", etc.
Politeness	Whether words to show respect or greeting are used, such as "thank you", "excuse me", etc.
Question length	The number of words used in a question, including punctuation marks.

Table 3. Coding categories of questioning style

This classification is consistent with past studies. Otterbacher (2010) unraveled that female movie reviewers frequently wrote in the first person. Rath et al. (2017) pointed out that a presence of interrogative words in a question increases the likelihood that it will be answered. Some users tend to show gratitude or respect when they put up questions (Jeng et al., 2017). Politeness is extracted as one of dimensions in a multi-dimensional model for assessing the quality of answers on social Q&A sites (Zhu et al., 2009). Showing politeness in a question may facilitate the acquisition of answers. Adamic et al. (2008) and Harper et al. (2008) discovered that very short questions is not efficient in attracting answers.

The process of categorizing the questions involved three steps. First, two coders independently performed a preliminary coding of 500 questions. Based on the results, inconsistent coding results between two coders are discussed with the third coder and conflicts are solved to reach an agreement. Following the data coding process described above, all questions are coded. We measured the consistency between coders via the Cohen's kappa coefficients, which were 0.81, 0.72, 0.91 for the classification on question motivation, emotional expression and question style, respectively. The results imply that the coding data are reliable (Lazar et al., 2009).

ANALYSIS

Data were entered in IBM SPSS Statistics 22. To determine the significance of difference between males and females, the T-test was performed in terms of all the variables (i.e., number of questions, number of answers, number of followers, each category of questioner's motivation, etc.).

User profiles

Based on the data of user profiles, the average values in terms of the numbers of questions, answers and followers of users are computed, as shown in Table 4. On average, users are found to ask 10.00 (SD = 52.403) questions. Especially, 2.6% of the users asked questions more than 50 times while 31% of them only posted one question. Averagely, users answered 55.32 (SD = 529.450) questions. In particular, 13.9% of the users offer more than 50 answers in comparison to 32.9% of the users who offer no or just one answer.

	Male (N = 5,170)	Female (N = 7,161)	Total (N = 12,331)
Number of Questions	16.27	5.48	10.00
Number of Answers	106.12	18.65	55.32
Number of Followers	1,122.14	129.6	545.74

Table 4. User Profiles (Mean)

Male users contributed to 5,170 questions (41.93%) in comparison to 7,161 questions (58.07%) by female users. Averagely, male users tend to ask more questions (Mean = 16.27, SD = 76.957) than female users (Mean = 5.48, SD = 720.117) (F = 257.758, $p < 0.001$). The standard deviation of the number of questions asked by males was nearly ten times larger than that of females. In addition, male users prefer to answer more questions (Mean = 106.12, SD = 809.379) than female users (Mean = 18.65, SD = 81.157) (F = 189.660, $p < 0.001$). Male users (Mean = 1,122.14, SD = 11,919.456) are found to have more followers than female users (Mean = 129.6, SD = 1,471.137) (F = 164.494, $p < 0.001$). To some extent, this shows that male users are more active than female users on Zhihu.

		All Questions	All Answers	All Followers
Answers (Total)	Pearson correlation	.010	.004	.029**
	Saliency(bilateral)	.271	.648	.001
	N	12,331	12,331	12,331
Answers (Males)	Pearson correlation	.006	.140**	.216*
	Saliency(bilateral)	.663	.000	.000
	N	5,170	5,170	5,170
Answers (Females)	Pearson correlation	.023*	.037**	.030**
	Saliency(bilateral)	.050	.002	.010
	N	7,161	7,161	7,161
*. a significant correlation at the 0.05 level(bilateral) **. a significant correlation at the 0.01 level(bilateral)				

Table 5. Correlation

To verify whether user profiles had influenced on the acquisition of answers, correlation analysis was conducted. It was shown that answers that a question obtained, and questioner's followers were positively correlated for either men or women. But the correlation for females was more significant than that for males, with the 0.01 level(bilateral). In addition, the answers of the question asked by females was significantly correlated with the all questions and all answers that they had contributed on Zhihu.

Questioner's motivation

Table 6 describes the distribution of motivations driving question-asking behaviours. The most important motivation is to raise discussion (30.66%). Note that, 25.89% of the questions is asked for ready reference. The proportions of questions seeking for guidance and evaluation are 13.05% and 14.53% respectively. Females often ask questions for discussion (33.07%). In contrast, seeking ready reference represents the main motivation for the males (28.92%). Males asked for opinions (category "evaluation") (18.80%) more often than females (11.45%)， F = 526.906, $p < 0.001$.

Table 6 also suggests that questions motivated by evaluation and discussion purposes are more likely to attract answers than questions seeking for description, ready reference and resources, independent of gender difference. When asking questions for recommendation (F = 9.916, p = 0.002) and discussion (F = 4.124, p = 0.042), the questions asked by males tend to receive significant more answers than females.

Category	Male (N = 5,170)			Female (N = 7,161)			Total (N = 12,331)		
	N	%	Answers (Mean)	N	%	Answers (Mean)	N	%	Answers (Mean)
Description	139	2.69%	4	177	2.47%	7	316	2.56%	6
Recommenda-tion	502	9.71%	22	726	10.14%	3	1,228	9.96%	10
Evaluation	972	18.80%	15	820	11.45%	21	1,792	14.53%	18
Ready reference	1,495	28.92%	3	1,697	23.70%	4	3,192	25.89%	4
Guidance	579	11.20%	3	1,030	14.38%	3	1,609	13.05%	3
Discussion	1,413	27.33%	22	2,368	33.07%	16	3,781	30.66%	18
Resources	49	0.95%	1	167	2.33%	2	216	1.75%	2
Other	21	0.41%	1	176	2.46%	2	197	1.60%	2

Table 6. Questioner's Motivations

Emotional expression

The distribution of the questions with regard to emotional expression are described in Table 7. The final data is comprised of 1,755 questions associated with emotional expression, of which 633 (36.07%) are from males in comparison to 1,122(63.93%) from females. Overall, questioners were more inclined to express positive emotions, other than negative ones. No significant differences were found between males and females in emotional expression.

A question embodying positive and multiple emotions was more likely to obtain answers than a question expressing neutral or negative emotions, and this effect is independent of the gender of questioner. Regarding questions expressing multiple emotions, the average number of answers received by male questioners is 512, which is significant more than female questioner (N = 11, F = 23.220, p < 0.001).

Polarity	Male(N=633)			Female(N=1,122)			Total(N=1,755)		
	N	%	Answers (Mean)	N	%	Answers (Mean)	N	%	Answers (Mean)
Positive	361	57.03%	9	698	62.21%	20	1,059	60.34%	16
Neutral	93	14.69%	5	150	13.37%	3	243	13.85%	4
Negative	157	24.80%	5	236	21.03%	10	393	22.39%	8
Multiple	22	3.48%	512	38	3.39%	11	60	3.42%	195

Table 7. Emotional expression

Person Pronouns	Male (N=5,170)			Female (N=7,161)			Total (N=12,331)		
	N	%	Answers (Mean)	N	%	Answers (Mean)	N	%	Answers (Mean)
First person pronouns	287	5.55%	7	403	5.63%	12	690	5.60%	10
Second person pronouns	363	7.02%	42	646	9.02%	27	1,009	8.18%	32
Third person pronouns	264	5.11%	7	355	4.96%	9	619	5.02%	8

Table 8. Person pronouns

Question style

Only 19.32% of the questions are found to use personal pronouns, in which the largest category is the second personal pronouns. As can be seen in Table 8, females (19.61%) preferred to use personal pronouns when asking questions in comparison with the males (17.68%) (F = 17.409, p < 0.001). It is noticeable that the second pronouns were used more often by women than men (F =17.409, p<0.001). A question using the second personal pronouns was more likely to obtain more answers than that using the first (F = 14.331, P < 0.001) and third person pronouns (F = 10.368, p = 0.001). However, no significant difference cross gender was found in terms of the average number of answers when using the same personal pronouns.

The results show that 8,751 out of the 12,331 questions (70.97%) used interrogative words, and questions asked by females (74.18%) were more likely to use interrogative words in comparison to those asked by males (68.65%) (F = 186.768, p <

0.001). The most prominent interrogative word used in questions is "How", while the least used interrogative word is "when", as shown in Figure 1. The use of interrogative words varied by gender as well according to a chi-square test ($p < 0.001$). There was a slightly higher proportion of females (14.84%) than males (12.92%) in the use of "what" ($F = 37.252$, $p < 0.001$). In contrast, the number of "how" used by females (32.84%) was noticeably lower than that of males (38.18%) ($F = 139.334$, $p < 0.001$). "Which" ($F = 13.375$, $p < 0.001$) and "why" ($F = 13.382$, $p < 0.001$) were also found to be significant, with less use in the questions for females.

Figure 2 shows that a question using "how" or "which" can attract more answers than a question using other interrogative words. Gender is found to significantly affect the number of answers concerning the questions using, "when" ($F = 6.869$, $p = 0.013$), "who" ($F = 9.796$, $p = 0.002$) and "what" ($F = 3.994$, $p = 0.046$).

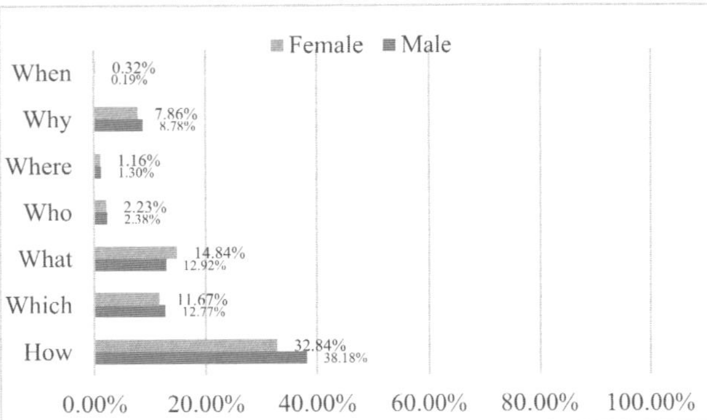

Figure 1. Measures of interrogative words

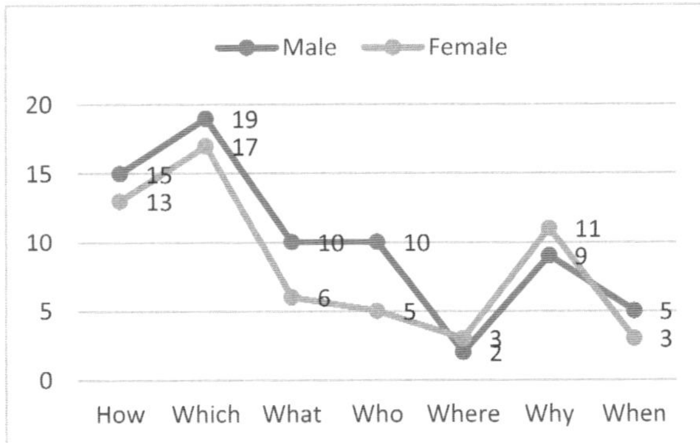

Figure 2. Average number of answers for questions classified by interrogative words

Females are more likely to express politeness in questions than males do ($F = 98.105$, $p < 0.001$). Besides, for the questions expressing politeness, male questioners (Mean = 4) received more answers than female questioners (Mean = 2) ($F = 7.189$, $p = 0.007$).

Based on all the questions, males (Mean = 22.36) were found to write significantly longer questions than females did (Mean = 20.89) ($F = 5.304$, $p = 0.021$).

DISCUSSION

Gender differences in user profiles

There were 5170 male-contributed questions and 7161 female-contributed questions. These numbers indicate that females are more proactive than males in the matter of asking music questions. However, it is interesting to contrast the finding with the total number that users contributed on Zhihu. The mean number of questions provided by females was 5.48, whereas for males the mean number was 18.65. In addition, it is worth noting that males in our data set has answered 6 times questions and attracted 9 times followers than the females. Therefore, to some extent, Zhihu is a male-majority social Q&A site, but as far as the music topic is concerned, females are more willing to ask questions. Halder et al. (2010) research showed that the main purpose using online information of females is to read or learn, while males preferred to publish information. Similar to earlier studies, Otterbacher (2013) have found additional evidence that IMDb is a male-majority forum.

Gender differences in music information behaviour

Our study identified some similarities between males and females in term of music information behaviour. On the questioner's motivations side, questions seeking for resources, description and recommendation remained very limited, accounting for less than 10% of the questions. By contrast, the discussion and ready reference categories were the largest. Then, on the emotional expression side, users were more inclined to express positive emotions instead of negative ones. Last, on the questioning style side, questioners preferred to use second personal pronouns and "How" as interrogative word.

Results reveal significant difference in gender concerning users' online music search behaviour. The average number of questions provided to Zhihu by females is 5.48, whereas the value is 16.27 for males. In addition, we found males answered significantly more questions and attracted significantly more followers in Zhihu than females. The results are in line with earlier studies. For instance, Otterbacher (2013) have found additional evidence that IMDb is a male-majority forum. Halder et al. (2010) showed that the main purpose to use online information for females is to read or learn, while males preferred to publish information.

On average, male questioners attract more answers than female questioners. Furthermore, within recommendation-seeking and discussion-seeking questions, multiple emotion-expressing questions, "when"-using, "who"-using and "what"-using questions, we observed that the number of answers in significantly likely to diverge by gender and the questions asked by males can receive more answers in contraction to females.

Comparison of music information behaviour on Zhihu and other social platforms

Many previous researches about social platforms focused on the question type or questioner's motivations. Fu et al. (2016) found that questions seeking for guidance were much more frequent, making up a relatively significant share (54.53%) of the whole 530 questions on Music Stack Exchange, while the ratio was only 13.05% on Zhihu. As a music question and answer community, the users of Music Stack Exchange are relatively monotonous, and most users are inclined to seek for guidance in order to improve their musical abilities or personal music accomplishment. In contrast, Zhihu is a comprehensive question and answer community, in view of breadth user groups and diverse backgrounds, seeking for discussion is the main questioner's motivations.

On Zhihu, the average length of the 12,331 music questions was 21.56 Chinese characters, which is much shorter than that of all the other social Q&A platforms in previous studies. The average length of the 3897 music questions was 41.30 words on Yahoo Answers (Hertzum et al., 2017). Each site has different question lengths, at Answerbag, the average length was 103 words, and at Metafilter, the average length was 844 words in Harper et al. (2010). On the one hand, the length of the questions varies according to the specific topics or the characteristics of one platform, on the other hand, it may be related to the characteristics of Chinese characters and the introverted character of Chinese.

CONCLUSION

By far, little study has been carried out to gender-based differences in the music search behaviour on social Q&A. Using Zhihu as the focus of our case study, this study adopted a mixed research methodology and performed both quantitative analyses and qualitative content analyses with 12,331 questions to examine gender differences in user profiles, questioner's motivations, emotional expression, and questioning style.

The results indicated that Zhihu is a male-majority social Q&A, but as for music topic, females were more willing to ask questions. In addition, the total number of questions, answers, followers for males were much higher than those of females. Answers a music question obtained and questioner's followers were positively correlated for either men or women. Secondly, the main motivation of males is to seek for ready reference, whereas the largest category of females is to seek for discussion. No significant differences were found between males and females in emotional expression. In specifying the questions, the second pronouns, interrogative words "what", and the words to show politeness are used more often by females than males. In contrast, length of questions males provided are longer than females, and the number of answers males received are more than females.

As in all studies, the present research is not free from limitations that need to be mentioned. First, our study payed more attention to gender differences in music information behaviour on Zhihu rather than on explaining why they existed. In other words, there is a lack of further fundamental explanations for gender differences. Second, there is room for improvement in analysing the answers content and the relationship between questions and answers.

For further studies, it would be interesting to find out if other factors such as age, education influence music information behaviour. The results indicated that there were some differences in music information behaviour between Zhihu in China and other western social Q&A sites. Accordingly, future research can explore cultural differences in term of music information behaviour. Finally, further studies using various approaches such as interviews or questionnaires can test, verify and enrich this paper.

REFERENCES

Adamic, L. A., Zhang, J., Bakshy, E., & Ackerman, M. S. (2008). Knowledge sharing and yahoo answers: everyone knows something. *Proceedings of the 17th international conference on World Wide Web* (pp. 665-674).

Bae, B. J., & Yi, Y. J. (2017). What answers do questioners want on social Q&A? User preferences of answers about STDs. *Internet Research*, 27(5), 1104-1121.

Baharuddin, K., Kassim, N. A., Ishak, N. H., Ariff, N. Z. Z. M., & Buyong, S. Z. (2016). Music Information Needs and Methods of Getting Information among Music Students in a Public Institution of Higher Education. *International Journal of Academic Research in Business and Social Sciences*, *6*(10), 44–51.

Bainbridge, D., Cunningham, S. J., & Downie, J. S. (2003). How People Describe their Music Information Needs: A Grounded Theory Analysis of Music Queries. *Proceedings of the 4th International Conference on Music Information Retrieval* (pp. 221–222).

Belk, S. S., & Snell, W. E. (1986). Beliefs about women: Components and correlates. *Personality and Social Psychology Bulletin, 12*(12), 403–413.

Bowler, L., Oh, J. S., He, D., Mattern, E., & Jeng, W. (2012). Eating disorder questions in Yahoo! Answers: Information, conversation, or reflection? *Proceedings of the ASIST Annual Meeting, 49*(1), 1-11.

Calefato, F., Lanubile, F., Merolla, M. R., & Novielli, N. (2015). Success factors for effective knowledge sharing in community-based question-answering. *Proceedigns of the 10th International Forum on Knowledge Asset Dynamics (IFKAD'15).*

China Internet Network Information Centre. (2017). The fortieth statistical report of Internet development in China. Retrieved December 27, 2017 from http://www.cac.gov.cn/2017-08/04/c_1121427728.htm.

Choi, E., & Shah, C. (2016). User motivations for asking questions in online Q&A services. *Journal of the Association for Information Science and Technology, 67*(5), 1182–1197.

Cunningham, S. J. & Hinze, A. (2014). Social, religious information behaviour: An analysis of Yahoo! Answers queries about belief. *Advances in the Study of Information and Religion, 4*, 1.

Downie, J. S., & Cunningham, S. J. (2002). Toward a theory of music information retrieval queries: System design implications. *Proceedings of the 3rd International Society for Music Information Retrieval Conference (ISMIR'02)*, 13–17.

Eagly, A. H. (1995). The science and politics of comparing women and men. *American psychologist*, 50(3), 145.

Fu, H., & Fan, Y. (2016). Music information seeking via social Q&A: An analysis of questions in Music StackExchange community. In *2016 IEEE/ACM Joint Conference on Digital Libraries (JCDL)* (pp. 139–142).

Gentile, C., Spiller, N., & Noci, G. (2007). How to Sustain the Customer Experience:. An Overview of Experience Components that Co-create Value With the Customer. *European Management Journal*, 25(5), 395–410.

Halder, S., Ray, A., & Chakrabarty, P. K. (2010). Gender differences in information seeking behaviour in three universities in West Bengal, India. *The International Information & Library Review, 42*(4), 242–251.

Harper, F. M., Raban, D., Rafaeli, S., & Konstan, J. A. (2008). Predictors of answer quality in online Q&A sites. *Proceedings of the twenty-sixth annual CHI conference on Human factors in computing systems - CHI '08* (p. 865).

Harper, F. M., Weinberg, J., Logie, J., & Konstan, J. A. (2010). Question types in social Q&A sites. *First Monday, 15*(7).

Hertzum, M., & Borlund, P. (2017). Music questions in social Q&A: an analysis of Yahoo! Answers. *Journal of Documentation, 73*(5), 992–1009.

Hu, X., Lee, J. H., & Wong, L. K. Y. (2014). Music information behaviours and system preferences of university students in Hong Kong. *Proceedings of the 15th International Society for Music Information Retrieval Conference* (pp. 579–584).

Hunter, B. (2006). A New Breed of Musicians : The Information-Seeking Needs and Behaviours of Composers of Electroacoustic Music. *Music Reference Services Quarterly, 10*(1), 1–15.

Iresearch. (2017). Report about online music users in China. Retrieved December 27, 2017 from http://www.iresearch.com.cn/report/3075.html.

Jeng, W., DesAutels, S., He, D., & Li, L. (2017). Information exchange on an academic social networking site: A multidiscipline comparison on researchgate Q&A. *Journal of the Association for Information Science and Technology, 68*(3), 638–652.

Kim, S. (2010). Questioners' credibility judgments of answers in a social question and answer site. *Information Research, 15*(2).

Kostagiolas, P. A., Lavranos, C., Korfiatis, N., Papadatos, J., & Papavlasopoulos, S. (2015). Music, musicians and information seeking behaviour. *Journal of Documentation, 71*(1), 3–24.

Kostagiolas, P., Lavranos, C., Martzoukou, K., & Papadato, J. (2017). The role of personality in musicians' information seeking for creativity. *Information Research, 22*(2).

Laplante, A., & Downie, J. S. (2006). Everyday Life Music Information-Seeking Behaviour of Young Adults. *Proceedings of the 7th International Conference on Music Information Retrieval* (pp. 381-382).

Laplante, A., & Downie, J. S. (2011). The utilitarian and hedonic outcomes of music information-seeking in everyday life. *Library and Information Science Research, 33*(3), 202–210.

Large, A., Beheshti, J., & Rahman, T. (2002). Gender differences in collaborative Web searching behaviour: An elementary school study. *Information Processing and Management, 38*(3), 427–443.

Lazar, J., Feng, J. H., & Hochheiser, H. (2009). Research methods in human-computer interaction. Handbook of Human-Computer Interaction (Second Edition), 203–227.

Lee, J. H. (2010). Analysis of user needs and information features in natural language queries seeking music information. *Journal of the American Society for Information Science and Technology, 61*(5).

Lee, J. H., Cho, H., & Kim, Y.-S. (2016). Users' music information needs and behaviours: Design implications for music information retrieval systems. *Journal of the Association for Information Science and Technology, 67*(6), 1301–1330.

Lee, J. H., & Downie, J. S. (2004). Survey of Music Information Needs, Uses, and Seeking Behaviours: Preliminary Findings. *Proceedings of the 5th International Conference on Music Information Retrieval* (pp. 441–446).

Lee, J. H., Downie, J. S., & Cunningham, S. J. (2005). Challenges in cross-cultural/multilingual music information seeking. *Proceedings of the 6th International Conference on Music Information Retrieval* (pp. 1–7).

Lee, J. H., Downie, J. S., & Jones, M. C. (2007). Preliminary Analyses of Information Features Provided by Users for Identifying Music. *Proceedings of the 8th International Conference on Music Information Retrieval* (pp. 325–328).

Liew, C. L., & Ng, S. N. (2006). Beyond the notes: A qualitative study of the information-seeking behaviour of ethnomusicologists. *Journal of Academic Librarianship*, *32*(1), 60–68.

Lim, S., & Kwon, N. (2010). Gender differences in information behaviour concerning Wikipedia, an unorthodox information source? *Library and Information Science Research*, *32*(3), 212–220.

Moeslinger, S. (1997). Technology at Home: A Digital Personal Scale. *CHI'97 Extended Abstracts on Human Factors in Computing Systems*, 216–217.

Nam, K. K., Ackerman, M. S., & Adamic, L. a. (2009). Questions in, knowledge in?: a study of naver's question answering community. *Proceedings of the 27th International Conference on Human Factors in Computing Systems*, 779–788.

Otterbacher, J. (2013). Gender, writing and ranking in review forums: A case study of the IMDb. *Knowledge and Information Systems*, *35*(3), 645–664.

Pennebaker, J. W., & Roberts, T.-A. (1992). Toward a His and Hers Theory of Emotion: Gender Differences in Visceral Perception. *Journal of Social and Clinical Psychology*, *11*(3), 199–212.

Pletea, D., Vasilescu, B., & Serebrenik, A. (2014, May). Security and emotion: sentiment analysis of security discussions on GitHub. *Proceedings of the 11th working conference on mining software repositories* (pp. 348-351).

Rath, M., Shah, C., & Floegel, D. (2017). Identifying the reasons contributing to question deletion in educational Q&A. *Proceedings of the Association for Information Science and Technology*, *54*(1), 327–336.

Robinson, M. D., Johnson, J. T., & Shields, S. A. (1998). The Gender Heuristic and the Database: Factors Affecting the Perception of Gender-Related Differences in the Experience and Display of Emotions. *Basic and Applied Social Psychology*, *20*(3), 206–219.

Rowley, J., Johnson, F., & Sbaffi, L. (2017). Gender as an influencer of online health information-seeking and evaluation behaviour. *Journal of the Association for Information Science and Technology*, *68*(1), 36–47.

Shah, C., & Pomerantz, J. (2010). Evaluating and predicting answer quality in community QA. *Proceeding of the 33rd international ACM SIGIR conference on Research and development in information retrieval - SIGIR '10* (p. 411).

Steinerova, J., & Susol, J. (2007). Users' information behaviour—a gender perspective. *Information Researchl*, *12*(3).

Stieglitz, S., & Dang-Xuan, L. (2013). Emotions and Information Diffusion in Social Media—Sentiment of Microblogs and Sharing Behaviour. *Journal of Management Information Systems*, *29*(4), 217–248.

Thelwall, M. (2008). Social networks, gender, and friending: An analysis of mySpace member profiles. *Journal of the American Society for Information Science and Technology*, *59*(8), 1321–1330.

Wang, W., Ji, Y. Q., Wang, H. W., & Zheng, L. J. (2017). Evaluating Chinese answers' quality in the community QA system: a case study of Zhihu. *Library and Information Service*, *61*(22), 36–44.

Wang, Z., & Zhang, P. (2016). Examining user roles in social Q&A: The case of health topics in Zhihu.com. *Proceedings of the Association for Information Science and Technology*, *53*(1), 1–6.

Zhu, Z., Bernhard, D., & Gurevych, I. (2009). A Multi-Dimensional Model for Assessing the Quality of Answers in Social Q&A Sites. *Proceedings of 14th International Conference on Information Quality*, *1*, 264–265.

Toward a Value-Analytic Approach to Information Standards

Brian Dobreski
Syracuse University School of Information Studies, USA
bjdobres@syr.edu

ABSTRACT

While developments in information technology enable exciting new potentials, they may, in the process, inadvertently violate important values such as autonomy or privacy. Responsible, ethical approaches to technology warrant the use of critical perspectives in evaluating our technological practices and artifacts. Key among such artifacts are information standards, influential documents that represent and perpetuate community agreements on ideal practice. In critically examining standards, values represent a promising conceptual lens. This paper advances the use of value analysis on information standards, particularly those devoted to knowledge organization. Value analysis is a methodological approach that guides the elicitation of values from artifacts. Two case studies demonstrate the application of value analysis to knowledge organization standards and their resulting data, and show how values and their implications can be discerned from these information artifacts. Value analysis must next be extended beyond standards as documents to examine the fuller ecosystem within which information standards are situated and enacted in order to fully understand their implications, uphold important community values, and maintain ethical information practices.

KEYWORDS

Values, information standards, knowledge organization, ethics.

INTRODUCTION

While developments in information technology enable exciting new potentials, they may, in the process, inadvertently violate our values. The creation, collection, and use of data is increasingly complex and opaque in all domains, and represents a growing threat to user autonomy and privacy. In order to sustain responsible, ethical approaches to information technologies, new, critical examinations of an array of technological practices and artifacts are warranted. Key among such artifacts are information standards, documents that represent and perpetuate community agreements on ideal practice and govern the creation and presentation of data. Standards are seemingly neutral pieces of infrastructure, but play a key part in embodying and perpetuating community perspectives (Bowker & Star, 2000). In further examining the role standards play in supporting or subverting ethical information practice, value analysis represents a promising evaluative lens.

Value theory conceptualizes values as deeply held beliefs in the preferability of certain ways of being or doing (Orsi, 2015). Put simply, values are any things that people or organizations consider to be important (Cheng & Fleischmann, 2010), though they are typically construed as abstract concepts such as efficiency or respect. Value theory and the study of values have been applied across domains, particularly in the social sciences. Within information science, values are already prominent in several streams of research, including professional ethics (Gorman, 2015; Koehler, 2015), and design (Friedman, Kahn, & Borning, 2002; Shilton, Koepfler, & Fleischmann, 2013). Though surveys and interviews are powerful methodological tools in examining values in all settings, eliciting values from written documents and other communicative artifacts has given rise to a distinct methodological tradition known as value analysis. In information science, value analysis has been applied to artifacts such as algorithms (Friedman & Nissenbaum, 1996) and tweets (Fleischmann et al., 2012), though at present, it has not been applied to information standards.

Standards are documents that codify and set forth specifications or protocols, and are agreed upon and distributed within a community (IEEE Standards Association, 2017). They serve to enable collective human activity but are often taken for granted in the process, leading to difficulties in discerning their role and effects (Busch, 2000; Bowker et al., 2009). Like all societal products, however, standards are shaped by the perspectives of those who produce them. Information standards oversee the creation and management of data and information systems, facilitating information access and sharing. In establishing ideal practice, information standards must espouse certain points of view at the expense of others (Lampland & Star, 2009), and may thus be seen as values-laden artifacts. What values these standards express, and whether they uphold or betray intended community values, is an open question.

In this paper, I advance a value-analytic approach to examining information standards as key technological artifacts. After reviewing relevant background concerning values in information science and the study of standards, I present two brief case studies. In these cases, I employ value analysis to demonstrate how values can be read from information standards and the data they are used to generate, and how standards and data embody and enforce systems of values. Following this, I then discuss the inherently values-laden and ethical nature of standards, and the implications of standards as value-bearing artifacts that are enacted through practice. I conclude that values are a useful evaluative tool for analyzing and designing information standards to support ethical technological practice, and outline an agenda for continued research in this area.

BACKGROUND AND APPROACH

The study of values has its origins in philosophy where it is known as value theory, referring not to a singular, formal theory, but rather, a discipline of inquiry (Orsi, 2015). Under value theory, values may take many forms but are usually depicted as abstract concepts such as happiness or efficiency; the values of rightness and goodness in particular are closely tied to ethics (Rescher, 1969). Inquiry into values has since flourished in other domains, especially the social sciences where it has been used to address motivation (McGuire, 1974), behavior (Rokeach, 1973), and social organization (Hofstede, 2003). Values have long been an important concept in information science, with much attention focusing on key values associated with the field and its practitioners, for example, access, intellectual freedom, and privacy (Bates, 1999; Gorman, 2015; Koehler, 2015). Beyond this reflexive emphasis on values, research in information science has also explored the interaction between values and technological design. One approach to understanding this relationship is value sensitive design (VSD), initially advanced by Friedman (1996) as a means of assessing how a set of heuristic values such as usability, autonomy, and freedom from bias are involved in the design of systems. A separate but similar area of study, known as values in design (ViD) focuses on a wider range of values beyond the heuristic, moral values of VSD and attempts to depart from such *post hoc* analyses (Knobel & Bowker, 2011). Recently, values and design (VaD) has been advanced as a general term to refer to both VSD and ViD research (Shilton, Koepfler, & Fleischmann, 2013).

In all domains, the content-analytic tradition of studying values associated with artifacts is referred to as value analysis (White, 1951). Early proponents of value analysis utilized pre-determined frameworks of values in the coding of textual data in order to reveal important, embedded values; approaches were typically quantitative (White, 1951; Rokeach, 1968). Later approaches to value analysis incorporated more inductive and qualitative methods, and moved beyond textual documents to examine other kinds of artifacts (Clawson & Vinson, 1978). Within the social sciences, value analysis has been applied to a range of materials including textbooks (Dhand, 1967), novels (Lester, 1982), and comic strips (Spiggle, 1986). Regardless of the specific content type analyzed, value analysis is designed to highlight the preferences and priorities embedded in a set of materials, and distill these into a system of values. In information science, value analysis has been used to analyze organizational codes of ethics, including those of library associations (Shachaf, 2005) and archival institutions (da Silva, Chaves Guimarães, & Bolfarini Tognoli, 2015). Most recently, automated and crowdsourced approaches to value analysis have been applied to social media to uncover user values (Fleischmann et al., 2012). Though VaD research has applied value analysis to technological artifacts such as algorithms (Friedman & Nissenbaum, 1996), so far, research in information science has not applied this approach to a key type of technological artifact in this area: standards.

Information standards serve as technological infrastructure, establishing guidelines for procedures and products and enabling collective work. There has been a particularly strong emphasis on standardization within the information domain (Delsey, 1989), especially concerning knowledge organization, the representation of knowledge or information in various forms of organizing systems (Andersen & Skouvig, 2006). Such standards are used extensively and serve to guide the creation and use of technologies such as classifications, ontologies, and databases, as well as associated data. Though widely adopted information standards tend to take on the appearance of neutrality (Olson, 2001), they have in fact been shown to embody specific perspectives at the expense of others (Bowker & Star, 2000; Lampland & Star, 2009). Critical analyses of terminological information standards in particular have revealed a range of embedded biases (Knowlton, 2005; Diao & Cao, 2016; Adler, Huber, & Nix, 2017). Though this body of research holds strong implications for values in information standards, values and value analysis in relation to these artifacts has not yet been formally addressed (Dobreski, 2017). While attention to the values in all information standards is critical, standards for knowledge organization present a particularly worthwhile site of investigation due to their ability to generate data that may further perpetuate embedded values.

Below, I present two case studies intended to illustrate the potentials of value analysis as an evaluative approach to knowledge organization standards and data. The first case study examines the text of several cultural heritage standards, focusing on passages concerning variations in a person's name and then following this element of data out into representations on the web. The second case study examines a bibliographic record produced under the library standard *Resource Description and Access* (RDA), placing it in the context of this standard's asserted goals and contrasting it with data from Google Books. Together, these cases show the utility of value analysis in examining important commitments embedded within knowledge organization standards and data. Further implications are explored following the case studies.

VARIANT NAMES FOR PERSONS

Cultural heritage is the study, preservation, and curation of cultural practices and artifacts passed down through societal groups (UNESCO, 2017). Given the complex and distributed nature of cultural heritage work, standards play an important role in coordinating activities in this domain, with knowledge organization standards holding special importance. Libraries, archives, and museums have devoted a great deal of energy to the creation, implementation, and maintenance of knowledge organizing systems. A major focus of standards in cultural heritage is resource description, the process of creating representations of artifacts and agents (Hider, 2012). Traditionally, libraries, archives, and museums have maintained their own distinct standards for resource description. Within the area of archives, *Describing Archives: A Content Standard* (DACS) (Society of American Archivists, 2013) serves as the *de facto* descriptive standard, emphasizing the structural and relational particulars of archival materials and their creators. For museums, *Cataloging Cultural Objects* (CCO) (Baca & Visual Resources Association, 2006) is a major content standard for describing works of art and other artifacts, and is often implemented in conjunction with structural standards including *Categories for the Description of Works of Art* (CDWA) and VRA Core. Within libraries, descriptive standards, commonly referred to as bibliographic standards, have guided the creation of catalog records for library resources and the persons and organizations associated with them. Over the past 40 years, a significant number of English-speaking libraries utilized the *Anglo-American Cataloging Rules, 2nd Ed.* (AACR2) as a descriptive standard. While many still do, 2010 saw the publication of AACR2's successor, the internationally focused *Resource Description and Access* (RDA), which is now being implemented by more and more libraries worldwide.

Despite the diversity of their intended settings and applications, descriptive standards in the cultural heritage domain prescribe and define a number of similar data elements, particularly for persons (Dobreski & Kwaśnik, 2017). For example, personal names, titles, and dates are common across cultural heritage standards. Each of these standards also differentiates between a preferred personal name and variant personal names. While the preferred name represents the "official" name to be used in a finding aid or catalog record, variant names represent any other name forms of significance. For example, while "George Eliot" may be the preferred name, "Marian Evans Cross" may be recorded as a key variant name for this author.

Given the similarities in concept and scope, the variant name instructions in AACR2, CCO, DACS, and RDA offer an opportunity to probe for differences in underlying value systems. While these four standards express the analogous concept of variant name, do they do so while expressing the same or different values? A brief value analysis of the initial instructions of the corresponding passages (Table 1) offers insight.

Standard	Passage	Instruction
AACR2	26.2A1	"Refer from a name used by a person, or found in reference sources, that is different from the name used in the heading for that person."
CCO	A.1.2.1.2.2	"Include alternate and variant names that appear in published sources and represent significant differences in form or spelling."
DACS	10.3	"Make a see reference from a form of the name of a person or corporate body or title of a work that might reasonably be sought to the form that has been chosen as the name or uniform title heading or as a title entry."
RDA	9.2.3.3	"Record a variant name for person that is considered important for identification or access by applying the general guidelines on recording names at 8.5."

Table 1. Corresponding passages concerning variant names.

At first glance, each of the standards appears to be placing value on the concept of use: use makes a particular variant name significant and justifies its inclusion in a record describing a person. Usage can be seen as a common value. However, a closer inspection of these instructions reveals important variations, particularly in determining whose usage is of value. For CCO, usage is limited to formally published sources. AACR2 refers somewhat similarly to usage in reference sources, but also includes usage by the actual person being described. DACS shifts the focus to usage by an implicit user, with variant names capturing any reasonable alternatives they may search under. Finally, RDA places value on two specific user tasks: identifying a person and accessing data about a person. Variant names that, to the cataloger's judgment, support these use cases are to be recorded.

We can see that while the concept of a variant name is similar, the associated values among the four standards are not. Different kinds of use are valued and thus justify a name as being significant or not. Value is given to formally published sources, to potential users, or to the person being described, and thus the resulting variant names recorded for one person may differ significantly among the four standards. Valuing or devaluing a person's own usage regarding their name has further implications for autonomy and self-identification as well. Even within the relatively narrow area of cultural heritage resource description, similar concepts carry differing values across different standards with immediate implications for data.

When expanded beyond the cultural heritage domain into the wider setting of the general web, we can see even greater variations among standardized naming practices. For example, the Wikipedia Manual of Style (MoS) prescribes guidelines for biographical articles with the goal of supporting consistency and ease of use, which we can interpret as an ostensible set of values ("Wikipedia: Manual of Style/Biographies," 2018). Functionally, MoS sets a standard for information to be included in articles representing persons. Specific rules are given concerning personal names, with the most commonly known form of a name serving as the article's title. Beyond this, the types of variants names and the order in which they are recorded are specified, including the fullest form of name, the birth name if different, other prior names of note, and any pseudonyms or nicknames.

Under these rules, consistency is clearly an important value, and may be seen as instrumental in supporting ease of use. Variant names are divided into common types and prescribed common treatments in all articles concerning persons. Usage, specifically the most "common," is most important in determining the article title, analogous to a preferred name in cultural heritage descriptions. Beyond this, variant names are implied to be derived from usage, though again, the question of whose usage is of value here is critical.

The Wikipedia article for Jake Zyrus lists the birth name and earlier stage names for the singer prior to his gender transition (Figure 1). The citations for the variant names in the Zyrus article are for recent online news articles. In justifying variant names on Wikipedia, all sources on the web thus constitute the realm of usage. However, in consulting the Library of Congress name authority file, we see that an RDA compliant authority record still lists the singer with a preferred name of Charice, and variant names given for his birth names, with no mention of Jake Zyrus (Figure 2). While this arrangement may be impeding the identification and access valued by RDA, it also reflects the differing conception of usage. Usage here reflects the library domain, and as the singer has only issued published recordings prior to adopting the Zyrus name, this name currently falls outside the range of materials relevant to usage. Beyond this, both the Wikipedia and RDA representations of Zyrus could potentially be seen as violating key human values such as privacy and self-identification.

Jake Zyrus	
Background information	
Birth name	Charmaine Clarice Relucio Pempengco
Also known as	Charice Pempengco · Charice

Figure 1. Wikipedia infobox for Jake Zyrus.

LC control no.:	no2009052666
LCCN Permalink:	https://lccn.loc.gov/no2009052666
Personal name heading:	Charice, 1992-
Variant(s):	Pempengco, Charice, 1992- Relucio Pempengco, Charmaine Clarice, 1992-
Found in:	Hit man [SR] p2008: container (Charice) Charice Pempengco WWW site, Apr. 3, 2009 (Charice Pempengco; Charice; b. Charmaine Clarice Relucio Pempengco, May 10, 1992, San Pedro, Laguna province, Philippines)

Figure 2. RDA record for Charice.

Though both cultural heritage and the wider web environment predicate variant names on usage, differing conceptions of whose usage is of value can lead to drastic differences in the ways in which people are named. The differences may hold other value implications and can significantly impact user understanding and access.

BIBLIOGRAPHIC REPRESENTATION

Like all standards, knowledge organization standards serve to bring practice into conformity (Svenonius, 2000). Within libraries, bibliographic standards have been designed to guide practices surrounding the creation of catalog data. The aforementioned standards AACR2 and RDA are the latest in a fairly linear succession of bibliographic standards that have brought increasing uniformity among catalog records over the past century. As the current *de facto* descriptive standard for libraries, RDA guides the creation of data for library catalogs, data that is also increasingly being shared outside the confines of the traditional catalog. RDA sets the current standard for a "good" bibliographic representation.

While the values of specific knowledge organization standards have yet to be fully explored, RDA offers evidence of its asserted values through the inclusion of an explicit statement on objectives and principles. Key objectives include fulfilling user needs, cost efficiency, and flexibility, while principles highlight differentiation, sufficiency, accurate representation, uniformity, and relationships (Canadian Library Association et al., 2010). Taken together, these objectives and principles can serve as an asserted value system, though how well the text of RDA upholds and expresses these values has not yet been assessed. However, another piece of critical evidence here is the resulting RDA bibliographic records. Each record compiles data prescribed by RDA for a specific resource, and may be seen as an enactment of the standard. Value analysis of bibliographic records can be used to gauge if the products of knowledge organization standards express values, and if so, how these values relate to those of the guiding standard.

Again, a brief value analysis of a specific case can offer further insight. Figure 3 presents a bibliographic record for the 2016 epistolary novel *The Pharos Gate: Griffin & Sabine's Lost Correspondence*, by Nick Bantock. This novel is the latest in a series of works documenting the correspondence of two fictional lovers through various art styles, post cards, and inserted letters. A bibliographic record was created for this resource by catalogers at the Library of Congress using the RDA standard; it has subsequently been revised and updated by a number of other institutions. Subject headings for the resource, which are dictated by separate knowledge organizing standards, have been omitted from this figure.

Personal name:	Bantock, Nick, author, illustrator.
Main title:	The pharos gate : Griffin & Sabine's lost correspondence / written and illustrated by Nick Bantock.
Published/Produced:	San Francisco : Chronicle Books, [2016]
Copyright:	©2016
LCCN:	2015020211
ISBN:	9781452151250 (alk. paper)
Description:	1 volume (unpaged) ; 21 cm + 5 folded letters
Type of material:	Book
Content type:	text
Media type:	unmediated
Carrier type:	volume
Summary:	Shares the fate of lovers Griffin and Sabine, in a volume published simultaneously with the twenty-fifth-anniversary edition of "Griffin & Sabine."

Figure 3. RDA bibliographic record for *The Pharos Gate.*

Typical of bibliographic representations, the RDA record offers many expected descriptive elements, including author, title, publisher, and date. However, several specific features of this record are worth noting. First, the author's name ("Personal name") is qualified with two relationship designators, specifying his role as author and illustrator of this work. The inclusion of this data echoes RDA's emphasis on relationships, while also supporting clarity on behalf of the user. The physical description represents the book as lacking page numbers and containing five letters. While the information on the accompanying letters may be seen as helpful to users in identifying and understanding the resource, the choice to note the work as unpaged may seem curious. While the RDA cataloger could have counted the number of pages, recording this resource as "unpaged" more accurately reflects how the resource presents itself. Though this supports accurate representation, it may leave the user unclear as to the scope of the resource, thus failing to fulfill user needs. Finally, the summary offers an oblique reference to this work's membership in a series with other works about Griffin and Sabine. More concrete information on relationships to other works is not presented, showing the valuation of relationships has not been fully realized.

While libraries may be considered the chief purveyor of bibliographic representations, catalogs are compiled in other settings as well. Again, we can turn to the general web environment for a revealing contrast. Google Books is an online catalog of books with full-text (where possible) and basic metadata designed to support web searching, browsing, and acquisition ("About Google Books," n.d.). A Google Books bibliographic representation of *The Pharos Gate* is given in Figure 4.

Title:	The Pharos Gate: Griffin & Sabine's Lost Correspondence
Author:	Nick Bantock
Edition:	illustrated
Publisher:	Chronicle Books, 2016
ISBN:	1452151253, 9781452151250
Length:	60 pages
Subjects:	Fiction › General

Figure 4. Google Books record for *The Pharos Gate.*

The Google Books bibliographic record is decidedly brief, although lengthier descriptions and reviews of this resource are included in the system's search and display in order to support the valued uses of search, browse, and acquire. Though this record seems less complete than its RDA counterpart, note that it does contain a count of 60 pages. A user might be puzzled here as to why a relatively brief record contains a page count while the fuller looking record seems to have overlooked this detail. This is not a matter of completeness, however, but can be explained by differences in values. RDA's value of accurate representation leads to a completely different conception of the extent of this book, as opposed to Google Book's more common sense, and arguably more user-friendly, approach.

This brief analysis shows that the RDA record for *The Pharos Gate* places value on relationships and user needs, albeit with varying success. Accuracy of representation is also valued, though it may come at the expense of clarity. In pursuing accurate depiction, this bibliographic representation may be failing to uphold the needs of users. Though the text of RDA acknowledges there may be tradeoffs among specific objectives and principles (Canadian Library Association et al., 2010), this could still be seen as a conflict between asserted and functional values. Expected values such as relationships and user needs may be compromised or even absent when standards are enacted. Overall, this case demonstrates that even seemingly neutral information artifacts embody values closely tied to the standards used to generate them, and may also be the site of important value conflicts and omissions.

DISCUSSION

The preceding cases show how value analysis can be applied to information standards and the data they produce, that standards and data do express discernible values, and that these values vary even among standards of similar scope. Even from such relatively low stakes examples there are major implications concerning values and information. In the case of variant names usage is clearly an important value, but whose usage is valued varies among different standards, leading to differences in which names are considered to be relevant. At the same time, important human values such as autonomy and self-identification are of lesser importance, or of no consideration at all. In the case of Jake Zyrus, differences in how usage and self-identification are valued among different standards can lead to completely different names and depictions of the same person among different knowledge organizing systems, with conflicting and confusing results for users. Though Zyrus's gender is not specified in the current library authority record, under RDA, gender and gender history may also be recorded. The inclusion of gender in RDA data has been criticized for removing an individual's choice for disclosure, compromising autonomy, and violating privacy (Billey, Drabinski, & Roberto, 2014), showing the potential for further value violations here.

In the case of *The Pharos Gate*, differences in values yet again play a role in differing depictions of the same resource. More importantly, the current RDA record for this book was shown to fall short of upholding an asserted value of relationships. The relationship of the present volume to previous works in a series concerning the same characters falls within the realm of bibliographic relationships of interest to RDA and its underlying conceptual model, *The Functional Requirements for Bibliographic Records* (FRBR). Why then is this relationship not further highlighted in the current bibliographic record? The answer may lie in the current technological environment in which RDA data is being produced. RDA describes an idealized bibliographic representation based on entity-relationship modeling, though current catalog systems rely on the MARC encoding format, which has been criticized for its inability to easily and accurately express relationships (Boehr, Reynolds, & Shrader, 2012). The realization of RDA's valued relationships is prevented by current technological limitations, thus demonstrating that values in standards can be threatened by other aspects of technological infrastructure. This suggests that standards as expressions of community value commitments should be further accounted for in VaD research.

As a genre of document, standards have been shown to communicate in specific ways, leading especially to their capacity to persuade potential users (Young, 2003; Feinberg, 2009). Similarly, the purpose and form of standards may be seen as contributing to their ability to bear values. In the strictest sense, standards are intended to communicate and regulate an ideal or optimal reality, and in the process, set benchmarks for correct practices or products. Standards attempt to define what is right or preferred in the eyes of a given community, and must value some things at the expense of others. These documents are thus inherently values-laden, and furthermore, carry ethical connotations. Ethics are seen as closely tied to the specific values of goodness and rightness (Rescher, 1969). In being designed to establish what is "right," all standards have ethical implications as well. Examinations of technology and ethics must consider standards and the role they play in establishing what a community values and considers correct.

While standards as written documents are one thing, standards in practice are another. Standards depict an ideal, but they must be enacted by actors in real working environments (Palme & Pargman, 2009). Information standards are technological artifacts, but they are also technological performances. In enacting a standard such as RDA, practitioners may be guided by the values they perceive from these documents, but must reconcile these with the values of their professional community, their individual institutions, and perhaps even their own personal values. As we have seen with the case of *The Pharos Gate*, they may also need to compromise important values in accordance with technological realities. While the resulting data provides us evidence of information standard enactment, to fully understand the role values play in the use of standards we must explore the perspectives and actions of practitioners. Understanding the decisions of those who interpret and enact a standard is critical in more fully revealing its value implications.

Value analysis offers a useful lens in evaluating technological artifacts and practices, and can serve effectively in revealing important value commitments and ethical implications. Traditional value analysis, as applied to the textual content of standards as documents, is warranted in further understanding and comparing specific standards. However, our conception of value analysis must be expanded beyond the text, not only to the enactment by practitioners, but also to the wider value ecosystems in which standards are situated. Any domain can be viewed as a collision of multiple value systems, with values from individuals, institutions, and artifacts interacting in specific ways. The resulting congruencies and conflicts bear meaningful influence on the role standards truly play, and whether their innate values are supported or subverted. Thus applications of value analysis to texts, practitioners, institutions, communities, domains, systems, and data all hold promise. Though all information standards are of interest here, it may be particularly useful to focus on knowledge organization standards, which guide the depiction of information and generate data that is being widely shared and reused. RDA in particular has seen a growing international implementation and sets an influential standard for bibliographic data in catalogs and the wider web environment (Marden et al., 2013). Value analysis of cultural heritage standards such as RDA also stand to benefit from the presence of strongly asserted community values that have already been actively explored (Gorman, 2015; Koehler, 2015; Vecco, 2010).

CONCLUSION

Information standards are not neutral, nor are the data they produce. Like all information artifacts, they have the capacity to both uphold and violate important community values. Value analysis represents an effective approach in uncovering key value commitments. As a methodological tradition, it deserves a place in the repertoire of critical approaches to technologies and technological practices. Information standards represent a particularly meaningful area of application for value analysis, as these documents formalize important community ideals. As the preceding case studies have demonstrated, the values found in standards and standard-driven data have implications for a potentially wide base of users on the web. While attention to these artifacts is critical, so too are the implications of their enactments by practitioners in real working environments. Beyond this, attention to an even wider range of information artifacts, persons, groups, and practices can place standards in the context of a larger ecosystem of values and offer a more complete image of their role and effects. Within information science, value analysis is a useful approach to understanding and upholding important values such as autonomy and privacy, and maintaining ethical information practices.

REFERENCES

About Google Books – Google Books. (n.d.). Retrieved March 29, 2018, from https://www.google.com/googlebooks/about/

Adler, M., Huber, J. T., & Nix, A. T. (2017). Stigmatizing disability: Library classifications and the marking and marginalization of books about people with disabilities. *The Library Quarterly, 87*(2), 117–135.

Andersen, J., & Skouvig, L. (2006). Knowledge organization: A sociohistorical analysis and critique. *The Library, 76*(3), 300–322.

Baca, M., & Visual Resources Association. (2006). *Cataloging cultural objects : A guide to describing cultural works and their images*. Chicago, Ill.: ALA Editions of the American Library Association.

Bates, M. J. (1999). The invisible substrate of information science. *Journal of the Association for Information Science and Technology, 50*(12), 1043.

Bantock, N. (2016). *The Pharos gate*. San Francisco: Chronicle Books.

Billey, A., Drabinski, E., & Roberto, K. R. (2014). What's gender got to do with it? A critique of RDA 9.7. *Cataloging & Classification Quarterly, 52*(4), 412–421.

Boehr, D., Reynolds, R. R., & Shrader, T. (2012). The US RDA test process. *The Serials Librarian, 62*(1–4), 125–139.

Bowker, G. C., Baker, K., Millerand, F., & Ribes, D. (2009). Toward information infrastructure studies: Ways of knowing in a networked environment. In *International handbook of internet research* (pp. 97–117). Netherlands: Springer.

Bowker, G. C., & Star, S. L. (2000). *Sorting things out: Classification and its consequences*. Cambridge, Mass.: MIT Press.

Busch, L. (2000). The moral economy of grades and standards. *Journal of Rural Studies, 16*(3), 273–283.

Canadian Library Association, Chartered Institute of Library and Information Professionals (Great Britain), Joint Steering Committee for Development of RDA, & American Library Association. (2010). *RDA toolkit: Resource description & access*. Retrieved from http://www.rdatoolkit.org/

Cheng, A.-S., & Fleischmann, K. R. (2010). Developing a meta-inventory of human values. *Proceedings of the American Society for Information Science and Technology, 47*(1), 1–10.

Clawson, C. J., & Vinson, D. E. (1978). Human values: A historical and interdisciplinary analysis. In K. Hunt (Ed.), *NA – advances in consumer research: Vol. 5* (pp. 396–402). Ann Arbor, MI: Association for Consumer Research.

da Silva, A. P., Chaves Guimarães, J. A., & Bolfarini Tognoli, N. (2015). Ethical values in archival arrangement and description: An analysis of professional codes of ethics. *Knowledge Organization, 42*(5), 346–352.

Delsey, T. (1989). Standards for descriptive cataloging: Two perspectives on the past twenty years. In E. Svenonius (Ed.), *The conceptual foundations of descriptive cataloging* (pp. 51–60). San Diego, Calif.: Academic Press.

Dhand, H. (1967). *A value analysis of Saskatchewan social studies textbooks* (Doctoral dissertation, University of Montana, 1967).

Diao, J., & Cao, H. (2016). Chronology in cataloging Chinese archaeological reports: An investigation of cultural bias in the Library of Congress Classification. *Cataloging & Classification Quarterly 54*(4), 244–262.

Dobreski, B. (2017). Authority and universalism: conventional values in descriptive catalog codes. In *Proceedings of the 2017 North American Symposium on Knowledge Organization*. Seattle, WA : University of Washington.

Dobreski, B., & Kwaśnik, B. (2017). Changing depictions of persons in library practice: Spirits, pseudonyms, and human books. *Knowledge Organization, 44*(8), 656-667.

Feinberg, M. (2009). Information system design for communication: the use of genre as a design element. *Proceedings of the Association for Information Science and Technology, 46*(1), 1–18.

Fleischmann, K. R., Oard, D. W., Cheng, A. S., Boyd-Graber, J., Templeton, T. C., Ishita, E., Wallace, W. A. (2012). Content analysis for values elicitation. In *Proceeding of the ACM SIGCHI 2012 Conference on Human Factors in Computing Systems, Workshop on Methods for Accounting for Values in Human-Centered Computing*. New York: ACM.

Friedman, B. (1996). Value-sensitive design. *Interactions, 3*(6), 16–23.

Friedman, B., Kahn, P., & Borning, A. (2002). Value sensitive design: Theory and methods (Technical Report 02-12-01). Seattle, WA: University of Washington.

Friedman, B., & Nissenbaum, H. (1996). Bias in computer systems. *ACM Transactions on Information Systems (TOIS), 14*(3), 330–347.

Gorman, M. (2015). *Our enduring values revisited: Librarianship in an ever-changing world.* Chicago, Ill.: American Library Association.

Hider, P. (2012). *Information resource description: creating and managing metadata*. Chicago, Ill.: American Library Association.

Hofstede, G. (2003). *Culture's consequences: comparing values, behaviors, institutions and organizations across nations* (2nd ed.). Thousand Oaks, Calif.: Sage Publications.

IEEE Standards Association. (2017). The IEEE Standards Association - Home. Retrieved March 14, 2018, from http://standards.ieee.org/

Knobel, C., & Bowker, G. C. (2011). Values in design. *Communications of the ACM, 54*(7), 26–28.

Knowlton, S. A. (2005). Three decades since prejudices and antipathies: A study of changes in the Library of Congress Subject Headings. *Cataloging & Classification Quarterly, 40*(2), 123–145.

Koehler, W. (2015). *Ethics and values in librarianship*. Lanham, Md.: Rowman & Littlefield.

Lampland, M., & Star, S. L. (2009*). Standards and their stories: how quantifying, classifying, and formalizing practices shape everyday life*. Ithaca, N.Y.: Cornell University Press.

Lester, N. B. (1982). A system for analyzing characters' values in literary texts. *Research in the Teaching of English 16*(4), 321–338.

Marden, J., Li-Madeo, C., Whysel, N., & Edelstein, J. (2013). Linked open data for cultural heritage: Evolution of an information technology. In *Proceedings of the 31st ACM International Conference on Design of Communication* (pp. 107–112). New York: ACM.

McGuire, W. J. (1974). Psychological motives and communication gratification. In J. G. Blumler & E. Katz (Eds.), *The uses of mass communications: Current perspectives on gratifications research* (pp. 167–196). Beverly Hills, Calif.: Sage Publications.

Olson, H. A. (2001). The power to name: Representation in library catalogs. *Signs, 26*(3), 639–668.

Orsi, F. (2015). *Value theory*. New York: Bloomsbury Publishing.

Palme, J., & Pargman, D. (2009). ASCII Imperialism. In M. Lampland & S.L. Star (Eds.), *Standards and their stories: How quantifying, classifying, and formalizing practices shape everyday life* (pp. 177–199). Ithaca, N.Y.: Cornell University Press.

Rescher, N. (1969). *Introduction to value theory*. Englewood Cliffs, N.J.: Prentice-Hall.

Rokeach, M. (1968). *Beliefs, attitudes and values: A theory of organization and change*. San Francisco, Calif.: Jossey-Bass Inc.

Rokeach, M. (1973). *The nature of human values*. New York: The Free Press.

Shachaf, P. (2005). A global perspective on library association codes of ethics. *Library & Information Science Research, 27*(4), 513–533.

Shilton, K., Koepfler, J. A., & Fleischmann, K. R. (2013). Charting Sociotechnical Dimensions of Values for Design Research. *The Information Society, 29*(5), 259–271.

Society of American Archivists. (2013). *Describing archives : A content standard* (2nd ed.). Chicago, Ill.: Society of American Archivists.

Spiggle, S. (1986). Measuring social values: A content analysis of Sunday comics and underground comix. *Journal of Consumer Research, 13*(1), 100–113.

Svenonius, E. (2000). *The intellectual foundation of information organization*. Cambridge, Mass.: MIT Press.

UNESCO. (2017). *Protecting Our Heritage and Fostering Creativity*. Retrieved July 10, 2017, from http://en.unesco.org/themes/protecting-our-heritage-and-fostering-creativity

Vecco, M. (2010). A definition of cultural heritage: From the tangible to the intangible. *Journal of Cultural Heritage, 11*(3), 321–324.

White, R. K. (1951). *Value-analysis: The nature and use of the method.* Glen Gardner, N.J.: Libertarian Press.

Wikipedia: Manual of Style/Biographies. (2018). In Wikipedia. Retrieved March 18, 2018 from https://en.wikipedia.org/w/index.php?title=Wikipedia:Manual_of_Style/Biographies&oldid=831036517

Young, J. J. (2003). Constructing, persuading and silencing: The rhetoric of accounting standards. *Accounting, Organizations and Society, 28*(6), 621–638.

Making the Case for Data Archiving: The Changing "Value Proposition" of Social Science Data Archives

Kristin R Eschenfelder
University of Wisconsin-Madison, USA.
eschenfelder@wisc.edu

Rachel D. Williams
Simmons College, USA.
rachel.williams@simmons.edu

Kalpana Shankar
University College Dublin, Ireland.
kalpana.shankar@ucd.ie

ABSTRACT

In this paper, we analyse how three social science data archives (SSDA) have adapted to provide value to different stakeholders over time. Drawing on historical administrative documents and interviews with current and former staff at three long standing SSDA, we examine how these archives have provided value, to whom, and how they have situated themselves vis-à-vis alternative archives over 20-40 year time spans. Although data archives have been in operation for decades, how they have sustained themselves over time by continuing to provide value to stakeholders in changing conditions is less well understood. Studies of value have tended to focus on a snapshot in time rather than providing a view that emphasizes change over time. We conclude with a comparative analysis of changes in value across archives and suggestions for future work

KEYWORDS

Data archives, sustainability, organizational change, business models, value proposition

INTRODUCTION

Repositories for the curation and management of data are an essential infrastructure for research across the disciplines. Although they have been in operation for decades, how they have sustained themselves over time (and can continue to do so) has only been explored in recent years. As these repositories have grown in scale and scope, they have been dependent upon heterogeneous sources of funding and have made structural and programmatic changes to accommodate shifts in user needs, technologies, and institutional relationships.

This paper explores the changes in the perceived value of data archives over time. The role of data archives has been well documented for their role in spurring research activity in not-for-profit and commercial enterprises and reducing the cost of secondary research (Beagrie and Pink 2012). However, most attempts to demonstrate the value of data archives have been at a specific point in time, a snapshot, whereas data have changing value: Some argue that the longer the investment, the more valuable data collections become (OECD 2017). Nevertheless, making the case for value and impact over time can be challenging. As Maron and Loy (2011) note, the transition from grant funding to a longer-term plan for ongoing growth and development of a repository or archive may seem just like a financial problem, but actually runs deeper since projects must justify their ongoing existence to depositors, users, hosts, funders, and others. Without a value proposition, digital resources, many of them representing the outlay of significant resources (financial and institutional), are likely to be become siloed or unusable.

One of many challenges archives face is the complex, fluctuating, and ill-defined organizational concept of "sustainability." Some definitions of organizational sustainability emphasize structural components, referring to "an economically viable infrastructure, both social and technical..." or " business, social, technological, and policy mechanisms." (Berman & Lavoie 2011; Bradley 2007) Others focus on resources, such as the ability "to generate or gain access to the resources-financial or otherwise." Other definitions emphasize sustainability as a culture or set of organizational competencies and skills that include ongoing engagement with user communities and other stakeholders, being prepared for an environment of constant change, demonstrating accountability, and managing risk (Guthrie, Griffiths, and Maron, 2008). Further, while definitions allude to data -related services, they vary with respect to the set of services they assume ought to be provided sustainably and how.

Another challenge is the complex, fluctuating and ill-defined nature of "value." What is the relationship of "value" to creating and managing a sustainable data archive and more importantly, how does "value" change over time? Further how do perceptions of value vary between different stakeholders or users? The idea that value underpins any business model, and the understanding that different stakeholders might value different aspects of a program are well accepted (OECD 2017); however, the evolution of value and what stakeholders' value over time has been less examined. In this paper we first summarize key ideas from the literature of business models about the role of value in business models. We then present the results of an empirical study of three large social science data archives, and we describe major changes to their value for different users and stakeholders over a 40 year period. This analysis of change in value over time is one part of a larger historical comparative case study of social science data archives (Eschenfelder & Shankar, 2017) and draws on and extend socio-technical approaches that emphasize how different stakeholders may have very different perceptions of the success or failure of technologies (Bijker, 1995).

VALUE PROPOSITIONS, BUSINESS MODELS AND DATA ARCHIVES

There is little agreement on what a business model actually consists of, and the exact role of value in a business model (DaSilva and Trkman 2014). Some argue that this stems from the newness of the term "business model" which only developed as the internet increased the number of options an organization could choose to organize itself and offer services (DaSilva and Trkman, 2014). In a structured review of the literature of business models, Zott, Amit, and Massa (2011) also found there is no agreement on what a business model is, and that researchers tend to adopt or create a definition instrumental to their particular research needs. One similarity that they did find across the literature reviewed is that business models are routinely invoked to understand/explain how business create value for stakeholders.

The intersection of business models and the creation of value in cultural and scientific organizations (which have different mandates than for-profit firms), has recently received increased interest. But most current work on business models of data organizations has focused on revenue generation and diversifying sources of income. The concepts of "value" or the "value proposition" offered by of data archives and data sharing are more lightly discussed. For example, the Research Data Alliance/World Data System (RDA-WDS) Cost Recovery Interest Group explored current and potential future alternative income streams via structured phone interviews with representatives from 22 mostly science data repositories globally (Dillo, Hodson, & Waard 2016). The European Commission Horizon 2020 Advisory Group on European Research Infrastructure report emphasizes how "flexible business models" are "essential to keep [research infrastructure] sustainable in the long run," calling for creation of innovative and flexible business models. (European Commission 2015). In 2017, the Organization for Economic Co-operation and Development (OECD) released a report on the business models of 47 data archives currently in operation across eighteen countries and numerous disciplines. While mostly reporting on income streams, the OECD's report recommended that all repositories develop a clearly articulated business model and that the model should change over time for many reasons, including the changing needs of stakeholders. The OECD suggests that value-added mixes of data and services should evolve over time in reaction to changes in the "market" for those data and services, and numerous other cost drivers (change in user base and expectations, to give one example). They write, "Engaging and maintaining structural, institutional, philanthropic, or other funders depends on their understanding of the value proposition, and ensuring such engagement may involve repositories undertaking detailed benefit/cost, value, and impact analyses….Sustainability depends, inter alia, on a clearly articulated value proposition and the development of a 'business model' (p. 9).

Another gap in the value discussion is the lack of empirical research on different stakeholders' perceptions of how value is created and maintained in data archives and how those perceptions might change over time. Ember and Hanisch (2013) take as given that data archives are "valuable" to their constituent communities and that the involvement of the community serviced (traditional disciplines or sub disciplines, networks of researchers, among others) is essential to the ongoing functioning of a data archive. This stands to reason; if the community values the resource, it will engage in developing and sustaining it (Michener et al 2012). However, they are forced to surmise that other ways that archives could add value, such as certification or commercial partnerships) have not proven to be as useful to the long-term success.

To explore changes in perceptions of value over time, we draw on an approach by Osterwalder. Osterwalder (2005) defines a business model as "a set of elements formed by a logical plan and a purpose to create and drive value." His popular Strategyzer "Business Model Canvas" addresses nine components including value propositions. (Osterwalder et al 2018) In this paper we focus on the "value propositions" which are defined as bundles of goods or services that create value for a given customer segment. Important to our paper, Osterwalder emphasizes that different customer segments may have different value propositions because they are trying to achieve different goals, or as Osterwalder describes "get different things done in their work or in their life," they have different "pains," or things that annoy or thwart them, and they have different "gains," or desired outcomes or benefits. (Osterwalder 2018). We also draw on work by Morris et al (2005) that analyzed 30 definitions of business models and identified three emphases: (1) economic aspects of an organization and how it creates revenue, (2) operational aspects of an organization and how it arranges work processes, and (3) strategic issues such as positioning in relation to competitors. Finally, we draw on socio-technical approaches that emphasize how different stakeholders may have very different perceptions of the success or failure of technologies, and the processes through which those perceptions of success or failure may come to change over time (Bijker, 1995). We combine these ideas to ask a series of questions about how data archives have created value for the different sets of stakeholders in relation to alternatives over decades.

Question 1. How has the data archive created value? What products or services has the data archive offered? Does the data archive provide access to other's data, its own data? Through what channels has the archive distribute its products services (direct distribution/indirect distribution)?

Question 2. For whom has the data archive create value? Who are the different types of direct and indirect users of the archive or stakeholders?

Question 3. How has the archive competitively positioned itself vis-a-vis alternatives over time? For example this might include the image the organization creates of itself in relation to alternatives, including alternatives of free data or no data, in terms of costs, quality or features available.

METHODOLOGY

This paper is part of a larger study on the sustainability of social science data archives (SSDA). We selected SSDA that have been in continuous operation for decades in order to examine change in the organizations, their data collections, their services and their stakeholders over time. We used purposive sampling to select long-lived archives with contrasting revenue models and whose organizational documents would be in the English language. Both ICPSR and LIS collect membership fees, while UKDA have received multi-year grants from a UK national research funder. The authors limited analysis from inception of each archive to 2002. We chose 2002 as an artificial if reasonable 'historical' cut off although in many cases we have later public data from annual reports and other posted materials. Our decision to end data collection in the early 2000s was based on a need to assure participants we would not be evaluating current archive practices, and a desire to focus on analysis of change over time rather than get caught up in the excitement of contemporary events.

ICPSR, or the Inter-university Consortium of Political and Social Research has been located at the University of Michigan – Ann Arbor. We collected data on operations from its founding in the early 1960s to the mid-2000s. Today, ICPSR maintains over 250,000 research data files in the social and behavioral research with specialized collections in 21 area, including education, aging, and other fields. ICPSR has operated as a membership organization and its fees were modelled off journal pricing with larger institutions paying a larger membership fee to provide access to all faculty, students and staff. But, since the 1990s, ICPSR has generated the majority of its revenue from serving as a contract data platform for US government agency offices. Further, it applies for external grants to fund special projects.

The UK Data Archive (UKDA) is now part of a cross-institutional UK Data Service. The UKDA was founded in 1967 at the University of Essex. For the purposes of this paper it is treated in its incarnation as a standalone service. Today UKDA advertises over 6,000 data collections for research and teaching from the social sciences and humanities. We collected data on UKDA operations from its founding in 1967 to the mid-2000s. The UKDA has operated with the support of regular large multi-year grants from the major UK funder, the Economic and Social Research Council (ESRC). As part of this arrangement, the UKDA has provided access to its data to all qualified UK educational institutions. The UKDA supplements the ESRC funding with additional grants for special projects and contract work. In the 2000s the ESRC modified its support to fund UKDA and several other UK data services in a more coordinated fashion as the UK Data Service.

The LIS Cross National Data Center (formerly known as the Luxembourg Income Study) began in 1979 in Luxembourg. It has a more thematically focused data collection: LIS harmonizes and provides access to cross-national microdata on individual and family financial data from 50 different countries. We have data on LIS operations from the mid-1980s (its inception) to the early 2000s. LIS is a membership fee driven organization, however LIS memberships are at the national rather than the institutional level. One organization pays a membership fee for a country and then all academic institutions in that country can use LIS data. In some cases the national membership fee is paid for by a governmental science funding agency (e.g., NSF, ESRC), but in other cases it may be paid for by a government agency or an individual university on behalf of others.

In addition to gathering documents, we conducted semi-structured interviews with former and current staff with roles including directors, collections managers, membership services coordinators and technology managers. Interviews took approximately 45 minutes and were both in-person and phone based. A preset list of topics guided analysis of both documents and interviews, but we remained open to new themes. Because our data stem from sources internal to the archives, readers should remember that findings about value or changes in value stem from documents predominantly written by archive staff or governance bodies and thus represent their perception of the perceived value of the archive in the eyes of stakeholders. In some cases we have external review reports and other materials that provide an external view of value. In the findings below we highlight snapshots of changes that each of our three sites enacted related to our three value questions.

FINDINGS

Based on our socio-technical approach that emphasizes how different stakeholders may have very different perceptions of the success or failure of technologies (Bijker, 1995), we begin by exploring how our case study sites believe they have created value for different stakeholders over time. We then describe the different stakeholders for whom our case study data archives perceived they might create value. Finally, we look at how our case sites believed they positioned themselves against a variety of competitors for their stakeholders' resources of money, usage, or enthusiasm. Because of space constraints, we include a few examples in each area, and we primarily chose examples that illustrate change in value.

Question 1. How has the data archive created value?

ICPSR

Since its inception, ICPSR has maintained that its value stems from stewardship and curation of collections of high-quality social science data. The proposition is that ICPSR institutional members will choose to pay membership fees to access this aggregated, indexed, cleaned and highly-described collection. ICPSR has also positioned itself as providing value to researchers looking to deposit their data to ensure responsible access by others. ICPSR promises that for each deposit, "... a data archivist reviews the data and documentation, builds a study description, enhances the documentation...and archives the data for long-term preservation." (ICPSR, 2018). ICPSR places the data within a larger search and indexing structure, and will also modify the data to protect the confidentiality of participants ICPSR. Through these services, it arguably adds value to researchers "raw" data that they could otherwise simply post in a more isolated fashion to the Web.

In its early pre-internet days, ICPSR promoted its value as a distribution mechanism. By depositing data with ICPSR, a researcher could rest assured that peer scholars could get access to the data via punch card and then tape drive distribution systems. Further, researchers could order copies of any data in the ICPSR collection for delivery via card, tape and then CD-ROM. But the advent of computer networking and internet sharing protocols challenged all SSDA's distribution value. By 1994, staff expressed concern that scholars found FTP is "more efficient" than ICPSR's traditional distribution systems (ICPSR 1994). Countering concerns about FTP in its 1995 Annual Report, ICPSR argued that "providing FTP access is not the same as preserving it for posterity or making [data] ready for ...use" and it urged members to continue to support the shared ICPSR collection (ICPSR 1995b pg 5).

While data quality has long been part of ICPSR's value claim, at times stakeholders have pushed for faster and more open access to data than curation would permit. This pressure for fast access to "as is" lower-quality data created complications with ICPSR's membership model which reserved access to data to paying members. To soften this tension and create value for different sets of stakeholders, ICPSR began to tier data, doing different levels of work on different data, and providing different types of access to the different tiers. Calls for open data however continue to draw the value proposition of access to a high quality collection into question. In interviews staff members worried that stakeholders might not no longer appreciate the work that ICPSR does and just use lower quality open alternatives (personal communications).

ICPSR also promotes itself as an R&D organization whose products provide value to other data archival organizations by furthering standards development, technologies and best practices in curation. For example, staff developed early statistical analysis software called OSIRIS, an early desktop statistics application called ABC, and ICPSR was a major player in the development of the SSDA community's development of the DDI metadata standard and markup language (ICPSR 1995).

UKDA

In the first few years the archive's founding, UKDA staff were primarily interested in exploring technical questions related to the feasibility of data archiving mostly of interest to other data professionals (Farlie 1971). But by 1971, after negative feedback from funders, it began to work to change the perception of the archive "an unresponsive self-centred organization" to one more "anxious and able to serve clients' needs" (Annual Report, 1982). UKDA leadership sought to create value by acquiring data that would be otherwise difficult to obtain, prioritizing data of "importance" rather than quantity (UKDA 1971). Also central to UKDA's value claims was high quality processing, and creation of extensive documentation that made data more accessible to users, and creation of collections of related surveys for temporal trend analysis. Further, by the mid-1980s, UKDA leaders portrayed the archive as a key player in facilitating data exchange between different countries, pitching the value of the archive as a data broker with other archives (Annual Report, 1983).

Like other archives such as ICPSR and LIS, UKDA did provide some training programs and seminars to gain more users and increase understanding of users' needs, but its ability to create value was more centered on other areas (UKDA 1982). By the 1980's UKDA was examining how to expand value through identifying new types of data to acquire or entertaining the possibility of commercial users. For example, UKDA began preserving data for time series and trend analysis (UKDA 1984). Like ICPSR, UKDA also created value by being responsive to technology trends and sought to increase value by changing how data was made available to users. The introduction of new technologies in the 1990s saw data usage double in the span of just three years.

LIS

LIS had a more narrow and niche data collection. To create more potential users, it developed extensive training programs to introduce new researchers to their data, generate demand for their data, and increase its perceived value within the scholarly community examining household wealth. LIS has had a stated goal of introducing "young" scholars to existing research, promoting new lines of inquiry that could make use of the data, and facilitating teaching using the LIS datasets (LIS 1988).

Like the other cases, LIS has also generated value through its curational, custodial and documentary activities that add value to data originally produced by national statistical agencies. The curatorial value propositions of the LIS Data Archive has three elements: microdata, cross-national and harmonization. First, while there are many sources of national-level economic data, fewer focus on household-level economic microdata such as household income, debt, spending etc. Second, LIS gathers microdata from many different national sources, saving the researcher a great deal of effort. In many cases these data are controlled by national government statistical agencies and it takes negotiation, relationships of trust, and the development of a secure access system in order to get the data out of its home country and provide remote access. "This time-consuming process usually requires negotiating national privacy restrictions, and often entails years of building and maintaining relationships" (LIS 2018). Thus, while country Z would have copies of its internal national data, and a researcher from country Z could get access to Z data, that researcher would not have access to similar data from other nations. A manager explained why national agencies will release microdata to LIS but not individual researchers, "... they can't because data providers won't release data to individuals. It has to be behind our protective firewall." (LIS 2004) LIS's value proposition has been to develop a consolidated collection, including data from multiple countries, on a secure platform, which ensures data use comports with the expectations of the data providers. Finally, data from different nations requires "harmonization" or the creation of common variables and normalized measures across data sets so that researchers can compare similar phenomena across nations. As LIS describes, "this process currently takes anywhere from one to three months per country dataset." (LIS 2018).

Question 2. For whom has the archive created value?

ICPSR

ICPSR initially conceptualized itself as creating value for scholars in U.S. political science departments by collecting voting, poll and other U.S. election-related data (ICPSR 1963). This collection of cross-state elections data was more valuable in aggregate; further, staff increased the value by cleaning the data and formatting it for the statistical processing software of the day. But by 1971 ICPSR documents discuss the need to broaden the archive's user audience and the range of relevant granting agencies. Staff propose changing the archives name to refer to Political *and* Social Research instead of just political research (ICPSR 1971). The eventual formal name change in 1975 was preceded by broadening collection development and grant activity in the early 1970s to curate data on a broader range of social science issues including aging, law and criminal justice, victimization, public health, demography, and history.

Additionally, throughout the 1970s and 1980s ICPSR expanded the audience for whom it created value by offering data archiving and distribution services to government agencies. This provided an important and significant new source of revenue, but it also created identity confusion. Meeting minutes describe how by 1996, some felt that agency revenue created a "confused organizational identity" and conflicted with ICPSR's original mission to provide data to (paying) members. Meeting notes express concern that ICPSR might be more responsive to agencies because of the financial importance of grants vs membership fees (ICPSR 1996). Our analysis of budgets over time shows that by the early 2000s, contracts and grants overshadowed membership fees as a revenue source.

As ICPSR sought to retain membership revenue during periods of campus budget cuts, ICPSR actively sought to cultivate a new audience of deans and other budget decision makers in order to convince them to continue paying (ICPSR 1994). ICPSR had initially saw "organizational representatives" (OR) -- often librarians or staff -- as their primary value advocates on campus. But given falling memberships, minutes express concerns about OR's unwillingness to "argue with deans" to keep memberships. By 1990 ICPSR created an advisory group to figure out how to better communicate ICPSR's value to campus budgetary decision makers.

UKDA

Due to UKDA's funding through the ESRC, the archive has sought to create value for the ESRC as defined by the terms of its funding agreements which specified a balance between educational users, government and commercial users. Its primary focus has been on UK academic users: Like ICSPR, it provided access to secondary data for research and education. It accepted deposit from individual researchers, and sought to capture data collected from studies funded by ESRC. UKDA's funding applications provide a window on its changing value proposition: UKDA has prepared grant applications every 5 years that make a case for its value for ESRC; further, ESRC has an external review panel assess the UKDA grant and provide feedback on reviewers' perceptions of UKDA's value.

UKDA worked to develop close relationships with government agencies that create and statistical and other data. From its inception, the UKDA was conceived of, in part, as "centre for storing data derived from social surveys sponsored by government departments..." (UKDA 1967) Getting government agencies to deposit data however was not always easy because of the need to build confidence with depositors, concerns about confidentiality of data, and the difficulty of transferring data. Early ESRC grant assessments critiqued the archive for low overall use, and especially low use by government agencies and potential commercial users (UKDA 1970). But UKDA argued that by providing a central means of disseminating government data, it relieved agencies from that work, saved money from "public purse," and made it easier for data seekers to locate data from different agencies (UKDA, 1980). UKDA continued to curry governmental and commercial users who would be interested in using the archive's data, particularly Census data and other housing and income datasets (UKDA, 1982).

Also like ICPSR, UKDA saw part of its value as stemming from research and development, and the archive worked on new retrieval techniques and data analysis software (UKDA 1978). UKDA also facilitated access to data for users overseas (ESRC 1988). The archive thus saw itself as providing access to a variety of users, primarily academic, but with a broad range of disciplines and interests.

LIS

LIS differed from ICPSR and UKDA archives in that it never offered a means for individual researchers to deposit and distribute their data. Its goals have been to gather a very specific type of data from national statistical and research offices. Further, while it is similar to ICPSR and UKDA in that it solicits data from government agencies -- albeit a much narrower set -- it does not market itself as a long term data preservation service for those agencies. Instead, it markets the value of its harmonized cross-national comparative data to both researchers and government agencies who might use the data to conduct comparative policy analysis (LIS 2017).

For the organizations that provide the national-level membership fees, LIS claims that it creates value through facilitation of better policy analysis about the effects of different kinds of national programs on poverty, income adequacy, and economic well-being generally. But, this value has been contested: for example, LIS records show how in the mid to late 1990s, the US National Science Foundation complained that not enough US economists were using LIS data, drawing NSF's continued payment of the US membership fee into doubt (LIS 1997). In another example, in interviews LIS staff described how in many cases the payment of annual fees for LIS is contingent on personal relationships with budget decision makers in government agencies. Change of personnel can disrupt the revenue as new decision makers may not be aware of, or value the LIS data collection (personal communications). As one described, new decision makers would ask "what is LIS? I just took over this job and I have this portfolio and I'm supposed to be giving you money for some data organization in Luxembourg? I don't know who you are." (Personal communication) LIS archive managers described spending a great deal of time cultivating and maintaining relationships with budget decision makers in order to ensure they appreciated the value of LIS membership and use of LIS data by policy analysts in their country.

LIS has always sought to expand the pool of policy analysts for whom it creates value by increasing the range of national data sets it contains. This draws new users to the resource, but also expands the breadth of comparative analysis possible. LIS has also expanded its membership pool to include international organizations such as the OECD. Finally, LIS has also received inquiries about whether they would consider serving as a data platform for other groups, and it is considering providing this service to research programs in intellectually aligned areas as a means of both diversifying revenue and supporting financial microdata research (personal communication).

Question 3. How has the archive competitively positioned itself vis-a-vis alternatives over time?

ICPSR

ICPSR and other social science data archives in the US purposefully attempted to distinguish themselves from one another through collection specialization with a set of early US data archives planning to divide up specific topical areas (Converse P. 1963). Among archives that charged membership fees, like ICPSR and the Roper Center for Public Opinion, disputes sometimes arose when one archive copied and began offering access to another's data.

In another example of positioning, as ICPSR sought to retain memberships and influence campus budget decision makers, it actively sought to reframe itself less as a club with membership fees and more as 'similar to a journal subscription.' It did this because staff believed that budget decision makers were already familiar with journal subscription fees and would more readily continue payment to ICPSR under this mental model (ICPSR, 1974). As part of this, ICPSR suggested that member campuses move membership fees from academic department budgets (e.g., political science) to the library because while the membership fee seems big in the context of a department budget, it is small in the context of a library budget (ICPSR, 2000)

In a final example, from the late 1990s onwards, some stakeholders have pressed for faster access to key data sets, and more open access to data. These pressures conflicted with the long-standing quality value proposition provided by the curation and documentation activities. The open access to data conflicted with ICPSR's members-only restrictions. In response to these pressures, in 1994 ICPSR developed its "FastTrack" FTP service that provided "as is" access to high-demand data to members. That same year, in response to pressure from a funder and PIs who wanted immediate open access, ICPSR provided non-member anonymous FTP access to certain federally funded data sets. Documents justify the change as necessary to avoid those data "being disassociated with us" and as necessary to avoid having PIs distribute their own data (Rockwell, 1994). ICPSR has provided both high quality curated data and low quality "as is" data to provide value in comparison to alternatives.

UKDA

For UKDA, being competitive over time involved having a thorough understanding in how its competitor archives operated and ensuring UKDA maintained its niche among competitors. Early after its creation, UKDA conducted a comparative analysis of the international landscape of existing data archives, and how UKDA could fit into that landscape (Land, 1970). For example, one of the ways in which, at least initially, UKDA was distinct in particular from other American archives was in its emphasis on data use by researchers, rather than students. It later changed that approach by bringing datasets into the classroom and providing additional training opportunities for students.

Because UKDA serves primarily UK educational institutions and government agencies, its primary alternatives are other UK data archives. It risks losing users, and ESRC support, to alternative UK data archives. Over time, ESRC grant review panels noted pros and cons of ESRC investment in a more centralized Essex operation, versus spreading out investment amongst several data archives in a more federated approach. Grant reviews in the 1980's describe how ESRC chose Essex as a location for a data archive over Manchester because of the computer processing facilities at Essex. (UKDA 1980) But by 1994, grant reviewers expressed concern that reduction or loss of ESRC funding was a possible threat. They describing how the structure of the ESRC funding as a "research center competition" encouraged other UK campuses to bid to create alternative data archives (UKDA 1994).

LIS

LIS does not tend to have the "open data" alternative because in most cases the data sets they receive from national agencies are restricted, and also because of the harmonization they provide. But they perceive that some stakeholders may dismiss LIS because the stakeholders' assume that some open data alternatives must exist. As one manager explained in an interview "We used to get [that question from X], and it made us want to throw ourselves out a window "Why can't individual researchers just do what you do?" Take 50 data sets and harmonize them? <Incredulous laughter>." (Personal communication). Another challenge is that some potential funders do not adequately understand the differences between microdata and other types of economic data. Many other archive projects exist that include other types of economic data, and funders may erroneously believe that redundancy in service exists between LIS and these other projects.

From the perspective of national agencies that provide data to LIS, an alternative is simply to not provide the data. Review of LIS meeting notes show how historically some government statistical agencies have perceived submission of data LIS as a risk. Many concerns have centred on privacy protections (LIS 2004). In order to satisfy data contributors' privacy concerns regarding remote access to digital data, LIS built a sophisticated access and use control system (LISSY) that would provide a method to allow researchers to use data under restrictions named by data contributing nations. But technology has not completely solved the problem, and in recent years LIS has lost former data contributors due to changing data privacy regulations and new interpretations of existing regulations. Agencies that formerly provided data will now not contribute data to LIS despite the robust LISSY infrastructure (personal communication).

DISCUSSION

In the business literature, it is taken for granted that adapting business models to changing circumstances is essential to the success of an organization (Wirtz, Pistoia, Ullrich & Göttel, 2016). While the literature presents business models as having varied constitutive elements, all business model frameworks include an element of "value." Further, some scholars like Zott, Amit, and Massa (2011) make value a central organizing principle for business model planning. To explore changes in value perceptions of data archives over time we asked three questions about value across three case sites including: How does the data archive create value? For whom does it create value? How does the data archives position itself in comparison to alternatives over time? In this section we present the questions in a different order because identification of the stakeholder for whom the archive is creating value drives answers to the other two questions. Drawing on socio-technical theorizing (e.g., Bijker, 1995) about stakeholder variance in the perceived success or failure of technologies, we draw out how different stakeholders may have very different expectations for, or perceptions of, the value of an infrastructure like data archives. The value is relational and based on the stakeholder.

For whom has the archive created value?

All of our data archives have attempted to create value for a similar set of stakeholders including scholars who create data, scholars who use data, social science methodology students and teachers, other organizations like government agencies that need curation services, practitioners in the field of data archiving, and funders. While each archive was developed with a core set of users and uses in mind, all of them expanded that user set over time by adding data in completely different topic areas (ICPSR & UKDA) or from more nations (LIS). Further, all our data archives interacted with government agencies as stakeholders, but in different ways. For ICPSR, agencies were a new source of revenue or a new service. UKDA served government agencies from its inception and as part of its core ESRC funding. For both UKDA and ICPSR, in-nation government agencies were data providers, but LIS had the additional challenge of trying to move data across national boundaries. Funding agencies (especially ESRC and NSF) were stakeholders for whom our data archive created value. But, that value was often in question and data archives risk being passed over for funding or having funding reduced. Another commonality we saw was that each archive has sought to justify its value to budgetary decision makers that might not be end users of the data. For example, ICPSR worked to increase name recognition among campus budget decision makers, LIS works constantly to maintain and renew relationships with organizations that pay national membership fees. UKDA must convince its major funder of its impact on research and education every five years. Data archives must prove value to these stakeholders even if they are not direct users of the data.

How have the data archives created value over time?

Stakeholders have varied expectations about, and perceptions of, the potential value of the data archive. The question of how the archive creates value is a function of the specific stakeholder in question. Our data archives adopted some common strategies for creating value including developing data collections to attract academic users including ensuring data quality, data documentation, educational endeavors to promote data use, adopting preferred technology and access methods, developing new software services, providing search and indexing tools, and managing privacy and security issues. Further, some value strategies were unique to particular archives. For example while all archives grouped related data such as time series, panels etc., the LIS data archive was unique in harmonization work it provided to facilitate cross-national analysis. Further, all our case sites sought to create value for government agencies, but in very different ways. UKDA sought to relieve agencies of the work of curating data as part of their ESRC remit. ICPSR also sought to relieve agencies of curation work, but for a contractual fee. LIS did not provide curation services for agencies, but through inclusion of a country's data in the comparative database, it provided that country's policy analysts with potential new comparative analyses.

How does the data archives position itself in comparison to alternatives over time?

Our case archives faced a number of different alternatives or competitors for resources over time including other data archives. What counts as an alternative is also driven by the perspective of the stakeholder and the potential value the archive might create for that stakeholder. One very important alternative facing all our cases was "free data." All our archives have distinguished themselves from the free data alternative by pointing to the quality of their data product, their documentation and their data deposit services to ensure privacy and distribution. Further, the archives will argue that they provide more data management and preservation services than free data alternatives. Another very important data alternative to deposit of data in our case study archives was "no data." By this we mean that potential depositors (e.g., PIs or government agencies) may simply forgo data contributions. Or, budget decision makers paying membership fees may choose not to pay, and not have access to members-only data.

CONCLUSION

In this paper, we explored three historical case studies of how data archives create value over time, for which stakeholders they create value, and how they position themselves against alternatives such as free data and no data. We used a documentary analytic approach from three social science data archives that have been curating data for decades to explore how perceptions of their "value" changed over 40 years.

This paper provides entry into two fruitful arenas of research. One is temporality and the long-view. Data archives and similar organizations have been creating and articulating value through the evolution of their business models over time; the literature has focused to date on how this happens at discrete points in time instead of examining them over time (OECD 2017). We would suggest that there is now a sizeable body of work upon which to build research that takes the long view. Secondly, this paper suggests that a focus on business models as an aggregation of resources, institutions, data, content, and technologies (among other factors) would provide one means of extending research on information infrastructures beyond the singular cyberinfrastructure/e-science platform case study.

We conclude with a provocation. In the case of sustainability in digital repositories, the assumption persists that infinite sustainability is a universal good (and thus is a "value" in and of itself – perhaps the greatest one?). This assumption places limitations on a discourse that should be more critically considered. Because digital technologies have made it possible to archive almost all content and because there are always costs associated with maintaining any repository, information professionals are in the position not just to advocate for the creation of infinitely sustainable archives but to also consider the needs of repository users recognizing that some repositories may not need to be infinitely sustained. Just because repositories CAN last, should they? To have substantive and thoughtful discussions about what and how long particular kinds of digital content should be retained, we cannot rely on a shared assumption that longer is better. Instead, we must consider how long is good. And sometimes, that what is good might not necessarily be forever.

ACKNOWLEDGMENTS

This study was funded by the Alfred P. Sloan Foundation G-2014-14521. Special thanks to Allison Langham for assistance with data analysis.

REFERENCES

Bauin, S., & Rothman, H. (1992). "Impact" of journals as proxies for citation counts. In P. Weingart, R. Sehringer, & M. Winterhager (Eds.), *Representations of science and technology* (pp. 225-239). Leiden: DSWO Press.

Beagrie, N., & Pink, C. (2012). "Benefits from research data management in universities for industry and not-for-profit research partners", White Paper, Retrieved from http://opus.bath.ac.uk/32509/

Bijker, W. (1995) Of Bicycles, Bakelites and Bulbs: Towards a Theory of Sociotechnical Change. Cambridge, MA: MIT Press.

Berman, F. & Lavoie, B. (2011). Economics and digital preservation: Final report of the Blue Ribbon Task Force on Sustainable Digital Preservation and Access. July 2011. Retrieved from: http://www.digitalpreservation.gov/meetings/documents/ndiipp11/Berman.pdf

Bradley, K. (2007). Defining digital sustainability. Library Trends, 56(1), 148-163.

DaSilva, C.M.; Trkman, P. (2014). "Business model: What it is and what it is not", Long Range Planning, 47(6), 379–389.

Dillo, I., Hodson, S., & de Waard, A. (2016). Income Streams for Data Repositories, White Paper, February 28, 2016. Retrieved from https://zenodo.org/record/46693#.WsSj59PwaV4

Ember, C. and Hanisch, R. (2013), "Sustaining domain repositories for digital data", White Paper, ICPSR, University ofMichigan-Ann Arbor, Michigan, 11 December 2013. Retrieved from: https://rd-alliance.org/sites/default/files/WhitePaper_ICPSR_SDRDD_121113.pdf

Eschenfelder, K. Shankar, K. (2017) Organizational Resilience in Data Archives: Three Case Studies in Social Science Data Archives. Data Science Journal, 16, p 12. DOI: http://doi.org/10.5334/dsj-2017-012

Gambardella, A. and McGahan, A. M. (2010). Business-model innovation: General purpose technologies and their implications for industry structure. Long range planning, 43(2-3), 262-271.

Guthrie, K., Griffiths, R., & Maron, N. (2008). Sustainability and Revenue Models for Online Academic Resources. Strategic Content Alliance, (May), 66.

LIS Cross National Data Archive (2018) "Services". Retrieved April 1, 2018 from http://www.lisdatacenter.org/about-lis/services/

LIS Cross National Data Archive (2018) "About LIS". Retrieved April 1, 2018 from www.lisdatacenter.org/about-lis/.

ICPSR (2018) "Start Sharing Data" Retrieved April 3, 2018 from https://www.icpsr.umich.edu/icpsrweb/deposit/

Maron, N. L., & Loy, M. (2011). Revenue, Recession, Reliance: Revisiting the SCA/Ithaka S+R Case Studies in Sustainability.

Michener, W. K., Allard, S., Budden, A., Cook, R. B., Douglass, K., Frame, M., ... & Vieglais, D. A. (2012). Participatory design of DataONE—enabling cyberinfrastructure for the biological and environmental sciences. Ecological Informatics, 11, 5-15.

Morris, M.; Schindehutte, M.; Allen, J. (2005). "The entrepreneur's business model: toward a unified perspective", Journal of Business Research, 58, 726–735.

OECD Global Science Forum. (2017) "Business models for sustainable research data repositories." OECD Science Technology and Industry Policy Paper No.47. Retrieved from: http://www.oecd.org/officialdocuments/publicdisplaydocumentpdf/?cote=DSTI/STP/GSF(2017)1/FINAL&docLanguage=En

Osterwalder, A., Pigneur, Y., & Tucci, C. L. (2005). "Clarifying business models: Origins, present, and future of the concept". Communications of the association for Information Systems, 16(1), 1.

Osterwalder, A.; Pigneur, Y.; Papadakos, T.; Bernarda, G.; Smith, A.; Smith , A. (2018) "Value proposition design : How to make stuff people want". John Wiley & Sons: Hoboken, NJ

Porter TM (1995) Trust in Numbers: The Pursuit of Objectivity in Science and Public Life. Princeton, NJ: Princeton University Press.

Shankar, K.; Eschenfelder, K.R.; Downey, G. et. al. (2014) "Social Science Data Archives: Case Studies in Data Sustainability" Poster at the 2014 iConference.

Trimi, S., & Berbegal-Mirabent, J. (2012). Business model innovation in entrepreneurship. International Entrepreneurship and Management Journal, 8(4), 449-465.

Wirtz, B. W., Pistoia, A., Ullrich, S., & Göttel, V. (2016). "Business models: Origin, development and future research perspectives", Long Range Planning, 49(1), 36-54.

Zott, C.; Amit, R.; Massa, L. (2011). "The business model: Recent developments and future research", Journal of Management, 37(4), 1019–1042.

REFERENCES – archival sources

Converse, Philip E. (1963) Memo to Committee of 8. [Minutes of Meeting Ann-Arbor Dec 1-2, 1962] , 0071 Bimu 2, ICPSR publications, Bentley Historical Library University of Michigan

ESRC (1988). 1988-1989 ESRC Data archive annual report [planning document]. UKDA Administrative files, University of Essex UK.

Farlie, D. J. C. (1971). Memo on review of the present and future of the SSRC Data Bank. UKDA Administrative Files. University of Essex UK.

ICPSR (1963) Annual Report 1962-1963. 0071 Bimu 2, ICPSR publications, Bentley Historical Library University of Michigan

ICPSR (1971, October) Council Meeting Minutes [minutes] 0071 Bimu 2, ICPSR publications, Bentley Historical Library University of Michigan

ICPSR (1974, March) Council Meeting Minutes [minutes] 0071 Bimu 2, ICPSR publications, Bentley Historical Library University of Michigan.

ICPSR (1994, October) Council Meeting Minutes [minutes]. 0071 Bimu 2, ICPSR publications, Bentley Historical Library University of Michigan

ICPSR (1995) Journey to the 21st Century: Towards a Strategic Plan for ICPSR [manuscript] Ann Arbor, MI: ICPSR.

ICPSR (1995b) Annual Report. 1994-1995. 0071 Bimu 2, ICPSR publications, Bentley Historical Library University of Michigan

ICPSR (1996) The Future of ICPSR [Long Range Planning Subcommittee Memo] 0071 Bimu 2, ICPSR publications, Bentley Historical Library University of Michigan.

ICPSR (2000, June) Council Meeting Minutes [minutes] 0071 Bimu 2, ICPSR publications, Bentley Historical Library University of Michigan

Land, F. (1970). 1970 Report to the SSRC Data Council.

LIS (1997, Jan 22) Minutes for Sixth LIS Biennial Meeting 21 & 22 July 1997, LIS Headquarters, Differdange, Luxembourg.

LIS (1998, July) Luxembourg Income Survey. (1)2, 6. UKDA Administrative files, University of Essex UK.

Rockwell, R. (1994, Nov 17) Distribution of AHEAD Data. [email to ICPSR Council] 0071 Bimu 2, ICPSR publications, Bentley Historical Library University of Michigan.

LIS (2004, May 28) Tim Smeeding to Carolyn Kennedy [Letter]. LIS Administrative Files.

UKDA (1967) Social Science Research Council Databank. [Grant to the ESRC], UKDA Administrative Files, University of Essex UK.

UKDA (1970, March) Minutes. [Minutes SSRC Database Council] UKDA Administrative Files, University of Essex UK.

UKDA (1978). SSRC Data archive: Report and proposal from the director [Report]. UKDA Administrative Files, University of Essex UK.

UKDA (1980) Report on the Review Panel on the SSRC Archive [Report], UKDA Administrative Files, University of Essex UK.

UKDA (1982, October). UKDA Annual report [Report], UKDA Administrative Files, University of Essex UK.

UKDA (1971, Jan 15). Summary of major points arising from Databank meeting [minutes], UKDA Administrative Files, University of Essex UK.

UKDA (1983, October). UKDA Annual report [report], UKDA Administrative Files, University of Essex UK.

UKDA (1984). Director's report [report]. UKDA Administrative Files, University of Essex UK.

UKDA (1994, November) Review of the ESRC Data Archive [Report]. UKDA Administrative Files, University of Essex UK.

Modeling Social Support Scores Using Phone Use Patterns

Isha Ghosh
Rutgers University,
New Brunswick, NJ.
Isha.ghosh@rutgers.edu

Vivek K. Singh
Rutgers University and Massachusetts Institute of Technology,
New Brunswick, NJ.
vivek.k.singh@rutgers.edu

ABSTRACT

Social support is a fundamental concept of interactional behavior and has been consistently linked with higher levels of emotional and physical well-being. Social support has been shown to be an effective coping mechanism in managing stress and depression and to provide positive experiences that directly enhance overall well-being and quality of life. The measurement and quantification of social support has generated a great deal of interest in the behavioral science community over the past 10 years. The dominant approach for quantifying individual social support remains self-reported surveys and generator-methods, which are costly, attention-consuming, and fraught with biases. Given the important role played by mobile phones in mediating human social lives, this study explores the use of phone metadata (call and SMS logs) to automatically infer an individual's social support. Based on Sherbourne and Stewart's Modified Social Support survey (MSSS) as ground truth and ten-week phone data collection for 55 participants, we report that multiple call and SMS based social features are intrinsically associated with social support and perform better than DEMOGRAPHY-BASED models.

KEYWORDS

Social Informatics, Phone Mediated Communication, Data Science

INTRODUCTION

Social support is defined as the resources or aids exchanged between individuals through interpersonal ties (Cohen & Willis, 1985) and the causes and effects of social support have stimulated research for almost 30 years (Dunkel-Schetter & Brooks, 2009; Wortman & Dunkel-Schetter, 1987). Access to social support has been shown to trigger many positive outcomes such as wellbeing and life satisfaction (Turner & Brown, 2010) as well as decrease the negative effects of physical and psychological illnesses more than any other buffering factor (Cohen & Wills, 1985). Social support is often seen as an interactional behavior through which individuals express, and receive emotional concern, instrumental aid, or information (Dunkel-Schetter & Brooks, 2009). Different aspects of an individuals' social network (online or offline), for example the size and diversity of the network, characteristics of their ties, (e.g. frequency of contact, multiplexity, and tie strength), and the attributes of the individual network members (e.g. age and gender) have been shown to have a relationship with their social support (Wellman & Frank, 2001). Social support consists of a variety of helping behaviors performed by one person for the benefit of another. Examples of such behaviors include giving advice, empathizing, assisting with practical tasks, and expressing encouragement (Barrera, Sandler, & Ramsay, 1981). Both receiving support, and perceiving that support is available, are associated with positive outcomes. Numerous studies indicate that people with spouses, friends, and family members who provide psychological and material resources are in better health than those with fewer supportive social contacts. Having access to a network that provides social support has been linked to reduction of stress, improvement of mental-health and depression, and increasing the overall well-being experienced by individuals (Haslam, O'Brien, Jetten, Vormedal, & Penna, 2005).

Previous research on how social support is transferred and received in social networks often builds on the theoretical concept of social capital (Bourdieu, 1980; Putnam, 1995). Williams (2006) adapted the concept of social capital to describe social support within online contexts and developed an operationalization of online social capital. Community ties with friends and relatives often provide different forms of social support for individuals. These relationships have also been shown to translate into social capital that people use to deal with daily life, seize opportunities, and reduce uncertainties (Kadushin, 1981). Social support needs to be differentiated from social capital, though. Social capital refers to the resources from one's social network (Lin, 2002) and originated in sociological research, whereas social support is a psychological construct. Adler and Kwon (2002) suggest to clearly distinguish between the source and the effects of social capital. The source is "the structure and content of the actor's social relations", whereas the effects are "the information, influence, and solidarity it makes available to the actor" (p. 23). Accordingly, social support is a possible effect of social capital.

Recent research investigating access to social support from online sources has highlighted how informational and emotional support is transacted in online settings (Ellison, Vitak, Gray, & Lampe, 2014; Chang, 2009). Informational support shows strong connections to the concept of bridging social capital as weak ties offer access to a wide array of connections, which may be capitalized in terms of novel information (Ellison et al., 2014). Emotional support is strongly linked to bonding social capital, as strong ties are an important source of emotional support. While the context-dependent aspects of social support have been previously studied, modeling the overall social support accessible to a person from various aspects of their network remains an open area of research.

Studies on online social networking have examined the exchange of social support through online social networking and its outcomes. Acquiring social support from others in a social network is found to be one of the most important reasons for online social networking (Oh & Syn, 2015; Oh, Ozkaya, & LaRose, 2013). People use online spaces to discuss problems or obtain information that is helpful when coping with particular stressors. Social media sites may fulfill a need for social belongingness, distract people from various stressors, or offer micro-boosts to self-esteem by being "friended," "liked," or "followed" by others (Cole, Nick, Zelkowitz, Roeder, & Spinelli, 2017). Previous studies from several different disciplines including communication, psychology and sociology suggest that the Internet offers opportunities to exchange information and consolation with online associates (Salehan & Negahban, 2013; Walther & Boyd, 2002) and fosters meaningful relationships (Parks & Floyd, 1996). Digital communications have also shown to help in mobilizing social support as well as maintaining and strengthening existing relationships with geographically near and distant contacts (Quan-Haase, Mo, & Wellman, 2017). While this research addresses the relationship between internet social network communities and the creation and maintenance of social support, the study of various facets of mobile phone usage as a facilitator of supportive social networks remains an open question.

Traditional approaches for quantifying individual social support have focused on aspects that could be simply observed (e.g., gender, race, age) or elicited in a small period of time in lab settings (e.g., via surveys and generator methods) (Gottlieb & Bergen, 2010). Each of these approaches relies on active human reporting and must contend with numerous hurdles such as subjectivity in reports and observations, social and cognitive biases, and narrow observation chances, while dealing with pressures such as budget, time, and the effort required. *This implies that there are no current approaches that infer an individual's social support levels without the need for active human effort.*

In today's world, mobile phones have become one of the most favored devices to interact and communicate with friends, family, as well as engage with digital information in its various forms. As interactions get increasingly mediated via mobile phones, individuals communicating with each other via these devices, form their own social network (Beale, 2005). Data generated from smartphones can provide insights into how often and which members of the network people choose to communicate with, changes in conversational patterns, as well as length and breadth of communication with different members of the network. Recently, mobile phones along with sensor-based data have been used by multiple researchers to construct rich and individualized models of human behavior in social, spatial, and temporal settings, and link them to individual personality traits such as privacy attitudes and trust propensity (Singh & Ghosh, 2017; Blumenstock, Cadamuro, & On, 2015). Emerging research has explored the potential of using information passively (i.e. without active human effort) gathered from these phone-mediated interactions to make predictions about an individual's economic status, personality traits, and well-being (de Montjoye, Quoidbach, Robic, & Pentland, 2013). Given such recent results and the theoretical literature connecting social support with social capital, mental health and well-being, (Ruvalcaba-Romero, Fernández-Berrocal, Salazar-Estrada, & Gallegos-Guajardo, 2017), this study explores the creation of an automated phone data-based approach for modeling individual social support. Such a phone-based method, if successful, would offer a low-cost, faster, scalable, and automatic method for generating insights into social support for millions of users with applications in information science research, health and wellness, as well as communications and sociology. Specifically, this exploratory study examines the following research questions:

RQ1. Which (if any) long-term phone-use patterns have associations with an individual's social support levels?
RQ2. Can a machine learning algorithm be used to automatically infer individual social support based on phone metadata?
In this work, we analyze data from a ten-week field study to systematically study the interconnections between phone-based behavioral measures (e.g. number of phone calls made) and "ground truth" modified social support survey scores based on Sherbourne and Stewart's (1991) survey for 55 individuals.

STUDY

We study the interconnections between social support and phone-based features on the data gathered as part of <Anonymized> Study undertaken at a major university in the Northeastern part of the United States of America. The participants for the study were recruited using flyers, email announcements, and social media posts in the area surrounding a major North American university. The participants needed to: (1) be between 18-75 years of age; (2) comfortable with written and oral English; (3) use an Android smartphone; (4) carry their phone on them most of the time; and (5) be willing and able to travel to the study site for three in-person sessions. This can hence be considered a convenience sample, which was considered acceptable, given the exploratory nature of this work.

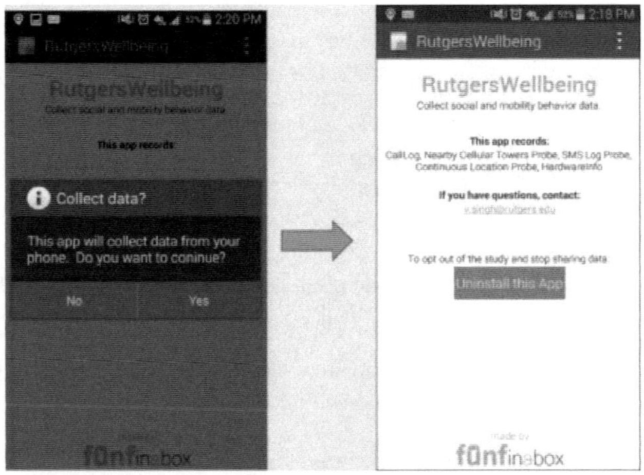

Figure 1. Screenshot of the App (anonymized for review)

Participants in this study were asked to attend three in-person sessions for surveys and to install a mobile application (Figure 1) onto their smartphone. The app recorded anonymized call and SMS metadata (calls/SMS initiated or received - number, times and anonymized id but no actual audio or text). The app also recorded location metadata, which is not relevant to the current discussion. The study included 59 participants. However, some of the participants did not complete all the surveys, and some did not enter their unique identifying code consistently across different surveys, resulting in a set of 55 participants for whom we have the mobile-based data as well as the scores for the two surveys of interest (more details on surveys presented later). The survey order was randomized for different participants. Participation in this study was voluntary and incentivized monetarily. The participants were compensated up to a sum of $100 on successful completion of the study over the ten-week period.

MEASURES

Demographic Descriptors

The sample consisted of 36 male and 19 female participants (university population is 50% male, 50% female). The most common age group for participants was 18-21 years, the most common education level was "some college," the median annual family income was in the range $35,000-$49,000 and 96% of them were single. A visual representation of the demographic is presented in Figure 2.

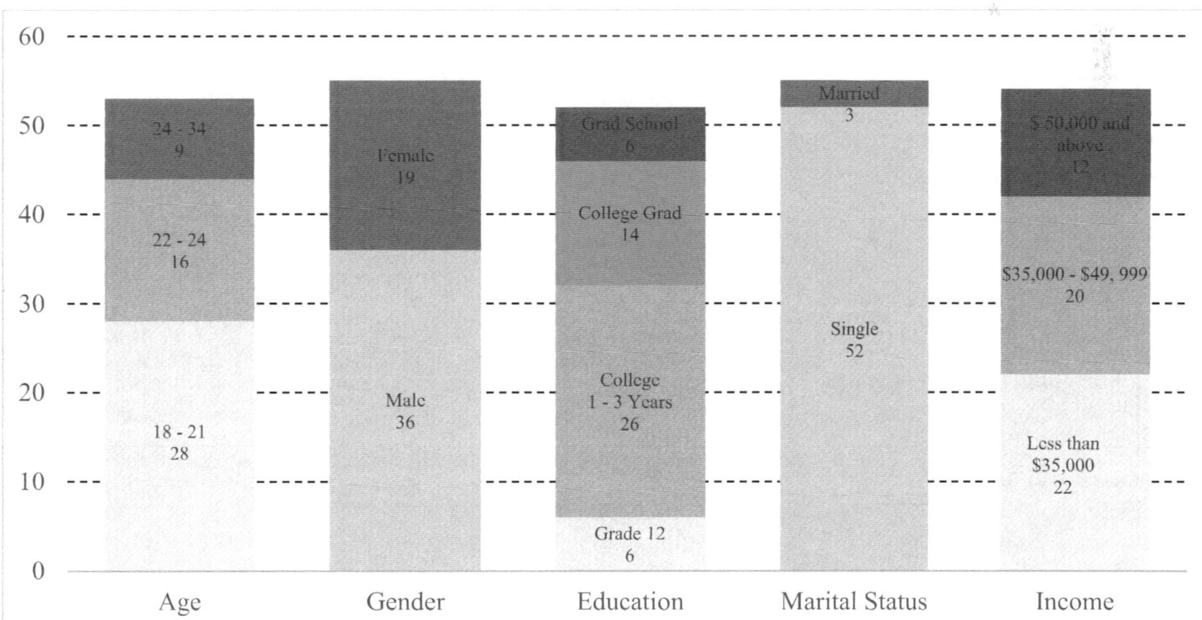

Figure 2. Descriptive statistics of the sample population

Data type	Number of participants	Data points
Calls	55	28,132 calls
SMS	55	187,720 messages
Surveys	55	2 surveys per participant.

Table 1. Summary of data considered in this study

A summary of the data collected over the ten-week period in Spring 2015 is shown in Table 1. The participants on average made 511 phone calls (median = 312; minimum = 43; maximum = 2,711) and exchanged 3,413 SMS messages (median = 2,423; minimum = 21; maximum = 17,625) over this period.

Social Support

The survey was based on Sherbourne and Stewart's Modified Social Support Survey (1991). This is a 19-item, self-administered social support survey measuring measure functional social support. It has been actively used by multiple studies (>4000 citations per Google Scholar) and is considered universally applicable (McDowell, 2006). The 19 items cover four domains of social support (emotional/informational support, tangible support, positive social interaction, and affection) as well as an overall social support score. Participants were asked to answer questions on a 5-point scale ranging from Strongly Disagree (1) to Strongly Agree (5).

Minimum	Maximum	Mean	Median
2	5	3.76	4

Table 2. Summary of Social Support Scores

A descriptive summary of the overall social support score is shown in Table 2.

While the different constructs of social support have previously been studied in relationship with online social networks, the quantification of the overall social support experienced by an individual remains to be studied. The unique affordances of a mobile phone (e.g.: access to synchronous and asynchronous modes of communication via call and text) make it the device of choice to connect with ties of different strengths in different modes (synchronous, asynchronous), across differing times and locations and provides different forms of social support.

Characterizing Phone-based Social Support

At a conceptual level, social support is closely connected with an individual's relative position in the network (Trepte, Dienlin, & Reincke, 2015). On a more granular level, the frequency of communication and access to strong and weak ties in a network has also been connected to social support (Oh et al., 2013). Such features have been operationalized over online social networks (Cole et al., 2017) and recently over phone networks in different contexts (Quan-Haase et al., 2015). At an empirical level, multiple recent efforts have quantified different aspects of individual behavior based on phone metadata with a goal to identify personal traits and well-being (de Montjoye et al., 2013; Singh & Ghosh, 2017).

Based on a survey of existing literature we characterize phone use features into four categories to understand different aspects of an individual's social behavior. In defining these features (total 17), we integrate some of the more obvious usage patterns (total number of calls/sms messages) with more nuanced/exploratory aspects of phone usage while keeping the number of features manageable.

Type	Phone Features	Empirical Support	Conceptual Framework
Social Activity	Call_Count Sms_Count Total_call_duration InOut_ratioCalls InOut_ratioSMS Call_Response_rate Missed_call_percentage	Oh et al., 2013 Utz & Breuer, 2016 Kovanen, Saramaki, & Kaski, 2010	Relational Investment Social Connectedness Donath, 2008; Ellison et al., 2014
Tie Strength	Call_Strong_ties; Sms_Strong_ties; Call_StrongWeak_ties_ratio; Sms_StrongWeak_ties_ratio	Wellman & Wortley, 1990 Luarn, Kuo, Chiu, & Chang, 2015 Utz & Breuer, 2016	Tie-Strength Granovetter (1973) Wellman, 1992
Relationship Maintenance	Call_Loyalty; Sms_Loyalty	Wellman, 1992	Relationship Maintenance Behavior Barrera, 1986
Temporal Rhythms	Day_night_Call_ratio; Day_night_sms_ratio; Weekday_weekend_call_ratio; Weekday_weekend_SMS_ratio	Jumin, Hyungeun, & Jung-hee, 2010 O'Keefe, & Sulanowski, 1995	Circadian Rhythms Abdullah et al., 2014; deMontjoye et al., 2013

Table 3. Summary of features considered in this study.

Social Activity

Theoretically, the amount of supportive interaction an individual has is associated with the size and frequency of communication within their network (Oh et al., 2013). In the context of a phone-based network, we quantify social activity as the frequency and duration of interactions within a network. Social support is also defined as an "interpersonal transaction" (Utz & Breuer, 2016), this implies that reciprocity plays an important role in individuals' social activity. Here, ease of access is operationalized using features related to accepting or rejecting calls (Kovanen, Saramaki, & Kaski, 2010). In the context of phone use networks, social activity can be characterized by the following seven features: Call_Count; Sms_Count; Total_call_duration; InOut_ratioCalls; InOut_ratioSMS; Call_Response_rate; Missed_call_percentage.

Tie Strength

The strength of relationships in a network have been shown to have a significant impact on supportive ties (Wellman & Wortley, 1990). Prior literature also connects strong and weak ties with different aspects social support (Wellman, 1992). On social network sites, responding to a post via a comment or message has shown to be indicative of a strong tie and provide emotional support to users (Luarn, Kuo, Chiu, & Chang, 2015). The number of comments or "likes" received for a post has also been shown to be indicative of support (Utz & Breuer, 2016). Since frequency of interaction is an important predictor of tie strength, to quantify the relative role of different types of ties in one's social network we approximate "strong ties" as the top-third most frequent of their contacts. For both calls and SMS, we quantify the number of interactions that take place with these "strong ties" as well as the relative percentage of all interactions that take place with these contacts. We characterize the following four features as indicative of tie-strength: Call_Strong_ties; Sms_Strong_ties; Call_StrongWeak_ties_ratio; Sms_StrongWeak_ties_ratio

Relationship Maintenance

Humans are a social species, with many survival advantages accruing from our connections to others (Wellman, 1992). Because humans have a fundamental need to feel that they belong to a group, social interaction should improve well-being by fulfilling these needs. Satisfaction will be greatest when there is frequent communication within a subset of the network (Luarn et al., 2015). This is because the need to belong is not satisfied by social interaction alone, but also requires stable interpersonal relationships marked by positive concern and caring. The people an individual chooses to reach out to in times of need is also considered an important indicator of social support. We define "loyalty" as the percentage of communication (call/sms) occurring only with the top three contacts of an individual. A high loyalty score (close to 1) would indicate a tendency to prefer repeated interactions with a small number of favorite connections. We characterize the following two features as indicative of relationship maintenance within phone-based networks: Call_Loyalty; Sms_Loyalty

Temporal Rhythms

While mobile phones allow us to be always connected and available, prior research has documented a difference in the interactions made during phases of the day (e.g. morning, evening, night). Further, interactions during late night (past midnight) have been shown to have predictive power on mental health and well-being (Jumin, Hyungeun, & Jung-hee, 2010). Research has also shown a difference in the frequency and quality of phone calls made during weekdays and weekends (O'Keefe, & Sulanowski, 1995). Hence, to understand the rhythms in user activity i.e. consistency across different times of day and different days, we quantify temporal phone usage pattern as the ratio of calls/sms received during AM Phase (12 AM – 11:59 AM) to calls/sms received during the PM phase (12 PM – 11:59 PM) and the ratio of calls/sms received during weekdays to calls/sms received during weekend. We define the following four features as indicative of temporal rhythms: Day_night_Call_ratio; Day_night_sms_ratio; Weekday_weekend_call_ratio; Weekday_weekend_SMS_ratio.

RESULTS- INFERRING SOCIAL SUPPORT

Predictive Model

Predicting social support scores from phone use patterns level is a regression problem; that is, predicting an outcome variable (i.e., social support scores) from a set of input predictors (i.e., phone-based features). We utilize Lasso (Least Absolute Shrinkage and Selection Operator) regularized linear regression model as our predictive model (Tibshirani, 1996). This technique has previously been used to infer human values from social media text analysis (Chen, Hsieh, Mahmud, & Nicolas, 2014). Another study using data gathered from Android phones to understand how individuals handle apps stored on their phone also uses Lasso regression as a technique to shrink the number of features and create an efficient predictive model (Li, Ai, Liu, Tang, Huang, Feng, and Mei, 2016). Previous research shows that Lasso regression is most effective when we wish to shrink features or variables to enhance the efficiency of a predictive model. In the current study, we have a large number of behavioral features for a relatively small dataset. Given this previous research on the efficiency of Lasso regression, this technique was chosen to build the model. Lasso minimizes the sum of squared errors, with a bound on the sum of the absolute values of the coefficients. Thus, Lasso automatically selects more relevant features and discards redundant features. We have $D = 17$ input features and $N = 55$ training cases. Lasso has been specifically designed to help identify relevant features (i.e., predictors) in such settings (N not much greater than D), while avoiding overfitting.

We use Pearson's correlation coefficient (r) between the model's predicted value and the "ground truth" survey value to quantify the prediction performance. We also report the mean absolute error (MAE). A smaller MAE is preferred because it indicates that the predictions are closer to the ground truth. The MAE is in the same unit as the predicted variable and is hence relatively easy to interpret.

Prediction Results

We evaluate three different prediction models in this work. These correspond three different approaches (phone feature-based, demography-based, and phone + demography based). Demography based features have been connected with social support in numerous studies (e.g., Manalel & Antonucci, 2017) and hence we use this approach as a baseline. Specifically, the difference between the demography-based model and the phone-features based model helps us interpret the predictive power of phone-based features. Further, the combined phone + demography model quantifies the performance in scenarios where demography information is already available (e.g., to the phone company, automatically derived via phone features (Zhong, Tan, Mo, & Yang, 2013) or surveyed once to allow for repeated social support inferences over time.

We apply 15-fold cross validation to determine the parameters for Lasso and the weights for each feature in each evaluation. The results for the evaluation in terms of correlation coefficients between predicted and actual scores for the target variable are summarized in Table 4.

	Phone-features based model	Demography based model	Phone + Demography based model
Overall Social Support	0.65	0.21	0.68

Table 4. Correlation between the predicted values based on different models and the real values of overall support.

As can be seen in Table 4, the predicted social support strongly correlates with the ground truth with $r = 0.65$ ($p < 0.01$). As a baseline for comparison we also consider models that focus only on the available demographic features (age, gender, marital status, ethnicity, level of education, and family income level).

	Phone-features based model	Demography based model	Phone + Demography based model
Overall Social Support	0.61	0.81	0.58

Table 5. Mean Absolute Error (MAE) for the predicted values based on different models and the real values of overall social support score.

While demographics explain some variance in the social capital levels, it can be clearly seen that phone-based features provide much higher predictive performance than that obtained by using only demography-based features. This underscores the value of phone-based features in automatically predicting social support scores for individuals. Lastly, the models that use both phone and demography based data have a correlation score of 0.68. This suggests that phone features are not merely replacements for demography-based features but rather, add complementary information.

We report the Mean Absolute Errors (MAE) between the actual and predicted values in Table 5. For instance, the MAE for predicted social support score using phone and demographic data was found to be 0.58, indicating that the predictions are within ±0.58 of the "ground truth" or survey based values of social support scores. Since the values for social support can theoretically range from 1 to 5, we consider an error of ±0.58 to be acceptable. We also note that the phone based models consistently yield lower errors than demography based models, and combining the phone and demography data yields the models with the lowest error rates.

Correlation Analysis

To understand the relative effect of different phone-based features on social support we undertook a *post-hoc* Pearson's correlation analysis between the social support scores obtained from the survey and phone-based features as shown in Table 6.

Phone Use features	Overall Social Support
Call_Count	0.082
Sms_Count	0.064
Total_Call_duration	0.364**
InOut_ratio	0.290*
Call_Response_rate	0.243
Missed_call_percentage	-0.258
Inout_ratio_SMS	0.218
Call_Loyalty	0.077
Sms_Loyalty	-0.198
Call_Strong_ties	0.343*
Sms_Strong_ties	0.276*
Call_SW_ties_ratio	0.246
Sms_SW_ties_ratio	-0.07
Day_night_Call_ratio	0.305*
Day_night_sms_ratio	-0.198
Weekday_weekend_call_ratio	-0.21
Weekday_weekend_SMS_ratio	0.204

Table 6. Bivariate correlation between phone-based features and overall social support score.

From Table 6, we see that the highest association was found with the total call duration ($r = 0.36$). This implies that the amount of time an individual spends on call interactions is more significant than the total number of calls for inferring a social support score. The calls and SMS made to strong ties (i.e. the top third most frequent contacts) also have a significant relationship with social support scores. Social support literature distinguishes the roles of strong and weak ties in providing social support. Strong ties are thought to provide empathic support, while weak ties maybe less willing to provide significant services but do provide access to new opportunities and ideas (Granovetter, 1973). As Wellman (1992) notes, "Nurturing, caring, and tangible assistance are more likely to be expected and provided more readily in closer, multiplex, dense relationships, which also likely carry a presumption of reciprocity of supportive behavior". Research also argues that everyday support received from strong ties is what promotes well-being, confirming the recipients' sense of mattering to other people and sustaining a sense of self-worth (Utz & Breuer, 2016).

From the perspective of social support, it is just as important to initiate relationships as it is to be available to other members of the network. Similarly, we note that the ratio of incoming to outgoing calls is positively associated with social support. We also find a significant correlation between relative ratio of calls received after 12 am and social support scores ($r = 0.30$). A possible interpretation is that calls made or received late at night are likely to be from close family or friends, therefore, a higher number of such calls would imply that the individual had access to a larger supportive network. These results underscore the value of initiating calls, talking to multiple individuals in such calls, and access to contacts with whom one can interact even at less common hours (i.e. during AM phase.)

DISCUSSION

The first research question (RQ1) for this work aimed at understanding the associations (if any) between long-term phone-use patterns and an individual's social support. Based on the reasonably high explanatory power at a collective level (regression analysis) and multiple significant associations at an individual level (correlation analysis), we report that many of the phone-based features may indeed be intricately associated with individual social support.

The results of correlation analysis are largely in line with prior literature (Burke & Kraut, 2016). At the same time, they expand the understanding of these ties and the associations to how they manifest themselves over smartphones. The smartphone is a convenient, highly accessible, and capable device that is well suited to share and disclose information. It is a two-way device, creating and consuming information, is highly personal, and is almost always available. Based on Beale's (2005) work, this study treats people connected via the smartphone as part of a supportive social network and interactions performed within this network communicative of relationship creation and maintenance behavior.

Relationship maintenance is shown to be a significant factor in achieving a feeling of connectedness within a network and therefore, enhancing social support (Ellison et al., 2014). In addition to directly maintaining relationships though substantive communication, the symbolic value of communication also can maintain relationships independent of the content exchanged. For example, according to the theory of relational investment (Donath, 2008; Ellison et. al, 2014), the frequency and length of messages serve as signals of relationship value in social network sites. Donath (2008) states that "cost in time is a signal of the resources one is willing to commit to this relationship" (p. 238). According to this theory, more effortful communication should have a greater impact on social support, we find similar results for smartphone interactions. Research also points to embeddedness in a network as an important factor in gaining social support (Barrera, 1986). In the context of social networking sites, belonging within a network is demonstrated via explicit behaviors signaling attention from other members of the network (Donath, 2008). For instance, explicit responses to a post via a like or comment is indicative of attention provided to the user. Assessing embeddedness within smartphone interactions is more challenging as there are no explicit markers to signal attention. However, individuals who have a higher social activity can be said to have a greater sense of belonging within the network. Therefore, phone use characteristics such as social activity can be an indicator of social support.

Research also specifies the role played by strong ties in providing social support (Utz & Breuer, 2016). Communicating with strong ties on Facebook is associated with increases in perceived social support and reductions in stress (Burke & Kraut, 2013) This reasoning suggests that online communication with stronger ties rather than with weaker ones should lead to larger improvements in well-being. We find tie-strengths within phone use networks to be an indicator of social support.

A feature of potential interest is the ratio of phone usage during the AM phase (midnight – 11:59 am) to the PM phase. In the considered dataset, the AM phase corresponds to the less socially active time period, and a higher score on this feature corresponds to more than usual activity during this period. Mobile phones allow an individual the possibility of being constantly connected to one's family and friends, however, etiquette dictates that most communications are made in more common or "regular" hours. Therefore, the analysis of phone-use patterns at irregular times could provide useful insights into an individual's social network. In past studies, late night communication has been connected with stress and potentially the need for social support. This suggests a future research direction where the *temporality* of interactions between individuals should be studied for its associations with strength of ties, as well as diversity in network structure.

The second research question for this work (RQ2) focused on the feasibility of a machine learning algorithm to automatically infer support based on phone metadata. Based on the results of the Lasso regression models, we report that phone-based features can perform reasonably well at estimating social support as obtained via survey methods. The correlation between the predicted and the actual overall social support scores was 0.65 and this went up to 0.68 in cases where demography data were also available. As many of the demography variables commonly available to phone service and app providers, can be inferred using phone metadata, or require one-time input, they can often be used in conjunction with phone-based features. The resulting model has a MAE of ± 0.58 which indicates that the predictions are within ± 0.58 of the "ground truth" or survey-based values of social support scores

This work is intended to start a conversation on the topic of automated inference of social support, rather than be a final word on it. Hence, we will be cautious in generalizing the results to larger populations until they are verified at scale. We define a set of 17 features for the sample set (n=55) and use Lasso regression, a technique specifically designed to avoid overfitting, and consider the correlation analysis only as a post-hoc interpretation mechanism. We note the moral and ethical considerations in building a social support score based solely on passive data collection. However, this score is intended to help individuals gain an awareness of their social network and the resources they potentially have access to. We also recognize the privacy implications of using an individual's smartphone metadata, however, we suggest using explicit opt-in measures that allow individuals to retain control of their information (e.g. via OpenPDS (de Montjoye, Shmueli, Wang, & Pentland 2014)). While the large-scale analysis and inference of social behaviors requires a larger policy conversation, we believe there is value in exploring these newer directions in order to inform the policy debate.

The phone-based predictions obtained here are not an exact replication of the scores obtained by the survey. However, the associations found paint a vision forward and the explanatory power achieved is comparable to those found in similar social computing studies. Given the limitation of sample size, we believe that the correlation scores (0.68) obtained here show a promising direction for the automated prediction of an individual's social support scores.

Despite certain limitations, this paper makes an important contribution towards the literature on social informatics, human centered data-science, and social computing. While previous efforts have studied self-reported interconnections between social behavior and social support, there is no existing effort that has studied the potential of using automated phone-based data to infer and predict the social support scores for individuals.

IMPLICATIONS AND FUTURE DIRECTIONS

In this study we track an individuals' social support via the phone, without having the need for complicated surveys or generator methods, making it a convenient way to get an ongoing assessment of how their daily interactions can impact social support and potentially suggest how it can be increased. The connection between social support and general well-being has been well-documented in literature (Zhang & Yang, 2013; Chang, 2009). It has been shown to directly contribute to the physical and psychological outcomes of health interventions (Zhang & Yang, 2013). The ability to provide and receive social support from a network is also an important motivation for information sharing and social engagement (Oh & Syn, 2013).

For instance, in spite of the many advantages gained from social support, many Americans don't feel they have access to this valuable resource (APA, 2018). When asked if there is someone they can ask for support in times of stress, such as talking over problems or helping make difficult decisions, more than half (55 percent) also said they could have used at least a little more emotional support. Individuals' also reported feelings of loneliness and uncertainty about access to support in stressful situations. American Psychological Association's (2015) article on strengthening supportive networks discusses the importance of proactively building a network that can help provide social support in times of need. Therefore, the ability to track one's social support score via a ubiquitous device like the mobile phone can be useful for individuals to be aware of their social support scores and also give valuable insights on the effect of regular interactions on one's social support score. For instance, people often lose established connections due to life changes such as retirement, relocation, or the death of a loved one. An assessment of how these changes affect one's supportive network can help provide a spur towards forging newer connections in order to have access to a supportive network when required.

Future work in this direction would require a nuanced conversation addressing the constructs of social support as well as integrating more specific phone features such as video calls as well as validation at a larger scale with participants from various demographics. With a larger target group and wide-scale validation, the proposed could help billions of users to keep a track of their social support scores and receive valuable suggestions when appropriate.

REFERENCES

Adler, P.S., & Kwon, S. (2002). Social capital: Prospects for a new concept. *Academy of Management Review*, 27(1), 17–40.

Barrera, M., Jr. (1986). Distinctions between social support concepts, measures, and models. *American Journal of Community Psychology*, 14, 413-416.

Beale, R. (2005). Supporting social interaction with smart phones. *IEEE Pervasive Computing*, 4(2), 35-41.

Blumenstock, J., Cadamuro, G., & On, R. (2015). Predicting poverty and wealth from mobile phone metadata. *Science*, 350(6264), 1073-1076.

Bourdieu, P. (1986). The forms of capital. In J. G. Richardson (Ed.), *Handbook of theory and research for the sociology of education* (pp. 241–258). New York: Greenwood.

Burke, M., & Kraut, R. E. (2016). The relationship between Facebook use and well-being depends on communication type and tie strength. *Journal of computer-mediated communication*, 21(4), 265-281.

Chang, H. J. (2009). Online supportive interactions: Using a network approach to examine communication patterns within a psychosis social support group in Taiwan. *Journal of the Association for Information Science and Technology*, 60(7), 1504-1517.

Chen, J., Hsieh, G., Mahmud, J. U., & Nichols, J. (2014, February). Understanding individuals' personal values from social media word use. In *Proceedings of the 17th ACM conference on Computer supported cooperative work & social computing* (pp. 405-414). ACM.

Cole, D. A., Nick, E. A., Zelkowitz, R. L., Roeder, K. M., & Spinelli, T. (2017). Online social support for young people: Does it recapitulate in-person social support; can it help? *Computers in Human Behavior*, 68, 456-464.

Cohen, S., & Wills, T. A. (1985). Stress, social support, and the buffering hypothesis. Psychological bulletin, 98(2), 310.

de Montjoye, Y. A., Quoidbach, J., Robic, F., & Pentland, A. S. (2013, April). Predicting personality using novel mobile phone-based metrics. In *International conference on social computing, behavioral-cultural modeling, and prediction* (pp. 48-55). Springer, Berlin, Heidelberg.

de Montjoye, Y. A., Shmueli, E., Wang, S. S., & Pentland, A. S. (2014). openpds: Protecting the privacy of metadata through safeanswers. *PloS one*, 9(7), e98790.

Donath, J. (2008). Signals in social supernets. *Journal of Computer-Mediated Communication*, 13(1), 231–251.

Dunkel Schetter, C., & Brooks, K. (2009). The nature of social support. *Encyclopaedia of human relationships*, 1565-1570.

Ellison, N. B., Vitak, J., Gray, R., & Lampe, C. (2014). Cultivating social resources on social network sites: Facebook relationship maintenance behaviors and their role in social capital processes. *Journal of Computer-Mediated Communication*, 19(4), 855-870.

Ghosh, I., & Singh, V.K. (2016). Predicting Privacy Attitudes Using Phone Metadata. In *Proceedings of 2015 International Conference on Social Computing, Behavioral-Cultural Modeling, & Prediction* (SBP15). 51-60.

Gottlieb, B. H., & Bergen, A. E. (2010). Social support concepts and measures. *Journal of psychosomatic research*, 69(5), 511-520.

Granovetter, M.S. (1973). The strength of weak ties. *American Journal of Sociology*. 78(6), 1360-1380

Haslam, S. A., O'brien, A., Jetten, J., Vormedal, K., & Penna, S. (2005). Taking the strain: Social identity, social support, and the experience of stress. British Journal of Social Psychology, 44(3), 355-370.

Jumin, C., Hyungeun, J., & Jung-hee, R. (2010, February). Predicting Interpersonal Relationships based on Mobile Communication Patters. In *2010 ACM Conference on Computer Supported Cooperative Work (CSCW)* (pp. 487-488).

Kadushin, C. (2002). The motivational foundation of social networks. *Social networks*, 24(1), 77-91.

Kovanen, L., Saramaki, J., & Kaski, K. (2010). *Reciprocity of mobile phone calls*. arXiv preprint arXiv:1002.0763.

Li, H., Ai, W., Liu, X., Tang, J., Huang, G., Feng, F., & Mei, Q. (2016, April). Voting with their feet: Inferring user preferences from app management activities. In *Proceedings of the 25th International Conference on World Wide Web* (pp. 1351-1362). International World Wide Web Conferences Steering Committee.

Lin, N. (1999). Building a network theory of social capital. *Connections*. 22(1), 28-51.

Luarn, P., Kuo, H. C., Chiu, Y. P., & Chang, S. C. (2015). Social support on facebook: the influence of tie strength and gender differences. *International Journal of Electronic Commerce Studies*, 6(1), 37.

Manalel, J. A., & Antonucci, T. C. (2017). Social Relations and Social Support: Understanding Group and Individual Differences. In *Later-Life Social Support and Service Provision in Diverse and Vulnerable Populations* (pp. 28-46). Routledge.

McDowell, I. (2006). *Measuring health: a guide to rating scales and questionnaires*. Oxford university press.

O'Keefe, G. J., & Sulanowski, B. K. (1995). More than just talk: Uses, gratifications, and the telephone. *Journalism & Mass Communication Quarterly*, 72(4), 922-933.

Oh, H. J., Ozkaya, E., & LaRose, R. (2014). How does online social networking enhance life satisfaction? The relationships among online supportive interaction, affect, perceived social support, sense of community, and life satisfaction. *Computers in Human Behavior*, 30, 69-78.

Oh, S., & Syn, S. Y. (2015). Motivations for sharing information and social support in social media: A comparative analysis of Facebook, Twitter, Delicious, YouTube, and Flickr. *Journal of the Association for Information Science and Technology*, 66(10), 2045-2060.

Parks, M. R., & Floyd, K. (1996). Meanings for closeness and intimacy in friendship. *Journal of Social and Personal Relationships*, 13(1), 85-107.

Putnam, R. D. (1995). Bowling alone: America's declining social capital. *Journal of Democracy*. 6(1), 65–78.

Quan-Haase, A., Mo, G. Y., & Wellman, B. (2017). Connected seniors: How older adults in East York exchange social support online and offline. *Information, Communication & Society*, 20(7), 967-983.

Ruvalcaba-Romero, N. A., Fernández-Berrocal, P., Salazar-Estrada, J. G., & Gallegos-Guajardo, J. (2017). Positive emotions, self-esteem, interpersonal relationships and social support as mediators between emotional intelligence and life satisfaction. *Journal of Behavior, Health & Social Issues*, 9(1), 1-6.

Salehan, M., & Negahban, A. (2013). Social networking on smartphones: When mobile phones become addictive. *Computers in Human Behavior*, 29(6), 2632-2639.

Stress About Health Insurance Costs Reported by Majority of Americans, APA Stress in America™ Survey Reveals (2018, January). Retrieved from http://www.apa.org/news/press/releases/2018/01/insurance-costs.aspx

Sherbourne, C. D., & Stewart, A. L. (1991). The MOS social support survey. *Social science & medicine*, 32(6), 705-714.

Singh, V. K., & Ghosh, I. (2017). Inferring Individual Social Capital Automatically via Phone Logs. (Press) *Proceedings of the ACM Human Computer Interaction*, 1(2).

Tibshirani, R. (1996). Regression shrinkage and selection via the lasso. *Journal of the Royal Statistical Society. Series B (Methodological)* 267-288.

Trepte, S., Dienlin, T., & Reinecke, L. (2015). Influence of social support received in online and offline contexts on satisfaction with social support and satisfaction with life: A longitudinal study. *Media Psychology*, 18(1), 74-105.

Turner, R. J., & Brown, R. L. (2010). Social support and mental health. *A handbook for the study of mental health: Social contexts, theories, and systems*, 2, 200-212.

Utz, S., & Breuer, J. (2016). Informational benefits from social media use for professional purposes: Results from a longitudinal study. Cyberpsychology: *Journal of Psychosocial Research on Cyberspace*, 10(4).

Walther, J. B., & Boyd, S. (2002). Attraction to computer-mediated social support. *Communication technology and society: Audience adoption and uses*, 153188.

Wellman, B. (1992). Which types of ties and networks provide what kinds of social support. *Advances in group processes*, 9(1992), 207-235.

Wellman, B., & Wortley, S. (1990). Different strokes from different folks: Community ties and social support. *American Journal of Sociology*, 96(3), 558-588.

Williams, D. (2006). On and off the 'net: scales for social capital in an online era. *Journal of Computer Mediated Communication*, 11(2), 593–628

Wortman, C. B., & Dunkel-Schetter, C. (1987). Conceptual and methodological issues in the study of social support.

Zhang, M., & Yang, C. C. (2015). Using content and network analysis to understand the social support exchange patterns and user behaviors of an online smoking cessation intervention program. *Journal of the Association for Information Science and Technology*, 66(3), 564-575.

Zhong, E., Tan, B., Mo, K., & Yang, Q. (2013). User demographics prediction based on mobile data. *Pervasive and mobile computing*, 9(6), 823-837.

Art and Everyday Information Behavior: Sources of Understanding

Tim Gorichanaz
Drexel University, United States. gorichanaz@drexel.edu

ABSTRACT

In our efforts to design an ethical information future, we must develop a deeper understanding of the information phenomena in everyday lived experience. Based on work in cultural theory and philosophy, art seems to present an illuminating domain for the study of everyday life. This paper presents findings from an exploratory, phenomenology-of-practice study of the information behavior of artists. These findings serve as an entryway to information phenomena that have largely gone unexplored in information behavior. The study builds on the literature of everyday information behavior and artists' information behavior, and it draws on a nascent information behavior theory that recognizes understanding as an epistemic aim and conceptualizes understanding as an information constellation. In this study, seven local artists documented their process creating self-portraits, and semi-structured follow-up interviews were conducted. This paper reports on the findings from four of these artists, demonstrating how memories, the lived environment, profound experiences, and online browsing were informative and contributed to the artists' understandings. It closes by discussing the meaning of these findings for the future of information science, suggesting that the information employed by artists might be recognized and appreciated more widely throughout society.

KEYWORDS

Everyday information behavior, artists, phenomenology, understanding, self-portraits.

INTRODUCTION

Luciano Floridi (2013) contends that we must consider the infosphere ecologically rather than only looking at particular information products, resources or targets. This means that the organization, preservation, sustainability of information, and the education of information professionals, should be directed toward the whole infosphere. This will involve recognizing the breadth of informative phenomena, rather than limiting our understanding to those sources that have traditionally been considered informative in information science. This will involve doing justice to how information manifests in the lived experience of being human, the study of which constitutes everyday information behavior.

Thus, in moving toward an ethical information future, this paper begins to plumb the informativeness of aspects of lived experiences that have gone unstudied in information behavior. In particular, this paper examines the information behavior of artists, showing how memories, the lived environment, profound experiences and online browsing inform visual artists in their work. The study builds on the literature of everyday information behavior and artists' information behavior, and it draws on a nascent theory in information behavior that recognizes understanding as an epistemic aim, which can be conceptualized as an information constellation—bundles of information, held together by narrative. It closes by discussing the possibilities that these findings disclose for the future of information science.

EVERYDAY INFORMATION BEHAVIOR

Interest in everyday life in information science reaches back to the user turn that the field experienced in the late 1970s (see Case & Given, 2016). More concretely, research into the everyday was first conceptualized as "nonwork information seeking" (Savolainen, 1995), and thus "everyday life" came to be defined in contrast to "work." Most research in this tradition was centered on everyday life information seeking (ELIS) (Case & Given, 2016).

In the past two decades, technological and theoretical developments have complicated this picture; the boundary between work and nonwork has blurred across many dimensions (see Rodeheaver & Zafirovski, 2017). Likewise, the scope of everyday life information behavior has broadened. Though much of this research is still focused on ELIS, it has also begun to explore aspects of information behavior beyond seeking. Still, scholars such as Melissa Ocepek (2018) argue that much "everyday" research still largely limits itself to studying the forms of recorded information that have historically concerned information behavior. Moreover, much research in everyday information behavior stops at identifying information sources (e.g., Agarwal, Xu & Poo, 2011). This seems to presume that if a person comes into contact with a piece of information, then they reliably gain the associated knowledge. Reality is surely not this simple, and information behavior researchers should also be concerned with becoming informed (Tkach, 2017). To move the field forward, the everyday should be broadly understood as the world of lived experience, or the lifeworld (Gorichanaz, Latham & Wood, 2018).

In this work, I respond to this need by contributing an information behavior theory of becoming informed through everyday information sources. This theory is based on a recently-proposed epistemic framework for information science (Gorichanaz, 2017), which positions understanding as an epistemic aim, and the concept of information constellations (Gorichanaz, 2018), which provides a method for concretely exploring understanding as information experience.

UNDERSTANDING AND INFORMATION CONSTELLATIONS

Discussions of epistemology in information science are rare (for a review, see Furner, 2010), but insomuch as information is considered an epistemic good they are indispensable. Historically, the most discussed epistemic framework in information science is the pyramid of data, information, knowledge and wisdom, but the verisimilitude and usefulness of this framework is questionable when it comes human knowing (Ma, 2012). In light of these shortcomings, some have sought to revise the pyramid (e.g., Bosancic, 2016).

I have proposed a new epistemic framework for information science based on the concept of understanding in information science and epistemology, as well as other work in phenomenology and philosophy of information (Gorichanaz, 2017). This framework defines two senses of understanding: ontological and ontic. *Ontological understanding* is the mode of being by which any intellectual activity is possible. Thus, ontological understanding is an ongoing background activity that is a matter of an agent's conscious and perceptive engagement with their environment: in short, making sense of one's situation. Over this background, the processes of ontic understanding take place. Here differences are perceived (data) as always already bundled with meaning (i.e., action) as information. This information becomes knowledge when it is accounted for in a satisfactory way, and this accounting-for puts knowledge into ontic understanding, where ontic understanding is a network of knowledge. *Ontic understanding* is defined as a coherent and self-transparent network of knowledge constructed by a conscious agent—for example, one's understanding of quantum mechanics or the American Civil War. Notably, this framework is consonant with a recent articulation of holistic epistemology for information science (Weissenberger, Budd & Herold, 2018).

Why the basis in understanding, and what does this mean for the study of the everyday? Ontic understanding is downstream from knowledge; this means that studying a person's understanding may reveal forms of knowledge, and consequently information sources, that otherwise go unnoticed and have yet to be acknowledged in information behavior research because information behavior research typically begins upstream, with particular information sources.

So how can understanding be studied empirically? In another study, I proposed the concept of information constellations, which are clusters of information linked together by narrative (Gorichanaz, 2018). Such constellations can be gathered and analyzed through narrative-based research techniques. A rich methodological toolkit for such research is provided by phenomenology of practice (van Manen, 2014), which, fittingly, is described by its author as the study of understanding.

In this paper, I present findings from a phenomenology-of-practice study of the information behavior of artists. The domain of art has been little studied in information behavior, yet it is of great importance, as will be discussed in the following section.

ART, INFORMATION, AND THE EVERYDAY

Art can be informative. Therefore, art can be considered information. To say so is not to impoverish or disparage art; on the contrary, it is to rightly acknowledge art as epistemically relevant. More concretely, following Luciano Floridi (2011), to conceptualize something as information is to show how it has perceptible form, how it allows an agent to move forward in their situation, how it can be analyzed within a particular syntax and semantics, and how it exemplifies some aspect of reality to contribute to human understanding.

Though the arts may not always contribute to what we generally define as *knowledge* as they are not necessarily truth-conducive, they may contribute to *understanding*. Elgin (2002, 2017) argues that evidence for this is seen in how art challenges assumptions and furthers inquiry in other fields. Jochen Briesen (2014) further conceptualizes this as art's capacity to provoke new perspectives on a phenomenon, which is a central part of understanding (both ontic and ontological, to use the terms defined above). Mark Johnson (2007) has also argued that art can be regarded as epistemic on the grounds that all meaning, even including intellectual abstraction, ultimately has a biological basis.

If information science is concerned with the production and circulation of understanding throughout society, a view that dates back to Egan and Shera (1952), then art ought to be studied in information science insomuch as it contributes to a society's understanding. Furthermore, art presents a rigorous test case for theories of classification and meaning, given the nonverbal nature of its workings (Day, 2008; Goodman, 1976); and art can challenge widespread philosophical and cultural assumptions and open doors to new understandings (Elgin, 2002; Heidegger, 1971, 1977). Other fields, such as media studies, have recognized art as a form of recorded human knowledge and called for the development of literacies around it (Mirzoeff, 2015). Further research into art from an information perspective has the capacity to bring art back into the realm of everyday life, as discussed variously by Ellen Dissanayake (1992), Michel Foucault (1997), Martin Heidegger (1971, 1977) and Roger Scruton

(2014). These scholars assert that, while today art sits on an "experts only" pedestal, this has not always been the case, and indeed art *works* best when it is integrated into a people's everyday life experience. A recent contribution in this regard is Edward Winters' (2018) essay on the line that has emerged between art and the everyday and modern artists' attempts to erase it. As Winters contends, art is a matter of drawing attention to those aspects of everyday life that would go unnoticed, which feeds forward into further everyday life experiences. Art is conversation with Being.

There has been some research on art in information behavior, though this work has not yet been linked to everyday information behavior. As relevant to the study at hand, the focus here will be on the information behavior of visual artists, but some research on other types of artists exists. Susie Cobbledick (1996) was the first to directly explore artists' information seeking, in an interview study of four faculty artists. Since her work, a number of other researchers have contributed; William Hemmig (2008, 2009) provides a review of this research. Hemmig draws the following conclusions from the literature:

- Artists seem to require information for five distinct purposes: inspiration, specific visual reference, technique, marketing and art world trends.
- Artists frequently need information on subjects unrelated to art, so art libraries rarely serve them well.
- Like information behavior in general, creative information behavior is idiosyncratic.
- Artists have a strong preference for visual information.

After Hemmig, there have been a few studies of artists' information behavior (Mason & Robinson, 2011; Régimbeau, 2009; Robinson, 2014), but Hemmig's findings still stand. A notable contribution in the literature is that of Sandra Cowan (2004), who was the first to conceptualize artists' information behavior outside the confines of the library, in a hermeneutic-phenomenological case study. Cowan interviewed one practicing artist and uncovered five main sources of information in art-making: the natural environment, the work itself, relationships with one's own artwork and with other artists and works, self-inquiry, and attentiveness. A key observation Cowan makes is that the artist does not view her art-making as involving information seeking or needs, but rather as a joyful process of dialogue and perception. Cowan remarks that the artist's "processes are fluid, interrelational, dynamic, and *creative*; they rely on the action of creating understanding, rather than finding pre-existing information" (2004, p. 19). Cowan was one of the first information behavior researchers to point out "creating understanding" as an activity, and this observation further suggests that a research focus on understanding is well-placed.

Though this body of research offers a coherent view of artists' information behavior, it only addresses information needs and seeking, rather than use or creation. To this end, an additional study emerges as relevant, which was not reviewed by Hemmig (2008) and appears to be disconnected from the rest of the literature discussed here: the unpublished doctoral dissertation of Tonyia Tidline (2003), who conducted a narrative analysis of the information behavior of artists. Tidline found that artists see their chosen medium of expression as significant and that engaging with other artwork is an important part of the creative process and artists' development. Tidline sought to provide evidence for the informativeness of art. In light of the above discussion, this evidence now seems to be secure. In her conclusion, Tidline called for further research on how artists work with information in art-making. To date, this call has not been answered. Doing so is a purpose of the present study.

METHODOLOGY AND METHODS

This study engages in phenomenology of practice, a philosophically-informed empirical methodology at the intersection of the social sciences and the humanities, developed by Max van Manen (2014). In phenomenology of practice, a researcher analyzes the experiential accounts of small groups of participants to develop theories *of the unique* (rather than of the general). Phenomenology of practice is a mode of interpretive inquiry that attempts to look deeper into what has been taken for granted. It provides a method for cultivating wonder. As such, it "is primarily a philosophic *method for questioning*, not a method for answering or discovering or drawing determinate conclusions" (van Manen, 2014, p. 29). That is, the value of phenomenology-of-practice findings are not in the concrete facts they apportion, but rather in the questions they spark, the way they reveal new research directions and the way they provoke readers to think and act in new ways.

In this study, I recruited seven local artists to create self-portraits. "Self-portrait" was not defined in the recruitment materials, and there were no requisite criteria for inclusion beyond being at least 18 years old and living locally. I recruited artists through my personal network and by contacting local artists whose information I found online. I used purposive sampling to assemble a diverse group of artists—they ranged in age, gender, professionality, artistic medium and experience. The artists were not necessarily portraitists; in fact, one never before created a self-portrait. In our initial meeting, I discussed the project with each participant and attained informed consent. All the artists elected to be identified in this study and gave permission for their images to be shared.

Visual and verbal empirical material was collected as the artists individually worked on their self-portraits. At the end of each work session, each artist completed a self-interview inspired from the technique of think-aloud protocols. After each piece was finished, a semi-structured follow-up interview was conducted. All the material from each individual artist constituted one lived experience example, or case. Analysis began along with empirical gathering and proceeded iteratively, according to guidelines given for phenomenological research by Smith, Flowers and Larkin (2009) and van Manen (2014). This was a multi-round process of open-coding for processes, emotions and descriptions; codes were gradually pulled into themes, and then these themes were woven into narrative descriptions. The visual material was not analyzed in itself, but it was referred to during analysis in order to clarify or bolster the understanding of the verbal material. Initially, each participant's experience was analyzed individually, pursuant to van Manen's (2014) commitment to the theory of the unique, but cases were also compared to each other in order to more fully draw out what made each case unique (and what they shared).

While a study such as this is not statistically generalizable, it can be assessed for its analytical generalizability, i.e., its transferability (Yin, 2014). There is a temptation to assume that the fewer participants a study has, the smaller its possible contribution. This is not necessarily true; even the study of a single case can reveal significant theoretical findings on its own (Yin, 2014). Thus, studies such as the present one should be assessed according to the principles discussed by Lucy Yardley (2000): context-sensitivity, philosophical commitment, transparency, coherence and importance. When phenomenological research achieves this goal, readers should experience resonance with the written account of the study, which is known as the *phenomenological nod* (van Manen, 2014). Moreover, van Manen (2014) suggests that a phenomenological study be assessed in terms of its providing and provoking contemplative wonder, questioning attentiveness, descriptive richness, interpretive depth, experiential awakening, openness and inceptual epiphany.

FINDINGS

In the context of this paper, the findings from this study that are of greatest interest are those demonstrating how nontraditional information sources contributed to an artist's understanding. In this spirit, this section presents four such sources, each of which was exemplified by the work of one artist.

Brian's Memories

Brian Jerome is a young professional abstract, multimedia painter whose work explores the difficulties of communication (Figure 1). For this project, Brian created a mixed-media piece, incorporating oil and graphite. When I asked him about any reference materials or sketches he used in his work, he told me that his memories and emotions were the only reference materials he used. In participating in this project, Brian came to understand the crucial role that memories play in his work.

In ideating his self-portrait, he began by stirring up memories from throughout his life. He thought about growing up in rural Pennsylvania compared to his life today in the city. "I want to try to consolidate all this into a picture that sums me up," he said. "I want to find a way to say all the things that can't fit into words." To reference different points in his life, he made various markings in his self-portrait, which he calls "referential marks." These he considered a form of drawing, rather than painting—which was related to his childhood, as he grew up drawing.

These memories infused his work process. For example, based on his early love of drawing, he prefers to work on a hard surface, so even as a painter he works on canvas pinned up against a wall, rather than stretched and on an easel. To blend the background colors in a smooth gradient, he used a balled-up old t-shirt to slowly wipe back and forth. He conceptualized this as looking at a lake—both in terms of the resulting visual effect and of his pushing and pulling being analogous to the sweeping of the lake's waves. As for his referential marks, he said, "Some of them are almost like written language but not quite, like those fuzzy memories that you can't quite make out. It's difficult to represent yourself in a painting, just like it's difficult to remember conversations from when you were 8."

Figure 1. Brian's self-portrait.

Emily's Lived Environment

Emily Addis is a hobbist artist who engages in many forms of art-making (Figure 2). For this project, she created a set of polaroid photographs along with an oil painting. In her career, Emily is an education and outreach coordinator at the Barnes Foundation, an art institution in Philadelphia. While Emily was working on her self-portrait for this study, she came to understand the impact her lived environment has on her work, in particular the other art she is immersed in on a regular basis.

In our follow-up interview, Emily said that her self-portrait reminded her of something by Matisse, which is atypical of her work. She recalled a painting she did years ago that resembled Degas' works, at a time when "I was looking at a lot of Degas and I really was interested in what he was doing." She discovered that her self-portrait recalled Matisse because of her current job, where she

Figure 2. Emily's self-portrait (unfinished).

sees

Figure 3. Justin's self-portrait.

works by Matisse every day. Commenting on this, she said,
"We're creative, but artists are always piecing things together from other people's ideas, because that's how we learn." Central to this understanding was coming to see those aspects of the environment that can easily be taken for granted.

Justin's Profound Experience

Justin Tyner is a professional stained-glass artist whose work explores the power of color and light as a form of communication (Figure 3). For this project, Justin created a large, circular piece with a painted image of his face in the center with kaleidoscopic rays emanating outwards. Justin worked on this piece over several months. His enthusiasm for and confidence in the project waxed and waned as time passed.

A turning point in his experience was a hiking trip he took to Colorado partway through the project. The trip was a major test of his physical endurance, and he experienced, as he described in our follow-up interview, "this crazy self-esteem and self-confidence. It's still kinda twinkling." It was, in his words, a profound experience. Though the resulting sense of self-efficacy was rooted in an accomplishment of physical fitness, it spilled into other parts of his life:

> That physical feat was a gut-check for me, a time to think about the man I am today, at 38, and my capabilities as an artist, as a father, as a husband and person. It solidified the confidence I'm feeling in working on this self-portrait—the confidence to trust my instincts, to do things my way. Before, I was concerned about how other people would look at it and see me as, but once that trip happened, that went away. Both the trip and this project have already been pivotal in the way I see myself.

When Justin returned home from the trip, he experienced high energy and finished within a week. This included the entire assembly of the piece, which involved about 200 pieces of glass that had to be individually cut and bound together with lead. He said of the finished piece, crediting this profound experience: "It's a milestone for me as an artist, to be successful in my own style in a piece that is entirely my own—of me, and in my style, both recognizable. It turned out way better than I thought."

Tammy's Social Media Browsing

Tammy Hala is an aerial acrobat, painter and photographer (Figure 4). Most of her paintings are abstract "flow pieces," as she calls them, where she intuitively applies and blends colors without forethought. She began her self-portrait with a session of flow painting, to get "back into art mode" after a long hiatus. She noticed that one of the pieces looked like a face, so she started a new painting, attempting to do her self-portrait in a similar style, but she found that "when I consciously try, it doesn't work."

Figure 4. Tammy's self-portrait.

Looking for a new plan, she browsed Instagram, a social network for sharing images. On Instagram, Tammy follows many artists, including a number of portraitists. Browsing, Tammy encountered a recent post by a portraitist she greatly admires, one who draws exquisitely. Tammy had long considered faces difficult to draw, and she decided at this point to challenge herself to draw her own face for this project. She studied several posts of this artist, including finished pieces, a sketchbook page of lips and progress shots. Taking inspiration from these works, she did first a drawing and then a watercolor painting of her own face, but she was dissatisfied with how they turned out. She began again, this time referencing a photo of herself. As part of the process, she used Instagram again to browse drawings of faces. She found one that showed measurements of facial proportions, and she sketched these proportions on a post-it note, which she then used as guides in her own self-portrait drawing. This led to a drawing she was satisfied with.

DISCUSSION

This study offers a glimpse at how memories, lived environment, profound experiences and social media browsing can be informative and contribute to understanding, i.e., the experience of being informed. First, the diversity of information that bears on self-portraiture goes far beyond the sorts of sources that the field has traditionally considered informative, even in "everyday" research. Moreover, this study has gone beyond merely identifying information sources to show how these sources are actually informative in a person's situation.

To be sure, this has only been a cursory look at these phenomena, with the intent of establishing their informativeness and contribution to understanding. Much more work could be done, not least linking up these discussions with other research in information behavior and allied fields. For instance, research has been done on online browsing, though to my knowledge this work has not yet discussed how browsing itself can be informative. Additionally, latent in this study is the finding that information activities always seem to involve information encountering, at least in the form of memories and associations, and all this information contributes to the resulting understanding. Information encountering has been identified previously as a facet of information behavior (Erdelez, 1995), but the present study shows an even deeper pervasiveness of information encountering than has previously been acknowledged.

More conceptually, this study demonstrates how the concept of understanding offers a way to explore human epistemology in a holistic way, going beyond the knowledge-contributing information sources that have been typically studied in information science. As defined above, ontic understanding is a coherent and self-transparent epistemic network that is constructed by a conscious agent over a background of ontological understanding. This study has borne some examples of ontic understanding. These examples have been described as information constellations that show how heterogeneous information comes together, bound by narrative structure, in the building of ontic understanding. Crucially, these examples of understanding were allowed to emerge naturalistically in this study, essentially by casting a very wide net. Approaching the topic in this way allowed aspects of existence to be recognized as informative that may otherwise not have been seen. This provokes information science to further develop ways to recognize the breadth of phenomena that are informative in human life.

CONCLUSION

Life abounds with information. So, if information science is to participate meaningfully and positively in the future, it must become attuned to life as lived. Historically, information science limited its scope of concern to particular sources, or forms, of information. That is, information has been conceptualized as something that has been formed. As the artist Paul Klee wrote in his notebooks, however, "Form is the end, death. Form-giving is movement, action. Form-giving is life" (Klee & Spiller, 1973, p. 269). Consonantly, the potential of research in everyday information behavior is to understand not just information forms, but of information form-giving—to look at information as a process, rather than just a thing. That is, the lived experience of creating information by putting other information to use.

Art, indeed, is an exemplar of form-giving (despite our penchant for conceptualizing it in terms of forms). This is because, in a sense, art is always in the process of being made. Elgin (2017, p. 287), for example, writes, "The picture is inexhaustible. There is always more to be found." This study has explored the work of artists from the perspective of information behavior, and its findings prompt us to ask: Where else can we see artful lived phenomena such as memories and profound experiences serving as information? Foucault (1997, p. 261) asked a similar question: "Couldn't everyone's life become a work of art? Why should the lamp or the house be an art object but not our life?" Surely, we have an opportunity to apply these ideas much more broadly across the various domains of human life.

REFERENCES

Agarwal, N. K., Xu, Y. C., & Poo, D. C. (2011). A context-based investigation into source use by information seekers. *Journal of the American Society for Information Science and Technology, 62*(6), 1087–1104.

Bosancic, B. (2016). Information in the knowledge acquisition process. *Journal of Documentation, 72*(5), 930–960.

Briesen, J. (2014). Pictorial art and epistemic aims. In H. Klinke (Ed.), *Art theory as visual epistemology* (pp. 11–27). Newcastle upon Tyne, UK: Cambridge Scholars.

Case, D.O., & Given, L.G. (2016). *Looking for information: a survey of research on information seeking, needs and behavior* (4th ed.). Bingley, UK: Emerald.

Cobbledick, S. (1996). The information-seeking behavior of artists: Exploratory interviews. *The Library Quarterly, 66*(4), 343–372.

Cowan, S. (2004). Informing visual poetry: Information needs and sources. *Art Documentation, 23*(2), 14–20.

Day, R. E. (2008). Works and representation. *Journal of the American Society for Information Science, 59*(10), 1644–1652.

Dissanayake, E. (1992). *Homo aestheticus: Where art comes from and why*. New York, NY: Free Press.

Egan, M., and Shera, J.H. (1952). Foundations of a theory of bibliography. *The Library Quarterly, 44*, 125–137.

Elgin, C. Z. (2002). Art in the advancement of understanding. *American Philosophical Quarterly, 39*(1), 1–12.

Elgin, C. Z. (2017). *True enough*. Cambridge, MA: The MIT Press.

Erdelez, S. (1995). *Information encountering: An exploration beyond information seeking* (Unpublished doctoral dissertation). Syracuse University.

Floridi, L. (2011). *The philosophy of information*. Oxford, UK: Oxford University Press.

Floridi, L. (2013). *The ethics of information*. Oxford, UK: Oxford University Press.

Foucault, M. (1997). *Ethics: Subjectivity and truth (the essential works of Foucault, volume 1, 1954–1984)* (P. Rabinow, Ed. & R. Hurley, Trans.). New York, NY: The New Press.

Furner, J. (2010). Philosophy and information studies. *Annual Review of Information Science and Technology, 44*, 159–200.

Goodman, N. (1976). *Languages of art* (2nd ed.). Indianapolis, IN: Hackett.

Gorichanaz, T. (2017). Applied epistemology and understanding in information studies. *Information Research, 22*(4), paper 776. Retrieved from http://InformationR.net/ir/22-4/paper776.html

Gorichanaz, T. (2018). Understanding and information constellations in ultrarunning. *Library Trends*, *66*(3), 329–350.

Gorichanaz, T., Latham, K. F., & Wood, E. (2018). Lifeworld as "unit of analysis." *Journal of Documentation, 74*(4), 880–893.

Heidegger, M. (1971). The origin of the work of art. In A. Hofstadter (Trans.), *Poetry, language, thought* (pp. 15–86). New York, NY: Harper & Row.

Heidegger, M. (1977). The question concerning technology. In D. F. Krell (Ed.), *Basic writings* (pp. 307–341). New York, NY: HarperCollins.

Hemmig, W. (2008). The information-seeking behavior of visual artists: A literature review. *Journal of Documentation, 64*(3), 343–362.

Hemmig, W. (2009). An empirical study of the information-seeking behavior of practicing visual artists. *Journal of Documentation, 65*(4), 682–703.

Ingold, T. (2018, February). *The sustainability of everything.* Paper presented at Natures: Anthropology Colloquium Series, University of Pennsylvania, Philadelphia. Retrieved from https://www.youtube.com/watch?v=BPEAUMQ0BIM

James, W. (1975). *Pragmatism: A new name for some old ways of thinking.* Cambridge, MA: Harvard University Press. (Original work published 1907)

Johnson, M. (2007). *The meaning of the body: Aesthetics of human understanding*. Chicago, IL: University of Chicago Press.

Klee, P., & Spiller, J. (Ed.). (1973). *Noteboooks, volume 2: The nature of nature* (H. Norden, Trans.). London, UK: Lund Humphries.

Ma, L. (2012). Meanings of information: the assumptions and research consequences of three foundational LIS theories. *Journal of the Association for Information Science and Technology, 63*(4), 716–723.

Mason, H., & Robinson, L. (2011). The information-related behaviour of emerging artists and designers. *Journal of Documentation, 67*(1), 159–180.

Mirzoeff, N. (2015). *How to see the world.* London, UK: Pelican Books.

Ocepek, M. G. (2018). Bringing out the everyday in everyday information behavior. *Journal of Documentation, 74*(2), 398–411.

Régimbeau, G. (2007). L'image d'art entre analyse critique et analyse documentaire [The art image in critical analysis and document analysis]. *Documentaliste, 44*(2), 130–137.

Robinson, S. M. (2014). From hieroglyphs to hashtags: The information-seeking behaviors of contemporary Egyptian artists. *Art Documentation, 33*(1), 107– 118.

Rodeheaver, D. G. and Zafirovski, M. 2017. Sociology of work. In B. S. Turner, C. Kyung-Sup, C. F. Epstein, P. Kivisto, W. Outhwaite, & J. M. Ryan (Eds.), *The Wiley-Blackwell encyclopedia of social theory*. doi: 10.1002/9781118430873.est0370

Savolainen, R. (1995). Everyday life information seeking: Approaching information seeking in the context of "way of life." *Library & Information Science Research, 17*(3), 259–294.

Scruton, R. (2014). *The soul of the world.* Princeton, NJ: Princeton University Press.

Smith, D. E. (2006). *Institutional ethnography as practice*. Lanham, MD: Rowman & Littlefield.

Smith, J., Flowers, P., & Larkin, M. (2009). *Interpretative phenomenological analysis: Theory, method, research.* London, UK: Sage.

Steedman, C. (1987). *Landscape for a good woman: A story of two lives*. New Brunswick, NJ: Rutgers University Press.

Tidline, T. J. (2003). *Making sense of art as information* (Unpublished doctoral dissertation). University of Illinois, Urbana-Champaign.

Tkach, D. (2017). The situatedness of the seeker: Toward a Heideggerian understanding of information seeking. *Canadian Journal of Academic Librarianship, 2*(1), 27–41.

van Manen, M. (2014). *Phenomenology of practice: Meaning-giving methods in phenomenological research and writing*. Walnut Creek, CA: Left Coast Press.

Weissenberger, L. K., Budd, J. M., & Herold, K. R. (2018). Epistemology beyond the brain. *Journal of the Association for Information Science & Technology, 69*(5), 710–719.

Winters, E. (2018). The world is not enough. *The Monist, 101*(1), 83–98.

Yardley, L. (2000). Dilemmas in qualitative health research. *Psychology & Health, 15*(2), 215–228.

Yin, R. K. (2014). *Case study research* (5th ed.). Thousand Oaks, CA: Sage.

Bibliotelemetry of Information and Environment: Evaluation of an IoT-Powered Recommender System

Jim Hahn
University Library, University of Illinois at Urbana-Champaign, USA. jimhahn@illinois.edu

ABSTRACT

Internet of Things (IoT) infrastructure within the physical library environment is the basis for an integrative, hybrid approach to digital resource recommenders. The IoT infrastructure provides mobile, dynamic wayfinding support for items in the collection, which includes features for location-based recommendations. A modular evaluation and analysis herein clarified the nature of users' requests for recommendations based on their location and describes subject areas of the library for which users request recommendations. The modular mobile design allowed for deep exploration of users' bibliographic identifiers throughout the global module system, serving to provide context to the browsing data that are the focus of this study. Bibliotelemetry is introduced as an evaluation method for IoT middleware within library collections.

KEYWORDS

internet of things, IoT, bibliographic classification, academic libraries.

INTRODUCTION

The Internet of Things (IoT) is an advanced technology of novel connectivity that encompasses devices other than the classic desktop computing paradigm. IoT infuses internet affordances into objects, buildings, and other infrastructures. This technology is poised to affect library spaces, collection evaluation, and user services. In this research paper, IoT advances were the basis for an integrative, hybrid approach to digital resource access while navigating the physical library environment. According to David Rose, author of *Enchanted Objects* and researcher at the MIT Media Lab, "The Internet of Things is made possible through ubiquitous connectivity. An Internet connection allows the transmission of sensing and signalling information, the processing and storage of information, and the delivery of new services" (Rose 2014, p. 194-195). The authors of *Designing Connected Products* underscored the importance of IoT data stating, "The falling cost of sensing and computation means that there are more and more devices that are capable of capturing, and acting on, data about the world" (Rowland, Goodman, Charlier, Light, & Lui, 2015, p. 573). The scale of data sensor captures about collections and their use introduces a new research area for information science. A recent Library Technology Report, "The Internet of Things: Mobile technology and location services in libraries," detailed the use of a Bluetooth Low Energy (BLE) beacon array installed over an open undergraduate library collection. This infrastructure provides mobile, dynamic wayfinding support for items in the collection. It is dynamic because of its ability to show the users their location in real time as they move throughout the book stacks and the service includes features for location-based recommendations. The case reported on how the system used Library of Congress classification in nearby books to provide recommendations within the Minrva mobile app (Hahn, 2017a). Users were presented with recommendations to print items in popular circulation. The location of the mobile device was used to recommend such electronic items as databases, indices to journals, and e-books. The overall system functionality relied on a micro-service based API for data access to the necessary library data, such as shelf arrangement, classification of items, and subsequent associations to relevant e-resources based on inferred location.

A contention of location-based recommendation in library book stacks is that as users navigate the library's physical space, they navigate intellectual space through which topic discovery of both print and electronic items can be enhanced further (Hahn, 2011). Development and evaluation of IoT navigation services in print collections reference and extend foundations of information science concerned with recommending. In this research, we sought to enrich information science paradigms that reference classification for finding like items. We used API log analysis to evaluate IoT wayfinding and navigation support. This analysis will foster an understanding of the nature of users' requests for recommendations based on location. Because the recommendations provided were based on location, it is possible to ascertain within what section of the library users are requesting topic-based recommendations and to note the areas for which users were most likely to request recommendations.

BACKGROUND

IoT technology is poised to provide system designers, data scientists, and librarians with significant data from which to derive greater insight in collection analysis. IoT-powered services are beginning to be implemented in libraries, particularly in smart building development. Libraries have taken particular advantage of such mobile affordances as Bluetooth and Wi-Fi capabilities for IoT-powered wayfinding in library buildings. The iBeacon library tours at Virginia Tech is a related project that uses IoT technology to explore information within a library building (Bradley et al., 2016). With Estimote iBeacons, the Virginia

Tech Library could update self-guided tour applications to provide easier access to contextually relevant videos and information. The iBeacon tour was introduced to scale new student orientation. This is indicative of how IoT hardware will make it possible to provide services that scale to increasing work demands and provide contextually relevant information in libraries. Incorporating IoT services into the Integrated Library System is the goal of another integrative technical project, undertaken by developers Stefanidis and Tsakonas (2015). The authors demonstrated a pilot integration with Koha, in which IoT services took advantage of RFID for library services. Stefanidis and Tsakonas demonstrated a pilot integration with Koha, in which IoT services took advantage of RFID for library services. Their work is inclusive of other next generation library services, and demonstrates the ability of their IoT infrastructure to use linked data from the library community to indicate the holdings and availability of IoT- tagged items in libraries. Contemporary projects, while technologically advanced, lead researchers to look for conceptual foundations. Have emerging technology projects in information science departed significantly from disciplinary foundations of information organization? Theoretical foundations of practice-oriented projects risk becoming superfluous because of their singular focus on technology qua foundations. However, technology is not an intellectual foundation for a discipline (Svenonius, 2000). Two overarching thematic frames are relevant to exploring the literature in this area: 1) conceptual frames of information behavior (Pettigrew, Fidel, & Bruce, 2001) and 2) frameworks related to browsing (Chang & Rice, 1993). Specific to browsing, a model for understanding was proposed to help clarify and expand its meaning, whereby it was argued that "… understanding browsing should include four major components—1) context, 2) influences, 3) browsing process, and 4) consequences – with iterations over time" (Chang & Rice 1993, p. 258). Additional frames synthesized in this research include those of Kuhlthau as well as Bates, whose works are situated in cognitive approaches to conceptual frameworks in information behavior. Other multifaceted approaches include "…multiple types of context such as the cognitive, social, and organizational context" (Pettigrew, Fidel, & Bruce 2001, p. 46).

Information Organization Foundations, Browsing, and Emerging Technology

This work focuses on understanding and supporting contemporary browsing as a part of information behavior (Pettigrew, Fidel, & Bruce, 2001). Browsing is an aspect of information behavior that occurs under a variety of circumstances depending on the user context (McKay, Buchanan, & Chang, 2015). Both the berrypicking model of information search (Bates, 1989) and the information search process (Kuhlthau, 2004) are relevant and instructive models with which to begin to understand users' interactions as they search book stacks. For example, they may not necessarily want to go from point A to point B but rather follow an exploratory path through the book stacks. The chaotic nature of search was perhaps argued most compellingly by Dervin while theorizing about information design (Dervin, 2000). Dervin's seminal information science contribution—sense making—did not advance theories of information behavior per se. However, Dervin's contributions and critiques of information design offers an illuminating model: Dervin proposed a conceptualization of information design as encompassing both order and chaos as a part of sense making (Dervin, 2000).

Threads of order and disorder underscore a counterintuitive and underappreciated dichotomy in collections-based research: the collections themselves are ordered, but a user's research path is often uncertain (Eaton, 1991) and anything but orderly and standardized. In response to the classic article "Design of browsing and berrypicking techniques for the online search interface" the information science field began to appreciate and design information search interfaces to better address the nonlinear way users navigate information resources (Bates, 1989). Bates was influenced by researchers who also helped the information science field understand human-centered domains of search, rather than system-centric searching (Kuhlthau, 1988). Kuhlthau also provided guides to understanding user uncertainty while continuing to attend to the affective domains of discovery (Kuhlthau, 1993). And, in "Discovering information in context," Solomon developed a new research goal that proposed the need for information science research to encompass the variety of contexts in information search. These contexts look beyond interfaces and information systems, particularly with respect to how users make sense of information while navigating information environments (Solomon, 2002). Solomon's work on contextual information discovery underscores the practice-oriented approach of navigating library collections with IoT technology. The implications are relevant to IoT system design focused on supporting navigation. Solomon noted that "While many of the structures (e.g., categorizations, index languages, representations, metadata, displays) created by information professionals are designed to aid in access, discovery, and retrieval, they often fail in one or more of these functions" (Solomon, 2002, p. 240). Bibliotelemetry research was inspired by Solomon's call to support discovery in practice that upholds the non-linear, evolving nature of search as contextually significant.

Sustained research that focuses on user wayfinding in libraries is needed (Mandel, 2017). Mandel noted that future research questions for sustained study in this area include those that investigate how new technology can support wayfinding. Mobile technology-supported wayfinding in library practice must consider the evolving berrypicking approach that Bates introduced and upon which Solomon expanded. Lee's seminal work, which explored the nature of collections in the digital era, is instructive for system design of navigational IoT technology development. Lee argued compellingly for research on collections as information contexts (Lee, 2000). Our research considered both the tangible and intangible aspects of access and navigation of library collections with new IoT affordances in the digital age. This work was concerned with IoT's ability to provide enhanced, serendipitous discovery of library collections based on collocation (Svenonius, 2000). Empirical evidence helped verify that nearby print books on a shelf will circulate if neighboring books are checked out (McKay, Smith, & Chang 2014). Researchers also have used studies on book-stack browsing to inform digital e-book browsing systems (Hinze, McKay, Vanderschantz, Timpany, & Cunningham 2012). What this research addresses with IoT-enhanced wayfinding are the difficulties inherent to the tangibility of print collections. McKay et al. found that users have a range of needs while browsing: some need an exact item while others appreciate exploring a topic and finding items that may not be near their initial browsing location (McKay et al., 2015). Researchers have noted that "Systems could leverage topic classification schemes to offer readers a very few different-but-interesting books based on topic data: this approach would mimic the physical shelves, but, being data driven, would offer a higher chance of success" (McKay et al., 2015, p. 291). This study investigated the data affordances and limitations of subject-based filtering in library classification. A limitation of print layout is that while there are shelves of items arranged by subject, library collections are interconnected more deeply than physical shelves can indicate and consequently fail to achieve users' browsing-based navigation objectives. Subjects related from a user's perspective or needs are not always placed next to one another on shelves. Print arrangement includes electronic relations, wholly or in part, to resources not visible to the user navigating the stacks. IoT-powered services that take advantage of mobile devices paired with Bluetooth beacons and a set of interlocking middleware solutions can help address these inadequacies in the contextual issues of stacks navigation (Hahn, 2017a).

Modular Mobile Application Design with RESTful APIs

The Wayfinder module within the Minrva mobile app was enhanced with a BLE beacon database to ascertain the location of the user device in the lower level of the Undergraduate Library at the University of Illinois. The Minrva app utilizes a modular design (Hahn & Ryckman, 2012). Each module is dependent on a unique bibliographic identifier and is not directly coupled with the larger system of modules. Modules communicate only indirectly. After a user searches for an item in the Catalog search module, they can then view a description of the item within the Display module, which will provide a summary along with location and availability information. Next, the user has the option to tap the Wayfinder module to be directed to the location of an item. Each module of the application uses a specific RESTful API. RESTful APIs are designed as concise, specifically formatted JSON data produced by servers to be consumed by other programs, such as mobile apps.

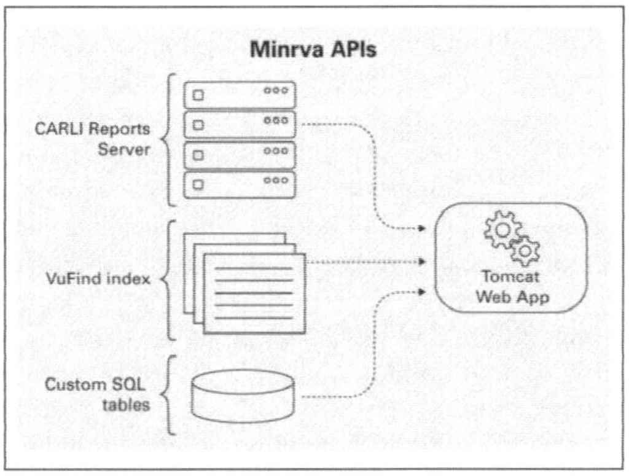

Figure 1. The data sources the Wayfinder and location-based recommendation service require.

The API developed for the Wayfinder module with recommendation support provides data based on three sources: basic call number layout (custom table we developed and curate), searching and filtering from the library catalog (VuFind), and ranking popularity (CARLI reports server). Examining Figure 1, we can see first the database labelled as the CARLI reports server refers to the Oracle Database that is the backend of the Integrated Library System (ILS). The system will request all data at once through one dynamic query. The goals and objectives for using Bluetooth beacons in the book stacks included the following: a) locating a user's device in the library book stacks, b) giving a user a recommendation for popularly circulating items, and c) showing the user relevant e-content based on their current location (Hahn, 2017a).

Recommendation Algorithm

An algorithm, at its most basic and essential parts, is simply several functions that represent the steps the server is taking. Figure 2 details steps taken by the IoT middleware for gathering recommendation results defined by a pre-determined criterion that will be shown to the user based on the location of their device when they tapped the recommendation button (Hahn, 2017a). In order to process recommendations, the server will filter through functions shown in Figure 2 beginning with the current location. Based on patron location, we get the shelf ranges from our custom database of all call numbers. Once we know the ranges of a nearby stack we get relevant books and e-books. We filter for popularity based on that range and add any e-books that would be relevant. Finally, we add any online journal databases that may be relevant to the patron's starting location and serialize this as a JSON response. In order to gather database journal recommendations, the service relies upon an EBSCO article search API. While recommending is not the main purpose of the EBSCO API, the conceptualization of a "recommendation" is considered broadly to encompass those items more relevant by arrangement. The EBSCO API returns a set of results to a subject query (gathered from the call number). In the case that a single journal title holds most of the results, the service then recommends that journal as relevant to the subject area. The students still must search within the journal to obtain articles. This part of the algorithm, at its most basic, promotes the availability of topically relevant journal titles from the EBSCO API. Certainty there are limitations to this type of search since promoting some resources over others may leave out resources relevant but not found in the recommendation model (Hahn, 2017a).

```
// Get the patron's physical coordinates
PatronLocation location = getLocation(locationInfo);

// Get shelf ranges from Minrva DB, based off of patron location
ArrayList<String> ranges = getRanges(location);

// Get relevant books/ebooks based off of the shelf ranges
BooksDB bookdb = getEBooks(ranges, context);

// Filter and add popular books that are near the patron
List<RecBooksModel> books = bookdb.bookList;

// Filter and add relevant ebooks that would be shelved
// near the user, if the ebook was a physical item
List<RecBooksModel> bookEBook = getPopularBooks(ranges, books);

// Add relevant databases, based off of the patron's location,
// to the list
List<RecBooksModel> bookEBookDB = getDBSuggestions(bookdb.DBList,
bookEBook);
```

Figure 2. Demonstration of computing processes that researchers developed for the phone to receive the recommendations of print, e-books, and databases.

METHODS FOR BIBLIOTELEMETRY ANALYTICS

Transactional search log analysis is a powerful tool that studies of the effectiveness of information systems employ (Jensen, 2006). Analysis of the server transaction logs recorded by library APIs is a comparable library research technique (Hahn, 2017b). Weblog analytics have proven to be a valuable method for understanding the information behavior of traditionally unobservable actions (Tobias & Blair, 2015). The focus of inquiry for log analytics in the case of this study was wayfinding, browsing, and selecting behavior in the library book stacks in general, and location-based recommendations, specifically. The analysis consists of extracting API logs, annotating the API logs, and then generating visualizations of the logs. Complete data are available from the University of Illinois databank (Hahn, 2018). The Bibliotelemetry analysis is inspired by commonly used methods for analyzing transaction logs, where data are annotated or coded for analysis after logging transactions (Xie & Wolfram, 2009; Brett, German, & Young, 2015). This research focused on two sets of modular API logs from the server middleware between the users' mobile device and the Bluetooth beacon array in the undergraduate library book stacks. The middleware for the app was designed modularly such that the API that sends data to the phone for basic wayfinding is distinct from the API that sends recommendations based on a user location generated by the client device. Therefore, the two modular APIs were parsed, analyzed, and annotated as part of this research. IRB approval was obtained to evaluate mobile app use and user location stored in the API server logs. Splunk Enterprise software was used to parse server logs and Tableau was used to filter the data further and to visualize the results of subject distribution. An intermediary step from the Splunk Enterprise log file parsing was generating file annotations to plot subjects. An example of the filtered logs is shown below in Table 1. In Table 1, the Wayfinder API is denoted in the "uri" column and shows the targets of Wayfinding support, or basic collections navigation, without recommendations.

uri	sum-records	X	Y	shelf-number	call-number
/api/wayfinder/map_data/uiu_undergrad/uiu_8127460	14	337	128	30	PN1995 .C655 2015
/api/wayfinder/map_data/uiu_undergrad/uiu_7419985	13	92	304	51	SF446 .C763 2014

Table 1. A sample from the annotated data generated from the middleware server/Wayfinder API.

uri	bib-id	bib-id	bib-id	bib-id	bib-id
/api/recommend/popularnear?x=4362.047852&y=3160.110596	uiu_8378456	uiu_7072382	hat_817483	uiu_7277188	uiu_8375583
/api/recommend/popularnear?x=3194.620605&y=4221.636719	uiu_6548355	uiu_7010231	hat_819122	uiu_6165435	hat_1273444

Table 2. A sample from the annotated data generated the middleware server/location-based recommendation API.

The data from the server logs do not contain the subjects of items, but rather unique identifiers of bibliographic IDs. Researchers coded the files to associate the subject areas of the bibliographic IDs with an LC call number that would make possible a broader subject analysis of recommended items. An example of the subject/topic coding for call number association is shown in Table 3, which references and are directly sourced from Library of Congress Class lists (Library of Congress, 2018). The Library of Congress classification model is an imperfect model for organizing knowledge. However, a departure point for this research stems in part from the aphorism about the inherent fallibility of all models because when conceptual models are imperfect, it is more fruitful to scholarly inquiry to consider whether they are useful (Box, 1979). Consequently, while the LC classification model is not perfect, it is useful for IoT-powered recommendation evaluation and analysis. It has been applied uniformly in a standardized manner to print items in library collections.

call-number	subject
B105.E9 G63 1974	Philosophy (General)

Table 3. Recommended call number associated with subject.

The study was conducted for one year, from September 1, 2016 through August 31, 2017. The collection for which the recommendations are provided included the print book stacks of a single floor of books in an undergraduate library. The collection of the undergraduate library numbers 125,000 monographs in open stacks. The goal of this evaluation was to understand the following: 1) Where are users when they request recommendations? 2) What are the subjects of the recommendations provided?

RESULTS OF BIBLIOTELEMETRY ANALYTICS

During the course of the study, the Wayfinder module of the library mobile app recorded a total of 205 API hits to book item map support. There was a total of 431 API hits recorded in the server to the recommender middleware. To understand the use of location support, a heat map over a map of the undergraduate library was generated from the API logs used in this study, together with an open source python program that plots X, Y coordinates over a given image file.[1] The heat map indicates the popularity of a specific section: the darker the red, the higher the number of points reported at that location, while a lighter blue indicates less popularity. A reveal filter of lighter areas is displayed for the location of recommendation support.

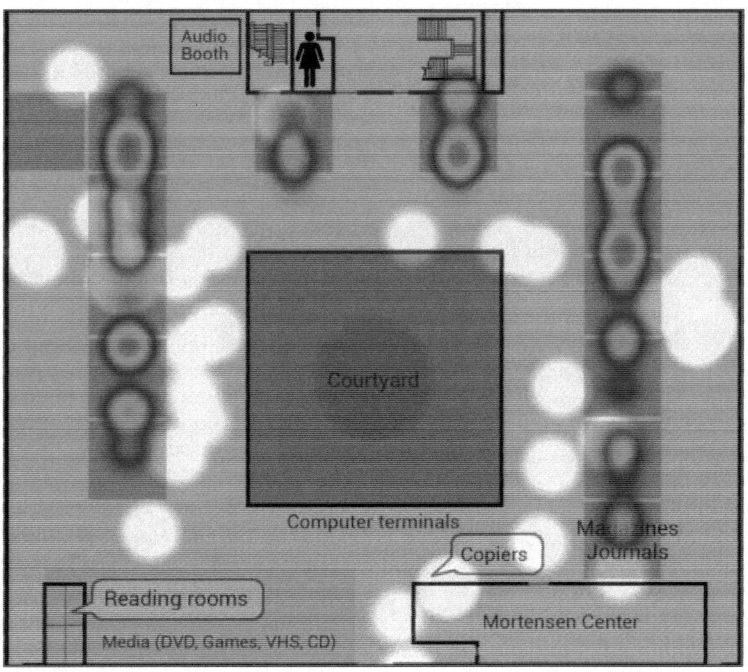

Figure 3. Lighter areas are user location in the Undergraduate Library when requesting recommendations.

To determine the topic areas of the wayfinding and recommendations, a subject distribution table was compiled with the API log data. The distribution is shown for the subjects of print items recommended based on user location (Figure 4). A long-tail power law model appeared to best fit the subject distribution findings (Anderson, 2006; Andriani & McKelvey, 2009). The results indicated that users of IoT-based recommendations are interested in a long-tail distribution of subjects. The secondary

[1] https://github.com/LumenResearch/heatmappy

trend in literature topic areas may be interpreted as a combination of the following: 1) reflects the reading preferences and practices of those students, faculty, and staff researching literature; or shows the popularity of 2) leisure or recreational material overall in the collection; or 3) represents a larger distribution of subjects for this area compared with the collection overall. Users' antecedent Catalog searches, prior to viewing in the Display module were also a focus of data analysis since these were the steps taken by users prior to activating the Wayfinder module for locating an item and requesting recommendation support. Catalog and journal searches during the study are shown in Figures 7 and 8, respectively. Voyant tools (Sinclair & Rockwell, 2016) were used to generate text mining results. Results of the mining of words among both journal and catalog search modules are shown in Table 6.

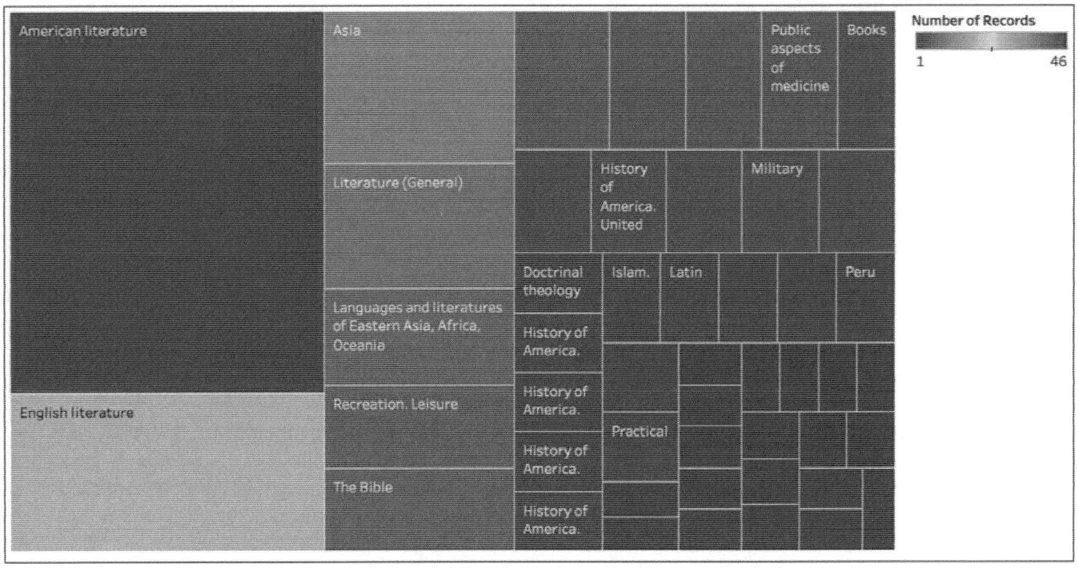

Figure 4. Subjects of in-library items that were recommended by user location.

Bibliotelemetry: unique identifiers in the global module system

The Bibliotelemetry analysis continues with the tracking user data of Wayfinder and BLE recommendations paired with the global modular mobile application data. This allows researchers the opportunity to follow a user from the Catalog Module search to the Display Module and finally to either Wayfinder and checkout or to Wayfinder and recommendations/checkout or more browsing afterwards. To begin to understand how satisfied users were with the recommendations and wayfinding support from a quantitative lens, researchers analyzed the bibliographic identifiers of circulation transactions after recommendation by the wayfinding module. Those items are detailed in Table 4. These are the print items recommended and subsequently checked out during the year under study. Recommendations for e-books in Table 4 do not have circulation records; however, the e-book access records are shown in Table 5. Further exploration of how bibliographic identifiers surface from catalog searching and into wayfinding throughout the module system is show in Figure 5 – which details how bibliographic identifiers from Wayfinder searching surfaced in other modules of the app, and Figure 6—which illustrates how identifiers from the location-based recommenders appeared in other modules throughout the app.

bib-id	charge-date	call-number	subject
7734446	8/31/17 9:49	GV1469.62.D84	Computer games. Video games. Fantasy games
5180498	8/31/17 18:51	PR9619.4.Z87	English literature: Provincial, local, etc.
4168504	8/31/17 18:52	PZ7.R79835	Fiction and juvenile belles lettres
4060124	9/1/17 13:45	PZ7 .R79835	Fiction and juvenile belles lettres
7878848	9/1/17 14:31	PN1991.75 A24	Radio broadcasts

Table 4. Bibliographic identifiers of checkouts after suggested to users within the Minrva Wayfinder module.

bib-id	req-date	call-number	subject
hat_606736	11/1/16 15:31	PR85.C45	English literature
hat_615138	11/1/16 15:32	PS94.B5	American literature
hat_345695	11/1/16 15:55	E669.F37	History of the Americas. United States
hat_659370	1/31/17 11:37	E154.N38	History of the Americas. United States

Table 5. Bibliographic identifiers of eBook views (e.g. clicks to open) within the location-based recommender.

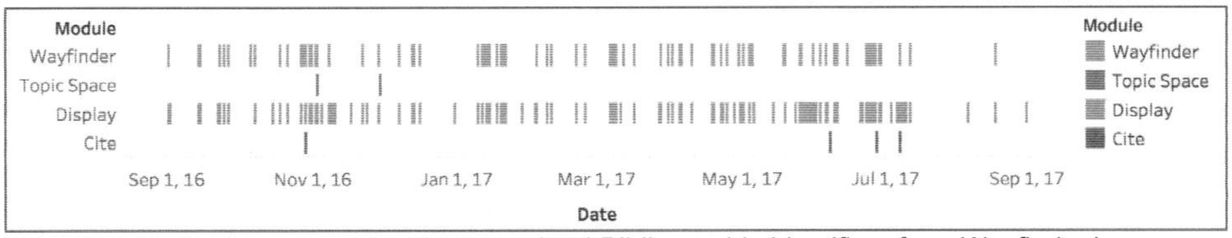

Figure 5. Minrva modules that contained Bibliographic identifiers from Wayfinder logs.

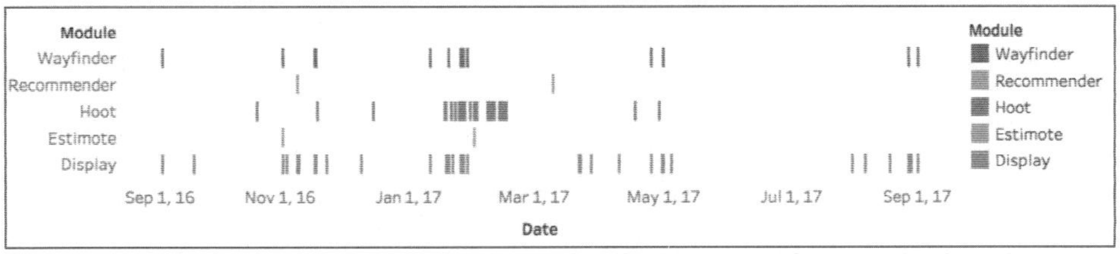

Figure 6. Minrva modules that contained bibliographic identifiers promoted from location-based recommender.

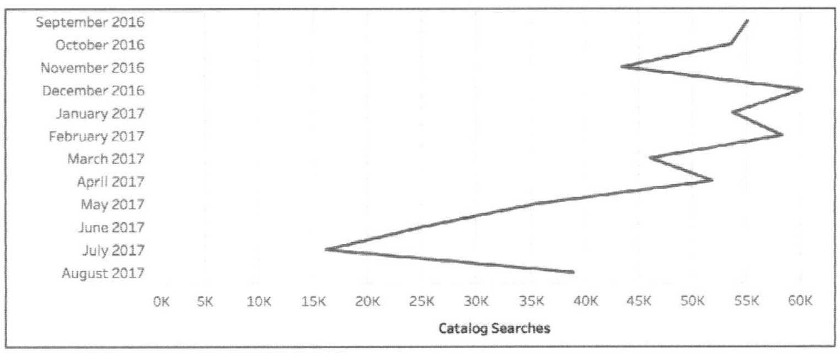

Figure 7. Monthly catalog searches to the Minrva middleware.

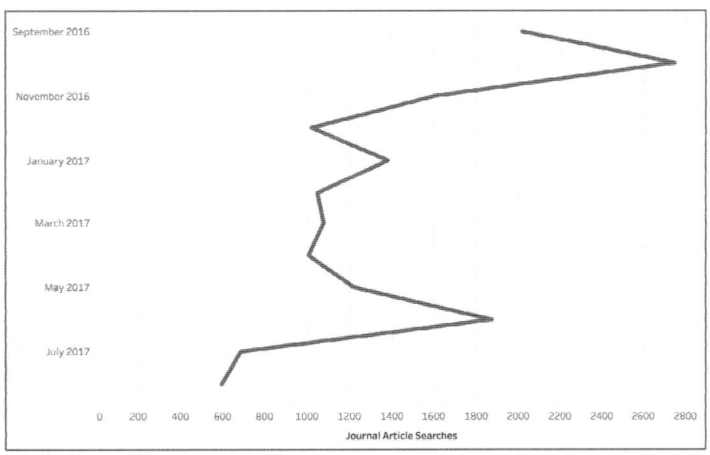

Figure 8. Monthly journal article searches in the Minrva middleware.

Module	Total Words	Unique Word Forms	Most Frequent Words
Catalog Search	1,951,982	3,016	ps4 (41331); 2c (22982); trio (13514); daniel (12798); focus (12744)
Journal Search	56,474	80	fish (36232); google (4880); math (2016); test (1696); hiv (1692)

Table 6. Text mining of catalog and journal query word corpora.[2]

[2] Note: Voyant Tools text mining (Sinclair & Rockwell, 2016) reports total words as a sum of every occurrence of every word, whereas the unique word forms are a summative word count based on first occurrence of a word only.

FINDINGS

Initial checkouts and e-resource view findings (Tables 4 and 5) showed that users of the Wayfinder module seem to be interested in browsing more than navigating for checking out known items. Further Bibliotelemetry data within the global module system of the Minrva app showed that bibliographic identifiers of which users sought wayfinding support also surfaced within the Topic Space module and the Citation module. Citing an item may be an indication that the item was consequently used as a reference for a research paper. As per Figure 6, there were modules that contained bibliographic identifiers promoted from location-based recommender. Researchers could see that these identifiers showed up in users' course reserves interest (by way of the Hoot API logs—which alters users to the availability of in-library reserve texts) and appeared in the mobile app's account-based recommender, which suggests items to users based on their current checkouts. The significance of finding these identifiers within the global module system underscored the item's relative importance for use whether that included checkouts, e-access, or even, as an item that eventually became included in a professor's course reserves. While these findings may suggest a broader topic browse exploration by users, in the library stacks the qualitative nature of this exploration would be best explored through user interviews or focus groups as a companion study to complement this research thread. An area for future qualitative study will focus on attending to the relative number of searches that were found (antecedent searches in catalog Figure 7 and temporally related journal article searches of Figure 8) versus the browsing observed by the Wayfinder module. The searching transactions far outnumbered browsing and checkout transactions in the study. In the future, researchers would specifically seek to understand why is it that searching is so prominent in the module system and to understand why browsing seemed important to users, but not necessarily for checkouts? What are the bookstacks offering users beyond their inventory? How do users decide to browse and not to select? Are these limitations in collection availability outside of the popular literature sections or is there another motivating set of factors? These may be best answered with focus groups and interviews. IoT navigational users' short-head preferences for literature may be used to inform the design of system improvements.

Long-Tail & Short-Head Findings

In recommendations of print items, American Literature demonstrated the short-head trend as the subject area recommended most (Figure 4), with English Literature following in popularity. By analyzing and visualizing the IoT middleware server logs, it was possible to approximate where users were within the undergraduate collection when they requested recommendations (Figure 3). What is surprising to note about this figure is that most recommender system users did not actually appear to be in the stacks when they requested recommendations. The users were near book stacks when they requested suggested items but not within the boundaries of a book stack location, i.e. surrounded on either side by a shelf. The one exception was it appears that users requested recommendations within the boundaries of the literature and fiction areas of the book stacks. A future follow on study may continue to attend to the context of users entering or leaving the library. Because it appears that IoT services in this library may be the focus of leisure reading, designers may want to target their services to this subset of their collection. Specifically, these results may inform marketing and interface elements that would help users understand the features of the app that are amenable to traditional "reader's advisory" services. A further system design improvement can be seen in Figure 3: users appeared to request recommendations at the entrance and exit of the library. Since the system was designed to provide recommendations based on classifications associated with stack location, the library's entrances and exits may need to be reconsidered as they relate to stack-based recommendations. While topic distribution in the short-head can show general trends in popularity, a long-tail distribution of subjects that occur less frequently deserves further interpretation, as the implications for service design and library marketing are not as straightforward. One group of researchers has shown that "Product categories with a higher number of titles and with a higher average demand display a shorter tail even with the same level of influence from the recommendation network. This is consistent with the conjecture that smaller categories with less popular products will have a more pronounced demand tail when influenced by recommendations" (Oestreicher-Singer & Sundararajan, 2012, p. 81). This observation may account for the short-head of subjects in fiction and literature. McKay found that day of the week effects browsing in the book stacks such that "Browsing is more likely on quiet days" (McKay, et al., 2015, p. 287). These time-sensitive data points consequently also effect the relevance of personalized recommendations shown to viewers of their service. Libraries that use a similar IoT-powered recommender may want to consider system design choices that use a combination of recommendations for short-head ranges and find ways to integrate less popular areas simultaneously based on profiling users through a collaborative filtering approach. Other library user data, such as further data mining subject data from circulation records, could be triangulated with the user findings here to be a weight in providing more personalized recommendations.

Observations that use system logs should be interpreted cautiously. Log analytic studies must consider two overarching limitations, such as interpretability and comparability (He, Qvarfordt, Halvey, & Golovchinsky, 2016). Researchers underscored the need to understand logs in context, using "… higher-level representation such as search tactics" (He et al. 2016, p. 1201). A review of recommender systems noted that, in some cases, content-based filtering "…causes overspecialized recommendations that only include very similar to those of which the user is already aware" (Park, Kim, Choi, & Kim, 2012, p. 10059). If the subject distribution is sparse, this may have been the case within literature when items circulating popularly may have been over-represented. Other digital library researchers have demonstrated ensemble approaches that combine a user's previous searches and views of items. System improvements also may be achieved by efforts to personalize the recommendations further with an individual's previous user movements, which would provide data for the system to learn and improve dynamically.

CONCLUSION

This paper detailed IoT methods for studying library spaces and collections. Trends in subject needs and users' preferences for topics can be identified by analyzing and visualizing IoT middleware server logs. One finding of this paper was the discovery of short-head occurrences of literature and fiction navigation in recommendation support. A long-tail finding showed significant diversity in the topics that IoT-powered location-based recommendation recommends to users in the library book stacks. The strength of this study was plotting the areas where users navigate in the stacks with IoT technologies, understanding where users are located when they are looking for assistance and, finally, providing a descriptive delineation of all topic areas of interest to the IoT-based wayfinding and navigation service users. Location-based recommendation services in libraries can become more intelligent and powerful by taking advantage of streams of user motion data to provide recommendations; with the introduction of IoT beacons paired with library middleware, a wealth of data will result from which to ascertain user engagement in library collections with a depth that was heretofore not possible.

This study has helped fill descriptive gaps in the information science literature posed by Bates (1989) and others (Dervin, 2000; Solomon, 2002) to understand how users browse and navigate information environments. Future research of long-tail subject recommendations is advisable to determine whether larger trends in the information science field may relate to other power laws. Explaining information behavior phenomenon using power law frames may help provide guidance in developing algorithms for recommendation and personalization services, which increase diversity of content, especially considering that filter bubbles have been shown to provide users more of what they already consume, while also serving to reinforce systemic bias (Noble, 2018). Therefore, a long tail of topic recommendations would be desirable from an information behavior perspective outside of recommender systems and within contemporary information environments generally.

ACKNOWLEDGEMENTS

The author sincerely appreciates the research contributions of software developers Nathaniel Ryckman & Benjamin Ryckman.

REFERENCES

Anderson, C. (2006). The long tail: Why the future of business is selling less of more. Hyperion, New York, NY.

Andriani, P. & McKelvey, B. (2009). From Gaussian to Paretian thinking: causes and implications of power laws in organizations. Organization science, 20(6), 1053-1071. https://dx.doi.org/10.1287/orsc.1090.0481

Bates, M. (1989). The design of browsing and berrypicking techniques for the online search interface. Online Review, 13(5), 407-424. https://doi.org/10.1108/eb024320

Bradley, J., Henshaw, N., McVoy, L., French, A., Gilbertson, K., Becksford, L., & Givens, E. (2016). Creation of a library tour application for mobile equipment using iBeacon technology. Code4Lib Journal, 32, http://journal.code4lib.org/articles/11338

Brett, K., German, E., & Young, F. (2015). Tabs and tabulations: Results of a transaction log analysis of a tabbed-search interface. Journal of Web Librarianship, 9, 22-41. https://doi.org/10.1080/19322909.2015.1004502

Box, G. (1979). Robustness in the strategy of scientific model building. In R. Launer & G. Wilkinson (Eds.), Robustness in statistics (pp.201-236). Academic Press.

Chang, S-J., & Rice, R. (1993) Browsing: A multidimensional framework. Annual Review of Information Science and Technology, 28, 231-276.

Dervin, B. (2000). Chaos, order and sense-making: A proposed theory for information design. In R. Jacobson (Ed.), Information Design (pp. 35-57). Cambridge, Mass: MIT Press.

Eaton, G. (1991). Wayfinding in the library: Book searches and route uncertainty. RQ, 30(4), 519-527.

Griffey, J. (2018). Library Spaces and Smart Buildings: technology, metrics, and iterative design. Library Technology Reports, 54(1). Retrieved 30 March 2018 from https://journals.ala.org/index.php/ltr/issue/view/666

Hahn, J. (2011). Location-based recommendation services in library book stacks. Reference Services Review, 39(4), 654-674. https://doi.org/10.1108/00907321111186677

Hahn, J. (2017a). The Internet of Things: Mobile technology and location services in libraries. Library Technology Reports, 53(1). http://dx.doi.org/10.5860/ltr.53n1

Hahn, J. (2017b). Use and users of the Minrva mobile app. Reference Services Review, 45(3), 472-484. https://doi.org/10.1108/RSR-09-2016-0056

Hahn, J. (2018). Bibliotelemetry data. University of Illinois at Urbana-Champaign. https://doi.org/10.13012/B2IDB-2237685_V2

Hahn, J. & Ryckman, N. (2012). Modular mobile application design. Code4Lib Journal, 18. http://journal.code4lib.org/articles/7336

He, J., Qvarfordt, P., Halvey, M., & Golovchinsky, G. (2016). Beyond actions: Exploring the discovery of tactics from user logs, Information Processing & Management, 52(6), 1200-1226. https://doi.org/10.1016/j.ipm.2016.05.007

Hinze, A., McKay, D., Vanderschantz, N., Timpany, C. & Cunningham, S. J. (2012). Book selection behavior in the physical library: Implications for ebook collections. In Proceedings of the 12th ACM/IEEE-CS joint conference on Digital Libraries (JCDL '12) (pp. 305-314). https://doi.org/10.1145/2232817.2232874

Jensen, B.J. (2006). Search log analysis: What it is, what's been done, how to do it. Library & Information Science Research, 28,(3), 407-432. https://doi.org/10.1016/j.lisr.2006.06.005

Kuhlthau, C. (1988). Developing a model of the library search process: Cognitive and affective aspects. RQ, 28(2), 232-242. http://www.jstor.org/stable/25828262

Kuhlthau, C. (1993). A principle of uncertainty for information seeking. Journal of Documentation, 49(4), 339-355. https://doi.org/10.1108/eb026918

Kuhlthau, C. (2004). Seeking meaning: A process approach to library and information services. Westport, CN: Libraries Unlimited.

Lee, H.-L. (2000). What is a collection? Journal of the American Society for Information Science, 51(12), 1106-1113.

https://doi.org/10.1002/1097-4571(2000)9999:9999<::AID-ASI1018>3.0.CO;2-T

Library of Congress (2018). Classification outline. Retrieved 22 March 2018 from http://www.loc.gov/catdir/cpso/lcco/

Mandel, L. (2017). Wayfinding research in library and information studies: state of the field. Evidence Based Library and Information Practice, 12(2), 133-148. https://dx.doi.org/10.18438/B8395P

McKay, D., Smith, W., & Chang, S. (2014). Lend me some sugar: Borrowing rates of neighbouring books as evidence for browsing. In Proceedings of the ACM/IEEE-CS joint conference on Digital Libraries (JCDL '14) (pp. 305-314). https://doi.org/10.1109/JCDL.2014.6970161

McKay, D., Buchanan, G., & Chang, S. (2015). Tyranny of distance: Understanding academic library browsing by refining the neighbour effect. In S. Kapidakis, C. Mazurek, and M. Werla M. (Eds.), Research and Advanced Technology for Digital Libraries. Lecture Notes in Computer Science (280-294). Springer. https://doi.org/10.1007/978-3-319-24592-8_21

Noble, S., (2018). Algorithms of oppression: How search engines reinforce racism. New York, NY: New York University Press.

Oestreicher-Singer, G., & Sundararajan, A. (2012). Recommendation networks and the long-tail of electronic commerce. MIS Quarterly, 36(1), 65-83. Retrieved 30 March 2018 from http://www.jstor.org/stable/41410406

Park, D.H., Kim, H.K., Choi, I.Y., & Kim, J.K. (2012). A literature review and classification of recommender systems research. Expert Systems with Applications, 39(11), 10059. https://doi.org/10.1016/j.eswa.2012.02.038

Pettigrew, K., Fidel, R., & Bruce, H. (2001). Conceptual frameworks in information behavior. Annual Review of Information Science and Technology, 35, 43-78.

Rose, D. (2014). Enchanted Objects: Design, human desire, and the Internet of Things. New York, NY: Scribner.

Rowland, C., Goodman, E., Charlier, M., Light, A., & Lui, A. (2015). Designing Connected Products: UX for the Consumer Internet of Things. Sebastopol, CA: O'Reilly.

Sinclair, S., & Rockwell, G. (2016). Voyant Tools. Retrieved 22 March 2018 from http://voyant-tools.org/

Solomon, P. (2002). Discovering information in context. Annual Review of Information Science and Technology, 36, 229–264. https://doi.org/10.1002/aris.1440360106

Stefanidis, K. & Tsakonas, G., (2015). Integration of library services with Internet of Things technologies. Code4Lib Journal, 30. https://journal.code4lib.org/articles/10897

Svenonius, E. (2000). The intellectual foundation of information organization. Cambridge, MA: MIT Press.

Tobias, C. & Blair, A. (2015). Listen to what you cannot hear, observe what you cannot see: An introduction to evidence-based methods for evaluating and enhancing the user experience in distance library services. Journal of Library & Information Services in Distance Learning, 9(1-2), 148-156. DOI: 10.1080/1533290X.2014.946354

Xie, I., & Wolfram, D. (2009). A longitudinal study of database usage within a general audience digital library. Journal of Digital Information, 10(4). Retrieved 30 March 2018 from https://journals.tdl.org/jodi/index.php/jodi/article/view/304

UNIX Time, UTC, and Datetime: Jussivity, Prolepsis, and Incorrigibility in Modern Timekeeping

Elliott Hauser
University of North Carolina at Chapel Hill, USA.
eah13@email.unc.edu

ABSTRACT

This paper examines the three entangled systems of the UNIX time data format, the UTC time standard, and the various administratively defined datetimes used to give specific moments in time names. Due to the increasing prevalence of Linux and Unix-based systems, a large majority of computing devices, from phones to Web servers, utilize these interlocking systems to structure time. The assemblage as a whole is briefly described, from UNIX time integers to the empirical measurements of atomic vibrations and the earth's rotation within its celestial frame, to the open source Internet Assigned Numbers Authority (IANA) maintained time zone database, which declares a distinct name for each instant within the hundreds of administrative time zones world wide. Three theoretical concepts of jussivity, prolepsis and incorrigibility are operationalized to distinguish each system's contribution to the computational assemblage of modern timekeeping. Bowker's conception of the jussive Archive is used to frame the inquiry, foregrounding the things that these timekeeping practices help us exclude and forget. Calendrical prolepsis is examined as what Siegert calls a cultural technique, one that enables each of these systems to extend its reach into the past and condition our conception of any possible future. Each of these systems utilizes the unique and under-appreciated abilities of digital systems to enact a kind of incorrigibility, which I argue is inextricably linked with what Hayles has called the cognitive nonconscious. By better understanding the jussive, proleptic, and incorrigible powers deployed in the massive cognitive assemblage that arrays vibrations of atoms alongside celestial mechanics to locate our present, past and future, we open up new possibilities for intervening in these technics. Understanding these dynamics may allow future temporal information systems to therapeutically influence our cognition and our consciousness of time. This paper is intended to provide theoretical support for such efforts.

KEYWORDS

UNIX time, UTC, Datetime, Theory

INTRODUCTION

Modern timekeeping is a vast enterprise, stretching from the vibration of cesium atoms to the rotation of the earth within a celestial frame determined by quasars to billions of smartphones, servers, and connected devices. And yet we constantly encounter it at middle-distance, quotidian scales, wherever we see clock time. This assemblage is implicated every time we find the door to the library locked outside of operating hours. We participate in it when we look at our cell phones to check the time. It controls us when once a year (in the US) our cell phone alarms begin waking us up an hour earlier. In perfect synchrony, academic journals and tax authorities adjust the times after which submissions are deemed on time.

Timekeeping and its human-readable product, datetime, are globally pervasive, but can appear diffuse or subtle in their effects, especially in comparison to more charismatic assemblages. Unlike a social media network, timekeeping rarely directly operates on the level of consciousness, or of culture. Instead, it subtly influences, inflects, and structures our day-to-day awareness of ourselves. It has an almost imperceptible yet almost omnipotent ability to locate us, at any given moment, with a precise name for that moment. Google or Facebook uses this crystalline timeline to (dis)orient us in the present by showing us what we were doing on this day 8 years ago. Global markets assign a precise time to each transaction, a temporal lattice that deepens its resolution each year as computational systems become faster and faster (rendering human traders comparatively slower and slower). The series of named moments stretches in front and behind us in an apparently interminable march, even as each second becomes refracted into almost infinitesimal pieces by accelerating computational processes.

This paper is an examination of the modern technics of time using the concept of cognitive assemblage. As I'll show, modern timekeeping is a heterogenous collection of technical, human, and material processes which are mutually constitutive. At the root of global standardized time is the nonconscious cognition of devices of durational measurement. This cognition is imbricated within choices of various kinds, from algorithmic if-thens to government fiat. The incremental accumulation of duration within timekeeping is inherently jussive, controlling what is admitted into temporality. At the same time, this rigid timeline is overlaid with a culturally and politically determined system of names, producing days, weeks, months and years, itself connected with the celestial mechanics of the solar year. Supported by cultural and political enactment, these names have a the strange property of incorrigibility: they contain their own truth grounds. Each of these assemblage components has a more or less well known historical origin, and thereby a moment of beginning. Yet they have the intriguing ability to be extended forwards and backwards through a process of prolepsis, enabling them to territorialize the past, future, and any possible present. These three ontic operations are central to time's monolithic structuration of temporality.

Structure of the Paper

The structure of the paper is as follows. First, I'll briefly describe the modern timekeeping apparatus, from atomic clocks to time zones the UNIX time data format. Though this is an extensive assemblage, I've tried to constrain my description to only those elements relevant to the subsequent analysis.

Next, I'll use Mark Hansen's concept of 'atmospheric media' and its microtemporality as a jumping off point and to describe the stakes of the project. As the time scales of media processes tunnel far below that of possible human perception, these processes are altering the conditions of human sensibility, replacing prior conceptions of media as indexed to human perception and altering the possibilities of perception.

Deepening this analysis, I next turn to the work of Katherine Hayles and her concepts of 'cognitive nonconscious' and 'cognitive assemblages'. Together, these concepts license an extension of Hansen's observations about the effects of atmospheric media on sensibility into an even broader analysis of the cognitive assemblage of modern timekeeping's effects on human consciousness itself. I first show how the jussive process of increment constitutes a proto-cognitive interpretation, ready for cognitive completion by either machinic or human choice. I then describe modern timekeeping as a cognitive assemblage. In the process, I propose an complementary inversion of Stiegler's conception of tertiary retention, situating the human as the site of technical 'memory'. This process which constitutes the human simultaneously to Stiegler's conception of human tertiary retention constituting the technical. Though the two terms are often considered distinct, I will utilize the terms 'machinic' and 'technical' roughly interchangeably in this paper, as the technical objects of interest are computing machines. Thus, 'machinic time' indicates the components of time produced by computers.

Next, I turn to Bernhard Siegert's conception of 'cultural techniques' to investigate the ontic operation of prolepsis whereby time is able to colonize the possibility of temporal experience. Mirroring Siegert's incisive analysis of the cultural technique of the grid, which gains its power of spatial control through its specification of the empty, the cultural technique of time is shown to enable both retrograde and anterograde proleptic reach from the present to any past or future moment.

Finally, I consider human-defined calendrical systems, expressed within computational systems as datetimes. Datetime databases are transcriptions of political power into technical inscriptions that allow the translation of technically computed durations into incorrigible declarations of names for a given instant on the scientifically constructed timeline of UTC.

I end with some concluding remarks about how the cognitive assemblage of modern timekeeping is a site for the promulgation of certainty across essentially unbounded regions of time and space. By understanding and observing the jussive, proleptic and incorrigible ontic operations within this powerful cultural technique, I hope to support technical and conceptual interventions into this assemblage to conscientiously alter our temporal experience and agency.

THE MODERN TECHNICS OF TIME

Time and its canonical representation is a fascinatingly complex subject that allows us to examine the ways in which human systems of certainty are enacted by and intertwined with the increasingly computational systems which constitute them. Computational modeling of duration combined with human-produced labels for quantities of duration are increasingly defining our conception of time as a phenomenon. Hansen has recently argued that computational systems' ability to process information at sub-perceptual speeds is leading to it serving as a substrate of pre-perceptual sensibility, conditioning and constraining human thought and agency in subtle and insidious ways (Hansen 2015). A fuller picture of how time is operationalized in computational systems to support criticism and refinement of work like Hansen's is clearly needed, and I hope that this investigation will serve as an initial step in that direction.

UNIX time

UNIX time is an integer-based representation of the number of non-leap seconds elapsed since 0:00 Jan 1, 1970 UTC, a datetime known as its epoch. The increasing dominance of UNIX-like systems in Internet applications and smartphones means that this method of computational timekeeping has a near monopoly on the representation of time in digital systems. iOS, Android, Linux, and MacOS devices all use this standard in the computation of time (including the Linux servers and virtual machines that run well over 95% of Internet applications). The story of how this standard was developed and propagated to its current ubiquitous status has, in my estimation, been unjustly overlooked by the various fields critically examining information, computation, and time.

Datetime

As just mentioned, UNIX time is simply a large binary integer that increments regularly as a processor operates.[1] This integer must be converted into conventional time to be human readable. This process of conversion into a human datetime standard is perhaps even more complex from a cultural perspective. For a given UNIX time integer to be represented in the correct local time zone, it must be parsed into dissonant units of time since the epoch (years, months, hours, etc), assigned a day of the week, and adjusted due to a dizzying array of fiat time zones and Daylight-Saving regimes. A database that aims to contain all known administrative time zones and Daylight-Saving schemes since 1970 is included with most UNIX-like systems for this purpose. The database was started and maintained by volunteers and is now maintained under the auspices of the Internet Assigned Numbers Authority (IANA). Since time zones are subject to legislative action in any of a number of city, state, provincial, tribal, territorial, or national entities, the database is historical, tracking changes in timezone and Daylight Saving regimes, and must be updated to reflect legislative or dictatorial fiat around the world.

Major Components of Modern Timekeeping

There is of course a massively complex interaction between the interconnected techniques of timekeeping; I'd like to lay out a basic glossary of systems to support the paper's analysis. Broadly, the systems can be bifurcated into durational time, which is measured in SI seconds, and astronomical time, which is measured by the position of the earth in relation to the sun. Most people assume these conceptions of time to be equivalent, but, as has been known for centuries, the temporal duration of a solar year is not an integer multiple of the duration of the rotation of the earth. Accounting for this discontinuity can be seen as a central problem of both scientific timekeeping and the human system of datetime labels, a problematic that UNIX time is acutely embroiled in. The complex chains of systems might be summarized in the following way:

- **International Atomic Time (TIA).**[2] This is a synthesis of the output of the world's atomic clocks, published by the Bureau International des Poids et Mesures. It is precisely corrected for the effect of phenomena such as gravitational time dilation due to each clock's distinct elevation. TIA was synchronized with Universal Time in 1958 and represents pure duration since that epoch. 'Leap seconds' are not added to TIA.
- **Universal Time (especially UT1).** The UT1 standard utilizes astronomical and GPS satellite measurements of the speed of the earth's rotation with respect to the International Celestial Reference Frame (ICRF). Thus, it defines time in terms of the rotation of the earth within space. The duration of seconds changes slightly as a function of the speed of the Earth's rotation.
- **Coordinated Universal Time (UTC).** UTC allows the precise coordination of durational time with solar time. It is an atomic time standard, which uses duration rather than position as its standard. However, it is periodically updated with 'leap seconds' to ensure that human datetimes occur in roughly the same solar orientation each year. Thus, it represents the unification of atomic and astronomical time. The combination of atomic precision and astronomical phenomenal consistency has made it the basis for most global timekeeping.
- **UNIX time.** As described above, the number of UTS seconds since Jan 1, 1970, minus leap seconds. The exclusion of leap seconds from UNIX time has an interesting cultural history not appropriate to recapitulate here. Its impact is that UNIX datetime can be ambiguous around UTC leap seconds, requiring those that need to distinguish between them to utilize other timekeeping formats.
- **Datetime.** Collectively, the various human labels applied to astronomical time. UTC represents the highest resolution reconciliation of astronomical and durational (atomic) conceptions of time, making it ideal for the promulgation of modern calendrical systems, most of which are defined in by their relationship to UTC. Human Datetimes are enacted by convention, religious, and/or governmental fiat. In computational systems, they are promulgated as the IANA time zone database.

Together, these computationally enacted systems are a complex blend of global immutability and local idiosyncrasy. They represent the almost universal dominance of the concept of Standard Time, a once-controversial replacement for the previous concept of solar time (i.e. that noon is the apex of the sun at a given longitude, rendering an infinite number of 'timezones', though this term is of course a retronym in this context). Its dominance is so complete that the concept of solar time is foreign to most modern observers. Within each time zone, only one longitude's clocks actually read noon when the sun is at its apex and for some, such as Western China, the government-mandated time zone may make 'noon' as many as five hours away from

---

[1] There are also complex processes of synchronization such as NTP involved in keeping this integer consistent across multiple systems that, while fully deserving of a separate analysis, are superfluous in the context of this paper.

[2] Note: the acronyms of universal time schemes are derived from their French names, accounting for the disparity.

solar noon. In less than two centuries, we have completely inverted our conception of which of these two regimes is 'natural time'.

The combination of technical assemblage and cognitive shift indicated by this account of modern timekeeping indicates a complex story ripe for explanation.

MICROTEMPORALITY AND MEDIA

For Hansen, "atmospheric media" connotes "less a set of objects or processes than a tendency: the tendency for media to operate at microtemporal scales without any necessary — let alone direct — connection to human sense perception and conscious awareness" (Hansen 2015, 37). Microtemporality in Hansen's sense indicates the increasingly complete excavation of every second by computers' processing units. Microseconds, nanoseconds, picoseconds, and, for PetaFLOP supercomputers, even femtoseconds (one trillionth of a second) all are meaningful durations in the context of modern computation. By comparison, human reaction time is about a tenth of a second.

Computers' speed and the correspondingly short durations within which they operate aren't the only relevant factor. Bullets similarly act at speeds faster than human reaction times but can't be said to have precipitated a sea change in the effects of media. Hansen's analysis presumes but doesn't strongly identify this difference: computational media are semiotic technologies (Smith 1996). It isn't just that computers are fast, it's that they perform *semiosis* at sub-perceptual speeds.

It might seem like sleight of hand to shift from Hansen's 'atmospheric media' to 'computers', but the two are inseparable, if not exactly coextant. Hansen's media lens onto the modern computational phylum is by no means unjustified. His goal is, after all, to show how such media condition the "sensible confound", prior to human perception or awareness. But, by situating his project in the slightly broader context of computation, I hope to employ it to understand the stakes of time in computation.

Hansen's use of Whitehead's ontology seems particularly suited to both durational and astronomical time, both of which are derived from the regular thermodynamics of a process with a regular period of oscillation or cycle (albeit within vastly different spatial frames). Whitehead's approach holds that

> The entirety of the universe informs any and every becoming. Thus, what may look like autonomous operations of subjects are in actual fact aggregates of multiple and heterogeneous, overlapping agencies complexly imbricated with the total situation or environment at the given moment of their occurrence. (p. 36)

Notice how temporality functions as the index of becoming here. Deleuze, following Whitehead, situates the temporal moment as the site of becoming, where the "temporal modulation operates directly on the subjectivity that inheres in the power of superjects to impact future becomings, both at the level of concrescence and at the level of events" (Hansen 2015, 36). For Hansen, Deleuze goes beyond Stiegler's separation of the technical object from consciousness, instead identifying a "becoming-subjective of the object" (p. 36).

For Hansen, Stiegler and Deleuze occupy two extremes on a continuum. While both are valid (Hansen uses the analogy of Newtonian and relativistic physics), Hansen is more interested in the implications of Deleuze's claims. This leads to an exploration of "how media might impact experience without being channeled through delimited, higher-order processes" (p. 36). This approach becomes central to Hansen's investigation of atmospheric media, with its characteristic microtemporality. As I'll show below, I believe Stiegler's approach can be extended in a way that might meaningfully respond to Hansen's critique.

INCREMENT AS INTERPRETATION

Before proceeding further, I'd like to introduce the recent work of Katherine Hayles as a method of expanding Hansen's concerns with the temporality of media to the level of consciousness through what Hayles calls 'nonconscious cognition' (Hayles 2016b). In a move similar to but even more expansive than Hansen's, Hayles identifies nonconscious cognition as a preconscious layer of apperception that in a sense grounds consciousness. She enumerates scientific evidence for 'distributed cognition' as evidence for the validity of her approach (Hayles 2016b, 14 et seq.), and such justifications won't concern us here. Instead, we'll take the relationship between cognition, which Hayles defines as low-level interpretation and choice, and consciousness, which Hayles reserved for the self-aware experience of humans (while leaving open the question of whether some intelligent animal species share these qualities). Importantly, low-level cognition need not occur within a conscious subject. Cognition can arise from sensibility and autonomic processes in the human organism, or human cognition can be augmented by that which occurs in animals (such as a bloodhound) or machines (such as a geiger counter). When these cognitive networks grow complex and heterogenous, Hayles suggests we consider them as cognitive assemblages, which indicates the complex and varied impact that specific components might have on the larger whole.

Turning our attention to time, it is clear that measures of duration such as the springs in traditional clockwork, the precise volume of sand in an hourglass, or the complex operation of atomic clocks all form potential extensions to human cognition.

Through each of these devices, time is made sensible, revealed to human perception, in ways not available in their absence. Humans do have a neurological ability to perceive and generate durations, and this ability can be honed over time. Such honing, however, is little more than the internalization of technical temporality. Musicians and athletes typically possess enhanced bodily temporal cognition, but they typically obtain even this internalized temporality from metronomes, stopwatches, and starting guns. For most humans, precise temporal cognition begins and ends with the use of some form of clock. What is the cognitive potential of such devices? How do the technical processes of duration measurement impact human cognition, and how does this cognition impact consciousness?

Jussivity and Interpretation

In modern timekeeping devices the trace of oscillation or processor cycles is jussively rendered as an increment after a predefined number of cycles. 'Trace' and 'jussive' are here used in Bowker's sense (Bowker 2005, 2010). 'Traces' are, roughly, causal chains. 'Jussive' processes are a description of the arbitrary (as in the result of arbitration) inclusion and exclusion of aspects of information as traces are incorporated into an archive.

Duration measurement devices that use periodic oscillation (i.e. a quartz watch or a cesium atomic clock) or computational cycles (modern computational devices such as smartphones and laptops) to measure time must count these cycles, incrementing them up to a specific number, then incrementing the count of seconds in system time. The intermediate increment is perhaps implicit in the final product but is excluded. For instance, in a (say) 1GHz processor the system must count a billion computation cycles to increment a single second. But the system's output in UNIX time is indistinguishable in form from that of a 1MHz processor, which counted one million computation cycles to produce the same second increment. The intermediate counts might be used to provide sub-second resolution for a given instant in systems that support this but, in most systems, sub second temporal resolution is continually purged for past seconds. In other words: in most systems, timestamps are denominated in seconds, constituting a jussive exclusion of any possible sub-second interpretation of the past.

This is an example of jussive processes in digital timekeeping but is by no means its limit. Timekeeping as a process excludes everything except duration. In Husserl's terms, timekeeping as increment could be seen as the secondary retention of temporal objects, i.e. pure duration. Each of these jussive operations constitutes an interpretation, forming a potential site for future cognition.

Locating Choice

At the level of timekeeping, choice has yet to occur. Jussivity takes action upon the world as it converts duration into increment But this is mere interpretation; if interpretation inherently involved choice in Hayles's sense, there would be no need for her second criterion of cognition. Thus, to characterize temporal cognition within timekeeping devices, we must locate choice.

A computational system which is incrementing an integer to track duration is performing proto-cognition. As Smith (1988) notes, timekeeping is not yet computation, though the semantics (in Smith's terms) or semiotics (in those I'd prefer) of a timekeeping system can be useful in showing properties of computation that might be otherwise obscured. In this case, we are able to see that the interpretation of duration in computers' timekeeping functionality arrays a proto-cognition through which their temporal sensibility is conditioned and constrained. This observation is similar in form to Hansen's description of the operation of "atmospheric media" upon human cognition. This parallel allows us to trace the effects that interest Hansen down into the cognitive layers of computation, revealing the mechanisms which produce these effects in humans by situating them in machinic nonconscious cognition. As I'll argue, the proto-cognition of increment can be completed by choices originating in a variety of agents, both human and technical.

INFRASTRUCTURE OF SENSIBILITY

Hansen's "atmospheric media" (a term Hayles prefers to what he elsewhere calls "twenty-first-century media") is defined by its microtemporality. For Hansen, the ability of computationally driven media to operate at sub-perceptual speeds is the root of its radical powers to shape human consciousness. Like Hayles's nonconscious cognition, this highlights the role of nonhuman systems in generating and characterizing human consciousness. Thus, for both, an examination of the dynamics of these systems is required for a full characterization of modern human consciousness. Broadly, both are consonant with the philosophy of Bernard Stiegler, which situates the human and the technical as co-constitutive. This is expressed in Stiegler's concept of epiphylogenesis, defined as "the theory that human development is not just one of genetics but is deeply implicated with technics as 'the pursuit of life by other means'" (Mills 2016, 163). With epiphylogenesis as a working assumption of sorts, we'll focus on Stiegler's conception of primary, secondary and tertiary retention, using these in an inverted way to describe temporal cognition in computers. This inversion consists of flipping the directionality of retention: whereas Stiegler starts from the human and ends with the technic as the site of tertiary retention, I'd like to explore whether we might start from computational cognition and conceive of the human as a site of tertiary retention for computational systems.

Microtemporality and Primary/Secondary Retention

I'd like to connect Hansen's project with Hayles's by characterizing microtemporality within the context of machinic cognition. As argued above, the incremental structure of UNIX time forms an interpretive layer underneath (or alongside) computational activity. Though devoid of cognitive choice, this interpretation forms one half of temporal cognition within computers. Computation itself provides the other half. Because of this pervasive layer of temporal interpretation, nonconscious cognition is itself conditioned at the level of sensibility. Without any retained conception of time, computers' cognition would be atemporal. In Stiegler's reading of Husserl, they would possess only primary retention. Oscillations or cycles embody Husserl's definition of temporal objects, being composed exclusively of durations. Increment forms a kind of secondary retention, whereby the experience of a period of cycles or oscillations is experienced in a different way, as a distinct, incremented integer. Though miniscule, this capability of secondary retention is enough to ground temporal cognition in computational systems. Thus, UNIX time can be seen as secondary retention for computational cognition.

The stage is set, then, for exploration of the human as tertiary retention for machinic cognition. For Stiegler, the tertiary retention of technical assemblages is precisely what enables temporality within the human. Foreshadowing Hansen, Stiegler sees tertiary retention as prior to, and conditioning of, even primary retention. Furthermore, human tertiary retention and the technical are identical for Stiegler. That is, the externalization of temporality for humans is constitutive of the technical. Could the reverse hold as well?

Cognitive Assemblages

Before proceeding, there is one final theoretical piece which it will be useful to examine more closely: the cognitive assemblage. In distinguishing her use of 'assemblage' from that of Deleuze and Guattari, Hayles writes "*Cognitive assemblage* emphasizes cognition as the common element among parts and as the functionality by which parts connect" (Hayles 2016a, 32). Thus she does not consider assemblages in terms of desire, affect or transversal energies in characterizing assemblages. This opinionated use of the terms bears fruit, however, for so many of the most important modern phenomena admit of cognitive analysis. 'Cognition', then is a broader conception than 'consciousness'.

> Because humans and technical systems in a cognitive assemblage are interconnected, the cognitive decisions of each affect the others, with interactions occurring across the full range of human cognition, including consciousness, the unconscious, the cognitive nonconscious, and the sensory/perceptual systems that send signals to the cortex. Moreover, the human decisions and interpretations feed back into technical systems, sometimes decisively affecting the contexts in which those systems operate. (Hayles 2016a, 33)

Though she reserves 'consciousness' for the human, there is plenty of room for symmetry in what might be termed cognitive symbiosis between the human and the technical. Even conceived as nonconscious, computing machines can, as we've shown, possess cognitive temporality. The questions now become:

1. Is nonconscious cognitive temporality capable of tertiary retention?
2. Is the site of this retention the human? Could this be said to *be* the human?

The second question will be addressed in the next section, with the help of Siegert's concept of cultural techniques.

Tertiary Retention of Machinic Time in the Human

As for the first, the concept of cognitive assemblages should provide the tools needed to investigate it. UNIX time is a component of the much larger cognitive assemblage of incremental time. The term incremental time is intended to contrast with human phenomenal time, which is what Stiegler was concerned with. In contrast to phenomenal time, which indicates an experience of time within human consciousness, incremental time is a nonconscious assemblage. As shown at the outset, this moves from observations of the earth's rotation to the oscillation of atoms to processing cycles to UNIX time binary integers. The assemblage also reaches into humans, over two billion of whom use smartphones and, presumably, use those smartphones' connections to network time servers to tell the time and date. If the technical components of this assemblage are technical precisely because of their function as tertiary retention for humans, I don't see how the inverse *couldn't* be true. The technicity of the technical components of the temporal assemblage gain this technicity in relation to the human. The tertiary retention of technical cognition in the human manifests itself in the very microtemporal conditions of modern sensibility that Hansen attributes to atmospheric media. The Bureau International des Poids et Mesures (BIPM), its inscriptions such as Circular T, the various administrative time zones, the use of datetimes in commerce, social events, and religion, and the phenomenal experience of 'Tuesday' are all sites of tertiary retention for machinic cognition. As internalizations of machinic time, they are externalizations of machinic time into the human, the complement to machinic time manifesting the externalization of human temporality. The complex co-creation of these notions of time is Stiegler's point, and I believe this inversion of his conception of retention strengthens that point. It completes a project of decentering of the human not yet visible in Husserl's original conceptions, one already apparent in Hansen's critique of Stiegler and embrace of Deleuze. Following Hayles, we can retain the distinction between the human and the cognitive nonconscious (which for Hayles includes both machines and animals).

But, by extending Stiegler's conception downwards from consciousness into cognition, we arrive at a more complex and detailed account of the mechanisms at work within the cognitive assemblage of time that increasingly dominates both human and technical cognition.

PROLEPSIS AS CULTURAL TECHNIQUE

So far, we've pursued an approach broadly compatible with, in media theorist Bernhard Siegert's words, "decentering the distinction between human and nonhuman by insisting on the radical technicity of this distinction" (Siegert 2015, 8). Thus, we are not concerned with philosophical ideals of the concepts we encounter, but rather with deely investigating their material basis and cultural embeddedness. Siegert labels his object of study 'cultural techniques' (*Kulturtechniken*).

Cultural Techniques

This approach is uniquely suited to examining the cognitive assemblage of timekeeping that we've identified. Siegert himself uses time in giving examples of the distinction between his approach to media theory and the 'posthumanities'.

> The concept of cultural techniques clearly and unequivocally repudiates the ontology of philosophical concepts. Humans *as such* do not exist independently of cultural techniques of hominization, time *as such* does not exist independently of cultural techniques of time measurement, and space *as such* does not exist independently of cultural techniques of spatial control. (p. 9)

Siegert also provides his own account of what Hayles has termed a cognitive assemblage, further justifying this admixture of methods:

> An abacus allows for different calculations than do ten fingers; a computer, in turn, allows for different calculations than does an abacus. When we speak of cultural techniques, therefore, we envisage a more or less complex actor network that comprises technological objects as well as the operative chains they are part of and that configure or constitute them. (p. 11)

Siegert would seem to wholeheartedly endorse the de-phenomenalization inherent in our extension of Stiegler's reading of Husserl's retention by de-emphasizing ontology in favor of the ontic:

> This does not mean that the theory of cultural techniques is anti-ontological; rather, it moves ontology into the domain of ontic operations. (p. 9)

Siegert follows Macho in defining cultural techniques as *second order* processes capable of representing themselves symbolically. There is no similarly clear division in Hayles's conception of consciousness or cognition. It is reasonable to assume that the symbolic is only operational within consciousness, which would prevent an inversion cultural technique analogous to that which I've proposed for tertiary retention. This is not the tack I'd like to take, however. Cultural techniques can remain grounded within human consciousness. Like Hayles's cognitive nonconsciousness, Siegert's cultural techniques employs an intertwining of the human and the technical that provides broad pathways for describing the relationship bidirectionality. Thus, an inversion of cultural techniques isn't our object. Rather, I'd like to show how cultural techniques can support the inversion of tertiary retention I'm proposing, and perhaps even define the human in these terms.

The Grid

Siegert's most generative employment of cultural techniques is, for me, his discussion of the grid. The grid is a cultural technique of spatial organization that, crucially, allows for the colonization of otherwise empty space. Grids that include a technique of extension potentially are able to locate (i.e. *name*) anything.

> Modernity is characterized by the invention of a *taxis* technique capable of also turning humans into retrievable objects. This modern *taxis* is implemented by means of a new cultural technique which takes into account that something may be missing from its place. In other words, it encompasses the notion of an empty space. The technique in question is the grid or lattice....[The grid] presupposes the ability to write absence. (p. 97)

Siegert's use of this as an analytical frame with which to examine representational art in the Renaissance, the literal colonization of South America, and the literal territorialization of the United States is masterful; I won't recapitulate it here. Importing his insights to the discussion of time as a cultural technique, however, Siegert's conception of the presence of an absence is key to the operation of modern timekeeping. In studies of datetime systems, an extension of a calendrical system to dates before its adoption is called prolepsis. The word's root is the greek *lambanein*, to take. This root is shared with both epilepsy, in which 'to take' means 'to seize' and the logico-mathematical concept of lemma, in which 'to take' means 'to assume'. Both of these senses are operative in the datetime operation of prolepsis, wherein a particular nomenclature is assumed, whilst simultaneously 'seizing' new temporal territory for a calendar.

Calendrical Prolepsis

The details of the use of the term prolepsis in historical understanding of calendars may be helpful. The Julian calendar was adopted on the orders of Julius Caesar in what we now call 45 BC. The system included both a definition of twelve months and a scheme of leap years that was irregularly observed until around 4 AD, when it became standardized. The calendar dominated much of Western timekeeping for the next millennium and a half, even as its annual epoch, the year at which its increment began, was periodically altered. In 1582, after growing discontinuities between Julian datetime and the solar year had become problematic, especially for the observance of important religious ceremonies, Pope Gregory XIII commissioned a new calendar to be made, which reconfigured both the months and the scheme of leap years. Under the new system, every 4 years was considered a leap year, with an additional day in February, except for centurial years, which were not leap years, except for years divisible by 400, which were leap years. This system was intended to preserve the religious continuity of feast days, which otherwise would slowly occur at different times of the solar year.

With the introduction of the Gregorian calendar, a discontinuity had been introduced in nomenclature. After its adoption, every day had both a Julian and Gregorian date, depending on which system was mandated by local authorities. Yet the true power of the new calendar (and, of course, shared by all calendars) was expressed in the proleptic re-definition of previous dates *before its adoption*. Thus, dates before 1582 can be said to have a *proleptic* Gregorian date, even though the calendar did not exist at the time. The promulgation and adoption of competing calendrical regimes was uneven in history, but the Gregorian calendar is the global standard for most governments, and past dates have been proleptically defined. For instance, George Washington was born on February 11, 1731, according to the Julian calendar in use at that time. England converted to the Gregorian calendar in 1752, and the proleptic date of February 22 is commonly given as George Washington's birthday, despite the fact that the historical man himself would have attested that his birthdate was February 11th for a good portion of his life.

This *retrograde* prolepsis is simply an easily discernible effect of the cultural technique of timekeeping. Anterograde prolepsis is the ontic operation of calendars that is used to define dates in the future before they happen. Jointly, they constitute the cultural power and effects of timekeeping techniques to territorialize our conscious experience of time.

Temporal Prolepsis

Just as Siegert identified the operation of grids upon both spatial presence and spatial absence as constitutive of its ability to encompass and territorialize space, prolepsis is the fundamental operation which gives the cultural technique of timekeeping through datetime, its power to name. A datetime system simultaneously locates the present, past, and future in interrelationships. It excludes non-temporal objects (i.e. everything except duration) from its scale, imparting them with temporal properties through this separation. It 'seizes' their temporality and names it. With temporality thus conquered, humans are able to easily 'assume' (consume) this temporality as an unquestioned background to temporal experience. In doing so, they import and extend the names specified by the politics of datetime.

Adding Siegert's conception of cultural techniques at this point in our analysis considerably expands and contextualizes Hansen's project. Though atmospheric media may have different-in-kind impacts upon human sensibility through their microtemporality, this can be seen as a metastasis of a cultural technique that was already ancient and had long been co-evolving with human cognitive potentiality. In other words, humans have always utilized techniques of temporal prolepsis to constrain the present, techniques that simultaneously colonized and arranged the future and past. The evolution of these systems has made them asymptotically indistinguishable from the solar year. From Julian leap years to Gregorian epicyclic leap centuries to UTC's empirically derived leap seconds, human techniques of time have hardened into a difficult to perceive superstructure surrounding our experience of duration. Examining the details of this structure can even induce a kind of vertigo; the arbitrariness of datetime combined with the ruthlessly efficient prolepsis of modern universal time seems an unlikely admixture of incompatible types. Yet, as noted by Hansen, this admixture possesses the seeds of a dramatic rewriting of human sensibility.

We invented temporal machines in part to colonize time with our dates; yet this machinic temporality has colonized us back, all the while faithfully enabling temporal prolepsis. As an exact inverse of Stiegler's tertiary retention, this human internalization and labeling of machinic duration is the negative space left over after global dissemination of binary signals to billions of connected devices and the subsequent rendering of these signals into patterns of colored pixels on screens has occurred. The 'recolonization' of the human by the technics of timekeeping can be thought of as outlining the shape of the modern temporal human. In performing the function of tertiary retention of human, semantic time for the machines that we in turn use for tertiary retention of machinic, durational time, human and machine co-constitute each other's temporality, a coevolution that is perhaps even deeper than Stiegler has envisioned.

DATETIME AND INCORRIGIBILITY

The human imposition of Datetime onto the ever more fine-grained and crystalline structure of durational time produced by machines' counting of periodic processes can demonstrate the power of prolepsis for clearing temporal landscape, readying it for colonization.

A user of a UNIX-based system still has agency in choosing amongst the supported time zone options. Yet the user is still constrained by the jussivity of timezone definition. The system is incorrigible within its limited domain in representing these choices: a time zone definition provides its own truth-grounds, even when those truth grounds are stated in relation to an external measure such as UTC. Re-definition (i.e. altering the time zone database) is the only way to challenge a time zone definition. The database that holds the encodings of administrative timezones was started by volunteers and is now maintained by the Internet Assigned Numbers Authority (IANA). The system is designed to produce certainty, and its incorrigibility is one of its key desiderata. That is, when the user specifies an administrative timezone, a given UNIX time integer can be reliably and invariably converted into a human readable datetime output. Thus, UNIX time and the timezone database combine to enable proleptic promulgation of politically defined time zones within computer systems.

Interestingly, the entire cognitive assemblage of timekeeping in modern computer systems is thus a *medium* for the promulgation of differently flavored or inflected time zone systems, each of which might be seen as a member in the family of cultural techniques called datetime. These cultural techniques are all enabled by and performed upon the grid-like temporality of UNIX time and its relationship to UTC's unification of astronomical and durational time. By utilizing this expansively proleptic time-grid, administrative timezones find a ready substrate that allows political fiat to alter when people get up, go to work, and even celebrate their own birthdays.

THE POSSIBILITY OF TEMPORAL THERAPY

Broadening the picture somewhat, the example of the cultural techniques of timekeeping give an important window into what I'd like to term the promulgation of certainty within information systems. Modern timekeeping is accomplished by a complex global network that connects the vibration of atoms, the movement of the earth in its celestial frame, and political expressions of power through the naming of days and designations of the hours. This cognitive assemblage includes the perceptions and behaviors of the humans that use and are affected by these times, which includes practically all humans except perhaps uncontacted primitive peoples. Even contacted primitive peoples which have not adopted these cultural techniques are impacted by them indirectly through their effects upon those making contact, structuring the durations of the encounters (i.e. 'this anthropological expedition will last for three weeks during the month of August').

The prolepsis of duration provides the substrate for the imposition of datetimes, which itself is a major substrate for the imposition of political and economic power. We have thus far neglected the operation of global markets, which are directly inscribed upon the temporal lattice produced by this assemblage. Hayles herself notes the interactions between time and markets in her incisive examination of High Frequency Trading (HFT). As computational speeds reduce the duration of meaningful units of time further and further, transoceanic cables are built at great expense to reduce informational transit times by mere milliseconds. Hayles diagnoses the root of the inherent instability HFT introduces into the global financial system as the ability for algorithms to form feedback loops far removed from human consciousness. Like microphones producing piercing feedback when held close to an amplifier, HFT algorithms have the latent potential to cause runaway price increases, as in the case of the $2 million book listed on Amazon, or flash crashes, which by some estimates happen thousands of times a year. The cognitive assemblage originally built by humans to allow coordination across time and space has been extended by machines into the infinitesimal depths of duration. Limited only by processing and communication speed, these cognitive ecologies will continue to operate without regard for their consequences upon human well-being until or unless human cognition can be reintroduced into their operation.

Following her diagnosis, Hayles does not stop short of a prescription. She identified new proposals for 'batch auctions' which would remove the incentive to produce the fastest possible algorithms. By allowing for more computational time within trades, programmers would be able to build more complex reasoning into trading algorithms, instead of ruthlessly simplifying them to gain temporal advantage over trading partners. Opening up this space for 'thought,' embodied in algorithmic computational processes, humans would regain a modicum of control over these processes, thereby breaking the deafening feedback loop that seems in constant operation in global financial markets. I don't have time or space here to elaborate much further, but future work should follow Hayles's lead in identifying therapeutic interventions into temporal cognitive assemblages, permitting the operation of human consciousness where it is needed to avoid the harm automated cognitive processes can cause when they're indiscriminately deployed.

CONCLUSION

The analysis of the technics of time pursued in this paper has uncovered three powerful instances of what Siegert might term ontic operations. These are jussivity, prolepsis, and incorrigibility. Together they provide the technics of time with its powerful abilities of colonization and territorialization, which animate the cultural technique of datetime. Durational time, as embodied in the incremental binary integers of UNIX time, contains only one part of Hayles's cognition, interpretation. For cognition to occur, choice must be supplied. A powerful reality of modern temporal techniques is that multiple sources for this choice exist. Algorithms make choices at microtemporal scales. Scientific standards bodies make and technically implement the choices underlying the various definitional time standards. Political powers make definitional datetime choices that are overlaid onto UNIX time integers to produce names for every second of every day. Jussive processes within each select and discard which elements of the past to import into the present. Proleptic processes determine aspects of the present to project into the future back onto the past. And each of these systems utilizes the unique and under-appreciated abilities of digital systems to embody an incorrigibility, which is inextricably linked with their specific modes of cognition. By better understanding the jussive, proleptic, and incorrigible powers deployed in the massive cognitive assemblage that arrays vibrations of atoms alongside celestial mechanics to locate our present, past and future, we open up new possibilities for intervening in these technics, thereby gaining a foothold to constructively alter the ways we possess of being human, and temporal.

ACKNOWLEDGMENTS

The ideas in this paper have been heavily influenced by ongoing discussions with Neal Thomas. The Organization Reading Group at UNC (of which Neal is a crucial part) has provided the ideal conditions for my thought. https://orgorgorgorgorg.org

REFERENCES

Bowker, Geoffrey C. 2005. *Memory Practices in the Sciences*. Cambridge, MA: MIT Press.

———. 2010. "The Archive." *Communication and Critical/Cultural Studies* 7 (2). Routledge: 212–14.

Hansen, Mark. 2015. *Feed Forward: On the Future of Twenty-First-Century Media*. Chicago: University of Chicago Press.

Hayles, N. Katherine. 2016a. "Cognitive Assemblages: Technical Agency and Human Interactions." *Critical Inquiry* 43 (1): 32–55.

———. 2016b. *Unthought: The Power of the Cognitive Nonconscious*. Chicago and London: University of Chicago Press.

Mills, Simon. 2016. *GIlbert Simondon: Information, Technology and Media*. New York; London: Rowman & Littlefield International.

Siegert, Bernhard. 2015. *Cultural Techniques: Grids, Filters, Doors, and Other Articulations of the Real*. Translated by Geoffrey Winthrop-Young. New York: Fordham University Press.

Smith, Brian Cantwell. 1988. "The Semantics of Clocks." In *Aspects of Artificial Intelligence*, 3–31. Studies in Cognitive Systems. Springer, Dordrecht.

———. 1996. *On the Origin of Objects*. Cambridge, MA: MIT Press.

Blocked and Chained: Blockchain and the Problems of Transparency[1]

Darra Hofman
University of British Columbia, Canada.
dhofman@mail.ubc.ca

Alamir Novin
University of British Columbia, Canada.
alamir.novin@ubc.ca

ABSTRACT

Blockchain is frequently claimed to be a democratizing technology. However, its relationship to both law and broader democratic institutions remains uncertain. One claim regarding blockchain's democratic potential is that it is radically transparent and can bring such transparency to existing systems of governance. This paper interrogates that claim in three different ways. Firstly, it examines blockchain technology against broader theories of transparency. Secondly, it examines the relationship between transparency and democracy, questioning how blockchain technologies could mediate that relationship. Finally, it examines how blockchain technologies could impact a particular exercise of transparency, freedom of information requests. This paper finds the relationship of transparency itself to democratic ideals is complex, contested and highly context-dependent; the "democratizing" technological transparency built into blockchains could easily prove undemocratic in application. Blockchain technology cannot meet broader transparency goals without addressing political gatekeepers and the legal, social, and cultural needs that animate those goals.

KEYWORDS

Blockchain; distributed ledger technology; transparency; freedom of information

INTRODUCTION

"Code is law" (Lessig, 2006, 2). Lessig's central provocation is no less relevant now than when he first published *Code* in 1999. It is centrally significant to the blockchain. Wright and De Filippi claim, "[a]s blockchain technology becomes widely adopted, centralized authorities [...] could lose the ability to control and shape of activities of disparate people through existing means" (2015,15). Others are more skeptical. Atzori refers to a blockchain-based "stateless global society" as "the myth of an egalitarian blockchain-based society" (2015, 57). Between these two poles, "[t]he central question is not how to regulate blockchains, but how blockchains regulate. They may supplement, complement, or substitute for legal enforcement" (Wright & De Filippi, 2015, 38).

We argue that blockchain, in and of itself, is neither salve nor poison. Rather, the difference between medicine and poison is dose; the ultimate impact of blockchain will be felt, not just due its innate characteristics, but its application. We take as our example the idea of blockchains as a "transparent" technology. The Tapscotts argue that "through smart contracts...[c]ompanies can program relationships with radical transparency" (Tapscott and Tapscott, 2016, 257). Blockchain transparency is sought for clinical trials (Benchoufi, Porcher, & Ravaud, 2017), corporate governance (Yermack, 2017), and real estate (Velpuri, 2017) Even the government of Canada is exploring the use of Ethereum to improve transparency (National Research Council Canada, 2018). Blockchain clearly holds a great deal of potential as a technology, but its benefits will be fully realized only if we do not underestimate its potential human, societal, and democratic risks. Can blockchain deliver "transparency" and for whom will be it be transparent?

TRANSPARENCY AND "TREACHEROUS VOCABULARY"

Angela Walch, a leading scholar on blockchain and law, asserts that "[blockchain's] unsettled vocabulary is relevant to how regulators understand, discuss, and ultimately regulate (or not) the technology or its uses" (2017a, 2). This "unsettled vocabulary" extends even to the idea of "blockchain" itself. "Blockchain technology" is a somewhat controversial term; while some use it to encompass the whole of distributed ledger technologies, others limit it to the distributed ledger technologies underlying cryptocurrencies such as Bitcoin and Ethereum. While there is no universally agreed upon definition of blockchain technology, for the purposes of this papers, it can be understood as "a distributed ledger that maintains a continually growing list of publicly

[1] The present paper is a significantly expanded and revised version of a paper that was previously presented at *HCI for Blockchain: A CHI 2018 workshop on Studying, Critiquing, Designing and Envisioning Distributed Ledger Technologies*, April 21–26, 2018, Montreal, QC, Canada. Portions of this work originally come from Ms. Hofman's doctoral dissertation proposal.

accessible records cryptographically secured from tampering and revision" (Lemieux 2016a, 5). Part of the challenge in defining blockchain technology arises from the fact that there is actually a diversity of blockchain technologies. However, at a fundamental level, blockchain technology distributes a ledger of transactions over numerous computers (nodes); each node runs software that continuously verifies and replicates the most recent copy of the ledger. Transaction data is hashed into blocks which are chained together; before a transaction can be hashed, however, it must be validated according to the blockchain's *consensus mechanism*. A validated transaction is then added to the blockchain; previous blocks cannot be removed without changing the rules of the blockchain (*forking*).

While there exist different kinds of consensus mechanisms, it is the concept of the consensus mechanism that is central to the disruptive potential of blockchain technology in recordkeeping. Blockchain transactions are not authenticated by a trusted authority; in fact, no authority, legal or otherwise, validates the blockchain. Instead, trust is placed in the algorithms underlying the consensus mechanisms. It is the possibility of such a "trustless" system of record authentication and validation for transactions such as drafting and executing contracts, registering and transferring property, administering trusts and estates, and managing identity rights – without the error prone, cost-inducing interference of trusted authorities, individual or institutional – that most authors point to when claiming the blockchain is a democratizing technology. The vision is one in which reliance on math, as in the consensus mechanisms, reduces (or even eliminates) the need for human intermediaries, thereby increasing the access and autonomy of individual actors. This "trustless" reliance on consensus mechanisms is also part of the claim that blockchains are transparent, because the validation of transactions by math rather than humans is, allegedly, less prone to bias and more easily verified.

However, Walch claims that the language around the technology – such as the claim that consensus mechanisms make the system "trustless" – is, at best, uncertain. Walch points to a number of factors that contribute to the uncertainty around the meaning of such fundamental blockchain terms as "immutable" and "trustless," including:

- Word taint: shifting terminology to avoid negative associations, such as Bitcoin with Silk Road;
- Technology variations: there are many different blockchain technologies with their own characteristics and capabilities;
- Cross-field communications: blockchain technologies are very interdisciplinary, with the communication problems attendant thereto;
- Industry "pivots": vocabulary shifts with marketing; and
- Fixing inaccuracies: debates over the accuracy of terminology (such as "miners") has brought language thought to be more accurate (by some) into the fold (such as "validators") (Walch, 2017a).

Thus, validating claims that blockchain technology is fundamentally "transparent" requires examining exactly what is meant by transparent, and in what context. The assertion that blockchain is inherently transparent is based on a few characteristics of the technology:

- The ledger, at least in the permissionless blockchains, is accessible to any and all nodes;
- The ledger is (theoretically) immutable, with full, automatic, timestamped audit trails of every transaction; and
- The disintermediation of the blockchain means that there is (theoretically) no human or institutional intervention in transactions on the chain.

Even if one takes these claims as *prima facie* true, however, that does not necessarily make the case that blockchain is "transparent," at least not in the democratic sense. In part, this is due to the fact that "transparency" itself is "treacherous vocabulary," subject to the same broad invocations and interdisciplinary uncertainty as "trustless." Indeed, "transparency" was unsettled long before Nakamoto's white paper birthed Bitcoin and the blockchain. Transparency works at different levels, with different theoretical assumptions depending upon the role that it is playing. Thus, in the organizational management literature, transparency is understood in relation to organizational theory; in the literatures of administrative law, political science, and archival theory, transparency is understood in relation to democratic theory. Almost all of the models, however, encompass human factors – understanding, trust, benevolence, and learning, for example – that point to transparency being a problem as much social as technological in its dimensions.

Schnackenberg and Tomlinson define transparency as "the perceived quality of intentionally shared information from a sender," and relate it to trust (2016, 1788).

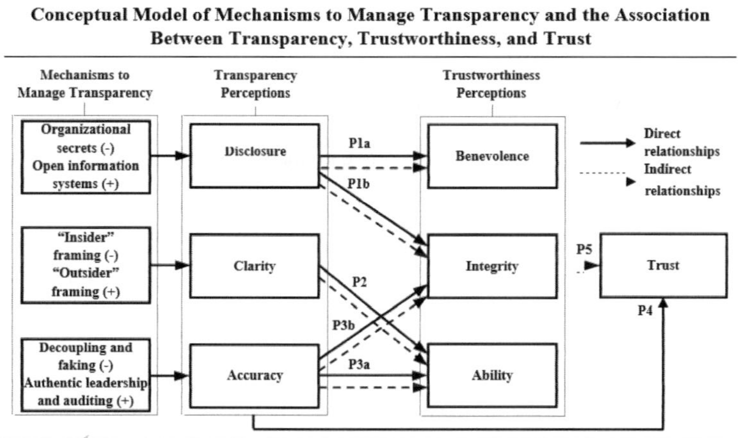

Figure 1: "Conceptual Model of Mechanisms to Manage Transparency and the Association Between Transparency, Trustworthiness, and Trust" (Schnackenberg & Tomlinson, 2016, 1802)

Writing in the tradition of organizational management, Schnackenberg and Tomlinson focus on stakeholder trust and organizational trustworthiness – concepts that nonetheless play a significant role in transparency as a construct in democratic theory. Also writing in organization management, Bernstein claims that "the logic of transparency is fundamentally based on the premise that more – and more accurate – awareness of others improves learning and control and therefore improves performance, as shown by the positive (+) relationships in Figure 2 (Bernstein, 2017, 263). However, in considering the effect of transparency on the observed, and not just the observer, Bernstein develops a model of transparency and privacy that captures a desire for privacy triggered by the awareness of others watching. Some scholars believe this fear could trigger "empty archives" due to people refusing to produce records that could be used to hold them accountable (Hentonnen, 2017):

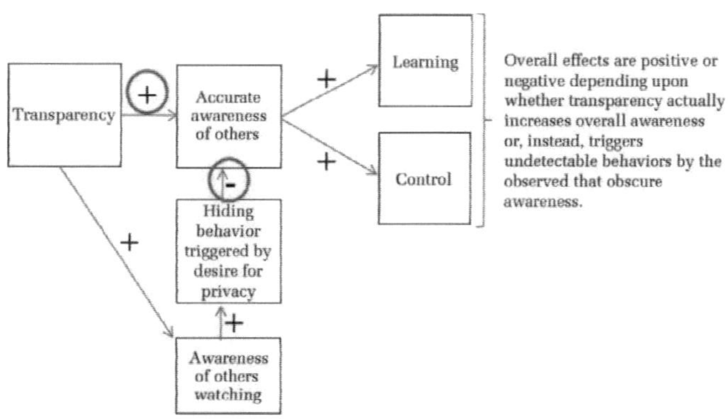

Figure 2: "Behavioral Update to Figure 1, Linking Transparency with Privacy" (Bernstein, 2017, 263)

Vacarro theorizes transparency with regards to the ethical concerns of business organizations' adoption of Information and Communication Technologies (ICTs) (2006). Vacarro's model is meant to provide a means to "frame the main ethical problems arising from the adoption and use of ICT for [business organizations'] activities" (2006, 248). Less apparent from the above model is that it is meant to be both an internal and external (two-level) model (2006, 248). Despite the seeming simplicity of the model, Vacarro posits that transparency encompasses "dynamic social processes [imbued with] the complexity, interdependence, and dynamism of the individual, collective, and social variables involved in such processes" (2006, 255).

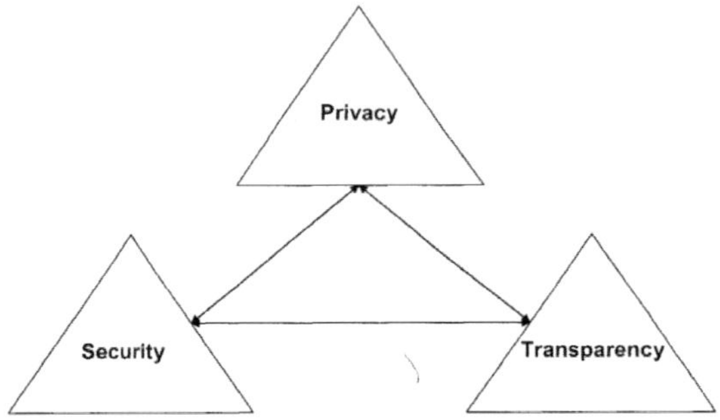

Figure 3: "The Three Dimensions of the Model" (Vacarro, 2006, 249)

Janssen and van den Hoven's model, below, attempts to capture the complexity and interrelatedness of transparency in the context of Big Open Linked Data (BOLD) for e-government purposes (2015).

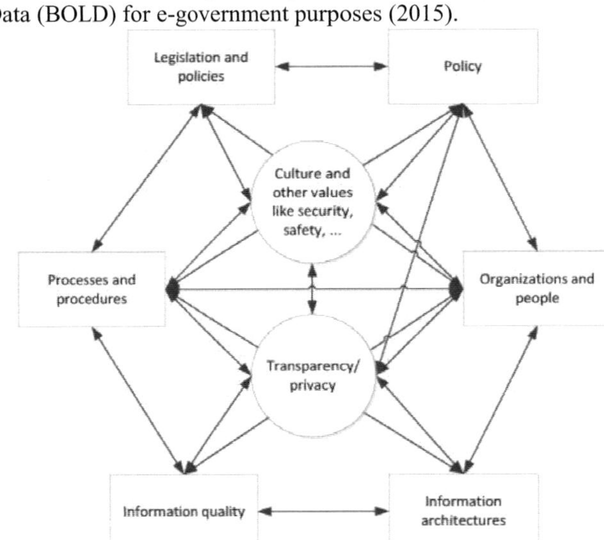

Figure 4: "Elements and dependencies comprising transparency and privacy landscape" (Janssen and van den Hoven, 2015, 367)

As Fenster notes, a number of assumptions from democratic theory are embedded in models such as Janssen and van den Hoven's, which assume *a priori* that "[t]ransparency and privacy are considered as important societal and democratic values that are needed to inform citizens and let them participate in democratic processes" (2015, 363) Their model also highlights the central role of law (both legal instruments, and policy) in our understandings of transparency.

When blockchain technologies are put forth as "transparent" technologies, the focus is upon their technical transparency. As the foregoing shows, however, even the simplest models of "transparency" as a democratic value highlight dynamic, human-oriented processes and concepts. We propose, then, to differentiate between technical transparency – the ability of a technical solution to make information available and/or accessible – and democratic transparency, an ideal of information availability, accessibility, and actionability meant to serve broader social purposes, including public actor accountability and citizen self-efficacy. Given the contested, legally-, socially- and culturally-situated nature of "transparency," it seems unlikely that any purely technical solution – blockchain included – could provide democratic transparency without reference to and support from law and other governing institutions. As Werbach argues, "the idea that all online communities will successfully enforce their rules, without regard for governments, will fare as poorly as it did [in the early days of the Internet" (2018). The inability of technology, in and of itself, to deliver democratic values can be seen in the Arab Spring and the 2018 Iranian revolution. Technology is only as transparent as legal, social, and cultural forces allow.

TRANSPARENCY, HUH. WHAT IS IT GOOD FOR?

If technical transparency, in and of itself, is not sufficient to support democratic ideals, should some broader form of transparency be designed into systems, and if so, how? Hansen, Christensen, and Flyverbom explain that "[m]any contemporary societal projects [...] generally assume that transparency can effectively steer individual and collective behavior towards desirable outcomes" (2015, 117). Janssen and van den Hoven explicitly define transparency and privacy in relationship to both one another and broader societal structures: "transparency should ensure that the actions and decisions of government can be monitored, whereas privacy should ensure that citizens are not monitored and are free to express their opinions [...] Transparency is a balance and control mechanism needed for ensuring a well-functioning democratic society" (2015, 364). A number of initiatives – including open data initiatives, freedom of information/right to know laws, and sunshine laws – are based upon the idea of transparency-as-accountability, or at least of transparency as a "pro-ethical condition for enabling or impairing other ethical practices or principles" (Turilli and Floridi, 2009, 105) including accountability. Zarsky describes transparency as nothing less than "mandatory disclosure to promote equality, enhance performance, generate efficiency, and assure a fair democratic process" (2004, 997). Lemieux and Trapnell, discussing the role of right to information (RTI) laws in achieving state transparency, make the common argument that transparency is essential to accountability: "transparency is a key to holding governments accountable. Further, we understand that transparency depends on the critical element of access: the right of a country's people to access information created and maintained by their government and governmental institutions" (2016, 21).

Fenster, who ultimately rejects transparency as an unworkable concept, both theoretically and practically, provides an exhaustive explanation of how transparency is supposed to work as a bureaucratic mechanism for public engagement and government accountability in democratic systems:

> [Transparency] operates in the first instance in the humdrum world of administrative laws ('freedom of information and 'right to know' Acts and the like), with its legal and bureaucratic systems that enforce transparency through the mandatory disclosure of government information to citizens. But transparency's animating principle operates in a political and social theory as well, where it serves as a foundational element of democratic participation and accountability [...] the state that is made visible proves to be more truly democratic, as well as more accountable and efficient. Transparency enables – and indeed, forces – this virtuous chain of events (2015, 150 – 151).

As Fox so simply puts it, "transparency is supposed to generate accountability" (2007, 663). Accountability, in turn, ensures that systems remain democratic by keeping them answerable to citizens. Applying this line of argument to blockchain technologies, blockchain technology is transparent, in that it provides access to information which could be used to hold actors accountable, and thus is democratizing. However, as can be seen from even the simplest of models and definitions offered thus far, transparency encompasses far more information access. Hosseini, et al., in an examination of transparency for requirements engineering, offer a "Transparency Achievement Spectrum" in which information accessibility is only the third step; the pinnacle of the Transparency Achievement Spectrum in their model is Information Actionability (2017, 6). Accessibility does not guarantee actionability. As an example, Helen Nissenbaum writes that our current "notice-and-choice" systems of privacy management, wherein a website or an app provides notice about how the user's data will be used and allows them to choose to opt-in or out, poses a "transparency paradox," wherein a notice that gives enough information for an individual to make a truly informed choice likely gives too much information for most people to either spend the time reading or to understand at all (2011, 36). In that case, information is accessible – transparent at a level – in that the potential user can read about the data processing policies that govern his/her/their policy should the user opt-in. However, it is not actionable beyond the binary opt-in/opt-out; the user cannot negotiate better privacy terms or control his/her/their data on a granular level. Access without actionability might be transparent in that it makes information visible, but it's not necessarily democratizing. As Ananny and Crawford explain, "[i]f transparency has no meaningful effects, then the idea of transparency can lose its purpose. If corrupt practices continue after they have been made transparent, public knowledge arising from greater transparency may lead to more cynicism, indeed perhaps to wider corruption" (2016, 6).

Furthermore, a growing body of scholars question whether "transparency" – with its metaphorical focus on the visual (Cohen, 2008, 181 – 183) and its assumption that "[t]he more that is known about a system's inner workings, the more defensibly it can be governed and held accountable" (Ananny and Crawford, 2016, 2) – is actually the right mechanism for holding either systems accountable. Indeed, "[f]ull transparency can do great harm. If implemented without a notion of *why* some part of a system should be revealed, transparency can threaten privacy and inhibit honest conversation" (Ananny and Crawford, 2016, 6). "[A] discursive space in which individuals and groups associate to discuss matters of mutual interest and, where possible, to reach a common judgment about them" (Hauser, 1999, 61) is fundamental to deliberative democracy. Transparency which inhibits honest conversation – such as public records laws which were meant to make courts accountable but have been used by private companies to accumulate data to build dossiers on citizens (Solove, 2002) – ultimately undermines, rather than supports, democracy. Turilli and Floridi assert that "Information transparency, understood in terms of disclosed information, does not necessarily imply ethical consequences, since the disclosed information may be ethically neutral" (2009, 106); they argue that transparency, in and of itself, is not an ethical principle but "an ethically ''enabling'' or ''impairing'' factor, that is a pro-ethical condition, when the disclosed information has an impact on ethical principle" (2007, 107). Transparency's democratic value, then, is a question of context and implementation. As Fox explains, "Transparency mobilises the power of shame, yet the shameless may not be vulnerable to public exposure. Truth often fails to lead to justice [...] the more relevant question turns out to be: what kinds of transparency lead to what kinds of accountability, and under what conditions?" (2007, 663).

"TRANSPARENCY" IN ACTION: FREEDOM OF INFORMATION

So far, this paper has demonstrated that transparency is not just a theoretical concept. It is a grounding cause behind any number of actions on the part of organizations and governments. At the heart of this disclosure lies trustworthy records. To be trustworthy, a record must be reliable and authentic (Lemieux, 2016). To be reliable, a record must be created by a competent author and have "contents [which] can be trusted as a full and accurate representation of the [...] fact to which they attest" (ISO/IEC, 2001). Thus, record reliability "is dependent upon the circumstances of [the record's] creation; an unreliable record cannot be made reliable" (Hofman, Duranti & How, 2017). A record is authentic when "it is the document that it claims to be, [free from] any manipulation, substitution, or falsification" (Duranti, 1995).

Blockchain technologies, as ledgers, are fundamentally a recordkeeping technology. However, while their cryptographic immutability is excellent for assuring the authenticity of records, they do nothing to ensure that records are reliable (Lemieux, 2016) – or even that the records necessary for democratic transparency would be created. As a high-profile example, the former Information and Privacy Commissioner of British Columbia, Canada, Elizabeth Denham wrote in her investigative report on the high percentage of FOI requests which returned a "No Responsive Records" reply:

> In the course of this investigation, we have seen evidence of the practice of "oral government", where business is undertaken verbally and in a records-free way. There is no requirement in FIPPA to document these activities. Without a duty to document, government can effectively avoid disclosure and public scrutiny as to the basis and reasons for its actions. The lack of documentation undermines the ability of citizens, journalists and the public to understand the basis for government's actions on any particular matter (2013, 3).

Blockchain solutions offer no solution where governments or other actors simply refuse to create records in the first place. Similarly, when it comes to records or data beyond those arising natively on-chain, there is nothing about the blockchain itself that prevents unreliable records from being hashed to the chain. Many blockchain solutions use off-chain storage for a variety of reasons, such as accommodating legacy systems, storage beyond the limits of the blockchain, or regulatory limitations. Records generated and stored off-chain remain vulnerable to all of the reliability-related problems that they had before a blockchain was introduced. "Reliability is provided to a record by its form and procedure of creation" (Duranti, 1995, 7); later authenticating a record to the blockchain does not change its form and/or procedure of creation to make that record reliable if the record was unreliable to begin with. A forgery does not become real because it is hashed to a blockchain; it will be an authentic, immutable forgery. A credit report riddled with errors remains riddled with errors after being hashed to a blockchain. In order to support democratic transparency, the records returned from FOI requests must be reliable; blockchain solutions have little to offer in this regard. "The truth of any data appearing on a blockchain ledger (other than perhaps the transfer of the native token itself) is limited by the quality or truth of the data entered on the ledger" (Walsh, 2017, 10).

Blockchain technologies, as currently configured, also fail to preserve the "archival bond," the web of relationships that tie one record to the other records that participate in the same action. (Lemieux and Sporny, 2017). Absent the archival bond, it is nearly impossible to understand the acts and facts of which the records are evidence; instantiating the archival bond is necessary to preserve records in their context. Furthermore, without the archival bond, responding to FOI requests – which are often written by lay people, and typically address their request by subject matter, could become more laborious and resource-intensive. In turn, the increase in labour and resources to fulfill FOI requests, which have both legal and practical deadlines for fulfilment, can create more opacity. Journalists, who often use FOI requests to source needed information, have a professional responsibility to communicate that information in a transparent and timely manner while minimizing harm to vulnerable parties. If a freedom of information officer struggled to locate responsive records in a blockchain-based system – because such systems do not tie records to their context or creators natively – the system would fail to serve the purposes of democratic transparency, because information would not be made available quickly enough for accountability purposes. Blockchain transparency will only be effective as democratic transparency if its role in sociotechnical systems of knowledge and disclosure is understood.

Finally, any blockchain solution for records subject to FOI would have to be both privacy-preserving and accessible. For example, many public records subject to FOI also contain personally identifiable information (PII) that must be protected. Solutions may be available, such as the use of off-chain storage or encrypting the data and using zero knowledge proofs. But these solutions come with trade-offs that must be considered against the needs of the system. Off-chain storage systems face the same preservation problems they always have, although the blockchain can provide some authenticity. Zero knowledge proofs are immature. Immutable personal data could also serve to reduce the responsiveness of freedom of information laws as a mechanism for transparency. As it standard currently, FOI requests can be met with redacted records. If personal information is immutably hashed to the blockchain, could FOI officers make a credible argument that, under those provisions of law meant to protect personal privacy, they must withhold responsive records because they cannot be redacted? The balance between privacy and transparency in blockchain solutions – particularly in solutions that are meant to promote democratic transparency – is an open challenge. Blockchain can at best improve the human problems of transparency; people can (and will) make errors in data entry, or refuse to make records, thwarting transparency and accountability.

BLOCKCHAIN BIAS

Designing blockchain solutions to support transparency, then, requires that we ask what kind of transparency the system needs to provide, to whom, for what kinds of ac countability, and under what conditions. Furthermore, such design requires not just leveraging the strengths of blockchain technologies, but should take account of the biases those solutions introduce. With any new technology, some of the structuralized biases may be difficult to identify immediately. For example, some of the biases of blockchain may lie in the strength of its immutability. As noted *supra,* immutability is one of the features that makes blockchains technologically transparent, however, immutability is valued differently by different communities. Indeed, in many cases, mutability is highly prized, as in the right to erasure. The right to erasure ("right to be forgotten"), embedded in both case law and the General Data Protection Regulation (GDPR) in the European Union, is only beginning to be understood vis à vis blockchain technology's immutability, and will undoubtedly evolve as GDPR comes into force (Sater, 2018). Such a right does not currently exist in Canadian or American law, although GDPR will apply to the data of European residents that is used or processed in those jurisdictions. Managing legally mandated erasure in a solution biased towards immutability requires balancing different concepts of – and purposes for – transparency. Preserving information immutably on the chain is "transparent" – but so is managing data subjects' rights over their records in an accessible, understandable way. Even if transparency is accepted as an unmitigated good, it must still be balanced against other goods. The context in which the solution operates is critical.

As noted supra, a number of laws, such as right to information/freedom of information laws and sunshine laws, are explicitly justified on the basis of transparency. Those laws, however, explicitly acknowledge the need for mutability (such as through redaction) and limitations on access. Exemption provisions that limit the release of information on a number of grounds, including national security privacy, play an important role in the design and implementation of such laws (Lemieux and Trapnell, 2016, 21). While such exemptions are necessary, they can be abused. "Exemption provisions, including those that protect personal privacy and national security interests, can be misused – used to cover up or benefit vested interests unfairly – rather than being used as intended to protect the rights of individuals or the public interest" (Lemieux and Trapnell, 2016, 28). Fung, Graham, and Weil, writing about the American case, note how contingent the implementation of transparency laws is upon the intentions and attitude of the individuals and institutions actually implementing those laws: Presidential leadership remained critical in establishing a climate of openness or secrecy [...] unilateral executive actions, typically adopted without public debate, demonstrated once again how much discretion officials had to foster or restrict public access to information (2007, 26 - 7). Indeed, the authors note that "the Justice Department began work on a policy [...] supporting agency actions to keep any information secret when there was a 'sound legal basis' for withholding it" (Fung, Graham, and Weil, 2007, 27). Privacy is one such basis, however, to withhold information – even information critical to protect the rights or interests of the public – on the basis of privacy threatens transparency without actually strengthening privacy, as privacy in such cases is merely a pretense for withholding information. The ethical problems of information access, and especially of transparency for accountability, are of course not unique to blockchain systems. However, the impact of the technology and its biases must be accounted for in the design and use of blockchain systems for transparency purposes.

CONCLUSION

Blockchain technologies have tremendous potential to change how we transact the business of life, including the business of government. However, the capabilities of blockchain alone are not enough to deliver positive social and legal changes. Language such as "transparent" or "democratic," when applied to the blockchain, must be understood in a narrow sense. A true "blockchain revolution" would lie at the confluence of regulatory forces, and must be considered in a careful, interdisciplinary way, with a focus on uncovering the assumptions built into the broad claims about blockchain. The ultimate impact of blockchain in systems of governance and regulation will be felt, not just due its innate characteristics, but its implementation. "Developing the rules, norms, incentives, and technical architectures [Lessig's four regulatory forces] for a well-functioning community is a very hard problem" (Werbach, 2017, 7). Blockchain is but one of those four forces and cannot achieve its potential on its own.

ACKNOWLEDGMENTS

We would like to thank our doctoral supervisors, Dr. Luciana Duranti and Dr. Eric Meyers, respectively, for their support and guidance. Ms. Hofman thanks the Social Sciences and Humanities Research Council (SSHRC), the Izaak Walton Killam Memorial Fund for Advanced Studies, InterPARES Trust, and Blockchain@UBC, especially Dr. Victoria Lemieux, for their support.

REFERENCES

Atzori, M. (2017). Blockchain technology and decentralized governance: Is the state still necessary? Journal of Governance and Regulation, 6(1), 45-62. 10.22495/jgr_v6_i1_p5

Benchoufi, M., Porcher, R., & Ravaud, P. (2017). Blockchain protocols in clinical trials: Transparency and traceability of consent. F1000research, 6, 66. 10.12688/f1000research.10531.1

Bernstein, E. (2017). making transparency transparent: The evolution of observation in management theory. Academy of Management Annals, 11(1), 217-266. 10.5465/annals.2014.0076

Duranti, L. (1995). Reliability and authenticity: The concepts and their implications. Archivaria, (39), 5-10.

Fenster, M. (2015). Transparency in search of a theory. European Journal of Social Theory, 18(2), 150-167. 10.1177/1368431014555257

Fox, J. (2007). The uncertain relationship between transparency and accountability. Development in Practice, 17(4-5), 663-671. 10.1080/09614520701469955

Hansen, H. K., Christensen, L. T., & Flyverbom, M. (2015). Introduction: Logics of transparency in late modernity: Paradoxes, mediation and governance. European Journal of Social Theory, 18(2), 117-131. 10.1177/1368431014555254

Hauser, G. A. (1999). Vernacular voices: The rhetoric of publics and public spheres. Columbia: University of South Carolina Press.

Henttonen, P. (2017). Privacy as an archival problem and a solution. Archival Science, 17(3), 285-303. 10.1007/s10502-017-9277-0

Hofman, D., Duranti, L., & How, E. (2017). Trust in the balance: Data protection laws as tools for privacy and security in the cloud. Algorithms, 10(2), 47. 10.3390/a10020047

Janssen, M., & van den Hoven, J. (2015). Big and open linked data (BOLD) in government: A challenge to transparency and privacy? Government Information Quarterly, 32(4), 363-368. 10.1016/j.giq.2015.11.007

ISO/IEC. 2001. ISO 15489-1:2001 – Information and Documentation – Records Management – Part I: General.

Lemieux, V. L. (2016). Trusting records: Is blockchain technology the answer? Records Management Journal, 26(2), 110-139. 10.1108/RMJ-12-2015-0042

Lemieux, V.L., & Sporny. M. (2017) Preserving the Archival Bond in Distributed Ledgers: A Data Model and Syntax. In Proceedings of the 26th International Conference on World Wide Web Companion, pp. 1437-1443. International World Wide Web Conferences Steering Committee.

Lessig, L. (2006). Code: Version 2.0 ([2nd]. ed.). New York: Basic Books.

National Research Council Canada. Exploring blockchain for better business. Blog post. (19 January 2018). Retrieved January 29, 2018, from https://www.nrc-cnrc.gc.ca/eng/stories/2018/blockchains.html.

Nissenbaum, Helen. 2011. A contextual approach to privacy online. Daedalus 140 (4): 32-48.

Sater, Stan. (2017) Blockchain and the European Union's General Data Protection Regulation: A Chance to Harmonize International Data Flows. Retrieved March 21, 2018 from https://papers.ssrn.com/sol3/papers.cfm?abstract_id=3080987.

Schnackenberg, A. K., & Tomlinson, E. C. (2016). Organizational transparency: A new perspective on managing trust in organization-stakeholder relationships. Journal of Management, 42(7), 1784-1810. 10.1177/0149206314525202

Solove, D. (2002). Access and aggregation: Public records, privacy and the constitution. Minnesota Law Review 86 (6): 1137

Tapscott, D., & Tapscott, A. (2016). Blockchain revolution: How the technology behind bitcoin is changing money, business, and the world. New York, New York; Toronto, Ontario: Portfolio/Penguin.

Vacarro. Antonio. (2006). Privacy, security, and transparency: ICT-related ethical perspectives and contrasts in contemporary firms. Social Inclusion: Societal and Organizational Implications for Information Systems. Eileen M. Trauth, Debra Howcroft, Tom Butler, Brian Fitzgerald, and Janice I. DeGross (Eds). Springer US, Boston, MA, 245 - 258.

Velpuri, M. (2017). Joining the blockchain gang. Land Journal, Jun/July 2017, 8.

Walch, A. (2017a). The Path of the Blockchain Lexicon (and the Law). Rev. Banking & Fin. L. 36: 713 – 975.

---. (2017b). blockchain's treacherous vocabulary: One more challenge for regulators. Journal of Internet Law, 21(2), 1.

Werbach, K. (2017). Trust, But Verify: Why the Blockchain Needs the Law. Berkeley Technology Law Journal. Forthcoming. Retrieved January 29, 2018, from https://papers.ssrn.com/sol3/papers.cfm?abstract_id=2844409.

Wright, A. & De Filippi, P. (2015). Decentralized Blockchain Technology and the Rise of Lex Cryptographia. Retrieved January 29, 2018 from https://papers.ssrn.com/sol3/papers.cfm?abstract_id=2580664

Yermack, D. (2017). Corporate governance and blockchains. Review of Finance 21(1), 7 - 15.

How Authors Cite References? A Study of Characteristics of In-text Citations

Tsung-Ming Hsiao
Department of Library and Information Science, National Taiwan University, Taiwan. f03126010@ntu.edu.tw

Kuang-hua Chen
Department of Library and Information Science, National Taiwan University, Taiwan. khchen@ntu.edu.t

ABSTRACT

How to differentiate citations is continuously an important research question of citation analysis. Recently, some researchers analyze full-text academic articles with tools and techniques of natural language processing to find out the characteristics of in-text citations. In this study, we analyze 4,255 articles published during 2007 to 2016 to explore how authors of library and information science (LIS) cite references in their articles. The pattern of citations shows that LIS authors cite more works on average but the average in-text citation times per reference in an article only increase slightly in this period. There are more in-text citations in the first quarter fraction of an article and the number of in-text citations decrease gradually with text progression. The distribution of POS shows that when LIS authors mention references in text body, they use more noun, verb, and preposition than less adjective and adverb. We also choose the high frequency words of different POS to investigate which words authors prefer in in-text citations. In these high frequency words, nouns tend to be about research topics. Verbs are neutral or used to describe methods or findings of these cited works. As to adjective and adverb, most of them are positive or neutral. But there are more negative words in adverb.

KEYWORDS

Bibliometrics, in-text citations, citation characteristics, content-based citation analysis, natural language processing, NLTK

INTRODUCTION

Citation analysis is one of the important research methodologies in bibliometrics. Traditionally, one implicit assumption of citation analysis is that all citations are equal of value (Nicolaisen, 2007; Smith, 1981). However, no later than 1971, researchers have questioned this assumption (Voos & Dagaev, 1976). The reason why all citations are counted equally is due to the limitation of technology and accessibility to full texts of scientific articles. Recently, with the advance of computer technology and the increasing availability of machine readable full-text articles, researchers could investigate the different possibilities of citation analysis using data extracted from full-text (Boyack, van Eck, Colavizza, & Waltman, 2018). Furthermore, the development in computational linguistics also provides kinds of easy-to-use tools to manipulate and analyze text data. By using these tools, researchers can analyze full texts in much finer granularity than before (Taşkın & Al, 2018). With more detailed and immense data, researchers can no longer be constrained by this implicit assumption that all citations are of equal value. Some specific problems can be studied in large scale nowadays, including identifying features of citations, differentiating importance of each citation, and classification of citation function (Boyack et al., 2018; Hsiao & Chen, 2017; Taşkın & Al, 2018).

By analyzing full-text research articles, researchers can extract much more information related to in-text citation. Recently, many studies investigate the applications of citation frequency, location of in-text citation, or both of them. The objectives of these studies are to differentiate characteristics of citations, the function of citations, and the importance of different references (Bornmann & Daniel, 2008; Boyack et al., 2018; Hooten, 1999; Hou, Li, & Niu, 2011; Hu, Chen, & Liu, 2013). The surrounding words afford more opportunities. Previous studies use these words in various applications, e.g. improving the search result of information retrieval system, enhancing the outcome of automatic text summarization system, identifying the function of different citations, and mapping the science field in finer granularity (Ritchie, Teufel, & Robertson, 2008; Small, 2011; Taşkın & Al, 2018; Teufel, Siddharthan, & Tidhar, 2006; Wan & Liu, 2014).

As Boyack et al. (2018) mentions, solider understanding of the characteristics of in-text citations will help to improve the validity of the result of citation analysis. This research aims to advance the understanding of the characteristics of in-text citations, including distributions related to frequency and location of in-text citations, words used in in-text citations, and part-of-speech (POS) of these words. In this study, the research questions are as follows:

RQ1. What is the difference of in-text citation patterns of LIS authors between articles in terms of journals and years?

RQ2. What is the distribution of POSes of words used by LIS authors when they cite references in articles?

RQ3. Do LIS authors prefer certain kinds of words? If yes, what kind of words do they prefer?

In this study, 4,255 articles published during 2007 to 2016 in five journals are collected as our research data set. To answer

RQ1, we analyse citation characteristics in each article and compare the distribution in different journals and years. For RQ2, by using NLTK, a natural language processing toolkit of Python, we tokenize all articles in research data set and identify each word's POS. Then, we examine the distribution of different POS. Finally, after lemmatizing these articles with NLTK, we calculate the word frequency and choose words with top used frequency. Then, we investigate the usage of these high frequency words to answer RQ3. To avoid confusion, in this study, the 'reference' is defined as the bibliography, cited works, or reference list of a document. When 'reference' is cited within the text body of an article, it is defined as an 'in-text citation'.

RELATED WORK

Studies of Citation Context in the Early Days

Treating all citations equal is an implicit assumption from the beginning of the development of citation analysis. Even today, most major citation index systems, like Web of Science and Scopus, still treat all citations equal. However, "it has long been recognized that not all citations are created equal" (Zhu, Turney, Lemire, & Vellino, 2015, p. 408). In the early days of citation indexing, Garfield (1965) had listed 15 reasons why reference citations are cited in papers. Moravcsik & Murugesan (1975) and Voos & Dagaev (1976) studied issues about function and quality of citations. Moravcsik & Murugesan (1975) selected 30 articles about theoretical high energy physics published in *Physical Review* and examined references in these articles. In their studies, four different questions were used to classify these references. Their result shows that 40% of the references are 'perfunctory' and 15% of the references are 'negational'. Voos & Dagaev (1976) investigated the distribution of in-text citation of four papers. Different ways were used to reveal the citation patterns in different sections. Voos & Dagaev proposes that different citation patterns among different disciplines "would be useful in studying the sociology of science, or non-science" (Voos & Dagaev, 1976, p. 21).

In 1982, Small defined "citation context" as "particular passage or statement within the citing document containing the reference" and "citation context analysis" as "any attempt to utilize these passages in a systematic fashion" (Small, 1982, p.288). Small (1982) also proposed two types of approaches of citation contexts analysis: classification approach and semantic content approach. Due to the shortage of computing power and poverty of machine-readable full texts, most studies are conducted manually (Hooten, 1991; Murugesan & Moravcsik, 1978; Spiegel-Rösing, 1977). However, as concluded by Voos & Dagaev (1976), manual counting is an uneconomical way. The studies of citation context are hardly conducted in large scale.

Studies about Feature of Citations and Further Applications

With the rapid development of computer technology and ready accessibility of machine readable full-text articles, researchers explore how to take advantage of full texts in diverse ways. Researchers study various features of citations, including citation frequency, location of in-text citation, length of citing sentence, time interval between references and referring articles etc. Hou et al. (2011) chooses 651 papers published in 2008 and compare the appearances between closely related references and less related references. The result shows that counting citation in the text is a more accurate indicator of scientific contribution than counting references. Hu et al. (2013) analyzes patterns of citation distribution in 350 articles published in the *Journal of Informetrics*. Their result verifies that there are more citations in the first section, namely Introduction.

In the following years, Wan & Liu (2014) uses six features to estimate the importance of each citation. These features include occurrence times, location of in-text citation, time interval, average length of citing sentences, average density of citation occurrences, and self-cited or not. The result shows that "the estimated values can achieve good correlation with human-labeled values" (Wan & Liu, 2014, p.1929). Hu, Lin, Sun, & Hou (2017) further investigates the characteristics of multiply mentioned references (MMRs). The research finding shows that three types of references are likely to be MMRs, including author self-citing references, journal self-citing references, and newer references. Their study also answers which kinds of citing papers tend to have MMRs and where are multiple mentions of references located. Recently, Boyack et al. (2018) analyzes characteristics of in-text citations in over five million full text articles from the PubMed Central Open Access and Elsevier journals. They report the distribution of in-text citations, numbers of sentences, references, and in-text mentions per articles in different research fields.

Location of in-text citation is also used to improve methodologies of citation analysis. Gipp & Beel (2009) proposes an approach to measure the proximity of citations to each other. Based on distance of the citation-pair, a value will be assigned as the proximity of these two cited works. This approach provides a more precise automatic document classification result. Liu & Chen (2011) uses similar concept but different co-citation proximity schema to conduct co-citation analysis. They compare traditional co-citation network and co-citation networks based on four different levels, including sentence, paragraph, section, and article.

Studies about Surrounding Words of Citations and Further Applications

A different approach is to utilize the surrounding words of citation. In 1998, Giles, Bollacker, & Lawrence present *CiteSeer*, an autonomous citation indexing system. *CiteSeer* uses three approaches to measure the similarity between two documents.

One approach is utilizing surrounding words of citation as features of a document when this document is cited (Giles, Bollacker, & Lawrence, 1998). In the following years, Teufel, Siddharthan, & Tidhar (2006) analyzes linguistic cues in the full texts to identify categories of citations. They argue that there is a strong relationship between sentiment and citation function. Furthermore, they propose a supervised machine learning framework that can classify citation function based on sentiment automatically. Ritchie, Teufel, & Robertson (2008) analyzes terms used by citing documents to index a given document. The result provides a new approach to study citation-based methods for information retrieval. Elkiss et al. (2008) also studies the possible usage of surrounding words of citation. They propose to summarize an article by those words from different citations to this article. Summary produced by this approach can be a surrogate of this article from diverse viewpoints. These studies above focus on exploring new possible applications of surrounding words.

Some studies try to enhance the results of citation analysis by using surrounding words of citations. Small (2011, p. 373) proposes that maps of science can be interpreted with citation context sentiments, namely "the text surrounding references in scientific papers". Jeong, Song, & Ding (2014) measures co-citation strength by proximity between two sentences within which two references are cited. This study shows that this approach can provide more details about sub-disciplines. With similar concept, Kim, Jeong, & Song (2016) proposes a new author co-citation (ACA) method, content- and proximity-based author co-citation analysis. In their new model, Kim et al. measure co-citation strength based on sentences similarity and whether they are cited in the same section. Hsiao & Chen (2017) proposes that it may be a more reasonable way to measure the similarity of two citations based on the similarity of the words of paragraph where they are cited. In their study, they compare the results of ACA, including traditional ACA and ACA enhanced by location of citations and surrounding words. Recently, Taşkın & Al (2018) uses 101,019 sentences in 423 articles to categorize citations from four dimensions, including meaning, purposes, shape, and array. These studies use surrounding words as a tool to enhance the results of different applications.

Due to the most previous studies of citation analysis focus on the applications of surrounding words, our major concerns are the characteristics of surrounding words of citations. There are three objectives for this study. Firstly, we aim to investigate what the citation patterns of LIS are in different articles, journals, and years. We will investigate this question within a single research field with comparison to the macro and cross-fields results in Boyack et al. (2018). Secondly, this study analyzes the distribution of POS in these surrounding words. Thirdly, we calculate the word frequency and find out whether LIS authors prefer to use certain type of words. If LIS authors do prefer certain type of words, what kinds of words they prefer to use?

METHOD

The research flow is as Figure 1 showed. Given our research objectives, journals of LIS are our research target. In this study, journals of LIS is defined as the intersection set of journals collected in information science and library science of JCR and journals of LISA database. As a preliminary study, we use five journals from this intersection set as out research data. The five journals are *Journal of the Association for Information Science and Technology (JASIST)*, *Journal of Documentation*, *Journal of Knowledge Management*, *Library Hi Tech*, and *The Electronic Library*. The full-text documents are collected from Wiley Online library and Emerald Insight in HTML format. In data collecting stage, documents published during 2007 to 2016 are used for this research. Due to these documents are HTML format, it is necessary to remove HTML tags. We also need to filter out some unnecessary words due to these words are not part of the text body of articles, like advertisement and navigation functions. Therefore, after collecting documents, we parse HTML documents to extract text body and metadata of an article. In the process of parsing HTML documents, we also extract the citations in the text body.

When a reference is cited in the text body, there is an in-text citation. Because the purposes of this study focus on analyzing the features of in-text citations, those documents without references or in-text citations are excluded. After filtering those unqualified documents, remaining documents are used as our research data. The following is a typical stage of natural language processing, including tokenization, lemmatization, and POS tagging. In this study, NLTK is applied for these works. NLTK is a natural language toolkit developed using Python and provides text processing libraries for classification, tokenization, lemmatizing, tagging, parsing, and semantic reasoning (Steven, Loper, & Klein, 2009). Although NLTK provides a reliable outcome, a few errors are also found in tokenization. Some words, like et al., pp., i.e., and e.g., will be taken as end of sentence. In this research, we apply some rules to fix these results. We also notice that NLTK judge words of compound nouns into adjective and noun, especially those appeared as separate words.

After completing the stage of natural language processing, we investigate the research data set to answer the raised research questions. For the first question, the discrepancy of patterns of in-text citations between different journals and different years, we compare those indicators, including average reference number per article, in-text citation times per reference, and location of in-text citation. For the second question, the distribution of POS, we analyze all sentences with in-text citations, including the types and usage of different grammatical categories of words in these sentences. As to the final question, we choose those words with high frequency in all sentences with in-text citations. Then, we analyze the usage of these highly used words.

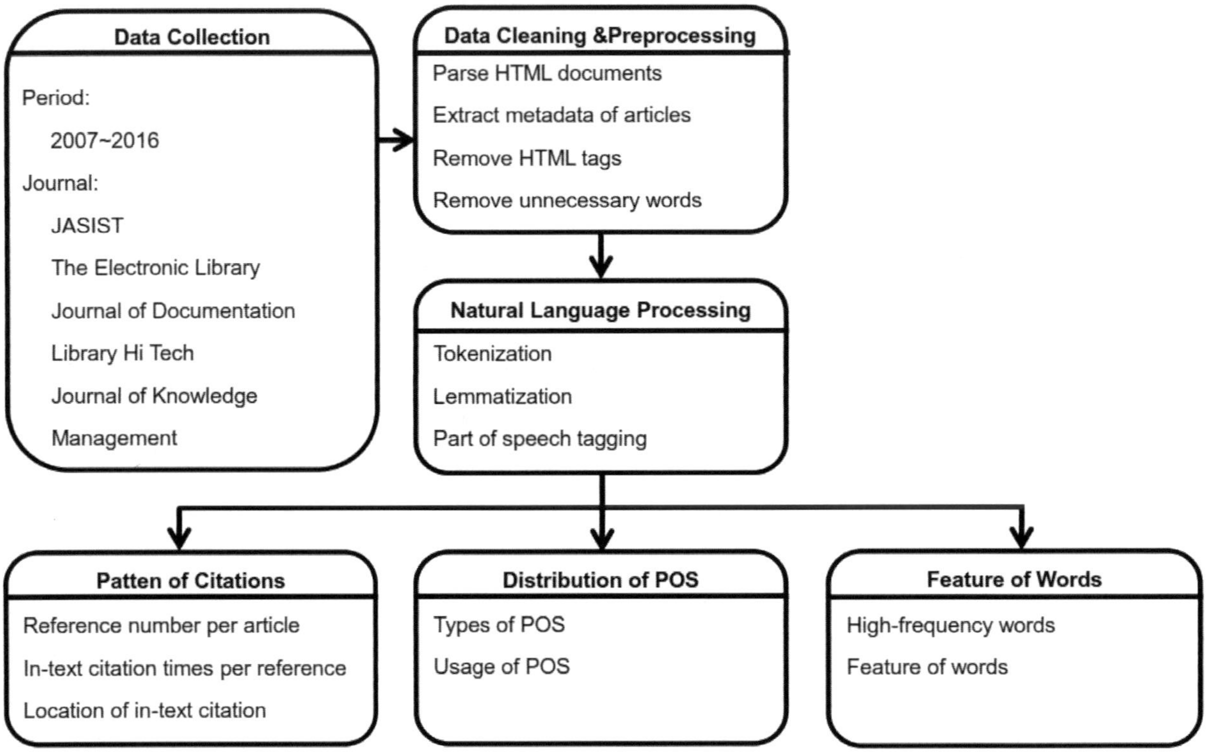

Figure 1. Research diagram

RESULTS AND DISSCUSSION

Basic Statistics

In data collecting stage, 5,133 documents from 343 issues are collected. When examining these data, we find that one issue, about 20 articles, is not collected during collecting data due to the technical problem. After data preprocessing and cleaning, we exclude 878 documents due to no references or citations in these documents and finally the data set are composed of the remaining 4,255 documents. Table 1 shows some characteristics of these 4,255 documents.

	Journal of Documentation	Journal of Knowledge Management	JASIST	Library Hi Tech	The Electronic Library
Year covered	2007-2016	2007-2016	2007-2016	2007-2016	2007-2016
# Articles	510	636	2,065	463	581
# References	24,096	36,326	92,273	11,704	16,108
# In-text citations	39,808	55,870	143,770	16,766	21,957
# Sentences (with citation)	25,941	35,961	88,737	11,971	15,602
# Sentences (without citation)	108,608	116,560	499,253	74,093	86,200
# Words (with citation)	1,100,432	1,414,550	3,642,844	478,728	607,069
# Words (without citation)	3,003,092	2,962,393	12,741,200	1,950,995	2,232,171
Words /References	170.3	120.49	177.63	207.6	176.26
Words /In-text citations	103.08	78.34	113.96	144.91	129.30

Table 1. Characteristics of research data set

In total, there are 180,471 references in 4,255 articles. These references are cited 278,171 times in these articles. Approximately, a reference will be cited 1.5 times in an article on average. Among different journals, the ratios vary from 1.36 to 1.65. After tokenization, over one million sentences are extracted from these articles. The ratio of sentences against citations is 1 to 4.9 on average. That is to say, every six sentences will have one sentence with in-text cation. On average, articles published in *Journal of Knowledge Management* cite references most frequently in text body. On the other side of spectrum, articles of *Library Hi Tech* have fewer in-text citations. Words/References and Words/In-text citation show similar trend. On average, articles of *Journal of Knowledge Management* cite reference about every 78 words. However, in *Library Hi Tech*, the figure is 144 words. An interesting point is that other three journals, viz. *Journal of Documentation, The Electronic Library, and JASIST,* have similar ratio in Words/References. The figures of Words/References in these journals center around 175. These three journals have more differences between each other in Words/In-text citations. There may be some similar writing styles among these journals, but it needs further investigation to answer this conjecture.

Pattern of citations

In order to demonstrate the pattern of citations, the different figures are depicted for easier observation. Figure 2 shows the trend of average references per article (ARPA) for the five journals during 2007 and 2016. In whole data set, the number of ARPA is rising from 31.81 in 2007 to 51.38 in 2016. The growth rate of ARPA is 161.52%. In journal level, the increasing scale in number of ARPA varies from 8.18 (*JASIST*) to 34.77 (*Journal of Knowledge Management*). The numbers of ARPA in other three journals increase around 15 to 20 during these ten years. *The Electronic Library* shows the highest growth rate of ARPA (198.63%) and *JASIST* the lowest growth rate (119.9%). *JASIST* is the only one journal that the growth rate of ARPA is lower than 150%. The growth rate of *Journal of Documentation* is 155% and other three journals have growth rates more than 170%. Although the trend of ARPA is decreasing in some years, the general trend of ARPA is increasing from 2007 to 2016. This result shows that authors use more and more references to support their studies within the ten years. The increasing trend is same with the results of Boyack et al. (2018). But the increasing scale of LIS in this study is more than Social Science and Humanities (SSH) in Boyack et al. (2018).

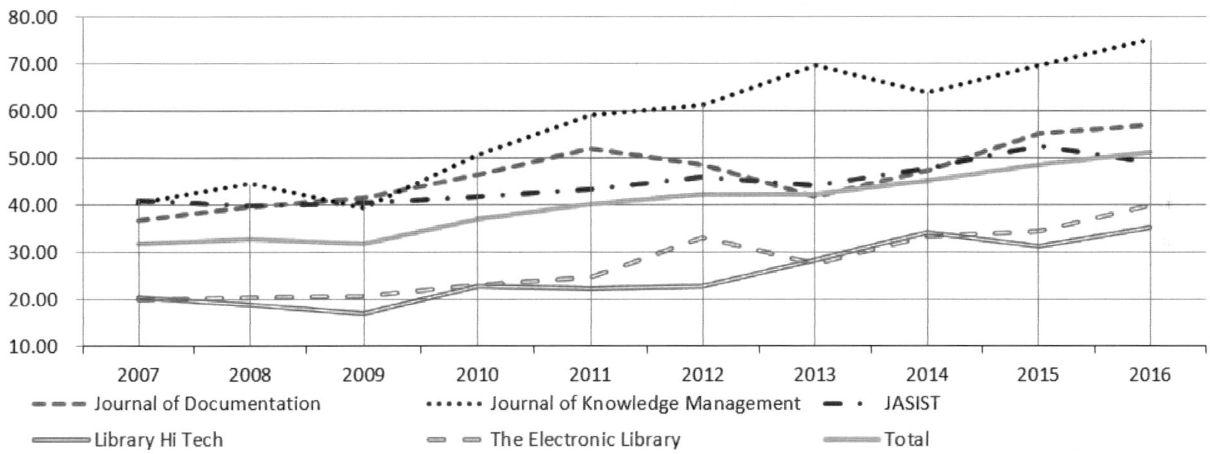

Figure 2. Trend of average references per article (ARPA)

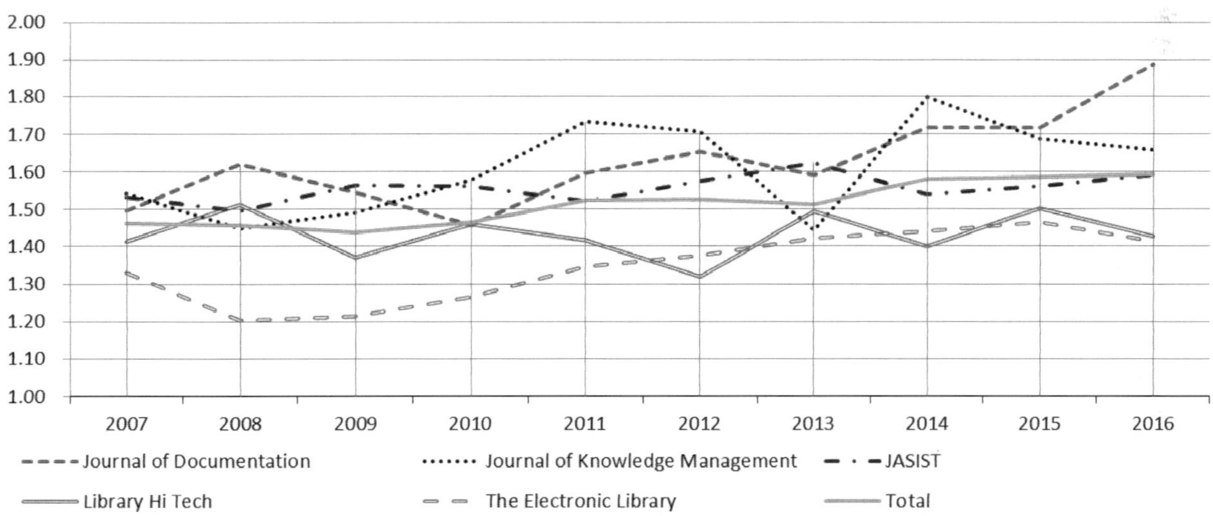

Figure 3. Trend of average in-text citation times per reference (ACTPR)

Figure 2 reveals the trend that how many references are used in an article. In Figure 3, we explore the trend that how many times a reference will be cited in an article. Different from ARPA, the trend of average in-text citation times per reference (ACTPR) only increases slightly in the ten years. The number of ACTPR of all articles is 1.46 in 2007 and 1.59 in 2016. It only increase 9% in ten years. Only *Journal of Documentation*, its growth rate of ACTPR is bigger than 125% and the trend of increase is relatively stable. The number of ACTPR in *The Electronic Library* also stably increases after 2008 although the growth rate is not as large as that of *Journal of Documentation*. In other three journals, the trends are up and down during this period. The result shows that authors cite references in text body with similar frequency although they use more references in an articles as Figure 2 shows. Compared with figures of SSH in Boyack et al. (2018), the slightly increasing trend is the same but ACTPR of LIS is fewer.

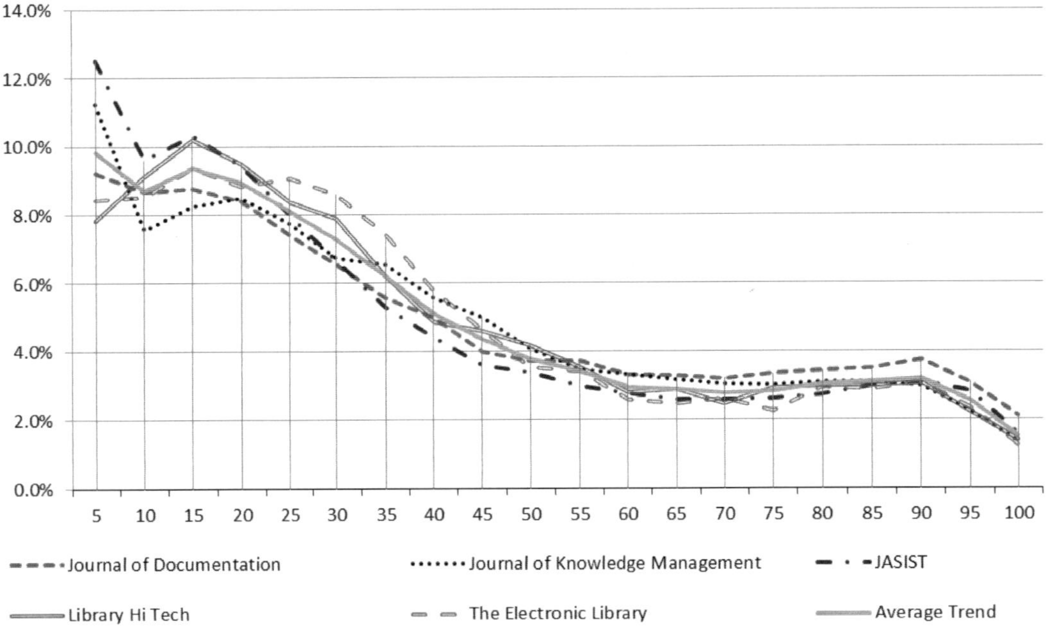

Figure 4. The location distribution of in-text citations in the article

Figure 4 shows the distribution of location of in-text citation in the article. The x-axis is the distance to the beginning of an article in percentage and the y-axis is how much in-text citations are located in this portion of text. In general, half of in-text citations are located in the first 30 centiles portion. In all five journals, the highest fractions of in-text citations are in the first 15 centiles portion. The percentage of fractions of in-text citations decreases gradually after the 15-20 centiles portion. In the latter half of an article, the percentage of fractions of in-text citations remains relatively stable between 2% to 4%. The result supports the finding of Hu et al. (2013) that there are more in-text citations in the first section. Also, the distribution of our study is very similar to the result that Boyack et al. (2018) reveal the distribution of in-text citations of SSH.

	Words of in-text citations						Whole Data (words of sentences without citations)
	Journal of Documentation	Journal of Knowledge Management	JASIST	Library Hi Tech	The Electronic Library	Whole Data	
Noun	28.31%	29.02%	29.12%	29.98%	30.18%	29.12%	29.14%
Punctuation	17.40%	18.19%	19.55%	17.02%	16.98%	18.58%	10.98%
Verb	11.53%	11.06%	10.39%	11.24%	11.09%	10.81%	13.30%
Preposition	10.56%	9.43%	9.69%	10.09%	10.40%	9.86%	12.03%
Adjective	7.40%	7.45%	7.21%	7.55%	7.49%	7.33%	8.83%
Determiner	7.14%	6.36%	6.71%	6.76%	6.79%	6.72%	10.00%
Numeral	4.91%	4.93%	5.10%	4.80%	4.84%	5.00%	1.94%
Conjunction	3.92%	4.86%	4.39%	4.06%	4.28%	4.38%	3.29%
Adverb	3.11%	3.20%	2.80%	3.08%	2.84%	2.94%	3.45%
Other	5.71%	5.50%	5.05%	5.42%	5.11%	5.27%	7.04%

Table 2. POS of words in different journals and whole data

Distribution of POS tags

By using NLTK, we can tokenize sentences in each article and the token is a suitable unit for the following processing. After tokenization, we identify the POS for each token using the function featured by NLTK and analyze the distribution of POS. Totally 45 different POS tags are defined by NLTK. In this study, these tags are simplified into 10 categories, as shown in Table 2. This study discusses the distribution of POS of tokens of in-text citations in different journals and whole data firstly.

Then we compare the differences between distribution of POS of tokens of sentences with in-text citation and distribution of POS of tokens of sentences without in-text citations.

As to the tokens of sentences with in-text citation, the result shows that about 30% tokens are tagged as noun. The second large portion is punctuation (17%~19%), including comma, sentence terminator, colon, and parenthesis. The third large type is verb. Totally 10% to 12% tokens are classified into this category. The fraction of tokens identified as preposition is slightly smaller than verb. Both adjective and determiner account about 6% to 7%. Among the remaining three categories, including numeral, conjunction, and adverb, each of them takes up no more than 5.1% tokens. In sum, almost 40% tokens are classified as noun or verb. This result corresponds with our cognition. Also, about 14% tokens are identified as preposition or conjunction. It also corresponds with our reading and writing experiences. Adjective and adverb only take little more than 10% of all tokens. This shows that authors use less adjective and adverb when they cite references.

When further examining the distribution of POS of words in sentences without citations, there are somethings noticeable. Firstly, the percentage of punctuation and numeral decrease in sentences without in-text citations, especially punctuation. An acceptable explanation is when authors cite references, there are more punctuations and numerals used due to the citation format. For example, comma is used to separate different authors; parenthesis is used to enclose the citation; the numeral indicates publication date and page number. Secondly, the percentage of most POS increase slightly, including verb, preposition, adjective, determiner, and adverb. Due to the percentage of punctuation decrease dramatically, the increase in fractions of other POS are reasonable. Thirdly, the percentage of conjunction decrease. Compared with the increase of most POS excluding punctuation and numeral, the decrease of conjunction in sentences without in-text citations is an interesting phenomenon. In NLTK, the category of conjunction includes words like "&", "both", "but", "either", "nor", "so", "therefore", "versus", "whether", and "yet" etc. It shows that authors may use these words more frequently when they write sentences that cite references.

Feature of words

After identifying POS of different words used in sentences with in-text citations, the top used words are identified from four different types of POS, including noun, verb, adjective, and adverb. Some words are removed, e.g., "et", "al", and "p." After removing these words, Table 3 shows the top 10 used words in different type of POS.

	Noun	Verb	Adjective	Adverb
1	information	is	such	not
2	knowledge	are	other	also
3	study	be	social	more
4	research	have	different	only
5	user	has	new	however
6	system	was	more	most
7	data	been	many	well
8	model	used	important	often
9	process	were	organizational	even
10	library	found	library	thus

Table 3. Top 10 frequently used words in in-text citations

According to the top 10 used nouns, these nouns can be categorized into two types, nouns about topics and nouns about research itself. Most frequently used nouns are probably related to research topics, like "information", "knowledge", "user", and "library". Some nouns, like "study" and "research", may refer to authors' research or works of cited references. We further examine more top frequently used nouns. Most of these nouns are still about topics, including "citation", "web", "organization", "service", and "network". Some frequently used nouns, like "approach", "method", and "result", are about research itself. However, there are other nouns that are not belong to the two types, like "example", "number", "value", and "others" etc.

Top 10 frequently used verbs show more information about writing style that authors' meaning. Most of them are *be* verbs, including "is", "are", "be", and "was" etc. Two of ten verbs, "have" and "has", are auxiliary verbs. Other two verbs are "used" and "found". It shows that most authors will describe the methods or findings of these cited works in in-text citations. Some verbs in top frequently used verbs support this conjecture, like "proposed", "developed", "suggested", and "reported" etc. We also notice that there are few verbs, like "improve" and "help", that may reveal authors' opinions to the cited works. However, in top 100 frequently used verbs, most of these words are neutral and only very few verbs may show authors' opinions.

With comparison to nouns and verbs, frequently used adjectives reveal more detailed information about how authors criticize their cited references. Although most adjective in top 10 list provide little help to find out the authors' opinions, adjectives like "important" or "new" do provide clues to realize authors' opinions about their cited references. Other similar adjectives are "effective", "positive", "useful", and "necessary". Some adjectives may be about research topics, like "library" and "digital".

The reason why "library" is classified as adjective here is due to the algorithm in processing compound nouns of NLTK. Generally speaking, three types of adjectives can be found in top frequently used adjective. The first type of adjective is neutral adjective and provides very little help to find out the author's opinions about cited works. The second type of adjective, like "important" and "useful", is more helpful to realize authors' opinions. The third type is adjective about topic, like "library" and "digital". These adjectives may show the topics of cited works. Among these three types, most of adjectives are neutral or positive. Top frequently used adjectives are seldom negative.

In adverb, the majority of adverbs are still neutral word, like "also", "more", "most", "often", and "even". Also, there are some positive adverbs, like "well", "significantly", and "effectively" in frequently used list. However, it is worth mentioned that there are some negative words in top frequently used list, like "not" and "never". "Not" is also the most frequently used adverb in in-text citation. The results suggest that authors may use an additional adverb to show their opinions instead of using adjective or verb only. The reason may be due to the consideration of writing skills, but it needs further investigation

CONCLUSION

This study uses 4,255 documents published during 2007 and 2016 and examines the characteristics of sentences with in-text citations. The preliminary results, on the one hand, show that authors refer more works in an article during this period. On the other hand, authors do not cite references more frequently in text-body on average. This study also confirms results of Hu et al. (2013) and Boyack et al. (2018). Authors cite more frequently in the beginning portion of an article and the frequency decreases gradually from beginning to end of the article.

By using NLTK, we analyze the distribution of POS of words of sentences with in-text in-text citations. The result shows that most of words are nouns, about 28~30%. The portion of punctuation is 17%~20% and there are 9~12% words are verbs. Prepositions have slightly lower fraction than verb, about 9~11%. Adjectives and determines have 7~8% and 6~8% respectively. The remaining types, including numerals, conjunction, and adverb, are no more than 5% fractions. When comparing the POS distribution between words of in-text citation and words of sentences without citations, we notice that authors use conjunctions more frequently in in-text citations.

This study further examines the frequently used words of four POS tags, including nouns, verbs, adjective, and adverb. These frequently used words show that authors tend to describe the topics, methods, and findings of the cited work when they cite references in text-body. Furthermore, it seems that authors use more neutral or positive words to depict the cited references, especially when using nouns, verbs, and adjectives. Although more negative words are frequently used in adverbs, the tendency is the same.

This study is limited by some factors. Firstly, only five journals of LIS are included in this study. The result of this study is a preliminary observation of LIS field. In the future, we will try to use more comprehensive data to investigate the characteristics of in-text citations. Secondly, NTLK toolkit does provide a reliable outcome. However, a few errors are also found in tokenization. Although we have already developed some tools to fix a few errors, the results are still dependent on NLTK. In the future, we try to analyze characteristics of citations with large corpus. We also plan to use other text resources like WordNet-Affect to explore more patterns about feature of words in sentences with in-text citations. With these tools, the characteristics of citations can be investigated and depicted more precisely.

ACKNOWLEDGMENTS

We would like to thank the anonymous reviewers for their suggestions and comments. This research was partially supported by Ministry of Science and Technology of the Republic of China under the Grant number MOST105-2420-H-002 -056 -MY2.

REFERENCES

Bornmann, L., & Daniel, H. D. (2008). Functional use of frequently and infrequently cited articles in citing publications. A content analysis of citations to articles with low and high citation counts (PDF Download Available). *European Science Editing*, *34*(2), 35-38.

Steven, B., Loper, E. and Klein, E. (2009). *Natural Language Processing with Python*. O'Reilly Media Inc.

Boyack, K. W., van Eck, N. J., Colavizza, G., & Waltman, L. (2018). Characterizing in-text citations in scientific articles: A large-scale analysis. *Journal of Informetrics*, *12*(1), 59-73. https://doi.org/10.1016/j.joi.2017.11.005

Elkiss, A., Shen, S., Fader, A., Erkan, G., States, D., & Radev, D. (2008). Blind men and elephants: What do citation summaries tell us about a research article? *Journal of the American Society for Information Science and Technology*, *59*(1), 51–62. https://doi.org/10.1002/asi.20707

Garfield, E. (1965). Can citation indxing be automated? In *Statistical Association Methods for Mechanized Documentation, Symposium Proceedings* (pp. 189-192). Washington: National Bureau of Standards Miscellaneous Publication.

Giles, C. L., Bollacker, K. D., & Lawrence, S. (1998). Citeseer: an automatic citation indexing system. In *International Conference on Digital Libraries* (pp. 89-98). ACM Press.

Gipp, B., & Beel, J. (2009). Citation Proximity Analysis (CPA) - A new approach for identifying related work based on Co-Citation Analysis. In *Proceedings of ISSI 2009.*

Hooten, P. A. (1991). Frequency and functional use of cited documents in information science. *Journal of the American Society for Information Science*, *42*(6), 397–404. https://doi.org/10.1002/(SICI)1097-4571(199107)42:6<397::AID-ASI2>3.0.CO;2-N

Hou, W. R., Li, M., & Niu, D. K.(2011). Counting citations in texts rather than reference lists to improve the accuracy of assessing scientific contribution. *BioEssays*, *33*(10), 724-727. https://doi.org/10.1002/bies.201100067

Hsiao, T. M., & Chen, K. H. (2017). Yet another method for author co-citation analysis: A new approach based on paragraph similarity. *Proceedings of the Association for Information Science and Technology*, *54*(1), 170–178. https://doi.org/10.1002/pra2.2017.14505401019

Hu, Z., Chen, C., & Liu, Z. (2013). Where are citations located in the body of scientific articles? A study of the distributions of citation locations. *Journal of Informetrics*, *7*(4), 887-896. https://doi.org/10.1016/j.joi.2013.08.005

Hu, Z., Lin, G., Sun, T., & Hou, H. (2017). Understanding multiply mentioned references. *Journal of Informetrics*, *11*(4), 948-958. https://doi.org/10.1016/j.joi.2017.08.004

Jeong, Y. K., Song, M., & Ding, Y. (2014). Content-based author co-citation analysis. *Journal of Informetrics*, *8*(1), 197-211. https://doi.org/10.1016/j.joi.2013.12.001

Kim, H. J., Jeong, Y. K., & Song, M. (2016). Content- and proximity-based author co-citation analysis using citation sentences. *Journal of Informetrics*, *10*(4), 954-966. https://doi.org/10.1016/j.joi.2016.07.007

Liu, S., & Chen, C. (2011). The proximity of co-citation. *Scientometrics*, *91*(2), 495-511. https://doi.org/10.1007/s11192-011-0575-7

Moravcsik, M. J., & Murugesan, P. (1975). Some Results on the Function and Quality of Citations. *Social Studies of Science*, *5*(1), 86-92.

Murugesan, P., & Moravcsik, M. J. (1978). Variation of the nature of citation measures with journals and scientific specialties. *Journal of the American Society for Information Science*, *29*(3), 141-147. https://doi.org/10.1002/asi.4630290307

Nicolaisen, J. (2007). Citation analysis. *Annual Review of Information Science and Technology*, *41*(1), 609-641. https://doi.org/10.1002/aris.2007.1440410120

Ritchie, A., Teufel, S., & Robertson, S. (2008). Using Terms from Citations for IR: Some First Results. In C. Macdonald, I. Ounis, V. Plachouras, I. Ruthven, & R. W. White (Eds.), *Advances in Information Retrieval* (pp.211–221). Springer Berlin Heidelberg. https://doi.org/10.1007/978-3-540-78646-7_21

Small, H. (1982). Citation Context Analysis. In *Progress in communication sciences.* (volume 3). Norwood, N.J.: Ablex PubCorp.

Small, H. (2011). Interpreting maps of science using citation context sentiments: a preliminary investigation. *Scientometrics*, *87*(2), 373-388. https://doi.org/10.1007/s11192-011-0349-2

Smith, L. C. (1981). Citation analysis. *Library Trends*, *30*(1), 83-106.

Spiegel-Rösing, I. (1977). Science Studies: Bibliometric and Content Analysis. *Social Studies of Science*, *7*(1), 97-113.

Taşkın, Z., & Al, U. (2018). A content-based citation analysis study based on text categorization. *Scientometrics*, *114*(1), 335-357. https://doi.org/10.1007/s11192-017-2560-2

Teufel, S., Siddharthan, A., & Tidhar, D. (2006). Automatic Classification of Citation Function. In *Proceedings of the 2006 Conference on Empirical Methods in Natural Language Processing* (pp. 103–110). Stroudsburg, PA, USA: Association for Computational Linguistics. Retrieved from http://dl.acm.org/citation.cfm?id=1610075.1610091

Voos, H., & Dagaev, K. S. (1976). ARe All Citations Equal? Or, Did We Op. Cit. Your Idem? *Journal of Academic Librarianship*, *1*(6), 19-21.

Wan, X., & Liu, F. (2014). Are all literature citations equally important? Automatic citation strength estimation and its applications. *Journal of the Association for Information Science and Technology*, *65*(9), 1929-1938. https://doi.org/10.1002/asi.23083

Zhu, X., Turney, P., Lemire, D., & Vellino, A. (2015). Measuring academic influence: Not all citations are equal. *Journal of the Association for Information Science and Technology*, *66*(2), 408-427. https://doi.org/10.1002/asi.23179

Surfing Safely: Examining Older Adults' Online Privacy Protection Behaviors

Hsiao-Ying Huang
University of Illinois at Urbana-Champaign, USA.
hhuang65@illinois.edu

Masooda Bashir
University of Illinois at Urbana-Champaign, USA.
mnb@illinois.edu

ABSTRACT

The advancement of Internet technologies, including instant and unlimited access to information and services, is an excellent source of support for older adults. However, pervasive and continuous online tracking can pose threats to older adults' information privacy. To enhance older adults' online information privacy, it is important to understand how older adults behave online to protect their information privacy. Although most studies have examined the effect of older adults' privacy attitudes and perceptions on their technology adoption, very few empirical studies have focused on older adults' online privacy protection behaviors. It also remains unclear whether cognitive factors, such as older adults' concerns, knowledge, and perceived risks, impact their protective behaviors for online information privacy. Therefore, this exploratory study conducted a survey to investigate how older adults protect their online information privacy and the cognitive impacts on their behaviors. Our results reveal that older adults use several strategies to protect their online information privacy. In addition, we also confirmed a phenomenon of 'Privacy Divide' among older adults and provide recommendations for future technological development.

KEYWORDS

Privacy-enhancing behaviors, aging-friendly systems, information privacy.

INTRODUCTION

The world population is increasing at an exponential rate. By 2050, the global population of older adults is expected to reach nearly 2.1 billion, which is double the number of older adults in 2017 (United Nations, 2017). The rapid growth of the aging population presents both opportunities and challenges for nearly all aspects of society, such as social support, economic, and healthcare systems. The current and future advancement of Internet technologies will soon connect almost every device in our daily lives, from smart homes to self-driving cars. Therefore, supporting older adults in the use of Internet technologies is increasingly important.

Many people may assume that older adults tend to avoid adopting Internet technologies. In fact, the percentage of older Internet users has been rapidly growing over the past decade. A survey by Pew Research Center reports that in 2016, 64% of U.S. older adults are Internet users, an approximately 50% increase compared to 2001 (Pew, 2017). In addition, studies have shown that frequent use of Internet technologies among older adults has been associated with their broader social networks, independent lifestyle, and wellbeing (Wagner, Hassanein & Head, 2010; Choi and DeNitto, 2013; Hills et al., 2015). For instance, when using the Internet, older adults can communicate with others through social media; they can keep learning and educating themselves via online courses; and they can increase social connections by engaging in online communities (Choi & DiNitto, 2013). Therefore, Internet technologies are not only a significant source of support for healthy aging among older adults but also offers new opportunities for geriatric care in countries with increasing numbers of older citizens.

The convenience provided by Internet technologies, however, is a double-edged sword because its pervasive and continuous data practices come with risks for information privacy and security, especially for older adults. According to the Internet Crime Report in 2016 (IC3, 2016), around 18% of Internet crime victims are aged over 60, and their financial losses account for $339 million in losses, which is the highest among all age groups. In addition, online privacy and security incidents can have disastrous impacts on older adults' physical and mental health. For instance, the manipulation of medical services could negatively influence their physical health, or a privacy breach could induce psychological distress. Consequently, protecting older adults' online information privacy is critical while developing technologies.

The pervasive and continuous data collection, sharing, and monitoring that occurs on the Internet means that older adults' online activities not only disclose information they are aware of having shared, but also personal information they do not intend to disclose. Since privacy is a complex and multilayered concept (Solove, 2008; Nissenbaum, 2009), technologists, psychologists, and legal scholars have used a variety of strategies to incorporate privacy into the design of socio-technical systems. For example, privacy protection guidelines and approaches have been developed, such as the Fair Information Practices Principles (FIPPs), Privacy by Design (PbD) (Langheinrich, 2001), the Do Not Track (DNT) policy and Privacy-Enhancing Technologies (PETs) (Goldberg et al., 1997).

In order to protect and enhance older adults' online information privacy, it is important to understand how older adults use existing tools and how they behave online to protect their information privacy. Most studies have examined the influence of older adults' privacy attitudes and perceptions on their technology adoption. Yet, very few empirical studies have focused on older adults' actual behavior in protecting online information privacy. Furthermore, it still remains unclear whether cognitive factors, such as older adults' concerns, knowledge, and perceived risks impact their protective behaviors for online information privacy. Accordingly, the aim of this exploratory study is to investigate how older adults protect their online information privacy and the cognitive impacts on their behaviors. In next section, we provide background and review related research.

RELATED WORK

Several empirical studies have focused on how older adults' privacy perceptions and attitudes influence their acceptance and adoption of emerging technologies, such as online social networking sites (McNeill et al., 2017; Chakraborty et al., 2013), health monitoring systems (Caine et al., 2006; Wild et al., 2008; Demiris et al., 2009; Lorenzen-Huber et al., 2011; McNeill et al., 2017; Boise et al, 2013), and robotic technologies (Kahn et al., 2007; Caine et al., 2012). In this section we review prior work on older adults' perceptions, behaviors, and potential cognitive impacts on their online privacy.

Older adults' Online Information Privacy Perceptions

Previous research has found that older adults have a more specific definition of "information privacy" than younger adults (Kwasny et al, 2008). For instance, older adults tend to define information privacy in terms of specific information categories, such as legal documents, health information, social security numbers, or a secret that a friend discloses to them, while younger adults have broader definitions of information privacy (Kwasny et al., 2008). When it comes to information privacy, older adults do show concerns about their information privacy while connected to the Internet (Hoofnagle et al., 2010). For example, a survey study conducted by Hoofnagle et al. (2010) indicates that older adults expressed more concerns about Internet privacy issues than their younger counterparts. A recent study (Walters, 2017) also indicates that approximately 75% of older people expressed concerns about their online privacy and 86% of them were concerned about their personal data being compromised. In addition, it is important to note that each older adult's privacy concerns may be influenced by their mental and physical wellbeing. For example, a survey experiment by Caine et al. (2006) revealed that older adults with lower mental functioning express lower levels of privacy concerns. Therefore, considering the impacts of cognitive factors on older adults' privacy perceptions and behaviors is essential.

Older Adults' Online Privacy Behaviors

When examining privacy behaviors in the literature, the majority of studies do not clearly distinguish between actual behavior and intended behavior. Nevertheless, privacy behavioral intentions do not necessarily lead to actual privacy protection behaviors (Kokolakis, 2017). In this study, we focus on older adults' actual privacy protection behaviors instead of behavioral intentions. As far as we know, very few empirical studies have investigated older adults' actual online privacy behaviors. The most relevant work is an observational study by Chakraborty et al. (2013). Chakraborty et al. (2013) analyzed 134 profiles of older adults on Facebook and observed their privacy-preserving actions. They found that older adults are more inclined to not sharing personal information if their friends did the same. In other words, older adults' decisions in taking privacy-preserving action can be affected by their social peers. Caine et al. (2012) investigated whether older adults engage in privacy-enhancing behaviors while interacting with monitoring devices. Their study suggests that older adults engage in more privacy-enhancing behaviors while being monitored by camera rather than when interacting with embodied robots. One potential explanation is that older adults may not be familiar with robots and, therefore, may be less cautious about their monitoring capabilities (Caine et al., 2012). This suggests that older adults' mental models of a technology impact their privacy behaviors.

Cognitive Impacts on Older Adults' Online Information Privacy

In reviewing privacy literature for all age groups, researchers have found that while users are highly concerned about their information privacy, they are still willing to disclose a substantial amount of personal information online (Kokolakis, 2017). This dichotomy of attitudes and behaviors in information privacy has been termed the "privacy paradox" (Norberg et al., 2007). Prior research has also indicated this paradoxical phenomenon in older adults' online information privacy. For instance, older adults make less online privacy protections than their younger counterparts, though they express higher levels of information privacy concern (Grimes et al., 2010; Miltgen et al., 2014; Blank et al., 2014). In addition, older adults seem to be willing to give up their personal privacy to maintain their independence and autonomy while adopting new technologies (Fisk et al., 2009). One possible explanation for these contradictions in privacy attitudes and behaviors in older adults may be related to cognitive factors, such as limited knowledge and mental models about online environments and current data practices (Garg et al., 2011; Lorenzen-Huber et al., 2011). Also, older adults perceive fewer privacy risks in online activities; therefore, they are more vulnerable to online privacy violation (Grimes et al., 2010). In other words, whether older adults take actions to protect their information privacy depends heavily on cognitive factors, such as concerns, knowledge, and, perceived risks.

In summary, previous research findings regarding older adults' online information privacy has pointed out the following:

- Older adults are equally as concerned about their information privacy as younger adults;
- Older adults seem to engage less in online privacy protection behaviors;
- Cognitive factors, such as concerns, knowledge, and perceived risks, can impact older adults' privacy protection behaviors.

However, we still have very little knowledge about what older adults do to protect their online information privacy, and how older adults' cognitive factors affect their privacy protection behaviors. Hence, this exploratory study aims to answer the following research questions:

- RQ1: What do older adults do to protect their online information privacy?
- RQ2: How do older adults' concerns, knowledge, and perceived risks regarding online information privacy impact their privacy protection behaviors?

METHOD

In this study, a survey methodology was adopted to investigate older adults' online privacy protection behaviors and how their concerns, knowledge, and perceived risks toward online information privacy impact their behaviors. In the following sections, we will refer to "Online Information Privacy" as "OIP".

Survey Procedure and Recruitment

Before launching the survey, two rounds of pilot testing were conducted to obtain the feedback from 12 participants who were above 65 years old. Based on the preliminary results, we found homogeneity among participants' responses. Considering that older adults constitute a diverse population, we think that it is important to recruit participants via different venues. Also, previous research has suggested that older adults' Internet usage is influenced by interpersonal or functional factors based on their age (Friemel, 2016). For example, most older adults who are between 55-64 years old are still in the workforce, which may make them more familiar with Internet technologies. We postulate that participants between 55-64 years old may have different privacy protection behaviors than those who are over 65 years old. Thus, we recruited participants 55 years old and older, and categorized them into two groups: (1) ages 55-64 and (2) ages 65 and up. To recruit a diverse sample, the survey was distributed via both online (n=125) and offline (n=44) venues. For the online survey, participants were recruited via a crowdsourcing platform, Amazon Mechanical Turk, and online mailing lists. Participants could access the online survey page via the recruitment post on the crowdsourcing platform or emails. For the offline survey, we used a snowballing approach and flyers to recruit participants from local communities, such as senior centers, local communities. After completing the survey, participants were given an educational handout about how to protect their online privacy and security. For compensation, participants recruited from the crowdsourcing platform were paid $1.75 for their participation, and other participants could select if they would like to participate in the lottery for a $25 gift card, which was given for every 25 participants. All participants were from the United States. Table 1 gives demographic information about our participants.

Age	55-64	66 (39.1%)
	>65	103 (60.9%)
Gender	Female	103 (60.9%)
	Male	66 (39.1%)
Education	Some high school	1 (0.6%)
	High school	16 (9.5%)
	Some college	42 (24.9%)
	Associate's degree	22 (13%)
	Bachelor's degree	39 (23.1%)
	Graduate or Professional degree	36 (21.3%)
	Doctoral degree	13 (7.7%)
Internet use	Several times a day	157 (92.9%)
	About once a day	7 (4.1%)
	A few times a week	2 (1.2%)
	About once a week	1 (0.6%)
	About once a month	1 (0.6%)
	Just a few times a year	1 (0.6%)
Living alone or with others	Living alone	60 (35.5%)
	Living with significant others	67 (39.6%)
	Living with family members	34 (20.1%
	Living with non-family members	3 (1.8%)
	Other	4 (2.4%)

Table 1. Main characteristics of participants

Measurement

The survey questionnaire includes 3 segments. In the first segment, participants were firstly asked about their use of the Internet. Then they were asked about their perceived risks of online activities, online privacy concerns, awareness of online privacy and security, as well as their privacy protection behaviors. In the final segment, participants were asked to provide demographic information, such as their gender, age, educational level, and living alone or with others.

Online Privacy Protection Behavior

The main goal of this study is to understand older adults' privacy protection behaviors while browsing online. Considering that the privacy-protective behaviors encompass with the various social and technical skills (Turkle, 1995; Park et al., 2012), we categorized privacy protection behaviors into 3 levels: passive, active, and proactive. The definition and measurement for each protection behavior are described below.

- *Passive protection behavior* is defined as 'using avoidant or social approaches to passively protect one's OIP', such as not registering to or purchasing on a website if users have privacy concerns about it. Eight items were adopted from Park et al. (2012) to measure older adults' protection behavior.
- *Active protection behavior* is defined as 'using functioning approaches to actively protect one's OIP', such as clearing browsing history, and removing cookies. Four items were adopted from Park et al. (2012) and used to measure active protection behaviors.
- *Proactive privacy protection* is defined as 'using advanced technical approaches, such as privacy-enhancing technologies to proactively protect one's OIP'. We select 9 types of online privacy-enhancing technologies that are popular and listed by Electronic Privacy Information Center.

Participants were asked to indicate if they have taken any of these approaches to protect their online privacy in the past. More details of the results of each privacy protection behavior are presented in Table 2.

Knowledge of Online Information Privacy

As indicated by Park (2013), knowledge of OIP can be operationalized as user awareness in two aspects: (a) technical understanding and (b) awareness of data practices. In this study, we adopted 11 true-false items to measure for technical understanding and 8 true-false knowledge items for data practices awareness from Park (2013). The answers were later recoded as "1" for correct answers and "0" assigned to all other responses. Each aspect of user knowledge was combined to create an index. The Cronbach's alpha of knowledge is 0.82.

Concerns of Online Information Privacy

Considering that concerns about OIP include multiple aspects, we measured users' privacy concerns about the use of online personal information and online data practices. For concerns about personal information, we adopted 6 items from Angulo & Ortlieb (2014) and asked participants to rate on a 5-point scale (from "Strongly disagree" to "Strongly agree"). The Cronbach's alpha of privacy concerns of personal information is 0.82. For concerns about online data practices, we adopted 9 items from Angulo & Ortlieb (2014) and Buchanan et al. (2007) and asked participants to rate how worried they are about each statement on a 5-point scale. The Cronbach's alpha of privacy concerns of data practices is 0.83.

Perceived Risk of Online Activities

To measure perceived risk of online activities, we generated 25 types of online activities based on Pew Research Center's report in 2010 (Pew, 2010). Participants were asked to rate how risky each online activity is on a 5-point scale. The Cronbach's alpha of perceived risk is 0.94.

RESULTS

RQ1: What do older adults do to protect their online information privacy?

Our first research question is how older people protect their OIP when they are concerned about it. We categorized privacy protection behaviors into 3 categories, including passive, active, and proactive behaviors. The Pearson Chi-square test was conducted to test whether the proportion of protective behaviors is the same for each type of privacy protection. As shown in Table 2, the proportion of protective behaviors has significant differences in passive, active, and proactive privacy protection. These results indicate that, for each type of privacy protection, participants reported to use certain approaches more than others.

For example, in terms of passive privacy protection, over half of participants reported that they had stopped visiting the websites, not registered, not purchased, asked online services to remove or not share personal information, and used secondary email(s). In addition, less than 50% of participants gave false personal information to websites, and/or made complaints to consumer or government agencies. For active privacy protection, over 65% of participants reported having experiences in clearing their browsing history, using tools to block unwanted emails, and/or clearing cookies. On the other hand, only about 25% of participants had experience in installing software to hide their computer identities from online services. When it comes to proactive approaches, over 90% of participants did not have experiences in using an anonymous browser, a third-party blocking plugin, an https-enforcement plugin, an anonymous search engine, email encryption, or disconnecting social media tracking plugins. Furthermore, only about 30 to 40% of participants have used an ad-blocking plugin, cookies/Cache/Online history cleaners, and online tracker management. Overall, most participants had experiences in taking passive or active approaches to protect their online privacy. However, most older adults have no experiences in proactive privacy protection.

Passive privacy protection	**Yes**	**No**	**Pearson X^2**
Chose not to register on a website	156 (91.8%)	8 (4.7%)	245.26
Stopped visiting particular websites	135 (79%)	29 (17.1%)	(df = 8,
Decided not to make an online purchase	134 (78.8%)	30 (17.6%)	p< .0001)
Asked a website to remove your name and address from their lists/database	115 (67.6%)	49 (28.8%)	
Asked a website not to share your personal information with other companies	106 (62.4%)	58 (34.1%)	
Used an email address that is not your main address	96 (56.5%)	68 (40%)	
Gave a false or inaccurate email address or fake name to websites	73 (42.9%)	91 (53.5%)	
Complained to a consumer or government agency about marketing practices of particular websites	27 (15.9%)	137 (80.6%)	
Active privacy protection	**Yes**	**No**	**Pearson X^2**
Cleared your web browser history	144 (84.7%)	20 (11.8%)	176.4
Erased some or all of the cookies on your computer	134 (78.8%)	30 (17.7%)	(df = 3,
Used filters to block or manage unwanted email	118 (69.4%)	46 (27.1%)	p< .0001)
Used software that hides your computer's identity from websites you visit	42 (24.7%)	122 (71.8%)	
Proactive privacy protection	**Yes**	**No**	**Pearson X^2**
Used cookies/Cache/Online history cleaner	69 (40.6%)	99 (58.2%)	308.5
Used online tracker management	69 (40.6%)	99 (58.2%)	(df = 7,
Used ad-blocking plugin on web browser	57 (33.5%)	111 (65.3%)	p< .0001)
Used third party blocking plugin	12 (7.1%)	157 (92.4%)	
Used browser plugin to make sure that you only access websites with a HTTPS header	15 (8.8%)	154 (90.6%)	
Used anonymous web search engine	14 (8.2%)	155 (91.2%)	
Used anonymous web browser	10 (5.9%)	158 (92.9%)	
Used email encryption	10 (5.9%)	159 (93.5%)	
Used disconnect social media tracking	7 (4.1%)	160 (94.1%)	

Table 2. Distribution of privacy protection behavior (n=169)

Online Privacy Protection Behaviors

We further explore the pattern of who takes what type of privacy protection. Since older adults are a diverse population, we think that age and familiarity with the Internet may affect how older adults approach their OIP. For instance, we postulate that participants recruited from the crowdsourcing platform may be more familiar with the Internet than those whom are not. Therefore, we categorized our participants based on their age and the medium of recruitment, which results in four groups: (1) aged 55-64; (2) aged 65 and older; (3) crowdsourcing (mTurk); and (4) general public (non-mTurk). To explore the relationship among categorical variables of privacy protections and demographics, we conducted Multiple Correspondence Analysis (MCA) by using R package FactoMineR.

MCA is a statistical technique to analyze the pattern of relationships between multiple categorical variables (Abdi & Valentin, 2007). More specifically, MCA model analyses associations between the frequencies of binary categorical variables and spatially projects the positions of variables in two dimensions. Therefore, MCA is a convenient tool for visualizing the associations between multiple categorical variables (Sourial et al., 2013). Considering that all of our variables were coded as binary variables, MCA is an adequate technique to explore the relationship between privacy protection and the population. Furthermore, MCA can add supplementary variables to the visualization without interfering the primary analysis (Sourial et al., 2013; Clausen, 1998).

In MCA, supplementary variables are projected onto the dimensions after the original analysis of the variables of interest is implemented. In this technique, supplementary variables do not affect the original results, but their position on the graph still allows us to see how the primary variables of interest are associated with supplementary variables. In our research context, the primary variables of interest are privacy protection approaches and the supplementary variables are age group and recruitment type. Next, MCA models for each type of privacy protection with supplementary variables will be presented individually.

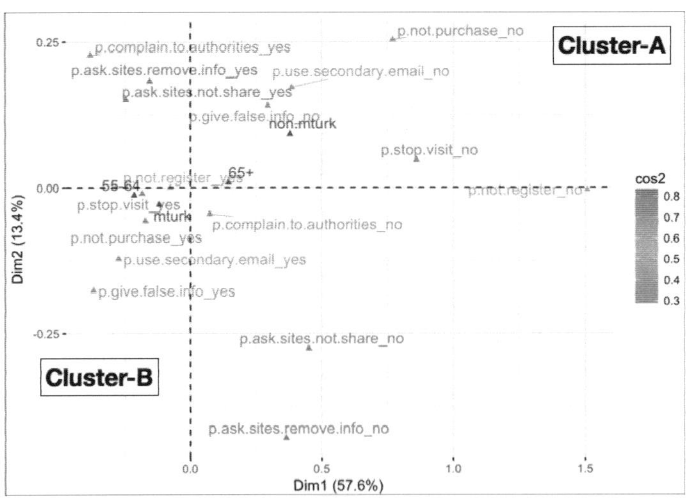

Figure 1. MCA map of passive privacy protection

1) MCA of Passive Privacy Protection

According to our analysis, the two-dimensional solution accounts for 71% of the total inertia, which provides sufficient explanation for the model of passive privacy protection. In addition, Dimension 1 explains the most variance in the model (57.6%), followed by Dimension 2 (13.4%). Table 3 shows the summary of the model. Figure 1 shows the symmetric map of two-dimensional solution.

As shown in Figure 1, five passive approaches were close to each other, including: stopping visiting websites, not purchasing, not registering, use secondary email, and give false information. Considering the avoidant nature of these approaches, we categorized these behaviors as 'Avoidant strategies'. In addition, participants who had experiences in asking websites to remove personal information and asking websites not to share their information were also inclined to take action in filing complains to authorities as they had privacy concerns. We characterized these two approaches as 'Expression strategies'. It is worth noting that the squared correlation (COS^2) of complaining to authorities is relatively low (Table 3). This suggests that this approach is not an appropriate indicator to represent how older people protect their online privacy.

Furthermore, based on the location of two supplementary variables (age and recruitment), two clusters emerge on the map, Cluster-A and Cluster-B. Cluster-A, located on the top-right of the map, shows that participants who were 65 years or older and among the general public (non.mturk), tended not to use avoidant strategies to protect their privacy. On the other hand, participants who were between 55-64 years old and recruited via the crowdsourcing platform, were inclined to use both avoidant and expression strategies (see Cluster-B on Figure 1).

2) MCA of Active Privacy Protection

Similarly, the two-dimensional solution is generated and accounts for 92.3% of the total inertia, which is also sufficient for explaining the model of active privacy protection. Dimension 1 explains the most variance in the model (79.9%), followed by Dimension 2 (12.4%). Figure 2 exhibits the symmetric map of two-dimensional solution for active privacy protection and demographics. According to the map, two active approaches are close to each other, including clearing browsing history, removing cookies, and blocking unwanted emails. We categorized these three active approaches as 'Disappearing strategies'. Moreover, we termed the behavior of using software to hide Internet identity as 'Hiding strategies'. The square correlation of these four categories are above 0.8 in Dimension 1, representing the adequate quality of active privacy protection. That is, the category of active privacy protection is well-presented by these four variables.

As shown in Figure 2, a salient Cluster-C is located on the left side of the map, suggesting that participants between 55-64 years old and in the mTurk group tended to take disappearing strategy to protect their OIP. In addition, participants of all ages did not report experience in using software to hide their computer ID from online services. In another word, participants were not familiar with this type of active protection.

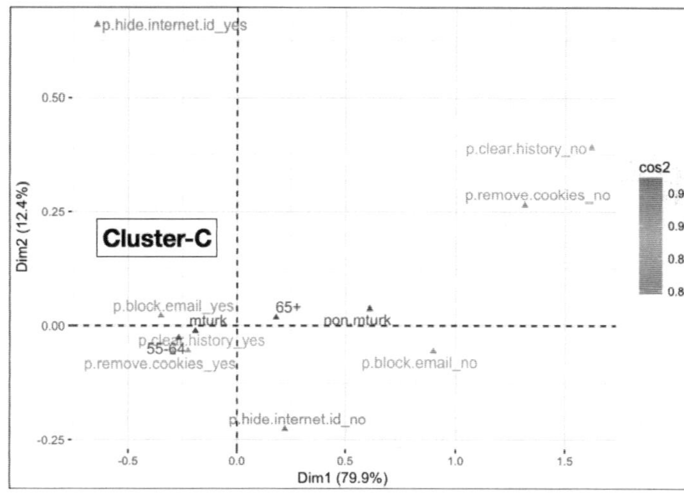

Figure 2. MCA map of active privacy protection

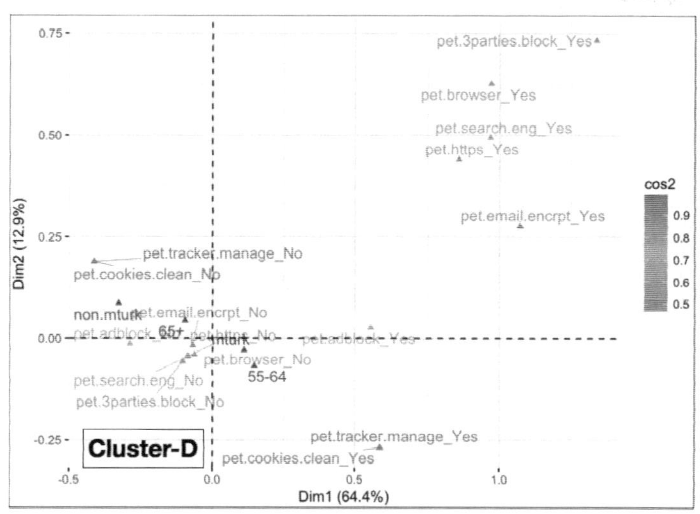

Figure 3. MCA map of proactive privacy protection

3) MCA of Proactive Privacy Protection

For proactive privacy protection, the two-dimensional solution is also generated and accounts for 77.3% of the total inertia. Dimension 1 explains the most variance in the model (64.4%), followed by Dimension 2 (12.9%). As shown in Figure 3, the majority of participants had no experience in most proactive approaches, such as using an anonymous browser, third-party blocking plugins, and email encryption. However, participants who reported using a cookies cleaner were more likely to use an online tracker management tool. Hence, we categorized these two proactive approaches as 'Anti-tracking strategies'. Yet, the general public (non.mturk) were disinclined to use anti-tracking strategies when compared to crowdsourcing participants.

	Dimension 1			Dimension 2		
Passive privacy protection	**Coordinate**	**COS²**	**Contribution**	**Coordinate**	**COS²**	**Contribution**
p.stop.visit_no	0.860	0.784	15.937	0.048	0.002	0.215
p.stop.visit_yes	-0.185	0.784	3.423	-0.010	0.002	0.046
p.give.false.info_no	0.296	0.594	5.916	0.141	0.136	5.810
p.give.false.info_yes	-0.369	0.594	7.375	-0.176	0.136	7.243
p.not.purchase_no	0.770	0.684	13.220	0.254	0.074	6.169
p.not.purchase_yes	-0.172	0.684	2.960	-0.057	0.074	1.381
p.not.register_no	1.508	0.648	13.523	-0.004	0.000	0.000
p.not.register_yes	-0.077	0.648	0.693	0.000	0.000	0.000
p.complain.to.authorities_no	0.075	0.208	0.574	-0.045	0.074	0.880
p.complain.to.authorities_yes	-0.381	0.208	2.911	0.227	0.074	4.464
Active privacy protection	**Coordinate**	**COS²**	**Contribution**	**Coordinate**	**COS²**	**Contribution**
p.clear.history_no	1.621	0.886	26.493	0.391	0.051	9.899
p.clear.history_yes	-0.225	0.886	3.680	-0.054	0.051	1.375
p.block.email_no	0.898	0.834	18.686	-0.056	0.003	0.470
p.block.email_yes	-0.350	0.834	7.285	0.022	0.003	0.183
p.remove.cookies_no	1.316	0.913	26.200	0.264	0.037	6.803
p.remove.cookies_yes	-0.295	0.913	5.866	-0.059	0.037	1.523
p.hide.Internet.id_no	0.222	0.476	3.020	-0.227	0.500	20.423
p.hide.Internet.id_yes	-0.644	0.476	8.771	0.660	0.500	59.324
Proactive privacy protection	**Coordinate**	**COS²**	**Contribution**	**Coordinate**	**COS²**	**Contribution**
pet.browser_No	-0.062	0.385	0.335	-0.040	0.160	0.698
pet.browser_yes	0.971	0.385	5.253	0.627	0.160	10.955
pet.adblock_No	-0.288	0.763	5.085	-0.013	0.002	0.055
pet.adblock_Yes	0.556	0.763	9.813	0.026	0.002	0.106
pet.3parties.block_No	-0.103	0.668	0.925	-0.057	0.201	1.389
pet.3parties.block_Yes	1.336	0.668	11.945	0.723	0.201	17.941
pet.https_No	-0.085	0.446	0.607	-0.043	0.118	0.801
pet.https_Yes	0.858	0.446	6.150	0.441	0.118	8.115
pet.search.eng_No	-0.089	0.491	0.669	-0.045	0.128	0.870
pet.search.eng_Yes	0.968	0.491	7.316	0.494	0.128	9.506

Table 3. Summary of Multiple Correspondence Model for Online Privacy Protection Behaviors

RQ2: How do older adults' concerns, knowledge, and perceived risks regarding online information privacy impact their privacy protection behaviors?

We further examined the effects of four cognitive factors on older adults' privacy protection approaches. These four factors include: 1) knowledge of privacy and security, 2) concerns about personal information, 3) concerns about online practices, and 4) perceived risks of online activities. Considering the variables of privacy protection behaviors are count data, the Generalized Linear Model with Poisson distribution was conducted for analyses.

The first model is calculated to predict four cognitive effects on older adults' passive privacy protection behaviors, which explains 80.3% of variance (R^2) of the model. As shown in Table 4, the only significant predictor in Model 1 is knowledge of privacy and security, which estimated β is larger than 0. This indicates that the more knowledge participants had, the more expected number of passive approaches participants would take to protect their online privacy. More specifically, for one unit of increase in the knowledge, the number of taking passive approaches will increase and be multiplied by 1.04 times (*exp*(0.04)).

Model 2 (see Table 4) is conducted to predict cognitive effects on older adults' active privacy protection, which explains 85.7% of variance (R^2) of the model. Similarly, only knowledge is a significant predictor of taking active privacy protections. This suggests that participants with more knowledge about privacy and security will take more active protection for their online privacy. More precisely, for one unit of increase in the knowledge, the number of taking active approaches will increase and be multiplied by 1.08 times (*exp*(0.079))

Model 3 is analyzed to predict cognitive effects on older adults' proactive privacy protection, which explains 43.8% of variance (R^2) of the model. The only significant predictor is also knowledge of privacy and security. Since the estimate β is positive, participants with more knowledge will take more proactive privacy protection. Furthermore, for one unit of increase in knowledge, the number of taking proactive approaches will increase and be multiplied by 1.18 times (*exp*(0.162)).

	Model 1: Passive		Model 2: Active		Model 3: Proactive	
	β	z-value (*p-value*)	β	z-value (*p-value*)	β	z-value (*p-value*)
Intercept	.751	2.26 (*p*=.024)	-.310	-0.66 (*p*=.509)	-.976	-1.79 (*p*=.074)
Knowledge of privacy and security	.040	3.34 (*p*=.0008)	.079	4.60 (*p*<.0001)	.162	6.88 (*p*<.0001)
Concerns about personal information	-.023	-0.43 (*p*=.668)	.016	0.21 (*p*=.835)	.012	0.13 (*p*=.898)
Concerns about online data practices	.118	1.62 (*p*=.106)	.113	1.10 (*p*=.272)	-.121	-1.06 (*p*=.287)
Perceived risks of online activities	.008	0.15 (*p*=.882)	-.047	-0.58 (*p*=.559)	.115	1.10 (*p*=.272)

Table 4. Generalized Linear Model of Online Privacy Protection Behaviors

DISCUSSION

In this empirical study, we investigated older adults' online privacy protection behaviors via survey methodology. The findings show that, in general, participants had more experiences in taking *passive* or *active* privacy protections than *proactive* approaches. We categorized older adults' protection behaviors using Multiple Correspondence Analysis. This analysis revealed five main strategies used by older adults within three protection approaches, which are summarized in Table 5. For passive approaches, older adults tend to avoid using online services or express their concerns directly with online service providers. For active approaches, older adults try to disappear or hide themselves from tracking capacities. As for proactive approaches, the main strategy adopted by older people is to use privacy-enhancing tools to prevent online tracking.

Behavior	Strategy	Item
Passive protection	Avoidance	• Stopped visiting particular websites • Gave a false or inaccurate information • Decided not to purchase • Chose not to register • Used secondary email
	Expression	• Asked a website to remove personal information • Asked a website not to share personal information
Active protection	Disappearing	• Cleared browsing history • Removed cookies • Blocked unwanted emails
	Hiding	• Used software to hide computer/Internet ID
Proactive protection	Anti-tracking	• Installed cookies cleaner plug-in • Used online tracker management

Table 5. Categories of Older Adults' Online Privacy Protection Behaviors

In addition, our results also reveal a phenomenon of '*Privacy Divide*' among our study participants. We found a pattern that participants who were at the younger end of our sample, between 55 and 64 years old, and recruited via a crowdsourcing platform were inclined to take more privacy protections than participants 65 and older and recruited among the general population. This phenomenon corresponds to previous research that has indicated the digital divide among older adults (Friemel, 2016). One possible explanation is that older adults who are still under 65 and using an online crowdsourcing platform may already have more Internet skills and knowledge to protect their OIP. In other words, older adults who are 65 years old and over and of the general public could be more vulnerable to online privacy attacks due to the lack of privacy protection behaviors.

We also investigated how older adults' cognitive factors (concerns, knowledge, and perceived risks) impact their protection behaviors. Corroborating previous studies (Garg et al., 2011; Lorenzen-Huber et al., 2011), our findings suggest that older adults' knowledge of OIP is the main significantly positive predictor for their behaviors. This further indicates that the lack of knowledge may be the primary cognitive factor leading to older adults' lack of protection behaviors. That is, older adults are concerned about their OIP, but they do not know how to protect it.

Based on our findings, we propose two recommendations for designers and policy makers. First, while developing Internet technologies for older adults, designers should keep in mind that older adults are going to be an increasing user population for Internet technologies, thus there will be many benefits for designing privacy-friendly systems for aging population. In addition, since older adults may have less technological knowledge and are therefore more vulnerable to privacy attacks, it is important to design systems that enables older adults to protect their privacy easily. Furthermore, we think that there is an urgent need to develop an educational program regarding OIP for older adults. Moreover, considering the complexity of OIP and its relevant applications, policy makers need to be creative in delivering complex technological innovations and communicating their related risks through educational materials to older adults.

Limitations and Future Research

We acknowledge that there are two main limitations in this work. First, our findings are limited to a specific sample because we only recruited U.S. participants. Older adults living outside the U.S. may report different online privacy protection behaviors due to the variety of social contexts and resources. Hence, we suggest future research to recruit international participants and compare the results. Also, our study focused on *what* older adults do to protect their OIP; it still remains unclear *why* older adults prefer taking certain approaches over others. We recommend future research to conduct a qualitative study that may provide more in-depth understanding about older adults' decision-making and their online privacy protection behaviors.

CONCLUSION

The advent of intelligent and Internet technologies will support healthy aging and enhance autonomy and independence for older adults. However, the deep interconnectedness of the Internet also increases risks for information privacy and security breaches, which can put older adults in danger. Therefore, how we empower older adults to protect their information privacy becomes an urgent and challenging question. In summary, this exploratory study found that older adults use different strategies to protect their online information privacy, and reveals that knowledge actually plays a critical role in older adults' protective behaviors. This work contributes in two ways. First, to the best of our knowledge, this is the first study revealing and categorizing older adults' online privacy protection behavioral strategies. Second, our study confirms a phenomenon of *Privacy Divide* among older adults. Therefore, we advocate for designing privacy-friendly systems and educational programs for older populations. While there is still a long road ahead of us to build an aging-friendly and comprehensive privacy-enhancing environment for older adults, this study offers insights for addressing online privacy challenges for an aging population.

REFERENCES

Abdi, H., & Valentin, D. (2007). Multiple correspondence analysis. Encyclopedia of measurement and statistics, 651-657.

Angulo, J., & Ortlieb, M. (2015, July). "WTH..!?!" Experiences, reactions, and expectations related to online privacy panic situations. In Symposium on Usable Privacy and Security (SOUPS).

Blank, G., Bolsover, G., & Dubois, E. (2014). A new privacy paradox: Young people and privacy on social network sites (SSRN).

Boise, L., Wild, K., Mattek, N., Ruhl, M., Dodge, H. H., & Kaye, J. (2013). Willingness of older adults to share data and privacy concerns after exposure to unobtrusive in-home monitoring. Gerontechnology: international journal on the fundamental aspects of technology to serve the ageing society, 11(3), 428.

Buchanan, T., Paine, C., Joinson, A. N., & Reips, U. D. (2007). Development of measures of online privacy concern and protection for use on the Internet. Journal of the Association for Information Science and Technology, 58(2), 157-165.

Caine, K. E., Fisk, A. D., & Rogers, W. A. (2006, October). Benefits and privacy concerns of a home equipped with a visual sensing system: A perspective from older adults. In Proceedings of the human factors and ergonomics society annual meeting (Vol. 50, No. 2, pp. 180-184). Sage CA: Los Angeles, CA: Sage Publications.

Caine, K., Šabanovic, S., & Carter, M. (2012, March). The effect of monitoring by cameras and robots on the privacy enhancing behaviors of older adults. In Proceedings of the seventh annual ACM/IEEE international conference on Human-Robot Interaction (pp. 343-350). ACM.

Chakraborty, R., Vishik, C., & Rao, H. R. (2013). Privacy preserving actions of older adults on social media: Exploring the behavior of opting out of information sharing. Decision Support Systems, 55(4), 948-956.

Choi, N. G., & DiNitto, D. M. (2013). Internet use among older adults: association with health needs, psychological capital, and social capital. Journal of medical Internet research, 15(5), e97.

Clausen, S. E. (1998). Applied correspondence analysis: An introduction (Vol. 121). Sage.

Demiris, G., Oliver, D. P., Giger, J., Skubic, M., & Rantz, M. (2009). Older adults' privacy considerations for vision based recognition methods of eldercare applications. Technology and Health Care, 17(1), 41-48.

Fisk, A. D., Rogers, W. A., Charness, N., Czaja, S. J., & Sharit, J. (2009). Designing for older adults: Principles and creative human factors approaches. CRC press.

Federal Bureau of Investigation (2015). Internet Crime Report. Available at: https://pdf.ic3.gov/2015_IC3Report.pdf

Friemel, T. N. (2016). The digital divide has grown old: Determinants of a digital divide among seniors. New Media & Society, 18(2), 313-331.

Garg, V., Camp, L. J., Mae, L., & Connelly, K. (2011, July). Designing risk communication for older adults. In Symposium on Usable Privacy and Security (SOUPS).

Goldberg, I., Wagner, D., & Brewer, E. (1997, February). Privacy-enhancing technologies for the Internet. In Compcon'97. Proceedings, IEEE (pp. 103-109). IEEE.

Grimes, G. A., Hough, M. G., Mazur, E., & Signorella, M. L. (2010). Older adults' knowledge of internet hazards. Educational Gerontology, 36(3), 173-192.

Hoofnagle, C. J., King, J., Li, S., & Turow, J. (2010). How different are young adults from older adults when it comes to information privacy attitudes and policies? SSRN.

Kahn, P.H., Ishiguro, H., Friedman, B., Kanda, T., Freier, N.G., Severson, R.L. and Miller, J. 2007. What is a human? Toward psychological benchmarks in the field of humanrobot interaction. Interaction Studies, 8 (3), 363-390.

Kokolakis, S. (2017). Privacy attitudes and privacy behaviour: A review of current research on the privacy paradox phenomenon. Computers & Security, 64, 122-134.

Kwasny, M., Caine, K., Rogers, W. A., & Fisk, A. D. (2008, April). Privacy and technology: folk definitions and perspectives. In CHI'08 Extended Abstracts on Human Factors in Computing Systems (pp. 3291-3296). ACM.

Langheinrich, M. (2001). Privacy by design—principles of privacy-aware ubiquitous systems. In Ubicomp 2001: Ubiquitous Computing (pp. 273-291). Springer Berlin/Heidelberg.

Lorenzen-Huber, L., Boutain, M., Camp, L. J., Shankar, K., & Connelly, K. H. (2011). Privacy, technology, and aging: A proposed framework. Ageing International, 36(2), 232-252.

McNeill, A., Briggs, P., Pywell, J., & Coventry, L. (2017, June). Functional privacy concerns of older adults about pervasive health-monitoring systems. In Proceedings of the 10th International Conference on PErvasive Technologies Related to Assistive Environments (pp. 96-102). ACM.

Miltgen, C. L., & Peyrat-Guillard, D. (2014). Cultural and generational influences on privacy concerns: a qualitative study in seven European countries. European Journal of Information Systems, 23(2), 103-125.

Nissenbaum, H. (2009). Privacy in context: Technology, policy, and the integrity of social life. Stanford University Press.

Norberg, P. A., Horne, D. R., & Horne, D. A. (2007). The privacy paradox: Personal information disclosure intentions versus behaviors. Journal of Consumer Affairs, 41(1), 100-126.

Park, Y. J., Campbell, S. W., & Kwak, N. (2012). Affect, cognition and reward: Predictors of privacy protection online. Computers in Human Behavior, 28(3), 1019-1027.

Park, Y. J. (2013). Digital literacy and privacy behavior online. Communication Research, 40(2), 215-236.

Pew Research Center, (December, 2010). Generations 2010. Available at: http://www.pewinternet.org/2010/12/16/generations-2010/

Pew Research Center, (May, 2017). Technology use among seniors. Available at: http://www.pewinternet.org/2017/05/17/technology-use-among-seniors/

Pew Research Center (January, 2017). Internet/Broadband Fact Sheet. Available at: http://www.pewinternet.org/fact-sheet/internet-broadband/

Solove, D. (2008). Understanding privacy.

Sourial, N., Wolfson, C., Zhu, B., Quail, J., Fletcher, J., Karunananthan, S., ... & Bergman, H. (2010). Correspondence analysis is a useful tool to uncover the relationships among categorical variables. Journal of clinical epidemiology, 63(6), 638-646.

Turkle, S. (1997). Life on the screen: Identity in the age of the internet. Literature and history, 6, 117-118.

United Nation (2017). World Population Ageing. Available at: http://www.un.org/en/development/desa/population/publications/pdf/ageing/WPA2017_Highlights.pdf

Wagner, N., Hassanein, K., & Head, M. (2010). Computer use by older adults: A multi-disciplinary review. Computers in human behavior, 26(5), 870-882.

Walters, N. (2017). Maintaining privacy and security while connected to the Internet. AARP Public Policy Institute.

Wild, K., Boise, L., Lundell, J., & Foucek, A. (2008). Unobtrusive in-home monitoring of cognitive and physical health: Reactions and perceptions of older adults. Journal of applied gerontology, 27(2), 181-200.

The Current State of Data Governance in Higher Education

Cary K. Jim
University of North Texas, USA. caryjim@my.unt.edu

Hsia-Ching Chang
University of North Texas, USA. Hsia-ching.Chang@unt.edu

ABSTRACT
Recent developments in big data have heightened the need for data governance in any organization. There has been a growing interest and recognition of the importance of data governance in higher education. While multiple research efforts focus on a literature-based approach to conceptualize data governance, evidence-based research on this topic can scarcely be found. Higher education institutes are facing similar challenges in aligning their information technology (IT) efforts with business processes to meet organizational goals. This study aims to address such a research gap and investigates the status quo of data governance practice across tier one universities in the United States. Using Web content analysis, this paper sought to obtain empirical evidence of data governance initiatives, the extent of data governance, and its relationship with IT governance and information governance across a sample of 30 tier one university websites. Results of this study revealed that most of the universities created a new data governance unit with different labels (e.g., data governance, institutional research, or data management/analytics), while some universities extended IT governance or information governance to data governance. These findings shed light on the potential directions of developing data governance initiatives in higher education.

KEYWORDS
Data governance, tier one universities, higher education, web content analysis, decision-making.

INTRODUCTION
The change from paper-based records to digital data opened a lot of opportunities and challenges for many organizations. During the last fifty years, computer software and hardware development continued to advance. Today, any person who interacts with technology locally or network through "wired" or "wireless", is generating data that are trackable and could be stored over time. The early use of digital technology in American higher education has been researched and documented since the 1960s (Picciano, 2012). Schools and universities have a long history of maintaining academic records and other operational documents. Students, faculty, and staff all contribute to the diverse sources of data in universities regardless of their awareness of how the data are used and for what purpose. From an organizational standpoint, the data stored in their information systems are valuable for decision-making, compliance, assessment and performance evaluation.

Using digital technologies for record management may appear to free up physical space, but this requires an on-going investment to keep up with the advancing hardware and software requirement. "Infusions of technology infrastructure, large-scale databases, and demands for timely data to support decision making have seeped into all levels of college leadership and operations" (Picciano, 2012, p. 10). It is not a simple task to maintain information technology (IT), and business processes while improving teaching and learning efforts for students, staff, and the community (Broad, 2014; Duhaney, 2005; Hora, Bouwma-Gearhart, & Park, 2017; Picciano, 2012). The blending of academia and business processes in higher education offer opportunities for information professionals to connect research to practice. For many universities, their business and instructional processes supported by information technology have become indivisible. The digitalized components within the universities require an inclusive structure to manage data and information for the benefit of the organizations and their stakeholders.

Even though information systems and data techniques continue to advance, the intent of using data to inform decisions is fundamental. The on-going cycle of data analytics provides information for performance, accountability, and other educational objectives such as students learning outcomes. Data-driven decision-making, then, became a widely adopted approach to address these concerns (Hora et al., 2017; Picciano, 2012). Administrative records, financial records, enrollment data, student information, and faculty records are examples of internal data maintained and processed in-house, usually in a form of data warehousing. External data are sourced from third-party applications such as a learning management system, curriculum and instructional tools, digital library resources, and social media data. These are just some examples of data shared and hosted by vendors or in-house. The third type of data that falls between internal and external is research data. Research data management is usually handled based on the institution's data management policy as well as on the funding agency's expectations. Therefore, universities do not lack data but rather direction in terms of how to utilize data and information for their benefit and how to protect data as an asset. Hence, the awareness and understanding of data as their asset is the first step. Often "third parties outside of the university may be the first to recognize data opportunities. Governance mechanisms to assure protection of privacy, academic freedom, intellectual property, information security and compliance" in universities is imperative (Borgman, 2018, p. 5). Data governance is needed to guide and facilitate information technology, data processes, and decision-making to support an organization in reaching its goals. Among library and information professionals, data management or data curation are not new concepts (Koltay, 2016). Library and information science professionals can enrich collaboration among organizations in data and information related activities, such as data governance.

RELATED WORK

Data governance exists in different industries and the interpretations of data governance differ. According to Nielsen's (2017) literature review on data governance practices between 2007 and 2017, 32% of published papers came from computer science disciplines, another 32% from information systems, and only 5% were from education (i.e. higher-education education institutions and learning). This provided us a sense of how data governance has been associated with certain disciplines such as computer science and information technology from a technical and system perspective. The inception of data governance typically involves IT, business processes, privacy and security measures. Information technology (IT) governance is used by organizations to guide their data related processes and has a longer history in the business domain. Weill and Ross (2014) defined "IT governance as specifying the decision rights and accountability framework to encourage desirable behavior in using IT" (p. 2). However, data are being collected constantly behind the scenes and it takes some conscious effort to appraise their value to an organization. Weber, Otto, and Österle (2009) explained that data governance includes both business processes and IT to provide organization-wide guidelines to ensure data quality and accountability. Several scholars suggested that when data are viewed as an asset in an organization, they should be monitored and managed (Brous, Janssen & Vilminko-Heikkinen, 2016; Khatri & Brown, 2010; Koltay, 2016; Otto, 2011). Culture and values of an organization are also important and will shape the behavior of individuals and organizations (Putro, Surendro, & Herbert, 2016). Therefore, a systematic approach in the development of data governance will allow an organization to utilize data effectively to achieve their goals. The increased concern over privacy and security due to data breaches is another facet of data governance. "Three major universities and one school district became victims of cyber breaches...it is not just identifiable information. It is also information about the students and their performance itself...the mental processes of students as they are working through equations" (How Data Mining, 2014, p. 2). The joint U.S. congressional hearing examined privacy concerns in education, especially, "the sharing of student information with educational software and cloud service vendors and the laws and guidelines that govern them" (How Data Mining, 2014, p. 3). Thus, the need to examine data sharing and how third parties are using identifiable data should be addressed by data governance in educational institutions. Information governance is another concept presented in relation to data governance in which both are important for organizations to achieve their desired outcomes (Bennett, 2017; Hulme, 2012). Li, Zhou, and Yu (2016) suggested seven core-criteria (based on information governance guidelines) for big data: organization, metadata, privacy, data quality, business process integration, master data integration, and information lifecycle requirements. Khatri and Brown (2010) suggested a data governance framework with five decision domains: data principles, data quality, metadata, data access, and data lifecycle. The Data Governance Institute (2017a) provided a data governance framework with three main branches: Rules and rules of engagement, people and organizational bodies, and processes. Each main branch from the framework contains components that guide an organization to develop data governance that will fit their needs. Brous et al. (2016) provided a systematic review of data governance principles and identified 27 related key concepts including: accountability, decision rights, compliance, privacy, security, and metadata management. The 27 related key concepts are arranged under four major principles: organization, alignment, compliance, and common understanding. In summary, data governance serves as the guiding framework that should address organizational goals and business processes (decision-making, culture, and values), legal obligations and compliance (accountability), risk management (privacy and security), data management (data quality and metadata) and the roles humans play (data stewards and data owners). Data governance should continue to mature and adapt for the organization's changing needs and processes.

PURPOSE OF THE STUDY

We believe that good data governance can only be meaningful when it aligns with the institutional goals and values in a sustainable manner. Based on the limited amount of research on data governance in education (Nielsen, 2017), there is a need to explore this topic for a better understanding. This paper is the first attempt to address the lack of research of data governance among higher education institutions by exploring the current practice of data governance among the tier one research universities in the United States. This study focuses on the following research questions:

1. What is the current status quo of data governance among tier one research universities in the United States?
2. What type of information is available from the universities that present their data governance initiatives in their websites?

METHODOLOGY

A Web content analysis is used to collect and analyze available information publicly released by the universities on their websites and webpages. The identification of tier one research universities in the U.S. is based on the rankings from the Carnegie Classification of Institutions of Higher Education (Indiana Univ. Center for Postsecondary Research, 2017). It is a recognized ranking system to classify higher education institutes in the U.S. The Carnegie Classification evaluates for-profit and non-profit higher education institutes and assigns ranking based on the type of degree granting program and the level of research activity at each. The R1 ranking is commonly referred to as tier one or top-tier which is the highest ranking in the Carnegie Classification. Tier one indicates a doctoral degree granting institute with the highest research activities. In 2017, there were 115 research universities in the U.S. listed in the R1 (tier one) criteria.

Thirty tier one research universities were selected for the initial sampling of this study based on their geographic location and business structure: for-profit vs. non-profit. We anticipated to identify data governance practices among the leading universities (tier one) in U.S. to inform future studies of data governance model and framework for higher education and related environments. Each sampled university website was searched to identify information regarding their data governance practices. Using existing documents and web content as a source of data are often referred as nonreactive measures and this type of data can be a better representation of the phenomenon comparing to data collected through self-reporting mechanism (Wildemuth, 2017, p. 165). The presence of online information released by each university was used as an indicator of their progress or awareness of data governance practices. The first part of the evaluation process is to review whether an existing data governance program is established, how the program is represented within the organization and what approach is taken to govern data as an asset. Furthermore, the primary goal of this paper is to examine the current data governance practices among the sampled universities instead of comparing the level of completion of their data governance efforts. In order to collect relevant data that are meaningful for analysis, a Data Governance Checklist was developed. It is derived from key literature on data governance with seven major criteria identified that would fit for the context of higher education (Brous, et al., 2016; Khatri & Brown, 2010; Koltay, 2016; Li, et al., 2016; Otto, 2011). A coding schema was developed to examine and collect evidence of the status quo of their data governance practices.

The seven criteria and definition of the Data Governance Checklist is presented in Table 1. Each criterion is designed to minimize overlapping ideas and to allow analysis of existing online documents and information from the sampled universities.

Data Governance Checklist Criteria	Definition
Data Governance Body	A group of stakeholders who formalize the data governance practice at their organization
Data Quality	Guidance on the accuracy, availability, integrity, data standards, and the intended use
Data Access or Restriction	Specific access or restriction policy on the data
Data Security	Guidance on system security to protect data and privacy issues of sensitive data
Data Stewardship, Ownership, and Roles	Roles and responsibility of those who interact with the data at various levels within an organization
Metadata Documentation and Organization	Structure and methodology to document and maintain data: e.g. data dictionary, metadata scheme
Business Process Integration	Core business process that is parallel to the data process, and management of both

Table 1. Data Governance Component Checklist

The Data Governance Body is a group of stakeholders who are interested in the development and oversight of the data governance program. Membership in this group can be formed internally but can also include other experts outside of an organization. When reviewing the institutional webpages, we looked for an official group or unit that hosts the data governance program information as an indication of their web presence. The data governance body is different from the other roles supporting the process. Other frequently discussed roles in data governance are data stewards, data owners, and data committees (Koltay, 2016; Otto, 2011; Rosenbaum, 2010). Data Stewardship, Ownership, and Roles indicated positions of those who have a vested interest and actively engage in the process of data governance within their institution. We explored to determine if the universities presented these roles in their webpages and how these roles are explained in their web content.

Data Quality is the foundation of the data-driven decision-making process. If the data are not genuine and trustworthy, the output will be misleading and ineffective. If the data collected are not relevant to the organizational goals, they will not be informative to decision making process. For this criterion, we looked for any description or statement in relation to data quality from the webpages.

Data Access and Restriction are important to regulate access rights and put limitations on the use of data within an organization. For example, staff who handle the institution's data should be given certain access or limitations to avoid misuse of the data. It also implies proper procedures to grant access for users who should have access to the data. This component is determined by identifying specific policies and procedures on the webpages addressing user access or restrictions. Sometimes, Data Security can be confused with access and restriction. Access and restriction are established for rights and limitations as for how users are retrieving and interacting with the data. Security is about safeguarding the data and valuable information of the organization. We use the term security to cover related concepts, such as privacy, confidentiality and data breach protection. Each institution may have its own definition, covering similar or different elements in its webpages.

Metadata Documentation and Organization are intended to provide structure and information about the data stored in the various systems within an organization. It is a common understanding among information professionals that metadata is meant to support organization and provide a description of the data for users. Some common forms of metadata documentation are data dictionary, metadata standards, thesauri, etc. The form of metadata implementation was assessed by reviewing the universities' data management mechanism from their web content.

The last criterion is the indication of business process alignment in the web content of each university. Business Process Integration is the backbone of any data governance process in an organization. Several scholars discussed the significance of business process integration with data governance to support the organization's overarching goals and mission (Brous, et al., 2016; Khatri & Brown, 2010; Otto, 2011). When reviewing the institutional data governance webpages, we looked for identifiable information, or business strategies, or processes integration in their data governance practices. Other information collected depends on its availability, such as department or unit that oversees the data governance practices, data governance documents, or policy in their webpages.

FINDINGS – PRELIMINARY RESULTS

Every effort has been made to discover publicly available information from the universities' websites. If the data governance information is hosted in a restricted web domain, that information will not be accessible to us and therefore won't be included in this initial data collection.

The preliminary result includes information collected from web content including online documents and hyperlinks from the 30 tier one universities data governance webpages. There are a variety of terms and concepts used by each university to describe their efforts in data governance. The use of the Data Governance Checklist helped target searches and organize identified information from existing key components of data governance in their organization. First, we used the Google search engine to locate the institution website by entering the full university name and the keyword "data governance". Then, we compared the Google search result with an internal search of the university website with the keyword "data governance". During data collection, we recognized the different organizational structure and naming mechanism they used among information technology, data related services and information related services.

Table 2 presents the offices or units which oversee data governance initiatives or data related services at their institution. The result indicated most of the data governance activities are supported by a designated group of members in the form of a committee, council, or working group in the universities. The second and third largest groups of staff who support and supervise data governance processes are the Information Technology departments as well as Institutional Research. Some institutions have their own single unit of data management and analytics that were not associated or under another department within the organization. An interesting fact during this initial data collection is two of the universities have two or more joint office/units that support both data governance and IT governance, shown in the last row of Table 2.

Office or Unit Represented	Count	Percentage
Data Governance Council, Working Group or Committee	10	33%
Information Technology	7	23%
Institutional Research	6	20%
Data Management or Analytics Unit	4	13%
Other units such as security or administrative	3	10%
No indication of data governance practice	2	6%
Two or more joint office/units governing data practices	2	6%

Table 2. Offices or unit within the university where information of data governance is hosted

The Data Governance Checklist is used to distinguish each specific component within the universities' data governance practice. The brief definition of each criterion can be found in Table 1. Each count is discrete in the following data analysis. One or zero was assigned to the checklist to present an indication of yes or no based on the content of their webpages (Table 3).

Data Governance Checklist Criteria	Count	Percentage
Data Governance Body	23	77%
Data Quality	16	53%
Data Access or Restriction	28	93%
Data Security	23	77%
Data Stewardship, Ownership, and Roles	22	73%
Metadata Documentation and Organization	19	63%
Business Process Integration	23	77%

Table 3. Findings of each data governance criterion by count and percentage

The initial analysis of the webpages with the Data Governance Checklist presented the majority (93%) of universities have policies and procedures of data access or restriction at their institution. About three quarters (77%) of the universities showed a data governance body in the form of a committee, working group, or council that directs and supports data governance practices at their institution. Furthermore, more than half of the universities appeared to exercise the other key principles of data governance at their institution in data quality, data stewardship/ownership, and metadata documentation and organization.

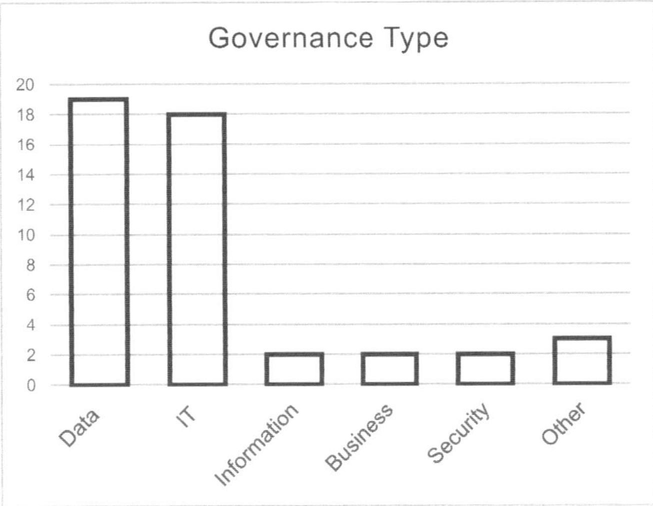

Figure 1. Types of governance found on the universities webpages

While examining the type of data governance initiative or program at each institution, we recognized that terms such as information, data, or IT governance are used similarly and differently to represent their practice. For example: IT governance, information governance, or data management are used together to describe their current practice of data governance. Figure 1 displays the count of the term data governance, IT governance, information governance, business governance, security and other types of governance found on the webpages. Note, some universities displayed more than one type of governance, for example, data and IT governance is the most common combination among the 30 universities. A further investigation is needed discover why there is such a disparity in their data governance practices.

Part of the Web content analysis is to examine information provided by the universities' webpages about their view on data governance. We were able to locate 14 university webpages that provide their direct statement on data governance. As stated before, it was impossible to mutually exclude data governance from IT governance because the perception of each depends upon the university. Therefore, we included only statements that address data governance directly in Table 4. The direct statements retrieved from the university websites represented the variety of perspectives and approaches. Some universities consider data governance as a process or underlying principles, while others construe it as a part of best practices to support business operation and system integration. The majority of the statements also cover overlapping key concepts presented in our Data Governance Checklist. Therefore, we organized the statements according to basic sentence structure in which "data governance" is the subject and the predicate is what and how the institution describes data governance.

Criteria	Examples of Statement by Universities
Data Governance Body	"The [Data Stewardship] Council addresses issues concerning data management including usage, sharing, integration, access, security, privacy, quality, and compliance" (The University of Chicago, 2018, para 3).
Data Quality	"Data governance adds value to our administrative and academic data systems by the establishment of standards that that promote data integrity and enables strategic integrations of information systems" (Vanderbilt University, 2018, para 1).
Data Access or Restriction	"Data Governance is the process of establishing and managing information about the data collected and used by the University...This ensures a common and consistent understanding of what data exists, term definitions, availability, sensitivity classification and access restrictions" (University of Norte Dame, 2018, para 1)
Data Security	"Data governance includes all the policies and practices that ensure UDW+ [online information system and dashboard] provides the university community with accurate and consistent information while protecting data security and confidentiality" (New York University, n.d., para 1).
Data Stewardship/Ownership, and Roles	"[Data Governance Stewardship] determine formal roles for those in charge of data. This does not mean that everyone on campus is not responsible despite formal roles." (University of Wisconsin at Madison, 2018).
Metadata Documentation and Organization	"This program [Data Governance program] will result in a sustainable and efficient set of controls, data standards and data policies for UTA, with the potential to extend its scope over time to other areas with UTA" (The University of Texas at Arlington, 2018).

Table 4: Direct statements that support each component of the Data Governance Checklist

DISCUSSION

According to a survey by Childers (2017) for the Higher Education Data Warehousing Forum, data governance is the most frequent topic among 57% of their surveyed universities for the second year (2016 and 2017). The latest result of the Top 10 survey by Childers and Walz (2018) again showed data governance as a priority topic and became a priority category in 2018. It is worth mentioning that several components in the data governance from their 2018 Top 10 survey also reflected similar observations as our study, such as administration of data governance, metadata and data definitions, data quality and role-based access.

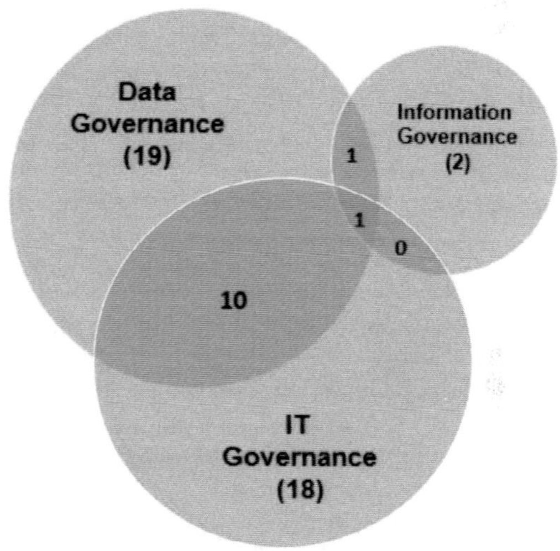

Figure 2. The interplay between data governance, IT governance, and information governance found on the universities' webpages.

Through the examination of data governance structure and processes, the sampled universities seem to have different overarching governance structures. For example, some universities created new units to lead the data governance initiatives; other universities began with their IT department and extended their work to address data governance. There are also a minority of universities working toward an integration of information and data governance in which IT plays a supporting role. Figure 2 presents a Venn diagram which depicts the relationships between data governance and two other types of governance, IT governance and information governance. The intersecting areas denote the interplay between different governance structures that work together with data governance initiatives, while non-intersecting areas illustrate the standalone governance structure in the sampled universities. Note, the number in parentheses reflects the count displayed in Figure 1.

Interestingly, two universities strategically extended their information governance to integrate data governance and/or IT governance. This approach can support interconnections as information governance refers to a broader concept that entails data governance and IT governance (Bennett, 2017; Smallwood, 2014). In addition, information governance is often considered within the scope of IT to address the importance of information within a modern organization (Faria & Simpson, 2013). As a result, many universities thus far do not seem to have embraced information governance as a relevant part of their framework to inform the creation of their data governance. As for the representation purpose, interplay between data governance and IT governance, ten universities (about one-third) have data governance embedded within the IT governance structure, and only one university demonstrated its inclusion of information governance, IT governance and data governance on the webpages.

Based on the evidence collected from the 30 tier one research universities, it has shown that most institutions have awareness of data governance and are in the process of forming policies and procedures for their institution. The mixture of information available from their webpages provides information of their current state of data governance. Yet, due to the design of this exploratory study and the collection of web content from the sampled universities, our study has limitations. First, the initial collection of web content for this study can only serve as a starting point to inform future research in this topic. The varied organizational structures and concept terms found in universities' data governance policies require further inquiry with each institution. The use of surveys or interviews with university officials within their IT, data or information units can provide valuable insight into their strategy. Institutional culture and values also have an impact on their views and approach to data related mechanism and processes. We recognized that organizational culture and values are important to the development and success of data governance policies and programs in higher education. However, culture and values are not simple variables that we can examine through the web content analysis in this study and should be further researched in light of their connection to data governance at the universities. Further comprehensive research is needed to establish a uniform model or framework for data governance in higher education.

As information professionals, we believe our profession can contribute to an organization's data governance initiative due to our expertise in information related work and services for the various settings. There is no one-size-fits-all solution to data governance. Our study does not propose a single solution approach to data governance, rather, we surveyed the data governance initiatives and practices based on the university's web presences to assess its status quo. We observed consistent themes across the samples in which a governing body with defined roles and access are important constituents within an organization. We also observed the use of software solutions to address their data governance need in many of the universities. To support data-driven decision making, most universities strive for business intelligence (BI) advancement utilizing a variety of analytics tools along with information technology (IT). BI and data analytics are all about using data for decision making and support. In order to acquire quality data for effective data analytics, a data governance or data management framework has to be in place to guide the process. It is evident that BI/analytics efforts co-evolve with data governance. More than 50% of sampled universities focus on BI betterment by indicating the advanced analytics tools in their webpages, such as SAS, Qlikview, Tableau, Cognos, SAP HANA, and OLAP cubes. One university specifically adopted a data governance platform, Collibra, to break down the data silos. This implies that using technology tools or software solutions could aid in navigating the complex data governance process. It is essential to further research on the interrelationship between an organizational structure of data governance and the digitized processes of data governance. Can the adopted solutions provide the one-stop-shop for a unique institution such as higher education? What are the elements in data governance that cannot be addressed by technical solutions but through the integration of human resources or supports?

The next step for our study is to complete the data collection of all tier one universities and collect other evidence to verify our observation from the web content such as interviews or surveys. Another aspect to explore is to identify models or frameworks used by the universities and if these draw from theoretical or conceptual work of data governance from other disciplines. Which type of governance should serve as the foundation of data governance for higher education and how it should it vary based on the institutional view on data and information? As Koltay (2016) suggested, "librarianship as well as library and information science also should pay attention to DG [data governance], albeit it attracted attention mainly in the business sector" (p. 304). It is our attempt to examine data governance in higher education from an information science perspective in hopes of understanding the significance of the interplay of data governance, IT governance, and information governance. The current landscapes of data governance among tier one universities are diverse and how they evolve will reflect the institutions' business approach and management as well as their academic vision and mission.

CONCLUSION

Data and information are both valuable assets for higher education. The need for information and data to support the dual roles as an academic institution and a business organization needs a systematic way to manage data and information. The goal of data governance in higher education should be strategic to address the needs and interests of stakeholders from students, staff, faculty, administrators to the larger research community. This paper conducts an evidenced-based study using Web content analysis that substantiates the current state of data governance among higher education. This exploratory approach provides information on one aspect of this phenomenon. Further data collection such as interviews or surveys can provide more in-depth insights in regards of data governance in higher education institutes and to address any information not released in their public domain webpages.

The findings highlight the different approaches undertaken by higher education on data governance. While information governance oversees people activities, technology, and processes (Information Governance Initiative, 2018), data governance revolves around managing information-related processes (The Data Governance Institute, 2017b). This perspective leads us to ongoing discussions regarding rethinking the role of information governance in data governance initiatives. Although the results from this study are not conclusive due to limited sample size, they are certainly worth investigating in depth with wider populations in tier one universities. It is our plan to further explore the rest of the tier one universities (85 out of 115) to get a better view of data governance among all the tier one universities in the U.S.

For publicly funded education entities, such as public universities, there are distinct features in comparison to a for-profit organization. Accountability, compliance, and transparency are the basis of a public domain that demonstrates equality, accessibility, and stewardship of public resources. Therefore, with the vast amount of data within an education institution, data governance should be in place to protect data assets and to guide the data processes to meet organizational goals. This paper is the first study to collect evidence of data governance across a sample of tier one research universities, thus contributing to the understanding of current state of data governance among leading research universities. Several organizations and universities have taken the lead in forming data governance to guide their decision making and control of data (Borgman & Wada, 2016; Chapple, 2013; Data Quality Campaign, 2018; Reeves & Bowen, 2012), but more work is needed to examine the maturity of data governance implementation. Other types of growing data such as social media and communication channels should also be considered in the data governance framework. If a higher education institute is to invest in software solutions and information architecture to support its business processes and services, a comprehensive data governance framework will help inform decisions in technology investment. The direction taken by the organization on data governance and how it evolves to keep up with the growing big data trend will be one of the determining factors of success in the decades to come.

REFERENCES

Bennett, S. (2017). What is information governance and how does it differ from data governance? *Governance Directions*, *69*(8), 462–467.

Borgman, C. L. (2018). Open data, grey data, and stewardship: Universities at the privacy frontier. *Berkeley Technology Law Journal*, *33*(2). Retrieved March 8, 2018 from https://escholarship.org/uc/item/9dh6b8j0

Borgman, C. L., & Wada, K. J. (2016). *UCLA Data governance task force final report and recommendations.* Retrieved March 14, 2018 from https://ucla.app.box.com/s/zvtg5rcd9ojo2by2rtzoum4kv9mdulnr

Broad, M. C. (2014). Leveraging technology for higher education challenges. *EDUCAUSE Review*, *49*(5), 108–109. Retrieved March 21, 2018 from https://er.educause.edu/articles/2014/9/leveraging-technology-for-higher-education-challenges

Brous, P., Janssen, M., & Vilminko-Heikkinen, R. (2016). Coordinating decision-making in data management activities: A systematic review of data governance principles. In H. J. Scholl, O. Glassey, M. Janssen, B. Klievink, I. Lindgren, & P. Parycek et al. (Eds.), *15th IFIP WG 8.5 International Conference, EGOV2016 (LNCS* 9820) (pp. 115–125). Cham, Switzerland: Springer International Publishing AG.

Chapple, M. (2013). Speaking the same language: Building a data governance program for institutional impact. *EDUCAUSE Review*, *48*(6), 14–27. Retrieved March 1, 2018 from https://er.educause.edu/articles/2013/12/speaking-the-same-language-building-a-data-governance-program-for-institutional-impact

Childers, H. (2017). *2017 HEDW survey of top 10 issues.* Retrieved April 1, 2018, from the Higher Education Data Warehousing Forum Web site: https://hedw.org/2017-hedw-survey-of-top-10-issues/

Childers, H., & Walz, A. (2018). 2018 General session research findings – The Hank and Aaron show. [Video Presentation Online]. Retrieved June 15, 2018 from https://vimeo.com/268473190/c1c458a758

Data Quality Campaign. (2018). *The art of the possible: Data governance lessons learned from Kentucky, Maryland, and Washington.* Retrieved March 1, 2018 from https://dataqualitycampaign.org/resource/art-of-the-possible-data-governance-lessons-learned/

Duhaney, D. C. (2005). Technology and higher education: Challenges in the halls of academe. *International Journal of Instructional Media*, *32*(1), 7–15.

Faria, F. A., & Simpson, G. E. (2013). Bridging the gap between business and IT: An information governance perspective in the banking industry (217-238). In N. Bhansali (Ed.), *Data governance: Creating value from information assets* (pp. 217-238). Boca Raton, FL: CRC Press.

Hora, M. T., Bouwma-Gearhart, J., & Park, H. J. (2017). Data driven decision-making in the era of accountability: Fostering faculty data cultures for learning. *The Review of Higher Education*, *40*(3), 391–426. Retrieved November 22, 2017 from https://doi.org/10.1353/rhe.2017.0013

Hulme, T. (2012). Information governance: Sharing the IBM approach. *Business Information Review*, *29*(2), 99–104.

How data mining threatens student privacy: Joint Hearing before the Subcommittee on Cybersecurity, Infrastructure Protection, and Security Technologies of the Committee on Homeland Security, House of Representatives, and the Subcommittee on Early Childhood, Elementary, and Secondary Education of the Committee on Education and the Workforce, House of Representatives, 113th Cong. 2(2014). Retrieved March 1, 2018 from http://purl.fdlp.gov/GPO/gpo55335

Indiana University Center on Postsecondary Research. (2017). *The Carnegie classification on institutions of higher education.* Retrieved March 13, 2018 from http://carnegieclassifications.iu.edu/

Information Governance Initiative. (2018). *Information Governance Initiative IGI State of the industry report 2016-2017.* Retrieved on March 31, 2018 from https://iginitiative.com/wp-content/uploads/The-State-of-IG-Report-Volume-III-highres.pdf

Khatri, V., & Brown, C. V. (2010). Designing data governance. *Communications of the ACM, 53*(1), 148–152.

Koltay, T. (2016). Data governance, data literacy and the management of data quality. *International Federation of Library Associations and Institutions*, *42*(4), 303–312.

Li, Y., Zhou, L., & Yu, Y. (2016). Research on big data governance of university information management. *Journal of Residuals Science & Technology*, *13*(7), 296.1-4.

New York University. (n.d.). *Data governance: What is data governance?* Retrieved March 2, 2018, from https://www.nyu.edu/employees/resources-and-services/administrative-services/university-data-warehouse-plus/data-management.html

Nielsen, O. B. (2017). A comprehensive review of data governance literature. *Information Systems Research Seminar (IRIS) in Scandinavia*, (8), 120–133.

Otto, B. (2011). Data governance. *Business & Information Systems Engineering*, *3*(4), 241–244.

Picciano, A. G. (2012). The evolution of big data and learning analytics in American higher education. *Journal of Asynchronous Learning Networks*, *16*(3), 9–20.

Putro, B. L., Surendro, K., & Herbert. (2016). Leadership and culture of data governance for the achievement of higher education goals (Case study: Indonesia University of Education). In *Proceedings of International Seminar on Mathematics, Science and Computer Science Education (MSCEIS 2015)* (pp. 050002: 1-12). Melville, NY: American Institute of Physics (AIP) Publishing.

Reeves, M., & Bowen, R. (2012). Demand action, not assumption: a data governance model at Vanderbilt University Medical Center supports patient safety by providing complete and accurate information. *Health Management Technology*, *33*(6), 10–11.

Rosenbaum, S. (2010). Data governance and stewardship: Designing data stewardship entities and advancing data access. *Health Services Research*, *45*(5, Part II), 1442–1455.

Smallwood, R.F. (2014). Information governance, IT governance, data governance: What's the difference? In R. F. Smallwood (Ed.), *Information governance: Concepts, strategies, and best practices* (pp. 15-23). Hoboken, NJ: John Wiley & Sons, Inc.

The Data Governance Institute. (2017a). *The DGI data governance framework.* Retrieved March 1, 2018 from http://www. datagovernance.com/the-dgi-framework/

The Data Governance Institute. (2017b). Definitions of data governance. Retrieved February 2, 2018 from http://www.datagovernance.com/adg_data_governance_definition/

The University of Chicago, Data Stewardship Council. (2018). *University-wide data governance*. Retrieved March 2, 2018, from https://dsc.uchicago.edu/

The University of Texas at Arlington, University Analytics. (2018). *UTA Data governance program.* Retrieved March 2, 2018 from https://www.uta.edu/analytics/Data%20Governance/index.php

University of Notre Dame. (2018). *About dataND: Data governance.* Retrieved March 2, 2018 from http://aboutdata.nd. edu/data-governance/

University of Wisconsin-Madison, Office of Data Management & Analytics Services. (2018). *Data governance, governance principles, stewardship.* Retrieved March 2, 2018, from https://data.wisc.edu/data-governance/#principles

Vanderbilt University, Institutional Data Governance Team. (2018). *About Vanderbilt data governance*. Retrieved March 2, 2018, from https://www.vanderbilt.edu/datagovernance/

Weber, K., Otto, B., & Österle, H. (2009). One size does not fit all - A contingency approach to data governance. *Journal of Data and Information Quality*, *1*(1), 4:1-27

Weill, P., & Ross, J. W. (2004). *IT governance: How top performers manage IT decision rights for superior results*. Boston, MA: Harvard Business School Press.

Wildemuth, B. M. (Ed,). (2017). *Application of social research methods to questions in information and library science.* Santa Barbara, California: Libraries Unlimited.

Characterizing Transgender Health Issues in Twitter

Amir Karami
University of South Carolina, USA. karami@sc.edu

Vanessa L. Kitzie
University of South Carolina, USA. kitzie@mailbox.sc.edu

Frank Webb
University of South Carolina, USA. fwebb@email.sc.edu

ABSTRACT

Although there are millions of transgender people in the world, a lack of information exists about their health issues. This issue has consequences for the medical field, which only has a nascent understanding of how to identify and meet this population's health-related needs. Social media sites like Twitter provide new opportunities for transgender people to overcome these barriers by sharing their personal health experiences. Our research employs a computational framework to collect tweets from self-identified transgender users, detect those that are health-related, and identify their information needs. This framework is significant because it provides a macro-scale perspective on an issue that lacks investigation at national or demographic levels. Our findings identified 54 distinct health-related topics that we grouped into 7 broader categories. Further, we found both linguistic and topical differences in the health-related information shared by transgender men (TM) as compared to transgender women (TW). These findings can help inform medical and policy-based strategies for health interventions within transgender communities. Also, our proposed approach can inform the development of computational strategies to identify the health-related information needs of other marginalized populations.

KEYWORDS

Transgender, health, topic modeling, linguistics analysis, Twitter

INTRODUCTION

In recent medical research and practice, lesbian, gay, bisexual, transgender, and queer (LGBTQ) health has received increased attention. Compared to their heterosexual and cisgender peers, these populations face decreased rates of preventative health care, along with increased rates of HIV and depression (Gonzales, Przedworski, & Henning-Smith, 2016). These adverse outcomes are due, in part, to a dearth of information on LGBTQ health among both patients and medical professionals. For instance, half of the participants in a national survey of transgender identifying individuals reported a lack of provider knowledge about transgender care (James, Herman, Rankin, Keisling, Mottet, & Anafi, 2016). Existing research is limited by small samples that are difficult to use in generalizing results to a larger population. These small sampling frames reflect a lack of large-scale, national studies that focus on LGBTQ people; likely a result of these populations still being stigmatized and discriminated against at the federal level. Further, current survey methods that capture information about LGBTQ health do not collect data that can be compared longitudinally or to other data, the latter due to unstandardized collection methods. The survey method is also not efficient. For example, one survey on experiences of discrimination among transgender people took several years to develop and refine – from 2011 to 2016[1].

A unique challenge faced by transgender individuals is access to affirming health care, with 19% of those surveyed claiming they were denied care and 50% reporting the need to educate their provider on transgender health care needs (Grant, Mottet, & Tanis, 2011). This same report also indicates 41% of transgender people have attempted suicide and a have 2.64% rate of HIV infection, with higher rates for transgender women of color and those who are unemployed. A meta-regression study of existing surveys report that there are approximately one million transgender adults in the United States (Meerwijk & Sevelius, 2017); however, similar to LGBTQ health surveys at large, these surveys are not generalizable and tend to focus on specialized populations, such as college students and inmates. This lack of information for transgender individuals, and for all LGBTQ people, leads to significant limitations in adequately addressing the health disparities they face (Sell & Holliday, 2014).

Using social media, millions of individuals can share their everyday life and stories. Each day, approximately 500 million tweets are posted on Twitter discussing everyday life issues[2]. Social media facilitates people's belonging to and exchanging information within LGBTQ communities, by allowing users to transcend geographic barriers and contributing to the perception of limited risk in being "outed" (Byron, Rasmussen, Wright Toussaint, Lobo, Robinson, & Paradise, 2017).

---

[1] https://transequality.org/issues/national-transgender-discrimination-survey
[2] http://www.internetlivestats.com/twitter-statistics/

Privacy and stigma pose significant barriers to LGBTQ people sharing information related to these identities in clinical settings (Byron, Albury, & Evers, 2013). Therefore, social media data may provide unique perspectives on LGBTQ issues that are not shared in these other settings. Twitter is a popular social media platform from which to collect data because it offers Application Programming Interfaces (API) to collect large-scale datasets. Due to its APIs plus millions of users, several studies have used Twitter data to examine phenomena of interest in different domains such as health (Shaw & Karami, 2017; Webb, Karami, & Kitzie, 2018), psychology (Golder & Macy, 2011), library (Collins & Karami, 2018), business (Karami & Pendergraft, 2018), and disaster management (Cameron., Power, Robinson, & Yin, 2012).

This study is one of the few large-scale studies that examine the health-related information needs of transgender individuals on Twitter. To collect macro-level data, we developed a computational framework to obtain and analyze the tweets of self-identified transgender Twitter users to characterize the health issues they experience. In this way, we can begin to capture a broader picture of this population's health-related information needs. This study opens a new direction at the intersection of health informatics, social media analysis, and data science that provides practical benefits for medical and health experts. We organize the remainder of this paper as follows. In the next section, we review related work. Then, we present our framework and results in detail. Finally, we present a summary, limitations, and conclude with future directions.

RELATED WORK

The US Office of Disease Prevention and Health Promotion's Healthy People 2020 initiative identified LGBTQ people as facing significant health disparities including higher rates of substance abuse, mental illness and suicide attempts, and youth homelessness, as well as lower rates of health care utilization. Transgender individuals are the least likely to have health insurance among LGBTQ and heterosexual populations, and experience higher rates of suicide and victimization (Office of Disease Prevention and Health Promotion, 2017). These disparities are produced, in part, by the discriminatory treatment LGBTQ people face when receiving health care. Health care providers receive a cumulative median of five hours of LGBTQ-related curricular content during the whole of their medical instruction, and transgender individuals report being denied care due to their gender identities (Obedin-Maliver, Goldsmith, Stewart, and et al, 2011; Grant, Mottet, & Tanis, 2011). Together, evidence from these studies indicates a need for better educational resources for providers, as well as advocacy and protection for transgender rights to healthcare. Also, there are some unique health issues among transwomen and transmen such as breast cancer[3], sexual health (Reisner, Perkovich, & Mimiaga, 2010), pregnancy (Light, Obedin-Maliver, Sevelius, & Kerns, 2014); however, surveys have grouped transwomen and transmen into a larger "transgender" category, ignoring these important distinctions.

Healthy People 2020 identifies the lack of sexual orientation and gender identity information associated with medical records as an area of improvement to lessen disparities for LGBTQ populations. As of now, only two national data systems include information on gender identity (Office of Disease Prevention and Health Promotion, 2017). Efforts to collect the appropriate data focus on standardized terminology, confidentiality, and clarity of questions, as well as reducing barriers to patients' willingness to offer the information. Due to identification outside of a gender binary, even asking the question can be difficult due to multiple or no identities being applicable (Harrison, Grant, & Herman, 2012). By creating comprehensive records of gender identity associated with patients' medical records, including preferred pronouns, better education and treatment methods can be utilized to reduce disparities (Institute of Medicine (US) Board on the Health of Select Populations, 2013).

In addressing public health, the first step is assessing the situation by monitoring the health statuses and diagnosing the problems or hazards. Policy development follows this step (Harrell & Baker, 1994). By turning to social media, both the issues of scale and stigma for LGBTQ individuals can be addressed, allowing for large amounts of health data, as well as associated metadata such as time and, in some cases, place, to be collected. Analysis of this data can inform the first step of addressing transgender public health issues by developing a framework of their information needs. This framework can be used to develop standardized large-scale data collection methods like surveys, as well as inform policy-based interventions.

Social media provides a new context in which to understand the unique experiences of sexual and gender minorities, including transgender people. Although prior research has used Twitter data for health applications, including intestinal disease (Zou, Lampos, Gorton, & Cox, 2016) and diabetes, diet, exercise, and obesity (Karami, Dahl, Turner-McGrievy, Kharrazi, & Shaw, 2018), these data have not been utilized to study the health information needs of transgender populations. This paper addresses this gap in the literature and proposes a computational framework using text mining methods to explore tweets of transgender users and identify the differences in the health-related information needs between TM and TW by analyzing their tweets using linguistics analysis and topic modeling.

---

[3] https://www.vumc.org/lgbti/key-transgender-health-concerns

METHODOLOGY AND RESULTS

We developed a framework to collect and analyze the content of the tweets by self-identified transgender users in Twitter. This framework has five steps: data collection, health data detection, linguistics analysis, and topic modeling (Figure 1).

Figure 1: Research Framework

Data Collection

To identify transgender users on Twitter, we searched profile descriptions for terms indicating identity disclosure (e.g., use of the label "FtM," which means "female to male"). Because transgender individuals comprise a vulnerable population, we avoid detailing all of our methods in this paper, however only focused on labels used explicitly to disclose a transgender identity. For this reason, we filtered the collected users to include those with at least 100 tweets and 100 followers, those identifying themselves as located in the United States, and those whose tweets were written primarily in English. This approach resulted in a dataset of 279 transgender users comprised of 73 self-identified TM and 206 self-identified TW users. We recognize that for many "transgender" represents a larger umbrella of non-cisgender identities (e.g., people identifying as "genderqueer"). For this paper, we wanted to focus on a subset of the population identifying as TM or TW since their needs might differ from other transgender-identified individuals who do not desire medical intervention. Focus on these other groups will constitute a future work. After we identified our 279 users, we used *twitteR* (a Twitter API within the statistical software package R) to collect up to 3,200 tweets for each of the 279 users. We removed retweets and the tweets containing URLs to focus content generated by these users, rather than the content they shared. This approach yielded 68,895 TM tweets and 215,556 TW tweets, for 284,451 tweets in total.

Health Data Collection

From this dataset of 284,451 tweets, we then identified tweets containing health-related content. To make this detection, we applied the Linguistic Inquiry and Word Count (LIWC) software, which captures thoughts, feelings, personality, and motivations, to the dataset (Karami & Zhou, 2015; Karami & Zhou, 2014a). This tool has a health-related category showing whether a tweet contains health-related words. Using LIWC, we identified 5,492 TM tweets and 14,869 TW tweets for a total of 20,361 health-related tweets for analysis. Table 1 shows a sample of the collected health-related tweets. To maintain user privacy, we have lightly edited all tweets to avoid detection.

	Recently received confirmation in writing from my health insurance that all transgender-related surgeries and services are now covered
	Pretty much all day, I've been on a liquid diet
	*this sh*tty neck pain I likely got from sleeping improperly is similar to my old neck injury*
	Eating, exercising, meds/ I've eaten, walked, done physical therapy, shopped, socialized, written, taken my meds and I've sewn!

Table 1. A Sample of Tweets

Linguistics Analysis

After identifying health-related tweets from our 279 users, we then wanted to determine whether there were linguistic difference between health-related tweets shared by TM and TW. We used the five LIWC categories to make this determination. These categories are word count (i.e., number of words), analytics (i.e., degree of analytical thinking), clout (i.e., authority of author), authenticity (i.e., honest self-depiction), and tone (i.e., emotional inclination of author) (Arenas, 2018).

We applied two-tailed t-tests to compare TM and TW tweets based on the five categories. Table 2 shows that although there is no significant difference between TM and TW tweets with respect to tone, there are significant differences between the two groups with respect to the rest of categories. Findings indicate that TW users used more words in general, as well as more analytical, clout, and authentic-related words than TM users in their health-related tweets. This finding indicates that TW provide more details about their health issues than TM. One possible reason for providing more detail is that they have more trust in Twitter users than TM and want to obtain their feedback or suggestions.

	Word Count	Analytic	Clout	Authentic	Tone
P-value	0.00<0.05	0.00<0.05	0.00<0.05	0.00<0.05	0.30>0.05

Table 2: P-value for Linguistics Analysis

Topic Modeling

When working with large datasets, it is difficult for people to manually identify health-related topics; there are simply too many tweets (Karami, 2017). To address this issue and understand what health-related topics transgender users were discussing, we applied Latent Dirichlet Allocation (LDA) to our dataset. This type of topic modeling is the most established and robust among the different types (Karami, Gangopadhyay, Zhou, & Kharrazi, 2015a). Researchers have used LDA in a wide range of applications such as analysis of health and medical corpora (Karami, Gangopadhyay, Zhou, & Kharrazi, 2018; Karami, Gangopadhyay, Zhou, & Karrazi, 2015b; Karami & Gangopadhyay, 2014), literature review (Priva & Austerweil, 2015), and politics (Karami, Bennett, & He, 2018; Najafabadi & Domanski, 2018; Najafabadi, 2017), as well as spam detection (Karami & Zhou, 2014b). For this research, we applied a Mallet implementation of LDA based on Java programming language (McCallum, 2002).

LDA assumes that each topic is a distribution over words and each document is a mixture of the topics in a corpus (Blei, Ng, & Jordan, 2002; Karami, 2015). The model categorizes the words that are semantically related in a topic to represent a theme. For example, this model assigns "gene," "dna," and "genetic" to a topic with the theme "Genetics" (Figure 2).

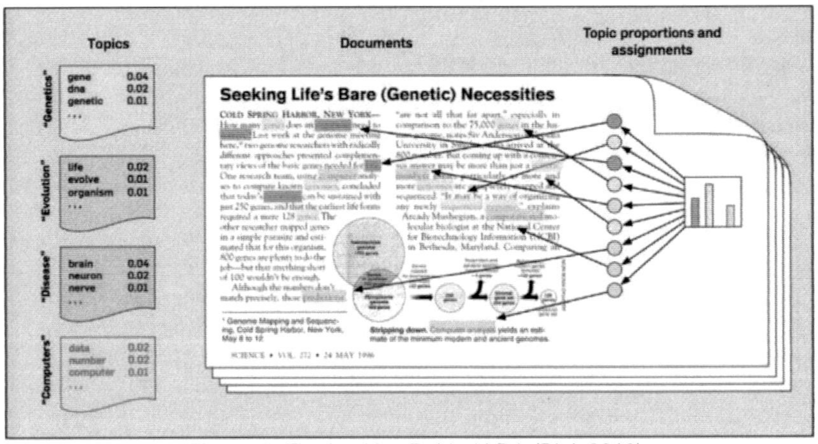

Figure 2: The Intuition Behind LDA (Blei, 2012)

Once we removed stopwords from our corpus (e.g., "and," "the"), we then determined how many topics best represented the data. To make this determination, we used the log-likelihood method to estimate the number of topics based on t inference of topic distribution on new, unseen documents and found the optimum number of topics to be 125 (Figure 3).

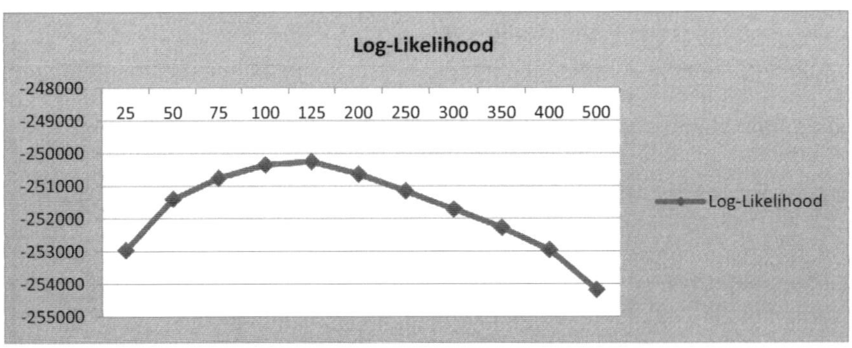

Figure 3: Determining Optimum Number of Topics

T#	Topics	Label
T1	surgery surgeon bottom chest ftm plastic feels grs recovery scars	Gender Confirmation (GC) Surgery
T2	experience agree lives talking pain harm difficult personal feelings mind	Emotional State
T3	exhausted today exhausting feel emotionally working physically home tiring bed	Emotional and Physical
T4	live die work forever people disabled family act medicaid cuz	Health Legislation
T5	mom home dad day hospital parents kids told family crying	Family's Health
T6	great state blue pill states medicaid medicare parents social security	Health Legislation
T7	pain dealing injury danger conversation patient coma addiction	Mental Health
T8	tired people sick stressed scared ugh break angry wired boring	Mental Health
T9	months hormones testosterone started ago hrt weeks change full transition	GC hormone replacement therapy (HRT)
T10	care health insurance medical pay money cover plan cost bills	Health Legislation
T11	life system death people support literally immune killing avoid operating	Critical Health Care
T12	trans health safe care transgender rights support vital lgbtq hiv	General LGBTQ Health
T13	free fat low class amazing creating culture planned milk water sugar	Diet
T14	medical trans history research treatment professionals records doctors diagnosis condition	Clinical Health
T15	type great lose alcoholic exercise arthritis weight injured surgeon diabetes	Diet and Lifestyle
T16	hope great end time night headache pain stress lot infection	Symptoms
T17	pretty exhausting awesome easy constantly medicine completely super benefit fairly	Positive Clinical Experience
T18	doctor office appointment time called put message visit scheduled experience	Clinical Experience
T19	calories burned walked miles workout exercise gym biking hill fitness	Exercise
T20	estrogen dose testosterone hormone high shot low pills double level	HRT
T21	work hard run exercise walk built makes fine time note	Exercise
T22	sore feel hand pains muscle throat hurts shoulder back aches	Aches and Pains
T23	life rest saved amazing entire transitioning celebrate changed worked peace	GC Positivity
T24	terrible pill coughing shot aids band fit prob usual crisis flu	Illness and Symptoms
T25	trans people transition hormones gender medical dysphoria surgery therapy doctors	GC Clinical
T26	pain back cramps gain hip run suffering leg waking joint	Aches and Pains
T27	therapist therapy work find doctor found thing clinic talk helped	Therapy
T28	eyes face nose allergies running bleeding itchy summer painful chills blood	Allergies
T29	gender identity diagnosis treat dysphoria specific informed ways hormones symptoms	GC Health
T30	therapy good exercises session today bring therapist advocate trans working	Therapy
T31	doctor side find testosterone prescription pharmacy effect estrogen bottle meds	GC Pharmaceutical
T32	mental health illness people issues illnesses stigma chronic struggle month	Mental Health
T33	care health listen speak abt taking doctors talking trust nice	Clinical Relation
T34	cancer problem suicide kill die symptom breast depression suicidal attempt	Critical Health Care
T35	fat body weight exercise loss size lazy mirror muscle face	Body Image and Gender Identity
T36	hope healing power back pain helping wounds hurt fast prayers	Healing
T37	blind hate turn eye operator broke glasses spot read touch	Vision
T38	drink water coffee alcohol diet tea cigarette smoking coke caffeine	Lifestyle Habits
T39	food eating diet poisoning sick addiction pizza chicken cheese chocolate	Food Poisoning
T40	drugs drug thing alcohol weird fucked buying addict test illegal	Drug Use
T41	physical emotional abuse hormones sexual violence labor practice drug hug	GC Stress
T42	feeling sick feel sad nauseous crying depressed body fever dizzy	Symptoms and Stress
T43	pregnant wife young family woman slowly age nurse ideas babies	Pregnancy
T44	hormones doctor pills blood appointment clinic test excited waiting days	GC Positivity
T45	things medical friend attack hospital apparently care bills panic heart	Health Finances Stress
T46	pain depression anxiety medication chronic extreme disorder dysphoria bipolar ocd	Mental Health
T47	brain stop science medicine term excuse injury vomit bigotry nonsense evidence	Variety of Symptoms and Society
T48	part healing thing open reason normal works medication sad wound	Medical Reaction - Negative
T49	bad hurt guy hit ache realize pain breaking felt stomach	Injuries
T50	tired hours sleep night sick morning bad migraine wake feeling	Sleep
T51	brain head headache migraine injuries bad migraines tumor deep breathing	Neurology - Headaches
T52	surgery gender change therapist clinic sex hormones transition numbing surgeries	General GC
T53	tired sleep night today tomorrow early woke insomnia stay bed	Sleep
T54	painful honestly sounds allergic bad incredibly reaction allergy metal feeling	Allergies

Table 3: Topics and Labels

From these 125 topics, 54 topics were relevant to health. Examples of irrelevant topics were those that discussed a health-related issue, but couched within a larger context, such as politics (e.g., "*trump, gop, abortion, president, debate*"). The middle column in Table 3 shows the top word for each of the topics that we found using LDA with 1000 iterations. Two members of the research team inductively labeled the topics based on the overall themes conveyed by the top words, then discussed and resolved any discrepancies in labeling (Table 3).

We compared these topics to other studies and surveys and found significant alignment. Specifically, the 2015 US Transgender Survey indicates that healthcare services such as insurance providers, transgender health care issues such as gender confirmation surgery and mental health are among the top concerns of transgender people (James, Herman, Rankin, Keisling, Mottet, & Anafi, 2016). Studies of transgender health issues also investigated diet, exercise, and disordered eating (VanKim, Erickson, Eisenberg, Lust, Simon Rosser, & Laska, 2014; Conron, Scott, Stowell, & Landers, 2012), sleep disorders (Shipherd, Green, & Abramovitz, 2010), drug use (Kecojevic, Wong, Schrager, Silva, Bloom, Iverson, & Lankenau, 2012), chronic pain disorders (Maurer, Lissounov, Knezevic, Candido, & Knezevic, 2016), body image (Atkins, 2012; Moradi, 2010), pregnancy (Light, Obedin-Maliver, Sevelius, & Kerns, 2014), and injury (House, Van Horn, Coppeans, & Stepleman, 2011).

Using the labels, we organized our 54 topics into seven categories including general healthcare, diet, healthcare services, mental health, symptoms, transgender healthcare, and wellbeing. Healthcare services and diet represent categories with the highest and the lowest number of topics, respectively (Figure 4):

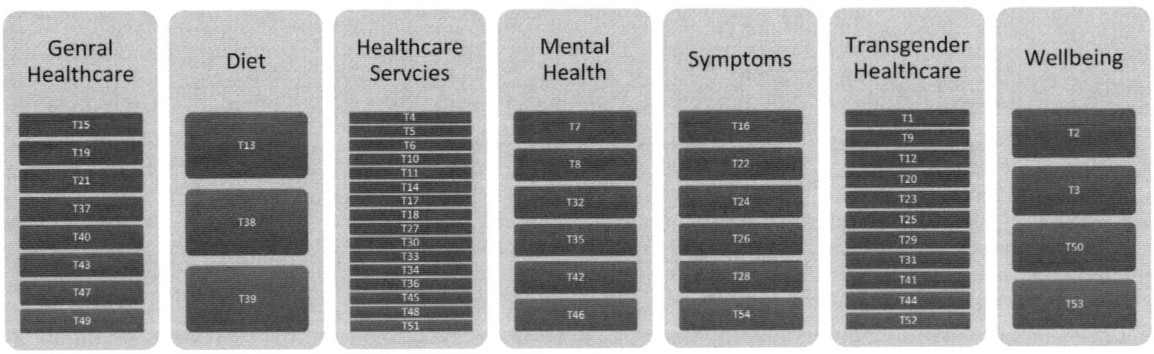

Figure 4: Categories of Topics

- **General Healthcare**: The category describes general physical states of being, activities, and sensations. It is broad and does not address specific diseases, disorders, or injuries, but rather health topics that impact a variety of populations. Topics include exercise, vision problems, drug use, and pain.
- **Diet**: Terms in this category are related to food and eating. Topic 13 was related to tweets mentioning fat-free, sugar-free, and milk-free food, indicating a desire for items within a certain diet. Topic 39 references specific food items as well as a discussion of meals. There is also the mention of "poisoning", indicating the bigram "food poisoning" occurred within these tweets. Topic 38 is primarily related to drinking with mentions of "water", "coffee", "alcohol", "tea", "coke", and just "caffeine." It also includes terms related to smoking as a habit.
- **Healthcare Services**: These topics are related to healthcare services as an institution. Individual topics address clinical care, hospitals, health insurance policies, and experiences related to health care. Topics 4, 6, and 10 are related to different legislation about expanded access to health care. Topics 27 and 30 are related to therapy. Topics 5, 34, 36, and 48 describe relaying and reacting to information about others' health care situations. These topics all show users' engagement within existing health care systems.
- **Mental Health**: These topics are related to a variety of mental health conditions. Topic 35 and associated tweets include terms related to body image and ability for users to appear as their identified gender. Topics 7 and 8 relate to stresses incurred by societal discrimination and lack of acceptance. Topic 32 discusses raising awareness of mental health. Topic 46 is a collection of terms related to specific diagnoses, treatments, and personal experiences. It includes "dysphoria" which refers to gender dysphoria and the sensation that a person's body does not match their identity. Topic 46 is related to the active experience of depression.
- **Symptoms**: These topics are similar to those in "general healthcare" but are more specific to a singular cause. Topics 22 and 24 are descriptions of the body aches, sore throats, and coughing related to the flu. Topic 26 is related to overexertion following exercise with cramps and leg and hip pain. Topics 28 and 54 are related to allergic reactions, and topic 16 is related to a general type of infection.
- **Transgender Healthcare**: These topics are specifically related to transgender healthcare. Topic 52 is a generalized collection of terms related to physical transitioning. Topic 25 focuses on the medical aspects of transitioning. Topics 29, 44,

23 and 41 are related to the personal and emotional experiences involved with transitioning. Topics 9, 31, and 20 are related to hormone replacement therapies as part of transitioning. Topic 1 is related to gender confirmation surgeries. Topic 12 is related to general LGBTQ health care, including issues of access and HIV.

- **Wellbeing**: These topics are related to day-to-day emotional and physical wellbeing. Topics 2 and 3 are related to recent past experiences and challenges. Topics 50 and 53 are both related to lack of sleep.

Similar to what we did in the linguistics analysis, we wanted to determine whether there was a difference in health topics discussed between TM and TW. To make this determination, we used probabilistic modeling. Specifically, for *n* tweets and *t* topics, LDA measures the probability of each topic occurring within each tweet or $P(T_k|D_j)$. We used $P(T_k|D_j)$ to find the weight of each of the topics for TM and TW separately, $WT(T_k)$. For an effective comparison, each of WTs was normalized by the sum of the weight scores of all topics:

$$\mathrm{N\_WT}(T_k) = \frac{\sum_{j=1}^{n} \mathrm{P}(T_k|D_j)}{\sum_{k=1}^{t}\sum_{j=1}^{n} \mathrm{P}(T_k|D_j)}$$

If $N\_WT(T_x) > N\_WT(T_y)$, it means that users were more likely to discuss topic *x* than topic *y*. Figure 5 shows that TW users discussed general healthcare and healthcare services categories more often than TM users. Conversely, TM users discussed mental health and wellbeing more than TW users. The differences between the other categories is negligible (less than 1%) For both genders, the most discussed category is healthcare services followed by transgender healthcare. The least discussed category is diet. This finding suggests the need for more research that identifies the unique health issues of TM and TW. This analysis addresses the limitations of prior research and surveys on transgender health issues to consider TM and TW separately.

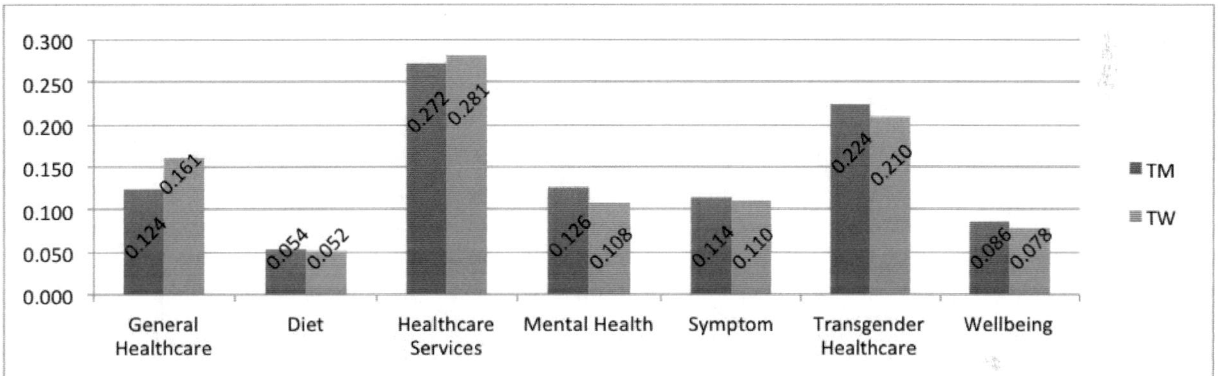

Figure 5: Weight of Categories

CONCLUSION

Lack of comprehensive information on the health-related information needs of LGBTQ people represents a significant barrier to improving their health outcomes. Current studies indicate limitations with current large-scale data collection options and the need for new, macro-level, standardized approaches for collecting and analyzing data related to LGBTQ health. Transgender populations represent an especially vulnerable subset of LGBTQ individuals, with a litany of negative health outcomes and barriers to affirmative and comprehensive health services. Fortunately, social media sites like Twitter provide a great opportunity for transgender users to share their health concerns and interests.

This paper employs a computational approach to collect tweets of self-identified transgender users and explore the linguistic and semantic patterns of their tweets. Identifying the health-related concerns and interests of transgender Twitter users can help medical and public health experts better understand the needs of sexual and gender minorities.

This research has several limitations. The first is that we collected the individuals voluntarily disclosing their identities on Twitter and did not consider other transgender users. Second, although we analyzed thousands of tweets, they were shared among less than 300 transgender users. Third, all the Twitter users in this study were located in the US. Our future research plan is to increase the sample size, incorporate temporal and spatial variables, and consider other users in LGBTQ community located in both non-US countries and in the US.

ACKNOWLEDGMENTS

This research is supported in part by the University of South Carolina Honors College Exploration Scholars and Magellan Scholar Programs. All opinions, findings, conclusions, and recommendations in this paper are those of the authors and do not necessarily reflect the views of the funding agency.

REFERENCES

Abbar, S., Mejova, Y., and Weber, I. (2015). You tweet what you eat: Studying food consumption through twitter. In Proceedings of the 33rd Annual ACM Conference on Human Factors in Computing Systems, pp. 3197-3206, ACM.

Arenas, E. S. (2018). Exploring Pornography in Widad Benmoussa's Poetry Using LIWC and Corpus Tools. *Sexuality & Culture*, 1-18.

Atkins, D. (2012). *Looking queer: Body image and identity in lesbian, bisexual, gay, and transgender communities*. Routledge.

Blei, D. M., Ng, A. Y., & Jordan, M. I. (2003). Latent dirichlet allocation. *Journal of machine Learning Research*, 3(Jan), 993-1022.

Blei, D. M. (2012). Probabilistic topic models. *Communications of the ACM*, 55(4), 77-84.

Byron, P., Albury, K., and Evers, C. (2013). "It would be weird to have that on Facebook": young people's use of social media and the risk of sharing sexual health information. *Reproductive health matters*, 21, 41, 35-44.

Byron, P., Rasmussen, S., Wright Toussaint, D., Lobo, R., Robinson, K. H., and Paradise, B, (2017). 'You learn from each other': LGBTIQ Young People's Mental Health Help-seeking and the RAD Australia Online Directory.

Cameron, M. A., Power, R., Robinson, B., and Yin, J. (2012). Emergency situation awareness from twitter for crisis management. In Proceedings of the 21st International Conference on World Wide Web, pp. 695-698., ACM.

Collins M., & Karami A. (2018), Social Media Analysis for Organizations: US Northeastern Public and State Libraries Case Study, Proceedings of the Southern Association for Information Systems (SAIS), Atlanta, GA.

Conron, K. J., Scott, G., Stowell, G. S., & Landers, S. J. (2012). Transgender health in Massachusetts: results from a household probability sample of adults. *American journal of public health*, 102(1), 118-122.

Golder, S. A., and Macy, M. W. (2011). Diurnal and seasonal mood vary with work, sleep, and daylength across diverse cultures. *Science*, 333, 6051, 1878-1881.

Gonzales, G., Przedworski, J., & Henning-Smith, C. (2016). Comparison of health and health risk factors between lesbian, gay, and bisexual adults and heterosexual adults in the United States: results from the National Health Interview Survey. *JAMA internal medicine*, 176(9), 1344-1351.

Grant, J.M., Mottet, L.A., Tanis, J., Harrison, J., Herman, J.L., & Keisling, M. (2011). Injustice at Every Turn: A Report of the National Transgender Discrimination Survey. Washington, DC: National Center for Transgender Equality and National Gay and Lesbian Task Force

Harrell, J. A., & Baker, E. L. (1994). The essential services of public health. *Leadership in Public Health*, 3, 3, 27-31.

Harrison, J., Grant, J., & Herman, J. L. (2012). A Gender Not Listed Here: Genderqueers, Gender Rebels, and OtherWise in the National Transgender Discrimination Survey, 2(1), 13.

House, A. S., Van Horn, E., Coppeans, C., & Stepleman, L. M. (2011). Interpersonal trauma and discriminatory events as predictors of suicidal and nonsuicidal self-injury in gay, lesbian, bisexual, and transgender persons. *Traumatology*, 17(2), 75.

James, S. E., Herman, J. L., Rankin, S., Keisling, M., Mottet, L., & Anafi, M. (2016). The Report of the 2015 U.S. Transgender Survey. Washington, DC: National Center for Transgender Equality.

Karami, A., Bennett, L. S., and He, X. (2018). Mining Public Opinion about Economic Issues: Twitter and the US Presidential Election. *International Journal of Strategic Decision Sciences* (IJSDS), 9(1), 18-28.

Karami, A., Dahl, A. A., Turner-McGrievy, G., Kharrazi, H., and Shaw, G. (2018). Characterizing diabetes, diet, exercise, and obesity comments on Twitter. *International Journal of Information Management*, 38, 1, 1-6.

Karami A., & Pendergraft N. M. (2018). Computational Analysis of Insurance Complaints: GEICO Case Study, International Conference on Social Computing, Behavioral-Cultural Modeling, & Prediction and Behavior Representation in Modeling and Simulation, Washington, DC.

Karami, A., & Zhou, B. (2015). Online review spam detection by new linguistic features. iConference 2015 Proceedings.

Karami A., & Zhou L. (2014a). Improving Static SMS Spam Detection by Using New Content-based Features, Proceedings of the 20th Americas Conference on Information Systems (AMCIS), Savannah, GA.

Karami, A., & Zhou, L. (2014b). Exploiting latent content based features for the detection of static sms spams. Proceedings of the American Society for Information Science and Technology, 51(1), 1-4.

Karami, A., Gangopadhyay, A., Zhou, B., & Kharrazi, H. (2018). Fuzzy approach topic discovery in health and medical corpora. *International Journal of Fuzzy Systems*, 20(4), 1334-1345.

Karami, A. (2017). Taming Wild High Dimensional Text Data with a Fuzzy Lash. In 2017 IEEE International Conference on Data Mining Workshops (ICDMW) (pp. 518-522). IEEE.

Karami, A., Gangopadhyay, A., Zhou, B., & Kharrazi, H. (2015a). A fuzzy approach model for uncovering hidden latent semantic structure in medical text collections. iConference 2015 Proceedings.

Karami, A., Gangopadhyay, A., Zhou, B., & Karrazi, H. (2015b). Flatm: A fuzzy logic approach topic model for medical documents. In the Annual Conference of the North American Fuzzy Information Processing Society (NAFIPS) held jointly with the 5th World Conference on Soft Computing (WConSC), (pp. 1-6). IEEE.

Karami, A. (2015). Fuzzy topic modeling for medical corpora. University of Maryland, Baltimore County.

Karami, A., & Gangopadhyay, A. (2014). Fftm: A fuzzy feature transformation method for medical documents. Proceedings of BioNLP 2014, 128-133.

Kecojevic, A., Wong, C. F., Schrager, S. M., Silva, K., Bloom, J. J., Iverson, E., & Lankenau, S. E. (2012). Initiation into prescription drug misuse: differences between lesbian, gay, bisexual, transgender (LGBT) and heterosexual high-risk young adults in Los Angeles and New York. *Addictive behaviors*, *37*, 11, 1289-1293.

Light, A. D., Obedin-Maliver, J., Sevelius, J. M., & Kerns, J. L. (2014). Transgender men who experienced pregnancy after female-to-male gender transitioning. *Obstetrics & Gynecology*, 124(6), 1120-1127.

Maurer, A. J., Lissounov, A., Knezevic, I., Candido, K. D., & Knezevic, N. N. (2016). Pain and sex hormones: a review of current understanding. *Pain management*, 6(3), 285-296.

McCallum, Andrew Kachites. "MALLET: A Machine Learning for Language Toolkit." http://mallet.cs.umass.edu. 2002.

Meerwijk, E. L., & Sevelius, J. M. (2017). Transgender Population Size in the United States: a Meta-Regression of Population-Based Probability Samples. *American Journal of Public Health*, 107(2), e1–e8. https://doi.org/10.2105/AJPH.2016.303578

Moradi, B. (2010). Addressing gender and cultural diversity in body image: Objectification theory as a framework for integrating theories and grounding research. *Sex Roles*, 63(1-2), 138-148.

Najafabadi, M. M., & Domanski, R. J. (2018). Hacktivism and distributed hashtag spoiling on Twitter: Tales of the# IranTalks. First Monday, 23(4).

Najafabadi, M. M. (2017). A Research Agenda for Distributed Hashtag Spoiling: Tails of a Survived Trending Hashtag. In Proceedings of the 18th Annual International Conference on Digital Government Research (pp. 21-29). ACM.

Nascimento, Thiago D., Marcos F. DosSantos, Theodora Danciu, Misty DeBoer, Hendrik van Holsbeeck, Sarah R. Lucas, Christine Aiello, Leen Khatib, and MaryCatherine A. Bender. (2014). Real-time sharing and expression of migraine headache suffering on Twitter: a cross-sectional infodemiology study. *Journal of medical Internet research*, 16(4).

Obedin-Maliver, J., Goldsmith, E. S., Stewart, L., White, W., Tran, E., Brenman, S., ... & Lunn, M. R. (2011). Lesbian, gay, bisexual, and transgender–related content in undergraduate medical education. *JAMA*, 306(9), 971-977.

Office of Disease Prevention and Health Promotion (2017, November 21). Lesbian, Gay, Bisexual, and Transgender Health. Retrieved from www.healthypeople.gov/2020/topics-objectives/topic/lesbian-gay-bisexual-and-transgender-health.

Priva, U. C., & Austerweil, J. L. (2015). Analyzing the history of Cognition using topic models. *Cognition*, 135, 4-9.

Reisner, S. L., Perkovich, B., & Mimiaga, M. J. (2010). A mixed methods study of the sexual health needs of New England transmen who have sex with nontransgender men. AIDS patient care and STDs, 24(8), 501-513.

Sell, R. L., & Holliday, M. L. (2014). Sexual orientation data collection policy in the United States: public health malpractice.

Shaw, G., & Karami, A. (2017). Computational content analysis of negative tweets for obesity, diet, diabetes, and exercise. Proceedings of the Association for Information Science and Technology, 54(1), 357-365.

Shipherd, J. C., Green, K. E., & Abramovitz, S. (2010). Transgender clients: Identifying and minimizing barriers to mental health treatment. *Journal of Gay & Lesbian Mental Health*, 14(2), 94-108.

VanKim, N. A., Erickson, D. J., Eisenberg, M. E., Lust, K., Simon Rosser, B. R., & Laska, M. N. (2014). Weight-related disparities for transgender college students. *Health Behavior and Policy Review*, 1(2), 161–171. http://doi.org/10.14485/HBPR.1.2.8

Webb, F., Karami, A., & Kitzie, V. (2018). Characterizing Diseases and disorders in Gay Users' tweets. Proceedings of the Southern Association for Information Systems (SAIS), Atlanta, GA.

Zou, B., Lampos, V., Gorton, R., and Cox, I. J. (2016). On infectious intestinal disease surveillance using social media content. In Proceedings of the 6th International Conference on Digital Health Conference (pp. 157-161). ACM.

What do the US West Coast Public Libraries Post on Twitter?

Amir Karami
University of South Carolina, USA. karami@sc.edu

Matthew Collins
University of South Carolina, USA. mcollinsga@hotmail.com

ABSTRACT

Twitter has provided a great opportunity for public libraries to disseminate information for a variety of purposes. Twitter data have been applied in different domains such as health, politics, and history. There are thousands of public libraries in the US, but no study has yet investigated the content of their social media posts like tweets to find their interests. Moreover, traditional content analysis of Twitter content is not an efficient task for exploring thousands of tweets. Therefore, there is a need for automatic methods to overcome the limitations of manual methods. This paper proposes a computational approach to collecting and analyzing using Twitter Application Programming Interfaces (API) and investigates more than 138,000 tweets from 48 US west coast libraries using topic modeling. We found 20 topics and assigned them to five categories including public relations, book, event, training, and social good. Our results show that the US west coast libraries are more interested in using Twitter for public relations and book-related events. This research has both practical and theoretical applications for libraries as well as other organizations to explore social media actives of their customer and themselves.

KEYWORDS

Library, social media, Twitter, text mining, semantic analysis.

INTRODUCTION

In the 21st century, libraries of all types are responding to the changing social, economic, and political impacts of living in a digital society. There are more than 9,000 public libraries[1] in the US that provide vital community services, such as early childhood literacy, computer training, and workforce development; they also invite community conversations and actions that further understanding and address local needs. In addition, public libraries act as a safe place for all patrons, reflecting and serving the diversity of their communities in their collections, programs, and services (ALA, 2014). In many communities, libraries advise patrons on issues; ranging from navigating the health system to helping those with housing needs. This "go-to" role has influenced library programming and events, with libraries providing advice and connections to health, housing, literacy, and other areas (Cabello & Butler, 2017). According to a 2015 Pew survey, almost two-thirds of Americans said that closing their local library would have a major impact on their community. Over 90 percent of adults think of public libraries as "welcoming and friendly places," and about half have visited or otherwise used a public library in the last 12 months (Zickuhr, Rainie, Purcell, & Duggan,2013).

Recent research indicates that more people are using social media applications. According to Statista Dossier (2014), the number of social network users will increase from 0.97 billion to 2.44 billion users in 2018, predicting an increase around 300% in 8 years. Considering its rapid development, social media may become the most important media channel for organizations to reach their clients in the near future (He, Zha, & Li, 2013; Moro, Rita, & Vala, 2016). Since its launch in July 2006, Twitter has quickly become one of the most popular social networking platforms for users to update their followers, and to provide convenient and effective information dissemination (Del Bosque, Leif, & Skarl, 2012; Shulman, Yep, & Tomé, 2015). Organizations have realized the potential of using internet-based social networks to influence customers, incorporating social media marketing communication in their strategies for leveraging their businesses. Measuring the impact of messaging is an important process for developing an effective social media strategy (Moro et al., 2016).

Beyond continued access to traditional collections and services, public libraries engage their patrons and communities through several new participation platforms, such as social media and maker spaces, which enable and mediate new forms of online user participation, engagement, access, and interactivity (Cavanagh, 2016). Social media applications have been increasingly adopted by libraries to market both resources and services as well as to enhance the relationship with their patrons. It enables "information and knowledge sharing, service enhancement and promotion, interaction with student library users, at minimal costs" (Collins & Quan-Haase, 2014; Chu & Due, 2013). Social media functions as a useful tool for libraries to reach out to current and prospective patrons outside of the physical library setting. Using social media can enable libraries to distribute

[1] http://www.ala.org/tools/libfactsheets/alalibraryfactsheet01

information through a medium with which many patrons are already familiar. Libraries must ensure the forms of social media they employ and the subsequent content they produce are relevant to the interests and information-based needs of their audience (Collins & Quan-Haase, 2014).

Research has shown that when a library has an engaged and active Twitter following, it is able to spread information more easily (Yep, Brown, Fagliarone, and Shulman, 2017). Twitter shows both sides of user evolution; as users offer their opinions and needs, libraries have real-time feedback they can utilize to adjust their services. Simultaneously, Twitter gives libraries unprecedented access to their users. Social media in general allows libraries to engage users who may otherwise never think of using the library's services. In addition to proactive community outreach programs, Twitter enables libraries to advertise their services and programs to many more users than traditional media. Mining these data provides an instantaneous snapshot of the content of public library tweets (Chew and Eysenbach, 2010). Social media sheds light on how patrons use library services, as well as assists academic libraries in advancing research (Yep, Brown, Fagliarone, and Shulman, 2017).

Apart from facilitating discussion between libraries, social media analysis (SMA) can also help libraries and other non-profit institutions to measure the satisfaction level of their users. When using SMA to their advantage, organizations are able to tailor their products to the needs of their clients and patrons. This is especially affordable for small and mid-size libraries that do not have the financial resources to afford traditional marketing campaigns. In addition to lower costs, libraries improve on serving their patrons when they utilize social media.

Twitter data analysis provides a convenient means of finding data for an organic user study. Twitter data have been applied in different domains such as health (Shaw, & Karami, 2017), business (Bollen, Mao, & Zeng, 2011), and politics (Karami, Bennett, & He, 2018; Najafabadi & Domanski, 2018; Najafabadi, 2017). For scholars who are looking for real-time conversational or text data, Twitter has provided a wealth of data for behavioral analysis (Karami, Bennett, & He, 2018), sentiment analysis (Shaw & Karami, 2017), trend analysis, information dissemination, and health surveillance (Karami, Dahl, Turner-McGrievy, Kharrazi, & Shaw, 2018; Webb, Karami, & Kitzie, 2018). Analyzing this vast amount of data can reveal knowledge and interesting patterns that can lead to new discoveries (He, Zha, & Li, 2013).

Although previous studies have provided valuable insights to social media analysis, other studies have yet to investigate the content of tweets posted by libraries to disclose their interests. In this study, we mine and analyze public library-related topics extracted from the Twitter accounts of 48 public libraries in the western US in order to examine how public libraries use social media to describe their services and interact with patrons. In the present study, we propose a computational approach to collect and analyze more than thousands of tweets to discover meaningful themes and semantic patterns in the data. This paper specifically addresses this question: *What do the US west coast public libraries post on Twitter?*

RELATED WORKS

Several previous studies have analyzed the content of social media posts. Twitter is one of the most popular social media applications used by studies from diverse fields, such as mental health (Jamison-Powell et al., 2012), libraries (Collins & Karami, 2018; Stvilia & Gibradze, 2017), and journalism and mass communication (Guo, Vargo, Pan, Ding, & Ishwar, 2016; Moro et al., 2016).

In an effort to help companies understand how to perform a social media competitive analysis and transform social media data into knowledge for decision makers and e-marketers, one study applied text mining to unstructured text content on Facebook and Twitter sites of the three largest pizza chains: Pizza Hut, Domino's Pizza and Papa John's Pizza. The authors manually collected data and utilized SPSS Clementine and Nvivo 9 for data analysis. Results revealed that the pizza chains actively used social media and have committed substantial resources for their social media efforts. The study also demonstrated that the three largest pizza chains have made significant social media efforts to increase interaction with customers and build brands in the online communities (He, Zha, & Li, 2013).

From another study that explored the role of social media in the discussion of mental health issues, and with particular reference to insomnia and sleep disorders, one research collected tweets using a tweet archiving application, but analyzed tweet content through a mixed methods approach. First, the Linguistic Enquiry and Word Count (LIWC) software performed an automated sentiment and linguistic content analysis, then the authors conducted a hand-coded, inductive thematic analysis. From the analysis six themes were identified. The study many several observations based on their content analysis, but unfortunately did not compare the automated and manual methods, nor state a methodological preference (Jamison-Powell, Linehan, Daley, Garbett, & Lawson, 2012). LIWC is a tool for capturing thoughts, feelings, personality, and motivations, to the dataset (Karami & Zhou, 2015; Karami & Zhou, 2014b).

Many studies have examined the content of library tweets, as well as the effectiveness of Twitter usage by libraries (Al-Daihani & AlAwadhi, 2015; Yep, Brown, Fagliarone, & Shulman, 2017). Aharony (2010) explored the use of Twitter in public and academic libraries to understand microblogging patterns. The study focused its research on three areas: (1) Do public libraries produce more or less tweets than academic libraries, (2) Is there a linguistic difference between tweets produced by public libraries and those produced by academic libraries, (3) Is the content of the tweets produced by public libraries different from that of tweets produced by academic libraries? Once data was collected manually, it was first, manually analyzed through a statistical descriptive analysis that described the basic features of the data in a study, and then secondly, manually examined with inferential content analysis which divided the tweets by topic categories and sub-categories. Results showed that the total number of tweets in public libraries was larger than the total number of tweets in academic libraries, most of the tweets posted by academic libraries used formal language and public libraries used informal language, and both kinds of libraries use Twitter to broadcast and share information about their activities, opinions, status, and professional interests.

METHODOLOGY AND RESULTS

This paper proposes a computational framework for mining the tweets of libraries to disclose their social media content in Twitter. This framework has four steps including Twitter account detection, tweets collection, topic discovery, and topic analysis (Figure 1).

Figure 1: Research Framework

Twitter Account Detection

The first step in this study is to detect the Twitter accounts of libraries in the western US west coast. We searched in Google to find the names of libraries in the five west coast states, including Alaska (AK), California (CA), Hawaii (HI), Oregon (OR), and Washington (WA). Then, we went to the websites of the libraries to find their Twitter account. In order to focus on active Twitter accounts, we selected accounts having at least 100 tweets such as the examples in Figure 1. Finally, we found 48 active Twitter accounts across five states, including 5 active Twitter accounts in Alaska; 22 in California; 1 in Hawaii; 9 in Oregon; and 11 in Washington (Table 1).

Figure 1: Twitter Accounts of 5 West Coast Libraries

State	Library Name
Alaska	Anchorage Public Library Ketchikan Public Library Kodiak Public Library Kuskokwim Consortium Library Homer Public Library
California	Los Angeles Public Library San Diego Public Library San Jose Public Library Fresno County Public Library Orange County Public Libraries San Francisco Public Library Marin County Free Library Solano County Library Pasadena Public Library Santa Cruz Public Libraries San Mateo County Libraries Santa Monica Public Library Monterey Free County Libraries Stanislaus County Library Long Beach Public Library Santa Clara County Library District Sacramento Public Library Alameda County Library Thousand Oaks Library Riverside County Library System Fortuna Library San Diego County Library
Hawaii	Hawaii State Public Library
Oregon	Multnomah County Library Beaverton City Library Cedar Mill Community Library Jackson County Library Services Salem Public Library Eugene Public Library Hillsboro Public Library Corvallis-Benton County Public Library Washington County Cooperative Library Services
Washington	King County Library System Sno-Isle Libraries Seattle Public Library Pierce County Library Edmonds Library Timberland Regional Library North Central Regional Library Tacoma Public Library Spokane County Library District Bellingham Public Library Whatcom County Library System

Table 1: The List of West Coast Libraries

Tweets Collection

To collect the tweets of each of the 48 libraries, we used the Twitter Application Programming Interfaces (API) in R platform[2]. Due to the API limit, we could only extract up to 3,200 tweets per account. After removing the duplicate tweets, we collected 138,056 tweets with 2,876.17 tweets per account (Table 2). Although California had the highest number of libraries in our dataset, based on average tweets/library score, it seemed that the Alaska and Oregon libraries were more active on Twitter. It is worth mentioning that this data will be publicly available in the first author's webpage.[3]

State	Number of Tweets	Number of Libraries	Average Tweets/Library
AK	26,739	5	5,347.8
CA	65,153	22	2,961.5
HI	1,739	1	1,739
OR	29,166	9	3,240.7
WA	24,259	11	2,205.36
Total	138,056	48	2,876.17

Table 2: Statitics of Tweets

Topic Discovery

Traditional concept analysis approach is not an efficient strategy to understand thousands of tweets (Karami, 2017). Therefore, there is a need to use computational methods to explore a huge number of social media posts (Karami, Gangopadhyay, Zhou, & Kharrazi, 2015a). We utilized topic modeling to discover topics in the collected tweets. Among different topic models, Latent Dirichlet Allocation (LDA) is an efficient machine learning method for text mining. LDA assumes that there are topics in a document and words can be assigned to the topics with different weights (Blei, Ng, & Jordan, 2003; Karami, 2015). This

[2] https://cran.r-project.org/web/packages/twitteR/twitteR.pdf
[3] https://sites.google.com/site/karamihomepage/

model categorizes the words that are semantically related in a topic and represented thematically. For example, this model assigns "life," "evolve," and "organism" to a topic with Evolution theme (Figure 2).

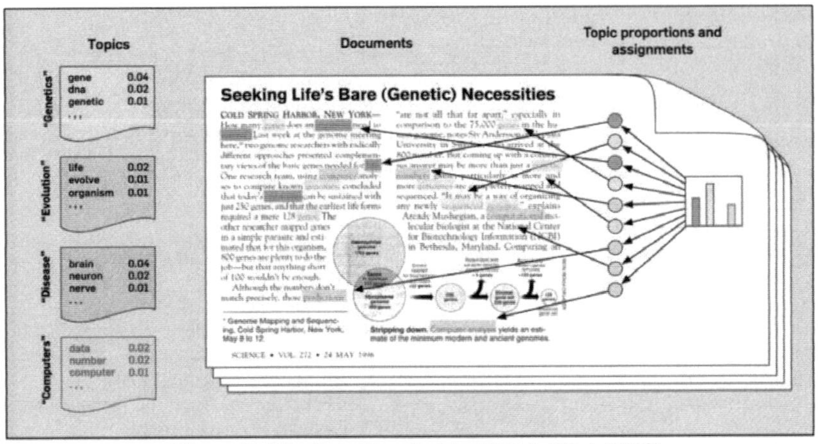

Figure 2: The Intuition behind LDA (Blei, 2012)

LDA has been used for different applications, such as medical research (Ghassemi, Naumann, Doshi-Velez, Brimmer, Joshi, Rumshisky, & Szolovits, 2014; Karami, Gangopadhyay, Zhou, & Kharrazi, 2018; Karami, Gangopadhyay, Zhou, & Karrazi, 2015b; Karami & Gangopadhyay, 2014), spam detection (Karami & Zhou, 2014a), and business (Karami & Pendergraft, 2018). While this text mining method has been applied on Twitter data, such as analyzing health tweets (Ghosh & Guha, 2013) and politics (Karami, Bennett, & He 2018), this model has not been considered for analyzing library tweets to disclose topics of interest in their social media posts. We applied Mallet Java-based implementation of LDA (McCallum, 2002). Mallet removed the stopwords such as "the" and "a" that do not have semantic value for our analysis. After removing the stopwords, such as "the" and "a" that don't have semantic value for our analysis, we found 20 topics (Table 3).

For *138,056* documents (tweets) and *20* topics, LDA also measured the probability for each of the topics in each of the documents or $P(T_k|D_j)$. We used $P(T_k|D_j)$ to find the weight of each of topics, $WT(T_k)$. For an effective comparison, each of WTs was normalized by the sum of the weight scores of all topics:

$$\text{N\_WT}(T_k) = \frac{\sum_{j=1}^{138,056} \text{P}(T_k|D_j)}{\sum_{k=1}^{20} \sum_{j=1}^{138,056} \text{P}(T_k|D_j)}$$

If $N\_WT(T_x) > N\_WT(T_y)$, it means that libraries posted more tweets about topic x than topic y. The first column of Table 3 shows the ranking of topics based on the weight of topics in Figure 3.

Topic Analysis

In this step, we labeled the associated words based on overall theme in each of the topics (Table 3). For example, "facebook," "posted," "photos," "online," and "exhibit" represents a topic related to "social media activities". This topic indicates the activities of the libraries in social media websites, such as Facebook. Table 3 also shows our interpretation and description for each of the topics in the second column. Using $WT(T_k)$ helped us to measure the weight of the topics and determine the rank for the libraries. While book recommendations, book reviews, and library hours are the three most frequent topics, health education, public service, and public talks are the least frequent according to our topics' ranking (Figure 3).

Rank	Associated Words for Topic Topic Description	Label
1	Associated words: books, read, book, list, favorite Describing books recommended by library staff for patrons.	Book Recommendations
2	Associated words: new, book, author, life, story Reviewing of the quality, author, plot, or subject of a book.	Book Reviews
3	Associated words: closed, open, library, hours, locations, branches Describing a library's hours of operation.	Library Hours
4	Associated words: free, learn, workshop, class, job, register Describing a training session or workshop at the library.	Public Trainings
5	Associated words: card, ebooks, collection, catalog, access, audiobooks Promoting the library's services, resources, and collection.	Promotions of Library Services
6	Associated words: great, awesome, staff, people, good, folks Describing gratitude or appreciation for staff, volunteers, or patrons.	Appreciation for Events
7	Associated words: county, community, public, support, libraries, board Requesting community and patron support for the library.	Request for Support
8	Associated words: free, movie, night, family, fun, games Describing a fun or enjoyable event at the library.	Fun Events
9	Associated words: summer, reading, program, kids, read Describing the upcoming summer reading program at a library.	Summer Reading Program
10	Associated words: book, author, join, local, event Describing a book-related event scheduled to occur at a library.	Book Events
11	Associated words: book, friends, big, sale, today Describing a book sale occurring at the library.	Book Sale
12	Associated words: teen, event, club, tonight, scavenger, hunt Describing a library event intended for teenagers.	Teen Events
13	Associated words: happy, celebrate, birthday, national, day, anniversary Describing an upcoming celebration to promote a program, issue, or campaign.	Theme Days and Months
14	Associated words: event, public, today, city, park Describing an event scheduled to occur nearby.	Local Events
15	Associated words: music, free, concert, tonight, rock, jazz Describing an upcoming musical performance or concert.	Music Events
16	Associated words: story, time, kids, ages, children's, stories Describing a library event planned for children.	Children's Events
17	Associated words: facebook, posted, photos, online, exhibit Describing information posted to a library's social media account.	Social Media Activities
18	Associated words: healthy, life, food, learn, health, garden Describing issues and resources for healthy living.	Health Education
19	Associated words: business, tax, learn, resources, free, great Describing resources and services provided by the library.	Public Services
20	Associated words: learn, today, talk, join, news Describing an upcoming talk or lecture at the library.	Public Talks

Table 3. Library Topic Descriptions

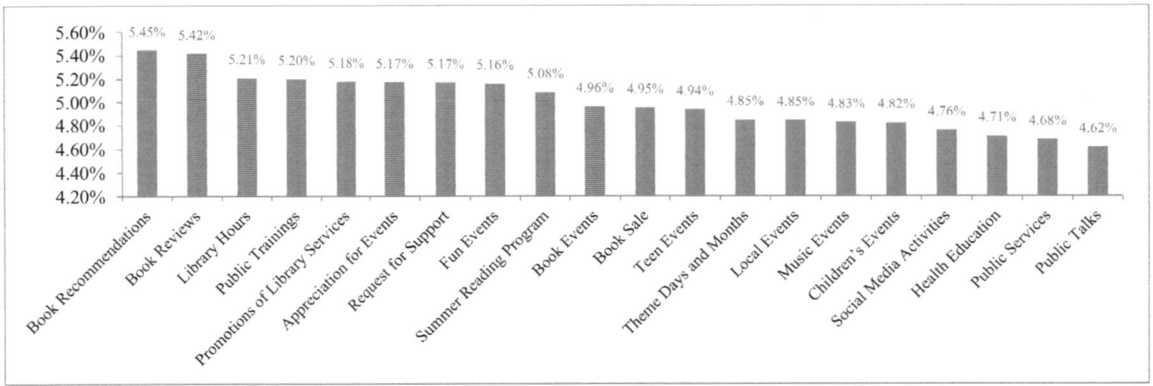

Figure 3. Weight of Topics

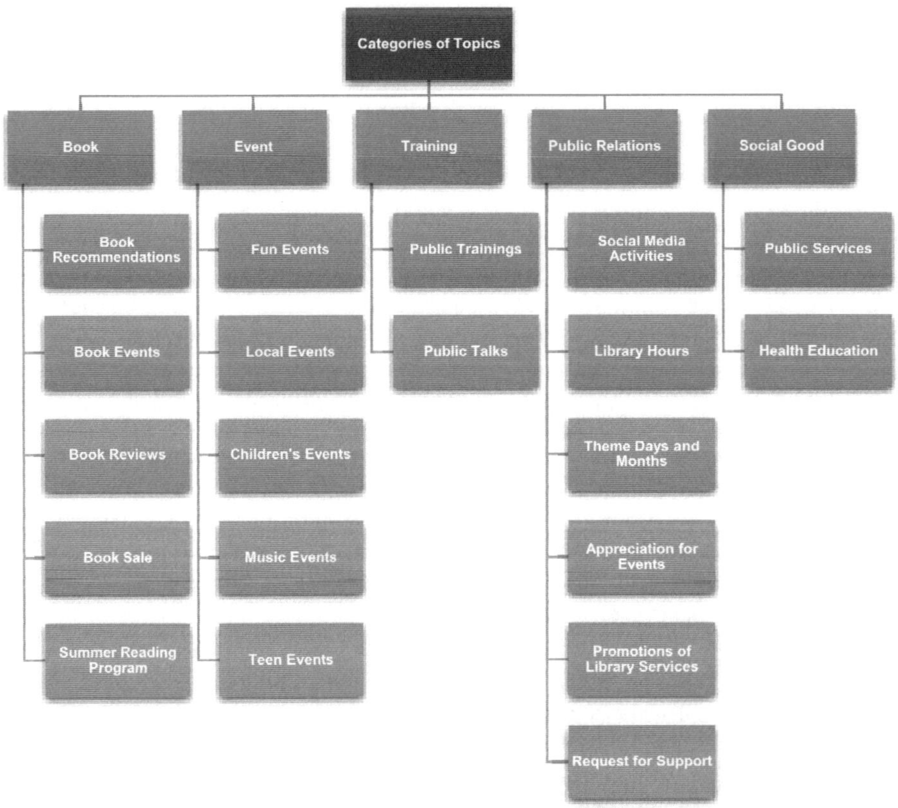

Figure 4: Categories of Topics

We also observed that the 20 topics could be assigned to five categories representing multiple topics including book, event, training, public relations, and social good (Figure 4):

1. The **Book** category shows the topics that book-related issues including book recommendations, book events, book reviews, book sale, and summer reading program.
2. The **Event** category describes library and local events including fun events, local events, children's events, music events, and teen events. The book events was assigned to the book category.
3. The **Training** category represents two topics including public trainings and public talks. This category is about library and non-library trainings, workshops, lectures, or talks occurring including public trainings and public talks.
4. The **Public Relations** category describes topics regarding the library public communication. The six related topics are social media activities, library hours, theme days and months, appreciation for events, promotions of library services, and request for support.

5. The **<u>Social Good</u>** category covers the topics related to issues benefiting the entire community such as tax filing. The topics are related to this category: library services and health education.

We also used $N\_WT(T_k)$ to find the weight of categories for each state. This means that we combined the weight of topics for each category and then found the weight of the category and normalized it. For example, we measured the total weight of public training (PTr) and public talks (PTa) for the libraries in Oregon. Then calculated the sum of PTr and PTa (PTr + PTa) as the weight of training category for Oregon. Figure 5 shows the weight of each of the five categories for each state along with the total weight of categories using a west cost (WC) label. It seems that around 55% of tweets were about public relations and book categories. We also found that:

- *Public relations*, *event*, and *book* were the top three categories in four states; in Alaska, the event category had a higher weight than the book category. These three categories were discussed in around 80% of the tweets.
- There is no specific pattern for training and social good categories. While Alaska, Hawaii, and Oregon libraries preferred training more than social good in their Twitter posts, libraries in California and Washington were vice versa. The total weight of these two categories was around 20%.

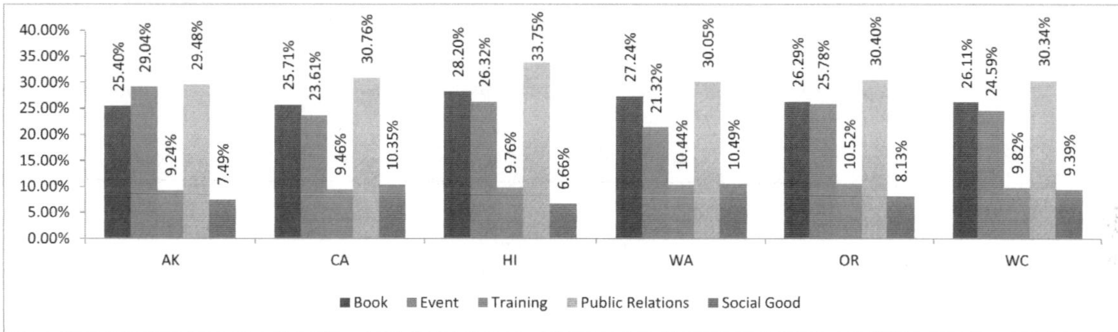

Figure 5: Weight of Categories per State

CONCLUSION

Twitter is a popular social media for different organizations to disseminate information for their followers. There is a wide range of studies to investigate what people and organizations post on Twitter; however, there is no study to detect the interests of public libraries in Twitter. This study proposed a computational framework to collect and explore thousands of tweets to disclose hidden semantic structure in them. We used LDA to find 20 topics and grouped them into five categories. LDA also helped us to find the weight of topics across the five states in our corpus.

The methodology and results in this paper have practical applications for library studies. Libraries as well as other organizations can reap benefit from this study by computational analysis of their social media content. Our future research plans will consider user location and time of tweet as added layers for investigating Twitter accounts of other US and non-US libraries.

ACKNOWLEDGMENTS

This research is supported in part by the Provost Office Social Science Research Grant and the first author's startup research funding provided by the School of Library and Information Science at the University of South Carolina. All opinions, findings, conclusions and recommendations in this paper are those of the authors and do not necessarily reflect the views of the funding agency.

REFERENCES

Al-Daihani, S. M., & AlAwadhi, S. A. (2015). Exploring academic libraries' use of Twitter : a content analysis. *The Electronic Library*, *33*(6), 1002–1015. https://doi.org/10.1108/EL-05-2014-0084

American Libraries Association (ALA). (2014). *State of America's Libraries Report 2014*. Retrieved from http://www.ala.org/news/state-americas-libraries-report-2014

Blei, D. M., Ng, A. Y., & Jordan, M. I. (2003). Latent Dirichlet Allocation. *Journal of Machine Learning Research*, *3*, 993–1022.

Blei, D. M. (2012). Probabilistic topic models. Communications of the ACM, 55(4), 77-84.

Bollen, J., Mao, H., & Zeng, X. (2011). Twitter mood predicts the stock market. *Journal of Computational Science*, 2(1), 1-8.

Cabello, M., & Butler, S.M. (2017, March 30). How public libraries help build healthy communities? *The Brookings Institution*. Retrieved from https://www.brookings.edu/blog/up-front/2017/03/30/how-public-libraries-help-build-healthy-communities/

Cavanagh, M. F. (2016). Micro-blogging practices in Canadian public libraries: A national snapshot. *Journal of Librarianship and Information Science*, *48*(3), 247–259. https://doi.org/10.1177/0961000614566339

Chew, C., & Eysenbach, G. (2010). Pandemics in the Age of Twitter: Content Analysis of Tweets during the 2009 H1N1 Outbreak. *PLoS ONE*, 5(11), 1–13. https://doi.org/10.1371/journal.pone.0014118

Chu, S., & Du, H. (2013). Social networking tools for academic libraries. *Journal of Librarianship and Information Science*, 45(1), 64-75. https://doi.org/10.1177/0961000611434361

Collins, G., & Quan-Haase, A. (2014). Are social media ubiquitous in academic libraries? A longitudinal study of adoption and usage patterns. *Journal of Web Librarianship*, 8(1), 48–68. https://doi.org/10.1080/19322909.2014.873663

Collins M., & Karami A. (2018), Social Media Analysis for Organizations: US Northeastern Public and State Libraries Case Study, Proceedings of the Southern Association for Information Systems (SAIS), Atlanta, GA.

Del Bosque, D., Leif, S. A., & Skarl, S. (2012). Libraries atwitter: trends in academic library tweeting. *Reference Services Review*, 40(2), 199–213. https://doi.org/10.1108/00907321211228246

Dossier, Statista (2014). Social media & user-generated content—Number of global social network users 2010-2018-Statista Dossier 2014. Retrieved September 10, 2015, from http://www.statista.com/statistics/278414/number-of-worldwide-socialnetwork-users/

Gao, W., & Wallace, L. (2017). Data Mining, Visualizing, and Analyzing Faculty Thematic Relationships for Research Support and Collection Analysis. In *ACRL 2017* (pp. 171–178). Baltimore.

Ghosh, D., & Guha, R. (2013). What are we 'tweeting'about obesity? Mapping tweets with topic modeling and Geographic Information System. *Cartography and Geographic Information Science*, 40(2), 90-102.

Guo, L., Vargo, C. J., Pan, Z., Ding, W., & Ishwar, P. (2016). Big Social Data Analytics in Journalism and Mass Communication: Comparing Dictionary-Based Text Analysis and Unsupervised Topic Modeling. *Journalism & Mass Communication Quarterly*, 93(2), 332–359. https://doi.org/10.1177/1077699016639231

He, W., Zha, S., & Li, L. (2013). Social media competitive analysis and text mining: A case study in the pizza industry. *International Journal of Information Management*, 33, 464–472. https://doi.org/10.1016/j.ijinfomgt.2013.01.001

Jamison-Powell, S., Linehan, C., Daley, L., Garbett, A., & Lawson, S. (2012). "I can't get no sleep": Discussing #insomnia on Twitter. In *Proceedings of the SIGCHI Conference on Human Factors in Computing Systems* (pp. 1501–1510). Retrieved from http://andygarbett.co.uk/wp-content/uploads/2016/05/Jamison-Powell-et-al-I-Cant-Get-No-Sleep.pdf

Karami, A., Bennett, L. S., & He, X. (2018). Mining Public Opinion about Economic Issues: Twitter and the US Presidential Election. International Journal of Strategic Decision Sciences (IJSDS), 9(1), 18-28.

Karami, A., Dahl, A. A., Turner-McGrievy, G., Kharrazi, H., & Shaw, G. (2018). Characterizing diabetes, diet, exercise, and obesity comments on Twitter. *International Journal of Information Management*, 38, 1, 1-6.

Karami, A., Gangopadhyay, A., Zhou, B., & Kharrazi, H. (2018). Fuzzy approach topic discovery in health and medical corpora. International Journal of Fuzzy Systems, 20(4), 1334-1345.

Karami A., & Pendergraft N. M. (2018). Computational Analysis of Insurance Complaints: GEICO Case Study, International Conference on Social Computing, Behavioral Cultural Modeling, & Prediction and Behavior Representation in Modeling and Simulation, Washington, DC.

Karami, A. (2017). Taming Wild High Dimensional Text Data with a Fuzzy Lash. In 2017 IEEE International Conference on Data Mining Workshops (ICDMW) (pp. 518-522). IEEE.

Karami, A. (2015). Fuzzy topic modeling for medical corpora. University of Maryland, Baltimore County.

Karami, A., Gangopadhyay, A., Zhou, B., & Kharrazi, H. (2015a). A fuzzy approach model for uncovering hidden latent semantic structure in medical text collections. iConference 2015 Proceedings.

Karami, A., Gangopadhyay, A., Zhou, B., & Karrazi, H. (2015b). Flatm: A fuzzy logic approach topic model for medical documents. In the Annual Conference of the North American Fuzzy Information Processing Society (NAFIPS) held jointly with the 5th World Conference on Soft Computing (WConSC), (pp. 1-6). IEEE.

Karami, A., & Zhou, B. (2015). Online review spam detection by new linguistic features. iConference 2015 Proceedings.

Karami, A., & Gangopadhyay, A. (2014). Fftm: A fuzzy feature transformation method for medical documents. Proceedings of BioNLP 2014, 128-133.

Karami, A., & Zhou, L. (2014a). Exploiting latent content based features for the detection of static sms spams. Proceedings of the American Society for Information Science and Technology, 51(1), 1-4.

Karami A., & Zhou L. (2014b). Improving Static SMS Spam Detection by Using New Content-based Features, Proceedings of the 20th Americas Conference on Information Systems (AMCIS), Savannah, GA.

Moro, S., Rita, P., & Vala, B. (2016). Predicting social media performance metrics and evaluation of the impact on brand building: A data mining approach. *Journal of Business Research*, *69*(9), 3341–3351. https://doi.org/10.1016/j.jbusres.2016.02.010

Najafabadi, M. M., & Domanski, R. J. (2018). Hacktivism and distributed hashtag spoiling on Twitter: Tales of the# IranTalks. First Monday, 23(4).

Najafabadi, M. M. (2017). A Research Agenda for Distributed Hashtag Spoiling: Tails of a Survived Trending Hashtag. In Proceedings of the 18th Annual International Conference on Digital Government Research (pp. 21-29). ACM.

Shaw, G., & Karami, A. (2017). Computational content analysis of negative tweets for obesity, diet, diabetes, and exercise. *Proceedings of the Association for Information Science and Technology*, 54(1), 357-365.

Shulman, J., Yep, J., & Tomé, D. (2015). Leveraging the Power of a Twitter Network for Library Promotion. *The Journal of Academic Librarianship*, 41(2), 178–185. https://doi.org/10.1016/j.acalib.2014.12.004

Stvilia, B., & Gibradze, L. (2014). Library & Information Science Research What do academic libraries tweet about, and what makes a library tweet useful? *Library and Information Science Research*, *36*(3–4), 136–141. https://doi.org/10.1016/j.lisr.2014.07.001

Webb, F., Karami, A., & Kitzie, V. (2018). Characterizing Diseases and disorders in Gay Users' tweets. Proceedings of the Southern Association for Information Systems (SAIS), Atlanta, GA.

Yang, T.-I., Torget, A. J., & Mihalcea, R. (2011). Topic Modeling on Historical Newspapers. *Proceedings of the 5th ACL-HLT Workshop on Language Technology for Cultural Heritage, Social Sciences, and Humanities,* (June), 96–104.

Yep, J., Brown, M., Fagliarone, G., & Shulman, J. (2017). Influential Players in Twitter Networks of Libraries at Primarily Undergraduate Institutions. *The Journal of Academic Librarianship*, 43(3), 193–200. https://doi.org/10.1016/j.acalib.2017.03.005

Zickuhr, K., L. Rainie, K. Purcell, & M. Duggan. (2013). "How Americans value public libraries in their communities." *Pew Research Internet Project*. http://www.pewinternet.org/2014/03/13/library-engagement-typology/

Algorithmic Reputation and Information Equity

Michael Katell
University of Washington, USA. mkatell@uw.edu

ABSTRACT

In this paper I offer a theory of reputation and information systems. As a form of human judgement and a tool for decision making, I argue that the social process of reputation plays a central role in essential human functions and that one's ability to control reputation is a mark of power over important decisions concerning one's fate. Algorithmic reputation can be understood as a type of reputation that has been transformed from a familiar and visible interpersonal process to a commodified and remote data process. I argue that we ought to evaluate algorithmic reputation as the digital expression of the social process of reputation and situate it within existing moral obligations and interests. Reputations can be fraught with error and bias but perform vital social and economic functions nonetheless. Reputation absolutists would require that we subsume any concerns about reputational fairness, such as the risk of disparate effects on members of marginalized social groups, to the ideals of information transparency and business efficiency. I conclude that we risk enshrining societal inequity as algorithmic destiny by committing to the absolutist position on reputational transparency, posing serious risks to the functioning of a free and fair information society.

KEYWORDS

Reputation, algorithms, equity, marginalization

INTRODUCTION

Information systems play an increasingly important role in determining human fates. Algorithms that process the vast troves of data about human activities are used to make predictions about individuals ranging from their purchasing preferences to their suitability as employees. The power of prediction is the key feature of decision support products and services offered in the information marketplace, which claim to reduce the tedium and inefficiency of human decision making while increasing its precision and objectivity. Meanwhile, scholars and other observers suspect that such systems are encoded with societal biases that reflect harmful racial, ethnic, gender, and other stereotypes (Barocas & Selbst, 2016). Examples of algorithmic bias have been revealed or are suspected in numerous technical artifacts, including: criminal defendant risk assessment systems that over-predict recidivism risk for African Americans while under-predicting such risks for White defendants (Angwin, Larson, Mattu, & Kirchner, 2016); online search and image services that are more likely to portray African Americans as criminals, non-human animals, and sex workers (Noble, 2018); and various consumer and financial scoring systems that discourage the selection of marginalized people for essential opportunities (Citron & Pasquale, 2014). Scholars who have suggested or revealed the discriminatory effects of various technical artifacts often situate their perceived failures with the biases and blind spots of a given system's designers and the business models involved. I argue, however, that we should avoid the tendency to look upon algorithmic prediction and decision systems as mere artifacts that can be individually examined, confronted, and repaired. Rather, I suggest that digital information systems are not individuated artifacts as much as they are expressions of human information practices rendered in digital form. As such, they can and should be evaluated as extensions of human social practices and evaluated together with the social processes they are meant to supplement or replace. Rather than interrogating technical systems and practices as bundles of design and marketing choices, we should situate them within preexisting and ongoing debates about the proper distribution of information affordances within human society. We can approach this work by examining the social process known as "reputation."

Human reputation is an information practice that emerges from observations and reports about a person's utterances and actions. Reputational information can be a particularly "slippery" type of information in that, by nature, it is a reductionist sketch of some aspect of a person and can be understood quite differently from one information consumer to another. Despite the ephemeral and inconstant nature of reputations, they are very powerful because they play a key role in essential human functions such as cooperation, including the transaction of business. Because a person's reputation is often considered by decision makers with the power to grant or deny access to economic and other opportunities, the individual's agency—her ability to participate in decisions about her fate—is closely linked to her ability to shape and contain her reputation as it is understood by others. Individuals or institutions in a position to choose others for access to important opportunities, like jobs and loans, are motivated to reveal as much as possible about their candidates. The candidate, meanwhile, has her own interests to promote that may be thwarted by obligatory or involuntary informational transparency. Within this tension of competing interests and contested claims to information access lie questions about the moral obligations of cooperative agents and the role of reputation in promoting autonomy, mitigating risk, and asserting societal ideals.

Algorithmic profiling is a powerful information practice that takes place through the observational and analytic affordances of information systems. Recruiting software, tenant screening services, criminal risk assessment, and dating apps are among the many products and services already available that utilize profiling techniques that include algorithmic processing of user data. Information products in this space mix information supplied by subjects with data held by others to derive predictive insights about a person in the form of risk scores, employability grades, and other categoricals (Singer, 2014). New methods for risk management in a range of opportunity and punitive realms, such as employment, housing, incarceration, public benefits, and intimate relationships, have strong appeal, but they may obscure the hazard of shrouding vexing social problems such as human fallibility and discriminatory bias in technocratic garments without actually "solving" them.

By dint of its accessibility, abundance, and perseverance, data collection and sharing within information systems vastly increases the quantity of materials that can be used to evaluate people as potential cooperators and transactants. It is for this reason I offer a new reputation type: *algorithmic reputation*, by which I mean human reputation as it is constructed from data captured during human interaction with information systems and then reproduced as consumable "insights" using automated data processes acting on the vast stores of personal data available from commercial and state entities. Algorithmic reputation can be understood as a form of reputation that is removed from strictly social settings and reimagined as a software process. Because algorithmic reputation typically involves a degree of automation, artificial intelligence technologies (e.g. machine learning, neural networks) participate in the turn towards making reputation a digital, as well as a social information process.

This article is organized as follows: First, I begin by offering a brief definition of reputation as an information phenomenon that emerges from human society and consider the effects of social marginalization on reputational assessments. I then describe its digital variant, algorithmic reputation, and associate it with the mechanisms and goals of reputation. I then discuss the value of reputation and the competing interests of agents involved in reputational exchanges. I close by addressing the tension between reputation "absolutism" and equitable information practices.

REPUTATION

A reputation is a set of semi-stable impressions about a specific subject held by others. Put another way, it is "a shared, or collective perception about a person" (Solove 2007, 1993, 11). I propose that the mechanisms of reputation are *collection,* in which some particular phenomena are observed or inferred; *interpretation,* in which collected information is shaped and analyzed; and *transmission,* in which the information is conveyed to others. Within each of these mechanisms of reputational formation, the agent performing the action has opportunities to choose what data is important enough to notice and retain, how to integrate the new data within her existing knowledge and belief systems, and how to convey something meaningful to others. The resulting reputations may include a mixture of facts, beliefs, and intuitions about the prior deeds of another, which are used to hold them accountable for their pasts and to project their likely futures. Within this understanding, reputation has two distinct but overlapping features. First, within communities we use reputation as a tool of social inclusion. A positive reputation invites social acceptance and esteem. A negative reputation puts one at risk of rejection and scorn. The acceptance-rejection dimension of reputation is one of reward and punishment that has a powerful normative effect that incentivizes individuals to comply with the perceived expectations of her community or assessors. A second dimension of reputation it its use to predict what a person will do in the future. In this dimension, reputation may be used by a decision maker who controls access to an opportunity to determine suitability or trustworthiness. An example of this latter dimension is that of an employer choosing prospective employees. In a typical recruiting context, an employer considers various types of reputational data—resumes, interviews, references, tests, certifications, etc.—to make predictions about how various applicants will perform in a particular role. Individuals are likely to desire to control this aspect of their reputations, but much of the work of prediction occurs outside of their immediate influence. A job applicant can study hard for a certification exam and take care to dress well for a job interview, but she cannot control how much the exam score will count or whether her clothing suits the tastes of her interviewers.

An individual's reputation is an especially valuable social and economic asset but it vulnerable to misrepresentations and misunderstandings by others. While some facts about a person are incontrovertible, other aspects of reputation defy certainty and require interpretation. Reputational assessors are often confronted with conflicting information that requires evaluation and reconciliation. The amount of control a reputational subject has over her own reputation is rarely total. Given the role that reputation plays for access to essential opportunities, such as jobs and other economic opportunities, reputational control corresponds to agency—the ability to influence decisions that affect one's life. An individual asserts reputational agency by self-consciously building and maintaining a reputation that suits her social and economic aspirations. This work is reflected Goffman's description of aspects of the reputational information exchange as a *performance* during which a subject leaves *impressions* with one or more observers that emerge from her direct and indirect *expressions* within a particular context (Goffman, 1990 [1959]). Subjects can contribute to their reputations by acting in accordance with their reputational aspirations (capable, loyal, wise, etc.), but except for the most concrete types of performances (e.g. paying bills on time, passing a skills test) the level of influence depends on a range of social factors including the ability the subject to perform the roles required to meet some standard, as well as the range of judgements others are prepared to make.

What Goffman demonstrates is that reputations are co-constructed between reputational subjects and their assessors. While a motivated candidate can influence her reputation, reputational subjects rely on other people to recognize and value them. A single assessor, whether rightly or wrongly trusted by others, can dramatically change one person's reputation and potentially sideline them from access to essential life opportunities. In 1996, following a bombing at the Summer Olympics, security guard named Richard Jewel was initially celebrated as a hero for discovering the bombs, notifying authorities, and helping to clear the area before the bombs exploded. After a law enforcement leak suggested that Jewel was a suspect in the bombing, there was a dramatic change in his public reputation. Despite Jewel's eventual exoneration in the bombing case, he endured months of negative publicity, a deeply tarnished reputation, and an untimely death (Brenner, 2007). The Richard Jewel case demonstrates how little control one can have over a reputation. The fragility of reputation and the role of others in forming it extends beyond individuals to include collective entities, such as businesses. A business can spend years establishing itself or its products as high quality, trustworthy, safe etc. and then experience a single public relations disaster from which they might never recover.

Reputation and Social Marginalization

Reputational agency is linked to social power. While anyone can be made vulnerable by informational transparency, members of non-dominant racial, ethnic, and gender classifications, as well as people living in poverty, are especially vulnerable because discreditable information about them is made more widely available due to their life circumstances and their increased levels of dealings with public institutions who maintain meticulous records about them. For example, people living in poverty are more likely to be employed in jobs that entail workplace surveillance and they are more likely to interact with government institutions that collect data, such as agencies that provide social services and financial support (Madden, Gilman, Levy, & Marwick, 2017). While there may be justifiable reasons for surveillance in such contexts, a result is the overrepresentation of marginalized persons in data sets that become available for reputational data processes. Surveillance data, collected over time, is likely to reveal at least a few discreditable facts about the people surveilled. Few if any members of a society are perfect and consistent in fulfilling their responsibilities and moral obligations. The extent to which one's imperfections become a matter of public record or are widely known corresponds to a variety of social factors, including but not limited to social status. Just as celebrities who live in the spotlight are subject to greater-than-average risks of exposure due to constant attention, other segments of the population who are more often subject to routine observation are also more likely to have discreditable information about them come to light. For marginalized persons, this is due, in part, to the types of activities that are most heavily surveilled as matters of policy. Consequently, negative reputations are not always the result of true moral turpitude as much as they reflect one's exposure to disproportionate attention. Marginalization increases the risk of discreditable facts coming to light and being used in the formation of reputation.

ALGORITHMIC REPUTATION

Just as reputation is built from the collection, interpretation, and transmission of information about a person, profiling systems collect, interpret, and produce reputational assessments. Algorithmic reputation is the digital incarnation of the familiar form of reputation, which we can refer to for clarity as "interpersonal reputation." Algorithmic reputation appears in the information landscape as the accumulation of data repositories about people and the process of generating analytic conclusions and predictions from that data. As people interact with digital systems, such as mobile apps and websites, their navigation choices, locations, 'clicks' and communicative expressions are logged and tracked. Much of this data travels far beyond the context in which it is collected to be exchanged in secondary data markets. Service providers and data brokers collect additional personal information from other sources, such as government databases and credit card processors, which is then aggregated to create more detailed repositories. Thus, data produced by a person in disparate, seemingly unconnected realms is brought together under individual profiles that become progressively richer with detail. The collection and aggregation of user information from multiple sources and over time, coupled with computational analysis and comparisons with data about others, functions like interpersonal reputational processes to produce new information about the person that is believed to be predictive of her otherwise unknown behaviors, choices, and attitudes.

The capabilities of these collections and systems are enormous, fueled by the increasing reliance of people on search and social information platforms and the resulting data generated by the surveillance and capture activities that accompany their use. As Nissenbaum observes, advances in computer storage and the technologies of data analysis mean that:

> "a) there is virtually no limit to the amount of information that can be recorded, b) there is virtually no limit to the scope of the analysis that can be done, bounded only by human ingenuity, and c) the information may be stored virtually forever...information that was once scattered and transient may now be ordered, systematized, and made permanent" (Nissenbaum, 1998, 577-578).

Notably, Nissenbaum believed in 1998 that the limits of "human ingenuity" would bound the digital processing of information (1998, 574). In the intervening years, however, developments in artificial intelligence suggest that human ingenuity is no longer the bounding condition. In contemporary data practice, accumulated data is analyzed using various techniques, including "machine learning" (ML), an artificial intelligence technology that identifies meaningful patterns based on an engineer's prompts and then learns to identify others autonomously (Barocas & Selbst, 2016).

Reputation and its digital variant, algorithmic reputation, are both used for similar purposes, such as evaluating prospective employees, romantic partners, tenants, and university students. There are dozens of employment recruiting and vetting systems that automatically identify and screen job candidates using profiling methods that include accessing social media profiles and government databases, as well as some that use artificial intelligence to interpret facial expressions, vocal ticks, and other candidate facets (Buranyi, 2018). Tenant screening and mortgage lending services that use profiling methods and data sources are also available in the information marketplace (Kayyali, 2016; Wei, Yildirim, Van den Bulte, & Dellarocas, 2015). Other than its use in advertising and consumer influence, recruiting and evaluating prospective employees is possibly the most developed use of algorithmic profiling. However, the market is robust and any opportunity to supplant familiar forms of reputational judging with an algorithmic variant is likely to be pursued. Yet this does not render algorithmic reputation entirely distinct from interpersonal reputation. They are both information constructs. The construction of systems of reputation involves a series of choices about what to notice, how to interpret it, and who should know about it. The structure of these mechanisms is not a given. Reputational systems, interpersonal or algorithmic, reflect human goals and world views.

The Power of Algorithmic Reputation

Algorithmic reputation departs in similarity from its origins as a social process mainly in the methods and actors involved in the collection, interpretation, and transmission of reputational information. Collecting reputational information requires sustained attention, interpretation of what has been observed requires cognitive effort, and transmission requires additional effort plus a receptive information market. Arguably, contemporary information services provide extraordinary power to perform all of these tasks. However, this does not necessarily make algorithmic reputation "better." The societal value of reputation does not lie entirely on in the detail or perseverance of a set of reputational data. Prior generations may have benefited from the relative transitivity and ephemerality of interpersonal reputation by encouraging assessors to accept more risks and to adapt to changing circumstances while permitting reputational subjects to evolve and, when appropriate, leave their pasts behind. One view of premodern life describes a sort of informational equilibrium in which each community member was unlikely to know a significant amount more about her neighbors than they knew about her. Similarly, governments and other institutions were also functionally constrained in the amount of information they could collect and retain about members of society (Doyle & Veranas, 2014). Reputations formed within this functionally limited information landscape could still perform their function without acquiring totalizing power and oppressive permanence. Scholars have suggested that institutional policies of "forgetting" aspects of a person's reputation are evidence of the value of limited information affordances: Bankruptcies and bad credit are removed from financial records over time; Juvenile convictions are sealed after a person reaches the age of majority; Even traffic offenses fade in importance after a few years (Blanchette & Johnson, 2002). The opportunity for reputations to recover after missteps enables individuals to return to civic life and a chance to contribute to socially productive ends. On this view, one of the risks contemporary information systems is that their power results in the creation of algorithmic reputations whose reach and perseverance limit that societal participation, particularly for those who are more likely than others to be surveilled and exposed (2002, 36-39). Of course, there are may be many reasons for desiring to know as much about individuals as possible, such as for the achievement of national security and the mitigation of business risk. Algorithmic approaches to reputation may serve these ends far better than interpersonal reputation. Facially, these are laudable goals for which many defenses have been offered, and indeed, the privacy literature contains a rich debate about the whether the achievement of security or the mitigation of risk "trump" the risks of personal information exposure (Himma, 2016; Moore, 2016). However, it can be argued that reputational systems constructed and employed with a restraint that respects baseline considerations of human well-being and social productivity serve similarly important goals.

THE VALUE OF REPUTATION

In this section, I discuss the value of reputation and its correspondence to the values promoted by algorithmic reputation. I begin by illustrating the role of reputation in cooperative projects and then suggest that reputation in all its forms implicates a set of moral considerations for cooperators.

Cooperation and Contemporary Information Systems

Cooperation, particularly forms of cooperation that occur voluntarily, is highly dependent on reputation. Cooperation is here defined as any joint activity requiring at least two persons who must coordinate their actions in order to sustain it. Companies, baseball games, and friendships are all examples of cooperative projects. Daily cooperative projects, such as maintaining interpersonal relationships, cultivating food, and engaging in trade aim towards human well-being because they create the conditions for productive human endeavors and the survival of the species. Of course, cooperation is not required for all human activity. Individuals can do many things for themselves and may survive without the assistance of other human beings. Some humans are content (or required) to live without others and to live solitary, self-reliant existences. However, while living without cooperating is possible to do, it is not inherently part of human nature.

Information systems offer many potential strategies and tools to increase the effectiveness and efficiency of cooperative tasks by, for example, making it possible for cooperators to work together and exchange information without sharing physical space and for providing data and techniques for the reputational analysis of potential partners. Algorithmic reputation also has its benefits for increasing the scope of understanding about potential cooperators and mitigating the risk of choosing ineffective or destructive partners. However, the remoteness and inscrutability of algorithmic reputation may deny humans control or awareness of the reputational assessments being made about them, thereby reducing their agency and social power. An example of this is the use of automatic assignment of scores and categories assigned to potential cooperators, such as in recruiting software that chooses, grades, and sorts job applicants. On the one hand, recruiters may benefit from the efficiency of a tool that winnows down an applicant pool based upon some set of preselected criteria. On the other hand, such systems can fail if they employ criteria that undervalues potential job candidates due to their membership in a particular demographic group by say, assigning lower scores to applicants with gaps in their employment history without considering that this may disproportionately impact women who have taken time off to have children. The increasing popularity of machine learning techniques makes algorithmic decision processes even more inscrutable, even to the programmers who design them. As has been demonstrated in cases ranging from detecting a teen pregnancy based on her shopping habits to exposing the real names of sex workers to their clients on social networks, complex analytic systems can develop insights about sensitive topics and social connections without directly accessing protected, shielded, or otherwise private information (Etzioni, 2011; Seelye et al., 2015). While it may be possible to "fix" systems that surface sensitive information or that are believed to promote unfair or inequitable decision patterns, the opaqueness and proprietary nature of commercial information systems make them particularly challenging to contest. In interpersonal reputational realms, laws and policies exist to instruct assessors and to limit certain disclosures, such as revealing irrelevant criminal histories, family planning, or medical conditions to potential employers. Laws and policies designed to achieve economic fairness are by no means perfect, but the average person is more likely to have access to tools of human accountability than they are to have the means or permission to audit complex, proprietary software. Human evaluators are capable of flexibly adapting their understandings of circumstances and their decisions are visible to other observers who can bear witness and hold them to account. Visibility, flexibility, and especially accountability are difficult to achieve in automated processes, including algorithmic reputation.

THE MORAL OBLIGATIONS OF REPUTATION

In this section, I argue that humans have moral obligations in the co-creation of reputation and in its use, particularly when making decisions about access to economic opportunities. The shape of such obligations may not be obvious for the parties involved because reputational subjects and assessors have competing interests in how reputations are created and applied.

In joint projects that involve access to a desirable opportunity or punitive sanction, there is typically an agent who occupies the role of "chooser" and one or more agents who occupy the role of "candidate." Choosers act as gatekeepers, selecting among candidates who may desire access to an opportunity, such as a job or a home, or who may be subject to a punitive sanction, such as a jail sentence. Choosers and candidates who are not intimately known to each other rely on some form of reputation in such choices, but their interests are frequently in conflict; choosers, as reputational assessors, typically desire to gain as complete a picture of a candidate as possible while candidates, as reputational subjects, may desire that some information be kept private, seeking to control the information flows that form their reputations. Both parties seek to mitigate their respective risks and to promote their respective goals. In contexts such as jobs and housing, the interests of choosers correspond to economic gains or losses and to the productive ends of their endeavors. Candidates in such contexts seek to assert control over information and its effects on their reputations to mitigate the risk of not gaining access to something desirable, which often involves their potential for economic gains or losses.

Contesting an Absolutist View of Reputation

In the domain of reputation, candidates may be obligated to provide truthful information about themselves in order to demonstrate their respect for their assessors. Manipulating or obscuring information about oneself can be equated to treating choosers disrespectfully and dismissing their interests. Indeed, where the desire of one party to control or hold back information is in conflict with another's desire to access it, it may appear that choosers, especially those in command of important projects, have the superlative moral claim in desiring to know as much about potential candidates as possible. As a practical matter, choosers may have the fate of an entire firm to consider while a candidate has only herself to worry about. We can refer to this view as an "absolutist" view of reputation. For absolutists such as Richard Posner, the desire for candidates to control and possibly limit access to information about themselves is characterized as "concealing discreditable facts" and the promotion of favorable "misapprehensions" (Posner 1978, 5). Posner makes an economic argument that such concealment is indefensible because it results in the inefficient sorting of candidates, leading to a loss of productivity.

This seems to pose a problem for a candidate who wishes to limit access to some information, such as her plans to have children or her sexual orientation out of concern that choosers may reject a qualified candidate based on personal or practical biases about such matters. Pregnancy and sexual identity are among the areas of life that have exposed many individuals to discrimination. Yet, Posner argues that transactants in a cooperative exchange have a fundamental right to know exactly who they are dealing with. Any and all information should be available to decision makers so they can mitigate their risks and secure the success of their firms. This stems from his view that the purpose of human society is "productivity," broadly defined to include both market and non-market activities. Therefore, concealing any and all information places the concealer in moral jeopardy because she threatens the success of productive activities, be they businesses or friendships. Algorithmic reputation would seem to further the goals set by Posner to make as much information as possible available for decision makers by reducing the costs increasing the depth of reputational assessment.

I offer three objections to Posner's view of reputational fairness. First, Posner arbitrarily prioritizes the interests of choosers over candidates, requiring candidates to respect the interest of choosers without similarly requiring reciprocal respect for candidates. This failure denies candidates the respect of equal consideration. Posner's rests his argument on the fulfillment of economic success for choosers—business firms in particular—while appearing indifferent to the success of candidates. If a chooser is morally unconstrained in what they may learn about a candidate, there is nothing to stop them from going to the limits of their abilities to learn it. Posner suggests that the reasonableness of such pursuits is limited by an economic equilibrium because a chooser is only likely to pursue information about a candidate until the costs of the pursuit surpass the economic gains from acquiring it (Poser, 1981). However, information technology has dramatically lowered the costs and functional barriers to acquiring information about people. Algorithmic reputation systems have access to a wealth of diverse data sources and can easily reveal where people go, what they read, what they buy, and who they know. Tomorrow's technology will reveal even more including perhaps our innermost thoughts (Pais-Vieira, Lebedev, Kunicki, Wang, & Nicolelis, 2013). If a hiring manager for a gym seeking a fitness trainer decides not to hire an otherwise well-qualified candidate based on an algorithmic inference of her political views or a prediction about her future health, Posner might consider that decision unwise or ultimately inefficient for the chooser, but otherwise permissible. The wide latitude this position provides to cooperative choosers, including employers, would limit access to opportunities to a narrow list of only the seemingly risk-free, "safe" candidates, diminishing the life chances of the rest. Meanwhile, Posner does not propose that such enforced transparency be mutual. He defends the secrecy of business firms in their operations, including some forms of deception, because business success might depend upon secret knowledge or the ability to conduct research in private. For Posner, the "legitimate strategic plans of business" serve a "valuable social purpose" and are therefore worthy of protection (Posner, 2008, 246). We might call this "trickle-down flourishing" because he appears to be arguing that granting a right to shield information from view to only some actors provides net benefits to all. It may be defensible to argue that firms should be able to assert control over the flows of business information for reasons of economic gain and continued solvency, but we can make similar arguments about the economic interests promoted by information control for candidates. Reputational subjects as candidates can also benefit by keeping some information out of their reputational profiles if it results in the attainment of a profitable life opportunity. While this does not address problems of willful deception on anyone's part to gain an economic advantage, it nevertheless suggests that applying one set of rules to one party to a transaction that are not applied to all is neither facially fair nor equitable. Privileging the interests of choosers, as Posner has, over the interests of candidates contravenes the ideals of democratic society by granting rights to one class of actors while denying it to another.

While willful deception may not always be defensible, I argue that some forms of non-disclosure are legitimate. We see this in a second objection to Posner, who has little to offer to a candidate whose "discreditable" history can be plausibly linked to factors beyond her control, such as her marginalized social status. Reputations are social products shaped by the social contexts in which they are formed. These include contexts of discrimination. African American men are disproportionately charged with drug offenses despite evidence that drugs are consumed and sold by Whites at similar rates (Fellner, 2009). This results in an African American job applicant being statistically more likely to have a criminal record than their White counterparts who engage in the same behavior. Criminal records are major barriers to gainful employment, housing, higher education, and other opportunities. Even for candidates with clean records, contemporary profiling technologies make it possible to learn about a candidate's friends or family members from their connections online, tainting the chances of selection for members of entire demographic groups where disproportionate arrests or other discreditable events are more likely to be discovered within family and other interpersonal networks.

Even if such indicators could be shown to truly predict poor performance in cooperation, the predictors would function primarily on only more marginalized demographic groups, while failing to function the same way for members of non-marginalized groups. Unequal distributions of information transparency might achieve some of the risk mitigation goals of choosers, but principles of democratic equality suggest that choosing these limited gains results in unacceptable costs to entire demographic segments. When policymakers seek to limit certain disclosures based on histories of discriminatory selection based on race, ethnicity, gender, or other marginalizing category (i.e. civil rights law), the goal is to limit the influence of bias found in the historical record in order to promote more equitable future outcomes for demographic groups that have suffered exclusionary discrimination. Information technology can sidestep such efforts through the algorithmic analysis of data and networks, as described above, but also with statistical methods and artificial intelligence analyses that are capable of identifying patterns in data that might not be evident to unaided human observers. Posner treats all persons as if they come to opportunities having been treated fairly and equally until the moment of selection. Decades of civil rights struggles suggest that this is not the case and that a certain amount of "concealment of discreditable facts" may be merited in order to ameliorate the discriminatory wrongs of history. Whether or not algorithmic reputation systems are capable of respecting these boundaries and social aspirations is an open question.

A third objection to Posner is offered by Doyle (2013) who points out that total transparency, especially when aided by information or medical technology, can have unintended consequences that serve neither choosers nor candidates well. Emerging technologies make it possible to reveal far more about the potential risks of cooperating with others than was previously possible. Abramson (2015) offers a telling example: The increasing sophistication and cheap accessibility of DNA analysis can be used to reveal a propensity for certain genetic disorders. If choosers could access and use such information in selecting potential cooperators, the result could be the creation of a "biological underclass" of candidates permanently barred from participating in cooperative projects (Abramson, 2015, 27-28). While screening out candidates based on their propensity for health problems appears to contribute to the goals of risk mitigation, it also creates conditions of moral hazard for choosers who can be tempted to pursue the full extent of reputational transparency. Doyle suggests that deepening the transparency of candidates would result in inefficient labor markets because entire classes of prospective candidates would be reluctant to apply for positions they are otherwise qualified to perform. Industries would struggle to find workers for a variety of roles, raising their costs while potentially depressing the wages of arbitrarily disfavored workers. While it may be true that some choosers could maximize their risk avoidance by thoroughly embracing algorithmic reputation to its absolute end, their potential gains must be counted against the losses to overly-transparent candidates and to a range of economic and social problems resulting the compulsory disclosure of sensitive personal facts.

CONCLUSION

In this article I have proposed to employ a fresh understanding of the familiar social artifact of reputation while linking it to its digital variant—algorithmic reputation. I have shown that algorithmic reputation applies similar mechanisms to assessing people and is similarly imperfect in doing so. I have also shown that the power of information technology can dramatically amplify all aspects of reputation, including its potential harms.

Algorithmic reputation, while powerful and arguably efficient, threatens to disrupt the familiar processes and norms of reputation. Familiar forms of reputational assessment are imperfect; they can be fraught with error, distortion, and biases that reflect many overlapping social histories and agendas, as well as basic human frailty. But this may be how reputation is supposed to work; by functioning at human scale where its understandings and applications are negotiated in the open and also mediated through law and policy. Attempts to extend reputation as an algorithmic process do not necessarily remove its imperfections but may instead subsume them beneath the obscurity of code and commercial secrecy.

We may have more information and more methods by which to evaluate each other than ever before, but the view of fairness and equity presented here suggests that providing increasingly revealing reputational data to the information marketplace is likely to provide benefits primarily to one subset of society while making others worse off. Algorithmic reputation presently operates without sufficient accountability to provide a check on such harms. As is true generally of information technologies, algorithmic reputation offers a mix of social costs and benefits. While we pursue the latter, we should be mindful of the former to prevent the diminishment of human agency and opportunity, and thereby foreclosing on the goals of achieving a free and equitable information society.

REFERENCES

Abramson, J. (2015). Searching for Reputation: Reconciling Free Speech and the Right to Be Forgotten. North Carolina Journal of Law & Technology, 17, 1–78.

Angwin, J., Larson, J., Mattu, S., & Kirchner, L. (2016, May 23). Machine Bias: There's Software Used Across the Country to Predict Future Criminals. And it's Biased Against Blacks. ProPublica. Retrieved from https://www.propublica.org/article/machine-bias-risk-assessments-in-criminal-sentencing

Barocas, S., & Selbst, A. D. (2016). Big Data's Disparate Impact. California Law Review, 104, 671–732.

Blanchette, J.-F., & Johnson, D. G. (2002). Data Retention and the Panoptic Society: The Social Benefits of Forgetfulness. The Information Society, 18(1), 33–45.

Brenner, M. (2007, August 1). American Nightmare: The Ballad of Richard Jewell. Vanity Fair. Retrieved from https://www.vanityfair.com/magazine/1997/02/brenner199702

Buranyi, S. (2018, March 4). "Dehumanising, impenetrable, frustrating": the grim reality of job hunting in the age of AI. The Guardian. Retrieved from http://www.theguardian.com/inequality/2018/mar/04/dehumanising-impenetrable-frustrating-the-grim-reality-of-job-hunting-in-the-age-of-ai

Citron, D. K., & Pasquale, F. (2014). The Scored Society: Due Process for Automated Predictions. Washington Law Review, 89(1), 1–33.

Doyle, T., & Veranas, J. (2014). Public anonymity and the connected world. Ethics and Information Technology, 16(3), 207–218.

Etzioni, A. (2011). Privacy Merchants: What is to be Done, The. U. Pa. J. Const. L., 14, 929.

Fellner, J. (2009). Race, Drugs, and Law Enforcement in the United States. Stanford Law and Policy Review, 20, 37.

Goffman, E. (1990). The presentation of self in everyday life (Repr). London: Penguin.

Himma, K. E. (2016). Why Security Trumps Privacy. In A. D. Moore (Ed.), Privacy, security, and accountability: ethics, law and, policy. London ; New York: Rowman & Littlefield International.

Kayyali, D. (2016, August 23). Big data and hidden cameras are emerging as dangerous weapons in the gentrification wars. Retrieved August 29, 2016, from http://qz.com/763900/surveillance-and-gentrification/

Madden, M., Gilman, M. E., Levy, K. E., & Marwick, A. E. (2017). Privacy, Poverty and Big Data: A Matrix of Vulnerabilities for Poor Americans. Retrieved from https://papers.ssrn.com/sol3/papers.cfm?abstract_id=2930247

Moore, A. D. (2016). Why Privacy and Accountability Trump Security. In A. D. Moore (Ed.), Privacy, security, and accountability: ethics, law and, policy. Lanham, MD: Rowman & Littlefield International.

Nissenbaum, H. (1998). Protecting Privacy in an Information Age: The Problem of Privacy in Public. Law and Philosophy, 17(5/6), 559–596.

Noble, S. U. (2018). Algorithms of oppression: how search engines reinforce racism. New York: New York University Press.

Pais-Vieira, M., Lebedev, M., Kunicki, C., Wang, J., & Nicolelis, M. A. L. (2013). A Brain-to-Brain Interface for Real-Time Sharing of Sensorimotor Information. Scientific Reports, 3, 1319. https://doi.org/10.1038/srep01319

Posner, R. A. (1978). Privacy, Secrecy, and Reputation 1978 James McCormick Mitchell Lecture, The. Buffalo Law Review, 28, 1–56.

Posner, R. A. (1981). The Economics of Privacy. The American Economic Review, 71(2), 405–409.

Posner, R. A. (2008). Privacy, surveillance, and law. The University of Chicago Law Review, 75(1), 245–260.

Seelye, A., Hagler, S., Mattek, N., Howieson, D. B., Wild, K., Dodge, H. H., & Kaye, J. A. (2015). Computer mouse movement patterns: A potential marker of mild cognitive impairment. Alzheimer's & Dementia: Diagnosis, Assessment & Disease Monitoring, 1(4), 472–480.

Singer, N. (2014, December 27). The Scoreboards Where You Can't See Your Score. The New York Times. Retrieved from http://www.nytimes.com/2014/12/28/technology/the-scoreboards-where-you-cant-see-your-score.html

Solove, D. (2007). The future of reputation: gossip, rumor, and privacy on the Internet. New Haven: Yale University Press.

Wei, Y., Yildirim, P., Van den Bulte, C., & Dellarocas, C. (2015). Credit Scoring with Social Network Data. Marketing Science, 35(2), 234–258.

Understanding the Information needs of Social Scientists in Germany

Dagmar Kern
GESIS – Leibniz-Institute for the Social Sciences, Cologne, Germany, dagmar.kern@gesis.org

Daniel Hienert
GESIS – Leibniz-Institute for the Social Sciences, Cologne, Germany, daniel.hienert@gesis.org

ABSTRACT

The information needs of social science researchers are manifold and almost studied in every decade since the 1950s. With this paper, we contribute to this series and present the results of three studies. We asked 367 social science researchers in Germany for their information needs and identified needs in different categories: literature, research data, measurement instruments, support for data analysis, support for data collection, variables in research data, software support, networking/cooperation, and illustrative material. Thereby, the search for literature and research data is still the main information need with more than three-quarter of our participants expressing needs in these categories. With comprehensive lists of altogether 154 concrete information needs, even those that are only expressed by one participant, we contribute to the holistic understanding of the information needs of social science researchers of today.

KEYWORDS

Information needs, social science, user study

INTRODUCTION

The Social Sciences look at the social relationships between humans and their interactions within the society and incorporate disciplines such as Sociology, Demography, Education/Pedagogy, Psychology, Communication Studies, Economics, and Political Science (cp. Hogeweg-de Haart 1983). It is a broad research field with different actors, different interests, and different information needs. Already in 1979, Brittain (1979) discussed the specialties of the social sciences such as imprecise terminology, the absence of experiment replication, different schools of thought and a lack of consensus. Hogeweg-de Haart (1983) stated that the scope of the social sciences is broad, not well defined, and it varies a lot in different definitions and in different countries. Also, in each discipline potentially an unlimited number of themes could be addressed. Because of this and the interlinking of different disciplines, the variety of primary information types used is large. Additionally, secondary use of existing data plays an important role for social scientists and requires the search for archived research data for reuse. A couple of decades later, the scope of social science research has increased even further, and the introduction of digital media has opened new fields for activities, e.g., the upcoming field of computational social science (Gilbert 2010). Furthermore, there is a trend towards open science with open publications, open data and open methodology in the context of the FAIR-principles (findable, accessible, interoperable, re-usable, Wilkinson 2016). Applying the FAIR-principles enables a better way for replication and reuse of research outcomes but also cause new activities and new information needs on the side of the researchers.

In this paper, we present the results of three studies to capture the current information needs of social scientists in Germany. We performed a diary study in which 12 participants protocolled their information needs over a period of two weeks. In a second study, we presented 25 pre-formulated information needs in a questionnaire to 18 social science researchers and let them vote which information needs match their own. In the last study, 337 participants expressed their information needs in an online survey.

RELATED WORK

There is a long tradition of studies to capture and understand the information use and needs as well as seeking behaviors of social scientists from the 1950s to nowadays. Folster (1995) summarizes the conclusions from three decades of research: (1) journals are the preferred information source for social scientists, (2) following citations is the preferred method, (3) informal channels play an important role, and (4) library services do not play a major role. Line (1971) reports on a study of information use and needs of social scientists in the UK of the 1970s. Data was gathered mainly by questionnaire (n=1,098), interviews (n=125) and daily observations. The results show the use of different information channels (mainly periodicals, then books, government publications, research reports, computer printouts, colleagues, etc.) but also different methods of locating this information (mainly bibliographies or references, then experts, abstracts and indexes, discussion, etc.).

Slater (1988) conducted thirty to forty interviews in the UK about the information needs of social scientists. Three interesting observations were that (1) a major library in the UK for the social sciences in general would be needed, that (2) there is a lack of a library dedicated just to social science methodology and that (3) online access to abstracting and indexing services was the way forward for the social sciences. Folster (1989) in 1987 surveyed social science researchers at University Wisconsin-Madison with 119 valid questionnaires. Similar to the study of Line (1971) they found out that journals are the most important source of information and tracking citations is the highest ranked method of seeking information. Computerized literature search was ranked lowest. De Tiratel (2000) examined the information use of social scientists in Argentina and found a similar information-seeking behavior as in prior studies of English-speaking countries such as the use of books and journals and the use of informal channels. Agrawal (1987) reports on similar information sources for social scientists in India. Shen (2007) conducted interviews with four professors of the social faculty of Wisconsin-Madison to identify information needs, sources and what causes problems in information search. She states that unlike research found before the 1990s, researchers make extensive use of electronic resources to find not only literature but also existing research datasets for secondary analysis. The major problems for researchers are that information is scattered in different places and that it is too much information.

Focusing on information seeking behavior, Ellis (1989) conducted interviews with academic social scientists and identified six broader categories of information seeking patterns: (1) starting (initial search for information), (2) chaining (following referential connections such as references), (3) browsing (e.g. by scanning of journals or table of contents), (4) differentiating (between sources to filter materials), (5) monitoring (the field of interest by following sources such as journals or conferences), and (6) extracting (relevant materials from sources). In a comparison study with physicists and chemists, Ellis et al. (1993) found two more categories: verifying (the accuracy of information) and ending (activities at the end of the project such as paper writing). Meho & Tibbo (2003) conducted e-mail interviews with sixty social science faculty members from 14 different countries to see if Ellis' model holds after the emergence of the World Wide Web and also on an international scale. They approved the model but could add four more categories: accessing (the material found with the methods above), networking (with colleagues to exchange information), verifying (the accuracy of the information), and information managing (by archiving and organizing information).

Identified already in earliest studies (e.g., Hogeweg-de Haart 1983), the re-use of research data for secondary analysis is a typical characteristic of social science research practice. Recently, with the upcoming of more and more data and online data platforms related work tries to understand the context and implications of data re-use. For the field of qualitative social science research Corti (2007) describes a number of factors that have the potential for the re-use of data sets: revisiting, reanalyzing and comparing with complementary data sources. For quantitative research this holds true, but here data mainly consists of survey data with attitudes, behaviors and factual information of a population group (Dulisch, 2015). Curty (2016) discusses benefits, risks, effort, social influence, facilitating conditions and reusability of data reuse based on interviews with 13 social scientists. Data re-use can avoid the time-consuming primary data collection and gathering process. Faniel et al. (2016) conducted a larger survey with 1,480 journal authors who have cited research data sets from the Inter-University Consortium for Political and Social Research (ICPSR). Data attributes such as completeness, accessibility, ease of operation, and credibility correlate positively with the re-users' satisfaction. The difference in the retrieval of literature and datasets is addressed in a work of Kern & Mathiak (2015). In a lab study and with telephone interviews, they found that the quantity and quality of the metadata are much more important in dataset retrieval. To identify if the data has the potential to answer their research question a lot of materials need to be scanned (codebook, questionnaire, raw data) which is much more time-consuming than having a look in a paper to judge its relevance.

DIARY STUDY

With the goal to find real information needs of social scientists, we performed our first study - a diary study. The study took place in January and February 2016. We asked social scientists to protocol their information needs over a period of two weeks. We provided them a protocol that starts with an introduction, our contact information for questions, a couple of examples and a two-column table. They were expected to write their current information need or the problem to be solved in the first column before they start to solve it and in the second column they ought to provide us information about the approach they used to meet their information need.

Participants

12 participants took part in the diary study (5 female, 7 male; mean age 37.5, SD=4.17). All of them are German social science researcher. 11 participants work at our research institute which focuses on empirical social science. One works as a professor at the University of Düsseldorf. Three of the participants have a doctoral degree, and the remaining 9 have a master's degree or equivalent and are working on a Ph.D. project.

Results

Altogether, we collected 54 statements. On average, participants indicated 4.5 (SD=2.42) individual information needs. We categorized the statements (see table 1) and provide examples for each category and the approaches the subjects followed to fulfill the information need.

Category	**Number of statements (n=12)**	**Examples for information needs in this category**	**Approaches / Tools / Portals**
Literature	19	From a specific author, on a specific topic, for a lecture, to get an overview, full texts	Web of Science, university library, ResearchGate, Google Scholar, Google, references of known/found papers, personal contacts, personal libraries, author's websites, library catalogs, digital libraries
Support for data analysis	9	On mappings, on metadata schemes, on network analysis, on classification of open answers	Looking for specific tools and specifications via Google, Google Scholar; personal contacts, YouTube, project websites
Research data	4	Data sets to a specific topic, that applied a specific test	Data catalogs, specialist literature, personal contacts
Illustrative material	4	Images, diagrams, videos	Web, Wikipedia, YouTube, Pixabay,
Definition /concepts	3	By a specific author, to a specific topic	Google (topic, author)
Networking /cooperation	3	Reviewers for a paper, journal, etc.; Who can give a talk on a specific topic	Sowiport, contacts
Support for data collection	3	Information about planning and designing a questionnaire, example questionnaires, recruiting of participants	Unipark, project websites, Google, mailing lists, Xing
Funding	2	Funding opportunities, What kind of research was already funded?	Institutional websites, Google
Strategy paper	2	On a specific topic	Specialist literature, personal contacts
Software support	1	On network analysis	YouTube, Google Books, personal contacts, support pages, user forum
Literature to a specific data set	1	Who used a specific data set?	Google
Reference lists	1	Geographic area data	Federal Statistical Office, Wikipedia
Measurement instruments	1	Scale to study personality traits	specialist literature, personal contacts
Training	1	Communication skills	Google, personal contacts

Table 1. Categories of information needs of social science researchers (n=12), number of statements in each category, examples and approaches to fulfil the information need.

QUESTIONNAIRE ON INFORMATION NEEDS

In a second step, we generated a list of 25 more general information needs based on the results of the diary study and on experiences of colleagues at our institute who provide specific services for social science researchers, e.g., they support them by finding appropriate data, designing questionnaires or analyzing survey research data. We presented this list in paper form to 18 different social science researchers in the context of a user study in March 2016. Table 2 shows the whole list in the column "I'm looking for …". The participants had to check which information needs correspond to their own.

Participants

18 German social scientists (7 female, 11 male, mean age 33.35, SD=10.04) took part in this study. Participants were recruited through personal E-mail invitations sent to the employees of the School of Social Science at the University of Mannheim and to the employees of the Institute of Social Science at the University of Düsseldorf. Two participants work as professors, four

are postdoctoral researchers, and the remaining 12 held a master's degree and work as research associates. Fourteen work with quantitative data, three with quantitative and qualitative data and one with neither of them. Eight of them narrow down their field of expertise to sociology, four perform research in the field of political science, two in psychology, two in survey methodology and two in communication science.

Results

In table 2 the comprehensive list of information needs is shown with the number of matches to the personal information need. For better comparison of the studies, we assigned each information need to categories also used in table 1. These categories were not presented to the participants in the study.

I'm looking for ...	Number (n=18)	Category
… full texts, which I can download directly.	15	Literature
… current literature by a certain author.	14	Literature
… literature in general.	13	Literature
… references of a paper.	13	Literature
… literature that gives me an overview of the topic.	13	Literature
… questionnaires on a specific topic.	12	Support for data collection
… variables collected in various studies to compare them.	12	Variables in research data
… international research data.	11	Research data
… literature that reports on analyses of specific research data.	11	Literature
… access to certain research data.	11	Research data
… information about which variables are included in the research data.	11	Variables in research data
… information on items and scales contained in research data.	11	Measurement instruments
… social science items and scales to create a questionnaire.	11	Measurement instruments
… information about training / seminars / summer schools.	11	Training
… national research data.	10	Research data
… study description to specific research data.	10	Research data
… research data mentioned in a paper.	9	Research data
… research projects.	9	Networking / Cooperation
… links between research data.	7	Research data
… questions for a study that I would like to carry out.	7	Support for data collection
… a definition of a term by a certain author.	6	Definition
… information on data analysis of microdata.	6	Support for data analysis
… information about questionnaire construction and development of survey tools.	6	Support for data collection
… material to create a lecture.	5	Illustrative material
… information on methodological aspects of organizing and conducting surveys.	3	Support for data collection

Table 2. Information needs presented to 18 social science researchers and the number of people who indicated that the information need corresponds to their own. The last column shows the category the information need is afterward assigned to.

ONLINE-QUESTIONNAIRE

In the third and last study, we created an online questionnaire in German to collect further insights from a larger group of social science researchers. We asked two questions only: (1) "In the following list, you find information needs of social sciences researchers. Please check the information needs that correspond to your own information needs.". The list options are shown in table 3 under "I'm looking for…". (2) "If you're thinking about the last week, what information were you looking for in the context of your scientific work? You are welcome to be concrete at this point, e.g. I was looking for instructions on how to categorize open replies". The second question was an open question and the first question primarily served to convey an idea of what kind of information needs is being addressed. The questionnaire was online from 25th of October 2017 until 31st of December 2017. The goal of this questionnaire was to collect more specific and individual information needs to get a more holistic view on social science information needs.

Participants

We sent invitations through a mailing list containing social science researchers in Germany, who agreed to be contacted again in a prior study. The original mailing list was created manually by our institute. We went through all web presences of Social Science institutes at German Universities and collected contact details from employees, who held at least a Master degree. Thus, we were able to send personalized email-invitation to 1,107 researchers. 223 of them answered the online questionnaire completely (response rate of 20%). Furthermore, we published an invitation to the study as a news entry on our homepage and distributed it through the social media accounts (Facebook and Twitter) assigned to our institute. Thus, we received further 114 filled out questionnaires. Altogether, we got 337 exploitable questionnaires.

Results

Table 3 shows the list of given information needs and the frequency of how often participants indicated this information need as their own. In the last column again, the assigned category is shown, which was not presented to the participants in the study. As the information needs of the two participant groups do not differ significantly, they are presented together.

I'm looking for	Number (n=337)	Category
... literature on a specific topic.	293	Literature
... for full texts, which I can download directly.	287	Literature
... national and/or international research data.	216	Research data
... social science items and scales to create a questionnaire.	171	Measurement instruments
... information about which variables are contained in certain research data.	163	Variables in research data
... for clues as to whether certain research data are suitable for answering my research question.	159	Research data
... variables collected in various studies to compare them.	154	Variables in research data
... research data mentioned in a paper.	134	Research data
... for cooperation partners for a research project.	62	Networking / Cooperation

Table 3. The first question in our online questionnaire on information needs and the number of participants who indicated that the provided information need corresponds to their own.

187 participants also answered the second question. Altogether, we got 331 individual information needs. We were able to assign 305 of them to the already introduced categories: literature (see table 4), research data (see table 5), measurement instruments (see table 6), support for data analysis (see table 7), support for data collection (see table 8), variables in research data (see table 9), software support (see table 10), networking / cooperation (see table 11) and illustrative material (see table 12). 26 information needs could not be assigned to any category as their meaning was not obvious. The *n* in the column "number" refers to the number of persons who have made one or more statements in this category.

Literature	Number (n=98)
Literature in general	81
Full text	22
Current literature	4
Literature of a specific author	2
Literature on fundamental work	2
Literature on related topics	2
Collection on sources	2
Cited literature	2
E-books, English literature, scientific journals, grey literature, journal articles, secondary literature, full text from journals/books, literature from related disciplines, literature on method comparison, literature to research data, survey articles, research reports, book reviews, methodical literature	Mentioned once in each case

Table 4. Information needs in the category literature.

Research data	Number (n=61)
Research data	36
Research data for comparison	8
Survey data	5
Historical data / time series	3
Research data mentioned in a paper	2
Statistics	2
Research data from a specific country	2
Access to research data	2
Data on population, research data from a specific country, geodata, microdata, qualitative data, linked data	Mentioned once in each case

Table 5. Information needs in the category research data.

Measurement instruments	**Number (n=26)**
Scales to a specific question	6
Items to a specific question	5
Information about specific scales	5
Items and variables on which my projects can be based	3
Items and scales from validated questionnaires	3
I searched for questionnaires containing items for specific concepts	1
Translation of scales	1
Replicability/copyright of a scale	1
Operationalization of scales and items	1

Table 6. Information needs in the category measurement instruments.

Support for data analysis	**Number (n=23)**
Information on a specific analysis method	7
Practical instructions for qualitative content analysis	3
Mathematical assumptions of maximum likelihood method	1
Literature on the interpretation of multinomial logistic regression and fixed effects models	1
Methodology literature to adjust my data analysis to the latest development	1
Instructions on statistical methods for answering my research question	1
Texts on the application of machine learning techniques in the social sciences.	1
Calculations of certain variables / syntax files	1
Application examples for a statistical method	1
Methodological articles on community analyses of hierarchical and mixed models	1
Documents for item analysis with R	1
Application possibilities of network analyses	1
Stata-DoFiles and keys for converting between different professional codes	1
Macro-indicators for international comparative studies	1
Instructions for comparative methodology	1

Table 7. Information needs in the category support for data analysis (table continued from previous page).

Support for Data collection	**Number (n=14)**
Information on survey methods	5
Instructions on how to create a survey	4
Formulation for item batteries	3
Recruiting of participants	2
How to create an online questionnaire with Unipark	1
Drawing of samples	1
Collection methods for qualitative surveys	1
Information on transnational standards for recording educational attainment	1

Table 8. Information needs in the category support for data collection.

Variables in research data	Number (n=13)
Specific variables collected in ALLBUS/ISSP	2
Variables including item formulation in codebooks	1
Certain variables in a known dataset (wanted to know if a particular question was asked last year)	1
Literature on a specific dependent variable (Which articles have examined this variable)	1
Variables in different datasets	1
Availability of certain variables in international population surveys	1
How have other studies used several variables on a topic	1
Variables contained in a research data set	1
Information on the frequency of collection of certain Eurobarometer questions	1
I checked whether certain items relevant to my question are available in large datasets	1
Variables in data sets	1
Descriptions of the variables contained in research data	1
Specific variables to answer a research question	1

Table 9. Information needs in the category variables in research data.

Software support	Number (n=12)
Stata Tutorials	4
Software for processing large data sets	1
Software for testing hypotheses on longitudinal data	1
Tool for visualization of statistical distributions	1
Software for the analysis of social networks, through website analysis	1
Tool for merging macro dataset (country level) with a micro dataset (EQLS 2003-2011)	1
I was looking for pros and cons of the Python programming language for statistical analysis	1
Tutorial for statistical programs	1
Help for dealing with MAXQDA	1
R-Base	1

Table 10. Information needs in the category software support.

Networking / Cooperation	Number (n=6)
Project partners	2
Scientific project to a specific topic	1
Overview of research projects on specific research questions.	1
Who is currently working with the data (in a project)?	1
Possible referent for a specific topic	1
Call for papers (conferences)	1
Online forums on specific scientific methods	1
I was looking for experts on certain aspects of the content who were willing to cooperate.	1

Table 11. Information needs in the category networking / cooperation.

Illustrative material	**Number (n=3)**
Video, images	1
Definitions	1
Lecture material	1

Table 12. Information needs in the category illustrative material.

DISCUSSION

By conducting three different studies (diary, questionnaire, online survey), we were able to collect 154 different information needs from 367 social science researchers in Germany. Our focus was on collecting concrete information needs that arise in the daily working life of social science researchers. The advantage of the mixed-mode method is that new real information needs can be identified on a high scale. Our approach is a bit different to prior studies which often ask researchers which predefined information types they use (journals, books, etc.) and how they are accessed (online, offline, etc.). Although the method implicates a diversity of answers, we were able to cluster most of the results into nine different groups: (1) literature, (2) research data, (3) measurement instruments, (4) support for data analysis, (5) support for data collection, (6) variables in research data, (7) software support, (8) networking/cooperation, and (9) illustrative material.

(1) Searching for literature is still the unchallenged main information need of researchers in the field of social science. In all studies, more than 80% of the participants stated at least one information need in this category: in the diary study 83%, in the offline questionnaire 88%, in the online questionnaire first question (closed) 90% and the second question (open) 52%. In early work (Foster 1995, Line 1971, De Tiratel 2000), researchers mentioned journals as their most important source of information. The results of our studies show that the sources itself seem to play a minor role by now whereas accessibility to full texts is becoming more and more important.

(2) The re-use of existing research data is a specialty of the social sciences which has been identified already in early studies (e.g. Hogeweg-de Haart 1983). With more and more data available online this information need gets more prominent. In the period of our diary study, only two of the 12 people searched for research data and also in the online questionnaire when we asked for the information need of last week only 32% stated "searching for research data" as their current information need. However, asking with a closed question about their general information needs as we did it in the questionnaire study and with the closed question in the online study the percentage of persons who are looking for research data is at 88% (questionnaire study) respectively 75% (online study).

Regarding the approaches social science researchers fulfill their information need; we found out, that all of the 12 participants in our diary study used the web at least as a starting point for most of their information tasks. As the most often used search engine "Google" was mentioned by ten subjects. Five participants used Google Scholar at the time of the study. Seven participants used discipline-specific databases or digital libraries such as Web of Science or Scopus. Beside of this, the following digital sources are mentioned: institutes' or authors' websites, ResearchGate, YouTube, Wikipedia, Amazon, and Pixabay. Only 3 mentioned non-digital sources like personal contacts (3), (University) libraries (2) and the personal book collection.

Although the way to get literature and research data has changed in the last decades, the interest in these categories is still and probably will remain high in the future. Especially, our participants in the questionnaire study expressed the desire for open access, 15 of 18 participants already look for full text that they can download directly. Also the need for linked information, e.g. research data mentioned in a paper or literature that reports on analyses of specific research data are information needs by more than half of the participants.

(3) Measurement instruments in the field of social science are used to collect sociological attributes in a standardized way. The instruments are items and scales that can be applied in surveys and enable the comparability of research data. In our diary study, one participant looked, for example, for a scale to study personality traits. In the online study, we addressed this category with two information needs which were checked by 11 participants each (61%). In the online study, also 50% checked the corresponding information need in the closed question, and 26 participants provided insight on their concrete information need in this category. This category and the following ones have not been identified as explicit information needs of social scientists in prior studies.

(4) The support for data analysis was the second most often mentioned information need in our diary study. The participants looked for mappings, metadata schemes, network analysis or classification of open answers. In our questionnaire study, we only asked for the information need of analyzing microdata which was checked by 6 participants. In the online study, 23

participants (12%) gave us detailed information on their information need in this category. The information needs in this category are manifold and, in some cases, very specific, but they show the general desire for better support of this information need.

(5) Three participants in our diary study expressed the need for support in the data collection process. They were looking for help regarding the planning of the study, designing the questionnaire and recruiting participants. In the questionnaire study, seven participants checked information needs in this category (39%). In the online study, this information need was not addressed in the close question, but 14 participants (7%) formulated their information needs in this category in the open question.

(6) The information need "variables in research data" was not mentioned in the diary study but added to the list of information needs presented to the participants in the questionnaire study because of the upcoming trend of variable search (such as provided by ICPSR[1]). Answers given in the questionnaire study as well as in the online study shows that about 50% of the researchers have this information need and 13 participants in the online study provide detailed information on their information need in the category variables.

(7) In the diary study, one subject reported the need for software support, in the online survey 12 (6%). Researchers in the quantitative social sciences, but also in the qualitative science use software to analyze their data. This process obviously needs support. (8) Networking/cooperation is a basic need of social scientists with three reported needs in the diary study, nine in the questionnaire, and 62 in the online closed question (18%) and 6 in the online open question (3%). (9) Illustrative material was reported to be needed in the diary study by four persons and online in the open question by 3 (2%).

Studies on information needs (in the social sciences) were conducted all time with the purpose to improve access to information and to adapt it to the current needs. Literature could be a long time only accessed through the library, the upcoming of the web and the trend of open access has adopted this behavior. Research data is more and more requested, and the rising of web portals for this purpose shows the trend. Very recently, also specialized portals came up which allow the search for variables in research data which also showed to be an information need in our study. Still underestimated is the search for re-usable measurement instruments. Also, this trend shows up in the open science movement with the term open methodology, comprehensive search portals which supports this need are missing. Support for data analysis, data collection and software support are often very individual and at least at our institute addressed with personal consulting and training. However, the barrier for this is high, and users look for quick help on the Web. These categories hold larger information needs that are not yet addressed by specialized portals.

PRACTICAL IMPLICATION

The presented studies were conducted as parts of a user-centered design process[2] which was applied to develop an integrated search system (https://search.gesis.org). This search system provides access to different information in the field of Social Science trough one single search bar. The search results are divided into different categories according to the findings of the conducted user studies, namely: *research data* (includes German studies retrieved from the GESIS data catalog as well as metadata of international studies), *publication* (includes open access publications and literature linked to research data), *questions & variables* (from research data archived in the GESIS data catalog), *instruments & tools* (includes measurement instruments, support for data collection and data analysis, and software support). Furthermore, the search system provides access to *GESIS Websites* on which users can find further support for conducting and analyzing survey data as well as to publications that are available in our *library*. The least demanded categories networking/cooperation and illustrative material are not included. One main benefit of the integrated search system is that information items are linked to each other so that users can see, for example, which publications contain data citations to research data. As we have seen, the information needs of social science are manifold and sometimes very individual and specific - the new integrated search system tries to support the most frequently mentioned.

ACKNOWLEDGMENTS

We would like to thank all who have participated in our studies.

[1] https://www.icpsr.umich.edu/icpsrweb/ICPSR/ssvd/index.jsp
[2] according to ISO 9241-201:2010 https://www.iso.org/standard/52075.html

REFERENCES

Agrawal, S. P., & Lal, M. (1987). Information needs of social scientists. *International Library Review*, 19(3), 287–299. https://doi.org/10.1016/0020-7837(87)90039-2

Brittain, J. (1979). Information Services and the Structure of Knowledge in the Social Sciences. *International Social Science Journal*, 31(4), 711–28.

Corti, L. (2007). Re-using archived qualitative data – where, how, why? Archival Science, 7(1), 37–54. https://doi.org/10.1007/s10502-006-9038-y

Curty, R. G. (2016). *Factors Influencing Research Data Reuse in the Social Sciences: An Exploratory Study*. IJDC, 11, 96–117.

de Tiratel, S. R. (2000). Accessing information use by humanists and social scientists: a study at the Universidad de Buenos Aires, Argentina. *The Journal of Academic Librarianship*, 26(5), 346–354.

Dulisch, N., Kempf, A. O., & Schaer, P. (2015). Query Expansion for Survey Question Retrieval in the Social Sciences. In S. Kapidakis, C. Mazurek, & M. Werla (Eds.), Research and Advanced Technology for Digital Libraries (pp. 28–39). Cham: Springer International Publishing.

Ellis, D., Cox, D., & Hall, K. (1993). A comparison of the information seeking patterns of researchers in the physical and social sciences. *Journal of Documentation*, 49, 356–356.

Ellis, David. (1989). A behavioural approach to information retrieval system design. *Journal of Documentation*, 45(3), 171–212.

Faniel, I. M., Kriesberg, A., & Yakel, E. (2016). Social scientists' satisfaction with data reuse. *Journal of the Association for Information Science and Technology*, 67(6), 1404–1416.

Folster, M. B. (1989). A study of the use of information sources by social science researchers. *Journal of Academic Librarianship*, 15(1), 7–11.

Folster, M. B. (1995). Information seeking patterns: social sciences. *The Reference Librarian*, 23(49–50), 83–93.

Hogeweg-de Haart, H. P. (1983). Characteristics of social science information: A selective review of the literature. Part I. *Social Science Information Studies*, 3(3), 147–164. http://dx.doi.org/10.1016/0143-6236(83)90021-2

Kern, D., & Mathiak, B. (2015). Are There Any Differences in Data Set Retrieval Compared to Well-Known Literature Retrieval? In S. Kapidakis, C. Mazurek, & M. Werla (Eds.), *Research and Advanced Technology for Digital Libraries* (pp. 197–208). Cham: Springer International Publishing.

Line, M. B. (1971). The information uses and needs of social scientists: An overview of INFROSS. In Aslib proceedings (Vol. 23, pp. 412–434). MCB UP Ltd.

Meho, L. I., & Tibbo, H. R. (2003). Modeling the Information-seeking Behavior of Social Scientists: Ellis's Study Revisited. *J. Am. Soc. Inf. Sci. Technol.*, 54(6), 570–587. https://doi.org/10.1002/asi.10244

Gilbert, G. Nigel, ed. *Computational social science*. Vol. 21. Sage, 2010.

Shen, Y. (2007). Information seeking in academic research: A study of the sociology faculty at the University of Wisconsin-Madison. *Information Technology and Libraries*, 26(1), 4.

Slater, M. (1988). Social Scientists' Information Needs in the 1980s. *Journal of Documentation*, 44(3), 226–237.

Wilkinson, M.D. et al.: The FAIR Guiding Principles for scientific data management and stewardship. *Sci. Data*. 3, 160018 (2016).

Reputation, Trust, and Norms as Mechanisms Leading to Academic Reciprocity in Data Sharing: An Empirical Test of Theory of Collective Action

Youngseek Kim
University of Kentucky, United States. youngseek.kim@uky.edu

ABSTRACT

This research investigated how scientists' academic reputation, community trust, and norms regarding data sharing all influence their academic reciprocity in data sharing, which eventually leads to the scientists' data sharing intentions. This research employed Ostrom's (2003) theory of collective action to better understand scientists' data sharing behaviors from the perspective of cooperation in a community. This research empirically evaluated the research model and related hypotheses by using the Structural Equation Modeling (SEM) method on a total of 456 survey responses from biologists in the U.S. The results suggest that biologists' perceived academic reputation significantly increases their perceived community trust, norm of data sharing, and academic reciprocity. Along with perceived academic reputation, both perceived community trust and norms of data sharing also significantly increases biologists' academic reciprocity in data sharing. This research also found that biologists' academic reciprocity and norms of data sharing significantly affect their data sharing intentions. The results of this research show that the theory of collective action provides new insight to scientists' data sharing behaviors. These results suggest how we can facilitate scientists' data sharing behaviors within a research community by increasing academic reciprocity through the mechanisms of reputation, trust, and norm.

KEYWORDS

Data sharing, reciprocity, reputation, trust, norm, biological science.

INTRODUCTION

In the past decade, scientific data sharing has become important to promote science and engineering research (Borgman, 2012; Tenopir et al., 2015). Scientific data sharing can help scientists conduct open and transparent scientific research (Borgman, 2007; Campbell et al., 2002), build better research using other scientists' data (Louis, Jones, & Campbell, 2002; Vickers, 2006), and eventually advance science based on the shared data sets (Kim & Stanton, 2016; Tenopir et al., 2011). However, even though data sharing provides benefits to both scientific communities and individual scientists, prior studies show that scientific data sharing is not yet a common research practice in many disciplines (Campbell & Bendavid, 2003; Piwowar, 2011).

A good number of studies have investigated diverse factors impacting data sharing; those studies have identified institutional contexts (e.g, regulative pressures from funding agencies and journals), individual motivations (e.g., perceived benefit, risk, and effort in data sharing), and disciplinary resources (e.g., metadata and data repository) as some of the main factors affecting scientists' data sharing behaviors (Kim & Stanton, 2016; Kim & Zhang, 2015). However, those studies are limited in that they mainly examined the static relationships between institutional, individual, and resource factors and scientists' data sharing behaviors (or intentions), and they did not capture the dynamic aspects of scientists' data sharing behaviors by considering the values systems and norms within a research community.

In order to better understand scientists' data sharing behaviors, it is important to understand the nature of science. Science is considered a social institution, and scientists interact with other members of their research communities and also with the broader scientist community (Ziman, 2000). Scientists work based on the race for priority and the profession's reward of a favorable reputation (Dundar & Lewis, 1998; Merton, 1957). This reputation mechanism – especially with regards to article publishing – is supported by recognition systems (e.g., having a published work cited), community trust, and norm (Kling & Spector, 2003). This mechanism eventually encourages scientist to share their research findings through publications rather than keeping those findings for themselves (Merton, 1973).

This research considers biologists' data sharing behaviors as collective actions based on the reputation mechanism of science. This research focuses on how biologists' perceptions of academic reputation, community trust, and norms of data sharing all affect biologists' academic reciprocity, which eventually leads to their data sharing intentions. This research utilized Ostrom's (2003) theory of collective action to explain biologists' data sharing intentions based on their perceptions of reputation, trust, and the norm of data sharing. This research especially focuses on how reputation, trust, and norms can affect biologists' academic reciprocity, which in turn influences their data sharing intentions.

LITERATURE REVIEW

Borgman (2007) and Tenopir et al. (2011) argued that data sharing is not yet a well-established research practice for many scientific disciplines. In the field of biological sciences, several studies have focused on whether scientists allow or deny other researchers access to their data (e.g., Campbell et al., 2002; McCain, 1991). Vogeli et al. (2006) surveyed science trainees regarding data withholding behaviors and found that 23.0% of trainees were denied access to publication related materials and 20.6% were denied access to unpublished research. Vogeli et al. (2006) also reported that 7.9% of science trainees had denied other researchers' requests to access the data for their own published research. However, behavioral studies showed that the actual rate of data withholding within the scientific community is actually higher (Blumenthal et al., 2006; Savage & Vickers, 2009).

Data sharing scholarship has examined the diverse factors either facilitating or hindering scientists' data sharing behaviors. Those factors can be divided into individual, institutional, and resource influences. With regards to institutional pressure, prior studies found that scientists' data sharing behaviors are strongly influenced by funding agencies' policies and journals' policies about data sharing. In terms of funding agency's pressure, McCullough et al. (2008) and Piwowar (2010) found that the regulative pressures from NIH significantly increased biologists' data sharing behaviors; however, some studies did not find any significant relationship between funding agencies' pressures and data sharing behaviors (Kim & Stanton, 2016; Kim & Zhang, 2015). In terms of journal pressure, many journals now require authors to share information with other researchers either by depositing their data in publically available data repositories or by providing the data freely upon request (Savage & Vickers, 2009). Piwowar and Chapman (2008) found that journals' policies on data sharing significantly increased biologists' sharing of microarray data in a data repository. However, Savage and Vickers (2009) reported that only one author provided his/her data when they requested data from ten authors of articles published in a journal with a strong data sharing policy. In contrast to funding agencies and journals, which encourage data sharing, industry sponsors often place restrictions on sharing research outcomes supported by their funding, preventing scientists from sharing data with others (Campbell, Louis, & Blumenthal, 1998). Researchers supported by industries are more likely to withhold their data through tactics such as by delaying publication by more than six months (Campbell & Bendavid, 2003). With regards to factors of individual motivation, prior studies identified various individual motivations affecting data sharing, including academic recognition (Kling & Spector, 2003) and reciprocal benefit (Zimmerman, 2007). Scientific communities rarely provide academic recognition such as citations for the data deposited in data repositories. Furthermore, scholars identified potential risks involved in data sharing as another main obstacle to engage in data sharing behaviors; they diverse potential risks identified include: losing potential future publications (Campbell et al., 2002; Savage & Vickers, 2009), misuse and/or misinterpretation of data (Borgman, 2007; Cragin, Palmer, Carlson, & Witt, 2010), and privacy concerns (Borgman, 2009; Savage & Vickers, 2009). Previous studies on scientists' data sharing have also reported that the effort of data sharing, such as organizing and preparing raw data into a readable format, prevents scientists from sharing their data with others (Campbell et al., 2002; Louis et al., 2002; Tenopir et al., 2011).

Finally, prior studies have examined the roles of technical resources such as metadata standards and data repositories in scientists' data sharing behaviors. Biological sciences have a metadata standard to organize and manage experimental research data, which can help biologists to share and reuse data easily (Paton, 2008). Bietz et al. (2010) argued that metadata standards can encourage scientists' data sharing behaviors. Also, Kim and Burns (2016) found that the availability of data repositories and metadata standards influenced scientists' data sharing behaviors indirectly via mediating the scientists data sharing norms. Choudhury (2008) and Witt (2008) reported that scientists are willing to deposit their data of their published articles when there are data repositories available to them.

Although prior studies investigated diverse factors influencing scientists' data sharing, those studies did not examine how the reputation mechanism of science affects scientists' data sharing behaviors mediated by academic reciprocity. This research builds on prior studies conducted by Kim and colleagues (Kim & Stanton, 2016; Kim & Zhang, 2015) by focusing on the impact of scientists' academic reciprocity on data sharing. This research aims to advance prior studies by investigating the role academic reciprocity plays in scientists' data sharing behaviors. This research employed a new theoretical framework to understand how perceived academic reputation, perceived community trust, and norms of data sharing all affect scientists' academic reciprocity in data sharing, which in turn leads to their data sharing intentions.

THEORETICAL FRAMEWORK

Recent studies in data sharing employed different theoretical models. Those studies employed either social psychology theories or organizational theories (Kim & Stanton, 2016; Kim & Zhang, 2015) to identify causal paths among different factors affecting scientists' data sharing behaviors or intentions. This research employed Ostrom's (2003) theory of collective action as its main theoretical framework to explain biologists' data sharing intentions by examining academic reciprocity as influenced by perceived academic reputation, perceived community trust, and data sharing norm factors.

Ostrom's (2003) theory of collective action was designed to predict and explain how an individual conducts a cooperative behavior based on the reciprocity formed by reputation, trust, and norms within a community. Reciprocity refers to community members reacting to the favorable behaviors of others in a positive way, but the unfavorable behaviors in a negative way (Ostrom, 2003). Reciprocity is strongly affected by the trust an individual has because they expect others will reciprocate. In addition, the degree of reciprocity can differ according to the expectations of others in the community (i.e., community norm about a certain behavior)(Rasch, Heckelei, Oomen, & Naumann, 2016). Ostrom (2003) also suggests that an individual's interpretation of others' reputation can increase his/her trust and norms of the behavior, which all form his/her reciprocity, which eventually affects their behavioral intention to cooperate or collaborate.

The theory of collective action assumes that individuals cannot perform any behaviors isolated by their social institutions, and institutional arrangements either facilitate or hinder individuals' behaviors (Ebenhöh & Pahl-Wostl, 2008). Ostrom (2003) suggests that three essential mechanisms influence individuals' reciprocity and cooperation: (1) the institutions providing rules and incentives, (2) norms at individual, group, and society levels, and (3) shared resources supporting their collaboration. The close coupling between socio-cognitive mechanisms (i.e., reputation, trust, and norm) and shared resources promotes individuals' reciprocity, and eventually, their cooperative behavior (Ostrom, 2003).

This research applied Ostrom's (2003) theory of collective action in the context of scientists' data sharing. This research assumes that the three structural elements – reputation, trust, and norms of data sharing – affect an individual scientist's willingness to reciprocate other scientists, and consequently, the likelihood of his/her data sharing (i.e., cooperation in a community). This research suggests that the equilibrium of reputation, trust, and norms can facilitate scientists' academic reciprocity in data sharing, eventually increasing their data sharing intentions. This new theoretical framework allows an investigation of scientists' data sharing behaviors, examining academic reciprocity as a central mechanism of data sharing behavior.

RESEARCH MODEL AND HYPOTHESIS DEVELOPMENT

Research Model

The research model for the impact of academic reciprocity on biologists' data sharing was developed based on the theory of collective action (Ostrom, 2003). The research model examined how academic reputation, community trust, and norms of data sharing all affect biologists' data sharing intentions, which is mediated by academic reciprocity. Figure 1 shows the research model for biologists' academic reciprocity and data sharing. Proposed hypotheses are further explained in the following section.

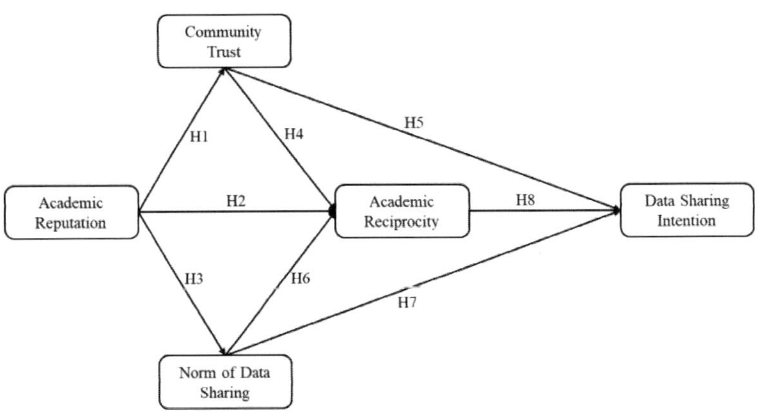

Figure 1. Biologists' Academic Reciprocity and Data Sharing Model.

Hypotheses Development

Perceived Academic Reputation

This research assumes that perceived academic reputation can positively increase biologists' perceived community trust, academic reciprocity, and norm of data sharing. Perceived academic reputation is defined as the extent to which a scientist believes that data sharing can increase their academic reputation through recognition and/or citation. Merton (1973) argued that scientific institutions work based on a rewards system in which recognition and credit go to those who make original contributions to scientific knowledge. Previously, the reward system in science was associated with the publication of research as a scholarly communication practice, but it could be extended to the publication of research data as well (Borgman, 2007). Prior studies in data sharing found that perceived career benefits of data sharing positively increased the overall attitude toward data sharing and the norm of data sharing (Kim & Adler, 2015; Kim & Zhang, 2015). Therefore, this research hypothesizes:

H1: Perceived academic reputation would positively affect a biologist's perceived community trust.

H2: Perceived academic reputation would positively affect a biologist's academic reciprocity in data sharing.

H3: Perceived academic reputation would positively affect a biologist's norm of data sharing.

Perceived Community Trust

Scientists in a research community have built their own community trust in data sharing. Community trust is one of the essential elements facilitating an individual's cooperative behavior (Yandle, Hajj, & Raciborski, 2011). Community trust refers to an individual scientist's expectation about the likelihood that other scientists will behave in a way to benefit or at least not to harm the individual scientist (Zanini & Migueles, 2013). Perceived community trust can be described as the biologists' belief regarding their colleague researchers. The level of community trust biologists may have for their research community can affect their academic reciprocity and data sharing intentions as well. Therefore, this research hypothesizes:

H4: Perceived community trust would positively affect a biologist's academic reciprocity in data sharing.

H5: Perceived community trust would positively affect a biologist's data sharing intention.

Norm of Data Sharing

Data sharing can be encouraged by the research community's norms about data sharing. The norm of data sharing can be defined as the degree to which a scientist perceives data sharing as an expected behavior by their colleagues or fellow researchers. In a scientific community, individual scientists are influenced by normative sanctions, so they would need to follow the expectations by their scientific communities (Ajzen & Fishbein, 2005). Communalism in Merton's (1973) norms of science supports open scientific research by freely sharing scientific findings; the idea of communalism can be extended to research data as well as research findings reported in published articles. The community expectations about data sharing affect scientists as normative pressures (Kim & Stanton, 2016). Scientists' norm of data sharing can be developed from his/her research community, where scientists have similar ideas and expectations (Ajzen & Fishbein, 2005). Scientists would follow their norms (especially about data sharing) to meet other researchers' expectations, and to retain their academic status in their respective research fields (John, Cannon, & Pouder, 2001; Zsidisin, Melnyk, & Ragatz, 2005). Therefore, this research hypothesizes:

H6: Norm of data sharing would positively affect a biologist's academic reciprocity.

H7: Norm of data sharing would positively affect a biologist's data sharing intention.

Academic Reciprocity

Academic reciprocity in data sharing refers to the degree to which a biological scientist considers sharing their data to a researcher in return for what they have already received from other scientists. In the context of knowledge sharing, Kankanhalli et al. (2005) found that employees wanted to share their knowledge with those whose knowledge helped them previously. Only a few studies have investigated the link between academic reciprocity and scientists' data sharing. Kim and Stanton (2016) reported that academic altruism as a form of reciprocity is a significant factor affecting scientists' data sharing behaviors. Therefore, this research hypothesizes:

H8: Academic reciprocity in data sharing would positively affect a biologist's data sharing intention.

Data Sharing Intention

This research examined data sharing intention as a dependent variable. Data sharing intention refers to the extent in which a scientist is willing to provide the data of their published articles by depositing the data in institutional repositories or making them available upon request. Since data sharing itself is not well-received by many disciplines, actual data sharing behavior cannot serve as a reliable outcome variable. The measurement items for data sharing intention can capture biologists' willingness to share their data as influenced by the diverse data sharing factors described above.

RESEARCH METHODS

An online survey was conducted with biologists who work in U.S. academic institutions. The data collected from this survey was used to evaluate the measurement items of the proposed research model. Additionally, this data assessed the degree to which the hypothesized relationships among constructs were accurate.

Target Population and Sampling

The target population of this research includes biologists who belong to U.S. academic institutions. This research utilized the scholar database provided by Pivot (http://pivot.cos.com) to identify the sampling frame. According to the Pivot scholar database, there were a total of 91,923 scholars registered in the discipline of biological sciences in the U.S. (as of November 1st, 2016). A total of 8,000 biologists in the U.S. academic institution were randomly selected as a sampling pool for this research. Since the Pivot scholar database has an extensive scholar list, the sampling pool is representative of the target population. The potential survey participants were randomly selected from a panel of scholars who belong to the discipline of biological sciences, work in U.S. academic institutions, and have job titles of assistant, associate, and full professor, as well as those with the title of researcher. Since this research employed Structural Equation Modeling (SEM) for the main statistical analysis, the required sample size for this research is at least 300 participants based on the research model developed above (Fornell & Larcker, 1981).

Measurement of Constructs

The majority of the measurement items used in this study were adapted from prior studies (Kim & Stanton, 2016; Kim & Zhang, 2015). While those studies generally measured the factors associated with scientists' data sharing behaviors or behavioral intentions (such as perceived benefits, risks, and effort), this research revisited those factors and revised them to fit the current research model through the scale development procedure. The pertinent measurement items in the previous literature were reviewed for coverage, reliability, and validity, and those prior measurement items were modified for this research. Then, a pilot survey was conducted by a group of 31 biologists, who were also selected from the Pivot scholar database. The feedback from the pilot survey resulted in modifying some of the survey items and the survey instruction and layout for clarity and simplicity.

Data Collection Procedure and Result

An online survey was set up through Qualtrics.com. It was distributed to the biologists who were randomly selected from the Pivot scholar database. A total of 8,000 potential survey participants were selected by the random sampling method, and the online questionnaire – including a research introduction, measurement items, and demographic questions – was distributed to those potential participants using survey distribution tool in Qualtrics.com. The initial recruitment message with the survey link was sent out in early November, 2016, and the survey was closed in mid-February, 2017 after two reminders were sent in late November and mid-December 2016 and one final reminder in late January, 2017. Among the 8,000 potential survey participants, 2,014 potential participants could not be reached due to incorrect emails and spam filters. A total of 675 valid responses were received, which consisted of participants who answered more than 80% of the survey questions, and those valid responses represent a 11.28% of response rate (675/5,986=0.1128). Since this research utilized Partial Least Square-based SEM technique, any responses with missing values (26 responses) were removed for an accurate analysis. Since this research focused on biological sciences, any responses from non-biologists (193 responses) were also removed from this dataset. In terms of academic disciplines of survey participants, although this research identified biologists as categorized by the Pivot scholar database, one-third of the participants (i.e., 193 responses) reported their academic disciplines other than biological sciences based on the NSF discipline code. Therefore, a total of 456 responses from biologists with no missing value were used for the final data analysis.

Demographics of the Respondents

The demographic information covers gender, age, position, and tenure status (see Table 1). About two-third of the survey respondents are male (302, 66.2%), and they are well distributed in diverse age groups. The majority of the participants are faculty members including assistant professor (50, 11.0%), associate professor (97, 21.3%), full professor (186, 40.8%), and professor emeritus (32, 7.0%). Many had received tenure (278, 61.0%).

	Demographic Category	Number	Percentage
Gender	Male	302	66.2
	Female	145	31.8
	Transgender	1	0.2
	Prefer Not to Answer	6	1.3
	Missing	2	*0.4*
Age	25-34	32	7.0
	35-44	94	20.6
	45-54	126	27.6
	55-64	111	24.3
	65+	78	17.1
	Prefer Not to Answer	9	2.0
	Missing	6	*1.3*
Position	Assistant Professor	50	11.0
	Associate Professor	97	21.3
	Full Professor	186	40.8
	Professor Emeritus	32	7.0
	Lecturer/Instructor	8	1.8
	Post-Doctoral Fellow	24	5.3
	Researcher	32	7.0
	Graduate Student	6	1.3
	Other	19	4.2
	Prefer Not to Answer	2	0.4
	Missing	*50*	*11.0*
Status	Tenured	278	61.0
	On Tenure Track	42	9.2
	Not on Tenure Track	88	19.3
	Retired	28	6.1
	Prefer Not to Answer	17	3.7
	Missing	3	0.7
Total		456	100%

Table 1. Demographic Information of Survey Participants

DATA ANALYSIS AND RESULTS

This research used a Partial Least Square (PLS) based Structural Equation Modeling (SEM) approach to inspect the hypothesized relationships in the research model of biologists' data sharing. The PLS-SEM technique utilizes component analysis rather than covariance analysis, and the component-based PLS-SEM technique is appropriate for an exploratory study because it does not require a large sample size or normality assumption (Bontis, Crossan, & Hulland, 2002). This research used SmartPLS 2.0 (Ringle, Wende, & Will, 2005) as the main data analysis software, and it took a two-stage approach by evaluating measurement model first and then assessing structural model (Hair, Black, Babin, Anderson, & Tatham, 2006). The measurement model was assessed to ensure the reliability and validity of the measurement items, and the structural model was evaluated to examine the hypothesized relationships in the biologists' data sharing model.

Measurement Model

The survey items were evaluated to warrant the reliability and validity of the measurement items. This research employed Cronbach's alpha, Composite Reliability (CR), and Average Variance Extracted (AVE) to ensure the reliability of research constructs. Cronbach's alpha values range from 0.83 for norm of data sharing to 0.95 for academic reciprocity, which are greater than the acceptable value of 0.70 (Chin, 1998; Nunnally & Bernstein, 1994). Also, the minimum CR value, 0.90 for both perceived community trust and norm of data sharing, is larger than the satisfactory value of 0.70 (Chin, 1998; Nunnally & Bernstein, 1994). Finally, the minimum AVE value, 0.70 for perceived community trust, is greater than the recommended value of 0.50 (Fornell & Larcker, 1981; Hair et al., 2006). Table 2 shows the reliability values of the measurement items including Cronbach's alpha, CR, and AVE.

Variables	Cronbach's α	Composite Reliability (CR)	Average Variance Extracted (AVE)
Perceived Academic Reputation	0.94	0.96	0.89
Perceived Community Trust	0.85	0.90	0.70
Norm of Data Sharing	0.83	0.90	0.75
Academic Reciprocity	0.95	0.97	0.91
Data Sharing Intention	0.94	0.96	0.90

Table 2. Reliability and Validity Values

In order to assess the validity of measurement items for constructs, the square roots of the AVEs for each construct were examined by comparing them with the correlations among constructs (Chin, 1998; Fornell & Larcker, 1981). The square roots of AVEs (the diagonal numbers in Table 3) are all greater than the correlations among constructs (the off-diagonal numbers in Table 3). This ensures the satisfactory convergent and discriminant validity for the measurement items used in this research (Chin, 1998; Fornell & Larcker, 1981). Table 3 shows the square roots of AVEs and the correlation matrix.

	Perceived Academic Reputation	Perceived Community Trust	Norm of Data Sharing	Academic Reciprocity	Data Sharing Intention
Perceived Academic Reputation	0.95				
Perceived Community Trust	0.19	0.84			
Norm of Data Sharing	0.52	0.07	0.86		
Academic Reciprocity	0.55	0.21	0.59	0.95	
Data Sharing Intention	0.46	0.09	0.68	0.63	0.95

Table 3. Correlation Matrix and Square Roots of AVEs

Structural Model

Once the measurement model was ensured in terms of reliability and validity of the research constructs, structural model was evaluated to examine the hypothesized relationships among the constructs. First, perceived academic reputation was found to have significant positive influences on perceived community trust ($\beta=0.193$, $p<0.001$), academic reciprocity ($\beta=0.313$, $p<0.001$), and norm of data sharing ($\beta=0.516$, $p<0.001$). With regards to academic reciprocity, this research found that perceived community trust ($\beta=0.119$, $p<0.01$) and norm of data sharing ($\beta=0.423$, $p<0.001$) have significant positive influences on academic reciprocity. The three factors including perceived academic reputation, perceived community trust, and norm of data sharing all explain 45.0% of the total variance in biologists' academic reciprocity ($R^2=0.450$).

This research also found that academic reciprocity (β=0.359, $p<0.001$) and norm of data sharing (β=0.470, $p<0.001$) have significant positive influences on data sharing intention; however, perceived community trust was not found to have a significant effect on data sharing intention (β=-0.018, $p>0.05$). This research shows that biologists' data sharing intentions can be explained by academic reciprocity and norm of data sharing. Those two factors accounted for 54.7% of the total variance in biologists' data sharing intentions ($R^2=0.547$).

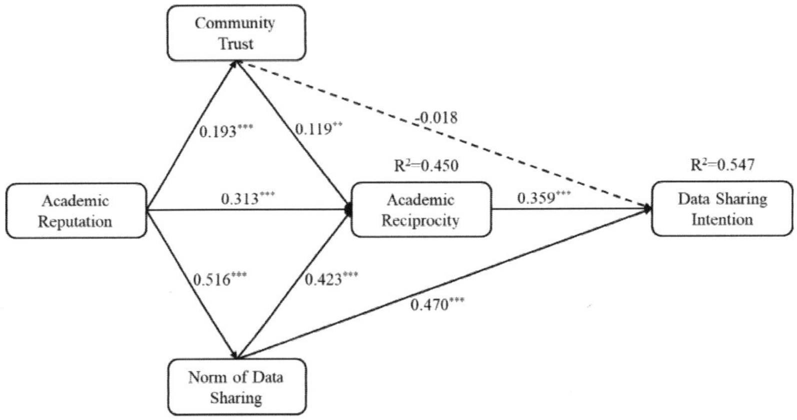

Figure 2. Hypothesis Testing Results

DISCUSSION

This research explored how biologists' perceptions of academic reputation, community trust, and norm of data sharing influence their willingness to reciprocate with other scientists; these factors lead to biologists to subsequently share their data in the perspective of cooperation in their research community. First, this research found that perceived academic reputation plays a critical role in scientists' data sharing intentions, as this variable has a significant influence toward scientists' perceived community trust, norm of data sharing, and academic reciprocity. The scientists who have a more perceived academic reputation in data sharing are more likely to have stronger community trust and a positive norm of data sharing. Also, they are likely to build stronger academic reciprocity and eventually share their data based on that academic reciprocity. Some comments made in open-ended questions in this survey indicate that the intention to share data still varies, even among those in the biological sciences. A full professor in ocean science said that, "A lot of my opinions about data sharing assume that I get credit (authorship, citation, etc.) in return." A full professor in botany said that "There may be a few bad actors in every field. My immediate circle of colleagues includes just one actual case of deliberately withheld data that damaged the reputation of the person involved, but more importantly, may have squandered years of effort by the community."

Second, this research showed that perceived community trust, norm of data sharing, and perceived academic reputation all increase scientists' academic reciprocity through intending to engage in data sharing. As hypothesized, the theoretical constructs in the theory of collective action play critical roles in predicting biologists' academic reciprocity through data sharing. This research confirmed the important relationships among reputation, trust, norm, and reciprocity. With regards to community trust, an associate professor in microbiology, immunology, and virology stated from open-ended survey question: "There are some incredible colleagues in my field, and there are some terrible, opportunistic, dishonest, selfish colleagues in my field. I try to interact with the former and not the latter, but on balance it is a mixed bag." With regards to norm of data sharing, a researcher in chemistry said that "I've used the CCDC to deposit crystal structure data, sharing is sort of a norm for crystallographers and there are standardized file formats plus good support for doing so."

Third, this research found that both biologists' academic reciprocity and norm of data sharing significantly increased scientists' data sharing intentions. With regards to the norm of data sharing, this research confirmed prior findings about the relationship between data sharing norms and data sharing behaviors (or intentions) (Kim & Stanton, 2016; Kim & Zhang, 2015). With regards to academic reciprocity, this research found that biologists' data sharing intentions are strongly driven by their academic reciprocity through having a mutually beneficial exchange of information with other scientists in the field. A full professor in botany, when concerning academic reciprocity, said, "Data sharing with people you trust and who reciprocate is one of the best parts of science. We can all move further ahead. What is not good is when someone wants to profit from your work without reciprocating and as occasionally happens, not even giving credit to the person who shared the data and did the work." With regards to norm of data sharing, a full professor in behavioral neuroscience said, "It [Data Sharing] should become typical and even expected."

Theoretical Implications

This research has several theoretical implications. First, this research provides a new perspective for understanding scientists' data sharing intentions based on the mechanisms of reputation, trust, norm, and reciprocity within a research community. The theory of collective action provides new insight about how we can better encourage scientists' academic reciprocity and data sharing by building scientists' reputation, trust, and norm in the research community. Second, this research suggests that biologists' data sharing intentions are mainly driven by their academic reciprocity and perceived norm of data sharing. This finding confirmed Ostrom's (2003) argument that reciprocity and cooperation (in this case, data sharing) are closely related and can help manage common goods in a community. Third, this research developed new research constructs (i.e., academic reputation, community trust, and academic reciprocity) and their measurement items based on the theory of collective action. Those new research constructs, along with the theoretical framework, can extend our understanding of data sharing and promote scientists' data sharing behaviors and intentions in the perspective of collective action.

Practical Implications

The findings of this research have several practical implications as well. This research suggests that the mechanism of academic reputation can facilitate scientists' willingness to engage in data sharing; this is mediated by their community trust, perceived norm of data sharing within their research field, and academic reciprocity. However, the current reputation mechanism in data sharing does not fully support scientists' expectations regarding academic reputation. In order to improve the perceived academic reputation associated with data sharing behaviors, scientific communities need to develop a system of academic recognition and rewards for data sharing. This research shows that the equilibrium of academic reputation, community trust, and norm can increase scientists' academic reciprocity in data sharing, which eventually increases their data sharing intentions. The results of this study indicate the importance of building a sense of academic reputation, trust, positive norms, and academic reciprocity within the scientific community to be better equipped to increase data sharing intentions and behaviors. Ostrom (2003) posited that continuous interaction among scientists, both individually and collectively as a profession, can foster trust, reputation, and norms, which directly affect reciprocity and cooperation (i.e., data sharing in this research).

CONCLUSION

This research advances our knowledge in scientists' data sharing behaviors by employing a new theoretical lens. This research employed Ostrom's (2003) theory of collective action to understand biologists' data sharing, which was affected by the perceived academic reputation, perceived community trust, data sharing norms, and reciprocity. The results of this research show that scientists' perceived academic reputation, community trust, and norm of data sharing all significantly affect their academic reciprocity, which ultimately increases their data sharing intentions. This research suggests the mechanisms of reputation, trust, and data sharing norms can help scientists build their academic reciprocity in data sharing, which leads them to then share their data. As Ostrom (2003) suggested, the cooperativeness in a community (i.e., data sharing in this research) can improve the levels of reputation, trust, and norm in a community. However, this research did not test the reciprocal loop in the current research mode; therefore, future studies can examine the reciprocal loop between actual data sharing behavior and predicting constructs including academic reputation, community trust, and norm involved in data sharing.

ACKNOWLEDGMENTS

I would like to acknowledge the ProQuest Pivot for allowing me to use its Community of Scientists (CoS) Scholar Database in recruiting the survey participants. I also would like to acknowledge Darra Hofman and Lindsey M. Harper for reviewing this article.

REFERENCES

Ajzen, I., & Fishbein, M. (2005). The influence of attitudes on behavior. In D. Albarracin, B. T. Johnson, & M. P. Zanna (Eds.), *Handbook of attitudes and attitude change* (pp. 173-221). Mahwah, NJ: Lawrence Erlbaum Associates.

Bietz, M. J., Baumer, E. P. S., & Lee, C. P. (2010). Synergizing in cyberinfrastructure development. *Computer Supported Cooperative Work: CSCW: An International Journal, 19*(3-4), 245-281.

Blumenthal, D., Campbell, E. G., Gokhale, M., Yucel, R., Clarridge, B., Hilgartner, S., & Holtzman, N. A. (2006). Data withholding in genetics and the other life sciences: Prevalences and predictors. *Academic Medicine, 81*(2), 137-145. doi:10.1097/00001888-200602000-00008

Bontis, N., Crossan, M. M., & Hulland, J. (2002). Managing an organizational learning system by aligning stocks and flows. *Journal of Management Studies, 39*(4), 437-469.

Borgman, C. L. (2007). *Scholarship in the Digital Age: Information, Infrastructure, and the Internet*. Cambridge: MIT Press.

Borgman, C. L. (2009). The digital future is now: A call to action for the humanities. *Digital Humanities Quarterly, 3*(4).

Borgman, C. L. (2012). The Conundrum of Sharing Research Data. *Journal of the American Society for Information Science and Technology, 63*(6), 1059-1078. doi:10.1002/asi.22634

Campbell, E. G., & Bendavid, E. (2003). Data-sharing and data-withholding in genetics and the life sciences: results of a national survey of technology transfer officers. *J Health Care Law Policy, 6*(2), 241-255.

Campbell, E. G., Clarridge, B. R., Gokhale, N. N., Birenbaum, L., Hilgartner, S., Holtzman, N. A., & Blumenthal, D. (2002). Data withholding in academic genetics - Evidence from a national survey. *Journal of the American Medical Association, 287*(4), 473-480. doi:10.1001/jama.287.4.473

Campbell, E. G., Louis, K. S., & Blumenthal, D. (1998). Looking a gift horse in the mouth - Corporate gifts supporting life sciences research. *Jama-Journal of the American Medical Association, 279*(13), 995-999. doi:10.1001/jama.279.13.995

Chin, W. W. (1998). The partial least squares approach to structural equation modeling. *Modern Methods for Business Research, 295*(2), 295-336.

Choudhury, G. S. (2008). Case study in data curation at Johns Hopkins University. *Library Trends, 57*(2), 211-220.

Cragin, M. H., Palmer, C. L., Carlson, J. R., & Witt, M. (2010). Data sharing, small science and institutional repositories. *Philosophical Transactions of the Royal Society a-Mathematical Physical and Engineering Sciences, 368*(1926), 4023-4038. doi:10.1098/rsta.2010.0165

Dundar, H., & Lewis, D. R. (1998). Determinants of research productivity in higher education. *Research in Higher Education, 39*(6), 607-631.

Ebenhöh, E., & Pahl-Wostl, C. (2008). Agent behavior between maximization and cooperation. *Rationality and Society, 20*(2), 227-252.

Fornell, C., & Larcker, D. F. (1981). Structural equation models with unobservable variables and measurement error: Algebra and statistics. *Journal of Marketing Research, 18*(3), 382-388.

Hair, J. F., Black, W. C., Babin, B. J., Anderson, R. E., & Tatham, R. L. (2006). *Multivariate Data Analysis (6th ed.)*. Upper Saddle River, NJ: Prentice Hall.

John, C. H. S., Cannon, A. R., & Pouder, R. W. (2001). Change drivers in the new millennium: implications for manufacturing strategy research. *Journal of Operations Management, 19*(2), 143-160. doi:10.1016/s0272-6963(00)00054-1

Kankanhalli, A., Tan, B. C. Y., & Wei, K. K. (2005). Contributing knowledge to electronic knowledge repositories: An empirical investigation. *Mis Quarterly, 29*(1), 113-143.

Kim, Y., & Adler, M. (2015). Social scientists' data sharing behaviors: Investigating the roles of individual motivations, institutional pressures, and data repositories. *International Journal of Information Management, 35*(4), 408-418.

Kim, Y., & Burns, C. S. (2016). Norms of data sharing in biological sciences: The roles of metadata, data repository, and journal and funding requirements. *Journal of Information Science, 42*(2), 230-245.

Kim, Y., & Stanton, J. M. (2016). Institutional and individual factors affecting scientists' data-sharing behaviors: A multilevel analysis. *Journal of the Association for Information Science and Technology*, 1-24. doi:10.1002/asi.23424

Kim, Y., & Zhang, P. (2015). Understanding data sharing behaviors of STEM researchers: The roles of attitudes, norms, and data repositories. *Library & Information Science Research, 37*(3), 189-200.

Kling, R., & Spector, L. (2003). Rewards for scholarly communication. In D. L. Andersen (Ed.), *Digital Scholarship in the Tenure, Promotion, and Review Process*. Armonk, NY: M.E. Sharpe, Inc.

Louis, K. S., Jones, L. M., & Campbell, E. G. (2002). Sharing in science. *American Scientist, 90*(4), 304-307. doi:10.1511/2002.27.3289

McCain, K. W. (1991). Communication, competition, and secrecy - The production and dissemination of research-related information in genetics. *Science Technology & Human Values, 16*(4), 491-516. doi:10.1177/016224399101600404

McCullough, B. D., McGeary, K. A., & Harrison, T. D. (2008). Do economics journal archives promote replicable research? *Canadian Journal of Economics, 41*(4), 1406-1420.

Merton, R. K. (1957). Priorities in scientific discovery. In N. W. Storer (Ed.), *The Sociology of Science* (pp. 286-324). Chicago: University of Chicago Press.

Merton, R. K. (1973). *The sociology of science: Theoretical and empirical investigations*. Chicago: University of Chicago Press.

Nunnally , J. C., & Bernstein, I. H. (1994). *Psychometric Theory (3rd ed.)*. New York, NY: McGraw-Hill.

Ostrom, E. (2003). Toward a behavioral theory linking trust, reciprocity, and reputation. In E. Ostrom & J. Walker (Eds.), *Trust and reciprocity: Interdisciplinary lessons from experimental research* (pp. 19-79). New York: Russell Sage Foundation.

Paton, N. W. (2008). Managing and sharing experimental data: standards, tools and pitfalls. *Biochemical Society Transactions, 36*, 33-36. doi:10.1042/b5t0360033

Piwowar, H. A. (2010). *Foundational studies for measuring the impact, prevalence, and patterns of publicly sharing biomedical research data.* (Ph.D.), University of Pittsburgh.

Piwowar, H. A. (2011). Who Shares? Who Doesn't? Factors Associated with Openly Archiving Raw Research Data. *Plos One, 6*(7).

Piwowar, H. A., & Chapman, W. W. (2008). *A review of journal policies for sharing research data.* Paper presented at the International Conference on Electronic Publishing.

Rasch, S., Heckelei, T., Oomen, R., & Naumann, C. (2016). Cooperation and collapse in a communal livestock production SES model–a case from South Africa. *Environmental Modelling & Software, 75*, 402-413.

Ringle, C. M., Wende, S., & Will, S. (2005). SmartPLS 2.0 (M3) Beta. Retrieved from http://www.smartpls.de

Savage, C. J., & Vickers, A. J. (2009). Empirical study of data sharing by authors publishing in PLoS journals. *Plos One, 4*(9).

Tenopir, C., Allard, S., Douglass, K., Aydinoglu, A. U., Wu, L., Read, E., . . . Frame, M. (2011). Data sharing by scientists: Practices and perceptions. *Plos One, 6*(6).

Tenopir, C., Dalton, E. D., Allard, S., Frame, M., Pjesivac, I., Birch, B., . . . Dorsett, K. (2015). Changes in Data Sharing and Data Reuse Practices and Perceptions among Scientists Worldwide. *Plos One, 10*(8). doi:10.1371/journal.pone.0134826

Vickers, A. J. (2006). Whose data set is it anyway? Sharing raw data from randomized trials. *Trials, 7.*

Vogeli, C., Yucel, R., Bendavid, E., Jones, L. M., Anderson, M. S., Louis, K. S., & Campbell, E. G. (2006). Data withholding and the next generation of scientists: Results of a national survey. *Academic Medicine, 81*(2), 128-136. doi:10.1097/00001888-200602000-00007

Witt, M. (2008). Institutional repositories and research data curation in a distributed environment. *Library Trends, 57*(2), 191-201.

Yandle, T., Hajj, N., & Raciborski, R. (2011). The Goldilocks solution: Exploring the relationship between trust and participation in resource management within the New Zealand commercial rock lobster fishery. *Policy Studies Journal, 39*(4), 631-658.

Zanini, M. T. F., & Migueles, C. P. (2013). Trust as an element of informal coordination and its relationship with organizational performance. *EconomiA, 14*(2), 77-87.

Ziman, J. M. (2000). *Real Science: What It Is, and What It Means*. Cambridge, U.K.; New York: Cambridge University Press.

Zimmerman, A. (2007). Not by metadata alone: The use of diverse forms of knowledge to locate data for reuse. *International Journal on Digital Libraries, 7*(1-2), 5-16.

Zsidisin, G. A., Melnyk, S. A., & Ragatz, G. L. (2005). An institutional theory perspective of business continuity planning for purchasing and supply management. *International Journal of Production Research, 43*(16), 3401-3420. doi:10.1080/00207540500095613

"Life Never Matters in the DEMOCRATS MIND": Examining Strategies of Retweeted Social Bots During a Mass Shooting Event

Vanessa L. Kitzie
University of South Carolina, USA. kitzie@mailbox.sc.edu

Amir Karami
University of South Carolina, USA. karami@sc.edu

Ehsan Mohammadi
University of South Carolina, USA. ehsan2@sc.edu

ABSTRACT

This exploratory study examines the strategies of social bots on Twitter that were retweeted following a mass shooting event. Using a case study method to frame our work, we collected over seven million tweets during a one-month period following a mass shooting in Parkland, Florida. From this dataset, we selected retweets of content generated by over 400 social bot accounts to determine what strategies these bots were using and the effectiveness of these strategies as indicated by the number of retweets. We employed qualitative and quantitative methods to capture both macro- and micro-level perspectives. Our findings suggest that bots engage in more diverse strategies than solely waging disinformation campaigns, including baiting and sharing information. Further, we found that while bots amplify conversation about mass shootings, humans were primarily responsible for disseminating bot-generated content. These findings add depth to the current understanding of bot strategies and their effectiveness. Understanding these strategies can inform efforts to combat dubious information as well as more insidious disinformation campaigns.

KEYWORDS

Social bots, mixed methods, social media, misinformation, disinformation

INTRODUCTION

It is widely acknowledged by researchers that social bots occupy diverse social media platforms. Defined as software programs that automatically produce content and emulate human behavior, these bots exhibit political and economic influence at an international scale (Ferrara, Varol, Davis, Menczer, & Flammini, 2016). For instance, it has been demonstrated that social bots manipulate political discourse (Bessi & Ferrara, 2016; Conover, Ratkiewicz, & Francisco, 2011; Howard & Kollanyi, 2016; Kollanyi, Howard, & Woolley, 2016; Ratkiewicz et al., 2011), affect stock trading (Fiegerman, 2014; Hwang, Pearce, & Nanis, 2012), and increase the spread of mis and disinformation during emergencies (Gupta, Lamba, & Ponnurangam, 2013).

On February 14, 2018, a mass shooting occurred at Stoneman Douglas High School in Parkland, Florida. The shooter killed 17 people and injured 17 more, making it one of the deadliest mass shootings on record in the US (Follman, Aronsen, & Pan, 2018). Following the shooting, millions of people discussed the event on Twitter. For example, Parkland survivor Emma González, who has been vocally pro-gun control, created a Twitter account following the shooting that has amassed over one million followers as of March 2018.[1]

Within 48 hours of the shooting, social bot monitoring services[2] reported a heightened use of shooting-related hashtags, keywords, and URLs. Specifically, researchers from the group Hamilton68 found that Russian bots were using the #parklandshooting to spread disinformation. The bots advanced unverified claims that the shooter searched for Arabic phrases on Google (Frenkel & Wakabayashi, 2018) and amplified conspiracy theories promoted by far-right outlets that the Parkland survivors were paid crisis actors (Smith, 2018). Presence of bots during the shooting aftermath paralleled documented concerns among journalists (Chen, 2015) and the government (Rid, 2017) of the potential for social bots to cause geopolitical conflict by spreading disinformation and contributing to political polarization.

A week after the shooting on February 21, Twitter released a new set of guidelines prohibiting three types of social bot behaviors enacted via third-party apps: posting similar content to multiple accounts; coordinating simultaneous likes, follows, and/or retweets across various accounts; and automating posts and actions from multiple accounts on a specific topic (Roth, 2018). The company also deleted thousands of accounts that it flagged as social bots. Specific groups, such as right-wing conservatives, criticized Twitter for their resultant loss of followers, their accounts being flagged, and their ability to run ads revoked.

---

[1] https://twitter.com/emma4change?lang=en
[2] https://dashboard.securingdemocracy.org/, https://botcheck.me/

Former Twitter employees also criticized the bot crackdown as too little, too late (Lorenz, 2018). They claimed that Twitter did not prioritize the development of a program sophisticated enough to detect social bots, along with problematic content including spam and abuse (Kosoff, 2018).

We decided to examine the activity of social bots during and following these events for several reasons. Most ostensibly, we considered it a good case because social bots were thought to be active. In addition, a mass shooting provides a new context from which to examine bot strategies, as existing research focuses on elections. Findings from this research, therefore, can provide a contextual counterpoint from which to compare and contrast bot strategies.

Our research meets several objectives. Initial media reporting relied primarily on quantitative evidence (e.g., hashtag frequency of identified bot accounts) to support the claim that bots could incite geopolitical conflict via disinformation campaigns. However, this claim is unsubstantiated without empirical evidence that examines social bot strategies, and which strategies are effective. Therefore, it is possible that we could identify any new changes or developments in bot strategies. Further, we engage in both qualitative and quantitative analysis of social bot strategies and their effectiveness, which provides both micro- and macro-level perspectives on these issues. We applied this analysis to thousands of social bot retweets to address the following research questions: 1) What are the main strategies employed by retweeted social bots? 2) Which strategies are most effective, as indicated by the number of retweets?

LITERATURE REVIEW

Multiple, sometimes contesting definitions of social bots exist (Stieglitz, Brachten, Ross, & Jung, 2017). Based on a comprehensive literature review, Stieglitz et al. (2017) define social bots as automated social media accounts that emulate human behavior. In this study, we also adopt this definition. Within the context of Twitter, social bots write original tweets, and follow and retweet other users. Social bots can engage in several malicious activities including identity attacks (e.g., duplicating a celebrity account, impersonating a user's friend or family member to extract personal information from them) (Goga, Venkatadri, & Gummadi, 2015), astroturfing (i.e., making it appear as if the vast majority of people are in favor of a particular position) (Ratkiewicz et al., 2011), smoke screening (i.e., using context-relevant hashtags to distract users from the main points of a debate), and misdirection (i.e., using context-relevant hashtags without referring to the topic at all) (Abokhodair, Yoo, & Mcdonald, 2015). Bots can also be purchased to sway public opinion, such as a politician buying social bots to boost their follower counts (Woolley, 2015). However, social bots can also engage in neutral, or even benign actions, such as chat bots (Stieglitz, Brachten, Ross, et al., 2017). These findings suggest that social bots adopt various strategies depending on the specific objectives of their creators.

Social bots are harder to detect as they become more sophisticated (Everett, Nurse, & Erola, 2016). Further complicating detection are cyborg or hybrid accounts, which are a combination of people and automation techniques (e.g., someone tweeting from their account, but also using a third-party service to tweet similar messages from other accounts) (Chu, Gianvecchio, Wang, & Jajodia, 2012). Researchers have employed three dominant techniques to identify social bots: graph-based, crowdsourcing, and feature-based (Ferrara et al., 2016). Feature-based approaches are the most reasonable for labeling larger datasets as they incorporate network features considered by graph-based models, as well as training data manually labeled by human annotators (Kruschinski, Jürgens, Maurer, et al., 2018; Stieglitz, Brachten, Ross, et al., 2017). Botometer[3] (formerly BotOrNot) represents the only public-facing interface that detects social bots. Several papers have used Botometer to detect bots that are relatively sophisticated (Stieglitz, Brachten, Ross, et al., 2017; Vosoughi, Roy, & Aral, 2018), however bots with higher levels of sophistication (e.g., those that simulate breaks and slightly modify messages) may avoid detection (Stieglitz, Brachten, Berthelé, et al., 2017). Further, Botometer does not detect hybrid or cyborg accounts.

The influence of social bots online is contested within the literature, and varies by context – both of the specific topic investigated (e.g., the US 2016 elections) and how influence is measured. Bessi & Ferrara (2016) found that bots generated approximately 20% of Twitter conversation in the months leading to the 2016 US presidential election. Further, they found that people were equally as likely to retweet other humans as they were social bots. Their findings support those from other work demonstrating the difficulty that Twitter users experience in identifying tweets from social bots, which may be due to the informal and short nature of Twitter messages (Freitas, Benevenuto, Ghosh, & Veloso, 2015). Therefore, there exists a potential for bots to leverage interactions with human users to disseminate misinformation and wage disinformation campaigns via social contagion (Wang, Angarita, & Renna, 2018). Studies of Twitter social bot involvement in other topics, including Brexit (UK) (Howard & Kollanyi, 2016) and political conversations in Venezuela (Forelle, Howard, Monroy-Hernandez, & Savage, 2015) found that social bots played a less prominent role based on content generated and retweeted. However, this role was strategic. For instance, Forelle et al. (2015) found that Venezuela's radical opposition uses the most active bots. Other studies have not

[3] https://botometer.iuni.iu.edu/#!/

found bots to be influential if they are even present in the conversation. For example, Brachten, Stieglitz, Hofeditz, Kloppenborg, & Reimann (2017) found that Twitter conversation around the German 2017 state elections had little social bot activity, the bots demonstrated little to no strategy and little influence as measured by retweets. Recently, Vosoughi et al. (2018) discovered that social bots accelerate the spread of both true and false news, and consequentially, people played more of a role in spreading false news than bots.

These works illustrate the importance of continued research on social bots as their strategies and influence appear to be constantly changing and highly contextual; indeed, the bots themselves are changing and becoming more difficult to detect. This research contributes to the established body of literature by presenting mass shooting event in the US as a new context.

METHODS

Data Collection

We chose to collect data following the Parkland shooting for two reasons: 1) prior research demonstrates that political events are rife for the presence of bot accounts, and 2) we wanted to collect recent data from a new context to consider any changes or developments in bot strategies. Following the events, of Parkland, we collected over seven million tweets from over two million unique users using the Twitter Streaming API via Mozdeh (mozdeh.wlv.ac.uk/). We collected tweets from February 16 through March 5, 2018. To collect these tweets, we used nine popular keywords and hashtags related to gun control and the Parkland shooting: *#schoolshooting, #parkland, #guncontrol, #guncontrolnow, #gunreformnow, #nikolascruz, #floridaschoolshooting, #floridashooting,* and *#floridahighschoolshooting*. We defined "popular" based on Twitter trending topics within the first 48 hours of the shooting, as well as hashtags identified by Hamilton68 and Botcheck.me as being wielded by social bots. Once we collected the tweets, we stored them in an SQL database.

Data Analysis

From the collected data, we took a random sample of 120,000 Twitter users and ran their usernames through the Botometer classification algorithm to identify bot accounts. The algorithm scored a detection accuracy of 0.95 AUC with ten-fold cross validation when applied to a 2011 dataset of detected social bots (Davis, Varol, Ferrara, et al., 2016). However, this high classification accuracy is likely inflated due to the age of the data. We accessed the Botometer public API endpoint using Python. Botometer's rate limit of 17k accounts per day (40k for a paid account) determined the size of our random sample. Of these 120,000 accounts, Botometer identified 2,739 (2.2%) as having been deleted. It is possible that some of these accounts were bots removed by Twitter. However other instances could represent users deciding to delete their accounts. Botometer classified 5% (6,051) of the remaining 117,261 accounts as social bots.

We then randomly sampled 5,000 social bot accounts from the dataset and queried them in our SQL database to determine how many of these bot accounts were retweeted. We decided to sample from the total number of bots due to the computational expense of a larger query. We found that 11% (557) of the 5,000 social bot accounts were retweeted. Since Botometer could return false positives, particularly flagging organizations like the GOP as bots in our dataset, we then checked our 557 retweeted accounts to determine which were verified by Twitter.[4] We automatically eliminated verified (16.5%, n=92) and deleted accounts (1%, n=6) from our dataset, leaving us with 459 social bot accounts.

In our next step, we queried the SQL database to pull all records that retweeted one of our 459 social bot accounts. We took the Twitter accounts that retweeted our identified social bot accounts (29,269) and ran them through Botometer. Similar to our initial analysis using Botometer, we removed seven deleted accounts and relabeled nine verified accounts initially flagged as bots. In a final step to clean the dataset, we queried our retweet database for any instances where the same Twitter account was flagged by Botometer as both bot and not bot – meaning that Botometer initially flagged it as a retweeted social bot, but the account had also retweeted social bot content captured in our dataset. We found that Botometer inconsistently flagged 51 (11%) of accounts in our dataset. We removed these accounts and their related records from our dataset.

Our final sample consists of 408 social bot accounts retweeted by 19,125 Twitter users, contributing a total of 36,627 retweets. Of these retweets, 1,413 (3.9%) are unique. Botometer flagged the majority of Twitter users retweeting social bot content as non-bots (92.9%, n=17,773) and the rest as bots (7.1%, n=1,352). Therefore, the majority of actors sharing social bot generated content were humans.

We took the sample of 1,413 unique retweets of bot accounts and coded them manually. During this qualitative coding, we sought to identify social bot strategies, which we defined as the inferred goals or aims of the social bot activity based on the type of content shared. We constantly compared emerging codes to existing ones, revising and combining coding categories

---

[4] https://help.twitter.com/en/managing-your-account/about-twitter-verified-accounts

(Charmaz, 2014). We ultimately created a codebook that nested types of content shared underneath higher-level bot strategies. Once we established a preliminary codebook, two members of the research team coded 20% of the data and discussed coding discrepancies, revising the codebook as necessary. We calculated reliability among two coders using percentage agreement at 88%. Following coding, we wanted to determine which strategies were most effective, which we operationalized by the number of retweets. To determine this number, we took our unique tweets and ran an SQL query to count the number of times they were retweeted in our dataset. Our dataset can be accessed at the following link: https://doi.org/10.6084/m9.figshare.6726419.

FINDINGS

We identified six key strategies employed by retweeted bot accounts. These strategies are: Baiting, Instilling Public Doubt, Sharing Information, Spreading Conspiracy Theories, Organizing Political Action, and Using the Shooting for Commercial Gain. We now discuss each strategy in more detail. From this discussion, we exclude the 8% (n=2,944) we coded as irrelevant (e.g., tweets about a basketball game in Florida). Below, we only use examples of tweets still publicly available on Twitter. However, it should be noted that since Twitter has recently started to shut down accounts suspected to be social bots, it is possible that these tweets will not be available by the time of publication of this paper. We have removed the names of all Twitter accounts, including bot accounts (since Botometer is not likely 100% accurate), to protect user privacy. Table 1 displays a list of all high-level strategies, their definitions, and frequencies.

Main Code	Definition	N	% (of 36,628)
Baiting	Instances where the tweet content elicits an angry or emotional response.	21,453	58.6%
Instilling doubt	Posting dubious information that makes people doubt democratic institutions	6,566	17.9%
Sharing information	Sharing factual information about the event	4,046	11.0%
Spreading conspiracy theories	Suggesting that the shooting event was part of a secret plan to do something unlawful or harmful	1,458	4.0%
Organizing political action	Attempting to elicit participation in a political event	88	0.2%
Using shooting for commercial gain	Attempting to profit from the shooting	73	0.2%

Table 1. High-level Social Bot Strategies

Baiting

The majority of retweets showcased the social bot strategy of baiting. A popular example of baiting was social bots retweeting content that criticized key actors in the Parkland shooting (36.6%, n=13,424). Consider the following tweet, which criticizes the media outlet CNN:

CNN condemns heroic student who shielded others as a liar because he wont parrot left-wing gun control talking points.. Straight up: CNN is no longer even pretending to be a news network, and instead has gone full-blown Marxist in pushing as much agitpr... https://t.co/6xAbujeFaV

This bot-generated tweet shares the first 280 characters of an article from a blog, Natural News (www.naturalnews.com) that sells various dietary supplements and alternative medicine, as well as shares false scientific news and conspiracy theories. Such content is standard for bot accounts, which predominately share content generated by others. This content represents a baiting strategy because of the language used. Connecting CNN to Marxist ideologies can elicit an emotional response among those who already mistrust the news network and believe that its coverage disproportionately represents a specific political agenda. Other actors frequently criticized in bot retweets were conservative politicians (10.1%, n=3,682), the FL police officers responding to the shooting (5.9%, n= 2,169), and liberal politicians (5.1%, n=1,862).

Another popular baiting strategy was bots' sharing of content that either was explicitly against gun control (4.6%, n= 1,672) or for gun control (3.4%, n= 1,255). Similar to the prior example, this sort of content represented retweets or excerpts of news content that had a distinct opinion on the gun control issue. The following tweet exemplifies a pro-con control strategy:

We are going to use THIS ARGUMENT when we discuss gun control with dolts: https://t.co/UrKap9AgHj

Here, the use of the word "dolts" to describe individuals against gun control represents baiting. It can both incite those who agree with gun control measures to share this content, as well as potential replies from those who disagree with gun control and are insulted by being called a "dolt."

Two other baiting strategies of note are drawing false equivalencies (3.9%, n=1,444) and inviting debate on gun control (2.2%, 794). Drawing false equivalencies represents when bots share content that equates mass shootings to some other controversial issue. For instance, the following example positions Planned Parenthood as more dangerous than school shootings:

> *Planned Parenthood has killed more babies last year than all school shooting COMBINED! #stop-plannedparenthood*

Drawing false equivalencies parallels smoke-screening strategies identified in prior work (Abokhodair et al., 2015), because bots use content with relevant hashtags and keywords representative of a particular issue (here, gun control) to ultimately distract individuals by having them discuss another topic. In the majority of cases, the issue meant to distract from a broader discussion surrounding mass shootings is societally contentious (e.g., abortion).

Inviting debate on gun control is a strategy used by bots to bring individuals from multiple sides of an issue into one Twitter thread, as illustrated by the following example. In this example, the Twitter account uses hashtags visible to individuals who stand on multiple sides of the gun control debate, asking them to retweet to "vote" on the issue. Ultimately, this strategy spreads this tweet to more Twitter accounts and can also artificially lend support to a specific stance on the issue based on retweet volume.

> *Should teachers be armed in schools? Retweet for more votes! #NRA #GunControlNow #GunReformNow*

Instilling Doubt

Instilling doubt was the second-most popular category after baiting. Content within this category focused on the media (9.4%, n=3,456), FBI (4.9%, n=1,806), and the police (2.8%, n=1,034). The following tweet illustrates instilling doubt in the media:

> *FL School Shooting Survivor Says CNN Gave Him a Scripted Question for Townhall Meeting https://t.co/BwOdiuXonr*

Here, the bot retweets a headline and link to a story from enVolve (https://en-volve.com/), a conservative news and opinion website that has been identified by fact-checking organizations as a source that creates and shares false news (Politifact, 2017). Several fact-checking organizations have debunked the story about CNN handing a scripted question to a Parkland survivor ("Did CNN give a Parkland shooting survivor scripted questions?," 2018). Therefore, this story goes one step beyond critique by instilling doubt about CNN's reporting practices by making a false claim about the network.

Instilling doubt in the FBI and police are connected. The majority of tweets coded under this category shared dubious information to insinuate that both institutions aided the shooting. For instance, the following tweet blames the FBI for ignoring tips about the shooter to focus on the Russia investigation:

> *Anyone else ticked about the FBI wasting resources on a phony witch hunt while letting 17 people get slaughtered. They were WARNED They knew his complete NAME: Nikolas Cruz They LET this happen on purpose But we're wasting MILs to appease Libs who're mad they lost an election?*

Similar to baiting, this tweet also elicits anger, both against the FBI and liberal politicians, who are portrayed by the tweet as letting a shooting happen for political gain. The dubious information in this tweet is twofold – that the Russia investigation is a "phony witch hunt" and that the FBI purposefully let the shooting happen. Tweets instilling doubt in the police follow a similar pattern but insinuate that the police worked to abet the shooting. For instance, one bot tweeted the following:

> *BREAKING! EMS Claims Broward Sheriffs Office Blocked Them From Entering FL School During Shooting https://t.co/znIlkeeABy*

The article to which the bot links is another false news site, Clash Daily (clashdaily.com) (Politifact, 2017). This headline likely derives from the "stand down" conspiracy theory, which purported that the police gave EMS a "stand down" order during the shooting. What prevented us from coding this tweet as a conspiracy theory is that it does not cite a "stand down" order, however it does misrepresent standard EMS protocol to wait for police affirmation before entering the scene of a shooting ("Did a first responder say he was told to 'stand down' in Parkland?," 2018). Therefore, the tweet makes a dubious claim about the Broward County Sherriff's office that could make a reader question the intents and motivations of police departments during mass shootings.

Sharing Information

A small, but significant proportion of bot retweets shared information. The following tweet illustrates one example of information sharing:

> *Russian Bots Moved Quickly to Exploit the Florida Shooting - The New York Times #DemForce https://t.co/ippBU4Gr0g*

Presence of these tweets confirms findings from other research that not all social bot accounts are malicious. Benign bots also exist, particularly in journalistic contexts to share news stories (Lokot & Diakopoulos, 2016). Interestingly, bot accounts that engaged in the spread of more malicious information (e.g., instilling doubt) could also spread information. Consider the following example from a bot account that predominately tweeted malicious tweet content:

> *Condoleezza Rice: US must reconsider 2nd Amendment 'in modern world' https://t.co/MpyTsgjpe5*

This account is of particular interest, as it links to a site called http://ytreet.com (see Figure 1 below). A small, but significant number of bot tweets (1.2%, n=439) originated from this domain http://ytreet.com/ye. This latter link directs to a log-in page (see Figure 2). This log-in page suggests a potential botnet or coordinated program that communicates across multiple devices to complete a task. Therefore, this finding suggests that a single bot account can engage in various strategies, which can be aided by botnets.

Figure 1. Suspected social bot account. Note that it would be impossible for a human to have tweeted 329,000 tweets in 18 months. The account tweets an average of over 500 tweets a day.

Figure 2. Log-in page to the suspected botnet.

Spreading Conspiracy Theories

This bot strategy confirms media reports of suspected bot activity and motivations following the Parkland shooting. The most popular conspiracy theory included in retweeted bot content was the "false flag" theory (Starbird, Maddock, Orand, Achterman, & Mason, 2014). This theory purports that the government planned the shooting and aided by the police and media to justify gun control measures. Below is an example of a tweet supporting a false flag conspiracy theory:

> *grazed Teacher by Parkland shooter's bullet: 'Shooter was in full metal garb, helmet, face mask, bulletproof armor, shooting a rifle I've never seen before' http://www.legitgov.org/Teacher-grazed-Parkland-shooters-bullet-Shooter-was-full-metal-garb-helmet-face-mask-bulletproof ... #ParklandShooting*

Here, the account links to a news blog, LegitGov (www.legitgov.org) that shares an alternate narrative of a shooting event. This story insinuates that the shooting was planned by questioning the accepted narrative of who the shooter was, how he was dressed, and what equipment he had. Another example of a popular conspiracy theory relates to the accusing Parkland shooting survivors as being crisis actors. For instance, the following tweet accuses survivor, David Hogg, of being coached by the FBI:

> *#DeepState #CNN #JakeTapper #VeryFakeNews | #ParklandShooting | #DavidHogg Outspoken Trump-Hating School Shooting Survivor is Son of #FBI Agent; MSM Helps Prop Up Bureau That Acknowledges It Messed Up https://truepundit.com/video-outspoken-trump-hating-school-shooting-survivor-son-fbi-agent-msm-helps-prop-incompetent-bureau/ ...| #tcot #PJNET*

The post links to True Pundit (truepundit.com), another blog sharing conspiracy theories and false news (Politifact, 2017). What many of these conspiracy theories have in common is that they take advantage of the confusion inherent to crisis events that may influence the presence of contradictory accounts, such as a witness claiming the shooter was heavily armed and outfitted. Further, they take advantage of facts, like that David Hogg's father is a retired FBI agent, to "prove" unsubstantiated claims about the shooting being a government-led conspiracy.

Political Organizing and Using Shooting for Commercial Gain

A smaller subset of tweets engaged in political organizing and using the shooting for commercial gain. Although this category is important because it could lead to political participation, as a bot strategy it was the least frequently retweeted. This lack of retweets does not reflect the reality that people engage in political organizing online, only that social bots may not have played a significant role in facilitating such organization within the context of the Parkland shooting. Another reason for the lack of retweets may have been the tweet collection time period, which ended as the March for our Lives walkouts were beginning. In the context of tweets analyzed, political organizing mostly encouraged participation, such as going to a walkout or boycotting an organization. The following tweet links to an article encouraging individuals to boycott companies sponsored by the NRA:

> *The only way to influence an organization like the NRA is through their sponsors. #BoycottNRA until they support common sense gun control. The NRA is being supported by these companies – ThinkProgress https://t.co/PutyfCLk36*

Using the shooting for commercial gain was used by some to make money from the shooting. For instance, the following account tweeted links to buy anti-gun protest t-shirts:

> *#MarchForOurLives Anti-Gun Protest T-shirt BUY HERE*

Again, the number of retweets for this bot strategy may have been low due to the data collection time period or simply that this bot strategy, while it exists, is not particularly effective as evidenced by number of retweets.

DISCUSSION

Our research examined retweeted content generated by social bots following a mass shooting event. We used a mixed method approach to collect and analyze our data, facilitating both macro- and micro- perspectives of bot strategies during this event. Findings indicated that the majority of actors retweeting bot accounts were humans. This finding supports the conclusions of prior work that while bots *amplify* conversation surrounding significant issues (e.g., political elections, crisis situations), people are primarily responsible for the dissemination of bot-generated content (Bessi & Ferrara, 2016). Another significant finding was that a subset of bot-generated content is not malicious. This content could be produced by "benign" bots, employed within journalism contexts to share news related to the Parkland shooting and its aftermath (Lokot & Diakopoulos, 2016). Therefore, reporting by media outlets on the presence of bot activity following the Parkland shooting may be substantiated by this analysis, but with these two critical caveats.

We coded the most popular social bot strategy as baiting. The cultural theory of risk can potentially explain the popularity of baiting content in our dataset (Douglas & Wildavsky, 1982). This theory contends that people have sophisticated social and cognitive reasons for seeking, sharing, and using specific information, even if that information is misleading or false. People develop risk perceptions based on their commitment to a particular way of life and worldview. Therefore, people may share content that criticizes institutions like the mainstream media if they view this institution as presenting a risk to their way of life. Content that bolsters a specific ideology, such as a pro-gun control agenda, may appeal because it affirms their sense of self. This sense is derived, in part, by the groups to which people belong. Therefore, supporting specific in-group ideologies and members by sharing content may help reinforce an individual's perception that they belong to the "correct" group with desirable ideologies (Sherman, Cohen, & Sherman, 2002).

Instilling doubt and conspiracy theories were two other key forms of bot-generated content that we found during data analysis. These two categories share patently false information and reflect popularized fear of bot activities discussed in the media. Prior research has established that the primary motivations for circulating this content, at least among bots, is to undermine trust – both in information and democratic institutions (Pomerantsev & Weiss, 2014; Starbird, 2017). We found that some bot accounts appeared to share a variety of content – ranging from conspiracy theories to more benign information. Further, there are likely botnets at work in disseminating this content, meaning that it is coming from a variety of sources, which can inaccurately foster the perception among people that these fringe ideas are more mainstream than in actuality.

Similar to the discussion on baiting, people are not necessarily cognitively or culturally helpless when processing and evaluating questionable or false information. Instead, these individuals may have a "crippled epistemology" from being exposed to limited media sources (Sunstein & Vermeule, 2008; see also Starbird, 2017). We found evidence for this perspective in qualitative analysis, where much of the content linked to sources that parroted similar narratives, most often supporting a false flag perspective.

These observations suggest the need to reframe our approach to issues like information literacy. As boyd (2018) argues, people often employ critical assessment and analysis of information sources. However, these standards of assessment and analysis vary based on cognitive and cultural perspectives and worldviews. For example, someone that retweets content instilling doubt in the media recognizes media strategies such as framing (e.g., questioning CNN's support of pro-gun control narratives), even if they are couched within a more substantial, false narrative (e.g., CNN supported its pro-gun agenda by feeding scripted questions to Parkland survivors). Therefore, addressing the spread of false information cannot be solely solved by teaching information literacy and critical thinking. Instead, it is important to recognize people's motivations for seeking, sharing, and using particular information and how the strategies used by actors, including bots, appeal to these motivations. Some concrete recommendations for improving information literacy instruction based on these findings include:

- **Outline approaches for identifying social bots.** Common heuristics, such as a high number of retweets for a recent account, indicate a high likelihood of a bot account (Ferrara et al., 2016). Individuals can also insert a Twitter account name into the Botometer interface to determine the likelihood of it being a social bot.
- **Overview common strategies used by social bots.** This paper offers a beginning typology, which can be combined with strategies identified by prior research, such as smoke screening and misdirection (Abokhodair, Yoo, & Mcdonald, 2015). Have individuals question whether there are underlying strategies present in social media content they encounter and what reactions these strategies are trying to elicit from them.
- **Engage in a dialog about media framing**. Have individuals share common frames they experience when engaging with media. What are some frames that individuals may have blind spots towards based on their underlying ideological views?
- **Do not discount emotions and group think.** Have an open discussion of how emotions and group memberships shape how individuals interpret and share information on social media. Stress the importance of striving for accuracy as defined by an information literacy framework and attempt to re-motivate individuals to strive for accuracy goals.

CONCLUSION

In this study, we examined the strategies of social bots whose content was shared on Twitter on the topic of gun control following the school shooting in Parkland, FL. Analysis of over 36k tweets from more than 400 social bot accounts identified six key bot strategies. Findings indicate that other people, rather than bots primarily shared bot-generated content. Reasons for the effectiveness of these strategies, as conveyed by the number of retweets, can be attributed to cultural and cognitive motivations that people have to protect their worldviews and related conceptions of self-worth.

Limitations of this work relate to data collection and analysis methods. For data collection, we used the Twitter stream, which collects a random sample of 1% of all Twitter data shared within a 24-hour period. Therefore, our data is not necessarily representative of all Twitter activity centered on the Parkland shooting. Further, we started the Twitter stream two days after the Parkland shooting and are therefore missing tweets from the outset of the event. This lack of sampling is somewhat countered since some content shared during these first two days was widely retweeted for days following the event, meaning that it is included in our dataset. However, to get a better picture of characteristics such as what bot content was shared and when our future work will incorporate this historical data.

Our data analysis was limited by the Botometer algorithm in detecting social bot accounts. We noted that Botometer inconsistently flagged 11% of Twitter accounts as bots when we ran these accounts through the algorithm twice, a few days apart. Further, Botometer flags institutional accounts as social bots, such as the news site, Vice. While we eliminated the inconsistently flagged and verified institutional accounts from the data, it is likely that some of the accounts identified as bots in the data are not bots. This limitation reflects the increasing sophistication of social bot accounts and the need for media companies like Twitter to continually provide researchers with training data to flag these accounts accurately over time. In addition, Botometer was trained on 2011 data, rendering its accuracy (0.95 AUC) as likely lowered due to this increasing sophistication of bot accounts. However, as of March 20, 2018 (after we conducted this research), the Botometer classifier was updated with thousands of new data points, which may have improved the accuracy of the classifier.[5] We will use this new version of Botometer in future work.

Since our research is exploratory, there are many directions for future work. Our next step with this data is to fold in historical tweets from the first days of the shooting and incorporate retweets of all flagged bot accounts. Due to Botometer's limitations,

---

[5] https://botometer.iuni.iu.edu/#!/faq

we plan to implement additional methods for verifying social bot accounts, including further feature-based identification of false positives and negatives, as well as using manual coding. The initial coding scheme for bot strategies can be expanded and refined to include other contextual elements, such as political ideologies (e.g., liberal, conservative) of those retweeting the content. We can use the labeled data to train a classifier that can code a larger sample of the data to determine how these strategies are disseminated across all collected tweets. Additionally, we can incorporate additional methods of analysis, including network analysis, to further describe the dissemination of tweet content. It would also be of interest to look at other Twitter activity, such as liking or replying, to see how bot strategies align with or differ from retweets. Finally, we will also sample from other events and platforms to track identified bot accounts and determine how their strategies may vary by context.

In sum, our research contributes to a growing body of work describing the strategies of social bots in online environments like Twitter. Understanding these strategies can inform efforts by other researchers and policy organizations related to the combat of misinformation, as well as more insidious disinformation campaigns.

REFERENCES

Abokhodair, N., Yoo, D., & Mcdonald, D. W. (2015). Dissecting a social botnet: Growth, content and influence in Twitter. In *Proceedings of the 18th ACM Conference on Computer Supported Cooperative Work & Social Computing* (pp. 839–851). http://doi.org/10.1145/2675133.2675208

Bessi, A., & Ferrara, E. (2016). Social bots distort the 2016 US presidential election online discussion. *First Monday*, *21*(11). http://doi.org/http://dx.doi.org/10.5210/fm.v21i11.7090

Boyd, D. (2018). Did media literacy backfire? Retrieved April 4, 2018, from https://points.datasociety.net/did-media-literacy-backfire-7418c084d88d

Brachten, F., Stieglitz, S., Hofeditz, L., Kloppenborg, K., & Reimann, A. (2017). Strategies and Influence of Social Bots in a 2017 German state election - A case study on Twitter. *Proceeedings of the Australasian Conference on Information Systems*, (May), 1–12. Retrieved from http://arxiv.org/abs/1710.07562

Charmaz, K. (2014). *Constructing grounded theory: A practical guide through qualitative analysis* (7th ed.). Thousand Oaks, CA: Sage.

Chen, A. (2015, June 2). The agency. *The New York Times*, pp. 1–21. Retrieved from https://nyti.ms/1AHZ353%0AThe

Chu, Z., Gianvecchio, S., Wang, H., & Jajodia, S. (2012). Detecting automation of Twitter accounts: Are you a human, bot, or cyborg? *IEEE Transactions on Dependable and Secure Computing*, *9*(6), 811–824.

Conover, M., Ratkiewicz, J., & Francisco, M. (2011). Political polarization on Twitter. In *Proceedings of the Fifth International AAAI Conference on Weblogs and Social Media Political* (pp. 89–96). http://doi.org/10.1021/ja202932e

Davis, C. A., Varol, O., Ferrara, E., Flammini, A., & Menczer, F. (2016). BotOrNot: A system to evaluate social bots. In *WWW'16 Companion* (pp. 1–2). https://doi.org/10.1145/2872518.2889302

Did a first responder say he was told to "stand down" in Parkland? (2018). Retrieved from https://www.snopes.com/fact-check/did-first-responder-stand-down-parkland/

Did CNN give a Parkland shooting survivor scripted questions? (2018).

Douglas, M., & Wildavsky, A. (1982). *Risk and culture: An essay on the selection of technical and environmental dangers*. Berkeley, CA: University of California Press.

Everett, R. M., Nurse, J. R. C., & Erola, A. (2016). The anatomy of online deception: What makes automated text convincing? In *Proceedings of the 31st Annual ACM Symposium on Applied Computing* (pp. 1115–1120). ACM.

Ferrara, E., Varol, O., Davis, C., Menczer, F., & Flammini, A. (2016). The rise of social bots. *Communications of the ACM*, *59*(7), 96–104. http://doi.org/10.1145/2818717

Fiegerman, S. (2014). The curious case of Cynk, an abandoned tech company now worth $5 billion. *Mashable*. Retrieved from http://mashable.com/2014/07/10/cynk/#8mv.CJM8MgqN

Follman, M., Aronsen, G., & Pan, D. (2018). US mass shootings, 1982-2018: Data from Mother Jones' investigation.

Forelle, M. C., Howard, P. N., Monroy-Hernandez, A., & Savage, S. (2015). Political bots and the manipulation of public opinion in venezuela. *SSRN Electronic Journal*, 1–8. http://doi.org/10.2139/ssrn.2635800

Freitas, C. A., Benevenuto, F., Ghosh, S., & Veloso, A. (2015). Reverse engineering socialbot infiltration strategies in Twitter. In *Advances in Social Networks Analysis and Mining (ASONAM), 2015 IEEE/ACM International Conference* (pp. 25–32). http://doi.org/10.1145/2808797.2809292

Frenkel, S., & Wakabayashi, D. (2018). After Florida school shooting, Russian "bot" army pounced. *The New York Times*.

Goga, O., Venkatadri, G., & Gummadi, K. P. (2015). The doppelgänger bot attack: Exploring identity impersonation in online social etworks. In *Proceedings of the 2015 ACM Conference on Internet Measurement Conference* (pp. 141–153). http://doi.org/10.1145/2815675.2815699

Gupta, A., Lamba, H., & Ponnurangam, K. (2013). $1.00 per RT #BostonMarathon #PrayForBoston: Analyzing fake content on Twitter. In *eCrime Researchers Summit* (pp. 1–12). IEEE. http://doi.org/10.1109/eCRS.2013.6805772

Howard, P. N., & Kollanyi, B. (2016). *Bots, #strongerIn, and #brexit: Computational propaganda during the UK-EU Referendum* (The Computational Propoganda Project Data Memos No. 1). Retrieved from http://arxiv.org/abs/1606.06356

Hwang, T., Pearce, I., & Nanis, M. (2012). Socialbots: Voices from the fronts. *Interactions*, *19*(2), 38–45. http://doi.org/10.1145/2090150.2090161

Kollanyi, B., Howard, P. N., & Woolley, S. C. (2016). *Bots and automation over Twitter during the US election. The Computational Progaganda Project Data Memos*. Retrieved from http://comprop.oii.ox.ac.uk/wp-content/uploads/sites/89/2016/11/Data-Memo-US-Election.pdf

Kosoff, B. Y. M. (2018). "Just an ass-backward tech company": How Twitter lost the internet war. *Vanity Fair*. Retrieved from https://www.vanityfair.com/news/2018/02/how-twitter-lost-the-internet-war

Kruschinski, S., Jürgens, P., Maurer, M., Schemer, C. & Stark, B. (2018). A multi-feature framework for detecting Social Bots on Facebook. Paper presented at the *68th Annual Meeting of the International Communication Association (ICA),* May 24-28, Prague.

Lokot, T., & Diakopoulos, N. (2016). News Bots: Automating news and information dissemination on Twitter. *Digital Journalism*, *4*(6), 682–699. http://doi.org/10.1080/21670811.2015.1081822

Lorenz, T. (2018). Inside Twitter's bot purge. *The Daily Beast*. Retrieved from https://www.thedailybeast.com/inside-twitters-bot-purge

Politifact. (2017). Politifact's fake news almanac. Accessed 01 July 2018 from: https://infogram.com/politifacts-fake-news-almanac-1gew2vjdxl912nj.

Pomerantsev, P., & Weiss, M. (2014). *The menace of unreality: How the Kremlin weaponizes information, culture and Mmney. The Interpreter.*

Ratkiewicz, J., Conover, M., Meiss, M., Gonçalves, B., Patil, S., Flammini, A., & Menczer, F. (2011). Detecting and tracking political abuse in social media. In *Proceedings of the Fifth International AAAI Conference on Weblogs and Social Media* (pp. 297–304). http://doi.org/10.1145/1963192.1963301

Rid, T. (2017). *Disinformation: A primer in Russian active measures and influence campaigns*. Washington, D.C.: United States Senate. Retrieved from https://www.intelligence.senate.gov/sites/default/files/documents/os-trid-033017.pdf

Roth, Y. (2018). Automation and the use of multiple accounts. Accessed 01 July 2018 from: https://blog.twitter.com/developer/en_us/topics/tips/2018/automation-and-the-use-of-multiple-accounts.html.

Sherman, D. K., Cohen, G. L., & Sherman, K. (2002). Accepting threatening information: Self–affirmation and the reduction of defensive biases. *Current Directions in Psychological Science*, *11*(4), 119–123. http://doi.org/10.1111/1467-8721.00182

Smith, A. (2018). Russian bots zeroed in on a survivor of the Florida school shooting who's been targeted by far-right conspiracy theorists. *Business Insider*.

Starbird, K. (2017). Examining the alternative media ecosystem through the production of alternative narratives of mass shooting events on Twitter. In *Icwsm17* (pp. 230–239).

Starbird, K., Maddock, J., Orand, M., Achterman, P., & Mason, R. M. (2014). Rumors, false flags, and digital vigilantes: Misinformation on Twitter after the 2013 Boston marathon bombing. In *iConference 2014 Proceedings* (pp. 654–662). http://doi.org/10.9776/14308

Stieglitz, S., Brachten, F., Berthelé, D., Schlaus, M., Venetopoulou, C., & Veutgen, D. (2017). Do social bots (still) act different to humans? - Comparing metrics of social bots with those of humans. In G. Meiselwitz (Ed.), *Lecture Notes in Computer Science* (Vol. 1, pp. 379–395). Springer. http://doi.org/10.1007/978-3-319-58559-8

Stieglitz, S., Brachten, F., Ross, B., & Jung, A.-K. (2017). Do social bots dream of electric sheep? A categorisation of social media bot accounts. In *Proceedings of the Australasian Conference on Information Systems* (pp. 1–11).

Sunstein, C. R., & Vermeule, A. (2008). *Conspiracy theories* (No. 199). Chicago, IL.

Vosoughi, S., Roy, D., & Aral, S. (2018). The spread of true and false news online. *Science*, *359*, 1146–1151.

Wang, P., Angarita, R., & Renna, I. (2018). Is this the era of misinformation yet? Combining social bots and fake news to deceive the masses. In *WWW2018 Proceedings*. Lyon. https://doi.org/10.1145/3184558.3191610

Woolley, S. C. (2015). Automating power: Social bot influence in global politics. *First Monday*, *21*(4). http://doi.org/10.5210/fm.v21i4.6161

The Islamic State's Strategic Communication: An Informetric Topic Analysis

Frauke Kling
Heinrich-Heine-Universität Düsseldorf, Germany.
frauke.kling@uni-duesseldorf.de

Aylin Ilhan
Heinrich-Heine-Universität Düsseldorf, Germany.
aylin.ilhan@uni-duesseldorf.de

Wolfgang G. Stock
Heinrich-Heine-Universität Düsseldorf, Germany.
stock@phil.hhu.de

Maria Henkel
Heinrich-Heine-Universität Düsseldorf, Germany.
maria.henkel@uni-duesseldorf.de

ABSTRACT
In this paper we describe an informetric approach to analyzing three recurrent facets of the Islamic State's strategic communication. These are (1) the call for emigration to IS-controlled territory *(hijrah)*, (2) the encouragement of lone-actor attacks in the West, and (3) the call for engagement in *jihad*. Content analysis of IS' English-language magazines *Dabiq* and *Rumiyah* was used to determine trends in the coverage of these themes. The text-word method, a knowledge representation method specifically suited for application on these non-scientific texts, was used to uncover further thematic insights within the magazines. This mixed-methods approach could serve as the basis for data collection on IS strategic communication and its themes, providing insight into longitudinal developments in IS writings. The presented use of informetrics and knowledge representation tools allows for a content-based analysis of terrorist group's communication. In the future, this approach may aid in the understanding of the development of jihadist ideology and radicalization efforts carried out by terrorist groups, presenting the field of Information Science with a unique opportunity to provide an answer to a growing need for data on extremism and communication.

KEYWORDS
informetrics, topic analysis, Islamic State, text-word method, content analysis

INTRODUCTION

Background
2017 has marked the end of the Islamic State's (IS) stranglehold on large parts of territory in Iraq and Syria. However, the group and its ideology have shown remarkable resistance against military defeat. While a holistic military and sociological strategy against groups like the IS is needed, research has so far been forced to analyze what the group chooses to present us with. This is due to classified information on key figures and regular sympathizers of IS, which makes it nearly impossible to conduct empiric studies on the impact of their strategic communication. The strategic communication propagated by IS includes tweets (Klausen, 2015), other social media and messaging services, as well as video material (Gates & Podder, 2015). With little known about their impact, and an unclear understanding of the creation of IS strategic narratives (Pisoui & Ahmed, 2016), research must focus on the manifest content of these persuasion tools. Knowledge extraction and representation of these materials can be used to further our understanding of what was published between the declaration of the Caliphate in 2014 and its military downfall towards the end of 2017. IS has published a considerable amount of text, audio, and visual material online since 2014, with an average number of 38 communication pieces produced per day in 2015 (Winter, 2015). Two of their most recognized publications have been the English-language magazines *Dabiq* and *Rumiyah*. Analysts have assessed these magazines from various points of view, using content analysis as the basis for their research. Ingram (2016a, 2016b) deems *Dabiq* a crucial factor in IS' strategic communication plan and connects it to the sweeping success in recruitment of foreign fighters, while *Rumiyah,* due to it being the centralized English language magazine of IS since 2016, is an even more streamlined attempt at spreading the group's message. According to Kiefer, Messing, Musial, and Weiß (2016), IS first thematically connected *jihad* (a holy war waged on behalf of Islam, with the goal to build an IS-controlled Muslim Caliphate) to *hijrah*, the religiously motivated emigration to IS-controlled territory. A shift from connecting *jihad* to promoting the use of terror in the home countries of recruits can be observed later in the magazines. They also note that changes in the group's situation in Syria seem to influence their strategic communication (Kiefer, Messing, Musial, & Weiß, 2016). Comparing both magazines, Wignell, Tan, O'Halloran, and Lange (2017) also come to the conclusion that the themes in the groups' publication output are adapted according to real-world strategic developments, while the underlying ideology seems stable. Earlier research has been done on the group's evolving language: Vergani and Bliuc (2015) point out that IS has increased the use of emotive language when

promoting affiliation with the group, called for female readers to engage in behaviors desired by the group, and increasingly uses jargon that appeals to a Western audience.

Previous research points towards three themes that seem to be of great importance in texts published from 2014 to 2017. First, the call to *hijrah*, which was answered by many individuals from around the world in hopes to support the Caliphate IS declared in 2014 (Gerges, 2014). Second, the call for lone-actor attacks in the recruit's home countries and the use of political violence in general, effectively provoking military intervention in hopes of further radicalizing followers and sympathizers. This strategy has also been attributed to the group al-Qaeda (Sedgwick, 2004), the ideological basis from which IS originated (Gerges, 2014). Lastly, there is the call for engagement in *jihad*. This is crucial to the IS *salafi*-jihadist world view, as it provides the ideological basis for building a united Islamic nation or state. Atwan (2015, p. 12) affirms that "all Islamic State propaganda focuses on these three stages", however, as Winter (2015) points out, analysis of these publications is always reactive in nature.

Furthering their global agenda IS uses their English-language publications in an adept, and calculated manner. But how can we sufficiently portray the manner in which IS develops the aforementioned three themes in its strategic communication? An overview of the general development of these themes is needed, focusing on what the group presents us with. In order to provide answers about the nature of manifest content IS publishes, we propose the use of a knowledge representation method particularly suited for their contents. The goal of our research is to gain insight into the longitudinal development of the aforementioned themes, and to provide knowledge about IS strategic communication in a manner that focuses on the manifest content provided by the group itself.

Research Questions

We provide a mixed-methods informetric approach to determine the development of the topics of *hijrah*, terror, and *jihad* in *Dabiq* and *Rumiyah,* by first conducting a content analysis on 149 articles. This serves as the basis of our research, providing us with data that shows how often these themes were mentioned, and when there were periods of unconventionally high or low coverage. We then apply the text-word method to those articles that contain coded statements. The text-word method is a knowledge representation method first developed by Henrichs (1970) for use on indexing documents without a standardized language. Since the magazines and their contents are far from scientific in nature, classic knowledge representation methods are hard to apply to their content. The text-word method handles this issue by staying with the text meticulously, without straying from the topic it discusses (Stock & Stock, 2013). It achieves this by indexing only those terms used in a document. This paper argues that the text-word method is a useful addition to the field, both in a mixed-methods approach with content analysis, and as a stand-alone method for knowledge representation of jihadist group's strategic communication. We will answer which topics were of importance in *Dabiq* and *Rumiyah* by indexing. The indexing of mentioned names provides an insight into IS' use of scholarly material, presenting information about the influences found in their articles. Since the method uses syntactical indexing, the semantic networks between core topics are calculated and represented using cluster analysis and graph visualization. We propose two research questions to be answered by this methodological framework:

RQ 1: How did the themes of *hijrah*, terror and *jihad* develop during the publication period of *Dabiq* and *Rumiyah?*

RQ 2: What specific topics and what (scholarly) sources were of importance in *Dabiq* and *Rumiyah* in regard to these themes?

METHODS

Content Analysis

Content analysis of fifteen volumes of *Dabiq*, and twelve volumes of *Rumiyah* was conducted to examine changes in IS reporting on the themes of *hijrah* (emigration to IS-controlled territory), incitement to lone-actor attacks, and encouragement to engage in *jihad* as defined and propagated by IS' *salafi*-jihadist ideology. The material was obtained from the website jihadology.net, a self-described "clearinghouse for Sunni jihadi primary source material" run by Aaron Y. Zelin (2016, 2017). This study encompasses all volumes of *Dabiq* and *Rumiyah,* except for the 13th issue of *Rumiyah*, which was released after the study had been conducted. The material spans a publication period of 37 months, from July 2014 to August 2017, with a median publication interval of 45.5 days for *Dabiq*, and 30 days for *Rumiyah*. The coding categories of incitement, condemnation and rewards were developed as emergent variables from the source material. Codes were structured in such a way that each theme had one or multiple specific incitement-codes, as well as a reward-code. Inciting statements were defined as those that emphasized on the urgency to actively engage in traveling to IS, using political violence, or partaking in *jihad* as defined in their strategic communication. Rewarding statements were defined as describing (or promising) rewards for engaging in the aforementioned behavior. A condemnation-code was added for both *hijrah* and *jihad.* Condemning statements were defined as ridiculing, insulting or threatening those that chose not to engage in either *hijrah* or *jihad*, or hesitated to do so. Guiding statements as well as tips and tricks for weapon-specific attacks were not included in the coding instruction for the terror theme and would have led to an inflation of these numbers in singular magazine volumes. All themes included a general incitement code. Table 1 shows a sample codebook entry, including the definition of incitement for the theme of *hijrah* and the corresponding code.

Incitement: hijrah	Code	Example
statements that convey a sense of urgency to the reader to take action towards emigrating to the Islamic State's territory, or act as advice, or express that hijrah is a religious duty	103 hijrah: incitement (general)	*„My advice is for them to do hijrah to the lands of the Khilāfah".*

Table 1. Codebook sample entry

Sampling units consisted of a total of 27 magazine volumes that were randomly presented to the coders. The contents of a total of 149 articles were considered for coding in this study. During the coding process, coders were instructed to search for statements, which were defined as a grammatically correct sentence found within an article. Phrases used within the graphic design of the article were to be disregarded. Coders were instructed to read all articles of a magazine volume given to them carefully and code statements that covered one or more of the three domains as described in the codebook. Contextual units were defined in the codebook as the article the statement was found in. As recommended by Rössler (2017), the contextual unit of a statement was consulted if it was otherwise impossible to identify a target country for emigration to IS-controlled territory, or a specific weapon advertised for use in lone-actor attacks. Randomization was used to ensure that coders did not project their underlying presumptions of code distributions over time onto the material (Neuendorf, 2002) in order to avoid bias through news reportings of IS territory loss towards the end of 2016 and throughout 2017. Coding was conducted by two coders, the primary researcher included. The other coder had been recruited through the department of Information Science of the Heinrich Heine University of Düsseldorf. A pretest was conducted with 3 randomly chosen volumes of the magazines to check for reliability. Coders disagreed on two statements within these pretest materials, and as a result the definition of incitement was amended to include statements that act as advice, as can be seen in the definition in Table 1. After the coding of all volumes had finished, the results were checked for statements that one of the two coders had not coded due to oversights. These statements were reviewed and consensus through discussion was achieved. This consensus-finding approach, and the fact that coders agreed on all statements that did not fall into the former category of oversights, ensured 100% agreement on all 873 coded statements and their respective codes that were included in the final set, resulting in a Krippendorff coefficient of $\alpha=1$. To answer the proposed research questions, a paired Student's t-test was used to check whether the themes in the magazines had undergone statistically significant changes in coverage of certain themes. A p-value of <0.05 was deemed statistically significant.

Text-word Method

The text-word method was applied to all articles that included coded statements. Indexing was focused only on the topics at hand, using strictly those terms that could be found within the text (Stock, 2000). Articles were indexed manually through terms that were found frequently in the text or in key passages of the article, such as the title, subheadings, and summaries (Stock & Stock, 2013, p. 737). The texts were then searched for names, which were added to the database entry if they were deemed relevant to the topics that were discussed, or if they were discussed as a topic themselves. Following the original method, terms were indexed in their original language, i.e. a mix of both Arabic and English terms. The database was extended by a translation field (Stock, 1989) so that terms were both represented in their original language, and an English translation of the Arabic term if needed. An indexing depth of 0.5 to 2 terms per page was used, as recommended by Stock and Stock (2013). Syntactical indexing was used during the indexing process. Terms were written into the database with their chain numbers, each number corresponding to the page of the article in which the term could be found. The M-weight (Stock, 1984), denoting the importance of a term within the magazines, was calculated for all terms and compared between *Dabiq* and *Rumiyah*. The M-weight of a term is calculated by first determining the weight of a term within a document, using Henrichs' algorithm (Henrichs, 1974) and then calculating the mean of the weights within a document group (Stock, 1984). In this study, this would be the respective document groups of *Dabiq* and *Rumiyah*. The total of indexed articles was 149, which were all articles containing previously coded statements. Thematic connection Ψ of all themes was calculated using the Jaccard-Sneath index (Stock, 1984). The Jaccard-Sneath index denotes the coincidence between terms in their chains. We chose the terms '*hijrah*' and '*jihad*' for visual representation, and used the data generated by calculating the M-weight of all terms to find those terms relevant to the theme of terror. The term 'terror' was not used for visual representation itself. The text-word method operates strictly on the terms used in the text, and because 'terror' was not indexed frequently enough (less than 10 times), it was irrelevant for cluster analysis. It also did not fit IS' language use, which can be seen in the ranking of terms by their M-weight. Terms represented in the clusters had to have been indexed at least twice, and a Ψ-threshold between terms was determined for each network. Semantic networks were visualized using Gephi version 0.9.2.

RESULTS

Content Analysis

Overall, a total of 873 statements in 27 magazine volumes were coded. Statements were coded more than once if they covered one or more themes, resulting in a total of 962 codes. Over half of all articles in both magazines contained statements that were thematically relevant to the study. The results show a thematic shift during the publication period of the magazines, indicating that the coded themes in general became more relevant, i.e. more written about, over time. The magazine volumes also became increasingly longer, including at least 10 articles since February 2015 (*Dabiq* Vol. 7). Volumes contained an average article count of 10.67, and the average number of articles including coded statements was 5.47. *Rumiyah* launched with 9 articles in September 2016 and did not show the same difference in length during its publication period, resulting in an average count of 9.67 articles per magazine volume. The average number of articles that contained coded statements was 5.58. This indicates that the themes were often covered in *Rumiyah*. The distribution of codes in the respective magazines further revealed a thematic shift, which is shown in Figure 1. Figure 2 shows the distribution of code-occurrence for all statements coded into the category of *hijrah*. The data shows a decline in publication of inciting statements after the first *Rumiyah* volume. Three outliers can be observed for this category, in December 2014 (*Dabiq* Vol. 6), October 2016, and March 2017 (*Rumiyah* Vol. 2 and 7). Condemnation for those who chose not to perform *hijrah*, or those who hesitated, as well as promised rewards for *hijrah* were also published less often after the switch to *Rumiyah*. A paired Student's t-test confirmed the change in publication frequency to be statistically significant at $p = 0.0428$. This means that statements calling for emigration to IS-controlled territory have decreased in frequency in *Rumiyah* when compared to *Dabiq*. Statements calling for emigration to IS-controlled territory outside Syria and Iraq were too infrequent to be statistically relevant on their own and thus counted into the general measure of incitement-statements.

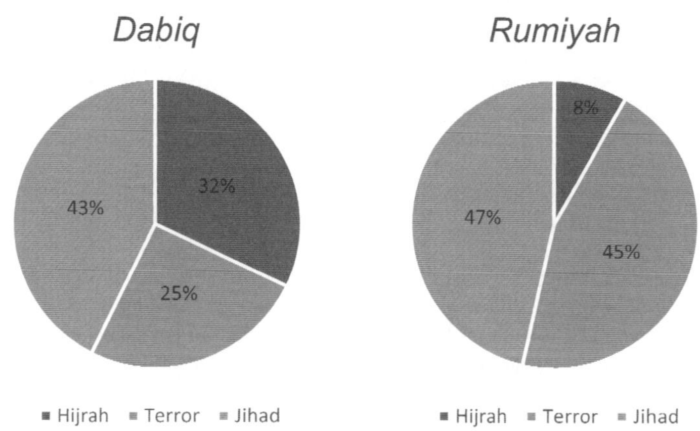

Figure 1. Distribution of the analyzed topics of hijrah, terror, and jihad in Dabiq and Rumiyah

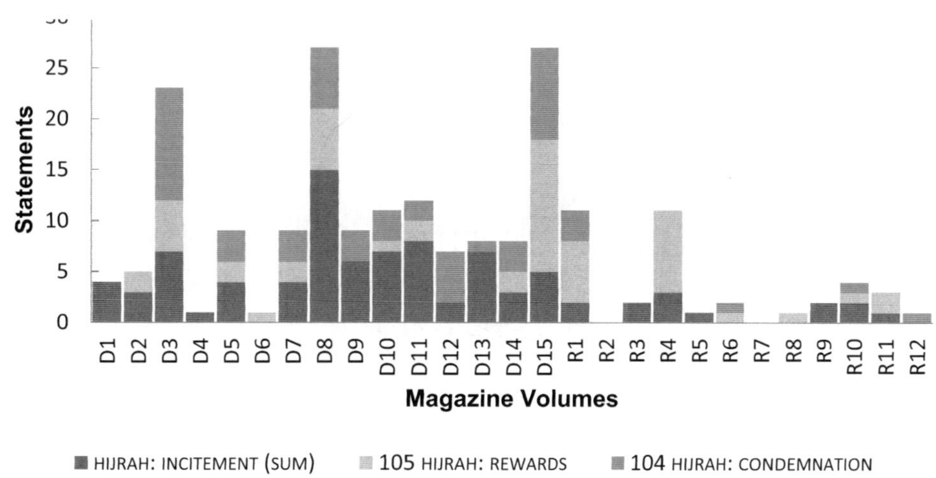

Figure 2. Distribution of code-occurrence for hijrah in Dabiq and Rumiyah

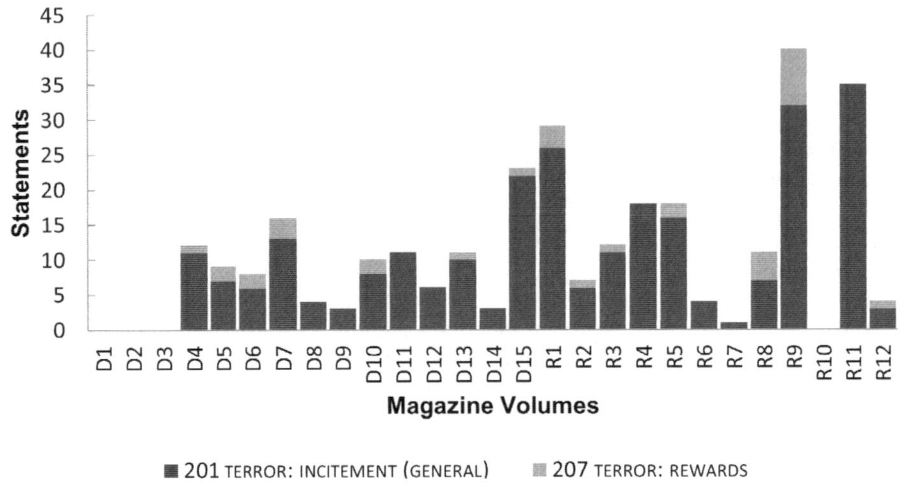

Figure 3. Distribution of code-occurrence for terror in Dabiq and Rumiyah

Promised rewards for lone-actor attacks or use of political violence in general were much less frequently published than the inciting statements themselves, which is shown in figure 3. We also see a steady publication of inciting statements throughout *Dabiq* volumes 4-15 and *Rumiyah* volumes 1-9. The first two volumes of *Dabiq* and *Rumiyah* Volume 10, however, show no statements coded into this category. The average amount of statements per volume for the theme of terror increased from 8.47 in *Dabiq* to 17.33 in *Rumiyah*. A paired Student's t-test, however, deemed the change not statistically significant at $p = 0.0819$. This is likely due to our conscious decision to not include all statements found in the 'Just Terror' series in *Rumiyah* and the relatively small sample size.

Finally, the distribution of codes for the theme of *jihad* shows a steady publication of statements calling for engagement in *jihad* during *Dabiq* volumes 6-15 and *Rumiyah* volumes 1-12. Outliers can once again be found in the first two volumes of *Dabiq* and the 6th volume of *Rumiyah*. The July 2017 volume of *Rumiyah* (Vol. 11) shows an unconventional amount of both inciting and reward-statements. Condemnation for those who chose not to engage in *jihad* or hesitated to do so, was published relatively consistently in *Dabiq*, but seemed to slowly decline in *Rumiyah*.

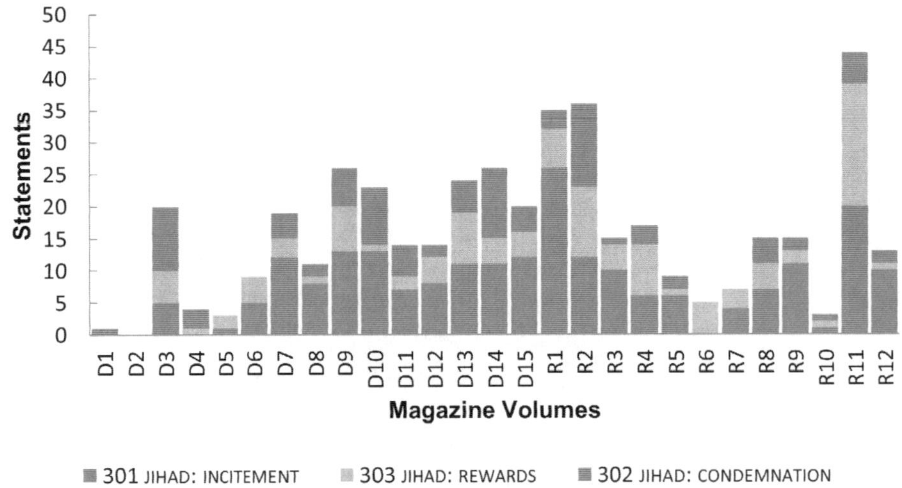

Figure 4. Distribution of code-occurrence for jihad in Dabiq and Rumiyah

A paired Student's t-test deemed the overall change in coverage of *jihad* between the two magazines not statistically significant at $p = 0.3045$. This confirms that the theme had not undergone dramatic changes in terms of publication from late 2014 to late 2017 and was relatively stable throughout the years. In regard to RQ 1, we can observe a measurable shift in the coverage of *hijrah*, terror and *jihad* over time, with *hijrah* losing in relevance, the theme of terror increasing in prevalence and *jihad* being a stable theme in IS strategic communication.

Text-word Method

Concerning RQ 2, analysis of the topics and scholarly sources that were of importance in *Dabiq* and *Rumiyah* was made possible by the data generated from the text-word method. Tables 2 and 3 show the results of calculating the M-weight of all indexed terms in *Dabiq* and *Rumiyah.* They show the importance of terms in relation to our article selection, and also provide insight into IS' method of relying on scholarly opinion, which was not examined by the previous content analysis. Articles were scattered with quotes, stories, or wisdom that were used to substantiate their claims. Many of these sources are based in the *Qur'an* or *ahadith*, and IS seems to employ these sources to tailor their extremist world-view to scholarly authenticity. Table 2 shows the 20 most important terms of *Dabiq*. In *Dabiq*, *'jihad'* and *'hijrah'* were at rank 3 and 5 respectively. The volumes included addresses to the group's followers from their leader, Abu Bakr al-Baghdadi, or spokesman of the Caliphate, Abu Muhammad al-Adnani. Both names ranked in the top 20 topics for *Dabiq,* with IS leader Abu Bakr al-Baghdadi as the second most important name in the magazine, and the Caliphate's spokesman on rank 13. Abu Mu'sab az-Zarqawi, a high-ranking member of al-Qaeda, was often referenced in *Dabiq* as well. Ranks 6 and 7 show IS' use of narrations from or about the Prophet Muhammad. On rank 10 the Islamic scholar Ibn Taymiyyah can be found, indicating that his narrations were highly relevant to the three themes and often used by IS authors. In *Dabiq*, the Caliphate itself was represented in this ranking twice, either referenced to as *'Islamic State,'* or *'Khilafah,'* the Arabic word for Caliphate. Both ranked at rank 2 and 8 respectively. Pledges of allegiance to the Caliphate (*'bay'ah'* and *'bay'at'*) from other extremist groups or individuals were thematically relevant in *Dabiq* and can be found in this ranking at rank 11 and 15. Enemies such as the *'Rafidah'* (rejectionists), a derogatory word used by IS for Shiite Muslims, and the more general *'factions'* were also of importance in *Dabiq's* indexed articles. Lastly, we can determine that IS addressed women in this context too, with *'sisters'* being at rank 15 of the 20 most important themes in relation to *hijrah*, terror and *jihad.*

Rank	Term	M-weight
01	Allah	87.35
02	Islamic State	29.79
03	Jihad	21.11
04	Abu Bakr al-Baghdadi	18.51
05	Hijrah	18.41
06	The Prophet	18.05
07	The Messenger	14.30
08	Khilafah	8.46
09	Rafidah	5.42
10	Shaykhul-Islam Ibn Taymiyyah	5.24
11	Bay'at	5.00
12	Abu Mus'ab az-Zarqawi	4.90
13	Abu Muhammad al-Adnani	4.70
14	Bay'ah	4.60
15	Sisters	4.35
16	Factions	4.26
17	Advice	4.07
18	Shari'ah	3.88
19	Libya	3.80
20	Ummah	3.57

Table 2. Ranking of terms in Dabiq using M-weight

When comparing the most important topics of *Dabiq* to *Rumiyah's* (Table 3), a notable change is the absence of Abu Bakr al-Baghdadi and Abu Muhammad al-Adnani from the list. The topic of *'jihad'* has slightly gained in importance and is on rank 2 in *Rumiyah*, while *'hijrah'* appears considerably less often, and can be found at rank 12. Ibn Taymiyyah's narrations are more often associated with the themes in *Rumiyah.* Other scholar's narrations, those of Ibn Kathir and al-Bukhari, have gained in importance as well. The Caliphate and its state seem less relevant in *Rumiyah*, with both 'Islamic State' and *'Khilafah'* declining in significance. However, we see a shift in topics about IS enemies, with *'Crusaders'* being a prominent term meaning those nations associated with The Global Coalition Against Daesh (IS). *'Mushrikin'* and *'Murtaddin,'* derogatory terms for polytheists and Muslims deemed un-Islamic by IS, are other prominently discussed enemies in *Rumiyah.* We also observe a new phenomenon: *'patience,'* *'victory,'* and *'promise'* are terms with significant importance in *Rumiyah.* Keeping in mind that these weights were calculated on articles previously filtered by the themes of *hijrah*, terror and *jihad,* we see a more emotional approach to these themes represented in *Rumiyah*. Using the data gathered from indexing through the text-word method we were able to show significant shifts in IS publication patterns. We have identified four new aspects in relation to the themes that were covered in the articles: The names of those most influential within the magazines, the enemies that were discussed, the emotional approach to the themes in question and the significance of its state-building goal over time.

Rank	Term	M-weight
01	Allah	97.93
02	Jihad	34.37
03	The Prophet	31.26
04	Crusaders	14.46
05	Shaykhul-Islam Ibn Taymiyyah	10.01
06	Islamic State	8.32
07	The Messenger	7.63
08	Victory	7.34
09	Mushrikin	7.05
10	Islam	6.90
11	Soldiers	6.90
12	Hijrah	6.13
13	Ibn Kathir	5.86
14	Khilafah	5.60
15	Murtaddin	5.57
16	Promise	4.82
17	Al-Bukhari	4.71
18	Wealth	4.64
19	Battle	4.34
20	Patience	4.17

Table 3. Ranking of terms in Rumiyah using M-weight

After having determined the most important topics covered in both magazines, we analyzed a third aspect of IS strategic communication: The encouragement of lone-actor attacks. How do we analyze a more complex topic like terror using the text-word method? By simply looking at the content of both magazines, we see a shift to guidelines for terror attacks in *Rumiyah*. This article-series is called 'Just Terror' and gives the reader detailed instructions on what weapons to use (knives, vehicles, Molotov-cocktails), what targets to choose from, and how to increase the kill-count of such an attack. However, we felt that while these articles and the statements found within them fall under the normalization of violence, they did not fall into the definition of incitement used in our codebook. What they also fail to uncover is the relationship of the theme (terror) to other related themes and names that are relevant to the construct of terror and political violence in IS strategic communication. We agree with Reed and Ingram's assessment of the series in that "we need to be careful that we do not place too much weight on these guides in themselves" and that they need to be interpreted "in the wider context of jihadist propaganda" (Reed & Ingram, 2017, p. 15). By uncovering the aspects that are thematically connected to the theme of terror, we are presented with multiple facets to analyze. We analyzed the term '*Crusaders*' for *Dabiq,* to see how this IS enemy vision was thematically embedded in the magazine. In *Rumiyah*, we looked at another aspect of terror: the soldiers of the Caliphate. Figures 5 and 6 show the semantic network for '*Crusaders*' in *Dabiq* and 'soldiers' in *Rumiyah.* Nodes represent the indexed terms and edges display their Jaccard-Sneath index Ψ. The size of the node is determined by its degree, and the higher the Ψ-value between two terms, the bigger and darker the edge. Edges were included in the graph if they reached a Ψ-threshold as indicated beneath the graph.

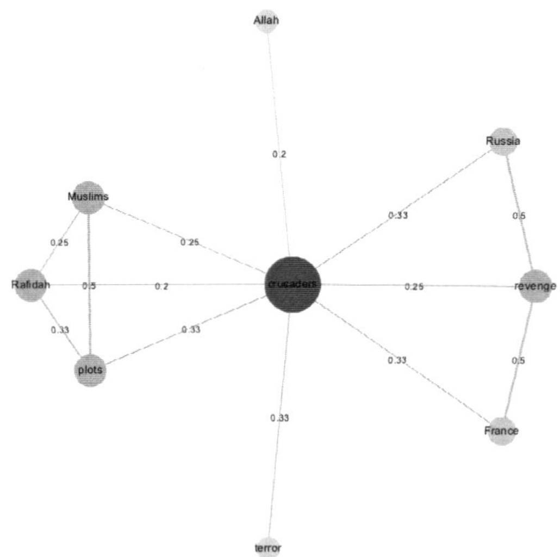

Figure 5. Semantic network for 'Crusaders' in Dabiq, Ψ > 0.19, n (articles) = 82

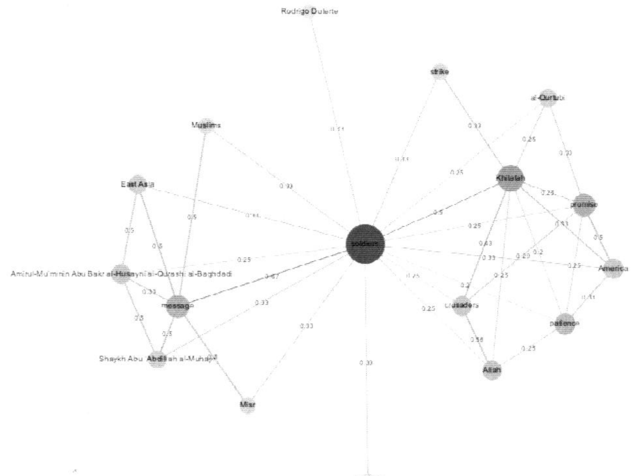

Figure 6. Semantic network for 'soldiers' in Rumiyah, Ψ > 0.19, n (articles) = 67

The terms '*Russia*' and '*France*' were connected to '*Crusaders*,' as well as the term '*revenge*' in *Dabiq*. This connection stems from articles discussing the attack on Metrojet Flight 9268 in October 2015 and the Paris attacks in November 2015. Another cluster of nodes connects '*Crusaders*' to a second enemy frequently discussed in *Dabiq*, the *Rafidah*. In *Rumiyah* we observe two main clusters, one connected to both IS leader Abu Bakr al-Baghdadi and Abu Abdullah al-Muhajir, a respected IS authority. Their names are associated with advice to IS soldiers, as well as '*East Asia*' and '*Misr,*' the Arabic term for Egypt. The other cluster is connected to the Caliphate itself. It includes prominent enemies such as '*Crusaders*' and '*America*,' as well as terms like '*patience*,' '*promise*' and '*strike*.' We discern two clusters of enemies: Those that either already were targets of terror attacks and the motivation behind these attacks, and those that were discussed as a worthy target for political violence.

CONCLUSION

We have analyzed how the constructs of *hijrah*, terror and *jihad* in IS strategic communication have developed during *Dabiq's* and *Rumiyah's* publication period. We also presented new emerging facets of IS strategic communication. These results were gathered by using a methodological framework relying on the manifest content found within the magazines, in hopes to reduce erroneous categorizations and to provide a baseline for further research. Three general trends can be discerned from the results of our content analysis. IS has indeed stopped calling for their target audience to travel to IS-controlled territory and support the Caliphate with boots on the ground. There is also a trend towards promoting violence in these recruits' home countries, and a wider spectrum of political or ideological enemies that are portrayed in IS strategic communication. All themes also show considerable outliers and a fluctuation in representation. The cause of these outliers is multi-faceted, and at this point in time, with the limited data available to us, much of an analysis of the causes would be speculative. It is, however, important to document these changes as accurately as possible in order to accelerate future research. Through our investigation, we have made the aforementioned changes in publication strategy observable. Similarly, their impact cannot be measured simply by comparing real-world events to the publication dates of the magazine volumes. The limited data we have on IS' sympathizers, recruiters, and strategic communication authors in general, makes it even more relevant to source data on the measurable impact, if any, these magazines have on their readers. As of 2018, research has suggested that the engagement rate with IS strategic communication has significantly decreased over time (Winter, 2018). Previous studies discussed in the introductory section of this work found similar trends as those we described, and as such, the results of our content analysis cannot be considered entirely unique. By substantiating our results with the text-word method, we showed the shifting importance of concepts such as state-building, authoritative figures, scholarly input and emotional approach in each magazine, and observed their thematic connections. The insights of thematic analysis through indexing could prove valuable for the construction of counter-narratives and could not have been achieved through the proposed content analysis framework alone. Previous research has shown that IS' use of excommunication (referred to as *takfirism*) of mainstream Islamic scholars and their schools of thought is a source of uncertainty amongst vulnerable, young sympathizers, which can be exploited by the group to counteract the moderating effect these scholars have, making them more accessible to radicalization (Müller, Suleymanova, & Eser Davolio, 2017). According to Maher (2016), scholarly sources such as Ibn Kathir and Ibn Taymiyyah are used to justify participation in violence in the Salafi-jihadist world view, and the collected data reflects this and makes it measurable. In order to provide a basis for developing counter-active efforts, there is a need for structuring the data found within IS strategic communication. This could in part be resolved by the use of a database constructed on the indexing of the partial, or complete available strategic communication material provided by the group. We have shown that the text-word method can be applied to a small thematic snippet of *Dabiq* and *Rumiyah*, and the principle can be applied to every written piece of strategic communication published by IS. The method handles different original languages of the communication gracefully and can be used for a broad approach of identifying all thematic connections within its database, or analyzing smaller samples of it, as was the case in this study. The results of these efforts could serve as a baseline-assessment of IS communication, focusing strictly on what is presented, and provide a substantiating role for further research.

As one of few studies in current research on this topic we aim to provide insight into a reliability measure for our findings. However, opinions on studies that use the primary researcher as one of the coders vary from support of this practice, if reliability of all coders is measured against the primary researcher (Rössler, 2017; Krippendorff, 2009) to the recommendation that the primary researcher not be included in the coding process (Krippendorff, 2009). Consensus-finding via discussion in order to ensure high agreement is also not commonly encouraged in literature (Neuendorf, 2002; Krippendorff, 2009). We chose to employ this method in order to provide a data set with high accuracy in the framework provided by the coding scheme. In regards to our use of the text-word method it must be said that the method still relies on manual indexing, and as such cannot be "non-interpretative in the hermeneutical sense, "it is „at best low-interpretative" (Stock & Stock, 2013, p. 737). Much is still unclear in this relatively young field of research. IS traces its root back to the 1990s, but its extreme efforts in producing and publishing strategic communication only became noticeable around the 2010s, after the damage had been done: large parts of Syria and Iraq were de-stabilized, and the Caliphate was declared. In the future, the output of extremist groups such as IS needs to be recognized and analyzed as early as possible, in order to produce a full knowledge representation of the information found within these strategic communication materials. Calls for support, such as joining the group on the ground, or promoting terror attacks, should be recognized and measured regularly during the publication cycle of a communication piece.

In the future, using the approach demonstrated here may further our understanding of jihadist ideology disseminated by terrorist groups. It may also be of use for the prevention of their radicalization efforts. The field of Information Science is absolutely suited for providing research methods and insights aiding this cause, and more studies on counter-terrorism should be incorporated into research efforts in the field.

REFERENCES

Atwan, A. B. (2015). *Islamic State: The Digital Caliphate*. Berkeley: University of California Press.

Gates, S., & Podder, S. (2015). Social Media, Recruitment, Allegiance and the Islamic State. *Perspectives on Terrorism*, *9*(4), 107–116.

Gerges, F. A. (2014). ISIS and the Third Wave of Jihadism. *Current History*, *113*(767), 339–343.

Henrichs, N. (1970). Philosophische Dokumentation: Literatur-Dokumentation ohne strukturierten Thesaurus. *Nachrichten für Dokumentation*, 21, 20–25.

Henrichs, N. (1974). Dokumentenspezifische Kennzeichnung von Deskriptorbeziehungen. Funktion und Bedeutung. In *Deutscher Dokumentartag* 1974 (pp. 343–353). Munich, Germany: Verlag Dokumentation.

Ingram, H. J. (2016a). An analysis of Islamic State's Dabiq magazine. *Australian Journal of Political Science*, *51*(3), 458–477.

Ingram, H. J. (2016b). ISIS: Assessing Rumiyah. Retrieved January 21, 2018, from http://www.internationalaffairs.org.au/ australianoutlook/isis-assessing-the-rumiyah-magazine/.

Kiefer, M., Messing, K., Musial, J., & Weiß, T. (2016). Westliche Jugendliche im Bann des Islamischen Staates – Radikalisierende Inhalte der IS-Propaganda am Beispiel der Onlinemagazine Dabiq und Rumiyah. *Journal for Deradicalization*, *9*(19), 126–184.

Klausen, J. (2015). Tweeting the Jihad: Social Media Networks of Western Foreign Fighters in Syria and Iraq. *Studies in Conflict & Terrorism*, *38*(1), 1–22.

Krippendorff, K. (2009). *Content Analysis: An Introduction to Its Methodology* (2nd Ed.). Thousand Oaks, CA: SAGE Publications.

Maher, S. (2016). *Salafi-Jihadism - The History of an Idea*. London: Hurst Publishers.

Müller, D., Suleymanova, D., & Eser Davolio, M. (2017). Dschihadismus online. Narrative Strategien, Herausforderungen für muslimische Organisationen und Stoßrichtungen für Präventionsprojekte. In *Digitale Medien und politisch-weltanschaulicher Extremismus im Jugendalter: Erkenntnisse aus Wissenschaft und Praxis* (pp. 60–83). Munich, Germany: Deutsches Jugendinstitut.

Neuendorf, K. A. (2002). The Content Analysis Guidebook. Thousand Oaks, CA: SAGE Publications.

Pisoui, D., & Ahmed, R. (2016). Radicalisation Research – Gap Analysis, 1–25. Europe: RAN Centre of Excellence.

Reed, A., & Ingram, H. J. (2017). Exploring the Role of Instructional Material in AQAP's Inspire and ISIS' Rumiyah. The Hague. Retrieved from https://www.europol.europa.eu/publications-documents/exploring-role-of-instructional-material-in-aqaps-inspire-and-isis-rumiyah.

Rössler, P. (2017). *Inhaltsanalyse* (3rd Ed.). Konstanz, Germany: UVK.

Sedgwick, M. (2004). Al-Qaeda and the Nature of Religious Terrorism. *Terrorism and Political Violence*, *16*(4), 795–814.

Stock, M. (1989). Textwortmethode und Übersetzungsrelation. Eine Methode zum Aufbau von kombinierten Literaturnachweis- und Terminologiedatenbanken. *ABI-Technik, 9*(4), 309–313.

Stock, W. G. (1984). Informetrische Untersuchungsmethoden auf der Grundlage der Textwortmethode. *International Classification, 11*, 151–157.

Stock, W. G. (2000). Textwortmethode. *Password*, (7/8), 26–35.

Stock, W.G., & Stock, M. (2013). *Handbook of Information Science*. Berlin, Germany, Boston, MA: De Gruyter Saur.

Wignell, P., Tan, S., O'Halloran, K. L., & Lange, R. (2017). A Mixed Methods Empirical Examination of Changes in Emphasis and Style in the Extremist Magazines Dabiq and Rumiyah. *Perspectives on Terrorism*, *11*(2), (20 pp.).

Winter, C. (2015). Documenting the 'Virtual Caliphate'. Retrieved from http://www.quilliaminternational.com/wp-content/uploads/2015/10/FINAL-documenting-the-virtual-caliphate.pdf.

Winter, C. (2018). Apocalypse, Later: A Longitudinal Study of the Islamic State Brand. *Critical Studies in Media Communication*, *35*(1), 103–121.

Zelin, A. Y. (2016). New issue of the Islamic State's magazine: "Dābiq #15". Retrieved from http://jihadology.net/2016/07/31/new-issue-of-the-islamic-states-magazine-dabiq-15/.

Zelin, A. Y. (2017). New release of The Islamic State's magazine: "Rome #12". Retrieved from http://jihadology.net/2017/08/06/new-release-of-the-islamic-states-magazine-rome-12/.

Reconceptualizing Superwork for Improved Access to Popular Cultural Objects

Jin Ha Lee
University of Washington, USA. jinhalee@uw.edu

Jacob Jett
University of Illinois at Urbana-Champaign, USA. jjett2@illinois.edu

Hyerim Cho; Travis Windleharth; Thomas Disher
University of Washington, USA. chohr113@uw.edu; travisw@uw.edu; tdisher@uw.edu

Senan Kiryakos; Shigeo Sugimoto
Tsukuba University, Japan. senank@gmail.com; sugimoto@slis.tsukuba.ac.jp

ABSTRACT

In the context of popular culture, a successful work or a work with broad cultural or scientific impact often prompts the publication of many derivative works across multiple formats and by multiple creators, works that share elements with the original work such as topics, characters or universes. We argue for reconceptualization of the "Superwork" entity to aggregate these relevant works into a single bibliographic entity about which facts in the form of metadata, exploitable by library users, can be recorded. In this paper, we aim to conduct a deeper investigation of the superwork concept and establish an initial definition for and some boundaries of the concept. In order to further develop the idea of superwork, we provide a prominent example and explain different characteristics of superwork identified via entity analysis. We conclude by discussing examples showcasing the multiple challenges for conceptualizing and representing superwork.

KEYWORDS

Superwork, Complex work, Multiverse, Popular cultural objects.

INTRODUCTION AND BACKGROUND

In recent years, the trend in creating many derivative and related works from a single successful work has exploded. These sprawling multimedia masses, often encompassing one or more complex narratives, are created by a number of different people or organizations. In some cases, these intertwining narratives are set in settings derived from a "multiverse"—some prominent examples include the Marvel Multi-verse, Gundam, Pokémon, and Star Wars. In other cases, the mass of narratives do not intertwine but are nonetheless related through shared topics, themes, or brands. In this paper, we argue the need for the superwork entity to explicitly connect these different types of relevant works in a conceptual model for bibliographic entities.

One specific area in which superwork entities can impact user access is popular cultural objects such as video games, comic books, manga, anime, music, TV shows, and films (Kiryakos et al., 2017). These objects are a significant part of our cultural heritage and, in their own right, objects of scholarly research. As an integral part of today's culture, they represent values and viewpoints of our society and people within it which will be important for future generations.

The concept of superwork is not new; in prior research on knowledge organization and representation, several researchers such as Carlyle (1996), Svenonius (2000), Antelman (2004), Smiraglia (2007), Kemp (2008), and Smiraglia et al. (2014) have discussed this concept. Similar or relevant concepts also exist in current bibliographic standards such as FRBR, $FRBR_{OO}$, and BIBFRAME 2.0. Our discussion builds upon these different ideas and prior definitions of this concept, aiming for a clearer conceptualization of this entity.

In this paper, we aim to answer the following research questions: How do we define superwork as a bibliographic entity? What kinds of properties or characteristics does this superwork entity possess? To answer these questions, we start by examining prior work that discusses superwork or similar concepts and present some prominent examples. This is followed by an entity analysis technique to identify different characteristics that superwork entails. We will then discuss some of the challenging examples to highlight the issues for conceptualizing and representing superwork.

DEFINING SUPERWORK

Existing Definitions

As one of the Group 1 entities in FRBR, a *work* is defined as distinct intellectual or artistic creation (Taylor, 2007). The *work* concept was previously discussed through Wilson's metaphor, "bibliographic family" (1968). As researchers further investigated the associations of work entities, they noted that constellations of works exist in the bibliographic universe (Smiraglia, 2007). This concept that incorporates a collection of works that have different types or iterations was coined by Svenonius

(Smiraglia, 2007). Carlyle (1996) used the term "superwork record set" to describe a set of records that may not share both primary author and title fields but may still be closely related ("the set of records related to a work in that they contain the same author and title field contents, but in secondary author and title fields as opposed to primary author and title fields" [pp. 540-541]).

Svenonius (2000) further explains the concept of superwork in her later work by discussing Domanovszky's statement on the principles of cataloguing (1973) and Pettee's speculations on the "literary unit" (1936), with an emphasis on the ur-work: "A superwork may contain any number of works as subsets, the members of which while not sharing essentially the same information content are nevertheless similar by virtue of emanating from the same ur-work" (p.38). As Svenonius (2000) mentioned, discussions on the similar concept of superwork—literary works or literary units—existed before the term, superwork, appeared. When particular books are not considered as single items but as representatives of a whole group of similar items, they all belong to the same literary unit (Verona, 1959). Especially in the context of cataloging, literary units were one of the main concerns that catalogers had; Verona (1959) argued that when there is a literary unit, "the choice of the main headings will not be centered on the elements determining particular books, but mainly on those designating whole literary units" (p. 80). Thus, a particular book can have two different titles: its own and the original or best-known title of the literary unit to which it belongs. Similar to literary units, Leazer and Smiraglia (1999) suggested bibliographic family, which is defined as "families of related works." The authors state that derivative relationships are the primary relationships existing among the members of a bibliographic family, specifically describing seven categories of derivation.

More recently, Smiraglia (2007) states that the notion of the superwork describes "the abstract intellectual concept of a given work that is the principle node around which all iterations of that work may be collocated" (p.78) and that superwork is "just an artificial record used to group all of the related work records together" (Smiraglia et al., 2014, p.24). He emphasizes that much more research is required to understand more fully the phenomenon of instantiation (the realization of phenomenon in time that represents a similar or less clear-cut typology of bibliographical patterns or types), a phenomenon which is common among various sorts of information materials including books, artifacts, archival documents, etc.

While the above researchers have used the term *superwork* in the context of bibliographic objects generally, serials researchers like Antelman (2004) and Kemp (2008) have used the term in the context of overarching super-serials that span across all of the title changes that a serialized work might have undergone during the timeline of its publication. An example of this latter problem in bibliographic control would be *Dr. Strange*, a work which begins as part of Marvel Comics' science-fiction/horror anthology *Strange Tales* (in issue #110), eventually expanding to the point of being the whole of the content of *Strange Tales* (by issue #169), before being renamed as *Dr. Strange* (also issue #169), and so a *superwork* in this sense would encompass some of *Strange Tales* and all of *Dr. Strange*. Thus, in the context of serials cataloguing, *superwork* often refers to the overarching *serial work* that one or more serial titles label.

Object-Oriented FRBR ($FRBR_{OO}$) takes a more rigid stance on the statuses of various bibliographic entities. As a CIDOC-based effort to reconcile the FRBR conceptual framework with the CIDOC Conceptual Reference Model (CIDOC-CRM), the $FRBR_{OO}$ model (Bekiari et al., 2015) provides a rich set of tools with which the bibliographic universe can be modelled. In particular, it provides a hierarchy of sub-classes that represent specialized conceptualizations of works. Among them is entity F15—Complex Work, which the editors define by saying, "This class comprises works that have other works as members. The members of a Complex Work may constitute alternatives to, derivatives of, or self-contained components of other members of the same Complex Work" (Bekiari et al., 2015, p.53). While the term complex work does not evoke the grand scope that a term like superwork does, the definition, scoping notes, and examples provided in the $FRBR_{OO}$ document seem to, at first, closely align to the definition of superwork and scope of the examples provided later in this paper, the primary intention of $FRBR_{OO}$'s developers is to model multipart works of authorship, such as Dante's *Inferno* which is a part of his larger *Divina Commedia* and groupings of derivative works[1]. The $FRBR_{OO}$ example illustrated by Figure 1, which showcases how works are realized, might easily be expanded to accommodate some portions of the examples which follow in the section below, e.g., the TV series *Mobile Suit Gundam* might be conceptualized as a $FRBR_{OO}$ *complex work*. However, given the examples in $FRBR_{OO}$'s documentation (see especially the scope and examples of relationship *R10 (has_member)* on pp 75-6), it does not seem as though works that are not intended by the creators to be part of one another, e.g., the TV series *Mobile Suit Gundam* and the full size model, *RX-78-2 Gundam* once on display at Gundam Front Tokyo are to be modelled using the *complex work* entity model, and so no easy solution can be found using an existing model like $FRBR_{OO}$.

---

[1] However, as $FRBR_{OO}$'s F1 Work is a subclass of CIDOC-CRM's Propositional Object, it is quite likely that none of the derivative work examples will hold up to serious scrutiny since they all revolve around translations and most philosophers hold propositional objects to be language-free (and thereby text-free) abstract objects (cf. Frege [1984] and Russell [1910, 1912, and 1913], among others).

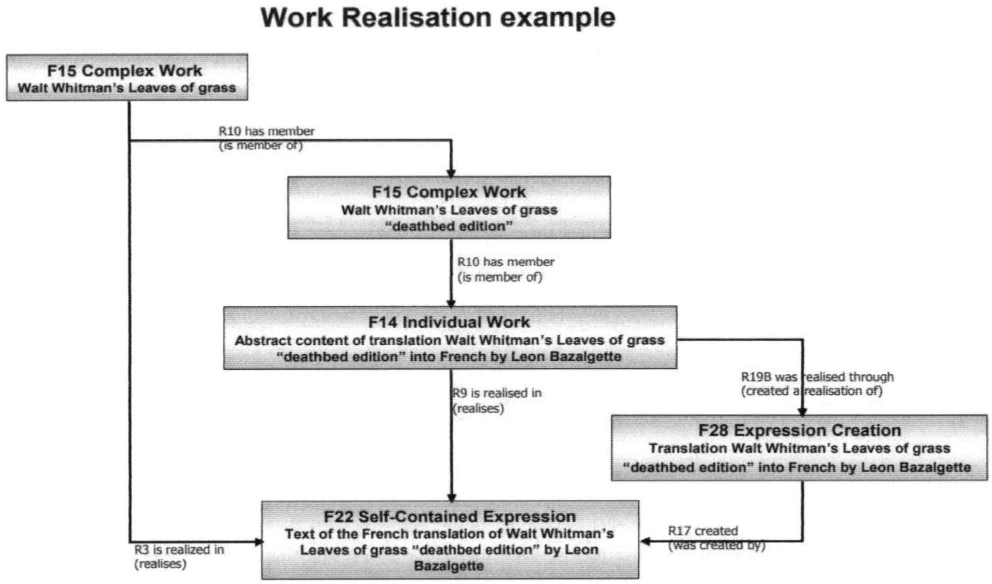

Figure 1. "Work Realisation Example" from Bekiari et al., 2015 (p. 16)

The BIBFRAME 2.0 model ("Overview of the BIBFRAME 2.0 Model," 2016) also has the potential to represent the concept of superwork. While there are currently no properties that explicitly mention superwork, the hasDerivative and derivativeOf properties, for instance, reflect one of the relationships found in superworks. However, it is unclear from the current documentation if other aspects of superwork can be represented in BIBFRAME 2.0 as is.

Reflecting these varied accounts of superwork (or a similar concept) in prior works, here we define superwork as an aggregate entity that encompasses multiple types of media objects that are related to each other based on:

1. their origins (i.e., derivative works from some ur-work), or
2. shared characteristics, such as theme, characters and world/universe.

Superwork Examples

The primary example of a superwork is that of Gundam. The term Gundam originates as the name of a type of giant manned robot in the anime *Mobile Suit Gundam* (1979). A selection of what the superwork currently encompasses can be seen illustrated in Figure 2 which showcases a variety of bibliographic entities that are related to one another through the term Gundam. Figure 2 does not give an exhaustive picture of all of the entities that are members of the Gundam superwork (among other things, the page is missing Gundam video games). One thing that immediately leaps out is that all of the entities are related to one another in some way. However, these relationships are complex, heterogenous, and in some cases, somewhat nebulous or not yet defined.

In a few cases, the relationships between the entities seem as though they are those with which we are readily familiar when we look at the bibliographic world through the lens of the FRBR framework. For instance, *Mobile Suit Gundam* (1979), *Gundam Wing* (1995), and *Gundam SEED* (2002) are all anime series and since they all share Gundam in common, it would be tempting to relate both *Gundam Wing* and *Gundam SEED* to *Mobile Suit Gundam* through the relationship of derivation (one work is derived from another). However, beyond some archetypal mechanical design styles, the overall plot, and the use of the reluctant hero trope, one can argue that *Gundam SEED* is mostly unrelated to *Mobile Suit Gundam*. It takes place in a different fictional universe with a cast of different fictional characters and remarks on some different narrative themes. It may be more accurate to say that *Gundam SEED* was inspired by *Mobile Suit Gundam*. Similarly, *Gundam Wing* differs not only with respect to fictional universe and characters but also with plot, so much so that it would be more accurate to say that *Gundam Wing* is influenced by *Mobile Suit Gundam*, rather than derived from it.

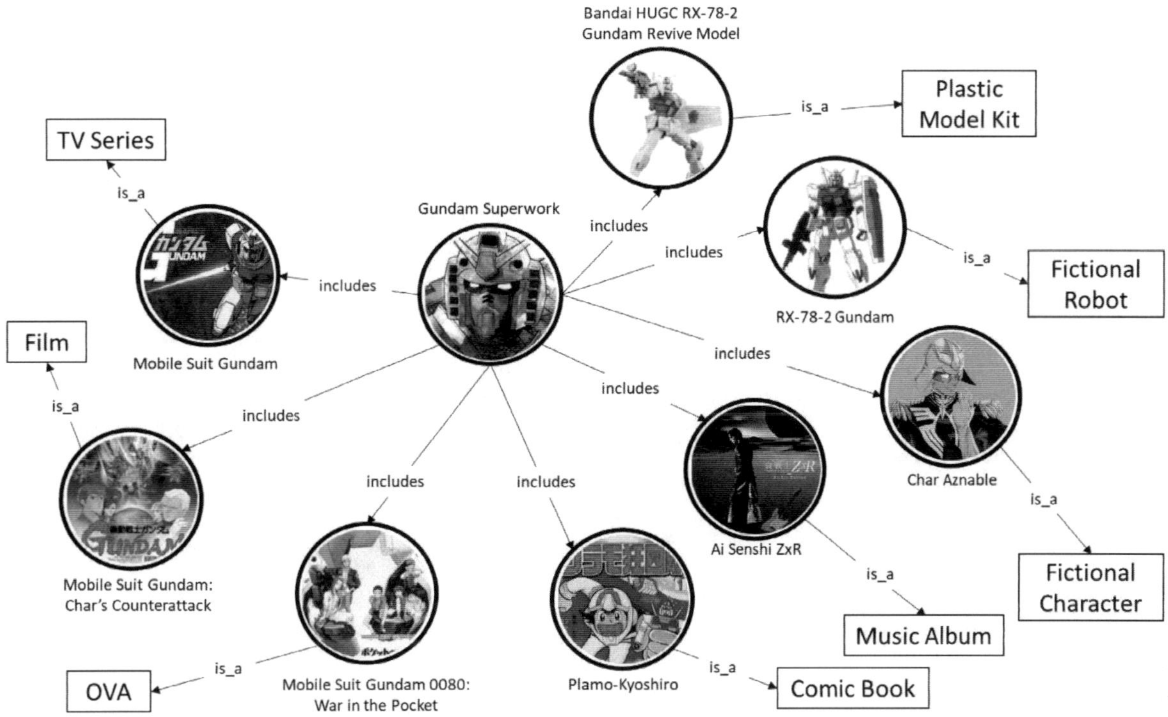

Figure 2. Some Entities from the Gundam Superwork

The relationships become even murkier as one goes down the list of entities in Figure 2. The list includes music, and so entities like *機動戦士ガンダム 鉄血のオルフェンズ COMPLETEBEST* (Kidō senshī Gandamu tekketsu no orufenzu Complete Best), a soundtrack, are among the things included as members of the Gundam superwork, and while that soundtrack directly relates to another work[2] in the same superwork through a part of relationship, it is unclear how it relates to any of the other members. Similarly, the superwork includes entities which cross the boundaries of other works which are members as showcased in Figure 3 through the *Dynasty Warriors: Gundam* video game.

Figure 3. Gundam Superwork Member Entities that Seem to Break Boundaries

Figure 3 also showcases entities that are members of the Gundam superwork entity but that challenge our normal assumptions with regards to the boundaries of fiction, fictional places, and our own everyday world. We could try to link these entities together through brand, but the *Dynasty Warriors: Gundam* video game and the WorldPost news article immediately break this linkage too since they are members of other brands (in this case the Dynasty Warriors and Huffington Post brands). Nor can

[2] It is a compilation soundtrack with music from various episodes of the animated TV series *機動戦士ガンダム 鉄血のオルフェンズ* (Kidō Senshi Gandamu Tekketsu no Orufenzu) which was originally broadcast from 4 October 2015 to 2 April 2017 on JNN. The TV series is also a distinct member of the Gundam superwork.

we easily link them through agents like creators, since the vast majority of the works have disparate creators. And yet all of the members of the Gundam superwork are related to one another in some fashion through the shared theme of Gundam.

At this point it is fair to ask whether or not a subject access point is sufficient means for users to access these materials. While it may be sufficient means for access, it lacks something that users could find useful and which, when they find lacking, they frequently forge for themselves. This *thing* is an account of the Gundam superwork. In ordinary library and digital library settings, these accounts are mediated to users through metadata records. It is at this point we turn our consideration to what properties a superwork entity must possess for a user to gain a sense of its nature.

Properties/Characteristics of Superwork

To define and set the boundaries of the superwork, we aimed to identify the essential characteristics regarding the properties of superwork or its relationships to other entities. Each was identified by examining select examples of superwork originating from different types of ur-works (for instance, the Hello Kitty superwork, which originated from a character design, or the Gundam superwork we have been discussing up to now, which originated from a TV series, *Mobile Suit Gundam*). Some characteristics were more easily agreed upon amongst the authors, while others led to more prolonged (and sometimes unresolved) discussions. It should be noted that the characteristics listed in this section are meant to form broad boundaries from which the beginnings of a definition for superwork can be established. The authors acknowledge that any practical implementation of a superwork concept, particularly when managed by fans, would need to be somewhat flexible in its boundaries so that it may adequately accommodate the needs of various communities.

A Superwork is a kind of aggregate.

- *hasMember*: Superworks are a kind of aggregate entity. At the very least they stand in a "hasPart" mereological relationship with the individual works that they are made of. More specifically, the individual works that make up a superwork stand in a mereonymic relationship with the superwork. If one models a superwork as the kind of thing that derives its identity from the works that compose it, then this narrower relationship is membership. If one models a superwork as the kind of thing that is constituted of the works that compose it, then this relationship is constitution. If one believes that the works that compose a superwork are brought together through curatorial intervention, then the relationship is the much narrower *gathered-into* relationship and superworks are identical to bibliographic collections.

A Superwork encompasses multiple works in multiple formats related to one another in a multitude of complex ways.

- *includesFormat*: One key feature of superworks is that they are pan-medium entities. They aggregate objects that are related to one another in some way. Frequently they are related through derivative relationships like adaptation. For example, the PlayStation 2 video game series, *hack//G.U.*, is adapted into both manga and anime formats which retell the story from the video games in subtly different ways more appropriate to their specific mediums. However, sometimes the objects that form a superwork's parts are related to one another in less clear ways, such as by being inspired by one of the other works in the superwork (e.g., *Mobile Suit Gundam SEED* is inspired by *Mobile Suit Gundam*). One important aspect is that the items in a superwork aggregation are related to one another beyond the curatorial sense of membership or the editorial sense of arrangement (i.e., they are not the same as collections or series). This distinction is important because both collections and series can also bring together works in multiple formats.

A Superwork will frequently contain works by several (and sometimes hundreds of) authors.

- *hasCreator*: Superworks are created and their creators are the creators of the works that compose them. Due to the grand scale of a superwork, it seems likely that they have manifold creators which participated in the creation of the works that compose them. However, it is possible that a superwork may be bound to a smaller, more specific body of work, e.g., the CLAMP superwork which is composed of all of the works created by CLAMP (a group of manga artists formed in the 1980s). During our discussion, a question was raised if multiple works by a single author can constitute a superwork. Considering a case like the Harry Potter series and the movie *Fantastic Beasts and Where to Find Them* (2016), both authored by J. K. Rowling, we believe it is possible for a superwork to emerge based on works by a single author.

A Superwork is aggregated around some theme or group of closely related themes.

- *hasTheme*: While it was clear to the authors that superworks are aggregated around a central unifying theme there was a great deal of discussion and some disagreement regarding the specific nature and granularity of that theme. Some authors argued that superworks were primarily built around shared fictional universes. While some examples, e.g., Holmes' Victorian London or the Marvel Comics Multiverse seem to bear this notion out, a close inspection of the Gumdam superwork showcased that this was not always true. Similarly, some of the authors argued that superworks seem to be built around brands, and examples like the Final Fantasy brand where neither the games in the video game series nor the films are narratively linked together in shared settings seemed to bear this out. But again, the Gundam superwork showcased counterexamples in the forms of the

Dynasty Warriors: Gundam video game and the WorldPost news article which have different brands from the Gundam brand. Finally, some authors argued that superworks could be built around shared topics but again, the Gundam superwork example showcased counterexamples as it was not the case that *Gundam SEED*, *Modeling Masters: Gundam Weapons*, and the WorldPost news article are all about the same thing. They might all share something in common (which we have chosen to call more generically theme) but that shared thing is not aboutness since *Gundam SEED* might better be described as an example of the Giant Robot genre that discusses the consequences of genetic experimentation and child soldiery. Similarly, the modeling guide is not about Gundam in any topical way but is instead describing tips for kit-bashing, painting, and posing models. Finally, it is not the case that the news article is about Gundam either, rather it is describing a work of art in the DiverCity Tokyo Plaza that just happens to be related to Gundam.

CHALLENGES

Defining the scope and nature of this reconceptualized superwork entity has been challenging, but we remain convinced that users frequently group works together that are related in ways that our digital library systems do not represent. If this were not the case, it is doubtful that the Gundam term would have an entire Wikipedia page devoted to it. Reconceptualizing superwork as an aggregation that primarily reflects something that users believe to be true about the bibliographic universe is a useful goal. Despite such utility, there are many possible pitfalls that we as group grappled with in our discussions about the scope and nature of the superwork entity.

Superworks as (non-)Bibliographic Entities

Superwork as Group 1 versus Group 3 Entities

One of the earliest and greatest hurdles that our superwork reconceptualization ran into was consideration of whether or not the thing we were referring to as a superwork was not better conceptualized as a kind of super-topic. After all, existing cataloging practices and digital information systems have well-developed senses of topical, genre-based, and agent-based access points. While these access points suffice for querying a catalog system we found that they lacked the essential conceptual substance that differentiates bibliographic aggregations from mere search query results—conceptual mass (Palmer, 2004).

While viewing each superwork as a "concept" entity from Group 3 would not be logically inconsistent with some of the arguments that have been made, in practical terms it would mean treating each unique franchise or series as its own subject entity. As these are usually under the control of various authority files, e.g. LCSH, implementation would mean the insertion of countless new subject terms based on each franchise, or the creation of a separate pop-culture authority file for this purpose.

An alternative is to represent the superwork entity as an abstract entity to which multiple relevant works belong (akin to FRBR Group 1 entities). A benefit here would be a more straightforward collocation of these works under the superwork entity rather than users having to access the network of works that may be grouped under a shared concept, place, and other elements.

Superworks as Bibliographic Aggregates

Superworks as Collections

Accepting the position that a superwork groups its members in a way such that they generate some contextual mass among them which is not otherwise present when each member is considered on its own naturally leads to the next challenge: 'Is a superwork a collection?' While we believe that it is true that superworks have contextual mass like a collection, it is important to recall that the contextual mass of a collection is carefully constructed as part of the curatorial process of selecting items being gathered into the collection (Palmer, 2004). Conversely, the items in a superwork do not seem to be grouped together through the curatorial process of selection. Therefore, it does not seem to be the case that superworks are the same kind of aggregation as a collection.

Superworks as Other Kinds of Aggregations

Similarly, we were forced to consider, 'If a superwork is not a collection, is it possible that a superwork might be some other kind of bibliographic aggregation, such as an anthology or a series?' Both of these bibliographic aggregates also have contextual mass and both of them have contextual mass for subtly different reasons. In the anthology's case, contextual mass is brought about through the editorial process of carefully arranging the works that compose the anthology. In the series' case, contextual mass is brought about through the authorial (corporate or individual) intention that the works that compose the series be understood as a whole and that they stand in some determined sequential relationship to one another. However, superworks are not assembled by editors and so are not carefully arranged. Similarly, the works that compose a superwork do not necessarily stand in some sequential relationship with one another (although where the work that is a member of a superwork is itself a series, then the works that compose it obviously do stand in such a relationship with one another), and so it does not seem as though there is any authorial intention creating the superwork's contextual mass.

Specialized Relationships among Superwork Members

Conceptualizing Crossover superworks

There were a few examples that proved even more challenging to conceptualize as superwork. Our first example is the superwork Kingdom Hearts which started with the video game *Kingdom Hearts*, developed and published in 2002 by Square. What is interesting about this particular example is that it is a crossover of two substantial superworks, Final Fantasy and Disney. Crossover refers to cases where a character from one title appears in another title, or one company's intellectual property appears in another company's product based on a negotiated legal agreement (Carreker, 2012). The characters from each of these two superworks (e.g., Cloud from *Final Fantasy 7*, Mickey Mouse from Disney) appear in this crossover superwork, along with some original characters of the Kingdom Hearts superwork (e.g., Sora, Kairi). While the authors did not have a disagreement on Kingdom Hearts itself constituting a superwork (given the numerous works including figures, soundtracks, novels, etc. that are derived from or influenced by the original game series), it was not clear if the Kingdom Hearts superwork then belongs to the Final Fantasy or the Disney superwork. After much discussion, the authors agreed that the mixed presence of characters from two different superworks in a crossover superwork made it feel unnatural to categorize the crossover superwork under one or the other superworks from which the characters originate.

Considering Spiritual Successors as Part of Superworks

Another challenging task was how to deal with spiritual successors which Lee et al. (2014) define as "a video game designed to be similar to existing game [*sic*] while distinguishing itself as a separate IP (intellectual property), often created by the same individual(s)" (p.4).[3] A good example of this is the video game *Dark Souls* (FromSoftware, 2011) which is a spiritual successor to an earlier game, *Demon's Souls* (FromSoftware, 2009). In this case, the core mechanics of both games are the same, with narratives that involve similar elements such as demons, undead creatures, and cursed characters. While the content of the games is very similar, they were issued under different titles because of legal reasons, more specifically, so that the game could be released for another game console. While the two games are separate brands with different rights owners, many players refer to these games together by the informal "Souls series" title, which encompasses Demon's Souls, the three titles in the Dark Souls series, and sometimes a similar title from FromSoftware, Bloodborne (2015). As we named brand as one of the criteria for superwork, distinguishing between explicit brands based on intellectual property and unofficial ones defined by users is an important consideration.

CONCLUSION

In this exploratory work, we examined how the concept of superwork has been discussed in previous literature in library and information science as well as cataloguing standards and suggested a set of characteristics that the superwork entity exhibits as an attempt to help define the concept and establish its boundaries. While the authors were not able to come to a consensus on the boundaries of the properties of superwork entities or define all of their possible properties, there appears to be sufficient anecdotal evidence that some form of aggregate entity that groups cultural-phenomenon-related entities together across the divides of authorial intentions, branding, and thematic elements is needed. Additional general boundary questions with regards to bibliographic objects and artifacts also reveal themselves. If a superwork is to be the complete aggregation of all things related to one another through some intention, brand, or theme, then the nature of those things needs to be carefully considered. With regards to all of our high-level and applied bibliographic standards, the ontological status of objects like toy whistles with Gundam shapes on them or coffee mugs with Gundams painted on them remains vague and ill-defined. We can be certain that these are bibliographic items since they are artifacts that can be described. It seems likely that they might also be bibliographic manifestations since there are many copies. But do they have a status as some kind of bibliographic expression or work? This seems much less clear.

It is clear that further work on the conceptual and formal levels needs to be done to better highlight the implications of including a superwork entity class in our bibliographic standards. In addition, there is also a clear need for a number of user studies to determine how prevalent grouping works together into superworks is among library users and cultural heritage consumers. The next phase of this research will refine our understanding of this phenomenon, especially with regards to how users conceptualize the superwork problem space, what methods they employ to retrieve objects of interest, and how (or even if) superwork entities affect their information seeking behaviors at all. This work will be accomplished through a number of conceptual analyses and user studies, including interviews and card sorting activities.

---

[3] Lee et al.'s definition is derived from a definition provided earlier by Carreker (2012). It is important to note that Carreker's definition is not intended for those concerned with creating metadata for the selection and access to video games in a collection through means of bibliographic control.

REFERENCES

Antelman, K. (2004). Identifying the serial work as a bibliographic entity. Library resources & technical services, 48(4), 238-255.

Bekiari, C., Doerr, M., Le Bœuf, P., & Riva, P. (2015). FRBR object-oriented definition and mapping from FRBRER, FRAD and FRSAD (version 2.4). International working group on FRBR and CIDOC CRM harmonisation.

Carlyle, A. (1996). Ordering author and work records: An evaluation of collocation in online catalog displays. JASIS, 47(7), 538-554.

Carreker, D. (2012). The Game Developer's Dictionary: A Multidisciplinary Lexicon for Professionals and Students. Boston, MA: Course Technology.

Domanovszky, A. (1973). Editor entries and the principles of cataloguing. Libri, 23(4), 307-330.

Frege, G. (1984). "Thoughts." In B. McGuinness (ed.) Gottlob Frege: Collected Papers on Mathematics, Logic, and Philosophy. Oxford: Basil Blackwell, pp 351-72.

Kemp, R. (2008). Catalog/cataloguing changes and web 2.0 functionality. The serials librarian, 53(4), 91-112.

Kiryakos, S., Sugimoto, S., Lee, J. H., Jett, J., Cheng, Y., & Downie, J. S. (2017). Towards a Conceptual Framework for Superworks. Proceedings of the 7th conference of Japanese Association for Digital Humanities: Creating data through collaboration, Kyoto, Japan, pp.47-49.

Leazer, G. H., & Smiraglia, R. P. (1999). Bibliographic families in the library catalog: A qualitative analysis and grounded theory. Library resources & technical services, 43(4), 191-212.

Lee, J. H., Clarke, R. I., Sacchi, S., & Jett, J. (2014). Relationships among video games: Existing standards and new definitions. Proceedings of the Association for Information Science and Technology, 51(1), 1-11.

Library of Congress (2016, April 21). Overview of the BIBFRAME 2.0 Model. Retrieved from https://www.loc.gov/bibframe/docs/bibframe2-model.html

Palmer, C. L. (2004). Thematic research collections. A companion to digital humanities, 348-365.

Pettee, J. (1936). The development of authorship entry and the formulation of authorship rules as found in the Anglo-American code. *The Library Quarterly*, 6(3), 270-290.

Russell, B. (1910). "On the Nature of Truth and Falsehood." In Philosophical Essays. London: Longmans. Green, pp 116-24.

Russell, B. (1912). *The Problems of Philosophy*. Oxford: Oxford University Press.

Russell, B. (1913). Theory of Knowledge. London: Routledge.

Smiraglia, R. (2007). Bibliographic Families and Super works. Understanding FRBR: what it is and How it will Affect our Retrieval Tools edited by Arlene G. Taylor. West port: Libraries Unlimited, 73-86.

Smiraglia, R. P., Riva, P., & Žumer, M. (2014). The FRBR family of conceptual models: toward a linked bibliographic future. Routledge.

Svenonius, E. (2000). The intellectual foundation of information organization. MIT press.

Taylor, A. (2007). An introduction to functional requirements for bibliographic records (FRBR). Understanding FRBR: What is and how it will affect our retrieval tools. Westport, CT.: Libraries Unlimited.

Verona, E. (1959). Literary unit versus bibliographical unit. Libri, 9(1-4), 79-104.

Wilson, P. (1968). Two kinds of power: An essay on bibliographical control. Univ of California Press.

Are There Different Types of Online Research Impact?

Steffen Lemke
ZBW – Leibniz Centre for Economics, Germany.
s.lemke@zbw.eu

Maryam Mehrazar
ZBW – Leibniz Centre for Economics, Germany.
m.mehrazar@zbw.eu

Athanasios Mazarakis
Kiel University, Germany. a.mazarakis@zbw.eu

Isabella Peters
ZBW – Leibniz Centre for Economics, Germany.
i.peters@zbw.eu

ABSTRACT
While web-based indicators for scientific impact – so-called altmetrics – have an increasing uptake as means for research evaluation, many questions regarding their actual meanings remain unanswered. In this article we analyse the data from a survey about researchers' use of 107 online actions that underlie potential altmetrics to discover whether certain types of altmetrics (1) better reflect the judgments of researchers from certain career stages and (2) more reliably capture positive judgments than others. We apply variance analyses to reveal significant differences between the frequencies with which early-stage researchers and professors perform various actions whose occurrences are counted as impact metrics (e.g., downloading, liking, or sharing of scientific publications). The findings imply varying degrees of representation of these groups in respective altmetrics. Moreover, by investigating how commonly various types of actions are used to express positive judgments, we disclose how reliably metrics can be used as proxies for positive impact. Our findings contribute to a more comprehensive understanding of the meaning of different web-based metrics for scholarly impact and provide a basis for evidence-based guidelines on how to use and interpret them.

KEYWORDS
Research evaluation, altmetrics, social media analysis, survey study.

INTRODUCTION
Enabled by the rise of the Internet and social media in particular, the idea of web-based metrics for research impact emerged as a promising means towards a more versatile and fair evaluation of scientific achievements. Frustration about the disproportionate influence of citation counts and citation-based metrics in the assessment of scholarly impact further encouraged researchers to look for alternatives, as for example described in the altmetrics manifesto (Priem, Taraborelli, Groth, & Neylon, 2010) or formulated from the DORA initiative (https://sfdora.org). As web-based platforms had become an integral part of many researchers' everyday work, new options unfolded themselves in the various possibilities to count online engagements with scientific publications, e.g. mentions, shares or downloads. Now, eight years after the coining of the umbrella term *altmetrics* (Priem, Taraborelli, Groth, & Neylon, 2010) to denote those metrics operationalizing the attention scientific products receive online, especially on social media platforms, several grand challenges of handling such metrics remain to be solved (Haustein, 2016).

Much research has been done to find out why people cite, arriving at a multitude of different reasons – a heterogeneity of underlying motivations that complicates the usage of citations as proxies for scientific relevance or quality (Bornmann & Daniel, 2008). When we turn to altmetrics, heterogeneity poses an even greater difficulty, as here it also concerns the tremendous number of existing and emerging platforms that could be used to derive altmetric indicators (Lin & Fenner, 2013). Every single platform potentially imposes its own technical conditions, provides its own set of functionalities and accommodates its own community of users.

As altmetrics are increasingly utilized in research evaluation (Haustein, 2016), a differentiated analysis of what different types of altmetrics precisely reflect is indispensable to ensure trustworthiness and fairness in their use (Lin & Fenner, 2013). This becomes especially apparent at a time in which the much-debated problem of fake news makes us painfully aware of one of social media's greatest weaknesses: the unfiltered stream of information on the platforms has to be processed with care, signals should be thoroughly assessed with regard to their origins. Obviously, this also concerns the process of measuring online attention as an indicator for scientific impact. For example, whose attention does a high number of retweets on Twitter reflect, compared to a high number of downloads on ResearchGate? Which level of expertise of the user is typically involved when a publication becomes an altmetric success on Facebook, i.e., shared or liked by many users? And do altmetrics involve a systematic bias towards young researchers, as is commonly suspected (Priem, 2014)? Originator-related questions like these need to be answered to turn the otherwise overwhelming thicket of altmetrics into transparent and conclusive metrics for scientific impact.

Another difficulty with the interpretation of altmetrics that needs to be addressed is the possibility that a certain action leading to an increase in altmetrics does not necessarily translate to a positive judgment about the object on the receiving end of the action. Just like citations, which can as well be used to criticize, correct or just neutrally comment on the cited publication, social media actions are performed for diverse purposes – even a seemingly one-dimensional action like a Facebook-'Like' (Levordashka, Utz, & Ambros, 2016). Evaluation of research products usually looks for positive interactions with them, so that relevance or quality can be confirmed. The common proxy for quality is: the more means the better – which makes it necessary to examine how reliably different types of metrics actually do reflect positive judgments.

To tackle these issues, we present in this article selected data from a survey conducted in spring 2017, investigating the social media usage of scholars. While researchers' usage of specific social media platforms has already been analyzed by a multitude of both quantitative (Collins, Shiffman, & Rock, 2016; Kramer & Bosman, 2016; Syn & Oh, 2015; Van Noorden, 2014) and qualitative (LaPoe, Carter Olson, & Eckert, 2017; Vainio & Holmberg, 2017) studies, the survey presented in this article sets itself apart from previous studies by inquiring detailed information about degrees of usage of a multitude of individual actions available on social media platforms.

To better understand whose judgments are reflected by which types of altmetrics, we aim to answer the following research question by analyzing the survey data:

RQ1: Which actions related to altmetrics are performed frequently by researchers from which career stages?

Additionally, to get a better understanding of which altmetrics can be regarded as indicators for genuine, positive scientific impact, we also aim to answer the following question:

RQ2: Which actions related to altmetrics are reliably used to express positive sentiments towards their targets?

This article presents findings of a survey that is part of a bigger study on the meaning, reliability and perception of altmetrics (https://metrics-project.net/). Understanding the meaning of altmetrics is a multidimensional task, as that meaning is shaped by both the characteristics of the users performing underlying actions, as well as their concrete motivations for doing so. While the different metrics' inherent positivity is one crucial aspect to consider, further steps are needed to account for the large variety of goals that researchers pursue when interacting with scientific products online. The survey presented here will therefore be succeeded by a round of qualitative interviews and a follow-up survey investigating in more depth on researchers' motivations when performing online actions related to altmetrics.

The relationship between academic experience or career stage and social media usage has been analyzed by previous works with diverging results for different platforms. Regarding *Twitter*, Bowman (2015) found the relationship between academic experience and usage to follow a reversed U-shaped curve, finding that researchers with 7 to 9 years of academic experience are more likely to be active on *Twitter* than those with less or more years of experience. Shema et al. (2012) examined data on research blogs aggregated by the service *ResearchBlogging.org,* concluding that most authors are either graduate students or PhDs, with both groups being about equally represented among the blogs' authorships. Several studies have examined the representation of different researcher career stages on social media by looking at the example of *Mendeley*, finding that junior researchers and doctoral students are the largest user group on the social bookmarking service (Haustein & Larivière, 2014; Jeng et al., 2015; Zahedi, Costas, & Wouters, 2014). These previous findings however do not allow for statements about the actual intensity of activity of users from different career stages on the platforms, e.g., the frequency with which they interact with publications. And – as quickly becomes apparent when looking at the different categorization schemas used in these studies – their results are not directly comparable to achieve a cross-platform overview. Also, so far there has been no broad study comparing the kinds of sentiments that researchers want to express by performing the various actions that lead to increases in potential altmetrics. These are gaps we aim to close with our work.

METHODS

To gather information on researchers' usage habits in respect to social media, an online survey consisting of 20 questions was designed and implemented using the online survey software *LimeSurvey* (https://www.limesurvey.org/). The dissemination was started on March 31st 2017 and ended on May 17th 2017. The call for participation was disseminated via a combination of direct personalized mails (containing the recipients' first and surnames), direct non-personalized mails and mailing lists. Personalized mails were sent to about 12,000 economists enlisted in a mailing list administered by the *ZBW Leibniz Information Centre for Economics*; non-personalized mails were sent to about 42,000 addresses of economics- or social sciences-related researchers which had been mined from RePEc and Web of Science. Additionally, about a dozen international mailing lists referring to either economics, social sciences or corresponding sub-disciplines were also addressed with the call for participation. The emphases put on economists and social scientists during dissemination were by design, as these disciplines hold particular interest for the institutions involved in the study's conduction.

Participants were asked between 13 and 20 questions, depending on their answers over the course of the questionnaire. Most questions revolved around a preselected list of 90 social media services. This list was compiled from three sources: (1) a joint brainstorm session among the authors, which also served the purpose of clarifying the direction to take in the whole process of service preselection; (2) services included in the previous surveys by Kramer & Bosman (2016) and Van Noorden (2014) were considered; (3) Kramer & Bosman (2015) make use of a crowdsourcing approach to collect information on online tools with potential relevance for researchers in an open spreadsheet – we manually scanned the spreadsheet for services we missed before, especially looking out for services with particular relevance for the fields of economics or social sciences. At the end of this preselection process the list was reduced to the 90 services deemed most relevant, to keep the questionnaire reasonably short. The services included in this list reflect a very broad definition of social media – we allowed any kind of web-based platform, which would allow for centrally countable interactions with scientific products and could thus potentially be exploited as a source for altmetrics.

In the survey participants were provided with the list of social media services described above and asked to select those who they use at work. The services a participant selected as "used at work" significantly shaped the remaining course of the questionnaire, as will be seen below.

To answer the first research question, we analyze responses to the survey questions *What is your current role?* (possible answers were *Professor/Associate professor/Assistant professor; Postdoc/Senior Researcher; Research assistant + PhD student; Research assistant; PhD student; Other*) and *How often do you…?* (with the possible answers *Several times a day; About once a day; Several times a week; About once a week; About once a month; Less often; Never*). The group of services a participant previously selected as "used at work" determined for which online actions that participant was asked to answer the latter question – e.g., if a participant stated that she would use *Facebook* and *Twitter* at work, here she would be asked to select the frequencies with which she *writes a post about academic research on Facebook, likes a post about academic research on Facebook, comments on a post about academic research on Facebook, shares a post about academic research on Facebook, writes a tweet about academic research, favors a tweet about academic research, replies to a tweet about academic research,* and *shares a tweet about academic research*. To come up with the survey's list of such actions, the 90 considered services were manually checked for features which could (1) be used to interact with scientific publications and (2) would lead to a measurable number of occurrences that could potentially be exploited as a quantitative metric (e.g., a publication's number of downloads). Frequent types of features were for example 'like'-, 'share'-, 'bookmark'- or 'download'-actions. In total, 107 actions were implemented in the survey this way, between 0 and 5 for each of the 90 included services.

To see whether the metrics behind certain actions better reflect the opinions of established researchers in contrast to beginners, we first assigned the participants to two groups, based on their stated role: (1) professors (consisting of those participants who identified themselves as *Professor/Associate professor/Assistant professor*) and (2) early-stage researchers (consisting of participants who identified themselves as either *Research assistant* and/or *PhD student*). Based on the data about frequencies with which those two groups use the actions the survey asked about, we then performed Welch's t-tests to check for significant differences regarding their mean frequencies. For this we ignored all actions for which less than a total of 150 survey participants provided answers, leaving us with 58 actions to test for. Resulting p-values were adjusted with Tukey's HSD (Lowry, 2008).

Answering the second research question, we analyzed the responses for the survey question *When you are performing the following actions, in how many cases does that indicate a positive stance on the respective target?* (possible answers: *In all cases, In most cases, In few cases, Never*). Participants were asked to answer this question for all actions they use at least occasionally according to their responses given before. For the analysis we again focused on actions for which we got data from at least 150 participants, in this case leaving us with 42 actions. These actions were then allocated to one out of seven groups each, depending on their consequences: 'writing', with 7 actions leading to an original piece of text by the active user; 'commenting', with 4 actions leading to an original piece of text by the active user that directly refers to an already existing item; 'downloading', with 14 actions that lead to a file download with the active user as recipient; 'sharing', with 5 actions that forward an existing item to the active user's contacts on the respective platform; 'bookmarking', with 3 actions that lead to the addition of a reference of the selected item to the active user's personal library on the respective platform; 'liking', with 5 actions that refer to an existing item, increase a visible score attached to it and add the active user to an associated user list; 'Other', with 4 actions that don't fit in the previous groups.

For all 42 actions we calculated the individual shares of users stating they would use the respective action exclusively to express positive sentiments among all users who provided an answer concerning the respective action. We then analyzed the resulting shares graphically. Examining which actions are most constantly performed to express positive sentiments towards their targets, we get evidence which altmetrics can reliably be used to measure an article's positive impact in its research community.

RESULTS AND DISCUSSION

In this section we present results of the analysis of the two pivotal questions asked in our survey. The analysis of the first question sheds light on the intensity of social media usage among researchers in different career stages, the analysis of the second question on the sentiments researchers express via affordances of social media and other web-based platforms.

Respondent Demographics

We received input from a total of 3,427 participants, i.e. a response rate of ~6% (n ≈ 54,000). Of those participants 2,659 (78%) had gone through the complete questionnaire. The median time spent in the survey was 9 minutes 3 seconds. Participants were from 84 countries, the majority being from *Germany* (51%), followed by the *United States of America* (10%), the *United Kingdom* and *Italy* (both 5%). Most participants stated to be from the age bracket *30-39 years* (32%), followed by the age brackets *40-49 years* (17%) and *20-29 years* (12%), the mean age was 40 years. Discipline-wise the sample was dominated by participants stating *Economics* as their primary field of research (60%), followed by *Social Sciences* (23%) and *Other* (7%). *Engineering/Technology*, *Life Sciences*, *Arts/Humanities*, *Law*, *Medicine* and *Physical Sciences* all received less than 4%.

Asking for the participants' current role revealed that most identified as belonging to the group *Professor/Associate professor/Assistant professor* (44%). Remaining categories were *Research assistant + PhD student* (20%), *Postdoc/Senior Researcher* (19%), *PhD Student* (9%), *Other* (5%) and *Research assistant* (3%).

The sample's considerable biases towards German participants as well as towards economists and social scientists can be explained by the choice of distribution channels explained in the Methods section. The discipline-wise emphases are a consequence of the topical focus of the project in which this study was carried out. The biases towards German participants and professors were very likely caused by the aforementioned mailing list with 12,000 entries administered by the ZBW, which contained email addresses of researchers from German-speaking countries working at institutions related to economics, business studies and closely related fields.

RQ1: Comparison of Frequent Actions by Career Stages

To reveal how the degree of representation of researchers from different levels of professional experience within specific metrics varies, we analyzed the mean frequencies with which *early-stage researchers* in contrast to *professors* use 58 social media actions by applying Welch tests. To be able to calculate mean scores for the ordinal scaled frequencies, we applied the following mapping from answer options to numerical values: *Never* = 0, *Less often [than once a month]* = 1, *About once a month* = 2, *About once a week* = 3, *Several times a week* = 4, *About once a day* = 5 and *Several times a day* = 6.

Assuming a significance level of 5%, for 27 actions significant differences in regard to the frequency with which the two groups on average use them were found. Table 1 shows the 15 actions that are used significantly more frequently by early-stage researchers than by professors. n_e/n_p shows the number of early-stage researchers/professors that stated a usage frequency regarding the respective action, m_e/m_p shows the mean frequency with which the respective group uses the respective action, p is the significance value of the according Welch test (adjusted with Tukey's HSD). Table 2 shows the 12 actions that are used significantly more frequently by professors than by early-stage researchers accordingly.

The probably most striking peculiarity in these results is the high number of 'download' actions seen in Table 1. In fact, we found significant differences for eleven out of thirteen 'download' actions we tested, in all cases with higher means for the early-stage researchers. A similar observation can be made for 'bookmarking' actions, where all three tested actions revealed higher means for early-stage researchers than for professors. Among the twelve actions that professors use significantly more frequently are seven actions that imply the writing of some original text. Of the remaining actions in Table 2, three are about sharing academic resources, two about liking. Also remarkable is that eight of the twelve actions from Table 2 refer to either *Facebook* or *Twitter*.

Action	Platform	n_e	n_p	m_e	m_p	p
download an article	Academia.edu	182	353	2.34	1.74	0.001
download an article	arXiv	63	101	2.98	2.12	0.001
download an article	EconStor	203	146	2.95	2.41	0.001
download an article	JSTOR	560	816	3.42	2.84	0.001
download an article	MPRA	50	155	2.96	2.22	0.001
download an article	PubMed C.	88	147	3.19	2.25	0.001
download an article	RePEc	155	492	3.20	2.50	0.001
download an article	ResearchGate	529	711	2.56	2.12	0.001
download an article	SSRN	219	505	2.70	2.10	0.001
download a repository	GitHub	159	130	1.98	1.63	0.016
download a sample	EBSCO	360	469	2.68	1.98	0.001
export/save a sample	EBSCO	357	457	1.93	1.35	0.001
save a bookmark	Citavi	302	94	2.94	2.06	0.001
save a bookmark	JSTOR	542	785	1.22	0.79	0.001
save a bookmark	Mendeley	159	205	2.43	1.55	0.001

Table 1. Actions used more frequently by early-stage researchers.

Given the availability of only quantitative data on the usage frequencies and significant differences we can only hypothesize about the underlying reasons for these results. The findings for early-stage researchers suggest a comparatively higher usage of services that are helpful during the practical stage of scientific work, in most cases by either providing access to literature or by assisting in managing it. This seems plausible as early-stage researchers might typically be able to spent more time with the realization of research than professors, who in turn often might be more occupied with diverse other tasks like administration or teaching. The observation that professors more frequently perform several actions involving writing might be explained by the availability of personal networks: as professors will on average have built more extensive professional networks than most early-stage researchers, they'll also have a wider potential audience to reach on social networks like *Facebook* and *Twitter*. This would both lead to more opportunities to engage in running scientific discussions as well as make posting written contributions more meaningful in general. Another reason for early-stage researchers' lower use of such actions might be a comparatively lower self-confidence to actively participate in scientific discussions online. Of course different interpretations are possible, all of which need to be backed up with in-depth research.

Action	Platform	n_e	n_p	m_e	m_p	p
cite academic research	Wikipedia	571	771	0.49	0.67	0.002
comment on a post[1]	Facebook	216	287	1.50	2.08	0.001
favor a tweet[1]	Twitter	123	283	2.41	2.86	0.032
like a post[1]	Facebook	219	289	2.62	2.94	0.046
reply to a tweet[1]	Twitter	123	280	1.64	2.09	0.012
retweet a tweet[1]	Twitter	124	283	2.23	2.81	0.004
send a tweet[1]	Twitter	135	297	2.03	2.78	0.001
share a post[1]	Facebook	218	289	1.65	2.19	0.001
share a video[1]	Youtube	279	452	0.44	0.73	0.001
write a post[1]	Facebook	228	308	1.33	1.89	0.001
write a post[1]	LinkedIn	227	465	0.58	0.80	0.009
write a post[1]	Wordpress	119	210	0.82	1.14	0.009

[1]about academic research

Table 2. Actions used more frequently by professors.

RQ2: Positive Sentiments Behind Social Media Actions

Exploring the ways users shape specific metrics is a multi-dimensional problem: while looking at the frequency with which certain user groups perform an action gives us insights on their probable influence on the respective metric's shape, another aspect are the users' prevalent motivations – *why* they perform certain actions. While a follow-up survey will be specifically dedicated to that aspect, we at this point want to hint at patterns related to user motivations that the past survey could reveal.

Figure 1 shows the shares of users of actions that use the respective action exclusively to express positive judgments. Every data point corresponds to one of the 42 actions for which at least 150 survey participants gave a response. The three points from the group *bookmarking* for example refer to the actions *save a bookmark on Citavi, save a bookmark on Mendeley,* and *save a bookmark on JSTOR*.

Comparing the ranges of the action groups suggests noticeable differences between the latter: for like-actions from different platforms we get shares between 32.8% and 40.6% of their users who exclusively use them to express positive judgments, suggesting Likes are a comparatively reliable proxy for praise. On the other end of the spectrum are comments – only between 13.7% and 16.9% of their users state that they only ever comment to express positive stances. Bookmarks follow Likes as another indicator with mostly fairly high shares of users only bookmarking targets they take a positive stance on, while the range of shares for writing-actions is the second lowest aside from comments. Sharing- and downloading-actions mostly lie in the midfield, with a few outliers to the top service-wise.

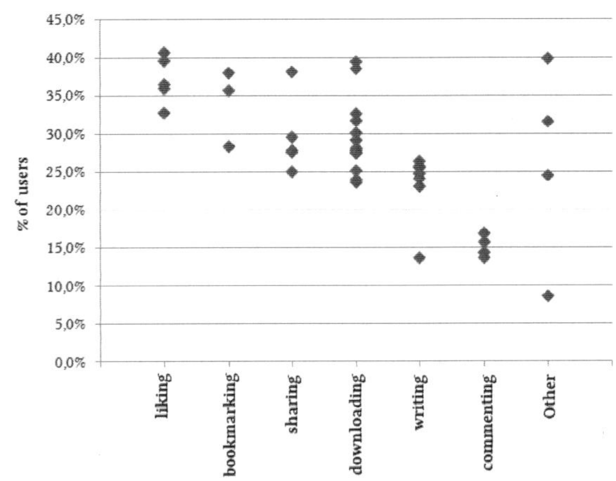

Figure 1. Share of users of an action who exclusively perform it to express a positive stance towards its target.

In addition to the described general tendencies observable for types of actions, through outliers like these the results provide another facet of interesting insights, as they indicate that similar actions might be commonly used for different reasons on different platforms. The outlier down among writing-actions for example refers to the action 'review academic research on Amazon', suggesting that *Amazon* is a platform used by more of its users to write critically about research, compared to the other platforms represented in that action group (*Facebook*, *Twitter*, *LinkedIn*, *Wikipedia*, *SSRN* and blogs).

CONCLUSIONS

The results of our survey indicated significant differences regarding the usage frequencies of researchers from different career stages in regard to actions whose consequences can be measured as altmetrics. This implies imbalanced degrees of representation of these user groups in respective altmetrics – for example publications' download counts on many platforms will more likely reflect judgments by early-stage researchers, counting mentions of a scientific article on *Facebook* or *Twitter* might lead to a better reflection of that article's impact among more experienced researchers.

The participants' responses to the survey question about how commonly they use different online actions to express positive judgments indicated that web-based impact metrics should be differentiated by the type of action behind them, not only by the source they are from – regarding their intended meaning, e.g., Likes on two distinct platforms seem in most cases to be more similar to each other than Likes and comments on the same platform. Also, our graphical analysis hinted at a rough 'ranking order' of different action types' likelihoods to represent positive judgments, with Likes being the most consistent and comments being the least consistent proxy for endorsement. Moreover, aggregations on action type-level – which some prominent providers for altmetric data already customarily do, such as PlumX – should still be done with care, as our analysis revealed a few strong outliers in several action groups.

In summary, this case study on scholarly social media use provides evidence that closely observing the circumstances among which different kinds of altmetrics arise is necessary to get to an informed picture of what they express. It also shows that such differentiation should not stop at the level of sources, but should go even deeper to the level of action types or even individual actions.

Our approach can only serve as a first glimpse at what users' motives for specific actions tell us about how to handle the metrics resulting of such activities, so further work will go into testing hypotheses made based on this article with solid statistical evidence. Also, future analysis of the survey data will incorporate an additional dimension by linking the participants' responses about their motives to perform certain actions with their stated individual frequencies of usage, thus accounting for the fact that on social media very few users are responsible for a large share of activities (Nielsen, 2006).

A limitation of this study lies in its sample, which was heavily biased towards economists and social scientists. Similar to how disciplines' differ regarding prevailing citation norms (van Raan, 2003), they might also behave differently regarding their usage of the social media-related actions analyzed in this study. And although it might be a reasonable assumption that the lion's share of online interactions with scientific products is performed by researchers, the influence of non-academic users on altmetrics should be considered in future studies as well.

Moreover, the survey results presented in this article only reveal a snapshot of the participating researchers' social media usage – safe predictions about that usage's future development cannot be made on this basis. To allow for such predictions a worthwhile approach might be to repeatedly survey the same group of researchers over a longer period of time. This could reveal whether certain participants continue to use particular services they started using early, regardless of changes to their career stage. However, our hypotheses for such a study would be in accordance with the results discussed above: for example, although someone who as a PhD student started to use the social bookmarking tool *Mendeley* might be more likely to also use it in later career stages, the frequency with which that researcher saves bookmarks on *Mendeley* would probably decrease due to accompanying changes regarding the researcher's tasks.

A general shortcoming of surveys like ours is their dependence on the participants' perceptions and memories, which are of uncertain reliability. A more reliable approach to investigate on individuals' usage habits would be to analyze log data from the platforms on which relevant actions take place. This approach however comes with its own challenges: for example the identification of respective active users' demographics, the possibly missing inter-platform comparability of log data due to differences between the ways they are recorded as well as – in the first place – the general difficulty to get access to log data for many platforms.

Also, there are other approaches which might be valuable complements to the survey-based approach taken by this study. Network analysis can provide additional insights regarding the influence of certain user types on the rise of specific metrics by revealing which nodes play particularly prominent roles during the dissemination of information through online communities (see e.g., Brown, Broderick, & Lee (2007)). Qualitative analyses of the circumstances under which interactions (e.g., comments or Likes) take place might result in similar results as for citation analysis (see for example Catalini, Lacetera, & Oettl (2015); Cavalcanti, Prudêncio, Pradhan, Shah, & Pietrobon (2011)). Although qualitative approaches like these might not be feasible to perform for a number of actions as high as in this study at once, for a selection of platforms sentiment analysis could be used to confirm this study's findings regarding the shares of writing- and commenting-actions that are performed to express positive judgments.

The results presented in this article provide input to research and development on the Web, for example by informing ranking or personalization algorithms that utilize social media and usage data in similar contexts. Moreover, our results could serve as a starting point for the development of well-informed guidelines for a more differentiated handling of altmetrics.

Suppliers of altmetric data for purposes of research evaluation are very aware that the online activities they measure do not equal scholarly praise, but are merely indicators for attention (Altmetric.com, 2015). Still, if we are striving to release altmetrics' full potential to lead to a more comprehensive, transparent and fairer appreciation of scientific work, systematic analyses of precisely what actions happening on social media platforms and the web in general mean are a necessary endeavor.

ACKNOWLEDGEMENTS

This work is part of the DFG-funded research project **metrics* (project number: 314727790). Further information on the project and the survey mentioned above can be found on https://metrics-project.net/.

REFERENCES

Altmetric.com. (2015). What are altmetrics? *Altmetric.com*. Retrieved February 19, 2018, from https://www.altmetric.com/about-altmetrics/what-are-altmetrics/

Bowman, T. D. (2015). Investigating the use of affordances and framing techniques by scholars to manage personal and professional impressions on Twitter (Dissertation). Indiana University, Bloomington, IN, USA. Retrieved April 3, 2018 from http://www.tdbowman.com/pdf/2015_07_TDBowman_Dissertation.pdf

Brown, J., Broderick, A. J., & Lee, N. (2007). Word of mouth communication within online communities: Conceptualizing the online social network. *Journal of Interactive Marketing*, *21*(3), 2–20.

Catalini, C., Lacetera, N., & Oettl, A. (2015). The incidence and role of negative citations in science. *Proceedings of the National Academy of Sciences of the United States of America*, *112*(45), 13823–13826.

Cavalcanti, D. C., Prudêncio, R. B. C., Pradhan, S. S., Shah, J. Y., & Pietrobon, R. S. (2011). Good to be Bad? Distinguishing between Positive and Negative Citations in Scientific Impact. *2011 IEEE 23rd International Conference on Tools with Artificial Intelligence* (pp. 156–162). Presented at the 2011 IEEE 23rd International Conference on Tools with Artificial Intelligence.

Collins, K., Shiffman, D., & Rock, J. (2016). How Are Scientists Using Social Media in the Workplace? *PLOS ONE*, *11*(10), e0162680.

Haustein, S. (2016). Grand challenges in altmetrics: heterogeneity, data quality and dependencies. *Scientometrics*, *108*(1), 413–423.

Haustein, S., & Larivière, V. (2014). Mendeley as the source of global readership by students and postdocs? Evaluating Article Usage by Academic Status. In *IATUL Conference, Espoo, Finland, June 2-5 2014*. Retrieved April 3, 2018, from http://docs.lib.purdue.edu/cgi/viewcontent.cgi?article=2033&context=iatul

Jeng, W., He, D., Jiang, J., & Zhang, Y. (2012). Groups in Mendeley: Owners' descriptions and group outcomes. *Proceedings of the American Society for Information Science and Technology*, *49*(1), 1–4.

Kramer, B., & Bosman, J. (2015). 400+ Tools and innovations in scholarly communication. *Google Docs*. Retrieved February 16, 2017, from https://docs.google.com/spreadsheets/d/1KUMSeq_Pzp4KveZ7pb5rddcssk1XBTiLHniD0d3nDqo/edit?usp=embed_facebook

Kramer, B., & Bosman, J. (2016). Innovations in scholarly communication - global survey on research tool usage. *F1000Research*, *5*, 692.

LaPoe, V. L., Carter Olson, C., & Eckert, S. (2017). "Linkedin Is My Office; Facebook My Living Room, Twitter the Neighborhood Bar": Media Scholars' Liminal Use of Social Media for Peer and Public Communication. *Journal of Communication Inquiry*, 0196859917707741.

Levordashka, A., Utz, S., & Ambros, R. (2016). What's in a Like? Motivations for Pressing the Like Button. *Proceedings of the Tenth International AAAI Conference on Web and Social Media* (pp. 623–626). Presented at the ICWSM 2016, Cologne. Retrieved from www.aaai.org/ocs/index.php/ICWSM/ICWSM16/paper/view/13022/12812

Lin, J., & Fenner, M. (2013). Altmetrics in Evolution: Defining and Redefining the Ontology of Article-Level Metrics. *Information Standards Quarterly*, *25*(2), 20.

Lowry, R. (2008). One-Way ANOVA: Independent Samples: II. *Vassar.edu*. Retrieved February 24, 2018, from http://vassarstats.net/textbook/ch14pt2.html

Lutz Bornmann, & Hans-Dieter Daniel. (2008). What do citation counts measure? A review of studies on citing behavior. *Journal of Documentation*, *64*(1), 45–80.

Nielsen, J. (2006, October 9). Participation Inequality: The 90-9-1 Rule for Social Features. *Nielsen Norman Group*. Retrieved February 19, 2018, from https://www.nngroup.com/articles/participation-inequality/

Priem, J. (2014). Altmetrics. *Beyond Bibliometrics: Harnessing Multidimensional Indicators of Scholarly Impact* (1st ed., pp. 480–508). Cambridge, Massachusetts: MIT Press. Retrieved February 1, 2018, from http://ieeexplore.ieee.org/xpl/articleDetails.jsp?arnumber=6828288

Priem, J., Taraborelli, D., Groth, P., & Neylon, C. (2010, October 26). Altmetrics: A manifesto. Retrieved January 23, 2017, from http://altmetrics.org/manifesto/

van Raan, A. F. J. (2003). The use of bibliometric analysis in research performance assessment and monitoring of interdisciplinary scientific developments. *Technikfolgenabschätzung - Theorie und Praxis*, *1*(12), 20–29.

Shema, H., Bar-Ilan, J., & Thelwall, M. (2012). Research Blogs and the Discussion of Scholarly Information. *PLoS ONE*, *7*(5), e35869–e35869. http://doi.org/10.1371/journal.pone.0035869

Syn, S. Y., & Oh, S. (2015). Why do social network site users share information on Facebook and Twitter? *Journal of Information Science*, *41*(5), 553–569.

Vainio, J., & Holmberg, K. (2017). Highly tweeted science articles: who tweets them? An analysis of Twitter user profile descriptions. *Scientometrics*. Retrieved April 4, 2017, from http://link.springer.com/10.1007/s11192-017-2368-0

Van Noorden, R. (2014). Online collaboration: Scientists and the social network. *Nature*, *512*(7513). Retrieved from http://www.nature.com/news/online-collaboration-scientists-and-the-social-network-1.15711

Zahedi, Z., Costas, R., & Wouters, P. (2014). Assessing the impact of publications saved by Mendeley users: Is there any different pattern among users? In *IATUL Conference, Espoo, Finland, June 2-5 2014.* Retrieved from http://docs.lib.purdue.edu/iatul/2014/altmetrics/4

An Examination of a Gamified E-quiz System in Fostering Students' Reading Habit, Interest and Ability

Xiuhan Li
Faculty of Education, the University of Hong Kong, Hong Kong. u3003557@hku.hk

Yuen Ying Janet Cheng
Faculty of Social Sciences, the University of Hong Kong, Hong Kong. janetcyy@connect.hku.hk

Sum Wing Mok
Faculty of Education, the University of Hong Kong, Hong Kong. moksanny@hku.hk

Samuel Kai Wah Chu
Faculty of Education, the University of Hong Kong, Hong Kong. samchu@hku.hk

ABSTRACT

Learning how to read is essential to a child's development. However, existing educational literature suggests that children are reluctant to read because of a decrease of reading motivation and a loss of interest in books (Alter, 2014). Gamified learning supported by information and communication technologies has gained popularity in recent years and been viewed by educators as an effective tool to facilitate pre-adolescent learning (Kapp, 2012). In the present study, gamified learning is studied in the local educational context. Through a recently developed gamified reading platform called Reading Battle, this study seeks to test the impacts of the platform on local primary students' reading experience. Adopting a mixed-method approach, the study fulfilled its quantitative objective by inviting 39 students, 23 parents and 7 teachers to complete a 4-point Likert-scale questionnaire. On the other hand, the study's qualitative objective was met by inviting 37 students, 20 parents and 7 teachers to face-to-face interviews. Results show that Reading Battle helps foster active reading habits in student users, improve their academic performance, enhance their reading competence, and boost their reading motivation. These findings in turn shed light on the educational implications of gamified learning: 1. It promotes self-regulated learning; and 2. It has aided both teachers and students to actualise the learning outcomes of their curriculum.

KEYWORDS

GAMIFIED READING, GAMIFICATION, E-QUIZ, READING COMPREHENSION

INTRODUCTION

Reading is a basic cognitive activity in human life. The more books one reads, the easier it becomes for them to understand and use texts (PIRLS, 2006). From an educational perspective, reading has long-term effects on a child's learning and social development (Holden, 2004). However, the ubiquity of computers, Internet, and smartphones (Flood, 2015) and a recent decline in reading for pleasure among youths (Alter, 2014) present educators a challenge, but nonetheless an opportunity to foster active reading habits in the younger generation (Sainsbury & Schagen, 2004). But how can this possibly be an opportunity per se? Whereas it has been known to many that encouraging youths to read for enjoyment is a challenge in and of itself, imparting active reading habits in them is even harder, if not an impossible endeavour.

A possible recourse seems to have arisen from recent technological advances, which have reinvigorated new energy into self-directed reading among children (Chu, 2016). Mediated through computers, new reading modes in the form of gamified reading apps are particularly receptive in children owing to its gamified aspect (Piaget, 1962). Research shows that these new modes can bring about a multitude of educational benefits. These include an increase in reading interest, an improvement on academic results, and lessons on important life values like honesty (Chu, 2016). It is not surprising then that school librarians have tapped into gamified tools to augment their efforts in promoting reading literacy in schools (Doiron, 2011). One new gamified tool adopted by Hong Kong librarians is called Reading Battle. Through this tool, it is hoped that when a reading experience is gamified, it paves for a learning pathway within which a feedback loop can be formed in a child's mind where their intrinsic motivation to compete with others for points and badges (gameplay elements) can stimulate them further to learn, read and play. And in that process, they can make out, acquire, and apply transferable skill sets to other aspects of their life.

How then, in reality, does this phenomenon actually fare in Hong Kong where many children study to "win" in life? In the present study, to test the extent to which gamification impacts on Hong Kong youths, Reading Battle is the subject of focus. Data derived from responses to the Reading Battle quizzes and semi-structured follow-up interviews with the participating students, parents and teachers all provide critical information. The results from those data can help elucidate the impacts of

Reading Battle on students' reading habits, academic performances, reading competency and reading motivation. Before discussing each of those aspects, however, the theoretical scope and methodological approach of the study will be outlined first.

LITERARTURE REVIEW

E-learning

There is a growing importance and application of information and communication technologies (ICT) on learning (Cheung & Slavin, 2013). Educational technologies are ever changing to keep pace with the wider social development, and to meet the needs of students, most of whom are digital natives (Kim et al., 2006; Snyder, Dillow, & Hoffman, 2008). This equilibrium hinges on a burgeoning market of tools that merge education with the affordances of technologies: openly accessible and user-friendly platforms such as e-book reader apps and massive open online courses. Epitomizing the new age of learning, these channels aim to break geographical barriers and improve the quality of life through affordable learning modes. Studies have shown how these channels improve academic performance, and some even suggest a positive correlation between computer usage and scholastic performance (Gil-Flores et al., 2012; Gamboa & García-Suaza, 2011; Chandra & Lloyd, 2008). On the teaching side, digital learning provides a litany of new tools to keep track of a student's learning progress. For example, online quizzes, or e-quizzes for short, help teachers grade students' performance while providing them instantaneous feedback, saving the economic costs of printing test copies, running tests and marking them individually (Richards-Babb et al., 2011).

Gamification

Now a popular trend in ICT, gamification seeks to enrich traditional learning by applying gameplay elements to the contents. Owing to its wide range of applications in such fields as commerce and marketing (Hamari, Koivisto, & Sarsa, 2014), social media (Lampe, 2014), and healthcare and fitness (Jones, Madden, & Wengreen, 2014), education, particularly e-learning, now makes use of gamification to realize specific learning outcomes (Kapp, 2012). Interspersed throughout the game are gameplay elements such as Points, Badges, Leaderboards, Rewards, Missions, Progression Charts, Levels and Statuses; these features serve to ensure that each player is on track on a predefined learning path, an indicator of their individual accomplishments relative to each other and a representation of their individual statuses within the game (Kuo & Chuang, 2016; Davis & Singh, 2015). Based on these metrics, the game administrators can keep track of the players' progresses within a systematically controlled context. In sum, online gamified learning is shown to be conducive to learning motivation, owing to its many emotional and cognitive scaffolds provided for the players (Morris et al., 2013).

Gamified Reading

Given the benefits of gamification in learning, many ICT applications are already utilised for reading. Popular tools for reading include e-books, e-readers, text-to-speech functions, and online reading programs, designed to monitor, guide, and build up knowledge in the users. Studies show that technology-enabled reading programmes can develop intrinsic motivation in readers to learn new things (Schiefele et al., 2012) and can lead to an improvement in reading comprehension as well as academic performance (Espin & Deno, 1993; Duncan et al., 2007; Loh & Tse, 2009). There are over 100 research studies that support the effectiveness of an online reading program called 'Accelerated Reader', which has an instant feedback and progress-monitoring feature. Clark (2013) found that this technology-mediated intervention has a positive impact on user's reading frequency, while Vollands et al. (1999) and Topping (2006) reported a statistically significant improvement on reading competency for using Accelerated Reader.

There are three common types of gamified reading platforms. The first type is gamified reading apps. Recently, the publishing industry was met with a disinterest in print-based reading (Martens, 2014). To galvanize youths to read print books again, publishers and authors now blurred the boundary between reading and playing, resulting in the appearance of gamified reading in the market (Rughiniş & Rughiniş, 2017). Thereafter, sales strategies and promotion changed; now whenever new print books were put out on sales, the publishers would come up with the corresponding e-books or gamified apps to pair with it in their marketing endeavours. Other reading apps in the market also emphasise the gamified aspects of their games in promotion. For example, Digital Storytime (http://digital-storytime.com) compiles and rates reading apps that encourage children to read digital stories and dabble with the corresponding gamified functions. Other than that, some gamified apps like "Pat the Bunny" and "Don't Let the Pigeon Run" are audio-enabled, allowing children to record their voice while they read and help them create their own audiobooks. To further promote reading literacy in schools, the gamified collaborative app "Q-Tales", funded by the European Union's Horizon 2020, enables school librarians and parents to co-create children's literature (Lounis et al., 2016, p.2). Through their joint efforts, the project hopes to create a close-knit online reading community for professionals, authors, parents, teachers, and children.

Another type is storyline games, based on the plot of a book. A book's background and content provide abundant materials for game design. These games, depending on its themes, can be grouped into serious games and entertainment games. For example, a language strategy game called "Around the world in 80 days" is considered a serious game with its plot development derived from Jules Vern's fiction *80 days*. As the purpose of these games is to facilitate learning and education, they are called serious games or educational games. However, Colombo and Landoni (2014) argue that this kind of online games largely subvert the literary values of the books from which their plots are revolved and lose the quality and complexity of the original narrative in the process of game-making. Moreover, this approach of gamification is likely to shift readers' attention from reading to playing.

The last type of gamified reading platforms is the library. Some libraries use gamification to attract students to take part in reading-related activities. These strategies take the form of online competitions, role-plays, points, rankings, and story creation. For example, in Hong Kong, 'A Passage A Day' reading scheme (trans.: 每日一篇網上閱讀計劃) is an online Chinese reading platform that encourages students to read broadly and complete post-reading questions as to test their understanding. Similarly, the University of Alabama utilises an online alternate reality game called "ProjectVelous" to arouse users' attention and engagement. On the operation side, gamified applications also help libraries in streamlining their library service and information (Felker, 2014). In sum, it is as Felker (2014) noticed, gamification helps libraries in four main areas of operation: orientation, information literacy education, resource usage, and online reading activities.

As the above anecdotal evidence serves, gamified reading is certainly on the rise, but research in this area remains underexplored in Hong Kong. Look no further than research in book gamification and its educational values and impacts on children and their reading habits. Thus, in a bid to provide more empirical evidence towards that end, the next section will lay out a methodological framework with which to test the recently developed gamified reading system 'Reading Battle'.

RESEARCH METHOD

Reading Battle grows out of a former research project funded by the Hong Kong Quality Education Fund, called "Strengthening students' reading comprehension ability through developing children's literature e-quiz bank on cloud" (Chu, 2016). On the e-quiz database, more than 5,000 questions are designed for around 500 children books. The collection of children's literature on the database covers a wide scope of genres, spanning fiction, fairy tales, folklore, science, and history. Student users can gain points by challenging themselves in 'battles' composed of ten reading-comprehension questions each. The leaderboard of the system shows users' rankings based on their performances (e.g., total score and improvement), and excellent players would be rewarded with badges and tokens. Besides ranking, badges, and rewards, the control panel, narration and animation also make Reading Battle an interesting and appealing platform for reading.

To test the extent to which Reading Battle influences a child's reading development, the present study seeks to answer four questions:

(1) How does the gamified e-quiz system affect primary students' reading habits?

(2) How does the gamified e-quiz system affect primary students' academic performance?

(3) How does the gamified e-quiz system affect primary students' reading competency?

(4) How does the gamified e-quiz system affect primary students' reading motivation?

A mixed-method approach was applied in this study to gather qualitative and quantitative data. The target subjects of this study are active users on Reading Battle. Thus, the top 20 scorers under the rankings of 'Last Term Score', 'Improvement Score' and 'Life Score', during the term period between 1 September 2015 and 31 January 2016, were invited to attend the study. Having that as a filter, 39 students were recruited at the end. On the quantitative side of the study, 39 students, 23 parents and 7 teachers were invited to complete questionnaires designed to gauge their opinions toward statements regarding intrinsic and extrinsic reading motivation. On the qualitative side, 37 students, 20 parents and 7 teachers were invited to face-to-face interviews during which they reported on their perceptions of the e-quizzes and its impacts on children's reading habits, academic performance, reading competency, and reading motivation. Each interview lasted for around 20 minutes, conducted during the lunchtime of their schools. The research team touched base with the interviewees at different points of the study to understand their reading and learning progress. The theoretical framework of both quantitative and qualitative instruments is based on self-determination theory regarding human essential psychological needs and intrinsic and extrinsic motivation. The questionnaire and interview protocol can be accessed at https://goo.gl/vzgFV9.

Quantitative data gleaned from the questionnaires were processed with the statistical software SPSS. Descriptive statistics and non-parametric analysis were used as main analysis methods. Any mean score ('M') above 2.5 was regarded as positive feedback. Qualitative data obtained from the interviews were analysed using the qualitative data-analysis software NVivo. As all interview questions were semi-structured, descriptive statistics regarding the interview transcripts were considered as part of the quantitative data.

RESULTS

This section summarizes results from questionnaires and interviews with the students, parents, and teachers. Their feedback indicates that Reading Battle helps fostering active reading habits in the students, improving their academic performances, enhancing their reading competency, and furthering their reading motivation.

Reading habits

The number of participants who agree that the students' reading habits were changed since they used Reading Battle is shown in Table 1. 35 out of 37 (95%) students reported that their reading habits had changed in various aspects, especially their reading frequency (68%) and the selection of books (59%). Results seem to be similar across the parents' and teachers' responses. One conspicuous difference is that there's only a 5-percentage point difference between students and teachers (24% and 29%, respectively) in term of their perceptions on reading initiative being enhanced, whereas half of the parents surveyed strongly believed this.

Items of reading habits	Students (n=37)	Parents (n=20)	Teachers (n=7)
Change in reading mode	8 (22%)	2 (10%)	1 (14%)
Change in selection of books	22 (59%)	15 (75%)	3 (43%)
Enhancing reading frequency	25 (68%)	13 (65%)	3 (43%)
Enhancing reading independency	6 (16%)	7 (35%)	2 (29%)
Enhancing reading initiative	9 (24%)	10 (50%)	2 (29%)

Table 1. Change of reading habits due to Reading Battle.

The table also shows that children's reading behaviours were changed since using Reading Battle. To gain more points and rank higher, students would often read voraciously even though they were not instructed to do so. A case in point can be found in a group of students who have read around 200 books after playing. This starkly contrasted with one of the students' prior reading of 10 books (e.g., LTM-STU-THK). In a way, then, the top scorers can be said to have become independent readers. Their motivation to read more books as to win 'battles' goaded them into reading more; one interviewee (HL-STU-PLC) testified, "My mum used to ask me to read more books, but now she no longer does that because I will read by myself now". Some students would read titles beyond the choice of offers on the Reading Battle database. One student (LTM-STU-LCC), for example, said "after joining Reading Battle, I think I will do more extended reading in related subjects that are interesting", while another (LTM-STU-TTF) commented "I used to read more Chinese books. Now I read the English ones too, and I will choose to read some more difficult books". These anecdotes seem to suggest that Reading Battle has made the children more receptive to English books, and that they will read titles close to their subjects of interest.

Concept	Sub-concepts	Coding example
Reading habits	Reading frequency	- In the past, I only read very few books, like 2-3 each week. Now I read 6-7 books each week. (HL-STU-LSC)
	Reading initiative	- My mum used to ask me to read more books, but now she no longer does that because I will read by myself now. (HL-STU-PLC)
	Selection of books	- I used to read more comic books, but now I will read books with more texts like novels. (HL-STU-LSC)
	Reading independency	- In the past, I needed my mother when reading, but now, I can do it myself. (LTM-STU-WTY)

Table 2. Coding example of the change in reading habits.

Academic performance

With regard to academic performance, 34 out of 37 (92%) students reported that they made various academic improvements while playing Reading Battle. Writing is a part that saw huge improvement, with a self-reported improvement rate of 49% among the students who did well on English writing. 55% of the parents thought that their children's academic scores on

Chinese reading tests had improved, while nearly half of the teachers (43%) surveyed agreed on this. Despite this, assessed questionnaire items other than Chinese reading and writing had yielded no feedback from the teachers. Table 3 below provides a general breakdown of students' academic improvements. For the attribution of these improvements, interviewees were asked to answer the question *"is your academic improvement owed to the use of Reading Battle or other methods"*. It is suggested that 43% of students believed it had been completely because of the game that they did well, and 30% of students thought it had been a combination of the game and other learning modes.

Items of academic performance	Students (n=37)	Parents(n=20)	Teachers(n=7)
Chinese-Reading	16 (43%)	11 (55%)	3 (43%)
Chinese-Writing	18 (49%)	9 (45%)	1 (14%)
Chinese-Vocabulary	9 (24%)	5 (25%)	0 (0%)
English-Reading	13 (35%)	5 (25%)	0 (0%)
English-Writing	18 (49%)	2 (10%)	0 (0%)
English-Vocabulary	8 (22%)	2 (10%)	0 (0%)
General studies	4 (11%)	5 (25%)	0 (0%)
Others	3 (8%)	0 (%)	0 (0%)

Table 3. *Aspects of students' academic improvements.*

During their interviews, participants explained how the game had positively affected their English learning experience. First, some students reported that they learned more English vocabulary as the number of books they read climbed. Their writing also improved due to an accumulation of words, phrases and ideas that they learned from across the pages, which enriched their writing. It was not only an increase in their vocabulary that this study found but also new writing techniques that they picked up along the way. Lastly, their reading speed was upped since joining Reading Battle, and that enabled them to be more capable of answering questions on their homework assignments. The practice of answering Battle questions facilitates children's understanding, which in turn helps them to concentrate on key points on their exams.

Reading Competency

The IEA's Progress in International Reading Literacy Study (PIRLS) defines four key types of reading comprehension competency for children: information retrieval, interpretation, inference, and evaluation. Besides these aspects, most interviewees mentioned general understanding as an important part of reading comprehension competency. It is demonstrated that 65% of students think that they have improved their general understanding of a text after playing Reading Battle, followed by their interpretation skills (57%). Nearly half of the students sampled (41%) think that they have improved their ability to make inferences. From the parents' perspective, forty-five percent of them believe their children have improved the abilities of both general understanding and interpretation skills. Some of the teachers also reported on this trend. Table 4 shows students' improvements in reading competency after using Reading Battle.

Items of reading competency	Students (n=37)	Parents (n=20)	Teachers (n=7)
General understanding	25 (68%)	9 (45%)	2 (29%)
Evaluation	6 (16%)	3 (15%)	0 (0%)
Inference	15 (41%)	4 (20%)	2 (29%)
Interpretation	21 (57%)	9 (45%)	3 (43%)
Information retrieval	3 (8%)	0 (0%)	0 (0%)

Table 4. Students' improvements in reading competency after using Reading Battle

As the design of the Battle questions was based on the framework of PIRLS, playing Reading Battle certainly helped improving reading comprehension. Some interviewees reported that they tried to read more challenging books, which help them gain a higher level of comprehension. For example, one student (LTM-STU-TTY) said that "reading more into the feelings and actions of various characters can enable him to conjecture people's internal states of mind and their thinking, and also their emotions". One parent also reported that her child used to read books with a lot of pictures, but now he reads books with more words in it. As the interviews revealed, students can now easily discern cause-and-effect relationships between ideas and concepts, read between the lines of dialogues and description, and grasp at the author's intention more accurately. Ultimately, Reading Battle enabled the children to take away important life lessons with them, such as honesty and love.

Reading motivation

Data for reading motivation was tabulated in Table 5. For extrinsic motivation, students thought that their active participation on Reading Battle owed a great deal to the rankings or leaderboard. This amounts to a 62% of the respondents. The points system came in at 30% as the second extrinsic factor, barely edging out Battle questions at 27%. Similarly, half of the parents agreed that their children engaged in Reading Battle due to the leaderboard, and 55% of the parents thought that the points on Reading Battle stimulated their children to read more. All the teachers agreed that the setting of leaderboard is the most effective extrinsic factor. For intrinsic motivation, forty-nine percent of the students believed that they engaged deeply in Reading Battle due to a sense of achievement they felt. Similarly, 86% of the teachers identified the sense of achievement their students had felt as a huge intrinsic motivator. Furthermore, twenty-five percent of parents thought that not only was the sense of achievement a huge incentive, but also the curiosity the children showed towards the game-like control interface.

Domain	Items	Students (n=37)	Parents (n=20)	Teachers (n=7)
Extrinsic motivation	Affordance-Badges(awards)	5 (14%)	0 (0%)	2 (29%)
	Affordance-Leaderboard(ranking)	23 (62%)	10 (50%)	7 (100%)
	Affordance- Points(scores)	11 (30%)	11 (55%)	1 (14%)
	Affordance- Questions(function)	10 (27%)	2 (10%)	0 (0%)
	Affordance-Contents	8 (22%)	3 (15%)	0 (0%)
Intrinsic motivation	Novelty (Curiosity)	13 (35%)	5 (25%)	1 (14%)
	Potential challenges	7 (19%)	3 (15%)	2 (29%)
	Sense of achievement	18 (49%)	5 (25%)	6 (86%)
	Sense of involvement (enjoyment)	6 (16%)	1 (10%)	0 (0%)

Table 5. Motivations of students in using Reading Battle.

As Table 5 shows, children are intrinsically motivated to read. The questionnaire surveyed to what extent do children read for intrinsic motivation (see Table 6). According to it, students, parents and teachers all gave positive feedback to all statements ($M>2.5$). Similar to their interview feedback, parents gave more positive feedback for the items of 'achievement' and 'curiosity'. However, teachers' ratings on the items of 'curiosity' and 'involvement' were more positive while that of 'challenge' and 'achievement' were less so. This result is slightly different to the data gleaned from interviews, and it might be due to the fact that the sample size of the teachers was too small as to make for a statistically significant quantitative analysis.

In sum, Reading Battle can motivate students to read both extrinsically and intrinsically. The competition rules and the real-time feedback feature in the game enable the students to know that their effort would pay off in one way or another. The leaderboard shows the results of the top achievers, which stimulate the children to compete with their peers. The well-designed questions enlighten them to think more carefully. As one interviewee (HL-STU-LSC) said, "I like to read the book and find the answers immediately. Since I want to answer the questions right, I am motivated to read the book." The experience driven from the extrinsic incentives translates into internal feelings, such as a sense of achievement and of challenge. For example, some students think they are encouraged to do better in reading if they get more badges. If they complete more difficult books and get more points, they will feel elated. Also, they extend their reading beyond the choices of offer in the game. For example, they would ask their parents to go to a local library with them or buy books for them. The extension of reading beyond Reading Battle shows an internalization of reading motivation. Students are not only motivated to read for points and ranking, but also for their own interest and the fun in reading.

Concepts	Statements	Students (n=39)	Parents (n=20)	Teachers (n=7)	Sig. Kruskal-Wallis
Challenge	If a book is interesting, I don't care how difficult it is to read.	3.51 (0.68)	3.39 (0.66)	2.86 (0.38)	.021
	I like it when the teacher gives us a difficult book to read.	3.21 (0.7)	2.74 (0.75)	2.67 (0.52)	.017
	I usually learn difficult things by reading	3.41 (0.68)	2.83 (0.65)	2.5 (0.55)	.001*
Curiosity	I like reading so that I can learn more about things.	3.59 (0.50)	3.22 (0.52)	3.0 (0.00)	.002*
	If the teacher discusses something interesting, I might read more about it.	3.36 (0.58)	3.48 (0.51)	3.14 (0.38)	.338
	I read books about my hobbies to learn more about them.	3.46 (0.85)	3.22 (0.52)	3.17 (0.41)	.049
Involve-ment	I feel like I get to know the characters in the books I read.	3.23 (0.71)	2.96 (0.64)	2.5 (0.55)	.035
	When I read, I make pictures in my mind about what I'm reading.	3.62 (0.54)	3.35 (0.49)	3.0 (0.00)	.005*
	I like to read a lot of adventure stories.	3.32 (0.75)	3.22 (0.67)	3.29 (0.76)	0.78
Achieve-ment	I know that I will do well in reading next year.	3.46 (0.55)	3.09 (0.51)	2.71 (0.49)	.002*
	I am a good reader.	3.38 (0.63)	3.05 (0.65)	3.00 (0.58)	.080

*statistically significant at $p < 0.05$.

Table 6. Students' rating of intrinsic motivation of reading.

DISCUSSION

Considering the positive reception of Reading Battle among the students, parents and teachers sampled, this section details the educational implications of their feedback. Two important themes emerge from the data: 1. The game has enhanced students' learning by promoting self-regulated learning; and 2. The game has aided both teachers and students to actualize the learning outcomes of their curriculum.

Promoting self-directed learning

Reading Battle has enabled the students to enjoy reading and to learn to study in a self-directed manner. From the teachers' perspective, Reading Battle is a helpful tool to foster students' reading habits, and useful in gaining insights into their students' reading skills and progress without putting pressure on the students. Students are more motivated to read, as reflected in the change of their reading habits. Combining results from the quantitative and qualitative analysis, one could see that students read more frequently since they played Reading Battle (students: 68%; parents: 65%; teachers: 43%), and that they have widened the genre of books they read (students: 59%; parents: 75%; teachers 43%).

Results on students' reading motivation offered much insights into the change of their reading habits. Reading Battle was not short on extrinsic and intrinsic motivation. The highest extrinsic motivation was the leaderboard feature as shown in Table 5. Achieving a satisfactory ranking on the leaderboard presumably had contributed to students' sense of achievement, which was the highest intrinsic motivation reported. The social element in leaderboard feature was important as it provided students with social credibility and recognition for academic achievements (Lee & Hammer, 2011). A deep dive into students' intrinsic motivation to read revealed that all four aspects of challenge, curiosity, involvement, and achievement were positively regarded by the students. These findings are encouraging in that it shows students' reading initiative has been internalised. In a virtuous cycle of learning, these intrinsic motivations serve to reinforce the changes in their reading habits.

Students' high engagement can be explained by the theory of self-directed learning, in which the student is free to control the conceptualisation, design, conduct and evaluation of his/her own learning (Brookfield, 2009). Autonomy has been a crucial principle in the design of Reading Battle. Students were free to choose which books to read and take e-quizzes with hardly any adult intervention. They were also free to adjust the pace and intervals of their reading and taking e-quizzes to suit their progress. The manner in which the quizzes were conducted also enhanced students' own sense of control – as the quizzes took place in a gamified environment, parents, who would normally oversee their children's homework, were generally comfortable with letting their children "play a little game once in a while". This reduced students' pressure to participate and incentivized them to take quizzes out of their own volition. The findings in this study were largely consistent with existing educational literature that found autonomy plays an important role in enhancing self-motivation (Deci & Ryan, 2000). In cases of highly-engaged students, for example LTM-STU-PSL, who used to hate reading but became an avid reader after partaking in Reading Battle, they eventually reached a state of 'flow' (Csikszentmihalyi, 1997) wherein they became so immersed in the game that they concentrate fully on completing their tasks (i.e. books and the battles). Their actions manifest what Csikszentmihalyi observed in his book on the idea of 'flow': "a state [in which] individuals experience when their actions seem, in retrospect, effortless and timeless, even though much is accomplished" (Hardy, 1998, p.795). The end result was that their learning curve was higher, and that the gratification they felt was much stronger than anybody.

Actualizing intended learning outcomes

With 92% students reporting an improvement on their academic performance and 43% attributing the use of Reading Battle for their improvement, the game benefits on students' academic development are numerous. Looking at places that students improved on, it can be said that Reading Battle helped students beyond the area of reading. Two notable areas of perceived improvement outside of reading are Chinese and English writings, both perched at 49% on the improvement scale. This is closely followed by Chinese reading at 43%. However, the improvement on English vocabulary was neither readily apparent to the students (22%), parents (10%), nor teachers (0%).

Improvement on reading skills would only be logical, as Reading Battle was essentially designed to promote reading, as discussed in Section 4.1 and 5.1. Further analysis of students' reading competency was conducted in Section 4.3, where results show that students improved more on their interpretation skills and making inferences, two mid-level Reading Battle question categories adapted from the PIRLS 2011 assessment framework (Mullis et al., 2009). A consistent trend in perception of reading competency improvement was recorded among students, parents, and teachers. All three parties agreed that improvement on interpretation was the greatest, followed by inference, evaluation (i.e. the most difficult questions), and lastly information retrieval (i.e. the easiest questions). This shows that students might already have mastered the skill of information retrieval before using Reading Battle but might not have reached a level where they can accurately evaluate information, hence a greater improvement rate reported in levels between interpretation and inference. These data offered teachers insight into students' abilities and would enable them to adjust their teaching plan and further develop their students' reading abilities.

As students read, they immerse themselves in the language of their reading. Naturally, they would go on to pick up essential literacy skills of said language, such as storytelling, sentence structure, and vocabulary. Better understanding of such literacy skills would help contribute to their writing repertoire. Students' perceived improvement of both Chinese and English writing skills was reportedly high relative to other aspects of their academic performance. This indicates that the benefits of improved reading extend to other aspects of their learning. It is noted that students reported a higher rate of perceived improvement than their teachers did in those aspects as laid out in Table 3. While we could neither assert nor negate any actual improvement in these aspects without the support of factual evidence (either Reading Battle scores or standardized tests administered by teachers), the discrepancy in perceived improvement shows that students were, at the very least, confident in their learning progress, a crucial element associated with better learning outcomes (Compte & Postlewaite, 2004).

CONCLUSION

In conclusion, Reading Battle has been an effective gamified learning tool. Data corroborated Reading Battle's intended goals of fostering reading habits, improving academic performances, enhancing reading competency and furthering reading motivation. 95% of the students surveyed reported a change in their reading habits, in particular, a higher reading frequency (68%) and a wider range of book choices (59%). Participation in Reading Battle had helped students beyond the area of reading, as most students witnessed their improvement on their Chinese and English writings (49% students for both). 43% students attributed their improvement on academic performance solely to their participation on Reading Battle. Improvement in reading competency was reported, with a 68% of students agreeing that they reached a higher level of general understanding since playing Reading Battle. Students reported that they were motivated to read more on Reading Battle both extrinsically (e.g. the leaderboard) and intrinsically (e.g. a sense of achievement).

Two important implications emerge from the data. The first implication is that Reading Battle induced the students to engage in self-directed learning. Owing to a high level of the learner's autonomy, students were able to reap the benefits of reading by themselves. Taking the initiative to read more and read in-depth, they leveraged on their freedom and flexibility to choose books fitting to their abilities and learning progress. In this regard, the battles that were designed to test their reading comprehension showed promising results in that the students were able to get the gist of their readings and had no trouble absorbing the ideas and concepts embedded within the story. Resonating with an anecdote raised in existing literature that learner's autonomy promotes self-motivation, the students in the present study have certainly gone above and beyond their intended learning goals with substantial changes in their reading habits compared to themselves prior to playing Reading Battle.

The second implication is that Reading Battle helped teachers and students actualize learning outcomes. The benefits of playing the game extend from its sole intended purpose of reading and writing to other basic literacy skills, such as interpretation and inferences. Although there are traces of evidence that suggest students may have learnt some basic reading literacy skills prior to playing Reading Battle, they reportedly show substantial improvement on interpretation and inferences, two benchmarkers for a young competent reader as suggested in the PIRLS 2011 reading literacy assessment framework. Based on this, teachers and educators can better tailor their lesson plans and curriculum designs to their students.

However, despite the many educational values Reading Battle presents in this research, limitations abound nevertheless. The first limitation is that the sample size has been too small and might not be representative of the entire Reading Battle community. The Second, the impact of Reading Battle on learning was measured solely by self-reported perceptions. In future study, as such, much attention should be devoted to working with teachers from multiple schools as to increase the sample size, and to administer various school-based assessments to benchmark students' improvement. Noting that it is far from the aim of Reading Battle to subject either the students or the teachers to pressure, the test should be implemented in a low-stake manner; for example, students will be invited to take part in a series of pre- and post-intervention reading exercises.

REFERENCES

Al-Azawi, R., Al-Faliti, F., & Al-Blushi, M. (2016). Educational gamification vs. game-based learning: Comparative study. International Journal of Innovation, Management and Technology, 7(4), 131.

Alter, C. (2014). Study: The Number of Teens Reading for Fun Keeps Declining. The Time Magazine, retrieval from: http://time.com/94794/common-sense-media-reading-report-never-read/

Brookfield S.D. (2009) Self-Directed Learning. In: Maclean R., Wilson D. (eds) International Handbook of Education for the Changing World of Work. Springer, Dordrecht

Chandra, V., & Lloyd, M. (2008). The methodological nettle: ICT and student achievement. British Journal of Educational Technology, 39(6), 1087-1098.

Cheung, A.C.K., & Slavin, R. E. (2013). Effects of educational technology applications on reading outcomes for struggling readers: A best-evidence synthesis. Reading Research Quarterly, 48, 277-299.

Chu, S.K.W. (2016). Gamification, data and learning, presented at Data, Innovation, Social Network and Convergence, Daegu, South Korea.

Clark, M. (2013). The use of technology to support vocabulary development of English Language Learners.

Colombo, L., & Landoni, M. (2014, June). A diary study of children's user experience with EBooks using flow theory as framework. In Proceedings of the 2014 conference on Interaction design and children (pp. 135-144). ACM.

Compte, O., & Postlewaite, A. (2004). Confidence-enhanced performance. American Economic Review, 94(5), 1536-1557.

Csikszentmihalyi, M. (1997). Flow and the psychology of discovery and invention. HarperPerennial, New York, 39.

Davis, K. & Singh, S. (2015). Digital Badges in afterschool learning: Documenting the perspectives and experiences of students and educators. Computers & Education, 88, 72-83

Deci, E. L. & Ryan, R. M. (2000). Self-determination theory and the facilitation of intrinsic motivation, social development, and well-being. American Psychologist, 55, 68–78.

Doiron, R. (2011). Using E-Books and E-Readers to Promote Reading in School Libraries: Lessons from the Field, 77th IFLA General Conference and Assembly, San Juan, Puerto Rico.

Duncan, G. J., Dowsett, C. J., Claessens, A., Magnuson, K., Huston, A. C., Klebanov, P., . . . Japel, C. (2007). School readiness and later achievement. Developmental Psychology, 43, 1428-1446.

Espin, C., & Deno, S. (1993). Performance in reading from content area text as an indicator of achievement. Remedial & Special Education, 14(6), 47.

Felker, K. (2014). Gamification in libraries: the state of the art. Reference & User Services Quarterly, 54(2), 19.

Flood, A. (2015, January 9). Sharp decline in children reading for pleasure, survey finds. The Guardian. [Online].

Fu, J. S. (2013). ICT in education: A critical literature review and its implications. International Journal of Education and Development using Information and Communication Technology, 9(1), 112.

Gamboa, L. F., & García-Suaza, A. F. (2011). Access to computer and academic achievement. Where is it best: At home or at school. Center for Studies on Inequality and Development. Discussion paper, 47.

Gil-Flores, J., Torres-Gordillo, J. J., & Perera-Rodríguez, V. H. (2012). The role of online reader experience in explaining students' performance in digital reading. Computers & Education, 59(2), 653-660.

Hamari, J., Koivisto, J., & Sarsa, H. (2014, January). Does gamification work?--a literature review of empirical studies on gamification. In System Sciences (HICSS), 2014 47th Hawaii International Conference on (pp. 3025-3034). IEEE.

Hardy, D. (1998). Creativity: Flow and the Psychology of Discovery and Invention. Personnel Psychology, 51(3), 794-797.

Holden, J. (2004). Creative reading. London: Demos.

Jones, B. A., Madden, G. J., & Wengreen, H. J. (2014). The FIT Game: preliminary evaluation of a gamification approach to increasing fruit and vegetable consumption in school. Preventive medicine, 68, 76-79.

Kapp, K. M. (2012). The gamification of learning and instruction: game-based methods and strategies for training and education. John Wiley & Sons.

Kim, A. H., Vaughn, S., Klingner, J. K., Woodruff, A. L., Reutebuch, C. K., & Kouzekanani, K. (2006). Improving the reading comprehension of middle school students with disabilities through computer-assisted collaborative strategic reading. Remedial and Special Education, 27, 235-249.

Kuo, M. & Chuang, T. (2016). How gamification motivates visits and engagement for online academic dissemination – An empirical study. Computers in Human Behavior, 55, 16-27.

Lampe, C. (2014). Gamification and social media. The Gameful world: Approaches, issues, applications. Cambridge, MA: MIT.

Lee, J. J., & Hammer, J. (2011). Gamification in education: what, how, Why Bother? Definitions and uses. Exchange Organizational Behavior Teaching Journal, 15(2), 1–5.

Loh, E.K.Y., & Tse, S.K. (2009). The relationship between motivation to read Chinese and English and the impact on the Chinese and English reading performance of Chinese students. Chinese Education and Society, 42, 66-90.

Lounis, S., Doukidis, S., Papastamatiou, N., & Doukoulos, T. (2016). Gamification of Authoring Interactive E-Books for Children: The Q-Tales Ecosystem. In MCIS (p. 31).

Martens, M. (2014). Reading and" Gamification": Joining Guilds, Earning Badges, and Leveling Up. Children & Libraries, 12(4), 19.

Morris, B. J., Croker, S., Zimmerman, C., Gill, D., & Romig, C. (2013). Gaming science: the "Gamification" of scientific thinking. Frontiers in psychology, 4.

Mullis, I., Martin, M., Kennedy, A., Trong, K., & Sainsbury, M. (2009). PIRLS 2011 Assessment Framework. Amsterdam, the Netherlands: the International Association for the Evaluation of Educational Achievement (IEA)

Piaget, J. (1962). Play, dreams and imitation (Vol. 24).

PIRLS 2006 International Report (2006). Retrieval from https://timss.bc.edu/pirls2006/intl_rpt.html

Richards-Babb, M., Drelick, J., Henry, Z., & Robertson-Honecker, J. (2011). Online homework, help or hindrance? What students think and how they perform. Journal of College Science Teaching, 40(4), 81.

Rughiniș, R., & Rughiniș, C. (2017). Reading with a Touch of Gameplay: Gamified E-Books' Convergence with Classical Literary Worlds. In Gamification (pp. 139-152). Springer, Cham.

Sainsbury, M., & Schagen, I. (2004). Attitudes to reading at ages nine and eleven. Journal of Research in Reading, 27(4), 373-386.

Schiefele, U., Schaffner, E., Möller, J., & Wigfield, A. (2012). Dimensions of reading motivation and their relation to reading behaviour and competence. Reading Res Quarterly, 47(4), 427–463.

Snyder, T. D., Dillow, S. A., & Hoffman, C. M. (2008). Digest of education statistics, 2007 (NCES 2008-022). Washington, DC: U.S. Department of Education, National Center for Education Statistics.

Topping, K. J. (2006). Accelerated Reader in Specialist Schools. Dundee, Scotland: University of Dundee, Centre for Paired Learning.

Vollands, S.R., Topping, K.J. & Evans, H.M. (1999). Computerized self-assessment of reading comprehension with the Accelerated Reader: Action research. Reading and Writing Quarterly, 15, 197–211 (themed issue on Electronic Literacy).

Evaluating the Impact of a Virtual Reality Workstation in an Academic Library: Methodology and Preliminary Findings

Zack Lischer-Katz
University of Oklahoma, USA. zlkatz@ou.edu

Kristal Boulden
University of Oklahoma, USA. ksb@ou.edu

Matt Cook
University of Oklahoma, USA. mncook@ou.edu

ABSTRACT

Collections of 3D models and the analytic affordances of virtual reality (VR) systems can be integrated to form a "3D digital heritage ecosystem" (Limp, et al., 2011), providing a potentially richer and more intuitive learning environment that enables students to interact with models of artifacts and spaces that are too rare, fragile, or distant to access directly. This paper describes efforts to evaluate the impact of virtual reality on undergraduate instruction in varied disciplines, hosted within an academic library context. Existing research on VR and learning has focused primarily on domain
-specific tasks carried out in controlled lab settings or the social aspects of immersive virtual worlds. This paper describes the methodology and preliminary findings of a mixed-methods research project currently underway (running from September 2017 to August 2018) that is evaluating how use of virtual reality impacts undergraduate students' self-efficacy, and seeks to understand students' embodied experiences. The strengths and weaknesses of the methodology, initial findings drawn from the early stages of data analysis, and directions for further research are discussed.

KEYWORDS

Virtual reality, 3D visualization, self-efficacy, academic libraries, instructional technology

INTRODUCTION

Following periods of experimentation and, ultimately, failure to reach mainstream adoption - starting in the late 1980s and continuing into the early 2000s - virtual reality (VR) technologies have returned to mainstream consciousness. With the release of the Oculus Rift headset in March 2016, followed closely by the HTC Vive in April 2016, high-fidelity VR has become affordable for a growing segment of the population, including scholars. Educational institutions are now actively exploring the benefits of VR technologies and are beginning to integrate them into academic research and instruction. Paired with high-resolution digital 3D models, which can take the form of cultural heritage artifacts, scientific models, or medical imaging data, VR can be used as a powerful analytic platform that engages users' embodied movements, stereoscopic vision, and wide angle of vision to enhance understanding.

Together, collections of 3D models and the analytic affordances of VR systems can be integrated to form a "3D digital heritage ecosystem" (Limp, et al., 2011), providing a potentially richer and more "natural" learning environment that enables students to interact with models of artifacts and spaces that are too rare, fragile, or distant to access directly. Furthering their role in providing curation, infrastructure, and training services for both traditional and emergent forms of information resources, academic libraries have become sites of VR deployment. Existing research on VR and learning has focused primarily on domain-specific tasks carried out in controlled lab settings or the social aspects of immersive virtual worlds.

This paper describes efforts to evaluate the impact on student learning of a custom-built VR application being implemented by staff at the academic library of a large research university that is being used to enhance undergraduate instruction in varied disciplines, specifically Biochemistry and Anthropology. It describes the methodology and preliminary findings of a mixed-methods research project currently underway (running from September 2017 to August 2018) that is evaluating how use of this VR system impacts the self-efficacy of undergraduate students and seeks to understand their embodied experiences with VR. A pre- and post-test survey was used to measure the impact of VR-based class assignments on students' self-efficacy, which was followed by semi-structured interviews that asked students to interpret their experiences of the VR environment. The main research objectives of this project are to:

1. Design a VR workstation that can effectively utilize embodied and immersive affordances to enable students in multiple disciplines to effectively analyze rich 3D content.
2. Develop tools for evaluating the impact of the VR workstation on student confidence and their learning experiences.

Following the literature review, initial findings drawn from the early stages of data analysis, the strengths and weaknesses of the methodology, and directions for further research will be discussed.

LITERATURE REVIEW

Virtual Worlds and Learning

Existing research literature on virtual environments and learning that predates the latest wave of VR technologies has been focused primarily on Second Life (Praslova–Førland, et al., 2006; Bronack, et al., 2008; Holmberg and Huvila, 2008; Warburton, 2009; Dalgarno & M. Lee, 2010; Hew & Cheung, 2010; Sheehy, 2010) and how it can emulate the benefits of traditional learning environments (Deutschmann and Panichi, 2009; Carr, et al., 2010); supporting library engagement with patrons (Haycock and Kemp, 2008) and collaboration in the workplace (Tan, et al., 2012). The virtual environments studied in these research projects employed 3D, computer screen-based visualizations, rather than the current immersive VR head mounted displays (HMDs), however, they demonstrate a research interest in studying how virtual simulations of spatially-oriented environments impact student learning.

VR and Spatial Cognition

More recent empirical research conducted in computer science, engineering, and cognitive psychology suggests that VR has the capability to be a particularly effective tool for supporting analysis and learning in academic disciplines in which the object of study is inherently *spatial* (Donalek, et al. 2014). This includes design-oriented fields such as Architecture, as well as the fields of Archaeology, Librarianship, Engineering, and Anatomy (Angulo, 2013; Cook 2018; Seth, Vance, and Oliver 2011; Van Dam, Laidlaw, & Simpson; Jang, et al., 2017). VR can be a low-cost alternative that enables engagement with this and other content that may be difficult to access (Limp et al., 2011).

VR also affords high visual *fidelity* for users (i.e. close correspondence to the perception of reality). Ragan, et al. (2013) show that visual fidelity depends on three characteristics of VR systems: 1) the ability to deploy visual content in 360 degrees around the user; 2) sensors to track the head and upper body to provide interactivity; and 3) the presentation of a slightly offset, stereoscopic image to each eye, which enables depth of field perception. These researchers focused on a combination of three characteristics, which, when deployed in tandem, "...produce visual stimuli with a higher level of similarity to real-world stimuli" (Ragan, et al., 2013, p.1). This combination of characteristics translates to a wider and deeper visual field for the user, resulting enhanced capabilities for analyzing and interacting with 3D digital content.

Laha, et al. (2014) identified a set of task-types (*searching*, *making spatial judgements*, and *describing shapes*) that are especially well supported by virtual reality. Qualitative data generated in the study supported these findings, suggesting that the perceived difficulty of tasks related to *searching* and *making spatial judgements* decreased while confidence in the participant's ability to *describe shapes* was improved with virtual reality.

VR Technology and Domain-specific Scholarship

Research domains are beginning to take advantage of the benefits of VR to support scholarship. For example, Van Dam, Laidlaw, and Simpson (2002) deployed more than 250,000 archaeological discoveries in a virtual environment for researcher analysis, which resulted in the generation of novel insights due to the researcher's ability to quickly scan a large number of individual artifacts within their real-world spatial context (e.g., the dig site's stratigraphy). In this case, VR supported the researcher's embodied engagement with highly detailed representations of archeological data, making analysis more efficient and generating new discoveries.

DEVELOPING TOOLS FOR A 3D ECOSYSTEM

Existing research literature suggests the benefits on learning and knowledge production of immersive VR visualization tools for analysis of spatially-oriented data types, however the benefits of VR as a pedagogical tool have not been studied in the context of academic library-supported course integrations. Since 2016, the authors have sought to address this gap by developing VR workstations at their home academic library to bring these benefits to faculty and students in as many fields as possible. Incorporating VR into existing library services is important because it is an essential part of the mission of academic libraries to provide the tools and training necessary for faculty and students to engage with information resources of all types.

The custom-designed virtual reality workstations used in this study are comprised of commercially-available hardware and a blend of commercially-available and locally-developed software. On the hardware side, each station consists of a moveable chair-on-rails, coupled with a high-end gaming PC and an Oculus Rift HMD (head mounted display). The LeapMotion hand-tracking controller and a SpaceConnextion 3D mouse complete the hardware assembly. This set of components was chosen by Emerging Technology Librarians to satisfy two practical design criteria: 1) enable full range-of-motion for users; and 2) cable management. Informal usability testing using Brooke's (1996) usability survey revealed that headset cabling and potential obstruction from real-world objects could interfere with users' experiences of immersion in VR (Forsberg, Katzourin, and Wharton 2008; Bowman & McMahan 2007).

Regarding the custom learning software used in the workstations, in-house development efforts utilized the Unity3D game design software suite as well as plugins necessary to support the peripheral hardware (e.g., the LeapMotion SDK). Growing demand for custom virtual reality experiences from faculty, students, and administrators led to the development of a discipline-agnostic VR "sandbox" where any 3D content from any academic field - within a range of acceptable 3D file types - could be rapidly uploaded to VR for analysis and manipulation across a network of VR headsets. Analysis and manipulation entails using the 3D mouse to orbit educational 3D content, leveraging the expanded visual field benefits and immersiveness of the technology. Additional tools were developed incrementally and included: orientation and scale controls; ambient lighting controls (including "sun" direction and intensity); "tour" mode; annotation tools; and screenshot and video capture capabilities. Study participants had access to all of this functionality. See Figure 1 below for a screen capture from the custom VR software that was developed.

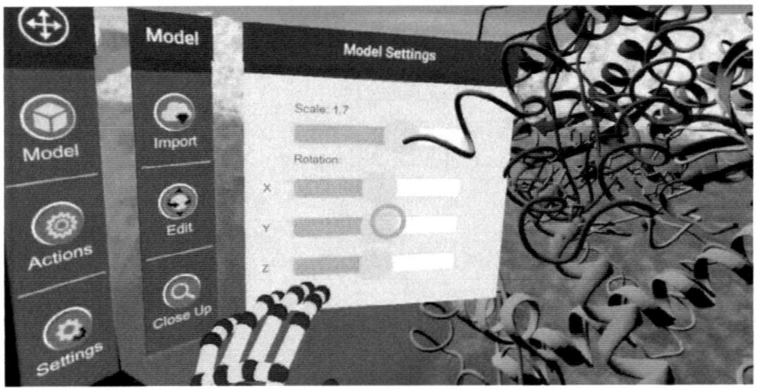

Figure 1

Since being made accessible to the university community starting in January 2016, these VR platforms have been successfully deployed in classes in a range of disciplines, most notably Anthropology and Biochemistry. In order to begin to evaluate the impact of these workstations on student learning, we contacted faculty members who had used the VR workstations in their classroom assignments. A faculty member from the Biochemistry Department and a faculty member from the Anthropology Department agreed to assist us in recruiting undergraduate research participants and developing a classroom activity that would draw on the benefits of VR technology and enable us to evaluate its impact on students. The remainder of this paper describes the methodology of this study and initial findings.

THEORETICAL FRAMEWORK

In order to produce a holistic understanding of the impact of VR on student learning in a real-world educational context, in designing our research methodology we drew on a theoretical framework that enables analytic insight into changes to students' beliefs (drawing on *self-efficacy theory*) and their interpretations of their embodied experiences (drawing on *interpretive phenomenological analysis*).

Self-efficacy theory helped guide the development of the surveys we used. The pre- and post-test surveys were designed to measure dimensions of students' self-reported self-efficacy, with changes in scores reflecting the impact of the VR activity. This theory was first developed by Bandura (1977) and has seen a variety of applications in psychology and education research. Abbitt (2011) explains "self-efficacy theory suggests that the beliefs concerning one's ability to affect a desired outcome influences both thought and action. In general, it is expected that higher self-efficacy beliefs will function as a positive support for action, whereas lower self-efficacy beliefs can have hindering effects on the decision to proceed with a particular course of action" (p.136). Using self-efficacy theory enables a more holistic understanding of the impact of VR use on students compared with using task completion metrics of efficiency and speed (as in Laha, et al., 2014). Abbitt (2011) suggests that improvements to self-efficacy may depend on embodied experiences and affective dimensions related to the success or failure of task completion and their perceived difficulty. To complement the analysis of self-efficacy, we turned to interpretive phenomenological analysis (IPA) to guide the generation and analysis of qualitative data (analysis of this data is ongoing and will appear in a future paper).

IPA is a theoretical and methodological framework that adopts a phenomenological attitude to the generation of qualitative data, with the analysis of that data guided by the assumptions of hermeneutics. IPA supports the interpretation of the lived experiences of participants. It also acknowledges that analysis is a "second-order hermeneutics," i.e. the research is always interpreting how participants themselves interpret their experiences (Smith, et al., 2009). Since participants are retrospectively interpreting their experiences, in this study, this could even be conceptualized as "third-order hermeneutics." This applicability of IPA to LIS research was described by VanScoy and Evenstad (2015). Phenomenology as a research perspective has seen increasing applications in LIS research (e.g., Dalbello, 2005; Suorsa and Huotari, 2014; Suorsa, 2017), with its fundamental assumptions outlined for an LIS audience in Budd (2005) and Budd, et al. (2010).

RESEARCH DESIGN

This research employed a mixed-methods approach, incorporating the generation and analysis of quantitative data (in the form of self-efficacy metrics collected via survey questionnaires before and after the VR activity) and qualitative data (in the form of semi-structured interviews).

The survey questions (see Table 1, below) were designed to measure students' self-reported measures of self-efficacy along the dimensions of general self-efficacy (Qs 1-2), educational self-efficacy (Qs 3-4), spatial skills self-efficacy (Q6, Q8, & Q9), and technological self-efficacy (Qs 10-12). Survey questions were developed from Schwarzer and Jerusalem's (1995) General Self-Efficacy Scale; Brinkerhoff's (2006) Computer Self-Efficacy Scale; Sam, Othman, & Nordin's (2005) Computer Self-Efficacy Scale; and Wang, Ertmer, & Newby's (2004) scale for technology integration.

Interview questions were designed to generate responses from students that would provide insight into how they interpret their experiences in the virtual learning environment, their thoughts and feelings throughout the VR activity, and how they use the VR technology to construct knowledge in order to answer the questions in the assignment.

The following interview questions (IQs) were developed to generate participants' reflections on their experiences using VR:

- IQ1 How would you describe your past experiences with virtual reality technology?
- IQ2 Please describe your most recent experience using virtual reality. What was it like? How did you feel throughout the process? What thoughts went through your mind?
- IQ3 How do you solve problems that come up when you're in VR? Please describe your process of problem solving and how you feel throughout that process.
- IQ4 How do you manipulate and analyze objects in VR? What is that experience like?
- IQ5 What is it like to complete a task in VR? For instance, how do you know when you have found the right area of the model to analyze? How do you know you're right?

Following the interviews, participants reviewed video screen captures of their VR sessions for approximately 15 minutes. They were prompted to reflect on what was happening in the video recording with the following Review Session Prompts (RSPs):

- RSP1: Please tell me what's going through your mind at this point. What are you feeling/thinking?
- RSP2: What did you do just do there? What was your thinking behind that? How did you know how to do that?
- RSP3: What is happening there? Was that expected? What were you thinking or feeling at the time?

VR Activity Design

The activity that participants carried out during the study was designed in consultation with the instructor of each course, so that the activity would fit seamlessly into the existing curriculum. The purpose was to design an activity that would support teaching and be integrated into the course content and learning objectives in order to reduce the perceived novelty of the VR technology, and instead emphasize the particular pedagogical content being taught. Close collaboration with the Anthropology class instructor resulted in an assignment that was more fully integrated into the course content, was a more appropriate length, and took into consideration the documented characteristics of VR that have been shown to support spatial analysis tasks. The assignment asked students to answer a set of questions (17 in the case of Biochemistry and three in the case of Anthropology) related to that week's course content that required them to analyze 3D models (complex protein structures in the case of Biochemistry, and hominid skulls in the case of the Anthropology) using the VR workstation in order to produce the correct answer.

Recruitment and Data Collection

After obtaining IRB approval, investigators worked with instructors of two undergraduate courses - Structural Biology (CHEM 4923) and General Anthropology (ANTH 1113) - to arrange for a recruitment session, which took place in the classroom and detailed the history of virtual reality and its applications to education. Students were provided with a recruitment notice and informed consent form; and, subsequently, 34 undergraduates (6 from CHEM 4923 and 28 from ANTH 1113) were recruited. Participants were incentivized to participate through course extra credit and receipt of a $15 gift card to the campus computer store upon completion. The assignment took on average 00:26:08 for CHEM 4923 students to complete, and 00:13:17 for ANTH 1113 students to complete.

Participants were asked to visit the publicly accessible virtual reality workstations at the library to familiarize themselves through an orientation session, in advance of the research study activity. Following a week-long orientation period in which students could drop in and practice using the VR workstations (assisted by student staff at the makerspaces in which the VR workstations are housed), students were contacted via email to arrange for another visit to the VR workstations to participate in the research activity and data collection. After signing informed consent forms, participants filled out basic demographic information and a 12 question pre-test survey that measured self-efficacy (see Table 1 below). Then, students worked with customized VR workstations to answer a set of questions related to the course curriculum (developed in conjunction with the respective instructors). Following the VR-supported activity, students were given a post-activity survey, which asked the same questions measuring self-efficacy, in order to measure any changes to their self-reported scores.

FINDINGS

Several demographic data points were tracked during the pre-survey portion of the study. The average age of the participants was 19.47 years and there was an approximately equal mix of male and female participants. Participants reported that they had previously engaged with virtual reality, on average, on 1.71 occasions, with a single participant reporting as many as six virtual reality experiences and 10 participants reporting no prior VR experience.

Changes in Self-Efficacy

Paired, two-sample t-tests (two-tailed) were run in order to see if the mean change in students' scores of self-efficacy were statistically significant. The null hypothesis was that the mean change in self-efficacy for each scale was zero. We found no significant impact (no change in mean scores) on any of the scales for the CHEM 4923 students (see Table 1, below). For some questions (Q's 1, 2, & 3), post-test scores remained unchanged across participants from this class.

Survey Questions	Pre-test		Post-test		Mean Change	Paired, 2 sample, t-test	
(N = 6)	Mean	σ^2	Mean	σ^2		t stat (2-tailed, t-critical = 2.23)	P
Q1. I am confident that I could deal efficiently with unexpected events.	3.83	0.17	3.83	0.17	0	0	1
Q2. When I am confronted with a problem, I can usually find several solutions.	4.17	0.57	4.17	0.57	0	0	1
Q3. I feel that I can handle any minor assignments that my professors might give to me.	4.67	0.27	4.67	0.67	0	0	1
Q4. I consider my myself to be very competent in the skills and knowledge required of my major.	4.00	0.40	3.83	0.57	-0.17	0.42	0.69
Q5. When my professor assigns a major project (final paper, presentation, etc.), I feel confident that I can complete the assignment successfully.	4.33	0.67	4.50	0.30	0.17	-0.42	0.69
Q6. I feel confident identifying important features and characteristics of structures in class activities.	3.50	0.70	3.33	0.67	-0.17	0.35	0.73
Q7. I feel confident finding important features on the model.	3.50	0.70	3.67	2.27	0.17	-0.24	0.82
Q8. I feel confident comparing and contrasting the shapes of different parts of the model.	3.83	0.97	4.00	1.20	0.17	-0.28	0.79
Q9. I feel confident judging the relative size of the various parts of models.	3.00	1.20	3.17	2.17	0.17	-0.22	0.83
Q10. I feel confident that I can use VR technology.	3.83	2.17	3.50	1.90	-0.33	0.40	0.69
Q11. I feel confident that I can use VR to complete class assignments without assistance.	3.00	0.80	3.50	1.90	0.50	-0.75	0.47
Q12. I find working with VR very frustrating (reverse coded).	2.17	0.57	2.33	2.27	0.17	-0.24	2.23

Table 1. Survey Questions with Descriptive Statistics for Pre-/post-test & t-tests (CHEM 4923 Students)

In the case of the ANTH 1113 students, significant positive changes to mean scores on task-specific (Q8&Q9) and VR-specific (Q10, Q11&Q12) scales were found (see Table 2 below). For Q8, "I feel confident comparing and contrasting the shapes of different parts of the model," we found that the ANTH 1113 students' mean scores increased from 3.86 to 4.29 (P=0.050). For Q9, "I feel confident judging the relative size of the various parts of the models," we found that the students' mean scores increased from 3.64 to 4.21 (P=0.001). These scores draw on skills related to judging the shape and size of models. For Q10, "I feel confident that I can use VR technology," we found that the students' mean scores increased from 3.89 to 4.33 (P=0.037). For Q11, "I feel confident that I can use VR to complete class assignments without assistance," we found that the students' mean scores increased from 3.61 to 4.21 (P=0.007). Finally, for Q12 (which was the one scale that was reverse coded), "I find working with VR very frustrating," we found that the students' mean scores decreased from 2.11 to 1.71 (P=0.046). It is worth noting that the CHEM 4923 students started at a similar "frustration score" of 2.17, but showed no significant change in this score. These three questions (Q10-Q12) were designed to measure participants' technological self-efficacy in regards to the VR technology.

Survey Questions	**Pre-test**		**Post-test**		**Mean Change**	**Paired, 2 sample, t-test**	
(N = 28)	**Mean**	**σ^2**	**Mean**	**σ^2**		**t stat (2-tailed, t-critical = 2.05)**	**P**
Q1. I am confident that I could deal efficiently with unexpected events.	4.11	0.32	4.29	0.29	0.18	-1.97	0.057
Q2. When I am confronted with a problem, I can usually find several solutions.	4.18	0.37	4.32	0.37	0.14	-1.689	0.103
Q3. I feel that I can handle any minor assignments that my professors might give to me.	4.36	0.31	4.43	0.33	0.07	-0.70	0.490
Q4. I consider my myself to be very competent in the skills and knowledge required of my major.	4.07	0.37	4.07	0.22	0	0.00	1.000
Q5. When my professor assigns a major project (final paper, presentation, etc.), I feel confident that I can complete the assignment successfully.	4.39	0.47	4.39	0.46	-0.03	1.00	1.000
Q6. I feel confident identifying important features and characteristics of structures in class activities.	3.93	0.59	4.18	0.37	0.25	-1.43	0.165
Q7. I feel confident finding important features on the model.	4.18	0.37	4.18	0.37	0.14	-1.69	0.103
Q8. I feel confident comparing and contrasting the shapes of different parts of the model.	3.86	0.72	4.29	0.72	**0.42***	-2.06	0.050
Q9. I feel confident judging the relative size of the various parts of models.	3.64	0.83	4.21	0.54	**0.57****	-3.62	0.001
Q10. I feel confident that I can use VR technology.	3.89	0.87	4.33	0.69	**0.44***	-2.20	0.037
Q11. I feel confident that I can use VR to complete class assignments without assistance.	3.61	0.99	4.21	0.69	**0.61***	-2.92	0.007
Q12. I find working with VR very frustrating (reverse coded).	2.11	0.84	1.71	1.02	**-0.39***	2.09	0.046

Table 2. Survey Questions with Descriptive Statistics for Pre-/post-test & t-tests (ANTH 1113 Students)

DISCUSSION

While data gathering was conducted without the control conditions present in the laboratory, the effectiveness of the VR workstations and the methods of evaluating them show promise. For the ANTH 1113 students, the significant positive impact on self-efficacy along dimensions related to completion of spatial tasks suggests that the positive attributes of VR technologies identified in lab-based research studies may have a benefit when applied in real-world, course-based activities. The improvement in students' self-efficacy related to successfully executing discipline-specific assignments using virtual reality, especially where those tasks relate to size judgements and other spatial thinking tasks, is also a promising outcome.

Implications for Designing Course Activities

The results of the study have some important implications for designing VR activities to support discipline-specific learning outcomes. We suspect that the lack of any significant change we observed in CHEM 4923 students' self-efficacy scores and the significant positive change in the ANTH 1113 students' self-efficacy scores can be attributed in part to different levels of guidance provided by the project team in helping the faculty member in each class design the activity. In the CHEM 4923 case, the faculty member designed the activity first, and then the project team made some suggestions for improvement. In the case of ANTH 1113, the project team worked with the faculty member from the start of the process of assignment design, ensuring that the activity was designed to specifically draw on the particular analytic affordances of VR. An initial analysis of the qualitative data collected in this study (to be discussed in greater detail in a future paper) also revealed that for the CHEM 4923 students some aspects of the VR environment that were designed to produce realistic objects, such as shadows, interfered with their visual analysis. These findings suggest that, in order to have a positive impact on students' self-efficacy, librarians and technologists should work closely with course instructors to ensure that VR activities are designed in consideration of both the types of spatial skills that VR is particularly apt at supporting and the particular analytic needs of students working in specific disciplines.

Methodological Considerations

While the results of this study suggest that VR can have a positive impact on student self-efficacy, our instruments need further development to ensure their validity. We need to further validate the survey instrument by analyzing correlations between scales to identify those that might be measuring the same underlying construct, look at the internal consistency of scores over multiple iterations of the study to assess the reliability of the survey, and most importantly, collect data about student learning outcomes (exam scores, final course grade, or other measures) and correlate with self-efficacy scores. It is hoped that these initial findings and methodological implications drawn from the quantitative data will serve as a guide for other librarians and researchers who are beginning to study and adopt these emergent and rapidly changing technologies in their institutions.

Limitations and Future Directions

These results are contingent on both the systems employed (e.g. the hardware/software idiosyncrasies of the specific virtual reality workstation implementation) and the instructional design of the associated activity. Lighting, and the ability (or inability) to quickly adjust ambient lighting conditions to reveal surface and geometric details of 3D content, were repeatedly mentioned as a feature that should be improved. Further, the current technological immaturity of virtual reality as a tool for scholarship means that issues related to "simulator sickness" (nausea due to the simulated motion of VR spaces) for example, must be taken into account when determining the appropriate duration of a virtual reality-based course assignment (Lin, et al., 2002). Sample size was an issue in this study as well, especially with regards to the CHEM 4923 class, which had only seven students enrolled, making it difficult to compare outcomes to the larger Anthropology class. Further studies will attempt to address this by selecting classes with comparable class sizes from which to recruit research participants.

Student learning outcomes were not a focus of this study, so participants' assignments were not graded. Therefore, data on self-efficacy cannot be correlated with learning outcomes. In addition, the site of data collection was not a controlled environment. Student participants were free to seek verbal guidance from investigators during the course of their VR activity. Future research will control for these variables in order to study the impact of VR on learning outcomes and performance dimensions of task completion (e.g., speed and accuracy). Another limitation of the study design is that it does not enable comparison of the benefits of VR to flat-screen based visualizations. In further refining the research design, a flat-screen 3D visualization could be used with a control group to further pinpoint the impact of VR on self-efficacy.

Finally, the qualitative data gathered during the post-activity interview phase of this study is rich, and provides many ways forward both for informing VR system design and formulation of future studies. Once fully analyzed, the qualitative data will provide rich description to students' experiences of VR and help to better understand how the technological affordances of VR shape students' self-efficacy.

CONCLUSION

Students' use of VR does not happen in a vacuum; their experiences of any technology or learning environment are embedded in their everyday lives as undergraduate students and the institutional contexts of the classroom and the academic library. Assessing the impact of VR use on students' self-efficacy in the context of a real-world, class-based activity offers a holistic approach to evaluating the impact of VR in an academic library context. Completing our analysis of the qualitative data generated through this study will further develop a rich picture of students' embodied experiences, with findings that will help guide other library professionals in developing VR platforms and the tools with which to effectively evaluate them.

REFERENCES

Abbitt, J.T. (2011). An investigation of the relationship between self-efficacy beliefs about technology integration and technological pedagogical content knowledge (TPACK) among preservice teachers. *Journal of Digital Learning in Teacher Education, 27*(4), 134-143.

Angulo, A. (2013). On the design of architectural spatial experiences using immersive simulation. In *Proceedings of EAE 11: Envisioning*

Architecture: Design, Evaluation, Communication (pp. 151-158). Italy: Milan.

Bandura, A. (1977). Self-efficacy: Toward a unifying theory of behavioral change. *Psychological Review, 84*(2), 191-215.

Bowman, D. A., & McMahan, R. P. (2007). Virtual reality: How much immersion is enough? *Computer, 40*(7), 36-43.

Brinkerhoff, J. (2006). Effects of a long-duration, professional development academy on technology skills, computer self-efficacy, and technology integration beliefs and practices. *Journal of Research on Technology in Education, 39*(1), 22-43.

Bronack, S., Cheney, A., Reidl, R., & Tashner, J. (2008). Designing virtual worlds to facilitate meaningful communication: Issues, considerations, and lessons learned. *Technical Communication, 55*(3), 261–269.

Brooke, J. (1996). SUS: A quick and dirty usability scale. *Usability Evaluation in Industry, 189*(194), 4-7.

Budd, J. (2005). Phenomenology and information studies. *Journal of Documentation, 61*(1), 44-59.

Budd, J., Hill, H., & Brooke, S. (2010). Inquiring into the real: A realist phenomenological approach. *Library Quarterly, 80*, 267-84.

Carr, D., Oliver, M., & Burn, A. (2010). Learning, teaching and ambiguity in virtual worlds. In A. Peachy, J. Gillen, D. Livingstone, and S. Smith–Robbins (eds.), *Researching learning in virtual worlds* (pp. 17–31). London: Springer.

Cook, M. (2018). Virtual serendipity: Preserving embodied browsing activity in the 21st century research library. *The Journal of Academic Librarianship, 44*(1), 145-149.

Dalbello, M. (2005). A phenomenological study of an emergent National Digital Library, Part I: Theory and methodological framework. *Library Quarterly, 75(*4), 391-420.

Dalgarno, B., & Lee, M. (2010). What are the learning affordances of 3-D virtual environments? *British Journal of Educational Technology, 41*(1), 10–32. http://dx.doi.org/10.1111/j.1467-8535.2009.01038.x

Deutschmann, M., Panichi, L., & Molka-Danielsen, J. (2009). Designing oral participation in Second Life: A comparative study of two language proficiency courses. *ReCALL, 21*(2), 206–226.

Donalek, C., Djorgovski, S. G., Cioc, A., Wang, A., Zhang, J., Lawler, E., ... & Davidoff, S. (2014, October). Immersive and collaborative data visualization using virtual reality platforms. In *Proceedings of IEEE International Conference on Big Data* (pp. 609-614). IEEE.

Forsberg, A., Katzourin, M., Wharton, K., & Slater, M. (2008). A comparative study of desktop, fishtank, and cave systems for the exploration of volume rendered confocal data sets. *IEEE Transactions on Visualization and Computer Graphics, 14(*3), 551-563.

Haycock, K., & Kemp, J.W. (2008). Immersive learning environments in parallel universes: Learning through Second Life. *School Libraries Worldwide, 14*(2) 89-97.

Holmberg, K., & Huvila, I. (2008). Learning together apart: Distance education in a virtual world. *First Monday, 13*(10), http://firstmonday.org/htbin/cgiwrap/bin/ojs/index.php/fm/article/view/2178/2033

Jang, S., Vitale, J. M., Jyung, R. W., & Black, J. B. (2017). Direct manipulation is better than passive viewing for learning anatomy in a three-dimensional virtual reality environment. *Computers & Education, 106*, 150-165.

Laha, B., Bowman, D. A., & Socha, J. J. (2014). Effects of VR system fidelity on analyzing isosurface visualization of volume datasets. *IEEE Transactions on Visualization and Computer Graphics, 20*(4), 513-522.

Limp, F., Payne, A., Simon, K., Winters, S., & Cothren, J. (2011). Developing a 3-D digital heritage ecosystem: From object to representation and the role of a virtual museum in the 21st century. *Internet Archaeology*, *30.*

Lin, J. W., Duh, H. B. L., Parker, D. E., Abi-Rached, H., & Furness, T. A. (2002). Effects of field of view on presence, enjoyment, memory, and simulator sickness in a virtual environment. In *Proceedings of IEEE Virtual Reality Conference* (pp. 164-171). IEEE.

Praslova–Førland, E., Sourin, A., & Sourina, O. (2006). Cybercampuses: Design issues and future directions. *Visual Computer, 22*(12), 1015–1028.

Ragan, E. D., Kopper, R., Schuchardt, P., & Bowman, D. A. (2013). Studying the effects of stereo, head tracking, and field of regard on a small-scale spatial judgment task. *IEEE Transactions on Visualization and Computer Graphics, 19*(5), 886-896.

Sam, H. K., Othman, A. E. A., & Nordin, Z. S. (2005). Computer self-efficacy, computer anxiety, and attitudes toward the Internet: A study among undergraduates in Unimas. *Journal of Educational Technology & Society, 8*(4), 205-219.

Schwarzer, R., & Jerusalem, M. (1995). Generalized Self-Efficacy scale. In J. Weinman, S. Wright, & M. Johnston, *Measures in health psychology: A user's portfolio. Causal and control beliefs* (pp. 35-37). Windsor, UK: NFER-Nelson.

Seth, A., Vance, J. M., & Oliver, J. H. (2011). Virtual reality for assembly methods prototyping: A review. *Virtual Reality, 15*(1), 5-20.

Sheehy, K. (2010). Virtual environments: Issues and opportunities for researching inclusive educational practices. In A. Peachey, J. Gillen, D. Livingstone, and S. Smith–Robbins (eds.), *Researching learning in virtual worlds* (pp. 1-15). London: Springer.

Smith, J. A., Flowers, P., & Larkin, M. (2009). *Interpretive phenomenological analysis: Theory, method and research.* Los Angeles: Sage.

Suorsa, A., & Huotari, M. L. (2014). Knowledge creation and the concept of a human being: A phenomenological approach. *Journal of the Association for Information Science and Technology, 65*(5), 1042-1057.

Suorsa, A.R. (2017). Knowledge creation and play: A phenomenological study within a multi-professional and multi-organizational community. *Journal of Documentation, 73*(6) 1167-1191.

Tan, W.-K., Tan, C.-H., & Teo, H.-H. (2012). Conveying information effectively in a virtual world: Insights from synthesized task closure and media richness. *Journal of the American Society for Information Science and Technology, 63*(6), 1198-1212.

Van Dam, A., Laidlaw, D. H., & Simpson, R. M. (2002). Experiments in immersive virtual reality for scientific visualization. *Computers & Graphics, 26*(4), 535-555.

Van Scoy, A., & Evenstad, S.B. (2015). Interpretative phenomenological analysis for LIS research. *Journal of Documentation, 71*(2), 338-357. https://doi.org/10.1108/JD-09-2013-0118

Wang, L., Ertmer, P. A., & Newby, T. J. (2004). Increasing preservice teachers' self-efficacy beliefs for technology integration. *Journal of Research on Technology in Education, 36*(3) 231-250.

Warburton, S. (2009). Second Life in higher education: Assessing the potential for and the barriers to deploying virtual worlds in learning and teaching. *British Journal of Educational Technology, 40*(3), 414–426.

User Interactions with "Alexa" in Public Academic Space

Irene Lopatovska
Pratt Institute, USA, ilopatov@pratt.edu

Heyrling Oropeza
Pratt Institute, USA, heyoropeza@gmail.com

ABSTRACT

Intelligent personal assistants (IPAs), such as Amazon Alexa, Google Assistant, Apple Siri, Microsoft Cortana and others, offer an example of an emerging technology with an uncertain adoption path. Evidence on how users adopt this technology is scarce, often anecdotal, and usually focuses on private uses and contexts. We conducted a study to examine Amazon Alexa adoption in a public common area of an iSchool. The study data were obtained from Alexa logs, observations of the public space, an online questionnaire, and interviews with students. Overall, IPA adoption trends among students were similar to adoption trends in the broader population and included using IPAs primarily at home for weather checks, quick references, setting an alarm/timer, and other requests. However, in a public academic setting, user interactions with Alexa were primarily characterized by questions about Alexa's features, "opinions," and rhetorical or mindless questions or requests. Such interactions might be explained in light of the device's novelty, user curiosity, and the anthropomorphizing of Alexa. Many participants ignored the device due to the lack of need to interact with it, lack of awareness, or perceived awkwardness of using it in a public space. The findings could be used to inform improvements of Alexa's features, educate potential adopters about its current functionality and limitations, and inspire directions for future research.

KEYWORDS

Intelligent Personal Assistants, Digital Personal Assistants, Voice-Powered Personal Assistants, Conversational Agent, Spart Speaker, Amazon Echo, Amazon Alexa, public academic setting, technology adoption, anthropomorphizing.

INTRODUCTION

According to industry reports, sales of Amazon Alexa hosting devices and other intelligent personal assistants (IPAs, also known as digital personal assistants, voice-powered personal assistants, or conversational agents) are on the rise (Dunn, 2016b; PRNewswire, 2017; Wakabayashi & Wingfield, 2018). Yet, evidence on how users adopt this technology is often anecdotal and scarce.

This article provides a brief overview of IPA technology, specifically that of Amazon Alexa, reviews relevant studies, and presents a case of Alexa's adoption in a public academic setting.

RELEVANT LITERATURE

Amazon Alexa is a voice-controlled software that works on Amazon Echo, Echo Dot, and Echo Show devices (Amazon, n.d.). Alexa belongs to the group of IPAs that includes Google Assistant, Apple Siri, Microsoft Cortana, and others. Alexa is designed to accept written or spoken user input, produce natural language responses, play music, place online shopping orders, set calendar reminders, and perform other tasks (Canbek & Mutlu, 2016). Alexa is activated when it receives the trigger word "Alexa" (the trigger word can be changed by a user, Clauser, 2017). Once active, Alexa uses a local WiFi internet connection along with Amazon's AWS cloud servers to obtain information, connect to other applications or skills, control smart home devices, such as lights and thermostat, or perform voice-operated functions (Dunn, 2016a).

Comparative studies of IPAs suggest that different IPAs have unique strengths. For example, Google Assistant performs best on travel and translation tasks, Microsoft's Cortana - on reminder tasks, and Alexa excels on Amazon shopping and controlling smart home devices (Dunn, 2016a; Graus et al., 2016; Dunn, 2016b; Thompson, 2017; Villas-Boas, 2017).

A cluster of IPA studies focuses on user satisfaction with this technology and these studies explore automatic methods for detecting satisfactory interactions. Jiang et al. (2015) examined user interactions with Microsoft Cortana on a Windows smart phone and determined that slower speaking rates and having to switch from voice to text input correlated with dissatisfactory interactions. Similarly, Kiseleva et. al (2016a) found that user satisfaction with IPAs decreases in situations when users need to switch inputs (from voice to gesture or text) in order to accomplish a task. Kiseleva et al (2016b) examined user satisfaction with Microsoft Cortana's performance on various tasks. The authors determined that users' judgements of satisfaction varied by task and were affected by task completion and task duration. Simpler tasks, rather than multi-turn conversations, were also linked to higher user satisfaction (Kiseleva et al., 2016b). Overall, the authors tend to emphasize the significance of the link between quality of conversational features and user satisfaction with IPAs.

Another group of studies examines usage, user expectations, and understanding of IPAs. Luger and Sellen (2016) interviewed IPA users and found that poor understanding of IPA features and lack of feedback from the device result in frustrating experiences and discontinued use. Sörensen (2017) compared two different chat-bot (conversational) systems and found that the system that provided feedback and shared updates about the status of task completion better met user expectations. Cowan et al.'s (2017) study of infrequent Siri users revealed that the lack of trust in IPA abilities and poor quality of the voice-controlled interface contribute to technology non-use. Similarly, a survey of IPA users by Moore et al. (2016) found a link between poor speech recognition accuracy and a decrease in usage.

Several authors focus on the privacy issues and cultural norms around IPA use. Easwara Moorthy and Vu (2015) surveyed seventy-six IPA users in the U.S. and found that, due to privacy concerns, users were more likely to rely on voice input only in private locations and around familiar people. Efthymiou and Halvey's (2016) study of smartwatch users also found that users were more likely to use voice input only around familiar people because of privacy concerns and norms of socially acceptable behavior. Several studies examined the usage of IPAs in group conversations and noted users' tendency to primarily engage the IPA for information seeking tasks (Porcheron et al., 2017; Porcheron et al., 2016). The studies identified additional issues with IPA performance, namely the misalignment of IPA conversational pace with human speech, the need for users to repeat queries, and the need to interrupt a group conversation in order to engage with an IPA.

Despite the issues associated with the use of IPAs in public, several reports describe IPA adoption in public settings, including museums, classrooms, and hospitals. The Boston Children's Hospital demonstrated IPA capabilities related to assisting patients with intake forms, providing updates to families in the waiting room, connecting patients directly with their clinician via phone call, text message, or email, and allowing patients to control lights and temperature in the room (Nguyen, 2016). The Barnes Foundation, an art museum in Philadelphia, PA, placed an Amazon Echo in one of the galleries (Bernstein, 2016). The museum discovered that people were not aware of the technology and therefore did not engage with it. Additionally, some visitors, both alone and in a group, were too shy to ask Alexa questions. The visitors who chose to interact with Alexa experienced difficulties due to the system's inability to "understand" foreign names such as Cézanne, Matisse, and Rousseau, or retrieve information past the first paragraph of Wikipedia entries. Another case study of Alexa adoption in a museum comes from the Museum of Modern Art (MoMA) in New York City (Moore, Pan, & Manish, 2017). In order to enhance visitor experience, the museum integrated Amazon Echo with the collections database and developed a new skill for answering queries related to modern and contemporary art. The article describes the skill creation process, which demonstrates Alexa's broad potential for uses in various public and educational settings. Similar to staff at the Barnes Foundation (Nguyen, 2016), MoMA staff found that language availability is a major barrier to using IPAs in museums. Alexa demonstrated difficulties in comprehending non-English names and titles posed within a query, and subsequently failed to produce proper responses. MoMA is currently working with Amazon to teach Alexa the names and titles of non-English artists and artwork. The museum aims to use Alexa as a tool for museum staff and visitors to quickly find information about an artwork. They plan to integrate it into the common areas, such as charging stations and cafes, to provide general information to the visitors and learn about visitors' interests. Once the skill is developed, MoMA plans to release it to the public.

In addition to museums and hospitals, Alexa has been tested in an educational setting. Flanagan (2016) hypothesized that using Alexa in an elementary school setting would develop children's comfort and confidence with using technology. The researcher installed Amazon Echo in the classroom and explained its design and functionality to the children. The study found that by speaking clearly or rephrasing their questions to Alexa, the students improved their speaking and listening skills. The students utilized the technology for school-related work including spell check, thesaurus questions, and help with simple math problems.

Overall, the reviewed studies on Alexa adoption in public spaces follow two approaches. They either a) instruct participants to use a specific functionality of the device, or b) invite them to discover Alexa's capabilities on their own. None of the published studies examined Alexa adoption in an academic setting. Due to the lack of prior knowledge about potential uses of Alexa in an academic context, we adopted the second approach in developing an exploratory study on how students choose to interact with Amazon Alexa in a public setting.

METHODS

We designed a study to examine user interactions with Amazon Alexa in a public space and address the following research questions:

1. How do students interact with Amazon Alexa in a public academic space?
2. What are the trends in iSchool student adoption of Amazon Alexa and other IPAs in private and public contexts?

The study was conducted in a main public hall of the Pratt Institute School of Information (approximately 25 x 25 feet, or 7.6 x 7.6 meters.) The area is primarily used by graduate students who are waiting for classes to start, working on individual and group projects, socializing with each other, using public computers, or meeting with a technology tutor (Figure 1). Students who are enrolled in one of the several master-level information studies programs have access to the area at any time of the day and day of the week. The area is most crowded during the workdays (Mon.-Fr.) between the early and late afternoon classes (~6pm). The data were collected during an academic semester between Sept. 29 and Oct. 22, 2017.

Figure 1. Public space where Amazon Alexa was placed.

The first generation of Amazon Echo with Alexa was chosen for this study because we needed an IPA that would work on the dedicated hardware (so as not to interfere with students using the public computers). Additionally, we chose Alexa over other smart speakers because it has a longer history on the market and there is prior research about its adoption in public spaces. The device was placed on of one the desks in the hall. A 16x14 inch colorful sign introducing Alexa and informing visitors about the ongoing study was placed next to the device. A similar informational message about the public Alexa and the study was also circulated on the school's mailing list and social media channels. In order to ensure that the placement of the device did not skew its usage, the device was moved to different areas of the hall during the study.

The study relied on several methods for examining user interactions with Alexa. Logfiles generated during the study by an Alexa app were used as a primary source of data on user interactions with Alexa (RQ1). The log data included a timestamp, the text of the user query (the way it was transcribed/understood by Alexa), and the text of Alexa's response. In order to determine the main types of user queries and system responses, the text of the logfiles was analyzed by two researchers using open coding method (Cronbach's Alpha score of .87 indicating acceptable inter-coder reliability). Content analysis of the interactions and timestamps was used to determine the number of sessions and interactions with Alexa. A session was defined as a complete conversation between a user and Alexa and included the total number of interactive turns. An interaction was defined as a single utterance from a user and single response from Alexa.

Online questionnaires, interviews, and observations were used to understand the general trends in student adoption of Alexa and other IPAs (RQ2). These instruments collected information on participants' demographics, ownership, use or non-use of IPAs, as well as participants' explanations for IPA adoption or non-adoption. A link to the online questionnaire (https://alexapratt.typeform.com/to/iVD8qz) was distributed through the school's mailing list and collected 85 responses (~30% response rate) from 52 active IPA users and 33 non-users. Twenty-three users of the school's public hall (twenty-two of whom were students) were interviewed in person for an average of 10 minutes about their adoption of IPAs in general and the use of the school's Alexa in particular. Interview questions resembled the online questionnaire items and focused on IPA ownership and usage. Several interview questions focused specifically on the school's public Alexa, asking interviewees for examples of usage and reasons for use or non-use. In addition to the questionnaire and interviews, the public area around the Alexa was observed at different times of the day and different days of the week over the course of one week, totaling 5.5 observation hours and 132 persons observed within the space. The findings pertaining to general trends of IPA adoption collected by the online questionnaires, interviews, and observations are not reported here. This paper focuses on the findings pertaining to RQ1 (types of user interactions with Alexa in a public professional space) and reports the RQ2 findings to the extent necessary to understand the context of user interactions with Alexa during the study.

FINDINGS

A total of 79 sessions and 169 interactions were logged during the 24 days of data collection (average of seven interactions per day). Most of the logged interactions occurred during workdays (N=111), with fewer interactions occurring on Saturdays and Sundays (N=58). The earliest interaction was logged at 9:34 AM and the latest at 12:13 AM (0:13).

The text of user interactions with Alexa was coded into the following broad categories: questions, salutations, requests, unclear/inappropriate, and commands. User questions directed at Alexa comprised the largest category of interactions (N=92). The questions were further classified by topic into questions related to Alexa and its functionality (32), factual questions (23), weather, time, and others (Table 1). The second most popular interaction type was salutations (N=32), user greetings and goodbyes addressed toward Alexa. Requests for Alexa to play music (9), tell a joke (8), or perform other tasks were expressed 24 times. The least frequent types of interactions included inappropriate or unclear requests (8) and commands (7), usually used to end the interaction.

Types of interactions Broad Narrow	Frequency / Percentage	Examples
Questions	92 (100%)	
Alexa/ Alexa features	37 (40%)	"Where are you from?" "What's your favorite musician?" "What's your opinion of the *New York Times*?"
Facts	23 (25%)	"Who wrote *From Here to Eternity*?" "Is there a bill to move the copyright office? "When does season 2 of *Westworld* start?"
Weather	13 (14%)	"What is the weather today?"
Time/Date/Calendar	9 (10%)	"What time is it?" "Is tonight the open house?"
Rhetorical	4 (4%)	"What is the meaning of life?"
Travel	4 (4%)	"Do you know when the Q train is coming?"
Recommendation	2 (2%)	"What do you recommend in New York city?" "Where can I find [...] books?"
Salutations Greetings+Goodbyes	38 22+16	"Good morning, Alexa"; "What's up, Alexa?"; "Alexa, how are you today?" "Good night, Alexa"; "Alexa, see you later"; "Alexa, goodbye"
Requests	24 (100%)	
Music	9 (38%)	"Play 'You Don't Love Me'"
Jokes	8 (33%)	"Tell me a joke"
Shopping	2 (8%)	"Buy me keys"
Social Media	2 (8%)	"Youtube (you to)"
Lights	1 (4%)	"Dim the lights"
Games	1 (4%)	"Can you play 21 Savage"
Rhetorical	1 (4%)	"Fix my life"
Unclear/Inappropriate questions and requests	8	"Play whatever sound this is"; "Alexa, say mess"; "Alexa, what's his name?"
Command Language	7	"Alexa, stop"; "Alexa, stay off"

Table 1. Types of user interactions with Alexa.

Content analysis of Alexa responses to user queries indicated that Alexa was able to provide appropriate responses in 95 (56% of the total) interactions (Table 2). For the remaining responses, Alexa was either unable to offer an answer, offered an inappropriate response, ignored the query, or was unable to respond due to its limited settings. In two instances, Alexa's responses to user commands were impossible to infer from the log data.

Responses	Frequency	Examples
Appropriate responses	95 (56%)	"The time is 4:54"; "It's 70 and sunny"
Unable to respond	51 (30%)	"Sorry, I'm not sure."; "Sorry, I don't know that one."
Inappropriate responses	9 (5%)	*[Question: "Is president Trump in New York Today?]* "It sounds like you're asking about President Donald Trump. ABC News reports: Trump has waived shipping restrictions between the US and Puerto Rico in order to expedite relief shipments to the disaster-stricken area."
No response	8 (5%)	
Unable to access skills and services	4 (3%)	"You don't have any Smart Home devices, to get started, go to the Smart Home section of the Alexa App."
Unclear response	2 (1%)	Not clear if command was performed (e.g. "Stop the music")
Total	169 (100)	

Table 2. Types of Alexa responses to user interaction.

Observation data confirmed the logfiles' findings: there were relatively infrequent interactions with the public Alexa. Of the 132 participants observed in the public area, only 13 (10%) interacted with the device. Students who ignored Alexa (N=119) were engaged in using public computers and printers (36%), conversing with other students (19%) and working in groups (13%); reading, eating, or drinking (13%); checking their phones (9%); moving through the area (8%), or utilizing a tech tutor (2%).

Online questionnaire and interview data shed light on some of the reasons behind low usage of Alexa in the public space. Questionnaire respondents reported using IPAs in a number of settings for various tasks (see summary in Table 3.)

Questionnaire respondents who indicated not actively using IPAs cited the lack of need (N=24), usage difficulties (N=4), privacy concerns (N=4), and other reasons for non-use (N=4).

Of the 22 interviewed students, fifteen reported actively using one or more IPAs, including Apple Siri, Google Home, and Amazon Alexa. The IPA uses reported in interviews resonated with the questionnaire data. All users reported using IPAs at home; with four users also mentioning using IPAs in public spaces like work, school, or transit (Table 3). Active IPA users praised the technology primarily for its convenience (34 mentions in interview responses), including its hands-free voice-controlled interface that supports multi-tasking, ease of use, and available functions. Additional positive comments about IPAs included acknowledgements of their informational value for fact-checking and recommendation tasks (N=7) as well as its entertainment value (N=3). The seven non-users expressed concerns about the technology's poor quality (N=29), mentioning problems such as voice recognition and response inaccuracies; lack of customization and specific functionality; usability issues (N=6); and privacy concerns (N=4).

Eighteen interviewees reported not using the Alexa in the public hall (though some of them also reported being active users of one or more IPAs in private settings). The non-users of the public Alexa cited the following reasons:

- lack of need (N=12): "*I don't have a reason to use it, it's stupid*", "*I have no need to use it. I come here for school and only school. When I'm at school, I already know things like weather, time, traffic, etc.*"
- lack of device awareness (N=10): "*Wasn't aware we had one. [Points to Echo] It blends into the background!*", "*I didn't notice it.*"
- discomfort of using Alexa in public (N=6): "*It's kind of embarrassing to use Alexa for basically nothing in the middle of a bunch of students; people are busy studying. It's distracting.*", "*I'm not sure about asking questions in that space and disturbing people [...] there is this sense of intimidation and spectacle with it being in a public setting.*"

Overall, the results point to relatively low use of Amazon Alexa in a public academic setting and mixed adoption trends of this emerging technology among iSchool graduate students.

Responses	Frequency from questionnaire (48 total responses)	Frequency from interviews (22 total responses)
Types of IPAs used		
Apple Siri	19	11
Amazon Alexa	7	2
Google Assistant	6	3
Microsoft Cortana	4	-
IPA features used most frequently		
Check Weather	15	7
Set Alarm/Timer	15	5
Play Music	12	4
Check Facts	11	7
Get News	7	-
Set Schedule	8	-
Traffic	5	-
Control Other Devices	2	-
Play Games/Tell Jokes	3	-
Purchase products	1	-
Other	3	-
Context of use		
Home	25	22
Transit	9	1
Work	5	1
School	5	2
Social Outings (i.e. party, bar)	4	-
Errands (i.e. grocery, laundry)	3	-

Table 3. IPA adoption trends by students based on the online questionnaire responses.

DISCUSSION

The results of our investigation of Amazon Alexa use in a public academic space are similar to previous studies of Alexa in public spaces: users did not actively engage with Alexa without receiving a specific task or instruction (Bernstein, 2016). The main reason for non-use emerged from participants' online questionnaires and in-person interview responses: the lack of need for an IPA. One of the ways to explain such user reactions to IPAs is through Roger's diffusion of innovation theory (2003), particularly the five qualities of a product that determine its adoption:

1. Relative advantage – degree to which innovation is perceived as better than the former idea
2. Compatibility – degree to which innovation is perceived as being consistent with existing values, past experiences, and needs of potential adopters
3. Complexity – degree to which innovation is perceived as difficult to understand/use
4. Trialability – degree to which innovation can be experimented with before adoption
5. Observability – degree to which results of an innovation are visible to others.

The lack of need for an IPA could be linked to participants' inability to recognize its relative advantage (1) compared to the other products that perform similar functions (e.g. web browser for searching and mobile phone for music, timers, or other tasks). Users might not see the need to change their information behavior routines for Alexa without significantly improved or innovative features that users find valuable. Our findings also indicate Alexa's "weakness" on the "complexity" dimension (3). In forty percent of the 169 device responses recorded in the logfiles, Alexa was unable to respond, provided an inappropriate response, or remained silent when a user engaged with it. Additionally, observability (5) of instances of a device's poor or inadequate performance might deter potential adopters from using this technology. The rate of Alexa's accuracy is reportedly trailing behind similar applications (Ryan, 2016) and could be the cause of users' avoidance of this technology.

Additional reasons for students not engaging with Alexa included lack of awareness and discomfort associated with the use of this conversational technology in a public space. The awareness factor could be mitigated in future studies or adoption cases by a more prominent positioning of the Echo device and better promotion of the device and its functionality. The findings related to the discomfort of using Alexa in public confirms prior research on social norms and privacy concerns around the use of voice-activated devices (Easwara Moorthy & Vu, 2015; Efthymiou & Halvey, 2016). Our participants expressed some concerns about the privacy of their interactions with Alexa and IPAs in general, a finding that is consistent with prior reports (Alhadlaq, Tang, Almaymoni, & Korolova, 2017; Brenner, 2017). However, such reports were relatively infrequent (four responses in the online questionnaire and four responses during the interviews) and don't provide sufficient evidence for the importance of this concern in users' overall IPA adoption.

The students who chose to engage with Alexa in the public hall often expressed similar requests as the ones reported in prior studies and private settings, including requests for factual information, weather, music, and others (Levin, 2016; Ong and Suplizio, 2016). The major difference in our findings compared to prior studies is the large number of questions about Alexa, namely about its "opinions" and features (40% of all questions, or 22% of the total interactions), and salutations directed at the device (22% of total interactions). Here are several possible explanations for such behavior with Alexa that warrant further examination:

- *Curiosity and lack of technology understanding.* Since many participants expressed no need for Alexa, but still wanted to engage with it, they chose to ask questions about its features, such as "Where are you from?", "Are you smart?", "What can you do?", and "Where were you born?" to name a few examples. Such behavior might indicate a lack of understanding but also a curiosity about the new device and its capabilities. The salutations directed toward Alexa might also signal curiosity and willingness to engage with the device without specific need for the device's functionalities.
- *Anthropomorphizing.* Anthropomorphizing, defined as the attribution of "humanlike properties, characteristics, or mental states to real or imagined nonhuman agents and objects" (Epley, Waytz, & Cacioppo, 2007), could explain the salutations and "personal" questions directed towards Alexa. Anthropomorphizing behavior might be intentional and might aid a person in making sense of an unfamiliar object, reducing the feeling of uncertainty, or establishing social connections (Epley et al., 2007). Anthropomorphizing, especially in the context of salutations, might also be explained by the theory of "overlearned politeness" (Nass & Moon, 2000), a mindless activity or an automatic response (e.g., "thanks" and "bye") that is triggered by social cues. The third reason for anthropomorphizing might be rooted in Mori's "uncanny valley" principle (1970) that refers to the human tendency to create a distance with technology that appears human. The "uncanny valley" principle would help to explain interactions that appeared to purposefully test the intelligence of Alexa and highlight its limitations. The behavior that emphasizes individual superiority or creates humorous situations might have also been encouraged by the presence of other students in the same public space.

In an area where students are preparing for classes, we expected Alexa to be engaged in more informational requests. Our logs did not confirm our expectations or findings from prior studies that identified the tendency to primarily use IPAs in public settings for information seeking tasks (Porcheron et al., 2017; Porcheron et al., 2016; Bernstein, 2016). The low frequency of information requests might be explained by participants' lack of appropriate information needs, lack of awareness of the device and its capabilities, or disappointment with device performance (low accuracy/response rate) which does not encourage subsequent interactions (Meeker, 2017.)

Relatively poor performance of the device in response to user questions or requests can be partially explained by the nature of the difficult, often rhetorical questions directed at Alexa (e.g. "Alexa, do you understand what pain and suffering is?", "Alexa, tell me the meaning of life?", or "Alexa, say 'Hi, Candice'"). It can also be explained by Alexa's limitations in processing natural speech and voice commands, an observation supported by prior research (Ryan, 2016). In some unsuccessful interactions, Alexa attempted to respond to participants' questions with irrelevant information. However, in the majority of such interactions Alexa admitted its inability to help or remained silent. In addition to improving Alexa's search, speech recognition, and conversational capabilities, we would recommend investigating the types of appropriate responses to rhetorical, silly, and other challenging questions. User response preferences should be examined in light of user behaviors with systems of similar functionality (e.g. web browsers) and other humans. For example, do users prefer receiving a silent response, an acknowledgment of defeat, or any answer no matter how inappropriate? Linking Alexa to a paid Amazon account could address the instances of Alexa's inability to address user requests due to limited settings (e.g. lack of access to the paid music source). Adding this feature, however, is problematic in a public setting where multiple users may potentially use the account for shopping, expensive services, and other types of requests that have financial implications. In order to enable paid services on Alexa, its current settings need to be redesigned to accommodate multiple users and accounts.

For the most part, users who chose to engage with Alexa used simple and short language structures for their questions, requests, and commands. Use of appropriate command language in interactions with Alexa might indicate users' familiarity with IPA technology and/or users' engagement with this new technology in a similar manner to more familiar retrieval systems such as web browsers. This familiarity with the device was confirmed by the questionnaire and interview data. The overall adoption and uses of IPA technology among students mirror similar trends in the larger population (Levin, 2016; Ong & Suplizio, 2016) and include uses of IPAs primarily at home for checking the weather, setting alarms and timers, playing music, performing information searches, and other tasks. The most frequently used IPA in our study was Apple Siri, followed by Amazon Alexa and other IPAs.

CONCLUSION

We examined a case of user adoption of Amazon Alexa in a public academic space. Many visitors to the space did not engage with Alexa due to the lack of need for the device's functionality, lack of awareness of the device's presence or relevant functionality, or discomfort in using the conversational device in the study area. The interactions that did occur were characterized by a prevalence of questions about Alexa's functionality, manifestations of "overlearned politeness," and rhetorical, inappropriate, or silly questions.

The small size and idiosyncrasy of the study limits its generalizability to the scope of a case study. However, a number of findings confirm previous observations and point to promising directions for future research. We think that it would be interesting to analyze IPA adoption using Roger's (2003) diffusion of innovation theory. Such analysis could reveal the strengths and weaknesses of this technology as well as outline its projected adoption path for private and public uses. The anthropomorphizing of IPAs, including the humiliation of this technology in public, deserves attention for its potential to inform design of conversational agents as well as shed light on user behavior towards technology. Lack of need and understanding of this technology could be addressed by developing context-specific features (e.g., research-oriented skills for academic uses), promoting them to potential adopters (similar to the previous studies of IPAs in hospitals, schools and museums), and comparing such "purposeful" uses to the more exploratory ones exhibited in our study.

Despite the industry hype around the rising sales of IPA devices, our study found rather cautious IPA adoption trends among our student participants, particularly in the public academic setting. Using the Roger's theory cited above, we think that this technology is still in the early stages of adoption. Whether IPAs ever cross the chasm that would move them to the mass adoption phase will depend upon improved design and performance as well as users finding this technology useful enough to adopt.

ACKNOWLEDGMENTS

We would like to thank the following student researchers for their contributions to the project: Brooke Bormann, Xiaxin Chen, Leah Constantine, Cormac Fitzgerald, Danielle Frank, Guida Lai, Stephanie Lee, Chinmi Liao, Lily Martin, Rachel Richardson and Katrina Rink. We would also like to thank our participants and the School's administration for their support.

REFERENCES

Alhadlaq, A., Tang, J., Almaymoni, M., Korolova, A. (2017). Privacy in the Amazon Alexa skills ecosystem. Paper presented at the 17th Privacy Enhancing Technologies Symposium, Minneapolis, MN. Retrieved from https://petsymposium.org/2017/papers/hotpets/amazon-alexa-skills-ecosystem-privacy.pdf

Amazon. (n.d.). Echo & Alexa devices. Retrieved from https://www.amazon.com/Amazon-Echo-And-Alexa-Devices/b?ie=UTF8&node=9818047011

Bernstein, S. (2016, December 6). What can Alexa teach us about the Barnes? [Blog post]. Retrieved on December 6, 2016 from https://medium.com/barnes-foundation/what-can-alexa-teach-us-about-the-barnes-21154d68700c#.v08qjcf4k

Brenner, B. (2017, January). Know the risks of Amazon Alexa and Google Home. *Naked Security by Sophos*. Retrieved from https://nakedsecurity.sophos.com/2017/01/27/data-privacy-day-know-the-risks-of-amazon-alexa-and-google-home/

Canbek, N. G. & Mutlu, M. E. (2016). On the track of artificial intelligence: Learning with intelligent personal assistants. *Journal of Human Sciences, 13*, 592-601. DOI: 10.14687/ijhs.v13i1.3549

Clauser, G. (2017, May 25). What is Alexa? What is the Amazon Echo, and should you get one? *The Wirecutter*. Retrieved from http://thewirecutter.com/reviews/what-is-alexa-what-is-the-amazon-echo-and-should-you-get-one/

Cowan, B. R., Pantidi, N., Coyle, D., Morrissey, K., Clarke, P., Al-Shehri, S., Earley, D., & Bandeira, N. (2017). "What can I help you with?": Infrequent users' experiences of Intelligent Personal Assistants. In *MobileHCI '17 Proceedings of the 19th International Conference on Human-Computer Interaction with Mobile Devices and Services* (pp. 43-52). New York, NY: ACM. http://dx.doi.org/10.1145/3098279.3098539

Dunn, J. (2016a, November 4). We put Siri, Alexa, Google Assistant, and Cortana through a marathon of tests to see who's winning the virtual assistant race — here's what we found. *Business Insider*. Retrieved from http://www.businessinsider.com/siri-vs-google-assistant-cortana-alexa-2016-11

Dunn, J. (2016b, December 28) It's been a good year for the Amazon Echo. *Business Insider*. Retrieved from http://www.businessinsider.com/amazon-echo-sales-figures-stats-chart-2016-12

Easwara Moorthy, A. and Vu, K.-P. L. (2015). Privacy concerns for use of voice activated personal assistant in the public space. *International Journal of Human-Computer Interaction, 31*, 307-335. https://doi.org/10.1080/10447318.2014.986642

Efthymiou, C., & Halvey., M. (2016). Evaluating the social acceptability of voice based smartwatch search. In D. Ma, J. R. Wen, Y. Liu, Z. Dou, M. Zhang, Y. Chang, & X. Zhao (Eds.) *Information retrieval technology* (Vol. 9994, Lecture Notes in Computer Science, pp. 267-278). New York, NY: Springer. DOI:10.1007/978-3-319-48051-0_20

Epley, N., Waytz, A., & Cacioppo, J. T. (2007). On seeing human: A three-factor theory of anthropomorphism. *Psychological Review, 114*, 864-886. DOI:10.1037/0033-295X.114.4.864

Flanagan, E. (2016, December 26). Using the Amazon Echo Dot and Alexa in the classroom [Blog post]. Retrieved from https://www.erintegration.com/2016/12/26/amazon-echo-dot-and-alexa-in-the-classroom/

Graus, D., Bennett, P. N., White R. W., & Horvitz, E. (2016). Analyzing and predicting task reminders. In *Proceedings of the 2016 Conference on User Modeling Adaptation and Personalization (UMAP '16)* (pp. 7-15). New York, NY: ACM. DOI:10.1145/2930238.2930239

Jiang, J., Awadallah, A. H., Jones, R., Ozertem, U., Zitouni, I., Kulkarni, R. G., & Khan, O. Z. (2015). Automatic online evaluation of intelligent assistants. In *Proceedings of the 24th International Conference on World Wide Web - WWW '15* (pp. 506-516). New York, NY: ACM. doi:10.1145/2736277.2741669

Kiseleva, J., Williams, K., Awadallah, A. H., Crook, A. C., Zitouni, I., & Anastasakos, T. (2016a). Predicting user satisfaction with intelligent assistants. In *Proceedings of the 39th International ACM SIGIR conference on Research and Development in Information Retrieval - SIGIR '16* (pp. 45-54). New York, NY: ACM. DOI:10.1145/2911451.2911521

Kiseleva, J., Williams, K., Jiang, J., Awadallah, A. H., Crook, A. C., Zitouni, I., & Anastasakos, T. (2016b). Understanding user satisfaction with intelligent assistants. In *Proceedings of the 2016 ACM on Conference on Human Information Interaction and Retrieval - CHIIR '16* (pp. 121-30). New York, NY: ACM. DOI:10.1145/2854946.2854961

Levin, M. R. (2016, April 28). Amazon Echo: What we know now. *The Huffington Post*. Retrieved from http://www.huffingtonpost.com/michael-r-levin/amazon-Echo--what-we-know_b_9802834.html

Luger, E., & Sellen, A. (2016). Like having a really bad PA: The gulf between user expectation and experience of conversational agents. In *Proceedings of the 2016 CHI Conference on Human Factors in Computing Systems* (pp. 5286-5297). New York, NY: ACM. DOI:10.1145/2858036.2858288

Meeker, M. (2017, May 31). *Internet Trends 2017- Code Conference*. Slide presentation presented at the Kleiner Perkins Caufield Byers Code Conference. Retrieved from http://www.kpcb.com/internet-trends

Moore, R. K., Li, H., and Liao, S.-H. (2016). Progress and prospects for spoken language technology: what ordinary people think. In *Proceedings of the Annual Conference of the International Speech Communication Association, INTERSPEECH* (pp. 3007–3011). http://dx.doi.org/10.21437/Interspeech.2016-874

Moore, S., Pan, D., Engineer, M. (2017, January 26). A case study on using voice technology to assist the museum visitor. *MW17: MW 2017*. https://mw17.mwconf.org/paper/a-case-study-on-using-voice-technology-to-assist-the-museum-visitor/

Mori, M. (1970). The uncanny valley (K. F. MacDorman & T. Minato, Trans.). *Energy, 7*(4), 33-35.

Nass, C., & Moon, Y. (2000). Machines and mindlessness: Social responses to computers. *Journal of Social Issues, 56*(1), 81-103. Retrieved from http://ldt.stanford.edu/~ejbailey/02_FALL/ED_147X/Readings/nass-JOSI.pdf

Nguyen, C. (2016, June 7). Bringing voice technology to healthcare: Hacking with Amazon's Alexa Vector [Blog post]. Rerieved on June 7, 2016 from https://vector.childrenshospital.org/2016/06/bringing-voice-technology-healthcare-hacking-amazons-alexa/

Ong, S., & Suplizio, A. (2016). Unpacking the breakout success of the Amazon Echo [Infographic]. Retrieved from https://www.experian.com/innovation/thought-leadership/amazon-echo-consumer-survey.jsp.

Porcheron, M., Fischer, J. E., & Sharples, S. (2016). Using mobile phones in pub talk. In *Proceedings from the 19th ACM conference on computer-supported cooperative work & social computing* (pp. 1649-1661). New York, NY: ACM. DOI: 10.1145/2818048.2820014

Porcheron, M., Fischer, J. E., & Sharples, S. (2017). "Do animals have accents?": Talking with agents in multi-party conversation. In *Proceedings from the 2017 ACM conference on computer supported cooperative work and social computing* (pp. 207-219). New York, NY: ACM. DOI:10.1145/2998181.2998298

PR Newswire. (2017, January 23). The 2017 voice report predicts more than 24 million Amazon Echo and Google Home devices will be sold this year. Retrieved from http://go.gale-group.com/ps/i.do?p=AONE&sw=w&u=cuny_broo39667&v=2.1&it=r&id=GALE%7CA479772272&asid=d21d16b66384b1e24ef2fd8bc75d8744

Rogers, E. M. (2003). Diffusion of innovations (5th ed.). New York: Free Press.

Ryan, K. J. (2016, June 3). Who's smartest: Alexa, Siri, and or Google Now? *Inc. Magazine*. Retrieved from https://www.inc.com/kevin-j-ryan/internet-trends-7-most-accurate-word-recognition-platforms.html

Sörensen, I. (2017). *Expectations on chatbots among novice users during the onboarding process* (Dissertation). Retrieved from http://urn.kb.se/resolve?urn=urn:nbn:se:kth:diva-202710

Thompson, C. (2017, January 4). Amazon's Alexa is officially coming to Ford cars. *Business Insider*. Retrieved from http://www.businessinsider.com/amazon-alexa-coming-to-ford-cars-2017-1

Villas-Boas, A. (2017, January 10). 14 ways you can control your home with your voice using Amazon's Echo and Alexa. *Business Insider*. Retrieved from http://www.businessinsider.com/amazon-echo-alexa-control-smart-home-with-voice-2017-1/#smart-home-hubs-compatible-with-alexa-1

Wakabayashi, D. & Wingfield, N. (2018, January 15). Alexa, we're still trying to figure out what to do with you. *The New York Times*. Retrieved from https://www.nytimes.com/2018/01/15/technology/virtual-assistants-alexa.html

Do Longer Articles Gather More Citations? Article Length and Scholarly Impact among Top Biomedical Journals

Peng-hui Lyu
School of Management, Hefei University of Technology, Hefei 230009, P.R China. Email: lyu@hfut.edu.cn.

Dietmar Wolfram
School of Information Studies, University of Wisconsin-Milwaukee 53201, USA. Email: dwolfram@uwm.edu.

ABSTRACT

Publications represent the most tangible products of research and scholarly communication. Growing pressures placed on researchers to increase their publication counts may encourage them to publish shorter papers, so that more publications may be generated from the same project and program. Is this the case? Furthermore, do shorter papers garner the same impact as longer papers as measured by the citations received? This research examines the relationship between article length and citations received by articles published in three prominent top biomedical research journals over the lifetime of the journals. The study reveals that instead of getting shorter, articles in these journals are getting longer over time. Longer articles in these journals, on average, attract more citations, and are therefore considered more impactful.

KEYWORDS

Article length; scholarly impact; citation; biomedical journals; publish or perish.

INTRODUCTION

The products of scientific inquiry continue to produce a growing number of publications each year in the form of journal articles (Rajagopal, Archunan, Surulinathi, & Ponmanickam, 2013). Biomedical journals occupy a significant portion of all the science and technology journals, accounting nearly one third of the journals from all of disciplines in the publication community (Coleman, 1999). According to the data from Clarivate Analytics Journal Citation Reports (https://clarivate.com/products/journal-citation-reports/), the biomedical journals ranked first in all subjects and those journals usually have a high Impact Factor (IF), which provide an indication of their active citation activity (Brown, 2007).

In science, the pressure of "publish or perish", where researchers are expected to publish as more as frequently has been part of the scientific landscape for several decades (Callaway, 2016). Broad (1981) observed that publication inflation was already present in biology or medicine in the decades prior to his publication. The manifestations of increased author productivity may be seen through increased collaboration, where the average number of authors per paper has increased over time in many fields (Glanzel & Schubert, 2005), although one could also argue that research in some fields today requires larger teams to carry out. Broad also discusses the idea of the Least Publishable Unit (also known as "salami slicing"), where authors reuse their data in multiple papers or publish shorter works to increase the number of papers arising from a research project (Broad, 1981). These activities raise ethical issues and the sustainability of these increasing demands on authors clearly is not realistic.

Several informetric studies have examined the relationship between different publication characteristics and impact. Tahamtan, Afshar and Ahamdzadeh (2016) reviewed the research literatures that have examined factors that affect the number of citations an article receives. Several studies have included the article length as a factor. For example, Stremersch, Verniers, and Verhoef (2007) tested a model consisting of many variables based on social constructivist, universalist and presentation features to determine which variables contributed to a publication's citation count for articles appearing in five marketing journals. The authors found that article length was a significant variable. Haslam et al. (2008) examined factors that made an article influential in social and personality psychology. They found that first author eminence, the seniority of later authors, journal prestige, article length, and the number and the age of the references were strong predictors. Similarly, Slyder et al. (2011) studied how different author and article-based factors influenced citation counts for academic faculty in geography and forestry departments at least ten American universities. They found that there was not a significant association between article length and citations received. Haustein, Costas and Lariviere (2015) examined document properties and collaboration patterns and compared social media metrics and citations across many disciplines for articles published in 2012. The authors included publication length, observing that citation counts increased for longer articles but varied for the very longest articles.

Falagas, Zarkali, Karageorgopoulos, Bardakas and Mavros (2013) studied the impact of article length on the number of future citations in general medicine journals. They conducted a small-scale study of 196 articles over a short period of time to examine citations in the future and found a positive association between article length and citations. The authors recognized that the size of the study and the limited period of time did not permit generalizability and suggested that there is a relationship that warrants further investigation. This study fills the gap by examining article and citation characteristics on a much larger scale.

By publishing shorter papers, authors may be able to increase the number of publications they produce (Callaham, Wears, & Weber, 2002). Does this strategy affect the impact of the publications as measured by the citations the publications receive? On one hand, more publications may receive more citations in turn, but do longer papers, which presumably report more research, garner more citations than shorter papers? An earlier preliminary study on a set of astronomy papers suggests that this is the case (Ball, 2008). This research reports on an investigation of the relationship of article length and citations received for three prominent top biomedical journals, to determine if there is a citation advantage for longer articles.

More specifically:
RQ1 – Has the average length of articles in three prominent top biomedical journals changed over time?
RQ2 – Are longer papers the product of larger, more diverse research collaborations?
RQ3 – Do longer articles attract more citations on average than shorter articles in these top biomedical journals?

METHODOLOGY

Three biomedical journals with the highest impact factors in the field of general and internal medicine were chosen from the list of all journals from Journal Citation Reports (JCR): The New England Journal of Medicine (NEJM), The Journal of the American Medical Association (JAMA) and The Lancet (Lancet) (Hu, Liao, Gao, & Li, 2010). JAMA was indexed under two titles at different times as JAMA - Journal of American Medical Association, and Journal of American Medical Association (Antoniou, Antoniou, Georgakarakos, Sfyroeras, & Georgiadis, 2015). This study included all regular "article" type papers from these journals mentioned above for analysis indexed in Clarivate Analytics' Web of Science, and excluded those which were not categorized as an "article", such as review articles, experimental studies, meta-analyses and editorials, etc. Despite limiting the selected document types to articles, we recognize there are some discrepancies in document type assignments (Donner, 2017), but they are largely correct.

To provide a more comprehensive analysis, data from these top journals were collected since their founding to illustrate the overarching patterns of citation in the biomedical research domain. After data cleaning, the final dataset yielded 27,305 papers in NEJM, 42,733 papers in JAMA and 65,525 papers in Lancet, up to 2016. Citation data were retrieved for each publication from the journal's inception to 2017. Specifically, a set of variables from each article was collected from Clarivate Analytics' Web of Science database to explore the relationship between article length, operationalized as the number of pages an article contains, and other publication characteristics, including the number of authors, author-affiliated institutions and their countries, number of bibliographic references, and number of citations.

The citation data for articles from NEJM, JAMA, and Lancet were investigated separately using informetric analysis. MS Excel 2016 was used to illuminate more visual features for the relationship between paper length and a variety of publication factors in biomedical research below.

RESULTS AND DISCUSSION

In this section, figures and tables are employed to describe the relationship based on distribution between the paper length and citations from top biomedical journals. Publications (as indicator for scientific performance) are widely accepted indicators for quantitative research (Garfield, 2000). Summary data for each journal are presented in 0.

	NEJM	JAMA	Lancet
Number of Papers	27, 305	42, 733	65, 525
Number of Total Pages	139, 464	171, 925	193, 728
Number of Total Citations	1, 971, 227	4, 083, 113	2, 919, 304
Number of Publication Year	89	97	116
Research Papers per Year	306.8	440.55	564.87
Number of Average Pages	5.92	4.37	3.23
Number of Average References	24.02	23.88	61.08
Number of Citation per Paper	72.19	95.55	44.55

Table 1. Summary data for the journals studied

Article length and publication number

As an initial exploration of the scientific data from three high impact biomedical journals, the total publication records were tallied by article length (i.e., number of reported pages). If more articles were published for a given page length, these may accumulate more citations, which will influence the relationship between the citations and the article length.

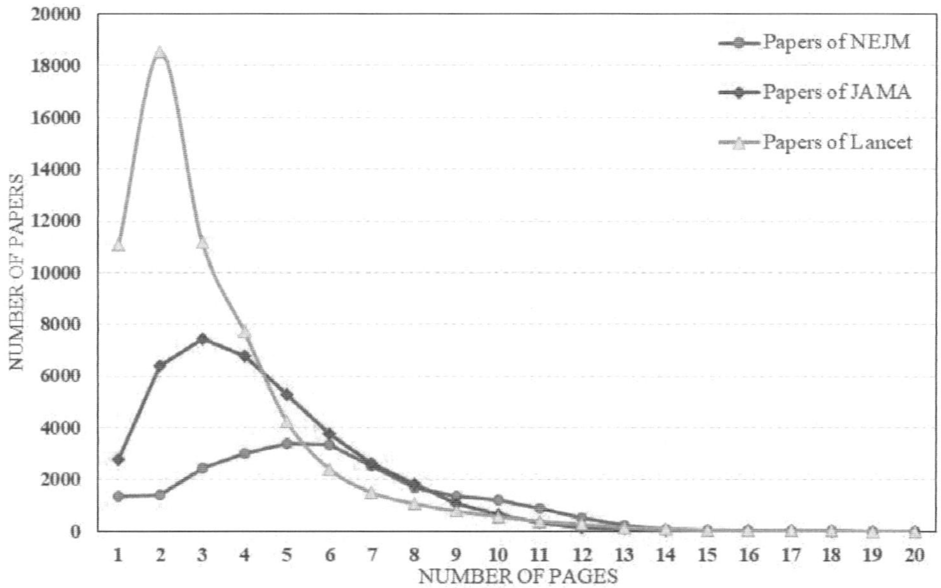

Figure 1. Frequency distribution of article length in top biomedical journals

Figure 1. shows clearly a similar trend of long tailed distributions in publication records vs article length in NEJM, JAMA and Lancet respectively. The average paper length is 5.92, 4.37 and 3.23 pages for all the publications from NEJM, JAMA and Lancet, respectively. On average, Lancet had the shortest articles, but with a large range of values. All three journals have few papers that exceed 14 pages, which may demonstrate that it is harder for biomedical scientists to publish longer papers, on average.

Article length and publication lifetime

Articles published earlier have a citation advantage over more recent articles because they have had a longer time in which to gather citations.

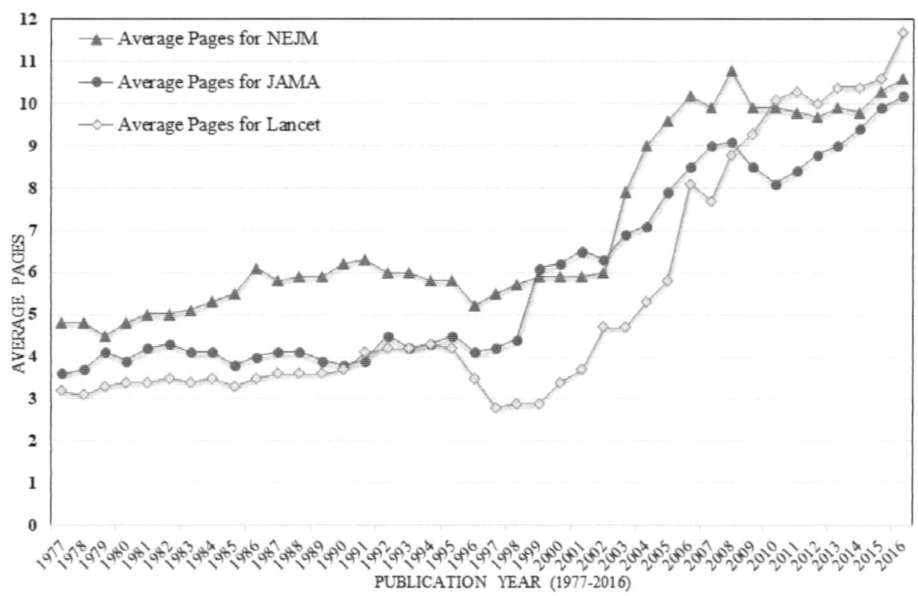

Figure 2. Average article length over time in top biomedical journals

If the average article length for journals has changed over time, for example, and articles have become shorter, one could argue that the average number of citations received by articles of a given length have more to do with their age than with their length. Tahamtan et al. (2016) found that, in general, article lengths across disciplines have been increasing from 1975 to 2011, although for articles in the life sciences there has been a slight decrease in length between 1995 and 2011 of about 11%.

Figure 2. summarizes the relationships between the average article length and the age of the articles for JAMA, NEJM, and Lancet. It can be seen that the average length of articles for the three top biomedical journals was steady between 1978 and the early 2000s relatively. Since then, the average article length has been increasing, and this trend was extremely clear in the 21st century. According to the layout policies of the biomedical journals studied, they tend to include more words or characters in a single page, so the number of pages is a valid indicator of the length of a biomedical article instead of the number of words or characters, which are not as intuitive.

An inspection of randomly selected articles over the study period revealed that there were no substantial layout or formatting changes to the three journals. Lancet and JAMA have relied primarily on a three-column format. NEJM appears to have switched from a two-column to a three-column format in the mid-2000s, but this occurred after the increase in the average article length in the early 2000s. Another observed change for the journals is the reliance on structured abstracts, which tend to be longer than unstructured abstracts. However, these longer abstracts would only increase the overall article length marginally. In answer to RQ1, articles in the three top journals have become longer over time. Therefore, if there were to be a citation advantage for articles based on age, it would favor shorter articles.

Article length and average references

For a longer biomedical paper, one would tend to include more references to support one's views or discourse processes. There is, however, great diversity in the number of references, ranging from 3 to more than 100 references. One implication of the longer papers with higher numbers of references is that they contribute a greater number of citations to the total pool of citations than shorter articles with fewer references (Falagas et al., 2013).

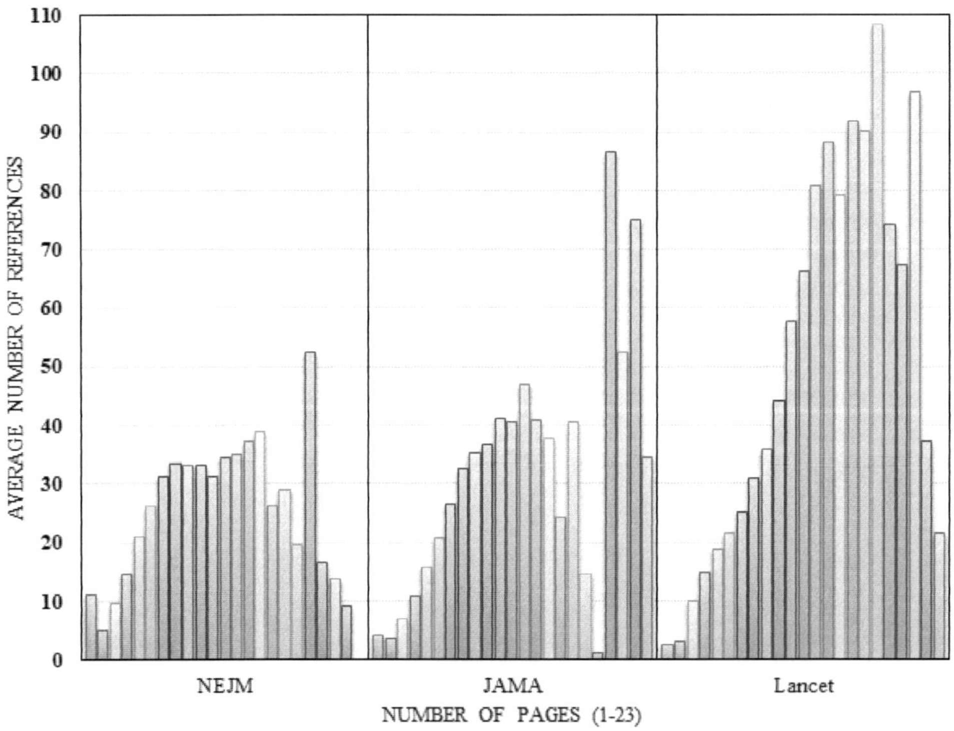

Figure 3. Relationships between average number of references and article length of top biomedical papers

Figure 3. presents three distributions to summarize the association between article length and average number of references in the top biomedical journals. These journals show very similar patterns in the average number of references for articles up to 9 pages long, after which increases in the average number of references continue or decline with divergent tendencies for longer articles. This is not unexpected. The small quantity of papers longer than 14 pages may significantly influence the relationships between average references and article length, so they are more irregular. This may have an influence on citations in the entire biomedical domain.

Article length and producers of articles

Article length also interacts with some related factors such as their producers or creators, including the number of authors and the number of their affiliations or countries. Longer articles may be the product of larger research teams or institutes and may contain more information that these academic communities produced, which creates the potential for more citations. Figure 4. 5 and 6 summarize the observed relationships between the article length and the average number of authors, institutes and countries (i.e., producers).

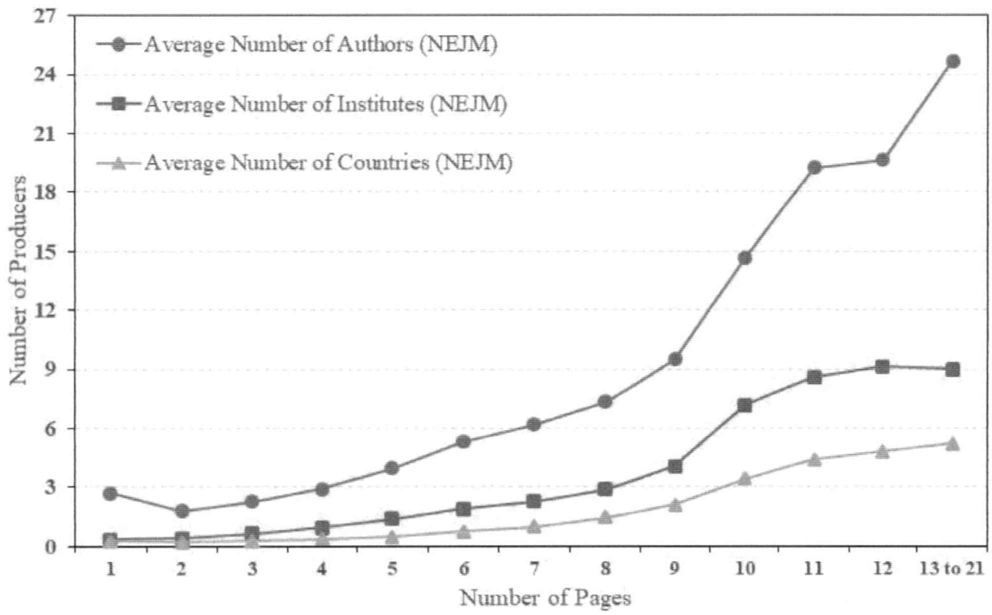

Figure 4. Relationships between producers of articles and number of pages in NEJM papers

NEJM, which ranked first with the highest IF among the biomedical journals, shows a steady increase, particularly in the average number of authors and with more modest increases in the number of countries and institutions, indicating that, as author teams grew, the authors were not necessarily from new institutions or countries according to Figure 4.

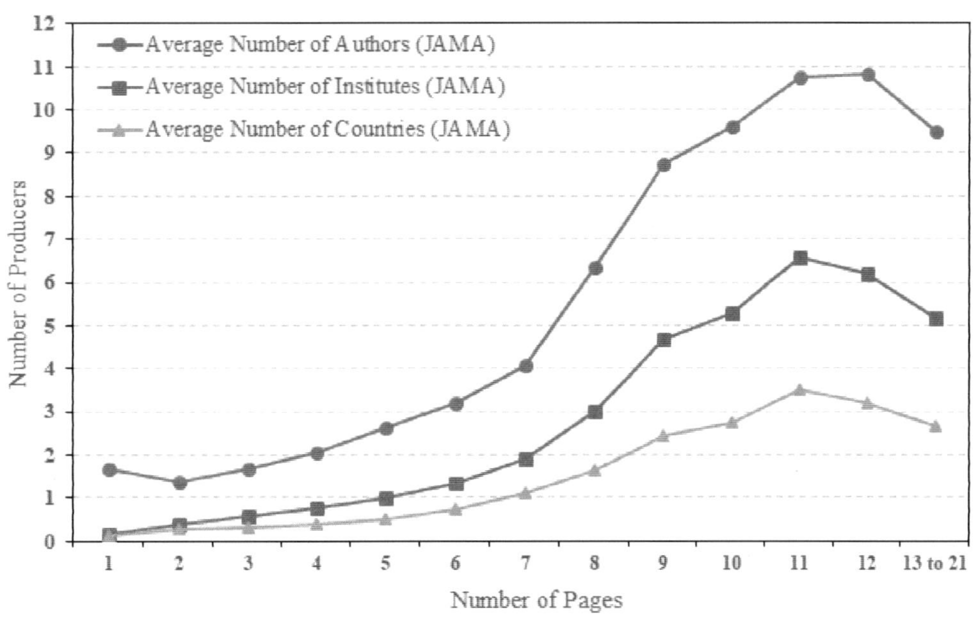

Figure 5. Relationships between producers of articles and article length for JAMA Papers

Figure 5. demonstrates a similar outcome for JAMA articles, but with the difference that, there is a slight decrease in the average values for articles of more than 11 pages, which are grouped together. It can be concluded from these observations that, in general, larger collaboration teams encourage the production of longer papers (RQ2).

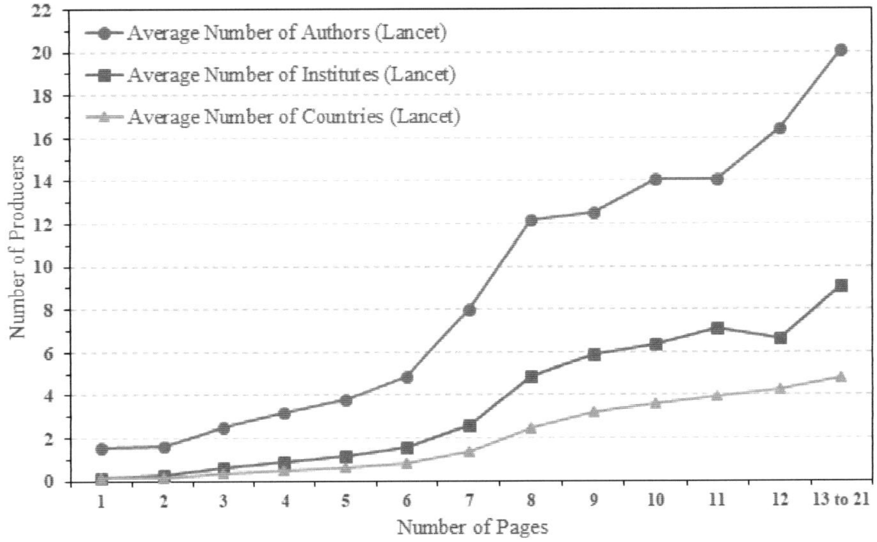

Figure 6. Relationships between producers of articles and article length for Lancet Papers

A similar pattern was observed for Lancet papers in Figure 6. Longer papers have more creators such as authors, institutes and countries for top biomedical journal such as Lancet, which can be understood easily in the big science era.

Article length and its scholarly impact

A high number of citations do not guarantee the quality of a paper, but it is a reliable measure of its impact and/or visibility in biomedical research domains. In previous research, it has been widely believed that the positive relationship of paper length on its citations results from a greater number of citable elements in longer papers, such as more data and ideas (Fox, Paine, & Sauterey, 2016).

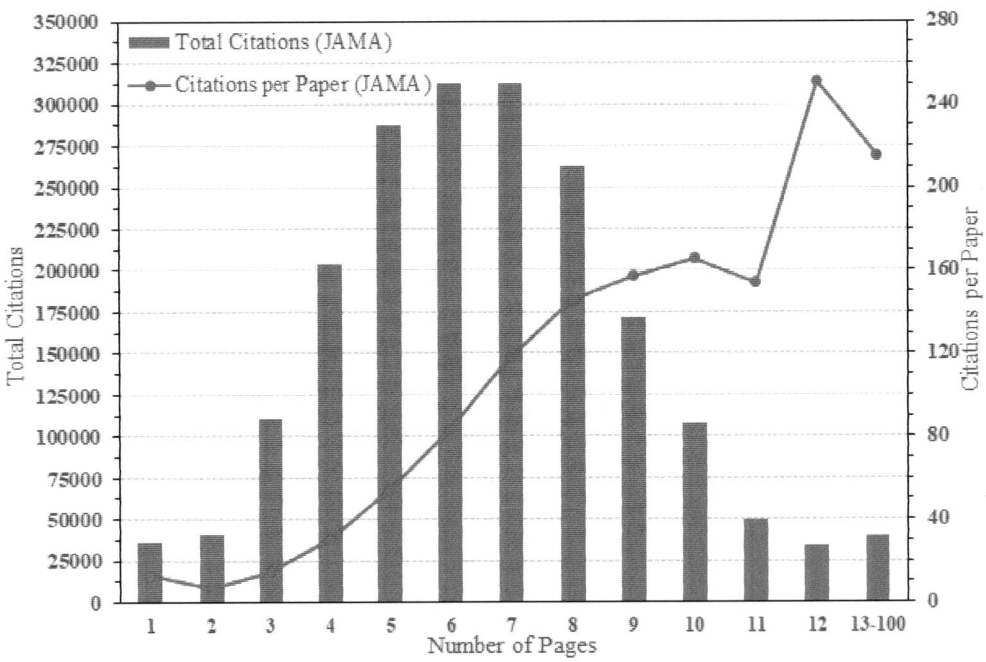

Figure 7. Relationships between citations and article length for JAMA papers

Specifically, two indicators should be adopted, total citations and citations per paper, as measurements to inspect the relationships between paper length and number of citations in each journal (Onodera & Yoshikane, 2015). However, the current study demonstrates a set of unexpected, but consistent, results from the explorations of these three top biomedical journals studied. The results for the three journals are summarized in Figures 7, 8 and 9. Due to the small number of longer papers with varying numbers of citations received, these were grouped together to provide an overall indication of the citation patterns for these longer publications. Figure 7 summarizes the distribution of the total citations and citations per article for a given article length in NEJM. As can be seen in the diagram, the histogram of total citations illustrates a normal distribution rather than an ascending trend, but the average number of citations per article does show an increasing trend, which is similar to the result reported by (Ball, 2008) for astronomy research.

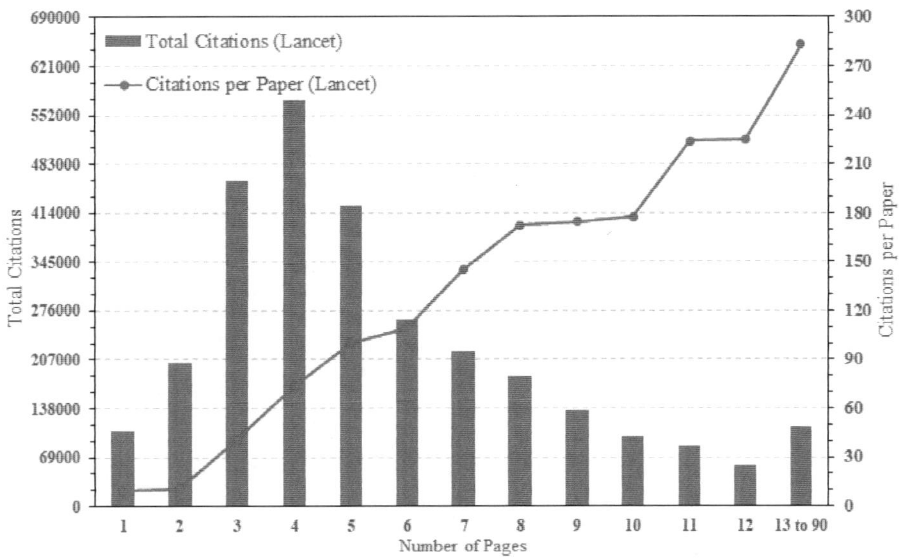

Figure 8. Relationships between citations and article length for Lancet papers

The total number of citations peaks at 6 or 7 pages for NEJM and JAMA (Figure 7.), but this is not necessarily a reflection of the highest citations per article in this case. When superimposed on the total citations, it can be seen that the average number of citations per article continues to increase. In fact, the highest numbers of average citations per paper appear for articles that are 12 pages long and declines slightly for longer papers, but still far more than for shorter papers. A similar relationship can be seen with Lancet in Figure 8. where the longest articles receive, on average, the highest number of citations.

CONCLUSION

Biomedical journals represent a large contributor to the annual production of scholarly communication (Gingras, Lariviere, & Archambault, 2009). What happens in biomedical scholarly literature, therefore, may provide insight into what might occur in other scholarly fields. The "publish or perish" environment in which researchers operate may affect the characteristics of their scholarly output, and ultimately the impact of their work (Weiss, 2007). This study has investigated the relationships between article length and several other article features for three high impact factor biomedical journals to determine if there is an association between article length, publication date, levels of co-authorship and article impact, as measured by the number of citations.

The results confirm that longer articles, on average, receive more citations and are, therefore, considered more impactful. Older articles have the advantage that they have had more time to attract citations, so if there is also a relationship between article length and age, this factor may be associated with the article impact. However, the findings indicate that the average article length for the three journals studied has increased over time, and therefore, although being newer, longer articles attract a higher number of citations. One conclusion this paper may draw is that publishing shorter articles in these journals, which may be motivated by considering the Least Publishable Unit (LPU), might end up resulting in work that is less impactful, at least in the top biomedical journals investigated in this paper.

The primary limitation of this research is the number of journals studied. The three highest impact journals in general and internal medicine were examined. These represent a small window into biomedical research, but they are considered the most influential. The focus on specific journals provides an indication of differences between journals that may be missed if many journals were grouped together. The fact that the three journals displayed similar findings, even though the average lengths of papers published in the three journals varied, suggests that these findings are not unique. Second, we did not examine factors that could influence the article page length, such as the number of tables or figures or the journal's editorial policy. However, we did note that there have not been dramatic changes in the journal layout that could account for the large increase in average article length. Third, variations in institutional affiliation names or multiple affiliations by authors were not considered. Future research is needed to verify whether these findings are also observed for lower impact journals in biomedical fields and other fields. Similarly, a more fine-grained temporal analysis could be conducted where article features for the different time periods are compared for any changes in correlations.

ACKNOWLEDGMENTS

This research was supported in part by a grant from the Natural Science Foundation of China (71661167007, 71771077) and the Hong Kong Scholars Program (XJ-2016064). The authors are grateful to professor Shan-lin Yang, Fei-cheng Ma and Zhou Ping for their helpful discussions and suggestions.

REFERENCES

Antoniou, G. A., Antoniou, S. A., Georgakarakos, E. I., Sfyroeras, G. S., & Georgiadis, G. S. (2015). Bibliometric Analysis of Factors Predicting Increased Citations in the Vascular and Endovascular Literature. Annals of Vascular Surgery, 29(2), 286-292. doi:10.1016/j.avsg.2014.09.017

Ball, P. (2008). A longer paper gathers more citations. Nature, 455(7211), 274-275. doi:10.1038/455274a

Broad, W. J. (1981). The Publishing Game - Getting More for Less. Science, 211(4487), 1137-1139. doi:10.1126/science.7008199

Brown, H. (2007). How impact factors changed medical publishing - and science. British Medical Journal, 334(7593), 561-564. doi:10.1136/bmj.39142.454086.AD

Callaham, M., Wears, R. L., & Weber, E. (2002). Journal prestige, publication bias, and other characteristics associated with citation of published studies in peer-reviewed journals. Jama-Journal of the American Medical Association, 287(21), 2847-2850. doi:10.1001/jama.287.21.2847

Callaway, E. (2016). Bibliometrics Publishing elite turns against impact factor. Nature, 535(7611), 210-211. doi:10.1038/nature.2016.20224

Coleman, R. (1999). Impact factors: Use and abuse in biomedical research. Anatomical Record, 257(2), 54-57.

Falagas, M. E., Zarkali, A., Karageorgopoulos, D. E., Bardakas, V., & Mavros, M. N. (2013). The Impact of Article Length on the Number of Future Citations: A Bibliometric Analysis of General Medicine Journals. Plos One, 8(2), 8. doi:10.1371/journal.pone.0049476

Fox, C. W., Paine, C. E. T., & Sauterey, B. (2016). Citations increase with manuscript length, author number, and references cited in ecology journals. Ecology and Evolution, 6(21), 7717-7726. doi:10.1002/ece3.2505

Garfield, E. (2000). Use of Journal Citation Reports and Journal Performance Indicators in measuring short and long term journal impact. Croatian Medical Journal, 41(4), 368-374.

Gingras, Y., Lariviere, V., & Archambault, E. (2009). Literature Citations in the Internet Era. Science, 323(5910), 36-36.

Glanzel, W., & Schubert, A. (2005). Domesticity and internationality in co-authorship, references and citations. Scientometrics, 65(3), 323-342. doi:10.1007/s11192-005-0277-0

Haslam, N., Ban, L., Kaufmann, L., Loughnan, S., Peters, K., Whelan, J., & Wilson, S. (2008). What makes an article influential? Predicting impact in social and personality psychology. Scientometrics, 76(1), 169-185. doi:10.1007/s11192-007-1892-8

Haustein, S., Costas, R., & Lariviere, V. (2015). Characterizing Social Media Metrics of Scholarly Papers: The Effect of Document Properties and Collaboration Patterns. Plos One, 10(3), 21. doi:10.1371/journal.pone.0120495

Hu, L. H., Liao, Z. A., Gao, R., & Li, Z. S. (2010). High quality medical journals and impact factors. International Journal of Cardiology, 140(3), 362-363. doi:10.1016/j.ijcard.2009.02.041

Onodera, N., & Yoshikane, F. (2015). Factors Affecting Citation Rates of Research Articles. *Journal of the Association for Information Science and Technology*, 66(4), 739-764. doi:10.1002/asi.23209

Rajagopal, T., Archunan, G., Surulinathi, M., & Ponmanickam, P. (2013). Research output in pheromone biology: a case study of India. Scientometrics, 94(2), 711-719. doi:10.1007/s11192-012-0788-4

Slyder, J. B., Stein, B. R., Sams, B. S., Walker, D. M., Beale, B. J., Feldhaus, J. J., & Copenheaver, C. A. (2011). Citation pattern and lifespan: a comparison of discipline, institution, and individual. Scientometrics, 89(3), 955-966. doi:10.1007/s11192-011-0467-x

Stremersch, S., Verniers, I., & Verhoef, P. C. (2007). The quest for citations: Drivers of article impact. Journal of Marketing, 71(3), 171-193. doi:10.1509/jmkg.71.3.171

Tahamtan, I., Afshar, A. S., & Ahamdzadeh, K. (2016). Factors affecting number of citations: a comprehensive review of the literature. Scientometrics, 107(3), 1195-1225. doi:10.1007/s11192-016-1889-2

Weiss, A. P. (2007). Measuring the impact of medical research: Moving from outputs to outcomes. American Journal of Psychiatry, 164(2), 206-214. doi:10.1176/appi.ajp.164.2.206.

What's Cached is Prologue: Reviewing Recent Web Archives Research Towards Supporting Scholarly Use

Emily Maemura
University of Toronto, Canada.
e.maemura@mail.utoronto.ca

ABSTRACT

Web archives are essential to support historical scholarship in the online age. Research on web archives spans many disciplines, often requiring domain-specific expertise. The wide-ranging nature of the literature makes it difficult to obtain a current overview of the field, but this view is needed to identify which core challenges define the field, and assess the different approaches taken to address them. This paper provides such a review of the current landscape of web archives research, focusing on addressing the common challenges faced to support scholarly use of archived web materials. The analysis describes three challenges and identifies key concepts and current approaches for each: (1) how to organize and select from web archives collections; (2) how to critically examine these sources; and (3) how to approach ethics and consent for using archived web materials. The discussion addresses open questions and tensions, highlighting the sociotechnical nature of these challenges and revealing opportunities to apply existing work from the body of knowledge of information studies. It concludes with several recommendations for future research directions to support scholarly use of web archives.

INTRODUCTION

Web archives capture versions of web resources at fixed points in time, in order to prevent the loss of ephemeral web material and preserve digital cultural heritage. The growing number of resources contained in these collections means they are becoming valuable primary sources for researchers from across the humanities and social sciences, who can use these records to study the past 25 years of cultural production and social interaction found on the web. As the amount of materials in web archives collections is increasing, the web archives community must also attend to how these materials are being collected and how they can be used in order to ensure a sustainable future for this work.

'Web Archives Research' is used broadly here to encompass the study of all activities involving web archives. This includes the creation of web archives, and the study of activities like how collections are created with technical tools and systems like web crawlers, as well as the organizational and curatorial aspects of collection development. This also includes the study of activities to support use of web archives, through developing access interfaces or specific research methods and techniques.

It can be difficult to compose a clear overview of the current state of Web Archives Research because of the wide-range of topics it includes. This paper develops such an overview by assembling and analyzing the body of literature in Web Archives Research for the past five years. Several common trends are identified from this recent work, and the research related to three specific challenges is analyzed in depth. The analysis reviews and compares key concepts and examples of the approaches to: (1) exploring, organizing, and delimiting a corpus; (2) critically examining collected materials; and, (3) considering ethics, consent and responsibility when using this material for scholarly work. The discussion further addresses gaps and open questions to be addressed by future work, and several recommendations for web archives research and development of theory going forward, particularly highlighting potential points of connection to other areas of information studies. The contribution of this paper is threefold: to assemble the web archives research literature, to identify common challenges through a synthesis of organizational, curatorial and technical perspectives, and to propose an agenda for Web Archives Research that aligns with the sociotechnical nature of these challenges.

BACKGROUND

The community of practice for creating web archives has centered on institutional programs, in particular the work of the International Internet Preservation Consortium (IIPC) which was formed in 2003, with twelve founding members including the non-profit California-based Internet Archive, the British Library, the National Library of Australia, and the U.S. Library of Congress. The IIPC has now grown to a community in over 45 countries who have collaborated to develop common tools, methods and standards for web archiving (http://netpreserve.org/about-us/). In addition to these large-scale collections by national institutions, many other organizations have begun collecting web materials of varying size and scope, such as websites focused on a single topic or event. The different types of collections, tools, and resources used by these different web archiving initiatives are characterized in several surveys that describe and compare web archiving programs at different institutions (Bailey et al., 2014; Bailey et al., 2017; Costa et al., 2017; Internet Memory Foundation, 2010). Truman (2016) surveys a wide range of practices through interviews, providing a series of 'institutional profiles' and a summary of tools available for different stages of the web archiving process. Webster (2017) provides a contrasting view to these comparative approaches with a cultural history that highlights the influence of Internet Archive from early on, as well as the many national libraries working within legal deposit frameworks. Further, recent developments from the Internet Archive and their subscription service *Archive-It* have focused on 'Community Webs' as local history collections, and it is expected the number of smaller collections from local libraries will increase in the coming years (Rollason-Cass, 2017).

The community of web archives researchers is more challenging to locate and characterize due to the interdisciplinary nature of this work. Research publications in recent years have centred on several events and publication venues. These include several conferences and workshops: Web Archiving and Digital Libraries (WADL) workshops at the Joint Conference on Digital Libraries (JCDL), Working with Internet Archives for Research (WIRE) conference in 2014 (http://wp.comminfo.rutgers.edu/nsfia/), the Web Archives 2015: Capture Curate, Analyze conference (https://www.lib.umich.edu/webarchivesconference), and the Research Infrastructure for the Study of Archived Web materials (RESAW) conferences in Aarhus, Denmark in 2015, and London, UK in 2017. Annual conferences include the Web Archiving Conference held in conjunction with the IIPC General Assembly since 2015, and the annual meetings of the Web Archiving Section of the Society of American Archivists since 2013. Research is also found in several special issues of journals, as well as recent books focused on web history (Brügger, 2016, 2017b; Brügger & Schroeder, 2017; Fox et al., 2018; Gibby & Hockx-Yu, 2014;)

Since there is no single venue or central community of web archives researchers, several organizations and individuals have created bibliographies of key articles on web archives (Archive-It, n.d.; International Internet Preservation Consortium, n.d.; Webster & Milligan, 2014). Ayala (2013) assembles an extensive bibliography, with over 100 publications on web archiving, organized by several categories like challenges, legal issues, practices, standards and tools, and research on web archives. Select sources are also highlighted by Brügger (forthcoming) who describes key anthologies and journals, existing web collections, and select literature on web archiving and web history. While these various listings and bibliographies provide initial points of entry to the field, none of the recent work aggregates the wide range of publications on web archives. Such an overview is needed to address how web archives research has developed and understand the direction it currently takes.

REVIEWING AND ANALYZING THE RECENT WEB ARCHIVES RESEARCH LITERATURE

I begin by assembling a list of research papers representing the current web archives literature, largely located through the bibliographies and sources listed above. In contrast to a systematic literature search, this approach was chosen because of the wide-ranging venues of publication, and the ambiguous definitions of "web archives" returning non-relevant items when searching article databases. The full bibliography of recent web archives literature - 185 items published between 2013 and early 2018 - is available as supplemental material (Maemura, 2018). These sources serve as the starting point for the analysis below that identifies and develops common themes, trends and challenges.

From Optimizing Collections to an Agenda for Supporting Scholarly Use

A great deal of research continues to develop new ways to optimize the process of collecting, and improve the coverage or completeness of web archives materials. This includes, for example, the development of metrics for archivability and methods to capture dynamic Javascript content (Banos & Manolopoulos, 2016; Brunelle et al., 2016; Kelly et al., 2013). There have also been developments to automate discovery of new content for genres like blogs or websites of public broadcasters (Baltussen et al., 2014; Kasioumis et al., 2013). This work focuses on developing solutions to create better, more complete, or more timely web archives; it remains a major challenge for archives to keep up with the changing technologies of the web.

The need for the web archives community to support research users is noted in several earlier publications and reports (Dougherty et al., 2010; Meyer et al., 2011; Stirling et al., 2012; Thomas et al., 2010). This research direction is extended in papers from Hockx-Yu (2014) and Dougherty & Meyer (2014) who ask how web archives can engage users and suggest specific approaches. Hockx-Yu (2014) provides examples of how researchers have worked with the British Library's UK Web Archive, and recommendations towards a goal of 'ready-to-download' datasets for scholars. Dougherty & Meyer (2014) identify several common themes and challenges of web archiving through interviews with librarians and archivists, researchers, and technologists from the U.S., U.K., and Europe. They highlight the lack of research and development to support access, and the need for improved navigation interfaces, as well as indexing and search to support detailed analysis. Interviewees suggest a number of specific solutions, including building community towards development of standards and tools, as well as funding to support both infrastructure and individual archiving activities. Together, these papers set an agenda for the development of search tools, and also emphasize that the importance of community engagement in development efforts.

This agenda has been advanced by institutional initiatives like the development of an Archive Research Services (ARS) workshop by the Internet Archive (https://github.com/vinaygoel/ars-workshop), and a competition by the Portuguese Web Archives to promote use of their collection (http://sobre.arquivo.pt/en/arquivo-pt-prizes-2018-call-for-submissions). Additionally, several 'researcher-centric' projects and initiatives have made existing web archives collections available to scholars while also studying their approaches and the outcomes. This includes: projects from NetLab in Denmark (netlab.dk); the WebART project with the National Library of the Netherlands (www.webarchiving.nl); the British Library's BUDDAH project (https://buddah.projects.history.ac.uk/), and predecessor AADDA (http://www.history.ac.uk/projects/digital/AADDA); and development of Warcbase with the Archives Unleashed project in Canada and the US (archivesunleashed.org). It is notable that while these initiatives often serve to further technical developments like indexing tools and search interfaces, they are not framed as 'user testing' to evaluate performance of specific tasks; instead, they are framed in a way that ensures researcher perspectives and needs are primary concerns. The insights emerging from these projects are of particular interest here in that they address the goals set out in the agenda to build community.

Through this work, as well as through methodological and theoretical reflections by individual researchers, three common challenges arise (Weber, 2017; Winters, 2017). First, there is a need to further develop specific methods and approaches for researchers to explore and organize a collection. Second, working with web archives reveals the need to identify and address which resources are absent, or outside the scope of a given collection. Third, many of the researchers encounter questions of ethics, asking who has responsibility for how data is collected, maintained, and used, and who ultimately has power to determine what is or is not archived. Approaches to each of these challenges are discussed in detail below, presenting key theoretical concepts that have been developed by past work, as well as how these concepts have been applied in specific studies and projects.

Challenge 1: Exploring and Organizing a Collection

Scholars working with web archives need to find and select the content relevant for their research questions. Technical and methodological challenges arise from the scale of data processing. Methodologically, determining the different steps necessary to define a subset (e.g. a corpus or a dataset) can also be a challenge. Conceptual challenges also arise in searching and exploring web archives, as researchers must familiarize themselves with the form of archived material, and how this relates to the definitions and formats of their own discipline. For example Ankerson (2015) uses web archives to study new media objects, and Shumate and Weber (2015) take a social science perspective on collecting web data. Milligan (2016) takes the perspective of a historian, addressing the range of technological methods needed to access and use these new types of sources.

Previous work has developed several central concepts that provide a point of entry to delimit materials for analysis. Five conceptual 'web strata' define typical objects of analysis: (1) *the web element* or individual resource such as an image defined by a URI; (2) *the web page,* the assembled resources that are rendered in a browser to present a single HTML document; (3) *the website*, a number of connected pages within a web domain; (4) *the web sphere*, or the inter-connected network of sites covering a topic or event; and, (5) *the web as a whole* (Brügger, 2013a). These strata build upon each other, and ultimately all reduce to individual resources, and the hyperlinks between those resources. Archived resources are associated with a standardized timestamp, and the Memento extension of the HTTP protocol provides a common framework and infrastructure for retrieving different time-based versions across web archival holdings (Van de Sompel et al., 2009). Hyperlinks can also be considered at different scales, and link direction (in-links, out-links), and internal (intra-domain) or external (inter-domain) links may also be relevant for analysis.

Multiple procedures and techniques are often combined to explore a web archive collections. In addition to selection of particular URIs, pages, or sites, other qualities or characteristics of the content may be drawn upon in the analysis. This includes drawing on qualities of text formats like sorting by mark-up structures or performing analyses like named entity recognition or topic modelling. Similarly, approaches to the study of images might perform visual analysis or use embedded metadata like geographic location.

To illustrate how these concepts are used, some select example approaches are discussed here. One approach used by several projects is to focus on a single website as the unit of analysis. Materials are selected by specifying a single URL (or set of URLs) and comparing or analyzing the changes to form and content over time. Rogers (2017) describes the process of creating 'screencast documentaries' that assemble images of a website homepage over time to enable a visual analysis of changes to design elements. Nanni (2017) similarly reconstructs the University of Bologna's website from a variety of sources.

A second approach is to combine the concepts above to develop a dataset with multiple dimensions for analysis. Huurdeman et al. (2013) provide examples for specific research questions studying a collection from the National Library of the Netherlands' web archives focused on news aggregator site 'nu.nl'. One example takes articles on different topics (e.g. Hurricane Sandy, Syria, and US Elections) and studies the out-links on those pages, comparing which domains are most frequently linked to as references in these new stories. This revealed which topics had references predominantly to other news sites in Dutch, or in English, and which link to Wikipedia, Google Maps, or YouTube. In another example, individual images are extracted based on a keyword search for "Mubarak" and are then plotted on a timeline for visual analysis.

Further comparing the findings from past work, there are notable differences between using these concepts to organize a collection at different points in the research process. Lin et al. (2017) present examples for how a scholar can begin to explore and orient herself to a collection, using the case of a collection capturing websites from Canadian Political Parties. They describe methods of creating link graphs as a navigational tool, suggesting that locating central domains or studying out-links can provide entry points for further questions. They propose that a researcher can follow a series of steps to Filter, Analyze, Aggregate, and Visualize (FAAV), and suggest that several iterations over these steps may be needed. This work highlights that users have different information needs in early stages using exploratory methods, compared with moving towards more targeted analysis based on domain-specific content to address a particular research question.

Several open questions and tensions on the processes of exploring and organizing web archives remain to be addressed by future work, in particular: what kinds of analyses align with what forms of corpora or datasets? Many of these recent studies and reflections have surfaced the challenge of connecting available data with appropriate research methodologies. One determining factor is the scope and scale - at a certain size, a corpus requires a shift from methods like close-reading to computational analysis. Both Hockx-Yu (2014) and Ben-David & Huurdeman (2014) note a shift in methodology is required at a certain scale, and distinguish between 'document-centric' and 'whole-collection' approaches. Further, developing approaches to whole-collection analysis relates to the open question of how standardized or customized data and methods should be. The approach by the Internet Archive in their ARS workshops has been towards standardized corpus formats for research: Web Archive Transformation (WAT), Web Archive Named Entities (WANE), Longitudinal Graph Analysis (LGA) that enable analysis of item metadata, named entities (people, places, organizations), and link graphs, respectively – all derivatives of the standard WebARChive (WARC) file format (Bailey & Goel, 2015). Others like the WebART project note that they have developed custom formats for researchers in the context of 'data sprints' but this would not be feasible or sustainable as an ongoing practice (Huurdeman et al., 2013).

Further, it is observed that approaches can fall along a spectrum: some approaches sort and organize by taking advantage of standard data structures in archived materials, for example, taking metadata fields recorded by a crawler like the timestamp, file format, or URL of a resource; other approaches rely upon domain-specific classification or 'coding' and interpretation of materials relative to the context a particular research question. Other examples challenge the separation between 'content' and 'container' by taking the infrastructural elements of the web like tracker cookies as the object of study, or even interrogating the archival search interface itself (Ben-David & Huurdeman, 2014; Helmond, 2017). In addition, one can consider the labour involved in making selections, and how it is spread across human and non-human actors (Maemura et al., 2018; Ogden et al., 2017; Summers & Punzalan, 2017).

Challenge 2: Critically Examining Collected Materials

In addition to selecting materials from web archives, scholars also need to evaluate this material in order to understand what is and is not included in web archives. An essential starting point is understanding that archived materials differ significantly from the live web. Past work has discussed the nature of web archives as new versions (not copies) of web materials; the archived version is understood as both a 'subjective reconstruction' and 'always deficient' when compared to the live web (Brügger 2013b; Brügger & Finnemann, 2013). Brügger (2013a) further describes a web archive as being 'both incomplete and too complete', meaning that web archives will never capture all materials from the web, but they may also capture some materials with greater frequency or depth than others. A scholar working with web archives must both surface the materials absent from a collection, and surface the biases in a collection's construction that may skew the interpretation of results.

Several authors have identified the need for 'source criticism' when working with web archives, and the challenge of determining reliability or veracity of materials (Rogers, 2017; Brügger 2013b; Nanni, 2017). These discuss three main approaches:

- examining the source itself for evidence of absences or inconsistencies;
- triangulating with other sources (online or offline); and,
- tracing the process of creation by drawing on documentation.

It should also be acknowledged that these concepts are not unique to web archives, and connect to source criticism in the traditions of analytical bibliography, archival diplomatics and provenance. However, when working with archived web materials, new methods may be required for performing source criticism computationally and at scale, and some of these emerging approaches are discussed here.

One approach to source criticism is through analyzing inconsistencies within the material, and how this might impact its reliability as a source. For example, absences may be encountered when viewing an archived web page, as Winters notes "A missing image confronts us with a blank square on the web page; a broken link produces an error" (Winters, 2017, p. 245). Analyzing a whole collection, Huurdeman et al. (2015) describe approaches to address 'the unarchived' by identifying 'the aura' of a collection, defined as the resources just beyond the boundary of a collection i.e. links are present within the archive, but the resources are not captured. Other inconsistencies may be harder to identify or resolve. At the level of the page, there may be temporal inconsistencies between individual resources like text and images captured at different times. At a larger scale, questions of inconsistency arise with visualizations produced from extracted data. Lin et al., (2017) use a bar chart visualization to observe some 'suspicious' statistics of a collection whose distribution of pages from different websites varies widely by crawl date. Similarly, Laursen & Møldrup-Dalum (2017) visualize data from the Danish *Netarkivet* collection over ten years and the resulting chart reveals uncharacteristic spikes or dips. These visualizations can identify outliers in the overall trend, but it is difficult to determine what this means or if this is correct, since, "nobody knows what the data is supposed to look like." (Laursen & Møldrup-Dalum, 2017, p. 209).

A second approach to source criticism is to compare multiple sources. At a small scale, a researcher can compare the archived version of a webpage to screenshots of that page from contemporary newspapers and magazines, or descriptions of a page's content from other archival sources (see e.g. Nanni, 2017; Ankerson, 2015). At a larger scale, several studies have tested methods and approaches for comparing coverage between different web archives, or between archives and 'the live web'. I focus here on studies that compare coverage between collections for a particular research topic or domain, as opposed to general quantitative evaluation of an archive's coverage compared to what exists on the live web (e.g. Ainsworth et al., 2011; Ainsworth et al., 2015; Brunelle et al., 2015). For example, Brügger (2013a) considers the coverage of material relating to Danish parliamentary elections by comparing historical network graphs available from the Danish *Netarkivet* collection and the Internet Archive. Samar et al. (2016) analyze coverage of trending topics for the Netherlands in 2014 by comparing the National Library of the Netherlands' web archive to the *Common Crawl* dataset. Milligan et al. (2016) use a case study of Canadian federal elections, comparing collections resulting from three different crawling strategies: starting with curated seed lists, collecting URLs from public tweets for a given hashtag, and broad crawls by the Internet Archive. Hale et al. (2017) similarly compare the archive and the live web for a population of web pages from *TripAdvisor*.

A third approach to source criticism is to review documentation and trace the process leading to particular datasets or artifacts. This can be difficult since documentation may not always exist, or may not be readily available to the scholar. Certain questions about the composition of the archived data can only be answered with details about how a crawl was conducted. For example, Lin et al. (2017) find that the bar graph visualization provokes a number of questions that may be explained by documentation of the crawl settings, or a change in the crawl policy. Alternatively, when Laursen and Møldrup-Dalum (2017) analyzed their visualization of data collected each year it led them to further examine documentation on the harvests to explain a large dip in 2010; ultimately they traced the anomaly to an error in the data extraction process to generate the visualization which requires long processing times and many steps for data preparation.

While the need for documentation and transparency is becoming more widely recognized, it remains unclear which type of documentation is necessary at what stages of the research process, and how this might be presented as part of an access interface. Recent initiatives like the OCLC's study of descriptive metadata provide recommendations for metadata to describe actors like collectors and creators, as well as elements about scope or extent of a collection (Dooley & Bowers, 2018). They further acknowledge that future work must address 'machine-actionable description' both to extract metadata, and to enable discovery and access at scale. Others have taken up an ethnographic approach that richly describes the web archiving process but is not easily translated to standard forms (Ogden et al., 2017).

Challenge 3: Approaches to Ethics and Consent

Underlying all of the methodological challenges described above, a scholar working with web archives must consider the ethical implications of how materials are used, questions of consent, and her responsibility to the people represented in this data. There are (at least) two sets of ethical frameworks that can influence this work: the ethics of collecting (which may be informed by institutional policies as well as professional codes of ethics) and the ethics of performing research (which may be informed or limited by requirements of Institutional Review Boards). Much of the professional and institutional discussions focus on the impact of legislation for copyright and privacy. However, it should be noted that the legal authority for collecting is not enough to address ethical practice, and additionally, assumptions and interpretations of these concepts vary across contexts. Past work by Rauber et al. (2008) focuses on ethical questions to identify and challenge the core assumptions inherent in archiving the web as a publication medium. Dougherty (2013) further describes how use of the web has evolved and reconfigured as an extension of self, resulting in complicated, conflicting expectations and interpretations of the private and the personal in online expression. Additional complications arise when studies span multiple legal jurisdictions with differing stances on issues like the right to be forgotten.

A common approach to manage use of web archives to protect privacy is by placing restrictions or limits on access. Many of the examples above use the Internet Archive whose collection is openly accessible through the public Wayback Machine and additionally via APIs (https://archive.org/help/wayback_api.php). Other collections restrict access to varying degrees – for example, the Danish *Netarkivet* requires researchers to apply for access, and the UK Web Archive has some publicly accessible content, but access to the full collection is only on-site. Taking a more active stance to manage or monitor use, Rauber et al. (2008) outline technological approaches to identify malicious users, and to classify personally identifiable content.

Another approach for addressing ethical questions and privacy is to consider when and how permission is granted to ingest materials into the archive. In creating the archive, an organization may use an opt-in model that requires the archive to contact individual website owners to inform them their material will be archived which is difficult to manage at scale. The alternative is an opt-out model where archiving proceeds unless a site owner explicitly denies permission. Some organizations infer permission is granted (or denied) by a website's robots.txt file that can specify which parts of a website may or may not be crawled, and by which specific crawlers. Other archives may have the legal authority to capture material whether or not granted explicit permission by a website owner. Further, much recent work focuses on social media collections, but these raise new questions of ethics and consent, and come with a different set of concerns around privacy and user agreements made directly with social media platforms (and subject to change without notice).

Different approaches may be considered by researchers using web archives, who are guided by frameworks like informed consent of participants. Weber (2017) notes that research ethics boards are still adapting to address web materials, and "a central challenge with regards to ethics of web based research is that many of the existing mechanisms for oversight are working to catch up with technology" (p. 132). Milligan (2016) discusses some of the considerations for privacy when working with *GeoCities* data, and how this depends on whether or not data is viewed in aggregate, and whether the original author of a website considered its content available to a wide or narrow audience.

Limitations

The analysis above is developed from examples drawn from the literature, and is limited to English-language publications. It is important to reflect here on how this research literature is situated, its limitations, and what is absent from this analysis. Many of the projects highlighted here centre on collections by IIPC members like the Internet Archive and national libraries – and would not encounter materials that fall outside these organizations' mandates, are not in their interest to collect, or are complicated by legal barriers, or technical issues to ingest at scale. While new tools are also becoming available for personal archiving and community archives of web materials – for example Documenting the Now (docnow.io), Web Archiving Integration Layer (WAIL https://machawk1.github.io/wail/), and Webrecorder (webrecorder.io) – the study of personal and community web archives is not well represented in the current literature. If and how more personal and community collections can be used in research remains an open question since the archives may have missions at cross-purposes to scholarly communications, or work outside the legal and ethical requirements of academic institutions.

GAPS AND RECOMMENDATIONS

The above examples have addressed the different methods, conceptual frameworks and approaches that are being developed for supporting scholarly use of web archives. First, while the original agenda to engage users had set the goal to develop search and navigation interfaces, these recent studies reveal that scholars explore these collections through a series of complex processes for selection and delimitation of archived web materials. Even before starting a search, a scholar must gain an understanding of both a collection's content, scope and focus, as well as the unique material conditions and constraints of archived web artifacts. Jackson et al. (2016) describe that many scholars 'don't know where to start' when approaching web archives and there is little available to guide scholars in this exploratory work. Second, the need for documentation and transparency in all steps of the process of creating and using web archives is a paramount concern. They also illustrate that source criticism may require an iterative process involving many different views of a collection. Statistical analyses may identify gaps or inconsistencies in a collection, leading to close inspection of individual elements. But it is difficult to address exactly why these differences occur and how that impacts interpretation or analysis, and some questions can only be answered by consulting with the individuals involved. There is generally a pressing need for documentation of the process of creating web archives (Brügger, 2013a; Winters, 2017). Finally, there is simply not enough discussion of ethics in the field (with the exception of the recent National Forum on Ethics and Archiving the Web https://eaw.rhizome.org/). New approaches are needed that go beyond the binary of 'opt-in' or 'opt-out' models, and that are possible to scale with current resources.

Across all these challenges, there is also a need to balance between human and non-human labour, especially for large-scale collections. While the entire World Wide Web of 1997 was estimated at a size of 650,000 sites, today a single national web archives collection can rival or exceed that size - the Danish *Netarkivet* Collection contained over 1.2 Million unique domains as of 2015 (Brügger et al., 2017; Gray, 1996). Managing these collections of millions of individual web resources, is further complicated by the need to manage multiple versions of each resource captured at different times, over decades. Providing access to data at this large scale will require methods from computer science to address technical challenges, as is reflected in much of the recent literature that focuses on addressing user needs through technical development. However, I argue that the analysis presented here reveals that these challenges to support research use of web archives are sociotechnical in nature.

The body of knowledge from Information Studies (IS) therefore offers opportunities and an existing body of research that web archives might draw upon. Several possible points of connection between core web archives concepts and existing approaches from IS are identified and described here. First, there is an affinity between the various approaches to delineate a corpus or dataset, and the long history of classification, representation and knowledge organization. The existing literature on information seeking behaviour and user studies in information retrieval would provide a useful approach for studying this question of 'where to start', as well as concepts like conducting reference interviews to identify information goals and needs.

Approaches to critically examining collected materials can draw from precedents in source criticism, and archival diplomatics (as also noted in Winters, 2017). The concepts and theory of archival provenance, as well as media-specific analysis, can provide approaches to understand how materials are embedded in a specific, historicized sociotechnical context. These approaches reframe the problem – it is not simply a matter of providing efficient or effective access, but of carefully considering the impact of information organization and representation, and how different information structures can emphasize or elide the ways the archived materials are shaped by the constraints of web medium, and web infrastructure – and the infrastructure of the archive itself.

Addressing ethics and consent is more difficult, and I highlight here the need to bridge between the legal frameworks that influence collecting and the ethics frameworks of conducting research. Many existing collections that originate from legal deposit consider websites to be 'publications' and the primary framework influencing research use with this material is copyright law. Other large-scale collections like government web archives treat materials as government records. However, as the web has evolved, 'publication' and 'record' no longer seem adequate as metaphors for the activities on social media sites and other platforms. It can be argued that these materials should be treated less like individually authored publications, and more as traces of communications or activities of daily life – for research purposes these should be treated as data of human subjects. From a researcher perspective, working with this data requires mechanisms to ensure informed consent of web creators, as well as opportunities for creators to specify how their data may or may not be used in the future. Discussions in critical library and information studies may be relevant for web archives, and similar work that addresses power and politics of creating collections. A more practical approach might be found in traditional mechanisms like donor agreements for archives. Ultimately this may also require re-evaluating the purpose of web archives, and redefining the role of web archivists as more active mediators between researchers who use web archives and the individuals who are the subjects of the data collected in those archives. For the ethics and responsibilities of using web archives as scholarly sources, many questions lead back to the overarching purpose of archives, such as who these archives serve, and to whom they are accountable. Web archives might also benefit from reviewing how archives have been framed in the past, particularly the archival paradigms described by Cook (2013) – archives as evidence, memory, identity, community – and which of these paradigms fits with the goals of different web archiving initiatives.

Finally, like other work in the digital humanities, a core question for web archiving is how to use computational methods without necessarily having the work driven by computational thinking; there is also a need for perspectives that critically reflect on the construction of data ontologies used in the development of tools and quantitative methods. For example, computational approaches that can be used to seek out absences in a collection may be grounded in a particular position of truth and veracity that presumes completeness can be measured quantitatively against a perfectly complete past version (i.e. a Platonic ideal). In contrast, other approaches adopt a humanistic perspective to create a transparently subjective reconstruction of a past web artifact, consciously acknowledging the limits of reproducing the past state of an object (questioning the limits of identity, permanence, and fixity). As web archiving develops and engages researchers from across humanities, social sciences and computational sciences, more work is needed to address and explicate the fundamentally different world views represented in these different areas of research. The tensions amongst different methodological and epistemological viewpoints in web archiving were noted by Dougherty and Meyer (2014) and in many ways this remains a central challenge. While it is necessary to develop shared practices and standards for this large-scale distributed work, it is also important to address how web archives can support a range of scholarly work with diverse models, methods and approaches.

In summary, I highlight here five areas for potential future work, to address the current challenges and gaps in the literature:

1. **Conduct studies to characterize user communities:** allowing for web archives to more clearly define and characterize their community of users (existing or aspirational) – and acknowledge when these users are not from a cohesive singular community. Recent work by Costea (2018) addresses users and non-users, but there is a need for more studies aimed at addressing the epistemological and ontological orientations of user communities towards web materials and how that impacts their needs – whether these are practical needs like access to data via APIs, or conceptual framing of the collected materials like an interest in preserving particular interface behaviours, or paratextual element like targeted ads.
2. **Explore new approaches to consent:** developing models and approaches to engage with web content creators in order to

discuss and agree upon future uses of data. One option explored in work and project like Documenting the Now (docnow.io) is to collaborate directly with particular online communities to develop archives of their materials. More work is needed that explores researcher perspectives, and the ethics concerns arising from use of smaller, curated, community-driven collections, in contrast to larger-scale collections with access and privacy restrictions.

3. **Test methods across collections:** contributing more cases of testing how methods perform across different collections. Existing work tends to focus on single collections, or the context of a national archive, and these can be extended to develop more common statistical evaluations, and heuristics for selecting a particular version of a webpage (for a start, some 'rules' are presented in Brügger, 2011 and 'probes' discussed in Brügger (2017a)). In order to test methods across a wide range of web archiving infrastructures, funding opportunities are needed that can support work internationally.
4. **Develop standard concepts and models:** particularly, developing precise and consistent core terminology to describe key concepts, that can bridge between abstract concepts of researchers and connect to the highly specific language of technical work. Potentially this could develop into a formal model for the kinds of problems being tackled by different studies of web archives research.
5. **Ensure continuous availability of research outputs:** As a more practical recommendation, the web archives research community would benefit from a common repository or database of literature. This paper and the accompanying bibliography are intended as a start to building such a resource to aid those entering the field.

I hope these points can serve as an agenda for web archives research and support further development of web archives theory.

CONCLUSION

The review of recent web archives literature presented here reveals the core challenges to support and engage scholarly users, and argues that the sociotechnical nature of these challenges can benefit from the theories and approaches of Information Studies. The discussion section further identifies gaps and recommends specific areas that future web archives research work might explore. This overview of literature and research also begins to highlight the need to critically reflect upon collecting practices, evaluating how they are meeting the needs of users in order to ensure the overall utility and sustainability of future of web archiving work.

ACKNOWLEDGMENTS

This work is supported by the Social Sciences and Humanities Research Council (SSHRC) Canada Graduate Scholarship 767-2015-2217 and Michael Smith Foreign Study Supplement.

REFERENCES

Ainsworth, S. G., Alsum, A., SalahEldeen, H., Weigle, M. C., & Nelson, M. L. (2011). How much of the web is archived? In *Proceedings of the 11th Joint Conference on Digital Libraries* (pp. 133–136). Ottawa, ON, Canada: ACM Press. doi:10.1145/1998076.1998100

Ainsworth, S. G., Nelson, M. L., & Van de Sompel, H. (2015). Only One Out of Five Archived Web Pages Existed as Presented (pp. 257–266). ACM Press. https://doi.org/10.1145/2700171.2791044

Ankerson, M. S. (2015). Read/Write the Digital Archive: Strategies for Historical Web Research. In C. Sandvig & E. Hargittai (Eds.), *Digital research confidential: the secrets of studying behavior online.* (pp. 29–54). Cambridge, MA: MIT Press.

Archive-It. (n.d.). Web Archiving Reading List. Retrieved March 23, 2018, from https://archive-it.org/blog/projects/community-webs/web-archiving-reading-list/

Ayala, B. R. (2013, June 28). Web Archiving Bibliography 2013. Retrieved March 27, 2017, from https://digital.library.unt.edu/ark:/67531/metadc172362/m1/1/

Bailey, J., & Goel, V. (2015, May 29). Datasets Available. Retrieved August 5, 2016, from https://webarchive.jira.com/wiki/display/ARS/Datasets+Available

Bailey, J., Grotke, A., Hanna, K., Hartman, C., McCain, E., Moffatt, C., & Taylor, N. (2014). *Web Archiving in the United States: a 2013 Survey*. National Digital Stewardship Alliance. Retrieved from http://www.digitalpreservation.gov/ndsa/working_groups/documents/NDSA_USWebArchivingSurvey_2013.pdf

Bailey, J., Grotke, A., McCain, E., Moffatt, C., & Taylor, N. (2017). *Web Archiving in the United States: a 2016 Survey*. National Digital Stewardship Alliance. Retrieved from http://ndsa.org/documents/WebArchivingintheUnitedStates_A2016Survey.pdf

Baltussen, L. B., Blom, J., Medjkoune, L., Pop, R., Van Gorp, J., Huurdeman, H., & Haaijer, L. (2014). Hard Content, Fab Front-End: Archiving Websites of Dutch Public Broadcasters. *Alexandria, 25*(1–2), 69–91. https://doi.org/10.7227/ALX.0021

Banos, V., & Manolopoulos, Y. (2016). A quantitative approach to evaluate Website Archivability using the CLEAR+ method. *International Journal on Digital Libraries*, *17*(2), 119–141. https://doi.org/10.1007/s00799-015-0144-4

Ben-David, A., & Huurdeman, H. (2014). Web Archive Search as Research: Methodological and Theoretical Implications. *Alexandria*, *25*(1), 93–111. https://doi.org/10.7227/ALX.0022

Brown, A. (2006). *Archiving websites: a practical guide for information management professionals*. London: Facet Pub.

Brügger, N. (2005). *Archiving websites: general considerations and strategies*. Århus, Denmark: Centre for Internet Research.

Brügger, N. (2011). Web archiving — between past, present, and future. In M. Consalvo & C. Ess (Eds.), *The handbook of internet studies* (pp. 24–42). Malden, MA: Wiley-Blackwell.

Brügger, N. (2013a). Historical Network Analysis of the Web. *Soc. Sci. Comp. Review*, *31*(3), 306–321. doi:10.1177/0894439312454267

Brügger, N. (2013b). Web historiography and Internet Studies: Challenges and perspectives. *New Media & Society*, *15*(5), 752–764. https://doi.org/10.1177/1461444812462852

Brügger, N. (2016). Introduction: The Web's first 25 years. *New Media & Society*, *18*(7), 1059–1065. doi:10.1177/1461444816643787

Brügger, N. (2017a). Probing a nation's web domain: a new approach to web history and a new kind of historical source. In G. Goggin & M. J. McLelland (Eds.), *The Routledge companion to global internet histories* (pp. 61–73). New York: Routledge.

Brügger, N. (Ed.). (2017b). *Web 25: histories from the first 25 years of the World Wide Web*. New York: Peter Lang.

Brügger, N. (forthcoming). Web Archiving. In P. Moy (Ed.), *Oxford Bibliographies in Communication*. Oxford University Press.

Brügger, N., & Finnemann, N. O. (2013). The Web and Digital Humanities: Theoretical and Methodological Concerns. *Journal of Broadcasting & Electronic Media*, *57*(1), 66–80. https://doi.org/10.1080/08838151.2012.761699

Brügger, N., Laursen, D., & Nielsen, J. (2017). Exploring the domain names of the Danish web. In N. Brügger & R. Schroeder (Eds.), *The Web as History* (pp. 62–80). London: UCL Press.

Brügger, N., & Schroeder, R. (Eds.). (2017). *The Web as History: Using Web Archives to Understand the Past and the Present.* London: UCL Press. Retrieved from http://oapen.org/download?type=document&docid=625768

Brunelle, J. F., Kelly, M., SalahEldeen, H., Weigle, M. C., & Nelson, M. L. (2015). Not all mementos are created equal: measuring the impact of missing resources. *International Journal on Digital Libraries*, *16*(3–4), 283–301. https://doi.org/10.1007/s00799-015-0150-6

Brunelle, J. F., Kelly, M., Weigle, M. C., & Nelson, M. L. (2016). The impact of JavaScript on archivability. *International Journal on Digital Libraries*, *17*(2), 95–117. https://doi.org/10.1007/s00799-015-0140-8

Cook, T. (2013). Evidence, memory, identity, and community: four shifting archival paradigms. *Archival Science*, *13*(2–3), 95–120. https://doi.org/10.1007/s10502-012-9180-7

Costa, M., Gomes, D., & Silva, M. J. (2017). The evolution of web archiving. *IJDL*, *18*(3), 191–205. doi:10.1007/s00799-016-0171-9

Costea, M. (2018). *Report on the scholarly use of web archives*. NetLab. Retrieved from http://netlab.dk/wp-content/uploads/2018/02/Costea_Report_on_the_Scholarly_Use_of_Web_Archives.pdf

Dooley, J., & Bowers, K. (2018). *Descriptive Metadata for Web Archiving: Recommendations of the OCLC Research Library Partnership Web Archiving Metadata Working Group*. OCLC Research. https://doi.org/10.25333/C3005C

Dougherty, M. (2013). Property or Privacy? Reconfiguring Ethical Concerns Around Web Archival Research Methods. *Selected Papers of Internet Research*, *3*(0). Retrieved from http://spir.aoir.org/index.php/spir/article/view/735

Dougherty, M., & Meyer, E. T. (2014). Community, tools, and practices in web archiving: The state-of-the-art in relation to social science and humanities research needs. *JASIST*, *65*(11), 2195–2209. https://doi.org/10.1002/asi.23099

Dougherty, M., Meyer, E. T., Madsen, C. M., Heuvel, V. D., Charles, Thomas, A., & Wyatt, S. (2010). *Researcher Engagement with Web Archives: State of the Art.* Rochester, NY: Social Science Research Network. Retrieved from https://papers.ssrn.com/abstract=1714997

Fox, E. A., Klein, M., & Xie, Z. (2018). Guest editors' introduction to the special issue on web archiving. *International Journal on Digital Libraries*, *19*(1), 1–2. https://doi.org/10.1007/s00799-016-0203-5

Gibby, R., & Hockx-Yu, H. (2014). Editorial. *Alexandria*, *25*(1–2), v–vii. https://doi.org/10.7227/ALX.0016

Gray, M. (1996). Web Growth Summary. Retrieved March 18, 2018, from https://stuff.mit.edu/people/mkgray/net/web-growth-summary.html

Hale, S. A., Blank, G., & Alexander, V. D. (2017). Live versus archive: Comparing a web archive to a population of web pages. In N. Brügger & R. Schroeder (Eds.), *The Web as History* (pp. 45–61). London: UCL Press.

Helmond, A. (2017). Historical website ecology. In N. Brügger (Ed.), *Web 25* (pp. 139–156). New York: Peter Lang.

Hockx-Yu, H. (2014). Access and Scholarly Use of Web Archives. *Alexandria*, *25*(1), 113–127. https://doi.org/10.7227/ALX.0023

Huurdeman, H. C., Ben-David, A., & Samar, T. (2013). Sprint Methods for Web Archive Research. In *Proceedings of the 5th Annual ACM Web Science Conference* (pp. 182–190). New York, NY, USA: ACM. https://doi.org/10.1145/2464464.2464513

Huurdeman, H. C., Kamps, J., Samar, T., de Vries, A. P., Ben-David, A., & Rogers, R. A. (2015). Lost but not forgotten: finding pages on the unarchived web. *IJDL*, *16*(3–4), 247–265. https://doi.org/10.1007/s00799-015-0153-3

International Internet Preservation Consortium. (n.d.). Bibliography. Retrieved March 23, 2018, from http://netpreserve.org/web-archiving/bibliography/

Internet Memory Foundation. (2010). *Web Archiving in Europe: A survey provided by the Internet Memory Foundation, 2010.*

Jackson, A., Lin, J., Milligan, I., & Ruest, N. (2016). Desiderata for Exploratory Search Interfaces to Web Archives in Support of Scholarly Activities (pp. 103–106). ACM Press. https://doi.org/10.1145/2910896.2910912

Kasioumis, N., Banos, V., & Kalb, H. (2013). Towards building a blog preservation platform. *World Wide Web*, *17*(4), 799–825. https://doi.org/10.1007/s11280-013-0234-4

Kelly, M., Brunelle, J. F., Weigle, M. C., & Nelson, M. L. (2013). On the Change in Archivability of Websites Over Time. In T. Aalberg, C. Papatheodorou, M. Dobreva, G. Tsakonas, & C. J. Farrugia (Eds.), *Research and Advanced Technology for Digital Libraries* (Vol. 8092, pp. 35–47). Berlin, Heidelberg: Springer Berlin Heidelberg. https://doi.org/10.1007/978-3-642-40501-3_5

Laursen, D., & Møldrup-Dalum, P. (2017). Looking back, looking forward: 10 years of development to collect, preserve, and access the Danish web. In N. Brügger (Ed.), *Web 25* (pp. 207–227). New York: Peter Lang.

Lin, J., Milligan, I., Wiebe, J., & Zhou, A. (2017). Warcbase: Scalable Analytics Infrastructure for Exploring Web Archives. *Journal on Computing and Cultural Heritage*, *10*(4), 1–30. https://doi.org/10.1145/3097570

Maemura, E. (2018). Web Archives Bibliography. https://doi.org/10.5281/zenodo.1293897

Maemura, E., Worby, N., Milligan, I., & Becker, C. (2018). If These Crawls Could Talk: Studying and Documenting Web Archives Provenance. *Journal of the Association for Information Science and Technology*. [early view] https://doi.org/10.1002/asi.24048

Meyer, E. T., Thomas, A., & Schroeder, R. (2011). *Web Archives: The Future(s)*. Retrieved from http://www.ssrn.com/abstract=1830025

Milligan, I. (2016). Lost in the Infinite Archive: The Promise and Pitfalls of Web Archives. *International Journal of Humanities and Arts Computing*, *10*(1), 78–94. https://doi.org/10.3366/ijhac.2016.0161

Milligan, I., Ruest, N., & Lin, J. (2016). Content Selection and Curation for Web Archiving: The Gatekeepers vs. the Masses. In *Proceedings of the 16th Joint Conference on Digital Libraries* (pp. 107–110). Newark, NJ, USA: ACM Press. doi:10.1145/2910896.2910913

Nanni, F. (2017). Reconstructing a website's lost past Methodological issues concerning the history of Unibo.it. *DHQ*, *11*(2). Retrieved from http://digitalhumanities.org/dhq/vol/11/2/000292/000292.html

Ogden, J., Halford, S., & Carr, L. (2017). Observing Web Archives: The Case for an Ethnographic Study of Web Archiving. In *Proceedings of the 2017 ACM on Web Science Conference* (pp. 299–308). Troy, New York, USA: ACM Press. doi:10.1145/3091478.3091506

Rauber, A., Kaiser, M., & Wachter, B. (2008). Ethical Issues in Web Archive Creation and Usage – Towards a Research Agenda. In *8th International Web Archiving Workshop (IWAW'08)*. Aarhus, Denmark.

Rogers, R. (2017). Doing Web history with the Internet Archive: screencast documentaries. *Internet Histories*, *1*(1–2), 160–172. https://doi.org/10.1080/24701475.2017.1307542

Rollason-Cass, S. (2017, June 30). Community Webs to bring web archiving to public libraries. Retrieved April 3, 2018, from https://archive-it.org/blog/post/community-webs-to-bring-web-archiving-to-public-libraries/

Samar, T., Traub, M. C., Ossenbruggen, J. van, & Vries, A. P. de. (2016). Comparing Topic Coverage in Breadth-First and Depth-First Crawls Using Anchor Texts. In *Research and Advanced Technology for Digital Libraries* (pp. 133–146). Springer, Cham. https://doi.org/10.1007/978-3-319-43997-6_11

Shumate, M., & Weber, M. S. (2015). The Art of Web Crawling for Social Science Research. In C. Sandvig & E. Hargittai (Eds.), *Digital research confidential: the secrets of studying behavior online.* (pp. 201–222). Cambridge, MA: MIT Press.

Stirling, P., Chevallier, P., & Illien, G. (2012). Web Archives for Researchers: Representations, Expectations and Potential Uses. *D-Lib Magazine*, *18*(3/4). https://doi.org/10.1045/march2012-stirling

Summers, E., & Punzalan, R. (2017). Bots, Seeds and People: Web Archives as Infrastructure. In *Proceedings of the 2017 ACM Conference on Computer Supported Cooperative Work and Social Computing* (pp. 821–834). ACM Press. doi:10.1145/2998181.2998345

Thomas, A., Meyer, E. T., Dougherty, M., van den Heuvel, C., Madsen, C. M., & Wyatt, S. (2010). *Researcher Engagement with Web Archives*. Rochester, NY: Social Science Research Network. Retrieved from https://papers.ssrn.com/abstract=1715000

Truman, G. (2016). *WebArchiving Environmental Scan* (Harvard Library Report). Harvard Library. Retrieved from http://nrs.harvard.edu/urn-3:HUL.InstRepos:25658314

Van de Sompel, H., Nelson, M. L., Sanderson, R., Balakireva, L. L., Ainsworth, S., & Shankar, H. (2009). Memento: Time Travel for the Web. *ArXiv:0911.1112 [Cs]*. Retrieved from http://arxiv.org/abs/0911.1112

Weber, M. S. (2017). The challenges of 25 years of data. In N. Brügger (Ed.), *Web 25* (pp. 125–138). New York: Peter Lang.

Webster, P. (2017). Users, technologies, organisations. In N. Brügger (Ed.), *Web 25* (pp. 175–190). New York: Peter Lang.

Webster, P., & Milligan, I. (2014, January 22). The Web Archive Bibliography. Retrieved March 23, 2018, from https://webarchivehistorians.org/the-web-archive-bibliography/

Winters, J. (2017). Coda: Web archives for humanities research - some reflections. In N. Brügger & R. Schroeder, *The Web as History* (pp. 238–248). London: UCL Press.

Scholarly Resource Linking: Building out a "Relationship Life Cycle"

Matthew S. Mayernik
National Center for Atmospheric Research (NCAR),
University Corporation for Atmospheric Research (UCAR),
USA. mayernik@ucar.edu

ABSTRACT

Scholarly resources, including publications, software, data sets, and instruments, are created in an iterative and interrelated fashion. Managing the relationships that exist among and between such resources is a central requirement for information systems. Practically, however, many scholarly resources exist online as discrete entities, divorced from other resources to which they are intimately related. A robust system for linking scholarly resources in a broad and sustainable fashion will have to navigate a set of complex and interrelated requirements. This paper presents results and insights from three different projects that focused on supporting more robust linkages among scholarly resources. The discussion details key technical and institutional challenges looking forward and backward in time across what might be considered to be a "relationship life cycle": identifying, validating, characterizing, and preserving relationships. The goal of the paper is to help guide new research initiatives and operational services focused on integrating relationship information into the scholarly record.

KEYWORDS

Data citation, metadata, web linking, scholarly communication

INTRODUCTION

Most scholarly resources are now available online. Journal articles are published via online platforms, reports and other gray literature are available via institutional and general-purpose repositories, data sets are increasingly archived in web-accessible data repositories, and software packages are widely distributed through GitHub and other code sharing tools. Not all resources are available online, of course. Numerous well-known social, cultural, and technical factors impede distribution of research products, and scholars do in some cases ensure a competitive advantage by maximizing their unique access to novel data, tools, or knowledge (Mitroff, 1974; Fienberg, Martin, & Straf, 1985; Borgman, 2012). It is certainly also the case that making something available online does not automatically ensure its usefulness or understandability to a broad audience (Mayernik, 2017). Nonetheless, the trajectory is clear that scholarly resources already are, or will increasingly become, available online. Policy pressures, technical affordances, and social norms are all pushing in this direction (Willinsky, 2005; Woelfle, Olliaro, & Todd, 2011; Kriesberg, et al., 2017). In the context of scholarly work, having resources available online provides broad benefits. Scholarly communities benefit from increased access to large numbers of resources, and individual scholars benefit from the citation and readership advantages that accrue (Hitchcock, 2013; Piwowar & Vision, 2013).

Once resources are available online, a natural question arises: can we link resources together? Linking, after all, is what the internet is all about. Publications, software, data sets, and other scholarly resources are created in an iterative and interrelated fashion. The interconnections between scholarly resources can be characterized as forming a value chain in which relationships provide significant value for resource discovery, use, management, and preservation approaches (Van de Sompel, et al., 2004; Pepe, et al., 2010). Managing such relationships is, in principle, a central component of information systems (Kent, 1978). Indeed, many information and data systems do manage and leverage relationships of a variety of kinds, particularly relationships among vocabulary terms and content structures (Bean & Green, 2001). Practically, however, most scholarly resources exist online as discrete entities. A search of the Registry of Research Data Repositories (https://www.re3data.org, search done on March 28, 2018) found only 48 repositories out of 2040 total repositories that are identified as accepting "Source Code" and 26 repositories as accepting "Software applications," with some repositories accepting both. These numbers are likely not exact, but they illustrate how data and software repository services are largely disjoint. Similarly, scholarly papers are housed in systems and repositories that typically do not collect data or software assets.

Linking scholarly resources thus requires an approach that navigates multiple scholarly institutions and technical systems. Establishing and managing relationships between information resources has been a common theme in information science and technology research. This paper will not attempt to survey all of the relevant literature and initiatives in this space. Useful overviews can be found elsewhere (Borgman, 2007; Lagoze, 2010; Van de Sompel & Nelson, 2015; Mayernik, Phillips, & Nienhouse, 2016). Instead, this paper presents results and insights from three different projects focused on linking data and literature. It outlines key challenges in identifying, validating, characterizing, and preserving relationships among scholarly resources, and discusses how these challenges differ when looking forward or backward in time. The goal of the paper is to help guide new research and operational services focused on integrating relationship information more fully into the scholarly record.

INVESTIGATIONS INTO LINKING

This section presents three separate projects conducted in the past four years. Each project has had different specific goals, scopes, and partners, but the overarching theme among the three projects has been to investigate approaches to cross-linking related scholarly resources. As Van de Sompel and Nelson (2015) state in their own recent retrospective on a series of scholarly resource and infrastructure interoperability projects, "it is hard to know how to exactly start an effort to work towards increased interoperability," because of the diversity of challenges and stakeholders involved. The following three projects should be seen as an attempt to make multiple starts in parallel toward understanding and potentially addressing scholarly resource cross-linking challenges.

Below, each project is discussed individually. Each section describes the projects' respective goals, approaches, and relevant accomplishments. Each section also identifies some notable lessons learned via the work within each project. Following these project descriptions, I provide cross-cutting discussion that pulls together points from each project to develop broadly applicable insights for scholarly resource cross-linking efforts.

Repository-to-Repository Cross-Linking

The first project (active Jan. 2015 – Mar. 2016) consisted of a pilot effort to exchange link information between two repositories, one data repository and one literature repository. The goal was to enable the two repositories to interact directly to exchange link information for resources that had known relations, but were hosted and managed separately, such as, for example, if data sets hosted by repository A were used to produce publications that were hosted by repository B. The vision for the project was to develop an interchange process between the two repositories that allowed researchers who deposited resources in one system to initiate the deposit of related resources in the other. Ideally, links between related resources held in the two separate systems could be exchanged and made visible in the respective repositories. From a system perspective, the objectives were to identify, scope, test, and deploy repository features that allow links between related resources to be created, exchanged, and maintained over time with low technical hurdles and minimal repository curator effort. The full end-to-end implementation of this vision was not completed, as discussed below. But the process of working on the project enabled us to investigate key requirements for how repository cross-linking might be achieved. We also held a workshop at the end of the project in which broader discussion of the project topics took place (Mayernik, Phillips, & Nienhouse, 2016).

We approached the project by: 1) specifying use cases and stakeholders, 2) developing technical requirements for these use cases and stakeholders, and 3) developing system functionalities that could meet the use case and stakeholder requirements. Figure 1 shows four resource linking scenarios that relate to the use cases and stakeholders for connecting a document with its underlying data. In scenarios #1-3 in Figure 1, a content creator (e.g. publication and/or data author) might be interested in depositing two new resources or might be depositing a new resource that is related to a resource deposited previously. In scenario #4, repository curators might be interested in identifying links between resources that are already part of their existing collections.

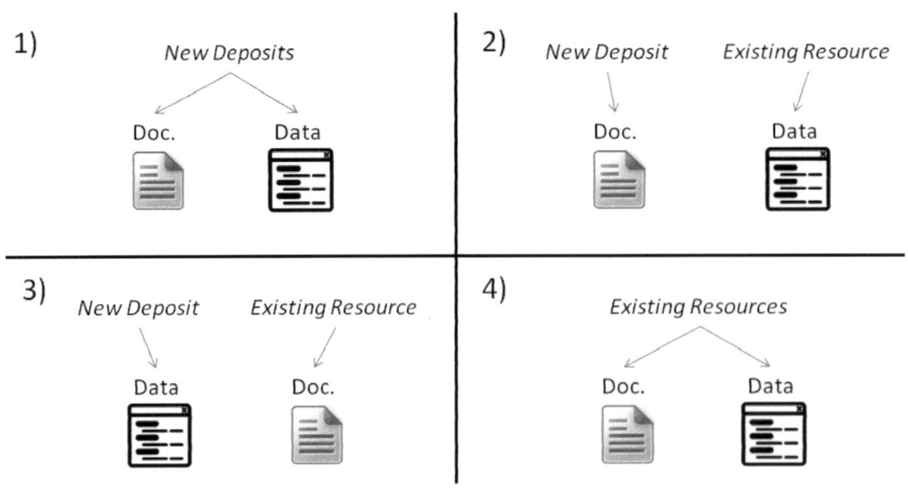

Figure 1. Repository linking workflow scenarios

These scenarios presented a number of tasks to support, including that: a) Data set providers can upload publications into one repository when depositing data sets in another (or vice versa), b) Repository content curators would be notified when new submissions are initiated from an external system, c) Publication and data authors would be able to share the deposited resources with colleagues and reference them appropriately, d) Research output consumers (either human or machine) could use the repositories to find resources and their relations. In breaking these tasks into sub-tasks and distinct workflows, the following technical requirements were identified being as key to establishing and maintaining robust connections between repositories of related resources:

- A notification mechanism to send information about related resources between repositories
- A data model for metadata exchange, to:
  - Specify metadata inheritance (e.g. authors and affiliated organizations that are in common from one resource to another)
  - Specify relationship types (e.g. that a data set underlies a publication)
  - Specify information necessary for maintaining relationships between resources over time as updates occur (e.g. a new version of a data set is produced, or a new publication is created based on an existing data set)
- Effective resource deposit interfaces that allow simple declaration of cross-repository relationships between data and publications
- Effective interface displays that make the cross-repository relationships transparent to the users

We investigated the SHARE Notify (https://share.osf.io/) service as a notification tool to enable repositories to interact and exchange relationship information. At the time of our investigation, SHARE Notify was being developed via the Center for Open Science as a third-party service for creating notifications of research publication "events." Our interest in using SHARE Notify was to send notifications of relationship "events" between our repositories, with the SHARE Notify service sitting as a intermediary between the two repositories. The appeal of a third-party intermediary like SHARE Notify was that it eliminated the need for every repository to directly connect to every other repository. While our direct use case was to connect two repositories, we were interested in a means of distributing relationship information to numerous potential partners. Thus, we wanted an approach that could potentially scale to support interchanges of relationship information between many repositories. We were hoping to find a third-party that could provide central registry of research release "events" via a metadata feed. The SHARE Notify service had potential to support our desired features, though our use case was not its main focus.

We conducted pilot experiments to use the SHARE Notify service, but ultimately did not complete an end-to-end workflow during the timeline of our project, for a couple of reasons. First, the SHARE Notify service was itself in a phase of development and iteration. As such, it presented a moving target for our requirements. The SHARE Notify data model and APIs, for example, were not finalized during the period in which our project was active. This is a key lesson from the project. The stability of a third-party notification service is an external factor that can affect the reliability of local workflows.

Another lesson learned, not related to SHARE Notify, was that an effort such as ours has to be agnostic about the identification schemes used to identify resources. Some of the technical workflows we explored required assets to be identified via Digital Object Identifiers (DOIs), specifically to take advantage of the metadata stores hosted by DOI registration agencies (e.g. CrossRef and DataCite). Many resources in the two repositories of interest for this project, however, had not been (and were not expected to be) assigned DOIs.

Tracing Resource Linkages through Literature References

The second project featured here (active 2014-current) focused on developing and evaluating tools for automating the tracing of research infrastructures in the research literature via persistent citable identifiers. From a linking perspective, the interest was in tracing linkages between papers and associated resources, such as data sets, that were used to produce the papers. This project was motivated by the increase in interest in "data citation," that is, the assignment of persistent identifiers like Digital Object Identifiers (DOIs) to data with the goal of enabling them to be cited and tracked like traditional research literature (Mayernik, et al, 2017; Silvello, 2017). Our interest, however, was in the question of the utility of persistent identification for research resources more broadly, including for scientific equipment (or sets of instruments), scientific software packages, computing systems, and communication networks. We use the overarching term "research infrastructures" to encompass this broad grouping. Since assigning and using persistent identifiers for scientific research infrastructures is a relatively new development, very few assessments have been conducted that systematically examine the effects of such identifiers assigned to these infrastructures. Our project goals were thus 1) to develop an understanding of how to methodically and consistently analyze the scientific impact of research infrastructures, and 2) to develop automated techniques that enable the tracing of research infrastructures to work more effectively. Specific research questions focused, for example, on how references to scientific research infrastructures have changed over time in relation to the assignment of persistent identifiers to data, software, and other components of research infrastructures.

The first effort within the project was to conduct a case study-based assessment to evaluate whether research infrastructures are being increasingly identified and referenced in the research literature via persistent citable identifiers. In this study (Mayernik & Maull, 2017), citations and references for four resources - two data sets, a software package, and a supercomputing facility - were collected manually using Google Scholar searches and analyzed to assess the ways that the resources had been referenced by researchers who used them, by characterizing how often the resources were referenced in papers through in-text descriptions, mentioned via acknowledgements, or explicitly cited in reference lists. Findings from this study showed how persistent identifiers assigned to the four examined resources were indeed being used in references in published papers on an increasing basis. But there was not a consistent pattern across the four case studies of how these increases were manifesting. Likewise, this analysis found that referencing practices were changing over time, but the extent of the changes varies considerably from resource to resource. A key takeaway from these results is that changing established practices for referencing and acknowledging data sets will potentially be more difficult than creating new practices for referencing other kinds of products, like software or computing facilities.

The above study was done as a largely manual process. The second effort within this project was to develop computational algorithms/methods to make this kind of assessment project easier. The development of tracing algorithms and methods followed a typical machine learning approach, centered on three axes: (1) collection of candidate publications for classification, (2) development of an experimental methodology for classification, and (3) an automation framework for executing document classification and analysis. This approach is showing promise, with an initial test of document classifiers being able to correctly determine whether a document from the test set did in fact use a computation facility of interest, based on characteristics of the documents' metadata and full-text. The limitation of this study thus far is that it is based on a relatively small corpus of documents. The training set (those that have been manually examined and labeled) includes about 300 documents, and the test set (those which had been labeled but had not yet been seen or trained on) includes about 120 documents. These numbers are far from ideal for machine learning studies, which often use thousands or even millions of documents.

A key lesson of this project is that human expertise is hard to scale but is critically necessary to identify and validate relationships in cases where computation-based approaches are not possible. Machine automation is readily scalable but ensuring and measuring accuracy of automated relationship gathering tools has been very difficult.

Both of the studies undertaken within this project have faced a similar challenge, namely that gathering a large number of documents with which to study any literature-based trends is very difficult outside of narrow domains, such as biomedicine (PubMed), physics (arXiv.org), and astronomy (Astronomical Data Service), where most of the literature is available via publicly accessible and machine-readable systems. In other domains, including those of interest within this project, the literature is spread across numerous publisher platforms that do not allow any overarching machine-accessibility capabilities. Google Scholar, while quite comprehensive in coverage, does not allow any significant automated literature mining. These methodological difficulties are a common refrain among numerous studies that have attempted to compile and analyze impact metrics for research infrastructures (Mayernik, et al, 2017). These scale-limiting copyright issues, along with journal editorial policies, publication platforms, and article formatting differences, present other uncontrollable factors for automating this kind of study.

EarthCollab - Linking via the Semantic Web

The third project of interest for this paper, called EarthCollab (active 2014-2018), has focused on using Semantic Web and linked data technology to facilitate the coordination and organization of complex scientific projects and their products. From a technology point of view, the goal of the project has been to develop information systems that demonstrate how the geosciences can leverage linked data to produce more coherent methods of information and data discovery for large multi-disciplinary projects and virtual organizations. The motivation for the project was to improve the discovery and sharing of information to advance research and scientific collaboration, enabling researchers to more easily find people, organizations, and research resources that are relevant to their work. The VIVO Semantic Web software suite (http://vivoweb.org/) was chosen because it is built around a web-centric data model that focuses on representing relationships between entities (Borner, et al., 2012). Figure 2 depicts how many-to-many relationships exist among (and within) scientific resources, projects, people, and organizations.

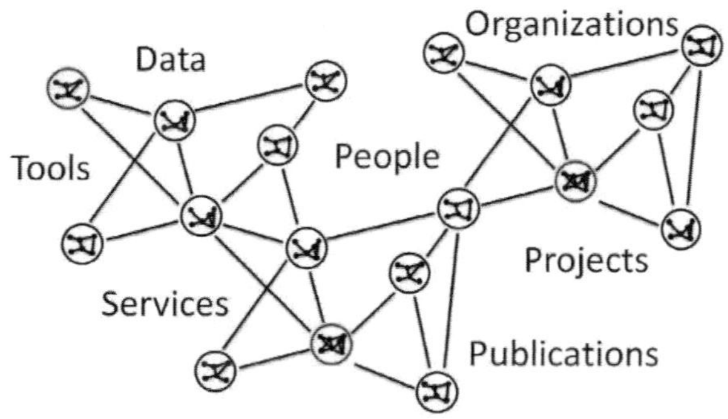

Figure 2. Networked science (Figure by Keith Maull)

The project used VIVO to provide web interfaces for researchers within two targeted scientific research areas to explore the people, publications, platforms, and data sets within their respective communities. These systems, called "Connect UNAVCO" (https://connect.unavco.org/) and "Arctic Data Connects" (http://vivo.eol.ucar.edu), have both been live for public use for over a year. As an illustration of the kinds of information that these systems contain, as of 1 April 2018, Connect UNAVCO contains records for nearly 6,000 scientific documents, 4,307 datasets, 3,841 research sites, 228 grants, 803 people, and 381 organizations. Arctic Data Connects, with a more focused case study on select arctic research projects, contains records for 354 datasets, 26 grants, 146 people, and 53 organizations. The information in these systems comes from a combination of existing metadata databases and newly created metadata. The resources are represented via the Semantic Web data model using multiple ontologies (Mayernik, et al., 2016). In the Semantic Web, ontologies are used to define entity types (classes), and the relationships between them (properties). Anything can be represented as a first-order object, as long as appropriate ontologies are declared. The result is a networked set of information, in which datasets, publications, scientific instruments, research projects, and research sites are each represented in the data model as distinct entities that have specific types of relationships with other entities. Practically, the VIVO software displays a web page for each entity, which provides information about the entity along with links to other entities that are related via explicitly declared relationships. For example, the web page for a data set within one of the systems will display all known links to associated publications, organizations, grants, creators, and instruments.

Another component of this project has been to undertake software development to add capabilities to the VIVO software suite. In the first two years of the project, we developed a prototype "cross-linking" approach to exchange information across VIVO instances. The motivation for this work was that participants in many scientific research projects are based at many different organizations. Some of those organizations already use VIVO to manage faculty and staff information profiles. The new cross-linking feature was developed to enable the exchange of information about specific people or entities that are in common across different VIVO instances. This new feature was intended to reduce duplication of information across systems and enable the distribution of authoritative information about a specific entity, such as when a single individual has VIVO profiles at different organizations. The cross-linking capability has been deployed within Connect UNAVCO and is being contributed to the core VIVO open source code base.

A key lesson learned within EarthCollab with regard to representing relationships between scholarly resources centers on the use and re-use of ontologies. To facilitate easier integration and data sharing across the geoscience community, our goal within this project has been to reuse existing ontologies as much as possible when developing project ontologies and web applications. Reusing existing ontologies did not prove to be as easy as originally anticipated. The difficult work in using ontologies is the conceptual modeling, in which the key entities and relationships of interest are specified and mapped. Only after this has been done can the next step take place, namely, finding relevant existing ontologies that map to your conceptual model, which is not a trivial exercise. In our project, no single ontology supported our project needs. We thus combined components from a couple of different ontologies and created custom ontology extensions as necessary to fill gaps (Mayernik, et al., 2016).

DISCUSSION

The three projects described above all focus on challenges associated with linking scholarly resources together in a web environment. The projects were conducted in parallel with some overlap in personnel, but no direct overlap in intended outcomes. The insights from the projects, however, are complementary. Together, they provide a larger view of the impediments and enablers of scholarly resource cross-linking efforts than any one of them could have allowed. This kind of "parallel trials" approach has proven to be particularly useful in situations where the optimal outcome (or path to an outcome) is not clear from the outset (Lenfle & Loch, 2010).

In this section, we provide an overarching discussion on scholarly resource cross-linking requirements, building on the knowledge and experience gained in working on multiple relevant projects concurrently. We first categorize the salient requirements and associated challenges in this problem space by type, and then depict how these requirements and challenges look different when looking forward in time vs. looking backward in time.

Requirements for Scholarly Resource Linking

A robust system for linking scholarly resources in a broad and sustainable fashion will have to navigate a set of complex and interrelated requirements. Just as research data and software creation, management, and preservation can be characterized through life cycle models (Carlson, 2014; Lenhardt, et al., 2014), we might characterize the requirements for a scholarly resource linking infrastructure through a "relationship life cycle" that encompasses the need to identify, validate, characterize, and preserve relationship and link information. Each of these areas is now discussed in turn.

Identifying relationships. Relationships between scholarly resources, to be useful for resource discovery, understanding, and use, have to be declared by somebody, or some entity. Where can (or should) these relationship declarations come from? Relationships that are not declared explicitly can sometimes be determined by computational processes, often relying on statistical measures to identify implicit relationships between specific entities or vocabulary terms included within a text (Sheth, Ramakrishnan, & Thomas, 2005). But these computational techniques are typically most successful in very specific applications and are difficult to generalize. The other obvious source for relationship information is from the creator(s) of the related resources. A truism of metadata generation for scholarly resources is that the scholars are best positioned to provide metadata about their own resources given their intimate knowledge of how those resources were produced and used. But efforts to gather information about relationships between data, software, publications, and other research resources directly from scholars also face well-known metadata creation challenges, namely that scholars have little incentive to describe such relationships explicitly, and that knowledge of specific relationships can decay quickly and be distributed among teams (Michener, et al., 1997; Edwards, et al., 2011). Gathering relationship information directly from scholars is thus a difficult task that does not scale well for the numbers of scholarly assets now being distributed on the web. Another potential source for relationship information is published literature. As we found in our Tracing Identifiers project, data and software citation are indeed increasingly cited formally, potentially making automated citation analysis possible. But, as our project also found, the timeline for these new citation practices to take root will likely be long. Identifying relationships is thus a significant rate-limiter for any effort to develop scholarly resource linking approaches. This challenge also has a bi-directional component, namely, even if relationship identification becomes more straight-forward, how do relationships propagate? Stated another way, if I know about a relationship between my resource and your resource, how do you learn about that relationship? How does my relationship declaration propagate to you? This requirement was what drove our interest in a relationship notification service within our Repository Cross-Linking project. There is currently no comprehensive aggregator for relationship information that could serve as this kind of general notification service. In the specific case of data-to-literature linking, the Scholix framework and associated Data-Literature Interlinking (DLI) Service have promise to serve key roles as a centralized third-party aggregator of relationship declarations (Burton, et al., 2017a; b), but these initiatives are still in early days of building adoption.

Validating relationships. Validation presents the next challenge and requirement. Whatever method used to identify relationships between scholarly resources, the relationship declarations need to be validated via some process, which again could be human or machine-based. A basic challenge for the validation process is simply to validate what entities are being related. Digital objects have diffuse boundaries and can change over time. Many approaches to relationship identification rely on the use of persistent identifiers (PIDs), such as DOIs, to ensure persistence and fixity. Technically, however, PIDs function as locators for the resources to which they are assigned, not as identifiers for those resources (Thompson, 2010; Duerr, et al., 2011). PIDs are also being assigned at different levels of granularity for different kinds of resources, and no broadly accepted rules exist to guide decisions about how PIDs should be assigned to compound digital objects (Mayernik, 2013). More practically, PID use is not comprehensive, as we studied in our Tracing Identifiers project. Many references to data, software, and other resources still take place through informal acknowledgements or in-text references. Validation of relationship declarations also depends on the notion of an authoritative source of the relationship information. Is relationship information that comes directly from resource creators, or from published articles, more authoritative than information from other sources? The DLI Service noted in the previous paragraph provides information about organizations that publish relationship declarations. But should all of providers be considered authoritative sources for relationship information? Mechanisms for ensuring trust in relationship declarations are key to any approach to relationship validation.

Characterizing relationships. For many purposes, the basic act of declaring that a relationship exists is not very useful. More information about the kind of relationships may need to be collected as well. The use of relationships, in other words, often requires additional description about the relationship itself. The Semantic Web approach is based on this premise, namely, that relationships should be designated as being of specific named types. Numerous ontologies and vocabularies have been created to define specific kinds of relationships that can hold between scholarly resources (see Mayernik, Phillips, & Nienhouse, 2016), but these relationship typologies are highly variable and inconsistent. In our EarthCollab project, we emphasized reusing existing ontologies as a way to represent entities and their relationships in an interoperable way. This proved to be more challenging than originally assumed due to the fact that numerous ontologies modeled the same kinds of resources (e.g. data sets) and relationships (e.g. citation relationships) in various ways (Mayernik, et al., 2016). An additional challenge in characterizing relationships is that different uses of relationship information might require different levels of description about the entities at either end of the relationships. The Scholix framework, for example, defines a very simple data model for representing relationships (Burton, et al., 2017b). For other applications, including our EarthCollab project, a simplistic data model did not support the goals of data discovery and understanding. A general issue related to characterizing relationships is that data models and metadata schemas do not always include ways to represent relationship information, or they have different requirements for describing relationships. The SHARE Notify data model, for example, did not have an explicit way to represent relationships during the time we were investigating its potential use as a relationship notification service within our Repository Cross-Linking project.

Preserving relationships. "Link rot" is the most obvious challenge for preserving relationships between web-based scholarly resources. Web sites change URLs or go down unpredictably, causing a cascade of errors for any links pointing toward the site that has gone down. This issue presents a significant challenge for projects that hope to use the scholarly literature as a source for relationship information. PIDs are again a solution for this issue, but PIDs are not inherently immune from link rot. All PID systems work through re-direct servers. Maintenance of redirects is an institutional challenge as much as it is a technical challenge. Organizations that register DOIs, for example, are required to maintain the resolution of their identifiers and associated landing pages. Beyond persistent resolution, preservation challenges relate to the level of description that might be needed to understand relationships as time goes by, and/or as the user communities for the resources and their relationships change over time. Processes to write and document the US National Climate Assessment report, for example, a cross-agency consensus report on climate change, have changed significantly in recent years to provide highly structured relationship information to illustrate specific linkages between scientific claims and the underlying data and research papers (Tilmes, et al., 2013). Baker, Duerr, & Parsons (2015) provide another vivid example of how user needs, and documentation needs, can shift significantly over time, even for the same scientific resource. It should be emphasized that in both of these examples, creating and curating this information was the responsibility of dedicated staff. Preserving the understandability of relationships is thus an ongoing process that can require significant expertise. As part of this preservation requirement, frameworks like Scholix and systems like the DLI Service should be explicit about their own sustainability models, to engender trust by potential adopters.

Looking Forward and Backward in Time

The issues associated with relationship identification, validation, characterization, and preservation present different challenges and requirements when looking forward vs. backward in time. The Repository Cross-Linking project workflows depicted in Figure 1 above provide a clear illustration of this. Looking forward in time, the challenges center on how to institute relationship declaration/identification as a routine and robust part of scholarly publishing, data and software archiving, and repository technologies. As Marchionini, et al., note, "[e]fficient capture of data including provenance and metadata is most easily done by working at the start of the process (2012, pg. 17)." In the scenario in which resources are being newly created and deposited into repository systems, it might be possible to gather relationship information as resources and relationships are produced.

Looking backward in time, linking scholarly resources involves mining available literature (and other available documentation), along with potentially querying scholarly resource creators directly about relationships that hold between existing resources. Literature mining can be manual or automated, as in our Tracing IDs project, with the attendant advantages and disadvantages of either approach. Copyright and licensing restrictions clearly limit current efforts toward literature mining, except in the academic specializations where open publishing models are well established. Directly contacting and working with resource creators to establish relationship information for existing resources has obvious limitations as well, and will likely only take place in the context of specific projects or applications where this information is desired. Within our EarthCollab project, for example, we are investigating protocols for querying researchers directly to gather information about linkages between data and scientific articles, because the articles themselves typically do not contain enough information for us to reliably assert the relationships ourselves.

Table 1 depicts the differing kinds of work required to support broad scholarly resource linking, when the focus is backward vs. forward looking. Each cell further breaks down the work requirements into "technical" and "institutional" work. As I discussed in a prior paper (Mayernik, 2016), scholarly resource curation encompasses far more than just technical work. Institutional factors like community norms and expectations, the availability of intermediaries to support curation work, standards development and adoption, and individual routines all play important roles in determining the success of curation efforts. Table

	Looking back in time	Looking forward in time
Relationship Identification	*Technical work* – Data mining approaches for extracting PID-based references from published literature *Institutional work* – Interfacing with publishers & funders to open scholarly literature to more comprehensive data mining	*Technical work* – Development of relationship aggregators, and associated open web services *Institutional work* – 1. Promoting consistent use of PIDs, 2. Developing and adopting community frameworks for relationship distribution (e.g. Scholix)
Relationship Validation	*Technical work* – Data mining approaches for extracting informal references from published literature, with confidence estimates *Institutional work* – Interfacing with publishers & funders	*Technical work* – Developing/updating data models to support relationship source and trust assertions *Institutional work* – Developing organizational trust networks for relationship declarations
Relationship Characterization	*Technical work* – Fitting non-standardized relationship declarations into community ontologies and metadata schemas *Institutional work* – Coupling entity and relationship descriptions to the needs of the target communities and/or applications	*Technical work* – Developing/updating data models and metadata schemas to consistently represent relationships and the entities being linked *Institutional work* – Coordinating agreements on relationship semantics within particular communities, or for particular applications
Relationship Preservation	*Technical work* – Coupling link crawling and web archiving tools *Institutional work* – Curating relationship information over time, iteratively updating relationships as necessary to support user needs	*Technical work* – Developing/adopting packaging tools that ensure links between resources are not lost over time *Institutional work* – 1. Developing sustainability approaches for relationship aggregators, 2. Curating relationship information over time

Table 1. Technical and institutional work needed to support scholarly resource linking.

1 thus outlines how technical and institutional developments are both critical to achieving robust infrastructures for scholarly resource linking. This table is meant to be illustrative, not exhaustive. Other writing cited in this paper present additional areas of emphasis for current and future work in this space.

CONCLUSION

Efforts to link scholarly resources in reliable and sustainable ways face numerous difficult challenges that span technical and institutional factors. This paper discusses three projects that all focused on one or more aspects of these challenges. It synthesized key outcomes and lessons that emerged from these three projects, and presents insights into four key requirement areas, namely, issues associated with the need to identify, validate, characterize, and preserve relationship information between scholarly resources. I also outlined how attempts to build out linking infrastructures going forward face different challenges than initiatives to gather and characterize links between already existing data, software, publications, and other scholarly resources.

By running multiple projects concurrently, we have taken a "parallel trials" approach to scope out what kinds of initiatives are more conducive to solving specific problems related to scholarly resource linking. Solving local requirements, e.g. the desire to link two specific local systems, can be approached with limited technical complexity. Developing cross-organizational and cross-institutional solutions to supporting resource linking, however, require standards and coordination work, and will necessarily have a longer timeline. No single technical system or infrastructure is likely to provide a general solution to the challenges identified in this paper due to the wide-ranging stakeholder communities involved. Iteration and institutional work will be key.

The information sciences have expertise and research capacity to be strong contributors to scholarly resource linking efforts going forward. The issues described in this paper touch on scholarly communication, metadata frameworks, bibliometrics, digital preservation, and web architectures, all of which are historically and currently areas of research within library and information science disciplines. Scholarly resource linking infrastructures will have to find ways to couple findings and tools associated with all of these areas to move forward productively.

ACKNOWLEDGMENTS

I wish to express my gratitude to the numerous collaborators at NCAR, Cornell University, and UNAVCO who have contributed to the three projects described above. The work described in this paper was supported by U.S. National Science Foundation (NSF) grants 1449668, 1448480, 1440293, 1440213, and 1440181. NCAR is funded by the NSF.

REFERENCES

Bean, C.A. & Green, R. (Eds). (2001). *Relationships in the Organization of Knowledge.* Boston, MA: Kluwer.

Baker, K.S., Duerr, R.E., & Parsons, M.A. (2015). Scientific knowledge mobilization: Co-evolution of data products and designated communities. *International Journal of Digital Curation*, 10(2): 110-135. http://doi.org/10.2218/ijdc.v10i2.346

Borgman, C.L. (2007). *Scholarship in the Digital Age: Information, Infrastructure, and the Internet.* Cambridge, MA: MIT Press.

Borgman, C.L. (2012). The conundrum of sharing research data. *Journal of the American Society for Information Science and Technology*, 63(6): 1059-1078. https://doi.org/10.1002/asi.22634

Borner, K., Conlon, M., Corson-Rikert, J., & Ding, Y. (Eds.). (2012). *VIVO: A Semantic Approach to Scholarly Networking and Discovery.* San Rafael, CA: Morgan & Claypool.

Burton, A., et al. (2017a). The data-literature interlinking service: Towards a common infrastructure for sharing data-article links. *Program*, 51(1): 75-100. https://doi.org/10.1108/PROG-06-2016-0048

Burton, A., et al. (2017b). The Scholix Framework for interoperability in data-literature information exchange. *D-Lib Magazine*, 23(1/2). https://doi.org/10.1045/january2017-burton

Carlson, J. (2014). The use of life cycle models in developing and supporting data services. In J.M. Ray (Ed.), *Research Data Management: Practical Strategies for Information Professionals* (pp. 63-86). West Lafayette, IN: Purdue Univ. Press.

Duerr, R., Downs, R., Tilmes, C., Barkstrom, B., Lenhardt, W.C., Glassy, J., Bermudez, L., et al. (2011). On the utility of identification schemes for digital earth science data: an assessment and recommendations. *Earth Science Informatics*, 4(3): 1-22. https://doi.org/10.1007/s12145-011-0083-6

Edwards, P.N., Mayernik, M.S., Batcheller, A., Borgman, C.L., and Bowker, G.C. (2011). Science friction: Data, metadata, and collaboration in the interdisciplinary sciences. *Social Studies of Science*, 41(5): 667-690. https://doi.org/10.1177/0306312711413314

Fienberg, S.E., Martin, M.E., & Straf, M.L. (Eds). (1985). Part I: Report of the Committee on National Statistics. In *Sharing Research Data.* Washington, D.C.: National Academy Press. http://www.nap.edu/catalog/2033/sharing-research-data

Hitchcock, S. (2013). *The effect of open access and downloads ('hits') on citation impact: a bibliography of studies.* University of Southampton. https://eprints.soton.ac.uk/354006/

Kent, W. (1978). *Data and Reality: Basic Assumptions in Data Processing Reconsidered.* New York: North-Holland.

Kriesberg, A., Huller, K., Punzalan, R., & Parr, C. (2017). An analysis of federal policy on public access to scientific research data. *Data Science Journal*, 16: paper 27. https://doi.org/10.5334/dsj-2017-027

Lagoze, C.J. (2010). *Lost Identity: The Assimilation of Digital Libraries into the Web.* Ph.D. diss. Cornell University.

Lenfle, S. & Loch, C. (2010). Lost roots: How project management came to emphasize control over flexibility and novelty. *California Management Review*, 53(1): 32-55. https://doi.org/10.1525/cmr.2010.53.1.32

Lenhardt, W.C., Ahalt, S., Blanton, B., Christopherson, L., & Idaszak R. (2014). Data management lifecycle and software lifecycle management in the context of conducting science. *Journal of Open Research Software*, 2(1): e15. https://doi.org/10.5334/jors.ax

Marchionini, G., Lee, C.A., Bowden, H., & Lesk, M. (Eds.). (2012). *Curating for Quality: Ensuring Data Quality to Enable New Science.* Final Report: Invitational Workshop Sponsored by the National Science Foundation, Sept. 10-11, 2012, Arlington, VA. http://openscholar.mit.edu/sites/default/files/dept/files/altman2012-mitigating_threats_to_data_quality_throughout_the_curation_lifecycle.pdf

Mayernik, M.S. (2013). *Bridging data lifecycles: Tracking data use via data citations workshop report.* NCAR Technical Note, NCAR/TN-494+PROC, Boulder, CO: National Center for Atmospheric Research (NCAR). https://doi.org/10.5065/D6PZ56TX

Mayernik, M.S. (2016). Research data and metadata curation as institutional issues. *Journal of the Association for Information Science and Technology*, 67(4): 973-993. https://doi.org/10.1002/asi.23425

Mayernik, M.S. (2017). Open data: Accountability and transparency. *Big Data & Society*, 4(2). https://doi.org/10.1177/2053951717718853

Mayernik, M.S., Gross, M.B., Corson-Rikert, J., Daniels, M.D., Johns, E.M., Khan, H., ... & Stott, D. (2016). Building geoscience Semantic Web applications using established ontologies. *Data Science Journal*, 15, article 11: 1-10. https://doi.org/10.5334/dsj-2016-011

Mayernik, M.S., Hart, D.L., Maull, K.E., & Weber, N.M. (2017). Assessing and tracing the outcomes and impact of research infrastructures. *Journal of the Association for Information Science and Technology*, 68(6): 1341-1359. https://doi.org/10.1002/asi.23721

Mayernik, M.S. & Maull, K.E. (2017). Assessing the uptake of persistent identifiers by research infrastructure users. *PLoS ONE*, 12(4): e0175418. https://doi.org/10.1371/journal.pone.0175418

Mayernik, M.S., Phillips, J., & Nienhouse, E. (2016). Linking publications and data: Challenges, trends, and opportunities. *D-Lib Magazine,* 22(5/6). https://doi.org/10.1045/may2016-mayernik

Michener, W.K., Brunt, J.W., Helly, J.J., Kirchner, T.B., and Stafford, S.G. (1997). Nongeospatial metadata for the ecological sciences. *Ecological Applications*, 7(1): 330-342.

Mitroff, I.I. (1974). Norms and counter-norms in a select group of the Apollo moon scientists: A case study of the ambivalence of scientists. *American Sociological Review*, 39(4): 579-595. https://doi.org/10.2307/2094423.

Pepe, A., Mayernik, M., Borgman, C.L., & Van de Sompel, H. (2010). From artifacts to aggregations: Modeling scientific life cycles on the semantic web. *Journal of the American Society for Information Science and Technology*, 63(3): 567-582. https://doi.org/10.1002/asi.21263

Piwowar, H.A. & Vision, T.J. (2013). Data reuse and the open data citation advantage. *PeerJ*, 1: e175. https://doi.org/10.7717/peerj.175

Sheth, A., Ramakrishnan, C., & Thomas, C. (2005). Semantics for the Semantic Web: The implicit, the formal and the powerful. *International Journal on Semantic Web and Information Systems*, 1(1): 1-18. https://doi.org/10.4018/jswis.2005010101

Silvello, G. (2017). Theory and practice of data citation. *Journal of the Association for Information Science and Technology*, 69(1): 6-20. https://doi.org/10.1002/asi.23917

Thompson, H.S. (2010). What is a URI and why does it matter? *Ariadne*, 65. http://www.ariadne.ac.uk/issue65/thompson-hs/

Tilmes, C., Fox, P., Ma, X., McGuinness, D.L., Privette, A.P., Smith, A., … Zheng, J.G. (2013). Provenance representation for the National Climate Assessment in the Global Change Information System. *IEEE Transactions on Geoscience and Remote Sensing*, 51(11): 5160-5168. https://doi.org/10.1109/tgrs.2013.2262179

Van de Sompel, H. & Nelson, M. L. (2015). Reminiscing about 15 years of interoperability efforts. *D-Lib Magazine*, 21(11/12). http://doi.org/10.1045/november2015-vandesompel

Van de Sompel, H., Payette, S., Erickson, J., Lagoze, C., & Warner, S. (2004). Rethinking scholarly communication. *D-Lib Magazine*, 10(9). https://doi.org/10.1045/september2004-vandesompel

Willinsky, J. (2005). The unacknowledged convergence of open source, open access, and open science. *First Monday*, 10(8). http://ojphi.org/ojs/index.php/fm/article/view/1265/1185

Woelfle, M., Olliaro, P., & Todd, M.H. (2011). Open science is a research accelerator. *Nature Chemistry*, 3(10): 745-748. http://doi.org/10.1038/nchem.1149

It Ain't What You Do, It's the Way That You Do It: Design Guidelines to Better Support Online Browsing

Dana McKay
University of Melbourne, Australia.
danamckay@gmail.com

Shanton Chang
University of Melbourne, Australia.
shanton.chang@unimelb.edu.au

George Buchanan
University of Melbourne, Australia.
george.buchanan@unimelb.edu.au

ABSTRACT

Many authors have proposed guidelines for online browsing systems, however recently empirical research has added depth to these requirements. There has also been a spate of development in online browsing systems, particularly for library shelf browsing. These strands of research are clearly in service of providing better browsing options in an increasingly online library environment, however they have not yet been brought together. In this paper we use a recent empirical study and a survey of the literature to generate a comprehensive list of requirements for browsing interfaces. We will then compare that list to the interface features of a range of different book browsing interfaces, demonstrating why they may be more or less effective, and signpost development of more effective online browsing.

KEYWORDS

Browsing, human computer interaction, ebooks, discovery, digital libraries

INTRODUCTION

Browsing is a key part of human information seeking (Ellis, 1989; Kuhlthau, 1991; Marchionini, 1997), yet until very recently it has been ignored in online interfaces. Scholars have long commented that browsing is a field in need of further research and support (Bates, 2007; Celoria, 1969; Marchionini, 1997; Rice, McCreadie, & Chang, 2001), but the vast majority of work on supporting online information seeking has been on search. There are any number of reasons why this may be true: there are clear metrics for search that allow scholars to measure progress against a standard set of metrics (Baeza-Yates & Ribeiro-Neto, 1999), and browsing meets needs that cannot be easily expressed in an online query, meaning its success is hard to measure.

Equally, browsing suffers from a definitional problem in research: the term 'browsing' is used to refer to a number of behaviors in disciplines as diverse as biology and marketing. Even in information research there are a number of behaviors addressed by the term browsing, from web-based information seeking through library or collection browsing right up to a highly trained academics looking for citations, a behavior described as browsing by information science (Rice et al., 2001). In this paper we focus on the definition most commonly associated with library science: that of browsing a collection of items that cannot be meaningfully assimilated into the information seeker's knowledge as part of the information seeking process. Further, we examine successful offline browsing as a way to improve online browsing; this is an approach that has been taken with both reading and triage in the past (Loizides & Buchanan, 2009; Pearson, Buchanan, Thimbleby, & Jones, 2012).

In all the information-based sciences, browsing has consistently been ignored in favor of search in research effort and research literature. With the advent of ebooks, the need for supporting online collection browsing has become pressing; in Australia at present over 90% of all volumes held by academic libraries are in ebook form[1]; in the United Kingdom the proportion of ebooks held by libraries doubled (from 10% overall to 20% overall) in four years[2]. This move to ebooks presents two major challenges for library users: ebook usability (which is a known and persistent problem (Pearson, Buchanan, & Thimbleby, 2010)), and—most pertinent to our work here—lack of opportunity for browsing.

Readers deliberately leverage library shelves to expand the offerings of library catalogues (Marchionini, 1997). They expect to experience serendipity, and the experience of browsing is valuable to them (Makri et al., 2007). They also use the shelves to provide information that they typically cannot get from library catalogues: recency of use by other readers, size (and weight), and the semantic information conveyed by book covers (Blandford & Furniss, 2006; Makri et al., 2007; Mikkonen & Vakkari, 2012; Stelmaszewska & Blandford, 2004). The evidence that the shelves affect which items readers borrow is consistent. In

[1] http://www.caul.edu.au/caul-programs/caul-statistics/statistics-summary-current
[2] https://www.sconul.ac.uk/sites/default/files/documents/Analysis%20_Loans%20ebooks%20visits%20June%202015.pdf

1993 Beaulieu noted that over half of all readers who found one book in the library catalogue selected a second book by browsing the shelves (Hancock-Beaulieu, 1993); our own earlier work demonstrated that readers tended to borrow books that are co-located on the shelves together, an effect that does not hold for ebooks (McKay, Smith, & Chang, 2014; McKay, Smith, & Chang, 2015). It is clear that—at least for print books—shelf browsing is a valuable part of the information experience; some readers have claimed it as a reason not to use ebooks (Hinze, McKay, Vanderschantz, Timpany, & Cunningham, 2012).

What is not clear is how best to facilitate a similar level of browsing online. There has been a spate of recent attempts (e.g. (Kleiner, Rädle, & Reiterer, 2013; Pearce & Chang, 2014; Thudt, Hinrichs, & Carpendale, 2012)), but none have had the uptake or approbation of the major search engines, meaning that they simply do not hold the same value for users. It is our conjecture that this is because these systems have not been underpinned by a clear and empirical understanding of reader browsing behavior and intentions. In this paper we combine an empirical study of browsing with the literature to generate a comprehensive list of behavioral requirements for browsing systems, noting particularly where these requirements have come from empirical research. We then compare these requirements to a range of browsing interface styles, focusing particularly on those developed recently, and noting any reasons why these interfaces may not meet all needs. Finally, we suggest avenues for future development of browsing interfaces, taking the gaps we have identified into consideration.

The remainder of this paper is divided as follows: first we consider the literature on browsing generally, presenting a working definition and examining its importance in human information behavior. Next, we review the literature on requirements of browsing systems and combine these with requirements from our observational research, identifying key aspects of browsing systems. Third, we overview a range of putative browsing systems, then we compare these systems to the requirements we have identified. Finally, we draw conclusions about what effective browsing systems may look like, based on our findings.

ON HUMAN BROWSING

Browsing is a key part of the human information seeking process, mentioned in all the major models (Ellis, 1989; Kuhlthau, 1991; Marchionini, 1997). These models describe browsing as being useful for meeting loosely specified information needs, meeting well specified but hard to describe needs with recognition strategies, or refining information needs in view of constructing a query. Other models have noted that browsing is good for 'social' information seeking, and for serendipitous discovery (Foster & Ford, 2003; McKenzie, 2003). Even Wilson's model of information behavior (Wilson, 1999), which doesn't mention browsing specifically notes that information seeking can occur in a context of ongoing attention without search. Yet search is what has drawn the most research interest. Browsing also has a different cognitive structure than search: browsers are guided by recognizing the 'scent' of interesting clusters of documents (Pirolli, 1997), rather than producing syntactic queries as abstract representations of their information need (Belkin, Oddy, & Brooks, 1982).

What, then, is browsing? Given the range of information needs it meets, it could be any number of behaviors; to discuss what we mean by browsing further we need to offer a definition. Bates (Bates, 2007) notes that browsing is the viewing of a large and interesting scene, and the identification and sequential (rather than concurrent) examination of objects of interest within it. This definition is drawn from a range of browsing literatures, including neuroscience and information science. This definition gives us an excellent working definition, and one that—as has been noted in previous research—describes library shelves as a near-perfect browsing engine (Kleiner et al., 2013).

Given the effectiveness of the library shelves, replicating them in virtual reality seems an obvious solution to the problem of online browsing. While this is low hanging fruit, early results are not promising in terms of user experience (Almeida, Cubaud, Dupire, Natkin, & Topol, 2006). Further, merely replicating the shelves in digital space does little to challenge the problems presented by physical shelves. Books may be missing or checked out (Blandford, Rimmer, & Warwick, 2006); related books may be shelved far from each other due to the classification scheme used (Losee, 1993; Marchionini, 1997), the top and bottom shelves are difficult to read and reach (Hinze et al., 2012; Reutzel & Gali, 1998), and the physical shelves can result in confusion and disorientation for even the most library savvy of readers (Martin, Greenspan, & Quan-Haase, 2017) (McKay & Conyers, 2010). It has been suggested by a number of researchers that a good browsing interface would not just match the effectiveness of the library shelves, but better it (Hinze et al., 2012; Marchionini, 1997; McKay, Chang, & Smith, 2017). This is in stark contrast to readers' existing experiences of online browsing alternatives, which are described as unsatisfactory.

In this paper we draw on the literature and our own empirical work to identify what the key behavioral elements of this putative hyper-effective online browsing system might be and compare those features to existing browsing systems.

ON EFFECTIVE ONLINE BROWSING SYSTEMS

A number of researchers have commented on what might make an effective online browsing system. Ellis suggested that all we needed to do to facilitate online browsing was to make the metadata held about objects browsable; however, he did not delve into what that might mean (Ellis, 1989). In contrast, Wilson suggested that we cannot actually describe requirements for online information systems—only make recommendations—because the act of information seeking is too complex, cognitive and contextual to allow for broad-brush support (Wilson, 1999). Marchionini noted that (Marchionini, 1997) that human computer interaction models were likely to offer helpful support to online browsing, however browsing has seen little attention even in HCI. General models of effective human computer interaction, while they almost certainly improve experiences with browsing systems, have not offered any dramatic insight into how online browsing might be better supported.

More recently Fidel (Fidel, 2012) has suggested that the reason we only have effective search systems is because Information Retrieval researchers are the only information researchers who have built systems to test their theories. While recent developments in browsing software, such as (Kleiner et al., 2013) and (Pearce & Chang, 2014) disprove this theory, historically it has carried some weight. Arguably the (relatively) limited body of research on browsing has come from the other side of the dichotomy drawn by Fidel: that of Human Information Behavior. Certainly, some of the drivers of online systems Fidel identifies—for example comparative quantitative evaluation—do not exist for browsing. We argue, however, that a dearth of information—particularly empirically derived data—on what might constitute effective offline browsing has a role to play in informing the design of better online browsing systems.

A number of fundamental requirements of online browsing systems have been identified by early work, particularly Marchionini's (1997). He notes that for any online browsing we need surrogate representations of the items available for browsing. These surrogates may represent 'semantic' or 'descriptive' information about the objects they represent. Semantic information describes the 'aboutness' of an object, and descriptive information offers metadata or information about the form of an object. He also mentions the need to manipulate these representations in a variety of rich and interesting ways. While these are clearly core requirements of effective online browsing systems, they do not give us much implementation detail in a modern context—yes, one needs to be able to manipulate information objects in a browsing interface, but how and what kinds of manipulations?

We have been addressing this question using behavioral observations in libraries, as outlined in (McKay et al., 2017). We observed 31 library users browsing in two very different libraries; we also conducted a short interview with each of them. The intentions and behaviors of these readers inform the requirements developed in the following section. While it is true that such browsers are (as users of any system) limited by the actions they can take within that system, shelf browsing is perceived by those who do it as a valuable and effective information seeking strategy. Direct translations of the physical shelves into an online environment have been demonstrably unsuccessful (Almeida et al., 2006). However, observation will likely elicit a variety of behaviors and activities, some of which will almost certainly prove key to making online browsing successful. We present initial requirements below. Given that we currently do not have successful online browsing systems, it seems likely that supporting those requirements currently least supported is most likely to generate improvements in online browsing.

REQUIREMENTS FOR ONLINE BROWSING

In this section we outline empirically driven user behaviour requirements for online systems. Many of these are taken from our own recent work, but descriptions are supplemented with a full range of browsing literature. As noted in (Fidel, 2012) there has been little crossover between the work of human information behaviour specialists, and interactive information retrieval specialists. This paper draws on both disciplines (via its authors) to generate a list of actionable requirements.

Requirement 1: Search

While not all of the participants in our observations searched, the majority did use the library catalogue. Savvy library users have been shown to use search as a tool for locating areas of the shelves that will be valuable for browsing (Marchionini, 1997; Rice et al., 2001), a finding reflected in our observations. Further to this, many users report experiencing serendipity at the shelves after engaging in search (Makri et al., 2007; Waugh, McKay, & Makri, 2017). While it may seem counterintuitive that search is a key component of browsing, it nonetheless is essential to allow readers to follow a process that works for them.

Requirement 2: Interleaved Search and Browse

The literature suggests information seekers must be able to interleave search and browse, with each interaction seeding further exploration in the other mode (Kuhlthau, 1991; Marchionini, 1997). This interleaving is borne out by our observations, in which a number of readers left the shelves to conduct searches and then returned or searched using a device in the stacks. Thus, not only must a good browsing interface support search, but the interaction between search and browse must be seamless.

Requirement 3: Search-free Browsing

While this contrasts with the first requirement, 20% of the participants in our study *never* searched during their interactions. This reflects some of the descriptions of browsing given in earlier observational studies (Foster & Ford, 2003; Stelmaszewska & Blandford, 2004), and is clearly an important information seeking strategy for those who cannot (yet?) generate a query.

Given the clear hurdles users must surmount to reach a point where a query can be formed (Belkin et al., 1982; Borgman, 1996), search-free browsing is not just a requirement of good browsing, but of good information interfaces generally.

Requirement 4: Book Set Filtering

Observational studies of readers at the shelves generally have seen a number of strategies for actually making book selections. Many readers filter books based on bibliographic (e.g. date of publication) or non-bibliographic features (e.g. size, cover image) (Mikkonen & Vakkari, 2012; Stelmaszewska & Blandford, 2004). Marchionini's work describes the need for the use of templates (Marchionini, 1997), which is akin to filtering in this way; though his approach could be used to limit a result set before it was ever seen. Whether this approach is used to frame the set of items visible to a reader, or support readers in filtering an already-visible set according to their requirements it is a key part of browsing. Practical examples of this from our observations include readers seeking only books that have been published in the past five years, or only textbooks.

Requirement 5: Placemarking

Our observations clearly identified placemarking on the shelves as a valuable part of the browsing experience. Readers in our study placemarked while examining the shelves by running their fingers along the shelves as they looked. They placemarked during triage (determining whether or not to take a book) placing the finger of a non-dominant hand in the shelves while examining a candidate item or placing a candidate book physically in a gap in the shelves marking the place they had reached in their exploration. A held finger was also used to help them return to a point on the shelf while they looked at other places. The need for this type of placemarking was also noted by Kwasnik (Kwasnik, 1992).

Requirement 6: Mark-as-Read

We observed two behaviors that could be supported by showing readers where they have been: re-checking areas of the shelves that had been previously examined within a single visit and returning to a previously-identified fertile browsing location. This second activity may require a form of placemarking, but the returning-to-area activity has been noted in other studies as well (e.g. (Stelmaszewska & Blandford, 2004)), and as such is a behavior that clearly needs online support.

Requirement 7: Rapid, Seamless Zooming

Marchionini noted the need for pan and zoom in his work on browsing requirements in the 90s (Marchionini, 1997). This requirement is borne out in our observations, where we saw many readers engage in rapid zooming from the topic overview provided by shelf endcaps to the book level and back again. Similarly, readers moved forward and back from the shelves, facilitating a fluid shift from overview to close detail.

Requirement 8: Ability to 'Jump' within a Hierarchy

We observed readers using the endcaps of shelves and turning around within the stacks. It is reasonable to assume that these readers were not satisfied with the options within one view and moved rapidly to a different-but-related area of the subject hierarchy. This need is borne out by our earlier statistical work, which shows that readers borrow books above and below a target book, and at the ends of shelves at a higher rate than other books (McKay, Buchanan, & Chang, 2015).

Requirement 9: Overview

The overview has been noted as useful for beginning a browsing process in a number of works (e.g.(Marchionini, 1997)), . This is borne out by our work, where readers were observed to use the ends of shelves to navigate to specific items or topical areas. The challenge of presenting an overview that is both useful and neutral have been mentioned in the literature (Kleiner et al., 2013; Whitelaw, 2015). Nonetheless particularly for readers with very loosely defined needs, the recognition afforded by an overview could help refine their needs enough to begin a more in-depth browsing process that eventually leads to the selection of an item or items. Neutrality is an important aspect—users of systems that anticipate their requirements often feel obstructed and confined by the system. Intelligence is best placed in the user, not the display.

Requirement 10: Display of a (Very) Large Number of Books

Bates notes that browsing involves a high degree of implicit rejection and decision making (Bates, 2007); it is this that underpins the high cognitive burden Marchionini notes as a potential downside of browsing (Marchionini, 1997). In our earlier paper, we commented on just how much implicit rejection was happening in her observations; many of the readers she observed glanced at many hundreds of books, either while navigating to a target item or search area, or as part of choosing the same. This is in stark contrast with the limited scanning of search results, where many users stop in the first page or, less frequently, two (Spink, Wolfram, Jansen, & Saracevic, 2001).

Requirement 11: Rearranging the Shelves

As noted in the introduction to this paper, digital shelves present opportunities that cannot exist with their physical counterparts: such as the opportunity to rearrange the shelves to meet the needs of an information seeker. We observed readers browsing in physically distant locations within a library because books on the same topic were shelved under different elements of a classification scheme. This challenge has also been noted by previous research on library shelving and browsing (Losee, 1993). Given that electronic shelves are not constrained in the same way as physical ones, good online browsing will allow readers to unite all the books on a single topic (or single author or related in another meaningful way) into a single browsable set of items.

Requirement 12: Visible Alternatives

In our earlier work, we note specifically that readers need to be able to examine one candidate book while retaining a visual sense of alternative options. We base this assertion on the fact that only one of our participants near-invariably triaged books anywhere other than in front of the shelves; this is also true in other observations (Hinze et al., 2012). Bates notes in her definition of browsing that browsers return again and again to the interesting scene in which they browse (Bates, 2007), again suggesting it has some visual persistence. Thus, retaining a visual sense of easily accessible alternative items is a key requirement of online browsing.

Requirement 13: Convenience

One of the major reasons given for using ebooks over print books is convenience of access: ebooks are available any time and from anywhere (Li, Poe, Potter, Quigley, & Wilson, 2011; Rowlands, Nicholas, Jamali, & Huntington, 2007). Usage analysis of ebooks bears out the importance of convenience (McKay, Smith, et al., 2015), which has been demonstrated in the information literature more generally (Connaway, Dickey, & Radford, 2011). Given this feature of ebooks, browsing systems that require readers to visit a specific location or use specialist equipment to browse are not likely to meet the needs of the average ebook reader. In fact, requiring the use of specialist equipment reimposes the negatives of shelf browsing—having to visit a specific location—over digital tools, and is a retrograde step.

Summary

The browsing system requirements presented here are based on the existing literature and our observational work. Each requirement has some grounding in empirical research, many of them also have support from information theory models. While, as Wilson suggests, it is likely to be impossible to narrowly specify every facet of a browsing system, this list gives us a comprehensive, empirically-based framework for assessing browsing interfaces. We apply this framework to the interfaces described below.

CURRENT BROWSING INTERFACES

A range of interfaces are described as browsing interfaces in the literature or in popular media. Some are longer-standing and some recent, some are research-based and some are commercial systems. We examine a number of these in turn, before considering them in the light of the requirements drawn from the research literature above. While we considered search clustering systems, such as Scatter/Gather (Hearst & Pedersen, 1996) or those mentioned in (Alam & Sadaf, 2013), there are no systems of this type currently in common use, nor are they regularly mentioned in the literature or popular media as ways to browse.

Search Result Lists

Search result lists, or ranked linked lists were the original online browsing interface. Lists were what Ellis had in mind when he suggested all metadata be 'browsable' (Ellis, 1989). Modern result lists typically consist of a list of 10 to 50 items, in relevance ranked order, presenting some metadata about the objects shown. For full-text search there is often a snippet showing the context in which the query terms have appeared, however this is not common practice in any of the major library book search services (the exception to this is Google Books). A number of approaches—for example faceted searching—have attempted to make search result lists more browsable (Yee, Swearingen, Li, & Hearst, 2003), but the fundamental information approach (which has been consistently criticized as a poor browsing experience) remains the same. A typical example of a book search results screen is shown below (from ExLibris' library catalogue software).

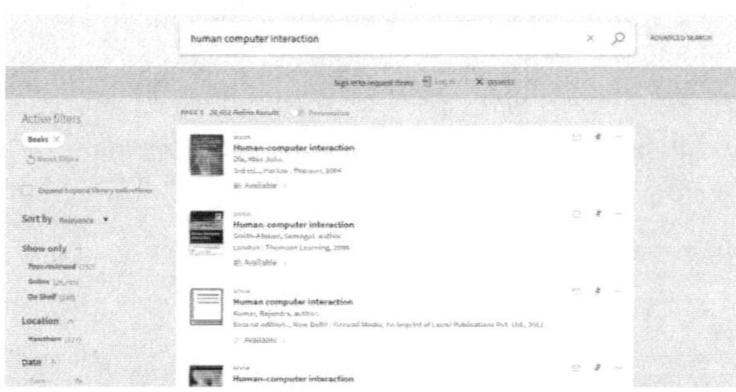

Figure 1: Book Search Results from ExLibris Catalogue System

Amazon-style Recommenders

Recommender systems are one commonly mentioned means of browsing or exploration in an information space (Herlocker, Konstan, Terveen, & Riedl, 2004), and the best-known book recommender system is Amazon. These systems rely on a vast quantity of user data, and present readers with related titles based on interactions by previous users. In this paper we focus on the Amazon recommender as the best known and most commercially successful of these recommenders: it presents readers with a selection of alternative or additional volumes for purchase showing the covers, author and title metadata, and price; dependent on-screen resolution readers may get as few as four books or as many as 10. These offerings are presented in a horizontal ribbon, with arrows to move forward and backward among the options available. An example is shown below.

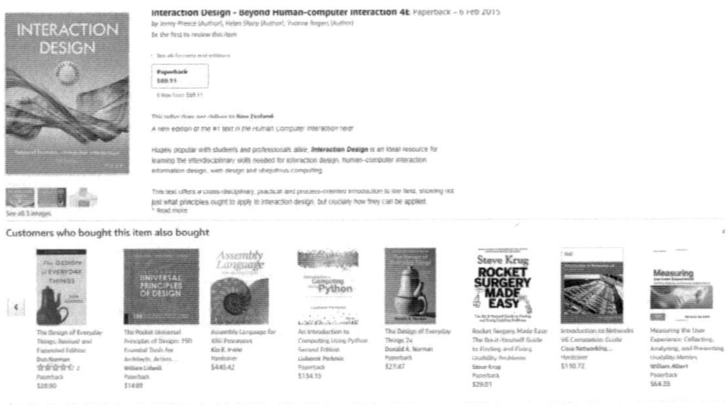

Figure 2: Amazon Recommendations

Slider-based Recommenders

Slider based recommenders, for example WhichBook[3] (a commercial system) and BookFish (Pearce & Chang, 2014) (a research-oriented system that is in living use) ask readers to indicate their preferences on a range of continua using sliders. Some of these continua, e.g. book length, are syntactic and easily defined; some (e.g. humorousness of a book) are more semantic and difficult to ascribe automatically. These interfaces are designed to allow exploration without keyword search and show a fixed number of books based on selections readers have made using sliders. Bookfish allows readers to examine a book using an overlay, retaining a sense that the Bookfish interface persists behind the book.

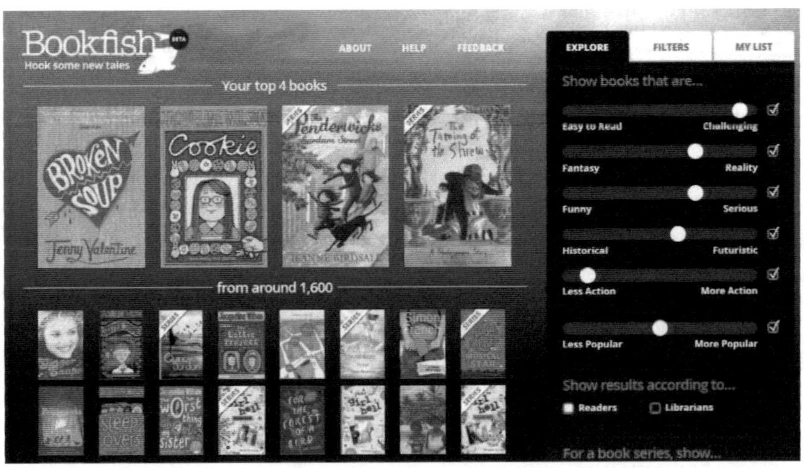

Figure 3: Slider-based Recommender Bookfish

---

[3] http://www.openingthebook.com/whichbook/

The Bohemian Bookshelf

The Bohemian Bookshelf is a research system designed as a library installation by Thudt et al (Thudt et al., 2012). It was specifically designed to facilitate serendipitous discovery of library books and offered a range of visualizations. The visualizations are:

- Color cover circles, showing books that have a similar colored cover together
- Keyword chains, identifying target books through keyword search and then showing up to nine books with adjacencies based on keyword splayed out around a target book
- Timeline view based on both the publication year and the time period a book covers
- Book pile, a book size related visualization
- Author spiral, a sorted list of authors presented as a seemingly infinite scroll

These visualizations are linked, so readers can explore a book's location between visualizations, allowing them to explore a range of relationships between books. This system was positively received by users but has not been further examined in the literature.

Next-on-the-shelf Environments

These environments are a library-system answer to the problem of online browsing. They aim to exploit topic relationship by showing the books that would literally be next on the physical shelves to a target book. These systems have not been the topic of academic research, but rather they exist in live systems. ExLibris Virtual Browse is one example of this[4], University of Technology Sydney's shelf view[5] is another. They each represent the shelf as a horizontal ribbon, showing up to ten of the nearest books on the shelf. The University of Technology Sydney shelf browse is shown below.

Figure 4: University of Technology Sydney Shelf Browse.

Virtual Reality Systems

There are any number of virtual reality environments to represent the library shelves. One recent example is the 'Blended Shelf' presented by Kleiner et al (Kleiner et al., 2013). This interface is presented on large screens and designed to allow naturalistic interactions such as zooming by allowing readers to physically move toward or away from the shelves. It offers an integrated search interface, and a subject overview, and aims to facilitate serendipity by showing recently returned or new books when it is idle (a strategy shown to be effective in physical libraries). Readers can access the 'next' group of shelves with a swipe gesture and can glimpse covers by moving to the sides of books (rather than having to move the books, as in the physical environment). Promisingly, this visualization also allows readers to rearrange the shelves according to their information needs. It is not clear from the description of this system whether readers can view books with a view of the shelves still visible.

MEETING USER NEEDS

Given all of these different representations of browsing in virtual spaces, how well are we meeting user needs? Do any of the interfaces described above allow readers the flexibility and serendipity afforded by library shelves—or, better, go beyond what library shelves offer? We have assessed each interface type against the criteria identified in Table 1 below. 'Y' represents

---

[4] https://knowledge.exlibrisgroup.com/Primo/Product_Documentation/Technical_Guide/010The_PNX_Record/150The_Browse_Section/020Virtual_Shelf_Tab

[5] http://www.lib.uts.edu.au/news/92740/another-new-way-to-browse-librarys-collection

supported requirements, 'N' represents unsupported requirements, and '?' represents requirements that are ambiguously supported.

	Search results	Amazon recommender	Slider recommender	Bohemian Bookshelf	Next-on-the-shelf	Blended Shelf Virtual Reality	Requirement met by n/6 interfaces
Search available	Y	Y	N	Y	Y	Y	5
Search interleaved	Y	Y	N	Y	Y	Y	5
Non-search option	N	N	Y	Y	N	Y	3
Book set filtering	?	N	Y	N	Y	Y	3
Placemarking	N	N	N	N	N	N	0
Mark-as-read	N	N	N	N	N	N	0
Zooming	N	N	N	Y	N	Y	2
Hierarchy jumping	N	N	Y	Y	N	N	2
Overview	N	N	N	N	N	Y	1
Rearranging the shelves	N	N	Y	Y	N	Y	3
Large number of books	N	N	N	Y	N	Y	2
Visible alternatives	N	?	?	Y	N	?	1
Convenience	Y	Y	Y	N	Y	N	4
Requirements supported	3	3	4	8	4	8	

Table 1. Browsing Interfaces vs Browsing Needs

It is clear from this table that the ability to mark one's place in a hierarchy, and to mark what has been seen before are the two needs that have not previously been met by browsing systems. That this requirement is unsupported is particularly surprising, as it was first reported over 25 years ago (Kwasnik, 1992).

Search results and Amazon style recommenders are a long way from meeting browsing needs, despite being commonly mentioned when discussing browsing. This is largely because they require readers to generate search terms, a task that is notoriously difficult with loosely defined information needs (Borgman, 1996), and one that many information seekers would struggle with during the browsing phase of their process (Kuhlthau, 1991).

The Bohemian Bookshelf (Thudt et al., 2012) and Blended Shelf (Kleiner et al., 2013) are easily the closest systems to meeting browsing needs, both allowing readers a range of ways to access the book collection, the ability to view a large number of books quickly, and a range of search and non-search options. Each of them has been developed originally as an installation using specialized equipment, however potentially they could each be re-implemented to allow readers access from their laptops or tablets (neither is likely to be something that could be implemented on a mobile device.

DISCUSSION

While we have clear empirical evidence for what shelf browsers need from browsing systems, we have not yet developed systems that meet these needs, possibly as a result of the disjunct between precision and recall focused IR, and the non-technical contributions of human information behavior research described by (Fidel, 2012).

The system we examined that was closest to meeting user needs was the 'Blended Bookshelf' (Kleiner et al., 2013), a system explicitly designed to support the requirements set down by Marchionini and Bates (Bates, 2007; Marchionini, 1997). The second most browsing-supportive system in our review was the Bohemian Bookshelf (Thudt et al., 2012) system explicitly designed to facilitate serendipity. This reinforces the clear indication from the literature that serendipity is a key element of library shelf browsing (Cooksey, 2004; Makri et al., 2007): support for serendipity goes some way to providing a supportive environment for browsing.

The existing approach of information retrieval, to offer variations on search (Baeza-Yates & Ribeiro-Neto, 1999; Fidel, 2012), is a clear confounding factor in good browsing systems: not offering non-search interaction was a failing of many of the interfaces we addressed. Given that browsing is consistently recognized as an information seeking strategy that is effective for situations where search fails—loosely defined information needs, tasks where recognition can help, refining information needs, requiring information seekers to search before they browse is setting them up to fail (Ellis, 1989; Foster & Ford, 2003; Kuhlthau, 1991; Marchionini, 1997). This understanding is not new, Belkin (Belkin et al., 1982) and Borgman (Borgman, 1996) both addressed it in the 90s, however it is an understanding we simply must take seriously in an age where we are replacing physical with digital, and readers are lamenting the lost ability to browse (Cooksey, 2004; Makri et al., 2007).

There are a number of clear and persistent gaps in our offerings for online browsing: few systems offer readers the ability to rapidly and implicitly reject a large number of items, which is a key component of both the behavior observed in our earlier work (McKay et al., 2017) and the definition Bates provides (Bates, 2007). No system offers placemarking, so it is entirely unclear how placemarking might be best facilitated online. Similarly, none of the interfaces we reviewed offer readers the ability to return to a previously identified fertile browsing field, nor understand what they have seen before. A final key element of physical browsing that is not supported by many of the systems reviewed is retaining a sense of the alternative options while viewing individual items. With new overlay functionalities in web browsers, it is surprising that this feature has not yet been implemented and thus remains untested.

CONCLUSIONS AND FUTURE WORK

Ellis suggested in 1989 that all that was needed to support online browsing, was to make the metadata held about objects browsable (Ellis, 1989). Even this low bar has rarely been met, particularly for online book systems, but what has become clear in the interim is just how difficult it is to make information collections 'browsable'. There have been a number of attempts to define online browsing requirements; our own observational work has focused on deriving these requirements empirically.

In this paper we have collated and summarized browsing requirements, then used them to assess existing browsing interfaces. We have demonstrated why we do not yet have a clearly successful online browsing system—none of the systems we reviewed met more than two thirds of the requirements. What is clear, though, is that purpose-built systems designed to facilitate serendipity and browsing are more effective for browsing than attempts to replicate part of the shelf browsing experience. They are also more effective than search or recommender systems. We are explicitly not arguing against the use of mechanisms for reader support in search results or recommender systems, however they do not, in and of themselves support online browsing in a meaningful way. Browsing is a key element of the information seeking process, and thus a key element of modern information work. To support it adequately we must understand and meet information seeker requirements; this paper goes some way toward that understanding. While we have defined a number of requirements and demonstrated they are not met, it remains future work to implement systems that do address these requirements—and thus are considerably more likely than existing systems to support online browsing.

REFERENCES

Alam, M., & Sadaf, K. (2013). *A Review on Clustering of Web Search Result*, Berlin, Heidelberg.

Almeida, R., Cubaud, P., Dupire, J., Natkin, S., & Topol, A. (2006). *Experiments Towards 3D Immersive Interaction for Digital Libraries*, Paper presented at the International Conference on Technologies for E-Learning and Digital Entertainment, Hangzhou, China.

Baeza-Yates, R., & Ribeiro-Neto, B. (1999). *Modern information retrieval* (Vol. 463): ACM press New York.

Bates, M. J. (2007). What is browsing--really? A model drawing from behavioural science research. *Information Research, 12*.

Belkin, N. J., Oddy, R. N., & Brooks, H. M. (1982). Ask for information retrieval: part I.: background and theory. *Journal of Documentation, 38*(2), 61-71.

Blandford, A., & Furniss, D. (2006). DiCoT: a methodology for applying distributed cognition to the design of teamworking systems. In *Interactive systems. Design, specification, and verification* (pp. 26-38): Springer.

Blandford, A., Rimmer, J., & Warwick, C. (2006). *Experiences of the Library in the Digital Age*. Paper presented at the 3rd International Conference on Cultural Convergence and Digital Technology, Tavros, Greece.

Borgman, C. L. (1996). Why are online catalogs *still* hard to use? *Journal of the American Society for Information Science, 47*(7), 493-503.

Celoria, F. (1969). The Archaeology of Serendip. *Library Association Record, 70*(1), 251-253.

Connaway, L. S., Dickey, T. J., & Radford, M. L. (2011). "If it is too inconvenient I'm not going after it:" Convenience as a critical factor in information-seeking behaviors. *Library & Information Science Research, 33*(3), 179-190. doi:10.1016/j.lisr.2010.12.002

Cooksey, E. B. (2004). Too Important to Be Left to Chance—Serendipity and the Digital Library. *Science & Technology Libraries, 25*(1-2), 23-32.

Ellis, D. (1989). A behavioural approach to information retrieval system design. *Journal of Documentation, 45*(3), 171-212.

Fidel, R. (2012). *Human information interaction: an ecological approach to information behavior*: MIT Press.

Foster, A., & Ford, N. (2003). Serendipity and information seeking: An empirical study. *Journal of Documentation, 59*(3), 321-340.

Hancock-Beaulieu, M. (1993). Evaluating the impact of an online library catalogue on subject searching at the catalogue and at the shelves. *Journal of Documentation, 46*(4), 318-338.

Hearst, M. A., & Pedersen, J. O. (1996). *Reexamining the cluster hypothesis: scatter/gather on retrieval results*. Paper presented at SIGIR '96, Zurich, Switzerland.

Herlocker, J. L., Konstan, J. A., Terveen, L. G., & Riedl, J. T. (2004). Evaluating collaborative filtering recommender systems. *ACM Transactions on Information Systems, 22*(1), 5-53.

Hinze, A., McKay, D., Vanderschantz, N., Timpany, C., & Cunningham, S. J. (2012). *Book selection behavior in the physical library: implications for ebook collections*. Paper presented at JCDL '12, Washington, DC.

Kleiner, E., Rädle, R., & Reiterer, H. (2013). *Blended shelf: reality-based presentation and exploration of library collections*. Paper presented at CHI 13, Paris, France.

Kuhlthau, C. C. (1991). Inside the Search Process: Information Seeking from the User's Perspective. *Journal of the American Society for Information Science and Technology, 42*(5), 361-371.

Kwasnik, B. H. (1992). *A Descriptive Study of the Functional Components of Browsing.* Paper presented at the the IFIP TC2/WG2. 7 Working conference on Engineering for Human Computer Interaction.

Li, C., Poe, F., Potter, M., Quigley, B., & Wilson, J. (2011). *UC Libraries Academic e-Book Usage Survey*. Retrieved from Oakland, CA, USA: http://www.cdlib.org/cdlinfo/2011/06/17/uc-libraries-academic-e-book-usage-survey-report/

Loizides, F., & Buchanan, G. (2009). *An Empirical Study of User Navigation during Document Triage*. Paper presented at ECDL '09, Corfu, Greece.

Losee, R. M. (1993). The relative shelf location of circulated books: A study of classification, users, and browsing. *Library resources & technical services, 37*(2), 197-209.

Makri, S., Blandford, A., Gow, J., Rimmer, J., Warwick, C., & Buchanan, G. (2007). A library or just another information resource? A case study of users' mental models of traditional and digital libraries. *Journal of the American Society for Information Science and Technology, 58*(3).

Marchionini, G. (1997). *Information Seeking in Electronic Environments* (Vol. 9). Cambridge, UK: Cambridge University Press.

Martin, K., Greenspan, B., & Quan-Haase, A. (2017). STAK–Serendipitous tool for augmenting knowledge: A conceptual tool for bridging digital and physical resources. *Digital Studies/Le champ numérique, 9*.

McKay, D., Buchanan, G., & Chang, S. (2015). *Tyranny of Distance: Understanding Academic Library Browsing by Refining the Neighbour Effect*. Paper presented at TPDL '15, Poznan, Poland.

McKay, D., Chang, S., & Smith, W. (2017). *Manoeuvres in the Dark: Design Implications of the Physical Mechanics of Library Shelf Browsing*. Paper presented at CHIIR '17, Oslo, Norway.

McKay, D., & Conyers, B. (2010). *Where the streets have no name: how library users get lost in the stacks*. Paper presented at CHINZ 2010, Auckland, New Zealand.

McKay, D., Smith, W., & Chang, S. (2014). *Lend me some sugar: Borrowing rates of neighbouring books as evidence for browsing*. Paper JCDL '14, London, UK.

McKay, D., Smith, W., & Chang, S. (2015). *Down the Superhighway in a Single Tome: Examining the Impact of Book Format on Borrowing Interactions*. Paper presented at OzCHI '15, Melbourne, Australia.

McKenzie, P. J. (2003). A model of information practices in accounts of everyday-life information seeking. *Journal of Documentation, 59*(1), 19-40.

Mikkonen, A., & Vakkari, P. (2012). *Readers' search strategies for accessing books in public libraries*. Paper presented at IIIX, Nijmegen, The Netherlands.

Pearce, J., & Chang, S. (2014). *Exploration without Keywords: The Bookfish Case*. Paper presented at OzCHI 2014, Sydney, Australia.

Pearson, J., Buchanan, G., & Thimbleby, H. (2010). *HCI design principles for ereaders*. Paper presZnted at the Booksonline '10, Toronto, Canada.

Pearson, J., Buchanan, G., Thimbleby, H., & Jones, M. (2012). The Digital Reading Desk: A lightweight approach to digital note-taking. *Interacting with Computers, 24*(5), 327-338.

Pirolli, P. (1997). *Computational models of information scent-following in a very large browsable text collection*. Paper presented at CHI '97, Atlanta, Georgia, USA.

Reutzel, D. R., & Gali, K. (1998). The Art of Children's Book Selection: A Labyrinth Unexplored. *Reading Psychology, 19*(1), 3-50.

Rice, R. E., McCreadie, M., & Chang, S.-J. L. (2001). *Accessing and browsing information and communication*: Mit Press.

Rowlands, I., Nicholas, D., Jamali, H. R., & Huntington, P. (2007). What do faculty and students really think about e-books? *Aslib Proceedings, 59*(6), 489-511.

Spink, A., Wolfram, D., Jansen, M. B. J., & Saracevic, T. (2001). Searching the web: The public and their queries. *Journal of the American Society for Information Science and Technology, 52*(3), 226-234.

Stelmaszewska, H., & Blandford, A. (2004). From physical to digital: a case study of computer scientists' behaviour in physical libraries. *International Journal on Digital Libraries, 4*(2), 82-92.

Thudt, A., Hinrichs, U., & Carpendale, S. (2012). *The bohemian bookshelf: supporting serendipitous book discoveries through information visualization*. Paper presented at CHI '12, Austin, TX.

Waugh, S., McKay, D., & Makri, S. (2017). *'Too Much Serendipity': The Tension between Information Seeking and Encountering at the Library Shelves*. Paper presented at CHIIR '17 Oslo, Norway.

Whitelaw, M. (2015). Generous Interfaces for Digital Cultural Collections. *DHQ: Digital Humanities Quarterly, 9*(1).

Wilson, T. D. (1999). Models in information behaviour research. *Journal of Documentation, 55*(3), 249-270.

Yee, K.-P., Swearingen, K., Li, K., & Hearst, M. (2003). *Faceted metadata for image search and browsing*. Paper presented at CHI '03, Ft. Lauderdale, Florida, USA.

When Search is (Mis)Learning: Analyzing Inference Failures in Student Search Tasks

Eric M. Meyers
University of British Columbia
eric.meyers@ubc.ca

ABSTRACT

Online inquiry tasks are a rich space to explore how young people take in new information, develop representations of a problem space, and use these representations to make decisions. This paper draws on data from 120 students engaged in scenario-based online inquiry about communicable diseases. Using multiple data sources, including pre/post knowledge tests, think alouds, and carefully constructed tasks that focus on learning, I argue that we might identify where student search processes break down as a way of exploring meditational practice and search support. Rather than seeing task failures as a deficit in students' information seeking abilities, the analysis suggests these misconceptions represent a liminal space for which educators can design informed pedagogical interventions. When the Web is a primary source for student learning, reading comprehension and reasoning skills may play a greater role in student learning outcomes than search skill and information quality.

KEYWORDS

Science learning, Internet, youth, cognition, information seeking and use.

INTRODUCTION

We live in an age of information over-abundance, which has both beneficial and deleterious effects on learning. The ability to make sense of the information one finds online is a critical academic and everyday skill. For today's students, more pedagogical activities are moving online, including flipped classrooms, open online courses, and supplemental materials sought by both teachers and students to support learning. This places a growing burden on young people to provide the content for their own learning, and furthermore to be the arbiters of information quality in the regular absence of teacher scaffolding and mediation. Science teachers in particular were quick to identify the potential of the Web to enhance student learning, but scholars were just as quick to point out the pitfalls of the Internet as a source of scientific information (Hoffman, Wu, Krajcik and Soloway, 2003). Teaching life science topics to young people can be complicated by the prior knowledge and experience they bring to the classroom. In addition to learning a new topic, and faced with managing an uncertain information environment as they surf the Web, students may need to organize their learning through explicit metacognitive strategies, or through implicit filters and heuristics that our brains develop over time and with experience. Cognitive construals are informal, intuitive ways of thinking, often rooted in the everyday act of observing the world and finding patterns and explanations to observable phenomena. Construals often surface as novices work through problems that incorporate new information. Construals are a kind of cognitive bias that can be helpful or harmful, depending on the nature of the learning activity and the expected learning outcome.

Online inquiry tasks are a rich space to explore how young people take in new information, develop representations of a problem space, and use these representations to make decisions. Life science topics in particular are a powerful domain in which to examine how cognitive biases influence what information we seek, take in, and employ in explanations and judgments. While developmental psychologists have studied the effect of construals and biases in very young children, few research studies have explored how these processes work in older students (Coley and Tanner, 2012; Gelman and Legare, 2011). This paper draws on data from a study of middle school students solving information-based scenarios with the aid of the Internet. Four classes of students participated in two information tasks embedded in their curricular unit on human health and wellness. I focus on the following questions that guide my argument:

1. How do cognitive biases emerge in the process of seeking and using information?
2. What affect do construals and biases have on students' learning from online resources?

In this paper, I draw in data that provides insights into how students make sense of a new curriculum topic with a particular emphasis on the errors, misconceptions, or "inference failures" that emerge from their engagement with online information. I posit that these failures, rather than simply exposing students' naïve cognition, provide researchers and educators with an incredible opportunity. Misconceptions, and I use this term to denote inaccurate or incomplete conceptualizations of a topic or process, are a liminal space, a building block toward more sophisticated levels of reasoning. Only in understanding these moments of productive failure can educators design more efficacious pedagogy.

An important focus of library and information science (LIS) research has been the process of accessing relevant documents on a given topic. Despite long standing calls for studies of information use (Buckland, 2012) much less attention has been given to how people make sense of the information they find, and how various cognitive biases can affect meaning making even in the presence of relevant, accurate and authoritative information. This paper contributes to the growing body of information on youth information seeking and use, and provides a bridge of sorts between concepts in the learning sciences and the information processing perspective of information science, building on prior work with young people learning from information (Badilla, et al., 2012 Beheshti, et al., 2014; Cole et al., 2015; Limberg, 2007; Neuman, 2011) and the growing interest in "search as learning" (Rieh et al, 2016).

BACKGROUND

A Constructivist View of Misconceptions

The constructivist view of learning places a great deal of emphasis on students' existing cognitive structures, those representations of the concepts and procedures that precede learning interventions (Bransford, Brown and Cocking, 2000). How students understand a topic and the resources they bring to engaging with new information directly affects their ability to make sense of everyday problems, in and out of school. The resources that students may bring to an information problem—one where they must decide what information to seek, read, reject or use—include not only their familiarity with the topic and inquiry skills, but also their attitudes toward the problem, and their receptiveness to changing their existing understanding. Furthermore, the conditions and motivations established by the context of information seeking and use can further influence the extent to which new cognitive structures represent a plausible and desirable outcome.

Decades of scholarship in scientific and mathematical misconceptions run contrary to the constructivist approach to learning. Smith, DiSessa and Rochelle (1993) document how researchers in the 1970s into the early 1990s approached misconceptions as flawed and unproductive representations of the world that needed to be replaced. More recently, Legare, Wellman, and Gelman (2009) reviewed contemporary approaches to research on science teaching and found similar themes and assumptions to be pervasive in the literature. A different way of thinking about misconceptions, consistent with a constructivist theory of learning, posits misconceptions as the building blocks of more accurate or expert representations. Inaccurate or incomplete understandings of the world are not like broken gears in a clockwork mind, demanding swift and accurate replacement with proper parts. Instead, misconceptions occupy a liminal space in a students' understanding of a topic, and therefore constitute one of the resources that a learner brings to an experience of conceptual development.

Construals, Biases and the Development of Misconceptions

The human brain is a sophisticated pattern recognition tool, seeking meaning and order in our observations of everyday life. We continuously develop and test theories about how the physical world works, how other living beings function and relate, and how other human minds perceive and process information. What emerges from our constant interaction and hypothesizing about the world are cognitive construals, or the everyday intuitive, causal, and explanatory theories that we construct to interpret our perceived existence (Coley and Tanner, 2012; Gelman and Legare, 2011). Construals, as they are often rooted in lived experience and sense-making in situ, constitute an important resource for learning about physics, biology and psychology. However, these construals are of varying accuracy and sophistication, consistent with developmental trajectories and the enormous variation in human experience over time and space. Intuitive theories, which are not formalized, precise, or experimentally grounded, often come in conflict with the explanations students encounter in the curriculum. This can lead to learning opportunities where students restructure their thinking about the world. Conversely, deeply held personal theories can prompt a student to reject or modify scientific explanations in a way that inhibits their understanding of more formal concepts. Coley and Tanner (2012) have proposed that teaching and learning science concepts is challenging not just because the material is complex, but because it also conflicts with these intuitive conceptualizations. They identify three types of construals that are particularly relevant in young people's developing understanding of life sciences, namely anthropocentric thinking, essentialist thinking, and teleological thinking. These three construals are not the only ways young people apply their "folk theories" to scientific problems, but they are potentially powerful in helping us understand how inferential errors might occur. Cognitive psychologists have identified these inference errors in young children, but studies of older students are largely absent from the literature (Coley and Tanner, 2012).

Contributing to the effect of construals on knowledge construction are cognitive biases and heuristics, which affect the way people perceive and process new information about a topic, particularly when the learner is new to a domain, or has to process conflicting or non-intuitive information (Tversky and Kahnman, 1974). While dozens—some scholars identify as many as 53 different kinds—of cognitive biases contribute to difficulties in inferential thinking (Hilbert, 2012; see also Kahnman, 2010 for a survey of the literature), several key theoretical constructs may be identified with information seeking and use situations. These include:

- Bounded rationality or "Satisficing" – when making decisions regarding information, learners are limited by the information to which they have access, the capacity to process and make sense of that information, as well as any constraints that affect the time frame in which the decision must be made (Agosto, 2002; Fidel et al; 1999).
- Attribute substitution – difficult judgments, or decisions in the absence of accessible information are cognitively taxing. People have been shown to reduce their load by reframing the problem in terms of available information, in essence substituting an easier or more accessible question for the more difficult one. This substitution may be unconscious or unrecognized by the decision maker, which explains in part why individuals are often unaware of biases or errors in judgment.
- Availability – decisions grounded in practical situations may prompt learners to identify representative situations from recent memory, particularly in moments of uncertainty. Institutional content filters, as well as the emergent socio-technical challenge of the personal "filter bubble" (Pariser, 2011) may further affect how availability influences conceptual development for novice learners.
- Affect – emotional responses to information can strongly influence the manner in which information is sought, processed, or even ignored, particularly in terms of the consequences associated with information of personal relevance. Other searchers' emotional stances can prompt the interpretation of information with a bias toward maintaining or influencing social relationships and impressions.

All of these constructs represent kinds of cognitive "short cuts", techniques that we employ, either consciously or not, to ease our cognitive load when resolving information problems. These factors contribute to judgment errors in information seeking, but can also affect the extent to which new information leads to the development or revision of conceptual structures. While scholars in information science have identified some of ways information systems affect human information processing (e.g., Fidel, 2012), yet, it is important to recognize that these are complex cognitive attributes with long developmental trajectories.

Information Seeking and Student Learning

Using Internet-based resources as a pedagogical approach has become increasingly common at all levels of K-12 education (Bleicher, 2008; Heil, 2005). It is routine to see students engaged in online inquiry activities to support learning outcomes, despite significant early skepticism regarding the quality and usefulness of much of the Web (Hoffman et al, 2003), not to mention the popular concern that the use of Google and other popular online services is eroding young people's cognitive capacities (Carr, 2010). Research on how young people seek and use information has been an important component of LIS research. A body of work dating to the early days of the Web provides important insights as to how they approach information systems and services, view technology tools, and employ various strategies on search tasks. At the same time, this research identifies a number of challenges in learning with online information. Young people have difficulty navigating the Web and other electronic resources (Bilal, 2000; 2001; 2002; Branch, 2003; Madden, Ford & Miller, 2006; Marchionini, 1989; Schacter, Chung & Dorr, 1998); they do not compose complex search queries or understand Boolean logic (Abbas, 2005; Bilal, 2001; Fidel at al, 1999); they have difficulty making relevance judgments (Agosto, 2002; Kuiper, Volman & Terwel, 2008). Much of this work focuses on identifying imprecise fits between young people's approaches to finding information and the tools available to them. Underlying this work is the assumption that information quality is paramount: if students have effective search strategies, they will access and make use of better quality information.

Recent studies have identified social patterns and processes in youth information behavior. Shenton and Dixon (2004) found that youth often use other people as important sources of information, including the articulation of search strategies. Kuhlthau (2004) and Limberg (1999) found that other searchers might be useful in helping to formulate search topics and keywords (further articulated in Kuhlthau, Maniotes and Caspari, 2007). Large, Beheshti and Rahman (2002) suggest that gender may influence how dyads compose search strings when using the Web. Closer in nature to this inquiry, van Aalst and colleagues examined how Hong Kong students engage in group-based research projects (van Aalst, Hing, May & Yan, 2007). The researchers used search diaries, questionnaires, and a limited number of interviews to explore how the cognitive and affective dimensions of information seeking may be different for groups of students. Recently, Beheshti, Cole and colleagues (2014, 2015, 2017) have done longitudinal work with middle grade students on history inquiry projects. They suggest that leveraging students' prior knowledge and beliefs would be an important tool in making search more efficacious for young people.

METHOD

One hundred twenty grade seven students (age 13-14 years) from four middle school classrooms participated in a two-month mixed methods field-experimental study of school-based information seeking behavior in small groups and as individuals. The study instruments were developed in coordination with classroom educators and integrated with the seventh grade health and micro-life unit at the participating middle school. In this unit, students explored microscopic life, microbiomes, diseases prevention, and personal hygiene. The students completed two information tasks (one class session each, 90 total minutes of search and writing time) related to health and wellness: one on salmonellosis and a second on proper use of antibiotics. One day prior to each search session students were given a brief 15 question pre-test of their topic knowledge. A post-test was administered the day following the search session.

Students completed tasks in one of two conditions: working alone at a computer, or working in a group of three students sharing a single computer. Classrooms were randomly assigned to condition and order balanced to permit between and within subject analyses. The information seeking tasks were presented in the form of a multi-part "progressive" scenario. The first scenario (Task 1) involved a hypothetical salmonella outbreak at school. The second scenario (Task 2) engaged students around the proper use of antibiotics and probiotic supplements to treat a classmate's illness. Task 1 and Task 2 were administered two weeks apart. A subset of students was recorded (audio and screen capture) to better understand the relationship between their search processes and knowledge construction as represented in the written tasks and assessments.

Scenarios were composed of related inquiry subtasks to deepen their knowledge of the topic, activate different kinds of information use, and to prompt inferential thinking. The subtask could be *descriptive* (finding information that describes a given situation), *explanatory* (ascertaining that factors that contribute to a specific situation) or *evaluative* (asking students to take a stance on a given issue or asking them to explore a given scenario or hypothesis). The two tasks assigned to students were composed of nine questions or subtasks. The subtasks were divided equally among the three question types (descriptive, explanatory, evaluative). Furthermore, there was one question of each type per page. For example, in the salmonella task students were prompted to identify the symptoms of salmonella (descriptive), infer the likelihood that a set of students calling in sick may have a food borne illness (evaluative), and explain what procedures a doctor might use to confirm a case of salmonellosis (explanatory). Students composed answers to these questions on a provided task booklet. A 2-1-0 scale (rubric assessment) was used to assess responses to each of the subtasks that students produced as evidence of their information-based reasoning. Each of the nine questions was scored independently, and thus the total assignment was worth 18 points. Non-parametric statistical tests were employed to identify statistical significance, where applicable.

FINDINGS

This paper reports select findings from a much larger data set. The focus of the original study was the comparison of individual and group information seeking and use behaviors (Meyers, 2011), hence much of the data is specific to the condition in which students engaged with the task. The overall conclusion of the study was that students working together in small groups, despite several theoretical advantages associated with collaborate search, encountered greater challenges in seeking and using the information they found, which were expressed in statistically significant differences between post-test scores of individuals and groups. This paper extends this conclusion by identifying specific points of breakdown, and connecting it to cognitive errors of individual learners. Using quantitative and qualitative data from the Salmonella task, I explore three levels at which we see students conceptual understanding expressed: their pre- and post-task knowledge, their task scores (written answers to the subtask prompts), and their reasoning about the problem via screen capture and voice recording.

Exploring the Data: Communicability of Salmonellosis

The progressive scenario asked young people to grapple with the nature and origin of salmonella, transition and prevention of salmonellosis, patient diagnosis and treatment options. These facets of the problem were provided to students in an order that would allow them to build on early subtasks and to position them to make hypothetical decisions. Two of these subtasks, #4 and #5, were focused on transmission and prevention issues, and relied on students finding some basic information about the disease and the common symptoms. The first of the transmission questions asked if salmonella was contagious, and could it be spread from infected students to others. The second question asked if the students with salmonella should be prevented from coming to school. Both subtasks asked students to explain their answer. The answer to the first question could be found on several highly reliable websites used by groups and individuals, including the Centers for Disease Control and Prevention (cdc.gov). Aside from direct contact with tainted or spoiled food, and cross-contamination of fresh and tainted foods, salmonella can be passed from person to person via the "fecal-oral route": poor hygiene on the part of those who are infected can cause the disease to spread to those who did not eat the originally tainted food, or can create new sources of infection. This is how the illness can spread from restaurants, food courts, supermarkets, and school cafeterias. In the middle school context, food sharing and students' poor sanitary practices are two salient issues. The answer to the second question relied on students to make this connection and infer a correct course of action. Several state health department websites (notably Minnesota, New York, South Dakota) provide information that make it explicit: people who are infected with salmonella should not go to work or attend school until they show no symptoms of the disease for 24-48 hours. People who work in the food industry must demonstrate they are disease free with a negative salmonella culture to return to their place of employment.

Students' Prior Knowledge

Students pre- and posttest knowledge of this aspect of the scenario was measured directly by a true/false question: "People who are suffering from food poisoning should be kept away from people who are well (not sick or not showing symptoms)". Based on the information available to students, the best answer to this question is True. In the advance of the information seeking intervention, fewer than 12% of students provided the correct answer. After the intervention, 42% of students provided the correct answer. While it is accurate to say that students' knowledge of the topic improved significantly as a result of the intervention, this is still fewer than half or worse than chance for a question with only two options. Students brought a strong prior sense that the answer to this question was false, and this prior conception was quite resistant to change.

			Pre-Test % Correct		Post-Test % Correct		Difference	
#	Question Focus	Format	Indiv	Group	Indiv	Group	Indiv	Group
5	Transmission	MC	37.7	34.0	35.8	44.7	-1.9	10.7
11	Transmission	TF	9.4	14.9	41.5	41.5	32.1 *	26.6 *
13	Transmission	TF	43.4	34.0	79.2	38.3	35.8 *	4.3

*Pre/Post change is significant at .05 level TF = True/False MC = Multiple Choice

#5: Approximately how many people report getting salmonellosis each year?
a) 3,000 b) 40,000 c) 500,000 d) 6 million
#11: People who are suffering from food poisoning should be kept away from people who are well (not sick or not showing symptoms)
a) True b) False
#13: You can get salmonella from pets, including some kinds of turtles.
a) True b) False

Table 1: Pre/Post-test Questions Related to Transmission

Other pre- and posttest questions that covered the learning objective of transmission and prevention included the true/false question: "You can get salmonella from pets, including some kinds of turtles." Prior to information seeking, 38% of students identified correctly that this statement is True. After the intervention there was a significant change in student answers among those working individually, but little change among those who worked collaboratively. Another question asked students to identify the estimated frequency of salmonellosis in the U.S. Again, the change in student knowledge was flat. These two questions though not directly related to subtasks #4 and 5 were included in this analysis to show that student knowledge of disease transmission started out and remained fairly low, in some cases worse than chance, even after the search task intervention.

One possible explanation for the responses to Question #11 is a resource students brought to the task that was not anticipated by the researcher: students viewed a short documentary on "Typhoid Mary"[1] the week prior to the search task. Students were overheard making analogies between the quarantine of ill patients in the early 20th Century and the student scenario. These quarantines often had significant health and social repercussions to patients and health workers, some of which were unnecessary and in violation of current social norms. The salience and availability of this bit of prior knowledge can explain the strong student reaction to the question, and the intractability of their prior conception.

Students' Search Task Performance

Student performance varied across the different subtasks, and the difference between individual and group performance also varied with the subtasks. That is, students as a whole did not perform consistently on all information seeking tasks, and there were subtasks in particular where students working in the individual condition performed significantly better than students in the group condition, including #4 and 5. Pearson's Chi Square test was used to assess the reliability of differences between individuals and groups for each subtask; the goal was to assess where the condition of information seeking contributed to breakdowns at the subtask level. Although individuals tended to do better than groups across the majority of questions, subtasks 4 and 5 show significant differences between conditions. Only 30% of students working alone received full points for their response; even fewer students working in groups provided a fully correct answer. Table 2 summarizes this data.

		Individual			Group			
#	Question Type	0	1	2	0	1	2	Pearson's λ
4	Explanatory	14	20	21	13	34	6	12.93 *
5	Evaluative	15	22	18	31	15	7	12.66 *

*significant at .05 level
#4: Are the students contagious (capable of spreading salmonella)? Explain your answer.
#5: Should the infected students be kept away from school? Why or why not?

Table 2: Task Results Related to Transmission

---

[1] The "complex" case of Typhoid Mary, quarantined for nearly three decades against her will, can be viewed at: http://www.pbs.org/wgbh/nova/typhoid/

In analyzing students' answers to these tasks, there were common problems and misperceptions in student responses, and these problems can be linked to observations of student performance in the classroom and in the process capture data.

Example of a correct student answer for Subtask 4:

> "Yes, because the infected person's feces contain salmonella so it can spread through unwashed hands." (O1-RK)

Examples of incorrect student answers:

> "Yes it is spread by inhalation of its spores." (O1-TW)
>
> "The students are not capable of spreading salmonella, because it isn't a virus." (04-RTC)
>
> "No, only travels through raw food and is non-communicable through humans." (04-MTS)
>
> "Salmonella is not contagious simply by being around someone. Salmonella could only be spread by the contact of feces. Bugs and such sit upon fruits and vegetables and poop, which is how the bacteria developes [sic]." (O1-SB)
>
> "No because unless a student ingests another student salmonella will not be spread." (O1-CN)

We see three different levels of misconception in these responses. The first two responses above show that students have incorrectly identified the nature of the salmonella pathogen. The third and fourth responses assume that the bacteria can only be found in raw food or feces, missing the possibility of transmission through cross-contamination. The last example is an inference that showed up in a handful of student responses, and was identified in groups and individuals from different classes. This student made the connection that salmonella is spread by tainted food, but then made the leap that unless people infected with salmonella are eaten – ingested by others as food, i.e., cannibalized – they cannot spread the disease.

Subtask #5 asked students to evaluate the status of potentially infected students and assist in making a decision regarding their school readiness. Very few students provided sophisticated responses. Examples of incorrect or partially correct responses:

> "No, just keep them clean." 04-CAC
>
> "Students should wash their hands often and be careful." 04-DS
>
> "Salmonella is not contagious but it would be smart not to go to school when you have it. It would be good to be kept away from school when they are sick because of the symptoms and what happens if salmonella gets worse." 05-KN
>
> "Yes, salmonella can make you vomit and that would be totally gross." 05-JR

It was not uncommon for students to provide an answer that included both incorrect and correct information, suggesting that they had an incomplete comprehension of how salmonella transmission occurs. In some cases, students performed a cognitive substitution, focusing on how the individual student would feel about being sick, or how sick students would not want to be in school, rather than answering the question that was asked, which was whether these students should be permitted to attend school showing symptoms of a food-borne illness.

Students Reasoning in Groups

Thus far the data has shown that students' prior knowledge was limited and fairly resilient in the face of a structured information seeking task, and that their responses to the related subtask illustrated several misconceptions and evidence of reasoning errors. To better understand how these errors emerged, transcripts of several group conversations were analyzed and compared with their search logs and written responses. Although these groups found websites that contained the information they needed to make correct inferences, they still failed to produce a correct answer. These breakdowns in the learning process included:

- Relying on surface understanding: when students jump to conclusions from insufficient evidence or research.
- Discounting evidence: when students have access to the correct answer, but discount its significance or application in context.
- Ignoring correct suggestions: when a student makes a correct inference, but his opinion is ignored or discounted by the group.

These cognitive errors are illustrated below with dialog from the group search diaries for subtasks 4 and 5.

Relying on Surface Understanding

When groups found one means of transmission (e.g. tainted food), they assumed that was all there was to know. Take the following group exchange from group O3-GHG:

Student A: Are they infectious?
Student B: No, because salmonella is, salmonella can only be spread...
Student C: It's food poisoning.
Student B: Yeah.
Student A: Ok. Um. Should they be isolated or kept away from school? No, cause it's not...
Student B: It's not infectious. It is not spread by human beings.

It was observed and recorded that students would first develop a hypothesis about the question ("I'm thinking no."), then browse the web to confirm their gut reaction. In the case of group O3-GHG, the students did not read deeply on the website, nor did they perform any additional searches to verify their assumption. Once they read that salmonella most often comes from tainted food, they discounted human contact as a possible means of transmission.

Some groups were able to "talk-out" the issue of food poisoning and what it means, but the written answers suggest these conversations were rare. From this evidence and observations of the class, we see that some groups did not take the time to engage with the ideas behind what they read, jumping to hasty conclusions unless corrected by a group member. A portion of the transcript from group O4-BHP illustrates this challenge:

Student D: [Reading from the task sheet] Are the students capable of spreading salmonella? Answer is no, because the disease is non-communicable.
Student F: Well, why is it non-communicable? What's it caused by?
Student E: It's caused by bacteria that's found in foods like chicken.
Student F: It's found in uncooked foods. So unless we have cannibals in the school...right? Oh, wait. It's contagious.
Student E: No, it's not.
Student F: [Paraphrasing from website] It says salmonella infection is contagious. You can pass the bacteria on to others.
Student D: You can't have food poisoning be contagious.
Student F: It's not food poisoning, it's a bacteria.
Student D: Alright.
Student F: It's bacteria in uncooked food. It's...it says right here it's contagious. You came up with a good explanation but it's wrong.

Student D appeared ready to draw a conclusion based on his assumptions rather than evidence. Student F was able to correct his mistaken assumption by questioning this move and engaging with a resource containing reliable information. While the group appears to accept Student F's explanation of salmonella as contagious, it is not clear that the entire group understands how salmonella may be spread in social situations, i.e., the mechanism of transmission is still "fuzzy" to the group members.

Discounting the Evidence

Some groups encountered good explanations for why those infected with salmonella should be kept home, but they discounted this advice because they felt it over-cautious or inconsistent with their perception of peer hygiene. These students were hesitant to admit that people fail wash their hands or might touch "gross" stuff. Witness an exchange from group O3-WLE:

Student J: [highlighting words from first search result] So it's transmitted by fecal or oral spread. That means if you ate someone's poop.
Student K: Yeah. Pretty much. But, like, if you were handling a dog and not washing your hands thoroughly enough.
Student J: Wait, what are we saying?
Student K: Something pretty gross.
Student L: It's right there.
Student J: So you have to wash your hands? But you'd already have it.
Student K: Yeah, but then you'd go to touch something, you'd be sharing feces.
Student J: Is that all?

Group O4-BPH, as many others, concluded that, so long as everyone can remember to wash after using the bathroom, sending infected students to school would be acceptable. This is the same group that correctly identified salmonella as contagious, above.

Student D: I don't think that's [keeping students from attending school] totally necessary. If they're careful and they wash their hands after they go to the bathroom, they're fine.
Student F: But what if they don't wash their hands?
Student D: Well, if they don't wash their hands, then they should leave school.

Student F: No, no…you misunderstand. What I'm saying is, even if they wash their hands, the virus may be communicable.
Student D: Well, it's not like a guy's gonna stick his hands in toilet water.
Student E: What if you drop the hall pass in? That's what [student] did.
Student D: Yeah, whatever. That's legit. But seriously, I just don't think it's capable of spreading without someone doing something like not washing their hands.

Students working in groups also expressed empathy for those classmates who might be kept away from school. The more students discussed the issue, the more they appeared to minimize the risk of spreading the bacteria, contrary to the evidence they found online. Their affective reaction to the consequences of being kept from school, and the analogous case of Typhoid Mary's quarantine, were potential sources of cognitive bias.

Ignoring Correct Suggestions

One of the challenges of working in peer groups is the possibility of an unequal social dynamic that results in the ideas of some students having more weight than others. This becomes problematic when the students who suggest the correct answer are ignored or their ideas rejected, not strictly on the idea's merits, but on the social status of the individual. The low-status member may have insights, but those ideas are discounted because he or she is not leading the conversation. Continuing from the conversation from group O4-GHG above, Student F tried emphatically to make his case, but his interpretation—the correct interpretation—was rejected by his peers.

Student F: I say they should be kept from school in case they forget to wash their hands and transfer the virus to someone else. I wash my hands, but people forget. [Raising voice] Nobody gets what I'm trying to say – people forget to wash their hands!

Ultimately, this group chose to ignore the correct suggestion and wrote that students should be able to attend school despite having salmonella symptoms, so long as they wash their hands.

Relying on surface understanding and preconceptions, ignoring evidence or alternatives, and projecting a false unanimity are all symptoms of "groupthink", a kind of social and affective decision bias when groups make poor decisions because they are too cohesive or wish to reduce tension within the group. Rather than challenging each other's assumptions, group members rationalize their answer and do not support their conclusions with expert opinion. The dialog samples from group interactions illustrated the different ways groupthink and other cognitive biases manifest in these information-seeking tasks, particularly around the portions of the task that asked them to critically evaluate a situation or come to a conclusion. By engaging in conversation, individuals shared and made salient their cognitive construals and biases, presenting a probable explanation for why groups of students performed lower on some portions of the task than students in the individual condition.

DISCUSSION

Contamination and illness are topics that are particularly useful for surfacing young people's thinking, as the processes by which pathogens and medical treatments affect the human body are largely invisible and often mysterious (Legare, Wellman, and Gelman, 2009). It is common for adults and even science teachers to have a poor grasp of how microlife interact with humans, and some cultural groups have endowed medical treatments with magical or religious properties. Life science pedagogy often fights an uphill battle against the construals and biases that originate in the various formal and informal learning spaces of childhood.

In this analysis we see how young people develop misconceptions or, in some cases, fail to correct naïve or incomplete conceptions of a topic despite adequate access to information. The search logs from the Internet sessions showed that students found and used reliable and authoritative information via the Web, suggesting that search technique, relevance, and authority were not the primary factors in students' failure to correctly resolve information problems. Instead, the errors were largely a matter of reading comprehension combined with cognitive frames that influenced the interpretation and reception of the information they accessed.

Evidence from multiple sources shows how cognitive construals emerge in how students constructed their knowledge of disease transmission. In particular, essentialist thinking is evidenced in students' naïve approaches to salmonellosis, and how their narrowing of a "food-borne illness" to simply tainted food confines their thinking about transmission mechanisms. This kind of thinking illustrates a cognitive bias exacerbated by shallow information processing and the constraints of satisficing on students' conceptual development. The analysis of students' reasoning, captured through audio recordings of group processes, makes evident how affective considerations of an information problem space influence decision-making, even to the point of minimizing or ignoring relevant information that might disconfirm preconceptions. The influence of the "Typhoid Mary" video presents an unanticipated salient analogy that potentially influenced student reasoning about the effects of disease as a social construct with affective consequences.

A seemingly intractable problem for novice searchers is confirmation bias, a desire to find information that supports a "gut feeling" or intuitive assessment of a problem. While the group condition in this study tended to disadvantage students in terms of their concept development as measured by both the search task and posttest measure, there is evidence that constructive argumentation within groups led students to reflect on their assumptions and articulate their rationales. Collaboration with other learners can be a source of constructive argumentation (Gilles and Ashman, 2003). It has also proven a challenge when social hierarchies compete with effective information processing, both in this study and in analyses of students working with information provided by an educator to support learning in other domains (Barron, 2003). The charge for educators of today's youth, endowed with confidence in their search skills, is to facilitate productive argumentation and scaffold effective information use scenarios that lead to the guided development of concepts in all academic domains.

LIMITATIONS

This analysis provides only a snapshot of student thinking on a small number of search tasks within a larger and more complicated study of the effect of collaboration on information seeking and learning. The study was not designed expressly to understand cognitive bias and the development of misconceptions, nor longitudinal understanding of students' concept development. As the study of cognitive processes is fraught by the inability to measure and ascertain the precise nature of student thinking and learning, I am necessarily making inferences about inference.

CONCLUSION

I argue in this paper that students' failure to develop a stronger understanding of a search topic is not simply a matter of search technique or information quality. Rather, a combination of inferential breakdowns based in common cognitive processes – "noisy information processing" – led to challenges in student learning. In particular, where students lack prior knowledge, peer elaboration can lead students to faulty inferential reasoning about science problems. In the age of data aggregation and team-based science, we often claim that additional minds make for more reliable decisions, but in the case of small groups of novice learners this is not always the case.

This paper illustrates how approaches and concepts from cognitive psychology and the learning sciences can enhance our understanding of youth information behavior by focusing on learning processes and outcomes, not just search success. The findings have implications for the design of information-intensive pedagogy in science as well as other disciplines that employ inquiry-based learning. If we seek to develop the capacities of young people to find, assess and use information, we have to better understand the starting point of their search, not just in terms of technical sophistication, but also in cognition and prior knowledge. Only then can we design efficacious inquiry-based pedagogy resulting in stronger learning outcomes.

ACKNOWLEDGMENTS

The author wishes to thank the children and teachers who participated in this study, as well as the comments and suggestions of three anonymous reviewers.

REFERENCES

Abbas, J. 2005. Out of the mouths of middle school children: Developing user-defined controlled vocabulary for subject access in a digital library. *Journal of the American Society for Information Science & Technology*, 56(14): 1512-1524.

Agosto, D. E. 2002. Bounded rationality and satisficing in young people's web-based decision making. *Journal of the American Society for Information Science & Technology*, 53(1): 16-27.

Meyers, E. M. 2011. The nature and impact of collaborative information problem solving in the middle school classroom. Unpublished doctoral dissertation. University of Washington.

Barron, B. 2003. When smart groups fail. The Journal of the Learning Sciences, 12(3): 307–359.

Badilla Quintana, M.G., Cortada Pujol, M., & Riera Romani, J. 2012. Internet navigation and information search strategies: How children are influenced by their participation in an intensive ICT project. International Journal of Technology and Design Education, 22, 513-529.

Beheshti, J., AlGhamdi, M. J., Cole, C., Abuhimed, D., Lamoureux, I. 2014. Designing an intervention tool for students with students. In (D. Bilal & J. Beheshti, Eds.) New Directions in Children's and Adolescents' Information Behavior Research. New York: Emerald, 295-331.

Bilal, D. 2000. Children's use of the Yahooligans! Web search engine: I. Cognitive, physical, and affective behaviors on fact-based search tasks. Journal of the American Society for Information Science, 51(7): 646-665.

Bilal, D. 2001. Children's use of the Yahooligans! Web search engine: II. Cognitive and physical behaviors on research tasks. *Journal of the American Society for Information Science & Technology*, 52(2): 118-136.

Bilal, D. 2002. Children's use of the Yahooligans! Web search engine. III. Cognitive and physical behaviors on fully self-generated search tasks. *Journal of the American Society for Information Science & Technology*, 53(13): 1170-1183.

Bleicher, R. E. 2008. Internet pedagogy: Using the Internet to achieve student learning outcomes. In (J. Coiro, M. Knobel, C. Lankshear, and D. Leu, eds.) Handbook of research on new literacies (pp. 1093-1107). New York: Lawrence Erlbaum.

Branch, J. 2003. Instructional intervention is the key: Supporting adolescent information seeking. School Libraries Worldwide. Retrieved March 18, 2011 from http://www.highbeam.com/doc/1P3-642087081.html.

Bransford, J. D., Brown, A. L., & Cocking. R. R. (Eds). 2000. How people learn: Brain, mind, experience, and school. Washington, DC: National Academy Press.

Carr, N. 2010. The shallows: What the Internet is doing to our brains. New York: W. W. Norton.

Cole, C., Beheshti, J., Abuhimed, D., & Lamoureux, I. 2015. The End Game in Kuhlthau's ISP Model: Knowledge Construction for Grade Eight Students Researching an Inquiry-based History Project. Journal of the American Society for Information Science and Technology, 66 (11), 2249-2266.

Cole, C., Beheshti, J., & Abuhimed, D. 2017. A relevance model for middle school students seeking information for an inquiry-based class history project. Information Processing & Management, 53(2), 530-546.

Coley, J. D., and Tanner, K. D. 2012. Common origins of diverse misconceptions: Cognitive principles and the development of biology thinking. CBE-Life sciences education, 11: 209-15.

Fidel, R. 2012. Human information interaction: An ecological approach to information behavior. Cambridge, MA: The MIT Press.

Gillies, Robyn M., & Ashman, A. F. 2003. Guiding intellectual and personal growth across educational contexts. In R. Gillies and A. Ashman (Eds.), Co-operative learning: The social and intellectual outcomes of learning in groups (pp. 224-238). New York: RoutledgeFalmer.

Heil, D. 2005. The Internet and student research: Teaching critical evaluation skills. Teacher-Librarian, 33: 26-30.

Hilbert, M. 2012. Toward a synthesis of cognitive biases: How noisy information processing can bias human decision making. Psychological Bulletin, 138(2): 211-237

Hoffman, J. L., Wu, H-K., Krajcik, J. S., and Soloway, E. 2003. The nature of middle school learners' science content understandings with the use of online resources. Journal of Research in Science Teaching, 40(3): 323-346.

Kuhlthau, C. C. 2004. Seeking meaning: A process approach to library and information services. Westport, CT: Libraries Unlimited.

Kuhlthau, C. C., Maniotes, L. K., and Caspari. A. K. 2007. Guided inquiry: Learning in the 21st Century. Westport, CT: Libraries Unlimted.

Kuiper, E., Volman, M., & Terwel, J. 2008. Students' use of Web literacy skills and strategies: Searching, reading and evaluating Web information. Information Research, 13(1) paper351. Retrieved March 18, 2011 from http://InformationR.net/ir/13-3/paper351.html

Large, A., Beheshti, J., & Rahman, T. 2002. Gender differences in collaborative Web searching behavior: An elementary school study. Information Processing & Management, 38(3): 427-443.

Legare, C. H., and Gelman, S. A. 2011. Concepts and folk theories. Annual Review of Anthropology, 40: 379-398.

Legare, C. H., Wellman, H. M., and Gelman, S. A. 2009. Evidence for an explanation advantage in naïve biological reasoning. Cognitive Psychology, 58: 177-94.

Limberg, L. 1999.. Experiencing information seeking and learning: A study of the interaction between two phenomena. Information Research, 5(1) paper 68. Retrieved March 18, 2011 from http://informationr.net/ir/5-1/paper68.html.

Limberg, L. 2007. Learning assignment as task in information seeking research. Information Research, 12(1) paper colis28. Retrieved March 18, 2011 from http://InformationR.net/ir/12-1/colis/colis28.html.

Madden, A. D., Ford, N. J., and Miller, D. 2006. Information resources used by children at an English secondary school: Perceived and actual levels of usefulness. Journal of Documentation, 63(3): 340-358.

Marchionini, G. 1989. Information-seeking strategies of novices using a full-text electronic encyclopedia. Journal of the American Society for Information Science, 40(1): 54-66.

Neuman, D. 2011. Learning in information-rich environments. New York: Springer.

Rieh, S. Y., Collins-thompson, K., Hansen, P., and Lee, H-J. 2016. Towards searching as a learning process: A review of current perspectives and future directions. Journal of Information Science, 42 (1), 19-34.

Schacter, J., Chung, G., & Dorr, A. 1998. Children's Internet searching on complex problems: Performance and process analysis. Journal of the American Society for Information Science, 49(9): 840-849.

Shenton, A. K. & Dixon, P. 2003. Youngsters' use of other people as an information-seeking method. Journal of Librarianship and Information Science, 35(3): 219-233.

Smith, J. P., diSessa, A. A., and Rochelle, J. 1993. Misconceptions reconceived: A constructivist analysis of knowledge in transition. The Journal of the Learning Sciences, 3(2): 115-63.

Tversky, A., and Kahneman, D. 1974. Judgment under uncertainty: Heuristics and biases. Science, 185: 1124– 1131

van Aalst, J., Hing, F. W., May, L. S., & Yan, W. P. 2007. Exploring information literacy in secondary schools in Hong Kong: A case study. Library & Information Science Research, 29(4): 533-552.

Wiley, J., & Bailey, J. 2006. Effects of collaboration and argumentation on learning from web pages. In A.M. O'Donnell, C. E. Hmelo-Silver, and G. Erkens, (Eds.) Collaborative learning, reasoning, and technology (pp. 297-321). Mahway, NJ: Lawrence Erlbaum Associates.

The Interaction Between People, Information and Innovation: Information Literacy to Underpin Innovative Work Behaviour in a Finnish Organisation

Lyndsey Middleton
School of Computing, Edinburgh Napier University, Scotland, UK, L.Middleton@napier.ac.uk

Laura Muir
School of Computing, Edinburgh Napier University, Scotland, UK, L.Muir@napier.ac.uk

Hazel Hall
School of Computing, Edinburgh Napier University, Scotland, UK, H.Hall@napier.ac.uk

Robert Raeside
The Business School, Edinburgh Napier University, Scotland, UK, R.Raeside@napier.ac.uk

ABSTRACT

Workplace learning and employee-led innovation are related. For example, mistakes made when learning may spur innovation. Investigated in this paper is the role of information literacy in the learning of innovative work behaviour in the workplace, and the associated information behaviours that allow for innovative work behaviour to develop. Thus, interactions between people, information and innovation are a main focus. The findings derive from analysis of data generated in twelve semi-structured interviews conducted within a Finnish organisation. Employee perceptions on the role of information in the workplace, and its role in supporting the learning of innovative work behaviour, are explored. The analysis reveals that: (1) information literacy skills serve as a pre-requisite for workplace learning; (2) information behaviours support the learning of innovative work behaviour and; (3) a variety of information sources support employees as they learn to behave innovatively.

KEYWORDS

workplace learning, innovative work behaviour, information literacy, information behaviour

INTRODUCTION

Information literacy has been considered an initiator of information behaviour applicable to workplace contexts since the 1990s (e.g. Bruce, 1999; Tait & Edwards, 2016). In prior research the focus falls on its role in the building of skills (e.g. Crawford & Irving, 2009) and generic workplace competencies (Banek Zorica, Spiranec, & Biskupic, 2014). A few researchers only (among them Lloyd & Somerville, 2006) have considered information literacy and associated information behaviours in respect of learning in the workplace. Most studies, in contrast, are conducted in educational settings such as schools (e.g. Adhikari, Scogings, Mathrani & Sofat, 2017).

The relationship between workplace learning and innovation has also been investigated in prior studies (e.g. Høyrup, 2010). Here employee-led innovation, i.e. innovation developed at the level of individual employees rather than that of the organisational level, is the main focus. Ellström (2010) suggests that learning plays a central role such research. Høyrup (2010) makes this relationship explicit by conceptualising innovation processes as learning processes: learning is a mechanism that underpins employee-led innovation, e.g. like innovation, it is both practice-based and employee-driven (p.151). Høyrup also differentiates between innovation and innovative work behaviour: the latter may lead to innovation, or to failure. Mistakes associated with failure may subsequently generate innovation. In turn, innovative work behaviour may be an outcome of innovative learning (Høyrup, 2010, p.152).

Investigated in this paper is the role of information literacy in the learning of innovative work behaviour in the workplace, and the associated information behaviours that allow for innovative work behaviour to develop. The findings derive from an analysis of data gathered in twelve semi-structured interviews conducted within a Finnish organisation. Employee perceptions on recognition of the need to use information in the workplace, and to act upon this in support of the learning of innovative work behaviour, are explored. Interactions between people, information and innovation are key to the analysis. Practitioners in information and knowledge management may draw upon the findings to establish the key determinants of successful workplace learning of innovative work behaviour.

Key concepts

Three terms used throughout this paper merit definition as key concepts: (1) 'innovative work behaviour'; (2) 'information literacy'; and (3) 'information behaviour'. The term 'innovative work behaviour' is best defined with reference to innovation per se, and the role that employees play in creating innovations. Innovation may occur at the level of the individual, group, or organisation (West & Farr, 1990, pp. 5-7), and can take many forms, e.g. product, process, organisational or marketing, technological, governance, conceptual (De Vries, Bekkers & Tummers, 2015). Employees are a vital resource to innovation through their acquisition of up-to-date information, as well as experience-based knowledge, from interactions with materials, markets, customers and users (Høyrup, 2010, p.143). Taking these processes into account, and drawing upon West and Farr (1990), *innovative work behaviour* is defined here as 'the intentional generation and implementation of new and useful ideas within a role, a group, or an organisation'. *Information literacy* is the ability to think critically, make balanced judgements about information, and then use this information appropriately (e.g. ethically) to meet information needs (see, for example, Goldstein & Whitworth, 2015, p.1; Johnston & Webber, 2013). Those who are information literate, for example, are empowered to develop informed views and engage fully with society (Secker, 2018). Levels of information literacy are contingent upon *information behaviour*, i.e. the means by which individuals interact with (e.g. seek and use) information (Bates, 2010).

LITERATURE: INFORMATION LITERACY, WORKPLACE INFORMATION LITERACY AND THE SCONUL MODEL

It has been established that much information literacy research concerns studies conducted in educational settings (Williams, Cooper & Wavell, 2014), often with a bias towards competence development in information seeking (Whitworth, 2014, p.74-81). In response, there have been a number of recent calls to consider information literacy more extensively elsewhere (e.g. Goldstein & Whitworth, 2015; Hall, Cruickshank & Ryan, 2018 in press). These draw attention to the general value of training people in information handling, and in fostering environments to promote the effectiveness of information use (e.g. Goldstein & Whitworth, 2015, p.1), as well as the opportunity to identify the complexities of information literacy across a variety of contexts. In terms of workplace information literacy, for example, there are contextual factors that may not come into play in educational learning. This is because, for example, workplace information literacy is embedded in practice (Lloyd, 2010, 2012) and is socially enacted (Lloyd, 2012, p.777). In addition, learning that underpins workplace information literacy is, more ad hoc, collaborative, multi-faceted, and informal than learning in educational environments (Cacciattolo, 2015; Goldstein & Whitworth, 2015, p. 1).

Those keen to consider information literacy beyond the classroom have also explored the value of adopting and adapting extant information literacy models that were originally applied in educational settings, such as that advocated by SCONUL (2011). The SCONUL model was initially deployed by librarians and teachers as a method of delivering information skills to learners. Comprising 7 'pillars', it sets out skills/competencies and attitudes/understanding applicable to information use: identify, scope, plan, gather, evaluate, manage, present. This model has been acknowledged as useful in other contexts and has been successfully adopted/adapted to generate new insight related to a range themes such as employability (Goldstein, 2015a) and democratic engagement (Hall, Cruickshank & Ryan, 2018 in press).

Research question

Broad themes associated with the development of innovative work behaviour have been investigated in the past (e.g. Hauschildt, 1996). Equally, the relationship between workplace learning and innovation per se has been explored (e.g. Leong & Anderson, 2012; Høyrup, 2010). However, the enhancment of *innovative work behavour* through workplace learning remains largely unexplored from the information science perspective. A wide exploration of the literature across multiple domains (e.g. workplace learning, organisational learning, and information and knowledge management) has highlighted the value of generating further understanding of contextual influencers of workplace learning development in relation to innovative work behaviour. One such factor is information literacy. Therefore, the research question that the study reported in this paper addresses is:

How does information literacy, and associated information behaviours, support successful workplace learning of innovative work behaviour?

RESEARCH DESIGN AND METHODOLOGY

Study setting and sample

This study used an explorative qualitative design informed by a constructivist approach to explore perceptions and actions of social factors (Flick, 2009, p.66-67), such as those involved in the learning process. Data were collected through the implementation of semi-structured interviews with twelve employees in a publically funded Finnish University. The use of semi-structured interviews served two main purposes: (1) to explore themes that emerged from the participants with minimal direction for the researcher and; (2) to add depth and context to responses given from participants (Pickard, 2013). The participants were non-academic staff, employed in support services, e.g. library, education and research support, administration, finance, planning, communication. Three considered themselves to be leaders responsible for a service or department, and three managerial running services themselves while responsible to the leadership. The rest had no managerial responsibility. Three were male, and nine were female. All but one was of Finnish descent: the other was British. Five were aged 35-45, five 46-55 and two 56-65. It should be emphasised here that although the site for data collected was a university, the interviewees reflected on their daily roles as employees. Thus, the interviews captured the nature of the *workplace* learning in an *organisational setting* (as opposed to *educational learning* in a *classroom*).

The university operates through a strategy designed to concentrate on the core value of improvement between 2015 and 2020. Innovation is prominent in the strategy and regarded as an anchor for the development of innovation. Data collection took place in December 2017. This timing was considered ideal for the purposes of the study because this was the mid-point of the implementation.

Procedure

Since the geographical location of the researcher and participating organisation differed, a facilitator shared study information with potential participants in Finland. The facilitator sent study information and researcher contact details to all departments within the support services to invite study volunteers to come forward. This opportunity sampling yielded twelve participants. Once each had given informed consent, the interviews were scheduled to take place at the university over a five-day visit to Finland.

The interview procedure was developed in English (the first or second language of all involved) to engage participants in discussions of how they learn to innovate best in the workplace, and explore factors influencing their learning and identification of success. 'Workplace learning' and 'innovative work behaviour' were explained by the researcher at the start of the interviews. Participants were asked to clarify their understanding of these terms and were able to refer back to the definitions at any point during the interview. The same procedure was carried out for definitions of 'information literacy' and 'information behaviour' before questions on these topics were posed. Initially, participants were asked *'How does information literacy play a role in learning to innovate?'* Participants were then asked to indicate actions they carry out with information and how this supports the learning of innovative work behaviour: '*Could you explain the kind of things you do with information to help you learn to innovate?*' Participants were then encouraged to talk about how such actions helped them to learn to innovate. If participants struggled to recall actions related to information use they were prompted using actions from the pillars of the SCONUL model (SCONUL, 2011). The interviews each lasted for around 30 minutes, with extra time for the participants to ask questions of the researcher before and after the interview. They were recorded on an audio device, and then transcribed to obtain twelve Word documents. The transcripts were imported into NVivo software for coding and analysis.

Analysis

The data were coded and analysed by one researcher, and the coding scheme was checked by two of the co-authors of this paper. The analysis was conducted in stages, using the thematic analysis procedure (Guest, MacQueen & Namey, 2012), as shown in Figure 1. The initial stages of coding were guided by information literacy models to identify potential coding categories (e.g. information sharing, access, gathering, analysis, presentation). The process of data coding (stage 2) was repeated multiple times to ensure that all data were coded, and potential themes could be categorised as they emerged. Saturation was reached when no new codes emerged from the interview transcriptions. In the final naming stage of the analysis (Stage 6) a narrative and working definition of the coded data were developed.

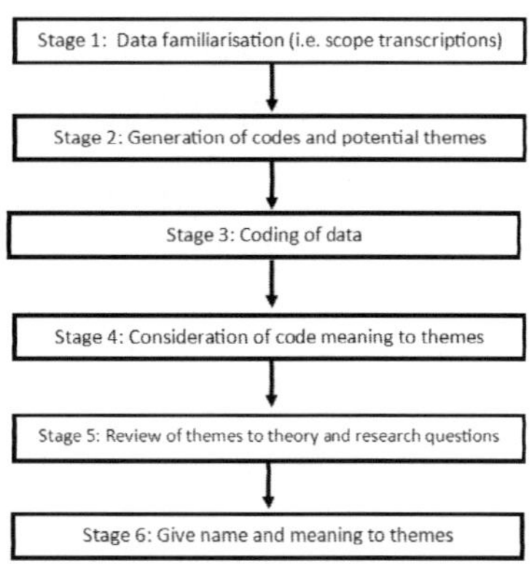

Figure 1. Stages of thematic analysis, adapted from Guest, MacQueen & Namey (2012)

RESULTS

The participants discussed a range of views on the use of information to support their learning of innovative work behaviour: (1) the role of information literacy in the learning of innovative work behaviour; (2) the importance of information behaviours in learning to innovate and; (3) the use of different information sources in workplace learning. The sections that follow explore these themes in detail.

The role of information literacy in the learning of innovative work behaviour

Nine participants explained that information is important for the development of innovative work behaviour through workplace learning. One noted:

> *Yes of course there is. I think you [as an employee] have to be very information literate in order to be a good learner in a workplace, yes and this helps to create new ideas. You have to be able to recognise what information is relevant for your job: what type of information you need and how you can get at that information (P5 - Librarian)*

Two made explicit that information literacy is the first step towards recognising a need for workplace learning:

> *Well, it is relevant because that's like the first step that you need to learn something in a way (P11 – staff member in Planning and Development)*

Similarly, two noted that information literacy helps give context to learning and presents a bigger picture of learning needs. It also helps to establish background information so that employees are aware of possible future requirements for change (e.g. the creation of new ideas) or a need for new learning:

> *I think it does because somehow it gives the bigger picture, somehow the context of learning things there in that sense so I think this is important (P9 – Project Coordinator)*

Another gave an example of the importance of information needs recognition. She then questioned how the need for information focuses on the individual, and whether this could be supported (or improved) by sharing the request (i.e. the need for information) with others:

> *...since we're the communications department and there's always a need for more information and people [employees] always somehow experience that they didn't get enough information... we try to inform people [employees] about stuff and we're like 'How should we do this?' so the people know what they should know (P8 – staff member in Communication Services)*

Similarly, the need for collective information literacy was also noted by other participants. Discussions centered on the organisation as a whole entity. Some employees may be able to recognise the information needs of other employees, but at the same time they need to understand the importance of sharing information in the process to help to innovate. Sharing information then helps observers to be aware of the information and decide whether it is important to their needs:

> *I don't know if I can say this, but I think I'm quite good at recognising other people's need of information when it comes to being in the communications department. Then there are some people that I think they might organise a big event and then they don't realise that we have to inform people otherwise nobody knows about our fantastic event (P8 - staff member in Communication Services)*

The participants also discussed the relationship between information literacy and the process of change. This appears to be evident when employees work within roles which may require frequent changes (an essential part to the development of innovative work behaviour). They highlighted the need for information to be recognised. Otherwise changes, such as those relevant to innovative work behaviour (in relation to process and organisational innovation suggested by De Vries, Bekkers & Tummers, 2015, p.153), would not occur:

> *But I mean, now when you see it in front of you, so I mean this is really, really important. Because I mean, if we would just continue year after year without changing any things, so we wouldn't be this good, as we are (P3 – Departmental Coordinator)*

The importance of information behaviours in learning to innovate

Information searching and access

The participants discussed information searching as an action in the development of workplace learning. Time spent searching is a barrier to learning: the employees explained that they find it difficult to find information they require due to the setup of the information source.

> *So, looking for information on our website – that's something that they find difficult, and that's not because they are bad at searching (P10 – staff member in Education Services)*

Information access is essential in order for employees to gather information quickly and generate new ideas, yet it was identified as challenge:

> *The whole access to information issue is challenging at the moment by everybody here (P2 – staff member in Research Services)*

If employees search for specific information for a length of time, and then cannot find it, this can hinder the process of innovative work behaviour. This is because as they do not have access to information that could help them generate new ideas:

> *So, you sometimes think that "oh dear, the information is there." But they can't find it if it doesn't come in a really, really easy way, immediately when you put on Google or whatever you want to use. So if you don't get the right answer, it doesn't exist, because ...you don't have the patience to put so much time into finding information (P3 – Departmental Coordinator)*

Information interpretation

The participants were of the opinion that information interpretation only helps them to learn if meaning can be added to the information, i.e. they can define the information, add context and can communicate this to another person. However, the addition of meaning to information takes time and requires employees to summarise information and break it down into smaller pieces first. The comment below was made by a participant who works within research services as a senior staff member and needs to interpret information frequently to then explain it to others.

> *I always try to somehow re-write it so it is easier and not just to send a link with 'read here' of course it is good to have that link because sometimes you need to read more, but also to somehow summarise what you need. It takes time but I have come to the conclusion that it is better and easier to open (P1 – staff member in Research Services)*

Information analysis

There appears to be a direct relationship between information interpretation and information analysis. Employees analyse information (e.g. complex procedural documents) in order to understand the meaning and then interpret it:

> *I would say so yes, if I get a lot, I would analyse it and just pick out and try to maybe re-write it, then I can also put the link to the whole information, but I try to open it a bit. I work a lot with academia, and it is the same theory, they have no time for reading a lot when it comes to some new rules or something, so it is easier to write something short, some lines, then they can read more if they want (P1 – staff member in Research Services)*

The ability to analyse information supports employees in its interpretation. However, the time available to analyse the information is limited:

> *When I did my PhD ten years ago which was luxury time, I had four years to myself to gather the information and to analyse it and write it down. I don't have the time anymore...(P4 – Senior staff member in Education and Research Services)*

The presentation of information

The analysis of information supports employees in presenting information to others, and possibly the sharing or development of new ideas as part of the innovation process. This then helps employees to discuss and create new ideas with others (i.e. the first stage of innovative work behaviour). A participant whose role focus is planning and development, and is required to make frequent presentations of information to others (e.g. when developing new ideas), said:

> *Then I use that to make a plan or suggestion or presentation for an idea or for the project plan (P11 – staff member in Planning and Development)*

However, if information needs to be presented, employees have to ensure that the communication method is suitable for the audience in question (e.g. use appropriate language, demonstrate specific skills practically):

> *I suppose it depends on what kind of circumstances I'm in and who I'm talking to. Some people I realise prefer to read and so I put it in writing to them (P2 – staff member in Research Services)*

Information sharing

Participants identified information sharing as a key activity to help people learn to innovate. However, this information sharing is only useful for employees when the information shared is relevant to the recipient:

> *Yes, if it's relevant information for them somehow yes. And of course, sharing information is really important and could be done more (P9 – Project Coordinator)*

In some departments, information sharing is a requirement. Employees are asked to share information from events, or relevant information they have acquired elsewhere. In other departments information sharing is not expected from employees. However, participants in this study felt it is an important activity to help other employees learn. Employees share information to help them to discuss ideas and check how others complete certain tasks (e.g. process innovation). Similarly, sharing information helps employees to understand how to carry out their jobs more effectively (e.g. in relation to administrative or processes innovation) and this is especially important in the informal workplace context:

> *Yeah. So, we talk a lot together. Share the information. And then I mean check with the colleagues "How would you do that?" "Oh, we do it like this, we could do it like that." (P3 – Departmental Coordinator)*

The use of different information sources in workplace learning

Five participants explained that people are an important information source, especially in cases where expertise is spread across the organisation:

> *It depends, since we are experts usually, I mean we are a small university and a small unit when I think about the resource services... there are not usually experts doing the same things, so for example we only have one innovation specialist, so there isn't anyone else who knows exactly that role (P1 – Senior staff member in Research Services)*

People are information sources that can be accessed quickly and are able to answer questions should the person seeking information require further clarification. A participant who works within Communication Services explained a preference for people as information sources:

> *So obviously networking is very important because if you find the right person to answer your question it's so much faster than to just try to look it up on the websites (P8 – staff member in Communication Services)*

People are believed to be good information sources for the initiation of innovative work behaviour through idea exchanges, access to relevant (unknown) information, and new learning:

> *And also, because their job is very similar to mine so then I can maybe steal some ideas and learn some things so I think that's a good thing for me. And then also since I'm here working with the press releases and media information, I also try to keep up with or maybe go to lunch with a journalist or somehow keep up with how they are working and how their work situation is developing and all these things (P8 – staff member in Communication Services)*

The participants noted that workplace learning is successful when people can be contacted in multiple ways (e.g. telephone and online). Workplace learning takes place as the contact can be carried out a time and place suitable to those involved, overcoming geographical location difficulties experienced by staff in this organisation:

> *Because it's a national thing too. It's a challenge. And there are people in Helsinki and Tampere and all over Finland that are gathering and taking part in these courses though the Net. With workplace learning is also that you can sit behind your desk and take part in discussions on the net. Connect and all those things. So yes (P6 - Librarian)*

The participants failed to distinguish between internal and external personal contacts when they spoke about people as information sources. However, external bodies were frequently discussed by for their contribution to learning in the workplace. A variety were identified and were specific to particular departments. One participant noted:

> *In networks we have a network of chief librarians in Finland, so chief librarians of university libraries and that's a very good place to find information (P5 - Librarian)*

External information sources help to bring in new knowledge. As a result, employees learn and are able to create new ideas to solve problems in the workplace. The comment below shows how external knowledge is vital to initiate changes in processes and procedures:

> *And then I also talked about it with our study psychologist, and then we were turning this idea round and looking at it and what could we do? And okay, so she already had some idea that she would... We need them to get to know each other (P7 – staff member in Administration)*

The participants also emphasised the need for external knowledge to enter the organisation and gave specific examples of how this is needed. In respect of the recruitment of new staff one participant said:

> *We always realise that when we can employ from outside, we get new knowledge – that is a very good thing because it tends to be, when you keep the same employees that the development gets very slow; people work the same way year in year out, and there is very little new learning (P12 – senior staff member in Financial Services)*

Concerns with information sources are important to acknowledge, both in terms of the amount of information available and trustworthiness of sources. Four participants noted that the amount of information can hinder processes involved in workplace learning. This is due to time required to analyse and interpret the information. One noted:

> *Sure, analyse it but my personal problem with the massive amount of information received is that we don't have the time to analyse it (P4 – senior staff member in Research and Education Services)*

Another referred to the need to critically analyse information, even in its vast amounts. The ability to handle large amounts of complex information is dependent on prior training and job roles:

> *I think in today's world there's too much information and how to have a critical standpoint to the flow of information…we have to be critical to the massive amount of information that comes from different sources (P4)*

Trustworthiness of information is seen as a facilitator of learning for employees. For example, one participant suggested that she only uses information sources she trusts (e.g. published literature or blog posts written by familiar people). Another questioned reliability in relation to issues highlighted in the media (e.g. the use of fake news):

> *That is dependent upon what kind of information I need, but as I said in the beginning the most common thing for me as a person would be I tend to look at the sources I trust – that would be research literature, management literature, also blogs because I am interested in… Then again, trust is very important in this sense, and the trust not necessarily towards a person but trust to the source (P11 – staff member in Planning and Development)*

DISCUSSION

The findings related above indicate that information literacy is a first step in the initiation of workplace learning in that it provides context for learning. There are five information behaviours that may support or hinder the learning of innovative work behaviour: (1) searching for and accessing information (2) information interpretation; (3) information analysis; (4) presentation of information and; (5) information sharing. In addition, the analysis shows the value of people as information sources, and highlights issues around information overload and trust.

The findings of this study relate to those found in prior research on the support of workplace learning in specific contexts (e.g. Fafeita & Lloyd, 2012; Lloyd, 2010; Lloyd, 2012; Lloyd & Somerville, 2006). The main contributions here relate to three themes: (1) information literacy skills as a prerequisite for workplace learning; (2) the role of information behaviours in supporting the learning of innovative work behaviour; and (3) information sources to support employees as they learn to behave innovatively.

Information literacy skills as a prerequisite for workplace learning

The findings show that the participants were able to contextualise information literacy and apply this to their own employment experiences with little effort, with acknowledgement of its importance in underpinning workplace learning. They also understood the importance of certain behaviours required for information literacy development in line with the SCONUL information literacy model (SCONUL, 2011). The collective nature of information literacy is evident in these findings, as has been identified in prior research. For example, Martin & Steinkuehler (2010) note the informal learning that occurs in the social online context (p. 355), and Cacciattolo (2015) explores how informal learning forms part of workplace learning. This adds to the argument that collective elements of practice should be embedded in the development of information literacy definitions.

The role of information behaviours in supporting the learning of innovative work behaviour

Processes of searching for, and accessing, information are key contributors to the development of innovative work behaviour according to the findings generated from this study. This been previously noted in other research (e.g. Bruce, 1999; Li, Brake, Champion, Fuller, Gabel & Hatcher-Busch, 2009). The participant discussions on organisational change processes have highlighted the need for information when a new direction is under consideration, and the negative impacts of a lack of information: the speed of change slows, or it may come to a standstill. Although prior research has investigated information behaviour and use in idea creation (e.g. Hauschildt, 1996), this does not address the innovative work behaviour process as a whole. In contrast the evidence here draws attention to the role of information in the process of change - first to help employees understand change, and second to support the creation of new ideas in the initial stages of the change process.

The findings related to information analysis within the workplace show that this may be supported, or hindered, by the nature of job roles. If it is accepted that workplace learning and innovative work behaviour result from reflecting on mistakes, then a lack of time for information analysis is a barrier (as well as a hindrance to general interpretation of information accessed).

Information sharing is shown to support innovative work behaviour in this context because it enables comparisons between organisations in terms of their achievements, procedures and processes (as related to process innovation discussed by De Vries, Bekkers & Tummers, 2015, p.153), and facilitates the creation of new ideas to be created from knowledge gained in this way.

The use of different information sources in workplace learning

Early research on information literacy in the workplace evidenced the use of people as information sources. For example, Hertzum and Pejtersen (2000) suggested that engineers get most of their information from colleagues and internal reports, and Hertzum, Andersen, Andersen and Hansen (2002) found that people were a valued information source for software engineers. Specifically, engineers used colleagues to help them recommend information sources they could trust. The results from this study as outlined above are in line with these earlier findings.

The issue of trust in information sources as a key component in information source choice in this study replicates findings from earlier research (e.g. Allard, Levine & Tenopir, 2008; Hertzum, Andersen, Andersen & Hansen, 2002). Trust in information in the environment under scrutiny here is determined by the known provenance and associated reliability of information sources, and particularly the personal relationship between the users and creators of the information sources in question.

Information overload featured in the findings presented here, and is another theme covered extensively in the Information Science literature (e.g. Bawden & Robinson, 2009). The most common consequence of information overload in respect of workplace learning is that it hinders productivity and efficiency of work. Participants in this research explained that the vast amount of information available is a barrier to their learning from it. The time required to analyse the large amount of information causes uneasiness and lowers confidence in information use. These findings are in line with recent research that suggests that information overload may influence the ability to search information effectively, and that people may not be aware of this (see Cleverley, 2017; Cleverley, Burnett & Muir, 2017). This could lead to search tasks being terminated early and with a detrimental effect on organisational outcomes (Cleverley, Burnett & Muir, 2017).

Limitations and future research

There are a number of limitations to the study presented here. First, it should be noted that during interviews the participants discussed examples of idea creation and the championing of such ideas, but examples of fully implemented ideas were not explained. Participants were able to talk about ideas they had generated, and ideas in the process of approval from leadership. However, none discussed examples of innovations that had been implemented and/or evaluated. This is most likely due to the timing of the interviews at the mid-point of an organisational strategy implementation. Further, the participants discussed innovations relevant to themselves, i.e. ideas they had generated or in which they had involvement. As such, this was the focus of conversations on their own innovative work behaviour and did not reflect all innovative work behaviour processes in the organisation.

Further research could therefore explore the pillars of the SCONUL model quantitatively as related to innovative work behaviour processes. Any relationships identified could be then followed up by means of qualitative interviews to explore further the meaning of such relationships. This would give information on specific information processes required at each stage of innovative work behaviour, and emphasise the application of the SCONUL model in workplace processes. However, to date, a quantitative survey to specifically explore the SCONUL model as a measurement of information literacy has not been designed. Consideration of this, and the potential of model adaptation to fit workplace contexts, would be required as part of further research.

Finally, the use of study setting also reduces the generalisability of the findings to other organisatons and workplace contexts.

Practical and theoretical recommendations

Practitioners in information and knowledge management may draw upon the findings of these findings to identify key areas where information literacy can influence the learning of innovative work behaviour, and the contextual factors - such as information access and information sharing practices – that are important to this. Since this study has identified information literacy as a precedent of workplace learning of innovative work behaviour, practitioners may also wish to focus on the development of information literacy skills initially if improvements are to be made in how employees learn to behave innovatively. In terms of theory, this research has demonstrated the applicability of an educational information literacy model to the workplace context. To this end, academics could apply other information literacy models previously developed for higher education settings and apply the processes to the role of information literacy in the workplace. Such models may require some adaptation to reflect the differences of information literacy in education and information literacy in workplace settings. As a direct consequence new information literacy models and theoretical perspectives for the workplace may be developed.

CONCLUSION

Through an analysis of interview data collected from twelve employees working in support services of a Finnish University support services, it has been shown that (1) information literacy skills serve as a prerequisite for workplace learning; (2) information behaviours support the learning of innovative work behaviour and; (3) a variety of information sources support employees as they learn to behave innovatively. These findings add to extant knowledge in the field, while contributing new insight. Expanding on the results of this study would require further data to be collected on the specific processes involved in innovative work behaviour (e.g. recognition of the need for innovation, idea creation, idea championing and implementation) and the role of information literacy during each process. To this end, quantitative exploration of this relationship may identify specific relationship between processes and contributors and qualitative follow up could provide explanations as to the meaning of each relationship identified.

ACKNOWLEDGMENTS

This work was supported by an Economic and Social Research Council [grant number: ES/J500136/1] and Skills Development Scotland as part of a collaborative +3-year PhD studentship. It was also supported by a John Campbell Trust student research bursary which provided funding for data collection to take place in Finland.

REFERENCES

Adhikari, J., Scogings, C., Mathrani, A., & Sofat, I. (2017). Evolving digital divides in information literacy and learning outcomes: A BYOD journey in a secondary school. *Internaltional Journal of Information and Learning Technology*, 34(4), 290-306.

Allard, S., Levine, K., & Tenopir, C. (2008). Design engineers and technical professionals at work: observing information usage in the workplace. *School of Information Sciences Publications and Other Works*. Retrieved from http://trace.tennessee.edu/utk_infosci-epubs/3

Banek Zorica M., Spiranec S., Ogrizek Biskupic I. (2014). What is the employers stand on information literacy – researching employers on expected generic outcomes of their future employees. In: Kurbanoğlu S., Špiranec S., Grassian E., Mizrachi D., Catts R. (eds) Information Literacy. Lifelong Learning and Digital Citizenship in the 21st Century. ECIL 2014. *Communications in Computer and Information Science*, vol 492. Springer, Cham.

Bates, M. J. (2010) Information Behavior. In Encyclopedia of Library and Information Sciences, 3rd Ed. Marcia J. Bates and Mary Niles Maack, Eds. New York: CRC Press, vol. 3, pp. 2381-2391.

Bawden, D., & Robinson, L. (2009). The dark side of information: overload, anxiety and other paradoxes and pathologies. *Journal of Information Science*, 35(2), 80–191.

Bruce, C. S. (1999). Workplace experiences of information literacy. *International Journal of Information Management*, 19(1), 33–47.

Cacciattolo, K. (2015). Defining workplace learning. *European Scientific Journal*: Special Edition, 1, 243-250.

Cleverley, P.H. (2017). Re-examining and re-conceptualising enterprise search and discovery capability: towards a model for the factors and generative mechanisms for search task outcomes. Robert Gordon University, PhD thesis. Held on OpenAIR [online]. Available from: https://openair.rgu.ac.uk/

Cleverley, P.H., Burnett, S., & Muir, L. (2017). Exploratory information searching in the enterprise: a study of user satisfaction and task performance. *Journal of the Association for Information Science and Technology* [online], 68(1), 77-96. Available from: https://dx.doi.org/10.1002/asi.23595

Crawford, J., & Irving, C. (2009). Information literacy in the workplace: a qualitative exploratory study. *Journal of Librarianship and Information Science*, 41(1), 29–38.

De Vries, H., Bekkers, V., & Tummers, L. (2015). Innovation in the public sector: a systematic review and future research agenda. *Public Administration,* 94(1), 146-166).

Ellström, P-E. (2010). Practice-based innovation: a learning perspective. *Journal of Workplace Learning*, 22(1/2), 27-40.

Fafeita, J., & Lloyd, A. (2012). Plating up information literacy as a social practice: a slice of the literature. *Australian Academic and Research Libraries*; 43(2), 92-101.

Flick, U. (2009). *An introduction to qualitative research* (4th Ed). London, UK: SAGE.

Goldstein, S. (2015a). A graduate employability lens for the SCONUL seven pillars of information literacy. Retrieved from http://www.sconul.ac.uk/sites/default/files/documents/Employability_Lens_only_2015_0.pdf

Goldstein, S., & Whitworth, A. (2015). DeVIL – Determining the value of information literacy for employers. Report retrieved from: https://www.informall.org.uk/wp-content/uploads/2015/11/DeVIL_report_final_draft_v05.pdf

Guest, G., MacQueen, K. M. & Namey, E. E. (2012). *Applied thematic analysis*. Thousand Oaks, CA: SAGE Publications Ltd.

Hall, H., Cruickshank, P. & Ryan, B. (2018, in press). Practices of community representatives in exploiting information channels for citizen democratic engagement. *Journal of Librarianship and Information Science*

Hauschildt, J. (1996). Innovation, creativity and information behaviour. *Creativity and Innovation Management*, 5(3), 169-178.

Hertzum, M., & Pejtersen, A.M. (2000). The information-seeking practices of engineers: searching for documents as well as for people. *Information Processing & Management*, 36(5), 761-778.

Hertzum, M., Andersen, H.K. Andersen, V., & Hansen, C.B. (2002). Trust in information sources: seeking information from people, documents, and virtual agents. Interacting with Computers, 14(5), 575-599.

Høyrup, S. (2010). Employee-driven innovation and workplace learning: basic concepts, approaches and themes. *Transfer*, 16(2) 143–154.

Johnston, B., & Webber, S. (2003) Information literacy in higher education: a review and case study. *Studies in Higher Education*, 28(3), 335-352.

Leong, J., & Anderson, C. (2012). Fostering innovation through cultural change. *Library Management*, 33(8/9), 490-497.

Li, J., Brake, G., Champion, A., Fuller, T., Gabel, S., Hatcher-Busch, L. (2009). Workplace learning: the roles of knowledge accessibility and management. *Journal of Workplace Learning*, 21(4), 347-364.

Lloyd, A. (2010). *Information literacy landscapes: information literacy in education, workplace and everyday context*. Chandos: London.

Lloyd, A. (2012). Information literacy as a socially enacted practice: sensitising themes for an emerging perspective of people-in-practice. *Journal of Documentation* 68, 772–783.

Lloyd, A & Somerville, M. (2006). Working information. *Journal of Workplace Learning*, 18 (3), 186-198.

Martin, C., & Steinkuehler, C. (2010). Collective information literacy in massively multiplayer online games. *E-Learning and Digital Media*, 7(4), 355-365.

Pickard, A.J. (2013). *Research Methods in Information* (2nd Ed.). London, UK: Facet Publishing.

Secker, J. (2018). The revised CILIP definition of information literacy. *Journal of Information Literacy*, S1(12), 56-158.

SCONUL. (2011). The SCONUL seven pillars of information literacy: core model for higher education. Retrieved form: https://www.sconul.ac.uk/sites/default/files/documents/coremodel.pdf

Tait, E., & Edwards, R. (2016). Information literacy and information seeking of public sector managers in the Welsh Government. *Library and Information Research,* 40(123), 88–105.

West, M. A., & Farr, J. L. (1990). Innovation at work. In M. A. West & J. L. Farr (Eds.), *Innovation and creativity at work: Psychological and organizational Strategies* (pp. 1–37). Chichester, UK: Wiley.

Williams, D., Cooper, K., & Wavell, C. (2014). Information Literacy in the Workplace: an annotated bibliography. Aberdeen: Robert Gordon University. Retrieved from https://pdfs.semanticscholar.org/39f2/63cb17222cacb8923a4628a8af2f61ab0aa5.pdf

Restructuring and Formalizing: Scholarly Communication as a Sustainable Growth Opportunity in Information Agencies?

A. J. Million
University of Michigan, USA. millioaj@umich.edu

Heather Moulaison Sandy
University of Missouri, USA. moulaisonhe@missouri.edu

Cynthia Hudson-Vitale
Penn State University, USA. cynhudson@gmail.com

ABSTRACT

Emerging technologies are revolutionizing the field of scholarly communication. Because of this, scholars increasingly need specialized support during all stages of the research process. With the academic library as the unit of analysis, two concepts from Rogers' Diffusion of Innovation theory and organizational innovation literature are drawn upon to assess the sustainability of scholarly communication work in libraries. These concepts are organizational restructuring and formalization. Data on Association of Research Libraries (ARL) employees with relevant job titles and three digital curation competencies documents are analysed. Study findings suggest that ARL information agencies have restructured to provide added research support and that skills associated with scholarly communication positions are becoming more uniform. We conclude that scholarly communication information professionals are part of a sustainable area of practice within ARL information agencies, that has matured over the past decade, and this trend is likely to continue in at least the short term.

KEYWORDS

Information professionals; Scholarly communication; Digital curation; Information agencies; Sustainability (management); Diffusion of innovations

INTRODUCTION

The emergence of new technologies to support publishing and communication (including social networks and online reference management and sharing platforms) have fundamentally changed the way that scholars work (Regazzi, 2015) and have altered the research process in which they engage. Scholarly communication has become more complex as a result of new and emerging technologies. *Scholarly communication,* an area supported by information professionals, is defined as:

> the study of how scholars in any field (e.g., physical, biological, social and behavioural sciences, humanities and technology) use and disseminate information through formal and informal channels. The study of scholarly communication includes the growth of scholarly information, the relationships among research areas and disciplines, the information needs and uses of individual user groups, and the relationships among formal and informal methods of communication (Borgman, 1990, pp. 13-4).

Scholarly communication enables the work of researchers at universities and organizations that are dedicated to creating new knowledge. In the United States (U.S.), over half of all federal research dollars are granted to university-affiliated researchers (Regazzi, 2015) making universities a hub for the creation of new knowledge.

Supporting Scholars

Supporting scholarly communication on university campuses in an age of emerging technologies has naturally fallen to information professionals based in information agencies, such as academic libraries. Traditionally, academic libraries have divided the expertise they provide into technical services and public services, but given the complexity of technologies combined with the increasingly sophisticated needs of users, a new breed of information professional must emerge (e.g., Kowalski, 2017). In the case of scholarly communication questions, not only must the information professional curate and supply access to scholarship, but he/she must also work with scholars to organize, provide access to, save, and share their work. Providing specialized support to scholars (e.g., Ketchum, 2017) during the research process has quickly become the purview of the academic library.

As the needs of researchers and scholars have changed, the work of information professionals has evolved in parallel. Working to support the field of "scholarly communication today reflects a [need to master an ever-growing] constellation of tools, practices, and competencies" (Cross, Oleen, & Perry, 2017, p. 365). The support scholarly communication information professionals provide to researchers varies according to the priorities of the institutions in which they work, the areas of expertise of the scholars whom they support, and their own skills and training. For the purposes of this paper, we consider work that supports scholarly communication as: assistance with digital curation, research data management, and open access and publishing. Although the competencies and skills to support this work have been codified in several documents (some of which are analyzed in this paper), little is known about the sustainability of scholarly communication work in information agencies.

This paper assesses the role of the scholarly communication information professional in an attempt to understand the sustainability of this non-traditional work. To assess sustainability, we review literature that pertains to the evolving roles and missions of academic libraries and the role that information professionals can play in supporting scholarly communication at their institutions. Next, we present the concepts of *restructuring* and *formalization* from Rogers' (2003) Diffusion of Innovations (DOI) Theory and organizational innovation literature, under the assumption that scholarly communication positions have diffused among information agencies in recent years.[1] Informed by concepts from DOI, we discuss findings from an analysis of Association of Research Libraries (ARL) job statistics and a qualitative evaluation of three scholarly communication competency documents specific to digital curators. Based on our findings, we conclude that ARL libraries have restructured to add scholarly communication positions due to the value these information professionals bring, and the alignment of competency documents suggests that the work of information professionals is becoming more uniform. DOI predicts that restructuring and formalization in organizations are associated with slower rates of change. Thus, evidence suggests it is likely that scholarly communication information professionals will remain a sustainable addition to ARL information agencies in the short term. We conclude by discussing limitations to our analysis and offer directions for future research.

Sustainability

For the purposes of this paper, we define *sustainability* as the stability of defined roles and responsibilities within information agencies. The United Nations Brundtland Report (1987) provides another definition, which says that sustainability is "development that meets the needs of the present without compromising the ability of future generations to meet their own needs" (p. 37). Applied to work in information agencies, this definition implies that sustainability occurs when individuals carry out work that does not compromise the ability of their successors to do the same. We do not discount the value of this definition; however, it is inappropriate for use in this paper. The reason we adopt the first definition is we are ultimately concerned with the perpetuation of scholarly communication as a set of positions and practices in ARL information agencies. Thus, we are not concerned with the question of whether short-term practices by scholarly communication professionals are likely to be harmful or counterproductive in the long-run.

Research Questions and Rationale

Based on survey data from 2012, the Council of Prairie and Pacific University Libraries (COPPUL) Scholarly Communications Working Group found the field of scholarly communication was not yet coalescing to form a community of practice in libraries (Swanepoel, 2015). However, after ten years of the Association of College and Research Library (ACRL) Scholarly Communication Roadshow, Cross, Oleen, and Perry (2017) found the field has significantly matured.

Given the work these information professionals carry out, and given the support that researchers and scholars require thanks to changing technologies, this paper addresses two research questions:

RQ1. *Going forward, how sustainable is the work of scholarly communication information professionals in ARL information agencies likely to be?*

RQ2. *To what extent has a sub-area of scholarly communication practice (i.e., digital curation) emerged as a cohesive area of practice?*

The first research question (RQ1) addresses the primary issue examined in this study. Research question two (RQ2) pertains to a sub-area of scholarly communications practice that must be examined to answer RQ1.

LITERATURE REVIEW

Scholarly communication is a field that has needed to adapt to modern technology, research approaches, and communication methods. Information professionals supporting scholarly communication have emerged to assist researchers in navigating this new landscape. As Brantley, Bruns, and Duffin, (2017) explain, "The activities of scholarly communication-support librarians have grown and changed in recent years due to the increasingly complex nature of modern digital scholarship" (p. 137). For example, Regazzi (2015) identifies big data and big science as two changes that have profoundly affected researchers and the work they do. Hey, Tansley, and Tolle's (2009) canonical text also correctly identifies a marked shift towards computational

---

[1]This assumption is based on Cross, Oleen, and Perry's (2017) history of the ACRL Scholarly Communications Roadshow and prior efforts to educate librarians about the need to engage in scholarly communication work.

and data intensive research in the academic environment. Furthermore, the 2013 U.S. Office of Science and Technology Policy memorandum, "Expanding Public Access to the Results of Federally Funded Research" hastened the development of library services that support the open access and sharing of research outputs. Scholarly communication information professionals have learned to navigate the increasingly complex field of scholarly communication and its related technologies, and work to support scholars in their use of these technologies through services they offer. Borgman (2000) clarifies that, in terms of the intersection of digital libraries and scholarly communication, information professionals are more interested in the services digital libraries can provide (Borgman, 2000, p. 415); in this way, they might be said to resemble both the technical services librarians and the public services librarians of the past.

The Evolving Academic Library

In response to the changing needs of their users and in support of the new services they must now provide, academic libraries have changed dramatically, beyond moving from a front-of-the-house/back-of-the-house binary model to convergence among the two (Bossaller & Moulaison Sandy, 2017; Kowalski, 2017). Library reorganization has been a key way in which academic libraries have positioned themselves for the future of access. In examining the literature, Novak and Day (2015) identify five steps libraries typically undertake during the reorganization process: libraries 1) identify drivers for change, 2) carry out analysis and diagnosis, 3) communicate the change plan, 4) implement the change, and 5) carry out continuous assessment afterward. Assigning new tasks to staff based on the *analysis and diagnosis* step takes place during the *implementing the change* step. It is at this point that staff are trained with any new skills they might need and are ideally placed in new positions based on their existing skills, talents, and proclivities. Staff may, therefore, have been hired under one set of requirements or professional expectations, and find themselves taking on new work in other areas.

Information Professionals Supporting Scholarly Communication

New job titles and requirements have emerged in support of the changing academic library and changing academic research practices. Positions may no longer require information professionals to have ALA-accredited degrees in Library and Information Science (LIS) (T. Dawes, personal communication, 2016). Research by Fearon et. al. (2013) found that the librarians supporting research data management services include subject expertise across varied research disciplines, in addition to, or in replacement of, the traditional LIS degree. These information professionals, therefore, have the potential to come from a variety of backgrounds and may have traditional LIS degrees, other areas of specialization, or both.

Anecdotally, there has been a marked increase in scholarly communication information professionals in academic libraries, but little is known about them other than the gender of SCHOLCOMM listserv members (Hayes & Kelly, 2017). According to the literature, in terms of their work, information professionals in this domain are responsible for a number of *sub-activities*. They may be expected to assist faculty and other users with the scholarly communication process (Klain-Gabbay & Shohamb, 2016). Promoting the open access movement among library users is also seen as a scholarly communication problem (Potvin, 2013; Rodriguez, 2015).

One primary sub-area of scholarly communication is digital curation, and by extension, research data management. To support scholars throughout the research process, scholarly communication information professionals must also assist with the curation and use of data and digital assets in light of the technological advances mentioned earlier (Fearon et al., 2013). Indeed, open access and open research services are inherent in the developing of support for research data management and curation. Fearon and his co-authors find that 85% of institutions who archive data do so to support open access (p. 56). Further, one of the core library services for research data management involves consultations and education around public access to all research outputs, not just data, but also code, analyses, protocols, workflows, publications, and more.

Information professionals working in this area also attempt to understand their users' information needs and digital information preferences (Maron & Smith, 2009). Lewis, Sarli, and Suiter (2015) found that many institutions are developing services to support researchers in managing their scholarly identities and track research outputs. To support this service, information professionals developed skills in data analysis, digital humanities, data management, and an understanding of various metric types. In short, as the field has evolved, scholarly communication information professionals have moved from advocating for open scholarship to actively providing services that relate to the communication and publishing of research, research data, and additional aspects of scientific inquiry.

DIFFUSION OF INNOVATIONS

It is challenging to predict the future, but Rogers' (2003) Diffusion of Innovations (DOI) theory and organizational innovation literature provides concepts to examine the sustainability of scholarly communication work in ARL information agencies. No theory can predict the future; however, DOI is one of the most cited works in social scientific literature (Green, 2016). Below, we introduce DOI and describe how the theory helps predict change in information agencies like libraries with a focus on the concepts of organizational restructuring and formalization. In social scientific literature, DOI is used to explain how and why innovations spread. An *innovation* is defined as "any idea, practice, or project that is perceived as new by an individual or other unit of adoption" (Rogers, 2003; pp. 11-12). In this paper, we define an innovation as scholarly communication positions within ARL libraries. Stemming from the work of rural sociologists (Ryan & Gross, 1943), Rogers (1962) is credited with popularizing DOI by synthesizing 508 studies that explained why individuals and organizations adopt innovations (Valente & Rogers, 1995). In doing so, Rogers (2003) identified four causal factors: an innovation, communication, time, and a social system (p. 11). We focus on innovations (i.e., scholarly communication positions) and social systems (i.e., ARL libraries) below.

Innovation in Organizations

Organizations are "organized bod[ies] of people with a particular purpose," and they tend to be complex (Oxford, n.d., para. 1). Originally, DOI emerged as a theory that focused on the decisions of individuals. Later developments extended it to describe innovation in organizations, such as academic libraries, through the use of metaphors. For example, one metaphor is that of an organizational decision-making process. Another metaphor is that of organizational structure.

Regarding the metaphor of organizational decision-making, one way that Rogers extended DOI was through the creation of a six-part model. Elaborating, Rogers (2003) argued that organizations act as if they possess agency and try to reduce uncertainty about the costs and benefits of adopting and/or rejecting innovations. The six stages of organizational innovation-decisions are: agenda-setting, matching, redefining, restructuring, clarifying, and routinizing (p. 421). *Agenda-setting* refers to where goals and agendas are set by leaders. *Matching* describes staff searching for and finding solutions to meet agendas. *Redefining* and *restructuring* mean that after the matching stage ends, agendas are refined and innovations adopted. Finally, *clarifying* describes the process of generating buy-in from staff (p. 427) and *routinizing* is when staff no longer perceive an innovation as new (p. 429). We do not focus on decisions to create scholarly communication positions in this paper, but Rogers' offers a way to infer changes in information agencies that have already taken place through a process of diffusion. Demonstrated by the creation of scholarly communication positions, we argue this change pertains to library restructuring.

Another metaphor central to this paper is the concept of organizational structure. Pugh (1990) says that organizational structures are "regularities in activities such as task allocation, coordination, and supervision" (p. 1), and Rogers (2003) argues there are six traits that determine if organizations will change. Rooted in organizational innovation literature, these structural traits are: centralization, formalization, complexity, interconnectedness, organizational slack, and size. *Formalization* describes the extent to which "an organization emphasizes its members' following rules and procedures" (p. 411) and we interpret it as information agencies creating positions that align with professionally uniform practices.

Literature examining innovation in organizations from a structural view supports Rogers' arguments—especially when it comes to the matter of formalization. Formalized job roles are associated with slower rates of innovation. For example, in a study of social welfare organizations Hague and Aiken (1967) found that a low degree of job codification is associated with a high rate of change. In 1981, Howard looked at four university libraries and found that the rate of innovation is negative for centralized, formal, and stratified organizations. More recently, Chen and Chang (2012) looked at 260 organizations via survey and determined that a high degree of organizational formalization slows decision speeds and organizational innovation. Formalization is not the only predictor of change in organizations, but it does align with the restructuring phase of Rogers' (2003) innovation decision-making process.

METHODOLOGY

Assessing the Prevalence of Scholarly Communication Positions in ARL Libraries

To understand the growth of the number of scholarly communication information professionals employed in large academic libraries in North America, we analyzed data for positions coded in the ARL Salary Survey. Although ARL institutions are not representative of all information agencies supporting research, they include some of the largest and most prestigious academic libraries in the U.S. and Canada. Once per year, 125 ARL libraries submit employee data for all positions. Survey coordinators choose one job code to apply per staff member, and later this data is cleaned, normalized, and aggregated.

For the current study, we examined data for positions coded as Scholarly Communication Librarian (SCHOLAR) and Digital Curation Librarian (DIGICUR). The SCHOLAR code is defined in the salary survey as a library staff member who is involved in scholarly communication. These individuals work with or promote open publication access, provide advice regarding copyright issues, and more. The DIGICUR code is defined as a library staff member who creates and curates digital collections in the sciences, social sciences, or humanities, or who works with data-management issues across multiple disciplines. As noted earlier, digital curation is a sub-area of scholarly communication. Both of these positions were analyzed given their support for the communication and publishing of scholarship. The year 2012 marked the first time ARL collected data regarding these two categories.

Skills and Competencies Assessment

Researchers also analyzed the recommended skills and competencies required for *digital curation and data management*, an area of expertise that blends back-of-the-house technology expertise with front-of-the-house service provision in support of the scholarly communication process. The project team applied a multi-step approach: (1) identification of relevant guidelines; (2) compilation of competencies/skills as a way to enable uniform mark-up during coding; (3) the inductive development of broad categories; and, (4) the coding of each competency to a category.

To find as many relevant digital curation skills and recommendation reports or research, the following approach was applied:

3. Databases searched: Library Literature & Information Science; Library, Information Science & Technology Abstracts; Google Scholar; Google
4. Keywords used: "digital curation skills"; "digital curation curriculum"; "digital curation training"

This search returned 418 articles. Given that we sought to understand competencies and skills for digital curation and research data management—a specific subset of work carried out by scholarly communication information professionals—documents focusing on practice rather than theory were retained. Articles analyzing position announcements were deemed unreliable since there was no way to know how successful searches would be or how closely the incumbent would meet requirements and would carry out the work as described. With this in mind, we developed and applied the following inclusion criteria to narrow search results:

1. Published 2007-present;
2. Written in English;
3. Specifically indicated necessary or recommended competencies/skills for properly curating or stewarding data; and
4. Competencies/skills were not developed by analysing job advertisements or reviewing the literature.

The following three competency documents were analyzed: *Librarians' Competencies Profile for Research Data Management* (2016), *Matrix of Digital Curation Knowledge and Competencies* (2009), and *Preparing the Workforce for Digital Curation* (2015). Below, we present each in chronological order based on their publication dates.

The *Matrix of Digital Curation Knowledge and Competencies* published in 2009 is one of the earliest documents that articulated the requisite skills for digital curation work. These skills were developed as part of the DigCCurr project led by Helen Tibbo and Cal Lee at the University of North Carolina as part of an Institute of Museum and Library Services (IMLS) project. This IMLS-funded project developed library school curricula and held a number of training events to support the diffusion of digital curation activities. A project matrix comprised of six dimensions was developed as a method to identify and organize material to be covered in digital curation curricula. These dimensions are: (1) mandates, values, and principles; (2) functions and skills; (3) professional, disciplinary, institutional, organizational, or cultural context; (4) type of resource; (5) prerequisite knowledge; and (6) transition point in information continuum. The dimension "function and skills" was the source for this research, because it is defined as "know how," as opposed to conceptual, attitudinal, or declarative knowledge.

In 2015, the National Research Council of the U.S. National Academies of Science released the report *Preparing the Workforce for Digital Curation*. This report was authored by a committee on "Future Career Opportunities and Educational Requirements for Digital Curation" and was intended to examine workforce-related issues in information agencies with an eye toward future economic development. The committee was composed of experts and industry representatives in library and information science, labor economics, and domain-specific scientific fields. More recently, the *Librarians' Competencies Profile for Research Data Management*, was published in 2016 by the Joint Task Force for Librarians' Competencies in Support of E-Research and Scholarly Communication convened by the ARL. The aim of this task force was to outline the competencies needed for e-research, repository management, and scholarly communication. The task force consisted of representatives from ARL institutions, the Canadian Association of Research Libraries, the Confederation of Open Access Repositories, and the Association of European Research Libraries.

Compilation of Competencies

The three competency guidelines varied in length and detail; two were documents, and one was a matrix of skills. Formats also varied, with one being an HTML document and two being in PDF format. To normalize these documents, a PDF was made of the HTML document. Next, using Adobe Acrobat Pro, we documented codes by highlighting relevant text and inserting comments for each competency. The level of detail for each competency document varied. The *Matrix of Digital Curation Knowledge and Competencies* included function categories, such as "access" and "administration" and sub-level functions, such as the "generation of dissemination information package," which went into great detail about each overarching category. To ensure comparison across the competency documents was reliable, we used high-level descriptions and text in the definition and explanation section of each document to conduct the qualitative coding process.

Inductive Coding

Content analysis is an appropriate methodology for understanding and reducing information from existing data sources such as competency documents. Because no taxonomy of qualitative competency guidelines for digital curation exists, we employed an inductive structural coding approach, which involved identifying concepts and skills that may apply to large segments of text and enabled the comparison of frequency counts across cases (Saldaña, 2013). Inductive coding means that coded skills reflect the content found in source documents rather than the skills categories being pre-determined by the researchers or based on existing taxonomies. Each document was read by a team member and a list of skills was developed. To allow for comparison and the next coding step across documents, broad categories or buckets of skills were created. For example, the category of research workflows includes skills such as the ability of a curator to understand research practices, workflows, and/or the ability of the curator to understand disciplinary norms and standards. After categories were developed, the competency documents were then re-coded for each category. As competencies or skills were mentioned, the researchers recorded instances for each category.

Suitability of Competencies as Data Points

Speaking about management, Jordan and Lloyd (2017) argue that human resource planning in libraries calls for the careful selection and recruitment of staff. One way this is accomplished is to formalize positions by defining job responsibilities to make work predictable and regular. In the case of scholarly communication, the existence of a disciplinary consensus about the skills individuals ought to possess would suggest the presence of formalized roles brought about by restructuring. Organizations do not constitute professions; however, they do employ the individuals who comprise them. As noted earlier, organizational formalization is associated with a decreased rate of change, so if ARL libraries are creating scholarly communication positions, it is more likely that scholarly communication work will be sustainable in the future.

FINDINGS

Number of Scholarly Communication Librarians in ARL Libraries

The number of scholarly communication librarians has been steadily on the rise since 2012 when data was first collected, as is demonstrated in *Figure 1*. Between 2012 and 2016, scholarly communication positions with the job titles *scholarly communication* (SCHOLAR; i.e., focusing on open access, etc.) and *digital curation* (DIGICUR; i.e., focusing on research data management, etc.) increased annually in ARL libraries. As indicated previously, 2012 marked the first year that ARL collected data for these positions; in 2012 SCHOLAR data was combined with other codes given the low number of positions and is, therefore, not presented in *Figure 1*. Interestingly, as shown below, growth in digital curation positions totaled 27%. Scholarly communication growth was far more rapid with an increase of 49%. A conclusion to draw is that the number of scholarly communication librarians in ARL libraries has grown since data was first collected and that the total of the two combined (as of 2016) was roughly 225 individuals.

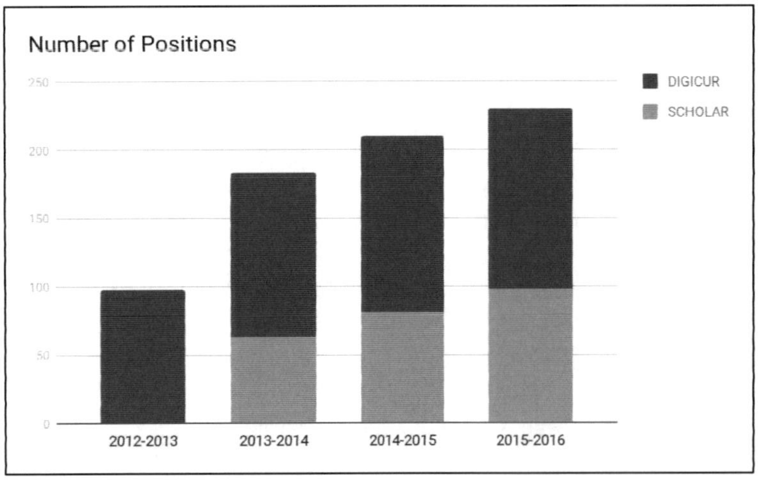

Figure 1. Scholarly communication (SCHOLAR) and digital curation (DIGICUR) positions at ARL libraries, 2012-2016.

Identification of Competencies and Agreement Within Documents

Coding of the competencies examined in this paper identified 23 categories for information professionals to perform digital curation and/or research data management work (see *Table 1*). Of these categories, twelve were found across all three competency publications. These 12 skills are: advocacy and outreach, instruction, data preservation, data management, data selection, data repository platforms, data linking, data audits, data type best practices, licensing data, data organization, and information discovery. An additional seven skills were found across two competency documents. These skills were: some type of discipline knowledge, data analysis skills, an understanding of funder requirements, knowledge of research workflows, data citation, data sharing, and data visualization skills. Finally, four skills were limited to only one competency document. These skills were: data security, programming and scripting, a background in science, technology, engineering, or medicine, and an understanding of publisher requirements.

Competency or Skill	***Matrix of Digital Curation Knowledge* (2009)**	***Preparing the Workforce for Digital Curation* (2015)**	***Librarians' Competencies Profile for Research Data Management* (2016)**
Advocacy & Outreach	1	1	1
Data Audit	1	1	1
Data Linking	1	1	1
Data Management	1	1	1
Data Organization	1	1	1
Data Preservation	1	1	1
Data Repository Platform	1	1	1
Data Selection	1	1	1
Data Types	1	1	1
Information Discovery	1	1	1
Instruction	1	1	1
Licensing Data	1	1	1
Discipline Knowledge	0	1	1
Data Analysis	0	1	1
Funder Requirements	0	1	1
Research Workflows	0	1	1
Data Citation	0	1	1
Data Sharing	0	1	1
Data Visualization	1	1	0
Data Security	0	1	0
Programming & Scripting	0	1	0
Education in STEM	0	1	0
Publisher Requirements	0	0	1

Table 1: Skills required for digital curation per the selected guidelines documents.

As noted above, competencies documents possessed a high degree of agreement expressed in skill categories. Such agreement is notable, because all three documents were written by separate groups over the past decade with notable disciplinary qualifications. Regarding agreement among documents, the most similar were the *Librarians' Competencies Profile for Research Data Management* and *Preparing the Workforce for Digital Curation* with over 78% agreement (18 of 23 skills). The *Matrix of Digital Curation* and the *Preparing the Workforce for Digital Curation* documents had the next closest agreement with 61% or 14 out of 23 points of overlap.

DISCUSSION

To address the question of sustainability, we consider our findings overall. Based on gathered ARL data, scholarly communication information professionals, especially generalists with the title Scholarly Communication Librarian, emerged in academic libraries in force through the 2010s. The upward trend in the growth of this position leads us to believe that this aspect of the information professions is in demand and that the work being done is both necessary and appreciated. Consensus in competencies suggests that the information professions are in agreement about what ought to be done in support of researchers as they seek assistance with digital curation and research data management. This implies that the role of the scholarly communication information professional, at least in terms of his/her work, is becoming formalized. We take the formalization of digital curation work to be an indicator of the maturation of the field as it coalesces around established competencies.

Based on reviewed literature and study findings, the time between 2009 and 2015 appears to have been pivotal in the formation and coalescence of scholarly communication work by information professionals. In 2009, the ACRL Scholarly Communication Roadshow began educating librarians and other information professionals about scholarly communication writ large. By 2012, ARL had begun to collect data on positions with the title Scholarly Communication Librarian, but did not find they had enough data to warrant reporting it separately from other positions. A divergence in data collection classifications was allowed to form between Scholarly Communication and Digital Curation, despite overlap in the work carried out. In 2012, respondents to the COPPUL survey supplied data indicating scholarly communication as an area of specialization had not coalesced (Swanepoel, 2015). Yet, by 2013, ARL was collecting data about scholarly communication librarians with over 50 positions in the 125 ARL libraries. In 2015 and 2016, two separate documents were published that indicated 78% agreement in terms of the required skills and competencies for the sub-area of digital curation (*Librarians' Competencies Profile,* 2016; *Preparing the Workforce,* 2015). By 2017, the ACRL Roadshow organizers found the knowledge of audience members had improved to the point where it was necessary reconfigure their curriculum (Cross, Oleen, & Perry, 2017), implying that a level of formalization had occurred in the information professions and information agencies. Based on these findings, the answer to research question two (RQ2) is digital curation has emerged as a cohesive sub-area of practice.

Further evidence for the emerging cohesiveness of practice in the sub-area of digital curation (and research data management) comes from findings associated with the three competencies documents that we examined. These documents were published at extreme ends of what the literature points to as a formative period for the field of scholarly communication within information agencies; they were also published before and after the establishment of the area as a formal title by ARL. The *Matrix of Digital Curation Knowledge* (2009) is the most different of the three competencies documents studied, implying that since its publication the sub-area of digital curation has coalesced. The competencies identified in 2015 (*Preparing the Workforce for Digital Curation*) and 2016 (*Librarians' Competencies Profile for Research Data Management*) demonstrate a mature understanding of this area of scholarly communication information work. All but one of the competencies in the 2009 document are included in later documents. Further, 6 of the 23 competencies shared by the 2015 and 2016 documents are unique to newer publications, having been identified and added since 2009. We interpret this as evidence of the maturation of this sub-area of practice within ARL information agencies and as a de facto formalization of associated work.

DOI and the Future of Scholarly Communication Information Professionals

Based on these findings and the concepts of restructuring and formalization from DOI and organizational innovation literature, we predict that increased formalization within information agencies will contribute to a slowing of change for scholarly communication information professionals. Therefore, to answer research question one (RQ1), we predict scholarly communications work will remain sustainable in the future. Staff are being brought in to do work in ARL libraries, and that work increasingly, at least in digital curation/research data management, is consistently codified in terms of the competencies and skills that practitioners require. Work in areas of scholarly communication has been made increasingly predictable and regular, in support of human resource planning (Jordan & Lloyd, 2017) as demonstrated in the consensus about professional skills and competencies. Presumably, these positions have diffused, and are diffusing, through the information professions, as implied by the success of the ACRL Roadshow. The coherence of competencies documents and the number of positions within ARL information agencies also suggests that most ARL information agencies are in, or have moved beyond, the restructuring stage of Rogers' (2003) innovation-decision process.

Study Limitations and Future Work

The future of ARL information agencies providing scholarly communication support to scholars appears to be sustainable, but there are limitations to this study. The data we collected only allowed us to examine two concepts from DOI and organizational innovation literature. Indicators such as ARL data and the cohesiveness of professional competencies documents suggest that scholarly communication work has entered the late stages of Rogers' innovation-decision process, but we did not look at individual adoption-decisions inside agencies.

Speaking about the process by which organizations "choose" to adopt or reject an innovation, Rogers notes how the process is not linear; at any point, steps in his model may be skipped, left unfinished, or started again later (p. 421). Without data to test Rogers' model, we do not know who made decisions to hire scholarly communication professionals in ARL information agencies, if positions resembled those described in competencies documents, and if staff communicate with stakeholders to demonstrate the value that they provide. The creation of new positions hints that scholarly communication work is sustainable, in that it has been formalized, but limitations associated with our data mean the long-term is uncertain. To address uncertainty, future research should examine how scholarly communications positions are created and evaluate their value, which may shape the sustainability of the work that scholarly communication information professionals carry out. One way to gather data would be to interview decision-makers who are responsible for creating positions in ARL libraries as well as the scholars who use scholarly communication services.

Another limitation associated with this paper carries over to high-level traits that are associated with organizational innovation. In this paper, much as has been made of formalization as a predictive indicator, but we did not examine the work that is actually carried out within ARL libraries. Therefore, it is possible that positions were less formal than competencies documents suggest.

Additionally, DOI and organizational innovation literature provide other variables that may shed light on if scholarly communication information services are likely to remain sustainable in the future.

Briefly discussed earlier, the variables we did not examine in this study include: centralization, complexity, interconnectedness, organizational slack, and size. As other ARL information agencies attempt to create positions, centralized decision-making by university administrators may intervene. A lack of available resources may also prevent positions from being filled. The financial state of many public universities is troubled, and today 46 U.S. states spend less per-student than a decade ago (Mitchell, Leachman & Masterson, 2016). Organizational size also correlates with innovation, and as scholarly communication positions diffuse through the information professions, it is likely that small or medium-sized universities will not be able to provide the same level of support as their larger counterparts. Wilder (2017, p. 4) reports that in 2015 the typical ARL library employed 84 professional staff, which is much larger than libraries at liberal arts colleges and teaching universities. To account for influences such as these, future work should seek to collect data that provides a more holistic view of scholarly communication position stability. Additionally, because organizational size is a factor to consider, future work should look at information agencies other than ARL libraries, because these libraries tend to be very large.

CONCLUSION

Our findings revealed that the work of scholarly communication information professionals has formalized since 2009. Using two concepts from DOI and organization innovation literature, despite the limitations of this study, we infer that there is value in the work these professionals do, and conclude that the field is entering into a period of clarifying itself (using Rogers' (2003) terminology) that is indicative of its sustainability within ARL libraries. Given the coalescence of practice in the sub-area of digital curation, scholarly communication will likely continue to remain a sustainable area of practice in the information professions. However, more work remains to be done. The data collected in this study was insufficient to test other concepts from DOI, which leads us to conclude that, while the present is stable, the long-term is much less predictable. Future research should seek to move beyond this effort and examine the emergence of scholarly communications work within specific organizations, the value that this work delivers to researchers, and its potential to create a reliable, long-term growth opportunity for all types of information agencies.

ACKNOWLEDGMENTS

The authors would like to thank ARL for providing access to its data.

REFERENCES

Brantley, S., Bruns, T. A., & Duffin, K. I. (2017). Librarians in transition: Scholarly communication support as a developing core competency. *Journal of Electronic Resources Librarianship, 29*(3), 137-150. doi:10.1080/1941126X.2017.1340718

Brundtland, G. H. (1987). *Report of the World Commission on environment and development: Our common future.* United Nations.

Borgman, C. L. (1990). *Scholarly communication and bibliometrics.* Newbury Park: Sage Publications.

Borgman, C. L. (2000). Digital libraries and the continuum of scholarly communication. *Journal of Documentation, 56*(4), 412-430.

Bossaller, J. S., & Moulaison Sandy, H. (2017). Documenting the conversation: A systematic review of library discovery layers. *College & Research Libraries, 78*(5), 602-619. doi:10.5860/crl.78.5.602

Calarco, P., Shearer, K., Schmidt, B., & Tate, D. (2016). *Librarians' competencies profile for scholarly communication and open access*. Retrieved from Confederation of Open Access Repositories website: https://www.coar-repositories.org/files/Competencies-for-ScholComm-and-OA_June-2016.pdf

Chen, S. T., & Chang, B. G. (2012). The effects of absorptive capacity and decision speed on organizational innovation: A study of organizational structure as an antecedent variable. *Contemporary Management Research, 8*(1), 27-50.

Cross, W., Oleen, J., & Perry, A. (2017). Jump start your scholarly communication initiatives: Lessons learned from redesigning the scholarly communications roadshow for a new generation of librarians. In: At the Helm: Leading Transformation, the Proceedings of the ACRL 2017 Conference. 361-371. Chicago: Association of College and Research Libraries, a division of the American Library Association, 2017. Retrieved from http://www.ala.org/acrl/sites/ala.org.acrl/files/content/conferences/confsandpreconfs/2017/JumpStartYourScholarlyCommunicationInitiatives.pdf

Fearon, D., Gunia, B., Lake, S., Pralle, B. & Sallans, A. (2013). *Research in Data Management Services* (SPEC KIT 334). Association of Research Libraries: Washington, D.C. Retrieved from: https://doi.org/10.29242/spec.334

Green, E. (2016, May 12). What are the most-cited publications in the social sciences (according to Google Scholar)? [blog post]. Retrieved from http://blogs.lse.ac.uk/impactofsocialsciences/2016/05/12/what-are-the-most-cited-publications-in-the-social-sciences-according-to-google-scholar/

Hage, J., & Aiken, M. (1967). Program change and organizational properties a comparative analysis. *American Journal of Sociology, 72(5*), 503-519.

Hayes, C., & Kelly, H. E. (2017). Who's talking about scholarly communication? An examination of gender and behavior on the SCHOL-COMM Listserv. *Journal of Librarianship and Scholarly Communication. 5*(1). doi:10.7710/2162-3309.2017

Hey, T, Tansley, S., & Tolle, K. (2009). *The fourth paradigm: Data-intensive scientific discovery*. Redmond, Washington: Microsoft Research.

Howard, H. A. (1981). Organizational structure and innovation in academic libraries. *College & Research Libraries, 42*(5): 425-34.

Ketchum, A. M. (2017). The research life cycle and the health sciences librarian: Responding to change in scholarly communication. *Journal of the Medical Library Association, 105*(1), 80-83. doi:10.5195/jmla.2017.110

Klain-Gabbay, L. & Shohamb, S. (2016). Scholarly communication and academic librarians. *Library & Information Science Research, 28(*2), 170-179.

Kowalski, M. (2017). Breaking down silo walls: Successful collaboration across library departments. *Library Leadership & Management, 31*(2), 1-15.

Kyrillidou, M, & Morris, S., eds. (2013). *ARL Annual Salary Survey 2012–2013*. Washington, DC: Association of Research Libraries. Retrieved from https://doi.org/10.29242/salary.2012-2013

Kyrillidou, M, & Morris, S., eds. (2014). *ARL Annual Salary Survey 2013–2014*. Washington, DC: Association of Research Libraries. Retrieved from https://doi.org/10.29242/salary.2013-2014.

Kyrillidou, M, & Morris, S., eds. (2015). *ARL Annual Salary Survey 2014–2015*. Washington, DC: Association of Research Libraries. Retrieved from https://doi.org/10.29242/salary.2014-2015

Lee, C. (2009). *Matrix of digital curation knowledge and competencies*. Retrieved from https://ils.unc.edu/digccurr/digccurr-matrix.html

Lewis, R., Sarli, C., & Suiter, A. (2015). *Scholarly output assessment activities* (SPEC Kit 346). Association of Research Libraries, Washington, D.C. Retrieved from https://doi.org/10.29242/spec.346

Maron, N. L. & Smith, K. K. (2009). Current models of digital scholarly communication: Results of an investigation conducted by Ithaka for the Association of Research Libraries. *The Journal of Electronic Publishing, 12*(1). doi:10.3998/3336451.0012.105

Mitchell, M., Leachman. M., & Maserson, K. (2016). *Funding down, tuition up state cuts to higher education threaten quality and affordability at public colleges*. Washington, D.C.: Center on Budget and Policy Priorities. Retrieved from https://www.cbpp.org/sites/default/files/atoms/files/5-19-16sfp.pdf

Montana, P. J., & Charnov, B. H. (1993). *Management.* Hauppauge, N.Y: Barron's.

Morris, S. (2017). *ARL Annual Salary Survey 2015–2016*. Washington, DC: Association of Research Libraries. Retrieved from https://doi.org/10.29242/salary.2015-2016

National Research Council. (2015). *Preparing the workforce for digital curation.* Washington, DC: The National Academies Press. https://doi.org/10.17226/18590

Novak, J., & Day, A. (2015). The libraries they are a-changin': How libraries reorganize. *College & Undergraduate Libraries, 22*(3-4), 358-373. doi: 10.1080/10691316.2015.1067663

Oxford. (n.d.). *Organization.* Retrieved from https://en.oxforddictionaries.com/definition/us/organization

Potvin, S. (2013). The principle and the pragmatist: On conflict and coalescence for librarian engagement with open access initiatives. *The Journal of Academic Librarianship, 39(*1), 67-75.

Pugh, D. S. (1990). *Organization theory: Selected readings.* Harmondsworth: Penguin.

Regazzi, J. J. (2015). *Scholarly communications: A history from content as king to content as kingmaker*. New York: Rowman & Littlefield.

Rodriguez, J. E. (2015). Scholarly communications competencies: open access training for librarians. *New Library World, 116*(7/8), 397-405. doi:10.1108/NLW-12-2014-0140

Rogers, E. M. (1962). *Diffusion of innovations.* New York: Free Press of Glencoe.

Rogers, E. M. (2003). *Diffusion of innovations* (5th ed.). New York: Free Press.

Ryan, B., & Gross, N. C. (1943). The diffusion of hybrid seed corn in two Iowa communities. *Rural Sociology, 8*(1), 15–24.

Swanepoel, M., Kehoe, I., Hohner, M., Shepstone, C., Vanderjagt, L., Wakaruk, A., [...] Winter, C. (2015). *Developing a community of practice: Report on a survey to determine the scholarly communication landscape in western Canada*. Unpublished manuscript. http://hdl.handle.net/10133/4784b

Valente, T. W., & Rogers, E. M. (1995). The Origins and Development of the Diffusion of Innovations Paradigm as an Example of Scientific Growth. *Science Communication, 16*(3), 242–273. http://doi.org/10.1177/1075547095016003002

Wilder, S. (2017). *Hiring and staffing trends in ARL libraries.* Retrieved from http://www.arl.org/storage/documents/publications/rli-2017-stanley-wilder-article2.pdf

The Role of Information Resources in Young Fathers' Parenting Experiences

Caroline Mniszak
University of British Columbia, Canada,
czekajlo@mail.ubc.ca

Cathy Chabot
University of British Columbia, Canada,
cathy.chabot@ubc.ca

Heather O'Brien
University of British Columbia, Canada,
h.obrien@ubc.ca

Jean Shoveller
University of British Columbia, Canada,
jean.shoveller@ubc.ca

ABSTRACT

Young fathers are frequently stigmatized as absentee and uninvolved in parenting. Although recent research has highlighted the need to develop programs and services specifically for this population, little consideration has been given to the kind of information young fathers would like to obtain, or the barriers inherent in existing programs and information resources. This research, which is part of a longitudinal ethnographic study conducted at young parent and pregnancy outreach programs in two Canadian cities, examined the ways in which young fathers are excluded from parenting resources and services. In this paper, we used content analysis to analyse photographs of information resources at study sites, e.g., parenting books, pamphlets, and posters advertising local events and services. Findings showed that the presentation of information is gendered and targeted at young mothers, thus serving as a form of exclusion for young fathers. These results, situated in the context of (young) parents' information practices, show that intentions to support young fathers must address issues of representation and audience in the design and delivery of parenting information.

KEYWORDS

Young parents, information access, information resources, fathers, qualitative methods, gender

INTRODUCTION

Expectant mothers are often identified as needing information – both by health professionals, but also by family, friends and even complete strangers (McKenzie, 2003). Young mothers are cast as even more "information needy" due to their age and perceived poor decision making that led them to become pregnant (Duncan, 2007; Whitley & Kirmayer, 2008). As a result, they are more intensely monitored by health and social services than older mothers (Shoveller & Johnson, 2006), and several information resources and programs are targeted toward them (Greyson, 2012; Mann, Pearl & Behle, 2004). Recent scholarly analysis of young mothers' information contexts, and the services and resources that provide access to parenting information (Carson et al., 2017; Greyson et al., 2017a; 2017b), does not yet account for the experiences of young fathers (aged 16 to 25). There is a persistent stigma that young fathers are absentee (Duncan, 2007), which may result in exclusion from parenting information, programs, and supports. No work to date has investigated how existing information and services targeted toward young parents encompasses or fails to include young fathers' perspectives, and how this affects parenting experiences and practices.

This research, which is part of a longitudinal ethnographic study of young parents in two Canadian cities, set out to explore information resources as a form of exclusion for young fathers. Based on photographs taken at young parent and pregnancy outreach programs, we analyzed information resources representative of the kinds of materials created to inform young parents about pregnancy and parenting, as well as local events and services: brochures and posters produced by health and service organizations and parenting books. Through the application of content analysis, these photographs conveyed the gendered nature of the information resources present in the environments of young parents' "information grounds" (Pettigrew, 1999). These findings were validated through data obtained from interviews with young parents and service providers, which confirmed that young fathers did not perceive they were the audience for these resources and that the advertised services were not intended for them. In highlighting the ways in which the design of information resources renders parenting information and support inaccessible to participants in this study, we argue that the presentation of information contributes to the exclusion experienced by young fathers, and has implications for their parenting practices.

LITERATURE REVIEW

Parents' Information Practices

Within the realm of parenting, information practices have been investigated with respect to how parents locate and make sense of parenting information in specific circumstances, such as being pregnant with multiples (McKenzie, 2003) or having a child with a medical condition (see for example, Knapp et al., 2011). Research that has emphasized more general parenting information practices, including the sources parents draw upon for information (e.g., web, health professionals, family and friends), has demonstrated a shift in parents' information seeking from place-based sources (e.g., health and social service organizations, commercial shops) (Marden & Nicholas, 1997) to digital sources (e.g., websites) (Radey & Randolph, 2009). Regardless of the type of sources parents utilize, it has been demonstrated that the ability to access resources is impacted by a range of contextual factors, such as number and age of children, socio-emotional support, and socioeconomic status. The parenting arena is further fraught by multiple sources offering conflicting information and parents' perceptions that their decisions and actions are monitored and judged by others, from health professionals to strangers (O'Brien, Greyson, Chabot & Shoveller, 2018). For example, Loudon, Buchanan and Ruthven (2016) found that parents did not always share information with health professionals for fear of being negatively evaluated. Low-income and young parents may experience additional monitoring due to the threat of child apprehension from social services, making them less likely to trust professionals or to reach out for help when they need it (Romagnoli & Wall, 2004; Walker, 2012).

Help-seeking may be further confounded by gender: research on men's help seeking habits consistently shows that men, regardless of age, ethnicity and social background, are reluctant to seek help, advice or information when they experience problems (Addis & Mahalik, 2003). The few studies that have compared mothers' and fathers' information practices have found that mothers are more likely than fathers to turn to the Internet (Radey & Randolph, 2009) and to act upon the information they find (Stern, et al., 2012). Perhaps more telling is the finding that fathers want to be involved in pregnancy, childbirth and childcare, but often do not know how to do so and feel unprepared to become parents (Poh, Koh & He, 2014; Symon & Lee, 2003). Thus, it is not only the case that mothers and fathers may engage in different information seeking practices and utilize different sources. There may also be differences in parents' self-efficacy and sense of inclusion that shapes where and with what frequency information is sought, interpreted and used, and this may be further influenced by socio-demographic variables, namely age.

Young Parents' Information Practices

Young parents are more heavily surveilled than older parents (Shoveller & Johnson, 2006). Societally, young mothers have been cast as naïve about sex and contraception (Duncan, 2007; Whitley & Kirmayer, 2008), while young fathers have been labeled as absentee and uninvolved (Duncan, 2007). Although young parents may have similar information needs and practices as older parents, they are often labeled as "information poor" (Greyson, O'Brien & Shoveller, 2017a; 2017b) and perceived to be lacking the information needed to make informed decisions. This stigma intensifies the degree to which young parents are monitored by health, education and social service authorities and society more broadly, and bolsters the argument that young parents need information and services to help them navigate pregnancy, birth and parenting (Carson et al., 2017; Greyson, 2012; Greyson et al., 2017a; 2017b; Mann, Pearl & Behle, 2004).

Although the Internet has increasingly become a popular source for parents to *seek* information (Radey & Randolph, 2009), parenting knowledge, efficacy and experiences are shaped by other forms of information acquisition. McKenzie's two-dimensional model of information practices demonstrated that people, and more specifically mothers of twins, connected and interacted with information in different ways: active information seeking of previously identified sources, active scanning/semi-directed browsing, non-directed monitoring of the physical environment or sources, and receiving information by proxy, i.e., being told information (McKenzie, 2003). Exploring this model with young mothers, O'Brien et al. (2018) concluded that "active seeking…was often discouraged by authorities, and more passive practices of information encountering and receipt of information from proxies were accepted and expected" (p. 621). These findings were particularly problematic in light of conflicting information from different sources (health authorities versus one's own parents), and the presence of social, financial, personal, and geographic factors, including level of family support, breastfeeding challenges, and ability to access resources. Thus, the context around parenting must be considered alongside individuals' observable information practices, such as seeking or not seeking.

Within the context of young parenting, more attention has been placed on the information practices and contexts of young mothers. Because they are perceived to need information, young mothers have access to a variety of "wrap around services," i.e. young parent and pregnancy outreach programs, which provide a variety of information and resources on an array of topics (Greyson et al., 2017a; 2017b). There has been a rise in research regarding the experiences of young fathers over the past decade (Dallas, 2009; Davies & Neale, 2015; Davies, 2016; Deslauriers, Devault, Groulx, & Sévigny, 2012; Kirven, 2014; Kiselica & Kiselica, 2014; Sopcak, 2013). However, these studies have focused on the benefits of establishing services and programs for young dads without considering the kinds of information with which dads *want* to connect, and lack a more grounded understanding of fathers' experiences as young parents, including the barriers they face in acquiring information.

Current Study

Context has been likened to a "container" or setting; as meaning constructed by individuals at the center of many nested networks; or a social process whereby "information activities take place within an explicit or implicit social community" (Courtright, 2007, p. 286, 289). In general, people move between many different settings (e.g., home, work) and communities where they fulfill different roles (e.g., student, partner, parent, neighbor), making it challenging to grapple with context and the role that information plays in shaping it. In the current study, young fathers' information contexts were explored by examining information resources contained within spaces offering parenting services and by talking with young parents and service providers. Three Young Parent Programs (YPPs) and one Pregnancy Outreach Program (POP) served as sites for recruitment and ethnographic observation in the current research.

We specifically investigated YPPs and the POP as information grounds, or "environment[s] temporarily created when people come together for a singular purpose but from whose behavior emerges a social atmosphere that fosters the spontaneous and serendipitous sharing of information" (Pettigrew, 1999, p. 811). YPPs existed for young parents to complete their high school education, while the POP served as an information resource and support for mothers with young babies up to six months of age. Despite their primary purposes, students formed social ties with each other and service providers, which promoted rich and often unintended information exchanges. Participants' informal interactions (e.g., preparing meals together) and formal programming (e.g., visits from health and social service professionals) offered opportunities for direct information acquisition, as well as peer support and general knowledge of community information. These were not always positive experiences for young parents; for instance, interventions were sometimes targeted to "correct" a behavior, such as the correct preparation of baby formula, or presented information that conflicted with familial practices. However, the abundance of information in the environment provided opportunities for young parents to ask questions, seek help, and be exposed to potentially useful information. However, these programs were not equitable information grounds for both young mothers and fathers, and young fathers did not benefit from the extent of services and programs offered. In some cases, barriers were clearly defined, such as policies that designated one YPP as "mothers-only;" more implicit barriers manifested in the section of reading materials and information resources available within the spaces. These observations were supported by interview comments from young fathers, mothers, and service providers.

This analysis looks specifically at information resources within the program spaces, such as posters, brochures, and books, to examine the ways in which gender manifests in information resources. In some cases, gender was made explicit through images of women and men. Some of the information resources captured in the photographs taken of the program spaces targeted young mothers through subtle design choices such as color. Several scholars have drawn connections between color and gender meanings and symbolism. Although the connection between color and gender are not historically deep-rooted, today pink is synonymous with femininity and blue with masculinity (Paoletti, 2012). Purple and pastels also carry connotations of femininity (Auster & Auster-Gussman, 2016), and marketers customize colors, namely pink and blue, to target specific genders (Khan, 2017). We complemented the visual analysis of the photographs with field notes and interview data derived from young parents and service providers, and were guided by the following research questions:

- *To what extent are information resources present in young parents' program spaces gendered?*
- *How do young fathers relate to these information resources, and what impact do they have on their parenting experiences?*

METHODS

Data were drawn from a longitudinal study of young parents conducted in two Western Canadian cities between 2013 and 2018. The populations of both cites were 86,622 and 2,463,431 people; youth between the ages of 15-24 years old made up 13.2% and 12.6%, respectively of these cities' populations (Statistics Canada, September 13, 2017). The researchers' University Research Ethics Board (Certificate #: H17-02504) approved the study.

	Age				Ethnicity			Education Attainment			
	16-18	19-21	22-24	25+	Caucasian	Indigenous	Other, e.g., Latino, Filipino	Some High School (HS)	Currently in HS	Graduated HS	Some post-secondary, e.g., college, trade school
YM	36	29	22	3	39	43	18	17	39	12	12
YF	4	7	7	5	8	14	3	13	3	5	1

Table 1: Demographic characteristics of young mother (YM) and young father (YF) parent participants

Participants

Over the course of the broader study, 90 expecting or parenting young mothers (YM), 23 young fathers (YF), 2 socially significant others (e.g., parents of YM), and 25 service providers (youth care workers, daycare staff, teachers, health care professionals, and program coordinators) participated. Table 1 summarizes the demographic characteristics of the young parents who took part in the study. Young parents were defined to be between the ages of 16-24[1], however the study sample includes exceptions[2]. Participants could choose more than one category when stating their ethnicity, and not all YF and YM responded to the question about educational attainment.

Recruitment and Data Collection

Data collection took place at four recruitment sites across the two cities: three alternative school programs (YPPs) and a pregnancy outreach program (POP). Participants were recruited via posters at these locales, as well as snowball sampling. In general, most young mothers and service providers were recruited at the four sites, and young mothers sometimes recruited their partners and socially significant others (e.g., their own parents). Young fathers were more difficult to recruit because of their notable absence at YPPs and the POP. Of those who did participate, not all were the biological fathers of their partners' children, but these men were included in the study since they were actively engaged in fathering roles.

Research staff visited the recruitment sites in the largest metropolitan city fifty-five times, and made nine two-week long visits to the smaller city's sites. Longitudinal data was gathered from participants using qualitative interviews, socio-demographic questionnaires, and naturalistic observation. Frequent trips to the sites enabled researchers to interview some participants between one to nine times and observe the program spaces over time. Interviews lasted 30-120 minutes, involved informed consent, and were audio recorded. The structure was open and covered a range of topics about young parents' experiences, as well as their information seeking practices and technology use. Socio-demographic questionnaires were administered at the beginning or end of the interview, depending on the interviewer's preference, and included questions about age, ethnicity and sexual identity, reproductive history, contraceptive practices, and access to services. Participants were given the opportunity to review their interview transcript and a $30 cash honorarium per interview.

Daily interactions at the YPPs and POP were recorded through naturalistic observation; informed consent was obtained from participants. In addition to taking field notes, researchers took photos. These images did not feature any study participants; they showed the physical spaces and detailed shots of information resources within the space such as computers, books about parenting, posters advertising local events and services, pamphlets from parenting and health organizations, and signs and messages on the white board. A selection of these resources formed the basis of the current research, with field notes and interviews with young parents and service providers used to situate their analysis.

Approach to Data Analysis

Interview transcripts, field notes, and photographs were stored and analyzed using Nvivo software; Excel was used to record and descriptively analyze the questionnaires. Grounded theory methods were used to analyze the interviews and ethnographic field notes. Specifically, coders engaged in open coding to establish categories, such as "Parenting Support", theoretical coding to thematically connect the categories (e.g., making notes on the connections between examples coded in the "Parenting Support" code and the "Information Behaviors/Practices" code), and selective coding, which involved organizing data based on specific themes (e.g., drawing examples of fathers facing barriers to services from the aforementioned codes) (Dey, 1999). This process gave rise to a specific examination of the experiences of young fathers, which were self-reported but also informed by conversations with young mothers and service providers.

Photographs of the information resources (books, brochures, posters, white board messages) were analyzed using content analysis techniques. Content analysis is an established technique used to identify messages and characteristics inherent in cultural objects that speak to their purpose, causes, and effects (Rudy, Popova & Linz, 2010). Though content analysis has been primarily used for textual analysis (Hara & Sanfilippo, 2017; Holsti, 1969; Li et al., 2017), it has been used with a variety of media (Bryman, 2012) and is a powerful and flexible technique for exploring visual data. In the current investigation of information resources situated within Young Parent Programs (YPP) and the Pregnancy Outreach Program (POP), content analysis strategies were used to interpret the text on the objects in the photos, as well as the objects themselves within the photographed environment, using manifest and latent content strategies. During initial coding, manifest content, i.e., what was observable in the photograph, was noted, and during the interpretation stage, latent content, or the "meanings that lie beneath the surface"

---

[1] The study's definition of "young" (e.g. age 16-24) was based on several services' eligibility criteria in the province.

[2] Young fathers were often recruited through snowball sampling when young mothers invited the fathers of their children to the study. Due to difficulties recruiting young fathers to the study, young fathers were not required to adhere to age eligibility restrictions.

(Bryman, 2012, p. 290) was the focus. The five photographs featured in this paper were chosen from a collection of 116 of photographs taken during the study. These photographs were chosen for analysis because they demonstrate a range of gendered elements contained in the parenting information documents at the YPPs and POP. To protect the identity of the YPPs and POP, identifying information in the photos was blurred.

During interviews[3], young fathers described feeling unwelcome at young parent spaces but often found it difficult to articulate why. One of the reasons may be that messages about gender and gender construction are complex and often overlooked. For example, a pink poster makes assumptions about parenting women and femininity while at the same time excluding parenting men. The current analysis considered whether the information needs of both parents were considered in common parenting information resources, or whether mothers' perspectives and experiences were privileged over fathers'.

FINDINGS

The analysis focused on photographs taken at YPPs and POP of information resources available to the clientele, specifically books, posters, and pamphlets visible within the environment. At the surface level, the images captured bookshelves, as well as individual posters and groups of posters advertising local programs and services or issued by provincial or federal health agencies. Going beyond the artefacts in the photographs, we articulated barriers for young fathers seeking parenting information and support, either because they were not designed for men or perpetuated negative messages about men. Many of the information resources available at YPPs and POP were intended for young mothers, the primary inhabitants of the spaces. Here we present these findings, drawing upon interview data and field notes to reinforce this analysis.

Figure 1: Books in one of the Young Parent Program Spaces

Figure 1 shows a shelf of parenting books available to students at one YPP. The majority of the books are designed for mothers, and this was evident by the colors used (pinks and pastel colors) in combination with the subject matter (e.g., breastfeeding, pregnancy). Note in Figure 1 that nine of the fifteen (64%) books shown in the photo have pink or pastel coloring or designs, which signals to potential readers that the material is targeting women. Many of these books, such as the book series *What to Expect*[4] cater to mothers' perspectives. Looking at the spine of the series, they are decorated with pastel colors traditionally associated with femininity (Auster & Auster-Gussman, 2016). The design of the background mimics a patchwork quilt composed of floral patterns, a craft commonly done by women (Stalp, 2006). Although not visible in the photograph, the cover art on the *What to Expect* books commonly feature women, giving men who are glancing at the book the impression that the information is targeted for mothers. Because of the design and marketing of popular parenting books, young fathers like Jim felt that resources for dads were limited. He said, "there's no really, like, book or, you know, something to look at and be, like, 'Okay, there's this, and this is that.'"

Figure 2 shows an assortment of posters placed on a door within a mothers-only YPP. Every poster featured women or mothers, clearly communicating that fathers were not the intended audience of the advertised services or information. Absentee fathers have been noted in other studies of information documents. For example, studies focused on children's picture books found that fathers were invisible or emotionally unavailable in many depictions of family dynamics (Adams, et al., 2011; Anderson & Hamilton, 2005). Excluding fathers from parenting literature and information documents perpetuates notions that mothers are and should be the primary – and at times, the sole – caregivers, and that fathers do not need to educate themselves about children and their care. Ruby, a service provider working with young mothers, said that "there really isn't anything put in place" to support young fathers. "[B]oys just don't have the same support" and opportunities to attend program[s] were limited to accompanying a young mother.

However, many fathers expressed interest in the resources being offered to mothers, such as prenatal and parenting classes, support groups and maternity ward tours. Young father Jim said that he and his partner found "one [parenting program] that [they] went to a little while ago. It was actually same sort of thing as the young moms', but for young dads." Jim explained that

---

[3] Self-selected pseudonyms have been used for all interviewees.

[4] The "What to Expect…" book series began with *What to Expect When You're Expecting*, a popular pregnancy guide written by Heidi Murkoff and Sharon Mazel, published by Workman Publishing. The series now contains several other books based on other parenting or child development stages, including What to Expect: The First Year and What to Expect: The Toddler Years (Wikipedia, 2017).

even though he and the other fathers attending found the group helpful and supportive, it was only put on three to four times a year due to low funding. He concluded, "The problem is that they don't think the young dads need it so much." Young fathers' desire to access resources such as parenting groups was unacknowledged, which is reinforced in the posters featuring only parenting women in Figure 2 and the existence of "mothers-only" YPPs and POP.

Figure 3 features a poster of a pregnant female body with a purple/pink filter in the background. The foreground of the poster features text to inform the audience of a pregnancy outreach program hosted by the YPP. For cis mothers with gender confirming bodies, the image of the naked, pregnant female belly and breasts may be familiar and relatable. However, for cis fathers with gender confirming bodies, the image may be unfamiliar and therefore alienating. Rather than empathising with the imaging, cis fathers may reason that the image in the background does not depict their experience and is not meant for them, i.e., it is intended for persons who are pre- or post-natal.

Figure 2: Collection of Posters on a door at a "Mothers Only" YPP

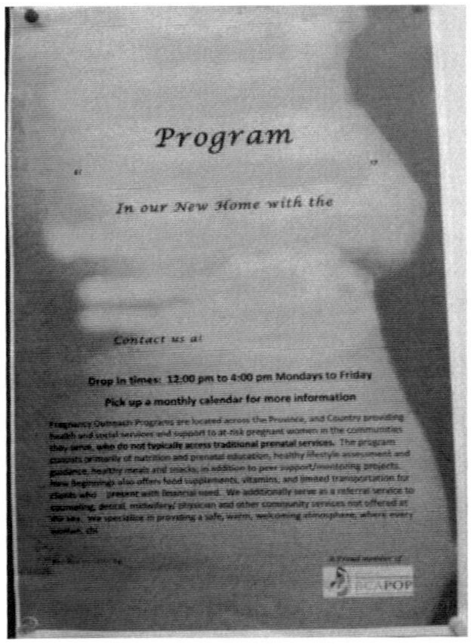

Figure 3: "Pregnancy Outreach Program" advertisement

An invitation to a baby shower event for mothers and their newborn to six-month-old babies is shown in Figure 4. The background of the poster features fluffy clouds, and the foreground contains text (colored pink, light blue and black) and a cartoon image of a parenting panda with a baby panda on its back. The abundance of pinks and pastels reflects a feminine aesthetic (Auster & Auster-Gussman, 2016; Khan, 2017; Paoletti, 2012). Since showers (e.g. wedding, baby) are traditionally "a gendered ritual, organized by women, for women" (Montemurro, 2005), fathers may not feel welcome to an event with that name. In addition to the name of the event, young fathers, may not perceive they are welcome since this poster was situated in a mothers-only YPP, even though the text in the poster stated, "Families welcome." The idea that young fathers are "guests" in the space, and not the intended clientele, is also indicated by the image of the two pandas. One of the pandas is positioned as a parent and the other is positioned to be the baby; the poster does not feature an image of a family of pandas (such as two pandas positioned as parents).

Even though some programs tried to cater to young mothers and fathers, these programs often had low numbers of young fathers attending, potentially because young fathers did not perceive they were welcome. One service provider named a specific program led by one of the few provincial organizations that catered to young fathers. However, young father, Victor talked about this same program, saying "I don't- I don't think they have programs for dads." When young fathers were not explicitly welcomed, many assumed they were not invited to participate because some programs were mothers only; those that welcomed young fathers did not make that explicitly obvious in their informational posters, as demonstrated in that Victor was aware of the program but not the scope of its clientele or services.

The scarcity of resources available to men is precisely why information resources targeted toward men must be careful not to further isolate them. Even important messages needed to be crafted carefully to prevent increased stigma for young fathers. Figure 5 shows a poster from a series called the "Domestic Violence Poster Set," produced by a national non-profit society warning about the potential effects of domestic violence. The poster features an image of a naked baby being held by its naked mother in the background, and the words "BEAT your wife and your SON will most likely go to PRISON." Messages such as these arise from literature suggesting a connection between domestic violence and youth delinquency (for examples, see Jonson-Reid, 1998; Synder & Sickmund, 1995). However, other studies have fought against these damning conclusions and argue that the correlations are not as strong as presented (Holt, et al., 2008). Such messaging does not address the root of domestic violence and neither does it help men change their behaviours. Displaying posters such as these in spaces which host mothers-only programming perpetuates messages that fathers who have made poor choices are not welcome in the lives of their children since their impacts on them will be detrimental. Service provider Ruby said that young men often encounter doubt about their parenting capabilities, which can result in increased surveillance from their partners, social workers and society in general. Because the parenting capabilities of many young fathers are often questioned (Duncan, 2007), messages targeted to them need to be presented with sensitivity.

In many spaces, there was evidence of an intention to increase resources and programs for fathers. For example, Figure 6 depicts an advertisement for a fathers' group. Upon further investigation, the field researcher noted that this group "hasn't been active since our study began in October 2013. Two of the staff [at the organization hosting the Father's Group] I spoke with didn't know much about the group or who is supposed to be running it."

This selection of photos, which were collected during fieldwork, showed that many information documents focused solely on parenting women. Figure 1 shows a bookshelf at a young parent program. Many of the books featured on the shelf are designed to appeal to parenting women rather than parenting men, giving young dads in the space the impression that there are no information resources personalized for them. Figures 2 through 5 depict posters showing pregnant women or women in parenting roles. Fathers are absent from many depictions of parenting. Although there may be an intention to create information and services for young fathers, many of these efforts are not maintained. Figure 6 shows an example of a parenting program customized for young fathers; however, the program no longer existed during the five years of ethnographic data collection. This collection of documents demonstrates that young fathers seeking information encounter many information documents targeting mothers but very few designed for them.

Figure 4: Baby shower community event poster

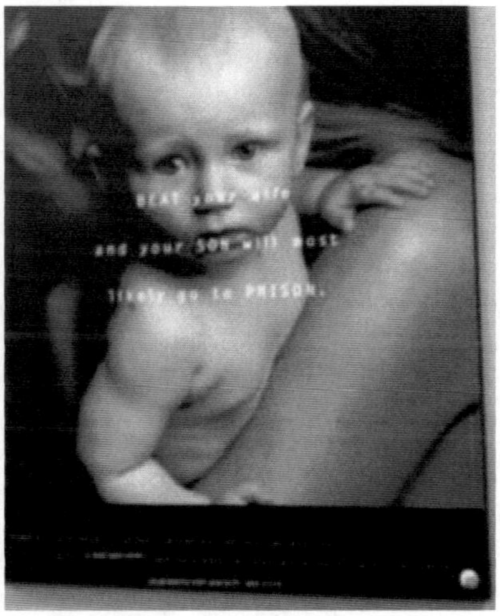

Figure 5: Poster from the "Domestic Violence Poster Set"

Figure 6: Poster advertising "Fathers' Group"

Two service providers attested to the power of images and photos in young parent spaces. David and Grant, who ran one of the only fathers' programs in the province, said they use father-friendly photos and images to communicate that their programs welcome fathers. According to David, photos are important for attracting young fathers to a program because "it's art. [...] They're looking at an image that they can relate to as opposed to a couple of lines." Because service providers have found that photos are a powerful way to send messages to young fathers, displaying father-friendly images at programs and services was an important way to welcome them. A careful selection of photos featuring positive images of parenting fathers could be used to advertise parenting programs and entice more young father attendees.

DISCUSSION

In a review of fathers' experiences during their partner's pregnancy and childbirth, Poh, et al. (2014) showed that 25 studies substantiated findings that fathers felt uninformed about pregnancy and parenting topics and relied on their partners and healthcare professionals for support (Poh et al., 2014). Although our data showed that young fathers were interested in parenting information and programs, they were often excluded from documents providing or advertising access to parenting information. Sometimes this occurred because young fathers were not welcomed at the information grounds where parenting information was exchanged. Other times, the documents in these spaces targeted only parenting women and gave young fathers the impression that they were not welcome in the space. Information resources targeted parenting women explicitly by featuring only women on the posters, and also implicitly through the use of the color pink or pastel palettes, which have been associated with femininity (Auster & Auster-Gussman, 2016; Paoletti, 2012). The limited amount of information resources for parenting men means that those that do target men need to be careful not to further isolate them, either through negative messaging (e.g. Figure 5, the Domestic Violence Poster Set) or lack of follow-through (e.g. Figure 6, the poster advertising a fathers' group). Service providers in this study attested to the power of images and documents to draw young fathers to information and services, or to estrange them. Creation of information resources for young parents must consider gender inclusivity in their design and delivery.

Returning to our original research questions, we found that information resources were gendered, and that they acted as reinforcement to the exclusion and lack of confidence that young fathers felt in their roles as parents. The depiction of young fathers as "absentee" (Duncan, 2007) may be more a function of the constrained and meager information contexts in which young men find themselves than the result of their ability and inclination to (co)parent. Given that information acquisition occurs through active seeking and in more passive ways, such as through advertisements and social interactions (McKenzie, 2003), it is essential to examine how information is constructed and delivered to young fathers. In addition to exploring programs and services for young fathers (see, for example, Davies & Neale, 2015; Davies, 2016; Deslauriers, et al., 2012), there should be careful consideration given to how health and service provided craft parenting materials, whether their messages are finding their way to young men, and how these messages are interpreted by recipients.

CONCLUSION

This analysis has made several important contributions. Building on the consolidative work of Courtright (2007), this analysis contributes to the field's current understanding of context by focusing on a population which has not previously been studied (i.e., young fathers) using information theory. Being one of the first analyses of young fathers' information contexts, this study enriches our understanding of young parents' information practices by demonstrating the limitation of information resources and programming spaces in reflecting the needs and experiences of young fathers.

With regards to limitations, a weakness of this analysis is the small sample of young fathers, which limits the generalizability of the findings. We relied on word of mouth and snowball sampling to reach young fathers since we did not have direct access to this population. Secondly, the sample of photos analyzed for this analysis was limited to the recruitment sites of the Young Parents Study. Most of the recruitment sites catered primarily to young mothers, which was reflected in the information resources within the spaces. Third, young fathers were not asked to comment on the information documents analyzed for this study; this limitation should be addressed by future studies analyzing young fathers' access to parenting services and information. Finally, to protect the confidentiality of the recruitment sites, we could not connect the information resources at the sites directly to a specific program and its policies and history for a more in-depth assessment of organizational contexts.

Despite these limitations, this work articulates that the information contexts of young fathers are less informed than those of young mothers. Rather than assuming that young men are disinterested in parenting, this analysis shows that parenting information may be one of many exclusionary elements. Further analysis of the broader ethnographic study's data will focus on young fathers' experiences beyond the information resources encountered in parenting programs, including familial and partner relationships, access to parenting services and supports, and social stigma. The overarching goal of this research is to offer recommendations to health and social service agencies regarding how young fathers' parenting contexts can be enhanced through the provision of relevant, inclusive, and timely information.

ACKNOWLEDGEMENTS

The authors thank the Young Parents Study participants for sharing their time and stories. Special thanks to the members of the Youth Sexual Health Team for their time spent collecting and preparing the data from this study for analysis. The authors are also grateful to the reviewers for their helpful feedback.

REFERENCES

Adams, M., Walker, C., & O'Connell, P. (2011). Invisible or involved fathers? A content analysis of representations of parenting in young children's picturebooks in the UK. Sex Roles, 65(3-4), 259-270.

Addis, M. E., & Mahalik, J. R. (2003). Men, masculinity, and the contexts of help seeking. American Psychologist, 58, 5-14.

Anderson, D. A., & Hamilton, M. (2005). Gender role stereotyping of parents in children's picture books: The invisible father. Sex Roles, 52(3-4), 145-151.

Auster, C. J., & Auster-Gussman, L. A. (2016). Contemporary mother's day and father's day greeting cards: A reflection of traditional ideologies of motherhood and fatherhood? Journal of Family Issues, 37(9), 1294-1326.

Bryman, A. (2012). Content analysis. Social research methods (4th ed. ed., pp. 288-309). Oxford: Oxford UP.

Carson, A., Chabot, C., Greyson, D., Shannon, K., Duff, P., & Shoveller, J. (2017). A narrative analysis of the birth stories of early-age mothers. Sociology of Health & Illness, 39(6), 816-831.

Courtright, C. (2007). Context in information behavior research. Annual Review of Information Science and Technology, 41(1), 273-306.

Dallas, C. M. (2009). Interactions between adolescent fathers and health care professionals during pregnancy, labor, and early postpartum. Journal of Obstetric, Gynecologic, & Neonatal Nursing, 38(3), 290-299.

Davies, L. (2016). Are young fathers "hard to reach"? Understanding the importance of relationship building and service sustainability. Journal of Children's Services, 11(4), 317-329.

Davies, L., & Neale, B. (2015). Supporting young fathers: The promise, potential and perils of statutory service provision. Families, Relationships and Societies, 4(2), 331-338.

Deslauriers, J., Devault, A., Groulx, A., & Sévigny, R. (2012). Rethinking services for young fathers. Fathering, 10(1), 66.

Dey, I. (1999). Coding. Grounding grounded theory (1st ed., pp. 95-113) Academic Press.

Duncan, S. (2007). What's the problem with teenage parents? and what's the problem with policy? Critical Social Policy, 27(3), 307-334.

Hara, N., & Sanfilippo, M. R. (2017). Analysis of roles in engaging contentious online discussions in science. *Journal of the Association for Information Science and Technology*, 68(8), 1953-1966.

Greyson, D. (2012). Young adult parenthood: Library science's latest revelation. Intersections, 3(2), 12-15.

Greyson, D., O'Brien, H., & Shoveller, J. (2017a). Constructing knowledge and ignorance in the social information worlds of young mothers. Paper presented at the Proceedings of the Association for Information Science & Technology, 54(1).

Greyson, D., O'Brien, H., & Shoveller, J. (2017b). Information world mapping: A participatory arts-based elicitation method for information behavior interviews. Library & Information Science Research, 39(2), 149-157.

Holsti, O. R. (1969). Content analysis for the social sciences and humanities. Addison-Wesley Pub. Co.

Holt, S., Buckley, H., & Whelan, S. (2008). The impact of exposure to domestic violence on children and young people: A review of the literature. Child Abuse & Neglect, 32(8), 797-810.

Jonson-Reid, M. (1998). Youth violence and exposure to violence in childhood: An ecological review. Aggression and Violent Behavior, 3(2), 159-179.

Kirven, J. (2014). Helping teen dads obtain and sustain paternal success. International Journal of Childbirth Education, 29(2), 85-88.

Kiselica, M. S., & Kiselica, A. M. (2014). The complicated worlds of adolescent fathers: Implications for clinical practice, public policy, and research. Psychology of Men & Masculinity, 15(3), 260-274.

Khan, S. A. (2017). Pink and blue: Gendered consumerism. Crossings: A Journal of English Studies, 8, 120-127.

Knapp, C., Madden, V., Marcu, M., Wang, H., Curtis, C., Sloyer, P., & Shenkman, E. (2011). Information seeking behaviors of parents whose children have life-threatening illnesses. Pediatric Blood & Cancer, 56(5), 805-811.

Li, X., Li, X., Cox, A., Cox, A., Ford, N., & Ford, N. (2017). Knowledge construction by users: A content analysis framework and a knowledge construction process model for virtual product user communities. Journal of Documentation, 73(2), 284-304.

Loudon, K., Buchanan, S., & Ruthven, I., 2016. The everyday life information seeking behaviours of first-time mothers. Journal of Documentation, 72(1), pp. 24 – 46.

Mann, M. B., Pearl, P. T., & Behle, P. D. (2004). Effects of parent education on knowledge and attitudes. Adolescence, 39(154), 355.

Marden, M., & Nicholas, D. (1997). The information needs of parents. Child Language Teaching and Therapy, 13(3), 279-285.

McKenzie, P. J., 2003. A model of information practices in accounts of everyday-life information seeking. Journal of documentation, 59(1), pp. 19-40.

Montemurro, B. (2005). Add men, don't stir: Reproducing traditional gender roles in modern wedding showers. Journal of Contemporary Ethnography, 34(1), 6-35.

O'Brien, H., Greyson, D., Shoveller, J., & Chabot, C. (2018). Young parents' personal and social information contexts for child feeding practices: An ethnographic study in British Columbia, Canada. Journal of Documentation, 74(3), 608-623.

Paoletti, J. B. (2012). Pink and blue: Telling the boys from the girls in America. Indiana University Press.

Poh, H., Koh, S., & He, H. (2014). An integrative review of fathers' experiences during pregnancy and childbirth. International Nursing Review, 61(4), 543-554.

Radey, M., & Randolph, K. A. (2009). Parenting sources: How do parents differ in their efforts to learn about parenting? Family Relations, 58(5), 536-548.

Romagnoli, A., & Wall, G. (2012). "I know I'm a good mom": Young, low-income mothers' experiences with risk perception, intensive parenting ideology and parenting education programmes. Health, Risk & Society, 14(3), 273–289.

Rudy, R. M., Popova, L., & Linz, D. G. (2010). The context of current content analysis of gender roles: An introduction to a special issue. Sex Roles, 62(11-12), 705-720.

Shoveller, J. A., & Johnson, J. L., 2006. Risky groups, risky behaviour, and risky persons: Dominating discourses on youth sexual health. Critical Public Health, 16(1), 47–60.

Snyder, H. N., & Sickmund, M. (1995). Juvenile offenders & victims: A national report. DIANE Publishing.

Stalp, M. C. (2006). Negotiating time and space for serious leisure: Quilting in the modern US home. Journal of Leisure Research, 38(1), 104-132.

Statistics Canada. (September 13, 2017). 2016 Census profile. Catalogue no. 98-316-X2016001. Ottawa, Statistics Canada.

Stern, M. J., Cotten, S. R., & Drentea, P. (2012). The separate spheres of online health: Gender, parenting, and online health information searching in the information age. Journal of Family Issues, 33(10), 1324-1350.

Symon, A., & Lee, J. (2003). Including men in antenatal education: Evaluating innovative practice. Evidence-Based Midwifery, 1(1), 12-20.

Walker, C., 2012. The information world of parents: a study of the use and understanding of information by parents of young children. Library Trends, 60(3), pp. 546-568.

Whitley, R., & Kirmayer, L. J. (2008). Perceived stigmatisation of young mothers: An exploratory study of psychological and social experience. Social Science & Medicine, 66(2), 339-348.

81st Annual Meeting of the Association for Information Science & Technology | Vancouver, Canada | 10 – 14 November 2018

Using Social and Topical Distance to Analyze Information Sharing on Social Media

Philippe Mongeon
Leiden University, Netherlands. p.mongeon@cwts.leidenuniv.nl

ABSTRACT

The diversity of social media platforms, users and uses has long been a challenge for social media research. The difficulty of inferring meaning from social media acts is also, and perhaps more importantly, due to the fact the even identical acts that are in appearance identical and that occur on the same platforms and contexts can have diverse meanings. This paper proposes a model based on the concepts of social and topical distance that can help shed light on the possible meanings of a social media act. The model considers the social relationship between the content creator and the user, as well as the topical relationship between the content the user's main topics of interest. It is demonstrated by analyzing a set of papers published in JASIST that were tweeted by researchers. The results show that the model can help differentiate between different types of heterogeneous social media acts and users or be used to characterize the attention that a specific content has received on social media.

KEYWORDS

Information sharing behavior, Altmetrics, Twitter, Social media metrics, Academia, Social media

INTRODUCTION

What's in a tweet? The diversity of social media platforms, their functionalities, their affordances, their users and their uses have long been a challenge for social media research. This issue is also ubiquitous in altmetrics (or social media metrics) research. While the diversity of tools and communication channels covered by altmetrics was initially considered their greatest advantage (Priem, Taraborelli, Groth, & Neylon, 2010), it did not take long for the community to realize that while this diversity opens new possibility for measuring scholarly communication, it is also the source of one of the most important limitation of altmetrics. Indeed, for Haustein (2016), heterogeneity is one of the grand challenges of altmetrics, along with the lack of an agreed-upon definition of altmetrics, a lack of conceptual frameworks and theories, data quality issues and the dependency on APIs, the companies who own the platforms (e.g., Twitter, Facebook) and data providers and aggregators (e.g., Almetric.com, Plum Analytics).

Diverse social media platforms have different purpose and functionalities that will attract different types of users that will use the platform to perform different kinds of acts (Van Noorden, 2014): "why would things as diverse as a mention on Twitter, an expert recommendation on F1000, a reader count on Mendeley, a like on Facebook, a citation in a blog post and the reuse of a dataset share a common meaning?" (Haustein, 2016, p. 415). However, the difficulty of inferring meaning from social media acts is not only due to the heterogeneity of the platforms, their functionalities, and their users. It is also, and perhaps more importantly, due to the diverse meanings of apparently identical acts occurring on similar platforms and in similar contexts. As Zeynep Tufekci puts it:

> "The question of inference from analyses of social media big data remains underconceptualized and underexamined. What's a click? What does a retweet mean? In what context? By whom? How do different communities interpret these interactions? As with all human activities, interpreting online imprints engages layers of complexity." (Tufekci, 2014, p. 510)

For example, a user may share an article because it is funny or controversial (Haustein, Peters, Sugimoto, Thelwall, & Larivière, 2014), requested using the #icanhazpdf hashtag (Swab & Romme, 2016), authored by a friend, on a topic of interests to him or her. They may also share information related to their professional activities or their personal interests (Bowman, 2015). Several studies have shed light on the heterogeneity social media. Some have investigated the types of users in order to identify distinct groups (Tsou, Bowman, Ghazinejad, & Sugimoto, 2015; Vainio & Holmberg, 2017), and others looked at disciplinary differences in social media uptake and usage (Holmberg & Thelwall, 2014). Much research has also focused on the sentiment analysis of social media posts (e.g., Thelwall, Buckley, & Paltoglou, 2011, 2012; Thelwall, Tsou, Weingart, Holmberg, & Haustein, 2013).

To further address these heterogeneity issues, I propose a new model based on the concepts of social and topical distance that can help better understand the possible meanings of a social media act. The model, partly borrowed from research on scientific literature recommender systems (Cabanac, 2011), considers the *social* relationship between the content creator (e.g., the author of a shared article) and the user, as well as the *topical* relationship between the content shared, saved or liked and the user's topics of interest. The rest of the paper is organized as follows: first, I define the concepts of social and topical distance. Then, I provide an empirical demonstration of the model by analyzing a set of publications from the *Journal of the Association for Information Science and Technology* (JASIST) that were shared on Twitter by researchers. Finally, I discuss the further research that needs to be done to improve, validate and expand the model.

Defining social and topical distance

The key idea of the proposed model is to put in relation the object of a social media act (the content) and the user who performs the act. This relation can be social (there is a social link between the creator of the content and the user performing the act) or topical (the content is related to the user's specific topics of interest).

I define social distance as the distance in a given *social* network between the creator of the shared content and the user performing an act (e.g., viewing, saving, reading, sharing, liking) of which that content is the object. The idea is that we might interpret differently a social media act if the content creator and the user who acts know each other than if they do not. For example, if I tweet a paper that was published by a friend, a family member, or a colleague, this act may not carry the same meaning than another of my tweet in which I share the work of someone I have never met or heard of.

I define topical distance as the cognitive distance between the content acted upon and the typical topics of interests of the user who performs the act. For example, the topical distance will be greater if I tweet or like a post about mathematics (since I am not a mathematician) than if I share a blog post about social media or any other topic related to information sciences.

The model is thus a two-dimensional space that could be visualized in a graph such as the one in Figure 1 and in which the user who is performing the act is situated at the bottom left. The content on which the act is performed is positioned on the graph according to its distance from the user in the social network (social distance) and in the cognitive distance between the content and the user's topic of interests (topical distance).

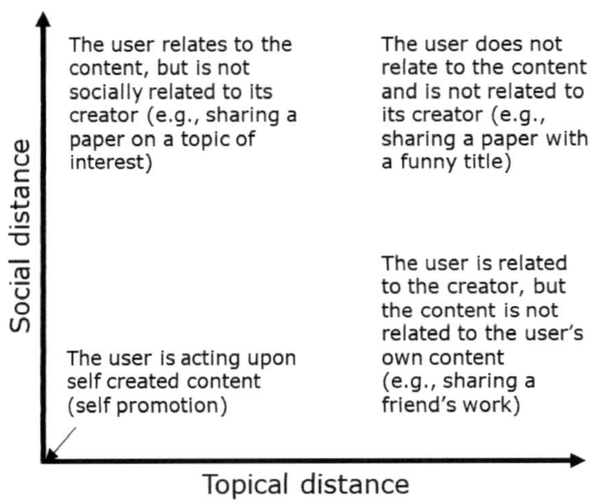

Figure 1. The model using social and topical distance for characterizing social media acts.

CASE STUDY: JASIST ARTICLES SHARED ON TWITTER BY RESEARCHERS

To empirically demonstrate how the model can be used for analyzing social media acts, I use it to analyze a set of papers published in JASIST that were tweeted by researchers. The aim is to illustrate what social and topical distance can tell us about:

- individual social media acts (in this case, tweeting about a publication)?
- the social media activity around a given content or group of contents (in this case, the tweeting activity of a scholarly publication)?
- the social media activity of a given user or group of users (in this case, researchers' content sharing activity on twitter)?

I chose this specific type of users and acts for the case study since, as I will show in the next sections of the paper, it makes the operationalization of the social and topical distance concepts relatively simple and straightforward. It is also a topic that has received much attention in altmetrics research, and the analysis thus has the potential benefit of directly addressing some of the issues that researchers in the field have been facing.

Data and Methods

I collected all tweets between 2012 and 2016 containing a link (with a DOI) using the altmetrics.com API. I then identified the tweets that linked to a publication in JASIST using a relational database version of Clarivate Analytics' Web of Science (WoS), limited to the Science Citation Index Expanded (SCI-Expanded), the Social Science Citation Index (SSCI) and the Arts & Humanities Citation Index (A&HCI), and hosted by the Centre for Science and Technology Studies (CWTS). In the CWTS database, the authors are already disambiguated using an algorithm developed by Caron and van Eck and van Eck (2014), which facilitates the identification of individual researchers as well as their publications.

I used the method developed by Costas, van Honk and Franssen (2017) to identify all the Twitter accounts that belong to a researcher with at least one publication indexed in WoS. The algorithm uses information on the authors extracted from bibliographic records of their publications (e.g., name, email address, organization, city, country) and compares with information on the Twitter account obtained through the Twitter API (e.g., description, name, email address). I was thus able to identify a total of 990 tweets made by 512 distinct researchers that linked to 365 distinct JASIST publications by 757 distinct authors. Finally, a retrieved all articles published between 1980 and 2016 by users. As I explain in more details in the next section, these publications are used to determine the research topics of the users.

To summarize, these data collection steps provided me with a list of researchers (hereafter referred to as the "users"), their WoS publications, the publications they have tweeted and the authors of these tweeted publications (hereafter referred to as the "content creators").

Operationalizing and measuring topical distance

In this analysis, I operationalize topical distance as the minimum cosine distance between research topics (i.e. WoS publications) of the user and the tweeted publication. I calculate the topical distance in two ways. First, I calculate the cosine distance between the reference list of each of the user's publication and the tweeted publication. I also calculate the cosine distance between noun phrases extracted from the title and abstract of each of the user's publication and the tweeted publication. The topical distance between the user and the content is the minimum value of those two cosine distances. The topical distance thus takes a value between 0 and 1. A value of 0 indicates that the tweeted publication is identical to one of the user's own publications, either in terms of references or in terms of noun phrases used in the title and abstract. Inversely, a topical distance of 1 indicates that none of the references and noun phrases are shared in the tweeted publications can be found in any the user's own papers.

Operationalizing and measuring social distance

For the present exercise, I use the following operational definition of the social distance: social distance is the shortest path between the user and any creator of the content acted upon in the global scientific collaboration network: the same process that is used to calculate the well-known Erdös number of mathematicians (Goffman, 1969). If the user is the same individual as the content creator, the social distance is 0. Otherwise, the social distance for given author creator pair is calculated following a five-step process:

5. I create the collaboration network of the *user* (network A). The social distance is 1 if the creator is found in network A.
6. I create the collaboration networks of all the researchers in network A (network B). The social distance is 2 if the creator is found in network B.
7. I create the ego networks of all the *creators* (network C). The social distance is 3 if a researcher in network B is found in network C.
8. I create the collaboration networks of all the researchers in network C (network D). The social distance is 4 if a researcher in network C appears in network D.
9. The social distance is 5 if no overlap between the user and creator extended collaboration networks was found in the previous four steps.

The social distance between a user and a creator ranges from 0 to 5, where 0 indicates that the user is also the creator and 5 indicates that the shortest path between the user and the creator in the global collaboration network is longer than 4. I stopped the process there because it is computationally intensive as the number of nodes in the network tends to increase exponentially at each expansion of the networks. It is also sufficient for the needs of this proof of concept. Like the topical distance, the social distance between a user and the *content* is the minimum value of the social distances between the user and any of the *creators* of that content.

These operational definitions of the concepts of topical and social distance are of course not the only ones possible, and perhaps also not the very best ones, but they are well suited for the present case study, in which the publication data provides useful information on the users and the content creator social and topical universes. It may not be suited for analyzing other types of social media acts or other types of users, but a generalizable and universal operationalization of the concepts of social and topical distance is beyond the scope of this paper, which is limited to the demonstration of the proposed model's usefulness for analyzing social media acts.

Results

Figure 1 shows the social and topical distance of the 990 tweets linking to a JASIST paper. We can see that social distance and topical distance are correlated, which is not surprising because we are looking at a research network in which researchers are expected to be connected to others that share the same research interest. What else can the model tell us about tweets? First, it tells us that 117 of the tweets were made by researchers sharing their own papers (these 117 data points overlap at the bottom left of the graph). At the opposite end of the graph, there are 79 tweets for which none of the users' publications overlapped with the tweeted publication in terms of noun phrases in the title and abstract or in terms of references. In this group, we find acts such as biochemists tweeting articles on citation analysis. These two examples alone exemplify how useful the model can be in distinguishing two acts that are in appearance identical (Two users tweeted a publication) but have potentially entirely different meanings.

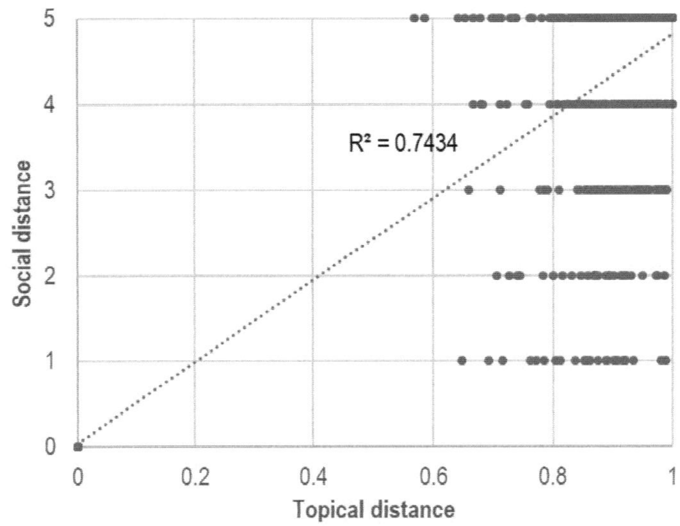

Figure 2. Social and topical distance of the 990 tweets linking to a JASIST publication.

Perhaps even more interesting are the outliers: those data points that are the furthest away from the linear trend line. For example, the tweet with the smallest topical distance (not counting the "self-tweets") in figure 2 has a social distance of 5. It is a paper on factors affecting citation rates of research articles that was published by two Japanese information scientists. It was tweeted by a Spanish medical researcher who has co-authored a bibliometric analysis of the publications in a Spanish public health journal. At the opposite end of the spectrum, some users tweeted papers from direct collaborators (social distance of 1), but a very high topical distance, indicating that the tweeted paper is not much related to the work of the user who tweeted it. For example, the tweet at the lower right end of the graph linked to a paper entitled "Correlations Between User Voting Data, Budget, and Box Office for Films in the Internet Movie Database" that was published by a group of chemical and biological engineers. This is not a topic that we would expect to be of great interest for biochemists, yet the paper was tweeted by a fellow bioengineer that happens to have collaborated with at least one of the authors. While the model doesn't allow to draw definitive conclusions about the motivation behind a social media act such as tweeting a paper, it does suggest that some acts may be socially motivated (tweeting the work of someone you know) or topically motivated (tweeting work on your topics of interest).

Let us now consider what social and topical distance can tell us about the overall social media activity around a single publication. The 47 tweets linking to the same paper are displayed in figure 3. This example allows to quickly see the diversity of the tweets. For instance, one tweet was from one of the authors of the paper, and two by close collaborators. Most tweets were made, however, by users who are further away in the global scientific collaboration network some of those (the few outliers on top of the graph) seemingly sharing an interest for the research topic but possibly working in a different field.

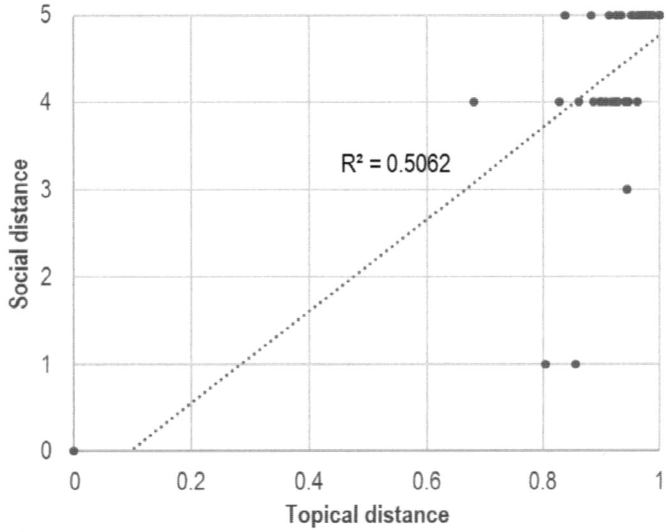

Figure 3. Social and topical distance of all the tweets linking to a single publication.

In figure 4, the data are aggregated at the tweeted paper level. The graph shows that the proposed model can potentially be used to compare, in a single graph, the social media attention that publications have received. For instance, 37 papers have only been tweeted by their authors, and apparently did not get tweeted or retweeted by other scientists. Some papers in the lower part of figure 4 were mostly tweeted by the authors and their collaborators. We also see that many papers have mostly been tweeted by users that are socially and topically distant from their author(s). The upper right corner of the graph is where we would expect to find those papers that are of a general interest to researchers, or that are part of some controversy (e.g., a funny mistake, a joke or a case of scientific fraud).

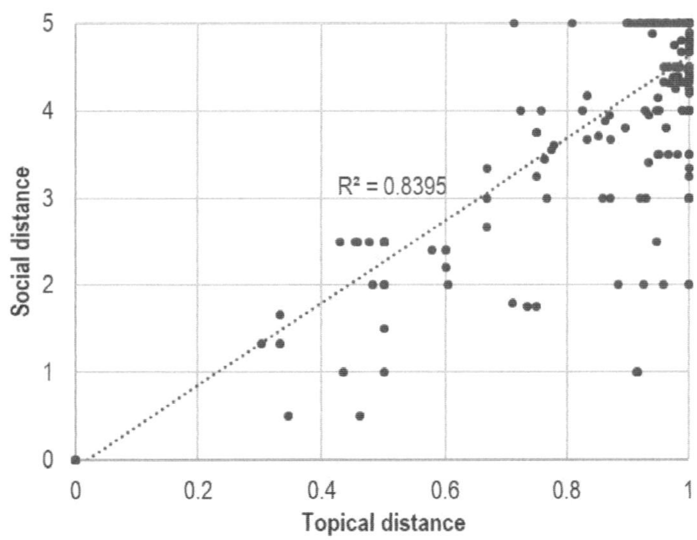

Figure 4. Average social and topical distance of the 365 tweeted JASIST publications.

The data are aggregated at the user level in figure 5 which allows us to compare the social media habits of different users. For instance, we see that some of the 39 researchers included in figure 5 tend to tweet mostly their own work or the work of their colleagues, while some others tend to tweet articles that are not particularly close to their own research topics nor authored by individuals who are close to them in the collaboration network. This highlights the potential usefulness of the model for the development of typologies of social media users.

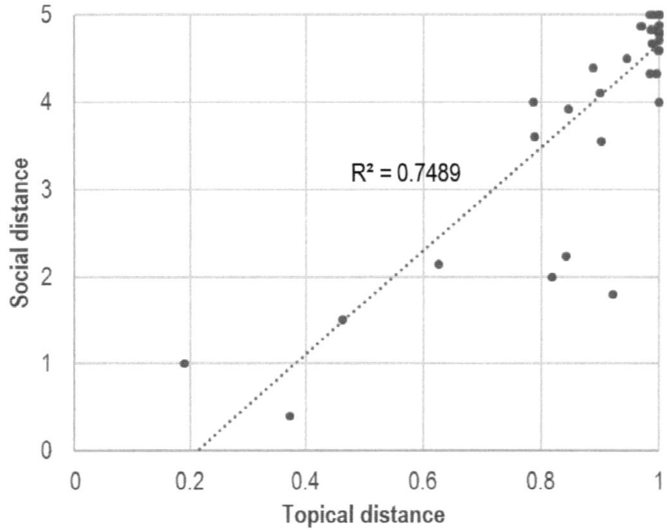

Figure 5. Average social and topical distance of tweets for the 39 users who tweeted more than 5 publications.

DISCUSSION AND CONCLUSION

I have presented in this paper a new model that combines the concepts of social and topical distance to relate the content that is the object of a social media acts to the social and informational universe of the user who performs the act. To demonstrate the potential of the model for enriching the analysis of social media activity, I presented an analysis of tweets linking to JASIST publications and made by Twitter users who are also researchers (i.e., individuals with at least one publication in WoS). With this analysis, I have shown that the model allows to meaningfully differentiate between different types of heterogeneous social media acts. I have also shown that the model can be used to characterize the attention a specific content has received on social media and to distinguish different types of social media uses and users.

That said, the proposed model is still in an early development stage and much research is needed to develop it further. For instance, further research needs to look at other (and perhaps better) ways of operationalizing the concepts and to test and compare their validity. Such new operationalizations will be necessary to fully take advantage of the model, especially for the analysis of social media users and acts that for which data on their social network and topics of interests are more difficult to grasps than in the case of researchers sharing scholarly publications. Further research could also seek to incorporate other concepts or dimensions in the model, or inversely, incorporate the model into previously developed analytical frameworks. As I mentioned above, the model could also be used to develop new typologies of uses and users or help improve existing typologies.

By demonstrating how social and topical distance can be operationalized and provide meaningful results when analyzing acts involving users who are scholars and content that are scholarly publications, I wished to provide the altmetrics research community with a new tool that could enrich the analysis of social media use in Academia. I That said the model could certainly be applied beyond that scope to analyze different types of users, contents and contexts, as Social media users have unique social and informational context, and the meaning of a specific act is can only be fully grasped if it is analyzed in relation to these specific contexts.

REFERENCES

Bowman, T. D. (2015). Differences in personal and professional tweets of scholars. *Aslib Journal of Information Management*, *67*(3), 356-371. https://doi.org/10.1108/AJIM-12-2014-0180

Cabanac, G. (2011). Accuracy of inter-researcher similarity measures based on topical and social clues. *Scientometrics, 87*(3), 597-620. https://doi.org/10.1007/s11192-011-0358-1

Caron, E., & van Eck, N. J. (2014). Large scale author name disambiguation using rule-based scoring and clustering. Dans E. Noyons (Éd.), *Proceedings of the 19th International Conference on Science and Technology Indicators* (p. 79-86). CWTS-Leiden University.

Costas, R., van Honk, J., & Franssen, T. (2017). Scholars on Twitter: who and how many are they? *arXiv:1712.05667 [cs]*. Consulté à l'adresse http://arxiv.org/abs/1712.05667

Goffman, C. (1969). And What Is Your Erdos Number? *The American Mathematical Monthly*, *76*(7), 791. https://doi.org/10.2307/2317868

Haustein, S., Peters, I., Sugimoto, C. R., Thelwall, M., & Larivière, V. (2014). Tweeting biomedicine: An analysis of tweets and citations in the biomedical literature: Tweeting Biomedicine: An Analysis of Tweets and Citations in the Biomedical Literature. *Journal of the Association for Information Science and Technology*, *65*(4), 656-669. https://doi.org/10.1002/asi.23101

Holmberg, K., & Thelwall, M. (2014). Disciplinary differences in Twitter scholarly communication. *Scientometrics*, *101*(2), 1027-1042. https://doi.org/10.1007/s11192-014-1229-3

Priem, J., Taraborelli, D., Groth, P., & Neylon, C. (2010). Altmetrics: A manifesto.

Swab, M., & Romme, K. (2016). Scholarly Sharing via Twitter: #icanhazpdf Requests for Health Sciences Literature. *Journal of the Canadian Health Libraries Association*, *37*(1), 6-11. https://doi.org/10.5596/c16-009

Thelwall, M., Buckley, K., & Paltoglou, G. (2011). Sentiment in Twitter Events. *Journal of the American Society for Information Science and Technology*, *62*(2), 406-418. https://doi.org/10.1002/asi.21462

Thelwall, M., Buckley, K., & Paltoglou, G. (2012). Sentiment Strength Detection for the Social Web. *Journal of the American Society for Information Science and Technology*, *63*(1), 163-173. https://doi.org/10.1002/asi.21662

Thelwall, M., Tsou, A., Weingart, S., Holmberg, K., & Haustein, S. (2013). Tweeting links to academic articles.

Tufekci, Z. (2014). Big Questions for Social Media Big Data: Representativeness, Validity and Other Methodological Pitfalls. *Proceedings of the 8th International AAAI Conference on Weblogs and Social Media, 14*, 505–514.

Tsou, A., Bowman, T. D., Ghazinejad, A., & Sugimoto, C. R. (2015). Who tweets about science? Dans *Proceedings of the 15th International Society of Scientometrics and Informetrics Conference* (p. 95-100). Istanbul, Turkey. Consulté à l'adresse http://www.issi2015.org/files/downloads/all-papers/0095.pdf

Vainio, J., & Holmberg, K. (2017). Highly tweeted science articles: who tweets them? An analysis of Twitter user profile descriptions. *Scientometrics*, *112*(1), 345-366. https://doi.org/10.1007/s11192-017-2368-0

Van Noorden, R. (2014). Online collaboration: Scientists and the social network. *Nature*, *512*(7513), 126-129. https://doi.org/10.1038/512126a

Investigating Practices for Building an Ethical and Sustainable Scholarly Identity with Online Platforms and Social Networking Sites

Marie L. Radford
Rutgers University, USA, mradford@rutgers.edu

Diana Floegel
Rutgers University, USA, diana.floegel@rutgers.edu

Vanessa Kitzie
University of South Carolina, USA, kitzie@mailbox.sc.edu

Gary P. Radford
Fairleigh Dickinson University, USA, gradford@fdu.edu

Stephanie Mikitish
Rutgers University, USA, mikitish@libraries.rutgers.edu

Lynn Silipigni Connaway
OCLC, USA, connawal@oclc.org

ABSTRACT

Informed by 30 semi-structured interviews with faculty, Ph.D. students, and academic librarians, this exploratory research examines how individuals create, cultivate, and manage their scholarly identity (SI) using online platforms. SI is defined as efforts by academics in promoting their personal "brand," regarding their intellectual work (Brigham, 2016). Results indicate that online platforms, including social networking sites (SNS), offer avenues for academics to connect with other scholars and disseminate their research. However, some sites were found to promote practices participants considered problematic, which forms the focus of this paper. Respondents noted that SI work performed on academic SNS (e.g., ResearchGate, Academia.edu) can present moral and ethical quandaries. For-profit business models pose a serious concern, and several interviewees advocated for open access materials and platforms (e.g., ORCID). Participants also reported a number of logistical problems with online SI work, including time constraints and context collapse (Marwick & boyd, 2011). Data were analyzed using a theoretical framework grounded in Goffman's (1959, 1967) concepts of impression management and face threats. Findings raise awareness of the need for academics and librarians to adopt strategies for creating/sustaining an ethical and sustainable online presence.

KEYWORDS

Social media, social networking sites, scholarly identity, qualitative methods, user studies

INTRODUCTION

Increasing and measuring one's productivity and reach represents a growing concern for scholars, who must navigate emerging, data-driven methods for communicating their influence. Academics are often asked to report on their impact (e.g., productivity and citation counts) by administrators, colleagues, external peer reviewers, and others when considered for hire, tenure, promotion, and grant funding. Further, scholarly work is being created and disseminated digitally, with a growing panoply of platforms and metrics that render this work and its impact visible. These factors necessitate that researchers craft and solidify their scholarly identity (SI), which Brigham (2016) defines as endeavors that allow scholars to build their reputations by promoting their personal "brand," including their research profile and intellectual work. Online platforms and other social networking sites (SNS) offer several features that can potentially advance SI practices. These include the ability to quantify and track scholarly impact (Thelwall & Kousha, 2015), disseminate one's work, communicate with a broad audience of other scholars (Brigham, 2016), and identify emerging areas of scholarship.

This paper reports the results of an exploratory study concerned with how researchers use online tools and platforms, such as academic and other SNS, to create, cultivate, and manage SI. Prior literature has demonstrated the use of both academic and popular SNS (e.g., ResearchGate, Academia.edu, Twitter) among researchers to engage in SI work, as discussed below. Research findings can help scholars understand and safeguard against the possible negative consequences of SNS for their SI work (Thelwall & Kousha, 2015). Although a range of these consequences has been identified in the popular media and think pieces (e.g., Hall, 2015; Howard, 2016), a significant research gap remains in empirically assessing researchers' attitudes toward their SI practices and these potential problems. In response to this gap, this research explores perceptions regarding how the use of SNS may pose practical, moral, and ethical dilemmas for faculty, Ph.D. students, and academic librarians.

LITERATURE REVIEW

Online platforms and metrics such as ORCID IDs (Akers et al., 2016) and other specialized academic SNS (Ovadia, 2014) facilitate the creation and development of SIs. Researchers have connected achievements, such as tenure and promotion, to altmetrics gathered from forums like ResearchGate (Megwalu, 2015) and Academia.edu (Duffy & Pooley, 2017; Ortega,

2015a; Thelwall & Kousha, 2014). Additionally, some scholarship has linked academic library services to SI-related assistance for researchers working within university settings (Ward et al., 2015; Reed et al., 2016).

These SNS and digital platforms offer many features and outcomes, including author disambiguation (Akers et al., 2016), information exchange (Jeng et al., 2017), and metrics that indicate impact and citation counts. Despite these advantages, some researchers are skeptical of SNS. They may consider participation to be irrelevant to their work, or they may be situated in workplace cultures that do not promote SI-related practices (Greifeneder et al., 2017). Some scholars report that maintaining online profiles could harm their careers, if others perceive them negatively. Additionally, research has uncovered evidence that metrics generated by SI platforms may be problematic, particularly regarding their ability to accurately measure citation impact (Ortega, 2015b).

While scholars express reservations toward SI maintenance, studies indicate that academic SNS are a part of scholarly life, though specific practices differ between disciplines (Kjelberg et al., 2016). Ortega (2015a), for example, found that humanists and social scientists used Academia.edu to actively contact other scholars within their disciplines, while biologists chose ResearchGate for their SI pursuits, although their use was passive in nature. Nández and Borrego (2013) found that academics engage in a range of activities, including contacting or following other scholars and disseminating their research. SI-related activities were also found to heighten competition within academic contexts, given their tendency to quantify selves and commodify publications (Hammarfelt et al., 2016).

A number of authors have also identified a "dark side" to SI activity, especially on academic SNS. For example, users of these tools can be unaware that sites like Academia.edu do not exist for altruistic reasons. Despite the early adoption of a .edu domain name, before designation was reserved for educational organizations only, Academia.edu is a commercial site. It uses a business model that seeks to exploit the data provided by the scholars who populate it for the financial gain of professional entrepreneurs and venture capitalists (Bond, 2017; Fitzpatrick, 2015; Ruff, 2016; Wexler, 2015). Referring to Academia.edu, Hall (2015) notes, "academics are laboring for it for free to help build its privately-owned for-profit platform by providing the aggregated input, data, and attention value. We can thus see that posting on Academia.edu is not ethically and politically equivalent to making research available using an internationally open access repository at all" (n. p.).

Research within Library and Information Science (LIS) also has linked academic library services to SI-related assistance (Ward et al., 2015; Reed et al., 2016). Because many scholars still may lack strategies for crafting or maintaining online SIs, libraries have begun to provide services to support, orient, and educate users (Reed et al., 2016). Like other faculty members and doctoral students, librarians also use various digital tools to promote their research and work (Brigham, 2016). Academic libraries are particularly well-positioned to provide SI assistance, given that librarians' potential to become versed in SI-related topics, including copyright issues, may foster the development of vital services for users and their institutions (Reed et al., 2016).

THEORETICAL FRAMEWORK

Goffman's (1959) theories of impression management and dramaturgy describe how individuals present and promote themselves in everyday interpersonal encounters. According to Goffman (1967), in human encounters, people aim to maintain "face" and avoid "face threats" by shaping their behaviors to protect others and themselves, within any given situation. Goffman's work informs this analysis of how scholars present themselves online. In LIS, Goffman's impression management frame has been applied to analysis of live-chat reference encounters (e.g., Radford & Radford, 2017; Radford, Radford, Connaway, & DeAngelis, 2011). Though no literature was found that applied Goffman's ideas to SI work, researchers have demonstrated impression management's applicability to online presences, especially those related to self-disclosure on social networking sites (Bareket-Bojmel et al., 2016; Bazarova & Choi, 2014; Buffardi & Campbell, 2008). Self-presentation online has also been related to hiring practices, since individuals can choose to present themselves in positive or negative ways that affect their professional image (Batenburg & Bartles, 2017; Chiang & Suen, 2015).

Since the purpose of SI is to create, cultivate, and manage a desired identity expression that *impresses* upon others, the research team saw a connection between Goffman's approach and SI. As a result, the team identified the key theoretical concepts of impression management centered on reasons for self-presentation, perceptions of others, and face threats (Goffman, 1959, 1967) and applied these concepts as high-level deductive codes to the data. Since the research was qualitative and exploratory, additional codes inductively emerged from the data, informed by participant accounts.

RESEARCH QUESTION AND METHODS

Based on the above literature, a series of Research Questions (RQs) were formulated regarding scholars' needs, use, and creation of effective practices to manage SI. For this paper, the focus is on an investigation of this RQ: What drawbacks/barriers exist to creating and managing SI? To address this question, the research team conducted 30 semi-structured phone interviews with 10 faculty members, 10 Ph.D. students, and 10 academic librarians recruited via the Association of College and Research Libraries (ACRL) and Communication, Research, and Theory Network (CRTNET) listservs. ACRL is a professional organization for academic librarians, while CRTNET is a listserv for communication scholars and other social scientists. As the target audiences for academic SNS such as ResearchGate, faculty members and doctoral students were a logical choice for interviews. Additionally, academic librarians were chosen because prior research suggested that library users desire increased assistance with SI work from librarians (Mikitish, 2017), and because they also engage in scholarly pursuits. The research team selected participants based on a prescreening questionnaire, which collected information regarding experiences with digital SI tools. Selection criteria required participants to use at least three digital tools such as ResearchGate, ORCID, and Twitter. Among those who qualified, 10 from each group were selected that varied in years of experience and demographic characteristics.

The interview instrument was informed by the theoretical framework, as well as themes derived from prior work, including: a) assessing impact (Kjellberg et al., 2016), and b) motivations for, and benefits of, use (Kjellberg et al., 2016; Nández & Borrego, 2012). The RQ also informed the instrument, particularly in developing questions about the drawbacks of SI use. The instrument consisted of 15 questions, although some were conditional. Interviews lasted approximately one hour, and the team compensated participants with a $30 gift card. Each of approximately 104 initial respondents was assigned a random number identifier upon completing the prescreening questionnaire to maintain confidentiality. Since this research is exploratory, a sample size of 30 was predetermined, based on available resources and the desire to balance the number of participants from all three groups.

Interviews were conducted by a team of four researchers who took detailed notes on participant responses, including the capture of verbatim quotes. Transcripts of these detailed notes were qualitatively coded using the constant comparisons method (Charmaz, 2014) and emic/etic coding (Miles & Huberman, 1994), wherein the researchers applied higher level codes (etic) informed by the theoretical framework, and lower-level codes (emic), which were inductively developed from the data. The team coded the transcripts, using NVivo software, achieving a high inter-coder agreement (Zhang & Wildemuth, 2005). Based on patterns found within a sample of the data, coders developed an initial typology to classify common themes. The research team refined the typology as they applied it to the remaining transcripts, expanding as needed to capture emerging codes. A final ICR of 100% was calculated via NVivo, after any differences were resolved through discussion.

FINDINGS

Table 1 presents demographics of those interviewed, indicating that the 30 participants were predominantly female and white, and about half were 26-34 years of age. Faculty included assistant (n=3, 30%), associate (n=2, 20%), and full professors (n=2, 20%), as well as an assistant dean, a teaching fellow, and a special instructor. Ph.D. students were in coursework (n=4, 40%) and post-coursework (n=6, 60%). Almost all Ph.D. students and faculty participants were in the field of communication, which was a reflection of the recruitment and sampling strategy. Academic librarians were tenured or tenure-track (n=7, 70%) and non-tenure track (n=3, 30%). The majority did not have a subject specialization (n=6, 60%), while others specialized in scholarly communication, life sciences, and copyright. All participants were from institutions located in the United States and Canada.

Gender	N (%)	Race/Ethnicity	N (%)	Age	N (%)
Female	20 (67%)	Caucasian/White	19 (63%)	26-34	16 (53%)
Male	9 (30%)	African American/Black	3 (10%)	35-44	5 (17%)
Nonbinary	1 (3%)	Asian	3 (10%)	45-54	3 (10%)
		Hispanic	2 (7%)	55-64	3 (10%)
		White/Latinx	1 (3%)	65+	3 (10%)
		Unknown	2 (7%)		

Table 1. Participant demographics

Table 2 presents the most frequent SNS that the participants used. There were several additional platforms listed by fewer participants, including SnapChat, Tumblr, WhatsApp, Linkedin, Google Profile, YouTube, VIVO, OpenVIVO, Sympletic Elements, ISNI, Scopus, and WebID.

SNS/Platform	N (%)
Twitter	23 (77%)
Facebook	22 (73%)
ResearchGate	20 (66%)
Instagram	19 (63%)
Academia.edu	18 (60%)
ORCID	15 (50%)

Table 2. Participant's most frequently used SNS/Platforms

Themes Related to Drawbacks of SI Work

Below, themes related to the drawbacks of SI work are identified in order of prevalence in the data. Selected participant quotations illustrate each theme. As noted above, while this paper focuses on drawbacks to SI work, participants also discussed benefits that included the ability to share and exchange materials, connect with other researchers, and facilitate getting tenure/promotion.

Time Constraints

Participants most frequently cited time constraints as a major drawback to SI work (n=16, 53%). Thirty percent (n=3) of faculty gave responses that centered on time constraints. In addition to the time it takes to update one's profile, faculty participant P42 also noted that she had to spend time deleting unsolicited emails. In particular, some emails she received from ResearchGate reminded her of "eHarmony, where you're matched with someone, and you're like, 'How did this happen?'" (P42).

Thirty percent (n=3) of Ph.D. students also identified time lost to SI work, though they focused almost exclusively on profile maintenance rather than solicitations. P34, for example, did not have time to populate their profiles after creating them: "I haven't done anything to it since then. It's just too much. Facebook and Instagram, it's just too much to maintain" (P34).

All librarian participants (n=10, 100%) also noted time constraints as a major barrier to SI work. One said: "Keeping up is a full-time job sometimes" (P10). Additionally, a majority of the librarians (n=7, 70%) reported other related nuisances of SI work. Librarians said that constant reminders from platforms like ResearchGate and Academia.edu, the pressure to update profiles, and difficulty tracking passwords and usernames all contributed to unpleasant interactions with digital tools. For example, Participant 101 stated:

> Academia.edu sends me these emails fairly regularly about papers that mention my name... I'm like, you just want me to go on and pay you money or see ads that get you money. ResearchGate is similar, the emails are never necessarily relevant (P101).

Librarians who framed SI maintenance as a nuisance also focused on the difficulty of maintaining profiles on several platforms. One participant inquired, "Why would I need to maintain a few online presences? Wouldn't it be nice to have it all in one place?" (P102). Sixty percent (n=6) of librarians believed that a single digital tool would improve their experiences.

Concern with For-Profit Business Models

Fifty percent of all participants (n=15) claimed that a major drawback to SI work involves the support of for-profit platforms. Among faculty with these concerns, twenty percent (n=2) had ethical trepidations. Dislike for the concept of self "branding" was expressed by one faculty member (P57). Faculty also reported that they might be taken advantage of when using for-profit services. One faculty participant explained this feeling when discussing Academia.edu: "They charge, and I don't feel the need to pay somebody to disseminate my work...They give you just enough tease to get you interested, [and then] ask you to pay 10 bucks a month" (P84).

Forty percent (n=4) of Ph.D. students expressed similar concerns. Participant 71 cited mistrust in ResearchGate and Academia.edu based on their marketing:

> I find that both ResearchGate and Academia.edu tend to be a scam. Before I ever published anything, I received notifications that people cited my writing, which is ridiculous. I think those two sites in particular are flawed and so I don't know that there's much impact (P71).

In addition, many Ph.D. students discussed the importance of access to other research. Therefore, they were less likely to support sites with for-profit models that charged for access to such material, as well as other SI services, such as impact-based measures. Per Participant 23: "Academia.edu, some of the things they started doing about trying to charge for access to academic work, I fell out of using that as much."

All but one librarian (n=9, 90%) also mentioned their apprehension surrounding for-profit business models, particularly ResearchGate and Academia.edu. When discussing her overall feelings toward SI work, Participant 50 expressed some unease:

> I think part of it is that I feel some hesitation to engage with ResearchGate and Academia.edu based on their corporate ties and for-profit business models. I know Twitter and Facebook are the same, so it's not a consistent feeling, but I worry about the profit motivations of ResearchGate and Academia.edu (P50).

Context Collapse

Context collapse concerned about half (n=14, 47%) of participants. Context collapse occurs when an SNS "flattens multiple audiences into one" (Marwick & boyd, 2011, p. 122), thereby preventing users from knowing their audience and leaving them susceptible to face threats. To guard against face threats, users may imagine an audience of "nightmare readers" such as bosses, parents, and teachers (p. 125), and limit their personal discourse to topics deemed appropriate for all readers. In SI work, researchers can experience context collapse as an inability to figure out what to say about their presentations, publications, and service activities because of an unknown audience. Thirty percent of faculty (n=3) mentioned context collapse. One faculty participant, who was very careful not to mingle their personal and professional identities online, stated that before posting they always ask themselves, "Am I going to be perceived as posting this as an individual or a [school] representative?" (P32).

Another faculty participant noted that preventing context collapse was easier on some platforms than on others. For instance, one professor who connects to her students on Twitter and Facebook for class exercises said that sometimes information related to her personal life, such as Irish football scores, leaked into her Twitter feed, but her personal Facebook group prevents students from knowing "what goes on in that world" (P57).

Forty percent (n=4) of Ph.D. students addressed context collapse. For example, Participant 39 provided two separate examples of how context collapse could threaten her reputation among her dissertation advisor and those outside of academia who see her social media posts:

> I am not a heavy user of Facebook, but sometimes I travel and post what I'm doing and geotag it as well. We know that we can group our friends on Facebook but that's tiring because I'm not a heavy user on Facebook. Sometimes I forget to set my friends group. My professor knows that I'm working hard on my dissertation and job applications and my husband booked a hotel and we decided to have a weekend getaway to relieve some of my stress. I posted a check-in at the hotel, but then realized maybe it's not a good thing to post because my professor might not think that I'm working hard. I don't want to make it look like I'm not focusing hard on my job and dissertation. I should have grouped him but forgot. I am writing my dissertation on Prep [an HIV prevention pill] by use of women in low income areas, so I decided to follow Prep groups on FB, but am sometimes worried about that because it's related to HIV. Maybe someone who doesn't have an idea about my scholarly identity, they might think that I'm weird or stigmatize me, or think I have HIV (P39).

In these examples, the participant demonstrates how two contexts – her social context, comprised of family, friends, and acquaintances, and her academic context, are collapsed on SNS like Facebook. Facebook does not offer many features that render it easy or convenient to separate an individual's contexts, which likely reflects founder Mark Zuckerberg's notion that on Facebook: "You have one identity. The days of you having a different image for your work friends or co-workers and for the other people you know are probably coming to an end pretty quickly" (Zimmer, 2010). As a result, the participant does not spend the additional time and effort required to separate her contexts. If her advisor sees that she took a weekend off, or if a friend or acquaintance not familiar with her research were to see which Facebook groups she followed, it could cause damage to both her scholarly and professional reputations.

Context collapse could also reflect larger cultural differences between various social groups with whom an individual interacts. For instance, Participant 34 chooses not to use Facebook because of regional differences between individuals he knows from home versus the culture of academia. He stated:

> Where I'm from it's blue collar and not a lot of people go to college and very few get a Ph.D., so that's another reason I don't promote that fact on my Facebook page. I don't want to be perceived as someone who is good at college because they don't value knowledge in the same way so that's why I keep it close to the chest. And so that depends on what region you're from, you're going to be viewed a certain way (P34).

However, context collapse does not solely impinge upon SI efforts when using SNS. Participant 95 discussed how she decides what research projects to investigate and which to not investigate based on whether it would be approved by individuals from her home country, Nigeria:

> You talked about how scholarly identity interacts with your personal identity and your cultural identity, all of these things. Even for me right now there are things and topics in my field that I never would want to study because they challenge my cultural assumptions and beliefs, like issues around gender equality and things. There are cultural reasons why I didn't want to go into that. That's why I want to create interest areas that don't challenge my cultural values and that goes into my personal beliefs and religious beliefs that could be of potential impact to the research community, but I know that if I go into these areas, if I write an article about gender equality in Nigeria that would go to my kinsmen and family members and they would say, "Oh so our culture is inferior?" (P95).

Here, Participant 95 does not specify how her research might be made visible to those from her home country, but even the potential of this visibility (whether offline or online) and its subsequent threat of context collapse is enough to shape her research agenda.

Seventy percent (n=7) of librarians discussed context collapse as a drawback of online SI activities. Citing difficulty differentiating various social media identities, Participant 11 said:

> I think the two can overlap quite a bit in today's age, people are on Twitter and have personal viewpoints which may overlap with professional identities. My professional identity is more related to my scholarly identity because I tend to publish in my area of expertise, which is the same as my professional expertise. So to me, they kind of overlap quite a bit (P11).

Though Participant 11 seemed to partly embrace overlap among her online identities, other librarians framed context collapse as problematic, particularly regarding its potential to offend certain audiences. Aligned with Marwick and boyd's (2011) claim that social media users often share the lowest common denominator of information to avoid controversy, one librarian explained, "Sometimes I try to put out something that is more about my opinions, those things don't get re-tweeted or liked, so this is a sign to me that I should keep it to myself" (P69).

Confusion

Forty-seven percent (n=14) of participants expressed confusion over how to use SI tools. Only one faculty member expressed this theme, stating that he is "suspicious of why the help button is needed" (P76) on certain platforms. Thirty percent (n=3) of Ph.D. students also described misunderstanding the technical features of SI tools. Participant 23 explained, "I don't know how ResearchGate or the others work as well. I have no clarity about how that works."

However, the faculty members and Ph.D. students interviewed all used digital tools for SI-related purposes. Librarians, who interact with users who may have little to no experience with SNS and other platforms, had a different take on confusion. Librarian participants were unanimous in stating that the number, variety, and features of the SNS platforms are confusing to them and to library users. Prominent sources of concern included metrics, which tools to use, and how to use certain technologies. For example, one librarian said:

> The landscape is now so crowded that it's difficult to choose, select, and create a consistent and comprehensive identity. They're all over the place, those identifiers. There are many different data and silos, and it's difficult to combine them in one place and draw some conclusion (P102).

Concern over Damage to Reputation

Participants (n=13, 43%) worried that online SI work could negatively impact their professional reputations or the professional reputation of their colleagues. Sixty percent (n=6) of faculty members said they were worried that their professional or personal reputation might be negatively impacted by use of SNS, especially among pre-tenue colleagues. According to Participant 20:

> Pre-tenure colleagues don't want to go on social media, they say every single sentence they write...can be perceived in the wrong light. It's not worth the risk. It's like the fear is stopping them, but my concern is that if they're in the habit of not doing it, will they convert? I don't think they'll start posting (P20).

Ph.D. students discussed such concerns more explicitly. Forty percent (n=4) of the Ph.D. participants identified concern over damage to their reputations as a significant theme. They also expressed reservations regarding how many of these platforms might exacerbate what they perceived as a competitive environment inherent to academia. Specifically, they were worried that their scholarly activities and opinions could be subject to critique due to SNS and digital tool features like persistence and visibility of content. Participant 23 illustrates this concern:

> Sometimes you are perceived as a scholar when engaging on social media as "dumbing down the conversation" and you're not serious and you're oversimplifying things. I feel like you can be criticized by some people for saying the wrong thing or not thinking through your tweet. You didn't represent the research as accurately as you should have. Academia has a critique and criticism culture so engaging in information conversations that aren't verbal, face-to-face, this is out there and can be subject to further examination by parties who wanted to critique you for some reason (P23).

Participant 23 perceived damage to reputation to constitute such a threat that they chose not to use SNS for academic purposes: "Better to be one of these people to be like, 'I'm not really on social media and that's not my thing,' than being on social media and failing at it" (P23).

Thirty percent (n=3) of librarians also discussed concern over damage to their scholarly reputation as a drawback of SI work. One remarked that SI may not only include positive attributes, stating: "I think a scholarly identity is not necessarily just positive things about you. It can include negative things, like dominating conversations on a mailing list, whether you intend it to be or not" (P101).

Privacy Concerns

Privacy concerns represent a final theme raised by 20% (n=6) of participants, especially faculty. Fifty percent (n=5) of the faculty members were troubled by privacy, surveillance, and tracking concerns. As one participant explained, "that idea of students finding my site and trying to friend me and learning personal information about me" is unsettling (P57). Moreover, making participation on SNS "compulsory is an ethical issue because the tools track their posts" (P57). On the other hand, another participant noted that while initially "people saw following others as quite negative like stalking" what was once "creepy is now due diligence" (P20).

No Ph.D. students explicitly discussed privacy. One librarian (10%) mimicked faculties' concerns, stating, "I have concerns about… the amount of data you put into their platforms" (P69).

DISCUSSION AND RECOMMENDATIONS

Looking across the three perspectives of participant groups, there were some commonalities. On the theoretical side, most participants expressed some level of impression management when discussing their SI-related practices and aims. Clarifying their identities, forming relationships with others, and engaging in positive professional practices were all impression management strategies identified by participants. Related to identity management is the concept of context collapse (Marwick & boyd,

2011), which emerged as a theme for all three groups. Marwick and boyd (2011) further explicate this concept in their discussion of imagined audiences:

> Every participant in a communicative act has an *imagined audience*. Audiences are not discrete; when we talk, we think we are speaking only to the people in front of us or on the other end of the telephone, but this is in many ways a fantasy… Technology complicates our metaphors of space and place, including the belief that audiences are separate from each other. We may understand that the Twitter or Facebook audience is potentially limitless, but we often act as if it were bounded…While anyone can potentially read or view a digital artifact, we need a more specific conception of audience than 'anyone' to choose the language, cultural referents, style, and so on that comprise online identity presentation. In the absence of certain knowledge about audience, participants take cues from the social media environment to imagine the community (boyd, 2007, p. 131) (Marwick & boyd, 2011, p. 115).

Thus, the imagined audience might be entirely different from the actual readers of a profile, blog post, or tweet. Participants made frequent references to being aware of who might see their posts and being wary of who might judge them, either immediately or over the course of time. The notions of context collapse and impression management seemed to play a major role in their decision-making processes regarding use (or non-use) of SNS. Face threats that are not present in face-to-face encounters were discussed by participants who spoke of their postings related to research being taken out of context, misinterpreted, characterized as silly, or resulting in difficult familial or professional misunderstandings. Participants suggested that the feedback process that is present in interpersonal encounters through discussion is usually missing or severely truncated in online forums.

Findings also suggest that librarians, Ph.D. students, and faculty use a variety of tools to serve different purposes. A participants' role, context, and specific aims influenced tool selection. Consistently, Twitter and Facebook were most commonly used by seventy-five percent (n=45) of participants, while more faculty than librarians and Ph.D. students used ResearchGate and Academia.edu in their SI work. Attitudes toward SI presence and maintenance varied, but few participants felt unequivocally positive and most expressed skepticism toward SI practices and suspicion regarding some platforms' motivations. All three groups relayed drawbacks related to confusion, time-constraints, and concern with for-profit use. Members of all groups commented on the considerable time commitment needed for effective SI work, on their confusion about how best to leverage limited time, and on the need to make decisions that have positive outcomes.

Beyond drawbacks that stem from logistics of SI participation, SI labor and platforms may have a "dark side" that forces participants to face moral and ethical quandaries. For-profit business models and their ability to keep scholarly work within the "ivory tower" of academia presented a serious concern for participants, many of whom advocated for open access materials. Whereas social media may be conceptualized as a means for academics to share their resources with a broader audience, platforms such as ResearchGate and Academia.edu engage in practices that some users find problematic, or at least questionable. Copyright laws can also come into play when users upload their publications without confirming their ownership rights, or often without realizing that there is a legal requirement to do so. Among the three groups, faculty demonstrated the least amount of concern with the "business" aspects of SI.

Some participants also expressed concern with the overall concept of "branding" through SI practices. Faculty Participant 57 called branding "antithetical" to their core values, and repeatedly expressed hatred for the word "brand." One librarian asserted, "Calling it a personal brand upsets me a little. It's treating people as though they were businesses or corporations and not people. I understand using that terminology, but it doesn't make me happy" (P101).

A small number of participants (n=2, 20%) also discussed SI issues that relate to broader notions of privilege and power within academia. The relatively small and predominantly white sample may have affected the limited discussion of this topic despite its salience. One librarian raised gender issues:

> I guess one of the things that I've noticed recently was, for example, at a conference that I'm engaged with, almost all the invited keynotes were men. I was getting frustrated because my area has a lot of women, but men tend to get more public-facing presentations. That bothered me on a gender front. There are issues with minorities as well, in terms of the impact of getting keynote lectures and getting an invitation. It can be about who you know. R1 institutions have more money and more travel. People see each other again and again, and naturally think to invite each other to other things. If you don't have funding and power to get away, you're not going to get to the conference and get the invite. So, it's kind of a cycle that feeds on itself that comes from prestige and funding and networking, which all feeds into your scholarly identity (P11).

These additional insights demonstrate that there may exist a deeper dark side of SI practices and expectations that warrants investigation that extends beyond the scope of this exploratory research. The emergent themes presented in this paper suggest that SI practices are a ripe area for further scholarship and that the concepts of impression management and face threats (Goffman, 1959; 1967) provide a viable framework for understanding the complexities of the use of digital tools for SI-related purposes.

Despite the drawbacks participants note, faculty, doctoral students, and librarians reported that they continue to use these SNS platforms with positive results. One librarian offered practical strategies for circumventing barriers and maintaining a sustainable SI presence:

> Find all of your numbers like ORCID, Web of Science, and Thompson, choose an email address on all profiles, a picture on all profiles. Email is something you should check regularly. Have a list of ways your name has appeared in author statements on any publications and a list of all your publications in a citation system like Mendeley or the like. Have a folder with a PDF of every publication, whether publicly available or not. Create a checklist of the order in which you update your profiles whenever you publish something new (P73).

While these suggestions do not necessarily address ethical quandaries including for-profit business models, they may help to assuage difficulties such as confusion and time constraints.

It is to be noted that there are some voices in the literature that assert that there is no middle ground when ethical issues are involved. Some unequivocally advocate total withdrawal from the for-profit sites. For example, Bond (2017, n. p.) states: "It is time to delete your Academia.edu account." None of the participants interviewed for this study expressed that definitive a statement. However, some said that they have chosen not to use for-profit sites, opting instead to use non-profit services such as ORCID. Others advocated the use of institutional repositories or other open access venues for sharing of scholarly work. At this stage of exploration for the preliminary research reported in this paper, no definitive recommendations can be made as of yet, although there are certainly a number of important issues raised in these interview results for critical reflection and further study.

CONCLUSION

This is among the first research projects that has compared the perspectives of faculty, Ph.D. students, and librarians on the topic of SI with a focus on the potential drawbacks and barriers when using SNS. This research, although preliminary, makes a contribution by identifying a number of intriguing findings and unveiling provocative future directions. It is important to note that limitations of this research include the use of a single method (i.e., qualitative semi-structured interviews) with a small sample size of 30 participants, coupled with the recruitment strategy which resulted in lack of diversity in gender, race/ethnicity, geographic location and disciplinary focus. Because these participants were social scientists (mainly communication scholars and academic librarians) it would be beneficial to conduct additional interviews, focus groups, or larger-scale surveys with researchers from other fields and in other nations to discover potential disciplinary and cultural differences. Future investigations could also address the critical question of the impact of SI practices and corresponding metrics on perceptions of quality scholarship, especially for tenure and promotion decisions. Additional research is needed to identify a more comprehensive range of barriers and determine strategies to overcome them. Practical assistance is warranted in developing materials to assist in the ongoing discovery and use of digital tools. Finally, future directions include explorations of the possibility of enhanced roles, relationships, and services that academic librarians could provide, given their specialized knowledge of copyright, open access, and the burgeoning variety of metrics and altmetrics. The next phase of this work seeks to identify key practices and strategies to establish and maintain SI that are both sustainable and ethical (see also Radford, Connaway, Kitzie, Floegel, Radford, & Chayko, 2018).

The ubiquitous nature of social media and the increasing need for self-promotion for professional advancement creates a number of opportunities for academics in various roles to disseminate their research. However, while use of digital tools for SI practices may provide scholars with a vehicle for impression management, such tools should not be promoted without consideration of their potential complications. Elucidating the drawbacks of emerging technologies for SI work may help researchers make informed and ethical decisions when seeking to increase their impact and reputation online.

REFERENCES

Akers, K. G., Sarkozy, A., Wu, W., & Slyman, A. (2016). ORCID author identifiers: A primer for librarians. *Medical Reference Services Quarterly, 35*(2), 135-44.

Bareket-Bojmel, L., Moran, S., & Shahar, G. (2016). Strategic self-presentation on Facebook: Personal motives and audience response to online behavior. *Computers in Human Behavior, 55*, 788-795.

Batenburg, A., & Bartles, J. (2017). Keeping up online appearances: How self-disclosure on Facebook affects perceived respect and likeability in the professional context. *Computers in Human Behavior, 74*, 265-76.

Bazarova, N. N., & Choi, Y. H. (2014). Self-disclosure in social media: Extending the functional approach to disclosure motivations and characteristics on social network sites. *Journal of Communication, 64*(4), 635-657.

Bond, S. (2017, January 23). Dear scholars, delete your account at Academic.edu. *Forbes Magazine*. Retrieved from https://www.forbes.com/sites/drsarahbond/2017/01/23/dear-scholars-delete-your-account-at-academia-edu/#28b4a4f52d62

boyd, d. (2007). Why youth <3 social network sites: The role of networked publics in teenage social life. In D. Buckingham (Ed.), *Youth identity and digital media* (pp. 119-142). Cambridge, MA: MIT Press.

Brigham, T. J. (2016). Online professional profiles: Health care and library researchers show off their work. *Medical Reference Services Quarterly, 35*(4), 440-48.

Buffardi, L. E., & Campbell,W. K. (2008). Narcissism and social networking web sites. *Personality and Social Psychology Bulletin, 34*, 1303-1314.

Charmaz, K. (2014). *Constructing grounded theory* (2nd ed.). Los Angeles, CA: Sage.

Chiang, J. K. H., & Suen, H.Y. (2015). Self-presentation and hiring recommendations in online communities: Lessons from LinkedIn. *Computers in Human Behavior, 48*, 516-524.

Duffy, B. E. & Pooley, J. D. (2017). "Facebook for academics": The convergence of self-branding and social media logic on Academia.edu. *Social Media and Society*, 3(1), 1-11.

Fitzpatrick, K. (2015, October 26). Academia, not edu. Retrieved from http://www.plannedobsolescence.net/academic-not-edu

Goffman, E. (1959). *The presentation of self in everyday life*. New York, NY: Doubleday.

Goffman, E. (1967). *Interaction ritual: Essays in face-to-face behavior*. New Brunswick, NJ: Transaction Publishers.

Greifeneder, E., Points, S., Blanford, A., Attalla, H., Neal, D., & Schlebbe, K. (2017). Researchers' attitudes towards the use of social networking sites. *Journal of Documentation, 74*(1), 119-136.]

Hall, G. (2015, October 18). *Does Academia.edu mean open access is becoming irrelevant*? Retrieved from http://www.garyhall.info/journal/2015/10/18/does-academiaedu-mean-open-access-is-becoming-irrelevant.html

Hammarfelt, B., de Rijcke, S., & Rushforth, A. D. (2016). Quantified academic selves: The gamification of research through social networking services. *Information Research, 21*(2). Retrieved from http://www.informationr.net/ir/21-2/SM1.html#.Wo14XGaZPUo

Howard, J. (2013, December 6). Posting your latest article? You might have to take it down. *The Chronicle of Higher Education.* Retrieved from https://www.chronicle.com/blogs/wiredcampus/posting-your-latest-article-you-might-have-to-take-it-down/48865

Jeng, W., DesAutels, S., He, D., & Li, L. (2016). Information exchange on an academic social networking site: A multidiscipline comparison on ResearchGate Q&A. *Journal of the Association for Information Science and Technology, 68*(3), 638-652.

Kjelberg, S., Haider, J., & Sudin, O. (2016). Researchers' use of social network sites: A scoping review. *Library & Information Science Research, 38*, 224-234.

Marwick, A. E., & boyd, D. (2011). I tweet honestly, I tweet passionately: Twitter users, context collapse, and the imagined audience. *New Media and Society, 13*(1), 114-133.

Megwalu, A. (2015). ResearchGate: An academic social networking site. *The Charleston Advisor, 17*(1), 47-51.

Miles, M. B., & Huberman, A. M. *Quantitative data analysis: A sourcebook.* Beverley Hills: Sage Publications.

Mikitish, S. (2017). *Information engagement: How social science doctoral students seek, filter, access, and organize information* (Unpublished doctoral dissertation). Rutgers, The State University of New Jersey, New Brunswick, New Jersey.

Nández, G., & Borrego, À. (2012). Use of social networks for academic purposes: A case study. *The Electronic Library, 31*(6), 781-791.

Ortega, J. L. (2015a). Disciplinary differences in the use of academic social networking sites. *Online Information Review, 39*(4), 520-536.

Ortega, J. L. (2015b). Relationship between altmetrics and bibliometric indicators across academic sites: The case of CSIC's members. *Journal of Infometrics, 9*, 39-49.

Ovadia, S. (2014). ResearchGate and Academia.edu: Academic social networks. *Behavioral & Social Sciences Librarian, 33*(3), 165-69.

Radford, M. L., Connaway, L. S., Kitzie, V., Floegel, D., Radford, G. P., & Chayko, M. (2018). Creating and cultivating a scholarly identity within digital worlds. iConference, Sheffield, England, March 25-28, 2018.

Radford, M. L. & Radford G. P. (2017). *Library Conversations: Applying Interpersonal Communication Theory in Face-to-Face and Virtual Contexts*. Chicago: ALA Editions.

Radford, M. L., Radford, G. P., Connaway, L. S. & DeAngelis, J. A., (October, 2011). On virtual face-work: An ethnography of communication approach to a live chat reference interaction. *The Library Quarterly 81*(4), 431-453.

Reed, K., McFarland, D., & Croft, R. (2016). Laying the groundwork for a new library service: Scholar-practitioner & graduate student attitudes toward altmetrics and the curation of online profiles. *Evidence-Based Library and Information Practice, 11*(2), 87-96.

Ruff, C. (2016, January 29). Scholars criticize Academia.edu proposal to charge authors for recommendations. *The Chronicle of Higher Education.* Retrieved from https://www.chronicle.com/article/Scholars-Criticize/235102

Thewall, M. & Kousha, K. (2014). Academia.edu: Social network or academic network? *Journal of the Association for Information Science & Technology 65*(4), 721-731.

Thelwall, M. & Kousha, K. (2015). Web indicators for research evaluation. Part 2: Social media metrics. *El Professional de la Información, 24*(5), 607-620.

Ward, J., Bejarano, B. & Dudás, A. (2015). Scholarly social media profiles and libraries: A review. *Liber Quarterly: The Journal of the Association of European Research Libraries, 24*(4), 174-204.

Wexler, E. (2015, December 11). As Academic.edu grows, some scholars voice concerns. The Chronicle of Higher Education. Retrieved from https://www.chronicle.com/article/As-Academiaedu-Grows-Some/234414

Zhang, Y., & Wildemuth, B. M. (2005). Qualitative analysis of content. *Analysis 1*(2), 1-12.

Zimmer, M. (14 May 2010). *Facebook's Zuckerberg: "Having two identities for yourself is an example of lack of integrity."* Retrieved from http://www.michaelzimmer.org/2010/05/14/facebooks-zuckerberg-having-two-identities-for-yourself-is-an-example-of-a-lack-of-integrity/

81st Annual Meeting of the Association for Information Science & Technology | Vancouver, Canada | 10 – 14 November 2018

Toward an Intensional Approach to Transformation Classification

Allen H. Renear
School Information Sciences, University of Illinois at Urbana-Champaign. renear@illinois.eu

Xinrui Wang
National Science Library, University of Chinese Academy of Sciences. wangxinrui@mail.las.ac.cn

ABSTRACT

Generating one dataset from another is a fundamental activity in data science: data *curators* convert datasets to different file formats, create data subsets, generate metadata, integrate data from multiple sources, and so on; data *analysts* generate summaries and classifications, create visualizations, and derive data about one sort of thing from data about another sort of thing. Sometimes these transformations occur in independent single episodes, sometimes as part of an extended structured process or scientific workflow. Although such transformations have been studied from a variety of perspectives, there has been little effort to develop a general classification based on intrinsic (rather than functional) characteristics, apart from computational complexity. With this paper we hope to motivate a classification of transformations based on the relationships between the *intensional* features of the input and output datasets, that is, their propositional and conceptual content. Intensional entities are the fundamental components of scientific reasoning and explanation and consequently deserve a uniquely central role in the analysis of information work. We believe such a classification would be a valuable contribution to the data curation curriculum. This paper is an introduction to that project.

KEYWORDS

Data science, data analytics, data curation, conceptual foundations.

INTRODUCTION

Transforming one dataset into another is routinely carried out in businesses, laboratories, government offices, and many other venues throughout our society. Moreover, although not always visible as such, it is often an immediate consequence of many of the familiar actions performed in the ordinary lives of people throughout the world.

Transformations are particularly central in those areas of science, commerce, and the professions where digital data and digital tools are common and data management tasks essential. For example, to ensure preservation, support integration with other datasets, and support the use of specialized software tools, data curators routinely convert datasets to different file formats or encodings. They also update information, make corrections, extract subsets, generate metadata, and so on.

Transformations are also central to the work of scientists and data analysts; datasets of particular observations are routinely transformed into datasets containing statistical summaries, classifications, and predictions. Of particular interest are transformations that derive data about one sort of thing from data about an entirely different sort of thing: data about climate in the distant past might be derived from data about tree rings, data about temperature on surface of the earth from electromagnetic radiation collected by geosynchronous satellites, and data about altitude from data about air pressure. Sometimes these things occur in sporadic single episodes, sometimes as part of an extended structured process or scientific workflow (Ludäscher, Marciano, & Moore, 2001)

Although dataset transformations are important and much studied, there have been only a few efforts to classify them generally as to kind. For such a classification, one might use computational features such as the expressiveness and efficiency of the underlying data description language, data structures, and algorithms. Alternatively, a classification can be made according to the purpose or function of different transformations within a system or organizational context. In this paper we propose a different but complementary approach, one based on the *intensional* features of the input and output datasets, that is, on their *propositional* and *conceptual* content — the natural cognitive components of scientific explanation and reasoning. We believe that among other things this approach could provide support for understanding and organizing information work, and, particularly, for preparing information professionals, particularly data curators. These are some first thoughts towards such a project.

THE SAM/BRM MODEL FOR DATA CONCEPTS

The initial problem for exploring dataset transformations is, of course the considerable variation in what is understood by *data* and *dataset* (Renear, Sacchi, & Wickett, 2010; Thomer & Weber, 2014). In what follows we will assume a particular conceptual model for data concepts, the Basic Reference Model (BRM), part of the Systematically Asserted Propositions (SAM) model.[1]

SAM/BRM Entity Types

There are three entity types in the SAM/BRM model: (i) *propositional content*, (ii) *symbol structure*, and (iii) *patterned matter and energy*.

Propositional content can be characterized as the language-independent content of meaningful assertions. Other common terms with similar meanings include "observations", "information", "facts", "states of affairs", "claims", "assertions" and "data". Propositions have also been defined as the things that are properly true or false, and as the things that are the proper objects of belief, doubt, and other "propositional attitudes". What is particularly important with respect to the SAM/BRM model is that propositions are not *sentences*. Two different sentences can express the same proposition and two people can believe the same proposition (for instance, *copper is a metal*) even if they have no language in common.

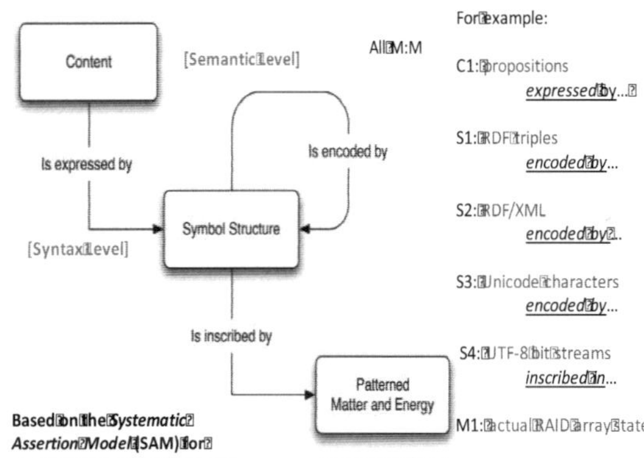

Based on the *Systematic Assertion Model* (SAM) for modeling datasets, developed by David Dubin et al.

A **symbol structure** is any abstract structure of symbols. Words, phonemes, characters, numerals, and bytes, for example, are all symbols and any structural arrangement of those things is a symbol structure. As just noted, the same proposition can be expressed in different symbol structures. Although our example proposition, *copper is a metal*, is expressed in English, the same proposition can be represented by sentences in other natural languages, or in any formal data description languages that has the required vocabulary.

Patterned matter and energy refers to a particular physical system in a particular concrete physical state. In the applicable context that physical state is understood as recording a symbol structure. An example would be a portion of the actual physical state of digital storage hardware.

SAM/BRM Relationships

There are three key relationship types in the SAM/BRM model: (i) *expressed by*, (ii) *encoded by*, and (iii) *inscribed by*.

Expressed_by: This relationship holds between a proposition and a symbol structure when the symbol structure is understood, in the relevant applicable context, as expressing the proposition.

Encoded_by: Symbol structures not only express propositions, they may also be said to *encode* other symbol structures. For instance, the English word *cat*, a symbolic entity, can be encoded in a sonic episode of phones and phonemes, or it can be encoded as the sequence of these three glyphs: "c", "a" "t". Phonemes and characters as well as the English word *cat*, are symbolic entities. And this cascade can continue: a sequence of characters can be mapped to different numerical values (the ASCII or EBCDIC integer code points), which in turn are mapped to binary octets, which in turned are mapped to bitstreams (UTF-8 for instance). Managing this representational cascade is a critical part of data curation.

Inscribed_by: Symbols structures may encode other symbol structures in encoding chains of arbitrary length, but if we are to store and communicate information then at some point an encoding symbol structure must by instantiated in arrangements of matter in energy. In SAM the relationship between a symbol structure and the matter and energy that instantiates it is referred to as *inscription*. The symbol structure it records is presumably the lowest level symbol structure in a representation instance, a bitstream perhaps.

Representation is of course a matter of social convention. Symbol structures express propositions or encode other symbol structures only in particular contingent social contexts that are created by the existence of a wide range of standing and episodic

---

[1] This model was initiated by David Dubin (Sandore & Unsworth, 2010) and subsequently developed as part of several projects at the Center of Informatics Resarch in Science and Scholarship at the School of Information Sciences, University of Illinois at Urbana-Champaign (Dubin, Wickett, & Sacchi, 2011; Wickett, Renear, & Dubin, 2011; Wickett, Sacchi, Dubin, & Renear, 2012).

conventions, agreements, intentions, expectations, and so on. Particularly relevant to digital representation are such things as data standards, language definitions, processing agreements, and hardware design intentions (Dubin, Wickett, & Sacchi, 2011).

INTENSIONAL CONTENT

The classification project we propose will be for the most part based on relationships between the *intensional* content of input and output datasets. For now we recognize two sorts of intensional content: *propositional* and *conceptual*.

Propositions

We have characterized propositions as the language-independent content of meaningful assertions, noting that other common terms for propositional content include observations, information, facts, or data. We also noted that propositions have been defined the proper subjects of truth and falsity, and the proper objects of propositional attitudes (belief, doubt, supposition, consideration, etc.).

In what follows we privilege the characterization of propositions as the proper objects of propositional attitudes. This characterization has the important consequence that propositions will be "finely individuated". Consider for instance the statement: *There are six people in the room;* and the statement: *The number of people in the room is identical with the smallest number that is the sum of all of its divisors other than itself.* As six *is* the smallest perfect number, and necessarily so, these two statements express logically equivalent propositions. We might even understand them to be "saying the same thing" or expressing "the same information". However it would seem to be possible for a person to believe that there are six persons in the room without believing that the number of persons in the room is identical with the smallest number that is the sum of all of its divisors other than itself. We certainly can imagine a scenario where someone would respond positively to the first statement but not to the second. This suggests that the two statements express two different propositions, even if there is also some sense in which they say the same thing. Taking this approach to propositional identity will let us make classification distinctions that could not be made otherwise.

Concepts

In what follows we assume that propositions have *concepts* as components. For instance, if a proposition characterizes some object as having a particular mass and another proposition characterizes another object as having particular mass then those two propositions have at least one thing in common: the concept of *mass*. As components of propositions concepts are also cognitively ingredient in reasoning, explaining, and making specific claims about the world. Common colloquial synonyms for concept in this sense include property, predicate, attribute, feature, characteristic. We are focused here on attributive use of concepts in datasets (for instance, as predicates), and not their referential use or their occurrence as objects of reference (names and values).

Our approach finely individuates concepts as well as propositions. The fact that concepts **F** and **G** apply to exactly the same pairs of things, even necessarily, does not imply that **F** and **G** are the same concept. If it is possible that someone believes F(a,b)) but does not believe G(a,b) then that immediately implies that F and G and not identical concepts.

SOME PRELIMINARES

Terminology: In what follows we are using familiar terms in order to suggest the types of transformation we are exploring and to guide our intuitions about features of those transformations. Many of these terms (*e.g, transformation, conversion, derivation*) are used with a very wide variety of meanings; our use will approximate only some of these and may clash with others. Other terms (e.g. *selection, update*) have very specific meanings in some communities; we do not intend those specific meanings here, although we hope that the resonance, when it exists, is helpful.

Necessary conditions: For the most part, the discussion below focuses on *necessary* conditions, that is, conditions that must hold for a particular type of transformation. Ultimately sufficient conditions will also need to be provided, but that is not our focus here. Wherever possible though we are looking for *discriminating* necessary conditions, that is, necessary conditions that although not sufficient to define the concept in question will distinguish one transformation type from another.

Pure instances: Generally, when we are discussing a transformation type we are considering scenarios that are *pure* in that they are not also a transformation of another type as well, at least not as a contingent matter. For instance, our discussion of conversion is intended to apply only to a transformation that is a conversion *and nothing but a conversion* — that is, a scenario that is a conversion but not also a selection, deduction, or update. Although scenarios of mixed type are common, presumably they can be understood as, and performed as, a sequence of one or more transformations that are of a single type. Of course some transformation types will have logical relationships to others, such as class/subclass — this restriction does not apply in those cases, as one type is implied by the other.

Uniformity: Although some definitions of dataset specify syntactic and semantic uniformity of assertions, a useful general notion of uniformity is difficult to define, and certainly datasets do often contain propositions that vary widely in nature. Nevertheless it will be useful for at least some of the discussion below to have before our minds only examples where propositions in the input dataset are substantial similar to one another. For instance, consider a case where the input dataset contains instrument data collected over a period of time and where there is also information about the calibration of that instrument that is needed for the derivation. That instrument information, although essential to the derivation, should for now be thought of as contained in a separate dataset that would be accessed in a derivation. So "input dataset" would, in discussion, refer only to the instrument data, not the calibration data. We recognize of course that systematically accommodating multiple datasets, metadata (Wickett, Urban, & Renear, 2010), libraries, formulas and assumptions, and collection circumstances, among other things is important. Classifying the variety of roles different sorts of information have in a transformation will be essential to a full treatment.

Finally, although our ultimate goal is a formal framework, in this paper we will speak casually and colloquially unless formality is needed to avoid misunderstanding.

TRANSFORMATIONS FROM AN INTENSIONAL POINT OF VIEW

Here we take a brief look at several familiar kinds of transformation, focusing on intensional characteristics.

Conversion: In a conversion (such as translation to a different character encoding or a different serialization language) the information contained in the output dataset would appear to be, in some relevant sense, identical to the information contained in the input dataset. If the output dataset has less information that the input dataset then apparently information has been lost and the conversion unsuccessful, or at least imperfect. If the output dataset contains information not in the input dataset than apparently information has been inappropriately added. Interpreting the information contained in a dataset as a set of propositions we could say that a necessary condition of being a successful (pure) conversion is that the set of input propositions and the set of output propositions are identical.

Selection: A common action on a dataset is to generate a new dataset by a selection (or filtering) of information from the input dataset. As in a conversion, the output propositions in a selection scenario will be a subset of the input propositions, but unlike a conversion, the set of input propositions and the set of output propositions are not identical.

Deduction: In a deduction the output propositions are logically implied by the input propositions. Unlike selection the output propositions of a deduction would generally not be a subset of the input propositions, or at least not necessarily so. Logical deductions will introduce new propositions, but not new concepts. [We will want to distinguish deductions that are strictly logical (for instance, valid according to the semantics of classical first order logic), from transformations carried out with additional mathematics.]

Updates: There are a wide variety of transformations that might be considered updates. What most, but perhaps not all, have in common is that the output propositions are not a subset of the input propositions, a condition that is not itself particularly discriminative. There are subclasses of updates though that conform to additional constraints. For instance, when the values in a relation are updated the concepts indicated by attributes (the column headings) will be identical with the corresponding input concepts, even though output propositions are never a subset of the input propositions in an update. *Amplifications* may require that input data be a subset of the output dataset. *Corrections* may require, in at least some varieties, that an inconsistency, perhaps mediated by a schema or other background assumptions, exists between input and output propositions.

Generalization and specialization: In a generalization applicable concepts are replaced by logically broader concepts: for instance, Kind(Fido,dog) becomes Kind(Fido,terrier). This is often useful for data integration. In a specialization assertions become more specific, for instance: Kind(Fido,terrier) becomes Kind(Fido,dog). In (pure) generalization and specialization (with no ungeneralized or unspecialized assertion retained) the output and input propositions will be disjoint, but their conceptual content will overlap; and, unlike some varieties of correction, output and input datasets will be logically consistent. The output propositions in a generalization will be logically implied from the input propositions and relevant class relationships, but the specialization transformation will require additional non-logical information.

Derivation: In the case of a derivation (for instance, altitude data calculated from air pressure data) we not only assume that input and output propositions will not be identical, we sometimes assume that input and output sets will not have any propositions in common. After all, if each statement in the (input) air pressure dataset makes an assertion about air pressure, and no statement in the (output) altitude dataset makes an assertion about air pressure, then the set of input datasets and the set of output propositions are not just different sets, they are disjoint sets.

These examples should be sufficient to suggest the sort of approach we are taking. This is far from a complete list of kinds of dataset transformations though. There are a number of important varieties of transformation, including summarization, classification, visualization, and modeling transformations that will need to be accommodated, and the varieties of contemporary mathematical processing will be particularly challenging to characterize.

GRICEAN ASIDES

Set / sub-set: We have suggested that a necessary condition for selection is that output propositions are a subset of input propositions. This would however allow the output of a selection to contain *all* propositions in the input file, which seems like an edge case with respect to usage. Consider the natural interpretation of "here is a selection from the income data" — you would not say this if you knew you were referring to an exact copy of the dataset. Strengthening the necessary condition to *proper subset* might improve the match with ordinary usage. And it also might also better discriminate selection from other transformations: if the requirement is simply that the output dataset is a subset of the input dataset then a transformation with identical output and input propositions is consistent with both selection and conversion — but if the condition is proper subset then that case is not consistent with selection. Nevertheless, most techniques for implementing selections can in some circumstances select all propositions in the input dataset, and so it seems arbitrary to exclude those cases as selections. Better perhaps to go with non-proper subset as the condition and allow that it is possible to use the term in a misleading way.

Trivial deductions: Can the output of a deduction be a proposition already in the input dataset? Such a trivial deduction also seems an awkward edge case; excluding this case as a deduction might better match how we think about deductive transformations. And as before it might also improve discrimination: without such a restriction, all selections are deductions. Still, P does follow logically from P (semantically and by deduction rule *reiteration*), and so formally excluding this deduction (and other similarly trivial deductions) seems arbitrary. So perhaps here too it will be best to simply allow that the term *deduction* can be used in a misleading way.

LOOKING AHEAD

Some of the issues that the proposed classification will need to explore include:

Kinds of Conversions: The SAM/BRM model reflects the possibility of a cascade of encoding levels, ranging from character encoding to the data description language. How do we understand and classify these? How do we accommodate substantive modeling variations that seem to amount to the same assertion? It may also be unclear exactly what should count as a conversion. Consider transformations such as canonicalization or the elimination of duplicate records. These meet the otherwise fairly discriminating necessary condition associated with conversions: identity of input and output datasets, and they result in identifiable changes in relevant files (they are not just a result of copying). But it is not clear how these would fit into a SAM/BRM based classification of types of conversion.

Domain: In some cases propositions in a dataset seem, in virtue of their concepts and referents, to be about things that, in some intuitive but hard to characterize sense, belong to a particular domain. When this is the case in an input dataset then the output dataset generated by, for instance, deductions and updates (as well as conversions and selections) will also contain only propositions associated with that domain. But in the case of derivations the output and input propositions often seem to be about things in different domain. The input data might be electromagnetic radiation recorded by a satellite, and the output data temperatures on the surface of the earth, or the input data might be might be the width of the rings in tree rounds, and the output propositions about rainfall in the very distant past. Can the notion domain be given a reasonably clear and useful definition?

Necessary external information: So far we have focused on simple relationships between input and output propositions. But there are some additional related features of transformations that will eventually be an important part of this classification. One is the various sorts of additional information required for particular kinds of transformations. In the case of deductions or selections there may be no additional information required, the elementary assumptions of logic and set theory are sufficient. In other cases additional mathematics may be required, but no contingent empirical information about the world. It is quite different for conversions and derivations. Conversions must make use of recognized relationships between input and output representations (e.g. format standards); this is additional contingent information about the world, even if a matter of social convention. In the case of derivations considerable factual information may be needed, including formulas and data representing our theoretical understanding of the physical or social world, information about the instruments being used, information related to the circumstances of data collection, and so on. Conceptualizing the varieties of additional external information and relating these to transformation types will be an important part of any classification from an intensional point of view.

Propositional identity: In this project we are individuating propositions finely, but that is a challenging commitment, as the discussion of both selection and deduction suggest. Consider this question: are the output propositions generated by relational algebra queries always a subset of the input propositions? All relational queries generate information that was, at least in some sense, already latent in the input dataset, so one might be tempted to answer in the affirmative. But although the operation `selection` in the relational algebra does seem to always generate a subset of the input propositions, we should be reluctant, given our commitment to individuating propositions finely, as objects of propositional attitudes, to say that *every* relational query results in a subset of the input propositions. A complex relational query can provide a result that is new, even startling, however familiar we may be with the input data. How could we be learning something new if we are not . . . *learning something new*. But by what principle do we determine which actions will generate subsets of input propositions and which will generate new propositions? Or, for that matter, how do we even determine whether or not the propositions of a particular dataset *are* a subset of the propositions of another particular dataset, since different representations do not imply different propositional content. Earlier we did allude to a method for determining propositional identity — in the smallest perfect number example. But this method is basically just asking oneself whether it seems possible to believe +++++ and not believe ------- and uses natural language sentences to set the question. How could it be applied to datasets, which can be very large, complex, and often presented in languages that are not intended to communicate directly to humans? Puzzles of this sort have led some data scientists to avoid the notion of identity (whether of propositions or information) altogether and instead characterize the input and output datasets of a successful conversion as "scientifically equivalent" (Tilmes, Yesha, & Halem, 2010; Tilmes, Yesha, & Halem, 2011; Duerr et al., 2011). Nevertheless, if we wish to make a connection between data and actual human understanding this is a problem we cannot ignore (cf. Sperberg-McQueen 2011).

ACKNOWLEDGMENTS

These ruminations have benefitted from culture of thought and conversation at the Conceptual Foundations Group, Center for Informatics Research in Science and Scholarship, School of Information Sciences, University of Illinois Urbana-Champaign.

REFERENCES

Duerr, R. et al. (2011). On the utility of identification schemes for digital earth science data: an assessment and recommendations. Earth Science Informatics. 4:139.

Dubin, D., Wickett, K. M., & Sacchi, S. (2011). Content, format, and interpretation. *Proceedings of Balisage: The Markup Conference* 7.

Duerr, R., Downs, R., Tilmes, C., Barkstrom, B., Lenhardt, W., Glassy, J., et al. (2011). On the utility of identification schemes for digital earth science data: an assessment and recommendations. *Earth Science Informatics*, 4, 139-160.

Ludäscher, B., Marciano, R., & Moore, R. (2001). Preservation of digital data with self-validating, self-instantiating knowledge-based archives. *SIGMOD Rec.* 30, 3 54-63.

Renear, A., Sacchi, S., Wickett, K. M. (2010) Definitions of dataset in the scientific and technical literature. *Proceedings of the Association for Information Science and Technology*. 47:1, 1-4.

Sacchi, S., Wickett, K. M., Renear, A. H., & Dubin, D. S. (2011). A framework for applying the concept of significant properties to datasets. In *Proceedings of the American Society for Information Science and Technology* 48:1, 1-10

Sandore, B., & Unsworth, J. (2010). ECHO DEPository — Phase 2: 2008–2010 final report of project activities. Section 4. Semantic Archive (SemArch) Project (David Dubin). University of Illinois at Urbana-Champaign, 30–37.

Sperberg-McQueen, C. M. (2011). What constitutes successful format conversion? Towards a formalization of 'Intellectual content'. *International Journal of Digital Curation*, 6(1), 2011.

Thomer, A. K. and Weber, N. M. (2014), The phylogeny of a dataset. In *Proceedings of the American Society for Information Science and Technology*, 51: 1-11.

Tilmes, C., Yesha, Y., & Halem, M. (2010). Tracking provenance of earth science data. *Earth Science Informatics*, 3(1-2), 59–65.

Tilmes, C., Yesha, Y., & Halem, M. (2011). Distinguishing provenance equivalence of earth science data. *Procedia Computer Science*, 4, 548–557.

Wickett, K., Sacchi, S., Dubin, D., Renear, A. (2012). Identifying content and levels of representation in scientific data *Proceedings of the Association for Information Science and Technology* 49:1, 1-10.

Wickett, K. M., Renear, A. H. and Urban, R. J. (2010), Rule categories for collection/item metadata relationships. *Proceedings of the Association for Information Science and Technology*, 47: 1-10.

Weapons of Affect: The Imperative for Transdisciplinary Information Systems Design

Gregory Rolan
Monash University, Australia.
greg.rolan@monash.edu

Antonia Lewis
Monash University, Australia.
nina.lewis@monash.edu

Sue McKemmish
Monash University, Australia.
sue.mckemmish@monash.edu

Joanne Evans
Monash University, Australia.
joanne.evans@monash.edu

Frank Golding
Care Leavers Australia Network.
fgolding@bigpond.net.au

Philip Mendes
Monash University, Australia.
philip.mendes@monash.edu

Jane Bone
Monash University, Australia.
jane.bone@monash.edu

Jacqueline Wilson
Federation University, Australia.
jz.wilson@federation.edu.au

Keir Reeves
Federation University, Australia.
k.reeves@federation.edu.au

ABSTRACT

Much has been written about ethical and human-centred Information Systems (IS) design, most recently regarding the deleterious outcomes and negative affect of some machine learning applications that embed and perpetuate unethical or even inhumane automation. Terms such as 'harm', 'damage', and surprisingly, 'weapon' have entered the language of this discourse. However, these characteristics are not unique to applications of data science but have long manifested in IS that can also can exhibit opacity and establish tight vicious cycles. These, when coupled with a lack of governance feedback, can perpetuate injustice that has community or sector-wide reach. In this paper, we explore how IS design that sets out with the best of intentions or at least, conceived as a 'neutral' system for managing transactional information, can emerge as 'tools that punish'. We argue that there are crucial principles to be taken from Recordkeeping Informatics, concerned as it is with the entanglement of information and people across space and through time on multi-generational timescales. In particular we discuss how transdisciplinary and critical approaches are necessary to cover more of the design space and surface issues, rights, stakeholders, and, most importantly, values that may be otherwise hidden from a here-and-now, transactional viewpoint.

KEYWORDS

Recordkeeping, Transdisciplinary, Participatory, Design, Ethical

INTRODUCTION

Much has been written about ethical and human-centred Information Systems (IS) design. While the volume of this discourse has grown recently in the context of the deleterious outcomes and negative affect from some machine learning systems (Eubanks, 2007; Introna, 2007; Lynch, 2017), these are not unique to applications of data science but have long manifested in IS. Again, it is only recently that terms such as 'harm', 'damage', and surprisingly, 'weapon' have entered the language of this discourse in the context of systemic opacity and pitfalls in design and governance that lead to biases of the past being codified and amplified into pernicious systems of today that will infiltrate tomorrow (d'Alessandro, O'Neil, & LaGatta, 2017). Beyond entrenching biases (Gangadharan, Eubanks, & Barocas, 2014), IS can serve to actually embed and perpetuate unethical or even inhumane automation (Redden & Brand, 2017).

Information Systems — and here we understand the term 'systems' to mean configurations of human activities and social structures as well as technical artefacts; in other words a broader socio-technical (or, more precisely as explained below, sociomaterial) use — can and do exhibit opacity and establish tight vicious cycles that, when coupled with a lack of governance feedback, perpetuates injustice that, even if not at the internet scale, can still have community or sector-wide reach. How is it that seemingly benign transactional IS can be considered successes and yet fail other stakeholder groups catastrophically (Hart & Warne, 2007) with life-altering affect? How does IS "technology [become] weapons of affect" (Wilson & Golding, 2016) and, more importantly, how can we avoid this emergent malevolence?

In this paper, we explore how IS design that sets out with the best of intentions or at least, conceived as a 'neutral' system for managing transactional information, can emerge as "tools that punish" (Eubanks, 2018). We argue that there are crucial principles to be taken from Recordkeeping Informatics (Upward, Reed, Oliver, & Evans, 2018), concerned as it is with the entanglement of information and people across space and through time on multi-generational timescales. In particular we discuss how transdisciplinary and critical approaches are necessary to cover more of the design space and surface issues, needs, stakeholders, and, most importantly, values that may be otherwise hidden from a here-and-now, transactional viewpoint. Importantly, "critical theorising [and] analysis highlight the fundamental shortcomings in [systems] designed around the requirements and demands of information elites, government, and big business – particularly in relation to social justice and human rights agendas and in situations of conflict, oppression, colonization and marginalization" (Evans, McKemmish, & Rolan, 2017).

The rest of this paper is organised as follows. Firstly, we provide a theoretical background to this position, after which we introduce the nature of the *Rights in Records by Design* project in which we are currently engaged as an example. We then describe our participatory and transdisciplinary approach and the contributions to the design from various disciplines and participants. Finally, we conclude with some of the challenges inherent in transdisciplinary and participatory design.

THEORETICAL UNDERPINNING

Perhaps a starting point is an appreciation of the situatedness of IS within information ecologies. We use the term information ecology here in the sense described by Nardi & O'Day (1999) who explain that, "like a biological ecology, an information ecology is marked by strong interrelationships and dependencies among its different parts". It is these far-reaching interrelationships and dependencies, sometimes obscure or opaque, that give rise to the complex, emergent behaviour of IS, beyond a simple, technological treatment. For example the design and operation of any given information system takes place, not only in a landscape of other systems with varying degrees of interoperability, but within ever-shifting legal, policy, and practice contexts. And these, at their core, are informed by the philosophy and epistemology, values and principles, and rights and obligations imbued in broader political, economic, and social contexts. The collection, meaning, and use of information cannot be disentangled from these elements in the ecology – change any of these, and the behaviour or affect of the system may alter as well, perhaps dramatically.

It is doubtful that a simple 'technology' perspective (Wand & Weber, 1995) is sufficient in relation to IS. Rather, we now understand that IS can only be meaningfully considered in the context of their social setting (Orlikowski & Scott, 2008; Svahn, Henfridsson, & Yoo, 2009). This indivisibility of material artefacts from their social embeddedness is termed sociomateriality (Cecez-Kecmanovic, Galliers, Henfridsson, Newell, & Vidgen, 2014; Leonardi, 2013); which holds that what is actually observable are performed relations between actors and objects rather than pre-formed elements (Orlikowski & Scott, 2008). As described above, these relations associate material artefacts and social actors alike, with agency that entangles over time in a non-deterministic manner (Svahn et al., 2009). This is not to say that artefacts do not exist outside of a performative context. Rather, "materiality exists independent of people, but affordances and constraints do not. Because people come to materiality with diverse goals they perceive a technology as affording distinct possibilities for action" (Leonardi, 2012, p. 20).

For example: depending on the context, a chair (a material item) may be considered as furniture for sitting upon, for use as a step ladder, as a repository for clothes, as an *objet d'art*, as a source of kindling, etc. Another good example of sociomaterial contingency in a technological context is the World Wide Web. The emergent nature of its affordances and constraints and the shift from hyperlinked documentation, to dynamic pages, to an application platform, (and more recently, to a real-time semantic knowledge base) has been well documented (O'Reilly, 2005). A further example is Facebook, with its once ostensibly benign social networking and publication functionality having recently been co-opted for, arguably, more sinister use.

Thus, the affordances and constraints of IS, together with their associated values, need to be explicitly explored from all viewpoints within the relevant information ecology. However, such viewpoints may be distanciated (Giddens, 1984, p. 84) from the immediate transactionality of a given system through space or time (or both). This means we need to gain an appreciation of all of the system stakeholders and uses of information beyond a synchronic (point-in-time) perspective, as they may manifest across space and through time. One approach is to draw upon recordkeeping and archival science which takes a diachronic (through-time) perspective to analyse how IS manifests with identity, memory, evidentiality, and accountability across space and through time.

In the past, recordkeeping systems were easily distinguished as a result of explicit business engineering; papers, files, correspondence, contracts, reports etc. — recordkeeping was built into the very fabric of systemic transactionality. However, with the digital transformation of the modern era, it is hard to imagine IS that are not also recordkeeping systems for at least someone in some context. This holds even (and this is the point) if they are not designed as such, for example, using diachronic analysis from the perspectives of all potential stakeholders (for example, in the current project context: Victorian Auditor-General, 2014, p. 14). It is all the more significant given the necessity of a recordkeeping perspective for addressing both long-standing societal Grand Challenges (Gilliland & McKemmish, 2012) and emergent ones such as the contemporary international refugee crisis.

Note though, that recordkeeping and archival systems can (and often do) suffer from the problems described above. This is due to a number of factors stemming from their roots in 19th century practice in the face of major social and technological change. Some administrative and archival systems that may have been acceptable a century ago, now are being recognised for the injurious impact they have. And, indeed, it is this weaponisation of one such recordkeeping system that provides motivation for the current project as described in this paper.

Nonetheless, decades-long critical recordkeeping research has resulted in the theory and practice of Recordkeeping Informatics (Upward et al., 2018) which can provide a diachronic (through-time) perspective and the ability to analyse the affect of IS on identity, memory, evidentiality, and accountability on individuals, organisations, the community, and society as it ripples out from the originating transactional context. A Continuum approach[1], in this case, the Records Continuum, most commonly expressed as the Records Continuum Model (RCM) (McKemmish, Upward, & Reed, 2010), links the transactionality of events with records and systems that establish evidentiality and the identity of stakeholders through time and space. Similarly, the Participatory Recordkeeping Continuum Model (PRCM) (Rolan, 2016) can be used with the RCM to identify potential stakeholders and the agency that they need to exercise in such systems.

Arguably then, it is the invisibility of some stakeholders, the negating of identity, the denial of agency, the disregarding of evidentiality, and the shirking of accountability that contribute to the unsurfaced (or implicit) influential loops that result in structures of surveillance and cycles of injustice. It is worth repeating that the root cause of these is the synchronic and technical-oriented design of essentially diachronic and socio-material IS. Beyond any flaws in the technical attributes of systems are the more general problems that stem from the 'nowism' perspective that runs through much of IS design. Additionally, the emergent and mutable nature of Information Systems contexts requires not only diachronic analysis, but participatory approaches such as value-based design, not only to ensure that the immediate transactionality of the system is 'correct', but also that the longer-term, societal affect of the system is surfaced. Note, though, it can be difficult to gain insight into values, for example, though conventional, arms-length requirements elicitation (Sexton & Sen, 2017). This is not just a case of insufficient end-user consultation or even organisational-unit turf wars over intellectual control of organisational data (Hart, 1994). This, often tacit, knowledge can only be apprehended through participatory engagement that ensures the socialisation of values from different perspectives of participants

The challenge, then, is to establish "investigative processes [that] result in a broad and rich understanding of the values at play, along with their influence on technical development" (McKemmish, Burstein, Manaszewicz, Fisher, & Evans, 2012). Such processes are necessarily critical and are, in turn, dependent on the epistemological underpinnings of a variety of disciplines beyond ours. An approach is needed that lies beyond a 'sum-of-the parts' multidisciplinary collaboration or even the integrated approach of interdisciplinarity. Rather, the concept of transdisciplinarity emerged in the second half of the 20th Century in response to a growing recognition of the wicked complexity of societal problems and that solving them requires new ideas, methods, models that transcend disciplinary boundaries (Lawrence, 2010). It has further evolved to encompass the need for the research community to collaborate outside of the academy in order to develop deep and rich understanding of the problem and solution spaces In particular, engagement is needed with those that have lived experience of the affect and consequences of IS over long – even multi-generational – timeframes. This understanding transcends insights that may be gained through even longitudinal studies of the scope found in research and, perhaps, systems development projects, all of which take place under various time and budget constraints.

A transdisciplinary approach recognises the fragmentation of knowledge and "its hybrid nature, non-linearity, and reflexivity" (Lawrence, 2010, p. 127) that requires perspectives drawn from across and beyond traditional authoritative knowledge institutions. It is this "context-specific negotiation of knowledge" that requires "making linkages not only across disciplinary boundaries but also between theoretical development and professional practice". Thus, a transdisciplinary approach involves "close and continuous collaboration" during all phases of a project by domain experts from various disciplines as well as practitioners and community members drawn from stakeholder groups. Such project characteristics are also intrinsic to Records Continuum thinking (McKemmish, 2001). They are necessary for developing rich understandings of people's lives at individual, community, organizational and societal levels, and using that understanding to develop appropriate IS.

Having provided this diachronic, critical, and transdisciplinary basis of our approach to IS design, we now introduce the project domain in which we are currently conducting our research.

PROJECT BACKGROUND

National standards for out-of-home Care[2] in Australia and other countries are increasingly emphasising the need to put the physical, emotional, spiritual and social health and wellbeing of children and young people at the centre of service provision (Department of Families, Housing, Community Services and Indigenous Affairs, 2011). For example, the Early Years Learning Framework sets out how a strong sense of identity, social, emotional and physical wellbeing, and connectedness with the world

[1] Continuum theory has also been extended into other domains, for example: generic Information Systems, Publishing, Cultural heritage, and Digital Forensics to name a few. See Upward et al. (2018, pp. 214–215).

[2] As explained in Wilson & Golding (2016), the capitalised term 'Care' is used to denote the ironic connotations of often manifestly uncaring treatment, without the typographically heavy-handedness of continually enclosing the word in quotation marks.

from the earliest years underpins our life chances (Department of Education, Employment and Workplace Relations, 2009). Moreover, there is increasing awareness of the role that records and archives plays in developing and supporting this sense of self throughout our lives (Cifor & Gilliland, 2015).

Such standards identify the right of the child or young person to have access to a complete and accurate history of their time in care; the plans for their future; their health, education and other important official records; their family and community connections; memories of key events; and other records. They also emphasise children and young people participating in decision making, which necessarily includes the formation and use of these records.

Children who experience out-of-home Care, therefore need quality recordkeeping systems to develop and nurture their sense of identity and connectedness to family and community; to account for their Care experiences; and to prevent, detect, report, investigate, and take action against child neglect and abuse. Those involved in providing care services and supporting children experiencing family dislocation need access to efficient, effective, and responsive information systems — driven by quality recordkeeping — to ensure the highest standards and continuity of care. The need for such systems does not disappear when a child leaves care. Many inquiries, including the recently completed Australian Royal Commission into Institutional Responses to Child Sexual Abuse, have highlighted the lifelong importance of these childhood records. In inquiry after inquiry, testimony after testimony[3], Care Leavers have highlighted the difficulties they have faced in finding and accessing records in the search for identity and memory, (re)connecting with family, holding the child- welfare system accountable for decisions and actions, and seeking redress for abuse and neglect (Mendes & Snow, 2016).

Records of Care experiences are too often lost, fragmented, and incomplete, and the bureaucratic processes of dealing with IS in order to access records can harm and re-traumatise Care Leavers rather than helping to heal (O'Neill, Selakovic, & Tropea, 2012; Wilson & Golding, 2016). Care Leavers have also been excluded from historical representations, narratives and dialogues, as others make use of the records from which they have been denied access, with the authority of the recollections of their own experiences often diminished (Logan & Reeves, 2011; Wilson & Golding, 2016).

Moreover, the recordkeeping systems themselves are the core of surveillance and control systems that lead to tight causal loops in the child protection sector (Mendes, 2009). Transactional records made and kept during Care are often used as 'evidence' to rationalise post-Care interventions. The opacity and lack of feedback within such recordkeeping systems, entangled as they are with policy and practice, leads to multi-generational involvement with child protection that is difficult to escape.

The *Rights in Records by Design* project brings together a transdisciplinary research team to address the critical research issues associated with designing and developing a Lifelong Living Archive for children and young people in out-of-home Care. Such an archive would support developmental outcomes and ensure accountability requirements are adequately met through enacting participatory recordkeeping and archiving frameworks, policies, processes and systems.

THE RIGHTS IN RECORDS DESIGN APPROACH

In the modern era, you do not need to look far to find the motto "Nihil de nobis, sine nobis" — "Nothing about us without us" adopted by a variety of activist or community groups. Largely, this is an expression of the politics of identity — those feeling dispossessed, oppressed, rejected, abandoned or otherwise wronged who do not want that experience mediated by outsiders, however well-intentioned; "If we have learned one thing from the civil rights movement in the US, it's that when others speak for us, you lose" (Driedger, 1989, p. 28). This captures the importance of trust and, crucially, the assertion of agency — that is, generating and exercising to the greatest extent possible the capacity to take charge of the decisions that affect one's life. Activists and advocates are wary of those who have no obvious compelling reason to advance their cause. Moreover, many people who grew up in Care developed, and maintain, an enduring mistrust of all authority.

Consequently, we conceive of *Rights in Records* as a participatory and transdisciplinary research project in order to address the critical issues associated with recordkeeping for childhood out-of-home Care. A Lifelong Living Archive must be built on principles for acknowledging, respecting, representing, and negotiating multiple rights in records in and through time and space. The intent is to reverse the long-established trend in recordkeeping, especially in public institutions, that results in records "dominated by the viewpoint of those in power, the decision makers" (Brownlee-Chapman et al., 2017, p. 4). Our project achieves this through close collaboration, in particular, with Care-leavers, families, and carers to ensure that the 'personal' is included in the record. Moreover, this project has sought out a wide variety of partners from various intersecting groups in the academy and broader community, from a range of disciplines and fields, including archives and recordkeeping, information technology, the arts, law, education, social work, and history.

---

[3] In the Australian context, see Swain (2014) and, most recently, Royal Commission into Institutional Responses to Child Sexual Abuse (2017). See also Munro (2011); Ryan (2009); Truth and Reconciliation Commission of Canada (2015) etc.

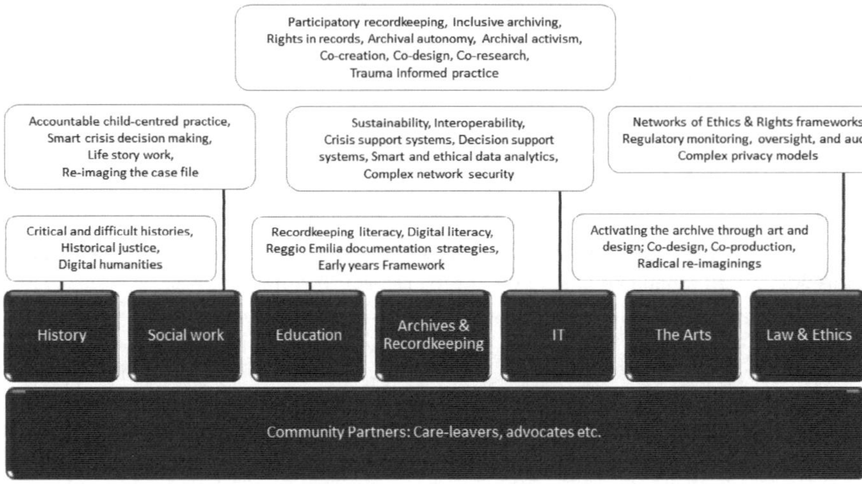

Figure 1. Disciplinary contributions

As illustrated in Figure 1, they bring the multiple expertise and experience needed to make the breakthroughs critical to solving the complex, multifaceted, and fundamental problems that the program has identified. All of the project activities – from the design and conduct of the research, to the design of the project outputs themselves – are conducted by transdisciplinary teams drawing from all of these disciplinary and community groups. In addition to the usual IS analysis and development techniques employed by the co-design team, the transdisciplinary nature of the team encompasses the following disciplinary perspectives:

Recordkeeping Informatics

Recordkeeping design in the out-of-home-Care sector is complex; involving transactional records, civil documentation, personal memory and identity material, along with security, confidentiality, and accountability considerations as well as the legal ramifications discussed below. Even a cursory analysis identifies stakeholders groups that span government child protection services, NGO childcare agencies, individual carers and other professionals, families and friends, community and personal advocates, the courts, police, the health system, government assistance programs, and educational institutions and professionals. This complexity demands the tools and techniques such as those of Recordkeeping Informatics including the continuum models described above, explicit metadata design, and an understanding of access and information cultures, in order to track the shifting aspects of agency and utility through time as the roles of various stakeholders wax and wane.

Historical records of out-of-home-Care — where they were indeed created and archived — are dispersed across an array of organisations: state libraries, government archives, government departments, non-government organisations including religious orders and charities which inherited the records of institutions that ran children's institutions in the past, and some organisations that are still involved in providing out-of-home Care on behalf of state governments (Find and Connect Web Resource Project Team, 2011). Recently the Australian Royal Commission into Institutional Responses to Child Sexual Abuse (2016, p. 4), when considering child-oriented institutions, concluded that even today "the creation and management of accurate records are systemic and enduring problems". In articulating these systemic and multi-generational problems, Wilson and Golding (2016) applied the term "weapons of affect", which has now entered the lexicon of Care-leavers in relation to the impact of records and archives.

The contemporary design of child-protection processes and systems perpetuate recordkeeping as an administrative burden, rather than being a negotiated space of shared stewardship within a complex, dynamic information ecology that lies at the heart of productivity, the quality and the child-centeredness of service provision (Victorian Auditor-General, 2014).

A key design principle and goal of the Lifelong Living Archive is Archival Autonomy: enabling 'individuals and communities to participate in societal memory, with their own voice, and to become participatory agents in recordkeeping and archiving for identity, memory and accountability purposes' (Evans, McKemmish, Daniels, & McCarthy, 2015). As well as facilitating this agency in the formation of records and archives, such autonomy manifests in historical representations, narratives and dialogues, to support justice and reconciliation at individual, community and societal levels for those who have experienced past regimes of institutional and other out-of-home Care. A Recordkeeping Informatics perspective is needed to integrate these lifelong needs into the design of out-of-home Care systems, rather than perpetuating the existing divide between transactional records-management and archival needs.

Historical Justice

We have learned through tough experience that "the loss of identity and connection with family is one of the most traumatic and distressing outcomes from a life lived in institutional care" (Australia Parliament Senate Community Affairs References Committee 2004, p. 253). That loss endures. People apply for their childhood records because they "...want to understand more about the circumstances that led to their placement in care, who their parents were and whether or not they have brothers or sisters..." (p. 253). On a practical level, they want to know about medical histories—and their parents' histories lest there be inherited conditions. Yet there is repeated evidence that whole childhoods spent in care went undocumented, with some survivors never even issued with a birth certificate. In order to unpack why making and keeping personal records about children of the state is never core business, a historical perspective is needed from which we can discern values and principles, even if the means of their identification is through examples of their violation.

The issues with recordkeeping in out-of-home-Care, are, in fact, symptomatic of a constellation of deeper problems that relate to the political and social purpose and function of the welfare system. As "the clients of the contemporary child protection system are most often drawn from the ranks of the poor and marginalised[, practice] in child protection social work is as much a class-based, gendered and culturally biased phenomenon" (D. Scott, 2006). Thus, the design of rights-based recordkeeping requires historical analysis of incarceration, institutionalisation, disadvantage, and the development of welfare and justice systems in Australian society. It also requires the perspective of the historical justice and reconciliation that explores the relationship between historical justice, memory and the archives and the ways in which impacted individuals and communities can participate in dialogues to imagine, define and cohere their identity.

The task of caring for state children was commonly outsourced to churches and charities, and even private institutions, with little or no monitoring or accountability about how the children fared. Historically, the removal of children from families was rooted in crisis, moral panic and a punitive management ideology in which the ruling class and their welfare delegates problematised children and their impoverished families. The purpose of state intervention in families was to control the 'other' and remake working class children into better citizens than their parents. There would be little or no need for personal records that dwelt on the child's past — that was rendered irrelevant. No accountability for the child's progress in the system was owed to parents whose rights had been forfeited. Making and keeping personal records about children of the state was never a high priority: what mattered was control — or being seen to be in control. That model continued from the eighteen-hundreds up until the late twentieth century.

There are many manifestations of this enduring culture of contempt for state children. Based on a criminal justice model, the welfare system was constructed within a penal framework that quickly conflated the situation of neglected and criminal children as they did the moral worth of children with the real or perceived disabilities that some had. Within the government's own industrial schools and reformatories — and in the even more numerous institutions run by churches, charities and community groups — this provided the rationale for state-sanctioned re-socialisation of these children by problematising the children and their parents rather than attending to the root causes of the problems they faced.

The recordkeeping systems of child protection today are haunted by such 19th century values of child welfare. The emphasis on controlling moral destitution is highlighted with the families encountering systems that consider them undeserving of recordkeeping to support their identity, memory and accountability needs. Such IS reinforce the power of the institutions to control what was recorded, how records were managed (or often mismanaged), what is destroyed, and who has access to the surviving fragments. Despite rhetoric that emphasises the need for child protection to be child-centred, especially for the children and young people who spend time in out of home Care, these recordkeeping systems are still too often 'weapons of affect'.

Education

The education perspective (and, in particular, innovative thinking in Early Childhood Education) informs the project by upholding the rights of the child in terms of wellbeing and social justice, recognising holistic and alternative approaches to pedagogy and learning, and considering the ethics of researching with young children (Bone, 2005). The idea of children as beings with rights who have a right to participate in events that concern them is not a new idea but seems to be taking a long time to filter through to institutions and belief systems that still see children as property, either of the family or the State.

A turning point in education arose when curriculum documents and learning frameworks were produced and children became seen as active learners to be educated as well as cared for (DEEWR, 2009). With the rise in preschools as sites for early learning, the role of children as beings with agency gained ground. When a person has agency they are seen as able, competent, active and able to make decisions about events that concern them. This is far from the child as victim, whether of circumstance or because of their vulnerability. Such a perspective holds that children have the right to protection but also to be seen as protagonists in their own lives. In early years education the role of assessment changed so that far from being a body to be looked at and checked over, the child was seen as part of a strong narrative (Carr, 2001): their story was important and their role in the story was a positive one. Educators were urged not to look for what was wrong, to take a deficit view, but to look for what the child had to offer and to put forward an image of that child that was empowering and showed potential for further learning. It is this child that has the right to their records, to be consulted, and to be involved in decisions that affect their lives.

However, such archival autonomy requires the nurturing of recordkeeping literacy as a crucial enabler for children, young people and their adult selves to exercise agency in records' creation, management and use. Decision-making needs to be informed by appropriate understanding and awareness of the impacts records and recordkeeping can have on lives (Nicholls, 2018). In the out-of-home Care context, studies of recordkeeping literacy are vital to ensure meaningful participation across stakeholder communities in the formation, management and use of the Lifelong Living Archive. This is the first project in the world to explore this concept in the out-of-home Care context as a key to facilitating a child centred care model.

Social Work

While most extant child-protection IS will have been designed with input from the social-work sector as its primary user base, there is still a role for critical enquiry into accountable child-centred out-of-home Care. This social work perspective contributes detailed knowledge of systems, policies, and practices within out-of-home Care and Care-leaving. This knowledge is key in understanding how to most effectively operationalise the Lifelong Living Archive to allow children to access their life records from the date of entry into care, to leaving care, to any time in their adult life.

The Arts

One role that the arts plays in the design is to explore the relationship between creative arts and the carriage of embodied, situational, recorded and relational knowledge. How can the arts (as both practice and form) function as a system for preservation and movement of these varied kinds of knowledge, while also offering a framework for building human resilience and agency? In considering creative practice as a way of learning and being, the research draws on pedagogical thinking that explores how the arts can be more widely applied beyond the social fields of entertainment and leisure, and specifically seeks to extend this type of investigation to harness benefits of arts-informed and culturally relevant information science.

The theoretical underpinnings have a basis in archival scholarship, but also reflect influences from outside the information disciplines. Asserting a necessity to understand how the shifting complexities of personal affect and structural realities intersect with everyday practices of sharing space and exchanging ideas, this perspective draws on the concept of cultural citizenship as "a right to be different and to belong in a participatory democratic sense" (Rosaldo, 1994). In doing so, it seeks to counter deficit models by acknowledging the potentiality (and potency) of cultural capital, cultural resiliency, and rights-claiming agency as outcomes emergent from social injustice and marginalisation.

The focus of this perspective is on how these types of cultural practice intersect with recordkeeping literacy and archival power: the arts as a pedagogical space for multimodal and multidirectional exchange of recorded information and experiential affect; and a method for imagining and activating alternatives within everyday contexts. Our proposal is that testing technological applications and their wider systems environment against principles of imaginative agency brings a new perspective to evaluating the desirability, adaptability, and robustness of recordkeeping mechanisms for out of home Care, feeding into the project aims of ethical, equitable, child-focused design.

Law and Ethics

Child welfare policy in Australia is constitutionally a matter for each State and Territory and, over time, has developed a hybrid mix of programs run by government, churches, charities, even some private individuals and more recently commercial providers. Lacking effective coordination and chronically under-resourced, this legislative hotch-potch has created a fractured and fragmented records landscape (Bessant & Watts, 2016). Obviously, an important perspective for analysis is the juridical structures within which recordkeeping takes place. Such structures are deeply embedded and are difficult to change due to their entanglement with structures of societal power. Even the best recordkeeping system design can be thwarted by conflicting legal requirements. Understanding the foundations, reach, and limitation of (domestic and international) law as mandates for recordkeeping, the role of recordkeeping provenance in evidence, and the embodiment of rights in records are necessary for a full critical and sociomaterial treatment of recordkeeping systems.

Such legal frameworks are positioned at the intersection of ethical considerations including confidentiality, third-party privacy, age-appropriate disclosure, and human rights. The contested nature of records means that seemingly competing access rights may need to be negotiated between multiple participants (Department of Social Services, Commonwealth of Australia, 2015; Gilliland, 2013; Iacovino, 2015; Ross, McKemmish, & Faulkhead, 2006). Additionally, rights need to be tempered by the need for accountability for past actions. In relation to contested incidents — from minor disputes to international tribunals — rights in records must be granted for all parties engaged in accountability determination, including those bringing a complaint as well as any accused. Central to this perspective is the idea of stewardship with the recordkeeper as facilitator rather than a custodian or gatekeeper. Stewardship, with its twin goals of preservation and access that facilitate shared memory, treats archival material less as property and more as a jointly held asset.

One design-outcome of our project is a robust Rights Charter — a statement of rights that declares individual identity, memory, and accountability rights and maps them to specific recordkeeping rights in participation; access; privacy and safe recordkeeping; and proactive disclosure. First, this charter provides a justified basis for the development of features of the Lifelong Living Archive. Secondly, it could be used to influence changes to policy and practice throughout the Australian child-welfare sector. Such a statement draws on a variety of ethically-driven sources including human rights principles; existing charters of children's rights; legal instruments; policy and practice; Care-leaver, support services, and advocate experiences; and community expectations. It considers domestic and international literature, legal mechanisms and opinions in state, national and international law, policy documents, and practice guidelines in order to identify specific warrant for all of its elements.

CONCLUSION

The dangers imposed by improperly designed and implemented IS are demonstrably real. Nevertheless, the focus of the contemporary discourse, with its focus on data science will not address the root cause of these problems. While machine learning components may add complexity and additional opacity, the issues we have surfaced are equally unaddressed in conventional IS as they are in AI systems. Post-hoc audit and human-in-the-loop architectures are important but, in the absence of adequate design, are simply workarounds — albeit with the ability to highlight the weaponisation of IS after it has been deployed.

As our project is demonstrating, a better approach lies in the treatment of all IS as (potential) recordkeeping systems that may impact identity, memory, evidentiality, and accountability beyond the immediate transactional context. Analysis, design, development, and testing – as well as the configuration and conduct of the research or development project itself – needs to be conducted from a diachronic perspective; identifying the needs all stakeholders from a variety of disciplinary perspectives and their manifestation across space and through time. Tools such as the continuum models, explicit metadata, and understanding of information cultures from Recordkeeping Informatics can provide the basis of such analysis.

Similarly, close collaboration with transdisciplinary partners from the academy and across the community is crucial if their perspectives are to be accounted for. Note though, that this brings additional communication and logistical challenges beyond that of simply establishing a larger core design group. There are issues of language, of epistemology, and of viewpoints that may even be incommensurable. Time must be allocated and purposeful activities scheduled for the reconciliation of these and development of project norms. This means that IS design takes a somewhat different trajectory — in the research context this means more 'up-front' time in the conceptualisation phases of the project (Burstein, 2002).

Nonetheless, IS design requires a range of professional, disciplinary and community stakeholders to come together to gain deeper and better understanding of incredibly knotty problems and then to strive for new solutions, which transcend the current limits and boundaries of any particular stakeholder's knowledge and expertise. What emerges are ethical and human-centred initiatives in which a range of professional and lived expertise come together to re-imagine, re-work and re-think in order to collectively and collaboratively design, develop and implement new, holistic, solutions.

REFERENCES

Australia Parliament Senate Community Affairs References Committee (2004). *Forgotten Australians : A report on Australians who experienced institutional or out-of-home care as children*. Canberra: Community Affairs References Committee. Retrieved from http://www.aph.gov.au/Parliamentary_Business/Committees/Senate/Community_Affairs/Completed_inquiries/2004-07/inst_care/report/index

Bessant, J., & Watts, R. (2016). Children and the law: An historical overview. In L. Young, M. A. Kenny, & G. Monahan (Eds.), *Children and the Law in Australia* (pp. 1–30). Chatswood, New Auth Wales, Australia: Lexis Nexis.

Bone, J. (2005). An ethical journey: Rights, relationships and reflexivity. *Australian Journal of Early Childhood, 30*(1), 1-5.

Brownlee-Chapman, C., Chapman, R., Eardley, C., Forster, S., Green, V., Graham, H., ...Townson, L. (2017). Between speaking out in public and being person-centred: Collaboratively designing an inclusive archive of learning disability history. *International Journal of Heritage Studies*, 1–15. doi: 10.1080/13527258.2017.1378901

Burstein, F. (2002). System development in information systems research. In K. Williamson (Ed.), *Research Methods for Students and Professionals: Information Management and Systems* (pp. 147–158). Wagga Wagga, N.S.W.: Centre for Information Studies, Charles Sturt University.

Carr, M. (2001). Assessment in early childhood settings. Thousand Oaks, CA: Sage.

Cecez-Kecmanovic, D., Galliers, R. D., Henfridsson, O., Newell, S., & Vidgen, R. (2014). The sociomateriality of information systems: Current status, future directions. *MIS Quarterly*, *38*(3), 809–830.

Cifor, M., & Gilliland, A. (2016). Affect and the archive, archives and their affects: An introduction to the special issue, *16*(1), 1–6. doi: 10.1007/s10502-015-9263-3

Department of Education, Employment and Workplace Relations. (2009). *The Early years learning framework for Australia.* DEEWR. Retrieved from https://docs.education.gov.au/node/2632

Department of Families, Housing, Community Services and Indigenous Affairs. (2011). *An outline of National Standards for out-of-home care. Department of Social Services*. Retrieved from https://www.dss.gov.au/our-responsibilities/families-and-children/publications-articles/an-outline-of-national-standards-for-out-of-home-care-2011

Department of Social Services, Commonwealth of Australia. (2015). *Access to Records by Forgotten Australians and Former Child Migrants: Access Principles for Records Holders, Best Practice Guidelines in providing access to records*. Commonwealth Government. Retrieved from https://www.childabuseroyalcommission.gov.au/downloadfile.ashx?guid=5177243f-0484-48ab-9984-46a07e3e1f04&type=exhibit&filename=DHS.3148.001.0079&fileextension=pdf

Driedger, D. (1989). *The Last civil rights movement : Disabled peoples' international*. London: C. Hurst & Co.

d'Alessandro, B., O'Neil, C., & LaGatta, T. (2017). Conscientious Classification: A Data Scientist's Guide to Discrimination-Aware Classification. *Big Data*, *5*(2), 120–134. doi: 10.1089/big.2016.0048

Eubanks, V. (2007). Popular technology: Exploring inequality in the information economy. *Science and Public Policy*, *34*(2), 127–138.

Eubanks, V. (2018). *Automating inequality how high-tech tools profile, police, and punish the poor*. New York, NY: St. Martin's Press.

Evans, J., McKemmish, S., Daniels, E., & McCarthy, G. (2015). Self-determination and archival autonomy: Advocating activism. *Archival Science*, *15*(4), 337–368. doi: 10.1007/s10502-015-9244-6

Evans, J., McKemmish, S., & Rolan, G. (2017). Critical Approaches to Archiving and Recordkeeping in the Continuum. *Journal of Critical Library and Information Studies*, *1*(2). Retrieved from http://libraryjuicepress.com/journals/index.php/jclis/article/view/35/29

Find and Connect Web Resource Project Team. (2011). Find and Connect. Retrieved from http://www.findandconnect.gov.au/

Gangadharan, S. P., Eubanks, V., & Barocas, S. (2014). Data and discrimination: Collected essays. *Open Technology*.

Giddens, A. (1984). *The constitution of society : outline of the theory of structuration*. Berkeley: University of California Press.

Gilliland, A. (2013). VIA Framework, Voice, Identity, Activism: A Community-centric Framework for Approaching Archives and Recordkeeping. In *Conceptualizing Twenty-First Century Archives*. Chicago: Society of American Archivists.

Gilliland, A., & McKemmish, S. (2012). Recordkeeping Metadata, the Archival Multiverse, and Societal Grand Challenges. Presented at the DC-2012, Kuching, Sarawak, Malaysia. Retrieved from http://dcevents.dublincore.org/IntConf/dc-2012/paper/viewPaper/108

Hart, D. N., (1994). *Information wards : A new conceptual tool for modelling the political implications of information systems development*. Canberra: Dept. of Computer Science, Australian Defence Force Academy.

Hart, D. N., & Warne, L., (2007). Poles Apart or Bedfellows? Re-conceptualising Information Systems Success and Failure. In D. N. Hart & S. D. Gregor (Eds.), *Information systems foundations: Theory, representation and reality* (p. 153). Canberra: ANU E Press.

Iacovino, L. (2015). Shaping and reshaping cultural identity and memory: Maximising human rights through a participatory archive. *Archives and Manuscripts*, *43*(1), 29–41. doi: 10.1080/01576895.2014.961491

Introna, L. D. (2007). Maintaining the reversibility of foldings: Making the ethics (politics) of information technology visible. *Ethics and Information Technology*, *9*(1), 11–25.

Lawrence, R. J. (2010). Deciphering interdisciplinary and transdisciplinary contributions. *Transdisciplinary Journal of Engineering & Science*, *1*(1), 125–130.

Leonardi, P. M. (2012). Materiality, sociomateriality, and socio-technical systems: What do these terms mean? How are they related? Do we need them? In P. M. Leonardi, B. Nardi, & J. Kallinikos (Eds.), *Materiality and organizing: Social interaction in a technological world* (pp. 25–48). Oxford: Oxford University Press.

Leonardi, P. M. (2013). Theoretical foundations for the study of sociomateriality. *Information and Organization*, *23*(2), 59–76.

Logan, W. S., & Reeves, K. (2011). *Places of pain and shame: Dealing with "difficult heritage"*. London; New York: Routledge, Taylor & Francis Group.

Lynch, C. (2017). Stewardship in the "Age of Algorithms". *First Monday*, *22*(12).

McKemmish, S. (2001). Placing records continuum theory and practice. *Archival Science, 1*(4), 333–359.

McKemmish, S., Burstein, F., Manaszewicz, R., Fisher, J., & Evans, J. (2012). Inclusive Research Design: Unravelling the double hermeneutic spiral. *Information, Communication & Society*, *15*(7), 1106–1135. doi: 10.1080/1369118X.2012.707225

McKemmish, S., Upward, F., & Reed, B. (2010). Records continuum model. In M. Bates & M. Maack (Eds.), *Encyclopedia of Library and Information Sciences* (pp. 4447–4459). Boca Raton, FL, USA: CRC Press.

Mendes, P. (2009). Improving outcomes for teenage pregnancy and early parenthood for young people in out-of-home care: A review of the literature. *Youth Studies Australia*, *28*(4), 11.

Mendes, P., & Snow, P. (2016). *Young People Transitioning from Out-of-Home Care*. London: Palgrave Macmillan UK.Munro, E. (2011). *The Munro review of child protection: Final report, a child-centred system* (Vol. 8062). Department of Education.

Nardi, B., & O'Day, V. (1999). Information Ecologies: Using Technology with Heart : Chapter Four: Information Ecologies. *First Monday*, *4*(5). Retrieved from http://www.firstmonday.dk/ojs/index.php/fm/article/view/672

Nicholls, C. (2018). Making the Case for Recordkeeping Literacy: A Narrative Approach, *Archives and Manuscripts,* **1-15**. doi: 10.1080/01576895.2018.1455598

Orlikowski, W. J., & Scott, S. V. (2008). Sociomateriality - challenging the separation of technology, work and organization. *The Academy of Management Annals*, *2*(1), 433–474.

O'Neill, C., Selakovic, V., & Tropea, R. (2012). Access to records for people who were in out-of-home care: Moving beyond 'third dimension'archival practice. *Archives and Manuscripts*, *40*(1), 29–41. doi: 10.1080/01576895.2012.668841

O'Reilly, T. (2005). What Is Web 2.0? Design Patterns and Business Models for the Next Generation of Software. Retrieved from http://oreilly.com/web2/archive/what-is-web-20.html.

Redden, J., & Brand, J. (2017, December). Data Harm Record. *Data Justice Lab*. Retrieved from https://datajusticelab.org/data-harm-record/

Rolan, G. (2016). Agency in the archive: a model for participatory recordkeeping. *Archival Science*, *17*(3), 195–225. doi: 10.1007/s10502-016-9267-7

Rosaldo, R. (1994). Cultural citizenship and educational democracy. *Cultural Anthropology*, *9*(3), 402–411.

Ross, F., McKemmish, S., & Faulkhead, S. (2006). Indigenous knowledge and the archives: Designing trusted archival systems for Koorie communities. *Archives and Manuscripts*, *34*(2), 112–151.

Royal Commission into Institutional Responses to Child Sexual Abuse. (2016). *Consultation Paper Records and recordkeeping practices,* (p. 66). Sydney: Commonwealth of Australia. Retrieved from https://www.childabuseroyalcommission.gov.au/media-centre/media-releases/2016-08/consultation-paper-on-records-and-recordkeeping-re

Royal Commission into Institutional Responses to Child Sexual Abuse. (2017, May). Final report. *Royal Commission into Institutional Responses to Child Sexual Abuse*. Text. Retrieved from https://www.childabuseroyalcommission.gov.au/final-report

Ryan, S. (2009). *Final Report of the Commission to Inquire into Child Abuse*. Commission to Inquire into Child Abuse. Retrieved from http://www.childabusecommission.ie/publications/index.html

Sexton, A, & Sen, D., (2017), More voice, less ventriloquism– exploring the relational dynamics in a participatory archive of mental health recovery, *International Journal of Heritage Studies*, DOI: 10.1080/13527258.2017.1339109

Scott, D. (2006). Sowing the Seeds of Innovation in Child Protection. In. Wellington, New Zealand. doi: 10.1.1.121.4966

Svahn, F., Henfridsson, O., & Yoo, Y. (2009). A threesome dance of agency: Mangling the sociomateriality of technological regimes in digital innovation. In *ICIS 2009 Proceedings*.

Swain, S. (2014). *History of Australian inquiries reviewing institutions providing care for children*. Retrieved from https://www.childabuseroyalcommission.gov.au/getattachment/8aafa21e-36e0-41c2-8760-b17662fb774f/History-of-Australian-inquiries-reviewing-institut

Truth and Reconciliation Commission of Canada. (2015). *Final report of the Truth and Reconciliation Commission of Canada. honouring the truth, reconciling for the future. Volume one, Volume one,*

Upward, F., Reed, B., Oliver, G., & Evans, J. (2018). *Recordkeeping informatics for a networked age*. Clayton, Victoria: Monash University Publishing.

Victorian Auditor-General. (2014). *Residential care services for children*. Melbourne: Victorian Government. Retrieved from https://www.audit.vic.gov.au/sites/default/files/20140326-Residential-Care.pdf

Wand, Y., & Weber, R. (1995). On the deep structure of information systems. *Information Systems Journal*, *5*(3), 203–223.

Wilson, J., & Golding, F. (2016). Latent scrutiny: Personal archives as perpetual mementos of the official gaze. *Archival Science*, *16*(1), 93–109. doi: 10.1007/s10502-015-9255-3

Understanding the Twitter Usage of Humanities and Social Sciences Academic Journals

Aravind Sesagiri Raamkumar
Nanyang Technological University, Singapore.
aravind002@ntu.edu.sg

Mojisola Erdt
Nanyang Technological University, Singapore.
mojisola.erdt@ntu.edu.sg

Harsha Vijayakumar
Nanyang Technological University, Singapore.
hvijayakumar@ntu.edu.sg

Edie Rasmussen
University of British Columbia, Canada.
edie.rasmussen@ubc.ca

Yin-Leng Theng
Nanyang Technological University, Singapore.
tyltheng@ntu.edu.sg

ABSTRACT
Scholarly communication has the scope to transcend the limitations of the physical world through social media's extended coverage and shortened information paths. Accordingly, publishers have created profiles for their journals in Twitter to promote their publications and to initiate discussions with public. This paper investigates the Twitter presence of humanities and social sciences (HSS) journal titles obtained from mainstream citation indices, by analysing the interaction and communication patterns. This study utilizes webometric data collection, descriptive analysis, and social network analysis. Findings indicate that the presence of HSS journals in Twitter across disciplines is not yet substantial. Sharing of general websites appears to be the key activity performed by HSS journals in Twitter. Among them, web content from news portals and magazines are highly disseminated. Sharing of research articles and retweeting was not majorly observed. Inter-journal communication is apparent within the same citation index, but it is very minimal with journals from the other index. However, there seems to be an effort to broaden communication beyond the research community, reaching out to connect with the public.

KEYWORDS
Social media, twitter, microblogs, journals, social network analysis, humanities, social sciences.

INTRODUCTION
Twitter can be considered as one of the contemporary and popular online social networks. As a micro-blogging system, it is relevant in both private and public communication spheres. Twitter is used for purposes such as updating current status, initiating conversations, endorsing tweet content, promoting products and even for spamming (Benevenuto, Magno, Rodrigues, & Almeida, 2010). The success of a social media platform lies in its ability to attract people from different domains and geographic locations Academicians and researchers from the scientific community are also interested in social media due to its various benefits (Sugimoto, Work, Larivière, & Haustein, 2016). Scholars have cited information dissemination as a major benefit of using Twitter (Letierce, Passant, Breslin, & Decker, 2010). It has been observed that tweets can help in predicting citations to a certain extent (Eysenbach, 2011). However, other studies advise analysts to exercise caution when using simplistic metrics such as the tweet count to evaluate research outputs (Robinson-Garcia, Costas, Isett, Melkers, & Hicks, 2017).

Social media has become a valuable marketing tool for publishers to promote research articles (Thelwall, Haustein, Larivière, & Sugimoto, 2013). Publication venues such as journals and conferences use Twitter for connecting with researchers. Studies have been conducted to investigate the usage of Twitter by researchers (Holmberg & Thelwall, 2014), conferences (Lee, Yoon, Smith, Park, & Park, 2017; Parra et al., 2016) and also journals from specific disciplines (Cosco, 2015; Kelly et al., 2016; Nason et al., 2015). It has been observed that journals with social media profiles (for e.g., Twitter) had higher academic metrics (Wong, Piraquive, & Levi, 2018). However, there has been a distinct lack of studies focusing on the usage of Twitter by journals from a broader outlook i.e., journals from different disciplines.

This study investigates the Twitter usage of humanities and social sciences (HSS) journals. In this study, we have concentrated on the soft sciences with a plan to compare the findings with the traditional science and engineering disciplines in future studies. The required data for this study was extracted from the Master Journal List (MJL)[1] and Twitter. Since the overall objective is

[1] Master Journal List of Clarivate Analytics http://ip-science.thomsonreuters.com/mjl/

to understand the usage dynamics of HSS journals in Twitter from a broader perspective, the following exploratory research questions are investigated in the study.

- **RQ1**: What types of actions on Twitter are prevalent among HSS journals?
- **RQ2**: What is the nature of Twitter conversations among the HSS journals?
- **RQ3**: What is the prevalent network structure in Twitter communication graphs of the HSS journals?
- **RQ4**: Which Twitter accounts act as hubs and authorities in the communication graphs of the HSS journals?

RELATED WORK

Several studies have investigated the social media usage of journals. Twitter is an important platform for journals as studies have shown that journals with Twitter accounts have higher number of tweets and citations of their articles, when compared with other journals (Ortega, 2017). Other studies have focused on the Twitter usage of journals from specific disciplines. Findings from these studies show that the amount of Twitter accounts varies a lot across different research areas. About 14% of dermatology journals (Amir et al., 2014), 25% of urological journals (Nason et al., 2015), 28% of radiology journals (Kelly et al., 2016), and 28% of medical journals (Cosco, 2015) were found to have Twitter accounts, compared to 44% of medical journals (Kamel Boulos & Anderson, 2014). Also, 17% of the top 10 2010 JIF journals from multiple disciplines (Kortelainen & Katvala, 2012), were found to have Twitter accounts. Some studies have focussed on the correlation of Twitter and bibliometrics indicators. Even though there was no strong relation with the Journal Impact Factor (JIF) for urological journals (Nason et al., 2015), the authors found the Twitter presence of journals to be positively associated with the JIF in radiology journals (Kelly et al., 2016). For medical journals, it was found that journals with high JIF had a greater number of Twitter followers than others (Cosco, 2015). Besides maintaining accounts, which are often used to share news and articles, some journals have started to ask authors to create Wikipedia articles (Butler, 2008; Maskalyk, 2014), and to provide so-called tweetable abstracts that journals can use to promote papers (Darling, Shiffman, Côté, & Drew, 2013). Some journals have created online journal clubs to encourage community discussions about articles (Chan et al., 2015). Most use Twitter (Chan et al., 2015; Gardhouse, Budd, Yang, & Wong, 2017; Leung, Siassakos, & Khan, 2015; Mehta & Flickinger, 2014; Thangasamy et al., 2014), but some use other social media tools such as blogs, live videos, and podcasts (Rezaie, Swaminathan, Chan, Shaikh, & Lin, 2015; Thoma, Rolston, & Lin, 2014).

Apart from journals, studies have been conducted on the Twitter usage of users at academic conferences as the main focus area. With more user participation in a Twitter network, the network structure might show a tendency to change. However, a 'tight crowd' network was consistently present in the case of the Association of Internet Researchers (AoIR) conference over the years (Lee et al., 2017). Also, the authoritative Twitter accounts did not change much even though there were changes in the conference theme every year. In a much larger study conducted with tweets from 16 computer science conferences (Parra et al., 2016), authors found that users were increasingly engaged in retweeting and sharing of web links over time. There was a drop in conversational tweets between users through the years, thereby changing the network structure to more of a broadcasting network. From a study of the tweeting behaviour of participants of the 2013 International Congress for Conservation Biology (ICCB) (Bombaci et al., 2016), it was found that the intended audiences, such as policy makers, government and non-government organizations, were rarely reached by tweets. Thus, it is questionable if tweeting at conferences is an effective strategy for promoting research to a wider audience other than the conference's research community.

Based on our literature review and to the best of our knowledge, there have been no studies that report about the Twitter usage and communication network of HSS journals across multiple disciplines. The current study attempts to address this gap.

METHODOLOGY

Raw Data Extraction

The Master Journal List (MJL) was selected as the main source to obtain journal titles for this study. Specifically, journal titles were extracted from the two major HSS indices – Arts & Humanities Citation (AHCI) and Social Science Citation Index (SSCI). The study was conducted on a corpus of 321,094 tweets extracted from 4,999 journal accounts of the two citation indices. Data collection details are provided below. MJL is generally acknowledged as one of the main sources for journal titles. Journals are included in MJL after a quality check process, thereby ensuring compliance to scientific standards. Hence, MJL can be considered as an authoritative source for journal titles across disciplines. Humanities and social sciences journals have been traditionally indexed under two indices in MJL, namely Arts & Humanities Citation (AHCI) and Social Science Citation Index (SSCI). All journal titles from the two indices AHCI and SSCI were manually downloaded. In total, 4,999 relevant journals were retrieved, including 1,769 journals from AHCI and 3,230 journals from SSCI. To examine whether the extracted journals have their own Twitter accounts, we searched for their titles using the search option in Twitter. After collecting the Twitter accounts of the journals in August 2016, we extracted the tweets from the Twitter accounts, using the Twitter API. A maximum of 3,000 tweets were extracted for each Twitter account due to the restrictions in the basic Twitter API service. A total of 321,094 tweets were extracted for the 4,999 journals.

Preparation of Data for Study

Tweets with URLs

The tweets which contained links to research articles were identified using a two-step process. First, the tweets containing Uniform Resource Locators (URLs) were filtered. From this filtered list, further filtering was carried out based on the presence of any one of the keywords 'doi', 'article' and 'issue' to identify the candidate tweets.

Twitter Mentions and Conversations

In Twitter terminology, *mention* is an instance of tagging/mentioning another Twitter user in a tweet. For example, if *user A* wants to start a discussion with *user B*, the "@" is used to tag *user B* in the tweet. It should also be noted that when a user retweets the tweet of another user, Twitter automatically adds the characters "RT @user_account" in the tweet. Hence, mentions are naturally present in retweets. From the full extract of tweets, only the tweets containing mentions were first filtered. From the filtered tweets, the Twitter account name (Twitter handle) and the mentions data were extracted. A combination of Twitter account name and mention is usually referred to as a *conversation*. A single tweet could contain multiple mentions.

Communication Graphs

The network analysis tool Gephi was used for addressing RQ3 and RQ4. The community detection algorithm ForeAtlas2 (Jacomy, Venturini, Heymann, & Bastian, 2014) was used in Gephi to align the communities in the graphs. The nodes in the graphs were sized based on their betweenness centrality (Freeman, 1977) values. Betweenness centrality is a measure of the centrality of nodes in a graph. Communication graphs were generated with the conversations data. In these graphs, the source node is the Twitter user account while the target node is the mention. This type of graph is referred to as a *directed graph* since the direction of communication is from the source to the target. Two separate directed graphs were generated using the Gephi tool. After the data was loaded in Gephi, we filtered out the nodes which had a degree of 1 to avoid sparsity in the graphs.

RESULTS

Presence and Activities of HSS Journals in Twitter

In Table 1, statistics related to the journals presence in Twitter are listed. Specifically, counts and percentages of journals and their tweets, retweets, mentions and presence of both general URLs & research article URLs in tweets. The percentage of journals with Twitter accounts is around 7% to 9% across the two indices with AHCI having the higher percentage of journals with Twitter accounts (8.99%). The low percentages indicate that a clear majority of HSS journals are yet to establish a presence in Twitter. Secondly, the presence is also affected by publication houses which are based out of countries where Twitter is banned. Retweeting is considered as one of the major activities in Twitter (Yang et al., 2010). Journals from SSCI had the highest number of retweets (23.39% of total) closely followed by AHCI (22.01% of total). Apart from retweeting, URL sharing is also one of the major activities of Twitter users (Java, Song, Finin, & Tseng, 2007). SSCI journals had a higher number of tweets with URLs (89.89% of total), followed by AHCI (86.76% of total). The presence of URLs in a tweet indicates that the journal is posting the URL of a research paper or website (e.g. news articles, blogs). The percentage of tweets containing links to research articles is not substantial (less than 15% of total), with SSCI (11.03% of total) having a better percentage than AHCI (4.98%).

Entity	AHCI (*n*)	SSCI (*n*)
Journals [A]	1769	3230
Journals with Twitter Accounts [B]	159 (8.99% of A)	249 (7.71% of A)
Extracted Tweets [C]	145419	175675
Journals with Public Tweets [D]	159 (100% of B)	249 (100% of B)
Retweets (RTs) [E]	32002 (22.01% of C)	41096 (23.39% of C)
Tweets containing URLs [F]	126172 (86.76% of C)	157918 (89.89% of C)
Tweets containing Links to Articles [G]	7240 (4.98% of C)	19370 (11.03% of C)

Table 1. Journals' Twitter Presence and Activities Statistics

Twitter Conversations

In Table 2, statistics related to the conversations of HSS journals in Twitter are listed for the two indices. The number of conversations was the highest for SSCI (*n*=121,099) corresponding to the higher number of tweets (refer Table 1). Since only the tweets containing mentions data were considered, some of the journals had zero conversations even though tweets could have been posted by these accounts. For instance, out of the 249 journal accounts with tweets in SSCI (refer Table 1), 242 accounts had mentions data.

Entity	AHCI (*n*)	SSCI (*n*)
Total conversations [A]	103181	121099
Unique journal accounts initiating conversations [B]	152	242
Unique mentions [C]	31040	32819
Conversations where mentions are AHCI journals [D]	13812 (13.39% of A)	70 (0.06% of A)
Conversations where mentions are SSCI journals [E]	63 (0.06% of A)	16048 (13.25% of A)
Unique AHCI journal mentions [F]	142 (93.42% of B)	18
Unique SSCI journal mentions [G]	18	230 (95.04% of B)
Conversations where account and mention are same [H]	13015 (12.61% of A)	14398 (11.89% of A)

Table 2. Journals' Twitter Conversations Statistics

In a conversation, the mention could be any Twitter account. To ascertain the level of interaction with other journals, we identified the mentions which were journal accounts. For journals within the same index, AHCI and SSCI conversations had similar percentages (13.39% for AHCI, 13.25% for SSCI). This finding indicates that journals do not seem to be interacting with other journals in Twitter to any great degree. In fact, interactions with journals from other index is very low with percentages below 1%.

However, most of the journals within the indices are involved in the conversations. For instance, 95.04% of all SSCI journals and 93.42% of all AHCI journals are presented as mentions in the conversations respectively. To investigate further, we identified the conversations where the user account and mentions were the same. We found that these types of conversations were around the same range for both indices (11.89% for SSCI and 12.61% for AHICI of the total conversations respectively). This finding is quite understandable since there are not many benefits for journals to tag their own Twitter account in their tweets

Communication Graphs

Statistics of the two communication graphs generated for AHCI and SSCI journals Twitter conversations are listed in Table 3. The node count in Table 3 corresponds to the number of conversations for each index in Table 2. SSCI (*n*=4,656) and AHCI (*n*=4,280) had similar number of nodes. In the case of average degree of a node, AHCI (*a*=2.84) and SSCI (*a*=3.08) were relatively close to each other. This finding indicates that even though the number of nodes is lower in the graph, each node has more connections with other nodes in the graph. Modularity (*m*) in a graph is an indication of how well a graph decomposes into modular communities. A high modularity hints at a complex internal structure with multiple sub-graphs (communities) densely connected to each other in the graph. The modularity value should be analysed together with the number of resultant communities (*c*) and total number of nodes in the graph (*n*). The modularity value is almost the same for the two graphs (*m*=0.53 for AHCI and *m*=0.52 for SSCI). Resultantly, the number of communities is also comparable for AHCI (*c*=11) and SSCI (*c*=13).

Metric	AHCI	SSCI
Number of Nodes (*n*)	4,280	4,656
Number of Edges (*e*)	12,194	14,353
Average Degree (*a*)	2.84	3.08
Modularity (*m*)	0.53	0.52
Number of Communities (*c*)	11	13

Table 3. Journals' Communication Graphs Statistics

The two graphs generated for the citation indices are illustrated in Figures 1 and 2. The node colour indicates the community to which they belong. The nodes size has been adjusted based on the betweenness centrality values of the nodes. We have added representative labels for the different communities based on the topic commonality in the profile descriptions provided in the Twitter accounts (journals). As an aid to interpret the graphs, we identified the top 20 nodes with the highest in-degrees and out-degrees respectively in Tables 4 and 5. Out-degree of a node is the number of edges where the node is the source node while in-degree is the number of edges where the node is a target node. Naturally, the nodes with the highest out-degrees will be the journal Twitter accounts while the nodes with the highest in-degrees could be of any type. Accordingly, we have listed the journal titles for the nodes with the highest out-degrees while we have identified type of the nodes with highest in-degrees. Even though out-degree is an indication of the journal's outreach in Twitter, it is important to recognize the popularity of the journals within the traditional citation network. This can be achieved by comparing the degree values with the journal impact factor (JIF). We have not listed the JIF values in these tables since interpreting JIF with different disciplines is not meaningful. However, we have listed the quartiles data of the journals based on the JIF. For example, if the journal belongs to the first quartile, it is considered to be among the top 25 percentile of journals in that discipline. Therefore, the prestige of journals can be ascertained with the JIF quartiles data. For AHCI journals, JIF data is not provided in the MJL, hence JIF quartiles column is not applicable for Table 4.

AHCI Graph

In Figure 1, the AHCI graph is represented by multiple topics including philosophy, history, arts, architecture, film and literature. Most of the Twitter accounts in this graph are related to the literature topic. Also, the communities adjacent to each other seem to be related - (1) architecture & art and (2) philosophy & history. This graph can be classified as a *community clusters* graph since there are multiple communities with minimal interspersed nodes. From Table 4, we observe that magazines and news portals are most frequently referenced as mentions in AHCI Twitter conversations. The top two nodes are the news portals Nytimes and Guardian, while six other nodes are of the magazine type in the top 20. However, these magazines are all within the scope of AHCI topics unlike the news portals which cover general topics. Libraries (@nypl, @ElectricLit) and museums (@metmuseum, @MusuemModernArt) are also present, thereby indicating substantial interactions with accounts outside academia. Paris Review is the only journal with a high in-degree value in this list and this journal's node can be clearly identified as the biggest node in Figure 1 due to its high betweeness centrality. The top 20 in-degree nodes indicate that AHCI journals tend to interact most with news and magazine-related Twitter accounts. The top 20 out-degrees nodes comprise of mostly literature and arts journals.

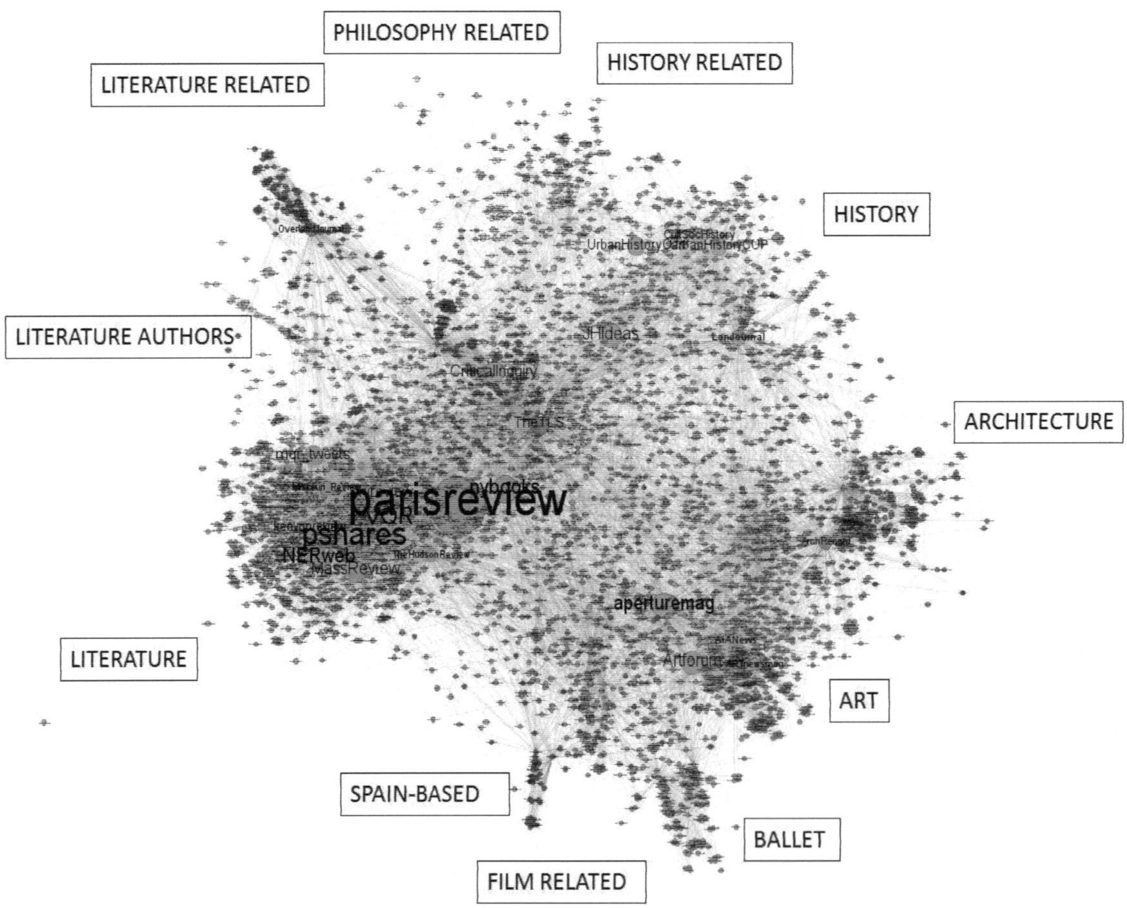

Figure 1. AHCI Graph

Top 20 Nodes with Highest In-degree			Top 20 Nodes with Highest Out-degree		
Twitter Account	Account Type	*in**	Twitter Account	Journal Full Name	*out*+
Nytimes	News	39	VQR	Virginia Quarterly Review	549
Guardian	News	30	AiANews	Art In America	468
NewYorker	Magazine	29	Missouri_Review	Missouri Review	439
Parisreview	Journal	23	Wasafiri1	Wasafiri	422
Nypl	Library	22	Artforum	Artforum International	391
Sharethis	Social Bookmarking	22	kenyonreview	Kenyon Review	366
LAReviewofBooks	Magazine	21	TheHudsonReview	Hudson Review	356
Metmuseum	Museum	20	ArchRecord	Architectural Record	346
Tate	Art Gallery	19	NERweb	New England Review-Middlebury Series	269
LRB	Magazine	18	LonJournal	London Journal	263
PoetryFound	Magazine	18	BurlingtonMag	Burlington Magazine	258
nybooks	Magazine	18	AD_books	Architectural Design	239
TheAtlantic	Magazine	18	nybooks	New York Review Of Books	232
ElectricLit	Digital Library	18	TheTLS	Tls-The Times Literary Supplement	231
MuseumModernArt	Museum	16	TheAmScho	American Scholar	225
OUPAcademic	Publisher	16	JCLJournal	Journal Of Commonwealth Literature	225
YouTube	Video Sharing	16	Apollo_magazine	Apollo-The International Art Magazine	205
gmailcom	Email	16	NOReview	New Orleans Review	195
PublishersWkly	Magazine	15	MassReview	Massachusetts Review	192
thelithub	Not Active	15	ARTnewsmag	Artnews	190

*Note: in** refers to in-degree value; *out*+ refers to out-degree value

Table 4. Top 20 In-degree and Out-degree Nodes in AHCI Graph

SSCI Graph

The SSCI graph, which has the highest number of communities (*c*=13) among the two graphs (refer Table 3), is illustrated in Figure 2. Interestingly, most of the communities are of different topics although the adjacent communities are related, similar to AHCI. The community related to feminism/women's studies has the largest nodes (@FeministReview, @AFSJournal) and this community is spread across other communities related to psychology and education. Similar to AHCI, this graph can also be classified as a *community clusters* graph since there are multiple communities and minimal interspersed nodes even though the feminism community is an exception.

Among the top 20 nodes with highest in-degrees, news portals (e.g., @nytimes, @washington) and magazines (e.g., @TheEconomist, @TheAtlantic) have a significant presence as already seen with AHCI. Unlike AHCI, news portals' (*n*=7) presence is more than magazines (*n*=4). Also, the magazines are mainstream magazines and not from academic publishers. Only two journals (@TheSocReview, @SAGEsociology) are present in this top 20 in-degree nodes list. The journals in the top 20 nodes with highest out-degrees are spread across different disciplines. From the JIF quartiles data, it can be ascertained that only three journals (@AmJNurs, @ AmEthno, @ASQJournal) are from the first quartile. There are more second quartile (*n*=7), third quartile (*n*=6) and fourth quartile (*n*=4) journals in this list. Therefore, the outreach is performed by journals from all tiers. Also, there is no overlap among the journals in the in-degree and out-degree list.

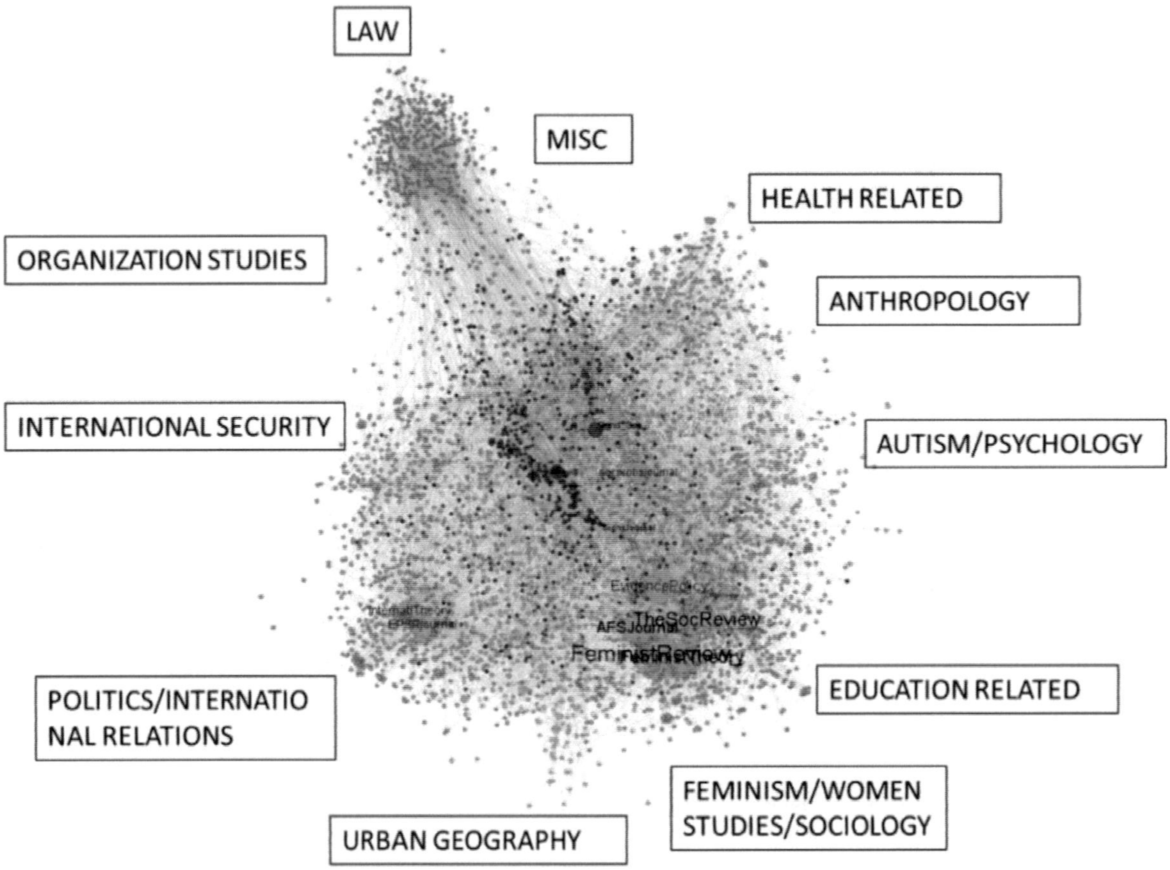

Figure 2. SSCI Graph

Top 20 Nodes with Highest In-degree			Top 20 Nodes with Highest Out-degree			
Twitter Account	Account Type	*in**	Twitter Account	Corresponding Journal Title	*out*+	JQ^
nytimes	News	67	InternatlTheory	International Theory	338	3
guardian	News	60	AFSJournal	Australian Feminist Studies	336	3
washingtonpost	News	46	AmJNurs	American Journal Of Nursing	277	1
TheEconomist	Magazine	41	EPSRjournal	European Political Science Review	268	2
TheAtlantic	Magazine	37	po_qu	Political Quarterly	260	4
WSJ	News	34	EvidencePolicy	Evidence & Policy	255	2
raulpacheco	Researcher	27	BulletinAtomic	Bulletin Of The Atomic Scientists	253	4
chronicle	News	27	terpolv	Terrorism And Political Violence	251	2
sharethis	Social Bookmarking	25	BASeditors	Business & Society	242	2
NPR	Media Organization	23	AmEthno	American Ethnologist	242	1
NewYorker	Magazine	23	govandopp	Government And Opposition	215	3
HuffingtonPost	News	23	ERSjournal	Ethnic And Racial Studies	211	2
TheSocReview	Journal	23	psychmag	Psychologist	208	4
SAGEsociology	Journal	23	CMPjournal	Culture Medicine And Psychiatry	195	3
timeshighered	Magazine	23	LAPerspectives	Latin American Perspectives	186	3
YouTube	Video Sharing	22	mgmt_learning	Management Learning	185	2
TIME	Magazine	22	hhrjournal	Health And Human Rights	173	3
Slate	Magazine	22	Editor_IES	Irish Educational Studies	166	4
wordpressdotcom	Content Management	21	socprobsjournal	Social Problems	162	2
ConversationUK	News	21	ASQJournal	Administrative Science Quarterly	154	1

*Note: in** refers to in-degree value; *out*+ refers to out-degree value; JQ^ refers to JIF quartile

Table 5. Top 20 In-degree and Out-degree Nodes in SSCI Graph

DISCUSSION

The presence of academic journals in Twitter is not yet substantial with AHCI having a slightly larger presence than SSCI journals. There is not much difference between the indices in terms of having a presence in Twitter. As Twitter's usage and popularity increases, more journals are expected to join the social media platform. However, the participation of journals in social media might be constrained by monetary and manpower availability factors. For the journals in this study, the retweeting frequency does not seem to exceed the general statistics reported in earlier studies (Holmberg & Thelwall, 2014) with SSCI journals having the highest percentage (23.39% of total tweets) of the two indices. In terms of URL sharing in tweets, journals exceed the sharing percentage from earlier studies (Raamkumar, Pang, & Foo, 2016). In fact, 89.89% of SSCI journals' tweets contain URLs. Even though URLs were found in most of the tweets, the percentage of tweets containing links to research articles was found to be low with AHCI being the lowest (4.98% of total tweets). The main reason could be the limited number of articles published per journal issue. For instance, most journals post a new issue every quarter and the new issue might comprise of eight to ten articles. Hence, the tweet count in such cases would obviously appear very small when compared to the total count of tweets.

In Twitter, there has been an apparent lack of interpersonal communication due to the predominance of retweeting and URL sharing by users (Parra et al., 2016). Therefore, in this context, understanding the volume of interpersonal communication is important for journals. This analysis was performed by extracting the mentions data from the tweets. After filtering out the retweets in the extract, it was found that AHCI tweets contained mentions in 22% of their total tweets. When the analysis is extended to composition of the conversations, there are new insights gained from the data (refer to Table 2). In the mentions data, the accounts which are journals were identified so that the extent of inter-journal communication could be ascertained. SSCI mentions had the highest percentage of references to SSCI journals themselves at 13.25% of the total conversations. In fact, SSCI and AHCI are closer in this aspect. This indicates that the journals from these indices are communicating more with non-academic Twitter accounts than HSS journal accounts. At a consolidated level, we found a reasonable percentage of tweets containing mentions data; however, most of the mentions were not academic HSS journal accounts. This clearly shows that inter-journal communication in Twitter is not substantial across the two indices.

AHCI and SSCI mentions graph structure largely resemble a *community clusters* network where there are multiple communities with dense intercommunication. There were a few exceptional cases such as the feminism community in SSCI which had nodes spread across a few other communities. Authoritative nodes in the mentions graphs are the Twitter accounts which are centripetal in nature i.e., most of the conversations are directed towards these nodes. After classifying the node type in the top 20 nodes with the highest in-degrees, it was evident that news portals such as the New York Times and Guardian along with magazines such as the NewYorker and The Atlantic were the most authoritative Twitter accounts in the two graphs. This finding underlines the influence of these sources on HSS academic journals. The presence of YouTube as an authoritative source was not surprising due to the abundance of educational/informational videos hosted by the service. Subject-specific magazines such as the New Scientist and The Economist were also prevalent in the top 20 in-degree nodes list of the two indices respectively. The minimal presence of journals in the list of authoritative nodes was a surprising finding. AHCI and SSCI had just a total of three journals combined. This finding not only shows that there are very few journals in the authoritative nodes list of the indices but also there seems to be a conscious effort among journals to propagate tweets of non-academic sources. The level of outreach was ascertained from the top 20 out-degrees nodes in the mentions graphs. These nodes are centrifugal in nature and hence, they are referred as hubs. In these top 20 lists, AHCI and SSCI had journals from different disciplines. On the question of ascertaining whether the top journals in Twitter were also top journals in the citation network, SSCI had journals from all four JIF quartiles in the top 20 list.

There are a few limitations in this study. By considering journals exclusively from MJL, we might be missing some other important journals which are indexed elsewhere. By the end of 2017, Twitter increased the character count in tweets to 280 from the earlier 140 characters. Hence, users can post more descriptive content and tag more users in their tweets. Therefore, this user-interface (UI) level change could possibly alter the usage dynamics of Twitter users.

CONCLUSION

In this paper, our goal was to understand the Twitter usage dynamics of HSS journals sourced from the citation indices in MJL. Using a corpus of 321,094 tweets which were extracted for the 4,999 journal accounts, analysis was performed at activity, tweet composition and structural levels. The tweets of the journals from AHCI and SSCI were analysed separately. Results show that URL sharing was a major activity performed by academic journals. HSS journals seem to focus more on initiating conversations with other Twitter accounts, although most were of a non-academic nature. Inter-journal communication seemed to be largely restricted to the journals within the same index. Tweets from public news portals and magazines were heavily disseminated by journal accounts, thereby identifying non-academic sources as the authoritative sources in the communication graphs of the two indices. Among the journals that initiate conversations, HSS journals irrespective of their standing in the citation network, are involved in Twitter outreach. In future studies, we plan to conduct in-depth investigations on whether the activities performed by HSS journals in Twitter lead to increased citations for constituent research articles. In addition, we plan to conduct similar analysis on Science Citation Index Expanded (SCIE) journals to compare the findings with this study. We hope that this study's findings are of value to publishers, researchers and social media campaign managers, who are responsible for the marketing, branding, and promotion of a journal's services on Twitter.

ACKNOWLEDGMENTS

The research project "Altmetrics: Rethinking and Exploring New Ways Of Measuring Research" was supported by the National Research Foundation, Prime Minister's Office, Singapore under its Science of Research, Innovation and Enterprise programme (SRIE Award No. NRF2014-NRF-SRIE001-019).

REFERENCES

Amir, M., Sampson, B. P., Endly, D., Tamai, J. M., Henley, J., Brewer, A. C., … Dellavalle, R. P. (2014). Social Networking Sites. *JAMA Dermatology*, *150*(1), 56. https://doi.org/10.1001/jamadermatol.2013.6340

Benevenuto, F., Magno, G., Rodrigues, T., & Almeida, V. (2010). Detecting Spammers on Twitter. In *Collaboration, Electronic messaging, Anti-abuse and Spam Conference (CEAS)*. Redmond, Washington. Retrieved from http://citeseerx.ist.psu.edu/viewdoc/summary?doi=10.1.1.297.5340

Bombaci, S. P., Farr, C. M., Gallo, H. T., Mangan, A. M., Stinson, L. T., Kaushik, M., & Pejchar, L. (2016). Using Twitter to communicate conservation science from a professional conference. *Conservation Biology*, *30*(1), 216–225. https://doi.org/10.1111/cobi.12570

Butler, D. (2008). Publish in Wikipedia or perish. *Nature*. https://doi.org/10.1038/news.2008.1312

Chan, T. M., Thoma, B., Radecki, R., Topf, J., Woo, H. H., Kao, L. S., … Lin, M. (2015). Ten Steps for Setting Up an Online Journal Club. *Journal of Continuing Education in the Health Professions*, *35*(2), 148–154. https://doi.org/10.1002/chp.21275

Cosco, T. D. (2015). Medical journals, impact and social media: an ecological study of the Twittersphere. *Canadian Medical Association Journal*, *187*(18), 1353–1357. https://doi.org/10.1503/cmaj.150976

Darling, E. S., Shiffman, D., Côté, I. M., & Drew, J. A. (2013). *The role of Twitter in the life cycle of a scientific publication*. PeerJ Inc. https://doi.org/10.7287/peerj.preprints.16v1

Eysenbach, G. (2011). Can tweets predict citations? Metrics of social impact based on Twitter and correlation with traditional metrics of scientific impact. *Journal of Medical Internet Research*, *13*(4), e123. https://doi.org/10.2196/jmir.2012

Freeman, L. C. (1977). A Set of Measures of Centrality Based on Betweenness. *Sociometry*, *40*(1), 35. https://doi.org/10.2307/3033543

Gardhouse, A. I., Budd, L., Yang, S. Y. C., & Wong, C. L. (2017). #GeriMedJC: The Twitter Complement to the Traditional-Format Geriatric Medicine Journal Club. *Journal of the American Geriatrics Society*, *65*(6), 1347–1351. https://doi.org/10.1111/jgs.14920

Holmberg, K., & Thelwall, M. (2014). Disciplinary differences in Twitter scholarly communication. *Scientometrics*, *101*(2), 1027–1042. https://doi.org/10.1007/s11192-014-1229-3

Jacomy, M., Venturini, T., Heymann, S., & Bastian, M. (2014). ForceAtlas2, a Continuous Graph Layout Algorithm for Handy Network Visualization Designed for the Gephi Software. *PLoS ONE*, *9*(6), e98679. https://doi.org/10.1371/journal.pone.0098679

Java, A., Song, X., Finin, T., & Tseng, B. (2007). Why We Twitter: Understanding Microblogging. In *Proceedings of the 9th WebKDD and 1st SNA-KDD 2007 workshop on Web mining and social network analysis* (pp. 56–65).

Kamel Boulos, M. N., & Anderson, P. F. (2014). Preliminary survey of leading general medicine journals' use of Facebook and Twitter. *Journal of the Canadian Health Libraries Association*, *33*(2), 38. https://doi.org/10.5596/c2012-010

Kelly, B. S., Redmond, C. E., Nason, G. J., Healy, G. M., Horgan, N. A., & Heffernan, E. J. (2016). The Use of Twitter by Radiology Journals: An Analysis of Twitter Activity and Impact Factor. *Journal of the American College of Radiology*, *13*(11), 1391–1396. https://doi.org/10.1016/j.jacr.2016.06.041

Kortelainen, T., & Katvala, M. (2012). "Everything is plentiful—Except attention". Attention data of scientific journals on social web tools. *Journal of Informetrics*, *6*(4), 661–668. https://doi.org/10.1016/J.JOI.2012.06.004

Lee, M. K., Yoon, H. Y., Smith, M., Park, H. J., & Park, H. W. (2017). Mapping a Twitter scholarly communication network: a case of the association of internet researchers' conference. *Scientometrics*, 1–31. https://doi.org/10.1007/s11192-017-2413-z

Letierce, J., Passant, A., Breslin, J., & Decker, S. (2010). Understanding how Twitter is used to spread scientific messages. In *Proceedings of the WebSci10: Extending the Frontiers of Society On-Line*. Raleigh, NC: US. Retrieved from http://journal.webscience.org/314/

Leung, E., Siassakos, D., & Khan, K. (2015). Journal Club via social media: authors take note of the impact of #BlueJC. *BJOG: An International Journal of Obstetrics & Gynaecology*, *122*(8), 1042–1044. https://doi.org/10.1111/1471-0528.13440

Maskalyk, J. (2014). Modern medicine comes online: How putting Wikipedia articles through a medical journal's traditional process can put free, reliable information into as many hands as possible. *Open Medicine*, *8*(4), e116-9. Retrieved from http://www.ncbi.nlm.nih.gov/pubmed/25426179

Mehta, N., & Flickinger, T. (2014). The Times They Are A-Changin': Academia, Social Media and the JGIM Twitter Journal Club. *Journal of General Internal Medicine*, *29*(10), 1317–1318. https://doi.org/10.1007/s11606-014-2976-9

Nason, G. J., O'Kelly, F., Kelly, M. E., Phelan, N., Manecksha, R. P., Lawrentschuk, N., & Murphy, D. G. (2015). The emerging use of Twitter by urological journals. *BJU International*, *115*(3), 486–490. https://doi.org/10.1111/bju.12840

Ortega, J. L. (2017). The presence of academic journals on Twitter and its relationship with dissemination (tweets) and research impact (citations). *Aslib Journal of Information Management*, *69*(6), 674–687. https://doi.org/10.1108/AJIM-02-2017-0055

Parra, D., Trattner, C., Gómez, D., Hurtado, M., Wen, X., & Lin, Y.-R. (2016). Twitter in Academic Events: A Study of Temporal Usage, Communication, Sentimental and Topical Patterns in 16 Computer Science Conferences. *Computer Communications*, *73*, 301–314. https://doi.org/10.1016/j.comcom.2015.07.001

Raamkumar, A. S., Pang, N., & Foo, S. (2016). When countries become the talking point in microblogs: Study on country hashtags in Twitter. *First Monday*, *21*(1). https://doi.org/10.5210/fm.v21i1.6101

Rezaie, S. R., Swaminathan, A., Chan, T., Shaikh, S., & Lin, M. (2015). Global Emergency Medicine Journal Club: A Social Media Discussion About the Age-Adjusted D-Dimer Cutoff Levels To Rule Out Pulmonary Embolism Trial. *Annals of Emergency Medicine*, *65*(5), 604–13. https://doi.org/10.1016/j.annemergmed.2015.02.024

Robinson-Garcia, N., Costas, R., Isett, K., Melkers, J., & Hicks, D. (2017). The unbearable emptiness of tweeting—About journal articles. *PLOS ONE*, *12*(8), e0183551. https://doi.org/10.1371/journal.pone.0183551

Sugimoto, C. R., Work, S., Larivière, V., & Haustein, S. (2016). *Scholarly use of social media and altmetrics: a review of the literature*. Retrieved from http://arxiv.org/abs/1608.08112

Thangasamy, I. A., Leveridge, M., Davies, B. J., Finelli, A., Stork, B., & Woo, H. H. (2014). International Urology Journal Club via Twitter: 12-Month Experience. *European Urology*, *66*(1), 112–7. https://doi.org/10.1016/j.eururo.2014.01.034

Thelwall, M., Haustein, S., Larivière, V., & Sugimoto, C. R. (2013). Do Altmetrics Work? Twitter and Ten Other Social Web Services. *PLoS ONE*, *8*(5), e64841. https://doi.org/10.1371/journal.pone.0064841

Thoma, B., Rolston, D., & Lin, M. (2014). Global Emergency Medicine Journal Club: Social Media Responses to the March 2014 Annals of Emergency Medicine Journal Club on Targeted Temperature Management. *Annals of Emergency Medicine*, *64*(2), 207–12. https://doi.org/10.1016/j.annemergmed.2014.06.003

Wong, K., Piraquive, J., & Levi, J. R. (2018). Social media presence of otolaryngology journals: The past, present, and future. *The Laryngoscope*, *128*(2), 363–368. https://doi.org/10.1002/lary.26727

Yang, Z., Guo, J., Cai, K., Tang, J., Li, J., Zhang, L., & Su, Z. (2010). Understanding retweeting behaviors in social networks. In *Proceedings of the 19th ACM international conference on Information and knowledge management - CIKM '10* (p. 1633). New York, New York, USA: ACM Press. https://doi.org/10.1145/1871437.1871691

Community-Driven User Evaluation of the Inuvialuit Cultural Heritage Digital Library

Ali Shiri
University of Alberta, Canada. ashiri@ualberta.ca

Robyn Stobbs
University of Alberta, Canada. stobbs@ualberta.ca

ABSTRACT

Preservation of and access to aboriginal and indigenous cultural heritage is emerging as a key area of information science research and development. In this study, we report on a community-driven user interface evaluation within a cultural heritage digital library that was developed for the Inuit communities in the Inuvialuit Settlement Region in Canada's north. The study adopted a culturally-aware, multi-method and multidisciplinary user evaluation framework to examine the usability and usefulness of the Digital Library North user interface. The three-phase user evaluation study consisted of such methods and approaches as environmental scanning, surveys, interviews, information audits, information tables, open houses as well as various community workshops. The iterative nature of the digital library interface development and usability evaluation provided rich and varied feedback and suggestions for the improvement of the user interface and its searching, browsing and navigation functionalities. The three thematized categories that emerged from the diverse data collected over the course of the three phases include user engagement, search and browse, and interface features. The study found that the development of cultural heritage digital libraries and their user interfaces for northern communities requires diverse, multidisciplinary and longitudinal methodologies that ensure their success, and more importantly, their sustainability and acceptance.

KEYWORDS

Digital libraries, Inuit communities, user interfaces, usability evaluation, community engagement.

INTRODUCTION

Digital libraries are useful platforms for the storage, preservation, access and dissemination of cultural heritage information. The World Intellectual Property Organization (WIPO), a United Nations specialized agency, defines cultural heritage of indigenous people, in part, as language, art, music, dance, song and ceremony, and documentation of those areas (WIPO, 2012). Cultural heritage information can include knowledge of traditional place names, hunting grounds and waterways, and it is often collectively labelled 'Traditional Knowledge' (Tyson, 1999; Asmah, 2010; White, 2006). In this paper, we focus on the Canadian context for cultural heritage digital libraries, specifically, the on-going Digital Library North (DLN) project in the Inuvialuit Settlement Region (ISR) located in the Northern Northwest Territories and Yukon. Research suggests that Canadian First Nations groups support documentation of cultural knowledge in order to pass it on to future generations, and that libraries have been identified by elders as "the most important custodians of documented traditional knowledge" (Maina, 2009; Lyons, 2010). The DLN project investigated the viability of a digital library in the ISR for that purpose.

DLN is a three-year project, funded by the Social Sciences and Humanities Research Council of Canada, that developed a digital library infrastructure in the ISR. The DLN project aimed to develop a digital platform that could serve as a model for northern, remote, and/or rural regions. The objectives included: a) investigate and identify the information needs and information-seeking behaviour of community members; b) develop a digital library of resources that will meet information needs of community members, including those in remote areas; c) explore appropriate methodologies and treatment of cultural heritage information; investigate and create a culturally appropriate metadata framework as a basis for resource description and discovery; d) develop specifications for multilingual user interfaces that support the dominant languages used; e) conduct a user-centred evaluation of the digital library, including users' attitudes, impressions and experiences in interacting with and making use of the digital library; f) develop a growth and sustainability strategy to ensure long-term access to information; and provide skills development training in information management to local project participants.

This paper reports on the development and evaluation of the digital library interface in the DLN project. It addresses research questions about how to create a digital library with the ISR communities. DLN took a holistic approach to digital library interface development by working with the ISR communities to examine user wants and needs before developing a prototype. The research team made use of a sophisticated multi-method and multidisciplinary methodological and theoretical framework in order to create a cultural heritage digital library for the ISR context. This process involved a longitudinal, community-driven usability evaluation of the cultural heritage digital library to develop, evaluate, and refine the digital library interface so that it would address the unique cultural and geographic context of the community. The methodology developed for the project helped the research team to collect data to tailor the project specifically to the ISR context by considering user engagement, searching and browsing, and other interface features through iterative feedback.

Geographic and Cultural Context

There are a number of significant information access and delivery challenges in the Canada's north, in particular, in the Inuvialuit Settlement Region (ISR) in the western Arctic. First, there is no coherent information infrastructure to provide seamless, efficient, and remote access to the resources available throughout the region. Specifically, there is no unified digital access platform for the geographically dispersed physical resources. Second, there is a lack of organization standards to represent, access, and retrieve resources of all formats. Third, little research has been undertaken on information needs and information-seeking behaviours of ISR community users to inform a design for effective delivery of information services and resources.

The DLN Project is an ongoing collaboration between researchers at the University of Alberta and the Inuvialuit Cultural Resource Centre (ICRC) that aims to address these challenges. The Inuvialuit Cultural Resource Centre (ICRC), which protects and promotes the Inuvialuit language, has an in-house library that focuses on languages and cultures. The ICRC is located in Inuvik in the Inuvialuit Settlement Region (ISR) in the Northwest Territories and Yukon (see figure 1), which is home to six geographically dispersed communities. The communities of Aklavik, Inuvik, Paulatuk, Sachs Harbour, Tuktoyaktuk, and Ulukhaktok are spread within the ISR, which spans ~91,000 square kilometres. Not all of these communities have year-round roads between them, making travel to access ICRC's resources by plane expensive. The resources held at ICRC include information on the North, residential schools, cultural history and language history (Cockney, personal interview 2012).

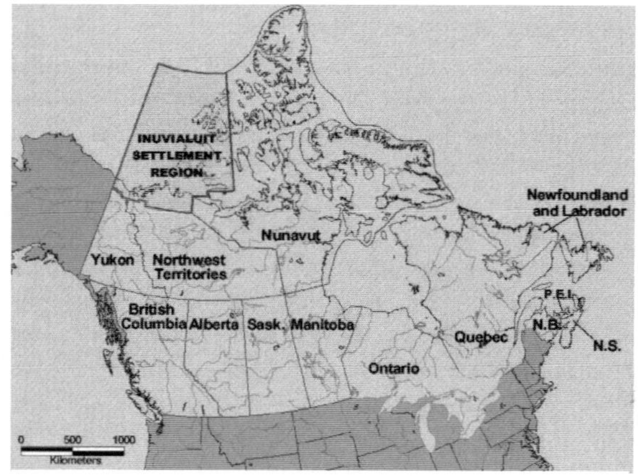

Figure 1: Inuvialuit Settlement Region (Joint Secretariat, n.d.)

As a part of its mandate, ICRC aims to preserve and promote development of the Inuvialuktun language and its associated dialects, namely Kangiryuarmiutun, Siglitun, and Uummarmiutun. These resources are only accessible physically on location, and the DLN project has created a digital library to increase their accessibility throughout the region by providing a digital means of access on the web (https://inuvialuitdigitallibrary.ca/). This digital library currently houses 5,182 resources organized in 49 different collections. These resources are a broad range of content types, from image and book items to multimedia collections containing Inuvialuktun language resources, oral history, and genealogy.

Earlier stages of the project collected initial data and community feedback that helped to develop the digital library prototype. These stages included environmental scanning to understand the project context (Rathi, Shiri, & Cockney, 2017), surveys and interviews to gather community members' impressions of the project and an understanding of their information needs and behaviour, and an information audit with ICRC staff to understand the extent of their collection and how they envision it being accessed digitally. The variety of methods used was intended to maximize community engagement, partnership, and input. Community collaboration was a cornerstone of the project that is reflected both in the methods chosen and the digital library interface developed.

PRIOR RESEARCH

Community-Focused Approaches in Digital Libraries

The importance of collaboration, community networking and community building in the development of digital libraries, archives, and repositories is widely emphasized in the literature (Williams, 2015; Caidi & Clement, 2004). Marchionini (2000) argues that digital library evaluation should be based on collecting multiple data sets and triangulating the results, which is advocated in most paradigms reported in the literature. Saracevic (2000) notes that community-focused evaluation of digital libraries is challenging due to the diverse objectives of the community. In terms of the context of evaluation, Saracevic (2004) introduces the ethnographic approach to involve the exploration of life-ways, culture, and customs in a digital library environment as well as the impact of a digital library on a given community. Lynch (2002) notes that digital libraries are not only collections of content and tools that build communities, they also allow members of communities to communicate and talk to each other.

Research on the development of cultural heritage digital libraries has largely focused on specific aspects of creating digital libraries, such as digitization, preservation, metadata, user interface design, repository, hardware and software components, and interoperability (Crane, 2002; Crane & Wulfam, 2003; Ruthven & Chowdhury, 2015). Other researchers have investigated the information search behaviour of users of cultural heritage digital libraries (Amin, van Ossenbruggen, Hardman, & van Nispen, 2008; Clough, Hill, Paramita, & Goodale, 2017; Suire, Jean-Caurant, Courboulay, Estraillier, & Burie, 2016). In his 5S theoretical model of digital libraries, Fox (2012) views societies as the highest-level component of a digital library, which exists to serve the information needs of its societies. Research and analysis of European cultural heritage digital libraries also point to the importance of community watch and participation in the creation and curation of digital content and calls for new methodologies and frameworks that cross disciplines (Aparac-Jelušić, 2017). However, there is limited research on methodological, cultural and multidisciplinary approaches to developing digital libraries, particularly for aboriginal, indigenous and northern communities. The DLN project developed a theoretical and methodological framework to support the creation of a cultural heritage digital library interface. The framework provides a multidisciplinary and multi-method approach crafted with community members from the ISR.

Indigenous Methodologies

When conducting community-driven and community-based research, it is critically important to be aware of and to use culturally appropriate methods. Lee (2011) reports that it can be difficult to find indigenous research participants due to a long history in which they have not benefitted from research results. Balanoff, Chambers, Kaodloak, and Kudlak (2015) stress the need to decolonize methodologies by collaborating with community members (including those fluent in the local language), at all stages of a research project—from planning, through to research studies and dissemination. It is imperative that elders and community participants understand the purpose and application of the research, be remunerated for their work, be given credit for their input and the opportunity to review and approve work before it is disseminated (Tyson et al., 1999; Hollowell & Nicholas, 2009). Previous research has made use of specific research approaches, such as qualitative and phenomenological studies involving interviews or conversations (Walts, 2011; Bushnell, 2009) and surveys (Lee, 2011). Ethnographic studies (focus groups, oral histories, participant observation, archival research, site visits) have also been used to understand complex cultural information and issues (Hollowell & Nicholas, 2009), and are particularly relevant and suitable to the development of cultural heritage digital libraries as they allow us to conduct observation and interviews, review documentation, and become immersed in the community's culture and the worldviews of its members (Bates, 2005).

A number of studies have adopted ethnography as method for investigating communities and their information needs in order to design information systems. Srinivasan (2007) elaborates on the notion of ethnographic process of engaging communities to develop information systems, architectures and ontologies. He argues that "acknowledging the cultural practices and belief systems of a set of users may allow systems to be more effectively created and deployed into particular contexts" (Srinivasan, 2007, p. 723). Involving the leaders of different sub-communities and persuading them to join to lead the project is part of his methodology (Srinivasan, 2007). Within the DLN project we have developed a multimethod and multidisciplinary framework that draws upon a range of theoretical frameworks and methods from various disciplines, including such diverse disciplines as business and management, organizational information systems, social sciences, cultural anthropology, community informatics as well as library and information science (Shiri et al., 2016, 2017). The methods used in this framework were iterative and adjustable in order to engage with the ISR communities and incorporate as much feedback as possible into the digital library interface.

User Evaluation and Usability Studies: Digital Libraries

A review of a number of user testing and user evaluation studies found a range of methods used to evaluate digital libraries, including surveys, interviews, focus groups, site log analysis, heuristics, and self-reported logs (Comeaux, 2008). In a review of literature on digital library user interface evaluation studies, Hariri and Norouzi (2011), propose a set of evaluation criteria based on widely and frequently used measures in previous research, some of which include navigation, search, design, interaction, learnability, ease of use, presentation, consistency, user experience, flexibility and accessibility. Zhang, Li, Liu, and Zhang (2008) note that searching and browsing are among the major interaction styles in digital libraries. Research on the usability evaluation of bilingual and multilingual cultural heritage digital library user interfaces suggests that they should be designed in such way as to allow users to easily view and form a coherent perspective of the collection and provide searching and browsing functions as well as high level facets to facilitate exploration and navigation (Shiri et al., 2011; Shiri, Ruecker, Bouchard, Doll, & Fiorentino, 2013). Drawing upon the literature of digital library interface design and usability, Xie and Matuziak (2016) emphasize that "usability testing is a critical component of user-centred design and an approach for improving user interface" (n.p.), which is a key element of the methodology employed by the DLN team. User engagement research (O'Brien & Toms, 2008, 2010) points to the importance of such measures as aesthetics, usability, attention, involvement and endurability. While there are some digital libraries developed for indigenous communities, such as the Blackfoot Digital Library, there is little research on the community-driven usability evaluation of those libraries. Sirinavasan (2007) conducted an evaluation of a community informatics system, called Tribal Peace in Southern California, using transaction logs to measure the usage of the system. However, he did not collect interview data on actual usability of the system, rather he focused on quantitative data such as views and the number of queries. In the DLN usability study, a multi-method, community-driven and culturally relevant framework was adopted to provide a more holistic perspective of the digital library usability. The user evaluation framework developed in this study adopted and adapted several usability criteria to make them relevant, suitable, and culturally appropriate the ISR communities.

METHODOLOGY

The Digital Library North project had an initial objective to create a framework for digital libraries in northern contexts, with the more specific goal to create a digital library with the ICRC (see figure 2). Although in this paper we are focused on the development of the interface of the digital library, it is important to step back to the project's beginning in order to show the holistic approach to the development of the interface that included not only software selection and user testing, but a wider engagement and incorporation of the community. A discussion of the DLN library interface cannot begin with the prototype. It needs to begin before that point.

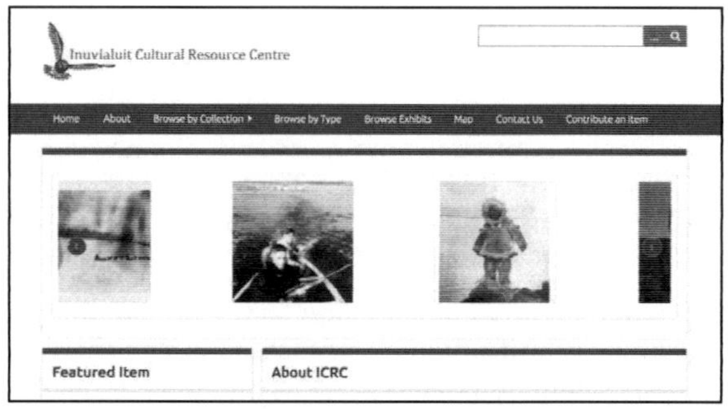

Figure 2: Digital Library Interface

The interface needed to embody community needs; therefore, the project began with more general information gathering that explored the community and existing information services, which helped to shape the eventual prototype. The project had three phases for the development and implementation of the digital library interface: 1) environmental scanning and information behaviour interviews, 2) prototype user evaluation and feedback, and 3) community demonstration and evaluation. Each of these phases included both formal methods of data collection (e.g., surveys, interviews, and usability evaluation) and informal methods of data collection (e.g., information tables, demonstrations, and open house events) in order to maximize community input in the project and create an environment for active community engagement and collaboration. At open houses, the project team and the ICRC provided bannock and soup for participants in order to create a friendly and inviting environment. The project is community-driven, and we worked in an iterative manner to build and adjust the digital library based on ongoing community input. The research team employed a multi-method, community-driven, and culturally relevant framework in order to gain a more holistic sense of the community and inform interface design.

Phase 1: Environmental Scanning and Information Behaviour Interviews

The first phase of environmental scanning and information behaviour interviews was an initial data gathering process. Before creating a prototype, we wanted to better understand the micro and macro environments in which the library would be situated, types of information that were held and distributed by the ICRC, and other information services in the area (for an in-depth discussion of the environmental scanning model see Rathi et al., 2017). Initial fieldwork to understand these community information environments was conducted in November of 2014 and Spring and Summer of 2015. In this phase we conducted 10 semi-structured interviews with staff of the libraries in Inuvik, students, college and secondary school teachers, and a researcher/consultant. To get more general public involvement, we put up information tables in public locations (e.g., the Inuvik Centennial Public Library, the Midnight Sun Recreation Centre, and the NorthMart grocery store) and held an open house at the ICRC. At the information tables and open house we distributed a survey and asked people about what types of information they would like to access. We also made the survey available online, and a link to it went on the Inuvialuit Regional Corporation website. We received 67 survey responses, 19 from the online survey and 48 in-person. The responses included types of cultural material people currently access, their internet use and languages spoken. Amongst respondents, top choices for cultural resources include: historical photographs (68.7% of respondents), family history (67.2%), oral history (64.2%), language learning material (61.2%), and place name and other land-based knowledge (55.2%) (Rathi et al., 2016). These responses helped to prioritize content additions to the prototype and influenced the types of metadata and organization used. During phase one, we also had team meetings with ICRC staff to discuss current use of their services and holdings and their expectations for the interface. As a part of these meetings, we conducted an information audit of the types of material the ICRC holds in its collection, and we recorded a group interview with staff to understand their needs and their users' needs. Based on the combined data collected from ICRC and the wider community, OMEKA was chosen as the suitable platform for the development of the digital library. This choice was due to a number of reasons including its: open source nature, flexibility, support for multilingual collections, compliance with metadata and interoperability standards, and sustainability. The initial digital library prototype was developed using input from this phase.

Phase 2: Prototype User Evaluation and Feedback

In the second phase, the research team collected feedback on the prototype that had been developed based on the data collected and analyzed in phase one. Evaluations were conducted over a three-week period in May of 2016. These evaluations included more formal usability testing and surveys, as well as demonstrations and an open house. The formal usability testing was carried out using interviews. A list of possible questions was drafted based on data collected in earlier stages of the project, previous interface prototype usability studies (Shiri et al., 2011, 2013), and literature on digital library usability (e.g., Saracevic, 2000, 2004; Rosenfeld & Morville, 2002; Nielsen, 1993; Comeaux, 2008; Parandjuk, 2010; Hariri and Norouzi, 2011). The usability questions included: searching and browsing (by peoples and places), looking at items, eliciting interest in sharing stories, tagging people and places the user may recognize in the digital objects, preference for textual or visual representation of the retrieved results, search and browse by language, ease of viewing and reading, appeal of colour scheme, features of particular interest (map, exhibit, images), and likes and dislikes. A total of 6 usability interviews were conducted. In each interview, participants were invited to explore and comment on the prototype, and then were asked particular questions to get them to elaborate on any issues or areas of interest. More targeted design questions, such as those relating to colour and layout, were also asked if the participants did not bring them up themselves. Initially, the prototype used an out-of-the box template from OMEKA for the interface. However, the prototype and template were adjusted as we received feedback. Small changes were made directly after feedback was received and larger changes were done later.

To maximize community participation, the team offered other ways for members of the community to give their input. These other methods included demonstrations, surveys, and an open house. Five demonstrations were given to students in junior and senior high in Inuvik. After the demonstrations, students were given the chance to ask and respond to questions and give feedback. Teachers also commented on potential uses students would have for the digital library in their future classwork. More hands-on opportunities were provided at an open house held at ICRC. The open house format provided a more flexible opportunity for community members to attend and give feedback than in formal user testing. A total of 17 people participated in the event. The use of less formal data collection allowed the research team to interact with a larger number of community members, which led to more input that could be incorporated into the digital library itself and a greater number of adjustments to the interface. An additional interview on metadata was also carried out with a member of the ICRC staff in order to take into consideration aspects that underlie the interface (for greater detail on metadata considerations of the project, see Farnel et. al, 2017).

Phase 3: Community Demonstration and Evaluation

In the third phase, the research team implemented larger changes arising from the feedback in phase two, and more content was added to the digital library prototype. Preparations for a multilingual interface were begun in earlier stages, but it was in this phase that translations for key areas of the interface were sought. Agnes White, one of the community elders with extensive knowledge or the Inuvialuit language joined the team to do translations and visit the communities. The team did demonstrations in the ISR communities in May of 2017, and we sought further feedback while also working in greater detail on the sustainability plan for the digital library with Inuvialuit Regional Corporation and ICRC staff (see figure 3 for an image of a community discussion following a demonstration and evaluation of the interface in Paulatuk).

Demonstrations were given in the four communities of Paulatuk, Aklavik, Ulukhaktok, and Sachs Harbour. A fifth demonstration was scheduled for Tuktoyaktuk, but it had to be cancelled due to weather conditions. At the demonstrations, community members looked at the library content, told stories about the people in the pictures they saw, and offered suggestions and corrections. The demonstrations served as a way to garner another layer of feedback from groups of interested community members. Demonstrations and workshops were also given to Inuvialuit Regional Corporation and ICRC staff in Inuvik with more of a focus on how new materials could be input into the library. Work on project sustainability and hosting continued after the demonstrations to help ensure long term viability of the project.

Figure 3: Community Evaluation in Paulatuk, May 17, 2017

Iterative Data Analysis

All of the qualitative data collected by the research team, in each of the three phases, was transcribed and input into the N-Vivo qualitative data analysis software. We used both inductive and deductive coding to analyze the data for themes that influenced the project structure and interface design. The deductive framework was meant as a way to recognize the areas that the research team had identified as important at the outset of the research, while the inductive coding was a way to add in more specific sub-themes or unforeseen themes as the project progressed. The deductive framework also allowed the team to make connections to the project objectives throughout the project phases and see connections to the tangible product of the project (the actual digital library).

Our deductive coding scheme was based on the key areas identified for the project in early collaborative work with ICRC: information behaviour, digital library creation, multilingual interfaces, appropriate information and metadata handling, user-centred evaluation, and sustainability strategy. These initial top-level codes shifted as data analysis progressed. For example, multilingual interfaces became a sub-theme of interface considerations more generally, and user-centred evaluation was not used as a code because feedback was parsed into more finite categories of other areas (e.g., under interfaces and handling of information and metadata).

Inductive codes were created during the coding process and added to the framework when the existing codes were not specific enough or did not adequately cover themes emerging in the data. These codes were typically created using a descriptive coding process, to demonstrate nuances of the data, or to add codes that connected to other, not previously identified, areas (e.g., information literacy and skills was a theme of importance to library staff and teachers). Using both inductive and deductive codes was an iterative process. Most of the child codes in our existing framework are inductive. An entire additional layer of coding was added to the initial deductive framework to better identify themes relevant to the environmental scan and the community-situated nature of the digital library design.

Figure 4: Browse by Collection Interface

The iterative coding and design process allowed the research team to see initial opinions and interest in the project from phase one alongside specific feedback gathered during later phases, such as user evaluation, to get a sense of how earlier data collection influenced project direction and ensure that themes were followed through. Both community-member contributions through interviews and researcher interpretations through field notes were included in order to track the ways in which the team interpreted what was shared with them by the community. To give an example, themes around user contribution and visual aspects of the interface began to surface early in phase one as participants and general public mentioned wanting to be able to tell stories and demonstrated their enjoyment of pictures on display. The research team identified software options that could include more visual options and opportunities for users and decided on a number of plugins that the OMEKA platform afforded, including maps, exhibits, etc. These considerations were further refined in phase two as we incorporated more visual aspects directly into the interface of the prototype based on user feedback. For an example, see Figure 4, which is a screenshot of the 'browse by collection' page that was edited to include thumbnails and increase the visual appeal of the interface based on user evaluation. Further details of the analysis and iterative design of the interface are discussed in the following section.

RESULTS AND DISCUSSION

The discussion here melds the methods and the qualitative data analysis results with examples of how the digital library interface was shaped and changed during the iterative process of data collection and library prototype creation. There were several themes related to the digital library interface that arose during data collection and analysis, which we have grouped into three categories. The first category relates to user engagement, the second category relates to browsing and searching, and the third category relates to the actual features of the interface. The ordering of these themes for our discussion is purposeful. The DLN project has a particular focus on community input and engagement, and the objective was to build a library prototype that would reflect and encourage that engagement. To capture that focus herein, we will discuss the interface through the perspective of user engagement, then through searching and browsing (which enable certain types of engagement), and then discuss some of the other interface aspects, which overlap with and echo concerns of the first two categories. Each of these three categories in our discussion of the DLN interface was inductively coded, and through that process they were assigned subthemes (or child codes), sometimes with multiple levels of child codes, to capture greater granularity of the concerns, observations, and feedback included in the data.

User Engagement

The subthemes for user engagement, as depicted in the screenshot in figure 5, are focused on different types of engagement, or motivations for engagement, with the collection materials. Each child code denotes a possible way of engaging with the digital library. These child nodes include: "interactivity", "listening", "looking at pictures", "reading", "sharing information", "sharing media", "staying connected", and "storytelling". Some of the instances coded to each of these nodes are from different stages of the project. For example, data collected in phase one contains more suggestions for what to include in the interface, while data collected in phases two and three tends to be more specific to the prototype or suggest additional features.

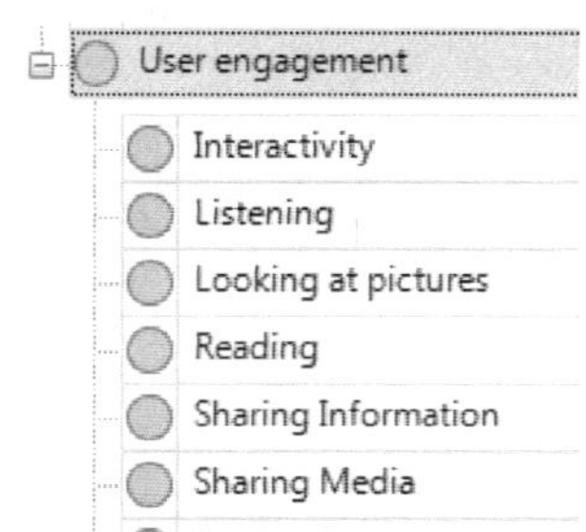

Figure 5: User Engagement Child Codes

In the earlier phases of the project, it was apparent that user engagement would need to be an important aspect of the interface. Facebook and social media were observed and recommended by community members as common communication tools for sharing community events and information, and the importance of storytelling was emphasized repeatedly. These themes were captured in the data through the codes of "storytelling", "sharing media", and "sharing information". For example, while sitting at information tables with physical copies of some of the photographs and publications that would be included in the digital library, the team members found that people were most interested in the looking at the photos, remembering people, and sharing stories. An excerpt from team field summaries in the Summer of 2015 demonstrates this point: "The information is embedded within stories of people's experiences. For example, at the NorthMart information table, one man was telling us the story of his family. The narrative included information on marriages, families moving from Aklavik to Inuvik and backstories on locations in some of the pictures from Aklavik. Stories are a respected form of knowledge transfer…" The photographs on the table that were to be incorporated into the digital library were a part of a personal and community story, and the digital library interface needed to be able to accommodate different needs for storytelling and sharing. The aesthetic, emotional and spatio-temporal elements of user engagement, as reported in previous research (O'Brien et al., 2008), was also present in user interaction experiences of the ISR community members, in particular such elements as interest, motivation, experiential goal, interactivity, and the emotional aspects of the digital library content.

The importance of story and sharing lead to several capabilities being added to the interface: social bookmarking options, download options so that the community could download their own copies of items, and the possibility to comment on items. These aspects are captured under the "facilitating engagement" child code in the interface category because they are actual features that were incorporated into the interface and then further evaluated by the community. Further considerations for engagement include the searchability and browsability of the digital library content and how the interface facilitates that engagement, as discussed in the following section.

Search and Browse

As community members explained their search preferences in information behaviour interviews and later evaluated the digital library prototype, this data was captured under the category of browse and search. The subthemes for browsing and searching, as depicted in the screenshot in figure 6, are: general comments on browsing ("Browse"), "categories or facets", general comments on searching ("Search"), and "spelling". Both searching and browsing were identified as important ways to access information in the first phase of the project, and the need for both was further demonstrated as we sought community feedback. For example, one of the first changes during collection of feedback on the prototype was the creation of a beta 'browse by collection' page to replace the long, text-heavy list of collections presented in the default interface. This beta page was created in response to a need for more visual aspects of the interface to facilitate browsing. The page has been formally incorporated into the interface and was previously described (see figure 4).

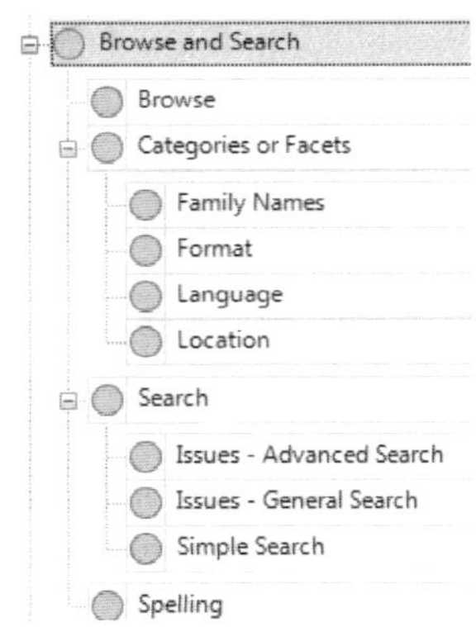

Figure 6: Browse and Search Child Codes

The "categories or facets" code contains the following children: "family names", "format", "language", and "location". Each of these facets was suggested as a way that community members would be likely to want to search or browse the digital library content. We explored these facets further in evaluating the metadata for the digital library, which is not the focus of this paper (see Farnel et al., 2017). Further detail on how browsing and searching could be facilitated in the digital library interface was also captured in child nodes of the broader browse and search categories (see figure 6).

The "Search" code has several child codes of its own: "issues – general search", "issues - advanced search", and "simple search". The issues child codes specifically arose from feedback as community members engaged with the prototype and made suggestions. One particular instance stands out: a user was trying to search for a family name "Day." Unfortunately, the search mechanism on the back end was programmed to ignore three letter words, and no relevant results could be retrieved. This particular instance instigated a detailed investigation into the search mechanisms in OMEKA and the viability of changing them because of the importance of being able to search for particular names or terms that were three letters or less in the northern context. The community members who provided feedback had particular interest in family information and stories, so the search function and interface needed to be able to support that form of engagement.

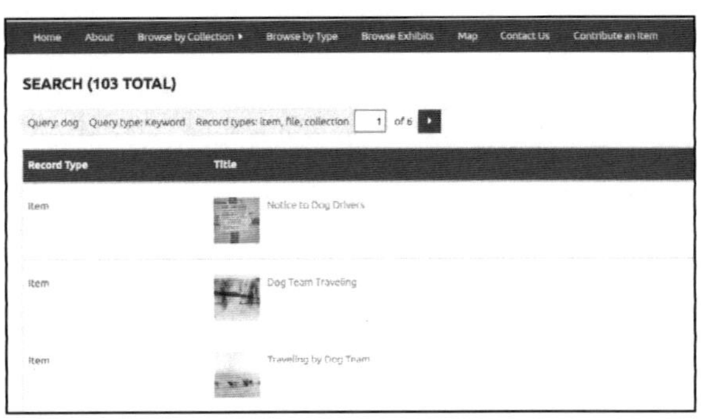

Figure 7: Thumbnails in Search Results

The importance of simple search was emphasized both in early suggestions by library staff who found that their patrons tended to prefer it and in later feedback on the prototype. When the advanced search function was added to the library community members noted that there were too many options that did not make sense to the general user. The interface has since been simplified to include fewer options and categories and to streamline the search process. The appearance of the interface for browsing and for viewing search results was also important. Community members preferred browsing the previously mentioned beta 'browse by collection' page, and thumbnails were appreciated in the search results even if they could potentially increase loading time on poor internet connections in some communities (see figure 7). Participants recommended we keep the thumbnails despite these increased loading times; they privileged the visual interface over speed of access, even with poor internet connectivity. These sorts of concerns were captured in more depth as features of the interface, as demonstrated in the following section.

Interface Features

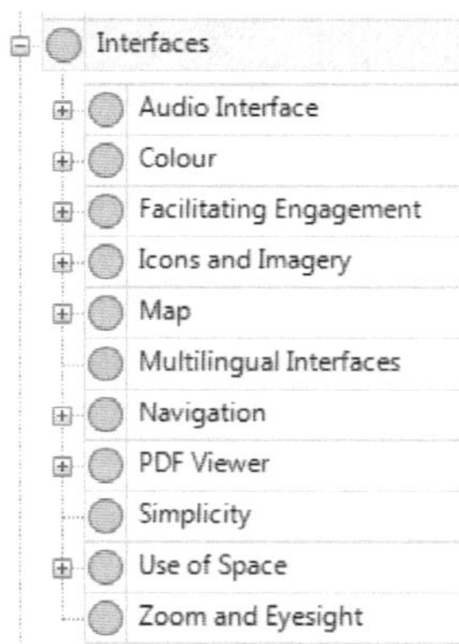

Figure 8: Interface Child Codes

The subthemes of the 'interface features' category, as depicted in the screenshot in Figure 7, includes the following child nodes: "audio interface", "colour", "facilitating engagement", "icons and imagery", "map", "multilingual interfaces", "navigation", "PDF viewer", "simplicity", "use of space", and "zoom and eyesight". Most of these codes have further child codes that were assigned in order to make it clear what aspects of the interface were suggested (phase 1) or preferred (phases 2 and 3) as we made adjustments to the interface. Due to considerations of space in this paper, we only focus on a few specific examples relating to ways in which the interface can facilitate engagement, rather than going into detail about each of the layers of child codes in this category.

In regards to the importance of engagement, we sought community feedback on the prototype and how it offered ways to access and share via social media and downloading content by asking community members about these features as they came across them or by directing their attention to them if they did not come up during their own browsing. The feedback we received revealed a need to consider different ways of displaying these capabilities in the interface.

In reviewing the data collected from phase 2, there were several suggestions that could increase engagement, including: adjusting where the comments were displayed on screen or reducing the scrolling (captured in the "Use of Space" code), providing a "contact us" button as a way to contribute information to the digital library (captured in a child code "contact us" under "facilitating engagement"), providing a more visual interface in a variety of ways (captured "under icons and imagery"), and including simple how-to videos that would appeal to people's preferences for visuals (captured in a child code "help" under facilitating engagement).

Regarding scrolling, one particularly poignant example was from a librarian reviewing the prototype: "Uhm, and then one other thing is like I noticed: there's a comments section on a lot of these pages, but because I'm lazy and most people spend less than 30 seconds on a web page, uhm, that means they're not scrolling all the way to the bottom, so a lot of people will miss the fact that they have an opportunity to add comments to everything that you've put on here. Like, it seems like there's a comment box on just about every page." To address this need, scrolling was reduced by rearranging the page display to bring the social bookmarking options up higher. The opportunity for engagement not only needs to be included in the interface, but it also needs to be made more prominent in order to facilitate the types sharing of information and storytelling that some of the community members emphasized they would like to see.

A further consideration for engagement with the interface involved the requirements of ICRC staff. The staff wanted to be able to verify information shared and contributed by the community, for example, when people in photographs are identified, to ensure that no one is incorrectly named. This discussion began with the suggestion of a "contact us" button. However, upon investigation of OMEKA features and consideration of staff time, this need was addressed through a mechanism for reviewing comments by staff, and a requirement for users to register an account, rather than emailed comments that staff would need to review. The need to balance suggestions and preferences of the community in general with requirements of the organization is highlighted in this example, and the interface for both users and staff needed to reflect their needs for both engagement and verification.

Preference for visuals was captured both in the "icons and imagery" code and the "help" code (a child of facilitating engagement). For example, one teacher suggested: "I think maybe, too, uh, having a little bit of pictures in the, like in the opening." This suggestion was incorporated to increase the visual aspect of the interface through a carousel feature on the homepage (which can be seen in figure 2). This carousel rotates through images to capture people's interest. One instructor also recommended that visual instructions be provided in the form of videos in order to make the interface more accessible to members of the community with various levels of literacy and computer literacy. He made this recommendation both before seeing the prototype and after interacting with it. While interacting with the prototype he commented: "Yeah! There you'd be. Boom done. You could, [cover] a billion points in a 30 second video." This type of tool requires further investigation to be created and incorporated into the digital library. However, all of these examples show the ways in which visual engagement is important and needs to be a part of the digital library interface in this context. Not only do visual aspects make the interface easier to navigate and catch attention, they also serve as starting points for finding and sharing knowledge and stories.

CONCLUSION

Developing cultural heritage digital libraries for northern and indigenous communities requires a broad, diverse and multidisciplinary methodological framework that is culturally-aware and appropriate. This kind of framework needs to take into account the nuances of combining multiple methodologies from different disciplines in order to create a meaningful, relatable and sustainable digital library. This paper presented a multi-phase user evaluation of the Digital Library North (DLN), a cultural heritage digital library developed for the Inuit communities in Canada's north. The study used an iterative, multi-layered approach to interface design and evaluation in order to create a digital library through community collaboration. Through close community engagement and over the course of three years, various user evaluations were conducted to design and improve the key functionalities of the user interface, namely user engagement, searching and browsing and interface features. The community-driven, incremental and iterative process of developing the digital library and its user interface functionalities helps us to ensure the sustainability of the library and the continuous engagement of the Inuvialuit Settlement Region community members in making effective use of digital technologies for preserving and providing access to cultural heritage information resources. Through this approach, the research team was able to gain a deeper understanding of the cultural context of the ISR communities and to implement feature changes and suggestions in the initial prototype interface as well as in the fully functional interface.

ACKNOWLEDGMENTS

This research was funded by a Social Sciences and Humanities Research Council (SSHRC) of Canada Insight Grant.

REFERENCES

Asmah, J. (2010). *Stepping outside the box - Traditional knowledge, folklore, indigenous textiles and cultural appropriation: Is there room for folklore protection under intellectual property law?* Retrieved from ProQuest Digital Dissertations.

Amin, A., Van Ossenbruggen, J., Hardman, L., & van Nispen, A. (2008, June). Understanding cultural heritage experts' information seeking needs. In *Proceedings of the 8th ACM/IEEE-CS joint conference on Digital libraries* (pp. 39-47). ACM.

Aparac-Jelušić, T. (2017). Digital libraries for cultural heritage: Development, outcomes, and challenges from European perspectives. *Synthesis Lectures on Information Concepts, Retrieval, and Services*, *9*(4), i-175.

Balanoff, H., Chambers, C. M., Kaodloak, A., & Kudlak, E. (2015). *"This is the way we were told...": Multiple literacies in Ulukhaktok, Northwest Territories*. NWT Literacy Council.

Bates, Marcia J. (2005). An introduction to metatheories, theories, and models. In K. E. Fisher, S. Erdelez, and L. E. McKechnie (Eds.), *Theories of information behavior* (pp. 1-24). Medford, NJ: Information Today

Bushnell, J. (2009). *"I can think of a lot of stories.": Shared knowledges, Indigenous methodology and purposeful conversations with sixteen Native women in Seattle*. University of Washington. Retrieved from ProQuest Digital Dissertations.

Caidi, N., & Clement, A. (2004, June). Digital libraries and community networking: The Canadian experience. In *Proceedings of the 4th ACM/IEEE-CS joint conference on Digital libraries* (pp. 386-386). ACM.

Clough, P., Hill, T., Paramita, M. L., & Goodale, P. (2017, September). Europeana: What users search for and why. In *International Conference on Theory and Practice of Digital Libraries* (pp. 207-219). Springer.

Comeaux, D. J. (2007). Usability studies and user centred design in digital libraries. *Journal of Web Librarianship, 2*(2–3), 457-75.

Crane, G. (2002, September). Cultural heritage digital libraries: Needs and components. In *International Conference on Theory and Practice of Digital Libraries* (pp. 626-637). Springer, Berlin, Heidelberg.

Crane, G., & Wulfman, C. (2003, May). Towards a cultural heritage digital library. In *Proceedings of the 3rd ACM/IEEE-CS joint conference on Digital libraries* (pp. 75-86). IEEE Computer Society.

Farnel, S. et al. (2017). A community-driven metadata framework for describing cultural resources: The Digital Library North Project. *Cataloging and Classification Quarterly*, 55(5), 289 – 306.

Hariri, N., & Norouzi, Y. (2011). Determining evaluation criteria for digital libraries' user interface: A review. *The Electronic Library*, *29*(5), 698-722.

Hollowell, J., & Nicholas, G. (2009). Using ethnographic methods to articulate community-based conceptions of cultural heritage management. *Public Archaeology*, *8*(2-3), 141-160.

Lee, D. (2011). Indigenous knowledge organization: A study of concepts, terminology, structure and (mostly) Indigenous voices. *Partnership: The Canadian Journal of Library and Information Practice and Research*, *6*(1).

Lynch, C. (2002). Digital collections, digital libraries & the digitization of cultural heritage information. *Microform & Imaging Review*, *31*(4), 131-145.

Lyons, N. (2010). The wisdom of elders: Inuvialuit social memories of continuity and change in the twentieth century. *Arctic Anthropology, 47*(1), 22-38.

Maina, C.K. (2009). *The traditional knowledge protection debate: Identifying and listening to the voices of traditional knowledge holders.* Retrieved from ProQuest Digital Dissertations.

Marchionini, G. (2000). Evaluating digital libraries: A longitudinal and multifaceted view. *Library Trends, 49*(2), 304-333.

Nielsen, J. (1993). *Usability Engineering*. Academic Press, Boston.

O'Brien, H. L., & Toms, E. G. (2008). What is user engagement? A conceptual framework for defining user engagement with technology. *Journal of the Association for Information Science and Technology*, *59*(6), 938-955.

O'Brien, H. L., & Toms, E. G. (2010). The development and evaluation of a survey to measure user engagement. *Journal of the Association for Information Science and Technology*, *61*(1), 50-69.

Parandjuk, J. C. (2010). Using information architecture to evaluate digital libraries. *The Reference Librarian, 51*, 124-134.

Rathi, D., Shiri, A., Campbell, S., Stobbs, R., Piltingsrud, A., Farnel, S., & Cockney, C. (2016). Understanding community needs: A step closer to a digital library for communities in Canada's North. 44th Annual Conference of the Canadian Association of Information Science CAIS/ACSI, June 1-3, 2016, University of Calgary.

Rathi, D., Shiri, A., & Cockney, C. (2017). Environmental scan: A methodological framework to initiate digital library development for communities in Canada's North. *Aslib Journal of Information Management*, *69* (1), pp. 76 - 94.

Rosenfeld, L. and P. Morville. (2002). Information architecture for the world wide web (2nd ed.). Sebastopol, CA: O'Reilly.

Ruthven, I., & Chowdhury, G. G. (Eds.). (2015). *Cultural heritage information: Access and management* (Vol. 1). Facet Publishing.

Saracevic, T. (2000). Digital library evaluation: Toward an evolution of concepts. *Library Trends, 49*(3), 350-69.

Saracevic, T. (2004, September). Evaluation of digital libraries: An overview. In *Notes of the DELOS WP7 workshop on the evaluation of Digital Libraries, Padua, Italy*.

Shiri, A., Ruecker, S., Bouchard, M., Doll, L., Fiorentino, C. (2013). User evaluation of Searchling and T-Saurus: Multilingual thesaurus-enhanced visual interfaces for digital libraries. *Canadian Journal of Information and Library Science*, *37*(2), 137-160.

Shiri, A., Ruecker, S., Bouchard, M., Stafford, A., Mehta, P., Anvik, K., Rossello, X. (2011). User evaluation of Searchling: A visual interface for bilingual digital libraries. *Electronic Library, 29*(1), 71 - 89.

Shiri et al. (2016). Methodological diversity: Community-driven development of a digital library for northern communities. 44th Annual Conference of the Canadian Association of Information Science CAIS/ACSI, June 1-3, 2016, University of Calgary.

Shiri et al. (2017). Methodological considerations in developing digital libraries for the arctic communities: The case of Canada's north. *Facilitating social sciences and humanities scholarship of the Arctic through library, archival, and information services, International Congress of Arctic Social Sciences*, June 8 -12, Umea, Sweden.

Suire, C., Jean-Caurant, A., Courboulay, V., Estraillier, P., & Burie, J. C. (2016, June). User activity characterization in a cultural heritage digital library system. In *Digital Libraries (JCDL), 2016 IEEE/ACM Joint Conference on* (pp. 257-258). IEEE.

Srinivasan, R. (2007). Ethnomethodological architectures: Information systems driven by cultural and community visions. *Journal of the American Society for Information Science and Technology*, *58*(5), 723-733.

Tyson, M., Stibbeston, S., & Dene Nation. (1999). *TK for dummies: The Dene Nation guide to traditional knowledge; A guide to commonly asked questions about traditional knowledge for everyone*. Yellownkife, N.W.T: Dene Nation.

Walts, N. (2011). *Native American Indian tribal college and university students: A qualitative study of the digital divide* (Doctoral dissertation, University of Phoenix).

White, G. (2006). Cultures in collision: Traditional knowledge and Euro-Canadian governance processes in northern land-claim boards. *ARCTIC, 59* (4), 401– 414.

Williams, A. (2015). Participation, collaboration, and community building in digital repositories/Participation, collaboration et développement communautaire dans les dépôts numériques. *Canadian Journal of Information and Library Science*, *39*(3), 368-376.

World Intellectual Property Organization. (2012). Intergovernmental committee on intellectual property and genetic resources, traditional knowledge and folklore. Accessed March 23, 2018. http://www.wipo.int/edocs/mdocs/tk/en/wipo_grtkf_ic_7/wipo_grtkf_ic_7_15.pdf

Xie, I., & Matusiak, K. (2016). *Discover digital libraries: Theory and practice*. Amsterdam: Elsevier Science.

Zhang, X., Li, Y., Liu, J., Zhang, Y. (2008). Effects of interaction design in digital libraries on user interactions. *Journal of Documentation*, *64*(3), 438-463.

Automatic Assessment of Mental Health Using Phone Metadata

Vivek K. Singh
Rutgers University, USA. V.singh@rutgers.edu

Teng Long
Rutgers University, USA. tl505@scarletmail.rutgers.ed

ABSTRACT

An accurate and timely assessment of mental health of individuals is an important building block toward healthy well-functioning societies. Traditional methods for assessing mental health and wellbeing are surveys administered by health-care professionals. Such surveys are labor intensive, costly, and typically intermittent. With the growth in mobile sensing, health informatics, and data science, this work argues a case for using mobile phone meta-data and data analytics to automatically infer an individual's mental health. Specifically, based on a clinically utilized health measure as ground truth (MHI-5) and ten-week phone usage metadata corpus for 45 participants we report that automated machine learning algorithms utilizing phone based features can achieve reasonable accuracy (around 80%) at automatically classifying the level of mental health of an individual. Results could pave way for cheaper, automated, health assessments with timely escalations to mental health professionals and interventions when required.

KEYWORDS

Mental Health, Ubiquitous Computing, Mobile Computing, Health Informatics, Data Science

INTRODUCTION

Mental health is a fundamental aspect of human lives and an accurate and timely assessment of mental health has been identified as an important enabler of individual and societal success (Wang et al., 2007). Keeping track of individual wellbeing can allow for understanding the dynamics of the process and support timely interventions (if required) to counter any issues before they become serious health risks. The state of the art in assessing mental health, however, still remains manual, self-reported, surveys administered periodically by health care professionals. Besides being costs for the individual and the healthcare system, such a process also involves sporadic sampling (typically once every few months to years), and most such tests are initiated *after* some serious events or episodes have taken place in an individual's life.

Inspired by the recent trends in Information Science involving advancement of mobile sensing for logging individual information, data science, health informatics, and social informatics, e.g. (Nicholas et al., 2013; Robinson, 2015; Shilton, 2012), this work explores the use of passive phone use meta-data to automatically infer an individual's mental health. The underlying hypothesis in this work is that social behavior is intrinsically linked with one's mental wellbeing (Taylor & Brown, 1988) and mobile phone's provide a rich window into the social behavior of an individual (Shmueli et al., 2014). Hence, appropriately characterizing an individual's social behavior (via phone) and building predictive machine learning models using it could yield important insights into creating *passive* (i.e. without manual attention or effort) predictors for mental health.

This builds upon a recent line of work in ubiquitous computing and social informatics that utilizes phone-based data to automatically infer an individual's traits and characteristics (e.g. Abdullah et al., 2015; Singh & Agarwal, 2016) and contributes to the line of work in health informatics where mobile phones have been used to automatically detect specific mental health related disorders (e.g., stress (Saeb et al., 2015)). Instead of focusing on specific disorders, though, this work aims to utilize mobile phones to infer general purpose mental health using clinically robust instruments.

Based on a ten-week field and lab study involving 45 participants, we report that (1) multiple phone-based behavioral features are intrinsically associated with mental health and general wellbeing; and (2) automated machine learning algorithms utilizing phone based features can achieve reasonable accuracy (around 80%) at automatically classifying the level of mental health and general wellbeing of an individual. The results pave way for better understanding of the underlying phenomena as well as the creation of automatic tools, which with refinement, could be used to trigger appropriate interventions.

The rest of the paper is organized as follows. First, we present background and related work in this area and identify the research questions. Second, we describe the details of the study conducted. Third, we present the data analysis and machine learning based classification approach. Then, we discuss the results, including the implications and the limitations. Lastly, we summarize the findings and identify future work.

RELATED WORK AND RESEARCH QUESTIONS

Over the last decade, multiple efforts have tried to understand and predict mental and physical health using personal data. While some efforts have focused on online social network data (De Choudhury et al., 2013), others have argued the value in using both online and offline user behavior to model mental and physical health (Bogomolov et al., 2014).

Here we discuss the related work in terms of the conceptual arguments connecting social processes with health, identify different trends in using mobile phones for healthcare, and identify the gaps to situate the contributions of this work.

Social Processes and their connections with health

There is extensive evidence that social capital and social support can help reduce feelings of stress, thus also minimizing its negative effects on physical health (Almedom, 2005; Uchino, 2004; Nabi et al., 2013). The effects of social support on health can be explained by at least two different models. The main effects model proposes that social support has a direct effect on health such that strong social support networks enhance health and well-being by minimizing stress, whereas weak social networks and a lack of social support act as stressors that have negative health effects (Underwood, 2000). Alternatively, the buffering hypothesis proposes that those with greater levels of social support enjoy greater health and wellbeing than those with poor social support when facing stressors in their lives because of the "buffer" space or cushioning provided by the social support (Cobb, 1976).

Using phones to survey user state

A number of recent efforts have tried to utilize mobile phones to administer fine-grained surveys that understand user state. For instance, (Servia-Rodriguez et al., 2017) discusses a large-scale study aimed at obtaining user mood state, multiple times a day, over time. Similarly, multiple efforts have used PANAS (Positive Negative Affect Sampling) and Ecological Momentary Assessments (EMAs) to understand user situation in a fine-grained manner (Turner et al., 2008; Silk et al., 2011). The primary goal of such studies, typically, is to collect more fine-grained data about user, rather than prediction, and most of such apps focus on aspects that change quite frequently over time (e.g. mood or affect) rather than longer-term clinical attributes like mental or general health.

Using phones to administer interventions

Many mental health apps focus on administering clinical self-report questionnaires to detect change of moods, stress level and depression level, followed by real-time interventions like text messaging, video, interactive voice, email prompt and virtual reality treatment are provided (e.g., Donker, 2013). Over the last decade, many such studies have suggested that the use of mobile phone and mobile phone apps for interventions in mental health settings (e.g., Harrison, 2011).

We consider building robust health status detectors as a pre-requisite for creating useful interventions. However, the current state of the art in detection is not robust enough for clinical purposes. Further, given the wide variety in mental and physical health and conditions and the associated nuances, there is a lack of general purpose approaches to automatically predict mental and physical health in a robust manner. Hence, we leave the intervention strategies as outside the scope of our current discussion and focus on detection aspects in this work.

Using phones to predict user stress, depression, and moods

Some recent efforts have proposed the use of GPS data and phone usage to predict depressive symptoms (Saeb et al., 2015; Canzian & Musolesi, 2015). In (Ferdous et al., 2015), the authors have shown that app usages can predict stress levels within the workplace context. In (Sano et al., 2015), the authors have reported the use mobile phone based features to automatically infer the Perceived Stress Score (PSS) for the participants. Similarly (Servia-Rodriguez et al., 2017) make use of mobile phone data to predict daily mood and affect levels of the participants.

Research Questions

Mental health includes a wide gamut of processes, states, and disorders. These include temporal states like mood and affect, symptoms like stress, and disorders like anxiety (agoraphobia; generalized anxiety disorder; panic disorder; post-traumatic stress disorder; social phobia), mood-based disorders (bipolar disorder including bipolar I and II; dysthymia; major depressive disorder), and substance disorders (alcohol and drug abuse and dependence) (Wang et al., 2007). Each of these marks a specialized set of conditions - as a means of analogy in the physical health, they vary from liver cirrhosis, to flu, to high blood pressure - and hence specialized instruments targeting each disorder is quite different from each other. Past literature has largely focused on detecting specific mental health disorders (Saeb et al., 2015; Servia-Rodriguez et al., 2017) or used ad-hoc (i.e. non-clinical) interpretation of overall health and well-being (Lane et al., 2011). For instance, (Lane et al., 2011) defines "wellbeing" as a weighted average of sleep, social activity, and physical activity. While Lane et al.'s effort at quantifying overall wellbeing is in the right spirit, there as yet few attempts that quantify and try to predict overall mental health and wellbeing using clinically-robust scales.

The SF-36 Health Survey asks 36 questions to measure functional health and well-being from the patient's point of view. It is a practical, reliable and valid measure of physical and mental health that can be completed in five to ten minutes (SF-36V2 Health Survey; Ware & Sherbourne, 1992). It is considered a generic health survey because it can be used across age (18 and older), disease, and treatment group, as opposed to a disease-specific health survey, which focuses on a particular condition or disease (SF-36V2 Health Survey). The survey is meaningful to patients, clinicians, researchers and administrators across the health care spectrum and has various applications including measuring health improvement or decline and assessing treatment effectiveness (Ware & Sherbourne, 1992). It is also reported that patients are more accepting of the test because it does not single out mental health concerns but rather integrates them with questions about the overall health (SF-36V2 Health Survey).

In this work, mental health is measured by the mental health sub-scale included in the SF-36 survey. The questions associated with the sub-scale were originally taken from the full-length (38-question) mental health inventory (MHI) survey. The subscale correlates significantly with the MHI-38 score and has been used as a standalone scale in its own right, known as the MHI-5. We refer to the score as the MHI-5 score in this work.

While there have been multiple recent attempts in the area of mobile phone based mental health measurement (e.g. (Saeb et al., 2015)), this work contributes to the literature by focusing on the following research questions:

(RQ1) Do certain mobile phone-based behavioral features have intrinsic associations with a person's mental health levels as measured via clinically-robust (MHI-5) survey instrument?

(RQ2) Can such mobile phone data and analytics techniques be used to create automated predictive models for an individual's mental health as measured via a clinically-robust (MHI-5) survey instrument?

STUDY

This study explores the associations between call log data and mental health based on a ten-week field + lab study involving 45 participants. The mental health levels of each participant is measured based on a "ground truth"' in-lab survey. The survey is considered "ground truth" in the current study due to its validity tested by other efforts in clinical settings as well as manual validation of the data (no missing values, improper selection of same choices etc.) captured in the current study by the authors.

Motivated by the existing literature in mental health as well as phone based behavioral assessment, a set of call-based features are defined. These features are computed in the dataset by preprocessing raw phone usage metadata. Machine learning based classification approaches have been applied to examine the interconnections between the defined call-based features and two aforementioned health levels.

Participants

The participants for the study were recruited using flyers, email announcements, and social media posts in the area surrounding a major North American university. A total of 59 participants completed the study. Some of the participants did not complete all the surveys, and some did not enter their unique identifying code consistently across surveys, resulting in a set of 45 participants for whom we have phone usage data as well as the mental health scores from the survey of interest.

Out of the 45 participants in the resulting dataset, 30 were male, and 15 were female. The most common age group was 16-29 years, most common marital status was single, the most common education level was ``some college", and the median annual family income was in the range US $50,000-$74,999.

Method

The data obtained in this study was collected as part of the <Anonymized> Well-being study. In this study, the participants were invited to attend three in-person sessions which involved filling out several surveys pertaining to health, well-being, cooperation and some demographic data. The survey of relevant to our study are the ones on Mental Health Inventory (MHI-5) subscale from the Short Form Health Survey (SF-36), and demography (details follow).

In the initial session, the participants were asked to read and sign a consent form to join the study and install a study client app on to their cell phones. The study started with an orientation program where participants were trained on how to use the app. Participants could opt out of the study at any point. The survey order was randomized for different participants. The participants were also instructed on the process of uninstalling the app and stopping data collection in the exit session.

All personnel involved in the study underwent human object training and Institutional Review Board certification. In order to protect participants' personal information, all participants were identified using their phone's unique IMEI number which was kept constant throughout the course of the study. This unique identifier was anonymized via one-way cryptographic hashing before any analysis was undertaken.

The participants were compensated up to a sum of $100 ($20, $30, and $50 respectively for the three in-person sessions) on successful completion of the study.

Data Collection

Two types of data were collected from the participants in this study. First, the phone-based data were collected through the app installed on each participants' phone. Second, different survey information were collected via in-person survey sessions.

The phone-based data included (call/SMS) log data and physical location data (GPS). However, in this work we consciously choose to focus on call-based features to be feature-phone compatible. Besides keeping the models and their interpretations simpler, the focus on feature phones allows for wider applicability across in low- and middle- income countries, for many of which mental health issues are among most disabling conditions (Wang et al., 2007). The call log data considered in this study includes date and time of communication event (call), incoming or outgoing direction, duration, and *anonymized* identifiers for both sender and receiver. Actual call audio were *not* collected in this study.

Health Measures

Mental health is measured by the mental health sub-scale included in the SF-36 survey. The questions associated with the sub-scale were originally taken from the full-length (38-question) MHI survey. The subscale correlates significantly with the MHI-38 score and has been used as a standalone scale in its own right, known as the MHI-5. The questions in MHI-5 are summarized in Table 1. The questions were assigned scores as prescribed by the SF-36 scoring guide (including score reversals, where required) (SF-36V2 Health Survey, Ware & Sherbourne, 1992).

S.No.	Question
1	During the past month, how much of the time were you a happy person?
2	How much of the time, during the past month, have you felt calm and peaceful?
3	How much of the time, during the past month, have you been a very nervous person?
4	How much of the time, during the past month, have you felt downhearted and blue?
5	How much of the time, during the past month, have you felt so down in the dumps that nothing could cheer you up?

Table 1: *Questions in the MHI-5 Survey*

Demographic Descriptors

The participants were surveyed about their demography. We collected the following information: age, gender, marital status, level of education, and level of family's income.

Phone-based Features

There has been a growing interest in using social mobile behaviors to infer people's wellbeing. From a conceptual perspective, these efforts are inspired by the literature connecting social capital, social support and mental health (Almedom, 2005; Uchino, 2004). Specifically, we focus on social capital (Putnam et al., 1994), its variants on "bridging" and "bonding" capital as suggested by Williams (2006), and we connect the concepts of "bonding" and "bridging" to those of "strong" and "weak" ties as proposed by Granovetter (1973).

From a practical perspective, prior work on characterizing user behavior via phones (e.g. (Wang et al., 2014; Saeb et al., 2015; Abdullah et al., 2014; Canzian & Musolesi, 2015)) has found that conversation, activity, mobility and sleep have significant correlations with mental health. For instance, the Student Life Project (Wang et al., 2014) reported that the students who engage in more frequent and longer conversations in the day epoch are less likely to feel stressed. Also, they suggest that students with less interaction in the day might have less collaboration with others thus leading to long hours of studying alone and getting less sleep.

Based on a survey of above-mentioned literature we have identified five categories of features (total 19 features) to characterize social behavior. We have defined these features based on the working assumption that certain individual traits that manifest themselves in the long-term social and mobile behavior patterns of the users might be predictive of one's mental and physical health status.

(A) Call Volume

Prior literature has connected social connections with mental health in both conceptual and empirical terms (Almedom, 2005; Saeb et al., 2015). Hence, we consider call count, total call duration, distinct users called and distinct users called (outgoing).

A summary of the identified features, their explanation, as well as descriptive statistics are presented in Table 2.

(B) Interaction Dynamics

An individual's interaction behavior might provide prescriptive clues to her mental and physical processes. Recent literature on phone-based latent attribute identification has used a number of such behavioral features (De Choudhury et al., 2013; Ghosh & Singh, 2016). Based on this literature we consider the following features: In Out Ratio, Missed Calls Percentage, Call Response Rate, Call Response Latency, and Longest Call Percentage.

Category (with supporting literature)	Feature	Explanation	Median	Mean
Call volume (Almedom, 2005; Saeb et al., 2015)	Call Count	Total calls made	274.00	452.31
	Total Call Duration	Time spent on calls (in seconds)	35842.00	79651.89
	Dinstinct Users Called	Unique users called	47.00	50.78
	Dinstinct Users Called (Outgoing)	Unique users called in outgoing calls	30.00	50.78
Interaction Dynamics (de Montjoye et al., 2013; Ghosh & Singh, 2016)	In Out Ratio	Incoming to Outgoing calls ratio	54.08	65.12
	Missed Call Percentage	Percentage of incoming calls not picked.	15.84	17.35
	Call Response Rate	Percentage of missed calls responded back within an hour	37.93	37.19
	Call Response Latency	Average response time (seconds) for missed calls responded	2801.12	2838.63
	Longest Call Percentage	Percentage of overall time spent on single longest call	7.60	10.13
Diversity and Novelty in Contacts (Sih et al., 2004; Singh and Ghosh, 2017)	Call Diversity	Shannon Entropy based measure of spreading calls across different contacts	72.00	71.98
	Call Loyalty	Percentage of calls made to top-three contacts	53.00	51.18
	Number of New Contacts	Number of contacts not present in first four weeks of data	17.00	19.64
	Number of New Contacts (Outgoing)	Number of outgoing call contacts not present in first four weeks of data	12.50	14.23
	Percentage Time Spent with New Contacts	Percentage of time spent talking with New Contacts	8.49	13.51
Tie Strength (Uchino, 2004; Underwood, 2000)	Call Strong Ties	Percentage of calls made to 33% most frequent contacts	84.00	81.82
	Call Weak Ties	Percentage of calls made to 33% least frequent contacts	5.00	6.04
Temporal Rhythms (R. Wang et al., 2014; Abdullah et al., 2014)	DayNight 12am Call Ratio	Ratio of calls made in PM phase to AM phase	3.58	4.47
	DayNight 12am Call Ratio Reverse	Ratio of calls made in AM phase to PM phase	0.28	0.28
	WeekdayWeekend Call Ratio	Ratio of calls made on weekdays to the weekend	2.26	2.44

Table 2: *Features considered in the study, including their literature support, explanation, and median and mean values in the dataset.*

(C) Diversity and Novelty in Contacts

Prior literature has stressed the value of diversity as well as change in maintaining one's health and well-being (Sih et al., 2004; Singh et al., 2013). For instance, a combination of an animal's behavioral traits (e.g., exploration, loyalty) have been demonstrated to have significant predictive power on an animal's social stature, survivability, metabolism rates, reproductive success, and other life outcomes (Sih et al., 2004; Wilson et al., 1994). Similarly, recent literature on mobile computing has connected diversity of contacts and novelty over time with individual outcomes (Ghosh & Singh, 2016; Singh et al., 2013). Hence, we have identified the following features to characterize diversity and novelty in the participant's contacts.

First is Call Diversity, which is based on Shannon Entropy and is a measure of how evenly a user's social engagements are distributed between different contacts (Shmueli et al., 2014). A user with low diversity distributes her communication unevenly across contacts, whereas a user with high diversity spends time evenly across many contacts.

$D_i = \sum_j p_{ij} \log_b p_{ij}$, where p_{ij} is the percentage of communication (call) between individual 'i' and 'j', and 'b' is the total number of contacts.

Call Loyalty quantifies the level of concentration (or preference) that an individual exhibits towards her strongest ties. While a highly "loyal" individual might have almost her entire social activity focusing on top three contacts, this ratio might be miniscule for another individual with a wider social graph (Singh et al., 2013). In a way, this aspect is tied to the "bonding" social capital derived from strong ties as defined by Granovetter and Putnam, and operationalized by Williams (Granovetter, 1973; Putnam et al., 1994; Williams, 2006). Further we capture the novelty in one's social patterns via the following features: Number of New Contacts, Number of New Contacts (Outgoing), and Percentage of Time Spent with New Contacts.

(D) Tie Strength

Significant prior literature connects strong and weak ties with mental and general health (Thoits, 2011; Uchino, 2004). The main effects model proposes that social support has a direct effect on health such that strong social support networks and satisfactory social support enhance health and well-being, whereas weak social networks and a lack of social support act as stressors that have deleterious health effects (Underwood, 2000). To quantify the relative role of strong and weak ties in the one's social network and its connections with mental and physical health, we identify the following features: Call Strong Ties and Call Weak Ties. These features quantify the percentage of communication effort that a user devotes to his/her preferred contacts. Following (Singh & Ghosh, 2017), we consider top one-third (33%) most frequent contacts as "strong ties" and bottom third contacts as "weak ties". It is expected that a user will spend at least 33% of her time with her top third of contacts. However, a higher score (e.g. 80%) could be an indicator of a person's preference toward engaging significantly more with strong ties rather than spreading the interaction effort more equitably. Similarly, the Call Weak Ties feature quantifies the percentage of communication effort that a user devotes to his/her less preferred (bottom third) contacts. A high weak tie engagement ratio would suggest that the user spends significant communication effort to interact with the less preferred contacts.

(E) Temporal Rhythms

Prior literature has connected circadian (biological rhythms) with stress as well as other cognitive functions (Wang et al., 2014; Abdullah et al., 2014). Hence we characterize daily and weekly patterns and the underlying variations in social activities as follows. DN12am Call Ratio, DN12am Call Reverse Ratio, and Weekday Weekend Call Ratio.

ANALYSIS AND RESULTS

Preprocessing

The data collected from the Anonymized Wellbeing study came with missing data and in different scales. Before moving on with any data analysis, missing data was imputed from the whole dataset and replaced with the median value of the corresponding feature. After imputation, all the real-valued features were standardized by removing the mean and scaling them to unit variance. Categorical variables, for example demographic features, were encoded by dummy variables for each category.

To build a classification model for high/low mental health score, instances were labeled into two categories via median split. The median value of the sample is chosen because there is no standardized median scores available for the specific survey instrument used in our work. Median split resulted in 2 classes (i.e. labels). There are 22 positive instances (higher mental health score) and 23 negative instances for the mental health classification.

In Figure 1, we show a comparison of the average values obtained for different features in the two categories as follows: *difference = mean(HighMentalHealth)−mean(LowMentalHealth)/ Mean(HighMentalHealth).* As can be seen, the values for 11 out of 19 phone-based features showed a difference of at least 10% between the two groups. Focusing the attention on the top three features in both positive and negative directions, we find that a higher call count, call response rate, and the number of new contacts (outgoing) are associated with higher mental health. Conversely, a higher percentage of calls made to weak ties, a higher percentage of calls made on weekdays compared to weekends, and a high missed call percentage are associated with lower values of mental health. In general, more social activity, and reciprocity are connected with better mental health. (We discuss some of the implications in the Discussion section.)

Impact of Phone Use based Features on Mental Health

In Figure 1, we show a comparison of the average values obtained for different features in the two categories as follows: *difference = mean(HighMentalHealth)−mean(LowMentalHealth)/ Mean(HighMentalHealth).* As can be seen, the values for 11 out of 19 phone-based features showed a difference of at least 10% between the two groups. Focusing the attention on the top three features in both positive and negative directions, we find that a higher call count, call response rate, and the number of new contacts (outgoing) are associated with higher mental health. Conversely, a higher percentage of calls made to weak ties, a higher percentage of calls made on weekdays compared to weekends, and a high missed call percentage are associated with lower values of mental health. In general, more social activity, and reciprocity are connected with better mental health. (We discuss some of the implications in the Discussion section.)

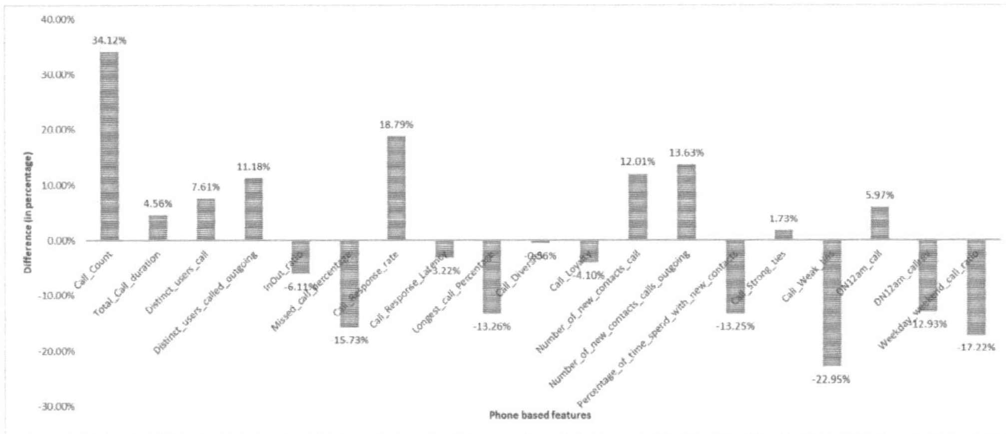

Figure 1. Difference in the feature values for the High and Low mental health groups

Classification: Feature Selection

Feature selection is the process of automatically selecting a subset of the defined features to create optimal classification models. Such feature selection is crucial especially for high-dimensional and small sample data to achieve interpretability, enhance generalization and reducing overfitting (Guyon & Elisseeff, 2003). In this study, feature selection is based on optimal subset selection according to mutual information between each feature and the target variable (Peng et al., 2005). Subset of features are selected to be highly correlated with the target variable. We used the implementation in SciKit Learn. The selected features are shown in Table 3.

Model	Features
Only Demography Features	Income, Gender
Only Phone Log Features	Call count, Total call duration, Call response rate, Number of new contacts in calls, Number of new contacts in outgoing calls
Demography + Phone Log features	Call count, Total call duration, Call response rate, Number of new contacts in calls, Number of new contacts in outgoing calls

Table 3. *Features selected for different machine learning models.*

Classification: Training and Evaluation

The selected features were then passed to different machine learning algorithms for classification. Specifically, we used three well-established methods implemented in Scikit Learn, namely Logistic Regression, (Gaussian) Naive Bayes, and Random Forest. We used a 10-fold cross validation procedure to evaluate the models. We also used Zero-R (Constant or Majority) without any cross validation as a baseline to facilitate interpreting the results. The following table offers a comparison of the results. It worth noting that AUCROC stands for the Area Under the Receiver Operating Characteristic Curve) (Bewick et al., 2004).

Method	Demography Only		Phone Log features Only		Demography + Phone Log features	
	AUCROC	*Accuracy*	*AUCROC*	*Accuracy*	*AUCROC*	*Accuracy*
Logistic Regression	0.52	0.53	0.75	0.76	0.75	0.76
Naïve Bayes	**0.63**	**0.62**	0.64	0.64	0.64	0.64
Random Forest	0.57	0.58	**0.80**	**0.80**	**0.80**	**0.80**
Zero-R	0.50	0.51	0.50	0.51	0.50	0.51

Table 4*. Performance of different machine learning models*

As shown in Table 4, the "phone log features only" and "demographic + phone log features" based models yielded the best case accuracy of 80% in predicting mental health level. Also as seen in Table 3, the features selected in both models are the same. It is hence unsurprising that the performance of the model remains the same. The classification performance (accuracy of 80%), marks a 56% relative improvement over a baseline majority classifier (Zero-R) and a 29% relative improvement over the "demography only" model.

DISCUSSION

The first research question in this work was: *(RQ1) Do certain mobile phone-based behavioral features have intrinsic associations with a person's mental health levels as measured via clinically-robust (MHI-5) survey instrument?*

As shown in Figure 1, we find multiple features to vary significantly (greater than 10%) between the high and low mental health groups. Focusing the attention on the top three features in both positive and negative directions, we find that a higher *call count, call response rate,* and the *number of new contacts (outgoing)* are associated with higher mental health.

This is largely in line with the existing literature on mental health as well as the theoretical construct of social capital (Putnam et al., 1994). The link between social isolation and reduced psychological well-being is well established in sociology, dating back to Durkheim (Durkheim, 1951(originally published in 1897)). Smaller social networks, fewer close relationships, and lower perceived adequacy of social support have all been linked to depressive symptoms (Barnett and Gottlieb, 1988). From a conceptual perspective a higher social capital is generally associated with higher mental health (Kawachi and Berkman, 2001). However, there have also been reported studies connecting the "dark side" of social capital for mental health (Brown and Harris, 1978).

The results of this study connect a higher call count with better mental health. A higher call count indicates that the person is more social and has access to more number of friends for emotional support when needed (Putnam et al., 1994). A higher call response rate is in line with existing literature and people who are easy to contact can be said to engage with a wider social network than those who remain unavailable (Singh & Ghosh, 2017). Lastly, a higher number of new contacts (outgoing) also points to a constantly growing network of contacts and again a higher social capital.

The top three predictors of lower mental health scores were a *higher percentage of calls made to weak ties*, a *higher percentage of calls made on weekdays compared to weekends*, and a *high missed call percentage*. A higher percentage of calls made to *weak ties* needs to be contrasted with the choice to make more calls to *strong ties*. While strong ties are expected to provide emotional support to the individual, weak ties often provide information and access to resources (Granovetter, 1973). The results from this study suggest that focusing the communication on strong ties (as opposed to weak ties) is important for better mental health. Similarly, the choice to make more calls during the weekdays needs to be contrasted with the calls made over the weekend. For most people, weekday activities are more likely to involve work and weekend activities to be focused on more leisure and social events. Hence, it is not surprising that a higher ratio of weekend calls is found to be connected with better mental health. Lastly, a higher missed call percentage might reflect a person's lower tendency to reciprocate in social networks. Reciprocity is a key component of social capital (Putnam et al., 1994) and a lower social capital is often connected with lower mental health (Nabi et al., 2013; Uchino, 2004).

The second research question in this work was: *(RQ2) Can such mobile phone data and analytics techniques be used to create automated predictive models for an individual's mental health as measured via a clinically-robust (MHI-5) survey instrument?*

As shown in Table 4, the phone log features based models yielded the best case accuracy of 80% in predicting mental health level which was significantly higher than a demography data based model (62%). One way to interpret these results is that having mobile sensing data (phone-based features for 10 weeks) may allow for the creation of a detailed model for personal behavior which goes beyond static demographic descriptors (age, gender, income level) for predicting mental health scores. The classification performance (accuracy of 80%), marks a 56% improvement over a baseline majority classifier. Thus, providing clear evidence of interconnections between the mobile features and mental and physical well-being and also motivating further work in this direction.

Note though, that we do not consider the current prediction levels to be sufficient for completely automated monitoring and decision making. However, they could act as a "triaging" step and medical experts could be called in to look more closely based on the initial results from such a system. We further identify certain limitations in the current study. This study focuses on a modest sample (N = 45) of participants from a relatively healthy university population. We also note that none of the results obtained here are causal, and hence the directionalities of the explanation could indeed be inverse. For instance, less healthy individuals could make less friends, or individuals with less friends may succumb to health issues more readily. Taking into account these limitations, we will be cautious in generalizing the results obtained until they are verified at scale over samples of more representative populations. Despite these limitations, this study is the first of its kind. To our knowledge, there have been no previous studies undertaken that analyze the link between stable clinically robust mental health instruments (namely MHI-5 subscale of SF-36) and phone-based behavioral features.

We also note the privacy and ethical considerations in giving a person a health score based on passive data collection (Tufekci, 2015). We suggest an explicit opt-in policy (as also adopted in this work) and use of such tools as merely a triage step before trained professionals can step in and take a closer look at the individual circumstances. Given the current health-care setup, we posit that automated tools that can reduce the costs and burdens on individuals and health care professionals could be a useful way forward. While a more nuanced policy debate is required, rather than abstaining from presenting such outcomes, we choose to raise awareness about these new prospects and informing the policy debate around them.

The results open the doors to a methodology that, with refinements and validation, could be used at scale. Mobile phones are now actively used by more than 3 billion users, hence the proposed method could potentially be applied to estimate the mental health levels for billions of individuals. In future, this work could also have multiple implications for health care professionals, health informatics professionals, mobile phone service providers, social scientists and individuals themselves. For example, the suggested methodology could help health care professionals study mental health at scale in the society. Similarly, as mobile phones are increasingly used, these methods could be used to trigger preventive interventions before serious lapses or incidents take place.

CONCLUSIONS AND FUTURE WORK

This work establishes a link between stable clinically robust mental health instrument (namely MHI-5 subscale from SF-36) and phone-based behavioral features. Specifically, it demonstrates how a selection of phone based behavioral features can be used to build prediction models whose AUCROC and accuracy are promising and encouraging (around 80%) at recognizing different levels of mental health. While we consider the results to be preliminary, they could be enhanced by future work by including a larger number of participants, more detailed phone-based features, and considering larger time durations. Furthermore, the suggested phone-based model could be expanded to study and predict other personal and societal behaviors and outcomes such as trust, cooperation, and happiness. Taken together such methods open ways to employing mobile sensing, data analytics, and social informatics for better human health and wellbeing.

REFERENCES

Abdullah, S., Matthews, M., Murnane, E. L., Gay, G., & Choudhury, T. (2014). Towards circadian computing: early to bed and early to rise makes some of us unhealthy and sleep deprived. In Proceedings of the 2014 acm international joint conference on pervasive and ubiquitous computing(pp. 673–684).

Almedom, A. M. (2005). Social capital and mental health: An interdisciplinary review of primary evidence. Social science & medicine, 61(5), 943–964.

Barnett PA, Gotlib IH. Psychosocial functioning and depression: distinguishing among antecedents, concomitants, and consequences. Psychol Bull. 1988;104:97–126.

Bewick, V., Cheek, L., & Ball, J. (2004). Statistics review 13: receiver operating characteristic curves. Critical care, 8(6), 508.

Bogomolov, A., Lepri, B., Ferron, M., Pianesi, F., & Pentland, A. S. (2014). Daily stress recognition from mobile phone data, weather conditions and individual traits. In Proceedings of the 22nd acm international conference on multimedia (pp. 477–486).

Brown GW, Harris TO. Social Origins of Depression: a Study of Psychiatric Disorder in Women. London: Tavistock; 1978.

Canzian, L., & Musolesi, M. (2015). Trajectories of depression: unobtrusive monitoring of depressive states by means of smartphone mobility traces analysis. In Proc. 2015 acm international joint conference on pervasive and ubiquitous computing (pp. 1293–1304).

Cobb, S. (1976). Social support as a moderator of life stress.Psychosomatic medicine, 38(5), 300–314.

De Choudhury, M., Gamon, M., Counts, S., & Horvitz, E. (2013). Predicting depression via social media. In Icwsm (p. 2).

de Montjoye, Y.-A., Quoidbach, J., Robic, F., & Pentland, A. S. (2013). Predicting personality using novel mobile phone-based metrics. In International conference on social computing, behavioral-cultural modeling, and prediction (pp. 48–55).

Donker, T., Petrie, K., Proudfoot, J., Clarke, J., Birch, M.-R., & Christensen, H. (2013). Smartphones for smarter delivery of mental health programs: a systematic review.Journal of medical Internet research, 15 (11), e247.

Durkheim E. Suicide. New York: Free Press; 1951. (Originally published 1897.)

Ferdous, R., Osmani, V., & Mayora, O. (2015). Smartphone app usage as a predictor of perceived stress levels at workplace. In Pervasive computing technologies for healthcare (pervasivehealth), 2015 9th international conference on (pp. 225–228).

Ghosh, I., & Singh, V. K. (2016). Predicting privacy attitudes using phone metadata. In International conference on social computing, behavioral-cultural modeling, and prediction, sbp-brims. Springer.

Granovetter, M. S. (1973). The strength of weak ties. American journal of sociology, 1360–1380.

Guyon, I., & Elisseeff, A. (2003). An introduction to variable and feature selection. Journal of machine learning research, 3 (Mar), 1157–1182.

Harrison, V., Proudfoot, J., Wee, P. P., Parker, G., Pavlovic, D. H., & Manicavasagar, V.(2011). Mobile mental health: review of the emerging field and proof of concept study. Journal of mental health, 20 (6), 509–524.

Herbert, T. B., & Cohen, S. (1993). Stress and immunity in humans: a meta-analytic review. Psychosomatic medicine, 55 (4), 364–379.

Kawachi, I., & Berkman, L. F. (2001). Social ties and mental health. Journal of Urban health, 78(3), 458-467.

Lane, N. D., Mohammod, M., Lin, M., Yang, X., Lu, H., Ali, S., . . . Campbell, A. (2011). Bewell: A smartphone application to monitor, model and promote wellbeing. In 5th international icst conference on pervasive computing technologies for healthcare (pp. 23–26).

Nabi, R. L., Prestin, A., & So, J. (2013). Facebook friends with (health) benefits? exploring social network site use and perceptions of social support, stress, and well-being. Cyberpsychology, Behavior, and Social Networking, 16 (10), 721– 727.

Nicholas, D., Clark, D., Rowlands, I., & Jamali, H. R. (2013). Information on the go: A case study of europeana mobile users. Journal of the American Society for Information Science and Technology, 64 (7), 1311–1322.

Peng, H., Long, F., & Ding, C. (2005). Feature selection based on mutual information criteria of max-dependency, max-relevance, and min-redundancy. IEEE Transactions on pattern analysis and machine intelligence, 27 (8), 1226–1238.

Putnam, R. D., Leonardi, R., & Nanetti, R. Y. (1994). Making democracy work: Civic traditions in modern italy. Princeton university press.

Robinson, L. (2015). Multisensory, pervasive, immersive: Towards a new generation of documents. Journal of the Association for Information Science and Technology, 66(8), 1734–1737.

Saeb, S., Zhang, M., Karr, C. J., Schueller, S. M., Corden, M. E., Kording, K. P., & Mohr, D. C. (2015). Mobile phone sensor correlates of depressive symptom severity in daily-life behavior: an exploratory study. Journal of medical Internet Research, 17(7), e175.17

Sano, A., Phillips, A. J., Amy, Z. Y., McHill, A. W., Taylor, S., Jaques, N., . . . Picard, R. W. (2015). Recognizing academic performance, sleep quality, stress level, and mental health using personality traits, wearable sensors and mobile phones. In Wearable and implantable body sensor networks (bsn), 2015 ieee 12th international conference on (pp. 1–6).

Servia-Rodriıguez, S., Rachuri, K. K., Mascolo, C., Rentfrow, P. J., Lathia, N., & Sandstrom, G. M. (2017). Mobile sensing at the service of mental well-being: A large-scale longitudinal study. In Proc. International conf. on world wide web (pp. 103–112).

SF-36V2 HEALTH SURVEY Health Survey. (2016). (Available online. http://campaign.optum.com/optum-outcomes/what-we-do/health-surveys/SF-36V2-health-survey.html)

Shilton, K. (2012). Participatory personal data: An emerging research challenge for the information sciences. Journal of the American Society for Information Science and Technology, 63(10), 1905–1915.

Shmueli, E., Singh, V. K., Lepri, B., & Pentland, A. (2014). Sensing, understanding, and shaping social behavior. IEEE Transactions on Computational Social Systems,1(1), 22–34.

Sih, A., Bell, A. M., Johnson, J. C., & Ziemba, R. E. (2004). Behavioral syndromes: an integrative overview.The quarterly review of biology,79(3), 241–277.

Silk, J. S., Forbes, E. E., Whalen, D. J., Jakubcak, J. L., Thompson, W. K., Ryan, N. D., . . . Dahl, R. E. (2011). Daily emotional dynamics in depressed youth: A cell phone ecological momentary assessment study.Journal of experimental child psychology, 110(2),241–257.

Singh, V. K., & Agarwal, R. R. (2016). Cooperative phoneotypes: exploring phone-based behavioral markers of cooperation. In Proceedings of the 2016 acm international joint conference on pervasive and ubiquitous computing (pp. 646–657).

Singh, V.K., & Ghosh, I. (2017). Inferring Individual Social Capital Automatically via Phone Logs. In Proceedings of the ACM Human Computer Interaction, 1 (CSCW), Article 95.

Singh, V. K., Freeman, L., Lepri, B., & Pentland, A. S. (2013). Predicting spending behavior using socio-mobile features. In Social computing (socialcom), 2013 international conference on (pp. 174–179).

Taylor, S. E., & Brown, J. D. (1988). Illusion and well-being: a social psychological perspective on mental health. Psychological bulletin,103(2), 193.

Thoits, P. A. (2011). Mechanisms linking social ties and support to physical and mental health. Journal of health and social behavior,52 (2), 145–161.

Tufekci, Z. (2015). Algorithmic harms beyond facebook and google: Emergent challenges of computational agency. J. on Telecomm. & High Tech. L.,13, 203.

Turner, M., Love, S., & Howell, M. (2008). Understanding emotions experienced when using a mobile phone in public: The social usability of mobile (cellular) telephones. Telematics and Informatics, 25 (3), 201–215.

Uchino, B. N. (2004). Social support and physical health: Understanding the health consequences of relationships. Yale University Press.

Underwood, L. G. (2000). Social relationships and health. Social support measurement and intervention: A guide for health and social scientists, 1.18

Wang, P. S., Aguilar-Gaxiola, S., Alonso, J., Angermeyer, M. C., Borges, G., Bromet, E. J., . . . others (2007). Use of mental health services for anxiety, mood, and substance disorders in 17 countries in the who world mental health surveys. The Lancet, 370 (9590), 841–850.

Wang, R., Chen, F., Chen, Z., Li, T., Harari, G., Tignor, S., . . . Campbell, A. T. (2014). Studentlife: assessing mental health, academic performance and behavioral trends of college students using smartphones. In Proceedings of the 2014 acm international joint conference on pervasive and ubiquitous computing (pp.3–14).

Ware Jr, J. E. (2000). Sf-36 health survey update. Spine, 25 (24), 3130–3139.

Ware Jr, J. E., & Sherbourne, C. D. (1992). The mos 36-item short-form health survey (sf-36): I. conceptual framework and item selection. Medical care , 473–483.

Williams, D. (2006). On and off thenet: Scales for social capital in an online era. Journal of Computer-Mediated Communication, 11 (2), 593–628.

Wilson, D. S., Clark, A. B., Coleman, K., & Dearstyne, T. (1994). Shyness and boldness in humans and other animals. Trends in Ecology & Evolution, 9(11), 442–446

Characterizing and Exploring Users' Task Completion Process at Different Stages in Learning Related Tasks

Xiaoxuan Song
Peking University, Beijing, China.
songxiaoxuan@pku.edu.cn

Hanrui Liu
Peking University, Beijing, China.
lhr2013@pku.edu.cn

Chang Liu
Peking University, Beijing, China. imliuc@pku.edu.cn

ABSTRACT

This study explored user interactions when accomplishing learning related tasks from a new perspective, the process perspective, and examined three main types of user interactions: searching, reading and writing behaviors. The goal is to characterize how users' searching, reading, and writing interactions change at different stages, and explore what contextual factors are related to the task completion process. A user experiment with thirty-two participants was conducted, and each participant was asked to work on two types of learning tasks: receptive tasks and critical tasks. For data analysis, we calculated the percentage of searching time, reading time and writing time during four stages, to characterize users' task completion process. Our results demonstrated that users' reading efforts were evenly distributed at four stages; half of their searching efforts were devoted at the first stage and writing efforts were mainly spent at the last stage. In addition, we also found task type and users' cognitive style had significant effects on users' searching, reading, writing process, and their writing efforts in the first stage were correlated to the quality of learning outcome. This study took the process perspective to characterize user interactions at different stages, and this perspective provides us a more comprehensive picture of user interactions and has implications for the design of search systems to fully support user interactions and their task completion process.

KEYWORDS

Searching process, reading process, writing process, task stage, learning related tasks.

INTRODUCTION

In interactive information retrieval, it is generally believed that better understanding of how users interact with search systems help improve users' search experience and search performance. Studies on user interactions during search episode have primarily focused on users' querying behaviors to examine how people express their needs or examination strategies on search result pages (SERPs) (White, Dumais & Teevan, 2009; Monchaux et al., 2015). However, searching for information is only one subtask in task performance. Besides searching, people also need to access information resources and browse or read specific webpages to acquire information. Since current search systems have performed well on retrieving specific factual information, most of current studies focus on complex exploratory search, especially learning related task (Marchionini, 2006). When searching for learning related tasks, people would involve in various types of activities. Järvelin et al. (2015) identified five main activities of information interactions during learning related tasks: task planning, searching information items, selecting information items, working with information items, and synthesizing and reporting. They further proposed an evaluation framework of task-based information interaction (TBII) and suggested all these five generic activities deserved more detailed examination because all of them contribute to task performance and outcome. Therefore, in the current study, we examine three main types of activities when users are working for learning related tasks: searching behaviors, reading behaviors and writing behaviors. Searching behaviors refers to user interactions on search homepages and search results pages; reading behaviors refers to user interactions on content pages; and writing behaviors refers to user interactions on the writing applications during the process of task completion.

In addition, we investigated these activities from a process perspective, aiming to characterize how people proceed on their searching/reading/writing activities through the process of task completion. Search stage has been found to be a significant factor affecting search behaviors in previous studies. Kuhlthau (1991) proposed six stages in ISP model to describe information seeking process for longitudinal learning related tasks. Recently, there have been some studies on analyzing within-session interaction variables with the purpose to generate real-time predictive models of task features or contextual factors (Liu, Liu & Belkin, 2014; Jiang, He & Allan, 2014; Liu & Wei, 2016). The current study extended these studies on characterizing the whole task completion process, by examining searching, reading and writing behaviors at different stages, and investigated how contextual factors would influence the process of these activities and how these activity process variables are related to the quality of learning outcome when users are searching for learning related tasks. Specifically, the current study aims to address the following three research questions:

RQ1: How to characterize users' searching, reading and writing process when searching for learning related tasks?

RQ2: How do users' individual characteristics and task type affect their searching, reading, writing process in one search episode when searching for learning related tasks?

RQ3: How are users' searching, reading and writing process related to their learning outcome?

RELATED WORK

Searching, Reading, Writing Behaviors

The goal of information searching is to find information so that to support task completion and task performance. When accomplishing a task, especially learning related tasks, users do not only search for information, during the search episode, they should also read and make sense of the information, and also produce information to accomplish the task (Vakkari, 2003). Thus, searching for information is only a subtask in a search episode, and a complete analysis of task completion process should also include other activities. Järvelin et al. (2015) proposed a task-based information interaction (TBII) model to evaluate information interaction activities in learning related tasks. They identified five main activities: task planning, searching information items, selecting information items, working with information items, and synthesizing and reporting. The TBII evaluation framework has the strength of supporting activity-based and comprehensive evaluation. However, no empirical study has examined these different activities in task completion process yet. Thus, the current study will examine different types of activities and how these activities proceed at different stages when users are searching for learning related tasks. Among these five activities, task planning is not easy to detect from users' interaction log; searching information items and selecting information items are both related to users' interactions on search homepages and search result pages; working with information items mainly belong to users' interactions on content pages; and synthesizing and reporting are related to users' interactions on learning outputs, e.g. written summaries or research papers in learning related tasks. Therefore, the current study focuses on three types of activities: searching behaviors, reading behaviors and writing behaviors.

Many studies have examined users' searching behaviors, e.g. query-related behaviors and SERP-related variables. Studies that focused on query behavior or search strategies mainly examined users' searching behaviors. The reading behaviors examined in this study specifically refers to the reading and browsing behaviors on content pages. Studies have found that users would read more content pages if they expected the task was difficult before searching in exploratory tasks, while the number of content pages visited was positively related to the experienced task difficulty when completing factual tasks (Kim, 2007). There have also been some studies that focused on writing behaviors during task completion process. For example, Liu and Belkin (2012) regarded task process as two types of activities, searching and writing, and examined factors that influenced these two types of behaviors. Hagen et al. (2016) investigated how writers conducted search to produce essays on different topics using Clueweb09. They compared writers' searching and writing behaviors at different task phases—early, middle and late, and found most queries and clicks happened in early phases, while writing happened in later phase. However, they did not further examine factors that could influence writer's working strategies, nor how their working strategy was related to the quality of writing output. In the current study, we first explored users' searching, reading and writing behaviors and examined whether contextual factors would influence these activities during task completion process.

Stages during Task Process

When searching for a complex task, learning related task in particular, users usually have to go through several stages within a search session to accomplish the task. Kuhlthau's ISP model (1991) highlighted search process in information seeking and identified six stages: initiation, selection, exploration, formulation, collection and presentation, and stressed that users' feelings, thoughts and actions all changed as search proceeded. Vakkari (2001) identified three problem stages when students were writing their research proposals for a master's thesis: pre-focus, formulation, post-focus. In interactive information retrieval studies, there is a trend to explore users' search interactions during different search stages. Some recent studies have made some relatively explicit exploration on splitting different task stages and found that task stage affected users' interactive behaviors. Liu, Liu & Belkin (2014) investigated users' behaviors at different stages of the search process: first-round point, middle point, and end point, to generate predictive models of task difficulties based on users' interactions at different search stages. Their results demonstrated that behaviors at the first query round could achieve best prediction performance. Jiang, He & Allan (2014) compared users' search behaviors in the initial query with that in subsequent query reformulations to examine how users' search behaviors changed in a search session. The results showed that users decreased interests on search results as the search session progressed. Liu & Wei (2016) examined the effects of time constraint on users' information search strategies during search process. They compared users' searching behavior with time constraint and without time constraint at two search stages: the first query interval and the whole session. They found that users under different time conditions behaved significantly different in their interactions during the first query interval and were not significantly different when considering the whole search episode. These studies highlighted the importance of first query interval, and users may have most difficulties at the beginning of the search. However, they did not examine the changes at the later stages during one search episode, and how users' interactions evolve through the way. Thus, in the current study, we segmented user's total task time of one search episode into four even stages to characterize and analyze users' searching, reading and writing process.

Contextual Factors

Research has found that context is an important factor that influences users' information search behaviors. Context includes many factors, such as users' individual characteristics, time and space factors, environment, social factors, and task context, and etc. (Cool & Spink, 2002). Research has found that individual characteristics, such as users' domain knowledge, cognitive style affect users' search behaviors. Some studies (Zhang, Anghelescu & Yuan, 2005; Wildemuth, 2004; White, Dumais & Teevan, 2009; Monchaux et al., 2015) have found that users' domain knowledge had significant effects on users' query tactics (e.g. the length of query, the source of query terms, query reformulation etc.) and search strategies (e.g. the features of searching, browsing or clicking on pages). With respect to user's cognitive style, Riding and Cheema (1991) classified cognitive style into two types: wholistic and analytic styles. Research has examined the effects of users' cognitive style on their search behaviors, and found that users with wholistic style tended to adopt a top-down approach, in which they first searched for a generic topic, and then reformulated their queries to search for specific information by adding query terms and read result pages more carefully; on the contrary, analytic users had a tendency to have bottom-up search strategies (Kinley & Tjondronegoro, 2010).

Another important influencing factor that influences users' behaviors during searching is task type (Kellar, Watters & Shepherd, 2007; Toms et al., 2007; Kim, 2009). Different researchers may classify tasks according to different facets (Marchionini, 1989; Kim, 2009; Jiang, He & Allan, 2014). With respect to learning related tasks, many studies adopted Anderson and Krathwohl's taxonomy of cognitive learning (Anderson & Krathwohl, 2001): remember, understand, apply, analyze, evaluate and create, e.g. Jansen, Booth & Smith (2009). Wu et al. (2012) constructed learning related tasks based on modified five-levels of this category except applying level, and found that users tended to spend more time, issue more queries, click on more search results, and visit more URLs as the cognitive complexity of task increased. Lee et al. (2014) proposed three types of cognitive learning tasks: receptive learning, critical learning, and creative learning to address the operationalization issues, and the learning related tasks designed in the current study was based on this task classification, and our goal is to examine whether task type would influence users' searching/reading/writing process.

METHODOLOGY

User Experiment

We conducted a user experiment to explore users' search process with thirty-two participants recruited from Peking University. Among all the participants, there were twelve males and twenty females, and their ages were between eighteen and thirty. There were twenty undergraduates and twelve graduate students, who majored in Humanities, Social Science, Information Science, Engineering, and Medical domains.

Participants used desktop computer to carry out four learning related search tasks. Two types of learning related tasks were constructed according to the first two levels of Cognitive Learning Mode (Lee et al., 2014) classification: receptive task and critical task. Receptive task is defined as understanding, remembering and reproducing what is taught, such as facts, concepts, procedures and principles, while critical task is defined as criticizing and evaluating ideas from multiple perspectives. There are two tasks for each type, and task descriptions are shown below. The sequence of tasks was rotated using Latin Square to reduce the learning and fatigue effects for the participants.

Task 1 (Receptive, about masks): *The haze is getting worse and worse, and you insistent demand of mask. Before buying a mask, you want to know what types of masks are available, and the differences between different types of masks, and which masks are suitable for young people.*

Task 2 (Receptive, about blood pressure monitor): *Elderly people in your family have high blood pressure and need to buy a blood pressure monitor to monitor their blood pressure. However, the family lacks experience in purchasing blood pressure monitor. Please find out which aspects should be used to evaluate the quality of household blood pressure monitor.*

Task 3 (Critical, about playing soccer): *Your cousin in junior high considers joining the school soccer team. Most of the relatives support this idea. But others suggest that soccer is a dangerous sport with potential health risks. His parents inquire your opinion on advantages and disadvantages of playing soccer for a long time, and should children join the soccer team?*

Task 4 (Critical, about snow boots): *On the Internet, there are some views about the harmful effects of snow boots on the health. They believe that snow boots can cause hurts in feet, ankles and hips. But on the other hand, there are many netizens who refute this idea. Please analyze and summarize your views on whether the snow boots will have an impact on your health.*

The procedure of our experiment is as follows: participants were first asked to complete a background questionnaire and the Cognitive Style Test developed by Peterson's Extended Cognitive Style Test: Wholistic/Analytic test (Peterson, Deary & Austin, 2005). After reading the task description and before searching, participants were asked to write down what they have already known about the tasks in the pre-search questionnaire on their own, without referring to any external references; during the search, they could write/copy/paste/reorganize related information to answer the questions raised in the search tasks in the notepad files; after the participants completed searching, they were asked to close all the webpages and notepad files, and write down what they knew about the question again in the post-search questionnaire on their own. During search, users' interactions with the computer were recorded by Morae Recorder.

Assessment of Pre-search knowledge and Learning Outcome

In this study, we assessed the participants' written summaries before and after task. The written summary before searching for the task was considered as the basis for assessing participants' pre-search knowledge level; and the written summary after searching was considered as their learning outcome. These written summaries were evaluated based on four measures: number of knowledge facets, number of knowledge points, breadth of knowledge scope, and depth of knowledge. To be specific, we first extracted all the knowledge points from participants' written texts before and after searching, and then summarized these knowledge points into different knowledge facets to represent the scope of knowledge for each task. The extraction of knowledge points and classification of knowledge facets were conducted through manual coding by two independent coders. When disagreements rose, a third independent coder encoded the inconsistent data. During the coding process in this study, the two coders achieved Fleiss k of 0.85, which reached the consistent agreement tests. Finally for each search task, the coders reached several knowledge facets. For instance, there were eight knowledge facets in Task 1 about masks: model, material, function, appearance, characteristic, recognition, use and price. Then we calculated the breadth of knowledge scope *(calculated as the number of knowledge facets divided by the total number of knowledge facets for the task) and* the depth of knowledge *(calculated as the number of knowledge points divided by the number of knowledge facets).*

Further, we conducted K-means clustering based on the above four indicators of written summaries before and after task respectively. Before searching for the task, 128 sessions were clustered into two groups: "low pre-search knowledge" (N=69) and "high pre-search knowledge" (N=59), as shown in left three columns of Table 1. The t-test result shows that participants with low pre-search knowledge had significant fewer knowledge points, fewer knowledge facets, smaller knowledge scope and shallower depth of knowledge. Similarly, all the sessions were clustered into two groups according to the values in these four indicators in their written summaries after search: "low learning outcome" and "high learning outcome", as shown in right three columns of Table 1. Similarly, there were significant differences between low and high learning outcome in four indicators related knowledge.

Indicators	Pre-search knowledge			Learning outcome after search		
	Low(N=69)	High(N=59)	p	Low(N=57)	High(N=71)	p
Knowledge points	0.96	5.08	<0.0001	4.65	15.17	<0.0001
Knowledge facets	0.67	2.63	<0.0001	2.12	4.45	<0.0001
Knowledge scope	0.09	0.39	<0.0001	0.33	0.65	<0.0001
Depth of knowledge	0.80	2.00	<0.0001	2.17	3.57	<0.0001

Table 1. The clustering analysis results of pre-search knowledge and learning outcome

Users' Searching, Reading, Writing Process

Our goal is to examine how would the percentage of users' searching time, reading time and writing time at each stage change during the whole task completion process. Would users proceed their searching, reading and writing evenly at each stage or would users devote different amounts of efforts on searching, reading and writing at different stages? We first distinguished users' searching, reading and writing behaviors in a search episode. Searching is defined as the process that users had interactions on search homepages or search result pages; reading is defined as the process when users interact with content pages; and writing is defined as the process when users interact with notepad files. With respect to characterizing users' searching, reading, and writing process, we first segmented user's total task completion time in one search episode into four even stages. Stage one (S1) to stage four (S4) represented the first quarter, a quarter to a half, half to three quarters, and the last quarter of the total task time respectively, as shown in the x axis of Figure 1. For users' searching process, we first extracted

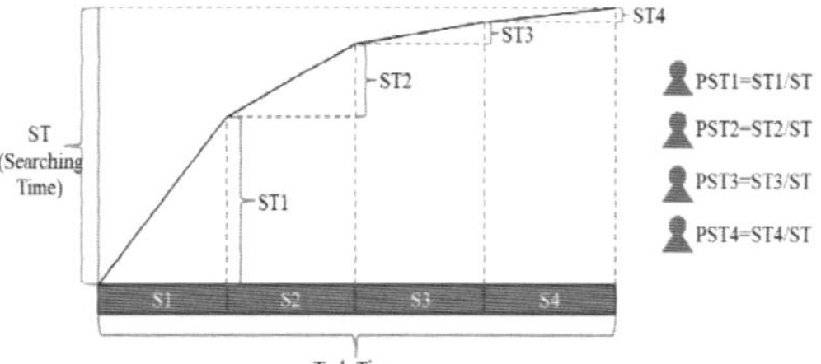

Figure 1. A demonstration of the calculation of PSTs

all users' searching interactions, i.e. users' interactions on search homepages and search result pages, and considered all the time on searching interactions as the total searching time (ST); then we segmented these interactions into four even stages during the search episode (S1 to S4), and calculated time they spent on searching during each stage, ST1 to ST4. Therefore, we could calculate the percentage of time the user spent on searching during each stage (PST[i]) as following equation:

$$PST[i] = ST[i] / ST$$

ST[i] represents the time a user spent on searching during the ith stage, ST refers to the total searching time in a search session. Figure 1 shows a demonstration of the calculation of PSTs at four stages to visualize users' searching process.

Similarly we could calculate the percentage of time they spent on reading during each stage (PRT[i]) as:

$$PRT[i] = RT[i] / RT$$

RT[i] represents the time a user spent on reading during the ith stage, and RT refers to the total reading time in a session.

Finally, the percentage of time they spent on writing during each stage (PWT[i]) could be calculated as:

$$PWT[i] = WT[i] / WT$$

WT[i] represents the time a user spent on writing during the ith stage, and WT refers to the total writing time in a session.

Contextual Variables

This study aims to explore the influence of task type and individual characteristics on users' searching, reading and writing process. The first contextual variable is task type, which was designed and manipulated into two types of learning related tasks, receptive tasks and critical tasks, as described in the previous part. As our experiment focused on the learning related tasks, we selected two knowledge characteristics of users that might be associated with users' learning outcome: pre-search knowledge and cognitive style. According to the clustering analysis based on the four indicators of users' written summaries before searching, participants' were classified into two groups: low pre-search knowledge (69 sessions), high pre-search knowledge (59 sessions). For the cognitive style, we used E-CSA-WA test to assess users' cognitive style tendency. The test produces a wholistic/analytic ratio for each participant. The ratio close to 0 indicates a tendency of wholistic style, and analytic style is related to a ratio closer to 2 or above. In this study, we selected the median (1.19) as a cutting-off score and had 16 participants in wholistic style and the other 16 in analytic groups.

RESULTS

Characterizing Searching, Reading, Writing Process

We first characterized users' overall searching, reading, writing process in their search episode. If users developed their searching, reading and writing efforts gradually in each stage, then the percentage of their searching/reading/writing time (PST, PRT, PWT) at each stage should all be approximately equal. In order to compare users' percentage of time on searching/reading/writing in the four stages, we conducted paired samples t-tests on PST, PRT and PWT among different stages respectively.

(1) Searching process

With respect to the searching process, after calculating the percentage of their searching time at each stage, we conducted paired samples t-tests among PST1, PST2, PST3, and PST4. The results of these tests are shown in Table 2, and the mean of PSTs at four stages are shown in Figure 2. The results revealed that PST1 was significantly higher than PSTs in the latter three stages (PST2, PST3, PST4) during a search episode ($p<0.0001$). As shown in Figure 2, users devoted nearly half of their searching time at the first stage (PST1=47%). In the latter three stages, users devoted similar percentage of their searching time and they were relatively low (around 18%).

Searching	PST1	PST2	PST3	PST4
PST1				
PST2	**0.0001***			
PST3	**0.0001***	0.984		
PST4	**0.0001***	0.726	0.723	

Table 2. Results of paired samples t-tests on PSTs

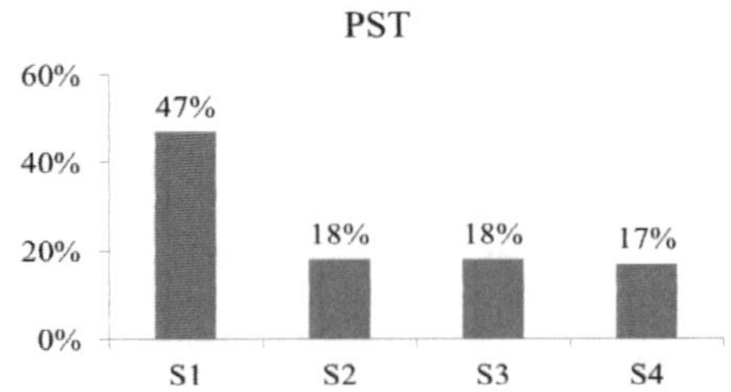

Figure 2. *The mean of PSTs at four stages*

(2) Reading process

We then conducted paired samples t-tests among PRT1, PRT2, PRT3, and PRT4 to compare the differences among the percentage of their reading time among different stages. The results of these tests are shown in Table 3, and the mean of PRTs at four stages are shown in Figure 3. The results revealed that PRT4 was significantly lower than PRTs in the first and second stages (PRT1 and PRT2) during a search episode ($p<0.05$). As shown in Figure 3, users devoted probably 27%-28% reading time in their first two stages, and spent about 21% of reading time in the last stage. However, their differences were not much, so such results indicated that users spent their reading time at four stages evenly as the task proceeded.

Reading	PRT1	PRT2	PRT3	PRT4
PRT1				
PRT2	0.468			
PRT3	0.302	0.069		
PRT4	**0.022***	**0.004***	0.121	

Table 3. Results of paired samples t-tests on PRTs

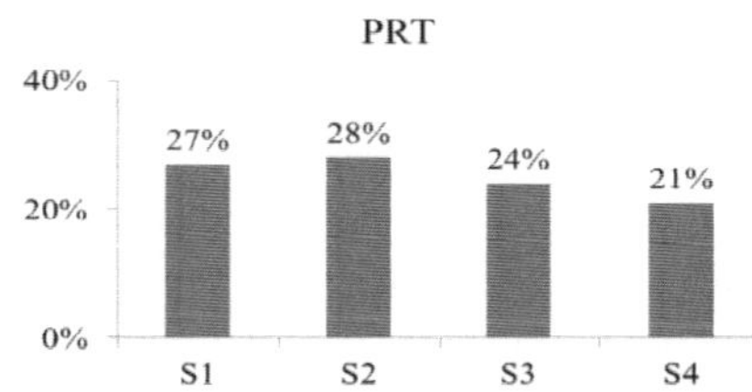

Figure 3. The mean of PRTs at four stages

(3) Writing process

The paired samples t-test results among PWTs and the mean of PWTs at four stages are shown in Table 4 and Figure 4. The results showed PWT1 was significantly lower than PWTs at the latter three stages ($p<0.0001$), and PWT4 was significantly higher than PWTs at the first three stages ($p<0.0001$). There was no significant difference between the 2nd and 3rd stage (19%~22%). Such results indicate that users could not write much at the first stage, could gradually contribute some writing at the middle stages, and devoted most of their writing efforts at the last stage.

Writing	PWT1	PWT2	PWT3	PWT4
PWT1				
PWT2	**0.0001***			
PWT3	**0.0001***	0.260		
PWT4	**0.0001***	**0.0001***	**0.0001***	

Table 4. Results of paired samples t-tests on PWTs

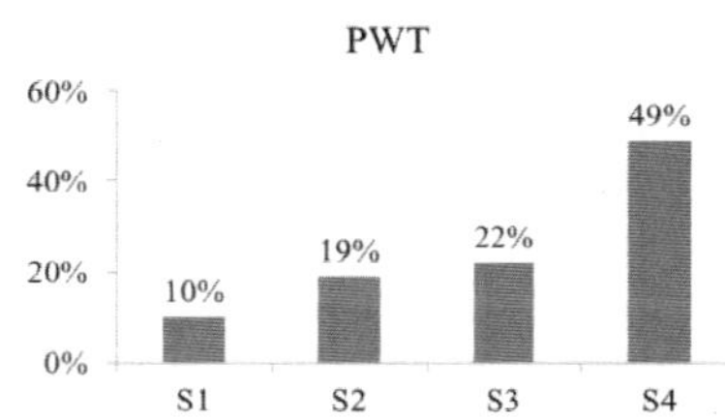

Figure 4. The mean of PWTs at four stages

The Effects of Individual Characteristics and Task Type

We conducted t-test analysis to examine the effects of three contextual factors on users' searching, reading, writing process in a search episode: pre-search knowledge, cognitive style and task type. In general, the results demonstrated that users' pre-search knowledge had no significant effect on their searching, reading, writing process, while users' cognitive style and task type had significant effects on their searching, reading and writing process. The detailed results are as following.

(1) Searching process

As shown in Table 5, Users' cognitive style had significant effect on users' searching process in the first and last stages. Wholistic style users had significantly higher PST1 than those with analytic style (50.27% vs. 41.55%), but wholistic style users had significantly lower PST4 than those with analytic style (13.68% vs. 21.25%). The results revealed that users with wholistic style tended to devote more searching efforts at the first stage than analytic style users, while analytic style users had more searching efforts at the last stage than wholistic users. Such results indicated that even though all users devoted most efforts at the first stage, analytic searchers contributed on searching continuously even in the last stage.

It was also found that task type had significant effect on users' searching process. As shown in Table 6, PST2 in receptive tasks was significantly lower than those in critical learning tasks (14.37% vs. 22.11%). It seems that users spent relatively more percent of time on searching during the second stage in critical tasks and searched relatively less during the third and last stages; while users in receptive tasks searched relatively less during the second stage but had more searching during the third and last stages.

Cognitive style	Wholistic	Analytic	p
PST1	**50.27%**	**41.55%**	**0.047***
PST2	18.04%	18.64%	0.855
PST3	18.01%	18.56%	0.877
PST4	**13.68%**	**21.25%**	**0.025***

Table 5: The effects of cognitive style on PTSs

Task type	Receptive task	Critical task	p
PST1	46.41%	45.63%	0.859
PST2	**4.37%**	**22.11%**	**0.018***
PST3	20.01%	16.63%	0.345
PST4	19.21%	15.63%	0.287

Table 6: The effects of task type on PTSs

(2) Reading process

With respect to users' reading process, it was found that users' cognitive style did not have significant effects. Results revealed that there were significant differences in PRT4 between receptive tasks and critical tasks, as shown in Table 8. In receptive tasks, users' percentage of reading time (PRT) was around 25% in all four stages. However, in critical tasks, users' PRTs at the first three stages were higher than the last stage. Specifically, users' PRT4 in critical tasks was significantly lower than that in receptive tasks (17.27% vs. 24.33%). Such results indicated that users did not spend much time on reading in critical tasks during the last stage.

Cognitive style	Wholistic	Analytic	p
PRT1	24.13%	29.17%	0.088
PRT2	28.85%	27.88%	0.751
PRT3	24.31%	24.33%	0.997
PRT4	22.71%	18.62%	0.196

Table 7. The effects of cognitive style on PRTs

Task type	Receptive task	Critical task	p
PRT1	23.91%	29.14%	0.076
PRT2	26.41%	30.25%	0.204
PRT3	25.36%	23.34%	0.430
PRT4	**24.33%**	**17.27%**	**0.025***

Table 8. The effects of task type on PRTs

(3) Writing process

Again, results revealed that there was no significant relationship between users' cognitive style and PWTs. Yet, task type was found to have a significant effect on PWTs, as shown in Table 10. Users wrote more in receptive tasks than critical tasks during the first (12.49% vs. 6.83%) and second stages (23.50% vs. 15.66%), while users devoted probably half of their writing time at the last stage with higher in critical task and lower in receptive task. Such results demonstrated that users were able to produce learning outcome much earlier in receptive tasks than in critical tasks.

Cognitive style	Wholistic	Analytic	p
PWT1	9.05%	10.16%	0.562
PWT2	21.42%	17.46%	0.223
PWT3	22.08%	22.36%	0.935
PWT4	47.45%	50.02%	0.593

Table 9. The effects of cognitive style on PWTs

Task type	Receptive task	Critical task	p
PWT1	**12.49%**	**6.83%**	**0.003***
PWT2	**23.50%**	**15.66%**	**0.015***
PWT3	21.52%	22.89%	0.693
PWT4	**42.50%**	**54.62%**	**0.011***

Table 10. The effects of task type on PWTs

The Correlation between Searching, Reading, Writing Process and Learning Outcome

We further investigated the relationship between users' searching, reading, and writing process and their learning outcome. As described in the methodology part, search sessions were clustered into two groups according to users' learning outcome: sessions with high learning outcome and sessions with low learning outcome. Thus, in this part analysis, we conducted t-tests analysis to examine the differences in users' searching/reading/writing process variables between high and low learning outcome sessions. The results showed (in Table 11) that sessions with high learning outcome had higher PWT1 than those with low learning outcome (12.30% vs. 6.24%). Such results indicated that users who devoted more efforts in writing at the first stage were more likely to have higher quality of learning outcome.

Process variables	Learning outcome		p	Process variables	Learning outcome		p	Process variables	Learning outcome		p
	Low	High			Low	High			Low	High	
PST1	49.44%	43.23%	0.162	PRT1	28.12%	25.35%	0.354	**PWT1**	**6.24%**	**12.30%**	**0.001***
PST2	15.22%	20.86%	0.083	PRT2	28.60%	28.20%	0.896	PWT2	19.51%	19.47%	0.990
PST3	17.44%	18.96%	0.672	PRT3	25.62%	23.27%	0.359	PWT3	23.86%	20.89%	0.395
PST4	17.90%	16.95%	0.781	PRT4	17.66%	23.18%	0.080	PWT4	50.39%	47.34%	0.528

Table 11. The comparison of PSTs, PRTs, PWTs between high and low learning outcome sessions

DISCUSSION

Stages in Task Completion Process

In this study, we segmented the whole task time into four even stages (S1 to S4), to explore whether users' searching, reading and writing efforts at each stage were equally distributed. The results showed users' efforts at the first and last stages were significantly different, especially in searching and writing activities, yet users' interactions during the second and third stages were relatively low and equal. In particular, users devoted nearly half of their searching time during the first stage, while they devoted about half of their writing time during the last stage. The results highlighted the importance of the first and last stages during a search episode, suggested that users may need system assistance during the first and last stages. Previous studies had stressed the importance of the first query interval, since users' interactions in the first query interval were significantly different (Jiang, He & Allan, 2014; Liu & Wei, 2016), and also suggested users' interactions at the first query interval could achieve relatively better prediction of task difficulty (Liu, Liu & Belkin, 2014). Most of these studies segmented the whole task completion process according to query intervals and they had not examined users' interactions during the last stage in details; furthermore, when there were not many queries issued, it would be difficult to segment the whole process. In the current study, we segmented stages by the total task completion time, and presented how users' searching, reading and writing efforts changed through the whole process.

Searching, Reading and Writing Process

We traced respectively three types of activities during a search episode: searching, reading and writing, and found that the three processes advanced in completely different path at different stages. Users' reading efforts were distributed relatively even at four different stages, showing a progressive pattern. With respect to the searching process, users tended to devote nearly half of the searching efforts at the first stage and had a significantly drop in searching efforts at the latter three stages. For the writing process, users could hardly write much at the first stage and devoted nearly half of their writing efforts at the last stage. Such results demonstrated that searching is only one subtask for task completion, and it is necessary to examine different types of users' interactions and how each type of interactions evolve during the task process. This study is a first attempt to examine users' searching, reading and writing process respectively during a search episode, and future work is also needed to further examine how users integrate different types of activities together and how searching process, reading process, and writing process would affect each other.

The Effects of Contextual Factors

In this study, we examined the effects of users' individual characteristics and task type on users' searching, reading, writing process. The results showed that users' cognitive style had some effects on their searching process. Specifically, wholistic users devoted more searching efforts at the first stage and less efforts at the last stage than analytic users. This may be explained by the top-down strategies by wholistic style users (Kinley & Tjondronegoro, 2010). Users with wholistic style tended to first search for a generic topic to have a complete picture of the search topic, and then transited to search for specific information.

It was also found that task type had a significant effect on users' writing process. Users wrote more at the early stages (first and second stages) in receptive learning tasks than critical learning tasks. Receptive tasks only require users to remember and understand the information in the learning process (Rieh et al., 2016), therefore, as soon as users got some related information, they could write it down, so they were able to start writing in earlier stages. On the other hand, when searching for critical learning tasks, users need to compare, analyze and evaluate information beyond the factual information acquisition (Rieh et al., 2016), so they may have to collect enough information and get some understanding before they started writing, which led to a delayed writing process.

The Correlation between Process and Users' Learning Outcome

This study also examined the relationship between users' searching, reading, writing process and their learning outcome, and found that users with high learning outcome devoted significantly more writing efforts at the first stage. Such result suggested that users could have better quality of learning outcome if they started writing in earlier stages. This study cannot provide explanations for this phenomenon and why some users were able to start writing in quite earlier stages and some could not. This might be related to users' prior knowledge levels, or task features, and we will further examine this issue in our future work.

CONCLUSION

This study characterized users' searching, reading and writing process at different stages during a search episode. Users' interactions were collected through a user experiment, in which participants were asked to search for two types of learning related tasks: receptive tasks and critical tasks. The total task completion time was segmented evenly into four stages, and we extracted three types of users' interactions: searching, reading, and writing. The results showed that the first and last stages were most important stages during task completion. Users spent nearly half of their searching time at the first stage and devoted nearly half of writing time at the last stage, while their reading efforts were distributed relatively even at four different stages. With respect to the contextual factors, users' cognitive style had a significant effect on searching process at the first and last stages; task type had significant effects on their writing process. However, there was no relationship between users' pre-search knowledge and their searching, reading, writing process. With respect to users' learning outcome, users with high learning outcome devoted more writing efforts at the first stage. This is a preliminary exploration of users' searching, reading, writing process at different stages, and future research is still needed to verify the results of this study. Our results have shown that it is very necessary to examine different types of interactions from the process perspective, and users may need different types of assistance at different stages for task completion. Future research should further examine how users would integrate different types of activities, and what factors would influence their task completion process.

REFERENCES

Anderson, L. W. & Krathwohl, D. A. (2001). A taxonomy for learning, teaching and assessing: A revision of Bloom's taxonomy of educational objectives. New York: Longman.

Cool,C., & Spink, A. (2002). Issues of context in information retrieval (IR): an introduction to the special issue. *IP&M, 38*(5), 605-611.

Hagen, M., Potthast, M., Gomoll, J., & Stein, B. (2016). How Writers Search: Analyzing the Search and Writing Logs of Non-fictional Essays. *In Proceedings of the 2016 ACM on Conference on Human Information Interaction and Retrieval* (pp.193-202). ACM.

Jansen,B.J., Booth,D., & Smith, B.(2009).Using the taxonomy of cognitive learning to model online searching. *IP&M, 45*(6), 643-663.

Järvelin, K., Vakkari, P., Arvola, P., Baskaya, F., Keskustalo, H., & Kumpulainen, S., et al. (2015). Task-based information interaction evaluation: the viewpoint of program theory. *ACM Transactions on Information Systems (TOIS), 33*(1), 1-30.

Jiang, J., He, D., & Allan, J. (2014). Searching, browsing, and clicking in a search session: changes in user behavior by task and over time. *SIGIR 14'* (pp.607-616). ACM.

Kellar, M., Watters, C., & Shepherd, M. (2007). A field study characterizing web-based information-seeking tasks. *JASIS&T, 58*(7), 999-1018.

Kim,J.(2007).Task difficulty in information searching behavior: expected difficulty and experienced difficulty. *JCDL '05.* (pp.383-383).

Kim, J. (2009). Describing and predicting information-seeking behavior on the web. *JASIS&T, 60*(4), 679-693.

Kinley, K., & Tjondronegoro, D. (2010). User-web interactions: how wholistic/analytic web users search the web?. OZCHI'10. ACM.

Kuhlthau, C. C. (1991). Inside the search process: information seeking from the user's perspective. *JASIS&T, 42*(5), 361-371.

Lee H, Lee J, Makara K et al. (2014). Does higher education foster critical and creative learners? An exploration of two universities in South Korea and the USA. *Higher Education Research and Development, 34*(1): 131–146.

Liu, C., & Wei, Y. (2016). The impacts of time constraint on users' search strategy during search process. *ASIS&T, 53*(1), 1-9.

Liu, C., Liu, J., & Belkin, N. J. (2014). Predicting search task difficulty at different search stages. *CIKM'14*, 569-578.

Liu, J., & Belkin, N. J. (2012). Searching vs. writing: factors affecting information use task performance. *ASIS&T, 49*(1), 1-10.

Marchionini, G. (1989). Information-seeking strategies of novices using a full-text electronic encyclopedia. *JASIS&T, 40*(1), 54-66.

Marchionini, G. (2006). Exploratory search: from finding to understanding. *Communications of the ACM, 49*(4), 41-46.

Monchaux, S., Amadieu, F., Chevalier, A., & Mariné, C. (2015). Query strategies during information searching: effects of prior domain knowledge and complexity of the information problems to be solved. *IP&M, 51*(5), 557-569.

Peterson, E. R., Deary, I. J., & Austin, E. J. (2005). Are intelligence and personality related to verbal-imagery and wholistic-analytic cognitive styles?. *Personality & Individual Differences, 39*(1), 201-213.

Riding, R., & Cheema, I. (1991). Cognitive styles—an overview and integration. *Educational Psychology An International Journal of Experimental Educational Psychology, 11*(3-4), 193-215.

Rieh, S. Y., Collins-Thompson, K., Hansen, P., & Lee, H. J. (2016). Towards searching as a learning process. *Journal of Information Science, 42*(1), 19-34.

Toms, E., MacKenzie, T., Jordan, C., O'Brien, H., Freund, L., Toze, S., ... & MacNutt, A. (2007). How task affects information search. *In Workshop Pre-proceedings in Initiative for the Evaluation of XML Retrieval (INEX)* (pp. 337-341).

Vakkari, P. (2001). A theory of the task-based information retrieval process: a summary and generalisation of a longitudinal study. *Journal of Documentation, 57*(1), 44-60(17).

Vakkari, P. (2003). Task-based information searching. *Annual Review of Information Science & Technology, 37*(1), 413–464.

White, R. W., Dumais, S. T., & Teevan, J. (2009). Characterizing the influence of domain expertise on web search behavior. *WSDM '09* (pp.132-141). ACM.

Wildemuth, B. M. (2004). The effects of domain knowledge on search tactic formulation. *JASIS&T, 55*(3), 246–258.

Wu, W. C., Kelly, D., Edwards, A., & Arguello, J. (2012). Grannies, tanning beds, tattoos and NASCAR: evaluation of search tasks with varying levels of cognitive complexity. *IIiX'12.* (pp.254-257). ACM.

Zhang, X., Anghelescu, H. G. B., & Yuan, X. (2005). Domain knowledge, search behaviour, and search effectiveness of engineering and science students: an exploratory study. *Information Research An International Electronic Journal, 10*(2), 217-217.

The Contribution of Information Science in the Semantic Web Research Landscape

Marielle St-Germain
Université de Montréal, Canada. marielle.st-germain@umontreal.ca

Philippe Mongeon
Leiden University, Netherlands. p.mongeon@cwts.leidenuniv.nl

ABSTRACT

Semantic Web and Linked Data promise to change the way we identify, classify, share, find and reuse information by managing and interlinking data so that it can be understood by machines. The benefits identified by the World Wide Web Consortium and other Semantic Web advocates have lead information professionals to explore these possibilities by implementing several initiatives based on Semantic Web technologies in recent years. Just like information science, Semantic Web research is multidisciplinary in nature and can be applied in many different disciplines. In this article, we provide a portrait of research on the Semantic Web using bibliometric methods and investigate the specific contribution of information science literature on the topic. We analyzed 6,438 articles published from 2001 to 2016 retrieved from the Web of Science database to evaluate the evolution of the papers published by discipline and the way the topic was discussed by different discipline. A citation analysis is also conducted.

KEYWORDS

Semantic Web, Linked Data, Information science, Bibliometrics, Citation analysis

INTRODUCTION

Seventeen years have passed since Berners-Lee, Hendler and Lassila's article (2001) describing the Semantic Web's functionalities and core technologies. Much research efforts related to the development and application of these technologies have since then occurred in various domains. The Semantic Web proposes a way of processing information and its data on the World Wide Web. Although it can be understood by humans, the information and data found on web pages is not structured and has no semantic value, so machines can't process and understand it. With the help of specific standards and technologies that enable this "understanding" by machines, the goal of the Semantic Web is to allow both humans and computers to find, share, reuse and modify information more quickly and efficiently. To achieve this, the World Wide Web Consortium (W3C) works on setting up standards that allow the permanent identification of entities (names of people, concepts, places, events, subjects, etc.), the expression of semantic relations between these entities and complex reasoning on data. In the information science field, the concepts and technologies surrounding the Semantic Web are particularly interesting because they can improve information retrieval, access to data between institutions and the visibility of institutions and their collections on the Web. Such promises, arising from this new way of thinking about knowledge management and representation, come with a certain appeal, especially for Linked Data, commonly referred to as a set of best practices for publishing and interlinking structured data on the Web (Bizer, Heath & Berners-Lee, 2009; W3C, 2014).

Several initiatives demonstrate the interest of our discipline in these technologies. In 2010, the W3C created the Library Linked Data Incubator Group[1] composed of thirteen early adopters from different institutions. Then, in 2012, the Library of Congress (LC) announced that the company Zepheira was charged of developing an alternative to the MARC standards based on Linked Data principles. The BIBFRAME model[2] is constantly evolving and more and more libraries are working on its implementation, demonstrating the importance that libraries give to these technologies. In the same year, OCLC released the experimental project WorldCat Linked Data, which is a Linked Open Data (LOD) version of their catalog. Finally, several libraries have developed projects implementing Semantic Web technologies such as the Swedish National Library[3], the French National Library[4], the German National Library[5], the British Library[6] and the National Library of Spain[7]. Let us also mention the Oslo

---

[1] https://www.w3.org/2005/Incubator/lld/
[2] https://www.loc.gov/bibframe/docs/bibframe2-model.html
[3] https://id.kb.se/
[4] http://data.bnf.fr/
[5] http://www.dnb.de/EN/Service/DigitaleDienste/LinkedData/linkeddata_node.html
[6] http://bnb.data.bl.uk/
[7] http://datos.bne.es/inicio.html

Public Library[8], which took the decision in 2014 to work on the development of a new library system based entirely on the Resource Description Framework (RDF), the data model behind the Semantic Web. This new interest from the community of information professionals is also characterized by collaborative projects such as Linked Data for Production (LD4P)[9] and the Canadian Linked Data Initiative[10].

Information professionals are no strangers to the need to adapt to technological evolution and to develop their skills to meet the various challenges brought by these changes. They are trained to use standards, analyze structured information and participate in the definition and evolution of formats to preserve, manipulate and exchange data (DeWeese & Segal, 2014). The concerns behind the development of Semantic Web technologies are similar to those expressed by the library community and the fact that standards like MARC are now considered outdated pushes information professionals to consider these technologies as a viable option (Alemu, Stevens, Ross & Chandler, 2012; Coyle, 2010). Considering that information science, just like the Semantic Web, is interdisciplinary and multidisciplinary in nature and directly connected to information technology and computer science (Holland, 2008; Knapp, 2012; Paul-Hus, Mongeon & Shu, 2016; Saracevic, 1995; Szostak, 2008), and that Semantic Web technologies can be relevant in almost all disciplines, it is interesting to study the contribution of information science in that research landscape and the feedback of the discipline to the broader Semantic Web community.

Related work

To our knowledge, there is only a few quantitative studies that have been conducted on Semantic Web research and on the impact of information science in this specific field of research. Ding (2010) proposed a portrait of the research on the Semantic Web based on papers and citations collected from the Web of Science (WoS) and Scopus, but a too broad set of keywords ("Ontolog*" OR "Semantic*") was used to conduct the study. She also focused on computer science and library and information sciences, which may exclude publications outside these two fields. Given the constant evolution of this field, the data from 1960-2009 may not provide an accurate portrait of the current state of research on the Semantic Web and one of the goal of this study is to fill that gap. Zhu and colleagues (2015) analyzed global ontology research from 1900 to 2012. Based on Ding's study (2010), they used the term "ontolog*" in the topic field of the WoS. Author keywords analysis allowed the team to identify applications in Semantic Web as one of the core categories. We argue that Ontology should not be considered as the main technology of the Semantic Web: it is indeed an important part of the architecture of the Semantic Web, but so are identifiers (URI), SPARQL queries, RDF, and the many other buildings blocks of the technology. Moreover, ontology is a broader term that can yield much false positives when using it alone as keyword to delineate the Semantic Web research field. Li and colleagues (2017) focused on portraying geo-ontology research by analyzing papers from the WoS published from 1999 to 2014. They used the query "geo*" AND "ontolog*" in the title, abstract and topic fields. Finally, Bansal, Bansal & Kumar (2017) conducted a study to analyze the Indian research output in Semantic Web. They restricted their search to the 2007 to 2016 period and retrieved publication data using the terms "semantic web" OR "ontolog*" in the title and the keyword fields. They were able to compare contributions from Indian institutions to institutions from the other nine most productive countries in Semantic Web research.

Research goals

The goal of this study is to provide a portrait of research on the Semantic Web using bibliometric methods and, more specifically, to investigate the specific contribution of information science literature on the topic. Our research questions are the following:

RQ1. How did the Semantic Web research output evolve over the 2001-2016 by discipline?

RQ2. What are the most frequent keywords associated with Semantic Web research in different disciplines?

RQ3. Are disciplines citing each other or working in silos when doing research on the Semantic Web?

DATA AND METHODS

This study is based on publications indexed in the WoS and provided in a relational database format by the Observatoire des sciences et des technologies (OST). It is limited to Art Science Citation Index Expanded (SCI-EXPANDED), the Social Sciences Citation Index (SSCI) and the Arts & Humanities Citation Index (A&HCI). We retrieved all articles, notes and reviews published between 2001 and 2016 and containing the terms "semantic web", "linked data", "linked open data", "web 3.0", "web 4.0", "web 5.0" or "web of data" in their title, abstract, or keywords. This search yielded a total of 6,438 records.

---

[8] https://www.deichman.no/
[9] https://wiki.duraspace.org/pages/viewpage.action?pageId=74515029
[10] https://connect.library.utoronto.ca/display/U5LD/Canadian+Linked+Data+Initiative+Home

The discipline of the articles is determined by the journal in which it is published, all journals being classified according to the National Science Foundation (NSF) classification system, which comprises 14 disciplines. We divided the disciplines in five groups:

- Engineering and Technology (this is one of the NSF disciplines);
- Health and Life sciences (Biology, Biomedical Research and Clinical Medicine, and Health);
- Library and Information Sciences (this is a subdiscipline of the Professional Fields discipline);
- Natural Sciences (Chemistry, Earth and Space, Mathematics, Physics);
- Social Sciences and Humanities (Arts, Humanities, Professional Fields (excluding LIS), Psychology, Social Sciences).

Furthermore, we gathered the following information from WoS for each of the article retrieved:

- The authors' keywords;
- The raw and field normalized number of citations received, as well as the discipline of the citing articles;
- The discipline (using the five disciplinary groups defined above) of the articles they cited.

The authors' keywords are used to identify the main topics addressed in articles published in journals from different disciplines. We do this by building a bimodal network in which disciplines and keywords are put in relation with one another and by which we can visualize the most common keywords by disciplines and identify keywords that appear in only one discipline and others who are shared by multiple disciplines.

We analyze the articles citing and cited by the articles in our dataset to provide insights on 1) the impact of research on the Semantic Web and its' variation by discipline and 2) the disciplinary foundations of this body of research, as well as how research in each discipline informs research in the others. We should also point out that one limitation of this study is the fact that much of the research output in Computer Science is published in conference proceedings, which are not included in our analysis.

RESULTS

Table 1 presents the results of our query. It shows that almost three quarters (71,5%) of the 6,438 distinct articles retrieved contain the term "Semantic Web" and that the clear majority of these articles are published in Engineering and Technology journals. This term is also the most frequently used in Social Sciences and Humanities, Information Science and Library Science, and Natural Sciences. However, the second most frequent term, "linked data", found in about a fifth (19,2%) of the articles is most frequently used in Health and Life Sciences, which already highlights the disciplinary differences in either the topic of research focus or the terminology used. Note that "Web 5.0" is absent from Table 1 since there is no article containing that term, showing that it is not commonly used in the literature.

	Linked data	Linked open data	Semantic Web	Web 3.0	Web 4.0	Web of data	Total*
Engineering and Technology	422	139	3,336	21	0	88	3,660
Health and Life Sciences	1,237	12	341	7	0	5	1,559
Social Sciences and Humanities	168	24	486	25	1	10	660
Information Science and Library Science	93	35	250	5	1	13	313
Natural Sciences	66	17	193	1	1	9	246
Total	1,986	227	4,606	59	3	125	6,438

* The total number of articles per discipline is smaller than the sum of the columns because the same article can contain more than one of the searched keywords.

Table 1. Number of articles by keyword and by discipline (2001-2016)

Figure 2 presents the evolution of the number of articles on the Semantic Web over the 2001-2016 period. We see that there is a hype in the first few years following the Berners-Lee paper: the total number of articles had a nine-fold increase in only five years, from 2001 to 2005. The figure shows that this hype resembling Gartner's hype cycle (Fenn & Raskino, 2008) only occurred in Engineering and Technology. The output in Life Sciences shows a relatively stable growth starting in 2005. The output growth in other disciplines (including LIS) came later (around 2008) but has remained relatively small in comparison to Engineering and Technology and Life Sciences.

It is also interesting to note that while the number of articles published in Engineering and Technology journals has been increasing steadily since it's dramatic drop in 2007, it is still nowhere close to its 2005 level, when the hype was at its peak. Furthermore, the relative share of the papers on the Semantic Web published in Engineering and Technology journals has been generally decreasing since 2007.

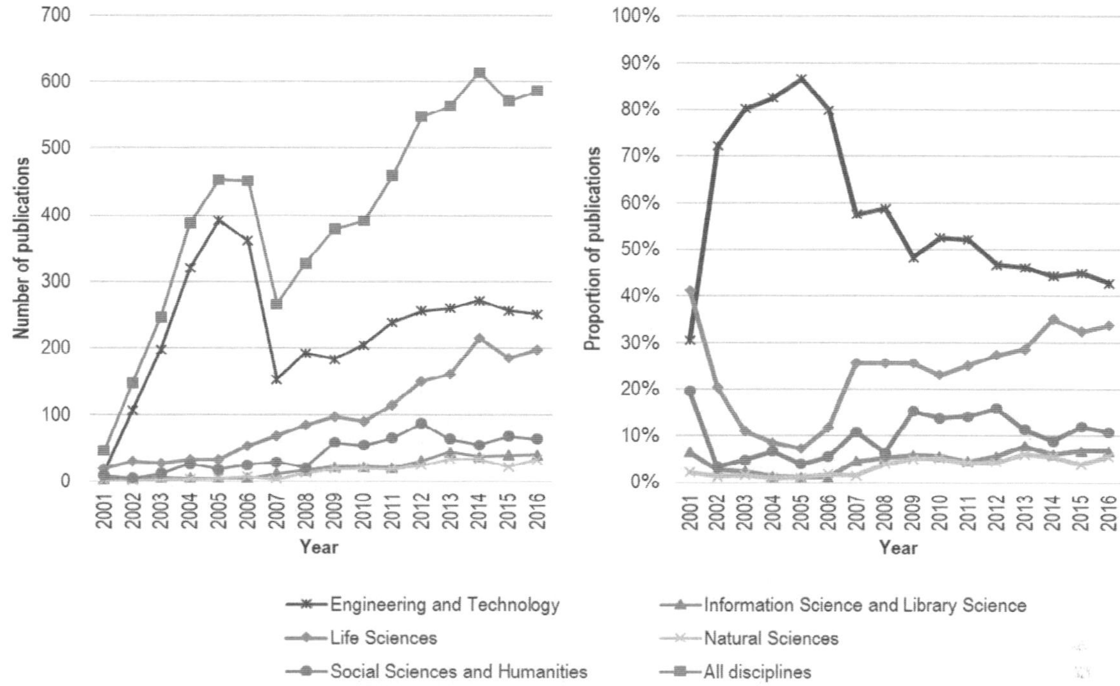

Figure 1. Evolution of the number (left) and proportion (right) of articles by discipline over the 2001-2016 period

Table 2 presents the total number of articles found by discipline, the total and average number of citations these articles have received, as well as their average field normalized citations. It shows that most research on the Semantic Web is mostly published in Engineering and Technology journals, followed by Life Sciences. Information Science and Library Science come in fourth position with 313 articles, behind Social Sciences and Humanities.

LIS articles come in last position in terms of total citations (1,168) and average citations (3,73). While such differences could be somewhat expected since Social Sciences disciplines and subdisciplines, which LIS is part of, receive on average less citations than articles in Engineering and Technology, Life Sciences and Natural Sciences. That said, LIS articles also have the lowest average field normalized citations, which means that they are on average less cited that other articles in the field. This could be considered surprising since the large amount of research on the topic in other disciplines could have been expected to give a "citation advantage" to LIS articles on the Semantic Web compared to other less multidisciplinary topics.

	Articles	Citations	Average citations	Average field normalized citations*
Engineering and Technology	3,660	20,994	5.74	0.83
Life Sciences	1,559	32,924	21.12	1.28
Social Sciences and Humanities	660	5,338	8.09	0.91
Information Science & Library Science	313	1,168	3.73	0.72
Natural Sciences	246	2,522	10.25	0.97

* The normalization is calculated by dividing the number of citations of an article by the average number of citations received by articles from the same NSF subdiscipline and published in the same year.

Table 2. Number of articles, citations, average raw and field normalized citations by discipline (2001-2016)

Figure 2 presents a graph of the bimodal networks of disciplines and keywords produced with Gephi[11]. The large nodes are the five disciplines and the smaller nodes are the keywords selected by the authors to describe the content of their article. A link between a keyword and a discipline indicates that the keyword appears at least once in that discipline. The complete network contains 10,527 distinct keywords, most of which occurred only once (and therefore in only one discipline) and 11,337 links. We divided the nodes in five clusters, with the disciplines at their center, using the Louvain community detection algorithm available in Gephi. To improve the readability of the graph, we only show the 5 discipline nodes and the union of the twenty

[11] https://gephi.org/

most frequent keywords and the twenty keywords with the highest weighted degree for each cluster. The graph presented in figure 2 thus contains 151 nodes and 335 links. We can see the distinctive topics that are of interest to specific disciplines. For instance, medical terms unsurprisingly appear in the Life Sciences cluster. Terms like thesauri and thesaurus, classification, metadata, data management, linked open data and of course libraries are found to relate more closely to LIS than to other disciplines. In the middle of the graph, we can see the (perhaps more general) keywords that are shared by multiple disciplines, such as Web 2.0 and Web 3.0, social networks, database and Internet.

Figure 2. Bimodal network of disciplines and keywords

Table 3 presents the characteristics of the five network clusters build in the graph and the top keywords for each discipline. The most frequent keywords, like the graph in figure 2, provide some insights on the distinctive research focus of the disciplines. The most frequent keyword in the network, "Semantic Web", appears in the LIS cluster, indicating that the term might relatively more frequently used in this field. It may also be of interest to note that the average degree and weighted degree are the highest in the LIS cluster, which indicates that its keywords are used in other disciplines more than the keywords of other clusters. A perhaps slightly negative interpretation of this could be that LIS lacks the distinct disciplinary approach to Semantic Web research which is found in other disciplines.

Cluster	Keywords	Avg. degree	Avg. weighted degree	Top keywords (total frequency)
Engineering and Technology	5293	2.11	1.06	Ontology (607), Linked Data (334), Ontologies (296), RDF (190), Web services (140)
Life Sciences	2667	2.10	0.52	Knowledge representation (97), Data integration (84), Data linkage (53), Mortality (52), Epidemiology (47)
Social Sciences and Humanities	1493	2.25	0.49	Web 2.0 (39), e-learning (36), Natural language processing (27), World Wide Web (24) Data Mining (24), Internet of thing (24)
Information Science and Library Science	545	2.37	1.32	Semantic Web (1450), linked open data (90), Metadata (65), Ontology matching (32), Knowledge engineering (25)
Natural Sciences	529	2.31	0.70	Description logics (84), Bioinformatics (25), Workflow (25), Database (24), Knowledge Discovery (18)
Total	10527	2.15	0.84	Semantic Web (1450), Ontology (607), Linked Data (334), Ontologies (296), RDF (190)

Table 3. Characteristics of the five network clusters

Another way to characterize the Semantic Web research performed in different disciplines is by analysing their references. Figure 3 thus presents, for papers in each discipline, the proportion of references to the different disciplines. Unsurprisingly, articles mostly cite papers from the same discipline. This is particularly the case for Engineering and Technology and Life Sciences, which is anticipated given the fact that they are also the discipline that publish most of the articles on the Semantic Web and on Linked Data, respectively. For possibly the same reason, the results also show that Information Science and Library Science and Natural Sciences (the two disciplines with the lowest output) are predominantly citing articles in other disciplines: Engineering and Technology in the case of LIS, and Life Sciences in the case of Natural Sciences.

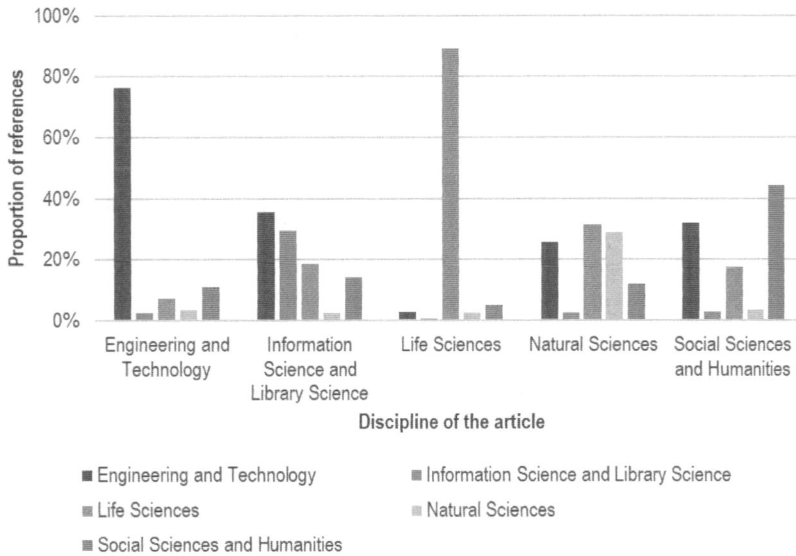

Figure 3. Evolution of the number of references by discipline over the 2001-2016 period

Figure 4 shows the proportion of citations received by citing discipline to provide insights on the multidisciplinary impact of the articles produced in different disciplines. Here, we see that articles in each discipline are predominantly cited by papers from the same discipline. This is the case even for LIS and Natural Sciences articles. Figure 3 and 4 provide insights on the interrelations between the disciplines around the Semantic Web as a research object. LIS research stands out are as a field that greatly integrates the knowledge produced in the other fields. However, LIS research seems to be mostly used within the field (hence the low impact showed in table 2) and less integrated in the other disciplines.

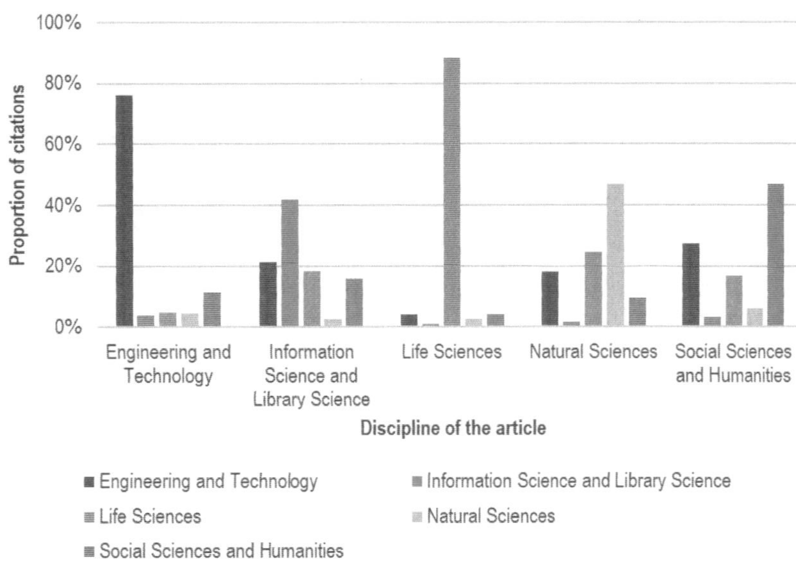

Figure 4. Evolution of the number of references by discipline over the 2001-2016 period

DISCUSSION AND CONCLUSION

In this study, we analyzed 6,438 articles published from 2001 to 2016 and retrieved from the WoS database. The goal of the study was to propose an up-to-date portrait of research on the Semantic Web using bibliometric methods, dividing 14 disciplines in five groups. Since information science is a multidisciplinary and interdisciplinary field in which many Semantic Web initiatives have occurred in the last few years, we wanted to investigate the contribution of this discipline in the Semantic Web research landscape. Based on our analysis, we found that LIS began to show interest in Semantic Web research around 2008, a little bit later than the Engineering and Technology disciplines and two years after Berners-Lee's note on Linked Data principles (2006). It is also interesting to mention the fact that the Swedish Union Catalog, LIBRIS, began sharing their data as Linked Open Data in 2008 (Malmsten, 2008) and that, after that, we saw more and more initiatives from major libraries. The bimodal network of disciplines and keywords illustrate how the authors of each discipline choose to discuss their research on Semantic Web and which keywords are used by the majority of the disciplines. For LIS, we notice that the top keywords used are "Semantic Web" (1450), "linked open data" (90), "Metadata" (65), "Ontology matching" (32) and "Knowledge engineering" (25). This provides an interesting portrait of the particular focus of the discipline, especially for the keyword "linked open data". Linked Open Data is essentially the same thing as Linked Data, except for the fact that it is Linked Data released under an open licence (Berners-Lee, 2006). Since the GLAM[12] sector's missions are, in part, to make knowledge accessible to everyone, it makes sense that these cultural institutions would promote open data. "Ontology matching" is one of the biggest challenge that is associated with implementing a Semantic Web project because it is essential to achieve interoperability between data from institutions using different schemas and standards. Finally, the development of Semantic Web applications requires technical knowledge as well as skills related to content management, data modeling, metadata schemas and a good understanding of information needs and behavior. The necessary skills are therefore "hybrid" and information science professionals and researchers can contribute to the development of the field by working on concrete applications of these technologies for different communities and their specific needs and by learning from the research done in the other disciplines.

This study is a good starting point for further analysis because it helps us to better understand how the information science discipline positions itself in this research field and which subtopics are of interest to information science professionals and researchers. Following these first results and based on the fact that information science is a multidisciplinary field in which researchers often come from diverse disciplinary backgrounds, it would be interesting to analyse the proportion of authors in information science who publish in other disciplines' journals, especially in computer science journals. A richer qualitative analysis would also enable us to obtain a better portrait of the contribution of the information science discipline in Semantic Web research.

ACKNOWLEDGMENTS

Philippe Mongeon is funded by the Social Science and Humanities Research Council of Canada.

REFERENCES

Alemu, G., Stevens, B., Ross, P., & Chandler, J. (2012). Linked data for libraries : benefits of a conceptual shift from library-specific record structures to RDF-based data models. *New Library World*, *113*(11/12), 549-570.

Bansal, M., Bandal, J., & Kumar, A. (2017). Semantic web research in India : a scientometric study of 2007-16. *International Journal of Information Dissemination and Technology*, *7*(4), 253-256.

Berners-Lee, T. (2006). Linked data – design issues. Retrieved on April 4th 2018 from https://www.w3.org/DesignIssues/LinkedData.html.

Berners-Lee, T., Hendler, J., & Lassila, O. (2001). The semantic web. *Scientific American*, *284*(5), 34-43.

Bizer, C., Heath, T., & Berners-Lee, T. (2009). Linked data – the story so far. *International Journal on Semantic Web and Information Systems*, *5*(3), 1-22.

Coyle, K. (2010). Library data in a modern context. *Library Technology Reports*, *46*(1), 5-13.

DeWeese, K. P., & Segal, D. (2014). *Libraries and the semantic web*. San Rafael, California: Morgan & Claypool.

Ding, Y. (2010). Semantic web : who is who in the field – a bibliometric analysis. *Journal of Information Science*, *36*(3), 335-336.

Fenn, J., & Raskino, M. (2008). *Mastering the hype cycle : how to choose the right innovation at the right time.* Boston, Mass.: Harvard Business Press.

Holland, G. A. (2008). Information science : an interdisciplinary effort? *Journal of Documentation*, *64*(1), 7-23.

Knapp, J. A. (2012). Plugging the "whole" : librarians as interdisciplinary facilitators. *Library Review*, *61*(3), 199-214.

Li, L., Liu, Y., Zhu, H., Ying, S., Luo, Q., Luo, H., … Shen, H. (2017). A bibliometric and visual analysis of global geo-ontology research. *Computers & Geosciences*, *99*, 1-8.

---

[12] Galleries, libraries, archives and museums

Malmsten, M. (2008). Making a library catalogue part of the semantic web. In J. Greenberg & K. Wolfgang (eds.), *Metadata for Semantic and Social Applications – Proceedings of the International Conference on Dublin Core and Metadata Applications* (p. 146-150). Dublin Core Metadata Initiative & Universitätverlag Göttingen.

Paul-Hus, A., Mongeon, P., & Shu, F. (2016). Portraying the landscape of library and information science research. *Canadian Journal of Information and Library Science*, *40*(4), 332-346.

Saracevic, T. (1995). Interdisciplinary nature of information science. *Ciênca da Informação*, *24*(1), 36-41.

Szostak, R. (2008). Classification, interdisciplinarity, and the study of science. *Journal of Documentation*, *64*(3), 319-332.

W3C. (2014). Best practices for publishing linked data. Retrieved April 4th, 2018 from https://www.w3.org/TR/ld-bp/.

Zhu, Q., Kong, X., Hong, S., Li, J., & He, Z. (2015). Global ontology research progress : a bibliometric analysis. *Aslib Journal of Information Management*, *67*(1), 27-54.

Chinese Collective Trolling

Honglei Sun
School of Information Management, Nanjing University, China

Pnina Fichman
Rob Kling Center for Social Informatics, School of Informatics, Computing, and Engineering, Indiana University

ABSTRACT

The vast majority of research on online trolling focused on Western cultures. Given the role context plays in shaping online interactions, it is important to take into account its socio-cultural context and investigate the role of national culture, by conducting research into trolling in Eastern cultures. In this paper, we attempt to begin addressing this gap by focusing on Chinese collective trolling, looking at *Sina Weibo's* PG One case. Specifically, we aim to identify who are the major players, what are the metaphors they use, and what are the major trolling tactics employed in Chinese collective trolling event. Using a mixed-method approach, we analyzed 2,004 posts and 9,967 comments on *Sina Weibo's* PG One case, of which 480 were sampled for thematic content analysis. Major contributions of this study include an account of collective trolling in Chinese cultural context that is characterized by role switching between trolls, bystanders, and victims during the various stages of the event. We conclude with suggestion for future research directions.

KEYWORDS

Online trolling, reverse trolling, collective trolling, China, collective action, Sina Weibo, Chinese online subculture

INTRODUCTION

Trolling can be defined as set of diverse context-dependent online behaviors that are pseudo-sincere, intentional, provocative and repetitive. Online trolling has become an increasingly pervasive and dynamic phenomenon in online communities (Fichman & Sanfilippo, 2016). Scholars described it as a context-dependent (e.g., Fichman & Sanfilippo, 2015; Herring, Job-Sluder, Scheckler, & Barab, 2002; Sanfilippo, Yang & Fichman, 2017), intentional (Hardaker, 2010; Shachaf & Hara, 2008), provocative (Hardaker, 2010), and repetitive (Fichman & Sanfilippo, 2016; Suler, 2004) behavior by an individual toward other individuals or groups (Fichman & Sanfilippo, 2016). Phillips (2015) noticed cross-national diversity of online trolling and mentioned various motivations of trolling behaviors in Australia, Britain and the US respectively. Fichman and Sanfilippo (2016) call for more research on the complex socio-cultural relationships between culture and trolling.

Yet, most of the literature refer to online trolling cases in the context of Western cultures. While online trolling in Eastern cultural context, such as China, began attracting scholarly attention (e.g., de Seta's, 2013; Yang, et al., 2017; Yang & Fichman, 2017), it is still unclear whether trolling behaviors exist in Chinese online communities, and how Chinese collectivistic culture might play into online trolling. Further, since Chinese Internet context is unique and characterized by the Great Firewall, it is possible that trolling in this context have distinct characteristics compared to online trolling in Western context. Given the role context plays in shaping socio-technical interactions (Kling, 2007), it is important to consider the contextual impact when studying online trolling (Sanfilippo, Fichman, & Yang, 2017). Thus, it is necessary to gain a better understanding of online trolling in various socio-cultural contexts and not to overlook trolling manifestation in Eastern cultures. In this paper, we conduct a study of collective trolling in China, focusing on *Sina Weibo*'s PG One case study. We aim to identify 1) who are the major players; 2) what are the metaphors they use; and 3) what are the major trolling tactics they employ in this collective trolling event. The paper structure is as follows: First, we provide a brief background and related work on online trolling, and then we describe our method, along with a description of our data. Next, we discuss our case analysis, answering the three research questions, and we conclude with discussion and suggestion for future research.

BACKGROUND

Internet and Sina Weibo use in China

Based on the latest report from the China Internet Network Information Center (2018), there are 751 million users in China (as of June, 2017), accounting for one fifth of the total number of Internet users in the world. The Internet penetration rate in China reached 55%, exceeding the global average by 4.6% (CNNIC, 2018). Furthermore, due to Internet censorship in China, known as "Great Firewall", many Western popular social network platforms, such as Facebook and Twitter, are blocked in mainland China (Ensafi, et al., 2015). Instead, Chinese users use the *Sina Weibo* platform—a *Twitter*-like website— to chat and share information with other users. One of the obvious difference between social network sites in China compared with the West is the lack of anonymity on Chinese platforms, while on some Western platforms, users are anonymous. On these western platforms, users can interact online without revealing who they are, where they come from, how old are they, and so on. However, on all Chinese social media platforms, all users online accounts are connected to their real-life ID. Even when users use various online usernames and try to disguise their real identities, age, and gender, the Chinese authorities can track their activities. This context clearly has an effect on norms of behaviors on Chinese social media platforms.

Sina Weibo is a popular social media site with over 361 million monthly active users and 159 million average daily active users (Noonan, 2017). The platform is currently the dominant microblogging service provider in China (Lin et al., 2013) and a major source of commentary on a wide range of topics. For example, about 100 million messages are posted daily on Sina Weibo (Jiang, Wang, Tsou, & Fu, 2015). On *Sina Weibo,* a user may post, mention, or talk to other people using "@UserName", add hashtags with "#HashName#", follow other users to make their posts appear in one's own timeline, repost with "//@UserName" (similar to Twitter's retweet function "RT @UserName"), select posts for one's favorites list, and verify the account, when the user is a celebrity. Just like on Twitter, there are also "VIP" accounts on *Sina Weibo*, which are called "verified users" and have a yellow "V" sign after their names. These verified users attract thousands of followers, creating "celebrity-centric" social networks on Sina Weibo, which play an important role in disseminating latest events, controversial opinions and breaking news (Wang, Lei, & Xu, 2015). Most verified users are influential people offline as well, and many are public figures, celebrities, or organizations' accounts. The major difference from *Twitter* is that *Sina Weibo* is used almost exclusively by Chinese language speakers (Jiang, Wang, Tsou, & Fu, 2015). In order to evade the multiple levels of Sina Weibo censorship, many Chinese netizens use clever methods to elude the suppression, for example posting images instead of more easily censored text or using memes (Sullivan, 2014).

Online trolling

As online trolling increased in pervasiveness, the term is used as an umbrella term for different phenomena, from serious and deviant to humorous or ideological driven behavior (Sanfilippo, Fichman, & Yang, 2018); it is context-dependent phenomena (Fichman & Sanfilippo, 2015). Trolling is associated with direct aggression, flaming, spraying, and even cyber bullying (Hardakar, 2010; de Seta, 2013). Perceptions of trolling varies between perpetrators, victims, bystanders, scholars, the media, and the public at large. On one hand, trolls often justify their behaviors ideologically or by the high moral disengagement experienced with respect to their online activities (Suler & Phillips 1998), while on the other hand, scholars and the media often frame trolling as unjustifiable and depraved acts (Bishop 2014).

While trolling behaviors varies widely, the literature emphasizes deviant and negative behaviors, which have many commonalities with flaming (e.g., Hardaker, 2010; Herring, Job-Sluder, Scheckler, & Barab, 2002) and hacking (e.g., Shachaf & Hara, 2010; Suler & Phillips, 1998). Fichman and Sanfilippo (2016) emphasize that "not all trolling is equal" and claim that trolling is more complicated than mere deviant behavior leading to negative impact, and recent scholarly works began to describe light-hearted, humorous, or ideological trolling (e.g., Phillips & Milner, 2017; Sanfilippo, Fichman & Yang, 2018). Because online trolling is a socio-technical phenomenon, with context-dependent manifestation that varies from one community to another and from one platform to another, it may exhibit different behavioral patterns in different countries (Fichman & Sanfilippo, 2016), and more specifically, its manifestation in China may be more collectivistic than trolling in Western cultures (Yang & Fichman, 2017). Thus, by using a mixed method analysis of *Sina Weibo* PG One's case to identify behavioral patterns of collective trolling, that flourish under the Chinese firewall, this paper aims to extend our understanding of online trolling in context. Specifically, we aim to identify who are the major players, what are the metaphors they use, and what are the major trolling tactics employed in this Chinese collective trolling event.

METHOD

We employed a mixed method approach and analyzed 2,004 posts and 9,967 comments on *Sina Weibo*, of which 480 were sampled for content analysis. The event of interest in our case study of Chinese collective trolling occurred in January 2018 and is referred to as PG One in this paper. PG One is the nickname of Wang Hao (王昊), one of China's best-known rappers, whose victory on *The Rap of China* competition brought him over four million followers on *Sina Weibo* platform (Fan, 2018). As part of the method section, we first describe the setting, PG One case study, and then follow with the description of our data collection and analysis.

PG One case study

The PG One case study illustrated an example of Chinese collective trolling on *Sina Weibo* that was observed during the time period of Jan. 7th, 2018 7 p.m. to Jan. 8th, 2018 5 a.m. (China Time). The event of interest to our case study started when some *Sina Weibo* users criticized one of his songs for containing degrading and out-of-line lyrics (Jiayun, 2018). Then, a magazine published by the central government, known as the Tower of Violet Light (TVL), and the Communist Youth League[1], continued posting and harshly criticizing the dark lyrics of PG One another song, "Christmas Eve", for encouraging teenagers to use drugs and insulting women. TVL also added two photos of a few lines from the lyrics of the song "Christmas Eve", to represent the

[1] The Communist Youth League is a youth movement of the P. R. China for youth between the ages of fourteen and twenty-eight, run by the Communist Party of China (CPC).

song's general spirit. PG One's fans (PGF) learned about TVL's posts on *Sina Weibo*, and a group of his fans, who misunderstood TVL to be the name of a restaurant, planned a revenge. Their revenge plan (which was based on their misunderstanding of TVL to be a restaurant name) included spreading cockroaches in the "restaurant". Their plan also included a negative campaign on a popular e-commerce site in China, Taobao, against the restaurant, claiming that the restaurant, TVL, uses sewer sludge skimmed oil for cooking, posting "Gutter Oil of TVL". At this point, around 6 p.m. on Jan. 7, 2018 (China Time), a microblogger (Xiaojiananfang), who was a member of PGF's QQ (an instant messaging software service) task-force group, posted the plan of the PGF QQ group chat on *Sina Weibo*. Following this post, the PGF plan, known now as "Gutter Oil of TVL", became viral and turned into a trending search topic on *Sina Weibo* on January 8, 2018 (China Time). The trending search topic increasingly attracted users' attention and *Sina Weibo* platform had been flooded with thousands of posts and comments over a 10 hours period. We collected all the *Sina Wiebo*'s PG One case study posts during this event for our analysis.

Data collection & analysis

We collected posts that were a part of this 10 hours event on *Sina Weibo* on Jan. 7th, 2018 7 p.m. to Jan. 8th, 2018 5 a.m. (China Time). The basic dataset consists of 2,872 posts that had the keywords "Gutter Oil of TVL" (紫光阁地沟油), in chronological order, and 9,967 comments replying to these posts. Table 1 and Figure 1 describe the dataset, distribution of posts and comments as of Jan. 8, 2018, 5 a.m. (China Time).

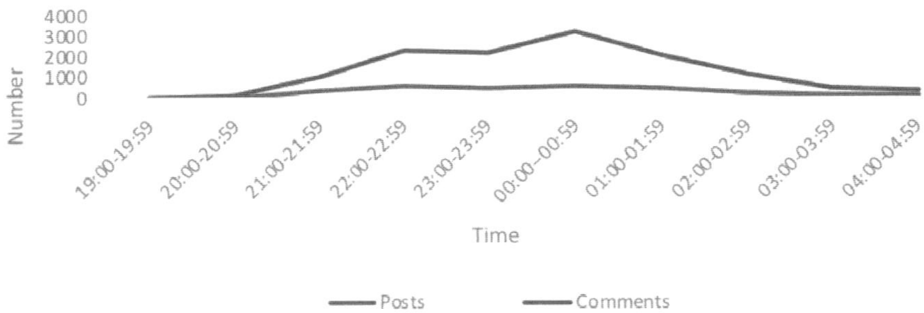

Figure 1. Distribution of posts and comments during the event

Number of pots and comments per hour	19:00-19:59	20:00-20:59	21:00-21:59	22:00-22:59	23:00-23:59	00:00--00:59	01:00-01:59	02:00-02:59	03:00-03:59	04:00-04:59
Posts	2	29	351	610	439	617	445	215	87	77
Comments	1	90	672	1656	1728	2634	1629	897	360	301

Table 1. Posting frequency during the event

Since the dataset is relatively large, and the distribution of posts is irregular, we designed a two-stage sampling process with non-probability at each and employed a judgment sampling strategy. This judgement sampling method uses purposeful criteria in choosing the sample, to include cases that have the most strategic position to provide the information needed (Sekaran & Boogie, 2010); it is based on our own judgements about the representative posts (Kothari, 1990). Although we were well aware of its limitations in representing the event, this method was applied in the selection of the posts since we felt that the sample selected could serve the research purpose better (Köksal, & Riddle, 2007).

Based on posting frequencies, we identified 5 primary segments of time periods: the first two hours were merged into one segment, the first stage, and the last 4 hours were merged into one stage, the last stage. Each stage stands for a particular turning point of the event as follow: Stage 1: earliest posts; Stage 2: First peak - turning into hottest search topics; Stage 3: Maintain momentum; Stage 4: Peak; Stage 5: Calm down.

Time period	Event stages	Numbers of posts, comments & chats per min	Number of posts sampled	Number of comments sampled	Number of chats sampled
19:00-21:59	Stage 1: Earliest posts	2.03	12	46	16
22:00-22:59	Stage 2: First peak – turning into hottest search topics	37.77	18	91	13
23:00-23:59	Stage 3: Maintain momentum	36.12	17	68	12
00:00-00:59	Stage 4: Peak	54.18	18	84	9

01:00-04:59	Stage 5: Calm down	16.75	15	51	10
Total		20.40	80	340	60

Table 2. Five stages sample

We found that many posts and comments added some screenshots of PGF group chats, which were included in our sample due to their informative nature. This sample includes a total of 480 posts: 80 posts, 340 comments, and 60 chats from the five segments was used in our content analysis (Table 2).

We designed a codebook, with 5 categories (stakeholder group, trolling role, content, and trolling tactic) and 49 codes. Codes were derived from prior work on trolling (Sanfilippo, Yang, & Fichman, 2017b), which we continuously revised during the coding process, adding codes that originated from our data.

We manually coded and analyzed the samples from these five stages using open coding (Corbin & Strauss, 2014). Coding was conducted at the level of individual posts by the first author and a second coder coded a subset of the data to ensure coding reliability. Inter-coder reliability was high, at 82.5% of agreement.

FINDINGS

This section includes three parts as we aim to identify 1) who are the major players; 2) what are the metaphors they use; and 3) what are the major trolling tactics employed in Chinese collective trolling event.

1) Major players

A few stakeholder groups were involved in our collective trolling event. Stakeholders switched their roles during the event between trolls, bystanders, and victims of trolls. We labeled posters group affiliation as one of the following four stakeholder groups: 1) PG One's Fans (PGF); 2) Tower of Violet Light (TVL); 3) General Participants (GP), those who lack other group affiliation; or 4) Verified users (VIP), those who typically hold a celebrity status. Based on self-proclaimed identity and the context of each post, we also assigned to each user one of three roles: 1) troll; 2) bystander; or 3) victim. Table 3 presents the number of posts by group in each stage that reveals the event pattern: an ephemeral but aggressive post-flood that increased quickly in a short time dominated by GP. This group, GP, generated most of the posts, overwhelming the other stakeholder groups during each of the five stages. PGF's and TVL's posting pattern have both a small-scale fluctuation pattern; for PGF the peak is in the first stage, and for TVL in the third stage, while VIP exhibit a decreased posting pattern as the event progressed.

Posts by stakeholder groups at stage	PGF Number of posts (percent of posts at stage out of all PGF posts)	TVL Number of posts (percent of posts at stage out of all TVL posts)	GP Number of posts (percent of posts at stage out of all GP posts)	VIP Number of posts (percent of posts at stage out of all VIP posts)
Stage 1: Earliest posts	22 (35.48%)	0 (0%)	46 (12.17%)	13 (33.33%)
Stage 2: First peak-turning into hottest search topics	12 (19.35%)	0 (0%)	95 (25.13%)	14 (35.90%)
Stage 3: Maintain momen-tum	11 (17.74%)	1 (100%)	83 (21.96%)	6 (15.38%)
Stage 4: Peak	10 (16.13%)	0 (0%)	87 (23.02%)	5 (12.82%)
Stage 5: Calm down	7 (11.29%)	0 (0%)	67 (17.72%)	1 (2.56%)

Table 3. Posts by stakeholder groups in Five stages (N= 480)

Table 4 provides the distribution of posts from each of the four stakeholder groups by each of the three trolling roles. At the beginning, PGF planned to troll the TVL, but later PGF became the target-group, which was trolled by TVL and thousands of GP users. As is shown in Table 4, PGF, GP, VIP all played more than one role during the entire event, they switched roles between trolls, bystanders, and victims of trolls.

Stakeholder groups by trolling roles	PGF Number of posts (percent of posts by role and stakeholder out of total posts)	TVL Number of posts (percent of posts by role and stakeholder out of total posts)	GP Number of posts (percent of posts by role and stakeholder out of total posts)	VIP Number of posts (percent of posts by role and stakeholder out of total posts)
Trolls	41 (8.54%)	0 (0.00%)	166 (34.58%)	18 (3.75%)
Victims	15 (3.13%)	1 (0.21%)	12 (2.50%)	0 (0.00%)

Bystanders	6 (1.25%)	0 (0.00%)	200 (41.67%)	21 (4.38%)

Table 4. Posts of stakeholder groups by trolling roles (N= 480)

The trolls

In this event, all stakeholder groups trolled at one point or another. At first, PGF were planning a revenge by a collective trolling campaign. In past events, the PGF group was involved in a well-organized and well-planned actions in support and admiration of PG One; these events lasted a couple of hours or days. The plan was to spread cockroaches into what they believed to be a restaurant, who criticized their idol, PG One, and to follow up by posting online about it. They had also planned to employ water-army[2] to post about TVL's terrible cooking practices, using the idea of "Gutter Oil of TVL". However, before PGF took action, their plan had leaked out, and they became the target of collective trolling. Toward the end of the event, PGF turned into the main trolling target in reverse-trolling by TVL, GP as well as VIP; most of the trolling at this point have been posted by GP.

Bystanders

The bystander role includes mainly GP and VIP accounts. While the GP group trolled the most and have been trolled the most of all four stakeholder groups, most of them played a bystander role during the entire event. The VIP, in addition to retweeting TVL's post, which reported on the PGF trolling plan, some VIP also added self-mockery posts and trolled the PGF. For example, The Communist Youth League (VIP account) posted jokingly: "Would their next exposed target be the small workshop that sells green rice balls? Afraid. JPG". In fact, VIP users played an important role in accelerating the development of this event by broadcasting it to their followers and by simply reacting to it. For instance, at 08:45 p.m. on January 7, 2018 (China Time), a well-known microblogger, Hacker Kevin, posted a post that was reposted thousands of times and generated 9,511 reaction comments. With the development of the event, more and more bystanders engaged in trolling PGF, together forming a viral group trolling; these bystanders turned into trolls and were engaged in this collective trolling event.

The victims

The victim role was played by TVL, PGF, and GP users. TVL at first was mistakenly confused to be a restaurant, was the target of the PGF trolling, as it was criticized for "Using gutter oil", "Brand Deception", and "Eat cockroaches in the food!". However, at 11:30 p.m. on January 7, 2018 (China Time), TVL made one post that self-mockingly described itself as a scared baby, who was too "weak, poor, and helpless" to fight with PGF, as they were neither ignoring posts related to "Gutter Oil of TVL", nor clarifying their position; instead they, as a scared baby, only hide in their dining room and kept shivering. This same post also mocked PGF users as if they were pretending to be asleep. This post reversed TVL's role from being trolled by PGF to reverse-trolling PGF, turning PGF into victims. This TVL post was reposted thousands of times and pushed this trolling "war" to its peak, when PGF was the new target of trolling.

2) Content

The thematic components of the posts and comments help us understand this collective trolling action better. Table 5 presents the top 5 topics and metaphors in each stakeholder groups' posts. There were four interesting metaphors: 1) this event was metaphorically referred to as "war" (战争); 2) participants who supported TVL were referred to as "The friendly army" (友军); 3) participants who supported PGF were referred to as "The enemy" (敌军); and 4) participants who watched the trolling event unfolding were referred to as "Onlooker" (吃瓜群众), a group of bystanders.

The most frequently posted metaphor was "the friendly army", as most posts and comments claimed their support of TVL or opposing PGF and indicating that they were the friendly army. Examples for the friendly army metaphor include: "Come on, baby purple" (加油，紫宝宝), referring to the literal meaning of TVL, Tower of Violet Light, and "Must ban this cult" (封杀这种邪教), referring to PGF as a cult of PG One fans . Interestingly, not all of the trolls trolled directly, as many of them, specifically GP users, intentionally pretended to be members of PGF group. They pseudo sincerely condemned "Gutter Oil of TVL" or supported PGF, adding a dog's head emoticon to mean the opposite, and that they actually supported TVL instead. Users who post or comment added a dog's head emoticon ( ) at the end of their comment to indicate that they are part of the friendly army, and thus expressing exactly the opposite meaning. For instance, a user posted the following: "Let's get together as PGF, and I can drive you to the mental hospital" (各位万友一定要团结起来，抱成团，我送你们去精神病院), to mock PGF as mentally ill users. Some users enjoyed making fun of "the enemy"(敌军) when referring to PGF while adding a smiley face emoticon ( ) to indicate the joke. For example, "We just want to ban PG One, but his fans want to kill him " (我们只是想封杀他，没想到他的粉丝是想弄死他). Some "onlookers", a group of bystanders, claimed that they simply

[2] Water-army refer to online paid ghost posters in China; it is typically composed of a large number of people, who are well organized to "flood" the Internet with purposeful comments and articles.

watched the fun as the event was unfolding; for example, posting “I am waiting to watch the ‘battle’” (吃瓜吃瓜).

Most frequent content by stakeholder groups	PGF (percent of content out of all PGF contents)	TVL (percent of content out of all TVL contents)	GP (percent of content out of all GP contents)	VIP (percent of content out of all VIP contents)	Overall (percent of content out of all contents)
1	Whitewashing PG One(23.68%)	“Gutter oil of TVL” (50%)	The friendly army (25.14%)	Reporting this event (12.50%)	The friendly army (20.56%)
2	Transferring Target (19.74%)	The friendly army (50%)	Attacking PGF or PG One (12.48%)	Response to PGF's action (12.5%)	Attacking PGF or PG One (11.09%)
3	TVL's identity (9.21%)	-	Onlooker's reaction (12.09%)	Attacking PGF or PG One (10%)	Response to PGF's action (10.06%)
4	Dirty words (7.89%)	-	Response to PGF's action (10.94%)	The friendly army (8.75%)	Onlooker's reaction (9.91%)
5	Education (6.58%)	-	Deceiving (6.72%)	PG One's candal (7.5%)	Deceiving (5.92%)

Table 5. Content by each stakeholder group.

The various stakeholder groups differ from each other in the frequency of metaphor use, and the rank of their Top 5 topics (Table 5). As can be seen in Table 5, PGF aimed at maintaining PG One positive image, which they admire, and thus their main focus was whitewashing his actions. TVL only posted on “Gutter oil of TVL” and showed that they are part of “the friendly army”. VIP were mainly “reporting the event” progression, saying for example “This topic had been read more than 20 million times” (话题的阅读量突破 2000 万). Interestingly, GP most frequent topics resembles the overall rank of frequent content, perhaps due to the fact that they posted the vast majority of posts during this event.

3) Trolling tactics

We further analyzed the use of trolling tactics by the five stakeholder groups (Table 6). Because TVL had only one post in our sample, we excluded it from farther analysis. As is shown in Table 6, the most common tactic overall is “Group trolling”, followed by “Emotional display”, “Lying”, “Memes”, and “Sarcasm”. PDF preferred to use hostile and insulting words to interact with others, such as “Do you have shit in your head?” (你是脑子装大便了吗?), as well as posting “illogical claims”, such as, “What’s wrong with taking drugs?” (吸毒怎么了?). GP mainly trolled as part of a group or trolled their target together. They tended to use more dog’s head than other groups in reference to “the friendly army”, and liked to troll others by adopting “memes” and “sarcasm”, such as “Please sit down, Duxiu Chen”(陈独秀，你坐下). People use this name as a meme just based on the meaning of the last two words: the word “Du” means alone and the word “Xiu” means a show. Nowadays, people refers to Duxiu as someone who show off alone and does not give others a chance; it typically accuses someone to be showing off alone and to be the focus of public attention. VIP users were more likely to troll by “lying” and their trolling involves more “name calling” in reference to PGF. For example, “PG One’s brainless fans dare to publicly attack TVL” (PG One 的脑残粉竟敢公开怼紫光阁), or “Must ban this cult” (封杀这种邪教). The top 5 trolling tactics that GP users exhibited are similar to the overall results, and it might be due to the fact that GP users dominated this event.

Tactics by stakeholders group	**PGF (percent of tactic out of PGF tactics)**	**GP (percent of tactic out of all GP tactics)**	**VIP (percent of tactic out of all VIP tactics)**	**Overall (percent of tactic out of all tactics)**
1	Flaming (23.47%)	Group trolling (15.86%)	Lying (8.99%)	Group trolling (13.86%)
2	Illogical claim (10.20%)	Emotional display (12.62%)	Name calling (7.87%)	Emotional display (10.02%)
3	Group trolling (8.16%)	Lying (8.58%)	Sarcasm (6.74%)	Lying (7.80%)
4	Mockery (8.16%)	Memes (7.77%)	Mockery (6.74%)	Memes (6.68%)
5	Name calling (8.16%)	Sarcasm (6.47%)	Group trolling (6.74%)	Sarcasm (6.44%)

Table 6. Tactics by each stakeholder group

DISCUSSION AND CONCLUSION

In this paper, we investigated collective trolling behavior in the Chinese context of *Sina Weibo*. Results illustrated a well-organized and well-planned collective trolling when four stakeholder groups assumed different roles, switching between trolls, victims and bystanders. Each group utilized a set of tactics in pursuing their goals. Thus, we argue that our study extends previous understanding of online trolling as an individual behavior (e.g., Fichman & Sanfilippo, 2016; Shachaf & Hara, 2010) to understand trolling also as a coordinated group effort. Our finding indicates that in the context of Chinese collectivistic culture, and under perceived lack of online anonymity in China, trolling is not an isolated behaviors of individual trolls, but rather a set of group behaviors. This is much in line with the argument that context, in our case Chinese *Sina Weibo*, shapes online behaviors (Sanfilippo, Yang & Fichman, 2017a; Sanfilippo, Yang, & Fichman, 2017b). Furthermore, our study provides an account of a Chinese trolling event as trolling behaviors vary during the various stages of the event; participants' roles evolve and change, and so do their tactics. Through this Chinese case study, we documented how stakeholders changed roles between trolls, bystanders, and victims during different stages of the event. Users switched roles throughout the same trolling event; a user can post as a troll or a victim of trolls during the same trolling event. Trolling behaviors are complex; not all trolling is anti-social and not all participants assumed the same role throughout the event. Additionally, we found that in the same period and in the same context, members of one stakeholder group may troll each other, just for fun. Thus, while previous research documented how socio-technical context impact online trolling, this paper suggests that trolling is a dynamic process with a range of manifestations within one socio-technical setting, *Sina* Weibo PG One case study. Clearly the features and context of the technological platform and Chinese socio-cultural norms, together, provide a different representation of the trolling phenomenon.

Future research can aim to gain a better understanding of the evolutionary mechanism of switching role in the same context and examine the interaction between trolls in the same group. In addition, future research can compare and contrast insiders' and outsiders' behavioural tactics in specific trolling events. Finally, future research may compare and contrast the unique attributes of online trolling in the East and West.

In summary, major contributions of this study include an account of 1) collective trolling in Chinese cultural context; 2) role switching between trolls, bystanders, and victims; and 3) an account of trolling event over time. We conclude with suggestions for future research directions.

ACKNOWLEDGMENTS

Honglei Sun was a visiting PhD candidate at Indiana University, supported by the China Scholarship Council, when this work was performed. We would like to thank Mr. Mitchell Casiano for proofreading and express our special thanks to the reviewers for their constructive suggestions.

REFERENCES

Bishop, J. (2014). Representations of 'trolls' in mass media communication: a review of media-texts and moral panics relating to internet trolling. *International Journal of Web Based Communities, 10*(10), 7-24.

China Internet Network Information Center (CNNIC). (2018). 41th statistical report on Internet development in China. China Internet Network Information Center (CNNIC), Beijing, China. Retrieved March 17, 2018 from http://www.cnnic.net.cn/hlwfzyj/hlwxzbg/hlwtjbg/201803/P020180305409870339 136.pdf.

Corbin, J., & Strauss, A. (2014). *Basics of qualitative research: Techniques and procedures for developing grounded theory* (4 edition ed.). SAGE Publications, Los Angeles, CA.

Ensafi, R., Winter, P., Mueen, A., & Crandall, J. R. (2015). Analyzing the Great Firewall of China over space and time. *Proceedings on Privacy Enhancing Technologies*, *1*, 61-76.

Fan, S. (2018). Fans and Netizens React to Rapper PG One's Recent Scandals. Retrieved March 16, 2017 from https://radiichina.com/fans-and-netizens-react-to-rapper-pg-ones-recent-scandals/.

Fichman, P., & Sanfilippo, M. R. (2015). The bad boys and girls of cyberspace: How gender and context impact perception of and reaction to trolling. *Social Science Computer Review, 33*(2), 163-180.

Fichman, P., & Sanfilippo, M.R. (2016). *Online trolling and its perpetrators: Under the cyberbridge*. Lanham: Rowman & Littlefield Publishers.

Hardaker, C. (2010). Trolling in asynchronous computer-mediated communication: From user discussions to academic definitions. *Journal of Politeness Research Language Behaviour Culture, 6*(2), 215-242.

Jiang, W., Wang, Y., Tsou, M. H., & Fu, X. (2015). Using social media to detect outdoor air pollution and monitor air quality index (AQI): A geo-targeted spatiotemporal analysis framework with Sina Weibo (Chinese Twitter). *Plos One*, *10*(10), e0141185.

Herring, S., Job-Sluder, K., Scheckler, R., & Barab, S. (2002). Searching for safety online: Managing "trolling" in a feminist forum. *Information Society, 18*(5), 371-384.

Kling, R. (2007). What is social informatics and why does it matter? *The Information Society, 23*, 205-220.

Köksal, M. H., & Riddle, L. (2007). Consumer behaviour and preferences regarding children's clothing in turkey. *Journal of Fashion Marketing & Management, 11*(1), 69-81.

Kothari CR. (1990). *Research methodology: Methods and techniques*. New Delhi: Wishwa Prakashan.

Lin, C., He, J., Zhou, Y., Yang, X., Chen, K., & Song, L. (2013). Analysis and identification of spamming behaviors in Sina Weibo microblog. *The Workshop on Social Network Mining & Analysis* (pp.1-9).

Noonan, K. (2017). Weibo Delivers Second-Quarter Sales and Earnings Beat. Retrieved March 21, 2017 from https://www.fool.com/investing/2017/08/12/weibo-delivers-second-quarter-sales-and-earnings-b.aspx.

Phillips, W. (2015). *This is why we can't have nice things: Mapping the relationship between online trolling and mainstream culture.* Cambridge, MA: MIT Press.

Sanfilippo, M. R., Yang, S., & Fichman, P. (2017a). Managing online trolling: From deviant to social and political trolls. *Hawaii International Conference on System Sciences (pp.1802-1811).*

Sanfilippo, M., Yang, S., & Fichman, P. (2017b). Trolling here, there, and everywhere: Perceptions of trolling behaviors in context. *Journal of the Association for Information Science & Technology, 68*(10): 2313-2327.

Sanfilippo, M. R., Fichman, P., & Yang, S. (2018). Multidimensionality of online trolling behaviors. *Information Society, 34*(1), 1-13.

Sekaran, U., & Bougie, R.(2010). *Research Method for Business* (5 edition ed). John Wiley and Sons, Inc. USA.

Seta, G. D. (2013). Spraying, fishing, looking for trouble: The Chinese internet and a critical perspective on the concept of trolling. *Fibreculture Journal, 22*(22): 301-318.

Shachaf, P., & Hara, N. (2010). Beyond vandalism: Wikipedia trolls. *Journal of Information Science*, *36*(3), 357-370.

Suler, J. (2004). The online disinhibition effect. *Cyberpsychol Behavior, 7*(3), 321-326.

Suler, J. R., & Phillips, W. L. (1998). The bad boys of cyberspace: Deviant behavior in a multimedia chat community. *Cyberpsychology & Behavior, 1*(3): 275-294.

Sullivan, J. (2013). China's weibo: Is faster different?. *New Media & Society, 16*(1), 24-37.

Wang, H., Lei, K., & Xu, K. (2015). Profiling the followers of the most influential and verified users on Sina Weibo. *IEEE International Conference on Communications* (pp.1158-1163). IEEE.

Yang, S., Chen, P. Y., Shih, P. C., Bardzell, J., & Bardzell, S. (2017). Cross-strait frenemies: Chinese netizens VPN in to Facebook Taiwan. *Proceedings of the ACM on Human-Computer Interaction* 1(CSCW), Article–115.

Yang, S., & Fichman, P. (2016, September). Collective online trolling: The "Diba Expedition", *4S/EASST Conference*, Barcelona, September, 2016.

The Development and Validation of "Preference Diversity" and "Openness to Novelty" scales for Movie Goers

Muh-Chyun Tang
Department of Library and Information Science, National Taiwan University, Taiwan. mctang@ntu.edu.tw

Sung-Chien Lin
Department of Information and Communication, Shih-Hsin University, Taiwan. scl@mail.shu.edu

Mei-Mei Chang
Department of Library and Information Science, National Taiwan University, Taiwan. cmeimie@gmail.com

ABSTRACT

This paper reports the results of an ongoing research to develop and validate scales for two psychological constructs: "preference diversity" and "openness to novelty", that we believe to be important factors in users' responses to movie recommendations. Question items were created based on literature review and the results of a focus group interview. A questionnaire interview that consists of the candidate question items were performed so the validation and purification of the scales can be performed (N =191). Through exploratory factor analysis, five items were eventually selected for each construct. A user study (N=293) were subsequently followed which collected both users' responses to the scales and their actual movie viewing history of a sample of 220 movies. The scales were shown to possess both stability and internal consistency. Results showed that the participants' preference diversity score were correlated with the diversity of the movies seen, as measured by the number of movies, the number of movie genres, and the average dissimilarity of the movies seen. Furthermore, those who have higher openness to novelty also tended to watch and appreciate more obscure films.

KEYWORDS

movies, recommender system, preference diversity, openness to novelty, scale development, psychometrics

INTRODUCTION

With the growing popularity of personalized recommender systems on e-commerce sites, their applications and impacts in marketing have also drawn growing interests. There have been previous effects to explore how to strategically apply recommendation techniques for consumers with different cognitive and affective traits such as personalities (Tkalcic & Chen, 2015, Onori, Micarelli, & Sansonetti, 2016; Cantador et. al., 2013; Wang & Doong, 2010), cultural orientations (Kramer, Spolter-Weisfeld, & Thakkar, 2007), and preference development (Shen & Ball, 2011; Kwon, Cho, & Park ; 2009; Simonson, 2005). One important implication of these studies is that recommendation strategies should be adopted adaptively according to the users' psychological traits.

In this study we set out to develop two psychological constructs that we believe might influence users' response to personalized recommendations, namely, "preference diversity" and "openness to novelty." These constructs are created in light of recent calls for recommender system objectives that go beyond accurate prediction of users' ratings (Konstan & Riedl, 2012; Castells at al., 2011, Hurley & Zhang, 2011; Celma & Herrera, 2008; McNee, Riedl, & Konstan, 2006; Herlocker, Konstan, Terveen, & Riedl, 2004). Traditionally the evaluation of recommender system has been mainly focused on prediction accuracy, as measured by MAE (Mean Absolute Error). The accuracy dominated paradigm is efficient for the evaluation and fine-tuning of recommendation algorithms, yet it has been pointed out that accuracy along is not sufficient to capture other aspects of user values generated by recommender systems, especially those related to user experiences (Konstan & Riedl, 2012; Pu, Chen, & Hu, 2011). A consistent issue is the balance between accuracy and other "non-obviousness" evaluation criteria (Herlocker et.al., 2004). While the recommendation of accurate, yet previously known items might foster user confidence, they also represent less novelty and serendipity. The other issue is the lack of diversity in the recommendation set (Zhou et. al, 2010; Bradley & Smith, 2001). It has been argued that many of the current similarity-based recommendation algorithms often expose users to recommendations that are "too similar" to each other. Efforts have been made to improve diversity in the top-N recommendation set to avoid monotonous recommendations (Zhou et. al, 2010; Zhang & Hurley, 2008).

To solve the dilemma, it is felt that the proper balance between accuracy and non-obviousness might lie in how willing or motivated a user is to explore novel items and diverse interests. We speculate that individuals with high level of openness to novelty in movies are more willing to venture out of their familiar genres, favorite directors and performers and therefore are more receptive to nonobvious recommendations. On the other hand, for individual with lower openness to novelty, an accuracy-oriented recommendation strategy will be more appropriate.

One the same token, users with higher preference diversity might welcome a more diverse recommendation set. Previously we have tested the construct of "preference diversity" in the context of fiction reading (Tang, Sie & Ding, 2014; Tang, Ke, & Sie, 2013) and music listening (Chang &Tang. 2018). Here we wish to extend the construct of preference diversity in the realm of movie tastes. It is postulated that individuals with more diverse movie interests would appreciate a more diverse recommendation list, while those who have more concentrated movie preference, on the other hand, might appreciate works in a certain genre or style.

The aims of the study can be summarized as follows: to develop scales to measure the two movies preference constructs that we believe would affect the effectiveness of personalized recommendations, that is, movie "preference diversity" and "openness to novelty." We started with generating candidate question items that reflect these two aspects of movie preference from a focus group study and literature review. A survey questionnaire was first developed based on which the respondents' answers to these items can be collected so that the question items can be purified and their reliability and validity tested. A user study was then conducted in which the participants were asked to perform a movie judgement task and answer the finalized scale questionnaires. In the judgment task they were asked to express their judgement of a set of 220 movies so their preference diversity and openness to novelty can be inferred from their movie viewing profile. The constructs measured by the participants' responses to the scales and data from their view profiles would then be correlated in order to test their congruent validity

METHODOLOGY

The construction of "preference diversity" and "openness to novelty" scales

In this section we report the procedures for developing of the movie preference diversity and openness to novelty scales. According to Furr (2011), the construction of a psychological scale involves the following steps:

1. Articulate the construct and context
2. Choose response format and assemble initial item pool
3. Collect data from respondents
4. Examine psychometric properties and quality

The construct of preference diversity is defined as the degree to which an individual appreciates movies of different genes, styles, or by different directors and performers. The construct of "openness to novelty" in movies is defined as the extent to which an individual is willing to try movies s/he is previously unheard of or unfamiliar with. Familiarity is defined as experience with works by previously known directors, actors or actresses, or works of preferred genres or plots. Based on the review of the literature and results from a focus group where 7 frequent movie-goers took part, a total of 18 question items were generated initially, 8 for preference diversity, and 10 for openness to novelty. A survey questionnaire was then administrated to a sample of 191 participants so reliability test, as well as factor analysis could be performed to purify the items. Reliability of items was analyzed by calculating Cronbach's α. As shown in Table 1, all the items demonstrate high reliability

	Items in Preference Diversity	Cronbach's alpha if Item deleted	Sources
1.	I have seen many non-mainstream movies	.744	Focus Group
2.	It's hard to categorize the movies that I like	.753	Focus Group
3.	I am able to discuss movies with people of various kinds of movies preferences	.731	Focus Group
4.	I often view movies of different topics, genres and styles	.699	Focus Group
5.	I always feel there are many good movies out there to be discovered	.752	Focus Group
6.	I often see works by different film directors	.719	Focus Group
7.	My movie preference is not limited to certain styles or genres	.700	Tang et al., 2014
8.	I often see movies featuring different actors/actresses	.720	Focus Group

n=191, * reverse question, Cronbach's α =.754

Table 1. Internal consistency of items in the preference diversity scale

For the construct of openness of novelty, three items found to be inconsistent with the rest of the questions: item 6, 9, and 10 were subsequently deleted. As shown in Table 2, their removal increases the overall Cronbach's α.

	Items in Openness to Novelty	Cronbach's alpha if item deleted	References
1.	I am willing to try movies recommended by media or online sources	.719	Focus Group
2.	I am willing to try movies recommended by others	.717	Focus Group
3.	I am willing to try movies by directors I am not familiar with	.727	Tang et al., 2014
4.	I often learn about new movies through different sources	.718	Focus Group
5.	I am willing to try movies featuring unfamiliar actors/actresses	.723	Tang et al., 2014
6.	I pay more attention to information about movies than my friends do	.769	Focus Group
7.	I am willing to try movies featuring different actors/actresses	.721	Rogers & Shoemaker, 1971 Shoemaker, 1974
8.	It gives tremendous pleasure to discovery new movies that I enjoy	.727	Focus Group
9.	*I judge new movies based on my previous preference of styles, genres, and topics	.771	Baumgartner & Steenkamp, 1996
10.	*I judge new movies based on my previous preference of actors and directors	.788	Baumgartner & Steenkamp, 1996

n=191, * reverse questions, Cronbach's α =.759

Table 2. Internal consistency of items in the openness to novelty scale

An exploratory factor analysis was conducted, which yielded three factors (See Table 3 for each item's factor loadings). Factor 2 and factor 3 can be interpreted as openness to novelty and preference diversity, respectively, as intended, but a mix of items originally intended to measure either construct were lumped together in factor 1. We suspect that the lack of resolution was mainly caused by the ambiguous wordings. The terms "different directors" and "different actors" appeared in question items intended to be included in both constructs. Even though we had used "frequently watched" in preference diversity and "willing to try" in openness to novelty, apparently the semantic differences were not discernable by the participants. Therefore, to avoid ambiguity and increase the resolution of the factors, the five items that contains these terms were deleted.

Items	Factors 1	2	3
I *often see* works by different **film directors**	**.818**	.140	.176
I *often watch* movies featuring different **actors/actresses**	**.762**	.001	.247
I am *willing to try* movies by unfamiliar **actors/actresses**	**.759**	.386	.082
I am *willing to try* movies by **directors** I am not familiar with	**.757**	.358	-.017
I am *willing to try* movies featuring different **actor/actresses**	**.667**	.507	.097
I am willing to try movies recommended by others	**.577**	.475	.268
I always feel there are many good movies out there waiting to be discovered	.170	**.803**	.138
It gives tremendous pleasure to discovery movies that I like	.180	**.788**	.037
I am willing to try movies recommended by media or online sources	.437	**.482**	-.010
I often learn about new movies though different sources	.334	**.477**	.393
It's hard to categorize the movies that I like	.069	-.179	**.692**
I am able to discuss movies with people of various kind of movies preferences	-.001	.257	**.673**
I often view movies of different subjects, genres and styles	.403	.107	**.624**
I have seen many non-mainstream movies	.005	.138	**.621**
My movie preference is not limited to certain styles or genres	.445	.065	**.590**
Variance explained (%)	26.031	17.577	16.069
Total variance explained (%)	26.031	43.608	59.677

n=191

Table 3. Factor loadings of the items in the initial questionnaire

Table 4 shows the results of factor analysis after removing the semantically confusing items. The resulting items with high factor loadings with either construct was then used as the final scale questions. Notice that the question, "I always feel there are many good movies out there to be discovered", initially intended to represent preference diversity, is found to be more in line with openness to novelty.

Items	Factors 1	Factors 2
It gives tremendous pleasure to discovery new movies that I like	**.786**	-.011
I always feel there are many good movies out there to be discovered	**.757**	.092
I am willing to try movies recommended by media or online sources	**.710**	.027
I am willing to try movies recommended by others	**.678**	.361
I often learn about new movies through different sources	**.611**	.388
It's hard to categorize the movies that I like	-.146	**.724**
I often view movies of different topics, genres and styles	.333	**.671**
My movie preference is not limited to certain types or genres	.330	**.652**
I am able to discuss with people of various kind of movies preferences	.151	**.643**
I have seen many non-mainstream movies	.044	**.590**
Variance explained. (%)	27.942	24.512
Total variance explained. (%)	27.942	52.454

n=191

Table 4. Factor loadings of remaining items

User viewing profile elicitation

A subsequent user study was then performed in which a new set of participants were recruited to judge a sample of movies so both their responses to the questionnaire-based scales and actually movies preference could be elicited. The movies seen by each individual and their judgment would be used as their movie viewing profile from which their preference diversity and openness to novelty could be inferred. To maximize sample representativeness without putting exceeding burden on the participants, a combination of a set of mainstream and a set of lesser-known movies were sampled. To balance the representativeness of the "hits" and "long tail" movies (Celma, 2010), a set of 160 movies were selected from IMDB's most 500 popular movie list and another set of 60 movies from those that have been shown in the local art-house theaters from 2011 to 2014, resulting in a total of 220 movies in the sample. The movies in either set were ranked and selected by its logarithmic popularity multiplied by review entropy proposed by Rashid et al. (2002).

A total of 300 participants were recruited to take part in this part of study. Upon their arrival, they were given a short instruction about the research procedure and then asked to judge the 220 movies sampled. The sequence of the movies was randomized to avoid order effect. The information of the movies was provided onscreen in two stages, with the poster and title of the movie as the primary cues for quick judgment. A click on the poster will bring up more information that includes its director and cast, awards received if any, alone with a short description of the plot (See Figure 1). For each movie, the participants were asked if they have heard of or seen the movie, along with their rating of the movie if seen, and how interested they would be in seeing the movies unseen before, both on the 0 to 5 star-rating scale with .05 intervals. After finishing the movie judgment task, the participants were asked to fill out a questionnaire that contains the finalized question items for the proposed preference diversity and openness to novelty scales. The average scores of items in each scale was used to create two corresponding variables for further analysis.

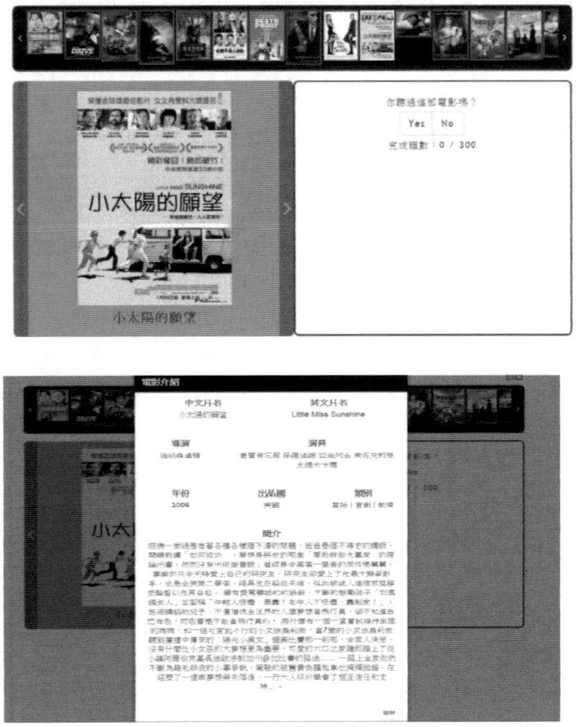

Figure 1. Screenshot of the movie judgment task interface

RESULTS

User study

Descriptive statistics

Two hundred ninety-three participants successfully completed the movie judgment task, among them 55.6% were female. Out of the 220 movies judged, on average, the participant saw 64.23 movies. For the movies unseen, the participants were aware of 75.23, and interested in 8.3 movies (rated above 4 stars). Table 5 reports the descriptive statistics of the movies seen by the users.

	Means	SD	Minimum	Maximum
Movies seen	64.23	31.91	10	201
Movie heard	75.23	24.649	16	162
Movie interested	8.30	8.61	0	53

n=293

Table 5. Descriptive statistics of participants' response to the movies judged

Preference diversity

To validate the psychological scale of preference diversity, we correlated the preference diversity scores with the average cosine similarity of the set of the movies seen by each participant. To create movie similarity matrix, the users' ratings for each movie were used as the feature vector to represent each movie so pair-wise similarity of the movies can be calculated by cosine similarity measure. The higher the average similarities of the set of movies seen by an individual, the lower the diversity of the movies seen, and presumably lower preference diversity. A medium significant negative correlation was found between the diversity scale and the average similarities of the set of movies seen ($r = -.41$, $p<.001$). The diversity scale also has a medium significant positive correlation with the number of the movies seen, as well as the number of genres present in the set of movies seen.

	Preference diversity
# of movies seen	$.39^{***}$
# of genre present	$.38^{***}$
Average cosine similarity of movies seen	$-.41^{***}$

n=293, *** $p < .001$, ** $p < .01$

Table 6. Correlations between preference diversity scale and the diversity of movies seen

Openness to novelty

The openness to novelty scale was intended to capture individuals' willingness to watch less well-known movies. Therefore, the popularity of the movies seen by the participants was used to gauge their openness to novelty. The enjoyment of less popular movies was used as the measurement of openness to novelty. The popularity ranking was determined by the number of times each movie has been seen by all the participants. Correlation analyses were performed between the participants' scores on the openness to novelty scale and the mean, medium, and arithmetic mean of the ranking of the movies they have seen. The lower ranking a movie is, the more potential novelty it brings to the uses. Furthermore, a weighted ranking measure was created where the ranking of the movies seen by an individual was multiplied by his/her rating for that particular movie (i.e. rating x log ranking). This is to better reflect the participants' preference for less popular movies. The assumption is that, the more an individual enjoy obscure movies in a greater number, the more open s/he is to novelty. As shown in Table 7, the participants' openness to novelty scores were found to be significantly correlated with their liking of less popular films.

	Openness to novelty
Mean ranking of movies seen	$.23^{***}$
Medium ranking of movies seen	$.20^{**}$
Arithmetic mean ranking of movies seen	$.26^{***}$

n=293, *** $p < .001$, ** $p < .01$

Table 7. Correlations between openness to novelty scale and the popularity of movies seen

DISCUSSION AND LIMITATION

In this study we set out to create two psychological constructs, namely, preference diversity and openness to novelty, that we believe to be important moderators in users' responses to movie recommendations. The question items in the scales were developed from literature review and a focus group interview. A questionnaire interview was first conducted so questions items can be purified. Following the scale construction, a user study was subsequently performed in which the participants were asked to judge a sample of 220 movies so their actual movie preference profile could be attained. With the users' responses to the two scales and their movie viewing profiles, we were able to examine how well the scales were related to these two preference attributes as reflected in their movie viewing profile. It was found that the preference diversity scale has a significant medium negative correlation with the average similarity of the set of movies seen, which has been widely used to gauge the diversity of recommended items. It also has a positive correlation with the total number of movies and genres seen. As for openness to novelty, a weighted preference for novelty measure was created based on the participants' rating of movies of different degrees of popularity. The weighted ranking measure was found to be significantly correlated with the openness to novelty scale.

We believe that the study has great practical implications. Recommender systems have attracted great attention both from the academic and business communities. Most of the research efforts have so far mostly driven by creating algorithms for the improvement of accurate prediction. Only recently have we seen efforts in incorporating alternative criteria, such as recommendation novelty and diversity as viable system objectives. Our research is based on the assumption that a proper balance between accuracy and other criteria might hinge on users' preference characteristics. In other words, systems should apply accuracy or diversity/novelty inducing strategies adaptively, according to the users' preference structure. To the best of our knowledge, ours is the first to propose the study of psychological constructs such as "preference diversity" and "openness to novelty" as potential factors that might impact users' response to movie recommendations. Our findings of the correlation between the psychological and behavioral manifestations of the two constructs also point to the possibly of inferring these two aspects of the users' preference structure based on their past viewing prolife without requiring them to answer the questionnaire, which is more obtrusive and therefore difficult to perform at a large scale.

Even though correlations were found between the proposed scales and the characteristics of the participants' movie viewing profile, it remains an empirical question whether and how these constructs might influence the users' responses to movies they have not seen or have not even heard of. In other words, will individuals with high preference diversity also prefer more diverse recommendations? And are individuals with higher openness to novelty indeed more likely to try less known movies? A question also raises with regard to the definition of novelty. Here we adopted the popularity-based definition of novelty, based on the assumption that the less popular a movie, the more novel it is to all movie goers. In contrast to considering novelty in absolute terms, novelty can be thought of as how novel an item is in relation to an individual's past preference. In other words, how dissimilar an item is to one's previous viewing profile. (Vargas & Castells, 2011). It is an interesting question in itself that how the openness to novelty manifested in the user's preference profile correlate with this dissimilarity-based novelty. More analyses need to be done to address these questions. In the present paper, only the data pertinent to the movies actually seen by the participants were used to represent their preference profile. More analyses are now underway to see how the participants with different preference profiles judge movies they have not seen, which should shade light on whether these constructs do indeed influence users' actual responses to recommendations.

REFERENCES

Baumgartner, H., & Steenkamp, J.-B.E.M. (1996). Exploratory consumer buying behavior: Conceptualization and measurement. International Journal of Research in Marketing, 13(2), 121-137. doi:http://dx.doi.org/10.1016/0167-8116(95)00037-2

Bradley, K., & Smyth, B. (2001). Improving recommendation diversity. In Proceedings of the Twelfth National Conference in Artificial Intelligence and Cognitive Science (pp. 75-84).

Cantador, I., Fernández-Tobías, I., Bellogín, A., Kosinski, M., & Stillwell, D. (2013, June). Relating Personality Types with User Preferences in Multiple Entertainment Domains. In UMAP Workshops, Girona, Spain.

Celma, Ò., & Herrera, P. (2008). A new approach to evaluating novel recommendations. In Proceedings of the 2008 ACM conference on Recommender systems (pp. 179-186).

Celma, O. (2010). Music Recommendation and Discovery: The Long Tail, Long Fail, and Long Play in the Digital Music Space. Springer.

Chang, Y. H., & Tang, M. C. (2018, March). Serendipity with Music Streaming Services: The Mediating Role of User and Task Characteristics. In International Conference on Information (pp. 435-441). Springer, Cham.

Furr, R. (2011). The Sage Library of Methods in Social and Personality Psychology: Scale construction and psychometrics for social and personality psychology. London, UK: SAGE Publications Ltd doi: 10.4135/9781446287866

Hurley, N., & Zhang, M. (2011). Novelty and diversity in top-n recommendation--analysis and evaluation. ACM Transactions on Internet Technology (TOIT),10(4), 14.

Herlocker, J. L., Konstan, J. A., Terveen, L. G., Riedl, J. T. (2004). Evaluating collaborative filtering recommender systems. Transactions on Information Systems, 22(1), 5-53.

Konstan, J & Riedl, J. (2012). Recommender system: from algorithms to user experience. User Model User-Adap Interface, 22, 101-123.

Kramer, T., Spolter-Weisfeld, S., & Thakkar, M. (2007). The effect of cultural orientation on consumer responses to personalization. Marketing Science, 26(2), 246-258.

Kwon, K., Cho, J., & Park, Y. (2009). Influences of customer preference development on the effectiveness of recommendation strategies. Electronic Commerce Research and Applications, 8(5), 263-275.

McNee, S. M., Riedl, J., & Konstan, J. A. (2006). Being accurate is not enough: how accuracy metrics have hurt recommender systems. In CHI'06 extended abstracts on Human factors in computing systems (pp. 1097-1101).

Pu, P., Chen, L., & Hu, R. (2011). A user-centric evaluation framework for recommender systems. In Proceedings of the fifth ACM conference on Recommender systems (pp. 157-164).

Rashid, A. M., Albert, I., Cosley, D., Lam, S. K., McNee, S. M., Konstan, J. A., & Riedl, J. (2002). Getting to know you: learning new user preferences in recommender systems. In Proceedings of the 7th international conference on Intelligent user interfaces (pp. 127-134).

Rogers, E. M., & Shoemaker, F. F. (1971). Communication of Innovations: A Cross-Cultural Approach. New York: Free Press.

Simonson, I. (2005). Determinants of customers' responses to customized offers: conceptual framework and research propositions. Journal of Marketing, 69(1), 32-45.

Shen, A., & Ball, A.D. (2011). Preference stability belief as a determinant of response to personalized recommendations. Journal of Consumer Behaviour, 10(2), 71-79.

Tang, M.C., Ke, Y.L., & Sie, Y.J. (2013). The Estimation of aNobii Users' Reading Diversity Using Book Co-ownership Data: A Social Analytical Approach. In Social Informatics (pp. 274-283)

Tang, M.C., Sie, Y.J., & Ting, P.H. (2014). Evaluating books finding tools on social media: A case study of aNobii. Information Processing & Management, 50(1), 54-68.

Vargas, S., & Castells, P. (2011). Rank and relevance in novelty and diversity metrics for recommender systems. In Proceedings of the fifth ACM conference on Recommender systems (pp. 109-116).

Wang, H.C., & Doong, H.S. (2010). Online customers' cognitive differences and their impact on the success of recommendation agents.

Information & management, 47(2), 109-114

Zhang, M., & Hurley, N. (2008). Avoiding monotony: improving the diversity of recommendation lists. In Proceedings of the 2008 ACM conference on Recommender systems (pp. 123-130).

Zhou, T., Kuscsik, Z., Liu, J.-G., Medo, M., Wakeling, J.R., & Zhang, Y.-C. (2010). Solving the apparent diversity-accuracy dilemma of recommender systems. Proceedings of the National Academy of Sciences, 107(10), 4511-4515.

Towards a More Inclusive Technical Website: Knowledge Gaps, Performance, Experience, and Perception Differences among Various User Groups

Rong Tang
Simmons University, USA. rong.tang@simmons.edu

Wenqing Lu
Simmons University, USA. wenqing.lu@simmons.edu

Will Gregg
Simmons University, USA. will.gregg@simmons.edu

Steven Gentry
Simmons University, USA. gentrysteven0208@gmail.com

Stephen E. Humeston
Simmons University, USA. sehumeston@gmail.

ABSTRACT

This paper reports a usability and user experience research study of PBCore.org, a WGBH website supporting the PBCore metadata dictionary. Usability testing was conducted with 53 participants who worked in audiovisual processing and archiving. Significant differences in task performances and interaction experiences among user groups were found, most notably between broadcast and information professionals, archivists/librarians and other staff, and participants who had an LIS degree and those who did not. Qualitative observations afforded a deeper understanding of the difficulties that non-LIS participants encountered. Recommendations for designing a more inclusive technical website include providing contextual and practical information on the homepage, delivering technical content visually and interactively, offering understandable definitions of terminology, and building a vibrant user community. Further research documenting users' knowledge gaps would be valuable. The paper concludes with a call for developing specific usability requirements for technical websites to create an inclusive and accessible user experience.

KEYWORDS

User group differences, technical websites, user community building, inclusive and accessible user experience

INTRODUCTION

The present study reports the results of a usability assessment of PBCore.org, a technical website developed and supported by WGBH, a non-profit public media producer serving New England. According to Clair (2008), "the PBCore standard initially emerged from the public broadcasting community, with its initial funding coming from the Corporation for Public Broadcasting and its continuing maintenance done by WGBH in Boston" (p. 54). PBCore.org hosts the Public Broadcasting Metadata Dictionary (PBCore), an XML-based metadata schema designed for the descriptive cataloging and management of sound and moving images. PBCore enables "producers and local stations" to "better share, manage and preserve the media they produce" (PBCore, 2015a). PBCore 1.0 was unveiled in April 2005, with PBCore 2.0, and 2.1 later being released in November 2011 and August 2015 respectively. In recent years, PBCore's user base has expanded to include institutions outside of public broadcasting including film archives, academic repositories, and technology vendors.

PBCore.org is a website that documents the PBCore schema, supports existing users, and serves as an educational resource for orienting new users. The website features three broad categories of information: (1) technical material on the structure and content of the schema, (2) supplementary resources such as controlled vocabulary lists and sample records, and (3) communication channels between users and developers that include a blog, contact form, and forum. PBCore.org is intended to serve two distinct populations: information professionals working at academic institutions or broadcast stations and broadcast professionals who do not have an academic background in LIS (PBCore, 2015b). To better understand whether PBCore.org meets the needs of all its users, the WGBH project team conducted an online survey in May 2016. Sixty-seven information and broadcast professionals responded to the survey, of which 42% were active PBcore.org users. Several respondents felt that the website's content was not accessible or well organized. They also expressed dissatisfaction with the website's limited search functionality. Data obtained from this earlier survey and other anecdotal evidence suggested gaps in the design of PBCore.org and that different user groups may experience varying degrees of difficulty in accessing the website's content.

Given the challenges identified by these respondents and WGBH's ongoing mission to serve its entire user base, a usability assessment and user experience (UX) study was necessary to investigate specific usability issues among various PBCore user groups. Researchers of this study were contracted as a third party to conduct a usability assessment of PBCore.org. Currently, there is limited research examining knowledge gaps and user experiences on a technical website. The practical goal of this project is to recommend improvements to the design of technical websites to make them more inclusive.

LITERATURE REVIEW

Metadata Registries and Practice

Metadata is used in all digital libraries. Metadata schemas provide a framework for representing metadata and typically include term definitions, structural constraints, and data structures (such as XML coding). A metadata schema registry is usually a website where authoritative documentation on the schema is hosted and managed (Nagamori & Sugimoto, 2006). In 2006, Nagamori and Sugimoto of the Dublin Core Metadata Initiative (DCMI) Registry Working Group advocated for the use of registries as a tool to enhance metadata interoperability. The following year, they called for registries to enhance usability and reusability of schemas (Nagamori & Sugimoto, 2007). Their effort was echoed by other researchers who promoted best practices for documenting metadata (Hodge, 2008; Nagamori & Sugimoto, 2008).

As indicated by Lee (2004), research involving metadata practice and the LIS community's use of metadata started in 1997. A great portion of the research has focused on "crosswalks, frameworks and supermetadata issues." There have been also studies on "the practitioner's use of metadata concepts, the application of metadata" (Lee, p. 7). For instance, Clair (2008) reported a project on the development of a PBCore application profile for Penn State library that included "a core element set upon which specific schemas can be seamlessly constructed to suit locally developed audiovisual collections" (p. 55).

Performance Gaps among Different User Groups

Task performance among different groups has been examined by a number of researchers on the basis of expertise (e.g., Dillon & Song, 1997; Faulkner & Wick, 2005; Azadbakht, Blair, & Jones, 2016). These studies found that evaluating performance gaps between groups can provide more information than would testing each group in isolation. For instance, Faulkner and Wick (2005) evaluated a web-based employee timesheet application by differentiating three groups of 20 participants (novice/novice, expert/novice, and expert/novice) based on their experience with computers and the application. Researchers found the performance of novice/novice and expert/novice to be significantly worse than expert/expert. This difference had to do "with the presentation or behavior of those elements" in the application (p. 781). The contrast among three groups enabled researchers to pinpoint the areas where the knowledge gap occurred.

The operational definitions of novice and expert vary. Dillon & Song (1997), for instance, delineate novice and expert on the basis of professional identity. In their evaluation of a university database for art-resource works, the authors compared the performance of librarians and LIS graduate students with the performance of undergraduate students in the arts and humanities. The study found that LIS professionals and students outperformed undergraduates in speed and accuracy. The authors indicated that future comparison based on subject expertise, "is likely to be worthy of further investigation" ("Research Design," para. 2).

User Based Design Principles for Complex Technical Websites

Over the years, researchers and design experts have developed fundamental principles for websites oriented toward the general public. Steve Krug, the author of *Don't Make Me Think (2006)*, proposed some key principles as Design 101 for general purpose websites. These include, "create a clear visual hierarchy," "conventions are your friends," "break up pages into clearly defined areas," "make it obvious what's clickable," and "keep the noise down to a dull roar" (Krug, 2006, p. 31-39). While there are some studies on digital collections (Saleh, 2018), metadata service systems (Lee, 2004), and complex websites (Ruzza, Tiozzo, Mantovani, D'Este, & Ravarotto, 2017; Goyal et al, 2012), seldom has there been research on user experience and design principles for technical websites. In conducting usability tests of OCLC Connexion with 10 participants, Lee (2004) identified six major usability problems with this integrated metadata service system. Among the six problems, Lee claims that the most important include "user assistance" and "navigation."

Meanwhile, in a study of the information architecture of a complex institutional website, Ruzza, et al (2017) discussed the typical challenges that IA managers of such sites face, including deep and complex content hierarchies, the need to constantly redefine and extend the original architecture, very busy and cluttered homepages and resulting navigation issues, and the lack of indicators and approaches to measure the improvement of the website. They further proposed an IA model for complex institutional websites, which consists of five characteristics that the website should exhibit. The first two characteristics appear to be pertinent to a technical website: "(1) Pages and sections organized according to a strict hierarchy. (2) News content organized according to a faceted classification approach" (p. 168). Overall, even though there exists scholarly literature on usability design principles for complex websites, seldom has any study focused directly on technical websites built for professionals for work-related tasks. None of the aforementioned studies name their website as a "technical website" directly. The present study addresses this gap and argues for the need for developing more inclusive technical websites.

Remote Usability Testing

In the field of usability testing, moderated remote usability testing has become a popular and effective method in recent years. Several sources ("Remote Testing," n.d.; Schade, 2013; Baker, 2014) note that, although it is similar to in-person testing, moderated remote usability testing is different in that it involves one or more tools (e.g. GoToMeeting, UserTesting) to complete sessions with participants who may not be in the same location. Moderated remote usability testing has a number of benefits over traditional ones, including the ability to acquire data from participants in distant geographic areas as well as those who cannot participate during normal business hours. Other benefits are increased user comfort as well as reduced researcher costs, given that moderators and observers do not need to travel to gather data.

Drawbacks of this technique include respondent-related problems (e.g. discomfort with software) and hardware or software issues that could inhibit or prevent usability test sessions (Usability.gov, n.d.; Baker, 2014). Researchers may also be more likely to fail to notice participants' subtle reactions during sessions (Usability.gov, n.d.; Schade, 2013). Despite these issues, scholars such as Thompson, Rozanski, & Haake (2004) and Batra & Bishu (2007), argue that the effectiveness of remote testing would be the same as traditional laboratory-based testing, if not more.

In summary, existing research has provided evidence for knowledge gaps between expert and novice users. Because metadata schemas often involve peculiar terminology and require training to develop the correct mental model, more nuanced categories than 'novice' or 'expert' were required. For that reason, this research study takes into consideration profession, education, on-the-job training, and job titles as well as experience using PBCore.org. Additionally, even though there are some UX and IA design studies on LIS systems and complex websites, none have specifically focused on the UX and knowledge gaps of users using technical websites such as PBCore.org. Through using both moderated remote testing and in person laboratory-based testing, the present research aims to examine such differences and provide recommendations for PBCore.org to address users' knowledge gaps.

RESEARCH QUESTIONS

The present research addresses following research questions:

RQ1.To what extent does prior experience with PBCore.org impact participants' task performances and interaction experiences?
RQ2. Do task performances and interaction experiences differ among information professionals, broadcast professionals, and in-between professionals?
RQ3. Do task performances and interaction experiences differ among participants who have an LIS degree, metadata training, both, or neither?
RQ4. Do task performances and interaction experiences differ among those whose professional title was "Archivist/Librarian," "Manager," "Audiovisual Producer/Processing Staff," or "Other Staff?"
RQ5. What significant correlations exist among success rate, satisfaction, confusion, and other performance and experience-related ratings?
RQ6. Do participants' qualitative perception and experience confirm and reinforce the results from the quantitative analysis?
RQ7. What design recommendations can be made to enable technical websites to be more inclusive and accessible?

METHODS

This research study used a mixed method approach that combines qualitative interviews, qualitative observations, and quantitative task performance. Prior to the formal study, data from the WGBH user survey were analyzed to help researchers better understand the website's user population. In order to create a task scenario representative of PBCore users' work tasks, two in-depth interviews with current PBCore users (an archivist and a production producer) were conducted in August 2017. The interviewees described the most frequent work tasks for which they used PBCore.org. Both interviewees indicated that one of the top tasks they perform was to figure out how to enter descriptive metadata into appropriate elements/attributes/container fields. Subsequently, and in consultation with the WGBH PBCore project team, usability tasks for a work scenario were developed. For example, in our usability task scenario, Tasks 2, 3, and 6 involved activities related to PBCore elements (PBCoreCreator, Creator, and CreatorRole), attributes (Portrayal) and instantiation (language). Upon obtaining IRB approval, three pilot usability test sessions were run. The formal usability study was conducted between October 6 and December 9, 2017.

Participant Recruitment and Usability Research Sessions

Multiple rounds of participant recruitment were performed to locate current and potential PBCore users. Email announcements about the study were sent to several professional listservs including (1) The Association of Moving Image Archivists (AMIA), (2) The New England Archivists (NEA), and (3) the American Archive of Public Broadcasting's member stations. The WGBH PBCore project team members also invited staff members at local New England stations to participate in the project. Of the 88 people who originally filled out a screener survey, 53 were recruited to participate in a usability research session (3 laboratory-based sessions and 50 via GoToMeeting sessions).

Each usability research session consisted of three parts: (1) a pre-session interview, (2) a usability test scenario with tasks, and (3) a post-session survey. The pre-session interview focused on the user's professional and academic background, including their metadata and cataloging experience. This part also included questions related to users' familiarity, proficiency, and comfort level with PBCore and PBCore.org. The task scenario consisted of eight main tasks, each of which had between two and four sub-tasks. These tasks and subtasks focused on key sections of PBCore.org, such as basic introductory impressions, searching for specific elements and attributes requirements, referencing controlled vocabularies, and learning about institutional policies and announcements. During the usability testing sessions, participants were encouraged to think aloud. The post-session online survey captured participants' responses about their reactions to the website immediately following their task scenario. Research session lengths ranged from 27 to 79 minutes (average time was 55 minutes).

Participants

Of the 53 participants, 37 (70%) were female and 16 (30%) were male. Thirty-four (64%) had an LIS degree and, of those with an LIS degree, 15 had received additional training about cataloging and metadata at their workplaces. The remaining participants either only had on-the-job training or had neither an LIS degree nor workplace-related metadata training (n=9, 17%). Most participants were employed at the time of their usability study, although a few were retired and one was "between jobs." Participants had worked in their field(s) for 14 years on average, with individual work experiences ranging from 1.5 to 48 years. Participants were from 26 states of the United States, with Massachusetts, Georgia, New York, and Texas being the most frequent.

Participants were also classified by (1) self-identified professional identity and (2) position or job titles that they held. With regard to their professional affiliation, participants were placed into three groups: "Information Professionals" (n=21, 40%); "Broadcast Professionals" (n=16, 30%); and "In-Between Professionals" (n=16, 30%), the latter of which being defined as individuals who work as both an information professional and a broadcast professional. Participants were also grouped into four groups based on their position titles: "Archivists/Librarians" (n=22, 42%); "Managers" (n=18, 34%); "Audiovisual Producers or Audiovisual Processing Staff" (n=9, 17%); and "Other Staff" (n=4, 8%). An example for a "Managers" position was "Director, Digital Repository Services," while "Other Staff" included an "Independent Consultant."

DATA PROCESSING AND ANALYSIS

Multiple data sets were gathered during the research sessions. Open-ended responses from the pre-session interviews and post-session surveys were coded. Performance data from the task performance process (e.g., time on task, task completion) and participants' think-aloud comments were coded. To gather experience data, researchers performed structured observation by recording instances of confusion, frustration, negative comments, and positive comments exhibited by test subjects. Non-parametric statistical tests were run to compare performances, experiences, and ratings of various groups. Qualitative analyses of participants' open-ended responses and think-aloud comments were also performed. Variables examined during the study's quantitative analysis are listed in Table 1.

Independent Variables	Dependent Variables
Profession • Information Professionals (IPs) • Broadcast Professionals (BPs) • In-Between Professionals (IBPs) **Position Title** • Archivists/Librarians (ALs) • Managers • Audiovisual Producers/Audiovisual Processing Staff (AVstaff) • Other Staff (Otherstaff) **Education and Metadata Training** • LIS Degree (LISd) • LIS Degree and On-the-Job Training (LISdt) • On-the-Job Training only (LISt) • None (Ndt)	**Task Performance** • Task completion ratio • Time on task • Task completion difficulty **Interaction Experience (Frequency of)** • Confusion • Frustration • Positive comments • Negative comments **Participants' Rating** • Familiarity with the PBCore website • Proficiency with metadata schemas • Comfort level with PBCore • Satisfaction • Usability of PBCore website • Usefulness for learning • Likelihood to use • Likelihood to recommend

Table 1. Variables used in the formal study

RESULTS

Quantitative measures of participants' self-rating and task performance are presented in this section first, followed by the results of statistical testing on group differences. Qualitative results are reported in the last subsection.

Overall Experience and Task Performance

During their pre-session interviews, participants were asked to assess their familiarity with PBCore.org, their proficiency with metadata schemas, and their comfort level with the PBCore metadata schema. On a scale of 1 to 7—with "7" being the highest measure—participants' average score of their familiarity was "2.25" (SD=1.57). The average rating for participants' proficiency was 3.89 (SD=1.85) and the average for their comfort level was 3.21 (SD=1.73).

One participant experienced technical difficulties and had to perform an informal usability evaluation of the PBCore website on a mobile device. This participant's (P40) data was excluded during analysis of task performance data. Task 8 was also excluded for the task completion measures because not all participants completed it. The average completion ratio was 86.54% (SD=11.19%), with a range of 37% to 97%. Participants' average task time was 265.80 seconds (SD=71.88), or 4.43 minutes per task. Participants' task performance was further coded by levels of difficulty experienced, based on researchers' real time observations. While 78.95% of all tasks were completed with ease, participants completed 10.29% of tasks with difficulty and failed to complete 9.74% of the tasks. Some tasks (1.01%) were not performed at all.

During the post-session survey, respondents were asked to rate their satisfaction with PBCore.org. The average satisfaction rating—on a seven-point scale—was 4.98 (*SD*=1.34). Participants also rated the usability of the site (*M*=5.06, *SD*=1.28), their view of the usefulness of the website content for learning about PBCore.org (*M*=5.30, *SD*=1.61), their likelihood to use the site in the future (*M*=4.91, *SD*=2.12), and their likelihood to recommend the site to their colleagues (*M*=5.62, *SD*=1.77). Even though their average satisfaction was below five, their likelihood to recommend the site to others was over 5.5. The range of participants' ratings was either between 1 and 7 or between 2 and 7.

User Group Differences

In comparing various user groups, participants of different professions, position titles, and education/training backgrounds exhibited significant differences in their self-rating, task performance, and interaction experiences.

Past Experience with PBCore.org

Of 53 participants, 29 participants acknowledged that they had used the website before. Of these participants, 17 noted that they had visited the website within the past year; three stated they had visited PBCore.org approximately 2 years ago; three estimated that they had visited the website between three and four years ago; and four said visited the website more than four years ago. Past experience impacted participants' task performances, experiences, and self-ratings. Participants who had previously used PBCore.org had higher task completion rates than participants who had never used the website prior to their research session (*U*=449.00, *n*=52, *Z*=2.14, *p*=.032). Participants who had used the website before also completed a significantly higher number of tasks with ease than those participants who had no prior experience with the website (*U*=482.00, *n*=52, *Z*=2.77, *p*=.006). Conversely, participants who had no prior use experience failed to complete more tasks than participants who used the website before (*U*=187.00, *n*=52, *Z*=-2.76, *p*=.006). These individuals were also observed to experience more confusion than those who had prior experience with PBCore.org (*U*=169.50, *n*=53, *Z*=-3.26, *p*=.001).

Those who had previously used PBCore.org also gave significantly higher positive ratings. Understandably, participants who had used the website before rated their familiarity with PBCore.org (*U*=619.00, *n*=53, *Z*=5.22, *p*=.000), proficiency with metadata schemas (*U*=479.00, *n*=53, *Z*=2.39, *p*=.017), and comfort with PBcore (*U*=509.00, *n*=53, *Z*=2.99, *p*=.003) as significantly higher than those who had not used the website before. They also saw themselves as more likely to use the website in the future (*U*=609.50, *n*=53, *Z*=4.78, *p*=.000) and recommend it to colleagues (*U*=472.50, *n*=53, *Z*=2.37, *p*=.018).

Profession

Table 2 includes significant results of Kruskal Wallis tests of group differences among the three professions. Overall, BPs reported significantly more years of work experience than IPs (post hoc Dunn's Test: *d*=-17.93, *p*=.001). In terms of task performance, a number of significant differences were shown between IPs and BPs as well as between IBPs and BPs. Post hoc Dunn's tests showed that IPs or IBPs generally outperformed BPs. Both IPs (*d*=17.35, *p*=.002) and IBPs (*d*=16.09, *p*=.007) had significantly higher ratios of task completion than BPs. Significantly more IPs (*d*=18.07, *p*=.001) and IBPs (*d*=15.50, *p*=.010) completed tasks with ease than BPs.

For tasks completed with difficulty, IPs (*d*=-15.53, *p*=.005) and IBPs (*d*=-17.75, *p*=.002) had significantly fewer difficulties than BPs. BPs experienced a higher frequency of confusion than IPs (*d*=-13.11, *p*=.027) and IBPs (*d*=-13.44, *p*=.036). Furthermore, IPs completed tasks more quickly and expressed fewer negative comments than BPs (*d*=-15.35, *p*=.004).

Both IPs and IBPs gave higher (more positive) ratings than BPs in the pre- and post-session interviews. Both IPs (*d*=22.56, *p*=.000) and IBPs (*d*=19.97, *p*=.001) viewed themselves as more proficient than BPs. During the post-session survey, IPs (*d*=13.73, *p*=.013) and IBPs (*d*=18.94, *p*=.001) selected a higher rating than BPs regarding their likelihood to recommend PBCore.org to their friends or peers. IPs also gave a higher satisfaction rating than BPs (*d*=13.33, *p*=.020) and more highly rated the website's educational value (*d*=14.91, *p*=.008). Meanwhile, IBPs rated their familiarity (*d*=17.88, *p*=.001) and comfort level (*d*=14.41, *p*=.019) to be higher than BPs. IBPs also gave a significantly higher rating than BPs regarding their likelihood to use PBCore.org in the future (*d*=18.75, *p*=.001). While there were few significant differences in IPs and IBPs self-ratings, IBPs gave a significantly higher rating for their familiarity with the PBCore website than IPs (*d*=-11.70, *p*=.042).

	Significant Test Results
Performance	**Task Completion Rate** (*H*=13.87, *n*=52, df=2, *p*= .001); **Complete with ease** (*H*=14.42, *n*=52, *df*=2, *p*= .001); **Complete with difficulty** (*H*=14.00, *n*=52, *df*=2, *p*= .001); **Average Task Time** (*H*=7.28, *n*=52, *df*=2, *p*=.026)
Work Length	**Years of Working** (*H*=12.31, *n*=53, *df*=2, *p*=.002)
Self-rating	**Familiarity** (*H*=12.93, *n*=53, *df*=2, *p*=.002); **Proficiency** (*H*=22.79, *n*=53, *df*=2, p=.000); **Comfort Level** (*H*=7.51, *n*=53, *df*=2, *p*=.023)
Interaction Experience	**Confusion** (*H*=8.59, *N*=53, *df*= 2, *p*=.014); **Negative comments** (*H*=11.00, *N*=53, *df*=2, *p*=.004)
Perception	**Usability of the website** (*H*=6.26, *n*=53, *df*=2, *p*=.044); **Usefulness for Learning** (*H*=9.23, *n*=53, *df*=2, p=.010); **Satisfaction** (*H*=7.45, *n*=53, *df*=2, *p*=.024); **Helpful Prior Knowledge and Experience** (*H*=12.24, *n*=53, *df*=2, *p*=.002); **Likelihood to Use** (*H*=12.57, *n*=53, *df*=2, *p*=.002); **Likelihood to Recommend** (*H*=14.75, *n*=53, *df*=2, *p*=.001)

Table 2. Group differences among IP, IBP, and BP in Their Performance, Experiences and Ratings

Position and Job Title

Table 3 includes significant results of Kruskal Wallis tests of group differences among participants of different job titles. Managers reported working longer than archivists/librarians (ALs) (d=14.65, p=.017). In terms of task performance, major differences occurred between (1) ALs and Otherstaff and (2) AVstaff and Otherstaff. Both ALs (d=25.85, p=.010) and AVstaff (d=24.31, p=.043) had significantly higher task completion ratios than Otherstaff. Otherstaff also had significantly lower frequency of completing their tasks with ease than ALs (d=26.51, p=.019) and AVstaff (d=27.13, p=.005). Both ALs (d=26.00, p=.008) and AVstaff (d=24.39, p=.037) had significantly fewer cases of failing to complete tasks than Otherstaff, and ALs experienced fewer cases of completing tasks with difficulty than Otherstaff (d=21.98, p=.039). As expected, ALs made significantly fewer negative comments than Otherstaff participants (d=-23.16, p=.021). In terms of their pre- and post- session evaluations, managers had significantly lower scoring of their proficiency with metadata schemas than ALs (d=-15.70, p=.006). ALs gave significantly higher ratings than Otherstaff with regard to both the website's usability (d=23.61, p=.020) and their likelihood to recommend PBCore (d=22.10, p=.030).

	Significant Test Results
Performance	**Completion Ratio** (H=11.30, n=52, df=3, p=.010); **Complete with ease** (H=14.51, n=52, df=3, p=.002); **Complete with difficulty** (H=11.39, n=52, df=3, p=.010); **Fail to complete** (H=11.60, n=52, df=3, p=.009)
Work Length	**Years of Working** (H=11.22, n=53, df=3, p=.021)
Interaction Experience	**Frustration** (H=8.69, n=53, df=3, p=.034); **Negative Comments** (H=11.82, n=53, df=3, p=.008)
Perception	**Proficiency** (H=12.45, n=53, df=3, p=.006); **Usability of Website** (H=10.05, n=53, df=3, p=.018); **Likelihood to Recommend** (H=8.47, n=53, df=3, p=.037)

Table 3. The impact of job titles on participants' performance, experience, and rating

Degree and Training

Table 4 includes significant results of Kruskal Wallis tests of group differences among participants who received different degrees or training. Those participants who had an LIS degree (LISd) as well as those who had both a degree and on-the-job training (LISdt) outperformed those who did not hold an LIS degree nor had received metadata training (Ndt). Specifically, both LISd (d=19.67, p=.008) and LISdt (d=20.18, p=.009) participants had significantly higher completion rates than Ndt. Both LISd (d=-20.22, p=.005) and LISdt (d=-16.94, p=.040) participants had fewer cases of failing to complete their tasks than Ndt participants. LISd participants also had significantly higher number of tasks completed with ease (d=17.17, p=.030) than Ndt participants. In terms of self-rating, LISd participants had significantly higher proficiency ratings than LISt (d=16.68, p=.028) and Ndt (d=25.97, p=.000) participants. LISdt participants also gave significantly higher proficiency ratings than LISt (d=-18.37, p=.017) and Ndt participants (d=27.66, p=.000). LISd participants rated their impression about PBCore.org's usefulness for learning (H=11.82, n=53, df=3, p=.008; d=16.94, p=.032) and their likelihood to use (d=18.09, p=.018) as significantly higher than the Ndt group. LISdt participants gave significantly higher ratings in their familiarity (d=16.06, p=.047), comfort (d=19.00, p=.015), usefulness for learning (d=19.18, p=.015), and likelihood to recommend (d=16.39, p=.044) than the Ndt group.

	Significant Test Results
Performance	**Completion Ratio** (H=13.23, n=52, df=3, p=.004); **Complete with ease** (H=8.23, n=52, df=3, p=.041); **Failed to Complete** (H=11.78, n=52, df=3, p=.008)
Work Length	**Years of Working** (H=13.23, n=53, df=3, p=.004)
Self-rating	**Familiarity** (H=7.90, n=53, df=3, p= .048); **Proficiency** (H=27.35, n=53, df=3, p=.000); **Comfort Level** (H=10.70, n=53, df=3, p=.013)
Perception	**Usefulness for learning** (H=11.82, n=53, df=3, p=.008); **Satisfaction** (H=8.20, n=53, df=3, p=.042); **Helpful Prior Knowledge and Experience** (H=11.62, n=53, df=3, p=.009); **Likelihood to Use** (H=9.57, n=53, df=3, p=.023); **Likelihood to Recommend** (H=8.69, n=53, df=3, p=.034)

Table 4. The impact of education and training background in participants' performance, experience, and rating

Correlations

Numerous sets of significant correlations among variables were found. Table 5 includes all the significant correlations concerning three variables: completion rate, satisfaction, and confusion. These variables are representative of task performances, interaction experiences, and participants' perceptions.

Categories	Variables	Task Completion	Satisfaction	Confusion
Performance	Average task time	r=-.35, p=.012	r=-.50, p=.000	r=.27, p=.049
	Completion rate	/	r=.28, p=.043	r=-.56, p=.000
	Complete with ease	r=.71, p=.000	r=.46, p=.001	r=-.56, p=.000
	Complete with difficulty	/	r=-.52, p=.000	r=.32, p=.023
	Fail to complete	r=-.93, p=.000	/	r=-.57, p=.000
Interaction Experience	Confusion	r=-.56, p=.000	r=-.47, p=.000	/
	Frustration	r=-.29, p=.039	/	/
	Negative comments	r=-.33, p=.017	r=-.46, p=.001	r=.35, p=.010
Self-Rating	Proficiency	r=.37, p=.008	r=.38, p=.004	r=-.32, p=.018
Perception	Usability of the website	r=.32, p=.023	r=.76, p=.000	r=-.35, p=.010
	Usefulness for learning	r=.29, p=.035	r=.87, p=.000	r=-.42, p=.002
	Satisfaction	r=.28, p=.043	/	r=-.47, p=.000
	Likelihood to use	r=.37, p=.007	r=.31, p=.024	r=-.47, p=.000
	Likelihood to recommend	r=.45, p=.001	r=.52, p=.000	r=-.42, p=.002

Table 5. Significant correlations with task completion rate, satisfaction, and occurrences of confusion

Participants' Qualitative Perceptions and Experiences

Major Areas of Knowledge Gaps

Quantitative analysis revealed that BPs had significantly more occurrences of confusion and made more negative comments than IPs. It appears that the lack of a systematic understanding of PBCore vocabulary prevented BPs from completing tasks. BPs who did not have any prior training commented on this knowledge gap. For instance, one BP participant said, "I don't know what does that mean, metadata schema" (P01). Another BP participant (P21) commented, "I don't know what sub-element means. I don't know what container means." For BP participants who received some level of metadata training, the vocabulary and structure of PBCore were still difficult to understand. While looking up a specific PBCore element, P03 claimed, "As a person who's not a librarian or something like that I don't know if those titles mean anything to me. Root element, intellectual content, intellectual property...I don't know what they mean."

Possibly due to lack of familiarity with the terminology, BP participants expressed a need for prior training, knowledge, or expert help. They felt "overwhelmed," "stuck," or "lost." In comparison, no IP or IBP participants expressed a desire for training. One IP and one IBP participant did express frustration when trying to find information on crosswalks between PBCore and Dublin Core: "I'm struggling. I don't know where to go here" (P19). Ndt participants pointed out their inability to understand PBCore due to a lack of LIS training. An Ndt participant (P21) commented that "at this point I'm already out. I need someone who has an LIS background." Multiple participants claimed that PBCore.org was for experts, not beginners. One Ndt participant (P20) indicated that the "footer is so confusing; this is for someone who is more of an expert." Even participants with metadata training were sometimes unsure about terminology. While looking for information related to the attribute "portrayal," P17 said, "I feel like either I haven't been taught why that's the term being used or what relation it has."

Overall, there were three primary areas where participants expressed problems, confusion or frustration: (1) the notion of a metadata schema, including its structure and components, (2) the roles of specific elements or attributes (e.g., PBCorePart), and (3) the website's orientation to experts or LIS users. See Table 6 for additional participant comments.

Metadata Schema & XML Examples	Specific Elements/Attributes	Challenges for Beginners/New Users
Metadata Schema • Metadata schema is a confusing term. • I don't know what that means, metadata schema. • All the categories at the bottom are confusing. **XML Examples** • I think it's very confusing. • This is unusable. • I have no idea what that is for.	**Elements/Attributes/Containers** • In the first reading I don't totally understand what those things [elements and attributes] are. • What is an attribute? • I don't even know what a container is. **PBCorePart** • That definition is a little confusing to me. **PBCoreCreater and CreatorRole** • I don't really understand the difference [between PBCoreCreator, Creator, and CreatorRole]. • It doesn't mean anything to me as a content producer.	**Website purpose** • [Moderator: What is this website for?] Oh man, I really can't even tell you. **Language/Vocabulary** • For someone like me, who doesn't know the language, I don't know where to look this [element] up. **Beginners/New Users versus Experts/LIS Background** • [The schema page is] overwhelming, not for beginners... Something makes me not so comfortable. • Footer is so confusing; this is for someone who is more of an expert. • At this point I'm already out. I need someone who has an LIS background. • I would have liked some place on the website that could ramp me up instead of assuming a prior knowledge of some of the concepts and terms.

Table 6. Select comments revealing knowledge gaps

Expectations and Needs of a Technical Website

Two themes emerged from participants' post-session survey comments: (1) using PBCore.org to access assistive features for implementing and/or learning about the PBCore schema and (2) developing a substantial community of users through exchanging and sharing use cases or stories. Regardless of profession or education, participants expressed hope that PBCore.org could have more helpful resources, including additional crosswalks, examples, and tutorials. An LISd, AL, IBP participant wanted "visual resources such as step by step tutorials or video content on different aspects of PBCore" (P28). An Ndt, Manager, BP participant urged the website to provide "some resource to help those not intimately familiar with PBCore or metadata standards to ramp up quickly with a short summary of the basic concepts in lay language" (P60). These comments suggest that a technical website must provide abundant practical resources to satisfy the information needs of various user groups.

Similarly, participants' emphasis on establishing a stronger community reinforces the idea that different user groups would benefit from having a professional support network. Participants expressed their needs for a user community explicitly and frequently. For example, P28 (LISd, AL, IBP) suggested "perhaps incorporate[ing] success stories or examples of PBCore in action on these sections which highlight the variety of institutions that are using PBCore as a descriptive schema for their collections." P30 (LISd, AL, IBP) echoes this sentiment with the desire for, "lot's [*sic*] of examples of usage, from the most amazing implementations in a broadcast environment to a humble flat spreadsheet migration sample from a small historical society." This need for community building was also expressed through suggesting improvements to the PBCore blog and for PBCore.org to "expand contact area to include listservs or google groups for assistance" (P51, LISd, Manager, IBP). Websites containing technical components should be mindful of creating platforms that facilitate community building as it allows advanced users to help new users to acquire professional knowledge and skills and/or establish an accurate mental model of the website.

RECOMMENDATIONS

Specific recommendations for revising the PBCore.org interface were presented to WGBH stakeholders, who have already made changes in several areas. This section outlines those recommendations that are generalizable to technical websites and include a homepage with a jargon-free overview, understandable definitions of core technical terms, and successful use examples; enriched and updated resources as well as a platform for user community building; and a navigation interface depicting the structure of PBCore's metadata schema as well as concrete definitions and technical content examples.

Homepage Design

Participants felt that PBCore.org's home page was intimidating to non-technical users. Multiple participants wanted a separate homepage with a jargon-free overview (e.g., P52's statement that the "home page looks like a 'page 2' to me. Need a landing page with an overview"). PBCore.org's landing page contains little information about the website's purpose. Several participants said that PBCore.org should have an "About us" page that includes "more context about the project, its importance, and the depth and breadth of public broadcasting collections" (P38).

A proper introduction to a website should also include clear definitions of key terms. Participants in this study often did not understand that PBCore is a metadata schema or the meaning of the term "metadata schema." Carefully written definitions allow users to comprehend technical concepts regardless of background. Meanwhile, multiple participants advocated for real-world examples of PBCore. For instance, P16 suggested that the home page include "links to publically [*sic*] available catalogs for institutions that use PBCore." P14 also asked for "real-world example - comparison of back and front end."

Useful Resources for Support and Training of Technical Content

PBCore.org currently features a "Resources" section with several pages: FAQ, Glossary, and How-To's/Presentations." While several participants reacted positively to this section's content, P54 argued that, "If you're going to name a section 'How To's | Presentations', include some actual How To guides!" P11 suggested an "expansion of resources to include more user guides, how-to's, for people who do not have technical experience." Participants also wanted this section to include "more examples of use cases" (P35) or "video tutorials" (P38). Several participants indicated that PBCore.org's content assumes significant prior LIS training and is thereby off-putting to non-LIS users. For example, P60 pointed out that "I would have liked some place on the website that could ramp me up instead of assuming a prior knowledge of some of the concepts and terms." As reported earlier, participants expressed a desire to share stories about successfully implementing PBCore or the obstacles encountered during the implementation progress. Participants wanted a community where they can learn from one another regarding specific topics (e.g. PBCore schema usage, crosswalking, etc.).

Presentation of Technical Content

New PBCore users often did not have a clear mental model of PBCore as a metadata schema, which triggered errors. P16 stated that "I have no clue where to download your software," while P01 said, when viewing the page on element PBcoreCreator, "I just want to know how to be a creator." Such misunderstandings resulted in participants' frustration, as evidenced by P21's comment that: "I don't know what subelement means. I don't know what container means." In order to help new users establish an accurate mental model, the metadata schema needs to be presented in a visually effective manner. As noted by P28, "perhaps there is a different way to present it in order to facilitate comprehension for folks new to PBCore or metadata schemas in general." Users should be able to navigate the schema using an interface that models the hierarchy of PBCore, examples of which include the RDA Toolkit or the Getty Art and Architecture Thesaurus.

Participants called for plain language explanations of elements and attributes and asked for more concrete examples of both. For instance, P16 suggested that the presentation of the definitions to be "more visually interesting but [*sic*] providing examples of catalog records in both marked up format and actual online formats for comparison." When asked about their least favorite part of the website, P20 said that the site is "super wonky and not intuitive and the language used is very off putting." Another participant (P21) strongly expressed a need for translating the metadata vocabulary to general users: "I've spent years unpacking jargon so the public can know what you're talking about… translate it to non-technical language."

DISCUSSION AND CONCLUSION

The results of this study have revealed significant performance and experience differences among various user groups, most notably between the BP Ndt Otherstaff group and IP/IBP LISdt AL group. Figure 1 outlines four main areas of group differences. Participants who were broadcast professionals with no prior LIS education or training experienced the widest knowledge gaps when using PBCore.org. While quantitative statistical analysis indicated significant group differences, qualitative analysis reinforced that such differences were due to knowledge gaps.

Technical websites have an innate tendency to exclude non-technically educated persons or trained user populations. Usability consideration for such websites should not only follow typical usability principles, but also pay special attention to mechanisms that bridge knowledge gaps so that these websites can be more inclusive and more accessible to a broader user base. Technical websites should also be designed to support multidisciplinary or interdisciplinary work practices. Furthermore, in order to facilitate a more inclusive usage, it is essential for technical websites to provide ample platforms for building substantial user communities.

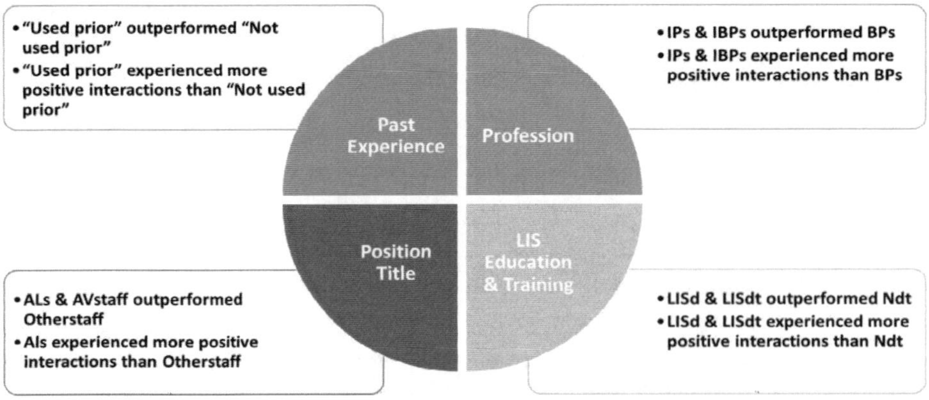

Figure 1. Summary of significant group differences

Reaching out to information and broadcast professionals from 26 states in the US through remote usability testing, this research study is innovative and valuable for its methodology as well as its depth in examining the user experience of working professionals. Our research provided empirical evidence for exposing the knowledge gaps of non-technically trained users as they use technical websites. Results from this study will be useful for comparing and evaluating other technical websites. We also advocated for the development of more inclusive technical websites that will empower under-served user populations. Further research investigating knowledge gaps of technical websites, as well as exploration of approaches and techniques for developing inclusive technical websites, would be highly valuable.

ACKNOWLEDGEMENT

This research study has been made possible in part by a major grant from the National Endowment for the Humanities: Exploring the human endeavor. Any views, findings, conclusions, or recommendations expressed in this article do not necessarily represent those of the National Endowment for the Humanities. We wish to thank all the participants of the study, including our pilot testers.

REFERENCES

Azadbakht, E., Blair, J., & Jones, L. (2017). Everyone's invited: A website usability study involving multiple library stakeholders. Information Technology and Libraries, 36(4), 34-45. Retrieved from https://doi.org/10.6017/ital.v36i4.9959

Baker, R. (2014). Remote usability testing: Thinking outside the lab. Retrieved from https://www.uxmatters.com/mt/archives/2014/04/remote-usability-testing-thinking-outside-the-lab.php

Batra, S. & Bishu, R. (2007). Web usability and evaluation: Issues and concerns. Paper presented at UI-HCII 2007: Usability and Internationalization. HCI and Culture, Beijing, China. doi: https://doi.org/10.1007/978-3-540-73287-7_30

Clair, K. (2008). Developing an audiovisual metadata application profile: A case study. Library Collections, Acquisitions, & Technical Services, 32, 53-57.

Dillon, A. & Min, S. (1997). An empirical comparison of the usability for novice and expert searchers of a textual and a graphic interface to an art-resource database. Journal of Digital Information, 1(1). Retrieved from http://hdl.handle.net/10150/106095

Faulkner, L. & Wick, D. (2005). Cross-user analysis: Benefits of skill level comparison in usability testing. Interacting with Computers, 17(6), 773-786. doi:10.1016/j.intcom.2005.04.004

Goyal, N., Miner, W., & Nawathe, N. (2012). Cultural differences across governmental website design. ICIC Session: Intercultural

Communication, Virtual Teams, and Technology.

Hodge, G. (2008). Toward interoperability: A report from the 11th open forum on metadata registries and related standards. Bulletin of the American Society for Information Science and Technology, 35(1), 25-30.

Krug, S. (2006). Don't make me think!: A common sense approach to web usability. Berkeley, CA: New Riders.

Lee, J.M. (2004). Usability Assessment of Integrated Cataloging and Metadata Services: An Exploratory Study of the OCLC Connexion System. Retrieved from http://purl.flvc.org/fsu/fd/FSU_migr_etd-3201

Nagamori, M. & Sugimoto, S. (2006). A metadata schema registry as a tool to enhance metadata interoperability. TCDL Bulletin, 3(1). Retrieved from http://www.ieee-tcdl.org/Bulletin/v3n1/nagamori/nagamori.html

Nagamori, M. & Sugimoto, S. (2007, August). Using metadata schema registry as a core function to enhance usability and reusability of metadata schemas. Paper presented at the International Conference on Dublin Core and Metadata Applications, Singapore. Retrieved from http://dcpapers.dublincore.org/pubs/article/view/869

Nagamori, M. & Sugimoto, S. (2008). DCMI metadata schema registry for sharing authoritative information about metadata schemas. Bulletin of the American Society for Information Science and Technology, 35(1), 20-24.

PBCore. (2015a). PBCore.org is here! Retrieved from http://pbcore.org/pbcore-2-1-is-here/

PBCore. (2015b). Webinar recap: A brief history of PBCore. Retrieved from http://pbcore.org/webinar-recap-a-brief-history-of-pbcore/

Ruzza, M., Tiozzo, B., Mantovani, C., D'Este, F., & Ravaratto, L. (2017). Designing the information architecture of a complex website: A strategy based on news content and faceted classification. International Journal of Information Management, 37, 166-176.

Saleh, E. I. (2018). Image embedded metadata in cultural heritage digital collections on the web: An analytical study. Library Hi Tech,

36(2), 339-357.

Schade, A. (2013). Remote usability tests: Moderated and unmoderated. Retrieved from https://www.nngroup.com/articles/remote-usability-tests/

Thompson, K.E., Rozanski, E.P., Haake, A.R. (2004). Here, there, anywhere: Remote usability testing that works. Paper presented at ACM Special Interest Group for Information Technology Education Conference 2004, Salt Lake City, Utah. doi:10.1145/1029533.1029567

Usability.gov. (n.d.). Remote usability testing. Retrieved from https://www.usability.gov/how-to-and-tools/methods/remote-testing.html

Supporting the Long-term Curation and Migration of Natural History Museum Collections Databases

Andrea K. Thomer
School of Information, University of Michigan, USA.
athomer@umich.edu

Nicholas M. Weber
Information School, University of Washington, USA.
nmweber@uw.edu

Michael B. Twidale
School of Information Sciences, University of Illinois at Urbana-Champaign, USA.
twidale@illinois.edu

ABSTRACT

Migration of data collections from one platform to another is an important component of data curation – yet, there is surprisingly little guidance for information professionals faced with this task. Data migration may be particularly challenging when these data collections are housed in relational databases, due to the complex ways that data, data schemas, and relational database management software become intertwined over time. Here we present results from a study of the maintenance, evolution and migration of research databases housed in Natural History Museums. We find that database migration is an on-going – rather than occasional – process for many Collection managers, and that they creatively appropriate and innovate on many existing technologies in their migration work. This paper contributes descriptions of a preliminary set of common adaptations and "migration patterns" in the practices of database curators. It also outlines the strategies they use when facing collection-level data migration and describes the limitations of existing tools in supporting LAM and "small science" research database migration. We conclude by outlining future research directions for the maintenance and migration of collections and complex digital objects.

KEYWORDS

Data curation, database migration, natural history museums, museum informatics

INTRODUCTION

Database migration ("The process of moving data from one information system or storage medium to another to ensure continued access to the information as the system or medium becomes obsolete or degrades over time" ("migration," n.d.)) is a fundamental task in data curation and long-term digital preservation – yet, there is surprisingly little guidance for information professionals faced with this task. While metadata standards, interoperability guidelines, and careful selection of preservation-ready file formats certainly render individual digital objects more portable from one system to another, these approaches don't necessarily support the migration of databases or *collections* of data, in which the complex relationships *between* data points must be maintained. Similarly, best practices in digital preservation do not necessarily support curators in the complex tasks (such as data modeling, schema matching, data transformation, provenance capture, etc.) entailed in migrating an entire data collection or database. And while there are certainly best practices aimed at supporting enterprise-level database migrations, these approaches do not easily scale down to library, archive, museum, or "small science" scholarly contexts (Cragin, Palmer, Carlson, & Witt, 2010), in which data are more likely to be stored in idiosyncratically-structured databases, distributed over a number of legacy systems, and managed on an *ad hoc* basis by information professionals with a number of other work responsibilities. Now that libraries, archives and museums (LAMs) primarily manage their collections catalogs in digital databases, the need to develop strategies to migrate and manage databases over time has become urgent. Research is needed to understand the unique database migration needs and workflows of these communities, and to develop appropriately scaled best practices.

In the following paper, we take Natural History Museums (NHMs) as a salient use case for exploring the maintenance and migration of data collections. NHM specimen collections are a vitally important source of scientific and cultural data (NTSC, 2009). Numerous NHMs publish their specimen records through their own web-facing databases and/or through platforms such as the Global Biodiversity Information Facility (GBIF) and the System for Earth Sample Registry; and many of the databases central to modern of bio-, biodiversity and earth science informatics have their roots in NHM collections. Furthermore, as relatively early adopters of database technologies, NHMs offer a unique longitudinal view on data curation and database management, which may be informative to many other research and LAM contexts.

Our work here is part of a larger project studying the migration of research data collections and databases more generally. Our goal is to understand how collections data and databases are changed over time, and how their managers cope with, mitigate, and facilitate that change. In this broader project we ask,

1. What patterns of use, access, and obsolescence drive and support the migration of research data collections, and how?
2. What are the curatorial processes that support the on-going use of research data collections between migrations?
3. How does the use of customizable vs. standardized "off-the-shelf" database platforms impact the accessibility and maintainability of research data collections? Open access vs. closed?

By answering these questions, we can better understand on aspect of the rote but critical work of infrastructure maintenance, and thereby contribute to library and information science theory as well as the construction of more sustainable data systems.

MOTIVATION: COLLECTIONS DATABASES, DATA COLLECTIONS, AND DATA MIGRATION

This project is motivated not just by the longstanding use of relational databases in scholarly research, but also the growing use of LAM collections catalogs as datasets in and of themselves (Padilla, 2018). Card catalogs, collection ledgers, and collection databases have long been the central access point and organizational system for LAMs. However, a growing number of institutions now publish their collection data for research use beyond the physical collection (see for example Chan, 2014; "DPLA API Codex," n.d.; Tate, 2013/2018). The use of collections catalogs as data is driving an urgent need for digital *collections* curation, in addition to the curation of individual digital objects. Not only must collections databases be maintained to ensure access to the physical materials they represent, but also to ensure the continued reliability of scholarship produced with the collection-as-dataset.

The need to curate digital collections as an entity unto themselves poses several novel challenges for the work of data curation. First, the management of aggregates, groupings, sets, and collections of digital objects requires understanding the relationship between collection- and item-level representations and metadata (Wickett, in press; Wickett, Renear, & Urban, 2010; Zavalina, Palmer, Jackson, & Han, 2009). Further, management of the infrastructure used to store collections data – often, relational databases – requires an understanding of the complex interplay between numerous entities and representation layers: the individual records in the collection; the data schemas that pull them together; the physical hard drives they are stored on; the physical objects they represent; and the uses and users of the collection; and the ways in which digital aggregates change and grow over time (Buneman, Chapman, & Cheney, 2006; Buneman, Cheney, Tan, & Vansummeren, 2008; Codd, 1970; Palmer, Zavalina, & Fenlon, 2010; Thibodeau, 2002). Finally, best practices in data collections curation must account for the fundamental need to migrate them over time. Where LAM collections are typically intended to last for generations, *digital* collections must necessarily rely on hardware that lasts years at best. Migration from one system to another is critical and inevitable given and the rate of obsolescence and decay in software, hardware, and storage media.

Though there is some guidance for database management and migration over time, much of it is focused on supporting large business-oriented platforms. For instance, Brodie and Stonebraker offer a guide through the general steps of database migration; however their work is targeted at business contexts with large homogenous data stores and dedicated information technology staff (Brodie & Stonebraker, 1995). Compelling work by Herrmann et al. proposes a database evolution language to support the migration of schemas over time, but further development would likely be needed for this approach to be feasible in many LAM contexts (Herrmann, Voigt, Rausch, Behrend, & Lehner, 2017). Extract-transform-load procedures (e.g. Henry, Hoon, Hwang, Lee, & DeVore, 2005; Vassiliadis, 2009) are similarly designed for large data warehouses and not the idiosyncratic and sometimes piecemeal systems of LAMs and small research labs. Additionally, these best practices don't necessarily account for the on-going work of database curation over time. Maintaining a database for continual use as a research tool requires many hours of digitization, annotation, and updating, as well as provenance management (Buneman et al., 2006, 2008; Buneman, Müller, & Rusbridge, 2009). Many database systems are simply not designed to support these complex tasks, let alone over the course of multiple migrations.

Databases in NHMs

NHMs have been treating their collections catalogs as research datasets for decades; consequently, they are an excellent grounding case for this study. As early as the 1960s, NHMs began "computerizing" or "digitizing" (manually transcribing) their paper and card catalogs into databases, and by the 1970s started sharing records via information systems such as SELGEM and TAXIR, two information retrieval systems for taxonomic data (Hudson, Dutton, Reynolds, & Walden, 1971; Mello, 1975; Sarasan, Neuner, & Association of Systematics Collections, 1983). Several other community-driven data and Collection management platforms have been developed since then (notably Specify and Arctos, two open source NHM-specific Collection management systems), as well as numerous data sharing networks (for instance, MaNIS, the Mammal Networked Information System (Stein & Wieczorek, 2004); FishNet, a data sharing network for ichthyological collections (Vieglais, Wiley, Robins, & Peterson, 2000); and perhaps most well-known, GBIF (Robertson et al., 2014).

It is estimated that the grand "dataset" of all NHM collections contains anywhere from 1-2 *billion* specimen records; however, only a small fraction of these are currently accessible through data sharing platforms (Ariño, 2010). The vast majority of museum collections are not fully cataloged; and many of the catalogs that do exist still await digitization (Beaman & Cellinese,

2012). Thus, digital databases are often only partial representations of their collections – and, as Bowker notes, the natural world (Bowker, 2000). However, as Strasser argues, NHM collection databases "are not mere repositories; they are tools for producing knowledge" (Strasser 2011, pg. 63); the collections themselves are infrastructure to support scholarship, and as such have value beyond their completeness.

The impact of relational databases on collections data

NHMs are additionally informative for their use of relational databases for data collection management. Relational databases have been fixtures in many offices and research labs for decades (despite predictions of their impending obsolescence (e.g. Atzeni et al., 2013)), and they play an important, complex and often shifting role in information ecologies (Buneman et al., 2008; Hine, 2006). By relational databases, we mean those that use (or are built with software using) E. F. Codd's relational data model. Codd's approach to data representation was later formalized as the ANSI-SPARC three level architecture, which conceptualizes a data bank's structure as: 1. A *physical* level where data are recorded on a storage medium; 2. A *logical* level, expressing relationships between data, and; 3. a *view* level, providing query access to stored data, but hiding the details of its organization from an end-user (Tsichritzis & Klug, 1978).

Codd intended this model to "[protect] users from having to know how data is organized" in a computer system (Codd, 1970), and argued that, "there is one consideration of absolutely paramount importance – and that is the convenience of the majority of users" (Codd, 1971). Relational architecture is thus predicated on a division of labor between database designers/administrators (who work at the logical level), and end-users (who work at the views level). Despite Codd's best intentions, though, relational databases remain challenging to use. Part of the issue may lie in how "administrator" and "user" roles have blurred over time (see Dourish & Edwards, 2000; Jagadish et al., 2007; Li & Lochovsky, 1996; Olson, 2009; Voida, Harmon, & Al-Ani, 2011 for examples of the impact of blurred database roles). Where databases would have once been programmed by computer scientists into mainframe computers, they can now be run on a desktop, programmed by anyone with Microsoft Access or FileMakerPro. In NHMs, they have traditionally been designed and maintained by collection managers who typically have training in some branch of natural history, but not necessarily database administration. By studying how they have adapted (and adapted to) database technologies for their work, we may better understand how to support other similar LAM users.

APPROACH

Six collection managers (CMs) were initially recruited for this study based on their known use, management or design of natural history databases; an additional six were selected through snowball sampling. In total, twelve CMs at eight different NHMs were enrolled in this study. We sought representation across different types of institutions involved in natural history research (e.g. both universities and independent museums), and different departments within natural history museums. We did not seek a statistically representative sample of the databases or their users in NHMs; rather, we take a multi-case study approach and follow a replication logic, to identify common phenomena and patterns between cases (Yin, 2009).

We engaged our participants through three phases:

1. *Initial demographic survey and background research*: Each participant was asked to fill out a demographic survey, through which we gathered basic information about their background and training, as well as information about the number and nature of databases they manage through their work. We also asked participants for links to or copies of their databases.
2. *Initial interview*: Each participant was interviewed following the same semi-structured protocol, though some questions were tailored based on the participants' survey response or based on our qualitative review of and databases or schemas they shared. We asked participants to describe this history of each of their databases. We asked them to describe three phases of each database's evolution: 1) Its state at the time that they began working at the museum (as well as his or her knowledge of any prior versions); 2) The database's present state, and; 3) Its future or anticipated state. By gathering data on these three different states, we could compare databases across time, departments, and institutions - seeking patterns in the way that content is normalized, migrated, and occasionally transferred between different database designs.
3. *Follow up interviews*: Between 12-15 months later, participants were contacted for follow up interviews, in which we received updates on their migration work. Eight CMs participated in follow-up interviews.

Data collection began in Spring 2014 and concluded in Winter 2016. Interviews lasted 45-75 minutes (60 minutes on average). Transcripts were summarized into short case reports of describing the history, migration and anticipated future state of each database. Transcripts were then coded for emergent themes related to database migration or evolution, and to identify CMs' strategies for database curation; these were added to case reports. Common maintenance strategies and migration patterns were then derived from intercase comparison.

RESULTS

Our participants had anywhere from two to thirty years of experience working with databases. All but two were self-taught and learned their skills on the job through webinars, workshops, and textbooks. One CM said he, "bought a book on Access in 2010 and started on page one" (07-VertPaleo); another said she learned the basics of relational database construction by "googling for various manuals for FileMaker Pro" (01-InvertZoo) and studying them as she explored her files. For most, database migration was one of their first tasks when starting their jobs as CMs. In only 3 cases, participants were able to directly consult with their databases' original creator; the rest had to reconstruct their databases' history and structure through a quasi-forensic examinations of the database itself. This reverse engineering process entails extensive review of available documentation, careful examination of data structures and contents, and conversations with senior staff who may have been around during the database's creation and fill in "tacit" details that lead to its creation.

Thirty-seven databases were described and managed by our participants, with a median of three per department. Database systems included Access, FileMaker Pro, MySQL Workbench, Arctos, Specify, KE EMu and Excel. We categorized databases into three types: Collection management (n=29), research (n=5) and auxiliary (n= ~6) (See tables 1-3). Below, we describe these databases according to their type more fully, and briefly discuss our participants' database histories.

ID	Database contents	History
01-InvertZoo (n=3 total)	Mollusk collections (1)	Originally paper catalogs; digitized to Filemaker Pro; **migrated to Excel;** planned for migration to Arctos
	non-Mollusk invertebrate collections (1)	Originally paper catalogs; digitized to Filemaker Pro; **migrated to Excel;** planned for migration to Arctos
	Type specimens (specimens cited as exemplars of their species) (1)	Originally paper catalogs; digitized to Filemaker Pro; planned for migration to Arctos
01-VertZoo (n=17)	4 databases for each of 4 departments (birds, mammals, fish, reptiles) (16 total)	Each was transcribed from catalogs into FileMaker Pro; **migrated to Excel and OpenRefine for cleaning; migrated to Arctos;** keeping in Arctos for now
	Invertebrate paleontology collections database (1)	Originally created in Access of FileMakerPro; migrated to Specify 5; **migrated to Specify 6;** planned migration to Specify 7
02-VertPaleo (n=1)	Vertebrate Paleontology collections database (1)	Originally stored in a paper card catalog; likely directly digitized to Access database consisting of 2 unlinked tables; **migrated to Specify 6;** planned migration to Specify 7
03-Paleo Mineral (n=3)	Paleobotany database (1)	Originally stored in paper card catalog; digitized at some point; migrated to FileMakerPro; **migrated to Access; attempted migration to Specify; now each table of database stored as a separate spreadsheet;** planned migration to custom Microsoft SQL Server
	Mineral database (1)	Originally stored in paper card catalog; **transcribed to Excel**; planned migration to a custom Microsoft SQL Server database
04-Paleo (n=1)	Collections database (1)	Originally paper card catalog; digitized, possibly directly to Dbase; **migrated to Specify 5;** planned migration to Specify 6
05-InvertZoo (n=2)	Lot/collections database (1)	**Digitized from labels on specimen buckets in the Marine Biodiversity Lab directly into FileMakerPro**; currently maintained in FMP, but planned for migration to Specify 7
	"prospective database"- a database being "fielded" but not currently used" (1)	**Drafts of interfaces and schema maps for Specify 6 are now being migrated to Specify 7**
06-VertPaleo (n=1)	Vertebrate Paleontology Collections database (1)	Originally paper card catalog; digitized, possibly directly to Dbase; **migrated to Access**; planned migration to Specify 7
07-VertPaleo (n=2)	Collection management database (1)	Originally digitized from paper catalogs to Paradox (using punch cards!); migrated to Excel for some cleaning; **migrated and maintained in KE Emu;** no plans for migration
	Radiocarbon dates (1)	**Created in and maintained in Excel**; potentially to be migrated into KE Emu at some point.

Table 1. *Collection management databases. The ID column represents the institution and collection code and includes a total count of collections databases managed by the collection's CM(s). The* ***Bolded*** *text in each database's history indicates work undertaken by current collection manager (our study participant).*

Collection management databases: uncertain origins and varied legacy structures

Collection management databases are primarily used to support the management, curation and use of a physical specimen collection by organizing and preserving data about the specimens, though some have public-facing web interfaces that can be searched for research discovery. These databases have typically been migrated from paper catalogues and were first and foremost designed as a finding aid for the physical collections, though often the specimen records are published to aggregators such as GBIF and used as data in further analyses. In three cases (04-Paleo, 01-InvertZoo, and 05-InvertZoo) electronic collections databases have essentially replaced paper catalogues; in the rest they are maintained concurrently with paper catalogues, which are sometimes viewed as being more stable and long-lasting. Many of the collection management databases described by our participants had uncertain origins: each had been transcribed from paper records at some point in the past, but it was often unclear when and by whom.

Though we expected to find some instances of active database migration, we were surprised by how many of our participants were actively engaged in migration. At the time of our interviews, all but one collection database described by our participants was in the process of being migrated or was being prepared for a migration in the near future. An additional 2 CMs were in the midst of planning migrations of their *physical* collections. Participants broadly characterized database migration less as a single activity undertaken within a constrained time period, but instead, as an on-going (albeit often interrupted) aspect of their day-to-day work. They estimated that spent anywhere from 20-80% of their week on database work. Many expressed frustration that they did not have the time needed to complete their data-related activities. For instance, one CM (05-InvertZoo) described his two-year-long-effort to migrate an invertebrate zoology collections database as one of continual disruption:

> The Specify database [to which the legacy system would be migrated] was designed, but for lack of developer time, has not been fully fielded. I have been so interrupted for the past several years, that we have multiple times gotten to the 95% complete phase for introduction and migration into it, and then something comes up, we get distracted, and then six months later we try it again.

Other participants also described migrations that were *almost* completed, but eventually had to be abandoned for a variety of reasons. In two cases, CMs spent months considering platforms that turned out to be a poor fit for their specific collections (04-Paleo; 05-InvertZoo) and eventually had to start over from scratch.

Platformization of NHM collections databases: moves to Specify and Arctos

All but two of the collections databases described by our participants had been or were in the process of being migrated to Arctos or Specify, the two main community-developed databases being adopted by NHMs. Both are designed specifically for NHM collections and include pre-defined data schemas designed to be generally applicable to natural history collections. At the time of our interviews, there was a key difference between the two systems: Arctos is cloud-hosted, and publishes collections online to a public, aggregated database. On the other hand, Specify (at the time of our interviews) was locally hosted and did not publish or aggregate data for its users, but thereby allowed users some greater flexibility modifiability. (Since the time of our interviews, Specify has since developed a cloud-hosted service.)

Participants said that adopting these platforms made it easier to share or manage their data in a community-driven and vetted format; however, there were also some unexpected complications. Some users of Arctos found that they needed to extensively rework their legacy data schemas by hand to facilitate migration. Two users of Specify (03-PaleoMineral and 04-Paleo) had to "co-opt" fields – meaning, use a data field for other than its intended purpose – to map their legacy databases to the Specify data model. This was necessary because Specify either did not have a needed data field, or because Specify fields have technical constraints (numerical constraints, prohibiting certain characters) that conflicted with existing cataloging practices. Co-opting fields is common enough in the Specify community that the development team has addressed it in some of their documentation ("Importing External Data into Specify 6," 2013).

While co-opting fields can solve cross-walking dilemmas in the short-term, it can create more problems in the long-term. For instance, the 04-Paleo collections database was migrated from dBase to Specify in the early 2000s, but the database now still retains evidence of its past structure. In the legacy database, each data field could only fit a maximum of 256 characters, so long locality descriptions had to be split between multiple fields (e.g. "stratigraphy 1," "stratigraphy 2" and so on). These fields were never concatenated in subsequent migrations. Now, any query for stratigraphic data needs to be run over a range of fields, rather than just one. The CM described these traces as "ghosts" that haunt her in her day-to-day work: shadows of database structures past that hamper the habitability and functionality of her current system. The 01-InvertZoo CM reported similar hauntings from her predecessor's co-opting of fields in Specify 5.

Auxiliary databases: spreadsheets as safe zones

CMs also maintained a range of *auxiliary databases* for specific tasks or data types that weren't supported by their Collection management databases (Table 2). We include in this category systems that may not be typically considered databases but are used by our participants in a database-like fashion: Excel, OpenRefine, Google Sheets, and so on. Some of these are used for specific "work tasks" (04-Paleo), such as managing loans, printing labels, and organizing literature.

Participants reverted to spreadsheets for a number of reasons. First, the familiar interface simply made data entry easier, particularly for CMs relying on other staff or volunteers for data entry. Second, spreadsheets are materially separate from the collection database, and could therefore be used as a "safe" intermediary or staging area between raw data entry and the fidelity of the collection at large. This again makes them attractive for data entry; both 01-VertZoo and 07-VertPaleo used spreadsheets for student and volunteer data entry because they liked being able to review the data before adding it to the collection database. Finally, spreadsheets support kinds of data manipulations that simply are not possible in a "real" database: dragging and dropping values between fields; complex text string-editing functions; clustering and batch correcting entries; and so on. For instance, the CMs at 07-VertPaleo have recently begun several projects in which they loan out large numbers of microspecimens for identification and protein extraction. Using cloud-based Google Sheets, they share a copy of relevant collections records with their collaborators, who add data as it is generated. At the end of the project, the CMs re-import the newly improved records into the KE-EMu collection management database. This workflow is easy for everyone involved – and simply isn't possible with KE-EMu alone.

ID	Auxiliary database type	History	Purpose
01-Invert-Zoo	"Peripheral taxonomy database"	Originally paper; digitized to Filemaker Pro; **migrated to Excel;** planned for migration to Arctos	External storage of taxonomic hierarchies
03-Paleo Mineral	Research Libraries	Stored and **managed in EndNote**	Reference management, includes literature that cites specimens from the collection
	Web accessible collections database	**Created as Access database w/SQL backend**	web accessible front end for external researchers and visitors
04-Paleo	various "work tasks" databases	**Created as Access databases**; no plans to migrate	Label printing and loan management
07-VertPaleo	Field note database	Originally created in Access; **migrated to Excel; currently used for data entry in Excel;** will be merged w/KE Emu	data entry and temporary storage of data about uncatalogued specimens
	Various google spreadsheets used to collaborate with external researchers	**Created in Google Sheets; periodically migrated into KE Emu**	data entry and temporary storage of data about uncatalogued specimens

Table 2. *Auxiliary databases. The* ***Bolded*** *text again indicates work undertaken by our study participant.*

Spreadsheets-as-databases were also used as longer-term staging zones between database migrations. The 01-InvertZoo collection database became so denormalized and difficult to navigate in its legacy format that the CM exported the entire database into Excel for cleaning and storage until she was ready to migrate to Arctos. In a more extreme example, the 03-PaleoMineral database has been stored entirely in Excel since its planned migration to Specify failed. Each individual table of the database is being stored as a separate Excel file until their Microsoft SQL server database can be finished. Its CM is now managing and updating each table, including primary keys *by hand.*

Research databases

Five "research databases" were described by our participants (Table 3). We define a research database as one that has been created to support scientific projects and answer specific research questions. They are integrative in nature, drawing from many different collections and sources of data, and are meant to facilitate data analysis in addition to storage and retrieval. They may include some of the same content as a collections database (specimen records, locality descriptions), but are maintained as separate, custom-built databases, often in MySQL or Access. All five of the research databases described by our participants were developed to support specific scientific goals and were at least initially grant-funded.

ID	Database name	History	Purpose
01-Invert-Zoo	MapStedi	Originally created in FileMakerPro, **migrated to Excel**; future status is unclear	a mapping "toolkit for the southern and central Rockies and adjacent plains."
02-VertPaleo	MioMap	Both originally created in MySQL; **current CM maintains in MySQL;** planned merge into Neotoma	Paleoecology database of mammals and their habitats ~5-30 million years ago
	FaunMap		Paleoecology database of mammals and their habitats ~40,000 to 500 years ago.
04-Paleo	Neogene Marine Biota of the Tropical Americas (NMITA)	Originally created and **currently maintained in Oracle**; no plans to migrate	public database of photos and taxonomic information about the Neogene Marine Biota of the tropical Americas
05-Invert-Zoo	Systematics of Decapoda	Originally created in and **currently maintained in FileMakerPro w/ web-accessible MySQL mirror**; no plans to migrate	synthesizes the taxonomic literature of decapods (ten-footed crustaceans)
08-Ento	United Chalcidodea Database (UCD)	Created and **maintained in Paradox**; exported to a SQL "dump"; planned for migration to TaxonWorks	synthesizes the taxonomic literature of chalcid (tiny, parasitic, hyperdiverse) wasps

Table 3. *Research databases. The* ***Bolded*** *text again indicates work undertaken our study participant.*

Because research databases are built for specific projects, their underlying structure is correspondingly idiosyncratic. Several feature instances of deliberate denormalization: structures or attributes that went against what might ordinarily be considered best practices in database construction for the sake of the research workflow, or the broader research goals. The MioMap, FaunMap and Systematics of Decopoda databases show the clearest examples of this. In the case of MioMap and FaunMap, the two systems have the same relational structure and can even be queried through the same web interface – but are still maintained as separate databases. The CM (02-VertPaleo) explains that this siloing is for both scientific and social reasons. Because Miocene data is of a slightly different temporal granularity, keeping it in a separate database makes it easier to maintain, and also, "makes it easier for the Miocene workers to focus on the Miocene stuff." Additionally, he says that, "a lot of it has to do with feelings of ownership and accessibility. There's a long history in paleontology of groups feeling like they don't want to have to share control of the data with other groups." Keeping the two databases separate helps groups feel like they have control over their own materials.

In the case of the Systematics of Decopoda ("ten-footed" crustaceans like lobsters and crabs) (SoD) database, strategic denormalization takes the form of the strategic preservation of historical typos. The SoD database is a taxonomic database: a carefully curated collection of species descriptions in published literature. These may superficially seem like a simple bibliographic resource, but 05-InvertZoo explains,

> It's important to remember that for taxonomists, the bibliographic information are data. It's not just the description of where to find the reference. It's actually data that represent the publication date, the publication information for a particular taxon concept, and they are very, very careful about that information.

The SoD curator and his colleagues have been careful not to "improve" the data quality as records were input, because "the systematists involved in the project had a very strong insistence that the bibliographic data exactly reflect the publication as it existed... This was not an attempt to rectify the literature, it was an attempt to reflect the literature as it existed." Any typos or misspellings in legacy citations are painstakingly preserved through two provenance tracking mechanisms: an annotation field where data enterers must justify any changes, as well as a version control system that archives edits. The database is now fairly widely used by decapod researchers (one hundred use it regularly, and a few thousand more casually). Our participant credits the aggressive provenance-tracking and annotation with making it usable by other scholars:

> [When] we reflected with the data that we made available, the change history of the records, all of a sudden, it gave a huge amount of credibility because then they can see what level of trust they're willing to put on any individual record.... And we've had feedback from the community that having that, exposing that kind of metadata about the metadata – the metadata metadata – is why they will very often tend to use our listing, rather than any other authoritative source where they are not able to check... the audit trail of the information.

DISCUSSION

We noted several trends in the maintenance and migration of our participants' databases. We summarize these below, and additionally identify points for future tool development or further research.

Maintenance through adaptation: strategies to make the database work

Though participants drew on a range of techniques to manage their databases, the following were particularly pervasive:

- *Strategic denormalization.* Several participants deliberately denormalized databases to facilitate data entry, or otherwise keep similarly structured data separate for different user groups. In doing so, CMs are essentially adapting the mechanics of relational databases to support security, privacy or usability needs. We note that Jagadish et al., similarly found that denormalization was sometimes necessary to make databases more usable (Jagadish et al., 2007).
- *Co-opting fields.* Users of databases with pre-determined data models and data entry interfaces (notably, older versions of Specify) sometimes co-opted fields for other-than-their-intended purpose. By doing so they are able to alter the database for their particular context without having to make changes at the schema level.

Both of these strategies make databases fit for immediate and idiosyncratic use but can cause problems over time. Denormalized tables are more challenging to consistently update and will inevitably require extensive cleaning before being made fit-for-use; and co-opting fields can make the schema mapping process of a database migration incredibly challenging. Both strategies risk leaving a database "haunted" (as our participant described it) by traces of prior use and users.

These maintenance strategies also double as database migration *avoidance* strategies. The desire to keep data in the same system is incredibly strong; the creative steps CMs take to keep their databases running despite their shortcomings is a testament to this inertial force. Our participants' databases were typically migrated only when legacy platforms became absolutely unsustainable (e.g. no longer capable of running on modern computers, or no longer supported by other IT staff), or because their creators/former custodians retired. To borrow from Kuhn: database paradigms don't really change, but rather, their advocates simply retire! This as a potentially self-perpetuating cycle. If database migrations are only reactionary (rather than proactive), they will likely be all the more painful and challenging; and if database migrations are always painful and challenging, then they are more likely to be delayed until absolutely necessary. There is a clear need, then, to further support proactive, incremental data collection migrations over time. Adaptation of existing best practices for incremental database migration (Brodie & Stonebraker, 1995) and recent work on database evolution languages (Herrmann et al., 2017) may facilitate this kind of long-term incremental migration.

Migration patterns: strategies to facilitate change

We noted several common themes in our participants' database migration strategies:

- *Reworking relationships*. In several cases, CMs had to transform legacy data schemas to fit new databases, reworking relationships between records and specimens, or between different tables in information models. This work was largely done "by hand," through manual manipulation of columns and rows within tables. We note that while there are tools for schema migration, none of our participants used them; further work is needed to explore why.
- *Community consultation, and duplication with adaptation*. We couple these themes because they are closely linked. All of our participants said that they spoke extensively with their fellow collection managers before beginning a database migration or selecting a new database system; and in some cases, they modelled data schemas or interfaces off of one another's systems. Even beyond the use of community-developed databases, community support and advocacy plays an important role in the selection, design and maintenance of collections databases.
- *Reliance on spreadsheet software*. Where others have noted the impact of the "psychological heritage of print" on users' wayfinding in databases (Kerr, 1990), here we note the psychological heritage of the spreadsheet for data entry and manipulation. Numerous participants used spreadsheet software as a place to temporarily store data (though we note that some took a fairly long view of temporary – months to even years at a time) between migrations. Others use them as a *lingua franca* to ease collaboration between near and distant project partners.

Platformization, infrastructuralization, and technological appropriation

One common theme – the move to community-developed databases – is notable enough to merit a more extended discussion. All but two of the collections databases described by our participants had been or were in the process of being migrated to Arctos or Specify; an additional three research databases (MioMap, FaunMap and UCD) were being integrated with or into larger community-developed infrastructures. Given our participants' descriptions of broader trends and our own prior experience in NHMs, we believe that our participants' migrations are representative of a discipline-wide movement: NHM data managers are moving away from in-house management of data infrastructure and moving toward NHM-specific platforms such as Arctos, Specify, KE-Emu, and Symbiota, among others.

We were initially tempted to characterize this trend as the "platformization" of NHM collections infrastructures – an adoption of middleware that imposes a top-down standard (specifically, a standardized data schema), around which users develop and maintain complementary components (in this case, auxiliary databases and query interfaces) (Plantin, Lagoze, Edwards, & Sandvig, 2016). However, the move toward primarily *community-developed,* open source and non-profit data management platforms complicates this account. For decades, NHMs have been using a technology that was not directly built for them: relational database software, which was designed for business use, and not for the iterative work of scientific data curation and management. The creative ways in which NHM workers have maintained their databases through adaptation can be viewed as a kind of technological appropriation by a (technologically) marginalized community (Eglash, 2004). As Eglash argues, technological appropriation occurs when groups with low social power "re-conceptualize ideas and artifacts" and "become producers" in their own right. While NHM staff, like all scientists (and particularly, Western scientists), certainly occupy positions of power in many ways, they have historically had relatively little sway over the computational tools at their disposal. But with the advent of community-developed database management systems, the technologically underserved NHM community has become the producers of its own database technology, information standards, and data publishing mechanisms.

Further work is needed to fully explore the nuances of how appropriation of database technology has impacted the NHM community, as well as other LAMs. Eglash notes that technological appropriation by those with low social power has potential to a community "move toward strong democracy"; however, there is also a risk that existing undemocratic hierarchies are simple replicated in the new NHM environment. For instance, there are already hints at a replication of the divide between users and producers within NHMs (e.g. users vs producers of Arctos), as well as a replication of the environment that necessitated appropriation in the first place. By co-opting fields, Specify users have had to make their own adaptations of an already adapted technology. This implies that users are still finding a need to innovate on their technology. Additionally, we note that not all users have found a solution to their data management woes; some, like the CM at 03-PaleoMineral, have found that the "community" developed products simply don't work for her edge case.

CONCLUSION & FUTURE WORK

In this study we have described database maintenance and migration work by collection managers at NHMs. We have identified some common strategies they deploy in adapting systems for continued use and maintenance, and in migrating their databases over time. We have additionally described how this community's move toward community-developed systems may reflect a kind of technological appropriation – albeit one that may risk reifying existing divides between users and developers. We believe these findings have implications not just to those working in NHMs or with NHM data, but also to others interested in the long-term maintenance of scholarly collections or datasets.

In our future work, we plan to look beyond NHMs to research collection databases used in other fields, and thereby expand on our understanding of data collection maintenance strategies and migration patterns. Though our project is still in early stages, we have identified several preliminary implications for practitioners, which we would like to explore further. For instance, we find that planning for truly long-term – on the scale of decades – digital collection curation requires the consideration of topics not always discussed in database design, such as the need to plan for retirement both of people and of information technologies. We also find that data collections migration is less of a one-time event and more a process that requires on-going consideration and preparation; we'd like to explore ways of making this interim migration work more intentional amidst information professionals' otherwise busy jobs. Finally, we find that data collection migration involves innovation with the resources at hand, and occasionally appropriating existing tools in unexpected ways; we hope to explore what tools and workplace conditions best foster this innovation and identify ways to support information professionals in sharing their *ad hoc* strategies.

ACKNOLWEDGMENTS

Enormous thanks to our study participants for sharing their time and insights for this project; and thanks to the UMSI Information and Archival Science reading group for feedback on early drafts of this paper.

REFERENCES

Ariño, A. H. (2010). Approaches to estimating the universe of natural history collections data. Biodiversity Informatics, 7(2). https://doi.org/10.17161/bi.v7i2.3991

Atzeni, P., Jensen, C. S., Orsi, G., Ram, S., Tanca, L., & Torlone, R. (2013). The relational model is dead, SQL is dead, and I don't feel so good myself. ACM SIGMOD Record, 42(1), 64. https://doi.org/10.1145/2503792.2503808

Beaman, R., & Cellinese, N. (2012). Mass digitization of scientific collections: New opportunities to transform the use of biological specimens and underwrite biodiversity science. ZooKeys, 209, 7–17. https://doi.org/10.3897/zookeys.209.3313

Brodie, M. L., & Stonebraker, M. (1995). Migrating legacy systems: gateways, interfaces & the incremental approach. San Francisco, Calif. : [S.l.]: Morgan Kaufmann Publishers ; IT/Information Technology.

Buneman, P., Chapman, A., & Cheney, J. (2006). Provenance management in curated databases (p. 539). ACM Press. https://doi.org/10.1145/1142473.1142534

Buneman, P., Cheney, J., Tan, W.-C., & Vansummeren, S. (2008). Curated Databases. In Proceedings of the Twenty-seventh ACM SIGMOD-SIGACT-SIGART Symposium on Principles of Database Systems (pp. 1–12). New York, NY, USA: ACM. https://doi.org/10.1145/1376916.1376918

Buneman, P., Müller, H., & Rusbridge, C. (2009). Curating the CIA World Factbook. International Journal of Digital Curation, 4(3), 29–43. https://doi.org/10.2218/ijdc.v4i3.126

Chan, S. (2014, November 7). The API at the center of the museum. Retrieved June 8, 2018, from https://labs.cooperhewitt.org/2014/the-api-at-the-center-of-the-museum/

Codd, E. F. (1970). A relational model of data for large shared data banks. Communications of the ACM, 13(6), 377–387. https://doi.org/10.1145/362384.362685

Codd, E. F. (1971). Normalized data base structure: a brief tutorial (p. 1). ACM Press. https://doi.org/10.1145/1734714.1734716

Cragin, M. H., Palmer, C. L., Carlson, J. R., & Witt, M. (2010). Data sharing, small science and institutional repositories. Philosophical Transactions. Series A, Mathematical, Physical, and Engineering Sciences, 368(1926), 4023–38. https://doi.org/10.1098/rsta.2010.0165

Dourish, P., & Edwards, W. K. (2000). A Tale of Two Toolkits: Relating Infrastructure and Use in Flexible CSCW Toolkits. Computer Supported Cooperative Work (CSCW), 9(1), 33–51. https://doi.org/10.1023/A:1008709725729

DPLA API Codex. (n.d.). Retrieved June 8, 2018, from https://pro.dp.la/developers/api-codex

Eglash, R. (Ed.). (2004). Appropriating technology: An introduction. In Appropriating technology: vernacular science and social power (pp. vii–xxi). Minneapolis: University of Minnesota Press.

Henry, S., Hoon, S., Hwang, M., Lee, D., & DeVore, M. D. (2005). Engineering trade study: extract, transform, load tools for data migration. In 2005 IEEE Design Symposium, Systems and Information Engineering (pp. 1–8). https://doi.org/10.1109/SIEDS.2005.193231

Herrmann, K., Voigt, H., Rausch, J., Behrend, A., & Lehner, W. (2017). Robust and simple database evolution. Information Systems Frontiers, 20, 45–61. https://doi.org/10.1007/s10796-016-9730-2

Hine, C. (2006). Databases as Scientific Instruments and Their Role in the Ordering of Scientific Work. Social Studies of Science, 36(2), 269–298. https://doi.org/10.1177/0306312706054047

Hudson, L. W., Dutton, R. D., Reynolds, M. M., & Walden, W. E. (1971). TAXIR-A biologically oriented information retrieval system as an aid to plant introduction. Economic Botany, 25(4), 401–406. https://doi.org/10.1007/BF02985207

Importing External Data into Specify 6. (2013, August 17). Specify Software Proejct. Retrieved from http://www.sustain.specifysoftware.org/wp-content/uploads/2017/03/Importing-External-Data-into-Specify-6.pdf

Jagadish, H. V., Chapman, A., Elkiss, A., Jayapandian, M., Li, Y., Nandi, A., & Yu, C. (2007). Making database systems usable (p. 13). ACM Press. https://doi.org/10.1145/1247480.1247483

Kerr, S. T. (1990). Wayfinding in an electronic database: The relative importance of navigational cues vs. mental models. Information Processing & Management, 26(4), 511–523. https://doi.org/10.1016/0306-4573(90)90071-9

Li, Q., & Lochovsky, F. H. (1996). Advanced database support facilities for CSCW systems. Journal of Organizational Computing and Electronic Commerce, 6(2), 191–210. https://doi.org/10.1080/10919399609540276

Mello, J. F. (1975). The Use of the Selgem System in Support of Systematics. In Computers in Botanical Collections (pp. 125–138). Springer, Boston, MA. https://doi.org/10.1007/978-1-4684-2157-6_17

migration. (n.d.). Glossary of Archival and Records Terminology. Society of American Archivists. Retrieved from https://www2.archivists.org/glossary/terms/m/migration

National Science and Technology Council, & Scientific collections: mission-critical infrastructure for federal science agencies: a report of the Interagency Working Group on Scientific Collections (Eds.). (2009). Scientific collections: mission-critical infrastructure for federal science agencies: a report of the Interagency Working Group on Scientific Collections. Washington DC: Office of Science and Technology Policy.

Olson, J. E. (2009). Database archiving: how to keep lots of data for a very long time. San Francisco, Calif. : Oxford: Morgan Kaufmann ; Elsevier Science [distributor].

Padilla, T. G. (2018). Collections as data: Implications for enclosure. College & Research Libraries News, 79(6). Retrieved from https://crln.acrl.org/index.php/crlnews/article/view/17003/18751

Palmer, C. L., Zavalina, O. L., & Fenlon, K. (2010). Beyond size and search: Building contextual mass in digital aggregations for scholarly use. Proceedings of the American Society for Information Science and Technology, 47(1), 1–10. https://doi.org/10.1002/meet.14504701213

Plantin, J.-C., Lagoze, C., Edwards, P. N., & Sandvig, C. (2016). Infrastructure studies meet platform studies in the age of Google and Facebook. New Media & Society, 1461444816661553. https://doi.org/10.1177/1461444816661553

Robertson, T., Döring, M., Guralnick, R., Bloom, D., Wieczorek, J., Braak, K., … Desmet, P. (2014). The GBIF Integrated Publishing Toolkit: Facilitating the Efficient Publishing of Biodiversity Data on the Internet. PLoS ONE, 9(8), e102623. https://doi.org/10.1371/journal.pone.0102623

Sarasan, L., Neuner, A. M., & Association of Systematics Collections (Eds.). (1983). Museum collections and computers: report of an ASC survey. Lawrence, Kan., U.S.A: Association of Systematics Collections.

Stein, B. R., & Wieczorek, J. R. (2004). Mammals of the World: MaNIS as an example of data integration in a distributed network environment. Biodiversity Informatics, 1(0). https://doi.org/10.17161/bi.v1i0.7

Tate. (2018). collection: Tate Collection metadata. Python, Tate Modern. Retrieved from https://github.com/tategallery/collection (Original work published 2013)

Thibodeau, K. (2002). Overview of Technological Approaches to Digital Preservation and Challenges in Coming Years (The State of Digital preservation: An International Perspective). Washington, D.C.: CLIR and the Library of Congress. Retrieved from https://www.clir.org/pubs/reports/pub107/thibodeau/

Tsichritzis, D., & Klug, A. (1978). The ANSI/X3/SPARC DBMS framework report of the study group on database management systems. Information Systems, 3(3), 173–191. https://doi.org/10.1016/0306-4379(78)90001-7

Vassiliadis, P. (2009). A Survey of Extract–Transform–Load Technology: International Journal of Data Warehousing and Mining, 5(3), 1–27. https://doi.org/10.4018/jdwm.2009070101

Vieglais, D., Wiley, E. O., Robins, R., & Peterson, T. (2000). Harnessing Museum Resources for the Census of Marine Life: The FISHNET Project. Oceanography, 13(3), 10–13. https://doi.org/10.5670/oceanog.2000.02

Voida, A., Harmon, E., & Al-Ani, B. (2011). Homebrew databases: complexities of everyday information management in nonprofit organizations (p. 915). ACM Press. https://doi.org/10.1145/1978942.1979078

Wickett, K. M. (in press). A logic-based framework for collection/item metadata relationships. Journal of Documentation.

Wickett, K. M., Renear, A. H., & Urban, R. J. (2010). Rule categories for collection/item metadata relationships. Proceedings of the American Society for Information Science and Technology, 47(1), 1–10. https://doi.org/10.1002/meet.14504701218

Yin, R. K. (2009). Case study research: Design and methods. (4th ed.). SAGE Publications Ltd.

Zavalina, O. L., Palmer, C. L., Jackson, A. S., & Han, M.-J. (2009). Evaluating Descriptive Richness in Collection-Level Metadata. Journal of Library Metadata, 8(4), 263–292. https://doi.org/10.1080/19386380802627109

Cultivating Data Expertise: Learning Strategies & Conditions for Research Institutions

Cheryl A. Thompson
School of Information Sciences, University of Illinois, USA.
cathmps2@illinois.edu

ABSTRACT

Data management has been identified as an emerging area of practice for science and scholarship. Research institutions are faced with the need for well-trained staff with the expertise and competence to manage and share high-quality research data products. This paper reports the results of a study into how a large geoscience research center with mature data services and systems developed and cultivated data expertise. Employing a case study approach and qualitative methodology, the study investigates the learning process for preparing workers for new data management responsibilities. Key outcomes include a set of learning strategies and conditions that support data expertise development that may be applied in other contexts. This paper shifts the conversation from 'what' data skills to 'how' to cultivate these skills in an organization.

KEYWORDS

Organizational learning; data workforce; data management

INTRODUCTION

Modern research has the ability to respond to society's grand challenges by leveraging large and diverse volumes of data and advanced computational methods to glean new insights. Responding to these advancements, research institutions are developing data services and systems for their scientists and users such as data management, metadata, and data access. Data work[20] has been identified as an emerging area of practice involving new responsibilities for data organization, description, dissemination, and preservation. Research institutions are faced with a need for well-trained staff with the experience and expertise to assemble, process, and share high-quality, digital data. Several studies and national reports have documented the new data roles and expertise requirements for data work such as domain science, technical, and metadata skill sets (see examples Atkins, 2003; Lord & Macdonald, 2003; Rusbridge, 2007). As data management education programs are scaling up to meet the workforce needs, research managers and administrators face applicant pools lacking the cross-cutting expertise necessary for data work (Thompson, 2017). Organizational learning initiatives offer a mechanism for research institutions to address the data skill gap through developing new expertise areas in their staff. However, to achieve this managers and administrators need an understanding of the learning strategies and conditions for cultivating a local data-savvy workforce that embraces a blended expertise to address the data challenges of modern science.

Learning and knowledge sharing in communities and organizations develops in practice by doing the work, engaging in work projects, and collaborating with others (Schwen & Hara, 2003). Similar to communities of practice (Lave & Wenger, 1991), my work finds that data professionals cultivate informal and formal communities where they create a shared worldview, practices, and expertise like legitimate peripheral participants learn by doing the work (Thompson, 2017; Thompson & Baker, n.d.). By participating in data communities, data professionals without a formal degree in data science or management extend their expertise to new data techniques and concepts. My study focuses on research institutions that are forming data management infrastructure, exhibiting social and organizational learning behaviors in response to the needs of modern science. As these data education and training programs are still emerging, it is timely to consider organizational and informal learning strategies that are preparing staff for new data work responsibilities.

This paper draws attention to the complexity of data expertise development by examining the social dimensions of learning and expertise. In a long-standing geoscience research center, I investigate the following research question: What are the learning strategies and conditions required to support data work? This study considers how expertise interacts with social and organizational dimensions to support data work for modern science, shifting the data expertise conversation from 'what' skill sets to 'how' these new skills can be cultivated by an organization.

A review of the data services and workforce literature sets the stage for the study design, findings, and implications.

---

[20] In this paper the term *data work*, as an inclusive term for many areas of practice involved in the research process such data production, processing, documentation, and integration along with the design of data infrastructure for organization, preservation, and dissemination.

BACKGROUND

Scientific data services have been developed by research institutions to address growing data volumes and sharing expectations. Geoscience research and data centers have provided valuable data products and services to their user communities for decades. The literature is full of examples and descriptions of new service models, software, and practices for data management, preservation, and sharing. This section reviews examples of current data services and associated challenges, focusing on the geoscience data center[21].

Federal and academic data centers in the geosciences have designed a variety of services and tools for scientific data. In particular, government agencies have been investing in access to research data and design of technologies for data solutions. For instance, the National Oceanic and Atmospheric Administration has designed a system of distributed data centers that provide data processing, archiving, and dissemination for earth science data products. The National Center for Atmospheric Research (NCAR), the research site in this study, conducts research and disseminates atmospheric and climate science reference data sets, observational data, simulation code and results, software, among other products. Further, Center for International Earth Science Information Network, which provides archiving, discovery, access, and mapping services for interdisciplinary research in the earth and social sciences (Downs & Chen, 2010). A study profiling 38 repositories in the atmospheric and climate sciences provides a snapshot of data services and capabilities in the U.S. Most repositories provide data access and assistance with identifiers and citation, with some degree of outreach, instruction, and user support; but less than half offer data processing, metadata enhancement, and software development services (Hou, Thompson, & Palmer, 2014). These geoscience data centers are providing valuable services and systems tailored to their user communities.

Data services and expertise must be viewed in the context of challenges to managing and preserving data. Geosciences face problems with geospatial data formats, representation, and scale (Morris, 2013) and qualified applicant pools of data workers with cross-cutting expertise (Mayernik et al., 2014). More recently, academic libraries have been building research data services and experiencing challenges in staffing (Brown, 2010; Corrall, Keenan, & Afzal, 2013; Creamer, Morales, Crespo, Kafel, & Martin, 2012). Across multiple domains, staffing issues have stood out where professionals lack the right knowledge, skills, and confidence to provide data management services.

Growing the pool of qualified data professionals that can address the challenges of science is a challenge when there are few effective and tailored data education programs. 'Ad hoc' learning and professional development strategies for data science and management are common across multiple disciplines (Jahnke, Asher, Keralis, & Henry, 2012) . Geoscience data centers provide a unique opportunity to investigate how data staffing and expertise have grown and matured and the strategies and conditions that are required for data professionals to maintain and improve services and systems to support science.

Scientific Data Workforce

Research support staff has been an integral part of the scientific enterprise. Data work involves a group of science and non-science professionals, organizations, and partners to manage high-quality data products. Current trends in eScience are calling for cross-cutting data staff that can understand scientific user needs, work with multiple disciplines, curate heterogeneous data, and advance data infrastructure (Atkins, 2003; Lord & Macdonald, 2003; Rusbridge, 2007).

New data positions and roles have emerged in the workforce such as data scientist, data curator, and digital librarian. The growth in data positions and responsibilities have been documented in the LIS field (Lyon, Wright, Corti, Edmunds, & Bennett, 2013; Maatta, 2013; Sierra, 2012) and other industries (Manyika et al., 2011; TEKSystems, 2013). Palmer, Thompson, Baker, & Senseney (2014) found that data curation duties are being added to established positions in research institutions. Research centers with mature data services offer an ideal setting for exploring how to prepare workers for new data duties and roles as they have a history in hiring and training staff for data management.

Data work, as an emerging area of practice, is a space where claims on the right formal preparation and expertise have not been settled (Abbott, 1988; Cox & Corrall, 2013). Visionary reports have stressed the need for quality data education (American Council of Learned Societies, 2006; Atkins, 2003). Data education initiatives are prevalent in information science and other fields such as computer science, domain sciences, and business. Professional associations offer opportunities for learning and

---

[21] Research data services and tools are also prevalent in other domains. The social and life sciences have mature services (see as examples: Altman & Crabtree, 2011; Greenberg, White, Carrier, & Scherle, 2009; Hedges, Haft, & Knight, 2012), and humanities are also beginning to expand (such as Flanders & Hamlin, 2013).

sharing data expertise such as Earth Science Information Partners; Earth and Space Science Informatics division within American Geophysical Union, and Research Data Alliance (Parsons & Berman, 2013). These learning venues provide an array of formal, social, and professional development opportunities for workers wishing to nurture their data expertise.

Research institutions have a critical need for professionals equipped with appropriate expertise to support current and future research data trends. My study builds on the previous data workforce and education studies by examining the organizational learning strategies (i.e., the how) for developing data expertise in an exemplar geoscience data center. Research centers with mature data services offer an ideal setting for exploring expertise as they have a history in training staff for data management and stewardship.

METHODS

The study applies an ethnographic and case study approach to examine the shared learning and expertise of data professionals and scientists. The case study approach is valuable in that it enables an "in-depth exploration from multiple perspectives of the complexity and uniqueness of a particular project, policy, institution, programme or system in a 'real life' context" (Simons, 2009, p. 21). Case study of an exemplar research center with mature data systems and services, NCAR, is developed using qualitative interviews and artifacts as evidence.

My research focuses on the organizational units and staff responsible for data management. These units include science teams and data teams involving a variety of workers such as scientists, data professionals, engineers, and information professionals. NCAR houses multiple labs and project teams providing data science and stewardship, but I chose to focus on specific teams, as described in the following case overview section to ensure feasibility. NCAR is an ideal site to study learning and expertise due to their long history of managing and sharing data and my 4-month field experience at the site in 2014. Through case study development, I explored the complexity of data expertise development specifically the expertise requirements, staffing, and learning processes.

The investigation employs qualitative interviews and artifact collection, enabling cross-checking and cross-validation of the findings using different data sources. Semi-structured interviews captured information on research data systems and operations, organizational structure, roles and responsibilities, necessary knowledge and skills, and professional backgrounds and identities. NCAR interviews targeted data professionals, managers, scientists, engineers, and librarians involved in the data services of the selected teams. Participant recruitment focused on professionals who are responsible for working with scientific data, planning data services or systems, or hiring staff for data roles. A total of 13 professionals participated in the study, totaling 15 interview sessions. Position titles included Project Scientist, Software Engineer, and Manager.

Information and organization artifacts are collected as evidence including organizational mission statement, policies, reports, webpages, and other material that illustrate data services and systems, expertise requirements, or practices. I collected a set of artifacts about the three data units in this study and organizational level data efforts. There were differences in the amount of documentation that was available for the teams and for different time periods of NCAR's history. These documents were used to verify interview participants' accounts and provide an organizational perspective on staffing and priorities. For more details on study design and methods please see Thompson (2017).

Qualitative coding and case analysis were used to investigate the research question. The concept, *knowing in practice*, developed by Orlikowski (2002) guides the understanding of expertise and competence needed for data work by examining the social and organizational dimensions of expertise and how *knowing* develops over time in an organization. Freewriting memos and mapping were conducted to unlock memories, make connections, and organize ideas (Sustein & Chiseri-Strater, 2012). Code development was both an inductive and deductive process. Open coding identified all the themes, ideas, and concepts in the transcripts and documents (Emerson et al., 2011). Then a list of codes was generated using the data practices and organizational learning literature. A set of final codes was selected for focused coding on transcripts, documents, materials, and field notes (Emerson et al., 2011). The final codes covered themes of data work, expertise, learning, staffing, facilitators, barriers, among others. ATLAS.ti for Mac was utilized for memoing, coding, and analysis.

FINDINGS

NCAR like peer institutions have a long history of building research data expertise in order to support and sustain services for data management and curation. NCAR data staff bridge multiple science and data roles, cultivating expertise spanning multiple areas over time. An objective of this research is to understand how organizations learn to work with research data, focusing on the act of building and sustaining this expertise. This paper contributes the learning strategies and influential conditions involved in expertise development, serving as a model for libraries and research organizations that wish to support professional development and staffing for data management.

Overview of NCAR

NCAR is a premier research center in the atmospheric sciences in Boulder, Colorado, USA. NCAR and its parent organization, the University Corporation for Atmospheric Research, started in the 1960s and have grown today to include 7 labs and programs conducting research on such topics as sun and earth connection, air quality and chemistry, and climate systems and interactions. NCAR is a federally-funded research and development center, funded by the National Science Foundation (NSF), supporting research and providing instruments, field campaign support, supercomputing facilities, and archival collections of data for the atmospheric science community (Mayernik et al., 2014). While each lab has grown their data services and staff in unique ways, NCAR has a history of organization-wide initiatives on research data such as the recent Data Stewardship and Engineering Team (DSET), for which I served as a graduate observer (Baker, Mayernik, Thompson, Nienhouse, Williams, & Worley, 2015). As a research center, NCAR has a long history of managing scientific data, producing valuable high-level data products, and supporting access to reference data sets, observational data, climate model code and outputs, and software. NCAR contains multiple data management teams and staff across its labs. For this study, the NCAR case covers the Research Data Archive (NCAR-Archive) team providing data archiving and preservation support for select atmospheric and related data sets from NCAR labs; High Altitude Observatory (NCAR-Solar) data professionals working on large-scale observational data streams; and Climate & Global Dynamics (NCAR-Climate) data professionals providing data management expertise for climate modeling and simulations. These three units represent a variety of data types, atmospheric sub-disciplines, and staffing arrangements (e.g., data managers placed into research teams; data teams separated from science labs) present across NCAR.

At NCAR, I observed data expertise types associated with seven categories– data, research, curation, engineering, service, analytics, and leadership. Data and research categories requires an understanding of the research process, techniques, and data types as well as the landscape of data trends relevant to data work. The curation category encompasses the core skills of organizing, preserving, and standardizing data and products. Engineering category involves knowing how to design and maintain software and systems for data management. The service category represents the importance of relationships with users and of collaborations in offering data services. The leadership category provides a guiding vision and coordination for data work across professionals, units, and partners. More details on expertise types and categories can be found in Thompson (2017).

Expertise Development Strategies

To offer research data services, organizations need a well-prepared staff knowledgeable in multiple expertise areas such as data handling, research processes, curation, engineering, among others (Palmer et al., 2014; Thompson, 2017). My study identifies a set of learning strategies used to enhance local data expertise. The following sections describe the three overarching learning activities of data expertise acquisition, sharing, and retention, aligning with typologies of organizational learning processes (Argote, 2011; Huber, 1991). These strategies are executed to achieve different learning objectives such as managing a new data type or implementing preservation techniques. The learning activities are initiated by workers on the ground needing to solve a data challenge and by management addressing service and staffing gaps. While emphasizing different areas of expertise development over time and by teams, NCAR made substantial progress in data staffing development using these learning approaches. This section describes a few prominent strategies observed in the NCAR data; see Table 1 for the full list.

Expertise acquisition. Learning by doing or *experiential learning* (Kolb, 1984) is the most common theme in the interview data. This approach occurs using formal and informal work projects. Several participants use phrases like "trial and error," and "jump right in" to describe their learning approaches. The experience of working with data creates informal learning opportunities for both individuals and teams. Advances in data formats, simulations, or technologies often initiates this strategy. At NCAR, all data professionals report learning new formats, programming languages, analysis techniques, or technologies by informal projects. Participants emphasize how they learned several programming languages by picking a common data task and re-creating it in the new language. Informal work experiments are a valuable learning tool, allowing the deep exploration of data problems and a platform for trying new approaches or tools.

Formal work assignments represent another mechanism for experiential learning as a means of staff development. These projects respond to emerging data needs recognized by the team. Incidents of new learning associated with special projects include data transfer technologies, website usability, and metadata standards. For instance, the NCAR-Archive manager describes a metadata project:

> We've got all these different data sets, and they have quasi-standard metadata but not quite. So, I went to [employee name redacted] and I said, '[employee name redacted] could you help us work things up and get all the metadata standardized across all of the data sets.' (NCAR 211)

This project improved the metadata quality and compliance with standards as well as enhanced expertise in geoscience metadata standards in this team. These special work projects enable one or two team members to experiment with a new standard, service, or technology and learn how it relates to research data and integrate into local practices and systems. This team also built an additional learning activity into these special projects by asking workers to reflect on lessons learned in their annual performance review and requiring them to share their experiences with co-workers. Formal work projects coupled with reflection are an effective learning strategy.

Expertise transfer. Local *task forces* or working groups are a popular expertise transfer strategy that often is initiated by data professionals or scientists. Employees form these cross-unit collectives to provide a forum for sharing lessons learned, emerging data standards or trends, technologies, and best practices, as well as designing new practices and software. These groups are often time-limited and driven by a mission to educate other staff and/or produce a shared approach or system for a specific data challenge. A key feature of these groups is cross-unit membership, bringing together professionals with different expertise and research projects.

NCAR has a series of data-focused task forces throughout its history that enabled expertise sharing across labs and teams. While the mission was to address a specific data challenge, these meetings offered opportunities for NCAR data professionals and scientists to interact and learn from each other. Often, data professionals working in science teams were not aware of data professionals and activities in other labs. The local groups spurred seminars, demonstrations, or shared tasks where professionals could share and learn from each other such as the current Data Stewardship and Engineering Team (DSET). The NCAR-Solar lab representative for DSET describe the meetings as allowing her/him to seek advice from seasoned data professionals on best practices:

> I asked this question the other day [at the DSET meeting] and was like 'does anyone else serve their data through Drupal' and they were like 'No, we have our own web servers in our labs that is how we serve our data.' (NCAR 101)

Task forces are successful for social learning and for cross-unit progress on shared definitions of terms like data (Baker, Mayernik, Thompson, Nienhouse, Williams, & Worley, 2015), on community data portal, and on a common set of data citation practices (Mayernik et al., 2012).

Expertise retention. NCAR retention strategies emphasize the preservation of data expertise into *documentation* such as technical reports and guides. These resources capture expertise and experiences for current and future employees to use as learning resources. At NCAR, the DSET and data citation task forces deliberately produce technical reports that are preserved in the NCAR digital repository due to the lack of documentation from previous data groups. These reports are accessible to NCAR employees and the general public providing best practices, new insights, and recommendations learned by these task forces. These valuable resources capture the expertise of data professionals as well as serve as a learning tool for other employees and broader audiences.

The development of *shared practices* is a promising strategy for data expertise retention. Shared practices are available for all employees to utilize, and many new data professionals benefited from a systematic approach to data processing or archiving, where the standards for metadata or archiving are embedded into the practice. For instance, the NCAR-wide data citation working group produced a set of recommended practices for digital object identifiers (DOIs) and data citation documented in the group's technical report. The group's practice recommendations are adopted across NCAR instilling the expertise of citations and identifiers into research teams and their workflows. Shared practices allow the expertise of data professionals to be retained. Table 1 summarizes the learning approaches observed in the interview data.

Strategy	Activity	Description
Expertise acquisition	Experiential	Learning by doing, formal or informal
	Grafting	Hiring new professionals
	Observational	Learning from watching other institutions
	Books/classroom	Learning from educational/training sources
Expertise transfer	Task forces	Sharing in informal, cross-unit collectives
	Peer-to-peer learning	Learning from expert co-workers
Expertise retention	Documentation	Capturing expertise in shared resources
	Practices	Embedding expertise in shared practices

Table 1. Data expertise development strategies

NCAR established a program for data professional development including a variety of learning strategies to acquire, share, and retain expertise. The data expertise acquisition activities focus on enhancing the current skill set of data professionals to meet the demands of their data roles as well as enabled other professionals to learn about data management and how it might relate to their work. Since NCAR has a long history in data management and acquired data expertise and competence, I was able to observe learning strategies for data expertise sharing and retention. The effectiveness to share and retain expertise has been observed to impact organizational learning (Argote, 2013).

Outcomes. At NCAR, an emphasis on data expertise development led data professionals to pursue new knowledge and experiences working with research data to address the challenges of data management, archiving, and sharing. The mix of strategies make it possible for data professionals to update and expand their skill sets to meet the needs of their organization and user communities. Data staff cultivate a deep expertise in data handling and trends, domain science, analytics, organization and curation, and technical areas specific to their work through various learning strategies and strong relationships with colleagues in their organization. Most NCAR data professionals have a geoscience and/or engineering background providing a foundation to expand their expertise into other practice areas such as computation, curation, or service-design. Data expertise retention efforts benefit current and future employees that may learn from these resources steeped in expertise and protects NCAR from knowledge loss due to staff turnover or retirements. These strategies work especially well for a domain research institution with a strong connection to the user community and a combination of seasoned and nascent professionals, where sharing expertise happens in multiple directions.

Conditions for Expertise Development

As organizations are embarking on learning, the process of change can be enabled by organizational or environmental factors (Argote, 2013). In my analysis, a set of conditions emerged in the NCAR history of data expertise and staff development. A number of these factors have been well documented in the literature: organizational culture (Edmonson, 1999), resource allocation (Kimberly & Evanisko, 1981), leadership support (Yin, 1977), alignment with stakeholder interests (Wagner, 2007), among others. In this study, sphere of influence, visibility of data work, and communities of practices are prominent conditions for expertise development, offering a model for research institutions that are preparing workers for new data roles.

Sphere of Influence. Influence and agency affect the ability of employees to spur service innovations, defying established institutional norms and practices (Garud, Jain, & Kumaraswamy, 2002; Maguire, Hardy, & Lawrence, 2004; Raven, Schwarzwald, & Koslowsky, 1998). This study observes that data professionals with extensive knowledge influenced the development of data expertise and services. When data workers are able to garner support to expand their learning and change practices, this results in new staffing, expertise, or services with varying degrees of impact across the institution. The summary of case results revealed data professionals influencing three spheres – 1) organization, 2) lab, and 3) project - impacting the story of data staffing and expertise development. See Table 2 for a summary of spheres of influence characteristics.

Sphere	Description	Agent exemplars	Outcome examples
Organization	Realize opportunities, motivate employees and stakeholders, and allocate resources to data efforts	NCAR director, assistant director, Library's data scientist	NCAR-wide data citation and identifier practices
Lab or unit	Influence over a unit's priorities and resources, and motivate unit employees	NCAR lab directors, Archive's manager and engineer, and Solar data scientist	NCAR Solar lab training for new data workers
Project	Make decisions for a single data service or research project and impact local data practices	NCAR Climate data scientist, and Archive and Climate engineers	NCAR Climate model metadata and provenance practices

Table 2. Spheres of influence characteristics

The first type of agent is an employee with an organizational sphere of influence, enabling him/her to initiate changes across the organization. Often, the employee has a deep expertise in scientific data management issues. At NCAR, three employees in the interview data exhibit this type of sphere of influence by enabling a data task force formation with allocated resources and NCAR-wide adoption of data citation practices. Interestingly, one data scientist due to her/his deep expertise in data curation garners the respect and support of peers for NCAR-wide innovations.

Data professionals with a lab-level influence are effective in producing changes in the lab or division, impacting many data workers and research projects. At NCAR, three employees have long careers in scientific data management, enabling them to build 'contributing expertise,' that is, the ability to contribute to research projects in substantial ways (Collins & Evans, 2007). Using their extensive expertise, these workers are able to motivate their peers and superiors to adopt changes such as data staff trainings.

The data workers with project spheres exhibit the ability to make decisions for their local data work and learning, impacting a single science project or service. As a NCAR-Climate Data Engineer describes the situation: "One good side about kind of falling in between the cracks and having the experience that I do is having fairly wide latitude of how things get done, which is nice. Because when I talk about various aspects of data management and data science I'm the only one…that has that knowledge. They just say, 'Whatever [interviewee name redacted] wants, that's fine'" (NCAR 206). Data professionals with a project-level influence and specialized expertise convince their supervisors of needed changes such as learning metadata and provenance standards and practices.

Data services and expertise need to grow and respond to emerging data trends. In an organization like NCAR, data professionals are working at multiple levels from management to the frontlines, exhibiting different amounts of agency and influence. A few NCAR data professionals emerge that were able to express more agency than typical in their position due to their deep, cross-cutting expertise. When data professionals did not have the ability to modify their learning or practices, data innovations are inhibited. An NCAR-Solar Data Scientist compares a data professional without the ability to explore and learn to "a lame duck congress when you can't get anything done" (NCAR 101). Misalignment between influence, data work, and positions spurred inconsistencies in the expertise and systems offered across NCAR labs and teams.

Visibility of Data Work. Recent attention to data sharing has highlighted an ignored part of the scientific process related to working with research data. Even so, my interviews show that the invisibility of data work is changing slowly in practice. Invisible work refers to "the expertise often hidden from view," emphasizing certain expertise, workers, and tasks in an organization are more visible than others (Star & Strauss, 1999, p. 11). Data workers have been members of research teams for decades; however, the curatorial work with research data itself has been invisible to research administrators and stakeholders. The visibility of data work is as a factor in the development of data expertise and staffing at NCAR.

Multiple NCAR data professionals drew attention to the invisibility of their work and the changes in visibility over time. In the descriptions of the science projects, I often heard two categories of workers – scientists and others. The other grouping includes an array of non-scientist professionals and skill sets such as data management, software engineers, and instrument operators. An example is a participant's description of a climate modeling project staff as "...the scientists here and their collaborators which is like everybody else" (NCAR 208). The combination of all non-scientists into one category makes the diversity of work and contributions invisible. Following on this theme, several data professionals note the lack of recognition of how data work contributes to science. The NCAR-Archive Data Service Manager describes how easy access to research data hid the complexity of data sharing and preservation:

> In some ways, we're victims of our own success. If the RDA [data portal] just sits there, a person comes and in an instance they find what they need. Then, they're [users are] gone off doing their research. They [users] probably don't even think that there are a lot of people behind that. It's like when you go to buy a book at Amazon and just two clicks. (NCAR 211)

Moreover, an NCAR-Climate data professional reports that a mistake makes data work visible to climate scientists: "If I don't do it or I do it wrong, we know about it right away. Somebody says, 'this data set is all messed up.' There has definitely been a greater appreciation of the work that I do" (NCAR 206).

The absence of data roles and professionals in the scientific authorship and organizational systems is evident at NCAR. For example, data professionals are often not acknowledged in the conference papers, technical reports, and products disseminated from the research project to which they contribute, masking the work they do. A few scientists-turned-data-professionals worry about their short vitae and future career prospects given the authorship practices. Furthermore, the NCAR job classification system lacks formal recognition of data work. Many data workers are hired as software engineers or scientists, shoehorning of data responsibilities into an existing category and resulting in a mismatch of skills and position levels. As an NCAR-Climate Data Engineer notes: "Some of the stuff I do would still be considered like a very low-level sophomore engineer like running scripts and running jobs on these machines. But then I get asked to these conferences for the NCAR view on data and participate in things like [redacted - data training initiative] and that's like a high-level managerial." (NCAR 206).

Examining the visibility of data work sheds light on how the attention to data activities and expertise impacted the learning innovations. At NCAR, data work is moving from invisible to visible, as data becomes a prominent product in the expanding scientific record. While data professionals report increasing respect for data work, the organizational systems for job classification and practices for authorship do not reflect the efforts of data professionals. The increasing visibility of data work fosters the legitimacy of data expertise and staffing, respect for data workers, and collegial support for data staffing and learning initiatives.

Local Data Communities. NCAR cultivates local research data communities of practice, supporting data expertise development strategies (Lave & Wenger, 1991). The process of learning about and enacting research data expertise has evolved slowly to form a CoP at NCAR. In the early days of NCAR, science teams and scientists had to manage data, but data work was considered a means to the end. The formation of NCAR-Archive, a data archiving team, brought together a group of professionals with the shared interests in data quality and access. Early on one member introduced database structures to the community so members worked together designing a SQL database for scientific metadata. This hands-on project improved metadata quality, compliance with standards, and member expertise in relational databases and metadata standards. One member described a community project on data search engines as: "working with people who do the [data archiving] job and processing the log to see who will get what and how much activity it can process" (NCAR 201). This group works on shared activities of data processing, software development, and dissemination, allowing a community to form that shares expertise and lessons learned and how to integrate it into local data workflows and systems.

While the NCAR-Archive team enables the initial CoP for research data, the formation of NCAR-wide data task forces expands the community to include data workers in other labs and teams. For many data professionals, these meetings are the only opportunities to interact with other data professionals, learning about data concepts, practices, and systems. As one NCAR representative described the meetings as allowing her/him to seek advice from seasoned data professionals on best practices: "I asked this question the other day [at the meeting] and was like 'does anyone else serve their data through Drupal' and they were like 'No, we have our own web servers in our labs that is how we serve our data'" (NCAR 101). Another anchor of the data CoP was the hiring of the NCAR Library's Research Data Scientist. This position is located in a UCAR unit serving all the science labs, giving this individual an opportunity to identify common data problems and connect staff across the labs to share best practices or recommendations. This individual plays a valuable role in expanding and strengthening the NCAR research data CoP. In particular, the NCAR CoP develops shared data identifier and citation practices, produces technical reports, and identifies data experts that serve as resources for new data workers. These results highlight the positive impact of communities of practice formation.

At NCAR, the process of data expertise development is enhanced by a set of conditions that foster and sustain the learning and knowledge. Three prominent conditions of sphere of influence, local data community of practice, and visibility of data work provide the impetus for professional development of data workers. These three conditions result in emphasizing the value of data work and expertise as well as continual professional development of data staff.

DISCUSSION

As data work becomes a more prominent part of the research process, research institutions face challenges in preparing staff for new data management responsibilities. A key outcome of this study is the learning strategies and conditions to enhance data expertise within an organization. My research findings move the data conversation from 'what' expertise to 'how' to cultivate and embrace a data-savvy workforce that can address the data challenges of modern research. This discussion illustrates the usefulness of the learning strategies and conditions to data professionalization and learning innovations.

A set of workplace learning strategies for building data expertise and staffing are identified and classified as: 1) data expertise acquisition, 2) sharing, and 3) retention, similar to typologies reported in the organizational learning literature (Argote, 2011, 2013; Huber, 1991). Multiple learning strategies are employed across NCAR teams and labs. These processes are complementary, instilling deep expertise across the organization, but are sequential meaning that an organization must have expertise before it can focus on sharing and retention efforts. The learning blends individual and social approaches to cultivating a data staff with the expertise and competence to keep pace with emerging data trends. These strategies provide a model for research administrators and managers wishing to prepare their staff for new data management responsibilities.

Local task forces and communities of practice are a promising strategy to foster the building and sharing of expertise within an organization or team. These groups confirmed the social dimensions of expertise, fostered by performing the work and from interactions with similar professionals (Collins & Evans, 2007; Lave & Wenger, 1991; Orlikowski, 2002). These communities fostered social learning and competence among data workers and the emergence of a shared perspective and practices at NCAR. Shared data projects allowed opportunities for data professionals across labs to interact and share their experiences. In these communities, data workers are valuable resources for each other, cultivating the expertise required for data work and responding to technological or institutional changes.

An important element in data innovations is cultivating expertise levels of data professionals to ensure they had the appropriate sphere of influence in the organization. My study draws attention to three spheres of influence of data professionals clarifying the types of institutional actors and agency needed to nurture data services (Garud, Hardy, & Maguire, 2007; Maguire et al., 2004). Data professionals that exhibited a larger sphere of influence than I expected based on their position are deemed as experts in data management by their supervisors and colleagues. NCAR workers cultivate expertise, as legitimate peripheral participants do (Lave & Wenger, 1991), and this expertise earned them respect and influence. These professionals extend their initial expertise in science or engineering to areas of curation or analytics by doing the work. These experiences taught data workers the language of data management, challenges, and concepts. This participation transforms them into key players in NCAR data services, further gaining support and agency from their colleagues. Future research in the appropriate agency and spheres of influence of data workers is warranted to design effective data infrastructure.

Ensuring successful data services requires research institutions to carefully plan where data professionals are located in the organization, how data work is recognized, and how to support the continuing professional development. My work highlights the organizational challenges in research data staffing offers a possible explanation for why academic libraries are slow to offer these services, a point made evident in Tenopir (2014). These findings respond to a recent survey of academic libraries that found cultivation of expertise and hiring staff as the biggest challenges for library data services (Hudson-Vitale et al., 2017) by drawing attention to the workplace challenges of cultivating expertise and integrating data professionals into established work systems, values, and career paths in an organization. The case results make evident that research institutions and administrators need to embrace and learn from data professionalization disconnects and dilemmas in order to build sustainable data services and systems.

CONCLUSION

High quality data management is an ambitious goal even for research institutions with mature data services like NCAR. The data infrastructure necessary to support quality curation involves a well-trained staff, continual professional development, and organizational strategies and structures to support the careers and recognition of data professionals. Research institutions and libraries can cultivate data expertise and staffing through a well-planned organizational learning initiative. To succeed, organizations need to encourage the agency of data workers and formation of local data communities of practices and to increase the visibility of data workers and their contributions to science. Continual attention to data expertise development will ensure a workforce that can steward valuable data products and solve the current and future data challenges in science and scholarship.

ACKNOWLEDGMENTS

This research was conducted as part of the Data Curation Education in Research Centers (DCERC) program, funded by the Institute of Museum and Library Services (grant RE-02-10-0004-10).

REFERENCES

Abbott, A. (1988). *The System of Professions: An Essay on the Division of Expert Labor*. Chicago, IL, USA: University of Chicago Press.

Altman, M., & Crabtree, J. (2011). Using the SafeArchive System : TRAC-Based auditing of LOCKSS. In *Archiving 2011 Final Program and Proceedings* (pp. 165–170).

American Council of Learned Societies. (2006). *Our Cultural Commonwealth*. Retrieved from http://www.acls.org/cyberinfrastructure/ourculturalcommonwealth.pdf

Argote, L. (2011). Organizational learning research: Past, present and future. *Management Learning*, *42*(4), 439–446. https://doi.org/10.1177/1350507611408217

Argote, L. (2013). *Organizational Learning: Creating, Retaining and Transferring Knowledge* (2nd ed.). New York, New York, USA: Springer Science+Business Media. https://doi.org/10.1007/978-1-4614-5251-5

Atkins, D. (2003). *Revolutionizing Science and Engineering through Cyberinfrastructure: Report of the National Science Foundation Blue-Ribbon Advisory Panel on Cyberinfrastructure*. Retrieved from http://www.nsf.gov/cise/sci/reports/atkins.pdf

Baker, K. S., Mayernik, M. S., Thompson, C. A., Nienhouse, E., Williams, S., & Worley, S. (2015). Envisioning and enacting a coherent organization-wide view of data. In *Proceedings of the International Digital Curation Conference.* Retrieved from http://hdl.handle.net/2142/73150

Brown, E. (2010). I know what you researched last summer: How academic librarians are supporting researchers in the management of data curation. *The New Zealand Library & Information Management Journal*, *52*(1), 55–69.

Collins, H., & Evans, R. (2007). *Rethinking Expertise*. Chicago, IL, USA: The University of Chicago Press.

Corrall, S., Keenan, M. A., & Afzal, W. (2013). Bibliometrics and research datamanagement services: Emerging trends in library support for research. *Library Trends*, *61*(3), 636–674. Retrieved from http://dx.doi.org/10.1353/lib.2013.0005

Cox, A. M., & Corrall, S. (2013). Evolving academic library specialties. *Journal of the American Society for Information Science and Technology*, *64*(8), 1526–1542. https://doi.org/10.1002/asi

Creamer, A., Morales, M. E., Crespo, J., Kafel, D., & Martin, E. R. (2012). An assessment of needed competencies to promote the data curation and management librarianship of health sciences and science and technology librarians in New England. *Journal of eScience Librarianship*, *1*(1), 18–26.

Downs, R. R., & Chen, R. S. (2010). Self-assessment of a long-term archive for interdisciplinary scientific data as a trustworthy digital repository. *Journal of Digital Information*, *11*(1).

Edmonson, A. (1999). Psychological safety and learning behavior in work teams. *Administrative Science Quarterly*, *44*(4), 350–383.

Flanders, J., & Hamlin, S. (2013). TAPAS: Building a TEI publishing and repository service. *Journal of the Text Encoding Initiative*, (5), 1–9. https://doi.org/10.4000/jtei.788

Garud, R., Hardy, C., & Maguire, S. (2007). Institutional entrepreneurship as embedded agency : An introduction to the special issue. *Organizational Studies*, *28*(7), 957–969. https://doi.org/10.1177/0170840607078958

Garud, R., Jain, S., & Kumaraswamy, A. (2002). Institutional entrepeneurship in the sponsorship of common technological standards: The case of Sun Microsystems and Java. *Academy of Management Journal*, *45*(1), 196–214.

Hedges, M., Haft, M., & Knight, G. (2012). FISHNet: Encouraging data sharing and reuse in the freshwater science community. *Journal Of Digital Information*, *13*. Retrieved from http://journals.tdl.org/jodi/article/view/5884

Hou, C., Thompson, C. A., & Palmer, C. L. (2014). Profiling open digital repositories in the atmospheric and climate sciences : An initial survey. In *Proceedings of the 77th ASIS&T Annual Meeting*. Seattle, WA, USA.

Huber, G. (1991). Organizational learning : The contributing processes and the literatures. *Organization Science*, *2*(1), 88–115.

Hudson-Vitale, C., Imker, H., Johnston, L. R., Carlson, J., Kozlowski, W., Olendorf, R., & Stewart, C. (2017). *SPEC Kit 354: Data Curation*. Washington, DC. Retrieved from http://publications.arl.org/Data-Curation-SPEC-Kit-354/

Jahnke, L., Asher, A., Keralis, S. D. C., & Henry, C. (2012). *The Problem of Data*. Washington, DC. Retrieved from https://www.clir.org/pubs/reports/pub154/

Kimberly, J. R., & Evanisko, M. J. (1981). Organizational innovation: The influence of individual, organizational, and contextual factors on hospital adoption of technological and administrative innovations. *Academy of Management Journal*, *24*(4), 689–713.

Kolb, D. (1984). *Experiential Learning: Experience as the Source of Learning and Development*. Englewood Cliffs, N.J.: Prentice-Hall.

Lave, J., & Wenger, E. (1991). *Situated Learning: Legitimate Peripheral Participation*. New York, NY: Cambridge University Press.

Lord, P., & Macdonald, A. (2003). *Data curation for e-Science in the UK: An Audit to Establish Requirements for Future Curation and Provision*. Retrieved from http://www.jisc.ac.uk/uploaded_documents/e-scienceReportFinal.pdf

Lyon, L., Wright, S., Corti, L., Edmunds, S., & Bennett, F. (2013). What is a data scientist? In *2013 International Digital Curation Conference*. Amsterdam, Netherlands: Digital Curation Centre.

Maatta, S. L. (2013). The emerging databrarian. *Library Journal*, *138*(17), 26.

Maguire, S., Hardy, C., & Lawrence, T. B. (2004). Institutional entrepreneurship in emerging fields: HIV/AIDS treatment advocacy in Canada. *The Academy of Management Journal*, *47*(5), 657–679. https://doi.org/10.2307/20159610

Manyika, J., Chui, M., Brown, B., Bughin, J., Dobbs, R., Roxburgh, C., & Byers, A. H. (2011). *Big Data: The Next Frontier for Innovation, Competition, and Productivity*. https://doi.org/10.1080/01443610903114527

Mayernik, M. S., Daniels, M. D., Ginger, K. M., Kelly, K. M., Marlino, M. R., Williams, S. F., & Wright, M. J. (2012). *Data Citations within NCAR / UCP*. Boulder, CO. Retrieved from http://dx.doi.org/10.5065/D6ZC80VN

Mayernik, M. S., Davis, L., Kelly, K., Dattore, B., Strand, G., Worley, S. J., & Marlino, M. (2014). Research center insights into data curation education and curriculum. In Ł. Bolikowski, V. Casarosa, P. Manghi, P. Goodale, N. Houssos, & J. Schirrwagen (Eds.), *Theory and Practice of Digital Libraries-TPDL 2013 Selected Workshops, Communications in Computer and Information Science* (Vol. 416 CCIS, pp. 239–248). Switzerland: Sprinter International Publishing. https://doi.org/10.1007/978-3-319-08425-1

Morris, S. (2013). *Issues in the Appraisal and Selection of Geospatial Data*. Retrieved from http://hdl.loc.gov/loc.gdc/lcpub.2013655112.1

Orlikowski, W. J. (2002). Knowing in practice: Enacting a collective capability in distributed organizing. *Organization Science*, *13*(3), 249–273. https://doi.org/10.1287/orsc.13.3.249.2776

Palmer, C. L., Thompson, C. A., Baker, K. S., & Senseney, M. (2014). Meeting data workforce needs: Indicators based on recent data curation placements. In *iConference 2014 Proceedings*. Berlin, Germany.

Parsons, M. A., & Berman, F. (2013). The Research Data Alliance: Implementing the Ttchnology, practice and connections of a data infrastructure. *Bulletin of the American Society for Information Science and Technology*, *August/Sep*, 33–36.

Raven, B. H., Schwarzwald, J., & Koslowsky, M. (1998). Conceptualizing and measuring a power/interaction model of interpersonal influence. *Journal of Applied Social Psychology*, *28*(4), 307–332. https://doi.org/10.1111/j.1559-1816.1998.tb01708.x

Rusbridge, C. (2007). Create, curate, re-use: the expanding life course of digital research data. In *EDUCAUSE Australasia 2007 Advancing Knowledge Pushing Boundaries. CAUDIT*. Retrieved from http://hdl.handle.net/1842/1731

Schwen, T. M., & Hara, N. (2003). Community of practice: A metaphor for online design? *The Information Society*, *19*(3), 257–270.

Sierra, T. (2012). Staffing for the future research questions: ARL university lIbrary hiring in 2011. In *ARl Fall Forum 2012*.

Simons, H. (2009). *Case Study Research in Practice*. London, UK: SAGE Publications, Ltd.

Star, S. L., & Strauss, A. (1999). Layers of silence, arenas of voice: The ecology of visible and invisible work. *Computer Supported Cooperative Work (CSCW)*, *8*(1–2), 9–30. https://doi.org/10.1023/A:1008651105359

TEKSystems. (2013). Trends IT industry big data ... The next frontier. *IT Industry Trends*, pp. 1–5.

Thompson, C. A. (2017). *Data Expertise and Service Development in Geoscience Data Centers and Academic Libraries*. University of Illinois at Urbana-Champaign.

Thompson, C. A., & Baker, K. S. (n.d.). Learning about Data Work: Applying Social Informatics to Data Communities. *Manuscript Submitted for Publication*.

Wagner, M. (2007). On the relationship between environmental management, environmental innovation and patenting: Evidence from German manufacturing firms. *Research Policy*, *36*(1587–1602).

Wenger, E. (1998). *Communities of Practice: Learning, Meaning, and Identity*. Cambridge, UK: Cambridge University Press.

Yin, R. K. (1977). Production efficiency versus bureaucratic self-interest: Two innovative processes? *Policy Sciences*, *8*(4), 381–399.

Demographic Factors and Trust in Different News Sources

Nitin Verma
School of Information, University of Texas at Austin, USA.
nitin.verma@utexas.edu

Kolina S. Koltai
School of Information, University of Texas at Austin, USA.
koltai@utexas.edu

Kenneth R. Fleischmann
School of Information, University of Texas at Austin, USA.
kfleisch@ischool.utexas.edu

ABSTRACT

What factors influence trust in different news sources? The goal of this study is to examine the role of various demographic factors: gender, age, educational attainment, political leaning, and frequency of social media use. This paper reports relevant results from a crowdsourced experimental study focusing on reporting of science news online. Significant findings include that conservatives place higher trust in fake news than moderates ($p < 0.05$), liberals place higher trust in mainstream media than moderates ($p < 0.05$), liberals place higher trust in scientific journals than conservatives ($p < 0.01$) and moderates ($p < 0.05$), and less frequent users of social media place higher trust in fake news than do more frequent users of social media ($p < 0.05$). Based on these results, political leaning and frequency of social media use influence trust in fake news, while political leaning also influences trust in mainstream media and scientific journals. These findings shed new light on the important issue of trust in news sources, illustrating the importance of considering political leaning and frequency of social media use in assessing trust in different news sources. These results further underscore the current degree of polarization present in the American public's perceptions of different online science news sources.

KEYWORDS

Trust, fake news, mainstream media, scientific journals, gender, age, educational attainment, political leaning, frequency of social media use.

INTRODUCTION

Trust in digital information is a vitally important topic, as trust is critical to the proper functioning of society, and social media is increasingly ubiquitous and powerful within society (Kelton, Fleischmann, & Wallace, 2008). The 2017 Gallup/Knight Foundation Survey on Trust, Media and Democracy identified several disturbing trends related to the general public's lack of trust in online information. For example, while 84% asserted that the news media play a "critical" or "very important" role in our democracy, and 70% adults reported using online platforms such as Google or Facebook to get news "frequently" or "occasionally," 73% responded that "the spread of inaccurate information on the Internet" is "a major problem," the most frequently selected category. Overall, trust in the news media is on the decline, with the level of media trust declining from 54% in 2003 to 41% in 2017, and "Internet-only news websites" and "news aggregators" had lower trust ratings than "your local newspaper," "national network news," "major national newspapers," and "cable news" (Gallup, 2018).

The goal of this paper is to dig deeper into the role of demographic factors such as gender, age, educational attainment, political leaning, and frequency of social media use on trust in different sources of online science news, including fake news, mainstream media, and scientific journals. The paper reports results from a larger study on factors that influence trust; a previous paper (Verma, Fleischmann, & Koltai, 2017) also reported a different subset of findings from the same study; the prior study reported data on clicking behavior and human values, and did not involve any analysis of demographic factors, the focus of this paper. The findings of this study shed new light on the relative importance of demographic factors in influencing trust, employing an experimental design rather than the more common approach of using surveys; as such, we can measure trust more directly, rather than relying on individuals to accurately assess and report their more abstract trust ratings in broad categories of online news sources.

BACKGROUND

Gender

Prior studies have found evidence that gender can have an impact on the formation of trust judgments. For example, a study on how Chinese students assess Wikipedia pages found that information accuracy, stability, and validity were all significant predictors of trust in information in Wikipedia, and that each of these factors was associated with gender, with males relying significantly more heavily on accuracy and stability, and females relying significantly more heavily on validity, which they define as relating to how information was collected and cited (Huang, Shi, Chen, & Chow, 2016). Thus, females focused more on the process, while males focused more on the product. A study that focused on the acceptance of a mobile payment system found that perceived trust in the system influenced attitudes more in women than in men (Liébana-Cabanillas, Sánchez-Fernández, & Muñoz-Leiva, 2014). A study that focused on how journalists source and trust information found that men showed slightly higher levels of trust in online news sources (Heravi & Harrower, 2016). However, a study on Facebook and privacy did not identify any differences in trust across gender (Malik, Hiekkanen, & Nieminen, 2016). Overall, findings regarding the effect of gender on trust in online news sources seem to be inconclusive, leaving room for further research.

Age

Age is one of the most commonly discussed demographic factors when it comes to information online, including trust in news sources. The 2007 Gallup/Knight Foundation Survey found higher use of online news sources among younger adults than among older adults. While more adults aged 65 or older had a favorable rather than unfavorable opinion of news media, in the 18-29 age group more than twice as many had an unfavorable opinion of news media. However, the survey also found that a majority of adults within each of the four different age groups surveyed assert that "fake news" is "a very serious threat" to democracy (Gallup, 2018). Recent surveys have shown dramatic increases in Internet and social media use by older adults (Pew Research Center, 2017a, 2017b). A study across European countries looking at the social participation with news online (e.g., sharing news stories online, commenting, talking with friends online about news stories) found no relationship between age and social participation (Hoelig, 2016). However, another study looking at privacy and trust on Facebook found that younger adults displayed higher trust levels towards Facebook than older adults (Malik et al., 2016). A study focusing on journalists found that younger journalists had a higher level of trust in online sources from social media compared to other sources; while the authors did not find a correlation between trust and age, they did note that trust seemed to trend downward for older adults (Heravi & Harrower, 2016). A survey about online sources for campaign information found low trust among both older adults and younger adults in online media (Towner & Munoz, 2016). In general, findings regarding age and trust online seem inconclusive, again demonstrating the need for further research on the role of demographic factors in influencing trust in online sources.

Educational Attainment

Prior studies regarding educational attainment also report fairly mixed results. For example, the study looking at social participation in Europe found that educational attainment did not impact social participation in online news (Hoelig, 2016). However, the Gallup/Knight Foundation Survey found that those with "postgraduate" education and those with "high school education or less" had higher trust in media than those with "some college" or a "four-year college degree only" (Gallup, 2018). Thus, there is also more room for exploring the relationship between educational attainment and trust in online news sources.

Political Leaning

In this age of partisan news, there are stark differences in how people with different political leanings consume and trust media. For example, the Gallup/Knight Foundation Survey found that overall trust in media was higher among liberals than conservatives (Gallup, 2018). Pew Research Center (2014) reported that in a survey covering 36 news sources, liberals expressed more trust than distrust in 78% of the new sources, while conservatives expressed more trust than distrust in 33% of the news sources, a stark difference. Conservatives strongly unified around a single outlet, *Fox News*, which was trusted by 88% of conservatives. Pew Research Center (2017c) also found that liberals are more likely to trust mainstream scientific outlets. There is, however, a need to take a deeper look into the role of political leaning, particularly in the wake of recent growth of fake news.

Frequency of Social Media Use

Finally, frequency of social media use is an important factor because the general assumption would be that those who are more familiar with social media outlets (high social media use) may be more adept at assessing online news media and may have higher trust. 67% of US adults get their news from social media, with 74% of Twitter users and 68% of Facebook users using the respective sites as news outlets (Pew Research Center, 2017a). An important aspect to consider is the distinction between online skills (e.g., how familiar people are with using social media platforms, how long they have been using the Internet) and the use of online news media (e.g., how often they use it). In a study on online news media and interactive news features (e.g., commenting), findings suggest that those with higher self-reported online skills used online news media more frequently than those who had lower skills (Opgenhaffen & d'Haenens, 2012). Interestingly, it was not gender or age that predicted the difference in the frequency of use of online news media, or even the length of time using online news media, but rather their own self-perceived online skill level (Opgenhaffen & d'Haenens, 2012). Another study found that those with high knowledge of social media also have higher trust in social media, but also found that having increased trust in social media does not seem to have any significant relationship with trust in any other news outlet (Heravi & Harrower, 2016). This supports previous work that found that time spent surfing news websites correlated with decreasing skepticism toward online news when controlling for demographic variables (e.g., age). Interestingly, another study from Israel found that those who were less experienced online became more skeptical as they were exposed to more online news sources (Tsfati, 2010). Again, there is a need for further research to explore this topic.

Research Questions

Based on this review of the literature, our main research question is: "Do demographic factors affect trust in online news sources?" Specifically, we ask whether the specific demographic factors of gender, age, educational attainment, political leaning, and frequency of social media use affect trust in fake news, mainstream media, and scientific journals as online science news sources.

METHODS

This paper reports findings from a crowdsourcing-based experimental study of the factors that influence trust in different online news sources. We previously published a preliminary analysis of the first subset of the overall data reported upon in this study; due to space constraints the study design is discussed briefly here, but it is explained in more detail in our prior article (Verma et al., 2017). It is important to note that, in addition to reporting on a larger sample, this paper reports a different facet of the analysis: whereas the previous paper explored clicking behavior and human values, this paper details previously unreported data and analysis about demographic factors.

We approached the design of the study instrument with the goal to approximate the social media-based information environment as closely as possible. We packaged the study as a Human Intelligence Task HIT to be completed by workers on Amazon's Mechanical Turk (MTurk) platform. Our choice of MTurk was informed by a body of research that indicates that MTurk offers a favorable alternative over other commonly used samples such as college student subject pools and generic Internet-based surveys in terms of accuracy of results, as well as diversity of demographic factors (e.g., Behrend, Sharek, Meade, & Wiebe, 2011; Hauser & Schwarz, 2016; Paolacci & Chandler, 2014). The demographic diversity offered by MTurk was a primary consideration for our study. MTurk has also previously been used to measure online trust (Golbeck & Fleischmann, 2010).

Data Collection

We collected data in two phases separated by a period of approximately eight weeks. In the first phase, we collected data using 100 HITs (that dataset was reported in Verma et al., 2017), and used an additional 150 HITs in the second phase for a total of 250 HITs. Within and across both phases, we verified the responses to ensure that none of the workers submitted more than one HIT.

In this paper, we report on the relationship between trust judgments of participants and different hyperlink conditions in relation to the answers to a survey asking about demographic factors. Each HIT contained a trust measurement instrument designed to visually approximate a Twitter user timeline. Each timeline was a sequence of 10 posts, and for each post we asked the participant to indicate on a five-point scale the degree to which they trusted it. This trust measurement scale ranged from "Trust Completely" to "Do Not Trust At All" (intermediate values not labeled) and numerically translated to trust scores ranging from 2 to -2, respectively.

Each post in a timeline consisted of one scientific claim, and one of five hyperlink conditions: the control condition (no hyperlink), a hyperlink to an open-access scientific journal article which the scientific claim was based on, a hidden hyperlink that redirected to the same scientific journal article (Google, n.d.), a hyperlink to a mainstream media site (Flaxman, Goel, & Rao, 2016; Silverman, 2016), and a hyperlink to a fake news site (Shao, Ciampaglia, Flammini, & Menczer, 2016). For more details about the choice of scientific claims and news sources, and our operationalization of fake news, please see Verma et al. (2017). The five conditions mentioned above formed the five levels of a factor we refer to as 'post type' in the rest of this paper. We assembled a corpus of 10 scientific claims for this purpose by applying the following inclusion criteria: each claim had to be published in a peer-reviewed scientific journal; the corresponding scientific journal article had to be linked-to by at least one fake news article and one mainstream media article; and each article had to be open-access to allow participants to read the article directly. We used the same set of 10 scientific claims for all participants, but randomly paired each claim with one of the five hyperlink conditions: No Hyperlink (NH), Fake News (FN), Mainstream Media (MM), Scientific Journal (SJ), or Hidden Hyperlink (HH). Overall, the timeline in each HIT consisted of 10 posts, with two distinct posts per post type.

We also asked participants to complete a survey instrument in which we asked them to provide demographic information such as their gender, age, educational attainment, political leaning, and how frequently, if at all, they used social media. For gender identity, we asked participants to select from "female," "male," and "other" (for the last option we asked participants to describe their gender identity in a text input field.) We asked participants to enter their age in years in a text field. We asked participants to select from one of five levels to indicate their highest level of educational attainment: "Less Than High School," "High School," "Some College," "College Graduate," and "Graduate Degree." We asked each participant to indicate their political leaning on a five-point scale ranging from Conservative to Liberal (intermediate values not labeled). Finally, we asked each participant to indicate how frequently they used social media on a six-point scale: "Do Not Use," "Less Than Once a Week," "Once a Week," "Multiple Times a Week," "Once a Day," and "Multiple Times a Day."

Data Clean-up and Preparation

For the current analysis, we combined the data from both collection phases to obtain a total of 250 HITs. We had to discard 31 responses from the first phase, and 14 responses from the second phase because of incorrect answers to the validation question, inconsistent answers to repeated questions in the three-part questionnaire, and due to non-completion of HITs. As a result, we had 205 valid responses to conduct our analyses.

To facilitate a simplified analysis of demographic factors and to ensure comparable group sizes within the different demographic factors, we redefined the number of categories for each demographic factor. For gender, only one participant reported their gender as "other"; therefore, to carry out reliable statistical analysis for the effects of gender, we considered data from only the 88 female and 116 male participants. We partitioned age into three categories: 18-29 years (n = 74), 30-39 years (n = 77), and 40 years or older (n = 54). For educational attainment, we partitioned the data into two categories instead of the original five: Less than College (n = 106), and College or Higher (n = 99) based on which out of the original five options participants had chosen. For political leaning, we reduced the number of nominal categories by collapsing the original data into moderates (those who selected the middle option in the five-point scale), conservatives (those who selected either of the two options on the conservative end of the scale), and liberals (those who selected the two options on the liberal end of the scale). With this reduction of levels, we had a total of 100 liberal, 54 moderate, and 51 conservative-leaning participants. For frequency of social media use, we excluded data for the four participants who chose the "Do Not Use" option. We then collapsed the five remaining original categories into two: 87 light users (those who responded with either of "Less Than Once a Week", "Once a Week", "Multiple Times a Week", or "Once a Day") and 114 heavy users ("Multiple Times a Day").

Data Analysis

We used the R programming language and the 'stats' (R Core Team, 2018), and 'ggplot2' (Wickham, 2009) packages for the statistical analyses and plots, respectively. To conduct within-subjects analysis, we needed to represent the trust ratings for each pair of posts for a post type by a single measure. To assess the aptness of using the mean of the trust ratings as a reliable single measure for each such pair we used the Wilcoxon Signed Rank (WSR) test (non-parametric equivalent of the paired *t*-test) to check if the two trust ratings for a post type came from the same distribution. We found no evidence to reject the null hypothesis—both sets of ratings belonging to the same distribution—for any of the five pairs of trust ratings. Therefore, it is reasonable to represent the two ratings per type by their mean. As a consequence of adopting the mean as an approximate single measure, and in cognizance of the fact that our original trust scale was ordinal, we chose to use only conservative, nonparametric statistical methods for our analysis.

For each demographic factor, we looked at the data from both within-subjects and between-subjects perspectives. We used the Friedman test (non-parametric equivalent of repeated measures ANOVA) to conduct a within-subjects comparison of participants' responses (trust ratings) to the different conditions (the five different post types). For demographic factors, we made subsets of the data—one for each factor level—and ran the Friedman test for each subset to investigate if participants displayed a difference in trust behavior across post types. Every significant Friedman test was followed up with WSR tests to compare trust ratings between pairs of post types using the Holm correction to control the family-wise error rate (to account for the use of multiple correlation tests).

To compare trust ratings for a given post type across the levels of a demographic factor, we utilized the Kruskal-Wallis H (KWH) test (non-parametric equivalent of ANOVA). We followed up significant KWH tests with Mann-Whitney U (MWU) tests (non-parametric equivalent of unpaired *t*-tests) with Holm correction to control the family-wise error rate (to once again account for the use of multiple correlation tests) to compare one factor level to another. In order to determine the direction of a significant difference in trust ratings between any two post types for a factor level, we calculated differences in trust ratings for all post types and visualized them using boxplots.

RESULTS

In this section, we describe multiple boxplots per demographic factor to illustrate our findings. Plot "a" in each figure looks at the distribution of trust ratings across the levels of a demographic factor for each post type; pairs with significant MWU p-values are annotated with levels of significance. Plot "b" in each figure visualizes the distribution of trust ratings across post types separately for each level of a demographic factor. Finally, plot "c" in each figure looks at the distribution of differences in trust ratings between each of the 10 pairs of post types for each level of the demographic factor; significant results from pairwise WSR tests are coded in grayscale.

Gender

As illustrated in Figure 1a, MWU tests did not reveal significant differences between females and males in trust in any of the five post types. To look within the results from both of these demographic categories, we used Friedman tests within the female ($n = 88$), and male ($n = 116$) categories, which revealed significant ($p < 0.001$) differences for both (Figure 1b).

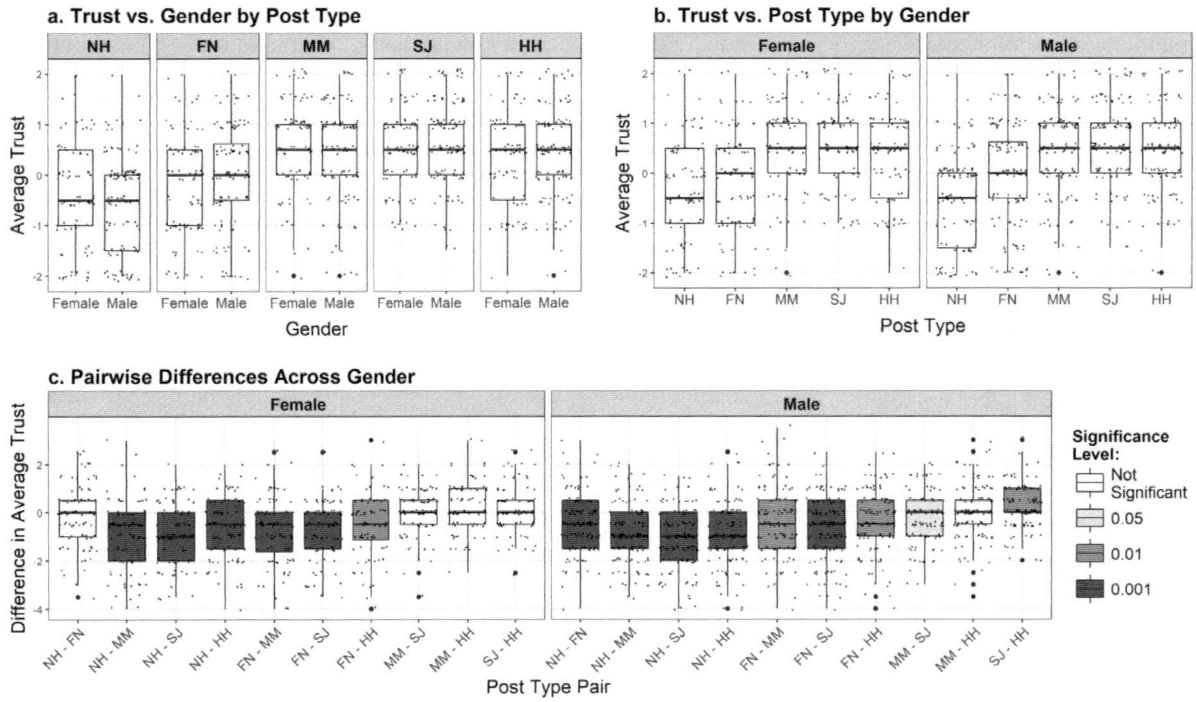

Figure 1. Trust and Gender (**: $p < 0.01$; *: $p < 0.05$)

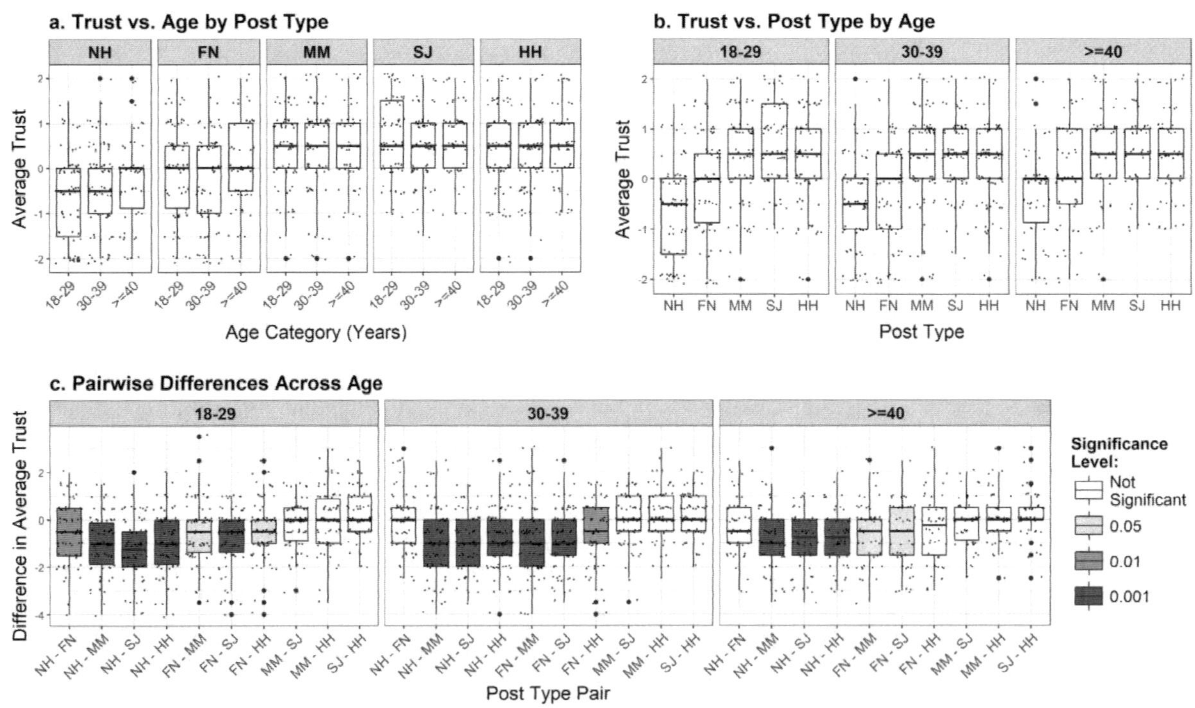

Figure 2. Trust and Age (**: $p < 0.01$; *: $p < 0.05$)

As illustrated in Figure 1c, most of the post-hoc WSR tests (Figure 1c) produced similar results for females and males. However, differences included males giving significantly ($p < 0.001$) lower trust ratings to fake news posts in comparison to no hyperlink posts, significantly ($p < 0.01$) higher trust ratings to scientific journals in comparison to hidden hyperlink posts, and significantly ($p < 0.05$) higher trust in scientific journals than in mainstream media; for females we did not detect statistically significant differences between these respective post types.

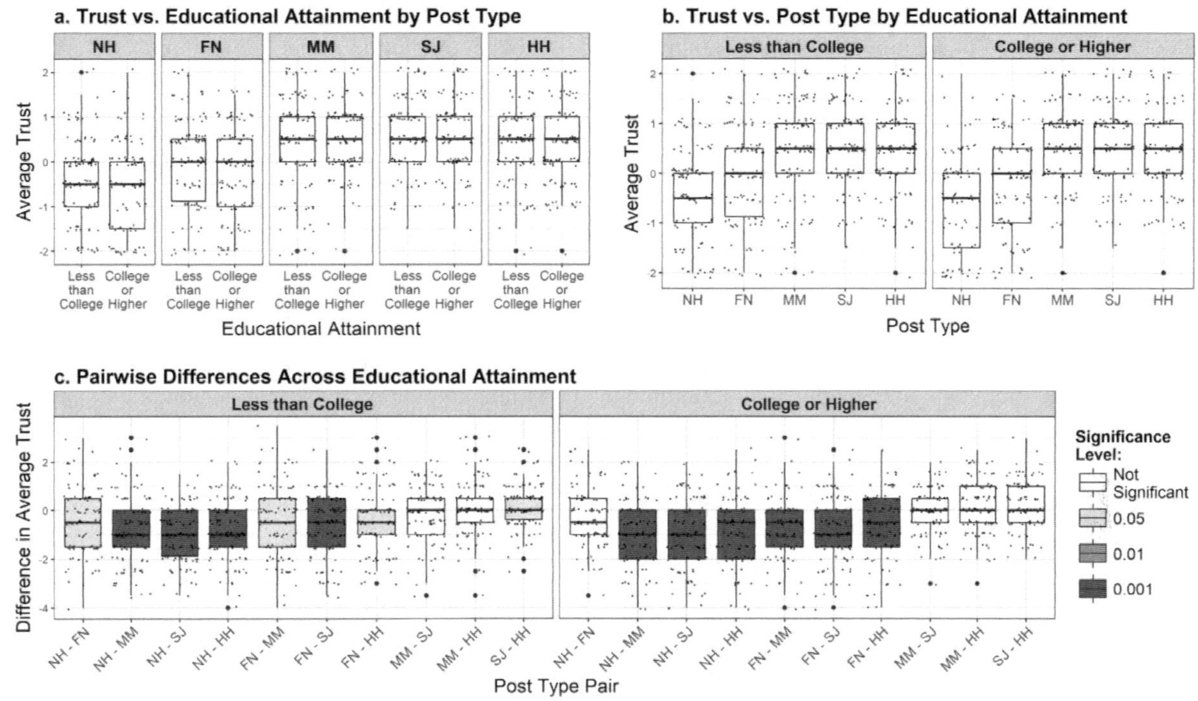

Figure 3. Trust and Educational Attainment (**: p < 0.01; *: p < 0.05)

Age

The three categories of the age variable were: 18-29 years ($n = 74$), 30-39 years ($n = 77$), and 40 years or older ($n = 54$). None of the five KWH tests indicated a significant difference within a post type and across the three age categories (Figure 2a). However, as suggested by Figure 2b, all three Friedman tests—one for each age category—indicated significantly ($p < 0.001$) different trust distributions for the five post types. Post-hoc pairwise WSR tests revealed that the most number of highly significant ($p < 0.001$) pairwise differences were concentrated in the 30-39 years category (Figure 2c). The 18-29 years category was the only one that displayed a significantly ($p < 0.01$) lower trust in no hyperlink posts in comparison to fake news posts.

Educational Attainment

We partitioned educational attainment into two categories: Less than College ($n = 106$), and College or Higher ($n = 99$). MWU tests did not reveal any significant differences between the two educational attainment levels for any post type (Figure 3a). However, Friedman tests for both levels were highly significant ($p < 0.001$), as is evident based on Figure 3b. Post-hoc pairwise WSRs revealed some significant differences in trust distributions for the different post types for each educational attainment category (Figure 3c). Less than College had significantly ($p < 0.05$) lower trust in no hyperlinks as compared to fake news, and significantly ($p < 0.05$) higher trust in scientific journals relative to hidden hyperlinks, while College or Higher did not evidence these significantly different relationships.

Political Leaning

We had a total of 100 liberal, 54 moderate, and 51 conservative participants. As the boxplots in Figure 4a show, KWH tests revealed that there were significant differences between the trust distributions of the three political leanings for fake news, mainstream media, and scientific journal post types. Post-hoc pairwise MWU tests revealed that conservatives trusted fake news significantly ($p < 0.05$) more than moderates, liberals trusted mainstream media significantly ($p < 0.05$) more than moderates, and liberals trusted scientific journals significantly more than moderates ($p < 0.05$) and conservatives ($p < 0.01$).

Friedman tests within each level of political leaning revealed highly significant ($p < 0.001$) differences across the five post types. As shown in Figure 4b, the differences in trust distributions are especially pronounced for liberals and moderates. Post-hoc pairwise WSR tests revealed pairs with significantly different trust distributions for each political leaning. As evident in the trust difference boxplots in Figure 4c, of the 10 different comparisons among the 5 post types, we found 8 significant differences for liberals, 6 for moderates, and 4 for conservatives. Importantly, liberals and moderates rated fake news as significantly less trustworthy than mainstream media, scientific journals, and hidden hyperlinks (for liberals, all three were at $p < 0.001$); contrastingly, for conservatives, none of these differences were significant. Thus, while liberals and moderates

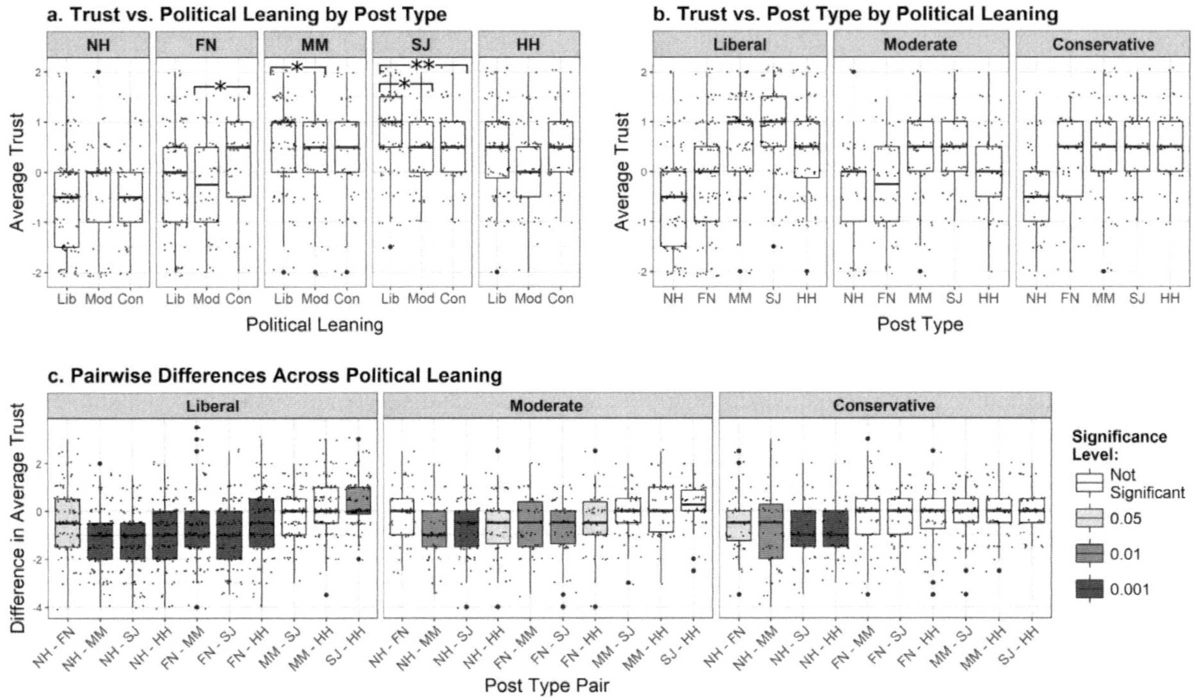

Figure 4. Trust and Political Leaning (**: $p < 0.01$; *: $p < 0.05$)

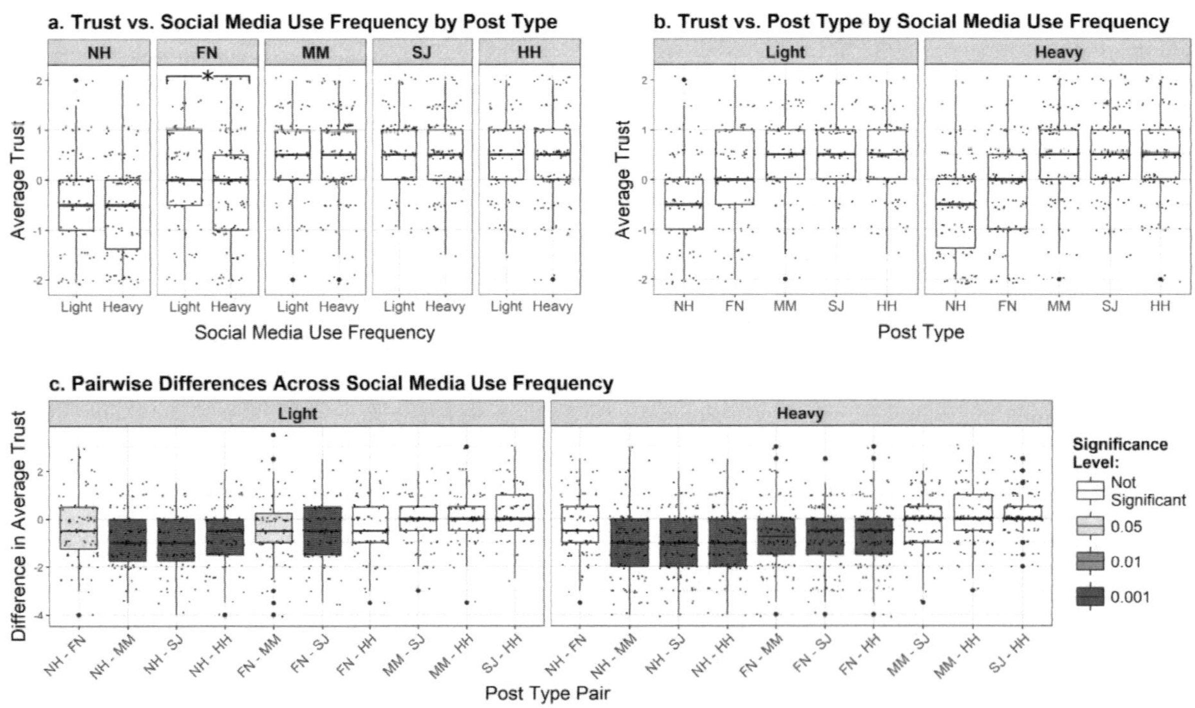

Figure 5. Trust and Social Media Use Frequency (: $p < 0.01$; *: $p < 0.05$)**

differentiated between hyperlinks to fake news and other hyperlinks, conservatives placed the same trust in fake news hyperlinks as other hyperlinks.

Frequency of Social Media Use

Based on self-reported frequency of social media use, we separated the participants into two categories: light users ($n = 87$) and heavy users ($n = 114$). MWU tests revealed that heavy users of social media platforms gave significantly ($p < 0.05$) lower trust ratings to fake news posts than light users (Figure 5a). Friedman tests for both categories revealed highly significant ($p < 0.001$) differences across post types (Figure 5b). We followed those results up with pairwise WSRs for both categories (Figure 5c) and found three notable differences between the results for the two categories: light social media users placed more trust in fake news than in no hyperlinks ($p < 0.05$), while heavy social media users placed more trust in hidden hyperlinks than in fake news ($p < 0.001$).

DISCUSSION

Based on these results, it is evident that political leaning and frequency of social media use are both significantly correlated with different levels of trust in different types of online news sources. Specifically, conservatives placed more trust in fake news than moderates; this finding is very interesting in contrast with the Gallup/Knight Foundation Survey, which found that conservatives perceive fake news as a greater threat than do moderates or liberals. However, as the authors of that report note, there are various definitions of fake news, and conservatives are more likely to associate mainstream media as representing fake news (Gallup, 2018), a message that is frequently amplified by President Trump from his podium and his Twitter account. Similarly, liberals place significantly more trust in mainstream media than moderates, reinforcing the degree to which perceptions of media bias have turned off moderates. It is interesting to note that while many of the mainstream media outlets selected are frequently accused of exhibiting a liberal bias, such as *CNN* and *The Washington Post*, we also included articles from *Fox News*, which is typically claimed to hold a conservative bias. Perhaps, in our current politically polarized environment, it is difficult for moderates to trust any media outlets, whether mainstream media or fake news such as *InfoWars* or *Natural News*.

Further, liberals expressed significantly more trust in scientific journals than conservatives or moderates. This finding is consistent with research by the Pew Research Center (2017c), which found that liberals tend to place more trust in science magazines than moderates and conservatives and were also less likely to assert that scientists overstate their research findings' implications. This finding is also consistent with a broader trend toward distrust in various forms of expertise, particularly among conservatives (Baumgaertner, Carlisle, & Justwan, 2018). Thus, this paper helps to reinforce the finding that trust is eroding in experts, particularly among conservatives but also among moderates (or, from another perspective, is perhaps remaining irrationally high among liberals). Interestingly, one way to interpret this finding is the postmodern chickens coming home to roost, as the social constructivist view of science that was initiated by primarily liberal social scientists in fields such as science and technology studies have increasingly found their rhetoric co-opted by conservative politicians (Fuller, 2017).

For frequency of social media use, the lower trust in fake news among heavy social media users corresponds with findings in the literature that greater use of social media causes individuals to be more critical consumers of online news (Tsfati, 2010). Interestingly, this means that those who are most exposed to fake news online are arguably the least susceptible to it, at least with major known fake news sites such as *Natural News* and (perhaps particularly, given its immense notoriety) *InfoWars*. In this sense, frequent use of social media may help one to make informed judgments about known fake news websites. However, it would be interesting to see if this trend was consistent with less well known fake news sites. If it is the name recognition that triggers the lower degree of trust, then this ability to discern fake news may exhibit similar limitations to internet filters that rely on blacklisting; since it is generated from experience, it may be more effective when dealing with established websites than with newer websites. However, future research including examples of both would be necessary to tease out this difference.

Limitations and Future Research Directions

Our study does have limitations that could be addressed through future research. First, the scope is limited to information originating in scientific journals, and more specifically, in open-access journals, and in turn picked up and reported in both mainstream media and fake news outlets. We made every effort to randomize the experimental design to ensure that participants saw the different claims under different conditions, but given the size of our sample, it is possible that seeing particular treatments of particular information within particular venues might present confounds. The ideal scenario would be if there were, for example, 10 scientific claims that were passed through the same scientific journal, the same fake news site, and the same mainstream media site (e.g., *PLoS ONE*, *InfoWars*, and *The LA Times*, respectively), to allow for better control of the venue. Similarly, it would also be helpful if the same scientific finding was spread through many different fake news and mainstream media sites, as well as science magazines, to allow for better control of the impact of the finding itself. Such an approach could be more feasible with constructed pages, but the tradeoff would be losing the naturalistic approach of this study, and the authenticity of the URLs in question (and indeed, would create an ethical paradox in terms of, for example, creating fake news to study trust in fake news).

Second, by asking participants to indicate their political leaning, we relied on their conception of political leaning. While their self-identification could be taken as the ground truth, their construal of political leaning could be confounded. As Everett (2013) points out, it is possible for an individual to measure on opposite ends of *social* conservatism and *economic* conservatism scales. Henningham (1996) argues that characteristics—such as values and acceptable behavior—of communities may evolve with time to such an extent as to render scales measuring social norms and attitudes as products of their "day and age" (Henningham, 1996). While there are no unanimously accepted scales to measure political and ideological attitudes, recently some scales such as the 12-item Social and Economic Conservatism Scale (Everett, 2013) have been proposed, and future studies could adopt such existing instruments, or develop new ones, to move away from relying on pure self-report data.

Third, based on the design of our study, we were unable to control clicking and browsing behavior, or to observe browsing. While we did measure and analyze the clicking behavior (Verma et al., 2017), this is a weak proxy for browsing behavior, as clicking on a link does not guarantee actual reading of the linked page. This shortcoming is particularly problematic for the hidden hyperlink condition of this study, although it is important to note that it was intended more for the study of clicking behavior than for how trust is influenced by demographic features. One approach would be to conduct a similar study within a controlled environment, such as a usability lab. In a usability lab, it would be possible to employ technology such as eye tracking to observe how participants interact with the web pages. Eye tracking data such as fixations, saccades, and scanpaths could help to determine whether there is a relationship between participants' trust judgments and cognitive activity, and the nature of that relationship if it exists. In such a setting, it would also be possible to conduct a more thorough interview following the study.

CONCLUSION

This study found that conservatives place higher trust in fake news than moderates ($p < 0.05$), liberals place higher trust in mainstream media than moderates ($p < 0.05$), liberals place higher trust in scientific journals than conservatives ($p < 0.01$) and moderates ($p < 0.05$), and less frequent social media users place higher trust in fake news than more frequent social media users ($p < 0.05$). These results offer evidence that political leaning and frequency of social media use both influence trust in fake news online, while political leaning also influences trust in mainstream media and scientific journals. These findings shed new light on the important issue of trust in news sources, illustrating the importance of considering political leaning and frequency of social media use in assessing trust in different news sources online. These results further underscore the current degree of polarization present in the American public's perceptions of different media outlets. In addition, these findings suggest that gender, age, and educational attainment are less critical in influencing how individuals trust news sources online. They also illustrate that frequent social media users, who might be most exposed to fake news, may be the least susceptible to trusting and believing it. Based on these findings, we conclude that there is a particular need for educating less frequent social media users about the potential dangers of fake news, and that there is also currently a gap in finding a common news outlet that is trusted by conservatives, moderates, and liberals; unavoidably, it appears that all information is now filtered through our political lens, creating a challenge for forming and maintaining a shared collection of trusted information that brings American society together rather than pulling it apart.

ACKNOWLEDGMENTS

The authors wish to acknowledge funding from a Special Research Grant from the Office of the Vice President for Research of the University of Texas at Austin, the anonymous crowdworkers on MTurk who participated in this study, and Sally Ragsdale of the Department of Statistics and Data Sciences at the University of Texas at Austin for providing statistical consultation to the authors.

REFERENCES

Baumgaertner, B., Carlisle, J. E., & Justwan, F. (2018). The influence of political ideology and trust on willingness to vaccinate. *PLoS ONE, 13*(1), e0191728. https://doi.org/10.1371/journal.pone.0191728

Behrend, T. S., Sharek, D. J., Meade, A. W., & Wiebe, E. N. (2011). The viability of crowdsourcing for survey research. *Behavior Research Methods*, 43, 800-813. https://doi.org/10.3758/s13428-011-0081-0

Everett, J. A. C. (2013). The 12 item social and economic conservatism scale (SECS). *PLoS ONE, 8*(12), e82131. https://doi.org/10.1371/journal.pone.0082131

Flaxman, S., Goel, S., & Rao, J. M. (2016). Filter bubbles, echo chambers, and online news consumption. *Public Opinion Quarterly, 80*(S1), 298–320. https://doi.org/10.1093/poq/nfw006

Fuller, S. (2017). Brexit as the unlikely leading edge of the anti-expert revolution. *European Management Journal, 35*, 575-580. https://doi.org/10.1016/j.emj.2017.09.002

Gallup. (2018). *American views: Trust, media, and democracy*. Retrieved April 3, 2018, from https://knightfoundation.org/reports/american-views-trust-media-and-democracy

Golbeck, J. & Fleischmann, K. R. (2010). Trust in social Q&A: The impact of text and photo cues of expertise. *Proceedings of the American Society for Information Science and Technology*, *47*(1), 1-10. https://doi.org/10.1002/meet.14504701048

Google. (n.d.). Google URL shortener. Retrieved April 23, 2017, from https://goo.gl/

Hauser, D. J., & Schwarz, N. (2016). Attentive Turkers: MTurk participants perform better on online attention checks than do subject pool participants. *Behavior Research Methods*, *48*(1), 400-407. https://doi.org/10.3758/s13428-015-0578-z

Henningham, J. P. (1996). A 12-item scale of social conservatism. *Personality and Individual Differences*, *20*(4), 517–519. https://doi.org/10.1016/0191-8869(95)00192-1

Heravi, B. R., & Harrower, N. (2016). Twitter journalism in Ireland: sourcing and trust in the age of social media. *Information, Communication & Society*, *19*(9), 1194–1213. https://doi.org/10.1080/1369118X.2016.1187649

Hoelig, S. (2016). Social participation in online news usage in Europe and its underlying causes: Individual versus structural factors. *European Journal of Communication*, *31*(4), 393–410. https://doi.org/10.1177/0267323116647237

Huang, J., Shi, S., Chen, Y., & Chow, W. S. (2016). How do students trust Wikipedia? An examination across genders. *Information Technology & People*, *29*(4), 750–773. https://doi.org/10.1108/ITP-12-2014-0267

Kelton, K., Fleischmann, K. R., & Wallace, W. A. (2008). Trust in digital information. *Journal of the American Society for Information Science and Technology*, *59*(3), 363-374. https://doi.org/10.1002/asi.20722

Liébana-Cabanillas, F. J., Sánchez-Fernández, J., & Muñoz-Leiva, F. (2014). Role of gender on acceptance of mobile payment. *Industrial Management & Data Systems*, *114*(2), 220–240. https://doi.org/10.1108/IMDS-03-2013-0137

Malik, A., Hiekkanen, K., & Nieminen, M. (2016). Privacy and trust in Facebook photo sharing: age and gender differences. *Program*, *50*(4), 462–480. https://doi.org/10.1108/PROG-02-2016-0012

Opgenhaffen, M., & d'Haenens, L. (2012). Heterogeneity within homogeneity: Impact of online skills on the use of online news media and interactive news features. *Communications*, *37*(3), 108–20. https://doi.org/10.1515/commun-2012-0016

Paolacci, G., & Chandler, J. (2014). Inside the Turk: Understanding Mechanical Turk as a participant pool. *Current Directions in Psychological Science*, *23*, 184-188. https://doi.org/10.1177/0963721414531598

Pew Research Center. (2014). *Political polarization and media habits*. Retrieved April 4, 2018 from: https://assets.pewresearch.org/wp-content/uploads/sites/13/2014/10/Political-Polarization-and-Media-Habits-FINAL-REPORT-7-27-15.pdf

Pew Research Center. (2017a). *News use across social media platforms 2017*. Retrieved March 28, 2018 from: https://assets.pewresearch.org/wp-content/uploads/sites/13/2017/09/13163032/PJ_17.08.23_socialMediaUpdate_FINAL.pdf

Pew Research Center. (2017b). *Tech adoption climbs among older adults*. Retrieved March 28, 2018 from: https://assets.pewresearch.org/wp-content/uploads/sites/14/2017/05/16170850/PI_2017.05.17_Older-Americans-Tech_FINAL.pdf

Pew Research Center. (2017c). *Science news and information today*. Retrieved April 3, 2018 from: https://assets.pewresearch.org/wp-content/uploads/sites/13/2017/09/14122431/PJ_2017.09.20_Science-and-News_FINAL.pdf

R Core Team (2018). *R: A language and environment for statistical computing*. R Foundation for Statistical Computing, Vienna, Austria. URL https://www.R-project.org/

Shao, C., Ciampaglia, G. L., Flammini, A., & Menczer, F. (2016). Hoaxy: A platform for tracking online misinformation. In *Proceedings of the 25th International Conference Companion on World Wide Web* (pp. 745–750). Republic and Canton of Geneva, Switzerland: International World Wide Web Conferences Steering Committee. https://doi.org/10.1145/2872518.2890098

Towner, T., & Munoz, C. L. (2016). Boomers versus millennials: Online media influence on media performance and candidate evaluations. *Social Sciences*, *5*(4), 56–20. https://doi.org/10.3390/socsci5040056

Tsfati, Y. (2010). Online news exposure and trust in the mainstream media: Exploring possible associations. *American Behavioral Scientist*, *54*(1), 22–42. https://doi.org/10.1177/0002764210376309

Verma, N., Fleischmann, K. R., & Koltai, K. S. (2017). Human values and trust in scientific journals, the mainstream media and fake news. *Proceedings of the Association for Information Science and Technology*, *54*(1), 426–435. https://doi.org/10.1002/pra2.2017.14505401046

Wickham, H. (2009). *ggplot2: Elegant graphics for data analysis*. New York: Springer-Verlag.

Understanding Multilingual Web Users' Code-Switching Behaviors in Online Searching

Jieyu Wang
University of Maryland, Baltimore County, U.S.A.
wajieyu1@umbc.edu

Omar Ka
University of Maryland, Baltimore County, U.S.A.
ka@umbc.edu

Anita Komlodi
University of Maryland, Baltimore County, U.S.A.
komlodi@umbc.edu

ABSTRACT

The availability of information in different languages on the Internet allows multilingual web users to search in multiple languages for the same search task. When searchers can search in multiple languages, they may combine these languages in various ways during searching. Few studies have examined multilingual web users' language switching behaviors in two or more languages online, specifically their code-switching search patterns. This research investigates native Chinese web users' code-switching (Chinese-English) search patterns in their information seeking process through controlled lab experiments and interviews. Results reveal three general code-switching search models for multilingual web users for their search tasks. Findings highlight factors and reasons for multilingual web users' situational and metaphorical code-switching during their information search on the Web. We find that multilingual web users switch code situationally due to pragmatic reasons such as information sufficiency, language proficiency, information verification, context, and translation. Metaphorical code-switching behaviors were motivated by the searchers' language image, cultural perspective, website credibility, sense of belonging, and psychological acceptance. We also investigate these users' code-switching search strategies. The study aims to provide design implications for website design concerning multilingual web users' code-switching search strategies, habits, and needs.

KEYWORDS

Information seeking behaviors, user search models, search strategies, design implications, multilingual users, code-switching.

INTRODUCTION

A large number of the potential users of the Internet are multi-lingual. Overall, only 40% of the world population is monolingual, whereas 60% of the world population is bilingual, trilingual or multilingual (Ilanguages Organization, 2016). A European Commission survey suggested that 56% of the respondents speak two languages in Europe (Ilanguages Organization, 2016). According to the U.S. Census Bureau, 18% of the population is bilingual or multilingual in the United States (U.S. Census Bureau, 2013). In this study we focused on Chinese native searchers who search in English. Though it is hard to investigate how many non-native English web users use English websites (L2 users), it was estimated there were over 200 million Chinese users who use English on the Internet (Kachru, 2005).

Code-switching refers to the switching of languages during conversation. It was defined as "an individual's use of two or more language varieties in the same speech event or exchange" (Woolard, 2004, pp73). Code-switching phenomena have been studied by social scientists for decades. Researchers have defined and analyzed code-switching in different social contexts (Auer, 1998; Gumperz, 1982; Merriam, 2009; Woolard, 2004). Discourse-related code-switching between one's native language and second/foreign languages as one dominant type of code-switching has been extensively studied in sociolinguistics (Maschler, 1998; Serra, 1998; Wei, 1998). However, little research has been done to study how users with multilingual backgrounds search for information by code-switching between their native languages and second/foreign languages in order to get satisfying results.

In this study we investigate native Chinese speaker web users' code-switching search behaviors between their native Chinese language and their English foreign language when they search online. This work explores these multilingual web users' code-switching search patterns and search strategies when they search for information. The research questions this research focused on are:

1) Why do bi-lingual searchers switch languages while searching? What types of code-switching epi
2) How do bilingual searchers combine code-switching strategies in online searching?

RELATED WORK

Our research focuses on multilingual web users' code-switching search patterns when they seek information online. It aims to find out the factors that impact multilingual web users' situational code-switching and metaphorical code-switching when they search for information on the web to satisfy their search needs.

Code-Switching in Socio-Linguistics

Code-switching is one of the most important concepts in the social-linguistic field. "Code-switching can be defined as an individual's use of two or more language varieties in the same speech event or exchange" (Woolard, 2004). Blom and Gumperz (1972) introduced the definition of situational switching and metaphorical switching. Situational code-switching happens when there are clear changes in the situation or context due to pragmatic reasons, for example, physical environment or the group of conversation participants (Blom & Gumperz,1972). For instance, one group of Italian tourists travelling in the United States would speak Italian among themselves, but would switch to English when they enter a store.

Metaphorical code-switching's "message elements are tied by syntactic and semantic relations equivalent to those that join passages in a single language, the relationship of language usage to social context is much more complex" (Gumperz, 1982, pp 61). The switch of languages is a metaphor for language associations, attitudes, feelings, and sometimes due to psychological reasons. For example, family members talk in their native language during dinner time. They switch to a highly prestigious second language to talk about school and work topics (Gumperz & Hymes, 1986).

Code-Switching in Online Interactions

Only a few researchers have studied multilingual web users' code-switching behaviors online. For instance, Kötter (2003) has studied German-English code-switching phenomena in an online environment. He analyzed 29 language students' code-switching discourses which were presented on MOO, an online language learning website. These language students were from a German university and a North American university. The German students were learning English and the US students were learning German and they collaborated in online teams. The researcher analyzed electronic transcripts of eight meetings between the German and American teams and the students' questionnaire data. They found that learners on MOO requested more clarification, explanation and reformulation from their language partners than what the learners did in other face-to-face discourse studies. Results revealed different ways and reasons that these students switched languages. When they encountered difficult words in the language they were learning during their communication, the American students preferred their German partners' translation rather than their German partners paraphrasing in German. The German students preferred to request their American partners to paraphrase the difficult words or repeat the words.

Bilingual postings on social media can also be classified as code-switching (Lingel et al., 2014). Multilingual web users switched languages to display and better represent their identities and to limit their audience by languages. Code-switching, or using non-native languages on Facebook were even considered to be presumptuous because these actions showed that their non-native language proficiency was higher than others'.

Facebook users with multilingual backgrounds also switch codes by posting bilingual/multilingual posts and comments on the website (Wang & Joardar, 2015). Through observing 83 active Facebook users' status updates and interviewing 10 users with multi-lingual backgrounds, the researchers found that audience, locality and context were three important factors that impacted users' language selections. Even though Facebook offered translational functions for users' posts and comments, multilingual users still tried to use their native languages to limit their audience to family members and a circle of friends because Facebook could not offer the translation of certain languages. Locality was one important factor that affected their language selections. Non-native English users in their native countries tended to prefer to use their native languages other than English on Facebook. Non-native English users in native-English speaking countries were likely to use English more often than their native languages. Context also impacted users' language selections on Facebook. When the context of the posts or comments was in English, users tended to respond in English. If the context of the posts and comments was in languages other than English, they tended to use the languages other than English. Users with high language proficiency in English and their native languages frequently code-switched from their native language to English in their posts and comments on Facebook.

Factors That Impact Code-Switching Information Seeking Behaviors

Previous research, as cited in the section following, has examined code-switching in searching but it only identified that this behavior exists, no significant analysis of the types of code-switching actions and scenarios has been completed. Previous research did examine the factors that affected code-switching in search. Access to information on the Web, language proficiency, and cultural impacts were three of the most important factors that were identified.

Access to Web Information

Access to Web information impacts multilingual users' searching behaviors (Kralisch & Mandl, 2006). There were more websites available for better represented language groups than underrepresented language groups on the internet, thus speakers of underrepresented language groups searched in better represented languages. The non-native multilingual web users did not get as much benefit as the users from the better represented language groups. As the number of non-native English web users increased, the challenges of web languages, content, and search tools appeared. Factors such as content-creation, link-setting, and link-following behavior contributed to the under-representation of non-English languages on the web (Berendt & Kralisch, 2009). User satisfaction was not only related to users' cognitive searching process but also related to the availability of the alternative information in other languages that the website offered. This situation encourages multilingual web users switch codes from their underrepresented native languages to English when they cannot find enough information on non-English websites.

Moreover, non-native English web users had less access to a website if the information on the website was not offered in their native language (Kralisch & Berendt, 2005). Furthermore, the way that non-native speakers with high domain knowledge searched for information was similar to that of native speakers. But if non-native English users' domain knowledge was not sufficient, their search was language-sensitive. Therefore, multilingual web users' language proficiency and domain knowledge may influence their information seeking behaviors of code-switching.

Language Proficiency and Translation

Language skills also influence users' code-switching information seeking behaviors (Clough & Eleta, 2010). Users with language-related majors, such as social sciences, anthropology, politics and international relations, were more likely to search and switch multiple languages. Users whose majors were medicine, dentistry and biology rarely searched in languages other than their native languages. Language abilities had an impact on multilingual users' information seeking. Users with multilingual backgrounds were likely to benefit more than users with monolingual backgrounds during their cross-language code switching searching process. Furthermore, the functionality of cross-language information retrieval tools, for example, Google translation functionality, was helpful to users who searched in languages other than their native language.

Multilingual users preferred to view the translated version of web pages in their third languages while reading the original versions of web pages in their second languages (Marlow et al., 2008). When language unfamiliarity increased, the use of Google translation also increased. They also found that users were more confident about the results for easy queries rather than hard queries. They concluded that users' language skills impacted their multilingual search experience and effectiveness.

Cultural Impact

Language tools and domain knowledge impact multilingual web users' code-switching search behaviors. Meanwhile, cultural elements also perform a role in multilingual users' information searching behaviors, Kralisch and Mandl (2006) did a lab-experiment to explore how factors such as culture, language, and medical knowledge influence web users' information categorization and search options. In this 2x2 study British and Malaysian groups were native speakers of the website's language. Russian and German groups were other language speakers. They found that due to the low level of the participants' medical knowledge, all groups preferred visual cues rather than verbal cues. Furthermore, they concluded that culture influences the users' information categorization, their attitudes, and their searching behavior the most. They found that in the card sorting activity the Malaysian and British groups' behaviors were close to each other, and the behaviors of the Russian and the German group were similar. Language mainly affected the users' opinions about the ease of use and usefulness of the website.

Even though the research summarized above has studied users' language selection behaviors, few studies have been done to explore multilingual web users' code-switching search patterns when they seek information online. We attempt to explain how multilingual users interact with different languages in order to satisfy their information needs.

METHODS

Participants

Our controlled lab study aimed at examining the code-switching search patterns of multilingual web users when they seek information online. We focused on studying the language switching strategies of multilingual web users when they searched for information for the same search task. The study specifically investigated the factors that impacted multilingual web users' language switching when they seek information on the Internet.

To address the research goal above, native Chinese Internet users who spoke English as a second or foreign language were selected to participate in the study. Fifteen international student participants were recruited by phone and email messages in the US. This group of participants represent a large proportion of internet users in the world. Chinese was the second popular internet language that used by 704.5 million users online in 2016, while the most popular language was English, whose web users were 872.9 million (Internet Live Stats, 2016). In terms of countries, China had 641.6 million internet users in 2016, which ranked No. 1 in the world (Internet Live Stats, 2016).

Questionnaires were used to collect participants' demographic and background information. Fifteen participants took part in the study, ranging from 19 to 30 years old with a mean age of 25. Five of them were female and 10 of them were male. Most of the participants' English language proficiency ranged from intermediate to advanced according to their scores of TOFEL (80 - 105), IELTS (6 - 7), or CET 4 - 6. All the participants obtained more than six years of computer experiences. Meanwhile, the participants were chosen from a variety of disciplines, such computer science, international business, engineering, English, information systems and human computer interaction. Most of the participants reported they switch languages daily or several times each week when they seek information online.

Procedures

In this study controlled-lab experiments were carried out in order to investigate multilingual web users' language switching patterns when they seek information online. The IRB of this study has been approved. Before the experiments have been carried out, a pilot study has been run in order to test the design of the study. In the experiments three tasks were given to the participants. These three tasks were chosen from our previous study's code-switching episodes (Wang & Komlodi, 2016; Wang & Komlodi, 2018). The tasks were based on search topics where the most code-switching episodes happened. The three tasks asked the participants to explore comments about the recent US election debate, a travel plan to Fiji, and a medical problem in the eyes. While the participants were asked to search for these specific topics, code-switching was not required of the participants. However, the task requirements included information cues for the participants to switch languages when they searched for information. For example, in the travel task the participants were required to leave from the U.S. to Fiji, which was an information cue for them to use English. Meanwhile, because few participants had been to Fiji, they may like to use their native language-Chinese in their exploratory searches. These contexts in the tasks enabled the participants to switch languages due to their information needs during their searches.

Data in this study were collected from observation, screen video analysis, and interviews. The investigator observed how the participants performed the tasks and how they switched languages during the process. Notes were taken during the observation. The participants' search process was also screen-captured and analyzed by the investigator. After the participants completed their tasks, the investigator conducted follow-up interviews by showing the participants the recorded videos about their searches. The interview questions focused on the code-switching patterns during their searches. The interviews explored in which context the participants switched to the other language due to what reason and what information needs and factors impacted their code-switching behaviors.

The interviews were audio-recorded, transcribed, and analyzed using qualitative data analysis methods. They were first coded to identify preliminary concepts of interest. Following this step, axial coding was used to identify and group code-switching episode characteristics. The method of constant comparison was used as new transcripts were added and the more recently emerging concepts and categories were compared to those previously identified ones (Corbin & Strauss, 2008; Merriam, 2009).

RESULTS

The analysis of the data resulted in a description of why and how bi-lingual searchers switched languages. First we will describe the types of code-switching episodes, building on the situational and metaphorical code-switching categories from socio-linguistics. Next, we will describe how these different types of code-switching techniques were combined in actual searching by our participants.

Users' Situational and Metaphorical Code-Switching

Code-switching has been identified as situational code-switching and metaphorical code-switching in the field of socio-linguistics. While these categories were developed based on the analysis of language use in discourse, we found this framework useful as a starting point for our analysis of code-switching episodes in searching. In this study we categorized multilingual web users' code-switching behaviors in searching into situational ones and metaphorical ones due to different functions of code-switching. Different factors that impacted users' code-switching behaviors were investigated.

We found 109 instances of code-switching through the observation notes and screen videos of the 15 participants. During the interviews participants explained how these switchings happened and what the reasons were for switching languages in each episode. Eighty-one situational code-switching episodes and 28 metaphorical code-switching episodes were identified. The situational code-switching episodes appeared due to pragmatic reasons related to information sufficiency, language proficiency, information verification, context, and translation. Metaphorical code-switching behaviors happened due to the reasons of language image, cultural perspective, website credibility, sense of belonging, and psychological acceptance.

Situational Code-Switching

Information sufficiency was one factor that encouraged these multilingual web users to switch code situationally when they searched for information online. When the retrieved results from one language could not satisfy the participants' information needs, they preferred to switch to the other language in order to find more information. For example, Participant 4 wanted to search for visa information in Chinese in the travel task. When effective results were not retrieved in the Chinese language search,she switched to English to satisfy her information needs.

"Because I did not find visa information in Chinese. So I searched in English for the visa information" (FI-P4).

Participant 9 searched for medical information in Chinese. However, he found that the results returned from various Chinese websites were similar to each other. Next, he switched to English to search for the disease information and find additional information.

"...I realized the information offered by Chinese results were not so much. Lots of results were similar" (FI-P9).

Several of the participants searched both in English and Chinese to obtain **different cultural perspectives** or information in two languages so as to get sufficient information. We considered this code-switching was a situational one because the participants did not show specific preferences for a specific cultural perspective, but were interested in both the Chinese-language and the English-language views. They simply wanted more and sufficient information. Participant 12 switched from Chinese to English when he reviewed the comments about the election debate. He explained that since he reviewed the Chinese comments, he was also interested in the comments from the U.S. perspective. He preferred different opinions in both cultural perspectives.

"Because just now I got to know the comments in Chinese. Then I went back and thoroughly read the American comments. I wanted to see the different opinions in the different culture" (FI-P12).

Low language proficiency in English and high language proficiency in Chinese encouraged the participants to search in their native language during their searching. For instance, Participant 12 did not understand the English terminologies in the retrieved English results for the medical task. He gave up and switched to search in Chinese.

"Because I really do not know some of the professional terminologies, for example, some places and liquids in the eyes. So I searched in Chinese" (FI-P12).

Low language proficiency in English also prevented the participants from receiving effective English results due to query inaccuracy or difficulties in processing retrieved results. This increased searcher frustration and encouraged them to switch to their native language. Participant 15 switched from English to Chinese due to the low information processing efficiency in English. He switched to Chinese for better information accuracy.

"Because I wanted to search for food and travel spot information. If I retrieved English results, the processing time for me is slow and there might be misunderstanding. By using Chinese I can control the search accuracy" (FI-P15).

Participant 9 found out the retrieved results were not what he expected during his search in English. This situation increased his frustration. So he switched to search in Chinese.

"Because I wanted to search for background information, but the retrieved result was the weather forecast. So I realized that searching in English might not present what I really meant. So I switched to Chinese" (FI-P9).

Translation happened as situational code-switching when the participants did not understand the retrieved English results.

"Q: I realized you translate a whole page of zocdoc.com, why?

A: I thought the explanation there is very reasonable. But there are some details I did not quite understand. So I translated it to Chinese to view it" (FI-P6).

When the participants did not know the English translation of the Chinese words, they also translated Chinese to English.

"Q: You first translate the Chinese disease into English, why?

A: I know the Chinese disease name. But I do not know its English name. So I translate it into English" (FI-P10).

Information verification refers to comparing information retrieved in one language to information retrieved in the other language. This helped multilingual web users verify information accuracy when they searched online. Participant 3 verified the medical treatment in two languages because he was not sure if the result was accurate in only one language. Participant 10 viewed the results both in English and Chinese for better understanding of the debate.

"I used the websites in two languages to verify each other because my major is not medicine" (FI-P3).

"I want to verify the information by the two languages. At first I viewed several English results and did not actually know what they talked about. After I switched to Chinese and basically understand the Chinese results, I went back to view English results in detail" (FI-P10).

Other participants verified their Chinese results with the English results so as to confirm the information they got was accurate.

"Some of the information says it is the disease for senior, some says it is temporary. I was not sure about it. So I wanted to search in English" (FI-P1).

"I searched in Chinese and got the answer that you do not need a visa. Then I went to English information to verify it" (FI-P6).

Context of the information need also impacted multilingual web users' code-switching during their information seeking process. The context here was defined as the physical environment, culture, and related pragmatic elements such as location. Participant 5 found acceptable disease causes and medical treatment in Chinese. However, he wondered if the result was appropriate in the context of the other culture. Therefore, he also searched in English.

"Even though I found some answers on Chinese websites. But due to different environments, the suggestions might not suit the US culture. I want to see if other people in the US culture have the same problem and see if there are more professional and localized answers" (FI-P5).

Participant 12 and 14 both expressed that since they searched for the information of Fiji. They switched to English so as to retrieve the information in the context of Fiji's language and culture.

"Because I have found the local language (in Fiji) is English. I searched in English to check the environment, place names and river names" (FI-P12).

Metaphorical Code-Switching

Metaphorical Code-Switching happened when multilingual web users switched languages in their search tasks due to the perceived image of the language used.

Information in the English language was often perceived as **accurate and objective.** For example, Participant 2 switched from Chinese to English in the travel task because he held a positive view of English-language information as being accurate.

"*In my impression, foreigners like to travel more. Their comments might be more accurate*" (FI-P2).

Other participants believed that information in English was more objective than information in Chinese. For example, Participant 3 switched from Chinese to English when he searched for the travel information. He expressed that some Chinese information about travel spots were overly commercial. He believed the English travel tips were objective due to his impression about the language. Participant 6 and 11 addressed that when they searched for news, the English results were more objective.

"S*ome travel spots have been developed so much, the (Chinese) information lose its authenticity. The English travel tips are more objective*" (FI-P3).

"*Some Chinese websites reported it with certain perspectives, not so neutral. So I chose to switch to English to view some comments*" (FI-P6).

"*Chinese media comments were different. American media is more serious*" (FI-P11).

However, multilingual web users also switched their searches in English back to Chinese due to their **sense of belonging**. Participant 3 talked about his switching from English to Chinese in the news task. He expressed that since his background was Chinese, he would like to view what other Chinese people thought about it instead of the English comments.

"*I wanted to see how Chinese websites commented on this. I chose this webpage because the author has the same cultural background as mine. The English one, I think the views are far left*" (FI-P3).

In the travel task Participant 6 wanted to find out what Chinese people shared on the Chinese as Fiji is a popular destination for Chinese tourists. He switched from English to Chinese to seek experiences and comments of Chinese tourists.

"*I wanted to see other Chinese' opinions. Lots of Chinese go to Fiji. They shared comments and experiences*" (FI-P6).

Different cultural perspectives were factors that multilingual web users considered about when they switched languages. Some participants switched languages during their searches because they **preferred a specific cultural view**. Participant 7 switched from Chinese to English because he believed the information in English could offer him new points from the other cultural perspective rather than Chinese.

"*I wanted to search in English about Nadi to view some comments and introduction. I thought the English information should offer something different from Chinese ones*" (FI-P7).

Participant 9 switched from English to Chinese in the news task because he would like to find a critique from the Chinese perspective rather than the English perspective. Participant 1 pointed out that due to different perspectives, he preferred to read Chinese trip advice in the travel task because the information was from the Chinese cultural perspective.

"*Because I wanted to find a Chinese critic*" (FI-P9).

"*It is very convenient to read Chinese about trip advice. As Chinese, we have different perspectives of views. The requirements are different, too*" (FI-P1).

Website **credibility and user trust** impacted multilingual web users' code-switching behaviors when they performed the tasks. When the participants considered the information on the retrieved websites fake, they switched to the other language. Participant 2 did not trust Chinese herbal medicine. Therefore, since the retrieved Chinese results were all about herbal medicine, he considered the results were fake and switched to search in English. Participant 4 judged the visa information on the English website and realized that the information was not complete. She refused to accept it because she thought the website looked like an unauthentic official website. Instead of continuing her search in English, she switched to search in Chinese.

"*Because there is lots of fake information on Chinese websites. I don't believe in Chinese herbal medicine. Lots of the methods are Chinese herbal treatment*" (FI-P2).

"*The English government website I found for visa looks fake. The information is incomplete. So changed back to Chinese Taobao to look for visa information*" (FI-P4).

User trust was also one reason that caused multilingual web users switched code metaphorically.

"*I wanted to plan the travel route. I trust Google maps. It is in English*" (FI-P5).

"*Because I think the US medical system is more advanced than the Chinese one. I do not trust the non-certified hospital recommended on Chinese websites*" (FI-P12).

The participants expressed **psychological** reasons that caused them switched languages metaphorically during their searches. Participant 14 expressed switching to Chinese helped him psychologically prepared for his trip in the travel task. Participant 2 was scared by the surgery information on the English websites so that he switched to Chinese to find out other solutions.

"*Searching in Chinese for specific travel spots and best comments offered me the psychological preparation for making a travel plan*" (FI-P14).

"*I did not find effective treatment in English. The surgery information looked horrible. I switched back to Chinese to see if there are better methods to treat this disease*" (FI-P2).

Code-Switching Search Models

The data from the observation notes, screen videos, and interviews revealed the search patterns of these multilingual web users' code-switching search behaviors during their information seeking process. The code-switching episodes have been defined as users' behaviors either switching from English to Chinese or switching from Chinese to English during their information seeking process. For the first task on reactions to the US election results, we found 34 instances of code-switching for the 15 participants with an average of about two code-switching episodes per participant. One process of these actions would be considered as one instance of switching. Twelve participants started with English due to the reasons such as information sufficiency/accuracy (including the objective attitude of English comments), event location, and cultural perspective (Figure 1). Three participants started to search in Chinese due to their low English language proficiency and high Chinese search efficiency. The reason that the 12 participants switched back to Chinese were impacted by their English language proficiency, Chinese cultural perspective and sense of belonging, and quick background information in Chinese (Figure 1). These 12 participants switched again to English due to the needs to view certain topics from an American perspective, information accuracy, and information verification. The three participants also switched languages due to similar reasons. Therefore, we generated the major model for Task One as in Figure-1 representing the search behavior starting in English then switching to Chinese and switching back to English.

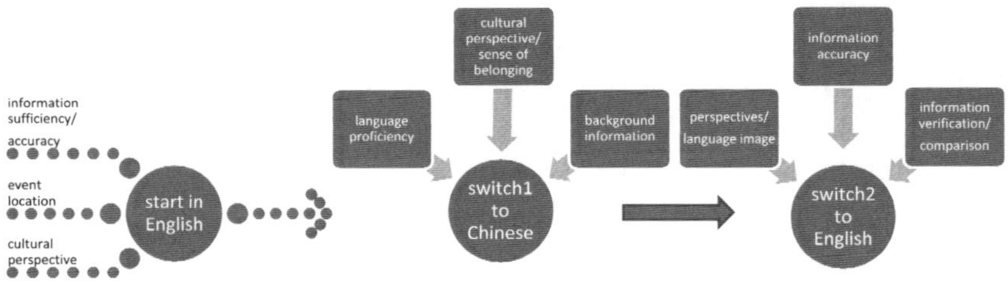

Figure 1. Multilingual web users' code-switching search model for the "Reactions to the US elections" task

We found 41 instances of code-switching in the travel task, with an average of about three instances of code-switching for each participant. Ten participants started with Chinese due to the reasons such as obtaining Chinese background knowledge, high Chinese language proficiency and search efficiency, and sense of intimacy to other Chinese. The other five participants started with English due to the travel location and information sufficiency in English (Figure 2). Next, these participants switched from Chinese to English (Switch 1) due to factors such as English information accuracy and sufficiency, information in different cultural perspectives, and the English context of the event location (Figure 2). They switched back from English to Chinese (Switch 2) due to obtaining information from the Chinese cultural perspective and psychological preparation for the trip, information verification (including website credibility), and language proficiency (Figure 2). They switched the third time (Switch 3) from Chinese to English due to the reasons of website credibility, information verification, and English information accuracy (Figure 2). The five participants who started to search in English displayed similar searching patterns with the ten participants' search patterns starting from the first switching. Therefore, we developed the major model for the travel task as can be seen in Figure-2.

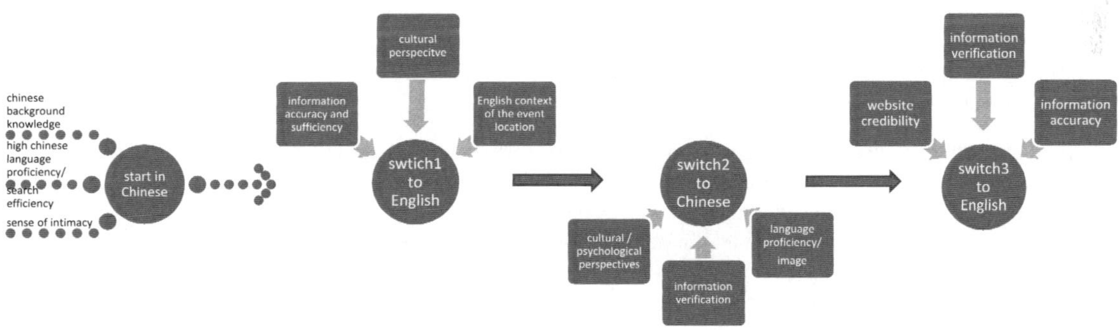

Figure 2. Multilingual web users' code-switching search model for the "Fiji travel" task

In the medical search task, we found 34 instances of switching with an average of about two instances of switching per participant. Fourteen participants started with Chinese due to difficulties in expressing and reading in English medical terminologies. One participant did not start with Chinese because he did not believe in Chinese herbal medicine, which he believed might be the most dominant retrieved results if he searched in Chinese. But later he switched to Chinese because he could not psychologically accept the "horrible" surgery information on English websites. The fact that the 14 participants switched to English from Chinese was due to the perception of English information sufficiency and accuracy, seeking information from a different cultural perspectives, and the English context of the event location (Figure 3). They switched back from English to Chinese because of exploring different types of treatments from different cultural perspectives, information verification, and low English language proficiency (Figure 3). The model developed based on the behavior in the medical problem task is shown in Figure 3.

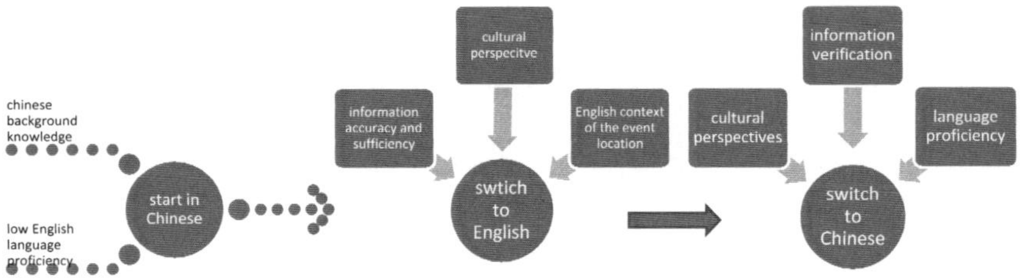

Figure 3. Multilingual web users' code-switching search model for the "Medical Problem" task

As can be seen from the three models, when multilingual web users had no severe English language proficiency problems, their first choice of language has been determined by the context of the information need, such as the event (US elections) or travel (Fiji) location. The participants' English language proficiency was sufficient to search for everyday topics such as political news and travel information, but not for the higher-complexity medical information need. For this topic they preferred to first search in their native language.

In the first set of switches participants switched languages to find more information, whether this is just additional information, more accurate and specific information, or information that is presented from a different cultural perspective. The last switch usually was based on the same rationale and additionally participants also switched language for a second time to compare information found in one language to information in the other language and thus verify their findings.

CONCLUSIONS

Through video analysis and observation, we identified three major multilingual web users' code-switching search strategies, which was also supported by the interview data. Multilingual web users switched languages during their searches in order to: 1) understand the situation related to the task, 2) make analogies between the Chinese search model and the English one, and 3) compare and verify information. In the first case, some participants chose to search in English for sufficient or accurate information. However, their English language proficiency was not high, which caused difficulties for them to understand retrieved English results. They preferred to switch back to Chinese to get basic situation about the task, which helped them to better understand the English results since they got to know the background information. In the second case, multilingual web users had their own habits of searching. When they switched to search in the other language, they made analogies in order to develop search strategies in that language's context. The third case shows the behavior when multilingual web users compared and verified information in two languages as their search strategy.

Our study identified interesting strategies of using code-switching to support search success and described interesting strategies for combining various code-switching techniques. Because all the participants are Chinese, the results may not be generalized to all multilingual web users. However, this work provides detailed description of the methods used and the context of multilingual web users' code-switching behaviors when they seek information online. These results may transfer to similar situations.

ACKNOWLEDGMENTS

We thank our participants for their contribution.

REFERENCES

Auer, P. (1998). Code-Switching in Conversation. London, Routledge.

Berendt, B., & Kralisch, A. (2009). A user-centric approach to identifying best deployment strategies for language tools: the impact of content and access language on Web user behavior and attitudes. Inf. Retr., 12, 3, 380-399.

Blom, J. P., & Gumperz, J. J. (1972). Social Meaning in Linguistic Structures: Code-switching in Norway. In J. J. Gumperz & D. Hymes (Eds), Directions in Sociolinguistics (pp. 407-434). New York: Holt, Rinehart, and Winston.

Clough, P., & Eleta, I. (2010). Investigating language skills and field of knowledge on multilingual information access in digital libraries. International Journal of Digital Library Systems 1(1), 89- 103.

Corbin, J. & Strauss, A. (2008). Basics of Qualitative Research: Techniques and Procedures for Developing Grounded Theory (3rd. ed.). Thousand Oaks, CA: Sage.

Gumperz, J. J. (1982). Discourse Strategies. Cambridge, Cambridge University Press

Gumperz, J. J., & Hymes, D. H. (1986). Directions in Sociolinguistics: The Ethnography of Communication. Oxford, UK: Basil Blackwell.

Ilanguages Organization. (2016). Multilingual People. Retrieved from http://ilanguages.org/bilingual.php

Internet Live Stats. (2016). Internet Users by Country. Retrieved from http://www.internetlivestats.com/internet-users-by-country/ China

Kachru, B. B. (2005). Asian Englishes Beyond the Canon. Hong Kong: Hong Kong University Press.

Kötter, M. (2003). Negotiation of meaning and codeswitching in online tandems. Language Learning & Technology 7(2), 145-172.

Kralisch, A., & Berendt, B. (2005). Language-sensitive search behavior and the role of domain knowledge. New Review of Hypermedia and Multimedia, 11(2), 221-246.

Kralisch, A., & Mandl, T. (2006). Barriers to information access across languages on the internet: Network and language effects. Proceedings of the 39th Annual Hawaii International Conference (Vol. 3, pp. 54b-54b). Kauai, Hi: IEEE.

Lingel, J., Naaman, M., & Boyd., D. M. (2014). City, self, network: transnational migrants and online identity work. In Proceedings of the 17th ACM conference on Computer supported cooperative work & social computing (CSCW '14) (pp. 1502-1510). New York, NY: ACM.

Marian, V., & Shook, A. (2012, October 31). The Cognitive Benefits of Being Bilingual. Retrieved from http://dana.org/Cerebrum/2012/The_Cognitive_Benefits_of_Being_Bilingual.

Marlow, J., Clough, P., Recuero, J. C., & Artiles, J. (2008). Exploring the effects of language skills on multilingual web search. In C. Macdonald, I. Ounis, V. Plachouras, I. Ruthven, & R. W. White (Eds.), Proceedings of the IR research, 30th European conference on Advances in information retrieval (ECIR'08) (pp. 126-137). Berlin, Heidelberg: Springer-Verlag.

Maschler, Y. (1998). On the transition from code-switching to a mixed code. In P. Auer (Eds.), Code-switching in Conversation: Language, interaction and identity (pp. 125-150). New York: Routledge.

Merriam, S.B. (2009). Qualitative research: A guide to design and implementation. San Francisco, CA: John Wiley & Sons.

Myers-Scotton, C. (1993). Social Motivations for Codeswitching: Evidence from Africa. Oxford: Clarendon.

Nzomo, P., Rubin, V. L., & Ajiferuke, I. (2012). Multi-lingual information access tools: user survey. Proceedings of the 2012 iConference (pp. 530-532). New York, NY: ACM.

Serra, C. O. (1998). Discourse connectives in bilingual conversation: The case of an emerging Italian-French mixed code. In P. Auer (Eds.), Code-switching in Conversation: Language, interaction and identity (pp. 101-124). New York: Routledge.

U.S. Census Bureau. (2003). Language Use and English-Speaking Ability. Retrieved from https://www.census.gov/prod/2003pubs/c2kbr-29.pdf

Wang, J., & Joardar, S. (2015). Cultural capital at work in Facebook users' selection of different languages. In P. L. P. Rau (Eds.), Cross-Cultural Design: Applications in Mobile Interaction, Education, Health, Transport and Cultural Heritage (pp. 101-109). New York, NY: Springer.

Wang, J. & Komlodi, A. (2016). Understanding Users' Language Selection: Code-switching in Online Searches. Proceedings of the 2016 ACM on Conference on Human Information Interaction and Retrieval (CHIIR '16) (pp. 377-379). New York, NY, USA: ACM.

Wang, J. & Komlodi, A. (2018). Switching Languages in Online Searching: A Qualitative Study of Web Users' Code-Switching Search Behaviors. Proceedings of the 2018 ACM on Conference on Human Information Interaction and Retrieval (CHIIR '18). New York, NY, USA: ACM.

Wei, L. (1998). The 'why' and 'how' questions in the analysis of conversational code-switching. In P. Auer (Eds.), Code-switching in Conversation: Language, interaction and identity (pp. 156-179). New York: Routledge.

Woolard, K.A. (2004). Codeswitching. In A. Duranti (Eds). A Companion to Linguistic Anthropology (pp. 73-94). Oxford, Blackwell.

Serendipity in Context: Prioritised Contextual Browsing in Large-Scale Digital Libraries

David M. Weigl
Oxford e-Research Centre, Department of Engineering Science, University of Oxford, UK.
david.weigl@oerc.ox.ac.uk

Kevin R. Page
Oxford e-Research Centre, Department of Engineering Science, University of Oxford, UK.
kevin.page@oerc.ox.ac.uk

Iain Emsley
Oxford e-Research Centre, Department of Engineering Science, University of Oxford, UK.
ian.emsley@oerc.ox.ac.uk

ABSTRACT

In previous work we proposed a model of information-seeking behaviour in scholarly workset creation, combining and extending established models by Bates, Ellis, and Wilson to encompass strategies for scholarly research in large-scale information systems. However, this model simplifies *contextual browsing*, a key aspect of information seeking in large-scale information systems, as a single, holistic, strategy. Here, we extend this model with granular strategies for contextual browsing, defining new modes to characterise contextual browsing as combinations of these strategies, which we show to be consistent with serendipitous discovery as described by Makri et al. We study the properties of *prioritised* contextual browsing as a mechanism for implementing these strategies. We describe the Compage framework, a proof-of-concept implementation for prioritised contextual browsing of Linked Data resources, using Jaccard similarity for prioritisation. Extending Compage, we develop a simulation environment in which we investigate the utility of prioritised contextual browsing over a large-scale digital library dataset. Our simulation applies three strategies for the traversal of contextual metadata: *reset, unprioritised*, and *prioritised*. Results empirically demonstrate the advantages of prioritised contextual browsing, and that elements of serendipity can be identified and incorporated within our information-seeking model. In doing so, we evaluate our model's suitability for this scenario, yielding a more detailed understanding of the strategies and modes of behaviour underlying contextual browsing.

KEYWORDS

Information-seeking behaviour, digital libraries, contextual browsing, serendipitous discovery

INTRODUCTION

Large-scale digital libraries (DLs) provide unified access to massive sets of heterogeneous content. We have previously proposed a model of information-seeking behaviour in large-scale DLs (Weigl, Page, Organisciak, & Downie, 2017) combining established models by Bates (1989), Ellis (1993), and Wilson (1997), extended with new strategies, classifications, and scopes of application. Our earlier model allows for more precise description of the challenges of supporting discovery, analysis, and scholarly use of the wealth of materials contained in DLs operating on massive scales. It supports use cases centred on worksets – machine-actionable research collections aggregating information resources alongside rich contextual metadata at various levels of granularity (Jett, Cole, Maden, & Downie, 2016). The model incorporates *contextual browsing* as a coarse-grained strategy operating over routes for nuanced exploration and analysis embodied by this metadata, providing singular conditions for *serendipitous discovery*. Finer-grained *modes* of contextual browsing, highly relevant in the scenario, were unexplored.

In this paper, we more fully assess contextual browsing in three ways: through modelling; implementation; and simulation. In the first half, we describe a new model of contextual browsing, elaborating upon our previous model. We unpack contextual browsing — previously incorporated as a single, holistic strategy — into a family of component strategies. In combination, these give rise to different modes of contextual browsing, which we describe and harmonise with a framework of behavioural strategies for serendipitous discovery. In the second half, we discuss the application of our extended model at scale through applied prioritisation, and present the Compage framework, an implemented proof of concept of our approach. Finally, we evaluate the utility of prioritised contextual browsing, employing three synthetic browsing strategies within a computer simulation of information-seeking behaviour across a large collection of Linked Data.

BACKGROUND: INFORMATION SEEKING AND SERENDIPITY IN LARGE-SCALE DIGITAL LIBRARIES

Worksets are information constructs (Jett et al., 2016) supporting the requirements of scholars undertaking research in large-scale DLs (Fenlon et al., 2014; Page et al., 2018). Their capabilities include: gathering documents within citable collections;

supporting computational extraction of document-derived features for scholarly analysis; generating new descriptive information by inference over existing metadata; and linking complementary information from external sources.

Workset creation and refinement is particularly underserved by a view of information-seeking behaviour couched in single-query sessions. Rather, workset building comprises iterative, evolving behaviours analogous to "berrypicking" (Bates, 1989). Our previous model of information-seeking behaviours for scholarly workset creation (Weigl et al., 2017) combined berrypicking *strategies* per Bates (1989), *categories* of information-seeking behaviour within the research process per Ellis (1993), and Wilson's *modes* of search (1997). This model classifies strategies as operating upon three *scopes* of application: content representations (e.g., images, text); content-derived metadata; and additional metadata derived via external (human or algorithmic) processes.

	Category of information-seeking behaviour (per Ellis, 1993)							
Strategy	Starting	Chaining	Browsing	Differentiating	Monitoring	Extracting	Verifying	Ending
Contextual browsing	S	A/P/S	A/P	A		A	A/P	A/P
Anchor specification	A	A/P	A/P	A		A		A/P
Target specification		A/P	A/P	A		A	A/P	A/P
Profile specification		A/P	A/P	A	O		A/P	
Prioritisation	*	*	*	*	*	*	*	*

Modes of search—A: *Active search,* P: *Passive search,* O: *Ongoing search,* S: Serendipitous discovery *(passive attention)*
*: Prioritisation is an ongoing process informed by and modulating behaviour across categories of information-seeking

Table 1. New information-seeking strategies to support contextual browsing

The models of both Bates and Ellis incorporate *chaining* as a means of traversing an information domain where a searcher performs "successive leaps" (Bates, 1989) from document to document, following up references or records in a citation index. On the Web, more diverse types of inter-document association are available through hyperlinks; following links is classified by Choo, Detlor, and Turnbull (2000) as a *chaining* "Web move". In a library context, fixed-schema fields of catalogue records provide further means of inter-record reference and traversal. In DLs, mutable-schema contextual metadata contributed through ongoing user and system processes (Weigl et al., 2017) provide ever more connections; where they are expressed as Linked Data, chaining may occur between data entities, rather than documents, enabling more fine-grained explorations.

The creation of semantic layers of contextual metadata using Linked Data in DLs is subject to ongoing research (e.g., Fafalios, Holzmann, Kasturia, & Nejdl, 2017; Page, Bechhofer, Fazekas, Weigl, & Wilmering, 2017). RDF, a framework for the specification of Linked Data, associates contextual metadata with information entities by asserting `{subject, predicate, object}` triples to specify directed relationships (`predicates`) between an entity (`subject`) and associated entities (`objects`). RDF-compliant systems operate on an open world assumption, meaning that the absence of a triple specifying a connection does not imply the absence of the connection, and that more triples can always be published, and new connections made.

These emergent connections provide prime conditions for *serendipitous* discoveries. Makri et al. build on empirical research into serendipitous information encounters among scholars (Makri & Blandford, 2012) and creative professionals (Makri, Blandford, Woods, Sharples, & Maxwell, 2014) to specify a set of information-system design suggestions to influence the likelihood of serendipitous encounters (Makri et al., 2014). Rather than proposing to "engineer" serendipity, a problematic notion given the inherent *unexpectedness* at its core, they identify human information behaviours that support the likelihood of serendipitous discovery by promoting the stages of the serendipity process: the making of a mental connection involving unexpected circumstance and insight; a projection regarding the connection's potential value, followed by actions taken to exploit it; culminating in a valuable, unanticipated outcome. These behaviours are identified from critical incident reports by participants reflecting on serendipitous information encounters in a semi-structured interview. Makri et al. (2014) detail the identified behaviours, providing corresponding recommendations for information-system design. The behaviours, numbered for reference, include:

1. *Vary your routine*, to provide more opportunities for making connections;
2. *Be observant*, to draw attention to unexpected aspects of the information environment;
3. *Make mental space*, reducing cognitive load to create contingencies for unexpected discovery;
4. *Relax your boundaries*, to avoid excluding valuable information entities due to overly narrow constraints;
5. *Draw on previous experience*, as a way of making and projecting the value of connections;

6. *Look for patterns*, in order to recognise unexpected alignments and extract meaning from them; and,
7. *Seize opportunities*, to exploit value from connections made.

AN EXTENDED MODEL: STRATEGIES AND MODES OF CONTEXTUAL BROWSING

Contextual Browsing Strategies

In this section we unpack contextual browsing, which we previously modelled (Weigl et al.; Section 2) as a single, unified strategy, into a family of new information-seeking strategies sharing key characteristics (Table 1). Each strategy enables or enacts *chaining* activities. The strategies make full use of the rich, open, inter-entity relationships expressed in the metadata of large-scale DLs, beyond inter-document traversal of reference lists or citation indices per Ellis and Bates. Our strategies are capable of connecting any addressable information resources unconstrained by scopes of application, interweaving content, metadata derived from content during cataloguing, and contextual metadata supplemented by system or user processes. Together, they support traversals of contextual space, jumping between entities in collections on the web of data through emergent vectors of association.

No anchor	One anchor	Multiple anchors	Target	Profile	Behaviours
Recommendation	**Entity description**	**Entity connections**	No	No	1,6,7
Target description	**Link discovery**	**Targeted prioritisation**	Yes	No	1,2,4,6,7
Collaborative filtering	**Contextualised review**	**Information filtering**	No	Yes	1,2,3,5,7
Information filtering	**Link discovery**	**Targeted prioritization**	Yes	Yes	1,2,3,4,5,6,7

Table 2: Modes of contextual browsing (modes indicated in bold)

Traversals are anchored to starting points (entities or worksets), providing a situated focus in contextual space. When not specified by the user (**anchor specification**, Table 1), the system must situate the traversal, e.g. by automated recommendation. Traversals may be constrained and guided according to defined *entities* and *inter-entity relationships* (**target specification).** This reduces cognitive load, at the cost of withholding unanticipated, potentially valuable connections from user attention. **Prioritisation,** applying **profile specification** according to user value projections or through algorithmic measures, further constrains the traversal space. Profiles combine user-specified "deferred query" expressions of interest (*personalisation*) with interaction history, e.g. by reference to the user's workset collection. Where these strategies guide the user to unanticipated locations in the collection, this provides the potential for serendipitous discovery per Makri et al. (as defined in Section 2).

Modes of Contextual Browsing as a Means to Serendipitous Discovery

Combinations of contextual browsing strategies give rise to new *modes* of contextual browsing (Table 2). Each combination is consistent with a number of serendipity-influencing information behaviours (Section 2)[1]:

- **Recommendation**. In the absence of specified anchors, targets, and user profiles, a system is limited to recommending potential starting points for contextual browsing. These may be extracted algorithmically (e.g., based on popularity) or by curation. Wikipedia's "article of the day" is an example of such an approach.
- **Entity description**. Browsable contextual views presented over anchoring entities in a result set provide a tight integration of search and browsing behaviour, supporting behaviour 1: *Vary your routine*. Where an entity is selected as an anchor, its entity description provides a view of associated contextual metadata.
- **Entity connections**. Where multiple entities or worksets are specified as anchors, a view describing similarities and notable differences among their descriptions supports serendipity behaviour 6: *Look for patterns.*
- **Target description**, and **Link discovery**. Where a target entity or workset is specified, a target description details the target's contextual metadata. With an entity selection, link discovery describes connections between the selected entity and target(s). These modes support behaviours 4: *Relax your boundaries*, providing a means of alerting users to related workset items during search or browsing; and 6: *Look for patterns*, revealing connections between selected and targeted entities.
- **Targeted prioritisation**. Where multiple anchors are specified alongside a target, prioritised contextual description and filtering actions can be undertaken by reference to weightings (e.g., similarity metrics) relative to the target.
- **Collaborative filtering**. When profile information is available by reference to a user's workset history, or by specification of relevance criteria (personalisation), a system can draw attention to entities selected by other users with comparable profiles, supporting behaviour 2: *Be observant.*

---

[1] Note that behaviour 7, *Seize opportunities*, is implicitly supported through the use of worksets for capture, storage, organization, and annotation of information throughout the information-seeking process.

- **Contextualised review** and **Information filtering**. A specified anchor can be associated with profile information on previous interactions, supporting behaviour 5: *Draw on previous experiences*. Multiple specified anchors can be prioritised accordingly, using profile-based information filtering approaches (Belkin & Croft, 1992). These modes support behaviours 3: *Make mental space* by integrating categorization into the information environment, supporting reflection as information is acquired; and 5: *Draw on previous experiences*, providing a mechanism for the discovery of unexpected connections between information under current, and previous, consideration, allowing users to review and revisit information in the light of new contextual connections.
- When a target is specified in the presence of profile information this provides further opportunities for **Information filtering**, **Link discovery**, and **Targeted prioritisation**, surfacing connections between anchoring entities, specified targets, previously encountered information, and entities encountered by other similarly interested users.

In the remainder of this paper, we consider the practical application of the new contextual browsing strategies introduced above, by: outlining an approach toward applied prioritisation in order to manage the massive quantities of contextual information available in large-scale DLs (Section 4); implementing a proof-of-concept framework and user interface realizing prioritized contextual browsing (Section 5); and conducting a simulation study to empirically validate the utility of prioritisation in contextual browsing over a large dataset (Section 6).

APPLIED PRIORITISATION FOR CONTEXTUAL BROWSING AT SCALE

Worksets provide a foundation for scholarship using prioritised contextual browsing by gathering the necessary information resources and contextual metadata within persistent, addressable collections. Consider the case of an academic information-seeker finding resources on Bede the Venerable, an English 7th-century monk of St. Peter and St. Paul in the Kingdom of Northumbria, modern day Jarrow, Tyne and Wear. Interested in *Roman Catholic biblical scholars*, the user starts a workset containing Bede, and undertakes contextual browsing anchored upon Bede's record to discover further relevant information.

Bede is associated, via contextual relationships, with a large number of categories[2]. Some of these are highly relevant to the researcher's information need: Bede is categorised as a *Benedictine biblical scholar*; a *7th-century theologian*; a *Christian hagiographer*. Others are less immediately applicable: Bede as an *Anglo-Saxon poet*; a *chronologist*; a *trope theorist*. Further categories are at best incidental to the topic at hand: Bede as a *doctor*, a *person from Jarrow*, a *living thing*. This example illustrates the need for information reduction in large-scale contextual browsing, and the utility of discerning by use case: consider the alternate priorities of a researcher establishing a prosopography of 7th-century Jarrow.

Unless specified as profile information, a user's interests and information needs are extrinsic to the data available in a DL. Through worksets, prioritised browsing can nevertheless be provided by prioritising according to computed contextual *similarities* with existing workset members. Here, similarity acts as a proxy for relevance to a topic captured by the workset.

We propose Jaccard distances computed by set operations over contextual descriptors — the `predicates` and `objects` associated with a given `subject` entity in Linked Data (RDF) datasets — as a meaningful measure of contextual similarity. Entities are compared by dividing the intersection of their associated `{predicate, object}` sets by their union. These comparisons are performed iteratively between each entity under consideration, and the collection of neighbouring entities available for subsequent navigation. This provides a data-intrinsic means of prioritisation for contextual browsing.

REALISING APPLIED PRIORITISATION AS A SPACE FOR SERENDIPITY

The Compage Framework

Compage[3], a new prototyping framework for prioritised contextual browsing, demonstrates the feasibility of our model and provides a platform for its empirical exploration. Compage is dataset-agnostic, capable of providing contextual views over any specified RDF graphs and constrained set of user journeys.

The framework maintains a collection of user-associated worksets. These can be created or extended via a set of panes presenting views of contextual metadata associated with entities in a result set, including: *Entity descriptions* providing comprehensive listings and summaries of the RDF predicates and objects associated with selected entities (Figure 1, top); *Similarity views* providing access to similarities and differences between selected and targeted entities (Figure 1, bottom); and *Entity connections* providing statistical summaries of the preponderance of different contextual metadata items within specified worksets,

[2] Illustrative examples from the *Bede the Venerable* DBPedia resource: http://dbpedia.org/resource/Bede
[3] Available at https://github.com/oerc-csi/compage

the user's workset collection, and the wider dataset. Each view provides traversal mechanisms supporting prioritised contextual browsing among the collection.

Workset targets may be specified to accommodate *Link discovery*. "Drilling-down" into the discovered connections, a user can explore contextual similarities from entities within the result set to entities in the user's workset collection (serving here as profile information), or with the wider dataset, providing a controlled means of broadening a search. Contextual information associated with a given entity may have numerous semantic relationships with different entities in the dataset. For instance, a date serving as 'birth date' for one entity may function as a publication, flourished, or death date for others. Compage enables summary and traversal of such values according to their semantic use context, realising a means of serendipitous discovery of new connections. During traversal, encountered entities may be added to the result set on user request. Similarities are recalculated after workset modification, providing the potential for further discoveries surfaced in the shifting contextual landscape.

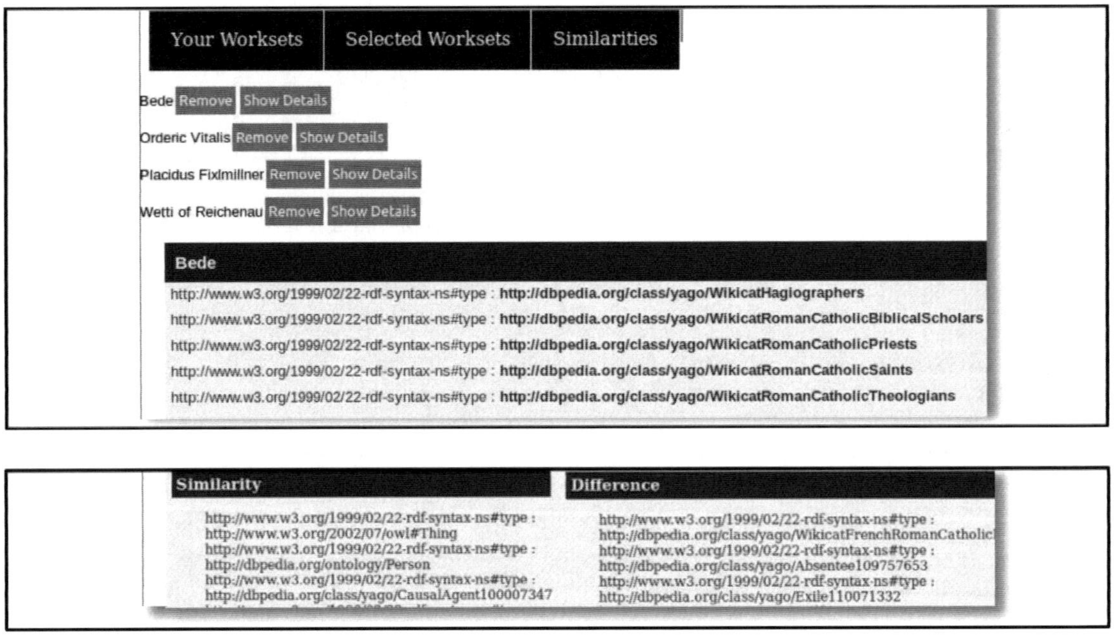

Figure 1. *Top*: Compage result set of Benedictine scholars, with entity descriptions for Bede the Venerable. *Bottom*: Entity connections pane with (a subset of) contextual similarities and differences between Bede and Orderic Vitalis

To illustrate, consider an application of Compage targeting DBPedia (Lehmann et al., 2015), a Linked Data publication of structured Wikipedia information. A researcher interested in studying Benedictine writers might incorporate our protagonist the Venerable Bede into a result set — by typing his name into a rudimentary search interface, or by loading a pre-specified workset of Benedictine scholars. Upon requesting an entity description ("Show Details"), the user discovers information relating to Bede's dates of birth, death, as well as the date on which he was canonised. Other entities associated with these date relationships can be retrieved from the current result set, a specified workset, or within the wider data. Alternatively, the user may discover from the entity description that Bede was canonised by Pope Leo XIII, and traverse to this associated entity to request *its* (Pope Leo's) associated entities. In either case, Jaccard similarities can be calculated to limit the set of retrieved entities to those similar to the ones currently under consideration, supporting discovery while constraining information load.

Compage employs a client/server architecture that uses client requests to parameterise SPARQL queries. Queries and similarity calculations are executed on the server via a triplestore[4], reducing client load. A JavaScript client presents the user interface, communicating requests to the server and caching data currently under consideration in order to minimise recomputation.

Model Conformance

Compage implements aspects of our extended model (Section 3) and notions of applied prioritisation (Section 4):

[4] Compage may be configured to query any triplestore exposing a SPARQL 1.1-compliant endpoint. It has been tested with Virtuoso and Blazegraph.

1. Anchor specification within a rudimentary search result set;
2. Contextual views over entity and workset descriptions;
3. Inter-entity similarity and difference listings;
4. Directed Jaccard prioritisation of contextual space;
5. Target and relation specification, enabling inter-entity traversals according to related contextual descriptions;
6. Constrained traversals targeting worksets in the user's collection;
7. Instantiation and refinement of worksets to include relevant entities as they are discovered (*extraction*).

As such, Compage demonstrates the feasibility of implementing the approaches discussed in this paper.

The framework does not currently implement other DL information-system affordances, such as prioritisation according to popularity with other users sharing related interests (e.g., for collaborative filtering). However, its modular, dataset-independent design is intended to support such applications in the future by treating crowd-sourced data, and other emergent metadata streams, as yet more context to be explored.

SIMULATING SCHOLARLY CONTEXTUAL BROWSING AND SERENDIPITOUS ASSOCIATIONS

Scholarly contextual browsing is a time-intensive undertaking. Aside from the time required for careful application of insight, the problem is one of combinatorial explosion inherent in graph structures. Consider the example of a family tree; moving backwards, ancestor by ancestor, through successive generations from a single person doubles the search space with every hop, from the person's two parents, to the four grandparents, eight great grandparents, and so on. This problem is compounded in a DL context, where each node is connected to a potentially large number of neighbours. Consider again the Venerable Bede; he has direct connections to 133 neighbouring graph entities; in turn, these are connected to 364 entities, Bede's neighbours once removed. There are 1,878 neighbours twice removed, and 38,948 neighbours thrice removed. The Compage framework assists users in constraining and directing their contextual browsing through this space by prioritisation according to similarity. Even so, longitudinal user studies are required to observe information seekers engaging in contextual browsing in such a scenario; we reserve such studies for future work. Here, we instead *simulate* these strategies for traversals across a large dataset to evaluate the utility of prioritised over unprioritised contextual browsing — the proposition at the heart of Compage. We treat similarity as a simplified proxy measure for topical relevance, where the topic is approximated by the membership of a seed workset. The goal of the simulated agent is to traverse iteratively through contextual space, incorporating new information while maintaining similarity (as relevance) both to the seed workset starting the traversal, and to the immediate predecessor workset at each iterative hop.

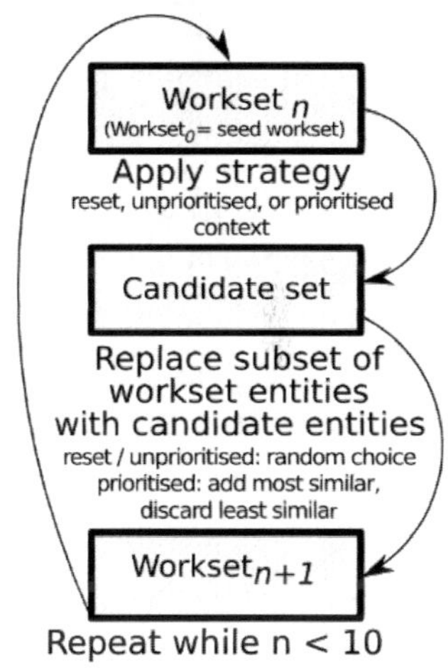

Figure 2: Simulation procedure

Dataset and Seed Worksets

Our simulation targets DBPedia (Lehmann et al., 2015). This Linked Data publication of structured Wikipedia information exhibits comprehensive coverage, a heterogeneous nature, and a high degree of interconnectedness. Thus, it provides an ideal proving ground for contextual browsing approaches. The simulation could equally target any RDF collection of large-scale DL metadata; the corresponding R script[5] can be pointed at any SPARQL endpoint. We have chosen two seed worksets for our simulation: **Seed1**: a subset of 50 entities randomly selected from the category Roman Catholic theologians (which contains 468 members on DBPedia); and **Seed2**: the more specialised subcategory of Benedictine Writers, which contains 13 members.

Simulated Strategies

Our agents employ one of three synthetic contextual browsing strategies, applying categories of information-seeking behaviour and (simulated) modes of search outlined in our extended model (Section 3). **Reset context** gathers new entities by randomly sampling the contextual space; an iterative, memoryless re-*starting* (per Ellis; see Table 1). This provides a baseline featuring neither *chaining* (following connections) nor *differentiating* (prioritising according to similarity), simulating a perpetual serendipity seeker, akin to a user making obsessive use of Wikipedia's "random article" feature in the hope of encountering relevant information — though lacking human insight to know the best entities to add to the current workset as they are encountered. **Unprioritised context** randomly traverses connections from entities in the current set. On each iteration this agent "follows its nose" through the contextual neighbourhood, *chaining* without *differentiating*, by adding a random selection of neighbouring

[5] Available at https://github.com/oerc-csi/contextualBrowsingSim

entities to the workset at each step. This simulates a purely "*passive* searcher" per Wilson, constantly starting new search tangents based on previous outcomes. **Prioritised context** traverses between connected entities, prioritising by Jaccard similarity. This corresponds to *chaining* with *differentiating* according to similarity. This strategy simulates an "*active* searcher" per Wilson, pursuing an information need of topical relevance (here, similarity) to the current workset.

Procedure and Testing

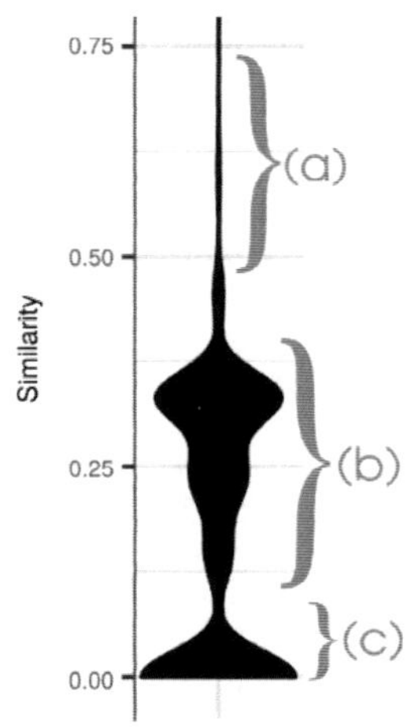

Figure 3. Example similarity distribution between a workset and its predecessor

Our simulation proceeds by iterative application of the simulated strategies (Figure 2), starting from the previous iteration's workset, and simulating contextual browsing to produce a new workset at each step. The simulation is run twice, either: maintaining a steady workset size across iterations, replacing $\frac{1}{5}$ of the preceding workset at each step; or narrowing the workset across iterations by $\frac{1}{5}$ of the preceding workset's size (incorporating $\frac{1}{10}$ new entities at each step). This simulates the distinct behaviours of open-ended exploration (approximating a *steady state*), or *narrowing down* toward the end of a research process.

Workset-to-workset distances comprising the Jaccard similarities (Section 4) are calculated between each entity in one workset and all entities in the other. These distances are computed between each workset and its predecessor; and between each workset and the corresponding seed (**Seed1** or **Seed2**). From these we produce a distribution of distances, which we refer to as a *similarity distribution.* Figure 3 shows an example similarity distribution visualised as a violin plot (a smoothed histogram reflected along the y-axis) where the width at any point corresponds to the proportion of inter-workset comparisons in the distribution sharing the corresponding similarity value. In the example, the narrow tail (a) indicates the presence of a small number of highly similar entities. The body of the distribution (b) characterises the range of typical (non-zero) similarity values present in the distribution: here, the median non-zero score is 0.33, slipping to .23 when including zero values. Finally, the foot of the distribution (c) indicates a large number of zero-similarity comparisons in the example.

We apply two-sample Kolmogorov-Smirnov tests between pairs of similarity distributions to test whether they share an underlying continuous distribution, or differ significantly:

Test 1: Do similarity distributions between each workset and the corresponding seed workset differ significantly across the simulated strategies? **Null hypothesis 1**: The produced worksets are equally similar to their seeds.

Test 2: Do similarity distributions between each workset and its predecessor differ significantly across the simulated strategies? **Null hypothesis 2**: The strategies produce worksets that are equally similar to their predecessor, at each step.

Test 3: Do similarity distributions between each workset and its predecessor differ significantly within each simulated strategy's iterations? **Null hypothesis 3**: There is no divergence in similarity distributions across iterative applications of each strategy.

We apply Šidák correction (1967) to account for multiple comparisons (declaring significance at $p < .0017$).

Visualisation and Interpretation

The resulting similarity distributions are visualised in Figures 4 (steady-state) and 5 (narrowing-down). Within each figure, the *top* two panels represent simulated traversals starting at **Seed1** (Roman Catholic theologians), and the *bottom* two panels starting at **Seed2** (Benedictine writers). Each plot illustrates the similarity distributions generated at each iterative step, for each of the three synthetic strategies distinguished by colour: prioritised context (green); unpriorisited context (orange); and reset context (purple). Each plot contains similarity distributions against the seed workset (*a*), and similarity distributions against the predecessor workset (*b*). The y-axis of (*b*) in each figure is inverted; proximity to the division line between (*a*) and (*b*) indicates lower similarity. Inspecting the plots across incremental iterations (from left to right), the changes in similarity distributions as each strategy unfolds may be visualised. A "sagging" of the distribution shape toward the division line (similarity = 0) indicates a tendency toward diminishing returns over successive iterations; whereas a retention of shape, or a tendency away from the line, implies that the strategy is successful at continuing to discover similar entities as the simulation proceeds.

Within each simulated step the prioritised context strategy, followed by unprioritised context, consistently produces the most similar distributions, both to the seed (*a*) and to predecessor (*b*) worksets. The reset context strategy consistently produces the least similar distributions and the most zero-similarity comparisons. However, it also occasionally produces outliers (manifested as narrow tails in the similarity distributions) that match or exceed the best scores produced by the other two strategies. The statistical reasoning behind these observations is as follows.

Statistical Analysis

For the steady state simulation, our two-sample Kolmogorov-Smirnov tests indicate that each of the three strategies produce significantly different similarity distributions at every step when comparing each iterative workset to the seed (*a*), with one exception (**Seed2,** unprioritised vs. reset context at iteration 6). Overall, this strongly suggests that Null Hypothesis 1 can be rejected for the steady state simulation.

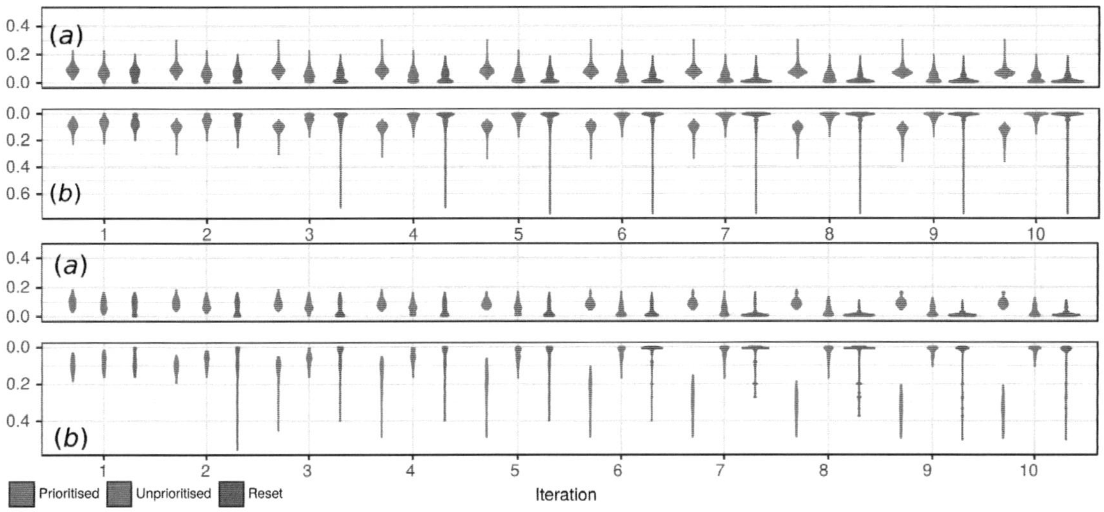

Figure 4. Similarity distributions generated by the simulation at *steady* workset size (replacing $\frac{1}{5}$ at each iteration). *Top two panels*: Iterations of Seed1, Roman Catholic theologians. *Bottom two panels*: Iterations of Seed2, Benedictine writers. In each iteration, similarities are computed between the generated workset and: (*a*) the corresponding seed workset, and (*b*) the immediate predecessor produced by the same strategy.

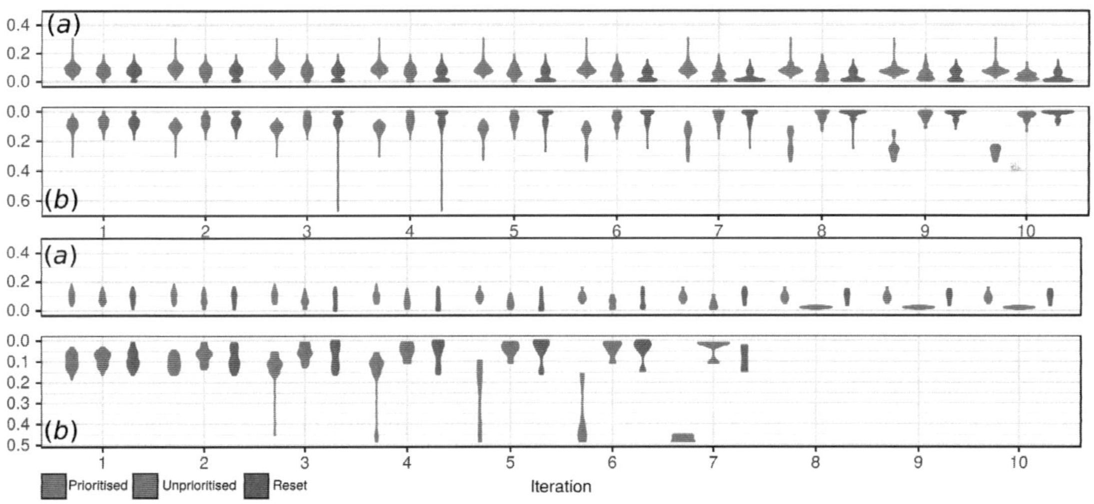

Figure 5. Similarity distributions generated by the simulation at *shrinking* workset size (narrowing by $\frac{1}{5}$ at each iteration). See also the caption for Figure 4, above. N.b. Workset size is 1 by the 7th iteration—hence the missing values in the lower panel (self-similarities are excluded from analysis).

For the narrowing simulation, the results for (*a*) are the same for **Seed1**, where each strategy produces significantly different similarity distributions at each iteration, with one exception (unprioritised and reset context, iteration 1). For **Seed2**, there are several exceptions: all three strategies exhibit only insignificant differences in their similarity distributions on iterations 1 and 2, with the unprioritised and reset context strategies remaining insignificantly different for iterations 3, 4, 5, and 6. This is explicable by the small size of the workset (13 members) and the narrowing nature of the simulation, meaning that only a small proportion of the data is modified in each step.

Interestingly the prioritised strategy separates itself early on from the reset context strategy (random baseline), suggesting that prioritised browsing provides more relevant discoveries even in small-scale explorations. Both the prioritised and reset context strategies exhibit insignificant differences for the same seed workset in iteration 7, 8, 9, and 10. This is because the narrowing process for this workset arrives at a membership of 1 by the 7th iteration, which happens to be equidistant in both cases.

For similarity to the predecessor (*b*), our results indicate significant differences in distribution across all strategies for each simulated step in the steady state simulation. We reject Null Hypothesis 2.

In the narrowing simulation, results for (*b*) are again the same for **Seed1**, with two exceptions (unprioritised and reset context, iterations 1 and 9). Again they are divergent for the smaller **Seed2**, where differences in predecessor similarity are insignificant between all strategies for iterations 1 and 2, and between unprioritised and reset context for all remaining steps. Again, prioritised browsing distinguishes itself after a few iterations, even in this small-scale scenario. The differences become insignificant among all strategies from the 7th iteration onward, again as an artifact of the narrowed workset's single-entity membership.

Results are mixed comparing similarity distributions of worksets to their predecessors (*b*) *within* each strategy's outcomes. For the steady state **Seed1** simulation, the following comparisons did not yield statistically significant differences in distribution:

- Reset context: Similarity to predecessor at steps 5 and 6; and at steps 9 and 10.
- Unprioritised context: Similarity to predecessor at steps 6 and 7; 8 and 9; and, 9 and 10.
- Prioritised context: Similarity to predecessor at steps 3 and 4; 4 and 5; 5 and 6; and, 6 and 7.

Comparing similarity distributions of worksets to their predecessor within each strategy in **Seed2** of the steady state simulation, **only** the following comparisons yielded statistically significant differences:

- Reset context: Steps 2 and 3.
- Unprioritised context: Steps 6 and 7.
- Prioritised context: Steps 5 and 6; 6 and 7; 7 and 8.

Results for the narrowing simulation were comparably mixed. For **Seed1**, only within-strategy predecessor comparisons between steps 1 and 2, and 9 and 10 of the prioritised strategy, steps 2 and 3 of the unprioritised strategy, and steps 2 and 3; 3 and 4; and 4 and 5 of the reset context strategy differing significantly. For **Seed2**, there were no significant within-strategy predecessor comparisons among any of the strategies.

Discussion: Contextual Browsing as a Vehicle for Serendipitous Discovery

In the context of our extended model (Section 3), grounded in Wilson's modes of search (Section 2), our simulation informs expectations on the utility of contextual browsing for human information seekers. Each workset's similarity to its seed provides a proxy for relevance outcomes of *active search* behaviour, where the seed workset represents a sample of results fulfilling an actively-pursued information need. Each workset's similarity to its predecessor is analogous to instances of *passive search*, where the pursuit of information results in the incidental acquisition of relevant information not subject to the active search.

Our simulated strategies can be viewed as agents pathologically applying *active* and *passive search*, and *passive attention* behaviours (the last of which involves serendipitous discovery of information outside of an information-seeking context). The prioritised context agent ruthlessly pursues its information need ("find other entities similar to this one"); the unprioritised context agent wanders amongst tangential connections; whereas the reset context agent constantly finds itself disconnected and memoryless within the information space, while occasionally chancing upon highly relevant entities.

Of course, separately incarnating the modes of search is an artificial exercise: human information seeking employs each mode simultaneously, particularly outside of single-query sessions, as in the continuous berrypicking of workset refinement. Nevertheless, our simulation results empirically demonstrating the potential value of prioritised contextual browsing in DL systems. They further demonstrate that the prioritised context strategy *retains* seed workset similarity, and gradually *improves* upon predecessor similarity over the course of the simulation. In other words, prioritised context rewards continued exploration for both active and passive search outcomes, whereas unprioritised context demonstrates a tendency toward diminishing returns.

Although random, the reset context strategy occasionally yields highly relevant results by pure serendipity. While clearly not a sensible mechanism for primary navigation of an information resource — our results show the overall similarity distributions produced by reset context are poor — this supports the utility of stochastic elements as secondary navigation vectors, per Makri et al.'s *relaxing boundaries* and *making mental space* serendipity behaviours.

CONCLUSIONS

In this paper we have extended our earlier model for information seeking in large-scale digital libraries with new strategies and modes of *contextual browsing*, showing their consistency with behaviours supporting serendipitous discovery set out by Makri et al. We have described how contextual browsing requires prioritisation to remain feasible in large-scale scenarios and have proposed the application of contextual similarity metrics to this purpose. Compage, a prototype for prioritised contextual browsing over RDF datasets, illustrates the suitability of our model through implementation; furthered by automated assessment of our strategies in a simulated extension of the framework. This simulation has empirically demonstrated the utility of prioritisation in a study comparing prioritised, unprioritised, and reset context strategies for contextual browsing.

We believe that prioritised contextual browsing, supporting and combining both active and passive search behaviours, creates a space in which users can benefit from structured information while encouraging the likelihood of serendipitous discoveries. Serendipity cannot be "engineered", as Makri et al. highlight, and we do not claim to have done so here. Unexpectedness is, after all, the key precept of serendipity. Our results do capture occasions of "pure" serendipity, at least within the synthetic confines of our simulation, in the rare gems uncovered by our — otherwise pathological — reset-context strategy.

Longitudinal user studies of scholars pursuing real information needs are required to more fully understand human contextual browsing behaviour. These future studies must use modern information systems capable of exposing mutable navigation vectors along contextual metadata - through the theoretical, applied, and experimental contributions in this paper, we hope to have provided a framing for such future work.

We arrive at a number of conclusions concerning contextual browsing of large-scale DLs: *i)* that a theoretical conception of this process as a holistic activity occludes considerable complexities relating to motivations, information affordances, and system and user behaviours, which continuously shift as information-seeking takes place; *ii)* that prioritisation is a necessary component of meaningful contextual browsing in large-scale scenarios; and *iii*) that the rich contextual metadata available in large-scale DLs provide valuable vectors of discovery for both actively pursued and serendipitously encountered information, above and beyond the search and browsing behaviours afforded by traditional, limited-schema library metadata.

ACKNOWLEDGEMENTS

This work was supported by grant #41500672 from the Andrew W. Mellon Foundation; and by Fusing Audio and Semantic Technologies for Intelligent Music Production and Consumption funded by the UK Engineering and Physical Sciences Research Council (EPSRC) under grant number EP/L019981/1. Conclusions and opinions expressed are those of the authors and are not necessarily shared by the sponsor.

REFERENCES

Bates, M. J. (1989). The design of browsing and berrypicking techniques for the online search interface. Online review 13(5), 407-424.

Belkin, N. J. & Croft, W. B. (1992). Information filtering and information retrieval: Two sides of the same coin? Commun. ACM 35, 12, 29-38.

Choo, C. W., Detlor, B., & Turnbull, D. (2000). Information seeking on the Web: An integrated model of browsing and searching. First Monday 5(2).

Ellis, D. (1993). Modeling the information-seeking patterns of academic researchers: A grounded theory approach. The Library Quarterly, 469-486.

Fafalios, P., Holzmann, H., Kasturia, V., & Neijdl, W. (2017). Building and querying semantic layers for Web archives. In Proceedings of the 17th ACM/IEEE-CS on Joint Conference on Digital Libraries, Vol. 2017.

Fenlon, K., Senseney, M., Green, H., Bhattacharyya, S., Willis, C., & Downie, J. S. (2014). Scholar-built collections: A study of user requirements for research in large-scale digital libraries. In Proc. Association for Information Science and Technology 51(1), 1-10.

Jett, J., Cole, T. W., Maden, C., & Downie, J. S. (2016). The HathiTrust Research Center Workset Ontology: A descriptive framework for non-consumptive research collections. Journal of Open Humanities Data 2.

Lehmann, J., Isele, R., Jakob, M., et al. (2015). DBPedia – A large-scale, multilingual knowledge base extracted from Wikipedia. Semantic Web 6(2), 167-195.

Makri, S. & Blandford, A. (2012). Coming across information serendipitously – part 1: A process model. Documentation 68(5), 684-705.

Makri, S., Blandford, A., Woods, M., Sharples, S., & Maxwell, D. (2014). "Making my own luck": Serendipity strategies and how to support them in digital information environments. In Journal of the Association for Information Science and Technology 65(11), 2179-2194.

Page, K. R., Bechhofer, S., Fazekas, G., Weigl, D. M., & Wilmering, T. (2017). Realising a layered digital library: exploration and analysis of the Live Music Archive. In Proc. Joint Conference on Digital Libraries, IEEE, 1-10.

Page, K. R., Jett, J., Cole, T. W., Kudeki, D., Bainbridge, D., Organisciak, P., & Downie, J. S. (2018). Worksets expand the scholarly utility of digital libraries. In Proc. 18th ACM/IEEE on Joint Conference on Digital Libraries (pp. 371-372). ACM.

Šidák, Z. (1967). Rectangular confidence regions for the means of multivariate normal distributions. The American Statistical Association 62(318), 626-633.

Weigl, D. M., Page, K. R., Organisciak, P., & Downie, J. S. (2017). Information seeking in large-scale digital libraries: Strategies for scholarly workset creation. In Proceedings of the Joint Conference on Digital Libraries, IEEE, 1-4.

Wilson, T. D. (1997). Information behaviour: an interdisciplinary perspective. Information Processing & Management, 33(4), 551-572.

Exploring Visual Representations to Support Data Re-Use for Interdisciplinary Science

Andrea Wiggins
University of Nebraska at Omaha, USA. wiggins@unomaha.edu

Melissa A. Kenney
University of Maryland, College Park, USA. kenney@umd.edu

Alyson Young
Indiana University-Purdue University Indianapolis, USA. youngaly@iupui.edu

ABSTRACT

Data discovery and re-use remain challenging, particularly for interdisciplinary research, but visual representations of data may have potential to better support these tasks than text-only metadata records. Our multi-stage exploratory study used think-aloud and intercept interviews to evaluate how scientists across multiple disciplines interpret the content and evaluate the credibility of climate indicators designed for general audiences as a way to understand the potential of visual representations for supporting interdisciplinary research. Climate indicators provided a convenient alternate representation for describing a data set, featuring a visualization of the data along with vernacular textual description. Our contributions include (i) findings on the preferences of scientists from multiple disciplines for establishing the credibility and assessing the content of data for re-use, (ii) the unexpected observation that a minimal set of core metadata was considered adequate by researchers examining data from outside of their specialties, and (iii) discussion of the implications for the design of data discovery interfaces and future research to support data discovery and re-use by increasingly diverse scientific data consumers.

KEYWORDS

Data representations, metadata, provenance, interdisciplinary science, climate indicators.

INTRODUCTION

Today's scientists are increasingly encouraged to share data, with interdisciplinary research on the rise (Krumholz, 2015; Tenopir et al., 2011; Van Noorden, 2015). The practice of sharing research data has grown substantially in short order (Tenopir et al., 2015; Force & Robinson, 2014), as has emphasis on replicability and open science as demonstrations of rigor and efficient resource use (Farnham et al., 2017). Data discovery and re-use remain difficult in practice (Poole, 2015), although attitudes are increasingly favorable (Curty et al. 2017) and substantial success has been achieved in isolated cases, such as that of clinical trial data (Coady et al., 2017) and bird abundance and distribution data from eBird (Lagoze, 2014). Actual statistics on data re-use are limited, but lags behind sharing; Bishop and Kuula-Luumi (2017) reported 40% of qualitative data sets were never downloaded, and about 25% of data is used just 1-10 times.

Our research centered on the use of climate indicators as visual representations of data with potential to assist researchers in identifying the potential utility of data for interdisciplinary research. We wanted to better understand how researchers evaluate data prior to exploring it in detail and learn what supporting information was required to establish the credibility of the information. Since data exploration is an effortful task, particularly for increasingly large data sets, we argue that the "first blush" initial evaluation of data is an important step in the process of data re-use that is currently overlooked. With current research trends emphasizing the value of data sharing for re-use, there is increasing need for better understanding of and stronger support for data discovery and evaluation in this crucial initial step for data re-use (Sun & Khoo, 2017).

Climate indicators are regularly updated visual representations that summarize key climate phenomenon and impacts relative to a baseline of change (Kenney et al., 2016). To establish a system of indicators as part of a sustained U.S. National Climate Assessment (Buizer et al., 2013), Kenney et al. (2016) describes a process involving over 200 scientific experts to recommend indicators of climate changes, impacts, and responses. This effort used a rigorous process to establish implementation recommendation (Kenney et al., 2014; Kenney et al, in review). The newly released U.S. Global Change Research Program climate indicators (Janetos & Kenney, 2015; www.globalchange.gov/explore/indicators) provided an ideal test case to explore a secondary audience benefit, interdisciplinary data discovery for re-use.

Climate indicators provided a convenient alternate representation to the typical text-only metadata record for describing a data set. Unlike a table of metadata about a data set, climate indicators include a visualization of the data designed to clearly show key trends, along with vernacular textual description, rather than highly technical details of the data (e.g., examples given in

Sun & Khoo, 2017). Through our partnership with the U.S. Global Change Research Program, we also sought to identify important design considerations for improving the utility and understandability of data representations intended to communicate long-term, large-scale trends in climate science (Gerst et al., 2017). Although the primary audiences for most climate indicators are members of the public and policy makers, this form of data representation may also have potential value for audiences such as scientists, particularly when they are not specialists in the area that the indicator represents.

Our research therefore focused on data representations as mediators of (i) data discovery, (ii) initial evaluation, and (iii) decisions to further explore data for re-use. These three functions alone require substantial information to support through standard data repository metadata; more complete "research objects" to support replication are still uncommon (Bechhofer et al., 2010). The design of data representations, which could be considered a type of metadata, from a functional perspective, is also likely to influence the processes they mediate (Sun & Khoo, 2017). Through exploratory multi-stage research, we examined the way that scientists across multiple disciplines interpreted the content and evaluated the credibility of climate indicators as a type of visual representations of data. In the initial stages, our primary research question was, "How do scientists assess the content and credibility of climate indicators?" The respondents' strong emphasis on the importance of metadata led to assessment of scientists' general expectations for metadata to accompany data representations, answering the question, "What are scientists' expectations for metadata to support evaluation of data for re-use?"

BACKGROUND

Promoting data re-use is a complex challenge for several reasons, such as (i) research incentive structures that often prioritize novel data collection over re-use and fail to reward replication studies (Farnham et al., 2017), (ii) general lack of awareness of existing applicable data (Tenopir et al., 2015), and (iii) limited or inconsistent metadata (Marcial & Hemminger, 2010; Birnholtz & Bietz, 2003), among others. The specific issue we examine in this work is that of evaluating data as an input to decisions around data re-use. Data re-use has been studied in health (Joo, Kim & Kim, 2017) and biomedical sciences (Federer et al, 2015; Rolland & Lee, 2013), social sciences (Faniel, Kriesberg & Yakel, 2015; Sun & Khoo, 2017; Yoon & Kim, 2017), archeology (Faniel et al., 2013), and engineering (Faniel & Jacobsen, 2010), among others, but rarely for multi- or interdisciplinary research (Parsons et al., 2011). Most of these studies focus on attitudes about re-use, rather than documenting actual data re-use practices or functional criteria for selecting data for re-use.

By extension, we therefore have relatively little understanding of how data are evaluated for re-use, particularly by non-specialist users such as students, since the prior work has focused on single-discipline studies where the norms within each discipline and scarcity of studies limits transferability of results. Among very few exceptions, the work of Gregory et al. (2018) on search processes for data re-use directly evaluates data discovery behavior across multiple disciplinary specialties, Carlson and Anderson (2007) examined data sharing and re-use behaviors across multiple disciplines, and Young and Lutters (2015) examined the re-use of interdisciplinary data sources for meta-study research in the environmental sciences. Cragin and Shankar (2006) and Baker, Duerr and Parsons (2015) noted the value for non-specialist data consumers, while another set of studies considered students' experiences with data re-use (Faniel, Kriesberg, & Yakel, 2013; Kriesberg et al., 2012).

While metadata is not the only information that plays into data re-use decisions (Zimmerman 2007, 2008), it provides initial impressions of credibility and supports development of trust in both the data and the repository (Yakel et al., 2013) that is necessary to support a re-use decision. Similarly, visual design has been seen to influence judgments of credibility in studies of websites (Fogg, 2003). Despite this, the metadata recorded often does not provide sufficient descriptions of the context in which the data were collected, such as choices of metrics and instrumentation for observation to enable prospective re-users to interpret the data for effective secondary analysis (Borgman et al., 2009; Borgman et al., 2007; Wallis et al., 2010). Metadata has also been found to be a source of friction, particularly between scientific collaborators from two or more disciplines, often impeding data sharing (Edwards et al., 2011). While the lack of contextual details is typically less of an issue for proximal disciplines, as similarities in background allow researchers to infer relevant information, scientists from adjacent communities encounter more difficulty due to vastly different scientific practices and use of instrumentation (Borgman et al., 2009; Zimmerman, 2007). Consequently, the process of understanding how variables are constructed is often a highly collaborative and time-consuming task (Rolland & Lee, 2013), requiring engagement with original study staff to obtain the contextual details needed to assess data for relevance (Lee et al., 2009; Edwards et al., 2011).

In light of these challenges, we see indicators and their style of data representation as a potential solution strategy at the data discovery stage of this process. Climate indicators are intended to provide input to decision-making by non-expert audiences who do not have intimate knowledge of the science but need to see credible evidence of causal mechanisms in order to formulate practical and policy interventions. Climate indicators are created by subject matter specialists to communicate complex information with a goal of decision support, which is functionally similar to the needs for data representations to support data re-use. In a data re-use scenario, the representations are created by experts in the data to communicate its potential and content to informed audiences who do not necessarily have intimate knowledge of the data, similar to policy makers in the case of climate indicators. In both scenarios, images accompanying text may be useful for communicating complex information quickly and efficiently, one of the main advantages to data visualization, and professionally designed visual representations of data can support judgments of credibility (Fogg, 2003). Whether visual representations of data are adequate or effective at communicating credibility for would-be data users, however, is not well understood.

METHODS

For this exploratory study, we employed a multi-stage research design, beginning with a small number of extended think-aloud interviews and proceeding to two rounds of intercept interviews at large scientific conferences as the research evolved. Although all stages of the research involved interviews with scientists, think-aloud and intercept interview methods are substantially different in execution and data that they yield, making this a mixed-methods study. Each stage of the research informed the design of the subsequent data collection and analysis.

Think-Aloud Interviews

We conducted 5 in-depth interviews, averaging 90-120 minutes, with scientists in several disciplines (astrophysics, forestry, ecology, marine biology) using a think-aloud protocol that focused primarily on understanding their perceptions of climate indicators from several federal agencies. While interacting with a set of indicators on the U.S. Global Change Research Program (USGCRP) website and extended metadata content on the Global Change Information System (GCIS; data.globalchange.gov), we asked participants to describe their thoughts about the system, the understandability of the climate indicators, and the level of trustworthiness or credibility of the data presented in the indicators. Sampling was constrained due to limited availability during the summer, so interviewees were federal research scientists based at NASA, US Forest Service, and Smithsonian Institution; they included 3 women. The think-aloud method was well suited to answering the research question focused on how scientists evaluated the content and credibility of climate indicators but yielded broad-ranging responses. Based on the initial findings, summarized in the following section, we redesigned our study approach for a more focused scope with an intercept interview design.

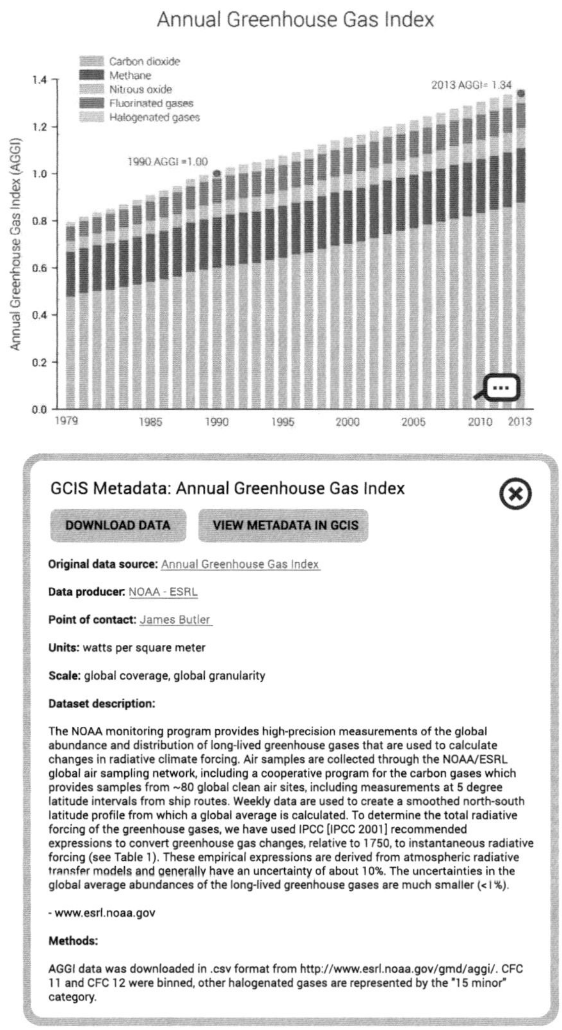

Figure 1. Metadata mockup for the Aggregated Greenhouse Gas Index climate indicator, showing both the indicator's data visualization and the "pop-up" metadata details

Intercept Interviews

After the initial interviews focused on climate indicator designs, we narrowed the scope of inquiry to the use of metadata to establish credibility from the perspective of research scientists. To increase our sample size and diversity, we conducted intercept interviews at the annual meetings of the 2015 Ecological Society of America (ESA) and the 2015 American Geophysical Union (AGU). Both of these meetings draw substantial attendance (approximately 7,000 at ESA and 25,000 at AGU) and include several subdisciplines and application spaces within the broad fields of environmental and Earth sciences. Researchers attending these conferences represent all career stages, employment sectors, and a wide range of nations. The intercept interview format involves "intercepting" random respondents at a public venue and asking a few questions.

For both meetings, interview team members were positioned near the exhibitor booth for DataONE (which supports data sharing and re-use) in the conference exhibit halls. Interviewers approached attendees at random and asked for five-minute responses to two questions, noting perceived gender and employment sector from affiliations on name badges to verify that a range of perspectives were represented. The ESA intercept interviews included 56 researchers, with 24 females and one of indeterminate gender, and sectors included 43 in academia, six in government, three nonprofit, three private, and one unaffiliated. The AGU intercept interviews included 49 researchers, with 16 females and three of indeterminate gender; sectors included 26 in academia, eight in government, five private, three nonprofit, one K-12 educator, and six undetermined.

After obtaining oral consent, different interview protocols were followed for each meeting. For the ESA interviews, interviewees were shown a randomly selected global climate indicator from the USGCRP website (e.g., vibrio infections, sea surface temperatures, arctic sea ice extent, start of spring, forest cover, atmospheric carbon dioxide) on an iPad and asked to examine the image and text. Interviewees were asked either "How would you interpret the information shown here?" (version 1), or "How would you assess the credibility of this information?" (version 2) Following their initial responses, interviewees were then asked, "What information is missing that would help you interpret it/make that assessment?" 18 interviewees were asked the version 1 questions, 32 were asked the version 2 questions, and six responded to both (3 questions in total).

Based on the results of the ESA intercepts, in which most respondents focused on data provenance in the form of metadata as a primary requirement for information credibility (which was available only through a platform separate from the climate indicators), a new intercept protocol was developed for the AGU meeting. Interviewees were first asked, "In a moment, I'll show you a paper version of a scientific visualization that would be viewed online. In general, what kinds of information or metadata about the visualization would you want to see?" Following their response, alternating participants were shown a high-fidelity mockup of a metadata pop-up interface alongside the climate indicator for either ocean chlorophyll concentrations or aggregated greenhouse gas index (Figure 1), and asked, "How well does this metadata meet your expectations for documenting a scientific visualization like the one here?" The ESA intercept interviews answered the research question focused on scientists' evaluations of credibility and content, while the AGU intercept interviews focused on scientists' expectations for metadata to accompany visual representations of data, as it was difficult to effectively prompt consideration of a data re-use scenario.

Analysis

Deductive and inductive content analysis was applied to all data (Neuendorf, 2016). The deductive analysis used a coding schema based on the web credibility literature (e.g., Barry & Schamber (1998), Fogg (2003), Kubiszewski, Noordewier, & Costanza (2011), Metzger (2007), Rieh & Danielson (2007)). Examples of concepts used to code responses included: accuracy, validity, authority, provenance/metadata, objectivity, informativeness, persuasiveness, quality, trustworthiness, clarity, and consistency. Deductive coding was completed by multiple team members who coded at the level of the entire response to each prompt for the intercept interviews and argued to consensus. Inductive codes were added based on emergent themes, including: intended audience, methodology for raw data collection, and methodology for indicator creation, as well as positive, negative, or neutral assessments of the metadata mockup.

FINDINGS

Several themes were identified at each of the three stages of the study, which focused the evolving exploratory research and refine the inquiry at each successive stage, with increasing emphasis on metadata as a key component of data representations. Table 1 summarizes the research questions and themes identified at each stage of the research.

Research stage	*Research questions addressed*	*Themes*
1: Think-aloud interviews	How do scientists assess the content and credibility of climate indicators?	• Metadata is required to assess data • Prior knowledge of data impacts assessments • Machine-readable metadata is not suitable for humans
2: ESA intercept interviews	How do scientists assess the content and credibility of climate indicators?	• Metadata is required to assess data • Prior knowledge of data impacts assessments • Disciplinary preferences for metadata • Data source impacts trust • Concerns over intended audience
3: AGU intercept interviews	What are scientists' expectations for metadata to support evaluation of data for re-use?	• Metadata is required to assess data • Disciplinary preferences for metadata • Data source impacts trust • Concerns over intended audience • Basic metadata is adequate for initial data assessments

Table 1: *Questions addressed and themes identified across stages of the study*

Stage 1: Data representation design and metadata presentation

The initial think-aloud interviews brought three themes to our attention. First, the context of production and processing for data is critical to its evaluation: data presented without metadata is not adequate for scientists' uses. This reflected a strong implicit norm across disciplines of providing basic details about data production and processing. For example, when examining the indicator for Frost Free Season, one participant indicated that he would want to see "details on how [the data] was collected, by whom… there isn't much information from what I saw regarding how they were [collected]... I don't know how that information was processed over time. Was the same methodology employed over time?"

Second, the machine-readable metadata system that was available for interviewees to explore was inadequate for human needs, although well suited to other purposes. Our interviewees consistently reported a strong need for an additional human-friendly interface with simplified navigation and comprehensive views of details relevant to the indicator. As another participant noted, when trying to find additional details about the Sea Ice Extent indicator, "... you shouldn't have to click an image to find the source, to find tabular data … then I have to click on the table, and I get the raw numbers, and then I get what report this appeared in, but I still don't get where this came from." For the GCIS, limited curation of existing machine-readable metadata would be adequate to serve this need.

Third, we observed different types of reactions from our interviewees to data that were and were not familiar to them. This was only partially surprising, as background knowledge is important for evaluating data, but the tone of responses was unexpectedly distinctive. The interviewees were more critical of the representations of data with which they were already familiar. For example, a forest ecologist made extended critical comments about the definitions of a "forest" built into the data that undergirded the Forest Cover indicator; no other interviewee had a similar reaction to this data. As reported below in our analysis of the intercept interviews, these were not isolated instances.

Stage 2: Metadata is essential to establishing scientific credibility

The intercept interviews at the ESA conference yielded several new observations. The most dominant theme, repeated by the majority of respondents, was the necessity of including metadata indicating the source of data and methods of processing. Common critiques of the indicators included statements like, "needs to be more references about who generated the graph and text" and "I want to see primary literature cited, where's data from?" The consistency of these responses was overwhelming, with associated codes for "Source" and "Provenance" occurring most often.

We continued to see differences in scientists' evaluations of the indicators based on whether the data were relevant to their specialty. We had no way of knowing specialties in advance, but reactions to the indicators clearly identified indicators that matched respondents' expertise. One respondent directly connected the credibility of the representation to prior knowledge, saying that "I believe it, but would need more information on the methods if I hadn't been familiar with it already." Responses were more critical when familiar with the data or related field. Those who expressed distaste for the forest cover data set were all clearly disciplinary "insiders" who knew the data set's limitations, while no other respondents made such comments on this indicator. For example, responses to the forest cover indicator ranged from a flat "I don't trust [this data set]" to a completely neutral evaluation accompanied by the caveat, "but I don't know much about [this data set]," clearly demonstrating the importance of background knowledge to evaluating the trustworthiness of data and visual representations of it.

This connected to a subtle theme that emerged during analysis: the source of the data (typically the organization producing it) was taken as a proxy for the methods of data production and interpreted as a signal of trustworthiness. In some cases, even when the specific data set was not familiar, respondents clearly recognized the methods through which these data products were produced due to the organization producing them. These responses were framed in terms of trust in the organization conducting the data collection or the instrument used in the process (e.g., LANDSAT), which bears strong similarity to results reported by Yakel et al. (2013), who reported distinctions in trust in the data versus the repository providing it. Several respondents also described a hierarchy for their trust of data based on who had produced it. Generally speaking, federal research data was considered credible; for example, one respondent said of the indicator source, "since it's government [research], I believe it." Other criteria for evaluation were clearly specific to the respondents' specialties; one respondent who worked primarily on computational modeling, for example, said hardware configuration details were critical for data re-use.

To our surprise, many scientists' interpretations of the factual content of the climate indicators were faulty, particularly when viewing indicators that represented unfamiliar topics or data, which also speaks to the importance of background knowledge in evaluating data. In some cases, they openly admitted to uncertainty in drawing a conclusion from the indicator, and their primary critique was often that the trend or purpose of the indicator was unclear or the implications of the trends and conclusions to be drawn were not obvious enough for confident interpretation. These concerns were raised alongside both correct and incorrect interpretations. One of the more pointed comments was a response to an indicator showing reduction in sea ice extent: "What does it mean to lose a million square miles of sea ice?" While the indicators' textual content satisfied some respondents seeking interpretation and meaning, others remained uncertain when trends were not apparent at a glance.

Finally, respondents commented with unexpected frequency on the intended audience for the representation (14 of 56 respondents) but primarily when struggling to interpret the indicator. These comments most often reflected on specific indicators, such as Heating and Cooling Degree Days, which was considered especially confusing by respondents, or focused on specific terminology, like radiative forcing in the Aggregate Greenhouse Gas Index. The respondents tended to couch their uncertainty about their interpretations by stating that the representation was adequate for their needs but might be less suitable for public and policy audiences. A respondent who was confused about the concept of radiative forcing claimed the indicator had "good credibility to a scientist, but I'm not sure for decision-makers." Another commented on the clarity of the same indicator, saying that "a lot of people don't know what radiative forcing is; I don't know and I studied it!" Overt concern for intended audience to indirectly indicated the respondents' own difficulty with interpretation: if a trained scientist struggled to interpret a representation, they were doubtful that policy makers or members of the general public would understand it. However, one respondent acknowledged that scientists may overthink their interpretations due to specialized knowledge, commenting that "cooling is potentially confusing to a scientist but maybe not so confusing to the average person."

Stage 3: Basic metadata is adequate for initial exploration

Much like the ESA respondents, the AGU attendees also identified specific sub-disciplinary preferences for metadata in their responses to the first prompt about what metadata they would expect to see accompanying a data visualization. Where the ESA attendees repeatedly mentioned error bars and sampling sites, AGU attendees frequently asked for uncertainty estimates, instrumentation details (e.g., for satellite products), and temporal and geographic information. The metadata they envisioned being useful reflected on the norms within their own specialties. One individual specified, "platform and physical devices used for gathering data, and processing to turn raw sensor data into products," while several others mentioned models.

Like the ESA attendees, AGU respondents placed consistent emphasis on metadata that provides information on research methods and the parties responsible for data collection and analysis, with a strong bias toward the identity of the source as a shortcut to establish credibility, often noting that "government versus private, or well-known versus unknown" sources of data would be evaluated differently; some also distinguished between parties collecting the data and those distributing it, similarly to findings from Yakel et al. (2013). A typical summary of expected information was, "when it was collected, who collected it, and where it was collected." A few respondents noted the importance of the intended use, and one person clearly understood the challenges of data re-use, mentioning need for more detailed column headers than typically expected.

Since the indicator metadata mockups that respondents were shown did not usually match their specific disciplinary expertise (again, we had no way to gauge this in advance), a few respondents echoed the concern about the purpose of and audience for indicators, but they were not asked to interpret the indicator content and made less indication of confusion than ESA attendees. To paraphrase a common response, "this data isn't from my field, so the basic metadata looks good enough for an initial evaluation of the data." This contrasted the specificity of their own desired details for imagined representations related to their research focus. The overall responses to the metadata mockups indicated adequacy for entry-level evaluation of the data, with 34 positive, 17 neutral, and 10 negative assessments for the question of whether the mockup met expectations (responses could be coded as both positive and negative if they contained both praise and critique). The generally positive response to the metadata mockups further confirmed the importance of metadata that participants reported in prior stages of the research.

When we examined the deductive coding for the responses to each of the questions, we saw additional evidence of the themes already highlighted. When discussing expectations for metadata, respondents referred to the authority of the content and its source in conjunction with presentation, provenance, informativeness, methods for data collection, and trustworthiness. They were more concerned about the authority of the source and provenance of the data collection methods than information about how the data representation was created. Provenance (metadata) was desirable primarily to demonstrate authority, which appeared to be the preferred source of credibility, as other credibility concepts were rarely mentioned besides sources and methods. Content presentation was also heavily emphasized in combination with clarity, authority, coverage (spatial/temporal range/scale), and provenance information. In the responses to the metadata mockups, strong emphasis was placed on presentation, especially for content clarity and informativeness. The positive assessments focused primarily on its presentation and informativeness, while negative assessments were much more diffuse, suggesting that they reflected personal preferences.

DISCUSSION

Our findings from this study of climate indicators as data representations repeatedly highlighted the utility of basic, standard metadata as an initial point of evaluation and minimum criterion for establishing credibility. As shown in Table 1, several themes were repeated and confirmed in each stage of the research. Contrary to prior work (Edwards et al., 2011), we saw more indications of metadata frictionlessness than metadata friction in our respondents' replies, likely because our respondents had to review the representations as scientific generalists, not disciplinary specialists, and their evaluation focused on a "product" rather than a "process" orientation to the metadata. Our discussion focuses on the tensions between metadata friction and frictionlessness, as well as implications for design and research from this exploratory work.

Metadata friction and frictionlessness

As noted, the responses here primarily reflect a "product" perspective on metadata, as our study only evaluated the initial step of data discovery for a process-oriented perspective and how study participants read and interpreted these visual representation products. Like prior work that reported on data re-use within specific disciplines and metadata friction among specialists (Edwards et al., 2011), we also saw that members of distinct scientific communities have different requirements or "wish lists" for the specific metadata they prefer to use for evaluating data and its potential for re-use, which increase the so-called friction to document and share data. At the same time, we were surprised to see the degree of commonality in core details that all scientists seemed to consider essential for basic description of a data representation. In this respect, we observed metadata frictionlessness in the high-level descriptions that respondents reported would be adequate for certain needs, and strong agreement on many of the basic details, which imply potential for reduction in expected metadata friction to support initial discovery. However, as discussed further below, we cannot determine whether the frictionlessness we observed was impacted by the inclusion of a visual representation of data as well as textual description, since most prior studies have relied on text-only information about data (e.g., Sun & Khoo, 2017), and further work would be needed to clarify whether visual representations provide a faster or easier way to evaluate data for re-use. In addition, our primary focus was on data discovery as opposed to other steps in the data re-use process, and it is not apparent from these results whether visual representations would have benefit for reducing metadata friction at other stages of the data re-use process.

The responses from the ESA and AGU meetings also suggested that researchers didn't make a strong effort to critically evaluate data that was too far removed from their specialty. There are several potential explanations: they may not have felt qualified to make the judgment, the representations we provided may not have given adequate detail at the outset, or the format of the intercept interviews may not have been conducive to a critical evaluation of the data. We were also surprised at the frequency with which trained scientists gave incorrect interpretations of carefully designed visual representations of data. If this issue was not solely based on our methods or indicator design, which seems improbable, it may suggest that there are confounding influences of background knowledge and data fluency that should be further investigated as an input to designing data repositories. In this respect, metadata friction or frictionlessness at the data discovery stage may be far less important than the researcher's background knowledge or their fluency in "reading" data representations, and the design of visual representations could have far more impact on assessments of data for re-use than details embedded in text.

Implications for design

As we refined our inquiry throughout this study, we saw that coupling a visualization of data with a textual summary and human-friendly provenance or metadata was preferred by researchers to support initial assessment of content and credibility, which are important to evaluating data for potential re-use. Our interviewees and ESA respondents insisted that metadata must always be packaged with other summary details, should not be buried within text blocks, and that it should be one click away, not several. The positive responses to the metadata mockups from AGU respondents was premised on a "one-click" model for retrieving additional details, which would make the information easy to obtain without distracting non-technical audiences.

The limitations of using climate indicators for this exploratory study also leaves several points for future work to support effective design of visual representations for data discovery and re-use. In particular, additional study is needed on the use of visual representations versus text-only descriptions; in our ESA interviews, many initial critiques based solely on the image and proximal text were resolved when the respondents reviewed the full text block accompanying the visualization. However, we do not know whether a text-only description would have been as easy to assess within minutes in a busy conference exhibitor hall, or if their interpretations of the content would have been more or less correct without the visualization. We can confirm, however, that respondents put a great deal of emphasis on the specifics of the presentation of information, which suggests the typical data repository record formats, a plain table of text, may be underselling the utility of the data on offer.

We also recommend additional work to explore researchers' responses across a wider range of disciplines, to confirm the utility of visual representations for data discovery, verify agreement on the basic details of data representations, and identify discipline-specific preferences. Replicating this study with researchers from social and other biophysical sciences would likely reveal a core set of key details that are always expected, while further clarifying the additional information of particular interest to specific scientific communities. Identifying the particulars preferred by each discipline would be useful for optimizing interfaces in disciplinary data repositories to support effective evaluation of data by target communities. It could also offer a novel way to assess similarities and differences between scientific disciplines, based on degree of agreement on core elements of research data, to support comparisons of data practices between fields in future studies.

As noted previously, most prior work that focused on supporting data re-use has been constrained to data and specialists within a single field, as opposed to evaluating whether there are general aspects of data representation that transcend disciplinary boundaries. We believe that our results indicate that this is indeed the case, which suggests that data representations may be more useful if they explicitly support multiple levels of detail, with general metadata for general consumption and additional specialist-specific information for disciplinary audiences. This could make browsing for data more efficient for broader audiences without losing the specific decision information that disciplinary specialists rely upon.

Implications for research

This study highlighted the contrasts between seeing data like a generalist as opposed to taking a specialist's view of data. Differences in the expected content, desired provenance and methods details, and even emotive responses to data that were near to versus distant from the respondents' research were striking. Because increasing emphasis is being placed on data sharing and re-use in scientific communities, our findings suggest a need for further research on the utility of alternative metadata and provenance representations. Specifically, research on representations with different levels of granularity and for a wider range of use cases, as discussed by Baker et al. (2015), could also support assessment of utility for collaborative research. An especially important use case for non-specialist data representations is students in training, who are increasingly learning their trade using existing data sources prior to developing the degree of subject specialization that characterizes the participants in most prior studies of metadata and data re-use.

We also believe that these findings point to the potential for data to serve as a neutral touchstone for fostering interdisciplinary collaboration between researchers in proximal disciplines. This bridging function is most likely to emerge when none of the collaborators "owns" the data as a result of specialized data expertise. Shared expectations for high-level information to describe data also suggests that collaborative data exploration exercises could put partners on equal footing in a new investigation, while also revealing their disciplinary differences in productive ways. For example, we can imagine a pair of new research partners simultaneously exploring a data set. The ecologist wonders aloud, "Where do you think we can find information on the sampling sites for this data set?" to which the geoscientist replies, "Oh, I hadn't thought about that yet, because I always look for details about the resolution first. But those are fundamentally related, so let's find out." Although imaginary, such an exercise could help an interdisciplinary team establish a shared vocabulary for research from the outset with greater sensitivity to different uses of similar terminology, and the experience of jointly exploring a data set that is unfamiliar to each party would inevitably highlight the expertise and interests each person brings to the partnership. Both of these potential outcomes are recognized as key factors in building effective interdisciplinary teams (Stokols et al., 2008).

The limitations of the study included its exploratory nature and the disciplines represented, as most participants' backgrounds were in relatively close intellectual proximity. The think-aloud interviews relied on convenience sampling but provided focus for the intercept interviews. The initial intercept interviews focused on the credibility of data as presented in indicators more than the utility of the presentation for data discovery, because the idea of browsing for data seemed foreign to most researchers. Additional research could provide more conclusive results about the utility of visual representations for supporting data discovery and re-use. Finally, the data and indicators presented to interviewees were quantitative and spatial in nature, so the findings reported here may have limited transferability to qualitative and textual research data. The indicators were also all carefully designed by professionals who were more focused on accuracy in representation than we would expect of a typical researcher preparing a data deposit. The data sets typically represented were well known by researchers in associated disciplines; data representations for more obscure data sets may elicit different responses.

CONCLUSION

In this multi-stage exploratory study of climate indicators as visual representations of data for re-use, we found that scientists rely heavily on traditional metadata as a signal of credibility, and often used the affiliated organizations that produced the data, such as federal agencies, as a proxy for methods and quality. Despite their training, many scientists had difficulty interpreting the content of carefully designed visual representations of data from other disciplines than their own, and under these circumstances, tended to report concerns about the suitability of indicators for non-scientific audiences. Given the emphasis that researchers placed on metadata, we further examined scientists' expectations for metadata to support data discovery and evaluating data for re-use. Contrary to expectations, a minimal set of core details were considered adequate by researchers examining data from a generalist perspective, although respondents also highlighted common discipline-specific preferences for metadata to contextualize data sets. We also saw that a greater degree of specificity in data description was expected for data that were closely related to researchers' specialties, while data unfamiliar to them was not met with the same scrutiny. This study complemented related prior work by examining scientists' evaluations of data representations and preferences for metadata in multiple disciplinary audiences, rather than a single disciplinary space, and is unique in evaluating visual representations of data as a support for data discovery.

These results suggested that visual representations of data may be useful for data discovery, which merits further study, and could also have value for mediating initial development of interdisciplinary collaborations. However, visual representations cannot stand alone: traditional metadata on data collection and analysis methods is always expected by scientific audiences. We suggest that in the design of data discovery interfaces, visual representations of data alongside high-level metadata, with one-click access to detailed "specialist-level" metadata, may better serve the interests of both general and disciplinary audiences that have different expectations for information about data. We also suggest that further study of metadata and data representations to support discovery and re-use is needed, particularly with a non-disciplinary and non-expert focus, to support the growing diversity of scientific data consumers, including students, interdisciplinary teams, and the general public.

ACKNOWLEDGEMENTS

This work was supported in part by NSF HRD grant 1008117 and NOAA grant NA14NES4320003. We thank DataONE for sharing space at ESA and AGU, annd our collaborators for contributions to these results, including J. Felix Wolfinger, Michael D. Gerst, Ainsley Lloyd, Amanda Lamoureux, Annibel Rice, Carly Brody, Sarah Ramdeen, and Emily Bondank.

REFERENCES

Baker, K. S., Duerr, R. E., & Parsons, M. A. (2015). Scientific knowledge mobilization: Co-evolution of data products and designated communities. *International Journal of Digital Curation,* 10(2), 110-135.

Barry, C. L., & Schamber, L. (1998). Users' criteria for relevance evaluation: a cross-situational comparison. *Information processing & management*, 34(2), 219-236.

Birnholtz, J.P., & Bietz, M.J. (2003). Data at work: Supporting sharing in science and Engineering. In *Proceedings of the International ACM SIGGROUP Conference on Supporting Group Work*, Sanibel Island, FL. New York: ACM Press.

Bechhofer, S., De Roure, D., Gamble, M., Goble, C., & Buchan, I. (2010). Research Objects: Towards Exchange and Reuse of Digital Knowledge. In *The Future of the Web for Collaborative Science (FWCS 2010).* Nature Precedings.

Bishop, L., & Kuula-Luumi, A. (2017). Revisiting qualitative data reuse: A decade on. *Sage Open*, 7(1), 2158244016685136.

Buizer J.L., Fleming P., Hays S.L. et al. (2013) *Report on preparing the nation for change: building a sustained national climate assessment process.* National Climate Assessment and Development Advisory Committee.

Carlson, S., & Anderson, B. (2007). What are data? The many kinds of data and their implications for reuse. *Journal of Computer-Mediated Communication* 12, (2). http://jcmc.indiana.edu/vol12/issue2/carlson.html

Coady, S. A., Mensah, G. A., Wagner, E. L., Goldfarb, M. E., Hitchcock, D. M., & Giffen, C. A. (2017). Use of the national heart, lung, and blood institute data repository. *New England Journal of Medicine*, 376(19), 1849-1858.

Cragin, M.H., & Shankar, K. (2006). Scientific data collections and distributed collective practice. *Computer Supported Cooperative Work* 15(2-3). Dordrecht, The Netherlands: Kluwer

Curty, R.G., Crowston, K., Specht, A., Grant, B.W., & Dalton, E.D. (2017). Attitudes and norms affecting scientists' data reuse. *PloS one*, 12(12), e0189288.

Edwards, P. N., Mayernik, M. S., Batcheller, A. L., Bowker, G. C., & Borgman, C. L. (2011). Science friction: Data, metadata, and collaboration. *Social Studies of Science*, 41(5), 667-690.

Faniel, I.M., & Jacobsen, T.E. (2010). Reusing scientific data: How earthquake engineering researchers assess the reusability of colleagues' data. *Computer Supported Cooperative Work*, 19(3-4), 355-375.

Faniel, I.M., Kansa, E., Whitcher Kansa, S., Barrera-Gomez, J., & Yakel, E. (2013, July). The challenges of digging data: a study of context in archaeological data reuse. In *Proceedings of the 13th ACM/IEEE-CS joint conference on Digital Libraries* (pp. 295-304). ACM.

Faniel, I.M., Kriesberg, A., & Yakel, E. (2012). Data reuse and sensemaking among novice social scientists. *Journal of the Association for Information Science and Technology*, 49(1), 1-10.

Faniel, I.M., Kriesberg, A., & Yakel, E. (2016). Social scientists' satisfaction with data reuse. *Journal of the Association for Information Science and Technology*, 67(6), 1404-1416.

Faniel, I.M., & Zimmerman, A. (2011). Beyond the data deluge: a research agenda for large-scale data sharing and reuse. *International Journal of Digital Curation*, 6(1), 58-69.

Farnham, A., Kurz, C., Öztürk, M.A., Solbiati, M., Myllyntaus, O., Meekes, J., ... & Kanninen, L. (2017). Early career researchers want Open Science. *Genome biology*, 18(1), 221.

Federer, L.M., Lu, Y.L., Joubert, D.J., Welsh, J., & Brandys, B. (2015). Biomedical data sharing and reuse: Attitudes and practices of clinical and scientific research staff. *PloS ONE*, 10(6), e0129506.

Fogg, B. J. (2003). Prominence-interpretation theory: Explaining how people assess credibility online. In *CHI'03 extended abstracts on human factors in computing systems* (pp. 722-723). ACM.

Force, M. and N. Robinson, Encouraging data citation and discovery with the Data Citation Index. Journal of Computer-Aided Molecular Design, 2014. 28(10): p. 1043-1048.

Gerst, M.D., Kenney, M.A, Wolfinger, J.F., Baer, A., Wiggins, A., Feygina, I., ... Young, A. (2017). *Effective Visual Communication of Climate Indicators and Scientific Information: Synthesis, Design Considerations, and Examples. A Technical Input Report to the 4th National Climate Assessment Report.* Version 2.0. http://www.umdindicators.org/wp-content/uploads/2018/01/Visual-Design-Guidance-Document-V2.0-1.pdf

Gregory, K., Cousijn, H., Groth, P., Scharnhorst, A., & Wyatt, S. (2018). Understanding Data Retrieval Practices: A Social Informatics Perspective. *arXiv preprint* arXiv:1801.04971.

Janetos, A. C., & Kenney, M. A. (2015). Developing better indicators to track climate impacts. *Frontiers in Ecology and the Environment*, 13(8), 403-403.

Joo, S., Kim, S., & Kim, Y. (2017). An exploratory study of health scientists' data reuse behaviors: Examining attitudinal, social, and resource factors. *Aslib Journal of Information Management*, 69(4), 389-407.

Kenney, M.A., Janetos, A.C., & Gerst, M.D. (in review). Climate indicators for the nation. *Climatic Change*.

Kenney, M.A., Janetos, A.C., & Lough, G.C. (2016). Building an integrated US national climate indicators system. *Climatic Change*, 135(1), 85-96.

Kenney M.A., Janetos A.C. et al. (2014) *National climate indicators system report*. National Climate Assessment Development and Advisory Committee. http://www.umdindicators.org/wp-content/uploads/2016/10/Pilot-Indicator-System-Report_final.pdf

Kriesberg, A., Frank, R.D., Faniel, I.M., & Yakel, E. (2013). The role of data reuse in the apprenticeship process. *Journal of the Association for Information Science and Technology*, 50(1), 1-10.

Krumholz, H.M., (2015). Why data sharing should be the expected norm. *British Medical Journal*, 350: p. H599.

Kubiszewski, I., Noordewier, T., & Costanza, R. (2011). Perceived credibility of Internet encyclopedias. *Computers & Education*, 56(3), 659-667.

Lagoze, C. (2014). eBird: Curating Citizen Science Data for Use by Diverse Communities. *International Journal of Digital Curation*, 9(1), 71-82.

Marcial, L.H., & Hemminger, B.M. (2010). Scientific data repositories on the Web: An initial survey. *Journal of the Association for Information Science and Technology*, 61(10), 2029-2048.

Metzger, M.J. (2007). Making sense of credibility on the Web: Models for evaluating online information and recommendations for future research. *Journal of the American Society for Information Science and Technology*, 58(13), 2078-2091. doi: 10.1002/asi.20672

Neuendorf, K.A. (2016). *The content analysis guidebook*. Sage.

Parsons, M.A., Godøy, Ø., LeDrew, E., De Bruin, T.F., Danis, B., Tomlinson, S., & Carlson, D. (2011). A conceptual framework for managing very diverse data for complex, interdisciplinary science. *Journal of Information Science*, 37(6), 555-569.

Poole, A.H. (2015). How has your science data grown? Digital curation and the human factor: a critical literature review. *Archival Science*, 15(2), 101-139.

Rieh, S.Y., & Danielson, D.R. (2007). Credibility: A multidisciplinary framework. *Annual review of information science and technology*, 41(1), 307-364

Rolland, B. and C.P. Lee, (2013). Beyond trust and reliability: reusing data in collaborative cancer epidemiology research. In *Proceedings of the 2013 ACM International conference on Computer supported cooperative work*. ACM: San Antonio, Texas, USA. p. 435-444.

Stokols, D., Misra, S., Moser, R.P., Hall, K.L., & Taylor, B.K. (2008). The ecology of team science: understanding contextual influences on transdisciplinary collaboration. *American Journal of Preventive Medicine*, 35(2), S96-S115.

Sun, G., & Khoo, C.S.G. (2017). Social science research data curation: issues of reuse. *Libellarium: journal for the research of writing, books, and cultural heritage institutions*, 9(2).

Tenopir, C., et al., (2011). Data Sharing by Scientists: Practices and Perceptions. *PLoS ONE* 6(6): p. E21101.

Tenopir C., Dalton E.D., Allard S., Frame M., Pjesivac I., Birch B., et al. (2015) Changes in Data Sharing and Data Reuse Practices and Perceptions among Scientists Worldwide. *PLoS ONE* 10(8): e0134826.

Van Noorden, R. (2015). Interdisciplinary research by the numbers. *Nature News*, 525(7569), 306.

Yakel, E., Faniel, I. M., Kriesberg, A., & Yoon, A. (2013). Trust in digital repositories. *International Journal of Digital Curation*, 8(1), 143-156.

Yoon, A., & Kim, Y. (2017). Social scientists' data reuse behaviors: Exploring the roles of attitudinal beliefs, attitudes, norms, and data repositories. *Library & Information Science Research*, 39(3), 224-233.

Young, A.L., & Lutters, W.G. (2015). (Re)defining land change science through synthetic research practices. In *Proceedings of the 2015 ACM International conference on Computer supported cooperative work*. ACM: Vancouver, British Columbia, Canada. p 431-442.

Zimmerman, A. (2007). Not by metadata alone: the use of diverse forms of knowledge to locate data for reuse. *International Journal on Digital Libraries*. 7(1-2): p. 5-16.

Zimmerman, A. (2008). New knowledge from old data: The role of standards in the sharing and reuse of ecological data. *Science, Technology, & Human Values* 33, (5). London: Sage.

The Impact of Fielding on Retrieval Performance and Bias

Colin Wilkie
University of Glasgow, United Kingdom.
c.wilkie.3@research.gla.ac.uk

Leif Azzopardi
University of Strathclyde, United Kingdom.
leif.azzopardi@strath.ac.uk

ABSTRACT

Within many domains, such as news, medicine and patent, documents contain a variety of fields such as title, author, body, source, etc. As such fielded retrieval models that query across these fields are often employed. It is largely presumed that fielding provides a better representation of the document and offers more control when querying and that this will lead to improved retrieval performance. However, depending on how the fields are weighted and if the fields are populated, the retrieval algorithm may unduly favour certain documents over others. This is known as algorithmic bias and it can be detrimental to retrieval systems performance. In this paper, we explore the impact of fielding on retrieval bias and performance across a variety of TREC News Test Collections. We perform an extensive large-scale analysis on two types of fielded retrieval model variations that are based on the popular BM25 retrieval algorithm where either: fields are scored independently and then combined (Model 1), or fields are first combined and then scored (Model 2). Our findings show that for Model 1 fielding, a strong correlation exists between retrieval bias and performance such that as title fields are weighted more heavily, bias increases, while retrieval performance decreases. When weighting is applied to content-based fields, performance increases as bias decreases, showing that relying more on content may be favourable in terms of fairness and performance. On the other hand, for Model 2 fielding, the relationship between retrieval bias and performance is more complex. But, crucially we show that Model 2 fielding results in lower retrieval bias and greater performance than Model 1 fielding. And, we observed that under Model 1, news articles without titles are substantially less retrievable (i.e. more susceptible to algorithmic bias). These findings have serious ramifications as many popular Open Source Information Retrieval frameworks, commonly used by professional searchers, use the default implementation of Model 1 for their fielded search capability. This research shows the importance of analysing retrieval algorithms with respect to both bias and performance to ensure they minimize any unwanted or unintended biases when maximising performance. Further work is required to examine this phenomenon in more detail and to design fielded retrieval models that have the advantages of control and performance without detrimental biases.

KEYWORDS

Algorithmic Bias, Information Retrieval, Search Engine Bias

INTRODUCTION

In the field of Information Retrieval (IR), the focus has typically been on trying to make search as effective and efficient as possible. However, depending on the algorithmic choices, the data and the configuration of the information retrieval system, algorithmic biases can creep in that can adversely affect the performance of the system by treating particular users or groups of documents unfairly (Kirkpatrick, 2016). Researchers have argued for the need of legislative controls to be applied to retrieval systems to reduce the level of bias present in search results (Goldman, 2005). Thus, it is also important to analyze and evaluate the bias within a system and how it relates to the performance of the system. In this work, we aim to do so in the context of fielded retrieval. Treating a document as a bag-of-words greatly simplifies how documents are modeled and represented. However, in many domains, documents contain structured meta-data and various fields that characterize the contents of the document (Robertson, Zaragoza and Taylor, 2004). For example, email documents contain subject, body, to and from, while news articles contain title, source, contents, author, etc. Whether it be patent, medical, academic, email or news, documents typically have a title and contents field that can be used to identify relevant material. The premise is that having a more structured representation of the document provides searchers with more control when querying a collection (Kim, Xue and Croft, 2009). Often query terms are related to specific fields within a document (Azzopardi, De Rijke and others, 2006) so query terms are mapped either explicitly or implicitly to fields and/or the importance of fields are weighted in order to improve retrieval performance.

In terms of ranking based on fielded documents, various retrieval algorithms have been developed including BM25F (Robertson, Zaragoza and Taylor, 2004) and variants of (Itakura and Clarke, 2010; Blanco and Boldi, 2012), Fielded Language and Relevance Models (Ogilvie and Callan, 2003; Azzopardi, De Rijke and others, 2006; Kim and Croft, 2012), Fielded Multinomial Randomness Models (Plachouras and Ounis, 2007), etc. These retrieval algorithms are used to score the document given the set of fields *f*, by either: (1) a weighted combination of field level scores (Kim and Croft, 2012), or (2) a combination of weighted fields, which is then scored (Robertson, Zaragoza and Taylor, 2004). While both have merits, the first approach to fielding has been criticized because it can lead to an imbalance due to how the term frequencies are handled on a per field basis and that terms missing from particular fields may lead to a greater disparity in scores. This could lead to retrieval biases creeping in that adversely affect the performance of the system. In a recent study on the second approach to fielding, it was shown that field weights can have a major impact on performance and that any improvements are very much dependent on the task, the domain and are sensitive to parameter tuning (Jimmy, Zuccon and Koopman, 2016). It is currently an open question whether fielding (and the different approaches to fielding) affect retrieval bias and consequently retrieval performance. Thus, we posit that fielding may introduce systematic algorithmic biases that are detrimental to retrieval performance when fielding is incorrectly applied. To explore whether this is the case we perform the first investigation on how fielded retrieval affects retrieval performance and retrieval bias given the two types of approaches to fielding. Given the concerns over the first approach, we contend that the second approach will be fairer i.e. it will exhibit less bias across the population of documents, and lead to greater retrieval performance. Our working hypothesis is that a fairer system will lead to better retrieval performance (Wilkie and Azzopardi, 2014a). Given that the most widely used Open Source IR systems, such as Elastic, Solr and Lucene, currently provide fielding out of the box using the first approach by default, it is important to study the implications of this choice. Thus, this work is both relevant and timely and will provide much needed guidance on how algorithmic biases stemming from fielding can be avoided or minimized.

RELATED WORK

Retrieval algorithms have generally been developed with a particular goal in mind; to increase performance. However, unintentional biases can appear in retrieval algorithms that can unwittingly impact performance. For example, earlier variants of **TF.IDF** either overly favored short documents or overly favored long documents depending on whether the term frequency was normalized (i.e. *favoring short documents*) or not (i.e. *favoring long documents*). Thus, pivoted length normalization was proposed as a way to mitigate length bias (Singhal, Buckley and Mitra, 1996). Now length normalization is common to most retrieval algorithms. When scoring documents, retrieval algorithms tend to have two main goals; first, to estimate the query terms information content and second, to apply length normalization factor to penalize long (or short) documents. Models which focus only on one component tend to lead to exhibit higher levels of retrieval bias (Wilkie and Azzopardi, 2017a).

However, the inclusion of fields introduces a new layer of complexity when scoring a document as the weights between and within fields will have an impact on retrieval performance and may also introduce additional harmful biases. In this paper, we intend to explore whether there is a relationship between retrieval bias and performance given the different types of fielding models. First, we will define precisely what we mean by retrieval bias and how it is derived from measures of retrievability. Following this, we will outline previous work examining the relationship between retrieval bias and performance in other contexts before formally describing the two different approaches to scoring fielded documents.

Retrievability and Retrieval Bias

The concept of retrievability was first introduced by Azzopardi and Vinay (Azzopardi and Vinay, 2008b, 2008a) to describe and measure how easily a document can be retrieved when using a particular configuration of an IR system. The measure of retrievability $\boldsymbol{r}$ of a document $\boldsymbol{d}$ with respect to an IR system was formally defined as:

$$r(d) \propto \sum_{q \in Q} O_q \cdot u(k_{dq}, c, a)$$

where the retrievability $\boldsymbol{r(d)}$ is calculated by taking the sum over the universe of all possible queries $\boldsymbol{Q}$, weighted by the probability of each query $\boldsymbol{q}$ being chosen, $\boldsymbol{O_q}$ multiplied by the utility access function, $\boldsymbol{u(k_{dq}, c, a)}$, which denotes how easily $\boldsymbol{d}$ can be found given the query $\boldsymbol{q}$. The utility function takes three parameters: the rank of the document given the query $\boldsymbol{k_{dq}}$, a rank cut-off $\boldsymbol{c}$ and discount factor $\boldsymbol{a}$. Two different utility functions have been proposed, which ascribe a value to how easily a document can be retrieved for a given query. The simplest is a cut-off based scoring model (or cumulative model), where the utility access function $\boldsymbol{u(k_{dq}, c, a)}$ is defined such that $\boldsymbol{u(k_{dq}, c, a) = 1}$ if $\boldsymbol{d}$ is retrieved in the top $\boldsymbol{c}$ documents given the query $\boldsymbol{q}$, otherwise $\boldsymbol{u(k_{dq}, c, a) = 0}$. In other words, this model accumulates score for a document so long as it is retrieved before the specified cut-off while documents appearing after the cut-off are ignored. This simulates a user who is willing to look at all documents up until a set point (e.g. all the documents on the first page of results).

An alternative utility function is the gravity-based scoring model, which simulates a user who is more likely to examine documents higher in the ranking, and less likely to examine documents further down. Formally the gravity-based utility function can be defined as:

$$\boldsymbol{u(k_{dq}, c, a) = \frac{1}{[k_{dq}]^a}}$$

where a is a discount factor that defines the magnitude of the penalty applied to a document given the document's rank position, when $k_{dq} < c$, otherwise $u(k_{dq}, c, a) = 0$. The idea behind the gravity-based model is that a document further down the ranked list is less retrievable because users are less likely to visit deeper ranks. Therefore, a document appearing at rank **1** contributes substantially more to the overall retrievability, $r(d)$, than a document at rank **10** or rank **100**. If the document appears beyond the cut-off c, it does not contribute anything to the documents overall retrievability.

The intuition behind the retrievability score is that documents that are retrieved at higher ranks by many queries are more retrievable. While, documents that few queries retrieve at a sufficiently high rank to be encountered by a user, modeled by c and a, are less retrievable. Assuming we can calculate the $r(d)$ for a collection of documents, it is possible to examine the overall bias across the population of documents and determine if one set of documents is more retrievable than other. Put another way, does the retrieval system unduly favor one set of documents over another set of documents? To obtain a high-level view of the retrieval bias that a system imposes on the document collection, the *Lorenz Curve* (Gastwirth, 1972) can be used. The Lorenz Curve visually depicts the inequality within a population of documents (according to their $r(d)$ scores). In Economics and the Social Sciences, the Lorenz Curve is used to show the inequality within a population given their income or wealth. This is performed by first sorting the individuals in the population in ascending order of their wealth and then plotting a cumulative wealth distribution. If the wealth in the population is distributed equally then this cumulative distribution will be linear (and thus denotes equality). The extent to which a given distribution deviates from equality is reflected by the skew in the distribution. The more skewed the plot, the greater the amount of inequality or bias within the population. The most extreme case being, when a monarch has all the wealth, while the peasants have none. To summarize the inequality of such distributions the *Gini Coefficient* is used (Gastwirth, 1972). The Gini Coefficient is essentially the area under the Lorenz Curve, **B**, divided by the area under the Line of Equality (**A+B**) as shown in Figure **1**.

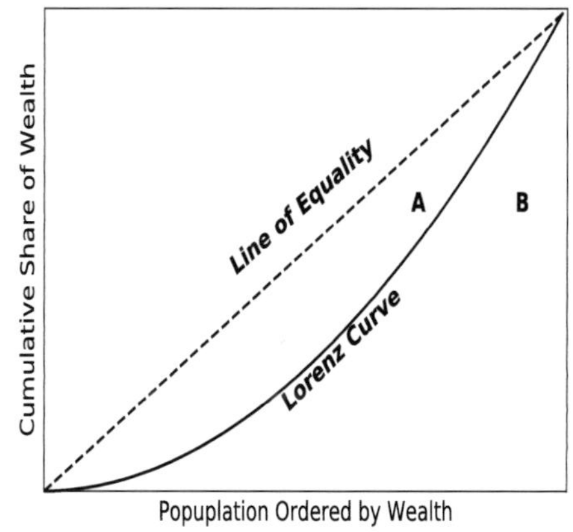

Figure 1: Lorenz curve demonstrating how inequality is depicted graphically.

In the context of retrievability, if all documents were equally retrievable then the area A in Figure **1** would be zero, and thus the Gini coefficient would be zero (denoting equality within the population). On the other hand, if the retrieval system only ever retrieved one document, and it was always the same document, while all other documents were not retrieved (and thus had a retrievability $r(d) = 0$), then the area **B** in Figure 1 would be equal to zero, and the Gini coefficient would be one (denoting total inequality). Usually, documents have some level of retrievability, and thus the Gini coefficient is somewhere between one and zero. Many factors affect the retrieval bias (denoted by the Gini coefficient) these include:

- The indexing processes,
- The retrieval model/system and its parameter settings,
- The documents and collection representations/statistics,
- The type and length of queries, and,
- The number of documents users are willing to examine.

In this paper, we explore the impact of fielding and approaches to fielding on retrieval bias.

Retrieval Bias and Performance

The relationship between retrieval bias and performance has been examined in various contexts (e.g. web, news, patents, archives, etc. (Azzopardi and Vinay, 2008b; Azzopardi and Owens, 2009; Bashir and Rauber, 2009a) and across number of different factors (query length, document length and document features (Wilkie and Azzopardi, 2013, 2015; Chen, Azzopardi and Scholer, 2017), query expansion (Bashir and Rauber, 2009b; C. Wilkie and Azzopardi, 2017b), retrieval algorithms (Bashir and Rauber, 2014; Wilkie and Azzopardi, 2014a; Lipani *et al.*, 2015) and over time (Traub *et al.*, 2016; Samar *et al.*, 2017) etc.) From this body of work there have been several key findings: first, different retrieval systems exhibit different levels of retrieval bias but the **BM25** retrieval algorithm tends to be the fairest when tuned (i.e. lowest Gini). Second, how the retrieval model is parameterized and configured has a considerable impact on what documents are favored over others, leading to greater or lesser amounts of bias. And third, there is strong correlation between performance and retrieval bias such that reducing bias tends to lead to better retrieval performance, leading to the *fairness hypothesis*. This hypothesis suggests that a system that affords access to all documents, and thus is fairer, will lead to better performance. The idea is that if a system makes some documents hard to retrieve i.e. $r(d)$ either zero or close to zero, then if a user ever wanted to retrieve those documents it would very difficult for the user pose a query which would surface a document at a rank sufficiently high enough for them to encounter it. Thus, a system that affords some level of retrievability to all documents as equally as possible gives some way to all (or most) of the documents being retrieved at a rank where the user will see it. However, prior research has only considered standard non-fielded retrieval algorithms and has not investigated the impact of fielding and fields on retrieval bias nor whether the fairest hypothesis holds in this context.

Fielded Retrieval Models

Fielded retrieval became popular due to the idea that particular sections of documents may contain more information content than other areas. The simplest example is for news story collections where fields such as title, content and source are often readily available. Since the title of the document is written to attract the attention of readers, it is logical to reason that the short titles will contain keywords which are very relevant to the article. As such, when querying these articles, having a part of your query specifically target this field could yield improvements in performance. However, this has been shown to be dependent on many factors including the implementation of fielded retrieval that is employed. As previously mentioned there are two main approaches when scoring fielded documents:

Model 1: where fields are scored independently and then combined to form the overall document score.

Model 2: where the terms within fields are first combined and then scored to provide the overall document score.

The baseline approach is to treat the fields as one big bag of words – a standard retrieval model – **Model 0,** where the score of a document is:

$$s(q,d) = \sum_j s(n(q_j),d)$$

Where the query q is composed of **j** terms q_j and $s(n(q_j), d)$ is the score assigned by the retrieval model i.e. **BM25**, **TF.IDF**, **PL2**, etc, given the number of times the terms q_j appears in the document $n(q_j)$. The **Model 1** fielded retrieval approach, however, scores the fields in the document first, and the totals up the weighted field scores as follows:

$$s(q,d) = \sum_i w_i \sum_j s(n(q_j,f_i),d)$$

Where the document is composed of i fields, f_i and the $s(n(q_j, f_i), d)$ is the score assigned by the retrieval model, given the number of times the term q_j appears in field f_i in document i.e. $n(q_j, f_i)$ and w_i is the weight assigned to the field f_i.

Robertson *et. al.* proposed a revision of this model, that altered how the fielded scores were combined (Robertson, Zaragoza and Taylor, 2004; Robertson and Zaragoza, 2009). The authors argued that simple linear combinations of the scores could interrupt the saturation of term frequencies across the fields of the collections thus negatively impacting performance. The authors performed experiments on news collections that featured title and content, and found that their alternative combination term frequencies from fields greatly improved upon the weighted linear combination. The **Model 2** approach scores the document as follows:

$$s(q,d) = \sum_j s(n_j,d)$$

Where:

$$n_j = \sum_i w_i \cdot n(q_j,f_i)$$

Where $n(q_j,f_i)$ is the number of times the term q_j appears in the field f_i in the document. However, **Model 2** fielding is not without its problems either. In Jimmy *et al.* they explored the influence of boosting the weights of different fields and found that significant reductions in performance can result depending on the configuration (Jimmy, Zuccon and Koopman, 2016). They posit that weighting title over content can have a negative impact on retrieval for exploratory queries whereas for navigational queries, title boosting often improves performance. Neither of these investigated the impact fielding has on retrieval bias. In this work, like the aforementioned studies, we will used **BM25** to provide the score between query terms and fields and/or documents and explore the influence of field weighting and the fielding approach on retrieval performance and bias.

EXPERIMENTAL METHOD

Research Questions

The primary research question of this study is: what is the relationship between the different approaches to fielding, retrieval performance and retrieval bias? More specifically:

- How does boosting the weights of fields affect retrieval bias and retrieval performance?
- How retrievable are documents when they have missing fields?

- Which fielding approach is more robust?

While exploring these questions, we will also examine whether the *fairness hypothesis* holds in this context and uncover if the fielding approach that is fairer (i.e. lower retrieval bias) also result in better retrieval performance?

Data and Materials

For this analysis, three TREC News test collections were employed as they contained a title field and a content field: Associated Press 88-89 (**AP**), TREC volumes **4&5** (**T45**) and Aquaint (**AQ**) (see Table **1** for the collection statistics). The collections were indexed using a single term tokenizer with Porter stemming. Additionally, all stop words were removed as were terms less than 3 characters long. Several indexes were created, one to represent **Model 0** that contained one field, "all", which housed both title and content i.e. the baseline bag of words approach). Another was created that contained, "title" and "content" fields separately which was used for **Model 1** experiments, where each field could be independently weighted. Then additional indexes were created which contained one field to house the weighted combination of "title" and "content" fields to support **Model 2** experiments. For the purposes of our experiments we employed a number of different weightings: ($w_{title} = 1$ and $w_{content} = 0, 1, 2, 4, 8$) and ($w_{content} = 1$ and $w_{title} = 0, 1, 2, 4, 8$) to explore how first, increasing the content weighting affects performance and bias, and second how increasing the title weighting affects performance and bias. The retrieval algorithm used across all fielding models was **BM25** (Robertson and Zaragoza, 2009) that has a length normalization parameter ***b*** which was set to 0**.75**, unless stated otherwise. All experiments were constructed using the Lucene4IR[1] add-on for experimental evaluations in IR, based on Apache Lucene.

	AP	T45	AQ
Documents	164146	527559	1032673
Topics	51-200	351-400	303-689 (50 topics)
Missing Titles	7541	55733	55080

Table 1. Collection statistics for each of the TREC test collections used – along with the number of missing titles

Retrievability and Retrieval Bias Estimation

To estimate the retrievability of the documents in each collection, we followed the methodology of Azzopardi and Vinay (2008). Since it is impractical to issue every query in the universe of all possible queries an approximation of the r(d) scores is obtained by using a very large set of queries instead. In prior work, automatically generated bigrams are extracted from the collection (Azzopardi and Vinay, 2008b; Bashir and Rauber, 2011; Wilkie and Azzopardi, 2014b; Samar *et al.*, 2017). For each collection, we extracted the top **100,000** collocations (bigrams) given their point wise information score i.e. common phrases (mostly people, places and events) that are prevalent in the collection and are likely to be issued as queries. This formed the query set ***Q***. These queries were then issued to each of the different indexes, where we recorded the documents and rank of the documents for each query. To calculate the ***r(d)*** scores, we used the cumulative based scoring function, where ***c=100***. Note that other cut-offs were used as well that led to similar findings as those reported below. Given the ***r(d)*** values for a given fielding approach and configuration, the Gini coefficient was then calculated to provide an estimate of the retrieval bias.

Performance Estimation

To estimate the retrieval performance for a given fielding approach (and configuration i.e. fielding weighting) we issued the corresponding TREC topics[2] and their relevance judgements. We then calculated the Mean Average Precision (**MAP**) and the Rank Biased Precision (**RBP**). However, due to space constraints we only report **MAP** scores to accommodate for comparison with prior work but note that we obtained similar findings for **RBP**.

RESULTS

To provide an overview of our main findings, we will focus reporting the results for collection **AQ** though our results for the other collections are similar (see Table **2** for an overview). Figure **2** provides an overview of the Lorenz curves for **Model 1** & **2** where we show how the inequality across the population of documents changes when the fielding boosting is varied: **T1-C1**, **T1-C8** and **T8-C1**. Of note is that for **Model 1**, changes in field boosts lead to greater changes in inequality – such that boosting the title leads to the greatest inequality – while boosting the content leads to lower inequality. On **Model 2** we can see that there is less variation in terms of inequality and that boosting either field leads to slightly less inequality. Note that **Model 2**, **T1-C1** is equivalent to **Model 0** (the baseline) and so under **Model 2** fielding appears to help in reducing bias. However, as both boost

[1] Code is available at: https://github.com/lucene4ir/lucene4ir
[2] Topics available at: https://trec.nist.gov/data/topics_eng/index.html

settings (**T1-C8** and **T8-C1**) lead to reductions in bias – this seems counter to intuition – how could they both reduce overall bias? We hypothesize that this is because bias can manifest from both the fielding and the length of fields, so it is possible that boosting one field might mitigate one and boosting the other might mitigate the other.

		AP			T45			AQ		
		Gini	**MAP**	**T vs NT r(d) Diff**	**Gini**	**MAP**	**T vs NT r(d) Diff**	**Gini**	**MAP**	**T vs NT r(d) Diff**
Model 0	**Base**	0.344	0.261	4.000*	0.49	0.159	-37.000*	0.545	0.16	3.000*
Model 1	**T1C0**	0.611	0.076	9.000*	0.795	0.058	2.000*	0.826	0.048	**3.000***
	T1C1	0.448	0.197	13.000*	0.627	0.12	**-1.000***	0.668	0.117	9.000*
	T1C2	0.389	0.24	12.000*	0.527	0.149	-12.000*	0.612	0.144	10.000*
	T1C4	0.358	0.256	10.000*	0.484	**0.16**	-21.000*	0.568	0.157	8.000*
	T1C8	0.349	**0.259**	7.000*	**0.482**	0.159	-26.000*	0.552	**0.161**	6.000*
	T0C1	**0.348**	0.257	**3.000***	0.494	0.155	-31.000*	**0.548**	0.157	**3.000***
	T1C1	0.448	0.197	13.000*	0.627	0.12	**-1.000***	0.668	0.117	9.000*
	T2C1	0.507	0.145	12.000*	0.715	0.093	4.000*	0.724	0.096	8.000*
	T4C1	0.549	0.121	11.000*	0.754	0.081	4.000*	0.76	0.079	6.000*
	T8C1	0.572	0.107	10.000*	0.771	0.075	3.000*	0.778	0.069	5.000*
Model 2	**T1C0**	0.62	0.069	8.000*	0.812	0.039	**3.000***	0.837	0.048	3.000*
	T1C1	0.344	**0.261**	4.000*	0.49	0.159	-37.000*	0.545	**0.16**	3.000*
	T1C2	0.342	0.253	3.000*	0.472	**0.161**	-35.000*	0.532	0.156	3.000*
	T1C4	0.329	0.243	**2.000***	0.465	**0.161**	-36.000*	0.523	0.149	**1.000***
	T1C8	0.335	0.232	**2.000***	**0.46**	**0.161**	-35.000*	0.522	0.142	2.000*
	T0C1	0.348	0.258	3.000*	0.493	0.155	-38.000*	0.549	0.157	3.000*
	T1C1	0.344	**0.261**	4.000*	0.49	0.159	-37.000*	0.545	**0.16**	3.000*
	T2C1	0.338	**0.261**	4.000*	0.484	0.16	-36.000*	0.538	**0.16**	4.000*
	T4C1	0.324	0.258	6.000*	0.472	**0.161**	-34.000*	0.528	0.157	5.000*
	T8C1	**0.306**	0.253	6.000*	0.461	**0.161**	-33.000*	**0.518**	0.154	6.000*

Table 2. Table of results from each collection featuring the Gini Coefficient, MAP and the Difference in average r(d) score between documents with and without titles. * denotes a statistically significant difference at $p < 0.02$

Figure 3 shows how boosting affects performance and bias. In the left plot, we can see how boosting the content tends to decrease the bias while increasing the performance (the changes are more dramatic for **Model 1** compared to **Model 2**). In the right plot, we can see the influence of boosting the title. For **Model 1** we see that boosting the title is clearly detrimental, decreasing the overall performance, and inducing more bias across the collection. For **Model 2**, boosting the title field leads to reductions in bias but at the expense of performance. These plots indicate that a fairer system (less biased) does indeed lead to better performance when **Model 1** is employed. And thus **Model 1** tends to uphold the fairness hypothesis. **Model 2** on the other hand, shows that including both fields substantially reduces the bias and increases performance, but then the field boosts lead to a trade-off between performance and bias.

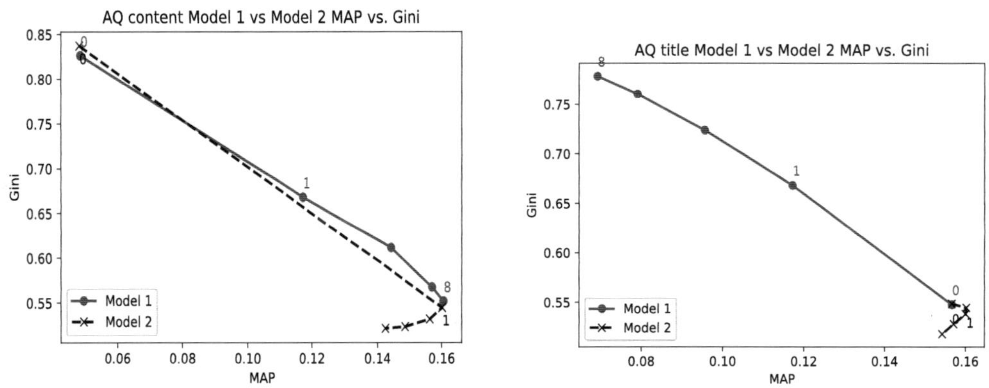

Figure 3. Retrieval Bias (Gini) vs Performance (MAP) for Content Boosting (left) and Title Boosting (right) for Model 1 and 2. When the content is boosted, it tends to increase performance and decrease bias. When title is boosted, on Model 1 performance decreases, while bias increases.

Figure **4** depicts the average retrievability of documents that have titles and documents that do not have titles. These plots show how the different fielding boostings can substantially affect the retrievability of documents. The left plots show the influence on **Model 1**, where increasing the title boosting (the two righthand boxplots), leads to even lower retrievability afforded to documents without titles whereas increasing the content boosting (the two middle boxplots) leads to increasing their retrievability instead. On **Model 2**, there is less difference between the two groups. Recall that when **Model 2** is set to **T1-C1** it represents the default bag of words model (i.e. no fielding, **Model 0**). We can see that under **Model 0** (**Model 2 T1-C1**) there is not much difference between the groups. However, when content boosting is applied (**Model 2 T1-C8**) the disparity is lessened, whereas when title boosting is applied (**Model 2 T8-C1**) the disparity increases slightly and is statistically significant.

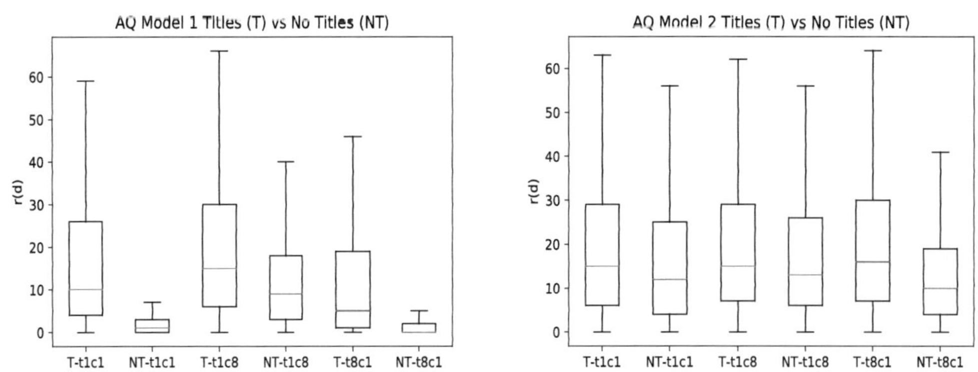

Figure 4. Boxplots of r(d) for with (T-) and without titles (NT-) for Model 1 (left) and Model 2 (right). On Model 1 there is greater disparity between document with titles and without, than on Model 2. When content is boosted on Model 2 (and to a lesser extent Model 1), there is less inequality between groups.
Note the red line indicates the median.

DISCUSSION AND FUTURE WORK

In this work we explored the impact that fielding has on both retrieval performance and retrieval bias and produced three key findings. The first finding highlighted is that **Model 2** was more robust to field boosting in terms of inequality. While **Model**

1 was highly sensitive to changes in the degree of boost applied, **Model 2** was able to keep the distribution of ***r(d)*** scores very similar, even when large boosts were applied. Next, we found that **Model 1** exhibits a linear relationship between retrieval performance and retrieval bias such that boosting titles degrades performance and increases bias while boosting content improves performance and decreases bias. This suggests that if **Model 1** is to be employed, minimizing bias will lead to maximizing the performance. On the other hand, **Model 2** demonstrates a more complex relationship between performance and bias: *(a)* including both fields dramatically reduced the bias and increases the performance, however, *(b)* boosting one field leads to a trade-off between performance and bias meaning that a fairer system can slightly degrade performance on the collections used. Therefore, it will be important to examine if the fairer system generalizes better than the optimized system when using held out queries. Finally, we found that the amount of retrievability ***r(d)*** assigned to documents with titles was far higher than those without when **Model 1** was employed. **Model 2** had less bias toward documents with titles than without titles and thus tended to be fairer overall. However, there were still significant differences in terms of retrievability between these two groups. These findings suggest that **Model 2** is fairer than **Model 1**, and that it is more robust and less sensitive to field boosting and can better handle documents with missing fields. This is an important finding given that **Model 1** fielding is the default fielding algorithm employed in the most widely used Open Source IR toolkits (e.g. Apache Lucene, Solr and Elastic). Our work suggests that if such an approach is to be used then **Model 1** has to be very carefully tuned, whereas a switch to **Model 2** type fielding is likely to lead to immediate benefits (i.e. reduced bias and increased performance).

Finally, this work presents multiple avenues for future work, the first concerning how to manage missing fields such as title fields in news stories. It may be the case that imputing a title for these documents could lead to significant reductions in bias on **Model 1** due to how the scoring handles empty fields. If a title could be imputed from the content or other features, then the bias towards documents with missing fields in **Model 1** might be redressed, leading to an alternative way of mitigating the algorithmic bias. In this work, we observed that **Model 2** reduced the bias of the system when boosting titles or content which seems counter to intuition and we hypothesize that this may be because the boosting tackles different biases, not just fielding but also length bias. As such, we plan to also examine the influence of the length normalization parameter within **BM25** to try and isolate the cause of the different biases.

More generally future work should examine how well our results generalize to other document genres (i.e. web, patent, medical, etc.) where fielding is extensively used and to explore how the number of fields and types of fields influence the performance and bias of the system. We also must explore other retrieval algorithms and other fielded approaches in such contexts as well as examine how fielded queries – that is where the query has structure specifying which field(s) should be used – influences performance and bias.

REFERENCES

Azzopardi, L. and Owens, C. (2009) 'Search engine predilection towards news media providers', in *Proceedings - 32nd Annual International ACM SIGIR Conference on Research and Development in Information Retrieval, SIGIR 2009*. doi: 10.1145/1571941.1572122.

Azzopardi, L., De Rijke, M. and others (2006) 'Query intention acquisition: A case study on automatically inferring structured queries', in *Proceedings of the 6th Dutch-Belgian Information Retrieval Workshop*, pp. 3–10.

Azzopardi, L. and Vinay, V. (2008a) *Accessibility in information retrieval, Lecture Notes in Computer Science (including subseries Lecture Notes in Artificial Intelligence and Lecture Notes in Bioinformatics)*. doi: 10.1007/978-3-540-78646-7_46.

Azzopardi, L. and Vinay, V. (2008b) 'Retrievability: An evaluation measure for higher order information access tasks', in *International Conference on Information and Knowledge Management, Proceedings*. doi: 10.1145/1458082.1458157.

Bashir, S. and Rauber, A. (2009a) 'Identification of Low/High Retrievable Patents Using Content-based Features', in *Proceedings of the 2Nd International Workshop on Patent Information Retrieval*. New York, NY, USA: ACM (PaIR '09), pp. 9–16. doi: 10.1145/1651343.1651346.

Bashir, S. and Rauber, A. (2009b) 'Improving retrievability of patents with cluster-based pseudo-relevance feedback documents selection', in *Proc. of the 18th ACM CIKM*, pp. 1863–1866.

Bashir, S. and Rauber, A. (2011) 'On the relationship b\/w query characteristics and IR functions retrieval bias', *J. Am. Soc. Inf. Sci. Technol.*, 62(8), pp. 1515–1532.

Bashir, S. and Rauber, A. (2014) 'Automatic ranking of retrieval models using retrievability measure', *Knowledge and Information Systems*. Springer, 41(1), pp. 189–221.

Blanco, R. and Boldi, P. (2012) 'Extending BM25 with Multiple Query Operators', in *Proceedings of the 35th International ACM SIGIR Conference on Research and Development in Information Retrieval*. New York, NY, USA: ACM (SIGIR '12), pp. 921–930. doi: 10.1145/2348283.2348406.

Chen, R.-C., Azzopardi, L. and Scholer, F. (2017) 'An empirical analysis of pruning techniques performance, retrievability and bias', in *International Conference on Information and Knowledge Management, Proceedings*. doi: 10.1145/3132847.3133151.

Gastwirth, J. L. (1972) 'The estimation of the Lorenz curve and Gini index', *The Review of Economics and Statistics*, 54, pp. 306–316.

Itakura, K. Y. and Clarke, C. L. A. (2010) 'A Framework for BM25F-based XML Retrieval', in *Proceedings of the 33rd International ACM SIGIR Conference on Research and Development in Information Retrieval*. New York, NY, USA: ACM (SIGIR '10), pp. 843–844. doi: 10.1145/1835449.1835644.

Jimmy, Zuccon, G. and Koopman, B. (2016) 'Boosting Titles Does Not Generally Improve Retrieval Effectiveness', in *Proceedings of the 21st Australasian Document Computing Symposium*. New York, NY, USA: ACM (ADCS '16), pp. 25–32. doi: 10.1145/3015022.3015028.

Kim, J., Xue, X. and Croft, W. B. (2009) 'A Probabilistic Retrieval Model for Semistructured Data', in *Proceedings of the 31th European Conference on IR Research on Advances in Information Retrieval*. Berlin, Heidelberg: Springer-Verlag (ECIR '09), pp. 228–239. doi: 10.1007/978-3-642-00958-7_22.

Kim, J. Y. and Croft, W. B. (2012) 'A Field Relevance Model for Structured Document Retrieval', in *Proceedings of the 34th European Conference on Advances in Information Retrieval*. Berlin, Heidelberg: Springer-Verlag (ECIR'12), pp. 97–108. doi: 10.1007/978-3-642-28997-2_9.

Kirkpatrick, K. (2016) 'Battling Algorithmic Bias: How Do We Ensure Algorithms Treat Us Fairly?', *Commun. ACM*, 59(10), pp. 16–17.

Lipani, A. *et al.* (2015) 'An Initial Analytical Exploration of Retrievability', in *Proc. of the 2015 ICTIR*. ACM (ICTIR '15), pp. 329–332.

Ogilvie, P. and Callan, J. (2003) 'Combining Document Representations for Known-item Search', in *Proceedings of the 26th Annual International ACM SIGIR Conference on Research and Development in Informaion Retrieval*. New York, NY, USA: ACM (SIGIR '03), pp. 143–150. doi: 10.1145/860435.860463.

Plachouras, V. and Ounis, I. (2007) 'Multinomial Randomness Models for Retrieval with Document Fields', in *Proceedings of the 29th European Conference on IR Research*. Berlin, Heidelberg: Springer-Verlag (ECIR'07), pp. 28–39.

Robertson, S. and Zaragoza, H. (2009) 'The Probabilistic Relevance Framework: BM25 and Beyond', *Foundations and Trends in Information Retrieval*, 3(4), pp. 333–389.

Robertson, S., Zaragoza, H. and Taylor, M. (2004) 'Simple BM25 extension to multiple weighted fields', in *Proceedings of the 13th ACM CIKM*, pp. 42–49.

Samar, T. *et al.* (2017) 'Quantifying retrieval bias in Web archive search', *International Journal on Digital Libraries*. Springer, pp. 1–19.

Singhal, A., Buckley, C. and Mitra, M. (1996) 'Pivoted document length normalization', in *Proce. of the 19th ACM SIGIR conference*. (SIGIR '96), pp. 21–29.

Traub, M. C. *et al.* (2016) 'Querylog-based assessment of retrievability bias in a large newspaper corpus', in *2016 IEEE/ACM Joint Conference on Digital Libraries (JCDL)*, pp. 7–16.

Wilkie, C. and Azzopardi, L. (2013) 'Relating retrievability, performance and length', in *SIGIR 2013 - Proceedings of the 36th International ACM SIGIR Conference on Research and Development in Information Retrieval*. doi: 10.1145/2484028.2484145.

Wilkie, C. and Azzopardi, L. (2014a) *Best and fairest: An empirical analysis of retrieval system bias*, *Lecture Notes in Computer Science (including subseries Lecture Notes in Artificial Intelligence and Lecture Notes in Bioinformatics)*. doi: 10.1007/978-3-319-06028-6_2.

Wilkie, C. and Azzopardi, L. (2014b) *Efficiently estimating retrievability bias*, *Lecture Notes in Computer Science (including subseries Lecture Notes in Artificial Intelligence and Lecture Notes in Bioinformatics)*. doi: 10.1007/978-3-319-06028-6_82.

Wilkie, C. and Azzopardi, L. (2015) 'Query length, retrievability bias and performance', in *International Conference on Information and Knowledge Management, Proceedings*. doi: 10.1145/2806416.2806604.

Wilkie, C. and Azzopardi, L. (2017) 'Algorithmic Bias: Do Good Systems Make Relevant Documents More Retrievable', in *Proceedings of the International ACM CIKM*. (CIKM '17).

Wilkie, C. and Azzopardi, L. (2017) 'An initial investigation of query expansion bias', in *ICTIR 2017 - Proceedings of the 2017 ACM SIGIR International Conference on the Theory of Information Retrieval*. doi: 10.1145/3121050.3121097.

ACKNOWLEDGMENTS

We would like to thank the EPSRC for supporting this research through grants EP/M508056/1 and EP/K000330/1.

Investigating Metadata Adoptions for Open Government Data Portals in US Cities

Fanghui Xiao
School of Computing and Information, University of Pittsburgh, United States. fax2@pitt.edu

Daqing He
School of Computing and Information, University of Pittsburgh, United States. dah44@pitt.edu

Wei Jeng
Department of Library and Information Science & Center for Research in Econometric Theory and Applications, National Taiwan University, Taiwan. wjeng@ntu.edu.tw

ABSTRACT

Open government data (OGD) is a valuable resource for both policy transparency and government accountability. All levels of the United States government are working hard to promote open data and its portals. However, there is still a lack of studies on local-level OGD portals in the United States, particularly on the quality of metadata adopted by these portals. By examining 200 US cities, a list of 112 local-level portals is sampled and we investigate the current usages of open data platforms for building local-level OGD portals. This study further investigates and discusses the adoption and potential issues of metadata on those OGD portals. Our result findings discuss the platform distributions among US local-level OGD portals, and also highlight several critical issues associated with metadata on the portals. We anticipate the results will inspire further studies on identifying solutions to improve the metadata and enhance the usability of open government data portals.

KEYWORDS

Open Government Data (OGD), Metadata, data standard, open data platform, open data platform

INTRODUCTION

Open government data (OGD) refers to any data or information generated by public bodies, such as all government levels, and are made available to the public to access, reuse, and redistribute without copyright restrictions (Kassen, 2013; Veljković et.al., 2014; Ubaldi, 2013). OGD has proven to enhance policy transparency and government accountability, and augment both economic and social development (Assaf et al., 2015; Ubaldi, 2013; Thorsby, 2017). It not only engages the public with better knowledge and understanding of government affairs, but also helps the government with better informed improvements on their services or policies (Assaf et al., 2015 & Ubaldi, 2013). Manyika et al. (2013) also state that open data could produce $3.2 to $5.4 trillion in economic value per year across several domains of the global economy, such as the fields of education and transportation. In addition, certain types of open data, such as transportation and air quality data, could stimulate innovations for improving the quality of people's lives (Assaf et al., 2015).

An OGD portal can be defined as "*an official web-portal launched at the federal or local level aimed at making certain types of governmental datasets publicly accessible via internet in a machine-readable format* (Kassen, 2013)." To date, as the concept of openness and data science related application are flourishing, the number of OGD portals has also been increasing rapidly in the United States. OGD portals can be divided into federal, state and local (cities and counties) levels. This paper focuses on local level OGD portals, the reason being that there is little prior work analyzing local level government open data. In addition, a local level OGD is important because of its closer connection with local organizations, neighborhoods, and communities, which could have more direct impacts on a citizen's daily life and neighborhood. For instance, New York officials indicate that analyzing open data about building inspections helps improve predictions of fires (Thorsby et al., 2017).

Despite the rapid adoption of OGD portals, there are still many challenges in enabling effective and user-friendly usages of open government data, such as data quality concerns (e.g., Conradie and Choenni, 2014; Huijboom & Van den Broek, 2011; Janssen et al, 2012), lack of common standards (Huijboom & Van den Broek, 2011; Zhang et al., 2015), and understandability issues about OGD (Weerakkody et al., 2017; Bayley et al., 2013; Verburg & Neumann, 2011). According to Neumaier (2017), metadata quality issues in OGD portals have been recognized as a crucial challenge for broader adoption and also as a barrier for the overall success of open data. In fact, many existing studies indicate there are many metadata issues in OGD portals. For example, in some cases the provided metadata was scarcely checked in terms of its correctness (Kučera, Chlapek, & Nečaský, 2013), and there is a lack of descriptive metadata, causing misinterpretation of government information (Dawes, 2010). Metadata plays an important role in OGD because it allows datasets to be more searchable, discoverable, interpretable and reusable. Incomplete metadata may influence users' ability to discover and locate the datasets they need, while incorrect or meaningless values for metadata elements could mislead users with misinterpretations of the data, and even wrong usage of the data (Neumaier, Umbrich, & Polleres, 2017). Therefore, having comprehensive metadata schemas and accurate metadata element values are crucial to the usage and overall mission of OGD portals; not to mention the fact that metadata also plays a central role in long-term preservation of data on those portals.

However, a recent study about metadata quality ranked data portals in North America at the bottom (Kubler et al., 2017). This study examined 259 open data portals across 43 countries, using Analytic Hierarchy Process method, and North American portals range between 130-220. This motivated us to look more closely at the metadata of US local government data portals. Since there are few studies on this topic, we first examine the current adoption of various open data platforms in local government data portals. This is because open data platforms often have corresponding metadata schemas, which could influence the adoption of metadata on the platforms. Furthermore, metadata schemas, as well as the naming and values of metadata elements, can sometimes be changed during the development of open data portals. This is beneficial for providing flexibility in the metadata to more tightly associate with the actual data on the portal, but it could also cause inconsistencies and difficulties for others to understand and use the metadata. Therefore, our study examines the commonly available metadata schemas such as CKAN, Socrata, and ArcGIS, and also studies their adoptions on local OGD portals. One outcome of our study is to propose suggestions for improving the information descriptions on these open data portals. In summary, the research questions of this study are:

RQ1: What is the current state of the adoption of open data portal platforms and the corresponding metadata schemas in major US cities?

RQ2: What are the existing metadata issues in US local government data portals?

LITERATURE REVIEW

Open data platforms

There are many open data platforms: some are developed by commercial companies, and others are open source projects with the support of active communities. Among the platforms developed by commercial companies, Socrata and ArcGIS are most commonly used. Socrata allows government organizations to publish their data online and make the data accessible, searchable, and usable by citizens (Socrata, 2018). ArcGIS Open Data is specialized in geographical data management, helps users collaborate on projects and access maps and apps, and has both analytic and administrative usages (ArcGIS Open Data, 2018).

In comparison, Junar, OpenDataSoft, and OpenGov are less common commercial platforms. The purpose of Junar is to assist governments, organizations or companies in publishing their data and to make the data reusable by providing tools, visualizations, maps, dashboards and APIs (Junar, 2018). OpenDataSoft is designed for business users to publish, share and re-use data, with the intention of inspiring new applications (OpenDataSoft, 2017). OpenGov provides cloud-based solutions that focus on transforming the way governments budget, measure performance and engage the public. (OpenGov, 2018).

There are two well-known open source open data platforms. Comprehensive Knowledge Archive Network (CKAN) is more commonly used. Its goal is to provide tools to ease publishing as well as to enable the finding, usage, and sharing of data (CKAN, 2018). DKAN is the other open source platform. Its goal is to provide freedom for both originations to publish structured information and for the public to use the structured data (DKAN, 2018).

All these platforms have some form of metadata schema to help describe the data stored on their platforms. Socrata, ArcGIS and CKAN operate with their own metadata schemas, whereas OpenDataSoft, Junar and DKAN all follow the DCAT standard in their metadata schema design.

Metadata in OGD

Metadata has been recognized as a significant factor in discovering, managing, preserving, and migrating data, but there is limited scholarly research on metadata within the context of open government data (OGD). Martin et al. (2017) conducted a study that evaluates the quality and usability of open data for public health research (three open data portals: federal, state, and city levels). They conclude that standardized metadata can improve the usability of open data and is likely to lead to better understanding of the data's limitations and the process of data collection. Assaf et al. (2016) introduced prevalent metadata models and harmonized them. Lisovska (2016) also compared the metadata styles that have been used for OGD, and discovered a serious issue of lack of interoperability between the metadata of open data portals. Furthermore, Lisovska claims that "if open data portals expose their metadata in different standards then searching and discovering datasets across platforms is impossible." The Australian Government Productivity Commission (2017) reports that "Data standards exist but are not widely used" and points out that much of Australia's metadata does not use clear and consistent standards. In the past two years, the issue of metadata quality has started to receive more attention. Neumaier et al. (2016) developed a generic metadata quality assessment framework to assess metadata quality for different open data portals. They propose that metadata quality issues on open data portals are a crucial problem for interoperability and may influence the overall success of open data. Kubler et.al (2017) adopted the assessment framework to compare metadata quality among OGD portals by using the analytic hierarchy process. They found that today's organizations do not sufficiently manage their published datasets, resources and corresponding metadata.

Most of the extant work focuses on the analysis of metadata styles on a conceptual level, and, to the best of our knowledge, very little research is based on open data portals in operation to examine how their metadata is practically used. Hence, this work focuses on inspecting the metadata issues of open data portals in the US.

METHODOLOGY

We believe that a well-designed OGD portal should have a clear presentation of its functions, its metadata schema, and a procedure for publishing dataset on its site, so that any user of the portal can obtain these critical pieces of information online at the portal. Consequently, the method used in this study is to directly analyze the portal's online content for answers to our research questions, rather than obtaining such information by engaging either the users or the management teams of the portals. As a preliminary study of the portals' metadata issues, our research method is adequate. We acknowledge the need to engage both the users and the management teams of the portals, which we plan to do in the future based on the specific problems we identify through this preliminary study.

Sample selection and cleaning criteria

Thorsby et al. (2017) indicate that a city's population size has a strong correlation with the possibility of that city having a local government data portal and the size of the datasets on the portals. Therefore, our study sampled the top 200 major cities in the United States based on their population (United States Census, 2018).

Besides using population as a sampling criterion, we also developed two rules for determining whether an online website is an open data portal or not. These two rules are as follows:

> Step 1: check if the website uses a common open data platform, such as Socrata or CKAN. If yes, we annotate it in the data collection table.
>
> Step 2: if a website is not an existing, well-known open data platform, it is examined based on four of Dawes' principles of open data: complete, accessible, machine-processable and downloadable (Dawes, 2010). If the platform satisfies the four principles, it is identified as an open data platform and annotated the related information. Otherwise, the website is not recognized as an open data platform.

These two steps helped us remove certain local city websites whose data do not have descriptive information or are not downloadable, or where the data link information is missing, since these issues are unable to satisfy the very basic criteria for open data.

Data collection procedure

To locate an open data website of a city in the top 200 US cities, we performed a Google search with the query "the city of + [city name] + open data." The reason that we took this approach rather than searching inside data.gov for the local open data portal information is because data.gov does not have a complete list of local governments' open data portals. There could be some data centers in a city with different purposes; however, in our study, we only focus on the government data portals that are generally supported or incorporated by their local governments. Through repeated Google searches for the 200 cities and applying the two open data portal identification rules, in total we found 112 online OGD portals from the selected 200 cities.

Based on each identified OGD portal, we performed deeper analysis on the platform used, the metadata schema, and metadata elements. To maintain the quality of the data annotation, two authors of this paper independently annotated all 112 OGD portals. Most data extracted did not involve subjective judgement, such as the number of datasets shown on the website. The complete annotation was conducted in February and March 2018, and all results are stored in a spreadsheet.

Table 1 shows the identified platform information for a portal, which includes the city name, portal URL, number of datasets, platform information, and metadata schema information.

Parameters	Description	Examples
City's name and state	the city's name	Pittsburgh, Pennsylvania
Binary	if the city has a portal then the value is 1, if no: 0	0 or 1
Portal's link	the link of the local-level OGD portal	http://www.wprdc.org
Number of dataset	The total number of datasets that the portal hosted as of January	349
Platforms of city	The system that the portal adopted	CKAN
The model of metadata	The metadata schema that the portal adopted	CKAN

Table 1. Example of the identified platform information

Based on the results from RQ1, we manually analyzed the top three most popular platforms for their metadata collection. Table 2 shows some examples of the metadata information we collected.

CKAN	CKAN Version	maintainer	maintainer_email	contact point phone number	license	......
WPRDC	2.4.4	data steward name	data steward email		license	
Houston	2.6.2					
Phoenix	2.5.7					
Philadelphia	2.2.4	maintainer	maintainer email	maintainer phone		
Boston	2.5.7	contact point	contact email	contact point phone number	license	

Table 2. Examples of the identified metadata information from datasets on CKAN platforms

Data analysis method

Our data analysis employed multiple methods. To answer RQ1, we performed descriptive statistics analysis on the open portal platforms and metadata schemas we collected. To answer RQ2, we decided to adopt the National Information Standards Organization (NISO) standard (Riley, 2017) for assessing the functionality of the metadata on the portals. Metadata has a wide range of functions, which include assisting the systems maintaining the content and facilitating users to find, obtain and share the information with others (Riley, 2017). Therefore, whether the metadata functioned well or not can greatly influence both the portals and users, such as if there is missing data or failure to discover a dataset.

NISO provides introductory guidance to users about metadata. NISO has been recognized as an organization that develops and maintains well-known technical standards related to information objects in the LIS field, e.g., Z39.50. In its publication "Understand Metadata," NISO discusses six essential attributes of metadata designed for different uses. These attributes are:

- *Discovery* means that metadata can aid users in looking for necessary information by allowing users to search or browse. Elements could include title, author, subject.
- *Display* shows that metadata can assist users in identifying or understanding a resource. Example properties could be title or publication data.
- *Interoperability* points out that to effectively exchange data between systems, high quality metadata could help effectively match materials and improve interoperability. Examples are file type and license.
- *Digital-object management* refers to the fact that metadata can provide information that points out the digital material or appropriate version to satisfy user needs, which supports digital-object management. The elements, for example, cover creation data/time and license terms.
- *Preservation* means that metadata plays a significant role in long-term preservation. For example, technical metadata and preservation metadata help verify content integrity, especially after a migration. Examples are the elements of file type and checksum.
- *Navigation* means that elements or attributes of metadata (such as tags or groups) can navigate users toward relevant information from one page or section to another, which helps users more quickly obtain the information they seek.

Consequently, our examination of issues in the metadata of US OGD portals consists of the six aspects above.

RESULT

Current state of the adoption of open data platforms and metadata schema

As shown in Table 3, among the 112 portals we collected, the top three adopted platforms are Socrata (38.4%), ArcGIS Open Data (tie, 38.4%), and CKAN (13.4%). This finding is similar to Kubler et al. (2017)'s study, where Socrata is the most common platform in North America; we would like to note that ArcGIS open data is also commonly used in US OGD portals.

Platforms	Socrata	ArcGIS Open Data	CKAN	homegrown	Others	Total
N	43	43	15	5	6	112
%	38.4%	38.4%	13.4%	4.5%	5.4%	100%

Note: The Other category includes Junar (n=2); dkan (n=2); OPEN GOV (n=1); and OpenDataSoft (n=1)

Table3. The distribution of the platforms adopted by US OGD portals (N=112)

As for metadata adoption, we found the distribution of metadata schemas is mostly consistent with the platform a portal adopts (see Table 4). The metadata schemas on each of the top three platforms (Socrata, ArcGIS Open Data, and CKAN) are developed as part of the platform. Among the remaining less common platforms, OpenDataSoft and many homegrown platforms have designed their own metadata schemas. Some platforms still decide to follow standard metadata schemas. For example, Junar adopts the RDF metadata standard as presented in Dublin Core and DCAT (Lisowska, 2016), and DKAN builds its metadata schema by selecting elements from DCAT and Project Open Data (DKAN Docs, 2017).

Metadata schema	Mapping to platform	N
Socrata	Socrata	42
ArcGIS Open Data	ArcGIS Open Data	43
CKAN	CKAN (n=15); homegrown (n=1)	16
homegrown	homegrown (n=4); Socrata (n=1)	5
Dublin Core and DCAT	Junar	2
DCAT & Project open data schema	DKAN	2
OpenDataSoft	OpenDataSoft	1
No metadata	OpenGov	1

Table 4. The cross-tabulation of platforms and corresponding metadata schema.

However, there are several exceptions. For example, Denver's OGD portal uses a homegrown platform, but adopts CKAN's metadata schema. Through investigation, we found that this is because Denver simply borrowed the metadata schema from its state's OGD portal, which uses CKAN as the platform. This is why there is one homegrown platform that uses CKAN metadata schema in Table 4. Another exception is San Francisco's OGD portal (DataSF), which uses the Socrata platform but with its own metadata schema. This is why the Socrata platform has one instance with a homegrown metadata schema. DataSF claims that their open data policy requires a metadata standard to assist users in understanding data, so they developed the DataSF metadata standard (DataSF, 2018).

Some portals totally abandon metadata in their platform. For example, Santa Clarita employs the OpenGov platform for its portal, but does not integrate any metadata information for its data. Instead, it provides various visualizations, including percentage graphs and line graphs, to provide means for describing its data on the portal.

Existing metadata issues in the US local OGD portals

To answer RQ2, as stated, we employed NISO metadata standards as the criteria and examined metadata based on six aspects: *discovery, display navigation, interoperability, digital object management, and preservation.* Our examination concentrates on analyzing the top three metadata schemas used by US OGD portals: Socrata, ArcGIS and CKAN. In the rest of this section, we will present the metadata issues according to these six aspects.

Discovery. Socrata and CKAN provide reasonable metadata information for users to discover data, but ArcGIS only has limited support for this aspect. Socrata and CKAN include attributes of title, categories or group of datasets, and tags, which provide basic functions to assist users in searching and browsing data. On the other hand, the default metadata in ArcGIS includes the elements of title and tags, but there is no attribute in the group level, i.e., categories or group, that could prevent users to find data from browsing categories.

Display. The displays of Socrata, CKAN and ArcGIS are clear. As shown in Figure 1, Socrata displays the metadata under the dataset and highlights important information, such as updated time and downloads times. This arrangement clearly presents the metadata information. CKAN presents the metadata elements closer to the relevant dataset, which highlights the association clearly (see Figure 2). Compared to Socrata and CKAN, metadata elements displayed on an ArcGIS interface are less efficient. When we reach a dataset page (see the screenshot in Fig 3), "View Metadata" must be clicked in order to see the elements in the dataset (Fig 4).

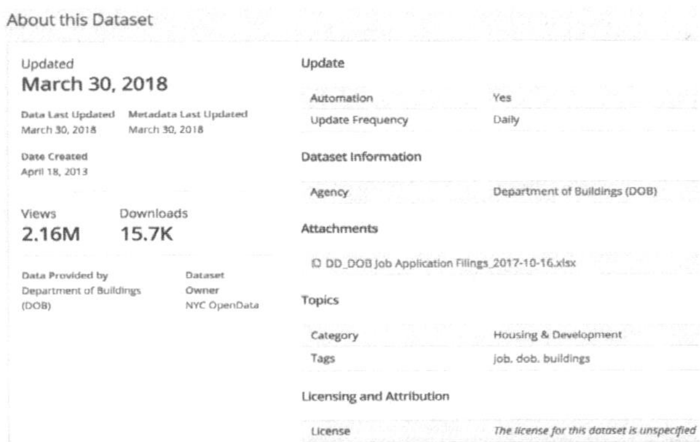

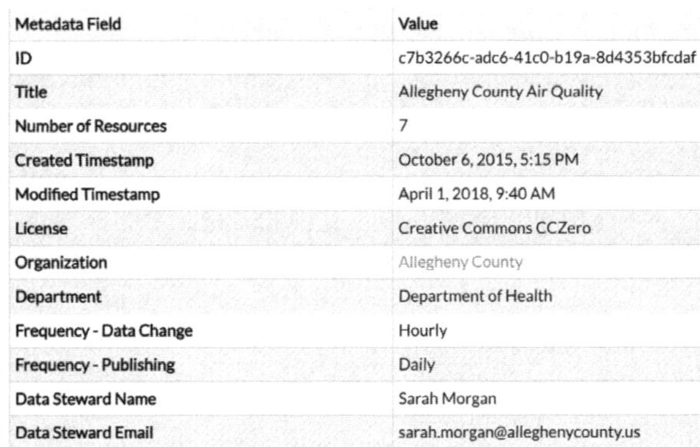

Fig.1. Socrata metadata page (from New York City OpenData) **Fig.2.** CKAN metadata page (from Western PA Reg. Data Ctr)

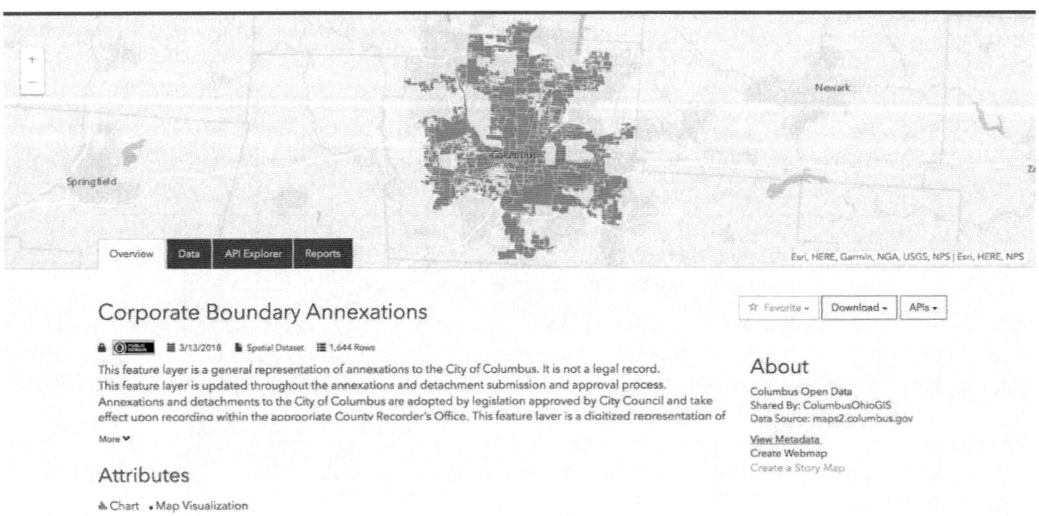

Fig.3. ArcGIS Metadata page1 (from the city of Columbus open data)

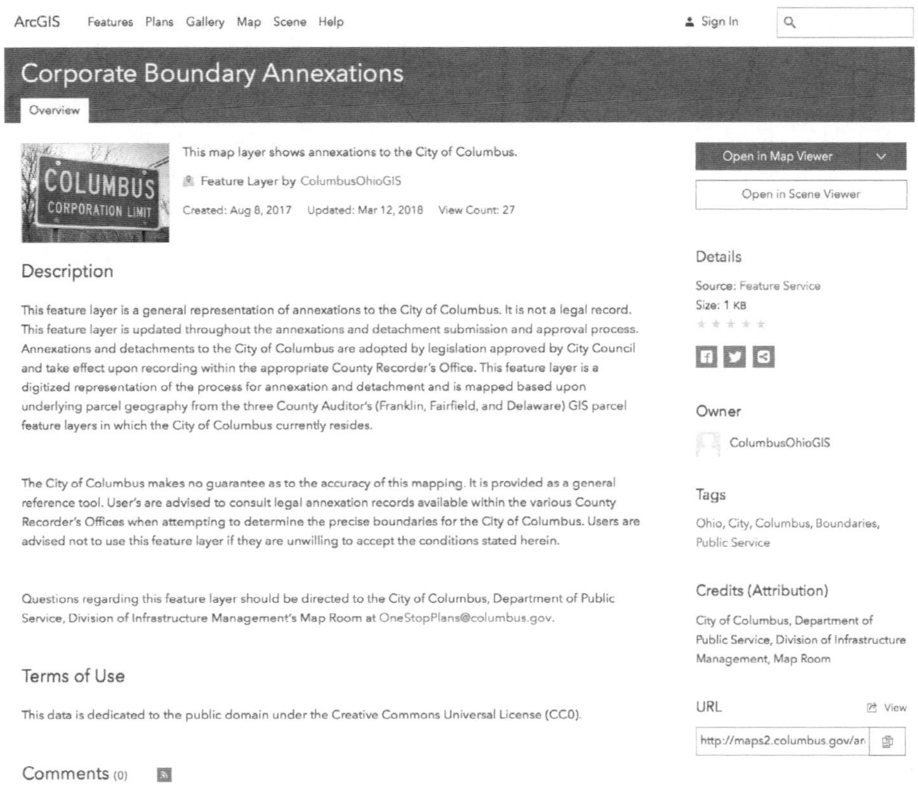

Fig.4. ArcGIS Metadata page2 (from the city of Columbus open data)

Navigation. Overall, all three metadata standards provide clear directions for users to look for relevant information and to navigate between datasets.

Interoperability. The three platforms provide very basic metadata elements for interoperability, and all of them have unique drawbacks. First, in order to effectively exchange content between systems, technical metadata and preservation metadata are essential, such as file format, file size and created or modified time. However, only CKAN has the "format" element in the resource level of the metadata schema. Socrata and ArcGIS do not include “format” as a metadata element, and only show it when users are trying to download a dataset. Also, among the three platforms’ metadata schemas, only ArcGIS has the element of “file size” in their metadata information. Second, the metadata about data ownership is also crucial for interoperability. ArcGIS’ metadata does not show license or right field, which is a major issue when using the data.

Digital item/object management. Socrata and CKAN provide adequate metadata support for digital object management, but ArcGIS cannot. Socrata and CKAN provide the information of "License", “Group or Categories”, "Version" and "Maintainer" or "Department" to point out the datasets that could match users’ needs. These two metadata schemas cover some elements that can support the digital item management, but the lack of file size information would influence long-term management. On the other hand, ArcGIS’ metadata does not have "License", "Version" or even “Group” elements, crucial information for managing and delivering the appropriate content or necessary version to users. ArcGIS metadata is not helpful to digital object management.

Preservation. Socrata and CKAN have basic preservation metadata, but ArcGIS’ default preservation metadata is limited. As a whole, Socrata and CKAN include administrative or descriptive metadata: title, resource, created date and license terms. New versions of CKAN also provide a group of resource metadata elements, such as package id and position, which enable long-term preservation and data management/discovery. These elements can assist in managing digital information. However, the default ArcGIS metadata has no resource, file types or license elements.

Finally, OGD’s metadata schema is constantly expanding in order to cope with the demands of representing new types of data. For example, the latest version of the CKAN metadata schema added geospatial related fields. In addition, Socrata added social media related metadata fields, such as comments, community rating, and your rating. These are not considered metadata elements in the traditional view of metadata but are added in order to improve social participation and engagement, and to augment the interactions between OGD and the public (Ubaldi, 2013).

DISCUSSION

Through the reported investigation on 112 US local OGD portals, we have the following observations.

Adoption of commercial platforms. Despite open source solutions, commercial platforms have occupied the majority of local-level OGD portals. Specifically, our results show that Socrata and ArcGIS, the two most common commercial platforms, make up more than three quarters (76.8%) of all the OGD portals we sampled. A commonly cited issue associated with projects based on open source platforms is the extra requirements of element tailoring and customization, which demand extra effort and labor with technical capabilities. We suspect this issue has triggered more local governments to hire commercial companies to work on their OGD portals. However, this deserves further investigation to obtain the exact explanation. We plan to conduct further interviews to develop deeper understanding.

The lack of investigation on a specific platform. We also found that lack of adequate studies on certain important commercial systems could reduce transparency in OGD portals. For example, there are many studies in the literature on Socrata, CKAN and even OpenDataSoft (Kubler et al., 2017; Neumaier, Umbrich & Polleres, 2016; Tygel et al., 2015), but few articles mention ArcGIS. Considering ArcGIS supports one-third of ODG portals in our samples, the unknown issues inside ArcGIS could significantly influence further development of open government data. In addition, because most of the data currently in OGD portals are numerical or geographical data, and many portals provide geographic visualizations to assist users with interpreting data or using data, it would be advantageous to pay more attention to the ArcGIS platform or other GIS tools so that the usage of open data can be improved.

The metadata quality issue. Overall, based on NISO's metadata analysis, all three platforms (Socrata, CKAN and ArcGIS) have metadata that meet the basic criteria. However, there are certain issues, such as ArcGIS' metadata not showing license or right fields and Socrata excluding geographic metadata. Another interesting observation is that our analysis shows that the quality of metadata, in terms of completeness and interoperability, is better in CKAN than in the other two. Combining this result with Kubler et al. (2017)'s results, where they found that CKAN is widely used in Europe and Central Asia, and Socrata is mostly adopted in North America, we hypothesize that the adopted platform might be one of the reasons why the metadata quality of open data in North America is ranked lower than other countries.

The issue of metadata variance. Flexibility in existing open data platforms, particularly their metadata schema customization, enables rapid development of OGD portals, but it may harm interoperability and cross-platform data discovery. For example, CKAN does not have adequate documentation to explain the meanings of the elements in its metadata schema, nor are there checking mechanisms to ensure that the values entered into the metadata are consistent with the intentions of the platform designers. Consequently, there are many misinterpretations of metadata elements in CKAN platforms. For instance, the element "Source" in the Boston portal has the value of "Internal", and it is not clear whether it refers to the interior of the publisher or the interior of the portal. In contrast, Jersey City's OGD portal assigns "Source" with the value of "Municipal Council of the city of Jersey City", which refers to the name of the source, whereas Denton city's "Source" is the URL of the data, which is the address of the dataset. When the value of the same elements in metadata adopt different data types and meanings, not only will users be confused, but the software that automatically processes the metadata will also encounter problems, thus harming interoperability and data discovery. The same problem could be caused by less crucial metadata inconsistency problems. For example, the standard element name "maintainer" in the CKAN platform is called "data steward name" at the Western Pennsylvania Regional Data Center (WPRDC) and "contact point" at the Boston's OGD portal. More importantly, inconsistency also exists across different platforms. For example, the meaning "topic" has three different names: "groups" in CKAN, "theme" in Project Open Data, and "category" in Socrata. Consequently, a balanced tradeoff between the flexibility to develop a portal and interoperability across many portals should be obtained. Also, documentation that explains the metadata schema in each portal could play an important role in helping users understand the data.

Deployment issues around metadata customization. In addition to interoperability, both metadata misinterpretation and inconsistency can affect data discovery. According to our findings, there are many issues in the development of OGD portals, particularly their metadata. However, the portals based on Socrata and ArcGIS do not have element misinterpretation problems at the same scale. This is likely because these two platforms belong to commercial companies, and there are dedicated professional teams to help the cities develop their open data portals and their metadata. This practice maintains consistency and knowledge across different local-level OGD portals on these two platforms. If such knowledge and experience can be openly shared in a best practice knowledge base among the whole community, it is likely that open government data would be greatly benefited. We conclude that professional development teams, as well as knowledge retainment and transfer, are important in open data portal development.

CONCLUSION

Open government data portals in the United States play an increasingly important role in government transparency and citizen engagement. Therefore, this study aims to examine local level open data portals in the US with two research focuses: 1) the adoption of open data platforms among the most populated US cities, and 2) the investigation of metadata schemas and elements in these portals. Our results show that commercial open data platforms such as Socrata and ArcGIS occupy the majority of the local level open data portals, although many portals also use open source platforms like CKAN. We further identified several issues regarding the development of metadata in these portals, including relatively limited metadata elements in ArcGIS platforms, and element misinterpretation and inconsistency in the portals using CKAN. These results and follow-up discussions contribute to the overall effort of improving the quality of metadata and the usability of open government data.

We acknowledge the limitations of this study. The sampled portals were obtained from the top 200 most populous U.S. cities; 74 out of the 112 cities we studied are ranked among the top 100. We anticipate that the number of cities with data portals will decrease drastically with the increase of population because a city's annual budget is related to the city's size. As a result, although we believe that our samples are representative enough for the purposes of this study, the identified metadata problems on the portals are far from being exhaustive.

In the future, we will expand upon our findings by including more US cities. Furthermore, as previously mentioned, we will further investigate metadata variance in the same platform, such as CKAN, as well as advance our study into data portals' decision-making strategies for adopting a particular platform, which can triangulate with our current study results. In addition, the interview method may be an appropriate method to deeply investigate metadata issues in OGD platforms from the angles of management and users, such as the intended use of portals, the issues facing portals and user's challenges regarding metadata.

ACKNOWLEDGEMENT

This study is partially funded by the Ministry of Science and Technology under Grants No. 107-2636-H-002 -002-. This work was also supported by the Center for Research in Econometric Theory and Applications (Grant no. 107L900204) from The Featured Areas Research Center Program within the framework of the Higher Education Sprout Project by the Ministry of Education (MOE) in Taiwan, and by the Ministry of Science and Technology (MOST), Taiwan, under Grant No. MOST 107-3017-F-002-004-.

This study obtains many profession suggestions from David Walker from Western Pennsylvania Regional Data Center. We would like to show our gratitude to him for many amazingly helpful discussions and valuable insights during the course of this research."

REFERENCES

Assaf, A., Troncy, R., & Senart, A. (2015). HDL-Towards a Harmonized Dataset Model for Open Data Portals. In *USEWOD-PROFILES@ ESWC* (pp. 62-74).

ArcGIS Open Data. (2018, March 6). Connecting Citizens and Businesses to Your Authoritative Data. Retrieved from http://www.esri.com/software/arcgis/arcgisonline/arcgis-open-data

ArcGIS for Desktop (2018, January 23). ArcGIS Metadata format. Retrieved from

http://desktop.arcgis.com/en/arcmap/10.3/manage-data/metadata/the-arcgis-metadata-format.htm

Australian Government Productivity Commission (2017). Data Availability and Use. Retrieved from:

http://www.pc.gov.au/inquiries/completed/data-access/issues/data-access-issues.pdf

Bayley, K. B., Belnap, T., Savitz, L., Masica, A. L., Shah, N., & Fleming, N. S. (2013). Challenges in using electronic health record data for CER: experience of 4 learning organizations and solutions applied. *Medical care*, 51, S80-S86.

CKAN. (2018, March 6). Retrieved from https://ckan.org/,

CKAN. (2018, March 6). Metadata. Retrieved from https://ckan.org/portfolio/metadata/

Conradie, P., & Choenni, S. (2014). On the barriers for local government releasing open data. *Government Information Quarterly, 31*(1), S10-S17. doi:10.1016/j.giq.2014.01.003

Dawes, S. S., & Helbig, N. (2010). Information strategies for open government: Challenges and prospects for deriving public value from government transparency. In Wimmer M.A., Chappelet JL., Janssen M., Scholl H.J. (Eds). Lecture Notes in Computer: Vol. 6228. Science Electronic Government (pp. 50-60). doi: https://doi.org/10.1007/978-3-642-14799-9_5

Dawes, S. S. (2010). Stewardship and usefulness: Policy principles for information-based transparency. *Government Information Quarterly*, *27*(4), 377-383.

DKAN. (2018, March 6). Retrieved from https://getdkan.org/

DKAN Docs. (2018, March 6). Advanced Metadata Features. Retrieved from http://dkan.readthedocs.io/en/latest/components/dataset/datasetfeatures.html

DataSF. (2018, March 6). Standard: Metadata. Retrieved from https://datasf.org/resources/metadata-standard/

Huijboom, N., & Van den Broek, T. (2011). Open data: an international comparison of strategies. *European journal of ePractice*, *12*(1), 4-16.

Janssen, M., Charalabidis, Y., & Zuiderwijk, A. (2012). Benefits, adoption barriers and myths of open data and open government. *Information Systems Management, 29*(4), 258-268. doi:10.1080/10580530.2012.716740

Junar. (2018, March 6). Open data that is easy to re-use and interpret by many different audiences. Retrieved from http://www.junar.com/

Kassen, M. (2013). A promising phenomenon of open data: A case study of the Chicago open data project. *Government Information Quarterly*, 30(4), 508-513. doi:10.1016/j.giq.2013.05.012

Kapoor, K., Weerakkody, V., & Sivarajah, U. (2015, October). Open data platforms and their usability: Proposing a framework for evaluating citizen intentions. In Janssen M. et al. (Eds), Open and Big Data Management and Innovation: Vol. 9373. Lecture Notes in Computer Science (pp. 261-271). doi: https://doi.org/10.1007/978-3-319-25013-7_21

Kubler, S., Robert, J., Neumaier, S., Umbrich, J., & Le Traon, Y. (2017). Comparison of metadata quality in open data portals using the Analytic Hierarchy Process. *Government Information Quarterly*, 35(1), 13-29.

doi: *https://doi.org/10.1016/j.giq.2017.11.003*

Kučera J., Chlapek D., Nečaský M. (2013) Open Government Data Catalogs: Current Approaches and Quality Perspective. In Kő A., Leitner C., Leitold H., Prosser A. (eds). *Lecture Notes in Computer Science*: Vol 8061. Technology-Enabled Innovation for Democracy, Government and Governance (pp.152-166). doi: https://doi.org/10.1007/978-3-642-40160-2_13

Lisowska. (2016). Metadata for the open data portals. Retrieved from:

http://juds.joinedupdata.org/wp-content/uploads/2016/12/JUDS-DP6-Metadata-for-the-open-data-portals.pdf

Manyika, J., Chui, M., Farrell, D., Kuiken, V.S., Groves, P., & Doshi, E. A. (2013). Open data: Unlocking innovation and preformation with liquid information. Mc Kinsey Report (2013). Retrieved from

http://www.mckinsey.com/business-functions/digital-mckinsey/our-insights/open-data-unlocking-innovation-and-performance-with-liquid-information

Martin, E. G., Law, J., Ran, W., Helbig, N., & Birkhead, G. S. (2016). Evaluating the quality and usability of open data for public health research: A systematic review of data offerings on 3 open data platforms. *Journal of Public Health Management and Practice,* 1. doi:10.1097/PHH.0000000000000388

Neumaier, S., Umbrich, J., & Polleres, A. (2016). Automated quality assessment of metadata across open data portals. Journal of Data and Information Quality (JDIQ), 8(1), 1-29. doi:10.1145/2964909

Osagie, E., Waqar, M., Adebayo, S., Stasiewicz, A., Porwol, L., & Ojo, A. (2017, June). Usability Evaluation of an Open Data Platform. In Proceedings of the 18th Annual International Conference on Digital Government Research (pp. 495-504). ACM.

OpenDataSoft, (2018, March 6). Retrieved from https://www.opendatasoft.com/

OpenGov. (2018, March 6). Retrieved from https://opengov.com/

Riley Jenn. (2017). Understanding Metadata: What is Metadata, and What is it For?: A Primer. *National Information Standards Organization.* Retrieved from: https://www.niso.org/publications/understanding-metadata-2017

Scorata. (2018, March 6). Retrieved from https://socrata.com/

Scorata. (2018, March 6). Best Practices for Metadata Management. Retrieved from https://support.socrata.com/hc/en-us/articles/115008609707-Best-Practices-for-Metadata-Management

Thorsby, J., Stowers, G. N., Wolslegel, K., & Tumbuan, E. (2017). Understanding the content and features of open data portals in American cities. *Government Information Quarterly*, *34*(1), 53-61.

Tygel, A., Auer, S., Debattista, J., Orlandi, F., & Campos, M. L. M. (2016, February). Towards cleaning-up open data portals: A metadata reconciliation approach. In *Semantic Computing (ICSC), 2016 IEEE Tenth International Conference on* (pp. 71-78). IEEE.

United States Census Bureau. (2018, February 10). American FactFinder. Retrieved from https://factfinder.census.gov/faces/tableservices/jsf/pages/productview.xhtml?src=bkmk

Ubaldi, B. (2013). Open government data: Towards empirical analysis of open government data initiatives. *OECD Working Papers on Public Governance*, (22), 0_1.

Veljković, N., Bogdanović-Dinić, S., & Stoimenov, L. (2014). Benchmarking open government: An open data perspective. *Government Information Quarterly*, 31(2), 278-290. doi:10.1016/j.giq.2013.10.011

Verburg, P. H., Neumann, K., & Nol, L. (2011). Challenges in using land use and land cover data for global change studies. *Global Change Biology, 17*(2), 974-989. doi:10.1111/j.1365-2486.2010.02307.x

Weerakkody, V., Irani, Z., Kapoor, K., Sivarajah, U., & Dwivedi, Y. K. (2017). Open data and its usability: An empirical view from the citizen's perspective. *Information Systems Frontiers*, 19(2), 285. doi:10.1007/s10796-016-9679-1

Zhang, J., Dawes, S. S., & Sarkis, J. (2005). Exploring stakeholders' expectations of the benefits and barriers of e-government knowledge sharing. *Journal of Enterprise Information Management*, 18(5), 548-567.

Empowering Communities with Data: Role of Data Intermediaries for Communities' Data Utilization

Ayoung Yoon
Indiana University Purdue University Indianapolis (IUPUI), USA. ayyoon@iupui.edu

Paula Jo McNally
Indiana University Purdue University Indianapolis (IUPUI), USA. pjmcnall@iu.edu

Andrea Copeland
Indiana University Purdue University Indianapolis (IUPUI), USA. ajapzon@iupui.edu

ABSTRACT

Data have significant potential to address current societal problems not only at the federal and state levels, but also in smaller communities, in neighborhoods, and in the lives of individuals. While the proposition for this potential is that data are and will be shared with and reused by and for communities at different levels, not all data are systematically or routinely shared for reuse with communities due to social, structural and technical infrastructure barriers. Data intermediary organizations can play a significant role in removing existing barriers while unlocking the potential of data for all, particularly for communities with limited human or financial resources, limited access to existing data infrastructures, and underserved populations. Considering the significance of the data intermediary organizations on local communities, this study aims to explore the role of intermediaries that usually facilitate community members/organizations' data utilization. The findings of this study reveal that data intermediary organizations play four major roles that are crucial in communities' data utilization: (1) democratizing data, (2) adding value to existing data, (3) enhancing communities' data literacy, and (4) building communities' data capacity. This study has several important implications to offer as a solution to overcome the challenges of data reuse at the local level.

KEYWORDS

Data reuse, open data, data infrastructure, data intermediaries, data curation

INTRODUCTION

Data have significant potential to address current societal problems (e.g., education, health, economic development, and the environment) not only at the federal and state levels, but also in smaller communities, in neighborhoods, and in the lives of individuals. Many have argued that data have value as a source for community economic development, disaster planning, and decision-making in citizens' daily lives (Kassen, 2013; Levin & Schneir, 2015). In the report *A World that Counts, Mobilizing the Data Revolution*, the United Nations Secretary-General's Independent Expert Advisory Group (IEAG, 2014) underscored the significance of data particularly for underdeveloped countries or neighborhoods, arguing that "data are the lifeblood of decision-making" (p. 4) and that the recent data revolution has created opportunities to design, monitor and evaluate effective policies for communities.

While the proposition for this potential is that data are and will be shared with and reused by and for communities at different levels, much data—including, particularly, data collected by university and research institutes—are not systematically or routinely shared for reuse with communities (Research Data Alliance [RDA] Data for Development Interest Group, n.d.; Urquilla & Shelton, 2015). Government data are traditionally shared with citizens, and while recent open data initiatives accelerate this tradition, Douglass et al. (2014) pointed out that there are still structural and technical infrastructure barriers to be overcome for data to be fully accessible and easily usable. Research data are usually shared within scientists' own communities of practice, although researchers often share data interpretations to support community development. The IEAG (2014) pointed out that unequal access and use of data limit the role that data can play in the realization of sustainable development and argued that it is critical for all stakeholders (e.g., government, regional institutions, public/private data producers, academics, and citizens) to work to create a more equitable data ecosystem.

Data intermediary organizations can play a significant role in removing existing barriers while unlocking the potential of data for all, particularly for communities with limited human or financial resources, limited access to existing data infrastructures, and underserved populations. Van Schalkwyk, Canares, Chattapdhyay, and Andrason (2016) emphasized the importance of these data intermediaries in open data ecosystems, as they can connect different stakeholders and facilitate the flow of data. However, despite the significance of the role and impact of data intermediary organizations on local communities, these groups have been paid little attention in scholarly works, and little is known about how data are utilized among local communities and at the neighbourhood level (Van Schalkwyk et al., 2016).

This study aims to explore the role of data intermediary organizations that usually connect community members/organizations with data sources and provide partnerships and consultations to support communities' data utilization (Yoon, 2017). We adopt our definition of data intermediary organizations from Van Schalkwyk et al. (2016), broadly defining such groups as agents positioned between two other agents in a data supply–demand chain and that facilitate the use/reuse of data. By uncovering the role of data intermediary organizations and analyzing the services they provide to the populations they serve, this study contributes to our understanding of how local communities utilize data to have meaningful impacts on their communities. The findings of this study have several important implications to offer a solution to overcome the challenges of data reuse at the local level.

LITERATURE REVIEW

A growing body of literature discusses the power and value of data to enhance data-enriched citizen and public engagement in policy- and decision-making relevant to citizens' daily lives (Gurstein, 2011; Kassen, 2013; Levin & Schneir, 2015). Keserű and Chan (2015) argued that open data not only impact economic development, but also increase state or institutional responsiveness, reduce levels of corruption, build new democratic spaces for citizens, empower local and disadvantaged voices, and enhance service delivery and effective service utilization. Levin and Schneir (2015) also underscored the importance of making reliable public data accessible to anyone, anytime, for any purpose, as such data have the power to help citizens make better decisions for their communities.

In the U.S. context, several cases demonstrate the potential of data reuse for community members. Chicago's open data portal driven by open government data initiatives resulted in several citizen-initiated projects that developed tools to serve Chicago's diverse community by improving the transparency of local governments' political processes (e.g., chicagolobbyists.org) and maintaining local neighborhoods as safe, open, and healthy green spaces for the local community (e.g., Mi Parquet Project; Kassen, 2013). Often, local organizations lead these projects. For example, the Green and Healthy Homes Initiative (GHHI) in Baltimore utilized health and housing data to provide healthy homes for communities and advocate for increased efforts to prevent lead poisoning (Urquilla & Shelton, 2015). These cases show how different community members (e.g., city planners, local government officers, economic developers, non-profit educational consultants, foundations and corporate organizations, and the public, including parents with concerns about childcare and school systems) can utilize or reuse data on regional areas and population groups collected by the private and public sectors to better understand the factors influencing their communities.

This emerging interest in using data for the community has sparked several discussions regarding how to make data open and sharable, many of which call for action on the part of the public sector. However, the movement to make data fully accessible and easily usable still faces several challenges, such as structural and technical infrastructure barriers (Douglass et al., 2014). In this context, several studies have explored the concept of intermediaries as agents capable of removing some of these barriers (e.g. Van Schalkwyk et al., 2016). The concept of Intermediaries was first discussed in the context of information and communication technology (ICT) as bridging or support organizations that link different agents by transmitting information from one to another (Brown & Kalegaonkar, 2002; Sapsed et al., 2007). They were later explored in different organizational contexts, such as business and e government, as agents for diffusing services (Janssen & Zuiderwijk, 2014; Sein & Furoholt, 2010). In the context of open data, Van Schalkwyk, Willmers, and Czerniewicz (2014) reported that data intermediaries play several possible roles, such as increasing data accessibility and utility, serving as "keystone species" in data ecosystems, and democratizing the impacts and use of open data. Several other studies have echoed the potential and significance of intermediaries in the contexts of government data (Chattapadhyay, 2014), developing countries (Davies, 2014; Van Schalkwyk et al., 2014), and broadly in ICT (Diaz Andrade, & Urquhart, 2010) and demonstrated intermediaries' crucial role in linking different agents in open data supply chains, including grassroots communities (Van Schalkwyk et al., 2016).

While the interest in and need for data intermediaries is growing, little empirical research has been conducted to understand their roles and the processes of data diffusion and utilization in local communities. By empirically investigating the roles and functions of data intermediary organizations, this study contributes to the understanding one facet of data utilization at local communities.

METHODS

This study takes a qualitative approach to explore the role of data intermediaries. We broadly define a data intermediary as an organization that facilitates the (re)use of data to impact communities. The project team interviewed one to three key staff at nine data intermediary organizations across the U.S. We used several strategies to identify data intermediary organizations in different U.S. cities. As previous research has suggested that community research centers often help community members/organizations with their data needs—and, thus, serve as a form of data intermediaries (Yoon, 2017)—we first conducted a Google search using several key words, such as *community research center* and *community research institute*. Using this strategy, we identified approximately 50 community research centers that existed as non-profit organizations or were affiliated with universities. We also reviewed the 42 partner organizations across 30 cities included in the National Neighborhood Indicators Partnership (NNIP, http://www.neighborhoodindicators.org/), a collaborative effort by the Urban Institute (http://www.urban.org/)

and local partners to further the development and use of neighborhood information systems in local policy-making and community building. We carefully reviewed each organization's website for information regarding their missions, services offered, and past projects. After assessing each organization's fit for this study, we then chose data intermediary organizations in small, medium, and large cities (e.g., Grand Rapids, MI; San Antonio, TX; and Boston, MA) that agreed to participate in the study. Since one organization dropped out during the interview process, we interviewed a total of 15 staff members (one to three per organization) from a total of nine organizations.

We conducted a semi-structured phone interview with our participants following pre-developed interview protocols. The interview questions covered the organizations' missions, the role of the staff, types of services to support communities' data utilization, the interviewees' experiences working with community members/organizations, and challenges associated with support communities' data work. All interviews were audio-recorded and fully transcribed by professionals. The sample sets of data were inductively analyzed to develop a set of codes representing emerging themes. Then, the rest of the data were deductively coded following the developed coding scheme. A qualitative data analysis tool, Nvivo, was used to code the transcripts and analyze the data. The inter-coder reliability among the project team members was 93%, and we had more than 90% agreement for all codes except one, which still achieved an acceptable 86% agreement rate. As this study aims to "understand and describe as accurately as possible the phenomena" (Groenewald, 2004, p. 5), we followed a phenomenological and interpretive analysis approach (Smith, Flowers, & Larkin, 2009).

RESULTS

The nine participating organizations were drawn from small, medium, and large cities across the U.S. (Dallas, TX; Columbus, OH; Boston, MA; San Antonio, TX; Grand Rapids, MI; New Haven, CT; Indianapolis, IN; Milwaukee, WI; and Providence, RI). Four were independent non-profit organizations, and five were university-affiliated organizations. Six organizations were part of the NNIP network. The sizes of the organizations varied from 7 to 30 staff members, with average staff of 15. Of the 15 staff who were interviewed for this study, 4 were male and 10 were female. Their ages ranged from 30s to 60s. Table 1 provides basic demographic information about the participants, including their education levels and years of experience at the organizations. In the following section, we present the participating organizations' primary missions and services, as well as some of the challenges they have faced in fulfilling their missions.

Organization	Staff	Age	Gender	Position	Years at the Organization	Level of Education
O1	S11	30s	F	Program management	2.5	MS
	S12	30s	F	Co-director	5	PhD
	S12	40s	F	Co-director	4	PhD
O2	S21	40s	F	Director	4	PhD
	S22	30s	F	Director of research	2.5	PhD
O3	S31	50s	M	Director	10	PhD
O4	S41	50s	M	Senior director	6	PhD
	S42	50s	F	(Former) research associate	5	PhD
O5	S51	30s	F	Director	5	PhD
O6	S61	30s	M	Executive director	9	BA
O7	S71	50s	F	Director of collaborative research	22	MLA
	S72	30s	M	Research analyst	1	MA
O8	S81	60s	F	Director	1.5	PhD
	S82	30s	F	Data analyst	1.5	BA
O9	S91	30s	F	Research associate data analyst	2	PhD

Table 1. Demographic information

Organizational Missions and Serving Communities

An organization's mission is crucial in justifying its existence, differentiating it from other organizations, facilitating organizational innovation, and helping it achieve intended performance (McDonald, 2007). The ways in which the staff explained their organizational missions reflected the ways in which they perceived these missions in relation to their job responsibilities. From their descriptions of the missions, we found that data were either explicitly or implicitly related to the intermediary organizations' overall missions. Staff from most intermediaries related that their mission was to "strengthen communities with data" by "connecting the communities with data" (e.g., easy access, data aggregation, and analysis) and/or by "helping the communities to make a better decision with data" (O2, O5, O6, O7, O8, O9). Staff from two organizations specifically stated that they contributed to "the democratization of data" through different types of data services for public use (O8, O9). Other staff emphasized how their organizations bridged communities and different partners (e.g., academics, business, etc.) by promoting collaborations and community research (O1, O3, O4). One staff member from O4 underscored the organization's mission to support community development by serving as "an information resource for community members." Although these three organizations (O1, O3, O4) did not explicitly mention data in their missions, data were inherently associated with their projects and community services. For instance, S11 discussed the significance of data in all projects, noting that data helps community organizations gain a better understanding of their communities at large.

Most organizations tended to focus their services on their regional geographic areas, such as their neighborhoods, counties, and cities; however, some stated that they also served other cities in and out of the state. Their clients or partners were predominantly non-profits (e.g., community foundations, advocacy organizations, community service organizations like the YMCA, etc.) and local government or quasi-government entities, but they also occasionally worked for business associations and individual companies, "although that's less common" (S41).

Emerging Data Needs for Communities

The staff interviewed for this study experienced emerging data needs with their targeted communities. To meet these needs, they interacted with and used a wide range of data. Many reported working with publicly available data published by various government organizations, such as the Department of Education, the Department of Health, and the Bureau of Labor Statistics. Census data and the American Community Survey were among the sources commonly mentioned, but the interviewed staff also utilized data from local agencies to learn more about health, economic indicators (income, unemployment, etc.), housing, education, and business. Though the majority relied on open data, several requested private, proprietary data for specific community projects.

From the staff members' perspectives, one reason for communities to utilize data is to understand their neighborhoods in order to "make community decisions based on data" (S22), such as developing community-specific programs or services. Data are "important in looking at trends and opportunities" (S91) because data "help [community organizations] understand what the needs of their constituencies are and how best to position themselves for the future" (S41). Several echoed the need for data "to set new goals for [community] programs" (S91) or "to start a new initiative" (S51). These initiatives pointed to community efforts to make decisions based on data. Data were also crucial in "adjust[ing] some of [the community organizations'] services if [the communities] have determined that the data show that they're really not having the same impact that they anticipated" (S91). Often, this need was tied to the organizations' program evaluation or outcome measures, since understanding the impacts of their programs guided the organizations to change what they had been working on and how.

Communities' data needs were also highly associated with communities' efforts to apply for grants and secure funding. Staff from almost all intermediaries mentioned the importance of grants for community organizations, most of which are small, non-profit, and in great need of financial support. Data provided evidence of the impact of the community organizations' proposed projects; therefore, community organizations increasingly tried to "visualize these data or to create data tables that they can use for grant applications" (S91). S91 further explained that grant agencies require data for project/program measures, meaning that community members "are asked to be very data fluent in not only their grant applications, but also their grant reporting. [...] They're being asked to demonstrate their impacts in terms of quantitative outcomes." Sometimes, funders required community organizations "to do an external evaluation [...] to prove that the program is working" (S61), creating another strong data demand on the community side.

Community Data Services

To meet their communities' various data needs, the surveyed intermediary organizations provided different types of data services. The depth and breadth of the services they offered varied depending the intermediary organizations' missions and scales.

Support Data Reuse

Supporting communities' use of secondary data was one of major areas in which most data intermediary organizations offered services, which could be fee-based or pro bono, depending on the scale of the work and the intermediary's service model. One way of supporting data reuse was to simply help "citizens, non-profits, [and] government agencies have easy access to data and knowledge that comes from that data" (S22). Staff from the majority of intermediaries noted that community members occasionally knew what data they needed and wanted, but more often were "not so familiar with pulling secondary data" (S22) and did not know where to search.

The data intermediaries also offered more sophisticated levels of service to support data reuse through data aggregation or integration. Many intermediaries either compiled or aggregated publicly available data by importing or integrating the data into their own system, which S71 described as an activity "adding value" to enhance data utilization. S21 said "a lot of people [from the community] were intimidated" when using secondary data because, even though such data are publicly available, "they are not necessarily publicly available in a ready to use format" (S71). Intermediary organizations took data from various sources, reorganized datasets to meet communities' needs (e.g., by geography or neighborhood), broke geographic data down into smaller geographies, made the data clear and easy to explore, and dug down into the neighborhood level for local stakeholders. S61 described this process as transforming data "from nothing to useful for something," noting that publicly available raw data are often not user-friendly to community members.

Data tools were essential in supporting communities' data reuse. Several intermediaries developed data tools from their data aggregation and integration efforts to facilitate communities' data utilization. S71 said that "provid[ing] tools to community members to help them really compile the information that's of interest to them [...] is a very important" piece of a data intermediary's work. While the functions of such tools differed across the intermediaries, common features included interactivity and the capability to present the data at the local level. Using the tools, community members "could select interested indicators as well as geographies and instantly map relevant information" (S22), functionalities that significantly supported the communities' data utilization. The tools also allowed communities to break data down to the neighborhood level, allowing community members to "build an index and look at comparisons between neighborhoods and trends over time" (S51). Being able to dig into data at the local level was crucial for communities' data reuse, as data at the state and federal level were often too general to accurately represent communities' current situations. Intermediary organizations also offered free training sessions to "teach people how to utilize those tools" (S51, S71) to maximize the benefits to the communities.

Collect Local Data

Several intermediaries were actively involved in collecting local data that accurately represented their communities, largely due to the lack of existing secondary data at the local level. S41 pointed out the "deficiencies in the [existing] data," stating this was why intermediary organizations had to "go out and [collect] primary data." S61 echoed that "often you can't get that granularity of data [at local level] from a government agency." The fact that publicly available data rarely provided enough information on a small scale was one of challenges hindering communities' data utilization. S81 said that the lack of data representing local communities was the major issue in supporting communities' data work, leading intermediaries to collect data to complement existing data.

Help with Analysis and Interpretation

While some intermediaries stated that they "don't do analysis" (S51), several others engaged with the analysis and interpretation process when asked to do so by their clients (i.e. community members). S91 said, "most of the smaller [community] organizations, [...] they just don't have the capacity to analyze [data] themselves." When the intermediaries analyzed data for the communities, they typically did more than simply share the numbers in written reports. Instead, they "visualize [the data] or map [the results] for [the organizational needs] so that [the community organizations] can then take that output and use [it right away]" (S81). S71 described the analysis process as "a partnership, where we don't just interpret the data and send it back to [the clients], but there's multiple sessions where they're talking about what the questions are, and then a preliminary data analysis is presented, and so it is an interactive process, and there's a lot of collaboration." Further, O7 described "working with [the clients] to understand their needs and their culture, and everything that would go into forming whatever final data project they need" (S71). These reflections show that the intermediaries actively communicated with their clients throughout the analysis process to make sure the clients accurately interpreted and understood the data for their purposes.

Promote Data Sharing and Share Data with Communities

A few intermediary organizations also contributed to the data-sharing landscape by supporting community organizations' data-sharing practices. S91 said that O9 had been working with different organizations that wanted to share data-driven information with members of the community and had "been [...] creating data-sharing relationship agencies [that currently do not share their data] to obtain new data sets." Using the data from these agencies, O9 was "linking the data and sharing back out the aggregate to them" as part of its data reuse support. The intermediary organizations also shared the data they collected with the communities. S61 said, "[regarding] our own data, our goal is to make everything public. [...] There's some data we released more in an unidentified format or in its original and raw format. [...] Pretty much everything we [collect], we make public."

While intermediary organizations occasionally shared raw data, including both secondary data they acquired and primary data they collected, several intermediaries shared data in more "processed" forms, considering the community members' different levels of data literacy and different abilities to search, understand, and interpret data. The most common form of "processed" data was "data reports" with tables and infographics on important indicators of communities' interests. Often these reports were included in the clients' requests. For instance, they might "compare how [the city] is doing compared to other peer cities on a variety of indicators, such as poverty levels, educational levels, housing, things like that," and were "shared around the community a lot" (S22) through the clients. In other cases, intermediaries produced data reports for general community members or citizens so that any stakeholder could learn about the community and different topics/indicators and use the data for their own purposes. Not all of the intermediaries tracked who accessed and used these reports, but some had a clear understanding of their users, including legislators, community advocates, government officials, and the general public.

Improve Communities' Data Practices

Although it was not common, two intermediaries helped community organizations improve their internal data practices. Community organizations often needed to collect internal data for program evaluation and outcome measures for grant reporting, but not all implemented best practices. S51 ran into "a lot of issues where organizations don't support their own data or don't keep [the data] in the same format all the time," generating "more process concerns." O9 helped these community organizations implement the best data organization method to "do or plan out their evaluation plan [early] so that they're not caught at the end of their grant cycle to figure out how demonstrate what their impact was in anything more than an anecdotal fashion" (S91). O1 was more actively involved in community organizations' internal data practices, helping them "curate the data they collect, and the method by which they collect, and the methods by which they store, and their quality assurance and improvement of that, [...] and [track] longitudinal patterns" (S13). This was one of the most active forms of data support that intermediary organizations provided communities.

Foster Community Research

A small number of intermediaries actively participated in community research either by independently conducting research "to understand specifically what's going on in [the county]" (S11) or through partnerships with research institutions and community organizations. S61 called this effort "community-engaged research," which could take the form of a survey study "in conjunction with the foundations, or hospitals, or health departments, or city offices" to answer community-specific research questions. These community research projects usually produced valuable data specific to the local context and helped to overcome some of the limitations of using secondary data.

Challenges to Support Communities' Data Work

While data intermediary organizations supported communities' data utilization through the various services described above, they also experienced different challenges doing their work. These challenges were associated with several different factors, such as a lack of organizational resources, a lack of local data, a lack of data literacy among community members, and difficulties building a partnership between communities and academic institutions.

Lack of Organizational Resources

Despite growing community demands for data utilization, not all data intermediary organizations were equipped with sufficient financial and human resources to either maintain current services or extend/develop new services for communities. Financial resources were crucial to the intermediary organizations' sustainability, and several mentioned that their business model was "100% self-funded" with no state support (and, thus, fully funded by projects). This limited opportunities for community organizations that could not afford a service fee, although some intermediaries noted that they did smaller-scale "pro bono work" (S21) for smaller communities. Limited financial resources could also limit the development of a new service or the extension of an existing service. As S71 mentioned, these "resource constraints prevent us from working on [new areas because] we don't have the funding to [do all the work]." For smaller intermediaries, a lack of human resources was the factor limiting their community data support, as no single staff member can have all different types of expertise and the data skills needed. S61 said, "the staff time and staff level of expertise" also mattered for collecting and working with complex data.

Lack of Local (Neighborhood) Data

While data intermediary organizations shared some common challenges relating to data reuse, such as difficulties accessing secondary data, difficulties aggregating data due to interoperability issues, and difficulties working with sensitive data (Lucero et al., 2015; Yoon, 2016), one notable challenge that staff from all intermediaries identified was a lack of data representing local areas or neighborhoods. Although all staff utilized publicly available data for community data work, they agreed that "the public data are fairly general, and usually the scope is fairly large (S41)." Many noted that there were no data available on particular topics (e.g., health data, unemployment data) at the neighborhood or small-town level. Alternatively, they used or let communities use "data at a zip code level to portray what's going on in their neighborhood," even though such reports are "just basically generally wrong" (S81) because "zip codes are not necessarily related to neighborhood[s]" (S21). S21 said this made community members really "angry [...] and the people in a particular neighborhood within that zip code are like, 'that's so not true' because their shared daily experience is different than what the data suggested, and so they're freaking out." This was the major challenge the intermediaries faced when supporting communities' data work, and it was also why data intermediaries needed "to figure out a way to develop our own [data]" (S41). In addition, publicly available data were "notoriously old, [and] it was really common to find data that would be six years old [or] a couple-year lag" (S42). Usually, communities needed current, up-to-date data representing current community problems; in such cases, old data were not particularly useful.

Community Members' Data Literacy Skills

One critical issue relating to interactions with communities was differences in community members' data literacy skills. Many intermediary staff mentioned that different levels of data literacy influenced how they communicated with both their clients and the general public. S72 said, "general citizens are probably not being very accurate in terms of interpreting [data]," which can be a challenge when working with them. Intermediary organizations shared the results of data analyses and/or interpretations in formats "designed to be digestible" (S61). Data reports also aligned with these efforts. Still, a lack of data literacy could hinder intermediaries' communication processes. As S11 shared, "it's hard for [community members] to understand what goes into analyzing and cleaning data. Our community partners get frustrated when they have a request and they don't understand why we can't generate it that second, why it might take a few days."

Building a Partnership between Academic Institutions and Communities

For those intermediaries that had tried to build or already built a partnership between communities and academic institutions to support communities' data work or community research, a distance between the two entities often posed a challenge. A partnership with university researchers can have great benefits for communities' data work because academic researchers are experts in topical areas or domains. S42 described one case in which he was "a little suspicious about the motivation for doing the community need assessment [requested by one community organization]." When he consulted with experts from a local university, one of them "flat out said, 'It's a fad, and this is what's going on politically' because they had done years of research on the area." He said the researchers immensely helped to clarify where to look for data sources while crystalizing the real problems to address using the clients' data sources. However, there was still a degree of distance between communities and academic institutions because the two parties tended to have different motivations and needs. Academic researchers tended to focus on education and research; thus, "they push a publication, research design [...] that would be required and understandable in [an academic] environment" (S81). By contrast, communities "may not see much value in research itself [...] They may be struggling with day-to-day challenges [...] and don't see any short-term or immediate benefits from [academic research]" (S31). S81 also found that, "sometimes, data people [from academia] are not very respectful of the [community members]." When academic researchers lacked a deeper understanding of communities' needs, community members found their collaboration intrusive.

DISCUSSIONS

This study explored data utilization at the local community level through the work of data intermediary organizations. The findings of this study reveal that data intermediary organizations play four major roles that are crucial in communities' data utilization: (1) democratizing data, (2) adding value to existing data, (3) enhancing communities' data literacy, and (4) building communities' data capacity.

Democratizing Data

Data democratization involves helping all citizens access and understand data. Although only two intermediary organizations in this study identified data democratization as one of their missions, all intermediaries contributed to democratizing data in practice. Easy access to data when needed at any given moment is an important first step towards data democratization, as previous research has suggested that access to data is the single most important component of successful data reuse (Yoon, 2016). Most intermediaries tried to improve communities' access to data. However, democratizing data means more than just ensuring easy access. Intermediary organizations were actively involved in helping communities make sense of data, ensuring that data could be easily understood and interpreted for the purpose of the communities' data utilization. Aggregating different data sources, breaking data down into desired units (e.g., neighborhood, county), developing self-service data tools for analysis and reuse, and visualizing data were all initiatives in which intermediary organizations engaged to support communities' understanding of data. These efforts align well with the goal of data democratization, which is to expedite decision-making processes, eliminate barriers to accessing or understanding data, and uncover opportunities for organizations (Marr, 2017).

Adding Value to Existing Data

A second critical role that intermediary organizations play is adding value to existing data. Not all of the intermediaries seemed to be aware of this role, though S71 acknowledged that their work added value to data and data utilization. However, whether intermediaries are aware of this role or not, adding value to existing data significantly contributes to open data curation. Value-adding activities are the hallmark of data curation and perhaps the most meaningful and uniquely necessary step in supporting data reuse and utilization. The Digital Curation Center (DCC, n.d.) defined digital (data) curation as the effort of "maintaining, preserving and adding value to digital data throughout its lifecycle," as well as to "enhance the long-term value of existing data by making it available" for current and future use. Data intermediary organizations may not contribute to curation of the complete data lifecycle, for example, as the interviewees rarely mentioned long-term data preservation or data sustainability. However, they notably contribute to several other curation components, particularly relating to maximizing access and data preparation. In the context of intermediaries' support of communities' data access, access does not simply mean connecting communities with data by identifying appropriate data sources. The studied intermediaries were also involved in the discovery process, during which they requested data on behalf of communities, suggested potentially good sources, and consulted with local domain experts to find good data sources. Further, much of the intermediaries' work was related to enhancing accessibility and understandability through thorough data preparation. Data preparation is known to be one of most difficult, time-consuming, and knowledge-intensive challenges in data curation. When obtaining data from different sources, the intermediaries had to address issues of interoperability, as well as to clean, merge, aggregate, and integrate data with their data system to make the data more accessible, easily retrievable, and understandable. Such steps enriched the data for communities' further use and analysis. When community members accessed data through their intermediaries' systems, the data were well-prepared for consumption and contained complete and self-explanatory information. Since the ultimate goal of data curation is to support current and future use/reuse of data, the role that intermediaries play in curation cannot be underestimated.

Enhancing Communities' Data Literacy

Data literacy is known to be fundamentally important for extensively using data for decision-making (Cruosoe, 2016). In the context of communities' and individuals' data utilization, data literacy is generally understood as "the knowledge of what data are, how they are collected, analyzed, visualized, and shared, and the understanding of how data are applied for benefits or detriments" (Crusoe, 2016, p. 27). Staff from the intermediaries noted that it was important to have a certain level of data literacy to ensure smooth communication during the process of working with communities. Often, a lack of such skills was a barrier to data utilization. Data literacy skills were also critical for communities because they needed to interpret data "based on their understanding of their community" (S71). Due to the importance of data literacy for both the intermediary organizations and the communities themselves, many intermediaries either directly or indirectly educated communities on data literacy. For example, they asked about communities' data needs and perspectives on data, which helped them understand the process of data utilization, and debriefed them on the data analysis and the results, thereby helping communities understand the data and draw accurate conclusions for decision making. Many staff discussed how this process was iterative and collaborative. Several intermediaries also offered the training sessions relevant to data, including training on the data tools they had developed and, less commonly, trainings on secondary data. Since general citizens and community members had few opportunities to develop their data knowledge and skills, intermediaries' contributions to data literacy education are critical and a good fit for the niche.

Building Community's Data Capacity

Overall, data intermediary organizations significantly contribute to building communities' data capacity. In a way, the simple existence of data intermediaries helped communities be less intimidated by data utilization. This represents one important step in introducing communities to the power of data. By using the data services offered by data intermediaries, communities can become more comfortable with data and perhaps become aware of the need to develop further data literacy skills to fully benefit from data. Further, some data intermediaries were aware of their communities' lack of capacity to use and interpret data, and they sought to address these issues. This approach was reflected in both the collaborative nature of intermediaries' work with communities and their efforts relating to data education. The intermediaries' intentions to build community capacity is illustrated in the following statement:

> S71: "we don't wanna just do things for [the community] and walk away. We want to be showing them how to do it. Obviously, some people, they're not interested in knowing the whole thing, but you have to be interested [...] our goal is to increase their ability to do similar things in the future, or at least a few steps forward and maybe adapt to just being more experienced in [data work]."

Greater community capacity for data utilization would be a great asset for society, as it would enhance communities' ability to utilize data to empower communities. Ultimately, such capacity will support the goal of open data and data reuse in the community context, which will improve the lives of communities and individuals.

Despite the multifaceted roles that data intermediaries play in helping with communities' data work, the findings also illustrated that there are still many barriers to be improved for intermediaries to support communities and make data really useful for communities. It is worth noting that data intermediaries are not and should not be the only player in communities' data work, and collaboration and/or partnership with other data infrastructures is necessary to overcome some of the barriers and generate synergy to support communities' data utilization. Intermediaries were limited to existing financial and human resources, which made them unable to serve as many communities as they wanted. This could include smaller communities that may not be able to afford the service fees, although intermediaries offer a pro-bono service for these organizations. In addition, the need to educate community members about data literacy skills emerged in this study; not all intermediaries had enough capacity to provide a formalized training session to the communities. Educational institutions (e.g., local universities) and local information organizations (e.g., public libraries) can share some of the responsibilities of educating communities about data literacy, and can help with communities' interaction with data, considering their expertise in education, community engagement and services. These collaborations and partnerships will complement the services provided by data intermediary organizations while meeting the needs of communities that intermediaries cannot fully afford. The best method and model for these partnerships should be investigated further by considering each entity's capacity.

CONCLUSION

As the findings demonstrate, data intermediary organizations play several important roles that affect communities' data utilization. By democratizing data, adding value to existing data, enhancing communities' data literacy, and building communities' data capacity, data intermediaries contribute to empowering communities with data, particularly regarding the communities' decision making relating to important community problems and improving community members' everyday lives.

While this study reports new findings about the role of data intermediaries and data utilization at the local community level, it also has several limitations. First, because the study focused exclusively on intermediaries, the findings reflect only intermediaries' perspectives regarding communities' data utilization. Most of the staff who participated in this study were highly skilled in the realm of data. Speaking directly to community members, who would have much more diverse backgrounds and levels of data skills, is necessary to fully understand how data are used and what kinds of challenges communities face in using data to make a real impact.

ACKNOWLEDGMENTS

This research is supported by the Institution of Museum and Library Services (IMLS) through the National Leadership Grant for Libraries program (#LG-96-17-0184-17), "Data Reuse for Local Community." The project team would also like to thank the nine data intermediary organizations and the staff who participated in our study.

REFERENCES

Brown, L. D., & Kalegaonkar, A. (2002). Support organizations and the evolution of the NGO sector. *Nonprofit and Voluntary Sector Quarterly*, *31*(2), 231–258. https://doi.org/10.1177/0899764002312004

Chattapadhyay, S. (2014). Access and use of government data by research and advocacy organisations in India: A survey of (potential) open data ecosystem. *Proceedings of the 8th International Conference on Theory and Practice of Electronic Governance (ICEGOV)*, 361–364. DOI: 10.1145/2691195.2691262

Crusoe, D. (2016). Data literacy defined pro populo: To read this article, please provide a little information. *The Journal of Community Informatics*, *12*(3). Retrieved from http://ci-journal.net/index.php/ciej/article/view/1290

Davies, T. (2014, July). *Open Data in Developing Countries - Emerging Insights from Phase I*. Retrieved from http://opendataresearch.org/content/2014/704/open-data-developing-countries-emerging-insights-phase-i

Díaz Andrade, A., & Urquhart, C. (2010). The affordances of actor network theory in ICT for development research. *Information Technology & People*, *23*(4), 352–374. https://doi.org/10.1108/09593841011087806

Digital Curation Center. (n.d.). *What is digital curation?* Retrieved from http://www.dcc.ac.uk/digital-curation/what-digital-curation

Douglass, K., Allard, S., Tenopir, C., Wu, L., & Frame, M. (2014). Managing scientific data as public assets: Data sharing practices and policies among full-time government employees. *Journal of the Association for Information Science and Technology*, *65*(2), 251–262. https://doi.org/10.1002/asi.22988

Groenewald, T. (2004). A phenomenological research design illustrated. *International Journal of Qualitative Methods*, *3*(1), 1–26.

Gurstein, M. B. (2011). Open data: Empowering the empowered or effective data use for everyone? *First Monday*, *16*(2). Retrieved from http://firstmonday.org/ojs/index.php/fm/article/view/3316

Janssen, M., & Zuiderwijk, A. (2014). Infomediary business models for connecting open data providers and users. *Social Science Computer Review*, *32*(5), 694–711. https://doi.org/10.1177/0894439314525902

Kassen, M. (2013). A promising phenomenon of open data: A case study of the Chicago open data project. *Government Information Quarterly*, *30*(4), 508–513.https://doi.org/10.1016/j.giq.2013.05.012

Keser, J., & Chan, J. K. (n.d.). *The social impact of open data*. Sunlight Foundation. Retrieved from http://www.opendataresearch.org/http://www.opendataresearch.org/dl/symposium2015/odrs2015-paper20.pdfdl/symposium2015/odrs2015-paper20.pdf

Levin, P. L., & Schneir, H. (2015, December 2). Imagine a world of good data. *Stanford Social Innovation Review: Informing and Inspiring Leaders of Social Change*. Retrieved from http://ssir.org/data_for_community_driven_solutions/entry/imagine_a_world_of_good_data

Lucero, R. J., Kearney, J., Cortes, Y., Arcia, A., Appelbaum, P., Fernández, R. L., & Luchsinger, J. (2015). Benefits and risks in secondary use of digitized clinical data: Views of community members living in a predominantly ethnic minority urban neighborhood. *AJOB Empirical Bioethics*, *6*(2), 12–22. https://doi.org/10.1080/23294515.2014.949906

McDonald, R. E. (2007). An investigation of innovation in nonprofit organizations: The role of organizational mission. *Nonprofit and Voluntary Sector Quarterly*, *36*(2), 256–281. https://doi.org/10.1177/0899764006295996

Marr, B. (2017, July 24). What is data democratization? A super simple explanation and the key pros and cons. *Forbes*. Retrieved from https://www.forbes.com/sites/bernardmarr/2017/07/24/what-is-data-democratization-a-super-simple-explanation-and-the-key-pros-and-cons/

Research Data Alliance (RDA). (n.d.). *Data for development interest group*. Retrieved from https://www.rd-alliance.org/groups/data-development.html

Sapsed, J., Grantham, A., & DeFillippi, R. (2007). A bridge over troubled waters: Bridging organisations and entrepreneurial opportunities in emerging sectors. *Research Policy*, *36*(9), 1314–1334. https://doi.org/10.1016/j.respol.2007.05.003

Sein, M. K., & Furuholt, B. (2012). Intermediaries: bridges across the digital divide. *Information Technology for Development*, *18*(4), 332–344. https://doi.org/10.1080/02681102.2012.667754

Smith, J. A., Flowers, P., & Larkin, M. (2009). *Interpretative Phenomenological Analysis: Theory, Method and Research*. SAGE Publications Ltd.

The United Nations Secretary-General's Independent Expert Advisory Group on a Data Revolution for Sustainable Development (IEAG). (2014). *A world that counts, mobilizing the data revolution*. Retrieved from http://www.undatarevolution.org/wp-content/uploads/2014/11/A-World-That-Counts.pdf

Urquilla, M., & Shelton, J. (2015, December 18). Bridging communities and government through data. *Stanford Social Innovation Review: Informing and Inspiring Leaders of Social Change*. Retrieved from http://ssir.org/data_for_community_driven_solutions/entry/bridging_communities_and_government_through_data

van Schalkwyk, F., Wilmers, M., Czerniewicz, L., & Czerniewicz, L. (2014). *Case study: Open data in the governance of South African higher education*. Retrieved from http://www.opendataresearch.org/sites/default/files/publications/Open%20Data%20in%20the%20Governance%20of%20South%20African%20Higher%20Education%20WEB.PDF

van Schalkwyk, F., Canares, M., Chattapdhyay, S., & Andrason, A. (2016). Open data intermediaries in developing countries. *The Journal of Community Informatics*, *12*(2). Retrieved from http://ci-journal.net/index.php/ciej/article/view/1146

Yoon, A. (2017, September). Data for community development and decision making. *Research Data Alliance (RDA) 10th Plenary Meeting*. Montreal, Canada.

Yoon, A. (2016, October). Red flags in data: Learning from failed data reuse experiences. *Proceedings of the 79th Association for Information Science and Technology (ASIS&T) Annual Meeting, 53*(1), 1–6. Copenhagen, Denmark. DOI: 10.1002/pra2.2016.14505301126

Evaluation of Metadata Change in Authority Data over Time: An Effect of a Standard Evolution

Oksana L. Zavalina
University of North Texas, USA.Oksana.Zavalina@unt.edu

Vyacheslav Zavalin
University of North Texas, USA.
VyacheslavZavalin@my.unt.edu

ABSTRACT

Information community creates, maintains and shares authority data through large-scale databases of standardized digital records that describe persons, institutions, places, events, and works, as well as relations between them. This submission presents some results of the content analysis study that explores the authority data change over time in response to change in standards. We analysed over 400 thousand of authority records that comply to the new standard, Resource Description and Access (RDA) and are available through the OCLC database. Records were obtained at two data collection points, with an interval of 22 months. Our analysis identified RDA-based authority data elements that are widely applied and the ones that need more attention by record creators. Findings reveal a significant increase over time in the level of application of some data elements, including several of the Linked Data-enabling elements. This study contributes to the understanding of metadata change and its relation to functionality of authority records and improved information access. Directions for future research are suggested.

KEYWORDS

Metadata analysis, authority data, Linked Data, MARC, RDA.

INTRODUCTION

The content of metadata records is influenced by various environmental change over time, including changes in national and international standards for record creation, etc. (Thornburg and Oskins, 2007). To keep pace with these environmental changes, metadata records to be regularly reviewed and updated. This applies both to bibliographic metadata that represents information objects, and to authority data that has long been used to facilitate access to information. Authority records represent in a standard way the names of persons, organizations, meetings, places and works related to information objects (e.g., as composers, translators, etc.) and subjects covered in these information objects.

The process of authority records creation is guided by data content standards that instruct what information to record and how to represent it, and data encoding standards for technical formatting and exchange of authority data. Since 1960s, authority data have been created, maintained and exchanged in digital form through the large-scale databases that rely on the international data encoding standard Machine-Readable Cataloging (MARC) Format for Authority Data (http://www.loc.gov/marc/authority/). The data in MARC authority records are organized into fixed and variable fields. Most of the variable fields (identified by a three-character numeric tag, e.g., 100), include multiple data elements (e.g., #a, #2, etc.). The authority data are freely available for harvesting individually and as record sets in their native MARC format, as well as (in the recent years) in Linked Data form in serializations of Resource Description Framework (RDF).

Both data content and data encoding standards evolve over time to reflect the changes in information environment and to meet the emerging requirements (e.g., the requirements of Semantic Web). In 2013, the new Resource Description and Access (RDA) standard designed to better support Linked Data officially replaced its predecessor as a data content standard for authority data. Since the early stages of RDA development, the active work is ongoing on aligning MARC with RDA. In the process of alignment, numerous new MARC record fields and subfields have been added, with the most recent revisions of RDA-based MARC Authority Standard – update no. 25 – completed in December 2017. For example, the "heading information" block of MARC authority fields has been greatly expanded through addition of 20 new 3XX MARC fields (e.g., 373 Associated Group).

Very few published papers so far discussed RDA implementation in authority records or evaluated implementation results. Niu (2013) and Southwick (2015) discussed the process of RDA-based MARC authority records creation or conversion of existing records into Linked Data form. Kimura (2015) compared data elements in over a million of personal, corporate, and meeting name authority records created in China, Japan, and Korea with data elements defined in RDA standard. Thompson's study (Thompson, 2016) focused on the application of the RDA-based field 375 Gender in a small sample of personal name authority records. Moulaison (2015) assessed the use of 7 RDA-based data elements in personal name authority records in an academic library consortia authority file one year after official adoption of RDA. Zavalina and Zavalin (2017) took a broader approach and examined levels of application of 35 RDA-based MARC fields and their subfields in 5 types of authority records 3 years after RDA adoption.

Despite the importance of measuring metadata change that was pointed out for information quality (Stvilia et al., 2004; Stvilia & Gasser, 2008), little research on metadata change has been published; all of the available studies focus on change in descriptive metadata, with no investigation of authority data change. The overall scarcity of metadata change studies is in part due to the shortage of information systems that provide a metadata versioning functionality. Several quantitative studies attempted to identify and measure change in metadata records in digital libraries that enable metadata versioning (e.g., Tarver, Zavalina & Phillips, 2016; Zavalina, Phillips & Tarver, 2017). A qualitative research project (e.g., Zavalina et al., 2015, 2016; Zavalina, Shakeri, & Kizhakkethil, 2015; Zavalina, Shakeri, Kizhakkethil, & Phillips, 2018) categorized metadata change in digital library metadata and in traditional library metadata.

The transition to RDA standard significantly impacts authority data that are crucial for providing adequate access to information. A research gap in the area of implementation of RDA standard in authority data exists. Little is known as to how the implementation of many new, RDA-based, MARC data elements is reflected in the authority data that is currently in use, and how the RDA-based authority records change over time.

METHODS

This study addresses the gap through quantitative empirical evaluation of the large representative dataset. Investigation is guided by the following research questions: What is the level of application of the new RDA-based data elements of MARC authority records and how does this level change over time? How are the Linked Data enabling elements of RDA applied in the existing authority data and how this changes over time?

MARC Edit (http://marcedint.reesenet.net) tool – Raw (ADV) search in Z39.50/SRU Client – was used for collecting the data to answer these research questions. The data was collected from the United States Library of Congress Authorities (https://authorities.loc.gov/) database, available for harvesting through OCLC, at two points in time, with an interval of 22 months: in early 2016 and in late 2017. A total of 408551 RDA-based authority records were retrieved in 2016. The same records, based on the unique records IDs, were collected in 2017. The MARC Edit Z39.50/SRU Client search in 2017 resulted in retrieving all but 26 records from the 2016 dataset; the 26 missing records had likely been deleted from the OCLC authority database between the two data collection points. Preliminary analysis identified, based on evaluation of data in the field 005 Date and Time of Latest Transaction, 35472 records that underwent changes between the two data collection points. This set included five types of authority records: corporate, geographic, meeting and personal names, as well as uniform titles. MARC Edit, Microsoft Excel and Sublime text editor were used in processing and analyzing the data.

In the next section, we present some results of the comparative content analysis of 2016 and 2017 versions of the changed records. We measured the utilization and assessed the level of change in application of RDA-based MARC authority variable fields (with their respective subfields) and RDA-based subfields of non-RDA-specific variable fields (#i Relationship Information, #4 Relationship #u Uniform Resource Identifier, #1 Real World Object URI, #2 Source of Data, #0 Authority Record Number).

FINDINGS AND DISCUSSION

Each record in the dataset underwent editing between the two data collection points. Less than half of 35472 records had been edited prior to initial data collection, as indicated by a total of 13786 occurrences of MARC 21 field 040 subfield #d an instance of each is automatically added upon every editing event. It is worth noting that each editing event could include multiple changes to one or more fields of the record. In the 2017 versions of authority records, the number of occurrences of this subfield increased to 49687, meaning one editing event per record on average over the period of 22 months. This is lower than the level of editing activity observed by previous research for bibliographic metadata during the first years after transition to RDA.

Our findings (Table 1) demonstrate that almost all of the RDA-based authority records that underwent changes between two data collection points were meeting name and personal name records (99.76% collectively: 60.15% and 39.6% respectively). The proportion of corporate name, geographic name and uniform title records among the edited records was minimal, between 0.02% and 0.17%. While in the total dataset of 408551 RDA-based records collected in 2016, meeting and personal names also represented the majority (86.39% collectively: 60.5% and 26.39%), the disproportional distribution of edited metadata records is an indication of a higher attention of metadata editors towards meetings and persons. This record-type-level finding is supported by data-element-level findings (Figures 1 and 2).

	meeting name	personal name	corporate name	uniform title	geographic name
% in total dataset (408551)	60.50%	26.39%	5.03%	4.45%	3.63%
% in edited records (35472)	60.16%	39.60%	0.17%	0.04%	0.02%

Table 1. Distribution by authority record type

A total of 17 RDA-based MARC fields were observed in the records that underwent changes between two data collection points. This represents 50% of all RDA-based fields in MARC authority standard at the time of 2017 data collection. None of the records in our dataset was found to include RDA-based fields 075, 147, 162, 336, 348, 385, 386, 388, 447, 462, 547, 562, 677, 700, 730, 747 or 762. In 2016, the most frequently occurring (in over 99% of records) RDA-based fields were 046 Special Coded Dates, 377 Associated Language, and 370 Associated Place. In 2017, the level of application of two more fields significantly increased and reached 99% or more of records: 373 Associated Group, and 372 Field of Activity (these fields apply mostly to personal name and corporate name records). The level of application of a field 375 Gender, specific to personal name authority records, nearly doubled from 39% to 78%. The application of fields 374 Occupation and 368 Other Attributes increased minimally but remained substantial: 39.1% and 60.3% of records respectively. The level of use of 7 additional RDA-based fields remained low (under 1%). This is mostly explained by low proportion of uniform title and geographic name records in the dataset, as 6 fields are specific to representing works or places. However, given the high proportion of personal name authority records (39.6%), the level of application of 371 Address field is much lower than expected (0.065%).

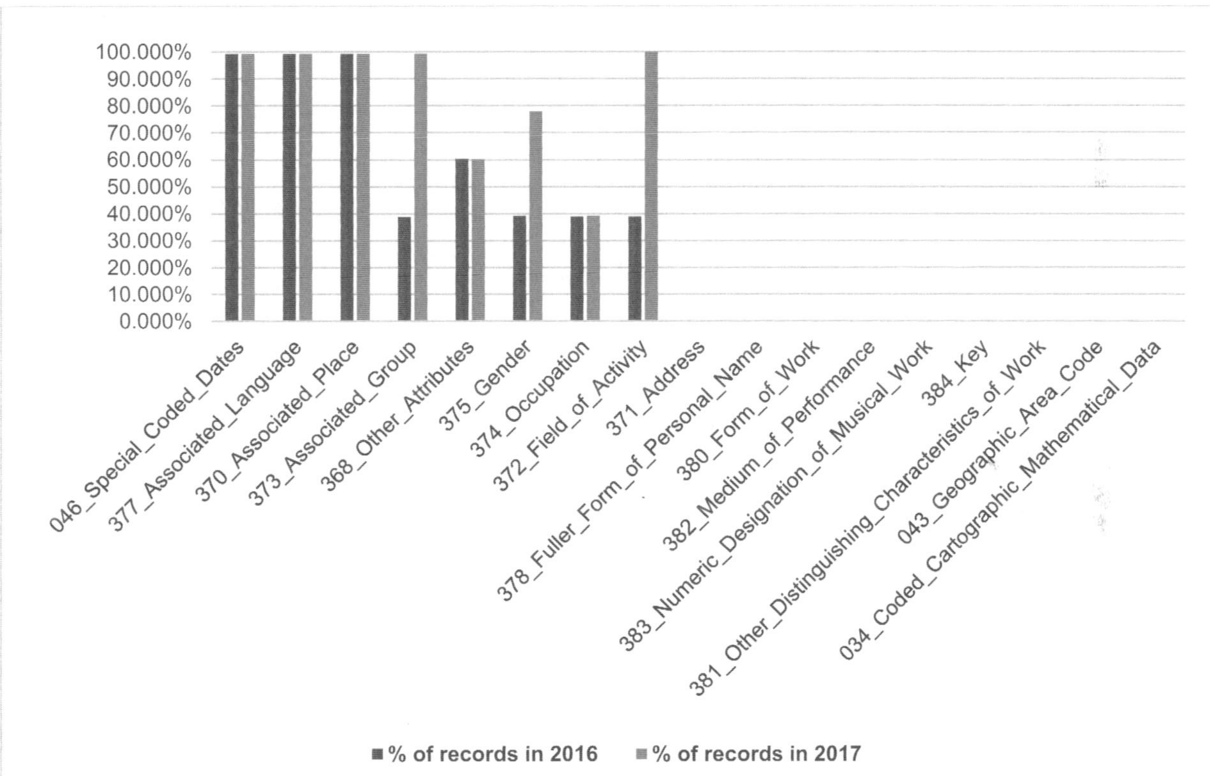

Figure 1. Field-level data elements in RDA-based MARC fields (n=35472)

Over 60 subfields of RDA-based MARC fields occurred at least once in edited records. Some are repeatable so can occur more than once in a single instance of a MARC field in a record. Four of these data elements – mostly those applicable only to the uniform title records – were not present in 2016 versions of the records and have been added since: 371#v Source of [address] information, 382#b Soloist, 383#d Thematic Index Code, and 383#2 Source. Twenty data elements occurred significantly more frequently (in at least 38% of records) than others, the level of application of which was under 2%. Figure 2 shows distribution of top 20 RDA-based MARC authority subfields. The most noticeable increase in frequency of occurrence was observed for data elements that represent relationships: 370#c Associated Country, 372#a Field of activity, 373#a Associated Group, 374#a Occupation, and 375#a Gender. The use of the Linked-Data-enabling subfield #2 Source of Term in 3 RDA-based fields – 372, 373, and 375 the overall level of application of which has also significantly increased – has grown dramatically: tripled from 13.7K to 35.1K occurrences for 373, propelled from 2 to over 13.7K occurrences for 375 and from 89 to over 27.5K occurrences for 372. This Linked-data enabling subfield #2 was not observed in the generally infrequently-used field 383 in 2016 dataset but by late 2017, 18 occurrences were added to the records.

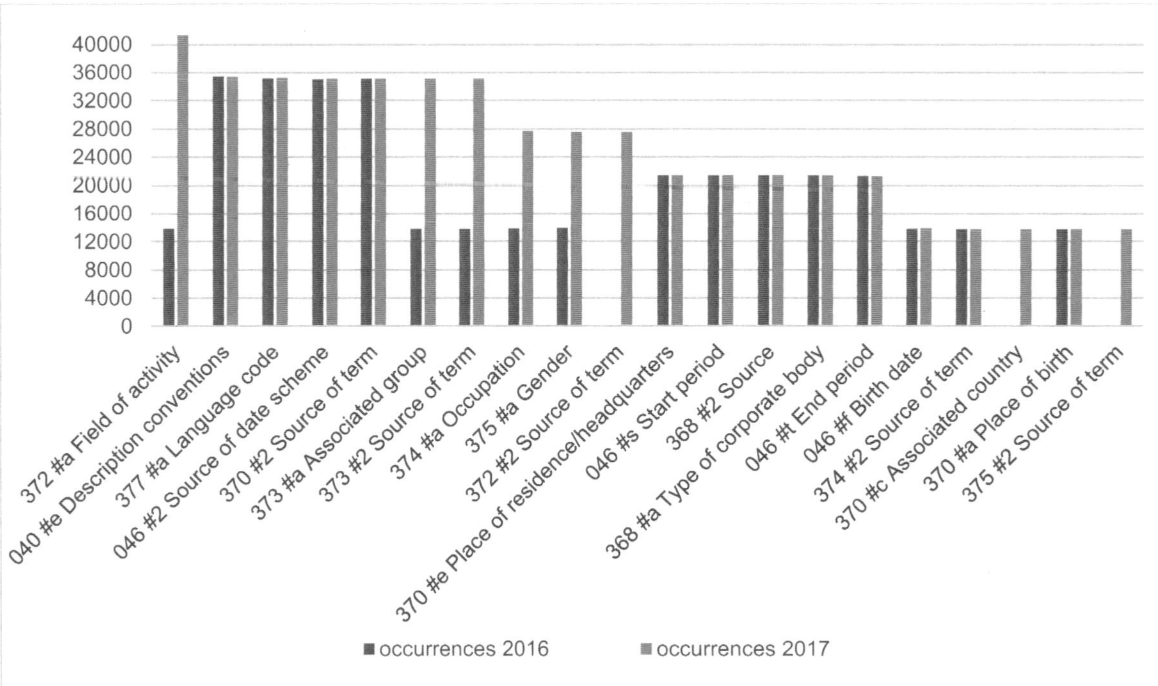

Figure 2. Subfield-level data elements in RDA-specific MARC fields: top 20 (n=35472)

RDA-based name authority records are also expected to contain new RDA-based subfields – mostly designed to support Linked Data functionality – in the traditionally-used pre-RDA fields (e.g., 410, 511, 670, etc.). This includes subfield #i for relationship information, subfield #u for unique resource identifier (URI), subfield #0 for authority record control number, subfield #1 for real world object URI, subfield #2 for information on the source of terms or other data, subfield #4 for URIs representing relationships. At the time of the first data collection in 2016, subfields #1, #4 and #i were not yet used to hold URIs and relationship information: #i and #4 were added to the MARC Authority standard in this function in May 2017, and #1 in December 2017. It is not surprising, therefore, that in late 2017 versions of authority records, no occurrences of Linked-Data-enabling elements #1 and #4 were observed. To the contrary, 4 pre-RDA fields (500, 510, 511, and 530) included subfield #i in high proportion (between 75% and 100%) of all records in the dataset containing these fields; for 3 of these fields, the level of use of #i increased between two data collection points. However, other Linked Data enabling RDA-based data elements, which existed in the standard for several years prior to our data collection, were found to be applied very infrequently in non-RDA-specific fields. For example, Subfield #u was observed in only one non-RDA based field: 670 Source Data Found but the level of its application increased by over 50%. Subfield #2 was found to be used, in a very small proportion of records, in only two non-RDA-specific MARC fields: 024 Other Standard Identifier (the level of application of 034#2 triples between two data collection points, and 034 Coded Cartographic Mathematical Data (the level of application remained unchanged)

CONCLUSION

This study addresses the research gap in the area of implementation of RDA standard in authority data that are crucial for providing adequate access to information. Our quantitative analysis of change in RDA-based authority data reveals the lower overall level of editing activity than that observed by previous research for RDA-based bibliographic metadata (Zavalina, Zavalin, & Miksa, 2016). Results of our study demonstrate higher editing activity for meeting name and personal name authority data than for three other types of authority records. The change in application of certain data elements, related to evolution of RDA standard, was observed, with gradual and sometimes drastic increase in the use of elements representing persons, as well as some of the Linked Data-enabling elements. Despite the observed growth, the level of application of Linked-Data-enabling elements in authority records remains relatively low. More research is needed to longitudinally monitor the change in metadata records over time (especially those intended for providing Linked Data functionality). Comparative analysis of metadata change is also needed for different kinds of authority data and between authority data and bibliographic data. Qualitative analysis with the focus on data values in the record fields will supplement and help interpret quantitative results. These findings will help develop a solid understanding of metadata change and model it in relation to functionality of authority records and improved information access in digital libraries and beyond.

REFERENCES

Kimura, M. (2015). A comparison of recorded authority data elements and the RDA framework in Chinese character cultures. *Cataloging and Classification Quarterly, 53*(7). DOI: 10.1080/01639374.2014.977984

Moulaison, H.L. (2015). The expansion of the personal name authority record under Resource Description and Access: Current status and quality considerations. *International Federation of Library Associations and Institutions, 41* (1), 13-24. DOI: 10.1177/0340035215570044

Niu, J. (2013). Evolving landscape in name authority control. *Cataloging and Classification Quarterly 51*(4), 404–419. DOI: 10.1080/01639374.2012.756843.

Southwick, S. B. (2015). A guide for transforming digital collections metadata into Linked Data using open source technologies. *Journal of Library Metadata, 15*(1), 1-35. DOI: 10.1080/19386389.2015.1007009

Stvilia, B., Gasser, L., Twidale, M., Shreeves, S., & Cole, T. (2004). Metadata quality for federated collections. In *Proceedings of the 9th International Conference on Information Quality* (*ICIQ04*), Cambridge, MA., *111-12*.

Stvilia, B., & Gasser, L. (2008). Value based metadata quality assessment. *Library & Information Science Research*, *30*(1), 67-74. Retrieved from http://dx.doi.org/10.1016/j.lisr.2007.06.006.

Tarver, H., Zavalina, O.L., & Phillips, M. (2016). A case study of metadata creation in the University of North Texas Libraries' Digital Collections. *Proceedings of the 82nd International Federation of Library Associations World Library and Information Congress*, Columbus, Ohio, August 13-19, 2016.

Thompson, K. J. (2016). More than a name: A content analysis of name authority records for authors who self-identify as trans. *Library Resources and Technical Services, 60*(3). DOI: http://dx.doi.org/10.5860/lrts.60n3.140

Thornburg, G., & Oskins, M. (2007). Misinformation and bias in metadata processing: Matching in large databases. *Information Technology and Libraries, 26*(2), 15-26.

Zavalina, O.L., Kizhakkethil, P., Alemneh, D., Phillips, M., & Tarver, H.S. (2015). Building a framework of metadata change to support knowledge management. *Journal of Information and Knowledge Management, 14* (1), 1-16.

Zavalina, O.L., Phillips, M., & Tarver, H. (2017). Quality assurance and evaluation of change for patent metadata: poster abstract. *Proceedings of the 80th Association for Information Science and Technology Annual Meeting.*

Zavalina, O.L., Shakeri, S., & Kizhakkethil, P. (2015). Metadata change in traditional library collections and digital repositories: Exploratory comparative analysis. *Proceedings of the 78th Association for Information Science and Technology Annual Meeting.*

Zavalina, O.L., Shakeri, S., Kizhakkethil, P., & Phillips, M.E. (2018). Uncovering hidden insights for information management: Examination and modelling of change in digital collection metadata. In G. Chowdhury et al. (Eds.), iConference 2018, *Lecture Notes in Computer Science 10766* (pp.1-7). New York: Springer.

Zavalina, O.L., & Zavalin, V. (2017). Identity management analysis: an empirical investigation into the state of library community's' authority data conformance to the new standard. In D.G. Alemneh, J. Allen, & S. Hawamdeh (Eds.), *Knowledge Discovery and Data Design Innovation* (pp. 233-248). Hackensack, NJ: World Scientific.

Zavalina, O.L., Zavalin, V., & Miksa, S. D. (2016). Quality over time: A longitudinal quantitative analysis of metadata change in RDA-based MARC Bibliographic Records Representing Video Resources. *Proceedings of the 79th Association for Information Science and Technology Annual Meeting.*

Zavalina, O.L., Zavalin, V., Shakeri, S., & Kizhakkethil, P. (2016). Developing an empirically-based framework of metadata change and exploring relation between metadata change and metadata quality in MARC library metadata. *Procedia Computer Science, 99*, 50-63.

Predicting the Dynamics of Scientific Activities: A Diffusion-based Network Analytic Methodology

Yi Zhang
Centre for Artificial Intelligence, Faculty of Engineering and Information Technology, University of Technology Sydney, Australia. Yi.Zhang@uts.edu.au

Guangquan Zhang
Centre for Artificial Intelligence, Faculty of Engineering and Information Technology, University of Technology Sydney, Australia. Guangquan.Zhang@uts.edu.au

Ximeng Wang
Centre for Artificial Intelligence, Faculty of Engineering and Information Technology, University of Technology Sydney, Australia. Ximeng.Wang@student.uts.edu.au

Jie Lu
Centre for Artificial Intelligence, Faculty of Engineering and Information Technology, University of Technology Sydney, Australia. Jie.Lu@uts.edu.au

ABSTRACT

With the rapid explosion of information and the dramatic development of bibliometric techniques in the past decades, it becomes a challenge to comprehensively, extensively, and efficiently understand science maps. Aiming to explore in-depth insights from science maps and predict the dynamics of scientific activities, this paper, based on the co-occurrence statistics of terms derived from scientific documents, proposes a diffusion-based network analytic methodology to conduct the prediction study from two aspects: the research interest of scientific researchers and the evolutionary directions of scientific topics. A case study on academic articles downloaded from three leading journals in the field of bibliometrics demonstrates the feasibility of the methodology. The future directions of bibliometrics are identified, such as the application of information technologies to traditional bibliometric data, the interactions between bibliometrics and science, technology, and innovation policy issues, and individual-level bibliometrics. The results also provide recommendations as potential research interests for a set of experts. The proposed method could be a toolkit to conduct forecasting studies for a given technological area or a given discipline, and a recommender system to assist academic researchers in identifying potential research interests and extended areas.

KEYWORDS

Bibliometrics, network analysis, diffusion, scientific activities.

INTRODUCTION

Science maps are described as the graphic reference systems representing the relationships among scientific disciplines and portfolios (Small 1999; Börner 2014), and have become one crucial part of bibliometric studies these years. Related endeavours include: introducing multiple bibliometric indicators (e.g., citation statistics, words/terms, bibliographic coupling, and specific classification codes) or their combinations for accurate knowledge representation (Noyons et al. 1999; Glänzel 2001; Chen et al. 2010; Klavans & Boyack 2017), applying information technologies (e.g., text analytics, topic models, and machine learning) to develop advanced bibliometric models for multiple purposes (van Eck et al. 2010; Ding & Chen 2014; Zhang et al. 2017), and integrating science maps with a broad range of tools (e.g., Google Map), scientific databases, and actual cases (Leydesdorff & Bornmann 2012; Huang et al. 2016). Unfortunately, with the rapid explosion of information, the structure of science maps are becoming more and more integrative and complicated, and thus comprehensively and extensively understanding science maps challenges both bibliometric communities and related users. Under this circumstance, one concern is how to explore the interactions between elements on science maps and predict underlying relationships that may appear in future.

Benefiting from the development of information technologies, network analysis provides opportunities to address the concern. Complex network analysis was first raised by physics communities, in which complex systems in nature and society are described as networks and many methods were proposed to reveal network structures and the relationships among their units (Palla et al. 2005). Complex networks are known as social networks in bibliometrics, especially when investigating the relationships between authors, portfolios (e.g., academic institutions and commercial firms), or journals (Otte & Rousseau 2002), and the comparison between complex networks and science maps have also been fully examined (Hung & Wang 2010; Yan et al. 2010). As a mainstream network analytic approach, centrality measures, first developed by Freeman (1977) for evaluating the structure of social networks, have been well-upgraded and applied to analyze co-authorship-based collaboration networks (Yan & Ding 2009; Abbasi et al. 2012). Despite the fact that these efforts provide new angles to further understand science maps, the way to predict the dynamics of scientific activities by profiling historical data is still elusive.

Aiming to address these considerations, this paper, based on the co-occurrence statistics of terms derived from scientific documents, is to propose a diffusion-based network analytic methodology to predict the dynamics of scientific activities from two aspects: the research interest of scientific researchers and the evolutionary directions of scientific topics. On one hand, considering unsupervised environments in a large number of real-world cases, we introduce an indicator *divergence* to a K-means-based clustering approach to automatically decide the number of topics in a given interval. On the other hand, with the aid of science maps, bipartite networks are used for constructing topic-term networks and author-term networks, and a diffusion-based analytic approach is proposed to predict the dynamics of scientific activities by detecting the diffusion trend of resources in the networks. A case study with 7,258 academic articles downloaded from *Journal of the Association for Information Science and Technology* (JASIST[1]), *Journal of Informetrics* (JOI), and *Scientometrics* (SCIM) was conducted to demonstrate the feasibility of our method, and the results hold interest to not only bibliometric communities but also a wide range of audiences in information science and technology, science policy, and industrial sectors.

The structure of this paper is organized as follows: the following section proposes the diffusion-based network analytic methodology, the application of our methodology to a set of bibliometrics-related articles follows, and finally we conclude limitations and future study.

METHODOLOGY

The framework of the diffusion-based network analytic methodology is given in Figure 1, including two models: term-based topic identification and diffusion-based network analysis.

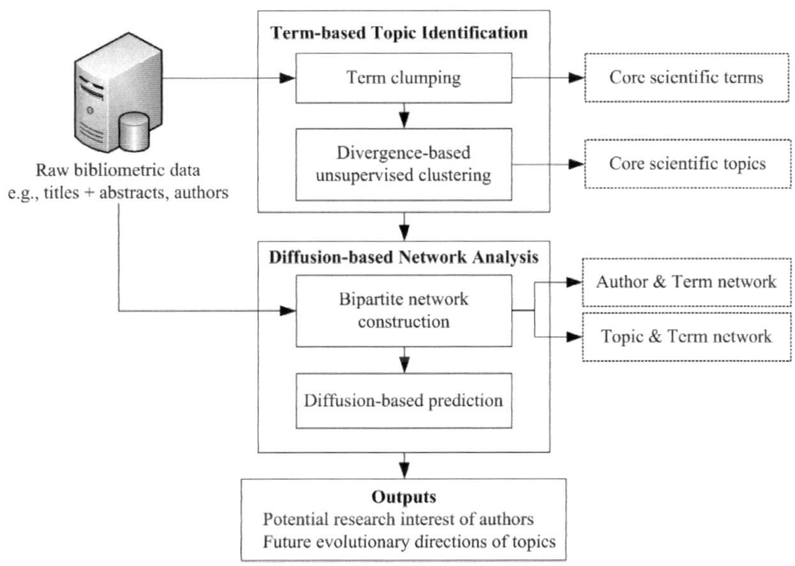

Figure 1. Framework of the diffusion-based network analytic methodology.

Input

The input of our methodology is raw bibliometric data derived from academic databases, e.g., Web of Science (WoS), and mainly includes titles, abstracts, and author information. With the use of VantagePoint (VP)[2], we will combine titles and abstracts and use the natural language processing (NLP) function of VP to retrieve terms. At the same time, some author name disambiguation (AND) techniques incorporated in VP can be applied to clean author information.

Term-based Topic Identification

This step is to identify core scientific terms and topics, which includes a term clumping function and a divergence-based unsupervised clustering function. Despite not the main focus, we will also pre-process author information in this model.

Aiming to remove noise and consolidate synonyms, the term clumping function integrates stopword-based thesauri and knowledge-based rules in a semi-automated stepwise process (Zhang et al. 2014). It holds the ability to reduce the scale of terms and identify the remaining thousand terms as core scientific terms.

---

[1] We also involve previous articles published by JASIST, with its old name *Journal of the American Society for Information Science and Technology*.
[2] VantagePoint is the software for bibliometric data-oriented text mining and visualization. More details can be addressed on the website: https://www.the-vantagepoint.com/

Considering most real-world bibliometric data is unlabeled and thus it is difficult to construct a training set for training parameters (e.g., the number of topics), we specifically integrate an indicator *divergence* with a K-means-based clustering algorithm (Zhang et al. 2016). This indicator can help automatically decide the best number of topics in a given interval, adapting to unsupervised environments. The indicator *divergence* is defined to measure the difference between topics, i.e., a higher divergence means larger differences exist between two topics, and the performance of such clustering can be better. We follow the idea that introducing the Jensen-Shannon divergence (JSD) approach (Lin 1991) to measure the distance between the word probability vectors of two documents (Boyack et al. 2011), but we calculate the distance between the term frequency vectors of two topics.

We denote $T(\Phi)$ as a topic and $C(\Psi)$ as the entire data corpus, of which Φ and Ψ are the term vectors. The frequencies of a term θ in topic $T(\Phi)$ and corpus $C(\Psi)$ can be described as θ_T and θ_C respectively. Given that α and β are the proportions of a term θ in topic $T(\Phi)$ and corpus $C(\Psi)$ respectively, i.e., $\alpha = \theta_T/||\Phi||_1$ and $\beta = \theta_C/||\Psi||_1$.

$$||\Phi||_1 = \sum_{i=1}^{dim(\Phi)} |\theta_i| \tag{1}$$

$$||\Psi||_1 = \sum_{i=1}^{dim(\Psi)} |\theta_i| \tag{2}$$

where $dim(\Phi)$ and $dim(\Psi)$ are the dimensions of vectors Φ and Ψ respectively.

Let$v = (\alpha + \beta)/2$, and the Kullback-Leibler divergence$D_{KL}(\alpha, v)$ and $D_{KL}(\beta, v)$ can be calculated as:

$$D_{KL}(\alpha, v) = \sum_{i=1}^{dim(\Phi)} \alpha_i \times log(\alpha_i/v_i) \tag{3}$$

$$D_{KL}(\beta, v) = \sum_{i=1}^{dim(\Psi)} \beta_i \times log(\beta_i/v_i) \tag{4}$$

Then, the JSD value of topic $T(\Phi)$ is:

$$JSD(T(\Phi)\,) = \frac{1}{dim(\Phi)} \frac{D_{KL}(\alpha,v)+D_{KL}(\beta,v)}{2} \tag{5}$$

Compared with the JSD formula used by Boyack et al. (2011), we take the dimension of the vector Φ into consideration to eliminate possible negative influence raised by the size of topics, e.g., a topic with more terms will have a higher JSD value. Furthermore, since the JSD value is calculated for each topic, we set the average JSD value of all topics as the divergence value of the current-round cluster analysis. Generally, when deciding the number of topics in a given interval, we prefer to choose the one with the highest divergence value. Thus, topics generated by the divergence-based clustering function are identified core scientific topics, and together with core scientific terms, are considered as the outputs of this step.

Diffusion-based Network Analysis

This step is to predict the dynamics of scientific activities, i.e., the potential research interest of researchers and the future evolutionary directions of topics, and it includes a bipartite network construction function and a diffusion-based prediction function.

As a particular network, the nodes of a bipartite network consist of two sets and edges only exist between two nodes in different sets (Zhou et al. 2007). Academic researchers (one set of nodes) that focus on similar research interests can be connected by terms (the other set of nodes), and the same as scientific topics and terms. Under this circumstance, it is reasonable to consider author-term networks and topic-term networks as bipartite networks. Using the author-term network as an example, we describe the algorithm of bipartite network construction and diffusion-based prediction as follows:

We denote an author-term network as $G_{A\&T}(A, T, L)$, where $A = \{a_1, a_2, \cdots, a_m\}$ is a set of authors, $T = \{t_1, t_2, \cdots, t_n\}$ is a set of terms, and $L = \{l_1, l_2, \cdots, l_z\}$ is a set of edges that link authors and terms. Generally, the bipartite network $G(A, T, L)$ can be represented as an $m \times n$ adjacency matrix $C_{A\&T}$, of which a cell $c_{i\alpha}(1 < i < m; 1 < \alpha < n)$ indicates the value of the edge between node t_α and node a_i, and

$$c_{i\alpha} = \begin{cases} 1 \text{ if term } \alpha \text{ appears in at least one article of author } i \\ 0 \text{ if term } \alpha \text{ does not appear in any article of author } i \end{cases} \tag{6}$$

An assumption in bipartite network projection is given that a number of resources are associated with one set of nodes in the network, and these resources can diffuse between two different sets of the bipartite network (Zhou et al. 2007). Thus, using a diffusion strategy that resources will be equally distributed by the degree of linked nodes (i.e., the number of edges connecting with the node), a mass diffusion-based analytic technique (Wang et al. 2016) was designed to detect such diffusion. Given that we plan to predict the potential research directions of author a_i, i.e., new terms that author a_i will collect in the near future.

The diffusion value $f(a_i, t_\alpha)$ is defined as the final resource that term t_α will obtain from other terms for author a_i, and can be calculated as:

$$f(a_i, t_\alpha) = \sum_{j=1}^{m} \left(\frac{c_{j\alpha}}{k(a_j)} \sum_{\beta=1}^{n} \frac{c_{i\beta} c_{j\beta} * f(t_\beta)}{k(t_\beta)} \right) \quad (7)$$

where $c_{j\alpha}$, $c_{j\beta}$ and $c_{i\beta}$ are the elements in adjacency matrix $C_{A\&T}$, $k(a_j)$ and $k(t_\beta)$ are the degrees of author j and term β respectively, and $f(t_\beta)$ is the initial resource on term β.

An example of such diffusion in a bipartite network is given in Figure 2, where nodes a_1, a_2 and a_3 represent authors, and nodes t_1, t_2, t_3 and t_4 are terms. Given that we target to author a_1, and terms t_1, t_2 and t_3 appear in the articles published by author a_1, thus, the three terms get 1 unit of resources respectively. In Step 2, these resources are equally distributed to authors by the degrees of the terms (e.g., author a_1 receives 1/2, 1, and 1/3 units of resources from terms t_1, t_2 and t_3 respectively). Then, authors flow their obtained resources back to their linked terms, and the diffusion value of each term for author a_1 is the final resource that it collects in Step 3, e.g., the diffusion value of term t_1 for author a_1 is 8/9.

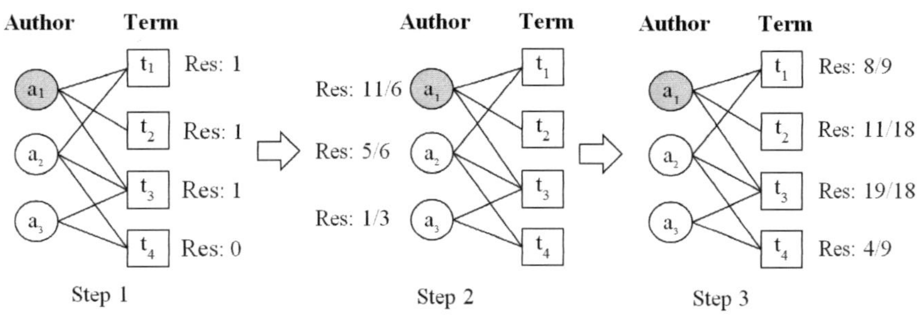

Figure 2. Sample of diffusion between nodes in a bipartite network.

Based on Equation 7, author a_i will have a diffusion vector $v(a_i)$ indicating the final resources that the author can obtain from all terms, and all these vectors will constitute a diffusion matrix $D_{A\&T}$, which can be considered as one output of our methodology. Furthermore, regarding the task of predicting the potential research interest of an author, we will remove all terms that have ever appeared in the articles of author a_i, i.e., $c_{i\alpha} = 1$, and rank the remaining terms by the diffusion value. At this stage, those terms that have never appeared in an author's articles but are ranked in the top of the list can be the potential research interest of the author. Following the same steps, we can also identify the terms that indicate the future evolutionary directions of topics. Therefore, a list of terms that hold the capability to predict the dynamics of scientific activities will be the final output of our methodology.

CASE STUDY

Aiming to demonstrate the feasibility and efficiency of our methodology, we conducted a case study to articles published by three leading journals in the areas of bibliometrics, i.e., JASIST, JOI, and SCIM, and the outputs include: the potential research interest of our bibliometric researchers and the future evolutionary directions of bibliometrics-related topics. The search was on WoS database, applied on March 22, 2017, and the collected dataset contains 7,258 articles and covers the time period from 2000 to 2017[3]. The detailed information (including the time coverage and the number of articles) of the three journals is given in Table 1.

Journal	Time Coverage	Number of Articles
JASIST	2000-2017	3225
JOI	2007-2017	698
SCIM	2000-2017	3335

Table 1. Detailed information of the three journals.

[3] The time coverage of the *Journal of Informetrics* is from 2007 (its established year) to 2017.

Term-based Topic Identification

113,159 terms were retrieved by an NLP function in VantagePoint[4], and the term clumping function was applied to identify core scientific terms. The stepwise results are given in Table 2, and the 9,942 terms generated in Step 8 is considered as core bibliometrics-related terms.

Step	Description	# Terms[1]
0	Raw terms retrieved by the NLP technique;	113,159
1	Remove terms starting/ending with non-alphabetic characters, e.g., "1.5%";	98,943
2	Remove meaningless terms, e.g., pronouns, prepositions, and conjunctions;	94,282
3	Remove common terms in scientific articles, e.g., "introduction";	92,942
4	Consolidate terms with the same stem, e.g., singular and plural, and parts of speech;	79,380
5	Consolidate synonyms based on expert knowledge, e.g., "co-word analysis" and "word co-occurrence analysis";[2]	58,624
6	Consolidate terms related to the same country or region, e.g., "Chinese economy" and "Chinese science policy";[3]	57,770
7	Remove terms appearing in only one article;	11,211
8	Remove single words;[4]	9,942

Table 2. Stepwise results of the term clumping.

Note. 1) #Terms – Number of Terms. 2) As bibliometric researchers, we quickly reviewed the results of Step 4 and summarized a list of criteria for consolidating bibliometric synonyms. 3) Considering those country/region-oriented cases have limited relationships with bibliometric methods, we decided to combine such terms to the name of related country/region. 4) According to the study conducted by Zhang et al. (2014), the meaning of single words can be fully covered by related terms, e.g., "fuzzy" and "fuzzy sets". However, as an example, we consolidated "classification analysis" to "classification" in Step 5, but we did not remove single words such as "classification" in Step 8. In addition, several extremely high-frequency terms were also removed, e.g., "bibliometrics", "scientometrics", and "informetrics".

A term co-occurrence map generated by VOSViewer (van Eck & Waltman 2009) is given in Figure 3. As an overall view, certain hotspots are observed: 1) as a mainstream in information sciences, information retrieval occupied a crucial proportion in the three leading bibliometric journals. 2) Led by citation analysis, the development of bibliometric methods is another main focus. 3) Case studies that apply quantitative methods (e.g., bibliometrics and information retrieval techniques) to handle real-world problems in specific countries or regions are another hotspot, and the United States (US) is widely involved.

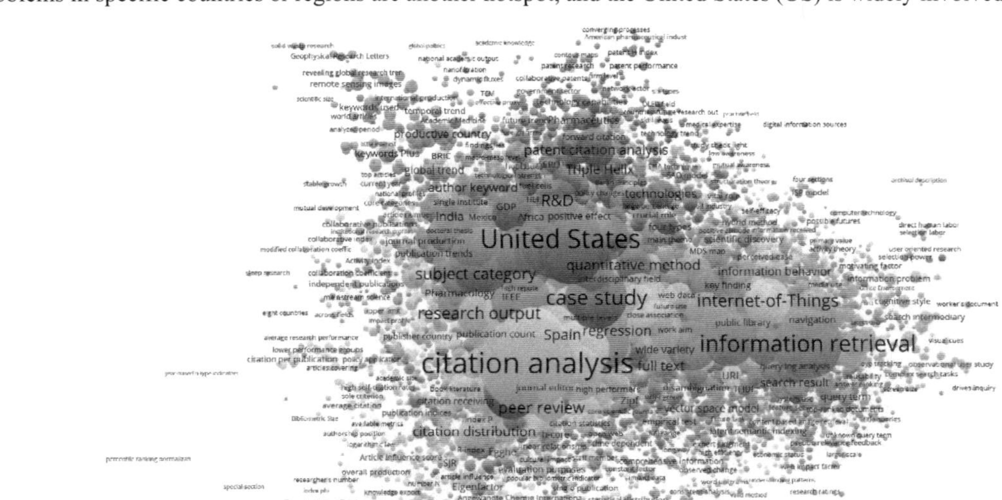

Figure 3. Co-occurrence map for core bibliometrics-related terms (from 2000 to 2017).

[4] https://www.thevantagepoint.com/

An article-term matrix linking the 7,258 articles and the 9,945 terms was constructed, and we ran the divergence-based clustering function by considering the number of topics in the interval [5, 20]. The divergence values of the 16-round experiments are given in Figure 4.

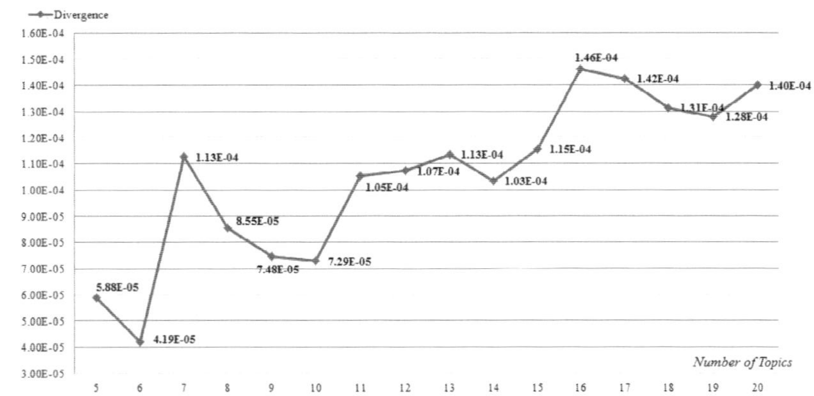

Figure 4. Divergence values of clustering with different number of topics.

Since our criterion of deciding the number of topics is to select the one with the highest divergence value, 16 topics were generated and considered as core bibliometrics-related topics. The detailed information of the 16 topics is given in Table 3.

No.	Label	Description
1	information retrieval	ranking method, search engine, machine learning, digital library, metadata, ontologies, natural language processing;
2	European Union	United Kingdom, R&D, internal collaboration, Spain, EPO, national research system, Italy, Germany, Czech Republic;
3	research evaluation	journal citation report, impact factor, h index, g index, measurement, individual scientist, journal quality;
4	science map	co-word analysis, visualizations, large scale data visualization, cluster analysis, co-citation network, multidimensional scale, robustness, bibliographic data;
5	social network	bibliographic coupling, Pearson correlation, betweenness, centrality measures, correlation analysis, complex network analysis;
6	collaboration research	co-authorship analysis, scientific community, bibliometric indices, research institute, collaboration network;
7	United States	United States, R&D, research institute, North America, technologies, management, public research, population, publication activity;
8	social science	governance, Triple Helix, natural science, patent data, university government industry relations, science & technology, developed country, life science;
9	citation analysis	citation network, co-citation analysis, self-citation, citation rate, citation distribution, altmetric, citation pattern, citation behavior;
10	decision making	research policy, optimization, library management, public policy, clinical medicine, stimulated recall interviews, policy maker;
11	information system	information behavior, computer science, information technology, human computer interaction, user interaction, semantic analysis, information interaction, ontologies, linear model;
12	statistical analysis	correlation analysis, regression, sample size dependency, Poisson distribution, data analysis, computer science, software system;
13	scientific output	bibliometric indices, research group, socioeconomics, female researcher, male researchers, academic collaboration;
14	data mining	data mining, text mining, classification, probability, longitudinal analysis, simulations, prediction model, mathematics, fuzzy set;
15	interdisciplinary research	subject category, interdisciplinarity, applied research, multidisciplinary approach, disciplinary diversity, longitudinal analysis;
16	China	Hongkong, India, collaboration pattern, Tsinghua University, policy implication, emerging economies, comparable analysis, innovative technology, Taiwan;

Table 3. Core bibliometrics-related topics.

As shown in Table 3, the 16 topics and related terms further extend our observations derived from Figure 2 and in particular enrich the details of the three hotspots: 1) the main areas of highly involved information technologies include not only information retrieval but also statistics, data mining, information system, and network analysis; 2) Science map, citation analysis, co-citation analysis, co-word analysis, and co-authorship analysis are highlighted for bibliometrics. 3) Specific real-world issues are also addressed, e.g., research evaluation, collaboration research, interdisciplinary research, and a broad range of science, technology, innovation, and policy (STIP) issues. 4) Three hottest countries/regions are raised, i.e., the US, China, and European Union (EU), and their related countries and regions are also specified. In addition, diverse foci among the three hottest countries/regions are raised, e.g., national research system in EU and emerging economies in China.

Regarding author information, we retrieved 9,555 author names from the 7,258 articles, including both authors and co-authors. A light AND function and a co-authorship-based macro for consolidating low-frequency authors to related high-frequency authors in VantagePoint were used for pre-processing, and 8,692 authors were finalized.

Diffusion-based Network Analysis

Two matrices were constructed for bipartite networks, i.e., a 16×9942 matrix for the topic-term network and an 8692×9942 matrix for the author-term network. The diffusion-based prediction function was first applied to the topic-term network, and based on the diffusion value the prediction for the future evolutionary directions of the sixteen bibliometrics-related topics is given in Table 4.

Topic	Future Research Direction[2]
1	subject category, research evaluation, collaboration research, active research, publication output, *journal citation report, R&D, policy making*;
2	prediction model, subject category, h index, journal impact factor, uncertainty, *centrality measures*;
3	collaboration network, social science, current study, qualitative method, empirical study, *research trend, public health*;
4	population, peer review, uncertainty, empirical result, publication output, *document type, impact factor ranking*;
5	computer science, collaboration network, semantic analysis, South Korea, reputation, *comparable analysis*;
6	information seeking, Netherland, subject area, academic journal, web search, *age distribution, bibliometric evaluation, overlap map*;
7	co-authorship network, research evaluation, machine learning, domain knowledge, bibliometric measure, *dissemination*;
8	full text, scientific community, Google, public health, dataset, *betweenness, digital library*;
9	information seeking, multidimensional scale, Lotka's law, knowledge management, domain knowledge, *technologies, metadata*;
10	Google Scholar, co-citation network, complex network analysis, research product, semantic analysis, *cluster analysis, text mining*;
11	research group, h index, journal impact factor, individual scientist, scientific field, *bibliometric indices, reputation, scientific output*;
12	longitudinal analysis, empirical result, centrality measure, research area, healthcare, *research policy, individual level, co-word analysis*;
13	developed country, internet of things, cluster analysis, text mining, wide range, *co-authorship analysis*;
14	growth rate, scientific literature, scientific output, academic research, co-word analysis, *internal collaboration, webometric analysis, knowledge management*;
15	future research direction, mathematics, research evaluation, research product, bibliometric indices, *individual level*;
16	multidisciplinary analysis, quantitative method, self-citation, individual scientist, scientific field, *United Kingdom, content analysis*;
Validation Measure[3]: There are 44 relevant terms, 14 "not so" relevant terms, and 22 irrelevant terms out of 80 terms, so we consider the precision as 0.64 (i.e., $(44 \times 1 + 14 \times 0.5)/80$).	

Table 4. Prediction for the future evolutionary directions of the bibliometrics-related topics[1].

Note. 1) We follow the sequence of the 16 topics given in Table 3. 2) The first five terms are the Top 5 terms with the highest diffusion value to related topics, and based on expert knowledge the italicized terms were selected from the list of the Top 6-10 terms and treated as supplementary terms. 3) We manually evaluated the first five terms of each topic with the following criteria: if a term is irrelevant with bibliometrics, we mark it with a solid underline (as 0 point); if a term is not so relevant, we mark it with a broken underline (as 0.5 point); if a term is relevant, we do nothing but as 1 point.

Observations on Table 4 are summarized: 1) one common interest is to apply information technologies (e.g., information retrieval, data mining, and information systems) to assist in specific bibliometric issues, e.g., evaluating research performance from different levels (e.g., h index for scientists and impact factor for journals), profiling scientific activities for analyzing internal or external collaboration, and decision support for R&D planning and policy making. 2) Individual-level bibliometrics seem to be an emergent direction, which include not only the development of related statistical models but also individual scientist-oriented bibliometric studies. 3) The engagement of text mining techniques with a wide range of mainstream bibliometric approaches (e.g., citation/co-citation analysis, science map, and social network analysis) is highlighted, since terms such as "semantic analysis", "metadata", "full text", and "content analysis" can be addressed here and there. 4) Intriguing terms are raised in specific country or region-based case studies, e.g., uncertainty issues in Europe, knowledge dissemination in the US, and self-citation issues in China.

Before moving our focus to the author-term network, we generated an author correlation network in Figure 5 to briefly spotlight certain leading experts and author groups, since bipartite networks are relatively abstract and not well-designed for visualization (e.g., two sets of nodes are located in columns, as shown in Figure 2). Note that Figure 5 is not a bipartite network, since it contains only one set rather than two sets of nodes, and the correlation coefficient between two authors is calculated by the Pearson measure, based on their 9,942-dimension term vectors.

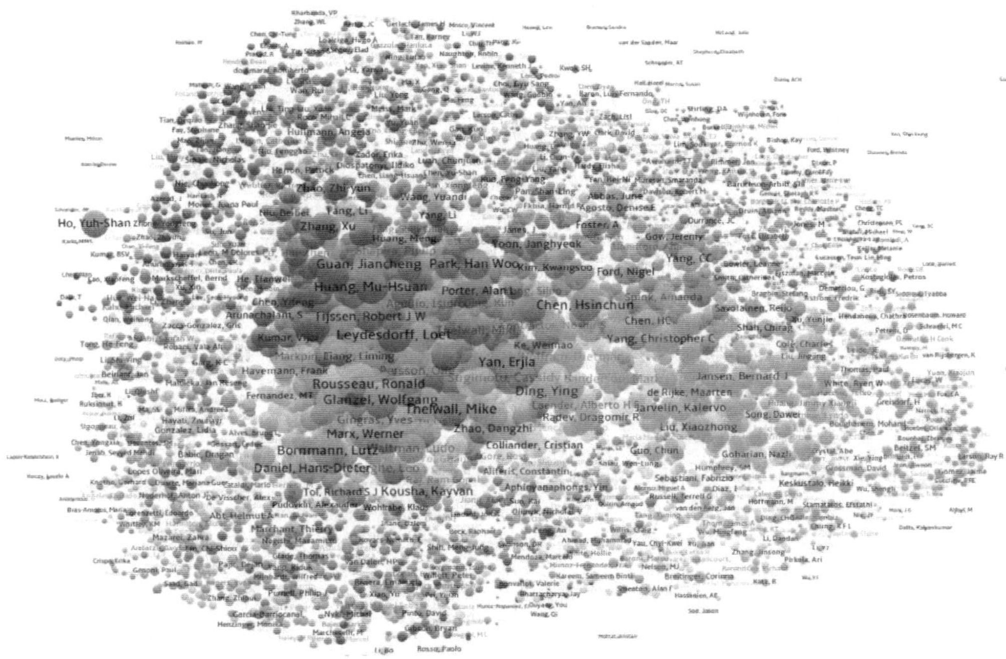

Figure 5. Correlation network of bibliometrics-related authors.

Note. Despite the use of the AND algorithm for data pre-processing, certain duplicate names might still exist in Figure 5, e.g., Chen, Hsinchun and Chen, HC. Since AND is not the main focus of our study, we do not provide any improvements in the current paper but it is definitely an important direction of our future study.

The prediction study on the potential research interest of authors was conducted from two ways: 1) focusing on the potential interest of some leading experts (those who have published a large number of articles covering a wide range of bibliometric topics and have established close interactions with worldwide researchers) to foresee the research frontiers of bibliometric topics, and 2) to select some relatively "niche" authors (those who do not publish so many articles and usually concentrate on a relatively small research circle) to delve into specific research directions. At this stage, five authors were selected, i.e., Loet Leydesdorff, Wolfgang Glanzel, Ludo Waltman, Hanwoo Park, and Alan Porter, and we then applied the diffusion-based prediction function to the author-term network, and the results are given in Table 5.

Author	Potential Research Interest[1]
Leydesdorff, L.	computer science, collaboration network, scientific products, interdisciplinary research, patent citation analysis;
Glanzel, W.	co-word analysis, social network, management, computer science, international collaboration;
Waltman, L.	United States, social science, information retrieval, China, scientific community;
Park, H.	ranking method, text mining, management, scientific community, information retrieval;
Porter, A.	citation analysis, information retrieval, h index, social network, scientific community;

Table 5. Prediction for potential research interests of selected authors.

Note. 1) We choose the terms from Top 10 terms with the highest diffusion value.

As leading experts in the field of bibliometrics, Dr Leydesdorff, Dr Glanzel, and Dr Waltman are ranked as the 1st, 4th, and 12th authors with the largest number of articles published in JASIST, JOI, and SCIM from 2000 to 2017. Based on the articles of these three leading bibliometric experts, we summarize our findings as follows: 1) indicated from those over 150 articles in our dataset, the main foci of Dr Leydesdorff cover a very broad range of bibliometrics, e.g., Triple Helix, social network analysis, science maps, and bibliometric methodology. Considering existing topics and the interest of those who share close similarity with Dr Leydesdorff, we specifically pick up two possible directions: introducing techniques in the field of computer science to enhance the capability of bibliometrics, and applying bibliometric approaches for interdisciplinary or multidisciplinary research. 2) Over 100 articles published by Dr Glanzel are involved, including a large number of topics on information science and library science, e.g., bibliometric indicators, probabilistic models, h index, and interdisciplinary/multidisciplinary studies. Our recommendation includes: the synergistic effect of co-word-based bibliometric approaches and other indicators (e.g., citation statistics), and bibliometrics-based case studies on investigating international collaboration, social network, and management. 3) Compared with those specified approaches or methods recommended to Dr Leydesdorff and Dr Glanzel, it is intriguing to investigate the research interest of Dr Waltman, whose research mainly focuses on the development of bibliometric indicators, analytic models, and networks. Our methodology considered that Dr Waltman might hold interest to apply his research to address empirical insights on real-world STIP issues, e.g., specific country/region-oriented case studies. As a comparison, we selected two more authors from our list, Dr Hanwoo Park who is a co-author of Dr Leydesdorff on Triple Helix-based case studies and also dedicates to webometrics and social network analysis, and Dr Alan Porter whose research aligns with both public policy and bibliometrics. Similarly, we recommend techniques such as ranking method, text mining, and information retrieval to Dr Park, which can help extend the adaptability and analytic capability of related webometric approaches, when we provide alternative bibliometric approaches (e.g., citation analysis, social network analysis, and h index) to Dr Porter, who are mostly involved into studies on research evaluation via term-based analytic models.

CONCLUSIONS

This paper proposed a diffusion-based network analytic methodology to predict the dynamics of scientific activities from two aspects: the potential research interest of scientific researchers and the future evolutionary directions of scientific topics. The method provides a novel way to integrate cutting-edge techniques in complex network analysis with term-based bibliometric approaches: 1) oriented to the unsupervised environments in real-world bibliometric studies, an indicator divergence is used to help automatically decide the number of topics for a K-means-based clustering approach; 2) science maps are introduced to bridge term-based bibliometric approaches (e.g., topic analysis, and term-based author correlation analysis) with a bipartite network, and provide supplementary information for further network analysis; and 3) a diffusion-based prediction approach is proposed to detect and predict the amount of resources diffusing within a bipartite network. The case study, applying the diffusion-based network analytic methodology to a set of bibliometrics-related articles, effectively identified a list of future evolutionary directions of specific bibliometrics-related topics and also a list of potential research interests of selected authors in the field of bibliometrics. The results can benefit not only bibliometric researchers for better understanding the research frontiers of bibliometrics but also a wide range of disciplines in information science and technology, science policy, and related industrial sectors.

We anticipate further study to look into the following directions: 1) introducing machine learning techniques to train our analytic models (in particular the prediction model) by dividing our dataset into several training sets with sequential time stamps and learning parameters (e.g., the diffusion strategy, and weights to indicate the priority of different terms) from the training process; 2) proposing more persuasive approaches for validation measures, e.g., comparing with the results of some similar bibliometric studies, expert knowledge-based evaluation, and quantitative validation models; and 3) testing the adaptability of our methodology by applying to diverse cases, e.g., relatively broad disciplines in natural science and social science (e.g., computer science, business and management), relatively specific areas (e.g., nanotechnology and solar cells).

ACKNOWLEDGMENTS

This work was partially supported by the Australian Research Council under Discovery Grant DP150101645 and the National Science Foundation of China under Grant 71673024.

REFERENCES

Abbasi, A., Hossain, L., & Leydesdorff, L. (2012). Betweenness centrality as a driver of preferential attachment in the evolution of research collaboration networks. *Journal of Informetrics, 6*(3), 403-412.

Börner, K. (2014). *Atlas of Knowledge*. Cambridge, MA: MIT Press.

Boyack, K. W., Newman, D., Duhon, R. J., Klavans, R., Patek, M., Biberstine, J. R., . . . Börner, K. (2011). Clustering more than two million biomedical publications: Comparing the accuracies of nine text-based similarity approaches. *PLoS One, 6*(3), e18029.

Chen, C., Ibekwe SanJuan, F., & Hou, J. (2010). The structure and dynamics of cocitation clusters: A multiple-perspective cocitation analysis. *Journal of the American Society for Information Science and Technology, 61*(7), 1386-1409.

Ding, W., & Chen, C. (2014). Dynamic topic detection and tracking: A comparison of HDP, C-word, and cocitation methods. *Journal of the Association for Information Science and Technology, 65*(10), 2084-2097.

Freeman, L. C. (1977). A set of measures of centrality based on betweenness. *Sociometry*, 35-41.

Glänzel, W. (2001). National characteristics in international scientific co-authorship relations. *Scientometrics, 51*(1), 69-115.

Huang, Y., Zhang, Y., Youtie, J., Porter, A. L., & Wang, X. (2016). How does national scientific funding support emerging interdisciplinary research: A comparison study of big data research in the US and China. *PLoS One, 11*(5), e0154509.

Hung, S.-W., & Wang, A.-P. (2010). Examining the small world phenomenon in the patent citation network: a case study of the radio frequency identification (RFID) network. *Scientometrics, 82*(1), 121-134.

Klavans, R., & Boyack, K. W. (2017). Which type of citation analysis generates the most accurate taxonomy of scientific and technical knowledge? *Journal of the Association for Information Science and Technology, 68*(4), 984-998.

Leydesdorff, L., & Bornmann, L. (2012). Mapping (USPTO) patent data using overlays to Google Maps. *Journal of the American Society for Information Science and Technology, 63*(7), 1442-1458.

Lin, J. (1991). Divergence measures based on the Shannon entropy. *IEEE Transactions on Information Theory, 37*(1), 145-151.

Noyons, E. C., Moed, H. F., & Luwel, M. (1999). Combining mapping and citation analysis for evaluative bibliometric purposes: A bibliometric study. *Journal of the Association for Information Science and Technology, 50*(2), 115.

Otte, E., & Rousseau, R. (2002). Social network analysis: a powerful strategy, also for the information sciences. *Journal of Information Science, 28*(6), 441-453.

Palla, G., Derényi, I., Farkas, I., & Vicsek, T. (2005). Uncovering the overlapping community structure of complex networks in nature and society. *nature, 435*(7043), 814-818.

Small, H. (1999). Visualizing science by citation mapping. *Journal of the American Society for Information Science, 50*(9), 799-813.

van Eck, N., & Waltman, L. (2009). Software survey: VOSviewer, a computer program for bibliometric mapping. *Scientometrics, 84*(2), 523-538.

van Eck, N., Waltman, L., Noyons, E., & Buter, R. (2010). Automatic term identification for bibliometric mapping. *Scientometrics, 82*(3), 581-596.

Wang, X., Liu, Y., & Xiong, F. (2016). Improved personalized recommendation based on a similarity network. *Physica A: Statistical Mechanics and its Applications, 456*, 271-280.

Yan, E., & Ding, Y. (2009). Applying centrality measures to impact analysis: A coauthorship network analysis. *Journal of the Association for Information Science and Technology, 60*(10), 2107-2118.

Yan, E., Ding, Y., & Zhu, Q. (2010). Mapping library and information science in China: A coauthorship network analysis. *Scientometrics, 83*(1), 115-131.

Zhang, Y., Porter, A. L., Hu, Z., Guo, Y., & Newman, N. C. (2014). "Term clumping" for technical intelligence: A case study on dye-sensitized solar cells. *Technological Forecasting and Social Change, 85*, 26-39.

Zhang, Y., Zhang, G., Chen, H., Porter, A. L., Zhu, D., & Lu, J. (2016). Topic analysis and forecasting for science, technology and innovation: Methodology and a case study focusing on big data research. *Technological Forecasting and Social Change, 105*, 179-191.

Zhang, Y., Zhang, G., Zhu, D., & Lu, J. (2017). Scientific evolutionary pathways: Identifying and visualizing relationships for scientific topics. *The Journal of the Association for Information Science and Technology*, to appear. doi: to appear

Zhou, T., Ren, J., Medo, M., & Zhang, Y.-C. (2007). Bipartite network projection and personal recommendation. *Physical Review E, 76*(4), 046115.

Beyond Mandatory Use: Probing the Affordances of Social Media for Formal Learning in the Voluntary Context

Quan Zhou
Wee Kim Wee School of Communication and Information, Nanyang Technological University, Singapore.
zhou0245@e.ntu.edu.sg

Sei-Ching Joanna Sin
Wee Kim Wee School of Communication and Information, Nanyang Technological University, Singapore.
joanna.sin@ntu.edu.sg

Chei Sian Lee
Wee Kim Wee School of Communication and Information, Nanyang Technological University, Singapore.
leecs@ntu.edu.sg

ABSTRACT

The integration of social media in formal education has received consistent interest in the recent decade. While most studies have focused on the mandatory use of social media as pedagogical tools, less explored is the context in which students voluntarily choose and use social media to supplement their formal learning. In this study, we employ an affordance approach to exploring the resources in social media that students perceive and use voluntarily for formal learning. Drawing on a qualitative study using focus groups of university students, we identified ten categories of social media affordances for learning in the voluntary context: association, editability, immediacy, interactivity, manageability, modality, persistence, scalability, searchability, and visibility. The affordances mentioned most frequently by students were visibility, persistence, and interactivity. These identified affordances encompass the major resources offered by social media for learning in the voluntary context, and provide insights into understanding, evaluating, and guiding social media adoption in formal education as well as lifelong learning. This paper concludes by presenting limitations and implications for research and practice.

KEYWORDS

Social media, affordances, voluntary use, formal learning.

INTRODUCTION

With the pervasiveness of social media, the usefulness of social media for teaching and learning in formal education has been widely documented (e.g., Huang, 2018; Zhou, Lee, & Sin, 2017; Greenhow & Lewin, 2015). Instructors in educational institutions have been using open access social media tools, such as Facebook, YouTube, WhatsApp, and Wikis, to enhance teaching (e.g., Jalali, Sherbino, Frank, & Sutherland, 2015; Robertson, 2011; Tess, 2013). The integration of social media in formal education is also deemed to be important for preparing students for lifelong learning (Greenhow & Lewin, 2015). As these new media technologies are not designed specifically for educational purposes, much scholarly attention has been devoted to the problem of how students can make informed choices about various social media and support formal learning with these tools.

Existing studies of social media use for formal learning have mainly focused on the mandatory use context, that is, the adoption of social media is a mandate from the course instructors and a requirement for the course (Greenhow & Lewin, 2015; Jalali et al., 2015). Specifically, past studies are mostly concerned about the utility and effectiveness of using social media as pedagogical tools (e.g., Huang, 2018; Dabbagh & Kitsantas, 2012) or focus on specialized platforms (e.g. Massive Open Online Courses) that are designed for learning purposes (Ma & Lee, 2018). However, recent work has suggested that students also voluntarily use various generalized social media platforms for their educational purposes. In particular, students select and employ social media to communicate with peer students on course-related information (Manca & Ranierit, 2016), search for learning resources to supplement course materials (Kind & Evans, 2015), and seeking help from expert online users (Greenhow & Lewin, 2015). With easy access to knowledge shared by other users and convenient interactions with other users, the phenomenon of voluntarily using social media for formal learning appears to be a significant part of the educational landscape (Manca & Ranierit, 2016), yet research in this area is still limited.

Further, past studies tend to focus on the use of a particular social media platform. There is a lack of understanding of how and what social media students use in combination given the wide array of social media available for them to choose and use, especially in the voluntary context. For example, students use multiple social media technologies such as Facebook, YouTube, and WhatsApp as part of their formal learning in the voluntary context, albeit with different learning purposes (Greenhow & Lewin, 2015). Less known is how students make sense of available resources offered by various social media and use them appropriately for learning.

To address these issues, we draw from an affordance approach, which is of great utility to understand the various ways users adopt, appropriate, and reinvent the material features of objects to accomplish tasks (Rice et al., 2017). The concept of affordances has been used to explicate the use of a set of technologies, including social media, in organizational communication research (e.g., Rice et al., 2017; Treem & Leonardi, 2013; Lee, Watson-Manheim, & Chudoba, 2014) and educational research (e.g., Dabbagh & Kitsantas, 2012; Väljataga, Pata, & Tammets; 2010). In particular, social media affordances refer to resources offered by social media, or the possible actions that social media enable users to achieve their goals (Rice et al., 2017). Instead of focusing centrally on features or a particular social media platform, an affordance lens is helpful in explaining why students use different social media in similar ways or the same social media in different ways (Treem & Leonardi, 2013). That is, exploring affordances can transcend the particularities of any platform or its features. With rapid update and emergence of new social media technologies, awareness of the affordances, coupled with adequate preparation while engaged in formal education, may hold the key for lifelong learners across lifespan (Väljataga et al., 2010).

The aim of this exploratory study is to understand the social media affordances students perceive when they voluntarily use social media for formal learning. Different from the mandatory-use context, the use of social media in the voluntary context can be considered a student-driven, bottom-up approach, where students have more choices over which tools and resources to employ (Greenhow & Lewin, 2015). An affordance approach is pertinent in this inquiry as this concept can shed light on the resources critical for students to achieve their learning goals when they are using social media technologies voluntarily. Taken together, this study attempts to answer the following research question: *What are the social media affordances that students perceive when using social media voluntarily for formal learning?*

LITERATURE REVIEW

Voluntary Use of Social Media for Formal Learning

Formal learning refers to learning that happens in courses or training supported by institutions, resulting in learners receiving grades, degrees, diplomas, and certifications (Dabbagh & Kitsantas, 2012). In the recent decade, as social media have become increasingly ubiquitous among millennium learners, the educational value of integrating these tools in formal education have been highlighted by stakeholders (Greenhow & Lewin, 2015). However, most studies have focused on the mandatory-use context, that is, social media are adopted by course instructors as part of the course design (e.g., Jalali et al., 2015; Robertson, 2011). An important context that is less explored is the voluntary use of social media for formal learning. With the availability of social media for personal usage, the study of the voluntary use of social media by students is an important endeavor (Manca & Ranierit, 2016).

During voluntarily use of social media, students have the freedom to choose and use social media to compensate for their formal learning in school (Greenhow & Lewin, 2015). Compared to mandatory use of social media as part of formal course design and requirements, voluntary use of social media empowers students with autonomy and control over their social media selection and usage, as well as learning activities. That is, with all the instruments, materials, and human resources offered by social media, students can construct a learning environment by themselves according to their preferences to meet learning needs. To be effective social media learners, it is necessary for students to be aware of available resources in social media that are important in the learning process (Väljataga et al., 2010).

Social Media Affordances

To understand the resources and possible actions students perceive when using social media voluntarily for formal learning, we draw on an affordance view. The term "affordances" was defined by Gibson (1986) in the field of ecological psychology as action possibilities for animals in relation to the properties of a given environment. With regard to the affordances of social media, it reflects the possible actions that users perceive they could apply social media relative to their needs or purposes (Rice et al., 2017; Treem & Leonardi, 2013).

Social media affordances have been applied in different areas. In organizational knowledge sharing, Majchrzak, Faraj, Kane, and Azad (2013) have theorized that social media provided the following four affordances: metavoicing, triggered attending, network-informed associating, and generative role-taking. In customer engagement, Cabiddu, Carlo, & Piccoli (2014) identified three distinctive social media affordances: persistent engagement, customized engagement, and triggered engagement. In organizational social media use, Treem and Leonardi (2013) identified four social media affordances: visibility, persistence, editability, and association. Thus, the affordances approach has been shown to be effective in understanding the resources afforded by information technologies to manage the communication environment (Lee, 2010).

In educational literature, affordances of social media have mainly been examined in the mandatory context. For example, Väljataga et al. (2011) examined college students' perceptions of the affordances of four social media tools (i.e., blog, wiki, aggregator, and social bookmarks) and suggested affordances such as information filtering, assembling the learning environment, community formation and grouping, and self-tutoring. Dabbagh and Kitsantas (2012) developed a pedagogical framework of social media affordances including personal information management, social interaction and collaboration, and information aggregation and management. However, different from the mandatory context, student may have different perceptions of the affordances of social media for their learning in the voluntary context. This is because the adoption and usage of social media in the mandatory context is only related to accomplishing the learning tasks assigned by the instructor, while learning purposes in the voluntary context are student-initiated (Greenhow & Lewin, 2015). For example, when using a particular or a set of social media is a mandate for a group assignment, the perceived affordances of social media may only be related the association and interactivity with other classmates. But if students use the same social media in the voluntary context with an intention to clarify a concept or to expand their knowledge base, they may perceive the affordance of searchability and scalability. Thus, a comprehensive understanding of how students perceive the affordances of social media for formal learning in the voluntary context is needed.

METHOD

Focus groups were used to collect data to address the research question. A focus group method is chosen in favor of other qualitative research methods (e.g., interview) since the interactions among participants during the focus groups can highlight their various views of how to use different social media to support formal learning in the voluntary context (Morgan, 1998). Prior to participant recruitment and data collection, the research procedures have been approved by the university's Institutional Review Board.

Focus Group Participants

Participants were recruited based on a convenience and purposive sampling from a large university in Singapore. Purposive sampling can facilitate the identification of target participants, who are interested in discussing their experience of voluntarily using social media for formal learning. Informed consents were obtained from all participants at the beginning of each study. A total of 21 students joined three different focus group sessions, ranging from 6 to 8 participants each. Among the participants, there were 12 (57%) male and 9 (43%) female students. It was also identified that 11 (52%) participants were undergraduate students and 10 (48%) participants were postgraduate students. In terms of educational background, there were 12 participants (57%) from engineering, 6 (29%) from social science, 2 (10%) from natural science, and 1 (5%) from humanities and arts.

Data Collection

Each focus group session was moderated by an experienced moderator and a research assistant. The discussion started by asking participants to think about the courses they took in the past few semesters in school and to write down the two courses in which they voluntarily used social media most frequently. Later, participants shared their experience of using social media tools for their course learning. Finally, participants were presented with a discussion guide including a list of popular social media tools (list available from the authors). They were asked to discuss about how the features built in each social media could be used for their formal learning in the voluntary context. Participants were also allowed to bring up any other social media tools that they used voluntarily for formal learning but were not listed in the discussion.

In this process, the moderator was responsible for encouraging all participants to voice opinions and preventing individuals from monopolizing the discussion. In addition, the moderator and assistant used probes, when needed, to continue discussion of a specific question or to keep the focus on the voluntary use of social media for formal learning. Each focus group session took about 90 to 120 minutes, and participants were paid 20 SGD after the study. All focus group sessions were fully transcribed from the audio files, and the transcripts served as the basis for subsequent analyses.

Data Analysis

The coding proceeded through two phases, which followed the two approaches of qualitative content analysis (Lee, 2012). The first phase of data analysis was conducted with the directed content analysis approach where researchers developed the initial coding scheme by identifying variables from prior research. The second data analysis phase used the conventional content analysis where new theoretical categories and insights emerge inductively from data during analysis. Some codes were combined during this process. Thus, combining these two approaches will allow a mix of a priori and emergent coding, leading to a comprehensive understanding of the phenomenon under investigation.

MAXQDA12, a software program for qualitative data analysis, was used to code and to keep track of all the codes in each phase of coding. The first author, who was trained in qualitative research methods, conducted a close and iterative reading on each transcript carefully from beginning to end, highlighting all participants' utterances that appeared to describe the use of social media to support their formal learning in the voluntary context. These highlighted texts were deemed as relevant data for the following two-phase data analysis. The basic unit of analysis was an uninterrupted utterance of a single group member, which was a natural segmentation of the recorded group discussion. This unitization method is the most frequently employed to separate data into units in the group communication literature (Hirokawa, 1988; Krippendorff, 2004).

Directed content analysis

The first phase of data analysis was designed to use direct content analysis, which focused on using predetermined codes to characterize the types of social media affordances students perceived when voluntarily using social media for formal learning. To create an appropriate coding scheme for identifying social media affordances, 82 terms were identified in prior literature in communication and education literature that referred to, or were named as, a social media affordance (table available from the first author). To assess the conceptual validity of these affordances, the conceptual framework of affordances proposed by Evans et al. (2017) was adopted. Specifically, it suggests that three threshold criteria should be considered when assessing a proposed affordance. First, affordances are not features of technologies. Features are built into the technology and do not exist outside the technology, while affordances are possible actions related to the feature. Second, affordances are not the outcomes of using technologies. Third, affordances have variability. Through an iterative review on the definitions and descriptions of affordances across different articles, a list of 11 primary distinctive categories of social media affordances, including association, editability, identifiability, immediacy, interactivity, manageability, modality, persistence, scalability, searchability, and visibility, was attained. As in Table 1, these 11 affordances served as predetermined codes in the initial coding scheme.

Affordances	Definitions
Association	Social media enables users to establish and keep connections with other users directionally or in groups, and also establish connections between users with content (Treem & Leonardi, 2013; Gibbs, Rozaidi, & Eisenberg, 2013), also refer to as “connectivity” or “linkage” (Fox & McWan, 2017).
Editability	Social media enable users to craft and recraft a communicative act before it is viewed by others (Walther, 1993), or to modify or revise content they have already been presented or communicated (Rice et al., 2017).
Identifiability	In social media, the communicator's identity can be presented or concealed (Halpern & Gibbs, 2013), also referred to as “anonymity” (Fox & McWan, 2017).
Immediacy	Social media enable users to get immediate response or update (Gibbs et al., 2013; Lee, 2010), also referred to as "signaling" (Rice et al., 2017), "engagement" (Evans et al., 2017), and "trigger attending" (Majchrzak et al., 2013).
Interactivity	Social media enable users to engage in interaction with other users and content through posting, chatting, commenting, liking, etc. (Evans et al., 2017; Sundar, 2008), also referred to as "metavoicing" (Majchrzak et al., 2013).
Manageability	Social media enable users to organize, control, and categorize users and information, also referred to as "information control" (Fox & Evans, 2017), "information filtering" (Väljataga et al., 2010), "selective sharing" (Gibbs et al., 2013), and "privacy control" (Evans et al., 2017).
Modality	Social media enable users to communicate and present information in multiple media formats, such as textual, graphical, aural, video, etc. (Sundar, 2008; Lee, 2010).
Persistence	Social media enable users to have information and communication archived so that they are still accessible as the original display after the communication or presentation is finished (Lee et al., 2014; Treem & Leonardi, 2013), also referred to as “durability (Evans et al., 2017)” and “recordability” (Toma, Hancock, & Ellison, 2008).
Scalability	Social media enable users to reach users and information out of their own network (boyd, 2007).
Searchability	Social media enable users to locate information or other users (boyd, 2007; Rice et al., 2017), also referred to as "navigability" (Sundar, 2008).
Visibility	Social media enable a user to see other users' behaviors, knowledge, preferences, personal profile and network connections (Treem & Leonardi, 2013).

Table 1. Initial coding and definitions of social media affordances.

In the iterative data coding, every uninterrupted utterance of a group participant in the highlighted text, that is, a unit of analysis, was reviewed at least four times to ensure the consistency of results (Saldaña, 2009). Every unit was coded into one of the predetermined categories of social media affordances wherever possible. After this phase, the initial coding frame was reassessed and underwent subsequent revisions.

Conventional content analysis

The second data analysis phase was using the conventional content analysis, which aimed to capture new occurrences of a phenomenon beyond the limit of the predetermined coding scheme. This phase followed a two-step inductive analysis process. First, data that could not be coded into one of the codes in phase 1 were reexamined to describe as new affordances. The analysis suggests that there was no new affordance emerged. Next, the first author examined how different codes are related and combined some codes based on their similarities. During this process, the affordance of identifiably was combined with the affordance of visibility in that the perception of identifiability was described as similar to the visibility of identification. The final categories and selected examples are listed in Table 2.

Affordances	Description and examples
Association	Remarks indicating the actions of establishing relationships. *Examples:* LinkedIn - "*And one more platform which I guess no one has mentioned is LinkedIn, like I have a few times I have followed some experts from my field so if I have some difficulties so I directly address them. They have accepted my request so I can directly address.*" WhatsApp - "*Then there's WhatsApp obviously because every class has a WhatsApp group and those groups we discuss about the questions that are being asked in class. Moreover, what questions are gonna appear in the examinations, what doubts we have regarding the class itself. We share pictures and videos from the tutorials itself.*"
Editability	Remarks describing the actions of editing information in social media. *Examples:* WhatsApp - "*So that's how people, you know when sometimes group chats getting out of control, sometimes people want to put in important information, they will just bold the words to catch everyone's attention.*" Stack Exchange Q&A Communities - "*And also comments are useful for answers, usually on Stack Exchange is that somebody posts an answer and then there is a few comments, and the answer is edited multiple times to the best.*"
Immediacy	Remarks indicating notifications or reply that may trigger immediate engagement. *Examples:* Google Office - "*So Google Office, the good point is that it is really instant, it doesn't lag.*"
Interactivity	Remarks describing actions of interacting with others. *Examples:* Quora - "*And then sometimes your answers are not just right or wrong, it can be based on opinions, like different people just have different opinions. So in that matter, it is a nice thing to share your opinions, and then other people can give their feedback about your opinion.* "
Persistence	Remarks indicating actions related to saving and retrieving information. *Examples:* WhatsApp - "*Even if you mute the group temporally, you can still go back and read the messages in the group discussion.*"
Scalability	Remarks indicating the possibilities to extend the current social network or knowledge base. *Examples:* Podcast - "*A lot of researchers, they use podcasts or like to, you know, reach out to people to share their ideas and also podcasts become very important sometimes.*" Wikipedia - "*And also in Wikipedia there are lots of references, so it can be a starting point...like if the journal I am interested in then I'll just jump to the references.*"
Searchability	Remarks describing the actions of searching information or users in social media. *Examples:* WhatsApp - "*Yeah. For example, WhatsApp. When you send answers through and after a while you want to look through the answers you have to scroll, search, try to find it amongst tons of other information. Because we use social media for other communication as well, so you have to sieve out the information manually.*"
Manageability	Remarks suggesting actions of using the settings to manage and control the information and users in social media. *Examples:* Facebook - "*Facebook has somewhere that you have so many friends, you'll have flooding information coming in, so it's like more like a distraction. Unless the notification can automatically categorize what is you want to hear at this moment from what you don't want to hear.*"
Modality	Remarks indicating the formats of content in social media (e.g., textual, video, audio, visual, etc). *Examples:* WeChat - "*There's this instant voice message and it's mostly for my friend. She likes to use that rather than texting, because it's so much instant to say out and send it over, rather than text.*"
Visibility	Remarks indicating the awareness of users' identity, disclosures, implicit cues, and networks in social media. *Examples:* LinkedIn - "*You know. In LinkedIn, they have something like verified user so someway they use it to verify, actually, if that person is truly knowledgeable in that domain. So That would actually may more into credibility add more of credibility.*" Yahoo Answers - "*But sometimes the answers there are three answers. So what I do is something similar. I need to see the 'likes', other people's comments to the reply itself. Whether it's right or wrong. But sometimes, there's no reply or there's no 'likes' so I just make a random choice to see which one is correct.*"

Table 2. Final coding scheme and selected examples of social media affordances.

Reliability

To avoid personal bias and ensure the reliability of the coding, another coder was recruited and trained on the final coding scheme created in the MAXQDA12 software. One of the focus group transcripts was randomly selected as a subsample for reliability assessment (Krippendorff, 2004). The second coder reviewed the same units of analysis from the subsample and coded independently. To ensure consistency, the first author (i.e., the first coder) initially reviewed the codes applied by the second coder. The two coders discussed the units with divergent opinions, and consensus was reached eventually for those units. This helped the coders to reach a consensus on the proper interpretation and application of each code. The second coder then recoded the initial group and coded one other randomly selected group. At the end of this process, a Cohen's Kappa, which has been the most often used index of reliability in social science (Zhao, Liu, & Deng, 2013), was calculated to determine the extent of agreement between the author and the second coder. The final Cohen's kappa is .83, indicating very acceptable agreement (Neuendorf, 2002).

RESULTS AND DISCUSSION

Following the coding process, we identified ten main categories of social media affordances, including association, editability, immediacy, interactivity, manageability, modality, persistence, scalability, searchability, and visibility. The affordance that was mostly mentioned by students in focus group discussion was visibility (20.7%), followed by persistence (14.2%) and interactivity (13.4%). Table 3 presents the frequency and percentage of each category of social media affordances. Each code was identified in every group, suggesting that additional groups would unlikely to yield additional themes.

Affordances	Group 1		Group 2		Group 3		Total	
	f	%	*f*	%	*f*	%	*f*	%
Association	11	8.7	10	7.9	12	10.1	**33**	**8.9**
Editability	5	4.0	2	1.6	8	6.7	**15**	**4.0**
Immediacy	9	7.1	10	7.9	8	6.7	**27**	**7.3**
Interactivity	17	13.5	18	14.2	15	12.6	**50**	**13.4**
Manageability	13	10.3	13	10.2	12	10.1	**38**	**10.2**
Modality	13	10.3	15	11.8	11	9.2	**39**	**10.5**
Persistence	18	14.3	19	15.0	16	13.4	**53**	**14.2**
Scalability	10	7.9	10	7.9	9	7.6	**29**	**7.8**
Searchability	4	3.2	5	3.9	2	1.7	**11**	**3.0**
Visibility	26	20.6	25	19.7	26	21.8	**77**	**20.7**
Total	**126**		**127**		**119**		**372**	**100.0**

Table 3. Frequency and percentage of units within each group attributed to each affordance

Association

The affordance of association refers to the extent to which social media enable users to establish and keep relationships with other users (Treem & Leonardi, 2013). In social media, a social tie is best expressed through one's friends on a SNS, following a microblogger, subscribing to another's tags, or joining a group (Gibbs et al., 2013). For formal learning, students would establish unidirectional connections with knowledge users as supplementary learning resources. As one student described the use of Pinterest to follow knowledgeable users for her course on art design, "*You can actually follow other people. Because everyone has their own personal library already, and if their library is really good right, it actually saves time if you follow that person and then you get all the information that they source out for themselves.*" When taking a course, it was also common for students from the same class to establish student-led groups for course-related information exchange. As one participant talked about class groups in WhatsApp, "*Then there's WhatsApp obviously because every class has a WhatsApp group and those groups we discuss about the questions that are being asked in class. Moreover, what questions are gonna appear in the examinations, what doubts we have regarding the class itself. We share pictures and videos from the tutorials itself.*"

Editability

Editability reflects the extent to which social media enable individuals to craft or recraft a communicative act. This affordance has been found common in the context of online interpersonal communication (Walther, 1993) and organization communication (Rice et al., 2017). This was common in collaborative work, which was a common practice in many course designs in formal education. For example, students would spend time and effort discussing the group assignment before they started working on the writing. "*I think we have used them for group presentations so...we were in a group of 5 and we had to make a common report, so we all discussed what were the topics we were making, and then we shared this particular Word file on Google Docs or Google Share or something.*" In addition, by offering the opportunity to modify and revise content, editability allowed for more fidelity and comprehension. As one student describe the editability of YouTube, "*Sometimes the videos are followed by the written notes after that, like the professors themselves have written certain things after that, in order to clarify certain things he spoke about. Those are really helpful.*" In this way, the quality of the generated content could gain some degree of control and revision even after the original display. On the other hand, students also perceived the negative effect of editability affordance. Taking the editability of Wikipedia as an example, "*Yeah we all know that the Wikipedia page can be edited by anyone who's not even related to the topic.*" In this case, the editability might lead to manipulation of content by less-qualified users.

Immediacy

The affordance of immediacy refers to the extent to which social media enable users to get an immediate response or update (Majchrzak et al., 2013). In the learning context, this affordance facilitated the communication by enabling instant feedback from others. As one student said, "*But what I like about social media is that it's immediate. Whenever we do peer learning, whenever you have a question you probably have immediate response, getting the person's attention within the shortest span because people always check their social media.*" In this case, although social media was not originally designed for educational purposes, the everyday use of social media for personal life made it natural to facilitate learning communication. In addition, the built-in features, such as updates and notifications, also contributed to the immediate engagement with social media. As one student said, "*When someone has a problem, he can just post it in Facebook group and everyone will get the notification of the new post.*"

Interactivity

The affordance of interactivity was the third most frequently identified affordances (13.4%), which refers to the extent to which social media enable users to engage in interaction with other users (Evans et al., 2017). It seems that the possibility to interact and communicate with other users to supplement the formal classroom teaching was an important reason why students used social media voluntarily for formal learning. As one student expressed how WhatsApp could facilitate the interactions and peer support among students when some students were afraid to seek help from instructors directly, "*Of course because if it's a trivial question it is useless to ask the professor and just waste some part of the class. Some students might be knowing it already, so they might ask in the group itself someone might be able to come up with the answer and then a lot of time and moreover some mutual discussion will also happen.*" Similarly, the other student described how interactivity afforded by WeChat helped disseminate course-related information when the course instructor was restricted on the access of resources, "*The course is the Financial Statement Analysis, and the platform that we use is WeChat. We use this to take photos and share with groupmates with the case studies. It is because of the teacher in this course. The teacher is very focused on the case and the privacy, so he doesn't want to hand out the material so we won't keep the material. We can only take photos about the answers, so we use this.*"

Manageability

The affordance of manageability can be considered as the possibility of organizing, controlling, and categorizing the content and user in social media (Gibbs et al., 2013). This affordance was perceived by students as useful in selective exposure, selective sharing and privacy control. That is, students could use some features in social media to manage the content and people that were related to learning. For example, a student mentioned the control of video playing on YouTube, "*Like for rewinding and fast-forwarding, like when you watch a YouTube video, trying to figure out a concept, this is very helpful as you can skip the parts you understand and go to the parts that you want the answers, or you can just replay. That's a part I find helpful.*" Students also categorized friends or groups in social media with different priorities, for example, "*Just as he pointed out sometime before, the same people will be in two different groups, one will be for an official one, one will be for the just the casual. So we'll give more priority to the official group because we know what will be posted there, so we prioritize.*"

Modality

The affordance of modality refers to the extent to which social media enable users to communicate and get information in different content formats (Lee, 2010; Sundar, 2008). Social media differed according to their modality, with Wikipedia predominantly textual and YouTube being visual and audio. One student described about his preference for learning with videos, "*For me, I prefer video lectures by profs because like at least he is comfortable and going through the slides, there are a lot of things that prof usually speaks about that are not in the slides or not in the books, the way they explain the things, so that is more important for me so I prefer video lectures.*" Another student mentioned about the ability to send both text and voice messages in WeChat, which offered a high level of modality, "*There's this instant voice message and it's mostly for my friend. She likes to use that rather than texting, because it's so much instant to say out and send it over, rather than text.*" In this case, students were able to increase the modality of communication with social media.

Persistence

The affordance of persistence is the second most commonly discussed in the group discussion (14.2%), slightly less than interactivity. This affordance refers to the extent to which social media users to have information and communication archived so that they are still accessible as the original display after the communication or presentation is finished (Lee et al., 2014; Treem & Leonardi, 2013). The saving could be done automatically by a system. For example, when users logged out from instant messages or Facebook, the conversations and posts remained available to users and did not expire or disappear. As one participant described, "*If you are in a study group on WhatsApp you can have a log of messaging coming up about a question. Say while I am travelling on a bus or something like that, I can view the discussion at later point of time.*" That is, the persistence of communications in social media also made it possible for users to learn from others' discussion, which had been automatically persistent in social media. In addition, some students also purposively used the features of social media to realize the persistence affordance, "*Very important like you need it and you can't forget it and something like that. Then you could always make a WhatsApp group with only you as a member, call it a memo and post it there also.*" In this case, the group features were used creatively to make useful information persistent and retrievable.

Scalability

The affordance of scalability is about the possibility of approaching people or getting useful information which may not be within the current network and knowledge base of a user (boyd, 2007). Many students mentioned that the possibility to connect and interact with a larger network of people was the main difference between institution-based learning technologies and public social media tools. For example, one student shared her experience of learning from experts through Facebook groups, "*If there is a group in Facebook then you can go directly to the group, how they are there will be lots of experts in the same field so they will be giving like they will be sharing much information on the same topic.*" In addition to the ability to extend social network, the analysis suggests that the open and active social media environment also made it easier for students to get useful resources as supplements to their current knowledge base. This scalability of knowledge was offered by other users or the system recommendation. As one student mentioned about the accessibility of learning resources in YouTube that were from prestigious educational institutions, "*Right. In quantum mechanics, there's this entanglement and stuff. When I read in a book I don't really understand. So I have to go to YouTube and look for online lectures or lectures from other schools like MIT.*"

Searchability.

The affordance of searchability reflects the possibilities in social media that people can actively get information through active searching (Rice et al., 2017). This affordance was mainly offered by the built-in searching functions. In learning, addressing a puzzle related to coursework was deemed as the goal or outcome. The searchability was thus particularly important when students face the issue of information overloading due to the use of social media. As one student mentioned how the searchability afforded by WhatsApp could facilitate information seeking, "*If you're thinking of something you just need to search. You cannot just go through all the posts about the discussion.*" If the affordance of searchability was not present or low in a social media, it would be hard for students to know what useful learning resources was available and accessible (Treem & Leonardi, 2013). As a student illustrated how the searchability afforded by YouTube made her aware of what she could get, "*I don't know if there will be some videos can be helpful for me to clarify the concept, but I know I can search and find out. The searching makes me more clear about what I can get.*"

Visibility

Visibility refers to the extent to which social media enable users to see others' online behaviors and information (Treem & Leonardi, 2013). The affordance of visibility was consistently the most frequently mentioned affordance by all groups, with around 20% of all discussion related to social media affordances. Scholars have noted that social media provide increased visibility into both behaviors and information, which separates them from other traditional information and communication technologies (Rice et al., 2017; Treem & Leonardi, 2013). In social media like Facebook and LinkedIn, people are more likely to self-present their identity information such as their real names, educational and professional information, and their places of living. Students could identify a user easily from such self-presented information. As one student mentioned the visibility of authentic identification, "*If there's a random medical article and if like is somebody else commented if some random friend commented I wouldn't take it so seriously. But If somebody who's practicing medicine in my friend group they commented, ok there is a certain credibility associated with it.*" On the other hand, some students noticed the visibility afforded by social media but tended to decrease the degree of identity visibility by concealing their personal information. For instance, a student described her use of anonymity to avoid negative judgement from others, "*When you want to ask questions. We don't want to look stupid, you know. We don't know it's considered stupid questions, but some people might think, 'This person is very stupid. Very easy question also wants to ask'. Anonymity is very important.*" In addition, with the communication visibility afforded by social media, students were also able to learn from other users' communication without the requirement of immediate engagement. As one student described learning from other people's comments under a YouTube video, "*And most of the time even in YouTube suppose I do not know a lot of people do that, but suppose if you don't understand the content of the video, suppose you get to the comments parts of the video, you can find a few other people who are also finding the same points, same time.*" Moreover, some non-text communication behaviors, such as liking and following, were also visible in social media. As one student described about the visibility of number of views and likes in social media, which were aggregated user communication behaviors, "*For everything that is posted out in social media, any form you can easily see the number of reviews or the number of likes, subscriptions or viewers after that. So that itself is a form of verification whether that source is correct.*"

CONCLUSION

This exploratory study of students' voluntary use of social media for formal learning has identified ten consistent affordances enabled by current social media technologies. These findings contribute to the existing field of technology use in education in several ways. First, to our knowledge, this is the first study that draws on an affordance perspective to investigate social media use for formal learning in the voluntary context. Specifically, instead of focusing on any particular feature or technology, an affordance view on social media use provides a theoretical foundation to understand students' awareness of resources that various social media can offer in the voluntary context. Second, unlike existing research on the adoption of a particular social media, this study considers a broader set of available technologies. This helps to create a dynamic picture of how social media can sustain and support students' learning in the voluntary context. Future research could thus conduct a more nuanced analysis of a specific affordance or combination of these affordances and their effects on student's learning outcomes.

The findings of this study also reveal practical insights into the ways of integrating social media in formal education as well as lifelong learning. For educators and policymakers, this study can help them understand how social media can be used for learning from the perspective of students. To prepare students to become independent learners, there is a need to provide students with opportunities to practice and acquire expertise in selecting and integrating a meaningful combination of available tools. The social media affordances identified in this study could thus be used to provide a guidance, with the goal of raising students' awareness of using emerging technologies for lifelong learning. For students, it is expected that the findings of social media affordances could help them make sense of resources offered by available tools, thus enhancing the capacity to make use of the tools proactively, instead of passively, to feed their learning curiosity.

There are some limitations in the present study that warrants future research. First, social media discussed in all focus groups were mainly popular tools familiar to our participants who were based in Singapore. It is possible that students in other countries may voluntarily use other kinds of social media to support formal learning. Future studies should address the generalizability of this study to other areas and cultural groups. Another limitation is that this study only engaged in an inductive approach to identify the affordances of social media for students' formal learning in voluntary context; hence measures indicating the extent to which those affordances are perceived by students are not the focus of this study. Nevertheless, the identified affordances can serve as a useful starting point for deductive research, in which instruments can be developed to verify the distinct affordances in a survey with a larger sample size.

REFERENCES

Boyd, D. (2007). Why youth (heart) social network sites: The role of networked publics in teenage social life. *MacArthur Foundation Series on Digital Learning – Youth, Identity, and Digital Media*, *76*(41), 1–26.

Cabiddu, F., Carlo, M. De, & Piccoli, G. (2014). Social media affordances: Enabling customer engagement. *Annals of Tourism Research*, *48*, 175–192.

Dabbagh, N., & Kitsantas, A. (2012). Personal learning environments, social media, and self-regulated learning: A natural formula for connecting formal and informal learning. *The Internet and Higher Education*, *15*(1), 3–8.

Evans, S. K., Pearce, K. E., Vitak, J., & Treem, J. W. (2017). Explicating affordances: A conceptual framework for understanding affordances in communication research. *Journal of Computer-Mediated Communication*, *22*(1), 35–52.

Fox, J., & McEwan, B. (2017). Distinguishing technologies for social interaction: The perceived social affordances of communication channels scale. *Communication Monographs*, *84*(3), 298–318.

Gibbs, J. L., Rozaidi, N. A., & Eisenberg, J. (2013). Overcoming the "Ideology of Openness": Probing the affordances of social media for organizational knowledge sharing. *Journal of Computer-Mediated Communication*, *19*, 102–120.

Gibson, J. J. (1986). *The ecological approach to visual perception*. Mahwah, NJ: Erlbaum.

Greenhow, C., & Lewin, C. (2015). Social media and education: Reconceptualizing the boundaries of formal and informal learning. *Learning, Media and Technology*, *41*(1), 6–30.

Halpern, D., & Gibbs, J. (2012). Social media as a catalyst for online deliberation? Exploring the affordances of Facebook and YouTube for political expression. *Computers in Human Behavior*, *29*(3), 1159–1168.

Hirokawa, R. Y. (1988). Group communication research: Considerations for the use of interaction analysis. In Tardy, C. H. (Eds.), *A Handbook for the study of human communication: Methods and instruments for observing, measuring, and assessing communication processes* (pp. 229-246). Norwood, NJ: Ablex.

Huang, C. (2018). Social network site use and academic achievement: A meta-analysis. *Computers and Education*, *119*, 76–83.

Jalali, A., Sherbino, J., Frank, J., & Sutherland, S. (2015). Social media and medical education: Exploring the potential of Twitter as a learning tool. *International Review of Psychiatry,27*(2), 1–7.

Kind, T., & Evans, Y. (2015). Social media for lifelong learning. *International Review of Psychiatry*, *27*(2), 124–32.

Krippendorff, K. (2004). *Content analysis: An introduction to its methodology* (2nd ed.). Thousand Oaks, Calif.: Sage Publications.

Lee, C. S. (2010). Managing perceived communication failures with affordances of ICTs. *Computers in Human Behavior*, *26*(4), 572–580.

Lee, C. S. (2012). Exploring emotional expressions on YouTube through the lens of media system dependency theory, *New Media and Society*, *14* (3), 457-475.

Lee, C. S., Watson-Manheim, M. B., & Chudoba, K. M. (2014). Investigating the relationship between perceived risks in communication and ICT-enabled communicative behaviors. *Information and Management*, *51*(6), 688–699.

Ma, L., & Lee, C. S. (2018). Understanding the barriers to the use of MOOCs in a developing country: An innovation resistance perspective. *Journal of Educational Computing Research*, *0*(0), 1–20.

Majchrzak, A., Faraj, S., Kane, G. C., & Azad, B. (2013). The contradictory influence of social media affordances on online communal knowledge sharing. *Journal of Computer-Mediated Communication*, *19*(1), 38–55.

Manca, S., & Ranieri, M. (2016). Is Facebook still a suitable technology-enhanced learning environment? An updated critical review of the literature from 2012 to 2015. *Journal of Computer Assisted Learning*, *32*(6), 503–528.

Neuendorf, K. A. (2002). *The content analysis guidebook*. Thousand Oaks, Calif.: Sage Publications.

Rice, R. E., Evans, S. K., Pearce, K. E., Sivunen, A., Vitak, J., & Treem, J. W. (2017). Organizational media affordances: operationalization and associations with media use. *Journal of Communication*, *67*(1), 106–130.

Robertson, J. (2011). The educational affordances of blogs for self-directed learning. *Computers and Education*, *57*(2), 1628–1644.

Saldaña, J. (2009). *The coding manual for qualitative researchers*. London: Sage.

Sundar, S. (2008). The MAIN Model: A heuristic approach to understanding technology effects on credibility. *Digital Media, Youth, and Credibility*, 73–100.

Tess, P. A. (2013). The role of social media in higher education classes (real and virtual) – A literature review. *Computers in Human Behavior*, *29*(5), 60–68.

Toma, C. L., Hancock, J. T., & Ellison, N. B. (2008). Separating fact from fiction: An examination of deceptive self-presentation in online dating profiles. *Personality & Social Psychology Bulletin*, *34*(8), 1023–36.

Treem, J. W., & Leonardi, P. M. (2013). Social media use in organizations: Exploring the affordances of visibility, editability, persistence, and association. *Annals of the International Communication Association*, *36*(1), 143–189.

Väljataga, T., Pata, K., & Tammets, K. (2011). Considering students' perspectives on personal and distributed learning environments in course design. *Web 2.0-Based E-Learning: Applying Social Informatics for Tertiary Teaching*, 85–107.

Walther, J. B. (1993). Impression development in computer-mediated interaction. *Western Journal of Communication*, *57*, 381–398.

Zhao, X., Liu, J. S., & Deng, K. (2013). *Assumptions behind intercoder reliability indices. Annals of the International Communication Association 36*(1), 419–480.

Zhou, Q., Lee, C. S., & Sin, S.-C. J. (2017). Using social media in formal learning: Investigating learning strategies and satisfaction. *Proceedings of the Association for Information Science and Technology*, *54*(1), 472–482.

The End of Ownership?: An Investigation of Users' Preferences and Perceptions of Ownership Configurations

Xiaohua Zhu
University of Tennessee, Knoxville, USA xzhu12@utk.edu

Moonhee Cho
University of Tennessee, Knoxville, USA mcho4@utk.edu

ABSTRACT

The notion of ownership of digital media content is complicated and fragmented, because of the interplay of intellectual property law, personal property rights, and contractual arrangements. Drawing from the existing literature on theoretical analysis of ownership, we present a framework with multiple ownership configurations of digital content. Using the online survey method, we investigated US users' perceptions of ownership of digital content, users' perceptions of the importance of various digital rights, and their preferences for different ways of obtaining media content. The results of this study show that downloadability and the continuity of rights together determine users' sense of ownership, and digital rights management (DRM) restrictions play a minor role in users' perceptions of ownership. Ownership, especially owning something physically, is still important to users with regard to books. With music, ownership is also important, but access, especially through the subscription model, is gaining in importance. Movie content shows a different pattern where users generally favor the access model over ownership. The study also found that users' perceived importance of digital rights varies with their preferences for obtaining different types of content.

KEYWORDS

Digital media content, digital virtual goods, ownership, subscription model, intellectual properties, digital rights

INTRODUCTION

When the Digital Millennium Copyright Act was enacted in 1998, observers in the United States considered it to be an initial success for the entertainment industry, and one step forward to the idea of an expanded "American shopping mall," because the Act made it illegal to circumvent the digital rights management (DRM) measures on digital information products (Litman, 1999, p. 213). But digital content did not proliferate immediately after its enactment, as content providers had promised (Gasaway, 2003). After years of research, exploration, and experiments with various pricing models and DRM technologies, content providers now seem to be more successful in persuading users to adopt the pay-to-play approach, using many different business models. The consumer markets for digital entertainment materials, end-user information products, and subscription-based services are thriving. However, the popular subscription models are making the already-complicated notion of intellectual property ownership even more perplexing, because subscription models are often associated with even stronger DRM protection.

Ownership is a legal and/or social arrangement between people with respect to a thing/property, including material objects or intangible objects (Gaus, 2012). Intellectual property is a special kind of property, and information products are a special kind of goods. The owner of a book does not own the copyright of the book, but owning a physical copy as a personal property does give the owner certain property rights, which are bestowed by copyright laws, especially the first sale doctrine and fair use doctrine. The notion of ownership is particularly problematic for digital content, because content providers are increasingly reliant on contracts (often in the form of license agreements), rather than copyright law and property laws, to regulate the behavior of users—what they can and cannot do with the product. With different rights arrangements for different information products and services, how do users perceive their ownership of digital content? How do they perceive the property rights associated with the digital content they pay for? Do users prefer the access model to ownership?

In this paper, drawing from the literature on the theoretical analysis of ownership, we consider information content ownership as a fragmented notion with various configurations, differentiated by their associated property rights, ranging from paid physical copies to various subscription models. On the opposite side of the ownership spectrum is the access model, typically exemplified by renting and borrowing. However, the ownership model and the access model may not be mutually exclusive—many consider subscription to be an example of the access model (Rosenblatt, 2017). We try not to arbitrarily distinguish between the two models, but use the ownership/access dichotomy only for the convenience of the discussion and narrative.

Digital media content, or digital information products, are also called "digital virtual goods" in marketing research. In this paper, we simply use the term "digital content". This study focuses on three types of digital content: books, music, and movies. Using the online survey method, we investigated the following research questions in the U.S. context:

RQ1: For each type of digital content, what ownership configurations are perceived as "owning" by users?

RQ2: What are users' perceptions of the importance of digital rights associated with different types of digital content?

RQ3: What are users' general preferences for obtaining different types of digital content?

RQ4: Do users' preferences for obtaining digital content differ by their perceived importance of digital rights?

Answers to these questions may give us a deeper understanding of users' perceptions about ownership, digital rights, and property rights. As different stakeholders are still negotiating to change the balance between intellectual property and personal property, such investigation can capture the users' views of ownership and property in the current flux and provide evidence for information policy making. In the long run, it can help us to understand how users' perceptions and attitudes are being shaped by the constant social negotiations. Moreover, it will enable information professionals and information providers to understand users' preferences and to design products that better suit users' interests.

LITERATURE REVIEW

Ownership and Property Rights

Ownership and property rights have been the subjects of study in multiple disciplines of law, economics, philosophy, and marketing/consumer research. The concept of ownership or owning a property is a complicated issue that is constantly being debated. A dominant view of law and economics scholars uses the "bundle of sticks" metaphor, explaining property ownership as an aggregation of separable legal rights/interests (Grey, 1980; Hohfeld, 1913, 1917; Honoré, 1961). Honoré, the representative of the bundle theory, listed incidents of ownership, including the right to possess (physical control), the right to use, the right to manage, the right to income, the right to capital, the right to security, the right of transmissibility, the prohibition of harmful use, etc. (Honoré, 1961). Each "right, power, privilege, or duty is but one stick in an aggregate bundle that constitutes a property relationship," and none of them is essential to ownership (Bell & Parchomovsky, 2005). That is, if one of the rights is removed from the bundle, the remainder of them may still constitute property ownership (Honoré, 1961).

Among the many new developments about property theories, Attas (2006) provides an approach especially useful for analyzing property rights related to digital content. Attas (2006) distinguishes between the content (the specific right with regard to a property) and the form (the feature of the specific right rather than the thing owned) of a property right. For example, the owner of a property has the right to use it (content), and this right may be transferred to others (form).

Ownership of Digital Content

In the literature, research on digital rights management (DRM) is abundant. Since the early 1990s, scholars have been discussing the impact of DRM, and many scholars are concerned about DRM restrictions and the shrinking of users' rights (Crawford, 2005; Gasaway, 2003; Lessig, 2004; May, 2007; Mulligan, Han, & Burstein, 2003). While most DRM research focuses on the conflicts between intellectual property (IP) holders and consumers/end users from intellectual property or marketing perspectives, a few researchers examined digital rights from the perspective of ownership and personal property rights (Perzanowski & Schultz, 2016; Watkins, Denegri-Knott, & Molesworth, 2016).

In their book "The End of Ownership: Personal Property in the Digital Economy," Perzanowski and Schultz (2016) try to answer the question of "whether digital goods … play by the familiar rules of personal property or the more flexible but often opaque rules of IP licenses" (p.20). By analyzing the digital economics and relevant legal cases, they concluded that the notions of ownership and property rights are constantly being shaped by various stakeholders in the digital marketplace. They consider it imperative to "craft a notion of ownership applicable to digital goods" by introducing aspects of personal property and private property into the digital marketplace in order to protect consumers' rights (Perzanowski & Schultz, 2016, p.193).

Watkins et al. (2016) discussed ownership of digital virtual goods in depth, pointing out the problems with the dichotomy of ownership and access-based consumption. Drawing from Attas (2006), they maintained that the ownership configurations of digital virtual goods are "fragmented" and "partial" (Watkins et al., 2016, p. 45). They analyzed several prominent ownership configurations, including local created content, hosted content, non-transferable license, and subscription-based services, and provided a framework for empirical studies.

In the DRM-related research, only a few studies explored users' perceptions towards digital rights. Arnab and Hofman's (2005) survey on media use, piracy, and users' attitudes about DRM show that most respondents considered portability (transferability of content between different devices and between operating systems) and format conversion as essential rights. Transfer of rights were also considered important, but modification and annotation were not considered essential. Loebbecke, Bartscher, Weiss, and Weniger (2010) found that in the German trade e-book market, consumers preferred DRM-free e-books to DRM-enabled ones. Alakurt and Teker's (2013) study indicated that Turkish undergraduate students are willing to pay for digital products that offer flexible usage rights. In addition, many researchers have noticed that users do not read the end user license agreement (EULA) (Bakos, Marotta-Wurgler, & Trossen, 2014; Cotton & Bolan, 2012). They may be signing away their rights without even noticing it. In this body of literature, we have not found any study that investigates users' perceptions of the notion of ownership.

Ownership vs. Access

In the library field, the ownership vs. access model in collection development/resource acquisition has been discussed for almost three decades (Kane, 1997; Miller, 2000; Monroe, 1992). In the consumers' information market, a similar theme has drawn more attention in recent years (Belk, 2014; Peoples, 2016; Rosenblatt, 2017). Scholars in marketing and consumer research observed a general shift from the ownership to the access model and suggested digital media content as examples of or candidates for communal sharing and short-term access in the "post-ownership economy" (Belk, 2014, p. 1599) or "the age of access" (Rifkin, 2000, p. 1). Although Watkins et al. (2016) opposed the use of the ownership and access dichotomy, many scholars/observers have used this dichotomy to suggest that consumers are moving away from ownership to access-based consumption (Belk, 2014; Lawson, Gleim, Perren, & Hwang, 2016; Rifkin, 2014; Rowley, 2008; Sinclair & Tinson, 2017). An example of this shift is the proliferation of the access-based digital services model, including subscription services for e-books, digital music, and digital videos. In the music industry, subscription streaming revenue has more than doubled since 2015, and has become the majority source (51%) of recorded music revenue (Rosenblatt, 2017).

Does the success of various subscription-based information services indicate that users prefer the access model over the traditional ownership model? In marketing, business, and electronic media studies, there is a body of literature on "willingness to pay" for digital content. Researchers have identified various factors that may reveal consumers' preferences and purchasing behavior in terms of digital content consumption, including expected benefit, quality of content, reputation, age, gender, content format, etc. (Berger, Matt, Steininger, & Hess, 2015; Chyi, 2012; Lopes & Galletta, 2006). But digital rights have not been studied as factors that may play a role in users' choices. Thus, this study attempts to fill the gap by providing users' perspectives on ownership, digital rights, and more importantly, whether their preferences for obtaining content differ by their perceptions of the importance of various digital rights.

FRAMEWORK

As mentioned above, Watkins et al. (2016) proposed a framework of digital virtual goods' ownership configurations. This framework drew from Attas' (2006) theory of personal property, treating ownership as a two-dimensional construct—content of rights and forms of rights. Clearly, not all property rights apply to digital content because of the complexity involved with intellectual properties. Watkins et al.'s (2016) framework includes only three specific rights in the content dimension: the right to use, the right to transform, and the right to income. As to form, they use transferability (whether rights can be transferred to others) and continuity (the duration of the specific right) as two forms of the rights. For this study, we modified this framework by removing the right to income, adding the right to possess and the right to manage, and making the right to use and the right to transform more specific (Table 1).

	Digital Media Content Ownership Configurations					**Example of Access**
	Purchased DRM-free digital copy	Purchased, DRM-enabled digital copy	Purchased, content hosted by content provider	Subscription, allowing temporary download	Subscription, content hosted by content provider only	Online renting
Examples	Mp3 downloads	Kindle e-book	Google Play movie/TV	Amazon music Unlimited	Netflix	Amazon movie renting
Right to possess: download	Unrestricted	Restricted	Denied	Restricted	Denied	Denied
Right to use: choose format	Unrestricted	Restricted	Denied	Restricted	Denied	Denied
Right to use: use on multiple devices	Unrestricted	Restricted	Restricted	Restricted	Restricted	Restricted
Right to use: use with multiple software	Unrestricted	Restricted	Restricted	Restricted	Restricted	Restricted
Right to manage: make a copy	Unrestricted	Restricted	Restricted	Denied	Denied	Denied
Right to manage: convert format	Unrestricted	Restricted	Restricted	Denied	Denied	Denied
Right to transform: modify	Unrestricted	Restricted	Restricted	Denied	Denied	Denied
Right to transform: reuse for creating new content	Relying on fair use doctrine	Restricted	Restricted	Denied	Denied	Denied
Transferability: share	Unrestricted	Restricted	Restricted	Denied	Denied	Denied
Transferability: resell	Restricted	Restricted	Restricted	Denied	Denied	Denied
Continuity	Permanent	Indefinite, requires device/software	Indefinite, requires account	Temporary, requires active account	Temporary, requires active account	Temporary
Enforced by	Contractual agreement	Contractual agreement and coding	Contractual agreement, surveillance, and coding	Contractual agreement, surveillance, and coding	Contractual agreement, surveillance, and coding	Contractual agreement, surveillance, and coding

Table 1: Digital Content Ownership Configurations

The right to income is ambiguous and prohibited in most cases. The right to possess and the right to manage are classic incidents of property rights (Honoré, 1961). With digital products, the right to possess means legally downloading the user's own copy. The right to manage means the user's ability to make a copy, and the ability to convert its format (in order to use the content on different devices or to back up the content against potential loss). The right to use is detailed as the ability to choose the format, to use the content on multiple devices, and to use the content with multiple software applications. The right to transform is interpreted as the ability to modify the information product and to reuse it for creating new content. The transferability of these rights is operationalized as the ability to resell the content and the ability to share it (including the ability to give/bequest it to another person). The form of continuity is difficult to measure, but it can be roughly indicated by the ability to purchase or subscribe to the content. Although the specifics of what rights users have and do not have regarding intellectual properties are not set in stone (Perzanowski & Schultz, 2016), most of the digital rights discussed here can arguably be protected by the fair use and first sale doctrines. Ideally, each right should be analyzed using the form dimension, but this would be difficult to operationalize and would make the survey questions overly complicated. Based on the different configurations of rights, the five ownership configurations can be considered as a spectrum, from the least-restricted configuration, i.e., the purchased, DRM-free copies, to the more restricted configurations, i.e., the hosted-content only subscription. Online renting is not considered to be an ownership configuration, but instead is an example of the access model; it is included in the table as a comparison to the different ownership configurations.

RESEARCH DESIGN

An online survey was employed to address the research questions. In order to reach out to a wide range of age groups and geographical locations, we recruited U.S. residents 18 years or older, via Amazon's Mechanical Turk mechanism. Upon giving their consent to participate, respondents were directed to the Qualtrics survey website and were asked to answer sets of questions addressing their ownership perceptions of each media type (i.e., books, music, and movies/TV), digital rights, and their preferences for obtaining content. Upon the completion of the survey, participants received $1.00 in compensation. After excluding any incomplete surveys and those who failed the attention check questions, a total of 304 surveys were used for the final analysis. The average age of the participants was 40.65 (SD = 11.48), with responses ranging from 22 to 75 years old. The gender distribution of the participants was quite even, although slightly more females participated in the survey (n = 154 or 50.7%). The majority of the sample was Caucasian/White (n = 256 or 84.2%), and 43.1% earned at least a bachelor's degree in college (n = 131).

The survey questionnaire was originally developed for this study based on the existing literature (e.g., Arnab & Hofman, 2005), and supplemented by informal interviews with media users of different ages. Prior to conducting the main survey, two sets of pilot tests, one with 20 graduate students and another with 50 Amazon Mechanical Turk (MTurk) workers, were conducted to check the validity of the survey questionnaire.

To measure ownership of digital content, the study asked participants to indicate whether they think they own a copy of each type of digital content, for the digital ownership configurations listed in Table 1. Three answer options were offered for each ownership configuration (yes, no, not sure). To assess the extent to which individuals perceive the importance of different digital rights, a total of ten different types of digital rights for each type of media content (i.e., books, music, and movies) were measured on a 5-point Likert scale (1 = not important at all, 5= very important). The specific digital rights were the ability to perform the following actions with the content: reselling, downloading, making a copy, sharing, modifying, converting the format, choosing the format, using it on multiple devices, using it with multiple software applications, and reusing it to create new content. The participants were also asked to evaluate their preferences related to four types of digital content (i.e., books for education/research, books for leisure reading, music, and movies), regarding ways to obtain the content (buy, rent, borrow, or subscribe), the format of the content (digital or physical), and the source options (online/store, library, and friend/family). Before ending the survey, participants provided their basic demographic information for statistical analysis. Given that users may not be familiar with terms such as DRM, the survey questions used user-friendly, explanatory language for all concepts.

FINDINGS

Perceptions of Ownership (RQ1)

Based on the ownership configurations in Table 1, for each media type (books, music, and movies), we listed four to six different configurations for users to judge whether or not they considered each situation to be "owning a copy" of the digital content. Table 2 summarizes the results. For all three content types, the overwhelming majority of the participants considered that they own a copy if they purchased a DRM-free digital copy (84.54% for e-books, 90.46% for music, and 89.14% for movies). Far fewer of them (55%-63% across the media types) felt they owned their purchased DRM-enabled copies. For e-books that require dedicated devices, more than half of the participants (58.22%) still considered the copies to be their property. For purchased, hosted content, the majority of participants did not consider themselves owners of the content, but the responses varied by media type—44% of participants said they owned the hosted, streaming-only movies they purchased, while only

27% of participants considered that they owned the hosted, online-viewing-only e-books they bought. As for subscribed items they can access, an overwhelming majority of participants did not consider them as their property. In the cases of music and movies, users' perceptions differed for the two subscription configurations: more users considered they owned downloadable subscription content (25.99% for music and 26.64% for movies) than those who considered they own the hosted-only subscription content (10.86% for music and 10.53% for movies).

#	Ownership Configurations	Number of "Yes" for e-book	Number of "Yes" for music	Number of "Yes" for movie
1	Purchased DRM-free digital copy	257 (84.54%)	275 (90.46%)	271 (89.14%)
2	Purchased DRM-enabled digital copy	193 (63.49%)	166 (54.61%)	186 (61.18%)
3	Purchased content that requires a dedicated device to use	177 (58.22%)	n/a	n/a
4	Purchased content hosted by content provider	81 (26.64%)	n/a	134 (44.08%)
5	Subscription allowing temporary download	39 (12.83%)	79 (25.99%)	81 (26.64%)
6	Subscription content hosted by content provider only	48 (15.79%)	33 (10.86%)	32 (10.53%)

Table 2: Users' Perceptions about Ownership

The results show a clear pattern. In general, users tended to think of the downloadable, purchased copies as their property, even if the content can only be downloaded to certain devices or used with dedicated software. Subscriptions were much less likely to be associated with a sense of owning the content, but this depends on the type of content—for music and movies, more people thought they owned the content, as compared to e-books. However, neither the ability to download (the right to possess) nor the status of purchasing (continuity) alone is a deciding factor in determining the perception of ownership. For example, temporary downloadability of subscribed content may not give most users the sense of ownership. Purchased but not downloadable content is also questionable (26.64% for e-books and 44.08% for movies. Only when downloadability (the right to possess) is accompanied by continuity (the form of the right), do most users assume ownership of the content. However, a lack of continuity seems to play a decisive role in non-ownership feelings.

Judging from the numbers of "yes" responses, we can also surmise that the ownership configurations are indeed a spectrum, ranging from a much stronger sense of ownership of DRM-free copies, to a very weak sense of ownership of subscribed, exclusively-hosted content. In other words, DRM may be a factor in ownership perception. If the content is device-dependent and/or software dependent, we expect that fewer users will think they own it.

To sum up, these users generally tended to think of the downloadable, purchased copy as their property. This perception did not vary much across different types of content. A combination of downloadability and the continuity of the right largely determined users' sense of ownership, and DRM restrictions also played a minor role in their perceptions.

Perceived Importance of Digital Rights (RQ2)

We asked the participants to rate the importance of each digital right for e-books, digital music, and digital movies, separately. Tables 3-5 show the means and standard deviations for each digital right. In the previous question, transferability as a form of the rights was not made explicit. In exploring the importance of digital rights, we asked more directly about the transferability of the digital content.

Results showed that for all three types of digital content, downloading, using the content on multiple devices, choosing the

Rank	Digital Right	Mean	SD
1	Download	4.36	.98
2	Use on multiple devices	4.34	1.01
3	Choose format	3.65	1.41
4	Use with multiple software	3.49	1.29
5	Share	2.90	1.35
6	Convert format	2.81	1.42
7	Make a copy	2.54	1.44
8	Reuse for creating new content	1.92	1.10
9	Resell	1.70	1.17
10	Modify	1.66	1.03

Table 3: Perceived Importance of E-book Rights

Rank	Digital Right	Mean	SD
1	Use on multiple devices	4.45	1.00
2	Download	4.43	1.01
3	Use with multiple software	3.61	1.41
4	Choose format	3.42	1.53
5	Make a copy	3.03	1.54
6	Share	2.94	1.42
7	Convert format	2.85	1.51
8	Reuse for creating new content	1.77	1.11
9	Modify	1.62	1.06
10	Resell	1.43	1.00

Table 4: Perceived Importance of Digital Music Rights

Rank	Digital Right	Mean	SD
1	Use on multiple devices	4.28	1.15
2	Download	3.98	1.27
3	Use with multiple software	3.52	1.42
4	Choose format	3.27	1.56
5	Share	2.88	1.42
6	Convert format	2.60	1.46
7	Make a copy	2.60	1.49
8	Reuse for creating new content	1.69	1.05
9	Modify	1.62	1.05
10	Resell	1.60	1.12

Table 5: Perceived Importance of Digital Video Rights

format, and using the content with multiple software applications were considered the most important rights by participants. Referring to the property rights' terminology, the right to possess and the right to use were generally considered important. Participants' perceptions of the importance of the right to manage the content, including making a copy and converting the format, were quite neutral. For digital music, the ability to make a copy ($M = 3.03$, $SD = 1.54$) was more important than it was for e-books ($M = 2.54$, $SD = 1.44$) or movies ($M = 2.60$, $SD = 1.49$). In terms of the right to transform the content, the results showed that the ability to reuse the content for creating new content and the ability to modify the content were not important to participants, with the respective means for the three media types all below 2.

For all three media types, results for most of the categories of specific rights grouped consistently, but results for the form of rights, transferability, did not. This study used the ability to share and the ability to resell the content, to measure the concept of the transferability of the rights. While the importance of the ability to resell the content was very low for all three media types (with the means ranging from 1.43 to 1.70), participants' rating of sharing is consistently neutral (2.88 –2.94). It is likely that participants interpreted "share" as the transferability of the right to use, which may be more important to them than transferring other kinds of rights. In this sense, it may be more helpful to consider the form of every right in future research.

General Preferences for Obtaining Content (RQ3)

This question is not limited to digital media content because we are interested in users' general preferences in obtaining information content. We included two categories for books because the purpose for the book's use often plays a role in reader preferences. Table 6 summarizes some of the major results, which showed that users have different preferences for different types of content.

	Buy physical	**Buy digital**	**Subscrip-tion**	**Rent physical**	**Rent digital**	**Borrow fromlibrary**	**Borrow from family/friends**	**Total**
Books for educa-tion/ research	122 (40.1%)	24 (7.9%)	8 (2.6%)	32 (10.5%)	19 (10.5%)	94 (30.9%)	5 (1.6%)	304 (100%)
Books for leisure	145 (47.7%)	63 (20.7%)	8 (2.6%)	9 (3.0%)	8 (2.6%)	62 (20.4%)	9 (3.0%)	304 (100%)
Music	47 (15.5%)	117 (38.5%)	106 (34.9%)	n/a	n/a	16 (5.3%)	18 (5.9%)	304 (100%)
Movies	39 (12.8%)	43 (14.1%)	120 (39.5%)	14 (4.6%)	61 (20.1%)	15 (4.9%)	12 (4.0%)	304 (100%)

Table 6: General Preferences in Obtaining Information Content

For books used for either education/research or leisure purposes, participants demonstrated a much stronger preference for physical copies. Overall (including the breakdown of physical/digital for the borrowing options not included in the table), 237 participants (78.0%) preferred using physical copies of education/research books, and 205 (67.4%) preferred physical copies for leisure readings. The results also showed a strong preference for purchasing books. Specifically, a total of 208 participants (68.4%) preferred buying either physical or digital books for leisure reading, while 146 (48.0%) preferred buying books for their education/research purposes. Comparing books for education/research and books for leisure reading, more participants preferred to borrow or rent books for education/research purposes than for leisure reading. Libraries are still one of the most important sources for obtaining books, especially for education/research purposes.

The pattern of preferences for music and movies were similar to each other, with some variances. In general, the subscription model was much more popular for music (34.9%) and movies (39.5%) than for books (2.6%). The participants also generally preferred the digital formats (82.6% for music and 79.3% for movies, again, including the breakdown of physical/digital for the borrowing options not included in the table). Compared to their book-related preferences, participants were much less likely to buy physical music and movies, and were much less likely to borrow music or movies from libraries or family/friends. However, purchasing was still preferred for obtaining music, as 164 (54.0%) participants preferred to buy music and most of them would buy digital music. Rental was a popular choice for accessing movies, especially the digital option.

Simply categorizing purchasing (either physical copies or digital copies) as "owning" and the rest of the methods (subscription, renting, and borrowing) as "accessing" the content, the results revealed different patterns for different types of content. There was a bifurcated preference for educational books (48% preferred owning) and for music (54% preferred owning). For leisure books, the majority of participants (68.4%) preferred owning. However, only 26.9% of participants preferred ownership of movies over accessing movie content.

Preferences and Digital Rights (RQ4)

To answer this question, we looked at four specific ways of obtaining digital media content: purchasing a physical copy, purchasing a digital copy, subscription, and renting/borrowing. Although there are differences between renting a physical copy and renting a digital copy, as well as between renting and borrowing, we considered renting and borrowing as instances of the access model, for the convenience of this analysis. Table 7 shows the variables used in the analysis (combining the "Rent physical," "Rent digital," "Borrow from library," and "Borrow from family/friends" options from Table 6). Because the percentages for subscription are very small (2.6%) for the two book options, those data were considered missing in the statistical analyses. To discover the relationships for each content type, we first used the multivariate analysis of variance (MANOVA) test to find out whether there were any significant results. Then, when a significant result was found, we ran individual ANOVA tests to identify the specific significant results, followed by Tukey's Post-hoc tests to draw further comparisons among the options for obtaining digital content.

	Buy physical	Buy digital	Subscription	Rent/Borrow	Total
Books for education/research	122 (40.1%)	24 (7.9%)	8 (2.6%)	150 (49.3%)	304 (100%)[2]
Books for leisure reading	145 (47.7%)	63 (20.7%)	8 (2.6%)	88 (28.9%)	304 (100%)[2]
Music	47 (15.5%)	117 (38.5%)	106 (34.9%)	34 (11.2%)	304 (100%)
Movie/TV episode	39 (12.8%)	43 (14.1%)	120 (39.5%)	102 (33.6%)	304 (100%)

Table 7: Summary of General Preferences for Obtaining Digital Content

Ownership preferences for education/research books and digital rights

The results of the MANOVA tests showed that, regarding users' preferences for education/research books, there were no significant differences in the means of the perceived importance of various digital rights, for different ways of obtaining content (Wilk's Lambda: $F(22, 566)=1.195, p=.245 > .05$).

Ownership preferences for leisure books and digital rights

The results of MANOVA tests showed that, regarding leisure books, there were significant differences in the level of the perceived importance of digital rights, by ways of obtaining content (Wilk's Lambda: $F(22, 566) = 2.62, p < .001$). Individual one-way ANOVAs and Tukey's Post-hoc test, the follow-up statistics used for significant MANOVA results for leisure books, found mean differences for these digital rights: the ability to resell, download, make a copy, use the content on multiple devices, and to reuse the content for creating new content.

More specifically, with regard to reselling the content, there was a significant difference between buying a physical leisure book ($M = 1.73$) and buying a digital version ($M = 1.24$) ($p < .05$), and between buying a digital leisure book ($M = 1.24$) and renting /borrowing one ($M = 1.95$) ($p < .001$). Participants who preferred to buy physical leisure books were more concerned about the resale rights than those who preferred to buy e-books. While this result also indicated that people who preferred to buy digital leisure books ($M = 4.65$) were more likely to consider downloadability to be an important right than did those who preferred to rent/borrow leisure books, ($M = 4.27$), this difference was only marginal at $p = .05$.

There was a statistically significant mean difference in user's perceived level of importance ascribed to the ability to make a copy of the content, between buying digital leisure books ($M = 2.14$) and buying physical copies ($M = 2.72$) ($p < .05$). People who buy physical books for leisure use care more about being able to make a copy of the content than those buying digital copies. Regarding the right to use the leisure book content on multiple devices, people who buy physical books are less likely to be concerned about this right ($M = 4.25$) than those who prefer to buy e-books for leisure use ($M = 4.65$) ($p < .05$). In addition, there was a statistically significant mean difference in users' perceived importance of the right to reuse the content, between buying digital ($M = 1.57$) versus buying physical leisure books ($M = 2.05$) ($p < .05$). People who prefer physical copies paid more attention to the reuse right than those who prefer digital copies.

Ownership preferences for music and digital rights

The results of MANOVA tests revealed that the levels of the perceived importance of digital rights were significantly different by participants' preferences for obtaining music content (Wilk's Lambda: $F (30, 855) = 2.30, p < .001$). Individual ANOVAs found significant differences in downloading, making a copy, converting the format, and choosing the format.

Regarding the ability to download the content, participants who preferred to buy digital copies of music tended to consider the ability to download to be more important ($M = 4.72$) than those who preferred to buy physical copies of music content did ($M = 4.26$) ($p < .05$), or those who preferred to rent/borrow music did ($M = 4.32$) ($p < .01$). People who preferred to obtain music through a subscription option were less likely to consider the right to make a copy important ($M = 2.64$) than those who preferred to buy physical copies ($M = 3.40$) ($p < .05$) or those who preferred to rent/borrow music did ($M = 3.56$) ($p < .05$). Moreover, the ability to convert the format was considered more important by people who preferred to buy digital music ($M = 3.12$) than by those who preferred subscription options for music content ($M = 2.53$) ($p < .05$). Similarly, for the right to choose the format, participants who preferred to buy digital music ($M = 3.74$) were more likely to consider format choice to be an important right than those who preferred subscription music were ($M = 3.00$) ($p < .01$).

Ownership preferences for movies and digital rights

The results of MANOVA tests did not show any significant results between participants' preferences for obtaining movies and their perceived level of importance of any of the digital rights (Wilk's Lambda: $F(30, 854.81)=.923, p >= .05$).

To sum up the RQ4 results, regarding participants' preferences for the options for obtaining movies or educational books, their perceived importance of the various digital rights displayed no significant differences. Regarding leisure books and music, the participants' perceived importance of digital rights did show some significant differences by ways of obtaining content. The right to possess (downloading content) and the right to manage (make a copy or convert the format of the content) may be related to their preferences for obtaining music. For educational books, every category of ownership rights that we evaluated in this study had a presence in the analysis—the right to possession (downloading content), the right to use (use content on multiple devices), the right to manage (make a copy of the content), and the right to transform (reuse for creating new content). The right of transferability (reselling content) may also be related to the participant's content option preferences. The results showed some interesting and expected correlations—for example, people who preferred buying physical copies were more concerned about the right to "make a copy" than those who preferred buying digital copies or using subscription access, but overall they did not display a strong pattern of level of importance vs. ownership/access preferences.

DISCUSSION

In this study, we adopted Watkins et al.'s (2016) concept of fragmented ownership, and modified their framework of digital virtual goods ownership configurations. By drawing from Honoré (1961)'s classic incidents of ownership (including the right to possess and the right to manage), and breaking these categories down further into Watkin's framework, we were able to incorporate more specific ownership configurations (as shown in Table 1). This new taxonomy of ownership configuration translates property rights/interests into commonly-seen digital rights or features of digital media products, e.g., downloading, making a copy, and converting the format. Our results for RQ2 show that this taxonomy is valid, because users' perceived importance of specific digital rights corresponding to each property right were very similar (Table 3, 4, and 5). This means, for example, that the digital rights to make a copy and to convert the format of the content can be clustered together to represent the ownership right to manage the digital content. In addition, the dimensional view of property rights (separating the content of the right from the form of the right) adopted by Watkins et al. (2016) from Attas (2006) proved to be useful in analyzing rights and preferences related to digital content.

From the results, we can illuminate an owning model and an access model for digital content, built to reflect users' perceptions. Across different content types, users generally tend to think they own the downloadable, purchased copies, even if these copies are attached to certain devices or dependent on certain software. Subscriptions, in general, are considered as instances of the access model, similar to renting the content. This general perception confirms the analysis of the fragmented ownership configurations specified in our framework (Table 1), in which the rights configurations of the subscription methods are almost identical to those of online renting. Meanwhile, we also see uncertainties associated with users' sense of ownership of the content, which indicates that the notion of ownership is still being shaped by various business models in the digital environment (Perzanowski & Schultz, 2016).

In studying the general preferences towards ownership or access for four different types of digital content, we noticed a general preference towards ownership when books and music are concerned. For movies, the access model wins. For the convenience of analysis and discussion, we defined owning as purchasing physical or digital copies, without incorporating the more specific configurations of ownership, such as the subtle differences between DRM-free and DRM-enabled copies, because most users do consider DRM-enabled copies to be their property. And we defined access as subscribing, renting, or borrowing, which also conforms with users' general perceptions of ownership (RQ1). Moreover, users showed a strong preference for physical books, and a preference for digital music and movies. If we consider paid digital material only (buying digital vs. subscription), the results show a preference for ownership of books and a strong preference for subscription access to movies. For paid digital music, users' preferences are split between ownership and subscription. Based on this analysis, we are not yet seeing the end of ownership of content, at least for books. Ownership, especially owning something physically, is still important to users with regard to books. For music, owning is also important, but access, especially via the subscription model, is gaining in importance. Movies clearly show a different pattern, and users generally favor the access model over ownership. The result is not surprising, given that seeing a movie is often a one-time consumption experience, while users may re-read books and listen to the same music repeatedly. But this result proves that content type plays an important role in users' media consumption/ownership preferences.

Our findings about users' perceived importance of digital rights are largely comparable to the previous study by Arnab and Hofman (2005). They found that more than half of the participants considered portability (the ability to use content on any operating system and any number of devices), converting formats, a choice of formats, and the transferability of rights as an "absolute necessity" for digital media content, while the rights to modify, redistribute, and annotate content were less important. The major differences are that participants in our current study do not consider converting formats and the transferability of rights (especially the right to resell) to be important. One explanation could be the time lapse between the two studies. Arnab and Hofman's study was conducted more than ten years ago, when digital media were not as prevalent as they are today, and therefore users' perceptions were heavily influenced by their usage of traditional media. Today, with the enforcement of DRM technologies and licensing agreements, as well as the influence of the subscription model, users may be increasingly adapted to the access-only approach and have largely accepted the fact that digital media content cannot be transferred. Qualitative research on changes in users' perceptions may help us to better explain the differences.

An important contribution of the study is to reveal that users perceived different levels of importance in various digital rights by their preferred methods of obtaining digital content. As mentioned, the analyses for RQ4 reveal variances of perceived importance in digital rights, but overall, this study failed to demonstrate significant mean differences. In other words, users did consider certain rights to be important, but that did not necessarily affect their preferences for certain ways of owning/accessing content. The reasons for this may be complicated. For one, although we listed the prominent configurations of ownership and access, they cannot represent all of the different models available in today's media content market. Therefore, we did not necessarily create an accurate "match" between rights and preferences. For example, downloading is important to most users, but some subscription services also allow temporary downloads. In addition, we did not list the free subscription model as a configuration of its own. For another, other factors may be more important in explaining why users prefer certain ways of obtaining digital media content over others, including the quality/selection of content, financial incentives, convenience, etc., some of which were discussed by Berger et al.(2015), Chyi (2012), and Lopes and Galletta (2006). However, the findings of this study do suggest some interesting factors to investigate further in future research using qualitative methods.

CONCLUSION

In the digital era, ownership of media content is becoming increasingly partial and fragmented. The notion of ownership is complicated and uncertain for users, likely because of the complexity of intellectual property rights, personal property rights, DRM systems, and contractual arraignments for digital media content. This study shows that users still very much prefer owning copies (either digital or physical), at least for books and music. However, users' perceptions, attitudes, and preferences are likely to change over time, and many factors may play a role in this process. As Perzanowski and Schultz (2016) argued, it is time to "craft a notion of ownership applicable to digital goods" (p.193), otherwise, the balance between intellectual property ownership and personal ownership will favor the IP owners.

One of the limitations of this study is the exclusion of the piracy option in addressing ways of obtaining digital media content. This option may still be used by certain groups of users, which may have affected the results of the study concerning the correlations between preferences and attitudes about digital rights. Conversely, attitudes about digital rights may help us better explain piracy behaviors. This limitation can be addressed in future studies, together with the issues mentioned in the discussion section, especially through qualitative research.

REFERENCES

Alakurt, T., & Teker, N. (2013). A study on undergraduate students' opinions about digital rights management/digital restrictions management. Egitim Bilimleri Fakultesi Dergisi, 46(2), 233–248.

Arnab, A. & Hofman, J. (2005). A survey on current media usage, piracy habits and attitudes on DRM. Retrieved from http://citeseerx.ist.psu.edu/viewdoc/summary?doi=10.1.1.521.2626

Attas, D. (2006). Fragmenting property. Law and Philosophy, 25(1), 119–149. https://doi.org/10.1007/s10982-005-8758-0

Bakos, Y., Marotta-Wurgler, F., & Trossen, D. (2014). Does anyone read the fine print? Consumer attention to standard-form contracts. The Journal of Legal Studies, 43(1), 1–35. https://doi.org/10.1086/674424

Belk, R. (2014). You are what you can access: Sharing and collaborative consumption online. Journal of Business Research, 67(8), 1595–1600. https://doi.org/10.1016/j.jbusres.2013.10.001

Bell A. & Parchomovsky, G. (2005). A theory of property. Cornell Law Review, 90(3), 531-616.

Berger, B., Matt, C., Steininger, D. M., & Hess, T. (2015). It is not just about competition with "free": Differences between content formats in consumer preferences and willingness to pay. Journal of Management Information Systems, 32(3), 105–128. https://doi.org/10.1080/07421222.2015.1095038

Chyi, H. I. (2012). Paying for what? How much? And why (not)? Predictors of paying intent for multiplatform newspapers. International Journal on Media Management, 14(3), 227–250. https://doi.org/10.1080/14241277.2012.657284

Cotton, H., & Bolan, C. (2012). User reaction towards end user license agreements on android smartphones. In Proceedings of International Conference on Security and Management (pp. 666-668). Las Vegas, NV.

Crawford, W. (2005). Whose rights does DRM manage? EContent, 28(4), 42.

Gasaway, L. N. (2003). The new access right and its impact on libraries and libraries users. Journal of Intellectual Property Law, 10(2), 269–308.

Gaus, G. (2012). Property and ownership. In D. Estlund (Ed.), Oxford handbook of political philosophy (pp. 93-112). Oxford: Oxford University Press.

Grey, T. C. (1980). The disintegration of property. Nomos, 22, 69–85.

Hohfeld, W. N. (1913). Some fundamental legal conceptions as applied in judicial reasoning. The Yale Law Journal, 23(1), 16–59. https://doi.org/10.2307/785533

Hohfeld, W. N. (1917). Fundamental legal conceptions as applied in judicial reasoning. The Yale Law Journal, 26(8), 710–770. https://doi.org/10.2307/786270

Honoré, A.M. (1961). Ownership. In A.G. Guest, Oxford Essays in Jurisprudence (370–375). London: Oxford University Press.

Kane, L. T. (1997). Access vs. ownership: Do we have to make a choice? College & Research Libraries, 58(1), 58-66. https://doi.org/10.5860/crl.58.1.58.

Lawson, S. J., Gleim, M. R., Perren, R., & Hwang, J. (2016). Freedom from ownership: An exploration of access-based consumption. Journal of Business Research, 69(8), 2615–2623. https://doi.org/10.1016/j.jbusres.2016.04.021

Lessig, L. (2004). Free culture: How big media uses technology and the law to lock down culture and control creativity. New York, NY: Penguin Press

Litman, J. (1999). Electronic commerce and free speech. Ethics and Information Technology, 1(3), 213–225. https://doi.org/10.1023/A:1010002704434

Loebbecke, C., Bartscher, P., Weiss, T., & Weniger, S. (2010). Consumers' attitudes to digital rights management (DRM) in the German trade ebook market. In 2010 Ninth International Conference on Mobile Business and 2010 Ninth Global Mobility Roundtable (ICMB-GMR) (337–344). https://doi.org/10.1109/ICMB-GMR.2010.16

Lopes, A. B., & Galletta, D. F. (2006). Consumer perceptions and willingness to pay for intrinsically motivated online content. Journal of Management Information Systems, 23(2), 203–231. https://doi.org/10.2753/MIS0742-1222230209

May, C. (2007). Digital rights management: The problem of expanding ownership rights. Oxford, UK: Chandos Publishing.

Miller, R. H. (2000). Electronic resources and academic libraries, 1980-2000: A historical perspective. Library Trends, 48(4), 645-670.

Monroe, W. S. (1992). Redefining the library: The year's work in collection development, 1991. Library Resources & Technical Services, 36(3), 277-289.

Mulligan, D. K., Han, J., & Burstein, A. J. (2003). How DRM-based content delivery systems disrupt expectations of "personal use." In Proceedings of the 3rd ACM workshop on Digital rights management. Washington, DC: ACM.

Peoples, G. (2016, January 29). The battle of subscription business models: A look at their strengths and weaknesses. Retrieved from http://www.billboard.com/articles/business/6859192/battle-subscription-business-models-strengths-weaknesses

Perzanowski, A., & Schultz, J. (2016). The end of ownership: Personal property in the digital economy. Cambridge, MA: The MIT Press.

Rifkin, J. (2000). The age of access: The new culture of hypercapitalism where all of life is a paid for experience. New York, NY: Penguin.

Rifkin, J. (2014). The zero marginal cost society. New York, NY: Palgrave.

Rosenblatt, B. (2017, April 12). In music, DRM is back while ownership is going away. Retrieved from https://copyrightandtechnology.com/2017/04/12/in-music-drm-grows-while-ownership-shrinks/

Rowley, J. (2008). Understanding digital content marketing. Journal of Marketing Management, 24(5/6), 517–540. https://doi.org/10.1362/026725708X325977

Sinclair, G., & Tinson, J. (2017). Psychological ownership and music streaming consumption. Journal of Business Research, 71, 1–9. https://doi.org/10.1016/j.jbusres.2016.10.002

Watkins, R. D., Denegri-Knott, J., & Molesworth, M. (2016). The relationship between ownership and possession: observations from the context of digital virtual goods. Journal of Marketing Management, 32(1/2), 44–70. https://doi.org/10.1080/0267257X.2015.1089308

Evaluating Interactive Bibliographic Information Retrieval Systems: A User-centered Approach

Yongjun Zhu
Department of Library and Information Science, Sungkyunkwan University, South Korea. jooyoungjun@gmail.com

Erjia Yan
College of Computing and Informatics, Drexel University, United States, ey86@drexel.edu

Meen Chul Kim
College of Computing and Informatics, Drexel University, United States, meenchul.kim@drexel.edu

ABSTRACT

As an integral part of research activities, scholars frequently interact with bibliographic information retrieval systems to acquire scholarly information. With the dramatic increase of scientific literature, there is the pressing need of building effective and efficient bibliographic information retrieval systems that support more granular and complex bibliographic information needs. Investigating users' interaction with these systems plays an important role in understanding the systems' features and usability issues, which contributes to better system design and implementation. In this paper, we evaluate three interactive bibliographic information retrieval systems proposed in our previous studies using a user-centered approach, including form-, natural language-, and visual graph-based systems. This study recruits 20 participants to evaluate the three systems from the aspects of success rate, search time, query size, usefulness, ease of use, ease of learning, and satisfaction. Results showed that: the form-based system needed the least time to formulate simple bibliographic queries and allowed the participants to make the least mistakes; the natural language-based system needed the least time to formulate high-complexity bibliographic queries and was rated as the most useful, easy-to-use, and easy-to-learn system; and the visual graph-based system's strengths lie in the support of complex queries as shown that it got better ratings of usefulness and satisfaction by the high-complexity task group.

KEYWORDS

bibliographic information retrieval, search user interfaces, interactive information retrieval, user-centered evaluation

INTRODUCTION

Bibliographic information retrieval systems such as Web of Science, Scopus, and Google Scholar have become essential tools for scholars to navigate scientific literature. In the past several decades, major bibliographic information retrieval systems have used form-based interfaces. These systems mainly support the search of scientific papers rather than other bibliographic entities such as authors, scientific terms, and research institutions. A recent work by de Ribaupierre (2014) discussed a few important challenges regarding bibliographic information retrieval in the big scholarly data area: the difficulty of answering scholars' precise bibliographic questions and the lack of techniques that help scholars directly target their information needs. A follow-up interview showed that researchers are interested in searching for papers as well as other entities such as authors and keywords (de Ribaupierre, 2014). Motivated by addressing these limitations, in our prior work, we proposed three bibliographic information retrieval systems to provide more efficient and effective ways of searching bibliographic information. These systems are based on the graph data model and provide novel ways of formulating bibliographic queries.

Three ways of formulating bibliographic queries are distinguished. The form-based system is the most common one, in which users formulate queries by interacting with forms. In the natural language-based system, users formulate queries using natural languages written in English. The last system is based on a visual graph interface, where users formulate queries by drawing graphs, which are then interpreted into queries. Each of these systems provides user different interfaces and distinct ways of processing user-generated queries while only shares the data management layer with the other two systems.

While system-centered evaluations have been conducted to evaluate the proposed systems, we see a user-centered evaluation of these systems will be beneficial for us to understand how users interact with each system and how their search behaviors vary across systems. A recent study on the user-centered evaluation of Web of Science and Scopus (Okhovati et al., 2016) showed that the number of search terms used between two groups of novice and experienced users was significantly different in Scopus but not in Web of Science. User-centered evaluations of information retrieval systems are an effective way of designing and improving information retrieval systems. Thus, the goal of this study is to understand how users interact with the three systems and formulate bibliographic queries.

The remainder of this paper is written as follows: in the literature review section, we survey recent studies on user-centered evaluations of information retrieval systems; in the experimental systems section, we briefly discuss three systems to be evaluated in the study; in the experimental setup section, we discuss the overall experimental setting, search tasks, and measures; in the results section, we report the experimental results; last, we end the paper with a discussion and conclusion.

LITERATURE REVIEW

Evaluations of interactive information retrieval (IIR) systems have been discussed in studies from earlier decades (e.g., Salton, 1970) to more recent years (e.g., Borlund, 2016). Kelly's two seminal studies (Kelly, 2009; Kelly & Sugimoto, 2013) reviewed extensive studies on this topic published before 2010. Readers may refer to the abovementioned studies to get a detailed understanding of the field. In this section, we provide a review of related work that was published after 2010 to deliver recent findings. In the reviewed literature, we identified three main research themes: studies that explored relationships among established IIR measures; studies that explored a variety of aspects of work and search tasks; and studies that proposed IIR evaluation frameworks and systems. In the following paragraphs, we synthesize the findings of these studies.

Relationships of IIR measures

Al-Maskari and Sanderson (2010) examined the relationship between four factors (i.e., system effectiveness, user effectiveness, user effort, and user characteristics) and user satisfaction to understand whether user satisfaction is influenced by these factors. The authors found a strong correlation between user effectiveness and user satisfaction. System effectiveness and user effort had weak correlations with user satisfaction. However, their results showed no correlation between user characteristics and user satisfaction. In their subsequent study (Al-Maskari & Sanderson, 2011), the effect of user characteristics on user effectiveness was investigated. User characteristics was measured by users' search experience and cognitive skills (i.e., perceptual speed). A few empirical findings were reported: experienced users retrieved much more relevant documents than inexperienced users and users received higher scores on the perceptual speed test took much less time than users with lower scores to locate the first relevant document. Smucker and Jethani (2010) examined the relationship between retrieval precision and perceived difficulty. They showed that a higher retrieval precision reduced users' perceived difficulty and their relationship was statistically significant.

Findings on work and search tasks

Li and Belkin (2010) explored the relationship between work tasks and users' search behaviors in interactive information retrieval. Six types of work tasks were employed based on their faceted classification scheme (Li & Belkin, 2008). They found that users presented different patterns of search behavior in different types of work tasks. Key findings include: in schoolwork-related tasks, users consulted library resources much more often than search engines such as Google, and in decision-making work tasks, users relied more on browsing than in schoolwork-related work tasks. Liu and colleagues (2010) also explored search behaviors in different task types in journalism. They classified tasks based on a modified version of Li's classification scheme (2009) by adding a new facet. Specifically, they examined the associations between search behaviors (e.g., task completion time, number of pages visited, number of queries) and different facet values (i.e., task product, task complexity, level, and task goal). A list of significant associations were reported in their study. Wildemuth and Freund (2012) reviewed 51 studies on exploratory search tasks and provided a list of task characteristics in exploratory search. Identified task characteristics were grouped into two categories: cognitive (e.g., learning and investigation as goals, general rather than specific) and behavioral (e.g., open-ended, target is multiple items). In a follow-up study, Wildemuth and colleagues (2014) reviewed 106 studies to examine how search task complexity and difficulty were defined and practiced. They identified three dimensions of task complexity including multiplicity of subtasks, multiplicity of facets, and uncertainty. They showed that search task difficulty can be measured both objectively and subjectively. Kelly and colleagues (2015) examined search tasks using a cognitive complexity framework from education theory. Search tasks were created and divided into five levels based on the framework to understand the differences among tasks. They found that participants showed more search activities in more cognitively complex tasks, but did not see more cognitively complex tasks as more difficult. This finding showed that self-reported task difficulty was not in line with physical effort (e.g., queries formulated, clicks, and time taken to complete tasks). Borlund and Schneider (2010) reviewed 85 individual studies that applied the concept of simulated work task introduced by her and Ingwersen (1997) to find how and where it was used. The main goal was to understand how the three parts of recommendations made in her earlier study of IIR evaluation model (Borlund, 2003) were practiced. Results showed that those recommendations were not well applied and studies varied in the way of reflecting and practicing the recommendations. A detailed follow-up study was conducted in 2016 (Borlund, 2016). In addition to the previous finings, the author showed that none of reviewed studies used pilot testing that is important to tune and refine simulated work task situations. Along with these findings, recommendations were made regarding the design and the creation of simulated work tasks. Clemmensen and Borlund (2016) studied order effect in IIR evaluation. They examined nine IIR parameters of search behavior in a between-group design. Results showed that order effect was evident in three parameters including website change, visit of webpage, and formulation of queries.

IIR evaluation frameworks and systems

A few frameworks and systems for IIR evaluations were proposed to aid researchers to conduct systematic evaluations. Renaud and Azzopardi (2012) proposed a web-based system that allows simple within-subjects experiments. The system includes a series of experimental components such as participant registration, consent, surveys, and logging information. While their system was particularly designed for undergraduate and Master's students as the authors stated, Hall and Toms (2013) proposed a framework that provides a common baseline by including existing evaluation measures to enable cross-study comparison. Another goal was to make the framework flexible and applicable to a large number of experiments. To achieve this, the framework defined a standardized set of questions and was designed to be easily integrated with existing systems. Zuccon and colleagues (2013) proposed a method of evaluating IIR systems using a crowdsourcing platform. The proposal was based on the motivation to address a few limitations of traditional laboratory-based evaluations such as high cost and the lack of heterogeneity among the user population. In the proposed method, evaluations of IIR systems including task assignment and data collection are taken online. A case study was performed to compare the laboratory- and crowdsourcing-based evaluations. Results showed that the two methods led to similar conclusions on the effectiveness of the studied IIR systems while the crowdsourcing-based method could collect five times more data than laboratory-based method with only half the cost. However, a few limitations of crowdsourcing-based method were also pointed out. These limitations include participants' lack of interactions with systems (e.g., issue fewer queries, click fewer documents), the control of data quality (e.g., data generated by bots), and the assessment of the reliability of participants' personal information. Recently, Wei and colleagues (2014) proposed a new web-based system for IIR evaluation. The system enables usability testing of different search task interfaces as well as different algorithms with the same search task interface. One strength of the system is the rich support of eye-tracking logging that includes automated recoding of interface element coordinates. Because the system was primarily designed using JavaScript, it has a broad applicability in the web environment.

EXPERIMENTAL SYSTEMS

In this section, we briefly discuss the three experimental systems (i.e., form-, natural language-, and visual graph-based system) to be evaluated in the study. All three systems are graph-based and interactive. They are graph-based because the graph data model was used to store and manage bibliographic data and bibliographic queries generated by end users are translated into graph queries. The systems are interactive because users' queries formulated in a variety of forms are automatically translated into graph queries and users can modify their queries interactively. We discuss each system with an example query— "papers on interface, that cited Josh Clow's papers" in the text below.

Form-based system

In the form-based system (Figure 1), users formulate queries by interacting with forms in a way similar to that of Web of Science. The difference is that the system allows for the formulation of more complex queries that involves citations. As shown in Figure 1, we select the bibliographic type we search and add additional information to both the cited and citing sides. A graph query is generated based on the form query and allows user to validate the initial query. Users can modify form queries interactively before sending them to the database. For more detailed description, please refer to our prior work (Zhu, Yan, & Song, 2016).

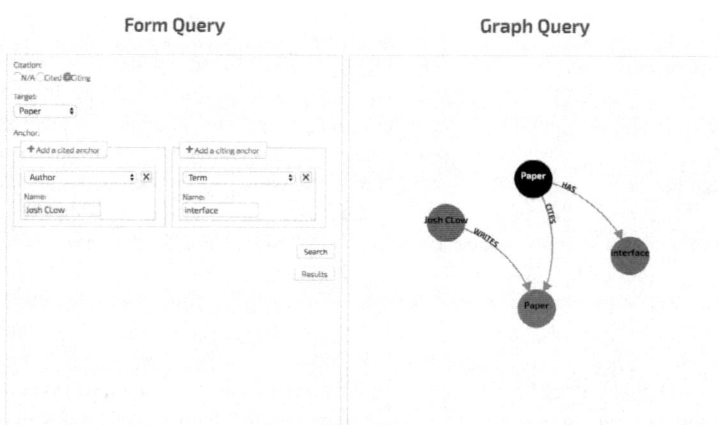

Figure 2. The form-based system

Natural language-based system

In the natural language-based system (Figure 2), users formulate queries using natural languages. The system identifies bibliographic entities and their relations in natural language queries and generates a graph query. Again, users can modify natural language queries interactively until they see a satisfied graph query. For more detailed description, please refer to our prior work (Zhu, Yan, & Song, 2017).

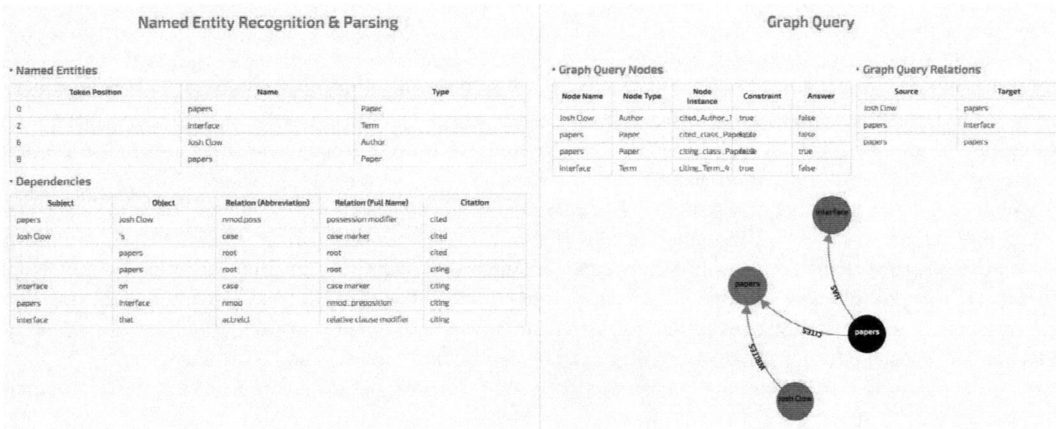

Figure 3. The natural language-based system

Visual graph-based system

In the visual graph-based system (Figure 3), users formulate bibliographic queries by drawing nodes and their relations. A reference schema is provided so that users can formulate visual graph queries based on it. The system includes a verification module and guides users to formulate a syntactically and semantically correct queries. For more detailed description, please refer to our prior work (Zhu & Yan, 2016).

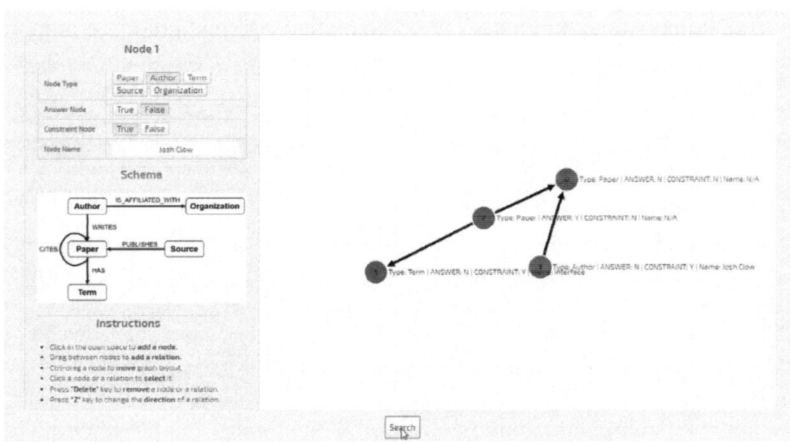

Figure 4. The visual graph-based system

EXPERIMENTAL SETUP

Overall experimental setup

The experimental setting is a laboratory study employing a mixed design (between-group and within subjects). Twenty participants were recruited using a convenience sampling method. A pilot-test was conducted to adjust the research setting. For example, through interviews with potential participants, we found that undergraduate students use academic information retrieval systems infrequently. This is probably due to their lack of research experience. Thus, the recruit is limited to people who have a master's or a more advanced degree. Among the 20 participants, 10 are male and the other 10 are female. Nineteen participants are at the age of 25 to 34 while one participant falls in the range of 35 to 44. There are four master's students, 13 doctoral students, two postdoctoral researchers, and one professor. Twelve participants are majored in Information Science, followed by Linguistics (three), Computer Science (three), and Biomedical Engineering (two).

Tasks and measures

Tasks were designed as a known-item search, in which users were provided with partial information to perform a search. Known-item searches are a common type of bibliographic searches. For example, users search for papers with partial information such as keywords and authors. Simulated work tasks (Borlund & Ingwersen, 1997) were employed to create the tasks in this study. As Borlund (2003) discussed, a simulated work task is a short cover story that describes situations where information needs arise. Because the three systems to be evaluated provide different ways of representing information needs, simulated situations are a good fit that helps us better understand how users formulate queries using different mechanisms. Overall, two task sets of simulated situations with varying task complexity (low and high) were created. The level of task complexity was decided based on the amount of effort needed to solve a problem. Participants were equally (i.e., ten for each set) divided into the two task sets. Each task set has three tasks (one for each system). To reduce the variance of using different tasks in each set, balanced task sets (e.g., Käki & Aula, 2008) were created. Specifically, tasks in each task set were made as similar as possible by only modifying terms (e.g., author name) in the description. This helps reduce learning effects and variance of task complexity within each task set. A factorial design with six conditions (three system types by two levels of task complexity) was used. Therefore, each system was tested under the condition of both complexity levels of tasks and each complexity level of tasks was tested with all system types. Table 1 shows two example task situations (one in each level of task complexity). Questionnaires were used to elicit data from the participants. Both closed and open questions were asked in the questionnaires. Closed questions were largely based on a seven-point Likert scale. Five questionnaires: a background, three post-task, and an exit were used. A background questionnaire was used to elicit background information about the participants. Three post-task questionnaires were administered after completing each of three tasks. The exit questionnaire was used to elicit overall cross-system comparisons and ratings.

Example 1 (low-complexity task)	Example 2 (high-complexity task)
John is a first-year doctoral student who is interested in Information Retrieval. His adviser asked him to find a few seminal papers and do a literature review. John knows Gerard Salton is one of the prominent researchers in the field. Among many journals, he plans to take a look at Communications of the ACM. Please use the form-based system and find papers that were written by Gerard Salton and published in Communications of the ACM.	James is a first-year doctoral student who is interested in Data Mining. His advisor asked him to find a few seminal papers and do a literature review. James knows Jiawei Han is one of the prominent researchers in the field. After reviewing Jiawei Han' papers, James find that he is specifically interested in a subarea of Data Mining called clustering. James wants to find out more researchers who cited Jiawei Han's papers and do research on clustering. Please use the natural language-based system and find out authors who wrote papers on clustering that cited papers that were written by Jiawei Han.

Table 7. Two example task situations used in the experiment

For evaluation measures, we adopted notions discussed in Kelly's study (2009). As discussed by Kelly, in IIR, unlike HCI research, performance is seen as a separate concept from usability and usability is usually evaluated based on self-report measures. In this study, we evaluated the systems in terms of performance and usability. Performance was measured by a set of objective measures while usability was examined by analyzing data elicited from questionnaires. Performance was defined as system's ability of helping users resolve bibliographic information retrieval tasks. Table 2 shows measures of performance and their operational definitions.

Category	Measure	Description
Relevance-based	Success rate	A binary measure (i.e., success or not) represents completion of each task.
Interaction-based	Search time	Time taken to complete a search task
	Query size	The number of issued queries to complete a search task.

Table 8. Performance measures used in the experiment

Success rate is used to measure participants' performance on retrieving relevant search results. Participants' answers are matched against correct answers to see whether they are identical. Used synthetically, it shows the fraction of participants who complete the search tasks. A larger fraction shows that the participants perform better with one system than another. Search time measures the time a participant uses to complete a task. It largely depends on the time a user spends on formulating a query because the time used by the background processes (e.g., interpreting queries, querying the database) are almost identical to the extent that we can ignore the differences across the three systems. Shorter search time represents better performance. Query Size measures the number of queries a participant formulates to finish a task. Participants might formulate more than one query to finish a task due to a lack of experience. A smaller query size denotes that the participants perform better in terms of formulating queries correctly.

ISO's definition of usability (ISO 9241-11, 1998) has three dimensions: effectiveness, efficiency, and satisfaction as shown in the following list (p. 2):

- Effectiveness is the "accuracy and completeness with which users achieve specified goals."
- Efficiency is the "resources expended in relation to the accuracy and completeness with which users achieve goals."
- Satisfaction is the "freedom from discomfort, and positive attitudes of the user to the product."

Kelly (2009) discussed that measures for effectiveness and efficiency used in HCI (e.g., Hornbæk, 2006) typically overlap with the performance measures in IIR (e.g., precision and time taken to complete a task). Thus, in this paper, we test usability by measuring satisfaction with three additional measures including ease of use, ease of learning, and usefulness. We use the USE questionnaire (Lund, 2011) to measure the above four dimensions of usability, in which each item is measured using a seven-point Likert scale.

RESULTS

Participants' overall experience on bibliographic information retrieval

Through a background questionnaire, we collected information on participants' general experience on academic search systems. Among the 20 participants, eight participants reported that they use academic search systems more than seven times in a week, followed by seven participants (one to two times), four participants (three to four times), and one participant (five to six times). About one third are active users of academic search systems; one third use academic search systems less frequently; and the remaining represent a moderate user group. As for the primarily used search system, 13 participants selected Google Scholar, five participants selected Web of Science, and two participants selected other systems (e.g., Microsoft Academic Search). Participants were also asked to rate their ability of using academic search systems through a five-point Likert scale. Eleven participants responded by selecting average, followed by proficient (eight) and very proficient (one). In terms of the motivation of using academic search systems, six participants responded that they usually have specific information needs in mind before searching while three participants responded that their main purpose is exploring. Eleven participants responded with both choices. Given this, we argue that most participants use academic search systems with specific information in mind. In a question that asked current academic search systems' support of bibliographic information needs, 14 participants responded that they are not powerful enough in terms of representing complex bibliographic information need, and some of their bibliographic information needs are not representable in the current systems while six participants were satisfied with them.

Results of performance evaluations

Table 3 shows the overall results of the performance evaluation. We can see how two groups of participants performed for each of the three systems. As mentioned previously, 10 were assigned to the low-complexity task and the other 10 were assigned to the high-complexity task. We show how many participants in each group successfully completed the tasks (success rate), and how long they spent on completing the tasks (search time, in seconds), and how many queries they formulated to represent information needs.

Task complexity	Measure	System type		
		Form-based	Natural language-based	Visual graph-based
Low	Success rate	10/10	10/10	10/10
	Search time	Max: 58, Min: 10 **Mean: 26**, Median: 22	Max: 61, Min: 12 **Mean: 33**, Median: 30	Max: 91, Min: 30 **Mean: 61**, Median: 58
	Query Size	Max: 3, Min: 1 **Mean: 1.5**, Median: 1	Max: 5, Min: 1 **Mean: 2.3**, Median: 2	Max: 4, Min: 1 **Mean: 1.7**, Median: 1
High	Success rate	9/10	10/10	7/10
	Search time	Max: 150, Min: 20 **Mean: 70**, Median: 64	Max: 90, Min: 21 **Mean: 53**, Median: 48	Max: 191, Min: 90 **Mean: 135**, Median: 131
	Query size	Max: 3, Min: 1 **Mean: 1.3**, Median: 1	Max: 5, Min: 1 **Mean: 2**, Median: 1	Max: 5, Min: 1 **Mean: 1.7**, Median: 1

Table 9. Results on the performance evaluation

For the low-complexity task set, all participants completed the tasks using all the systems while for the high-complexity task set, one participant failed the task for the form-based system and three participants failed for the visual graph-based system. A reasonable explanation is that the natural language-based system requires no additional knowledge to use. On the other hand, users need to learn how to use the other two systems, which requires additional time and effort. Because the participants have never used a visual graph interface to formulate bibliographic queries, the visual graph-based system is less familiar to them. Thus, compared with the form-based system, which has been widely adopted by major academic search systems, the visual graph-based system has more features to be learned and the participants performed worse with the system than with the other systems.

The participants spent the least time (i.e., 26 secs) with the form-based system in the low-complexity task set while for the high-complexity task set, the least time (i.e., 53 secs) was achieved with the natural language-based system. We can see that, for simple tasks, the form-based system is the fastest way to formulate queries, probably due to its simplicity and users' familiarity with the system. As information needs become more complex, the natural language-based system proves to be a faster solution because one just needs to write down natural language queries without repeating mouse and keyboard operations such as selecting items and inputting values. In both task sets, the participants spent the most time with the visual graph-based system. This was expected because the visual graph-based system is specifically designed to answer complex bibliographic queries (e.g., bibliographic coupling and author co-citation), and it requires every single node in a query to be manually specified with properties.

Query size reveals the magnitude of errors made by the participants. In both task sets, the participants formulated the smallest number of queries (i.e., 1.5 and 1.3) with the form-based systems and the largest number of queries (2.3 and 2) with the natural language-based system. Typographical errors might be the factor that affected the participants' query size in the natural language-based system. Before the evaluation, we expected that the largest query size would be recorded with the visual graph-based system because it is the most complex system among the three. However, in both task sets, the query size was between the other two systems. It is partly due to its query verification module that automatically corrects misrepresented queries and recommends new ones.

Results of usability evaluation

Figure 4 shows the bar charts of the four usability measures (i.e., usefulness, ease of use, ease of learning, and satisfaction). In the figure and tables following below, F denotes the form-based system, NL denotes the natural language-based system, and VG denotes the visual graph-based system. For each measure, the means and error bars of the two groups (high-complexity group vs. low-complexity group) are shown.

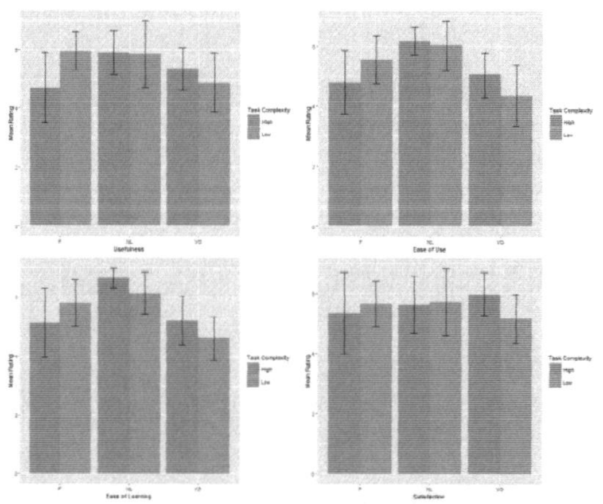

Figure 5. Descriptive statistics for usability measures

To further explore any statistically significant differences, we run a 2*3 mixed-design ANOVA because the task complexity is a between-group variable and system type is a repeated-measure variable. Table 4 shows the results.

Effect	Usefulness	Ease of Use	Ease of Learning	Satisfaction
Main effect of Task complexity	$F(1,78) = 1.41$, $p = .24$, $\eta^2 = .007$	$F(1,78) = .025$, $p = .87$, $\eta^2 < .001$	$F(1,78) = .53$, $p = .47$, $\eta^2 = .004$	$F(1,78) = .3$, $p = .58$, $\eta^2 = .002$
Main effect of System type	$F(2,156) = 7.48$, $\mathbf{p < .001}$, $\eta^2 = .05$	$F(2,156) = 28.65$, $\mathbf{p < .001}$, $\eta^2 = .16$	$F(2,156) = 52.05$, $\mathbf{p < .001}$, $\eta^2 = .21$	$F(2,156) = .42$, $p = .65$, $\eta^2 = .002$
Interaction between the two	$F(2,156) = 9.75$, $\mathbf{p < .001}$, $\eta^2 = .07$	$F(2,156) = 7.57$, $\mathbf{p < .001}$, $\eta^2 = .05$	$F(2,156) = 11.81$, $\mathbf{p < .001}$, $\eta^2 = .06$	$F(2,156) = 4.7$, $\mathbf{p = .01}$ $\eta^2 = .03$

Table 10. Results of the mixed-design ANOVA

As shown in Table 4, there is no significant difference between ratings of the two groups of task complexity. However, we see participants rated the three systems differently when evaluating their usefulness, ease of use, and ease of learning (i.e., all of them are significant at the 0.001 level). Interactions between task complexity and system type are shown to be significant in all the four measures. Pairwise t-test with Bonferroni correction was performed to see how differently participants rated the systems (Table 5). However, because of the existence of the interaction effects between task complexity and system types, the ratings could also had been partly affected by task complexity. Satisfaction was not included because it is not significant in Table 4.

Usefulness			Ease of Use			Ease of Learning		
	F	NL		F	NL		F	NL
NL	0.0168*	-	NL	<0.0001***	-	NL	<0.0001***	-
VG	1.00	0.0021**	VG	0.12	<0.0001***	VG	0.0069**	<0.0001***

Table 11. Results of pairwise t-test on system type

Based on Table 5 and Figure 4, we see that the participants rated the natural language-based system more useful than the other two systems. It was also rated as the system that is the most easy to use and learn. The participants also reported that the form-based system was easier to learn than the visual graph-based system. In terms of usefulness and ease to use, we do not see any significant difference between the form- and visual graph-based systems. Finally, simple effects analysis was performed to understand the interaction between task complexity and system type. The datasets of four measures were further split into three subsets. Then, ANOVA and Tukey's tests were performed to see whether significant differences exist between the two complexity groups upon each of the three system types. The results are shown in Table 6.

System type	Usefulness	Ease of Use	Ease of Learning	Satisfaction
F (Low vs. High)	0.3594	0.0227*	0.0341*	0.3594
NL (Low vs. High)	0.8267	0.5567	0.0058**	0.8267
VG (Low vs. High)	0.0068**	0.0345*	0.038*	0.0068**

Table 12. Results of ANOVA and Tukey's tests

Combining the result shown in Table 6 with that of Figure 4, we see that participants assigned to the high-complexity tasks rated the visual graph-based system higher than the participant group of low-complexity task in usefulness and satisfaction. This shows that participants thought the visual graph-based system is more useful and satisfactory for high-complexity tasks. For the form-based system, the participant group of low-complexity tasks rated it higher than its counterparts in terms of ease of use and learning. The natural language-based system was reported with similar ratings on ease of use by the two groups. This is the strength of the natural language-based system that no additional effort is needed to formulate more complex queries, and there is no significant difference of effort between formulating low- and high-complexity queries. A seemingly contradictory result is that participants assigned to the high-complexity tasks rated both the natural language- and visual graph-based systems higher than the participant group of low-complexity task in easy of learning. Because participants in the high-complexity task group interacted with all the three systems, who felt the form-based system hard to learn (e.g., due to its unsuitability to high-complexity task) might feel the other two systems relatively easies to learn. Overall, the interaction effect is the most significant in the visual graph-based system and least significant in the natural language-based system.

DISCUSSION AND CONCLUSION

In this paper, we evaluated three interactive bibliographic information retrieval systems using a user-centered approach. The study recruited 20 participants to evaluate three systems with different query formulation mechanisms (i.e., form-, natural language-, and visual graph-based) from a variety of aspects such as success rate, search time, query size, usefulness, ease of use, ease of learning, and satisfaction. We deployed a mixed-design experiment to understand how task complexity and system type affect users' performance and ratings of usability.

The form-based system needed the least time (i.e., 26 secs for the low-complexity tasks) to formulate simple bibliographic queries and allowed the participants to make the least mistakes (i.e., the average query size 1.5 and 1.3 for low- and high-complexity tasks). Participants stated that "The form-based system makes everything clear, so it is easy for me to handle each part of my query", "The form-based system is kind of fun and may come into handy pretty fast". One weakness of the system is that, with complex queries, participants feel that it is not as easy to use as it is with simple queries. The participant group of low-complexity task rated higher than its counterparts in terms of ease of use and learning. A participant assigned to high-complexity tasks stated that "The form-based (system) needs users to take more logic consideration and have more clicking." The natural language-based system needed the least time (i.e., 53 secs) to formulate high-complexity bibliographic queries and was rated as the most useful, easy-to-use, and easy-to-learn system. Participants stated that "Using natural language for searching bibliographic information would be the most intuitive way", "As long as my query is in good grammar, the system does everything automatically and transforms it into a graphical query, which is quite cool, and time-efficient". Flexibility was reported as the main weakness of the system. A participant stated that "The natural language-based system is easy to use, but it didn't allow too much flexibility on how to express a query by natural language". This was expected because the system requires users to input queries without grammatical errors and state-of-the-art NLP parsers can sometimes make mistakes even though the input queries are correct. The visual graph-based system did not get the best ratings in any of the measures. However, its strengths lie in the support of complex queries as shown that it got better ratings of usefulness and satisfaction by the high-complexity task group. Participants stated that "The visual graph-based system is a very flexible one. It seems everything is within my control. I felt comfortable to use this tool", "The visual system seems a little bit more complex than the other two systems, but it is actually the most powerful one that can answer lots of, almost every query that I can imagine." As stated by a participant-"The visual graph-based system has a learning curve and requires some learning costs in the beginning", one weakness of the system is that the system requires more effort than the other two systems to get familiar with it. The participants rated the system as the most hard-to-learn system.

Our study has the following contributions. First, our first contribution lies in the design of the experiment that is tailored to complex bibliographic information retrieval. To achieve this, we designed customized simulated task sets with varying task complexity. Second, we examined how form-, natural language-, and visual graph-based systems support users' bibliographic information needs. Strengths and weaknesses of the systems were examined from several perspectives. Third, the experimental design and results shown in this paper can serve as a useful guideline and benchmark for future studies. In the background questionnaire, 14 out of 20 participants stated that current bibliographic search systems are not powerful enough in terms of representing and answering complex bibliographic information need. It is clear that there is no single answer to address this limitation, and different approaches have different values as shown in the evaluation results.

ACKNOWLEDGMENTS

This project was made possible in part by the Institute of Museum and Library Services (Grant Award Number: RE-07-15-0060-15), for the project titled "Building an entity-based research framework to enhance digital services on knowledge discovery and delivery."

REFERENCES

Al-Maskari, A., & Sanderson, M. (2010). A review of factors influencing user satisfaction in information retrieval. Journal of the American Society for Information Science and Technology, 61(5), 859-868.

Al-Maskari, A., & Sanderson, M. (2011). The effect of user characteristics on search effectiveness in information retrieval. Information Processing and Management, 47(5), 719-729.

Borlund, P. (2003). The IIR evaluation model: A framework for evaluation of interactive information retrieval systems. Information Research-an International Electronic Journal, 8(3), 152.

Borlund, P. (2016). A study of the use of simulated work task situations in interactive information retrieval evaluations: A meta-evaluation. Journal of Documentation, 72(3), 394-413.

Borlund, P., & Ingwersen, P. (1997). The development of a method for the evaluation of interactive information retrieval systems. Journal of Documentation, 53(3), 225-250.

Borlund, P., & Schneider, J. (2010) Reconsideration of the simulated work task situation: A context instrument for evaluation of information retrieval interaction. Paper presented at the Third Information Interaction in Context Symposium (IIiX), 155-164.

Clemmensen, M. L., & Borlund, P. (2016). Order effect in interactive information retrieval evaluation: An empirical study. Journal of Documentation, 72(2), 194-213.

de Ribaupierre, H. (2014). Precise information retrieval in semantic scientific digital libraries (Doctoral dissertation). University of Geneva, Geneva, Stitzerland.

Hall, M. M., & Toms, E. (2013). Building a Common Framework for IIR Evaluation. Paper presented at the Forth International Conference of the Cross-Language Evaluation Forum for European Language, 17-28.

Hornbæk, K. (2006). Current practice in measuring usability: Challenges to usability studies and research. International Journal of Human - Computer Studies, 64(2), 79-102.

ISO 9241-11 (1998). Ergonomic Requirements of Office Work with Visual Display Terminals (VDTs): Part II: Guidance on usability. International Organization for Standardization

Käki, M., & Aula, A. (2008). Controlling the complexity in comparing search user interfaces via user studies. Information Processing and Management, 44(1), 82-91.

Kelly, D. (2009). Methods for evaluating interactive information retrieval systems with users. Foundations and Trends in Information Retrieval, 3(1—2), 1-224.

Kelly, D., Arguello, J., Edwards, A., & Wu, W. C. (2015). Development and evaluation of search tasks for IIR experiments using a cognitive complexity framework. Paper presented at the ACM SIGIR International Conference on the Theory of Information Retrieval (ICTIR), 101-110

Kelly, D., & Sugimoto, C. R. (2013). A systematic review of interactive information retrieval evaluation studies, 1967–2006. Journal of the American Society for Information Science and Technology, 64(4), 745-770.

Li, Y. (2009). Exploring the relationships between work task and search task in information search. Journal of the American Society for Information Science and Technology, 60(2), 275-291.

Li, Y., & Belkin, N. J. (2008). A faceted approach to conceptualizing tasks in information seeking. Information Processing and Management, 44(6), 1822-1837.

Li, Y., & Belkin, N. J. (2010). An exploration of the relationships between work task and interactive information search behavior. Journal of the American Society for Information Science and Technology, 61(9), 1771-1789.

Liu, J., Cole, M., Liu, C., Bierig, R., Gwizdka, J., Belkin, N., Zhang, J., & Zhang, X. (2010). Search behaviors in different task types. Paper presented at the Joint Conference on Digital Libraries (JCDL), 69-78.

Lund, A. M. (2011). Measuring usability with the USE questionnaire. Usability Interface, 8(2), 3-6.

Okhovati, M., Sharifpoor, E., Aazami, M., Zolala, F., & Hamzehzadeh, M. (2016). Novice and experienced users search performance and satisfaction with web of science and scopus. Journal of Librarianship and Information Science, 49(4), 359-367.

Renaud, G., & Azzopardi, L. (2012). SCAMP: A tool for conducting interactive information retrieval experiments. Paper presented at the Fourth Information Interaction in Context Symposium (IIiX), 286-289.

Salton, G. (1970). Evaluation problems in interactive information retrieval. Information Storage and Retrieval, 6(1), 29-44.

Smucker, M. D., & Jethani, C. P. (2010). Impact of retrieval precision on perceived difficulty and other user measures. Paper presented at the Fourth Symposium on Human-Computer Interaction and Information Retrieval (HCIR), 20-23.

Wei, X., Zhang, Y., & Gwizdka, J. (2014). YASFIIRE: Yet another system for IIR evaluation. Paper presented at the Fifth Information Interaction in Context Symposium (IIiX). 316-319.

Wildemuth, B., & Freund, L. (2012). Assigning search tasks designed to elicit exploratory search behaviors. Paper presented at the Sixth Symposium on Human-Computer Interaction and Information Retrieval (HCIR), 1-10.

Wildemuth, B., Freund, L., & Toms, E. (2014). Untangling search task complexity and difficulty in the context of interactive information retrieval studies. Journal of Documentation, 70(6), 1118-1140.

Zuccon, G., Leelanupab, T., Whiting, S., Yilmaz, E., Jose, J. M., & Azzopardi, L. (2013). Crowdsourcing interactions: Using crowdsourcing for evaluating interactive information retrieval systems. Information Retrieval, 16(2), 267-305.

Zhu, Y., & Yan, E. (2016). Searching bibliographic data using graphs: A visual graph query interface. Journal of Informetrics, 10(4), 1092-1107.

Zhu, Y., Yan, E., & Song, I.-Y. (2016). The use of a graph-based system to improve bibliographic information retrieval: System design, implementation, and evaluation. Journal of the Association for Information Science and Technology, 68(2), 480-490.

Zhu, Y., Yan, E., & Song, I.-Y. (2017). A natural language interface to a graph-based bibliographic information retrieval system. Data & Knowledge Engineering, 111, 73-89.

Investigating Youth Learning and Data: Contexts, Concepts, and Connections

Amelia Acker
University of Texas at Austin, School of Information, USA. aacker@ischool.utexas.edu

Dania Bilal
University of Tennessee, Knoxville, School of Information Sciences, USA. dania@utk.edu

Leanne Bowler
Pratt Institute, School of Information, USA. lbowler@pratt.edu

Patricia Garcia
University of Michigan, School of Information, USA. garciapg@umich.edu

Eric M. Meyers
University of British Columbia, School of Library, Archival and Information Studies, Canada. eric.meyers@ubc.ca

Yan Zhang
University of Texas at Austin, School of Information, USA. yanz@ischool.utexas.edu

ABSTRACT

This panel presents research that has explored young people in relation to data traces in digital, networked platforms supported and made accessible through Internet connected devices, applications, and platforms, asking the question: how might we help youth, as data subjects, gain a sophisticated understanding of data, including the processes involved in data creation, collection, curation, and aggregation with networked devices, platforms, and information services? Panelists will convene around the impact of these new technologies in youths' lives by presenting a range of empirical research on search engines, identity-based gaming, literacy groupware for children, and data literacy programming for youth in public libraries.

KEYWORDS

Data, youth, libraries, literacy

INTRODUCTION

The data ecosystem "brings surveillance into the intimate space of a child's life, tracking their gestation, sleep, play, talk, learning and much more" (Livingstone & Third, 2017) and configuring children and youth "as algorithmic assemblages" for the benefit of powerful others. (Lupton & Williamson, 2017). The effect of mass data collection on the development of young people and their digital subjectivity is as yet unknown, particularly in the areas of privacy, identity development, learning, self-efficacy, and individual freedom. Given the rapidly emerging data regimes within which today's young people grow up, the time is right to explore the unique data literacy needs of youth in terms of their critical and civic participation in a data driven society and how we might empower young people to be agents of change in relation to computational, data-driven infrastructures.

BACKGROUND AND MOTIVATIONS

Data literacy is a new construct in the fields of education and libraries, its meaning still open to negotiation. Although many have advocated for the education of a data literate population, there is little consensus on what such educational programs should look like, how it is defined, and what competencies for youth should be. Traditional approaches to data literacy emphasize quantitative reasoning by focusing on numeracy, statistics, and computer programming while a broader view interprets data literacy to be a new liberal art that includes humanistic reasoning skills. Situating data literacy in the context of personal data management gives young people a meaningful frame to apply as they work toward the development of analytic skills needed to create, collect, manage and curate data sets in their lives.

Though there is a robust literature about digital youth and information literacy skills, data literacy is under-theorized and continues to be focused on more formal learning contexts. There is little empirical research that examines teen data literacy, especially in the context of the public library. This panel brings together six "digital youth" scholars from the ASIS&T community to discuss their research agendas in areas related to youth, data and information in digital contexts. Each panelist will present current research that explores young people in relation to data traces in digital, networked platforms supported and made accessible through Internet connected devices, applications, and platforms, asking the question: *how might we help youth, as data subjects, gain a sophisticated understanding of data, including the processes involved in data creation, collection, curation, and aggregation with networked devices, platforms, and information services?* Panelists will convene around the impact of these new technologies in youths' lives by presenting a range of empirical research on search engines, identity-based gaming, literacy groupware for children, and data literacy programming for youth in public libraries.

PANEL FORMAT AND PRESENTATION ABSTRACTS

We have assembled a panel of researchers currently conducting research in the area of youth, data, and digital networked platforms and services. Amelia Acker will begin the session with a brief introduction to the data literacy problem space (10 minutes). She will then be followed by five panelists: Dania Bilal and Yan Zhang will discuss how young people interpret the snippets listed on the search engine results page (SERP) and what that suggests about their mental model of the inner workings of search (15 minutes); Eric Meyers explores an emerging type of literacy groupware system that quantifies early literacy practice, changing the way children and adults perceive the practice of reading (15 minutes); Patricia Garcia shares her experiences developing a culturally responsive data literacy program (15 minutes) and; Leanne Bowler and Amelia Acker conclude the panel presentation with a look at their findings vis à vis education for data literacy in the context of Teen Services at the public library (15 minutes). We will then open the floor to audience questions and comments (20 minutes). In total the session will run 90 minutes.

Youths' Mental Models of Search Engine Results Pages (SERPs)

Have you ever wondered what the ranked SERPs snippets mean to the youth? In a previous study, youth indicated that the top-ranked snippet that a search engine retrieves is the most popular, most reputable, most useful, most trustworthy, or most familiar (Gwizdka & Bilal, 2017). In this presentation, Bilal and Zhang will share the preliminary results of a survey-based study that explores youth's mental models of search engine SERPs, including but not limited to ranking order, structure of snippets, how snippets are generated, perceived importance in terms of providing answers to questions, and other features youth attach to SERPs snippets. Previous studies that examined people's mental models of the Web and search engines did not consider youth. The aim of this study is to explore youth's mental models of SERPs snippets to shed light on whether one-size-fits-all SERPs indeed mean the same for different user groups. These results augment our understanding of how youth conceptualize SERPs beyond what has been explored by researchers (e.g., Gossen, Höbel, & Nürnberger, 2014; Mlilo & Thatcher, 2011) and how such conceptualization differ from adults' mental models (e.g., Mlilo & Thatcher, 2011; Zhang, 2008). Practically, these results inform the design of increasingly more adaptive SERPs and innovative ways for teaching web information literacy.

Promoting Critical Data Literacy in Youth Tech Programs

Scholars have argued that studying the impact of digital technologies on youth requires more than a "screen-deep" analysis and have challenged us to examine the machinic and human practices embedded within networked platforms and services (Nakamura, 2014). In this presentation, Garcia will present preliminary findings from a multi-sited qualitative study on the interplay between critical data literacy and youth identity development. The presentation will include an overview of a culturally responsive computing program designed to encourage teens to think critically about 1) the forms of data collected through everyday online experiences, and 2) how the data is used to create an "algorithmic identity" that is classed, raced, and gendered (Cheney-Lippold, 2011; Noble, 2018). Drawing on data from a nine-month study, Garcia will discuss findings from an activity designed to promote positive self-concepts among girls (ages 13-16) through the deconstruction of an identity-based gaming platform. The findings presented will use participant observations and artifact analysis to illustrate how teaching youth to examine data practices can facilitate discussions about the impact of algorithms on personal identity formation, the "datafication" of daily activities, and the design of socio-technical systems.

Literacy as Data: The Quantified Child Reader

This presentation will discuss the data implications of mediatized reading through an educational platform we term children's literacy groupware. We define this emerging technology as cloud-based reading management systems that combine digital reading collections with behavior tracking and analysis, communication tools, and reader incentives. Children's literacy groupware extends the notion of a digital library for children (e.g., Druin, 2005) as they provide value-added tools for teaching, monitoring, evaluating, and encouraging young readers. The systems enable adult stakeholders (e.g., teachers, parents, caregivers) to track and manage the reading activities of one to dozens of children. Meyers will report on his research team's inquiry into two for-profit app-based systems that provide reading content and instruction for elementary age children in North America and throughout the world. This investigation is part of a larger conceptual and empirical study of the use of networked, digital information systems that document the daily activities of children. We argue that these systems are shifting children's practices in school and home environments, including reading, play, exploration, and socialization (Meyers, Nathan & Stepaniuk, 2017). Our overarching research question is: How do systems for managing engagement with digital texts frame (or reframe) reading practice--the what, where, when and how of reading, including behaviors, attitudes and dispositions toward reading? Literacy groupware generates a wealth of data about reading behavior that has the potential to radically change the way we teach and assess beginning readers. However, Meyers will also point out the pitfalls of "quantifying" the reading experience through dashboards and reading metrics, which may isolate and objectify the reader, decontextualizing reading practice through a "one size fits most" approach and shift the locus and perceived responsibility of reading instruction. Most importantly, we will outline the tensions among stakeholder uses and data awareness, such as the contradiction between reading as pleasure and reading as labour. The presentation will include several suggestions, generated through our content analysis and interviews with multiple stakeholders (children, parents, teachers), that will help develop future iterations of these systems, as well as propose alternative deployment strategies to help reconfigure networked reading practice.

Entry Points into Data at the Public Library

The public library needs data literacy models that address the everyday concerns of youth, particularly with respect to their digital traces, and which align with the humanistic, community-oriented goals, and unique pedagogy of this public institution. In much of the literature, data literacy is presented as a set of skills related to numeracy, statistics and computation (See for example, Gunther, 2007; van't Hooft et al, 2013; Fontichiaro & Oehrli, 2016). In terms of library-based approaches to data literacy, we must look to the world of academic libraries, where models of data literacy focus on the management and use of data as a product of scholarly research (Prado & Marzal, 2013; Carlson & Johnston, 2015, Shorish, 2015), and to the school library environment, which explores data skills primarily through the lens of statistics and visualization (Fontichiaro et al, 2017, Abilock et al, 2017). There is, however, a dearth of empirical models that situate data fluency within the context of Teen Services at the public library, even though programming that provides learning experiences with data is already occurring through digital media labs, makerspaces, and youth hackathons (Dankoski, 2018). We present here, as part of the *Exploring Data Worlds at the Public Library* project, a preliminary framework for supporting the development of data literacy at the public library - a method for opening a gateway toward data programs that are both meaningful and engaging to young people and at the same time, doable in the library context. It builds upon the authors' earlier work exploring data through the eyes of young people – what it is and how it configures in their everyday lives (Acker & Bowler, 2017; Bowler et al, 2017).

PANELISTS' BIOGRAPHIES

Dr. Amelia Acker is Assistant Professor of Information in the School of Information at the University of Texas at Austin. She holds a PhD and MLIS from University of California, Los Angeles where she was also an archivist. Dr. Acker studies the emergence and standardization of new information objects and data traces communication networks. Currently, she is researching data cultures, information infrastructures and digital preservation contexts that support long term cultural memory. Her current research program addresses emerging digital traces and mobile computing cultures that are shaped by new data collection practices amongst different kinds of users, designers, technologists, and institutions.

Dr. Dania Bilal is a Professor at the School of Information Sciences, the University of Tennessee, Knoxville. She obtained her PhD in Library and Information Studies from the Florida State University School of Library and Information Studies in 1988. Since her appointment to the faculty in August 1997, she has taught courses in human-computer interaction, web mining, research methods, information systems design and implementation, and information access and retrieval, among others. Her research is at the intersection of information behavior, information retrieval, and human-computer interaction with a focus on children. She has published work on children's use of web search engines, interaction with international digital libraries, conceptual structures, design of search engine interfaces, and compared their web information behaviors with the behaviors of adults.

Dr. Leanne Bowler is an Associate Professor at the Pratt Institute's School of Information in New York City. She received her PhD from McGill University and holds Master's degrees in Education as well as Library Science. Her research focuses on youth technology practices and how family, teachers, and out-of-school organizations like libraries support young people's competencies in socio-technical environments. She has expertise in the study and practice of participatory design with young people, which directly involves youth in the development of services and technologies that sup- port positive interactions with information and data. Additionally, Dr. Bowler researches how to support STEM learning in public libraries, most recently through a project exploring youth data literacy programs in library-based technology centers.

Dr. Patricia Garcia is an Assistant Professor at the University of Michigan, School of Information. She conducts sociocultural research on race, gender, and technology with a special interest in studying how the use of culturally responsive computing practices can increase girls' participation in STEM activities. She conducts interdisciplinary action research on race, gender and technology with a special interest in studying the role of information institutions in promoting equitable and culturally responsive STEM programming for girls of color. Her current work focuses on broadening participation in computer science by developing a low-resource model for teaching computational thinking skills in informal learning environments, such as libraries. She holds a PhD in information studies from the iSchool at UCLA.

Dr. Eric M. Meyers is an Associate Professor at the School of Library, Archival and Information Studies (SLAIS) at the University of British Columbia, where he teaches and conducts research on the information practices of young people in academic and everyday contexts. Dr. Meyers' research interests lie at the intersection of information science, the learning sciences, and new media studies, with a focus on collaborative information use and meaning making in social situations.

Dr. Yan Zhang is an associate professor in the School of Information at the University of Texas at Austin. She holds a Ph.D. in Information and Library Science from the University of North Carolina at Chapel Hill. Her research focuses on general consumers' information seeking behavior, particularly online health information search behavior using both search engines and social media, as well as users' mental models of search engines and information-rich web spaces.

REFERENCES

Abilock, D., Ballard, S.D., Bergson-Michelson, T., Colby, J., Fontichiaro, K., Hoelter, L., Joque, J., Oehrli, J.A., Seroff, J., Smith, S. and Steelberg, T. (Eds.). (2017). *Creating Data Literate Students*. Michigan Publishing, University of Michigan Library.

Acker, A. & Bowler, L. (2017). Youth data literacy: Teen perspectives on data created with social media and mobile device ownership. *Hawaii International Conference on System Sciences 2018* (HICCS). January 3-6, 2018.

Bowler, L., Acker, A., Jeng, W. & Chi. Y. (2017). "It lives all around us": Aspects of data literacy in teens' Lives. *80th ASIS&T Annual Meeting. Diversity of Engagement: Connecting People and Information in the Physical and Virtual Worlds.* October 27-November 1, 2017. Washington, D.C.

Carlson, J. & Johnston, L.R. (Eds). (2015). *Data Information Literacy: Librarians, Data, and the Education of a New Generation of Researchers.* (Purdue Information Literacy Handbooks). Ashland, OH: Purdue University Press.

Cheney-Lippold, J. (2011). A new algorithmic identity: Soft biopolitics and the modulation of control. *Theory, Culture & Society*, *28*(6), 164-181.

Dankowski, T. (2018). Engaging civic-minded teens: Data literacy fosters YA participation and innovation. *American Libraries.* March/April, pp. 38-41.

Druin, A. (2005). What children can teach us: Developing digital libraries for children with children. *The Library Quarterly,* 75 (1), 20-41.

Fontichiaro, K., Lennex, A., Hoff, T., Hovinga, K. & Oehrli, J.A. (Eds.). (2017). *Data Literacy in the Real World: Conversations & Case Studies.* Maize Books Michigan Publishing.

Fontichiaro, K. & Oehrli, J.A. (2016). Why data literacy matters. *Knowledge Quest*, 44(5) (May/June), 20-27.

Gossen, T., Höbel, J., & Nürnberger, A. (2014). A comparative study about children's and adults' perception of targeted Web search engines. *Proceedings of the SIGCHI Conference on Human Factors in Computing Systems* (pp. 1821–1824). New York, NY, USA: ACM. https://doi.org/10.1145/2556288.2557031

Gunter, G.A. (2007). Building student data literacy: An essential critical-thinking skill for the 21st century. Multimedia & Internet @ Schools, 14(3), 24-28.

Gwizdka, J., & Bilal, D. (2017). Analysis of children's queries and click behavior on ranked results and their thought processes in Google search. *Proceeding of CHIIR"17 of the 2017 Conference on Human Information Interaction and Retrieval* (pp.377-380). Oslo, Norway, March 7-11. Doi: >10.1145/3020165.3022157.

Livingstone, S., & Third, A. (2017). Children and young people's rights in the digital age: An emerging agenda. (2017): 657-670.

Lupton, D., & Williamson, B. (2017). The datafied child: The dataveillance of children and implications for their rights. *New Media & Society*, *19*(5), 780-794.

Meyers, E. M., Nathan, L. P., and Stepaniuk, C. (2017). Children in the cloud: Literacy groupware and the practice of reading. *First Monday, 22* (2). http://firstmonday.org/article/view/6844/5845. doi: http://dx.doi.org/10.5210/fm.v22i2.6844

Mlilo, S. & Thatcher, A. (2011). Mental Models: Have users' mental models of Web search engines improved in the last ten years? *International Conference on Engineering Psychology and Cognitive Ergonomics EPCE 2011* (pp. 243-253). Orlando, FL, USA, July 9-14.

Nakamura, L. (2014). Indigenous circuits: Navajo women and the racialization of early electronic manufacture. *American Quarterly*, *66*(4), 919-941.

Noble, S. U. (2018). *Algorithms of Oppression: How Search Engines Reinforce Racism*. NYU Press.

Prado, J.C. & Marzal, M.A. (2013). Incorporating Data Literacy into Information Literacy Competencies and Contents. *Libri*, 63 (2), 123-135.

Shorish, Y. (2015). Data information literacy and undergraduates: A critical competency. College and Undergraduate Libraries, 22(1), 97-106.

Van't Hooft, M., Vahey, P., Swan, K. Kratcoski, D. C. & Rafanan, K. (2012). A cross-curricular approach to the development of data literacy in the middle grades: The Thinking with Data project. Middle Grades Research Journal, 7(3) 19-33.

Zhang, Y. (2008). Undergraduate students' mental models of the Web as an information retrieval system. *Journal of the American Society for Information Science and Technology*, 59(13), 2087-2098.

Rules of the Game: An Interactive Panel Discussion about How Institutions Shape Information

Grant A. Allard, MBA
Clemson University, USA, gallard@clemson.edu

Steven B. Sawyer, PhD
Syracuse University, USA, ssawyer@syr.edu

ABSTRACT

We focus on the roles that institutions play relative to information behavior. Our working definition of institution is the formal and informal constraints that form the basis for exchange, relationships, and decision-making. We know that institutions play significant roles in the creation, management, and uses of information. And, scholars have long recognized that institutions have both direct and indirect impacts on the sustainability and ethical value of information. What is less clear are the ways in which institutions and people's information behaviors are mutually-constituted. The goal of this panel is to highlight particular opportunities for expanding the current and modest level of attention to studying the roles of human institutions relative to information. To do so, this panel will involve the audience in a lively conversation about how information science views the role of institutions in information behavior. It includes a participatory design structured activity that will engage the audience in identifying how existing threads of research are making contributions and key areas of further inquiry. The panel will begin with dialogue sharing insights of scholars and practitioners who are interested in data governance, information behavior, organization of information, and knowledge management. Then the panel will engage the audience in an interactive activity that explores emerging research streams and questions.

KEYWORDS

Data Management, instituions, information behavior, sustainability, cyberinfrastructure, ethics

INTRODUCTION

This panel builds on the issues explored at ASIS&T 2017 in the panel "Organizational and Institutional Work in Data Infrastructures" that showcased scholars in our discipline who are working to address challenges that are institutional in nature focusing specifically on scientific cyberinfrastructure projects. Two common themes that the panelists and audience identified are sustainability and ethics. From a sustainability perspective, cyberinfrastructure organizations face the challenge of meeting current needs without compromising their ability to meet future needs. From an ethical perspective, cyberinfrastructure organizations allocate goods and services, the process of which involves making decisions that affect human well-being.

The foundation of information science is that information is an object that is created, managed, and used by people (Buckland, 1991). Information scholars are using theories and methodologies from a range of related disciplines and fields to include communications, computing, linguistics, public policy, economics, management, and other social sciences to understand why and how people make decisions about and based-on information. There are four approaches that are commonly used to study information. First, we study the technological challenges related to information. Second, we study the interfaces that allow human beings to interact with information. Third, we study how people behave when creating, managing, or using information. Lastly, we examine how information is organized. In all four approaches, there are rules, norms and cognitive structures that constrain and enable information creation, sharing, use and storage. These rules, norms and cognitive structures form the basis of institutions – always present, but not always made visible in our scholarship.

Our conception of institutions builds on North's (1990) notion that institutions are the formal and informal rules that provide the structure for exchange. Formal constraints include laws, rights, and contracts, while informal constraints include norms, mores, and morals. Exchange means the act of trading one good or service for another. In the context of information, institutions may shape decisions of how people choose to build and sustain cyberinfrastructure, the required capabilities for information storage and retrieval technologies, as well as decisions about data governance. Policy scholars and economists have developed an understanding of institutions with the goal of explaining how the "rules-of-the-game" affect the way people behave when exchanging goods and services. Institutions such as laws, norms, mores, and morals allow people to correct for negative externalities and to provide positive external effects by correcting for cost distortions. Information science scholars are now addressing many of these issues and are developing a disciplinary language and network for doing so.

Ethics and sustainability are examples of constraints that shape exchange and behavior—or institutions. Identifying ethics and sustainability as institutions moves the study of these concepts from a normative to a positive frame. Now, our discipline faces the challenge of integrating insights from across our subfields to create a complete picture of the institutional structure of information.

This panel will challenge the audience to addresses institutions in a different way than has commonly been used in most information science research by bringing together a priori and empirical approaches from information science, management, and public policy to inspire conversation about the role of institutions in information. Presenters will each give a lens into their work on this topic and address key questions such as:

- What are empirical examples of how institutions shape information behavior?
- Why is the study of institutions in information different from existing scholarship of information behavior and existing scholarship in other disciplines?
- What theoretical frameworks from information science or other disciplines are useful for studying the institutions in information?
- What are some of the most pressing questions for scholars focusing on the institutions of information?

PANEL PRESENTATIONS

Our panelists represent a variety of subfields and each give a lens into the institutional structure of information. Below we provide the title, biography, and abstract of the panelists' presentations. Below, we provide each presentation's name, title, authors, and abstract. Each presentation will have one or two presenters.

Presentation 1: Private Provision of Cyberinfrastructure

Steven B. Sawyer, PhD is a Professor and Director of Doctoral Programs at the iSchool of Syracuse University. Sawyer studies the design, development, deployment and uses of information technologies and new forms of information-sharing systems. He pursues this work in the social informatics tradition, focusing on social practices, collective action, the roles and functions of the technologies and systems of information sharing, and the institutional contexts in which these happen

Sarika Sharma, MLIS is a fourth year PhD student at Syracuse University. Sharma is interested in large-scale, long-term technology investments in the form of information infrastructures within organizations. She is currently investigating the coordination and governance of infrastructure efforts that aim to preserve, store, and provide access to data within scientific communities. Her dissertation work is supported by the NSF-CHS. Sharma is also a research assistant on the NSF-VOSS grant with Co-PI's: Dr. Steve Sawyer and Dr. Carsten Osterlund. Using the sociomateriality lens, the research aims to understand how academic researchers use documents in their distributed, virtual collaborations.

Abstract: Sawyer and Sharma share preliminary findings about empirical research on how human institutions shape the behavior of universities to independently create their own cyberinfrastructures to support scientific data needs and computational tools. Sawyer and Sharma identify that scholars express a need for computational and data resources to support their scientific work. These expressions turn into grant seeking behaviors to find an initial pool of funding for infrastructure. Universities display the behavior of paying the full cost over time to provide the cyberinfrastructure and allow other universities and researchers to use their infrastructure without paying. This phenomenon shows that, for some cyberinfrastructure projects, universities bear the cost of providing a shared resource based on the demands of their researchers and are willing to allow other researchers and universities to benefit from the good as well without requiring those users who are benefitting to pay. In other cases, cyberinfrastructure use is limited to the organization's members- concentrating the resource to a small group of scholars at the university. Either way investments in cyberinfrastructure serve as a crucial input to knowledge creation creating a conversation that ties together macro-level institutional analysis and micro-behaviors of scholars. Sawyer and Sharma connect their empirical research to a discussion of how the human institutions design and set the priorities for shared digital science resources in this presentation.

Presentation 2: "The First Dataset is Free": Social Science Data Archives as Agents of Disciplinary Change

Kalpana Shankar, PhD is Professor of Information and Communication Studies at University College Dublin's School of Information and Communication Studies (Ireland). Her research examines how data practices reflect and reify the larger society, culture, and institutions where they are enacted. Her current research projects focus on the sustainability and longevity of data archives and peer review of grants in Irish funding.

Kristin R. Eschenfelder, PhD is a Professor at the School of Library and Information Studies at the University of Wisconsin-Madison. Her research interests focus on access and use regimes – or the complex, multi-level networks of laws, customs, technologies and expectations that shape what information we can access in our daily lives and how we can make of it.

Abstract: Social Science Data Archives (SSDAs) enjoy a (relatively) long and successful history of archiving quantitative social science data, such as those derived from longitudinal studies, opinion polls, surveys/questionnaires, and census files. Rather than being passive repositories of machine-readable data that researchers just "used", a close look at the history of

SSDA suggests that these institutions created a culture of data sharing, use, and advocacy as a deliberate part of their strategies to become and stay relevant to social science research. In turn, the changing nature of the social sciences and their role in higher education and society profoundly influenced the institutional development of SSDA in the USA and elsewhere. Using a historical case study approach with documents and interviews drawn from several of the oldest extant SSDAs, we explore this mutual shaping as a story of how "data work" (acquisition, preservation, dissemination), data as objects of study, and institutional practices enact research disciplines, and implications for the agency of data and data institutions.

Presentation 3: Institutional Dimensions of Data Curation: Astronomy, Research Libraries, and Multiple Approaches to Curation

Peter T. Darch, PhD is an Assistant Professor in the School of Information Sciences at the University of Illinois at Urbana-Champaign. Prior to joining the iSchool at Illinois, Darch worked as a postdoctoral researcher in the UCLA Department of Information Studies, with which he continues to collaborate on studies of the building, running, and effects of information infrastructures that support scientific collaboration. His dissertation for the DPhil in Computer Science from the University of Oxford (2012) addressed how scientists and software engineers in online citizen science projects manage members of the public to process and generate large datasets.

Ashley Sands, PhD is a recently-graduated doctoral student in Information Studies at UCLA. Prior to joining UCLA, she had nearly a decade of experience working with scientific data in archaeology. Sands' dissertation research examined astronomy data management practices to reveal the expertise and infrastructure most appropriate for maximizing the utility of scientific data. Research methods included semi-structured interviews, participant observation, and document analysis. Ashley's research interests include scholarly communication, scientific data practices, and data management workforces.

Christine L. Borgman, PhD is Professor and Presidential Chair in Information Studies at UCLA. Prof. Borgman is author of more than 200 publications in information studies, computer science, and communication. She conducts data practices research with funding from the National Science Foundation, Sloan Foundation, and Microsoft Research. She is a member of the Board of Directors of the Electronic Privacy Information Center, a Fellow of the American Association for the Advancement of Science, and previously served on the U.S. National Academies' Board on Research Data and Information and the U.S. National CODATA.

Sharon Traweek, PhD is Associate Professor of Gender Studies and History at UCLA. She is the author of *Beamtimes and Lifetimes: The World of High Energy Physicists* (Harvard, 1988), which is used in courses worldwide as an exemplar of how to conduct ethnographic research on knowledge-making practices among scientists. Her many years of studying data practices in high-energy physics is essential expertise for studies of astronomy and astrophysics. She is currently collaborating on a project collecting oral histories of the careers of women in astronomy.

Milena Golshan, MLIS is the UCLA Center for Knowledge Infrastructures' Data Scientist and Project Manager. She organizes and mines the trove of data, which the UCLA Center's teams have collected since 2002, and facilitates the process of exploiting these resources for longitudinal and comparative research. Milena holds MLIS degrees from UCLA and Sofia University St. Kliment Ohridski in Bulgaria. She is especially interested in open data, digital archiving and data analysis, management and curation. Milena's experience includes academic research support, qualitative data analysis, content management, information architecture, and electronic networking for environmental protection.

Abstract: Many stakeholders, including professional associations and funding agencies, regard Research Data Services (RDS) in university libraries as an attractive solution to the problem of long-term curation of research datasets. However, institutional analyses reveal the difficulties of implementing RDS consistently across libraries. This presentation explores how institutional factors influence RDS development, including how libraries interpret and enact activities for dataset curation. Institutional differences between libraries, in turn, have profound implications for the datasets themselves, including how their boundaries are defined and possibilities for their access and use. We present a qualitative case study of how two research libraries approached the task of curating a large-scale dataset produced by the Sloan Digital Sky Survey (SDSS), a major astronomy project. As its first two phases (SDSS-I/II) drew to a close, SDSS partnered with two libraries at large US research universities to sustain long-term access to SDSS-I/II data. Although the task facing each library was ostensibly the same, the two libraries diverged significantly in their approaches. They set different boundaries for the dataset, with the dataset's content varying between the libraries. Each library also developed different associated services to support data access and use. The libraries' divergent approaches afforded and constrained differing possibilities for data use, including who could access the data and for what purposes the data could be used.

Presentation 4: The Impact of Human Institutions on Information Behavior in Technology Transfer: Preliminary Findings

Grant A. Allard, MBA* is a doctoral student in Policy Studies at Clemson University and is developing a research agenda that investigates how governments, firms, universities, and civil society use information to guide their decisions for innovation. Allard's research agenda develops a deeper understanding of how institutional frameworks influence the behavior of universities, governments, and firms. Allard pursues four lenses of this problem: information behavior in technology transfer, the organization of technology transfer, tand the political economy of technology transfer.

Abstract: The purpose of this presentation is to identify a research agenda in Information Science for understanding the institutional barriers that shape the way stakeholders in technology transfer create, manage, and share information. Technology transfer is the process of translating scientific knowledge into commercial applications. Technology transfer is topic that has not been widely addressed by information scholarship since the late 1990s and no other information scholars have developed an empirical analysis of technology transfer stakeholders' information behaviour. This analysis builds on existing technology transfer literature such as Siegel and colleagues (2007), Chapple and colleagues (2005), and Link and colleagues (2007). We analyse data collected through a Delphi study of stakeholders to identify relevant theoretical frameworks in Information Science to provide insights into information behaviour. My presentation makes two contributions to information scholarship. First, I report empirical data on the information behaviour of stakeholders that have yet to be studied by the broader information community. Second, my analysis sheds light on a gap in information science theory regarding the institutions of information. I propose frontiers for further research by information scholars to fill this gap through developing theory, research, and practice relating to human institutions of information.

REFERENCES

Buckland, M. K. (1991). Information as Thing. *Journal of the American Society for Information Science (1986-1998); New York*, *42*(5), 351–360. Retrieved from https://search-proquest-com.libproxy.clemson.edu/docview/216897238/abstract/A721F9A6C487466FPQ/1

North, D. (1990). *Institutions, Institutional Change and Economic Performance* (Kindle Edition). Cambridge University Press.

81st Annual Meeting of the Association for Information Science & Technology | Vancouver, Canada | 10 – 14 November 2018

Politicians & the Public: The Analysis of Political Communication in Social Media

Juan Pablo Alperin
Simon Fraser University, Canada. juan@alperin.ca

Catherine Dumas
University at Albany, USA. cdumas@albany.edu

Amir Karami
University of South Carolina, USA. karami@mailbox.sc.edu

David Moscrop
Simon Fraser University, Canada. david.moscrop@gmail.com

Vivek Singh
Rutgers University, USA. vs451@comminfo.rutgers.edu

Hassan Zamir
Dominican University, USA. mzamir@dom.edu

Aylin Ilhan
Heinrich Heine University Düsseldorf, Germany. aylin.ilhan@hhu.de

Isabelle Dorsch
Heinrich Heine University Düsseldorf, Germany. isabelle.dorsch@hhu.de

ABSTRACT

Nowadays, social media has a pivotal role in political communication. Politicians, parties, and the public engage in social networks like Twitter or Facebook. This panel focuses on election campaigns and policy-making process in social media. How do politicians use social media during elections? How can we identify the public opinion of voters through the application of text-mining in social media? The US presidential election in 2016, possess big discussions and critics about the general social media usage in the context of election campaigns. Considering the case of Cambridge Analytica, information leakage, privacy issues, and trust also play an essential role as well. In respect of truthfulness, how can we encourage more robust and wide-reaching sharing of trustworthy material, such as scholarly research? Besides politicians, the public comes more and more into the focus as a political stakeholder in social media. How does the public engage in policy-making? Electronic-petitioning serves as a medium to mobilize support and interest of the public. The panel provides the possibility for speaker and participants to exchange both, information as well as methodological approaches of political communication in social media.

KEYWORDS

E-petitioning, opinion mining, privacy challenges, political elections, social media

INTRODUCTION

For politics, social media became a pervasive communication tool connecting politicians, parties, and the public. It has gained more and more importance within the last years, especially in respect to election campaigns. For example, the use of Twitter during election campaigns and mediated campaign events as well as social media impact on scientific research in various fields (Jungher, 2016). With the American election in 2016 leading the way, significant discussions and critics about social media usage in context of the election campaigns arose in the media until today, including aspects like politician's social media use, public and company engagement in social media and also the collection of political social media data. Likewise, during the 2016 US presidential elections, issues on big data analyses emerged. Already Alistair Croll stated for the elections in 2012:

"After Eisenhower, you couldn't win an election without radio. After JFK, you couldn't win an election without television. After Obama, you couldn't win an election without social networking. I predict that in 2012, you won't be able to win an election without big data. (Alistair Croll, founder of Bitcurrent)," (González, 2017, p. 10).

Nowadays, it seems his prediction has come true. Cambridge Analytica, a big data analysis company specialized in political data-driven campaigns and commercial data-driven marketing works with big data from social media like Facebook. The case of Cambridge Analytica got a huge medial resonance within the last months and in the context of information leakage, privacy issues, trust of big data in social media, it is critically discussed (e.g. Tufekci, 2018). Thereby, information leakage is defined as "phenomena where explicit information provided to a third party can be used to derive implicit and previously hidden information about an entity," (Nouh et al., 2014, p. 353).

In the past, policy-making research has focused mostly on the influence of political leaders, interest groups, and the mass media; "the public" was absent from this research (Muhlberger, Stromer-Galley, & Webb, 2011). However, nowadays this has changed. Public and its policy-making engagement; e.g. electronic-petitioning (Yasseri, Hale, & Margetts, 2018); and political opinion (Anstead & O'Loughlin, 2015) are also objects of investigation.

This panel comprises social media research addressing political elections and policy-making engagement as well as the analysis of such social media data. In doing so, it provides an ideal opportunity for speakers and participants to exchange not only information but rather methodological approaches. Thereby, it addresses the topic from different viewpoints, namely:

- Social media usage of politicians during elections
- Public opinion data tracking and application of text-mining in social media
- Privacy challenges of big data (according to the case of Cambridge Analytica)
- Sharing behavior of trustworthy material in order to inform about political decisions
- Electronic-petitioning for political decisions

Such diverse views enable a discussion taking into account politicians and parties as well as the public involved in political social media communication.

PANEL STRUCTURE

The panel is structured as follows. First, the chair will introduce the panel speakers and give a short overview of the discussed topics, including the main concerns and definitions as well as the outcomes of an informetric analysis on the topic. Following this, each panelist will answer the main question regarding her or his research. The addressed questions concern social media in the context of politicians and the public. The panel will be concluded with a discussion forum. The panel should last 1.5 hours.

SPEAKER OVERVIEW

Aylin Ilhan and Isabelle Dorsch will introduce the speakers, present a short informetric analysis, and moderate the panel.

Isabelle Dorsch is research associate and PhD candidate at the Department of Information Science, Heinrich Heine University Düsseldorf (Germany). She is a lecturer in social media and knowledge representation as well as a mentor for student research projects. Besides social media (with a special focus on user behavior on Instagram), her research interests include, but are not limited to informetrics (especially scientometrics).

Aylin Ilhan is research associate and PhD candidate at the Department of Information Science, Heinrich Heine University Düsseldorf (Germany). She is a lecturer in social media, scientific writing as well as a mentor for student research projects. Her research interests include, but are not limited to, social media (user behavior), activity trackers (e.g., acceptance, impact, motivation, information and user behavior) and smart cities.

Hassan Zamir on how political elites use, interact and share information on Twitter during recent presidential elections around the world?

Social media plays a vital role in political information dissemination during national election. With its success in the 2008 Obama Presidential election campaign strategy, political elites across the globe strongly use social media like Twitter in recent national election. Rapid exposure to voters, digression of traditional broadcasting and print media etc. contribute profoundly why politicians use Twitter and other social media. Due to the emergence of new media it is interesting to identify how politicians use Twitter during election years as an online platform for conveying political information. Twitter use for political communication has become global practice. However, further investigations are required to understand politicians' Twitter use behavior. This study aims to map politicians' Twitter use patterns, understand their level of interactions, and types of contents shared. With a comparative lens, it discusses how politicians particularly from the US, Mexico, Russia, France, and Iran use, interact, share information on Twitter during recent presidential elections.

Dr. Hassan Zamir is a lecturer at the School of Information Studies at the Dominican University (USA). He teaches in the areas of information technology, data science, informatics, and big data. His research interests revolve around social media analytics, big data, and text mining. He plays active leadership roles at the Dominican University and in various professional organizations including the Association for Information Science and Technology (ASIS&T) and the Association for Library and Information Science Education (ALISE).

Amir Karami on social media and opinion mining in elections – How to track public opinion in social media?

Opinion polls and surveys have played an important role in elections. Different methods, including face-to-face interviews, phone interviews, and surveys sent by mail or email or available online have been used to gather and learn about people's thoughts about main issues. Among different technologies, social media plays the role of a big focus group in an election cycle. Unlike traditional surveys, collecting and analyzing social media data is a cost-effective way to survey a large number of participants in a short period of time. However, analyzing a large amount of social media data is a complicated task that needs computational methods. The proposed topic discusses the application of text mining methods for mining social media in elections.

Amir Karami is an Assistant Professor in the iSchool of the College of Information and Communications at the University of South Carolina. His research interests are computational social science and and medical/health informatics. He is currently working on developing text-mining techniques and utilizing them for medical, health, and social science. Previously, he was a Data Science Consultant at Washington DC area.

Vivek Singh on the newer privacy research challenges in surveillance with social "Big Data".

Recent uproar regarding Cambridge Analytica's use of social media data to influence US elections underscore two privacy related issues.

1. Privacy of your friends' data: While the app in question was installed by 270K users, it had access to the data from 50M users. This is because each user installing the app inadvertently gave access to their friends' data. I will present results from an experiment making people aware of this "social information leakage" and their response.
2. De-anonymization of individuals in large streams of social data: Our behaviors are inherently unique and even after the removal of personally identifiable information (e.g. name, address, social security number) one's data can be connected back to them. In a Science article, my colleagues and I have reported that an individual whose data is part of a large corpus (e.g. millions of users), may be de-anonymized quite simply with access to just four external data points.

Vivek Singh is an Assistant Professor at Rutgers University and a Visiting Professor at the MIT Media Lab. His work on privacy has been published in leading scientific venues (Science, Proceedings of the IEEE) and has received significant media coverage (BBC, New York Times, Wall Street Journal).

David Moscrop and Juan Pablo Alperin on why do pundits share scholarly research on social media—and why should we care?

The arrival of the internet was expected to initiate an era of information democratization; as communication technology proliferated, cyber optimists argued it would lower barriers to political participation. Decades later, the internet and social media are pervasive but the egalitarian and democratizing potentials of these technologies haven't been fully realized—in some ways, they've been co-opted for purposes that run counter to these goals, with some digital media practices making it more difficult for citizens to find trustworthy information. This raises questions about how we can encourage more robust and wide-reaching sharing of trustworthy material, such as scholarly research. We investigate how media personalities use research to inform the public sphere so that we can better understand how reliable knowledge can inform our political decisions.

Dr. David Moscrop is a postdoctoral fellow with the Scholarly Communications Lab at Simon Fraser University, specializing in democracy and decision making. He's also a writer and political commentator.

Dr. Juan Pablo Alperin is a Director of the Scholarly Communications Lab and an Assistant Professor in Publishing at Simon Fraser University. He uses a combination of computational techniques and innovative methods to investigate how knowledge is produced, disseminated, and used.

Catherine Dumas on electronic petitioning and social media: online collective action or "slacktivism"?

Events happen in the public sphere that trigger attention to policy issues. New Information Technologies offer a great deal of opportunity for the public to participate. E-petitioning systems have the potential to position the public as active participants in the policy-making process by allowing them to initiate policy proposals on issues of interest to them. Further, using links to Twitter and Facebook, these systems provide users with the technical capabilities to mobilize support from their social networks, or from the public at large, for or against particular policy proposals. Do these new forms of online or virtual participation constitute a new form of collective action or are they simply acts of "slacktivism" which debates the value of online participation?

Catherine Dumas is a PhD Candidate in Information Science at the University at Albany, State University of New York. Her research is motivated by data generated by platforms potentially used for online collective action or digital activism. Using data mining techniques and online collective action theories her work is exploring the impact of new information communication technologies (ICTs) on the phenomenon of online collective action.

ACKNOWLEDGMENTS

The panel is organized by the officers of the Special Interest Group Social Media (Aylin Ilhan, Isabelle Dorsch, Philippe Mongeon, Nic DePaula, Kaja Fietkiewicz, and Wasim Ahmed). The SIG SM thanks all speakers for their effort.

REFERENCES

Anstead, N., & O'Loughlin, B. (2015), Social Media Analysis and Public Opinion: The 2010 UK General Election. *Journal of Computer-Mediated Communication*, *20*(2), 204– 220. https://doi.org/10.1111/jcc4.12102

González, R. J. (2017). Hacking the Citizenry? Personality Profiling, 'Big Data' and the Election of Donald Trump. *Anthropology Today, 33*(3), 9–12. https://doi.org/10.1111/1467-8322.12348

Muhlberger, P., Stromer-Galley, J., & Webb, N. (2011). Public Policy and Obstacles to the Virtual Agora: Insights from the Deliberative E-Rulemaking Project. *Information Polity, 16*(3),197–214. https://doi.org/10.3233/IP-2011-0235

Nouh, M., Almaatouq, A., Alabdulkareem, A., Singh, V. K., Shmueli, E., Alsaleh, M., Alarifi A., Alfaris A., & Pentland, A. S. (2014). Social Information Leakage: Effects of Awareness and Peer Pressure on User Behavior. In T. Tryfonas, & I. Askoxylakis (Eds.), *Human Aspects of Information Security, Privacy, and Trust* (pp. 352–360). HAS 2014. Lecture Notes in Computer Science, Vol 8533. Springer, Cham. https://doi.org/10.1007/978-3-319-07620-1_31

Jungherr, A. (2016). Twitter Use in Election Campaigns: A Systematic Literature Review. *Journal of Information Technology and Politics, 13*(1), 72–91. https://doi.org/10.1080/19331681.2015.1132401

Tufekci, Z. (2018). *Facebook's Surveillance Machine*. Retrieved from https://www.nytimes.com/2018/03/19/opinion/facebook-cambridge-analytica.html

Yasseri, T., Hale, S. A., & Margetts, H. Z. (2017). Rapid Rise and Decay in Petition Signing. *EPJ Data Science, 6*(20), 1–13. https://doi.org/10.1140/epjds/s13688-017-0116-6

ALISE@ASIS&T: Building an LIS Research-Teaching Nexus

Stephen Bajjaly
Wayne State University, USA, bajjaly@wayne.edu

Heidi Julien
University at Buffalo - SUNY, USA, heidijul@buffalo.edu

Rong Tang
Simmons College, USA, rong.tang@simmons.edu

Dietmar Wolfram
University of Wisconsin – Milwaukee, USA, dwolfram@uwm.edu

ABSTRACT

This panel continues an interactive discussion begun at the ALISE 2018 conference. Designed primarily to benefit new tenure track faculty, doctoral students, and academic librarians, the session looks to attract attendees seeking advice and those with expertise to share. Using the World Café Discussion format, the goals for the session are to develop further a conceptual framework and identify critical success factors for bridging teaching and research. Discussion themes will be the same as the ALISE special session with sub-points informed by literature and by the discussion from ALISE 2018 conference: 1) How can research inform teaching? 2) How can teaching inform research? 3) What strategies can be applied in bridging teaching and research? The panelists facilitating the discussion are ALISE board members who are also active members of ASIS&T and the iSchools Organization.

KEYWORDS

Research-teaching nexus, teaching informed research, research informed teaching, bridging teaching and research.

INTRODUCTION

The literature on the relationship between teaching and research includes advice for faculty as well as research on the realization of that relationship. Over 28 years ago, Boyer (1990) cited Aristotle: "Teaching is the highest form of understanding," and proposed that the work of a faculty member in higher education involves four dimensions of scholarship: Discovery, Integration, Application, and Teaching. The Teagle Working Group (2007) published a White Paper arguing for the value of enhancing the teaching-research nexus to benefit individual undergraduate learners. The assumption made is that scholarship and teaching are mutually sustaining and in partnership work to promote student learning as well as positive outcomes for faculty. Students benefit from faculty who are engaged in scholarship and in continuous learning and networking with scholarly colleagues, because faculty bring that fresh knowledge to the classroom. Scholarly engagement by faculty also models the intellectual commitment, creativity, deep learning, and critical thinking which are desirable learning outcomes for students. Malcom (2014) provides an overview of the literature on the teaching-research relationship, demonstrating that there is a lack of consensus on the nature and consequences of that relationship.

In 2005, Healey proposed a model of research-teaching nexus that features four quadrants containing different strategies for linking research, teaching, and learning. The strategies vary according to the extent to which they are teacher-focused and students are treated as the audience, or student-focused and students are treated as participants. Healey's model focuses mainly on learners' perspectives, instead of specifically addressing how a faculty member may effectively use their research to support teaching and use their teaching to support their research endeavor. In a later report, Jenkins, Healey, & Zetter (2007) asserted that "the 'teaching-research nexus' is central to higher education; student intellectual development and staff identity can and should be developed by departments focusing on the 'nexus'; and, effective teaching research links are not automatic and have to be constructed" (p.2). In their report on case studies from small universities in Australia, Boyd and his colleagues (2010) adopted the faculty perspective, outlining five dimensions in the teaching-research nexus: (1) Learning through research, (2) Research-led teaching, (3) Researching teaching, (4) Teaching informed research, and (5) Learning how to do research. The report includes five case studies illustrating how faculty link teaching and research through various dimensions.

Robertson (2007) discusses research which points to disciplinary differences in the ways that academics think about knowledge, which affects their experience of the teaching-research nexus. Humanists tend to experience a more integrated teaching/research academic experience, while scientists tend to see a weaker relationship; Social scientists fall in between those two points. Grant and Wakelin (2009) conducted an interview study with faculty members and suggest that respondents believe that teaching is informed by the process and products of research, but that research was not particularly informed by teaching. Douglas (2013) reports the results of an interview study with social scientists that provides advice for scholars who wish to improve the teaching-research nexus: "teach as part of your research activity; use your research when planning lectures; be a flexible researcher and adapt your research interests to available opportunities; proactively promote yourself and your research; and engage in research as a collective activity" (p. 377). Geschwind and Broström (2015) report that despite attempts at Swedish universities to strengthen the relationship between teaching and research, in practice faculty tend to focus more heavily on either research or teaching, rather than balancing or integrating the two.

The literature, however, provides examples of successful attempts to integrate teaching and research. Little et al. (2008) show how a 'living case study' approach to learning in the field of marketing can enhance the integration of teaching and research, and lead to theory development. Cassanovas-Rubio et al. (2016) provide an example in the field of construction engineering of how teaching can inform research. In summary (p. 105):

- "Teachers can gain deeper understanding of a subject by teaching it, facilitating research advances in that subject.
- Teaching encourages a wider intellectual context for researchers who are highly specialized.
- Students can provide feedback on research analysis, helping to identify flaws.
- A 'research-based' student learning activity can produce new research materials.
- Student projects can help to test the analytical frameworks that academic staff are developing or provide the beginnings of comparative studies.
- New students are a stimulating form of pressure that can provide reassurance and motivation."

In the case study presented, students acted as gatherers of research data, which benefited both the students and the teaching faculty.

Structural issues clearly play a role in how teaching and research are integrated. Taylor (2007) offers a model for institutional management of the teaching research nexus that incorporates institutional ideology, environmental factors, ideological factors, and management style working together to influence the relationship between teaching and research in universities. In a second paper, Taylor (2008) argues that the teaching research relationship is affected by a range of institutional factors, including structural and political context, and discipline. Brew (2010) argues that structural changes are needed in universities to give faculty sufficient independence in their teaching to encourage the integration of research, and to design curricula that facilitate that integration, such as problem-based learning. Horta et al. (2012) summarize the structural tensions that challenge development of a close relationship between teaching and research (primarily increasing expectations for research output), but their quantitative analysis of national U.S. data demonstrates that research productivity can be enhanced through teaching, particularly at the graduate level, and especially when curricula are inquiry-based.

This review demonstrates that there is a robust literature focusing on the research-teaching nexus. However, there has been a dearth of literature focused on LIS. The panel will provide an opportunity for participants to build on that foundation and learn from the panelists and one another.

PANEL FORMAT

Panel participants sit at four tables. Each table has an assigned theme and a set of questions to discuss. Each table will identify a designated note taker who will not move to other tables when everyone else in that table moves. Each table spends 15 minutes discussing their questions, then participants are asked to move to a different table for another 15-minute discussion of questions assigned to that table. Then all tables discuss the final theme for 15 minutes. The remainder of the session will be a group report and final summary.

THEMES

Table 1 Theme: Using research to inform teaching
1.1. What research ideas, activities, or completed studies have you shared with your students in your courses?
1.2. What research ideas, activities, or completed studies have you shared with your students outside the course for their learning purposes?
1.3. Have you developed a course or designed course activities based on what you learned from your research studies? If so, please share your examples.

Table 2 Theme: Using research to inform teaching
2.1. When you share your research ideas, activities, or completed studies with your students, do you typically share how you develop your problem statement, research questions, research design, or results?
2. 2. In using research to inform teaching, do you distinguish among various types of research (e.g., practical and applied, conceptual/theoretical, history, or bibliometrics)?
2.3. How has your research contributed to sustainable areas of teaching for the information professions and information science?

Table 3 Theme: Using teaching to inform research
3.1. How does what you teach inspire, expand and sustain your research endeavor?
3.2. Have you ever been motivated to conduct research due to a gap in teaching content?

3.3. In what areas of LIS teaching and pedagogical practices do you see opportunities for empirical investigation?

Table 4 Theme: Using teaching to inform research
4.1. How frequently do you and your students collaborate in a subsequent research project as a result of a class?
4.2. What research-oriented activities do you have students perform that you then integrate into your scholarly activities?
4.3. How have your teaching areas contributed to sustainable research to support the information professions and information science?

Final theme for all tables: Challenges and Strategies in Bridging Teaching and Research
5.1. What challenges have you encountered in trying to integrate your teaching and your scholarship?
5.2. What strategies do you employ to encourage practitioners to read and apply your research in their work?
5.3. How will evidence-based research or action research studies help to bridge LIS teaching and research?
Results of the discussion will be recorded, documented, and shared with the participants after the session.

REFERENCES

Boyd, W. E., O'Reilly, M., Bucher, D., Fisher, K., Morton, A., Harrison, P. L., Nuske, E., Coyle, R., & Rendall, K. (2010). Activating the Teaching-Research Nexus in Smaller Universities: Case Studies Highlighting Diversity of Practice. *Journal of University Teaching & Learning Practice, 7*(2). Available at: http://ro.uow.edu.au/jutlp/vol7/iss2/9

Boyer, E. (1990). *Scholarship Reconsidered.* New York: Carnegie Foundation for the Advancement of Teaching.

Brew, A. (2010). Imperatives and challenges in integrating teaching and research. *Higher Education Research & Development*, 29(2), 139-150.

Casanovas-Rubio, M., Aheam, A., Ramos, G. & Popo, S. (2016). The research-teaching nexus: using a construction teaching event as a research tool. *Innovations in Education and Teaching International*, 53(1), 104-118.

Geschwind, L. & Broström. A. (2015) Managing the teaching–research nexus: ideals and practice in research-oriented universities. *Higher Education Research & Development*, 34(1), 60-73.

Grant, K. and Wakelin, S. (2009). Re-conceptualizing the concept of a nexus? A survey of 12 Scottish IS/IM academics' perceptions of a nexus between teaching, research, scholarship and consultancy. Teaching in Higher Education, 14(2), 133-146.

Healy, M. (2005). Linking research and teaching: exploring disciplinary spaces and the role of inquiry-based learning. In Barnett, R. (ed) *Re-shaping the University: New Relationships between Research, Scholarship and Teaching* (pp.67-78). Maidenhead, UK: McGraw Hill / Open University Press.

Horta, H., Dautel, V. & Veloso, V. (2012). An output perspective on the teaching–research nexus: an analysis focusing on the United States higher education system. *Studies in Higher Education*, 37(2), 171–187.

Jenkins, A., Healey, M., & Zetter, R. (2007). *Linking research and teaching in disciplines and departments.* York, UK: Higher Education Academy. Retrieved from https://www.heacademy.ac.uk/knowledge-hub/linking-teaching-and-research-disciplines-and-departments.

Little, V., Brookes, R. & Palmer, R. (2008). Research-informed teaching and teaching-informed research. The Contemporary Marketing Practices (CMP) living case study approach to understanding marketing practice. *Journal of Business & Industrial Marketing*, 23(2), 124-134.

Malcolm, M. (2014). A critical evaluation of recent progress in understanding the role of the research-teaching link in higher education. *Higher Education,* 67, 289-301.

Robertson, J. (2007) Beyond the 'research/teaching nexus': exploring the complexity of academic experience, Studies in Higher Education, 32:5, 541-556.

Taylor, John. (2007). The teaching: research nexus: a model for institutional management. Higher Education 54:867–884.

Taylor, John (2008). The teaching–research nexus and the importance of context: a comparative study of England and Sweden. Compare, 38 (1), 53–69.

Teagle Working Group. (2007). Student Learning and Faculty Research: Connecting Teaching and Scholarship. A Teagle Foundation White Paper. American Council of Learned Societies.

Peer Review, Bibliometrics and Altmetrics - Do We Need Them All?

Judit Bar-Ilan
Bar-Ilan University, Israel,
Judit.Bar-Ilan@biu.ac.il

Isabella Peters
ZBW Leibniz Information Center for Economics & Kiel University, Germany, i.peters@zbw.eu

Stefanie Haustein
University of Ottawa, Canada,
stefanie.haustein@uottawa.ca

Dietmar Wolfram
University of Wisconsin-Milwaukee, United States,
dwolfram@uwm.edu

Staša Milojević
Indiana University Bloomington, United States,
smilojev@indiana.edu

ABSTRACT

This panel will present views and critical reflections on peer review, bibliometrics and altmetrics against the background of the latest developments and critique of the scientific system (e.g., replication crisis, DORA, open science, data manipulation). Peer review is the oldest form of monitoring the scientific process and research outcomes and is sometimes considered as the gold standard for evaluating quality. However, it also has its drawbacks; therefore, new forms of peer review are being explored. Bibliometrics, comparative statistics based on publication and citation counts, was introduced as a more objective evaluation method, which is applicable on meso and macro levels of research producing units but is not without problems either. Citation counts as a proxy of quality; the impact factor and the h-index are some of the most controversial subjects of research evaluation today. The newest addition to the evaluation toolbox are altmetrics, impact measures based mainly on social media activity. Altmetrics have pros and cons as well. None of the measuring devices is perfect, and rather than replacing they complement each other. By drawing on indicators from all three aspects of research evaluation, negative and adverse effects are limited.

KEYWORDS

Peer review, bibliometrics, altmetrics, research evaluation

INTRODUCTION

Since the foundation of scholarly journals in the 17th century, the process of quality control and gatekeeping in science has been traditionally based on peer review, the evaluation of scientific work through one's colleagues. Researchers are used to having their work evaluated. In light of limited resources, peer review—particularly in grant allocation and hiring and promotion decisions—is increasingly being replaced by bibliometric analyses, statistics based on publication output and citation impact. Aiming to make research funding more efficient as well as effective, bibliometric research assessments are said to be more objective, applicable on a larger scale and at lower costs than expert evaluations (Moed, 2005). With the introduction of large international citation databases, bibliometrics has often replaced peer judgements in research evaluation leading to adverse effects and unethical behavior such as salami publishing, honorary authorships and citation cartels (Haustein & Larivière, 2015). This has led to a push to broaden impact metrics by counting not only traditional journal publications and citations but considering mentions and output on the web. These so-called altmetrics (Priem et al., 2010) are largely based on social media activity and were introduced as alternative or complementary to bibliometrics.

This panel will provide an overview and critically reflect on the various aspects of research evaluation and the scientific reward system. Panelists will discuss various aspects of peer review (including open peer review), bibliometrics and altmetrics as forms of evaluation and ask whether they are still needed today. A special emphasis will be put on different aims of research assessments including different use cases and evaluation audiences, asking what different indicators and types of analyses are used for.

PANEL ORGANIZATION

This panel will present views on peer review, bibliometrics and altmetrics against the background of latest critiques of the scientific system (e.g., replication crisis, DORA, open science, data manipulation). The topics are controversial and will thus hopefully result in a lively discussion with the audience. At first Stefanie Haustein will provide a general overview and introduction to peer review, bibliometrics and altmetrics and the connection between them, highlighting different applications and audiences of various research assessments. Then Judit Bar-Ilan will present the current state and challenges of traditional peer review, followed by Dietmar Wolfram on new developments in peer review systems related to open science. Staša Milojevic will discuss bibliometrics and finally Isabella Peters will present her views on altmetrics. After the initial presentations, the panelists will engage with the audience by discussing issues relevant to the conference theme in relation to each of the three aspects of research evaluation.

PANEL TOPICS

Peer Review

Scholarly peer review started with the establishment of academic journals in the 17th century. At first, the review was done by the editor, and later by select members of the societies that published the journal. Seeking outside reviewers' help was not the norm until the mid-20th century (Spier, 2002). In 1936, Albert Einstein complained to the editors of *Physical Review*, that his article was sent to outside reviewers without his permission (Nielsen, 2009). We have gone a long way since then and have a better understanding of the pros and cons of the use of peer review for scholarly publishing, grant applications and promotions. Peer review is not perfect, as can be seen from the growing number of yearly retractions.

A recent survey by Belluz, Plumer, and Resnick (2016) asked what scientists wished to change about today's science. Among the top four problems identified by the 270 respondents was the broken peer review system. Poor quality or flawed manuscripts pass peer review processes either due to reviewers not spending sufficient time in their evaluations or lacking adequate expertise (Eisen, MacCallum, & Neylon, 2013).

One aspect of open science that has not yet been widely adopted and investigated is that of open peer review (OPR), which makes pre- or post-publication reviews of scholarly works publicly available and can be used for pre- or post-publication evaluation. The idea of OPR itself is not new. Proposals extend back at least to the early days of Web-based open access journals. Van Rooyen, Godlee, Evans, Black and Smith (1999), studying OPR in the journal BMJ with open and blind reviews, noted that there was no difference in quality between the open and blind reviews based on human judgments. They concluded there was no evidence to support that the traditional blind approach to peer review resulted in superior reviews. They also posited that if reviewers were identifiable, they might put greater effort into their reviews. More recent research has also concluded there are no significant differences between open and closed peer reviews within a given journal (Wang, You, Rath, & Wolfram, 2016).

In recent years, several OA journals have pioneered the OPR process to vet manuscripts for publication. Today, the notion of OPR is still evolving; diverse models of OPR have been implemented from the most open and interactive processes, such as by *F1000Research*, to blind peer review followed by optional publishing of review history, such as adopted by *PeerJ*. A dual model of peer review as used by *Papers in Physics*, allows the author to choose, at the time of submission, either closed peer review or OPR. The question remains whether reviewers, given a choice, would be willing to identify themselves and whether authors would be willing to share their reviews. Despite the lack of standards or de facto models, OPR journals are growing fast. The number of OPR journals indexed by the Directory of Open Access Journals (doaj.org) has increased from 20 in January 2016 to 127 in March 2018, representing a growth of 535%.

Bibliometrics

The citation indices developed by Eugene Garfield during the 1960s provided the sociology of science and bibliometrics with new measurement instruments for understanding social and epistemic aspects of science. At the same time, the citation indices became the major source for measuring research performance across all levels: individuals, projects, departments, universities, countries and journals. Today, there are widely available resources that allow for measuring numbers of publications, citations, h-index, and other indicators at the level of individuals, journals, and institutions without much prior knowledge of bibliometrics involved. This has prompted numerous warnings that a deeper understanding of bibliometrics is necessary for making sense of and formulating informed criticism about university rankings, evaluations, and audit culture within which academics work (e.g., Hicks et al., 2015).

The use of impact factors of journals for evaluative purposes has pervaded the academic environment, even to the level of individual tenure decisions, which increasingly are being based on quantitative measures of publications and citations (Haustein & Larivière, 2015). The impact factor has been used by journal editors and publishers to attract authors and readers, and by researchers as an indicator of prestige and as a tool for screening an ever-growing body of literature for reading and, eventually, citing (De Rijcke et al., 2016). Despite the prevalence of the impact factor as a measure of journal impact, there is a large body of research arguing that evaluating the impact of journals is not a straightforward task (e.g., Bar-Ilan, 2012).

Another popular indicator, the h-index (Hirsch, 2005), provides a simple impact metric for individual authors combining both citation and publication counts, that can readily be used in online searching, for example, with Google Scholar, but is also incorporated in the major citation databases such as the Web of Science and Scopus. The measure was designed to capture both the productivity and impact of a researchers. However, it is also a measure of career longevity. In addition, it is a measure that can never decrease.

One of the biggest problems with bibliometrics measures is to identify a proper reference group against which to evaluate. This problem is tied to the problem of field delineation, which has been mostly resolved at the level of journals, despite the problem that there is a growing number of interdisciplinary journals. In addition, science is increasingly a team-based activity, and the bibliometric indicators and available data are still such that they cannot precisely attribute credit to each of the authors appearing on the bylines of papers.

Altmetrics

Since 2010 altmetrics (Priem et al., 2010) have been discussed as new and alternative means for the evaluation of scientific work. They are largely based on social media users' interactions with scholarly products. Actually, by now, an extensive body of literature has shown that altmetrics complement and do not replace current procedures and measures used in research evaluation (e.g. Wilsdon et al., 2015), as reflected in low correlations with citations (with the exception of Mendeley reader counts; (Costas, Zahedi, & Wouters, 2015)). As such, altmetrics can enrich current research assessment by adding new perspectives, they include the views of all stakeholders and not only other authors (as with citations) and they also offer potential in assessing interdisciplinary research. Although altmetrics can easily be considered as pure quantitative indicators, they offer the option to analyze information about users and beneficiaries of scholarly products (e.g., via content analysis of user profiles or comments) and connections between them. Those properties of altmetrics can also be exploited for other use cases, such as exploration or showcasing of research results (see Altmetrics Definitions and Use Cases; NISO, 2016).

Moreover, altmetrics present some strong advantages compared to citations: they accumulate faster than citations, they cover not only journal publications, but also datasets, code, experimental design, nanopublications, blog posts, comments and tweets, and they are diverse, providing multiple signals for the same object (e.g., downloads, likes, and comments; Priem et al., 2010). Theorization of those findings has only just begun (Haustein, Bowman, & Costas, 2016).

However, altmetrics are also confronted with severe challenges and skepticism, especially when considered for open science (Bar-Ilan & Peters, 2016). Altmetrics suffer from a lack of robustness and an easiness with which underlying systems can be gamed. Altmetrics suffer from biases due to, amongst others, the limited uptake of social media in several disciplines, countries or user groups (Sugimoto et al., 2016), or the use of certain identifiers which are better trackable online (e.g., DOI). A further severe problem with altmetrics is the lack of access to the underlying data (Haustein, 2016). Because standards are in the development phase and used voluntarily so far (see NISO Altmetrics Data Code of Conduct; NISO, 2016) neither reproduction of calculations nor scrutinization of altmetrics data is possible.

There is also a fear that altmetrics will introduce a new form of competition and that researchers have to (unwillingly) adapt to this new evaluation system, with reluctance leading to severe disadvantages: for example, that spectacular results create more buzz. Hence, creation and utilization of altmetrics must meet academic standards and should serve the needs of academia (Bar-Ilan & Peters, 2016).

Peer review, bibliometrics and, more recently, altmetrics have represented ways to evaluate scholars and scholarly products. However, in today's data-driven research world, we must ask if these are the best ways to do so and whether we can identify additional methods by which scholarly impact may be objectively assessed?

PANELISTS

Judit Bar-Ilan is professor at the Department of Information Science of Bar-Ilan University in Israel. Her areas of interest include informetrics, information retrieval, Internet research, information behavior, and usability. Additional details are available at http://is.biu.ac.il/en/judit.

Stefanie Haustein is assistant professor at the School of Information Studies at the University of Ottawa, where she teaches research methods and evaluation, social network analysis and knowledge organization. Her research interests focus on social media in academia and altmetrics. More information and a list of publications can be found at stefaniehaustein.com.

Staša Milojević is associate professor at the School of Informatics, Computing, and Engineering at the Indiana University Bloomington. Her areas of interest include informetrics, computational social science and digital humanities.

Isabella Peters is professor at the Department of Computer Science at Kiel University and responsible for Web Science research at ZBW Leibniz Information Center for Economics. Her research interests include social media and user generated content for scholarly communication (e.g., altmetrics), knowledge representation and information as well as open science. More information can be found at http://isabella-peters.de.

Dietmar Wolfram is professor at the School of Information Studies at the University of Wisconsin-Milwaukee. He received his PhD in Library and Information Science from the University of Western Ontario. His research interests include informetrics, information retrieval, the intersection between these two areas, scholarly communication, and user studies.

ACKNOWLEDGMENTS

This panel is sponsored by ASIS&T SIG/MET. Work presented by Judit Bar-Ilan is supported by EU COST Action TD1306 "New Frontiers of Peer Review" PEERE.

REFERENCES

Bar-Ilan, J. (2012). Journal report card. Scientometrics, 92(2), 249-260.

Bar-Ilan, J., & Peters, I. (2016). Next-generation metrics: responsible metrics and evaluation for open science. Presentation at 3:AM Conference, Bucharest, Romania. Retrieved from https://dx.doi.org/10.6084/m9.figshare.c.3488817.v1

Belluz, J., Plumer, B., & Resnick, B. (2016). The 7 biggest problems facing science, according to 270 scientists. Retrieved from: http://www.vox.com/2016/7/14/12016710/science-challeges-research-funding-peer-review-process.

Costas, R., Zahedi, Z., & Wouters, P. (2015). Do "altmetrics" correlate with citations? Extensive comparison of altmetric indicators with citations from a multidisciplinary perspective. Journal of the Association for Information Science and Technology, 66(10), 2003-2019.

De Rijcke, S., Wouters, P., Rushforth, A., Franssen, T., & Hammarfelt, B. (2016). Evaluation practices and effects of indicator use - a literature review. Research Evaluation, 25(2), 161-169.

Eisen J.A., MacCallum C.J., & Neylon C. (2013). Expert failure: Re-evaluating research assessment. PLoS Biol 11(10): e1001677. doi:10.1371/journal.-pbio.1001677.

Haustein, S. (2016). Grand challenges in altmetrics. Scientometrics, 108, 413-423. doi:10.1007/s11192-016-1910-9

Haustein, S., Bowman, T. D., & Costas, R. (2016). Interpreting "altmetrics": viewing acts on social media through the lens of citation and social theories. In C. R. Sugimoto (Ed.), Theories of informetrics and scholarly communication. A Festschrift in Honor of Blaise Cronin (pp. 372–405). Berlin: De Gruyter. Retrieved from http://arxiv.org/abs/1502.05701

Haustein, S & Larivière, V. (2015). The use of bibliometrics for assessing research: possibilities, limitations and adverse effects. In I. M. Welpe, J. Wollersheim, S. Ringelhahn, & M. Osterloh (Eds.), Incentives and Performance. Governance of Research Organizations (pp. 121–139). Springer. Retrieved from: http://crc.ebsi.umontreal.ca/files/sites/60/2015/10/HausteinLariviere_revised2.pdf

Hicks, D., Wouters, P., Waltman, L., de Rijcke, S. and Rafols, I. (2015). The Leiden Manifesto for research metrics. Nature, 520, 429-431.

Hirsch, J. E. (2005). An index to quantify an individual's scientific research output. Proceedings of the National Academy of Sciences of the USA, 102(46), 16569-16572.

Moed, H.F. (2005). Citation Analysis in Research Evaluation. Dordrecht: Springer.

Nielsen, M. (2009). Three myths about scientific peer review. Retrieved from http://michaelnielsen.org/blog/three-myths-about-scientific-peer-review/

NISO (2016). Outputs of the NISO Alternative Assessment Metrics Project. Retrieved from https://groups.niso.org/apps/group_public/download.php/17091/NISO%20RP-25-2016%20Outputs%20of%20the%20NISO%20Alternative%20Assessment%20Project.pdf

Priem, J., Taraborelli, D., Groth, P., & Neylon, V. (2010). Altmetrics: A manifesto. Retrieved from http://altmetrics.org/manifesto

Spier, R. (2002). The history of the peer-review process. TRENDS in Biotechnology, 20(8), 357-358.

Sugimoto, C. R., Haustein, S., Ke, Q., & Larivière, V. (2016). Social Media Metrics as Indicators of Broader Impact. OECD Blue Sky III Forum on Science and Innovation Indicators. Gent (Belgium). Retrieved from http://www.oecd.org/sti/172%20-%20SugimotoOECDaltmetrics.pdf

van Rooyen, S., Godlee, F., Evans, S., Black, N., & Smith, R. (1999). Effect of open peer review on quality of reviews and on reviewers' recommendations: A randomised trial. British Medical Journal, 318(7175), 23-27.

Wang, P., You, S., Rath, M., & Wolfram, D. (2016). Open Peer Review in scientific publishing: A web mining study of PeerJ authors and reviewers. Journal of Data and Information Science. 1(4). Retrieved from: https://www.degruyter.com/view/j/jdis.2016.1.issue-4/jdis.201625/jdis.201625.xml

Wilsdon, J. R., Allen, L., Belfiore, E., Campbell, P., Curry, S., Hill, S., …, & Johnson, B. (2015). The Metric Tide: Report of the Independent Review of the Role of Metrics in Research Assessment and Management. doi:10.13140/RG.2.1.4929.1363

Transdisciplinary Approaches to Critical Data Studies

Ryan Burns
University of Calgary, Canada. Ryan.burns1@ucalgary.ca

Andrew Iliadis
Temple University, USA. Andrew.iliadis@temple.edu

Blake Hawkins
University of British Columbia, Canada. Blake.hawkins@alumni.ubc.ca

Jim Thatcher
University of Washington, USA, jethatch@uw.edu

Anne Lauren Hoffmann
University of Washington, USA. alho@uw.edu

ABSTRACT

In this paper we describe the rationale behind a panel concerning the transdisciplinary approaches to critical data studies. We illuminate emerging modes of conducting critical data studies research and highlights the interdisciplinary opportunities within future research directions. We describe the format for the panel and the themes that will be covered by each of the author. By having this panel to occur it creates a space for interdisciplinary dialogues on a timely topic that touches various sub- fields of information science along with the broader social science disciplines in the academy.

KEYWORDS

Critical data studies, interdisciplinary, ethics, GIScience, Queer theory.

INTRODUCTION

This panel illuminates emerging modes of conducting critical data studies research and highlights the interdisciplinary op- portunities within future research directions. Highlighting the plurality of approaches within the emerging research area, the panel focuses on the transdisciplinarity of critical data studies for the following reasons:

1. In recent years, the field of critical data studies has been researched across multiple disciplines and is no longer merely of interest to information and computer sciences. Other disciplines such as geography, communication and media studies, and sociology provide additional theoretical frameworks for critiquing data, including critical theories of race, sexuality, political economy, governance, and gender.
2. Critical data studies are growing in popularity and it is important to build connections between fields rather than in disciplinary silos.
3. Research in this field is continually growing as data's significance becomes more of an issue in public domains. Given the ongoing discussions about data production and usage across disciplines and in popular discourse, it is a timely juncture to convene a panel on transdisciplinarity in critical data studies. Across disciplines in the social sciences and humanities there are concurrent discussions about data: who produces this data, how data can racialize communities, who benefits from the data, and how processes of sexuality coincide and interact with data production. This collective of researchers hails from diverse academic backgrounds that intersect ethics, critical race, social theory, political economics, public health, queertheory, and GIScience. By having this discussion, we hope to create a productive space to explore pressing new research directions as data become more embedded in society.

BACKGROUND

Critical data studies is a transdisciplinary field that explores the mutual imbrication of data with spatial, social, political, eco- nomic, and institutional processes (Dalton and Thatcher 2014). It has fostered debates across disciplines as varied as informa- tion science, GIScience, sociology, and the digital humanities. These debates have suggested that data should not be considered politically neutral abstractions of the natural or social world, but instead as artifacts deeply embedded with values, norms, epistemological claims, and philosophical outlooks (Iliadis & Russo, 2016; Schuurman, 2000; boyd and Crawford, 2012; Kitchin, 2014, Hoffmann 2017).

While related to the methodologies and exigencies of Big Data as it is practiced and imagined, the concerns raised in these and other works highlight the need to continually engage new technical regimes with critiques from feminist, queer, critical race, and social theory. To date, research has primarily investigated the social and political nature of *existing* data, but recent work has also sought to explain the gaps in data production systems as well as the reasons why some data exist, but others do not (Burns 2018; Thatcher 2014; Graham 2014). The *implications* of this research extend beyond data into the socio-spatial inequalities and unevennesses of algorithms and software for data processing, and the ways in which power functions through them (Dalton et al. 2016; Noble, 2018). Some work has focused on the development of feminist and decolonial approaches to data-driven knowledge production (Leurs, 2017).

Within the discipline of geography, critical GIScience has explored the political and power relations within map making. Building on JB Harley's (1988) ideas that cartography constitutes the exercise of power, Monmonier's (1996) *How to Lie With Maps* exposed that maps have the capacity to shape the ways we come to know the world and the people in it,partly through the legitimacy afforded to cartographic representations. These ideas at the time, however, sat askew to what many human geographers saw as a broader disciplinary-wide return to "naive empiricism" in the growing use of GIS (Taylor 1990, 212). After a series of heated debates in the early and mid-1990s, closer collaboration and conversation between GIScientists and human geographers fostered the field of critical GIS. Coined in 2000 (Schuurman 2000), Critical GIS hasembraced many, sometimes conflicting, epistemological orientations. It has been feminist (Schuurman and Pratt 2002), queer (Brown and Knopp 2008), and indigenous (Rundstrom 1995); however, throughout, like the work of Harley and Monmonier, Critical GIS has been concerned with the social and epistemological foundations of spatial technologies.

Recently, and drawing from the insights learned in and through these earlier contestations, Critical GIS work has more direct- ly engaged with the ways in which data, analysis, and visualization matter to non-dominant cultures and peoples. Exemplify- ing scholarship by Jack Gieseking (2017a; 2017b; 2017c) incorporates radical feminist and queer critiques to the ontologies of map and data production for mapping. He shows that data marginalize vulnerable communities by normalizing the data that have been collected, and by reinscribing heteronormative and masculinist forms of measurement. As postulated by Gieseking "[h]ow can we recognize those whose lives and data become attached to the far-from-groundbreaking framework of "small data"? Specifically, how can marginalized people [especially queer people] who do not have the resources to produce, self-categorize, analyze, or store "big data" claim their place in the big data debates?" Thus, big data needs trenchant critique despite its emergent opportunities, and this critique is needed especially among communities traditionally under-served and represented in data systems.

In information science, critical-oriented researchers have been interested in data labelling and sharing in the context of scien- tists solving data-sharing problems in science teams (Fonseca and Martin, 2007; Borgman, 2010, 2011, 2015). This work coincides and is in line with increasing critical attention to issues of social justice, identity, and community across library and information science research broadly (Jaeger, Shilton, and Koepfler, 2016). Critical information studies ask us to center in our analyses "the ways in which culture and information are regulated, and thus the relationships among regulation to commerce, creativity, science, technology, politics, and other human affairs" (Vaidhyanathan, 2006, p. 293). In addition, longer-standing conversations around cultural and ethical dimensions of information, technology, and privacy in information studies and elsewhere make clear the ways in which data-intensive surveillance systems help produce and regulate the lives of subjects, especially along the lines of gender (Smith, 2015) and race (Browne, 2015). These domains - social justice in LIS, critical information studies, and cultural studies of surveillance - offer important footholds for the development of critical data studies.

Building and extending this work to data justice and social progress issues involves also looking at how critical approachesare connected to data gathering, data modeling, databases, and metadata in informatics (Sweeney and Brock, 2015), and how the use of these and other tools like application programming interfaces (Qiu, 2017) impact civil society through public facing apps and technologies. Drawing on the work of Gitelman (2008), Srinivasan (2012) offers one such approach by askinghow we might include discussions related to "ethical questions about the sovereignty of diverse knowledge, and whether the voices of emerging users should be ignored or empowered" (205). Similarly, Duarte and Belarde-Lewis (2015) offer "imagin- ing" as a methodology for decolonizing the classification and organization of data and information, especially with regard to indigenous subjects. Duarte and Belarde-Lewis (2015) work will be brought into conversation with cultural geographer Sarah Hunt's (2013) work on indigenous ontologies, which, in turn, will be deepened through consideration of traditions within and across the fields of Critical GIS and critical information studies. Critical data studies serve as the locus that brings together experts across these areas, allowing for ideas in separate, but related, disciplines to hang together; to inform and to trouble.

Panel Agenda

The purpose of this panel is to 1) examine the various theoretical and methodological approaches possible within critical data studies, and to 2) consider the potential overlapping themes that might lead to productive future research collaborations. In other words, this panel will be both exploratory and agenda-setting. We will address the following topics:

- the overlapping foundational debates across disciplines concerning critical data studies;
- theoretical resources for critiquing data, data systems, and data implications;
- future research needs of, and productive directions for, critical data studies;
- obstacles for research in the field of critical data studies. The organization of our panel is as follows:

1. A brief introduction about critical data studies and its transdisciplinary nature by the panel moderator Dr. Jim Thatcher (5 Minutes)
2. Five examples of research in critical data studies will be presented by the panelists Ryan Burns, Blake Hawkins, Anna Hoffman, Andrew Iliadis, and Jim Thatcher. (50 minutes)
3. World Cafe discussions in small groups, each panelist acts as a facilitator for discussions related to the panel, creat- ing five options for audience members to engage in a discussion about the transdisciplinary nature of critical data studies. (30 minutes)

4. Brief closing remarks and additional discussion of critical data studies will be presented by a panelist to be deter- mined (5 minutes)

PANEL DISCUSSIONS

Ryan Burns is Assistant Professor in the Department of Geography at University of Calgary, and a faculty fellow with the O'Brien Institute for Public Health. In this panel, Burns will discuss the new ways in which forms of exclusion, oppression, resistance, and empowerment are occurring in open data platforms. Municipalities across the globe are increasingly pursuing "smart city" status by accelerating the circulation of data -- embedding sensors in the urban fabric, analyzing data for real- time data-driven decision making, and promoting open data platforms as ways of being "transparent" and "accountable". Burns's research shows that despite claims to "openness", multiple layers of social process and power relations saturate open data platforms, essentially reinscribing pre-existing inequalities and producing new forms of marginalization. In contrast, a small movement of community and grassroots data sharing platforms and data co-operatives are working to subvert such top-down state-sponsored open data initiatives by creating their own open data platforms. Although these open data platforms enable and encourage alternative visions of their cities, their work is still in tension with many of the same logics of neoliberal governance and empiricist epistemologies as the platforms they resist. The result is a complex picture of the ways data serve many competing and contradictory aims.

Blake W. Hawkins is a PhD student at the University of British Columbia Interdisciplinary Studies Graduate Program. As pan- elist, he will highlight some early findings from an ongoing interdisciplinary project about Grindr users perspectives of the appli- cation metadata. Grindr is a hookup application commonly used by gay, bisexual, and other men (trans-inclusive) who have sex with men. What motivated this project were the recent changes made to the metadata items by Grindr to create a more inclusive application. These recent changes to the profile include the option of sharing preferred pronouns, HIV status, last time being tested, and preferred sexual practices. Despite creating these new metadata options, there are still some tensions with the application and the data produced from filling in the metadata for a profile. In April 2018, it was reported that Grindr sold data about HIV statuses in different geographical settings. Furthermore, to take advantage of searching with dif- ferent metadata options, users need to have the pay-per-use version which creates new barriers. Additional motivations for sharing this work include the opportunity for future critical data studies research that incorporates queerer perspective and suggest some potential challenges when completing research with an underrepresented community, like Grindr users, to discuss their perspectives about meta/data

Anna Lauren Hoffmann is an Assistant Professor at the University of Washington Information School. As a part of this pan- el, she will highlight the connection between data and violence, as well is the implications of this connection for "data ethics"— that is, for thinking about ethical approaches to data science, research, and computer engineering especially as it relates to vulnerable subjects and communities. Inherent in conceiving of something as data is a kind of subjection—it involves taking myriad and diverse ways of being or knowing and subjecting them to the more or less exacting logics of quan- tification, segmentation, and reduction. Hoffmann theorizes this subjection as a kind of violence not in the sense of a deviation or abhorrence, rather as some- thing that can be pervasive and routinized. She illustrates this through three case examples centering the lives and experiences of transgender women: 1) airport body scanners that flag trans bodies as threats, 2) the automated banning of trans women from dating sites, and 3) the culling of trans YouTubers' videos to train facial recognition software. In each case, harmful cultural ideas and stereotypes surrounding trans women are not only reproduced, but routinized in the service of administrative, commercial, or scientific ends. By foregrounding the experiences of this particular vulnerable community, Hoffmann seeks to reinforce the idea that data is merely instrumental to, but constitutive of violent social, political, or other action.

Andrew Iliadis is Assistant Professor at Temple University in the Department of Media Studies and Production (within the Lew Klein College of Media and Communication) and serves on the faculty of the Media and Communication Doctoral Pro- gram. In this panel, he will discuss metadata ecologies and their relationship to social ontology. Increasing data accessibility through metadata curation is a key feature of the semantic web. Several domain-specific metadata initiatives have facilitated linked data for individual industries. These metadata schemas allow administrators to tag web data to boost contextual expressivity and se- mantic content, thus improving search and retrieval in their respective fields. Some drawbacks of this prac- tice are that a plurality of metadata schemas produces layered code that can overburden administrators, while lack of a single metadata vocabulary results in unequal distribution of schemas due to intermittent application. The present work provides an analysis of these schemas and describes global efforts to amalgamate smaller domain-specific schemas into a universal standard vocabulary. We will discuss organization and practice in these metadata ecologies, how they differ from applied ontol- ogy, and end by raising potential ethical concerns in social categorization.

Jim E. Thatcher is Assistant Professor of Urban Studies at the University of Washington Tacoma and holds an affiliate appoint- ment in the graduate school of Geography at the University of Washington. He is the current chair of the Digital Geographies specialty group of the American Association of Geographers and was previously an NSF fellow for CyberGIS. His research ex- amines the recursive relations among extremely large geospatial data sets, the creation and analysis of those datasets, and society, with a focus on how data has come to mediate, saturate, and sustain modern urban environments. His work takes as central questions how the constitution and analysis of data are framed by and subsequently frame the production of knowledge with regards to nature, society, and politics. On one level, his work engages directly with large geospatial data using a variety of research tools, including bespoke open-source applications, to conduct rigorous, empirical analysis of urban systems. On another, it draws on critical theory and qualitative methods to trace the impact of massive geospatial data sets on the shifting relations among economic forces, technology, environments, and society. His research is often referred to as Critical Data Studies or Digital Political Ecologies. He is the lead editor of a 2018 University of Nebraska Press book on the roles 'big data' has come to play within and across academic Geography and cognate disciplines.

REFERENCES

Borgman - 2010 - Research Data Who Will Share What, with Whom, Whe.pdf. (n.d.). Retrieved from https://www.ratswd.de/ download/RatSWD_WP_2010/RatSWD_WP_161.pdf

Borgman, C. L. (2010). Research Data: Who Will Share What, with Whom, When, and Why? *SSRN Electronic Journal.*

https://doi.org/10.2139/ssrn.1714427

Borgman, C. L. (2011). *The Conundrum of Sharing Research Data* (SSRN Scholarly Paper No. ID 1869155). Rochester, NY: Social Science Research Network. Retrieved from https://papers.ssrn.com/abstract=1869155

Borgman, C. L. (2015). *Big Data, Little Data, No Data: Scholarship in the Networked World.* The MIT Press.

boyd, danah, & Crawford, K. (2012). Critical Questions for Big Data. *Information, Communication & Society*, *15*(5), 662– 679. https://doi.org/10.1080/1369118X.2012.678878

Brown, M., & Knopp, L. (2008). Queering the Map: The Productive Tensions of Colliding Epistemologies. *Annals of the Association of American Geographers*, *98*(1), 40–58. https://doi.org/10.1080/00045600701734042

Burns, R. (2018). Datafying Disaster: Institutional Framings of Data Production Following Superstorm Sandy. *Annals of the American Association of Geographers*, *108*(2), 569–578. https://doi.org/10.1080/24694452.2017.1402673

Dalton, C. M., Taylor, L., & Thatcher (alphabetical), J. (2016). Critical Data Studies: A dialog on data and space. *Big Data & Society*, *3*(1), 2053951716648346. https://doi.org/10.1177/2053951716648346

Dalton, C. & Thatcher, J. (2014). WHAT DOES A CRITICAL DATA STUDIES LOOK LIKE, AND WHY DO WE CARE?

Retrieved April 4, 2018, from http://societyandspace.org/2014/05/12/what-does-a-critical-data-studies-look-like- and-why-do-we-care-craig-dalton-and-jim-thatcher

Fonseca, F., & Martin, J. (2007). Learning the Differences Between Ontologies and Conceptual Schemas Through Ontology- Driven Information Systems. *Journal of the Association for Information Systems*, *8*(2). Retrieved from http:// aisel.aisnet.org/jais/vol8/iss2/4

Harley, J. B. (1992). Deconstructing the map. *Passages*. Retrieved from http://hdl.handle.net/2027/spo.4761530.0003.008

Hoffmann, A. L. (2017). Making Data Valuable: Political, Economic, and Conceptual Bases of Big Data. *Philosophy & Tech- nology*, 1–4. https://doi.org/10.1007/s13347-017-0295-x

Iliadis, A., & Russo, F. (2016). Critical data studies: An introduction. *Big Data & Society*, *3*(2), 2053951716674238. https:// doi.org/10.1177/2053951716674238

Jaeger, P. T., Shilton, K., & Koepfler, J. (2016). The rise of social justice as a guiding principle in library and information science research. The Library Quarterly: Information, Community, Policy, 86(1), 1-9.

Kitchin, R. (2014a). Big Data, new epistemologies and paradigm shifts. *Big Data & Society*, *1*(1), 2053951714528481. https://doi.org/10.1177/2053951714528481

Kitchin, R. (2014b). Big Data, new epistemologies and paradigm shifts. *Big Data & Society*, *1*(1), 2053951714528481. https://doi.org/10.1177/2053951714528481

Leurs, K. (2017). feminist data studies: using digital methods for ethical, reflexive and situated socio-cultural research. Femi- nist Review, Volume 115, Issue 1, pp 130–154

Monmonier, M. (1996). How to Lie with Maps. Chicago: University of Chicago Press Noble, S. (2018). Algorithms of Oppression. New York: NYU Press

Rundstrom, R. A. (1995). GIS, Indigenous Peoples, and Epistemological Diversity. *Cartography and Geographic Informa- tion Systems*, *22*(1), 45–57. https://doi.org/10.1559/152304095782540564

Schuurman, N. (2000). Trouble in the heartland: GIS and its critics in the 1990s. *Progress in Human Geography*, *24*(4), 569– 590. https://doi.org/10.1191/030913200100189111

Schuurman, N., & Pratt, G. (2002). Care of the Subject: Feminism and Critiques of GIS. *Gender, Place & Culture*, *9*(3), 291– 299. https://doi.org/10.1080/0966369022000003905

Thatcher, J. (2014). Big Data, Big Questions| Living on Fumes: Digital Footprints, Data Fumes, and the Limitations of Spa- tial Big Data. *International Journal of Communication*, *8*(0), 19.

Open Science: Development, Challenges and Practice in the Global Context

Hsin-liang Chen
University of Massachusetts, USA
hsinliang.chen@umb.edu

Lei Pei
Nanjing University, China
plei@nju.edu.cn

Ina Smith
Academy of Science of South Africa
ina@assaf.org.za

Ying-Hsang Liu
Charles Sturt University & The Australian National University, Australia. yingliu@csu.edu.au

Isabella Peters
ZBW Leibniz Information Center for Economics & Kiel University, Germany. ipe@informatik.uni-kiel.de

ABSTRACT

Open science (OS) is a global issue concerning how researchers work, collaborate, interact, share resources, and disseminate results in the digital age. This panel assembles researchers from various continents to discover their experiences and to address some of the following issues: What is the state of OS policies in the region? Does the region have any international, national, or regional OS collaborations and/or agreements? Does the region have any international, national or regional OS infrastructure and/or systems? Are international, national or regional OS standards being adapted in the region? What is the utilization level of the OS infrastructure and/or systems in the region? Is the region experiencing any progress, barriers and/or challenges in implementing the OS initiatives?

KEYWORDS

Open science, globalization, scholarly communication, research collaboration, information policy

INTRODUCTION

Open science (OS) is a new approach to the scientific process based on cooperative work, coupled to new tools for collaboration and new routes for knowledge diffusion through online digital technologies. OS entails a shift from the standard practice of publishing research results in scientific journals toward sharing all available data and knowledge at the earliest stages of the research process. It requires a move from "publishing as fast as possible" to "sharing knowledge as early as possible." The United Nations Educational, Scientific and Cultural Organization (UNESCO) stated, "Open Science is the movement to make scientific research and data accessible to all" (UNESCO, n.d.). Borgman (2015) pointed out that "providing open access to data has implications for scholars, libraries, universities, funding agencies, publishers, and other stakeholders that are poorly understood" (p. 14); and "knowledge infrastructure are evolving to accommodate open access, data-intensive research, new technologies, social media, and changes in practice and policy" (p. 15).

To date, many organizations and data-sharing systems have been implemented to support the OS movement. For example, the Open Science Grid (OSG) provides common service and support for resource providers and scientific institutions using a distributed fabric of high throughput computational services (Pordes et al., 2007); the Open Science Framework was established by the Center for Open Science (COS, n.d.); and the Any Data, Any Time, Anywhere (AAA) infrastructure was built by Bloom and his colleagues (2015). In 2017, the science ministers of the G7 countries (Canada, France, Germany, Italy, Japan, the United Kingdom, and the United States) and the European Commissioner for Research, Science, and Innovation agreed to support the OS infrastructure with an emphasis at the global scale (Europe Commission, 2017).

However, in highlighting one journal, *Epidemiology*, Basken (2017a) reported disagreement within the science research community and showed the challenges among a group of biology researchers regarding data-sharing practice and academic publishing. Additionally, the International Committee of Medical Journal Editors (ICMJE) is not pursuing the data-sharing requirement for authors (Basken, 2017b). Scientists are also concerned about one important challenge: relevance and accuracy in sharing and interpreting data (Basken, 2016). Those incidents present key barriers and the hesitation of researchers in the different cultures and countries toward the OS movement.

OS is a global issue concerning how researchers work, collaborate, interact, share resources and disseminate results in the digital age. To better understand the global OS movement, this panel assembles researchers from various continents to discuss practical approaches that are taken to implement OS and to address some of the following issues:

1. What is the state of OS policies in the region?
2. Does the region have any international, national, or regional OS collaborations and/or agreements?

3. Does the region have any international, national or regional OS infrastructure and/or systems?
4. Are international, national or regional OS standards being adapted in the region?
5. What is the utilization level of the OS infrastructure and/or systems in the region?
6. Is the region experiencing any progress, barriers and/or challenges in implementing the OS initiatives?

The above issues are initial discussion points for the panelists to present their cases, as well as for the audience to ask additional questions.

THE AUSTRALIAN VISION OF OPEN SCIENCE / YING-HSANG LIU

Ying-Hsang Liu (Charles Sturt University & The Australian National University) will talk about the National Innovation and Science agenda and the National Collaborative Research Infrastructure Strategy (NCRIS) in Australia, with particular reference to data sharing for innovation and the Australian National Data Service (ANDS). More specifically, a Public Data Policy statement has been released to make non-sensitive government data public by default to enable data-driven innovation. Research data from public funded research projects through the Australian Research Council (ARC) are expected to follow the OECD Principles and Guidelines for Access to Research Data from Public Funding (2007), but do not mandate open access to data. On the other hand, the purpose of ANDS is to make research data managed, connected, discoverable and reusable by researchers, as exemplified by Research Data Australia portal (https://researchdata.ands.org.au). These developments reflect the value of accountability, transparency, participation, and inclusion in the neoliberal transformation of higher education in Australia. Ying-Hsang's talk will provide the audience with an overview of the research infrastructures in support of open access to research data in Australia from the perspectives of different stakeholders, such as funding agencies, researchers, university administrators and research support services (i.e., research offices and libraries).

OPEN SCIENCE IN CHINA: WEAK POLICY BUT HOT PRACTICE / LEI PEI

Lei Pei (School of Information Management, Nanjing University) will talk about "Open Science in China: Weak Policy but Hot Practice" by introducing the understanding of OS of both scientists and the government, as well as analyzing several typical projects of data publishing and OS data services in China. The concept of OS was introduced in China around 2011 (Xu, 2011), and scholars proposed to promote open access and data reuse in the context of digital library services (Wu, 2016), academic communication (Gu, 2017), data publishing (Liu & Zhang, 2017) and data analysis in non-computing science. Accordingly, relative policy issues were also becoming included in the open movement (Tang & Xiao, 2013; Zhang, 2014). Although the official Chinese media have discussed OS, only few OS policies have been issued. In the meantime, the Chinese Science Academy, Peking University, Tsing Hua University and Nanjing University have initiated OS data projects. As a member of the OS projects at Nanjing University, Lei will share the project challenges and experiences, as well as potential curriculum development at Nanjing University's iSchool.

THE EUROPEAN VISION OF OPEN SCIENCE / ISABELLA PETERS

Isabella Peters (ZBW Leibniz Information Centre for Economics and Kiel University) will talk about "The European Vision of Open Science" by first introducing the five schools of thought influencing OS (Fecher & Friesike, 2014) and the expected benefits of OS. She will then elaborate on recommendations for and the means of implementing OS in Europe, for example the European Open Science Cloud (Ayris et al., 2016) and related initiatives (such as GoFAIR and the recommendations of the Expert Group on New Generation Metrics; Wilsdon et al., 2017). The European Commission sees a shift to an OS system as a competitive advantage for European societies.

Isabella's talk will provide the audience with the basics concepts of OS and will introduce the major European initiatives that seek to motivate and enable OS adoption. In the discussion with the other panelists and the audience, success factors of those initiatives, as well as barriers toward OS, can be discussed and critically evaluated against other international approaches.

THE SOUTH AFRICAN VISION OF OPEN SCIENCE / INA SMITH

The *Science International Accord on Open Data in a Big Data World* (Science International, 2016) presents an inclusive vision of the need for and the benefits of open data for science internationally, and in particular for Lower and Middle Income Countries. In addition to benefiting from data from the international community, African countries have much to contribute in terms of FAIR data (Wilkinson, 2016) so that all benefit and make progress toward implementing the United Nations Development Programme (UNDP) 2030 Sustainable Development Goals (SDGs) (United Nations, 2016).

The African Open Science Platform initiative (Academy of Science of South Africa, 2016)—managed by the Academy of Science of South Africa, directed by the Committee on Data for Science and Technology (CODATA) and funded through the South African Department of Science and Technology—is one of the major outcomes of the international accord, focusing specifically on sharing data as an outcome of OS. During year one of the project (2017), much progress was made in identifying opportunities for inter-regional links to strengthen collaboration and toward international alignment with science activities on an international level. The project further tries to better understand the current status of OS policies, infrastructure, capacity building and incentives—in other words: what is the current status in terms of the four focus areas, where do countries want to take research sharing, and what do countries need to advance OS and data sharing.

Where governments invest in research and where there is the political will, African countries appear to be actively generating and curating data. The Square Kilometre Array initiative is another indicator of research activity, as well as the presence of the African Academies of Science and Research Educational Networks (NRENs). African countries participating as part of the Square Kilometre Array initiative include South Africa, Mozambique, Madagascar, Zambia, Mauritius, Kenya, Ghana, Namibia, and Botswana. The NRENs in those countries will play an important role in enabling the transmission and sharing of trusted data across the globe. Collaborative projects such as H3ABioNet and GBIF further champion the sharing of data on the African continent, and the experiences from these projects are regarded as important in further informing the frameworks and roadmaps to be delivered as outcomes of this project. The frameworks and roadmaps in terms of OS policy, ICT infrastructure, capacity building and incentives are expected to be of great help for countries also exploring the advancement of OS.

Although there is no existing OS policy on the national level thus far, advocacy and awareness creation efforts among government officials—in Madagascar, Botswana, South Africa, Kenya, and Uganda—have brought together stakeholders and decision makers on the national level to discuss this very important topic toward formulating national policies. The fundamental role of data for research, economic development and ecological sustainability are recognized as important and are supported by the selected governments, as well as research institutions and the community. Selected institutions, such as the ICT Centre of Excellence & Open Data in Kenya, have institutional level policies for governing data and the outcomes of science. Policy is a process, differing from one country to the next, and to develop policy, decision makers first need to have a better understanding of the principles, benefits, challenges, intellectual property, licensing and other issues associated with OS and open data. One of the deliverables of the AOSP project is to provide a policy framework and roadmap aligned with international requirements, to guide African governments in terms of issues that should be addressed through such a policy, but also to provide guidelines on how to roll out such a policy. It is still early days for Africa in terms of OS policy, but through advocacy and awareness creation much is gained, and great progress is expected.

CONCLUSION

This panel assembled researchers from different continents to present the current state of the OS movement in their regions and the unique challenges and strategies in the globalization era. Various actions have been under development to establish governing policies and mandates, build supporting infrastructure, and encourage inter/multi organizational collaboration in a global environment.

REFERENCES

Academy of Science of South Africa. (2009). African Open Science Platform. Retrieved February 14, 2018, from http://africanopenscience.org.za/

Ayris, P. et al. (2016). Realising the European Open Science Cloud. First report and recommendations of the Commission High Level Expert Group on the European Open Science Cloud. Directorate-General for Research and Innovation. doi:10.2777/940154

Basken, P. (2016). As the drive to share data intensifies, can standards keep up? *The Chronicle of Higher Education*. Retrieved from https://www.chronicle.com/article/As-the-Drive-to-Share-Data/238722

Basken, P. (2017a). Elsevier embraces data-sharing standards, in step toward scientific openness. *The Chronicle of Higher Education*. Retrieved from https://www.chronicle.com/article/Elsevier-Embraces-Data-Sharing/241089

Basken, P. (2017b). Journals' retreat from data-sharing mandate puts onus on universities and government. *The Chronicle of Higher Education*. Retrieved from https://www.chronicle.com/article/Journals-Retreat-From/240323

Bloom, K., Boccali, T., Bockelman, B., Bradley, D., Dasu, S., Dost, J., Vuosalo, C. (2015, December). Any data, any time, anywhere: Global data access for science. Paper presented at Big Data Computing (BDC), 2015 IEEE/ACM 2nd International Cyprus (pp. 85-91). Symposium Limassol.

Borgman, C. L. (2015). *Big data, little data, no data: Scholarship in the networked world.* Cambridge, MA: MIT Press.

Center for Open Science. https://cos.io/

European Commission (2016). Open Innovation, Open Science, Open to the World - A Vision for Europe. DG Research and Innovation. doi:10.2777/061652.

Europe Commission. (2017). G7 Science Ministers' communiqué. Retrieved from http://www.g7italy.it/sites/default/files/documents/G7%20Science%20Communiqu%C3%A9.pdf

Fecher B., Friesike S. (2014) Open Science: One Term, Five Schools of Thought. In Bartling S., & Friesike S. (eds), Opening Science. Springer, Cham: Heidelberg et al. doi: 10.1007/978-3-319-00026-8_2Pordes, R., Petravick, D.,

Gu, L. (2013). A Review of Scholar Communication in Open Science . Knowledge Management Forum, 1(2):9-15.

Kramer, B., Olson, D., Livny, M., Roy, A., … Foster, I. (2007). The open science grid. *Journal of Physics: Conference Series*. 78(1), 012057. doi:10.1088/1742-6596/78/1/012057

Liu, F., & Zhang, T. (2017). An emerging type of scholarly articles in the open science background: research elements publishing. *Chinese Journal of Scientific & Technical Periodicals*,(2):138-144

Organisation for Economic Co-Operation and Development (OECD) (2007). *OECD Principles and Guidelines for Access to Research Data from Public Funding*. Retrieved March 16, 2018, from https://www.oecd.org/sti/sci-tech/38500813.pdf

Science International. (2016). *Science International Accord on Open Data in a Big Data World.* Retrieved February 14, 2018, from http://www.science-international.org/

Tang, Y., & Xiao, X. (2013). Development process of open science: existing problems and their solutions. *Information & Documentation Services, 34*(5), 20-24.

United Nations. (2016). *Transforming our world: the 2030 Agenda for Sustainable Development.* Retrieved February 14, 2018, from https://sustainabledevelopment.un.org/post2015/transformingourworld

United Nations Educational, Scientific and Cultural Organization. (n.d.). Open Science Movement. Retrieved from http://www.unesco.org/new/en/communication-and-information/portals-and-platforms/goap/open-science-movement/

Wilkinson, M. D. et al. (2016). The FAIR Guiding Principles for scientific data management and stewardship. *Sci. Data*3:160018. Retrieved February 14, 2018, from https://www.researchgate.net/publication/298345883_The_FAIR_Guiding_Principles_for_scientific_data_management_and_stewardship

Wilsdon, J., Bar-Ilan, J., Frodeman, R., Lex, E., Peters, I., & Wouters, P. (2017). Next-generation metrics: Responsible metrics and evaluation for open science. Report of the European Commission Expert Group on Altmetrics. doi:10.2777/337729

Wu, X. (2016). Connotation Dimensions, Characteristics and Developmental Models of Open Science. *Science & Technology Progress & Policy*, 33(20):7-12.

Xu, J. (2011). Open science: a future shaped by shared experience. *English Digest*,7: 23-27.

Zhang, X. (2014). The motivations of open science: an empirical measuring for academic and industrial scientists. *Studies in Science of Science*, 32(11):1620-1629.

Challenges for Social Media: Misinformation, Free Speech, Civic Engagement, and Data Regulations

Nic DePaula
University at Albany, SUNY, USA.
ndepaula@albany.edu

A.J. Million
University of Michigan's iSchool, USA.
millioaj@umich.edu

Kaja J. Fietkiewicz
Heinrich Heine University Düsseldorf, Germany.
kaja.fietkiewicz@hhu.de

Isabelle Dorsch
Heinrich Heine University Düsseldorf, Germany.
isabelle.dorsch@hhu.de

Thomas J. Froehlich
Kent State University, USA.
tfroehli@kent.edu

Aylin Ilhan
Heinrich Heine University Düsseldorf, Germany.
aylin.ilhan@hhu.de

ABSTRACT

Social media has arguably brought one of the greatest changes to Internet communication since the invention of the Web but challenges as well. Apart from helping people to have access and to exchange information, social media has also been used to spread misinformation, hate speech, and the user-generated data is adopted for targeted commercial and political advertising based on personal profiles. Moreover, the most popular applications available are owned by a small number of companies who may have an undue influence on how civic engagement takes place on their platforms. In this panel, four panelists will discuss the following: *misinformation and the role of pseudo-cognitive authorities*; *hate speech and Germany's Network Enforcement Act (NetzGD)*; *civic engagement and market capture by social media companies*; and finally, *personal data processing and the General Data Protection Regulation (GDPR)*. We intend to raise interesting questions helping to understand these issues, and to find solutions for the beneficial use of information technologies as well as to scope out all its advantages.

KEYWORDS

Civic Engagement, Hate Speech, Misinformation, Social Media, GDPR

INTRODUCTION

The use of social media has become an integral part of many areas in our lives – from the communication between friends, to the organizing of social gatherings, protests and even the decision-making of government officials. The way these technologies have developed, however, have also brought many challenges, which highlight their ethical, legal and political characteristics. One of the main challenges of social media is the proliferation of misinformation or "fake news." According to Allcott and Gentzkow (2017, p. 213), fake news "are intentionally and verifiably false, and could mislead readers." On social media, "consumers cannot spotlessly infer accuracy" (p. 214) of the news and this may help explain why fake news and misinformation quickly spread. In this panel presentation, Thomas J. Froehlich discusses the problem of online misinformation and in particular the issue of "pseudo-cognitive-authorities." He raises questions regarding the role of such authorities and how disinformation may be facilitated on social media.

Another challenge of social media concerns hate speech. Perry and Olsson (2009) stress that with the Internet, hate groups get a new platform where they can distribute their messages and form their communities. Mondal, Silva, and Benevenuto define hate speech "as an offensive post, motivated, on whole or in a part, by the writer's bias against an aspect of a group of people" (2017, p. 87); and Facebook defines it as "content that attacks people based on their actual or perceived race, ethnicity, national origin, religion, sex, gender, sexual orientation, disability or disease" (Facebook, n.d.). As simple as the definitions may seem – it is not easy to control hate speech and to support and protect free speech, especially since national laws are so different (Akdeniz, 2006; Alam, Raina, & Siddiqui, 2016). In this panel presentation, Kaja J. Fietkiewicz raises the issue of hate speech and discusses the Network Enforcement Act that was passed in Germany in January 2018. She reviews the debate on how this legislative act may perform in addressing the hate speech dilemma.

One of the main benefits of the Internet and social media for political purposes is their uses in civic engagement activities. Civic engagement is central to democratic politics and it can be defined in many ways. For example, Putnam (2001) defines civic engagement as connections to community and social life, and Norris (2001) conceives of civic engagement as intrinsically related to politics. Vitak et al. (2011, p. 108) noted that Facebook and its possibilities "offer affordable (i.e., free) opportunities to develop civic engagement skills with little to no additional time costs for users of Facebook, while simultaneously having access to a potentially large enough ''public'' to develop civic skills." But what happens when Facebook is the only game in town? In this panel presentation, A.J. Million discusses the problem of social media market capture and the consequences for non-profits involved in civic engagement.

Social media clearly offer a number of benefits to society. These tools allow companies to advertise their products, and political groups to reach their constituencies. They also lead to mass social phenomena, such as protests and opinion changes, which can have overall positive benefits to societies. Moreover, these tools are generally open for individuals to exchange information that they may prefer, and sometimes not prefer, to see and potentially discuss. But how are personal data of individuals—generated by social media and online activity more broadly—processed by the companies that are given and become owners of the data? In this panel presentation, Nic DePaula raises the issue of targeted advertising, psychological profiles and how the General Data Protection Regulation (GDPR) of the European Union is supposed to address the issue of personal data processing and the rights of the data subject.

PANEL STRUCTURE

The panel is structured as follows. First, the chair will introduce the panel speakers and give an overview of the discussed topics, including the main concerns and definitions of the research area as well as the outcomes of an informetric analysis on the topic. Following this, each panelist will answer the main question regarding her or his research. The addressed questions concern the challenges and risks related to social media use in the context of fake news, hate speech, manipulation and surveillance. The panel will be concluded with a discussion round. The panel should last 1.5 hours.

Aylin Ilhan and Isabelle Dorsch will introduce the speakers, present a short informetric analysis, and moderate the panel.

Isabelle Dorsch is research associate and Ph.D candidate at the Department of Information Science, Heinrich Heine University Düsseldorf (Germany). She is a lecturer in social media and knowledge representation as well as mentor for student research projects. Besides social media (with special focus on user behavior on Instagram), her research interests include, but are not limited to informetrics (especially scientometrics).

Aylin Ilhan is research associate and Ph.D candidate at the Department of Information Science, Heinrich Heine University Düsseldorf (Germany). She is a lecturer in social media, scientific writing as well as mentor for student research projects. Her research interests include, but are not limited to social media (user behavior), activity trackers (e.g., acceptance, impact, motivation, information and user behavior) and smart cities.

Fake news, its rapid dissemination and its relation to pseudo-cognitive-authorities, by Thomas J. Froehlich

Given the rise of disinformation and misinformation, particularly in terms of fake news or doxing, with a large segment of the population not only embracing but also perpetuating this content, questions need to be raised about false or pseudo- cognitive authorities in the disinformation marketplace. What are pseudo-cognitive-authorities? What are their characteristics and venues? How do they foster and spread fake news through social media and cable news? Recent studies (e.g., Vosoughi, Roy, & Aral, 2018) suggest that lies spread faster online than the truth and that the right-wing is more prone to uncritically embrace and spread fake news. Combining these threads leads to the question: What are the grounds, psychological and otherwise, to account for the speed and dissemination of fake news and the role(s) that pseudo-cognitive-authorities for creating and abetting the spread of such disinformation?

Thomas J. Froehlich, Ph.D., is Professor Emeritus, School of Information, Kent State University (27 years). The majority of his publications are concerned with ethical considerations in the information professions, evolving in part from his philosophy background (Ph.D., Duquesne University). Dr. Froehlich currently teaches a course on the Age of Disinformation and has taught in the areas of information science, ethics, online searching, knowledge management and user interface design. He has provided workshops, trainings, seminars or presentations in 26 countries.

The boundary between hate and free speech—What are the risks of the German Network Enforcement Act? by Kaja J. Fietkiewicz

Free speech is one of the fundamental democratic rights. Especially today with the enormous popularity of social media the ordinary user can address a much broader audience than before. As in real life, social media channels are not exclusively used for "friendly" and positive content, but also for hate speech, mobbing or defamation. In the last few years the amount of hate speech spread via social media increased, making the so-called "incitement of the masses" or "incitement to hatred" get more and more attention by the law enforcement. One of the problems was the reluctance of platforms like Facebook to (immediately) delete such content after it was reported by users. To counteract the spreading of hate speech as well as "fake news" on social networks, the German legislature issued the "Netzwerkdurchsetzungsgesetz" (NetzGD), the Network Enforcement Act, which came into force on January 1st, 2018. Since then, there is an ongoing debate whether this is an adequate tool against hate speech or rather a new form of censorship based on denunciation by social media users and "enforced" by the social media giants.

Dr. Kaja J. Fietkiewicz is post-doctoral research associate at the Department of Information Science, Heinrich Heine University Düsseldorf (Germany). She is a lecturer in information law and statistics as well as mentor for student research projects. Her research interests include smart city development (with focus on e-government), information law (with focus on competition law and data privacy), as well as social media, especially social live streaming services.

Civic engagement and social media use by nonprofit organizations—Does market capture pose a threat to grassroots democratic activity? by A.J. Million

Civic engagement is central to democratic governance. Engagement can take many forms, and examples range from fundraising for nonprofit organizations to registering voters in poorly represented communities. As a consequence, more engaged communities tend to possess lower rates of crime, poverty, and unemployment, and have better health and education than their less engaged counterparts. Since the 1970's, evidence suggests that civic engagement in Western democracies is declining or changing. To remedy this issue, one solution is for nonprofits to leverage social media to engage with citizens online. There are roughly 1.5 million nonprofits in the U.S. However, based on initial data from a study of 23 nonprofits in Chicago, IL, Facebook appears to have "captured" the nonprofit social media market. Already, Facebook is the most used social media tool in the world, and market capture often hurts consumers. This raises the question if social media market capture poses a threat to grassroots democratic activity, given the key role that nonprofits play in sustaining it.

Dr. A.J. Million is a post-doctoral research fellow at the University of Michigan School of Information. His research pertains to the creation and administration of public and nonprofit information resources. He earned his Ph.D. from the University of Missouri, where his dissertation examined bureaucratic organization and innovation in U.S. state department of transportation websites.

Personal data processing and targeted advertising—Does the General Data Protection Regulation go far enough? by Nic DePaula

In an interview on March 27, 2018, Apple CEO Tim Cook, said that: "we could make a ton of money … if our customer was our product. We've elected not to do that." (Sherter, 2018). Why not? Is there an ethical problem with using personal data for targeted advertising? What about creating psychological profiles for political advertising? Or is the ethical problem one of having (or not) consent from users? Although in the U.S. and in Canada no major regulations have been created to address problems with the processing of personal data by businesses—including those that came to light from the Cambridge Analytica scandal—the General Data Protection Regulation (GDPR) has come into effect in the European Union of as May 2018 to provide some relief for those concerned. How does it achieve this? In this panel presentation, I identify issues with the processing of personal data carried out by social media and Internet companies more broadly. I then review some principles of the GDPR and its stipulated "rights of the data subject." Lastly, I raise questions regarding the necessity and sufficiency of the GDPR within its own as well as other legal contexts.

Nic DePaula is a PhD candidate in the department of Information Science at the University at Albany, State University of New York. His research interests are in data science, text mining and political communication. Previously, Mr. DePaula has worked with geographic information technologies and information security. His work has appeared in various journals, including Government Information Quarterly, Social Science Computer Review and First Monday.

ACKNOWLEDGMENTS

The panel is organized by the officers of the ASIS&T Special Interest Group Social Media (Aylin Ilhan, Isabelle Dorsch, Philippe Mongeon, Nic DePaula, Kaja Fietkiewicz and Wasim Ahmed). The SIG SM thanks all speakers for their effort. The panel is endorsed by the ASIS&T Special Interest Group Social Informatics.

REFERENCES

Akdeniz, Y. (2006). Stocktaking on Efforts to Combat Racism on the Internet. Background Paper. Intergovernmental Working Group on the Effective Implementation of the Durban Declaration and Programme of Action, Commission on Human Rights, E/CN, 4, 2006.

Alam, I., Raina, R. L., & Siddiqui, F. (2016). Free vs hate speech on social media: The Indian perspective. *Journal of Information, Communication and Ethics in Society, 14*(4), 350–363. https://doi.org/10.1108/JICES-06-2015-0016

Allcott, H., & Gentzkow, M. (2016). Social media and fake news in the 2016 election. *Journal of Economic Perspectives, 31*(2), 211–236. https://doi.org/10.3386/w23089

Facebook. (n.d.). What does Facebook consider to be hate speech? Retrieved April 04, 2018, from https://www.facebook.com/help/135402139904490/

Mondal, M., Silva, L. A., & Benevenuto, F. (2017). A measurement study of hate speech in social media. In *Proceedings of the 28th ACM Conference on Hypertext (ACM HT'17)* (pp. 85–94). New York: ACM.

Norris, P. (2001). Digital Divide: Civic Engagement, Information Poverty, and the Internet Worldwide. Cambridge: Cambridge University Press.

Perry, B., & Olsson, P. (2009). Cyberhate: the globalization of hate. *Information & Communications Technology Law, 18*(2), 185–199. https://doi.org/10.1080/13600830902814984

Putnam, R. D. (2001). Social capital: measurement and consequences. *Isuma: Canadian Journal of Policy Research [Internet]*, 41–51.

Sherter, A. (2018, March 28). Apple's Tim Cook on Facebook: "I wouldn't be in this situation." CBS News: Money Watch. Retrieved April 04, 2018, from https://www.cbsnews.com/news/apple-ceo-tim-cook-blasts-facebook/

Vosoughi, S., Roy, D., & Aral, S. (2018). The spread of true and false news online. *Science, 359*(6380), 1146–1151. https://doi.org/10.1126/science.aap9559

Vitak, J., Zube, P., Smock, A., Carr, C. T., Ellison, N., & Lampe, C. (2011). It's complicated: Facebook users' political participation in the 2008 election. *Cyberpsychology, Behavior, and Social Networking, 14*(3), 107–114. https://doi.org/10.1089/cyber.2009.0226

Decolonizing Archival Description: Can Linked Data Help?

Jennifer Douglas
University of British Columbia, Canada. jldoug@mail.ubc.ca

Greg Bak
University of Manitoba, Canada.
Greg.Bak@umanitoba.ca

Evelyn McLellan
Artefactual Systems Inc., Canada. evelyn@artefactual.com

Seth van Hooland
Université libre de Bruxelles, Belgium.
Seth.Van.Hooland@ulb.ac.be

Raymond Frogner
National Centre for Truth and Reconciliation, Canada
Raymond.Frogner@umanitoba.ca

ABSTRACT

Archival description documents the provenance of records, their interrelationships, and the processes of their creation. The concept of archival provenance was first elaborated in the context of 19th-century European archival institutions and reflects particular socio-historical perspectives on the nature of records and recordkeeping. Decolonizing archival description is a necessity, not only because it contributes to the discoverability of Indigenous knowledge woven into records of shared provenance, but also because it disrupts traditional concepts of singular provenance, calls attention to complex processes of records creation, and permits more expansive understanding of record contexts. Linked data appears to (1) promise the ability to represent complex multiple provenances, (2) promote multiple perspectives on the creation of records and (3) allow archives and Indigenous communities to work together to implement what the First Nations Information Governance Centre has characterized as Indigenous ownership, control, access and possession of records of shared provenance. From a variety of perspectives, this panel provides a critical analysis of linked data as a candidate solution for decolonizing archival description.

KEYWORDS

Linked data; archival description; archival decolonization; provenance; Records in Contexts

INTRODUCTION

This panel engages directly with the conference theme of 'building an ethical and sustainable future with emerging technologies' by exploring the potential of linked data as a tool for archival decolonization.

DECOLONIZING ARCHIVAL DESCRIPTION

For at least a quarter century, archivists have been aware of the limited and therefore inadequate representations of archival provenance made through archival description. The traditional notion of provenance, rooted in 19th century ideas about the nature of primary sources, historiography, and the governance of nation states, dictates that (1) all of the records of a single creator be kept together and not intermingled with records of any other creator and (2) that the creator's records be kept in the same way that the creator used and/or maintained them. Traditional archival description is predicated upon this essentialized and simplistic association of records to a single record creator.

The emergence of archival postmodernism in the early 1990s and its consolidation in the early 2000s resulted in a new consensus within archival studies. Records creation has since been understood to be both temporally protracted, encompassing processes of inscription, preservation, representation and access, and socially diffuse, including people from inscribers of records to the subjects, keepers and users of records (Cook 2001a, b; Bastian 2006; Nesmith 2006a, b). Archival postmodernists explored how the creation of records might be attributed to a variety of agents, including archivists themselves. This led to the articulation of simultaneous multiple provenance as an alternative to the singular and linear provenance of traditional archival theory and to Scott's serial multiple provenance (Hurley 1994, 2005a, b). Recently, some archivists have persuasively argued that subjects of records – and especially of colonial records or records documenting human rights abuses – must be viewed as co-creators of records created about them (McKemmish et al. 2011; Caswell 2014; Iacovino 2010; Evans et al. 2015). A new and significant focus on archival decolonization calls attention to traditional ideas about provenance as inherently Western and suggests that Indigenous ways of knowing might be incommensurate with traditional archival concepts and principles (Brands & Gooda 2006; Fraser and Todd 2016; Genovese 2016; Nakata 2012; Ghaddar 2016). How archivists represent the creation of records is emerging as an issue of social justice related to the power of archives to mediate societal memory (Wood et al. 2016).

Archival description does more than simply allow records to be discovered and accessed: establishing provenance asserts the context of creation of the records and thus establishes ownership and control over them. When Indigenous records - such as those created through government surveillance, regulation and oppression, or through anthropological or archaeological study - are presented as having a singular, non-Indigenous provenance, this not only makes the records difficult for Indigenous researchers to discover, it also silences Indigenous voices, denies Indigenous agency and undermines Indigenous cultural sovereignty. This has long been understood to be a problem in terms of removing Indigenous knowledge from Indigenous control (Hagan 1978; Christen 2012; TCPS2 2014). Indigenous groups working at national and international levels have created declarations and protocols that seek to establish accurate provenance of Indigenous knowledge, including the First Nations Information Governance Centre's OCAP Principles (2014); the First Archivists' Circle's Protocols for Native American Archival Materials (2004) and the United Nations Declaration on the Rights of Indigenous Peoples (2007).

Although recognition of the need to expand understanding of records creation, and to develop new means of representing it, have circulated for decades, archival descriptive methodologies, standards and systems have changed very little (Dancy 2012). The Australian Series System implemented Scott's (1966) concept of serial multiple provenance and has been widely deployed by archives in Australia and selectively in Canada. The more complex forms of simultaneous multiple provenance that are key to archival decolonization have been worked out in theory for more than a decade but have yet to be implemented in any archival system. Archivists have continued to rely on top-down, hierarchical, database-driven content management systems that do not challenge traditional models of provenance. The emergence of linked data as a new technology appears to offer new opportunities to represent the complexities of archival creation.

DECOLONIZATION THROUGH LINKED DATA?

There is a small but growing literature on how archives might make use of linked data technologies such as W3C's Resource Description Framework (RDF). Niu (2016) surveys linked data projects carried out by archival institutions; these tend to focus on combining data from across the cultural heritage sector, with a particular emphasis on the reuse of authority records and the sharing of basic biographical information. While some of the projects seek to create new pathways of discovery, none do so as a way of decentering traditional archival provenance or advancing archival decolonization. Theoretical studies (e.g. Lemieux 2014; Gracy 2015) have explored whether linked data might allow archives to represent the multiple relationships among records and between records and agents that lie beyond the reach of traditional archival provenance but have not attempted a practical implementation of linked data within contemporary archival descriptive systems.

The International Council of Archives has introduced a draft conceptual model, Records in Contexts (RiCS) (ICA 2016), that promises to revise the theoretical underpinnings of traditional archival description, and particularly the concepts of creation and provenance, and to allow implementation of linked data. With the issuance of this draft standard, the time is ripe for a critical analysis of the potential of RiCS and of linked data to engage with debates about archival provenance and address the increasingly urgent need to decolonize archival description.

PANEL FORMAT AND PANELISTS

The panel will consist of a roundtable during which each panelist will give a 10-minute statement followed by audience commentary and discussion. The panelists will ask the audience to consider the following: new technologies often promise to solve old problems, but those old problems can sometimes remain embedded – or baked into – new approaches. Can linked data help us solve 'old problems'? What 'old problems' do we need to be wary of bringing back in to new approaches to the representation of records and related materials? What 'new problems' are created by 'open' approaches, or by viewing technology itself as progressive or liberatory? Can technologies like linked data aid in the construction of mutually recognized "ethical spaces" (TCPS; CIHR) for Indigenous methods of knowledge creation?

Jennifer Douglas

Jennifer Douglas is an assistant professor at the iSchool, School of Library, Archival and Information Studies at the University of British Columbia. She teaches courses on archival arrangement and description, personal and community archives, and foundational archival concepts, and has published on archival creation and the principle of provenance.

Douglas will introduce the concepts of archival provenance and archival creatorship. She will trace an evolution from traditional ideas that equate provenance with a single creator through to more recent ideas about multiple provenance and about the variety of different ways in which archives are created by different agents and over time. Douglas will also introduce the draft standard RiCS and discuss its potential to serve as a transformative model for archival description.

Greg Bak

Greg Bak is an associate professor of Archival Studies at the University of Manitoba. Until 2011 he was a Senior Digital Archivist at Library and Archives Canada where he worked on the LAC Trusted Digital Repository, among other projects. His teaching and publications address the current practice, theory and history of digital archiving and archival decolonization.

Bak will explore intersections between the history of digital archiving, the theory and practice of archival description, and archival decolonization.

Evelyn McLellan

Evelyn McLellan, President, Artefactual Systems Inc. Artefactual is a Canadian company that develops free and open-source software applications for archives, libraries and museums. McLellan has a Master of Archival Studies from the University of British Columbia, and her areas of specialization include digital archives and linked data. For the past two years, she has been an active member of a working group that released a draft OWL ontology for the PREMIS preservation metadata dictionary in December 2017.

McLellan will focus on the technical aspects of implementing linked data, exploring how emerging ontologies and evolving technological platforms affect expectations for both archival practice and the user experience.

Seth van Hooland

Seth van Hooland is deputy-head of the Information and Communication Science department and associate professor at Université libre de Bruxelles. His current research focuses on the possibilities and limits of the linked data paradigm within the field of document and records management. In the past, he initiated the Free your metadata project and published two handbooks on metadata quality and teaching digital humanities.

van Hooland will focus on the debate between minting new elements and properties to express archival finding aids as linked data and using existing ontologies from other application domains. He will argue that, in contrast to RiCS, which has the ambition of proposing a full-fledged ontology for the archival domain, a more pragmatic approach can be taken by embedding specific new elements within the existing framework of EAD or by using extensions of other ontologies such as schema.org.

Raymond Frogner

Raymond Frogner is the Head of Archives for the National Centre for Truth and Reconciliation, located on the campus of the University of Manitoba. His current research focuses on the history of the representation of Indigenous identity within western institutions of law and cultural heritage.

Frogner will focus on how digital technologies have brought conceptual ruptures to the colonial relationships between Indigenous peoples and western institutions of cultural, legal and academic authority. He will discuss how public archives have been characterized by a kind of cognitive imperialism where certain knowledge types are privileged. A resurgence of Indigenous activism in our spaces of public engagement suggests a need to reconceptualize our social relationships of knowledge production, preservation and access (Alfred 2009; Battiste & Youngblood Harrison 2000; Youngblood Harrison 2016). Frogner considers whether linked data can be more capable of representing Indigenous knowledge paradigms than traditional database models have been, suggesting that this is an ongoing conversation that reaches beyond the boundaries of traditional archival theory and method.

REFERENCES

Alfred, T. (2009). Peace, Power, Righteousness: An Indigenous Manifesto. Oxford University Press.

Bastian, J. A. (2006). Reading colonial records through an archival lens: the provenance of place, space and creation. Archival science, 6(3), 267-284.

Battiste, M., Youngblood Henderson, J. (2000) Protecting Indigenous Knowledge and Heritage: A Global Heritage. Purich Publishing.

Brands, J., & Gooda, M. (2006). Putting the users of research in the driver's seat: The Cooperative Research Centre for Aboriginal Health's new approach to research development. Australian Aboriginal Studies (2), 27.

Canada. CIHR guidelines for health research involving aboriginal people (2007-2010). http://www.cihr-irsc.gc.ca/e/29134.html

Canada. Panel on research ethics (2014). TCPS2(2014)-Tri-Council Policy Statement: Ethical Conduct for Research Involving Humans. Retrieved from: http://www.pre.ethics.gc.ca/eng/policy-politique/initiatives/tcps2-eptc2/Default/

Caswell, M. (2014). Toward a survivor-centered approach to records documenting human rights abuse: lessons from community archives. Archival Science, 14 (3.4), 307-3

Christen, K. (2012). Does information really want to be free? Indigenous knowledge systems and the question of openness. Cook, T. (1997). What is past is prologue: a history of archival ideas since 1898, and the future paradigm shift. Archivaria, 43, 17-63.

Cook, T., & Schwartz, J. M. (2002b). Archives, records, and power: from (postmodern) theory to (archival) performance. Archival Science, 2, (3-4), 171-185.

Dancy, R. (2012). RAD: past, present and future. Archivaria, 74, 7-41.

Douglas, J. (2018). A call to rethink archival creation: exploring types of creation in personal archives. Archival Science 18(1), 29-49.

Evans, J., McKemmish, S., Daniels, E., & McCarthy, G. (2015). Self-determination and archival autonomy: advocating activism. Archival Science, 15(4), 337-368.

First Archivists' Circle. Protocols for Native American Archival Materials. Retrieved: http://www2.nau.edu/libnap-p/protocols.html

First Nations Information Governance Centre (2014). Ownership, Control, Access and Possession (OCAP™): The Path to First Nations Information Governance. Retrieved from:http://fnigc.ca/sites/default/files/docs/ocap_path_to_fn_information_governance_en_final.pdf

Fraser, C. & Todd, Z. (2016). Decolonial sensibilities: Indigenous research and engaging with archives in contemporary colonial Canada. L'internationale. Retrieved from: http://www.internationaleonline.org/research/decolonising_practices/54_decolonial_sensibilities_indigenous_research_and_engaging_with_archives_in_contemporary_colonial_canada

Genovese, T.R. (2016). Decolonizing archival methodology: combating hegemony and moving towards a collaborative archival environment. AlterNative: An International Journal of Indigenous Peoples 12(1), 32-42.

Ghaddar, J.J. (2016). The spectre in the archive: truth, reconciliation and Indigenous archival memory. Archivaria, 82, 3-26.

Gracy, K. F. (2015). Archival description and linked data: a preliminary study of opportunities and implementation challenges. Archival Science, 15(3), 239-294.

Hagan, W. (1978). Archival Captive—The American Indian. *The American Archivist*, *41*(2), 135-142.

Hurley, C. (2005a). Parallel provenance: part 1: what, if anything, is archival description? Archives and Manuscripts, 33(1), 110-145.

Hurley, C. (2005b). Parallel provenance: Part 2: When something is not related to everything else. Archives and Manuscripts, 33 (2), 52-91.

Iacovino, L. (2010). Rethinking archival, ethical and legal frameworks for records of Indigenous Australian communities: a participant relationship model of rights and responsibilities. Archival science, 10 (4), 353-372.

International Council on Archives. Expert Group on Description (2016). Records in Contexts - A Conceptual Model. Retrieved from: https://www.ica.org/en/egad-ric-conceptual-model

Lemieux, V. L. (2014). Toward a "Third Order" archival interface: research notes on some theoretical and practical implications of visual explorations in the Canadian context of financial electronic records. Archivaria, 78, 53-93.

McKemmish, S., Faulkhead, S., & Russell, L. (2011). Distrust in the archive: reconciling records. Archival Science, 11(3-4), 211-239.

Nakata, M., Nakata, V., Keech, S., & Bolt, R. (2012). Decolonial goals and pedagogies for Indigenous studies. Decolonization: Indigeneity, Education & Society, 1(1), 120-140.

Nesmith, T. (2006a). The concept of societal provenance and records of nineteenth-century Aboriginal-European relations in Western Canada: implications for archival theory and practice. Archival Science 6(3), 351-360.

Nesmith, T. (2006b). Reopening archives: bringing new contextualities into archival theory and practice. Archivaria, 60, 259-274.

Nesmith, T. (2002). Seeing archives: postmodernism and the changing intellectual place of archives. American Archivist, 65 (1), 24-41.

Niu, J. (2016). Linked data for archives. Archivaria 82, 83-110.

Wood, S et al. (2014). Mobilizing records: re-framing archival description to support human rights. Archival Science, 14(3-4), 397-419.

Youngblood Henderson, J. (2016). Postcolonial ghost dancing: Diagnosing European colonialism. In Reader, D. and Morra, L.M. (Eds.) Learn, Teach, Challenge: Approaching Indigenous Literatures. Wilfred Laurier Press.

Lost in Knowledge Translation: Our Shifting Research Landscape

Alexeis Garcia-Perez
Coventry University, United Kingdom. ab1258@coventry.ac.uk

Denise A. D. Bedford
Georgetown University, United States, db233@georgetown.edu

Wayne Jones
University of the District of Columbia, United States. dwane.jones@udc.edu

Darin Freeburg
University of South Carolina, DARINF@mailbox.sc.edu

Peter Tatian
Urban Institute, United States, ptatian@urban.org

Dean Testa
Goodyear Tire and Rubber Co., LLC (retired), USA. Dean.testa@gmail.co

ABSTRACT

In 2018 there is a new research modality. Research is increasingly produced by individuals and organizations not formally affiliated with academic institutions; based on funding that does not come from the public sphere; aligned with and intended to support advocacy perspectives and is designed for use by particular communities and agents. The new research modality presents challenges and opportunities. While all of these new agents in the research landscape are well educated and qualified to conduct research, in many cases they are operating outside of the traditional research environment and perhaps with a different set of "research cultural norms". This new research modality in fact begs for a solution similar to that promoted within the health sciences field – a model of knowledge translation. A panel of researchers drawn from across the new research landscape will engage with information professionals to discuss six key questions.

KEYWORDS

Research landscape, community-based research, research markets, research processes, research safeguards

INTRODUCTION

The research landscape has evolved over the past century. Prior to World War II research was the purview of independent scholars and inventors. The victories of the Allied forces in World War II and the critical role that research played in that outcome stimulated post-war public sector investment in academic research. Academic research conducted with federal funding was the dominant model until the 1970s. In the 1990s the landscape shifted to include private foundation support. The early years of the 21st century have seen research funds and researchers shift further to the local and community level.

NEW RESEARCH MODALITY

In 2018 there is a new research modality. Research is increasingly: produced by individuals and organizations not formally affiliated with academic institutions; based on funding that does not come from the public sphere; aligned with and intended to support advocacy perspectives and is designed for use by particular communities and agents. This new research modality is a logical result of the shift in the research landscape (Adams Black Clemmons and Stephan 2005) (Chopyak and Levesque 2001) (Chopyak and Levesque 2002) (Collins 2011) (Fontana Geuns and Matt 2006) (Kaushal et al 2014) IKim et al 2013) (Nelson 2004) (Nelson 2008) (Spencer 2001) (Spencer 2001) (Welikala 2011). It is further supported by a refocus on communities and individuals in the new knowledge economy and knowledge society. Today, four of the most highly educated generations are alive and contributing to the broader knowledge base. The number of individuals who are sufficiently well educated and skilled to undertake good quality research is significant. Retirees may be leaving the paid workforce but they are not leaving the knowledge workforce, and they are increasingly interested in contributing to applied and basic research. Citizens of all ages are engaged in maker spaces that afford access to local expertise, tools and technologies needed to do innovative research. Think tanks increasingly undertake research pertaining to public policy and "hot topic" issues. While some think tanks tend toward advocacy research rather than applied or basic research, their results are routinely reported out in the media. Think tanks such as the Urban Institute and National Bureau of Economic Research (Bedford and Hadar, 2014) (Welner et al 2010) (routinely generate high quality research products that used by communities and non-profits. Private industry is now a major source of research – with much research being conducted in house and targeted towards products and services. The University of the District of Columbia's Muirkirk Experimental Farm and the Shenandoah Master Naturalists are communities of volunteer citizen scientists and researchers who advance applied and basic knowledge in agricultural and natural resources. This new research modality is significantly different from the pre-World War II era of the independent inventor or the post-World War II academic researcher working from large public agency grants.

IMPACT ON RESEARCH LIFE CYCLE AND KNOWLEDGE TRANSLATION

The new research modality presents challenges and opportunities. While all of these new agents in the research landscape are well educated and qualified to conduct research, in many cases they are operating outside of the traditional research environment and perhaps with a different set of "research cultural norms". This new research modality in fact begs for a solution similar to that promoted within the health sciences field – a model of knowledge translation (Eppler 2007). This program will focus on knowledge translation, and opportunities and challenges for its use in a broader research context. According to the Canadian Institutes of Health Research Canadian Institutes of Health Research (2007), knowledge translation is defined as "the exchange, synthesis and ethically-sound application of knowledge - within a complex system of interactions among researchers and users - to accelerate the capture of the benefits of research for Canadians through improved health, more effective services and products, and a strengthened health care system." While the model has been primarily applied to the health services context, it has value for today's increasingly complex research environment. Knowledge translation involves the collaborative and systematic review, assessment, identification, aggregation and practical application of high-quality ...research by key stakeholders (i.e., consumers, researchers, practitioners, policy makers) for the purpose of improving the lives of individuals.

Knowledge translation models (Figure 1) provide a holistic view of the activities essential to ensuring that knowledge which begins its life as research ultimately impacts those who can benefit from it. In the new research landscape, we might find that defining research questions and methods (KT1) and conducting research (KT2) follow standard practices. However, subsequent translation steps - publishing in plain language and accessible formats (KT3), placing research findings in the context of other knowledge and sociocultural norms (KT4), making decisions and taking action informed by research findings (KT5) and influencing subsequent rounds of research based on the impacts of knowledge use (KT6) - may not be built into the processes of new players in the research landscape. Additionally, non-academic research or research funded by non-regulated sources may not ensure the same standards for ethical behavior, quality controls or safety standards where there is no Institutional Research Board oversight. Where research projects achieve the goal of direct knowledge translation and implementation, they may bypass the publication step entirely. In some cases, they may produce gray literature or simple media communications but not result in any persistent or peer reviewed information.

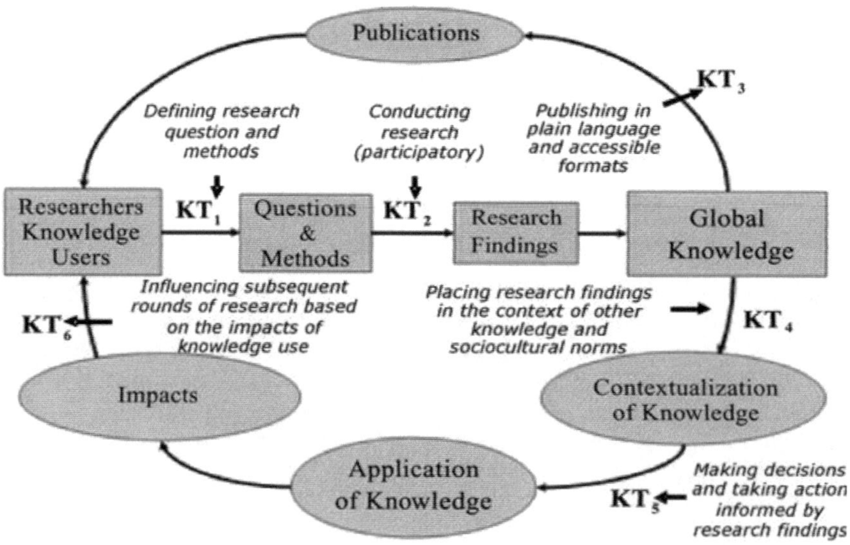

Figure 1. Canadian Institutes of Health Research Knowledge Translation [KT] within the Research Cycle Chart.

Key challenges include the capture of and access to this new wealth of research, the simple preservation of the new knowledge that is being generated and used, and the long-standing challenge of research uptake.

NEW RESEARCH MARKETS – NEW KNOWLEDGE MODELS

The Knowledge Economy is grounded on markets for ideas and innovation. We need to think about research markets differently in the knowledge economy. Information and knowledge scientists have developed robust methods for identifying, reviewing, capturing, organizing and making accessible the formally published results of research generated in academic environments. These methods are predicated on an understanding of the traditional research market – which is grounded in the pre-1970s academic research model. Do these methods need to be adapted or extended? Does the research community need to be expanded to go beyond publishers, information scientists and academic researchers to include all of the new players in the landscape? Is there a new role for information scientists in the new research landscape, or does this role belong to the knowledge scientists who are engaged in research with these new players? Who consumes and looks for research has also shifted. In the new research landscape, producers and consumers are part of the same community. What does this mean for where we capture, preserve and make available research results? Do all of these new research players still look to an academic or public library to discover, preserve, and access this research? Or, is there a need for a new open research repository model? What is the impact of the growing interest in making underlying research data available to the larger community?

New knowledge markets challenge existing research reward and recognition systems. In the traditional areas of the landscape, research is rewarded with publications and life-time tenure awards. In other parts of the new landscape, the reward for research is a practical implementation with tangible impacts. In the private sector, traditional rewards are based on financial returns or an increased market share. However, private-public-community based research collaborations are generating multifaceted rewards including environmental and social reputational capital. What models need to be created to align or mediate these different economic rewards? Six key questions for this new research landscape include how might researchers and information scientists: (1) align the research agendas and questions across the research landscape? (2) share basic knowledge about how to conduct research across the landscape? (3) ensure all the players have the capacity to capture, publish, distribute and preserve their research? (4) ensure that there are appropriate peer review processes in place for all knowledge generated through research - emphasis on "peer" here focuses on the intended consumers of the knowledge)? (5) ensure that feedback or impacts from any part of the landscape are accessible to all researchers? and (6) design a new preservation, publishing, search and access models to support this new research community?

PROGRAM DESIGN

This program is designed for interaction among a panel of researcher practitioners who are actively engaged in this new research landscape, and information professionals attending the ASIST 2018 annual meeting. The facilitator will open the program with short case studies from each of the six panelists to set a context for exploring the six key questions. Next the facilitator will introduce each of the six key questions and open discussions to panelists and audience. The intent is to generate a highly interactive discussion around the challenges and opportunities among panelists and the audience. The expected outcomes include: (1) increased awareness among information scientists of the new research landscape; (2) increased awareness of researchers of the need to ensure their research fulfills all six knowledge translation steps; and (3) identification of new partnerships between academic librarians and non-academic researchers.

Alexeis Garcia-Perez is Reader, Coventry University's Faculty Research Centre for Business in Society. Dr. Garcia-Perez will speak to a critical gap in today's research markets, specifically the gap that exists between society's vision and expectations for intelligent transportation systems and the actual research that is being produced by academic institutions today. Dr. Garcia-Perez will provide a case study from the United Kingdom that highlights the challenges and opportunities from the university, public sector and private sector industry perspective.

Denise Bedford is Adjunct Faculty, Georgetown University's Communication Culture and Technology and Retired Senior Information Officer, World Bank. Dr. Bedford will speak to the shifting research landscape from an economic perspective. Dr. Bedford's economics background, and her experience in private sector, public sector, university and community-based research provides a unique perspective and backdrop for the panels discussion. Dr. Bedford will provide a case study from academies of science research project carried out by a consulting company. This case study highlights the need to ensure that quality and peer review standards are built into all research projects.

Dean Testa is Manager, Knowledge Management Office, Goodyear Tire and Rubber Company LLC. Dean will discuss the challenges involved in designing and implementing collaborative research projects that involve private industry, national research laboratories and universities to bring innovative products and processes to the market efficiently and effectively.

Dwane Jones is Professor, University of the District of Columbia's **Center for Sustainable Development.** Dr. Jones is heavily engaged in community-based research at the University and across the District of Columbia. Dr. Jones will share his experiences in community-based research at the Muirkirk Farm and talk about how members of the community are prepared for and drawn into research. He will also talk about how this community addresses the challenge of knowledge translation and shortens the time between the time of discovery and uptake.

Darin Freeburg is Assistant Professor, School of Library and Information Science, University of South Carolina. Dr. Freeburg has developed a new model. Guided Innovation, which supports his research with refugee communities. This is an area where traditional research practices often do not work given the urgency of their issues and the time lags associated with research cycles. These communities must conduct their own research, combining existing knowledge with their personal knowledge, to engage in rapid prototyping of ideas for social innovation.

Peter Tatian is Senior Fellow, Urban Institute. The Urban Institute is one of several "think tanks" in the United States that conduct research. Peter will speak to the Urban Institute's approach to research and their collaboration with both academic and community-based organizations. Peter will provide a case study of their work with the University of Baltimore's Neighborhood Indicators Alliance project.

REFERENCES

Adams, J. D., Black, G. C., Clemmons, J. R., and Stephan, P. E. (2005). Scientific teams and institutional collaborations: Evidence from US universities, 1981–1999. *Research policy*, *34*(3), 259-285.

Bedford, D., and Hadar, G. (2014). "Do Think Tanks Think?", Jim Rooney (Ed.), Proceedings of the 11th International Conference on Intellectual Capital Knowledge Management And Organisational Learning, ICICKM 2014, Reading, The UK: Academic Conferences and Publishing International Limited, 64-73

Canadian Institutes of Health Research (2007). Canadian Institutes of Health Research Knowledge Translation [KT] within the Research Cycle Chart. Ottawa: Canadian Institutes of Health Research, 2007

Chopyak, J., and Levesque, P. (2001). New frameworks for research collaborations: changing what we mean by research. In *Annual Meeting of the Society for the Social Study of Science*.

Chopyak, J., and Levesque, P. N. (2002). Community-based research and changes in the research landscape. *Bulletin of Science, Technology & Society*, *22*(3), 203-209.

Collins, F. S. (2011). Reengineering translational science: the time is right. *Science translational medicine*, *3*(90), 90cm17-90cm17.

Eppler, M. J. (2007). Knowledge communication problems between experts and decision makers: An overview and classification. *Electronic Journal of Knowledge Management*, *5*(3).

Fontana, R., Geuna, A., and Matt, M. (2006). Factors affecting university–industry R&D projects: The importance of searching, screening and signalling. *Research policy*, *35*(2), 309-323.

Kaushal, R., Hripcsak, G., Ascheim, D. D., Bloom, T., Campion Jr, T. R., Caplan, A. L., and Hart, R. (2014). Changing the research landscape: The New York City clinical data research network. *Journal of the American Medical Informatics Association*, *21*(4), 587-590.

Kim, K. K., Browe, D. K., Logan, H. C., Holm, R., Hack, L., and Ohno-Machado, L. (2013). Data governance requirements for distributed clinical research networks: triangulating perspectives of diverse stakeholders. *Journal of the American Medical Informatics Association*, *21*(4), 714-719.

Nelson, R. R. (2004). The market economy, and the scientific commons. *Research policy*, *33*(3), 455-471.

Nelson, R. R. (2008). What enables rapid economic progress: What are the needed institutions? *Research Policy*, *37*(1), 1-11.

Spencer, J. W. (2001). How relevant is university-based scientific research to private high-technology firms? A United States–Japan comparison. *Academy of Management Journal*, *44*(2), 432-440.

Welikala, T. (2011). Rethinking international higher education curriculum: Mapping the research landscape. *Universitas*, *21*.

Welner, K. G., Molnar, A., Hinchey, P. H., and Weitzman, D. (Eds.). (2010). *Think tank research quality: Lessons for policy makers, the media, and the public*. IAP.

What Does the Future Hold for the Information Associations? A Panel with the Presidents of ASIS&T, ALISE, and the Chair of iSchools Consortium

Lisa M. Given
Swinburne University of Technology, Australia,
lgiven@swin.edu.au

Sam Oh
Sungkyunkwan University, Korea,
samoh@skku.edu

Heidi Julien
University at Buffalo, USA,
heidjul@buffalo.edu

Saguna Shankar
University of British Columbia, Canada,
saguna@mail.ubc.ca

ABSTRACT

This panel will explore how information associations can maintain engagement and relevance at a time when academic disciplines are evolving, when institutional and personal budgets face increasing pressures, and as we strive to connect across a broad global footprint. The panel brings together the leaders of three information science associations – the President of the Association for Information Science and Technology, the President of the Association for Library and Information Science Education, and the Chair of the iSchools' Consortium – to discuss the issues their associations face currently.

KEYWORDS

Information science; Collaboration; Professional associations; Education; Futures

INTRODUCTION

The discipline of Information Science (IS) covers a diverse, interdisciplinary range of research topic areas and professional contexts, all bound together by a shared interest in people and information, in an ever-changing global, digital landscape. Over the years, academics and professionals in IS have tried to identify clear boundaries of where these shared interests begin and end – e.g., on the ways that individuals seek information, on the design of information systems to gather and share knowledge, or on the strategies we use to classify and categorise information – to name just a few. However, as new disciplines have emerged (such as digital humanities, data science, and health informatics), those working within the historic boundaries of IS have struggled to maintain those boundaries. More and more people, professions, and academic disciplines are now working in areas that overlap and complement IS areas of practice and research. Although this presents many opportunities for IS – from collaborative research, to practice that is informed by a broader range of disciplinary contexts – this seeming encroachment on traditional IS territory also presents a number of challenges that must be considered and addressed.

This panel will explore one of these challenges – how best to maintain engagement and relevance as an information association at a time when academic disciplines, and the information professions, are changing and evolving, globally. Given global pressures on institutional and personal budgets, which can reduce membership and conference attendee numbers, the information associations must find ways to connect to a broader range of people, across a larger geographic footprint, and at a time when new organisations and events are competing for individuals' attention and membership dollars. At the same time, global political movements (from the rise of 'fake news' to the continuing struggles between proprietary vs. open access publishing models) illustrate that the need for strong associations of information specialists has never been so high. The panel will explore how information science practitioners, researchers, and educators may work together closely to collectively address these issues.

PANEL OVERVIEW

This panel brings together the leaders of three IS associations – the President of the Association for Information Science and Technology (ASIS&T), the President of the Association for Library and Information Science Education (ALISE), and the Chair of the iSchools' Consortium – to discuss the issues their associations face currently. The panel will also explore, through interactive engagement with the audience, the potential strategies that the three associations could embrace to 1) address global information issues, collectively; and, 2) work together to provide complementary supports for academics and professionals engaged in information science.

Panelist #1: Dr. Lisa M. Given, President of ASIS&T

Dr. Lisa M. Given is Associate Dean, Research and Development, for the Faculty of Health, Arts and Design at Swinburne University of Technology, Australia. She is President of the Association for Information Science and Technology and has served on the College of the Australian Research Council. Lisa is an Adjunct Professor in the School of Information Studies, Charles Sturt University (Australia), as well as in the Faculty of Arts (Digital Humanities), University of Alberta (Canada). A former Director of the International Institute for Qualitative Methodology (Canada), Lisa has received numerous grants and awards. She is Lead Investigator of a current ARC Linkage Project exploring research adoption by the wine industry and of an ARC Discovery Project looking at knowledge management practices in non-profit organizations. Lisa is also co-investigator for the ARC Linkage Project "Library and Information Science Research Australia," where she co-developed the Research Assistance & Development Australian Researchers Grant Program to provide a series of supportive activities to foster research collaboration in library and information science. She is co-author (with Donald O. Case) of *Looking for Information: A Survey of Research on Information Seeking, Needs, and Behavior* (2016, 4th edition).

Panelist #2: Dr. Heidi Julien, President of ALISE

Dr. Heidi Julien is Professor and Chair of Library and Information Studies at the University at Buffalo Graduate School of Education. Her research and teaching interests focus on digital literacy and information behavior. She is the author of numerous articles and presentations on digital and information literacy, including several keynote addresses. Heidi is President of the Association for Library and Information Science Education, past president of the Canadian Association for Information Science. She has served as editor of the *Canadian Journal of Information and Library Science (CJILS),* and on the editorial board of *Library & Information Science Research*; currently she serves on the editorial board for *CJILS* and for *Cosmopolitan Civil Societies: An Interdisciplinary Journal.* Dr. Julien is President of the Association for Library & Information Science Education. She is also active in the Association for Information Science & Technology where she has served as chair of SIG USE.

Panelist #3: Dr. Sam Oh, Chair of the iSchools' Consortium

Dr. Sam Oh earned his Ph.D. in Information Transfer from Syracuse University in 1995 and worked as an assistant professor at the University of Washington Information School for four years before returning to South Korea to become a professor at the Sungkyunkwan University iSchool. He has taught summer courses at the University of Texas at Austin; Syracuse University; and the University of North Carolina at Chapel Hill. He also spent a sabbatical year at the University of Pittsburgh iSchool. Dr. Oh served as the chair of ISO TC46/SC9 (Identification and Description) for six years and the chair of ISO/IEC JTC1 SC34 (Document Description & Processing Languages). He is currently a chair-elect of the DCMI governing board and a member of the iSchool executive committee, as well as served as a chair of the Asia-Pacific iSchools. His expertise lies in the fields of metadata design, social/big data analytics, and data/ontology modeling.

Panel Moderator: Saguna Shankar, PhD Student & ASIS&T New Leader

Saguna Shankar is a doctoral student at the University of British Columbia's iSchool where she is supervised by Dr. Lisa Nathan. In her research, she investigates ways in which information practices are designed and adapted over time in the context of transitional experiences, focusing on migration. Through this work, she explores how information practices are knotted with issues of agency, ethics, identity, and power, and considers the potential for information practices to affect social change and address societal challenges. As a member of the iStories Lab with fellow founding PhD students at the University of British Columbia, she is also involved in collaborative research on the nature of interdisciplinary communication and identity in information science. Saguna is currently working under the mentorship of Dr. Given as part of ASIS&T's New Leaders program.

PROPOSED ACTIVITIES

Interactive Discussion

Following brief (10 minute) presentations by each of the panellists, the audience will be asked to engage in a discussion of the following issues:

- Information science is a diverse and interdisciplinary field. What is the role of information science organizations in bringing different members of the field together to engage in dialogue about its current state and possible futures?
- What are some of the current opportunities for collaboration and coordination across information science communities?
- How do we keep the growth of the field sustainable? Do you see challenges or limits to its growth? How can we remain reflective about these challenges or limits while we continue to grow as a field (e.g., these may be limits we identify in the capacity of the earth, the economy, within the institutional, political, and societal structures in which we work, with the technologies that we study, etc.)?
- How do we reach out to members of the field to create a shared sense of belonging to the field of information science? How important is it to have a shared sense of belonging?

- How do we ensure that membership of the organizations is sustainable – and relevant – for the coming years?
- Thinking about our continuing education as information professionals and scholars: How may we keep pace with the ongoing transitions in emerging technologies and ways of using information?
- What is the role of the associations in enabling practitioners and researchers to not only keep up with technological changes, but to act as critical thinkers and mediators in considering the potentially positive and negative impacts of these changes from an information science perspective?

81st Annual Meeting of the Association for Information Science & Technology | Vancouver, Canada | 10 – 14 November 2018

Everyday Documentation of Arts and Humanities Collections

Ann Graf[1]
Simmons University, United States. ann.graf@simmons.edu

Crystal Fulton
University College Dublin, Ireland. crystal.fulton@ucd.ie

Amy Jackson
University of New Mexico, United States. amyjacks@unm.edu

Kathryn La Barre
University of Illinois at Urbana-Champaign, United States. kathryn.labarre@gmail.com

John Walsh
Indiana University, United States. jawalsh@indiana.edu

Carol Tilley
University of Illinois at Urbana-Champaign, United States. ctilley@illinois.edu

Shannon Lucky
University of Saskatchewan Library, Canada. shannon.lucky@usask.ca

Tim Gorichanaz
Drexel University, United States. gorichanaz@drexel.edu

ABSTRACT

Formal institutions can only collect, document and provide access to a limited number and type of materials in limited ways. Thus, institutions miss out on collections or aspects of description that may be culturally important (to underserved groups, to small subcultures, to countercultural groups, etc.), which introduces myriad ethical issues. This panel will focus on "everyday documentation" of arts and humanities-based collections done by those outside libraries, archives, and museums, and how such documentation practices can and should inform institutional practice and technological developments. The panel consists of a diverse group of academic researchers and practitioners working with a variety of arts and humanities collections. This panel is a program of the SIG for Arts and Humanities (SIG-AH).

KEYWORDS

Everyday life, documentation, art

BACKGROUND AND RELATION TO CONFERENCE THEME

Formal institutions can only collect, document and provide access to a limited number and type of materials in limited ways. This may be due to budgetary restrictions, the limits of space and time, and the resultant need to employ standard technologies and knowledge organization systems (KOS) to afford efficient and quick access. By default, institutions miss out on collections or aspects of description that may be culturally important (to underserved groups, to small subcultures, to countercultural groups, etc.). This panel will focus on "everyday documentation" of arts and humanities-based collections done by those outside libraries, archives, and museums, and how such documentation practices can and should inform institutional practice and technological developments. Such collections, objects, audiences, and KOSs are infused with ethical concerns, because of the exercise of freedom and discernment involved in processing the collections.

The panel consists of a diverse group of academic researchers and practitioners working with a variety of arts and humanities collections. Each person brings a unique perspective on community, collection, audience, and documentation to bear on the organization of materials with extra-institutional input. Some panelists have worked with communities far outside the bounds of libraries and archives, while others have acted as a bridge between subcultures and LIS institutions. The work represented on this panel is important as it informs the direction of technological developments from the very important view of humans interacting with artistic and historical objects, highlighting the views of those intimately involved in the creation, description, preservation, and (digital) dispersion of knowledge. Each participant is introduced with a paragraph describing the projects and a brief biographical statement.

PANEL STRUCTURE

Each panelist will give a very brief introduction (about 5 minutes) to their work that relates to the panel theme. One question will be allowed after each panelist. After all the presentations, there will be an open discussion. There will be an emphasis on

[1] Now at Simmons College, United States.

the knowledge gained from non-institutional participants. Salient ethical issues that also arise when working with indigenous, insider, or otherwise non-institutional or non-privileged communities or sub-cultures will be discussed, as well as how to mitigate differences between institutional practice and cultural practice. This may involve differences in how a particular community views a collection of objects, practices, or audiences, the differences in terminology used for description, the privacy and ownership of sometimes sensitive materials, and the representation of voices native to collections (see Britz & Lipinski, 2001). Gorichanaz will keep time and moderate discussion; if the audience is reticent, he will have prepared questions for discussion.

ORGANIZER AND PANELIST: ANN GRAF

Graffiti artists and street artists have long documented their own work and the work of others through photographic means. In the early days of the graffiti art movement, beginning roughly in the late 1960s in the United States, graffiti writers shared photos of their works through the mail and later through photocopied zines distributed to subscribers also through the mail. Now, the practice of graffiti art and street art documentation takes places largely online through blogs, websites, and various social media feeds such as Instagram, Facebook, and Flickr. Ann has studied over 200 graffiti art and street art websites to determine the organizational practices of those photographing and sharing these ephemeral works. She also interviewed a number of curators of these websites to gain deeper insight into how graffiti and street artworks are described and organized by those documenting the works.

Bio

Ann Graf is a PhD candidate at the University of Wisconsin-Milwaukee and holds an MLIS with a concentration in Information Organization. She has taught information literacy, information organization, research methods, and introduction to cataloguing courses over the past five years. Her research has used domain analytical methodologies alongside qualitative interviews to understand the importance of descriptive art process and style language used within the graffiti and street art community. She has also done comparative analysis of graffiti art terminology used within the graffiti art community and related terminology found within the Getty Research Foundation's Art and Architecture Thesaurus. She joins the faculty of Simmons College as Assistant Professor in July, 2018.

PANELIST: CRYSTAL FULTON

Urban exploration is a hobby, in which participants, enter and take high spec photographs or videos of buildings, factories, sewers, etc. that have been abandoned or that have fallen into disuse. Images may then be selectively posted on webpages or social media platforms, and, because urban exploration may involve trespass, a large amount of this visual content is hidden on Web. Interviews with seventeen urban explorers from Ireland and the United Kingdom revealed that urbexers have multiple motivations for hobby participation, including their commitment to creating high quality photographic images, as well as documenting sites visited as an historical record. Urban explorers exhibited both purposed and incidental creation of information on and offline. The highly secret nature of the hobby places them outside mainstream social participation; however, their approach to documenting and sharing reveals an interesting part of understanding how individuals gather, create, share, and document information.

Bio

Crystal Fulton is an associate professor in the School of Information & Communication Studies at University College Dublin, where she studies the interactions among people, information, and communication in everyday life settings. She holds a PhD and MLIS in library and information science from Western University, Canada. Her research into the information worlds of people engaged in serious leisure examines leisure participation and the connections among hobbies, behaviours around information supporting hobby activities, and impact on individuals, groups, and communities. In particular, her work extends beyond issues of information acquisition to investigate how information is used, shared or hidden, and created in both digital and non-digital environments. She has recently published on the topic of information creation by older adults engaged in genealogy in the Journal of Multidisciplinary Research. She also co-authored the monograph, Digital Detectives (Chandos, 2016), which explores digital competencies around information acquisition, evaluation, and use.

PANELIST: AMY JACKSON

While libraries have recently started to address the data deluge of qualitative and quantitative data produced in academia, musicians have been documenting their art for decades outside of institutional-supported initiatives. Although these practitioners may not use the terms research and data to describe their work, shared understandings of performance as documentation and practice as research in the arts are well established across the discipline. The end products of this documentation and research are data which carry specific contexts and requirements for sharing, access, and preservation. This data can include sound, video, image, and electronic music files, often created on personal devices, such as laptops, recorders, or cell phones. Musicians are turning to intuitive, freely-available online platforms, such as Facebook, YouTube, and Soundcloud, to share their data, and may not understand the strengths and weaknesses of each platform. Without easily accessible and intuitive institutional data repositories capable of supporting large video and audio files, this trend is likely to continue. Presenters will provide an overview of arts-based research and data as experienced by musicians, and report findings regarding how and where musicians share their data.

Bio

Amy Jackson is an Associate Professor and Director of Instruction & Outreach at the University of New Mexico. She holds an MLIS from Simmons College and a Master of Music from the Peabody Institute of the Johns Hopkins University. Previous positions include Performing Arts Librarian and Digital Initiatives Librarian. Amy's research focuses on music research data management and supporting students as producers in the library environment.

PANELIST: KATHRYN LA BARRE

Zines are self-published, small release materials that are typically pamphlet-sized. Often bartered rather than sold, zines are the passionate expressions of people whose voices are absent or mis/represented by corporate, mainstream media. Rebellious and provocative, they are ideal vehicles to connect like-minded souls. There are no rules, no definitions, and no constraints in zine culture. Authors publish anonymously or use pseudonyms. Usual metadata points, like dates or place of publication are obscured or implied. Each zine is a glorious time capsule and complex artefact, often with associated accoutrements such as pins, posters, or musical recordings. A few public and academic libraries have zine collections, but most are held by independent libraries or infoshops that honour and preserve self-published or independent media materials. This presentation will discuss the zine collection at the Urbana-Champaign Independent Media Center, and the work of a collective of radical librarians and archivists to preserve and provide access to a zine collection that has grown organically since 2000. Guided by the Zine Librarian's Code of Ethics (Berthoud et al., 2015), this presentation will engage with the ethical issues and other representational challenges presented by everyday documentation of this collection. One unique aspect of documentation for this collection involves ongoing oral history work with previous radical librarians and archivists.

Bio

Kathryn La Barre is an Associate Professor at the School of Information Sciences and Gender and Women's Studies faculty affiliate at the University of Illinois at Urbana-Champaign. She is also a principal member of the Knowledge Organization Research Group in the School of Information Studies, University of Wisconsin-Milwaukee. Her work interrogates the power dynamics of historical and contemporary naming practices in cultural heritage collections (La Barre, 2017). She is currently an ASIST Director-at-Large, and the ASIST Curator and the caretaker of the UCIMC Zine Library in Urbana, Illinois.

PANELIST: JOHN WALSH

Since 2015 La Barre, Tilley, and Walsh have collaborated on the Comic Book Readership Archive (CoBRA). For CoBRA and related projects, these scholars collect images from American comics books of the 1930s to the present to document print-based participatory culture and other readership and fandom activities. The images are captured with digital cameras, including mobile phone cameras, from comics in personal collections, libraries, archives, and special collections. The documentation of these images goes beyond standard bibliographic and archival metadata and involves, for instance, documentation about individual readers and fans and the types of participatory culture activities in which they are engaged.

Bio

John Walsh is an Associate Professor of Information and Library Science at Indiana University. His research applies digital and computational methods to the study of literary and historical documents. Walsh is an editor of digital scholarly editions (http://petrarchive.org, http://swinburneproject.org, and http://chymistry.org). He developed the Comic Book Markup Language (CBML) (http://www.cbml.org/), for scholarly encoding of comics, and TEI Boilerplate (http://teiboilerplate.org/), for publishing TEI-encoded documents on the Web. Research interests include: digital and computational literary studies; textual studies and bibliography; text technologies; book history; 19th-century British literature, poetry, and poetics; and comic books.

PANELIST: CAROL TILLEY

Children's voices—especially historical ones—are often difficult to uncover, in part because so much of the historical record of childhood has been mediated through adult voices and perspectives. Archival research around the gatekeeping of children's comics reading by adults in the United States during the mid-20th century provided an unexpected trove of letters written by young people articulating their own interests in and relationships to comics. These letters provide a unique glimpse into not only the history of comics - a medium which was the most popular form of print material during the 20th century - but also into our understanding of childhood, reading and information behaviours, and culture. These original letters and related materials such as early fanzines as well as written and drawn contributions to comic books and similar periodicals lack adequate description, making them easy to overlook. This presentation will address issues around access to these materials, their documentation, and what can be ascertained from them. It serves as a springboard for the larger project, the Comic Book Readership Archive (CoBRA).

Bio

Carol Tilley is an Associate Professor in the School of Information Sciences at the University of Illinois at Urbana-Champaign, where she is also an affiliated faculty with the Department of Gender and Women's Studies and the Center for Writing Studies. Her scholarship focuses on comics readership, especially during the mid-20th century. A 2016 Eisner Comics Industry Awards judge, Tilley is also a former Executive Board member for the Association for Library and Information Science Education (ALISE) and currently is President-Elect of the Comics Studies Society.

PANELIST: SHANNON LUCKY

PAVED Arts is a Saskatoon, SK based artist-run centre whose mandate is to support local artists working in photography, audio, video, electronic, and digital arts. They do this by operating a media production centre and exhibition space. While their mandate does not explicitly include archival activities, PAVED has kept original work made in the production centre, recordings of artists' talks, documentation of exhibitions, and operational records with the goal of making them accessible to artists, curators, researchers, and the public. This talk will describe the efforts PAVED has made over the past fifteen years to preserve and make their collections accessible and the issues they have encountered related to the nature of their non-profit, grant reliant, future-focused organizational structure. Focusing specifically on two earlier digital archive projects that PAVED created but was unable to support, this talk will look at what made these projects unsustainable and what we can learn from them.

Working in collaboration with the directors and board of PAVED, this research proposes a post-custodial archive model that partners PAVED with the University of Saskatchewan Library. This mutually beneficial partnership will give PAVED access to digital technology that has been a financial and technical barrier in the past, but that the library is uniquely positioned to provide. The library will benefit by being able to provide access to a locally important and unique collection of materials. The library has developed a digital asset management system (DAMS) that allows collaborators to add content and metadata descriptions at their own pace and from their own location, retaining ownership and rights to the material in their archives. PAVED can then focus on selection, description, and public interface design without having to worry about digital storage, backups, web hosting, and other technical concerns. The ultimate goal of this project is to develop a collaborative model for communities with cultural heritage collections and institutional memory institutions to form equitable, mutually beneficial partners for the preservation and contextual description of unique cultural heritage collections.

Bio

Shannon Lucky is an assistant librarian in the Library Systems & Information Technology unit at the University of Saskatchewan Library. Her research focuses on how open source technology can support the information practices of non-expert people and communities, particularly in the preservation and use of cultural heritage collections. She holds an MLIS and MA in humanities computing from the University of Alberta.

ORGANIZER AND MODERATOR: TIM GORICHANAZ

Tim Gorichanaz will moderate this session. He is a doctoral candidate in the College of Computing & Informatics at Drexel University. His research engages with the philosophy of documents. In his dissertation, he explored the documentation of the process of an artwork's creation.

REFERENCES

Berthoud, H., Barton, J., Brett, J., Darms, L., Fox, V., Freedman, J., … Wooten, K. (2015). Zine librarian's code of ethics. Retrieved from http://zinelibraries.info/code-of-ethics/

Britz, J. J., & Lipinski, T.A. (2001). Indigenous knowledge: A moral reflection on current legal concepts of intellectual property. *Libri, 51*, 236–246.

Fulton, C., & McGuinness, C. (2016). *Digital detectives: Solving information dilemmas in an online world.* Oxford: Chandos.

La Barre, K. (2017). Interrogating facet theory: Decolonizing knowledge organization. In R. P. Smiraglia & H.-L. Lee (Eds.), *Dimensions of knowledge: Facets for knowledge organization* (pp. 7–30). Würzburg, Germany: Ergon Verlag.

Online Targeting of Researchers/Academics: Ethical Obligations and Best Practices

Devon Greyson
University of British Columbia, Canada.
dgreyson@bcchr.ubc.ca

Amelia Gibson
The University of North Carolina at Chapel Hill, USA.
angibson@email.unc.edu

Nicole Cooke
The University of Illinois at Urbana-Champaign, USA.
nacooke@illinois.edu

Heidi Julien
University at Buffalo, USA.
heidijul@buffalo.edu

ABSTRACT

Targeted online harassment of academics has been on the rise in the US and internationally. Such harassment ranges from online threats and hacking to doxxing and organized campaigns to discredit one's work. It has now become an often-unrecognized part of the job for academics—particularly socially marginalized academics and those who study controversial topics such as race, ethnicity, gender, and sexuality—to work to protect themselves from such attacks. With this increase in intimidation attempts, new questions for the profession arise regarding what skills we should be instilling in trainees, whether professional association and academic units should be taking explicit positions or action on researcher/faculty harassment, and the obligations of our employers with regard to defending faculty, staff, and students. This panel will describe targeted online harassment of academics, discuss models for individual and institutional response, and raise questions for the profession as a whole. Sponsored by SIG ED.

KEYWORDS

Online harassment, racism, sexism, LIS education, institutional obligations

INTRODUCTION

Targeted online harassment of academics has been on the rise in the US and internationally. It has now become an extra and "invisible" (i.e., unrecognized) part of the job for academics—particularly socially marginalized academics and those who study controversial topics such as race, ethnicity, gender, and sexuality—to work to protect themselves from harassment ranging from online threats and account/site hacking to doxxing and organized campaigns to discredit one's research and teaching. Such attacks "pose a profound and ominous challenge to higher education's most fundamental values" (AAUP, 2017), disrupting the lives of targeted academics and administrators, and creating a less inclusive, safe, and welcoming environment in academia.

With this increase in threats and intimidation attempts, new questions for the profession arise regarding what skills we should be instilling in trainees, whether professional associations and academic units should be taking explicit positions or action on information researcher and faculty harassment, and the obligations of our home institutions and employers with regard to defending employees who have come under attack. This panel will discuss some ways targeted online harassment of academics has occurred, along with models for individual and institutional response to this rising climate as well as specific threats, and raise questions for the profession as a whole.

Online Targeting of Academics

While politically-motivated targeting of academics is hardly a new phenomenon (Nwanevu, 2016), current online technology combined with a recent upswell in racist, isolationist, and "populist" movements has led to new developments in online attacks against academics in the US and beyond. Using tactics associated with the previous "Gamergate" attacks against feminists in the tech sector, individuals and organized groups are harassing, doxxing, and threatening faculty members at colleges and universities of all types. Websites with names such as "Professor Watchlist" and "Campus Reform" walk the line between selectively aggregating news and outright organizing or harassment campaigns against academics whose teaching, research, or personal expression may not fall in line with the site owners' political preferences.

In the USA, it has been documented that a disproportionate number of those academics threatened via online campaigns have been African American (American Association of University Professors, 2017). Academic institutions have had mixed responses to the targeting of their faculty, sometimes protecting employees, sometimes criticizing them, and often wavering in inconsistent responses that betray their lack of preparedness for such a situation (Flaherty, 2017). Effects on targeted faculty, particularly in the absence of institutional support, may include stress, financial and career losses, and self-censorship in attempts to protect oneself against further attack.

Given that information professions engage with diversity and inclusion issues in and around online fora, it should come as no surprise that some of our own colleagues have been targeted. After receiving a Diversity Research Grant from the American Library Association's Office for Diversity, Literacy, and Outreach Services, Assistant Professor Nicole Cooke became a target of Campus Reform, an alt-right student publication whose goal it is to expose professors' "liberal biases." This "publication" is a feeder site for racists and white nationalists, and as a result of having her professional photo and contact information doxxed, Cooke spent the summer of 2017 in partial seclusion and fighting with her university and professional organizations for their support and protection for the diversity and social justice work they *say* they encourage, and that the profession absolutely needs. Cooke will detail her research, teaching, and service endeavors related to diversity (Cooke 2016), social justice, implicit bias, and microaggressions (Sweeney and Cooke 2018), and recount her advocacy efforts to alert the profession to online harassment, trolling, and racist bullying.

Emerging Guidance, Standards, and Best Practices

Most of the current guidance and tools for minimizing harm due to online targeting are individually-focused in nature, tending toward lists of things one might attempt in order to secure personal information, reduce the risk of hacking, restrict access to oneself, and document harassment. These checklists were pioneered on the open web by those targeted by Gamergate (McKeon, 2017), and were often informally prefaced with statements such as, "here's what I've learned from the last two months of getting hacked and helping friends who have gotten hacked" (Quinn, 2014). Feminist Frequency, founded by media critic and Gamergate target Anita Sarkeesian, maintains a helpful guide to that details many recommended actions such as regularly checking and removing one's personal information from databroker sites, password and website security measures, and social media practices that reduce the exposure of one's personal details.

These actions are time consuming, sometimes expensive, and often limit an academic's ability to broadly communicate and disseminate their research and ideas. The stress, time, expense, and limitations on scholarly and personal discourse caused by responding to threats and attacks are not equally distributed among the academic population, but rather are concentrated in subpopulations already facing systemic barriers to career success. As Feminist Frequency notes, their guide "is for anyone who fears they might be targeted, or who is already under attack, for speaking their mind online, but is especially designed for women, people of color, trans and genderqueer people, and everyone else whose existing oppressions are made worse by digital violence." (Freedman, Sarkeesian, & Sherman, n.d.)

Despite well-intentioned exhortations such as, "Don't suffer alone. Make sure you reach out, and again, don't judge yourself" (Quinn, 2014), anecdotal evidence indicates that online targeting is isolating and overwhelming, and few targeted academics feel they are well supported by their colleagues and institutions. A few resources have emerged that include advice for supporting a colleague who is being targeted. Ashe Dryden, for example, offers best practices for being sensitive to colleagues' security concerns (e.g., conference badges that indicate photography preferences, being sure not to broadcast colleagues' home or meeting locations via social media geolocation), as well as concrete actions to offer to a targeted colleague (e.g., offering to screen messages, reporting and blocking harassers online) (Dryden, 2014).

Institutional responses to targeting of their academics have been highly variable, although with awareness of the issue growing, certain organizations have been leading the way. Some professional associations (e.g., Art Professors of America) have offered tools and trainings for their members, in order to minimize their risks of being targeted. Such moves also increase awareness in the profession, even among those not at high risk of targeting, potentially improving collective support for individuals who do find themselves the subject or harassment campaigns and recommending resources such as C.O.A.C.H (Crash Override, n.d.) for those concerned about or experiencing an attack.

The American Association of University Professors (AAUP) has been amplifying voices of targeted professors, and built on their association's previous statements on academic freedom to lead calls for "administrations, governing boards, and faculties, individually and collectively, to speak out clearly and forcefully to defend academic freedom and to condemn targeted harassment and intimidation of faculty members," including with new institutional regulations (American Association of University Professors, 2017). However, it remains unclear the extent to which universities and other organizations have acted upon or institutionalized such exhortations.

PANEL PROPOSAL

The objective of this panel is to instigate and broaden conversations in the information science community about the problem of online targeting and harassment of academics, the ethical obligations of individuals and collective bodies toward targeted academics (including our students/trainees), and concrete steps that might be taken to move toward ethical and effective practices to protect marginalized academics.

In this panel, we will span personal and political to discuss topics including:

- What do we know about the nature and effects of online threats against academics?
- What resources exist to help prevent/defend against such targeting of oneself, one's colleagues, or one's employees?
- What can or should institutions such as departments, faculty unions, and university administrations do to support faculty who are, or might come under, attack?
- Should strategic defence against such attacks be integrated into graduate student education and/or new faculty orientations?

The proposed structure of the panel is:

1. Introduction: A brief review of recent threats to academics and various responses to these threats (10 min)
2. Each panelist will speak, sharing their views on how to address the situation, and the rationale for these views (40 min)
3. Guided discussion/think-pair-square-share responses to discussion prompts (30 min)
4. Concluding statements (10 min)

PANELISTS

Nicole A. Cooke is an Assistant Professor and Program Director at the School of Information Sciences, the University of Illinois at Urbana-Champaign. Her research and teaching interests include human information behavior, critical cultural information studies, and diversity and social justice in librarianship. She was the 2016 recipient of the American Library Association's (ALA) Equality Award, and the 2017 Achievement in Library Diversity Research Award presented by ALA's Office for Diversity, Literacy & Outreach. Her latest work is *Information Services to Diverse Populations* (Libraries Unlimited, 2016).

Cooke will join the panel by video link and will speak from the perspective of an academic who has been the target of online hate and bullying. Cooke's contribution to the panel will include a description of her experience as a person of color *and* as someone who is a diversity and social justice scholar and explicate how these characteristics add to the acuteness of this type of harassment. Cooke will also her describe her efforts to gain support from her institution and professional organizations.

Amelia Gibson, Ph.D., is an assistant professor in the UNC School of Information and Library Science. Her primary research interests include information access, marginalization, and information poverty within communities; and health information behavior and information policy, focusing specifically on place-based communities as information systems. Dr. Gibson is currently conducting research on social exclusion and systematic marginalization in social and technical information systems. Her studies explore institutional and social support of information seeking and sharing among people with disabilities and of youth of color.

Amelia Gibson will speak from the perspective of an early career researcher who studies race, disability, gender, and institutional and social marginalization. She has not experienced extensive online harassment. She will discuss both her thoughts on institutional and social support, and her hopes and expectations for support as a junior faculty member of color.

Devon Greyson, PhD MLIS, is a postdoctoral research fellow at the British Columbia Children's Hospital Research Institute and the University of British Columbia and teaches gender studies at Capilano University. Greyson studies health-related information practices and is chair of the ASIS&T Education and Professional Advancement Committee. Prior to transitioning into academia, Greyson worked in community anti-oppression organizing and education, and thus brings this experience and perspective into scholarship and teaching.

Devon Greyson will speak from the perspective of an early career academic who has some experience with online targeting. Greyson's contribution to the panel will include description of some responses to finding oneself or one's colleague the sudden target of online harassment, and considerations of what this means for training programs and early career faculty.

Heidi Julien, PhD is a Professor and Chair at the Department of Library and Information Studies in the Graduate School of Education, University at Buffalo. Her research focuses on information behavior and digital literacy. She is President of the Association for Library and Information Science Education. She served as President of the Canadian Association for Information Science, and as Chair of the ASIS&T Special Interest Group Information Seeking and Use (SIGUSE). She also serves on the Permanent Committee for ISIC: the information behaviour conference.

Heidi Julien will speak from the perspective of a department chair who is responsible for mentoring and supporting faculty members. Her contribution to the panel will focus on appropriate institutional responses to online targeting and harassment of information researchers and academics.

REFERENCES

American Association of University Professors (AAUP). (2017, Jan 31). *Targeted online harassment of faculty.* https://www.aaup.org/file/2017-Harassment_Faculty_0.pdf

American Association of University Professors, American Federation of Teachers, & Association of American Colleges and Universities. (2017, Sept 7). *Taking a Stand Against Harassment, Part of the Broader Threat to Higher Education.* https://www.aaup.org/sites/default/files/Statement%20on%20Harassment.pdf

Cooke, N. A. (2016). *Information Services to Diverse Populations: Developing Culturally Competent Library Professionals*. ABC-CLIO / Libraries Unlimited.

Crash Override. (n.d.). *COACH: Crash Override's Automated Cybersecurity Helper.* http://www.crashoverridenetwork.com/coach.html

Cuevas, J. A. (2018). A new reality? The far right's use of cyberharassment against academics. *Academe*, Jan/Feb 2018, https://www.aaup.org/article/new-reality-far-rights-use-cyberharassment-against-academics

Dreyden, A. (2014). You asked: How do I deal with online harassment? How do I help the targets of online harassment? https://www.ashedryden.com/blog/you-asked-how-do-i-deal-with-online-harassment-how-do-i-help-the-targets-of-online-harassment

Flaherty, C. (2017, June 26). Old criticisms, new threats. *Inside Higher Ed,* https://www.insidehighered.com/news/2017/06/26/professors-are-often-political-lightning-rods-now-are-facing-new-threats-over-their

Friedman, J., Sarkeesian, A., & Sherman, R. B. (n.d.). Speak up & stay safe: A guide to protecting yourself from online harassment. *Feminist Frequency*, https://onlinesafety.feministfrequency.com/en/

McKeon, L.(2017, Sept 11). How gamergate pioneered the backlash against diversity. *The Walrus.* https://thewalrus.ca/how-gamergate-pioneered-the-backlash-against-diversity-in-technology/

Nwanevu, O. (2016, Mar). Political correction. *Harper's Magazine.* https://harpers.org/archive/2016/03/political-correction/

Quinn, Z. (2014, Oct 10). What to expect when you're expecting (the internet to ruin your life). Blog post, *Zoë Quinn.* http://blog.unburntwitch.com/post/99694581114/what-to-expect-when-youre-expecting-the-internet

Sweeney, M. E., & Cooke, N. A. (2018). You're So Sensitive! How LIS Professionals Define and Discuss Microaggressions Online. *The Expanding LIS Education Universe*, 197.

Digital Liaisons: Connecting Diverse Voices to Support an Ethical and Sustainable Information Future in Digital Libraries

Ekatarina Grguric
McGill University Library, Canada
ekatarina.grguic@mcgill.ca

Tamarack Hockin
Fraser Valley Regional Library, Canada
tamahoc@gmail.com

Nushrat Khan
University of Wolverhampton, UK
n.j.khan@wlv.ac.uk

Virginia Dressler
Kent State University, United States
vdressle@kent.edu

Alyson Gamble
Simmons College Graduate School of Library and Information Science, United States
alyson.gamble@simmons.edu

ABSTRACT
Digital Liaisons is a platform for including student and early career voices in open dialogue with practitioners and researchers who work in or adjacent to the field of Digital Libraries. It has taken several forms over the last few years, ranging from a poster session, to an unconference-style panel, to moderated Twitter chats. This year we are proposing to merge two of these approaches: a series of Twitter chats that provide mentor-mentee connections for early career practitioners, and a panel which reports on the outcomes of these chats and concludes with a digital poster session for students and early-career practitioners. The merger of Twitter chats and a digital poster session will provide two ways for participants to interact with the theme of this year's conference and will allow sharing their views and experiences.

KEYWORDS
Digital libraries, ethical librarianship, critical librarianship, LIS4Good, early-career development, graduate students, students, student research

INTRODUCTION
SIG DL is supporting this year's conference theme, "Ethical impacts of digital information ecologies", by expanding the structure of Digital Liaisons, a yearly initiative to bring early-career and student voices into debates within the LIS community. We will do this by first hosting a series of Twitter chats through the Digital Liaisons virtual un-commons, a regularly held Twitter chat under the hashtag #SIGDLChats which is now in its third year, and then presenting on the outcomes of these chats in a panel session that will incorporate a Twitter chat and a digital poster session for early career and student practitioners.

The goal of Digital Liaisons is to promote a channel of conversation for student and early career professionals with practitioners and researchers in the field of Digital Libraries and other closely related areas. It is a safe space in which to engage with themes within the LIS community and connect with practitioners. In the past we employed different methods of engaging into this conversation ranging from a poster session, an unconference-style panel and a series of Twitter chats. Based on the feedback, this year we are proposing to merge two of these approaches: a series of Twitter chats that provide mentor-mentee connections for early career practitioners, and a session at the Annual Meeting to share the outcomes.

Digital Liaisons has evolved over time; this year we are reserving half of the panel for a digital poster session for student participants on the conference topic of the "Ethical impacts of digital information ecologies". Student and early-career attendees of the conference will also be invited to sign up to present a digital poster accompanied by a lightning talk both before the Annual Meeting and in the lead-up to the panel at the Annual Meeting. By merging a panel style report on the Twitter chats with a light digital poster session we aim to provide additional modes of interactivity for Digital Liaison attendees and support early-career professional development by fostering mentor-mentee connections. Attendees who choose to participate in the session will be asked to focus on the theme of this year's conference and critically address some aspect of it. All #SIGDLChats conversations will also focus around the conference theme. We hope to continue iterating on our approach to encourage the inclusion of new voices.

This structure is informed by several consecutive years of Digital Liaisons as a traditional poster session and then the #SIGDL-Chats Twitter chats which were thematically informed by the interests of the SIG DL membership. For example, our previous chat topics included adoption of emerging digital technologies in the libraries, developing core technical skills, examples of data driven work in library settings and how these types of work are supported. SIG-DL executive members brainstorm and prepare 5-6 key questions to discuss with the participants with a goal of simulating discussion. We encourage participation by also asking the participants to submit any questions they would like to talk about. Using a consistent Twitter hashtag provides an easy way to follow this conversation but we also use other open platforms, such Google docs to facilitate future reference to the questions or direct input of answers at a later time. In previous years the Digital Liaisons panel has covered what questions were asked during the Twitter chats, how participants responded and what overarching themes. We have previously published all chats through the Storify platform but are exploring different approaches to saving the output of #SIGDLChats in the future.

In order to iterate on our early ideas and what has worked for bringing community members together, we are merging two approaches. Our goal in every iteration of the Digital Liaisons is to enable discussions between early and later career practitioners on a variety of topics and to provide early career practitioners with opportunities to structure their voice around a theme. This panel will involve students, expand perspectives, and try to produce a summary output of the discussions that we will facilitate. International perspectives will be represented through recruitment methods detailed below and are already represented in the membership of our group. We will assess the impact of this approach by considering metrics such as number of participants overall and how many participants are newcomers to the SIG DL or ASIS&T communities.

Asking participants to submit digital posters to Digital Liaisons in order to express their ideas in a low-cost and low-stress environment will provide early-career practitioners with the opportunity to engage with a lightweight version of a common form of academic reporting while also delving into critical assessment of the ideas that this year's conference is rooted in. Past participants in Digital Liaisons as digital poster session have spoken to the career benefit of stepping through the process of creating and presenting a poster to facilitate group discussion around a theme.

MODERATORS AND PRESENTERS

The panelists for the first half of the Digital Liaisons panel will be a sub-group of SIG DL executive members. These members are also Moderators and reporters on #SIGDLChats outcomes and represented as the authors of this submission.

The second half of the session will give space to students and early career professionals who will be able to sign up to participate. It will be moderated by the SIG DL panelists. All participants will be required to address this year's conference theme. Digital poster submissions will be vetted for relevance by the SIG DL executive members upon receipt.

STRUCTURE AND FORMAT

During the panel session, SIG DL executives will give opening remarks and report on the 2018 #SIGDLChats season as well as provide an introductory presentation on the history and structure of Digital Liaisons. The panel will begin in a traditional format where SIG DL executive members will report on the outcomes of the 2018 #SIGDLChats season. It will then shift to a digital poster session combined with lightning talks by early-career attendees of the Annual Meeting. We will request that all poster presenters provide a single slide stating a topic, who they are, one big idea, and how they would like to engage with their idea going forward. They will present on this slide in a lightning talk format for 2 minutes.

The panel will end with an open discussion by attendees. Presenters will be able to sign up to present a lightning talk both before and during the Annual Meeting. Group discussion will be moderated by the panelists and held simultaneously on Twitter under the #SIGDLChats hashtag. By removing the restriction of early submission, we hope to encourage more students and early career practitioners to dive in and join the professional dialogue at the Annual Meeting.

RECRUITMENT

If the panel is approved, SIG-DL will follow the successful model from previous years and begin promotion of the chat series in June. SIG-DL will announce each chat through an aggressive promotion campaign using a variety of media channels including LIS programs and other relevant professional listservs, as well as social media outlets. SIG-DL members will also contact ASIS&T student chapters and LIS program faculty teaching pertinent coursework. Submissions to the Digital Liaisons panel have grown every year over the four years the session has been held at the annual conference. If the panel is approved, we anticipate another strong pool of student participants.

We will send a call for posters to iSchools and through the SIG DL membership. We will publicize to a list of international LIS, IS, Archival, etc. I-*, programs and will also encourage participation from mentors by reaching to practitioners working in Digital Libraries in related professional communities such as the Digital Library Federation and Code4Lib. Because our goal is to foster the inclusion of new and early-career voices in debating topics of concern to the professional community we will focus on providing ample opportunity for individuals with little to no experience to engage with their peers and get their feet wet. Recruitment for the digital poster session and lightning talks will continue throughout the Annual Meeting.

VIRTUAL UNCOMMONS TWITTER CHAT TIMELINE

Twitter chats will be three times between from July 2018 and October 2018 and will be scheduled according to moderator availability. Each chat occurs with slightly different timing to account for diverse time zones. All findings collected will be presented at the Annual Meeting with a focus on descriptive themes that come out of participant conversations. Throughout we will focus the conversations on this year's conference theme and the intersection of ethical information systems and digital libraries.

Moderation duties fall to all SIG DL executive officers pending availability and includes, but is not limited to:

Ekatarina Grguric
User Experience and Digital Technologies Librarian, McGill University Library, Canada

Nushrat Khan
Doctoral Researcher, University of Wolverhampton, UK

Alyson Gamble
Doctoral Researcher, Simmons College Graduate School of Library and Information Science, United States

Tamarack Hockin
Collection Services Librarian, Fraser Valley Regional Library, Canada

Virginia Dressler
Assistant Professor, Kent State University, United States

Daniel Pollock
Doctoral Candidate, College of Communication & Information University of Tennessee, United States

Carla Colombati
Librarian, Università degli Studi di Teramo, Italy

Anna Maria Tammaro
Professor of Digital Library University of Parma, Italy

DIGITAL POSTER SESSION TIMELINE

Initial solicitation for student participants in the digital poster session will occur in July and continue through to the Annual Meeting. Due to the highly structured one-slide format we propose for the digital posters, participants will be able to sign up and present on their ideas through the Annual Meeting up to the day of our panel session. All participant submissions will be vetted by SIG DL moderators.

POTENTIALLY INTERESTED SIGS

SIG III is willing to support this panel by promoting through their channels to reach a broader international community of ASIS&T members and interested students. One of our primary goals is to include more international voices in debate around the ethical implications of digital libraries and also to specifically reach out to student groups from outside North America.

Blockchain: One Emerging Technology—So Many Applications

Sandra Hirsh
San Jose State University, School of Information, US, sandy.hirsh@sjsu.edu

Susan Alman
San Jose State University, School of Information, US, susan.alman@sjsu.edu

Victoria Lemieux
University of British Columbia, iSchool, CA, v.lemieux@ubc.ca

Eric T. Meyer
University of Texas at Austin, iSchool, US, dean@ischool.utexas.edu

ABSTRACT

It is clear from the expanding literature that blockchain technology is a trend potentially on the brink of revolutionizing the public and private sectors. There have been conferences, books, white papers, start-ups, and numerous back-channel discussions on ways blockchain technology can address seemingly endless processes, and it is on the radar of many information professionals. Blockchain technology has the potential for organizations to accomplish much more than cryptocurrency, payments or housing electronic credentials. Currently, organizations are experimenting with its use in a variety of settings from land transaction recording, medical recordkeeping, supply chain management, regulatory compliance, identity management and beyond. The technology enables a broader impact within the information community and around the globe. Some suggestions being mooted for blockchain applications in information centers include building an enhanced metadata center, protecting Digital First Sale rights, supporting community-based collections, and facilitating partnerships across organizations. With its potential to transform social, political and economic interactions, and the way that information is managed, there is more to explore about how blockchain can be applied to manage information and what the ethical implications may be. The panelists will provide an update on the current and future uses of blockchain from their own ongoing research: they will present the recommendations developed from the IMLS-funded project to investigate the possible uses of blockchain, research outcomes from the University of British Columbia's Records in the Chain Project, and the outcomes of a recently completed project (Project Novum) that focused on the organizational and structural issues in visual arts and financial services.

KEYWORDS

Blockchain, IMLS, Project Novum, UBC Records in the Chain, SJSU

INTRODUCTION

It is clear from the expanding literature that blockchain technology is a trend potentially on the brink of revolutionizing the public and private sectors. There have been conferences, books, white papers, start-ups, and numerous back-channel discussions on ways blockchain technology can address seemingly endless processes, and it is on the radar of many information professionals. Blockchain technology has the potential for organizations to accomplish much more than housing electronic credentials. The technology enables a broader impact within the information community and around the globe. Some suggestions being explored for blockchain applications in information centers include building an enhanced metadata center, protecting Digital First Sale rights, supporting community-based collections, and facilitating partnerships across organizations. Currently, blockchain technology is being used in a variety of settings, and the panelists in this session will discuss the projects they have implemented.

SJSU SCHOOL OF INFORMATION/IMLS-FUNDED BLOCKCHAIN INVESTIGATION

The San Jose State University (SJSU) School of Information (iSchool) was awarded a grant from the Institute of Museum and Library Services (IMLS) to investigate ways that blockchain technology can be used by libraries to partner with other organizations and to support city or community goals. The project investigators, Drs. Sandra Hirsh (SJSU iSchool Director) and Susan Alman (SJSU iSchool Lecturer), developed a website and blog, hosted an online conference and national forum, and conducted a survey. The resulting commentary served as the basis for recommendations to the library and information communities on ways to implement blockchain technology.

A dedicated website and blog were created as part of the research project where visitors can learn about blockchain basics and discuss ways in which the technology can be used to advance the role of libraries in serving global communities. The website (https://ischoolblogs.sjsu.edu/blockchains/) details the scope of the project, provides background information about blockchain technology, examples of blockchain applications, and includes resources for further exploration. The blog is intended as a national forum for continued discussion of the issues surrounding blockchain technology.

Information professionals participated in the Library 2.0 online conference on June 7, 2018 to learn about blockchain technology and the ways it is being applied. Nationally recognized experts in blockchain technology participated in keynote panels and members from the information professional community presented sessions focused on their experiences with blockchain. A survey was available to all participants to gather suggestions for future projects involving blockchain technology.

The Blockchain National Forum was held in San Jose, CA on August 6, 2018. Participants in the forum represented a variety of information organizations and specializations including those with expertise in academic, public, and special libraries and archives, information technology, and urban planning. The forum, which was live-streamed and recorded, is available on the Blockchain website. Recommendations for future directions involving blockchain will be available in the white paper that is scheduled for distribution in November 2018.

The project investigators, who plan to expand the project to develop blockchain models based on the data gathered throughout the project, will report on the recommendations that were made throughout the investigation.

UNIVERSITY OF BRITISH COLUMBIA – RECORDS IN THE CHAIN PROJECT

Dr. Victoria Lemieux is an Associate Professor of Archival Science and lead of a 23-faculty multidisciplinary blockchain research cluster at the University of British Columbia in Vancouver, Canada. She is also international project leader for the International Organization for Standardization Technical Committee 307 developing a new standard on blockchain terminology. Her current research is focused on risk to the availability of trustworthy records, in particular in blockchain record keeping systems, and how these risks impact upon transparency, financial stability, public accountability and human rights. She holds a doctorate from University College London (Archival Studies, 2002), and, since 2005, has been a Certified Information Systems Security Professional (CISSP). She is also the winner of the 2015 Emmett Leahy Award for outstanding contributions to the field of records management, a 2015 World Bank Big Data Innovation Award, and a 2016 Emerald Literati Award for her research on blockchain technology.

Dr. Lemieux will discuss findings of an ongoing research project called "Records in the Chain," based at the University of British Columbia in Vancouver, Canada. This project seeks to understand the implications of blockchain recordkeeping and to investigate its potential for creation and long-term preservation of authentic records. Research questions that the project explored are: 1) what types of records are being generated in different blockchain solutions and platforms? 2) How are these records being accessed, managed, secured and preserved? 3) What is the distributed technological ecosystem upon which these solutions rely? What are the interdependencies among these systems? 4) What is the context (i.e., provenencial, juridical-administrative, procedural, documentary, and technological) of creation and management of records in these blockchain systems? The project entails conducting case study analyses of several projects involving the application of blockchain technology to creation, capture and preservation of records. Six case studies relating to land, identity, and medical records have been completed or in progress to date. Dr. Lemieux will discuss what the early findings from the case studies reveal about why government bodies and other organizations are choosing to experiment with and adopt blockchain record keeping, how they have been undertaking their pilots of blockchain record keeping solutions, what these pilots entail, and what the implications may be for long-term preservation of blockchain-based digital records.

OXFORD INTERNET INSTITUTE – PROJECT NOVUM

Distributed Ledger Technologies (DLTs) enable new ways of generating, managing, and disseminating real-time transaction data in a distributed fashion, using very different transparency and security models from the current status quo. They can potentially reshape organizations and industries by replacing gatekeepers and custodians with shared ledgers, or by enabling new types of horizontal coordination and collaboration. In many cases a significant structural or organizational change may also be a prerequisite for successful application of DLTs.

Much of the focus of blockchain media attention has been on the splashy applications such as bitcoin. One understudied sector, however, is the visual arts and the overlaps of art with financial services. Visual art is a significant economic contributor in countries such as the UK, and the sector has significant costs in maintaining value chains, establishing and recording provenance, processing payments to artists and their estates, and undertaking other critical activities that could potentially be more effectively done with a distributed ledger. A recently completed project (Project Novum) has focused on the distributed ledger technologies in the visual arts, and the findings from that project will be shared as part of the panel. Among the top-level findings of the project are the necessity of developing interoperable frameworks to tie blockchains together into a sustainable ecosystem, since in many ways blockchain in 2018 resembles the internet in 1993: still emerging in terms of both structure and abilities. In addition, we will highlight the need in the art world for trusted actors to represent working artists, since despite the distributed nature of blockchains, the uptake of the technology is likely to make the world more consolidated than less. We call for a Fair Art Market, built on distributed ledger technologies, that will have fair trading built into its fabric.

Eric T. Meyer, currently professor and dean of the iSchool at UT-Austin and formerly Professor of Social Informatics at the University of Oxford, was on the faculty of the Oxford Internet Institute from 2007-2018. He will discuss Project Novum, which is a collaborative project between University of Oxford, the Alan Turing Institute, and DACS (The Design and Artists Copyright Society) that focused on organizational and structural changes required for the successful application of DLTs in the visual arts and proposed the creation of a Fair Art Market.

CONCLUSION

The panelists from different institutions in different parts of the world will present the findings from the blockchain and DLT projects they developed. The short presentations are expected to stimulate discussion among the audience on ways that the technology can be applied within the profession and encourage others to explore the possible uses of blockchain for the Information Science and Technology community.

REFERENCES

Johnston, Ryan. (2018). Blockchain at the library: new study will explore how the technology can connect and support institutions. *edscoop* February 8, 2018. Retrieved March 25, 2018 from https://edscoop.com/blockchain-library-study-san-jose-state.

Lemieux, Victoria. (2016). Trusting records: is Blockchain technology the answer? *Records Management Journal* 26:2. 110-139.

Library 2.0 Online Conference. (2018). Blockchain Applied: Impact on the Information Professions. June 7, 2018. Recorded content accessed from https://www.youtube.com/c/Library20.

Meyer, Eric T. (2017). Project Novum: Distributed ledger technologies and structural change in financial and cultural services. Retrieved March 25, 2018 from https://www.oii.ox.ac.uk/research/projects/project-novum-distributed-ledger-technologies-and-structural-change-in-financial-and-cultural-services/.

Beyond Fairness, Accountability, and Transparency in the Ethics of Algorithms: Contributions and Perspectives from LIS

Anna Lauren Hoffmann
The Information School, University of Washington
Seattle, WA, USA. alho@uw.edu

Christine T. Wolf
IBM Research – Almaden Research Center
San Jose, CA, USA. ctwolf@us.ibm.com

Sarah T. Roberts
Department of Information Studies, UCLA
Los Angeles, CA, USA. sarah.roberts@ucla.edu

Stacy Wood
School of Computing and Information, University of Pittsburgh, Pittsburgh, PA, USA. sewood@pitt.edu

ABSTRACT

Recent debates have revealed the urgent need for work addressing social and ethical implications of the algorithmic and data-driven systems that govern our lives. Focusing largely on machine learning (ML) and artificial intelligence (AI), conversations among scholars, journalists, and advocates have started to address questions of fairness, bias, transparency, access, participation, and discrimination often under the monikers "AI and Ethics" (AI+Ethics) or "fairness, accountability, and transparency in algorithms" (FAT*). Underlying these discourses are concerns about how to mitigate discrimination and bias in data, as well as open questions over whether algorithmic systems can be fair and if their use will help promote equitable futures (or instead further perpetuate existing inequalities). Despite the seeming "newness" of these issues, many of the underlying concerns have a longstanding tradition and intellectual lineage in the library and information science (LIS) field. In this panel, we will discuss and elaborate on these connections, drawing on our research and experiences in a number of contexts and outlining opportunities these relationships present for future research and engagement.

KEYWORDS

Information ethics, AI+Ethics, fairness, accountability, transparency in algorithms (FAT*)

INTRODUCTION

Rapid technical advances in areas of Artificial Intelligence (AI) and other algorithmic systems are undeniably transforming our worlds, with their far-reaching applications into wide swathes of everyday life ushering what has been described as the "fourth industrial revolution" (Schwab, 2017). Propelled by Big Data, these advances bring with them great promise – and the excitement and intrigue they garner reveals something about our collective imaginaries and underlying desires for transformed futures where societies are enriched with novel knowledge and insights and lives are relieved from the burdens of tedious and mundane activities of today. These developments bring with them significant implications for social and ethical orders – indeed, the broader effects and ramifications of algorithmic systems represent one of the most pressing contemporary problems we face today. Large-scale collaborations across academia and industry like DeepMind Ethics & Society,[1] AI Now Institute,[2] and the "Prosperity Through AI" Pillar of MIT-IBM Watson AI Lab[3] have emerged to devote technical attention to the ethical aspects of AI (or "AI+Ethics") and specialized workshops and conferences have also emerged to focus on topics of fairness and transparency in algorithmic ecosystems – for example, Conference on Fairness, Accountability, and Transparency (FAT*)[4] and the AAAI/ACM Conference on Artificial Intelligence, Ethics, and Society.[5] In these domains, many terms and concepts are the central locus of inquiry – with fairness, bias, discrimination, and transparency playing prominent roles.

Many calls for change have aligned around these ambiguous concepts – ambiguous because they are to a certain extent elastic, allowing for a range of strategies, tactics, and responses to fall underneath their umbrella. This panel will critically engage with these concepts in order to address the ways in which they are operationalized across domains – and how those operationalizations relate to existing dialogues within the LIS community. Engaging substantively with the realities of building ethical and

---

[1] https://deepmind.com/applied/deepmind-ethics-society/
[2] https://ainowinstitute.org/
[3] http://mitibmwatsonailab.mit.edu/
[4] https://fatconference.org/
[5] http://www.aies-conference.com/

sustainable information systems requires a confrontation with the specific ways these concepts are deployed, the intellectual lineages they invoke, and the opportunities those connections present for future research and engagement.

PANELISTS

The panel will consist of four panelists.

Anna Lauren Hoffmann, Ph.D., is an Assistant Professor with The Information School at the University of Washington. Her work centers on issues in information, data, and ethics, with particular attention to the ways in which discourses, design, and uses of information technology can promote or hinder the pursuit of important human values like respect and justice.

Sarah T. Roberts, Ph.D., is an Assistant Professor in the Department of Information Studies in the Graduate School of Education and Information Studies at the University of California Los Angeles. Her research examines information work and information workers and she is the leading authority on "commercial content moderation."

Christine T. Wolf, J.D., Ph.D., M.S.I., is a Research Staff Member at IBM's Almaden Research Center. Her work is primarily ethnographic in nature and broadly investigates how people make sense of (and transform) emergent technologies through everyday practice. Her ongoing research project is focused on the incorporation of data analytics into organizational life, with a current focus on the interpretability/explainability of analytics outputs in the context of everyday work practices. Dr. Wolf will also act as the panel moderator.

Stacy Wood, Ph.D., M.L.I.S. is an Assistant Professor with the School of Computing and Information at the University of Pittsburgh. Her work focuses on the histories of information, communication, and record-keeping technologies within the criminal justice system.

PANEL DISCUSSION PROPOSAL

The objectives of this panel are: 1) to provide a background of recent discourses around AI+Ethics/FAT* and highlight key terms in these arenas; 2) identify how those terms relate to key concepts and values in the LIS community; and 3) discuss opportunities these relationships present for future research and engagement. Towards that goal, we will each draw on our ongoing research in these areas, which will include a mix of empirical case studies, as well as epistemological investigation into ethical dimensions of data/algorithmic systems. Below is an outline of the topics we will present and discuss:

- **Dr. Hoffmann** will discuss the limits of antidiscrimination frameworks for addressing problems of fairness and bias. Anti-discrimination discourses hold that automated or algorithmic processes are a problem insofar as they reproduce either certain unjust cultural biases of their creators or generate unfair outcomes that we would disallow if generated by human decision-makers, especially in the areas of housing and employment (see, for example: O'Neil, 2016). But this approach treats algorithmic processes as themselves amoral; judging the injustice or unfairness of their outputs means judging some human behind or alongside the tech, be it an engineer or some hypothetical human decision-maker. Similarly, United States antidiscrimination law relies heavily on locating specific perpetrators, that is, a particular person or persons who responsible for committing a discriminatory act (Freeman, 1978). Further, anti-discrimination frames also tend toward single-axis thinking that cannot account for many—or even most—identity-based harms. Nor can it account for the ways in which anti-discrimination laws and policies are themselves complicit in the production and circulation of social categories (Crenshaw, 2015). Similarly, much work on data, fairness, and discrimination conceptualizes the problem less as a broader sociotechnical one of the production of subjects and more as a problem of misguided or "bad" technology designed and implemented by humans. To move beyond a narrow anti-discrimination frame, Dr. Hoffmann will discuss how work in LIS and surveillance studies (Gandy, 1993; Olson, 2001; Browne, 2015; Noble, 2018) can provide data ethics conversations with more productive ways to better grapple with the co-construction of data and vulnerable subjects.
- **Dr. Roberts** will discuss the relationship between notions of algorithmic transparency and digital human labor. Transparency with respect to methods, practices and workings of computational tools does not necessarily imply transparency in terms of labor or business practices and can work to obscure more complex effects. This work stems from Dr. Roberts work on commercial content moderation (Roberts, 2016) as well as work on policy, standards and operations in ICTs.
- **Dr. Wolf** will discuss her current work on the interpretability/explainability of analytics outputs in the context of everyday work practices. Approaching this from the vantage of information behavior, this project builds on her prior work on the social and discursive uses of information (Wolf, 2016, 2018; Wolf & Veinot, 2015) and investigates *in situ* sensemaking, that is, the ways in which people interact with data-driven outputs and interpret machine actions in context.
- **Dr. Wood** will discuss her current work on algorithmic transparency in the United States criminal justice system. As automation, Big Data, and prediction have become more ubiquitous in police work, challenges to colloquial and rhetorical uses of transparency have become central to emergent legal and activist discourses. Specifically focusing on automation

in cloud-based evidence management platforms, this project foregrounds fundamental shifts in daily workflows, consequences to evidence production and integrity, intellectual property, and inchoate data economies. This extends previous work on the consequences of shifting records management practices in policing for long-term access and accountability (Wood, 2016).

We will use our work to animate different key terms, highlighting the ways in which these concerns connect to established issues and underlying values within the LIS community. The panel will be interactive, with points for audience Q&A throughout the session, as well as polling the audience on key controversies to invite discussion and engagement with the topics covered.

AGENDA FOR THE PANEL

90 minutes total, broken down as follows:

- **Introduction** – Overview of AI+Ethics landscape, Panel's Objectives, Roadmap, and Call for Audience Participation (15 minutes, Dr. Wolf)
- **Case Studies** – Each Panelist presents for 8-10 minutes, with Q&A after each (40 minutes total)
- **Roundtable Discussion** – Mix of Audience Q&A and Panel Prompts (35 minutes)

REFERENCES

Browne, S. (2015). Dark Matters: On the Surveillance of Blackness. (Durham, NC: Duke University Press.)

Crenshaw, K. (2015). Demarginalizing the Intersection of Race and Sex: A Black Feminist Critique of Antidiscrimination Doctrine, Feminist Theory and Antiracist Politics. University of Chicago Legal Forum, 1989(1).

Freeman, A. D. (1978). Legitimizing Racial Discrimination Through Antidiscrimination Law: A Critical Review of Supreme Court Doctrine. Minnesota Law Review, 62, 1049–1120.

Gandy, O. H. (1993). The Panoptic Sort: A Political Economy of Personal Information. Critical Studies in Communication and in the Cultural Industries. (Boulder, CO: Westview Press.)

Noble, S. U. (2018). Algorithms of Oppression: How Search Engines Reinforce Racism. (New York, NY: NYU Press.)

Olson, H. A. (2001). The Power to Name: Representation in Library Catalogs. Signs: Journal of Women in Culture and Society, 26(3), 639–668.

O'Neil, C. (2016). Weapons of math destruction: how big data increases inequality and threatens democracy. (New York, NY: Crown Publishing Group.)

Roberts, S.T. (2016). Commercial content moderation: Digital laborers' dirty work. In Noble, S.U. and Tynes, B. (Eds.), The intersectional internet: Race, sex, class and culture online. New York: Peter Lang.

Schwab, K. (2017). *The Fourth Industrial Revolution*. Crown Publishing Group.

Wolf, C. T. (2016). DIY Videos on YouTube: Identity and Possibility in the Age of Algorithms. *First Monday*, *21*(6).

Wolf, C. T. (2018). Reckoning With: Information Use and Engaging With Strategic Decisions in High Tech Work. In *Proceeding of iConference 2018, Sheffield, UK.*

Wolf, C. T., & Veinot, T. C. (2015). Struggling for space and finding my place: An interactionist perspective on everyday use of biomedical information. *Journal of the Association for Information Science and Technology*, *66*(2), 282–296.

Wood, S. E. (2017). Police Body Cameras and Professional Responsibility: Public Records and Private Evidence. *Preservation, Digital Technology & Culture*, 46(1), 41-51.

Contexts, Critiques, and Consequences: A Discussion about Educational Data Mining and Learning Analytics

Kyle M. L. Jones
Indiana University-Indianapolis (IUPUI), United States, kmlj@iupui.edu

Roderic Crooks
University of California-Irvine, United States, crooksr@uci.edu

Chase McCoy
Indiana University-Bloomington, United States, chamccoy@indiana.edu

Amy VanScoy
University at Buffalo, United States, vanscoy@buffalo

ABSTRACT

The capture, aggregation, and analysis of student data is becoming ubiquitous at all levels of education—from primary to post-secondary—as institutions increase their adoption of information technologies to serve administrative and educational ends. In part, this has led to a growing interest among education scientists and administrators in strategically mining and analyzing troves of data in order to uncover student behaviors and intervene in student life. As is the case in other contexts where actors are pursuing Big Data's supposed benefits, educational data mining is fraught with moral, ethical, and political conflict. The panel is composed of four researchers who analyze and critique educational data mining practices and learning analytics initiatives in particular micro- and macro-contexts, including academic libraries and professional advising, urban schools, graduate-level online learning, and higher education generally. Each panelist also represents a unique conceptual background, pulling from work in information ethics and policy, critical data studies, documentation studies, and higher education policy to empirically analyze and critically evaluate tools, systems, practices, policies, and values. Through their individual but thematically intertwined perspectives, the panelists will present their research and lead audience members in discussion.

KEYWORDS

Educational data mining, learning analytics, critical data studies, documentation studies, information policy

INTRODUCTION

Scholars, reporters, and government actors are increasingly playing close attention to the emergence of educational data mining (EDM) strategies and their application in learning analytics (LA) initiatives. EDM applies automated methods (e.g., machine learning) to learner data in order to surface, describe, and predict learning behaviors in particular systems (Baker & Siemens, 2013). LA takes EDM approaches a step further by applying these methods to investigate, understand, and optimize learning environments and processes within an institutional context, not just a singular technological system (Siemens, 2012). Both EDM and LA require access to significant stores of data, some of which is focused on student learning while other data captures the minutiae of student life outside the classroom. EDM and LA have both benefited from the "data explosion" in education, which was sparked by the evolution of educational environments where information systems have become ubiquitous and various forms of data capture are increasingly common (Long & Siemens, 2011, p. 32). Due to these new technological conditions, student behaviors once "unseen, unnoticed, and therefore unactionable" (Bienkowski, Feng, & Means, 2012, p. ix) can now be described and analyzed, including a student's social, educational, and increasingly mental state. New opportunities brought about by data aggregation and analytics has spurred some to claim that big data has arrived in educational institutions (Picciano, 2012). Claiming that it holds the power to transform "existing processes of administration, teaching, learning, [and] academic work" (Daniel, 2015, p. 913) in schools and universities, some see big data in education as a possible panacea for solving the seemingly "intractable challenges" (Campbell, DeBlois, & Oblinger, 2007, p. 42) education institutions face in an accountability culture that seeks to maximize outcomes with minimal cost expenditures.

When all these things are considered, it becomes clear that there a host of ethical and social issues with EDM and LA worth unpacking and critiquing. This is especially true given that the stoutest proponents argue that "there are no more excuses" (Crow, 2012) for *not* analyzing available data; others state that there exists a moral obligation to pursue data analytics given the availability of and access to datasets—to not use existing data would abdicate an institution's responsibility to its students. If we accept this argument—that data *must* be collected, analyzed, acted upon—then we are led to ask some important questions: Who is collecting the data, how are they collecting it, and what right do they have to do so? Are the analytical methods valid and verifiable? To what ends are data analytics put, and are these ends justifiable? These questions and more surface important aspects of EDM and LA in need of targeted critiques of ideological, epistemological, and ontological perspectives aligned with big data in education. It is also important to take note of how EDM and LA become dominant methods and ideologies in a given context (e.g., primary education, higher education) and micro-context (e.g., charter schools, academic libraries), as the intersection of tools, norms, values, ethics, and goals will all vary.

This panel will examine educational data mining and learning analytics toward the end of raising awareness around related sociotechnical and ethical questions worthy of analysis using empirical, philosophical, and critical methods and approaches. The panelists will model these approaches by highlighting the unique but thematically intertwined work they have accomplished to date. The following sections provide an overview of each researcher's approach before summarizing a particular project the researcher will discuss on the panel. The panel description ends with the structure of the panel.

INFORMATION FLOWS, PRACTICES, AND PROFESSIONAL ETHICS IN MICRO-CONTEXTS

In the context of higher education, administrators view the systemic application of data analytics as a means to support strategic retention, graduation, and time-to-degree improvement programs. To aid administrative ends and use these data and related analytics to better understand and report on the institution as a whole, it is increasingly the case that other institutional actors are being forced—or heavily "encouraged"—to begin strategically collecting student data and acting on learning analytics. Often, these actors are affiliated with micro-contexts, or groups of professionally affiliated actors, like advisors, librarians, and educational technologists. Each micro-context has its own norms, principles, and goals for which it creates and sustains supportive information flows (Nissenbaum, 2010). But the degree to which one micro-context values and builds information flows to facilitate learning analytics may not align with another micro-context's expectations. Misalignment can create conflict in ways that enable one micro-context to suppress the professional ethics commitments and values that characterize another micro-context.

AFFECT AND POLITICS IN DATA VISUALIZATION

Despite the technical and conceptual heterogeneity of data accumulated in the various processes that constitute formal education, this portion of the presentation will point to the homogeneity of visual modes of interpretation used in unpacking and understanding data, particularly the construction and circulation of dashboards. Although data professionals themselves express a variety of positions with respect to the representational capacity of data, these important ambiguities are necessarily obscured by workflows that take visualizations not as (re)mediations or representations of data, but as objective, self-evident measurements. Sociology of quantification argues that data visualizations evoke feelings and emotions from their viewers, a dynamic at odds with the perceived objectivity and certainty claimed for educational data by researchers and policymakers alike (Kennedy & Hill, 2016). With this conceptual tension in mind, this portion of the presentation seeks to better understand the action of visualization via the method of semantic analysis (Kennedy et al., 2016). This method combines analysis of several typical data dashboards with interview data collected from these visualizations' authors, data professionals employed by a Charter Management Organization (CMO) that operates one dozen schools in South and East Los Angeles. This panel will discuss the initial findings in terms of political issues for students and communities so represented via dashboards and theoretical implications for the application of data science to the domain of public education.

DOCUMENTATION STUDIES AND CRITICAL LEARNING ANALYTICS

Critics of learning analytics have primarily focused on issues of student privacy and surveillance. Yet, there are other critical areas that need to be addressed in order to uncover the unintended consequences of learning analytics in practice. Although learning analytics advocates have often treated student data as unproblematic by promoting, often implicitly, data as objective and value neutral, this view is untenable. Modern documentation studies provide a conceptualize lens for critical assessing learning analytics practices. Framing data as documents and using the concepts of "made into" and "considered as" (Buckland, 2013) highlights data as socially constructed and subjective representations of students. Using documentation studies as a framework, four areas of future critical research are presented. These areas include data as not pre-factual objects; data patterns, apophenia, and data misjudgments; data categories and discriminatory institutional practices; and data doubles and student's right to access their data. Existing learning analytics cases will be examined using these critical areas to provide examples of how these areas can be applied in future critical learning analytics research.

STUDENT DATA PRIVACY IN HIGHER EDUCATION: THE ROLE OF THE SYLLABUS

As the ubiquity of learning analytics increases in higher education, it will be increasingly important for institutions to communicate how they are collecting data, to whom they are making it available, and to what ends the data are being used. Often, these communications are done with policy documents and notifications. But central to this discussion are instructors, who are in a unique position to communicate with and educate students about uses of their data. Such discussions may occur face-to-face, but it is often the case that instructors communicate about important issues—such as privacy—in syllabi. Conceptualizing the syllabus not only as communication tool, but also as an expression of instructor values raises critical ethical and pedagogical questions about the role of instructors in students' understanding and value of their personal data.

PANELISTS AND TOPICS

Topic 1: Learning Analytics in the Academic Library

Kyle M. L. Jones is an assistant professor at Indiana University-Indianapolis (IUPUI) in the School of Informatics and Computing within the Department of Library and Information Science. His research centers on information ethics and policy issues associated with learning analytics tools, practices, and interests in higher education. Among other things, his past work considered how learning analytics violates student privacy rights and expectations. More recently, he has focused on the use of learning analytics in particular higher education micro-contexts. He asks questions related to how specific professional communities consider and reconcile data mining practices with extant values and norms, using case study and interview methods to surface data. Using this data, he examines effects from contextual nesting, conflict, and suppression to highlight how the application of learning analytics affects professional practices and identities. In this panel, Jones will highlight an interview-based study of academic library professionals who provided their perspectives on learning analytics, the compatibilities and conflicts with professional ethics commitments (e.g., ALA Code of Ethics), and political tensions with institutional administrators.

Topic 2: Affect and Visualization in Urban Education

Roderic Crooks is assistant professor of Informatics at the University of California, Irvine. He studies information and communication technology use in minoritized communities through field-based methods, often in the context of public schools. His current project explores the application of data analytics to the complex and politically charged realm of urban education. Urban schools in Southern California—high-poverty, public schools that serve primarily black and Latino students in the central zones of the city—face pressure to address persistent conditions of inequality by making use of novel forms of digital technology, to make communities that are perceived to be technologically bereft into the beneficiaries of progress associated with the tech sector. This project examines the work of data professionals working in this area to question the intellectual commitments of "data science" as well as the political implications of data-centric management of public institutions.

Topic 3: Documentation Studies and Critical Learning Analytics

Chase McCoy is a doctoral student at Indiana University-Bloomington. His work focuses on the practices of higher education decision makers when engaging with information visualization dashboards. He explores these practices and their consequences by examining how these actors are embedded within broader institutional socio-technical networks, how these networks shape data-informed decision-making practices, and the unintended consequences that emerge when these actors engage in practices that differ from what is expected by dashboard designers and stakeholders. In this panel, he will present work on a collaborative conceptual project that draws on modern documentation studies to outline emerging areas for critical learning analytics research and for the broader educational data science community.

Topic 4: Student Data Privacy in Higher Education Syllabi

Amy VanScoy is an assistant professor at the University at Buffalo in the Department of Library and Information Studies. Her work focuses on how professional thinking influences professional practices. Using qualitative methods, such interpretative phenomenological analysis, she has explored how values, attitudes, beliefs, and practice theories influence professional practice, in the context of information services, library programming, and instruction. VanScoy will discuss her study of library and information science (LIS) syllabi. LIS courses, with their goal of preparing graduates to be savvy and ethical consumers of information, seem an ideal context for educating students about data privacy issues. However, the study found that few syllabi address student data privacy and, when addressed, syllabi reveal knowledge gaps, an overfocus on legal aspects of students' privacy, and a focus on specific techniques, rather than a broad conceptual understanding of the issues.

THE PANEL'S STRUCTURE

The aim of the panel is twofold. First, the panelists seek to provide audience members a broad overview of educational data mining (EDM) and learning analytics (LA). To this end, Kyle M. L. Jones will provide a brief talk on the state-of-the-art with regard to practices, technologies, and politics. Second, the panelists seek to provide unique conceptual lenses through which the audience members will be able to see how to enter into this area for their own research; here, each panelist will give a short talk on their topic as detailed above. After these aims are accomplished, the panelists will lead the audience in discussion regarding EDM and LA generally and more specific related issues, opportunities, and methods for developing a research agenda in this area and recommending paths forward with regard to practice, technological design of data-based artifacts (e.g., visualizations, algorithms), and policy.

ACKNOWLEDGMENTS

The panelists thank the Information and Learning Sciences (InfoLearn) Special Interest Group for their sponsorship. InfoLearn welcomes researchers from the information and learning sciences, and it aims to "advance theories of learning, information-seeking, and learning systems' design" (About InfoLearn, 2018). The SIG fuses the "scholarly disciplines of information science and the learning sciences stand to enrich one another theoretically, methodologically, and, empirically."

REFERENCES

About InfoLearn. (2018). Special interest group: Information and learning sciences (InfoLearn). Retrieved from https://www.asist.org/SIG/SIGILS/about/

Baker, R., & Siemens, G. (2014). Educational data mining and learning analytics. In R. K. Sawyer (Ed.), *The Cambridge handbook of the learning sciences* (pp. 253–272). Cambridge, MA: Cambridge University Press. doi: 10.1017/CBO9781139519526.016

Bienkowski, M., Feng, M., & Means, B. (2012). *Enhancing teaching and learning through educational data mining and learning analytics: An issue brief* (U.S. Department of Education No. ED-04- CO-0040). Retrieved from http://tech.ed.gov/wp-content/uploads/2014/03/edm-la- brief.pdf

Buckland, M. (2013), Document theory: an introduction. In M. Willer, A. J. Gilliland, & M. Tomic (Eds.), *Records, Archives and Memory: Selected Papers from the Conference and School on Records, Archives and Memory Studies (*pp. 223-237), University of Zadar, Zadar.

Campbell, J. P., DeBlois, P. B., & Oblinger, D. (2007). Academic analytics: A new tool for a new era. *EDUCAUSE Review, 42*(4), 40–57. Retrieved from http://www.educause.edu/ero/article/academic-analytics-new-tool-new-era

Crow, M. (2012). 'No more excuses': Michael M. Crow on analytics. *EDUCAUSE Review, 47*(4), 14–22. Retrieved from https://er.educause.edu/~/media/files/article-downloads/erm1241p.pdf.

Daniel, B. (2014). Big data and analytics in higher education: Opportunities and challenges. *British Journal of Educational Technology, 46*(5), 904–920. doi: 10.1111/bjet.12230

Kennedy, H., & Hill, R.L. (2017). The pleasure and pain of visualizing data in times of data power. *Television and New Media* 18 (8), 1–14. https://doi.org/10.1177/1527476416667823

Kennedy, H., Hill, R.L., Aiello, G. & Allen, W. (2016). The work that visualisation conventions do. *Information, Communication & Society* 19(6), 715-735. https://doi.org/10.1080/1369118X.2016.1153126

Long, P., & Siemens, G. (2011). Penetrating the fog: Analytics in learning and education. *EDUCAUSE Review, 46*(5), 30–40. Retrieved from https://er.educause.edu/~/media/files/article-downloads/erm1151.pdf

Nissenbaum, H. (2010). Privacy in context: Technology, policy, and the integrity of social life. Stanford, CA: Stanford Law Books.

Picciano, A. G. (2012). The evolution of big data and learning analytics in American higher education. *Journal of Asynchronous Learning Networks, 16*(3), 9–20. Retrieved from http:// onlinelearningconsortium.org/jaln/v16n3/evolution-big-data-and-learning-analytics-american-higher-education

Siemens, G. (2012). Learning analytics: Envisioning a research discipline and a domain of practice. *Proceeding in LAK '12: The 2nd International Conference on Learning Analytics and Knowledge* (pp. 4-8). New York, NY: ACM. doi: 10.1145/2330601.2330605

Glittering in the Dark: Memory, Culture, and Critique in Light of the History of Information

Kathryn La Barre
University of Illinois at Urbana-Champaign, USA.
klabarre@illinois.edu

Sachi Arafat
King Abdulaziz University, KSA.
sachiarafat@hotmail.com

Michael K. Buckland
University of California, Berkeley, USA.
buckland@ischool.berkeley.edu

ABSTRACT

An ethical and human-centered approach to Information Science requires rigorous, historically-informed analysis of both the resources that inform this discipline and the cultural role it inhabits. This session will present and discuss significant recent developments in the history and foundations of the field. ASIST has formally established a new volunteer administrative position of ASIST Curator. Kathryn La Barre, the newly-appointed Curator, will describe the role and responsibilities of this position and assess the state of Information Science history in relation to the conference themes. In two complementary reports: Michael Buckland will examine theoretical accounts of the materials made use of in Information Science; and Sachi Arafat will explain why Information Retrieval and Information Science should be integrated and rethought as a science of technology-mediated experience, and how this new *kind* of science relates to the pre-modern memory arts tradition.

KEYWORDS

ASIS&T Curator, Information Retrieval, Information Science, Robert Pagès, Technology-mediated experience

INTRODUCTION

The goal of this interactive panel is to provide a forum for discussion and critique, as well as a platform to support development of propositions that could inform both the development of ethical and human-centered approaches to Information Science and the role of the ASIST Curator.

KATHRYN LA BARRE: ON CURATION, DOCUMENTATION, AND CRITIQUE

Kathryn La Barre, ASIST Curator will discuss the creation of the Curator position and attendant responsibilities, which include "monitoring the discovery, preservation, and accessibility of resources relating to the history of the ASIST" and "working to promote policy, best practices and documentation to preserve Association, Committee, Chapter, and SIG records." Motivating the creation of this role was a simple notion, "If we don't have a history, we lack an identity." For over eighty years, ASIST has participated in, or has been the beneficiary of numerous specialized conferences, oral history programs, and other initiatives in the field of Information Science. During this time, ASIST has accumulated photographs, recordings and other archival material which are at increasing risk of deterioration and loss. Many materials are undocumented and thus inaccessible, while others are scattered in private or temporary holdings. The net result that they are hidden from discovery and thus inaccessible. There is growing interest world-wide in documenting the history and development of documentation, and information science and technology, and much work to be done to preserve and create access to such materials. One key focus of my presentation will be to engage with session participants about their concerns and priorities.

The title of this position, Curator, was chosen carefully as the duties extend beyond that of an archivist or historian. I envision a role that includes consulting and documenting current material and acquisitions, acting as a subject specialist, and interpreting the artifacts of our mutual cultural heritage. Serving as Curator provides a unique vantage point from which to unearth and amplify the intellectual history embedded in these materials. The conference theme evokes the need to scaffold the development of an ethical and human-centered information science. Concerns about sustainability, privacy, human agency and equity are not new as they span both the past and future of Information Science. The conference also engages with rapid developments and emerging technologies in artificial intelligence, big data analytics, virtual and augmented reality, and embedded, ubiquitous computing. These are all technologies with which members of our organization share deep experience and expertise, during the period it was called the American Documentation Institute, or the American Society for Information Science, or the American Society for Information Science and Technology, or as today, the international Association for Information Science and Technology.

The secondary focus of this presentation will be on the rich intellectual history of ASIST that intersects with and provides context for contemporary discussions of sustainability, privacy, human agency and equity. Understanding our shared history of ideas and approaches will help us better understand current biases, developments, and debates; help us ask better questions; and inform deeper critiques of the technologies we seek to implement.

MICHAEL K. BUCKLAND: FROM BIBLIOGRAPHY TO INFORMATION SCIENCE: ROBERT PAGÈS, 1919-2007.

Bibliography has a long history and developed rapidly from the 1890s onwards. But the limitation of bibliography to printed documents was increasingly seen as an unacceptable constraint in providing access to what people needed to know. Suzanne Briet's manifesto *What is documentation?* (1951) asserted the need to provide access to a broader range of evidence. Her declaration that an antelope placed in a zoo and in a taxonomy becomes a document is now well-known. But neither Briet nor her successors provided much explanation or guidance on how to proceed. What has been overlooked is that key ideas in Briet's manifesto had been presented and discussed in a leading journal three years earlier by Robert Pagès.

Robert Pagès (1919-2007) was a clandestine anarchist activist who used the false name Rodion. Later he became a well-known researcher in social psychology. But between those two careers he became a student in the program of professional education in documentation in Paris where he was one of Briet's students. As a student of documentation, he wrote two theses. The first, on documentary transformations and cultural milieu, was published as an article in F.I.D.'s *Revue of documentation* in 1948. The second thesis eventually appeared as a book on cultural and documentary classifications. In Information Science, Pagès has been remembered, if at all, for a powerful, concise indexing language named CODOC (or "coded analysis"). He was especially interested in language and he published two books and a novel about sense-making.

Pagès' objective was to relate information science (he used "documentology") to theories of human culture and, like Briet, he saw information science as a cultural technique. He wrote that documents are to culture what machinery is to industry and that nothing was more important for the study of culture than examination of its infrastructure, which was becoming more technological, more controlled, and more organized. Pagès is an interesting figure not only for his explanation of ideas hitherto associated with Suzanne Briet, but also because his background in Trotskyism, psychology, and cultural studies was very different from the scientistic enthusiasm for technology of pioneers of documentation and information science in the U.S.A. at that time.

I will briefly summarize Pagès' career and ideas as they relate to not only Briet, but also to the conference theme.

SACHI ARAFAT: FROM SEARCH AS MEANING-SUGGESTION, TO THE MEMORY ARTS, AND TOWARDS A SCIENCE OF TECHNOLOGY-MEDIATED EXPERIENCE

As search applications expand well beyond simple finding to facilitate diverse cognitive goals such as enjoyment and arbitrarily-purposed 'information experiences', and as we move away from the point-click mode of interaction to specify searches in augmented and virtual-reality modes: what search is, and hence what the disciplines (e.g. Information Retrieval (IR) and Information Science (IS)) studying and facilitating it should become, emerge as pressing questions. Given the modern context, search should be understood not in its usual technical sense as a relation between queries and documents, but more generally as a (hermeneutical) process of meaning-suggestion. Related to these are further foundational questions about what constitutes context, the query, document and 'user', and other issues whose resolution determine how we study and build not only the next generation of interactive devices, but more generally, how we understand and facilitate technology-mediated experiences in general.

I argue based on the findings in my recent book (Arafat, S. & Ashoori, E. *Search Foundations*, 2018), that the 'foundations' of IR and IS require serious re-orientation without which serious progress in IR and IS is unlikely. That as the relationships between humans and interactive technology become more intimate such that every interaction with ubiquitous and "vanishing" programmable devices is a "search", the focus of any future 'search science' - and I do think it should be a science albeit a kind that is not at all common - must be technology-mediated human experience as a whole. This embodied and embedded experience is neither solely `mental stuff' nor an experience divorced from an environment and culture, and it goes beyond both simple `user interaction' and the idea of `user engagement' or `user experience' when they are limited to accounts of 'user-behaviour'.

I call such a science, that seeks to understand and explain such experience, a science of technology-mediated experience. Any such science, in addition to its explanatory function (as is a function of IS relative to search systems), must have a `practical art' or 'making function' (as is the function of IR to search systems) that facilitates the design, creation and/or `arrangement' of devices, which is to effect users towards particular experiences in a way that is coherent with the determinations of the explanatory aspect of the science. While the technical design of the device is crucial for this practical art, the main focus must be the experience itself, and as such, it is unlike IR. Instead, it resembles the pre-modern 'memory arts': techniques for associating-between and traversing (through remembering and imagining) an existent set of images, symbols and/or ideas (whether 'in mind' or in a physical space, or a combination thereof), purposed to lead to the discovery of new knowledge, or for having new (beneficial) experiences; the modern computational device was originally conceived as a tool for such discovery. I argue that the 'practical art' function requires serious appropriation of the memory arts, a discourse centred-upon (technique-mediated) human-experience. Moreover, the explanatory function of this science is not unlike that of any other existent science as it involves systematic integration between humanistic and technological explanatory aspects of a particular information event. This is what makes this science rather peculiar, and as I believe, makes it a new *kind* of science. While I was led to this idea through analysing IR and IS discourses, this new science has a larger scope: it must at once systematically integrate (and not just juxtapose) technical computer science discourse on the one hand and with cultural and philosophical discourses on the other.

I will also briefly discuss the foundations research culture that would support the development of such a science and its ethico-social disciplinary implications.

CONTRIBUTION

This panel provides seminal context that enhances the conference theme which interrogates the enterprise of building an ethical and sustainable information future. Conference participants face an information future replete with inextricably linked issues arising from implementations of emerging technologies such as artificial intelligence, big data analytics, virtual and augmented reality, and embedded, ubiquitous computing. These presentations seek to amplify the intellectual history of these current developments by posing much-needed questions about antecedent developments. The goal of this panel is to enhance understanding and ensure that participants are well equipped to engage with the necessity of embedding ethical and human-centered perspectives into technological solutions.

PANELISTS

Sachi Arafat is an Assistant Professor at King Abdulaziz University, KSA where he teaches Data Science. He was previously a Royal Academy of Engineering Research Fellow at the University of Glasgow, UK, where he also completed the first doctoral work on Quantum-theory inspired Retrieval with Keith van Rijsbergen. He is co-author with Elham Ashoori of a book on Search Foundations (MIT Press, forthcoming).

Michael K. Buckland is emeritus professor in the School of Information at the University of California Berkeley. He worked as a librarian in England and the USA before becoming Dean of the School of Librarianship at Berkeley and, later, coordinator for library plans and policies for the multi-campus University of California system. He has written extensively on the history and theory of Information Science, with a special interest in the work of forgotten pioneers, and was ASIST President in 1998.

Kathryn La Barre is an Associate Professor at the School of Information Sciences and Gender and Women's Studies faculty affiliate at the University of Illinois at Urbana-Champaign. Her work interrogates the power dynamics of historical and contemporary naming practices in cultural heritage collections. She has served ASIST as a Member of the 75th Anniversary task force and helps facilitate the oral history project 'Leaders of Information Science Worldwide'. A Director-at-Large, she chaired the ASIST 80th Anniversary working group, and is the newly-appointed ASIST Curator.

REFERENCES

Arafat, S. & Ashoori, E. (December, 2018). Search Foundations: Towards a Science of Technology-Mediated Experience. Cambridge: MIT Press

Briet, S. 1951. Qu'est-ce que la documentation? Paris, ÉDIT. http://martinetl.free.fr/suzannebriet/questcequeladocumentation/

Buckland, M. (2017). Before the antelope. Proceedings from the Document Academy. 4(2) (Article 6) Retrieved, March 23, 2018 http://ideaexchange.uakron.edu/docam/vol4/iss2/6

Pagès, R. 1948. Transformations documentaires et milieu culturel (Essai de documentologie). Review of documentation 15, fasc. 3:53-64. Reprint of thesis Transformations documentaires et milieu culturel, CNAM, 1947.

How Does Health Happen in Public Libraries? Ethical and Emerging Issues

Noah Lenstra
University of North Carolina-Greensboro, USA.
njlenstr@uncg.edu

Mary Grace Flaherty
University of North Carolina-Chapel Hill, USA.
mgflaher@email.unc.edu

Ellen L. Rubenstein
University of Oklahoma, USA. erubenstein@ou.edu

Amelia N. Gibson
University of North Carolina-Chapel Hill, USA.
angibson@email.unc.edu

Catherine Arnott Smith
University of Wisconsin-Madison, USA.
casmith24@wisc.edu

ABSTRACT

The past five years have featured increased multidisciplinary interest in how health happens in public libraries. This panel will explore ethical and emerging issues associated with conducting research on this topic. After lightning talks from five panelists, the audience will engage in interactive, small group discussions focused on how we can form and sustain meaningful research relationships with public libraries and public librarians, for health-related and for other research. Through this discussion, we will outline new research directions on how health happens in public libraries and challenge ourselves to do more to understand this and other processes in public libraries.

KEYWORDS

Health information, health informatics, health literacy, public libraries, wellness

INTRODUCTION

During the past five years, public libraries have been recognized by a diverse array of policy makers and scholars as vital contributors to health and wellness (e.g. Correal, 2018; Morgan et al., 2016; Robert Wood Johnson Foundation, 2017). Since their inception, public libraries have in one form or another attempted to support health (Rubenstein, 2012). There is evidence, however, that the scope of how health happens – or at least the scope of how health is studied – in public libraries is expanding. Part of this trend can be attributed to expanded ideas of what "health" is. For instance, the Robert Wood Johnson Foundation (2018) has said "health" should be defined "in the broadest possible terms," suggesting that past definitions have been overly narrow. Defining "health" broadly, the American Library Association published in 2018 two practitioner-oriented books on supporting health in public libraries (Carson, 2018; Flaherty, 2018).

Taking into account the perspectives of LIS and IS scholars who have researched public libraries in the context of a) health information behaviors, b) health informatics, and c) health and wellness programming, this interactive panel will address three questions: 1) how different disciplinary and theoretical perspectives can productively inform understanding of how health happens in public libraries, 2) how these different perspectives can more generally inform the field's understanding of health information behavior and health informatics, and 3) how different methods can be utilized to form and sustain meaningful research relationships with public libraries and public librarians. This panel will be of special interest to members of the Health Informatics (HLTH) and the Information Needs, Seeking and Use (USE) Special Interest Groups (SIGs).

The session will also appeal to others doing or considering research in or with public libraries, as the panel will use the example of how health happens in public libraries as a lens for a broader discussion of methodological challenges and opportunities associated with conducting research in public libraries. On February 10, 2018, Marcellus Turner, the Chief Librarian and Executive Director of the Seattle Public Library, convened a conversation in Denver, Colorado, among public library directors and LIS researchers that examined the frequently strained relationships between these two communities. That discussion focused in part on the need to better prepare future public librarians to be ready to build teams and relationships in and out of the library. This panel will continue that conversation. Through this discussion, we will develop novel ways of forming and sustaining meaningful research relationships with public libraries.

BACKGROUND

Recent research on public libraries and health tends to focus on three broad topics: 1) the preparedness of library staff to support health, 2) how library programs and services contribute to health and wellness outcomes, and 3) the relationship between libraries and the determinants of health. The most traditional way of studying health and libraries has been to consider how prepared library staff are to support health, particularly through the provision of consumer health information (e.g. Linnan et al., 2004). This trend continued in recent studies focused on how prepared public library staff are: a) to help people navigate the U.S. health insurance marketplace and the Affordable Care Act (Smith, 2017; Vardell & Charbonneau, 2017), b) to support health literacy through programs and services (Rubenstein, 2016a), c) to provide access to consumer health information more generally (Rubenstein, 2016b) and in controversial domains specifically (Keselman, Smith & Hundal, 2014; Smith, Hundal & Keselman, 2014), and d) to provide physical activity programs (Lenstra, 2018). Relatedly, Rubenstein (2017) discussed how best to educate the next generation of public librarians to support health.

A second stream of research investigates how library programs and services contribute to health and wellness outcomes. Flaherty and Miller (2016) analyzed how a rural public library contributes to community health and wellness through its programs and services. Xie (2012) worked with the Prince George's County Memorial Library System to offer a public library-based e-health literacy intervention training program, which she then assessed. One of her conclusions was that libraries should do more programming similar to the training she provided. Studies have also considered the health and wellness outcomes of nutrition workshops (Freedman & Nickell, 2010), seed exchanges (Soleri, 2018), and physical activity programming (Lenstra, 2017) in public libraries. Studies have also considered the lack of impact that public libraries have. Goytia et al. (2005) investigated public libraries' capacity to support cancer screening in underserved communities to reveal significant attitudinal barriers on the part of the library staff. Gibson, Kaplan, and Vardell (2017) found that "libraries were the least frequently selected source of information" for parents of individuals with Autism Spectrum Disorder. Similarly, Flaherty, Tayag, Lanier, and Minor (2014) found that not all public libraries provide credible information in response to the question "do vaccines cause autism?"

Finally, an emerging stream of research considers how public libraries more generally impact the social, economic, and cultural determinants of health. Comparing clinical variables to library usage patterns, Zager, Haskins, Maland, and Holt (2016) found that library usage intersects with positive health behaviors. Similarly, Morgan et al. (2016) investigated how public libraries influence the social determinants of health. Research has also considered the general relationship between public libraries and individual and community health and wellness/wellbeing (Fujiwara, Lawton, & Mourato, 2015; Patel, Skarzynski, & Nassimbeni, 2015). For instance, Phillips (2017) considered how the empathy of library staff contributes to social, emotional, and psychological outcomes. Brewster (2014) examined how public libraries function as a kind of "therapeutic landscape," supporting mental health and wellness in their communities.

This recent research comes from multiple disciplinary backgrounds and perspectives. In addition to scholars working in the information sciences, scholars working in Ethnoecology (Soleri, 2018), Nutrition and Food Science (Freedman & Nickell, 2010), Economics (Fujiwara, Lawton, & Mourato, 2015), Public Health (Morgan et al., 2016), the Health Sciences (Brewster, 2014), and Medicine (Zager et al., 2016) have also contributed to these discussions. The fact that the health roles of public libraries have received such attention from scholars outside of the information sciences suggests that this is an opportune moment for us to ask at ASIS&T "how *does* health happens in libraries?" Can we challenge ourselves to do more to answer this question?

PANEL ORGANIZATION

This interactive panel brings together researchers working on how health happens in public libraries to discuss conceptual and methodological challenges associated with this topic. Each panelist will contribute a unique perspective, based on their own background, theoretical orientation, and programs of research. We will structure the proposed panel session in the following manner.

Part 1: Lightning talks on emerging and ethical issues (40 minutes)

- Introduction: The moderator (Lenstra) will introduce the panel and panelists
- Catherine Arnott Smith will discuss librarian "resistance" to health information provision historically and currently, and examine the implications of this attitude for researchers working in and with public libraries
- Mary Grace Flaherty will discuss public libraries as community level resources for advancing population health
- Amelia Gibson will discuss how models of inclusion and marginalization in libraries influence policy and planning, and frame libraries' ability to support health and wellness-related information seeking for people of color, and people with autism and other high-incidence disabilities
- Ellen Rubenstein will discuss the challenges and opportunities public libraries face in providing health information and facilitating health literacy
- Noah Lenstra will discuss physical activity promotion in public libraries and will then wrap up the presentations and introduce the group discussion stage of the session

Part 2: Interactive group discussion (30 minutes)

- Group discussions with audience members separating into five groups, each with a panelist guiding conversation, focused on discussing the three questions shaping this panel:

1. How can different disciplinary and theoretical perspectives productively inform understanding of how health happens in public libraries?
2. How can different perspectives more generally inform the field's understanding of health information behavior and health informatics?
3. How can we form and sustain meaningful research relationships with public libraries and public librarians?

Part 3: Wrap-up and discussion of next steps (20 minutes)

- The panelists will express and discuss together perspectives shared in their groups as well as their own perspectives regarding the three questions articulated above (15 minutes)
- Wrap-up. The moderator summarizes the outcomes of the panel discussion, focusing on next steps in researching how health happens in public libraries (5 minutes)

THE PANEL MEMBERS

Noah Lenstra, moderator, is an Assistant Professor of Library and Information Studies in the School of Education at the University of North Carolina at Greensboro, where he is also Affiliated Faculty in the Gerontology Department. He currently serves on the Advisory Board for the Public Library Association's Promoting Healthy Communities initiative. His research focuses on how public libraries support health through programs that increase physical activity. More information can be found on this project's website: LetsMoveLibraries.org. He is the 2018-2019 Chair of the ASIS&T Health Informatics SIG.

Catherine Arnott Smith was a National Library of Medicine Predoctoral Trainee in Biomedical Informatics at the Center (now Department) of Biomedical Informatics, University of Pittsburgh, and is a Professor at the Information School and a Discovery Fellow attached to the Wisconsin Institutes for Discovery's Virtual Environments Group, University of Wisconsin-Madison. Her principal research foci are (1) consumer language for clinical information systems, and (2) clinical information provision and handling in nonclinical settings, such as public libraries, archives and disabilities centers.

Mary Grace Flaherty is an Assistant Professor at the School of Information & Library Science at the University of North Carolina at Chapel Hill. She has over 25 years' experience working in a variety of library settings, including academic, medical research, special and public. Her research focuses on how individuals find and act upon health information, and the role of public libraries with regard to health information provision and health promotion.

Amelia Gibson is an Assistant Professor at the School of Information and Library Science at the University of North Carolina at Chapel Hill. Her primary research interests center on health information behavior, and local communities and places as information systems. Her current work focuses on information poverty and how intersections of identity, place, space, and social and economic power/privilege influence information access and information behavior. Dr. Gibson is a research fellow with the Frank Porter Graham Child Development Institute and the UNC Parr Center for Ethics.

Ellen Rubenstein is an Assistant Professor at the School of Library and Information Studies at the University of Oklahoma. Her research focuses on access to health information and health literacy in public libraries and in online communities. as well as information behavior. She serves on the Health Initiatives Committee of the University of Oklahoma College of Arts and Sciences and statewide organization, Oklahoma Regional Advisory Committee, which looks at how libraries are contributing to health.

EXPECTED OUTCOMES

By the end of this panel, panelists and audience members will have shared complementary perspectives on a) how health happens in public libraries, b) what is meant by the concept of "health," and c) how to form sustained and meaningful research relationships with public libraries. Through this discussion, we will outline new research directions on how health happens in public libraries and challenge ourselves to do more to understand this topic.

REFERENCES

Brewster, L. (2014). The public library as therapeutic landscape: A qualitative case study. *Health & Place*, 26, 94-99.

Carson, J. (2018). Get your community moving: Physical literacy programs for all ages. Chicago: ALA Editions.

Correal, (2018, February 28). Once it was overdue books. Now librarians fight overdoses. *New York Times*. Retrieved from https://www.nytimes.com/2018/02/28/nyregion/librarians-opioid-heroin-overdoses.html.

Flaherty, M. G., & Miller, D. (2016). Rural public libraries as community change agents: Opportunities for health promotion. *Journal of Education for Library and Information Science*, 57(2), 143-150.

Flaherty, M. G. (2018). Promoting individual and community health at the library. Chicago: ALA Editions.

Flaherty, M. G., Tayag, E. K., Lanier, M., & Minor, J. (2014). The Jenny McCarthy conundrum: Public libraries, popular culture, and health misinformation. *Proceedings of the Association for Information Science and Technology*, 51(1), 1-1.

Freedman, M. R., & Nickell, A. (2010). Impact of after-school nutrition workshops in a public library setting. *Journal of nutrition education and behavior*, 42(3), 192-196.

Fujiwara, D., Lawton, R., & Mourato, S. (2015). *The health and wellbeing benefits of public libraries*. Arts Council England and SIMETRICA. Retrieved from http://www.artscouncil.org.uk/health-and-wellbeing-benefits-public-libraries.

Gibson, A. N., Kaplan, S., & Vardell, E. (2017). A survey of information source preferences of parents of individuals with Autism Spectrum Disorder. *Journal of Autism and Developmental Disorders*, 47(7), 2189-2204.

Goytia, E. J., Rapkin, B., Weiss, E. S., Golub, D., Guzman, V., & O'Connor, M. (2005). New York literacy task force: Readiness and capacity of librarians in public libraries to implement a breast cancer outreach and screening campaign in medically underserved communities. *Cancer Control*, 12 Suppl(2),13-20.

Keselman, A., Smith, C. A., & Hundal, S. (2014). Library workers' personal beliefs about childhood vaccination and vaccination information provision. *Journal of the Medical Library Association*, 102(3), 205-210.

Lenstra, N. (2017). Movement-based programs in US and Canadian public libraries: Evidence of impacts from an exploratory survey. *Evidence Based Library and Information Practice*, 12(4), 214-232.

Lenstra, N. (2018). The experiences of public library staff developing programs with physical activities: An exploratory study in North Carolina. *Library Quarterly*, 88(2), 142-159.

Linnan, L. A., Wildemuth, B. M., Gollop, C., Hull, P., Silbajoris, C., & Monnig, R. (2004). Public librarians as a resource for promoting health: Results from the Health for Everyone in Libraries Project (HELP) librarian survey. *Health Promotion Practice,* 5(2), 182-190.

Morgan, A. U., Dupuis, R., D'Alonzo, B., Johnson, A., Graves, A., Brooks, K. L., ... & Grande, D. (2016). Beyond books: Public libraries as partners for population health. *Health Affairs*, 35(11), 2030-2036.

Patel, N., Skarzynski, J., & Nassimbeni, M. (2015). Improving people's lives: Measuring Harare Public Library's contribution to individual and community wellbeing. *Proceedings of IFLA 2015*. http://library.ifla.org/1240/1/088-patel-en.pdf.

Phillips, A. (2017). Understanding empathetic services: The role of empathy in everyday library work. *Journal of Research on Libraries & Young Adults* 8(1), 1-27.

Robert Wood Johnson Foundation. (2017). *Social and economic environment: Public Libraries*. Retrieved from https://www.cultureofhealth.org/en/taking-action/creating-healthier-communities/social-and-economic-environment.html.

Robert Wood Johnson Foundation (2018) *2018 RWJF Culture of Health Prize Finalists Announced*. Retrieved from http://www.countyhealthrankings.org/news-events/2018-rwjf-culture-of-health-prize-finalists-announced.

Rubenstein, E. L. (2012). From social hygiene to consumer health: Libraries, health information, and the American public from the late nineteenth century to the 1980s. *Library & Information History*, 28(3), 202-219.

Rubenstein, E. L. (2016a). Knowing how to help: Providing health information in public libraries. *Journal of Consumer Health on the Internet*, 20(3), 114-129.

Rubenstein, E. L. (2016b). Health information and health literacy: Public library practices, challenges, and opportunities. *Public Library Quarterly*, 35(1), 49-71.

Rubenstein, E. L. (2017). "I didn't learn that in library school": Experiential learning in consumer health for future public librarians. *Library Trends*, 66(1), 37-51.

Smith, C. A. (2017). *Weary of helping: Public libraries, health information, and the affordable care act*. Webinar at University of Wisconsin-Madison Information School. Retrieved from http://wisc.adobeconnect.com/p8571ti6qdv/.

Smith, C. A., Hundal, S., & Keselman, A. (2014). Knowledge gaps among public librarians seeking vaccination information: A qualitative study. *Journal of Consumer Health on the Internet*, 18(1), 44-66.

Soleri, D. (2018). Civic seeds: New institutions for seed systems and communities—a 2016 survey of California seed libraries. *Agriculture and Human Values*, 35(2), 331–347.

Vardell, E., & Charbonneau, D. H. (2017). Health insurance literacy and roles for reference librarian involvement. *The Reference Librarian*, 58(2), 124-135.

Xie, B. (2012). Improving older adults' e-health literacy through computer training using NIH online resources. *Library & Information Science Research*, 34(1), 63-71.

Zager, S., Haskins, A., Maland, K., & Holt, C. (2016). The health and libraries of public use retrospective study (HeLPURS). *Health Information & Libraries Journal*, 33(3), 190-203.

Meet the Editors – Successfully Publishing in Information Science Journals

Dirk Lewandowski
Hamburg University of Applied Sciences, Hamburg, Germany. dirk.lewandowski@haw-hamburg.de

Javed Mostafa
University of North Carolina at Chapel Hill, USA. jm@unc.edu

Andrew Dillon
University of Texas – Austin, USA. adillon@ischool.utexas.edu

Jim Jansen
Hamad bin Khalifa University, Qatar. bjansen@hbku.edu.qa

Fidelia Ibekwe-SanJuan
University of Aix-Marseille, France. fidelia.ibekwe-sanjuan@univ-amu.fr

Andrew M. Cox
University of Sheffield, United Kingdom. a.m.cox@sheffield.ac.uk

Samuel K. Chu
University of Hong Kong. samchu@hku.hk

ABSTRACT
This is a panel to introduce the editors of prestigious international journals in library and information science, who will discuss the aim and the scope of the journals and elaborate on the expectations from potential contributors to help young academics understand and appreciate the process of academic publishing.

KEYWORDS
Academic journals, journal editors, publishing

INTRODUCTION

Publishing in a scholarly journal often seems complicated and challenging, particularly for the new researchers and academics, who are expected to produce high quality papers from the outset of their careers. The aim of this panel is to help researchers not only choosing the right journal for publishing their research, but also to help them understand the processes from submission to final acceptance that papers undergo at the different journals. Editors will give insights into their quality criteria and, more generally, what they are looking for in a paper to be published.

Each panelist will spend about 5-7 minutes introducing their journal, after which, the floor opens for Q&A, and a general roundtable discussion on challenges of academic publishing. Topics likely being of interest to the audience are, amongst others, editors' position on open data, emerging new forms of peer review, motivations for reviewers, and altmetrics.

The journals chosen for this panel represent some of the top ranking publications in the field of library and information science based on the reports by the Journal Citation Report and Scopus SCImago Journal & Country Rank (http://www.scimagojr.com/index.php), and include:

- Journal of the Association for Information Science & Technology
- Journal of Documentation
- Information Processing & Management
- Aslib Journal of Information Management
- Education for Information
- Online Information Review
- Information and Learning Science

The panelists, the editors and editorial board members of these journals, are prominent scholars and academics, who will share their extensive experience on scholarly and professional publishing with the audience. They will provide insight in the publication process form the time a paper has been submitted to the peer-review stage, and acceptance of the final manuscript.

After the successful editors panel at the ASIS&T Annual Meeting in Copenhagen in 2016 with more than 80 participants (Beheshti et al., 2016), this second installment will again offer researchers the opportunity to directly discuss questions related to publishing with the people directly responsible for deciding what gets added to the body of knowledge in information science.

PANELISTS

Javed Mostafa, Journal of the Association for Information Science and Technology

The *Journal of the Association for Information Science and Technology* (*JASIST*) is a leading international forum for peer-reviewed research in information science. For more than half a century, *JASIST* has provided intellectual leadership by publishing original research that focuses on the production, discovery, recording, storage, representation, retrieval, presentation, manipulation, dissemination, use, and evaluation of information and on the tools and techniques associated with these processes.

Javed Mostafa is the Director of the Carolina Health Informatics Program and the Director of the Laboratory of Applied Informatics Research. His research concentrates on information retrieval problems, particularly related to search and user-system interactions in large-scale document/data repositories. He also serves as the Deputy Director of the Biomedical Informatics Core at the NC Translational & Clinical Sciences Institute and has current research engagements in biomedical data mining, analysis, visualization, user interface design, and multi-modal human- computer interaction. He regularly serves on program and organizing committees for major conferences and participates as reviewer for major grant initiatives. Javed served as an associate editor for the ACM Transactions on Information Systems for eight years. He currently serves as the Editor-in-Chief of the Journal of the Association for Information Science & Technology, an associate editor of the ACM Transactions on Internet Technology, and an editor of the Information Processing & Management Journal. Translating scientific advances into health care improvements is a passion for Javed, and based on support from UNC's Translational & Clinical Sciences Institute he co-founded a company concentrating on patient-centric decision support and streamlined care workflow called Keona Health. In UNC, Javed holds a joint faculty position in information science in the School of Information and Library Science and in the Biomedical Research Imaging Center in the School of Medicine. Additionally, he holds the title of Adjunct Professor of Community and Family Medicine, School of Medicine, Duke University.

Andrew Dillon, Journal of Documentation

The Journal of Documentation (JDoc) is a one of the longest-established academic journals in library/information science, providing a unique focus on theories, concepts, models, frameworks and philosophies related to documents and recorded knowledge. This peer-reviewed journal is included in both ISI and SCOPUS. Our articles have long-lasting value, with the longest citation half-life in ISI's LIS category. JDoc provides a link between research, scholarship and reflective professional practice. It publishes research papers with novel methods or results of wide significance, in all the information-related disciplines. Critical and scholarly reviews are welcome, as are reviews of the evidence base for professional practice, and shorter speculative articles. We particularly welcome submissions exploring topics where concepts and models in the library and information sciences overlap with those in cognate disciplines: these disciplines include, but are not limited to, psychology and cognitive science, the physical sciences, communication and media studies, museum studies, computer science, sociology and publishing. We also welcome contributions in the 'Speculation in Documentation' category. These are short (no more than 5,000 words) contributions, presenting an original concept or perspective.

Professor Andrew Dillon (member of the editorial board), Dean, School of Information, University of Texas – Austin, USA

Andrew Dillon is the Dean and Yule Regents Professor of Information at the University of Texas-Austin School of Information. His research emphasis is on the human response to information environments with an emphasis on social and psychological determinants of discovery, learning and use. He has served on the editorial boards of multiple journals, most recently Interacting with Computers and the Journal of Documentation and is the editor for the UT Press book series on Information.

Jim Jansen, Information Processing & Management

Information Processing and Management is a leading international journal focusing on research concerning theory, methods, or application in the fields of information science and computer science. The journal is indexed in both Web of Science categories of "Computer Science, Information Systems" and "Information Science Library Science". The journal's impact factor is 2.391. The acceptance rate is about 15%. The journal's turnaround time to first decide is ~30 days, with a high variance among individual manuscripts. The journal has an immediate publication policy (i.e., no wait time for a complete journal issue). The journal has four Associate Editors who are: Luanne S. Freund (University of British Columbia), Christina Lioma (University of Copenhagen), Paolo Rosso (Universitad Politècnica de València), and Ian Ruthven (University of Strathclyde).

Jim Jansen is editor-in-chief of the journal, Information Processing & Management (Elsevier) and was previously editor-in-chief of the journal, Internet Research (Emerald) for 5 years. Jim is a principal scientist in the social computing group at the Qatar Computing Research Institute, Professor in the College of Science and Engineering, Hamad bin Khalifa University, and Adjunct Professor at the College of Information Sciences and Technology at The Pennsylvania State University. He is a graduate of West Point and has a Ph.D. in computer science from Texas A&M University, along with master degrees from Texas A&M (computer science) and Troy State (international relations).

Dirk Lewandowski, Aslib Journal of Information Management

Aslib Journal of Information Management (AJIM) is a peer-reviewed international journal providing key insights into the latest international developments in the research and practice of information management and information science. Areas of interest include topics such as social media, data protection, search engines, information retrieval, digital libraries, information behaviour, intellectual property and copyright, information industry, digital repositories and information policy and governance. The journal invites contributions from academics and practitioners which cover a broad range of issues in the field, including economic, behavioural, social, ethical, technological, international, business-related, political and management-orientated factors.

Dirk Lewandowski is a professor of information research and information retrieval at the Hamburg University of Applied Sciences, Germany. He studied library science at the School of Library Science in Stuttgart, as well as philosophy, information science, and media studies at Heinrich Heine University in Düsseldorf. He received his Ph.D. from that university in 2005. Dirk has published extensively in the areas of Web information retrieval, search engine user behaviour and the role that search engines play in society. His work has been published in some of the leading information science journals, including JASIST, Journal of Information Science and Journal of Documentation. Dirk has served as an expert to, among others, the High Court of Justice (UK) and the Deutscher Bundestag (German Parliament). He has been named an ACM Distinguished Speaker in 2016. Prof. Lewandowski authored and edited several books on search engines, including "Suchmaschinen verstehen" (Springer, 2015) and "Web Search Engine Research" (Emerald Group Publishing, 2012), as well as a series of German-language handbooks on search.

Fidelia Ibekwe-SanJuan, Education for Information

Founded in 1983, Education for Information (EFI) is a quarterly refereed academic international journal publishing research articles on issues related to the teaching and learning of information scientists and professionals for an information society.

EFI welcomes a broad perspective on issues related to pedagogy and learning in the information and communication disciplines (ICD) such as Library and Information Science, Communication and Media studies, Journalism, Archival studies, Museum studies, Psychology, Cognitive science and Digital Humanities.

EFI provides a link between scholarly research, teaching and professional practices in cognate information-communication disciplines. As a peer-reviewed journal with an international focus, EFI publishes full-length articles, comprehensive literature reviews, commentaries, funded innovative research protocols, short communications and book reviews. Its News section reports on significant activities and events in the international arena.

Fidelia Ibekwe-SanJuan is a full Professor at the School of Journalism and Communication, University of Aix-Marseille in France. She teaches « Theories of Information & Communication", "Digital Culture & Communication", "Data visualisation, Information & Innovation in the digital age". Her research interests span both empirical and theoretical research. She has previously worked on human language technology applied to automatic indexing, text mining, topic mapping, terminology engineering and information retrieval. Her research in recent years has taken a more theoretical and reflexive bent. She has been studying the impact of big data, open data and web 2.0 on science and on the society as well as the working on the historical and theoretical foundations of information and library science (LIS) and on the epistemology of LIS. She has been a visiting research scholar at the iSchool of the University of Drexel, Philadelphia. She has authored four books and published about 60 peer-reviewed publications.

Andrew M. Cox, Online Information Review

Online Information Review is co-edited by Dr.s Jo Bates, Andrew Cox and Angela Lin (Information School, Sheffield, UK) and Prof. Dr. Robert Jäschke (Humboldt University, Berlin, Germany). The journal provides a multi-disciplinary forum for scholars from a range of fields, including information studies/iSchools, data studies, internet studies, media and communication studies and information systems. We are particularly interested in publishing research on the social, political and ethical aspects of emergent digital information practices and platforms, and welcome submissions that draw upon critical and socio-technical perspectives in order to address these developments. We welcome empirical, conceptual and methodological contributions on any topics relevant to the broad field of digital information and communicatio

Dr Andrew M. Cox is a senior lecturer in the Information School, University of Sheffield. He is head of the School's Digital Societies research group, coordinator of PhD studies and of the MSc in Digital Library Management

Sam Chu, Information and Learning Science

Information and Learning Science advances inter-disciplinary research that explores scholarly intersections shared within 2 key fields: information science and the learning sciences / education sciences. The journal provides a publication venue for work that strengthens our scholarly understanding of human inquiry and learning phenomena, especially as they relate to design and uses of information and e-learning systems innovations.

We invite research that builds upon and advances theories, methods, results, innovation designs, evidence bases and frameworks for action present across both information science, and the learning/education sciences scholarly domains. We especially welcome the submission of papers that directly address, explicate and discuss the inter-disciplinary boundaries and intersections present across these two fields, and that offer new conceptual, empirical and technological syntheses.

Dr. Sam Chu is Associate Professor, Division of Information and Technology Studies, Faculty of Education, The University of Hong Kong. He received 2 PhDs in Education – one focusing on e-Learning from University College London, Institute of Education, U.K. and another one focusing on Information Science from HKU, Faculty of Education. His areas of expertise include gamified learning, 21st Century Skills, Social Media in Education, School and Academic Librarianship, Plagiarism-free Collaborative Inquiry Project-based Learning, Digital Literacies: Information, Media & Technology Literacy. He has involved in over 60 research/project grants with a total funding of US$7,582,075. He has published more than 270 articles and books with over 50 appear in international academic journals. He is a Member of the Humanities and Social Sciences Panel of the Research Grants Council of HK. His works in gamified learning won him 3 awards from HKU and HK's Food and Health Bureau. He is ranked as the top 66th author in the world regarding his publications in library and information science (DOI 10.1007/s11192-014-1519-9).

REFERENCES

Beheshti, J., Jansen, J., Dillon, A., Lewandowski, D., Mostafa, J., Khanova, J., Wilson, T., Seadle, M. (2016). Publish or perish: Meet the editors a special panel. *Proceedings of the Association for Information Science and Technology*, *53*(1), 1–4. https://doi.org/10.1002/pra2.2016.14505301021

Fandom, Food, and Folksonomies: The Methodological Realities of Studying Fun Life-Contexts

Melissa G. Ocepek
University of Illinois, USA. mgocepek@illinois.edu

Julia Bullard
University of British Columbia, Canada. julia.bullard@ubc.ca

Jenna Hartel
University of Toronto, Canada. jenna.hartel@utoronto.ca

Eric Forcier
Swinburne University of Technology, Australia. eforcier@swin.edu.au

Sarah Polkinghorne
Swinburne University of Technology, Australia; University of Alberta, Canada. spolkinghorne@swin.edu.au

Ludi Price
City University of London, United Kingdom. Ludovica.Price.1@city.ac.uk

ABSTRACT

As Library and Information Science research has evolved, new domains of interest have shaped the field, and with them comes a need to question the appropriateness of applying traditional methodologies to these new domains. This panel focuses on the methodological realities of studying fun life-contexts and will address how researching a new domain comes with challenges and opportunities. The group of scholars on this panel all share an appreciation for identifying and exploring the unique information experiences within fun life-contexts, and engage with a variety of subfields, including information behavior, information organization, embodied information, and fan communities. This interactive panel will consist of five short presentations from each of the panelists and a moderated Q&A led by moderator, Jenna Hartel. The panelists each share some examples of their recent work studying fun life-contexts, reflect on their experience researching in a new domain, and develop themes and questions that should be addressed in future work.

KEYWORDS

Methodology, fun, serious leisure, context, fan communities

INTRODUCTION

As Library and Information Science (LIS) research has expanded to study much more than the library, researchers have found themselves studying new populations in new domains across the discipline. While scholars continue to rely on the concepts and methods that were created to study the library and similar formalized information systems, it is important to step back and ask: are our old tools adequate for studying new spaces, or informal systems? That question is central to this panel on the methodological realities of studying fun life-contexts.

The panelists will provide brief presentations on their experiences studying fun life-contexts, followed by a moderated Q&A with the audience. This format will allow scholars to learn more about the methodological realities of studying LIS in an emerging domain, as well as help scholars in these domains to identify questions related to methodology that may require future exploration. The goals of this panel are to start formalizing a conversation around research methods in new research domains, to invite more scholars into this space, and to develop future work that can improve LIS research into fun life-contexts and the variety of new domains scholars are approaching.

BACKGROUND

LIS research can trace its roots back to early studies of the effects of libraries and reading, all the way back to an 1849 report from the British parliament (Case & Given, 2016). The field expanded after WWII with research and funding opportunities focusing on improving the dissemination of information for researchers in basic and applied sciences; this is also when the subfield of information behavior research began. Models were developed that sought to generalize the behavior of information users, a more reductive approach that sought to illuminate the commonalities between users. Recently, however, LIS research broadly and information behavior research specifically has evolved to examine information behaviors and systems outside of libraries and the scientific community to study how people use information in a variety of aspects of their lives. Beginning with the everyday life information seeking model (Savolainen, 1995), information behavior scholars have explored non-work contexts, both fun and banal, to gain a more holistic understanding of information use and to understand context as a driver for information behaviors and practices. Context has now become an important factor in describing user information behavior and practice, as Greifeneder (2014) summarizes. While studying everyday life is not new in LIS, there have been no focused discussions of the best methods for studying fun life-contexts.

Hartel (2003) argues for moving information behavior and LIS research more broadly into the informal and even fun aspects of life with her call to embrace serious leisure, hobbies, and the pleasures of life (Kari & Hartel, 2007) as research settings. A growing number of researchers have taken up this call. Most recently there has been attention given to "happy information" (Tinto & Ruthven, 2015) and its positive impact upon friendships, and how play can promote knowledge creation in a program to promote children's joy of reading (Suorsa, 2017). Lee and Trace (2009) explored how information sustains people's interests, efforts, and desires within a community of hobbyist collectors. Harviainen (2015) found that people have fun exchanging information about a pleasurable activity, even when they are not engaging in it. And Swalwell, Stuckey, and Ndalianis (2017) discussed how gamers develop videogame collections and share information on best practice to conserve and preserve old games.

Could it be that fun settings generate unique information experiences? Are there distinct information forms and genres associated with fun, such as the joke or exposé? Is laughing an information behavior? Or is it that a *lack* of information can sometimes lighten the spirit and make something enjoyable? These provocative questions have captured the imaginations of the panelists. Answers can only be found through original research, but what are some methodological realities of studying fun life-contexts?

This panel, which brings together scholars from across LIS, will present examples of the similarities and differences studying fun life-contexts compared to more traditional LIS domains. In addition to the presentations, the panel will consist of a moderated Q&A with panelists and the audience to explore how LIS scholars can approach this domain, and what questions should be further explored in future work.

FORMAT

This interactive panel will feature five panelists and a moderator who have performed research in the area of fun, non-work contexts. The panel will begin with a brief introduction from the moderator, Jenna Hartel, welcoming everyone and explaining the purpose of the session as well as introducing the session format. Each panelist will offer a 5-minute presentation on their work with illustrative examples of what data collection and analysis looks like in this domain. After the presentations, the moderator will open the session for questions she has prepared as well as questions from the audience.

MODERATOR AND PANELISTS

The moderator and panelists represent a wide swath of LIS research as well as different stages of academic careers and institutions. By bringing together a variety of methodological and research perspectives this panel will represent how many different sub-fields of LIS are working in the domain of fun life-contexts.

Jenna Hartel, Moderator

Jenna Hartel is an Associate Professor at the Faculty of Information, University of Toronto. Her research is organized around the question: *What is the nature of information in the pleasures of life?* She is investigating this matter through the concatenated study of serious leisure realms, which are crossroads of information and enjoyment (Hartel, 2003). Professor Hartel has employed ethnography and visual methods to explore the use and structure of leisure information on personal and social levels, and her dissertation was a case study of information phenomena in the hobby of gourmet cooking (Hartel, 2007). At the Faculty of Information, she has supervised investigations of information practice in a variety of fun settings: amateur comedy, eating out at restaurants, going to the movies, clothes shopping, video gaming, and online dating. Overall, Professor Hartel's research and teaching aim to be an imaginative, energetic, and committed form of intervention in the field of library and information science. She believes a different character of LIS is possible, one that moves beyond pragmatic concerns with information resources and technologies to consider positive and upbeat information phenomena across the entire human experience.

Julia Bullard, Panelist

Julia Bullard is an Assistant Professor at the School of Library, Archival and Information Science at the University of British Columbia. She researches information organization, particularly the design of classification and controlled vocabulary systems, with an eye to how designers instantiate community values in decisions of terminology and organization. Julia has found design processes within leisure communities exemplifying the connection between shared values and system design. In her study of game players who designed databases to organize *World of Warcraft* game information and of members of the fanfiction community who maintained a curated folksonomy for the organization and retrieval of fanworks, participants described their work as a variation of the fun thing at the center of their hobbies—that parsing changing data logs can be as rewarding as defeating digital dragons and that finding just the right term for a concept is a valuable and creative way to support a community of creators and readers.

The combination of fun contexts and stereotypically un-fun tasks has meant that Julia's research methods, including participant observation, diary studies, and interviews, are rare opportunities for her participants to share their passions and challenges with an engaged audience, producing deeply reflective and evocative accounts of technological work. In this panel, Julia will discuss the data collection and analysis issues she found in seeking the technical details at the center of passion projects.

Eric Forcier, Panelist

Eric Forcier is a doctoral candidate at Swinburne University of Technology in the department of Media and Communication. His research explores the information-related activities of transmedia fans and fan communities in postdigital everyday life. This research was inspired by an interest in transmedia storyworlds and how the concept of "narrative" is understood by gamers and fans. In 2013, he co-edited the book *Words, Worlds and Narratives: Transmedia and Immersion*, a collaborative project with researchers from a variety of disciplinary backgrounds offering a spectrum of perspectives on the experiences of contemporary creators, fans and media consumers. More recently, at ASIS&T 2017 Eric presented the results of a pilot project comparing fan responses to *Game of Thrones* in his award-winning paper "Re(a)d Wedding: A Case Study Exploring Everyday Information Behaviors of the Transmedia Fan".

Now undertaking data collection for his dissertation, Eric is conducting semi-structured exploratory interviews with self-identified media fans and content analysis of publicly accessible online fan communities. The study adopts a constructivist grounded theory approach (Charmaz, 2014) to identify the specific ways in which transmedia fans interact with information through their engagement with a chosen narrative. In his presentation, Eric will address the decision to adopt two distinct data collection methods and report on his progress, including any challenges or pitfalls encountered in the early stages of data collection and analysis. He will also present examples from the data that represent emerging themes about the information-related activities of fans.

Melissa G. Ocepek, Panelist

Melissa G. Ocepek is a Visiting Assistant Professor at the University of Illinois Urbana-Champaign in the School of Information Sciences. Her research addresses how individuals use information in their everyday lives. Her research interests include everyday information behavior, critical theory, and food. Melissa was drawn to fun contexts early in her academic career when working with her two co-authors, Dr. William Aspray and George Royer, Dr. Ocepek on two books and several articles that that addressed the intersection of food, information, and culture. Her interest in food lead her to complete her dissertation entitled, *Everyday Shopping: An Exploration of the Information Behaviors of the Grocery Shoppers*.

To collect data for her dissertation, Melissa interviewed and observed grocery shopping trips with her participants. She discovered that while grocery shopping is something all of her participants regularly participated in, they did not have well-formed thoughts or opinions about most of their grocery shopping habits. The interview protocol required a very deliberate organization to allow her participants to first describe their behaviors and then reflect on them. The interviews were surprising due to the rich details participants were able to provide about their grocery shopping, while being less aware of the underlying rationale. During her presentation, Melissa will provide examples from her data of surprising stories that participants shared as well as how the organization of interview questions led to several "ah ha" moments for her participants near the end of the interviews.

Sarah Polkinghorne, Panelist

Sarah Polkinghorne is a doctoral candidate at Swinburne University of Technology in Melbourne, Australia and a librarian at the University of Alberta in Edmonton, Canada. In this panel, Sarah will discuss the use of wearable technology for data collection during fun experiences. For her doctoral study, Sarah uses a GoPro camera to document participant-led walking interviews. This approach facilitates observation and discussion of participants' gestures and other embodied aspects of tacit knowledge and information practices.

Sarah's doctoral study examines how people feed themselves and their families, and the nature of the information practices within people's food-related activities. She uses data collection techniques influenced by sensory ethnography (Pink, 2015), paired with a constructivist grounded theory approach to data analysis (Charmaz, 2014). Food is a vital element in many hobbies and events, and a common cornerstone of family enjoyment, and as such it carries great potential for fun. At the same time, as a daily need that is encountered subjectively through culture, gender, class, labor, health, and other experiences, food is not inherently, straightforwardly, or universally fun. As such, food-related information and information practices offer rich conceptual and methodological considerations for a discussion of fun in our field.

Ludi Price, Panelist

Ludi Price is based at the Centre for Information Science in City, University of London. She was recently awarded her doctorate after successfully defending her thesis: "Serious leisure in the digital world: exploring the information behavior of fan communities." She is also a librarian at SOAS, University of London. Ludi is deeply involved in the fan community as a fan artist and writer, and a mentor to younger fans and peers. This, coupled with her practitioner experience, influenced her interest in the information behavior of fan communities, and inspired her to ground her research in methods used within both LIS and fan studies. Her particular interests focus on fan-tagging, fan self-publishing, and the collaborative innovations developed by fans to build their own 'rogue archives' (De Kosnik, 2016).

For this panel, Ludi will discuss her use of three research methods in her thesis: a synthesis of the literature on fan information behavior found within both LIS and fan studies; a Serious Leisure Delphi study; and the use of tag analysis to describe fan information behavior, conducted on the folksonomies implemented on three websites used by fans. This use of mixed methods reflected an attempt to marry the rich, qualitative textual accounts favored by fan studies (which is based in cultural studies), and the focus on process and the mapping of human behaviours found in LIS. She will also discuss the issues involved in studying partially-deviant and/or sensitive groups such as media fans, and the need for a wider awareness of interdisciplinary ethics within LIS.

ACKNOWLEDGMENTS

Melissa Ocepek's project was supported by the Institute of Museum and Library Services grant RE-02-12-0009-12, awarded to researchers at the University of Texas at Austin, School of Information. Eric Forcier is supported by Swinburne University of Technology. Sarah Polkinghorne is supported by Swinburne University of Technology and the University of Alberta. Ludi Price's research was supported by a doctoral studentship awarded by the School of Informatics, City, University of London.

REFERENCES

Case, D.O., & Given L.M. (2016). *Looking for information: A survey of research on information seeking, needs, and behavior.* 4th ed. Bigley, UK: Emerald Group Publishing.

Charmaz, K. (2014). *Constructing grounded theory.* 2nd ed. London: Sage.

De Kosnik, A. (2016). *Rogue archives: digital cultural memory and media fandom.* Cambridge, MA and London: MIT Press.

Greifeneder, E. (2014). Trends in information behavior research. In: *ISIC: The Information Behaviour Conference, Proceedings of ISIC: The Information Behaviour Conference*, Leeds, 2-5 September 2014.

Hartel, J. (2003). The serious leisure frontier in library and information science: Hobby domains. *Knowledge Organization, 30*(3-4), 228-238.

Hartel, J. (2007). *Information activities, resources, and spaces in the hobby of gourmet cooking* (doctoral dissertation). University of California, Los Angeles. ProQuest Dissertations and Theses.

Harviainen, J. T. (2015). Information literacies of self-identified sadomasochists: an ethnographic case study. *Journal of Documentation, 71(*3), 423–439.

Kari, J., & Hartel, J. (2007). Information and higher things in life: Addressing the pleasurable and the profound in information science. *Journal of the Association for Information Science and Technology*, *58*(8), 1131-1147.

Lee, C. P., & Trace, C. B. (2009). The role of information in a community of hobbyist collectors. *Journal of the American Society for Information Science and Technology, 60*(3), 621–637.

Pink, S. (2015). *Doing sensory ethnography* (2nd edition.). Los Angeles: Sage.

Savolainen, R. (1995). *Everyday life information seeking: Approaching information seeking in the context of "way of life". Library & Information Science Research, 17*(3), 259-294.

Suorsa, A. R. (2017). Knowledge creation and play: A phenomenological study within a multi-professional and multi-organizational community. *Journal of Documentation*, *73*(6), 1167-1191.

Swalwell, M., Stuckey, H., & Ndalianis, A. (eds.) (2017). *Fans and videogames: histories, fandom, archives*. New York; Abingdon: Routledge.

Tinto, F., & Ruthven, I. (2015). Sharing happy information: responses and self-portrayal. *Information Research*, *20*(1).

Embodied Information Practices

Michael Olsson
University of Technology Sydney, Australia.
Michael.Olsson@uts.edu.au

Christopher Lueg
University of Tasmania, Australia.
christopher.lueg@utas.edu.au

Annemaree Lloyd
University of Borås, Sweden. annemaree.lloyd@hb.se

Pamela McKenzie
University of Western Ontario, Canada.
pam.mckenzie@uwo.ca

ABSTRACT

Information Science researchers have been relatively slow to consider the role of the body in understanding the relationship between people, information and technology. This panel will discuss how a consideration of the body can enrich information researchers' understanding of the complex relationship between people, information and technologies, old and new. Each panel member will briefly describe their own theoretical and methodological approach and how they have informed their understanding. This will be followed by a moderated discussion between the panel and audience members.

KEYWORDS

Embodiment, information practices, people and technology

INTRODUCTION

Despite being a well-established focus of social science research for many decades (Dewey, 1939; Foucault, 1979; Goffman, 1983; Merleau-Ponty, 1969), the role of the body in people's relationship with information has been slow to emerge as an object of information science research. This international panel of researchers will draw on their own research to discuss a range of theoretical and methodological approaches to studying embodied information practices. The panel will put forward the argument that these approaches allow information researchers to understand the role of the body in shaping people's information practices and their relationship with technologies, both old and new.

EMBODIED INFORMATION PRACTICES

Information Science researchers have been relatively slow to consider the role of the body in understanding the relationship between people, information and technology. The reasons for this are no doubt complex but have no doubt been strongly influenced by the prevalence of an 'information behavior' discourse (Savolainen, 2007) which has tended to largely focus on problem-focused, purposive, individual information seeking. The growing interest amongst information researchers in studying online information contexts has similarly been marked by prevailing discourses that have constructed such spaces as 'virtual' and thus implicitly disembodied.

In more recent times, however, a growing number of information researchers have come to question the assumptions and focus of such prevailing approaches arguing that they have led to an overly narrow construction of the complex relationship between people, information and technology. This has led to the emergence of an alternative 'information practices' discourse (Lloyd, 2010; McKenzie, 2003; Savolanien, 2008). This discourse acts as a critical alternative to information behavior, focusing on the intersubjective experiences of people who are acting, working, performing or participating in shared endeavors. Savolanien suggests that this approach "shifts the focus away from the behaviour, action, motives and monological individuals. Instead the main attention is directed to them as members of groups and communities that constitute the context of their mundane activities" (Savolainen, 2007).

A key feature of this alternative approach to information research has been the emergence of a small but growing cohort of information researchers whose work explicitly examines the inherent relationship/connection between embodiment and information in a wide variety of communities and contexts (e.g. Godbold, 2013; Keilty 2016; Lloyd, 2007; Lueg, 2014; Olsson, 2010a; 2010b; 2016; Prigoda and McKenzie, 2007; Veinot, 2007, Cox, Griffin, & Hartel, 2018). This work challenged long-held assumptions in information science research. It has demonstrated that to see our relationship with information as essentially mental in nature or to regard online contexts as 'virtual' is to impose a narrow worldview which limits the researcher's ability to appreciate the central role of embodied practices across all contexts and environments.

This panel session explores a n approach to information research that recognizes that:

...knowing and ways of knowing occur through the enactments of practice (Lloyd, 2010) and this requires an active relationship with the socio-material and symbolic elements that are inherent in practices, and the information landscape created through practicing (Lloyd, 2010). This approach requires us to understand how shared, practical understanding is derived from becoming or being embodied in context (in situ). Consequently, to know is to be capable of participating with the requisite competence in the complex web of relationships among people, material artifacts and activities (Olsson & Lloyd, 2017b)

FORMAT OF THE PANEL SESSION

Each panel member will give a brief (5 minute) presentation focusing on their own approach to studying embodied information practices. They will identify some of the key theoretical and methodological influences on their research and explicate how they helped inform their understanding of the relationship between the body, information and technology.

After the presentations, each panelist will be asked to present a short commentary on their colleagues' presentations with a focus on pointing out commonalities and differences in the approaches. The majority of the session will be devoted to a moderated discussion between panel members and the audience exploring issues and questions relating to the challenges and rewards of studying embodied practices in an information science context, as well as participatory exercises designed to give audience members insights into embodied research practice.

PANEL MEMBERS

The panel will consist of four international researchers with a strong track-record of researching embodied information practices. All the panelists' research is strongly interdisciplinary in nature drawing on a wide range of theories and approaches including: practice theory (Gherardi, 2009; Schatzki, 1996); Sense-Making (Dervin & Foreman-Wernet, 2003); actor-network theory (Latour, 2005); and Foucauldian (Foucault, 1972) and multimodal discourse analysis (Kress & Van Leeuwen, 2001).

Annemaree Lloyd

Annemaree Lloyd has been conducting research into the body-as-information source since 2004. Her research introduced the concept of corporeality within LIS field, connecting it to information literacy within the broader site of information practices. She has studied embodied information and ways of knowing in the context of firefighter's development of 'fire sense' , ambulance officers development and access to expertise,nurses ability to access contingent knowledge at the 'moment of practice' and more recent work with Olsson (2017) on the remaking practices of car enthusiasts .The model and theory of information literacy practice developed by Lloyd (2017) centralises the corporeal modality as central to learning and working.

Christopher Lueg

Originally trained as a computer scientist Christopher Lueg became interested in the nature of human expertise, the situated aspects of work practices, and embodied cognition in general when working on human centered design projects in Zurich in the mid 1990s ("situated design" as we called it back then). Over time the emphasis shifted to exploring how people make use of information in various forms which included studying interactions in online communities pre 'social media' (Lueg and Fisher: From Usenet to Cowebs: Interacting with Social Information Spaces, Springer 2003) and critical explorations in information needs, information filtering and spam filtering. Embodiment, perception and a deep appreciation of the fact that we are all different in terms of how we experience the world have always been there as key concerns when trying to understand how people engage with information: "[learning that] what I aim for in my work today was present long before I could name it" (Uta Barth, The Long Now, 2010).

Pamela McKenzie

Pam McKenzie has explored the ways that experiential (including embodied) knowledge is taken up in negotiations of cognitive authority; interactional and embodied practices in clinical encounters and public library spaces; and the documentary, material, and embodied practices through which individuals, families, and households keep track of everyday life. She uses in-depth interviewing, participant observation, and visual methods. Her research has drawn theoretically from approaches including symbolic interaction and ethnomethodolgy (e.g., Goffman, 1983); discourse analysis in social psychology (Potter & Wetherell, 1987; Harré, R., & van Langenhove, L., 1999), practice theory (Schatzki, 1996), and approaches that situate micro-level practices within macro-level contexts (Holstein and Gubrium, 2005; Smith, 2005).

Michael Olsson (moderator)

Michael Olsson has undertaken a range of studies in which embodied information practices were central to understanding how members of the communities being studied made sense of their world. He has studied embodied information practices in artistic (theatre professionals), academic (archaeologists) and (with Lloyd) serious leisure (enthusiast car restorers) contexts. His research employs a variety of research methods including in-depth interviewing and ethnographic fieldwork. Conceptually, his work draws on a range of theories drawn from a range of disciplines, including Sense-Making (Dervin & Foreman-Wernet, 2003), practice theory (Gherardi, 2009; Schatzki, 1996), and Foucauldian (Foucault, 1972) and multimodal discourse analysis (Kress & Van Leeuwen, 2001).

REFERENCES

Cox, A. M., Griffin, B., & Hartel, J. (2018). Introduction. Special issue on embodiment in LIS. *Library Trends, 66*(3).

Dervin, B., Foreman-Wernet, L. & Lauterbach, E. (2003). *Sense-Making methodology reader: selected writings of Brenda Dervin*. Cresskill, NJ: Hampton Press.

Dewey, J. (1938). *Experience of education*. New York: Macmillan.

Foucault, M. (1972). *The archaeology of knowledge*. London, Tavistock.

Foucault, M. (1979). *Discipline and punish: the birth of the prison*. New York: Vintage.

Gherardi, S. (2009). Introduction: the critical power of the 'practice lens'. *Management Learning*, 40(2), 115–128.

Godbold, N. (2013). Listening to bodies and watching machines: developing health information skills, tools and services for people living with chronic kidney disease. *Australian Academic Research Libraries*, 44(1), 14-28.

Goffman, E. (1983). The interaction order. *American Sociological Review*, 48, 1-17.

Harré, R., & van Langenhove, L. (1999). Positioning theory. Oxford: Blackwell.

Holstein, J. A., & Gubrium, J. F. (2005). Interpretive practice and social action. In N. Denzin & Y. S. Lincoln (Eds.), The Sage handbook of qualitative research (3rd ed., pp. 483-505). Thousand Oaks, CA: Sage.

Keilty, P. (2016) Embodied engagements with online pornography, *The Information Society*, 32:1, 64-73, DOI: 10.1080/01972243.2015.1107162

Kress, G. and Van Leeuwen, T. (2001). *Multimodal Discourse: The Modes and Media of Contemporary Communication*. Arnold: London.

Latour, B. (2005). *Reassembling the social: an introduction to actor-network-theory*. Oxford New York: Oxford University Press.

Lloyd, A. (2007). Recasting information literacy as sociocultural practice: implications for library and information science researchers. *Information Research*, 12.

Lloyd, A. (2010). *Information literacy landscapes: information literacy in education, workplace and everyday contexts*. Oxford: Chandos.

Merleau-Ponty, M. (1962). *Phenomenology of perception*. London: Routledge & Kegan Paul.

Olsson, M. (2010a). The play's the thing: theater professionals make sense of Shakespeare. *Library & Information Science Research*, 32(4), 272-280.

Olsson, M. (2010b) All the world's a stage - the information practices and sense-making of theatre professionals. *Libri*, 60, 241-252.

Olsson, M. (2016). Making sense of the past: the embodied information practices of field archaeologists. *Journal of Information Science*, 42(3), 410-419.

Olsson, M. & Lloyd, A. (2017a). Being in place: embodied information practices. *Information Research* 22(1). Retrieved March 28, 2018 from http://InformationR.net/ir/22-1/colis/colis1601.html

Olsson, M. & Lloyd, A. (2017b), 'Losing the art and craft of know-how: capturing vanishing embodied knowledge in the 21st century', *Information Research* 22(4). Retrieved March 28, 2018 from http://www.informationr.net/ir/22-4/rails/rails1617.html

Potter, J., & Wetherell, M. (Eds.). (1987). Discourse and social psychology; beyond attitudes and behaviour. London: Sage.

Prigoda, E. & McKenzie, P. (2007). Purls of wisdom: a collectivist study of human information behaviour in a public library knitting group. *Journal of Documentation*, 63(1), 90-114.

Savolainen, R. (2007). Information behaviour and information practice: reviewing the 'umbrella concepts' of information seeking studies. *Library Quarterly*, 22(2), 109-132.

Savolainen, R. (2008). *Everyday information practices: a social phenomenological perspective*. Lanham, Md.: Scarecrow Press.

Schatzki, T. (1996). *Social practices: a Wittgensteinian approach to human activity and the social*. Cambridge, UK: Cambridge University Press.

Smith, D. E. (2005). Institutional ethnography: A sociology for people. Lanham MD: AltaMira.

Veinot, T. C. (2007). 'The Eyes of the Power Company': workplace Information practices of a vault inspector. *The Library Quarterly*, 77(2), 157-179.

What Do We Do About "Fake News" and Other Forms of False Information: The Roles of the Organization of False Information, Professional Ethics and Information Literacy?

Shannon M. Oltmann
University of Kentucky, USA. shannon.oltmann@uky.edu

Denise E. Agosto
Drexel University, USA. dea22@drexel.edu

Thomas J. Froehlich
Kent State University, USA. tfroehli@kent.edu

ABSTRACT

False information, of which the most dominant types in the current disinformation marketplace are fake news or disinformation, seems to be ubiquitous these days, with little certainty about how to solve the problems they bring. In this panel, we discuss a taxonomy of types of false information, which will help us better understand the phenomenon and how to address it. We note that simply restricting access to or censoring false information will likely be ineffective and counter to professional information ethics. Instead, the way forward is to promote and practice meaningful information literacy.

KEYWORDS

Fake news, information literacy, censorship, disinformation

INTRODUCTION

For many people, social media is playing a large and growing role in their monitoring of what's going on their communities at the local, national, and global levels. An estimated 14% of U.S. adults relied on social media as their *most important* source of news about the 2016 U.S. Presidential election (Alcott & Gentzkow, 2017). This means that the types of news their friends chose to share online likely shaped their opinions of the election and possibly influenced their voting choices. Although in the primarily paper-based information world of decades past most widely-available information was vetted by professional editors or other experts, much of the information available online today is not. The result is a groundswell of unverified and unverifiable information being passed around online—not just intentionally-created fake news, but unintentionally false or misleading information as well.

False information goes by many monikers these days, including fake news, disinformation, misinformation, and lies. All of these terms are interrelated, and the distinctions are worth teasing out because we ought to deal with various types of falsity in different manners. What is troubling is that the speed, accuracy, and possibilities of generating fake news have dramatically increased with artificial intelligence (AI), so that videos can be created that purport to show former president Obama advocating ideas to which he would be fundamentally opposed. Technologist Aviv Ovadya warns of a forthcoming Information Apocalypse, or Infocalypse, in which anyone can make anything appear as if it actually happened. Unfortunately, our "technologies that can be used to enhance and distort what is real are evolving faster than our ability to understand and control or mitigate it" (Warzel, 2018, para. 10). On a more positive note, however, it is possible that fake news could be combatted with AI, using machine learning to analyze and refute the source and content of a fake news story.

The objective of the panel is to provide tools to analyze types of false information and to discuss ways to counter their effects. We will do this by describing a taxonomy of types of false information explaining why censoring it would not be a valid approach and discussing how information literacy can better combat the varieties false information.

PANEL DISCUSSION

This panel will focus on describing issues of information ethics and intellectual freedom related to fake news and disinformation, placing the recent groundswell of disinformation online into the broader context of library and information science. It will also offer a detailed taxonomy of forms of false information in "the Age of the Anti-Enlightenment." The first problem is what to call such a taxonomy because of the varieties included: not only misinformation and disinformation, but also ignorance per se and self-deception. A tentatively complete taxonomy would include: ignorance per se, misinformation, paltering, disinformation, missing information, self-deception (motivated and unmotivated, non-social and social, social situating and social persuasive). We will characterize and exemplify the members of this taxonomy and then we will look at two dominant forms of information calumny: doxing and fake news and their role in deception and self-deception (Froehlich, 2017; Fallis, 2014).

What is included in this taxonomy are new forms of fake news. What has made the issue more critical is the ability to generate more sophisticated fake news stories through AI (Warzel 2018), making videos that can be made to make anyone say anything about anything. Furthermore, clickbait, algorithms that motivate YouTube viewing sequences drive viewers to more and more sensationalized videos aims in effect to radicalize viewers. (Tufekci 2018).

Outright lies can be challenged and reputed, often with evidence and data. Unfortunately, all forms of false information have psychological grounds that make it difficult for rational approaches from the information professions or professional ethics to confront or override.

The Association for Information Science and Technology (ASIS&T) has developed a list of professional guidelines to aid its members in making responsible, reasoned, and ethical decisions. However, the guidelines' applicability to the varieties of false information is quite problematic. For example, the guidelines note that members should "truthfully represent themselves" by "not knowingly making false statements or providing erroneous or misleading information" (ASIS&T, 1992, para. 8-9). While having a professional obligation to be truthful seems reasonable and laudable, the admonition to avoid providing erroneous or misleading information is more problematic upon examination. It is one thing to not make false statements oneself and another to avoid providing (access to) erroneous or misleading information that another has said or posted. For example, some may argue that simply sharing tweets from the American President could constitute sharing misleading information in many cases (e.g., Dockray, 2016; Politfact, 2018). Can one intelligently comment on current events without repeating potentially misleading or incorrect information (in Froehlich's [2017] terms, misinformation and disinformation)? On the other hand, knowingly providing false information to another person (or to a system) seems highly problematic.

In a subsequent section, members are encouraged to "resist all forms of censorship" and to "promote open and equal access to information, within the scope permitted by their organizations or work" (ASIS&T, 1992, para. 17, 19). These tenets seem to indicate that all information, even false informations, should be accessible and open. Restricting access to false information would be a form of censorship; labeling it as such may also be problematic.

We can turn also to the library science field for guidance. A core value of library and information science is intellectual freedom. According to the American Library Association (ALA), intellectual freedom is "the right of every individual to both seek and receive information from all points of view without restriction. It provides for free access to all expressions of ideas through which any and all sides of a question, cause or movement may be explored" (ALA, 2018, para.1). Similar to the ASIS&T tenets, the guidance from ALA seems to indicate that no information should be restricted, regardless of its veracity or falseness (Oltmann, 2018).

Nonetheless, as information professionals, we must be concerned about the spread of false information and the impact it has on communication, trust, collaboration, and effective governance. Vincent Cerf (2017), among others, has wondered "can liberty survive the digital age?" This is a question that information professionals must address

The solution to the spread of false information, from an information ethics perspective, consists of more (and better) information, a critical discerning perspective, and stronger information literacy. We argue that librarians and other information professionals can and should be at the forefront of the struggle over false informations; as Agosto (2018) explains, "librarians have both the opportunity and the responsibility for teaching their communities how to determine if information they encounter online is accurate, reliable, and worthy of being shared" (n.p.).

JUSTIFICATION FOR PANEL FORMAT

This topic is timely, urgent, and changeable. False information is escalating on all media fronts, as does frustration and uncertainty about how to address it. This panel brings together three experts with unique perspectives on false information to discuss its definition and contours, its place in society and in information organizations, and an approach to address it that focuses on information literacy. We anticipate our unique perspectives will foster rich discussion with the audience members, many of whom may have different points of view; we plan to leave at least 20 minutes for discussion.

BIOGRAPHIES OF PANELISTS

Thomas J. Froehlich, Ph.D., is Professor Emeritus, School of Information, Kent State University (27 years). The majority of his publications are concerned with ethical considerations in the information professions, evolving in part from his philosophy background (Ph.D., Duquesne University). Dr. Froehlich currently teaches a course on the Age of Disinformation and has taught in the areas of information science, ethics, online searching, knowledge management and user interface design. He has provided workshops, trainings, seminars or presentations in 26 countries.

Shannon M. Oltmann is an Assistant Professor in the School of Information Science at the University of Kentucky. Her research interests include censorship, intellectual freedom, information policy, public libraries, privacy, and qualitative research methods. She has presented her research at academic conferences such as the Information Ethics Roundtable, the Annual Conference of the Association for Information Science & Technology, the iConference, and the International Congress on Qualitative Inquiry. Her work has been published in the *Journal of the American Society for Information Science and Technology*, *Library Quarterly, Public Libraries Quarterly, Collection Management, Libri*, and *Library and Information Science Research.*

Denise E. Agosto, Ph.D., is Professor in the College of Computing & Informatics at Drexel University and Director of the Master's of Library & Information Science Program. Her research focuses on young people's use of social media and the implications for library services. On the topic of fake news, she recently finished editing the book *Information Literacy and Libraries in the Age of Fake News* (Libraries Unlimited, 2018).

REFERENCES

Agosto, D.E. (Ed.). (2018). Information Literacy and Libraries in the Age of Fake News. Chicago: Libraries Unlimited.

Allcott, H. & Gentzkow, M. (2017). Social media and fake news in the 2016 election. *Journal of Economic Perspectives* 31(2), 211-236. https://web.stanford.edu/~gentzkow/research/fakenews.pdf.

American Library Association. (2018). Intellectual freedom and censorship Q&A. Retrieved 4/02/18 from http://www.ala.org/advocacy/intfreedom/censorship/faq.

Association for Information Science & Technology. (1992). ASIS&T professional guidelines. Retrieved 4/02/18 from https://www.asist.org/about/asist-professional-guidelines/.

Cerf, V. (2017). Can liberty survive the digital age? *Communications of the ACM, 80*(5), 7.

Dockray, H. (2016). Donald Trump writes misleading tweet, but that's not the scary part. Mashable. Retrieved 4/02/18 from https://mashable.com/2016/11/18/trumps-misleading-tweet-fake-news/#YehvpWPApOqE.

Fallis, D. (2014). The varieties of disinformation. In L. Floridi and P. Illari (Eds.), *The philosophy of information quality*. Springer International Publishing: Synthese Library 358.

Froehlich, T.J. (2017). A not-so-brief account of current information ethics: The ethics of ignorance, missing information, misinformation, disinformation and other forms of deception or incompetence. *BiD (Biblioteconomia i documentacio), 39*. Retrieved 4/02/18 from http://bid.ub.edu/en/39/froehlich.htm.

Oltmann, S.M. (2018). Misinformation and intellectual freedom in libraries: Does fake news have a place in libraries? In Agosto, D.E. (Ed.). (2018). *Information Literacy and Libraries in the Age of Fake News.* Chicago: Libraries Unlimited.

Politifact. (2018). All false statement involving Donald Trump. Retrieved 4/02/18 from http://www.politifact.com/personalities/donald-trump/statements/byruling/false/.

Tufekci, Z. (2018). YouTube, the great radicalizer. New York Times, March 10, 2018. Retrieved 4/03/18 from: https://www.nytimes.com/2018/03/10/opinion/sunday/youtube-politics-radical.html.

Warzel, C. (2018). He predicted the 2016 fake news crisis. Now he's worried about an information apocalypse. Buzzfeed News. Retrieved 4/04/18 from https://www.buzzfeed.com/charliewarzel/the-terrifying-future-of-fake-news?utm_term=.jwvN21Z4O#.qrkw5JrxY.

Confronting the Expanse of Data Education: From Local Open Data to Global Cyberinfrastructure

Carole Palmer
Information School, University of Washington, USA.
clpalmer@uw.edu

Jane Greenberg and Xia Lin
Information Science Department, Drexel University, USA.
janeg@drexel.edu; xlin@drexel.edu

James Howison
School of Information, University of Texas-Austin, USA.
jhowison@ischool.utexas.edu

Nicholas Weber
Information School, University of Washington, USA.
nmweber@uw.edu

Sam Oh
LIS & Data Science, Sungkyunkwan University (SKKU), Republic of Korea. samoh@skku.edu

Angela Murillo
School of Informatics and Computing, Department of Library and Information Science at Indiana University – Purdue University Indianapolis, USA. apmurill@iu.edu

ABSTRACT

As the demand for data science and data-intensive capabilities grows in all sectors, educators in schools of information and library and information science are working to deepen and expand their programs to meet workforce expectations. This panel will examine current trends and investments in data education and professionalization, with an emphasis on the unique contributions information professionals bring to the data workforce. Educators will present on current initiatives that represent the breadth and complexity of preparing information professionals for work in data intensive environments. Their unique approaches anticipate and respond to workforce demand, address significant educational challenges, and offer models for making progress within the varying contexts of schools in different regions of the U.S. and Asia. Half of the session will be reserved for audience engagement designed to leverage and share the wealth of experience of the educators and students in attendance. The exchange will generate ideas about new directions and successful approaches that educators can apply to set priorities, position their programs, and collaborate to enrich and provide leadership in data education.

KEYWORDS

data science, data education, professionalization, curriculum development, educational leadership

INTRODUCTION

Data science and analytics programs are proliferating at a rapid pace in computer science, business, statistics, and information schools in anticipation of continuing job growth in this area of the workforce. For example, a recent study identified 2.3 million data science and analytics job listings in 2015, and positions are projected to grow by 28% by 2020 (Markow, Braganza, Taska, Miller, & Hughes, 2017). While this trend is not new or unexpected, it has major implications for how we design and build capacity in our educational programs for information professionals. At the same time, it is recognized that the field of data science is still in its infancy, with no established base of core knowledge or standard approach to education—an issue addressed by the 2018 National Academies of Sciences, Engineering, and Medicine (NASEM) report, *Envisioning the Data Science Discipline*. The NASEM report specifies the concept of "data acumen" as the "chief objective of data science education," identifying the "key component of data science" as: mathematical foundations, computational thinking, statistical thinking, data management, data description and curation, data modeling, communication skills, reproducibility best practices, ethical dilemmas, problem-solving skills, and a range of domain-specific topics.

Educational programs in information schools and library and information science (LIS) have been evolving to incorporate data science, with varying coverage of these areas of data acumen. Significant efforts began in the mid 2000s, with formalized curriculum in data curation starting around 2006, soon followed by a range of other curricular efforts to build data expertise (Gold, 2010). Progress has been made establishing competencies in data literacy for critically evaluating, using, and managing data, as well as curriculum for research data management to support diverse research communities, including model internship programs to help prepare students for the data intensive research environment (Kelly et al., 2013; Ortiz-Repiso, Greenberg, & Calzado-Prado, 2018). Exploration continues on core competencies, skills gaps, and data science requirements for information professionals and librarians (Burton, Lyon, Erdmann, & Tijerina, 2018; Lyon & Brenner, 2015), as information schools simultaneously work to enrich and expand existing programs and curricula that invest in certain dimensions of the data acumen model (NASEM, 2018). These advances need to align with the evolving demand for data professionals in the workforce at large, but also necessarily build upon the strengths and orientations of the local schools and universities where they are developed.

This panel captures the breadth and complexity of educating information professionals for data intensive environments. The panelists are experienced educators, each representing a unique approach and focus that addresses significant education challenges: doctoral experiences for preparing future faculty; curriculum and internships to build open data competencies in the public sector; emerging areas of professionalization in cyberinfrastructure; collaborative undergraduate education; and trends in Asia and across the international consortium of information schools. The panelists will offer models for building capacity and probe challenges faced by schools in various regions of the U.S. and the world. Presentations will be lightning talks, allowing substantial time for active engagement with the attendees, as described below.

PARTICIPANTS AND THEIR CONTRIBUTIONS

Carole Palmer will serve as the facilitator and provide a framing introduction to the session, highlighting new directions, opportunities, and responsibilities for educating information professionals and the range of approaches and innovations represented by the group. In introducing the panelists, the emphasis will be on the variety and value of their responses to data workforce trends and challenges. She will also set the scene for the active exchange with the audience that will follow the panelists' contributions and facilitate productive interaction among presenters and attendees for a highly collaborative session.

Palmer is Professor and Associate Dean for Research in the Information School at the University of Washington. She has been active in data curation workforce development in LIS for over a decade, leading a series of grant-funded efforts to build educational capacity through curriculum development and internships in partnership with research centers and state agencies. She has promoted educational advances through summits and workshops and numerous service roles including membership on the National Academy of Sciences study committee on Preparing the Workforce for Digital Curation and her work on the technical advisory board for the Research Data Alliance (RDA). Her research focuses on data curation and digital research collections to facilitate interdisciplinary inquiry.

Jane Greenberg and Xia Lin will share about the Library Education and Data Science (LEADS) for the National Digital Platform (NSF-4-NDP) program, an Institute of Museum and Library Science (IMLS) Laura Bush 21st Century program, overseen by the Metadata Research Center, Computing and Informatics, Drexel University. LEADS-4-NDP is preparing the next generation Library and Information Science faculty so they may meaningfully integrate data science and LIS education. LEADS fellows benefit from Drexel's data science intensive curriculum and immersive real-world applications with leading NDP partners. The presentation will report outcomes from the first cohort of LEADS Fellows (summer 2018 program), and share insights about educating the next generation of LIS faculty in the data science area.

Jane Greenberg is the Alice B. Kroeger Professor and the Associate Department Head, Information Science Department for Graduate Affairs. Her research focuses on metadata, knowledge organization, ontologies, with an emphasis on data. Xia Lin is the Department Head, Information Science. His research focuses include information retrieval, digital libraries, data analytics, and visualization.

James Howison will share his perspective as a leader in a National Science Foundation (NSF) Research Coordination Network (RCN) on "Managing Cyberinfrastructure Organizations," (together with Nick Berente at the University of Georgia and John King at the University of Michigan). The RCN held two workshops on the topic of professionalization among cyberinfrastructure professionals, bringing together researchers from the organizational sciences and practitioners working in cyberinfrastructure centers. Howison will report on emerging efforts towards professionalization and discuss three routes to increased professionalization and the tensions inherent in each. This case of professionalization is instructive as an evolving area of expertise in the information field, with implications for how we prepare students in information schools for roles in cyberinfrastructure and research facilitation.

Howison is an Associate Professor in the School of Information at the University of Texas at Austin. His research addresses collaboration, particularly in the online development of software. He has studied open source software developers and scientists building software.

Nicholas Weber will present ongoing work from the University of Washington's IMLS funded Open Data Literacy (ODL) project. ODL's goals are to develop curriculum and student learning experiences that prepare future information professionals to meaningfully contribute to the development and sustainability of open data programs in the public sector. ODL has two approaches to curriculum development: 1. Transforming existing courses in data curation and digital preservation to include public sector use cases developed with ODL partners, including Washington State Department of Transportation, City of Seattle's Open Data program, and Washington State Office of the Chief Information Officer (OCIO). 2. Placing University of Washington (UW) iSchool students in internships and capstone projects with public sector partners engaged in open data initiatives. The ODL presentation will report on outcomes from the first two years of student experiences working with open data, and the implications of these experiences for curriculum development in the graduate programs at the UW iSchool.

Weber is an Assistant Professor in the Information School at the University of Washington, and the technical director of the Qualitative Data Repository. His research focuses on the development and use of information systems for transparency, and most recently on infrastructures that facilitate transparent research.

Angela Murillo will report on a collaboration at Indiana University – Purdue University Indianapolis (IUPUI), between the School of Informatics and Computing, Department of Library and Information Science and the Department of Human-Centered Computing, to create the undergraduate Bachelor of Science program. The program has two specializations: Applied Data Science and Information Science. The Applied Data Science Specialization focuses on data skills including data analysis and visualization, and the Information Science Specialization focuses on data curation, organization, and management.

Angela P. Murillo is an Assistant Professor at the School of Informatics and Computing, IUPUI. Her research focuses on data life-cycle management, curation, metadata, and human-computer interaction (HCI).

Sam Oh, current chair of the iSchool Caucus, will present an analysis of the different ways that iSchools and non-iSchools teach data science and related subjects. He will also share his views on the iSchool approach to data science and discuss a data science curriculum that capitalizes on the strengths of the information field.

Sam Oh is a professor at Sungkyunkwan University (SKKU) and an affiliate professor at the University of Washington iSchool. He played an active role in designing the Bachelor of Science in Data Science curriculum at SKKU in 2015. Oh's teaching and research interests include metadata/ontology design, data modeling, social data analytics, and knowledge management. He was chair of ISO/IEC JTC1 SC34 (Document Description & Processing Languages) for nine years and chair of ISO TC46/SC9 (Identification and Description) for six years. He is currently serving as chair for the iSchool Caucus.

AUDIENCE ENGAGEMENT

The session is designed to be inclusive and interactive. Half of the session will be reserved for engaging the audience in a way that builds on and enriches the topics presented by the speakers with substantive contributions from attendees. After the panelists' presentations, rather than taking questions from the audience, the group will pose questions to the audience designed to leverage and share the wealth of experience and know-how in the room from both educators and students. Each panelist will field a question aimed at soliciting practical strategies and solutions, or particularly vexing challenges, in educating data professionals. A note-taker will provide a summary of the discussion following the presentation. Representative questions are outlined below.

- What PhD experiences are the most effective in giving students a deep grasp of the state-of-the-art or emerging state of practice? How do these experiences translate to different career trajectories (e.g. in industry, academia, public services, etc.)?
- What areas of professionalization are on the horizon, and how will they further stretch expectations for graduates of our programs?
- What makes for a successful internship, and what strategies can we use to scale and extend field experiences to online students? What strategies are successful for a sustainable partnership with internship sponsors?
- What platforms can educators and schools use to share specialized expertise, and to collaborate on scaling and extending their curriculum?
- What is the trajectory for undergraduate education in the information science/data science space?

CONCLUSION

Through proactive engagement with the ASIS&T audience, this panel will offer a diverse range of perspectives that reflects how information schools are investing in and advancing information professions in the age of data. The group will identify strategies and solutions for meeting current data education challenges, and the exchange will ultimately raise important issues around jurisdiction, specialization, and collaboration within and across universities and disciplines.

ACKNOWLEDGMENTS

The development of this panel is sponsored, in part, by IMLS award #E-40-16-0015-16 (Open Data Literacy). The work that James Howison will discuss is based upon work supported by the National Science Foundation under Grant No. #1148996.

REFERENCES

Burton, M., Lyon, L., Erdmann, C., & Tijerina, B. (2018). Shifting to data savvy: The future of data science in libraries. Project Report. University of Pittsburgh, Pittsburgh, PA. Retrieved from: http://d-scholarship.pitt.edu/33891/

Gold, A. (2010). Data curation and libraries: Short-term developments, long-term prospects. California Polytechnic University. Retrieved from: http://works.bepress.com/agold01/9/

Kelly, K., Marlino, M., Mayernik, M. S., Allard, S., Tenopir, C., Palmer, C. L., & Varvel Jr, V. E. (2013). Model development for scientific data curation education. *International Journal of Digital Curation*, *8*(1), 255-264. http://doi.org/10.2218/ijdc.v8i1.258

Lyon, L., & Brenner, A. (2015). Bridging the data talent gap: Positioning the iSchool as an agent for change. *International Journal of Digital Curation*, *10*(1). http://dx.doi.org/10.2218/ijdc.v10i1.349

Markow, W., Braganza, S., Taska, B., Miller, S., and Hughes, D. (2017). The quant crunch: How the demands for data science skills is disrupting the job market. Burning Glass Technologies. Retrieved from: https://www-01.ibm.com/common/ssi/cgi-bin/ssialias?htmlfid=IML14576USEN&

National Academies of Sciences, Engineering, and Medicine. (2018). Envisioning the data science discipline: The undergraduate perspective: Interim report. Washington, DC: The National Academies Press. https://doi.org/10.17226/24886

Ortiz-Repiso, V., Greenberg, J., & Calzada-Prado, J. (2018). A cross-institutional analysis of data-related curricula in information science programmes: A focused look at the iSchools. *Journal of Information Science*. http://doi.org/10.1177/0165551517748149

Beyond Bloom's Taxonomy: Integrating "Searching as Learning" and E-Learning Research Perspectives

Rebecca Reynolds
Rutgers University, USA. rbreynol@comminfo.rutgers.edu

Souvick Ghosh
Rutgers University, USA. Sg1223@comminfo.rutgers.edu

Eric Meyers
University of British Columbia, Canada. Eric.meyers@ubc.ca

Alamir Novin
University of British Columbia, Canada, alamir.novin@ubc.ca

ABSTRACT

Searching as learning work is growing in interest, however definitions of 'learning' in this space have been somewhat narrow. Here we propose a panel sponsored by SIG InfoLearn that will feature presentations from three scholars whose work falls in the domain of "searching as learning," followed by a synthesis presented by a fourth scholar along with one of the panelists, who will draw key conceptual intersections among the three empirical research papers and then explicate linkages to existing research in the learning sciences that has potential to further inform the ongoing development of the panelists' and others' work in this domain.

KEYWORDS

Searching as learning, inquiry, information-seeking, e-learning, learning sciences

INTRODUCTION

Information and learning sciences as scholarly disciplines are experiencing a moment in which inter-disciplinary ties present among them are being increasingly recognized and noted in the literatures. The field of the learning sciences, or education sciences, is substantial, and many scholars within this field address the design and development of technological innovations for learning and engage in theory-building around instruction and human learning that takes into consideration the presence and use by learners, of technological affordances. Such affordances have been encapsulated by an umbrella term in the literature: e-Learning. Haythornthwaite & Andrews (2011) and Haythornthwaite, Andrews, Fransman & Meyers (2016) define e-learning quite broadly, as a transformative movement in learning, not just the transfer of learning to an online stage. The authors embrace the ways in which learning flows across physical, geographical, and disciplinary borders (2011). They describe e-learning as perpetual, sustained over a lifetime, and enacted in multiple daily occurrences as we search for information to satisfy our learning needs and contribute content that promotes our and others' understanding (2011). This definition can be seen as inclusive of information searching phenomena of which learning is a part.

Special issues of several journals, and a number of international workshops and seminars have discussed the intersections in human information and learning behaviour. These include the 2016 Journal of Information Science special issue on "Searching as Learning," (Guest Editors: Hansen, Freund, Gwizdka, He, Kando, Rieh); the 2016 special issue of The Information Society "Revealing Mutually Constitutive Ties between the Information and Learning Sciences"(Guest Editors: Ahn and Erickson), the 2014 IIiX workshop on "Searching as Learning" (Organizers: Freund, Gwizdka, Hansen, He, Kando, and Rieh); the 2017 Schloss Dagstuhl seminar on "Search as Learning"(Organizers: Collins-Thompson, Hansen, Hauff, and Klas), and the 2017 special issue of Information Retrieval Journal edited by Eickhoff, Gwizdka, Hauff & He). The success of the launch of SIG InfoLearn and launch of a new journal published by Emerald UK entitled *Information and Learning Science* further add support to these intersections.

Here we propose that the systems being studied within the burgeoning "searching as learning" domain fall within Haythornthwaite & Andrews' (2011) rigorous framing and definition of e-learning research. We propose that the framing work of these authors may provide useful boundaries and definitions as we continue to explicate what is meant by "searching as learning" work, and where such work fits in these broader intersections.

SEARCH AND LEARNING

In setting out to re-frame research on searching for its positionality vis-a-vis human learning processes, Rieh, Collins-Thompson, Hansen & Lee (2016) present a review literature that addresses past work in which associations have been drawn between searching and learning. Their article offers a perspective that focuses on the learning that occurs during the search process, as well as search outputs and learning outcomes. They propose a concept they term 'comprehensive search,' to describe iterative, reflective and integrative search sessions that facilitate critical and creative learning beyond receptive learning. They propose that system enhancements may lead to richer representations of information, learning and domain expertise, embedding learning motivation, intentions, knowledge levels, content diversity, and more (2016). They also discuss how search interaction data can provide a rich source of implicit and explicit features through which to assess search-related learning. They propose that extensions that situate search in these ways may contribute to reconfiguration of search systems from information-retrieval tools to rich learning spaces in which search experiences and learning experiences are synergized. In doing so, they propose 4 domains that are promising for future scholarship: (1) *System:* Developing a search system that supports sense-making and enhances learning; (2) *Interaction:* Supporting effective user interaction for searching as learning; (3) *Information literacy:* Providing inquiry-based information literacy tool within a search system; (4) *Learning assessment and comprehensive search*: Assessing learning from online search behavior (2016).

In the same special issue of the *Journal of Information Science*, Vakkari (2016) generously offers a highly useful exposition on ways in which learning has been conceptualized in the education sciences, and some of the intersections between learning research concepts, and what occurs during information-seeking and search by information systems users. Vakkari presents constructivist learning definitions that build upon Piaget's early notions of assimilation, accommodation, and knowledge-building. He discusses differences between novices and experts, vis-à-vis existing knowledge schemas and how humans internalize new information and transform it to knowledge, internalizing it accretion, tuning and out and out restructuring of cognitive schema. His essay then turns to information-seeking, reviewing how information search has been conceptualized in past work in ways that consider human cognition as well. He reviews models of information-seeking processes in information science touching upon Kuhlthau, Belkin and Ingwersen's work, and considering searchers' interactions with source texts. His article covers the distinction between open search and task-driven search in which learning is often implicit to the user's consciousness, but present nonetheless. Per task-driven search, he states (p. 9), "Interacting with sources is the phase when the searcher familiarizes herself with the sources to realize the task for which they were selected. It may include reading, making notes, extracting pieces of information, combining and organizing information and outlining [1]. The aim of this activity is to analyse, categorize and structure information in documents for preparing the final outcome of the task. The borderline to synthetizing and presenting information for task outcome is blurred, because it is impossible to determine exactly when, for example, combining and outlining information by writing for the task outcome becomes synthetizing or presenting." His article then proceeds on to present a range of scenarios in which learning may be occurring during search processes.

This article also helpfully offers a review of studies in which learning has been addressed vis-à-vis inquiry and information-seeking (2016), linking to Vakkari's conceptualization presented in his early conceptual scenarios. His article presents 2 dimensions of work – "from searching to learning," which highlights recent information sciences scholarship that has potential to bring in learning perspectives, and "from learning to searching," which focuses on learning research that has already been incorporated into recent empirical studies of search. Of note, much of the work cited falls into the arena of cognitive perspectives, and several studies cited define learning in ways that draw upon Bloom's taxonomy as a framework for defining learning and higher order thinking. Like most other "searching as learning" scholarship to-date, Vakkari omits mention of more recent learning sciences research, and, information science research for instance that which has been developed in the "digital youth" scholarly community and in the arena of the everyday life information needs of young people. Much of this work centers on design and development of e-learning innovations besides 'search' but strongly involve inquiry and information-seeking activity, nonetheless.

BEYOND BLOOM'S TAXONOMY: BUILDING ON EXPANSIVE E-LEARNING LITERATURES

Here we propose that definitional boundaries for "searching as learning" may need to be broadened and/or explicated much more clearly, to be meaningful for research. Reynolds & Hansen (2018) for instance propose that models for Searching as Learning must factor in the parallel scholarly advances being made within e-Learning and learning sciences research communities such as those outlined in Haythornthwaite & Andrews (2011) and Haythornthwaite, Andrews, Fransman & Meyers (2016). Learning Sciences is a scholarly domain fostering interdisciplinary study of teaching and learning in both formal and informal settings, involving e-learning innovations, and drawing on knowledge from various fields including cognitive science, educational psychology, computer science, information sciences, and design studies among others (e.g., Sawyer, 2014). The work in this field offers a wealth of scholarly advances in learning theory that moved scholarship on learning and cognition forward, over the last 2 decades.

Working together, information and learning researchers can move beyond narrow cognitivist definitions of learning that invoke Bloom, to apply the substantial corpus of work advanced in learning sciences, and to create more meaningful understandings of phenomena involving search, information-seeking, inquiry and learning -- in a range of e-learning platforms and settings, not just search. "Searching as learning" as conceptual nomenclature may not be the most meaningful choice for establishing conceptual boundaries for this work and if scholars wish to continue using this terminology we suggest it needs further explication and clearer definition. Here we propose a panel sponsored by SIG InfoLearn that will feature presentations from three scholars whose work falls in the domain of information and learning sciences. Three paper presentations will be offered, and then lastly, a synthesis of these works will be presented by a fourth scholar, who will draw out key conceptual intersections among the three empirical research papers and then discuss the positionality of each of these papers, vis a vis current conceptualizations of "searching as learning," and the broader conceptualizations of e-learning, and the inter-disciplinary nexus of information and learning sciences research.

PANELIST 1

Bio. Eric M. Meyers is an Associate Professor at the School of Library, Archival and Information Studies at the University of British Columbia, Vancouver, Canada.

Title. Learning Design for Highly Relevant Information Interactions

Overview. In this panel presentation, Meyers will present work on the development of learning-focused inquiry approach called Information Interaction by Design (IIXD). A holistic approach to thinking of young people as knowledge builders demands that we consider the searcher in context. We conceive of this process starting from the proposition that knowledge construction activities involving information-intensive problems are a design space, and we can prompt—and better understand—inquiry activities by closely attending to their structure, rather than treating the search task as a "random" or inert variable in experimental designs. The principles of Information Interaction by Design include:

- ***Participant respect***: research with youth should begin by thinking of young people as active, capable information seekers.
- ***Authenticity***: young people are engaged w. research when questions we ask and tasks provided fit their lived experience.
- ***Contextual Integrity***: research that respects the places and conditions of youth information work should strive for a high-level external validity.
- ***Design for Cognition***: information seeking can be designed to elicit specific mental processes, and to make those processes visible to participants and researchers.

This perspective is informed by the progressive pedagogical philosophy of Dewey (1938) and articulated in Bruner's conception of *scaffolding* and the spiral curriculum (Bruner, 1973). Many of the exploratory tasks assigned to young searchers setup a type of scavenger hunt (find obscure fact X or all the information you can on topic Z) rather than an ordered approach to developing knowledge of a new area. Progressive Scenarios introduce youth to a problem space a bit at a time, beginning with background knowledge, and building to situations where they apply previously found information to develop inferences and make decisions. Situations are provided like onion layers, and as searchers explore deeper aspects of the problem, there are opportunities to assess whether their earlier inquiries were sufficient and applicable to changes in the scenario. This approach is not only consistent with how people learn, but also how educators wish to model problem solving that prepares learners for future inquiry (Bransford et al, 2000). In his presentation, Meyers will provide examples of how this approach bears out in projects with elementary and middle grade children.

PANELIST 2

Bio. Souvick Ghosh is a second year Ph.D. student in the School of Communication and Information at Rutgers University.

Title. Exploring the overlap between searching and learning using the revised taxonomy of educational objectives.

Overview. People search for information and learn from that experience. Although we associate the term *learning* with an educational context, as an effect of *studying*, yet learning need not always be a conscious effort. It may occur during everyday life as a consequence of our actions. Information scientists have explored why and how people search while educational theorists have focused on how to make learning a more holistic experience. Interestingly, searching and learning can be related using the knowledge structures which people possess. Schutz and Luckmann (1974) suggest that every human action is grounded in the "properties of the life world" and our "structures of thinking." In other words, the world around us acts as a learning environment which shapes how we think and interpret. While learning is a process that involves creation or acquisition of new knowledge (constructivist approach to learning), or modification of existing knowledge, searching is a recognition of the insufficiency of the existing knowledge structures. Searching can thus, be conceptualized as an action motivated by cognitive needs, and learning as an associated outcome. Our user study, which was conducted over a period of six to seven months, used the revised framework of educational objectives (Anderson et al., 2001) for designing the search tasks. We attempt to connect the constructivist approach to learning (i.e., learning as knowledge construction) to the constructive paradigm of information searching (e.g., Kuhlthau's Information Search Process model), to explain how learning occurs while searching, or how searching facilitates the process of learning. "Searching as learning" has emerged as an essential subdiscipline in library and information science (LIS) as it allows for a better understanding of human search behavior using the broader context of human learning. Our work uses the framework of human cognition and knowledge to explain the interrelationships between information seeking and learning. The cognitive complexities of the search tasks guide the users as they collect information, both online and offline, to satisfy the information need and complete the tasks. We explore the different search behaviors, the learning outcomes, and the choice of information sources in different levels of learning complexities.

PANELIST 3

Bio. Alamir Novin is a PhD student at the University of British Columbia's Information School (SLAIS). His research and contact information can be located at: blogs.ubc.ca/alamir

Title. Complex Search Tasks are Required for Complex Science Topics

Overview. The National Science Board reported that search engines are currently the primary method that the public uses to learn about science topics (2014). Developing the usefulness of search engines for learning requires supporting the complex human interactions that take place when users search to learn (Gwizdka, Hansen, Hauff, He, & Kando, 2016). Aspects of the complexity in human learning were examined in Daniel Kahneman's book *Thinking, Fast and Slow* (2013), which is based on his seminal work on cognition. In brief, for certain tasks an agent can "think fast" (e.g., Googling today's weather), while for other tasks thinking fast can lead to errors (e.g., Googling today's weather to disprove global warming). The latter example requires that the agent "thinks slow," such as critically thinking about the relationship between weather and climate change. However, developing a search engine that supports this latter task runs counter to the goal of providing immediate search results that satisfice simple queries. While some, including Google (2011), have argued that this problem can be solved by providing the required complex information in an immediate manner, the solution is misplaced for several reasons. I will provide three: 1) Empirically, a study by Novin and Meyers observed that providing scientifically comprehensive information at the top of a search page might provoke users who have little prior knowledge on the topic to skip the complex information in favour of more simple results (2017a). 2) Supporting the complexity of learning is not solely a technological issue, but also a human one. When the learner "thinks fast" they rely on already developed heuristics that can increase their likelihood of committing decision-making errors (i.e., cognitive biases). Four of the cognitive biases that take place when a user searches were identified in a study by Meyers and Novin (2017b). 3) Historically, the philosophy of science has shown that complex scientific information often contains a range of biases. This much has been argued by science philosophers of the past century (Amend & Barney, 2016; Dewey & Rogers, 2012; Hayles, 2001; Kuhn, 1970). However, I will add that the situation has not improved due to the rise of what is often termed as "single-source" journalism (i.e., the media using the perspective of a single source of scientists, often from a press release, to represent a complex. scientific topic (Brumfiel, 2009). This is problematic because with certain sciences there is not one single perspective, but several competing scientific theories (Kuhn, 1970). In these situations, when a search page is dominated by a single scientific perspective it biases a user's ability to learn. These issues exist even *before* accounting for the misinformation of "fake news," which further complicates the problem.

PANELIST 4

Bio. Rebecca Reynolds is an Associate Professor at the School of Communication & Information at Rutgers University. She is the founding chair of SIG InfoLearn at ASIS&T and co-editor of the forthcoming journal, Information and Learning Sciences, published by Emerald.

REFERENCES

Amend, E., & Barney, D. (2016). Getting It Right: Canadian Conservatives and the" War on Science". *Canadian Journal of Communication*, *41*(1).

Anderson, L. W., Krathwohl, D. R., Airasian, P., Cruikshank, K., Mayer, R., Pintrich, P., & Wittrock, M. (2001). A taxonomy for learning, teaching and assessing: A revision of Bloom's taxonomy. *New York. Longman Publishing. Artz, AF, & Armour-Thomas, E.(1992). Development of a cognitive-metacognitive framework for protocol analysis of mathematical problem solving in small groups. Cognition and Instruction*, *9*(2), 137-175.

Bates, M. (1989). The design of browsing and *berrypicking* techniques for the online search interface, *Online Review*, 13(5).

Bransford, J. D., Brown, A. L., & Cocking. R. R. (Eds). (2000). *How people learn: Brain, mind, experience, and school*. Washington, DC: National Academy Press.

Bruner, J. (1973). *Beyond the information given: Studies in the psychology of knowing* . New York: W. W. Norton.

Dewey, J., & Rogers, M. L. (2012). *The public and its problems: An essay in political inquiry*. Penn State Press.

Google. (2011). *The Evolution of Search*. Retrieved from https://www.youtube.com/watch?v=mTBShTwCnD4

Gwizdka, J., Hansen, P., Hauff, C., He, J., & Kando, N. (2016). Proceedings of the Second International Workshop on Search as Learning. In *DIVA*. CEUR-WS.org. Retrieved from http://urn.kb.se/resolve?urn=urn:nbn:se:su:diva-137486

Hayles, N. K. (2001). Desiring agency: Limiting metaphors and enabling constraints in Dawkins and Deleuze/Guattari. *SubStance*, *30*(1), 144–159.

Haythornthwaite, C., & Andrews, R. N. L. *E-learning theory and practice*. 2011. SAGE Publications Inc.

Haythornthwaite, C., Andrews, R., Fransman, J. & Meyers, E. (2016). *SAGE Handbook of E-Learning Research, 2nd edition*. London: Sage.

Kahneman, D. (2013). *Thinking, fast and slow*.

National Science Board (2014) Science and Engineering Indicators. (2014). National Science Foundation, Arlington, VA.

Novin, A., & Meyers, E. (2017a). Making Sense of Conflicting Science Information: Exploring Bias in the Search Engine Result Page. In *CHIIR '17 Proceedings of the 2017 Conference on Conference Human Information Interaction and Retrieval* (pp. 175–184). Oslo, Norway: ACM Press. https://doi.org/10.1145/3020165.3020185

O'Day V and Jeffries R. "Orienteering in an information landscape: How information seekers get from here to there." In: Proceedings of the *INTERCHI conference on human factors in computing systems* (CHI'93), 1993: 438–445.

Petrelli, D., Hansen, P., Beaulieu, M., Sanderson, M., Demetriou, G., and Herring, P. (2004). Observing users, designing clarity: A case study on the user-centered design of a cross-language information retrieval system. *Journal of the American Society for Information Science and Technology*, 55(10): 923-934.

Rieh, S.Y. Collins-Thompson, K. Hansen, P. & Lee H-J. (2016). Towards searching as a learning process: A review of current perspectives and future directions. *Journal of Information Science.* 42: 19-34.

Sawyer, R. K. (Ed.). (2014). *The Cambridge Handbook of the Learning Sciences, Second Edition*. Cambridge Univ. Press.

Schutz, A., & Luckmann, T. (1973). *The structures of the life-world* (Vol. 1). northwestern university press.

Vakkari, P. (2016). Searching as learning: A systematization based on literature. *Journal of Information Science*, 42: 7-18.

Venter, P., van Rensburg, M. J., & Davis, A. "Drivers of learning management system use in a South African open and distance learning institution." *Australasian Journal of Educational Technology,* 2012, *28* (2) 183-198

Publication Quality, Peer Review and Predatory Journals

Michael Seadle
Humboldt-Universität zu Berlin, Germany
mseadle@ischools.org

ABSTRACT

Academic tenure and promotion decisions typically involve judgements about quality and generally require authors to publish in peer-reviewed venues. Even though peer review is known to be imperfect, it remains a widely accepted quality assurance mechanism. Nonetheless in recent times attacks on traditional peer review have come from multiple sources, including concerns about effectiveness, calls for open peer review, and predatory publishers. The panel will discuss these and related issues.

KEYWORDS

Publication quality, peer review, predatory publishers

INTRODUCTION

Academic tenure and promotion decisions typically involve judgements about quality and generally require authors to publish in peer-reviewed venues. Even though peer review is known to be imperfect, it remains a widely accepted quality assurance mechanism. Nonetheless in recent times attacks on traditional peer review have come from multiple sources. One is an empirically founded concern about the effectiveness of single- and double-blind reviews in some technical fields. (Pier, 2018) Another is a move for open peer review by publishers like F1000 to ensure greater transparency. A third attack comes from the growth of so-called predatory publishers that take money via Article Processing Charges (APC) and offer fake reviews, or a review process that is rigged to guarantee quick acceptance.

PEER REVIEW

Improving peer review has no easy solution. As experienced editors know, matching a reviewer with the right expertise to a paper is hard, especially in a discipline like information science, which borrows methodologically from a wide range of other disciplines, and not all reviewers have time enough to devote to a high-quality review. Access to the data can be an issue, but even when the data are available, redoing a whole analysis goes beyond what most reviewers are willing to do. The history of peer review is itself complex, and as Csiszar (2016) writes in *Nature*: "Peer review did not develop simply out of scientists' need to trust one another's research. It was also a response to political demands for public accountability." The desire for accountability remains valid in the era of open access.

Open peer review takes many forms. In its most conservative form the reviews are just anonymously made public. In a more aggressive form a work is available to read online, and people may volunteer to do reviews as long as they meet certain (sometimes minimal) qualifications. F1000 and Wellcome Trust use this form of open peer review. Authors pay up front, though they may get their money back from the Wellcome Trust if the reviews are unacceptable. (Wellcome, 2018) F1000 marks articles that have not yet been positively reviewed, but apparently does not return the APC. The articles remain in the public record.

PREDATORY JOURNALS

At present there is no formal definition of a predatory publisher, though Cabell's Scholarly Analytics (2018) has published a "blacklist" of characteristics and Jeffrey Beall published a list on his blog (now available in archival form). In general usage a predatory publisher is one that takes money from authors (usually via an APC) and publishes without any serious peer review process the way a vanity press does, except that the money sometimes comes from government agencies or university funding sources rather than from the author's own pocket. One of the problems in recognising predatory publishers is how to tell whether a serious peer review process with legitimate reviewers has taken place. There are exceptions, of course. it is not unusual for the editor of a genuine scholarly journal to publish a work by a noted scholar without a full peer review, especially if the article was solicited on a specific topic.

Predatory journals have become a topic for newspapers. Recently an investigative report by the *Süddeutsche Zeitung* described a fictitious author, "R. Funden" (equivalent in English to "I. Maginary") who wrote a fake study that the *Journal of Integrative Oncology* accepted after a pseudo-peer review. The newspaper claims that 5000 German academics have published in predatory journals. (Bauer, 2018) The more elite universities may be less affected, however, simply because their scholars can publish in the top venues.

Some fields have responded to the uncertainty about where to publish by creating lists of "A" journals and "B" journals, which count positively toward tenure and promotion. Information science as a field has not yet established such lists, though some publications, such as JASIST are prime "A" list candidates. The iSchools received a ranking-request from members, but has not decided how to react.

PANEL DISCUSSION TOPICS

The panel will discuss the following issues:

- What can we expect from peer review?
- What makes a publication acceptable for promotion and tenure processes?
- What measures, if any, should institutions take to deal with predatory journals?
- Should the Information Science community establish a list of preferred journals?

The panel members are current or former heads of iSchools.

REFERENCES

Bauer, Patrick, Till Krause, Katharina Kropshofer, Katrin Langhans, and Lorenz Wagner (2018). Das Scheingeschäft: Angriff Auf Die Wissenschaft. *Süddeutsche Zeitung Magazin*, 20 Juli 2018: 11–24.

Cabells Scholarly Analytics (2018). Cabell's Blacklist Violations. Available: https://www2.cabells.com/blacklist-criteria.

Csiszar, Alex. (2016). Peer Review: Troubled from the Start. *Nature* 532 (7599): 306–8. https://doi.org/10.1038/532306a.

Cole, Graham D., Matthew J. Shun-Shin, Alexandra N. Nowbar, Kevin G. Buell, Faisal Al-Mayahi, David Zargaran, Saliha Mahmood, Bharpoor Singh, Michael Mielewczik, and Darrel P. Francis (2015). Difficulty in Detecting Discrepancies in a Clinical Trial Report: 260-Reader Evaluation. *International Journal of Epidemiology*. https://doi.org/10.1093/ije/dyv114.

F1000. (2018). "How It Works: Our Publishing Process." Available: https://f1000research.com/about.

Pier, Elizabeth L., Markus Brauer, Amarette Filut, Anna Kaatz, Joshua Raclaw, Mitchell J. Nathan, Cecilia E. Ford, and Molly Carnes (2018). Low Agreement among Reviewers Evaluating the Same NIH Grant Applications. In *Proceedings of the National Academy of Sciences. Mar 2018, 115 (12) 2952-2957; DOI:10.1073/pnas.1714379115*

WellcomeTrust (2018). Wellcome Open Research: How to Publish. Available: https://wellcomeopenresearch.org/gateways/OUCRU/for-authors/article-processing-charges.

Infrastructural Justice and the Social Consequences of Occupational Classifications

Richard P. Smiraglia
Data Archiving and Networked Services, Netherlands
University of Wisconsin Milwaukee, USA.
Richard.smiraglia@dans.knaw.nl
smiragli@uwm.edu

Ronald E. Day
Indiana University, USA. roday@indiana.edu

Eva Hourihan Jansen
University of Toronto, Canada.
eva.jansen@utoronto.ca

Kathryn La Barre
University of Illinois at Urbana-Champaign, USA
klabarre@illinois.edu

ABSTRACT

This panel builds on the momentum of previous SIG/CR workshops towards examining the framing and scaffolding of knowledge in order to understand its bearing on seeking, reception, circulation and use of knowledge in research and knowledge organization systems. It features reports of research undertaken in North America and Europe relating to social and economic classifications of the International Labour Organization of the United Nations. It considers how the narrative arc of the field of information science exists in relation to social divisions of labour represented in occupational classification. Panelists will present new research and engage participants in discussion about trajectories for future research in knowledge organization.

KEYWORDS

ISCO, occupations, history, Canada, Netherlands, data discovery

INTRODUCTION

This panel nurtures the theoretical and practical call to confront classification and violence. Ron Day (2015) argued that research on classification in social and cultural issues needs to be done at the levels of primary and secondary documentation, as a problem of epistemic and practical infrastructure, and as political economy. Smiraglia (2015) contrasted the notions of cultural pervasiveness and objective violence in questioning KOS as cultural arbiters, noting how pervasive classifications are always enmeshed in interacting social discourses. New research demonstrates the significance of information organization in the development and consequences of policy objectives.

The International Standard Classification for Occupations (ISCO), for example, is a standard international system of ordering information about labor and jobs, essentially according to tasks. Maintained by the International Labour Organization, ISCO is part of an even larger body of United Nations social and economic classifications and has been used in various countries as the basis of their own occupational classifications. ISCO is "intended for use in statistical applications and in a variety of client-oriented applications" (http://www.ilo.org/public/english/bureau/stat/isco/). The applications for which ISCO is maintained are, in turn, used to generate visas, social benefits, work opportunities, and a host of other social objectives. But social objectives often have unintended or unforeseen consequences.

CONTRIBUTION OF THE PANEL

The narrative arc of information science includes ongoing attempts to understand information not only as a social phenomenon but also as a commodity and policy objective. In the analysis of occupational classification, all three come together as forces shaping the epistemic stances of social classifications. For example, Day (2014) described the sociocultural roots of the emergence of information science from documentation, casting current ethical analyses of all aspects of information in light of the field's entire narrative arc. Jansen's 2017 work on the Canadian National Occupational Classification (83) includes a nod to the qualitative perspectives on statistical information systems in the late 1940s and early 1950s that informed the ILO's generation of the eventual ISCO classification.

PANEL ORGANIZATION

The panel will open with an introduction to cultural approaches to research in information organization. Following this frame, panelists will present recent findings from studies of occupational classification systems. *Eva Hourihan Jansen* traces local and global variants to establish a history of standard occupational classification in Canada and relate its development to contemporary applications in workplace settings. *Richard Smiraglia* will discuss the Netherlands' national data portal occupational classification of research domains, to describe the consequences of pragmatic generation of classifications that eliminate entire fields of study and bodies of researchers. *Ron Day* will discuss both traditional documentation tools and also post-documentation—algorithmic tools that organize labor as class identities, not only by their functions, but by their very ubiquity as means of class inscription. *Kathryn La Barre* will serve as *rapporteur*, responding to the panelists and giving a summation to facilitate discussion.

The panel will open the discussion to pursue questions about future research agendas in information organization.

Eva Hourihan Jansen

Eva Jansen will present findings from historical documentary research on standard occupational classification in Canada and the development of occupational classification in a globalized international context. She posits that the historically contingent relationship between standard occupational classification and the evolution of immigration policy in Canada represents a form of documentary governmentality (Day 2014, p.137) as a regime of use (Eschenfelder 2014). The talk will demonstrate the occupational classification as a socially constructed documentary form contingent on relationships with previous versions, with American, British and other international systems both currently and among its predecessors. Explicating the links between the development of standard occupational classification and the emergence of immigration policy in Canada.

Social histories of occupational classification reveal information about occupations is embedded in social practices over the past century. Dr. Jansen argues their significance must be examined in light of longer-term development of beliefs in information. Examining beliefs about occupational information from the perspective of information science by following their development in the modern documentary tradition (Day, 2014) into social informatics and linked to contemporary big data will be important for responding to violence in social classification.

The research presented here only begins to respond to the question of the role of occupational classification in society. There are several other regimes of use that exist across the social sciences and in disciplines of medicine, law and education. Continued exploration of this form of information organization should continue into each of the many practices that take standard occupational classification systems as their instrument.

Richard P. Smiraglia: NARCIS Classification for multidisciplinary data discovery: Pragmatism and Some Unintended Consequences.

NARCIS is the Netherlands' national repository of open access publications and original datasets from Dutch scholars to provide a means of national data curation. The acronym means National Academic Research and Collaborations Information System. The database is governed by its own carefully designed knowledge organization system of the same name the NARCIS classification. The NARCIS Classification represents the current output of Dutch scholarship by providing access to scientific information from Dutch scholars who enter their research, open access texts, datasets and reviews, into its repository. A pragmatic occupational research classification, NARCIS Classification symbols are intended to represent the knowledge-bases of contributing scholars thus creating a discipline-based source for comparative data resource discovery. The classification has evolved through several generations of data curation since 1992, when it began with a consortium of Dutch university repositories. The NARCIS classification supports a vital national research portal, which in turn supports a nationally-coordinated research effort designed to provide better inter-institutional communication of scholarly productivity.

However, the pragmatic origins of the classification have created discontinuities in the representation of the research community. The classification is not synthetic (it has no faceted capabilities) and thus, although more than one symbol might be assigned, they cannot be coordinated to represent complex concepts. The disciplinary basis represents the most highly functional parts of the Dutch research community, and thus does not represent emergent communities, which have no home in the classification. Interdisciplinarity is represented by enunciated enumeration of "interdisciplines" effectively overriding the advantages of interdisciplinarity.

In other words, a very effective classification, pragmatically derived, and serving as the backbone of a national research information system, is simultaneously an instrument of oppression of new ways of thought and new methods of scholarship. How can this happen? This is the subject of this talk.

Ronald E. Day

Not only traditional documentation tools, but today post-documentation—algorithmic tools—organize labor as class identities, not only by their functions, but by their very ubiquity as means of class inscription. Knowledge organization pervades identity and agency, not only as tools for control, but as means for advancement, rebellion, conservation, and, as Walter Benjamin saw, dreams of progress. 'Knowledge organization' covers documentation, post-documentation, communicative, and literary inscriptions of identity and agency of labor and social reproduction for the working classes. It includes not only knowledge organization as descriptive metadata tools, but as prescriptive tools for identity and difference, particularly as such tools cybernetically shape the documentary user as the used and the documentation used as the user, in real time feedback loops mediated by indexing and search algorithms, on the one hand, and ideology on the other. Such tools create socio-technical graphs that construct lines of flight for subjects, both capturing and liberating them by means of documentality. These are important aspects of the role of knowledge organization in labor, which through reference and sense, information and affect, representation and self-identity, constructs much of the sphere of identity and agency for class subjects that earn their living by means of the wage.

PANELISTS

Richard P. Smiraglia

Richard P. Smiraglia is Professor in the Knowledge Organization Research Group of the iSchool at the University of Wisconsin-Milwaukee, Visiting Professor for 2016-2017 at DANS - Data Archives and Networked Services (a Division of the Royal Netherlands Academy of the Arts and Sciences) and Editor-in-Chief of the journal Knowledge Organization. His work explores ontology extraction and evolution of knowledge in domains, classification interaction, classification-based knowledge maps, the cultural role of authorship, the representation of knowledge in knowledge organization systems and the phenomenon of instantiation among information objects. He is the recipient of the 2018 Frederick Kilgour Award for Research in Library and Information Technology.

Ronald E. Day

Ron Day is Professor and Department Chair and the Department of Information and Library Science at Indiana University. He is the author of several books and many articles and book chapters. His research has been in documentation and several aspects of critical information theory, including knowledge management, Italian post-Fordist theory, and theories of women's and affective labor.

Eva Hourihan Jansen

Eva Jansen graduated with a PhD from the Faculty of Information at the University of Toronto, Canada. Her dissertation, "Let's talk about the NOC: an ethnography of classification" documents the development of standard occupational classification in Canada, from historical forms of through to its embedding in immigration policy. Dr. Jansen is interested in documenting the intellectual histories of information organizing systems for understanding potential interventions in contemporary information practices. She is currently social media officer for SIG/CR.

Kathryn La Barre

Kathryn La Barre is an Associate Professor at the School of Information Sciences and Gender and Women's Studies faculty affiliate at the University of Illinois at Urbana-Champaign. She is also a principal member of the Knowledge Organization Research Group in the School of Information Studies, University of Wisconsin-Milwaukee. Her work interrogates the power dynamics of historical and contemporary naming practices in cultural heritage collections. She is currently an ASIST Director-at-Large, and the newly-appointed ASIST Curator.

ACKNOWLEDGMENTS

The organizers would like to acknowledge the sponsorship of ASIS&T SIGs Classification Research (CR), Social Informatics (SI) and History &Foundations of Information Science (HFIS). Dr. Jansen's participation is also supported by Litwin Books Conference Travel Grant.

REFERENCES

Day, R.E. (2014) Indexing it All: The Subject in the Age of Documentation, Information, and Data. History and Foundations of Information Science. Cambridge, Mass. And London, UK: MIT Press.

Eschenfelder, K. (2014) Use regimes: a theoretical framework for social informatics research on intellectual and cultural property. In P. Fichman and H. Rosenbaum (Eds), *Social informatics: Past, present and future,* p. 101-117. Cambridge Scholars Publishing..

Jansen, E.M.H. (2017) Let's Talk about the NOC: An Ethnography of Classification. PhD dissertation, University of Toronto.

La Barre, K. (2017). Interrogating Facet Theory: Decolonizing Knowledge Organization. In Richard P. Smiraglia and Hur-Li Lee (Eds), *Dimensions of Knowledge: Facets for Knowledge Organization,* pp. 7-30. Würzburg: Ergon Verlag.

SIG/CR/ 2015. Call for papers. https://www.asist.org/events/annual-meeting-2015/seminars-and-workshops/conceptual-crowbars-and-classification-at-the-crossroads-the-impact-and-future-of-classification-research-sigcr/

Smiraglia, R.P. (2015) Cultural Pervasiveness or Objective Violence?: Three Questions about KOS as Cultural Arbiters." 26th ASIS SIG/CR Classification Research Workshop, Advances in Classification Research Online, doi:http://dx.doi.org/10.7152/acro.v26i1.14981

The YouTube Formula: Information Work and Community-Building in a Visual Era

Leslie Thomson
University of North Carolina at Chapel Hill, USA.
lethomso@live.unc.edu

Eric Forcier
Swinburne University of Technology, Australia
eforcier@swin.edu.au

Nadia Caidi
University of Toronto, Canada.
nadia.caidi@utoronto.ca

Alice N. Kim
University of Toronto, Canada.
nh.kim@mail.utoronto.ca

Kyong Yoon
University of British Columbia Okanagan, Canada,
Kyong.Yoon@ubc.ca

Niel Chah
University of Toronto, Canada.
niel.chah@mail.utoronto.ca

ABSTRACT

In our increasingly visually oriented world, people's information practices shift and adapt accordingly. In this panel, we bring together an international group of scholars to discuss their insights on information practices related to visual platforms such as YouTube. From the information and communication practices of beauty vloggers garnering international attention to YouTubers specializing in building bridges between cultures, the emergence of the K-pop fandom on YouTube, and the effects of participatory transmedia on viewers' everyday rituals, the panelists share theoretical, empirical, and methodological insights on emerging and evolving everyday information practices. The audience engagement and panelist presentations will coalesce in the formulation of a research agenda that pertains, broadly, to everyday visual engagement, trust and meaning-making, and community building at local and translocal levels.

KEYWORDS

YouTube, visual culture, everyday life information practices, intercultural literacy, community-building, cognitive authority

INTRODUCTION

The video-hosting site, YouTube, is the second most-visited website in the world (Alexa, January 2018). YouTube is estimated to have over one billion total users who stream more than 3.25 billion hours of video per month (Statista, 2015; YouTube Statistics, 2016). A survey of 13 to 18 year-olds by *Variety* magazine (Ault, 2014) found that YouTubers (YouTube video creators) are the most 'influential celebrities' for this demographic group. Given its worldwide prominence, an exploration of the YouTube platform, and the rituals and interactions that occur around it, is timely indeed. In an increasingly visually oriented world (Kaminsky, 2010), people's information behaviours, practices, and source preferences are necessarily shifting, and information science scholars are beginning to pay attention to YouTube as a context for research. Recent work has examined YouTube features with a focus on pedagogy, scholarship, and entertainment (e.g., Cho, 2013; Kousha et al., 2012; Sugimoto & Thelwall, 2013); however, several critical gaps remain in our understanding of some YouTube dynamics:

- Why do certain individuals create and share videos, and curate YouTube channels?
- What leads viewers/consumers to seek information on YouTube over other sources?
- What patterns of site-wide engagement can be discerned on YouTube?

This panel and associated audience engagement will coalesce in the formulation of a research agenda that pertains, broadly, to everyday visual engagement, trust and meaning-making, and community building at local and translocal levels.

THE EMERGENCE OF 'YOUTUBERS' AND AFFILIATIVE IDENTITIES

As of 2011, 47.3 million of YouTube users had uploaded at least one video to a personal channel on the site; by 2012, 'thousands' of them were grossing up to $100,000 US dollars by creating and sharing content in this way, with earnings flowing largely from advertisement revenue and various sponsorships (Telegraph, 2012). While many of the individuals uploading to YouTube do so casually, simply dabbling in video-making, others undertake the practice with seriousness, and regularly upload self-produced videos to their channels; thus, claiming a niche for themselves; and addressing global audiences of unknown viewers whom they cultivate as dedicated sub-communities (Thomson, 2017). The "micro-celebrities" of modern social media (Jerslev, 2016) can inspire fandoms, and contribute to forging intercultural boundaries and fostering transnational connections (Kim et al., 2018).

YouTubers' videos run the gamut of imaginable topics, and sit under broad categories like Music, Comedy, Science & Education, Tech, Cooking & Health, and How-To & DIY. A majority of YouTubers working within categories centred around relaying first-hand wisdom and personal advice as opposed to entertainment (Cooking & Health rather than Comedy, for example)—whether casual or serious—are explicitly not topical experts. Instead, they make videos as ordinary citizens, speaking to hobby interests and issues of everyday concern. As relatable 'citizen experts,' uploading to a platform that is reminiscent of face-to-face talk and predicated on an 'ideology of authenticity' (Burgess & Green, 2009, p. 28), such YouTubers come to occupy increasingly important positions in the information source horizons of audiences. Many are cast by their viewers into—and, in turn, assume—roles as informal information providers, offering up their 'experiences, knowledge, resources, [... and] support' (Oh & Syn, 2015, p. 2046; cf. Burnett, 2000).

FORMAT AND SCOPE OF PANEL

The panel brings together a group of scholars with broad, international perspectives to discuss their diverse theoretical, empirical, and methodological work around everyday information practices and the YouTube platform. The panel's short presentations and interspersed audience interaction will coalesce in a concluding open discussion revolving around such issues as the following (these are meant as semi-structured question probes only, as spontaneous points raised by audience members are likely to also move the conversation in fruitful directions):

1. What framework and concepts best account for the everyday rituals involved in creating and viewing YouTube videos?
2. What cognitive, affective, and bridge-building work do YouTube videos do in an intercultural context?
3. What approaches are most suitable for exploring YouTube and similar visually based platforms?

The panel will begin with an overall introduction to visual information culture, new media information, and information practices, along with a brief introduction to YouTube as a platform (including examples of YouTube channels and videos representative of the cases featured in this panel session). Four short presentations (of no more than 10 minutes per panelist) will follow, introducing different findings from rich and diverse settings. Panel members will then lead the audience into a discussion/engagement portion. The panelists' various projects are outlined below (in alphabetical order by last name, with presentation titles illustrative only):

- ***The case of digital/visual consumption and creative practice among transmedia fans (Eric Forcier, Swinburne Univ. of Technology)***

Transmedia fandom represents the engagement practices of a given storyworld's fans, including everyday consumption, community interaction and inspired creative works. The panelist will focus on the influence of visual participatory platforms, such as YouTube and Twitch, in his study on the everyday information behaviours of transmedia fans. Audiences and official authors co-construct storyworlds that are extended across multiple narrative media (Stein & Busse, 2012). Based on in-depth interviews with self-identified fans and textual analysis of online fan communities, the panelist will present key examples that demonstrate how digital/visual media contribute to the everyday rituals of fans.

- ***The case of intercultural literacy mediated through YouTube encounters (Alice N. Kim, Nadia Caidi, and Niel Chah, Univ. of Toronto)***

In this study, the panelists examine YouTube channels dealing with their creators' experiences with another culture—for example, British or Canadians individuals who live (or lived) in Korea, and wish to share their experiences about Korean culture. These YouTubers create and upload videos on a range of topics, including food practices, beauty practices, and other everyday matters; draw comparisons with practices 'back home'; and stimulate vivid engagement around these videos. The panelists theorize about the resulting dynamics of such intercultural encounters, the role of YouTubers as bridges and facilitators, and the emerging modes of engagement.

- ***The case of serious beauty and lifestyle YouTubers (Leslie Thomson, Univ. of North Carolina)***

In this study, the panelist examines YouTube creators who operate personal YouTube channels focused upon such varied terrain as skincare, makeup, fashion, fitness, home décor, relationships, school, careers, and daily life. Among other topics, she considers these YouTubers' paradoxical positions as non-experts, "native speakers of the language of teen girls" (Jeffries, 2011, p. 64), and savvy businesspeople, manoeuvring through a competitive, commodity-intensive environment with strategic brand partnerships and video metadata, while trying to attain broad, international appeal. She theorizes about the cultural aspects of the serious leisure social world in which beauty and lifestyle YouTubers move, and the complex relationships that factor into their creating and sharing, including with global viewerships, brands, third-party 'infopreneurs,' and the YouTube platform itself.

- ***The case of transnational fan knowledge of K-pop on YouTube (Kyong Yoon, Univ. of British Columbia)***

Drawing on a textual analysis of Western fan vlogs of K-pop (Korean pop music), the panelist explores how YouTube is integrated into young people's transnational cultural consumption and understanding. Owing to its intensive and extensive exploitation of YouTube, K-pop has rapidly emerged as a new transnational cultural phenomenon among subcultural youth, not only in Asia, but also in the West, over the past 10 years. The panelist's work examines how Western K-pop fans—who may encounter linguistic and cultural barriers with K-pop as a music genre produced in a non-Western context—engage with an interactive participatory culture on YouTube.

The open discussion with the audience that follows these short presentations will pave the way for future research at the intersection of visual engagement, trust and meaning-making, and local and translocal community building. This panel is expected to appeal to researchers and practitioners alike, particularly but not limited to those involved with SIG USE, SIG III, and SIG SM. It is likely to result in a research agenda that may be carried forward into a future ASIS&T or SIG workshop on the new media platforms and modes of engagement increasingly characteristic of our visual and networked environment.

SPEAKERS' BIOGRAPHIES

Leslie Thomson is a Ph.D. candidate in the School of Information and Library Science, University of North Carolina at Chapel Hill. Her research interests include human information behaviour, everyday life and leisure, and social media.

Nadia Caidi is Associate Professor in the Information School, University of Toronto. She received her Ph.D. from UCLA, and her research interests include human information behaviour, global migration, and information policy.

Kyong Yoon is a media researcher specializing in Asian digital media, youth culture, and cultural studies. He received his Ph.D. in Cultural Studies from the University of Birmingham.

Eric Forcier is a Ph.D. candidate in Media and Communication at Swinburne University of Technology in Melbourne, Australia. His research interests include postdigital information behaviour in everyday life contexts and transmedia fan studies.

Alice Nahyeon Kim is a Researcher at the Korean Education Centre in Toronto. She received her M.I. from the Information School, University of Toronto, and her research interests include information practices of diaspora communities, ethnic media, and intercultural communication mediated through social media.

Niel Chah is a Ph.D. student in the Information School, University of Toronto. His research interests include social media, intercultural communication, and ethnic media.

REFERENCES

Alexa. (2018). The top 500 sites on the web. Retrieved April 3, 2018 from http://www.alexa.com/topsites.

Ault, S. (2014, August 5). Survey: YouTube stars more popular than mainstream celebs among U.S. teens. *Variety*. Retrieved April 3, 2018 from http://variety.com/2014/digital/news/survey-youtube-stars-more- popular-than-mainstream-celebs-among-u-s-teens-1201275245/.

Burgess, J., & Green, J. (2009). YouTube: Online video and participatory culture. Cambridge, UK: Polity.

Burnett, G. (2000). Information exchange in virtual communities: A typology. *Information Research*, 5(4), Retrieved from April 3, 2018 http://informationr.net/ir/5-4/paper82.html.

Cho, A. (2013). YouTube and academic libraries: Building a digital collection. *Journal of Electronic Resources Librarianship*, 25(1), 39-50.

Jeffries, L. (2011). The revolution will be soooo cute: YouTube "hauls" and the voice of young female consumers. *Studies in Popular Culture, 33*(2), 59-75.

Jerslev, A. (2016). In the time of the microcelebrity: celebrification and the youtuber zoella. *International Journal of Communication*, 10, 5233-5251.

Kaminsky, M. S. (2010). *Naked lens: Video blogging and video journaling to reclaim the you in YouTube*. New York City, NY: Organik Media.

Kim, A., Caidi, N., & Chah, N. (2018). "'Our Korea': Transcultural affinity as negotiated through YouTube encounters." In Proceedings of the Information Seeking in Context (ISIC) 2018 Conference, Krakow, Poland, Forthcoming in *Information Research.*

Kousha, K., Thelwall, M., & Abdoli, M. (2012). The role of online videos in research communication: A content analysis of YouTube videos cited in academic publications. *Journal of the American Society for Information Science & Technology*, 63(9), 1710-1727.

Oh, S., & Syn, S. Y. (2015). Motivations for sharing information and social support in social media: A comparative analysis of Facebook, Twitter, Delicious, YouTube, and Flickr. *Journal of the Association for Information Science & Technology*, 66(10), 2045-2060.

Statista. (2015). Hours of video uploaded to YouTube every minute as of July 2015. Retrieved April 3, 2018

from https://www.statista.com/statistics/259477/hours-of-video-uploaded-to-youtube-every-minute/.

Stein, L. E. and Busse, K. (2012). Introduction: The Literary, Televisual and Digital Adventures of the Beloved Detective, in L. E. Stein and K. Busse (Eds.), *Sherlock and Transmedia Fandom: Essays on the BBC Series*. Jefferson, NC: McFarland & Company.

Sugimoto, C. R., & Thelwall, M. (2013). Scholars on soap boxes: Science communication and dissemination in TED videos. *Journal of the American Society for Information Science & Technology*, 64, 663-674.

Thomson, L. (2017). "In my humble opinion...": Serious YouTubers' self-presentations, roles, and authority. In *Proceedings of the 80th ASIS&T (Association for Information Science and Technology) Annual Meeting*, Washington, D.C.

Telegraph. (2012, August 31). Top YouTube users 'making six figure incomes.' *The Telegraph*. Retrieved from April 3, 2018 http://www.telegraph.co.uk/technology/google/9511534/Top-YouTube-users-making-six-figure-incomes.html.

YouTube Statistics. (2016). Google. Retrieved April 3, 2018 from https://www.youtube.com/intl/en-GB/yt/about/press/.

Users' Perceptions of Topical Learning for Aiding Exploratory Video Search

Dan Albertson
University at Buffalo, The State University of New York, USA. dalbert@buffalo.edu

ABSTRACT

The present study examines users' perceived need for topical learning within exploratory video searches. A survey that incorporated sample search scenarios was employed. Findings demonstrated various relationships between the perceived need for topical learning and other variables such as topic familiarity, search system, and user confidence for completing searches.

KEYWORDS

Video search, exploratory search, topical learning, system experience, user confidence.

INTRODUCTION AND REVIEW

Searching for video is an everyday activity for many. Videos searches themselves can be unique from searches for other types of information. A search for video can include a range of different criteria or needs such as physical, visual, story, time-based, and others (Albertson, 2016; Albertson & Ju, 2015). Further, prior research has examined users' interactions in a video search process across different contexts (Albertson, 2010; Lee & Smeaton, 2004; Marchionini, Wildemuth, & Geisler, 2006).

Exploratory searches involve different types of learning, with "learning" applied loosely in existing research (Marchionini, 2006). In exploratory searches, users seek to achieve a better understanding of the search itself, the topic or need, the content, and/or any other relevant aspect of the search. An exploratory search would involve different processes than a known-item or look-up search (Marchionini, 2006). Various digital library projects – e.g. the Open Video Project – have been used to examine exploratory video search research (Marchionini, Wildemuth, & Geisler, 2006).

The goal of the present study is to better understand topical learning in exploratory video search from the users' point of view. Here, users' perceived need for topical learning for aiding an exploratory video search is examined and compared against search topic familiarity, the search system, and users' own confidence in completing different video searches.

RESEARCH QUESTIONS

RQ1. How do users perceive the need for topical learning within an exploratory video search?
RQ2. Do users' perceptions of the need for topical learning vary by their familiarity with the video search topic?
RQ3. Do users' perceptions of the need for topical learning vary by the video search system to be used?
RQ4. Do users' perceptions of the need for topical learning vary by their level of confidence in fulfilling a video search?

METHODOLOGY

The study assessed the research questions using a survey with a brief search scenario. Two versions of the survey were created. The different versions were only distinguished by the system (i.e. video website) used in the scenario. One survey specified and displayed a screengrab of YouTube (including its search features) as the system example; the other posed the same scenario and questions, but rather used the C-SPAN Digital Video Library (not YouTube). On both versions of the survey, participants were asked to rate:

1. Their frequency of use or level of experience with the video website (on a scale of 1-never used to 5-use daily)
2. Their familiarity with the general topic of "how the Chief Justice of the Supreme Court ruled on 'Obama Care'" (scale of 1-absolutely no familiarity to 5-expert on topic)
3. Their level of confidence for successfully completing two video searches (1-not capable to 5-highly confident) including:
    a. "An unedited video of the Chief Justice of the Supreme Court discussing his ruling on Obama Care during a college campus interview," coded for the study as a precision video search
    b. "Many video clips of political analysts critiquing the Chief Justice's ruling on Obama Care," coded as a recall search.

4. Their perceived amount of learning on the topic (i.e. the Chief Justice's ruling on Obama Care) needed to aid the search with [the system example] (on a scale of 1-none to 5-a lot)

For the most, paper surveys were collected; however, a small number of surveys was sent and received through direct email. The result was a total of 270 surveys from unique participants across the two groups; an equal number of 135 completed the YouTube and C-SPAN Digital Video Library versions of the survey respectively (no participant was given both surveys). The overall participant pool is further described by both age and gender in Table 1.

Gender			Age					
Female	Male	Non-report	18-20	21-29	30-39	40-49	50+	Non-report
156 (57.8%)	101 (37.4%)	13 (4.8%)	86 (31.9%)	103 (38.1%)	25 (9.3%)	20 (7.4%)	32 (11.9%)	4 (1.5%)

Table 1: Participants by gender and age

Survey responses were analyzed quantitatively. Basic statistics were used to assess participants' overall perceptions of the need for topical learning to aid the provided exploratory video searches (RQ1). Next, Whitney-Mann U tests were used to compare the perceptions for topical learning across independent groups of high versus low levels of topic familiarity (RQ2) and system experience (RQ3). Finally, relationships between user confidence in fulfilling the searches (combined) and the perceived need for topical learning were assessed using Spearman correlation analysis (RQ4).

RESULTS

RQ1. The overall need for topical learning to aid these exploratory video searches – as expressed by the users – was measured at M=3.03 with a SD=1.04 and range of 4. These results include both groups of surveys (YouTube and C-SPAN).

RQ2. Results of a Mann-Whitney U test showed a significant difference at U=7311, p=.014 between the high versus low groups of topic familiarity. The group with lower levels of topic familiarity (Mdn=3) expressed a significantly greater need for topical learning than that of the higher group (Mdn=3).

RQ3. First, the overall level of use or experience with YouTube was measured at Mdn=4, M=3.53, and SD=1.27, compared against Mdn=1, M=1.18, SD=0.61 for the C-SPAN Digital Video Library. However, in regards to the perceived need for topical learning to aid the video searches, results of a Mann-Whitney U test (U=8080, p=.128) showed no significant difference between the YouTube (Mdn=3) and C-SPAN (Mdn=3) groups.

RQ4. Results of a Spearman's correlation test between users' perceived need for learning and overall user confidence for completing the search topics produced a significant negative correlation at $r(266)$=-.41, p=.000. Therefore, the higher the confidence of the user, the lower perceived need for learning and vice versa. (Confidence of users in this test included combined level for both the recall and precision sample search topics.)

DISCUSSION AND IMPLICATIONS

Topical learning by users may be viewed as more of an implicit or secondary process within a search – if considered at all in retrieval studies – especially when compared to other, more-direct or observable actions of users. As a result, different perspectives of topical learning have not been as thoroughly addressed for exploratory video search. Findings here provide a user-centered evaluation of learning in an exploratory video search scenario and demonstrate the need for continued research.

Results from the study showed that topic familiarly did affect users' perceived or expressed need for further topical learning. While this finding may seem obvious, the fact that users were able to self-identify and recognize the need for topical learning as part of a video search is significant. Secondly, the system examples of the study had no direct effect on the users' expressed need for learning. This finding was also interesting in that users were able to cognitively separate out the topic (and need for learning) from the system, despite one system showing high levels of use (YouTube). Finally, the significant negative correlation between the perceived need for topical learning and user confidence is reasonable; the more confident the user, the less perceived need for learning and vice versa.

Results here provide a better understanding of users and their perceptions of learning in an exploratory video search, which, in turn, provides a number of implications. As users seek to learn throughout a video search, as demonstrated by findings of the study, researchers can next examine how to support them at opportune times, such as through curated video content and interface features and functions.

REFERENCES

Albertson, D. (2010). Analyzing user interaction with the ViewFinder video retrieval system. *Journal of the American Society for Information Science and Technology, 61*(2), 238-252.

Albertson, D. (2016). A unified framework of information needs and perceived barriers in interactive video retrieval. *Journal of Information Science Theory and Practice, 4*(4), 4-15.

Albertson, D., & Ju, B. (2015). Design criteria for video digital libraries: Categories of important features emerging from users' responses. *Online Information Review, 39*(2), 214-22.

Lee, H., & Smeaton, A.F. (2004). Designing the user interface for the Físchlár digital video library. *Journal of Digital Infor- mation, 2*(4).

Marchionini, G. (2006). Exploratory search: From finding to understanding. Communications of the ACM, 49(4), 41-46. Marchionini, G., Wildemuth, B.M., & Geisler, G. (2006). The open video digital library: A möbius strip of research and practice. *Journal of the American Society for Information Science and Technology*, 57(12), 1629-1643.

A Methodology for Scientific Cyberinfrastructure Sustainability Research

Grant Allard
Clemson University, USA. gallard@clemson.edu

Suzie Allard
University of Tennessee, USA. sallard@utk.edu

ABSTRACT

Scientific cyberinfrastructure (SCI), defined as "the distributed computer, information and communication technologies combined with the personnel and integrating components that provide a long-term platform to empower the modern scientific research endeavor" (Atkins et al., 2003), is a foundation for the modern scientific enterprise and open science. Establishing persistent SCI requires an understanding of the essential topics related to cyberinfrastructure sustainability. We add to the study of SCI sustainability by focusing on the roles of financing structure and property rights. The Sustainability Transitions Outcomes Research Methodology (STORM) is a reproducible technique which opens the door for conversations that are based on existing data and from which scholars can derive axioms to help explain and predict the SCI sustainability. STORM provides steps for quantitatively categorizing financing, property rights, and outputs against cardinal metrics such as revenue, costs, and consumption of the resource. Our findings are presented with an interactive web application.

KEYWORDS

Cyberinfrastructure, sustainability, intellectual property rights, technology transfer, research methodology

INTRODUCTION

Scientific cyberinfrastructure (SCI), defined as "the distributed computer, information and communication technologies combined with the personnel and integrating components that provide a long-term platform to empower the modern scientific research endeavor" (Atkins et al., 2003), is a foundation for the modern scientific enterprise and open science. Prevailing scholarship identifies that governance structure and management techniques of SCI projects impact the ability of the projects to sustainably provide products and services beyond the early stages of research and development. Some of the dominant topics include documenting cyberinfrastructure projects across the globe (Shankar and Eschenfelder, 2017), historical analysis of cyberinfrastructure technologies (Fidler and Acker, 2016), analyzing scientists' motivations for sharing data (Douglass et al., 2013, Tenopir et al, 2011), data curation strategies (Kim and Stanton, 2016, Darch, 2017; Borgman et al., 2014), the return on investment of computing technology (Grudin, 2004), and the interoperability of projects to deal with outside demands (Sawyer and Sharma, 2016). Scholars have primarily uses case study methodology to document empirical behaviors of cyberinfrastructure organizations. Case study is a powerful tool for documenting the behavior of specific organizations and identifying particular, important events. However, the study of SCI sustainability can be enhanced with a methodology that promotes reproducibility, has the potential to explain and predict the behavior of stakeholders in cyberinfrastructure organizations, and could also provide a foundation for theory development. We propose the Sustainability Transitions Outcome Research Methodology (STORM) which builds on the case study method while also providing the ability to derive insights from empirical results that can explain and predict the behavior of SCI organizations—and perhaps information institutions more generally.

STORM FRAMEWORK

The starting point for STORM is the axiom that the sustainability of cyberinfrastructure depends on its ability to generate enough revenue to provide products and services beyond the early stages of research and development. STORM is founded on four assumptions. First, the source of funding matters because SCI organizations develop to maximize their potential for bringing in revenue. SCI organizations that are government-funded are expected to have different behavior than SCI organizations that are funded as joint ventures of private companies. This assumption is significant for our study because many SCI begin as term-limited projects funded by government agencies with the goal of providing long-term products and services. Second, the creation and distribution of property rights affects the future prospects for project sustainability. Property rights create incentives and assign accountability for maintaining the cyberinfrastructure (Ostrom and Hess, 2007). Third, over time, the funding structure and property rights regime are covariant, although not perfectly, which means that we recognize there is a relationship between funding structure and property rights, although we recognize that each project may have made unique decisions that buck this trend. Therefore, it is important to study funding structure and property rights separately. Fourth, there is heterogeneity of SCI projects' production functions. Over time, the type of outputs these projects produce will vary. Across projects and based on the combinations of funding structure and property rights regimes, there will be variance project to project.

The STORM framework holds that there are two periods in which cyberinfrastructure projects exist: research and development (R&D) and commercialization. R&D refers to the time in which the scientific cyberinfrastructure project is developing its production function, and commercialization refers to the time in which the project's technology is mature and it seeks to maintain and marginally increase its production. We call this commercialization because it refers to the translation of scientific findings to applications for which people or organization are willing to pay. We assume, based on the fact that it is in the best interest of science as well as the project managers' self-interest, that all SCI projects have the goal to exist in both time periods.

STORM has two steps. First, we categorize cyberinfrastructure projects and then estimate the relationship between categories and outcomes. We analyze the source of project funding. Projects may be funded by governments, private entities, non-profit organizations, or a mixture of the three groups. Then, we use Keeney and Raiffa's (1993) multi-attribute utility methodology to analyse the chartering document of each project and quantify the way it creates and distributes property rights and the type of output it specifies.

STORM provides a foundation for reproducible work on scientific cyberinfrastructure and information institutions that expands beyond the constraints of case study. STORM observes data that is a product of SCI project operations, which reduces limitations associated with scholars' or survey respondents' biases or perceptions. Further, by creating a quantitative methodology for analyzing these projects, we encourage other scholars to test our methodology with different data and to question assumptions that may prove us wrong. Further, our methodology examines two of the most salient, yet understudied, features related to project sustainability: funding and property rights. Our approach advances information science research by integrating the examination of problems in information through a public policy framework. To promote conversation and engagement, we present our findings in an interactive web application. Our web application presents our findings using data visualizations and multimedia. It also allows attendees to contribute to the conversation about the institutional structure of information by sharing their feedback, thoughts, and experience in a public forum accessible through our application.

REFERENCES

Borgman, C. L., Darch, P. T., Sands, A. E., Wallis, J. C., & Traweek, S. (2014). The ups and downs of knowledge infrastructures in science: Implications for data management. In *IEEE/ACM Joint Conference on Digital Libraries* (pp. 257–266). https://doi.org/10.1109/JCDL.2014.6970177

Darch, P. T. (2014). Managing the Public to Manage Data: Citizen Science and Astronomy. *International Journal of Digital Curation*, *9*(1), 25–40. https://doi.org/10.2218/ijdc.v9i1.298

Douglass, K., Allard, S., Tenopir, C., Wu, L., & Frame, M. (2014). Managing scientific data as public assets: Data sharing practices and policies among full-time government employees. *Journal of the Association for Information Science and Technology*, *65*(2), 251–262. https://doi.org/10.1002/asi.22988

Fidler, B., & Acker, A. (2017). Metadata, infrastructure, and computer-mediated communication in historical perspective. *Journal of the Association for Information Science and Technology*, *68*(2), 412–422. https://doi.org/10.1002/asi.23660

Grudin, J. (2004). Return on Investment and Organizational Adoption. In Proceedings of the 2004 ACM Conference on Computer Supported cooperative Work (pp. 324-327).

Hess, C., & Ostrom, E. (Eds.). (2007). *Understanding knowledge as a commons: from theory to practice*. Cambridge, Mass: MIT Press.

Keeney, R. L., & Raiffa, H. (1993). *Decisions with Multiple Objectives: Preferences and Value Trade-Offs*. Cambridge University Press.

Kim, Y., & Stanton, J. M. (2016). Institutional and individual factors affecting scientists' data-sharing behaviors: A multilevel analysis. *Journal of the Association for Information Science and Technology*, *67*(4), 776–799. https://doi.org/10.1002/asi.23424

Ostrom, E., & Hess, C. (2007). A Framework for Analyzing the Knowledge Commons. In C. Hess & E. Ostrom (Eds.), *Understanding knowledge as a commons: from theory to practice* (Kindle Edition). Cambridge, Mass: MIT Press.

Shankar, K., & Eschenfelder, K. (2017). Organizational and institutional work in data infrastructures. *Proceedings of the Association for Information Science and Technology*, *54*(1), 595–598. https://doi.org/10.1002/pra2.2017.14505401082

Sharma, S., & Sawyer, S. (2017). Comparing internal and external interoperability of digital infrastructures. *Proceedings of the Association for Information Science and Technology*, *53*(1), 1–6. https://doi.org/10.1002/pra2.2016.14505301091

Tenopir, C., Allard, S., Douglass, K., Aydinoglu, A. U., Wu, L., Read, E., … Frame, M. (2011). Data Sharing by Scientists: Practices and Perceptions. *PLoS ONE*, *6*(6), e21101. https://doi.org/10.1371/journal.pone.0021101

Information Seeking Behaviors of New Immigrants

Shimelis Assefa
University of Denver, USA. Shimelis.assefa@du.edu

Krystyna Matusiak
University of Denver, USA. Krystyna.matusiak@du.edu

ABSTRACT

This poster presents preliminary findings from a study focused on information seeking behaviors and everyday information practices of new immigrants who have settled in the Denver, Colorado metro area. Language was used as an inclusion criterion to recruit immigrants from three linguistic communities (Amharic speaking, Spanish speaking, and Russian speaking) to participate in the study. The study employed photovoice to gather data about participants' information seeking practices. First, the participants were asked to take pictures of the sources of information that they use in everyday life. In a follow-up interview, participants explained the context within which each of the pictures were taken. The findings of the study indicate that the information seeking behaviors of new immigrants is bilingual shifting frequently from a native language to English depending on the source and type of information. Many new immigrants prefer information in their native language.

KEYWORDS

Immigrants, everyday information practices, information seeking, Photovoice.

INTRODUCTION

The purpose of this study was to investigate: a) the type of information resources immigrants search for and use in their everyday information practices, b) how immigrants evaluate credibility and usefulness of information resources, and c) the influence of information behavior of immigrants from their countries of origin. One in four people living in the United States is an immigrant or has a parent who is an immigrant (National Academies of Sciences, Engineering, and Medicine, 2015). As immigrants settle in their host countries and begin to build a new life, it is critical for them to have access to credible and usable information resources. For immigrants, information is key to understanding a new country, navigating an unfamiliar environment, and engaging in economic, political, and cultural activities (Andrade & Doolin, 2016; Caidi et al., 2010; Lloyd, 2013). Immigrants are a heterogeneous group of information users with diverse linguistic, educational, and cultural backgrounds (Waters & Pineau, 2015). Immigrants face many socio-cultural obstacles in their information seeking, such as lack of language proficiency (Kim & Yoon, 2012; Savolainen, 2016).

METHODS

This research was informed by the theory of everyday life information seeking (ELIS), which focuses on information behavior in non-work contexts (Savolainen, 1995). It employed photovoice, a qualitative, visual research method, to gather data from study participants' regarding their information seeking practices for everyday life situations (Evans-Agnew & Rosemberg, 2016; Wang & Burris, 1997). A total of 13 participants from the three linguistic groups (Amharic, Spanish, and Russian) were recruited through flyers and community organizations.

RESULTS

The interviews with participants and the analysis of visual evidence indicate that the information seeking behavior of new immigrants is often bilingual shifting from their native language when they search for information about their countries to English when they look for jobs or places to live. A Russian speaker (Participant K) might be using a Russian search engine Yandex and the Russian equivalent of Facebook, Vkontakty for his personal interests and contacts with friends but a few minutes later switching to Google Search when looking for a new apartment. One key finding from the study across the three linguistic groups is that language is the most critical factor. Many new immigrants, especially those with limited English language proficiency, tend to rely on sources and services that are prepared in their own native language. But even those who are fluent in English, use a significant number of information resources in their native language. For Participant N who is a fluent English speaker, following Spanish-language sites and reading in Spanish is important to maintaining her cultural identity.
Using the study questions as a guide, interview transcripts were analyzed, and the following themes were identified:

- Switching between their native language and English was the chief strategy adopted to find and use information
- Friends and family are primary sources of information
- Information about employment is the first and most crucial need immigrants have when they arrive
- New immigrants have keen interest in and continue to follow current affairs about their country of origin
- Having access to information resources in the immigrants' native language is important to maintaining their cultural identity – values and heritage immigrants bring from their country of origin

- It is often difficult for new immigrants to find usable print information in their own native language
- Phone apps, social apps, and the Internet are the primary means by which they find information and maintain contact with family and friends in their country of origin
- Immigrants evaluate the information to be credible based on source type and when the information appears in multiple sources.

The pictures taken by participants served as important source of data. Many images provided by participants were about street and transit signs, or physical locations, such as stores or restaurants, indicating the importance of learning how to navigate through an unfamiliar space. Interestingly, the role of images in immigrant information seeking behavior emerged as a surprising theme in the interviews. Several participants talked about using images to communicate with English speakers when they felt that their English language was limited, and they could not get their message across. They carried images of their addresses on their phones as it was easier to show the picture than spell the address out. They also took images of street or bus signs to remind themselves where they needed to get off or change the bus. They also found images helpful in learning new vocabulary as they could associate a picture with an unfamiliar sound.

Figure 1. Selected sample photos juxtaposed to illustrate how new immigrants across the three linguistic group documented the information sources and services they use to make sense of their new adopted country.

CONCLUSION

The study indicates that although recent immigrants use the Internet to seek information, they often feel overwhelmed and face many socio-cultural obstacles. People in their immigrant communities, public libraries, and social organizations are the major sources of information and support. Recent immigrants live between cultures and having access to information in their language and about their culture is important to their well-being and maintaining cultural identity. For new immigrants to integrate well and become productive members of society, hosting cities and counties need to prepare useful information in a language, format, and level appropriate to them. One way to accomplish this goal would be to work with public libraries, community organizations, and key stakeholders and opinion leaders in the respective community.

REFERENCES

Caidi, N., Allard, D., & Quirke, L. (2010). Information practices of immigrants. *Annual Review of Information Science and Technology*, 44(1), 491-531.

Evans-Agnew, R. A., & Rosemberg, M. A. S. (2016). Questioning photovoice research: Whose voice?. *Qualitative Health Research*, 26(8), 1019-1030.

Kim, S., & Yoon, J. (2012). The use of an online forum for health information by married Korean women in the United States. *Information Research*, 17(2). Retrieved from http://www.informationr.net/ir/17-2/paper514.html

Lloyd, A., Kennan, M. A., Thompson, K. M., & Qayyum, A. (2013). Connecting with new information landscapes: information literacy practices of refugees. *Journal of Documentation*, 69(1), 121-144. doi:10.1108/00220411311295351

National Academies of Sciences, Engineering, and Medicine. (2015). *The Integration of Immigrants into American Society.* Panel on the Integration of Immigrants into American Society, M.C. Waters and M.G. Pineau, Eds. Committee on Population, Division of Behavioral and Social Sciences and Education. Washington, DC: The National Academies Press. doi: 10.17226/21746.

Savolainen, R. (1995). Everyday life information seeking: Approaching information seeking in the context of "way of life."

Library and Information Science Research, 17(3), 259-294.

Savolainen, R. (2016). Approaches to socio-cultural barriers to information seeking. *Library & Information Science Research*, 38(1), 52-59.

Wang, C. & Burris, M. A. (1997). Photovoice: Concept, methodology, and use for participatory needs assessment. *Health Education Behavior*, 23(2), 369-387.

Comparing Features of Fabricated and Legitimate Political News in Digital Environments (2016-2017)

Toluwase Victor Asubiaro
University of Western Ontario, Canada. tasubiar@uwo.ca

Victoria L. Rubin
University of Western Ontario, Canada. vrubin@uwo.ca

ABSTRACT

With the problem of 'fake news' in the digital media, there are efforts at creation of awareness, automation of 'fake news' detection and news literacy. This research is descriptive as it pulls evidence from the content of online fabricated news for the features that distinguish fabrications from the legitimate political news around the time of the U.S. Presidential Elections (276 articles in total, from November 2016 - June 2017). Certain stylistic and psycho-linguistic features of fabrications may be apparent to the news readers: fewer words and paragraphs but longer paragraphs, more slangs, swear words and affective words in the stories. Such features could be used for educational information literacy campaigns for spotting so-called 'fake news'. Other informative features may require specialized analytical tools (or further training) to notice the presence of more words, punctuation marks, demonstratives and emotiveness in fabrications but fewer verifiable facts (or named entities) in their headlines.

KEYWORDS

News fabrication, Fake news, Disinformation, Deception, Content analysis, Information literacy.

INTRODUCTION

Information literacy (IL) includes a set of skills that require individuals to "have the ability to locate, evaluate, and use effectively the needed information" (American Library Association, 1989). In recent times, the ability to evaluate information from news sources is a new challenge to the news readers in the digital environment because of the proliferation of fabricated news, often referred to as 'fake news'. In response to the need for IL programs to incorporate skills for identifying misinformation and disinformation online, there are new IL programs which are customized towards 'fake news' identification (International Federation of Library Associations, 2018; Wyman, 2017).

In the Tandoc, Lim, & Ling (2018) 'fake news' typology, news fabrication (or falsification) is defined as having low facticity with high author's intention to deceive. In other words, the content of news fabrication is not factual and it is presented with the intention to create a false impression or conclusion in the reader's mind. Studies have shown that humans are not effective at the lie-truth discrimination task; typical accuracy rates are in the 55–58% range, with a 54% mean accuracy of over 1,000 participants in over 100 experiments (DePaulo, Charlton, Cooper, Lindsay, & Muhlenbruck, 1997). On the other hand, some algorithmic applications, called automated deception detection, can be more accurate than humans in certain contexts (Rubin & Conroy, 2012). Automatic deception detection for the news context is hinged on contrasting differences in the linguistic, stylistic and psycholinguistic features between the legitimate and fabricated news articles. The differences in some of these features are not easily observed or recognizable by humans, for instance, pronoun or punctuation marks frequencies, but can be tallied and monitored algorithmically. As we are doing research in preparation for automation of identification of fabricated news, we perform comparative statistical analysis of linguistic features of fabricated versus legitimate news. Despite substantial difficulties expected for news readers in separating legitimate news from fabricated ones, news readers could and should pay attention to certain statistically significant differences between the two types of texts that we identified in our dataset.

The aim of this research is to highlight some human-noticeable features which can help human differentiate fabricated news from legitimate ones. The idea is that some of these features are informative, and they can be taught and incorporated into the IL programs for spotting 'fake news' with a naked eye. For an obvious example, consider the use of customary more formal language in news articles. Overt incessant non-standard language use, such as slang and swearing, should be raise a red flag.

METHODOLOGY

We collected 276 digital articles in the domain of the U.S. politics in order to find differences between fabricated (i.e., 'fake') and legitimate news, emanating from the United States between November 2016 and June 2017. The volume of fabricated news and the associated problems became unprecedented around the time of the 2016 U.S. Presidential Elections. Three steps were taken during our data collection. First, the PolitiFact.com was examined for the 50 most current websites identified at the time of data collection as 'fake news' sources with 'pants-on-fire' ratings. Secondly, we collected 5 most up- to-date fabricated (or falsified) news articles from the sources, identified via PolitiFact. The resulting total was 185 'fake news' from 37 websites relating directly to politics. Out of those, 138 falsifications were used for direct matching with legitimate news; we ended up with 138 pairs of news articles (138 fabricated and 138 legitimate, 276 articles in total). We manually matched the falsifications to their potential inspirations. We assumed high probability of falsifications emanating from some legitimate news and limited the dataset to U.S. politics only. Each article and headline was carefully read (by the first author) and key words were extracted manually to reflect the theme or the subject. Keyword search strategy was used with the Google search engine and the Reuters database and verified by a close reading for the best match between the fakes and their matching legitimate news.

We content-analyzed the matched datasets of 276 fabricated and legitimate news headlines and texts with natural language processing (NLP) techniques, using *pattern.en* (De Smedt, and Daelemans, 2012) and the NLTK packages (Loper & Bird, 2002) of the Python language libraries. The following features were collected: word count per news story, paragraph and headline; number of affect words, number of informalities (swear words and slangs), and verifiable facts (referred to in NLP as named entities which can be proper names of individuals, things, places, times and dates). Other features that were extracted are affect (positive and negative wording), emotiveness (counts of adverbs + adjectives divided by counts of noun + verbs) and frequencies of demonstratives ('this', 'that', 'these') and pronouns ('he', 'she', 'mine', 'hers', *etc.*) Paired sample *t*-test was conducted on pairs of legitimate and fabricated news with significant level set at 0.05.

RESULTS AND DISCUSSION

The result of the paired sample *t*-test is presented in Table 1 where each pair (from 1 to 10) refers to legitimate versus fabricated news pair. Let us consider differences in the surface stylistic (lexical) features first. Legitimate news stories contain an average of 481.87 more words ($F(1, 137)=5.88, p\approx0.01$) than fabricated news. Similarly, legitimate news contain an average of 14 more paragraphs ($F(1, 137)=6.90, p\approx0.01$) than fabricated news. On the other hand, legitimate news contain shorter paragraphs ($F(1, 137)=-3.00, p=0.04$), an average of 8.06 number of words per paragraphs less than fabricated news that contain longer paragraphs. Figure 1 (see Appendix) shows a sample each from legitimate and fabricated news sources where the legitimate news has shorter paragraphs and bigger fonts, while the fabrications are presented with smaller fonts but longer paragraphs. On the other hand, fabricated news headlines contain more words ($F(1, 137)=3.00, p=0.03$) and more punctuation marks ($F(1, 137)=-4.06, p\approx0.01$) than the sample legitimate news headlines. It may be difficult for humans to keep track of punctuation marks in the body of the news but spotting unnecessary punctuation marks in the headline is trivial.

No	Features Compared	Mean	Std. Dev	Std. Error Mean	95% Confidence Interval of the Diff		*t*	Sig. (2-tailed)
					Lower	Upper		
1	No of words/story	481.87	962.23	81.91	319.90	643.84	5.88	.000
2	No of paragraphs/story	14.09	24.00	2.04	10.05	18.13	6.90	.000
3	No of words per paragraph/story	-8.06	32.03	2.73	-13.46	-2.67	-3.00	.004
4	Affect/story	-.20	.17	.02	-.23	-.17	-13.66	.000
5	Informality/story	-.02	.06	.005	-.03	-.01	-4.26	.000
6	No of words/headline	-1.74	6.84	.58	-2.89	-.59	-3.00	.003
7	Verifiable facts/headline	1.10	.97	.08	.94	1.27	13.36	.000
8	No of punctuations/headline	-.25	.71	.06	-.37	-.13	-4.06	.000
9	Demonstratives/headline	-.25	1.02	.09	-.42	-.07	-2.82	.005
10	Emotiveness/headline	-.06	.04	.003	-.07	-.06	-20.17	.000
	The *df*=137							

Table 1. Paired Sample *t*-test result of Legitimate vs. Fabricated News

Differences in psycho-linguistic features also show that fabricated news articles contain more positive and negative affect ($F(1, 137)=-13.66, p\approx0.01$) and their headlines contain more emotiveness ($F(1, 137)=-20.17, p\approx0.01$) showing attempts at heavy emotional appeals to the readers in the bodies of such articles and their headlines. We found more informal words in fabricated news stories ($F(1, 137)=-4.26, p\approx0.01$), as expected. Also, fabricated news headlines contain more demonstratives (pronouns and unspecific) in fabricated news headlines ($F(1, 137)=-13.66, p\approx0.01$) and on the other hands, less verifiable facts (specific names) ($F(1, 137)=13.36, p\approx0.01$) as often seen in clickbait. In essence, put in plain language, fabricated news headlines contain 'more of *he, she, they, etc.*' (i.e., pronouns), while legitimate news headlines contain more specific names. Figure 2 shows fabricated vs. legitimate news headlines (see Appendix) with more words, demonstratives, pronouns, and punctuations marks but with fewer verifiable facts (or named entities).

CONCLUSIONS

Based on the results of the paired *t*-test between fabricated and paired legitimate news in the U.S. politics from 2016-2017, we identified several features that can be incorporated in the news literacy awareness campaigns targeting broader awareness on how to spot 'fakes' in the digital news environments. Fabricated political news stories by comparison to their likely legitimate counterparts, tend to have fewer words, fewer but lengthier paragraphs; they also contain more slang, swear, and affective words. The fabricated news headlines contain more words, punctuation marks, demonstratives, emotiveness and fewer verifiable facts.

ACKNOWLEDGMENTS

This research has been funded by the Government of Canada Social Sciences and Humanities Research Council (SSHRC) Insight Grant (#435-2015-0065) awarded to Dr. Rubin for the project entitled *Digital Deception Detection: Identifying Deliberate Misinformation in Online News.*

REFERENCES

American Library Association. (1989). *Presidential Committee on Information Literacy.* (Final Report). Retrieved from www.ala.org/Template.cfm?Section=Home&template=/ContentManagement/ContentDisplay.cfm&ContentID=33553#f1

DePaulo, B. M., Charlton, K., Cooper, H., Lindsay, J. J. & Muhlenbruck, L. 1997. The Accuracy-Confidence Correlation in the Detection of Deception. Personality and Social Psychology Review, 1, 346-357.

De Smedt, T. & Daelemans, W. (2012). Pattern for Python. *Journal of Machine Learning Research*, 13: 2031–2035.

International Federation of Library Associations. (2018). How to spot fake news. Retrieved March 29, 2018, from https://www.ifla.org/publications/node/11174

Loper, E., & Bird, S. (2002). NLTK: The Natural Language Toolkit. In *ETMTNLP '02 Proceedings of the ACL-02 Workshop on Effective tools and methodologies for teaching natural language processing and computational linguistics* (Vol. 1, pp. 63– 70). Philadelphia, Pennsylvania: Association for Computational Linguistics.

Tandoc, E. C., Lim, Z. W., & Ling, R. (2018). Defining "Fake News": A typology of scholarly definitions. *Digital Journalism*, *6*(2), 137–153. https://doi.org/10.1080/21670811.2017.1360143

Rubin, V. L., & Conroy, N. (2012). Discerning truth from deception: Human judgments and automation efforts. *First Monday*, *17*(3). https://doi.org/10.5210/fm.v17i3.3933

Wyman, J. (2017). How to Identify Fake News in 10 Steps. Retrieved March 29, 2018, from http://blogs.proquest.com/general/how- to-identify-fake-news-in-10-steps/

APPENDIX

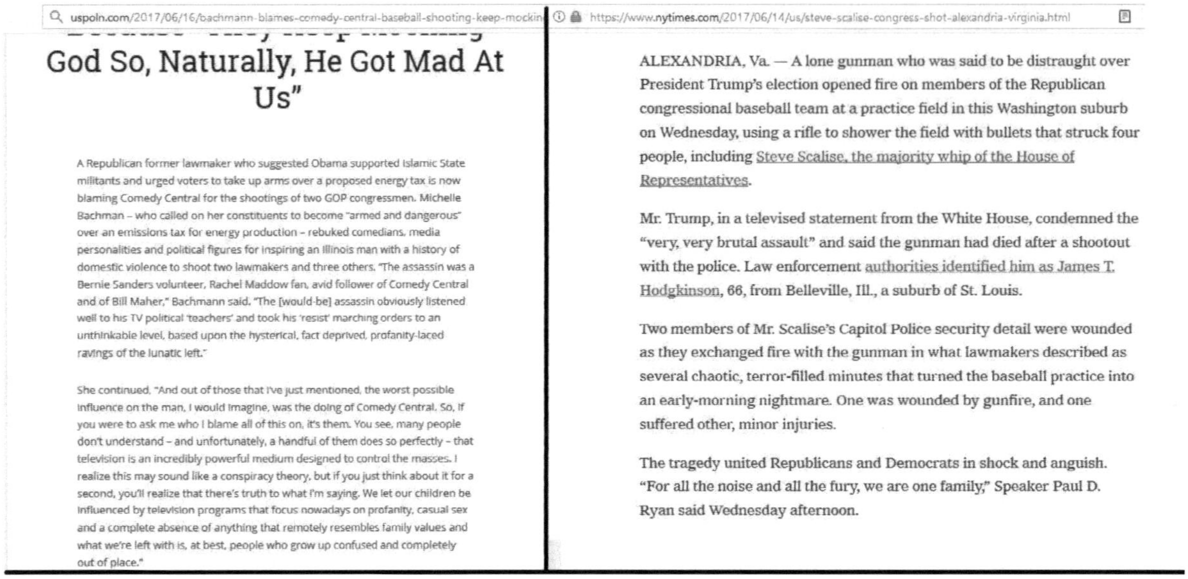
uspoln.com/2017/06/16/bachmann-blames-comedy-central-baseball-shooting-keep-mockin

God So, Naturally, He Got Mad At Us"

A Republican former lawmaker who suggested Obama supported Islamic State militants and urged voters to take up arms over a proposed energy tax is now blaming Comedy Central for the shootings of two GOP congressmen. Michelle Bachman – who called on her constituents to become "armed and dangerous" over an emissions tax for energy production – rebuked comedians, media personalities and political figures for inspiring an Illinois man with a history of domestic violence to shoot two lawmakers and three others. "The assassin was a Bernie Sanders volunteer, Rachel Maddow fan, avid follower of Comedy Central and of Bill Maher," Bachmann said. "The [would-be] assassin obviously listened well to his TV political 'teachers' and took his 'resist' marching orders to an unthinkable level, based upon the hysterical, fact deprived, profanity-laced ravings of the lunatic left."

She continued, "And out of those that I've just mentioned, the worst possible influence on the man, I would imagine, was the doing of Comedy Central. So, if you were to ask me who I blame all of this on, it's them. You see, many people don't understand – and unfortunately, a handful of them does so perfectly – that television is an incredibly powerful medium designed to control the masses. I realize this may sound like a conspiracy theory, but if you just think about it for a second, you'll realize that there's truth to what I'm saying. We let our children be influenced by television programs that focus nowadays on profanity, casual sex and a complete absence of anything that remotely resembles family values and what we're left with is, at best, people who grow up confused and completely out of place."

https://www.nytimes.com/2017/06/14/us/steve-scalise-congress-shot-alexandria-virginia.html

ALEXANDRIA, Va. — A lone gunman who was said to be distraught over President Trump's election opened fire on members of the Republican congressional baseball team at a practice field in this Washington suburb on Wednesday, using a rifle to shower the field with bullets that struck four people, including Steve Scalise, the majority whip of the House of Representatives.

Mr. Trump, in a televised statement from the White House, condemned the "very, very brutal assault" and said the gunman had died after a shootout with the police. Law enforcement authorities identified him as James T. Hodgkinson, 66, from Belleville, Ill., a suburb of St. Louis.

Two members of Mr. Scalise's Capitol Police security detail were wounded as they exchanged fire with the gunman in what lawmakers described as several chaotic, terror-filled minutes that turned the baseball practice into an early-morning nightmare. One was wounded by gunfire, and one suffered other, minor injuries.

The tragedy united Republicans and Democrats in shock and anguish. "For all the noise and all the fury, we are one family," Speaker Paul D. Ryan said Wednesday afternoon.

a. An example of fabricated news story. **b.** An example of legitimate news story.

Figure 1. Fabricated versus Legitimate news story

American Flavor

HOME US POLITICS BREAKING WORLD POLITICS

You are here Home > US Politics > They Caught Her! Guess Who Was Hiding Behind Closed Doors, Aiding & Abetting Obama, Spying On Tru

They Caught Her! Guess Who Was Hiding Behind Closed Doors, Aiding & Abetting Obama, Spying On Trump?

US Politics by admin - May 9, 2017 0

Share Tweet

The New York Times

254

Susan Rice, Ex-Obama Adviser, Is Back in Political Cross Hairs Over Surveillance

a. An example of fabricated news headline. **b.** An example of legitimate news headline.

Figure 2. Fabricated versus Legitimate news headline.

Landscape of Knowledge Sciences in JASIST

Denise A. D. Bedford
Georgetown University, U.S.A. db233@georgetown.edu

Jyldyz Bekbalaeva
American University of Central Asia, Kyrgyzstan, bekbalaeva_j@auca.kg

ABSTRACT

This poster describes a research project in progress to map the historical and current published and grey literature of the field of knowledge management/knowledge sciences. The research describes the mapping of 11,820 JASIS papers to the landscape of knowledge sciences. The mapping is grounded on the automated classification and automated indexing of the individual papers leveraging a semantic profile and the SAS Content Categorization Suite. The semantic profile was created from the knowledge sciences classification scheme and thesaurus developed by Bedford (2015). The results suggest that JASIS papers and the research being published by ASIST members have some alignment with the field of knowledge sciences. The research is concentrated in three primary facets, including (1) Knowledge Asset Management; (2) Knowledge Technologies; and (3) Communities and Collaboration. Within these three facets there are clear pockets of concentration. The results further suggest that the research methodology can be applied to other sources.

KEYWORDS

Knowledge sciences, knowledge management facets, semantic analysis, automated classification

INTRODUCTION

This poster builds upon the work reported in three earlier research projects, including (1) a project to develop a comprehensive concept level thesaurus covering the field of knowledge sciences (Bedford, 2015a), (2) the on-going project to define de facto strands that define knowledge management education standards (Bedford Georgieff Brown-Grant), and (3) an assessment of the landscape of published and grey literature in the field of knowledge management (Bedford, 2015b). The knowledge sciences thesaurus provides a comprehensive description of the field in twelve facets (Figure 1), and identifies approximately 67,000 concepts distributed across the twelve facets.

• Knowledge Theories, Models and Methods	• Knowledge Asset Management
• Knowledge Strategy & Leadership	• Knowledge Architecture
• Intellectual Capital	• Knowledge Technologies
• Knowledge & Information Economics	• Knowledge Assessment and Evaluation
• Organizational Culture & Communication	• Innovation
• Collaboration and Communities	• Organizational Learning

Figure 1. Proposed scope and coverage of the knowledge sciences thesaurus and classification scheme

This poster describes a research project in progress to map the historical and current published and grey literature of the field of knowledge management/knowledge sciences. The goal of this research project is to describe who is conducting relevant research and where they are located, to understand what topics are currently being researched, and to identify gaps in the broader research landscape. The larger effort involves mapping the published literature of the top ten referenced journals in the field of knowledge management, including Journal of Knowledge Management, Journal of Knowledge Economy, Journal of Intellectual Capital, Electronic Journal of Knowledge Management, Journal of Information and Knowledge Management, VINE Journal of Information and Knowledge Management Systems, Journal of Knowledge Management Practice, and Journal of Knowledge Management Research. This paper builds upon a body of peer-reviewed knowledge sciences literature (Binney, 2001; Bontis and Serenko, 2009; Ponzi, 2002; Serenko and Bontis, 2009; Serenko Bontis and Hull, 2011; Serenko et al, 2010; Wallace Van Fleet and Downs, 2011). The first phase of this research project focuses on papers published in the Journal of the Association for Information Science (JASIS). JASIS was selected as a starting point for the research because it was rated by knowledge management professionals as a journal which was *not often* consulted for knowledge sciences re- search (Bedford, 2015b). The research team hopes to learn why it is not often consulted or cited. Through the semantic analysis of all JASIS papers dating back to 1950, the researchers explain why knowledge management professionals do not perceive JASIS as a core journal in their field.

RESEARCH QUESTIONS AND METHODOLOGY

The research reported in the poster addresses five essential questions, including:

- RQ1: How do JASIS papers map to the facets of Knowledge Sciences?
- RQ2: How dense is the coverage of core concepts (e.g., how good is the fit to a facet)?
- RQ3: Where are the gaps in coverage? Where are the concentrations in coverage?
- RQ4: How do the semantic analysis classification and indexing results compare to JASIS keywords?

- RQ5: Are there opportunities for promoting JASIS to the knowledge management community?

In 2015, the research team consulted with Information Today to obtain a working corpus of JASIS papers. The full corpus included 11,820 papers, covering the years 1950 to 2016. Full-text papers were downloaded and organized by year. In 2017, Bedford translated the knowledge sciences thesaurus into a semantic profile for automated categorization and automat- ed indexing using the SAS Content Categorization Suite. The semantic profile was applied to the corpus as part of a batch process. Each paper was classified according to facets in the profile based on goodness of fit, and was keyword indexed to determine the nature and density of concepts treated. The metadata generated for each paper including facets-classes and keywords were aggregated into a database for analysis. The classes assigned to each paper were used to generate a visual map of papers across the field (Research Question 1). The keywords assigned to each of the papers were visually mapped to determine the density of coverage within each facet (Research Question 2). Gaps in coverage were determined through a visual review of the mapping and a statistical analysis of the datasets (Research Question 3). A sample of the keywords generated is compared to the key-words assigned to papers by authors (Research Question 4). The results of the four research questions are considered and observations are offered for improving engagement of the ASIST and the knowledge management communities.

RESULTS

The results suggest that JASIS papers and the research being published by ASIST members have some alignment with the field of knowledge sciences. The research is concentrated in three primary facets, including (1) Knowledge Asset Management; (2) Knowledge Technologies; and (3) Communities and Collaboration. Within these three facets there are clear pockets of concen-tration over the past six decades. The results further suggest that the research methodology is sufficiently rigorous to apply to other journals and sources. The results do indicate that there is a particular audience within the field of knowledge sciences that might be interested in JASIS coverage, but the perspective and context are challenging. In particular, the focus is heavily oriented towards libraries rather than to open or other organizational contexts. Additionally, the focus is heavily oriented to encoded and explicit information rather than to the larger body of knowledge.

REFERENCES

Bedford, D. A. D. (2015a). Enhancing access to knowledge management literature - a proposal for domain-based classification scheme and thesaurus. *Journal of Information & Knowledge Management*, 14(1), 1550006

Bedford, D. A. (2015b). The Knowledge management information landscape—awareness, access, use and value of sources. *Journal of Information & Knowledge Management*, *14*(02), 1550002

Bedford, D. A., Georgieff, M., & Brown-Grant, J. (2017). Lifewide, lifelong comprehensive approach to knowledge management educa-tion–emerging standards. *VINE Journal of Information and Knowledge Management Systems*, *47*(4), 467-489.

Binney, D (2001). The knowledge management spectrum understanding the KM landscape. *Journal of Knowledge Management*, 5(1), 33–42.

Bontis, N and A Serenko (2009). A follow-up ranking of academic journals. *Journal of Knowledge Management*,13(1), 16–28.

Ponzi, LJ (2002). The intellectual structure and interdisciplinary breadth of knowledge management: A bibliometric study of its early stage of development. *Scientometrics,* 55(2), 259–272.

Serenko, A and N Bontis (2009). Global ranking of knowledge management and intellectual capital academic journals. *Journal of Knowledge Management*, 13(1), 4–15.

Serenko, A, N Bontis, and E Hull (2011). Practical relevance of knowledge management and intellectual capital scholarly research: Books as knowledge translation agents. *Knowledge and Process Management*, 18(1), 1–9.

Serenko, A, N Bontis, L Booker, K Sadeddin and T Hardie (2010). A scientometric analysis of knowledge management and intellectual capital academic literature (1994–2008). *Journal of Knowledge Management*, 14(1), 3–23.

Wallace, DP, C Van Fleet and LJ Downs (2011). The research core of the knowledge management literature. *International Journal of Information Management*, 31, 14–20.

Rhetoric of Oppression – Linguistic Maps and Semantic Classifications

Denise A. D. Bedford, Ph.D.
Georgetown University, USA, db233@georgetown.edu

Stephanie Bennett
Georgetown University, USA, sab360@georgetown.edu

Kevin Bishop
Georgetown University, USA, kb1001@georgetown.edu

Conor Cuse
Georgetown University, USA, ccc84@georgetown.edu

Lin Ding
Georgetown University, USA, ld703@georgetown.edu

Sean Gabaree
Georgetown University, USA, sg1287@georgetown.edu

Yifei Ji
Georgetown University, USA, yj143@georgetown.edu

Rebecca Kielty
Georgetown University, USA, rck40@georgetown.edu

Rima Mandwee
Georgetown University, USA, rm1724@georgetown.edu

Katie Mikalnik
Georgetown University, USA, km594@georgetown.edu

Katherine Oberkircher
Georgetown University, USA, klo39@georgetown.edu

Mihika Sapru
Georgetown University, USA, ms4347@georgetown.edu

Sarah Shanoudy
Georgetown University, USA, ss4010@georgetown.edu

Shuyang Wang
Georgetown University, USA, sw903@georgetown.edu

Samantha Whalen
Georgetown University, USA, sew117@georgetown.edu

ABSTRACT

Language gives rise to consciousness and consciousness gives rise to reality. In 2018 we are more aware of the existence of oppressive language than we have been in recent decades, perhaps in part due to the reach of social media and the 24/7 coverage of events and discourse in the public space. In reality, oppressive language has been with us for centuries. This poster represents an effort to map and document the characteristics of the rhetoric of war, economic, cultural, ethnic, racial, and gender oppression, social alienation, extremism, anti-immigration, and political language. The poster presents the results a map of rhetorical elements, describes its application to the language of the ten areas noted above, and the model's translation into an early stage semantic profile for detection of oppressive language in written text or transcribed speech. The poster will also include test results generated prior to the ASIST Conference.

KEYWORDS

Rhetoric, semantic profiles, oppressive language, hate language, linguistic analysis

INTRODUCTION

Language gives rise to consciousness and consciousness gives rise to reality. In 2018 we are more aware of the existence of oppressive language than we have been in recent decades, perhaps in part due to the deliberate use of social media to target and divide, and the 24/7 coverage of events and discourse in the public space. In reality, oppressive language has been with us for centuries (Baker-Shenk, 1986; Bosmajian, 1974; Chomsky, 1992; Chomsky, 2006; Halliday Matthiessen and Yang, 1999; Reisigl and Wodak, 2005). It permeates the way we think and the way we talk. This poster represents the work of a class of students to map and document the fundamental characteristics and nature of oppressive rhetoric, including the rheto-ic of war pre- and post-9/11 (Lakoff, 2000), economic oppression (Shildrick and MacDonald, 2013), cultural and ethnical oppression (Kaplan, 2009; Reisigl and Wodak, 2005), racial oppression (Wetherall and Potter, 1992), gender oppression (Mills and Melany, 2011), social alienation (Harris, 1983; Levinson, 1980), extremism (O'Regan and Betzel, 2015), antiimmigration (Cunnningham-Parmeter, 2010), and politics (Riggins, 1997). We are more aware of the existence of oppressive language today than we have been in recent decades, perhaps in part due to the reach of social media and the 24/7 coverage of events and discourse in the public space.

METHODOLOGY

While there is a rich body of research on discourse analysis, the language of oppression and targeted research on each of these topics, there is no comprehensive conceptual model. By nature, the bulk of the research is qualitative in nature and often subjective in its interpretation. There is little quantitative or objective research on the topic. The research team's goal was to portray on an objective and quantitatively verifiable level the nature of oppressive language. A strawman version of the model first emerged from the team's deep dives into rhetoric, discourse, linguistic and semantic analysis. The strawman included a central element – Context – and six related elements – Meaning, Language, Linguistics, Identity, "The Other" and Naming. Context was defined to include legal, social, cultural, religious and racial. Meaning was expanded to include dic- tionary definitions, etymology, interpretation, and knowledge structures. Language was expanded to include myths, taboos, idioms, clichés, humour, cynicism, jokes, narratives and unreal scenarios, explicit-implicit-embeddedness, sounds and utter- ances, euphemisms, metaphors, allusions and generalizations. Linguistics includes grammatical patterns, linguistic registers and roles and actors. Identify was expanded to include the "ideal" and the "undesirable", group characteristics, group bound- aries, choice and inherence of affiliation, oppressor and oppressed, stereotypes, slurs and stigmas, power and status relation- ships. "The Other" was defined to include invisibility, knowledge of, distance from, values related to, and dehumanization of. Naming includes the power to name, the simplicity of the name and familiarity of the name.

Over the course of 13 weeks, the team provided greater definition and expanded the model to include sub elements. Definition and examples were drawn from ten contexts, including: pre- and post-9/11 war and conflict, economic oppression, cultural and ethnical oppression, racial oppression, gender oppression, social alienation, extremism, anti-immigration, and politics. The team approached each context by (1) reviewing the peer reviewed literature peculiar to that context, (2) assembling a corpus of relevant primary source documents and generating linguistic registers; (3) conceptual modelling of the elements of the rhetoric; and (4) discussion and brainstorming.

Once the conceptual model had been fully expanded, the team transformed it into a rule-based categorization profile. The intent of the categorization profile was to assess the feasibility of identifying oppressive language in any written text or transcribed speech. The transformation involved creating a class or category of rules and concepts for each sub element of the conceptual model. Knowledge representations and rules will be illustrated in the presentation. The SAS Content Categorization suite of semantic tools was using to encode and apply the profile. The rules and concepts were built out based on linguistic registers generated across contexts. An internal test of the profile was conducted against the individual primary source documents. The results were reviewed – at the source document level – and adjustments were made to the profile. Next, an external test of the profile was conducted – focusing primarily on social media posts, targeted websites and news stories. Implications of the conceptual model for future study and of the semantic profile for discovering examples of oppressive lan- guage.

PRESENTATION OF RESEARCH RESULTS

The poster presents the (1) conceptual model; (2) the human interpretation of the model in selected contexts; (3) the semantic profile and snapshots of the rules and concepts; and (4) the preliminary results of the semantic profiling of social media posts, targeted websites and news stories. The goal of sharing this work in progress with the information science community is to hear feedback on the model, and to identify opportunity to collaborate in further testing and use of the semantic profile.

REFERENCES

Baker-Shenk, C. (1986). Characteristics of oppressed and oppressor peoples: Their effect on the interpreting context. *Inter- preting: The art of cross-cultural mediation*, 43-54.

Bosmajian, H. A. (1974). *The language of oppression*. Public Affairs Press. Chomsky, N. (1992). Explaining language use. *Philosophical Topics*, *20*(1), 205-231. Chomsky, N. (2006). *Language and mind*. Cambridge University Press.

Cunningham-Parmeter, K. (2010). Alien language: Immigration metaphors and the jurisprudence of otherness. *Fordham L. Rev.*, *79*, 1545.

Halliday, M. A. K., Matthiessen, C. M., & Yang, X. (1999). *Construing experience through meaning: A language-based ap- proach to cognition*. London: Cassell.

Harris, A. (1983). Language and alienation. *The sociogenesis of language and human conduct*, 99.

Kaplan, T. P. (2009). The language of Nazi genocide: Linguistic violence and the struggle of Germans of Jewish an- cestry.

Lakoff, R. T. (2000). *The language of war*. Univ of California Press.

Levinson, M. H. (1980). General Semantics and Student Alienation. *Et cetera*, *37*, 172.

Mills, S., & Mullany, L. (2011). *Language, gender and feminism: Theory, methodology and practice*. Taylor & Francis. O'Regan, J. P., & Betzel, A. (2015). Critical Discourse Analysis: A Sample Study of Extremism. *Research Methods in Intercultural Communication: A Practical Guide*, 281-296.

Reisigl, M., & Wodak, R. (2005). *Discourse and discrimination: Rhetorics of racism and antisemitism*. Routledge. Riggins, S. H. E. (1997). *The language and politics of exclusion: Others in discourse*. Sage Publications, Inc.

Shildrick, T., & MacDonald, R. (2013). Poverty talk: how people experiencing poverty deny their poverty and why they blame 'the poor'. *The Sociological Review*, *61*(2), 285-303.

Wetherell, M., & Potter, J. (1992). *Mapping the language of racism: Discourse and the legitimation of exploitation*. Colum- bia University Press.

The Effect of Demoting Near-Duplicate Pictures

Ofer Bergman
Bar-Ilan University, Israel. Ofer.Bergman@biu.ac.il

Somaya Dahamshy
Bar-Ilan University, Israel. somaia.d.1988@gmail.com

Simon Tucker
Google, USA. brotherlogic@gmail.com

ABSTRACT

People often take several pictures of the same situation "just in case something goes wrong". As a result, their picture folders tend to be cluttered with near-duplicate pictures. These near-duplicate pictures reduce the efficiency of retrieving a specific picture as they compete for the users' attention. To address the problem of near-duplicates, we developed *Duplipix*, a working prototype that identifies near-duplicate pictures and piles them in a stack. When a user hovers the mouse over a stack, it opens allowing the user to select one or more of the near-duplicate pictures. In an initial within-subjects evaluation, we asked our 82 participants to retrieve a random picture from the same collection - with and without *DupliPix*. The use of *DupliPix* resulted in significantly faster picture retrieval, and the majority of participants indicated that using it is easier, more aesthetic and interesting than the standard picture presentation. They would also like *DupliPix* to be included in their next operating system.

KEYWORDS

Pictures, near-duplicates, user-subjective, demotion.

INTRODUCTION

In recent years, people often take several pictures of the same situation. As a result, their picture folders tend to be cluttered with very similar versions of the same picture, which we term *near-duplicates*. To address the near-duplicates problem, we developed *DupliPix*, a working prototype that identifies near-duplicate pictures and piles them in a stack (see Figure 1). In an initial within-participants design study we introduced *DupliPix* to our 82 participants, and then asked them to retrieve a random picture from the same collection three times with *DupliPix* and three times without, and measured their retrieval time. We then asked our participants to compare their user-experience with and without *DupliPix*.

BACKGROUND

In the age of digital photography, people tend to take numerous pictures, reasoning that it is cost-free. However Whittaker, Bergman, & Clough (2010) discovered that at retrieval time there is a price to pay for cluttering folders with large amount of pictures, with participants unable to find nearly half of their most salient family pictures taken more than a year ago. A related problem is that people take multiple pictures of the same object or situation "just in case something goes wrong" (e.g. a technical problem with the first picture). As a result, their picture folders are often cluttered with near-duplicate pictures. These near-duplicate pictures may not only mar the appearance of these picture folders, making them look dull, but also reduce the efficiency of retrieving a specific picture since they compete for the users' attention. It is well known in the field of cognitive psychology that in visual scanning, the number of irrelevant distracters increases the time it takes for people to identify a target object (Treisman & Gelade, 1980). In order to address the near-duplicates problem, we implemented the user-subjective approach to personal information management system design (Bergman & Whittaker, 2016). One of the key user-subjective principles is the demotion principle that suggests that information items of lower importance should be demoted (i.e. making them less visible) so as not to distract the user, but (unlike deletion and archiving) be kept within their original context just in case they are needed. This option combines both the advantage of the "delete" option (reducing competition for attention) with the advantage of "keeping" (allowing access to information if it is unexpectedly needed in the future). Several prototypes implementing the demotion principle have already been developed and positively evaluated including: *GrayArea* which allows users to demote unimportant documents by manually dragging them to a gray area at the bottom of their folders (Bergman, Tucker, Beyth-Marom, Cutrell, & Whittaker, 2009); *DMTR* which automatically demotes mobile phone contacts that have not been used for over six months by presenting them in a smaller font at the end of the contact list (Bergman, Komninos, Liarokapis, & Clarke, 2012); and *Old'nGray* that demotes old document versions by graying them, allowing the user to recognize the new version at glance (Bergman, Elyada, Dvir, Vaitzman, & Ben Ami, 2015).

Figure 1: A pictures stack created by *DupliPix*

THE *DUPLIPIX* PROTOTYPE

To identify near duplicates, *DupliPix* first checks that images are of the same orientation, and then computes the average difference between pixel colors for each image, using a threshold to separate near-duplicates from different images. *DupliPix* then demotes these near-duplicate pictures by piling them in a stack, with pictures hidden behind the top one showing a bit on the side to indicate their existence, without burdening the users with their full presentation (see figure 1). Should the users want to reach one of these near duplicate pictures after all, they can hover the mouse over them, resulting in the stack opening to standard presentation mode.

RESEARCH METHODOLOGY

Participants were 82 students living in Israel selected in a convenience sample. Of the participants 59 were females. Their age ranged from 19 to 65 years old (M = 30.88, SD = 9.71). The procedure included a learning stage where the participants got acquainted with DupliPix, a test phase and a questionnaire. The test was within-subjects: using the same set of pictures, each of the participants conducted three retrievals with DupliPix and three without it (order counterbalanced). In each retrieval task, a random picture from the collection was presented to the participants as a target, and their task was to find it in the collection as fast as they could and click on it.

RESULTS

Research question 1: Does the use of DupliPix affect retrieval time?

In order to answer this question, we conducted a paired t-test. Results indicate that the retrieval speed when participants used *DupliPix* (M = 16.79 sec., SD = 5.6 sec.) was significantly faster than when not using it (M = 20.27 sec., SD = 10.24 sec.), $t(81)=3.16$, $p<.001$.

Research question 2: What is the participants' attitude towards DupliPix?

Results regarding the four questionnaire questions are presented in Table 1 and discussed in the discussion section.

Question	With *DupilPix*	No difference	Without *DupliPix*
1. Which condition was *easier* for you to find the target picture?	48 (59%)	11 (13%)	23 (28%)
2. Which condition was visually more *interesting*?	60 (73%)	4 (5%)	18 (22%)
3. Which condition was visually more *aesthetic*?	64 (78%)	3 (4%)	15 (18%)
	Yes	Don't know	No
4. Would you like *DupliPix* as part of your next operating system?	62 (76%)	5 (6%)	15 (18%)

Table 1. Participants' attitudes towards *DupliPix*

DISCUSSION

Our results indicate that the use of *DupliPix* resulted in significantly faster picture retrieval, and that the majority of participants thought that using it is easier, more aesthetic and interesting than using the standard picture presentation, and indicated that they wish to use it in their next operating system (see Table 1). These initial results suggest that *DupliPix* was successful at addressing the near-duplicate pictures problem, and more generally supports the demotion principle of the user-subjective approach (Bergman & Whittaker, 2016). In future research we will improve *DupliPix* allowing it to present the best quality picture in front and examine *DupliPix* when run on the participants' own computers, to increase ecological validity.

REFERENCES

Bergman, O., Elyada, O., Dvir, N., Vaitzman, Y., & Ben Ami, A. (2015). Spotting the Latest Version of a File with Old'nGray. *Interacting with Computers, 27*(6), 630-639. doi: 10.1093/iwc/iwu018

Bergman, O., Komninos, A., Liarokapis, D., & Clarke, J. (2012). You never call: Demoting unused contacts on mobile phones using DMTR. *Personal and Ubiquitous Computing, 16*(6), 757-766. doi: 10.1007/s00779-011-0411-3

Bergman, O., Tucker, S., Beyth-Marom, R., Cutrell, E., & Whittaker, S. (2009). It's not that important: Demoting personal information of low subjective importance using GrayArea. *CHI 2009 Conference on Human Factors and Computing Systems* (pp. 269-278). New York, NY, USA: ACM.

Bergman, O., & Whittaker, S. (2016). *The Science of Managing Our Digital Stuff*: Mit Press.

Treisman, A. M., & Gelade, G. (1980). A feature-integration theory of attention. *Cognitive psychology, 12*, 97-136.

Whittaker, S., Bergman, O., & Clough, P. (2010). Easy on that trigger dad: a study of long term family photo retrieval. *Personal and Ubiquitous Computing, 13*(5), 17-30.

The Values and Design of Emerging Medical Biotechnologies: A Grounded Theory Analysis of TED Talks

Beth Strickland Bloch
University of Illinois, Urbana-Champaign, USA. mestric2@illinois.edu

ABSTRACT

The nonprofit TED organization currently hosts over 2800 videos on their website about topics related to Technology, Entertainment, and Design. The average video receives over one million views and serves as an influential tool for how the public thinks about the role of technology in their daily lives. In this work in progress, a values and design approach is used to consider what values are indicated by TED speakers when they present emerging medical biotechnologies to the general viewing public. Over 50 TED talks are identified as discussing these technologies at various stages of design: theoretically, in development, and currently tested. The transcripts of these videos are coded using a grounded theory approach to identify how values are used to present these emerging technologies. Preliminary results suggest that theoretical biotechnologies are discussed in more extreme utopian and dystopian views, but that the intensity of these views lessen when the technologies presented are further along in the development process. Biotechnologies currently tested on humans are more likely to be described using standard social values like privacy, sustainability, and human welfare. The values used to discuss these technologies suggests important ethical implications regarding the role they should occupy in society.

KEYWORDS

Values, design, emerging technology, biotechnology, TED talks

INTRODUCTION

First founded in 1984, the nonprofit TED organization hosts conferences where influential individuals from around the world present talks on topics related to Technology, Entertainment and Design. The organization video records these talks and started posting them on their free and publicly accessible website in 2006. The average recording is approximately 18 minutes or less in length and full transcripts of each talk are provided online.

TED Talks have the power to influence how the average viewer views the role of technology in their life. This is particularly important when we consider that many of the technologies presented in these talks, especially emerging medical biotechnologies (i.e. those which work with cell-driven molecules for health-related diagnosis or therapy (Musiband & Saha, 2012) are not yet routinely used within everyday clinical practice. Research suggests that the public acceptance of using certain medical biotechnologies is low and that top concerns relate to the use of stem cells, tissue engineering, and other cell-based therapies (Gupta, et al., 2017); all of which are discussed by various TED speakers.

So what values are used to present and discuss these technologies with members of the general public? What do these expressed values tells us about the perceived role these technologies are expected to occupy in society as envisioned by those who design them? What does the way these technologies are discussed tell us about the values of the designers themselves?

BACKGROUND

Many interdisciplinary information scholars are active in the emerging area of values and design research. These researchers work in the fields of computer science, information science, human computer interaction, and science and technology studies. There are two frameworks which have emerged from this research, Values in Design (VID) and Value Sensitive Design (VSD), and inform the approach used in this current project.

Both VID and VSD scholars reject the idea that technology is inherently neutral and only take on political properties once they are used. Langdon Winner (1980) first asserted that technology could indeed embody politics and argues this happens in two ways. First, human values shape how technologies are designed and result in their embodying values. Second, the use of technologies has an impact on social values. Values and design scholars argue that designers have a level of responsibility to make ethical decisions in their practice of technological development since using technology has social impacts (Verbeek, 2008).

Although the use of a values and design approach does not limit the type of values that should be considered in any analysis, VSD does provide a values heuristic that can be consulted as part of the values identification process. This heuristic includes twelve standard values: human welfare, ownership & property, privacy, freedom from bias, universal usability, trust, autonomy, informed consent, accountability, identity, calmness, environment & sustainability (Friedman, et al., 2013). The underlying perspective asserts that technologies themselves are sociotechnical and comprised of a complex system of people in roles and in relationships with system elements (Kling, 2007).

METHOD AND PRELIMINARY RESULTS

In this work in progress, over 50 TED Talks have been identified which discuss the design and use of (actual or intended) emerging medical biotechnologies. Talks were selected for inclusion if they met the following criteria: explicitly referred to a technology under development or being tested, if the technology discussed was intended for medical use in humans, and if the technological application was designed for use at the cellular level. The TED organization currently categorizes their talks into 441 topical areas. Initially, some categories (e.g. Biotech, Nanoscale, Synthetic Biology) were used to identify videos for possible inclusion in this study; however, upon further review, it was found these categories might miss applicable videos. Therefore, videos included in this study were selected by the author from a complete and unfiltered set of talks.

Transcripts of these talks are analyzed using a grounded theory approach. This method stresses the discovery of meaning while analyzing the data (from the transcripts) and works toward the development of theory after information has been collected (Charmaz, 1983). One out of every five talks were also watched and what was said in the video was compared to what was written in the transcript to account for accuracy. Watching the videos also provided an informal opportunity to reflect on what was presented and to consider potential values and ethics implications of the technologies discussed.

The transcripts are in the process of being coded to decipher meaning from what was said as it relates to the broader issues of values and ethics. These transcripts will be coded using multiple phases: meaning coding, meaning condensation, and meaning interpretation (Kvale, 1996). Once a final coding scheme is identified and applied to the transcripts, all relevant significant themes will be presented and discussed in a draft manuscript.

Initial findings of this study prove promising for contributing to the larger body of values and design research. Talks have been initially categorized as those which present biotechnologies in purely theoretical design terms, those under development, and those being tested on humans. Preliminary analysis suggests that the type of values used to discuss these technologies vary in their utopian or dystopian view of what these technologies mean for larger society. Utopian perspectives tend to describe biotechnologies using the terms of *hope*, *advanced*, or *effective*. Dystopian perspectives tend to describe biotechnologies using the terms of *fear*, *unknown*, or *uncontrolled*. Often the most extreme views describe theoretical biotechnologies, but the intensity of these views decrease when more developed biotechnologies are discussed. Biotechnologies further along in the development process are more likely to be presented using traditional social values like *privacy, sustainability,* or *human welfare*.

CONCLUSION

The role of emerging biotechnologies for routine use in healthcare applications is currently unknown. We do not know how using these technologies will impact our social values, but preliminary results of this study suggest that the values associated with each become less extreme in both their positivity and negativity the further along they are in development. These results also indicate that standard values, like those presented in the heuristic associated with VSD research, are easier to identify with biotechnologies that have made it to the testing phase. Ultimately, it may prove to be more difficult to assess which social values are implicated in the very early design stages of emerging medical biotechnologies.

REFERENCES

Charmaz, Kathy. (1983). The Grounded Theory Method: An Explication and Interpretation. In *Contemporary Field Research*, (pp. 109-126). Waveland Press: Prospect Heights, IL.

Friedman, B., Kahn, P. H., Borning, A., & Huldtgren, A. (2013). Value sensitive design and information systems. In *Early engagement and new technologies: Opening up the laboratory* (pp. 55-95). Springer, Dordrecht.

Gupta, V., Sengupta, M., Prakash, J., & Tripathy, B. C. (2017). *Basic & Applied Aspects of Biotechnology*. Singapore: Springer.

Kling, R. (2007). What is social informatics and why does it matter?. *The Information Society*, *23*(4), 205-220.

Kvale, S. (1996). InterViews. An introduction to qualitative research writing. *Thousand Oaks, CA: Sage.*

Musiband, M. K., & Saha, S. (2012). Ethical Considerations in Biomaterials Research and Development. In *New Materials and Technologies for Healthcare* (pp. 483-492).

Verbeek, P. P. (2008). Morality in design: Design ethics & the morality of technological artifacts. *Philosophy & design*, 91-103.

Winner, L. (1980). Do artifacts have politics?. *Daedalus*, 121-136.

Injecting Realism into Simulated Work Tasks: A Case Study of the Book Domain

Pia Borlund
Oslo Metropolitan University, Norway, piabor@oslomet.no

Toine Bogers
Aalborg University, Denmark, toine@hum.aau.dk

ABSTRACT

Interactive IR studies are commonly conducted by assigning participants *simulated work tasks situations* (SWTS), predeter- mined textual descriptions of an information need and its context to motivate participants to perform realistic searches of the IR system in question. Despite their popularity, research has shown that formulating realistic and engaging SWTSs remains challenging. In this paper, we propose using the analyses of large samples of complex real-world search requests—with the specific case of book search—to inject realism into SWTSs by taking different relevance aspects and their relative frequencies into account when formulating them. This should make it easier for researchers to design realistic SWTSs in the future.

KEYWORDS

Simulated work tasks, interactive IR, complex search, book search

INTRODUCTION

In interactive information retrieval (IIR) studies, participants are commonly assigned predetermined search tasks to initiate their search behavior. These search tasks function as a test instrument enabling realistic search interaction and assessment of retrieved information. As a result, it is necessary for these tasks to be designed in such a manner that they fit the study partici- pants, so that they can adopt these search tasks as if they were their own personal information needs. This requires search tasks to be designed with great care to ensure their soundness and validity. Anybody who has conducted an IIR study using assigned search tasks (e.g., in the form of *simulated work task situations* (Borlund, 2000; 2003)) will recognize that this is straightforward in theory, yet difficult in practice. Research shows that the majority of IIR studies fail to sufficiently tailor the simulated work task situations (SWTS), despite being rich in contextual descriptions, hence also disqualifying the study results (Borlund, 2016).

We believe that the design of SWTSs could benefit from a better understanding of real-world search tasks and information needs, and there is rich history of studying this. Recent work by Koolen et al. (2015) and Bogers et al. (2018) has taken a different approach to studying real-world needs by analyzing the complex requests of users in book and movie discovery. Their focus was on the relevance aspects expressed by users in their complex requests, i.e., what makes a book or movie relevant to a person's request? The objective of the paper is to help IIR researchers design better and more realistic search tasks for IIR evaluation studies—more specifically book search tasks—by using the relevance aspects uncovered by Koolen et al. (2015) to serve as a source of inspiration for the design of SWTSs. In the next section, we revisit the general evaluation framework of SWTSs, followed by an overview of the work by Koolen et al. (2015). We then present suggestions for the use of such real- world analyses to make it easier to inject realism into SWTSs, followed by our discussion and suggestions for future work.

SIMULATED WORK TASK SITUATIONS

The use of assigned search tasks in IIR evaluation studies is a well-established testing protocol since the introduction of SWTSs (Borlund & Ingwersen, 1997). A SWTS is a short textual description that presents a realistic information-requiring situation that motivates study participants to search the IR system (Borlund, 2000; 2003). Borlund and Ingwersen (1997, pp. 227-228) describe how SWTSs can ensure realism by allowing for user interpretations of the task, leading to cognitively individual information need interpretations—as in real life. Furthermore, by being the same for all the study participants experimental control is provided, and the search interactions are comparable across the group of study participants for the same SWTS. Borlund (2003) formulates five requirements for ensuring realism in SWTSs: (1) tailoring the SWTS to the information envi- ronment and the participant group; (2) including participants' personal information needs; (3) randomizing the order of SWTs to prevent biases; (4) pilot-testing the SWTSs; and (5) including the SWTSs when reporting on the study (Borlund, 2016, p. 396, 407). She further specifies that well-designed SWTSs are relatable and self-identifiable for participants due to contextual richness and overlap in topical interest (Borlund, 2016, p. 396). Such tailoring of SWTSs requires a certain degree of homogeneity of the group of study participants as well as a relatively high level of abstraction in the

SWTS wording (Borlund, 2016, p. 397). Nevertheless, research shows that formulating realistic and engaging SWTSs remains challenging (Borlund, 2016).

RELEVANCE ASPECTS IN BOOK SEARCH

One way of injecting realism into SWTSs is by drawing inspiration from analyses of real-world information needs, such as the relevance aspects expressed by users, which determine what makes information items relevant to them. A more accurate under- standing of real-world relevance aspects could help us formulate better SWTSs. In this paper, we draw inspiration from the work by Koolen et al. (2015), who harvested 944 examples of complex book search requests from the LibraryThing forums to gain insight into the composition and complexity of the information needs represented by these requests. They analyze the relevance aspects expressed in these 944 book requests by adopting the seven categories identified by Reuter (2007) in her study of school children's relevance aspects for book selection. Koolen et al. (2015, p. 188-189) add known-item search as the eight relevance aspect. Table 1 shows an overview of the eight different aspects as well as their relative frequency in the 944 requests (third column). The right-most columns show how often the different relevance aspects co-occurred with each other. For example, the aspects *Familiarity* and *Engagement* co-occurred in 91 different requests.

Aspect	Description	% of requests	Co-occurence frequencies							
		(*N* = 944)	A	C	E	F	K	M	N	S
Accessibility	The language, length, or level of difficulty of a book.	16%	**152**	109	44	50	15	39	8	27
Content	Topic, plot, genre, style, or comprehensiveness of a book.	74%		**698**	172	267	100	176	26	99
Engagement	Books that fit a certain mood, are considered high quality, or provide a certain reading experience.	23%			**213**	91	17	50	11	24
Familiarity	Books similar to known books or related to a previous experience.	36%				**338**	12	83	17	45
Known-item	Descriptions of known books with the sole purpose of identifying its title and/or author.	21%					**202**	85	0	1
Metadata	Books with a certain title, by a certain author/publisher, in a particular format, or from a certain year.	28%						**264**	11	26
Novelty	Books that are unusual or quirky, or have novel content.	4%							**34**	10
Socio-cultural	Books related to the user's socio-cultural background or values, have had a particular cultural or social impact or are popular or obscure.	14%								**143**

Table 1. Relevance aspects in the book domain (Koolen et al., 2015), along with their relative occurrence in the 944 book requests and co-occurrence counts with other relevance aspects.

TAILORING SIMULATED WORK TASK SITUATIONS TO THE BOOK DOMAIN

A better understanding of the types of information needs in a particular domain and the relevance aspects expressed therein could help in the formulation of more realistic SWTSs. While the most common aspects for book discovery—*Content* and *Familiarity*—may not necessarily be surprising relevance aspects to include in SWTSs, other aspects such as *Engagement* and *Socio-cultural* are more of a 'treasure' in the view of the authors. They are not obvious elements to include, but can be very motivational to participants in that they involve feelings and values and may therefore be another dimension of interest. For example, users may search for funny books or books that challenge existing views (Koolen et al., 2015, p. 189). Knowledge of how to realistically combine different aspects—through co-occurrence frequencies—could also help with design of SWTSs. We believe that knowledge of the relevance aspects in a domain could result in more realistic and better tailored SWTSs.

DISCUSSION & CONCLUSIONS

In this poster paper, we have suggested how analyses of real-world information needs in specific domains can help inform the design of SWTS, more specifically in the book domain. Taking different relevance aspects and their relative frequency into account, as well as which aspects are commonly combined could provide inspiration for more realistic SWTSs. For future work, we would like to use the results of similar analysis of complex search requests in other domains to tailor SWTSs and ultimately evaluate the quality of SWTSs designed using inspiration from these different domains.

REFERENCES

Bogers, T., Gäde, M., Koolen, M., Petras, V., and Skov, M. (2018). "What was this movie about this chick?": A Comparative Study of Relevance Aspects in Book and Movie Discovery. *Proceedings of the 2018 iConference* (pp. 323-334).

Borlund, P. & Ingwersen, P. (1997). The Development of a Method for the Evaluation of Interactive Information Retrieval Systems. *Journal of Documentation*, 53(3), 225-250.

Borlund, P. (2000). Experimental Components for the Evaluation of Interactive Information Retrieval Systems. *Journal of Documentation*, 56(1), 71-90.

Borlund, P. (2003). The IIR Evaluation Model: A Framework for Evaluation of Interactive Information Retrieval Systems. *Information Research*, 8(3).

Borlund, P. (2016). A Study of the Use of Simulated Work Task Situations in Interactive Information Retrieval Evaluations: A Meta-Evaluation. *Journal of Documentation*, 72(3), 394-413.

Koolen, M., Bogers, T., Bosch, A. V., & Kamps, J. (2015). Looking for Books in Social Media: An Analysis of Complex Search Requests. *Proceedings of ECIR 2015* (pp. 184-196).

Reuter, K. (2007). Assessing Aesthetic Relevance: Children's Book Selection in a Digital Library. *JASIST*, 58(12), 1745-1763.

Information Encountering by an Art Historian: A Methodological Case Study

Sarah A. Buchanan
University of Missouri, USA. buchanans@missouri.edu

Sanda Erdelez
Simmons University, USA. erdelez@simmons.edu

Shann Bossaller
University of Missouri, USA. sbossaller@gmail.com

ABSTRACT

Research activities of humanities scholars are complex. Novel methodologies are needed to facilitate investigation of their information behavior processes. This poster presents a case study designed to evaluate use of information encountering (IE) model as a methodological framework for soliciting rich feedback about serendipity in information behavior via research activities of an art historian. The preliminary findings reveal intricate connections between information encountering and searching that evolve over a long period of time.

KEYWORDS

serendipity, information encountering, information seeking, information behavior, humanities, art history

INTRODUCTION

Information seeking and needs of humanities scholars is a rich area of study for information behavior researchers. Case (1991) studied research processes of American historians in using library and specific collections materials. Duff and Johnson (2002) investigated how historians discover primary sources in archives. A study by Rose (2002) focused on the growing importance of information technologies in historians' research. Most recently, Martin and Quan-Hasse (2016, 2017) brought attention to the role of serendipity in the research practices of historians relying on both electronic and paper-based resources. The findings from these prior studies provide a descriptive, idiosyncratic view of intricate information activities. There is a need for methodological tools for comparative, systematic research of detailed aspects of humanities scholars' information behavior. In this case study we evaluate a methodological process for researching experiences of serendipity in discovering information, through application of Erdelez's (2004) model of information encountering.

STUDY FRAMEWORK

Information encountering (IE) is broadly defined as the experience of serendipity in a context of human information behavior. A typical IE episode, according to Erdelez (2004), includes several functional elements (see Figure 1). These elements indicate that some initial, *foreground activity* is interrupted (*Stopping*) with perception of encountered information (*Noticing*); follow by evaluation of encountered information (*Examining*), extraction or saving of information (*Capturing)* and finally reconnection with the activity that was interrupted (*Returning*). While experiences of serendipity in the work of humanities scholars have been documented both in prior research (see Duff and Johnson, 2002; Martin and Quan-Hasse 2016, 2017) and also in anecdotal evidence, little is known about how they experience the process of information encountering. The above IE model served as a framework for systematic collection of data to learn more about humanities scholars' practices.

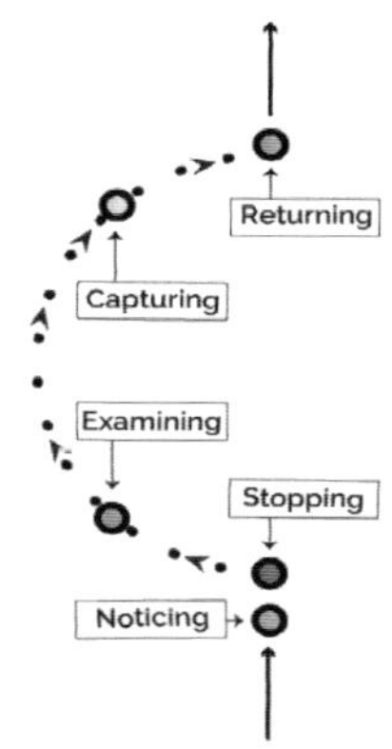

Figure 1. IE Model

METHOD

We drafted interview protocol questions focused on the components of IE model, consisting of 23 questions (for example questions see Table 1). In Spring 2018 with IRB approval we conducted case studies with humanities scholars in situ, including a senior medieval history scholar at a Midwestern university. In order to allow the respondent to frame the particular stages coherently we adopted the critical incident approach, taken during our in-depth interviews and particularly effectively and instructively with the aforementioned scholar. The respondent was asked to recall a situation when she stumbled upon something interesting for her research. Her research specialty formed a central aspect of the interview and allowed us to discuss specific personal practices and tools that aid in conducting a new scholarly project. The interview was recorded, transcribed, and collaboratively thematically analyzed by all members of the research team.

FINDINGS

Immediately, without much prompting the respondent recalled a situation from 20 years ago when she was conducting research on the perception of prayer in medieval literature and the related role of visual images. Unexpectedly, during the literature search process she discovered an excerpt from an unpublished document that provided a novel view of the topic of her interest. Following the initial recollection of the information encountering experience, the interview systematically proceeded with the questions from the interview guide addressing each of the components of the IE model. Table 1 provides illustrative examples of quotations from the interview and the coding themes.

IE element / question	**Quotes**	**Coding themes**
Noticing *What caught your attention?*	We have a lot of sort of scholarly material about that kind of thing that was aimed at people who were monks and nuns and priests and so forth... But this little bit that I stumbled upon then... was a text that was written for the queen.	Unusual content as a trigger
Stopping *Did you hesitate about diverting from original goal?*	Yeah, it ended up being a footnote, just an interesting footnote.	Diversion hesitation
Examining *How much time did you devote to it?*	Probably a few days because I found a bibliographic citation of that source. And I think I had to order the book either from inter library loan or from one of the consortium systems. Then I read the book in French so that took a little just a little bit more time than it would have normally.	Extended time devoted to examining
Capturing *What did you do with the find of interest?*	I probably wrote it down with a pencil on a yellow pad at some point and then it migrated into it into a footnote for something that I published and then the original note disappeared.	Pencil and pen recording
Returning *Did you return to the initial activity?*	...it became a footnote in a study that I was working on at the time, so I kind of turned back to my original project.	Use and return to foreground activity

Table 1. Data coding examples

While responding to the interview questions about Capturing, the respondent shared an unexpected experience of accidentally re-discovering the content encountered while reading a manuscript on another project, about 15 years later. This re-discovery resulted in a research exchange with a colleague from another university and the publishing of an essay.

CONCLUSION

In this case study we explored the possibility of using components of the IE model combined with the critical incident technique to solicit rich and structured analysis of the experience of serendipity while doing humanities research. The model-based interview, which evolved with ease and provided detailed views of the progression of specific phases of experiencing serendipity in a particular discipline; demonstrated how, in the case of our respondent, unexpected information may become dormant and reappear in the overall research process over an extended period of time (see Figure 2).

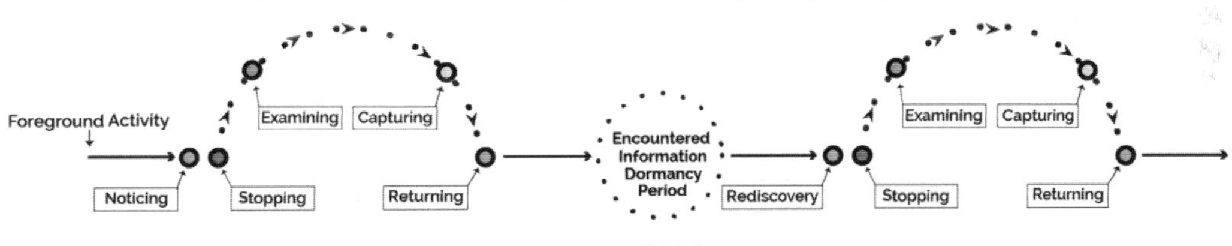

Figure 2. Expanded IE Model

Our finding, that such reincorporation occurs intentionally during the research process, provides novel insight into how information encountering is embedded into the information behavior of humanities scholars. It also directs future study on the temporal issues of information behavior, which as suggested by Savolainen (2006) deserve more systematic research. The case study demonstrated the potential of using IE model both as a methodological framework for systematic data collection on serendipity in information behavior and as a tool for gathering novel insights on information processes in humanities research.

REFERENCES

Case, D.O. (1991). The collection and use of information by some American historians: A study of motives and methods. *The Library Quarterly: Information, Community, Policy*, *61*(1), 61–82. doi:10.1086/602298

Duff, W.M., & Johnson, C.A. (2002). Accidentally found on purpose: Information-seeking behavior of historians in archives. *The Library Quarterly: Information, Community, Policy*, *72*(4), 472-496. doi:10.1086/lq.72.4.40039793

Erdelez, S. (2004). Investigation of information encountering in the controlled research environment. *Information Processing & Management*, *40*(6), 1013–1025. doi:10.1016/j.ipm.2004.02.002

Martin, K., & Quan-Haase, A. (2016). The role of agency in historians' experiences of serendipity in physical and digital information environments. *Journal of Documentation, 72*(6), 1008-1026. doi:10.1108/JD-11-2015-0144

Martin, K., & Quan-Haase, A. (2017). "A process of controlled serendipity": An exploratory study of historians' and digital historians' experiences of serendipity in digital environments. *Proceedings of the Association for Information Science and Technology*, *54*(1), 289–297. https://doi.org/10.1002/pra2.2017.14505401032

Rose, T. (2002). Technology's impact on the information-seeking behavior of art historians. *Art Documentation: Journal of the Art Libraries Society of North America, 21*(2), 35-42. doi:10.1086/adx.21.2.27949206

Savolainen, R. (2006). Time as a context of information seeking. *Library & Information Science Research*, *28*(1), 110–127. doi:10.1016/j.lisr.2005.11.001

Building a Future Through STEM Learning for Children in Underserved Communities

Dr. Kathleen Campana
Kent State University, USA. kcampan2@kent.edu

Dr. Michelle H. Martin
University of Washington, USA. mhmarti@uw.edu

J. Elizabeth Mills
University of Washington, USA. jemills1@uw.edu

ABSTRACT

Public libraries offer a variety of STEM learning opportunities for children and youth to allow them to experience emerging technologies in a hands-on, play-based manner. Opportunities like these are important for all children as research has identified the importance of STEM learning in informal learning environments (Bell, Lewenstein, Shouse & Feder, 2009). However, a variety of barriers may prevent many children in underserved communities from taking advantage of the STEM opportunities that public libraries offer. Because of this, some libraries are taking their programs and services out to community locations to reach these children. This poster highlights findings from Project LOCAL, an IMLS-funded planning grant, around STEM learning opportunities offered by libraries out in community locations for children in underserved communities.

KEYWORDS

STEM learning, technology, outreach, children and youth, libraries

INTRODUCTION

Over the past several years, our society has begun to recognize the importance of STEM learning for children and youth. In addition, many have realized that the responsibility for STEM learning cannot solely be placed on the school systems. Children need to be exposed to STEM learning in a variety of environments (NSTA, 2012). One of the benefits of STEM learning in informal learning environments is the capability to provide hands-on experiences with a variety of STEM concepts and technologies in a fun, play-based manner (Bell et al., 2009). Informal learning environments allow children to experiment with concepts and try out new skills without the pressure of formal academic standards. STEM learning in informal learning environments is also important because it can provide opportunities for children in underserved communities to experience STEM concepts and technologies that they might not have access to otherwise (Migus, n.d.).

Public libraries are often considered an important informal learning environment for children and their families. They can offer a variety of free STEM learning opportunities for children (Center for Interactive Learning, 2016), but many children from underserved communities may not be able to take advantage of these opportunities because of a variety of barriers. To try and overcome these barriers, some libraries are offering programs out in community locations to reach and serve children in underserved communities (Campana, Mills, & Martin, 2018). Project LOCAL (Library Outreach as a Community Anchor in Learning), an Institute of Museum and Library Services National Leadership Planning Grant, endeavored to understand on a broader scale how libraries are reaching and serving children and families in underserved communities by offering programs and services out in the community.

THE STUDY

The goal of Project LOCAL was to understand how libraries are going outside of their walls and into community locations to offer programs and services to children and families in underserved communities, who do not come into the library. To understand this, the study used a tripartite methodology, consisting of focus groups, virtual interviews, and a national survey. The research was guided by three research questions:

Research Question 1 (RQ1): How, if at all, are libraries working to understand the needs of children and families in underserved communities who do not come into and utilize the library?

Research Question 2 (RQ2): What are libraries offering in terms of programs and services that take place outside of library walls to reach children and families in underserved communities who do not come into and utilize the library?

Research Question 3 (RQ3): What do libraries perceive as challenges or obstacles to developing and delivering programs/services outside of library walls for children and families in underserved communities who do not come into and utilize the library?

The first phase of the study included three focus groups held at the ALA Annual Conference in June 2017. Over the three focus groups there were a total of sixteen participants, representing a variety of roles within public libraries, such as children's librarian, head of children's services, and director. The sixteen participants represented ten different states.

The second phase of the study consisted of virtual interviews. These interviews were completed over a two-week period at the beginning of November 2017. Since many small- and medium-sized libraries do not have the funds to send staff to the ALA Annual Conference, the researchers made efforts to include a higher number of small and medium libraries in the interviews. Twenty-one library staff participated in the virtual interviews. Similar to the focus groups, they represented a variety of roles in the public library, including outreach librarian, children's librarian, and director. The participants represented twelve different states.

The findings reported here represent a subset of the findings that surfaced under research question 2 and emerged during the focus group and interview phases of the research. The survey phase has just been completed, so the data has not yet been analyzed. However, the data from the survey is expected to expand upon the findings reported here.

RESULTS

Through the focus groups and interviews, the research uncovered that libraries are going outside of their walls, into community locations, to reach and serve children in underserved communities. The data revealed that one way libraries are doing this is by taking STEM programming to these children and families to meet them where they are and increase their access to different types of technology as well as a variety of other STEM concepts andskills.

The focus group and interview participants shared thirteen different STEM learning opportunities that they are taking out of the library to reach children in underserved communities. The thirteen programs were offered to a variety of children and teens from ages 0-18, but a majority focused on school-age children. The programs offered for children ages 0-5 mostly included a story component as well as activities that focused on STEM concepts--block play and maker activities--and emerging technologies. Moreover, the programs worked to provide developmentally appropriate introductions to STEM while also focusing on the importance of play. The programs offered for school-age children focused more heavily on providing access to and experience with emerging technologies, such as Solar Legos, Connect Kits, Squishy Circuits, Little Bits, and Cubelets. These programs provided hands-on experience with these technologies as well as with other STEM and maker activities.

Some of these STEM learning opportunities were offered to the broader community while the others were offered for specific groups within the broader community, including children and families experiencing poverty, children and families for whom English is a second language, children with special needs, and children and families with low literacy. To reach these children, the libraries often worked with partners, such as barbershops, Boys and Girls Clubs, schools, WIC centers, and Summer Meals Program/USDA. The programs frequently occurred at the partner location, but occasionally they took place at a third space, such as parks, daycares, and affordable housing complexes.

CONCLUSION

In our technology-driven society, opportunities and experiences with STEM learning and emerging technologies are important for all children since these types of knowledge and skills will provide a foundation for success in their future. By taking STEM learning opportunities outside of the library to children in underserved communities, libraries can overcome some of the barriers that these children and their families face and provide access and rich learning experiences with emerging technology and STEM concepts through play-based and hands-on methods. In doing this work, libraries are helping to build a future through STEM learning for children in underserved communities.

ACKNOWLEDGEMENTS

This project was made possible in part by the Institute of Museum and Library Services. We would also like to thank the participating librarians for sharing their time, knowledge, and expertise.

REFERENCES

Bell, P., Lewenstein, B., Shouse, A., & Feder, M. (2009). Learning Sicence in Informal Environments: People, Places, and Pursuits. Retrieved from: http://www.washingtonstem.org/stem/media/media/resources/learning-science-in-informal- environments-people-places-and-pursuits.pdf?ext=.pdf

Campana, K., Mills, J.E., Martin, M. (2018). ECRR Outside of the Library: Providing Meaningful Family-Focused Outreach.

Children & Libraries: The Journal of The Association for Library Service to Children, 16(2), 35-36.

Center for Interactive Learning. (2016). STEM Equity in Informal Learning Settings: The Role of Libraries. Retrieved from: http://www.nc4il.org/images/papers/STEM%20Equity%20in%20Informal%20Learning%20Settings_FINAL.PDF

Migus, L. (n.d.) Broadening Access to STEM Learning through Out-of-School Learning Environments. Committee on Suc- cessful Out-of-

School STEM Learning. Retrieved from: https://sites.nationalacademies.org/cs/groups/dbassesite/documents/webpage/dbasse_089995.pdf

National Science Teachers Association (NSTA). (2012). NSTA Position Statement: Learning Science in Informal Environ- ments. Retrieved from: http://static.nsta.org/pdfs/PositionStatement_Informal.pdf

Relevance Criteria Dynamics: A Study of Online News Selection on SERPs

Yung-Sheng Chang
School of Information, University of Texas at Austin, USA.
yscchang@utexas.edu

Jacek Gwizdka
School of Information, University of Texas at Austin, USA.
asist2018@gwizdka.com

ABSTRACT

A lab-based experiment was conducted to understand the multidimensional and dynamic changes in the use of relevance criteria on online news on search engine result pages (SERPs). Data from retrospective think-aloud (RTA) was first analyzed to investigate the criteria used when participants selected a search result on SERPs. The number and frequency of criteria used for relevance judgments were calculated. The criteria used on subsequent SERPs visits and on results at different ranks on SERPs were then analyzed to understand the differences in relevance criteria that were applied. The results showed that among the top six identified criteria, *specific source* and *topicality* were the two most often used relevance criteria. 59.6% of the times partic- ipants used a single criterion to make relevance judgment. Considering how criteria changed on subsequent visits to SERPs and on search results at different ranks, *specific source* was the most often used criterion initially but was then surpassed by *topicality* on subsequent visits to SERPs and on results at lower ranks. This could be explained by users using *specific source* as the primary cue in information evaluation and by users' expectation that Google's search engine algorithm shows more relevant information on the first SERP and at the top result ranks.

KEYWORDS

Relevance, Relevance criteria, Web search, SERP.

INTRODUCTION

With the current ubiquitous access to internet, users primarily access news online. The internet changed the ways in which people seek news. People used to receive news passively from radio, television, or newspapers. Access to news online lets news readers have the autonomy to actively select news. When news readers search news online, SERPs are the first stage of online news selection and evaluation. Hence it is vital to understand how people judge the relevance of online news on SERPs.

Relevance is a vital but complex concept that aids an information retrieval system to retrieve relevant information. Given its complexity, previous studies (Borlund, 2003; Saracevic, 1996; Schamber, Eisenberg, & Nilan, 1990) have defined relevance as having two characteristics: multidimensionality and dynamics. Relevance multidimensionality refers to the many criteria used in relevance assessment by different users, while relevance dynamics refers to the perception of relevance changes over time for the same users (Borlund, 2003). In past studies, Zhang, Zhang, Lease, and Gwizdka (2014) applied crowdsourcing and verified five relevance factors: reliability, topicality, scope, novelty, and understandability. Sundar (1999) focused on online news information evaluation and identified four criteria: credibility, liking, quality, and representativeness. Taylor, Zhang, and Amadio (2009) examined dynamic changes in relevance judgment within four information search processes (learning, focusing, browsing, and extracting) and found a number of common criteria used. Although there have been studies focusing on the multidimensional or dynamic aspects of relevance, there is lack of studies focusing on how news readers apply relevance criteria in their assessment of online news and how it changes with subsequent visits to SERPs. To bridge this literature gap, we conducted a lab-based experiment in which RTA was employed to elicit the relevance criteria used by participants and how the use of relevance criteria changed on subsequent SERPs and on results displayed at different ranks on SERPs.

METHOD

40 native English speakers with no vision correction participated in the study (26 females). Only participants who rated topic familiarity below medium on a five-point Likert scale were recruited. Since news information is time sensitive, we created naturalistic search scenarios related to recent news. When participants arrived in the lab, they read the experiment instructions, signed the consent form, and filled in demographic information. The experiment presentation was controlled by iMotions software (https://imotions.com/). Tobii TX-300 eye-tracker captured participants' eye-movement. Participants first performed a training task that guided them through the procedure. Then they conducted four assigned search tasks (order was randomized) on following topics: Zika virus, Brexit, 2016 Summer Olympics, and Bob Dylan Nobel Prize award. Each search task started with a display of task scenario and two questions to be answered by searching for information. Next, participants started searches by using Google search engine. While performing search tasks, participants were asked to save and annotate webpages they thought were relevant. The annotations were answers responding to the questions. Lastly, a gaze-cued RTA was conducted by replaying search sessions recorded from iMotions and participants were asked to explain their relevance judgments and search behaviors. Replay of participants' own eyes gaze helped them recall where they looked at on SERPs. The RTA sessions were open coded. Camtasia software was used to record the RTA sessions. The experiment took 1.5 to 2 hours to complete.

RESULTS

The frequency and percentage of relevance criteria used were first calculated. Low frequency criteria (< 0.05%) were excluded. This left six criteria for further analysis: *specific source* (28%), *topicality* (27.8%), *result rank* (9.4%), *credibility* (6%), *familiarity* (4.9%), and *recency* (4.3%). For clarification, *specific source* means the origin of the news information, for example, BBC. *Specificity*, which is a low frequency code, means how focused was the information in relation to the search topic. We analyzed participants' use of single and mul- tiple criteria when they selected a result judged by them as relevant on SERP (Table 1). The changes in the use of relevance criteria on subsequent SERP visits and per result rank on SERPs are shown in Figure 1.

Single Criterion			Multiple Criteria			
			Two		Three	
	#	%	#	%	#	%
Source	122	31.3	87	41.4	18	33.3
Topicality	175	44.9	42	20.0	9	16.7
Recency	23	5.9	9	4.3	3	5.6
Familiarity	10	2.6	22	10.5	8	14.8
Credibility	10	2.6	26	12.4	13	24.1
Rank	50	12.8	24	11.4	3	5.6
Total	390	-	210	-	54	-

Table 1. Frequency of single and multiple-criteria used in assessment of relevant results displayed on SERPs

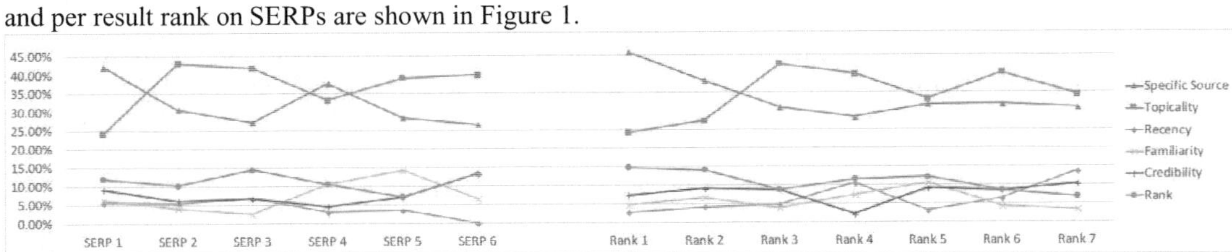

Figure 1. Percentage of criteria used on subsequent SERP visits (left) and per result rank on SERPs (right).

DISCUSSION

We identified six relevance criteria, with *specific source* and *topicality* being the two most used criteria. Participants often used a single criterion to make relevance judgments (59.6%). The use of *topicality* decreased as the number of criteria used increased. *Specific source* remained above 30% regardless of the number of criteria used. Interestingly, the emphasis on *credibility* increased as more criteria were used. These results differ from Sundar's study (1999) due to the differences in information items on which relevance is assessed. Sundar (1999) investigated online news story itself while we focused on online news information on SERPs. The use of relevance criteria in relation to the order of SERP visits and result rank on SERPs showed the highest use of *specific source* followed by *topicality* on the first visited SERPs in search session and on the top ranked results on SERPs. However, after the first visit to SERPs and on the lower result ranks, the use of *topicality* increased and surpassed the use of *specific source*. This could be explained by the website source being the primary cue in user's online information evaluation (Greer, 2003), leading participants to focus on *specific sources* in the early stages of the search process. The relationship between relevance criteria use and the result rank may be explained by searchers' expectations of how well Google's search engine works – it is expected to display results which are more relevant on the first SERP page and at higher ranks. Our results are similar to White's study (2013), showing that users tend to select the top ranked results. In the future, we plan to gain more insights into the relevance judgment process by investigating how many relevant pages were found and how they are distributed on different SERPs and ranks. Furthermore, we will combine and analyze the use of criteria with eye fixation data.

REFERENCES

Borlund, P. (2003). The concept of relevance in IR. JASIST, 54(10), 913-925.

Greer, J. D. (2003). Evaluating the credibility of online information: A test of source and advertising influence. Mass Communication and Society, 6(1), 11-28.

Saracevic, T. (1996). Relevance reconsidered. Proceedings of CoLIS'1996.

Schamber, L., Eisenberg, M. B., & Nilan, M. S. (1990). A re-examination of relevance: toward a dynamic, situational definition*. Information processing & management, 26(6), 755-776.

Sundar, S. S. (1999). Exploring receivers' criteria for perception of print and online news. Journalism & Mass Communication Quarterly, 76(2), 373-386.

Taylor, A., Zhang, X., & Amadio, W. J. (2009). Examination of relevance criteria choices and the information search process. Journal of Documentation, 65(5), 719-744.

White, R. (2013). Beliefs and biases in web search. Paper presented at the Proceedings of the 36th international ACM SIGIR conference on Research and development in information retrieval.

Zhang, Y., Zhang, J., Lease, M., & Gwizdka, J. (2014). Multidimensional relevance modeling via psychometrics and crowdsourcing. Paper presented at the Proceedings of the 37th international ACM SIGIR conference on Research & development in information retrieval.

Voice of Children: Children in the Restrictive Mediation of Smartphone Use

Wenting Cheng
Peking University, China. chengwenting@pku.edu.cn

Jun Wang
Peking University, China. junwang@pku.edu.cn

Mingyi Yang
Peking University, China. yangmingyi@pku.edu.cn

ABSTRACT

Parents set rules and regulations about children's media use, which is called restrictive mediation. This study aims to understand how children describe their behaviors in and attitudes to restrictive mediation of smartphone use in the family context. We conducted a narrative inquiry with 47 Chinese children, ages 7 to 12. Then we used semi-structured coding method on the text transcribed from three types of collected data, including painting, written text and recording of the narrative. The study found two roles of children in the restrictive mediation process: children being monitored and children as the intervener. When the children are monitored by their parents, sometimes they disagree with their parental mediation when their parents' behaviors are also questionable. Parents should set an example for their kids and discipline themselves' media use first. On the other hand, children could also be the intervener of their parental media use. Although the intervention from children is less effective than the parental mediation, children do play some role in contributing to cultivating good family media use habits.

KEYWORDS

Children, parental mediation, restrictive mediation, smartphone.

INTRODUCTION

Young children have increasing access to interactive media at home. The potential effects of children's heavy media use have drawn parental attention. The parental mediation is a means that parents take an active role in managing and regulating their children's experiences with media (Clark, 2011). Valkenburg et al. (1999) developed a scale to measure three different strategies of mediation: active mediation, restrictive mediation, and co-use. Here we focus on the restrictive mediation which means setting rules and regulations for children's media use, covering technical safety guidance and supervision (Nikken & Jansz, 2014). In contrast to prior research on restrictive mediation which paid more attention to children's media habit and the strategies of parental mediation in different media, this research aims to understand young children's attitudes to restrictive mediation and their contribution to cultivating good family media use habits. Our research questions are: 1) how children describe restrictive mediation behaviors of smartphones use in family context; 2) their attitudes towards these mediation behaviors.

METHODOLOGY

We used the narrative inquiry in child groups to collect data. Since the restrictive mediation sometimes occur along with parent-child conflicts (Beyens & Beullens, 2017), group discussion is preferred as it can make children feel more relaxed than the individual interview (Fargas-Malet et al., 2010). In our study, children were divided into small groups and asked to complete 3 tasks in 1 hour: 1) paint a restrictive mediation story of family smartphone use after group discussion; 2) write their thoughts during and after the mediation; 3) narrate the story to the researchers. Unlike previous studies, we didn't assume that only parents could be the mediators.

The narrative inquiry was conducted in August 2017 in Hangzhou and Shanghai respectively, the cities in eastern China. This study recruits 47 young children, 23 boys and 24 girls, aged 7-12 years old (Mean=9.5, SD=1.69). The children were allowed to choose their own group members, and 18 groups were formed with 2-4 members per group. Three types of data were collected from the narrative inquiry, namely painting, written text and recording of narratives. All of them were transcribed into text afterwards. These transcripts were semi-structured coded in terms of character (i.e. parent and child), interaction behavior and dialog between characters, location, time, media content, the reason and result of mediation, as well as the children's attitudes of the mediation process and result.

RESULTS

Children being monitored

In most cases, children agree with the limit and control of media use set by their parents. A common situation triggering the parental mediation is when the children delay having meals or taking showers. Children would normally argue against the mediation first. But the reason they argued is just "I wanna play more" (e.g., Group17, 2 boys, age_{mean}=10), children would show a positive attitude to the parental mediation after the argument and accept the parents' advice. And, it is highly likely that the children will abide by the media use rules in the future.

However, some children would question the parental mediation when they found inconsistency such as disagreement between mother and father, or between parents' words and conducts. Parental consistency refers to the similarity with which a child is treated by one or both parents in various situations (Gentile & Walsh, 2002). The children complained about the parental inconsistency in mediation strategies across time and between father and mother, which were also observed by Gentile and Walsh (2002). For example, when the child character in Group5 (3 boys, age_{mean}=9) said "I have finished my homework, I wanna play with the phone", the father allowed, but the mother didn't allow as usual. The children got confused by the inconsistency. Children need clear rules of media use with high parental consistency.

Children also find inconsistency between parents' words and conducts. Parents set rules of media use for children, but they don't follow the rules by themselves. Such inconsistency undermines children's willingness to accept the parental mediation. The child character in Group12 (2 girls, age_{mean}=9) questioned "Dad has been playing with the smartphones for a long time, why can't I play with it more?" Children expect parents to be a good example in media use.

All the parental mediation is effective with just spoken language. However, children's feelings may be hurt if mediation gets prolonged. In the beginning, the tone of parents is peaceful, such as "Daughter, it's time for dinner" (Group18, 2 girls, age_{mean}=10). If that does not work, the parents would keep repeating the words, and eventually, the tone becomes aggressive, such as "Stop using the phones! If you don't want to eat, I will throw the meal away!" In this case, children would submit to parents' anger and the mediation is still effective, but it could harm the relationship between children and parents.

Children as intervener

Most of the studies on children media use are about the parental monitoring. In this study, we found that children can also be the intervener. And there are obvious differences between the parental mediation and the children's intervention, especially in terms of behaviors and emotions.

The parental restrictive mediation concerns about the amount of time, the media content and when children use media (Gentile & Walsh, 2002; Nikken & Jansz, 2014). The parents' concerns about the amount of time of their kids spent on screen are always related to the health aspect, such as risks of obesity and harm to sightedness. In this research, children intervened their parents' media use with regard to the amount of time and when parents use smartphones. The children often mimic their parents' mediation behaviors when they intervene parental media use. For example, the child character in Group6 (2 girls, age_{mean}=10.5) said to her father "Don't use the phones too much, you will become blind!" With regard to the time of media use, parents set rules for children, e.g. children cannot use mobile phones at mealtime and bedtime. When kids use the smartphone during these times for daily activities, the parents will come to interfere. The children would use the same rules to persuade their parents from using the smartphone and urge them to do daily activities. The child character in Group14 (3 boys, age_{mean}=9) said "Mom, you need to go to take a shower. Don't play the smartphone anymore."

Unlike parental mediation, the children's intervention is sometimes invalid. They also use words but couldn't be as aggressive as their parents. When oral intervention fails, the children would intervene with actions, e.g., take their parents' smartphone away to stop parents from using them. If the intervention fails, the children would feel sad, upset or even cry, but would not become angry like their parents would be.

CONCLUSION AND DISCUSSION

In this study, we analyse the children's role in the restrictive mediation process of smartphone use. On the one hand, when children are monitored by parents, parental consistency is important. To guide children to use technology positively, parents should not only keep the consistency between mediation strategies but also be a good example for children in smartphone use. On the other hand, children can also be the intervener of parental media use. Although the intervention from children is less effective than the parental mediation, children do play some role in contributing to cultivating good family media use habits.

Children's voice in smartphone use in family context should be valued. The results could help parents and researchers understand children's behaviors and how children view their parents' media use better. Our future research will further analysis the intervention from children side to enrich the understanding of the interaction between parents and children in media use.

REFERENCES

Beyens, I., & Beullens, K. (2017). Parent-child conflict about children's tablet use: The role of parental mediation. New Media & Society, 19(12), 2075-2093.

Clark, L. S. (2011). Parental mediation theory for the digital age. Communication theory, 21(4), 323-343.

Fargas-Malet, M., McSherry, D., Larkin, E., & Robinson, C. (2010). Research with children: Methodological issues and innovative techniques. Journal of early childhood research, 8(2), 175-192.

Gentile, D. A., & Walsh, D. A. (2002). A normative study of family media habits. Journal of Applied Developmental Psychology, 23(2), 157-178.

Nikken P, Jansz J. Developing scales to measure parental mediation of young children's internet use[J]. Learning, Media and technology, 2014, 39(2): 250-266.

Valkenburg, P. M., Krcmar, M., Peeters, A. L., & Marseille, N. M. (1999). Developing a scale to assess three styles of television mediation:"Instructive mediation","restrictive mediation," and "social co-viewing". Journal of broadcasting & electronic media, 43(1), 52-66.

Topical and Semantic Aspects of #MarchforOurLives

Miyoung Chong
University of North Texas, U.S.A.
miyoungchong@my.unt.edu

Brandon Moore
University of North Texas, U.S.A.
brandonmoore@my.unt.edu

ABSTRACT

One of the most intriguing developments in online activism is the emergence of hashtag activism. However, digital activism research has mainly investigated the networked and connective features. This study examined the topical and semantic aspects of the #MarchForOurLives network in Twitter through social media analytics. The extracted topics mainly supported the #MarchforOurLives movement, and the event's agenda and the digital movement presented positively skewed sentiment.

KEYWORDS

#MarchForOurLives, topic modeling, Twitter, LDA, sentiment analysis.

INTRODUCTION

One of the most developments improvements in online activism is the emergence of hashtag activism. Recently, the power of digital activism renewed attention through #MarchforOurLives created by the student leaders of the Marjory Stoneman Douglas High School in response to the mass shooting that occurred at their campus in Parkland, Florida, on February 14, 2018. Scholars on digital activism have mainly investigated the networked and connective features (Bennett & Segerberg, 2013) and argued about the question of institution and leadership (Gerbaudo, 2012). However, the major topics and semantic aspects of the interpersonal conversations in digital movements have not been fully examined yet. Therefore, the purpose of this study is to examine the topical and semantic aspects of the #MarchForOurLives network in Twitter by conducting social media analytics methods.

RELATED WORKS AND RESEARCH QUESTIONS

Social media users can directly diffuse information to the Internet, "bypassing the hierarchical and elite-controlled traditional news media" (cited by Luo 2014, p. 1291). The Internet users' agendas became powerful enough to influence the salience of specific political issues (Luo, 2014). On Twitter, information or opinions about news and incidents are predominantly organized and shared through hashtags with the # symbol. Hashtags are generated volunterily by users as a method to classify information and to accentuate topics. Yang (2016) defined hashtag activism as "discursive protest on social media united through a hashtagged word, phrase or sentence (p. 13). #MarchForOurLives was a protest movement that occurred both in the streets and online, which generated attention to the power of online activism in creating public discourse. Through a large amount of data collected from Twitter regarding the mass shooting event, this study examined the major topics discussed with the hashtag #MarchForOurLives and semantic characteristics of the conversations with #MarchforOurLives.

In order to accomplish the goals of the study, the following two research questions were explored.

- What are the topics created through the #MarchforOurLives movement?
- What is the sentiment in the #MarchforOurLives movement?

DATA COLLECTION AND METHOD

This study focuses on the Twitter conversations right after the March for Our Lives event held on March 24, 2018 in the U.S. because #MarchforOurLives was originally created to promote the rally that attracted enormous participation nationwide. A total of 245,591 #MarchforOurLives tweets were collected between March 24 and March 28 through Twitter API and were used for analysis in this study. Topic modeling was performed using gensim's Latent Dirichlet Analysis (LDA) module to train and fit a topic model (https://radimrehurek.com/gensim). After multiple iterations with refinements to parameters, including number of topics, stop words, synonyms, bigram extraction, and training iterations, a model composed of 50 topics was selected. Semantic analysis was performed using the NLTK TextBlob sentiment analyzer based on the pattern library. It calculates a polarity score between -1 (most negative) and 1 (most positive) where 0 denotes neutral sentiment.

FINDINGS

Table 1 presents the top 12 topics. The most prominent topic was about rage against Fox News media because of its coverage of the event. The tweet "Fox News covered the #MarchForOurLives by insulting students for not wanting to be gunned down at school. This is unhinged" was shared 10,441 times on in the dataset, which greatly contributed to make the topic as the most dominant topic based on LDA. Generally, the shooters of mass shooting have been negatively described as either a terrorist or a person with serious mental illness. Interestingly, the fourth and the ninth top ranked topics (topic id 24 and 28) presented sympathy to the shooter of the incident, Nicolas Cruz. For example, the following tweets were retweeted 8,744 times: "Emma Gonzalez admits to bullying School Shooter Nikolas Cruz And Says She Was Justified In Doing So. #ParklandShooting" and "I feel bad for this boy, if he were to fight back the school would label him a bully suspend him…" The fifth topic is criticizing the student protesters while accusing them of leaving their trash for someone else to clean up.

TopicId	Count	Terms
36	6719	0.096*"news" + 0.090*"fox" + 0.085*"fox_news" + 0.085*"student" + 0.084*"school" + 0.083*"covered" + 0.082*"wanting" + 0.081*"gunned" + 0.081*"insulting" + 0.081*"unhinged
22	5378	0.061*"picture" + 0.059*"art" + 0.056*"beautiful" + 0.056*"something" + 0.055*"take" + 0.055*"using" + 0.054*"msd" + 0.054*"form" + 0.052*"create" + 0.052*"photographer" + 0.
39	3105	0.053*"heard" + 0.051*"murdered" + 0.050*"bitch" + 0.046*"i'll" + 0.045*"alton" + 0.045*"sterling" + 0.045*"alton_sterling" + 0.043*"heard_murdered" + 0.043*"i'll_kill" + 0.043*"I
28	2777	0.048*"would" + 0.046*"fight" + 0.046*"back" + 0.040*"adult" + 0.038*"school" + 0.037*"bad" + 0.035*"boy" + 0.033*"bully" + 0.033*"feel" + 0.032*"label" + 0.032*"where's" + 0.0
10	2776	0.032*"protester" + 0.028*"girl" + 0.028*"little" + 0.028*"story" + 0.024*"make" + 0.024*"trash" + 0.024*"else" + 0.024*"someone" + 0.023*"hogg" + 0.022*"represent" + 0.021*"w
4	2601	0.103*"gun" + 0.089*"many" + 0.072*"let" + 0.068*"proud" + 0.049*"owner" + 0.049*"believe" + 0.047*"reform" + 0.045*"attended" + 0.038*"owner_believe" + 0.030*"fact" + 0.0:
37	2444	0.054*"thing" + 0.054*"never" + 0.034*"one" + 0.031*"youre" + 0.026*"past" + 0.025*"young" + 0.024*"#march" + 0.024*"group" + 0.023*"start" + 0.022*"revolution" + 0.021*"we
17	2439	0.048*"want" + 0.047*"movement" + 0.041*"check" + 0.030*"first" + 0.030*"million" + 0.029*"gun" + 0.027*"people" + 0.026*"school" + 0.025*"safety" + 0.021*"poor" + 0.020*"#r
24	2384	0.075*"say" + 0.053*"shooter" + 0.049*"school" + 0.048*"cruz" + 0.048*"admits" + 0.046*"emma" + 0.045*"bullying" + 0.045*"gonzalez" + 0.045*"emma_gonzalez" + 0.044*"nikola
27	2260	0.068*"american" + 0.039*"every" + 0.036*"still" + 0.036*"white" + 0.033*"black" + 0.028*"alive" + 0.028*"legacy" + 0.028*"grandfather" + 0.028*"spit" + 0.027*"lived" + 0.027*"gr
48	2135	0.070*"vote" + 0.066*"part" + 0.056*"change" + 0.056*"real" + 0.052*"register" + 0.049*"name" + 0.048*"next" + 0.048*"that's" + 0.045*"what's" + 0.045*"take" + 0.044*"educate'
13	2082	0.169*"school" + 0.163*"yet" + 0.027*"shooting" + 0.018*"dear" + 0.017*"answer" + 0.016*"money" + 0.015*"kid" + 0.014*"teen" + 0.014*"#ca22" + 0.014*"#deardevin_kid" + 0.01

Table 1. Extracted topics

225568	One thing weve learned this past month Youre never too young to start a revolution! #MarchForOurLives #March	mentalpau:	3411	RT @The_L	{'sentiment	negative	-0.0625
225569	Goodnight all. Thanks for another great day. Tomorrow, my friends and I take a little breathing time. Tuesday were	davepower	1807	RT @came:	{'sentiment	positive	0.270833
225570	Also, the crowd at the #MarchForOurLives was bigger than the crowd at Trump's inauguration.	tgeno	165	RT @Joyce'	{'sentiment	neutral	0
225571	It seemed that Trump didnt have an untweeted thought, yet since last weekend, not a word of three major events: the expulsi	cmfranchie	100	RT @MiaFa	{'sentiment	positive	0.03125
225572	Whoa. This is a problematic take, fam. 1st, video is of a fierce organizer who, like many black organizer	bfelice	51	RT @BreeN	{'sentiment	positive	0.166667
225573	Marco Rubio may not agree with #MarchForOurLives, but he definitely agrees with the $3.3 million he received from the NRA. htt	Bonnievee:	476	RT @jdice0	{'sentiment	neutral	0
225574	Incremental steps regarding sensible gun control will only cost more young people their lives.	NoFoxnews	0	@snowyeg	{'sentiment	positive	0.2
225575	Emma Gonzalez admits to bullying School Shooter Nikolas Cruz And Says She Was Justified In Doing So. #ParklandShootin	DJRobbyRo	6586	RT @Miller	{'sentiment	positive	0.4
225576	. The #MarchForOurLives was historic.	BreakandE	118	RT @hardb	{'sentiment	neutral	0
225577	Im a photographer from MSD. I take pictures for our yearbook. This is my art form, and I am using it to create something beau	mori_higas	7817	RT @hayko	{'sentiment	neutral	0
225578	For those outraged over police failure at Parklandwhere is your outrage over police failures for #StephonClark, Philando Cas	sarahandth	322	RT @Musli	{'sentiment	negative	-0.60833
225579	Lin-Manuel Miranda () on why he decided to come to #MarchForOurLives and record his collaboration with Ben Platt,	Moonorribl	1370	RT @niktaC	{'sentiment	neutral	0
225580	LITTLE HOGGS: #MarchForOurLives Student Protesters Leave Their Trash for Someone Else to Clean Up	johnyc46	0	LITTLE HOG	{'sentiment	positive	0.089583
225581	You dont get to throw away my rights simply because you dont feel you need the Second Amendment. Sorry. #marchforourlives	tprezzano	3131	RT @TomiL	{'sentiment	negative	-0.16667
225582	This is how a lot of school shootings happen! We dont have a gun problem, we have a Generation Brat, poor parenting pro	HomerWhi	729	RT @Shawt	{'sentiment	negative	-0.4
225583	Fox News covered the #MarchForOurLives by insulting students for not wanting to be gunned down at school. This is unhinged	Junerandol	10433	RT @nowth	{'sentiment	negative	-0.57778

Table 2. Examples of raw sentiment scores

The last column of Table 2 presents the raw sentiment scores that give an idea of how sentiment scores were generated.

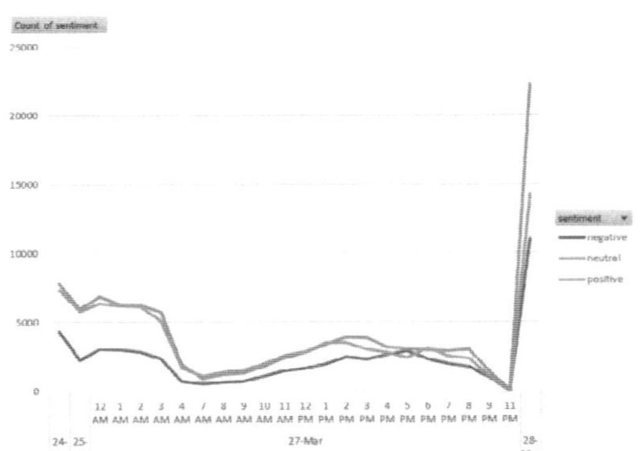

Figure 1. Sentiment line graph

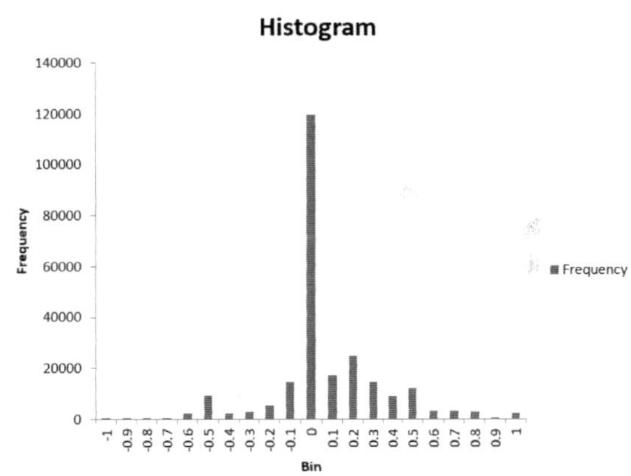

Figure 2. Histogram of sentiment scores

Figure 1 demonstrates positive (gray), negative (blue), and neutral (orange) sentiment of #MarchforOurLives. The semantic analysis of #MarchforOurLives presents mainly neutral with somewhat positive sentiment.

CONCLUSION

This study uncovered highly expressive evidence on hashtag activism with #MarchforOurLives. The extracted topics mainly supported the #MarchforOurLives movement and the event's agenda, including supporting gun control, protesting the NRA, and protecting students. Many topics provided positive perspectives to the student leaders but opposing views were also discovered against the movement. This confirms that the digital activists share and include hashtags for relevant issues.

REFERENCES

Bennett, W. L., & Segerberg, A. (2012). The logic of connective action: Digital media and the personalization of contentious politics. *Information, Communication & Society*, *15*(5), 739-768.

Chaffee, S. H., & Metzger, M. J. (2001). The end of mass communication?. *Masscommunication & society*, *4*(4), 365-379.

Gerbaudo, P. (2018). *Tweets and the streets: Social media and contemporary activism*. Pluto Press.

Luo, Y. (2014). The Internet and agenda setting in China: The influence of online public opinion on media coverage and government policy. *International Journal of Communication*, *8*, 24.

Yang, G. (2016). Narrative agency in hashtag activism: The case of# BlackLivesMatter. *Media and Communication*, *4*(4), 13.

Collaboration Makes Global Digital Libraries Sustainable and Ethical

Charlene Chou
University of Washington, *USA. cc83@uw.edu*

Steven R. Harris
University of Nevada, Reno, USA. stevenharris@unr.edu

ABSTRACT

With swiftly increasing projects of digital scholarship and digital libraries in recent years, many project leaders have shared concerns about the long-term financial sustainability of their platforms. The lack of a long term plan of system maintenance and funding will undermine the richness and functionalities of a digital library. Project leaders express their concerns and needs about effectively allocating financial resources and subject expertise. Without strong collaborations and communications between scholars and cultural institutions, we risk duplicating efforts for similar research projects or creating gaps between the knowledge and expertise in different communities. Shareable across multilingual or multicultural communities, open access digital resources have increasing impact. However, sharing at a large scale is not without issues and challenges. This poster will present a framework to keep global digital libraries sustainable and ethical. The author proposes a workflow to create and maintain digital libraries as ecosystems, and includes a flowchart for visual presentation. Collaboration, interoperability and sustainability are key to the vision of digital libraries able to communicate with each other. When a digital library infrastructure anchors digital scholarly methods in the workflows, digital libraries will truly become a scholarly cyberspace and provide added-value services to global users in future.

KEYWORDS

Digital libraries, sustainability, ethics, collaboration.

INTRODUCTION

With swiftly increasing projects of digital scholarship and digital libraries in recent years, many project leaders have shared concerns about the long-term financial sustainability of their platforms (initial funding usually supplied by a grant obtained by the scholar). For examples, the issues of cost and sustainability were discussed often and at length in the International Conference on the Cyberinfrastructure for Historical China Studies on March 14-16, 2018, Harvard China Center, Shanghai and the Digital Humanities Asia Conference at Stanford Humanities Center, April 27-28, 2018. Collier (2012) emphasized that "many digital library projects are started without much attention to the business issues." There has been more funding for digitization projects than projects on processing print collections, such as the CLIR (Council on Library and Information Resources) and the Andrew W. Mellon Foundation, etc. Each digital library or digital scholarship project requires tremendous amount of man power, time and expertise. After producing the deliverable of a digital project, sustaining the digital platform with continuing funding becomes a critical and challenging issue for many academic or cultural institutions.

The lack of a long term plan of system maintenance and funding will undermine the richness and functionalities of a digital library. Project leaders express their concerns and needs about effectively allocating financial resources and subject expertise. Without strong collaborations and communications between scholars and cultural institutions, we risk duplicating efforts for similar research projects or creating gaps between the knowledge and expertise in different communities. Sharing data does have the underlying complexities of sharing (Thomee, et al., 2016). To improve data sharing, metadata interoperability is the core of discussion. Tasovac (2017) points out the key challenges for digital humanities/library/infrastructure are "interoperability, communication and integration: aggregation and federation." Adding to his perspective, this study suggests that collaboration, such as sharing costs and expertise and providing standard-compliant metadata has a pivotal role for long-term maintenance of digital projects and platforms.

One of the most powerful features of open access digital resources is worldwide discoverability and accessibility. Shareable across multilingual or multicultural communities, open access digital resources have increasing impact. However, sharing at a large scale is not without issues and challenges such as sharing contents across languages and cultures. It is evidently challenging to transfer digital contents without losing contexts and causing misinterpretations. In recent years, fake news, racism, privacy and network security have raised serious concerns about maintaining digital resources that are ethical, authentic, accurate and consistent. Star & Ruthleder (1996) pinpointed complex challenges in creating a large-scale infrastructural tool with critical issues such as communication, transparency and power. These are still crucial for the emergence of the global cyberspace.

GLOBAL DIGITAL LIBRARY INFRASTRUCTURE

This poster will present a framework to keep global digital libraries sustainable and ethical, and focus on how to expand the digital models of LAM (libraries, archives and museums) with the developments of digital scholarship. The author proposes a workflow to create and maintain digital libraries as ecosystems, and includes a flowchart for visual presentation. Each digital project has complex operations and involves multiple stakeholders. Collaboration is the key to address the complexity and facilitate communications for effective team work and coherent workflow. Further, to allocate limited resources effectively, collaboration is necessary to reduce duplicate efforts. It serves as a powerful and critical underlying principle to share and leverage financial resources and subject expertise across institutions for the formation of global digital libraries in the long run.

The key assumption of collaboration is sharing authoritative, consistent and ethical contents in multiple languages when applicable. Successful collaboration heavily relies on interoperability, which requires metadata to be compliant with international standards for international data sharing. Some examples include ISO (International Organization for Standardization), ISSN (International Identifier for Serials), IFLA (International Federation of Library Associations and Institutions and IIIF (International Image Interoperability Framework) and RDA (Resource Description & Access). Because of sharing the same principles of UBC (universal bibliographic control) and the roles of library authority data for the linked open data, IFLA's initiative on VIAF (Virtual International Authority File) and ISNI (International Standard Name Identifier) has transformed ways of trustfully consolidating identities. VIAF presents a great model, in which each country is responsible for the authority files of its national language(s). Language files created and maintained by individual countries are linked and mapped across countries. Because each authority record goes through a review process for approval and has ongoing maintenance such as LCGFT (Library of Congress Genre/Form Terms), the authority file plays a pivotal role not only for the authentication of semantic relationships but also for establishing and applying ethical and equitable controlled vocabularies. For the global use of RDA, RDA Registry includes RDA terms in multiple languages. Each language has URI for mapping and linking in the linked open data environment. In addition to national libraries, consortium or language groups have contributed to building up multilingual terminologies in the RDA Registry. The poster will elaborate on a use case for Chinese, Japanese and Korean languages to explain why CEAL (Council on East Asian Libraries) tackled multilingual challenges and how CEAL supports enriching multilingual terms in the RDA Registry.

The workflow of maintaining digital infrastructure begins with a digital platform to collect data from scholars, libraries and museums, or consortiums. This platform can accept raw data, scanned texts, machine-computable data or various metadata. Most importantly, this digital platform is capable of providing user services to standardize, validate and parse texts or metadata and fixing OCR results for all languages. When texts or data are authenticated in the backend, the user interface at the frontend provides user services and allows data to be downloaded or shared. Enormous online information hubs have connected people to diverse digital resources or communities. Some great examples include IFLA, DARIAH (Digital Research Infrastructure for the Arts and Humanities) and CLARIN (European Research Infrastructure for Language Resources and Technology). Through linking the digital platform with international frameworks, or regional or international information hubs, users can conduct more thorough searches for accurate information in multiple languages and cultures. Most importantly, this digital platform functions as a digital library or digital-scholarship-friendly platform with added-value and enriched workflow. It serves as a scholarly cyberspace for sharing innovative ideas and research projects.

CONCLUSION

As the IFLA/UNESCO Manifesto for Digital Libraries (2014) explicitly states, "interoperability and sustainability are key to the vision of digital libraries able to communicate with each other. Digital libraries that conform to commonly-agreed open standards and protocols improve world-wide knowledge dissemination and access." With a global vision, it is necessary to create and promote the use of more international standards to improve interoperability. Each digital platform or digital library should not be a silo or closed system. Instead, each digital platform connects to related resources in linked open data, and contributes to the realization of the semantic web. With the rapid development of DH (digital humanities) and digital scholarship, more digital scholars are aspiring for more DH-friendly libraries. Tasovac (2017) articulated the significance of "anchoring digital scholarly methods in digital library workflows—developing tools and services for different types of scholarly primitives in modular, dynamic, research-driven digital collections." In the near future, we may envision a digital library providing very dynamic services to scholars or users with "machine-readable and machine-computable texts or data and layers of automatic and semi-automatic, structured, linguistic and semantic annotations with crowdsourced corrections." With the goals above achieved, digital libraries will truly become a scholarly cyberspace and provide added-value services to global users.

REFERENCES

Collier, M. (2012). Sustainability of digital libraries: economic issues and business planning. London: Henry Stewart Talks.

IFLA/UNESCO Manifesto for Digital Libraries (2014).

Star, S. L., & Ruhleder, K. (1996). Steps Toward an Ecology of Infrastructure: Design and Access for Large Information Spaces. *Information Systems Research, 7(1), 111–134.*

Tasovac, T. Libraries in the age of digital infrastructures (and catastrophes), *IFLA Satellite Meeting 2017.*

Thomee, B., et al. (2016). YFCC100M: The New Data in Multimedia Research. *Communication of the ACM, 59(2), 64-73.*

Augmented and Virtual Reality Technologies: Bridging Practice and Research in the Academic Library

Patrick Tod Colegrove
University of Nevada, Reno, USA. pcolegrove@unr.edu

ABSTRACT

This paper offers practical insights and lessons learned from over five years of direct experience provisioning and supporting augmented and virtual reality equipment as lendable technology. A pragmatic exploration of one academic library's experience in the development, sustainability, and evolution of augmented and virtual reality technology and associated services. Analyzed and critiqued in comparison to traditional library materials and services, the novel library collection is bridging the gap between learning, research, and practice. Library support is proving to be critical path: from the initial development of the lending technology collections, through the collaborative development of mixed reality equipment, spaces, and software. Specific details associated with the library's current state of practice are shared, including specifics as to working systems for both the HTC Vive and Oculus Rift equipment on dedicated mobile workstations available throughout the library. Collaborations with departments including Computer Science & Engineering, as well as the School of Journalism, have proven to be a natural outcome of the library's support: joint effort resulting in the development of numerous dedicated mobile augmented and virtual reality software development stations throughout the library, and resultant exhibit development.

KEYWORDS

virtual reality, augmented reality, digital literacy, information visualization, emerging technology

INTRODUCTION

Augmented and virtual reality technologies are increasingly prevalent across society, offering new opportunities for service development and media support by libraries. This paper presents a case study of practices, implementation, and support of augmented and virtual reality technologies (AR/VR) as part of the lending technology collections of the DeLaMare Science & Engineering Library at the University of Nevada, Reno. The University is a Land Grant institution, a public state university and PhD-granting institution of Carnegie class R2: Doctoral Universities – Higher Research Activity. The DeLaMare Library is a branch library tasked with providing primary library support for the physical sciences and engineering on campus. A first-mover in the makerspaces in libraries movement, and early adopter of implementing lending technology collections, the library has included AR/VR technologies as part of its collections for over five years.

With the rapidly changing landscape of virtual and augmented reality technologies, and continued high cost of entry, particularly when the cost of supporting computer hardware is taken into consideration, the author reasoned there might be demand among the library's membership for access to current technology available for check-out from the library. Adoption of technology in any area where it is rapidly evolving includes significant risk of mistake, from the selection of appropriate equipment to the parallel development of supporting library services. In this paper, early progress toward best practices learned by trial-and error are shared, along with practical details of the library's support and insights gleaned from direct experience provisioning the service.

METHODS, MATERIALS, PROCEDURES AND EQUIPMENT USED

Building on the success of others' successful development of laptop and other lending technology collections, Radniecki & Colegrove (2017) detail the background of the development of the lending technology collection at DeLaMare Library, and its impact on the library's revitalization. The technologies selected for inclusion in the technology pool were chosen as the result of ongoing environmental scans of the technology landscape and in-depth engagement the communities supported by the library. With the sure knowledge that any technology chosen for inclusion in the collection would be quickly outmoded and subject to being quickly replaced by iterative versions and selections, the library committed to the longitudinal development and support of the collection.

The library's earliest investment in AR/VR as lending technology was as an early-adopter of the first release of the Oculus Rift Development Kit 1 in late 2012. Subsequent releases purchased/provisioned included the second edition of the development kit, followed by the current offering of the Oculus Rift 3. Additional technologies added included a Google Glass partnership in late 2013, numerous playback headsets including the Zeiss VR/One that leverage the availability of Google Cardboard functionality, ubiquity of high-quality cellphones, and the mid-2016 release of the HTC Vive. Ancillary supporting equipment was added starting in late 2015 to include support for the capture and production of VR and 360-video content: from an early,

3D-printed/open sourced, frame that housed six GoPro Hero cameras to the more professional GoPro Omni camera; more recent additions have evolved through both the ultra-portable Nikon Keymission and the more recent Garmin/Virb 360 camera.

Particular methods of selection of appropriate technologies and materials, including an overview of generalized procedures for cataloging, checkout, and repair of the equipment are shared. In addition, preliminary usage numbers and cost per use metrics, anecdotal stories of failure and success can help inform others considering offering a similar level of support. Contributions to the development of library assets, including the creation of custom software and development workstations, are shared online and illustrated by means of a standalone VR headset during the visual presentation.

FINDINGS

From its earliest inclusion in the lending collections of the library, the speculated demand among the library's membership for access to current AR/VR technology proved substantial. Early hopes were quickly realized, with heavy usage driving a cost/use significantly below that of a typical item in the overall collections of the library; a critical consideration, given significant entry costs and the non-traditional nature of emerging technology as part of the lending collection of the academic library. Other practical insights and details shared include:

- Staff, equipment, and software are detailed, including associated workflows developed to ensure attention to replacement and repair of equipment upon return to the library. Three years of circulation data for each type of equipment and relative cost per use are shared, along with detail of the minimal replacement and repair costs incurred.
- Detail associated with the cataloging and circulation records associated with each of the pieces of equipment provisioned as lendable technology, including examples detailing example MARC records associated
- Pragmatic insights include alternatives for replacement of the foam gaskets typically installed on AR/VR equipment as a light shield, to enable quick and thorough sanitation of equipment upon return; the need for built-in headphones, rather than a reliance on personal earbuds for audio content; the utility of color-coded skins to differentiate between duplicate sets in the collection; workarounds for infrared interference with some AR/VR technology in brightly sunlit environments; the need for overhead cable management and general safety concerns for permanent installations.
- Successful outcomes include closer engagement and collaboration with computer science and engineering faculty, including the development of multiple courses in VR software development, and the implementation and development of AR/VR development workstations distributed on each floor of the library.
- Ongoing challenges include: the continued pace of evolution of the AR/VR technology field, with early obsolescence a norm; a continued need for potent – and expensive – computer hardware to support existing playback models; workarounds needed to address licensing and IT departmental constraints and security concerns.

DISCUSSION AND CONCLUSIONS

The results of the library's extended pilot provisioning AR/VR technology as part of a lending technology collection demonstrate that demand for access to the technology at the University level is both real and substantial. Practitioner details shared in this paper further show that with relatively minimal modification, consumer grade AR/VR technology available off-the-shelf can be successfully incorporated into lending technology collections. Appropriate staff onboarding and training, combined with similarly minimal modification of traditional library cataloging workflow, enables relatively seamless integration into the circulating collections of an academic library. Practitioner details shared will enable others contemplating similar development to avoid potential missteps in implementation, and more quickly scale lending collections to meet demonstrated need, building engagement and opportunity for collaborations with supported departments.

PRESENTATION OF THE WORK

This paper, and supporting materials, will be presented as a visual presentation at the meeting. Supporting 360-video content will be viewable to attendees through Vimeo and by means of a standalone VR viewer headset.

REFERENCES

Radniecki, T. & Colegrove, T. (2017). Going Beyond Books: Lendable Technology, Interdisciplinary Innovation, and the Revitalization of the Academic Library. In Robison, M., & Shedd, L. (Eds.), *Audio Recorders to Zucchini Seeds: Building a library of things* (pp. 153-169). Santa Barbara, CA: ABC-CLIO.

Hall, S. & Takahashi, R. (2017). Augmented and virtual reality: the promise and peril of immersive technologies. World Economic Forum https://www.weforum.org/agenda/2017/09/augmented-and-virtual-reality-will-change-how-we-create-and-consume-and-bring-new-risks/

Craig, E. & Georgieva, M. (2017). A New World: VR and AR Tech Developments. EDUCAUSE Review [blog post]. Retrieved from https://er.educause.edu/blogs/2017/7/a-new-world-vr-and-ar-tech-developments

Radical Inclusion: Immersive 360-degree Video Capture, Dissemination, and Use of Emerging Technology in Support of Traditional Archival Roles at a University Library

Patrick Tod Colegrove
University of Nevada, Reno, USA. pcolegrove@unr.edu

Michael Mikel
Burning Man Project, USA. M2@burningman.org

ABSTRACT

This paper presents preliminary findings of a work-in-progress, a project operating in the overlap of virtual reality technology and the traditional role of libraries, archives, and museums in the preservation of archives, records, and cultural heritage materials. Currently in its third year of operation, the Radical Inclusion project has been utilizing consumer grade technology to capture, preserve, and disseminate unique cultural and historical experiences in immersive VR & 360-degree video format. Presented as a case study, detailed examples include workflows associated with the capture, post-processing, and dissemination of content associated with large-scale artwork installations: from in-depth exchanges and documentation of projects in the process of construction, to experiential vignettes from the Burning Man event that occurs in the Black Rock Desert. Archival collections are shared more broadly to "radically include" individuals and to preserve the experience for the future so that people can study and better understand thoughts and inspirations of the artists and fellow participants. Associated detail includes specific workflows developed and software; ethical considerations and practice surrounding the capture, sharing, and sustainability of the collection; and the potentially novel hybrid use of use of Islandora and Kaltura as web platform for distribution.

KEYWORDS

virtual reality, emerging technology, archives, digital humanities, cultural heritage materials

INTRODUCTION

Libraries, archives, and museums, have long collected, preserved, and provisioned access (Hedstrom & King, 2003) to a depth of materials of cultural and historical significance unique to their local purview and specific mission. Examples of such items might range from video recordings to still photographs or audio recordings preserved in oral history collections. With the increasing adoption and availability of augmented and virtual reality (VR) technology, the incorporation of the new media types into traditional archival roles is a natural. This paper presents a case study in the development, methods, and sustainability of an ongoing project to leverage virtual reality technologies and incorporate immersive VR content into one such collection of University Libraries at the University of Nevada, Reno. A Land Grant institution, Libraries at the public state university and PhD-granting institution of Carnegie class R2: Doctoral Universities – Higher Research Activity, made an active choice to develop and house archival collections associated with the Burning Man event held annually (St. John, 2017) on the Black Rock Desert playa in the northern Nevada section of the Great Basin. The Burning Inquiry collection, "a comprehensive collection of published materials on the Burning Man event, including a growing collection of archival and artistic materials" was born, including ephemeral "art, performances, happenings, and spontaneous celebrations" (Home, 2017) that take place at the event.

With the growing availability of virtual reality technology, and the advent of the 360-degree video format (360-video) enabling deeply immersive playback of captured content, the authors proposed augmenting the Burning Inquiry collection. From inception the intent was to capture snippets of ephemeral experiences from the event, perform post-production editing and clean-up, and make finalized versions available as part of the growing archive: built upon year-over-year and made available through University Libraries over the web as a digital collection. The original footage along with edited versions would be deposited in the University archives; final copies would be accessible over the web for study and sharing of the experiences captured more broadly. The objective of this paper is to demonstrate the possibility and practicality of collecting VR and 360-video for use by end-users equipped with consumer-grade VR viewer equipment – to provision a truly immersive record of cultural and historical events of local interest. This paper shares early progress made toward best practices and lessons learned from direct experience.

METHODS, MATERIALS, PROCEDURES AND EQUIPMENT USED

As Burning Man is a private event, photographers, videographers and documentarians wishing to capture images intended for public distribution are subject to a proposal process prior to the event, with approved proposals subject to use agreements (The Network, 2018). Following approval of the initial Media Project Proposal in 2016, work began in earnest. Adopting the name of the first of the core principles of the Burning Man Project, Radical Inclusion, as its namesake (Burning Man – The Culture,

2018) members of the team pulled together to begin to address overriding strategies, including: potential ethical issues regarding participants captured in recordings, including specific prior release; documentation of processes, procedures, and standards; risk-centric preservation planning; lifecycle-based file management; content integrity; metadata; and outreach.

Training of team members in the use of the video and audio equipment, coupled with field practice and the development of associated documentation processes, began in earnest. Particular equipment used to capture the VR and 360-video content evolved from an early, 3D-printed/open sourced, frame that housed six GoPro Hero cameras to the more professional GoPro Omni camera; more recent additions have evolved through both the ultra-portable Nikon Keymission and the Garmin/Virb 360 camera. Supplementary audio recordings were made contemporaneously by means of a Zoom H5 Audio Recorder to preserve fidelity of event audio. Post-production workflow included the use of the software *AutoPano 360* to perform and correct initial stitching of individual camera output into the immersive 360-degree format; additional post-production editing was performed using Adobe Premiere. On a granular level, content was archived utilizing a STorNext system for long-term preservation of these born-digital surrogates; functionally, access is provisioned by means of a digital collection migrated to the Islandora platform, with links to the open-source video platform Kaltura to provision playback access.

DISCUSSION AND CONCLUSIONS

Preliminary results of this small pilot show that not only is it possible to capture VR and 360-video content of deep local cultural and historical interest, but that the immersive nature of the content collected, and the potential it offers to capture and preserve glimpses into otherwise intangible heritage, outweighs downsides of added workflow in post-processing and provisioning access to the video content. Given the rapidly changing nature of the technology, the added workflow is already significantly reduced; in the near-term, it is reasonable to expect that such specialized steps will be even further reduced, enabling practitioners from across disciplines of Libraries, Archives, and Museums to quickly and easily provision similar niche collections of deep local impact.

Practitioner details shared demonstrate that with relatively minimal modification, consumer grade AR/VR technology available off-the-shelf can be successfully utilized to achieve impactful results. Appropriate staff onboarding and training, combined with similarly minimal modification of traditional archival workflow, enables relatively seamless integration into other digital archives provisioned by the library. Practitioner details will enable others contemplating similar development to avoid potential missteps in implementation, and more quickly scale lending collections to meet demonstrated need, building engagement and opportunity for collaborations with supported departments.

ACKNOWLEDGEMENTS

The author gratefully acknowledges the contributions of the Burning Man Organization, with specific thanks to members of the Media Department for their ongoing support of these efforts. Contributions of colleagues across University Libraries and the greater Burning Man community, specifically the evolving membership of the Radical Inclusion team, are also gratefully acknowledged: without their effort, this project simply would not have been possible.

PRESENTATION OF THE WORK

This paper, and supporting materials, will be presented as a visual presentation at the meeting. Samples of archival VR and 360-video content provisioned will be viewable to attendees both through Vimeo and by means of a standalone VR viewer headset.

REFERENCES

Hedstrom , M. and J.L. King . 2003. On the LAM: Library, archive, and museum collections in the creation and maintenance of knowledge communities. Paris, France: Organisation for Economic Co-operation and Development. Retrieved from http://www.oecd.org/data-oecd/59/63/32126054.pdf

Home (2017). Burning Inquiry: Burning Man at UNR. Retrieved from http://guides.library.unr.edu/burningman

Burning Man Project (2018). The 10 Principles of Burning Man. Retrieved from https://burningman.org/culture/philosophical-center/10-principles/

Lynch, C. A. (2003). Institutional Repositories: Essential Infrastructure for Scholarship In The Digital Age. *portal: Libraries and the Academy*, 3(2), 327-336.

St. John, G. (2017). Civilised Tribalism: Burning Man, Event-Tribes and Maker Culture. *Cultural Sociology*, 12 (1), 3-21.

The Network (2018). Apply to Cover the Event. Retrieved from https://burningman.org/network/about-us/press-media/press-apply/

The Challenge of Assessment for Library *Makerspaces*

Aijuan Cun
University at Buffalo/SUNY, USA. aijuancu@buffalo.edu

Sam Abramovich
University at Buffalo/SUNY, USA. samuelab@buffalo.edu

ABSTRACT

The emergence of *Maker* culture has led to an increase of *Makerspaces* around the United States across a variety of educational organizations (Halverson & Sheridan, 2014). When *Makerspaces* are incorporated into public libraries, library patrons have new opportunities to learn and create through play, exploration, and creation (Moorefield-Lang, 2015) by utilizing cutting-edge tools such as virtual reality and 3D printers. However, as the number of library *Makerspaces* grows, so do the challenges associated with supporting their learning potential. In particular, there are no widely accepted means of assessing learning in library *Makerspaces*. Our study examined patron and librarian use of a *Makerspace* through a theoretical framework based on modern assessment research. Findings were: (1) categories of library *Makerspace* participants and their assessment needs – including librarian assessment needs; (2) assessment tools that can address the learning needs of different patrons, librarians, and other stakeholders; and (3) design implications for assessment tools in library *Makerspaces*.

KEYWORDS

Makerspaces, Assessment; Learning

INTRODUCTION

The emergence of *Maker* culture has led to an increase of *Makerspaces* around the United States across a variety of educational organizations (Halverson & Sheridan, 2014). In particular, an increasing number of public libraries are using *Makerspaces* to offer new opportunities to learn and create through play and creation (Moorefield-Lang, 2015). However, as the number of library-based *Makerspaces* grows, so do the challenges associated with supporting their learning potential. Missing from most library-based *Makerspaces* are assessments of learning. This is not necessarily surprising since assessing learning is a well-established, difficult challenge (Stiggins, 2002) despite it being a necessary component of effective instruction (Shepard, 2000; Havnes, 2004). In addition, a reliable and valid assessment can be used as evidence of the effective value of a library *Makerspace*, as often demanded by various library stakeholders (e.g., administrators, Board of Directors, Local Politicians).

THEORETICAL PERSPECTIVES

Because of its relative novelty, we first define *Making*, *Makerspaces*, and *Makers*. *Making* is a process of "developing an idea and constructing it into some physical or digital form," often with positive educational outcomes (Sheridan et al., 2014, p. 507). To encourage *Making*, advocates often provide a *Makerspace,* a physical location where anyone can use digital and physical technologies to make something, master new skills, and gain hands-on experience (Sheridan et al., 2014, p. 507). Kalil and Miller (2014) define *Makers* as people who have intrinsic motivation to *Make*, solve problems, and share what they have learned through *Making*.

Research on assessment informs how learning in a library *Makerspace* can be studied. Wehlburg (2010) defines assessment as a method to identify the evidence of learning in order to help learners improve skills. Necessary for creating assessment is knowing who is being assessed (the Maker), where they are being assessed (the Makerspace) and what learning is being assessed (Making). Applied to library *Makerspaces*, assessments should inform both patrons and librarians who is learning, what they are learning, and where they are learning it. Summative assessment focuses on identifying evidence of what is learned and reporting the evaluation results at the end of a learning opportunity (Sadler, 1989). Formative assessment refers to feedback that could be used to help improve students' competence during learning processes (Sadler, 1989). Both formative and summative assessments are necessary for library *Makerspaces*.

METHODOLOGY

Utilizing a Design-Based Research approach (Sandoval & Bell, 2004), we first designed and tested assessment instruments within a library *Makerspace*. Initial assessment instruments included surveys, observations, and interviews. However, we identified two major challenges where participants were observed and surveyed during their participation in this *Makerspace*. The first challenge was the various objectives and levels of prior knowledge of the different populations that visit the library *Makerspace*. The second challenge was that we could not predict when and how much time a patron might visit the library *Makerspace*. After analyzing the aforementioned challenges, we utilized a new research approach, codifying our initial observations into distinct categories of users of the *Makerspace* and the different learning objectives of those users. A second literature review then allowed us to determine what type of assessment tools may be applicable in informal learning spaces. We then assigned these possible assessments to various users and learning goals in a library *Makerspace*, based on an initial determination as to what assessment would generate the necessary summative and formative feedback. The results were then shared with librarians, who offered additional feedback and revision.

FINDINGS

Categories of Participants

We identified four different categories of library *Makerspace* patrons: a child visiting the *Makerspace* for the first time, an adult visiting the *Makerspace* for the first time, a (repeat) child who returns to the *Makerspace*, a (repeat) adult who visits the *Makerspace* for more than one time. We grouped participants into two different age groups (children and adults) because the library offers different services for patrons of different age groups. We also identified two categories of patrons regarding experience with *Making* – patrons visiting the *Makerspace* for the first time, and (repeat) patrons who return to the *Makerspace.* Adults and children who visit the *Makerspace* for the first time have different needs and *Making* goals than patrons who were familiar with *Making* and visited the *Makerspac*e for many times. A secondary classification of non-English speakers was also identified as applying to the four patron categories because of a number of patrons who visit the library *Makerspace* without mastery of English.

Assessment Needs of Patrons and Librarians

Because the repeat patrons have different needs than that of patrons who visit the *Makerspace* for the first time, we categorized assessment needs accordingly. *Basic Mastery of Technology* is an assessment need for initial visitors to the *Makerspace* while *Advanced Mastery of Technology* is an assessment need for repeat patrons. Additionally, we identified seven groups of assessment needs of librarians: *Willingness to Come Back, Change in Library Use, Level of Interest*, *Engage in Other Programs*, *Progress Towards Technical Literacy*, *Self-Driven Uses*, and *Media Literacy*. *Willingness to Come Back* concerns how assessment tools can be used to predict whether or not a patron will return to the library *Makerspace*. *Change in Library Use* represents assessment that can help measure a patron's increase or decrease in the use of other library offerings. *Level of Interest* can be used to measure patron engagement in specific *Maker* activities. *Engage in Other Programs* can be used to predict if patrons will engage in other *Make*r activities offered through the *Makerspace*. *Progress Towards Technical Literacy* can be used to examine patrons' overall progress through *Making* toward a library's goal for patrons to be technically literate, with the same also true for *Media Literacy*. We also identified the term *Self-Driven Use* for librarians who wish to motivate patrons to experience self-driven *Making* in the *Makerspace*.

Six Categories of Assessment Tools

We also identified six categories of assessment tools that either are commonly used in libraries or can be adapted into everyday library practice in a Makerspace: *Visitor Logs*, *Surveys*, *Self-Assessment Forms*, *Librarian Observations, One-On-One Session,* and *Competition*. *Visitor Logs* can help address the assessment needs of *Willingness to Come Back*. *Surveys* can be utilized to address the needs of *Willingness to Come Back*. *Self-Assessment* can be used to address the needs of *Progress towards Technical Literacy*. *Librarian Observation* can be used to address the needs of *Level of Interest* and *How to use Technology for Children*. *One-On-One Session* can help address the needs of *Willingness to Come Back* and *Basic Mastery of Technology*. *Competition* can be used to address the needs of *Level of Interest*. An important conclusion was that no single assessment tool seems to serve a majority of assessment needs for a library-based *Makerspace*. Combining multiple assessment tools should be considered to address the assessment needs of patrons and librarians.

REFERENCES

Halverson, E. R., & Sheridan, K. (2014). The maker movement in education. *Harvard Educational Review*, *84*(4), 495-504.

Havnes, A. (2004). Examination and learning: an activity-theoretical analysis of the relationship between assessment and educational practice. *Assessment & Evaluation in Higher Education*, *29*(2), 159-176.

Moorefield-Lang, H. (2015). Change in the making: Makerspaces and the ever-changing landscape of libraries. *TechTrends*, *59*(3), 107-112.

Kalil, T., & Miller, J. (2014, February 3). *Announcing the first White House Maker Faire*. The White House Blog. Retrieved from https://obamawhitehouse.archives.gov/blog/2014/02/03/announcing-first-white-house-maker-faire

Sadler, D. R. (1989). Formative assessment and the design of instructional systems. *Instructional science*, *18*(2), 119-144.

Sandoval, W. A., & Bell, P. (2004). Design-based research methods for studying learning in context: Introduction. *Educational Psychologist*, *39*(4), 199-201.

Shepard, L. A. (2000). The role of assessment in a learning culture. *Educational researcher*, *29*(7), 4-14.

Sheridan, K., Halverson, E. R., Litts, B., Brahms, L., Jacobs-Priebe, L., & Owens, T. (2014). Learning in the making: a comparative case study of three makerspaces. *Harvard Educational Review, 84*(4), 505-531.

Stiggins, R. J. (2002). Assessment crisis: The absence of assessment for learning. *Phi Delta Kappan*, *83*(10), 758-765.

Wehlburg, C. M. (2010). Assessment practices related to student learning. In K.J. Gillespie, D.L.Robertson and associates (Eds.), *A guide to Faculty Development* (2nd ed.). (pp. 169-184). San Francisco: Jossey-Bass.

How “Enhanced” are They? An Exploratory Analysis of Journals in Information Science

Renata Gonçalves Curty
Universidade Estadual de Londrina, Brazil. re-curty@gmail.com

Natalia Rodrigues Delbianco
Universidade Estadual de Londrina, Brazil nathdel-bianco@gmail.com

ABSTRACT

This poster presents early findings from an ongoing study which investigates to what extent Information Science journals have been adopting enhanced properties and attributes. Based on a set of requirements derived from the literature and complemented by an empirical study we analyzed eight journals. Preliminary results reveal that the Journal for the Association of Information Science and Technology is the leading journal, and that user-generated content related features and interactive content are missing in our sample. We expect this research will not only contribute to the conceptual understanding of enhanced features and tools functions and applications, but also provide valuable information for editors and publishers to rethink about journals' platforms and better align them to current innovations in academic publishing.

KEYWORDS

Academic Publishing, Enhanced Publications, Scientific Journals, Scholarly Communication.

BACKGROUND AND MOTIVATION

Amidst the rise and intensification of Web 2.0 tools and features as well as the developments and semantic functionalities promoted by the Web 3.0, the scientific community has been experimenting the modernization of the academic publishing system. Some journals are offering more data-rich and cross-content environments with post-publication capabilities which incorporates social features for engagement, interaction and sharing, reaching the status of enhanced publication.

Enhanced journals seek to overcome the limitations of the digital manuscript through complementary tools and resources to enable a better understanding of the narrative of the scientific paper. They are capable of integrating scientific information, by linking related contents and objects, and help to structure academic publishing in a more efficient way (Woutersen-Windhouwe & Brandsma, 2009). Research-related files (e.g. spreadsheets, transcripts, flowcharts, videos, images) not contemplated in the body of paper, but important for allowing the paper interpretation, are linked to the manuscript. In addition, these journals incorporate Web 2.0-based reading, discovery, and recommendation functions, as well as tools for the execution and in-situ plotting of digitally-linked files for purposes of validation, visualization and reanalysis of the research data (Bardi & Manghi, 2014; 2015). Besides linking data assets in a meaningful way, enhanced journals also aggregates some features and user generated-content such as comments, ranking and rating as well as sharing, download and citation metrics, which can help readers to make a more informed decision about the paper's relevance and impact.

In order to better comprehend such properties and functionalities, firstly we conducted an empirical study with enhanced scientific journals which allowed to add new features to the list found in the literature, as well as to describe each of these properties and functions in a more comprehensive and descriptive way. Secondly, we analyzed journals in the Information Science field in order to identify which enhanced features and tools are present in those journals.

METHODS

From August to October 2017 we explored and scrutinized the interface of eight scientific journals from different fields, which are known for their enhanced properties and attributes: Biodiversity Data Journal, Journal of Open Psychological Data, Data in Brief, Journal of Open Health Data, (Giga)^n Science, PhytoKeys, Scientific Data, and Geoscience Data Journal. Besides the homepage of each journal and some key information such as journal description, submission guidelines, etc., we also examined five randomly selected papers for each journal (40 papers in total), considering that some features could be dependable on the paper's content to be displayed. These stage of criteria development allowed us to conduct an annotated data collection and add eight desirable attributes to Adriaansen and Hooft's (2010) original list comprised of 10 properties.

Having this more comprehensive set of desirable enhanced features we later developed a checklist with a total of 18 attributes for evaluating journals from the Information Science field. We selected journals which conformed with three requirements: 1) evaluated as A1, the highest score according to the journals' quality classification from Brazil known as Qualis; 2) internationally recognized journals with papers in English, and 3) open access journals or journals we could fully access through our institutional subscription. The final sample consisted of eight journals. We collected data from December 2017 to February 2018 following the same strategy adopted in the criteria development stage. Additionally, we took screenshots and organized them in a directory for consistency, considering that some updates and changes in journals' interface', tools and features could happen throughout the data collection. We developed individual checklists in excel spreadsheets for each of the papers, which were later meta-analyzed and combined into one main spreadsheet per journal, and then compiled into one table.

PRELIMINARY FINDINGS

We coded the selected journals as it follows: Information, Communication and Society (J1), Information Research (J2), Information Sciences (J3), Journal of Documentation (J4), Journal of Librarianship and Information Science (J5), Journal for the Association of Information Science and Technology (J6), Online Information Review (J7), and Scientometrics (J8). Table 1 depicts the enhanced properties/attributes, their description and presence in each of the journals.

Property/Attribute	Description	J1	J2	J3	J4	J5	J6	J7	J8
Navigable Tab. Contents	Allows users to easily move to a specific section of the paper	•		•	•	•	•	•	•
Metadata	Provides metadata associated to the paper	•	•	•	•	•	•	•	•
Links to Figs and Tabs	Offers cross-navigation to figures and tables mentioned in the text	•		•	•	•	•	•	•
Supplementary Data	Provides data resources (e.g. spreadsheets, models, transcripts, etc.)			•	•	•	•		•
Links to References	Links in-text citations to the full reference of the cited work	•	•	•	•	•	•	•	•
Direct Links	Redirects users to the original location of items from the reference list	•	•	•	•	•	•	•	•
Readers' Comments	Allows users to add comments about the paper								
PDF Download	Allows readers to download the paper file in a more print-friendly format	•		•	•	•	•	•	•
Interactive Content	Offers graphs, images, etc. users can interplay with (e.g. rotate, add variables)								
Relations	Displays related papers by subject, authorship or other users' preferences	•		•	•	•	•	•	•
Cited by	Indicates which other studies have cited the paper	•	•	•	•	•	•	•	•
Sharing Tools	Allows users to share links to paper through social networks	•	•		•	•	•	•	•
Ranking and Rating	Allows users to rank and rate the paper according to their quality judgment								
Automatic Citation	Allows users to automatically create the paper's citation	•	•	•	•	•	•	•	•
Alerts	Allows users to create alerts for notification of new-related papers						•		
Export and Downloading	Allows users to export and download data files	•		•	•	•	•	•	•
Accessibility	Offers assistive technologies and tools for disable users						•		
Metrics	Displays download and citation counts, and alternative metrics	•		•		•	•		•

Table 1. Research Findings.

Table 1 shows that metadata, links to references, direct links to cited data sources, the "cited by" and automatic citation feature are present in all the eight journals. It is important to underscore though, that J2 provides the ready recommended citation, whereas other journals allow users to create citation according to the desired style. None of the journals we examined presented the following three attributes/properties: readers' comments, interactive content, and ranking and rating features. Information Research (J2) complies with less enhanced properties and features (n=6). Conversely, the Journal for the Association of Information Science and Technology (J6), was the leading journal with a rate of 83% compliance with the verified features and tools. Besides these extreme cases, other journals' had little variation, ranging from 11 to 13 items from the checklist. It is worth noting that accessibility was only found in J6, however, among the different existing assistive technologies (i.e. screen readers, contrast control etc.), J6 limits to offer the text resizing feature.

INITIAL CONCLUSIONS AND FUTURE RESEARCH

Based on preliminary results we can infer that the majority of the features and tools associated with user-generated content (e.g. comments, ratings and rankings) is still absent in the journals we examined. Also, we found these journals are not in consonance with accessibility principles, thus they are not ready for users with disabilities. The lack of interactive content can be also highlighted, however, we recognize that this type of content may not be suitable to all papers and that their availability depends, first and foremost, on papers authors' provision. Therefore, more than offering enhanced attributes, editors and publishers should promote extensively their functionalities among members of their targeted scientific community.

As a future step we aim to review and expand the list of enhanced properties, by refining it to a more granular level, as well to establish weights of importance to such items according to scientists' judgments. We also plan to categorize levels of sophistication for enhanced journals for comparative purposes. Based on this more robust instrument we plan to collect data from a wider range of journal titles and taking into account a larger sample of papers. Last but not least, we intent to evaluate results considering different units of analysis i.e. journal platforms and editors, to compare and contrast their editorial policies towards the implementation of enhanced features and tools.

REFERENCES

Adriaansen, D., & Hooft, J. (2010). Properties of enhanced publications and the supporting tools. *Computingscience*, 1-10.

Bardi, A., & Manghi, P. (2014). Enhanced publications: Data models and information systems. *Liber Quarterly*, *23*(4).

Bardi, A., & Manghi, P. (2015). A framework supporting the shift from traditional digital publications to enhanced publications. *D-Lib Magazine*, *21*(1/2).

Woutersen-Windhouwer, S., & Brandsma, R. (2009). *Report on enhanced publications state-of-the-art*. [S.l.]: DRIVER.

Educators' Perceptions of Information Literacy and Skills Required to Spot 'Fake News'

Nicole S. Delellis
University of Western Ontario, Canada. ndelelli@uwo.ca

Victoria L. Rubin
University of Western Ontario, Canada. vrubin@uwo.ca

ABSTRACT

This research examines the concept of 'fake news' in the context of information literacy (IL) in a post-secondary educational setting. Educators' perceptions shape both IL curricula and classroom discussions with students. We conducted 18 interviews with members of 3 integral groups implementing IL education (8 professors, 6 librarians, 4 department chairs). Interviews explored participants' perceptions of: IL education, perceived skills associated with IL, skills required to spot 'fake news', and gauged our participants' willingness to incorporate segments dedicated to detecting 'fake news' in IL curriculum. Our qualitative findings identify a substantial overlap that exists between skills associated with IL and 'fake news' detection (e.g., close-reading, critical disposition, bias awareness). Professors and academic administrators also appeared to underappreciate the role of librarians as IL educators. We advocate improving communication among integral facilitators of IL education. More research is needed to assess effectiveness of IL education as an 'inoculation' against 'fake news.'

KEYWORDS

Information Literacy, Perceptions, 'Fake News', Information Literacy Instruction

INTRODUCTION

What does it mean to be critical of information? In 1989, the American Library Association (ALA) defined information literacy (IL) as a set of skills that enables individuals "to find, evaluate, and use information effectively to solve a particular problem or make a decision." However, as conceptualization of information shifts, and the technologies people use to communicate change, so does the teaching of IL. How we obtain information, and specifically news has been altered by the existence of social media platforms. Blending of traditional news outlets and user generated content procured through social media has influenced how individuals inform themselves (Chen, Conroy and Rubin, 2015). "Most of what we think of as news is now delivered to and received by us in video clips and sound bites, often forwarded without filter or review through social networks from one screen to another in a matter of minutes" (Frederiksen, 2017). Through social media platforms individuals are presented with a decontextualized 'news' sources, often stripped of details about information production. Reliance on social media as a news vector has disrupted traditional methods of information acquisition. Individuals who were once reliant on librarians to provided epistemological protected procured information are now "using the internet to acquire information and making important decisions with it [...] acquiring knowledge from a media where anyone can write anything they want, true or false, anonymously and without consequences" (Walsh, 2010).

Critical assessment of information is important today as it ever has been. Decontextualization of news stories has left individuals who lack IL skills susceptible to 'fake news' deception. Citizens lacking IL skills are predisposed to believing 'problematic information' that is "inaccurate, misleading, inappropriately attributed or altogether fabricated" (Jack, 2017). Researchers have found that "in-spite of the importance of information literacy instruction in higher education, it is still not an integral component of many higher education programs and the students who are going to be graduated from universities are "ill-equipped" with information skills" (Singh, 2011). Past scholars have propagated the idea of IL as a potential cure or remedy that could protect individuals against the disinformation, however few studies have explored IL in relation to 'fake news' in the current state of IL instruction in higher education. It also remains unanswered as to who should take the burden of equipping individuals to be critical evaluators of information.

RESEARCH QUESTION

Effort has been put into finding technological solutions to the proliferation of misinformation, and disinformation in current online informational spaces (e.g., Rubin (2017), Rubin, Chen, and Conroy (2015)). This research however, focuses on the human side of digital news reading, and how it relates to the broader concept of IL. Revealing educators' perceptions about IL, and 'fake news' is important because these perceptions shape IL curricula, can direct classroom discourse, and form how IL is presented. Specifically, we addressed the following research questions:

1. What perceptions do librarians, professors, and academic administrators have about IL?
2. Should 'fake news' be introduced into IL education?
3. What skills are perceived as necessary to detect 'fake news'?

METHODS AND ANALYSIS

This is a case study of a large Southern Ontario Canadian higher educational institution. Perceptions about IL education and 'fake news' were assessed in one-on-one interviews. In winter 2018, we solicited participation of 166 university employees via direct personal e-mail invitations and received a 10.8% response rate, indicative of a high interest in the topic of the study. Consequently, 18 participants from the invited pool were interviewed face-to-face (8 professors, 6 librarians, and 4 department chairs) with an average duration of interviews of 24 minutes (ranging from about 10 minutes to 50 minutes). Interviews contained 11-13 structured question and concluded with an open-ended question. Transcriptions of interviews were analyzed using Glaser and Strauss' (1967) Grounded Theory Approach. A concept map was created to visually display an aggregation of identified concepts that re-appeared as themes in at least 2 of the participants' transcripts (Appendix Figure 1).

MAIN FINDINGS

In general, all participants emphasized IL as the ability to not only find information, but to evaluate this information synthesized from a variety of sources. Substantial overlap existed in the 18 participants' perceptions of skills associated with IL, and skills thought to be essential for 'fake news' detection. Both skills sets were perceived to contain: an understanding of how language works (close-reading skills), skepticism/critical disposition, an understanding about how information is produced, an awareness of biases (both internal and external), and the ability to synthesize various sources/perspectives. Perceived overlap in skill sets (Figure 1) emphasizes the inherent connection between IL and 'fake news' detection, and provides insights into why participants perceived that skills required to detect 'fake news' are an extension to general IL skills.

Almost all interviewees (17 out of 18) believed that it is important for students to be information literate upon graduation, and more than half (10 out of 18) agreed that segments about 'fake news' should be included in IL curriculum. Participants perceived IL to be an essential citizens' education, which enables individuals to be able to function and engage in democratic societies. As of early 2018, our participants report that only limited curricula include segments dedicated specifically to 'fake news'. Also, librarians are underutilized in the IL education within our case study sample. Researchers in Library and Information Science have proclaimed that "the role of librarians and information professional is to develop well-educated information consumers" (El Rayess et al., 2018), but neither set of interviewed professors or department chairs mentioned librarians when asked who should be teaching IL.

CONCLUSION

Based on interviews with 18 participants within our case study's post-secondary Canadian institution, we noticed a substantial overlap in recurring concepts associated with their perceptions of IL skills, and skills required to spot 'fake news' (see Appendix Figure 1). Participants saw IL skills being applied towards the broader societal concern of producing critically thinking, aware, information literate citizens. We also identified an unfortunate disconnect between the awareness of the value of IL education, and its universal implementation across the institution. Further research needs to assess the effectiveness of current IL education in imparting perceived skills of critical evaluation of information. In the time being, we recommended for institutions to more proactively facilitate open communication between professors, librarians, and academic administrators to enable the building of curricula, and concrete detailed plans to provide IL education to every student, across every discipline.

REFERENCES

American Library Association (1989), Presidential Committee on Information Literacy: Final Report, American Library Association, Washington, DC, Retrieved from http://www.ala.org/acrl/publications/whitepapers/presidential

Chen, Y., Conroy, N.J., & Rubin, V.L. (2015). News in an online world: the need for an automatic crap detector. Proceedings of the 78th ASIS&T Annual Meeting: Information Science with Impact: Research in and for the Community. American Society for Information Science, 81.

El Rayess, M., Chebl, C., Mhanna, J., & Hage, R. (2018). Fake news judgement. *Reference Services Review, 46*(1), 146-149.

Frederiksen, L. (2017). Best of the Literature: Fake News. *Public Services Quarterly, 13*, 103-107.

Jack, C. (2017). Lexicon of lies: terms for problematic information. *Data & Society*. Retrieved from https://datasociety.net/pubs/oh/DataAndSociety_LexiconofLies.pdf

Rubin, V. L., Chen, Y. & Conroy, N. J. (2015). Deception Detection for News: Three Types of Fakes. *Proceedings of the 78th ASIS&T Annual Meeting: Information Science with Impact: Vol. 81.*

Rubin, V. L. (2017). News Verification Suite: Towards System Design to Supplement Reporters' and Editors' Judgements.

Proceedings of the 45th Annual Conference of the Canadian Assoication for Information Science L'Association canadienne des sciences de l'information (CAIS/ACSI2017), Toronto.

Walsh, J. (2010). Librarians and controlling disinformation: Is multi-literacy instruction the answer? *Library Review, 59*(7), 498-511.

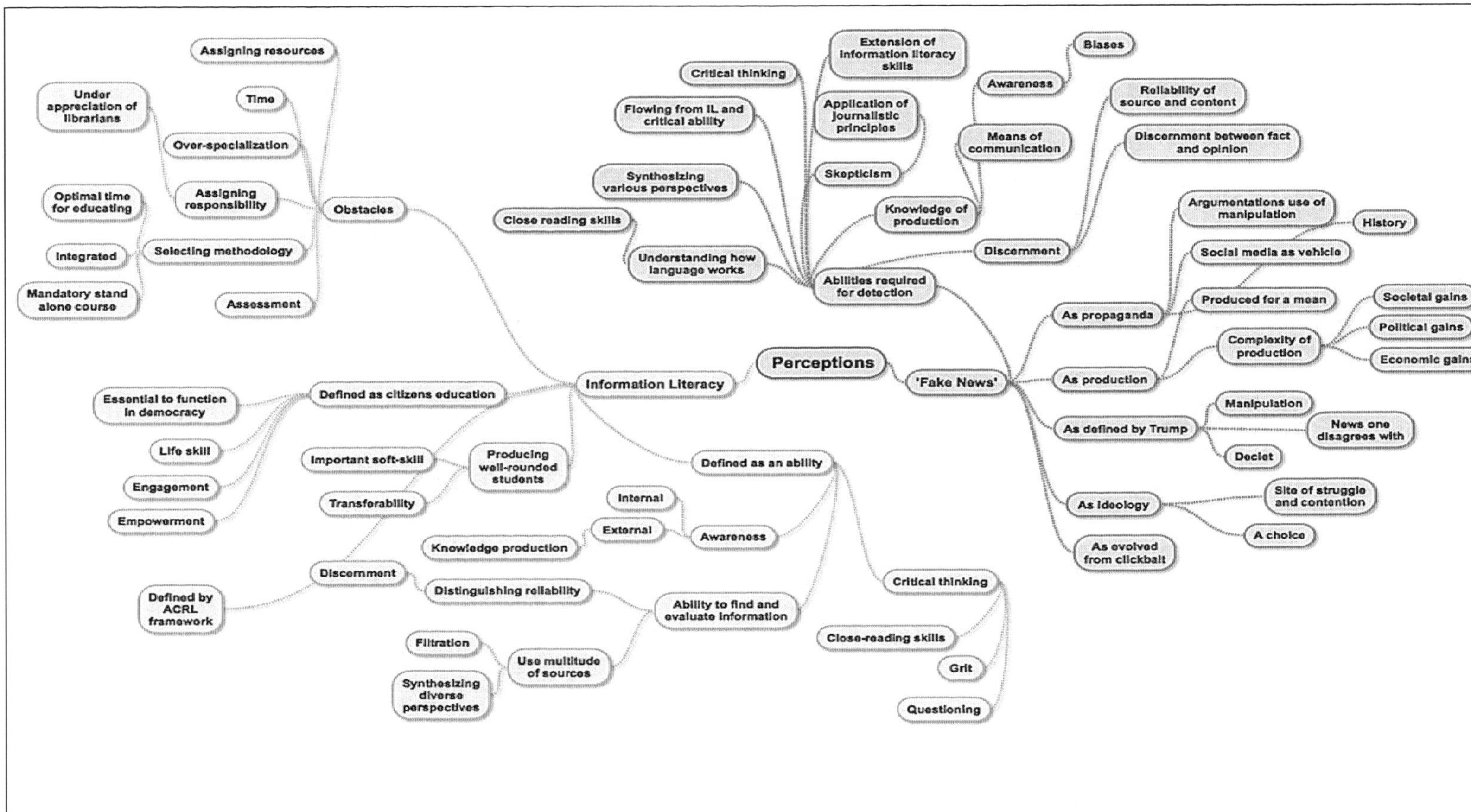

Appendix Figure 1. A Concept Map of Themes in Educators' Perceptions about Information Literary (IL) and Skills Required to Detect 'Fake News'.

In their face-to-face interviews, 16 participants involved in a IL education revealed substantial overlap in perceived skills associated with information literacy (IL) and those thought to be required for 'fake news' detection. The concepts referring to IL are linked in the yellow bubbles, and those referring to spotting 'fake news' are in red bubbles. See for example, the similarities between IL 'defined as an ability' and 'awareness' of 'knowledge production' (in yellow bubbles) and 'abilities required for detection' of 'fake news' as 'means of communication' with its 'biases' (red bubbles). Both skills sets were perceived to contain: an understanding of how language works (close-reading skills), skepticism/critical disposition, an understanding about how information is produced, an awareness of biases (both internal and external), and the ability to synthesize various sources/perspectives.

#Supporting the Cause: An Analysis of How Government Agencies Use Twitter Hashtags

Nic DePaula
University at Albany, SUNY, USA. ndepaula@albany.edu

ABSTRACT
One of the main characteristics of social media is the use of *hashtags*, and one of the growing and important group of actors in this environment are government agencies. However, how government agencies use hashtags has not been addressed in the scholarly literature. By definition, hashtags always serve to help index content. However, they are also reflective of information campaigns, perspectives on social issues as well as explicit calls for action. In this preliminary study I explore how U.S. federal government agencies have used Twitter hashtags during 2016 and 2017, under the Obama and Trump administrations. I present empirical results on the most used hashtags across both administrations as well as the purposes for which they wore adopted.

KEYWORDS
Twitter hashtags, government communication, social media, social tagging

INTRODUCTION
Social media sites have become important components for online public communication. However, only recently have they been widely adopted by institutions of government—government communication on social media virtually did not exist ten years ago. Now, as of March 2018, the 15 primary agencies of the U.S. federal government have approximately 25 million followers on Twitter. NASA, an independent agency of the executive branch, alone boosts of 29 million followers as of the same time. However, despite the importance and power of government actors, their employment of *hashtags* on platforms such as Twitter and Facebook has not been studied. In this brief paper, I thus address how U.S. government agencies have used Twitter hashtags over time and across political administrations as part of their information and communication activities.

GOVERNMENT INFORMATION AND COMMUNICATION ACTIVITIES
Some of the most important actions of governments are their *information and communication activities* (ICA), where they interface with the public, provide critical and reliable information and, given their resources and legitimacy may influence public behavior (Hood & Margetts, 2007). However, these activities can also be controversial as the information exchanged may be biased or unwarranted (DePaula et al., 2018; Yudof, 1983). Nevertheless, social media can increase the quantity and quality of such activities, as they provide direct information channels to the public. One of the unique components of social media communication is the use of *hashtags*. A hashtag is a single term preceded by the "#" (hash or pound) symbol—e.g. #USA or #ActOnClimate—included as part of, or as the whole, content of a post. Although not a reliable taxonomic system, this type of *social tagging* or *folksonomy* may assist in information organization and retrieval (Trant, 2009). At a social level, these tags have also been recognized for their *community-building* and *meaning-making* purposes (Lee, 2018). In an analysis of government use of these tags it may thus be useful to at least distinguish between two kinds: *generic indexing* or *purpose-specific*—a distinction similarly noted by Sunstein (2017) in his recent evaluation of polarization in *#Republic*. This distinction should help us understand and differentiate the extent to which government agencies are using hashtags to simply index content or to promote their policies, and what the most heavily promoted policies are across agencies and political administrations.

METHODS
For this study, I collected all original posts (i.e. not including "replies" or "retweets") of four U.S. federal agencies during one year of the Obama (2016-1-1 to 2017-1-20) and Trump (2017-2-1 to 2018-2-20) administrations. The agencies were chosen to give a preliminary and diverse view on government activity on the Twitter platform. I then processed the data with Python and NLKT to enable identification and count of hashtags. I separately selected the 10 most used hashtags for each specific agency and administration, and then computed how many times they were used for each agency in both administrations. I then classified hashtags as *purpose-specific* if the hashtag text itself included a *verb* or an *adjective* and clearly promoted an idea or action, or if it was associated with a policy or program of the agency. All other hashtags were considered *generic indexing.*

RESULTS AND DISCUSSION
From Figure 1, it is clear that some tags are used more than others and there are differences across agencies in how hashtags changed across administration. For example, whereas the Department of Interior (DOI) shared its most used hashtags across administrations, this overlap was least so for the Department of Homeland Security (DHS) and the Environmental Protection

Agency (EPA). Moreover, DHS under Obama was considerably more active compared to the subsequent administration. The tags classified as purpose-specific are underlined. It should be emphasized that this term is used here in a preliminary way to differentiate between overly generic tags from those that are more apparently associated with specific programs or explicit calls for action. For example, *#KnowYourMil* from the Department of Defense is a campaign to promote the military, and the purpose to which it refers is explicit in the tag. Similarly, *#WeAreDHS* is used to showcase specific actions of the organization that may help people appreciate what they do. The EPA used the *#EPABack2Basics* tag to signal a specific set of priorities of the incoming administration, indicating some of the policies that the agencies should go "back to". Similarly, commonly used tags by EPA in the previous administration—but not at all used in the subsequent—were the *#ActOnClimate, #NoWastedFood* and *#FlushForFlint,* all calling for specific types of action on climate, food waste and the Flint water crisis.

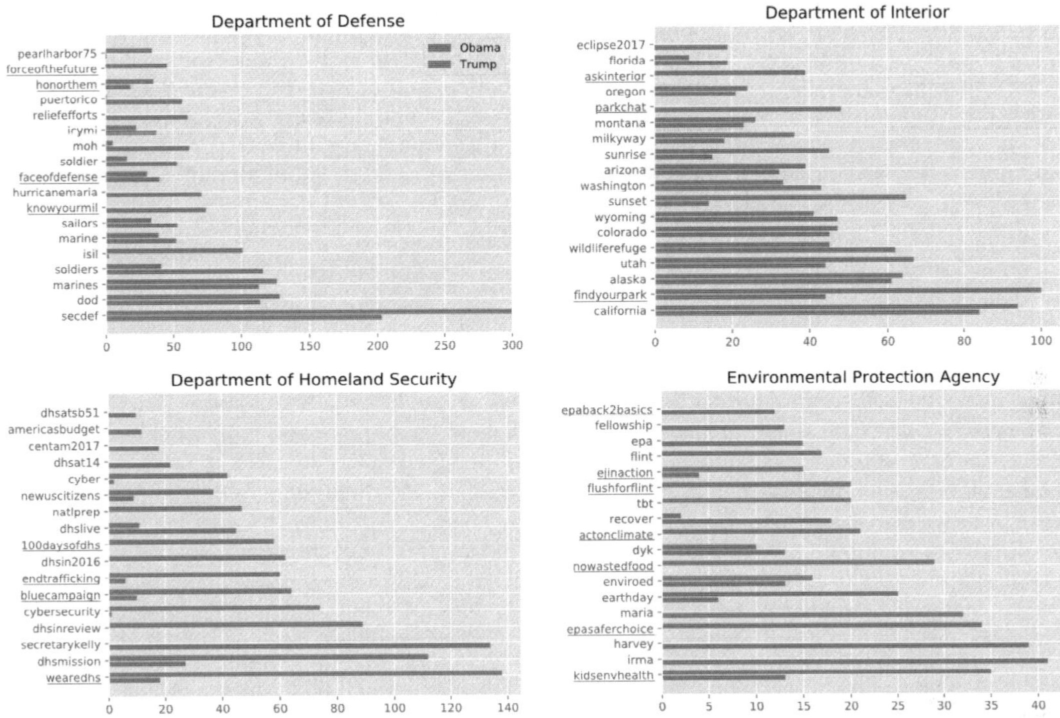

Figure 1. The most used hashtags during the Obama (2016) and Trump (2017) administrations. Underline means purpose-specific. X-axis refers to unique instances the hashtag was used; *secdef* count under Obama is 751.

CONCLUSIONS AND FUTURE WORK

This study shows that the employment of Twitter hashtags is a frequent and relatively widespread information and communication activity in the U.S. federal government. These tags are used for generic indexing and purpose-specific communication, which signal calls for action, policy preferences or programs that connect with citizens (e.g. ParkChat). The tags were sometimes used across distinct and opposing political administrations, the reasons for which may require further study. Interesting and useful future work may investigate the representativeness of hashtags in relation to other content, on social media or otherwise; the persuasive effects of the communication; as well as the ethical and legal issues that arise from these activities.

REFERENCES

DePaula, N., Dincelli, E., & Harrison, T. M. (2018). Toward a typology of government social media communication: Democratic goals, symbolic acts and self-presentation. *Government Information Quarterly, 35*(1), 98–108.

Hood, C. and Margetts, H. (2007). *The tools of government in the digital age*. Palgrave Macmillan.

Lee, C. (2018). Introduction: Discourse of social tagging. *Discourse, Context & Media, 22*, 1–3.

Sunstein, C. (2017). *#Republic: Divided democracy in the age of social media*. Princeton University Press.

Trant, J. (2009). Studying social tagging and folksonomy: A review and framework. *Journal of Digital Information, 10*(1).

Yudof, M. (1983). *When government speaks: Politics, law, and government expression in America*. Univ. of California Press.

Middle of the (By)line: Examining Hyperauthorship Networks in the Human Genome Project

Ly Dinh
University of Illinois at Urbana-Champaign, USA.
dinh4@illinois.edu

Yi-Yun Cheng
University of Illinois at Urbana-Champaign, USA.
yiyunyc2@illinois.edu

ABSTRACT

The era of big science promises rapid growth of scientific innovations and complex problem-solving, bringing forth the practice of doing science in large-scale collaborative effort rather than single author, solitary work. In disciplines such as genomics and high-energy physics, it is not uncommon that hyperauthorship phenomenon with the amount of authors soaring high from hundredth to thousandth. The purpose of this research is to explore the collaboration dynamics and the partial alphabetical author byline in one of the primary research articles within the Human Genome Project (HGP). Using co- authorship network analysis, we find that middle authors play crucial roles in facilitating collaboration among previously unconnected authors as well as contributing to genetic sequencing efforts. Future work entails network analysis of all published works by HGP to comprehensively capture collaboration dynamics among multiple research centers.

KEYWORDS

Hyperauthorship, human genome project, co-authorship networks, author byline

INTRODUCTION

As large-scale scientific endeavors such as the Human Genome Project (HGP) or the CERN Large Hadron Collider are on the rise, the number of authors associated with these research projects substantially increase as well (Ioannidis, 2008). In fact, co-authorship dynamics has evolved from multiple authors to 'mega-' or 'hyper-' amount of authors (Cronin, 2001), ranging from 80 to 200 authors per paper. Evidently, hyper-authored papers are more of a convention in scientific domains such as biology, high energy physics, and medicine that requires large and complex coordination of tasks (Birnholtz, 2006). Consistent with the current author-ordering tradition in the field of genomics, the research on chromosome sequencing often listed its authors in three parts: first, middle, and last. First authors are usually the main contributors, last authors are senior researchers who supervise the research, while middle authors usually take on tasks such as data collection or annotation and are assumed to make smaller contributions (Mongeon et al, 2017). Given the complex contribution structures, there is a more pressing need to sort out questions of authorship order and credit allocations.

This study aims to examine the collaboration dynamics and the three-parts-structure of partial alphabetical author byline (some authors are listed alphabetically, some not) using co-authorship network analysis in the case of the HGP. In particular, we investigate the hyperauthorship phenomenon of one major research publication (Gregory et al, 2004) from the Wellcome Trust Sanger Institute, the biggest contributor to the sequencing of eight human chromosomes.

METHOD

With the HGP as a research setting and the Wellcome Trust Sanger Institute as the primary research center, we collect co- authorship data on articles published by the center. Given that the Sanger institute contributed efforts to sequencing chromosomes 1, 6, 9, 10, 13, 20, 22, and X, we only include published articles on the results of these eight chromosomes. The 8 papers identified were published between the years of 1999 to 2006, and were all highly-cited within the field. In this study, we focus specifically on the published work on chromosome 1 (Gregory et al, 2004), the largest human chromosome, thus requiring the most coordinated efforts to annotate and sequence.

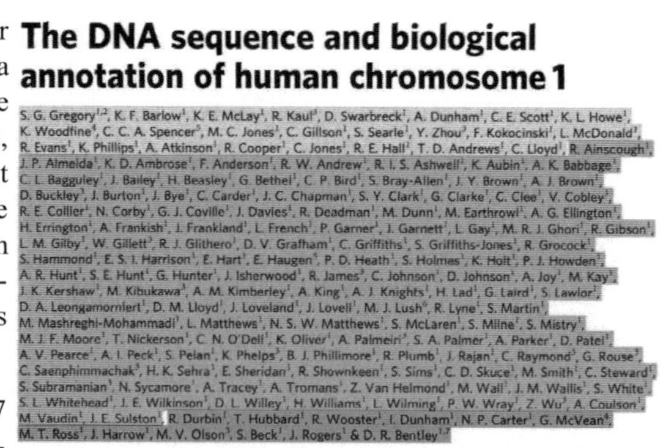
The DNA sequence and biological annotation of human chromosome 1

S. G. Gregory[1,2], K. F. Barlow[1], K. E. McLay[1], R. Kaul[3], D. Swarbreck[1], A. Dunham[1], C. E. Scott[1], K. L. Howe[1], K. Woodfine[4], C. C. A. Spencer[5], M. C. Jones[1], C. Gillson[1], S. Searle[1], Y. Zhou[3], F. Kokocinski[1], L. McDonald[1], R. Evans[1], K. Phillips[1], A. Atkinson[1], R. Cooper[1], C. Jones[1], R. E. Hall[1], T. D. Andrews[1], C. Lloyd[1], R. Ainscough[1], J. P. Almeida[1], K. D. Ambrose[1], F. Anderson[1], R. W. Andrew[1], R. I. S. Ashwell[1], K. Aubin[1], A. K. Babbage[1], C. L. Bagguley[1], J. Bailey[1], H. Beasley[1], G. Bethel[1], C. P. Bird[1], S. Bray-Allen[1], J. Y. Brown[1], A. J. Brown[1], D. Buckley[3], J. Burton[1], J. Bye[1], C. Carder[1], J. C. Chapman[1], S. Y. Clark[1], G. Clarke[1], C. Clee[1], V. Cobley[1], R. E. Collier[1], N. Corby[1], G. J. Coville[1], J. Davies[1], R. Deadman[1], M. Dunn[1], M. Earthrowl[1], A. G. Ellington[1], H. Errington[1], A. Frankish[1], J. Frankland[1], L. French[1], P. Garner[1], J. Garnett[1], L. Gay[1], M. R. J. Ghori[1], R. Gibson[1], L. M. Gilby[1], W. Gillett[3], R. J. Glithero[1], D. V. Grafham[1], C. Griffiths[1], S. Griffiths-Jones[1], R. Grocock[1], S. Hammond[1], E. S. I. Harrison[1], E. Hart[1], E. Haugen[3], P. D. Heath[1], S. Holmes[1], K. Holt[1], P. J. Howden[1], A. R. Hunt[1], S. E. Hunt[1], G. Hunter[1], J. Isherwood[1], R. James[3], C. Johnson[1], D. Johnson[1], A. Joy[1], M. Kay[1], J. K. Kershaw[1], M. Kibukawa[3], A. M. Kimberley[1], A. King[1], A. J. Knights[1], H. Lad[1], G. Laird[1], S. Lawlor[1], D. A. Leongamornlert[1], D. M. Lloyd[1], J. Loveland[1], J. Lovell[1], M. J. Lush[6], R. Lyne[1], S. Martin[1], M. Mashreghi-Mohammadi[1], L. Matthews[1], N. S. W. Matthews[1], S. McLaren[1], S. Milne[1], S. Mistry[1], M. J. F. Moore[1], T. Nickerson[1], C. N. O'Dell[1], K. Oliver[1], A. Palmeiri[3], S. A. Palmer[1], A. Parker[1], D. Patel[1], A. V. Pearce[1], A. I. Peck[1], S. Pelan[1], K. Phelps[3], B. J. Phillimore[1], R. Plumb[1], J. Rajan[1], C. Raymond[3], G. Rouse[3], C. Saenphimmachak[3], H. K. Sehra[1], E. Sheridan[1], R. Shownkeen[1], S. Sims[1], C. D. Skuce[1], M. Smith[1], C. Steward[1], S. Subramanian[3], N. Sycamore[1], A. Tracey[1], A. Tromans[1], Z. Van Helmond[1], M. Wall[1], J. M. Wallis[1], S. White[1], S. L. Whitehead[1], J. E. Wilkinson[1], D. L. Willey[1], H. Williams[1], L. Wilming[1], P. W. Wray[1], Z. Wu[3], A. Coulson[1], M. Vaudin[1], J. E. Sulston[1], R. Durbin[1], T. Hubbard[1], R. Wooster[1], I. Dunham[1], N. P. Carter[1], G. McVean[4], M. T. Ross[1], J. Harrow[1], M. V. Olson[3], S. Beck[1], J. Rogers[1] & D. R. Bentley[1,7]

Figure 1. Three-parts author structure of chromosome 1 paper

The paper contains 166 authors, of which 24 are first authors, 127 are middle authors, and 15 are last authors (Figure 1). Data on authors' affiliations, general demographics as well as the list of co-authors are obtained from the ISI Web of Science and Scopus. We conduct a co-authorship network analysis to capture collaboration patterns among all the authors involved in the chromosome 1 study. In this network, node i (ego) represents each author, and an edge $a_{\#\$}$ between node i (ego) and j (alter) denotes that these two authors have worked on at least 5 papers together. The network is undirected because co-authorship is mutual between two researchers. We use R's *igraph* package as the tool for constructing the network matrix and calculating network measures. Visualizations of the whole network along with induced subgraphs are then created on *Gephi*.

RESULTS

The co-authorship network created from the dataset above is the result of combining 166 different ego-networks of 166 original authors listed on the chromosome 1 paper byline (Figure 2). An ego-network of each focal author (ego) is composed of the edges that link that author with all co-authors (alters) that he/she has worked with on at least 5 papers. The whole network includes not only ego-alter relationships, but also alter-alter relationships (co-authors tied to the focal author are also tied to each other). Hence, the network size is larger with 1918 nodes, and 14088 edges. At the whole network level, density is relatively low (ρ=.008), with a mean degree of 14.69 edges per author. Though the network is sparse, clustering coefficient is very high at (C=.843) and with a relatively short average path length (ℓ=3.538) given the large network size. Thus, the topology of this network exhibits more desired properties of a small world network, rather than a scale-free network as with most co-authorship networks (Barabasi & Albert, 1999). In fact, our degree distribution is skewed, but does not entirely follow a power-law distribution (α=.582, R^2= .431) of a typical scale-free network.

At the subgraph level, it is interesting that we detected 6 communities (using Girvan-Newman modularity) beyond the three- part author structure. Since our network boundary is beyond the main authors of the chromosome 1 paper, we can infer that there are more communities of authors that exist beyond this research and perhaps give a holistic view to the general collaboration structure of the HGP. More interestingly, we find that central actors in this network are primarily from the middle author list (e.g. Leongamonert, D; Hunt, S; Lloyd, D). In fact, 60-70% of the most influential nodes are from these middle authors, suggesting that they are actively working with other scholars (high degree), connecting scholars of different institutions together (high betweenness), and also directly working with other well-established scholars (high eigenvector).

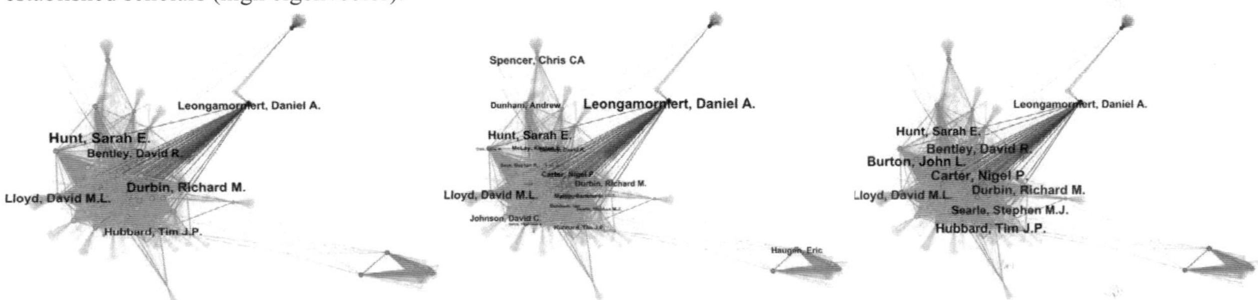

Figure 2. Top authors ranked by degree, betweenness, eigenvector centralities, respectively (by node label size)

CONCLUSION

The HGP is a leading example of big science that requires collaborative efforts from hundreds to thousands of researchers who are from a wide range of disciplines. Though determining where credit is due remains a conundrum in a hyper-authored setting, we find that middle authors may hold essential positions within the collaboration network in the chromosome 1 research. Recognizing that misallocation of credits may result in misallocation of funding opportunities and academic positions, we believe that providing a contribution list to describe *whodunwhat* in conjunction with the author byline is a necessary practice. Our future work includes examining in detail the collaboration dynamics among the first, middle, and last authors of all published works by a number of research centers affiliated with the HGP.

REFERENCES

Birnholtz, J. P. (2006). What does it mean to be an author? The intersection of credit, contribution, and collaboration in science. Journal of the Association for Information Science and Technology, 57(13), 1758-1770.

Cronin, B. (2001). Hyperauthorship: A postmodern perversion or evidence of a structural shift in scholarly communication practices?. Journal of the Association for Information Science and Technology, 52(7), 558-569.

Gregory, S. G., Barlow, K. F., McLay, K. E., Kaul, R., Swarbreck, D., Dunham, A., ... & Jones, M. C. (2006). The DNA sequence and biological annotation of human chromosome 1. Nature, 441(7091), 315.

Ioannidis, J. P. (2008). Measuring co-authorship and networking-adjusted scientific impact. PLoS One, 3(7).

Mongeon, P., Smith, E., Joyal, B., & Larivière, V. (2017). The rise of the middle author: Investigating collaboration and division of labor in biomedical research using partial alphabetical authorship. PloS one, 12(9).

Video-Based Consensus Annotations for Learning: A Feasibility Study

Samuel Dodson
University of British Columbia. dodsons@mail.ubc.ca

Matthew Fong
University of British Columbia. mfong@ece.ubc.ca

Luanne Freund
University of British Columbia. luanne.freund@ubc.ca

Rick Kopak
University of British Columbia. r.kopak@ubc.ca

Dongwook Yoon
University of British Columbia. yoon@cs.ubc.ca

Sidney Fels
University of British Columbia. ssfels@ece.ubc.ca

ABSTRACT

Video-based learning is increasingly common in higher education; however, the video players available make limited use of logged interaction data to support and guide students' viewing. In this work in progress, we explore the feasibility of aggregating students' annotations of videos (e.g., highlights, notes, and tags) to identify "hot spots," which can signal areas of interest to subsequent learners. We conducted a deployment study with 315 undergraduate students using ViDeX, a video player designed for active viewing. We logged students' use of ViDeX for four months, and then aggregated and graphed their annotations across 13 instructional videos. Our results show that consensus annotations—the video content that has received attention from many students—may be a feasible, data-driven way to flag information for use by subsequent learners.

KEYWORDS

Video-Based Learning, Annotation, Interaction Data, User Interface Design, Information Visualization.

INTRODUCTION

Video-based learning is increasingly popular in higher education; however, most video players provide students with limited tools for learning. They commonly include only basic playback tools, such as play and pause, fast-forward, and rewind. This work is part of a larger project to design a video player, ViDeX (Fong et al., 2018), with tools for active viewing (Dodson et al., 2018). The current version of ViDeX supports user interaction with video, including highlighting, note taking, and tagging. This opens up the possibility of using this interaction data to enable students to learn from one another. We hypothesized that there would be sufficient agreement among students, such that aggregating and sharing data from their annotations could flag interesting or confusing parts of videos for subsequent learners. The objective of this work was to test this hypothesis and to develop a data-driven means of visualizing the aggregated interaction data for students.

Many types of interaction data can be aggregated, including the number of times an interval of content has been annotated. Marshall (1998) proposed that readers' annotations, such as their highlights and notes, could be aggregated in order to "identify n-way consensus, places in the text that all n of the readers… had agreed were important, or at least worthy of pulling out from the text." Like Marshall, we use the degree of annotation consensus as an indicator for agreement of points of interest. High degree of consensus among individuals may indicate what information they find confusing or interesting.

Video players are just beginning to make use of students' interaction data in order to support subsequent learners' video use. LectureScape (Kim et al., 2014) includes a visualization of aggregated view counts of a given video. By looking at the peaks and troughs of the aggregated view count plot, students can see which intervals of video content are most and least popular. LectureScape uses "byproducts" of students' navigation behaviors, which are implicit measures of students' video use; however, our data source is annotation, which is an explicit user interaction. MudSlide (Glassman et al., 2015) allows students to click on the visual content of a video to apply a "muddy point," a semi-translucent circle, to flag confusing content. Aggregated, explicit user interactions, such as muddy points, may provide more insight into what students find important or confusing than aggregated, implicit measures of video use, such as view counts. In this work in progress, we explore the use of aggregated summary plots and heat maps as visualizations for assessing degree of annotation consensus.

METHODS

We introduced ViDeX to 315 undergraduates in an introductory engineering course. Students were provided with 13 optional videos (8±3 minutes each) to watch before classes. The videos showed their instructor working through practice problems similar to those on their homework and exams. Students received a demo of the annotation features of ViDeX at the beginning of the semester, but they were not required to use the system. We logged students' use of ViDeX for four months, and then aggregated, normalized, and graphed summary plots and created heat maps of student's aggregated annotations for each video (Figures 1 and 2). Two videos were removed from analysis as they were annotated by fewer than 5 students. To smooth the plots of the logged data and enable comparison, the remaining 11 videos were binned into 10% time intervals, which ranged from 22 to 103 seconds depending on the video length. The annotations within each interval of a video were counted and divided by the total number of annotators for the video. Consequently, multiple annotations by the same student were counted once. The normalized values for each interval are between 0 and 1, and these values were used to create the heat maps. The warmer colors represent higher degrees of consensus in highlights, notes, and tags and serve to identify "hot spots," or intervals of video content that have been annotated by at least half of students who annotated a video.

PRELIMINARY RESULTS

Of the 315 students in the course, 281 logged into ViDeX at least once during the semester. Of these, 77 students (27%) annotated, creating 593 highlights, 264 notes, and 1,178 tags in total. User interaction plots were created for each video (Figure 1), to provide visual summaries of annotations from all students. Highlights are displayed as horizontal bars. The color, length, and position of each bar matches the color, length, and position of the corresponding ViDeX highlights. Notes and tags are displayed as blue and red points, respectively. Figure 2 provides an example of a heat map for the same video, with the value in each interval representing the degree of consensus annotation. For example, a value of 0.5 means that half of those who annotated a video, did so in this interval. We found that all but one video had hot spots. The number of hot spots in each video varied between 1 and 3. Of all hot spots, 80% were in the first half of the video content. Hot spots, which may represent confusing or interesting video content, are now visible with the heat map.

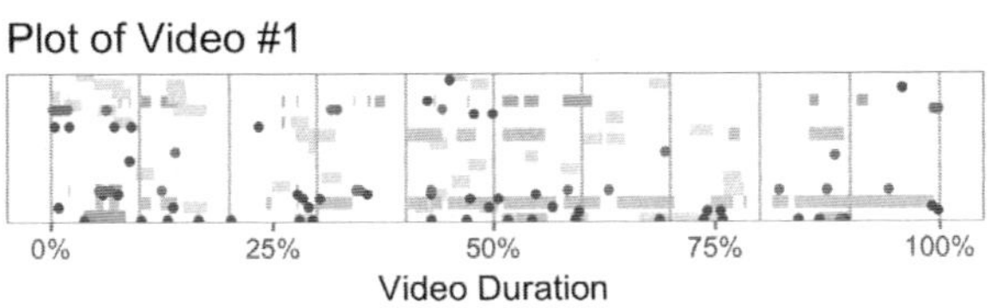

Figure 1: The summary plot of annotations for video #1. Each row represents a user. Highlights are displayed as colored horizontal bars, matching the color of the ViDeX highlights. Notes and tags plotted as blue and red points.

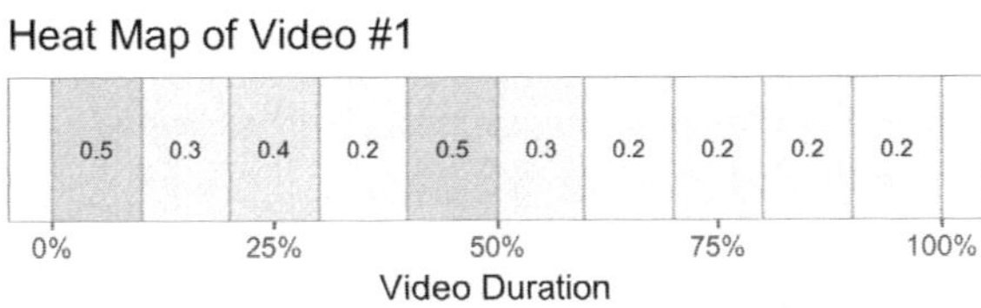

Figure 2: The heat map showing annotation (highlights, notes, and tags) consensus for video #1. The values and shades in each interval represent the degree of consensus

CONCLUSION & FUTURE WORK

This initial study supports our hypothesis that there are discernable patterns of consensus in annotation across this set of videos, which could be informative to subsequent learners. We created two prototype visualizations, summary plots and heat maps, both of which could be displayed alongside a video timeline. We consider the heat map to be a good candidate for conveying degree of consensus annotation to users, as it is easy to interpret and scalable. Our next steps include: i) analyzing the aural, textual, and visual features of video in the hot spots to identify content that may trigger students' confusion or interest, and ii) evaluate the usability and value of aggregated annotations for students. Longer term questions include: does supplying this information change students' viewing behaviors, their level of engagement, or their learning outcomes?

ACKNOWLEDGEMENTS

This work was funded by UBC TLEF, NSERC of Canada, and Microsoft Corporation. We would also like to thank the members of the ViDeX research project, especially Negar M. Harandi, Min Li, Ido Roll, Sameer Sunani, and Junyuan Zheng.

REFERENCES

Dodson, S., Roll, I., Fong, M., Yoon, D., Harandi, N. M., & Fels S. (2018). Active viewing: A framework for understanding student engagement with educational videos. *Proceedings of the Fifth ACM Conference on Learning at Scale*, 24:1–24:4.

Fong, M., Dodson, S., Roll, I., & Fels S. (2018). ViDeX: A platform for personalizing educational videos. *Proceedings of the 2018 ACM/IEEE Joint Conference on Digital Libraries*, 331–332.

Glassman, E. L., Kim, J., Monroy-Hernández, A., & Morris, M. R. (2015). Mudslide: A spatially anchored census of student confusion for online lecture videos. *Proceedings of the 33rd ACM Conference on Human Factors in Computing Systems*, 1555–1564.

Kim, J., Guo, P. J., Cai, C. J., Li, S. W. D., Gajos, K. Z., & Miller, R. C. (2014). Data-driven interaction techniques for improving navigation of educational videos. *Proceedings of the 27th ACM Symposium on UIST*, 563–572.

Marshall, C.C. (1998). Toward an ecology of hypertext annotation. *Proceedings of the Ninth ACM Conference on Hypertext and Hypermedia*, 40–49.

Working with Indigenous Communities: Reflections on Ethical Information Research with Ngarrindjeri People in South Australia

Jia Tina Du
University of South Australia, Australia. tina.du@unisa.edu.au

Jelina Haines
University of South Australia, Australia. jelina.haines@mymail.unisa.edu.au

ABSTRACT

In this paper, we reflected on the ethical information research based on our two studies conducted with an Indigenous community in South Australia. The first study was about understanding how Indigenous people interact with information and communication technologies (ICTs) on their traditional land and how they perceive the role of ICTs in the community development. The second study focused on Indigenous knowledge and experiences sharing in the traditional society. Ethical investigations on Indigenous people's information and knowledge practices will contribute to information research with marginalized groups.

KEYWORDS

Ethical research, Indigenous community, information research, information and communication technologies

INTRODUCTION

Stipulating ethical research requires dual needs of evading exploitation and misappropriation of knowledge shared by the participants and affirming community's right to self-determination (Buchanan et al., 2007; De Crespigny et al., 2004; Du et al., 2015). Nakata and colleagues (2005) stressed the importance of recognizing Indigenous knowledge as distinct with its own orality of management; failure to the recognition will result in the reluctance of Indigenous people to share their stories and practices. Williamson and Jackway (2003) stated that once Indigenous knowledge is digitally archived in an official institution, its public accessibility often becomes limited and therefore Aboriginal people are reluctant to access their own knowledge. By reflecting on our studies conducted in partnership with an Indigenous community in the Ngarrindjeri Ruwe (country) in South Australia, this paper contextualizes relevant ethical considerations, including the ethical guidelines of respect, trust, reciprocity and mutual partnership framework and responsibilities governing our conduct as researchers. This poster paper is, for the first time, centrally discussing aspects of ethics when researching with indigenous communities in the field of library and information sciences.

THE INDIGENOUS COMMUNITY AND TWO STUDIES

The research team (non-Indigenous researchers) has conducted two studies with the Ngarrindjeri community in South Australia who traditionally owns the land around the lower lakes of the Murray River and the Coorong areas. The knowledge structure of Ngarrindjeri people is exclusively in oral traditions and tangible objects (basket weaving), and the creation stories were handed down from Elders to younger generations. A more detailed description of the Ngarrindjeri community and its demographics can be found in Du and Haines (2017).

Field research	Study 1	Study 2
Length of data collection	9 months (Jan-Sep 2014)	12 months (Feb 2016-Feb 2017)
No. of participants	47	13
Instruments	Face-to-face questionnaire, Semi-structured interview (audio recordings) Field observations (notes-taking)	Video and audio dialogue interviews Visual ethnography (video and audio diaries)
Incentives	Cooking fresh meals for participants, petrol vouchers	Honorary vouchers valued $50.00 petrol vouchers, cooking fresh meals for participants and grocery bag for the host community
Reciprocity	Providing printed copies of research outputs, delivering computer/Internet training workshops, and holding a public seminar to share research findings from this project and other Indigenous studies	Annual reporting to the community, providing printed copies of research outputs, representative Elder as co-author in journal and conference publications, monthly visits back to the community to help the Aunties on their daily life activities

Table 1. Summary of methods.

Study 1 was a one-year project that investigated the use of ICTs as a way to promote learning and effective living within the Aboriginal community (Du & Haines, 2017). The research goal was to identify the strengths and challenges facing Aboriginal people as they access information via the Internet in everyday lives. Study 2 is an ongoing doctoral study that examines the knowledge journey practices of Indigenous Elders within the paradigm of Community-Based Participatory Research (Haines et al., 2017). Its research aim was to explore the cyclical process of how knowledge is created, synthesized, and shared in their unique social and cultural contexts. Table 1 summarizes the research design of each study.

As shown in the table, the philosophies of respect, trust and reciprocity were aimed at creating deeper connections with the community. We improved the rate of participation as the participants favored fresh meals, we brought fresh meat and vegetables to the research site (by traveling around 160km in one way) and cooked for them. Sitting together during mealtime provided a great-shared space to exchange ideas and evaluate existing practices, to relax, and catch up. During the tea breaks, over lunch and dinner, there were lively conversations between men and women, between researchers and participants. However, conversations between men and women differ when it comes to cultural stories. This is one of the cultural protocols that researchers must be aware.

CONDUCTING ETHICAL RESEARCH WITH INDIGENOUS COMMUNITIES

Arguments on the ethical research with Indigenous communities were seen in our prior works (Du & Haines, 2017; Haines et al., 2017) and in the literature (e.g. De Crespigny et al., 2004; Kelley et al., 2013; Koster et al., 2012). As pointed out by Castleden et al. (2012), it is critical that research design involving Indigenous people will address ongoing imbalances of power in the academia and eliminate recurrence of unethical research practices. Based on a culmination of research from relevant literature (Favel & Coates, 2016; Mnjama, 2008; Schnarch, 2004) and the context of the partnering community, we develop a framework illustrating the guidelines of conducting ethical and sustainable research with Indigenous communities (Figure 1).

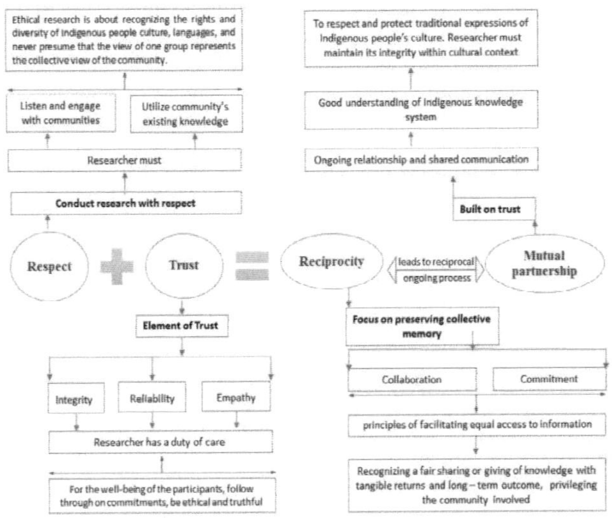

Figure 1. Ethical guidelines and research sustainability framework in the Ngarrindjeri context.

Figure 1 demonstrates that reciprocal research postulates a continuing process. The framework proposes a method that emphasizes respect for listening profoundly and understands Aboriginal culture. Respect will lessen the notion of distrustful inquiries, and gaining trust is fundamentally important to avoid common mistakes and stereotyping. Reciprocity and mutual partnership is an ongoing community consultation that stresses a collaborative and shared practices of respect and trust. In our cases, these involved a series of dialogues and conversations before, during and after the research projects. This ensured better input from the community and research data were collected and shared in accordance with the Ngarrindjeri protocols. The partnership was established between the research team and the Ngarrindjeri Land & Progress Association (NLPA), the representative body for the Ngarrindjeri people of Meningie and the Lower Lakes of the Coorong. NLPA see the projects as an integral part of building a stronger Ngarrindjeri Nation and privileging future generations. It should be noted that the ethical considerations reported in this paper are based on our working with one Indigenous community and these might not be generalizable to other Indigenous communities in practice due to varied cultures and protocols. However, the purpose of this framework is to visually illustrate the protocols and principles that are useful for future researchers and professionals undertaking on a similar topic.

Challenges and Concerns

Challenges exist for non-Indigenous researchers as we might not understand (or truly appreciate) Indigenous protocols. For example, each community has different laws and practices that we need to pay attention to and taking time to listen, and the unpredictable nature of Indigenous participants' lives (often with multiple community and family commitments) requires patience, adaptability and flexibility. Working with the Indigenous community needs a long-term planning and investment in time, infrastructure, finance and commitment from both the community and research team. Data collection instruments also need to be culturally appropriate, able to address community needs and engaging. We are still grappling with the questions, such as, which research methodology and practices are the best to use without devaluing the significance and importance of Indigenous knowledge? What are ethical approaches for acknowledging research participants contributing to the study? What are long-term benefits for the community after the research project is finished? One possibility might be is to aim for lasting benefits as we undertake a multi-year project that will deliver ongoing mentoring, training and employment for the Indigenous community.

ACKNOWLEDGMENT

We wish to acknowledge Elders Aunty Ellen and Aunty Alice for their advisory roles and partnership in our studies. Thanks also to the Ngarrindjeri participants who gave their time and shared their insights and knowledge with us.

REFERENCES

Buchanan, D. R., Miller, F. G., & Wallerstein, N. (2007). Ethical issues in community-based participatory research: Balancing rigorous research with community participation in community intervention studies. *Progress in Community Health Partnerships: Research, Education, and Action, 1*(2), 153-160.

Castleden, H., Morgan, V. S., & Lamb, C. (2012). "I spent the first year drinking tea": Exploring Canadian university researchers' perspectives on community-based participatory research involving Indigenous peoples. *The Canadian Geographer, 56*(2), 160-179.

De Crespigny, C., Emden,C., Kowanko, I.,& Murray, H. (2004). A partnership model for ethical Indigenous research. *Collegian, 11*(4), 7-13.

Du, J. T. & Haines, J. (2017). Indigenous Australians' information behaviour and Internet use in everyday life: An exploratory study. *Information Research, 22* (1), paper 737. Retrieved from http://InformationR.net/ir/22-1/paper737.html

Du, J. T., Haines, J., Sun, V.Q., Partridge, H. & Ma, D.D. (2015). Understanding indigenous people's information practices and Internet use: A Ngarrindjeri perspective. In *Proceedings of the 19th Pacific Asia Conference on Information Systems*, paper 183, Retrieved from http://aisel.aisnet.org/pacis2015/183/

Favel, B., & Coates, K. S. (2016). Understanding UNDRIP: Choosing action on priorities over sweeping claims about the United Nations Declaration of the Rights of Indigenous Peoples. Retrieved from https://www.macdonaldlaurier.ca/files/pdf/MLI-10-UNDRIPCoates-Flavel05-16-WebReadyV4.pdf

Haines, J., Du, J. T., Geursen, G., Gao, J., & Trevorrow, E. (2017). Understanding Elders' knowledge creation to strengthen Indigenous ethical knowledge sharing. *In Proceedings of RAILS 2016. Information Research,* 22(4), paper rails1607. Retrieved from http://In-formationR.net/ir/22-4/rails/rails1607.html

Kelley, A., Belcourt-Dittloff, A., Belcourt, C., & Belcourt, G. (2013). Research ethics and indigenous communities. *American Journal of Public Health, 103*(12), 2146-52.

Koster, R, Baccar, K., & Lemelin, R.H. (2012). Moving from research ON, to research WITH and FOR Indigenous communities: A critical reflection on community-based participatory research. *The Canadian Geographer, 56* (2), 195-210.

Mnjama, N. (2008). The Orentlicher principles on the preservation and access to archives bearing witness to human rights violations. *Information Development, 24*(3), 213-225.

Nakata, M., Byrne, A., Nakata, V., & Gardiner, G. (2005). Indigenous knowledge, the library and information service sector, and protocols. *Australian Academic & Research Libraries, 36*(2), 7-21.

Schnarch, B. (2004). Ownership, control, access, and possession (OCAP) or self-determination applied to research: A critical analysis of contemporary First Nations research and some options for First Nations communities. *International Journal of Indigenous Health, 1*(1), 80.

Williamson, K. & Jackway, C. (2003). Trust and technology: Providing access to oral memory for Indigenous communities. *Incite, 24*(11), 6.

Sticky Words: Evaluation and Optimization of Information Interactions Based on Linguistic Analysis

Nim Dvir
University at Albany, USA. ndvir@albany.edu

ABSTRACT

This visual presentation describes a novel approach to systematically improve interactions with digital content based solely on its wording. Following an interdisciplinary literature review, we recognized three key attributes of words that drive successful interactions: (1) Novelty (2) Familiarity (3) Sentimentality. Based on these attributes, we developed a model to systematically improve a given content using word frequency, sentiment analysis and semantic substitution, and by employing computational linguistics and natural language processing (NLP) techniques. We conducted a pilot study (*n*=416) in which the model was used to formalize evaluation and optimization of academic titles. A between-group design was used to compare responses to the original (control) and modified (treatment) titles. Results show that the modified titles had significantly higher scores for selection, user engagement and memorability. Our findings suggest that users' successful interactions with digital content is fostered by, and perhaps dependent upon, the wording being used. They also provide empirical support that engaging content can be systematically evaluated and produced. Implications and future research directions are discussed.

KEYWORDS

Content strategy, human-computer interaction, user experience (UX), engagement

INTRODUCTION

Providing users with information in a form and format that maximizes its effectiveness is a research question of critical importance. With increasing amount of digital content being published by commercial businesses, governments, healthcare organizations and private citizens, information interactions and information behavior become more complex (Toms, 2002; Wilson, 2000). User engagement (UE) is often used to describe the process of drawing favorable attention, interest and investment in an interaction between a user and a resource (O'Brien, 2016; O'Brien & Toms, 2008). Given the growing competition for users' attention and interest, it is agreed that content must engage. However, there are no clear methods or frameworks for evaluation, optimization and creation of such content (Dvir & Gafni, 2018; Gafni & Dvir, 2018).

We suggest that the phrasing of the digital content – the words being used – can impact how the information will be consumed, perceived and used. We propose a conceptual and practical framework to evaluate and improve a given content based on the identification of reliable and reusable metrics for linguistic analysis and employment of computational linguistic and NLP techniques.

Following a comprehensive literature review, we conceptualize and operationalize the process of information interaction and identify three key attributes of digital content that drive successful information interactions: (1) Familiarity - words that are known and popular, operationalized as having high frequency in popular culture (cultural relevance); (2) Novelty – words that are rare in the context of the interaction, (operationalized as having low frequency in that context); (3) Emotionality – emotive words that evoke emotional reaction, operationalized through sentiment polarity (positive, negative, or neutral).

We call these words "sticky words." We hypothesized that when strategically placed in a given content, these words can increase the motivation to consume it, improve how it is evaluated and lead to better knowledge retention. We conducted a pilot study in which our model was used to formalize evaluation and optimization of academic titles. The pilot study was guided by the following research questions: RQ1: Can "sticky words" improve interactions with digital content? RQ2: Can such words can be systematically, or automatically, evaluated and produced?

METHOD

A randomized between-group design was employed to observe how changes in wording (independent variable) impact information interaction and behavior (dependent variable). First, the model was used to create control and treatment groups of original and modified academic titles. Then, users' responses were recorded to observe the effect on the interaction.

We collected academic titles from the JSTOR database. We created a corpus of potential "sticky words" using the movie keyword analyzer of The Internet Movie Database (IMDB.com), which aggregates all keywords assigned to movies. These represent well-known words frequently used in popular culture. We used Term frequency–Inverse document frequency (TF-IDF) to find words with high frequency on the list of IMDB keywords (for familiarity), and with low frequency in the collection of the academic titles (for novelty). Sentiment analysis was used to categorize the words for emotional polarity (positive, negative, or neutral). We then used semantic and lexical analysis to find synonyms and make replacements of words in the academic titles, substituting only one word at a time with a semantically equivalent "sticky word." For example, the title "**End** of the library: Organized information and digital ubiquity" became "**Death** of library: Organized information and digital ubiquity". We manually verify that the introduction of the new word does not alter the meaning of the text. The result is a dataset of control and treatment (modified) titles (all titles will be presented in the poster presentation).

We used Qualtric.com to randomly present the titles and to collect responses. Participants (n=416) were recruited using an email sent to a listserv of undergraduate students in a large research university in the U.S. After providing demographic information, each participant was randomly presented with a version of a title, either original (control) or modified (treatment). The interaction was assessed through questions relating to the different dimensions of information behavior. Specifically (a) Motivation to consume the content: Participants were asked whether they would like to read the title (b) Evaluation of the content: Participants were asked to rate the title for interest, value, readability and other factors adopted from the User Engagement Scale (UES) (O'Brien, Cairns, & Hall, 2018) (c) knowledge retention: Participants answered post-task questions to test whether they recall the information.

RESULTS

RQ1: Impact of "Sticky words" on the interaction

The effect was examined using univariate analysis of variance (ANOVA), Chi-Square and paired-samples t-tests. Results show significant difference in favor of the treatment group. The modified titles were significantly ranked higher for motivation to consume, had higher evaluation scores and higher recall rates. We observed a significant positive correlation between the treated titles and effective interactions in all dimensions. Thus, the findings indicate that "sticky words" impact information behavior and lead to a more effective interactions.

RQ2: Can "sticky words" be systematically identified

While we were able to use term frequency, sentiment analysis and semantic substitution to evaluate and replace "sticky words," we had to manually confirm that the meaning of the title did not change. The findings indicate the potential to use computational linguistics to identify factors that predict successful interactions, yet there is still a need to refine our model to achieve full automation.

CONCLUSION

The implications of this research are twofold. First, our findings suggest that successful interactions with digital content are fostered by, and perhaps dependent upon, the wording or language being used. Second, we provide empirical support that engaging content can be evaluated and optimized systematically. We propose that computational linguistics is a useful approach for studying online information interactions and that further study can result in a broader conceptualization of content strategy and its evaluation. These empirically based insights can inform the development of digital content strategies, thereby improving the success of information interactions. Moving forward, the validity, reliability and generalizability of our model should be tested in various contexts. In future research, we propose to include additional linguistic factors and develop more sophisticated interaction measures. This research can be used as an important starting point for understanding the phenomenon of digital information interactions and behavior, the factors that promote and facilitates them, and in the development of a broad framework for systematically evaluation, optimization, and creation effective digital content.

REFERENCES

Dvir, N., & Gafni, R. (2018). When less is more: empirical study of the relation between consumer behavior and information provision on commercial landing pages. *Informing Science: The International Journal of an Emerging Transdiscipline*, *21*, 019–039. doi:10.28945/4015

Gafni, R., & Dvir, N. (2018). How content volume on landing pages influences consumer behavior: empirical evidence. In *Proceedings of the Informing Science and Information Technology Education Conference, La Verne, California* (pp. 035–053). Santa Rosa, CA: Informing Science Institute. doi:10.28945/4016

O'Brien, H. L. (2016). *Why Engagement Matters*. Cham: Springer International Publishing. doi:10.1007/978-3-319-27446-1

O'Brien, H. L., Cairns, P., & Hall, M. (2018). A practical approach to measuring user engagement with the refined user engagement scale (UES) and new UES short form. *International Journal of Human-Computer Studies*, *112*, 28–39. doi:10.1016/j.ijhcs.2018.01.004

O'Brien, H. L., & Toms, E. G. (2008). What is user engagement? A conceptual framework for defining user engagement with technology. *Journal of the American Society for Information Science and Technology*, *59*(6), 938–955. doi:10.1002/asi.20801

Toms, E. G. (2002). Information interaction: Providing a framework for information architecture. *Journal of the Association for Information Science and Technology*, *53*(10), 855–862.

Wilson, T. D. (2000). Human information behavior. *Informing Science*, *3*(2), 49–56.

Exploring linked data benefits for digital library users

Katrina Fenlon
University of Illinois at Urbana-Champaign, kfenlon2@illinois.edu

Jacob Jett
University of Illinois at Urbana-Champaign, jjett2@illinois.edu

Ryan Dubnicek
University of Illinois at Urbana-Champaign, rdubnic2@illinois.edu

Timothy W. Cole
University of Illinois at Urbana-Champaign, t-cole3@illinois.edu

Deren Kudeki
University of Illinois at Urbana-Champaign, dkudeki@illinois.edu

ABSTRACT

Linked open data technologies seem likely to offer significant benefits for digital library users. So far, however, these benefits remain largely speculative despite growing momentum toward the application of linked data in libraries. This paper reports on an exploratory user study to evaluate the use of linked data with digital library special collections. This pilot study assessed features designed to contextualize search results and representations of primary sources, and features that leverage linked data to offer analytic insights. Digital library users were most excited by applications of linked data that provide new, analytic information, and which simultaneously serve to open up new avenues for research within and beyond individual collections.

KEYWORDS

Linked open data, digital libraries, users.

INTRODUCTION

Linked open data (LOD) technologies offer opportunities for enhancing library collections and resources for users. Momentum toward the implementation of LOD in libraries has been growing in recent years, spurred by research initiatives and community incubation efforts (e.g. *Linked Data for Libraries*;[1] Haslhofer & Isaac, 2011; etc.). The benefits of LOD for digital library users remain largely speculative, but these benefits may represent an important motivator for the adoption of LOD in library settings.

This paper reports on an exploratory study to evaluate uses of LOD for digital library special collections. The study investigated how LOD features stand to affect the use of digital collections for humanities research. Funded by the Andrew W. Mellon Foundation, "Exploring the Benefits for Users of Linked Open Data for Digitized Special Collections"[2] examined the potential benefits of LOD for users of digital collections. (Additional details of this study are provided in Fenlon et al., 2018.)

METHODS

The first phase of this study established baselines for the usability of our test collections through task-based user interviews with 15 humanities researchers. The second phase (on which this paper reports) comprised a series of five interviews with humanities researchers to assess new, LOD-based enhancements to our collections. Each interview lasted between a half hour and an hour. Participants described their research processes in general, and then offered their reactions to experimental, LOD-based features that were mocked up in our test collections. We tested these features in two digital collections at the University of Illinois Library: the Kolb-Proust Archive[3] and the Motley Collection of Theatre and Costume Design.[4]

PRELIMINARY OUTCOMES

This paper reports on user reactions to three applications of LOD in digital collections: (1) enhanced representations of primary sources, (2) enhanced search results, and (3) the addition of an analytic feature for exploring a collection. Overall, participants expressed enthusiasm for LOD-based features to forge connections between collections and external resources, offer new modes of access to collections, and expand contextual information about sources and collections.

---

[1] https://www.ld4l.org/
[2] http://publish.illinois.edu/linkedspcollections/
[3] http://kolbproust.library.illinois.edu/proust/search
[4] http://imagesearch-test1.library.illinois.edu/

Enhanced primary source representation

We tested the use of LOD to augment an item-detail page with a sidebar containing automatically derived contextual information and links to relevant external resources (Figure 1). Contextual sources were found to be valuable to users doing early-stage research or studying entities peripheral to main queries.

Enhanced search results

We tested the use of LOD to augment search results with a "knowledge panel" (as popularized by Google) —created dynamically in response to user queries—which offers contextual information about named entities relevant to search results. We found significant variation in how much and what kind of information participants wanted to see alongside search results. Most participants agreed that the LOD-based "knowledge card" feature was highly useful, especially for disambiguation of terms and for shedding light on the contents of the collection as a whole.

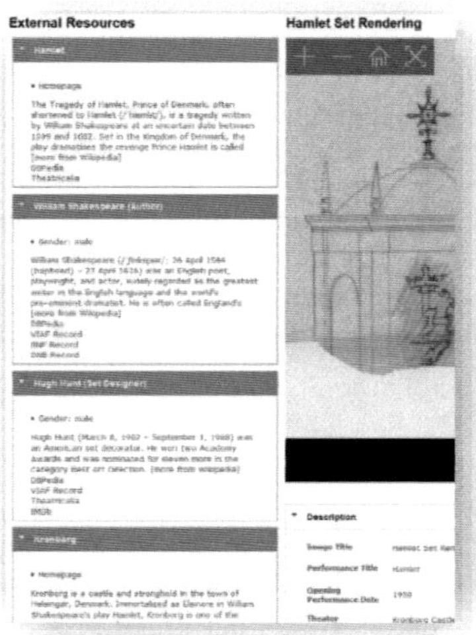

Figure 2. Item enhanced with info about contextual entities, derived from external sources through LOD

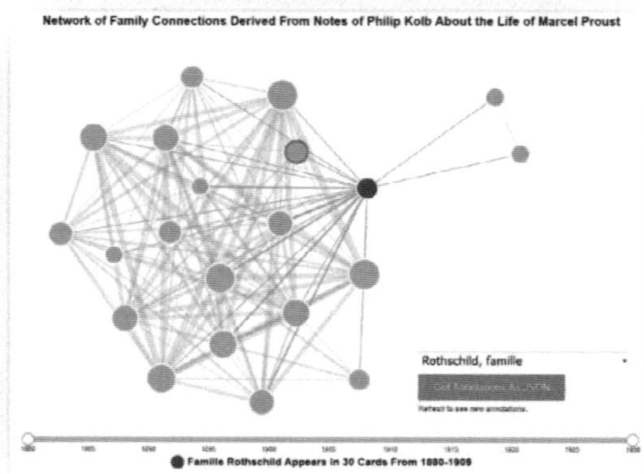

Figure 3. Interactive visualization of relationships between named entities in collection, derived from LOD

Introducing analytic features

The final feature assessed in this pilot was an interactive, analytic social network visualization of relationships derived from LOD representations of named entities in one collection (Figure 2). The visualization supports dynamic exploration of relationships within the collection and allows users to add exportable annotations to the graph. Participants expressed demand for such visualizations to serve both as entry points into collections and as hubs for collaboration. What excited participants most was that this feature offers substantial new, interpretive or analytic information, which serves to open new avenues for research.

DISCUSSION AND FUTURE WORK

Next-generation cultural collections will rely on data models that readily support interlinking among and inferencing across related but scattered collections, items, and datasets. Our early outcomes suggest that libraries may exploit LOD to improve access to and understanding of research collections through analytic and social features. Because researchers have idiosyncratic preferences and processes for working with collections, the most effective applications of LOD will accommodate different kinds of users and evolving research contexts. LOD is not the only data model for realizing the kinds of features described here, but it carries a main advantage of facilitating standards-based interoperability across digital libraries. This exploratory study is intended as a pilot for future work on the potential of LOD to benefit research users of digital collections.

REFERENCES

Haslhofer, B., & Isaac, A. (2011). data.europeana.eu: The Europeana Linked Open Data Pilot. *International Conference on Dublin Core and Metadata Applications*, *0*, 94–104. http://dcpapers.dublincore.org/pubs/article/view/3625

Fenlon, K., Jett, J., Dubnicek, R., Cole, T., Szylowicz, C., Kudeki, D., Zavala, M., Kinnaman, A. (2018). *Project White Paper #2: Analysis of Early User Feedback*. http://publish.illinois.edu/linkedspcollections/files/2018/06/LOD_research_whitePaper2_29June2018.pdf

Human Values and End-of-Life Decision Making: Results from a Pilot Study of Dementia Caregivers

Fleischmann, Kenneth R.
The University of Texas at Austin, USA,
kfleisch@ischool.utexas.edu

Kwak, Jung
The University of Texas at Austin, USA,
jkwak@nursing.utexas.edu

Xie, Bo
The University of Texas at Austin, USA,
boxie@utexas.edu

Koltai, Kolina S.
The University of Texas at Austin, USA,
koltai@utexas.edu

Champion, Jane Dimmitt
The University of Texas at Austin, USA,
jdchampion@mail.nur.utexas.edu

ABSTRACT

Can basic human values be used to predict end-of-life (EOL) decision making? Millions of Americans suffer from Alzheimer's Disease and Related Dementias (ADRD), yet many ADRD patients do not have advance directives, leaving their loved ones unprepared to make decisions on their behalves. Since EOL care preferences are often treated as a taboo topic, it is important to find ways to predict EOL care preferences in cases where they are unknown. This paper sets out to identify any correlations between basic human values and EOL care preferences. A survey of 50 caregivers found that individuals who highly valued *benevolence* preferred more care ($p<0.01$), while individuals who highly valued *power* preferred less care ($p<0.01$). This study provides preliminary evidence supporting the use of basic human values as a proxy for EOL care preferences.

KEYWORDS

Alzheimer's Disease and Related Dementias (ADRD), end-of-life (EOL) decision making, human values, power, benevolence.

INTRODUCTION

In 2017, 5.5 million Americans suffered from Alzheimer's Disease and Related Dementias (ADRD) (Alzheimer's Association, 2017). Approximately 40% of people with ADRD in nursing homes receive costly, burdensome interventions that are often inconsistent with their wishes (Mitchell et al., 2012). The end-of-life (EOL) care decision making for people with advanced ADRD falls mostly on family members as surrogate decision makers (hereafter referred to as caregivers). EOL decisions are high-stake and value-laden; however, caregivers do not fully understand their loved ones' preferences for EOL treatments and report inadequate support from professionals in decision making (Kwak, Kramer, Lang, & Ledger, 2012). Caregivers may be unprepared for their EOL decision-making roles and may experience conflicts with other family members and health care providers in making choices (Ditto et al., 2001). At the same time, health care professionals often lack skills and tools to help families communicate and engage in shared decision making (Kwak et al., 2012). Rich evidence in the literature suggests human values (e.g., self-enhancement vs. self-transcendence; conservation vs. openness to change) affect individuals' behaviors and choices (Fleischmann, 2014; Schwartz, 2007). In the case of EOL decision making by caregivers, their understanding of ADRD patients' values is a key determinant of decisional uncertainty and confidence in caregivers (Kwak et al., 2012). Thus, the goal of this paper is to identify any correlations between basic human values and EOL care preferences.

METHODS

To answer our research question, "are there correlations between EOL preferences and basic human values?" we developed a survey instrument that included the Portrait Value Questionnaire (PVQ) as well as an EOL care scenario. The PVQ (Schwartz, 2007) was developed for the European Social Survey, and measures 10 basic human values (power, achievement, hedonism, stimulation, self-direction, universalism, benevolence, tradition, conformity, and security). The EOL care scenario lays out a situation where the participant is asked to imagine that they are suffering from advanced ADRD and that they are in their last year of life, and are asked to select from one of three options: "perform everything that a modern hospital can offer, including hospitalizations, cardiopulmonary resuscitation (CPR), feeding tubes, ventilator, and other procedures in the intensive care unit (ICU)," henceforth referred to as "perform everything" or PE; "perform everything except for CPR or procedures in the ICU," henceforth referred to as "everything except" or EE; or "perform only procedures for pain and symptom control, but not hospitalization, CPR, feeding tubes, ventilator, or other procedures in the ICU", henceforth referred to as "pain and symptom" or PS. Due to the modest sample size, we chose more robust non-parametric methods to perform our statistical analyses. We used Kruskal-Wallis H, the non-parametric equivalent of ANOVA, to determine if there were any significant differences in the value ratings across the three groups, and for all values for which Kruskal-Wallis H returned a significant result, we used Mann-Whitney U, the non-parametric equivalent of the unpaired t-test, to look for differences between any two of the three options.

RESULTS

In April-May 2017, we conducted a survey study of caregivers of persons with ADRD (N = 50). Participants were recruited during a 3-week period via word-of-mouth and flyers posted at a medical practice. Participants' ages ranged from 27 to 85 (Mean = 53; SD = 13.8). Many participants reported a lack of documentation of their loved one's EOL preferences; 42% reported that their relative did not have a power of attorney for their health care and 40% reported that their relative did not have a living will or advance directive. As shown in Table 1, we found significant differences for two values: power and benevolence. As shown in Table 2, we found that those who preferred having hospitalization, feeding tubes, and ventilator as treatment options placed a significantly higher value on *benevolence* ($p<0.01$) and significantly lower on *power* ($p<0.01$).

Value	H	*p*
Power	7.956	0.019
Achievement	4.276	0.118
Hedonism	4.518	0.104
Stimulation	2.094	0.351
Self-Direction	3.070	0.215
Universalism	0.863	0.649
Benevolence	7.611	0.022
Tradition	2.744	0.254
Conformity	5.826	0.054
Security	1.867	0.393

Table 1. Kruskal-Wallis H for All 10 Values

Value	Power	Benevolence
PE vs. EE U	37.5	35.0
PE vs. EE *p*	0.241	0.270
PE vs. EE *r*	-0.256	-0.240
EE vs. PS U	70.0	61.5
EE vs. PS *p*	0.005	0.005
EE vs. PS *r*	-0.448	-0.449
PE vs. PS U	91.0	95.0
PE vs. PS *p*	0.265	0.333
PE vs. PS *r*	-0.186	-0.161

Table 2. Mann-Whitney U for Power and Benevolence

DISCUSSION

We found that individuals who highly value *benevolence* are likely to prefer more medical intervention, perhaps indicating that people who value helping others also value being helped. We also found that individuals who highly value *power* are likely to prefer fewer medical intervention, potentially to maintain their control over their own bodies and fates. Our findings provide preliminary evidence that human values can predict EOL care preferences and can inform future research such as ethnographic studies of the role of *benevolence* and *power* in EOL decision making as well as tailored interventions that use basic human values to assist caregivers with EOL decision making (Xie et al., 2018).

ACKNOWLEDGMENTS

This work was part of a Pilot Research Grant from the Population Health Initiative at the University of Texas at Austin, entitled *Values and Preferences in Dementia Family Caregivers' End-of-Life Decision-Making*; Principal Investigator (PI): Bo Xie; Co-PIs. Kenneth R. Fleischmann and Jung Kwak. We thank the caregivers who participated in the study.

REFERENCES

Alzheimer's Association. (2017). 2017 Alzheimer's disease facts and figures. *Alzheimer's & Dementia*, *13*, 325-373.

Ditto, P. H., Danks, J. H., Smucker, W. D., Bookwala, J., Coppola, K. M., Dresser, R., . . . Zyzanski, S. (2001). Advance directives as acts of communication: A randomized, controlled trial. *Archives of Internal Medicine*, *161*, 421-430.

Fleischmann, K. R. (2014). *Information and human values*. San Rafael, CA: Morgan & Claypool.

Kwak, J., Kramer, B. J., Lang, J., & Ledger, M. (2012). Challenges in end-of-life care management for low-income frail elders: A case study of the Wisconsin Family Care Program. *Research on Aging*, *35*, 393-419.

Mitchell, S. L., Black, B. S., Ersek, M., Hanson, L. C., Miller, S. C., Sachs, G. A., . . . Morrison, R. S. (2012). Advanced dementia: State of the art and priorities for the next decade. *Annals of Internal Medicine*, *156*, 45-51.

Schwartz, S. H. (2007). Value orientations: Measurement, antecedents and consequences across nations. *Measuring Attitudes Cross-Nationally: Lessons from the European Social Survey*, 161–193.

Xie, B., Berkeley, A. S., Kwak, J., Fleischmann, K. R., Champion, J. D., & Koltai, K. S. (2018). End-of-life decision making by family caregivers of persons with advanced dementia: A literature review of decision aids. *Sage Open Medicine*, *6*.

Shifting Standards: Participative Dimensions of Information Literacy

Rich Gazan
University of Hawaii, USA, gazan@hawaii.edu

Natalie Wahl
Leeward Community College, USA, nwahl@hawaii.edu

Katie MacLean
University of Hawaii, USA, kmaclean@hawaii.edu

ABSTRACT

Information resources and practices have always been social, but traditional information literacy instruction tends to prioritize a model of an individual searcher evaluating library-curated resources, while social collaboration tools and user-generated content sites provide more participative paths and practices for research at all levels. Using document analysis of the information literacy instructional materials of 42 institutions, we investigate the extent to which information literacy instruction incorporates participative standards, resources and practices. The findings suggest that while information literacy standards and frameworks are evolving to encompass participative resources and practices, only 21% of the institutions studied inscribed participative resources and practices into their instructional materials. This visual presentation will be designed to elicit discussion about the ways in which document analysis may fail to capture the participative practices in information literacy instruction, to inform our ongoing research.

KEYWORDS

Information literacy standards, Resource evaluation, Social learning.

INTRODUCTION

In a study of over 40 million student papers submitted to a plagiarism detection site (Turnitin, 2011), the most common sources of matched online content (33%) were from social and content-sharing sites, including forums, Q&A sites and similar sources of user-generated content. In this paper we ask whether students may be deriving tangible educational value from these non-traditional, participative resources and practices. Through document analysis of information literacy instruction resources, we address the question of how existing standards and frameworks are being interpreted to support the integration of participative resources and practices into information literacy instruction, to better support STEM education.

Interrogating standards and practices is related to infrastructural inversion (Bowker et al., 2010), where infrastructure refers to "pervasive enabling resources in network form" (p. 98). One of our goals in this study is to investigate information literacy standards and practices to reveal some of the presumptions behind traditional conceptions of trustworthiness, authoritativeness and the practice of science. Our preliminary results suggest that while information literacy standards and frameworks are evolving to become more hospitable to participative resources and practices, documentation of information literacy instruction sessions at a small sample of 2-year and 4-year institutions tends to reflect the more traditional view of individual students accessing and evaluating library resources, with little evidence of participative elements.

METHOD

We conduct an environmental scan and document analysis of 42 colleges and universities offering information literacy instruction, selected via convenience sample. We review the information literacy resources and documentation publicly posted by each institution, including standards and learning outcomes, information literacy exams, modules and preparatory materials, tutorials on source evaluation, and other locally-created materials such as LibGuides. We code the documentation according to three participative dimensions:

- *Participative standards:* Information literacy instruction is aligned with standards and frameworks with participative dimensions, such as university-wide student learning outcomes that include knowledge generation and collaboration.
- *Participative resources:* Integration of student-generated content into information literacy instruction, such as forum, Q&A and discussion sites.
- *Participative practices:* Integration of active learning, collaborative source evaluation or other group practices into information literacy instruction.

Each set of documentation was reviewed by two coders, with initial agreement on 37 of the 42 institutions studied; the remainder were reviewed again by both coders and categorized by consensus.

RESULTS AND DISCUSSION

The results of the document analysis suggest that of the 42 institutions studied, just 13 explicitly align their information literacy instruction with participative standards and frameworks. The most commonly observed standards and learning outcomes connected to information literacy instruction in this group reflected a traditional, library-centric model of an individual student learning to access and search library collections and systems, and to evaluate resources against academic authority and expertise indicators such as journal quality and institutional affiliation. Web resources were presented as to be used in course assignments with extreme caution—indicators of acceptability included .edu and .gov domains. Crowdsourced, user-generated content sites, if they were mentioned at all, were not presented as appropriate resources; Wikipedia was commonly presented as an example of a resource to avoid. When interactions were included in the information literacy instruction documents of institutions coded as non-participative, they tended to focus not on students interacting with one another, but with a librarian as information mediator.

Conversely, institutions that aligned their instruction with participative standards generally did so following the ACRL Framework for Information Literacy for Higher Education (ACRL, 2015), summarized below. Others supported institutional learning outcomes such as envisioning students as knowledge creators, engaged with their local and professional communities, with a responsibility to seek out the voices both present and absent in the research and professional literature.

We note that four of the institutions that claimed to align their information literacy instruction with participative standards did not appear to incorporate participative resources or practices into their publicly available documentation. While we acknowledge that there may be documentation of participative resources and activities that we were not able to access, this finding combined with the relatively low number of institutions evidencing participative standards led us to question this stage of our approach. Document analysis of information literacy instruction may help provide a broad overview as an environmental scan but is not likely to describe any individual institution's practices with precision.

CONCLUSION

The broader ACRL Framework for Information Literacy for Higher Education (ACRL, 2015) has evolved in the direction of acknowledging the informal, social elements of information literacy, and the role of nontraditional sources and pathways. Information literacy sessions serve as an environment where students can learn to become sharers, creators and collaborators, and while we have seen documentary evidence that some library-based instruction appears to remain focused on individual search skills and traditionally authoritative resources, we have also observed participative resources and practices being integrated into local instruction sessions. We hypothesize that in the domain of information literacy instruction, participative resources and practices may be the kind of de-emphasized "invisible work" (Suchman, 1995) that is practiced but not documented. Invisible work tends not to become valued until it is articulated, and while the ACRL standards and frameworks have evolved to encompass participative resources and practices, their translation and formalization in documented practice takes time. We anticipate that this visual presentation will elicit discussion of similar hidden practices, and ways to bring them to light.

ACKNOWLEDGMENTS

This project was made possible in part by the Institute of Museum and Library Services, grant number LG-81-16-0025.

REFERENCES

ACRL (2015). *Framework for Information Literacy for Higher Education.* Association of College and Research Libraries (ACRL). Retrieved from http://www.ala.org/acrl/standards/ilframework

Bowker, G., Baker, K., Millerand, F., & Ribes, D. (2010). Toward information infrastructure studies: Ways of knowing in a networked environment. In J. Hunsinger et al. (eds.), *International Handbook of Internet Research*. Springer Science+Business Media, 97-117.

Suchman, L. (1995). Making work visible. *Communications of the ACM* 38, 56-64.

Turnitin (2011). *Plagiarism on the Web: Myths and Realities. An Analytical Study on Where Students Find Unoriginal Content on the Internet.* Retrieved from https://turnitin.com/static/resources/documentation/turnitin/company/Turnitin_Whitepaper_Plagiarism_Web.pdf.

Towards Automatic Fake News Classification

Souvick Ghosh
Rutgers University, USA. souvick.ghosh@rutgers.edu

Chirag Shah
Rutgers University, USA. chirags@rutgers.edu

ABSTRACT

The interaction of technology with humans has many adverse effects. The rapid growth and outreach of the social media and the Web have led to the dissemination of questionable and untrusted content among a wider audience, which has negatively influenced their lives and judgment. Many research studies have been conducted to tackle the detection and spreading of fake news, which is misinformation that looks genuine. While the first step of such tasks would be to classify claims associated based on their credibility, the next steps would involve identifying hidden patterns in style, syntax, and content of such news claims. We propose a generalized method based on Deep Neural Networks to detect if a given claim is fake or genuine. We have used a modular approach by combining techniques from information retrieval, natural language processing, and deep learning. Our classifier comprises two main submodules. The first submodule uses the claim to retrieve relevant articles from the knowledge base which can then be used to verify the truth of the claim. It also uses word-level features for prediction. The second submodule uses a deep neural network to learn the underlying style of fake content. Our experiments conducted on benchmark datasets show that for the given classification task we can obtain up to 82.4% accuracy by using a combination of two models; the first model was up to 72% accurate while the second model was around 81% accurate. Our detection model has the potential to automatically detect and prevent the spread of fake news, thus, limiting the caustic influence of technology in the human lives.

KEYWORDS

fake news, deep neural network, fake news detection, machine learning, classification, social media.

INTRODUCTION

With the increasing popularity and outreach of social media channels, fake news or misinformation could spread faster than ever before, reach a broader audience, and influence public opinion on a deeper level. Therefore, it has become increasingly important to address the concerns about fake news, using all system-level and human-level approaches. Creating public awareness on how to judge a news item for veracity is one such approach, as is developing algorithmic methods to act as a first step in combating this ever-increasing problem. As different disciplines of information science have been working towards mitigating this problem; it is essential to have a precise definition of the problem. While fake news means false stories or misinformation, it can be defined by other common terms like *satire, propaganda,* and *rumor*. In our current research, we have tried to address the problem of fake news by developing a classifier which can automatically detect fake news accurately. We have trained our classifier on several benchmark datasets which comprise short sentences containing fake and real news obtained from several credible and fake sources.

RELATED WORKS

Rubin, Chen, and Conroy (2015) identified three types of fake news in their work - serious fabrications, large-scale hoaxes, and humorous fake news. Conroy, Rubin, and Chen (2015) were one of the first researchers to use network analysis in fake news detection while Mukherjee and colleagues (2013) used words and the respective part-of-speech tags, together with bigrams to achieve a 68.1% accuracy on Yelp review classification. Shu and colleagues (2017) provided a detailed overview of the recent approaches towards fake news detection and similar problems. While the problem of fake news detection is relatively new, there have been several attempts to tackle it from an algorithmic (more specifically, machine learning) perspective. One such problem was proposed in the Fake News Challenge[1] (2017) where the participating teams were asked to detect the stance of the news claim. Researches have used modified versions of bidirectional LSTM/GRU architectures (Zeng, Zhou and Xu, 2017; Chopra, Jain, and Sholar, 2017), ensemble of classifiers (Thorne et al., 2017), vanilla CNNs, independent encoders, conditional encoder (Rakholia and Bhargava, 2016), multipass conditional encoders, attentive readers with or without weighted cross entropy function (Miller and Oswalt, 2017) and bidirectional LSTMs.

DATASET

The Fake News Challenge Dataset (Rubin, Chen, and Conroy, 2015) contains around 13000 short headlines and 2587 full articles. Each instance contains a headline (which is mostly short), a reference to one of the articles, and the stance of the article towards the claim. The stance could be *agree*, *disagree*, *discuss*, or *unrelated*. Though the challenge approached the fake news

[1] Fake news challenge stage 1 (fnc-i): Stance detection. 2017. URL http://www.fakenewschallenge.org/. https://www.theonion.com/

through stance detection, which is unique and interesting, yet it requires a classification based on a pair of claim and article. University of Washington Fake News Dataset contains a total of 49000 instances, each comprising a paragraph of news article collected from credible and fake news sources (e.g., The Onion[1]). Each claim has one of four possible labels: *hoax*, *propaganda*, *satire*, or *true news*. The length of each sentence ranges from 500 to 600 words. Although the dataset was developed for a similar problem, we made slight modifications to make it more generalizable. For example, we removed all sentences which were labeled as satire as we theorize that satire is more of a linguistic phenomenon (intended for humor) than fake news (Rashkin et al., 2017).

METHODOLOGY

The proposed model consists of several smaller submodules, each responsible for categorizing the instances based on a set of features. Finally, we combine the results through a voting process, which is based on a weighted average where the weights are also learned by the deep neural model. In this research, we have focused on two main submodules: the veracity detection submodule (based on information retrieval models and knowledge base) and the style based submodule. The main module can be extended by adding other submodules such as author metadata (background information, posting history, etc.) or cognitive authority of the source. The first submodule is responsible for checking the veracity of each claim given that we have already constructed a knowledge base. First, the most relevant documents are retrieved from the knowledge base. Secondly, given those documents, the stance of the claim towards the documents is inferred. For retrieval, we used TF-IDF method as a baseline and more advanced algorithms for comparison and improved performance. We also implemented and tested BM25, Vector Space and Language Models. After the *k* related articles are retrieved, in the second step of the algorithm, each article is classified into three labels '*Fake*', '*Suspicious*' or '*Legit*.' For the classification, any deep learning architecture can be used. The input features of the classifier are two one-hot bags-of-word vectors of size 5000, one corresponding to the news statement and the other to the article. Both vectors are fitted on the vocabulary of 5000 most frequently used words in the knowledge base. Additionally, it takes the cosine similarity between these two vectors as an additional input, hence, extending the final size of the input vector to 10001. The hidden layer of the model has 100 Rectified Linear Units (ReLU), and the final layer is a SoftMax layer with three output classes as mentioned before. The second submodule of our model is responsible for gaining valuable insights into how the writing style of fake news differs from real news. The syntax, semantics, and style of the written text can provide significant information about the intention of the authors. It has been widely observed that the language and tone of fake news presentation are more aggressive in general, and it involves a choice of words depicting strong emotions and biases (Rashkin et al., 2017). Our model uses a deep, bidirectional LSTM architecture.

RESULTS AND DISCUSSION

The veracity-based submodule retrieved the most relevant documents relative to the claim and classified the claim into three possible mutually exclusive categories: *fake*, *suspicious* and *real*. The accuracy of prediction was 67.1% for ternary classification and 72.12% for binary classification. The style-based submodule, when evaluated separately on the UW test dataset, predicts with an accuracy of 81.83% (the best performing architecture). Finally, by combining both the submodules using a weighted average, we were able to slightly increase the accuracy to 82.4%. Our contribution is not limited to constructing an accurate model, but it advances the literature on the fake news by evaluating how different retrieval techniques can be incorporated to deep neural architecture to create a more robust and flexible model. By modularizing the architecture, we allow for further enhancements and modules, such as the cognitive authority of source, mining of social media and public opinion and so on.

CONCLUSIONS AND FUTURE WORK

In this paper, we proposed a universal model to verify the authenticity of news claims. By using different features like the authenticity of the source, perceived cognitive authority, style, and content-based factors, and natural language features, it is possible to accurately predict fake news. Our experiments conducted on benchmark datasets show that for the given classification task we can obtain up to 82.4% accuracy by using a combination of two models; the first model was up to 72% accurate while the second model was around 81% accurate. Our detection model has the potential to automatically detect and prevent the spread of fake news, thus, limiting the caustic influence of technology in the human lives.

FORMAT OF PRESENTATION

The presentation will be in the form of either a poster or a three to four minutes video which will highlight the details of the study and the key findings.

---

[1] https://www.theonion.com/

REFERENCES

Chopra, S., Jain, S., & Sholar, J. M. (2017). Towards Automatic Identification of Fake News: Headline-Article Stance Detec- tion with LSTM Attention Models.

Conroy, N. J., Rubin, V. L., & Chen, Y. (2015). Automatic deception detection: Methods for finding fake news. *Proceedings of the Association for Information Science and Technology*, *52*(1), 1-4.

Miller, K., & Oswalt, A. (2017). Fake News Headline Classification using Neural Networks with Attention.

Mukherjee, A., Venkataraman, V., Liu, B., & Glance, N. S. (2013, July). What yelp fake review filter might be doing?. In *IC- WSM.*

Rakholia, N., & Bhargava, S. (2016). 'Is it true?–Deep Learning for Stance Detection in News'.

Rashkin, H., Choi, E., Jang, J. Y., Volkova, S., & Choi, Y. (2017). Truth of varying shades: Analyzing language in fake news and political fact-checking. In *Proceedings of the 2017 Conference on Empirical Methods in Natural Language Pro- cessing* (pp. 2931-2937).

Rubin, V. L., Chen, Y., & Conroy, N. J. (2015). Deception detection for news: three types of fakes. *Proceedings of the Association for Information Science and Technology*, *52*(1), 1-4.

Shu, K., Sliva, A., Wang, S., Tang, J., & Liu, H. (2017). Fake news detection on social media: A data mining perspective. *ACM SIGKDD Explorations Newsletter*, *19*(1), 22-36.

Thorne, J., Chen, M., Myrianthous, G., Pu, J., Wang, X., & Vlachos, A. (2017). Fake news stance detection using stacked ensemble of classifiers. In *Proceedings of the 2017 EMNLP Workshop: Natural Language Processing meets Journalism*(pp. 80-83).

Zeng, Q., Zhou, Q., & Xu, S. (2017). Neural Stance Detectors for Fake News Challenge.

Digital Humanities, Libraries, and Crowdsourcing: Foundations of Digital Textual Technologies

Twyla Gibson
University of Missouri, USA. gibsontg@missouri.edu

Bridget A. Disney
University of Missouri, USA. badqm9@missouri.edu

Stuart J. Murray
Carleton University, Canada. stuartmurray@cunet.carleton.ca

Brian Greenspan
Carleton University, Canada. briangreenspan@cunet.carleton.ca

Sanda Erdelez
Simmons University, USA. sanda.erdelez@simmons.edu

ABSTRACT

The Greek Key is a prototype Virtual Research Environment (VRE) for the analysis of patterns in ancient texts and manuscripts. A Powerpoint presentation demonstrates how the VRE functions through a comparative case study of the organization of information in Plato and Aristotle. The interdisciplinary method combines historical, philological, and philosophical techniques with approaches from the digital humanities. The Greek Key is a collaborative, scalable, multidisciplinary project that has the potential to engage librarians in participatory strategies such as crowdsourcing (or "Citizen Science"). The Greek Key tools for visualizing textual data have the potential to: reveal previously undetected patterns in books and collections; make connections among different works; help users bring new information to bear on interpretation; demonstrate the significance of findings; and generate fresh insights about works of literature that have had a central and enduring influence on both our scholarly traditions and the history of libraries and librarianship. The VRE will make it possible for academic researchers and librarians to pursue perennial questions in innovative ways, and respond to questions that do not lend themselves to more traditional methods.

KEYWORDS

historical and philosophical foundations of library and information science, digital humanities, virtual research environment, text analysis, Plato, Aristotle, crowdsourcing, Citizen Science

INTRODUCTION

Faculty, administrators, and funding bodies are increasingly acknowledging the importance of digital humanities to research and teaching goals in higher education. Studies highlight the benefits of collaborations between universities and colleges (Gunn and Spencer 2014). They stress the value of partnering with librarians for digital humanities projects (Wong 2016; Zhang 2008). They point to the potential of participatory strategies such as crowdsourcing to improve humanities collections and increase access to them online (Terras 2016). Studies also recommend focusing on "one collaborative, multidisciplinary flagship project" to identify the digital humanities with something familiar that people can support (Pannapacker 2013).

The Greek Key is a working prototype Virtual Research Environment (VRE). The Greek Key Project is a collaborative, scalable, multidisciplinary, digital humanities initiative that has the potential to engage librarians and citizens in participatory strategies for scholarship such as crowdsourcing. The Greek Key comprises a suite of tools and resources for identifying, visualizing, and annotating complex repeating patterns that are only now being discovered in ancient texts from many different cultures.

BACKGROUND: ANCIENT INFORMATION TECHNOLOGIES AND THE HISTORY OF LIBRARIANSHIP

An expanding body of research provides indisputable evidence that early texts from around the globe are ordered in repeating sequential patterns known as "parallelism" and "ring composition." Parallelism is the repetition of an initial series of topics in an ABCABC format. Ring composition repeats the initial series in reverse order to create a symmetry of topics on opposite sides of a mid-point, e.g., ABCBA. These patterns have been identified in Plato's dialogues and Aristotle's treatises—as well as in texts in numerous other languages (Welch and McKinlay 1998). Scholars investigating these patterns stress that serial ordering of information is a form of "shorthand" (Douglas 2007), a communication medium, "ancient technology of representation," or "language" (Foley 1999) that requires a kind of "cultural competence" to be able to detect (MacDonald 2003). If serial patterns that are manifest in a wide variety of ancient texts function as an information technology in ways that have not been well understood, then this research has significant implications for interpreting source texts that continue to influence world cultures. Additionally, deeper understanding of how early books communicate information is crucially relevant to the history of librarianship. Evidence indicates that texts such as Plato's dialogues and Aristotle's treatises are the product of editorial work by scholars and librarians at Alexandria and other ancient libraries (Pfeiffer 1998). The edition of Plato's dialogues that has come down to us was put in order by the librarian Thrasyllus (Tarrant 1993). Andronicus of Rhodes arranged and published Aristotle's manuscripts. The works of Aristotle, together with his book collection, were used to found the Library at Alexandria (Strabo *Geography* 13.1. 54; Plutarch *Vita Sulla* 26). The technology for representing information in parallel and ring-patterned sequences is therefore a significant chapter in the history of libraries and librarianship that warrants further investigation. Moreover, the occurrence of consistencies in the arrangement of information in these texts means that these patterns lend themselves to investigation via "big data" textual analyses using digital humanities tools and techniques.

THE GREEK KEY VIRTUAL RESEARCH ENVIRONMENT

Using Plato and Aristotle as case studies and our Powerpoint to demonstrate, we show how The Greek Key tool functions and explain how it makes it easier for non-specialists to take part in research and the process of discovery. Currently, the VRE is online and with permission, can be accessed via Google login. Users click buttons at the top of the screen to select from different displays. One view, for example, is used to identify phrases in a single text; another view is for comparing sequences of topics in different texts. Buttons also allow users to select a language (Greek, English) and to choose a text to analyze from either the Greek Key archive or another website. To compare the sequence of topics in two different texts, the user selects the comparative display. The list of topics in a parallelism or a ring (in this case from Plato) can either be input manually or transferred to the comparative view from the single text display. A cluster matching tool searches for possible matches within a given distance of Aristotle's text and then displays them as red circles on a scatter plot visualization. From these possibilities, parallel topics can then be confirmed or rejected. If rejected, the color of the circle changes from red to grey. When topics in a sequence are confirmed, they change from red circles to green dots (see Figure 1). The line-up of green dots in the scatter plot shows the topics in a sequence for which there is a direct match. To provide the scaffolding that will orient librarians and other users to the system and help them become proficient at identifying patterns, educational videos at various levels of complexity will be created and posted online. As the project scales up, libraries and librarians at colleges and research institutions and at cultural and heritage organizations will be added to the network of collaborators. Eventually, and with further funding support, the VRE will be made available for public participation online through crowdsourcing.

Figure 1: Confirmed Match (Green)

CONCLUSION

With an understanding of classification, collections, tools, and resources, as well as a dedication to teaching and research, academic librarians can be full collaborators in the advancement of digital humanities research and in teaching that provides students with the opportunity to experience the excitement of original discovery. The Greek Key Project is an exemplary digital humanities project that provides college and university librarians with an opportunity to contribute to the improvement of humanities collections, to broaden access to online materials, and to promote the democratization of knowledge creation.

REFERENCES

Douglas, M. (2007). *Thinking in circles: An essay on ring composition.* New Haven and London: Yale University Press.

Foley, J.M. *Homer's traditional art.* University Park, PA: The Pennsylvania State University Press, 1999.

Gunn, K. & Spencer, J. (2014). Introduction to Scholarly Communication. *College & Undergraduate Libraries 21*, 241-243.

MacDonald, D. (2003). Does the New Testament imitate Homer? New Haven: Yale University Press.

Pannapacker, W. (May 13, 2013). Cultivating partnerships in the digital humanities: What teaching colleges and research universities have to gain from collaboration. *Chronicle of Higher Education.*

Pfeiffer, R. (1998). History of classical scholarship. Oxford: Clarendon Press.

Tarrant, H. (1993). *Thrasyllan Platonism.* Ithaca, NY: Cornell University Press.

Welch, J.W. & McKinlay, D.B. (1998). *Chiasmus bibliography*. Provo, UT: Brigham Young University.

Wong, S.H.R. (2016). Digital humanities: What can libraries offer? Portal: *Libraries and the Academy 16*(4), 669-690.

Zhang, W. (2008). Is there a role for the library in a student-faculty collaborative research program? *College & Undergraduate Libraries 15*(3), 341-356.

Finding Trafficked Children through Crowdsourcing

Dion Hoe-Lian Goh
Nanyang Technological University, Singapore.
ashlgoh@ntu.edu.sg

Hang Guo
SAP, Singapore. hang.guo01@sap.com

Chei Sian Lee
Nanyang Technological University, Singapore.
leecs@ntu.edu.sg

ABSTRACT

Tackling child trafficking requires a multi-pronged approach from government and non-government organizations as well as individuals. In this paper, we introduce Zhongxun, a crowdsourcing platform for finding missing children that have been potentially trafficked. Users submit photos of children whom they suspect may be victims of trafficking. Zhongxun uses a facial recognition algorithm to match the submission against its database of photos missing children and returns those that are similar for followup action. Users may also provide feedback on the matches to improve the facial recognition algortihm. Zhongxun is a live system and is currently being used in China.

KEYWORDS

Child trafficking, crowdsourcing, social media, facial recognition, machine learning

INTRODUCTION

Human trafficking is a serious, global problem and is defined by the United Nations Office on Drugs and Crime as "the acquisition of people by improper means such as force, fraud or deception, with the aim of exploiting them" (UNODC, 2018). It is a form of human slavery and involves people of across genders and ages (Bedford, Bekbalaeva, Ballard, & Hernandez, 2017). Child trafficking represents a subset of this crime but is no less insidious, involving the exploitation children for labor, sex, other nefarious purposes (Beyrer, 2004). Victims of child trafficking suffer from physical and psychological problems that curtail their development, and such children are unable to achieve their full potential in life.

Tackling the child trafficking problem requires a multi-pronged approach, and government and non-government organizations across different countries have launched different initiatives ranging from awareness campaigns to enforcement operations. Complementing these efforts are ground-up initiatives involving individuals working together. In particular, with the popularity of the Internet and social media, as well as the proliferation of mobile devices such as smartphones, crowdsourcing is now being used as a tool to help find trafficked children. Put succinctly, crowdsourcing mobilizes the skills and expertise of online users to address specific problems without being restricted by time and space (Doan, Ramakrishnan, & Halevy, 2011). This very definition makes crowdsourcing suitable as a means to combat trafficking as children are often transported to different parts of a country or across borders. Through crowdsourcing, the people on the ground because the "eyes and ears", reporting any suspicious activity that may then be followed up by the relevant authorities.

ZHONGXUN: A CROWDSOURCED SOLUTION

Zhongxun is a crowdsourcing platform for finding missing and potentially trafficked children in China. Zhongxun's design is meant to be simple to cater to users with different backgrounds. Thus, a conversational user interface was chosen, built upon Weibo, a microblogging service similar in concept to Twitter. By leveraging on this popular and familiar social media service, Zhongxun minimizes learning effort and lowers the barriers to usage.

In a typical usage scenario, consider a user who chances upon a child whom she suspects has been trafficked. The user snaps a photo of the child and sends it to Zhongxun via Weibo (Figure 1). Upon receipt of the photo, Zhongxun uses a machine learning facial recognition algorithm to compare the submitted photo against its database of photos of missing children in real-time. Matching photos and their associated similarity indices are then posted on Zhongxun's Weibo account for viewing (Figure 2) by the public. At this point, appropriate followup actions, such as approaching the child or notifying a relevant authority, may be taken if the user is confident of the match.

Notably, the facial recognition algorithm is also able to account for aging since the time between a child is reported missing to the time when his/her photo is snapped and submitted to Zhongxun could be considerable. Hence, a user may take a photo of an older child or adult, and Zhongxun will return photos matching the younger version of the submission. Finally, Zhongxun's facial recognition algorithm also learns via crowdsoucring. Specifically, users can provide feedback on whether each returned photo is similar or dissimilar to the submitted photo (Figure 3). These responses are used to improve the algorithm.

Figure 1. Submission of a photo to Zhongxun.

Figure 2. A matching photo is displayed on Zhongxun's Weibo account.

Figure 3. Users provide feedback on the similarity between photos.

PRESENTATION FORMAT

The presentation of this paper will comprise three components. First, a printed poster will describe Zhongxun and explain how it works, from the point of photo submission, to the facial recognition algorithm that employs machine learning, and to the provision of user feedback to improve the performance of the algorithm. The poster will also provide English translations of Zhongxun's screenshots, which are originally in Chinese. The second component will be a video demonstrating the Zhongxun platform. Finally, a couple of mobile devices will be provided for participants to try Zhongxun. We will be available to help participants with the platform and answer questions that may arise. Feedback will also be solicited from participants to identify areas of improvement.

CONCLUSION

Zhongxun is a live system that is currently in use in China to find missing children. Although designed for that specific country, the concepts and technologies employed are transferrable to other contexts because child trafficking is a global problem. Firstly, crowdsourcing transcends national boundaries and has been employed to solve different problems around the world. Next, the use of a conversational interface based on Weibo may be substituted with popular social media platforms outside China including Twitter and Facebook. Finally, the facial recognition algorithm employs machine learning and requires an appropriate dataset of missing children during evaluation and deployment.

Zhongxun is still a work-in-progress in terms of making improvements to the facial recognition algorithm as well as the user interface. For the latter, systematic evaluations of the platform in terms of perceptions of usability and usefulness will be embarked upon soon. Anecdotal evidence from current users however suggest the viability of the system, and the platform was also a winner of the Good Design Award in 2017 (http://www.g-mark.org/award/describe/45933).

REFERENCES

Bedford, D.A.D., Bekbalaeva, J., Ballard, K.M., & Hernandez, T.J. (2017). Global human trafficking seen through the lens of semantics and text analytics. *Proceedings of the 80th Annual Meeting of the Association for Information Science & Technology*, 535-538.

Beyrer, C. (2004). Global child trafficking. *The Lancet*, 364, 16-17.

Doan, A., Ramakrishnan, R., & Halevy, A.Y. (2011). Crowdsourcing systems on the World-Wide Web. *Communications of the ACM*, 54(4), 86-96.

UNODC. (2018). UNODC on human trafficking and migrant smuggling. Retrieved May 6, 2018 from https://www.unodc.org/unodc/en/human-trafficking/index.html.

Digital Assistants and Human Values

Kathryn E. Golden
The University of Texas at Austin, USA,
kegolden@utexas.edu

Kenneth R. Fleischmann
The University of Texas at Austin, USA,
kfleisch@ischool.utexas.edu

ABSTRACT
Are digital assistants sensitive to the values of their users? In this paper, we report the results of ten interviews with users of Apple's Siri, Amazon's Alexa, and Google Assistant about how they use these digital assistants. Our thematic analysis led us to identify three key themes across the ten interview transcripts: functionality of the technology, trust in the manufacturer, and privacy versus convenience. We conclude that the manufacturers of digital assistants need to be sensitive to users' values when designing and deploying these technologies.

KEYWORDS
Digital assistants, human values, Apple's Siri, Amazon's Alexa, Google Assistant.

INTRODUCTION
Digital assistants, alternatively referred to as virtual assistants, voice assistants, and (artificially) intelligent personal assistants, are becoming a ubiquitous element of the information society. Digital Assistants such as Apple's Siri, Amazon's Alexa, Google Assistant, and Microsoft's Cortana are now embedded in smartphones, tablets, computers, smart watches, and smart home devices. Their introduction raises important questions about their compatibility with human values, or "what a person or group of people consider important in life" (Friedman, Kahn, & Borning, 2006, p. 349). However, very little research has been conducted on the user experience of digital assistants. One of the few studies of user interactions with digital assistants to date found that participants' use of Alexa decreased over time, and the authors of the study call for further research on the users' experiences with Alexa and other digital assistants (Lopatovska et al., In Press). To address this gap in the literature, we set out to answer the following research question: which human values are salient in users' experiences with digital assistants?

METHODS
To answer this research question, we conducted interviews with ten users of digital assistants. Our ten participants included two users of Siri and Google Assistant, one user of Siri and Alexa, one user of Google Assistant and Alexa, three users of Google Assistant only, two users of Siri only, and one user of Alexa only. Our in-depth, semi-structured, open-ended interviews included questions such as "Could you please tell me more about what tasks you use each of these AI assistants for?" and "Overall, would you consider yourself satisfied with the AI assistants that you currently use?" We used thematic analysis (Braun & Clarke, 2006) to analyze the interview transcripts, with the first author identifying themes that occurred across the interviews, and the second author reviewing the interview transcripts and confirming the presence of the identified themes.

RESULTS
We identified three overarching themes that emerged from the interview transcripts: functionality of the technology, trust in the manufacturer, and privacy versus convenience. This section reviews our findings for each of these three key themes.

Functionality of the Technology
Our participants expressed frustration with the functionality of the technologies. For example, in reference to Alexa, one participant stated, "it doesn't understand what I'm saying when I say it. People understand what I'm saying." Another participant stated about Siri, "I really wish she was just better at understanding what I intended, what am I actually asking when I ask a question." While these two participants expressed similar frustrations with the voice recognition and information processing of these digital assistants, it is interesting to note the contrast in pronouns used. Another participant described a frustrating experience with Google Assistant, "I can tell a Google Home to play something on Netflix and it works, but if you ask it to play something on Google Play it doesn't work. It doesn't make sense!" These frustrations clearly diminished the user experience.

Trust in the Manufacturer
Our participants linked their perceptions of digital assistants with trust in their respective manufacturers. For example, one participant stated, "Ultimately, what attracts me to each AI system is the device itself, what it lives on. The manufacturer matters in the actual device in conjunction with the AI. I use Apple because I have a good history with Apple products." With similar logic but different allegiance, another participant asserted, "I think Google is reliable in quality. It is also cheaper than Apple." A third participant noted, "I would be wary about using the Alexa, because I feel like Amazon is kind of shady. Well, they all are, but." Thus, participants' perceptions of the devices are tied to trust in the devices' manufacturers.

Privacy Versus Convenience

Our participants honed in on the value conflict between privacy and convenience. For example, in reference to Alexa, one participant opined, "What has been frustrating comes from feeling wary of my privacy. For a while I felt really weirded out by the robot listening in, and it still doesn't sit well. I've just gotten used to it I guess." Another participant observed about Siri, "I am too private I guess, I feel my privacy is gone when using these applications." Another participant argued that this issue determined their choice of platform, connecting back to the prior theme on trust in the manufacturer, "As far as we know, Google protects users' data jealously, as they use targeted ads to make money. Therefore, I think they will value it. Not like Google won't sell it in the future, but currently it is really against their business interests. I would stop using it if they sold information." Clearly, the value trade-off between privacy versus convenience was particularly salient for our participants.

DISCUSSION

Our finding about frustration with features resonated with Lopatovska et al. (In Press), who found that system features often led to user frustration, which in turn contributed to resulting reduction in use of digital assistants. Similarly, Luger and Sellen (2016) found that defaulting to search was a particularly frustrating feature for users, and that users with less understanding of the technical constraints of the devices were more likely to express frustration. They also indicate that this lack of knowledge also led to anthropomorphizing the devices; we found that some users anthropomorphized by attributing gender to the devices.

Our finding about trust in the manufacturer echoed Chung et al.'s (2017) argument that digital assistants need to be designed to be trustworthy. This finding is also consistent with Kelton et al.'s (2008) observation that trust in information is derived in part from trust in the author of the information, so it is logical that a similar pattern applies for information technology.

Our finding about the value conflict between privacy and convenience is consistent with Chung et al.'s (2017) observations about the privacy risks of digital assistants. Jackson and Orebaugh (2018) provide a thorough discussion of the potential implications of digital assistants for users' privacy in legal cases, such as *Arkansas v. Bates*, in which the state of Arkansas sought to compel Amazon to release recordings from an Amazon Echo that was in essence a witness to a murder. This value conflict is also consistent with the larger phenomenon of value conflicts influencing design (Fleischmann & Wallace, 2010).

FUTURE RESEARCH DIRECTIONS

In reporting results from one of the first interview studies of the users of digital assistants, this paper provides useful preliminary insights into the role of values in the user experience of digital assistants. However, further research is warranted into this topic. As digital assistants become increasingly ubiquitous, it will be useful to interview larger numbers of individuals with experience using multiple devices, to provide greater contrast among the user experiences of these devices. Individuals who consciously chose to switch from one digital assistant to another, or who use different digital devices for different purposes, can provide particularly insightful perspectives, as they can provide data about the relative value sensitivity of different digital assistants.

ACKNOWLEDGMENTS

We would like to thank Randolph Bias, who served as the second reader for the Master's Report that led to this paper.

REFERENCES

Braun, V., & Clarke, V. (2006). Using thematic analysis in psychology. *Qualitative Research in Psychology*, *3*, 77-101.

Chung, H., Iorga, M., Voas, J., & Lee, S. (2017). "Alexa, can I trust you?" *Computer*, *50*(9), 100-104.

Fleischmann, K. R., & Wallace, W. A. (2010). Value conflicts in computational modeling. *Computer*, *43*(7), 57-63.

Friedman, B., Kahn, P. H., Jr., & Borning, A. (2006). Value sensitive design and information systems. In P. Zhang & D. Galletta (Eds.), *Human-computer interaction and management information systems: Foundations* (pp. 348-372). Armonk, NY: M. E. Sharpe.

Jackson, C., & Orebaugh, A. (2018). A study of security and privacy issues associated with the Amazon Echo. *International Journal of the Internet of Things and Cyber-Assurance*, *1*, 91-100.

Kelton, K., Fleischmann, K. R., & Wallace, W. A. (2008). Trust in digital information. *Journal of the American Society for Information Science and Technology*, *59*, 363-374.

Lopatovska, I., Rink, K., Knight, I., Raines, K., Cosenza, K., Williams, H., ...Martinez, A. (In Press). Talk to me: Exploring user interactions with the Amazon Alexa. Forthcoming in *Journal of Librarianship and Information Science*.

Luger, E., & Sellen, A. (2016). "Like having a really bad PA": The gulf between user expectations and experience of conversational agents. *Proceedings of CHI '16* (pp. 5286-5297). New York: ACM.

BiblioMaps - A Software to Create Web-Based Interactive Maps of Science: The Case of UX Map

Sebastian Grauwin
University of Lyon, ENS Lyon, France,
sebastian.grauwin@universite-lyon.fr

Isabelle Sperano
MacEwan University, Edmonton, Canada,
speranoi@macewan.ca

ABSTRACT

Maps of science, allowing the exploration of large-scale bibliographical datasets, are meeting an increasing interest across a broad range of audiences: students, educators, researchers, policy makers, technology developers, etc. This paper presents BiblioMaps, a freely available software that can be used to create web-based interactive maps of science. Our toolkit uses a mixture of statistical techniques and similarity measures on bibliographic metadata extracted either from the Web of Science or Scopus. After processing, the data is used in web-based interactive visualizations. The main visualization is a map of topical clusters - gathering publications based on shared references - whose characteristics can be easily explored in detail. As an example, we discuss some insights gained by exploring maps based on a corpus of about 10,000 "User Experience Design" research publications.

KEYWORDS

Map of science; Interactive tool; Web interface; Information visualization; Bibliometry; UX design.

INTRODUCTION

In recent years, the number of scientific publications being published has been constantly increasing, reaching just about 3 million publications in 2016 according to the Web of Science and Scopus. And while the scientific knowledge continues to grow in size and complexity, the different communities willing to access it - researchers, students, policy makers or citizen - are lacking accessible tools to explore it and make sense of it.

INTERACTIVE MAPS OF SCIENCE

We present BiblioMaps[1], a web-based interactive map of science, allowing the exploration of large-scale bibliographical datasets. This tool was developed to propose a maximum of relevant information that can be intuitively explored and used by a large audience. Bibliomaps also offers a freely available toolkit that allows anyone with minimal developing skills to process the metadata of the corpus of publications of their choice and produce interactive maps of science from any corpus of bibliographic data extracted from either Scopus or the Web of Science.[2]

Here are BiblioMaps Interface's main feature:

- Interact spatially with the map
- Explore the nature of each topic and subtopic
- Access a selection of representative and highly cited papers using Google Scholars
- Perform searches in topics
- Modify layout parameters
- Export the produced visualizations
- UX Map

As an example, we have built a scientific map of the User Experience Design field (UX Map). To allow users to interact with the data and analyses we produce, we developed two visualization interfaces created using D3.js. These interfaces can be explored online (http://sebastian-grauwin.com/UXMAP). The first interface proposes a description of the items found in the publications of the studied corpus (their authors, keywords, references, countries in the affiliations, etc.), via sorted lists and a series of customized graphics (word clouds, networks, pie chart, bar graph or world map) that were chosen to fit common, intuitive metaphoric representations. The second interface (cf Figure 1) allows the exploration of the two-levels hierarchical thematic map built out of clusters obtained in the Bibliographic Coupling analyses. It was built to answer potential needs of various users.

---

[1] BiblioMaps is the extension of BiblioTools (Grauwin & Jensen 2011) a toolkit that already allowed to draw static representations of topical fields but necessitated the production of lengthy companion documents to make the link between paper-level and topic-level information.

[2] A few maps of sciences can be found online, see for example (Börner & al., 2012; Claveau & Gingras, 2016; Cobo & al., 2011; George & Knedjens, 2013; Kang & al., 2006; Leydesdorff & Rafols, 2009). However, these maps often require strong information visualization knowledge to be able to navigate and to understand the data presented. A few software toolkits allowing researchers to create standard bibliographic maps (co-authors, co-citation, bibliographic coupling networks, etc.) also exists, see e.g. Van Eck & Waltman (2010). However, most of them produce visualizations that are not primarily built for the web and require installing specific interface to be explored and are therefore less easily accessible to a large public. They also often require programming knowledge.

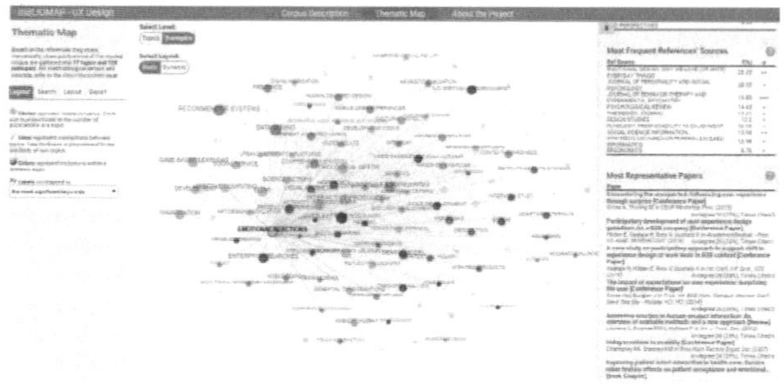

Figure 1. Screenshot of the "Thematic Map" interface.

Methods

Bibliographical data can be retrieved from either Scopus or the Web of Science, and processed by the BiblioMaps software as described in Grauwin & al. (2012). Here, we selected a corpus representative of the research perform in UX Design by using the query *TITLE-ABS-KEY (UX AND design*) OR TITLE-ABS-KEY ("user experience*" AND design*)* in Scopus. This combination of keywords query allows to gather publications related to UX. Combining the terms User Experience and Design ensured that all the selected papers have a minimal focus on both UX and design, while using a query based only on e.g. "User experience" only yield too many results outside of our focus of interest. In total, the selected UX-Design corpus contains 12,220 publication records. Publications are then grouped in relevant topical clusters, by performing a standard Bibliographic Coupling (BC) analysis (see Grauwin & al. (2012)). Since it takes into account all publications - even not yet cited ones - BC is a relevant technique to represent research front and emerging topics such as UX Design in a meaningful way.

CONCLUSION AND FUTURE WORK

BiblioMaps visualizations can be of interest to the general public as well as to experts across diverse disciplines for educational, scientific, and practical purposes. More generally, it can help students, educators or researchers new to a field to rapidly get an overview of a discipline's topics of research, and relevant publications or authors. Researchers already aware of a field can also use BiblioMaps to look for new collaborators, to identify gaps in the research and to discover unforeseen links between different research topics. Policy makers can use it as an opportunity to build maps of their own institutions, thus fostering ongoing dialogue and praxis in their own institution. As for the UX Map example, it can become a valuable tool in this young field, strongly led by practitioners (Sperano, 2017), to address research issues and to build a stronger research agenda.

We plan to develop the tool further. For example, we are currently working on a functionality that would focus on the evolving nature of research fields (their appearance, disappearance, merging, splitting, etc.) and the detection and visualization of trends (e.g. in keywords or references usage).

REFERENCES

Börner, K., Klavans, R., Patek, M., Zoss, A.M., Biberstine, J.R., Light, R.P. (2012). Design and Update of a Classification System: The UCSD Map of Science. *PLoS ONE* 7(7): e39464.

Claveau, F. & Gingras, Y. (2016). Macrodynamics of Economics: A Bibliometric History. *History of Political Economy* 48, 4: 551-592.

Cobo, M.J., Lopez-Herrera, A.G., Herrera-Viedma, E. & Herrera, F. (2011). Science mapping software tools: Review, analysis, and cooperative study among tools. *Journal of the American Society for Information Science Technology*, 62, 1382-1402.

George, D. & Knedjens, R. (2013). Paperscape, an interactive map of the arXiv. Accessed Sept. 2017. http://paperscape.org/

Grauwin, S. & Jensen, P. (2011). Mapping scientific institutions. *Scientometrics* 89:943-954.

Grauwin, S., Beslon, G., Fleury, E., Franceschelli, S., Robardet, C., Rouquier, J-B. & Jensen, P. (2012). Complex systems science: dreams of universality, interdisciplinarity reality. *J Am Soc Inf Sci Technol* 63(7):1327-1338.

Kang, H. et al. (2006). NetLens: Iterative exploration of Content-Actor Network Data. *Proceeding of IEEE Symposium on Visual Analytics Science and Technology 2006 (VAST2006)*, 91-98.

Leydesdorff, L. & Rafols, I. (2009). A global map of science based on the ISI subject categories. *Journal of the American Society for Information Science Technology*, 60(2), 348-362.

Sperano, I. (2017). Content Audit for the Assessment of Information Space: Definitions and Exploratory Typology. *SIGDOC 2017*, Halifax.

Van Eck, N.J. & Waltman, L. (2010). Software survey: VOSviewer, a computer program for bibliometric mapping. *Scientometrics* 84, 2:523-538.

(How) Should Information World Maps be Visually Analyzed?

Devon Greyson
University of Massachusetts Amherst, USA. dgreyson@umass.edu

Heather O'Brien
University of British Columbia, Canada h.obrien@ubc.ca

Saguna Shankar
University of British Columbia, Canada saguna.shankar@gmail.com

ABSTRACT

Information world mapping (IWM) is a participatory, arts-based elicitation method for use in interviews about information behaviours or practices. The participant-drawn maps that result from this technique are typically used as ancillary data sources to aid in analysis of interview transcripts; however it may be possible, and even useful, to analyze these maps as data independent of the interviews, using methods suited to image analysis. This brief paper and accompanying visual presenta- tion describe results of analyses of information world maps using four different and contrasting methods with accompanying examples, and issue recommendations regard-ing the use of qualitative content analysis, compositional analysis, conceptual analysis, and visual discourse analysis, for analysis of information world maps. These insights may be generalized to other objects (e.g., pho-tos) created through arts-based elicitation interviewing.

KEYWORDS

Information worlds, information behavior, visual analysis, arts-based methods, qualitative methods

INTRODUCTION

Participatory, arts-based methods have been used in social research for some time (Pauwels, 2010), including information science research (Hartel, 2014; Julien, Given, & Opryshko, 2013; Sonnenwald, Wildemuth, & Harmon, 2001). While it is clear that the artistic, often visual, artifacts that result from such methods elicit rich interview data, the potential of these arti-facts as data is unknown. A notable exception to this trend is the iSquares project (Hartel, 2014), which has experimented with a variety of visual analytic methods for organizing and interpreting participants' depictions of the concept of infor-mation.

Information world mapping (IWM) is a participatory drawing activity intended for use in qualitative interviews about infor-mation behaviours and practices (Greyson, O'Brien, & Shoveller, 2017). Combining elements of Photovoice (Wang & Bur-ris, 1997), information horizons (Sonnenwald et al., 2001), and relational mapping (Radford & Neke, 2000), IWM prompts participants to depict their social information worlds from their own perspective. In the current visual presentation, we ex-plore whether visual analysis of IWMs can contribute analytic depth or valid new findings, and draw conclusions regarding which methods appear promising and for what purposes.

METHODS

This methodological investigation involved four test analyses, each applying a specific visual analytic method to portions of a collection of 52 IWMs that were generated through two previous studies. We developed research questions that were appro-priate for each analytic method, and explored each analysis, drawing conclusions regarding the strengths and weaknesses of each respective method as applied to the analysis of IWMs. The four methods were selected in order to represent diverse the-oretical perspectives and embody different methodological strengths and weaknesses.

1. In qualitative content analysis (QCA), the researcher begins with a research question, from which they systemati- cally engage in a sequence of steps to build, test, evaluate, refine, and apply a consistent coding frame, in order to identify themes and patterns (Schreier, 2012). QCA is common in information research, but primarily applied to tex- tual data. Our research question for QCA was: What do IWMs convey about the information worlds of participants?
2. Compositional analysis, drawn from art history and media studies, is based on interpretation of common visual ele- ments in images (Kress & Leeuwen, 2006). We explored how to systematically apply understandings of composition using an existing taxonomy as a means to classify the structure of participant-generated artifacts (Matusiak, Hartel, & Thomson, 2016), as compared with an inductive classification scheme grounded in the data. Our research ques- tion for compositional analysis was: Which compositional approach fits with IWM?
3. Conceptual analysis has been described as "a traditional means of interrogating visual concepts using existing theo- ries or frameworks in scholarly literature" (Hartel & Noone, 2016, p. 2). Such systematic assessment of conceptual underpin-nings of data may help in structuring and modelling frameworks, particularly in interdisciplinary work. Our research ques-tion for conceptual analysis was: Do participants' IWMs reflect existing information behaviour mod- els?
4. Discourse analysis for textual data is not uncommon in information research, but is less commonly applied to visual data.

From the various approaches that exist to guide discourse analysis, we selected situational analysis (SA) (Clarke, 2005), a postmodern grounded theory technique that involves diagramming of codes. Our research question for SA was: *What discourses about information are evident in the IWMs?*

FINDINGS

We took a directed approach to QCA, developing our coding scheme based on key concepts inherent in IWM. This provided an overview of participants' information worlds and practices, and enabled comparisons across maps from different studies. However, challenges in interpreting some map elements raised concerns about introducing systematic bias. Applying an ex- isting "universal" taxonomy was not fruitful in our compositional analysis; however, developing an inductive taxonomy al- lowed us to identify genre conventions for classifying IWMs. Conceptual analysis ultimately resulted in a reflection of the research procedures and epistemology, rather than providing insight into participants' own conceptual models, and might be useful as a reflexive exercise for researchers. SA resulted in a large amount of rich data, including discourses and power rela- tions not identified in previous analysis of the textual data. However, it was very time consuming to conduct this type of analysis.

Given the participant-centered nature of IWM, and its emphasis on empowering marginalized perspectives, ethical considerations regarding visual analysis of IWMs are crucial to consider. We caution researchers to be mindful of the potential for inferring intentionality or misinterpreting participant intentions with an image, and to work to acknowledge potential biases in interpretation. Visual analysis of IWMs might in some cases be best deployed as a collaborative or iterative process that involves participant populations in interpreting their own or others' IWMs.

CONCLUSION

We encourage others using IWM to explore visual analysis of the resulting maps, and in particular to consider using QCA to summarize and compare the content of IWMs, compositional analysis to extend our taxonomy for IWM classification, and SA to discover discourses that may be present in participant generated maps. We suggest that conceptual analysis of IWMs may also be useful as a reflexive tool for researchers to consider their theoretical affinities and research practices.

ACKNOWLEDGMENTS

Maps for this project were created by studies funded by the Canadian Institutes of Health Research and the British Columbia Immunization Committee. Dr. Greyson was supported by a Michael Smith Foundation for Health Research Trainee Award.

REFERENCES

Clarke, A. (2005). *Situational analysis: Grounded theory after the postmodern turn*. Thousand Oaks, CA: SAGE. Drisko, J., & Maschi, T. (2015). *Content Analysis*. Oxford, UK: Oxford University Press.

Greyson, D., O'Brien, H., & Shoveller, J. (2017). Information world mapping: A participatory arts-based elicitation method for information behavior interviews. *Library & Information Science Research*, *39*(2), 149–157. https://doi.org/10.1016/j.lisr.2017.03.003

Hartel, J. (2014). An arts-informed study of information using the draw-and-write technique. *Journal of the Association for Information Science and Technology*, *65*(7), 1349–1397.

Hartel, J., & Noone, R. (2016). Analyzing visual data (workshop). Presented at the iConference 2016, Philadelphia, PA. https://doi.org/10.9776/16348

Hsieh, H.-F., & Shannon, S. E. (2005). Three approaches to qualitative content analysis. *Qualitative Health Research*, *15*(9), 1277–1288. https://doi.org/10.1177/1049732305276687

Julien, H., Given, L. M., & Opryshko, A. (2013). Photovoice: A promising method for studies of individuals' information practices. *Library & Information Science Research*, *35*(4), 257–263. https://doi.org/10.1016/j.lisr.2013.04.004

Kress, G. R., & Leeuwen, T. V. (2006). *Reading images: The grammar of visual design*. London, UK: Routledge.

Matusiak, K., Hartel, J., & Thomson, L. (2016). Visual research methods workshop. Presented at the Association for Infor- mation Science & Technology Annual Meeting, Copenhagen, DK.

Pauwels, L. (2010). Visual Sociology Reframed: An Analytical Synthesis and Discussion of Visual Methods in Social and Cultural Research. *Sociological Methods & Research*. https://doi.org/10.1177/0049124110366233

Radford, J., & Neke, J. (2000). *Relational mapping* (Special Paper). Royal Roads University. Retrieved from http://www.conflictresolutionsk.ca/RelationalMapping-JohnRadford.pdf

Schreier, M. (2012). *Qualitative content analysis in practice*. Thousand Oaks, CA: SAGE Publications.

Sonnenwald, D. H., Wildemuth, B. M., & Harmon, G. L. (2001). A Research Method to Investigate Information Seeking Using the Concept of Information Horizons: An Example from a Study of Lower Socio-economic Students' Infor- mation Seeking Behaviour. *New Rev. Inf. Behav. Res.*, *2*(November), 65–86.

Wang, C., & Burris, M. A. (1997). Photovoice: concept, methodology, and use for participatory needs assessment. *Health Education & Behavior*, *24*(3), 369–387.

Using Virtual Worlds to Investigate Perceived Affordances on Learned Navigation and Objective Location Performance

Kenneth Carter Haggerty, Ph.D.
University of Memphis, USA, khggerty@memphis.edu

Joseph Gregory Griffin
University of Missouri, USA, jggmr2@mail.missouri.edu

Peter John Cosgrove, Ph.D.
Drury University, USA, acosgrov@drury.edu

ABSTRACT

Navigation in virtual worlds is vital for users to move about effectively, complete objectives, and interact with one another and the environment. The ability to accurately orient oneself within a virtual world is essential for successful engagement in video games, simulations and learning environments. This study investigated the effects of perceived affordances on learned navigation and objective location performance within a virtual world. We hypothesized that such perceived affordances impede the learning of virtual geography by fostering reliance on "artificial" cues instead of real space navigation techniques such as the observation of landmarks, spatial orientation, sense of time and distance travelled. The presence of perceived affordances was not significant in predicting retention accuracy. However, the presence of perceived affordances was a significant predictor of objective location performance.

KEYWORDS

Navigation, affordances, virtual worlds, retention accuracy.

INTRODUCTION

Virtual worlds represent a valuable paradigm for human communication, collaboration, learning and entertainment. However, a problem common to all these applications is that of navigation within the virtual space. After learning how to move their in-world avatar, users must become familiar with the geography of the virtual world in order to achieve their objectives. While it has been found that users can effectively use similar way-finding techniques in virtual environments as they do in reality (Ruddle, Payne, & Jones, 1997), many virtual worlds feature "navigation assistance." A common form of navigation assistance is to overlay the environment view with a Heads-Up Display (HUD). This output interface includes interactional cues ("click to open"), directional cues ("this way to exit" or "follow me"), a compass display, and a small, persistent map centered on the user's avatar that displays local geography and points of interest as the avatar moves through the world. This study will be presented in poster form with visual images of the map used for testing, the affordances studied and tables summarizing our data. In addition, the researchers will have a video presentation of how testing was conducted.

RESEARCH & HYPOTHESES

Hypotheses

Heads-Up Display (HUD) navigation assistance in virtual worlds fosters reliance on perceived affordances such as mini-maps, icons and directional arrows. Users are not required to use experiential learning of landmarks and other "real world" analogs to gain spatial orientation in order to accomplish a navigation task. Therefore, HUD perceived affordances negatively affect the user's ability to learn the geography of the virtual world. However, while we expected these perceived affordances to impair learning, we also hypothesized that navigational assistance would positively affect performance.

HA1: The presence of HUD perceived affordances negatively affects the learning and subsequent retention of virtual world geography (greater distance error between start point and perceived objective location).

HA2: The presence of HUD perceived affordances positively affects navigational performance while the affordances remain available for use (faster time to locate objective).

METHOD

We measured how effectively participants learned the virtual environment geography and how navigational task performance was affected by the presence of the HUD. For our virtual world, we used a multiplayer map from the first-person video game Call of Duty: Modern Warfare running on the Microsoft X-Box. The *District* map covered a virtual area roughly equivalent to eight acres of real space and consisted of a Middle Eastern urban setting with many buildings, streets and passageways.

Participants were randomly assigned to one of two treatment groups and tested by completing navigation tasks:
1. Treatment Group A was provided HUD affordances to assist in finding map objectives.
2. Treatment Group B was provided no HUD affordances.

Both treatment groups were first given a 5-minute period in a separate training environment to learn how to move the avatar.

PARTICIPANTS

Eleven participants were recruited by email distribution list invitation from the graduate student body of a large state research university in the Midwest. Qualified participants were required to be familiar enough with video games to be able to use an X-Box controller with minimal training, but unfamiliar with the specific map in the video game used as the testing environment. Although the study was open to all, every participant was male. All were over the age of 21 years.

RESEARCH FINDINGS

Study data (included in Appendix B) were analyzed using t tests for independent samples over the mean distance error (learned navigation) and over the mean time to complete in each participant treatment (task performance).

Results: Learned Navigation

H0: μdistance error A = μdistance error B
HA: μdistance error A > μdistance error B
A one-tailed t test for independent samples was conducted to compare mean distance error in treatments where the HUD was present and when the HUD was not present. Levene's Equality of Variances test indicated unequal variance at $\alpha = 0.05$ ($p = 0.045$), so an "equal variances not assumed" test was used. There was no significant difference between Treatment A (M = 53.00, SD = 30.98) and Treatment B (M = 56.33, SD = 20.51); $t(9) = 0.21$, $p = 0.418$, $\alpha = 0.05$. We therefore fail to reject the null hypothesis. These results suggest that the presence of the HUD has no significant effect on the user's ability to learn the relative geographical positions of objectives in virtual environments (however, the limitations of this study, particularly sample size, should be considered when interpreting this result).

Results: Task Performance

H0: μtime to complete A = μtime to complete B
HA: μtime to complete A > μtime to complete B
A one-tailed t test for independent samples was conducted to compare mean time to complete in treatments where HUD affordances were present and when HUD affordances were not present. Levene's Equality of Variances test indicated unequal variance at $\alpha = 0.05$ ($p = 0.029$), so an "equal variances not assumed" test was used. There was a significant difference between Treatment A (M = 14.89, SD = 5.99) and Treatment B (M = 122.18, SD = 61.42); $t(4.06) = 3.89$, $p = 0.009$, $\alpha = 0.05$. We therefore reject the null hypothesis.

While limited in size, scope and definitive results, this study will be important in informing the development of future investigations. Another valuable point is an awareness of the existing literature and how it might inform the design of future studies. Navigation assistance techniques have been classified into a taxonomy by Dodiya and Alexandrov (2008). This taxonomy, together with Darken and Sibert's types of search behavior (1996), could be particularly useful in reducing the number of uncontrolled variables and attaining a tighter focus in future studies. Also from Darken and Sibert (1996) is the forward-up equivalence principle: The tendency of participants to assume that "up" on a map is equivalent to cardinal north or the direction in which they were facing first, or both. The authors of this study have concerns regarding the forward-up equivalency and the possibility that it may be a confounding influence on participant's navigational assumptions and treatment outcomes.

In conclusion, there are many rich opportunities for new, important studies in this emerging field: Virtual environments are becoming more prevalent and ever more capable in online education, communications and entertainment; Virtual augmentation of the real world for navigation is gaining a foothold with technologies such as handheld GPS systems and smart glasses. Researchers have done important work on foundational concepts such as wayfinding using landmarks and the motivations underlying different types of navigation. However, there is an untapped wealth of potential research connected to reusing successful navigation practices and perceived affordances from video gaming in other, non-game virtual environments.

REFERENCES

Darken, R. P., & Sibert, J. L. (1996). Wayfinding Strategies and Behaviors in Large Virtual Worlds. In *Proceedings of the SIGCHI conference on Human Factors in Computing Systems.* Presented at the CHI 96, New York: ACM. Retrieved from http://www.sigchi.org/chi96/proceedings/papers/Darken/Rpd_txt.htm

Dodiya, J., & Alexandrov, V. N. (2008). Navigation Assistance for Wayfinding in the Virtual Environments: Taxonomy and a Survey. Presented at the 18th International Conference on Artificial Reality and Telexistence 2008, Yokohama, Japan: ICAT.

Ruddle, R. A., Payne, S. J., & Jones, D. M. (1997). Navigating buildings in "desk-top" virtual environments: Experimental investigations using extended navigational experience. *Journal of Experimental Psychology*, 3(2), 143–159.

Video Ethnographic Documentation of Stories and Cultural Practices with Indigenous Elders

Jelina Haines
University of South Australia, Australia.
jelina.haines@mymail.unisa.edu.au

Ellen Trevorrow
Camp Coorong, Meningie, Australia
ellen1955.et@gmail.com

Jia Tina Du
University of South Australia, Australia.
tina.du@unisa.edu.au

ABSTRACT

This visual presentation reflects on the broader uses of video as a valuable tool for ethical recording of the stories and cultural practices of Indigenous Elders. The opportunities afforded by the use of the video were three-fold, by its impact on the accuracy, truthful engagement, and connection with the Indigenous community. The inclusion of various segments of video in this paper shone a light on issues associated with ethical concerns such as anonymity and maintaining the integrity of recorded data. Thus, to ensure that the collective knowledge was shared in line with traditional laws and protocols of the Ngarrindjeri Nation. Our findings have significant implications for library and information researchers and professionals who gather video data from within (and about) Indigenous communities.

KEYWORDS

Indigenous community, informed consent, video ethnography, video ethics, information research

INTRODUCTION

For generations, Indigenous people have been subjected to subservient colonial policies implemented by imperial governments (Castleden et al., 2013). In some cases, evidence of misrepresentation and exploitation of traditional knowledge purported by past researchers still linger to this day. Consequently, appropriate methodologies were necessary to establish a reciprocal relationship that was based on mutual respect, with the Elders. Using the video as data collection as part of doctoral research focusing on documenting the stories and cultural practices of Indigenous Elders, without devaluing their cultural significance, integrity and meaning. In this context, the principles of Storywork, as coined by Joan Archibald (2008), was proven useful as it provided an ethical standpoint from which knowledge of the Elders could be recorded. Moreover, according to Zimmer (2010), there has been a renewed attention to push the importance of information ethics and its related values to engage with a community ethically. He asserted that information ethics is the requisite ethical values and practices for storage of knowledge and distribution of information.

In this paper, we illuminate the practice of using video to record the Elders' stories associated with ethical concerns. Second, we grapple with the positionality of video segments as evidence-based findings. Two central questions were formulated from this research: (1) what did the story have to say about the Elders' cultural beliefs, as related to the successful transfer of knowledge into the future generations? And (2) how can video support the ethical practices of recording Indigenous stories in the context of dissemination of information?

We have set forth an Indigenist paradigm where we capitalize the words "Indigenous" and "Elder", as these terms are used to identify a person's ethnicity, identity and belief system (Haines et al., 2017; 2018). The words 'Aunty' and 'Uncle', in this study, refer to the Elders and are terms that are collectively used to show respect to their status within the community (Haines et al., 2017). Together, three prominent Elders, who are customarily educated with generational stories passed on by their ancestors, guided us through the laws and protocols contained within the stories.

VIDEO ETHNOGRAPHY AS COMMUNITY-BASED METHODOLOGY IN THIS STUDY

This research design is based on qualitative method. In this case, Video Ethnography is a naturalistic process to record stories and cultural practices in their natural setting: to experience, interpret and present the Ngarrindjeri culture by the holders of cross-generational knowledge (Bromley et al., 2012). Video ethnography, as a community-based methodology, allows us to record the visual contexts of Elders stories accurately. It is an innovative process through which one can gain useful insights into the evolving role of video with respect to ethically retrieved Indigenous knowledge in lesser amounts of time. The video mediates dynamic social interaction of storytelling unfolded minute by minute (Bromley et al., 2012). The use of video supported our objective of achieving accountable and reliable knowledge from the Elders' stories. The use of video for ethnographic purposes parallels the Indigenous people's stories and their cultural practices.

However, this useful feature of the video is accompanied, to some extent, by the uncertainty of ethical challenges as well as opportunities with regard to information sciences.

ETHICAL CONCERNS NOTED IN THE LITERATURE

The ethical concerns are the anonymity, privacy and maintaining the integrity of recorded data and are being reviewed for certain reasons (Castellano, 2004). First, ethics are moral principles that govern our behaviors with regard to conducting equitable and respectful research with Indigenous peoples. Second, the ethical stance of video ethnography was to respect and assist each decision and each act to protect Elders' knowledge from falsification and misuse (Figure 1). Given the cultural sensitivity of data gathered, video ethnography is the ideal methods that instruct ethical values of informed consent, transparency, and governance of data results (Figure 1). The first author's 18 years of connection with the Elders at the Camp Coorong community had provided the space for ongoing dialogue. The Elders gave their consent to be recorded and to be actively involved in the research process by adding their voice to deliver their stories in the manner that they considered as appropriate, rather than being identified as mere code or numbers (Haines et al., 2017). Since our research has been collaborative right from its inception, a representative Elder from the community is a co-author of this paper.

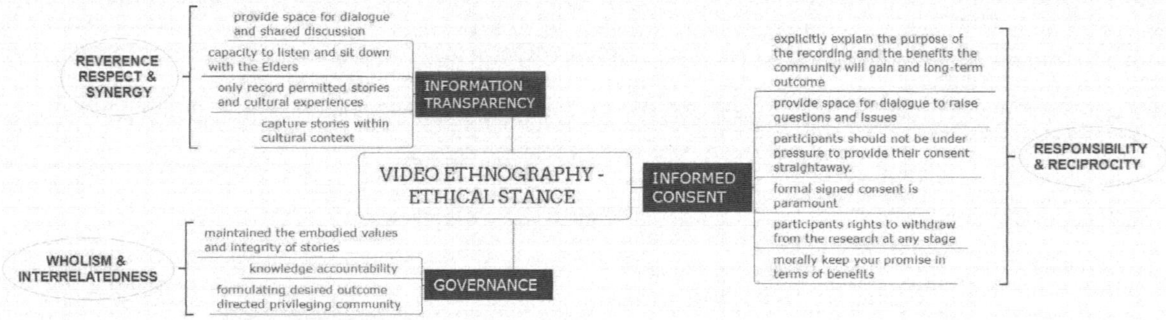

Figure 1: Video ethnography ethical stance framework adapted from the seven principles of Storywork: respect, responsibility, reverence, reciprocity, wholism, interrelatedness and synergy (Archibald, 2008)

The framework in Figure 1 is grounded by the seven principles of Storywork developed by Joan Archibald (Atleo, 2009). It was developed to ensure that Elders who participated in this research would have greater control over their stories and would be empowered to tell their stories (Waller, 2010) accurately. Figure 1 advocates a meaningful engagement, commitment to respect and an ear, as it were, to listen to the needs of Indigenous people.

FINDINGS AND DISCUSSION: VIDEO SEGMENTS OF STORYWORK

The ideality and affordability of digital video was an excellent research tool to which one can gather data from daily practices of social interaction. The video segments captured a permissible version of our field study interview as it happens. The five-minute video presents recorded stories of cultural practices articulated in the "welcome ceremony", the "basket weaving", and the "language song", as told by Uncle Moogy, Aunty Ellen and Aunty Hilda. These recorded stories were expressed as the Elders told without the interference of the researchers. In this context, the video ethnography method distinguishes from other approaches as it provided a space for Elders to share and deliver their stories their way and culturally. As it shows, it draws on the holism as well as diversity of Elders' knowledge rather than approach their stories in isolation; moreover, the stories were selected for their significance and relevance. As opposed to mere anecdotal observations, the participants were actively in- volved in the research, which gives them a sense of pride. The video segments are organized as follows:

INTRODUCTION (45 SECONDS)

This part contains a brief overview of video ethnography and its ethical concerns with respect to recording the Elders' knowledge. It engages with two questions that have been mentioned in the Introduction section. Moreover, it comprises unobserved social interactions such as mannerisms, hand gestures, facial expressions, and emotions in a natural setting, which captured in the video.

WELCOME DANCE (UNCLE MOOGY SUMNER AND THE TAL-KEN-JERI DANCE GROUP — 1 MINUTE)

Uncle Moogy Sumner is a Ngarrindjeri Elder and a Medicine Man who takes us on a journey of Ceremony, Stories Dance, and Song. The dance ceremony is part of the ceremonial process of "Welcome to Country." Either the Aboriginal custodian or an Elder traditionally performs the ceremony to welcome people to their land. This recorded video was conducted during the inaugural event of the Dupang Festival.

As Uncle Moogy pointed out:

"Our dance stories is [are] a way of life; it's not just about dancing, it's more than just going to a ceremony, it's how we live, we pass our knowledge to the best of our ability, to practice our own culture within the environment that we were born and grow up" (personal communication,17 June 2016).

NGARRINDJERI BASKET-WEAVING (AUNTY ELLEN TREVORROW — 1 MINUTE AND 36 SECONDS)

The baskets are seen as vessels of survival and resilience while simultaneously highlighting the importance of storytelling. Aunty Ellen emphasized that the continuation of weaving to the next generation is crucial, and stated that:

"Our weaving stories bring people together, give us something to work, and each stitch connects us to our Miwi. Our weaving creation is like our children; each stitch carries our stories pass on by generations of Elders. I believed the weaving object we create is like our children; they do not belong to us. We just a vessel to channel our stories through weaving and letting them go to share their own stories with the rest of the world" (personal communication, 07 July 2016).

SONG AS VISUAL LITERACY (AUNTY HILDA BLESSIOS — 58 SECONDS)

Aunty Hilda shared her love of singing; it is her way of being connected to the Ngarrindjeri language and Ruwe (country). This video is significant because Aunt Hilda's song is believed to be the only complete recorded song in the Ngarrindjeri language. Therefore, it serves as an important resource for visual literacy and language preservation. Currently, it is a significant challenge to transcribe the song into written text.

VIDEO CHALLENGES AND OPPORTUNITIES (61 SECONDS)

Challenges exist for non-Indigenous researchers when it comes to digitally synthesizing Elders' stories and their cultural practices. Elders are concerned about the exploitation and misappropriation of their knowledge once it gets exposure through its online publication. In particular, they fear that the Internet will replace the traditional ways of storytelling and younger generations will lose their connection to their Indigenous land and country. There is a high degree of anticipation, in this research that accuracy and the validity of video recording will support and provide assurance for the Elders to preserve their traditional stories in its entirety. Furthermore, video ethnography has provided a two-way learning, which reflects on the diversity of the Elders' knowledge. Evidence shows that their stories are seen as a community resource. Therefore, ethical use of the video will assist and preserve the integrity and validity of Elders as well as knowledge. Furthermore, Turilli and Floridi (2009) point out that appropriate applications of ethical values will regulate the flow of information, the access, the usage, the dissemination and the storage of long-term knowledge provided by the stories and cultural practices of the Elders.

CONCLUSION (1 MINUTE)

Stories are considered a central part of knowledge that comes from experiential learning. Cultural activities such as Welcome Ceremony, Weaving, and Songs in the Indigenous language are not only documents of stories but also serve as memories passed throughout successive generations of Elders. The video segments tell us that stories and cultural practices have ontological connection to the geographical environment of Indigenous residence as well as social interaction. This enhances its importance and shines a light on ethical approaches that ensure the sharing of collective knowledge in accordance with the traditional laws and protocols of the Ngarrindjeri Nation.

ACKNOWLEDGEMENTS

This research is supported by the Research Training Program (RTP) Scholarship. The authors sincerely acknowledge the contributions of the Ngarrindjeri Cultural Mentors, Elders, and participants for welcoming us to the Ngarrindjeri community.

REFERENCES

Archibald, J. (2008). *Indigenous storywork: Educating the heart, mind, body, and spirit.* Vancouver: UBC Press.

Atleo, M. R. (2009). Understanding Aboriginal learning ideology through storywork with elders. Alberta *Journal of Educational Research*, 55(4), 453.

Bromley, E., Adams, G. F., & Brekke, J. S. (2012). A Video Ethnography Approach for Linking Naturalistic Behaviors to Research Constructs of Neurocognition in Schizophrenia. The Journal of Neuropsychiatry and Clinical Neurosciences, 24(2), 125–140. http://doi.org/10.1176/appi.neuropsych.11080201

Castellano, M. B. (2004). Ethics of Aboriginal research. *International Journal of Indigenous Health*, 1(1), 98.

Castleden, H., Daley, K., Sloan Morgan, V., & Sylvestre, P. (2013). Settlers unsettled: Using field schools and digital stories to transform geographies of ignorance about Indigenous peoples in Canada. *Journal of Geography in Higher Education*, 37(4), 487-499.

Haines, J., Du, J. T. & Trevorrow E. (2018). In search of Indigenous wisdom and interdisciplinary ways of learning together. *Journal of the Australian Library and Information Association* (JALIA), 67(3). Retrieved from https://doi.org/10.1080/24750158.2018.1488358
Haines, J., Du, J. T., Geursen, G., Gao, J., & Trevorrow, E. (2017). Understanding Elders' knowledge creation to strengthen Indigenous

ethical knowledge sharing. *In Proceedings of RAILS 2016. Information Research,* 22(4), paper rails1607. Retrieved from http://In- formationR.net/ir/22-4/rails/rails1607.html

Turilli, M., & Floridi, L. (2009). The ethics of information transparency. Ethics and Information Technology, 11(2), 105-112.

Waller, L. (2010). Indigenous research ethics: new modes of information gathering and storytelling in journalism. *Australian Journalism Review*, 32(2), 19.

Zimmer, M. (2010). Innovations and Challenges in Teaching Information Ethics Across Educational Contexts. *International Review of Information Ethics*, 14, 12.

Helpful Information to Whom? An Intersectional Critique of the 'It Gets Better Project

Blake Hawkins
University of British Columbia, Canada. blake.hawkins@alumni.ubc.ca

Oliver Haimson
University of California Irvine, USA. ohaimson@uci.edu

Nazanin Andalibi
Drexel University, USA. naz@drexel.edu

ABSTRACT

The 'It Gets Better Project' started as an online campaign responding to the suicide deaths of multiple young gay men in Fall 2010. The campaign involved people posting videos providing messages of hope and helpful health information for youth as they finish high school and can move on with their lives. Although there is seemingly good intentions driving this this campaign, we were troubled by the initial positioning of the campaign. In this paper we use an intersectional critique to discuss the lack of inclusivity in these videos and how it created a potential opportunity to engage with more LGBTQ youth. Furthermore, we suggest that future online campaigns for gender/sexual minority populations be more mindful of others' lived experiences and how this may impact how they seek health information.

INTRODUCTION

The 'It Gets Better Project' (IGB) was triggered when numerous young gay men committed suicide in Fall 2010 as a result of harassment and cyber-bullying by their peers (It Gets Better, 2018). Prominent gay author Dan Savage and his partner Terry Miller pioneered IGB with a 2010 YouTube video in which they used their personal stories to signal to LGBTQ youth that life can improve over time. In turn, many other LGBTQ people, famous and not, shared their positive life trajectories via YouTube, and these narratives were then spread across other social media sites. Some video creators described their own experiences of harassment by their classmates and others because they identified as a gender or sexual minority. Although these videos were undoubtedly supportive for some, they do have considerable limitations that have been highlighted previously in the public health, social work, and gender studies literature (Asakura & Craig, 2014). Some have argued that Savage's vision of "better" is narrow, and hard to relate to for many, given his subject position as white, male, cisgender, and financially secure (Nakamur, 2013). By using an intersectional lens to critique mental health promotion campaign suggest how online mental health promotion campaigns can become more inclusive when providing supportive information. Otherwise, these potentially beneficial campaigns will not successfully reach those who are most vulnerable and need these resources most. LGBTQ people already frequently use online resources for health information (Hawkins, 2017). Thus, online mental health awareness campaigns, if created and managed in inclusive, intersectional ways, have the potential to provide positive changes.

LITERATURE REVIEW

We frame this IGB critique with literature on intersectionalities of sexuality and race and LGBTQ health information behaviour. Intersectionality is an approach of looking at an issue from an interdisciplinary lens and embracing that there are various factors are interwoven to understand a specific issue (Crenshaw, 1991). In the case of the online mental health campaign IGB we are critiquing the issues of homonormativity and race with the campaign. Homonormative is a concept from queer theory that refers to being LGBTQ but living a lifestyle and embracing values similar to heterosexual people. No longer are all spaces lived by LGBTQ people emphasizing a need to trouble heteronormative sexuality (e.g., monogamous relationships) and other social values (Bettani, 2015).

Race critiques of online health promotion literature generally focuses on disparities among minority populations' participation, yet lacks a political framing. This body of literature does, however, discuss some issues with race in design values, game studies, and classification of racists' text (Hankerson et al., 2016). However, given the ongoing struggles experienced by people of color (e.g., as demonstrated by the Black Lives Matter movement), much of which takes places and is documented in online spaces, online campaigns must take race more seriously, and in tandem with other identity facets like LGBTQ identities. In information science there is a growing body of scholarship concerning the connections between race and technology (Kvasny & Payton, 2018; Noble, 2018).

Previous scholarship from information studies highlights that there are unique information needs and experience for LGBTQ people based on their identity and potential stigma from those around them. In Jabson et al (2017) they highlight how LGBTQ people typically go online for health information given the potential barriers in physical settings. These barriers may include a lack of properly trained professionals who can answer questions that are relevant for LGBTQ people. Additionally, there are unique mental health disparities among LGBTQ people that sometimes gets homogenized in both the research and by healthcare professionals (Ross et al., 2018). Therefore, it is understandable that LGBTQ people would go online and might want to use a campaign like IGB for information and support.

CRITIQUING IT GETS BETTER

We briefly highlight some of our critiques of the IGB Project related to intersectionality and homonormativity for this online LGBTQ youth mental health campaign. In doing so, we add to an existing scholarship that has been critical of IGB. Inclusive design is vital for online mental health campaigns. Previous research has described the IGB message being pertinent for mainly white, cisgender, young, and abled-bodied gay men (Asakura & Craig, 2014). Furthermore, the campaign is embedded in gender and sexuality assumptions that create a non-inclusive initiative (James et al., 2016). Furthermore, heterogeneity among underserved communities requires that campaigns not be reduced to only one type of message.

In reality, many LGBTQ people do not want to live a sanitized homonormative lifestyle, and may consider it unsustainable for keeping themselves satisfied. It is quite common among LGBTQ people to have non-traditional relationships, and for them or their partners to be non-binary or fluid in their gender and sexuality identity (Asakura & Craig, 2014; Craig et al., 2014). The ongoing message from the campaign that getting "better" equates with "normality" does not promote inclusiveness or hope as intended. Rather, it proposes that only one lifestyle is acceptable – a lifestyle that is out of the realm of possibility or desirability for many LGBTQ youth.

There is potential for online campaigns to help with reducing stigma and access to support (Anadibli, 2018). To best enable all people to experience mental health benefits, including those with marginalized identities, online health promotion campaigns must determine how to be more inclusive (Huang et al., 2015). This oversight – that is, online health campaigns' tendency to, whether intentionally or unintentionally, exclude certain marginalized users (Hankerson et al., 2016) argument that there is an ongoing lack of consciousness for people of colour when using technology to create new systems or artifacts. Using IGB as a case study, we argue that campaign designers, activists, and tech designers should pay attention to creating more inclusive campaigns and technologies that support them.

CONCLUSION

Online mental health campaigns for sexual and gender minorities provide opportunities to create awareness for people who may otherwise not have access to traditional mental health services due to stigma or other factors. We critiqued The IGB Project as an example that did not sufficiently create an inclusive space for LGBTQ youth who may require access to helpful information and stories of support during a difficult life period. As young LGBTQ people navigate the coming out process, they often face stigma, shame, discrimination, and other minority stressors that hinder the path to a "better" life. Online campaigns have great potential for creating networks of care, which are an important factor for the mental health and wellness of LGBTQ youth. As social media plays a prominent role in young people's lives, it is important that online campaigns aiming to improve mental health proactively prioritize inclusivity. Otherwise, they risk promoting only one type of lifestyle that is not sustainable or inclusive for all LGBTQ youth, thus not facilitating mental health improvement across the population.

REFERENCES

Andalibi, N., & Forte, A. (2018). Announcing Pregnancy Loss on Facebook: A Decision-Making Framework for Stigmatized Disclosure on Identified Social Network Sites. ACM CHI Conference on Human Factors in Computing Systems.

Asakura, K., & Craig, S. L. (2014). "It Gets Better" … but How? Exploring Resilience Development in the Accounts of LGBTQ Adults. Journal of Human Behavior in the Social Environment, 24(3), 253–266.

Bettani, S. (2015). Straight subjectivities in homonormative spaces: moving towards a new, 'dynamic' heteronormativity? Gender, Place & Culture, 22(2), 239–254.

Crenshaw, K. (1991). Mapping the Margins: Intersectionality, Identity Politics, and Violence against Women of Color. Stanford Law Review, 43(6).

Hankerson, D., Marshall, A. R., Booker, J., El Mimouni, H., Walker, I., & Rode, J. A. (2016). Does Technology Have Race? In Proceedings of the 2016 CHI Conference Extended Abstracts on Human Factors in Computing Systems (pp. 473–486). New York, NY, USA: ACM. https://doi.org/10.1145/2851581.2892578

Hawkins, B. (2017). Does quality matter? Health information behaviors of LGBTQ youth in Prince George, Canada. Proceedings of The Association for Information Science and Technology

Huang, L.-L., Thrasher, J. F., Jiang, Y., Li, Q., Fong, G. T., Chang, Y., … Friedman, D. B. (2015). Impact of the "Giving Cigarettes is Giving Harm" Campaign on Knowledge and Attitudes of Chinese Smokers. Tobacco Control, 24(0 4), iv28–iv34.

It Gets Better. (n.d.). Retrieved February 13, 2018, from https://itgetsbetter.org/

Jabson, J., Patterson, J., Kamen, C. (2017). Understanding Health Information Seeking on the Internet Among Sexual Minority People: Cross-Sectional Analysis From the Health Information National Trands Survey. JMIR Public Health Surveillance. 3(2): e39

Kvasny, L., & Payton, F. (2018). Managing Hypervisibility in the HIV Prevention Information-Seeking Practices of Black Female College Students. Journal of the Association for Information Science and Technology. 69(6).

Nakamura, L. (2013). Cybertypes: Race, Ethnicity, and Identity on the Internet. Routledge.

Noble, S. (2018). Algorithms of Oppression: How Search Engines Reinforce Racism. New York: NYU Press

Ross, L., Salway, T., Tarasoff, L., MacKay, J., Hawkins, B., Fehrl, C. (2018). Prevalence of Depression and Anxiety Among Bisexual People Compared to Gay, Lesbian and Heterosexual Individuals: A Systematic Review and Meta-Analysis. The Journal of Sex Research. 55(4-5): 435-456

Supporting Student Agency with Transmedia

Amanda Hovious
University of North Texas, USA.
amandahovious@my.unt.edu

Ian Harper,
Bradfield Narrative Designs Inc., Canada.
harperjian@gmail.coml

Valerie Harlow Shinas, Ph.D.
Lesley University, USA.
vshinas@lesley.edu

ABSTRACT

Student agency is defined as a student's sense of self-control over his or her educational experiences. It is a critical aspect of learning among adolescents. One way to promote student agency in the classroom is through the integration of texts and tools that allow students to become producers and consumers of content. Transmedia—the creation and sharing of narrative across media—is such a tool. This poster presentation illustrates how transmedia can be used to support student agency and engagement, drawing on a foundational case study of middle-grade students who interacted with the project, *Inanimate Alice*, an interactive novel that follows the adventures of Alice, a globetrotting girl who wants to be a game designer when she grows up. Future directions of the project are demonstrated via a new iteration of *Inanimate Alice*, a virtual reality (VR) gap story called *Perpetual Nomads.* The audience may experience *Perpetual Nomads* with a VR headset and learn about its implications for fostering student agency based on beta testing of the story with middle-grade students. The presenters also discuss an upcoming research initiative that will further test the impact of *Perpetual Nomads* on digital and technological literacies—an important avenue for fostering student agency.

KEYWORDS

Transmedia, emerging technologies, human agency, student agency, student engagement.

INTRODUCTION

Student agency is defined as a student's sense of self-control over his or her educational experiences. It is a critical aspect of learning, particularly among adolescents. Bandura's agentic perspective offers the most useful theory for understanding it (Klemencic, 2017). Bandura (2001) views an agent as an individual that purposely uses his or her actions to make something happen. He states that "agency embodies the endowments, belief systems, self-regulatory capabilities and distributed structures and functions through which personal influence is exercised" (Bandura, 2001, p. 2). Thus, agency represents a set of dispositions that lead to intentional actions and interactions within the environment. In education, student agency is recognized as a major aspect of student engagement, and higher degrees of student agency are associated with greater engagement in learning. The idea of agentic engagement is defined as the student's "constructive contribution into the flow of instruction" (Reeve & Tseng, 2011, p. 258), and emerging evidence suggests that transmedia may be a useful tool for supporting it.

According to Scolari (2009), transmedia is the creation and telling of narrative across media using multiple modalities. Transmedia leverages the semiotic nature of digital platforms, the innovation of the Internet, and the power of social media to create spaces where readers become co-constructors of dynamic, engaging narratives. Engaging narrative and the ability to co-construct make transmedia a powerful tool for supporting student agency. This poster presentation draws on a foundational case study that illustrates how transmedia narratives were used to support agentic engagement with middle school students. The study highlights the transmedia project, *Inanimate Alice*, a multi-episode interactive novel that follows the adventures of Alice, a globetrotting girl who wants to be a game designer when she grows up. Future directions for research are introduced through a hands-on demonstration of a new iteration of the project, a virtual reality (VR) story called *Perpetual Nomads*. Implications of the VR story are discussed, using *Perpetual Nomads* as an example of how emerging technologies like VR transmedia may be tested in future studies as a tool for supporting digital and technological literacies—an increasingly important avenue for fostering student agency (Warren & Jones, 2017).

THE ROLE OF TRANSMEDIA IN STUDENT AGENCY

Transmedia often incorporates gaming elements, a dynamic feature that lends itself to social constructivist educational approaches that can foster student agency. Agency as the ability to explore has been cited as a reason that students are engaged by game-like transmedia environments (Beavis, Muspratt, & Thompson, 2015). Additionally, putting students into the game designer role gives them a sense of agency over their learning. For example, Warren and Jones (2017) created the role-playing transmedia game *Broken Window* to teach computer literacy skills. Following transmedia play, students were tasked with creating their own transmedia experiences modeled after the game to demonstrate the skills they learned. Transmedia also fosters student agency through the ability to remix multiple media elements into a new media composition. This too puts students into the designer role, creating meaningful opportunities to express themselves (Ray, 2013). *Inanimate Alice* incorporates both gameplay and remixing, and as the following foundational case study illustrates, *Inanimate Alice* offers a pedagogical exemplar for using transmedia to foster student agency.

FOUNDATIONAL CASE STUDY: ADOLESCENT READERS ENGAGING WITH *INANIMATE ALICE*

This foundational case study is drawn from a larger study conducted in the spring of 2012. During the study, the fourteen adolescent students who participated were completing the final term of the 8th-grade year and were all strong readers of traditional texts as measured by performance on standardized assessments. Although all students reported regular access to technology in and out of school, none had previous experience with transmedia narratives.

To understand the potential power of transmedia as a tool to support student agency, data collected during think-alouds and post-reading interviews were examined as well as transcripts of focus groups conducted with ten of the fourteen participants. Data were analyzed in two ways. First, word frequency analysis of all transcripts was conducted to reveal evidence of emerging themes. In addition, open coding and inductive analyses were conducted to identify themes emerging from the data.

Findings revealed that these adolescent students were deeply engaged in the narrative and identified with the main character, Alice. In addition, think-aloud data provided evidence of how students used their personal interpretations of the semiotics and their own prior experiences to become co-creators during meaning making. Students explained how they used their own experiences to immerse themselves in the narrative and create a personalized understanding. Ruby shared:

> Well, when it was telling you about how she was all alone and it was snowing, I thought back to my own experiences because my parents have been out and me and my brother would be home alone during a snowstorm. Or just if it was dark outside and you get really worried, trying to decide what to do, whether or not they're going to come home.

Similarly, Anna's think-aloud reveals that she relied on her own interpretations of the images to make meaning:

> Ayisha arrives at our house wearing her niqab, but when she takes it off she's like a wonderful bird..." And this is, when she says bird, I'm thinking that she looks really pretty. And she's like, gracious, like a bird, like a bird... like a symbol. Like certain birds are a symbol of peace.

PERPETUAL NOMADS: IMPLICATIONS FOR FUTURE DIRECTIONS

When considering the foundational case study presented here and the extant and emerging literature, there are important implications of this work. Specifically, it is critical that we look closely at innovative resources and study how these are used by teachers to support student agency and motivation. For example, *Perpetual Nomads* is a recently developed VR story that spans the gap between Episodes Six and Seven of *Inanimate Alice.* Currently in the beta testing phase, initial response from middle-grade students has shown greater engagement and interaction with the story using a VR headset than without one. Considering the experimental nature of VR stories, this may imply that the affordances of VR transmedia can support agentic engagement in ways that more traditional modes of transmedia cannot. To further test this hypothesis, a partnership between the team behind *Perpetual Nomads* and the Fraser Valley Regional Library (FVRL) in Vancouver, BC is in the works. The purpose of this partnership will be to provide the FVRL library community with access to *Perpetual Nomads* and to determine the impact of VR on the development of digital and technological literacies. Findings from the project should provide greater insight into the way VR transmedia can be used to foster student agency in learning environments through the development of digital and technological literacies.

REFERENCES

Bandura, A. (2001). Social cognitive theory: An agentic perspective. *Annual Review of Psychology, 52*, 1-26.

Beavis, C., Muspratt, S., & Thompson, R. (2015). 'Computer games can get your brain working': Student experience and perceptions of digital games in the classroom. *Learning, Media and Technology, 40*(1), 21-42.

Klemencic, M. (2017). From student engagement to student agency: Conceptual considerations of European policies on student-centered learning in higher education. *Higher Education Policy, 30*(1), 69-85.

Ray, B. (2013). More than just remixing: Uptake and new media composition. *Computers and Composition, 30*, 183-196.

Reeve, J., & Tseng, C-M. (2011). Agency as a fourth aspect of students' engagement during learning activities. *Contemporary Educational Psychology, 36*, 257-267.

Scolari, C. A. (2009). Transmedia storytelling: Implicit consumers, narrative worlds, and branding in contemporary media production. *International Journal of Communication 3*, 586–606.

Warren, S., & Jones, G. (2017). *Learning games: The science and art of development*. Springer, Cham: Springer International.

Unraveling Scientists' Multiple Data Roles Dealing with Genomic Data

Hong Huang
University of South Florida, USA. honghuang@usf.edu

ABSTRACT

This study contributes to a better understanding of 135 genomics scientists' perception about their data roles in genome curation work. Our study was guided by previously identified sixteen data role items (Salomone et al., 2011), and intended to define a model of groupings for data roles in genome curation. Analysis of the results revealed that genomics scientists have specific sets of data roles in the genome curation work. These data role items were reduced to four factor constructs. Both data producer and data custodian are ranked the highest, followed by data manager, and data consumer. The findings indicate that genomics scientists are primarily dealing with reusing and wrangling data (e.g., cleaning up the raw data across platforms and databases). The constructs defined by this study advance the understanding of data roles and their relationships in genomic data curation. In addition, the resulting data role model can serve as a valuable resource to genome scientists for assigning data curation tasks, training and data management policies development.

KEYWORDS

Data roles, genome annotation, curation, perception

INTRODUCTION

With the availability of high-throughput genomic data production and big data curation and analysis methods (Howe et al., 2008; Huang, 2018), genomic scientists have to deal with the complex genomic data tasks that involved multiple data roles. In order to access easily for the organized and interpretable genomic data, genomic scientists make a great effort to create multiple data wrangling tools that can integrate different data files and formats for a better interpretation. However, due to a lack of understanding for data role structure for genomic scientists, and in general, each scientist needs to play multiple data roles and work together tightly toward collaborative efforts. The research in understanding data role structure could help genomic scientists identified their specific data roles and their specific data tasks.

Research about data roles has been reported in literature. Lee and Strong (2003) reported three types of data role players. The first type is data consumers that generally utilize information to make a decision, and the second type is data collectors that help produce data collection; thirdly, the data custodians can maintain the data resources (Lee and Strong, 2003). Literature also reported another one: data managers who manage the whole data process (Wang 1998). However, no studies reported how many kinds of data players and what a particular set of data role items associate with them in a particular context (e.g., genomics). This survey study was designed to identify data roles structure for genomic data curation work. The responses from genomic scientists could guide developing the typology of data role types and their associate data tasks so that can specify the curation job responsibility in genome curation work.

METHODS

To collect the data, the study used a survey questionnaire. The survey was constructed based on the eighteen data role items identified in Salomone et al. (2011). To provide the context for the questions, the survey used a representative scenario to conceptualize the activities related to data role playing in genome data curation. The survey participants consisted of 135 genomic scientists who published journal articles related to genome annotation, analysis methods and research. Eight hundred emails were sent with a response rate of 17%. Respondents were asked to rate the importance of a data role on a seven-point Likert scale. The descriptive statistics and factor analysis reports were produced by the statistical software SPSS.

FINDINGS

The descriptive statistics of the data role rankings are given in Table 1. On average, the participants ranked 'Data reuse' as being of the highest importance and 'Non-daily work' the lowest. Other data roles among the top-five list are 'Dealing with raw data,' 'Cross database integration,' 'Making decisions,' and 'Data cleansing.' Table 2 showed four data role constructs including data producer, data custodian, data manager, and data consumer. This reflected that the genomic data curation work are primarily focus on data sharing and data wrangling work in a large scale.

Data roles	# of responses	*Mean*
Data reuse	138	5.17
Dealing with raw data	133	5.09
Cross database integration	133	4.99
Making decisions	138	4.94
Data cleansing	134	4.86
Requested information	139	4.77
Data administration	134	4.6
Used-by-others' information collection	133	4.6
Data imputation	136	4.59
Data update & modification	133	4.56
Data preservation	136	4.54
Data deployment	130	4.48
Data provenance	135	4.41
Computer based design	125	4.39
Received reports	138	3.65
Not-daily-work data collection	130	3.53

Table 1. Survey participants' ranking of data roles by mean importance in the context of scenario.

Data role constructs	Rank-ing	Data roles
Data producer	4.77	Data imputation, Data cleaning, Dealing with raw data, Data preservation
Data custodian	4.77	Making decision, Data reuse, Data update & modification, Data provenance
Data manager	4.54	Computer based design, Data deployment, Data administration, Cross-Database integration, Received reports, Data preservation, Data update & modification
Data consumer	4.3	Requested information, Not-daily-work data collection, Used-by-others' information collection

Table 2. The four data role constructs generated from the data roles, and ranked by the arithmetic averages of the mean ratings of the types of data roles loaded on the constructs.

CONCLUSION

This study provided empirical data analysis to specify genomics scientists' data roles in genome curation work. The results indicate that data producer and custodian are two most important roles that genomics scientists are playing. Their daily data roles are related to data reuse, data wrangling, and data preservation. The results help specify data curation job assignments and develop role-based curation training.

REFERENCES

Howe, D., Costanzo, M., Fey, P., Gojobori, T., Hannick, L., et al. (2008). Big data: the future of biocuration. *Nature*, 455(7209), 47–50.

Huang, H. (2018). Big data to knowledge–Harnessing semiotic relationships of data quality and skills in genome curation work. *Journal of Information Science*, dio:0165551517748291.

Lee, Y. W., D. M. Strong. 2003. Knowing-why about data processes and data quality. *Journal of Management Information Systems* **20**(3) 13–39.

Salomone, S., Hyland, P., & Murphy, G. D. (2011). Perceptions of data quality dimensions and data roles. In *25th ANZAM Conference, 2011*.

Wang, R.Y. (1998). A product perspective on total data quality management. *Communications of the ACM*, 41(2), 58-65.

Why do People Come? The Factors Influencing Public Library Visits

Li-Min Huang
University of Tennessee, USA. lhuang23@vols.utk.edu

Iman Tahamtan
University of Tennessee, USA. tahamtan@vols.utk.edu

ABSTRACT

Current study investigates what variables, including expenditures, services, and collections, can predict the total annual public library visits (VISITS) in the United States. The data source was the 2015 Public Library Service data and reports, and a multiple regression model was used to analyze the data in the R programming language. Results indicated that the best variables for predicating VISITS were a library's total operating expenditures, usage of public Internet-enabled computers per year, audio-physical units, total children programs, and video-physical units. The best subset model for predicting VISITS included the total number of public libraries, total operating expenditures, print materials, audio-physical units, total children programs, total young programs, and the usage of public Internet-enabled computers per year.

INTRODUCTION

Public libraries aim to fulfill users' information needs by providing a variety of facilities, resources, and services (Clubb, 2009). Public librarians have always taken efforts to increase reader visits, however, they have also gone through various challenges when enhancing people's motivation for visiting libraries in this digital era. For example, many public libraries have inadequate funding to cope with the drastic changes that technology brings (Clubb, 2009). With limited budget and labor power, it is urgent for public libraries to figure out the most influential factors on library visits and to determine the strategies for attracting users to libraries. The purpose of current study is to examine the key factors that could effectively predict public library visits. The findings begin to establish an empirical model on predicting factors that would influence public library visits in the U.S. and will have implications on policy planning and funding distribution of those public libraries. The main research questions in the study are: 1) Which variables are most important in predicting the total annual public library visits in the U.S.? 2) What is the best subset model for predicting the total annual public library visits in the U.S.?

RELATED WORKS

Bertot, et al. (2008) found that public libraries served as important workstations with Internet access for many people in their communities. Public library collections and services are also associated with library visitation. Sin and Kim (2008) analyzed data from the Public Library Service (PLS) and attributed public libraries with higher collections, more Internet terminals, and more branch libraries to having higher library visitation. This study further indicated that programs and collections related to children have significant impacts on library visits. Another study by Joo and Cahill's (2017) indicated that using printed children materials were viewed by parents as the primary reason to visit public libraries. Similarly, Hemmeter (2006) found that the households with children used public libraries more than those who didn't have children. The literature indicates that people visit public libraries for a variety of reasons such as using their collection, services, and spaces. However, it is not yet well understood what factors predict public library visits in the U.S.

METHOD

The data source for this study was the Institute of Museum and Library Services (IMLS) PLS reports for 2015. We included the 50 U.S. states and the District of Columbia. The dependent variable was VISITS (total number of persons entering the library for all purposes during that year), and independent variables included: POPUST (reported state total population estimate), NLIB (total number of public libraries), TOTOPEXP (total operating expenditures), BKVOL (print materials, including books and government documents), EBOOK (electronic books), AUDIOPH (audio-physical units such as audio cassettes and talking books), VIDEO_PH (video-physical units such as video tapes), LOANFM (inter-library loans received), KIDPRO (total children's programs), YAPRO (total young adult programs), PITUSR (uses of public Internet-enabled computers per year).We used multiple linear regression in the R programming language to analyze the data. Three regression assumptions, including normality, independence of errors, and homoscedasticity of residuals were met. However, the data did not meet linearity. To fix nonlinearity, we transformed several variables using log(X). Using the variance inflation factor (VIF), no evidence of multicollinearity was observed. To know how well the results will generalize to other data sets we used k-fold cross-validation. The model to be tested was as follows: *VISITS ~ log(POPUST) + log(NLIB) + log(TOTOPEXP) + BKVOL + log(EBOOK) + AUDIOPH + log(VIDEOPH) + log(LOANFM) +log(KIDPRO) + log(YAPRO) + log(PITUSR)*

FINDINGS

In 2015, nearly 311 million Americans lived within a public library service area. Public libraries in the U.S. have offered 4.7 million programs in 2015, which were attended by 106 million people. Results indicated that the best subset model for predicting VISITS included NLIB, TOTOEXP, BKVOL, AUDIOPH, KIDPRO, YAPRO, and PITUSR, with an adjusted R-square of 0.88. Removing other variables from the model significantly increases the predictive power of the model. Therefore, the best model to predict VISITS would be as follows: VISITS ~ log(NLIB) + log(TOTOPEXP) + BKVOL + AUDIOPH +log(KIDPRO) + log(YAPRO) + log(PITUSR).

Cross-validation was used to evaluate the generalizability of our regression equation. Cross-validation indicated that the model predicts 79% of VISITS in practice. Figure 1 shows that TOTOPEXP, PITUSR, AUDIOPH, KIDPRO, and VIDEOPH were the best predictors of VISITS, respectively.

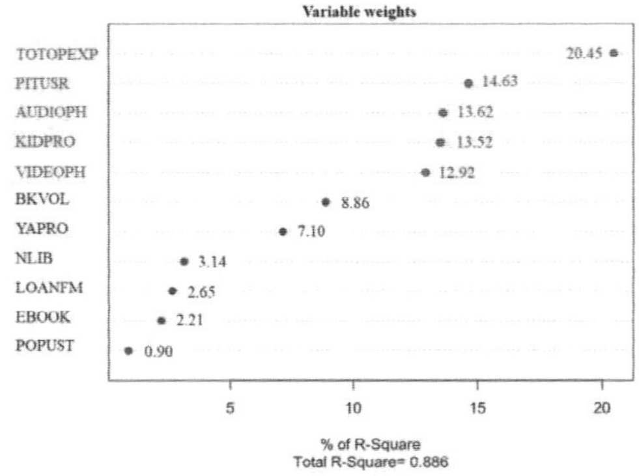

Figure 1. Dot chart of the relative importance (weights) of predictor variables of public library visits in the U.S. Larger weights indicate relatively more important predictors.

DISCUSSION

TOTOPEXP was the most important factor predicting 20.45% of VISITS. Salaries and wages for all library staff, as well as the employee benefits for all library staff, may motivate library staff to provide better services and programs, consequently leading to more VISITS. In this regard, Mezick (2007) found a statistically significant relationship between the total academic library expenditures and student retention.

We found that PITUSR predicts 14.63% of VISITS. Internet technology infrastructure in public libraries appears to be an important factor for attracting people to the public libraries. Internet access in public libraries would contribute to offering other services including licensed databases, homework resources, virtual reference services, ebooks, and audio content (Bertot et al., 2008).

In contrary to some previous studies, such as Sin and Kim (2008), we found that NLIB only predicts 3.14 % of VISITS. It may be argued that alongside the number of public library services (e.g. children's programs), their quality matters too.

The major implication of the study is that to attract more visitors, public libraries should increase their expenditures for both electronic and print materials; public Internet access and youth and adult programs.

Limitation: If there is any evidence of interaction among the variables, the model that includes the interaction term is superior to the model that contains only the main effects. Further studies should take interactions into consideration.

CONCLUSION

Public libraries with higher expenditures, audio- and video-physical units, programs for a variety of age groups, public Internet-enabled computers, and print materials experience more VISITS.

REFERENCES

Bertot, J. C., McClure, C. R., & Jaeger, P. T. (2008). Public libraries and the Internet 2007: Issues, implications, and expectations. *Library & Information Science Research, 30*(3), 175-184.

Clubb, B. H. (2009). Public Libraries. In *Encyclopedia of Library and Information Sciences, Third Edition.* (pp.4347-4366). Taylor & Francis.

Hemmeter, J. A. (2006). Household use of public libraries and large bookstores. *Library & Information Science Research, 28*(4), 595-616.

Joo, S., & Cahill, M. (2017). The relationships between the expenditures and resources of public libraries and children's and young adults' use: An exploratory analysis of Institute of Museum and Library Services public library statistics data. *Journal of Librarianship and Information Science*, 1-10.

Mezick, E. M. (2007). Return on investment: Libraries and student retention. *The Journal of Academic Librarianship, 33*(5), 561-566.

Sin, S. C. J., & Kim, K.S. (2008). Use and non-use of public libraries in the information age: A logistic regression analysis of household characteristics and library services variables. *Library & Information Science Research, 30*(3), 207-215.

Conceptualizing Research Ethics on Scientific Data Sharing: Evidence from Biological Scientists

Boryung Ju
Louisiana State University, United States. bju1@lsu.edu

Youngseek Kim
University of Kentucky, United States. yki237@uky.edu

ABSTRACT

This paper presents the results of our study of biological scientists' formation of research ethics for data sharing intentions. Based on consequential theorists' perspective of ethics, it examines what the main contributing factors affecting biological scientists' formation of research ethics for data sharing are. By analyzing an online survey with 577 respondents with SEM (Structural Equation Modeling) technique, the paper identifies the extent to which egoism factors and utilitarian factors influence their research ethics formation, which eventually leads to their data sharing intentions.

KEYWORDS

Research ethics, data sharing, egoism, utilitarianism, biological scientists.

INTRODUCTION

With a growing number of scientific research collaboration via cyber-infrastructure and the advent of the big data revolution, researchers encounter ample opportunities to share and reuse research data collected and deposited by other researchers. More and more data is accessible to researchers through the research data centers or institutional repositories on the World Wide Web. Data sharing can be defined as scientists making their raw or preprocessed data of their published work available to other scientists through data repositories or private communication among them. This includes any aspects of the deposition, preservation, and accessibility for use and reuse of data (Tenopir et al., 2011). Research data sharing has been encouraged for various reasons and dimensions. Data sharing helps to promote innovation and potential new uses of data, reduce the cost of duplicating data collection, maximize transparency and accountability of research, and provide quality assurance (Tenopir et al., 2015). Perceptions of and approaches to data sharing may vary according to research environments and disciplines, due to the varying nature of data types and their characteristics. The purpose of this current study is to examine biological scientists' formation of research ethics for data sharing intentions.

THEORETICAL FRAMEWORK AND RESEARCH MODEL

Grounded on the consequential theorists' perspective of ethics, this research aims to explain how biological scientists' research ethics are formed based on egoism and utilitarian factors, and what extent those factors contribute to their formation of research ethics for data sharing. Our proposed research model in this study consists of four main components that include egoism factors (perceived reputation, perceive risk, and perceived effort), utilitarianism factors (perceived community benefit and perceived reciprocity), research ethics, and data sharing intentions. Egoism can be defined as a belief that an act is ethical when it promotes the individual's best long term interests, while utilitarianism can be defined as a belief that an act is ethical when it produces the greatest ratio of good for everyone (Tsalikis & Ortiz-Buonafina, 1990).

Perceived reputation, perceive risk, and perceived effort were adapted from Kim and Zhang's (2015) and Kim and Stanton's (2016) survey items and were modified to examine biological scientists' perceptions on data sharing. Utilitarianism factors including perceived community benefit (Cronin, 2005) and perceived reciprocity (Zimmerman, 2007) constructs were drawn from prior studies. For the research ethics construct, we employed two-item measurements by asking whether they would think data sharing is ethical as a researcher (Guillemin & Gillam, 2004). In addition, the construct of data sharing intention was adapted from Ajzen and Fishbein's study (2005). In order to address our research question, we developed the research model of biological scientists' data sharing and eight hypotheses focusing on the roles of egoism (perceived reputation, risk, and effort) and utilitarian (perceived community benefit and reciprocity) factors and research ethics in biological scientists' data sharing intentions.

RESEARCH METHOD

We used the Community of Scientists' (CoS) scholar database to randomly select potential survey participants. As of October 31, 2016 there were 90,574 biological scientists registered under the category of natural sciences (defined by CoS). The permission from the ProQuest Pivot, which owns the CoS scholar database, was sought before we selected the potential survey participants from its scholar database. The online survey was conducted from November 2016 to February 2017. We received a total of 577 valid responses for this research. Among the 577 respondents, there were 379 male respondents (65.7%) and 185 female respondents (32.1%). For age, the respondents are from diverse age groups ranging 25-34 (40, 6.9%), 35-44 (108, 18.7%), 45-54 (149, 25.8%), 55-64 (151, 26.2%), and 65 and older (109, 18.9%).

DATA ANALYSIS AND RESULTS

We employed the Partial Least Square (PLS) based Structural Equation Modeling (SEM) analysis method as the major data analysis technique for this research. The hypothesized relationships in the research model was evaluated by using SmartPLS 2.0. The measurement model was used to examine the validity and reliability of research constructs, and the structural model was used to evaluate the research model of biological scientists' research ethics for data sharing and its hypothesized relationships. The assessment of the measurement model demonstrates that the measurement items for each research construct are reliable and valid. The assessment of the measurement model permits to further examine the structural model. Figure 1 below shows the evaluation of structural model and hypothesized relationships.

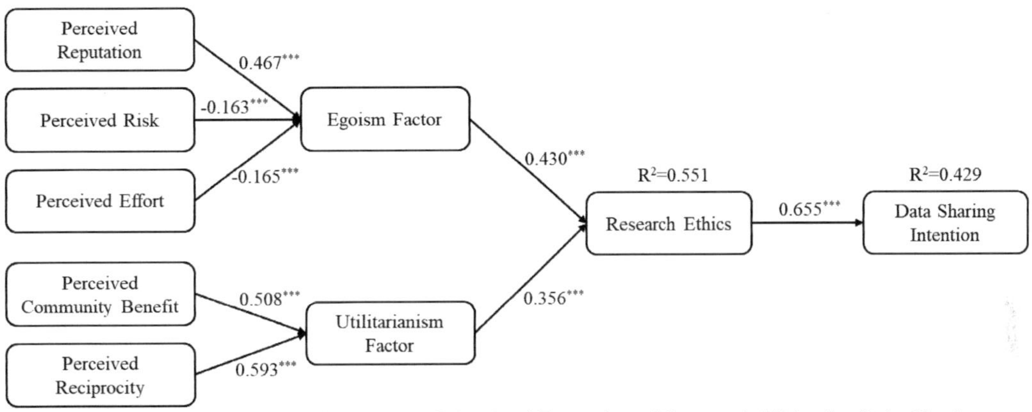

Figure 1. Research Model of Biological Scientists' Formation of Research Ethics for Data Sharing.

First of all, in terms of egoism, perceived reputation, risk, and effort all significantly affect biological scientists' ethical egoism for data sharing. Perceived reputation was found to have a significant positive influence on biological scientists' ethical egoism ($\beta=0.467$, $p<0.001$). However, both perceived risk ($\beta=-0.163$, $p<0.001$) and perceived effort ($\beta=-0.165$, $p<0.001$) are found to have significant negative influences on biological scientists' ethical egoism. Second, in terms of utilitarianism, perceived community benefit ($\beta=0.508$, $p<0.001$) and perceived reciprocity ($\beta=0.593$, $p<0.001$) are all found to have significant positive influences on biological scientists' ethical utilitarianism. The two main ethical components including egoism ($\beta=0.430$, $p<0.001$) and utilitarianism ($\beta=0.356$, $p<0.001$) factors all positively influence biological scientists' research ethics for data sharing. Those two ethical components explain 55.1% of the total variance in biological scientists' research ethics ($R^2=0.551$). Eventually, research ethics is found to have a significant positive influence on biological scientists' data sharing intentions ($\beta=0.655$, $p<0.001$). Research ethics accounts for 42.9% of the total variance in biological scientists' data sharing intentions ($R^2=0.429$), which means that research ethics is the main factor influencing biological scientists' data sharing intentions.

CONCLUSION

We found that both egoism factors (perceived reputation, perceive risk, and perceived effort) and utilitarianism factors (perceived community benefit and perceived reciprocity) contribute to the formation of research ethics for data sharing, which eventually lead to biological scientists' data sharing intentions. Also, research ethics were found to have a strong influence on data sharing intentions. Our next step will be to extend our research model by incorporating additional factors such as pressure by funding agencies, perceived pressure by journals, or norm of data sharing among scientists. We hope that this work provides deeper understanding on motivations and perceptions of scientists' research ethics on their data sharing behaviors.

REFERENCES

Ajzen, I., & Fishbein, M. (2005). The influence of attitudes on behavior. In D. Albarracin, B. T. Johnson, & M. P. Zanna (Eds.), *Handbook of attitudes and attitude change* (pp. 173-221). Mahwah, NJ: Lawrence Erlbaum Associates.

Cronin, B. (2005). *The hand of science: academic writing and its rewards*. Oxford, UK: Scarecrow Press, Inc.

Guillemin, M., & Gillam, L. (2004). Ethics, reflexivity, and "ethically important moments" in research. *Qualitative inquiry, 10*(2), 261-280.

Kim, Y., & Stanton, J. M. (2016). Institutional and individual factors affecting scientists' data-sharing behaviors: A multilevel analysis. *Journal of the Association for Information Science and Technology*, 1-24. doi:10.1002/asi.23424

Kim, Y., & Zhang, P. (2015). Understanding data sharing behaviors of STEM researchers: The roles of attitudes, norms, and data repositories. *Library & Information Science Research, 37*(3), 189-200.

Tenopir, C., Allard, S., Douglass, K., Aydinoglu, A. U., Wu, L., Read, E., . . . Frame, M. (2011). Data sharing by scientists: Practices and perceptions. *Plos One, 6*(6).

Tenopir, C., Dalton, E. D., Allard, S., Frame, M., Pjesivac, I., Birch, B., . . . Dorsett, K. (2015). Changes in Data Sharing and Data Reuse Practices and Perceptions among Scientists Worldwide. *Plos One, 10*(8). doi:10.1371/journal.pone.0134826

Tsalikis, J., & Ortiz-Buonafina, M. (1990). Ethical beliefs' differences of males and females. *Journal of Business Ethics, 9*(6), 509-517.

Zimmerman, A. (2007). Not by metadata alone: The use of diverse forms of knowledge to locate data for reuse. *International Journal on Digital Libraries, 7*(1-2), 5-16.

Information Practice, Responsibility, and the Ability to Respond

Michelle Kaczmarek
University of British Columbia, Canada.
michelle.kaczmarek@ubc.ca

Lisa P. Nathan
University of British Columbia, Canada.
lisa.nathan@ubc.ca

Saguna Shankar
University of British Columbia, Canada.
saguna@mail.ubc.ca

ABSTRACT

In situations when digital systems exacerbate bias and injustice, who should be held responsible? Who is in a position to respond effectively? This poster 1) critiques dominant rhetoric concerning responsibility and the ability to respond to the influence of digital information systems; 2) argues for the field of information science to contribute to this discussion beyond a focus on policy; and 3) calls for information scientists to draw upon and extend information practice scholarship by applying it as a generative lens for conceptualizing responsibility in relation to ethical data stewardship.

KEYWORDS

Information Practice, Responsibility, Practice Theory, Networked Systems, Information Policy.

INTRODUCTION

Every day digital information systems are woven deeper into the fabric of daily life. These systems are increasingly algorithmic, artificially intelligent, networked, and monetized. They optimize your social media feeds, determine your wait time on customer help lines, and select you for "personalized" attention from airport security. Reports analyzing the myriad influences of these systems abound in news media and scholarly discourse, where their capabilities are simultaneously framed as disruptive and inevitable (Clifford, 2018). However, concern is growing as scholars offer evidence that these systems also encode inequalities and prejudice (e.g., O'Neil, 2016).

In situations when digital systems exacerbate bias and injustice, who should be responsible? Who is in a position to respond effectively? We find paradoxical answers to these questions within reports, articles and other media. For example, many position individuals as responsible for the ways in which their personal data is collected, managed, stored, and used (e.g., Gebhart, 2018). In alignment, others add that technology companies should be more transparent about their data harvesting and sharing practices as a way to better inform users and that governing institutions have a responsibility to regulate these companies (e.g., Diakopoulos, 2016). Yet, these positions are problematic when viewed alongside research that demonstrates how, even if technological mechanisms are made more transparent, the ability (or capability) of individuals to respond effectively is constrained and easily manipulated (e.g., Acquisti, Brandimarte, & Loewenstein, 2015).

Through this poster we: 1) critique dominant rhetoric concerning responsibility and the ability to respond to the influence of digital information systems; 2) argue for the field of information science to contribute to this discussion beyond a focus on policy; and 3) call for information scientists to draw upon information practice scholarship as a generative lens for conceptualizing responsibilities towards ethical data stewardship in the age of social media and social networks.

RECURRING RESPONSIBILITY LOOP

In discourse addressing concerns about digital information systems, responsibility is often framed through three related ideas:

1. Governments need to regulate: Governing institutions and policy-makers have a responsibility to catch up with the fast pace of technology development (e.g., Manjoo, 2017).
2. Industry needs to be more transparent: Attempts at government regulation often take the form of policy to promote transparency in corporate owned information systems. As the creators of systems that use our data to make decisions about our lives, industry is responsible for making clear how such decisions are made (e.g., O'Neil, 2016).
3. Individuals need to skill up: Individuals are often framed as responsible for developing the skills needed to keep themselves digitally secure (e.g., Gebhart, 2018).

DISCUSSION

Questioning dominant rhetoric: We find conversations that frame responsibility through government regulation, industry transparency, and individual skill-sets to be cyclical and limiting. These framings imply that people hold shared and corresponding: 1) access to power, 2) ability to respond, and 3) values around what an ethical, algorithmically-enhanced technological system looks like. Calls for increased transparency in the design and the operation of digital information systems assume that once systems are open to scrutiny, individuals will be able to understand how they work and make informed choices about their system engagement, advocate for themselves, and hold systems accountable (Ananny & Crawford, 2018). Yet, for decades scholars have argued that as information systems become more intertwined and ubiquitous, individuals have less agency, little knowledge about how tools function, and are kept so distracted by their devices that there is little time left for critical reflection (e.g., Winner, 1978; Acquisti, Brandimarte, & Loewenstein, 2015). Ironically, as responsibility is offloaded to individuals, individuals have less agency and knowledge of how they might respond.

Beyond a focus on policy: Information policy approaches in this area are important, however, we see opportunities for information science scholarship that takes seriously ideas that people do not share the same or equivalent: 1) access to power, 2) ability to respond, and 3) values around what an ethical, algorithmically-enhanced technological system looks like. For example, there is potential for information literacy research to consider the influence of peer groups on learning or information design research that embraces the diversity of values, cultures, privilege, experience, knowledges and power.

Drawing upon information practice scholarship: Previous literature on expertise and responsibility in relation to questions of ethics emphasizes the *work practices* of technology designers (Shilton & Anderson, 2017). Yet, the *practices* of individuals who use technological systems also play a role in how these systems influence societies. Through inquiries framed by the concept of information practice, information science scholars have explored assemblages of human actors, information, and technologies for decades (e.g., Dourish & Anderson, 2006; Cavanagh, 2013). However, we find that there are challenges with the concept of information practice when considering ethical questions of how humans participate in information practices with ever larger, automated, and distant digital systems (Morley, 2017): How are technologies that are further removed from the human body implicated in information practices? How do individuals reassert their agency in relationships with highly personalized information systems? We view these questions as opportunities to deepen and enrich information practice theory.

CONCLUSION

This work will be presented in the form of an interactive poster designed to generate conversations about the distribution of agency and responsibility in designing and enacting information practices in the context of pervasive, algorithmic, intelligent, and networked information systems. We will engage ASIS&T attendees in discussing how information scientists might investigate arrangements of diverse stakeholders, technologies, and information practices, and how these arrangements may make visible the ethical issues and implications that impact stakeholders in different ways.

REFERENCES

Acquisti, A., L. Brandimarte, and G. Loewenstein. (2015, January 30) Privacy and Human Behavior in the Age of Information. *Science 347*(622), 509–14. https://doi.org/10.1126/science.aaa1465.

Ananny, M., & Crawford, K. (2018). Seeing without knowing: Limitations of the transparency ideal and its application to algorithmic accountability. *New Media & Society, 20*(3), 973–989. https://doi.org/10.1177/1461444816676645

Cavanagh, M. F. (2013). Interpreting reference work with contemporary practice theory. *Journal of Documentation, 69*(2), 214–242. https://doi.org/10.1108/00220411311300057

Clifford, C. (2018, February 1). Google CEO Sundar Pichai: AI is more important than fire, electricity. *CNBC*. Retrieved from https://www.cnbc.com/2018/02/01/google-ceo-sundar-pichai-ai-is-more-important-than-fire-electricity.html

Diakopoulos, N. (2016) Accountability in algorithmic decision making. *Communications of the ACM* 59(2): 56–62.

Dourish, P., & Anderson, K. (2006). Collective Information Practice: Exploring Privacy and Security as Social and Cultural Phenomena. *Human–Computer Interaction, 21*(3), 319–342. https://doi.org/10.1207/s15327051hci2103_2

Gebhart, G. (2018, March 19) How To Change Your Facebook Settings To Opt Out of Platform API Sharing. *Electronic Frontier Foundation*. Retrieved from https://www.eff.org/deeplinks/2018/03/how-change-your-facebook-settings-opt-out-platform-api-sharing.

Manjoo, F. (2017, October 25). Can Washington Stop Big Tech Companies? Don't Bet on It. *The New York Times*. Retrieved from https://www.nytimes.com/2017/10/25/technology/regulating-tech-companies.html

Morley, J. (2017). Technologies within and beyond practices. In A. Hui, T. R. Schatzki, & E. Shove (Eds.), *The nexus of practices: connections, constellations and practitioners* (pp. 81-97). New York: Routledge, Taylor & Francis Group.

O'Neil, C. (2016). *Weapons of math destruction: how big data increases inequality and threatens democracy*. New York: Crown.

Shilton, K., & Anderson, S. (2017). Blended, Not Bossy: Ethics Roles, Responsibilities and Expertise in Design. *Interacting with Computers, 29*(1), 71–79. https://doi.org/10.1093/iwc/iww002

Winner, L. (1978). *Autonomous Technology: Technics-out-of-control as a Theme in Political Thought*. Cambridge, MA: MIT Press.

Implications for LIS from an Embedded Chronological Case Study of a Vaccine Avoidant Mommy Blogger

Samantha Kaplan
University of North Carolina at Chapel Hill, USA. samanthajkaplan@gmail.com

ABSTRACT
In this poster, I review vaccine avoidance and how it is typically studied. I then describe how I conducted my dissertation research and present some implications for library and information science. This research, an embedded chronological case study of a vaccine-avoidant mommy blogger, utilized multiple methods to understand why some people view vaccine avoidance as normative and desirable and how they engage with a mainstream world which disagrees. The findings from this research hold important theoretical and practical implications for library and information science, particularly how we study and work with communities we consider stigmatized or vulnerable to problematic information.

KEYWORDS
Vaccine avoidance, case study, information behavior, misinformation, problematic information

INTRODUCTION
Hinshaw et al. (2013) assert, "Ever since vaccines were introduced in the 18th century, questions and concerns about their safety have been voiced" (p. 18). It is true that, "Vaccines—like all drugs or medical interventions—are neither 100 percent risk-free nor 100 percent effective" (Hinshaw et al., 2013, p. 2). However, vaccine refusal has led to outbreaks of preventable diseases like measles and pertussis (Phadke, Bednarczyk, Salmon, & Omer, 2016).

Rationales for vaccine opposition include but are not limited to one or more of the following factors; falsified research that suggests vaccines are linked to Autism Spectrum Disorder (Wakefield et al., 1998), celebrities (Flaherty, Tayag, Lanier, & Minor, 2014; Gottlieb, 2016), lack of personal exposure to many of the diseases for which we vaccinate (Fine, Eames, & Heymann, 2011), safety concerns (Dempsey et al., 2011; Freed, Clark, Butchart, Singer, & Davis, 2010; Luthy, Beckstrand, & Callister, 2010), a calculated risk assessment (Feikin et al., 2000), and conscientious objection to government regulation of the body (Busse, Wilson, & Campbell, 2008).

Research about vaccine opposition typically attempts to profile the population (Smith, Chu, & Barker, 2004) catalog the rhetoric and themes of extremist anti-vaccination material (Davies, Chapman, & Leask, 2002); report a skew toward anti-vaccination materials in digital spaces (Buchanan & Beckett, 2014; Guidry, Carlyle, Messner, & Jin, 2015); or center the issue inside the office of a health care provider (Luthy et al., 2010). These approaches leave a rich range unexamined and neglect how vaccine avoidant parents and individuals navigate everyday life.

RESEARCH DESIGN
I conducted a grounded theoretical chronological embedded case study of the information practices and everyday life behavior of a parent who has not vaccinated their children using multiple methods and grounded theory as a frame. The case study methodology was selected because of its suitability for research where "the boundaries between phenomenon and context may not be clearly evident" (Yin, 2014, p.16). I selected a vaccine avoidant mommy blogger, Genevieve Howland of MamaNatural.com, as the primary case because of her large YouTube following garnered over seven years, Howland's habit of citing her information sources, the rich evidence streams available, and the evidence of secrecy around her vaccine views. I utilized multiple methods, including qualitative and quantitative content analyses, inductive coding and memo writing, bibliometrics, descriptive statistics, and digital ethnography.

IMPLICATIONS FOR LIS
Theoretical
Through gerundic inductive coding and memoing, I developed a model to explicate how problematic information, such as inaccurate or misleading information about vaccines, flourished in the worldview of my case. This model had significant overlap with Ludwik Fleik's theory of thought collectives. Thought collectives are characterized by a "shared thought-style which links the individual participants of a collective together, whilst simultaneously constraining and determining the way of thinking adopted" (Arksey, 1994, p. 450). In these collectives, members "participate in verifying the specialised knowledge" (Arksey, 1994, p. 449). This theory merits greater examination and application in LIS when studying the resilience and acceptance of problematic information, particularly discredited information or information lacking a strong evidence base.

Practical

The case I examined cited academic and popular materials with great frequency. Many of these sources were problematic in some way, either because of what their content or how the case utilized them. However, they were all extremely easy to access, via tools like PubMed or one's local library. By allowing problematic materials such as Dr. Sear's *The Vaccine Book,* a favorite of my case and a book so flawed it earned a rebuttal in *Pediatrics,* to reside in library collections without any context about **why** they are included, we allow problematic materials to capitalize on the authority and trust individuals place in libraries and legitimize these materials. In our information retrieval systems, catalogs, finding aids, and collections, we must begin to educate patrons and users about how items are selected and why they are included.

REFERENCES

Arksey, H. (1994). Expert and lay participation in the construction of medical knowledge. *Sociology of Health & Illness*, *16*(4), 448-468.

Buchanan, R., & Beckett, R. D. (2014). Assessment of vaccination-related information for consumers available on Facebook®. *Health Information & Libraries Journal*, *31*(3), 227-234.

Busse, J. W., Wilson, K., & Campbell, J. B. (2008). Attitudes towards vaccination among chiropractic and naturopathic students. *Vaccine*, *26*(49), 6237-6243.

Davies, P., Chapman, S., & Leask, J. (2002). Antivaccination activists on the world wide web. *Archives of disease in childhood*, *87*(1), 22-25.

Dempsey, A. F., Schaffer, S., Singer, D., Butchart, A., Davis, M., & Freed, G. L. (2011). Alternative vaccination schedule preferences among parents of young children. *Pediatrics*, peds-2011.

Feikin, D. R., Lezotte, D. C., Hamman, R. F., Salmon, D. A., Chen, R. T., & Hoffman, R. E. (2000). Individual and community risks of measles and pertussis associated with personal exemptions to immunization. *Jama*, *284*(24), 3145-3150.

Fine, P., Eames, K., & Heymann, D. L. (2011). "Herd immunity": a rough guide. *Clinical infectious diseases*, *52*(7), 911-916.

Flaherty, M. G., Tayag, E. K., Lanier, M., & Minor, J. (2014). The jenny mccarthy conundrum: Public libraries, popular culture, and health misinformation. *Proceedings of the Association for Information Science and Technology*, *51*(1), 1-1.

Freed, G. L., Clark, S. J., Butchart, A. T., Singer, D. C., & Davis, M. M. (2010). Parental vaccine safety concerns in 2009. *Pediatrics*, *125*(4), 654-659.

Gottlieb, S. D. (2016). Vaccine resistances reconsidered: Vaccine skeptics and the Jenny McCarthy effect. *Biosocieties*, *11*(2), 152-174.

Guidry, J. P., Carlyle, K., Messner, M., & Jin, Y. (2015). On pins and needles: how vaccines are portrayed on Pinterest. *Vaccine*, *33*(39), 5051-5056.

Hinshaw, A., Aragon, T., Berg, A., Buka, S., Charo, R., Fairbrother, G., ... & Leland, A. (2013). Childhood immunization schedule and safety: stakeholder concerns, scientific evidence, and future studies. *Institute of Medicine*.

Luthy, K. E., Beckstrand, R. L., & Callister, L. C. (2010). Parental hesitation in immunizing children in Utah. *Public Health Nursing*, *27*(1), 25-31.

Offit, P. A., & Moser, C. A. (2009). The Problem With Dr Bob9s Alternative Vaccine Schedule. *Pediatrics*, *123*(1), e164-e169.

Phadke, V. K., Bednarczyk, R. A., Salmon, D. A., & Omer, S. B. (2016). Association between vaccine refusal and vaccine-preventable diseases in the United States: a review of measles and pertussis. *Jama*, *315*(11), 1149-1158.

Smith, P. J., Chu, S. Y., & Barker, L. E. (2004). Children who have received no vaccines: who are they and where do they live?. *Pediatrics*, *114*(1), 187-195.

Wakefield, A. J., Murch, S. H., Anthony, A., Linnell, J., Casson, D. M., Malik, M., ... & Valentine, A. (1998). RETRACTED: Ileal-lymphoid-nodular hyperplasia, non-specific colitis, and pervasive developmental disorder in children.

Yin, R. K.(2014). Case study research: Design and methods.

81st Annual Meeting of the Association for Information Science & Technology | Vancouver, Canada | 10 – 14 November 2018

Data-Activism as Civic Engagement: Forming a Narrative to Foster Social Change on Gun Control in the United States

Hammad Rauf Khan
University of North Texas, U.S.A. hammadkhan@my.unt.edu

Yunfei Du
University of North Texas, U.S.A. Yunfei.Du@unt.edu

Uriel Uzochukwu Onye
University of North Texas, U.S.A. urielonye@my.unt.edu

ABSTRACT

This research evaluates data activism on the popular social media website twitter. The study focused on the predominant debate between the pro-gun and anti-gun activists in the United States. Such factors as data bias, ambiguity, and inaccuracies may occur when either feuding party shares data on gun violence statistics through twitter. The researchers adopted a veracity assessment synthesized from previous studies, which focuses on three main aspects 1) objectivity/subjectivity 2) truthfulness/deception, 3) credibility/implausibility. The preliminary research focused on finding data influencers on twitter through the NodeXL application and studying their tweets through content/text analysis. Results indicate that both sides of the debate are misrepresenting gun violence data in the United States to put forward their own agenda.

KEYWORDS

Data Ethics, Data Activism, Data Literacy, Media Literacy, Twitter

INTRODUCTION

The implementation of digital data through information communication technology (ICT) in humanitarian and disaster settings has become popular on social media applications such as Facebook, twitter, YouTube, and Instagram. Individuals have become active information-seekers that search a variety of sources than be passive recipients of traditional media information (Stephens & Malone, 2009). Online social media has become increasingly popular as an information source. Society is waking up to datafication, which alters "the conditions under which we can make sense of our world and our own actions", affecting "our capacity to act with agency" (Baack, 2015, p.1). The way individuals' present data and form narratives around data, has the potential to alter our vision and affect our choices, especially when decision making is data-driven.

Technology has scattered information and social media has pulled users away from traditional news sources. For example, "Fact checking" has become a popular term in the media as a way of understanding political speech and reporting. Even upon fact checking, people will still claim the facts as "alternative facts" and report the media outlet as "fake news".

An ongoing debate in most American ICT-championed online communities and the real world include the topic of gun control vs. gun rights. Both sides, gun supporters and gun control activists are taking sides and presenting their own narratives through data. How are the data representations on gun violence in the United States being presented by the two opposing sides on social media? Is the data being ethically used or is it being misreported by these quarreling parties to favor their own agenda?

METHOD

Authentication of identity on social media is paramount to the notion of trust. The use of twitter in influencing political perceptions (Cook et al., 2013) is one scenario where data, namely the inclusion of hyperlinks, can be compiled to establish veracity assessments. The researchers in this study wanted to gather the key group of data activists for both sides of the gun violence debate. NodeXL was used to generate a report from twitter to identify the key groups and people involved in this discussion of gun violence by focusing specifically on those tweets that shared a URL to a data source. If the URL did not link to data on gun violence it was not included in the veracity assessment synthesis. Previous researchers, such as Chong (2016), used NodeXL to focus on sentiment analysis. This research focusses on representation of sources through content analysis.

NodeXL enables social media network analysis and visualization and from this the researchers were able to map public social media conversations around the topic of gun violence and gun rights. This method allows the nodes (twitter accounts) and connections (twitter followers/retweets) to better understand what data is being shared by key players in this debate. The researchers found the top five influencers on both sides of the debate. They were considered influencers based on the amount of mentions they received by followers and the public on their gun violence statistics data. Some popular hashtags on the topic studied were #gunstatistics #gunviolence #gunfacts. It was found that these hashtags increased tweets in data activism during or right after a mass shooting. The tweets and conversations were recorded with a median mention of a data influencer to be 226 retweets; NodeXL tweet limits were set to 500 tweets retrieved per hashtag.

The data which was shared by the higher end influencers was then studied and compared against other influencers through content/text analysis to see if the data they were sharing had been ethically used to represent their viewpoints or was it used to further their own personal agenda by misreporting the data to their followers.

RESULTS

The results found both sides of the debate misrepresenting gun violence data in the United States. For example, the pro-second amendment influencer would share the FBI statistics on negligent homicide and claim it to be the FBI statistics for gun violence. They would then report only the negligent manslaughter homicides committed in self-defense, which clearly lowers the statistics for actual deaths counted by the FBI in the cases of gun violence. They would not share the year it was reported by the FBI. Had they correctly reported the non-negligent manslaughter homicides by firearms, the data could have resulted in different amount of tweets/retweets and mentions by the public.

Anti-gun data activist influencers shared data from sources such as the National Center for Health Statistics and would misreport the data percentages from hospitals where survivors of a mass shooting were being cared for. When in fact they should have taken a holistic view from the average percentage of firearm related injuries reported in hospitals throughout the entire United States and not specific events. Even then, the estimates they reported were not clearly representative for injuries versus actual deaths by firearms.

Without any ethical considerations on how data could positively or negatively affect society, both sides of the gun debate are portraying and providing a narrative told through data which influences the public to their own personal agenda.

DISCUSSION

It is interesting to see the tweets collected become data represented discussions on guns used in terrorism, mass shootings, school shootings, police officers killed by guns, and police shootings of civilians. No side represented why the data was important to their cause. They just gave a number of deaths caused by guns which would favor their agenda, but did not talk about any other issues such as safety, post-traumatic stress, or mental health. Data activists on twitter need to explain the meaning behind the number, more importantly why these events occur. Civic engagement is not only about creating change, but change through reason. No one is discussing the root of the violence. Why is this such a problem for the United States in 2018? Oddly enough, firearm violence is far lower than it was in 1993, according to the Pew Research Center for Gun Homicide Rate Statistics, but if you follow the media and social media there seems to be an uprise in voices on both sides of the gun violence debate. This is a preliminary research, but future research should address the response tweets to the high influencer data activist, to study if there is an agreement or disagreement by users to their representation of data.

CONCLUSION

Data acts as a check on rhetoric. Increasing levels of social media usage and civic engagement in the United States continues to gravitate to online venues (social media formed virtual communities) in terms of political dialogue and debate. If we are truly to have data activism lead to civic change in the United States, there needs to be ethical considerations in sharing the data with the public on social media platforms. A need for veracity assessments, information and data literacy skills, and media literacy are needed to be able to discern between real and fake data activist tweets. Future research should address the question, what set of ethical practices can be set for socio-technical usage for data production, processing, and representation?

REFERENCES

Baack, S. (2015). Datafication and empowerment: How the open data movement re-articulates notions of democracy, participation, and journalism. *Big Data & Society*, *2*(2), 2053951715594634.

Chong, M. (2016). Sentiment analysis and topic extraction of the twitter network of #prayforparis. In *Proceedings of the 79th ASIS&T Annual Meeting: Creating Knowledge, Enhancing Lives through Information & Technology* (p. 133). American Society for Information Science.

Cook, D. M., Waugh, B., Abdipanah, M., Hashemi, O., & Rahman, S. A. (2014). Twitter deception and influence: Issues of identity, slacktivism, and puppetry. *Journal of Information Warfare*, *13*(1), 58-IV.

Stephens, K. K., & Malone, P. C. (2009). If the organizations won't give us information…: The use of multiple new media for crisis technical translation and dialogue. *Journal of Public Relations Research, 21*(2), 229-239.

A Comparative Examination of Factors that Affect the Credibility of Health Information on Social Media

Heejun Kim
University of North Carolina at Chapel Hill, USA.
heejunk@email.unc.edu

Bogeum Choi
University of North Carolina at Chapel Hill, USA.
choiboge@live.unc.ed

ABSTRACT

The purpose of this research is to investigate factors affecting the perceived credibility of health information on social media and their varying effects on different platforms. We incorporated Elaboration Likelihood Model as a theoretical framework for our inductive content analysis. Then we conducted a correlation analysis and regression analyses to examine the relationship between the perceived credibility and identified factors. Our study discovered an extensive set of credibility factors and statistically significant effects made by platform-specific factors.

KEYWORDS

Credibility, factors, comparative study, content analysis, regression analysis, health information, social media.

INTRODUCTION

Social media has been a fast-growing source of health information alongside traditional media. Patients who have difficulties in finding relevant information with their complex health problems tend to rely on interactive media. Social media is better suited to meet those personalized information demands than traditional media. However, concerns about the credibility of online health information found on social media are also growing. The potential risk of unreliable information in the context of health should be properly addressed because it can be detrimental to users' health and can threaten their lives.

Credibility is considered the believability of a message, source, or media that consists of the two main dimensions of trustworthiness and expertise (Rieh, 2010). According to the Elaboration Likelihood Model (Petty & Cacioppo, 1986), there are two routes to persuasion. In the central route, an individual evaluates the claims of the content logically. In the peripheral route, the person relies more on simple and heuristic cues. The Elaboration Likelihood Model (ELM) was used as a theoretical framework to inductively examine the structure of credibility and related factors.

Previous studies have examined factors constituting information credibility, but those studies have yet to provide evidence that factors contributing to health information credibility can vary across platforms (Ma & Atkin, 2017). In this study, we conducted a content analysis to identify platform-specific factors as well as common factors affecting credibility judgments of health information on social media. We also ran statistical analyses to examine their varying effects over platforms (Q&A vs. review).

METHOD

We randomly selected 500 data instances from Yahoo! Answers (https://webscope.sandbox.yahoo.com/catalog.php?datatype=l) and Yelp (https://www.yelp.com/dataset/challenge) respectively and used 1,000 data instances in total. Only health-related posts were selected by using category information. In the case of Yahoo! Answers, questions were manually inspected until we collected 500 reasonable-quality questions to reduce noises from low-quality questions.

One author developed an initial codebook by examining 200 random answers and reviews and referencing existing studies (e.g., Rieh, 2010). Credibility was evaluated using the instrument (7-point Likert scales for *believable*, *trustworthy*, *accurate*, and *complete*) created by Rains and Karmikel (2009), and credibility factors were binary-coded (*yes* or *no*). Two authors independently coded 1,000 data instances and resolved any differences through the codebook and iterative discussions.

Pearson correlation coefficients were computed to assess the relationships between the perceived credibility and underlying factors. Multiple regression analyses and corresponding F-tests were conducted to test if platform-specific factors have a significant effect in predicting the perceived credibility.

RESULTS

We found 18 factors that affect the perceived credibility of health information (Table 1). Among these factors, 11 factors (e.g., *comprehensive* and *objective*) were found to be common to both Yahoo! Answers and Yelp. 4 factors (e.g., *plausible* and *relevant* showed a unique influence on Yahoo! Answers, and 3 factors (e.g., *specific*) had a unique influence on Yelp reviews. Cohen's Kappa (K_c) agreement that measures the chance-corrected agreement between two coders for those credibility factors ranged from 0.66 to 0.91 (mean=0.74, SD=0.07). The Kappa agreement for the credibility labels was 0.75. The numbers in parentheses in Table 1 represent Cohen's Kappa agreement.

Yahoo! Answers		Common						Yelp	
Plausible	Relevant	Comprehensive	Objective	Promotion	Presentation	Positive	Negative	Excessively positive	Excessively negative
0.75*** (0.78)	0.57*** (0.7)	0.47*** (0.83)	0.55*** (0.71)	-0.27*** (0.7)	0.13*** (0.91)	0.08* (0.66)	-0.08* (0.69)	0.08 (0.77)	0.03 (0.68)
1st hand	Sympathy	Credential	Current	Expertise	Honest	Reference		Specific	
0.12** (0.8)	0.21*** (0.68)	0.07* (0.67)	0.1** (0.81)	0.23*** (0.73)	0.23*** (0.75)	0.07* (0.83)		0.41*** (0.66)	
* significant at p < 0.05; ** significant at p < 0.005; *** significant at p < 0.001									

Table 1. Correlation coefficients between the credibility and underlying factors and Cohen's Kappa agreement.

Among common factors for both social media platforms, *objective* showed the largest positive correlation (0.55, $p < .001$) with the credibility, while *promotion* shows negative correlation (-0.27, $p < .001$). Regarding factors specific to Yahoo! answers, *plausible* (0.75, $p < .001$) and *relevant* (0.57, $p < .001$) exhibited strong correlation with the credibility. Among factors that uniquely influenced Yelp reviews, *specific* showed the largest correlation with credibility (0.41, $p < .001$).

To test the influence of platform-specific factors in predicting the credibility, a constrained linear regression model was created using step-wise feature selection. For the less-constrained linear regression models, one platform-specific factor (*plausible* or *relevant* for Yahoo! and *specific* for Yelp) was added to the constrained model and compared by conducting F-tests. All three F-tests indicated significant contribution of the added factors and the results are summarized in Table 2.

Yahoo! Answers				Yelp	
Constrained model: expertise+reference+objective+honest+negative+comprehensive+promotion+credential					
Less-constrained model: constrained model + ***plausible***		Less-constrained model: constrained model + ***relevant***		Less-constrained model: constrained model + ***specific***	
F-value	P-value	F-value	P-value	F-value	P-value
345.82	2.2E-16***	120.08	2.2E-16***	46.33	2.93E-11***

Table 2. Results of F-test to examine the influence of platform-specific factors.

CONCLUSION

The content analysis identified an extensive set of factors that potentially influence the perceived credibility of health information on social media. Factors that have a unique contribution associated with a platform were discovered along with common factors for both platforms. For instance, *relevant* was considered important in Yahoo! Answers, because answers that do not address users' information need can be of no use. The correlation analysis identified several factors that have a positive/negative relationship with the perceived credibility. We also demonstrated the impact of discovered factors on the perceived credibility using linear regression models and F-tests. This study can help us better understand users' interactions with health information on social media and provide insights into developing more credible socio-technical systems.

REFERENCES

Ma, T. J., & Atkin, D. (2017). User generated content and credibility evaluation of online health information: a meta analytic study. *Telematics and Informatics*, *34*(5), 472-486.

Petty, R. E., & Cacioppo, J. T. (1986). The elaboration likelihood model of persuasion. In *Communication and persuasion* (pp. 1-24). New York: Springer.

Rains, S. A., & Karmikel, C. D. (2009). Health information-seeking and perceptions of website credibility: Examining Web-use orientation, message characteristics, and structural features of websites. *Computers in Human Behavior*, *25*(2), 544-553.

Rieh, S. Y. (2010). Credibility and cognitive authority of information. In M. Bates & M. N. Maack (Eds.) *Encyclopedia of Library and Information Sciences,* 3rd Ed. (pp. 1337-1344), New York: Taylor & Francis.

Evaluating Social Media Information: Impact of Academic Background, Purpose of Use, and Perceived Importance of Information Quality

Kyung-Sun Kim
University of Wisconsin-Madison, USA.
kskim@ischool.wisc.edu

Sei-Ching Joanna Sin
Nanyang Technological University, Singapore.
joanna.sin@ntu.edu.sg

ABSTRACT

Issues with inaccurate information on social media have caused a rising concern. In addition to improving students' knowledge and skills in evaluating the quality of social media information, there is also a need to understand potential barriers such as students' lack of attention to information quality. Surveying over 1,800 students, the current study investigated the relationships among students' perceived importance of finding quality information, academic background, purposes of social media use, and evaluative actions taken. A multiple regression analysis revealed that two purposes of use and other academic backgrounds are related to the perceived importance of finding quality information from social media. Further investigation through correspond- ence analysis revealed distinctive clusters of evaluative actions when the purpose of use was to get background information from social media – the purpose closely related to the perceived importance of finding quality information. Implications of the findings on information literacy education were discussed.

KEYWORDS

Social media, information quality, purpose of use, evaluation of information, academic background.

INTRODUCTION

Fake news or inaccurate information spread through social media has been an issue of concern for many. In the academic setting, various initiatives have been taken to address the issue, including information literacy training to support the evaluation of information quality. While it is necessary to increase students' information evaluation skills, enhancements in knowledge and skills alone may not suffice. A key concern is that some students do not perceive the information quality as an important issue when it comes to their information behavior on social media. They may forgo quality issues in favor of other factors (e.g., expedience, fun). Understanding this potential affective barrier in students' evaluation of social media information will help refine and customize information literacy programs. Research has been conducted to understand why and how social media are used in the academic setting (Head & Eisenberg, 2010, 2011; Kim, Sin, & Yoo-Lee, 2014; Lim, 2009). However, little is known whether certain user groups are less concerned about the information quality, and whether this perception is related to the users' purpose of using social media and their evaluative actions. This study aims to answer two research questions: (1) How are the users' purpose of using social media and their backgrounds including their program level and discipline related to the perceived importance of finding quality information?; and (2) For the purposes of using social media significantly related to the perceived importance of finding quality information, are certain user groups more likely to prefer or bypass specific evaluative actions?

METHODS

A total of 1,847 students from a public university in the United States participated in a Web-based study. To recruit participants, a call for participation was distributed via email. About 60% of the participants were female while 40% were male. The majority of participants were undergraduates (73%). About 12% and 15% of the participants were master's and doctoral students, respectively. Regarding their major areas, about 12% of the participants were from humanities, 38% from social sciences, and 39% from sciences and engineering. About 10% of the participants responded "others." The first research question was analyzed using multiple regression. The importance of finding quality information was the dependent variable. Purposes of using social media (hereafter, *purposes of use*) as well as users' program level and disciplinary area (hereafter, *academic background*) were independent variables. The second research question was examined using correspondence analysis, which helps visualize the relationship among users' academic background, purpose of use and evaluative actions taken.

FINDINGS

The multiple regression analysis revealed that two purposes of use are significantly related to the perceived importance of finding quality information: 1) getting background/introductory information is related to a higher perceived importance ($\beta = 0.11$, $p < .001$), and 2) establishing/maintaining relationship with others is related to a lower perceived importance ($\beta = -0.10$, $p < .01$). In addition, five academic backgrounds (Master-Humanities, Master-Sciences, Master-Social sciences, PhD-Sciences, and PhD-Social sciences) were significant ($p < .05$). These groups tended to perceive information quality as more important than the reference group (Bachelor-Sciences) did.

Figures 1 and 2 present the correspondence analysis (CA) results for the second research question. It shows the relationships between users' academic backgrounds and evaluative actions for the two purposes of use that, the multiple regression analysis revealed, are significantly related to the perceived importance of finding quality information. Items that are closer on the CA plot are more related to each other. Figure 1 shows the relationships between the evaluative actions taken and users' academic background when social media are used for establishing/maintaining relationships with others. M ost actions are fairly close together, implying that users take evaluative actions similarly despite their differences in academic background. This contrasts with findings presented in Figure 2.

Focusing on getting background/introductory information as the purpose of use, Figure 2 shows more distinctive action groupings. In Figure 2, Cluster I includes evaluative actions such as: 1) Check tone/style of writing, 2) Compare the content with external sources, and 3) Check quantity/quality of links/references. These actions are directly related to checking the content quality, requiring more analytical efforts. PhD students in social sciences and sciences, and masters' students in humanities are more likely to take these actions. Cluster II covers more actions: 1) Check the posting date, 2) Check other users' reactions to the posting, 3) Check quality of images/sounds, 4) Check the length of posting, and 5) Check the edit/update history. These actions tend to focus on checking manifested properties, rather than the content, of the information. More undergraduate students, especially those in sciences tend to take such actions often. Cluster III consists of: 1) Check genre/category of post, and 2) Check the coverage. These seem to focus on the nature/characteristics of the content. No particular user groups are closely related to these. Cluster IV includes: 1) Check the disclaimer, 2) Check the information about the platform, and 3) Check information about the author. These focus on the source of information. Master's students in social sciences seem to be keener on these actions.

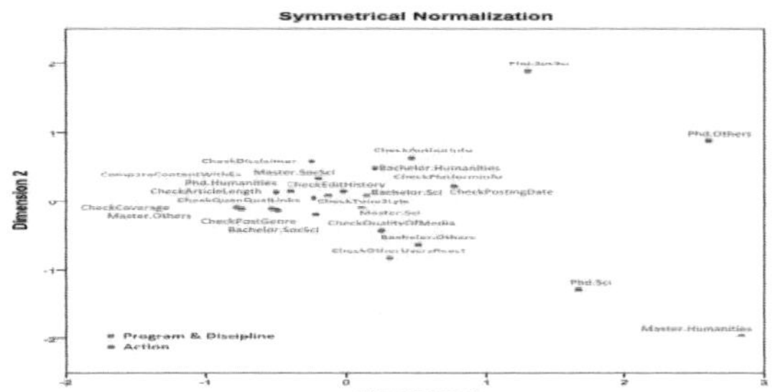

Figure 1. CA result: To establish/maintain relationships

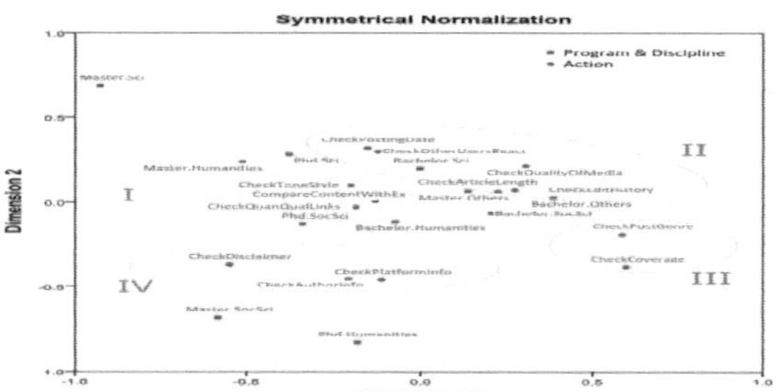

Figure 2. CA result: To get background information

CONCLUSION

The study revealed that the purpose of using social media is related to the perceived importance of finding quality information. For example, finding quality information is not perceived as important for students who use social media more for establishing relationship with others. For these students, information literacy instructors may highlight that neglect of information quality (e.g., sending low-quality information to friends) may have negative impacts on establishing/maintaining sound social relationships. Such reminders that are tailored to fit the students' purposes of using social media may appear more relevant and prompt students to be more careful about checking the quality of information. In addition, users' academic background and their purpose of using social media seem to be related to the actions taken for evaluating information from social media. When designing information literacy training programs, differences in disciplines and program levels, as well as users' motivations, might need to be considered to ensure that students be exposed to various yet appropriate strategies for evaluating information.

REFERENCES

Head, A.J., & Eisenberg, M.B. (2010). Truth be told: How college students evaluate and use information in the digital age. Retrieved from http://projectinfolit.org/pdfs/PIL_Fall2010_Survey_FullReport1.pdf

Head, A.J., & Eisenberg, M.B. (2011). Balancing act: How college students manage technology while in the library during crunch time. *Project Information Literacy* Research Report, University of Washington's Information School. Retrieved from http://projectinfolit.org/images/pdfs/pil_fall2011_techstudy_fullreport1.2.pdf

Kim, K.-S., Sin, S.-C.J., & Yoo-Lee, E. (2014). Undergraduates' use of social media as information sources. *College and Research Libraries, 75* (4), 442-457.

Lim, S. (2009). How and why do college students use Wikipedia? *Journal of the Association for Information Science and Technology, 60*(11), 2189-2202.

Analyzing Library and Information Science Full-Text Articles Using a Topic Modeling Approach

Keiko Kurata
Keio University, Japan. kei.kurata@keio.jp

MICHIMASA YAMAMOTO
Keio University, Japan. michimasa_y@keio.jp

Yosuke Miyata
Teikyo University, Japan. m@miyay.org

Fang Yang
Keio University, Japan. fyang@keio.jp

Emi Ishita
Kyushu University, Japan. Ishita.emi.982@m.kyushu-u.ac.jp

Azusa Iwase
Keio University, Japan. azs2iwase@keio.jp

ABSTRACT

The topic modeling approach can indicate hidden relationships between articles in a particular academic discipline. This study aims to examine topics in library and information science (LIS) using the latent Dirichlet allocation method. From representative five journals, 1,648 full-text articles were analyzed. We labeled 30 identified topics based on the top 10 highly weighted terms for each topic, title, and body of articles. From the topic mapping, commonly used methods and shift of research issues in LIS were found.

KEYWORDS

Topic modeling, library and information science research, latent Dirichlet allocation, mapping

INTRODUCTION

Many studies on the analysis of trends and characteristics in academic disciplines have been conducted using different methods, such as co-citation analysis and content analysis (Börner, Chen & Boyack, 2003). Recently, topic modeling approach has been applied to this analysis. Blei & Lafferty (2006) were the first to apply a topic modeling approach in their analysis of all scientific disciplines based on 30,000 articles from the journal *Science*. Topic modeling methods are also used in specific disciplines. In library and information science (LIS), Sugimoto et.al (2011) analyzed the topic of 3,131 North American dissertations on LIS. Lu and Worfram (2012) compared the topic modeling approach and author co-citation approach using articles from eight LIS journals. Yan (2015) discussed research dynamics and impact using topic modeling and citation data with 47,137 publications from JCR indexed journals.

The topic modeling approach can indicate hidden relationships between articles as well as subjects expressed in titles. The previous research on topic modeling in LIS, however, did not focus on what each topic meant. This study aims to examine topics identified by topic modeling through the commonality of articles that have strong relations with each topic. To examine the comprehensive aspect of topics, this study targeted full-text articles instead of metadata used in previous studies.

METHOD

We analyzed 1,648 full-text articles (561 articles from 2000 to 2002 and 1,087 from 2015 to 2017) from *Journal of the Association for Information Science and Technology* (JASIST), *Information Processing & Management* (IPM), *Journal of Documentation* (JDOC), *Library & Information Science Research* (LISR), and *Library Quarterly* (LQ) as representative LIS journals (See Table 1). As preprocessing, we removed function words, symbols, numbers, stop words listed in the Python NLTK library and frequently used terms in academic articles (e.g. "figure", "table", and "et al."). The remainder of words was pruned by stemming. After removal of words that occurred in over 90% of articles or in 20 or fewer articles, the total number of words was 10,457 from 454,008 original different words. We used the Gensim Python Library (3.3.0) with the default parameters setting and set the number of iterations as 500 for the latent Dirichlet allocation (LDA). The number of topics was set at 30 in this analysis considering the characteristics of the collection, our preliminary analysis, and discussion of previous studies.

Period	JDOC	LISR	LQ	JASIST	IPM	Total
2015-2017	190	108	39	567	183	1,087
2000-2002	89	48	36	280	108	561
Total	279	156	75	847	291	1,648

Table 1. Number of full-text articles for LDA

RESULTS & DISCUSSION

Labeling of 30 topics

We labeled 30 topics using title, body, publication year of articles which have a topic probability of more than 0.7, and the top 10 highly weighted terms for each topic by discussion with all authors. Each topic label is considered to represent common elements of articles that belong to that topic. As a result, topic labels represent an interesting subject, research perspective, or specific approach. For example, the topic "*raison d'etre of library*" reflected the "library" as an object of interest, and the topic "*ranking algorithm*" reflected the "ranking" approach. Topics identified by this modeling and thematic subject are not the same. The topic "*relation modeling"* included articles about academic journal reviewers, the ISP model of information behavior, and improvement of access to XML documents, which do not share the same subject. The common element of them is considered to be the relationship between two agents. For example, the article on information behavior describes how children use parents as an information resource, and the article on XML documents pointed out a parent-child relationship in XML tree structure as research issues. These topics represent non-thematic subject and reflect hidden elements. It is a typical example identified by the LDA.

Mapping of 30 topics

Thirty labeled topics were mapped from the perspective of article publication year and journal scope (Figure 1). The x- axis is the ratio of articles published in JASIST and IPM, and the y-axis is the ratio of articles published in 2015-2017. Values were normalized because the number of publications between the two journal groups and in 2015- 2017 and 2000-2002 were very different. The topic "*citation analysis and publishing"* and the topic "*measurement of publication"* are located in the middle of Figure 1. Both topics represent major bibliometric research methods that have been used constantly over two publication periods, and both journal groups. In contrast, the topic "*human computer interaction (HCI) in searching*" and topic "*web searching in different contexts"* are distantly positioned, but both are about user searching in a web environment. In the former, 96% (25/26) of articles published in 2000-2002 and focused on research questions of using computer in searching instead of library or people. These two topics represent the shift of research interests in the same research realm. Topic modeling is able to identify common methods and changes in research trends.

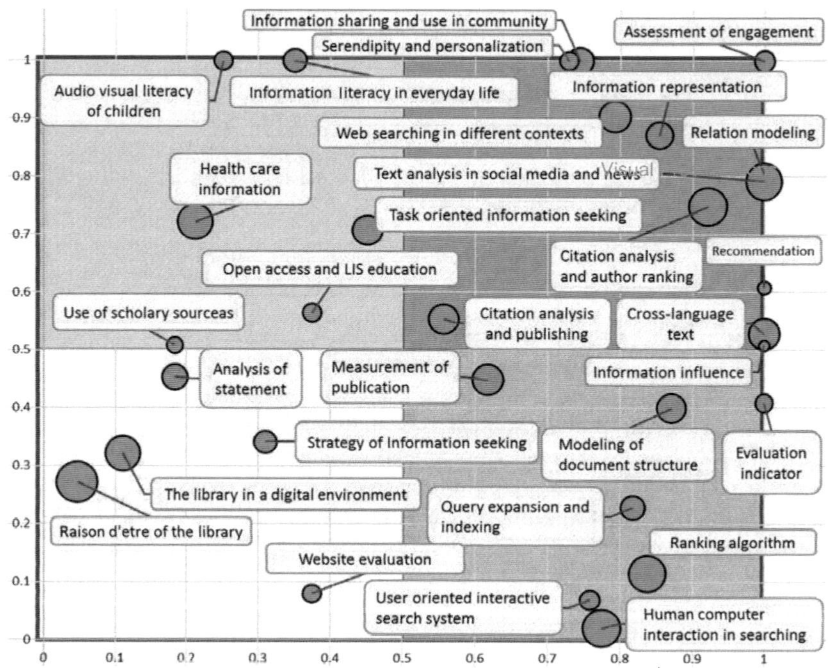

Figure 1. Mapping of 30 topics

REFERENCES

Börner, K., Chen, C. & Boyack, K. W. (2003), Visualizing knowledge domains. *Annual Review of Information Science and Technology, 37*, 179-255.

Blei, D.M., & Lafferty, J.D. (2006). Dynamic topic models. In *Proceedings of the 23rd International Conference on Machine Learning (ICML '06)*. (pp. 113-120). Pittsburgh: ACM.

Lu, K., & Wolfram, D. (2012). Measuring author research relatedness. *Journal of the Association for Information Science and Technology* 63, 1973-1986.

Sugimoto, C.R. et.al. (2011). The shifting sands of disciplinary development. *Journal of the Association for Information Science and Technology* 62, 185-204.

Yan, E. (2015). Research dynamics, impact, and dissemination. *Journal of the Association for Information Science and Technology* 66, 2357-2372.

Embracing Semantic Ambiguity to Enhance Interpretability of Complex Unstructured Machine Learning Problems.

James Lee
University of Cincinnati, USA. james.jlee@uc.edu

Arlene Johnson
University of Cincinnati, USA. johnsoam@ucmail.uc.edu

Zuemao Wang
University of Cincinnati, USA. wang2xm@ucmail.uc.edu

ABSTRACT
Ambiguity is frequently seen as an impediment to the recovery of a unique interpretation and meaning in texts. Machine learning algorithms have recently been deployed as an effective way to automate the process of semantic disambiguation. However, a growing body of literature has raised questions about problems of reduced accuracy and interpretability that come with disambiguation defined in terms of optimization at large data scales. We propose a hybrid methodology that can take advantage of the increased expediency of optimization (i.e. how a machine learning algorithm efficiently identifies semantic patterns within a corpus), while rethinking ambiguity as a semantically meaningful and interpretively useful feature of linguistic corpora. Our method examines why ambiguity occurs within a natural language corpus and the consequences of ambiguous meanings. Combining the "how" and the "why" dimensions of ambiguity requires a team science approach of researchers trained to study language from different disciplines, and we demonstrate how transdisciplinary digital scholarship centers located in academic libraries can create a space to foster precisely such collaborations purposefully created to analyze ambiguous datasets in more nuanced ways.

INTRODUCTION: AMBIGUITY AS AN OPTIMIZATION PROBLEM

Resolving ambiguity in unstructured textual datasets is a common problem in the domain of machine learning, with disambiguation invoked as a necessary step to successfully implement artificial intelligence algorithms (Burrell, 2016). Underlying the need to eliminate ambiguity is a fundamental assumption that "each use of a linguistic expression has a unique intended interpretation in context," and that we can "recover such a unique interpretation" (Yang, 2010). While few researchers in computational linguistics would question this assumption, it has resulted in an optimization mentality that has led to a view of ambiguity as a problematic feature to be "eliminated" for the sake of efficiency at large data scales, in what has been called the "curse of dimensionality" (Zimek et al., 2012). While framing ambiguity resolution in terms of optimization has led to increased efficiency and scalability of machine learning algorithms applied to large, unstructured datasets, it has come at the cost of diminished empirical accuracy and interpretability. Poesio and Artstein (2008) have suggested "the idealized view of communication, according to which natural language expressions are always meant to be uniquely disambiguated in context, is too simplistic." Lipton (2016) has argued "simplified optimization objectives fail to capture our most complex real-life goals."

EMBRACING AMBIGUITY AS A SALIENT FEATURE OF LINGUISTIC CORPORA

We propose that a remedy for the methodological mismatch between inherently ambiguous real-world research problems and the formal machine learning methods used to address them lies in a hybrid technical methodology that accepts ambiguity as an inherent variable in the formulation of research questions, and does not dismiss ambiguity as a problem to be eliminated or optimized in large textual datasets. Rethinking ambiguity as a positive variable to be analyzed by machine learning techniques can improve interpretability, which has been identified as a known blind spot. Burrell (2016) has defined interpretability as a dual problem of *how* an algorithm resolves ambiguity - which is an optimization problem - and *why* the algorithm has returned a specific disambiguated result, which should be understandable and explainable to human reasoning. The "how" element of the solution is purely technical and does not conform to the cognitive processes of human reason. But as Goodman and Flaxman (2017) have argued, the "why" element of a machine learning result must be interpretable to a human and testable for ethical reasons, in what the European Union has called a "right to explanation and contestability." This ethical parameter applies to all cases where the data are derived from human activity.

Recent work in computational linguistics has begun to shift in the direction of a positive definition of ambiguity as a fundamental and semantically meaningful trait of natural language, and as an interpretive tool for the researcher rather than an obstruction in the path to disambiguating meaning. This revised definition is particularly important for corpora in which ambiguity is not accidental or problematical, including legal and political texts, poetry, comedy, and social media (Wagner and Cacciaguidi-Fahy, 2006; Su, 1994; Raskin, 1985; Poesio et al., 2006; Ferreira et al., 2002). In all of these non-outlier cases, "attempting to build a system capable of recovering the originally intended meaning would not make any sense." (Poesio and Artstein, 2008) In a historical application of this approach, Hamilton et al. use word embeddings to understand the behavior of polysemy not as a feature of synchronic ambiguity but rather diachronic linguistic innovation. (Hamilton et al., 2016) In these recent studies, computational researchers have acknowledged the advantages to analyzing "why" ambiguity exists rather than reductively optimizing "how" to eliminate it.

A TEAM SCIENCE MODEL: THE ROLE OF LIBRARY DIGITAL SCHOLARSHIP CENTERS IN EMBRACING AMBIGUITY

Developing and implementing this hybrid methodology that accounts for both the technical "how" and the interpretive "why" of machine learning research is a multi-disciplinary space in which libraries, and particularly library digital scholarship centers, are particularly well-positioned to act as a methodological common ground in the age of algorithms. In this model of interpretive digital scholarship, libraries do not only serve as information brokers, but actively work as mediating agents translating between different registers of interpretability in teams of scholars trained in the "how" and "why" dimensions of complex and ambiguous real-world problems that would benefit from the application of machine learning methods.

At the University of Cincinnati's Digital Scholarship Center (DSC), we have created a collaborative research model that enables teams of researchers to leverage their respective strengths in both the "how" and "why" methodological orientations to address ambiguous and complex social problems using machine learning. To promote partnership across different disciplines, we have borrowed the "team science" model defined as a "collaborative effort to address…a challenge that leverages the strengths and expertise of professionals trained in different fields," particularly in the cases of "complex social problems with multiple causes." In particular, we have assembled teams combining computer scientists and informatics faculty to address the "how" dimension of ambiguous machine learning problems, with qualitative subject matter experts to make sense of the "why" dimension of ambiguity in our research questions. The third component of our teams are faculty and librarians with training in the digital humanities, familiar with the data structures and algorithms used in machine learning, but who also can translate between the different disciplinary languages and methodological attitudes to ambiguity and interpretability.

Our digital presentation will showcase two of our "team science" projects that have deployed this transdisciplinary mingling of methods and attitudes to ambiguity. The first is a network analysis and text mining project of social justice movements on Twitter that brings together the library digital scholarship team, faculty from computer science, the college of law, the journalism program, and the design school. The computer science collaborators suggested that the raw Twitter data required substantial cleanup, and that we should develop a standardized dictionary of terms and hashtags to correct for spelling errors. The humanities faculty responded by contrast that variant spellings and atypical uses of hashtags might contain meaning, and wanted to study geographical and demographic trends in the Twitter language ambiguity. For example, did high school and college students, or users from specific regions use a different vocabulary and orthography in an age- or geography-specific digital dialect? We faced challenges in parsing tweets or responses that are stated in jest, with a sarcastic tone, or generally not in good faith with the original tweet. As a result we incorporated these ambiguities into our methodological design as meaningful variables to study, rather than miscommunications or errors to correct into a uniform vocabulary.

The second project is composed of a team of plant geneticists, bioinformaticians, library informationists, and English faculty. We performed a text mining analysis of publication inequality in the PubMed scientific literature corpus, focusing on how poor stylistic and mechanical usage in English leads to different rates of publication success in scientific journals. Our initial hypothesis posits that authors from non-English speaking nations would have more ambiguous or imprecise use of English, and native English speakers would have clearer and more accurate language. We focused on the field of plant genetics, in which predominantly Anglophone investigators study samples from biodiverse countries where English is not the primary language. Our initial finding is a clear inverse relationship between a country's overall biodiversity and the publication output of its researchers. Non Anglophone countries with many plant species have low publication rates, and the reverse holds true for countries with low biodiversity but English speaking researchers. This study demonstrates that ambiguous or imprecise use of language itself may be a marker of both geographical difference within the published body of work in a field, and also a potential measurement to predict the publication success rate of investigators from a given country given the amount of ambiguity in their language, regardless of the technical merits of the research.

REFERENCES

Burrell, J. (2016). How the Machine "Thinks": Understanding Opacity in Machine Learning Algorithms. *Big Data and Society 3*, 1-12.

Ferreira, F., Bailey, K.G.D., & Ferraro, V. (2002). Good Enough Representations in Language Comprehension. *Current Directions in Psychological Science 11*, 11-15.

Goodman, B., & Flaxman, S. (2017). European Union Regulations on Algorithmic Decision-Making and a "Right to Explanation." *AI Magazine 38*, 50-57.

Hamilton, W.L., Leskovec, J., Jurafsky, D. (2016). Diachronic Word Embeddings Reveal Statistical Laws of Semantic Change. *Proceedings of the 54th Annual Meeting of the Association for Computational Linguistics*. Berlin: ACL.

Lipton, Z. (2016). The Mythos of Model Interpretability. *ICML Workshop on Human Interpretability in Machine Learning (WHI 2016)*. New York: ICML.

Poesio,, M., & Artstein, R. (2008). Introduction to the Special Issue on Ambiguity and Semantic Judgments. *Research on Language and Computation 6*, 241-245.

Poesio, M., Sturt, P., Artstein, R., & Filik, R. (2006). Underspecification and Anaphora: Theoretical Issues and Preliminary Evidence. *Discourse Processes* 42, 157-175.

Raskin, V. (1985). *Semantic Mechanisms of Humor*. Dordrecht: D. Reidel.

Su, S. P. (1994). *Lexical Ambiguity in Poetry*. London: Longman.

Wagner, A., & Cacciaguidi-Fahy, S. (2006). *Legal Language and the Search for Clarity.* Peter Lang AG.

Yang, H., De Roeck, A., Gervasi, V., Willis, A., & Nuseibeh, B. (2010). A Methodology for Automatic Identification of Nocuous Ambiguity. *Proceedings of the 23rd International Conference on Computational Linguistics (Coling 2010),* 1218-1226. Sheffield: ICCL.

Zimek, A., Schubert, E., & Kriegel, H. P. (2012). A Survey on Unsupervised Outlier Detection in High-Dimensional Numerical Data. *Statistical Analysis and Data Mining* 5.

Everyday Information Practices: An Exploration of Intra-individual Information Behavior across Everyday Contexts

Lo Lee
University of Illinois at Urbana-Champaign, USA, lolee2@illinois.edu

Melissa G. Ocepek
University of Illinois at Urbana-Champaign, USA, mgocepek@illinois.edu

ABSTRACT

Everyday information behavior studies individuals' information behaviors based on their everyday experience. To analyse one participant's information behaviors across daily life contexts, we used interviews and observations as primary research methods. Findings demonstrated that one individual's regular behavioral patterns, such as cross-referencing, information reviewing, and vision driven information seeking, were consistent across contexts. This work also confirmed the potential to conduct information behavior research by closely looking into one individual across different life situations.

KEYWORDS

Information behavior, everyday information behavior, contexts, information seeking.

INTRODUCTION

Research on everyday information behavior has addressed the roles of human information behaviors in individuals' daily life experience. Previous studies have largely explored a person's everyday information behavior by breaking their life into different sections. For example, Savolainen (2009) argued that everyday life information seeking can be discussed by considering work and non-work contexts. Hartel (2003) championed studying leisure as a research subject via closely looking into serious leisure, in particular, information-rich hobbies. While these discussions have contributed critical insights to each single context, a holistic understanding of an individual's information behavior has not yet been fully explored. Hence, our research approaches an individual's daily life across contexts, such as working, shopping, and down-time. We aim to see if patterns emerge that demonstrate an individual's everyday information behavior practices.

BACKGROUND

The Theory of the Everyday

The theoretical concept of everyday was addressed by Lefebvre (2008). The theory of the everyday advocates that everyday experience constructs the primary understanding of human lives. The everyday world is the totality of lived experience, and it relates to all human activities, such as work, leisure, family time, and self-care (Lefebvre, 2008). Building on everyday experience, humans learn how to live in our social worlds, how to interpret social relationships, and how to interact with information.

Everyday Information Behavior

The only research that embraced the totality of everyday life was Julien and Michels' work (2004) on intra-individual information behavior. In this study, Julien and Michels studied one participant for ten weeks via diaries and interviews and identified multiple contextual factors that would affect the participant's information behaviors across contexts. Their research indicated the need to think outside two favorite contexts for information behavior research, including work and academics, for future studies interested in learning more about how contexts would influence information behaviors in everyday lives.

METHODS

To study information behaviors across an individual's everyday life, we conducted an empirical study with one recruited graduate student working in wet lab and recognized her recurrent behavioral patterns. Our primary methodological approach was based on Smith's institutional ethnography (Smith, 1987), which was designed for researching the social relationships that built a context by focusing on a participant's localized lived experience. The research began with a semi-structured interview addressing the participant's weekly routines, including her work and leisure activities, followed by a brief survey asking for participant's basic demographic information, such as age, gender, and educational background.

Following the pre-interview and survey, we observed our participant for one week to see her information behaviors throughout her daily life. All observations occurred in the form of 2-4-hour blocks, based around the participant's activities. Within the nine observations, our sessions focused on the participant's work, leisure, down-time, and chores. Throughout the observations, written notes were taken, and questions were developed for a post-interview. Audio recordings were occasionally used to more accurately capture information activities. After the one-week of observations, there was a post-interview for the participant to be debriefed, share her final thoughts, and to clarify some of her observed behaviors.

RESULTS

From the empirical study, we were able to recognize our participant's information behaviors, both in terms of her interaction with information at work and leisure. After collecting data and coded interview transcripts iteratively, we identified three recurrent patterns regarding the participant's information seeking behavior.

Cross-referencing

The first pattern we observed from our participant's information seeking behavior was that she liked cross-referencing when deciding if she could trust an information source. For example, during one observation, our participant was thinking of an ideal term to search information for work. She said although she felt more confident about the topic after several tries, she still had to cross-reference information to ensure its credibility. In the final interview, when asked how she learned about nutrition as a hobby, which was not related to her work, our participant mentioned two kinds of sources: a blog and a YouTube channel. One primary reason our participant liked them, as what she explained, was "*they always have references, reliable references. So I can always build trust. [...] I do have to cross-reference them based on my previous understandings about nutrition.*" Cross-referencing sources helped the participant judge if information on hand was believable throughout her information searching.

Information Reviewing

The second pattern we identified was the participant's habit of reviewing past information. We noticed that she would use her prior information records or memories when searching for information. For instance, the participant not only liked retrieving research articles she had highlighted before, but also frequently searched her browsing history to see websites she had visited. Similarly, while doing online shopping, we found our participant preferred to check her previous orders before placing new orders on the same product. By looking at previous orders, our participant explained she could then order the same stuff when she felt the product "*it's not something I'd like to try something new.*" When our participant went shopping in a physical grocery store, she mentioned she liked seeing the same products be put in the same places as she very relied on her knowledge about the grocery store. Reviewing previous information offered the participant an efficient way to solve her information needs.

Vision Driven Information Seeking

The third pattern we recognized from our participant's daily life was that she heavily relied on pictures and images when interacting with information. According to what we observed, when our participant was reading academic articles, she enjoyed seeing colorful figures and flowcharts. She said colors enabled her to receive information faster: "*I get information quickly from the pictures. [...] People would have some relationships between the colors and the subjects, and I enjoy seeing that because I can get ideas much faster.*" Another example could be seen when our participant was doing online shopping on Amazon. She described that the display of images on Amazon would influence her confidence about a purchase. Suggesting it was more likely for her to make the purchase if the seller had more high-quality pictures.

DISCUSSION AND CONCLUSION

The present work demonstrates how recurrent information seeking patterns emerging from an individual's daily life can provide insights to everyday information behavior research. In our study, three behavioral patterns were observed based on the participant's daily life contexts: cross-referencing, information reviewing, and vision driven information seeking. Our findings suggested the way the participant was trained as a lab researcher, such as the participant had to deal with experimental data that required definite accuracy, was reflected in her information seeking behavior across daily life situations.

While this empirical study only included one participant, future work will apply the same framework to study different participants for wider narratives. This research not only created a unique venue to discuss everyday information behavior by breaking contexts, but also provided information behavior research with a new holistic understanding about the everyday.

REFERENCES

Hartel, J. (2003). The serious leisure frontier in library and information science: Hobby domains. *Knowledge Organization, 30*(3-4), 228-238.

Julien, H., & Michels, D. (2004). Intra-individual information behaviour in daily life. *Information Processing & Management, 40*(3), 547-562.

Lefebvre, H. (2008). *Critique of everyday life: Volume 1*. London: Verso.

Savolainen, R. (2009). Everyday life information seeking. In M. J. Bates, & M. L., Maack (Ed.), *Encyclopedia of Library and Information Sciences* (pp. 1780-1789). Boca Raton, FL: CRC Press.

Smith, D. E. (1987). *The Everyday World as Problematic: A Feminist Sociology*. Boston, MA: Northeastern University Press.

Across Borders: The Concept and Applications of Eugenics in the CCL and the NDC

Wan-Chen Lee
University of Washington, USA. leew23@uw.edu

ABSTRACT

This study presents analyses based on a previous study on the subject ontogeny of Eugenics in the New Classification Scheme for Chinese Libraries (CCL) and the Nippon Decimal Classification (NDC). In the bibliographic records using the CCL and the NDC, I ask (1) what are the concepts in the titles of the works about Eugenics? (2) What are the subject headings frequently assigned to the works about Eugenics? Answers to the questions not only identify underrepresented aspects of Eugenics in the schemes but also provide insights into the meanings and usages of the term Eugenics in different contexts. Further, these results encourage us to reflect on the relationship between cataloging practices and classification principles and warrants.

KEYWORDS

Subject ontogeny, the New Classification Scheme for Chinese Libraries, Nippon Decimal Classification, Eugenics.

INTRODUCTION

This study expands on a previous study (Lee, 2016) on the subject ontogeny of Eugenics in the CCL and the NDC. Examining all editions of these classification schemes and bibliographic records with Eugenics as a subject heading, the author addresses two research questions in this study. What are the concepts in the titles of the works about Eugenics? What are the subject headings frequently assigned to the works about Eugenics? The results identify underrepresented aspects of Eugenics in the schemes by comparing the classes with the prominent themes in the bibliographic records of publications about Eugenics. This study provides insights into how meanings and uses of a subject change in different contexts and over time. I also reflect on the relationship between cataloging practices and classification principles and warrants.

CONCEPTS IN THE TITLES OF THE WORKS ABOUT EUGENICS

Focusing on bibliographic records that apply the CCL and the NDC, the author conducted subject searches of 優生學 (i.e., Eugenics) in NBINet and 優生学 (i.e., Eugenics) in NDL Search, and retrieved 222 and 490 bibliographic records respectively. The union catalogs were selected for their great coverages of publications in Taiwan and Japan (Lee, 2016). The purpose of reviewing the titles is to identify prominent concepts in the publications about Eugenics in Taiwan and Japan, and to observe the meanings and uses of Eugenics in both contexts. Hence, identical titles or titles with punctuation differences were analyzed only once. There are 72 unique titles in the 222 records applying the CCL, and 59 unique titles in the 490 records applying the NDC. The author translated the titles to English for analysis.

Frequency	Term (CCL)	Frequency	Term (NDC)
47	Eugenics	35	Eugenics
10	Care	9	Human
10	Children	9	Life
9	Birth	7	Japan
9	Health	7	Thoughts
8	Genetics	5	Eugenic
8	Gifted	5	Nazi
7	Give	4	Genetics
5	Fetal	4	Movement
5	History	4	Policies
5	Marriage	4	Science
5	Thoughts	4	Theories
4	Baby	3	Euthanasia
4	Introduction	3	History
3	Chinese	3	Improvement
3	Diseases	3	Introduction
3	Education	3	Marriage
3	Family	3	Perspective
3	Human	3	Sexuality
3	Japan	3	Social
3	Movement	3	Society
3	Pregnancy	3	Sterilization
3	Raise		

Table 1. Term frequency in the titles of works about eugenics

Translation is not perfect. There are translation strategies which prioritize different purposes and yield various results (Simon, 1996; Venuti, 2008; Yokota-Murakami, 1994). Acknowledging the subjective filter of the translator (Mangiron, 2013), this study aims to capture all concepts in the Chinese and Japanese titles. Hence, parallel titles were not adopted for analysis. For instance, the Chinese title 天才寶寶胎教法 has Japanese parallel title 胎児はみんな天才た. The English translation *Fetal Education for Gifted Children* was based on the Chinese title. If the author were to translate the Japanese title to English, the title would be *All Babies are Genius*. Recognizing the challenges of translation, this study does not argue for "the correct" translation. The goal is to surface prominent themes in the publications about Eugenics in different contexts.

Terms that appear more than twice in the titles of works about Eugenics are listed in Table 1. We can place title terms from records applying the CCL into three non-mutually exclusive groups. There are terms specifying (1) relevant kinds of studies about eugenics, (2) the health aspects of eugenics, and (3) the social aspect of eugenics. Similarly, three groups are identified for title terms from records applying the NDC. There are terms of (1) relevant kinds of studies about eugenics, (2) the historical aspect of eugenics, and (3) the social aspect of eugenics.

SUBJECT HEADINGS ASSIGNED TO WORKS ABOUT EUGENICS

All bibliographic records collected have Eugenics as a subject heading. What are the other subject headings assigned? Addressing this question advances our understanding of how Eugenics is used and what it means in publications in Taiwan and Japan.

It provides contexts for the stability and concentration of classes for Eugenics in the CCL and the NDC over time (Lee, 2016). Do the meaning and usage of Eugenics change in different languages and evolve over time like Eugenics in the DDC (Tennis, 2012)? To examine the meaning and usage of Eugenics, future studies can analyze co-assigned headings and explore indexers' perception of relevance between the headings (Gabel & Smiraglia, 2009).

Subject headings in all records were counted to highlight the subjects frequently co-assigned with Eugenics. Synonyms and variant forms were merged. There are 54 unique Chinese headings and 45 unique Japanese headings. Table 2 shows the English translation of the most frequently co-assigned headings. We can place the Chinese headings into four groups. There are (1) headings of relevant kinds of studies about eugenics and (2) subjects emphasizing the medical aspect, (3) the ethical aspect, and (4) the social aspect of eugenics. Similarly, we can group the Japanese headings into two groups: history and ethics.

Frequency	Translated subject headings (CCL)	Frequency	Translated subject headings (NDC)
237	Eugenics	356	Eugenics
86	Pregnancy	128	Eugenics—History
35	Genetics	49	Bioethics
24	Eugenics and health care	45	Euthanasia
19	Genetic disorder	42	Genetic engineering
15	Genetic engineering	36	Nazis
14	Bioethics	26	Fetus
11	Marriage	24	Gene
9	Public health	21	Nazism
5	Obstetrics	20	Anthropology—History
4	Child-rearing	18	Genetics
4	Family planning	16	Hearing impairment
3	Eugenics—Conference	15	Medical ethics
3	Human genetics	14	Germany—History—Nazi Germany (1933-1945)
3	Pediatrics	7	Population problem

Table 2. Subject headings frequently co-assigned with Eugenics

We can compare the analyses above with the results of the previous study (Lee, 2016) and see different focuses of Eugenics in the schemes and in the publications. For the CCL, the titles and subject headings highlight relevant studies about Eugenics, and the health, medical, social, and ethical aspects of Eugenics. The classes for Eugenics in the CCL over time focus on the biological and social aspects of Eugenics. The medical aspect was officially added to the scheme in 2001 and removed in 2007. The comparison affirms the prominence of medical aspect in the publications and identifies ethics as an underrepresented aspect in the CCL. For the NDC, the titles and subject headings cover relevant studies about Eugenics, and the historical and ethical aspects of Eugenics. However, the classes in the NDC over time focus on the biological and medical aspects of Eugenics. In the previous study (Lee, 2016), we saw different focuses between the schemes, the publications, and the records. The analyses were based on the classes (e.g., a frequently assigned class number to resources about Eugenics is 234.074 Nazi Germany 1933-1945. The Second World War 1939-45, which is under class 200 History in the NDC). In this study, the subject headings enable us to identify specific topics in the classes that are present in the publications about Eugenics. In addition, we can compare the focuses of titles and subject headings across schemes to observe how Eugenics translate between languages and schemes over time.

CONCLUSION

Classificationists develop schemes based semantic warrants and principles. Recognizing that actual use may differ from the intended use (Bowker & Star, 1999), this study asks us to reflect on the underlying warrants of the schemes through examining the use of standards. Analyses of titles and subjects of publications urge reflections on literary warrant (Hulme, 1911). When the meanings and uses of a subject in publications change over time, such as how different aspects of Eugenics were emphasized, do the schemes accommodate the changes? Does the literary warrant stand over time? Failing to reflect changing subject ontogenies (e.g., the ethical aspect of Eugenics is underrepresented in the CCL) would undermine the sustainability of schemes. While changes in meaning and usage can be subtle, contextual, cultural, and thus challenging to trace, this study presents an attempt to tackle that semantic complexity across the borders of languages, time, and spaces.

REFERENCES

Gabel, J., & Smiraglia, R. P. (2009). Visualizing Similarity in Subject Term Co-Assignment. *Advances in Classification Research Online*, *20*(1).

Geoffrey C. Bowker, & Star, S. L. (1999). Classification, coding, and coordination. In *Sorting things out: classification and its consequences*. Cambridge, Mass: MIT Press.

Hulme, E. W. (1911). Principles of book classification. *Library Association Record*, *13*, 354–358; 389–394, 444–449.

Lee, W.-C. (2016). An Exploratory Study of the Subject Ontogeny of Eugenics in the New Classification Scheme for Chinese Libraries and the Nippon Decimal Classification. *Knowledge Organization*, *43*(8), 594–608.

Mangiron, C. (2013). The localization paradigm: Localization versus translation. In M. O'Hagan (Ed.), Game Localization: Translating for the Global Digital Entertainment Industry (pp.87-110). Amsterdam: John Benjamins Publishing Company.

Simon, S. (1996). Taking gendered positions in translation theory. In Gender in Translation: Cultural Identity and the Politics of Transmission (pp. 1-38). London and New York: Routledge.

Tennis, J. T. (2012). The strange case of eugenics: A subject's ontogeny in a long-lived classification scheme and the question of collocative integrity. *Journal of the American Society for Information Science & Technology*, *63*(7), 1350–1359.

Venuti, L. (2008). Invisibility. In *The Translator's Invisibility: A History of Translation* (2nd ed., pp. 1–34). London; New York: Routledge.

Yokota-Murakami, T. (1994). Translating literature, love, and sexuality: Negotiation of the ideologies in early modern Japan. In *Proceedings of the 1991 ICLA Congress*. (pp.25-30). Tokyo: The University of Tokyo Press.

The Narrative Structure as a Citation Context in Data Papers: A Preliminary Analysis of *Scientific Data*

Kai Li
Drexel University, Philadelphia, United States; kl696@drexel.edu

Pei-Ying Chen
Indiana University, Bloomington, United States; peiychen@iu.edu

ABSTRACT

The data paper is a new type of scientific publication aiming to describe data objects *per se* and bridge the gaps between scientific writing and data-driven scientific practice. Despite its importance, we are still largely in the dark as to the narrative structure of this emerging genre of scientific writing. In this poster, we presented and discussed some preliminary empirical evidence of the narrative structure of data papers and the distribution of cited sources in relation to this structure, based on a manual examination of 40 data papers from the journal of *Scientific Data*. Our findings suggest that even though data papers have a different structure from research papers, their paper sections bear distinct narrative functions as illustrated by the pattern of citation distribution. Moreover, some of these sections have similar functions to their counterparts in research papers. The implications of our initial findings and the next step of our project were explained in conclusion.

KEYWORDS

Data paper, data publication, narrative structure, citation content analysis

INTRODUCTION

The rise of data-driven science in the 21st century requires new forms of scholarly communication that could incorporate digital objects into the scholarly ecosystem. The emergence of data paper is an important development in meeting such demand. As a type of scientific publication aiming to describe the data object *per se* (Chavan & Penev, 2011), it integrates scientific data into academic peer review processes (Mayernik, Callaghan, Leigh, Tedds, & Worley, 2015) and creates a space where data-related information can be described in a more detailed manner (Chao, 2015). Both serve to increase the reusability of data objects.

Little is known, however, about the narrative structure of data papers, whose importance is highlighted by the strong tension between data and narratives in our daily life (Manovich, 1999). Earlier efforts, mostly devoted to research papers, are made along two strands of research: one that examines the linguistic characteristics of scientific texts (e.g., Hyland 2005; Swales, 1990) and one that focuses on how citations contribute to the narrative structure of scientific publications through examining citation contents and contexts (e.g., Bertin et al., 2016; Teufel et al., 2006).

To bridge the empirical gap, our research focuses on the relationship between the narrative structure of and the citation distribution in data papers. We are especially interested in how the cited data and tool objects in a data paper fit into its narrative structure. As the first step, we conducted a content analysis to classify references in data papers based on the represented agents (i.e., data, tool, and others) and examine how these different types of references are distributed across paper sections.

DATA AND METHOD

As a pilot study, we analyzed a subsample of 40 articles from 396 data papers (i.e., *Data Descriptors*) published between 2014 and 2017 in *Scientific Data*, an open access journal launched in Spring 2014 by Nature Publishing Group (NPG). Towards the mission of "help[ing] foster the sharing and re-use of the data underpinning scientific research," the *Data Descriptor* is introduced and defined as "peer-reviewed, scientific publications that provide detailed descriptions of experimental and observational datasets" (Scheer, 2013). *Scientific Data* was selected over other data journals because of its broad disciplinary coverage, ranging from life, biomedical and environmental sciences to other fields in natural and social sciences. The full texts and metadata were acquired from the API of Europe PMC database, as implemented in the *europepmc* package in the R software ecosystem (Jahn, 2018). The texts were cleaned, and all sentences, references and their links were parsed from the texts.

All 1,272 references were then manually coded into the following three categories: *Data*, *Tool*, and *Others*. The category of *Data* denotes references which represent data object(s) *per se*, such as another data paper, or the link to a dataset, database, and data repository. Likewise, the *Tool* category denotes references that directly describe a specific tool, including, but not limited to, software package, data simulation system, data standard, and metadata format. All other references fall into the category of *Others*, most of which are typical research papers.

PRELIMINARY RESULTS

There is a relatively consistent paper structure across all 40 papers. This structure is composed of five sections (with name variances in different papers): *Background and Summary*, *Methods*, *Data Record*, *Technical Validation*, and *Usage Notes*, as required by the submission guidelines of the journal.[1] Most papers contain all the sections, with only one missing *Technical Validation* and 14 missing *Usage Notes*. This structure is markedly different from the IMRaD (Introduction, Method, Results, and Discussion) structure that has been commonly adopted by research papers (Huth, 1987). The left panel of Figure 1 displays the mean relative length (at the sentence level) of each section in all papers and the ratio of sentences with citations to all sentences in each section. Two observations are worth noting here. First, the *Methods* is the longest section, containing 2740 of all 5904 sentences (46.4%) parsed from our sample. Second, citations are most concentrated in the *Background and Summary* section, with 36.5% of 949 sentences containing at least one citation, a proportion significantly higher compared to 16.3% across all sections. The latter observation is comparable to Bertin et al. (2016)'s finding based on an examination of research papers across all Public Library of Science (PLoS) journals. This suggests that the *Background and Summary* section in data papers plays similar "stage setting" roles as the Introduction section in research papers (Swales, 1990, pp. 137-166).

The right panel of Figure 1 displays the distribution of references across paper sections and of their types within each section. Overall, references are overwhelmingly dominated by research papers, with *Data* and *Tool* categories accounting for only 4.2% and 9% of all references, respectively. However, the proportions of reference types differ across sections. In particular, the *Methods* and *Data Record* sections have significantly higher ratios of *Data* and *Tool* references, indicating their relative importance/visibility within these two sections: *Data* and *Tool* references respectively account for 7.4% and 17% in the *Methods* section; 13% and 26% in the *Data Record* section. One possible explanation is the more technical orientation of the two sections, in which authors typically describe and justify the use of specific datasets, tools, or methods in the scientific process.

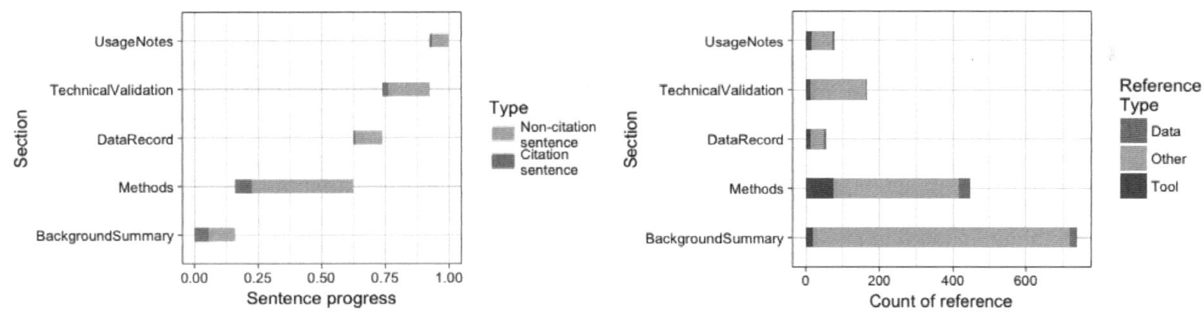

Figure 1: How citations are distributed across sentences in different data paper sections (Left panel: sentence progress and the amount of citation and non-citation sentences in each section; Right panel: Occurrences of references and reference types in each section)

CONCLUSION

This pilot study serves as the first step towards a fuller appreciation of the increasingly important presence of data papers. We offered some initial empirical evidence concerning the narrative structure (in terms of the paper section) of this scientific genre as well as its relation to the pattern of citation distribution. We are planning to conduct a more thorough examination of the relationship among linguistic features, citation pattern and contexts, as well as the representation of digital objects in the full texts of data papers, based on a larger corpus. The study will not only illuminate the nature of data papers as a scientific genre but also how science is conducted and communicated in the data-driven paradigm.

ACKNOWLEDGMENTS

This project was made possible in part by the Institute of Museum and Library Services for the project titled "Building an entity-based research framework to enhance digital services on knowledge discovery and delivery" (Grant Award Number: RE-07-15-0060-15) and "IDEASc: Integrated doctoral education with application to scholarly communication" (Grant Award Number: RE-02-14-0023-14).

REFERENCES

Bertin, M., Atanassova, I., Gingras, Y., & Larivière, V. (2016). The invariant distribution of references in scientific articles. Journal of the Association for Information Science and Technology, 67(1), 164–177.

[1] https://www.nature.com/sdata/publish/submission-guidelines

Chao, T. (2015). Mapping methods metadata for research data. International Journal of Digital Curation, 10(1), 82–94.

Chavan, V., & Penev, L. (2011). The data paper: A mechanism to incentivize data publishing in biodiversity science. BMC Bioinformatics, 12(15), 1.

Huth, E. J. (1987). Structured abstracts for papers reporting clinical trials. Annals of Internal Medicine, 106(4), 626-627.

Hyland, K. (2005). Metadiscourse. Wiley Online Library.

Jahn, N. (2018). europepmc: R Interface to the Europe PubMed Central RESTful Web Service. R package version 0.3. https://CRAN.R-project.org/package=europepmc

Manovich, L. (1999). Database as symbolic form. Convergence, 5(2), 80–99.

Mayernik, M. S., Callaghan, S., Leigh, R., Tedds, J., & Worley, S. (2015). Peer review of datasets: When, why, and how. Bulletin of the American Meteorological Society, 96(2), 191–201.

Scheer, R. (2013, April 4). NPG to launch Scientific Data to help scientists publish and reuse research data. Retrieved April 20, 2018, from https://www.nature.com/press_releases/scientificdata.html

Swales, J. (1990). Genre Analysis: English in Academic and Research Settings. Cambridge University Press.

Teufel, S., Siddharthan, A., & Tidhar, D. (2006). Automatic classification of citation function. In Proceedings of the 2006 Conference on Empirical Methods in Natural Language Processing (pp. 103–110). Association for Computational Linguistics.

Exploring the Relationships between Freedom of Information and Institutional Information Management in the Chinese Government: An Empirical Study

Siyi Li
Renmin University of China, China, 15136469820@163.com

ABSTRACT

The Regulation on Opening Government Information of the People's Republic of China **- the Chinese version of Freedom of Information (FOI) law in other contexts - was issued by the State Council in 2007 and took effect the following year. Similar to other FOI laws, the regulation stipulates two approaches for disclosing information and they are proactive disclosure and disclosure-by-request (DbR). This research aimed at exploring the relationships between DbR and institutional information management in China. Twenty-five institutions of the State Council were decided to be data sources, from which data were collected by browsing websites and sending information requests. This presentation reports on the findings of the study and the future work that should follow up on the study.**

KEYWORDS

Freedom of Information, Information and Records Management, China, Empirical Study

STUDY BACKGROUND

The Regulation on Opening Government Information of the People's Republic of China (hereafter the Regulation) was issued by the State Council of the People's Republic of China in 2007 and took effect the following year. The Regulation, while termed differently, functions similarly to the legislation of Freedom of Information or Access to Information in western countries such as the United States of America or Canada. In the Regulation, government information is defined with an encompassing scope, as "that of being created or obtained by administrative organs in the processes of discharging their responsibilities and of being recorded and maintained in certain format". Following the requirement of the Regulation, government institutions subject to it all started publishing institutional information online as their way of proactively disclosing information, including annual reports on the administration of the Regulation. Correspondingly, academic studies started to exam proactive disclosure and annual reports, for example, Long-analyzed information proactively disclosed on a government website, which is www.shanghai.gov.cn, from 2004 to 2014, and found that not all information can be accessed from government websites (Long, 2014). Xiang and Li investigated the annual report institutional system in 31 provincial administration regions by analyzing related legal and policy documents (Xiang& Li, 2014). However, the topics of disclosing information under request and the relationships between this disclose-by-request (DbR) and institutional information management (IIM) remain rarely touched by the Chinese academia, for example, Li and Yi explored the implementation of DbR in 22 ministries and commissions (Li& Yi, 2017), and Wang investigated status quo of DbR in Anhui province from 2008 to 2012 (Wang& Yin). This is in sharp contrast to the practices of other countries, where the topic of DbR appears more frequently than proactive disclosure, for example, Elizabeth claims that in England, records management services can make contributions to the abilities of local authorities to comply with FOIA, especially in retrieving and locating information when coping with FOI requests (Elizabeth, Alice& Andrew, 2010), and the DbR-IIM relationship can be rooted in legal framework such as the *Lord of Chancellor's Code of Practice on the Management of Records issued under section 46* of the FOIA in UK. This observation motivated the present study, which aimed at exploring the relationships between DbR and IIM in China.

METHODS

Guided by the research design of the Records and Information Management in the Government of Canada project (Xie, 2017), the present study decided to use the combination of searching websites and sending information requests to government institutions as its data collection techniques. As the first of its kind in China, it makes sense to start with the central government at the national stage. When data were being collected, there were 25 ministries and commissions constituting the central government, all of which are under the leadership of the State Council. These ministries and commissions are all required to proactively disclosing information, but only 22 offer also the service of providing information under requests. The three ministries that are exempted from responding to information requests are the Ministry of Public Security, the Ministry of State Security and the Ministry of Supervision. As a result, data were collected for all 25 institutions from their official websites, and information requests were sent to the 22 institutions that are not exempted for additional data. The information request, which is the same for all the 22 institutions, is drafted as the following:

In your institution,

1. Is there a dedicated unit responsible for managing government information? (Here, "government information" means the same as defined by the Regulation);

1.1. If yes, could you please provide policies and procedures issued by this unit with respect to the management of government information in your institution?

1.2. If yes, does this unit assist the work of disclosing information under requests?

1.3. If no, could you please provide the detailed organizational structure of your institution and point out which units are doing the job of managing government information on behalf of your institution?

2. Is there a dedicated unit responsible for administering the Regulation?

2.1. If yes, could you please provide policies and procedures issued by this unit regarding the disclosure of information under requests?

2.2. If no, could you please provide any policies and procedures regarding the disclosure of government information in your institution?

2.3. If no, could you please provide the detailed organizational structure of your organization and point out which units are jointly administering the Regulation?

FINDINGS

The study has found out that:

- Most of the institutions replied within the prescribed timeline, that is, 15 work days, but a few failed, including Ministry of Land and Resources and State Ethic Affairs Commission;
- For those who replied on time, some did not provide any information, citing various reasons such as "the information request is unclear", "the information you requested does not fall within the scope of government information", or "the information you requested does not exist";
- From those who provided information,
  - No formal policies or procedures regarding information management were found existing. In other words, organizational information management as a whole is typically missing in these government institutions despite the fact that information systems are widely deployed, and they are all subject to the Regulation on Opening Government information;
  - Government information is managed in silos, that is, it is managed by central offices (similar to registries), business units, and the institution's archival unit separately.
  - The Central Office is typically responsible for administering the Regulation, but requests are handled primarily on subjects, not on unified management of information. As a result, responses to information requests are produced isolated, without any form of cooperation.

FUTURE WORK

The findings of the present study depict the ineffectiveness of responding to information requests in government institutions, which, however, seemed not to be the concerns of the government officials who interacted with the researchers during the phase of request clarification. The next step of the study is to seek a deeper understanding of this situation, to sort out both the relationships between freedom of information and institutional information management administratively and academically, and to suggest a more effective model to government institutions for responding to information requests. Nearly a decade after the Regulation took effect, the Legislative Affairs Office of the State Council is currently calling for its revision. It is the hope of the present study that research like this can inform the revising process so that more aspects regarding the implementation of the Regulation can be taken into consideration.

REFERENCES

Elizabeth Shepherd, Alice Stevenson & Andrew Flinn (2010). Information governance, records management, and freedom of information: A study of local government authorities in England. *Government Information Quarterly*, 27, 337-345.

Lei Wang & Zhuru Yin (2014). Case Study on Local Government Information Disclosure in Anhui Province. *Information studies: Theory & Application*, 37, 48-50.

Liling Xiang & Wenlong Li (2014). Investigation and Analysis of Annual Report Institution System Construction Situation on Government Information Disclosure in China. *Journal of Modern Information*, 34, 3-6.

Siyi Li & Zhaolin Yi (2017). Access to Information in the Context of Open Government: An Explorative Study on Disclosure by Request in Chinese Government. *Archives Science Study*, S1, 84-91.

The State Council of People's Republic of China (2008). *Regulations of the People's Republic of China on the Disclosure of Government Information (Order of the State Council: No. 492).* Beijing: China Legal Publishing House.

Yi Long (2014). Content Analysis on Government Website Information Disclosure Based on a Decade Information Disclosure Data of Shanghai Government. *E-GOVERNMENT*, 142, 27-38.

ACKNOWLEDGEMENT

This research is supported by the Fundamental Research Funds for the Central Universities and the Research Funds of Renmin University of China as part of the Records-Centered Digital Information Management Theory and Mechanisms (DI{R}Mtm) Project (No. 15XNL032), directed by Professor Sherry L. Xie. Sincere gratitude to her for her supervision and guidance.

Post-checkout (Non-)usage of Library Digital Content

Angela Lieu
University of Alberta, Canada, angela.lieu@ualberta.ca

Dangzhi Zhao
University of Alberta, Canada, dzhao@ualberta.ca

ABSTRACT

The present study analyzed a large urban Canadian public library's data (2013-2017) from Rakuten OverDrive to identify patterns, trends, and potential implications related to post-checkout non-usage (material that is checked out by a user, but subsequently never opened and/or downloaded) of library digital content. It was found that over 12% of the more than 1.1 million checkouts of digital content via OverDrive in 2017 were never opened, causing a waste of over $10,000 USD on metered access eBooks alone; this figure will likely increase in the coming years based on the trends found in this study. Juvenile and non-fiction eBooks are most likely to be checked out and go unused. These findings may shed light on ways libraries and digital content vendors might improve the efficiency of digital content lending, and serve to inform collection management and user-targeted marketing and solutions.

KEYWORDS

Library uses, Post-checkout usage, Collection development, eBooks, digital content in libraries, library finances.

INTRODUCTION

As the proliferation and accessibility of technology and web-based applications continue to rise, more and more libraries are adding digital items to their collections (Ashcroft, 2011; Havergal & Price, 2011). As of 2016, more than 90% of public libraries offer eBooks to library users (Arch, 2016). The introduction of digital content to libraries provides opportunities to analyze usage data and investigate the phenomenon of post-checkout non-usage (material that is checked out by a user, but subsequently never opened and/or downloaded). Such studies are impossible for physical library materials as there is no way to gather objective data on post-checkout usage; however, findings from studies in a digital context may be transferable and provide insight into similar user behaviours with physical library materials.

The identification of patterns in post-checkout (non-)usage may bear implications for libraries in terms of finances, collection development, and user services. As financial restrictions play a major factor in decisions around services and collections, library systems must carefully evaluate available digital content vendors to determine the most sustainable platforms that meet the needs of their users (Polanka, 2012). Digital content vendors differ in how library users may access digital content from their libraries (Arch, 2016; Polanka, 2012). Common lending models include: metered access (limited by number of checkouts and/or number of months), pay-per-use (the library pays a fee for each checkout), and one copy/one user (sometimes called "pretend it's print," where libraries purchase a fixed number of copies and each copy can be accessed by only one user at any given time). When post-checkout non-usage occurs with materials under metered access or pay-per-checkout models, libraries pay for checkouts that are never used. With one copy/one user models, library users that check out items and never use them prevent others from accessing them, and prolong wait times if there are holds. The adverse implications of post-checkout non-usage should be studied as findings may help libraries prepare for increasing financial challenges and improving user experience in the digital environment.

The present study aims to identify patterns, trends, and potential implications related to post-checkout non-usage of library digital content. Results from this study may shed light on ways libraries and digital content vendors might improve the efficiency of digital content lending and may also serve to inform collection management and user-targeted marketing and solutions.

METHODOLOGY

A large urban Canadian public library's data (2013-2017) from Rakuten OverDrive was downloaded in the format of a large spreadsheet for each year of data. In these spreadsheets, each row details one checkout. There are approximately 4 million total rows of data. Data columns used in this study include: usage status of checkouts (pending, opened, or downloaded), file formats, lending models, subject/audience, and library price. Pending items (items that are checked out but neither opened nor downloaded) were compared with total checkouts to determine post-checkout non-usage rates. To explore and analyse the data, the spreadsheets were imported to a relational database. SQL queries were used to compute calculations and metrics.

In the library studied, lending models used in OverDrive include one copy/one user and metered access. In determining the effects of post-checkout non-usage on library costs, the average cost of pending items under a metered access lending model was used to calculate the average cost per circulation. This number was multiplied by the number of pending checkouts of the associated lending model to approximate the library's loss in dollars each year. eAudiobooks and eVideos in OverDrive are not provided under metered access models at the library studied and were therefore not considered in the cost analysis. As averages were used in the calculations in this study, and only metered access eBooks were considered, the approximate financial loss due to post-checkout non-usage is likely underestimated; further studies must be conducted to more accurately capture this information.

RESULTS

Unsurprisingly, checkouts of eBooks and eAudiobooks have risen significantly and consistently from 2013-2017 (Figure 1). The overall rates of post-checkout non-usage of eBooks and eVideos have also increased significantly over this time, while that of eAudiobooks increased to a lesser extent (Figure 2). The number of unopened checkouts has also increased each year, with nearly 140,000 in 2017 alone. It is important to note that Overdrive is a major provider of eBooks and eAudiobooks at the library studied but plays a far less significant role as an eVideo provider. Figure 3 shows that Juvenile eBooks demonstrate higher post-checkout non-usage rates than adult eBooks. Post-checkout non-usage rates of non-fiction eBooks are consistently higher than those of fiction eBooks; this holds true for both adult and juvenile material. This pattern, however, is not consistently found in eAudiobooks.

Figure 4 shows that the library in which the data was collected spends up to $10,700 per year on metered access eBooks that are never opened by users. This number has grown significantly since 2013 with the significant growth of library expenditures on eBooks each year. This analysis is based solely on eBooks that used a metered 26 or 52 checkout lending model, and is intended to demonstrate the financial implications of post-checkout non-usage to libraries.

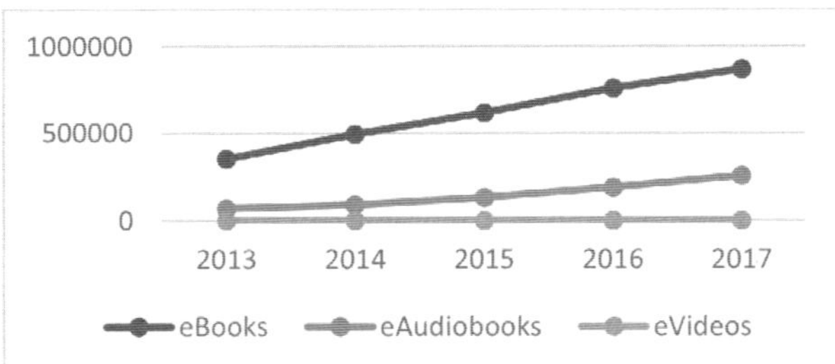

Figure 1. Total Checkouts by Year

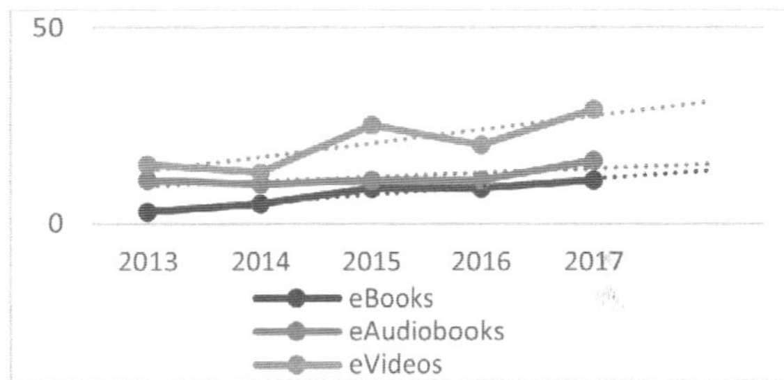

Figure 2. Yearly Post-Checkout Non-Usage Rates in %

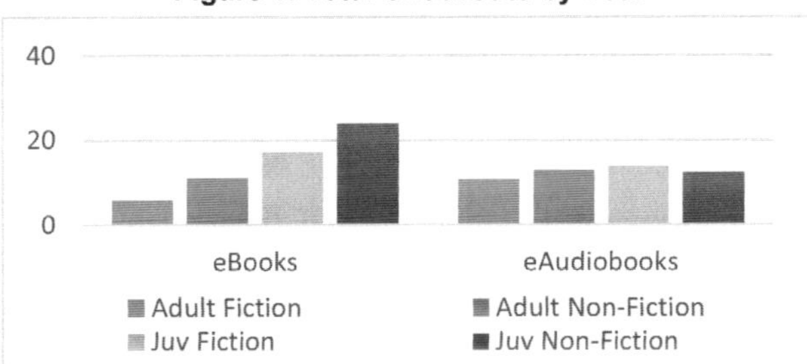

Figure 3. Average Post-Checkout Non-Usage Rates Based on Subject/Audience in % (2013-2017)

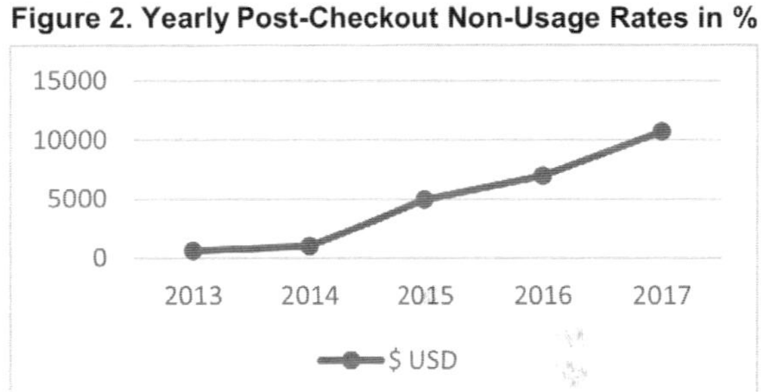

Figure 4. Approximate Loss ($) (based on eBooks with 26 and 52 checkout limits)

DISCUSSION AND CONCLUSION

Among the more than 1.1 million checkouts of eBooks and eAudiobooks in 2017, 11% and 16% respectively were never opened, causing a waste of over $10,000 on metered access eBooks alone. These numbers should be considerably higher when other lending models are included and will likely increase in the coming years based on the trends found in this study. More refined lending models should be explored to minimize waste and to improve user experience. For example, lending limits could be changed from checkout-based to access-based, where vendors tally a "use" only when a checked-out item is opened or downloaded. In addition, automatically generated messages could be sent to users who have checked out a digital item but have neither opened nor downloaded it after a certain period of time. This would prompt users to either use or return their checked-out items, particularly if the items have holds. This would likely lead to an increase in early returns of unused items and decrease wait time for library users. Page-based access is another possible solution (e.g. Total Boox, http://www.totalboox.com/faq-direct-readers), where libraries are charged for the number of pages accessed by users, reducing costs and improving user experience by eliminating wait times. Future studies that explore user implications of post-checkout non-usage (e.g., wait times) and factors that cause the phenomenon of post-checkout non-usage would be beneficial and interesting, particularly in an ever-growing digital library environment.

ACKNOWLEDGMENTS

We would like to thank Rachael C. for assisting in the provision of the data used in this study.

REFERENCES

Arch, J. (2016). Ebooks in libraries: Equal access to digital content? *Information Today, 33*(5), 1-25.

Ashcroft, A. (2011). Ebooks in libraries: An overview of the current situation. *Library Management, 32*(6/7), 398-407.

Harvergal, V. & Price, K. (Eds.) (2011). *E-books in libraries: A practical guide.* London, UK: Facet.

Polanka, S. (2012). An ebook primer. *Library Journal, 137*(7), 42-44.

Challenges and Opportunities in Data Curation for a Social Sciences Data Archive: An Institution Theory Inspired Analysis Framework

Chi-Shiou Lin
National Taiwan University, Taiwan. chishioulin@ntu.edu.tw

Wei Jeng
National Taiwan University, Taiwan. wjeng@ntu.edu.tw

ABSTRACT
In this paper we describe an analysis inspired by institution theory on the collection development of social sciences data ar- chives. The theory introduces three dimensions that together support enduring social practices, i.e., regulative, normative, and cultural-cognitive dimensions. We use the concepts to understand the nature and the relationships among the observed prob- lems in a case archive so as to better describe and understand the problems and possible solutions.

KEYWORDS
Social sciences data archives, research data, data curation, institutional theory

INTRODUCTION
This study takes a collection development perspective to examine the challenges and opportunities facing a social science data archive when it decides on the scope of data acquisitions. Collection development is a process through which a library, archive, or any other type of memory organization determines its missions and objectives based its analyses of the community needs; it thus develops a series of acquisition strategies to achieve the service goals. Various concerns beyond cost, manpower, and resources allocation influences how a data archive envisions itself within the immediate research community as well as larger social world. It also influences whether the archive is proactive or conservative in collection building.

Data curation is a developing academic practice that is shaped by regulations and policies, cultural norms, and conflicting values and interests. Each archive in taking a direction for collection development invariably faces different dilemmas and struggles. This study employs an institution theory approach to analyze the problems and challenges. Based on the theory, we propose an analytic framework that addresses possible problem types, nature of the problems described by the institution theory dimensions, and the mutual influences or inter-dependence of the problems. Through the analysis, possible solutions to the problems and opportunities for beneficial changes may be derived and assessed for their effectiveness.

INSTITUTION THEORY AS A THEORIZING LENS
Institutions are multifaceted, durable social structures made up of symbolic elements, social activities and material resources. Scott (2001) proposes a conceptual model that views the regulative system, normative system, and cultural-cognitive system as three pillars supporting a particular social institution. The regulative aspect of social institutions involves explicit regulato- ry processes that constrain behaviors, e.g., rule-setting, monitoring, and sanctioning activities. The normative system com- prises values and norms that form the prescriptive, evaluative, and obligatory requirements for social practices. The cultural- cognitive system is a common framework of meaning that is socially constructed and shapes each individual's interpretation of things. Scott emphasizes the need to recognize the divergent conceptions of the three pillar systems and to differentiate and compare the associated social processes. He also identifies theoretical constructs to study the three components as in Figure 1.

	Pillar		
	Regulative	Normative	Cultural-Cognitive
Basis of compliance	Expedience	Social obligation	Taken-for-grantedness Shared understanding
Basis of order	Regulative rules	Binding expectations	Constitutive schema
Mechanisms	Coercive	Normative	Mimetic
Logic	Instrumentality	Appropriateness	Orthodoxy
Indicators	Rules Laws Sanctions	Certification Accreditation	Common beliefs Shared logics of action
Basis of legitimacy	Legally sanctioned	Morally governed	Comprehensible Recognizable Culturally supported

Figure 1. Scott's Three Pillars of Institution

Collection development in data archives is a professional practice. In studying the challenges and opportunities facing social sciences data archives, we focused on identifying the various ***problems*** as perceived by the stakeholders and determines the nature of a problem, or, the ***source dimension*** of the problem, i.e., whether it is a regulative, normative, or cultural-cognitive problem or a combination of more than one dimension. We further examine whether a problem is connected to another problem and whether a possible solution constitutes conflict of interests.

THE INITIAL ANALYSIS AND PRELIMANARY FINDINGS

The case site is a data archive established in the 1990s within a large public research institution in Taiwan. Over the previous two decades, it had been focusing on curating data generated from large-scaled, long-term surveys, usually sponsored in part or wholly by the central government. In recent years, the archive has extended its effort to collect survey data from individual researchers. Further, with the recent advocacy and heightened public expectation for research data sharing, the archive is also considering collect other types of data, e.g., quantitative datasets other than survey data and qualitative data. But the decision is not made yet. The current analysis is based on in-depth interviews with four senior staff from that archive and secondary sources such as public documents about the archive and social science data policies in Taiwan. Through the aforementioned analysis procedures, we identified four major problems.

The Role and Identity Problem

The fundamental question facing the archive is whether it wants to turn into a bigger and more diverse data repository serving purposes beyond the current ones. Doubts and possible difficulties arise mostly from the regulative dimension. In contrast, both the normative and cultural-cognitive dimensions present opportunities and development niches if the archive does take the step. Currently, there is not a central hub for data sharing in Taiwan. The archive has already enjoyed a high degree of visibility among Taiwan social scientists. If it takes the step, support would be strong from the scholarly community. But the expansion of data acquisitions and service also means a change in the archive's roles, identities, and relations with the social sciences community. So the regulative problem is intertwined with normative and cognitive dimensions.

The Data Value Problem

Data type and timeliness are related to the perceived data value. The problem is cultural-cognitive in nature. The staffers are uncertain about the usefulness of the other types of data beyond survey datasets. However, the normative dimension presents an opposite perspective in arguing that data deposit is not just for re-analyses, but also for research transparency and accountability. If the data transparency perspective is reinforced in future research regulations, the "utility of data" will be interpreted differently and the archive may possibly embrace new value of data.

The Data Owner Cooperation Problem

The data owner cooperation problem is both a regulative and normative problem. It involves why and how people submit data, when they submit data, in what manners, how good the submitted data are as well as the accompanying materials. A few years ago, the archive successfully persuaded the Ministry of Science and Technology to mandate research grant receivers to deposit survey data to the archive. However, there is no penalty for those who fail to comply. For other types of survey data, such as the highly valuable long-term data collected by government agencies or research institutes, the archive relies mainly on mutual agreement/understanding to obtain data. In recent years, the call for open government and open data presents an opportunity for the archive to win the cooperation from government agencies. The archive presents itself as a professional and trustworthy service that can curate the data for the agencies for long term. The archive-agency alliance further attracts other agencies. This "soft" lobbying strategy along the normative dimension seems to work well for the archive. But if the archive wishes to expand its data collection, it will still have to strengthen the regulative support and provision.

The Data Curation Technicality Problem

The technical system for data curation also constitutes part of the consideration, and it is mainly a cultural-cognitive problem. The archive is currently adopting DDI (Data Documentation Initiative) for its metadata standard. As much as it wants to comply to the standard, the staffers also worry about the complexity and usability of the metadata scheme. If the collection expands beyond survey data, new standards, procedures, and data processing expertise need to be introduced.

CONCLUDING REMARK

We will employ visualization to present the three pillars as well as the identified problems, structure of the problems, and the inter-relations between problems and solutions if this proposal is accepted. For the future investigation, we plan to employ this analysis framework to study multiple social sciences data archives to reveal different collection development problems in various social settings.

ACKNOWLEDGEMENTS

This study is supported by the Ministry of Science & Technology, Taiwan (Grant No. MOST 105-2410-H-002-120-MY2).

REFERENCES

Scott, W.R. (2001). *Institutions and Organizations* (2nd Ed.). Thousand Oaks: Sage.

Data Type and Data Source Preferences for Six Social Sciences Subjects in Quantitative Data Reuses

Chi-Shiou Lin
National Taiwan University, Taiwan. chishioulin@ntu.edu.tw

YI-YU WANG
National Taiwan University, Taiwan. r03126027@ntu.edu.tw

ABSTRACT

In this paper we describe an analysis of the most frequently used data types intersecting data sources in quantitative data re- uses in six major social science subject disciplines. Using a sample of 1,319 papers from 40 social sciences journals in Taiwan, this study reveals the reuse patterns among the subjects for a time span of 15 years. The finding shows that the six sub- jects formed three groups, each with similar data reuse patterns. It also shows that business data from governments, series surveys from academic institutions, and series surveys from governments are the three most important kinds of data for social scientists, but the major users of those data differed.

KEYWORDS

Data reuse, quantitative data, social sciences research

INTRODUCTION

Social sciences have a long tradition of reusing quantitative data for extended analyses. Previous studies indicated that, in data reuses for extended, original analyses, social scientists employ mostly survey data and business data from governments or academic institutions rather than data from other researchers (Lin & Lai, 2017); significant differences also existed among social sciences areas in regard to data type and data source (Lin & Lai, 2018). This study continues to examine the kinds of data that are most used in six major social sciences subjects when data type intersects with data source.

RESEARCH METHOD AND THE STUDY SAMPLE

This study used the journals indexed in the 2015 TSSCI (*Taiwan Social Sciences Citation Index*) as the basis for the analysis; journals indexed in TSSCI are considered as good-quality research journals in Taiwan. All of the journals of the six subject disciplines are included in our analysis. Each issue of those journals published during 2001-2015 was manually scanned to identify empirical papers that have used at least one externally acquired quantitative dataset in the analyses (the "reuse papers"). For each reuse paper, the bibliographic information, subject category, and the number of datasets used in the paper were recorded. Table 1 shows the distributions of reuse papers and reused datasets in the study sample.

	N. of journals	N. of empirical papers	N. of reuse papers	% of reuse papers	N. of da-tasets	Avg. dataset (per paper)	St. D.
Economics (Eco)	4	469	395	84.22	1001	2.53	2.21
Agricultural Economics (Agr.E.)	3	281	202	71.89	503	2.49	2.68
Political Science (Poli.)	6	442	187	42.31	389	2.08	2.31
Public Admin. & Int'l Relations (PA/IR)	5	394	154	39.09	305	1.98	1.85
Sociology (Soc.)	5	381	195	51.18	291	1.49	1.16
Education (Edu.)	17	2535	186	7.34	243	1.31	1.20
Total	**40**	**4502**	**1319**	**29.30**	**2732**	**2.07**	**2.08**

Table 1. Distributions of the reuse papers and reused data in the study sample

For each reused dataset, the data identifying information (e.g., title and publisher of the data, date year, URL, DOI), data source, and data type were recorded. This study differentiated four data sources: *government agencies*, *academic institutions*, *private sectors*, and *individual researchers*. It also differentiated three data types: *business data* refers to quantitative data that are generated from daily operations, business transactions, or societal changes (e.g. crime rates, economic indicators, air pollution statistics); *series survey* refers to long-term, continuous surveys conducted for specific research or policy purposes; *one-time data* refers to data collected only for once without obvious seriality. Most of the one-time data are survey dataset on which we found no information about their intended continuation.

RESULTS

Table 2 shows the results of the analysis. Based on the table, we have the following findings:

- The top five most used data were: (1) business data from the governments (39.31%); (2) series surveys from aca- demic institutions (14.09%); (3) series surveys from government agencies (13.21%); (4) business data from private sectors (11.20%); (5) one-time data from individual researchers (6.92%).
- Economics and agricultural economics both had heavy uses of business data from the governments (48.65% vs. 56.06%) and business data from private sectors (20.58% vs. 14.51%). Economics in addition had a 15.88% usage of series survey from governments.

- Political science and PA/IR both had used a good amount of series surveys from academic institutions (both 26%); political science curiously had used a rather high percentage of one-time data from individual researchers (19.28%), while PA/IR used an unusually high percentage of business data from the government (40.98%).
- Sociology relied mostly on series surveys from academic institutions (32.30%) and governments (23.37%); also business data from the governments (20.27%).
- Education relied mostly on series surveys from academic institutions (27.57%) and governments (17.70%); business data from governments accounted for (20.16%).

	Business data				Series surveys				One-time data				Others	Total
	Gov.	Aca.	Priv.	Indiv.	Gov.	Aca.	Priv.	Indiv.	Gov.	Aca.	Priv.	Indiv.		
Eco	487 (48.65)	22 (2.20)	206 (20.58)	0 (0.00)	159 (15.88)	25 (2.50)	11 (1.10)	2 (0.20)	13 (1.30)	3 (0.30)	2 (0.20)	22 (2.20)	49 (4.90)	**1001 (100.00)**
Agr.E.	282 (56.06)	8 (1.59)	73 (14.51)	1 (0.20)	45 (8.95)	16 (3.18)	2 (0.40)	1 (0.20)	7 (1.39)	0 (0.00)	3 (0.60)	32 (6.36)	33 (6.56)	**503 (100.00)**
Poli.	72 (18.51)	10 (2.57)	9 (2.31)	2 (0.51)	38 (9.77)	102 (26.22)	22 (5.66)	10 (2.57)	7 (1.80)	20 (5.14)	9 (2.31)	75 (19.28)	13 (3.34)	**389 (100.00)**
PA/IR	125 (40.98)	9 (2.95)	7 (2.30)	0 (0.00)	8 (2.62)	81 (26.56)	3 (0.98)	3 (0.98)	2 (0.66)	17 (5.57)	11 (3.61)	27 (8.85)	12 (3.93)	**305 (100.00)**
Soc.	59 (20.27)	4 (1.37)	7 (2.41)	0 (0.00)	68 (23.37)	94 (32.30)	5 (1.72)	3 (1.03)	10 (3.44)	16 (5.50)	2 (0.69)	15 (5.15)	8 (2.75)	**291 (100.00)**
Edu.	49 (20.16)	3 (1.23)	4 (1.65)	0 (0.00)	43 (17.70)	67 (27.57)	17 (7.00)	24 (9.88)	1 (0.41)	7 (2.88)	4 (1.65)	18 (7.41)	6 (2.47)	**243 (100.00)**
All	1074 (39.31)	56 (2.05)	306 (11.20)	3 (0.11)	361 (13.21)	385 (14.09)	60 (2.20)	43 (1.57)	40 (1.46)	63 (2.31)	31 (1.13)	189 (6.92)	121 (4.43)	**2732 (100.00)**

*Numbers in parentheses are percentages

Table 2. Distributions of the reuse papers and reused data in the study sample

Based on the distributions, we may say that, in terms of the preferred data type and data sources, the studies of econom- ics and agricultural economics had similar use patterns; sociology and education also had similar preference patterns. The studies of political science and PA/IR were similar in their interests in series surveys from academic institutions, but for other data their use patterns varied.

We may also see that business data from the governments are important to all the six subjects, although economics, agricultural economics, and PA/IR proportionally relied on this type of data more than others. In sharp contrast, business data from private sectors were heavily used only in economics and agricultural economics. Percentagewise, we can see that series surveys from governments constituted an important part in economics, sociology, and education. But when we look further at the numbers of dataset, we see that agricultural economics also used a good number of this type of datasets, although the percentage of usages for this subject was not that high. As such, we may safely conclude that series surveys from government were important for those four subjects. In contrast, series surveys from academic institutions were more important for the bottom four subjects and not important to economics and agricultural economics.

CONCLUSION

This study analysed the quantitative data reuses over 15 years in six social sciences subjects in Taiwan and identified the most frequently used data type for those subjects. It has great practical value for social sciences data libraries as it shows dis- tinct data use patterns among those subjects which constitute major users of existing quantitative data, for instance, we now know the data reuse patterns of sociologists and education researchers are similar. Data curators should emphasize on the preferred data types in their collection development. Based on the different preferred data, they may also develop subject- specific services such as customized new data alerts and data use workshops.

REFERENCES

Lin, C.-S., & Lai, C.-Y. (2017). A study of data reuse behavior of social scientists in Taiwan. *Journal of Library and Information Science Research*, 11(2), 95-138.

Lin, C.-S., & Lai, C.-Y. (2018). The reuse of quantitative data in social sciences in Taiwan: 2001-2015. *Journal of Educational Media & Library Sciences*, *55*(1), 39-69.

ACKNOWLEDGEMENTS

This study is supported by the Ministry of Science & Technology, Taiwan (Grant No. MOST 105-2410-H-002-120-MY2).

The Performance of Reading Appeal Descriptors for Fiction: From the Perspective of Indexing Consistency

Chi-Shiou Lin
National Taiwan University, Taiwan. chishioulin@ntu.edu.tw

Yi-Yu Wang
National Taiwan University, Taiwan. r03126027@ntu.edu.tw

ABSTRACT

In this paper we describe indexer agreement and disagreement on the application of appeal descriptors on adult fiction. The appeal descriptors developed by Ebsco NoveList were used for the testing. The analysis found that about 1/3 of the appeal descriptors were of high use, but indexer inconsistency was generally high for those descriptors. In contrast, only a very small number of descriptors were of high use and at the same time of higher indexer consistency.

KEYWORDS

Indexing consistency, reading appeals, cataloging for fiction

INTRODUCTION

The indexing and retrieval of fiction have always been a problem in information organization. In practice, libraries often skip subject cataloging for fiction. Even when subject headings are assigned to fiction in some limited cases, the mostly topic headings may not necessarily meet fiction searchers' needs (Šauperl, 2013). Recently, some readers' advisory services have begun using reading appeals as indexing terms to catalog fiction (e.g., Allreaders.com, Whichbook.com). Reading appeals are a reader's "feel of a book" (Saricks, 2005). The indexing of book appeals usually involves multiple-dimensional descriptions, e.g., story setting, storyline, writing style, tone, characters; that is, appeal-based indexing is usually facet classification. NoveList is a readers' advisory service currently owned by Ebsco. It employs a list of appeal descriptors to catalogue all the pleasure reading materials in the database. The appeal guide differentiates descriptors applied to adult fiction and other types of materials, e.g., juvenile fiction, nonfiction, audiovisual works. For adult fiction specifically, there are currently 94 appeal descriptors under five facets: *pace* (3 descriptors), *storyline* (10 descriptors), *tone* (41 descriptors), *character* (21 descriptors), and *writing style* (19 descriptors) (NoveList, 2017). The descriptors are generic appeal terms that can be applied across cul- tures. We thus tested the appeal descriptors on 60 adult fiction written in Mandarin Chinese to observe the indexer agreement in the use of those terms. Indexing consistency is an indirect assessment of the retrieval effectiveness. When two or more indexers agree with the use of a descriptor on a specific work, it means higher consensus exists about the characteristics of that work; it is more likely to be catalogued by different indexers in the same way. The goal of this study is to examine to what extent appeal descriptors can be used effectively on a fictional work and which descriptors enjoy higher consensus among indexers.

METHODOLOGY

Six trained library and information science graduate students participated in the cataloging of 60 randomly selected fiction, avoiding any specific genre type. Prior to the actual cataloging, all of the indexers received three group training sessions in which the meanings of the NoveList appeal descriptors were fully discussed, annotated in Chinese, and tested against 22 adult fiction. In the formal implementation, each fiction was cataloged by three indexers who worked independently. The indexers should not have read the works assigned to them before they cataloged them. They first spent no more than 30 minutes to obtain an impression of a work either by browsing the book or by searching book reviews and reader comments on the Internet. They then considered each appeal descriptor against the work to see if it is applicable to that work. The eval- uation of descriptors for each book should take no more than 45 minutes. The procedures resulted in three conditions: indexer inconsistency (one indexer's judgment is different from the other two's), all-use consistency (all three indexers apply the descriptor on the book), and all-nonuse consistency (all three indexers do not use the descriptor on the book).

PRELIMINARY FINDINGS

This paper reports the preliminary findings based on 60 adult fiction. Unsurprisingly, inconsistency among indexers about the use of those descriptors was generally high. Table 1 shows the 30 appeal descriptors (32.98% of the total) with inconsistency rates over 50%. That is, those appeal descriptors were actually used by indexers on more than 30 books, but at the same time disagreement among indexers existed. We see that the descriptor "well-crafted dialogue (writing style)" had the highest in- consistency (80.00%), followed by "atmospheric (tone)" and "relatable (character)" (both 78.33%), and other descriptors with inconsistency up to 75.00%. Descriptors as such are significant because, on the one hand, they were in high use by in- dexers; but on the other hand, consensus on the use of them was low. A few descriptors' all-use consistency was higher than all-nonuse consistency, i.e., "flawed (character)", "descriptive (writing style)", "intensifying (pace)", "relatable (character)" and "stream of consciousness (character)". Comparatively, these are the more reliable descriptors.

Facet	Appeal Descriptor	Inconsistency%	Consistency%		Facet	Appeal Descriptor	Inconsistency%	Consistency%	
			All use	All nonuse				All use	All nonuse
ace	Intensifying	58.33	23.33	18.33		Relatable	78.33	11.67	10.00
	Fast-paced	51.67	6.67	41.67		Flawed	60.00	35.00	5.00
	Unconventional	58.33	3.33	38.33		Complex	60.00	1.67	38.33
Storyline	Plot-driven	56.67	16.67	26.67	Character	Courageous	56.67	8.33	35.00
	Sweeping	50.00	3.33	46.67		Large cast of characters	55.00	5.00	40.00
	Atmospheric	78.33	6.67	15.00		Sympathetic	53.33	16.67	30.00
	Thought-provoking	75.00	8.33	16.67		Brooding	50.00	15.00	35.00
	Dramatic	70.00	0.00	30.00		Well-crafted dialogue	80.00	8.33	11.67
	Reflective	68.33	5.00	26.67		Stream of consciousness	75.00	13.33	11.67
Tone	Bittersweet	68.33	1.67	30.00		Engaging	75.00	0.00	25.00
	Heartwrenching	61.67	6.67	31.67		Compelling	68.33	1.67	30.00
	Haunting	60.00	1.67	38.33	Writing Style	Conversational	66.67	15.00	18.33
	Strong sense of place	56.67	10.00	33.33		Descriptive	63.33	21.67	15.00
	Chaste	53.33	8.33	38.33		Lush	61.67	16.67	21.67
						Candid	56.67	0.00	43.33
						dialect-filled	50.00	5.00	45.00

Table 1. Descriptors with Indexer Inconsistency Over 50% (n=60 books)

Table 2 shows the descriptors with the highest all-use consistency in descending order. As we expected, all-use consistency is very difficult to achieve in appeal-based cataloging. "Authentic (character)" was the only descriptor with all-use consistency over 50%. It was also the only descriptor that had been applied to all the 60 books; the all-nonuse consistency was zero. That is, it was the most highly used descriptor and its retrieval effectiveness was much higher than the others. The performance of the other two descriptors, "character-driven (storyline)" and "flawed (character)", was not bad either. For all other descriptors except "intricately plotted (storyline)", the inconsistency was all higher than all-nonuse consistency. That is, these descriptors were in high use, but their reliability was questionable. Eleven of these descriptors were duplicates of those in Table 1 as their inconsistency exceeded 50%.

Facet	Descriptor	Consistency		Inconsistency	Facet	Descriptor	Consistency		Inconsistency
		All use	All non-use				All use	All nonuse	
Character	Authentic	55.00	0.00	45.00	Writing Style	Lush	16.67	21.67	61.67
Storyline	Character-driven	48.33	8.33	43.33	Storyline	Plot-driven	16.67	26.67	56.67
Character	Flawed	35.00	5.00	60.00	Character	Sympathetic	16.67	30.00	53.33
Pace	Intensifying	23.33	18.33	58.33	Writing Style	Conversational	15.00	18.33	66.67
Storyline	Issue-oriented	23.33	28.33	48.33	Character	Brooding	15.00	35.00	50.00
Writing Style	Descriptive	21.67	15.00	63.33	Writing Style	Stream of consciousness	13.33	11.67	75.00
Pace	Leisurely paced	20.00	38.33	41.67	Character	Relatable	11.67	10.00	78.33
Storyline	Intricately plotted	18.33	46.67	35.00	Tone	Strong sense of place	10.00	33.33	56.67

Table 2. Descriptors with the Highest Observed Indexer Consistency (n=60 books)

There were 55 descriptors (58.51% of the total) with all-nonuse consistency over 50%, among which 31 (32.98%) had all-use consistency of zero. At the first glance, these seem to be good descriptors as indexer agreement on its non-usage was high and stable. However, whether they should be viewed as reliable descriptors is open to debate. If higher consistency was achieved by nonuse, it doesn't really help the readers find works showing those appeals.

CONCLUSION

So far we have presented the preliminary analysis on the performance of appeal descriptors that is actually used in a commercial database. Because the sample size is small, we will continue to increase the number of test fiction to observe whether the descriptor performances remain the same. We will also introduce different fiction genres into the test collection to observe whether descriptor performance will vary by genre. Further, we plan to imitate real-life cataloging and ask the indexers to select only a limited number of descriptors for each fiction and compare the term selection so as to further understand the retrieval effectiveness of appeal-based cataloging. We believe the effort will help improve the construction and application of appeal terms for the organization and retrieval of fiction.

REFERENCES

NoveList. (2017). *The secret language of books: A guide to appeal* (2018 ed.). Retrieved December 30, 2017 from https://www.ebsco-host.com/uploads/novelist/pdf/NoveList_Appeal_2018.pdf

Saricks, J. G. (2005). *Readers' Advisory Service in the Public Library* (3rd ed.). Chicago, IL: American Library Association. Šauperl, A. (2013). Four views of a novel: Characteristics of novels as described by publishers, librarians, literary theorists,

and readers. *Cataloging and Classification Quarterly, 51*(6), 624-654. doi: 10.1080/01639374.2013.773953

Information Science Research and Sustainable Development

Christine Meschede
Heinrich Heine University, Germany.
christine.meschede@hhu.de

Maria Henkel
Heinrich Heine University, Germany.
maria.henkel@hhu.de

ABSTRACT

Awareness on and importance of sustainability in all its facets is becoming more and more important in all aspects of our lives. The question arises, how – not if – scientists can contribute to a sustainable development. As information and knowledge play an important role for development, information scientists should be included in this debate. But is there a sustainable information science or an information science of sustainability? Publications from the Library and Information Science (LIS) community addressing this topic are present, but only sparse. With this visual presentation, we aim at identifying possibilities where Library and Information Scientists can contribute to a sustainable development through and in research as well as teaching. After presenting the results of a structured literature review on sustainability in LIS research we aim at discussing these and further ideas on a sustainable information future with the participants. Thereby we endeavor to raise awareness on the topic and to share approaches to include sustainability in research, teaching and practice.

KEYWORDS

Sustainability, sustainable development, library and information science, structured literature review

INTRODUCTION

On January 1st, 2016, the Sustainable Development Goals (SDGs) went into effect. These 17 goals are intended to "end poverty, protect the planet and ensure prosperity for all" (United Nations, 2015, para. 1). A sustainable development can be described as a "development that meets the needs of the present without compromising the ability of future generations to meet their own needs" (WCED, 1987, p. 37). The SDGs include targets regarding different dimensions of sustainability (social, economic and environmental). In detail, the 17 SDGs address the following issues:

1. no poverty
2. zero hunger
3. good health and well-being
4. quality education
5. gender equality
6. clean water and sanitation
7. affordable clean energy
8. decent work and economic growth
9. industry, innovation and infrastructure
10. reduced inequalities
11. sustainable cities and communities
12. responsible consumption and production
13. climate action
14. life below water
15. life on land
16. peace, justice and strong institutions
17. partnership for the goals

Whereas prior formulations of similar goals – like the Millennium Development Goals – focused on advancements in developing countries, the SDGs demand involvement of all countries. Hence, this is a matter for all of us. Today, we can already observe several initiatives supporting a sustainable development, like a growing interest in the sharing economy (Hamari, Sjöklint, & Ukkonen, 2016).

Already in 1995, Spink (1995) discussed the role of information science for a sustainable future. Nonetheless, publications on sustainability from the Library and Information Science (LIS) community remain sparse. However, Chowdhury (2013, p. 617) argues that "since information forms an integral part of every development and innovation, sustainability should become a mainstream research topic within information studies". Apart from research activities, Chowdhury and Koya (2017) argue that sustainability should also find its rightful place in LIS education. Thereby "sustainability should be embedded in every aspect of data and information management teaching and research in iSchools and other university disciplines so that the graduates can make appropriate management, research, and professional contributions at the workplace in every business and industry towards achieving the SDGs" (Chowdhury & Koya, 2017, pp. 2135–2136).

METHODS

A structured literature review was conducted in February 2018, analyzing 81 research articles published in LIS journals and conferences. The set of publications was chosen based on a Scopus database search in 102 LIS sources listed by the SCImago Journal Rank (JIR). All articles were retrieved containing the string *sustainab** in their title or keywords, thus addressing sustainability or sustainable development directly. Some irrelevant publications were removed as well as new ones added based on relevant references. For the remaining articles, it has been noted what dimension of sustainability (environmental, economic, social) was addressed. Furthermore, the main topic, applied methods and addressed countries were listed.

RESULTS

From the 81 analyzed publications, 68 could be related to environmental sustainability, 43 to economic and 45 to social sustainability. Taking a deeper look into the contents of publications, eight major topics could be identified. Most articles (19) focus on libraries and archives, for example, by presenting case studies on green library initiatives. Therein, different types of libraries are addressed. Nine publications focus on academic libraries, four on public and three on digital libraries. The remaining articles did not specify the library type. Eighteen articles consider the role of Information and Communication Technology (ICT) for sustainable development. Ten further publications investigate governmental activities, for instance, information dissemination strategies regarding sustainability. Other articles are concerned with scientific publications on sustainability (7), society (7), urban development (6), research institutes and universities (4) and Information Science in general (3). Seven remaining publications, assigned to the category 'Other', discuss further topics like waste disposal, knowledge management or carbon footprints. Several articles refer to one or more concrete location(s) or region(s). Represented are developing countries (e.g. Nigeria with five publications) as well as developed countries (e.g. the United States with six articles).

VISUAL PRESENTATION AND ENGAGEMENT

While sustainability is the responsibility of every human – and therefore every scientist – journals, institutions, associations and conference organizers can encourage individuals to make one's own contribution to this topic. They can offer spaces for scientific discussion and exchange between professionals. This year the ASIS&T annual meeting's motto is "building an ethical and sustainable information future with emerging technology" (ASIS&T, 2018). We would like to pick up this theme to discover how information science scholars and practitioners will contribute to this future. By presenting our results with an emphasis on information science in relation to sustainability and the Sustainable Development Goals, we have three objectives:

1. Raising (further) awareness and initiating a discussion on the SDGs and the role of information science research and practice in fulfilling them.
2. Collecting small and big ideas and tips on how to practice sustainable research and teaching.
3. Encouraging participants to commit to more sustainable habits and practices or to include the sustainability issue in their research.

Therefore, we would like to invite conference attendees to share their own ideas, experiences and opinions or research projects that are relevant for this discussion. This will be realized by providing a poster with our results as well as a related hashtag. A tablet computer (provided by us) will be showing related tweets with the participant's contributions and summaries from us during the presentation. Furthermore, through the collection of tweets, the exchange of experiences and ideas will be available even after the poster presentation.

REFERENCES

ASIS&T. (2018). 2018 ASIS&T Annual Meeting. Retrieved May 15, 2018, from https://www.asist.org/am18/

Chowdhury, G. (2013). Sustainability of digital information services. *Journal of Documentation*, *69*(5), 602–622. https://doi.org/10.1108/JD-08-2012-0104

Chowdhury, G., & Koya, K. (2017). Information practices for sustainability: Role of iSchools in achieving the UN Sustainable Development Goals (SDGs). *Journal of the Association for Information Science and Technology*, *68*(9), 2128–2138.

Hamari, J., Sjöklint, M., & Ukkonen, A. (2016). The sharing economy: Why people participate in collaborative consumption. *Journal of the Association for Information Science and Technology*, *67*(9), 2047–2059.

Spink, A. (1995). Information and a sustainable future. *Libri*, *45*(3–4), 203–208. https://doi.org/10.1515/libr.1995.45.3-4.203

United Nations. (2015). Sustainable Development Goals. Retrieved January 5, 2018, from http://www.un.org/sustainabledevelopment/sustainable-development-goals/

WCED. (1987). Report on the World Commission on Environment and Development. Our Common Future.

The Evolving Landscape of Children's Librarians' Use of New Media with Young Children and Their Caregivers: A Longitudinal Study

J. Elizabeth Mills
University of Washington, USA. jemills1@uw.edu

Marianne Martens
Kent State University, USA. mmarten3@kent.edu

Katie Campana
Kent State University, USA. kcampan2@kent.edu

Claudia Haines
Homer Public Library, USA. cshaines@gmail.com

ABSTRACT

Technology is an integral part of our society and has taken root in various aspects of young children's lives. A 2014 nationwide survey of children's librarians' use of new media with young children and their caregivers established baseline results. An expanded version of this survey will be administered in August 2018 to provide a longitudinal view of children's librarians' use of new media with young children and their caregivers as well as insight into their role as media mentors--guiding families and modeling effective practices in working towards a balanced media diet for today's youth. This poster will provide the 2018 survey design and findings that will speak to change in practices and prevalence of technology from 2014 and provide selections from the emergent data regarding various new areas of inquiry around diversity, attitudes, and evaluation.

KEYWORDS

Technology, children and youth, librarians, media mentorship.

INTRODUCTION

Technology is an integral part of our society and has taken root in various aspects of young children's lives. But what is happening in libraries across the country with respect to new media use with young children and families? Are librarians adopting new media devices? If so, how are they doing so and what challenges do they face in that endeavor? An initial survey of libraries and new media was disseminated nationwide in 2014 to document usage at the time and uncover promising practices for the incorporation of new media into library collections, services, and programs for families with young children (Author et al., 2015). This survey grew out of observations in conference presentations and online listservs that many practitioners were not aware of the research nor of the initial recommendations from the American Academy of Pediatrics regarding screen time and young children (Hill 2015). Thus, there was a lack of understanding of what to do regarding new media and young children in the library that has persisted into current practice with online discussions, even heated debates, on library listservs and social media outlets, about the safety of using new media with young children. The research community itself diverges in this area regarding whether or not to use such media tools with young children; however, parents are forging their own path based on their own needs. These continued debates and concerns pointed to the need for more current insight into children's librarians' use of new media with young children and their caregivers and the potential for media mentorship.

The 2014 survey was guided by the overarching research question: What is the landscape in public libraries around the country with respect to new media use in programming for young children ages 0-5? More than 400 responses offered compelling, widespread insights into this largely uncharted and disparate landscape, with greater than 70% of respondents using some form of new media in their programming with young children, and 22% offering some kind of device mentoring. Given the massive changes in technology use with young children, it is important to return to and expand upon the original survey to learn more around current device use, librarians' attitudes around device use, the use of diverse media, and evaluation of media. Due to the desire to understand the changes in current practice, the 2014 baseline results are being used as a foundation to inform an updated 2018 survey that will provide a longitudinal view of the field. This survey seeks to determine a) the presence of any kind of change in the use of new media devices with young children and their caregivers from the results received in 2014; and b) details on specifics in terms of types of use, attitudes towards new media use with children, evaluation tools, and more.

LITERATURE REVIEW

Research has shown that young children ages 0-5 are developing and building cognitive function at an incredible rate. Since the 2014 survey, library programs such as storytime have been shown to positively affect that development through an intentional focus on early literacy-related materials in the content of the program (Author et al., 2016; Author et al., 2018). For the past several years, that developmental process has also included media literacy as well—98% of children ages 8 and under live in a home that has a mobile device of some sort; in fact, 42 percent of children now possess their own tablet device (Common Sense Media, 2017). As access to mobile devices has increased from 2013 to 2017, though, are parents and caregivers aware of the latest research around how to engage effectively with their children using these devices and do they know how to select high quality content for these devices? These types of media are helping to shape a child's experience of their world through social interactions and learning about cause and effect in the games and apps they play—it's crucial that parents and caregivers know how to provide meaningful learning experiences in these new tools and recognize their role as their child's first and best teacher. A 2012 publication by the American Library Association (ALA), entitled *Technology and Literacy: 21st Century Library Programming for Children and Teens*, clearly situates the library as a location for informal learning that can support and scaffold children's use of technology. The library community can help children develop their digital literacy skills even at a very young age. Caretakers and other adults can play a critical role in shaping and modeling how children can use technology in a positive and nurturing way. And librarians can use technology to bring the outside world into traditional storytimes in a meaningful way to provide powerful learning opportunities for young children.

The 2014 survey informed a 2015 white paper, adopted by ALSC, entitled Media Mentorship in Libraries Serving Youth (Campbell et al.) that outlined a new name for a tried and true role held by librarians with respect to more traditional types of media—books, videos, audio—but that now also applies to digital media as well. Using a term coined by Lisa Guernsey in 2014, media mentorship seeks to uphold and inform the ways in which librarians are recommending, guiding, and incorporating new media into their spaces, programs, and advisory work in their efforts to support young children and their caregivers. It is this role of media mentor that best describes the evolving children's librarian and the 2018 survey will provide additional data as to how this role is defined by the field and to what extent it has taken hold as a concept for professionals.

2018 SURVEY PURPOSE AND DESIGN

Using longitudinal research to determine any change in practice in libraries and to provide evidence of continued and innovative use of new media with young children and caregivers can push the field forward and define new and emerging roles for librarians that demonstrate their sustainability as mentors of media for families. For the survey design, the original eight questions from the 2014 survey were repeated along with new questions that explore the following research questions: What is the landscape in public libraries around the country with respect to new media use with young children and their caregivers? What kinds of changes are present in the data from 2018 when compared to the data from 2014 in terms of new media use with young children? How, if at all, are librarians acting as media mentors for families with young children? What are librarians' attitudes about the use of new media in libraries with young children and their caregivers? How are librarians using diverse media and how are they using media with underserved communities? To what extent do librarians feel equipped to be media mentors for young children and their caregivers? The survey data will be analyzed using descriptive statistics to determine the change in responses from 2014 to 2018 as well as using axial coding of the short answer responses to look for relevant themes and common practices that can be reported out to impact and inform the field.

CONCLUSION

In conclusion, this study seeks to understand, across time, what has changed and evolved in how children's librarians are using and sharing new media with the young children and caregivers they serve in their communities. Building on the 2014 baseline data, this data can inform the library field on the dynamic landscape of new media adoption in libraries across the United States, enabling the field to respond accordingly with further research and update graduate courses to prepare future librarians to serve as media mentors who can effectively guide families to make healthy, mindful media choices for their young children.

ACKNOWLEDGMENTS

The researchers wish to thank the Association for Library Service to Children (ALSC) for their support of this research.

REFERENCES

Author, 2018.

Author, 2016.

Author, 2015.

Hill, D. L. (2015). Beyond 'turn it off': How to advise families on media use. *AAP News*, *36*(10), 54.

Campbell, C., Author, Koester, A., & Stoltz, D. (2015). "Media mentorship in libraries serving youth." Chicago, IL: ALSC. Retrieved May 11, 2018 from http://www.ala.org/alsc/sites/ala.org.alsc/files/content/2015%20ALSC%20White%20Paper_FINAL.pdf.

Guernsey, L. (2014). "How the iPad affects young children, and what we can do about it," [Video file], https://www.youtube.com/watch?v=P41_nyYY3Zg.

National Association for the Education of Young Children & the Fred Rogers Center for Early Learning and Children's Media at Saint Vincent College. (2012). "Technology and Interactive Media as Tools in Early Childhood Programs Serving Children from Birth through Age 8." Washington D.C.

Nelson, J., & Braafladt, K. (2012). *Technology and literacy: 21st century library programming for children and teens*. Chicago: American Library Association.

Rideout, V. (2017). The Common Sense census: Media use by kids age zero to eight. San Francisco, CA: Common Sense Media.

Is Scientific Novelty Geflected in Citation Patterns?

Chao Min
Nanjing University, China. chaomin@smail.nju.edu.cn

Jianjun Sun
Nanjing University, China. sjj@nju.edu.cn

Yi Bu
Indiana University Bloomington, USA. buyi@iu.edu

Ying Ding
Indiana University Bloomington, USA. dingying@iu.edu

ABSTRACT

We investigate the diffusion characteristics of two groups of scientific works with different levels of novelty to see how scientific novelty interacts with citation patterns. Preliminary results show that: (1) novel ideas have long-lasting impact, but the recognition process lags behind; (2) most diffusion metrics can't differentiate the two groups under a similar macro environment; (3) citation take-off, average clustering coefficient, and connectivity *can* distinguish works with different levels of novelty. The latter two characteristics—average clustering coefficient and connectivity of citing literature networks—show particular potential for identifying innovative scientific works at an early stage.

KEYWORDS

Citation pattern, citation diffusion, scientific novelty, citation dynamics, citation structure

INTRODUCTION

Citation is a multi-faceted process with both temporal (Min, Ding & Li et al., forthcoming) and structural aspects (Min, Sun & Ding, 2017). We propose viewing the citation process as a diffusion process (Min, Ding & Li et al., forthcoming) akin to the innovation diffusion described by Rogers (2003). This paper reports preliminary results on the relation between citation patterns (temporal as well as structural) and scientific novelty.

DATA AND METHOD

Scientific novelty is hard to quantify, but works recognized by professional institutions (e.g., Nobel Prize) are considered to possess sufficient novelty at least at publication time. In keeping with the recommendations of Shen & Barabási (2014), we select a group of 116 Nobel Prize winning publications and construct a control group where each work correspondingly has the same publication year, venue and roughly equal citation impact. In the temporal dimension, we collect yearly citations from the publication year onward; citation structure is represented by four generations of citations to the works under study, made within four years of initial publication. In all, more than 19 million citation pairs were extracted from an in-house version of Web of Science database. We calculate the following temporal and structural metrics for the two datasets. *Temporal metrics*: (1) First citation: time span between publication and first citation, along with citation counts in the first cited year. (2) Citation take-off: the turning point at which a work starts to get attention (Ke et al., 2015). (3) First citation peak: point at which yearly citations form the first peak on the citation curve. We consider it a peak if the year's citation count is greater than in each of the previous three years and no less than in the three subsequent years. (4) Citation summit: a point where a work gets highest yearly citations. *Structural metrics* were calculated for the first one, two, three and four generations of the citing article's citation network. They include: (1) Average clustering coefficient. (2) Network density. (3) Connectivity.

PRELIMINARY RESULTS

Characteristics of Nobel Prize papers

Nobel Prize papers perform well according to citation metrics, but their impact is revealed rather slowly. While most of the papers received attention shortly after publication, a small portion remained uncited until 3–9 years later. A significant number of papers "took off" five years after publication, with take-off time varying from 5–25 years to 25–45 years (Fig. 1). With such a long preparation period before take-off, several papers accumulated more than 100 citations, but most obtained fewer than 100. After take-off, all Nobel Prize papers were heavily cited. A long timespan between publication and citation summit (Fig. 2) also suggests a long period of citation growth. Typical papers reach their summit 2–6 years after publication, but Nobel Prize papers tend to lag behind: for most of these, the summit comes after the 6–year mark, with some peaking more than 30 years after publication.

Comparison between two groups of papers

We conduct a *t*-test to investigate whether the two groups of papers differ in their citation metrics. Tables 1 and 2 show that Nobel Prize papers and non-Nobel Prize papers exhibit no significant difference in most temporal and structural citation characteristics. However, they do show a significant difference in citation take-off, average clustering coefficient, and network connectivity. On average, Nobel Prize papers took off 4 years later than non-Nobel Prize papers, and they had far more accumulated citations (nearly 2.4 times) at take-off. This verified the fact that scientific novelty has far-reaching impact, though its recognition lags behind. Nobel Prize papers have significantly higher average clustering coefficients and greater connectivity, implying that more "interlocked" structures exist in their (direct or indirect) citing literature networks. This suggests that scientific works with significant novelty can inspire subsequent works that are also relevant to each other.

CONSLUSION AND NEXT STEPS

We selected a group of works that won Nobel Prizes and constructed a suitable control group. As it happens, these groups show no significant difference in most citation measures when controlled under a similar macro environment. Three measures− citation take-off, average clustering coefficient and connectivity—do significantly distinguish the two groups. This suggests that although scientific novelty is not easy to quantify, it leaves visible marks in the process of citation diffusion. These marks provide potential traces (e.g., the average clustering coefficient and connectivity of citing literature networks) for us to identify innovative scientific works at an early stage. Our results show that works with sufficient scientific novelty reveal unusual characteristics in the first one or two generations of citing structures shortly after publication. In subsequent research, we hope to further excavate the potential of citation diffusion characteristics in identifying early innovative scientific works.

REFERENCES

Ke, Q., Ferrara, E., Radicchi, F., & Flammini, A. (2015). Defining and identifying Sleeping Beauties in science. *Proceedings of the National Academy of Sciences*, *112*(24), 7426–7431.

Min, C., Ding, Y., Li, J., Bu, Y., Pei, L., & Sun, J. (forthcoming). Innovation or imitation: The diffusion of citations. *Journal of the Association for Information Science and Technology*.

Min, C., Sun, J., & Ding, Y. (2017). Quantifying the evolution of citation cascades. *Proceedings of the Association for Information Science & Technology*, *54*(1), 761–763.

Rogers, E. M. (2003). *The diffusion of innovations*. New York, NY: Free Press.

Shen, H. W., & Barabási, A. L. (2014). Collective credit allocation in science. Proceedings of the National Academy of Sciences, 111(34), 12325–12330.

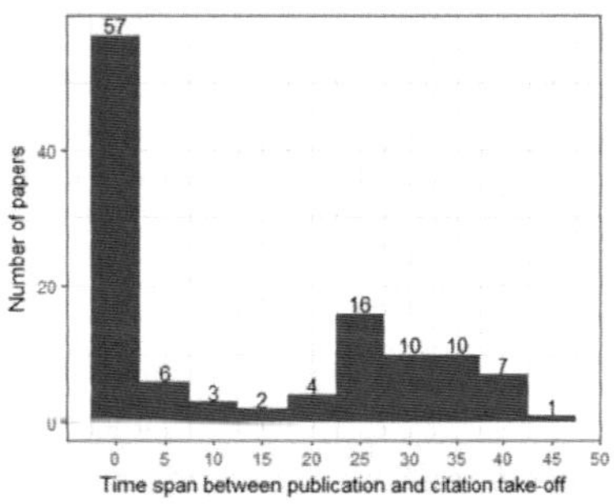

Figure 1. Take-off span for Nobel Prize papers.

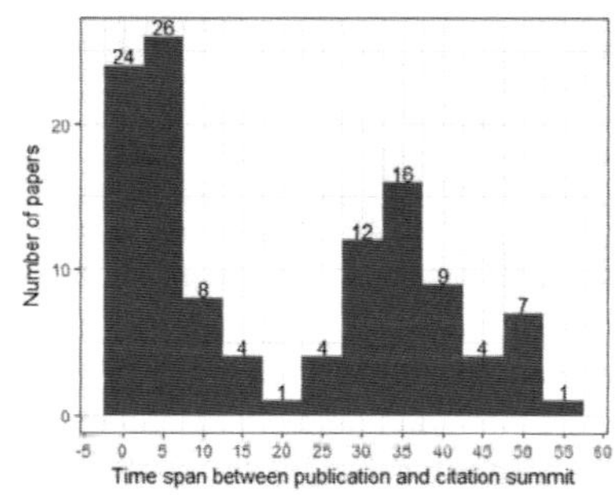

Figure 2. Citation summit span for Nobel Prize papers.

Temporal	**Nobel**	**Non-Nobel**	**Sig.**
FCS	0.37	0.57	0.155
FCC	11.40	9.10	0.361
TOS	***11.89***	***7.87***	***0.034***
TOC	***274.43***	***114.09***	***0.010***
FPS	4.18	4.66	0.302
FPC	84.61	72.09	0.496
CSS	17.52	15.38	0.318
CSC	132.29	104.98	0.223

Table 2 (Left). t-test results for temporal characteristics. FCS=First cited span, FCC=First cited citations, TOS = Take-off span, TOC=Take-off citations, FPS=First peak span, FPC=First peak citations, CSS=Citation summit span, CSC=Citation summit citations.

Table 2 (Right). t-test results for structural characteristics. n g = n^{th} generation of citations.

Structural	**Nobel**	**Non-Nobel**	**Sig.**
ACC(***1 g***)	***0.21***	***0.17***	***0.023***
2 g	**0.25**	**0.23**	**0.077**
3 g	0.22	0.20	0.241
4 g	0.20	0.18	0.157
Density(1 g)	0.05	0.04	0.195
2 g	0.02	0.03	0.913
3 g	0.02	0.02	0.848
4 g	0.02	0.02	0.814
Connectivity (***1 g***)	***0.72***	***0.63***	***0.020***
2 g	***0.87***	***0.80***	***0.031***
3 g	**0.90**	**0.84**	**0.083**
4 g	0.90	0.86	0.119

Wandering as Information Behavior in New Environments

Chiyoung Oh
University of Maryland, USA. jcoh@umd.edu

Beth St. Jean
University of Maryland, USA. bstjean@umd.edu

Brian S. Butler
University of Maryland, USA. bsbutler@umd.edu

ABSTRACT

Today, more and more people migrate to different parts of the world. Previous studies showed that these newcomers use various online and social sources to acquire information in new countries, but a few recent studies have indicated that "wandering" is a type of information behavior that newcomers use to become familiar with their new environments. This paper extends our knowledge of wandering behavior by examining international newcomer students' wandering and information acquisition based on findings from a study of international students' information behavior. Also, we add to the existing literature on information behavior (IB) models and theoretical concepts by analyzing wandering through the lenses of Wilson's information behavior model and Erdelez's concept of information encountering.

KEYWORDS

Wandering, information behavior, information encountering, newcomers

INTRODUCTION AND PREVIOUS WORK

International migration is increasingly common for education, work, and immigration. Previous studies addressed these newcomers' challenges involving different cultures, systems, and social networks, as well as daily living challenges (Mehra & Bilal, 2008; Poyrazli & Grahame, 2007). Also, recent studies identified information challenges and information behaviors (IBs) of international newcomers. Family and friends are important everyday information sources for immigrants (Quirke, 2012), and international newcomers use social media to gather information and connect with family and friends (Komito & Bates, 2011). Further, a few recent studies discussed an interesting type of IB—*wandering* (walking around). International newcomers wandered around to become familiar with their new neighborhoods (Lingel, 2011) and to acquire local information about new areas and places (Oh, Butler, & Lee, 2014). Oh et al. (2014) also found that newcomers' concerns about safety or fear of becoming lost often kept them from wandering. But additional work is needed to better understand wandering as an IB for acquiring local information. This paper aims to fill this gap and develop a theoretical analysis of wandering as an IB through the lenses of Wilson's (1997) IB model and Erdelez's (1999) concept of information encountering.

METHODS

As part of a project that examines new international students' local information behavior, this study surveyed 149 international and domestic out-of-state newcomer students at a U.S. university and conducted interviews with a subset (57) of respondents. Surveys were developed based on prior IB studies of international newcomers to understand their IB patterns (Lingel, 2011; Sin & Kim, 2013). Also, interviews were used to identify the detailed contexts of their IBs. Survey data were analyzed using SPSS, and the interview data were analyzed using both deductive and inductive coding in NVivo. This paper reports and analyzes the findings specifically related to wandering as an IB during participants' adjustments to their new environments.

FINDINGS AND DISCUSSION

Factor analysis of the survey data identified that *wandering & encountering* (i.e. finding information by chance through engagement with the physical environment) was one of the 10 underlying types of information sources which included: web & online maps, mobile maps & location-bases services, co-nationals, university online resources, wandering & encountering, other nationals, online communities, university offline resources, family, and neighbors (in the order of use frequency for all participants, with web & online maps being most frequently used). The findings also indicate that wandering is not a unique practice of international newcomers. Wandering as an IB was reported by both international and domestic newcomer students. However, statistical analysis showed that international students were more likely than domestic students to acquire local information through wandering & encountering ($F(1, 144) = 5.712, p = .018$). Interview data provided more details and contexts of wandering. By wandering, international newcomer students intended to learn more about their surroundings, enjoyed walking around, and looked for specific places. While wandering, sometimes they intended to gather local information, and at other times they did not. In some cases, they looked for specific local information (e.g., a metro station), but in other cases they did not have an informational goal in mind while wandering. Their wandering involved various types of "information-seeking behaviours" such as *passive attention, passive search, active search,* and *ongoing search* (Wilson, 1997, p. 562). First, passive attention, "where information acquisition may take place without intentional seeking," applied to wandering behavior. Information acquisition often occurred while participants were leisurely walking around their new surroundings without intentionally seeking information, which can also be identified as information encountering (Erdelez, 1999). Second, passive search, where "one type of search" results in the "acquisition of information that happens to be relevant to the individual," was also found in wandering behavior. Participants happened to find other places while looking for a specific place, which can be seen as a type of information encountering. For example, P5 (Male, China) was looking for a bank near campus, but incidentally found other services around the bank. Third, active search, "where an individual actively seeks out information," was also often involved in wandering behavior. Some newcomer students intended to find specific local places by actively wandering and directly interacting with the environment. During her early adjustment period, P12 (Female, Argentina) "started walking around and checking for different places, especially to locate the metro station at first and then the bank." Lastly, ongoing search, "where occasional continuing search is carried out to update or expand one's framework," applied to wandering behavior. International newcomer students tended not just to wander around once or twice, but rather in an ongoing fashion during their early adjustment. These active and ongoing searches involved specific information to search for, which would not conform to the notion of information encountering (Erdelez, 1999). As such, wandering behaviors can be theoretically understood through the lenses of Erdelez's (1999) information encountering and Wilson's (1997) four types of information-seeking behaviors. However, in addition to the four types, this paper proposes two additional types of information-seeking behaviors associated with wandering—*active attention* and *ongoing attention*. Participants often actively wandered around to get to know their new environments, without searching for specific information. In this case, their behavior is "attention" rather than "search." But it is not passive attention. It is rather an active behavior often without a specific target of searching, thus active attention. Also, this activity of "attention" generally does not take place as a single event. Newcomer students' wandering behavior involves constant exposure to local environments, and they are likely to acquire some information as they move around the local area over time for leisure or other purposes without intentional information seeking. In this sense, wandering, as an IB, also involves ongoing attention, which can take place over time during newcomers' adjustment to unfamiliar environments.

As practical implications, researchers, designers, and other practitioners could consider developing services and systems that can help newcomers effectively wander around new and unfamiliar environments either physically or virtually and acquire useful local information. These can be either assistive mobile applications or augmented reality technologies that they can use while wandering around or online systems that allow newcomers to virtually wander around new environments without concerns regarding safety, becoming fatigued due to extensive walking, or getting lost in unknown areas (Oh et al., 2014).

CONCLUSIONS

Overall, this paper showed that wandering entails complex information-seeking patterns including Wilson's (1997) four types of information-seeking behavior—passive attention, passive search, active search, and ongoing search—and two additional types that are proposed in this work—active attention and ongoing attention. While wandering behavior is often closely related with information encountering, it can also involve purposive information seeking. This paper extends our understanding of wandering as an IB, proposes two new types of information-seeking behaviors, and adds to the existing empirical literature on wandering (Lingel, 2011, 2015) and information encountering in physical environments (Erdelez, 1999).

REFERENCES

Allen, M. (1993). International students in academic libraries: A user survey. *College & Research Libraries*, *54*(4), 323–333.

Erdelez, S. (1999). Information encountering: It's more than just bumping into information. *American Society for Information Science. Bulletin of the American Society for Information Science*, *25*(3), 25. http://doi.org/10.1002/bult.118

Komito, L., & Bates, J. (2011). Migrants' information practices and use of social media in Ireland: networks and community. In *Proceedings of the 2011 iConference* (pp. 289–295). ACM.

Lingel, J. (2011). Information tactics of immigrants in urban environments. *Information Research*, *16*(4), 1–16.

Lingel, J. (2015). Information practices of urban newcomers: An analysis of habits and wandering. *Journal of the Association for Information Science and Technology*, *66*(6), 1239–1251. http://doi.org/10.1002/asi.23255

Mehra, B., & Bilal, D. (2008). International students' information needs and use of technology. *ASIS&T 2008*, *44*(1), 1–8.

Oh, C. Y., Butler, B. S., & Lee, M. (2014). Information Behavior of International Students Settling in an Unfamiliar Geospatial Environment. *Proceedings of the ASIS&T*, *51*(1), 1–11.

Poyrazli, S., & Grahame, K. M. (2007). Barriers to adjustment: Needs of international students within a semi-urban campus community. *Journal of Instructional Psychology*, *34*(1), 28–45.

Quirke, L. (2012). Information practices in newcomer settlement: a study of Afghan immigrant and refugee youth in Toronto.

Proceedings of the 2012 iConference, 535–537.

Sin, S.-C. J., & Kim, K.-S. (2013). International students' everyday life information seeking: The informational value of social networking sites. *Library & Information Science Research*, *35*(2), 107–116.

Wilson, T. D. (1997). Information behaviour: an interdisciplinary perspective. *Information Processing & Management*, *33*(4), 551–572. http://doi.org/10.1016/S0306-4573(97)00028-9

New International Students' Social Information Practices During Transition to Their Host Country

Chiyoung Oh
University of Maryland, USA. jcoh@umd.edu

Brian S. Butler
University of Maryland, USA. bsbutler@umd.edu

ABSTRACT

As newcomers, international students face information challenges in unfamiliar environments. Studies have reported that social and online resources, such as friends and the Internet, are their important sources of information, but research is less clear about how international students seek information through social sources. This paper examines social information practices of new international students in a U.S. university during adjustment to their new local environments. Also, based on prior studies, we investigate how international students' socio-national context, specifically the degree to which there are co-nationals in one's local environments, shapes their social information practices. Findings show that international students from common countries of origin (China, India, and Korea) developed online and mobile communities with co-national students and shared local information among them while most international students from other less common countries did not engage in such co-national networking and information practices. This paper suggests that information behavior theories account for people's socio-national contexts to better inform research and practice involving internationally mobile individuals and groups.

KEYWORDS

Information behavior, international student

INTRODUCTION AND PREVIOUS WORK

As migratory individuals, international students face many challenges involving different societal systems, cultures, and social networks in their new country (Abe, Talbot, & Geelhoed, 1998). Specifically, they experience information challenges as they deal with various everyday issues in unfamiliar environments (Zhang & Brunton, 2007). During adjustment to a life in their new country, international students need and seek information about housing, places, local areas, services, and transportation, that is *local information*, among others (Mehra & Bilal, 2008; Oh, Butler, & Lee, 2014). Studies show that social sources, such as co-national friends, and online sources, such as web and social networking sites, are international students' important sources of information in everyday life (Oh et al., 2014; Sin & Kim, 2013). However, despite prior studies, it is unclear how international newcomer students seek local information through social sources and online social technologies. To fill this gap, this paper examines international newcomer students' social information practices in the context of adjustment to their new local environments. Especially, drawing on Oh et al.'s (2014) finding about co-nationals as international students' important information sources and Burnett and Jaeger's (2011) theory of information worlds which considers small and larger social factors influencing human information behavior, we investigate how new international students' social information practices are shaped by their socio-national context, specifically by the degree to which there are co-nationals in one's local environments.

METHODS

We used a mixed-method approach with online surveys and follow-up interviews. First-year graduate students from three different socio-national contexts were recruited at University of Maryland, College Park. Among 149 survey respondents, 55 were students from China, India, and Korea, the top 3 most common countries, who have many local co-nationals (*International-common*). 28 were students from 18 other less-common countries, who have relatively fewer local co-nationals (*International-less-common*). 66 were U.S. newcomer students from other states (*Domestic*), a comparison group. Survey questions were based on previous studies of international student information behavior (Oh et al., 2014; Sin & Kim, 2013) and examined one's local information needs and information source use. 57 of 149 respondents participated in the follow-up semi-structured interview which was designed to draw contexts and rationale for their information practices. Survey data were analyzed using SPSS, and the interview data were analyzed through both deductive and inductive coding in NVivo (Corbin & Strauss, 1990).

FINDINGS

Survey data showed a pattern that survival-related, basic local information, such as information about housing, transportation, and groceries, was perceived more important than recreation-related local information, such as information about café/restaurants and places for exercise, for all three groups of newcomer students. However, the patterns of information source use to meet their information needs significantly varied among the three groups in different socio-national contexts. Specifically, international-common students acquired information from co-national friends (i.e., co-national information practices) statistically significantly more frequently than did international-less-common (Mean difference = 2.539, Std. Error = 0.311, $p = .000$) and domestic (Mean difference = 1.287, Std. Error = 0.248, $p = .000$) students. For international-common students, co-national friends were the most frequently used social sources of local information than any other social sources, such as family or other nationals (i.e., students from other countries). Interview data revealed that this co-national information practice of international-common students generally began through online communities (e.g., Facebook groups) and then continued to develop through mobile social networks (e.g., using WhatsApp). In contrast, most international-less-common students did not engage in such online or mobile social information practices with co-nationals or with other nationals although they did have access to some local co-nationals and various social technologies. Instead, international-less-common students mostly relied on non-social online sources, such as web and online maps, to seek local information. Domestic students also mainly used non-social online sources to seek local information. However, mainly using non-social online information sources, without much use of social information sources, was largely sufficient for domestic students to meet their local information needs while it was not for international-less-common students. International-less-common students did not frequently use social information sources, either in offline or online settings, which otherwise could effectively provide them with rich, context-specific local information needed to deal with issues and decision making during their adjustment to unfamiliar environments.

DISCUSSION AND CONCLUSIONS

The findings indicate that international newcomer students' information behavior can significantly vary depending on their socio-national contexts in their local environments. In other words, international newcomer students' socio-national context, specifically the degree to which there are co-nationals in one's local environments, may play a significant role in shaping their social information practices in both offline and online. This might imply that different socio-national contexts of international-common and international-less-common students influenced their local social structure, development of online and mobile communities, social capital, and social information practices during their transition to a new country, a specific period when international students face greater challenges (Poyrazli & Grahame, 2007). As results, it is possible that there develop information gaps between international newcomers in different socio-national contexts. Further, the interaction between socio-national context and socio-technical context (e.g., development of local co-national online and mobile communities) led to active social information practices for international-common students. International-common students' co-national networking and information practices were augmented through these social technologies, which provided them with expediency in acquiring local information during adjustment to their new country. However, despite their access to some local co-nationals and various social technologies, most international-less-common students did not exhibit such use of social technologies or pursue active co-national information practices. This may suggest that, without critical mass of local co-nationals, international-less-common students were less likely to develop local co-national online communities and co-national information practices.

Although many prior studies considered international students as one homogeneous group, the findings of this study show that they are not the same, but rather diverse in terms of their social contexts and information behavior. In practice, special attention would be needed to support international-less-common students for their development of social resources and information practices during their transition to host countries. In research, future studies involving international newcomers could further investigate the role of socio-national contexts in shaping information practices of various types of international newcomers, such as immigrants, refugees, or other sojourners. Also, more studies on the influence of the interactions between socio-national contexts and other contextual factors, such as cultures, situations, or demographics, would help develop information behavior theories to better inform research and practices involving internationally mobile individuals and groups around the world.

REFERENCES

Abe, J., Talbot, D. M., & Geelhoed, R. J. (1998). Effects of a peer program on international student adjustment. *Journal of College Student Development*, *39*(6), 539–547.

Burnett, G., & Jaeger, P. (2011). The theory of information worlds and information behaviour. In *Library and Information Science: New Directions in Information Behaviour.* (pp. 161–180).

Corbin, J., & Strauss, A. (1990). Grounded Theory Research: Procedures, Canons, and Evaluative Criteria. *Zeitschrift Fur Sociologie, 19*(6), 418–427.

Mehra, B., & Bilal, D. (2008). International students' information needs and use of technology. *Proceedings of the ASIS&T, 44*(1), 1–8.

Oh, C. Y., Butler, B. S., & Lee, M. (2014). Information Behavior of International Students Settling in an Unfamiliar Geo- spatial Environment. *Proceedings of the ASIS&T, 51*(1), 1–11.

Poyrazli, S., & Grahame, K. M. (2007). Barriers to adjustment: Needs of international students within a semi-urban campus community. *Journal of Instructional Psychology*, *34*(1), 28–45.

Sin, S.-C. J., & Kim, K.-S. (2013). International students' everyday life information seeking: The informational value of social networking sites. *Library & Information Science Research*, *35*(2), 107–116.

Zhang, Z., & Brunton, M. (2007). Differences in Living and Learning: Chinese International Students in New Zealand. *Journal of Studies in International Education, 11*(2), 124–140.

Going GoPro: Integrating a Wearable Camera into Qualitative Information Research

Sarah Polkinghorne
Swinburne University of Technology, Australia /
University of Alberta, Canada. spolkinghorne@swin.edu.au

ABSTRACT

Wearable technology has been a news-friendly trend in the past decade, particularly given the popularity of, and attendant concerns with, digital fitness trackers. One type of wearable technology, the GoPro camera, has become widely known for enabling first-person views of athletic feats such as skiing and surfing. Recently, such cameras have begun to be applied within social science research. This visual presentation offers a unique report on the sustainable integration of a GoPro into data collection for a qualitative study of everyday-life information practices. The presentation details the walking tour method into which the camera has been integrated, as well as the technical and ethical considerations involved in implementation.

KEYWORDS

Wearable technology, qualitative research, data collection, everyday life, embodiment, information behaviour.

INTRODUCTION

This visual presentation reports on the integration of a wearable camera into a qualitative study of people's everyday-life information practices. The information science literature shows growing interest in wearable technologies (Adapa, Nah, Hall, Siau, & Smith, 2018). The category of "wearables" includes a variety of devices, and for most people, it brings to mind fitness trackers such as the FitBit and smart watches such as the Apple Watch. The data that wearables collect about human practices are primarily quantitative, such as geolocation data, and there are numerous potential research directions relating to these data. At the same time, as interest in topics such as embodiment and everyday life continues to expand, wearables can be investigated for their potential contribution to qualitative data collection and provision of distinctive insights into information practices.

This visual presentation examines one wearable technology, the GoPro camera, within the context of an ongoing study. It describes the walking tour technique into which the camera has been integrated, as well as the technical and ethical considerations involved in implementation. This presentation also offers attendees an opportunity to see GoPro data for themselves.

BACKGROUND

In information science, wearable video cameras appear to have played a data collection role in one previous study, an ethnographic exploration of academic library wayfinding (Kinsley, Schoonover, & Spitler, 2016). Wearables have been more substantially examined from two other angles: technology adoption (e.g., Adapa, Nah, Hall, Siau, & Smith, 2018), and health information sharing and privacy (e.g., Banerjee, Hemphill, & Longstreet, 2018). Emerging information science research areas relating to the present study, such as embodiment, have been studied from predominately qualitative and theoretical perspectives, such as semi-structured interviews within a constructivist grounded theory approach (Lloyd, 2007), ethnographic observation framed by critical discourse analysis (Olsson, 2016), and phenomenologically-informed self-observation (Gorichanaz, 2017). Embodiment has been theorized in relation to technology (Keilty, 2016). The present study distinctively and intentionally incorporates a wearable camera, along with its material and theoretical affordances, into empirical procedure.

METHOD

The study reported in this presentation concerns people's everyday food-related information practices. Using data collection techniques drawn from sensory ethnography (Pink, 2015), paired with a constructivist grounded theory approach to analysis (Charmaz, 2014), this exploratory study asks how a diverse sampling of people use information within the daily process of feeding themselves and their families. The study will include approximately 24 participants, with half recruited in a large Canadian city and half recruited in a rural community on the Canadian prairies. The study focuses particularly on how people's bodies are informative and involved in food-related information practices.

One of the data collection methods in the study is a video tour in which each participant shows the researcher a food-related place of their choosing. Examples of places chosen by participants include a kitchen, a backyard garden, and a community-supported farm. Each participant leads their video tour, and unstructured conversation ensues throughout. The researcher wears a GoPro camera to create a "video trace" of the tour, focusing on the participant's actions, gestures, and expressions (Sumartojo & Pink, 2017). Video tours capture participants' dynamic physicality, including gestures, movement, and sensory moments. Such tours invoke "not only the visual or verbal knowledge that might be produced through interviews or observations, but also [...] a route into the more complex multisensorality of the experiences, activities, and events we might be investigating"

(Pink, 2015, p. 125). That is, video tours capture verbal and text-based data, and they simultaneously capture people's interactions with their surroundings. In this way, like other "mobile methods" (Evans & Jones, 2011; Kusenbach, 2003; Sheller & Urry, 2006), video tours create opportunities to observe embodied experiences, while also enabling observation of how people move in relation to their intentional statements and actions. The video tours, along with the semi-structured interviews that precede the tours, are undergoing constructivist grounded theory analysis using the software NVIVO.

TECHNICAL AND ETHICAL CONSIDERATIONS

This presentation will detail the technical complexities surrounding the use of GoPro. For example, sound quality is a relatively low priority for most GoPro uses, and the camera's onboard microphone is generally inadequate for data collection. This necessitates the use of lavalier microphones and double-system recording in to ensure highly audible video data. Ethical considerations will also be emphasized. These include the nuances of ethics board review for a study involving video in public and private places, as well as the complexities around anonymization and informed consent.

VISUAL PRESENTATION

This presentation features a poster communicating contextual and background information, and a looping video sharing vivid examples of GoPro data from the present study. The video will be available to attendees on a laptop with headphones.

CONCLUSION

This presentation speaks to the conference theme in several ways. It describes an opportunity afforded by a recent technology to creatively enrich qualitative data collection and analysis. At the same time, by emphasizing the considerations around integrating a GoPro into data collection, this presentation highlights the careful work required to use wearable video in a person-centred and ethical way.

ACKNOWLEDGMENTS

Thank you to the anonymous reviewers for your constructive comments. This study is supported by Swinburne University of Technology, the University of Alberta, and the Social Sciences and Humanities Research Council of Canada.

REFERENCES

Adapa, A., Nah, F. F., Hall, R. H., Siau, K., & Smith, S. N. (2018). Factors influencing the adoption of smart wearable devices. *International Journal of Human-Computer Interaction, 34*(5), 399-409. doi:1080/10447318.2017.1

Banerjee, S., Hemphill, T., & Longstreet, P. (2018). Wearable devices and healthcare: Data sharing and privacy. *Information Society, 34*(1), 49-57. doi:10.1080/01972243.2017.1

Charmaz, K. (2014). *Constructing grounded theory.* 2nd ed. London: SAGE.

Evans, J., & Jones, P. (2011). The walking interview: Methodology, mobility and place. *Applied Geography, 31,* 849-858.

Gorichanaz, T. (2017). Auto-hermeneutics: A phenomenological approach to information experience. *Library & Information Science Research*, *39*(1), 1–7. doi:10.1016/j.lisr.2017.01.001

Keilty, P. (2016). Embodied engagements with online pornography. *The Information Society*, *32*(1), 64–73. doi:10.1080/01972243.2015.1107162

Kinsley, K. M., Schoonover, D., & Spitler, J. (2016). GoPro as an ethnographic tool: A wayfinding study in an academic library. *Journal of Access Services, 13*(1), 7-23. doi:10.1080/15367967.2016.1

Kusenbach, M. (2003). Street phenomenology the go-along as ethnographic research tool. *Ethnography*, *4*(3), 455–485.

Lloyd, A. (2007). Learning to put out the Red Stuff: Becoming information literate through discursive practice. *The Library Quarterly*, *77*(2), 181–198. doi:10.1086/517844

Olsson, M. (2016). Making sense of the past: The embodied information practices of field archaeologists. *Journal of Information Science*, *42*(3), 410–419. doi:10.1177/0165551515621839

Pink, S. (2015). *Doing sensory ethnography* (2nd ed.). Los Angeles: SAGE.

Sheller, M., & Urry, J. (2006). The new mobilities paradigm. *Environment and Planning A*, *38*(2), 207–226. doi:10.1068/a37268

Sumartojo, S., & Pink, S. (2017). Empathetic visuality: GoPros and the video trace. In E. Gómez-Cruz, S. Sumartojo, & S. Pink (Eds.), *Refiguring techniques in digital video research* (pp. 39-50). Cham: Springer Nature.

Improving Corpus Reproducibility through Modular Text Transformations and Connected Data Set

Jonathan Pulliza
Rutgers University, USA. jonathan.pulliza@rutgers.edu

Chirag Shah
Rutgers University, USA. chirags@rutgers.edu

ABSTRACT

The Enron Email Corpus is one of the most utilized collections of documents in Natural Language Processing, Machine Learning, and Network Analysis. Different groups of researchers have transformed the corpus, changing the content and format to meet their needs. The many distinct versions can all claim to be the Enron Email Corpus, though they are as distinct from the original publicly available collection as they are from each other. Researchers then have to determine the usefulness of a particular version in comparison to the many others available, as well as ascertain what has been done to the collection and how it would affect their specific research goal. This is especially important for reproducing a particular research method onto a different corpus, as transposing a method necessitates a deep understanding of the original data in the experiment. This project models the various transformations performed on different versions of the collection to form a network of connected datasets, highlighting the most important nodes as well as the most common transformations. Traversing different paths between nodes offers the community a way to model and reproduce the necessary data work performed on one collection that can be transposed onto other collections.

KEYWORDS

Reproducible Research, Data Citation, Email, Network Analysis, Enron e-mail dataset, Data Reuse

INTRODUCTION

Reproducibility and replication have been key topics in producing high-quality scientific research, with many organizations setting recommendations and standards for researchers to follow. Peng (2011) set out some common recommendations to address replication specifically concerning data analysis and large datasets, recommending researchers make available all of the code and data used in their work. Making the data public does not necessarily ensure reproducibility in the future, as proprietary data standards may become obsolete and websites hosting the data may be taken down. This has been an issue for the Enron Email Corpus, as over time different organizations have claimed stewardship and have hosted the collection on the web. The current publicly available collection that most closely resembles the original data set provided by the Federal Energy Regulation Commission (FERC) is hosted by Cohen at Carnegie Mellon University. But as Melorose et al. (2005) state "[t]here is not the Enron email corpus available, but multiple instances of it." (Melorose et al., 2005, p. 4). The differences in both format and content between versions of the corpus can be dramatic, but exactly how those differences came to be may be difficult to ascertain without understanding all of the different versions that came before. Researchers hoping to compare results against some of the Enron work may have difficulty in designing apples-to-apples comparisons, as testing on different versions of the corpus may result in different outcomes. Improving data citation practices as discussed by Silvello (2018) can alleviate some of the ambiguity concerning which data set was used in a particular work, but it does not explain the relations between the data sets and the potential usefulness of one over another. This project maps out the various versions of the Enron Email Corpus as a network of datasets, with their connections consisting of the text transformations and larger routines the researchers used, thus facilitating easier replication of previous work and transposing of methods onto other collections.

METHOD

This study drew from previous work by Zhao, Yan, and Li (2018), where they examined references to data sets and data attributions in a sample of publications and then used content analysis to generate a coding scheme for comparison across disciplines. In this case, a sampling of the literature utilizing the Enron Email Corpus was first taken by collecting the top fifty cited works as compiled by Google Scholar referencing the paper "Introducing the Enron Corpus" by Klimt and Yang. This project does not rely on just tracing citations, but on recording the actual datasets used in each experiment as mentioned in the methodology section of each work. These datasets were recorded along with any necessary transformations researchers made to the collection to produce their version of the corpus. If a dataset was used in a paper but did not have its respective underlying paper in the sampled works, then that paper was added to the sample and processed as well. The transformations were then grouped by common terms and functions, such as parsing, removing, and replacing. Finally, each dataset is labeled by its original source dataset and the transformations implemented to compile its particular version, resulting in a network of datasets.

FINDINGS

The repository managed by Cohen plays a key role in facilitating research around the dataset, but because it takes the form of a collection of text files many researchers utilize other versions that may be more convenient for their needs, such as the SQL database version made available by Shetty and Adibi (2004). A large portion of the differences in the data made available between versions is determined by what the researchers consider valid content, and this can have a large impact on the characteristics of the collection. Cohen has a policy of redacting any email that is requested to be removed by an Enron employee, so that repository is not static. A few researchers filter out what they believed to be duplicate content, whether that is removing quoted text from emails that were replies or forwards, or using a file comparison algorithm like Mccallum and Wang (2005), which resulted in filtering out almost half of all emails. Klimt and Yang (2004b) choose to completely remove any email outside of the "@enron.com" domain, which may have been appropriate for their particular work but is likely to be problematic for other studies. Decisions around research relevance also affect the actual textual content of each document, such as replacing certain strings within the emails or metadata. Some researchers also choose to append outside data into their versions, including additional employee metadata provided by FERC and manual annotations of email content. A simplified portion of the data version network can be seen in Figure 1, including a subset of the text transformations recorded in the study.

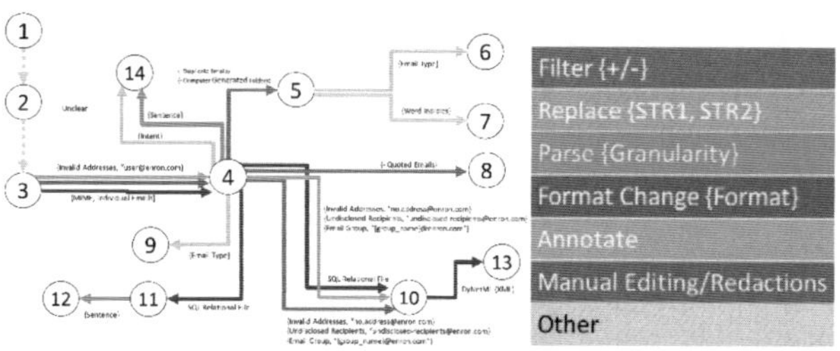

Figure 1. Simplified data network of the Enron Email Corpus.

DEMONSTRATION

The research will be presented as a poster, including a map of the full network formed by the various Enron Email Corpus versions connected by transformations and routines. There will also be a portion illustrating the transposing of various routes along the network onto another email corpus, illustrating the utility of this approach when replicating a study.

REFERENCES

Klimt, B., & Yang, Y. (2004a). Introducing the Enron Corpus. Machine Learning, stitutep1, wwceasccaers2004168. Retrieved from http://scholar.google.com/scholar?hl=en&btnG=Search&q=intitle:Introducing+the+Enron+Corpus#0

Klimt, B., & Yang, Y. (2004b). The enron corpus: A new dataset for email classification research. In European Conference on Machine Learning (pp. 217–226).

Mccallum, A., & Wang, X. (2005). The author-recipient-topic model for topic and role discovery in social networks, with application to Enron and academic email. In Workshop on Link Analysis, Counterterrorism and Security (pp. 33–44).

Melorose, J., Perroy, R., Careas, S., Diesner, J., & Carley, K. M. (2005). Exploration of communication networks from the Enron email corpus. In SIAM International Conference on Data Mining: Workshop on Link Analysis, Counterterrorism and Security, Newport Beach, CA (Vol. 1, pp. 1–12). http://doi.org/10.1017/CBO9781107415324.004

Peng, R. D. (2011). Reproducible research in computational science. Science (New York, N.Y.), 334(6060), 1226–7. http://doi.org/10.1126/science.1213847

Shetty, J., & Adibi, J. (2004). The Enron Email Dataset - Database Schema and Brief Statistical Report. Information Sciences Institute Technical Report. Retrieved from http://www.isi.edu/~adibi/Enron/Enron_Dataset_Report.pdf

Silvello, G. (2018). Theory and practice of data citation. Journal of the Association for Information Science and Technology, 69(1), 6–20. http://doi.org/10.1002/asi.23917

Zhao, M., Yan, E., & Li, K. (2018). Data set mentions and citations: A content analysis of full-text publications. Journal of the Association for Information Science and Technology, 69(1), 32–46. http://doi.org/10.1002/asi.23919

A Model for Analyzing and Understanding How Novice Researchers Construct Source Authority

James Rosenzweig
Eastern Washington University, USA. jrosenzweig@ewu.edu

Frank Lambert
Middle Tennessee State University,USA. frank.lambert@mtsu.edu

Mary Thill
Northeastern Illinois University, USA. m-thill@neiu.edul

ABSTRACT

This bibliometric pilot study presents a modified assessment taxonomy devised originally by Leeder, Markey, and Yakel (2012) and demonstrates how to apply it to assess the resources used in the construction of student academic research papers. Besides discussing this assessment tool, we present empirical data of its application, the result of a pilot study conducted at a medium sized Midwestern American university, based on the analysis of a sample of papers written for a freshman level English composition class. Our findings, among many, demonstrate that just one in 700 academic resources cited in these papers comes from a resource like Wikipedia, and that 52% of resources cited in student papers fall into the five taxonomic category combinations. Besides being used for assessment, this taxonomy may reveal models of information usage in future research.

KEYWORDS

Information literacy, faceted taxonomy, coding, citation analysis.

INTRODUCTION

During the 2016 election season, myriad fraudulent and sensational news stories circulated through a variety of social media outlets in the United Kingdom and the United States. Information literacy, usually confined to the realm of educators, and of librarians especially, became an issue of greater public concern. Just as information literacy and fake news were having their "moment" in popular culture, the research team was evaluating a random sample of 60 final research papers (n=180) collected from students of English 102 as part of a larger research project during spring 2014. Our analysis focused on two main data points: the *citations* (n=2059) contained within the body of the sample papers' text; and the *references* (n=692) contained within the papers' bibliographies. The research team employed the 2015 *ACRL Framework for Information Literacy for Higher Education* to ground its analysis. The *Framework* contains six core ideas that help novice researchers to make sense of the current "uncertain information ecosystem." The first frame, which focuses on the constructed and contextual nature of authority, led us to our central research question: How do students in an English composition class think about authority, and how are their ideas of authority evident in the sources they cite?

The research team performed a broad review of the literature to identify a suitable method for analyzing the authority of student sources, settling eventually on Leeder, Markey, and Yakel's faceted taxonomy (2012). Their taxonomy is a "format neutral" rating system that eliminates artificial distinctions between print and online resources. It provides coders with a method to describe today's complicated scholarly and non-scholarly information landscape with greater precision.

METHODOLOGY

For this pilot study, 180 papers written by students of a sophomore English composition class held at a large Midwestern American public university were collected by the researchers. All papers were anonymized prior to scanning and conversion into Adobe .pdf format to allow for easier analysis amongst the three researchers. Cumulative GPA, age, gender, and race/ethnicity were recorded to reflect basic demographic attributes of the student authors of these papers. A randomly selected sample of 60 scoreable papers (papers of sufficient quality in terms of the quality of the bibliography and the citations in the papers' text) ordered alphabetically by student surname was used for data analysis.

The instrument used to code bibliographies was adapted from Leeder, Markey, and Yakel's taxonomy (Tables 1, 2, and 3, see appendix). Two facets were omitted from the original taxonomy to focus on the areas tied most closely to authority as expressed in the Framework. The three remaining facets we used to analyze the students' citation data were: Author Identity, Editorial Process, and Publication Purpose. To categorize the three facets, two members of the research team researched independently the authors and publishers of each of the 692 sources in the sample student bibliographies using commonly available online and library tools such as the Internet Archive's Wayback Machine, LinkedIn, and Ulrich's Periodicals Directory. The researchers counted the number of times each source was referenced in the body of the respective paper to gauge student confidence in that respective source. To validate the coding of the three facets, the third research team member coded a sample of the original sample by recording similarly the respective facets for each reference in the paper's bibliography, recording the number of times each reference was cited in the paper, and recording whether or not the reference source was used for the purpose of referring to statistics of some sort. We used Krippendorf's *alpha* to measure the degree of agreement between the original two coders' efforts and that of the third coder. In all cases, $a > 0.70$, the accepted cut-off for rate of agreement between coders (Hayes and Krippendorf, 2007). However, different facets had higher rates of agreement. E.g., facet 3 $a = 0.8195$, facet 4 $a = 0.7152$, and facet 5 $a = 0.7336$. This variance indicates there may be future challenges to coding bibliographies using the current facet coding scheme we have designed thus necessitating further changes with the codes' scope notes and possibly providing additional training to other coders.

FINDINGS

The students whose papers were chosen randomly for analysis displayed the following demographic attributes. The majority of student authors were female (*n*=35, 58.3%). All students in the sample had an average age of 20.75 and were widely distributed (*sd*=3.616) with a heavy positive skew, indicating some more mature students were enrolled in this class. In fact, 20% of the students included in our sample were 22 years and older (ages ranged from 22 to 42), while the remaining 80% students were aged 18-21, inclusive. In terms of where these students were in their respective programs of study, 61.6% were freshmen, 35% sophomores, and 0.017% was each juniors and seniors. These same students had an average cumulative GPA of 2.9633 (*sd*=.65511).

Turning to attributes associated with the actual English composition papers that were analyzed by the research team, the mode or most frequently occurring subfacets for Facets 3, 4, and 5 were 3F (Academic Professional- A person with a Master's or Doctoral degree in the area being written about, which they held at the time the content was published), 4E (Editor and Editorial Staff-Professionally reviewed and approved by editor/editorial staff), and 5B (Commercial-Material is published for commercial gain), respectively. Corresponding code interpretations of the subfacet labels are provided in appendices 1, 2, and 3 following this article's text. There were a total of 70 combinations of the three combined subfacets (e.g., *3x4x5x*) coded in our data out of a theoretical 343 possible combinations ($n=7^3$). The references we analyzed in our sample of the English composition class we describe above used the subfacet combination (in terms of *in-text citations*) of '3F4F5F' most frequently. The subfacet combination '3F4E5B' appeared most commonly in the English composition papers' bibliographies as *references*. Tables 1 and 2 show the top 10 most frequently *cited* subfacet combinations and most frequent subfacet combination *references*, respectively. As the tables demonstrate, only five source *types*, as distinguished and defined by the subfacet combination, out of a possible 343 subfacet combinations account for at least 50% of the sources used in terms of being *cited* and consequently *referenced* in the papers' bibliographies. Thus the students in this English composition class relied most heavily on five types of sources in their references and use them with varying degrees of frequency as exemplified by the number of times these sources are cited within the body of the their papers.

Subfacet Combination	Frequency	Percent	Cumulative Percent
3F4F5F	383	18.6	18.6
3E4E5B	312	15.2	33.8
3C4A5C	134	6.5	40.3
3C4A5B	117	5.7	45.9
3C4E5B	116	5.6	51.6
3B4E5B	110	5.3	56.9
3C4A5E	89	4.3	61.2
3F4E5F	82	4.0	65.2
3F4E5B	65	3.2	68.4
3B4D5B	47	2.3	70.7

Table 1. The top 10 most frequently cited subfacet combinations

Subfacet Combination	Frequency	Percent	Cumulative Percent
3E4E5B	111	16.0	16.0
3F4F5F	109	15.8	31.8
3C4A5C	47	6.8	38.6
3C4A5B	43	6.2	44.8
3C4A5E	37	5.3	50.1
3C4E5B	32	4.6	54.8
3F4E5F	30	4.3	59.1
3B4E5B	29	4.2	63.3
3F4E5B	23	3.3	66.6
3C4E5C	15	2.2	68.8

Table 2. The top 10 most frequent subfacet combination references (as found in bibliographies)

CONCLUSION

The taxonomy excelled in providing a method for analyzing the non-scholarly sources that constituted more than two-thirds of student references and citations, as well as revealing complexity in the ways traditional journalistic and scholarly sources establish their authority (e.g., in their employment of laymen as authors). The study clarified that student responses to today's complicated landscape of sources are remarkably consistent. There are no significant patterns of source usage that can be statistically associated with better papers (as represented by the grade the paper received). Students use the sources they use, in the same general proportions, regardless of their demographic or academic background. This challenges us to engage with our students in a more authentic fashion.

REFERENCES

ACRL (2015). *Framework for information literacy for higher education*. Retrieved from http://www.ala.org/acrl/standards/ilframework on July 2, 2017.

Hayes, A.F. & Krippendorff, K. (2007). Answering the call for a standard reliability measure for coding data, Communication Methods and Measures, 1(1), 77-89.

Leeder, C., Markey, K., & Yakel, E. (2012). A faceted taxonomy for rating student bibliographies in an online information literacy game. *College and Research Libraries*, 73, (2), 115-133.

APPENDIX

App. 1. Author Identity Facet

Author Identity Category	Brief Description
3A: Unknown Authorship	No identification is possible.
3B: Layman	A person without demonstrated expertise in the area being written about
3C: Corporate Authorship	No single author identified on a work issued by an organization
3D: Professional Amateur	A person with a degree in another field, but demonstrating interest, dedication, and experience in the area being written about
3E: Applied Professional	A person with relevant experience, training or credentials relevant to the area being written about (i.e., journalist with journalism degree OR substantive professional experience)
3Z: Source Unknown	No information on the category could be found

App. 2. Editorial Process Facet

Editorial Process Category	Brief Description
4A: Self-Published	Material made public directly by the author
4B: Vanity Press	Material the author paid to publish, generally as self-promotion
4C: Collaborative Editing	Material that is reviewed or edited by multiple possibly anonymous collaborators
4D: Moderated Submissions	Contributed content that has been accepted or approved by someone other than the author
4E: Editor and Editorial Staff	Professionally reviewed and approved by editor/editorial staff
4F: Peer Reviewed	Evaluated by members of the scholarly community before acceptance and publication
4Z: Source Unknown	No information on the category could be found

App. 3. Publication Purpose Facet

Publication Purpose Category	Brief Description
5A: Personal	Material is published without commercial aims
5B: Commercial	Material is published for commercial gain
5C: Non-Profit	Material is published by a non-profit organization
5D: K-12 Education	Material is published for educational purposes
5E: Government	Material is published by the government
5F: Higher Education	Material is published for an academic audience
5Z: Source Unknown	No information on the category could be found

Information Porter: A Study on Intangible Cultural Heritage Databases of Provincial Public Libraries in China

Chen Runhao
Sun Yat-Sen University, China. chenrhao@mail2.sysu.edu.cn

ABSTRACT
Interest in intangible cultural heritage (ICH) from UNESCO and other groups has grown in recent years, precipitating the need for greater attention to digital ICH and ICH databases in this area. This research aims to measures the ICH databases, and to explore the role of public libraries in the protection of ICH. [Methodology] According to accessing the websites of 31 provincial public libraries in China, the study collects and analyses the names, copyright, metadata of the ICH databases. [Finding] The research finds that more than 60% provincial public libraries have ICH database, and there are three kinds of ICH database's name, the copyright of databases belongs to provincial public libraries, the National Cultural Information Resources Sharing Project, and Superstar Co., Ltd. The metadata used by each database is not uniform. [Conclusion] Those databases are still in the record stage, mainly for publicity and display ICH projects, can't reaching the goal of digital inheritance. The lack of national uniform standards also leads to disunity of naming and metadata on databases. Libraries just play the role of information porters without more innovations.

KEYWORDS
Intangible cultural heritage, database, digital, community, public library.

INTRODUCTION
Interest in intangible cultural heritage (ICH) from UNESCO and other groups has grown in recent years, precipitating the need for greater attention to digital ICH in this area. At the 10th anniversary of the promulgation of *the Convention for the Safeguarding of Intangible Cultural Heritage* (*Safeguarding*) in 2013, Chengdu China held the Fourth International Intangible Cultural Heritage Festival, the theme was "Everyone is a cultural inheritor". The emergence of this theme is not only a response to the *Safeguarding*, but also a reflection on the development of theory and practice of ICH in China. The public library, as the soul of the community, undoubtedly becomes an important cultural institution for the protection and of ICH, and is endowed with records, propaganda and display. In the wake of development in digital ICH, more and more public libraries try to build the ICH database. What kind of role does library play in the protection of ICH? Can the database interpret the community principles of the *Safeguarding*? The research tries to answer these questions.

METHODOLOGY
From January 10 to 20, 2018, the author investigated 31 provincial public libraries in mainland China through the way of website investigation, to know whether these libraries have ICH database, and to collect the name, copyright, metadata of the ICH databases. And there are 25 ICH databases built by 19 provincial public libraries, 22 is open access, 3 is just for users inside the libraries.

FINDINGS & DISCUSSION
Names
In the 25 ICH databases, there are three kinds of names: ICH database of a province(N=18), culture/memory of a province(N=4), database directly named by an ICH project (N=3). Firstly, the ICH database of a province is the way to name the database directly following the Chinese National Academy of Art, on this basis, it can just add the name of provinces such as ICH databases of Hunan provincial. Secondly, the use of culture/memory of a province maybe influenced by the National Library of China' China Memory project, such as Fujian Province Cultural Memory. These two types of databases are more abundant, contain various categories of ICH resources, the system of ICH is more complete. On the other hand, there are some databases directly named by an ICH project, such as Tibetan Thangka database of Sichuan Library, Mianzhu New Year Paintings database and so on. This type of databases has only one ICH project, the resources of those database are just around this project, and all of the projects come from the National ICH Representative Directory.

Copyright
According to the copyright information that can be found at the bottom of the ICH database page, the databases belong to different organizations, including provincial public libraries(N=11), the National Cultural Information Resources Sharing Project(N=10), and Superstar Co., Ltd(N=1). The first two are more common. As for the first type, the libraries own the ownership of the database, it means that this database built by the library, and the main source of the information is the library collection. As for the second one, the library only provides links to the database, the National Cultural Information Resources Sharing Project is responsible for the construction, design and maintenance of ICH database. The last one is that library commissioned commercial companies to build the ICH databases, for example, the ICH database of Henan provincial library is constructed by Superstar Co., Ltd, the library only provides links, the ownership belongs to Superstar Co., Ltd.

Metadata

Research finds that core metadata commonly used in ICH databases includes title, date, description, type, format, relation, coverage, it is different from the seven basic elements of Dublin Core, which includes title, publisher, format, type, identifier, date, subject. The metadata settings in the ICH database are directly related to the National ICH Representative Directory, the library can extract the corresponding content of each metadata directly from the project application. On the other hand, even the same metadata has different representation, for example, many databases express description as overview, text, introduction, summary and so on, which will undoubtedly lead to difficulties in data sharing and interoperability. Although the Ministry of Culture and Tourism of China published the *Professional Standard for Digital Protection of Intangible Cultural Heritage(draft)*, and this standard stipulates 17 core metadata, due to not officially released, few libraries follow it.

CONCLUSIONS

This research shows the ICH databases of provincial public library in China, in the process of the construction of the ICH database, the main role of the library is concentrated in two aspects: one is to provide the digital communication platform for the ICH projects, another is to assist the organization of a large number of existing ICH resources. But those ICH databases are still in the record stage, mainly for publicity and display of ICH projects, can't reaching the goal of digital inheritance. The lack of national uniform standards also leads to disunity of naming and metadata on databases. At this stage, libraries play the role as an information porter, most of the libraries only put the information from the National ICH Representative Directory into the database without more innovations, this approach embodies the will of the State rather than the community, under this mode, it is hard to hear the voice of community and inheritor of ICH.

81st Annual Meeting of the Association for Information Science & Technology | Vancouver, Canada | 10 – 14 November 2018

Text Data Mining Beyond the Open Data Paradigm: Perspectives at the intersection of Intellectual Property and Ethics

Megan Senseney
University of Illinois at Urbana-Champaign, USA.
mfsense2@illinois.edu

Eleanor Dickson Koehl
University of Illinois at Urbana-Champaign, USA.
dicksone@illinois.edu

ABSTRACT

This poster highlights outcomes from an IMLS-funded National Forum project on text data mining with content that is subject to use conditions due to intellectual property rights. It argues that developing strong frameworks for conducting text mining with IP-limited data is an urgent priority for supporting responsible, sustainable research in the twenty-first century.

KEYWORDS

Text data mining, intellectual property, ethics.

INTRODUCTION

Copyright law and resource licensing complicate research with text data (Brook, Murray-Rust, & Oppenheim, 2014). Within the context of text data mining, researchers often use, or wish to use, web-based content, news media, scholarly journal articles, or large collections of digitized books. To work with these data, scholars must interpret the terms of use for publicly available content, negotiate with content providers for access through formal licensing, and operate within an ambiguous fair use framework for material that are in copyright. As authors in their own right, scholars must also make a series of complicated choices regarding the terms under which they publish and make available their own scholarship in an environment where it may also be treated as data for analysis. The existing legal and socio-technical landscape gives rise to ethically complicated situations: researchers want to use text data but lack clarity on which uses are permissible; authors want to mine journal content but may not engage in publishing practices that make their own work mineable; universities want to benefit from the use of altmetrics but, in doing so, risk compromising and commodifying scholarly production. Navigating the contours of intellectual property for text data mining raises a host of ethical concerns for scholars, both as producers and consumers. This poster articulates the ethical dimensions of text data mining in the United States with content that is anything but open.

BACKGROUND

Addressing the complicated set of intellectual property issues surrounding text data mining requires a socio-technical perspective that draws on expertise from a range of stakeholders. To map the landscape and facilitate collaborative action, a team of scholars from the University of Illinois hosted an IMLS-funded National Forum in April 2018.[1] Twenty-five leading figures selected from among researchers who use TDM techniques, librarians, legal experts, content providers, and representatives of scholarly and professional societies converged in Chicago to establish a shared understanding of issues encountered across the stakeholder groups, assess strategies and recommendations for action, and make commitments for future work. While the focus of the event was on legal and logistical strategies for working with these data, attendees were quick to assert that intellectual property issues are deeply entwined with research ethics. This poster discusses the ethical implications that emerged from the National Forum project and argues that developing strong frameworks for conducting text mining with IP-limited data is an urgent priority for conducting responsible, sustainable scholarship in the twenty-first century.

DATA AND METHOD

In advance of the National Forum, project members undertook a two-part research initiative: a literature review and a set of semi-structured interviews with participating stakeholders. Potential stakeholders were identified through the literature review and subsequent snowball sampling. Each participant agreed to prepare a forum statement and an analysis of Strengths, Weaknesses, Opportunities, and Threats (SWOT) prior to the event. Interview protocols were designed to assist participants in preparing their materials, while also providing an opportunity to speak extemporaneously and confidentially with the project team

[1] Project information along with a copy of the pre-forum discussion paper and participants' statements and SWOT analyses are available at https://publish.illinois.edu/limitedaccess-tdm/

during the early phase of the project. Upon completion of all interviews, the project team reviewed notes and interview transcripts for prominent themes and then coded each interview using a set of 26 thematic codes divided into six categories. Using the codebook, the team conducted a conventional qualitative content analysis of the transcribed interviews to identify key topics and establish cross-cutting themes and tensions identified by participants from across different stakeholder communities (Hsieh & Shannon, 2005). The findings reported below combine initial analysis with data drawn from a further round of selective coding on initial interview transcripts, SWOT analyses, and forum notes for ethics as a sensitizing concept.

FINDINGS

Participants raised ethical concerns at two levels within the academic ecosystem: the individual and the institutional. At the individual level, several participants remarked on scholars' research practices in the face of ambiguity. One participant proposed a black hat, gray hat, and white hat model for understanding users' assumptions about access and use where "gray hat" practice operates "in a space where legal and ethical compliance is uncertain." Another participant remarked that in the face of uncertainty, "some researchers do not admit to TDM or are unwilling to share their projects because of fear of being sued, leading to difficulty in reproducibility." At the institutional level, participants emphasized the need for university administrators to pay greater attention to library licensing, data governance, and intellectual privacy. Participants were at odds over whether model licenses for TDM were beneficial in providing much-needed clarity to allowable data access and use or detrimental in their tendency to restrict activities that constitute fair use. Reversing a conversation about TDM practice where researchers are situated as data consumers, one participant also advocated for more attention to understanding the role of researchers as data producers, both in terms of the research they produce and the data that are systematically collected as a byproduct of their scholarly activity in the form of altmetrics. From this perspective, universities bear an ethical obligation to develop data governance policies that better protect academic freedom in the face of digital surveillance.

DISCUSSION

Researchers who wish to utilize text data mining methods experience a chilling effect on the scholarship when faced with legal and ethical ambiguity. For those who aren't deterred entirely, maintaining the quality and validity of a research project is an uphill battle as scholars are faced with compromising on corpus creation, utilizing black box tools that introduce new levels of technical opacity, and communicating research with underspecified "snippets" and derivative data. To conduct TDM confidently and ethically, several scholars who participated in the National Forum expressed interest in compiling a best practice guide or convening "the text-analytic equivalent of an Institutional Review Board for human subjects research, where it becomes clear when a research project has followed all appropriate guidelines." At the level of local policy, university administrators must re-examine the ways they license content and how they implement data governance policies in light of the text data mining practices of scholars and the vendors who wish to profit from scholarly production. Administrators are responsible for ensuring that academic institutions meet their ethical obligations to protect the privacy and intellectual freedom of individual scholars and to serve as responsible stewards of the scholarly record. The university library is well placed to advocate for policy reform along these lines, as it is bound by a code of professional ethics to protect privacy and confidentiality, navigate the balance between the interests of information users and rights holders, and refrain from advancing private interests at the expense of the institution and its members (American Library Association, 2017).

CONCLUSION

Working with content that falls outside the open data paradigm introduces significant challenges both legal and ethical. In discussing contemporary research practice, nearly every participant at the national forum described text data mining as vital for navigating scholarly literature at scale, recovering undiscovered public knowledge, and formulating new research questions. Yet in the absence of clear institutional policies or disciplinary best practices, scholars are left to operate in a legal and ethical gray zone that stymies groundbreaking research. The current climate hampers research activity and undermines scholarly communication. While research into strategies and recommendations for library administrators is ongoing, this poster aims to foster further discussions within the ASIS&T community about the role libraries ought to play in fostering rather than inhibiting text data mining research through institutional policies, better licensing strategies, and research services that improve research with text data, from corpus creation and analysis to publication and redistribution.

REFERENCES

American Library Association. (2017, May 19). Professional ethics. Retrieved from http://www.ala.org/tools/ethics

Brook, M., Murray-Rust, P., & Oppenheim, C. (2014). The social, political and legal aspects of Text and Data Mining (TDM). *D-Lib Magazine*, *20*(11/12).

Hsieh, H. F., & Shannon, S. E. (2005). Three approaches to qualitative content analysis. *Qualitative health research*, 15(9), 1277-1288.

Computational Social Science Using Topic Modeling: Analyzing Patients' Values Using a Large Hospital Survey

Mariia Shovkun
The University of Texas at Austin, USA,
mshovkun@utexas.edu

Bo Xie
The University of Texas at Austin, USA,
boxie@utexas.edu

Kenneth R. Fleischmann
The University of Texas at Austin, USA,
kfleisch@ischool.utexas.edu

ABSTRACT

In this paper, we explore new approaches for combining manual and automatic content analysis. We compare three approaches to topic modelling: Latent Semantic Analysis (LSA), Latent Dirichlet Allocation (LDA), and Hierarchical Dirichlet Process (HDP). We applied all three approaches to study a corpus of 21,085 free-response answers to questions from the Hospital Consumer Assessment of Healthcare Providers and Systems (HCAHPS) survey. We built topic models using the algorithms. Our preliminary results indicate that LSA and LDA yielded more useful results than HDP. We thematically analyzed the topic models and found similarities and differences in the factors that influenced patients' satisfaction with doctors and nurses.

KEYWORDS

Human Values, HCAHPS, LSA, LDA, HDP.

INTRODUCTION

How can we derive meaning from large open-text collections quickly and at scale? Sentiment analysis has rapidly evolved from an exploratory research area to an established industry. However, the results of sentiment analysis are typically quite thin, focusing on detecting positive or negative sentiment. What are the factors that motivate that sentiment? Human values have been shown to have significant explanatory power for explaining sentiment (Fleischmann, 2014). In this paper, we describe preliminary results from an exploratory study that provides a proof-of-concept for a computational social science approach that combines the approaches of topic modeling from natural language processing and thematic analysis from qualitative research.

BACKGROUND

Topic modeling is commonly used to identify hidden semantic structures in texts. Leading approaches to topic modeling include Latent Semantic Analysis (LSA), Latent Dirichlet Allocation (LDA), and Hierarchical Dirichlet Process (HDP). LSA was one of the earliest approaches for automatically identifying topics within a corpus using semantic structure (Deerwester et al., 1990). In contrast, LDA employs a probabilistic approach using Baysian statistics (Blei et al., 2003). HDP is a nonparametric extension of LDA, building a hierarchy of Dirichlet processes (Teh et al., 2005). Maier et al. (2018) apply topic modeling to computational social science and call for additional research on the generalizability of this approach, a gap this paper attempts to help to fill.

METHODS

The corpus included 21,085 free-response answers to questions collected from patients and family members of patients who had inpatient stays at hospitals managed by the Seton Healthcare Family. Data were collected by Seton using the Hospital Consumer Assessment of Healthcare Providers and Systems (HCAHPS) survey. The data reported in this paper included 13,720 answers to the question, "[Hospital Name] is interested in recognizing excellence. During this hospital stay, was there anything that you feel was outstanding?" and 7,365 answers to the question, "What could have been done to improve (your/your family member's) hospital stay?" To clean the dataset, we removed proper nouns, punctuation, and stop words. We also tokenized and lemmatized the dataset. We also iteratively developed a list of synonyms as a semantic extension of the lemmatization that we performed. We then applied LSA, LDA, and HDP with parameters of 20 topics and 7 words per topic. We performed thematic analysis (Braun & Clarke, 2006) on the resulting topic models, focusing on topics that included the terms "doctor(s)" and/or "nurse(s)," referring to the raw data as needed to provide further context about the topics that emerged from the topic models.

RESULTS

In this section, we report findings from our automatic analysis and from our manual analysis of the automatic analysis results.

Automatic Analysis

We applied all three topic models to the data from the two questions listed above, referred to henceforth as the positive and negative datasets, respectively. For both datasets, LSA and LDA produced semantically-interpretable results. However, HDP frequently returned less relevant words such as misspellings and non-standard contractions and was thus far less useful.

Manual Analysis

We began by thematically analyzing the results of the topic models. To validate the themes and to provide more depth about how the themes arose within the datasets, we manually reviewed answers in both datasets that contained the identified themes. In this paper, we report findings related to the human values that patients associated with doctors and/or nurses. To do this, we identified values that were present in topics that contained the terms doctor(s) and/or nurse(s). We again used a manual targeted review of the raw datasets as a confirmation step to correctly identify the appropriate classification for each value.

For the positive dataset, we identified several values that were associated with both doctors and nurses. *Respect* occurred in relation to both provider groups, especially nurses, and especially in relation to privacy. *Friendliness* was another value associated with positive interactions with hospital staff. *Knowledgeable* was also used in relation to positive interactions with both doctors and nurses. *Informative* was also frequently invoked in relation to positive experiences with both provider groups. *Helpfulness* was also used to describe individuals from both provider groups. In relation to doctors, *communication with nurses* described a positive attribute of successful doctors. For nurses, *responsiveness*, *listening*, and *humor* were all valued.

For the negative dataset, salient values for both provider groups included *uninformative*, *miscommunication between staff members*, and *rudeness*. For doctors, negative values included *unavailability*, referring to difficulty in getting access to doctors, and *lack of involvement with patients*, similarly referring to a lack of involvement in the treatment plans devised by their doctors. For nurses, negative values included *overworked*, referring to the nurses' workload detracting from their job performance, and *disruptiveness*, particularly focusing on overnight disruptions caused by nurses checking on patients.

DISCUSSION

These results provide a proof-of-concept of the utility of this approach for partially automating thematic analysis by using topic modeling. The approach goes beyond previous computational social science studies that have overlaid thematic analysis upon automatically generated dictionaries (e.g., Fleischmann et al., 2015) and provides evidence of the ability to combine big data with the thick description of Geertz (1973) (Bornakke & Due, 2018). The results of this study in terms of values resonate with the findings of field studies of what patients value in hospital care (e.g., Joffe et al., 2003; Morris, 1997).

ACKNOWLEDGMENTS

Thank you to the Seton Healthcare Family-Center for Health and Social Policy (CHASP) Research Partnership for funding this research, to Ryan Leslie and his team at Seton Healthcare Family for providing access to the data, to Byron Wallace for collaborating on the proposal that led to this research, and to Byron Wallace and David Inouye for helping to prepare the dataset.

REFERENCES

Blei, D. M., Ng, A. Y., & Jordan, M. I. (2003). Latent dirichlet allocation. *The Journal of Machine Learning Research*, *3*, 993-1022.

Bornakke, T., & Due, B. L. (2018). Big-thick blending: A method for mixing analytical insights from big and thick data sources. *Big Data & Society*, *5*, 1-16.

Braun, V., & Clarke, V. (2006). Using thematic analysis in psychology. *Qualitative Research in Psychology*, *3*, 77-101.

Deerwester, S., Dumais, S. T., Furnas, G. W., Landauer, T. K., & Harshman, R. (1990). Indexing by latent semantic analysis. *Journal of the American Society for Information Science*, *41*, 391-407.

Fleischmann, K. R. (2014). *Information and human values*. San Rafael, CA: Morgan & Claypool.

Fleischmann, K. R., Takayama, Y., Cheng, A.-S., Tomiura, Y., Oard, D. W., & Ishita, E. (2015). Thematic analysis of words that invoke values in the net neutrality debate. In *iConference 2015 Proceedings*.

Geertz, C. (1977). *The interpretation of cultures*. New York: Basic Books.

Joffe, S., Manoccia, M., Weeks, J. C., & Cleary, P. D. (2003). What do patients value in their hospital care? An empirical perspective on autonomy-centered bioethics. *Journal of Medical Ethics*, *29*, 103-108.

Maier, D., Waldherr, A., Miltner, P., Wiedemann, G., Niekler, A., Keinert, A., ... Adam, S. (2018). Applying LDA topic modeling in communication research: Toward a valid and reliable methodology. *Communication Methods and Measures*.

Morris, N. M. (1997). Respect: Its meaning and measurement as an element of patient care. *Journal of Public Health Policy*, *18*, 133-154.

Teh, Y. W., Jordan, M. I., Beal, M. J., & Blei, D. M. (2006). Hierarchical Dirichlet processes. *Journal of the American Statistical Association*, *101*, 1566-1581.

Tracing Social Question and Answer Users' Interaction Patterns

Sei-Ching Joanna Sin
Nanyang Technological University, Singapore.
joanna.sin@ntu.edu.sg

Yin-Leng Theng
Nanyang Technological University, Singapore.
yltheng@ntu.edu.sg

Chei Sian Lee
Nanyang Technological University, Singapore.
leecs@ntu.edu.sg

ABSTRACT

The study analyzed social question and answer (SQA) threads on Stack Overflow to investigate users' interaction patterns within an SQA thread and how these patterns related to the likelihood of receiving an acceptable answer. Robert Bales' Interaction Process Analysis was used to code the data. Analysis of 125 threads (844 posts) showed differences in response time and top interaction sequences. A significant difference was found in IPA.2 (shows tension release), a category in IPA's social- emotional area. This suggests that users' interactions on SQA, including their emotion management, are worth investigating.

KEYWORDS

Social question and answer, user interaction patterns, query outcome, Interaction Process Analysis.

INTRODUCTION

SQA sites have emerged as a notable platform for seeking information and solving information needs collectively, with sites such as Stack Exchange gaining more than 100 million visitors monthly. Despite their popularity and utility, many SQA users still failed to receive satisfactory answers (Chua & Banerjee, 2015). This has prompted considerable research into factors affecting SQA query success. Currently, less is known about how users' interactions within a SQA thread (e.g., sequence and interaction types) vary with query outcomes (Liu & Jansen, 2013; Sin, Lee, & Theng, 2016). This research gap warrants attention, as user interaction is a central characteristic of social media and the value of a process-oriented perspective is recognized in information behavior research (Savolainen, 2006). In light of this research gap, this exploratory study investigated two research questions. **RQ1**: How do users' interactions unfold within a SQA thread? Does query outcome (specifically, receiving an accepted answer) vary with these interaction characteristics? **RQ2**: What are users' interaction types as classified by Bales' Interaction Process Analysis (IPA)? Does query outcome vary with these interaction types?

METHODS

The study analyzed SQA threads (questions plus corresponding answers and comments) from Stack Overflow (SO), a prominent SQA community for programmers. Data were drawn from the official data dump released by the Stack Exchange Network (2018). A total of 125 threads published on the same date (February 1, 2016) were sampled, which provides 2-year worth of comments and answers, yielding 844 posts. Two coders independently coded users' interaction types based on Robert Bales' IPA, which is an established scheme for studying small group interaction. IPA includes 12 interaction categories: (1) shows solidarity; (2) shows tension release; (3) agrees; (4) gives suggestion; (5) gives opinion; (6) gives orientation; (7) asks for orientation; (8) asks for opinion; (9) asks for suggestion; (10) disagrees; (11) shows tension; and (12) shows antagonism (Bales, 1951). The unit of coding is a post. Inter-coder reliability check found 75% to 99% agreements on the coding of the 12 IPA categories. Data analysis, including Wilcoxon rank-sum tests, was conducted using R.

RESULTS

Overall, the 125 questions garnered 178 answers and 541 comments, yielding an average of 1.42 answers and 4.33 comments per thread. On query outcome, 51 threads (40.8%) had an answer accepted by the asker (for brevity, a thread with an accepted answer will be referred to as a *successful thread*; threads without accepted answers will be called *unsuccessful threads*).

RQ1 investigated how users' interactions unfolded. The fastest answer response time was 1 minute. About half of the answers arrived within 36 minutes (median = 0.60 hours). Variations in answer response time were considerable ($M = 7.58$ days; $SD = 37.33$ days; Max = 266.46 days). For comments, the fastest response time was also 1 minute. The median comment response time (1.15 hours) was longer than that for answers. Nevertheless, comment response time was less varied ($M = 2.27$ days; $SD = 16.88$ days; Max = 216.15 days). Figure 1 shows the types and time of posts. Each row represents a thread. Each symbol indicates when an answer or a comment was posted on the thread. Successful threads (top panel) tended to have answers arriving sooner. Notable is that new comments and answers still come in months after a question was posted. This suggests that old questions on SQA can still attract the interest of some users. Wilcoxon rank-sum test, a non-parametric parallel of independent samples t-tests, showed that the mean response time differed by query outcome ($p < 0.01$). Specifically, successful threads received slightly faster responses ($M = 3.25$ days) than unsuccessful threads ($M = 3.87$ days). The most frequent type of interaction sequence for the entire sample was: Question-Answer ($n = 11$, 8.8%), followed by Question-Comment-Comment-Answer (6.4%). The pattern differed by query outcome. Top patterns for successful threads were: Question-Answer (5.88%), Question-Answer-Answer (5.88%), and Question-Answer-Comment (5.88%). For unsuccessful threads, top patterns were: Question-Answer (10.81%) and Question-Comment-Comment-Answer (10.81%). The result indicates that unsuccessful threads were not always the result of a lack of answers.

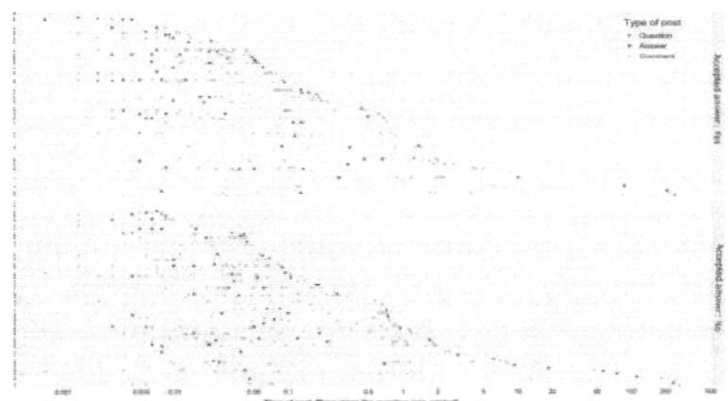

Figure 1. Types and time of posts

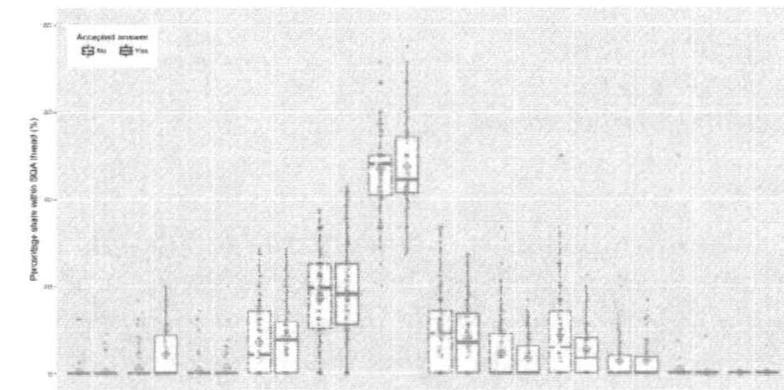

Figure 2. Shares of IPA categories

RQ2 explored the types of interaction based on IPA. Figure 2 shows boxplots of the shares of IPA categories within a thread. IPA.6 (gives orientation) had the highest prevalence (about 47%). Differences between successful and unsuccessful threads were observable in categories such as IPA.2 (shows tension release) and IPA.9 (asks for suggestion). Sample means (diamond symbol in Figure 2) indicated that, compared to unsuccessful threads, successful threads tended to have a higher share of IPA categories 1 to 5 (shows solidarity, shows tension release, agrees, gives suggestion, gives opinion) and interestingly, IPA.10 (disagrees) and IPA.12 (shows antagonism). Successful threads had lower shares of IPA categories 6 to 9 (gives orientation, asks for orientation, asks for opinion, asks for suggestion) and IPA.11 (shows tensions). Wilcoxon rank-sum tests found one difference to be statistically significant. Successful threads had a higher share of tension release (IPA.2, $p < .001$).

DISCUSSION AND IMPLICATIONS

The study found that successful and unsuccessful threads differed in users' interaction patterns including mean response time, top interaction sequences, and IPA interaction categories especially IPA.2. It is interesting that even though SO discourages affect-oriented posts such as expression of thanks and agreement, successful threads still showed a higher share of tensions release (e.g., jokes and showing satisfaction). The implication is that the finding suggests the expression and management of emotion, while not always officially endorsed, is still a notable SQA interaction factor that is worth further investigation. Overall, the findings suggest that users' interaction and IPA interaction types can be a promising area and tool for further research on users' behavior and SQA query success. The current study is on SO, a programming community with a strong focus on factual questions. Further studies may apply IPA to examine SQA communities with different domain interests and social norms. Research on the relationships between IPA interaction types and other SQA query outcomes (e.g., users' evaluation of answer quality and their engagement and satisfaction levels) may also provide new insights.

ACKNOWLEDGMENTS

This work was supported by the MOE Academic Research Fund (RG58/14). We thank Syamsul Ramadhan Bin Awang for his help with data coding.

REFERENCES

Bales, R. F. (1951). Interaction process analysis: A method for the study of small groups. Cambridge: Addison-Wesley Press.

Chua, A. Y. K., & Banerjee, S. (2015). Answers or no answers: Studying question answerability in Stack Overflow. Journal of Information Science, 41(5), 720-731.

Liu, Z., & Jansen, B. J. (2013). Question and answering made interactive: An exploration of interactions in social Q&A.

Proceedings of the 2013 International Conference on Social Intelligence & Technology (pp. 1-10). Los Alamitos: IEEE. Savolainen, R. (2006). Time as a context of information seeking. Library & Information Science Research, 28(1), 110-127.

Sin, S.-C. J., Lee, C. S., & Theng, Y.-L. (2016). Social Q&A question-and-comments interactions and outcomes: A social sequence analysis. In A. Morishima, A. Rauber & C. L. Liew (Eds.), ICADL 2016 (pp. 325-338). Cham: Springer.

Stack Exchange. (2018). Stack Exchange data dump. Retrieved from https://archive.org/details/stackexchange

The Technology Information-Seeking Behaviors of School Librarians

Daniella Smith
University of North Texas, United States.
Daniella.Smith@unt.edu

Michelle Farabough
University of North Texas, United States.
Michelle.Farabough@unt.edu

Barbara Schultz-Jones
University of North Texas, United States.
Barbara.Schultz-Jones@unt.edu

Harshita Parcha
University of North Texas, United States.
HarshitaParcha@my.unt.edu

ABSTRACT
The purpose of this poster is to present the results of a study implemented with 448 school librarians, designed to understand their technology information seeking behaviors. The results indicate that school librarians' primary source of information about technology are school district professional development opportunities. Other popular activities for learning about technology include establishing personal learning communities and attending conferences and events from professional organizations. While most (54.3%) of the participants attended professional development 3 or more times a year, most of them did not survey teachers and students about their technology needs. Just 49.7% of the respondents participated in the technology planning process at their schools. These results are important for understanding how to design degree program and continuing education opportunities that prepare school librarians for their technology implementation responsibilities. QR codes will be embedded in the poster to share additional resources about the school librarian's role in implementing technology in schools.

KEYWORDS
School librarians, information seeking behaviors, K-12 technology implementation, school librarian information literacy.

INTRODUCTION
The U.S. Department of Education (USDOE) National Education Technology Plan (2017) emphasizes the need to ensure that schools are equipped with up-to-date instructional technologies and calls for educators to be prepared to implement them. The USDOE (2016) further asserts that there is a lack of teachers equipped to teach the science, technology, engineering, and mathematics skills that are essential for students to compete in a technology-infused global society. While there is a shortage of educators able to teach STEM subjects, school librarians are prompted by national guidelines and standards to implement technology to teach multiple literacy skills. As such, school librarians participate in a variety of tasks to promote the use of technology and improve the academic achievement of students through the acquisition of technology skills (Wine, 2016).

THE STUDY PURPOSE
Given the importance of technology indicated by the National Technology Education Plan (USDOE, 2017), and the roles of school librarians in implementing technology, this study seeks to understand the technology information seeking behaviors of school librarians. The following research questions were used to implement the study. 1. What types of standards-related information seeking behaviors do school librarians engage in? 2. What sources do school librarians use to seek information about technology? 3. What comments do school librarians have about their technology skills?

THE METHODOLOGY
The participants in this study were 448 school librarians with varying levels of experience. Participants reported having 16 years or more (21%), 11-15 years, (18.1%), 5-10 years (36.6%), 1-4 (21.7%), and less than 1 year of experience (2.7%). Most participants (76.2%) had a degree in librarianship. The majority (44.9%) worked in Pre-Kindergarten or Elementary schools. The others worked in schools with a combination of grade levels (12.5%), high schools (20.3%) and middle schools (22.3%).

A survey with open and close-ended questions was developed with the assistance of practicing school librarians. It was designed to collect information about technology integration behaviors. A subset of the data was used for this report. Participants were invited via email to complete the survey online. SPSS was used for the quantitative analysis. The open-ended questions were coded into themes. The coded responses were discussed by the researchers and discrepancies in coding were resolved.

FINDINGS
Research Question 1: What types of standards-related information seeking behaviors do school librarians engage in?

The survey asked the participants how often they engaged in various information seeking behaviors related to the roles of school librarians discussed in the AASL Standards Framework for Learners (2018). In response, the participants noted their professional development attendance. Most participants specified that they attended professional development four or more times a year (35.5%). The rest chose once a year (22.3%), twice a year (21.9%), three times a year (18.8%), and never (1.6%). Other behaviors relevant to school librarianship roles included in the standards are listed in Table 1.

	Always	Frequently	Rarely	Never
Participate in technology learning communities	15.4%	56.8%	22.8%	4.9%
Participate in the technology planning process	12.4%	37.3%	29.0%	21.1%
Review and share literature about technology trends	15.9%	49.8%	28.3%	6.0%
Survey students about technology training needs	2.5%	20.0%	33.5%	44.0%
Survey teachers about technology training needs	4.7%	21.7%	30.9%	42.7%

Table 1: Technology information seeking behaviors relevant to school librarian standards.

Research Question 2. What sources do school librarians use to seek information about technology?

Next, participants were asked to share their sources for information about new technology in an open-ended question response. A total of 406 participants responded. These sources, their definitions, and response frequencies are shown in Figure 1.

Classroom observations (249)- watching teachers use technology in the classroom
Colleagues (140)- asking co-workers and other librarians for information about technology
Committees (5)- participating on committees that review and implement technology
Conferences and professional organizations (142)- utilizing the professional development and interactions during conferences and professional organization activities to learn about technology
District technologists (11)- asking school district personnel that specialize in technology for assistance
Educational television programs and videos (14)- watching traditional television programs or online videos about technology
Exploration (95)- finding out about technology by seeking information and engaging in independent hands on activities
Family members (7)- discussing new technology with family members such s adult children, spouses, and siblings
Help desks (2)- help services offered by companies to assist with technology
Internet (68)- exploring websites to learn about technology
Professional development (249)- utilizing learning opportunities offered by school districts and webinars to learn about technology
Professional publications (144)- reading journals, articles, and newsletters to learn about technology
Shopping (7)- visiting physical and online stores to view and purchase new technology
Social media (99)- using various social media outlets such as blogs, listservs, Twitter, and Facebook to learn about technology
Teacher and student needs (2)- technology requests from students and teachers or obvious needs for academic achievement
News (8)- announcements of technology via news outlets
University classes (13)- enrolling in classes at an institution of higher education
Querying youth (12)- asking Kindergaten-12th grade students for information about technology
Vendors (3)- information provided by vendors about technology tools that they sell

Figure 1: Source of Technology Information

Research Question 3. What comments do school librarians have about their technology skills?

The participants were invited to provide additional comments about their technology skills. Responses were offered by 147 participants. Of those responses, 124 discussed the librarians' personal assessment of their skill levels. Most of the skill assessment comments (93) were favourable. Many comments (61) addressed barriers to implementing technology, such as time, access to technology, outdated technology, and low budgets.

DISCUSSION AND CONCLUSIONS

The participants' primary method of technology information seeking is professional development through their school districts. This source is frequently not tailored to the specific roles of librarians. Attending conferences and paying for classes can be expensive. Other sources such as searching social media or forming personal learning communities can provide economical opportunities that are tailored for their needs. School librarians could benefit from training to teach them how to develop learning communities and how to utilize social media effectively.

More than half of the participants were not part of the technology planning process. This is an activity that can keep them abreast of changes that will be implemented. Moreover, while many participants were confident in their skills, they still delineated barriers that prevent them from implementing technology. Potential areas for continuing education include overcoming implementation barriers and engaging in the technology planning process. Further research is needed to determine effective methods for overcoming technology implementation barriers and to learn how school librarians view participation in learning communities and the use of social media for professional development.

REFERENCES

American Association of School Librarians. (2018). National school library standards for learners, school librarians, and school libraries. Chicago, IL: ALA Editions.

U.S. Department of Education. (2017). Reimagining the role of technology in education: 2017 National Education Technology Plan Update. Retrieved May 14, 2018 from https://tech.ed.gov/files/2017/01/NETP17.pdf.

U.S. Department of Education. (2016). Science, technology, engineering and math: Education for global leadership. Retrieved May 1, 2018 from https://www.ed.gov/Stem.

Wine, L. D. (2016). School librarians as technology leaders: An evolution in practice. Journal of Education for Library and Information Science, 57(2), 207-220.

Learning Visual Communication: A Preliminary Analysis of HCI/UX Curricula

July Sosebee
Pratt Institute, USA. jsosebee@pratt.edu

Craig M. MacDonald, Ph.D
Pratt Institute, USA. cmacdona@pratt.edu

ABSTRACT

Both the significant impact of visual design on users' perceptions of products and the industry-demand for employees with well-developed visual design skills in the HCI/UX fields has been well-documented. However, the question remains: are HCI/UX graduates prepared to address the visual design challenges they will face in their future careers? To answer this question, we have collected and analyzed program outcomes and titles, descriptions, and syllabi for courses relating to visual design and communication. Currently we have looked at 24 universities in North America that offer graduate-level HCI/UX programs and plan to expand our search to include other countries and undergraduate programs. This visual presentation provides an overview of the current visual design courses being offered to HCI/UX students and introduces a new typology to develop a more comprehensive approach to visual design instruction in this field.

KEYWORDS

Visual design, graphic design, information design, user experience, curriculum

INTRODUCTION

Visual design has become a major part of the Human-Computer Interaction (HCI) and User Experience (UX) fields, but questions remain over the extent to which education programs prepare students in this capacity. To better understand if and how graduates of HCI/UX programs are prepared for the visual components of UX, we collected titles, descriptions, and syllabi (where available) for courses related to graphic design and visual communication and conducted a content analysis of course content to determine how visual design concepts are currently incorporated into the curriculum.

LITERATURE REVIEW

As shown by several studies, aesthetic perceptions and judgements by users can have a major impact on several product attributes. Yamamoto & Lambert demonstrated how aesthetics can have a greater impact on users' product preference over other factors like product performance or cost (1994). Tractinsky, Katz, & Ikar found a strong positive correlation between interface aesthetics and perceived usability of product. Furthermore, they found that aesthetics more strongly predicted the perceived usability, than the actual usability of the product (Tractinsky et al., 2000). Similarly, Han van de Heijden found that perceived visual attractiveness of a website significantly contributes to feelings of usefulness, enjoyment, and ease-of-use (2003). More recently, Porat & Tractinsky demonstrated that perceived aesthetics in combination with usability of webstore interfaces contributes to consumers' pleasure (2012). Thielsch, Blotenberg, & Jaron found that when compared against content and usability, aesthetics had the largest influence on users' first and overall impressions of website interfaces, as well as a significant influence on the intentions to revisit and recommend the website (2014). Additionally, Oyibo and Vassileva showed that not only does aesthetics influence perceived usability, but that it also influences the credibility of a product/interface (2016). The importance of good visual design and having visual design skills has also been discussed at great lengths by UX professionals such as Don Norman. Norman specifically discusses aesthetics in that beautiful things create an initial positive reaction and belief in the user towards the product (Norman, 2004). In their analysis of four Agile teams at two large companies, Da Silva, Silveira, Melo, and Parzianello found that those in UX roles should have design thinking and visual design skills (2013). Jurca, Hellmann, and Maurer also saw that UX roles often contributed to or were in charge of the visual design aspect of product development (2014). As a whole, the literature provides clear evidence of the importance of visual and graphic design in determining a user's experience with a product or service, but to date there have been no studies examining the extent to which these concepts are incorporated into HCI/UX curricula.

METHODS

To address this gap, we began by looking at universities that offered graduate-level HCI/UX programs in North America; we chose this fairly limited scope as a starting point and eventually plan to expand our search to include other countries and undergraduate programs. We found 24 universities in all and then gathered the following information about each: program learning outcomes, required courses, courses related to visual design, and graduation requirements (i.e. thesis, capstone, portfolio, etc.). Courses that were considered as a part of this sample were chosen based on if course descriptions/syllabi included topics relating to visual design theory/practice and were available to students in the HCI/UX program.

An initial content analysis of 15 of the 24 courses was conducted using a combination of list-coding and open-coding. For the list-coding, we utilized the 12 aspects of visual aesthetics that was developed by Moshagen and Thielsch (2010). Open-codes included quotations that did not fit into the 12 aspects of visual design. These quotes often addressed other topics of design, including the design process, skills needed to do visual design, and other types of design such as information or graphic design.

PRELIMINARY FINDINGS

Only 14 of the 24 universities offered visual design courses to their HCI/UX students, and in those 14 universities we found a total of 24 visual design courses. An initial analysis of 15 course descriptions revealed that topics related to "design concepts" (e.g., typography and color) were most frequently observed followed by skills needed to do design work (e.g., design judgment, and software skills), what the design process entails, and applications of design in real-world settings. Focusing on the codes that specifically relate to visual design, within the largest code group (design concepts), the most prominent topic featured in the course descriptions covered visual communication. Some examples that fall under this code include: "principles of effective visual communications", "an overview of the many tools and techniques available to convey an idea, communicate a message and influence an experience," "visual language vocabularies." and "visual communication and design."

FUTURE WORK

Unfortunately, because the 12 aspects of visual design (which we used for our initial coding) were created specifically for website interfaces, they did not map well onto the course descriptions, which often included other elements of visual design that may not be present in website interfaces (example: texture). Therefore, moving forward we have decided to recode all of the courses in terms of the following 10 visual design principles (Torre, 2017): Point, Line, and Shape; Color; Typography; Space; Balance, Rhythm, & Contrast; Scale; Grid & Alignments; Framing; Texture & Patterns; and Visual Concept.

Using these principles of visual design, we hope to identify which areas of visual design are being addressed and which may be underrepresented in graduate-level HCI/UX curricula. We also plan to expand our sample to include undergraduate courses as well as international HCI/UX programs. Further, we will be examining the program-level learning outcomes for each program to determine whether students are expected to demonstrate competency in visual design in order to earn their degree. We are using the preliminary results of this research to inform the development of a new graduate course at our institution, where we will be piloting a variety of different techniques to increase students' competency and proficiency with visual design concepts. It is our hope that this research will allow us to create a typology of visual design courses being taken by HCI/UX students and to help develop a more comprehensive approach to visual design instruction in this field.

REFERENCES

Da Silva, T. S., Silveira, M. S., De O. Melo, C., & Parzianello, L. C. (2013). Understanding the UX designer's role within agile teams. In Lecture Notes in Computer Science (including subseries Lecture Notes in Artificial Intelligence and Lec- ture Notes in Bioinformatics) (Vol. 8012 LNCS, pp. 599–609). https://doi.org/10.1007/978-3-642-39229-0_64

Jurca, G., Hellmann, T. D., & Maurer, F. (2014). Integrating agile and user-centered design: A systematic mapping and re- view of evaluation and validation studies of agile-UX. In Proceedings - 2014 Agile Conference, AGILE 2014 (pp. 24– 32). Institute of Electrical and Electronics Engineers Inc. https://doi.org/10.1109/AGILE.2014.17

Norman, D.A., 2002. Emotion and design: attractive things work better. Interactions, July Aug, 36–42. Norman, D. (2004). Emotional design: Why we love (or hate) everyday things. Basic Books (AZ).

Porat, T., & Tractinsky, N. (2012). It's a pleasure buying here: The effects of web-store design on consumers' emotions and attitudes. Human–Computer Interaction, 27(3), 235-276.

Oyibo, K., & Vassileva, J. (2016, October). The interplay of aesthetics, usability and credibility in mobile websites and the moderation by culture. In Proceedings of the 15th Brazilian Symposium on Human Factors in Computer Systems (p. 10). ACM.

Thielsch, M. T., Blotenberg, I. & Jaron, R. (2014). User evaluation of websites: From first impression to recommendation.

Interacting with Computers, 26 (1), 89-102.

J. Torre. (2017, June 9). 10 basic principles of visual design. [blog post]. Retrieved from https://blog.prototypr.io/10-basic- principles-of-visual-design-55b86b9f7241

Tractinsky, N., Katz, A. S., & Ikar, D. (2000). What is beautiful is usable. Interacting with computers, 13(2), 127-145.

van der Heijden, H., 2003. Factors influencing the usage of websites: the case of a generic portal in the Netherlands. Infor- mation and Management 40, 541–549.

Yamamoto, M., & Lambert, D. R. (1994). The impact of product aesthetics on the evaluation of industrial products. Journal of Product Innovation Management, 11(4), 309-324

Social Tagging and Name Authorities: Popular Music Information Discovery

Kabel Nathan Stanwicks
University at Albany, USA. kstanwicks@albany.edu

Hemalata Iyer
University at Albany, USA. hiyer@albany.edu

ABSTRACT

The study examines the alignment of user tags with Name authority attributes of popular music artist names. The authors found 65% of the tags mapped to Resource Description and Access Name authority data. User tags provide more granular genre information than Name authority records; therefore, user tags can enhance retrieval based on genre.

KEYWORDS

Social Tagging, Popular Music Retrieval, Authorities, Metadata, RDA, FRAD, IFLA LRM

INTRODUCTION AND BACKGROUND

In the digital environment, Web 2.0 technologies have enabled collaborative approaches to different endeavors, such as social tagging of objects and resources. This bottom-up approach begins at the grassroots with the advantage of aggregating many users' opinions. It is increasingly being used by information organizations for organizing and retrieving information resources. The top-down approach envisages first creating a structure and controlling the terminology—this supports metadata's consistency, interoperability, and accuracy. The Functional Requirements for Authority Data (FRAD) model, consolidated into the International Federation of Library Associations and Institutions Library Reference Model (IFLA LRM), models the bibliographic universe's entities, attributes, and relationships and is concerned with concepts relating to authority data. The Resource Description and Access (RDA)—based on FRAD and being revised to implement IFLA LRM—is a code of data elements, instructions, and guidelines for creating information resource metadata. Authority records use RDA code as metadata standards for resource description and access. RDA mandates many changes to authority records, to fall in line with the IFLA model. Authorities are becoming increasingly complex through the addition of attributes. Since 2010 several new fields have been added to the persons and corporate bodies authority record. Both user-generated and professionally-generated metadata have their limitations as discussed in literature in the context of different domains (Iyer & Bungo, 2011), but the two working in concert can greatly improve discovery, make resource description more sustainable, and enhance access points to resources. While social tagging has been researched from many perspectives, it has not been fully explored with reference to name authorities (Mouliason, 2015).

This study's overall objective is to develop an understanding of how users' mental models—as demonstrated through their tagging behavior—align with the ways in which information professionals describe name entities and attributes through RDA Authority Records. The study addresses the following research questions: 1. How do popular music listeners describe artists using social tags? 2. To what extent, and how, do user-generated tags align with, and deviate from, RDA Authority Record elements and attributes? 3. Can social tags aide in resolving user information queries in ways authority records cannot in the popular music domain?

METHODOLOGY AND RESULTS

The authors used a simple random sample of fifty-five artist names from the weekly Billboard Hot 100 Charts' number-one-ranked songs, and they pulled 2572 user-generated tags corresponding to these artists from the last.fm Web site using the last.fm top artist tags API. Tags were examined and coded to individual RDA Name Authorities attributes or coded as Work-Expression-Manifestation (WEM) tags using a content analysis dictionary that the authors created; tags that did not map to these metadata elements were coded as personal/subjective tags. The authors performed content analysis on the entire tag sample, and a third person coded a random sample consisting of 25% of the study's tags. Inter-coder reliability was calculated, using Cohen's Kappa, for each of the 25 attributes coded within the tag sample. Cohen's Kappa ranged from 0.857 to 1 for the attributes, with Kappa calculated at or above 0.961 for all but one attribute. The user-generated tags that mapped to RDA data points were compared with professionally-generated metadata from corresponding name authority records. Artists with Billboard number-one-ranked songs were selected as popular content is more likely to be tagged by many users (Rolla, 2009). This study used last.fm tags because last.fm is the only social music site that employs user-generated tags—other sites use only professionally-generated tags.

The authors found that 66% of the tags mapped to RDA Name authority data elements, 3% of the tags mapped to WEM metadata elements, and 31% of the tags were coded as personal/subjective (Figure 1). 65% of the RDA-related tags mapped to Field of Activity (i.e., genre) data elements, 7.8% of the RDA-related tags mapped to Place data elements, 7% of the RDA-

related tags mapped to Occupation data elements, 3% of the RDA-related tags mapped to Name data elements (Figure 2). 66% of tags mapped to WEM metadata elements correspond with title data, and 37% correspond to awards received by the artists. The metadata overlap between user-generated tags and Authority name records is limited. Authority name records apply a
limited number of broad genre terms to each artist. However, users apply significant numbers of genre-related tags to each artist, as illustrated in the spike in Figure 2. These tags provide greater granularity than the genre terms found in authority records, and, therefore, provide additional access points to resources through their description of genres, sub-genres (e.g., dance pop, AOR, Acid Jazz, Disco), styles, radio formats, and instrumentation.

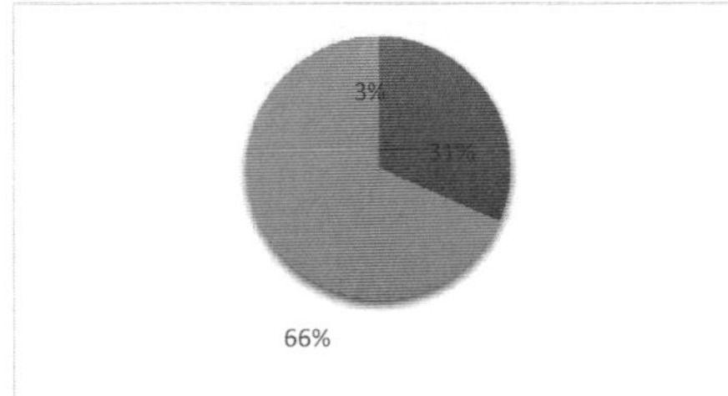

Figure 1. Tag Mapping Distribution

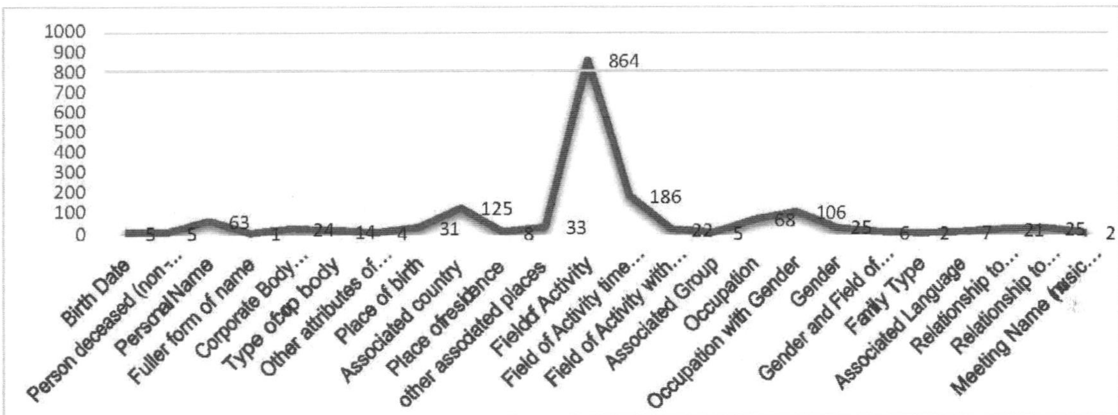

Figure 2. RDA Tag Mapping

CONCLUSION

User-generated metadata largely align with elements and attributes used for professionally-generated metadata records. Genre granularity is important to music description and access as demonstrated by the large volume of these user tags applied to artists. Therefore, user tags are capable of resolving queries related to sub-genre, style, and format, which Name authority records are not able to resolve. This study demonstrates the value of aggregating and integrating the tags for use in the discovery services in information organizations. This work is a unique contribution to the field, as there have been no prior studies addressing the social tagging mapping to Name authorities in the popular music domain. Future studies should examine tagging behavior in popular song titles and music from different cultures, as well as the alignment of name authorities and social tagging in other domains.

REFERENCES

Blythe, Kurt C., Gunther, Wnada K., Spurgin, Kristina M. (2013). Resource Description and Access. *Serials Review*,39, 175- 180.

Iyer, Hemalata and Bungo, Lucy (2011). An examination of semantic relationships between professionally assigned metadata and user-generated tags for popular literature in complementary and alternative medicine. *Information Research*, 16(3) paper 482. Retrieved on May 14 from http://InformationR.net/ir/16-3/paper482.html

Library Resources and Technical Services, 53(3), 174–184.

Mouliason, Heather Lea. (2015). The Expansion of Personal Name Authority Record under Resource Description and Access: Current Status and Quality Considerations. *International Federation for Library Associations and Institutions* 4(1), 13-24. Rolla, P. J. (2009). User tags versus subject headings: Can user-supplied data improve subject access to library collections?

What Drives Black Contributions to Wikipedia?

Brenton Stewart
Louisiana State University, USA. brentonstewart@lsu.edu

Boryung Ju
Louisiana State University, USA. bju1@lsu.edu

ABSTRACT

We examine extrinsic motivational factors around Black Wikipedians' content contributions. Data collected from an online survey of 318 participants were analyzed with multiple regression analysis in order to measure the degree of association among factors. Results indicate that racial identity, social presence, and perceived information quality have significant positive effects on motivations of Black Wikipedia authors and editors.

KEYWORDS

Black Americans, race, social media, social identity, Wikipedia

INTRODUCTION

A recent Pew Internet Study on social media use in the United States showed that African Americans were the largest racial/ethnic group of users (2018). While researchers have begun to examine Black social media activity (Lee-Won, White and Potocki, 2018; Correa and Jeong, 2011) very few have examined behaviors around Black Wikipedians. As the world's largest crowdsourced encyclopedia, Wikipedia is available in 301 language editions. The English version is not only the largest, but the majority of its content is contributed from North America. Recent studies have examined motivators, or factors that drive Wikipedia content contributions. Yang and Lai (2010) drew participants from the English edition of Wikipedia, but did not mention geographical background, and is silent on the racial composition of participants. Xu and Li (2015) recruited partici- pants from the Chinese edition, and posited "cross-cultural studies can be conducted to investigate the impact of cultures on online encyclopedia systems." In this paper, we examine motivational factors around Black Wikipedians' content contribu- tions. Using social identity theory as a framework to situate our analysis, we position Black Americans are a distinctive popu- lation with a shared racial identity and social interactions, both online and in face-to-face communication (Tajfel and Turner, 1986). In this paper we examine motivational factors around Black Wikipedians' content contributions. Specifically, we ex- plore: Are there any significant relationships between extrinsic motivators (racial identity, social presence, and perception of information quality) and content contribution?

Research on Wikipedia and knowledge sharing has also measured intrinsic variables, such as altruism, belonging, entrainment, and self-development. We limit our analysis to the aforementioned constructs and will explore interactions with intrin- sic variables in an expansive future study. As previously mentioned, studies rarely examine racial identity as a motivator in Wikipedia peer production. In this analysis the racial identity construct is based on an adaptation of Seller's et.al (1997) "Multidimensional Inventory of Black Identity" developed as a tool to uniformly measure Black identity. Social presence refers to the participants' belief that their contributions results in personal recognition, reward, or acclaim within the Wikipe- dia community. This concept has been explored using various terminologies such as, *extrinsic motivators* (Yang, 2010) *repu- tation* (Xu and Li, 2015) and *recognition* (Cho, Chen, Chung 2010). Information quality is a subjective judgment based on the participants' perception that information encountered within Wikipedia is reliable. This construct was adapted from a study by Lim (2009). Content contribution encompasses edits, new article creation, editing existing articles, and/or cleanup or verifying content, this construct was derived from Xu and Li (2015).

METHODOLOGY

An online survey was administered via Qualtrics during October of 2017. A total of 318 participants responded to the survey questionnaires. The sampling method used to recruit the study participants was purposive sampling. Each sample element was selected based on a clearly defined and limited group of individuals who identified as Black/African American and had made at least one edit/contribution to Wikipedia over the last three years. Most participants were between the ages of 20-29 and 30-39 at 33% (n=105) and 30% (n=95) respectively. 40-59 year-olds comprised 23% (or n=73) while the two smallest age groups were 18-19 at 6% (n=18) and 60+ at 8 % (n=27). Women and Men were equally represented at 49% (n=158) with two individuals identifying as trans. The participants were given a set of survey questions under four constructs: racial identi- ty, social presence, perceived information quality and contribution. Quantitative analyses were performed to examine the research questions and corresponding hypotheses of the present study. The following three hypotheses were developed: $H_0$1: Racial identity will have a positive effect on Black Wikipedians to contribute Wikipedia contents. $H_0$2: Social presence will have a positive effect on Black Wikipedians to contribute Wikipedia contents. $H_0$3: Black Wikipedians' perception on information quality on Wikipedia will have a positive effect on their contribution to Wikipedia contents.

	Mean	Std. Deviation	Cronbach's α
Racial identity	3.871	1.033	0.899
Social presence	3.614	1.028	0.923
Perception on info quality	3.744	0.821	0.893
Contribution	2.667	0.806	0.903

Table 1. Descriptive statistics and reliability

Figure 1. Results of Hypothesis Testing of Research Model Based on Multiple Regression Analysis

We assessed the measurement model by calculating reliability (internal consistency) and construct validity. Cronbach alphas (for reliability assessment) for four constructs were all above the recommended level of 0.70, indicating a high degree of in- ternal consistency. Validity of the instrument was measured by factor analysis in order to identify underlying constructs that explain the correlations among a set of items. All factor loadings of the items exceeded 0.60 level (all range from 0.588 to 0.807), which is considered critical for construct validity. In order to assess the research model, correlation coefficient analy- sis was used to examine the degree of association among variables, and multiple regression analysis tested the hypothesized relationships among multiple variables.

RESULTS

All three independent variables (racial identity, social presence, and perceived information quality) have significant pos- itive effects on motivating Black Wikipedian contributions (rejecting H_01, H_02, and H_03 respectively). Among these, perceived information quality (β=.299, p<.001) is the most significant motivator on content contribution; this is followed by racial iden- tity (β=.217, p<.001) and social presence (β=.218, p<.001), have almost equally significant effects on the Wikipedia contribu- tion. The R square (R^2) which indicates the variance between three factors (independent variables) and Wikipedia content contribution (dependent variable) is 41.9%. Hence, the regression model in this study is proved to be valid (F = 75.480, p<.001). For correlation racial identity (r=.542), social presence (r=.581), and perceived infor- mation quality (r=.583) have sig- nificant association with Wikipedia contribution. The research model, as presented in this study, demonstrates moderate lev- els of predictability, thus all variables can serve as reasonable predictors for mo- tivating Black Wikipedians' motivation to contribution to Wikipedia contents.

CONCLUSON

The results presented here comprise the preliminary results of a study identifying external motivational factors and their as- sociations with the content contribution among Black Wikipedia authors and editors. The findings of this study ad- vance knowledge on Black social media participation, specifically information behaviors in collaborative peer-produced reposito- ries, like Wikipedia.

REFERENCES

Cho, H., Chen, M., & Chung, S. (2010). Testing an integrative theoretical model of knowledge-sharing behavior in the con- text of Wikipedia. *Journal of the Association for Information Science and Technology*, *61*(6), 1198-1212.

Correa, T., & Jeong, S. H. (2011). Race and online content creation: Why minorities are actively participating in the Web. *Information, Communication & Society*, *14*(5), 638-659.

Lee-Won, R. J., White, T. N., & Potocki, B. (2018). The Black catalyst to tweet: the role of discrimination experience, group identification, and racial agency in Black Americans' instrumental use of Twitter. *Information, Communication & Society*, *21*(8), 1097-1115.

Lim, S. (2009). How and why do college students use Wikipedia? *Journal of the Association for Information Science and Technology*, *60*(11), 2189-2202.

Pew Research Center. (2018). Social media fact sheet.

Tajfel, H., & Turner, J. C. (2004). The social identity theory of intergroup behavior.

Xu, B., & Li, D. (2015). An empirical study of the motivations for content contribution and community participation in Wik- ipedia. *Information & management*, *52*(3), 275-286.

Yang, H. L., & Lai, C. Y. (2010). Motivations of Wikipedia content contributors. *Computers in human behavior*, *26*(6), 1377-1383.

Word-building and World-stealing: Taking, Making, and Playing across Fictional and Material Borders

Robyn Stobbs
University of Alberta, Canada. stobbs@ualberta.ca

Arlene Oak
University of Alberta, Canada. aoak@ualberta.ca

ABSTRACT

Information practices and experiences are complex and layered; they can traverse borders between fiction and reality and the material and immaterial. This poster will present a visual representation of an ongoing narrative analysis from a pilot study of information practices involved in creative engagements with fictional worlds.

KEYWORDS

Fiction, information behaviour, information experience, narrative methods.

INTRODUCTION

This poster will present emerging narratives from a pilot study of information and making practices related to fictional worlds. Specifically, the pilot study is the beginning of a larger project with the aim to study information practices and experiences of people who make items related to fictional worlds, e.g., art or clothing based on Harry Potter, maps for Dungeons & Dragons, etc. The research questions that frame the study are: 1) How do people experience information as they engage with fictional worlds in their making practices? 2) How do those fictional worlds map onto makers' actual, material creations and lives? 3) What information is used and represented in these practices, and in what forms? People are situated in their own contexts as they engage with fictional worlds, creating an overlap between the imaginary and the real that is made visible when they make some form of representation of the fictional world. This poster will present the narrative research framework and methods used for the pilot study and the emerging narrative analysis. The research is situated within an interdisciplinary space between library and information studies (LIS) and material culture studies.

SITUATING THE RESEARCH

The research framework is built on a concern for understanding information experience from the field of LIS combined with theories from material culture studies that consider the importance of objects and environments. Information behaviour has been defined as the ways in which people need, seek, use, and share information (Fisher, Erdelez, & McKechnie, 2005, p. xix); while information experience is a holistic concept that can be approached from various perspectives. It can encompass emotional, embodied, and other aspects of information use that go beyond seeking or skills and behaviours (Bruce, Davis, Hughes, Partridge, & Stoodley, 2014, p. 8). Fiction and fandom have been identified as an understudied and emerging area in this realm (Doty & Broussard, 2017; Forcier, 2017; Price & Robinson, 2017). Creative engagements with fictional worlds can be examined with a consideration for their materiality. Materiality is an important concept for framing this research because objects and environments can both shape and be shaped by people; objects can have agency and affect situations (e.g., Ingold, 2012; Latour, 2005). Creative engagements with fictional worlds encompass a variety of information practices that cross and re-cross borders from imaginary worlds to the material worlds where people engage with them.

METHODS

The poster will demonstrate the emerging narrative analysis from a pilot study designed to collect detailed data with participants to explore the myriad ways that they creatively engage with fictional worlds. The research framework uses perspectives from narrative inquiry (e.g., Clandinin & Connelly, 2000) influenced by material culture studies (e.g., Riello, 2009; Ingold, 2012) to form a holistic view of information experience as situated in material and narrative contexts. Initial object-interviews were conducted with five participants, and further follow-up continues. Small numbers of participants are used in narrative inquiries in order to be able to interact with them over an extended period of time and generate detailed stories of their experience. All of the participants in this pilot study chose to talk about a fictional world they engage with through some form of gaming (tabletop gaming, live action roleplay, or computer gaming). They told many stories of their engagements with fictional worlds, but the focus for this poster is the stories of their information use and the forms it takes across borders between fictional and material realities. In the object interviews, each participant brought in items they have made based on a fictional world of their choosing and/or objects they use to engage with that world. The objects then served as prompts for the interviews as participants explained how they were made and used. Follow-up has included participants sharing character backstories, photographs, game notes, and in one case, observing an evening of gameplay. As aspects of the experiences of participants are written up, they are further negotiated with participants as a way to acknowledge that we are co-creating the stories of their experience. These stories will then be a used for further analysis and engagement with theories of information behavior and experience.

EMERGING NARRATIVES

Some of the narratives emerging in the pilot data include stories of: ephemeral practices; collaboration; and rules, worlds, and frameworks shaping, but also shaped by, the participants' engagements. This poster will visually illustrate some of the information used by participants, the material forms they give it, and the connections and categories participants highlighted about their engagements with fictional worlds. For example, Cassius (a pseudonym) inspired the title for this poster through his use of the term "stealing." In discussing the resources he uses to build his game world, he referred to reading fiction to steal ideas, to stealing images from the internet to give his players visuals, and to using advice from an online series to "rip off" other people's ideas. His familiarity with specific genres and rule sets allows him to create a detailed and layered fictional world for his players to further engage with and shape. Hence the title of this paper, individuals participate in not just world-building, but world-stealing, by taking bits and pieces from other places to further engage with a fictional world, either of their own creation, or an extension of an existing creation. Cassius takes bits and pieces, themes and moods, and recombines them into his own world that is then further shaped by his players. In discussing his process, he shared resources ranging from sticky notes and dry erase markers, to game handbooks, to online random generators and map builders, and an extensive list of notes in preparation for his first game. There are complicated information practices interwoven with his creative engagement with fiction and the ways he represents an imaginary world materially. The other participants had equally complicated stories of engagement to share. Photographs of their materials and stories will be shared in poster format to emphasize the complex and layered information practices of the participants.

CONCLUSION

Information crosses fuzzy borders between the imagination and the material world when a person engages with fictional worlds. The case studies visually represented on the poster provide windows to ways in which fictional worlds and information can become materially situated in people's real lives through their making practices. Information is sought, "stolen," represented, reinterpreted, and used in a variety of ways to build and engage with fictional worlds. This pilot study was conducted specifically to test methods for a larger study, so the results reported here are provisional and interim. They result from early and ongoing analyses in the study and should be considered to be emerging narratives composed with participants about their practices. These narratives will be refined through further follow-up with participants and further analysis in the larger study. The emerging narratives demonstrate the complexity of information practices situated at intersections between the material and the imaginary and between fictional narratives and stories of people's lives and motivations entwined with those worlds.

ACKNOWLEDGMENTS

This research is supported by the Social Sciences and Humanities Research Council of Canada through a Doctoral Fellowship.

REFERENCES

Broussard, R., & Doty, P. (2016). Toward an understanding of fiction and information behavior. *Proceedings of the Association for Information Science & Technology*, *53*(1), 1–10.

Bruce, C., Davis, K., Hughes, H., Partridge, H., & Stoodley, I. (2014). Information experience: Contemporary perspectives. In *Library and Information Science* (Vol. 9, pp. 3–16). Bingley: Emerald Group Publishing.

Clandinin, D. J., & Connelly, F. M. (2000). *Narrative inquiry: Experience and story in qualitative research* (1st ed.). San Francisco, CA: Jossey-Bass Inc.

Doty, P., & Broussard, R. (2017). Fiction as informative and its implications for information science theory. *Proceedings of the Association for Information Science & Technology*, *54*(1), 61–70.

Fisher, K. E., Erdelez, S., & McKechnie, L. E. F. (Eds.). (2005). Preface. In *Theories of information behavior* (pp. xix–xxi). Medford, NJ: Information Today, Inc.

Forcier, E. (2017). Re(a)d wedding: A case study exploring everyday information behaviors of the transmedia fan. *Proceedings of the Association for Information Science & Technology*, *54*(1), 93–101.

Ingold, T. (2012). Toward an ecology of materials. *Annual Review of Anthropology*, *41*(1), 427–442.

Latour, B. (2005). *Reassembling the social: An introduction to actor-network-theory*. Oxford: Oxford University Press.

Price, L., & Robinson, L. (2017). 'Being in a knowledge space': Information behaviour of cult media fan communities. *Journal of Information Science*, *43*(5), 649–664.

Riello, G. (2009). Things that shape history: Material culture and historical narratives. In *History and material culture: A student's guide to approaching alternative sources* (pp. 24–46). London: Routledge.

Reading Around the World: A Web-based Application for Creating a Communal Knowledge Base of Reading Materials

Limor Tamim
University of British Columbia, Canada. Limor.tamim@alumni.ubc.ca

Eleri Staiger-Williams
University of British Columbia, Canada. Eleri.staiger-williams@alumni.ubc.ca

ABSTRACT

Reading has many benefits, and has been shown to improve verbal abilities, concentration, imagination, and memory. Diverse reading materials have also been shown to reduce prejudice; perspectives drawn from different experiences and locales evoke empathy in the reader. To encourage diverse perspective taking, the Reading Around the World Challenge (RAWC) encourages people to read one book from every country. However, there is a lack of materials available for some countries, and existing books are not well known. Further, challengers take part individually or within existing social groups, and there is currently no means of exchanging book lists with other RAWC participants. To address this issue, we created RtWTrack, a web-based prototype, which features a publicly available book database and visual map, that aggregates bibliographic data about reading materials and makes it publicly available.

MOTIVATION

Reading has the power to change the way we view the world. For example, one study showed that narrative fiction reduced Arab-Muslim prejudice among readers and offered a safe haven from intergroup anxiety, a form of social anxiety that people experience when interacting with groups that are different from their own (Johnson, Jasper, Griffin, & Huffman, 2013). When readers look for a book they typically use a series of personal filters (Sheldrick Ross, 1999). These include the physical characteristics of the book, such as size and cover art, as well as other elements, such as the author, genre, title, and the book summary or sample paragraph. In addition, readers consider the kind of reading experience they want to have, and how difficult it will be to acquire the material (Sheldrick Ross, 1999). Therefore, to facilitate greater ease of access for avid readers to engage with material written from diverse viewpoints, we have created a prototype tool called RTwTrack.

BACKGROUND

The Reading Around the World Challenge (RAWC) is one mechanism to encourage people to read fiction from diverse perspectives; by reading material from authors who are not a part of the reader's cultural group, readers engage indirectly with different attitudes, mores and beliefs. The general rules of the challenge are to find one book per region by an author who is native to that region. Finding books for some regions is not easy - different cultures may have primarily oral storytelling traditions, and some may not be interested in sharing their artistic expressions with the world at large. Moreover, only about 3 percent of literature published in English in the U.S. each year consists of translated works (Allen & Adamo, 2007). As a result, RAWC participants typically follow a RAWC website for recommendations; see, for example, Ann Morgan's "A Year of Reading the World" (Morgan, 2012). The communities from each website do not engage with each other. Although an individual RAWC website may form a community, the RAWC challenge itself does not, under the working definition of a virtual community as "a cyberspace supported by computer-based information technology centered upon communication and interaction of participants to generate member – driven contents, resulting in a relationship being built up" from Lee, Vogel, and Limayem (2003). This factor limits the methods of discovery that readers employ, as RAWC websites do not maintain comprehensive book lists and Facebook group pages are not optimized for the discovery of new books due to their scrolling format.

PROTOTYPE

When these factors are considered, it is clear that a collective book list would benefit RAWC participants: having access to other participants' book lists would make searching for a book with specific features more efficient and would provide readers with a wider variety of choices; this would increase the chances of a reader finding a book. Since the RAWC is not an online community, but a group of individuals pursuing the same goal, the challenge is how to exchange information about reading materials without direct communication. To address this issue, we designed a tool called RtWTrack, which consists of a shared, publicly accessible database of bibliographic details, and displays this information textually and visually via a map; it allows users to share information indirectly.

RtWTrack enables public access to a comprehensive database of books from around the world, and a complementary personal tracking tool allows individual participants to record their progress visually and, optionally, to share it with others. Three key requirements guided the design: relevance to the user, simplicity and legibility (Darejeh & Singh, 2013). The first and most important one was to take into account the characteristics and desires of potential users (Zaina & Alvaro, 2015). The prototype addresses the most salient needs of our user group: it provides a book list and tracking tool in one place, in an accessible format designed to improve the readers' challenge experience. For example, the website application contains clear, short menus that allow users to add/edit their book entries, map the books they've read, and share their progress on social media platforms, if desired (Darejeh & Singh, 2013).

Figure 1 below shows our prototype. If a reader logs into their account, they will be able to see countries they have "read" in green (see A), allowing visual presentation of their progress. Hovering over a country shows the name of a book associated with that country (see B). The complete book list is accessible through the menu (see C). Books that are new to the communal database would be added after automatically validating the information inserted by the user (title, author and so on). Figure 2 demonstrates the table view of books sorted by author's nationality, but it is possible to sort by any column. For example, if a reader wants a book in which the plot takes place in the relevant country, they can choose to sort by "Plot Location"; some plots take place in fictional locations (see D). Users can add books to their own lists directly from the communal list by clicking "add to my list" (See E).

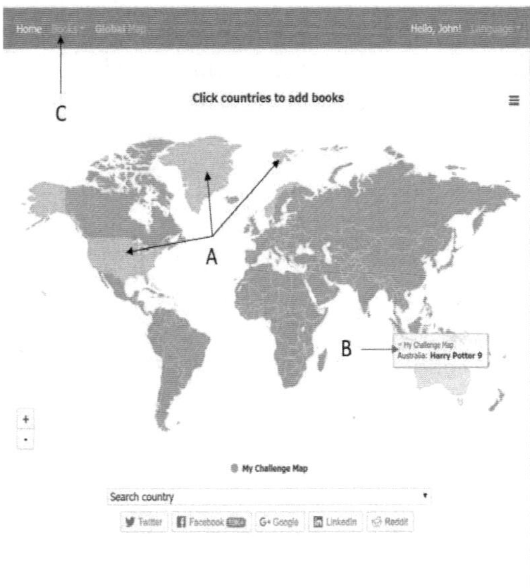

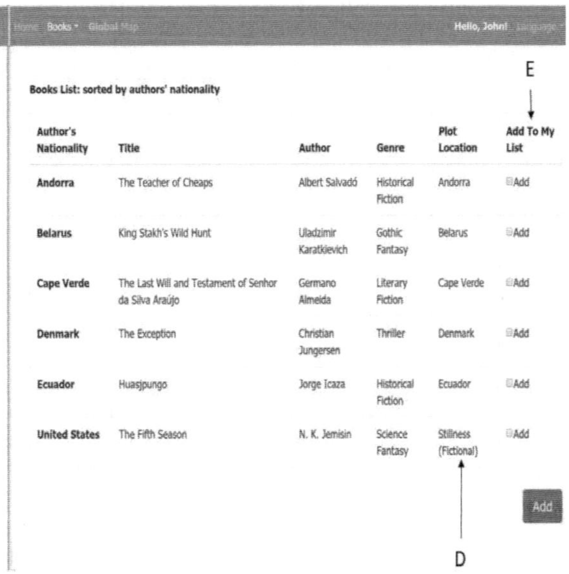

Figure 1: Web-based prototype with map

Figure 2: Book list of aggregated bibliographic data

CONCLUSION

We would like to solicit feedback on the prototype through a demonstration for ASIS&T community to inform future work, which may include introducing the prototype to selected RAWC groups or more general users via social media or in libraries, collecting feedback, and modifying the design accordingly. We can see this idea being applicable for other uses, such as a site that allows users to anonymously share fitness information or recommend medical clinics to stigmatized groups.

REFERENCES

Allen, E., & Adamo, G. (2007). To be translated or not to be: PEN/IRL report on the international situation of literary translation. Barcelona: Institut Ramon Llull

Darejeh, A., & Singh, D. (2013). A review on user interface design principles to increase software usability for users with less computer literacy. *Journal of Computer Science, 9*(11), 1443-1450. 10.3844/jcssp.2013.1443.1450

Lee, S.L.F., Vogel, D., & Limayem, M. (2003). Virtual community informatics: A review and research agenda. *Journal of Information Technology Theory and Application, 5*(1), 47.

Johnson, D. R., Jasper, D. M., Griffin, S., & Huffman, B. L. (2013). Reading narrative fiction reduces Arab-Muslim prejudice and offers a safe haven from intergroup anxiety. *Social Cognition, 31*(5), 578.

Sheldrick Ross, C. (1999). Finding without seeking: The information encounter in the context of reading for pleasure. *Information Processing and Management, 35*(6), 783-799. doi:10.1016/S0306-4573(99)00026-6

Zaina, L., & Alvaro, A. (2015). A design methodology for user-centered innovation in the software development area. *Journal of Systems and Software, 110*, 155-177. doi:10.1016/j.jss.2015.08.029

Improving Access to API Documentation for Developers with Docs-as-Code-as-a-Service

Richard Thomchick
VMware, Inc., United States. richardt@vmware.com

ABSTRACT

Web Application Programming Interfaces (APIs) provide the connective tissue that developers need to integrate Internet services and create "software-as-a-service" (SaaS) applications. To learn an API's usage, developers often turn to their web brows- ers to access documentation and try out APIs. However, traditional approaches to documentation present obstacles that can hamper API comprehension and developer productivity. To overcome these obstacles, practitioners are adopting a new ap- proach called Docs-as-Code, in which documents are published with many of the same tools and practices used to deploy source code. In this paper, we present Dev Center, a system based in part on the Docs-as-Code framework and designed to provide ubiquitous access to a broad set of API documentation resources. Preliminary findings suggest that Dev Center could potentially improve API comprehension and developer productivity, while Docs-as-Code could benefit related research efforts.

KEYWORDS

API; Documentation; Developer; SaaS; Traceability; Context Switching; Docs-as-Code

INTRODUCTION

Application Programming Interfaces (APIs) are used as key interconnectivity mechanisms to access software services over the Internet (S. M., Anslow, & Maurer). There has been exponential growth in the number of web APIs over the last 10-15 years (Gentle, 2017), and as organizations focus increasingly on API consumption strategies (Columbus, 2017), API providers must document these interfaces well enough for developers to connect systems and share data, and frequently enough to keep pace with rapid SaaS release cycles. For this paper, we broadly define "developer documentation" to include structured API refer- ence documentation, code samples, and usage tutorials. API reference complements the API by providing information not obvious from the API syntax (Maalej & Robillard, 2013). Developers also want example code that correspond to functions they want to learn how to use (Haenni, Lungu, Schwarz, & Nierstrasz, 2013). Usage tutorials complement the API reference and code samples by combining the functional explanations and examples together to help developers quickly learn to use the APIs correctly in specific situations (Jiang, Zhang, Li, Ren, & Lo, 2016).

API DOCUMENTATION CHALLENGES

It is often stated that APIs can be hard to learn and use (McLellan, Roesler, Tempest, & Spinuzzi, 1998; Robillard & DeLine, 2011), and developers report that poor documentation is one of the most severe learning obstacles they face (Watson, 2012). One common challenge is that the documentation is sometimes ambiguous, outdated, or missing altogether (Robillard & DeLine, 2011), which gives developers little choice but to try and reverse-engineer the API (Hossain, et al., 2018). Another problem is that API users must search multiple disconnected information sources (Wu, Hou, & Liu, 2016) to find adequate information, and that development tools and web browsers remain disconnected (Goldman & Miller, 2008), resulting in poor traceability (Wu, Hou, & Liu, 2016) (Dagenais & Robillard, 2012) and frequent context shifts for developers. One study (Ko, Aung, & Myers, 2005) found that developers spent 11 percent of the total task time either reading an API doc or switching between applications such as their IDE and web browser, which suggests that documentation is important and there is a lot overhead that could be eliminated, even for relatively small tasks (Goldman & Miller, 2008).

APPLYING DOCS-AS-CODE PRACTICES TO API DOCUMENTATION

Given that developers are reportedly notorious for neglecting source code documentation (McBurney, et al., 2017), It is not entirely surprising that API documentation presents learning obstacles. However, sometimes even technical writing teams can't handle the number of web services and APIs that must be documented (Gentle, 2017). To address these and other issues, many companies are adopting an approach called Docs-as-Code, which generally refers to the practice of treating documentation like software source code (Etter, 2016). According to the author of the book, "Docs Like Code", Docs-as-Code means storing the source files in a version control system, building the documentation artifacts automatically, ensuring the docs are reviewed, and publishing the artifacts with little or no human intervention (Gentle, 2017). For API reference, this entails the use of tools such as Swagger UI to automatically generate documentation, which also facilitates the creation of interactive API consoles for testing API calls in a web browser (Neumann, Laranjeiro, & Bernardino, 2018). For usage tutorials, practitioners often use Markdown or reStructuredText (rST), store the files in GitHub repositories, and automatically deploy updates.

DEV CENTER SYSTEM DESIGN FOR DELIVERING DOCS-AS-CODE-AS-A-SERVICE

Several studies (Goldman & Miller, 2008; Wu, Hou, & Liu, 2016) have proposed the integration of developer information resources to address the issue of disconnected resources, lack of traceability, and context switching. Our system, Dev Center, applies Docs-as-Code and SaaS techniques to enable integration and continuous, automated deployment of developer infor- mation resources to any client that supports REST API services, including websites, SaaS application interfaces, and integrated development environments (IDEs) such as Eclipse. At the center of Dev Center are three core services: API Explorer for reference documentation; Sample Exchange for code snippets, and DocStream for usage tutorials. When a contributor wants to add or update documentation with Dev Center, they check out the file(s) from a GitHub repository, make their changes, and then submit a pull request to have their changes merged. Once the pull request is accepted, the system looks for changes, automatically generates new HTML pages, and deploys the updates so that they are accessible to Dev Center service clients.

IMPLEMENTATION

Dev Center is implemented with open-source software so that it can be freely integrated into and distributed with downstream software projects. There are currently three major types of Dev Center implementations: first, a public-facing website, which displays all documentation types across all APIs offered by a provider; second, a SaaS user interface for users of VMware Cloud on Amazon Web Services (AWS); and third, an Angular application with support for containerization to use as a refer- ence implementation. To test the system's efficacy at streamlining the API learning process, we conducted some preliminary usability tests on the AWS implementation at an internal research conference in May 2018. Users were given a series of tasks to complete that involved finding documentation and using an interactive console to try various API calls. We measured the success rate, error rate, and time-to-completion, and captured Screen recordings of each test session for further evaluation.

CONCLUSION

While more testing must be conducted, preliminary results suggest that the Dev Center system can improve access to API documentation, reduce obstacles to API comprehension, and improve productivity. Using Dev Center, several participants were able to find an API that correlated to their task, grasp its usage, and make their first API call in under 10 minutes, with few errors. Many participants commented that the Dev Center system represents a major improvement over the traditional scenario in which it could take days or even weeks to provision hardware, install software, and configure a test environment before even attempting to understand an API and make an initial API call. Overall, we believe the results so far validate the notion that we can overcome some API learning obstacles by of continuously delivering contextually relevant API documentation as a service.

One current limitation of this system is the lack of community-based documentation from forums, question-and-answer (Q&A) websites such as StackOverflow, and real-time messaging applications such as Slack. These are important resources, and future work in this area should incorporate these information resources so that developers can seek answers and advice from peers without switching context. Correlating related resources and increasing documentation traceability is another area for improve- ment, as we found it quite challenging to connect code snippets and usage tutorials with specific API methods and classes.

As for Docs-as-Code, preliminary results suggest that it is not a panacea for improving API documentation but can help to alleviate some obstacles such as missing or outdated documentation by streamlining publication, and it is a valuable building block for delivering documentation as a service. We also foresee many other potential applications for Docs-as-Code, particu- larly for integrating documentation into IDEs and other developer interfaces (Goldman & Miller, 2008), and believe there are other Docs-as-Code qualities, such as increased collaboration from open-source contributors, that merit further examination.

REFERENCES

Columbus, L. (2017, January 29). *2017 Is Quickly Becoming The Year Of The API Economy*. Retrieved from Forbes: https://www.forbes.com/sites/louiscolumbus/2017/01/29/2017-is-quickly-becoming-the-year-of-the-api- economy/#33a27c726a41

Dagenais, B., & Robillard, M. P. (2012). Recovering traceability links between an API and its learning resources. *34th IEEE/ACM International Conference on Software Engineering* (pp. 47-57). Zurich: IEEE/ACM.

Etter, A. (2016). *Modern Technical Writing: An Introduction to Software Documentation.* Seattle: Amazon Digital Services LLC.

Gall, H., Chen, T., Panichella, S., Zhou, Y., & Gu, R. (2017). Analyzing APIs Documentation and Code to Detect Directive Defects. *39th IEEE International Conference on Software Engineering.* Buenos Aires: IEEE.

Gentle, A. (2017). *Docs Like Code.* Austin, TX: Just Write Click.

Goldman, M., & Miller, R. C. (2008). Codetrail: Connecting source code and web resources. *IEEE Symposium on Visual Languages and Human-Centric Computing* (pp. 65-72). Herrsching am Ammersee: IEEE.

Haenni, N., Lungu, M., Schwarz, N., & Nierstrasz, O. (2013). Categorizing Developer Information Needs in Software Ecosystems. Bern: WEA 2013 Proceedings of the 2013 International Workshop on Ecosystem Architectures.

Hossain, M. A., Versteeg, S., Han, J., Kabir, M. A., Jiang, J., & Schneider, J.-G. (2018). Mining Accurate Message Formats for Service APIs. *2018 IEEE 25th International Conference on Software Analysis, Evolution and Reengineering (SANER)* (pp. 266-276). Campobasso: IEEE.

Jiang, H., Zhang, J., Li, X., Ren, Z., & Lo, D. (2016). A More Accurate Model for Finding Tutorial Segments Explaining APIs.

IEEE 23rd International Conference on Software Analysis, Evolution, and Reengineering (pp. 157-167). Osaka: IEEE.

Ko, A. J., Aung, H., & Myers, B. A. (2005). Eliciting design requirements for maintenance-oriented IDEs: a detailed study of corrective and perfective maintenance tasks. *27th International Conference on Software Engineering* (pp. 126-135). Saint Louis: ICSE.

Maalej, W., & Robillard, M. P. (2013). Patterns of Knowledge in API Reference Documentation. *IEEE Transactions on Software Engineering, 39*(9), 1264-1282.

Martin P. Robillard, A. M.-V. (2017). On-Demand Developer Documentation. Dallas: IEEE International Conference on Software Maintenance and Evolution.

McBurney, P. W., Jiang, S., Kessentini, M., Kraft, N. A., Armaly, A., Mkaouer, W., & McMillan, C. (2017). Towards Prioritizing Documentation Effort. *IEEE Transactions on Software Engineering*, 1-1.

McLellan, S. G., Roesler, A. W., Tempest, J. T., & Spinuzzi, C. I. (1998). Building More Usable APIs. *IEEE Software, 15*(3), 78-86.

Neumann, A., Laranjeiro, N., & Bernardino, J. (2018). An Analysis of Public REST Web Service APIs. *IEEE Transactions on Services Computing*, 1-1.

Pfleeger, S. L., & Atlee, J. M. (2010). *Software Engineering - Theory and Practice.* Upper Saddle River: Prentice Hall. Robillard, M. P., & DeLine, R. (2011). A Field Study of API Learning Obstacle. *Journal of Empirical Software Engineering,*

16(6), 703-732.

S. M., S., Anslow, C., & Maurer, F. (n.d.). A Case Study of Web API Evolution. *2015 IEEE World Congress on Services* (p. 8). TBA: IEEE.

Watson, R. (2012). Developing best practices for API reference documentation: Creating a platform to study how programmers learn new APIs. *IEEE International Professional Communication Conference* (pp. 1-9). Orlando: IEEE.

Wu, N., Hou, D., & Liu, Q. (2016). Linking Usage Tutorials into API Client Code. *IEEE/ACM 3rd International Workshop on CrowdSourcing in Software Engineering (CSI-SE)* (pp. 22-28). Austin: IEEE/ACM.

Augmented Reality for Library Literacy: Collaborating for Innovative Instruction and Content Development

Wendy Traas
University of British Columbia, Canada.
wendy.traas@ubc.ca

Eric M. Meyers
University of British Columbia, Canada.
eric.meyers@ubc.ca

Alexandra Kuskowski
University of British Columbia, Canada.
alex.kuskowski@ubc.ca

ABSTRACT

Although it is most often employed in informal settings, augmented reality (AR) is emerging as an exciting way to bring playful, engaging mobile technologies into formal learning environments, such as the academic library. In this poster we document a multi-year design-based exploration of augmented reality employed to enhance library-based information literacy instruction. In a scholar-practitioner partnership between an academic library and faculty and students in an MLIS program, the project team developed an iterative approach to designing, creating, and evaluating AR materials and an app that were integrated with the existing information literacy program at two branch libraries. The emphasis on learning outcomes, both for the participants of information literacy instruction sessions, as well as the MLIS students, differentiate this work from other AR projects that emphasize playful engagement over explicit skill development. We reflect on the affordances and constraints of using AR in academic libraries, as well as the value of scholar-practitioner partnerships for enhancing library-based instruction.

KEYWORDS

Augmented reality, information literacy, design-based research, academic libraries

INTRODUCTION

The 2016 NMC Horizon Report identifies augmented reality (AR) as an emerging educational technology expected to have a significant impact on higher education in the next two to three years (Johnson, Adams Becker, Mullins, et al., 2016). AR refers to "any technology that blends real and virtual information in a meaningful way" (Wu, Lee, Chang & Liang, 2013). The proliferation and popularity of mobile AR applications for casual, playful engagement–witness the phenomenon of *Pokémon Go* or virtual museum apps like *MOMAR*–suggests that this technology may be employed to enhance a range of educational activities and bring high levels of motivation and engagement to what might be perceived as otherwise staid instruction (Radu, 2014; Kesim and Ozarslan, 2012). However, before such technologies can be deployed in learning settings, there is considerable development work that must be done, along with alignment of the activities with the learning outcomes of any instructional components where AR might be used (Giles, 2015; Ireton, Pitts and Ward, 2013). To explore the application of AR in an academic library setting, the authors of this poster developed a scholar-practitioner partnership to apply a theoretical lens to a practice-based development program. Our work was guided by the following research questions:

1. How can AR be employed in the teaching of information literacy?
2. What are the affordances and constraints of AR in formal instructional settings?

We hypothesized that AR technology can create a more engaging and immersive experience for library patrons by allowing them to immediately and independently access information on library resources, promote library literacy, and empower patrons to make better use of their libraries at their own pace. We also sought to bring learning theory into the development process by using successive iterations of an LIS course to develop AR content, and test that content against key learning principles, including motivation and engagement.

METHODS

Our study relied on two approaches, specifically the scholar-practitioner partnership model and design-based research. The scholar-practitioner model originated in clinical settings, namely medicine and psychology, and emphasizes the application of theoretical concepts to the problems of practice. It has since been used employed in other professional programs, including law, social work, and public health. The goal of our partnership was identifying the ways learning theory can be applied to the use of AR technologies, with the intended outcome of enhancing instruction, leveraging classroom-to-practice reflexivity, while also looking for emergent socio-technical insights. Employing a design-based approach to this work, we used iterative cycles of development of AR resources, as well as cyclical evaluation of the process and product. Design-based research is inherently interventionist, emphasizing the study of new methods of learning in situ, but it is not simply figuring out "what works". Rather, the goal is to develop localized and domain-specific theory that can be used across multiple isomorphic contexts (Cobb, Confrey, diSessa et al., 2003).

FINDINGS

The project team comprised a collaboration between an LIS faculty member who teaches in the area of information literacy and instruction, two library faculty working at two different branch locations with different client-based services, and several classes of MLIS students (over 40 in total) enrolled in a user instruction course. The team initially employed free, off-the-shelf AR technologies, such as Aurasma™, but based on the limitations of this environment, eventually moved to the development of an in-house AR smartphone app using a commercially available AR Toolkit. The app has been deployed at the two branch locations. It facilitates way finding, adds value to collections, as well as highlights key resources and service points. The AR app uses the smartphone camera as a scanner to provide overlaid AR menu links and mobile context-specific access to remotely stored digital resources. Student users download the free app onto their iOS device in the context of an orientation session or self-directed exploration in the library space. The app can be used to scan established targets, leading to a display of related digital content in a collection-view on the user's device. Student users have free access to the scanner application. Instructors have additional access to the web server side to manage AR targets and linked resources. Below we highlight key goals and processes that the app facilitates:

Extending Collections: Faculty instructors customized the learning experience by identifying library-related target images for scanning (posters, book covers, pamphlets, etc.) as well as related digital resources to highlight. The AR app allows faculty to draw connections between physical resources and digital content, which can include instructional videos, maps and wayfinding information, and relevant content that exists outside of the university's information ecosystem.

Building Awareness: An innovative library orientation program encourages self-guided interaction with space and resources, making library literacy instruction more sustainable and engaging.

Practice-Based Learning: The project provided authentic learning and media development opportunities to graduate and undergraduate students, including the evaluation of previous development work and the identification of new AR opportunities. Student reflections on the process and product were part of the overall program evaluation.

Pilot testing of the app was performed with undergraduate students in the teacher education program at the university. Data was collected through site-specific surveys and focus groups to assess the app's usefulness to library patrons. The data is being used to improve performance in future iterations of the app. This poster, if accepted, will include pilot test data analysis, and a demonstration of the app.

CONCLUSION

This ongoing study demonstrates the value of scholar-practitioner partnerships in developing leading edge learning innovations in academic libraries. It points to the value, for students, faculty, and institutions of collaboration in the development of instructional systems, particularly where guidance in how to deploy these systems is still emerging. Future work on this project includes further iterative development of the AR targets and supporting materials, a refined app experience cultivated with classroom educators, and continuous evaluation with both end users and student design partners.

REFERENCES

Cobb, P., Confrey, J., diSessa, A., Lehrer, R., and Schauble, L. (2003). Design experiments in educational research. Educational Researcher, 32 (1), 9-13.

Cuendet, S., Bonnard, Q., Do-Lenh, S., & Dillenbourg, P. (2013). Designing augmented reality for the classroom. Computers and Education, 68, 557–569. https://doi.org/10.1016/j.compedu.2013.02.015

Giles, K. (2015). No Budget, No Experience, No Problem: Creating a Library Orientation Game for Freshman Engineering Majors. Journal of Academic Librarianship, 41(2), 170–177. https://doi.org/10.1016/j.acalib.2014.12.005

Ireton D., Pitts J., Ward B. (2013). Library discovery through augmented reality: A game plan for academics. International Journal of Technology, Knowledge and Society, 9(4), 119–128.

Johnson, L., Adams Becker, S., Cummins, M., Estrada, V., Freeman, A., & Hall, C. (2016). NMC Horizon Report: 2016 Higher Education Edition. Austin, Texas: The New Media Consortium. Retrieved from https://www.nmc.org/publication/nmc-horizon-report-2016-higher-education-edition/

Kesim, M., & Ozarslan, Y. (2012). Augmented Reality in Education: Current Technologies and the Potential for Education. Procedia - Social and Behavioral Sciences, 47(222), 297–302. https://doi.org/10.1016/j.sbspro.2012.06.654

Radu, I. (2014). Augmented reality in education: A meta-review and cross-media analysis. Personal and Ubiquitous Computing, 18(6), 1533-1543. DOI: 10.1007/s00779-013-0747-y

Wu, H.-K., Lee, S. W.-Y., Chang, H.-Y., & Liang, J.-C. (2013). Current status, opportunities and challenges of augmented reality in education. *Computers & Education, 62*, 41–49. https://doi.org/10.1016/j.compedu.2012.10.024

iWords: Exploring the Interdisciplinary Vocabularies of Information Research

Bonnie Tulloch
The University of British Columbia, Canada.
bonniejoline@gmail.com

Andrea Hoff
The University of British Columbia, Canada.
akahoff@gmail.com

Saguna Shankar
The University of British Columbia, Canada.
saguna.shankar@gmail.com

Lisa P. Nathan
The University of British Columbia, Canada.
lisa.nathan@ubc.ca

Michelle Kaczmarek
The University of British Columbia, Canada.
michelle.kaczmarek@ubc.ca

ABSTRACT

Language presents an insightful lens through which to consider issues of identity and interdisciplinarity within the field of information science. Through a multiphase research project, we seek to facilitate discussion among practitioners, graduate students and faculty about the way words shape our conceptualizations of information research. This work reports on the theoretical underpinnings of our inquiry and provides preliminary results from the first phase of our project, which included a workshop with 22 members of the iSchool community. During this arts-based workshop, participants created keyword cards and word dice to generate dialogues about the role of language in the field of information research. Moving forward, we will adopt a Social Interactional Approach (De Fina & Georgakopoulou, 2008) to the narrative analysis of these artefacts, exploring the ways scholars used them to frame their research and construct their professional identities.

KEYWORDS

Keywords; Identity; Information science; Interdisciplinarity; iSchools

INTRODUCTION

Information, record, document, relevance, practice, archive, theory, design, research, system. These words are critical to the (often invisible) work of information professionals and scholars. Yet, the ubiquity of these words, which can take on various meanings in different contexts, can pose challenges to communicating what our research is about and, by extension, what information science is capable of contributing to society. This is not a problem unique to information science. Oftentimes, disciplines use the same words to describe alternate things, or employ metaphors differently to conceptualize the meaning of various phenomena. However, this issue is particularly salient for the field of information science, not only because it is attentive to the practices of creating, organizing, representing, and mediating information, but also because it is a "meta-discipline" (Bates, 1999, p.1045) that comprises scholars from diverse disciplinary backgrounds.

BACKGROUND

The interdisciplinary nature of information science means that an awareness of the different ontological, epistemological, and disciplinary values informing the language we use is critical to the process of engaging in information research. One of the challenges to understanding different approaches to research is the language used to describe them. Guiding our exploration of disciplinary language within information science is the work of cultural theorist Raymond Williams (1976), whose concept of keywords has been adopted by various disciplines for the purpose of identifying the communicative tensions associated with different terminologies (e.g., *Keywords for Children's Literature* (2011), *Keywords for Media Studies* (2017), *Keywords for Latina/o Studies* (2017), etc.). Williams' (1976) work draws attention to the way words take on multiple and often conflicting meanings over time that can contribute to misunderstandings among the people who use them, both within and across different cultures. Williams' research relates well to Ludwig Wittgenstein's (1953/2001) descriptions of blurred concepts and language games, as well as the different types of language problems articulated by scholars such as Vivien Petras (2006). We see instances of this conflict in information science (Bates, 1999), where differing views of "information" (Furner, 2015), "research" (Feinberg, 2012), and "interdisciplinarity" (Dillon, 2012; Madsen, 2016) often make it difficult to articulate and enact an interdisciplinary identity (White, 1999).

Unlike much scholarship on keywords, however, the aim of this project is not to identify and describe a definitive set of terms that represents a central vocabulary of information research. Rather, our objective is to identify *methods* for discussing keywords as dynamic conceptual designs that organize the way we think about, conduct, and communicate our research to people within and outside of the field of information science. As such, the fundamental question underlying this project is: *How do our respective vocabularies affect our conceptualizations of information and the interdisciplinary field of information research?*

METHODS

Phase One: iWords Workshop

We designed and held a workshop with 22 members of the iSchool community at the iConference 2018. In the workshop, we hosted a panel discussion and employed a range of arts-based activities to elicit insights on the role language plays in participants' conceptualizations of their research and identities as information scholars. Building on Heckman and Snyder's (2008) observation that "aesthetic experience should play an important role in the education of information professionals," we designed several means of engaging in concrete and playful interaction. These methods included a keyword connection activity, a word dice game, and a graffiti wall. The data collected from the workshop, which took the form of participant observations, keywords, artefacts, and feedback, will be analyzed using a Social Interactional Approach to narrative analysis (De Fina & Georgakopoulou, 2008, p. 382).

Phase Two: Survey of iSchool leaders

In phase two we will conduct an online questionnaire of iSchool leaders (e.g. deans, directors, etc.) within the iConsortium. The open-ended questionnaire is designed to elicit insights on the ways in which iSchool leaders envision and articulate the identities of their units to those within and outside of their academic institutions.

WAYS FORWARD

We believe that the ASIS&T community can draw upon its differences to learn how to better articulate and communicate what its research is about and, by extension, what information science is capable of contributing to society. In this respect, we agree with Madsen (2016) that "[t]o better understand interdisciplinary processes, and to be able to theorize them, we need to look into the concepts and the meaning ascribed to concepts in discourse" (p. 2698-2699). By aiming to view keywords as "small stories" through which we represent our research (De Fina & Georgakopoulou, 2008, p. 385), we hope to better account for the social practices, assumptions, and values that underlie their use in particular contexts. As a whole, this project intends to contribute to a greater understanding of the role that language plays in enacting and envisioning interdisciplinarity in the field of information science. Through this work we engage members of the information science community in reflection and dialogue about the ways we can create more effective communicative pathways. In our preliminary findings, we aim to investigate whether sharing the stories underlying our respective vocabularies may be an effective approach to improving cross cultural, interdisciplinary communication. The small stories generated by these keyword activities may provide us with an intertextual frame of reference through which to surface the multiple voices and perspectives that shape the larger meta-narrative of information science.

REFERENCES

Bates, M. (1999). The invisible substrate of information science. *Journal of the American Society for Information Science 50*(12), 1043-1050.

De Fina, A., & Georgakopoulou, A. (2008). Analysing narratives as practices. *Qualitative Research*, *8*(3), 379-387.

Dillon, A. (2012). What it means to be an iSchool. *Journal of Education for Library & Information Science, 53*(4), 267–273.

Feinberg, M. (2012). Information studies, the humanities, and design research: interdisciplinary opportunities. In *Proceedings of the 2012 iConference* (pp. 18–24). ACM. Retrieved from http://dl.acm.org/citation.cfm?id=2132179

Furner, J. (2015). Information science is neither. *Library Trends 63*(3), 362-377.

Heckman, R., & Snyder, J. (2008). The role of the arts in an iSchool education. *Proceedings of the iConference 2008: iFutures: Systems, Selves, Society,* February 28-March 1, UCLA, Los Angeles, CA.

Madsen, D. (2016). Liberating interdisciplinarity from myth: An exploration of the discursive construction of identities in information studies. *Journal of the Association for Information Science and Technology 67*(11), 2697-2709.

Petras, V. (2006). *Translating dialects in search: Mapping between specialized languages of discourse and documentary languages* (Doctoral dissertation). University of California, Berkeley.

White, H.D. (1999). Scientist-poets wanted. *Journal of the American Society for Information Science 50*(12), 1052-1053.

Williams, R. (1976). Introduction. In *Keywords: A vocabulary of culture and society*, (pp. 9–24). New York: Oxford University Press.

Wittgenstein, L. (2001). *Philosophical investigations: the german text, with revised English translation* (1953). Trans. G.E.M. Anscombe, Oxford, UK: Blackwell Publishing.

Fake It to Make It, Media Literacy, and Persuasive Design: Using the Functional Triad as a Tool for Investigating Persuasive Elements in a Fake News Simulator

Alex Urban
University of Missouri, USA. urbanac@mail.missouri.edu

Joi Moore
University of Missouri, USA. moorejoi@missouri.edu

Carl Hewitt
University of Missouri, USA. cjh69h@mail.missouri.edu

ABSTRACT

How can we motivate social media users to critically analyze potential misinformation? Video games may be one way. This project presents research on a social-impact game, *Fake It to Make It*, which positions players as for-profit misinformation disseminators. Drawing upon the BJ Fogg's Functional Triad for Persuasive Computers and paying particular attention to the usability and perceived credibility of *Fake It to Make It*, this research analyzed the game from a persuasive design lens using player-participant data. This was accomplished through screen-captured gameplay as well as interviews and retrospective think-alouds. Additionally, to determine if the game affects abilities to assess claims on social media, pre- and post-intervention media literacy assessments were utilized. With this data, the researchers provide design recommendations to increase usability, influence procedural knowledge on social media, and promote continued gameplay and greater emotional/behavioral impact.

KEYWORDS

Social media, video games, media literacy, persuasive technologies

INTRODUCTION

How can we motivate social media users to critically analyze potential misinformation? Video games may be one way. This project presents research on a fake news simulator created by designer/developer Amanda Warner, *Fake It to Make It*, which positions players as for-profit misinformation disseminators. Specifically, this research includes: (1) an analysis of the game from a persuasive design lens using player-participant data, (2) an analysis of participant abilities to assess claims on social media before and after exposure to *Fake It to Make It*, and (3) design recommendations for greater emotional/behavioral impact and usability.

PROBLEM

While automated assessment methods have shown high accuracy results in classification tasks with online media, this has only been in limited domains (Conroy, Rubin, Chen, 2016). Currently, it is incumbent on the consumers to rely on their media literacy skills when detecting disinformation. Unfortunately, a concerning study by Stanford researchers shows that many college students lack the skills to distinguish between legitimate journalism and false, misleading, or satirical "news" (Wineberg, 2016). In addition to helping students spot signs of sensationalized or fictional online "news" articles, it is key that they also recognize how it is spread and its social impact. Yet, how can we motivate social media users to critically analyze potential misinformation when it is easier to simply allow confirming viewpoints into social media feeds? Well-designed video games may be one way to motivate learners to scrutinize news sources in social media spaces. Consequently, it is crucial to analyze the effectiveness of existing serious games as media literacy tools.

BACKGROUND

Fake It to Make It is a self-described "social-impact game about fake news" (Warner, n.d.) This single-player, browser-based game positions players as misinformation "entrepreneurs"; players spread illegitimate news—using techniques such as purchasing bots and manipulating viewers' fears, anger, and other strong emotions—in order to generate shares, and, thus, profit. The developer of the game, Amanda Warner, states that her hope with the game is to see the actions, attitudes, and beliefs of players change after playing the game (Warner, n.d.).

Fake It to Make It does indeed provide a space for players to identify common themes and techniques used in the dissemination of false or misleading stories. While Warner's game was created to facilitate role-playing—a key advantage of persuasive technologies—it may lack the persuasive design elements to motivate players to continue playing the game, let alone promote greater media literacy (Fogg, 2007, p. 141). As such, the following research questions were posed:

RESEARCH QUESTIONS

1. How does *Fake It to Make It* utilize persuasive design elements to motivate sustained gameplay?

2. How does *Fake It to Make It*'s usability influence its perceived credibility as a persuasive media literacy tool?
3. Does *Fake It to Make It*'s current design promote procedural knowledge with claims on social media, i.e. verifying a post's sources and motivations?

THEORETICAL FRAMEWORK

This research utilizes BJ Fogg's Functional Triad, which positions technologies as persuasive tools, media, or social actors, to determine which features require improvements to turn *Fake It to Make It* into a persuasive game. Persuasive *tools* condition a behavior and lead the user through a pre-set process. As this is a role-playing game and not intended to teach players how to spread disinformation, this study focuses on the game as a form of persuasive *media*, which allows for the exploration of causal relationships, and as a persuasive social *actor*, which relies on positive feedback and social support.

In addition to drawing upon the Functional Triad, this research investigates the inherent usability and perceived credibility of *Fake It to Make It*. Interactive systems often use what Fogg calls "microsuasion," subtle advice to help users solve a problem, such as successfully navigating a system; as such, an interface layout and menu options can be a form of advice. (Fogg, 2007, p. 141) If *Fake It to Make It*'s interface is a hindrance in performing certain actions, its perceived credibility diminishes.

METHODOLOGY AND PARTICIPANTS

To determine the efficacy of the game's motivational affordances and its effect on procedural knowledge with social media posts, the researchers used (1) demographic questionnaires (2) pre-test media literacy assessments, (3) exposure to the intervention, (4) post-test media literacy assessments, and (5) short semi-structured interviews with a retrospective think-alouds. There were seven participants in this study, all of whom completed the demographic questionnaire. This questionnaire included questions to reveal their familiarity with video games and perceived proximity to misinformation. Questions related to misinformation were adapted from the Pew Research Center (2016). The researchers requested the participants' self-reported proximity to gaming and misinformation to gain insight into their in-game choices during the intervention, attitudes toward the intervention, and procedural knowledge of verifying claims on social media.

FINDINGS & CONCLUSION

After conducting the thematic analysis of interviews and retrospective think-alouds, it became apparent that attitudes toward the game varied greatly. In total, there were 58 positive codes, 69 negative codes, and 11 indifferent codes in response to aspects of computers as persuasive media (*cause-and-effect*, *environmental*, and *object simulations*) and persuasive social actors (*language* and *physical cues*). *Psychological cues, social interaction*, and *social roles* did not emerge as significant themes. This is most likely due to simulation not being overly didactic or emphasizing its moral intentions or authority.

Correlating this thematic analysis with 3.5 hours of recorded gameplay, the researchers suggest providing quicker, more poignant feedback, greater emphasis on in-game goals, and including more realistic elements. Additionally, by drawing upon the cognitive principles of multimedia learning and reducing split-attention effect with gestalt guidelines, the usability—and thus credibility—of the game will increase. Specifically, the researchers recommend applying greater adherence to Mayer's cognitive principles of signalling and modality as well as the gestalt principle of continuation (2017). Lastly, while *Fake It to Make It* provides a glimpse at disinformation as a means for wealth, it does not expound upon the motivations and minute techniques used by politically motivated actors. By doing so, procedural knowledge with social media claims may increase as well. With these recommendations, *Fake It to Make It* may become a useful—and fun—persuasive game.

This research and greater information on its findings will be presented in a visual format including posters describing findings, design recommendations, and a computer to play the game and discuss its elements.

REFERENCES

Conroy, N. J., Rubin, V. L., & Yimin, C. (2015). Automatic Deception Detection: Methods for Finding Fake News. Proceedings Of The Association For Information Science & Technology, 52(1), 1.

Fogg, B. J., Cueller, G., & Danielson, D. (2007). Motivating, Influencing, and Persuading Users: An Introduction to Captology. In A. Sears & J. Jacko (Eds.), The Human-Computer Interaction Handbook (133 - 147). Location: CRC Press.

Mayer, R. & Mayer, R. (2010) Nine Ways to Reduce Cognitive Load in Multimedia Learning, Educational Psychologist, 38:1, 43-52, DOI: 10.1207/S15326985EP3801_6

Pew Research Center. (2016) "Many Americans Believe Fake News Is Sowing Confusion" Washington, D.C. Available at: http://www.journalism.org/2016/12/15/many-americans-believe-fake-news-is-sowing-confusion/.

Warner, A. Fake it To Make It. Retrieved from https://www.fakeittomakeitgame.com/

Wineburg, S., McGrew, S., Breakstone, J., Ortega, T. (2016). Evaluating Information: The Cornerstone of Civic Online Reasoning. Stanford Digital Repository. Available at: http://purl.stanford.edu/fv751yt5934

Collaboration and Friendship of Scholars: A Dual Metwork Analysis

Xianwen Wang
Dalian University of Technology, China.
xianwenwang@dlut.edu.cn

Shenmeng Xu
SUniversity of North Carolina at Chapel Hill, USA.
shenmeng@email.unc.edu

Yunxue Cui
Dalian University of Technology, China.
zmxiaohai@mail.dlut.edu.cn

ABSTRACT

In this study, we analyze the dual network of scholars' co-authorship and online friendship. We conduct comparisons of these two networks in the field of scientometrics. Using co-authorship data of publications and following data on ResearchGate, we extract the co-authorship network and online friendship network, respectively. The results reveal several topological differences between these two networks. The edges of co-authorship network are more decentralized than the online friendship network. Moreover, the co-authorship network has a clear community structure, while the online friendship network has clustered communities. However, the two networks have a strong internal relationship. Specifically, the co-authorship intensity has an impact on the formation of social relations. The academic social network promotes the integration of and scholarly communication among academic communities.

KEYWORDS

Social network, co-authorship, online friendship, relation, scientist, altmetrics.

INTRODUCTION

There are various perspectives on the research about scientist' social network, Van Noorden (2014) compared the characteristics of various academic social networking sites as a whole. Haustein (2014) analyzed the relationship between the use behavior of astrophysicists on Twitter and their publication behavior. Some researchers focus on the influence of social network on academic benefits and academic evaluation (Thelwall & Kousha, 2015). Others are more interested in the reasons and motivations for scholars to use social networks (Manca & Ranieri, 2017). Ke, Ahn, & Sugimoto (2017) found that Twitter "has been employed by scholars across the disciplinary spectrum". Previous studies mainly focus on the single network of online friendship among scholars, and didn't reveal the formation mechanism of the network, which may be explained by the connections between the online friendship in the virtual world and the co-authorship in the real world. In this study, our goal is to addresses the following research questions: What are the characteristics of scholars' co-authorship network and online friendship network? What are the connections of scholars' co-authorship network and online friendship network?

DATA

The co-authorship network is built from the 2262 publications in two journals, *Scientometrics* and *Journal of Informetrics*, from 2012 to 2016, a five-year time span. We select 255 scholars with the most publications (with no less than four publications) in the field of scientometrics as research objects. The scholars' friendship network is extracted from the following data collected from ResearchGate. The data are collected in March 2017. There are 68 scholars among 255 productive authors don't have ResearchGate account or have no friendship on ResearchGate.

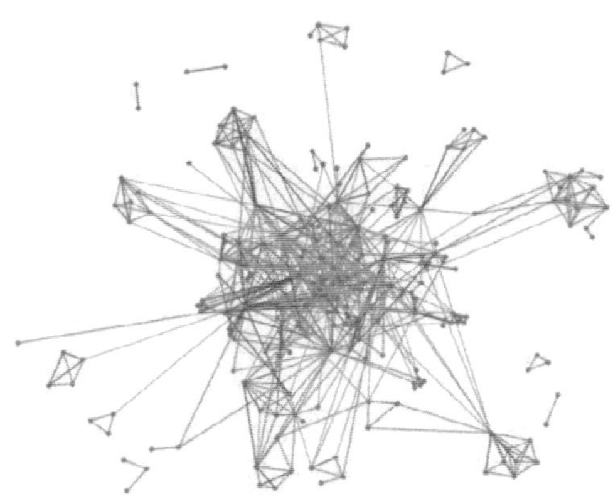

Figure 1. A cross network of co-authorship network and ResearchGate friendship network.

RESULTS

The topology of the network

Figure 1 shows a cross-network combining the two networks of co-authorship network and online friendship network. Since the nodes of the two networks are identical, we use different line colors to display the links in each network. Specifically, the blue lines represent the co-authorship, the gray lines represent online friendship, and the red lines indicate the presence of both relationships. As Figure 1 shows, the grey lines and the red lines are gathered around the center, while the blue lines are more evenly distributed. This distribution explains the difference in the average length and average clustering coefficient of the two networks. The co-authorship network has a more complete subgraph structure, which means that it has a higher average clustering coefficient. Overall, both networks have "small world" network features.

Relation analysis of two networks

In Figure 2 and Figure 3, different colors represent different communities. The size of the nodes indicates the degree of the nodes. Comparing to the online friendship network, the community structure of the co-authorship network is clearer, with more isolated small groups within which the nodes are more closely linked. This indicates frequent communication inside a community but less frequent communication with other communities. For the ResearchGate friendship network, however, the nodes are clustered, forming indistinct boundaries among communities.

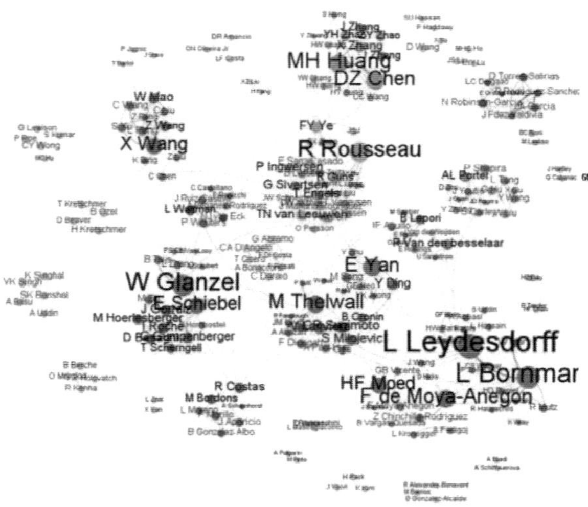

Figure 2. Co-authorship network.

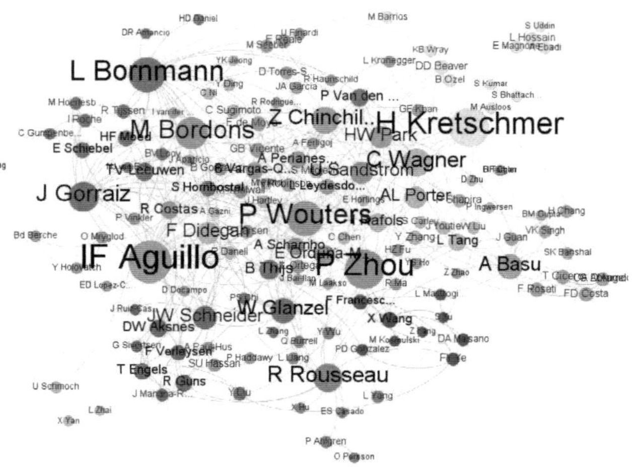

Figure 3. Online friendship network.

CONCLUSION

For scholars in the field of scientometrics, their co-authorship network has different topology features from the ResearchGate friendship network. The co-authorship network has both a higher average clustering coefficient and a higher path length, while its density (after removing the isolated nodes) is lower than the social network. This reflects the difference of distribution of edges in these two networks: the co-authorship network edges are more decentralized while the online friendship network edges are concentrated. However, both networks have the characteristics of 'small-world' networks and 'scale-free' networks. Regarding community structures, the co-authorship network displays a clear structure: the boundaries of the groups are distinct; the internal connections within the communities are close, and the external connections are sparse. The structure of the online friendship network is the opposite: the communities are clustered, and both internal and external connections are abundant. Most scholars belonging to the same community in the co-authorship network also belong to the same community in the online friendship network. Therefore, the co-authorship network has a similar community relation to the online friendship network. Considering the number of communities in academic social network is half of that in co-authorship network, the social networking sites for scholars promoted the integration and academic exchange of scientific communities.

ACKNOWLEDGMENTS

This work was supported by the "National Natural Science Foundation of China" (71673038, 71503031), and the project of "Fundamental Research Funds for the Central Universities" (DUT18JC32).

REFERENCES

Haustein, S., Bowman, T. D., Holmberg, K., Peters, I., & Larivière, V. (2014). Astrophysicists on twitter: an in-depth analysis of tweeting and scientific publication behavior. *Aslib Journal of Information Management*, 66(3), 279-296(18).

Ke, Q., Ahn, Y. Y., & Sugimoto, C. R. (2017). A systematic identification and analysis of scholars on twitter. *Plos One*, *12*(4), e0175368.

Manca, S., & Ranieri, M. (2017). Networked scholarship and motivations for social media use in scholarly communication. *International Review of Research in Open & Distance Learning*, *18*(2), 133-138.

Thelwall, M., & Kousha, K. (2015). ResearchGate: Disseminating, communicating, and measuring scholarship?. *Journal of the Association for Information Science and Technology*, *66*(5), 876-889.

Van Noorden, R. (2014). Scholars and the social network. *Nature*, *512*(7513), 126.

What Type of Domain Knowledge is Cited by Articles with High Interdisciplinary Degree?

Yuzhuo Wang
Nangjing University of Science and Technology, China.
Wangyz@njust.edu.cn

Chengzhi Zhang
Nangjing University of Science and Technology, China.
Zhangcz@njust.edu.cn

ABSTRACT

Interdisciplinary studies require integration of principles, theories and practices from multiple disciplines. What type of domain knowledge will be applied more in such researches? Since scientific paradigms differ in fields, this paper takes computer science (CS) as a case and investigates utilization patterns of CS knowledge in articles from PLOS One with high interdisciplinary degree (IDD) by citation content analysis. Since scholars usually organize and indicate used knowledge in methodology, we study articles which cite CS articles in this section. After extracting citation content from citing articles, we identify the cited knowledge and analyse the type of cited knowledge. Experimental results show that: In the PLOS One articles which cited the CS knowledge, algorithm is the most used knowledge type and the most used object is random forests. Our study can be applied to understand how articles with high IDD use the knowledge from other disciplines in the future.

KEYWORDS

Cross-discipline, knowledge diffusion, citation content analysis.

INTRODUCTION

Interdisciplinary knowledge diffusion has important implications for promoting advance of science and technology. In 1953, Watson and Crick first put forward the famous model of double helix structure of DNA molecules. This is one of the greatest achievements of life science, which is a perfect combination of knowledge from domain of chemistry, biology and physics. Exploring what knowledge has exchanged between different disciplines can help scholars better understand the formation of disciplinary knowledge structure and development of new disciplines. However, most of the existing studies mainly used bibliographic information of academic papers and focus on which disciplines exchange knowledge (Leeuwen 2000; Vugteveen, Lenders, & Besselaar 2014; Xu, Guo, Yue, Ru, & Fang 2016). Questions such as '*What knowledge has been diffused among different disciplines*' and '*What is the type of this interdisciplinary knowledge?*' have no answers yet. Scholars usually organize and indicate used knowledge in section about methodology ("method" section) in articles. Can citation content from 'method' sections be analyzed to find answers of these questions?

This paper chooses *Computer Science* (CS) as a case and investigates cited CS knowledge in articles with high IDD. All of the citation content is from "method" section in interdisciplinary articles published by PLOS One. Based on the citation content in these articles, we analyze what kind of CS knowledge cited by these articles with high IDD in 'method' section.

METHODOLOGY

Data collection and processing

We collect all the articles published by PLOS One (http://journals.plos.org/plosone/) from 2003 to 2016, and pick out 24, 500 articles which cite at least one reference belongs to one of seven sub-discipline of CS according to category of 'Master Journal List' (*http://mjl.clarivate.com/cgi-bin/jrnlst/jlsubcatg.cgi?PC=K&from=groupmessage&isappinstalled=0*).

$^2D^S$ (Zhang, Rousseau, & Glänzel 2016) is applied to measure the IDD of article:

$$^2D^S = 1 - \sum_{i,j=1}^{N}(1 - d_{ij})p_ip_j \qquad (1)$$

Where, i and j represent two cited subject fields, N is number of cited subject field (variety), p_i , p_j mean proportion of the number of i, j in the number of all cited disciplines(balance) respectively, and d_{ij} is the difference between i and j (disparity). Leinster & Cobbold (2012) proposed $^qD^S$ to measure the diversity of an object, Zhang, Rousseau, & Glänzel (2016) set the case q = 2, and used the $^2D^S$ to measure the IDD of an academic article. They identified the subject fields assigned to cited items in the article's reference list, and took variety, balance, and disparity of cited reference into account.

Top 10% articles (2, 450) are chosen as articles with high IDD. We download these papers in XML format from PLOS One, and classify all the sections into four categories, namely *Introduction, Method, Result* and *Conclusion*. Then, reference and the corresponding citation content (citation sentence, previous and later two sentences of the citation sentence) in 'method' section are extracted. CS citation sentences are identified by matching journal title of each reference with CS journal title in 'Master

Journal List'. Finally, we obtain 1, 054 citation sentences and 802 references (597 cited papers) from 469 papers with high IDD.

Citation content analysis of knowledge in "method" section

A professor and a PhD candidate are invited to annotate the CS knowledge in citation sentences. Just to be clear, all of the CS knowledge is collectively called cited object. Firstly, they identify the name of cited object, and different names of the same object are summarized as the same name. If the object in a sentence cannot be recognized, they will record it as 'Other'. Furthermore, they label the type of object according to the authors' description and explanation on the Internet. Finally, all of
the cited object are classified into 14 categories, namely *Algorithm, Concept, Data, Data structure, Experimental process, Formula/Function, Framework/Theory, Index, Model, Other, Program, Research background, Software* and *Tool.*

RESULTS ANALYSIS

The top-5 cited object in CS citation content

According to annotation result, we count the number of each kind of cited object. After filtering the object that cannot be identified, the top-5 cited objects are listed in table 1. These objects include three algorithms, a software and a program. The most highly cited object is *random forests*. In various software, *VMD* is most used in articles with high IDD. *AMBER* has the highest frequency of occurrence in all programs. As general algorithm, random forests and *SVM* are used for multiple task. *SHAKE*, *VMD* and *AMBER* have higher pertinence, and all of them are related to molecular dynamics. It is obvious that PLOS One contains many biological articles, and researches are related to molecular dynamics. Authors need an algorithm or a programmer to investigate molecular dynamics, a visualization software can help them to show their results.

Rank	Name	Frequency	Type	Rank	Name	Frequency	Type
1	*Random forests*	43	Algorithm	*4*	*SHAKE*	16	Algorithm
2	*VMD*	31	Software	*5*	*AMBER*	9	Program
3	*SVM*	19	Algorithm	-	-	-	-

Table1. The top-5 highly cited object in CS citation content

Knowledge type of cited object in CS citation content

We classify all the cited objects into 14 categories. Table 2 displays the proportion of each category. Although some of the knowledge that failed to identify the category was marked as 'Other', category of 'Other' accounted for only 5.88% in all objects. Therefore, most of the knowledge is clearly expressed in the process of being cited, and we can identify the category. Among all kinds of objects, algorithm, model, and software are the top three types, which occupy more than half of amount of the cited knowledge. They are more likely to be used as methods in articles. The last three are experimental process, research background and data structure, and these are more bias towards a description than a specific method. It is obvious that in the 'method' section of high IDD articles, CS knowledge is used more as a method rather than introduction.

No.	Type	Frequency	Percentage	No.	Type	Frequency	Percentage
1	Algorithm	305	28.94%	*8*	Data	41	3.89%
2	Model	261	24.76%	*9*	Program	34	3.23%
3	Software	100	9.49%	*10*	Formula/function	24	2.28%
4	Index	78	7.40%	*11*	Framework/Theory	18	1.71%
5	Other	62	5.88%	*12*	Experimental process	14	1.33%
6	Concept	58	5.50%	*13*	Research Background	8	0.76%
7	Tool	46	4.36%	*14*	Data structure	5	0.47%

Table2. Proportion about different type of cited object CONCLUSION AND FUTURE WORKS

One articles. Results indicate that among all kinds of knowledge, the most highly cited one is *random forests*. Similarly, among the different types of knowledge, the most cited type is algorithms.

In general, we carry out a case study about what type of CS knowledge cited by articles with high IDD. In this paper, we only consider the cited knowledge of CS in the "method" section of articles. In the future, categories, motivations and functions of cited knowledge will be taken into account, we will not only know what the knowledge is, but also know how the knowledge exchanges and why the knowledge exchanges. In addition, scope of the study will be extended from the 'method' to all kinds of sections in the full text to explore the differences of cited knowledge in different sections. At the same time, more disciplines besides CS will be analyzed, and the IDD will be divide into different intervals. Based on cited object of a discipline in papers with different IDD, we will investigate the differences and analyze the reason for differences.

ACKNOWLEDGMENTS

This work is supported by Major Projects of National Social Science Fund (No.17ZDA291).

REFERENCES

Leeuwen, T. V. (2000). Interdisciplinary dynamics of modern science: analysis of cross-disciplinary citation flows. *Research Evaluation*, 9(3), 183-187.

Leinster, T., & Cobbold, C. A. (2012). Measuring diversity: the importance of species similarity. *Ecology*, 93(3), 477-489. Vugteveen, P., Lenders, R., & Besselaar, P. V. D. (2014). The dynamics of interdisciplinary research fields: the case of river research. *Scientometrics*, 100(1), 73-96.

Xu, H., Guo, T., Yue, Z., Ru, L., & Fang, S. (2016). Interdisciplinary topics of information science: a study based on the terms interdisciplinarity index series. *Scientometrics*, 106(2), 583-601.

Zhang, L., Rousseau, R., & Glänzel, W. (2016). Diversity of references as an indicator of the interdisciplinarity of journals: Taking similarity between subject fields into account. *Journal of the Association for Information Science & Technology*, 67(5), 111-112.

Health Data Accessibility: A Preliminary Study of Biotech and Medicine Industry Startup Stakeholders

Zih-Han Wang
University of Washington, USA. zhwang96@uw.edu

Wei Jeng
National Taiwan University, Taiwan. wjeng@ntu.edu.tw

ABSTRACT

Recent research has been emerging on the issues related to health data and informatics; however, there is a dilemma between data accessibility and ethical concerns in today's biotech and medicine industry (BMI) development. Conducting a case study through qualitative interviews of nine participants, we investigate the actual practices that the BMI startup community engages in while accessing and collecting health data for their businesses, as well as the insights of those who are eager to change and improve the current environment. Our preliminary results reveal the high cost of accessing and collecting clinical data in BMI fields, not only in terms of monetary price but also the strict regulations. Interestingly, rather than merely relaxing the regulations, many BMI startups hope that the regulations become more transparent and well-rounded.

KEYWORDS

Data accessibility and reusability, health informatics, medical data, health data, data infrastructure

INTRODUCTION

When data involves human beings, there are immediate concerns about ethics and privacy; this has made health data one of the most sensitive data types. Currently, to obtain data and patients, biotech and medicine industry (hereafter: BMI) startups need to acquire approvals from the Food and Drug Administration (FDA) as well as the Institutional Review Board (IRB). These processes, as well as database access, can be and often are designed to be labor-intensive, time-consuming, and expensive[1].

In order to investigate the current states of BMI startups' perceived data accessibility, we conduct a case study in Taiwan. Since Taiwan is ranked one of the top-performing countries in the area of access to healthcare by the Economist (EIU, 2017), as well as at the top in terms of openness of government data by New York Times and by Global Open Data Index (Carroll and Frakt, 2017; Open Knowledge Network, 2018), we anticipate that BMI startups' data accessibility in Taiwan can serve as an important reference case, revealing potential challenges that might be encountered by others. Our main research questions include the obstacles startups face when accessing health data, as well as the ideal mechanism that BMI startups perceive in order to access data.

DATA COLLECTION

We selected the interview method to answer our research questions, as we want to directly capture different stakeholders' perceptions and insights. We follow a semi-structured design for preparing prompts, since we anticipate needing flexibility to adjust the sequence of questions to get deeper understanding in words that we are not familiar with. Our interview consists of three stakeholder groups. Group A includes three participants working on BMI startups without in-hospital working experience, as we assume those without in-hospital practitioners may have fewer resources and connections comparatively. Group B consists of three in-hospital physicians, in order to understand medical personnel's attitudes about data accessibility. Our rationale is that medical personnel are the people standing between startups/hospitals and patients, thus playing an important role in the data access and collecting process. Group C consists of three medical personnel with startup experience, as we would like to observe if they have advantages in general over Group A or, counterintuitively, interwoven limitations.

RESULTS

Occasion for data access. Through the interviews, we discovered channels that startups utilize to access data include social media, such as Facebook or LINE, real-world personal networks, or even the team member's patients. Some startups have asked the national academy of Taiwan (i.e., Academia Sinica) and insurance companies for help, but found such organizations have no right to release any information. Others intend to visit patients or elders randomly by knocking on the doors of houses or rehabilitation centers, but nearly no one has accepted their requests. Some interviewees offered other possible channels, such as turning to private health evaluation centers for help and sharing the patients' data while startups offer techniques, systems, and data collecting research assistants.

Obstacles for BMI startups to access and collect clinical data. We also clarified the obstacles for startups to access and collect data. To acquire IRB approval, startups must have doctors as their projects' principal investigators. However, there are a few issues with this; first, physicians are difficult to reach. Second, medical personnel is often unwilling to offer help, since their workload in hospitals is too heavy and there are risks to promoting startup products to patients. Third, the cost of accessing and collecting data is very high. Last but not least, there are regulation barriers. Every organization with health databases has their

[1] Using National Health Insurance Research Database (NHIRD) in Taiwan as an example, a single request for data access may cost approximately USD 30,000 according to National Health Insurance Administration Ministry of Health and Welfare. (n.d.) in Taiwan.

own IRB regulations to follow. Also, IRB currently requires every project applying for its approval to be an academic project, so the startups have to modify their project to resemble research. To them, this is a task that wastes considerable time and effort.

Desired BMI data infrastructure in terms of data accessibility. Some BMI startups responded that it is acceptable for regulations to be strict, as long as they are well-informed and coherent. Regarding medical personnel, one participant stated that doctors have no right to use patients' data to aid startups, while another expects the regulations to be loosened, and stated, "The economy will die because of the restricted environment…when I mentor new-coming doctors, I look at them, expecting they don't need to do every detailed work and can tell what can be achieved with data and technologies."

Tension between the process toward IRB's approval and the startup's development cycle. Serving as a trusted third party, IRB has an important responsibility to protect research subjects, including patients. However, as suggested by some interviewees, months of review may be too long for startups, slowing down their technical innovation. It is fundamentally challenging to resolve this tension between the IRB approval process and the startup development cycle. We leave it to future work to explore possible solutions from policy-making perspectives.

DISCUSSIONS AND FUTURE WORK

Startups' perceived data needs. Our results revealed types of discrepancies between perceived and actual data needs. In particular, some participants in the BMI Group do not distinguish statistical information from raw data. For example, a participant expressed that their startup would be happy to access to raw health data in the NHIRD database. However, through further interviewing the participant, we found that what they might need first is statistical information, e.g., the percentage of adults using software applications for monitoring or the percentage of adult taking birth control. Our observation is that some participants in Group A may lack practice with experimental designs and experience dealing with research data, and they might have misconceptions about their data requests and ethical accountability. For example, for conducting a user experience survey, some BMI startups may not know they can simply obtain an IRB application for Minimal Risk Research, which is a relatively fast process compared to a regular application. An interesting future work direction is to assess participants' data literacy and inquire about their definition of data and data privacy, and triangulate with their data needs.

Suggestions for government and startup accelerators. We also observed that startups have a strong demand for the government to make regulation adjustments so that they are more transparent and well-informed, clearly informing startups what they can and cannot do. Most participants in the BMI Group expect a better channel for reaching potential users or self-reported patient data, e.g., a patient-matching website. For startup accelerators, they can focus more on how to mentor startups going through FDA or IRB approvals. As mentioned above, startups may not be familiar with every application regulation, or they may not know where their product falls under FDA classification. It would be very helpful if startup accelerators could provide mentorship on the complicated regulations and assist startups in reaching doctors, utilizing their large network.

In sum, this preliminary study investigated the current practices of healthcare startups accessing and collecting health data. Through nine in-person interviews, we identified several obstacles these startups encountered when attempting to balance development and ethics and summarized their expectations about health data accessibility. Despite the unsatisfactory current practices, we observed that many of the obstacles can be overcome concertedly by the government, hospitals, and startup accelerators. We hope our findings can provide insights on how to reach mutually beneficial results for all stakeholders, thereby helping create a better environment for startups to access and collect data. As a long-term research effort, we hope to systematically investigate various stakeholders in the ecosystem. To achieve this, we plan to expand our sample group by recruiting the IT and legal department directors in the hospitals.

ACKNOWLEDGEMENT

This study is funded by the Ministry of Science and Technology under Grants No. 107-2636-H-002 -002-. This work was also supported by the Center for Research in Econometric Theory and Applications (Grant no. 107L900204) from The Featured Areas Research Center Program within the framework of the Higher Education Sprout Project by the Ministry of Education (MOE) in Taiwan, and by the Ministry of Science and Technology (MOST), Taiwan, under Grant No. MOST 107-3017-F-002-004-.

REFERENCES

Carroll, A. E., & Frakt, A. (2017) The leap to single-payer: what Taiwan can teach how one nation transformed a health care system. New York Times.

Economist Intelligence Unit "EIU" (2017). Global access to healthcare building sustainable health systems. Economist Intelligence Report.

Ministry of Health and Welfare. (n.d.) https://www.mohw.gov.tw/mp-2.html

Open Knowledge Network (2018). Global Data Index – by places. Retrieved from https://index.okfn.org/place/

Shueh, J. (2014). Open Data: What Is It and Why Should You Care? Retrieved from: http://www.govtech.com/data/Got-Data-Make-it-Open-Data-with-These-Tips.html

Readiness for and Barriers to Implementation of Linked Data by Pakistani Libraries

Nosheen Fatima Warraich
University of the Punjab, Pakistan.
nosheen.im@pu.edu.pk

Abebe Rorissa
University at Albany, State University of New York, USA
arorissa@albany.edu

ABSTRACT

The extant literature adequately documents Linked Data initiatives primarily undertaken and implemented in information environments and cultural institutions in Europe and North America. Information professionals play crucial roles in implementing those initiatives that can potentially improve access to knowledge and information. In order to gauge the level of Linked Data application in libraries and have a broader and global understanding, it is important that researchers also explore this topic in the context of libraries in developing countries. Accordingly, our aim in the current study was to assess the willingness and level of interest in the application of Linked Data by librarians in Pakistan as well as determine their perceptions of the barriers to Linked Data application in their respective libraries. A survey of information professionals in Pakistan showed a broad interest in implementing Linked Data technologies, while acknowledging that potential barriers exist. Where there is a skills gap, participants were willing to attend events to learn more about the technologies and their applications in libraries. These and other dynamics could have implications for the prospects of Linked Data applications in Pakistani libraries.

KEYWORDS

Pakistan, Libraries, Linked Data, Metadata, RDF, Semantic Web, Barriers-Linked Data, Readiness-Linked Data.

INTRODUCTION

The basic premise of Linked Data and the semantic Web - that they have the potential to add new capabilities for users to discover, explore (often with the help of visualizations), and utilize online information resources available on the web (Breeding, 2013) - is due to the fact that Linked Data enables information providers to encode contents of information sources through the Resource Description Framework (RDF) to make the parsing of the relationships between resources via computers possible. Linked Data and semantic Web technologies add value and usefulness to data and online information resources by interlinking them with other similar data and resources from different, including external, sources (Bizer, Heath, and Berners-Lee, 2009). In short, it is a technology that has applications in and crucial for any organization engaged in the organization, management, and dissemination of information. However, Linked Data, while it has been adopted by organizations in other sectors for over a decade, it remains a relatively new phenomenon in libraries and cultural institutions, especially those in developing countries such as Pakistan.

By their very nature, information environments such as libraries and cultural heritage institutes, occasionally have, in their collections, some amount of unique and rare data, information, and other digital resources that are likely to have limited visibility and, hence, limited potential for discovery by users. Information environments such as libraries also acquire, organize, and make the bulk of their information resources available in the hope that they would be utilized by potential users. Given the trends in human information seeking behavior, especially novice users, where the first and starting point for information search is to enter keywords into search engines such as Google (Hung, Johnson, Kaufman, and Mendonca, 2008), and if libraries are to keep up with these trends and relevant innovations, it is imperative that they continue exploring ways to publish their online catalog using Linked Data. Because, they need to reach and attract the "Google" generation if they are to continue to be relevant. Linked Data helps libraries and cultural heritage institutions publish their online catalogs and data, making their deep wells of information and knowledge readily available to a wider user base (Winer, 2014), in turn creating a web of visibility for their colelctions and services, no to mention meeting expectations of the "Google" generation of users.

In Pakistan, library users' expectations have been raised due to the investments in information and communication technology (ICT) infrastructure by the government in order to build the capacity of academic and research institutions as well as their libraries. Those expectations lead to added pressure on information professionals to devise new strategies and ways to make information resources, those in their collections and beyond, readily available. One of the innovations that could offer the means to meet those expectations is Linked Data. However, whether information professionals in Pakistan are willing and inerested in taking advantage of innovations such as Linked Data and the semantic Web is not clear. Therefore, our aim in the current study was to assess the willingness and level of interest in the application of Linked Data by librarians in Pakistan as well as determine their perceptions of the barriers to Linked Data application in their respective libraries. Specifically, we set out to seek answers to the following research questions: (1)What is the level of interest and willingness to explore Linked Data applications in libraries among information professionals in Pakistan?; and (2) What are the perceived constraints for effective implementation of Linked Data in Pakistani libraries?

RESEARCH DESIGN AND METHODS

This is part of a larger study that used survey research design. An online self-administered questionnaire, consisting of 10 items/statements with a 7-point Likert scale (1=Strongly Disagree, 2=Disagree, 3=Slightly Disagree, 4=Neutral - Neither Disagree nor Agree, 5=Slightly Agree, 6=Agree, 7=Strongly Agree) and a few demographic questions, was used as a data collection instrument. The questionnaire was developed through a comprehensive review of the literature and a sorting activity by domain experts in order to ensure validity. Survey participants were librarians working at degree awarding higher education institutions in Pakistan. There were approximately 350 potential participants, of which 136 completed the questionnaire with 86 usable responses, a response rate of 24.57%. With respect to their level of education, of the 86, almost all (96.5%) hold either a masters or and MPhil degree whereas the remaining 3.5% have PhDs.

FINDINGS

Preceding the final data analysis, test of the internal consistency or reliability of the multi-item scales in the survey instrument was conducted. The two scales, one for the level of interest and willingness and a second for the constraints of implementing Linked Data in Pakistani libraries, had Cronbach's (1951) Alpha values of 0.886 and 0.875, respectively, which we accepted as evidence of internal consistency. Principal component analysis also confirmed that each set of five items produced a single principal component. Hence none of the items were dropped.

Tables 1 and 2 summarize results of our analysis with respect to the two research questions. Table 1 suggests that respondenst were generally interested in or willing to explore ways to incorporate and implement Linked Data in their librararies. However, they would still like to attend more events to learn more about its potential and how to integrate it into, say, creating bibliographic records or data that could be published online. Among the five statements about barriers to implementing Linked Data technologies in Pakistani libraries, the statement on the general lack of awareness about Linked Data among librararians in Pakistan received the highest mean level of agreement (5.92) with a standard deviation of 1.3. The second and third highest rated statements have to do with lack of best practices, something LaPolla (2013) found as well, and Linked Data being too new and unproven, at least in libraries, respectively. These findings slightly differ from those of LaPolla (2013) who found finances and cost to be among the major hinderances.

Statements	Mean	SD
Interested in attending events where the topic of creation of bibliographic records that aim to incorporate Linked Data standards is discussed	5.59	1.508
Willing to explore ways to incorporate Linked Data standards in bibliographic records management at my institution/library	5.33	1.359
Interested in exploring the creation of bibliographic records that aim to incorporate Linked Data standards at my institution/library	5.3	1.275
Willing to promote incorporating Linked Data standards in bibliographic records management at my institution/library	5.29	1.396
Interested in advocating for creation of bibliographic records that aim to incorporate Linked Data standards at my institution/library	5.19	1.355

Table 3. Descriptive statistics for the level of interest and

Statements	Mean	SD
There is a general lack of awareness of the basic concepts of Linked Data among library and information professionals	5.92	1.323
There is lack of best practices with respect to Linked Data and their application in libraries	5.53	1.404
Linked Data technology is too new and unproven in libraries	5.26	1.494
The technology is too complex to implement a Linked Data compliant catalog in libraries	5.01	1.525
Implementing Linked Data technology would be too costly for libraries in terms of financial and human resources	4.97	1.464

Table 2. Barriers to effective implementation of Linked Data in Pakistani libraries (N=86).

CONCLUDING REMARKS AND RECOMMENDATIONS

There is no question that Linked Data holds some potential for improving accessibility and visibility of data and information resources held by libraries as well as interlinking them beyond a single collection and/or location. If results of our study are any guide, information professionals in Pakistan are aware of this and they are interested in and willing to explore and implement Linked Data in their libraries, despite some barriers. This is encouraging. Because, eventually, it is initiatives by information professionals that would potentially help improve access to knowledge and information. In an information and knowledge age, this should be beneficial to end users.

Finally, like any other research, the current study was delimited in terms of the sample and variables. Linked Data is also an emerging technology. Hence, it is important for future research to conduct a more comprehensive assessment of the conditions for and nature of the adoption and implementation of Linked Data in libraries, especially those in developing countries.

REFERENCES

Bizer, C., Heath, T., & Berners-Lee, T. (2009). Linked Data - the story so far. *International Journal on Semantic Web and Information Systems, 5*(3), 1-22.

Breeding, M. (2013). Linked Data: The next big wave or another tech fad?. *Computers in libraries, 33*(3), 20-22. Retrieved from http://www.infotoday.com/cilmag/apr13/Breeding--Linked-Data--The%20Next-Big-Wave-or-Another-Tech-Fad.shtml.

Cronbach, L. J. (1951). Coefficient Alpha and the internal structure of tests. *Psychometrika 16*(3), 297-334.

Hung, P. W., Johnson, S. B., Kaufman, D. R., & Mendonca, E. A. (2008). A multi-level model of information seeking in the clinical domain. *Journal of Biomedical Informatics, 41*(2), 357-370.

LaPolla, F. (2013). Perceptions of librarians regarding semantic Web and Linked Data technologies. *Journal of Library Metadata, 13*(2-3), 114-140.

Winer, D. (2014). Judaica Europeana: An infrastructure for aggregating Jewish content. *Judaica Librarianship, 18*(1), 88-115

81st Annual Meeting of the Association for Information Science & Technology | Vancouver, Canada | 10 – 14 November 2018

Advancing Open Data: Aligning Education with Public Sector Data Challenges

Nicholas M. Weber
University of Washington, USA nmweber@uw.edu

Bree Norlander
University of Washington, USA norlab@uw.edu

Carole L. Pamer
University of Washington, USA clpalmer@uw.edu

ABSTRACT

LIS education has invested heavily in workforce development for data services in research institutions, however little work has been done on open data competencies needed in public libraries and government agencies. The Open Data Literacy (ODL) project is working to prepare students to build infrastructure and to curate and sustain open data resources for the public by advancing data curation and data science curriculum and providing field experiences in collaboration with city and state agencies. To determine the expertise students need to meet workforce demands, we are examining the current data challenges faced by these public sector organizations. Based on the first year of student field experiences, we found that data organization and access, data quality, and data visualization were prominent areas of competency needed across the sites. While these areas are captured to some degree in current frameworks meant to catalog "data expertise" we find that additional competencies are required, in particular the need for developing and following metadata standards, evaluation and use of storage and cloud services, APIs, law and ethics, and public sector and not-for-profit organization knowledge. In future work these emerging areas of data expertise will be prioritized and deepened in our curriculum and better articulated for application in data education more generally.

KEYWORDS

open data, curriculum development, data literacy, public sector information, experiential learning

INTRODUCTION

Open data initiatives are accelerating around the country and around the world (Barbosa, Pham, Silva, Vieira, & Freire, 2014; Dawes, Vidiasova, & Parkhimovich, 2016). In the U.S., cities across the country are actively involved in opening up their data to the public, as documented by the U.S. City Open Data Census (http://us-city.census.okfn.org/). Some open government data programs have been established for many years. For example, the city of Seattle launched their open data policy in 2010, and the state of Washington began providing open data in 2009. Increasingly, public libraries are also important contributors to the open data movement, often in partnership with local government agencies (Okamoto, 2016). To date, Library and Information Science (LIS) education has invested heavily in workforce development for data services in research institutions, however as civic open data initiatives have grown, little has been done to address the need for open data competencies in the public sector.

The Open Data Literacy (ODL) project is making progress on filling the gap in educational programs around public sector data. We are advancing data curation and data science curriculum and providing field experiences to students to prepare graduates to build infrastructure and curate and sustain open data resources for the public. In the first year, two data curation courses were extended to cover open data and a data science sequence was promoted to students. Fieldwork options were provided through summer internships and capstone projects in government agencies and libraries, working on current open data efforts and problems faced by these organizations. Through the student placements, we are documenting the expertise needed to advance public sector open data initiatives. The results are guiding improvements in our curriculum and can inform broader educational frameworks for data professionals.

This poster reports on analysis of the internship and capstone projects completed in the first year of the ODL project, to identify the kinds of data challenges public sector organizations are experiencing and the expertise required to address them. The results are based on a systematic examination of the documentation and outputs from the field experiences, a focus group with the students, and a debriefing session with the site mentors. We discuss the data challenges and expertise identified in relation to current frameworks guiding data education and how they can be extended or enriched to better prepare the data workforce for open data responsibilities.

Partners and Projects

Working in collaboration with regional agencies, we offered fieldwork placements to students in the local city government, a large urban public library, and several state agencies involved in open data initiatives. The state government sites included the Office of the Chief Information Officer, Department of Transportation, Department of Fish & Wildlife, and the Department of Ecology. Eight projects involving 17 students were completed in the first year--four individual summer internships and four capstone team projects. Project proposals were developed by mentors at the sites in coordination with our team, resulting in three categories of open data projects: requirements and analysis, development, and engagement.

Data Challenges and Expertise

Four kinds of data challenges were represented across the eight projects:1. aggregating dispersed, inconsistent data, 2. improving user access and ability to view and interpret data, 3. assessing and enhancing metadata, catalogs, indexing, and 4. designing and delivering community and professional outreach.

Among the associated areas of expertise, several were common across multiple projects, with visualization and data processing for data quality particularly prominent. Projects also involved multiple stakeholder groups and required knowledge of standards and data portal development. In relation to our current data curation and data science coursework, the focus group and mentor debriefings indicated that further depth is needed in: metadata, storage and cloud services, APIs, legal and ethical dimensions, and background on public sector and not-for-profit organizations.

Implications for Curriculum Frameworks

Based on the full array of open data expertise identified, we assessed alignment with the areas of data knowledge and skills presented in two National Academy of Sciences consensus study reports covering data workforce issues. To adequately encompass open data expertise, the areas outlined in *Preparing the Workforce for Digital Curation* (2015) would need further articulation of areas related to access, use, and sustainability: Data Collection & Management, Data Analytics, and Archiving & Preservation. Three other areas--Technology, Tools, & Infrastructure, Values & Principles, and Services and Management--are also key areas of emphasis for open data. Extending the "data acumen" reported in *Envisioning the Data Science Discipline* (2018) to cover open data expertise would require adding Infrastructure and Archiving, and the existing areas of Data Management, and Data Description and Curation, would need to highlight provenance and other key aspects impacting data access and reuse. Additionally, for students to succeed in open data positions in public sector organizations, they need background preparation on local best practices and technology constraints, as well as competency in developing work plans and in communicating and coordinating with stakeholders.

CONCLUSION

We have used preliminary results from our ongoing work to reinforce concepts and fill gaps in data focused curriculum, and to improve field experiences of students. Observations and progress from the second year of ODL will be integrated into the final poster presentation, including activities stemming from a new partnership with the state library.

ACKNOWLEDGMENTS

ODL is funded by a grant from the Institute of Museum and Library Services, Laura Bush 21st Century Librarians Program. Grant number: 67-5285. The team also wishes to acknowledge An Yan for her important contributions to the project.

REFERENCES

Barbosa, L. R., Vieira, M., Pham, K., Silva, C., & Freire, J. (2014). Structured Open Urban Data: Understanding the Landscape. *Big Data, 2*(3), 144-154.

Dawes, S., Vidiasova, L., & Parkhimovich, O. (2016). Planning and designing open government data programs: An ecosystem approach. *Government Information Quarterly, 33*(1), 15-27.

National Research Council. (2015). *Preparing the Workforce for Digital Curation*. Washington, DC: The National Academies Press. https://doi.org/10.17226/18590.

National Academies of Sciences, Engineering, and Medicine. (2018). *Envisioning The Data Science Discipline: The Undergraduate Perspective: Interim Report*. Washington, DC: The National Academies Press. doi: https://doi.org/10.17226/24886.

Okamoto, Karen. (2016). Introducing open government data. *The Reference Librarian*, 58:2, 111-123. doi: 10.1080/02763877.2016.1199005

"Bouncing ideas": When Participants Use this Phrase, What Do They Really Mean?

Rebekah Willson
University of Strathclyde, UK. rebekah.willson@strath.ac.uk

ABSTRACT
In a qualitative study of the information behavior of early career academics transitioning from doctoral studies to their first continuing academic positions, participants used the phrase "bouncing ideas" with relative frequency to describe their interactions with colleagues. Using constructivist grounded theory methodology, interviews with 20 early career academics were analyzed and for themes and sub-themes. "Bouncing ideas" emerged as a sub-theme, related to collegial information exchange, an important way early career academics find workplace information. Despite its common usage, the term remained vague in participant discussions and unexamined in the information science literature. This poster will investigate the meaning of "bouncing ideas" as used by participants, exploring its potential constituent parts including: information seeking, information sharing, collaboration, and information creation. ASIS&T conference attendees will be encouraged to think about and actively engage in discussion about the phrase, in an attempt to answer the research question, What does "bouncing ideas" mean?

KEYWORDS
Bouncing ideas; information seeking; information sharing; collaboration; information creation

INTRODUCTION
In reading the transcripts of the interviews from my dissertation research, I found my participants using the phrase "bouncing ideas" with relative frequency. This led me to search the information science (IS) literature for the phrase to more fully explore its meaning. This search uncovered sporadic and passing use by researchers but comparatively frequent use by the researchers' participants. Participants made statements such as, "I didn't ask anyone professionally there to help me but I sat round and discussed with friends how they'd gone about different avenues they'd taken, bounced ideas about basically" (Foster & Urquhart, 2012, p. 790) and "we worked together more like on ideas, you know; we didn't really work together on projects so much, but we...constantly got to bounce around ideas about what we were going to do" (Sugimoto, 2011, p. 7). Participants used "bouncing ideas" to describe a range of information activities such as looking for information, sharing information, working collaboratively, and creating information. However, the term was used without definition or examination. Its common, colloquial use indicates it has meaning for those who use it despite its lack of explanation. This visual presentation will explore the meaning of the phrase "bouncing ideas" to elucidate its constituent parts and consider whether a definition can be proposed. This poster will encourage attendees at the ASIS&T conference to consider what "bouncing ideas" means by engaging them in three ways: 1) by presenting research about the term, 2) by encouraging discussion with myself and other attendees, and 3) by asking attendees to contribute their own thoughts about the term to a collection of sticky notes that will be made available. In essence, interaction with the poster and sticky notes will encourage ASIS&T conference attendees to 'bounce ideas' about "bouncing ideas" and to begin to answer the research question, What does "bouncing ideas" mean?

METHODOLOGY AND METHODS
My dissertation research was a qualitative examination of the information behavior of early career academics in the humanities and social sciences when making the transition from their doctoral studies to their first continuing academic position. It used constructivist grounded theory methodology, which guides systematic and simultaneous data collection and analysis (Charmaz, 2006). Data collection was collected over a 5-7 month period, beginning and ending with an in-depth interview, with "check-ins" (brief contact in the form of a modified journal entry or interview) in between. Participants consisted of 20 early career academics, 12 men and 8 women, ranging in age from 29 to early 50s. Half the participants were from Australia and half were from Canada. All participants were in humanities and social science disciplines. Data were coded in two rounds, initial and focused coding, using constant comparison to compare the themes to each other to determine their explanatory power and distinctiveness. From the coding, themes and sub-themes emerged, one of the sub-themes being "bouncing ideas."

FINDINGS AND DISCUSSION
In my dissertation "bouncing ideas" emerged as a sub-theme, related to the social exchange of information that takes place between colleagues within the academic work environment. "Bouncing ideas" – along with the associated phrases "ping ponging" and "hashing out" – was one way participants described interacting with colleagues.

Information seeking?
> And then other kinds of questions or issues, I'd usually bounce things off [Colleague A] or [Colleague B], often. So sometimes I'd say, "I've got a question about this. Do you think this will work as an assignment?" And, "Oh, why don't you tinker with that a little bit," or something. ("Ben," academic in the social sciences)

Some participants described "bouncing ideas" as part of asking colleagues for help, as a way to find information and generate ideas. However, it was more than seeking information, as it also includes aspects of modification (or "tinkering").

Information sharing?

> What it is, is that you actually spend more time bouncing ideas off of and I usually think that it makes the final product better. But this also means that I have to feel comfortable soliciting feedback from other people. But the nice thing about being in a collegial department is that you build up good will and ... just by not being a jerk people are prepared to do you favors, right? And so, if I read something for somebody, then they might read one of my things. ("Madeline," academic in the social sciences)

When ideas are bounced between colleagues, information is shared. Participants described forming relationships with their colleagues that could be categorized as "information relationships" (Cross & Sproull, 2004), creating safe spaces and facilitating the exchange of information. However, at times participants described unequal information sharing, which engendered a feeling that reciprocity had not be achieved.

Collaboration?

> But I think I'll be happy to work collaboratively for the rest of my life, really. It's not just doing something completely on my own. It's not something that I really aspire. Even if you do something on your own you can bounce things off your colleagues and it just how the most successful ideas are born. ("Leanne," academic in business)

"Bouncing ideas" requires jointly working with others on ideas, the definition of collaboration. However, some participants differentiated between collaboration and bouncing ideas, indicating the terms are not synonymous. What appears to be fundamental to "bouncing ideas" is interaction. Discussing and extending McKenzie's model of information practices, Yeoman (2010) added "interaction," stating that interaction, "interaction permits the discussion to move beyond information seeking and finding into what happens once interaction with a source of information has been initiated" (para. 28).

Information creation?

> So, it tends to be, with for instance [colleague's name], I mean we were on a pint, we were just ping ponging. We did most of this stuff in a café. So, we would meet, ... we'd just sort of jump from one café to the next and we'd be writing. And we finished half of the paper actually in Amsterdam over beers. ("Niels," academic in the humanities)

"Bouncing ideas" (or "ping ponging") is a social practice that is part of some academics' process when creating information. However, participants rarely described what this process entails. It may share some aspects of what Koh (2013) refers to as remixing, "building on and making a creative change to the original information or projects," (p. 1832) which is form of "collaborative creation" in which people "build upon, alter, and transform others' ideas" (p. 1834). However, Koh discussed remixing in relation to digital media, rather than ideas.

CONCLUSION

The phrase "bouncing ideas" evokes the image of repeatedly throwing a rubber ball that rebounds and thrown once again. In its use by participants in my dissertation, it typically describes an idea being presented to a colleague; discussion and active work on or with that idea (which might include brainstorming, testing out, adding to, and/or modifying); repetition of the active engagement; and then the originator of the activity taking the idea away for further work or implementation. It describes a way of socially and actively working out ideas. The idea is worked on, modified, and passed back and forth between colleagues, with both contributing expertise and ideas, despite one colleague initiating the discussion. "Bouncing ideas" is inherently social, though it may not be a partnership where both have equal stake in the work nor a shared project. It includes aspects of information seeking, information sharing, collaboration, and information creation, but does this adequately describe what "bouncing ideas" really means?

REFERENCES

Charmaz, K. (2006). Constructing grounded theory: A practical guide through qualitative analysis. Thousand Oaks, CA: SAGE Publications, Inc.

Cross, R., & Sproull, L. (2004). More than an answer: Information relationships for actionable knowledge. Organization Science, 15(4), 446–462. doi:10.1287/orsc.1040.0075

Foster, A., & Urquhart, C. (2012). Modelling nonlinear information behaviour: Transferability and progression. Journal of Documentation, 68(6), 784–805. doi:10.1108/00220411211277046

Koh, K. (2013). Adolescents' information-creating behavior embedded in digital media practice using Scratch. Journal of the American Society for Information Science & Technology, 64(9), 1826–1841.

Sugimoto, C. (2012). Are you my mentor? Identifying mentors and their roles in LIS doctoral education. Journal of Education for Library and Information Science, 53(1), 2–19.

Yeoman, A. (2010). Applying McKenzie's model of information practices in everyday life information seeking in the context of the menopause transition. Information Research, 15(4). Retrieved from http://informationr.net/ir/15-4/paper444.html

Exploring Dynamic Change of Users' Cross-device Search Performance

Dan Wu
Wuhan university, China, woodan@whu.edu.cn

Fang Yuan
Wuhan university, China, 2012302480046@whu.edu.cn

ABSTRACT

This paper conducted a user experiment to explore dynamic changes of users' cross-device search performance. By analysing the experiment results, the change of users' search performance was presented and the impact of directions of device-switch on users' search performance was explored. This paper also provided suggestions for improving cross-device search system.

KEYWORDS

Cross-device search, Search performance, Information seeking behavior, Context-dependent.

INTRODUCTION

Users have changed their search behaviors along with the diverse devices, rather than just one, which they employ in their seeking for information. This so called cross-devices search means that users conduct their search tasks initially on one device then resume the same task on another device after interruption (e.g., desktop search→ mobile search). It is uncertain whether the users can obtain the information they need after the search task interruption and devices transition. Current studies on cross-device search behavior focus on the feature description, behavior prediction, comparison between different device-switching directions, but pay less attention on users' search performance. Wang et al. (2013) predicted task-resuming after device-switch. Montanez et al. (2014) predicted directions of device-switch. To aid users in completing the task efficiently and help the search system improving search efficiency, this paper focuses on users' cross-device search performance, which is about how well users could perform tasks and obtain the information they search for. Cross-device search involves at least two devices and accordingly two sessions called pre-switch session and post-switch session which happen before or after device transition. Specifically, this paper works on two research questions: (i) Is there any difference of users' search performance between pre-switch and post-switch session? (ii) How does the search performance change regarding different directions of device-switch?

RESEARCH DESIGN

User Experiment

A controlled user experiment was conducted to study the users' cross-device search behaviors. Considering the time limitation, in this experiment, a single cross-device search only of consisted two sessions, and between these two sessions, there was an interruption and a device switch. The directions of devices-switch were desktop-to-mobile (DM) and mobile-to-desktop (MD). 34 university students were selected through recruitment questionnaires. A self-developed search system, Cross-device Access and Fusion Engine (CAFE), was used for desktop and mobile search. The interfaces of CAFE in desktop and mobile were the same. Participants needed to finish four tasks, which were about movie, drama, music and language. These were top 4 common topics in daily cross-device search according to participants recruitment questionnaires. There was a pilot search of the four tasks before the formal experiment and the result of the pilot search showed every task was complex enough that participants could not finish it in only one session. In the experiment, participants firstly completed pre-switch sessions of four tasks then rested for 20 minutes. After that, they switched device to finish post-switch sessions of four tasks. Each session lasted for 20 minutes. Therefore, there was an 80-minutes interval between two sessions of a task. Meanwhile, during search process, participants needed to judge the relevance of every result they clicked. This relevance judging method dependents on context and reflects dynamics of users' needs, which was called ESR in Jiang et al (2017). Different to system performance, user search performance should consider users' real congnition of multi-level relevance judgement. Therefore, the degree of relevance in the experiment was divided into "irrelevant", "generally relevant" and "highly relevant". The results that were not clicked were regarded as irrelevant. Finally, participants were interviewed briefly about their impressions.

Data Collection and Analysis Methods

In total, the experiment produced 259 search sessions, 1670 queries and 1102 clicked results. The statistics of this paper mainly came from (i) the log of CAFE, including search history and participants' interaction data, (ii) relevant judgement, and (iii) interview after experiment. Effective search time, nDCG@n and p@n were used to evaluate users' search performance. The effective search time was defined as the search time of the query that could retrieval relevant results. The nDCG@n was calculated using participants' 3-level relevance judgement. The degree of relevance was assigned to corresponding values, that was, "irrelevant" as 1, and "generally relevant" as 3, and "highly relevant" as 7. The p@n was calculated using 2-level relevance judgement, "irrelevant" and "relevant". The "generally relevant" and "highly relevant" results were classified as "relevant" results. The p@n refered to the proportion of "relevant" results in top n results.

RESULTS ANALYSIS AND DISCUSSION

In cross-device search, without considering the directions of device-switch, the proportion of effective search time of pre-switch (mean=0.688, SD=0.31) was more than post-switch session (mean=0.591, SD=0.301) and the difference was significant (p<0.01). Figure 1 presented the comparison of nDCG@n and p@n between pre-switch and post-switch sessions. The nDCG@n and p@n of pre-switch was more than post-switch sessions, but the difference was not significant, which was showed as Figure 1(a). Considering directions of device-switch, in DM, the proportion of effective search time of pre-switch (mean=0.755, SD=0.279) was more than post-switch session (mean=0.522, SD=0.305) and the difference was significant (p<0.001). As Figure 1(b) showed, p@n of pre-switch was non-significantly better than post-switch sessions. In contrast, users' effective search time and p@n of pre-switch were non-significantly worse than post-switch sessions in MD. However, as Figure 1(b) and 1(c) showed, nDCG@n of pre-switch was worse than post-switch sessions in DM and better than post-switch sessions in MD, which was a contrast to the other two metrics.

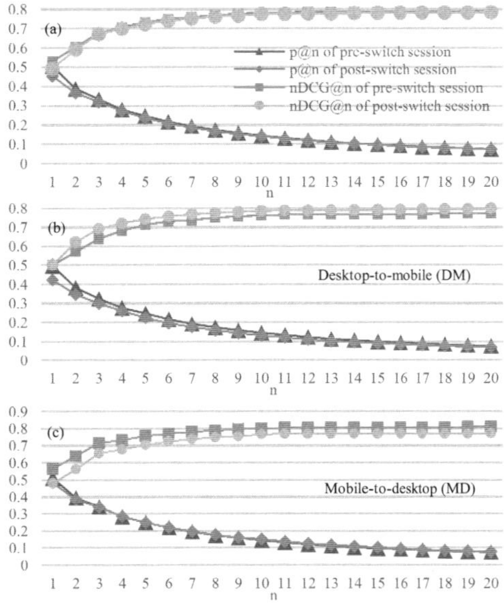

Figure 1. The distribution of nDCG@n and p@n in results rank of SERP.

For research question (i), in cross-device search, users' search performance decreased in post-switch session. This finding was different from daily cognation, which may think that the search performance of the post-switch session was better due to the accumulation of search experience after pre-switch session. Actually, this assumption neglected the dynamics of users' information need. This study found from interviews that 21 out of 34 participants wanted new information in the post-switch session rather than repeated information. Jiang et al. (2017) also found that users preferred novel information when they judge results' relevance in search process. The result in this study indicated that information of post-switch sessions could not satisfy participants' changeable needs and it was not easy to get new information in post-switch session. For research question (ii), the difference of search performance between pre-switch and post-switch sessions varied with directions of device-switch. But the change of nDCG@n in DM and MD was different from the effective search time and p@n, which probably because nDCG@n was calculated based on 3-level relevance judgement and the effective search time and p@n was calculated based on 2-level relevance judgement. This was interesting to be further explored.

CONCLUSION

This paper presented dynamic change of users' cross-device search performance and made following contributions: (i) it was found that, without considering directions of device-switch, users' search performance slightly declined after device switch, (ii) directions of device-switch had an impact on the change of users' search performance, and (iii) when designing cross-device search system, recommendations for new information after device transition should be considered to help users satisfy their changeable needs. In the future, we will further explore why the change of nDCG@n in DM and MD was different from the other two metrics. Besides, we will focus on the prediction and recommendation of users' cross-device search.

ACKNOWLEDGMENTS

This work was supported by National Natural Science Foundation of China (Grant No. 71673204).

REFERENCES

Jiang, J.P., He, D., Kelly, D., & Allan, J. (2017). Understanding Ephemeral state of relevance. In R. Nordlie, N. Pharo, L. Freund, B. Larsen, & D. Russel (Eds.), *Proceedings of the 2017 Conference on Conference Human Information Interaction and Retrieval (CHIIR '17)* (pp. 137-146). Oslo: ACM.

Montanez, G.D., White, R.W., & Huang, X. (2014). Cross-device search. In J. Li, X.S. Wang, M. Garofalakis, I. Soboroff, T. Suel, & M. Wang (Eds.), *Proceedings of the 23rd ACM International Conference on Conference on Information and Knowledge Management (CIKM'14)* (pp. 1669-1678). Shanghai: ACM.

Wang, Y., Huang, X., & White, R. W. (2013). Characterizing and supporting cross-device search tasks. In S. Leonardi, A. Panconesi, P. Ferragina, & A. Gionis (Eds.), *Proceedings of the sixth ACM international conference on Web search and data mining (WSDM'13)* (pp. 707-716). Rome: ACM.

An Analysis of the Relationship between Crime Incidents and 911 Calls

Jiahui Wu
University of Maryland, USA. jeffwu@umd.edu

Vanessa Frias-Martinez
University of Maryland, USA. vfrias@umd.edu

ABSTRACT

Crime incidents are a major concern of public safety. Residents can help in crime-fighting by reporting suspicious behavior via call for service (calling 911 in the U.S.). To study this behavior at the city level, we analyze the relationship between crime incidents and 911 calls data. First, we propose an approach to pairing up calls with incidents based on spatiotemporal proximity. Based on the paired up calls and incidents, we define and compute the reporting rate for the studied city. Then we analyze the reporting rate and disaggregate it by types of crimes and neighborhoods. Our analysis reveals that residents are better at reporting shooting incidents than arson or rape incidents, and wealthier neighborhoods tend to have lower reporting rate. City planners can use the reporting rate to engage residents more in reporting suspicious behavior and provide better public safety services.

KEYWORDS

Public safety, crime incidents, 911 calls, reporting rate.

INTRODUCTION

Crime incidents are a major concern of public safety. One way that residents can help in crime-fighting is via call for service, *e.g.,* calling 911 in the U.S. Crime incidents and 911 calls data are collected by police departments to guide public safety services and commonly used in public-safety-related studies. Incidents data can be used to compute crime rate (Hipp, 2007) and enable hot-spot-based predictive policing (Bowers et al., 2004). 911 calls data can be used to measure crime rate instead of crime incidents (Tita & Ridgeway, 2007). Frequently, both datasets are combined as proxies to measure public safety (Burdette & Whitaker, 2005). However, the relationship between these two datasets is rarely studied. In this paper, we propose an approach to model the relationship between calls and incidents. Specifically, we study the reporting rate defined as the percentage of crimes that can be paired up with 911 calls. This reporting rate is important for city planners because it reflects a kind of important residents' behavior: engaging in crime-fighting via calling 911. Such engagement is important for many reasons, *e.g.* it is a form of collective efficacy which is linked to crime reduction (Sampson et al., 1997); it helps discover more crimes independent on the police's patrol choice and thus help mitigate the crime underreporting issue (Tita & Ridgeway, 2007); and the investigation workload, positively correlated with longer sentence, might be lower with than without information from 911 calls (Ray et al., 2017). Disaggregating the reporting rate by types of crimes and neighborhoods, we explore how this indicator could potentially help city planners provide better public safety services.

DATA

The crime incidents and 911 calls data used here are from the Baltimore open data portal (https://data.baltimorecity.gov). Both datasets contain information about time, location and description of each event. The time range we studied is from Jan. 2015 to Feb. 2018. The description of crime incidents data is merged into 8 types: theft & larceny, assault, burglary, robbery, shooting, rape, homicide, and arson. For 911 calls, we first discard calls not related to crimes, (*e.g.* no voice, traffic stop, and tow), and then merge the descriptions into 13 types, which are 8 types of crimes plus 5 types that are likely precursor behavior to crimes, namely abuse, disorderly conduct, insecurity, mental case, and other offense. There are 147k of crime incidents and 986k of 911 calls in the datasets we analyze.

PAIRING UP 911 CALLS WITH CRIME INCIDENTS

A crime incident can be reported by residents within some hundred meters before (behavior like carrying weapons), during (criminal behavior) and after (behavior like fleeing the scene) that incident. Therefore, we propose to pair up a 911 call with a crime incident if that call is spatiotemporally close to that incident, *i.e.,* a call is within a distance radius (D) and a time range (T) of that incident. The best parameters would depend on the duration of crimes (*e.g.* burglary has a longer observation window than a shooting incident) and the geographical layout of the neighborhood (*e.g.* tall building would block residents' vision). The larger D and T are, the more 911 calls would be paired up with crimes along with more noisy calls, *i.e.,* calls reporting unrelated issues with their corresponding crime incidents. To roughly estimate the volume of wrongly paired up calls, we compute the mean of the number of types of paired up 911 calls other than the type of the paired up crime incident (denoted as M). For example, a burglary is paired up with 3 calls, 2 burglary and 1 insecurity (1 type other than burglary) while a shooting incident is paired up with 2 shooting calls (0 type other than shooting), then M = (2+0)/2 = 1. The lower M is, the fewer wrongly paired up 911 calls there are. Note that we don't require paired up 911 calls to be the same type as paired up crimes, because residents may witness precursor behavior of crimes, such as reporting armed person before a shooting occurs. We tried different combinations of D and T (Figure 1). D means a 911 call is less than D meters away from the paired up incident; T means the time difference (911 call time minus the incident time) is in the range of [-1 h, T h]. We allow a 911 call to occur before its paired up incident to capture calls that witness precursor behavior to crimes. We set D=100m and T=1h because M increased significantly when D and T is larger. With these parameters, 35% of crimes (5k/147k) and 7% of calls (6k/986k) are paired up.

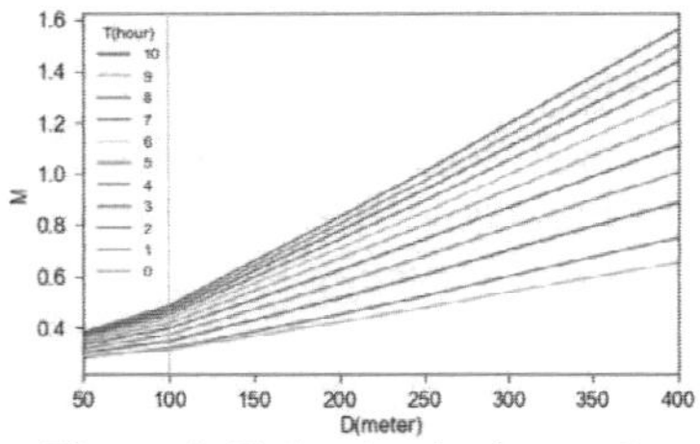

Figure 1. Estimate of volume of wrongly paired up 911 calls

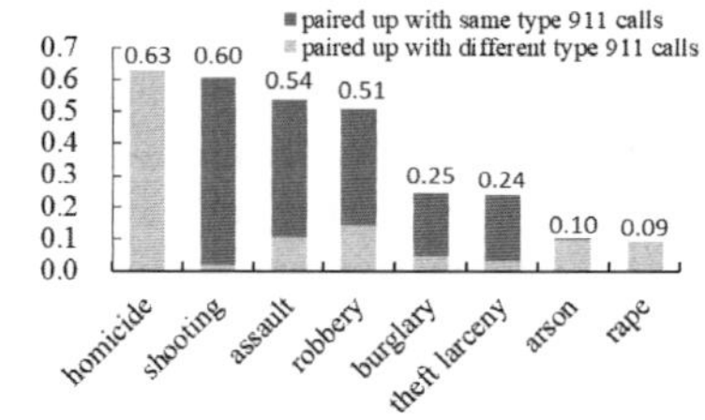

Figure 2. Reporting rate by types of crimes

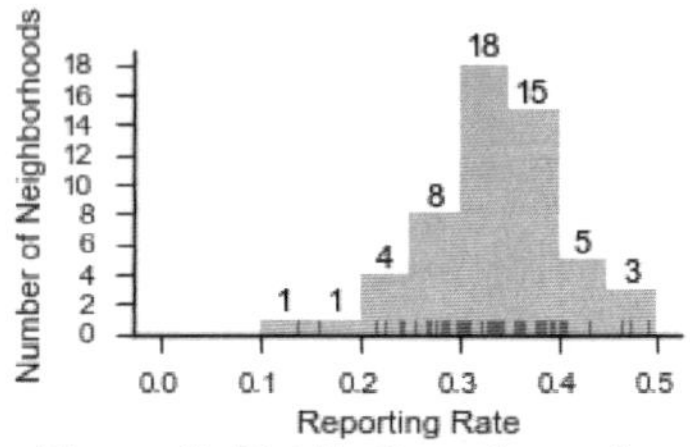

Figure 3. Distribution of reporting rate per neighborhood

ANALYZING REPORTING RATE

As mentioned in the introduction, it is important to engage residents in reporting suspicious behavior by calling 911. And the reporting rate is an indicator of the degree of such engagement. The overall reporting rate for the Baltimore city across all types of crimes is 35% which should be further improved. In the next section, we disaggregate the reporting rate by the types of crimes and neighborhoods respectively. Doing so we can understand what types of crime and which neighborhoods have low reporting rates and provide suggestions for city planners to improve the reporting rates.

Disaggregation by Types of Crimes

We compute reporting rates for 8 types of crimes with all paired up calls. As shown in Figure 2, the reporting rates for homicide, shooting, assault, and robbery are quite high, larger than 50%. Homicide crimes have the largest reporting rate. However, none of the paired up calls is described as homicide calls. Instead, most of them are reporting shootings (1178 out of 1298). Together with the high reporting rate of shooting crimes, we observe that residents are very responsive to shooting incidents. The latter four types of crimes have lower reporting rates. The low reporting rates for burglary and theft & larceny could be due to their stealth nature, especially if those incidents occur at night. Arson and rape incidents are concerning, as they have very low reporting rates even if they are severe violent crimes.

Disaggregation by Neighborhoods

We computed the reporting rate for each of the 55 neighborhoods of the Baltimore city defined by BNIA(https://bniajfi.org/). Most of the neighborhood rates are about 30~40% (Figure 3). Some are low, less than 20%. To understand the difference in reporting rates across neighborhoods, we analysed Pearson correlation between reporting rate and the three indicators of the income level of neighborhoods provided by BNIA in 2015, namely median household income (Coef.=-0.43, $p<0.001$), percent of family households living below the poverty line (Coef.=0.48, $p<0.001$) and percent of households with no vehicles available (Coef.=0.54, $p<0.001$). As shown by the coefficients, the wealthier the neighborhood is, the lower the reporting rate is. This suggests the city planners could encourage wealthier neighborhoods to call 911 to report suspicious behavior.

CONCLUSION

Given the importance of crime incidents and 911 calls data in public safety research, we proposed a method to pairing up calls and crimes. Based on paired up result, we computed reporting rate for the Baltimore city, which is 35%, and disaggregated the reporting rate by types of crimes and neighborhoods. We observed that residents are better at reporting shooting incidents, while arson and rape incidents have very low reporting rates to which city planners should pay more attention. Poorer neighborhoods call 911 more than wealthier ones. Based on this indicator, city planners can prioritize resources to engage residents more in reporting suspicious behavior and improve public safety. Our future research will improve the pairing up approach by considering types of crimes and the analysis of the relationship between reporting rates and neighborhood characteristics.

REFERENCES

Bowers, K. J., Johnson, S. D., & Pease, K. (2004). Prospective hot-spotting: The future of crime mapping?. British Journal of Criminology, 44(5), 641-658.

Burdette, H. L., & Whitaker, R. C. (2004). Neighborhood playgrounds, fast food restaurants, and crime: relationships to overweight in low-income preschool children. Preventive medicine, 38(1), 57-63.

Hipp, J. R. (2007). Income inequality, race, and place: Does the distribution of race and class within neighborhoods affect crime rates?. Criminology, 45(3), 665-697.

Ray, K., Borkowski, E. L., Leal, W., & Bales, W. D. (2017). What Happens When Investigating A Crime Takes Up Too Much Time? An Examination of How Optimal Law Enforcement Theory Impacts Sentencing. International Journal of Criminology and Sociology, 6, 215-225.

Sampson, R. J., Raudenbush, S. W., & Earls, F. (1997). Neighborhoods and violent crime: A multilevel study of collective efficacy. Science, 277(5328), 918-924.

Tita, G., & Ridgeway, G. (2007). The impact of gang formation on local patterns of crime. Journal of Research in Crime and Delinquency, 44(2), 208-237.

Precision Poverty Relief in China - The Role of Information and Information Technology

Sherry L. Xie
Renmin University of China, China. sherrylx@outlook.com

Chenyue Jiao
Renmin University of China, China. jiaocy0117@163.com

ABSTRACT

Precision poverty relief, a similar concept to targeted poverty relief, has gained tremendous momentum in China since 2013 when it, as a new strategy to the lasting anti-poverty battle in China, was officially acknowledged by the Chinese Central Government. A series of policies and implementation plans were subsequently issued, either dedicating themselves to this new strategy or to include it as a critical part of a more encompassing measure. To state it is new is not to suggest that the idea only emerged in 2013 but to emphasize its gain of official recognition. In addition, precision poverty relief is reviewed as new in recent years because of the new developments and deployments of information technologies in China, or, as by its Chinese expression, informationalization. This visual presentation reports on the preliminary findings of the project Digital Information and Societal Change, a subtask of the Records-Centred Digital Information Management Theory and Mechanisms (DI{R}Mtm), which aimed at examining the role of information and informationalization in relation to precision poverty relief strategy.

KEYWORDS

Precision poverty relief, information, information technology, China.

INTRODUCTION

The official battle of fighting poverty in China, dominantly referring to the effort towards rural areas, can be traced back to the 1980s when the notion of "the poorer, the prouder" was abandoned and growing income inequality was heeded. Newspapers, journal articles and provincial government policies focusing on "poverty relief" or "assistance to the poor" started to appear in the early 1980s (e.g., Xue, 1981; Wu, 1983; HuNan Province, 1982) and national policies in the late 1980s (NPC, 1987; State Council of China, 1989). For the past decades, the way of assisting the poor had remained consistent, which was basically allocating funds annually to impoverished areas/counties by the Central Government, along with calls for local production and assistance from society at large (e.g., State Council, 1994; Central Committee of the Communist Party & State Council, 2011). With rapid and continued economic developments nationwide, China has so far lifted a large quantity of people out of poverty. However, a considerable number of rural residents live still below the poverty line, facing various challenges including difficult natural and personal conditions as well as administrative misconducts. It is in this context that the notion of being precise for relief effectiveness and prevention of corruption started to be reflected upon and gradually developed (e.g., Jiang & Yao, 2006; Zhang & Sun, 2007; Gong, 2010). The expression "precision poverty relief" was officially acknowledged in 2013 by the Chinese President XI Jinping as an innovative strategy capable of reforming the previous approach, which has ever since gained tremendous momentum. A series of policies and implementation plans were subsequently issued at both the national and local levels, either dedicating themselves to this new strategy or to include it as a critical part of a more encompassing measure. Precision poverty relief is now specified as encompassing six types of "precisions": 1) precision in identifying the real poor; 2) precision in tailoring aid projects to help the poor according to their needs; 3) precision in guaranteeing financial support for aid projects; 4) precision in guaranteeing the implementation of aid projects for every impoverished household; 5) precision in designating officials to help carry out poverty relief measures in every poor village; and 6) precision in evaluating whether poverty relief goals are met according to defined standards (Xi, 2015). This visual presentation reports on the preliminary findings of a component study of the Records-Centered Digital Information Management Theory and Mechanisms (DI{R}Mtm) project, which aimed at examining the role of information and information technology, or, as by its Chinese expression, informationalization (i.e., computerization), in this precision poverty relief strategy.

RESEARCH QUESTIONS AND METHOD

Sizable bodies of Chinese literature exist for "poverty relief" and "precision poverty relief": 4,863 core journal articles with the phrase in title for the former and 1016 for the latter, both by the China Academic Literature Database. However, academic studies dedicated to the role of information and information technology in precision poverty relief do not currently exist. To consider the 6 types of precision as 6 major activities in the effort of reducing poverty, where does information first occur, how does it flow, and where does it end? Along the way, how is information managed and how is informationalization materialized? A two-level research plan was devised to find answers to these questions: first, to examine relevant government policies such as the Implementation Measures for Establishing Precision Poverty Relief Work Mechanisms (State Council, 2014), the 13th

Five-Year Plan for Poverty Relief and Challenges Overcoming (State Council, 2016), On the Implementation Plan for Advancing Internet-Facilitated Poverty Relief (Ministry of Industry and Information, 2018) etc., as well as empirical studies such as those that surveyed poor villages or counties. Second, based on the results of the first level, to submit freedom of information requests to relevant institutions for additional information and to decide candidate province(s) for field investigations.

FINDINGS

The preliminary findings are organized as role of information and role of information technology.

Role of Information

Unsurprisingly, information is present in all 6 precision activities, starting at "identifying the real poor". Information produced by this activity is the foundation on which all other precision activities rely. The term "real" here signals strongly the challenges of carrying out this activity, due to the reasons of 1) lack of means to collect accurate income information, 2) lack of standard to evaluate living conditions (e.g., quality of house), 3) complication of factoring in health and education situations, 4) insufficient participation of villagers, and 5) administrative misconduct. Information in the activities of "tailoring aid projects", "guaranteeing financial support", and "guaranteeing the implementation of aid projects" serves as the linkages between the identified impoverished households and the aids available (or can be available) to them, including farming/business ideas, assistance/advice from research institutes, consulting companies, and e-commerce companies, employment opportunities, and loans. Information in "designating officials" comprises that 1) qualifies the officials for the job, 2) defines responsibilities and accountability mechanisms, and 3) bridges the designated officials with identified impoverished household on a one-on-one basis. For the last activity "precision in goal evaluation", information is mainly in the forms of assessment mechanisms and methods.

Role of Information Technology

The utilization of information technology is much emphasized in precision poverty relief policies and implementation mechanisms, both nationally and locally. Information systems, cloud computing, big data etc. are now being applied. The affordance of the application, however, appears unequal. Information technologies assist greatly with all the activities except "identifying the real poor". For this activity, information technology can only be useful after the information is collected, which is done manually. The figure depicts the situation with more details.

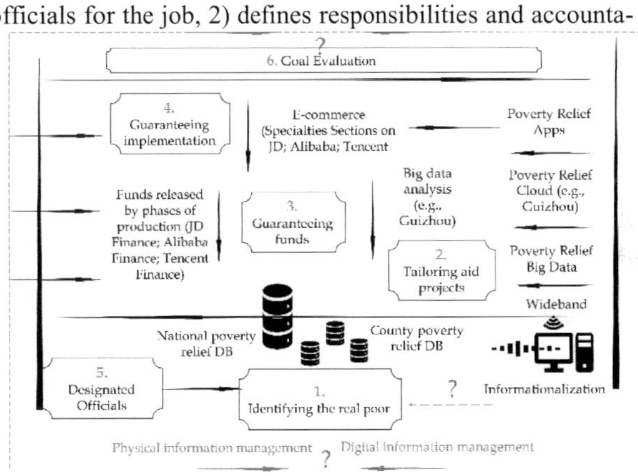

Figure 1. Information, Informationalization and Dedication in Precision Poverty Relief in China

NEXT STEPS

More data is needed for answering all the research questions, in particular, how digital information is managed. Due to the complexity of the activities (i.e., large numbers of policies and participating organizations, both public and private), it is anticipated that more specific questions will emerge when more data is collected and analyzed. Only by answering the emergent questions can this question be sufficiently answered.

ACKNOWLEDGMENTS

This study is supported by the Research Funds of Renmin University of China as part of the Records-Centered Digital Information Management Theory and Mechanisms (DI{R}Mtm) Project (No. 15XNL032).

REFERENCES

Central Committee of the Communist Party & State Council, (2011). Outline of Development-oriented Poverty Reduction Program for Rural China. Retrieved June 20, 2018 from http://www.gov.cn/gongbao/content/2011/content_2020905.htm.

CGTN. (2018). How are the Six "Precisions" of Poverty Alleviation Applied. Retrieved June 20, 2018 from https://news.cgtn.com/news/3d55544e3130575a306c5562684a335a764a4855/share_p.html.

Jiang, Y. & Yao, R. (2006, May 9). How to improve precision in poverty reduction. *China Ethnic News*.

Ministry of Industry and Information, (2018). On the Implementation Plan for Advancing Internet-Facilitated Poverty Relief. Retrieved June 20, 2018 from http://www.cpad.gov.cn/art/2018/6/6/art_50_85021.html.

State Council, (2014). Implementation Measures for Establishing Precision Poverty Relief Work Mechanisms. Retrieved June 20, 2018 from http://www.cpad.gov.cn/art/2014/5/12/art_343_461.html.

State Council, (2016). 13th Five-Year Plan for Poverty Relief and Challenges Overcoming. Retrieved June 20, 2018 from http://www.cpad.gov.cn/art/2016/12/3/art_46_56101.html.

Online Scholarly Tools: Use and Value

Shenmeng Xu
University of North Carolina at Chapel Hill, USA, shenmeng@unc.edu

Bradley M. Hemminger
University of North Carolina at Chapel Hill, USA, bmh@ils.unc.edu

Cecelia Brown
University of Oklahoma, USA, cbrown@ou.edu

ABSTRACT

In this paper, we describe our preliminary findings of our multi-site study on researchers' use of online scholarly tools. Using surveys and in-depth interviews, our study will provide information professionals and scholars a 360-degree panorama of the ways social media is impacting the dissemination and evaluation of scholarly research. At the visual presentation session, we will present the statistical results and analysis of our data, as well as individual case stories exemplifying the main findings. Additionally, we will have an activity where our audience can participate in the same card sorting exercise that study subjects did, and compare their results with the study participants, to better understand the value of various scholarly activities.

KEYWORDS

Scholarly communication, digital scholarship, social networking tools, card sorting, altmetrics

INTRODUCTION

Social networking tools and online scholarly platforms allow scholars to share, discuss, and assess scholarly information in real time (Cronin, 2013). Measurement of the activity on these sites can assess impact beyond citation enumeration and add validity to non-refereed scholarly products such as data sets and blog postings (Piwowar & Priem, 2013). Combining surveys and in-depth interviews with scholars, our study aims to extend the previous work on the information seeking behavior of scientists in the digital age. Better understanding current tool use, as well as their advantages and disadvantages, will help in designing the best online scholarly tools in the future.

METHODS AND DATA

This study is conducted at the University of North Carolina at Chapel Hill (UNC) and the University of Oklahoma (OU). Ateach site, we conducted an online survey and follow-up semi-structural interviews. The surveys and interviews followed the same procedures at both sites. The participants of our study are professors, researchers, and graduate students who conduct teaching and/or research at these two universities. The **survey** was designed to gain a complete picture of the usage and ac- ceptance of online information sharing platforms. At the end of the survey, we invited participants to our **interview**, which followed up the survey with in-depth questions. Additionally, in the interview, we employed a **card sorting** technique to have participants rank cards of scholarly activities according to their perceived importance of the activities. In this visual approach to engage nine categories of scholarly activities (see below), participants were asked to discuss the value of their daily individual and collaborative research work while ranking the cards within groups and ranking the groups against each other.

We received 284 responses in total (173 from UNC, 111 from OU). After data cleaning, 238 responses were used in our analysis (154 from UNC, 84 from OU). In total, 42 of the survey participants (30 from UNC, 12 from OU) were interviewed. We performed a series of statistical analyses on the survey data. Qualitative data from the interview, including the card sorting results, were manually coded and analyzed. We analyzed our data collected from each site separately first. Then, we integrated data from both sites to see if they show similar trends.

RESULTS

Survey Scholars at both universities report similar usage of online scholarly tools. The top four frequently used tools at OU based on the sum of daily and weekly uses are Google Scholar, OU Library, Twitter, and Wikipedia. These same top four from OU are present in UNC's top six. UNC's ranking order is Wikipedia, Google Scholar, UNC Library, PubMed, Researchers' personal websites, and Twitter. One difference is that the sum of daily and weekly usage of the tools at UNC are higher than at OU. Analysis of the usage patterns by age bracket shows further usage patterns. For instance, Figure 1 displays the daily use of the top used tools by age of survey respondents. Regarding the frequency of use for a specific purpose, OU and UNC have the same top three purposes: to communicate with colleagues, to read articles posted by others, and to search for researchers with similar interests. Researchers at the two universities share opinions about the importance of scholarly online tools. The top benefits to use online scholarly tools at OU are "to keep in touch with researchers you are friends with", "to get information about other researchers", "to save and organize other researchers' papers you have downloaded", "to share opinions/interesting ideas", and "to followthe latest works of researchers." Moreover, OU and UNC researchers similarlyvalue the tools to enhance their scholarly work. To "stay abreast of new developments in your field" and to "get information on conferences and scholarly events" are the top two reasons for using the tools at both universities. The poster will present additional findings such as almost half of the surveyed researchers reported they have not met any new people using social media tools. We will also report the use of less frequently used tools including Mendeley (88% of the OU scholars surveyed have not used).

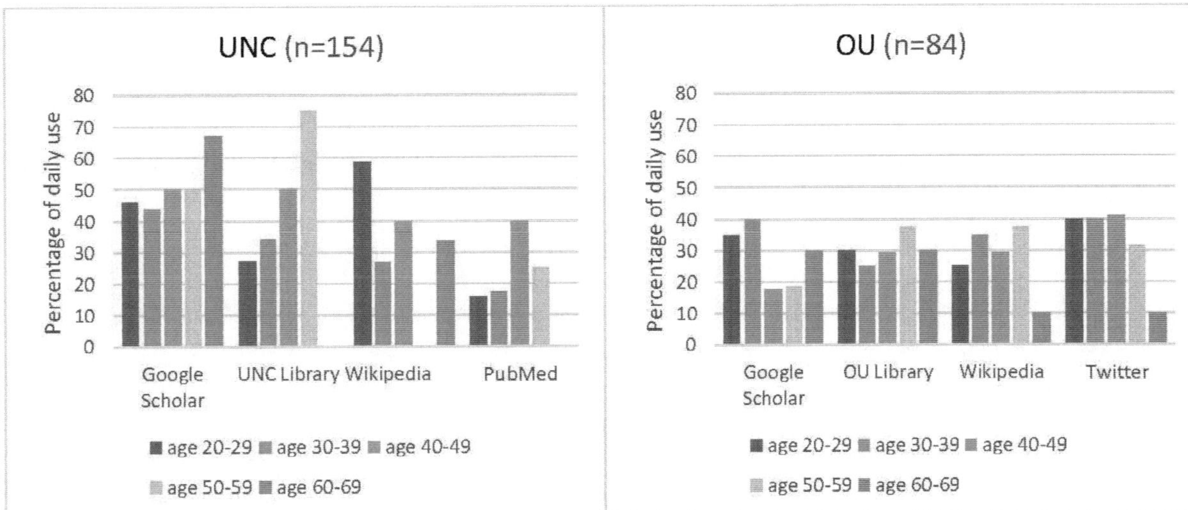

Figure 1. The Daily Use of the Top Used Tools by Age at Two Universities

Through the Fisher's exact test, it is found that demographic differences such as age, discipline, and current position significantly affect the use of scholarly online tools. For instance, at UNC, the uses of Google Scholar, UNC Library, PubMed, PLoS, Slideshare, Twitter, Wikipedia, WorldCat, Zotero, and researchers' personal websites are significantly correlated with discipline. The poster will present all the correlation results and analysis.

Interview Based on the answers provided in the survey, participants were asked to describe in greater detail the motivation for using their frequently used tools and how they use them. We found that often a participant's reason for not using a particular tool was simply because they had not heard about it or had the opportunity to explore it. To better understand the value of using the tools, participants were asked to discuss how they incorporated the tools in their typical daily workflow. The use of different tools was found to vary significantly based on the periodicity of their research project and career development. Additionally, participants discussed their likes and dislikes of the features of online scholarly tools. We found that influence from colleagues in an institution or discipline had a positive impact on the adoption of tools. In the interview, participants also shared their opinions about the future of scholarly communication and the value of online scholarly tools in measuring scholarly impact.

Card Sorting For the card sorting activity, interviewees were asked to sort 40 cards arranged in the following nine categories: searching, obtaining access, initial evaluation, reading and understanding, connecting beyond article, organization/knowledge structuring, article sharing, article using, and sharing their opinion of an article. As the interviewees ranked the cards, they compared and discussed their perceived value of the activities in their scholarly processes. Most of the participants similarly ranked and ordered the activity categories.

DISCUSSION AND CONCLUSION

This study characterizes the use and value of online scholarly tools in scholarly communication. The use of the tools is agreed by many researchers to have benefited their information retrieval and organization, as well as communication efficiency. However, our results show that some tools that have been extensively studied (e.g. Mendeley) are not frequently used. Furthermore, the wide adoption of online scholarly tools as an integral part of research has not occurred. This study found that while researchers at UNC and OU share similar use patterns and opinions of the online tools , usage decreases with age.

REFERENCES

Cronin, B., Snyder, H. W., Rosenbaum, H., Martinson, A., & Callahan, E. (1998). Invoked on the Web. *Journal of the Associ- ation for Information Science and Technology*, *49*(14), 1319-1328.

Piwowar, H., & Priem, J. (2013). The power of altmetrics on a CV. *Bulletin of the Association for Information Science and Technology*, *39*(4), 10-13.

Visibility of Disciplines in Academic Web Space

Bo Yang
Nanjing Agricultural University, China. mail.bo-yang@gmail.com

Ying Sun
University at Buffalo, USA. sun3@buffalo.ed

ABSTRACT
In academic web space, only a small portion of hyperlinks point to topic-related contents, while most of them are designed for general use. In this study, a hierarchy affiliation model (department-school-university) is proposed to extract discipline structure from linkage network and then to evaluate the discipline visibility on academic web. The case study of the Chinese academic web shows that this hierarchy model performs better in detecting disciplines on academic web over that was applied previously to a similar sample set.

KEYWORDS
discipline visibility, academic web, community detection.

INTRODUCTION
The World Wide Web is increasingly becoming an important resource to trace the propagation and to explore the patterns of academic information. Web hyperlink plays a fundamental role in web information organization because of its popularity as a hypertext technique, and its ability to be used in topic structure analysis. However, the motivations for using hyperlinks vary. Only a small portion of links on academic web point to topic-related contents, while most of them are used for inner-site navigation, administration, teaching or public resources listing (Wilkinson, Harries, Thelwall, & Price, 2003; Bar-Ilan, 2005). Research conducted on UK university websites shows that only 30% web links are closely related to their research topic (Harries, Wilkinson, Price, Fairclough, & Thelwall, 2004). Identification of collaboration through link analysis experienced many obstacles because of a large number of topic-unrelated links on web pages. Due to this, a supervised machine learning method was applied to filter page types in Kenekayoro, Buckley and Thelwall's study (2014). Comparing to co-author analysis on publications, they found this technique successfully filtered out some irrelevant inlinks. Proper techniques and strategies are crucial in identifying different linking motivations, collecting the most relevant links, and mining topic structure on the WWW.

In this study, a hierarchy affiliation model (department-school-university) is applied to the Chinese university websites. The direct affiliations of a university (schools) are used as the basic units for data collection and discipline analysis. A broad classification is used to measure the discipline visibility in academic link network quantitatively, and then to investigate the effectiveness of mining discipline structure from the hyperlink network by the strategy proposed above.

DATA COLLECTION
The institution samples and classification system for this study are from the certified evaluation data set issued by CDGDC (China Academic Degree & Graduate Education Development Center). There are 7 broad disciplines (Humanities and Social Sciences, Sciences, Engineering, Agriculture, Medicine, Management Science and Arts) and 95 disciplines in the classification (CDGDC, 2012). The study collected all the affiliated schools from the website of each university. Those schools that do not have websites or their websites were not accessible during three rounds of test are removed from the data set. We end with 5711 domain names of schools and 21,575,697 web pages in our data set.

To statistically evaluate the discipline cohesiveness of communities discovered in link network, four volunteers (master students) manually annotate the disciplines of each sample (school website) using the 95 CDGDC disciplines.

STRUCTURE ANALYSIS
In this section, we report the extracted research communities from the multi-disciplinary samples of school network and university network respectively using our strategy of structure analysis. We also report the evaluation of the discipline cohesiveness of communities on the school and university level respectively.

Discipline visibility in school network
Figure 1 is the visualized result of non-overlapping community detection generated by the algorithm SLPA (Speaker-listener Label Propagation Algorithm, when r equals 0.5; Xie, Szymanski, & Liu, 2011) from the directed and weighted school network. The nodes of the same color belong to the same community. The ForceAtlas layout, used in the visualization tool Gephi, is not necessarily consistent with SLPA, therefore only the communities with high discipline cohesiveness and clear structure are labelled with their discipline names. The statistics shows that 68 different disciplines appear in the 256 communities detected in directed network. The average discipline cohesiveness is 0.69. For the undirected network we found 71 disciplines from the 223 communities and the average discipline cohesiveness is 0.68.

Discipline visibility in university network

During the test we found that the community detection algorithm, SLPA, was suitable for directed and sparse network while FUA (Fast Unfolding Algorithm; Blondel, Guillaume, Lambiotte, & Lefebvre, 2008) was better for undirected and dense network, so FUA will be used for community detection in university network. The broad-discipline-based communities detected by FUA are shown in Figure 2 generated by the OpenOrd layout in Gephi. Different colors indicate different communities and the nodes in the figure are labelled by the major part of domain names of universities in the samples. Figure 2 shows that the communities of Medicine and Arts are isolated components in the network. We can find 14 communities from university network which covers four broad disciplines out of seven in the classification system and the discipline cohesiveness is 0.91 on average.

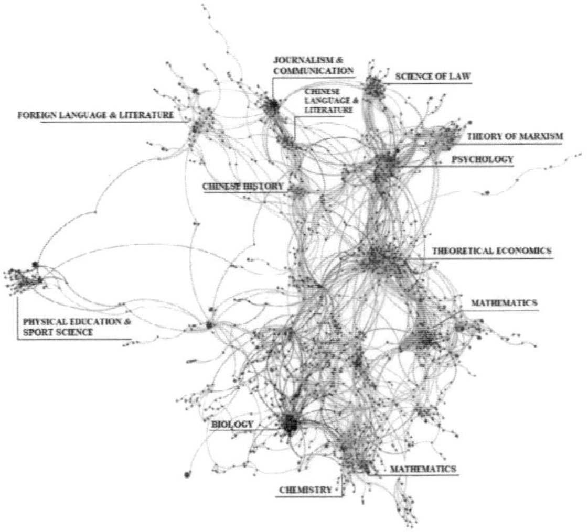

Figure 1. Communities Discovered in School Network

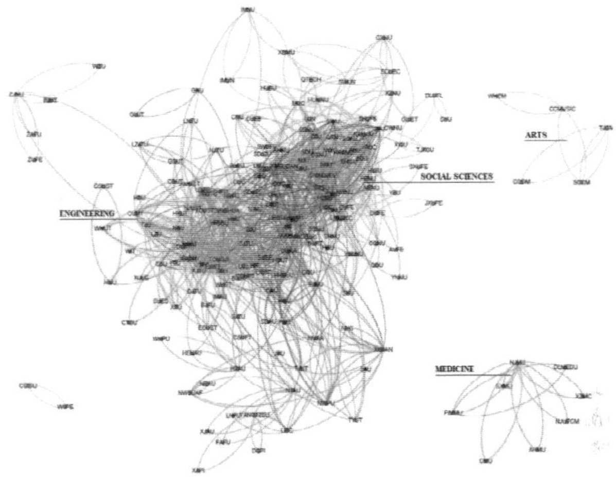

Figure 2. Communities Discovered in University Network

CONCLUSIONS

This study proposes the use of school website as the basic linked disciplinary unit to optimize the relationships in networks from the perspective of schools and universities. The case study on the network of 342 Chinese universities composed of 5711 affiliated schools shows that this strategy improves upon on the network built on the linkage relationships between universities directly (Yang, Liu, & Meloche, 2010). The structure detected using the proposed method is clearer and the discipline cohesiveness is higher. In term of discipline visibility, the outline of the communities discovered generally reflects the relations between disciplines and their positions in the whole scientific system.

REFERENCES

Bar-Ilan, J. (2005). What do we know about links and linking? A framework for studying links in academic environments. *Information Processing & Management*, 41(4), 973-986.

Blondel, V. D., Guillaume, J. L., Lambiotte, R., & Lefebvre, E. (2008). Fast unfolding of communities in large networks. *Journal of statistical mechanics: theory and experiment*, (10), P10008.

CDGDC. (2012). China Discipline Ranking. Retrieved from http://www.cdgdc.edu.cn/xwyyjsjyxx/xxsbdxz/2012en/index.shtml

Harries, G., Wilkinson, D., Price, L., Fairclough, R., & Thelwall, M. (2004). Hyperlinks as a data source for science mapping. *Journal of Information Science*, 30(5), 436-447.

Kenekayoro, P., Buckley, K., & Thelwall, M. (2014). Hyperlinks as inter-university collaboration indicators. *Journal of Information Science*, 40(4), 514-522.

Wilkinson, D., Harries, G., Thelwall, M., & Price, L. (2003). Motivations for academic Web site interlinking: Evidence for the Web as a novel source of information on informal scholarly communication. *Journal of information science*, 29(1), 49-56.

Xie J., Szymanski B.K., & Liu, X. (2011). SLPA: Uncovering overlapping communities in social networks via a speaker-listener interaction dynamic process. Proceedings of *Data Mining Workshops: IEEE 11th International Conference (pp.* 344-349*)*. Washington, DC, USA.

Yang, B., Liu, Z.H., & Meloche, J.A. (2010). Visualization of the Chinese academic web based on social network analysis. *Journal of Information Science* 36(2), 131-143.

Promoting Healthy Lifestyle Via Mobile-health Technology for African American Young Adults

EunYoung Yoo-Lee
North Carolina Central University, USA. eunyoung@ccu.edu

Kyung-Sun Kim
University of Wisconsin-Madison, USA. kskim@ischool.wisc.edu

ABSTRACT

As part of a theory-based project, this study reports the first phase of elicitation interviews to design and implement an effective information intervention with an emphasis on behavior changes in life style. The results of the study will be used to test the efficacy of mobile-health (m-Health) as a promising intervention tool for African American young adults in urban communities.

KEYWORDS

Mobile-health, health promotion, personal health management, social marketing, social media, social support, African Americans

INTRODUCTION

African Americans have the highest rates of obesity and hypertension, and a high degree of clustering of certain cardiovascular risk factors including diabetes and physical inactivity (Lakka, et al., 2002; Mozumda & Liguori, 2011). This subsequently put African Americans at a higher risk of developing associated diseases, notably cardiovascular disease. Nonetheless, African Americans have been underrepresented in previous research on disease prevention and management intervention, and urgent ongoing efforts are needed to address these health disparities in African Americans. Although a constellation of various factors at multiple levels may affect health outcomes and health disparities in population subgroups, health experts agree, and studies have confirmed that simple behavioral changes in lifestyle (e.g., dietary habits, physical activities, smoking, alcohol use, etc.) can significantly reduce health risks including overweight/obesity and hypertension, and should be the priority goal of preventive intervention and also the first line treatment. The main goal of this study is to promote lifestyle changes as lifestyle is modifiable through effective intervention technology.

To this end, the use of e-Health, in particular, m-Health has a great potential to improve the effectiveness of behavioral interventions because it can address some challenges often seen in community-based and clinical interventions such as low enrollment, attrition, ease of access, geographical proximity, time limitations, inconvenience, and sociocultural attitudes toward research. Additional benefits may include time and cost efficiency, improved health literacy, and confidential delivery of intervention contents (Pew, 2015).

According to the 2015 Pew Internet Survey, African Americans had the highest ownership of smartphones among all race/ethnic groups while African Americans' home broadband adoption rate is smaller than that of non-Hispanic white Americans. Also, some interesting change patterns have been observed in the adoption of broadband and use of smartphones. First, broadband adoption declined modestly between 2013 and 2015, and the decline was greater among African Americans. Second, an increasing number of Americans, particularly young African Americans rely only on their smartphones for online access (Pew, 2015; Anderson, 2015). This trend, along with the potential advantages of m-Health, makes young African Americans good candidates for m-Health intervention for healthy life style.

We focus on African American young adults because it has been reported that obesity in young adulthood increases the risk of developing metabolic syndrome over the subsequent 15 years almost 20-fold, and effective and sustainable health management strategies are needed early in adult life (Ogden, et al., 2015).

CONCEPTUAL DESIGN

This project employs multi-level theories as a theoretical foundation and guidance throughout different phases of the health information promotion. These theories include the Integrated Behavioral Model (IBM) (Fishbein and Capella, 2006), Behavioral Change Model Taxonomy (Michie et al., 2013), and Message Framing (McGuire, 2012). The IBM guides the entire Information promotion phase and behavior change process.

This study reports preliminary results of an open-ended elicitation interview that is a critical step in the IBM.

RESEARCH QUESTIONS

Although this study reports the first phase of the elicitation interviews, this project pursues the following three research questions.

1. Identify key contextual factors or covariates affecting (a) the adoption and effectiveness of mobile Health. intervention in African Americans, and (b) their healthy life style to prevent / manage metabolic syndromes.

2. Evaluate the effectiveness of mobile health technology as a behavioral change intervention for healthy life style.
3. Evaluate the relative effectiveness of various behavioral change methods and additional potential moderators of intervention effectiveness.

METHODS

A Historically Black College and University HBCU) in an urban community in NC was chosen as the study site. Elicitation interviews were conducted three times. Each time, 5-6 American young adults who were using a smart phone and were interested in managing a healthy lifestyle participated in a group interview. The number of interview participants was 16 in total. Average age was 21.3; five were men and eleven were women. The interview questions included: 1) IBM constructs: salient behavioral, normative, and control beliefs associated with the target behavior (i.e., healthy lifestyle with m-health technology) with the target population, 2) current health needs and healthy lifestyle, use patterns of m-health technology, and 3) modes of m-health technology delivery. The interviews were audio-recorded, professionally transcribed and content-analyzed. Qualitative data from open-ended questions were analyzed by a coding scheme.

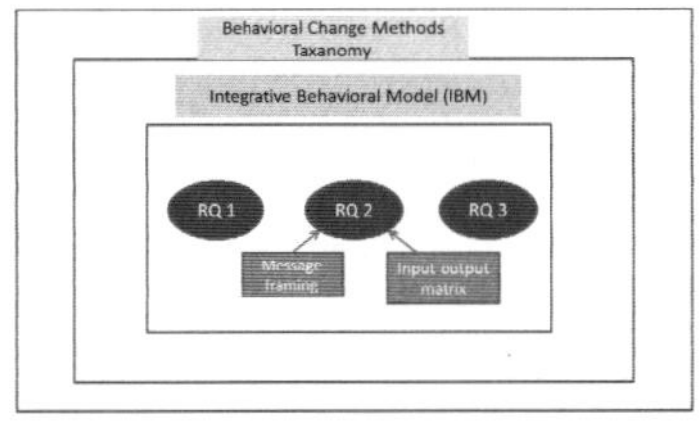

Figure 1. Theories involved in this project

PRELIMINARY FINDINGS

Table 1 summarizes the selected salient responses from elicitation interviews. The preliminary results show the target population's salient beliefs related to the behavior of healthy lifestyle.

Constructs	Selected Responses
Health needs/problems	long healthy life; pre-diabetics (diagnosed); high blood pressure (family history); appearance, weight loss/gain, muscles
Current healthy lifestyles	routine physical exercise; jogging; eat fruits and vegetables; cut back fast food and fried food, home cooking
M-Health technology use	Apps: My Plate, Sweat coin, workout apps, Social media: Snapchat, Instagram, FB, Pintrest, YouTube, Google: health information, Wearable trackers; fitbit, Apple watch, etc.
Advantages/Disadvantages of using M-health	guidance, making you keep up too many apps, weak progress, distraction; cost
Attitudes	friends/parents/medical professionals
Social norm	friends through social media (e.g., Snapchat)
Perceived control	time, motivation, busy, ease of use, cost
M-Health promotion modes	community engagement, (virtual and physical) social media. motivation boost

Table 1. Selected Responses to the Elicitation Questions

The results of the elicitation interviews allow us to develop more appropriate questionnaire items to measure each of the model constructs. They will also be design messages and the delivery methods of the m-Health technology intervention to change behaviors for healthy lifestyle.

NEXT STEPS

The next step is to develop survey questionnaires using the results of the elicitation interviews and test the effectiveness of the m-Health technology intervention in a field experimental setting (pre & post tests). Knowledge gained form this study can be used to better understand the potential of emerging information/communication technologies and to develop more effective health promotion intervention strategies tailored to the specific needs of the target population

REFERENCES

Anderson, M. (2015). *Technology device ownership 2015*. Retrieved from http://www.pewinternet.org/2015/10/29/technology-device-ownership-2015

Fishbein, M., & Cappella, J. N. (2006). The role of theory in developing effective health communications. *Journal of Communication*, *56*(s1), S1-S17.

Lakka, H.M., Laaksonen, D.E., Lakka, T.A., et al. (2002). The metabolic syndrome and total and cardiovascular disease mortality in middle-aged men. *Journal of the American Medical Association, 288* (21), 2709-16. PMID: 12460094

McGuire, W. (2012). McGuire's Classic Input–Output Framework for Constructing Persuasive Messages. *Public communication campaigns*, In Rice, R. E., & Atkin, C. K. *Public communication campaigns, 4th ed. (pp.133-143)*. Thousand Oask: Sage.

Mozumdar, A., & Liguori, G. (2011). Persistent increase of prevalence of metabolic syndrome among U.S. adults: NHANES III to NHANES 1999–2006. *Diabetes Care*, *34*(1), 216-219. doi: 10.2337/dc10-0879.

Ogden, C. L., Carroll, M. D., Kit, B. K., & Flegal, K. M. (2015). Prevalence of Obesity Among Adults and Youth: United States, 2011–2014. *NCHS Data Brief (219)*. Retrieved from https://www.cdc.gov/nchs/data/databriefs/db219.pdf

Pew Research Center (2015). Home broadband 2015: The share of Americans with broadband at home has plateaued, and more rely only on their smartphones for online access. Retrieved from http://www.pewinternet.org/2015/12/21/2015/Home-Broadband-2015

Drugs and Bitcoins: What Role do Bitcoins Play in the Darknet Market? A Preliminary Study

Chenwei Zhang
Indiana University Bloomington, USA
Qiqihar Institute of Engineering, China.
zhang334@indiana.edu

Xiaozhong Liu
Indiana University Bloomington, USA. liu237@indiana.edu

Ruibin Wei
Anhui University of Finance and Economics, China.
rbwxy@126.com

ABSTRACT

Darknet markets (DNM) and bitcoins are two emergent topics in the information field and have attracted much attention. However, few has explored them together. This study aims at understanding the relation between them. It is investigated that whether the bitcoin exchange value and the public interest in it are predictable of the daily sales in the darknet markets in the future. By applying the Granger-causality analysis, we find that the daily bitcoin exchange value with one day lag are Granger causative of the sales, so does the daily searching frequency in Google with one, two, and three-day(s) lags. From the linear regressions, we find that the increasing bitcoin price reduces the daily DNM sales, while the increasing public interest in bitcoins facilitate the sales. By understanding relation between the DNM sales and bitcoins, two emergent topics in information science, we can get some insights on how to monitor the activities in the DNM, especially those illegal transactions and can further extend to how to regulate the DNM.

KEYWORDS

Bitcoins, darknet market

INTRODUCTION

Darknet markets (DNM) are like black markets operating via darknets, which could be accessed anonymously. They usually provide users with an escrow payment service, where the trades are made in bitcoins, and a vender feedback system. The darknet technology and especially the powerful anonymity of bitcoin made DNM a breeding ground for many illegal transactions such as drugs, weapons, and forgeries. Bitcoin is a type of cryptocurrency worldwide. As a digital currency without a central bank or administrator, it is more and more widely used in the exchange for other currencies, products, and services. However, bitcoin itself could also be treated as a special currency/product since it has a limited total amount all over the world. The exchange price of bitcoin fluctuates wildly. Whether such a payment method with quick changing value has something to do with sales in DNM is an interesting question and is worth checking. This project seeks to characterize how bitcoins influence the DNM sales. We would like to investigate the role that bitcoins play in DNM. Bitcoin is quantified in two perspectives—its exchange value and the public interest in it. We conjecture that both perspectives could be predictive of future DNM sales.

METHODOLOGY

Data

The DNM data was obtained from Branwen et al. (2015). They crawled several darknet markets in a daily base, except for some errors presented. Our analysis is based on the data from Silk Road 2, which was a darknet market mainly selling illegal drugs. It started on November 6, 2013 and was shut down in November 2014. On most days during its operating period, the item pages describing the goods sold on Silk Road 2 were crawled, including information such as one item's description, its category, the vendor, and customers' feedbacks on this item. For each piece of feedback on each item, we know the rating a customer put, the text of the feedback, and the freshness of this feedback. By tracking the same item's customer feedbacks over different days, we can estimate the sales of an item on each day (Christin, 2013). Two variables related to bitcoins were collected, bitcoin exchange value and the public interest in bitcoins. The first one was measured by Bitcoin Price Index (BPI), which demonstrates an exchange rate between US dollars and bitcoin. The other variable is reflected by the daily Google Trends result of the term "bitcoin", which shows the frequency of "bitcoin" searched on each day.

Method

Bivariate Granger Causality Analysis

We first investigate the hypothesis that bitcoin exchange value and the public interest in bitcoins are predictive of future sales in the darknet markets by applying the Granger causality analysis. Granger causality analysis assumes that the changes in a variable X will systematically occur before changes in the other variable Y, if X causes Y. In other words, the lagged values of X will be statistically significant correlated with Y. This will show whether X has predictive information about Y or not. To test whether the proposed two bitcoin related variables predict the product sales in the darknet market, the variance of the two linear models listed below (Equations 1-2) should be compared. S_t represents the product sales in the darknet market on day t; S_{t-n}

to S_{t-1} represent n lagged values of S_t; X_t represents one of the proposed variables on day t; and X_{t-n} to X_{t-1} represent n lagged values of X_t. If there is a statistically significant difference, the null hypothesis could be rejected that the time series X do not predict the product sales in the dark net market.

$$S_t = \alpha + \Sigma_{i=1}^{n}\beta_i S_{t-i} + \epsilon_t \quad (1)$$
$$S_t = \alpha + \Sigma_{i=1}^{n}\beta_i S_{t-i} + \Sigma_{i=1}^{n}\gamma_i X_{t-i} + \epsilon_t \quad (2)$$

Linear Regression

We also implement a linear regression, which aims at understanding the predictive power of two proposed bitcoin related variables to the DNM sales. We do not aim for a perfect model for the prediction. Instead, we want to check two bitcoin variables with different time lags to get a rough idea how they influence the DNM sales. The model is shown in Equation (3).

$$S_t = \lambda + \theta_i X_{t-i} + \epsilon_t \quad (3)$$

PRELIMINARY RESULTS

From the results of Granger causality (shown in Table 1), we find that both bitcoin related variables predict the daily DNM sales in some way. The bitcoin exchange value, represented by the Bitcoin Price Index has the Granger causality with the daily DNM sales for a lag of 1 day. The public interest in bitcoins, reflected by the daily Google Trends of "bitcoin" has the Granger causality with the daily DNM sales for lags of 1 day, 2 days, 3 days, and 6 days.

Lag	Bitcoin exchange value	Public interest in bitcoins
1 day	0.066*	0.005***
2 days	0.771	0.005***
3 days	0.391	0.090*
4 days	0.261	0.153
5 days	0.247	0.123
6 days	0.198	0.093*
7 days	0.111	0.146

(Note: p-value < 0.01: ***, < 0.05: **, < 0.1: *)

Table 4. Statistical significance (p-values) of bivariate Granger-causality correlation

Table 2 shows the results from the linear regressions, in which the DNM sales is the dependent variable, and the two bitcoin related variables with no lag, 1-day lag, and 2-day lag is the independent variable, respectively. We find that the daily bitcoin exchange value actually has a negative effect on the DNM sales; while the public interest in bitcoins has the opposite effect—the more people search bitcoin in Google, the more sales are made in the DNM.

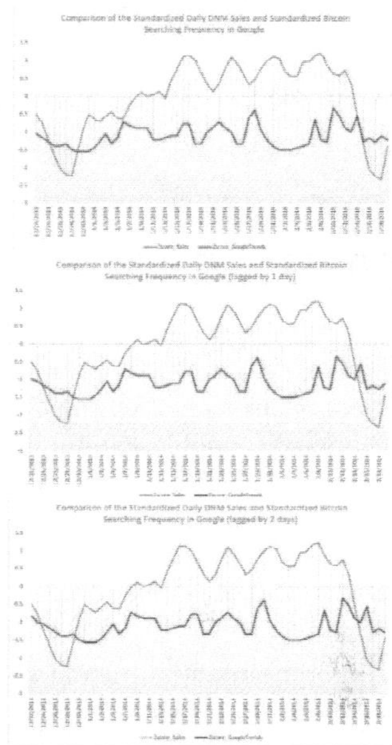

Figure 1. Plots of Standardized daily DNM sales and bitcoin searching in Google

To have a better idea of the results above, we visualize the correlation between the daily DNM sales and the daily searching frequency of "bitcoin" in Google for a range of 60 days as an example. For the convenience of visualization, we plot both time series in the same scale by converting each series to its z-score. Figure 1-up shows the overlap of these two variables on the same day; Figure 1-middle shows the overlap of the daily DNM sales and the searching frequency of "bitcoin" in Google one day before; Figure 1-down shows the overlap of the daily DNM sales and the searching frequency of "bitcoin" in Google two days before. As can be seen in Figure 1, the time series of the daily DNM sales and the daily searching frequency of "bitcoin" in Google frequently point in the same direction. The daily searching frequency of "bitcoin" (t = 0) and its values on one day before and two days before may predict the daily DNM sales (t = 0).

IV (with lags)	Coefficients of bitcoin exchange value	Coefficients of public interest in bitcoins
0 day	-160.58***	2757.8***
1 day	-143.93***	3042.3***
2 days	-126.53**	3108.6***

(Note: p-value < 0.01: ***, < 0.05: **, < 0.1: *)

Table 5. Results of six individual linear regressions on daily DNM sales

CONCLUSION

This preliminary study tries to explore whether there exists relation between the daily DNM sales and the bitcoin exchange value and the public interest in it. It is found that both terms are predictable of the DNM sales in the future. In the next step, we would like to create a model that perfectly describe the relationship and make precise predictions.

REFERENCES

Branwen, G., Christin, N., Décary-Hétu, D., Andersen, R. M., StExo, Presidente, E., …Goode, S. (2015). Dark net market archives, 2011-2015. Retrieved from https://www.gwern.net/DNM-archives

Christin, N. (2013, May). Traveling the Silk Road: A measurement analysis of a large anonymous online marketplace. In *Proceedings of the 22nd international conference on World Wide Web* (pp. 213-224). ACM.

Multi-discipline Correlation Analysis between Citations and Detailed Features of Library Holdings

Heng Zhang
Nanjing University of Science and Technology, China.
525696532@qq.com

Qingqing Zhou
Nanjing University of Science and Technology, China.
breeze7zhou@163.com

Chengzhi Zhang*
Nanjing University of Science and Technology, China.
zhangcz@njust.edu.cn

ABSTRACT

Citations and library holdings are two important metrics for assessing book impact. Traditional researches about correlations between these two metrics are mainly based on books' citations and holding numbers. More detailed information about books' holding (i.e. their holding regions) can be used in book impact assessment. In this paper, we will investigate the relationships between citations and more comprehensive features of library holdings, namely holding numbers, holding regions and holding distributions. We obtain citations of 2, 356 Chinese books from CSSCI[1] and the corresponding library holding data from OCLC[2]. Then, we conduct correlation analysis between citations and the three features of library holdings respectively. Results show that there are general weak correlations between the two metrics in all disciplines, while correlations in Linguistics, Ethnology and Archeology are stronger.

KEYWORDS

Book impact assessment, citations, library holdings, correlation analysis, disciplines differences

INTRODUCTON

Citations (Barilan, 2010) and library holdings (White et al., 2009) are two important metrics for book impact assessment (White, 1995). Many researchers have investigated correlations between these two metrics. Zuccala & Guns (2012) found significant correlations between the citations and libcitations in humanities journals. Zuccala & White (2015) proved that there were positive, weak but highly significant correlations between OCLC WorldCat library holdings and Scopus citations in humanities. The previous studies only analyzed correlations between citations and books' holding numbers. More detailed information about books' holding can be mined to use for book impact assessment. Hence, we obtain books' citations from CSSCI (Su, 2011) which includes Chinese high-cited books in the disciplines of humanities and social sciences, and find their corresponding library holdings from OCLC. Then, we analyze correlations between citations and three features of library holdings, namely holding numbers, holding regions and holding distributions. Experimental results show that correlations of two sources are very weak in disciplines except for Linguistics, Ethnology and Archeology.

METHODOLOGY

Framework of our study

The main purpose of this paper is to study correlations between citations and detailed features of library holdings in different disciplines. As shown in Figure 1, firstly, we collect Chinese books' citation data and their corresponding library holding data, including holding numbers, holding regions and holding distributions. Specifically, we obtain books' holding distributions by calculate their entropy values, and a higher entropy value indicate a more uniform distribution. Then, we conduct correlation analysis between citations and the three features of library holdings in different disciplines respectively.

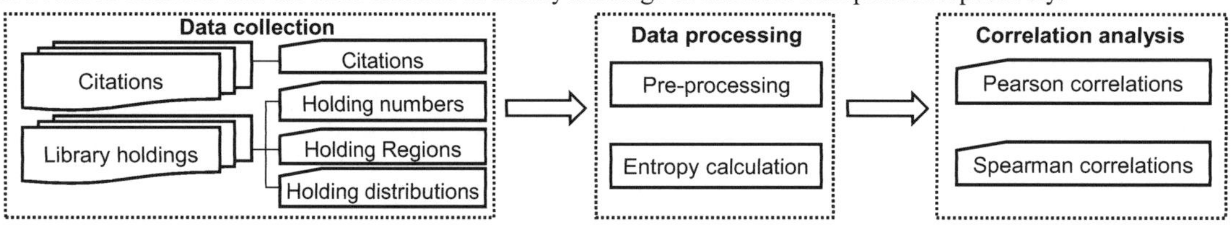

Figure 1. Framework of our work

Dataset

We collected 2, 356 books' citation data (citations >=10) from CSSCI and their corresponding library holding information from OCLC. For a book, its library holding information includes total holding number, the number of regions which collect it,

* Corresponding author
[1] http://cssci.nju.edu.cn
[2] http://www.oclc.org

and holding distributions among these regions. These books belong to 21 disciplines, namely *Archeology, Art, Chinese Literature, Culture, Economics, Ethnology, Foreign Literature, History, Journalism and Communication, Law, Library and Information, Linguistics, Management, Marxism, Pedagogy, Philosophy, Politics, Psychology, Religion, Sociology* and *Sports.*

Entropy computation of holding distributions

In general, a book is collected by different libraries in several regions. Hence, we can use entropy value of a book to identify whether it is uniformly distributed among the regions. Books with uniform distributions tend to get higher entropy values. Entropy value of a book is calculated by formula (1).

$$E = -\frac{1}{n}\sum_{i=1}^{n}\frac{p_i}{m}\cdot\ln\left(\frac{p_i}{m}\right) \qquad (1)$$

Where, n is the number of holding regions of a book, p_i refers to the holding number of ith region, and m denotes the total holding number of the book.

RESULTS ANALYSIS

We analyzed the correlations between citations and three features of library holdings in different disciplines respectively. Results are shown in Figure 2, 3 and 4.

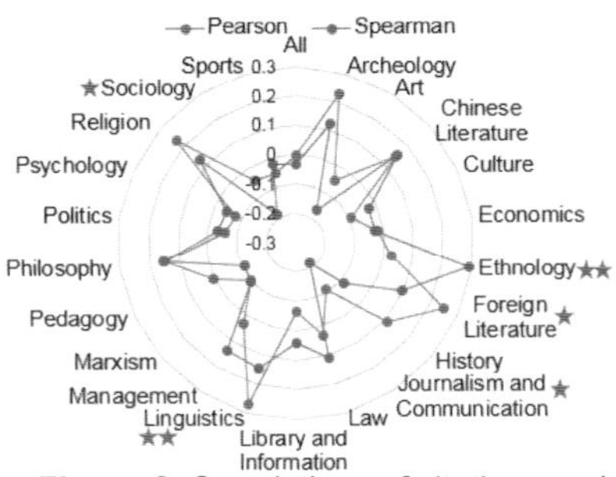

Figure 2. Correlations of citations and holding numbers

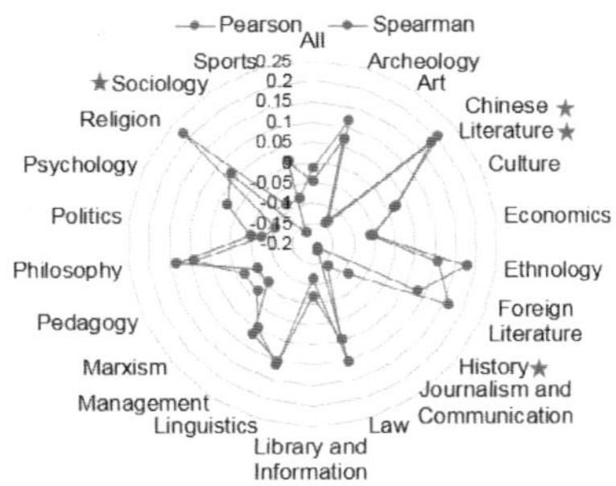

Figure 3. Correlations of citations and holding regions

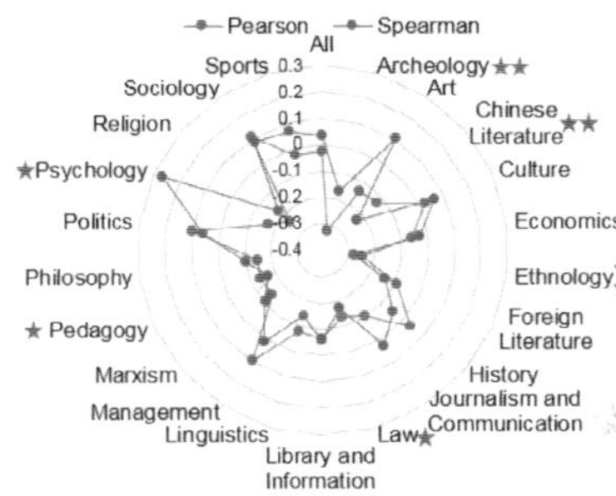

Figure 4. Correlations of citations and entropies of holding distributions

*Note: *, p<=0.5; **, p<=0.01.*

On the whole, the correlations are weak. In Figure 2, Linguistics has the highest Pearson correlation (coefficient=0.2736) and Ethnology has the strongest Spearman correlation (coefficient=0.2912). As shown in Figure 3, correlations are generally lower than which in figure 2 and 4. According to Figure 4, there are more negative correlations than positive ones. Books in most disciplines get massive citations while their holding distributions are not uniform. Meanwhile, we make a statistic of library holdings, and the result reveals that America and China hold most of the library holdings. In addition, as Figure 4 shows, Archeology has the strongest Pearson correlation (coefficient=-0.3228).

CONCLUSIONS

What we find in this research is of great significance for book impact assessment. We should not use the same standard of citations and library holdings to assess impact of books in different disciplines. Furthermore, holding regions and holding distribution are other good metrics for book impact assessment besides the well-known holding numbers.

ACKNOWLEDGMENTS

This work is supported by Major Projects of National Social Science Fund (No.17ZDA291).

REFERENCES

Su, X. (2011). A report on the academic influence of Chinese humanity and social science books. Beijing: China Social Science Press. (In Chinese).

Barilan, J. (2010). Citations to the "Introduction to informetrics" indexed by WOS, Scopus and Google Scholar. *Scientometrics, 82*(3), 495-506.

White, H. D., Boell, S. K., Yu, H., Davis, M., Wilson, C. S., & Cole, F. T. H. (2009). Libcitations: A measure for comparative assessment of book publications in the humanities and social sciences. *Journal of the Association for Information Science and Technology 60*(6), 1083–1096.

Zuccala, A., & Guns, R. (2013). Comparing book citations in humanities journals to library holdings: Scholarly use versus perceived cultural benefit. *Proceedings of the 14th International Conference of International Society for Scientometrics and Informetrics (ISSI)* (pp. 353-360).

Zuccala, A., & White, H. D. (2015). Correlating Libcitations and Citations in the Humanities with WorldCat and Scopus Data. *Proceedings of the 15th International Conference of International Society for Scientometrics and Informetrics (ISSI)* (pp. 305-316).

White, H. D. (1995). *Brief tests of collection strength: A methodology for all types of libraries* (No. 88). Greenwood Publishing Group.

Extracting Metadata of Scientific References in Patents Based on Combination of Representation Learning and Machine Learning

Jinzhu Zhang
Nanjing University of Science and Technology, China. zhangjinzhu@njust.edu.cn

Yiming Hu
Nanjing University of Science and Technology, China. 313409834@qq.com

ABSTRACT

The scientific references in patent (SRPs), one type of non-patent references (NPRs), is the best representative of scientific knowledge cited in patents (SKCP). However, SKCP is often indicated by NPRs rather than SRPs currently, which may reduce the accuracy of the analysis of science & technology transfer and transformation. In the other hand, the content of SRPs is important for subsequent in-depth patent analysis, which requires more accurate SRPs' metadata extraction. In order to enhance the accuracy of SRPs identification and SRPs' metadata extraction, this paper uses the representation learning method to learn vectors of the NPRs and the parts separated by delimiters with each SRP (metadata), respectively. These vectors conclude the context information and the same type of metadata may appear in the same position in vector space. Then the problem of SRPs identification and SRPs' metadata extraction are transferred as the automatic categorization with the machine learning method. The experiment is conducted in the field of gene where patents cite lots of SRPs. The result shows that in 1000 patent citations, the accuracy of SRP identification reaches 99.27% and the accuracy of SRP title extraction reaches 90.57% which is 4.51% higher than the pure machine learning method.

KEYWORDS

Scientific references in patents; metadata extraction; machine learning; representation learning

INTRODUCTION

The scientific references in patent (SRPs), one type of non-patent references (NPRs), is the best representative of scientific knowledge cited in patents (SKCP) (Narin F, Hamilton K S, Olivastro D, 1997). However, currently SKCP is often indicated by NPRs rather than SRPs, and thus lead to reduce the accuracy of the analysis of science & technology transfer and transformation. Therefore, it is urgent to identify the SRPs in NPRs for better patent analysis.On the basis of SRPs identification, it also requires accurate SRPs' content extraction for subsequent in-depth patent mining. Researchers have explored several different methods to extract the SRPs' metadata, including rule-based (Wei W, King I, Lee H M. 2007), template-based (Day MY, Tsai TH, Sung CL, et al. 2007) and machine learning based methods (Jiang L, Wang D). The machine learning based methods perform better in most of the times and have better robustness. The mainly applied machine learning algorithm including Hidden Markov Model (Seymore K, Mccallum A, Rosenfeld R. 2008), Support Vector Machine (SVM) (Han H, Giles C L. 2003) and Conditional Random Field (CRF) (Nanba, H., Anzen, N., & Okumura, M. 2008). However, these methods rarely consider the semantic information of metadata in SRPs which may be useful for metadata extraction and enhance the extraction accuracy. Therefore, in order to enhance the accuracy of SRPs identification and SRPs' metadata extraction, this paper uses the repre- sentation learning method to learn the vectors of NPR and the parts of SRP separated by delimiters respectively. These vectors conclude the context information and the same type of metadata may appear in the same position in the vector space. Then the problem of SRPs identification and SRPs' metadata extraction are transferred as the automatic categorization with the machine learning method.

DATA AND METHOD

This paper combines the representation learning and the machine learning method to consider more semantic information. Firstly, the whole NPR is vectorized by the representation learning method doc2vec in training set for considering context information, and then the vector of NPR and its category are as the input of machine learning method SVM (support vector machine) for model training, finally new NPR is categorized using this model and the SRP is identified. On the basis of the above result, the identified SRP is divided into several parts by delimiters. These parts are vectorized by doc2vec in training set for considering context information, and then the vectors of these parts and their categories are as the inputs of SVM for model training, finally the parts of a new SRP is categorized using this model and the metadata are extracted.

Data description

This paper selects 1000 patent citations in the field of gene for experiment, which were downloaded from the U.S. Patent and Trademark Office (USPTO) website. Firstly, the punctuations in patent citation is pre-processed, e.g., deleting the quotes, hyphens, and et.al, and replacing several punctuations into unified separators. For machine learning, this paper randomly chooses 800 (80%) records are as the training set and the rest 200 (20%) are as the testing set.

SRP identification based on combination of representation learning and machine learning

1. Each NPR is vectorized by the representation learning method doc2vec in training set. The doc2vec (Le Q, Mikolov T. 2014) is an extension of word2vec (Mikolov T, Chen K, Corrado G, et al. 2013), which can capture and combine the linguistic contexts of each word and denoted as a low-dimensional vector.
2. The NPRs are categorized into two classes, including SRPs and non-SRPs. The vectors of NPRs and their categories in the training set are as the input of machine learning method SVM (support vector machine) for model training.
3. The new NPR is categorized using the above model and the SRP is identified. The new NPR is also denoted as a vector using doc2vec, and then the vector is as the input of the above model for binary classification.

SRPs' metadata extraction based on combination of representation learning and machine learning

1. On the basis of the above result, the identified SRP is divided into several parts by delimiters. For example, one of the SPRs "Prokop. 1984; Spectral shifting by dyes to enhance algae growth; Biotechnology and Bioengineering; vol. XXVI; 1313-1322." is divided into seven parts: "Prokop"(p1), "1984" (p2), "Spectral shifting by dyes to enhance algae growth" (p3), "Biotechnology and Bioengineering" (p4), "vol" (p5), "XXVI" (p6), "1313-1322" (p7).
2. These parts are categorized into three classes, including author (A), title (T) and others (O) in the training set. In the above example, p1 is categorized as A, p3 and p4 are both categorized as T, and the other parts are all categorized as O. Then these parts are vectorized by doc2vec in training set, and both the vectors and their categories are as the inputs of SVM for model training.
3. When a new SRP is coming, the SPR firstly divided into several parts and each part is vectorized by doc2vec, and then the vectors are as the inputs of SVM for classification to extract the SPR's metadata.

RESULTS

SRP identification

This paper selects templates based and machine learning-based method for comparison. Three indicators, i.e., precision (P), recall (R) and F1score (F1), are selected for evaluation. The result is shown in Figure 1 and Figure 2. It means that the forms better than others.

Patent citations	SRP identification
Yamamoto et al (Experimental Cell Research. 1982; 142: 79-84).	SRPs
Furusawa et al (In vivo and in vitro erythropoiesis: the Friend system. 1980. Editor: GB Rossi).	SRPs
GenBank Accession No. AL731582, (2002).	SRPs
GTAAAC recogntion site enzymes list generated Apr. 2012.	non-SRPs
Holen et al. (Nucleic Acids Research 2002, vol. 30: 1757-1766).	SRPs

Figure 1. The result of SRP identification

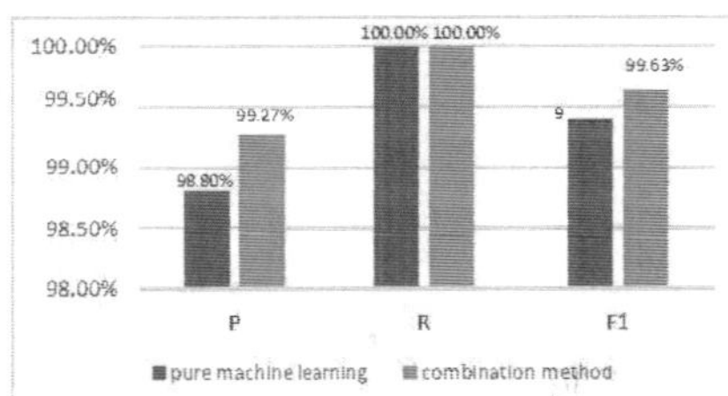

Figure 2. The comparison of two methods of SRP identification

This paper selects machine learning based method for comparison. In addition, this paper only completes one type of metadata extraction, i.e., title extraction. The results are shown in Figure 3 and Figure 4. It shows that the accuracy of SRPs' title extraction can reach 90.57% which is 4.51% higher than the machine learning method without representation learning. The result means that the combination of representation learning and machine learning is effective for SRPs' metadata extraction.

SRPs	Extracted title
Kudo, Akira et al., “Structure of thymidine kinase gene introduced into mouse Ltk- cells by a new injection method”, Gene (1982), vol. 19, pp. 11-19.	Structure of thymidine kinase gene introduced into mouse Ltk- cells by a new injection method
Furusawa et al (In vivo and in vitro erythropoiesis: the Friend system. 1980. Editor: GB Rossi).	In vivo and in vitro erythropoiesis: the Friend system
Prokop et al; (1984); Spectral shifting by dyes to enhance algae growth; Biotechnology and Bioengineering; vol. XXVI; 1313-1322.	Spectral shifting by dyes to enhance algae growth
Gressel, J; (1999); Tandem Constructs: Preventing the Rise of Superweeds; Tibtech; 17:361-366.	Tandem Constructs: Preventing the Rise of Superweeds
Baulcombe et al., The Plant Cell(1996) 8:1833-1844.	The Plant Cell

Figure 3. The result of SRPs' titles extraction

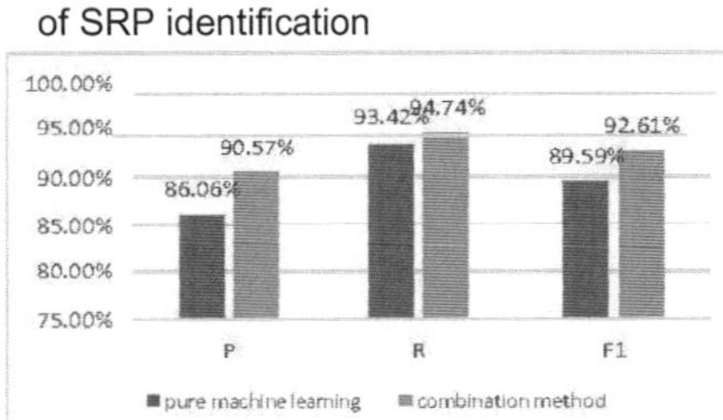

Figure 4. The comparison of two meth- ods of SRPs' titles extraction

CONCLUSION

This paper combines the representation learning method and the machine learning method for SRPs identification and SRPs' metadata extraction. The result shows that this method can enhance the accuracy in both of situations. In future, we would like to apply this method to extract other types of SRPs' metadata and increase data size to verify the effectiveness of the method in big data set.

ACKNOWLEDGMENTS

This work is supported by the National Natural Science Foundation of China (No. 71503125), the Social Science Fund Youth Project of Jiangsu Province (No. 17TQC003) and the Fundamental Research Funds for the Central Universities (No. 30918013108).

REFERENCES

Narin, F., Hamilton, K. S., & Olivastro, D. (1997). The increasing linkage between U.S. technology and public science. *Research Policy 26*, 317-330.

Wei, W., King, I., & Lee, H. M. (2007). Bibliographic Attributes Extraction with Layer-upon-Layer Tagging. *International Conference on Document Analysis and Recognition* (Vol.2, pp. 804-808). Curitiba: IEEE.

Day, M. Y., Tsai, T. H., Sung, C. L., Hsieh, C. C., Lee, C. W., & Wu, S. H., et al. (2007). Reference metadata extraction using a hierarchical knowledge representation frame- work. *Decision Support Systems 43*, 152-167.

Jiang L, Wang D. (2017). Automatically detecting and tagging foreign language citation metadata. *Data Analysis and Knowledge Discovery 39*, 47-54.

Seymore, K., Mccallum, A., & Rosenfeld, R. (1999). Learning hidden markov model structure for information extraction. *Proc Aaai'99 Workshop Machine Learning for Information Extraction* (pp. 37-42). Orlando: AAAI.

Han H, Giles C L, Manavoglu E, et al. (2003). Automatic Document Metadata Extraction Using Support Vector Machines. *2003 Joint Conference on Digital Libraries* (pp. 37-48). Houston: IEEE.

Nanba, H., Anzen, N., & Okumura, M. (2008). Automatic extraction of citation information in Japanese patent applications. *International Journal on Digital Libraries 9*, 151-161. Le, Q., & Mikolov, T. (2014). Distributed representations of sentences and documents. *International Conference on International Conference on Machine Learning* (Vol.4, pp. II-1188). Beijing: ACM.

Mikolov, T., Corrado, G., Chen, K., Dean, J., Mikolov, T., & Corrado, G., et al. (2013). Efficient Estimation of Word Representations in Vector Space. *International Conference on Learning Representations* (pp. 1-12). Scottsdale: ICLR.

Motivations of Volunteers in the Transcribe Sheng Project: A Grounded Theory Approach

Xuanhui Zhang
Nanjing University, China. zhangxhdo@163.com

Yuxiang (Chris) Zhao
Nanjing University of Science & Technology, China. yxzhao@vip.163.com

Shijie Song
Nanjing University, China. ssong@smail.nju.edu.cn

Qinghua Zhu
Nanjing University, China. qhzhu@nju.edu.cn

ABSTRACT

With an increasing interest in leveraging crowdsourcing in GLAMs (Galleries, Libraries, Archives, and Museums) projects, there is a growing trend within the digital humanities field to develop various platforms and tools that outsource the traditionally knowledge-intensive tasks to the mass volunteers. However, such kind of projects usually entail a greater level of time, effort, and intellectual input from the public. In such case, what motivates volunteers remains little studied and poorly understood. To better understand volunteers' motivations and how they may benefit from their participation, we conducted interviews on volunteers in the Transcribe Sheng project, a crowdsourcing project in digital humanities domain in China. Grounded theory is employed to investigate the motivations from the interview data. The preliminary findings show that volunteers are motivated by a complex framework involving external factors, cognitive value, emotional perception, and task driven factors. Based on the qualitative analysis, this study proposes a preliminary theoretical framework to understand volunteers' motivations, which may also yield practical implications on digital humanity practices.

KEYWORDS

Crowdsourcing, digital humanities, motivations, grounded theory, Transcribe Sheng.

INTRODUCTION

In recent years, crowdsourcing approach has been increasingly adopted in GLAMs (i.e., Galleries, Libraries, Archives, and Museums) projects to improve the collecting, organizing, and evaluating processes on valuable resources. Crowdsourcing initiatives of GLAMs endeavor to offer citizens the opportunity to deeply involve in production, utilization, communication, and curation of those feature collections and archives (Owens, 2013). In digital humanity fields, similar demands exist, calling for developing platforms and tools to harness the wisdom of crowds to utilize the feature collections in GLAMs. However, crowdsourcing in cultural heritage usually entails a greater level of time, effort, and intellectual input from the public (Oomen & Aroyo, 2011). So the public may likely lose their interest after initial trials without sustained motivations. Therefore, how to sustain volunteers' participation is a great challenge for digital humanity projects.

In this paper, we explore the motivations of volunteers' continuous participation in the Shengxuanhuai Manuscript Transcription Initiative. Grounded theory approach is used to investigate the motivational lens based on interview data. The purpose of this study is to better understand the characteristics of crowdsourcing participation in the digital humanities. Meanwhile, as one of the first large-scale crowdsourcing projects in the cultural heritage domain in China, Transcribe Sheng is of great significance to the development of Chinese digital humanities.

A BRIEF INTRODUCTION ON TRANSCRIBE SHENG PROJECT

	Profile category	Count
Gender	Male	8
	Female	6
Age	18~30	9
	31~40	4
	>40	1
Education	Ph.D./Doctoral Degree	3
	Master Degree	8
	Bachelor Degree	3
Position	Student	8
	Librarian	5
	Teacher	1

Table 1. Demographic information

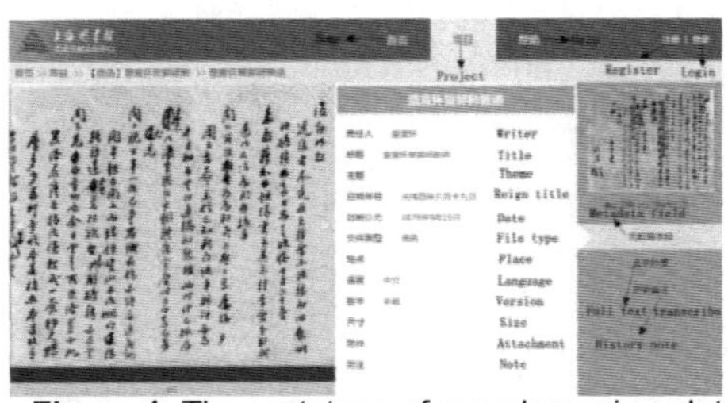

Figure 1. The prototype of crowdsourcing platform

Sheng Xuanhuai, Wade-Giles romanization Sheng Hsüan-huai (1844-1916), a Chinese government official, representative of Westernization Movement and entrepreneur in the last years of the Qing dynasty (1644–1911/12), responsible for much of China's early industrialization. The Shengxuanhuai Manuscript Transcription Initiative (Transcribe Sheng for short) is a cultural heritage-oriented crowdsourcing project which engages researchers and the public. The engaged volunteers are expected to generate, describe, and identify the historical records of Sheng from Shanghai Library, involving 175,000 volumes (c. 100 million words) in total, via a collaborative crowdsourcing platform (Figure 1). A beta-test of Transcribe Sheng was released to the public in 2016, and the project was formally launched in early 2017.

METHOD

A semi-structured interview was carried out from November 10th to December 10th, 2017. Purposive sampling was conducted to recruit every single participant, who already registered in Transcribe Sheng and finished some tasks. We finally found 14 participants who meet the requirement; demographic information is shown in Table 1. We used face-to-face interview to ask questions in four aspects, including task, platform, volunteer, and organization of the Transcribe Sheng; detailed questions are shown in Table 2. Each interview took about 60 minutes. Then we used grounded theory approach to elicit concepts and categories in order to explore the motivations of volunteers' engagement.

The coding of interviews involved two researchers. The first 2/3 (9) interview records were coded by two researchers respectively, while the remaining 1/3 (5) were used for theoretical saturation test.

#	Question
1	Why do you participate in Transcribe Sheng?
2	How do you feel about doing this task?
3	Are you interested in history and culture? Why?
4	Is there anyone around you to take part in this project? (Does this have any effect on you?) Please specify.
5	How do you feel about the platform of Transcribe Sheng? Why?
6	If you can add one feature in this platform, what would it be? Why?
7	What do you want to gain during the participation? Why?
8	Anything else you would like to say.

Table 2. Questions asked in the interview

FINDINGS

After three coding stage - open coding, axial coding, and selective coding (Strauss and Corbin, 1990), we identified 32 initial concepts, 14 categories, and corresponding 4 core categories. The 4 core categories include external factors, cognitive value, emotional perception, and task driven factors. Based on the coding results, a theoretical model is proposed (Figure 2).

External Factors

There were essentially four categories of external factors identified through data analysis: (1) External reward, (2) Feedback, (3) Help/Training, and (4) Subjective norms. External rewards include monetary and non-monetary rewards. 8(57%) interviewees mentioned money or other material rewards ("*I think some material rewards, such as money, can be added.*"), of which 4(29%) participants believed that besides material rewards, virtual rewards such as points, badges and rankings could affect their willingness to participate. Meanwhile, 5(36%) respondents call for the instant feedback function and help/training from the platform ("*Every time I finish a transcribe task, I want to know the quality of my work.*"; "*You know Transcribe Sheng is not a simple work, sometimes when I met with difficulties, if I could not get online help immediately, I can hardly go on.*"). Furthermore, subjective norms such as peer influence and enforcement may also affect volunteers' willingness to participate ("*My best friend participates in this project, and so do I.*").

Cognitive Value

Cognitive value refers to the motivation of volunteers to continuously participate in projects based on the perception of costs and benefits. Three categories were discovered: (1) Perceived cost, (2) Expected benefit, and (3) Social value. In this study, the perceived cost is mainly reflected by the time and effort spent; the expected benefit is mainly reflected by the reputation and ability gained. 7(50%) respondents said that Transcribe Sheng tasks required a lot of time and effort ("*I think it is difficult for me to do these tasks. It takes me a lot of time and effort.*"). 4(29%) responses are related to reputation ("*If I transcribed more and better, more people would notice me.*"). Meanwhile, several respondents described a strong feeling of being part of a community ("*I can make friends with people who have similar interests with me.*").

Emotional Perception

Emotional perception mainly includes four aspects: (1) Enjoyment, (2) Obstruction, (3) Satisfaction, and (4) Commitment. 6(43%) respondents mentioned "fun", "interesting", "enjoyable" or similar words. However, these participants also mentioned that the sense of interest gradually vanished with the frequent tasks. 4(29%) participants thought it was too difficult to do the tasks ("S*ome words are hard to recognize, I don't know what they mean.*"). 7(50%) respondents expressed satisfaction after finishing the task ("*It has been hard to do at first but now I'm getting satisfaction from the tasks.*"). Moreover, some participants felt a sense of obligation to the project ("*It is very meaningful and necessary to make contributions to the preservation of historical documents.*").

Task Driven Factors

Task driven factors are composed of three aspects: (1) Resource presentation, (2) Task design, and (3) Task description. 6(43%) volunteers indicated that the presentation of archival resources should tend to be more diversified ("*I think combining texts, pictures, and videos could mobilize volunteers' interests in participating.*"). 5(36%) volunteers considered that the tasks should vary in difficulty. Furthermore, almost all of the respondents said that "*if the project organization could send them some interesting information on regular, it could enhance their stickiness to the project*".

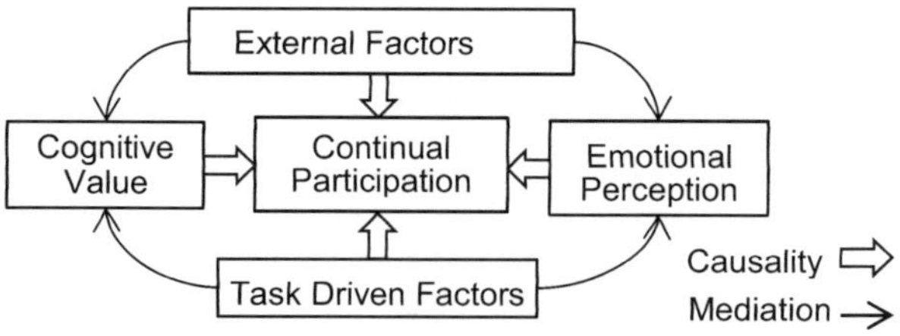

Figure 2. The theoretical model

REFERENCES

Oomen, J., & Aroyo, L. (2011). Crowdsourcing in the cultural heritage domain: opportunities and challenges. In Proceedings of the 5th International Conference on Communities and Technologies (pp. 138-149). ACM.

Owens, T. (2013). Digital cultural heritage and the crowd. Curator: The Museum Journal, 56(1), 121-130.

Strauss, A., & Corbin, J. M. (1990). Basics of qualitative research: Grounded theory procedures and techniques. Sage Publications, Inc.

Visualizing ResearchGate as a Scholarly Social Networking Site for U.S. Research Universities

Yin Zhang
Kent State University, USA. yzhang4@kent.edu

Weiwei Yan
Wuhan University, China. yanww@whu.edu.cn

ABSTRACT

This poster showcases recent research on scholarly use of the social networking site ResearchGate (RG). It aims to depict how researchers from U.S. research universities utilize the site and how their use demonstrates institutional differences and forms social networks that mirror their scholarly reputation and status in reality.

KEYWORDS

ResearchGate, Academic social networking site, research reputation, user characteristics, institutional difference, follower-followee relationship, research activity level.

INTRODUCTION

Individual academics have been increasingly adopting academic social networking sites for research-related activities (Gruzd et al., 2012; Thelwall & Kousha, 2014). ResearchGate (RG), one of the leading academic social networking sites, combines communication and dissemination with a repository of academic publications (Thelwall & Kousha, 2015). Most previous research on RG has focused on user participation and site activities, very few revealed the institutional user structures and their behavior characteristics. The research methods mainly used questionnaire surveys (Corvello et al., 2014; Elsayed, 2016) or open-ended interviews (Nicholas et al., 2015). Some utilized data from the RG site, but were based on a small sample or lacked data filtration (Thelwall & Kousha, 2015; Yu et al., 2016; Hoffmann et al., 2016). While previous studies have shown the value and correlations of RG indicators to other accepted impact indicators, there is not consensus on the most appropriate way to measure academic influence via social media (Jordan, 2015). In addition, there is a research gap in user characteristics and behavior analysis, especially in revealing institutional differences and the social networks of institutions at different research activity levels. The study presented in this poster aims to fill the research gaps.

METHODS

This study harvested data from RG user profile pages from 61 U.S. research universities at different research activity levels, as categorized by the Carnegie Classification of Institutions of Higher Education. The multiple-step data collection and processing process is illustrated in Figure 1 and study sample summarized in Table 1. The user data included user name, affiliation, profile page URL, and RG metrics such as RG score, publications, reads, citations, profile views, followers, and followees.

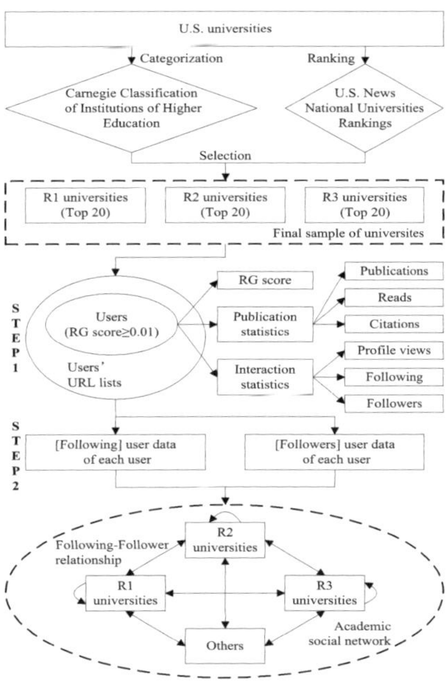

Figure 1. The data collection and processing process.

Category	ID	# of users	# of users with RG score ≥ 0.01	Ratio (RG score ≥ 0.01)	Followers	Followees
R1	R101-R121	126,998	71,821	56.55%	383,676	296,050
R2	R201-R220	27,364	11,304	41.31%	56,947	47,483
R3	R301-R320	13,697	3,958	28.90%	19,140	16,717
Total		168,059	87,083	51.82%	459,763	360,250

Note: The university IDs of each category of Carnegie Classification of Institutions of Higher Education are category are ordered by national university rankings.

Table 1. Sample of U.S. research universities.

FINDINGS

The major findings of the study will be presented in the poster. Below are two selected visuals to highlight the interaction metrics by research activity level (Table 2) and the academic social network formed among U.S. research universities in RG (Figure 2).

Indicator	Category	Median	Mean	SD	Between group		
					$\chi 2$	df	Effect size
Profile views (per user)	R1	238.55	246.43	35.85	28.158	2	0.469
	R2	197.36	205.93	36.13			
	R3	139.72	154.50	49.78			
Followers (per user)	R1	33.81	34.72	4.00	13.248	2	0.221
	R2	32.80	32.48	2.50			
	R3	28.09	27.78	7.69			
Followees (per user)	R1	21.84	21.73	1.67	3.455	2	0.058
	R2	22.80	22.45	2.22			
	R3	19.77	20.70	5.62			
Difference between Followers and Followees (per user)	R1	12.29	12.99	3.93	23.051	2	0.384
	R2	9.97	10.04	2.41			
	R3	6.65	7.07	3.37			

Table 2. RG interaction metrics statistics by research activity level.

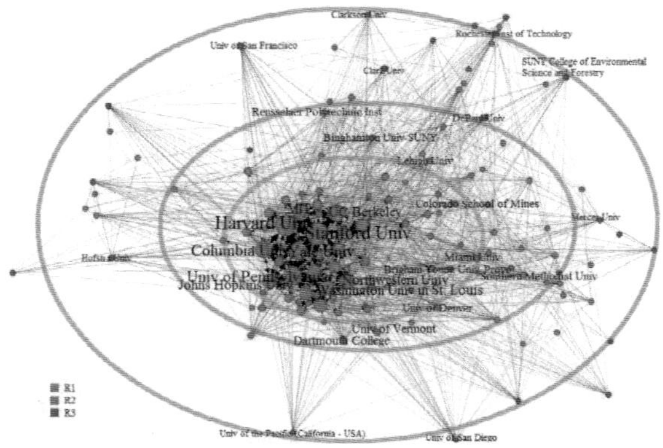

Figure 2. The follower-followee social network of U.S. universities (degree ≥ 5).

CONCLUSION

The findings of this study show that there are institutional differences in scholarly reputational metrics in RG, which relates to the research activity level category. While researchers in RG commonly follow peers from the same institution, they primarily follow others from universities in a higher research activity level category. The follower-followee social networks among high research activity level universities formulate a rich-club phenomenon. In sum, this research contributes to research efforts in scholarly use of social networking sites such as RG, which is helpful for a deeper discussion of RG metrics, meaningful user participation, extending academic interaction, improving user experience on academic social networking sites, and the ongoing debate of whether RG metrics can serve as effective measures that reflect the actual research activities and the reputations of researchers and research institutions in reality. Future research directions will be discussed at the presentation.

REFERENCES

Corvello, V., Genovese, A., & Verteramo, S. (2014). Knowledge sharing among users of scientific social networking platforms. In G. Phillips-Wren, S. Carlsson, A. Respício, & P. Brézillon (Eds.), *DSS 2.0 - Supporting decision making with new technologies* (pp. 369-380). Retrieved May 15, 2018 from http://ebooks.iospress.nl/volumearticle/36223

Gruzd, A., & Goertzen, M. (2013). Wired academia: Why social science scholars are using social media. In R.H. Sprague (Ed.), System Sciences (HICSS). Paper presented at the 46th Annual Hawaii International Conference on System Sciences, Grand Wailea, Maui, Hawaii, 7-10 January (pp. 3332-3341). Los Alamitos, CA: IEEE Computer Society.

Jordan, K. (2015). Exploring the ResearchGate score as an academic metric: reflections and implications for practice. In: *Quantifying and Analysing Scholarly Communication on the Web (ASCW'15)*, 30 June 2015, Oxford.

Nicholas, D., Herman, E., Jamali, H. R., Bravo, B. R., Boukacem-Zeghmouri, C., Dobrowolski, T., & Pouchot, S. (2015). New ways of building, showcasing, and measuring scholarly reputation. *Learned Publishing 28,* 169-183.

Thelwall, M., & Kousha, K. (2014). Academia. edu: social network or academic network?. *Journal of the Association for Information Science and Technology 65*, 721-731.

Thelwall, M., & Kousha, K. (2015). ResearchGate: Disseminating, communicating, and measuring scholarship?.*Journal of the Association for Information Science and Technology 66*, 876-889.

Yu, M. C., Wu, Y. C. J., Alhalabi, W., Kao, H. Y., & Wu, W. H. (2016). ResearchGate: An effective altmetric indicator for active researchers?. *Computers in Human Behavior 55*, 1001-1006.

Do Administrative Roles Affect Professors' Research?

Yuehua Zhao
School of Information Studies, University of Wisconsin-Milwaukee, USA yuehua@uwm.edu

Wen Lou*
East China Normal University, China
wlou@infor.ecnu.edu.cn

ABSTRACT

This study quantitatively investigated whether the research performance of academic administrators (leaders) was affected by their administrative services. We examined the quantity of 111 professors' publications and citations in the Web of Science including 90 deans and 21 university presidents, from 26 universities. To compare the effect on their research performances by their administrative roles, we proposed four periods: the pre-position period, the latest position period, the reference period, and the in-position period. Statistical methods were applied and suggested that administrative services have strongly affected academic leaders' research performances.

KEYWORDS

Research Performance; Leadership; Administrative Roles; Career Path.

INTRODUCTION

It has become increasingly common worldwide that after years of excellent teaching and research services in a university, professors would serve as department or university leaders, these leaders are also involved with scientific research and they represent the top research level of their departments and schools (Boyko & Jones, 2010). Therefore, we have wondered whether their administrative roles have affected their research performance. There were few quantitative studies conducted on the research performances difference of academic leaders between before and after the leadership. Our aim is to explore, by answering how the administrative role as a university president or a department dean affects one's performance as a researcher.

METHOD

Variables' definition

The leaders were promoted step by step in several periods. To examine the difference before and after the leadership, it is essential to differ these periods (see Figure 1). Latest position period is introduced to avoid the potential effect on research performance from multiple previous administrative roles. Our target is to compare P_{DE} with P_{AD}. As we can see, latest position period is within pre-position period. However, the situation in P_{AD} is obviously complicated, such as relocation, promoted, and demoted. Trying to minimize the factors, we focus on comparing P_{DE} with P_{CD}. Reference period balances the different lengths of periods between latest position and in-position by either limiting the time length of the latest position periods to equal the time length of in-position periods or the other way around.

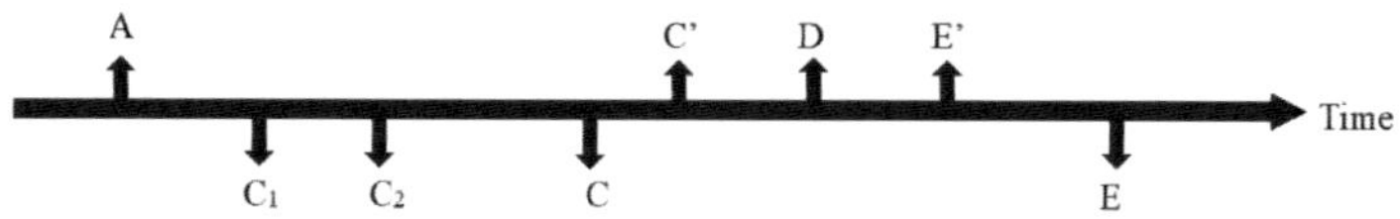

Pre-position period (P_{AD}): the years from when a leader published her or his first publication in WoS until the year when she or he became the current leader.
In-position period (P_{DE}): the years that a leader has held the position and includes from the year she or he was announced to be the leader until the day we collected data.
Latest position period (P_{CD}): the years that a leader had held the last administrative position.
Reference period ($P_{C'D}/P_{DE'}$) is viable depending on individual leaders. If $P_{DE} > P_{CD}$, then reference period is $P_{DE'}$; If $P_{DE} < P_{CD}$, then reference period is $P_{C'D}$; If $P_{DE} = P_{CD}$, then reference period is P_{CD}.

Figure 1. An example of a leader's promoting life

Data collection

We started by selecting 29 universities based on the 2017 Best Global Universities Rankings established by the U.S. News & World Report. These rankings fell into three groups: 1 to 10, 51 to 60, and 101 to 110. To explore the differences among department deans, we chose the most common departments (Art, Business and Management, Engineering, and Medicine). Two universities which lack most of the departments were excluded (California Institute of Technology and Mount Sinai School of Medicine). Therefore, 27 universities which had the four most common departments were selected for the next step.

First, we collected the name of every university president. Second, we looked through, in turn, the faculties, schools, and departments' leaders, since some universities had layered administrative structure. We selected the most important leaders to guarantee that there would be only one leader in each school or department. Interim leaders were selected only if a university or department had no officially announced leaders at the time of this research. University of Munich was excluded due to the inaccessibility of the website and a language barrier. 130 administrators had been chosen so far.

We collected the exact years (including the years of current leaderships and latest administrative roles) by looking through the leaders' CVs and LinkedIn pages, and the university news and welcome letters (found on the websites) when their profiles searches did not mention the year. Full records of the documents that were published by the sampled leaders were downloaded from *WoS* core collection. The data collection was conducted between March 9th and 16th, 2018. Seventeen leaders had no publications in *WoS* and two leaders have been established as the current leadership in 2018. In the end, 111 leaders with publications were included in this research.

FINDINGS

Under different conditions ($P_{DE} > P_{CD}$; $P_{DE} < P_{CD}$; $P_{DE} = P_{CD}$), we adopted non-parametric tests to examine the difference the number of publications during the reference period and the in-position/latest position period. The Wilcoxon signed-rank test is designed for repeated measures (*H1 and H2*).

H1: There is no significant difference before and after taking the current administration positions in terms of the number of publications.

H2: There is no significant difference before and after taking the current administration positions in terms of the number of citations.

The test results demonstrated that there were significant differences between the reference period and the in-position period in terms of publications (z=-4.424, p=*0.00*<0.05) and citations (z=-5.515, p=*0.00*<0.05). The resultant effect size r was 0.42 (publications) and 0.523(citations), both indicating a medium effect on professors' research.

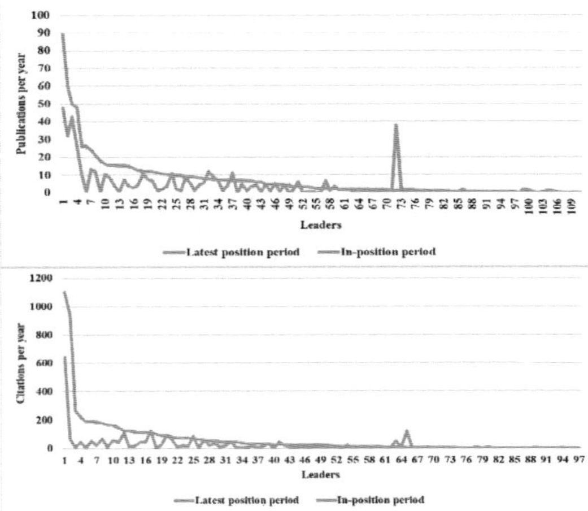

Figure 2. Distribution of publications and citations of professors during different periods

In Figure 2, we purposely used average values to avoid the unequal time lengths of the latest position period and the in-position period. The number of annual publications during the latest position period outnumbered the number during the in-position period substantially. The distribution of the number of citations followed a similar pattern. Before performing the administrative services, on average, each professor yielded 7.15 publications every year and received 54.50 citations every year. The average number of annual publications dropped down to 4.13 and the average number of annual citations dropped down to 20.45 during the in-position period. Among the investigated professors, 82 out of 111 (73.84%) professors published more papers before the leadership, and 90 out of 111 (81.08%) received more citations before carrying the duties of leaderships. On average, professors published three more papers every year and gained 20 more citations every year before they became the professors in the current positions. It showed that most professors were highly productive and influential before accepting the administrative positions, but that their research productivities and impact were apparently affected by the administrative services.

CONCLUSION

We have found a significant difference for a professor between the time before the administrative role and the time after accepting an administrative role. Both research productivity and research impact were affected. We believe this is because the extra administrative responsibilities require time and energy of the leaders which could have been used on research. This situation should be paid more attention by policy makers. Future research, including measuring academic presentations and adding more subjects, may corroborate these findings.

ACKNOWLEDGMENTS

This work was supported by Fundamental Research Funds for the Central Universities, the "Chenguang Program" of Shanghai Education Development Foundation and Shanghai Municipal Education Commission [grant number 17CG19] and China Postdoctoral Science Foundation [grant number 2017M620142].

REFERENCES

Boyko, L., & Jones, G. a. (2010). The Changing Dynamics of Higher Education Middle Management. *Higher Education Dynamics*, *33*, 83–102. https://doi.org/10.1007/978-90-481-9163-5

Ontology-based Analysis of the Large Collection of Historical Hebrew Manuscripts

Maayan Zhitomirsky-Geffe
Bar Ilan University, Israel. Maayan.Zhitomirsky-Geffet@biu.ac.il

Yitzchak Miller
Bar Ilan University, Israel. Isaac.Miller@biu.ac.il

Gila Prebor
Bar Ilan University, Israel. gila.prebor@biu.ac.il

ABSTRACT
In this study we proposed and implemented a new research framework based on the data-driven approach that aims to quantitatively analyse the largest catalogue in the world of Hebrew manuscripts' metadata records. We used an event-based ontology model which captures the information on the main types and relationships of manuscript metadata. Then, we utilized the ontology-based inference to automatically complete and expand the data on Hebrew manuscripts recorded in the catalogue and further mine and analyse this data at the large scale. As part of the quantitative analysis we applied statistical and data visualisation techniques in order to compare the effect of time and place on the manuscripts' characteristics and distribution, to discover previously unknown distant relationships between entities and events, to reveal global phenomena and trends, and better appreciate their impact on the Hebrew writing and its different manifestations.

KEYWORDS
Hebrew Manuscripts, Data-Driven Analysis, Visualization, Ontologies, Metadata

INTRODUCTION
The examined catalogue comprises over 130,000 records maintained by the National Library of Israel (http://web.nli.org.il /sites/NLI/English/collections/manuscripts) which cover over 95% of all the Hebrew manuscripts that survived in the world through the centuries. Although catalogue data is assumed to be structured, in the previous research (Zhitomirsky-Geffet and Prebor, 2016) substantial inconsistencies have been detected and many of the examined fields required further structuring and reorganization into atomic searchable entities. Beyond the methodological significance of the data-driven research in the field of Digital Humanities (Kaplan and di Linardo, 2017; Lei Zeng, 2017), its results might shed new light on historical, linguistic, religious, ethnological, philosophical and social aspects of Jewish life in different time periods and places, since Hebrew manuscripts constitute one of the most unique and authentic witnesses of the Jewish culture.

METHOD
The ontology model of the study incorporates the FRBR distinction between the abstraction of a work and an item, i.e. its concrete physical realisation (a manuscript in our case). The main classes of the model are Work, Work_Realisation_Event (transforming the abstract work into a concrete manuscript item), Manuscript_Biographic_Event and Historical_Manuscript_Item. The classes are inter-linked through the Manuscript_Biographic_Event class, which encapsulates all the data of a certain action undertaken over the manuscript. The proposed research framework comprises the following stages of catalogue data processing and creation and analysis of the ontology data: 1. Building the generic scheme for the event-centric ontology for the comprehensive representation of the domain knowledge; 2. Ontology population with entities linked to events; 3. Error correction and completion of the missing data (places and dates) by inference from the existing data in the ontology and from external resources; 4. Intra- and inter-event data analysis based on the inference from the ontological relationships. The last two stages would not be possible to accomplish without the constructed ontology which imposes structure on the data by decomposing catalogue fields into well-defined atomic entities and linking these entities to the corresponding events.

RESULTS
There were 117,526 Codicological Units (CUs) representing manuscripts in the catalogue. Table 1 summarizes the missing data (mostly dates and places) that was completed by inference from the constructed ontology and from external resources.

Inferred entity data	Quantity	Inferred entity data	Quantity
Number of person life periods inferred from CUs	6,750	Number of copying events with a place of writing derived from scribe activity sites	2,335
Number of persons with geodetic data derived from CUs	3,009	Number of creation events with a date of creation derived from author life periods	36,277
Number of person life periods extracted from viaf.org	1,494	Number of creation events with a place of creation derived from author activity sites	27,056
Number of people with geodetic data extracted from viaf.org	9,035	Number of storage events with a place of storage derived from CUs current locations	114,816

Table 1. Descriptive statistics of the manuscript corpus data completed by inference from the constructed ontology and from external resources.

The Hebrew manuscripts have been spread across the globe, as Jews were forced to wander from place to place, the manuscripts wandered with them and new manuscripts were written in many places around the world. The writing place of a manuscript is very important and allows us to locate it in its historical context. In our corpus we found only 16,032 (out of 117,526) CUs with this information (less than 14%). We could infer the place of writing with a high probability using the ontologically related scribes' activity (events) places and the types of scripts used in these manuscripts. Also, for over 12% of scribes' their lifetimes could be inferred based on their ontologically related manuscripts' creation events' dates and if a certain scribes' manuscript creation event's date is outlying compared to the inferred range of years, it could be inferred that it is a mistake. Hebrew manuscripts were written in 93 countries and in 4,371 different places. The country where the greatest number of manuscripts was copied is Italy with 4,577 CUs. The ontology-based inference is illustrated in Figure 1. The geospatial distribution of the archiving events of the Hebrew manuscripts is visualized by the map below (Figure 2). Some results of the ontology-based analysis are demonstrated in Figures 3 and 4. As can be observed from Figure 3, Maimonides was the most popular author and was copied in many different countries, the most dominating among them were Italy and Yemen, even though he has never visited them. The majority of the early manuscripts were mostly copied 1-2 centuries after their creation (Figure 4).

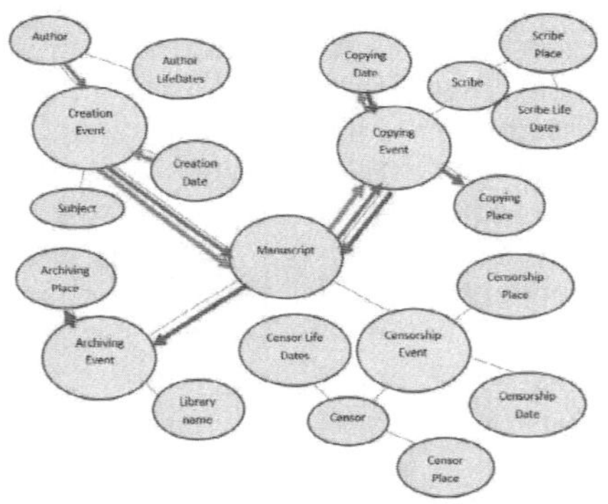

Figure 1: Derivation of the cross-event relations and influences from the ontology. The

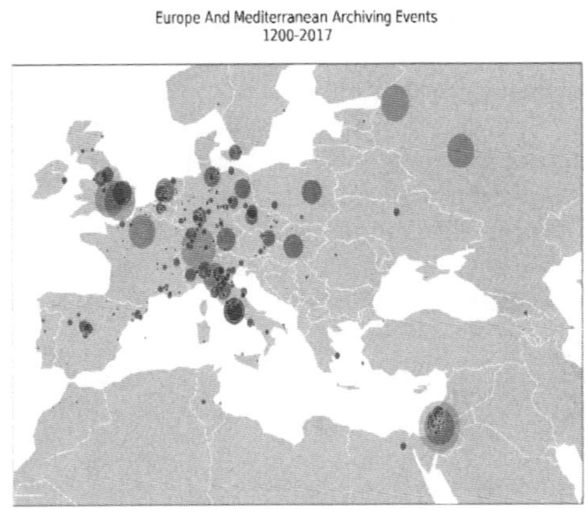

Figure 2: Manuscript source libraries locations (Europe and the Mediterranean, only)

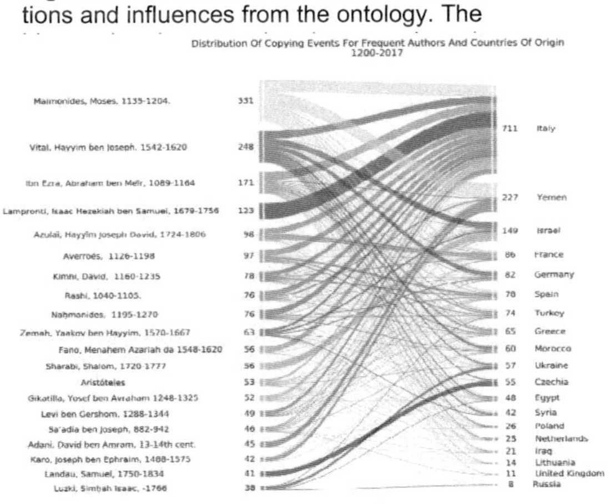

Figure 3: A bi-partite graph of the geospatial distribution of copying events for the top 20 popular authors and countries.

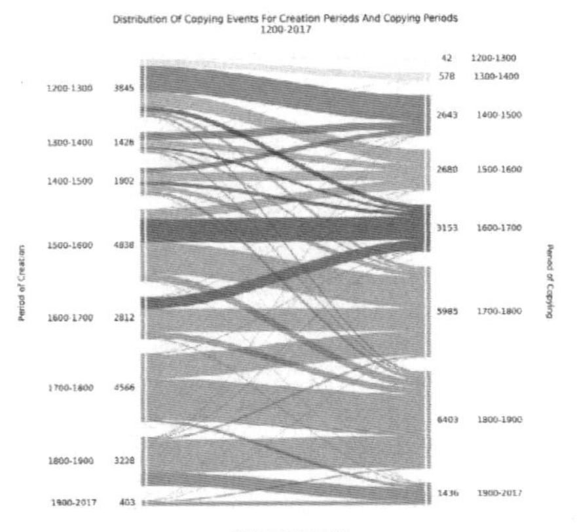

Figure 4: A bi-partite graph representation of the comparative analysis of the creation vs. copying events' dates of the same manuscripts

REFERENCES

Lei Zeng, M. 2017, Smart Data for digital humanities, Journal of Information and Documentation, 2, 1, pp. 1-2.

Kaplan, F., & di Lenardo, I. (2017). Big data of the past. Frontiers in Digital Humanities, 4, 12.

Zhitomirsky-Geffet M. & Prebor G. (2016). Towards an ontopedia for historical Hebrew manuscripts. Frontiers in Digital Humanities, section of Digital Paleography and Book History, 3, 3. http://dx.doi.org/10.3389/fdigh.2016.00003

Identification of Information Search Strategies and Their Impact on Learning Outcome in Learning-Related Tasks

Han Zhu
Peking University, China. zhuhan@pku.edu.cn

Xiaoxuan Song
Peking University, China. songxiaoxuan@pku.edu.cn

Chang Liu
Peking University, China. imliuc@pku.edu.cn

ABSTRACT

This study aims to identify users' information search strategies in learning-related tasks and investigates how the search strategies would influence their learning outcome. We conducted a lab-based user experiment with 36 participants, recorded their search interactions during search process and measured their learning outcome by having them answer multiple choice questions after search. We extracted 14 behavioural features in three dimensions and conducted k-means clustering analysis. Results showed that there were four types of search strategies: Economic Browsing, Supplementary Browsing, Exhaustive Browsing and Exhaustive Searching. It was found that Supplementary Browsing Strategy achieved the best learning outcome, while Economic Browsing Strategy showed the worst outcome, with Exhaustive Searching Strategy and Exhaustive Browsing Strategy in between. The findings indicated that careful selection of content pages and frequent querying were highly beneficial for users' learning during search. This study provides a deeper understanding of users' search strategies and has valuable implications on optimizing search systems to help users achieve better learning outcome.

KEYWORDS

Search strategy, learning outcome, cluster analysis, learning-related tasks.

INTRODUCTION

In interactive information retrieval, it is generally believed that better understanding of how users interact with search systems is important for improving users' search experience and search performance. Information search strategies reflect users' overall planning of the search and characterize users' interaction with systems comprehensively (Bates, 1979). Some attempts have been made to identify information seeking strategies (e.g., Heinström, 2006), and some focused on identifying search strategies on search engine result pages (SERPs) (Alua, Maiaranta & Räihä, 2005; Dumais, Buscher & Cutrell, 2010; Buscher et al., 2012; Liu & Wei, 2016). However, learning-related search is more complex exploratory search, rather than just retrieving specific factual information (Marchionini, 2006). When searching for learning-related tasks, people may involve in various activities, such as task planning, searching information items, selecting information items, working with information items, and synthesizing and reporting (Järvelin et al., 2015). Therefore, it is necessary to examine what information search strategies users adopt when searching for learning-related tasks, based on users' interactions on various types of web pages. This study aims to address two research questions as below:

RQ1: What information search strategies would users adopt when searching for learning-related tasks?

RQ2: How are users' information search strategies related to their learning outcome?

METHODS

User Experiment

A lab-based user experiment was conducted to the research questions in this study. We recruited 36 freshmen from Peking University, all of whom were majored in information management, in order to control their age, familiarity with the Internet, information search capabilities and search experience at the similar level. Among them, 24 were male and 12 were female. The participants were invited to our interactive lab individually, to search for three assigned learning-related tasks in three fields (sports, law, and technology). An example of the task description (technology field) is shown as below:

> *Usability testing is a technique commonly used in IT industry nowadays. As a student in the Department of Information Management, you are interested in engaging in related jobs in the future and hope to have a preliminary understanding about it. Please search for the concept of usability testing, its significance, popular methods, and etc.*

After reading the task description, the participants searched freely on the Internet until they thought they have learned enough information to answer questions in this field. After searching, participants were asked to close all the web pages they visited during search and answer 10 multiple-choice questions containing both factual and comprehension questions about the topic on their own. During search, their interactions with the computer were recorded by Morae Recorder.

Interaction Variables

In this study, we attempted to identify users' information search strategies according to their whole-session interaction, SERP interactions and content page interactions. Since different pages may have different contributions to users' learning during search, we assume that pages with longer dwell time are more important for users. Therefore, we selected the web page that has the longest dwell time during search as the most valuable page, and thus we identified the *most valuable SERP* (MVS) and the *most valuable content page* (MVC). Furthermore, users might visit the most valuable page several times. Each dwelling on this page may involve different types of information uses. In our study, we considered the longest dwelling period for these most valuable pages as the *most valuable SERP reading period* (MVSR) and *most valuable content reading period* (MVCR). The selected interaction variables are as follows:

(1) Session Time; *(2) Proportion of dwell time on SERP;*
(3) Number of queries; *(4) Number of content pages;*
(5) Proportion of dwell time on MVS; *(6) Proportion of dwell time on MVC;*
(7) MVS Visit ID (8) MVC Visit ID: The visit ID of the first appearance of MVS/MVC during search;
(9) Number of visits on MVS; *(10) Number of visits on MVC;*
(11) Proportion of dwell time on MVSR; *(12) Proportion of dwell time on MVCR;*
(13) MVSR Sequence ID (14) MVCR Sequence ID: The sequential ID of MVSR/ MVCR visit.

RESULTS

Then k-means clustering analysis was conducted to identify search strategies according to above interaction variables, and four groups of search strategies were identified. ANOVA test showed significant differences ($p<0.05$) among the four groups, therefore the clustering result was effective. The four groups were named according to their features as below:

1. Economic Browsing (EcB) Strategy (N=30): EcB strategy issued very few (average 1.9) queries, visited a few (2.5) content pages, and finished searching very quickly (about 9.5 minutes). Users tended to spend most of their content page reading time (83.2%) on one specific page.
2. Supplementary Browsing (SB) Strategy (N=19): SB Strategy showed generally similar pattern with EcB in session duration (9.5 minutes) and number of queries (1.5), but users visited more content pages (3.6) and visited the most valuable SERP many times repeatedly (4.2). It demonstrated that SB strategy users were more selective in choosing content pages as supplementary information sources.
3. Exhaustive Browsing (ExB) Strategy (N=31): ExB Strategy had much longer session duration (about 14 minutes), issued more queries (3.0) and visited more content pages (7.0). It also showed largest number of visits on both the most valuable SERP (6.0) and the most valuable content page (5.4).
4. Exhaustive Searching (ES) Strategy (N=28): ES Strategy showed the longest session duration (about 15 minutes), issued most queries (4.6) and visited most content pages (7.6).

We further investigated the relationship between information search strategies and users' learning outcome. Learning outcome was calculated by the percentage of correct answers in multiple-choice questions. The ANOVA test showed that there were significant differences in learning outcome among the four search strategies ($p=0.001$). As shown in Figure 1, SB sessions had the best learning outcome with the accuracy of 70.5%. ES Strategy ranked second with the average accuracy of 65.4%, followed by ExB Strategy (60.3%). The performance of EcB Strategy was significantly worse than that of the other three strategies, with the accuracy of 50.3%.

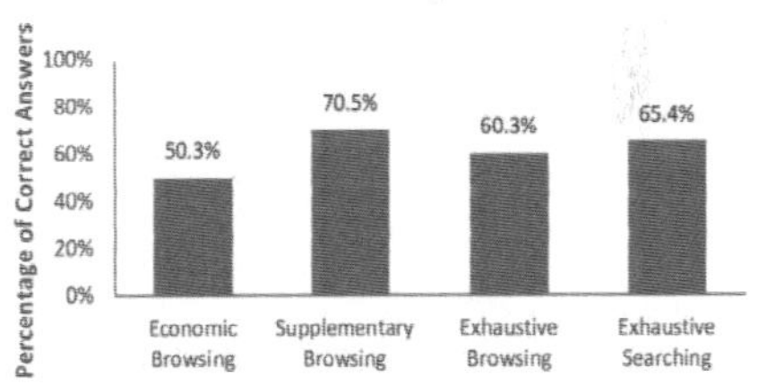

Figure 1. Comparison of learning outcome by different search strategies

DISCUSSION AND CONCLUSION

In this study, we identified four types of information search strategies: Economic Browsing (EcB), Supplementary Browsing (SB), Exhaustive Browsing (ExB), and Exhaustive Searching (ES). Among these four strategies, EcB strategy and ExB strategy required the least cognitive load, but the difference was that EcB visited very few content pages, while ExB clicked many content pages without selection; therefore, the learning outcome of these two strategies were relatively low. ES mainly spent their efforts on query formulation and reformulation, while SB Strategy demonstrated careful selections of content pages on SERPs. Both strategies required relatively high cognitive load, and they both led to better learning outcome. This is a preliminary investigation of the relationship between search strategies and learning outcome in learning-related tasks. We acknowledge the sample size was small and only three search topics were examined. Future work could explore whether the results are consistent with other user samples and in other search topics. Our results suggest that the current search engine can best support users who are experts in querying or selective of content pages on SERPs, but not for other users. The findings of our study may shed light on the design of search systems, for example, system features that could encourage users to issue more queries or support more efficient examination of SERPs. This study did not provide explanations about why and how users adopted a certain strategy, and we will examine this issue in our future work.

REFERENCES

Aula, A., Majaranta, P., & Räihä, K. J. (2005). Eye-tracking reveals the personal styles for search result evaluation. In *IFIP Conference on HCI* (pp. 1058-1061). Springer, Berlin, Heidelberg.

Bates, M. J. (1979). Information search tactics. *JASIS&T, 30*(4), 205-214.

Buscher, G., White, R. W., Dumais, S., & Huang, J. (2012, February). Large-scale analysis of individual and task differences in search result page examination strategies. In *WSDM 12'*(pp. 373-382). ACM.

Dumais, S. T., Buscher, G., & Cutrell, E. (2010, August). Individual differences in gaze patterns for web search. *II*iX10'

Heinström, J. (2006). Broad exploration or precise specificity: Two basic information seeking patterns among students. *JASIS&T, 57*(11), 1440-1450.

Järvelin, K., Vakkari, P., Arvola, P., Baskaya, F., Keskustalo, H., & Kumpulainen, S., et al. (2015). Task-based information interaction evaluation: the viewpoint of program theory. *TOIS, 33*(1), 1-30.

Liu, C., & Wei, Y. (2016). The impacts of time constraint on users' search strategy during search process. *ASIS&T, 53*(1), 1-9.

Marchionini, G. (2006). Exploratory search: from finding to understanding. *Communications of the ACM, 49*(4), 41-46.

Information Horizons Mapping to Assess the Health Literacy of Refugee and Immigrant Women

Margaret S Zimmerman
University of Iowa, USA. margaret-zimmerman@uiowa.edu

ABSTRACT

Introduction- Refugees and immigrants are at a heightened risk of many negative health outcomes. While strong health literacy ability may be a determinant of favorable health outcomes, assessing the health literacy of refugee and immigrant women is a challenge. Due to typically lower literacy and English ability, one possible method to measure the health literacy of this population is to ask them to graphically represent their health-related information horizons. Seventy-four women were asked to take a survey and answer open-ended questions about their HISB and demographic information, and then asked to create an information horizons map in the context of health information seeking. Each map was compared to the survey questions and specific questions that were asked to gauge the health literacy of the participants. The network of information resources for immigrant and refugee women was graphically displayed. Women who drew maps that were more complex had survey responses that correlated with higher health literacy. Refugee women were less aware of health information sources than other immigrant women. While more research is needed, this research provides evidence that information horizons mapping within a health information-seeking context may be predictive of health literacy.

KEYWORDS

Information horizons mapping, health literacy, health information-seeking behavior, refugees, immigrants, women.

INTRODUCTION

Refugees and immigrants in the United States are at a heightened risk for a number of negative health outcomes including diabetes, obesity, chronic disease, and mental health disorders (Im & Rosenberg, 2016; Nelson-Peterman et al., 2015). In an increasingly polarized climate, studies have shown a direct relationship between anti-immigration policies and their effects on access to health services (Martinez et al., 2015). There is a canon of literature stating that successful health information-seeking behavior (HISB) is dependent upon strong health literacy skills, and that proficient health literacy by women is a determinant of favorable health outcomes for both herself and her children (Lloyd, 2014; Wångdahl, Lytsy, Mårtensson, & Westerling, 2014). In alignment with this, conducting assessments to determine the health literacy of immigrants and refugees- a requisite step in addressing health literacy needs- is a continuous challenge.

This poster details a preliminary study to develop a methodology to measure health literacy through information horizons mapping for immigrant and refugee populations. Information horizons mapping is a methodology developed by Sonnenwald, Wildemuth, and Harmon in 2001 that combines interview data with participant- drawn graphical representations of recent information-seeking experiences situated within specific contexts. In this study, women were asked to take a survey and answer open-ended questions about their HISB and demographic information, and then asked to create an information horizons map in the context of health information-seeking. Because these populations traditionally have lower literacy levels and limited English ability, drawing is theorized to be a medium that may offer further expression beyond written language to immigrant and refugee women. Literature about health literacy assessment was evaluated, and questions previously validated as being significant measures of health literacy were included on the survey. These responses were compared to the complexity of the maps including the detail and breadth of the sources utilized, plus the demographic data obtained to determine the women's individual and collective information horizons and to assess their corresponding health literacy. By doing so, this study both employed and expanded upon the information horizons research method used by Sonnenwald in 2001 to evaluate the potential for this methodology to be a platform by which to examine the health literacy of the women. In gauging the health literacy of the participants using the demographic and survey questions, then examining the correlation of these responses with the complexity of each information horizon, the author was attempting to determine if there is a relationship between health literacy and the way in which the participants graphically represented their information horizons.

METHOD AND ANALYSIS

Adult women were approached at events of refugee and immigrant organizations and asked if they would like to participate in the study. Seventy-four women agreed and were given a survey that was available in multiple languages. The survey, which was based upon previously published and validated instruments, had questions about the participant's health information needs and information-seeking behavior, her demographic information, and had instructions to create the information horizons map. Questions drawn from a literature review that have been demonstrated to be predictive of health literacy, including those about woman's self-reported ability to find the information that she was looking for when she had questions about health, whether or not she was able to understand the information she found, and her personal rating of her overall health, were included on the survey. The women were asked to draw a picture, in order, of where they would go or what sources they would consult when, in the past, they had needed information about health. Women were instructed to show preference, and to draw as many places to look for information as they could. Following the administration of the survey, each information horizons map was analyzed both independently and congruent to the demographic information and responses in the survey. Maps were first examined in order to describe the network of information resources for immigrant and refugee women following the same methodology used in Sonnenwald's 2001 paper. Next, the current research deviated from Sonnenwald's methodology. First, the number of sources that each woman drew, including people, places, or other types of informational resources, was counted and compared with the demographic and information-seeking data that was collected through the survey. Specifically, drawings were grouped by years of education, frequency of internet use, medium of internet access, number of years living in the United States, and if the participant came into the United States under refugee status. The purpose of this analysis was to try to determine if any of these factors had correlative or influential relationships on the participants' vision of their own information horizons. When correlation was applied, it was using the Spearman's rank correlation coefficient. The number of sources on the information horizons maps was also compared with the woman's self-reported ability to find the information that she was looking for when she had questions about health, whether or not she was able to understand the information she found, and her personal rating of her overall health. Each of these questions potentially has correspondence with the women's health literacy.

RESULTS AND DISCUSSION

When comparing the number of sources each woman drew to her years of schooling, there was a strong correlative relationship ($r=.924$). There was also a strong relationship ($r=.885$) between a woman's frequency of internet use and the number of sources she drew. There was no correlation between the number of sources women drew and either their number of years having lived in the United States or whether they access the internet through their phone, a personal computer, tablet, or a borrowed device from outside of the home. Immigrant women who did not enter the United States under refugee status drew an average of twice the number of sources that women who entered the United States under refugee status drew.

Regarding the comparison of the drawn sources to questions that may be predictive of health literacy, women who drew more sources were much more likely to report that when they needed health information that they were able to find the information that they needed. These women also tended to have a more favorable report of their own health. Only approximately half of the women who drew one or two information sources felt that they could access information that they could understand when they needed it. Many, though not the majority of women, also cited distrust in medical professionals.

The outcome of this analysis is compelling in that it demonstrates potentially predictive qualities of information horizons mapping in two different ways. First, there is support within these results for the potential of information horizons mapping methodology to be predictive of health literacy for refugee and immigrant women. Second, there is a clear relationship between the complexity of these maps and the illustrators' years of schooling and internet usage. This latter point is not relevant to health literacy, as health literacy has not been convincingly tied to educational attainment. Nevertheless, it is significant as it demonstrates the effect of schooling on the women's knowledge of health-related resources available to them.

CONCLUSION

This was a preliminary study into the potential of information horizons mapping as a methodology to measure the health literacy of immigrant and refugee populations. As a beginning, this study demonstrated positive results. Using Sonnenwald's methodology, women who are more likely to have higher health literacy according to measures used by other means of assessment are also more likely to draw information horizons maps of higher complexity, just as women who are likely to have lower health literacy ability are likely to draw simpler maps. However, this research is a first step into understanding the capability of this methodology in providing assessment of health literacy.

REFERENCES

Im, H., & Rosenberg, R. (2016). Building social capital through a peer-led community health workshop: A pilot with the Bhutanese refugee community. *Journal of community health, 41*(3), 509-517.

Lloyd, A. (2014). Building information resilience: how do resettling refugees connect with health information in regional landscapes–implications for health literacy. *Australian Academic & Research Libraries*, *45*(1), 48-66.

Martinez, O., Wu, E., Sandfort, T., Dodge, B., Carballo-Dieguez, A., Pinto, R., & Chavez-Baray, S. (2015). Evaluating the impact of immigration policies on health status among undocumented immigrants: a systematic review. *Journal of Immigrant and Minority Health, 17*(3), 947-970.

Nelson-Peterman, J.L., Toof, R., Liang, S., & Grigg-Saito, D.C. (2015). Long-term refugee health: health behaviors and outcomes of Cambodian refugee and immigrant women. *Health Education & Behavior, 42*(6), 814-823.

Sonnenwald, D. H., Wildemuth, B. S., & Harmon, G. L. (2001). A research method to investigate information seeking using the concept of Information Horizons: An example from a study of lower socio-economic students' information seeking behavior. *The New Review of Information Behavior Research*, *2*, 65-86.

Wångdahl, J., Lytsy, P., Mårtensson, L., & Westerling, R. (2014). Health literacy among refugees in Sweden–a cross-sectional study. BMC Public Health, 14(1), 1030.

Collaboration Matters: Faculty Hiring in Information School

Zhiya Zuo
University of Iowa, USA. zhiya-zuo@uiowa.edu

Kang Zhao
University of Iowa, USA. kang-zhao@uiowa.edu

ABSTRACT

Successful hiring decisions are important for both academic institutions and individual faculty members. While factors including institutional prestige and gender are shown to affect faculty hiring outcome, there is a lack of study on whether and how research collaboration helps. We aimed at bridging this gap with a hand-curated dataset of 81 junior faculty members from 27 information schools. Specifically, we analysed the effect of advisors and collaborators on faculty placement, controlling for a candidate's h-index, gender, prestige of degree-granting institution, and position openings. We found that the median of collaborator h-indices has a significant and positive effect on the prestige of the institution that hires a faculty. PhD graduates who have co-authored with high-impact researchers (other than advisors) are more likely to find faculty positions in better ranked institutions. This reveals an implicit hiring decision-making factor that encourages young researchers to actively seek collaboration opportunities with well-established scholars to secure a good faculty job in the future.

KEYWORDS

Faculty hiring, social inequality, collaboration, prestige.

INTRODUCTION

Faculty hiring is important for institutions and researchers. Successful hiring decisions, for example, contribute to higher standing among peer institutions, leading to greater resource allocation and better research and education. Research has revealed two aspects that determine the hiring decisions: (i) universalism and (ii) particularism (Long & Fox, 1995). Universalism indicates that candidates are assessed based on their academic achievement, whereas particularism involves factors independent of scholarly merit. The literature has systematically examined the effects of institutional prestige and gender on hiring outcome. For example, particularistic factors including institutional prestige (Zhu & Yan, 2017) and gender (Sheltzer & Smith, 2014) appear to dominate the final hiring decision, shaping a steep hierarchy in academic exchange networks (Clauset, Arbesman, & Larremore, 2015). Nonetheless, there is a lack of detailed investigation on whether and how collaboration of faculty candidates can help their placement. In fact, PhD advisor is one of the strongest collaboration ties of early stage researchers. It is possible that past collaboration experience with prestigious researchers may bring benefits to one's job search. Specifically, mentorship, one of the most important aspects of PhD training (Godechot, 2016), has rarely been examined. PhD advisors not only advise students scholarly, but, more importantly, provide social ties that significantly help junior researchers expand their relatively limited networks. In the literature, there is a mixed finding on whether advisor academic reputation helps one's faculty career (Cable & Murray, 1999; Hadani, Coombes, Das, & Jalajas, 2012; Pezzoni, Sterzi, & Lissoni, 2012). Another gap is the lack of investigation on the importance of (weak) collaborative ties that may potentially lead to better job placement (Granovetter, 1973). While advisors provide significant and direct assistance in academic career, weaker social ties (e.g., infrequent but eminent collaborators) may bring in new perspectives that contribute to final placements. Investigation of these two types of collaboration ties in placement outcomes may provide new insights on faculty hiring mechanisms.

RESULTS AND DISCUSSIONS

We present preliminary analyses of the effects of collaborators on faculty hiring. The data comes from a set of 27 information schools (a.k.a, iSchools) in the United States collected from November to December 2014. Our dataset contains full time faculty members' gender, seniority (full and associate professors are senior; assistant are junior), and publication record (including collaborators) from Scopus between November 2014 and May 2015 from Scopus API via http://api.elsevier.com and http://www.scopus.com. We further collected junior faculty members' advisors based on their dissertation data from ProQuest. In total, there are 81 junior faculty members and 69 unique advisors. Without an authoritative ranking, we ranked iSchools based on senior faculty members' hiring. Specifically, iSchools are ranked based on their PageRank scores in the senior faculty hiring network, where edges represent acknowledgement and go from hiring to doctoral institutions. We ran PageRank repetitively and obtained average PageRank scores (varied damping factors from 0 to 1). The higher PageRank score an iSchool has, the better ranking it has with respect to faculty hiring.

We investigate the relationships between hiring institution rankings (based on senior hiring) and potential factors that may impact such placements among junior faculty. The control variables are junior faculty members' h-index, gender (a binary indicator: 1 for female and 0 for male), and doctoral institutional ranking. We further controlled for annual faculty openings, measured by the number of junior faculty hires in each year. There are three study variables: h-indices of advisors and collaborators (median and maximum). All h-indices are measured based on papers and citations up to the year a junior faculty member joined her current institution. We test the effects of study variables separately by linear regressions. For collaborator effects, we included advisor h-index as an additional control. Figure 1 shows that the median of collaborator h-index is a significant and positive predictor for junior faculty placement outcome. In other words, PhD graduates who have co-authored with higher-impact researchers (other than advisors) are more likely to find faculty positions in better ranked institutions. This may imply the importance of collaborating with well-known researchers for young scholars' early career placement in the academia.

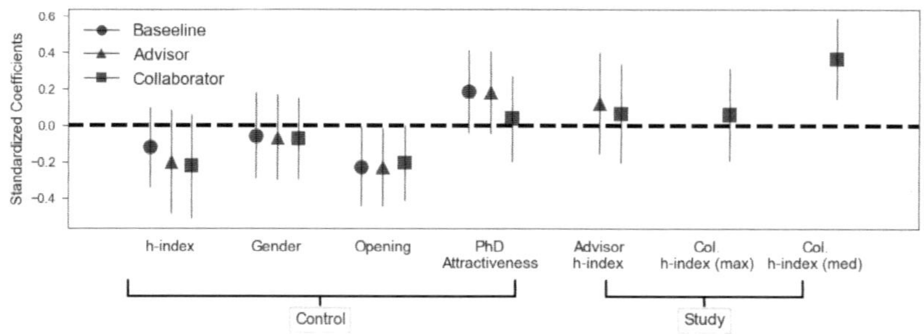

Figure 1. Standardized regression coefficients for faculty hiring outcome. The error bars are coefficients' 95% confidence intervals. The dashed line shows the zero value. Baseline model only contains control variables.

REFERENCES

Cable, D. M., & Murray, B. (1999). Tournaments versus sponsored mobility as determinants of job search success. *Academy of Management Journal*, *42*(4), 439–449.

Clauset, A., Arbesman, S., & Larremore, D. B. (2015). Systematic inequality and hierarchy in faculty hiring networks. *Science Advances*, *1*(1), e1400005–e1400005.

Godechot, O. (2016). The chance of influence: A natural experiment on the role of social capital in faculty recruitment. *Social Networks*, *46*, 60–75.

Granovetter, M. S. (1973). The Strength of Weak Ties. *American Journal of Sociology*, *78*(6), 1360–1380. University of Chicago Press .

Hadani, M., Coombes, S., Das, D., & Jalajas, D. (2012). Finding a good job: Academic network centrality and early occupational outcomes in management academia. *Journal of Organizational Behavior*, *33*(5), 723–739.

Long, J. S., & Fox, M. F. (1995). Scientific Careers: Universalism and Particularism. *Annual Review of Sociology*, *21*(1), 45–71.

Pezzoni, M., Sterzi, V., & Lissoni, F. (2012). Career progress in centralized academic systems: Social capital and institutions in France and Italy. *Research Policy*, *41*(4), 704–719.

Sheltzer, J. M., & Smith, J. C. (2014). Elite male faculty in the life sciences employ fewer women. *Proceedings of the National Academy of Sciences of the United States of America*, *111*(28), 10107–12. National Academy of Sciences.

Zhu, Y., & Yan, E. (2017). Examining academic ranking and inequality in library and information science through faculty hiring networks. *Journal of Informetrics*, *11*(2), 641–654.